REBELLION IN AMERICA

REBELLION IN AMERICA:

A Contemporary British Viewpoint, 1765–1783

David H. Murdoch, *editor*

CLIO BOOKS
Santa Barbara, California • Oxford, England

Library of Congress Cataloging in Publication Data

Rebellion in America.

   "Reproduces the Annual register's account of the Anglo-American conflict as it appears in the volumes from 1765–1782 inclusive."
   Includes bibliographical references and index.
   1. United States — History — Revolution, 1775–1783— Foreign public opinion, British.   2. Public opinion — Great Britain.   3. United States — History — Revolution, 1775–1783 — Sources.   I. Murdoch, David H.   II. The Annual register of world events.
E249.3.R43   973.3   77-16302
ISBN 0-87436-225-3

American Bibliographical Center—Clio Press
Riviera Campus, 2040 A.P.S., Box 4397
Santa Barbara, California 93103

Clio Press, Ltd.
Woodside House, Hinksey Hill
Oxford OX1 5BE, England

Manufactured in the United States of America

Design and Production: Graphics Two, Los Angeles

CONTENTS

Acknowledgements

For their help in the preparation of this work, I should like to express my thanks to Mr. Dennis Cox, Librarian, Mr. Peter Morrish, Keeper of the Special Collections, and the staff of the Brotherton Library; to Mr. Eric Daniels of the Photography Department, for his expertise in the difficult task of photographing the selections from the Brotherton Library's first editions of the *Annual Register;* to Miss Irene Cassidy for her assistance in the editing; to Mr. Robert Collison for the preparation of the index; and most particularly to Prof. David N. Dilks for his constant interest and encouragement and to my colleague Dr. John A. Woods for his most helpful advice and criticism.

D. H. Murdoch
University of Leeds
May 1977

Chronological Survey

1763	February	Treaty of Paris ends Seven Years' War
	April	Grenville ministry takes office
1764	March	American Revenue ('Sugar') Act
1765	March	Stamp Act
		New York Assembly refuses to comply with the Quartering Act
	May	Virginia Resolutions
	June	Grenville dismissed; Rockingham ministry takes office
	August	Boston and Newport Riots
		Newport Resolves
	October	Stamp Act Congress
	November	Sons of Liberty nullify Stamp Act
	December	Nonimportation agreements reduce Anglo-American trade
1766	January	British towns petition Parliament for repeal of Stamp Act
	March	Repeal of Stamp Act
		Declaratory Act
	July	Rockingham dismissed; Chatham ministry takes office
1767	July	Townshend Revenue Acts

viii

The Annual Register—Chronological Survey

	December	Grafton assumes leadership of ministry on semi-retirement of Chatham
1768	January–May	Colonies protest against Townshend Acts
	February	Massachusetts Assembly sends circular letter to other colonies appealing for resistance to taxation without representation
	March	Boston nonimportation agreement
	June	Massachusetts Assembly attempts to force recall of Governor Bernard
		Boston disturbances over Custom's seizure of Hancock's *Liberty*
	October	Chatham resigns leadership in favour of Grafton
	December	House of Lords condemns activities of Massachusetts
1769	February	Henrician Treason Act extended to America
	May	Virginia leads extension of nonimportation associations
1770	January	Grafton resigns; replaced by North Affray at Golden Hill, New York
	March	Boston 'Massacre'
	April	Repeal of Townshend Acts, except Tea Act
	May–December	Collapse of colonial nonimportation agreements
1771		Parliament concentrates on dispute with Spain over the Falkland Islands and on emerging East India Company crisis
		Declining influence of radicals in America
1772	June	Revenue schooner *Gaspée* destroyed by Rhode Islanders

The Annual Register—Chronological Survey

	October	Boston radicals set up Committee of Correspondence to mobilise public opinion in Massachusetts
1773	March	Virginia establishes first intercolonial Committee of Correspondence
	May	New Tea Act permits export of tea direct to America, free of duty in Britain but paying old duty in colonies
	June	Massachusetts Assembly attempts to force recall of Governor Hutchinson and Lieutenant-Governor Oliver
	December	Boston Tea Party
1774	April	Burke's speech on American taxation
	March–May	The Coercive (Intolerable) Acts
	May	Quebec Act
		Boston Committee of Correspondence calls for new nonimportation agreement
	June	Extension of Quartering Act to all the colonies
	September	Massachusetts Suffolk County Meeting Resolves
		Dissolved Massachusetts Assembly meets as a Provisional Congress
		Continental Congress meets in Philadelphia
	October	Continental Congress calls for trade boycott toward Britain, petitions Crown for redress of grievances and forms Association
1775	February	Chatham's conciliation plan rejected by Parliament
		Parliament declares Massachusetts to be in rebellion
		North's Conciliation Resolution

	March	Burke's speech on conciliation
		New England Restraining Act
	April	Restraining Act extended to all colonies save New York and North Carolina
		British troops and Americans clash at Lexington and Concord
		British forces besieged in Boston
	May	Ticonderoga captured by Americans
		Reinforcements reach British army in Boston
	May–June	Continental Congress reassembles, appeals for support to Quebec settlers, orders raising of troops and appoints Washington Commander-in-Chief
		Battle of Bunker Hill
	July	Congress issues Declaration of the Causes of Taking Up Arms, petitions the Crown and appeals to the people of Britain; rejects North's Conciliation Resolution and intensifies trade boycott
	August	American forces invade Canada
	December	Prohibitory Act
		American assault on Quebec fails
1776	March	British army evacuates Boston for Halifax, Nova Scotia
	May	North establishes first Peace Commission
		Carleton defeats Americans besieging Quebec and advances into New York.
	June	British attack on Charleston fails
	July	Declaration of Independence
		British army occupies Staten Island
	August	Battle of Long Island
	September	Americans reject Peace Commission

The Annual Register—Chronological Survey

		British capture New York
	October	Carleton retires to Quebec
	November–December	British enter New Jersey, force Washington into Pennsylvania, and occupy Rhode Island
	December	Battles of Trenton
1777	January–April	Rockingham Opposition 'secedes' from Parliament
	February	Parliament authorizes privateers against Americans
		Habeas Corpus Act suspended for treason in America and for piracy
	May	Chatham's motion for repeal of post-1763 American legislation rejected by Parliament
	July	British recapture Ticonderoga
	August	Battle of Oriskany
		Battles of Hubbardton and Fort Stanwyx
		British forces land at Chesapeake Bay
	September	Battle of Brandywine Creek
		Battle of Freeman's Farm
		Battle of Paoli
		British capture Philadelphia
		Battle of Germantown
	October	British capture Verplancks and Fort Montgomery on the Hudson River
		British army under Burgoyne surrenders at Saratoga
	October–November	British capture forts on the Delaware River
	November	Congress adopts Articles of Confederation
	December	Battle of Whitemarsh
		Washington retires to Valley Forge
1778	February	Treaties of Commerce and Amity between France and America

March	British naval weakness revealed to Parliament
	North's ministry secures new Conciliation Acts and establishes second (Carlisle) Peace Commission
	Rockingham opposition call for recognition of American Independence
March–April	North ministry challenged by demands for 'economical' reform of Parliament and by discontent in Ireland
April	Death of Chatham
	John Paul Jones raids Whitehaven
June	British forces evacuate Philadelphia for New York
	Battle of Monmouth Courthouse
	Carlisle Peace Commission arrives in New York
July	American raid into the Ohio Valley; capture of Kaskaskia
	Wyoming Valley Massacre
	British fleet under Keppel fails to defeat French at Ushant
	French fleet arrives on American coast
	War declared between Britain and France
	Peace Commission approaches Congress and appeals to the American people
	Tory raid on German Flats, New York
July–August	French fleet fails to blockade New York, abandons American siege of Newport, Rhode Island
September	French capture Dominica
	British raid Bedford and Martha's Vineyard

	October	Peace Commission returns to Britain
	December	British expedition captures St. Lucia
		British forces capture Savannah
1779	January	British capture Augusta
	January–February	Keppel courtmarshalled and exonerated
	March	Battle of Briar Creek
	April	Franco-Spanish Alliance
	April–June	Parliamentary Committee of Enquiry into the Conduct of the war fails to shake North's ministry
	May–November	Sullivan's expedition against Tories and Indians
	May–June	British raids on Virginia coast; capture of Stony Point, Verplancks Point and Fort Lafayette on the Hudson
	June	Spain declares war on Britain; besieges Gibraltar and Minorca
		French capture St. Vincent
	July	Americans recapture Stony Point
		British raid Connecticut; evacuate Rhode Island
		French capture Grenada
	August	American raid on Paulus Hook
	August–September	Threatened French invasion of Britain
	September	John Paul Jones wins engagement with H.M.S. *Serapis*
		General Election fails to improve support for North Ministry
	October	British raid Omoa, Honduras
		Spanish capture West Florida
		Failure of Franco-American siege of Savannah
	November	Yorkshire Movement increases pressure for parliamentary reform

		Irish discontent increases
1780	January	Gibraltar re-supplied by British fleet
	January–April	Major pressure from County Associations and the Opposition for reform of Parliament
	February–March	Irish crisis
	April	British begin siege of Charleston
		British fleet fails to defeat French off Martinique
		Abortive British raids on Nicaragua and the Mosquito Shore
		League of Armed Neutrality formed
	May	Americans surrender Charleston
		Battle of Waxhaws; British capture Fort Ninety-Six
	June	Gordon Riots in London
		British raid into Connecticut; battles of Connecticut Farms and Springfield
		French army arrives in Newport, Rhode Island
		Hyder Ali War begins in India
	July	Tory-Patriot Civil War in the Carolinas
	August	Battle of Camden
		Battle of Fishing Creek
	September	Defection of Benedict Arnold; execution of Major André
	October	Battle of Kings Mountain
	December	Britain declares war on the Netherlands
		Collapse of Congressional finance; states in serious arrears with quotas for the Continental Army
1781	January	British capture St. Eustatius
		Battle of Cowpens

The Annual Register—Chronological Survey

		British raids on Virginia
		Mutinies in the American army
	March	Battle of Guilford Courthouse
		British fleet drives off French at Chesapeake Capes
		British raids into Virginia
		Articles of Confederation ratified
	April	Battle of Hobkirk's Hill
	May	Spanish capture Pensacola
		Weathersfield Conference
	June	French capture Tobago
		British lose Augusta and other posts in Georgia
	July	Battle of Green Spring
		British defeat Hyder Ali at Porto Novo
	August	British naval defeat of the Dutch off Dogger Bank
		British army occupies Yorktown
	September	Battle of Eutaw Springs
	October	British army surrenders at Yorktown
	November	British seize Negapatam in India
1782	January	French capture St. Kitts, Montserrat, Nevis
		British capture Trincomalee in Ceylon
		British defeat American expedition sent to recapture Georgia
	February	Parliament votes to end the American War
	March	North resigns; second Rockingham ministry takes office
	April	British fleet defeats French off the Iles des Saintes
		Britain begins peace negotiations with France and America
	May	Parliament passes economical reform bills; faces demands for

		legislative independence from Ireland
	July	Death of Rockingham; Shelburne ministry takes office
		British evacuate Savannah
	August	French recapture Trincomalee
	October	America, France and Spain present draft peace terms
		Gilbraltar relieved
1783	February	Parliament discusses peace preliminaries with France and Spain and accepts draft treaty with America
		Shelburne resigns
	March	Political crisis in Britian over appointment of new ministry
	April	Fox-North ministry takes office
		American Intercourse Bill rejected
		Repeal of Prohibitory Acts
	July	Negotiations for Anglo-American Trade treaty fall through
	September	Peace preliminaries between Britain and the Netherlands agreed
	November	Definitive treaties with France and Spain approved by Parliament
	December	East India Company Bill precipitates fall of Fox-North ministry; Pitt ministry takes office

Selected Bibliography
Reference and Bibliographical

Bellot, H. Hale. "General Collections of Reports of Parliamentary Debates for the Period Since 1660." *Bulletin of the Institute of Historical Research* 10 (1933–34): 171–77.

Boatner, Mark M. *Biographical Dictionary of the American Revolution.* London, 1966.

The Commissioned Sea Officers of the Royal Navy, 1660–1815. Admiralty Handlist. 3 vols. London, 1955.

Dictionary of American Biography. Edited by Allen Johnson (vols. 1–6) and Dumas Malone (vols. 7–21). 21 vols. New York, 1943.

Dictionary of American History. Edited by James Truslow Adams. 5 vols. 2nd ed., rev. New York, 1942.

Dictionary of National Biography. Edited by Lesley Stephen, Sidney Lee, et al. 63 vols., with supplements. London, 1885–1901.

Dictionnaire de biographie francaise. Edited by J. Batteau, M. Barroux, and M. Prevost. 14+ vols. Paris, 1933–76+.

Ford, Worthington C. *British Officers Serving in the American Revolution, 1774–1783.* Brooklyn, 1897.

Gipson, Lawrence H. *The British Empire before the American Revolution.* Vol. 14: *A Bibliographical Guide to the History of the British Empire, 1748–1776.* New York, 1968.

Harvard Guide to American History. Edited by Frank Friedel and Richard K. Showman. 2 vols. Cambridge, Mass., 1974.

Heitman, F. B. *Historical Register of the Officers of the Continental Army*. New ed., rev. Washington, D.C., 1914.

Smith, Dwight L., ed. *Era of the American Revolution: A Bibliography*. Clio Bibliography Series 4. Santa Barbara, Calif. and Oxford, 1975.

Tercentenary Handlist of English and Welsh Newspapers, Magazines, and Reviews. London, 1920.

Todd, William B. *A Bibliography of Edmund Burke*. London, 1964.

Printed Sources

Acts of the Privy Council of England: Colonial Series. Edited by William L. Grant and James Munro. 6 vols. Hereford, 1908–12.

Adair, Douglas, and Schutz, John A., eds. *Peter Oliver's Origin and Progress of the American Rebellion: A Tory View*. San Marino, Calif., 1961.

Adams, John. *The Adams Papers*. First Series: *Diary and Autobiography of John Adams*. Edited by Lyman H. Butterfield et al. 4 vols. Cambridge, Mass., 1961. *Supplement to the Diary and Autobiography of John Adams*. Edited by Lyman H. Butterfield. Cambridge, Mass., 1966. Second Series: *Adams Family Correspondence*. Edited by Lyman H. Butterfield et al. 2 vols. Cambridge, Mass., 1963. *Letters of John Adams Addressed to His Wife*. Edited by Charles Francis Adams. Boston, 1841. *Familiar Letters of John Adams and His Wife Abigail Adams during the American Revolution*. Edited by Charles Francis Adams. New York, 1876.

Adams, Samuel. *The Writings of Samuel Adams*. Edited by Harry Alonzo Cushing. 4 vols. New York, 1904–08.

[Almon, John], ed. *A Collection of Interesting, Authentic Papers Relative to the Dispute between Great Britain and America: Sharing the Causes and Progress of that Misunderstanding from 1764 to 1775*. London, 1777.

———. *The Debates and Proceedings of the British House of Commons . . . [1743–1774]*. 11 vols. London, 1766–75.

———. *The Parliamentary Register. . . .* 17 vols. London, 1775–80. Second Series. Edited by John Debrett. 45 vols. London, 1782–96.

Barlyn, Bernard, and Garrett, Jane N., eds. *Pamphlets of the American Revolution, 1750–1776*. Cambridge, Mass., 1965.

The Annual Register—Selected Bibliography

Beccaria Bonesana, Marchese Cesare di. *An Essay on Crimes and Punishments, Translated from the Italian, with a Commentary attributed to M. De Voltaire, Translated from the French.* London, 1767.

Beloff, Max, ed. *The Debate on the American Revolution, 1761–1783.* London, 1949.

Brown, Lloyd A., and Peckham, Howard H., eds. *Revolutionary War Journals of Henry Dearborn, 1775–1783.* Chicago, 1939.

Burke, Edmund. *The Correspondence of Edmund Burke.* Edited by Thomas W. Copeland. 9 vols. Cambridge and Chicago, 1961–70.

————. *The Select Works of Edmund Burke.* Edited by E. T. Payne. 3 vols. New ed., rev. Oxford, 1878–88, vol. 1.

————. *Speeches of the Right Honourable Edmund Burke.* 4 vols. London, 1816.

Burnett, Edmund C., ed. *Letters of Members of the Continental Congress.* 8 vols. Washington, D.C., 1921–36.

Clinton, Sir Henry. *The American Rebellion: Sir Henry Clinton's Narrative of His Campaigns, 1775–82, with an Appendix of Original Documents.* Edited by W. B. Willcox. New Haven, Conn., 1954.

Cobbett, William, and Hansard, T. C., eds., *The Parliamentary History of England from the Earliest Period to 1803.* 36 vols. London, 1806–20.

Commager, Henry Steele, and Morris, R. B. *The Spirit of 'Seventy-Six: The Story of the American Revolution as Told by Participants.* 2 vols. Indianapolis and New York, 1958.

[Debrett, John], ed. *The History, Debates and Proceedings of Both Houses of Parliament of Great Britain, from the Year 1743 to the Year 1774. . . .* 7 vols. London, 1792.

Dickinson, John. *Letters from a Pennsylvania Farmer to the Inhabitants of the British Colonies.* Philadelphia, 1768.

Fonblanque, E. B. de. *Political and Military Episodes in the Latter Half of the Eighteenth Century, Derived from the Life and Correspondence of the Right Honourable John Burgoyne.* London, 1876.

Fox, Charles James. *The Speeches of the Right Honourable Charles James Fox in the House of Commons.* Edited by John Wright. 6 vols. London, 1816.

Franklin, Benjamin. *The Examination of Doctor Benjamin Franklin before an August Assembly Relating to the Repeal*

The Annual Register—Selected Bibliography

of the Stamp Act. Philadelphia, 1766; Boston and London, 1767.

———— . *The Papers of Benjamin Franklin.* Edited by Leonard W. Labaree (vols. 1–14) and William B. Willcox (vol. 15+). 19+ vols. New Haven, Conn., 1959–76+.

Gage, Thomas. *Correspondence of General Thomas Gage with the Secretaries of State and with the War Office and the Treasury, 1763–1775.* Yale Historical Publications, Manuscripts and Edited Texts, xi–xii. Edited by C. E. Carter. 2 vols. New Haven, Conn., 1931–33.

Garth, Charles. "Correspondence of Charles Garth." Edited by Joseph Barnwell. *South Carolina Historical and Genealogical Magazine* 28 (1927)–33 (1932).

———— . "Stamp Act Papers." *Maryland Historical Magazine* 6 (1911): 283–86, 291–302.

George III. *The Correspondence of King George the Third from 1760 to December 1783: Printed from the Original Papers in the Royal Archives at Windsor Castle.* Edited by Sir John W. Fortescue. 6 vols. London, 1927–28. See also Lewis B. Namier, ed. *Additions and Corrections to Sir John Fortescue's Edition of the Correspondence of King George the Third.* Manchester, 1937.

———— . *The Letters of King George III.* Edited by Bonamy Dobrée. London, 1935.

Gipson, L. H. "The Great Debate in the Committee of the Whole House of Commons on the Stamp Act, 1766, as Reported by Nathaniel Ryder." *Pennsylvania Magazine of History and Biography* 86 (1962): 10–41.

Henry, Patrick. *Patrick Henry: Life, Correspondence and Speeches.* Edited by William W. Henry. 3 vols. New York, 1891.

Historical Statistics of the United States: Colonial Times to 1957, A Statistical Abstract Supplement. Bureau of the Census. Washington, D.C., 1960.

Hull, C. H., and Temperley, H. W. V., eds. "Debates on the Declaratory Act and Repeal of the Stamp Act." *American Historical Review* 17 (1911–12): 543–86.

Hutchinson, Thomas. *The Diary and Letters of His Excellency Thomas Hutchinson.* Edited by Peter Hutchinson. 2 vols. London, 1883–86.

Jefferson, Thomas. *The Papers of Thomas Jefferson.* Edited by Julian P. Boyd et al. 19+ vols. Princeton, N.J., 1950–70+.

The Annual Register—Selected Bibliography

Jensen, Merrill, ed. *English Historical Documents.* Vol. 9: *English Colonial Documents to 1776.* London and New York, 1955.

Johnson, William Samuel. "Letters of William Samuel Johnson to the Governors of Connecticut." *Collections of the Massachusetts Historical Society.* 5th ser. 9 (1885): 211–490.

Journal of the Commissioners for Trade and Plantations from April 1704 to May 1783: Preserved in the Public Record Office. 14 vols. London, 1920–38.

Journal of the House of Commons.

Journal of the House of Lords.

Journals of the Continental Congress, 1774–1789. Edited by W. C. Ford. 34 vols. Washington, D.C., 1904–37.

Lee, Henry. *Memoirs of the War in the Southern Department of the United States.* Edited by R. E. Lee. Rev. ed. New York, 1869.

Mackenzie, Frederick. *The Diary of Frederick Mackenzie, Giving a Daily Narration of His Military Service as an Officer of the Regiment of Royal Welsh Fusiliers during the Years 1775–81.* 2 vols. Cambridge, Mass., 1930.

[Mitchell, John]. *The Present State of Great Britain and North America with Regard to Agriculture, Population, Trade and Manufactures, Impartially Considered. . . .* London, 1767.

Montesquieu, Charles de Secondat, Baron de. *Oeuvres de Monsieur de Montesquieu. Nouvelle Edition, revue, corrigé et considérablement augmenti par l'auteur.* Amsterdam and Leipsig, 1757.

Morgan, E. S., ed. *Prologue to Revolution: Sources and Documents on the Stamp Act Crisis, 1764–1766.* Chapel Hill, N.C., 1959.

Morison, Samuel E., ed. *Sources and Documents Illustrating the American Revolution, 1764–1788, and the Formation of the Federal Constitution.* Oxford, 1923.

Paine, Thomas. *The Complete Writings of Thomas Paine.* Edited by Philip S. Foster. 2 vols. New York, 1945.

Pendleton, Edmund. *The Letters and Papers of Edmund Pendleton.* Virginia Historical Society, Documents, vols. 7 and 8. Edited by David J. Mays. 2 vols. Charlottesville, Va., 1967.

Pickering, Danby, ed. *The Statutes at Large from Magna Charta to . . . 1761.* 24 vols.; continued to 1806, vols. 25–46. Cambridge, 1762–1807.

Pitt, William, Earl of Chatham. *Correspondence of William Pitt, Earl of Chatham.* Edited by William S. Taylor and John H. Pringle. 4 vols. London, 1838–40.

———. *The Speeches of the Right Honourable the Earl of Chatham in the House of Lords and Commons.* Edited by W. S. Hathaway. New ed. London, 1848

Pitt, William [the Younger Pitt]. *The Speeches of the Right Honourable William Pitt in the House of Commons.* Edited by W. S. Hathaway. 4 vols. London, 1806.

Pownall, Thomas. *The Administration of the Colonies.* 2 vols. 5th ed. London, 1774.

Reed, Joseph. *Life and Correspondence of Joseph Reed.* Edited by W. B. Reed. 2 vols. Philadelphia, 1847.

Ruffhead, Owen, and Runnington, Charles, ed. *The Statutes at Large from Magna Charta to the Twenty-Fifth Year of the Reign of George the Third.* 10 vols. New ed., rev. London, 1786.

Sandwich, John Montagu, 4th Earl of. *The Private Papers of John, Earl of Sandwich, First Lord of the Admiralty, 1771–1782.* Edited by G. R. Barnes and J. H. Owen. 4 vols. London: Naval Records Society, 1932–38.

Sir Henry Cavendish's Debate of the House of Commons during the Thirteenth Parliament of Great Britain, Commonly Called the Unreported Parliament. . . . Edited by John Wright. 2 vols. London, 1841.

Smith, William. *Historical Memoirs, from 16 March 1763 to 9 July 1776, of William Smith, Historian of the Province of New York.* Edited by H. W. Sabine. New York, 1956.

Thomas, P. D. G., ed. "Parliamentary Diaries of Nathaniel Ryder, 1764–67." *Camden Miscellany* 23 [Camden 4th ser., vol. 7]: 241–320. London, 1969.

Treaties and Other International Acts of the United States of America. Edited by D. H. Miller. 8 vols. Washington, D.C., 1931–48.

Tucker, Josiah. *The True Interest of Great Britain Set Forth in Regard to the Colonies and the Only Means of Living in Peace and Harmony with Them.* Norfolk, Eng., 1774; Philadelphia, 1776.

Uhlendorf, B., ed. *Revolution in America: Confidential Letters and Journals, 1776–84, of Adjutant General Major Baurmeister of the Hessian Forces*. New Brunswick, N.J., 1957.

———. *The Siege of Charleston with an Account of the Province of South Carolina: Diaries and Letters of Hessian Officers, from the Von Jungkenn Papers in the William L. Clements Library*. Ann Arbor, Mich., 1938.

Van Alstyne, Richard, ed. "Europe, the Rockingham Whigs, and the War for American Independence: Some Documents." *Huntington Library Quarterly* 25 (1961–62): 1–28.

———. "Parliamentary Supremacy versus Independence: Notes and Documents." *Huntington Library Quarterly* 26 (1962–63): 201–33.

Walpole, Horace. *Last Journals of Horace Walpole, 1771–83*. Edited by Dr. Doran. 2 vols. London, 1859.

———. *Memoirs of the Reign of George III*. Edited by Denis Le Marchant, Bart. London, 1845.

———. *The Yale Edition of Horace Walpole's Correspondence*. Edited by W. S. Lewis et al. 39 vols. London and New Haven, 1937–73.

Washington, George. *The Writings of George Washington from the Original Manuscript Sources 1745–1799*. Edited by J. C. Fitzpatrick. 39 vols. Washington, D.C., 1931–44.

Watson, D. H. "Joseph Harrison and the *Liberty* Incident." *William and Mary Quarterly* 3rd ser. 20 (1963): 585–95.

———. "William Baker's Account of the Debate on the Repeal of the Stamp Act." *William and Mary Quarterly* 3rd ser. 24, no. 2 (1969): 259–65.

Wraxall, Nathaniel William. *The Historical and Posthumous Memoirs of Sir Nathaniel William Wraxall*. Edited by H. B. Wheatley. 5 vols. London, 1884.

Wright, John, ed. *Debates of the House of Commons in the Year 1774 on the Bill for Making More Effective Provision for the Government of the Province of Quebec*. London, 1839.

Secondary Works

Abernethy, Thomas P. *Western Lands and the American Revolution*. University of Virginia Institute for Research in the Social Sciences, Monograph no. 25. London and New York, 1937.

Alden, John R. *The American Revolution*. New York, 1954.

———. *A History of the American Revolution*. New York, 1969.

———. *Pioneer America*. New York, 1966.

———. *The South in the Revolution, 1763–1789*. Baton Rouge, La., 1957.

Allen, Gardener W. *A Naval History of the American Revolution*. 2 vols. Boston, 1913.

Anderson, Troyer S. *The Command of the Howe Brothers during the American Revolution*. London and New York, 1936.

Andreano, Ralph L., and Werner, Herbert D. "Charleston Loyalists: A Statistical Note." *South Carolina Historical Magazine* 60 (1959): 164–68.

Andrew, Charles McLean. *The Colonial Period of American History*. 4 vols. New Haven, Conn., 1934–38.

Arnold, Isaac N. *The Life of Benedict Arnold: His Patriotism and His Treason*. Chicago, 1880.

Aspinall, A. "The Reporting and Publishing of the House of Commons Debates, 1771–1834." In *Essays Presented to Sir Lewis Namier*. Edited by Richard Pares and A. J. P. Taylor. London, 1950.

Auger, Helen. *The Secret War of Independence*. New York, 1955.

Bailyn, Bernard. *Ideological Origins of the American Revolution*. Cambridge, Mass., 1967.

———. *The Ordeal of Thomas Hutchinson*. London, 1974.

Bargar, B. D., ed. "Charlestown Loyalism in 1775: The Secret Reports of Alexander Innes." *South Carolina Historical Magazine* 63 (1962): 125–36.

———. *Lord Dartmouth and the American Revolution*. Columbia, S.C., 1965.

Barker, Charles A. *The Background of the Revolution in Maryland*. Yale Historical Publications, Miscellany, 38. London and New Haven, Conn., 1940.

Barrow, Thomas C. "Background to the Grenville Program, 1757–1763." *William and Mary Quarterly*, 3rd ser. 22 (1965): 93–104.

————. *Trade and Empire: The British Customs Service in Colonial America, 1660–1775.* Cambridge, Mass., 1967.

Bell, W. J., Jr. "Thomas Auburey's 'Travels through America': A Note on Eighteenth Century Plagiarism." *Papers of the Bibliographical Society of America* 37 (1943): 23.

Bemis, S. F. "The British Secret Service and the French-American Alliance." *American Historical Review* 29 (1923–24): 474–95.

————. *The Diplomacy of the American Revolution.* Edinburgh and London, 1957.

Bezanson, Anne, et al. *Prices and Inflation during the American Revolution: Pennsylvania 1770–1790.* Philadelphia, 1951.

Bill, Alfred H. *New Jersey and the Revolutionary War.* New Jersey Historical Series, 11. Princeton, N.J., 1964.

Billias, George A., ed. *The American Revolution: How Revolutionary Was It?* Magnolia, Mass., 1965.

————. *George Washington's Generals.* New York, 1964.

————. *George Washington's Opponents: British Generals and Admirals in the American Revolution.* New York, 1969.

Black, Eugene C. *The Association: British Extraparliamentary Political Organization, 1769–1793.* Cambridge, Mass., 1963.

Bowen, Catherine Drinker. *John Adams and the American Revolution.* Boston, 1950.

Bowler, R. Arthur. *Logistics and the Failure of the British Army in America, 1775–1783.* Princeton, N.J., 1975.

Boyd, Julian P. *The Declaration of Independence: The Evolution of the Text as Shown in Facsimiles of Various Drafts by Its Author, Thomas Jefferson.* Princeton, N.J., 1945.

Brooke, John. *The Chatham Administration, 1766–68.* London, 1956.

————. *King George III.* London, 1972.

Broomfield, J. H. "Lord Sandwich and the Admiralty Board: Politics and the British Navy, 1771–1778." *Mariner's Mirror* 51 (1965): 7–17.

Brown, Gerald S. *The American Secretary: The Colonial Policy of Lord George Germain, 1775–1778.* Ann Arbor, Mich., 1963.

Brown, Peter. *The Chathamites: A Study of the Relationship Between Personalities and Ideas in the Second Half of the Eighteenth Century.* London and New York, 1967.

Bryant, Donald C. *Edmund Burke and His Literary Friends.* Washington University Studies, New Series, Language Literature, no. 9. St. Louis, 1939.

————. "New Light on Burke." *Quarterly Journal of Speech* 39 (1953): 351–53.

Butterfield, Herbert. *George III and the Historians.* London, 1957.

————. *George III, Lord North and the People, 1779–80.* London, 1949.

Cannon, J. *The Fox-North Coalition: Crisis of the Constitution, 1782–84.* Cambridge, 1969.

Champagne, Roger. "The Military Association of the Sons of Liberty." *New York Historical Society Quarterly* 41 (1957): 338–50.

————. "New York and the Intolerable Acts, 1774." *New York Historical Society Quarterly* 45 (1961): 195–207.

————. "New York Politics and Independence, 1776." *New York Historical Society Quarterly* 46 (1962): 281–303.

————. "New York's Radicals and the Coming of Independence." *Journal of American History* 51 (1964): 21–40.

Christie, I. R. *The End of North's Ministry, 1780–82.* London, 1958.

————. *Wilkes, Wyvill and Reform: The Parliamentary Movement in British Politics, 1760–1785.* London and New York, 1962.

Clark, Dora Mae. *British Opinion and the American Revolution.* Yale Historical Publications, Miscellany, 20. New Haven, Conn., 1930.

————. *The Rise of the British Treasury: Colonial Administration in the Eighteenth Century.* Yale Historical Publications, Studies, no. 20. New Haven, Conn., 1960.

Clowes, William Laird, et al. *The Royal Navy: A History from the Earliest Times to the Present.* 7 vols. London, 1897–1903, particularly vols. 3 and 4.

Coleman, Kenneth. *The American Revolution in Georgia, 1763–1789.* Athens, Ga., 1948.

Collins, A. S. "The Growth of the Reading Public during the Eighteenth Century." *Review of English Studies* 2 (1920): 284–94, 428–38.

The Annual Register—Selected Bibliography

Cone, Carl B. *Burke and the Nature of Politics: The Age of the American Revolution.* Lexington, Ky., 1957.

Copeland, Thomas W. "Burke and Dodsley's *Annual Register.*" *Publications of the Modern Language Association* 54 (1939): 223–45.

——— . *Edmund Burke: Six Essays.* London, 1950.

——— . "Edmund Burke's Friends and the *Annual Register.*" *Transactions of the Bibliographical Society: The Library* (March 1963): 29–39.

Curtis, Edward P. *Organisation of the British Army in the American Revolution.* Yale Historical Publications, Miscellany, 19. London and New Haven, Conn., 1926.

Dabney, William M., and Dargan, Marion. *William Henry Drayton and the American Revolution.* Albuquerque, N.M., 1962.

Davidson, Philip. *Propaganda and the American Revolution, 1767–1783.* Chapel Hill, N.C., 1941.

Derry, John W. *Charles James Fox.* London, 1972.

Dickerson, Oliver M. *The Navigation Acts and the American Revolution.* Philadelphia, 1951.

Donaghue, Bernard. *British Politics and the American Revolution: The Path to War, 1773–75.* London, 1964.

Downes, Randolph C. *Council Fires on the Upper Ohio: A Narrative of Indian Affairs in the Upper Ohio Valley until 1795.* Pittsburgh, Pa., 1940.

Dull, Jonathan R. *The French Navy and American Independence: A Study of Arms and Diplomacy, 1774–1787.* Princeton, N.J., 1975.

East, Robert A. *Business Enterprise in the American Revolutionary Era.* New York, 1938.

Eelking, Max Von. *Die Deutschen Hülfstruppen im nordamerikanischen Befreiungskriege, 1776 bis 1783.* 2 vols. Hanover, 1863. Translated and abridged by J. G. Rosengarten as *The German Allied Troops in the North American War of Independence.* Albany, N.Y., 1893.

Egnal, M., and Ernst, J. A. "An Economic Interpretation of the American Revolution." *William and Mary Quarterly* 4th ser. 29, no. 2 (1972): 1–32.

Ehrman, John. *The Younger Pitt.* London, 1969.

Einstein, Lewis. *Divided Loyalties: Americans in England during the War of Independence.* Boston, 1933.

Ellefson, L. Ashley. "Loyalists and Patriots in Georgia during the American Revolution." *Historian* 24 (1961–62): 347–56.

_____ . "The Stamp Act in Georgia." *Georgia Historical Quarterly* 46 (1962): 1–19.

Ernst, Joseph A. "Genesis of the Currency Act of 1764: Virginia Paper Money and the Protection of British Investments." *William and Mary Quarterly* 3rd ser. 22 (1965): 33–74.

Evans, Emory. "Planter Indebtedness and the Coming of the Revolution in Virginia." *William and Mary Quarterly* 19 (1962): 511–33.

Ferguson, E. James. *The Power of the Purse: A History of American Public Finance, 1776–1790.* Chapel Hill, N.C., 1961.

Flick, Alexander, ed. *History of the State of New York.* 10 vols. New York, 1933–37, particularly vol. 3.

Foord, Archibald S. *His Majesty's Opposition, 1714–1830.* Oxford, 1964.

Foran, William. "John Marshall as Historian." *American Historical Review* 43 (1937–38): 51–64.

Fortescue, John W. *History of the British Army.* 13 vols. London, 1899–1930.

Freeman, D. S. *George Washington.* 7 vols. New York, 1948–57.

French, Allen. *The Day of Concord and Lexington: The Nineteenth of April, 1775.* Boston, 1925.

_____ . *The First Year of the American Revolution.* Boston, 1934.

Fryer, W. R. "King George III: His Political Character and Conduct, 1760–1784." *Renaissance and Modern Studies* 6 (1962): 68–101.

Gerlach, Don R. *Philip Schuyler and the American Revolution in New York, 1733–1777.* Lincoln, Neb., 1964.

Gipson, L. H. *The British Empire before the American Revolution.* 15 vols. New York, 1936–70.

_____ . *The Coming of the American Revolution, 1763–1775.* New York, 1954.

_____ . "Virginia Planter Debts before the American Revolution." *Virginia Magazine of History and Biography* 69 (1961): 259–77.

The Annual Register—Selected Bibliography

Gottschalk, Louis R. *Lafayette and the Close of the American Revolution.* Chicago, 1942.

———. *Lafayette Comes to America.* Chicago, 1935.

———. *Lafayette Joins the American Army.* Chicago, 1937.

Graham, Gerald S. *Empire of the North Atlantic: The Maritime Struggle for North America.* Toronto, 1950.

Greene, Jack P. "Foundations of Political Power in the Virginia House of Burgesses, 1720–1776." *William and Mary Quarterly* 3rd ser. 16 (1959): 485–506.

Gruber, Ira D. "The American Revolution as a Conspiracy: The British View." *William and Mary Quarterly* 3rd ser. 26 (1969): 360–72.

———. "Lord Howe and Lord George Germain: British Politics and the Winning of American Independence." *William and Mary Quarterly* 3rd ser. 22 (1965): 225–43.

Hanna, William S. *Benjamin Franklin and Colonial Politics.* Stanford, Calif., 1965.

Harlow, Ralph V. *Samuel Adams, Promoter of the American Revolution: A Study in Psychology and Politics.* New York, 1923.

Harlow, V. T. *The Founding of the Second British Empire 1763–1793.* 2 vols. London, 1952.

Hatch, Lewis C. *The Administration of the American Revolutionary Army.* New York, 1904.

Hawke, David. *In the Midst of a Revolution.* Philadelphia, 1961.

Higginbotham, Don. "American Historians and the Military History of the American Revolution." *American Historical Review* 70 (1964): 18–34.

———. *The War of American Independence.* New York and London, 1971.

Hinkhouse, Fred J. *The Preliminaries of the American Revolution as Seen in the English Press, 1763–1775.* Columbia University Studies in History, Economics and Public Law, no. 276. New York, 1926.

The History of the Times. Edited by Stanley Morison. 4 vols. London, 1935–52. Vol. 1: *"The Thunderer" in the Making, 1785–1841.*

Jacobson, David L. *John Dickinson and the Revolution in Pennsylvania, 1764–1776.* University of California Publications in History, 78. Berkeley and Los Angeles, 1965.

The Annual Register—Selected Bibliography

James, Janus A. *The Life of George Rogers Clark.* Chicago, 1928.

Jensen, Merrill. *The Founding of a Nation: A History of the American Revolution 1763–1776.* New York and London, 1968.

Johnson, Cecil. *British West Florida, 1763–1783.* Yale Historical Publications, Miscellany, 62. London and New Haven, Conn., 1943.

Kallich, Martyn, and Macleish, Andrew, eds. *The American Revolution through British Eyes.* Evanston, Ill., 1962.

Kammen, Michael. *A Rope of Sand: The Colonial Agents, British Politics and the American Revolution.* Ithaca, N.Y., 1948.

Ketcham, Ralph L. *Benjamin Franklin.* New York, 1965.

Klingelhofer, Herbert E. "The Cautious Revolution: Maryland and the Movement toward Independence, 1774–76." *Maryland Historical Magazine* 60 (1965): 261–313.

Knollenberg, Bernard. *Growth of the American Revolution, 1766–1775.* London, 1975.

————. "John Dickinson vs. John Adams." *Proceedings of the American Philosophical Society* 107 (1963): 138–44.

————. *The Origin of the American Revolution, 1759–1766.* New York, 1960.

Labaree, Benjamin W. *The Boston Tea Party.* New York, 1964.

Labaree, Leonard W. *Royal Government in America: A Study of the British Colonial System before 1783.* Yale Historical Publications, Miscellany, 6. London and New Haven, Conn., 1930.

Lanctot, Gustave. *Canada and the American Revolution, 1774–1783.* Translated by Margaret M. Cameron. Cambridge, Mass., 1967.

Land, Aubrey C. *The Dulanys of Maryland: A Biographical Study of Daniel Dulany, the Elder, and Daniel Dulany, the Younger.* Baltimore, Md., 1955.

Langford, P. *The First Rockingham Administration 1765–1766.* London, 1973.

Lee, E. Lawrence. "Days of Defiance: Resistance to the Stamp Act in the Lower Cape Fear." *North Carolina Historical Review* 43 (1966): 186–202.

The Annual Register—Selected Bibliography

Leslie, William R. "The Gaspée Affair: A Study of Its Constitutional Significance." *Mississippi Valley Historical Review* 39 (1952–53): 233–56.

Libby, Orin G. "A Critical Examination of William Gordon's History of the American Revolution." *Annual Report of the American Historical Association* 1 (1899): 367–88.

———. "Ramsay as a Plagiarist." *American Historical Review* 7 (1902): 697–703.

———. "Some Pseudo Histories of the American Revolution." *Transactions of the Wisconsin Academy of Sciences, Arts and Letters* 13 (1900): 419–25.

Love, Walter D. "Burke's Transition from a Literary to a Political Career." *Burke Newsletter* 6, no. 2 (1964–65): 376–90.

Lovejoy, David S. *Rhode Island Politics and the American Revolution, 1760–1776.* Brown University, Studies, vol. 22. Providence, R.I., 1958.

Lundin, Leonard. *Cockpit of the Revolution: The War for Independence in New Jersey.* Princeton History of New Jersey, 2. London and Princeton, N.J., 1946.

Lutnick, Solomon. *The American Revolution and the British Press 1775–1783.* Columbia, Mo., 1967.

Mackesy, P. "British Strategy in the War of American Independence." *Yale Review* 52 (1963): 539–57.

———. *The War for America, 1775–83.* London, 1964.

Madariaga, I. de. *Britain, Russia and the Armed Neutrality of 1780: Sir James Harris's Mission to St. Petersburg During the American Revolution.* London, 1962.

Mahoney, Thomas H. D. "Edmund Burke and the American Revolution: The Repeal of the Stamp Act." *Burke Newsletter* 8 (1965–66): 503–21.

Maier, Pauline. "John Wilkes and American Disillusionment with Britain." *William and Mary Quarterly.* 3rd ser. 20 (1963): 373–95.

Malone, Dumas. *Jefferson and His Time.* Vol. 1: *Jefferson the Virginian.* Boston, 1948.

Marcus, Geoffrey J. *A Naval History of Britain.* 2 vols. London, 1961–71. Vol. 1: *The Formative Years.*

Marshall, Peter. "Lord Hillsborough, Samuel Wharton and the Ohio Grant, 1769–1775." *English Historical Review* 80 (1965): 717–39.

Mason, Bernard. *The Road to Independence: The Revolutionary Movement in New York, 1733–1777.* Lexington, Ky., 1966.

Mays, David J. *Edmund Pendleton, 1721–1803: A Biography.* 2 vols. Cambridge, Mass., 1952.

Minchinton, Walter E. "The Stamp Act Crisis: Bristol and Virginia." *Virginia Magazine of History and Biography* 73 (1965): 145–55.

Montross, L. *Rag, Tag and Bobtail: The Story of the Continental Army, 1775–1783.* New York, 1952.

Moomaw, W. H. "The Denouement of General Howe's Campaign of 1777." *English Historical Review* 79, no. 3 (1964): 498–512.

Morris, Richard B. *The American Revolution Reconsidered.* New York, 1967.

———. *Government and Labour in Early America.* New York, 1946.

———. *The Peacemakers, the Great Powers and American Independence.* New York, 1965.

Mott, Frank L. "The Newspaper Coverage of Lexington and Concord." *New England Quarterly* 17 (1944): 489–505.

Mowat, Charles L. *East Florida as a British Province, 1763–1784.* University of California Publications in History, 32. Berkeley and Los Angeles, 1943.

Mullen, J. C. "Lecky as Plagiarist: The *Annual Register* and the American Revolution." *Studies on Burke and His Time* 13, pt. 3 (1972): 2193–202.

Murdock, Harold. *Nineteenth of April, 1775.* Boston and New York, 1923.

Namier, L. B. *England in the Age of the American Revolution.* 2nd ed. London, 1963.

———. *Structure of Politics at the Accession of George III.* 2nd ed. London, 1957.

Namier, L. B., and Brooke, J. *Charles Townshend.* New York, 1964.

———. *The History of Parliament: The House of Commons 1754–90.* 3 vols. London, 1964.

Nelson, William H. *The American Tory.* New York, 1961.

Newcomb, Benjamin H. "Effects of the Stamp Act on Colonial Pennsylvania Politics." *William and Mary Quarterly.* 3rd ser. 23 (1966): 257–72.

The Annual Register—Selected Bibliography

Newmyer, R. Kent. "Charles Stedman's History of the American War." *American Historical Review* 63 (1958): 924–34.

Noailles, Vicomte Amblard de. *Marins et soldats francais en Amérique pendant le guerre de l'independence des Etats-Unis, 1778–1783.* 2nd ed. Paris, 1903.

Norris, J. *Shelburne and Reform.* London, 1963.

O'Gorman, Frank. *The Rise of Party in England: The Rockingham Whigs 1760–82.* London, 1975.

Olson, Alison G. *The Radical Duke: Career and Correspondence of Charles Lennox, Third Duke of Richmond.* Oxford, 1961.

Pace, Jacob M. "The Economic Growth of the Chesapeake and the European Market, 1697–1775." *Journal of Economic History* 24 (1964): 496–511.

Palmer, R. R. *Age of the Democratic Revolution: A Political History of Europe and America, 1790–1800.* 2 vols. Princeton, N.J., 1959.

Pares, Richard. "Economic Factors in the History of the Empire." *Economic History Review* 1st ser. 7 (1936–37): 119–44.

————. *George III and the Politicians.* The Ford Lectures, 1951 and 1952. Oxford, 1953.

————. *Limited Monarchy in Great Britain in the Eighteenth Century.* Historical Association, General Series, no. 35. London, 1957.

————. *War and Trade in the West Indies.* Oxford, 1936.

Patterson, A. Temple. *The Other Armada: The Franco-Spanish Attempt to Invade Britain in 1779.* Manchester, 1960.

Patterson, S. E. *Political Parties in Revolutionary Massachusetts.* Madison, Wis., 1973.

Peckham, Howard W. *The War for Independence: A Military History.* Chicago, 1958.

Pennington, Edgar L. "East Florida and the American Revolution, 1775–1778." *Florida Historical Quarterly* 9 (1930): 24–46.

Phillips, Paul C. *The West in the Diplomacy of the American Revolution.* University of Illinois Studies in the Social Sciences, 2. Urbana, Ill., 1913, reprinted 1966.

Rea, Robert R. *The English Press in Politics 1760–1774.* Lincoln, Neb., 1963.

Ripley, R. B. "Adams, Burke and Eighteenth Century Conservatism." *Political Science Quarterly* 80 (1965): 216–35.

Ritcheson, C. R. *British Politics and the American Revolution.* Norman, Okla., 1954.

Robson, Eric. *The American Revolution in Its Political and Military Aspects, 1763–1783.* London, 1955; Hamden, Conn., 1965.

Rutman, Darrell B., ed. *The Old Dominion: Essays for Thomas Perkins Abernethy.* Charlottesville, Va., 1964.

Sabine, Lorenzo. *Biographical Sketches of Loyalists of the American Revolution.* 2 vols. New ed. Port Washington, N.Y., 1966.

Sarason, Bertram D. "Edmund Burke and the Two *Annual Registers.*" *Publications of the Modern Language Association* 68 (1953): 496–508.

Savelle, Max. "Nationalism and Other Loyalties in the American Revolution." *American Historical Review* 67 (1962): 901–23.

Scheer, George F., and Rankin, Hugh F. *Rebels and Redcoats.* New York, 1957.

Schlesinger, Arthur M. *Prelude to Independence: The Newspaper War on Britain.* New York, 1958.

———. "Political Mobs and the American Revolution, 1765–1776." *Proceedings of the American Philosophical Society* 99 (1955): 244–50.

Schutz, John A. *Thomas Pownall, British Defender of American Liberty: A Study of Anglo-American Relations in the Eighteenth Century.* Glendale, Calif., 1951.

Seitz, R. W. "Goldsmith and the *Annual Register.*" *Modern Philosophy* 31 (1933–34): 183–94.

Siebert, F. S. *Freedom of the Press in England 1476–1776: The Rise and Decline of Government Control.* Urbana, Ill., 1965.

Sheridan, R. B. "The British Credit Crisis of 1772 and the American Colonies." *Journal of Economic History* 20 (1960): 161–86.

———. "The Wealth of Jamaica in the Eighteenth Century." *Economic History Review* 18 (1965): 292–311.

Shy, John. *Toward Lexington: The Role of the British Army in the Coming of the American Revolution.* Princeton, 1965.

Smith, Page. *John Adams, 1735–1826.* 2 vols. Garden City, N.Y., 1962.

Smith, Paul H. *Loyalists and Redcoats: A Study in British Revolutionary Policy.* Chapel Hill, N.C., 1964.

Sosin, Jack M. *Agents and Merchants: British Colonial Policy and the Origins of the American Revolution 1763–1775.* Lincoln, Neb., 1965.

————. "The Massachusetts Act of 1774: Coercive or Preventative?" *Huntington Library Quarterly* 26 (1962–63): 235–52.

————. "A Postscript to the Stamp Act: George Grenville's Revenue Measures: A Drain on Colonial Specie?" *American Historical Review* 63 (1957–58): 918–23.

————. *The Revolutionary Frontier, 1763–1783.* New York, 1967.

————. "The Use of Indians in the War of the American Revolution: A Re-Assessment of Responsibility." *Canadian Historical Review* 46 (1965): 101–21.

————. *Whitehall and the Wilderness: The Middle West in British Colonial Policy, 1760–1775.*

Spector, Margaret M. *The American Department of British Government, 1768–1782.* Columbia University Studies in History, Economics and Public Law, no. 466. New York, 1940.

Stanley, George F. S. "The Six Nations and the American Revolution." *Ontario History* 56 (1964): 217–32.

Stanlis, Peter J. "The Basis of Burke's Political Conservatism." *Modern Age* 5 (1960–61): 263–711.

————. "Burke's *Annual Register* and American History." *Burke Newsletter* 4, no. 2 (1962–63): 179.

Steele, I. K. "Time, Communications and Society: The English Atlantic, 1702." *Journal of American Studies* 8 (1974): 1–21.

Stephenson, O. W. "The Supply of Gunpowder in 1776." *American Historical Review* 30 (1925–26): 271–81.

Stinchcombe, William C. *The American Revolution and the French Alliance.* New York, 1969.

Stirling, A. M. W. *Coke of Norfolk and His Friends.* 2 vols. London, 1908.

Stone, William L. *Border Wars of the American Revolution.* 2 vols. New York, 1900.

The Annual Register—Selected Bibliography

Strauss, Ralph. *Robert Dodsley*. London, 1910.

Sutherland, Lucy S. *The City of London and the Opposition to Government 1768–1774*. The Creighton Lecture 1958. London, 1959.

————. *The East India Company in Eighteenth-Century Politics*. Oxford, 1952.

————. "Edmund Burke and the First Rockingham Ministry." *English Historical Review* 48 (1932): 46–72.

Swiggett, Howard. *War Out of Niagara: Walter Butler and the Tory Rangers*. New York, 1933.

Sydnor, Charles S. *Political Leadership in Eighteenth Century Virginia*. Oxford, 1951.

Syrett, D. *Shipping and the American War, 1775–83: A Study of British Transport Organisation*. London, 1970.

Tate, Thad W. "The Coming of the Revolution in Virginia: Britain's Challenge to Virginia's Ruling Class, 1763–1776." *William and Mary Quarterly* 3rd ser. 19 (1962): 323–43.

Thayer, Theodore. *Nathaniel Greene: Strategist of the American Revolution*. New York, 1960.

————. *Pennsylvania Politics and the Growth of Democracy 1740–1776*. Harrisburg, Pa., 1933.

Thomas, P. D. G. "The Beginning of Parliamentary Reporting in Newspapers, 1768–1774." *English Historical Review* 74 (1959): 623–36.

Thomas, R. P. "The Sugar Colonies of the Old Empire: Profit or Loss for Great Britain?" *Economic History Review* 21 (1968): 30–45.

Thompson, Mark E. "The Ward-Hopkins Controversy and the American Revolution in Rhode Island: An Interpretation." *William and Mary Quarterly* 3rd ser. 16 (1959): 363–75.

Tunstall, Brian. *William Pitt, Earl of Chatham*. London, 1938.

Ubbelohde, Carl. *The Vice-Admiralty Courts and the American Revolution*. Chapel Hill, N.C., 1960.

Valentine, Alan. *Lord George Germain*. Oxford, 1962.

Van Alstyne, Richard. *Empire and Independence: The International History of the American Revolution*. New York, 1965.

———— . "Great Britain, the War for Independence and the 'Gathering Storm' In Europe, 1775–1778." *Huntington Library Quarterly* 27 (1963–64): 311–46.

Van Doran, Carl. *Benjamin Franklin.* New York, 1938.

———— . *Mutiny in January: The Story of a Crisis in the Continental Army Now for the First Time Fully Told from Many Hitherto Unknown or Neglected Sources, Both American and British.* New York, 1943.

———— . *Secret History of the American Revolution: An Account of the Conspiracies of Benedict Arnold and Numerous Others Drawn from the Secret Service Papers of the British Headquarters in North America Now for the First Time Examined and Made Public.* New York, 1941.

Van Every, Dale. *A Company of Heroes: The American Frontier 1775–1783.* New York, 1962.

Van Tyne, Claude H. *Loyalists in the American Revolution.* New York, 1902.

Wallace, Willard M. *Appeal to Arms: A Military History of the American Revolution.* New York, 1951.

Walsh, Richard. *Charleston's Sons of Liberty: A Study of the Artisans, 1763–1789.* Columbia, S.C., 1959.

Ward, Christopher. *The War of the Revolution.* Edited and compiled by J. R. Alden. 2 vols. New York, 1952.

Watson, D. H. "Barlow Trecothick." *Bulletin of the British Association for American Studies* n.s. no. 1 (September 1960): 36–47; n.s. no. 2 (March 1961): 29–39.

———— . "The Rockingham Whigs and the Townshend Duties." *English Historical Review* 84 (1969): 561–65.

Watson, J. Steven. "Parliamentary Procedure as a Key to the Understanding of Eighteenth Century Politics." *Burke Newsletter* 3 (1962): 107–29.

———— . *The Reign of George III, 1760–1815.* London, 1960.

Weir, Robert M. "North Carolina's Reaction to the Currency Act of 1764." *North Carolina Historical Review* 40 (1963): 183–99.

Western, John R. *The English Militia in the Eighteenth Century: The Story of a Political Issue, 1660–1802.* London and Toronto, 1965.

Wickwire, Franklin B. *British Subministers and Colonial America 1763–1783.* Princeton, N.J., 1966.

Wickwire, Franklin B., and Wickwire, Mary. *Cornwallis: The American Adventure*. New York, 1970.

Willcox, W. B. "The British Road to Yorktown." *American Historical Review* 52 (1946): 1–35.

_____ . "British Strategy in America, 1778." *Journal of Modern History* 19 (1947): 97–121.

_____ . *Portrait of a General: Sir Henry Clinton in the War of Independence*. New York, 1964.

_____ . "Rhode Island in British Strategy, 1780–1781." *Journal of Modern History* 17, pt. 4 (1945): 304–31.

_____ . "Too Many Cooks: British Planning before Saratoga." *Journal of British Studies* 2 (1962): 59–90.

Wish, Harvey. *The American Historian*. New York, 1960.

Wood, Gordon S. *The Creation of the American Republic*. Chapel Hill, N.C., 1969.

Wright, Esmond. *Fabric of Freedom, 1763–1800*. New York, 1961.

Wright, Esmond, ed. *A Tug of Loyalties: Anglo-American Relations, 1765–85*. Institute of United States Studies Monographs, 2. London, 1974.

Young, Henry J. "Agrarian Reactions and the Stamp Act in Pennsylvania." *Pennsylvania History* 34 (1967): 250–30.

Zobel, Hiller B. *The Boston Massacre*. New York, 1970.

General Introduction

The only contemporary account of the American Revolution providing a detailed record of the progress of the conflict between Britain and America, year by year as it developed, is in the English periodical the *Annual Register*. This unique historical source provides a British view of those events in extensive and generally accurate detail; it also reveals the role played by American affairs in British politics, particularly the way in which the parliamentary opposition took up the cause of America during the period 1765 to 1782. The *Register* was edited throughout this period by men connected with a section of that opposition—the Rockingham Whigs —and that inevitably suggests the possibility of bias in its reporting. However, the popularity of the *Register* with the reading public is demonstrable, and therefore its basically consistent, critical attitude toward the American policies of Lord North's government raises a question about public support for these policies outside Parliament.

The value of the *Register* as an historical source was recognised shortly after its first publication in 1759. Oliver Goldsmith made extensive (and unacknowledged) use of it for his *History of England*[1] as early as 1764, and most of the early histories of the Seven Years War relied exclusively on the *Register*'s first six volumes. It was also of course used by the first historians of the American Revolution, but the striking feature of these accounts, written before 1800 and long regarded as original sources, is their shameless plagiarism of the *Annual Register*. This plagiarism was first exposed by Orin G. Libby in 1899 and is apparently still being studied.

Libby showed that the hitherto valued histories of the revolution by William Gordon and David Ramsay, as well as several other accounts written between 1779 and 1781, were all copied more or less closely from the *Register*.[2] Later, it was revealed that John Marshall's biography of Washington and Thomas Anburey's *Travels through the Interior Parts of America* 'owed much to the same unacknowledged source. More recently Charles Stedman's history of the war was similarly exposed.[3] (Even this does not exhaust the entire list of plagiarists. A century after these accounts, William Lecky's much respected *The His-*

tory of England in the Eighteenth Century borrowed from the *Register* at length and without attribution.)[4]

The discovery that so many contemporary sources for the revolution period largely plagiarised the *Register* simply means, as Stedman's critic remarks, that "... the *Annual Register* emerges as a source of the first importance." At the beginning of this century, Libby asked (somewhat prematurely in view of later investigations), "Will it not be profitable, now that the last of the contemporary historians yields his place of authority, to compile from the *Annual Register* a history of the American Revolution which shall be known for what it is under its true colours."[5] This work is a belated attempt to produce precisely such a history.

The *Annual Register* began with an agreement dated 24 April 1758 between London publishers Robert and James Dodsley and Edmund Burke for the latter to "... write collect & compile from such materials as may arise a work entitled the Annual register or Retrospections on men & things for the year 1758...." The agreement indicates this was intended to be the first of a series of annual volumes; the work was to be printed in octavo, making between thirty and thirty-four sheets (240 to 272 pages) and was to be ready for publication on Lady Day of the new year (25 March). Burke was to be paid £100, in two equal instalments, for his services, and the agreement was to be terminable on three months' notice by either side.[6]

This agreement presumably formalised the results of discussion which had already established format and method of presentation, since it refers to this aspect of the work as "... according to a plan agreed upon." The preface for the first volume specified what the *Register* intended to offer its readers:

Not confined to a monthly publication we have an opportunity of examining with care the products of the year, and of selecting what may appear most particularly deserving of notice; we are better able to rank the several kinds under their proper heads, at least with as much exactness as the nature of a miscellany will permit.[7]

The original plan, as revealed in the first volume, involved eight sections: "History of the Present [Seven Years] War"; a chronicle, or list of news items, domestic and foreign, listed month by month; a selection of state papers which would "... serve to illustrate and confirm the facts in the historical part...";[8] "Characters" (biographical notes, essays, and extracts on figures past and present); "Extraordinary Adventures"; "Literary and Miscellaneous essays"; poetry; and a book review section. As the editor explains: "Endeavouring to be as extensively useful as possible, we aimed at uniting the plan of the Magazines with that of the Reviews."[9] In 1762, the arrangement was modified—"Extraordinary Adventures" were dropped and three new sections added: "Natural History" (essays actually covering the broad field of scientific interest); "Projects" (short essays dealing with new and useful processes); and "Antiquities." Another new section, "Appendix to the Chronicle," in which news items were illustrated by documents which could not properly be included among state papers, was added in 1763.

After 1762, with the end of the war, the historical section was renamed "History of Europe," and the editor expressed worry about a future deficiency of material. The 1763 preface however prophetically noted:

In reality, Europe may be said to be perfectly quiet; but the extent of the commercial empire of Great Britain is such, and it engages her in such a vast variety of difficult connections, that it is almost impossible for any considerable length of time to pass over, without producing an abundance of events of a very interesting nature.[10]

Ironically, the 1764 preface in referring to the general warrants issue judiciously praised occasional challenges to the state, and concluded that "there are times when the spirit of liberty must owe something to the spirit of faction."[11] During the next two decades, accounts of imperial crisis eventually dominated a vastly extended historical section as the connection between faction and liberty became tragically complex, and the crisis became civil war.

The format that had emerged by 1763 remained basically unchanged until exactly a century later. The *Annual Register* acquired a wide readership, and its success as a publishing venture was assured. That success is easily understood when the *Register* is viewed in the context of eighteenth-century journalism. There was an extraordinarily rapid expansion of the reading public, and more people sought both news (i.e., reports of current, particularly political, affairs and matters of general interest) and general knowledge (popular views of history, philosophy, science, and literature). A vast increase in the number of newspapers and periodicals met the demand, beginning in the first decade of the century—though their mortality rate was high.[12]

London had three daily newspapers in 1724, seven published three times per week, and six weeklies.[13] The tri-weeklies (often titled "Posts," since they were published on Tuesday, Thursday, and Saturday to coincide with the despatch of mail from the London General Post Office) were widely read, together with the weeklies, in the provinces. The 1730s saw the emergence of a number of new papers (often titled "Advertisers") which aimed to supplement sales profits by advertisement revenue. By 1784, London had eight dailies (five "Advertisers" and three papers concentrating on news—the *London Chronicle*, the *Morning Post*, and the *Morning Herald* and nine tri-weeklies (the most important was probably the *London Evening Post*).[14] As early as 1758, Dr. Johnson noted that the provincial paper was well established and ". . . almost every large town has its weekly historian."[15]

Newspaper growth was parallelled by that of periodicals. The literary essay was established early by the *Spectator* and the *Tatler*. The first really successful magazine, providing a selection of the best writing in the London press each month, was Edward Cave's *Gentleman's Magazine*, founded in 1731. It had a circulation of 10,000 by 1739, and provoked over sixty imitators (most short-lived) by 1780. By mid-century, reviews emerged to bring the public rapidly into contact with current literature. The earliest success was Griffith's *Monthly Review*, first published in 1749, and it was soon rivalled by Smollett's *Critical Review* from 1756. The rapidly increasing public call for works of general knowledge is evidenced by the success of Chambers's *Cyclopaedia*, first published in 1728, fifth edition by 1746; the popular science of John Hill; and above all, the histories of Smollett, Hume, Robertson, and Gibbon.[16]

Government viewed the rise of the Fourth Estate with disfavour because matters of state were treated as though they were matters of concern to the public at large and, more important, because the press rapidly became a vehicle for attacks by the Opposition. The Government therefore devised ways to control the press. The stamp tax, when added to taxes on paper and advertisements in 1712, reduced newspaper profits to the point where peripheral journals went out of business and the remainder were financially precarious. The stamp and advertisement taxes were increased in 1757, and a graduated stamp tax (1773), based on the size of the paper, maintained the pressure. A direct result of newspapers' financial instability was to make them susceptible to subsidisation, so that concealed subsidies involving a complex organisation of ministerial writers and an unofficial Government press were matched by an equivalent Opposition press. The system of direct ministerial subsidisation reached a peak in Sir Robert Walpole's era, declined by the 1760s, and was revived in 1782. Papers could always depend heavily on the support of politicians and factions.[17] Inevitably, the term journalist was equated with hackwriter at best and libeller at worst; political reporting was always assumed to be partisan.

The core of political news was the reporting of parliamentary debates, though Parliament forbad such reporting under standing orders and sporadically attempted to enforce the ban. Magazines began reporting debates in summary form during parliamentary recesses, but in 1738, the House of Commons ruled publication of debates out of session a breach of privilege. In 1747, the House of Lords ordered the *Gentleman's Magazine* and *London Magazine* to cease publication of debates entirely. The spate of new journals which appeared in the late 1750s created so much competition, however, that the tri-weeklies and dailies began reporting current debates to attract readers. The House of Commons reacted by reprimanding four printers in 1760 and by holding a printer

in custody in 1761; the House of Lords fined three printers in 1765 and one in 1768. By 1770, most newspapers were reporting debates despite the ban (though not comprehensively and often by pirating each other's material), and the magazines were producing summaries of the newspapers' reports each month.

The result was the debacle of 1771. The House of Commons summoned eight offending printers to the Bar of the House; three printers, aided and abetted by the City of London, defied arrest, and the conflict escalated into a major political struggle. The House committed the Lord Mayor and an alderman to the Tower for compounding a breach of privilege but the City officers became popular heroes as a result, and the papers of the three defiant printers continued publishing debates throughout the crisis. Parliament reaffirmed its privileges but recognised that it had lost the real battle,[18] and made no further move to stop publication of debates. It was still possible however to limit public access to debates, for the Standing Order of 1705 prohibited "strangers" in the House. Thereafter, until 1875, the speaker was obliged to clear the galleries on the motion of a single member, and that procedure was used regularly during debates on American legislation in the 1770s. Note-taking was prohibited until 1783 and had to be done surreptitiously. Reliance on such notes, augmented by memory and hearsay, inevitably resulted in inaccuracy and misrepresentation. Parliament could defend itself against this by invoking prosecution for libel in the House itself, or by petitioning the Crown for a prosecution at common law.[19]

The popular press did not offer comprehensive and accurate reports of parliamentary proceedings until the 1780s, and the significant growth of informed public opinion which exerted regular pressure on Parliament dates from that period. A smaller politically educated public *had* emerged thirty years earlier, but contemporary journalism did not provide accurate and measured summaries of each year's events or appropriate reports of parliamentary debates. The *Annual Register* filled the gap. As an annual publication, the *Register* offered, in its opening section, not news but an essay on contemporary history. It thus avoided attracting the hostility of Parliament for reporting debates, and the time available for completion of each essay permitted research and revision, to ensure accuracy. For the same reason, the *Annual Register* was able to maintain its impartiality, for it offered little attraction to politicians aiming at immediate political impact through the popular press and because the *Register* also avoided the higher stamp tax rates borne by newspapers it was thus less amenable to subsidisation. The reputation it established within a short time of its first publication (1759) ensured the *Register* a steadily increasing popularity; some of the early volumes were published in several editions while in later years, the *Annual Register* sold well outside Britain.[20]

There is much information about the *Annual Register* that remains obscure; for example, the identity of its eighteenth-century editors is not clear. Like many of their contemporaries, the editors of the *Register* remained anonymous largely because of the stigma attached to journalism. The borderline between a man of letters and a journalist was shadowy (Dr. Johnson wrote for the periodicals), but it was also real. Horace Walpole paid Burke no compliment when he noted in 1766 that "his best revenue had arisen from writing for booksellers."[21]

Edmund Burke's editorship of the *Annual Register* is clearly established up to 1764 by receipts for his £100 annual payment from Dodsley, and other evidence.[22] Some historians maintain that Burke gave up the main editing work sometime around 1765 or 1766, when he became secretary to the Marquis of Rockingham and entered Parliament. Thomas English is the next person known to have been paid for work on the *Register*. Receipts for his payment, first £140, later £150 per annum, exist for the period 1766 to 1791.[23] English was probably a fellow Irishman, certainly a friend, and later a neighbour of Burke,[24] his obituary in the May 1798 *Gentleman's Magazine* stressed English's devotion to Burke.[25] As part of the campaign in 1795 to defend the *Annual Register* published by Rivington as the legitimate successor to Dodsley's (as opposed to the rival published by Otridge from 1791) English had declared: "I have conducted the Annual Register ever since the year 1765 down to the present moment, for some time entirely by myself; but from a period prior to [1780] . . . with the aid of occasional assistance."[26] The identity of those assistants is not readily established. The first may have been John Campbell, 1773 to 1774. Campbell was a respected minor writer, some of whose works had been published by Dodsley; he died in 1775. Dr. Walker King may have worked on the *Register* from 1775, and it can be proved that he did so in the 1780s. Walker King and his brothers were disciples of Burke and Walker King was politically associated with the Rockingham Whigs and became Bishop of Rochester in 1809. Later collaborators, during the late 1780s and early 1790s, probably included Walker King's brother John, Richard Lawrence, and certainly Richard's brother French Lawrence.[27]

Most of this is not a matter of controversy. But there is a difference of opinion concerning the role played by Edmund Burke after about 1766. Bertram D. Sarason contends that Thomas English was (as English stated in 1795) the principal editor, occasionally assisted by others, from 1765 to 1791. Burke simply retired from the editorship in 1765.[28] Thomas W. Copeland, however, argues that Burke remained the "principal conductor" of the *Register* from its inception in 1758 to 1789, when he retired from the post, and that Burke continued to exert some influence until his death in 1797. Copeland stresses that "... every person we *know* to have been employed by Dodsley on the *Register* can be fairly described as a close friend or professed disciple of Burke," thus it was both easy and natural for Burke to retain controlling influence over editorial policy.[29] Donald C. Bryant agrees with Sarason that Thomas English became principal editor in 1765 or 1766, and he accepts part of Copeland's argument. At least, Bryant concurs that Burke maintained a close connection with the *Register* until his death by writing many of the book reviews and prefaces, while English and the other assistants wrote the historical section.[30]

All this, as Copeland himself says, is very much a question of interpreting the evidence, which is fragmentary, often indirect, and rarely explicit. Burke may have found the burden of compiling the *Register* more than he could carry alone, once his political career began. However, the material provided by the publishers and the range of information produced through writing the historical section would have been useful to a man aiming to make his mark in Parliament through thoroughly prepared and well-informed speeches. The *Register* might well have provided Burke a "creative outlet,"[31] if he was uncertain whether he had wholly abandoned a

literary for a political career.[32] But if English and the other assistants compiled the historical section, the most useful part of the *Register*, from this point of view, was not written by Burke, though it may well have been revised by him. Copeland indeed argues that the increased size of the historical article in 1769 indicates the new hand of English, and the increase in 1775 the hand of Walker King.[33] Copeland draws attention to the coincidence of Burke's ill health in 1765 and 1774, and the appointment of English and possibly Walker King, and he also suggests that delays in the publication of the *Register* were "a barometer of pressure" in Burke's life.[34]

These delays increased steadily beginning in 1775; the 1783 volume was not published until December 1785. From 1775, the editor regularly blamed delays on the growth in the number of significant events, "... the abundance of matter which is now necessarily discussed."[35] The 1780 preface provided a more detailed explanation. The first delay was caused by a "long and dangerous illness," which under ordinary circumstances would have made recovering lost ground difficult, given the nature of the *Register*'s composition. An "unexpected and extraordinary accession of business" ensued and continued, so that the "original difficulty was not only rendered insurmountable, but the evil itself became of necessity greater."[36] These reasons may be conceded, but the much-enlarged, historical articles—particularly after 1777—were extremely detailed in contrast to the concise summaries of earlier years and this therefore suggests a different hand at work in the preparation.[37]

The controversy would merely be a matter of minor interest were it not for the significance of the *Annual Register* as an historical source, and specifically for the period of the American Revolution. The *assumption* that Burke was closely connected with the *Register* throughout this period raises queries about the objectivity of its treatment of the American conflict, in view of the well-defined views of Burke and the Rockingham Whigs on that issue. As one historian writes:

> *The Annual Register* . . . was not, strictly speaking, a Rockinghamite production. . . . But a perusal of the historical article in each issue during these years [1760 to 1782] shows that the writer generally took a Rockinghamite view of national and world events. It is impossible to judge the effect of these articles upon contemporary opinion, but easy to see why the party received such favourable treatment from historians who regarded the *Register* as unbiased.[38]

The question of possible bias in the writing of the historical section will remain, like that of the editorship with which it is so closely associated, a matter of interpretation. In 1763, the editor wrote:

> As to our domestic dissensions, we have stated as fairly as we could the points in contest between parties. Little heated ourselves, we have not endeavoured to heat others. We have carefully adhered to that neutrality, which, however blameable in an advocate, is necessary in an historian, and without which he will not represent an image of things, but his own passions.[39]

Whether this high-minded impartiality was constantly practised is a matter of judging the evidence. For example, in 1766 the dismissed Rockingham ministry is awarded a minor eulogy (and the entire text of Burke's *Short Account of a Late Short Administration* is reprinted among the miscellaneous essays). Yet in the previous year, despite Burke's dislike of George Grenville and the Rockinghams' opposition to the bulk of the Grenville ministry's measures, the *Register* generously assessed that ministry's merits. The reporting of parliamentary debates rarely overem-

phasises the Opposition's arguments—indeed, the relatively partisan account of the Stamp Act debates in the 1765 volume is unusual. Comment on the apparent invincibility of North's majority in the 1770s clearly echoes the despair of the Rockinghams, but the *Register* also sharply criticises the debilitating effects of Opposition disunity, and it impartially discusses the merits and demerits of the Rockingham "secession" from Parliament (1776–1777). Burke's major speeches were invariably given close attention, but usually not more than their real importance warrants.[40]

The *Register*'s war reporting from 1776 to 1782 was impartial, with few exceptions. Indeed, the *Register* reported military and naval engagements from the role of spectator-commentator, distributing praise and blame with an even hand to both sides. Nor did the *Register* convey obvious propaganda. The atrocity stories circulated after Lexington and Concord were dismissed with the implicit assumption that truth was the first casualty. American propaganda however was given credence in two areas, both matters of specific concern to Burke and the Rockinghams. The Opposition violently attacked the hiring of German mercenaries for a variety of reasons, including fear of a military power independent of Parliament. The reports of alleged brutality on the part of Hessians and Brunswickers in America were more readily believed than accusations against British troops.[41] The Opposition also expressed outrage at the use of Indians and the deliberate employment of redskin barbarity as an ingredient of military policy. American versions of torture and massacre practised by Tory-Loyalists and their Indian allies in upstate New York and on the "dark and bloody ground" of the Ohio Valley were accepted by the *Register* (most notably in the case of the

1778 Wyoming Valley massacre).[42] Apart from these instances, the *Register*'s impartiality was weakened only by the entry of France into the war, which led to an occasional indulgence of British prejudice against the traditional enemy.

Taken as a whole, the *Register*'s historical articles were accurate and free of blatant bias. However, it is difficult to avoid the conclusion that the *Register* projected a view of the conflict between Britain and America which was consistently aligned with that of Burke and the Rockinghams. The *Register*'s reports of debates generally presented the ministerial position fairly and clearly, but the overall tenor of the commentary was critical of every government's American policy save that of the two Rockingham administrations. Its treatment of the development of the conflict with the colonies implicitly defended the American position. From 1765 to 1775, American reaction to British policy was condemned when it involved disorder and violence; nonetheless, it was presented as a natural and inevitable response of Englishmen to the erosion of their rights under the constitution. The solemn preface to the 1775 volume poignantly comments on the difficulties of reporting a civil war, but stresses the division of public opinion in Britain. Actually, the *Register* overestimated opposition to policies of coercion in 1774 and to punitive military action in 1775. It was forced to return to regular expressions of regret over the steady support for the Government's prosecution of the war up to 1780–1781. Comment also regularly tended to overestimate the unity within and between the colonies, most obviously in 1767–1768 and 1774–1776, much in line with the Opposition's contention that coercion had merely united Americans in disaffection. Throughout the war, the *Register* em-

phasised (and indeed exaggerated) American patriotism and sustained a picture of popular heroic resistance to British military power.

The effect of the *Register*'s attitude toward the conflict on historians writing in the first century following the revolution was that

> . . . [Burke's] Whig viewpoint satisfied the patriotic and partisan feelings of the American historians who took over his ideas and even his language. Burke's interpretation of the American Revolution, and of the character of George III and his Tory ministers, became generally standard among American historians of the nineteenth century.[43]

American historiography however is characterised by periodic shifts of viewpoint and relatively complete replacements of one approach and interpretation by another. American historians tend to believe (and their beliefs are often well founded) that the great issues in American politics are permanent and thus need to be periodically reexamined in the light of new evidence and as the issues themselves reemerge. The "patriotic and partisan" historians of the nineteenth century saw themselves as the architects of national unity, charged with instructing the nation in its heritage. Accordingly, they expressed the Anglo-American struggle in terms of ideology and principles—specifically, political liberty versus an attempted despotism. These historians ultimately succumbed to a new school which emerged with Herbert Osgood and George Louis Beer and finally dominated the field with Charles Andrews, Claude van Tyne, Arthur Schlesinger, Sr., and Carl Becker. The new interpretation centred on the clash of great impersonal economic forces which drove Britain and America apart, and on a seething social and political conflict in America. As Harvey Wish notes, ". . . the standard Whig interpretation of the Revolution held by Burke and his imitators had almost disappeared among scholars"[44] by the 1920s. This new orthodoxy was first challenged by consensus historians during the Cold War era, and then both their revisions and the remnants of the new orthodoxy were nibbled to death by fresh critical attacks from John Carey, Jackson T. Main, J. P. Greene, and Jack Pole. A new and unifying interpretation was begun in the 1950s by Charles Ritcheson and Edward Morgan, and was developed by Bernard Bailyn, Richard Buel, and Gordon S. Wood. Ironically, the new approach brought the process of reinterpretation of the revolution full circle, for once more the conflict between Britain and America was seen as a clash of rival political ideologies over issues of principle. Of course, the "new idealists" see more complexity than did the nineteenth-century historians, and they emphasise different aspects of the issue. However, the currently fashionable interpretation of the era has more in common with the views of Burke and the version of events presented in the *Annual Register* than any treatment since the mid-nineteenth century.

It is logical to speculate whether the *Register*'s undoubted popularity was clearly connected to its Rockingham views. It is impossible to measure precisely its influence, but there are good reasons to suppose it did not play a decisive role in the formation of public opinion. First, the *Register*'s generally measured tone diffused the impact of its Rockingham attitude. The really effective writings of the period are well-argued polemics, like those of Israel Mauduit and Thomas Paine.[45] Second, the *Register* lacked the immediate impact needed to become a decisive opinion-former. As the delays in publication grew, the *Register* dealt less and less in "news,"

so it may have had an incremental effect at most, helping to confirm views already in the process of change for other reasons.

It is also impossible to establish with certainty that the *Register*'s disapproval of the Government's policies toward America reflected a section of public opinion, not least because it is also far from clear how many Britons disapproved of those policies. The views of many prominent Englishmen who opposed coercion and the war were well known; the attitudes of Chatham, Burke, Fox, and others were public knowledge. Amherst and Keppel refused to command forces against the Americans; the Earl of Effingham, Lord Pitt, and Peregrine Bertie, M.P. for Oxford, resigned their commissions rather than serve in a civil war. But did that solid majority which supported North for so long truly represent the political nation at large? Few men would perhaps have gone as far as Thomas Coke, who declared in 1821: "Every night during the American War I did drink to the health of General Washington as the greatest man on earth."[46] Many people probably shared the view expressed by Horace Walpole in 1775: "Our stake is deep . . . yet it is that kind of war, in which even victory may ruin us"[47] and by 1777, many Britons recognised that American ". . . alienation from this country is incredible and universal; so that instead of obtaining a revenue thence, the pretence of the war, the conquest would only entail boundless expense to preserve."[48] The Rockinghams' despair over their failure to secure extraparliamentary support for their attacks on the Government suggests that the American issue alone was never sufficient to create politically significant public pressure—in contrast to their involvement in the economical reform movement. In sum, it is likely that the *Register*'s Rockingham outlook was mostly incidental to its popularity, which was essentially based on its copious and accurate reporting and the wide range of material it presented in each volume.

The value of the *Register* as a contemporary record of events is clear, but just as the identity of the editors remains controversial, so it is not at all certain what sources the editors used to construct each of the sections. Much of each volume was simply a matter of compilation. The agreement between the Dodsleys and Burke mentions that the publishers will, on behalf of the editor, "... find him all Books & Pamphlets necessary for his carrying on the said work."[49] But what exactly these "books & pamphlets" were, and how the comprehensive and authoritative historical section was composed, are largely matters of speculation.

Up to 1775, we may reasonably assume that Burke's connections, through the Rockingham group, with the merchant element trading with America, his work as agent for New York from December 1770, and his many American contacts all provided him with a fund of information on American affairs which would have been available for the *Register*.[50] After 1775, the historical section contains much less information on the progress of American politics in those colonies with established revolutionary governments. The *Register*'s reports of the proceedings of the Continental Congress were apparently derived almost entirely from the published resolutions of the Congress, and where they are not are in error.[51] The war inevitably made details of domestic American politics more difficult to acquire as the peacetime channels of communication became constricted. But the *Register* also clearly considered these politics less relevant, since the war induced a more anglocentric viewpoint. Therefore, the reader will not find

information in the *Register* on the establishment of the new state governments, the progress toward confederation or the problems besetting the Congress. The appalling difficulties which faced Washington in supplying and paying the Continental Army, and the depreciation of state and continental currency, received serious attention only in the 1781 volume.

Instead, the reader will find detailed accounts of military campaigns, often derived from the reports of British commanders and not infrequently compared with those of the American commanders which appeared in the transatlantic press. In the fashion of the time, comment in these accounts tended to treat the honour of victory and the courage of the troops rather than to analyse strategy or tactics. Even so, transparent incompetence, as in the American defeat on Long Island in 1776, was castigated. On the other hand, the accounts include perceptive judgements regarding the results of campaigns fought to achieve dubious objectives; for example, the capture of Philadelphia in 1776 was judged as having the sole value of providing comfortable winter quarters for the British army.

The *Register* is a useful supplement to other available reports of parliamentary debates from 1765 to 1783. It is particularly valuable on those occasions when alternative reports of debates in closed session are few or incomplete (for example, in 1765 and 1774). Initially, the speakers were not identified by name in order to avoid action for libel,[52] but from 1774 some Opposition speakers are regularly named, ministers are identified indirectly by office and other M.P.'s by a distinguishing phrase. Finally, it should be noted that the *Register* reports the parliamentary year from the beginning of the pre-Christmas session to the following summer recess, so that, for example, the 1766 volume reports debates from December 1765 to June 1766 and the 1767 volume from November 1766 to June 1767. and so on.

The *Register* excluded many matters simply because they could not be public knowledge. The inner workings of the Cabinet, interministerial discussion, the role of the King, and all the detailed origins of policy were naturally inaccessible, and even if some of these matters had been accessible, as during the Rockingham administrations, it would have been improper to print them. The *Register* also chose not to deal in rumour when speculating on the motivating factors behind events; though its speculations are often sound, as on North's reasons for calling the 1774 general election. Occasionally, rumour was dismissed even though based on facts, as in 1781, when official backing for the establishment of the Board of Associated Loyalists was denied. In this case, the *Register* could know nothing of ministerial instructions to army and navy commanders unless the orders were placed before Parliament or reported in the press, as were Germain's orders to Burgoyne in 1777.

The *Register*'s account of each year's ·events was also limited by time and communication lags.[53] News of American affairs might reach London within two months, and was then added to the materials the editor was compiling for the annual volume. This usually meant that events which occurred after the late summer were discussed in the historical section of the next year's volume, though some documentary items were included in the *Appendix to the Chronicle* and in *State Papers* for the current year. It might be supposed that, what the *Register* lost in topicality it gained in inclusivity as the delays in publication grew longer. The in-

crease of military, naval, and political activity however soon overwhelmed the editor, and ensured that sections of the historical article were regularly devoted to reviewing events not recorded in the previous volume.

In addition to being a valuable contemporary record of events, the *Register*'s historical section provides a necessary sense of perspective in the study of the American Revolution. The nineteen volumes from 1765 to 1783 not only trace the development of the crisis with America and the progress of the war, but also reveal the importance of the war at each stage, for contemporary observers, through the context of the historical section read as a whole. In 1765 and 1766, the Stamp Act crisis takes up about one-third of the text. By 1771, American affairs earned only a paragraph, and received no mention at all in the next two years—but from 1775 to 1779 American affairs entirely dominated the historical article. From 1779, as the impact of the Bourbon intervention was felt, the *Register* relegated America to the sidelines where it strategically belonged, the single exception being 1781, the year of Yorktown and disaster. The historical article was recording the progress of the third of the eighteenth-century struggles between Britain and France, and described a global war in which Britain's position as a maritime and commercial power was at stake.

An analysis of the volumes through this period clearly shows the part played by America in British domestic politics, and in particular the connection between American issues and the Opposition in Parliament. The Opposition's attacks on the North administration had for years only the Government's handling of the American problem as a means of attracting support. When other issues emerged which provided tactically better points of assault, such as economical reform and India, the intensity of attention on America diminished; that attention increased again only when other issues failed to capture sufficient votes from the independent group to bring down the Government. In this sense, the *Register*'s account of parliamentary affairs unwittingly supports the view that the Opposition used America as a convenient lever to achieve its basic goal—the end of North's ministry and the influence of the Crown which underpinned it.

This work reproduces the *Annual Register*'s account of the Anglo-American conflict as it appears in the volumes from 1765 to 1783 inclusive. The material is selected from the historical article, the *Appendix to the Chronicle*, the *State Papers*, and from the prefaces when they are particularly appropriate. The reader will appreciate that it was not easy to separate the parts of the text dealing with purely American issues, particularly as those issues became a factor in domestic political battles and as the war broadened into a global struggle. The choice of extracts ultimately involved

some arbitrary judgements which doubtless merit some disagreement.

The introductions to each volume-year are intended to place the extracts in the context of their overall historical setting and within the *Register*'s total coverage of events for the year. The scope of this work does not provide answers to many of the intriguing questions about the sources and methodology of the *Register*'s compilation so the editing of the *Register* in this volume is therefore confined to identifying persons, measures, and similar items not clear from the text. Additional commentary is provided where extra information seems called for. References to secondary works will direct the reader to the most relevant account for detailed discussion of the point in question. The dates of publication for each volume are taken from Professor Copeland's carefully calculated list.[54] The original pagination of the extracts is appended; the reader should note that since the *Register* was usually set up by the printer in stages, pagination is not always continuous and the treatment of page numbers varies within each volume.

1. R. W. Seitz, "Goldsmith and the *Annual Register*," *Modern Philosophy*, 1933–34, vol. 31, pp. 183–94.
2. Orin G. Libby, "A Critical Examination of William Gordon's History of the American Revolution," *Annual Report of the American Historical Association*, 1, 1899, pp. 367–88; "Ramsay as a Plagiarist," *American Historical Review*, 1902, vol. 7, pp. 697–703; "Some Pseudo Histories of the American Revolution," *Transactions of the Wisconsin Academy of Sciences, Arts and Letters*, 1900, vol. 13, pp. 419–25. The histories analysed are William Gordon, *The History of the Rise, Progress and Establishment of the Independence of the United States of America*, 4 vols. (London, 1788) and 3 vols. (New York, 1789); David Ramsay, *History of the American Revolution*, 2 vols.

(Philadelphia, 1789; London, 1793); the appendix to William Russell, *The History of America*, 2 vols. (London, 1778) by James Murray: *Impartial History of the Present War in America*, 3 vols. (Newcastle upon Tyne, ?1778); and three anonymous accounts: *The History of the War in America between Great Britain and Her Colonies from Its Commencement to the End of the Year 1778*, 2 vols. (Dublin, 1779; London, 1780; Boston, 1781); *An Impartial History of the War in America between Great Britain and Her Colonies from Its Commencement to the End of the Year 1779* (London, 1780); *The History of the Origin, Rise and Progress of the War in America between Great Britain and Her Colonies, from Its Commencement in the Year 1764 to the Time of General Gage's Arrival in Bos-*

ton in 1774 (London, n.d.; Boston, 1780). Libby also notes similar plagiarism in the serial accounts of the revolution and war in the Philadelphia *Columbian Magazine and Monthly Miscellany*, 1790–92, and the South Carolina *Monthly Register*, 1804–05.

3. John Marshall, *The Life of George Washington, Commander in Chief of the American Forces during the War Which Established the Independence of His Country, and First President of the United States*, 5 vols. (London, 1804–07); [Thomas Anburey], *Travels through the Interior Parts of America: In a Series of Letters, by An Officer* (London, 1789). Charles Stedman, *The History of the Rise, Progress and Termination of the American War*, 2 vols. (London, 1794). The works of Anburey and Stedman, particularly, were long regarded as of considerable significance as original sources; their work and that of Marshall is reassessed in William Foran, "John Marshall as Historian," *American Historical Review*, 1937–38, vol. 43, pp. 51–64; W. J. Bell, Jr., "Thomas Anburey's 'Travels through America': A Note on Eighteenth Century Plagiarism," *Papers of the Bibliographical Society of America*, 1943, vol. 37, p. 23–26; R. Kent Newmyer, "Charles Stedman's History of the American War," *American Historical Review*, 1958, vol. 63, pp. 924–34.

4. J. C. Mullen, "Lecky as Plagiarist: The *Annual Register* and the American Revolution," *Studies on Burke and His Time*, 1972, vol. 13, pt. 3, pp. 2193–202.

5. Libby, "Ramsay as a Plagiarist," p. 703.

6. Ralph Strauss, *Robert Dodsley* (London, 1910), pp. 257–58, quoted in Thomas W. Copeland, *Edmund Burke: Six Essays* (London, 1950), p. 96.

7. *Annual Register*, 1758, p. iv. (Hereafter cited as *AR*.)

8. *AR*, 1758, p. vi.

9. Ibid.

10. *AR*, 1763, p. iii.

11. *AR*, 1764, p. iv.

12. The mortality rate of eighteenth-century newspapers and periodicals is easily checked in *Tercentenary Handlist of English and Welsh Newspapers, Magazines and Reviews* (London, 1920).

13. A. S. Collins, "The Growth of the Reading Public during the Eighteenth Century," *Review of English Studies*, 1920, vol. 2, pp. 284–94, 428–38.

14. *The History of the Times*, vol. 1: *'The Thunderer' in the Making, 1785–1841* (London, 1935), ch. 2.

15. *The Idler*, no. 30.

16. Collins, "The Growth of the Reading Public."

17. F. S. Siebert, *Freedom of the Press in England 1476–1776: The Rise and Decline of Government Control* (Urbana, Ill. 1965), chs. 15, 16. A good example of a politician's support for a particularly virulent paper is Earl Temple's backing of the *North Briton*. See Robert R. Rea, *The English Press in Politics 1760–1774* (Lincoln, Neb., 1963), p. 30.

18. As the *Annual Register* stated: ". . . the House had been drawn to show a disposition to the use of the strongest measures in support of these privileges; but . . . all their exertion had tended only to lower the opinion of their power in the estimation of the world. Their commands were not followed by obedience; their menaces were not accompanied by terror; their punishments being marks of honour with the people, were converted into rewards." *AR*, 1771, p. *70.

19. A. Aspinall, "The Reporting and Publishing of the House of Commons Debates, 1771–1834," in *Essays Presented to Sir Lewis Namier*, ed. Richard Pares and A. J. P. Taylor (London, 1950), pp. 227–57.

20. The volumes for the years 1758–63 appeared in seven, eight, or nine editions. The historical sections were reprinted as histories of the Seven Years War, including one in Dutch and two in German. William B. Todd, *A Bibliography of Edmund Burke* (London, 1964), pp. 44–68 gives full details of all editions of the *Register* for 1758 to 1766. In 1782, the editor notes in the preface:

   The increasing favour we experience from the public at home, and the distinguished reception which our work meets with abroad, not only in those extensive parts of the world where the English language is vernacular, but wherever the general affairs of mankind are so far known as to be interesting, and are admitted to become subjects of free discussion, have fully qualified all our apprehensions, and amply repaid our labours.

21. Horace Walpole, *Memoirs of the Reign of George III*, ed. Denis Le Marchant, Bart. (London, 1845), vol. 2, p. 273.

22. Thomas W. Copeland, "Burke and Dodsley's *Annual Register*," *Publications of the Modern Language Association*, 1939, vol. 54, pp. 223–45; *Edmund Burke: Six Essays*, ch. 3.

23. Ibid.

24. *The Correspondence of Edmund Burke*, ed. Thomas W. Copeland, 9 vols. (Cambridge and Chicago, 1961–70), vol. 2 (ed. Lucy S. Sutherland), p. 314.

25. *Gentleman's Magazine*, 1798, vol. 68, pt. 2, pp. 448–49.

26. *Gentleman's Magazine*, 1795, vol. 65, pt. 2, pp. 734–35.

27. Thomas W. Copeland, "Edmund Burke's Friends and the *Annual Register*," *Transactions of the Bibliographical Society: The Library*, March 1963, pp. 29–39.

28. Bertram D. Sarason, "Edmund Burke and the Two *Annual Registers*," *Publications of the Modern Language Association*, 1953, vol. 68, pp. 496–508.

29. Copeland, "Edmund Burke's Friends," p. 38.

30. Donald C. Bryant, "Edmund Burke and His Literary Friends," *Washington University Studies, New Series, Language Literature*, no. 9 (St. Louis, 1939); "New Light on Burke," *Quarterly Journal of Speech*, 1953, vol. 39, pp. 351–53.

31. Copeland, *Edmund Burke: Six Essays*, p. 109.

32. Walter D. Love, "Burke's Transition from a Literary to a Political Career," *Burke Newsletter*, 1964–65, vol. 6, no. 2, pp. 376–90.

33. Copeland, *Edmund Burke: Six Essays*, pp. 109–10.

34. Copeland, *Edmund Burke: Six Essays*, p. 116.

35. *AR*, 1776, p. iv.

36. *AR*, 1780, pp. v–vii.

37. This is particularly noticeable in the reporting of parliamentary debates, where the earlier pattern of grouping separately the arguments for and against a motion gives way to a more narrative style.

38. Archibald S. Foord, *His Majesty's Opposition, 1714–1830* (Oxford, 1964), p. 351. This question takes on an extra dimension when the role played by the *Annual Register* in the early histories of the revolution is considered. For example, Harvey Wish writes: "An almost unfailing ingredient in the writing of American history for this era [1780–1810] was the ghost-writing of Edmund Burke, Whig leader of the pro-American faction in Parliament." *The American Historian* (New York, 1960), p. 40.

39. *AR*, 1763, p. iv.

40. Since many of Burke's speeches were published in pamphlet form, the *Register*'s editor would in any event tend to give a more detailed summary when he had an exact text in hand.

41. Some evidence suggests that the Germans had a worse reputation than the British in the early campaigns. However, one sixth of the 30,000-odd Germans who served in America deserted and were presumably absorbed into local populations. Thus, resentment against them could scarcely have been as violent as the propaganda implied.

42. It should be noted that few rival accounts of the frontier war were available in many cases for a considerable period.

43. Peter J. Stanlis, "Burke's *Annual Register* and American History," *Burke Newsletter*, 1962–63, vol. 4, no. 2, p. 179.

44. Wish, *American Historian*, p. 152.

45. Mauduit's pamphlet, *Considerations on the Present German War* (1760), apparently persuaded a significant number of M.P.s that the cost of the Seven Years War was driving Britain into bankruptcy; Paine's *Common Sense* (1776) clearly influenced a large number of Americans to accept the necessity of declaring independence.

46. A. M. W. Stirling, *Coke of Norfolk and His Friends*, 2 vols. (London, 1908), vol. 1, p. 190.

47. Walpole to Horace Mann, 7 May 1775, *The Yale Edition of Horace Walpole's Correspondence*, ed. W. S. Lewis et al., 39 vols. (London and New Haven, 1937–73), vol. 24, p. 98.

48. Walpole to Mann, 1 September 1777, ibid., p. 324.

49. Strauss, *Robert Dodsley*, pp. 257–58, quoted in Copeland, *Edmund Burke: Six Essays*, p. 96.

50. His correspondence, however, provides a relatively small amount of evidence for this assumption. See *The Correspondence of Edmund Burke*, ed. Thomas W. Copeland, vols. 2 (ed. Lucy S. Sutherland), 3 (ed. G. H. Guttridge), and 4 (ed. John A. Woods).

51. As, for example, the adoption of the Articles of Confederation. See "Notes, 1776," n. 97.

52. See "General Introduction," p. 4.

53. See "Introduction, 1775," n. 6.

54. Copeland, *Edmund Burke: Six Essays*, p. 117, n. 37.

Original Pagination of the Extracts

1765, pages: 18]–26]; [33–38]; [49–56];
[263.

1766, pages: [31–[47; [173; [182–194];
216]–[217.

1767, pages: 48].

1768, pages: [67*–*74]; [235–[255; 272]–
[273.

1769, pages: 52*]–[*61; [215; [227–228].

1770, pages: [73*–[77*; *90]–*92]; [211–
[219; 224]–[225; 230]–[231.

1771, pages: [17.

1774, pages: [43–50]; 58]–78]; [201–240];
[271–278].

1775, pages: preface; [1–*142]; [247]–
266]; [267–272].

1776, pages: preface; 1]–[75; 86]–124*];
128*]–140*]; 142*]–184*];
[252]–270].

1777, pages: preface; [13–[25; [31–66];
[113–176*]; [231]–232];
[261–264]; [275]–[281; [289–
[313.

1778, pages: preface; [35–52]; [53–[81;
[82–172*]; [*175]; [*195–

**207]; 210*]–236*]; 264]–
274]; [286–[295; 298]–[301;
304]–305]; [315–334].

1779, pages: preface; [1–[35; 50]–54];
[75–[91; [105–107]; [137–
[153; [179–*198]; *206]–
*214]; [297–312]; [317–318];
[336]–342]; [345–348]; 390]–
[412; 429]–442].

1780, pages: [33–36]; [*207–[*211; 216*]–
[*225; 230*]–234*]; [356–
374]; 384]–[399.

1781, pages: preface; [13–[25; 28]–30];
36]–[97; 118]–136]; 142]–
[145; [149–[156; [251–[261;
[263–266]; 320]–[323.

1782, pages: 126]–[133; 142]–148]; [155–
[157; [167–[175; [177; [190]–
194*]; [281–282]; 296]–[297;
[301–[307; [315–324].

1783, pages: [129–136]; 138]–146]; 148]–
[167; [175; [241]–244]; 262]–
[279; 310]–312]; 339]–342];
346]–350].

1765

Introduction

The *Annual Register* for 1765 is the first volume since the close of the Seven Years War in which Britain's relationship with the empire receives extensive treatment. In part, this was because " . . . Europe seems in general, to wear a much more serene appearance, than from history there is any reason to judge she ever did."[1] An unnewsworthy peace therefore diverted attention to British imperial activity, as the editor earlier predicted it would.[2] Even without a dearth of interesting material from Europe, the development of the clash between Britain and her North American colonies would have commanded attention, for the events of 1765 were an imperial crisis of the first magnitude.

The Seven Years War had doubled Britain's national debt[3] and increased direct and indirect taxation to an unprecedented level; yet the cost of administration and defence of Britain's vast territorial gains at the Peace of Paris in 1763 promised little chance of tax reductions.[4] On the contrary, by 1764 there was a budget deficit, so that the government led by George Grenville, which took office in April 1763, was forced to look for fresh sources of revenue.

1. *AR*, 1765, p. 6].
2. *AR*, 1763, preface.
3. The methods for calculating the debt were complex; the *Register* itself gives the total as £129, 586, 789 10s. O¼d. *AR*, 1764, pp. [169–170].
4. The resentment of the landowning interest, which was powerfully represented in Parliament, against the land tax staying at four shillings in the pound was a factor no government could ignore.

The decision to station ten thousand British troops in America for permanent defence, at an estimated annual cost of £350,000,[5] seemed to suggest an obvious solution: America should contribute revenue to her own defence.

Between May and December 1763, consultations between the Treasury, the Board of Trade, and customs commissioners suggested this might be done by strict enforcement of the Navigation Acts. Dissatisfaction with American evasions of trade regulations had been growing for some time and the recent war had focussed attention on illegal American trade with foreign colonies. New efforts at enforcement had been made since 1761. British duties on colonial trade were, however, generally designed to control and channel the pattern of commerce rather than to produce revenue. On 9 March 1764, Grenville introduced proposals to be embodied in the forty-six articles of the American Revenue Act. The enforcement of that act was to be prosecuted by the Courts of Vice-Admiralty and not by local colonial courts. Central to the Act (which was passed on 17 March by the House of Commons exhausted by debates on the general warrants issue) was effective collection of a reduced rate of duty on foreign (usually French) molasses and sugar imported into America. The legislation tended to ignore the fact that New England's ability to pay for extensive imports of British goods rested in part on the profits of trade in rum made from cheap foreign molasses. The act was a revenue failure and by 1766 it was clear that evasion was rendering it nugatory.

Grenville hinted in his budget speech of 9 March that he was considering extending the stamp tax (operative in England and Wales since 1694) to the colonies. After consultations with colonial agents on 17 May 1764 and again in the first week of February 1765, during which the colonies were offered an opportunity to suggest alternatives, Grenville introduced the stamp bill (on 3 February 1765). The ensuing debate was lengthy and there was some sharp opposition, but the bill was passed by a large majority, who clearly assumed that the right to tax the colonies was an essential attribute of the imperial legislature.

The act received royal assent on 22 March (by a special

5. P. D. G. Thomas, ed., "Parliamentary Diaries of Nathaniel Ryder, 1764–67," *Camden Miscellany*, vol. 23 [Camden 4th ser., vol. 7]: 241–320 (London: Royal Historical Society, 1969), p. 235.

commission because the King was ill) though it was not to become effective until 1 November. Between March and November the imperial crisis erupted. Colonial protests against the American Revenue Act (1764) had been voiced, and petitions from several colonies against the stamp bill were sent to Parliament. On 29 May, a list of resolutions was prepared in the Virginia House of Burgesses which claimed that taxation of Americans by Parliament denied their right as British subjects to be taxed by their own representative assembly. Versions of these resolutions were printed in the major newspapers of most of the colonies. On 6 June (before the Virginia resolutions were published) the Massachusetts Assembly called for a congress of colonial delegates to frame a petition to the Crown for relief from the Stamp Act. This congress finally met in October, framed a set of declarations asserting American rights under the constitution, and forwarded rather more moderate petitions to the King and Parliament.

Protests had become violent before the petitions were sent. Rioting mobs in Boston on 14–15 and 26 August, and in Newport, Rhode Island, on 27–29 August, destroyed the houses of prominent locals who had supported the Stamp Act and forced government-appointed stamp distributors to resign. These mobs were led by artisans and shopkeepers, but they were probably promoted by merchants and encouraged by radicals. No serious attempt was made in either colony to punish the rioters. Following the Newport riot, the Rhode Island Assembly passed six resolves declaring any act of Parliament imposing internal taxation to be invalid in the colony. Between September and December, several other colonies produced similar resolutions, indicating a clear unanimity of American opinion.

Unanimity also emerged at another level. A semisecret paramilitary society calling itself the Sons of Liberty originated in the radical eastern counties of otherwise conservative Connecticut.[6] The society rapidly grew into an intercolonial network which forced the resignation of stamp distributors and blocked the distribution of stamps and stamped paper. By 1 November, the Sons of Liberty had effectively nullified the Stamp Act, and this poten-

6. Their title is almost certainly taken from a phrase in Colonel Isaac Barré's second speech in the debate on the stamp bill. See Jared Ingersoll to Governor Thomas Fitch, 11 February 1765, in E. S. Morgan, *Prologue to Revolution: Sources and Documents on the Stamp Act Crisis, 1764–1766* (Chapel Hill: N.C., 1959), p. 32.

tially revolutionary element then attempted (with varying success) to force commercial and legal activity to continue in defiance of the act.

The ministers and the majority of Parliament entirely underestimated American reaction to the Stamp Act because they failed to realise the fundamental division of opinion between Britain and the colonies on the nature of the imperial constitution. The parliamentary majority thought it necessary to distribute more fairly the costs of empire, which were borne almost entirely by Britain, in the interests of the whole, through the constitutional authority of Parliament. The Americans interpreted the constitution as a guarantee that no British subject could be taxed without his consent. They believed that such consent could only be expressed through their own representative assemblies, and that no British financial problem justified parliamentary taxation of the colonies, which they considered an act of tyranny.

The *Register*'s treatment of the origins and growth of the Stamp Act crisis reveals its extensive sources of information and its editor's sharp perception of the key issues. The account, nonetheless, is partial; some material was compressed and omitted, and therefore the account is not comprehensive. It also shows some signs of deliberately partisan reporting.

The historical section for 1765 consists of eleven chapters, fifty-six pages in all, of which twenty-one are devoted to the conflict between Britain and America. European affairs are treated in Chapters I and II, British conquests in Bengal take up Chapters III and IV. Chapters V to XI deal with British and colonial politics, but these chapters tend to emphasize the way events were presented to Parliament. Thus, the critical review of the Grenville ministry (Chapter V) links enforcement of the Navigation Acts to the growing economic recession in Britain. Chapter VI accurately measures the extension of the Grenville programme by relating its economic effects on both the colonies and Britain, but the programme is not judged at all in terms of Britain's national debt nor against the costs of imperial defence. Nor does the lengthy criticism of the use of the navy in customs enforcement mention the resentment of Americans against the role of Vice-Admiralty Courts.

Chapter VII begins with a précis of the King's speech opening the January 1765 parliamentary session, which asserted the legislative authority of Britain. The chapter proceeds to the major issue of that session—the question of the legality of general warrants, which originally arose over the case of John Wilkes and the publication of the notorious Number 45 (1763) of the *North Briton*. Chapter VIII is devoted exclusively to the debates over the stamp bill and the passage of the act. The *Register*'s account of the arguments raised against the bill, with some editorial additions, is a good résumé of the views expressed in the House of Commons debate of 6 February by Alderman William Beckford (ex–Lord Mayor, sugar millionaire, and vocal defender of "liberty"), Richard Jackson (one of Grenville's secretaries, he had also acted as agent for Pennsylvania and Connecticut in London), and Colonel Isaac Barré (who served in the colonies during the Seven Years War and was strongly pro-American), and by General Henry Seymour Conway (a supporter of Wilkes and a pro-Rockingham politician) in his speech on 15 February, the date of the bill's second reading. The account fails to emphasize that the House as a whole strongly favoured Britain's constitutional right to tax the colonies, or that the bill was passed in the Commons by a large majority and was approved in the House of Lords without a division. The *Register*'s account thus carefully stresses the view of the Rockinghamite opposition.

The next two chapters are concerned with British domestic issues—the passage of the Regency Act, consequent on the King's illness; the silk weavers' riots in Spitalfields; and the King's resentment over Grenville's handling of the regency issue, which led to the formation of a new government, led by the Marquis of Rockingham,[7] in June 1765.

The final chapter describes in detail the colonial reaction to the Stamp Act. The critical importance the *Register* attributes to New England contrasts with the emphasis historians usually give to the effects of the Virginia resolutions. Overall, the treatment of the lead taken by Massachusetts in calling the Stamp Act Congress; the breakdown of order in Boston and Newport; the influence of the Rhode Island resolves; and the origins of the Sons of Liberty in Connecticut seems to properly emphasise those events. The *Register*'s account of official and popular protests indicates that it was very well informed and

7. Charles Watson-Wentworth, 2nd Marquis of Rockingham (1730–82).

clearly apprised of the unity and extent of defiance in the colonies and of the serious commercial consequences.

State Papers consists of speeches from the throne at the opening of parliamentary sessions, the replies from both Houses, and an abstract of the Regency Act and similar items. The royal speech of 17 December 1765, which directed Parliament's attention specifically to the American situation and the coming battle for repeal of the Stamp Act, is extracted here.

But however negatively the want of employment, which most of the working people now began to complain of, might at first seem to be owing to the want of a real concern for their subsistence, in those who had taken upon them to be the champions of their liberty, it soon appeared to be positively owing to the ministry, allowing the ministry to [1] be chargeable with the ill consequences of every measure they propose, however sanctified by the approbation of the privy council and parliament, and enforced by the latter; a way of judging, which, by the bye, is attended with no small degree of injury to our honour, and even of danger to our well-being, since it not only tends to make foreigners believe, that we consider ourselves as the property of a few individuals, but to render us actually so, by exempting those, whose business it is to examine into the proposals of ministers, from the infamy of not doing their duty properly in that respect.

But to abide by the common mode of speech on these occasions, a mode which ministers, however, cannot justly complain of, since they have so long acquiesced in it, this great decline of the means of subsistence, as we have been just saying, soon appeared to be their own work. At the same time that they thought it expedient to fit out armed cutters, **under the command of sea officers, to prevent smuggling on** the coasts of Great Britain and Ireland, they obliged all sea officers stationed on those of our [2] American colonies, to act in the capacity of the meanest revenue officers; making them submit to the usual custom house oaths, and custom house regulations for that purpose; by means of which the nature of their own important and exalted character was debased, and that irregular vivacity of theirs, and contempt of common forms, which had been so lately, and with such advantage, exerted against the common enemy, was now inconsiderately played off upon the subject.

If these gentlemen did not understand all those cases, in which ships were liable to penalty, they as little understood those, in which ships were exempt even from detention; and, of course, hurt the interests of trade in the same proportion, that they disappointed the expectations of the treasury; so that, through the natural violence of their disposition, and their unacquaintance with the revenue business, (and, how could it be expected they should all at once become acquainted with a business, which requires, at least, as much study, as that they had been bred to?) the trade still carried on between British subjects, in spite of that vast number and intricacy of bonds, clearances, cockets, affidavits, stamps, certificates, registers, manifests, &c. with which the heart has been so unskilfully oppressed to benefit the members, was very much injured.

What served greatly to aggravate this evil, was its being, in a great measure, without prevention or redress; or at least that speedy prevention and redress, which so great an evil required. Those, who did the mischief, lived on an element, where civil justice is well known to have but little influence; or, if they sometimes ventured on shore, it was in bodies too numerous not to intimidate the civil officers; or in places, where their blunders, to call them by no worse a name, were not cognizable, or where, at least, they ran no risk of being met by those, whose business it was to prosecute them. The lords of the admiralty, or of the treasury, in Europe, could alone remove the evil; so that, considering the time an application to these boards must have taken in reaching them, and the orders of these boards in reaching the transgressors, it may fairly be accounted one of the greatest blessings Great Britain has had for a long time past to boast of, that the trade of her colonies, as far as it depended upon these new-fangled custom house officers, was not, in the mean time, totally annihilated.

Bad as this evil was, there sprung one still worse from the same source. A trade had been for a long time carried on between the British and Spanish colonies in the new world, to the great advantage of both, but especially the former, and likewise of the mother country; the chief materials of it being, on the side of the British colonies, British manufactures, or such of their own produce, as enabled them to purchase British manufactures for their own consumption; and, on the part of the Spaniards, gold and silver in bullion and in coin, cochineal and medicinal drugs; besides live stock, and mules, which in the West India plantations, to which places alone these last articles were carried, from their great usefulness justly deserved to be ranked in the same predicament with the most precious metals.

This trade did not clash with the spirit of any act of parliament made for the regulation of the British plantation trade, or, at least, with that spirit of trade, which now universally prevails in our trade acts; but it was found to vary from the letter of the former, enough to give the new revenue officers a plea for doing that from principles of duty, which there were not wanting the most powerful motives of interest to make them do. Accordingly, they seized, indiscriminately, all the ships upon that trade both of subjects and foreigners, which the custom house officers stationed a shore, through fear of the inhabitants, a juster way of thinking, or an happy ignorance, had always permitted to pass unnoticed. Probably, those at the head of affairs did not suspect that there was any such variance between the letter of our old laws and the present spirit of trade.

And, how weak soever this excuse may appear, it is the best that can be made for occasion being given to an evil, to which it was not in the power of any board to apply an adequate remedy; since all naval officers, though not sworn and particularly directed to act, *professedly*, as tide surveyors and tide waiters, may, notwithstanding, do both occasionally, in virtue of their rules of war; and it is hardly probable, [3] that, having once tasted the sweets of making rich prizes, they should all, and all at once, shun those opportunities, which before it had been their business to seek; and sacrifice their interests to the barren honour of complying with the orders of superiors, however enlightened, and actuated by a regard to the welfare of their country. Nay, how could these superiors venture to issue such orders, considering what jealousy the representatives of the people have ever shewn to secure to the law its full course; and how severely they have sometimes animadverted upon the highest characters, that happened to avow a design of dispensing with it?

It might even be doubted, if the supreme authority of the nation could apply such a remedy, considering the offence, which the making of a law for that purpose might give the court of Spain, in consequence of some treaties [4] made with her at a time, when we did not understand the principles of commerce so well; or did not apprehend such advantages from trading with the Spaniards in the new world; and, consequently, neglected to make these treaties sufficiently explicit; not but that they have been since often and often implicitly renewed in more enlightened periods. But, perhaps, it was this very consideration, that prevented any attempts being made to amend them.

Besides this trade carried on between the British American colonies in general, especially those in the West Indies, and the Spanish, there had for a long time subsisted one, equally extensive, between the British North American colonies in particular, and the French West India ones, as it consisted chiefly in such goods, as must otherwise have remained a drug, if not an incumbrance, upon the hands of the possessors; so that it united, in the strictest sense, all those benefits, which liberal minds include in the idea of a well-regulated commerce, as tending, in the highest degree, to the mutual welfare of those who carry it on.

In these benefits the respective mother countries had, no doubt a very large share, though it may be impossible to determine, which, upon the whole, had most. We had enough to engage those in power to wink at it, for it was not strictly according to law, in consideration of the vast quantity of manufactures it enabled our North American colonies to take from us; and this, too, in spite of all the clamours, which those concerned in our West India trade and possessions could raise against it, as enabling the French to undersell them, in West India produce at foreign markets. Probably, this clamour was found to arise in a great measure from another consideration, which it was not so proper in these gentlemen openly to avow, that of their not getting as good a price, as otherwise they might expect, for such part of their produce, as they sold in the markets of the mother country; and which, considering the vast demand for it, even by the poor, to whom from long habit it is become one of the chief necessaries of life, it would have savoured of oppression to permit the raising any higher. Be that as it will, this trade was permitted to be carried on for a long time into the last war between Great Britain and France; directly, by [5] means of flags of truce; and, in a roundabout way, through the Dutch and Danish islands; and, at length, through the Spanish port of Monte Christi in the island of Hispaniola; till, at last, the vast advantages the French received from it above what the English could expect, in consequence of our having in a manner laid siege to all their West India islands, determined the government to put a stop to it.

In doing this, however, they did not think proper to consider it so much in the light of a contraband trade, as in that of a treasonable practice, supplying the enemy with necessaries, without which it would have been impossible for these valuable islands to hold out so long against our attempts to reduce them. Accordingly, as soon as the conclusion of the last war had taken the sting of treason from this trade, it returned again to its pristine flourishing condition, and remained so, till it sunk under the same blow with the trade between us and the Spaniards, whose history we have already related.

This trade not only prevented our North American colonies from being drained of their current cash by the calls of the mother country upon them, but added greatly to it, so as to make it in some measure keep pace with their domestic trade, which could not but increase greatly from day to day in proportion to the remarkable increase of mankind in that part of the world, where the cheapness of land determines the greater part of the inhabitants to the exercise of the rural arts, so favourable to population.

It is, therefore, no way surprising, if the inhabitants of these colonies, immediately on a stop being put to this trade, came to a resolution not to buy any cloathing they could possibly do without, that was not of their own manufacturing. They were already too much in debt to the mother country to expect the usual supplies from her without making the usual returns; and, not having the usual returns to make, they wisely began the plan of retrenchment, which necessity dictated, by renouncing finery, to the no small disappointment of many wise politicians, who had, rather prematurely, concluded, that, because the wool of the colonies was not as good as that of the mother country, it would be impossible for them not to depend upon her.

Injury to the North American colonies considerably increased by ill-timed laws in England. North American colonies obliged thereby to manufacture for themselves. Mischiefs to be apprehended from that spirit to the mother country. Opinion of a great minister concerning the expediency of the British parliament's taxing the colonies.

THOUGH, therefore, that suppression of trade, of which we have been speaking in the last chapter, instead of barely intercepting the supply of the necessaries and conveniences of life, which our North American colonies before used to receive in return for their superfluities and incumbrances, tended visibly, by obstructing their internal commerce, to deprive them in a great measure even of those blessings, the sources of which lay within themselves; [6] yet was a law made in the beginning of the last year, 5th Apr. 174. which, whilst it rendered legal, in some respects, their intercourse with the other European colonies in the new world, loaded the best part of it with duties so far above its strength to bear, as to render it contraband to all intents and purposes. Besides, it ordered the money arising from these duties to be paid, and in specie too, into the British exchequer, to the entire draining off of the little ready money which might happen to be still remaining in these colonies. As though, however, the best way to cure an emaciated body, whose juices happened to be tainted, was to leave it no juices at all, within [7] a fortnight after another law was passed to hinder these wretched colonies from supplying the demand of money for their internal wants, by preventing such paper bills of credit, as might afterwards be issued in them, from being made legal tender in payment; and the legal tender of such paper bills, as were actually subfisting, from being prolonged beyond the periods already limited for calling in and sinking the same.

It is true, indeed, that all the money arising from the above duties was to be reserved for defraying the charges of protecting the colonies on which it was levied; and that, at the same time with the law for restraining the increase of paper money, several new laws were made to encourage and increase, as well as regulate, the commercial intercourse of our North American colonies with the mother country; such as a bill [8] for granting leave, for a limited time, for carrying rice from the provinces of South Carolina and Georgia to other parts of America on paying British duties; a bill for granting a bounty upon the importation of hemp, and rough [9] and undressed flax, from the American colonies into Great Britain; and a bill to encourage the whale [10] fishery on their coasts; but, unfortunately, the effects of all these laws to restrain the foreign trade of the colonies, and cramp their domestic trade, by not only hindering money to flow in upon them for the supply of their growing calls, or their making any at home, was certain and instantaneous; whereas the effect of the laws made for their benefit, which might compensate these evils, was, if not uncertain, at least remote; so remote as to require, perhaps, many years after its coming to compensate the delay.

We know it has been alledged, that the greatest part, if not the whole, of the money arising from these duties, could not fail of returning back into the colonies to pay the troops actually quartered there for their defence. But the colonies had no assurance, that these troops would continue amongst them, as, if it was intended by the legislature they should, the act would certainly have directed the money to be paid them at firſt hand, without the riſk and expence of making ſo long a voyage, and paſſing through ſo many hands, merely to have the honour of viſiting the Britiſh exchequer. The ſubjecting the colonies unneceſſarily to that additional burthen, would have been too wanton and unwiſe an exerciſe of power for a Britiſh parliament ever to be guilty of. And as to the miniſter's giving directions, that the money ſhould be iſſued on the ſpot, contrary to the plain letter of the act, we reſpect him too much to believe it true, however confidently ſome pretended well-wiſhers of his have aſſerted it. [11]

Thus were our North American colonies, (for the Weſt India colonies were, upon the whole, much more benefited than hurt by theſe laws, ſo much more, perhaps, as to receive, in ſome meaſure, amends for their loſs of trade with the Spaniards) put to the ſevereſt trial of their love and reſpect for the mother country, and it is but doing them juſtice to ſay, that, though ſome of them had been very lately quarrelling with their proprietary, and others with their royal, governors, moſt of them bore this ſtroke of the ſupreme legiſlature of Great Britain with all that patience and ſubmiſſion, which the moſt indulgent parent could have expected from the moſt dutiful children. For, if ſome preſumed to call in queſtion her authority, they were excited thereto, not ſo much by any actual laws or regulations concerning them, as by a vote of the houſe of commons paſſed at the time of laying the new duties upon their foreign trade, " that, towards further defraying the neceſſary expences of protecting the colonies, it may be proper to charge certain ſtamp duties upon them."

The inhabitants, indeed, of moſt of the North American colonies, inſtead of barely reſolving, every man for himſelf, as they had before done in conſequence of the interruption given to their foreign trade by the naval cuſtom houſe officers, not to buy any cloathing they could poſſibly do without, that was not of their own manufacturing, now entered into aſſociations, not only to abide by their former reſolution, but otherwiſe encourage as much as poſſible all kinds of manufacture within themſelves. The heavier the burthen, the greater exertion and unanimity ſeemed requiſite to bear it. It could not, ſurely, be expected, that, merely out of a compliment to the mother country, they ſhould ſubmit to periſh for thirſt, with water in their own wells. They ſuffered enough, as it was, by being obliged to make bricks without ſtraw; to carry on manufactures and trade, without either metal or paper money to acilitate the courſe of them.

Much, however, as theſe reſtrictive laws tended to hurt the Britiſh North American colonies, they tended ſtill more to hurt Great Britain herſelf; for, in conſequence of the general aſſociation of all ranks and orders of people in theſe colonies, not only to conſume as few Britiſh manufactures as poſſible, but to manufacture as much as poſſible for themſelves, they might, in ſpite of their preſent want of money, bring many commodities, the means and materials of which they enjoy in a much greater plenty than Great Britain, to ſuch a degree of perfection and cheapneſs before they could pay her for any, as, by the time they could, to want but little, and deſire ſtill leſs. And, when things once came to this paſs, what ſhould hinder their being, in a little more time, able to ſerve their neighbours, the American Portugueſe and Spaniards, with many articles, now the ſtaple commodities of Great Britain, on ſo much better terms than Great Britain herſelf, as might tempt both parties to force an intercourſe with each other, and enable them to maintain it, to the irreparable loſs of Great Britain; ſince the maritime ſtrength ſhe requires as a maritime country, and particularly as an iſland, cannot be ſupplied in any eminent degree, or at leaſt without ſacrificing to her ſecurity ſo great a ſhare of her ſubſiſtence, as hardly to retain enough to be worth fighting for, but by a trade carried on in ſhips belonging to, and navigated by, her own ſubjects; circumſtances ſhe cannot pretend to command in any trade with countries under a different head.

But allowing, that the ill adviſed meaſures we have been ſpeaking of were to be attended with no other ill conſequence, than a temporary interruption in the commercial intercourſe between Great Britain and her North American colonies, that alone could not fail of being very prejudicial to the former. It is computed, that theſe colonies, not to mention the foreign goods they receive through our hands, take off yearly of our produce and manufactures to the amount of three millions. Now, almoſt all the perſons concerned in the preparation, the buying and the ſelling, and the tranſportation of theſe manufactures, from the ſowing of the ſeeds of them in the fields of Great Britain to the landing of them on the ſhores of North America, muſt, during ſuch ceſſation, be ſupported at the expence of the reſt of the community, ſince they have nothing elſe but the labour of their hands to live upon, and it is ſcarce poſſible they ſhould in the mean time be able to find any new kind of labour to put them to. The revenue, too, muſt proportionably ſuffer by the want of the export duties payable on the goods ſent to the colonies, and the import duties payable on the goods we receive from foreign countries in return for what the colonies fend them; which duties, inconfiderable as the firft may be, cannot but amount to a great deal more, than thofe to raife which a ftop was now unhappily put to them.

This laft is the moft favourable idea, that could poffibly be formed of thefe meafures. It is, therefore, very furprifing, how a miniftry compofed of perfons, one of whom had fo long and with fuch [12] applaufe prefided at the board of trade and plantations, and another at that of the treafury,[13] fhould well come to think of them. It is ftill more furprifing, that thefe meafures fhould meet with the approbation of a Britifh privy council and parliament. But that, after almoft the worft idea, that could well be formed of them, had been in a great degree realifed, another meafure, the bare propofal of which had given fo much more offence, fhould be approved even with oppofition, inftead of the firft being repealed, if not ftigmatized, argues fuch want of reflection, as can fcarcely be parallelled in the public councils of any country.

Sir Robert Walpole is faid to have had much clearer and jufter notions concerning the means of making the Britifh colonies pay the mother country for their defence, and even contribute to her opulence. A fcheme for taxing them having been mentioned to him during that war with Spain, which broke out in the year 1739, he fmiled and faid. "I will leave that for fome of my fucceffors, who may have more courage than I have, and be lefs a friend to commerce than I am. It has been a maxim with me during my adminiftration, to encourage the trade of the American colonies in the utmoft latitude (nay it has been neceffary to pafs over fome irregularities in their trade with Europe) for by encouraging them to an extenfive growing foreign commerce, if they gain 500,000l. I am convinced that in two years afterwards full 250,000l. of their gains will be in his majefty's exchequer by the labour and product of this kingdom, as immenfe quantities of every kind of our manufactures go thither; and as they increafe in their foreign American trade, more of our produce will be wanted. This is taxing them more agreeably both to their own conftitution and to ours."

As to the legality of thefe laws, if we may be allowed the expreffion, we fhall poftpone the confideration of it to the following chapters, in which it will arife of itfelf out of the fubject.

THOUGH the miniftry could not fee the glaring inexpediency of thefe laws, they could, it feems, forfee the oppofition, that was likely to be made to meafures of the fame kind. The fpeech made from the throne at the opening of the next feffion, Jan. 10th. 1765. though it recommended the eftablifhing of fuch regulations, as might beft connect and ftrengthen every part of his majefty's dominions, for their mutual benefit and fupport, it mentioned no amendment in any former regulations relating to that fubject; but, on the contrary, a reliance on the firmnefs and wifdom of parliament in promoting the proper refpect and obedience due to the laws, and *the legiflative authority of Great Britain*; the bringing of which into queftion had been much better avoided, fince fuch a debate could have no iffue, but what muft be highly prejudicial to the mother country, efpecially after an unqueftioned exercife of fuch authority. Decided in the affirmative, it muft tend to alienate the affections of the colonies; in the negative, to increafe their prefumption; and left undecided, breed in them a complication of both thefe evils.

. . .

Opportunity given the colonies to offer a compensation for the stamp duty, and to establish a precedent for their being consulted, before any tax was imposed upon them by parliament ; rejected. Vote of last session for the propriety of laying a stamp duty upon them taken up again. Debates concerning the right of the British parliament to tax the British colonies without their concurrence, and the expediency of taxing them in the way now proposed. Bill for laying the stamp duty on the colonies passes both houses, and receives the royal assent by commission. Act for encouraging the importation of lumber from the British colonies into Great Britain. King's illness.

THE right hon. gentleman,[14] to whom has been attributed the framing of all the regulations and laws relating to the British colonies, which we treated of in our fifth and sixth chapters, though not aware, it seems, of any injury, with which they could be attended to the mother country, in point of honour, safety, or subsistence, contrived, however, that all further proceedings upon the resolution of last session for adding a stamp duty to them should be postponed to the present, in order that the colonies might have time to offer a compensation for the revenue such a tax might produce. Accordingly, when the agents of these colonies waited upon him to thank him for this mark of his confideration, he told them, that he was ready to receive proposals from the colonies for any other tax, that might be equivalent in its produce to the stamp tax; hinting withal, that their principals would now have it in their power, by agreeing to this tax, to establish a precedent for their being consulted, (by the ministry, we suppose) before any tax was imposed on them by parliament.

Many persons at this side of the water, and perhaps the agents themselves, looked upon this as a generous and humane proceeding. But the colonies seemed to consider it as an affront rather than a compliment. No doubt, they viewed the minister in the light rather of a servant than a protector. At least, not one of them authorized its agent to consent to a stamp duty, or to offer any compensation for it; and some of them went so far as to send over petitions, to be presented to the king, lords, and commons, positively and directly questioning the authority and jurisdiction of parliament over their properties. Two of the agents, indeed, answered for the colonies they served bearing their proportion of the stamp duty by methods of their own ; but, when questioned, confessed, that they had no authority to undertake for any particular sum.

This sullenness in the colonies should alone, one would imagine, have prevented the laying of any additional burthen on them. At least some measures should have been previously taken effectually to prevent the opposition, which that sullenness but too plainly indicated, and save Great Britain the mortification of seeing her laws publickly despised, and even her right to make them flatly contradicted, by those, whom the world had hitherto considered as her most dutiful subjects.

It must be owned, however, to the honour of parliament, that, however smoothly the vote concerning the propriety of laying a stamp duty on the colonies might have passed the lower house in the preceding session, the final laying it on in the present was attended with no small debates, both as[15] to the British legislature's right to tax the colonies without their concurrence, and the expediency of exercising that right, if any, for the present purpose ; though the petitions questioning the jurisdiction of parliament were not suffered to be read in the house, and the agents for the colonies refused to concur in another petition, which might have established a precedent for their being heard in behalf of their respective colonies against the tax. Possibly, these gentlemen imagined, that the petitioning for a suspension of the vote, as a favour, might be deemed an acknowledgment, that their principals had no right to oppose the execution of it when passed into a law ; or a surrender of that right, allowing they ever had any.

It was urged in favour of the colonies, that those, who first planted them, were not only driven out of the mother country by persecution, but had left it at their own risk and expence ; that, being thus forsaken, or rather worse treated, by her, all ties, except those common to mankind, were dissolved between them ; they absolved from all duty of obedience to her, as she dispensed herself from all duty of protection to them ; that, if they accepted of any royal charters on the occasion, it was done through mere necessity ; and that, as this necessity was not of their own making, these charters could not be binding upon them ; that, even allowing these charters to be binding, they were only bound thereby to that allegiance, which the supreme head of the realm might claim indiscriminately from all its subjects.

That it was extremely absurd, that they should be still thought to owe any submission to the legislative power of Great Britain, which had not authority enough to shield them against the violences of the executive ; and more absurd still, that the people of Great Britain should pretend to exercise over them rights, which that very people affirm they might justly oppose, if claimed over themselves by others.

That it cannot be imagined, that, when the same people of Great Britain contended with the crown, it could be with a view of gaining those rights, which the crown might have ufurped over others, and not merely recovering thofe, which the fame crown arbitrarily claimed over themfelves; that, therefore, allowing their original charters to be binding, as they had been deprived of them in an arbitrary and tyrannical manner, fuch as the people of Great Britain would not now by any means fuffer, they fhould be confidered as ftill intitled to the full benefit of them; that their being bound by thefe charters to make no laws, but fuch as, allowing for the difference of circumftances, fhould not clafh with thofe of England, no more fubjected them to the parliament of England, than their having been laid under the fame reftraint with regard to the laws of Scotland or any other country would have fubjected them to the parliament of Scotland, or the fupreme authority of any other country; that, by thefe charters, they had a right to tax themfelves for their own fupport and defence.

That it was their birth-right, even as the defcendents of Englifhmen, not to be taxed by any but their own reprefentatives; that, fo far from being actually reprefented in the parliament of Great Britain, they were not even virtually reprefented there, as the meaneft inhabitants of Great Britain are, in confequence of their intimate connection with thofe, who are actually reprefented; that, if laws made by the Britifh parliament to bind all except its own members, or even all except fuch members and thofe actually reprefented by them, would be deemed, as moft certainly they would, to the higheft degree oppreffive and unconftitutional, and refifted accordingly, by the reft of the inhabitants, though virtually reprefented; how much more oppreffive and unconftitutional muft not fuch laws appear to thofe, who could not be faid to be either actually or virtually reprefented?

That the people of Ireland were much more virtually reprefented in the parliament of Great Britain, than it was even pretended the people of the colonies could be, in confequence of the great number of Englifhmen poffeffed of eftates and places of truft and profit in Ireland, and their immediate defcendents fettled in that country, and of the great number of Irifh noblemen and gentlemen in both houfes of the Britifh parliament, and the greater number ftill conftantly refiding in Great Britain; and that, notwithftanding, the Britifh parliament never claimed any right to tax the people of Ireland, in virtue of their being thus virtually reprefented amongft them.

That, whatever affiftance the people of Great Britain might have given to the people of the colonies, it muft have been given either from motives of humanity and fraternal affection, or with a view of being one day repaid for it, and not as the price of their liberty and independence; at leaft, the colonies could never be prefumed to have accepted it in that light; that, if given from motives of humanity and fraternal affection, as the people of the colonies had never given the mother country any room to complain of their want of gratitude, fo they never fhould; if given with a view of being one day repaid for it, they were willing to come to a fair account, which, allowing for the affiftance they themfelves had often given the mother country, for what they muft have loft, and the mother country muft have got, by preventing their felling to others at higher prices than they could fell to her, and their buying from others at lower prices than they could buy from her, would, they apprehended, not turn out to her advantage fo much as fhe imagined.

That their having heretofore fubmitted to laws made by the Britifh parliament, for their internal government, could no more be brought

as a precedent againft them, than againft the Englifh themfelves their tamenefs under the dictates of an Henry, or the rod of a ftarchamber; the tyranny of many being as grievous to human nature as that of a few, and the tyranny of a few as grievous as that of a fingle perfon.

That, if liberty was the due of thofe who had fenfe enough to know the value of it, and courage enough to expofe themfelves to every danger and fatigue to acquire it, they were better intitled to it than even their brethren of Great Britain, fince, befides faceing, in the wilds of America, much more dreadful enemies, than the friends of liberty they left behind them could expect to meet in the fields of Great Britain, they had renounced not only their native foil, the love of which is fo congenial with the human mind, and all thofe tender charities infeparable from it, but expofed themfelves to all the rifks and hardfhips unavoidable in a long voyage; and, after efcaping the danger of being fwallowed up by the waves, to the ftill more cruel danger of perifhing afhore by a flow famine.

That, if in the firft years of their exiftence one of them was guilty of fome intemperate fallies, and all expofed to enemies, which required the interpofition and affiftance of an Englifh parliament, they were now moft of them arrived at fuch a degree of maturity in point of polity and ftrength, as in a great meafure took away the neceffity of fuch interpofition and affiftance for the future. At leaft, that interpofition and affiftance would not be the lefs effectual for the colonies being reprefented in the Britifh parliament, which was all the indulgence thofe colonies contended for.

That, allowing the Britifh parliament's right to make laws for the colonies, and even tax them without their concurrence, there lay many objections against all the duties lately imposed on the colonies, and more still and weightier against that of the stamps now proposed to be laid upon them; that whereas those stamp duties were laid gradually on the people of Great Britain, they were to be saddled all at once, with all their increased weight, on those of the colonies; that, if those duties were thought so grievous in England on account of the great variety of occasions in which they were payable, and the great number of heavy penalties to which the best meaning persons were liable for not paying them, or not strictly conforming to all the numerous penal clauses in them, they must be to the last degree oppressive in the colonies, where the people in general could not be supposed so conversant in matters of this kind, and numbers did not understand even the language of these intricate laws, so much out of the course of what common sense alone might suggest to them as their duty, and common honesty engage them to practise, the almost only rule of action, and motive to it, compatible with that encouragement, which it is proper to give every new settler in every country, especially foreigners, in such a country as America.

Such were the principal arguments now urged in Great Britain, most of them within doors, against the justice of laying any tax at all, and the inconveniency of laying the stamp tax in particular, upon the British colonies in America. And they must be owned, to carry great weight with them. At least, little or nothing worth notice, except what we have added to every argument, and the absurdity of their pretending to be exempt from the taxation of parliament, because authorized by charter to tax themselves, since at that rate all the corporations of Great Britain might claim the same exemption, was said, as far as we have

been able to learn, to invalidate them; unless we are to admit claims for titles, assertions for proofs, fictions in law for substantial arguments, the statutes of England for the dictates of nature, and the private opinions of the gentlemen of Westminster-hall for the general sense of mankind; and even allow conveniency to be the only measure of right and wrong; a doctrine, which the inhabitants of Great Britain should of all people be the last to adopt, since of all people they are those, who would suffer most by its being enforced against themselves. Nay, conveniency itself seemed to dictate other measures, as must appear but too obvious from what we have already said ourselves upon the subject; and which the enemies to this measure did not fail to urge against it.

When we say, that we have not heard of any thing material being brought to invalidate the arguments alledged against the British parliament's right to tax the British colonies without their concurrence, we are very far from meaning, that nothing was or could be brought to invalidate these arguments. We are still further from admitting the claim of the British colonies to be represented in the British parliament, at least as fully as the people of Great Britain are. Common sense, nay self-preservation, seem to forbid, that those, who allow themselves an unlimited right over the liberties and lives of others, should have any share in making laws for those, who have long renounced such injust and cruel distinctions. It is impossible, that such men should have the proper feelings for such a task. But then we could wish, that, since it was resolved to make the colonies contribute to their defence by taxes imposed on them without their concurrence, instead of abiding by the good old methods heretofore pursued for that purpose, these disqualifications in them to be fully represented in a British parliament had

been assigned as the reason for the mother country's taxing them unrepresented. Then her doing so, instead of carrying an appearance of arbitrariness, considering her own claims to liberty, would manifest her best title to that invaluable blessing, and even of absolute empire over her colonies. For, though a strict regard to private independence may not be such a title to political dominion, as to justify an attempt to acquire that dominion by force, it must, certainly, be allowed a sufficient reason for the holding of it when of long standing, and never controverted, like ours over our colonies, coeval with their existence, and never before disputed by them.

But though nothing of this kind was, we believe, said to forward the bill, it made its way through both houses, with the same disagreeable injunction for having the money arising from it paid into the British exchequer; and, at last, his majesty being indisposed, received the royal assent by commission on the 22d of March, 1765.

Besides this bill's enacting, that the money arising from the duties imposed by it should be reserved for defraying the charge of protecting the colonies, there passed another to encourage the importation of all kinds of timber from [16] them; which, considering how plentiful that article is in most parts of North America, and the little time necessary to cut down trees, to what is requisite to raise flax and hemp, might in some places compensate the operations of the stamp duty, at least much more readily, than the douceurs allowed in the preceding session could counteract the effects of the import and export duties laid on at the same time. But it seems the colonies were by this time too much soured for the most powerful sweeteners to have any salutary effects upon them. Interesting however as the consequences have been, it would be unpardonable in us, after mentioning the king's illness, not to lay aside the thoughts of them and every thing else, till we have considered those of an event, which, independent of that gratitude, to which his majesty's constant attention to the happiness of his people so justly intitles him, could not but fill their breasts with the greatest anxiety for their own welfare, considering the infancy of his majesty's children, and the tempest expected in North America, the weathering of which might require that dispatch and vigour incompatible with a divided or delegated command.

• • •

Proceedings against the stamp act and stamped papers by the populace of the old North American colonies. Better sort of people gradually mix with them. Provincial assemblies countenance these proceedings, assert their independence, and resolve on a general congress. Petitions conformable thereto. Measures taken to elude the act, or force a repeal of it. Behaviour of the other North American colonies and the West India plantations.

HAD the stamp duty been laid on the colonies, at once, and without any previous mention of it to them, they would, perhaps, have submitted to it, if not without grumbling, at least without that open opposition, the consequences of which it may be more easy to guess than safe to expatiate on. The principal people amongst them would not then have had an opportunity of making the lower sort foresee in that act of the British legislature, when merely held out to them, much greater evils, than they, probably, were liable to feel from it, when actually inflicted; much less would they have had time to animate each other against it to such a degree, that every news concerning it, that reached any one part of the wide extended British dominions in America, almost instantaneously flew over the rest, like fire put to the well laid trains of a vast but well combined mine, exciting every where such heartburnings amongst all ranks, and such commotions, in most of them, amongst the populace, as were sufficient to destroy all differences in religious sentiments or forms of government, the best security the people of Great Britain can have for a ready submission, on the part of the people of the colonies, to their decrees; and the best tie, by which they can, at any rate, hope to keep them united, till they shall think proper to adopt them as fellow subjects, and bind them by the considerations of common and equal interest, the strongest and most durable of all bands.

But, how generally soever the people of the colonies were indis-

posed against this tax, it is to be presumed, that they were not, all, equally so; and, therefore, it was of no small consequence, what colony any interesting news of it first reached. The example of passiveness, or even moderation, in one colony might have been of some service to induce the rest to submit quietly to it. But, unfortunately, the account of its having passed into a law got first to New England, that colony, the inhabitants of which considered their ancestors, who had first settled it, as the most injured of all those Englishmen, who had fled to America from civil or spiritual persecution in their native country; and some of whose progenitors, accordingly, had, so early as the year 1642, spirit enough to assert their independence, and the happiness of seeing the best title they could have to that dependence, if not expressly owned, at least greatly countenanced by the vote of an English house of Commons, that the plantations in New England had succeeded in their enterprize without any charge to the state, and were likely to prove beneficial and commodious to the mother country.

Accordingly, the news of the stamp act having received the royal assent no sooner reached that province, than the melancholy, which had taken possession of every countenance on their receiving the first account of the vote for the propriety of laying it on having been resumed, and which had afterwards visibly increased on the arrival of that of its having passed both houses, turned to fury, and every where broke out into action. The ships in the harbour hanged out their colours half mast high, in token of the deepest mourning; the bells rang muffled; the act itself was printed, with a death's head to it in the place where it is usual to fix the stamps, and cried publicly about the streets by the name of the "Folly of England, and Ruin of America." Essays soon followed, not only against the expediency, but even the equity, of it, in several news papers, one of which bore the significative title of "The Constitutional Courant, containing matters interesting to liberty, and no wise repugnant to loyalty, printed by Andrew Marvel, at the sign of the Bribe refused, on Constitution Hill, North America;" and wore a still more significative head-piece; a snake cut in pieces, with the initial letters of the names of the several colonies, from New England to South Carolina inclusively, affixed to each piece, and above them the words JOIN or DIE. To these were added caricatures, pasquinades, puns, bons mots, and such vulgar sayings fitted to the occasion, as by being short could be most easily circulated and retained, at the same time that, by being extremely expressive, they carried with them the weight of a great many arguments.

It were needless to dwell much upon the contents of these newspaper essays. Two things excepted, they said little more, than what we ourselves have already said, on the occasion, from the mouths of others at this side of the water. But these were things of the most serious nature, and such as the most despotic tyrant might expect to see remonstrated against by the most abject vassals. The first was, that the person acting under this act had it in his power to bring an action, the cause of which had arisen at one extremity of the North American colonies, to the other, at almost two thousand miles distance, without the trader's being enti-

tuled to recover damages, in case the judge certified that there was any probable cause for the prosecution. The second was, the judge's having an interest in giving a decree in favour of the party suing for the penalties of the act, by being allowed, by way of commission, a very large share in these penalties.

These proceedings were followed by such others, as might naturally be expected from them. By the time the act itself, as printed at the king's printing-house, reached the colonies, the populace were every where exasperated against it, to such a degree, that they treated it with all that contempt and indignation, which could be expressed by public authority against the most offensive libel of a private person. It was publickly burnt by them, in several places, along with the effigies of those, who where supposed to have had any hand in bringing it about, at the same time that it was voted in some meetings of persons in higher rank, that thanks should be given to general Conway and colonel Barré, two gentlemen whom they considered as the most strenuous opposers of it in the British house of Commons; that their speeches against it, and their pictures should be requested; their pictures to be hung up in their places of meeting; and their speeches to be inserted in the books destined to record their principal transactions.

Upon the arrival of the news of this discontent in England, several masters of ships refused to take any stamps on board for the colonies; and it soon appeared, that their precaution was well founded; for such as ventured to take them had great reason to repent it on their arrival at their destined ports, where, to save their vessels from fire, and their persons from the gallows, they most of them were obliged to surrender their execrated cargoes into the hands of the enraged multitude, to be

treated in the same ignominious manner, in which the act itself had been treated; and the rest to take shelter under such of the king's ships, as happened to be at hand to protect them.

Those gentlemen, who came from England with commissions to act as distributors of the stamps, fared still worse. Many of them were made to renounce, now and for ever, publickly and upon oath, all manner of concern in them; others thought proper to return from whence they came; whilst some, who were suspected of obstinately persisting, as it was termed, in endeavouring to enslave their country, or of having spoken too freely concerning the behaviour of the people on this occasion, had their houses burnt to the ground, and their most valuable effects plundered or destroyed. Even those, who had been named without their sollicitation or knowledge, or were obliged to superintend the distribution of the stamped paper, in virtue of the offices they already filled, (governors and chief justices, who had been most unaccountably pressed into this odious service, not excepted,) were treated in the same manner, and one much worse. The populace, suspecting him of having written to England in disrespectful terms concerning their proceedings, surrounded his house, and obliged him, in spite of tears and prayers, to deliver up the copies of his letters, and thereby turn evidence against himself. Nay ships bringing stamped merchantile or custom-house papers, merely in their own defence, from such of the colonies, as had thought proper to submit to the stamp act, were forced to part with them to be stuck up in derision in coffee-houses and taverns, and then publicly committed to the flames.

Many of the better sort of people gradually mixed with the populace in these tumults; and one of them was not afraid to set the act openly at defiance, by advertising, under his hand, that those, whose business it was to enforce it, might save themselves the trouble of calling upon him for that purpose ; for that he was resolved to pay no taxes, but what was laid by his representatives. The provincial assemblies themselves not only declined giving the governors any advice concerning their behaviour on this critical occasion, but, convinced how little the wisest heads must avail without able hands to execute what they have projected, though they disavowed these riotous proceedings, and even bid rewards for apprehending the rioters, especially on a chief justice being so[19] plundered by them as to be obliged to appear on the seat of justice, without those ensigns of office so wisely calculated to procure respect to authority, yet could not be brought to condemn them further than decency required ; and absolutely refused, when exhorted to it by the governors, to make any compensation to the injured parties ; much less could they be brought to strengthen the hands of the executive powers so far as to prevent any future commotions ; which, as levelled entirely at the stamp act, and as having no particular leaders, whose ignorance and brutality might be attended with worse consequences than what they wished to avoid, they did not, it seems, think proper to consider as objects of military restraint. And, indeed, it does not appear, that a single sword was drawn, or a single musket fired, on the occasion ; though some persons, very early, thought it no improper caution privately to spike up the cannon belonging to the forts and ship yards, left any use should be made of them on either side.

This behaviour of the general assemblies was openly approved, if not encouraged, by assemblies of the freeholders and principal inhabitants of some places, who directed their representatives not to agree to any steps for the protection of stamped papers, or stamp officers, though they owned there had been already some tumults and disorder, relating to them ; and likewise cautioned them against all unconstitutional drafts on the public treasury, for fear, no doubt, that the governors might endeavour to strengthen their hands that way without their consent.

But the general assemblies went still further. Instead of barely conniving at the people's asserting their independence by tumultuous acts, they proceeded to avow it themselves in the most expressive terms, grounding it on the same arguments, which their friends at this side of the water had already used to prove it. And, if at the same time they came to a resolution to petition the legislature of Great Britain against the stamp act, it was in such terms, as served to express weakness rather than acknowledge submission, and what one independent body, in cases of great distress, might use in applying for assistance to another

Considering, at the same time, that unanimity is the chief source of strength, they established committees to correspond with each other concerning the general affairs of the whole, and even appointed deputies from these committees to meet, in congress, at New York. But it seems, there already prevailed such harmony in the sentiments of the general assemblies of the several provinces, that the deputies, when met, had little more to do than congratulate each other upon it, and put their hands to one general declaration of their rights, and grievances they laboured under, and to one general petition, expressive thereof, to the king, lords, and commons, of the mother country.

At length, those invested with the subordinate executive powers began to join the legislative. The justices of the peace for the district of Westmoreland in Virginia gave public notice under their hands, that they had declined acting in that capacity ; because, in consequence of their judicial oath, they were, they said, liable to become instrumental in the destruction of their country's most essential rights and liberties. The gentlemen of the law soon after caught the fire of patriotism to such a degree, that they resolved rather to give up their business than carry it on with stamped papers.

By the 1st of November, the time the act took place, not a sheet of stamped paper was to be had throughout the several colonies of New England, New York, New Jersey, Pensilvania, Virginia, Maryland, or the two Carolinas, except a small parcel, which the governor of New York, terrified by the threats of the enraged populace, had surrendered into the hands of the corporation of that place, on condition of their not being destroyed like the rest, so that all business, which could not be legally carried on without stamps, was at once put to a stand, except that of news-printing, which the printers still continued, pleading in excuse, that, if they did not, the populace would serve them as they had done the stamp-masters themselves ; at least those, who, for that purpose, made use of stamped paper in Canada, where the act was received, could find no sale for their news. The courts of justice were closed, and the ports were shut up. Even in those colonies, where stamps were to be had, the people of the best fortunes submitted to be called in church, rather than take out licences for private marriages.

But the consequences of this stagnation soon began to be so severely felt, that the inhabitants, who, though probably cooled not a little by them, were yet unwilling to submit to the act, began to think how they could effectually elude it. To this end, some one or another, fruitful in expedients, sent to the printers at Boston, a thin piece of bark, on which he had written, that, it being neither paper, parchment, or vellum, he would be glad to know, if instruments written on such stuff might not be valid, though not stamped; in which case, he was ready to supply with good writing bark all those, whose consciences were bound by the late act. At last, the governors of some of the provinces, though bound by the act to swear to see it observed, under the severest penalties, thinking the total stoppage of all public business of such bad consequence to the community, as to render lawful the non-compliance with any injunctions laid on them, or even the breach of any oath taken by them, in consequence of injunctions, merely for the sake of that community, thought proper so dispense with the use of stamps, grounding their dispensation on the absolute impossibility of procuring any; and, accordingly, granted certificates of that impossibility to all outward bound vessels, to protect them from the penalties of the act in other parts of his majesty's dominions.

On this occasion, the commons house of assembly of South Carolina, whose lieutenant governor [20] was one of those who still refused their consent to the transacting of any public business without stamps, took a very proper course with him. They addressed him to know, if the stamp act had been transmitted to him by the secretaries of state, the lords of trade, or through any other authentic channel; and, on his answering, that he had received it first from the attorney general of the province on that gentleman's arrival from England, and since from Mr. Boone, the governor of the province, they replied, that neither of these ways of receiving any act was such a notification thereof, as to oblige him to enforce the execution of it; as the governor, whilst out of the province, or the attorney general, even while in it, could not, at least with regard to this communication, be considered in any other light than private gentlemen. At the same time, they put him in mind, that there were several instances of the province's having suffered peculiar and very great hardships, and for no small length of time, even from the accidental detention or miscarriage of govermental informations, enough to prove, that certain forms were absolutely necessary in all matters of government, especially such, as related to the authentication of new laws of such immense consequence.

But these arguments seem to have made little or no impression on the governor or his council,; and, indeed, it could hardly be expected they should, as the colonies may well be supposed to have submitted to many laws made in the mother country, though transmitted through channels that were not more authentic.

The best methods, therefore, of avoiding any injury from this act, appear to be those, which we have yet to relate. The merchants of all those colonies, which ventured to oppose it openly, entered into the most solemn engagements with each other, not only not to order any more goods from Great Britain, let the consequences be what they would, and recall the orders they had already given, if not obeyed by the 1st of January 1766, but even not to dispose of any British goods sent them on commission, that were not shipped before that day; or, if they consented to any relaxation from these engagements, it was not to take place, till the stamp act, and even the sugar and paper-money acts, were repealed. The people of Philadelphia likewise resolved, though not unanimously, that, till such repeal, no lawyer should put in suit a demand for money owing by a resident in America to one in England; nor any person in America, however indebted in England, make any remittances there; a resolution, in some degree, unnecessary, as by the late restraints laid on their trade, and the almost total stagnation of it in consequence of their opposition to the stamp act, it was almost impossible for the best meaning people to make any remittances. These resolutions were adopted by the retailers, who unanimously agreed not to buy or sell any British goods shipped contrary to them.

Ireland benefited greatly by these proceedings, as what goods the colonies could not possibly do without, they took from that country in exchange for their hemp-seed and flax-seed, of which they yearly send her very large quantities. In the mean time they omitted no methods to free themselves even from this dependence. A society of arts, manufactures, and commerce, on the plan of the London society, was instituted at New York, and markets opened for the sale of homemade goods; by which it soon appeared, that neither the natives, nor the manufacturers whom the natives had for some time past been inviting from Great Britain by very large encouragements, had been idle. Linens, woollens, the coarser but most useful kinds of iron ware, malt spirits, paper hangings, &c. were produced to the society, and greatly approved; and, when brought to market, as greedily bought up. At the same time, lest the new woollen manufacturies should come short of materials, most of the inhabitants came to a resolution not to eat any lamb; and, to extend the influence of their resolution to those, who did not join them in it, not to deal with any butcher that should kill or expose any lamb to sale. In a word, the spirit of industry and frugality universally took place of the spirit of idleness and profuseness. The most substantial and even fashionable people were foremoft in fetting the example to their countrymen, by contenting themfelves with home-fpun or old cloaths, rather than make ufe of any thing Britifh, which they before ufed to be fo madly fond of. And fuch were the efforts of all ranks, and fo prudent their meafures, that many now began to be convinced of what they had till then thought impoffible, that the colonies would foon be able to fupply themfelves with every neceffary of life.

One would be apt to imagine, that it was impoffible for the colonies to go greater lengths againft the mother country. But the contrary foon appeared. A refolution began to be talked of, of ftopping the exportation of tobacco from Virginia and South Carolina to Great Britain ; by which, confidering the great quantities of that article re-exported from Great Britain, and the immenfe fum fo imperceptibly raifed by what fhe herfelf confumes of it, her trade, and efpecially her revenue, could not fail of being confiderably affected.

Such have been, according to the beft accounts we have been able to procure, the principal proceedings of the fix greateft Britifh colonies of North America, New England, New York, New Jerfey, Philadelphia, Virginia, the two Carolinas, and Maryland, in confequence of this famous act, from the time of their firft hearing of its being voted proper in parliament, till they heard of the abfolute repeal of it ; an event, upon which it cannot be expected we fhould now enlarge. The other North American colonies, more, poffibly, from a confcioufnefs of weaknefs, than a principle of duty, though they could by no means form the fame pretenfions to independence, as being either conquered countries, or countries fettled at the expence of the Britifh government, thought proper to fubmit to it, but not all with equal grace. The Weft

India plantations bowed their heads to it with that readinefs, which their condition as iflands feemed to require, all to the iflands of St. Chriftopher's and Nevis, whofe populace fuffered themfelves to be fo far impofed on by the crews of fome New England veffels in their harbours, as to go even greater lengths than the New Englanders themfelves ; particularly the populace of St. Chriftopher's, who, not content with burning the ftamped papers of their own ifland, and making thofe appointed to diftribute it renounce that office, went over in a body to affift their neighbours of Nevis in taking the fame riotous precautions againft it.

. . .

His majefty's moft gracious fpeech to both houfes of parliament, on Tuefday the 17th of Dec. 1765 ; with the humble addrefs of the houfe of Commons on the occafion, and his majefty's moft gracious anfwer.

My Lords and Gentlemen,

THE prefent general ftate of tranquillity in Europe, gave me hopes, that it would not have been neceffary to affemble my parliament fooner than is ufual in times of peace.

But, as matters of importance have lately occurred in fome of my colonies in America, which will demand the moft ferious attention of parliament ; and as further informations are daily expected from different parts of that country, of which I fhall order the fulleft accounts to be prepared for your confideration ; I have thought fit to call you now together, in order that the opportunity may thereby be given, to iffue the neceffary writs on the many vacancies that have happened in the houfe of commons, fince the laft feffion ; fo that the parliament may be full, to proceed immediately after the ufual recefs, on the confideration of fuch weighty matters as will then come before you.

Notes, 1765

1. This typically Burkean digression continues the theme, stressed in the 1764 volume, of warning against threats to the freedom, authority, and responsibility of Parliament as a whole.

2. It is not entirely clear from the text which measure is referred to. A policy of stricter enforcement of the Navigation Acts had, of course, been emerging for some years. The act of 1762 (3 Geo. III c. 22), intended to reduce smuggling ". . . on the Coasts of Great Britain and Ireland, and of the other Dominions and colonies belonging to the Crown of Great Britain," permitted the use of naval officers and vessels. This act was implemented by the Order in Council of 1 June 1763; on 9 July, the Secretary of State for the Southern Department wrote to all governors in America deploring the loss to the Treasury from illegal trade in American waters, and this was followed by a letter from the Board of Trade enjoining strict enforcement of the Navigation Acts. The American Revenue Act (1764) implicitly regarded the navy as the instrument of enforcement and restated the disposition of rewards from seized contraband; the confused wording required clarification by the Privy Council (order of 12 October 1764).

3. The Admiralty ordered naval commanders in colonial waters to suppress illegal trade as early as 1740. See also note 5, below.

4. The two old treaties governing commercial and maritime regulations between Britain and Spain dated from 1667 and 1670. Both were in a sense markedly inexplicit. The treaty of 1667 was not specifically applicable to the Americas, except for Article 8, which implied that Spain would not interfere with Britain's trade to British colonies. The 1670 treaty was meant to apply to America but Article 15 was vague regarding Britain's rights of navigation in American waters, leaving a loophole for trade with the Spanish American Colonies. The acquisition by Britain of the Asiento in 1713, at the end of the Spanish Succession War, also left points vague, and British merchants hoped to exploit that vagueness to their considerable advantage. For the most part, they were disappointed (hence the war in 1739), but by the 1760s a steady and profitable trade had developed between the Spanish colonies and the British in North America and the West Indies.

5. The North Americans used these and other expedients to continue a flourishing trade with the French West Indies, until Pitt decided to suppress it in 1761. The navy gained its first experience of continuous, determined enforcement of trade regulations against the Americans during this period.

6. The American Revenue Act (1764, 4 Geo. III c. 15) contained one article which imposed new duties (reduced from those of 1733) on sugar, molasses, and rum imported into North America; five articles on imported wines, textiles, and foodstuffs; and forty-one articles deriving from recommendations to prevent evasion of the Navigation Acts and to ensure their enforcement. The act was not strictly an innovation of the Grenville ministry, but the culmination of a long-standing dissatisfaction with American customs returns dating from at least 1759.

7. 4 Geo. III c. 34; an extension of the principles of the New England Currency Act (1751).

8. 4 Geo. III c. 27.

9. 4 Geo. III c. 26.

10. 4 Geo. III c. 29.

11. Article 11 of the American Revenue Act specifically stated that money raised by the new duties "... shall be paid into the receipt of his Majesty's Exchequer, and shall be entered, separate and apart from all other monies ... and shall be there reserved to be from time to time disposed of by Parliament towards defraying the expenses of defending, protecting and securing the British colonies and plantations in America."

12. George Montagu Dunk, 2nd Earl of Halifax (1716–71), President of the Board of Trade, 1748–61; Secretary of State for the Southern Department in the Grenville ministry.

13. George Grenville (1712–70), First Lord of the Treasury, April 1763–July 1765.

14. George Grenville.

15. These arguments appear to be those advanced by opponents of the Government's measure in the debate of 6 February (when Grenville reintroduced the notion of an American stamp tax, first raised during the debates on the Sugar Act), and those made on the second reading of the actual bill on 15 February. The views of those who supported the bill, for example, Grenville, who opened the debate on 6 February, and Charles Townshend, are not mentioned here at all. One report suggests the House of Commons division on the bill was about 250 in favour and 50 against.

16. 5 Geo. III c. 45. This act made other concessions: American bar iron could be imported free into any British port (not just London, as hitherto), and North Carolina was permitted to export rice on the same terms as laid down in 4 Geo. III c. 27. However, the act also imposed more regulations intended to reduce illegal trade.

17. George III's illness in 1765 indicated the need to establish a regency of those who would rule in the event of his death or incapacity during the minority of his heir. This apparently simple issue caused the fall of the ministry. Grenville's regency bill excluded the King's mother (probably on the advice of the Duke of Cumberland, who thought his sister-in-law was a baleful influence). The bill was amended to include the Princess Dowager with the other members of the royal family who might be appointed to the Regency Council, but Grenville never recovered the confidence of the King, who rapidly sought to replace him.

18. It is not clear who is referred to here. The Boston rioters (26 August) believed local Crown officers had sent critical reports of the colony to London, hence their attacks on the marshall and registrar of the Vice-Admiralty Court and the comptroller of customs. The stamp distributor for New Hampshire, George Meserve, when forced to resign, was also obliged to hand over his commission and instructions, by the local Sons of Liberty.

19. Thomas Hutchinson (1711–80), Lieutenant-Governor and Chief Justice of Massachusetts, whose house was sacked in the Boston riot of 26 August.

20. William Bull (1710–91) put the first consignment of stamps to South Carolina under military guard and indicated his determination to enforce the act.

21. Of the Thirteen Colonies, Georgia alone saw a temporary enforcement of the Stamp Act, until opposition forced the governor to permit ship clearances without stamped paper, in February 1766. In the provinces of Nova Scotia, Quebec, and East and West Florida, the act was apparently enforced without much opposition.

Introduction

1766

News of the real extent of American opposition to the Stamp Act was becoming widespread by the time Parliament reassembled for its short session in December, 1765. Reports of the riots in Boston and Newport, the effective nullification of the act by the Sons of Liberty, and resolves rejecting Parliament's authority to legislate for internal colonial affairs all presented an alarming picture. The virtual stoppage of trade between Britain and America was equally serious, and its effects were apparent before an official report of the colonial nonimportation agreements was actually received. British merchants trading with America were hard hit, and manufacturers supplying goods for the trade lost orders and were forced to lay off workers. In addition, the refusal of American merchants to pay outstanding debts threatened a major credit crisis.

The Rockingham ministry was thus faced with a dilemma. The Rockinghams disliked the Stamp Act, were dubious about its constitutional basis, and were worried by its commercial consequences; their sympathies lay with the Americans. The logical policy was to repeal the act. However, they were shocked by reports that public order had collapsed in the colonies, and feared that repeal in the face of violence might deal a mortal blow to imperial authority. Moreover, the act had been passed by a large parliamentary majority, so repeal would require skillful political tactics.

Rockingham used the Christmas recess to seek political

support and devise an acceptable formula for repeal. Attempts to induce William Pitt, who was still a formidable and widely popular figure despite his ill health, to join the ministry were unavailing. However, significant support came from outside Parliament. Rockingham's close friend, Barlow Trecothick, a vastly wealthy London merchant raised in Boston and heavily involved in the American trade, led an association of London merchants to pressure the Government into restoring amicable relations with the colonies. A committee representing the London merchants circularised thirty other ports and major manufacturing towns suggesting combined action to push the Government into a policy which would prevent, as they put it, the commercial ruin of the nation. The result was a battery of petitions presented to Parliament when it reconvened in January 1766. Meanwhile, Rockingham and his closest colleagues failed to agree on a repeal formula; consequently, the King's speech opening the new session on 14 January was designed to hit a carefully neutral note. The speech prompted a major debate.

Pitt began by declaring that Parliament's attempt to tax America directly was unconstitutional, and he concluded:

> ... my opinion ... is, that the Stamp Act be repealed absolutely, totally, and immediately. That the reason for repeal be assigned, because it was founded on an erroneous principle. At the same time, let the sovereign authority of this country over the colonies, be asserted in as strong terms as can be devised, and be made to extend to every point of legislation whatsoever. . . .[1]

Pitt's view was strongly contested, most notably by Grenville, who argued that he could see no difference in principle between internal taxation (i.e., taxes designed to raise revenue) and external taxation (i.e., those imposed to regulate trade).

Rockingham's tactics developed from the debate. The ministry hoped to play down the constitutional issue, and concentrate Parliament's attention on the commercial aspects, by using the petitions from British towns and evidence of experts on American affairs (most notably, Benjamin Franklin). The aim was to show the necessity for repeal and that Americans were objecting only to internal taxation. However, the distinction between inter-

1. *The Parliamentary History of England from the Earliest Period to 1803* eds. William Cobbett and T. C. Hansard, 36 vols., (London, 1806–20), Vol. 16, 108. Hereafter *Parliamentary History*.

nal and external taxation was probably already untenable in America.

On 28 January, the House of Commons resolved itself into a comittee of the whole to discuss the petitions, hear evidence, and debate the repeal issue. Between 3 February and 24 February, when the House met again in open session, the House adopted a series of resolutions; the most important were intended to repeal the Stamp Act and to declare Parliament's absolute sovereignty over America "in all cases whatsoever." Bills were accordingly prepared, despite opposition particularly in the House of Lords, where the constitutional aspects of repeal were hotly debated; and finally became law on 18 March. The ministry believed it had produced a solution, acceptable in both Britain and America, which would permit a rapid return to a harmonious imperial relationship.

The *Register's* treatment of these events in the historical section reflects their significance; about one-third of the text is devoted to them. Chapters I, II, and III describe continental European affairs, noting a spate of insurrectionary activity which stretched from Spain to the Caucasus. Ironically, Chapter III refers to Spain's appeasement of a "revolution" in Quito as suggesting that ". . . the Spaniards perhaps hold but a precarious power in the new world."[2] The fourth and fifth chapters cover events in India and indicate a growing public uncertainty in Britain about the ambiguous role of the East India Company as both a commercial and governing body. Chapters VI, VII, and VIII deal with British politics and America.

The emphasis given the Stamp Act crisis and the difficulties the ministry faced might well be expected from the *Register*, given Burke's attachment to Rockingham. But the King himself referred to the crisis as ". . . undoubtedly the most serious matter that ever came before Parliament."[3]

Rockingham's acute dilemma over repeal of the Stamp Act is clearly indicated at the end of Chapter VI, and the stress given the commercial aspects of the crisis at the beginning of Chapter VII reflects Rockingham's deliberate attempt to divert Parliament's attention from the con-

2. *AR*, 1766, p. [29.

3. George III to Henry Conway, 5 December 1765, in Bonamy Dobrée, ed. *The Letters of King George III*, (London, 1935), p. 33. The King also doubted Parliament's ability to handle the crisis.

The Annual Register—1766

stitutional implications of repeal. But although Parliament was clearly influenced by the commercial evidence,[4] the constitutional issue was also vigorously debated.

An argument unreported in the *Register* was perhaps even more important. On 7 February, in reply to Grenville's proposal for a resolution to recommend enforcement of the Stamp Act, and again on 21 February, in pressing his own resolution for repeal, Conway warned that enforcement in America would lead to war and such a war would give France and Spain an opportunity to recoup the losses they sustained by the Treaty of Paris in 1763. Fear of a Bourbon war of revenge while Britain was embroiled in a transatlantic conflict may therefore have been significant.[5]

The *Register*'s account does not distinguish between the debates at the opening of the new session on 14 January and those which followed the decision of the House of Commons to resolve itself into a committee of the whole in closed session for the crucial February debates,[6] for which contemporary reports exist. It is usually claimed that the *Register*'s account refers to the January debates alone. It is clear that the *Register*'s description is a reconstruction after the event: the arguments are summarised and grouped to indicate a point of view, rather than narrating the debates in order of speaker. A comparison of the text of the *Register* with the major accounts of the

4. The *Register* makes no reference to the examination of witnesses by the House. Franklin's influential testimony was published in the fall of 1766 in America, and anonymously by John Almon in England in 1767.

5. See L. H. Gipson, "The Great Debate in the Committee of the Whole House of Commons on the Stamp Act, 1766, as Reported by Nathaniel Ryder," *Pennsylvania Magazine of History and Biography*, 1962, vol. 86, pp. 10–41.

6. These are the letters of Charles Garth, London agent for Maryland and South Carolina, to the Maryland delegates to the Stamp Act Congress, 26 February and 5 March 1766, in *Maryland Historical Magazine*, 1906, vol. 11, pp. 282–305; Horace Walpole, *Memoirs of the Reign of George III*, ed. Denis Le Marchant, Bart. (London, 1845), vol. 2, pp. 277–307; P. D. G. Thomas, ed., "Parliamentary Diaries of Nathaniel Ryder, 1764–67," *Camden Miscellany*, vol. 23 [Camden 4th ser., vol. 7]: (London: Royal Historical Society, 1969), pp. 241–320; C. H. Hull and H. W. V. Temperley, eds. "Debates on the Declaratory Act and the Repeal of the Stamp Act," *American Historical Review*, 1911–12, vol. 17, pp. 543–86 (based on the notes of Grey Cooper); D. H. Watson, "William Baker's Account of the Debate on the Repeal of the Stamp Act," *William and Mary Quarterly*, 1969, 3rd ser., vol. 24, pp. 259–65. A complete list of all the material relating to the debates can be found in P. Langford, *The First Rockingham Administration 1765–1766* (London: 1973), pp. 290–91.

February debates does suggest that some portion of them are described in the latter part of Chapter VII and the beginning of Chapter VIII, though the method of presentation precludes easy comparisons and conclusions. In any event, the extended analysis of the arguments for and against repeal presented by the *Register* appears to accurately reflect the main positions taken during the debates and thus the *Register* makes a useful additional source.

The historical section reviews the year to the end of the summer session of Parliament and concludes with a brief account of the fall of the Rockingham ministry and its replacement by that headed by Pitt, who was created Earl of Chatham, on 30 July 1766. The American issues which emerged after 3 June (notably New York's resistance to the Quartering Act) therefore appear in the 1767 volume.

The *Appendix to the Chronicle* includes, however, material relating to the dispute between the governor and the assembly of Massachusetts in June. This conflict, which dragged on until December 1766, centred on the question of compensating those who had suffered material losses during the Stamp Act riots and raised serious constitutional issues. The attitude of the Massachusetts Assembly threatened Parliament's hopes that repeal of the Stamp Act and trade concessions[7] would restore America to submissive loyalty.

In the aftermath of anti–Stamp Act activities, radical elements in the Massachusetts Assembly were determined to secure political control of the House of Representatives and the Governor's Council. The particular object of the radicals' attack in the ensuing struggle was Thomas Hutchinson. Governor Francis Bernard viewed the radicals' attack as part of a concerted manoeuvre to oust from office those who had supported the British position in 1765. The radicals claimed that Hutchinson's tenure as both lieutenant-governor and chief justice for the province combined executive and judicial powers, and was thus a threat to political liberty. Hutchinson had been active in enforcing the Grenville trade and revenue measures, though he had opposed implementation of the Stamp Act. Hutchinson's house was sacked in the Boston riot of 26 August 1765, and Parliament particularly had his case in mind when considering the question of compensation for those who had suffered in the King's service. The Mas-

7. See "Notes, 1766," n. 14.

sachusetts Assembly was reluctant to vote compensation, despite the Secretary of State's instruction, but finally did so in December 1766—on condition that all those responsible for the riots be automatically pardoned. (The Privy Council eventually vetoed this act on the grounds that it usurped the royal prerogative.) The assault on the power of the governor and on the extent of Parliamentary authority over the colony was to continue.

Diſtreſſed ſtate of the nation and colonies : both involved in the greateſt difficulties by the new laws reſpecting the colonies. Critical ſituation of the miniſtry. State of parties. A powerful oppoſition formed. Parliament meets. The king in his ſpeech takes particular notice of the American affairs. Addreſſes thereon. Both houſes adjourn for the holidays.

AT the concluſion of our laſt volume, we ſaw the nation involved in the moſt diſtreſsful circumſtances that could well be imagined ; our manufactures at a ſtand, commerce almoſt totally annihilated, proviſions extravagantly dear, and a numerous populace unemployed, without the means of procuring a livelihood. Such, and ſo gloomy was the proſpect that opened at home upon us along with the year : nor did the view become more pleaſing by extending it acroſs the Atlantic, where the colonies exhibited nothing but ſcenes of anarchy and confuſion ; where licentiouſneſs was carried almoſt to the higheſt pitch that it could poſſibly admit, without aſſuming another name : whilſt the profligate and abandoned (as is uſually the caſe in civil commotions) under the ſpecious pretext and maſk of liberty, and the common cauſe, gave a looſe to their own unruly paſſions, and committed all thoſe exorbitances which the vulgar are ſo prone to, when under any pretence they are allowed to aſſemble in bodies, and through any relaxation of the laws, they have not the fears of immediate puniſhment upon them. We have before obſerved, that thoſe of an higher rank amongſt them did not take any pains to allay the ferments

it is probable, that many of the more ſerious of them condemned inn their own minds ſeveral acts that were committed ; but did not think proper to damp a ſpirit, which, however irregularly or improperly exerted, they perhaps at that time thought it conducive to their deſigns to keep alive.

But though a violent reſentment ſupported the ſpirit of the coloniſts, they could not but ſenſibly feel the inconveniencies, which an entire ſtoppage of trade muſt occaſion among a people who had hitherto ſubſiſted by commerce. However their warehouſes were full of Britiſh goods, for which they had not paid. And the many reſources of ſo vaſt an extent of country, abounding in the moſt eſſential articles of life, prevented them from feeling ſo much immediate diſtreſs, as our own manufacturers and labouring poor at home.

It muſt be obſerved, that the enormous ſums owing to our merchants, in the colonies, added greatly to the difficulties the public were under, and ſeverely affected the trading and manufacturing part of the community. Theſe debts, amounting to ſeveral millions ſterling, the Americans abſolutely refuſed to pay, pleading in excuſe their utter inability : which

plea, it appears, the merchants admitted to be reaſonable.

As the nation was never perhaps in a more critical ſituation, ſo of conſequence no adminiſtration ever had greater difficulties to encounter than the new one. They were under an immediate neceſſity of enforcing the ſtamp act by fire and ſword, or elſe of moving its immediate repeal in parliament. In the former caſe, though there was no doubt of the ability of Great Britain to cruſh, or even extirpate the colonies ; yet ſuch a deciſion, if not looked upon as abſolute ſuicide, muſt at leaſt be conſidered as making uſe of one arm to cut off the other.

Fatal were the conſequences, which it was foreſeen and foretold would attend ſuch an attempt, and it was obvious, that if ſuch conſequences ſhould enſue, the firſt framers and promoters of the obnoxious laws, would have been entirely forgot in the general odium and execration, which would have fallen ſolely upon the miniſters, who, by enforcing ſuch ruinous meaſures, had wrought the deſtruction of their country.

On the other hand, if the act ſhould be repealed, a colourable appearance was not wanting to charge them with ſacrificing the dignity of the crown, together with the honour and intereſt of the nation to their own irreſolution, or elſe to a cauſeleſs animoſity, which it would be ſaid they bore to their predeceſſors, and a blind oppoſition to all their meaſures.

The loss of their illustrious friend and patron, the Duke of Cumberland, seemed at this nice[2] period to be truly critical to the ministry : his influence, his authority, his good sense, his patriotism, and the high regard the public held him in, would have added greatly to their strength and security.

Thus situated, they had an opposition to encounter, consisting of gentlemen, several of whom had held the first employments in the kingdom, and who, for abilities, experience, knowledge of business, property, and connections, were very respectable, and therefore truly formidable.

Some of these gentlemen seemed obliged in honour, as well as thro' opinion, and a spirit of opposition, to embark warmly in vindication and support of measures which had originally been their own, for which it may be supposed they had the natural partiality of a parent, and in defence of which they were determined to dispute every inch of ground with the ministry. Some also joined them through principle.

They thought that the insolence of the Americans deserved chastisement, where otherwise the hardship of their circumstances might merit relief. Others there were who gave themselves no trouble as to the rectitude of the American taxation, but who would have been very glad that their own burdens at home could be at all lightened, by any sums, that could be drawn in any manner, out of the pockets of the colonists : and in general it may be supposed that the lovers and assertors of high prerogative, naturally chimed in with the rest, upon their own principles.

There were not a few also who first kept aloof from, and in due time declared against the ministry, upon some symptoms which appeared early, of their wanting that countenance, which, as it hath been favourable or adverse, has determined the good or ill fortune of the several successive systems of administration for some years past. This part of the opposition was, for very obvious reasons, by much the most dangerous.

To balance this powerful opposition, the administration consisted of gentlemen, who, though many of them were young in office, were yet extremely high in estimation ; whose characters were clear; whose integrity was far above suspicion, and whose abilities seemed to grow with the difficulties of the business they were engaged in ; their constant adherence also to the cause of liberty had procured them the confidence and good will of the public, both of which they enjoyed in a very eminent degree. They had besides some other advantages : as they were not bound to the support of measures at all events, merely because they had planned or advised them ; so they could weigh matters with coolness and impartiality, and judge without prejudice or passion ; at least they had the happiness not to be obliged to act systematically wrong.

They appear accordingly to have avoided, as well as in matters so critical perhaps they could be avoided, the two extremes, on one of which it was apprehended they must inevitably have struck : they neither precipitated affairs in America by the rashness of their councils, nor did they sacrifice the dignity of the crown or nation, by irresolution or weakness; and the[3] firmness, as well as temper, which appeared in their dispatches to the different governors, when examined by the house, did them the greatest honour. By preserving this medium, by suspending their own judgment in a matter of so great importance, till they had obtained that of the representatives of the nation, they still left it in the power of the supreme legislature, to use healing measures, and did not urge their fellow-subjects, through desperation, to the committal of such acts as could not be forgiven.

Notwithstanding the prudence of this conduct, it was severely animadverted on by the opposite party. These gentlemen would have the most coercive means made use of, for enforcing the new laws and regulations in which themselves had so great a share ; fully sensible of the disgrace that must be reflected on them by a repeal, it is not unnatural to suppose, that they wished to see the executive power so deeply engaged before the meeting of parliament. that the legislative could not then in honour recede from the support of it. Upon this principle, the plan of moderation that had been adopted, was opposed with the greatest acrimony, and the severest invectives pointed at administration, for not having immediately employed troops and ships of war, to enforce the laws in such a manner, as the outrageousness of the resistance, and the importance of the authority which was resisted, did, as they asserted, indispensably require.

In the mean time, the American affairs were become a general subject of discussion, and numberless pamphlets were wrote on both sides of the question : in general both sides were guilty of the same fault, though in the most opposite extremes ; the advocates for the colonies carried the idea of liberty to the highest pitch of enthusiasm, while their antagonists seemed to imagine, that a person forfeited every birthright and privilege of an Englishman by going to live in America. They both also proved a great deal too much, while the former seemed to consider the colonies rather as independent states in a sort of equal alliance with the mother country, than as dominions depending upon and belonging to her ; they furnished the strongest reasons, why that irregular spirit of enthusiasm should be timely checked, by making them sensible of their dependence.

On the other hand, the enemies of the colonies, by exaggerating their power, opulence, and population, sufficiently proved the necessity of treating them with tenderness; as, if their calculations were allowed to be well founded, it must be impossible to retain them long in subjection by any other means.

In this situation were affairs 27 Dec. when the parliament met in the latter end of the year 1765. Particular notice was taken from the throne of the importance of the matters which had [4] occurred in North America, and which were given as a reason for assembling the two houses sooner than was intended, that they might have an opportunity to issue the necessary writs on the many vacancies that had happened since the last session; and proceed immediately after the recess to the consideration of the weighty matters that should then be laid before them, for which purpose the fullest accounts of the American affairs should be prepared for their inspection.

Most of the friends to administration had vacated their seats in consequence of the late changes, so that by deaths and promotions there were 41 seats now vacant. Some thought it would be ungenerous to make any strictures upon the conduct of the ministers, till they should be in a situation to vindicate or explain it, in their proper persons as members of the house: it appears however that others were of a contrary opinion. An address having been resolved in answer to the king's speech, a motion was made by the opposition, that his Majesty might be addressed to give orders, that copies of all letters, papers, orders, or instructions, sent from the secretary of state's office, or the other principal departments, to the governors and officers of the crown in North America, together with copies of all answers thereto, and

of all other papers relative to the late disturbances there, to the execution of the stamp-duty, to the enforcing of the laws, and to the quelling of riotous and tumultuous disorders, should be laid before the house.

This motion seemed the more extraordinary, as it had been declared from the throne, that the fullest accounts of these affairs should be laid before parliament.

The house probably thought the proposition not very decent with regard to the crown, nor candid with regard to the ministry, in their situation at that time. So that on a sharp debate the previous question being put, it was carried in the negative by a majority of 70 to 35. The house having then issued the necessary writs, adjourned for the holidays.

Parliament meet after the holidays. The American affairs again particularly recommended from the throne; addresses thereon. Petitions sent from the trading and manufacturing towns. Great debates upon the right of taxation. The right of taxation confirmed and ascertained.

THERE scarce was ever any affair debated in a British parliament, in which the public thought themselves more deeply interested, or for the result of which they felt a more impatient anxiety than the present. Nor was the rest of Europe, especially the commercial part, inattentive to the event.

The second speech Jan. 14. from the throne, as well as the first, pointed out the American affairs to parliament, as the principal object of its deliberations: both houses by their addresses shewed that they looked upon them in the same important light. Petitions were re-[5]ceived from the merchants of London, Bristol, Lancaster, Liverpoole, Hull, Glasgow, &c. and indeed from most of the trading and manufacturing towns and boroughs in the kingdom. In these petitions they set forth the great decay of their trade, owing to the new laws and regulations made for America: the vast quantity of our manufactures, (besides those articles imported from abroad, which were purchased either with our own manufactures, or with the produce of our colonies), which

the American trade formerly took off of our hands: by all which, many thousand manufacturers, seamen, and labourers had been employed, to the very great and increasing benefit of the nation. That, in return for these exports, the petitioners had received from the colonies, rice, indico, tobacco, naval stores, oil, whale-fins, furs, and lately potash, with other staple commodities, besides a large balance in remittances by bills of exchange and bullion, obtained by the colonists for articles of their produce, not required for the British market, and therefore exported to other places.

That from the nature of this trade, consisting of British manufactures exported, and of the import of raw materials from America, many of them used in our manufactures, and all of them tending to lessen our dependence on neighbouring states, it must be deemed of the highest importance in the commercial system of this nation. That this commerce so beneficial to the state, and so necessary for the support of multitudes, then lay under such difficulties and discouragements, that nothing less than its utter ruin was apprehended without the immediate interposition of parliament.

That the colonies were then indebted to the merchants of Great Britain, to the amount of several millions sterling : and that, when pressed for payment, they appeal to past experience in proof of their willingness ; but declare, it is not in their power at present to make good their engagements, alleging that the taxes and restrictions laid upon them, and the extension of the jurisdiction of the vice-admiralty courts, established by some late acts of parliament, particularly by an act passed in the 4th year of his present Majesty, for granting certain duties in the British colonies and plantations in America, and by an act passed in the 5th year of his Majesty, for granting and applying certain stamp-duties, &c. in the said colonies, &c. with several regulations and restraints, which, if founded in acts of parliament for defined purposes, they represent to have been extended in such a manner, as to disturb legal commerce and harass the fair trader : and to have so far interrupted the usual and former most fruitful branches of their commerce, restrained the sale of their produce, thrown the state of the several provinces into confusion, and brought on so great a number of actual bankruptcies, that the former opportunities and means of remittances and payments were utterly lost, and taken from them.

That the petitioners were, by these unhappy events, reduced to the necessity of applying to the house, in order to secure themselves and their families from impending ruin ; to prevent a multitude of manufacturers from becoming a burden to the community, or else seeking their bread in other countries, to the irretrievable loss of the kingdom ; and to preserve the strength of this nation entire, its commerce flourish-

ing, the revenues increasing, our navigation, the bulwark of the kingdom, in a state of growth and extension, and the colonies, from inclination, duty, and interest, firmly attached to the mother country.

Such a number of petitions from every part of the kingdom, pregnant with so many interesting facts, stated and attested by such numbers of people, whose lives had been entirely devoted to trade, and who must be naturally supposed to be competent judges of a subject which they had so long and so closely attended to, (besides that it shewed the general sense of the nation), could not fail of having great weight with the house.—There was also a petition from the agent for the island of Jamaica, setting forth the ill consequences that had attended a stamp-tax, that had been laid on in that island by the assembly, and which was suffered to expire, it having been found *unequal* and *burdensome* in a very high degree. And he conceived the present law for a stamp-duty in the colonies, would be attended with the same, if not greater inconveniencies.

There were also petitions received from the agents for Virginia and Georgia, setting forth their inability to pay the stamp-duty, &c. It is remarkable that these three were the only petitions delivered this session in the name of any of the colonies : which must be imputed to the reception their petitions met with the last year, of which we have already taken notice.

But neither the arguments nor facts contained in the petitions could prevail on the party who had resolved on the support of the stamp act at all events, to remit in the least of their ardor.

They represented the petitions as the effects of ministerial artifice. And they argued, even if [6] the distress of trade, from a due exertion of the authority of parlia-

ment, had been as real and as great as it was represented ; yet it were better submit to this temporary inconvenience, than, by a repeal of the act, to hazard the total loss of the just superiority of Great Britain over her colonies.

Those who contended for the repeal were divided in opinion as to the right of taxation : the more numerous body, of whom were the ministry, insisted that the legislature of Great Britain had an undoubted right to tax the colonies ; but relied on the inexpediency of the present tax, as ill adapted to the condition of the colonies, and built upon principles ruinous to the trade of Great Britain.

Those who denied the right of taxation, were not so numerous ; but they consisted of some of the most distinguished and popular names in the kingdom, among which was that of a noble lord at the head of one of the first departments of the law, who, by [7] some decisions favourable to liberty, stood high in the esteem of the public ; and a right honourable commoner, who had long enjoyed the most unbounded popular applause, together with other lords [8] and gentlemen of the first character.

Though the urgency of the matter occasioned the house to attend to it with the most unwearied application, and twelve, one, or two o'clock in the morning, were become common hours of dining with the members, so late it frequently was before they broke up from the public business ; yet the nature of their inquiries, the number of petitions they received, and the multitude of papers and witnesses they had to examine, occasioned a delay which could not be remedied. During which time there were continual debates, and the opposition made the most strenuous efforts for enforcing the stamp act, and by every means to prevent the repeal. There were two questions arose in the course of this debate, upon which the whole turned. The first was, whether the legislature of Great Britain had a right of taxation over the colonies, or not? The second was confined to the expediency, or inexpediency of the late laws. We shall give some of the arguments that were made use of on both sides, without presuming to give any opinion of our own, which in this case will be the easier excused, as it has already been decided to general satisfaction, by the highest authority.

As to the right of taxation, the gentlemen who opposed it, produced many learned authorities from Locke, Selden, Harrington, and Puffendorff, shewing, *that the very foundation and ultimate point in view of all government, is the good of the society.*

That by going up to Magna Charta, and referring to the several writs upon record, issued out for the purpose of raising taxes for the crown, and for sending representatives to parliament, as well as from the bill of rights, it appears throughout the whole history of our constitution, that no British subject can be taxed, but *per communem consensum parliamenti,* that is to say, of himself, or his own representative; and this is that first and general right as British subjects, with which the first inhabitants of the colonies emigrated: for the right does not depend upon their charters: the charters were but the exterior modelling of the constitution of the colonies; but the great interior fundamental of their constitution is this general right of a British subject: which is the very first principle of British liberty,—No man shall be taxed, but by himself, or by his representative.

That the counties Palatine of Chester, Durham, and Lancaster, were not taxed but in their own assemblies or parliament; till at different periods in our history, they were melted into our present form of parliamentary representa-tion. That the body of the clergy, till very late, taxed themselves, and granted the king benevolencies.

That the Marches of Wales, had a right of taxing themselves till they sent members of parliament, and from this circumstance has continued the style of the king's proclamations, and of our acts of parliament to this day, although unnecessarily, to name especially the principality of Wales, and the town of Monmouth, as they do that of Berwick.

That many people carry the idea of a parliament too far, in supposing a parliament can do every thing; but that is not true, and if it were, it is not right constitutionally: for then there might be an arbitrary power in a parliament, as well as in one man.— There are many things a parliament cannot do. It cannot make itself executive, nor dispose of offices that belong to the crown. It cannot take any man's property, even that of the meanest cottager, as in the cases of inclosures, without his being heard. The lords cannot reject a money-bill from the commons, nor the commons erect themselves into a court of justice. The parliament could not tax the clergy, till such time as they were represented in parliament. Nor can the parliament of England tax Ireland.

The charters of the colonies, which are derived from prerogative, and are in fact only so many grants from the crown, are not the only rights the colonies have to being represented before they are taxed: they, as British subjects, take up their rights and liberties from a higher origin than their charters only. They take them up from the same origin and fountain, from whence they flow to all Englishmen, from Magna Charta, and the natural right of the subject. By that rule of right, the charters of the colonies, like all other crown-grants, are to be restricted and interpreted, for the benefit, not the prejudice of the subjects. Had the first inhabitants of the colonies renounced all connection with their mother country, they might have renounced their original right; but when they emigrated under the authority of the crown, and the national sanction, they went out from hence at the hazard of their lives and fortunes, with all the first great privileges of Englishmen on their backs. But at the same time they were not, and could not be bound by penal laws of this country, from the severity of which they fled, to climates remote from the heavy hand of power; and which they hoped to find more friendly to their principles of civil and religious liberty. It is upon this ground, that it has been universally received as law, that no acts of parliament made here, and particularly those which enact any penalty, are binding upon the colonies, unless they are specially named.—The inhabitants of the colonies once removed from the domestic legislation of the mother country, are no more dependent upon it in the general system, than the isle of Man is, or than, in the feudal system of Europe, many subordinate principalities are dependent on the jurisdiction of the seigneur suzerain, or lord paramount; but owing only a limited obedience.

It is not meant by what has been said, to affect the case of any external duties laid upon their ports, or of any restrictions which by the act of navigation, or other acts, are laid upon their commerce; for they are in the same case, as all other colonies belonging to the rest of the maritime powers in Europe, who have shut up their colonies from all intercourse with foreign countries, in the very first establishment. What is spoken of are internal taxes, to be levied on the body of the people. And that, before they can be liable to these internal taxes, they must first be represented.

Many other arguments were made use of, and instances were brought from ancient history of the conduct of some of the most famous republics, with respect to their colonies, as well as of colonies, which outgrew their mother countries, such as Carthage, the northern emigrants, &c. Precedents were quoted from what happened in the United Netherlands, and other places, which should serve as a beacon, to warn us from pursuing such measures, as brought about those revolutions.

These arguments were answered with great force of reason, and knowlege of the constitution, from the other side. They observed it was necessary to clear away from the question, all that mass of dissertation and learning, displayed in arguments which have been brought from speculative men, who have written upon the subject of government. That the refinements upon that subject, and arguments of *natural* lawyers, as Locke, Selden, Puffendorff, and others, are little to the purpose in a question of constitutional law. That it is absurd to apply records from the earliest times, to our present constitution ; because the constitution is not the same : and nobody knows what it was at some of the times that are quoted : that there are things even in Magna Charta which are not constitutional now, and that those records are no proofs of our constitution as it now is.

The constitution of this country has been always in a moving state, either gaining or losing something : nor was the representation of the commons of Great Britain formed into any certain system till Henry the 7th. That with regard to the modes of taxation, when we get beyond the reign of Edward the 1st, or King John, we are all in doubt and obscurity. The history of those times

is full of uncertainties. In regard to the writs upon record, they were issued, some of them according to law ; and some not according to law ; and such were those concerning ship-money ; to call assemblies to tax themselves, or to compel benevolencies. Other taxes were raised by escuage, fees for knights service, and other means arising from the feudal system. Benevolencies are contrary to law, and it is well known how people resisted the demands of the crown in the case of ship-money, and were prosecuted by the court. And if any set of men were to meet now, to lend the king money, it would be contrary to law, and a breach of the rights of parliament.

With respect to the marches of Wales, who were the borderers privileged, for assisting the king in his wars against the Welch, in the mountains ; their enjoying this privilege of taxing themselves, was but of a short duration, and only during the life of Edward the first, till the Prince of Wales came to be king : and then they were annexed to the crown, and became subject to taxes like the rest of the dominions of England ; and from thence came the custom though unnecessary, of naming Wales and the town of Monmouth in all proclamations, and in acts of parliament. Henry the 8th was the first who issued writs for it, to return two members to parliament. The crown exercised the right *ad libitum*: from whence arises the inequality of representation, in our constitution of this day : Henry the 8th issued a writ to Calais to send one burgess to parliament. One of the counties palatine was taxed 50 years to subsidies, before it sent members to parliament.

The clergy at no time were unrepresented in parliament. When they taxed themselves in their assemblies, it was done with the concurrence and consent of parliament, who permitted them to tax themselves upon their petition, the

convocation sitting at the same time with the parliament ; they had their representatives too, always sitting in the house of lords, bishops and abbots : and in the other house, they were at no time without a right of voting singly for the election of members. So that the argument fetched from the case of the clergy, is not an argument of any force, because they were at no time unrepresented.

The reasoning about the colonies of Great Britain, drawn from the colonies of antiquity, is a mere useless display of learning : for the colonies of the Tyrians in Africa, and of the Greeks in Asia, were totally different from our system. No nation before ourselves formed any regular system of colonization, but the Romans : and their system was a military one, by garrisons placed in the principal towns of the conquered provinces. But the right of jurisdiction of the mother country over her colonies was, among the Romans, boundless and uncontrollable. The States of Holland were not colonies ; but they were states dependent on the house of Austria, in a feudal dependence. Nothing could be more different from our colonies, than that shock of men (as they have been called) who came from the North, and poured into Europe. Those emigrants renounced all laws, all protection, all connection with their mother countries. They chose their leaders and marched under their banners, to seek their fortunes and establish new kingdoms upon the ruins of the Roman empire ; whereas our colonies, on the contrary, emigrated under the sanction of the crown and parliament. They were modelled gradually into their present forms, respectively by charters, grants, and statutes : but they were never separated from the mother country, or so emancipated as to become *sui juris*.

There are several sorts of colonies in British America : the charter-colonies, the proprietary governments, and the king's colonies. The first colonies were. the charter-colonies, such as the Virginia company, and these companies had among their directors, members of the privy council, and of both houses of parliament; they were under the authority of the privy council, and had agents residing here responsible for their proceedings. So much were they considered as belonging to the crown, and not to the king personally, (for there is a great difference, though few people attend to it), that when the two houses in Charles the first's time, were going to pass a bill concerning the colonies, a message was sent to them by the king, that they were the king's colonies, and that the bill was unnecessary; for that the privy council would take order about them : and the bill never had the royal assent.

The commonwealth parliament, as soon as it was settled, were very early jealous of the colonies separating themselves from them ; and passed a resolution or act, (and it is a question whether it is not now in force), to declare and establish the authority of England over her colonies. But if there was no express law, or reason founded upon any necessary inference from an express law ; yet the usage alone would be sufficient to support that authority. For have not the colonies submitted, ever since their first establishment, to the jurisdiction of the mother country ? In all questions of property, the appeals of the colonies have been to the privy council here : and such causes have been determined, not by the law of the colonies, but by the law of England. The colonies have been obliged to recur very frequently to the jurisdiction here, to settle the disputes among their own governments. New Hampshire and Connecticut, have been in blood about their differences : Virginia and Maryland were in arms against each other : this shews

the necessity of one superior decisive jurisdiction to which all subordinate jurisdictions may recur. Nothing could be more fatal to the peace of the colonies at any time, than the parliament giving up its authority over them : for in such a case there must be an entire dissolution of government. Considering how the colonies are composed, it is easy to foresee, that there would be no end of feuds and factions among the several separate governments, when once there shall be no one government here or there, of sufficient force or authority to decide their mutual differences : and government being dissolved nothing remains, but that the several colonies must either change their constitution, and take some new form of government, or fall under some foreign power. At present the several forms of their constitution are very various, having been produced, as all governments have been originally, by accident and circumstances. The forms of government in every colony, were adapted from time to time according to the size of the colony, and so have been extended again from time to time, as the numbers of the inhabitants, and their commercial connections, outgrew the first model. In some colonies at first, there was only a governor assisted by two or three council : then more were added : then courts of justice were erected, then assemblies were created.

Somethings were done by instructions from the secretaries of state : other things were done by order of the king and council, and other things by commission under the great seal. It is observable in consequence of these establishments from time to time, and the dependency of these governments upon the supreme legislature at home, that the lenity of each government in the colonies, has been extreme towards the subject ; but if all these governments which are now

independent of each other, should become independent of the mother country, it is to be feared the inhabitants would soon find to their cost, how little they were aware of the consequences. They would very soon feel in that case, the hand of power much heavier upon them in their own governments, than they have yet done, or than they have ever imagined.

As the constitutions of the several colonies, are made up of different principles ; so they must remain dependent (from the necessity of things and their relations) upon the jurisdiction of the mother country, or they must be totally dismembered from it. No one ever thought the contrary, till the trumpet of sedition has been lately blown. Acts of parliament have been made, not only without a doubt of their legality, but with universal applause, the great object of which has been ultimately to fix the trade of the colonies, so as to center in the bosom of that country, from whence they took their origin. The navigation-act shut up their commerce with foreign countries. Their ports have been made subject to customs and regulations, which cramped and diminished their trade, and duties have been laid, affecting the very inmost parts of their commerce, and among others, that of the post ; yet all these have been submitted to peaceably ; and no one ever thought, till now, of this doctrine, that the colonies are not to be taxed, regulated, or bound by parliament. A few particular merchants then, as now, were displeased at restrictions, which did not admit them to make the greatest possible advantage of their commerce, in their own private and peculiar branches ; but though these few merchants might think themselves losers, in articles which they had no right to gain, as being prejudicial to the general national system ; yet, upon the whole, the colonies were benefited by these laws, because these restrictive laws, founded upon principles of the most solid policy, flung a great weight of naval force into the hands of the mother-country, which was to protect the colonies, and without an union, with which the colonies must have been entirely weak and defenceless; instead of which they became relatively great, subordinately and in proportion, as the mother-country advanced in superiority over the rest of the maritime powers in Europe, to which both mutually contributed, and of which both have reaped the benefit, equal to the natural and just relation in which they both stand reciprocally, of dependency on one side, and protection on the other.

There can be no doubt but that the inhabitants of the colonies are as much represented in parliament, as the greatest part of the people of England are, among nine millions of whom, there are eight [9] who have no votes in electing members of parliament: every objection therefore to the dependency of the colonies upon parliament, which arises to it upon the ground of representation, goes to the whole present constitution of Great Britain. A member of parliament chosen for any borough, represents not only the constituents, and inhabitants of that particular place, but he represents the inhabitants of every other borough in Great Britain; he represents the city of London, and all other the commons of the land, and the inhabitants of all the colonies and dominions of Great Britain, and is in duty and conscience bound to take care of their interests.

The distinction of internal and external taxes, is as false and groundless as any other that has been made. It is granted, that restrictions upon trade, and duties upon the ports, are legal, at the same time that the right of the parliament of Great Britain to lay internal taxes upon the colonies is denied. What real difference can there be in this distinction? A tax laid in any place, is like a pebble falling into, and making a circle in a lake, till one circle produces, and gives motion to another, and the whole circumference is agitated from the centre; for nothing can be more clear, than that a tax of ten or twenty per cent. laid upon tobacco, either in the ports of Virginia, or London, is a duty laid upon the inland plantations of Virginia a hundred miles from the sea, where-ever the tobacco grows.

Many other arguments were made use of. It was urged, that protection is the ground that gives a right of taxation. That the obligation between the colonies and the mother-country, is natural and reciprocal, consisting of defence on the one side, and obedience on the other; and that common sense tells, that they must be dependent in all points upon the mother-country, or else not belong to it at all. That the question is not, what was law, or what was the constitution? but the question is, what is law now, and what is the constitution now? That if a matter of right has been generally exercised, and as generally held to be law, as has been proved in numberless instances, without its ever having been questioned before, it is now the constitution. It was also observed, that the colonies had gone very great lengths; and it was even insisted, that by appointing deputies from their several assemblies to confer together, that they had absolutely forfeited their charters.

No matter of debate was ever more ably and learnedly handled in both houses. It was argued too with moderation and temper. The subject was of the highest importance, and it was not without difficulties both constitutional and political, in the discussion, and in the consequences.

Upon the question being put, the power of the legislature of Great Britain over her colonies, in all cases whatsoever, and without any distinction in regard to taxation, was confirmed and ascertained, without a division. And this was, perhaps, the only question that could have been thought of, upon which the ministry, and their antagonists in the opposition, would have gone together on a division.

A bill brought in and passed for securing the dependency of the colonies, &c. Bill brought in for the total repeal of the stamp-act; great debates thereupon; the bill passed by a great majority. Bill of indemnity passed. Repeal of the cyder-act. Bill for opening free ports in the West Indies. Parliament breaks up; change in the ministry, &c.

THE grand committee who had passed the resolutions, on which the foregoing question was debated, had also passed another for the total repeal of the stamp-act; and two bills were accordingly brought in to answer these purposes. By the resolutions on which the former was founded, it was declared, that tumults and insurrections of the most dangerous nature had been raised and carried on in several of the colonies; in open defiance of government, and in manifest violation of the laws and legislative authority of this kingdom. That these tumults and insurrections had been encouraged and inflamed, by several votes and resolutions which had passed in the assemblies of the said colonies, derogatory to the honour of government, and destructive to their legal and constitutional dependency on the crown and parliament, &c. By the bill itself, all votes, resolutions, or orders, which had been passed by any of the general assemblies in America, by which they assumed to themselves the sole and exclusive right of taxing his Majesty's subjects in the colonies, were annulled, and declared contrary to law, derogatory to the legislative authority of parliament, and inconsistent with their dependency upon the crown.

The opposition, far from being dispirited, seemed to gather fresh vigour, and still opposed the repeal in every part of its progress. So many instances of the inexpediency of the stamp-duty had already occurred, that the question was scarcely controvertible; they accordingly changed their ground, and instead of entering into the merits of that part of the controversy, rested their principal defence upon the resolutions, on which the late bill for securing the dependency of the colonies had been founded.

They argued from thence, that the total repeal of the stamp-act, while such an outrageous resistance continued, would for the future lessen the authority of Great Britain, and make it appear even contemptible. That such a submission of the supreme legislature, would be in effect a surrender of their ancient unalienable rights, to subordinate provincial assemblies, established only by prerogative; which in itself had no such powers to bestow. That a concession of this nature carried with it such an appearance of weakness and timidity in government, as may probably encourage fresh insults, and lessen the respect of his Majesty's subjects to the dignity of his crown, and the authority of the laws.

It was further advanced, that the power of taxation is one of the most essential branches of all authority; that it cannot be equitably or impartially exercised, if it is not extended to all the members of the state, in proportion to their respective abilities; but if a part are suffered to be exempt from a due share of those burdens, which the public exigencies require to be imposed upon the whole, such a partiality, so directly repugnant to the trust reposed by the people in every legislature, must be absolutely destructive of that confidence, on which all government should be founded.

The inability of the colonists to comply with the terms of the stamp-act was also denied; and it was asserted as an instance to the contrary, that the debt contracted by them in the last war, 1,755,000 l. has been already discharged, in the course of three years only; and that the much greater part of their remaining incumbrances, amounting in the whole to 760,000 l. will be discharged in two years more.

Many other arguments were made use of; the general scope and tendency of which were to shew the heavy burthens with which the mother country was loaded; the ability of the Americans; their exemption from all manner of taxation; and their peremptory and refractory refusal, to contribute in any degree to the public expences.

It was said on the other side of the question, that the three first objections bore no manner of weight, as every consequence, they presumed, was already guarded against, by the bill for securing the dependence of the colonies; which had also sufficiently provided for the honour and dignity of Great Britain, and its constitutional superiority over them.

The propriety of all the parts contributing to the expences of the whole, is readily admitted; the fact alleged by the other side, of the heavy debt contracted by the Americans, in the course of the war, sufficiently shews they contributed largely to the public expence; as their being repaid a part of it since, is also a convincing proof, that the parliament were of opinion, they had contributed beyond their abilities.

That nothing could be more remote from fact, than the assertion, that they paid *no* taxes. They even paid many which had been laid on by act of parliament; as they then paid a great variety of port-duties, imposed previous to the stamp-act; which lay very heavy upon their trade, and tended much to inflame their minds against that law. That they paid many port-duties imposed by provincial authority;——many *excises*;—a *land-tax* in many provinces;—an heavy *poll-tax*; besides a *faculty-tax* upon all personal estates and acquisitions, amounting in some provinces to 5 er 6 s. in the pound. So that the assertion of their not contributing to the public expence, being false in fact, every argument, built upon so baseless a foundation, must of course fall to the ground.

It was also shewn, that most of the provinces in North America are notoriously poor: — that they were upwards of four millions in debt to the merchants of Great Britain; who being creditors to such an amount, are in reality the proprietors of a great part of what the Americans *seem* to possess.

That the suppression of manufactures in that country, and obliging them to take every sort which they use from Great Britain, comprizes all species of taxes in one, and makes them in reality the supporters of a great part of the public burdens.

That their great distance from hence, and the difficulty of making us thoroughly acquainted with the minute circumstances of every colony, renders us liable to great mistakes, and consequently to the hazard of great oppression, whenever we attempt to levy internal taxes in that country. That our true policy is to acquiesce in the great commercial advantages we derive from the Americans, rather than to attempt a revenue from thence; which, by disabling the people to make returns to our merchants, will put them under a necessity to set up manufactures of their own.——That by the former policy, America has been advantageous to us, and quiet in itself; but that the present state of things shews too evidently the ill effects of a contrary mode of acting.

These and many other arguments were made use of both within doors and without upon this interesting occasion; notwithstanding the vigour with which the opposition was supported, the bill passed upon a division by a majority of 275 to 167, and was carried up[10] to the lords by above two hundred members of the house of commons. The eclat with which it was introduced in the upper house, did not prevent its meeting with a strong opposition there; 33 lords entered a protest against it at the second reading; as 28 did at the third; it was however carried through by a majority of 34 lords, and in three days after received the royal[11] assent. An event that caused more universal joy, throughout the British dominions, than perhaps any other that can be remembered.

Mar. 18.

A bill was also brought in June and passed; to indemnify 6. those who had incurred penalties on account of the stamp-act, &c. and a requisition was made by government to the North American provinces, to indemnify such persons as had suffered in their property by the late riots; by making them a proper compensation for the losses they had sustained: which after some time was accord-[12] ingly done.

• • •

During the long debates that had attended the repeal of the stamp-act, the ministry had frequent conferences with the North American and West India merchants, by which means they had acquired great knowledge of the trade, and the manner of conducting it, in those parts of the world. In consequence of these informations, and of petitions from several of the most trading towns in England, a bill was passed, for open-[13] June ing free ports, under certain 6. restrictions, in different parts of the West Indies.

Several new and important regulations were also made in the general commercial system of the colonies, and some restrictions taken off, which had been long com-[14] plained of, as heavy clogs upon it.

This conduct gained the administration a great weight with the mercantile part of the nation, who could not avoid being pleased at the attention that was paid to their interests, and the regard to their opinions; so different from what had been generally practised by preceding administrations.

• • •

Extract of a letter from the Right Hon. Henry Seymour Conway,[15] *Esq; one of his Majesty's principal secretaries of state, to Governor Bernard, dated at St. James's*[16] *Oct. 24. 1765.*

IT is with the greatest concern his Majesty learns the disturbances which have lately arisen in your province; the general confusion that seems to reign there, and the total languor, and want of energy in your government to exert itself with any dignity or efficacy, for the suppression of tumults, which seem to strike at the very being of all authority and subordination amongst you.

Nothing can certainly exceed the ill-advised and intemperate conduct held by a party in your province, which can in no way contribute to the removal of any real grievance they might labour under, but may tend to impede and obstruct the exertion of his Majesty's benevolent attention to the ease and comfort, as well as to the welfare of all his people.

It is hoped and expected that this want of confidence in the justice and tenderness of the mother country, and this open resistance to its authority, can only have found place among the lower and more ignorant of the people; the better and wiser part of the colonies will know that decency and submission may prevail, not only to redress grievances, but to obtain grace and favour, while the outrage of a public violence can expect nothing but severity and chastisement.

These sentiments you and all his Majesty's servants, from a sense of your duty to, and love of your country, will endeavour to excite and encourage; you will all in a particular manner call upon them not to render their case desperate. You will in the strongest colours represent to them the dreadful consequences that must inevitably attend the forcible and violent resistance to acts of the British parliament, and the scene of misery and destruction to both countries inseparable from such a conduct.

For however unwillingly his Majesty may consent to the exertion of such powers as may endanger the safety of a single subject; yet can he not permit his own dignity and the authority of the British legislature to be trampled on by force and violence, and in avowed contempt of all order, duty, and decorum.

If the subject is aggrieved, he knows in what manner legally and constitutionally to apply for relief; but it is not suitable either to the safety or dignity of the British empire, that any individuals, under the pretence of redressing grievances, should presume to violate the public peace.

Extract from Mr. Secretary Conway's circular letter; which has been printed in America.

IF by lenient persuasive methods you can contribute to restore the peace and tranquillity to the province, on which their welfare and happiness depend, you will do a most acceptable and essential service to your country: But having taken every step, which the utmost prudence and lenity can dictate in compassion to the folly and ignorance of some misguided people; you will not on the other hand fail to use your utmost power for repelling all acts of outrage and violence, and to provide for the maintenance of peace and good order in the province, by such a timely exertion of force, as that occasion may require; for which purpose you will make the proper application to General Gage, or Lord Colvill, commanders of his Majesty's land and naval forces in America, &c.

Secretary Conway's letter to Governor Bernard, of New England.

St. James's March 31. 1766.

SIR,

HErewith I have the pleasure of transmitting to you the copy of two acts of parliament just passed; the first for securing the just dependency of the colonies on the mother country; the second for the repeal of the act of the last session granting certain stamp duties in America; and I expect shortly to send you a third for the indemnity of such persons as have incurred the penalties imposed by the act just repealed; as such bill is now depending, and has made a considerable progress in the house of Commons.

The moderation, the forbearance, the unexampled lenity and tenderness of parliament towards the colonies, which are so signally displayed in those acts, cannot but dispose the province committed to your care, to that return of chearful obedience to the laws and legislative authority of Great Britain, and to those sentiments of respectful gratitude to the mother-country, which are the natural, and I trust will be the certain effects of much grace and condescension, so remarkably manifested on the part of his Majesty and of the parliament, and the future happiness and prosperity of the colonies will very much depend on the testimonies they shall now give of these dispositions. For, as a dutiful and affectionate return to such peculiar proofs of indulgence and affection may now, at this great crisis, be a means of fixing the mutual interests and inclinations of Great Britain and her colonies, on the most firm and solid foundations, it cannot but appear visible that the least coolness or unthankfulness, the least murmuring or dissatisfaction, on any ground whatever of former heat, or much prevailing prejudice, may fatally endanger that union, and

give the most severe and affecting blow to the future interest of both countries.

You would think it scarce possible, I imagine, that the paternal care of his Majesty for his colonies, or the lenity and indulgence of the parliament, should go further than I have already mentioned; yet so full of true magnanimity are the sentiments of both, and so free from the smallest colour of passion or prejudice, that they seem not only disposed to forgive, but to forget those most undeniable marks of an undutiful disposition, too frequent in the late transactions of the colonies, and which, for the honour of these colonies, it were to be wished had been more discountenanced and discouraged by those who had knowledge to conduct themselves otherwise.

A revision of the late American trade laws is going to be the immediate object of parliament; nor will the late transactions there, however provoking, prevent, I dare say, the full operation of that kind and indulgent disposition prevailing, both in his Majesty and parliament, to give to the trade and interests of America, every relief which the true state of their circumstances demands or admits.

Nothing will tend more effectually to every conciliating purpose, and there is nothing therefore I have in command more earnestly to require of you, than that you should exert yourself in recommending it strongly to the assembly, that full and ample compensation be made to those, who, from the madness of the people, have suffered for their deference to the acts of the British legislature. And you will be particularly attentive that such persons be effectually secured from any further insult, and that, as far as in you lies, you will take care, by your example and influence, that they may be treated with that respect to their persons, and that justice in regard to all their pretensions, which their merits and sufferings undoubtedly claim.

The resolutions of the house of Commons, which, by his Majesty's commands, I transmit to you, to be laid before the assembly, will shew you the sense of that house on these points: and I am persuaded it will, as it most certainly ought, be the glory of that assembly, to adopt and imitate those sentiments of the British parliament, founded on the clearest principles of humanity and justice.

I must mention the one circumstance in particular, that should recommend those unhappy people, whom the outrage of the populace has driven from America, to the affection of all that country; which is, that, unprovoked by the injuries they had suffered to a forgetfulness of what they owed to truth and their country, they gave their testimonies with knowledge, but without passion or prejudice; and those testimonies had, I believe, great weight in persuading the repeal of the stamp-act.

I have only to add, which I do with great pleasure, that every part of your conduct has had the entire and hearty approbation of your sovereign; and that the judicious representations in favour of your province, which appear in your letters laid before both houses of parliament, seem to have their full weight in all those parts of the American interests, to which they relate. And as his Majesty honours you with his fullest approbation, both for the firmness and temperance of your conduct, so I hope your province will cordially feel what they owe to the governor, whom no outrage could provoke to resentment, nor any insult induce to relax in his endeavours to persuade his Majesty to shew his indulgence and favour even to the offending part of his people.

I am,
With great truth and regard,
Your most obedient,
Humble servant,
H. S. CONWAY.

The speech of his Excellency Francis Bernard, Esq; Captain-general and Governor in chief, in and over his Majesty's province of Massachuset's Bay in New England, and Vice-admiral of the the same

To the great and general court of the said province,
Tuesday, June 3. 1766.

Gentlemen of the Council, and Gentlemen of the House of Representatives,

I Have received a letter from the Right Honourable Mr. Secretary Conway, inclosing two acts of parliament; the one, securing the dependency of the colonies on the mother country, and the other for the repeal of the stamp-act. At the same time he is pleased to signify what his Majesty and his parliament expect from the colonies in return for the indulgencies shewn to them. I am also ordered to recommend to you, that full and ample compensation be made to the late sufferers by the madness of the people: and for that purpose I am directed to lay before you the votes of the house of Commons, expressing their sense upon that subject; whose humanity and justice, it is hoped, it will be your glory to imitate. The whole of this letter is conceived in such strong, patriotic, and conclusive terms, that I shall not weaken it by a representation of my own, other than this short recapitulation, necessary to introduce what I have to say on the subject.

I cannot but lament that this letter did not arrive before the meeting of the general court: if it had, I flatter myself it would have prevented a transaction which must now be more regretted than ever. I mean, your excluding from the king's council, the principal crown-officers; men not only respectable in themselves for their integrity, their abilities, and their fidelity to their country, as well as to their king, but also quite necessary to the administration of government, in the very station from which you have displaced them. By this you have anticipated the expectations of the king and parliament, and disappointed them, before they have been communicated to you. It is not now in your power in so full a manner as will be expected, to shew your respectful gratitude to the mother country, or to make a dutiful and affectionate return to the indulgence of the king and parliament. It must and will be understood, that these gentlemen are turned out for their deference to acts of the British legislature. Whilst this proceeding has its full effect, you will not, you cannot avoid being chargeable with unthankfulness and dissatisfaction on ground of former heat and prevailing prejudice.

It is impossible to give any tolerable colouring to this proceeding: if it should be justified by asserting a right, that is, a legal power to chuse whom you please, without regard to any considerations whatsoever; the justification itself will tend to impeach the right. But if your right is ever so absolute, the distinction between a right, and the propriety of exercising it, is very obvious; as this distinction has so lately been used with great effect to your own interest. Next to wishing that this had never happened, it is to be wished some measures might be found to draw a veil over it, or at least to palliate it, and prevent its bad effects; which surely must be very hurtful to this province, if it should be maintained and vindicated. If any expedients can be found out for this purpose, I will heartily concur in them; and in general I will make the best use of all means which you shall put into my hands to save the credit of the province upon this unhappy emergency; and I will set off to the best advantage I can, all other methods which you shall take to demonstrate those sentiments which are expected from you in the most effectual manner.

Gentlemen of the house of representatives,

The requisition contained in this letter is of a most singular nature, and the only one of the kind that I have known since I have served his Majesty in America. It is founded upon a resolution of the house of Commons, formed after a full consideration of the matter, and represented to his Majesty by the address of that house. The justice and humanity of this requisition is so forcible, that it cannot be controverted; the authority with which it is introduced should preclude all disputation about complying with it. I hope therefore, you will add to the merit of compliance by the readiness of it, and assume to yourselves the honour, which now offers itself, of setting the first example of gratitude and dutiful affection to the king and parliament, by giving those proofs of it, which are now pointed out to you. I must observe, that it is from the provincial assembly that the king and parliament expect this compensation should be made to the sufferers, without referring them to any other persons whatsoever. Who ought finally to be charged with this expence, may be a proper consideration for you; and I shall readily concur with you in your resolutions thereon after the sufferers have been fully satisfied.

Gentlemen,

Both the business and the time are most critical; and let me intreat you to recollect yourselves, and consider well what you are about. When the fate of the province is put in a scale, which is to rise or fall according to your present conduct, will you suffer yourselves to be influenced by party animosities or domestic feuds? Shall this fine country be ruined, because every person in the government has not been gratified

with honours or offices according to the full of his pretensions? Shall the private interests, passions, or resentments of a few men deprive this whole people of the great and manifold advantages which the favour and indulgence of their sovereign, and his parliament, are even now providing for them? There never was at any time whatsoever, so fair a prospect of the improvement of the peace and welfare of this province, as is now opening to you. Will you suffer this pleasant view to be intercepted or overclouded by the ill-humours of particulars? When wealth and happiness are held out to you, will you refuse to accept of them? Surely after his Majesty's commands are known, and the terms in which they are signified, well considered, the very persons which have created the prejudices and prepossessions, which I now endeavour to combat, will be the first to remove them, and prevent their ill effects.

It is now declared that such is the magnanimity of the king and his parliament, that they seem disposed not only to forgive, but to forget those unjustifiable marks of an undutiful disposition, too frequent in the late transactions of the colonies. It is my desire to render this grace as beneficial and extensive within this province as it can well be made. But it must be expected, that whosoever intend to take the benefit of it, should intitle themselves to it by a departure from that offensive conduct which is the object of it. Here then will it be necessary to draw a line, to distinguish who are, and who are not the proper objects of the gracious intentions of the king and parliament. And if after this proffered grace, any person should go beyond this line, and still endeavour, directly or indirectly, to foment a division between Great Britain and her colonies, and prevent that connection of policy and union of interests,

which are now in so fair a way of being established to perpetuity, surely that man will have much to answer for to both countries, and will probably be called to answer.

But I hope it will not be so, not in a single instance; but that every person, even they who have given the greatest offence, will embrace this opportunity to restore peace to their country, and obtain indemnity for themselves. And all such who shall really desire to reconcile themselves to the king's government, either at home or here, may assure themselves, that, without a future delinquency, every thing past, will, as far as it can, be buried in total oblivion. No one can suspect me of want of sincerity in making this declaration; as too ready a forgetfulness of injuries hath been said to be my weakness: however, it is a failing which I had rather suffer by, than be without.

I have spoke to you with sincerity, openness, and earnestness, such as the importance of the subject deserves. When the fate of the province seems to hang upon the result of your present deliberations, my anxiety for the event, I hope, will make my warmth excuseable. If I have let drop any word which may seem severe or unkind, let the cause I am engaged in apologize for it: and where the intention is upright, judge of what I say, not by detached words and syllables, but by its general purport and meaning. I have always been desirous of cultivating a good understanding with you: and when I recollect the former happy times, when I scarce ever met the general court without giving and receiving testimonies of mutual approbation, I cannot but regret the interruption of that pleasant intercourse by the successful artifices of designing men, enemies to the country, as well as to me. But now that my character for affection to the province, and attention to its interests, is confirmed by the most authentic testimonials, I hope that at the same time you renew your duty to the King, you will resume a confidence in his representative.

In the House of Representatives, of Massachusets Bay, New England, June 5. 1766,

Voted, that the following address be presented to his Excellency, in answer to his speech to both houses, the 3d instant.

May it please your Excellency,
THE house have fully considered your Excellency's speech of the third instant, and beg leave to observe, that as, on the one hand, no consideration shall ever induce us to remit in the least of our loyalty and gratitude to the best of kings, so, on the other, no unprovoked asperity of expression, on the part of your Excellency, can deter us from asserting our undoubted charter rights and privileges. One of the principal of those is that of annually chusing his Majesty's council for this province.

Had the most excellent letter from one of his Majesty's principal secretaries of state, which has been communicated to the house, arrived sooner, it could not have prevented the freedom of our elections; nor can we, on the strictest examination of the transactions of the day of our general election, so far as the house was concerned, discover the least reason for regret. —So long as we shall have our charter-privileges continued, we must think ourselves inexcusable, if we should suffer ourselves to be intimidated in the free exercise of them. This exercise of our rights can never with any colour of reason be adjudged an abuse of our liberty.

Lest we should be at a loss for the proceedings and transactions which have given your Excellency so much uneasiness, you have been pleased to inform us in express terms, that you mean the excluding from the king's council the principal crown-officers, men not only respectable in themselves for their integrity, their abilities, and their fidelity to their country, as well as to their king, but also quite necessary to the administration of government in the very station from whence we have displaced them. Had your Excellency thought fit to have favoured us with your sentiments and opinion of the candidates previously to the election, it could not have more arrested our attention as a breach of our privileges; and it would surely be as proper to give intimations of this kind before, as now the business is past a remedy, for this year at least. The assembly of another year will act for themselves, or under such influence and direction as they may think fit. The two crown-officers, who were of the honourable board of the last year, and not chosen this, are the lieutenant-governor and secretary. The other gentlemen of the board last year who are not chosen this, hold only provincial commissions. This province has subsisted and flourished, and the administration of government has been carried on here entirely to the royal approbation, when no crown-officers had a seat at the board, and we trust this may be the case again. We find not in the secretary of state's letter the least intimation that it was expected by his Majesty or his ministry, that we should elect into his Majesty's council the principal, or indeed any other crown-officers. For any thing that appears in the letter, we are left entirely to the exercise of our own judgment and best discretion in making our elections, agreeably to the royal charter.

If it is not now in our power, in so full a manner as will be expected, to shew our respectful gratitude to the mother country, or to make a dutiful, affectionate return to the indulgence of the king and parliament, it shall be no fault of ours; for this we intend, and hope we shall be able fully to effect.

We cannot persuade ourselves that it must and will be understood, that those gentlemen were turned out, as your Excellency is pleased to express it, for their deference to acts of the British legislature. We have given the true reason of this proceeding in our answer to your Excellency's first speech of this session. We are under no apprehension that when the true grounds and reasons of our proceedings are known and candidly considered, we shall be in the least degree chargeable with unthankfulness and dissatisfaction, on ground of former heat and prevailing prejudice, or on any other ground.

Your Excellency says, it is impossible to give any tolerable colouring to this proceeding. The integrity and uprightness of our intentions and conduct is such, that no colouring is requisite, and therefore we shall excuse ourselves from attempting any. We hold ourselves to be quite free in our suffrages; and provided we observe the directions of our charter, and the laws of the land, both which we have strictly adhered to, we are by no means accountable but to God and our own consciences for the manner in which we give them. We believe your Excellency is the first governor of this province that ever formally called the two houses of assembly to account for their suffrages, and accused them of ingratitude and disaffection to the crown, because they had not bestowed them on such persons as in the opinion of the governor were quite necessary to the administration of government. Had your Excellency been pleased in season to have favoured us with a list and positive orders whom to chuse, we should, on your principles, have been without excuse. But even the most abject slaves are not to be blamed for disobeying their master's will and pleasure, when it is wholly unknown to them.

Your Excellency says, "If it should be justified by asserting a right, that is, a legal power to chuse whom we please, without regard to any considerations whatever, the justification itself will tend to impeach the right." We clearly assert our charter-rights of a free election; but for your Excellency's definition of this right, viz. "A legal power to chuse whom we please, without regard to any considerations whatever," we contend not. We made our elections after the most mature and deliberate consideration, and had special regard to the qualifications of the candidates, and all circumstances considered, chose those we judged most likely to serve his Majesty, and promote the welfare and prosperity of his people. We cannot conceive how the assertion of our clear charter right of free election can tend to impeach that right or charter. We would hope that your Excellency does not mean openly and publicly to threaten us with a deprivation of our charter-privileges, merely for exercising them according to our best judgment and discretion. As dear to us as our charter is, we should think it of very little value, if it should be adjudged that the sense and spirit of it require the electors should be under the absolute direction and control of the chair even in giving their suffrages. For whatever may be our ideas of the wisdom, prudence, mildness, and moderation of your administration, and of your forgiving spirit, yet we are not sure your successor will possess those shining virtues.

We are very sensible, that be our right of election ever so clear and absolute, there is a distinction between a right and the propriety of exercising it. This distinction, we

hope, will apply itself with full force, and all its advantage, to your Excellency's reluctant exertion of the prerogative in disapproving six of the gentlemen chosen by the two houses of assembly: but this being a matter of discretion, is solely within your Excellency's breast, and we are taught by your just distinction, that such is the gift of our suffrages. It therefore gives us great pain to have our discretion questioned, and our public conduct thus repeatedly arraigned.

Your Excellency has intimated your readiness to concur with us in any palliative or expedient to prevent the bad effects of our elections, which you think must surely be very hurtful to the province, if it should be maintained and vindicated. But as we are under no apprehensions of any such effects, especially when we reflect on the ability and integrity of the council your Excellency has approved of, we beg leave to excuse ourselves, from any unnecessary search after palliatives or expedients.

We thank your Excellency for your kind assurances of "using all means to save the credit of this province;" but we conceive, that when the true state of the province is represented and known, its credit can be in no kind of danger.— The recommendation enjoined by Mr. Secretary Conway's letter, and in consequence thereof made to us, we shall embrace the first convenient opportunity to consider and act upon. In the mean time we cannot but observe, that it is conceived in much higher and stronger terms in the speech than in the letter. Whether in thus exceeding, your Excellency speaks by your own authority, or a higher, is not with us to determine.

However, if this recommendation, which your Excellency terms a requisition, be founded on "so much justice and humanity, that it cannot be controverted;" if

"the authority with which it is introduced should preclude all disputation about complying with it," we should be glad to know what freedom we have in the case.

In answer to the questions which your Excellency has proposed with so much seeming emotion, we beg leave to declare, that we will not suffer ourselves to be in the least influenced by party animosities or domestic feuds, let them exist where they may: that if we can possibly prevent it, this fine country shall never be ruined by any person: that it shall be through no default of ours, should this people be deprived of the great and manifest advantages which the favour and indulgence of our most gracious sovereign and his parliament are even now providing for them. On the contrary, that it shall ever be our highest ambition, as it is our duty, so to demean ourselves in public and in private life, as shall most clearly demonstrate our loyalty and gratitude to the best of kings, and thereby recommend this people to further gracious marks of the royal clemency and favour.

With regard to the rest of your Excellency's speech, we are constrained to observe, that the general air and style of it favours much more of an act of free grace and pardon, than of a parliamentary address to the two houses of assembly; and we most sincerely wish your Excellency had been pleased to reserve it (if needful) for a proclamation.

• • •

Abstract of the late act of parliament for the better securing the dependence of his Majesty's dominions in America, on the crown of Great Britain.

THE preamble sets forth, "That several of the houses of representatives in his Majesty's colonies in *America* had of late, against the law, claimed to themselves, or to the general assemblies of the same, the sole and exclusive right of imposing duties and taxes on his Majesty's subjects in the said colonies, and have passed certain votes, resolutions, and orders, derogatory to the authority of parliament, inconsistent with the dependency of the said colonies upon the crown of Great Britain; it is therefore declared, That the said colonies have been, are, and of right ought to be subordinate unto, and dependent on the imperial crown and parliament of Great Britain; and that the king and parliament of Great Britain had, hath, and of right ought to have full power and authority to make laws and statutes of sufficient force to bind the colonies, and his Majesty's subjects in them, in all cases whatsoever.

" And it is further declared, That all resolutions, votes, orders, and proceedings in any of the said colonies, whereby the power and authority of the king, lords, and commons of Great Britain, in parliament assembled, is denied, or drawn into question, are, and are hereby declared to be utterly null and void to all intents and purposes whatsoever."

Abstract of an act for repealing the stamp-act.

THIS act sets forth, that as the continuance of the former act would be attended with many inconveniences, and may be productive of consequences greatly detrimental to the commercial interests of these kingdoms, it is therefore, from and after the 1st day of May, 1766, with the several matters and things contained in it, hereby repealed and made void, to all intents and purposes whatever.

...

His Majesty's most gracious speech to both houses of parliament, on Tuesday the 14th day of January, 1766; with the humble addresses of both houses upon the occasion, and his Majesty's most gracious answer.

My Lords, and Gentlemen,

WHEN I met you last I acquainted you, that matters of importance had happened in America, which would demand the most serious attention of parliament.

That no information which could serve to direct your deliberations in so interesting a concern might be wanting, I have ordered all the papers that give any light into the origin, the progress, or the tendency of the disturbances which have of late prevailed in some of the northern colonies, to be immediately laid before you.

No time has been lost, on the first advice of these disturbances, to issue orders to the governors of my provinces, and to the commanders of my forces in America, for the exertion of all the powers of government in the suppression of riots and tumults, and in the effectual support of lawful authority.

Whatever remains to be done on this occasion I commit to your wisdom; not doubting but your zeal for the honour of my crown, your attention to the just rights and authority of the British legislature, and your affection and concern for the welfare and prosperity of all my people, will guide you to such sound and prudent resolutions, as may tend at once to preserve those constitutional rights over the colonies, and to restore to them that harmony and tranquillity, which have lately been interrupted by riots and disorders of the most dangerous nature.

If any alterations should be wanting in the commercial oeconomy of the plantations, which may tend to enlarge and secure the mutual and beneficial intercourse of my kingdoms and colonies, they will deserve your most serious consideration. In effectuating purposes so worthy of your wisdom and public spirit, you may depend upon my most hearty concurrence and support. The present happy tranquillity, now subsisting in Europe, will enable you to pursue such objects of our interior policy with a more uninterrupted attention.

Gentlemen of the house of Commons,

I have ordered the proper estimates for the current service of the year to be laid before you. Such supplies as you may grant shall be duly applied with the utmost fidelity, and shall be dispensed with the strictest oeconomy.

My Lords, and Gentlemen,

I earnestly recommend to you to proceed in your deliberations with temper and unanimity. The time requires, and I doubt not but your own inclinations will lead you to those salutary dispositions. I have nothing at heart but the assertion of legal authority, the preservation of the liberties of all my subjects, the equity and good order of my government, and the concord and prosperity of all parts of my dominions.

Notes, 1766

1. The petition of the London merchants to the House of Commons, read on 17 January 1766, estimated the debt to be "... in the Sum of several Millions Sterling." Some recent work suggests that major shifts in the economic relationship between Britain and the Thirteen Colonies had produced a critical state of American indebtedness to British merchants well before the Stamp Act and that opposition to the latter should be examined with this in mind. See M. Egnal and J. A. Ernst, "An Economic Interpretation of the American Revolution," *William and Mary Quarterly*, 1972, 4th ser., vol. 29, pp. 1–32.

2. William Augustus, Duke of Cumberland (1721–65), second (surviving) son of George II and uncle of George III, over whom he had considerable influence. The King sought his help in 1765 in dismissing Grenville, and he was instrumental in the formation of the Rockingham ministry.

3. See, for example, pp. [173–74].

4. The King's speech referred to the anti–Stamp Act riots and the ensuing erosion of orderly government as "Matters of Importance [which] have lately occurred in some of My Colonies in America"—a calculated understatement vigorously protested by Grenville. *Journal of the House of Commons*, vol. 30, pp. 437–38, gives the text of the King's speech and Grenville's proposed amendments.

5. Petitions to Parliament came to be an accepted method for expressing grievances by that part of the nation not directly represented under the restricted franchise. In 1669, Parliament had resolved that presentation of petitions was an inalienable right of the subject.

6. There is good evidence to suggest collusion between Rockingham and the leader of the London merchants' committee, Barlow Trecothick (c. 1719–75), in the organization of the petitions from the other ports and industrial areas. See, for example, D. H. Watson, "Barlow Trecothick," *Bulletin of the British Association for American Studies*, September 1960, n.s. no. 1, pp. 36–47, and March 1961, n.s. no. 2, pp. 29–39.

7. Charles Pratt (1714–94), created Baron Camden, 1765, Attorney-General, 1757–61; Chief Justice of the Common Pleas, 1761–66; Lord Chancellor, July 1766–January 1770. He earned considerable popularity for his judgements declaring general warrants to be illegal; the decisions arose from the case of John Wilkes and number 45 of the *North Briton* (1763). His opposition to the Stamp Act made him something of a popular hero in America also; the towns of Camden, South Carolina, in 1768, and Camden, New Jersey, in 1773, were named in his honour. Both were battlegrounds during the War of Independence.

8. William Pitt (1708–78). His acceptance of the earldom of Chatham in July 1766 markedly reduced his popularity. See *AR*, 1766, p. 48].

9. An electorate of one million is probably a considerable exaggeration; a closer estimate is 245,000. See L. B. Namier, *Structure of Politics at the Accession of George III*, 2nd ed. (London: Macmillan, 1957), pp. 65, 81.

10. The voting figure of 275 to 167 is that for the division on the resolution for repeal of the Stamp Act, taken at the end of the closed debate, in the early hours of the morning of 22 February 1766. The bill for repeal received its third reading on 4 March and was passed 250 votes to 122. See *Journal of the House of Commons*, vol. 30, p. 627. The bill was taken up to the House of Lords the following day. However, in reporting the vote on the resolution of 21 February, the *Register* correctly stressed by implication that this was the crucial division; after this point, the Opposition's efforts, though maintained, were in vain.

11. The Repeal Act was 6 Geo. III c. 11, and the Declaratory Act, 6 Geo. III c. 12.

12. 6 Geo. III c. 51. The matter was not so simple; see *Appendix to the Chronicle*, extracts, pp. 174]–182].

13. 6 Geo. III c. 49.

14. A broad range of concessions, mostly involving elimination or reduction of duties affecting American trade, was embodied in 6 Geo. III c. 52.

15. Henry Seymour Conway (1721–95), brother of the Marquis of Hertford, cousin of Horace Walpole, M.P. for various boroughs, 1741–84; served in the Austrian Succession and Seven Years wars; promoted to Lieutenant-General, 1759. His opposition to the use of general warrants lost him his civil and military posts in 1763, but by 1765, he became attached to the Rockingham group and was appointed Secretary of State for the Southern Department in July. He had consistently opposed the Stamp Act, and he introduced resolutions for the Declaratory Act and the Repeal Act during the February 1766 debates.

16. Francis Bernard (1712–79), Governor of Massachusetts, 1760–69.

1767

Introduction

The *Register* for 1767 devotes virtually no attention to America. Of the eight chapters and fifty-four pages comprising the historical section, only two paragraphs in the last chapter suggest that the "factious and turbulent spirit" of the colonies in the previous year had not been reduced by British concessions and lenience.

The *Register*'s account of these events is an admirable précis of a complex issue. The New York Assembly refused to comply with some of the provisions of the act of 1765 for providing temporary quarters for British troops in America. The presence of the soldiers themselves was not opposed: leading landowners were glad to have military support against the anti-rent movement among their tenants, which was amounting to a minor insurrection by midsummer 1766. The assembly was, however, determined to quarter British soldiers on its own financial and political terms and so substituted its own act which was disallowed by the Privy Council in May 1767.[1]

On 13 May, the House of Commons, in a committee of the whole, debated American affairs and paid special attention to New York. Parliament viewed the defiance of the colony as a particularly serious matter, since it had received a petition in February from New York merchants protesting trade regulations, a petition which seemed almost a claim for commercial autonomy. During the May debates, Parliament was divided only over the degree of

1. *Acts of the Privy Council, Col. Ser. 1766–83*, p. 581.

severity to use in restoring the province to obedience. The Government finally gained a majority on 30 June (the Opposition pressed for a much harder line) for the New York Restraining Act. When the act was forwarded to Governor Sir Henry Moore by the new Secretary of State for the Southern Department (the Earl of Shelburne), he stressed its leniency. On 6 June, the New York Assembly had already abandoned its stand and voted funds in conformance with the requirements of the Quartering Act (without actually acknowledging the act in its own measure). The matter still rankled, and New York was soon to protest parliamentary interference with its legislature and attempts to raise revenue in America.

The *Register*'s failure to report the 1767 attempt at raising revenue in the colonies seems a remarkable omission. The disunited and faltering Chatham administration's Chancellor of the Exchequer was the brilliant, erratic, and irresponsible Charles Townshend.[2] In the debates on 13 and 15 May, Townshend introduced proposals for a new set of duties to be imposed on a range of goods imported into the colonies. The revenue raised was to pay the salaries of Crown officials in America and finance the American Board of Customs Commissioners, to be set up in Boston. In addition, a drawback of all British duties was permitted on tea exported to America, and an extra import duty of three pence per pound was to be levied in the colonies.[3]

Townshend used the colonists' distinction between internal and external taxes and elected to raise revenue by imposing external duties only. He then ensured effective enforcement by establishing an expanded system of Vice-Admiralty Courts.[4] The resultant revenue was earmarked to meet defence costs and to render salaries of Crown officials independent of the colony's control. The bills passed both Houses of Parliament without major debate on the principle of taxing America and received the royal assent on 29 June and 2 July. But Townshend's

2. Charles Townshend (1725–67), M.P. for Harwich from 1761 to his death, had great abilities and equally great defects; he was "... a political adventurer delighting in chaos and confusion." John Brooke, *The Chatham Administration, 1766–1768* (London: 1956), p. 93.

3. 7 Geo. III c. 46; 7 Geo. III c. 41; 7 Geo. III c. 56.

4. The new system of Vice-Admiralty Courts was simultaneously established at Boston, Philadelphia, and Charlestown, as well as Halifax, though it was not implemented until 1768.

cleverness had outreached itself, and Parliament's acquiescence indicated its poor judgement regarding the state of colonial opinion, as the reaction of America was soon to show.[5]

The *Register*'s omission of this episode and concentration on other matters may reflect Parliament's concern with two issues which dominated domestic politics. A major corn shortage created serious disturbances in the fall of 1766, and since Parliament had just been prorogued, royal proclamations were issued to restrain grain profiteers and embargo ships exporting grain. The ministry's attempts to prove the legality of these actions (by implying that the King still held the power to dispense with the normal processes of law in an emergency) provoked a minor constitutional crisis. The attention of Parliament was also focussed on the affairs of the East India Company. The company's new role as a governing power was problem enough, but that was exacerbated by its estimate of profits from the dewanni revenue of £2 million per annum. Stockholders demanded an increase in dividends, the Government expected part of the profits to be paid to the Treasury, and the company pleaded huge debts. Direct government intervention aroused bitter parliamentary debate over the constitutionality of such action, which culminated in one act restraining the dividend and another regulating an annual payment to the state.[6]

The constitutional and legal implications of these issues seem to have been more significant than the American revenue legislation to the editor of the *Register*. The balance had to be redressed in the 1768 volume.

5. See "Introduction, 1768." Townshend did not live to reap the whirlwind; he died suddenly on 4 September 1767.
6. 7 Geo. III c. 48; 7 Geo. III c. 57. The concession permitting drawback of the British duty on tea exported to Ireland and America provides, of course, a link with Townshend's American revenue legislation, since tea importers could now afford to pay an American import duty of three pence in the pound.

The factious turbulent spirit, which seemed to have taken possession of the minds of some of our North American colonies on occasion of the stamp-act, was far from being mollified by the lenient concessions in their favour, and the great consideration shewn to their circumstances by the legislature. Not content with the private acts of outrage that were too often repeated, and marks of disrespect to government which were too frequently shewn; the assembly of New York had, in direct opposition to the act of last session, for the providing of the troops[1] with necessaries in their quarters, passed an act of assembly, by which these provisions were regulated and settled in a mode of their own, without any regard to that prescribed by parliament.

This affair being brought before the house, occasioned many debates; and some rigorous measures were proposed. The general opinion, however, was rather to bring them to temper and a sense of their duty, by acts of moderation, which should at the same time sufficiently support the dignity of the legislature, than by rigorous measures to inflame still farther that spirit of discontent which was already too prevalent among them. Upon these principles, a bill was passed, by June 15th[2] which the governor, council, and assembly of New York, were prohibited from passing or assenting to any act of assembly for any purpose whatsoever, till they had in every respect complied with all the terms of the act of parliament. This restriction, though limited to one colony, was a lesson to them all, and shewed their comparative inferiority, when brought in question with the supreme legislative power.

Notes, 1767

1. 5 Geo. III c. 33.
2. 7 Geo. III c. 59.

1768

Introduction

Organised protest by Americans against the Townshend Acts gained momentum through 1768. The lead was taken by Massachusetts. In January, the House of Representatives petitioned the Crown to repeal the acts; on 11 February, it issued a circular letter to all the other colonial assemblies calling for them to take similar action. Reaction in the other colonies varied in timing and degree, partly influenced by the effect of a circular letter sent to all the colonial governors by the new Secretary of State for the Colonies, Lord Hillsborough. On 21 April, Hillsborough directed the governors to frustrate attempts by their assemblies to cooperate with Massachusetts and to dissolve assemblies of the royal and proprietary colonies should they persist in cooperating. Georgia and South Carolina had already instructed their London agents to press repeal of the Townshend Acts. More significantly, the Virginia House of Burgesses voted on 14 April to petition Parliament in order to protest the new revenue legislation and the New York Restraining Act, and on 9 May, Virginia sent its own circular letter to the other colonies recommending similar action. Despite Hillsborough's letter, every other colony voiced a protest against taxation without consent between early summer and the year's end.

Formal protests were not the only pressure directed at Britain. In October 1767, Boston merchants attempted to organise a nonimportation agreement against British goods. They revived this tactic on 17 March 1768, and

New York merchants agreed in April to join them, providing Philadelphia merchants joined on the same terms. The Pennsylvania merchants however cautiously delayed action until the spring of 1769.

What had disturbed the British government was the rapid growth of collusion among the colonies to defy parliamentary authority and the significant leadership of Massachusetts.

Events in Massachusetts were a specific cause for alarm. Elements dominating the Massachusetts House of Representatives, like Speaker Thomas Cushing, James Otis, Samuel Adams, and John Hancock, were determined to assert the power of the assembly over the executive authority of Governor Bernard. These men opened their attack in February. On 30 June, following Bernard's presentation on 21 June of Hillsborough's 21 April letter requiring the assembly to repudiate its circular letter, they attempted to petition the Crown for Bernard's recall. They were frustrated only when Bernard dissolved the assembly.

The situation in Massachusetts had already reached a new level of instability. Customs officers seized John Hancock's ship *Liberty* on 10 June and provoked a mob reaction in Boston, fomented by the radicals. There followed a town meeting which sent to the governor a petition virtually asserting the legislative autonomy of the colony. The customs commissioners, claiming that the local authorities were impotent, then appealed to the commander-in-chief of British forces in North America, Thomas Gage, for military support. Despite Bernard's reluctance to accede to this step, six warships arrived at Boston on 28 September with transports which promptly disembarked two regiments. News of their impending arrival had already resulted in a convention of delegates from ninety-six towns in the colony (since the assembly was still dissolved). The convention assured the public on 22 September that the rights and liberties of the colony would be protected, but the troops remained, and the *Register* remarked that "the town and province have been in general very quiet." Nevertheless, when John Adams defended Hancock at his trial on the smuggling charge in October he vigorously attacked the constitutionality of Britain's legislation for America and of the jurisdiction of the Vice-Admiralty Courts. The attorney-general dropped the case against Hancock in 1769.

The *Register*'s account of these events is, as far as it goes, full and generally accurate. It concentrates almost exclusively on Massachusetts, and mirrors (it probably helped to confirm) the contemporary British opinion that Massachusetts, with Boston as the centre of disaffection, was the major challenge to imperial authority. Yet, the *Register*'s account tends to overestimate the degree of unanimity in the colonies. The Massachusetts circular letter probably received general support in the colonies, but the nonimportation agreement of October 1767 did not, hence its revival in March 1768. The revolutionary movement spread slowly during 1769, hampered by inter-colonial suspicion and by the reluctance of many merchants to sacrifice improving business prosperity. Indeed, the *Register* barely hints at the growing differences between conservatives, moderates, and radicals which later became a significant feature of American politics.

In the 1768 *Register*'s historical section, only eight pages out of eighty-four deal with American events. This part of the *Register* was increased in 1768,[1] and nine chapters (sixty-five pages) are devoted to European affairs. Chapter X describes the activities of "that bold adventurer," Hyder Ali, whose exploits in the Deccan caused the East India Company new difficulties, and then analyses the American situation. Chapter XI recounts British politics from the November 1767 parliamentary session to the end of the short summer session in May 1768. The key issues were seen as the high cost of provisions, the new act for restraining East India Company dividends, and the dispute over a motion for the introduction of a nullum tempus bill.[2]

The editor notes in the preface that "as the present year has been uncommonly productive of remarkable events that do not properly come within the line of History, the Chronicle and its Appendix have, on that account, been extended to an unusual length." The *Chronicle* therefore recounts in fragments John Wilkes's successful contest in

1. See "General Introduction."
2. The old maxim "nullum tempus occurrit regi," i.e., no length of time in possession by a subject can prevent the Crown from asserting a claim to lands which could be part of the royal domain, reemerged in a legal struggle over part of the Duke of Portland's estate. The 1768 bill sought to allay the fears of the landed interest by preventing the Crown from raising a claim to a property alienated longer than sixty years. Though strongly supported by Rockingham, the motion was defeated. It eventually passed, in 1769.

the Middlesex election and the accompanying popular disorders,[3] which increased with Wilkes's commitment to prison on the old charges of publishing a seditious and obscene libel (number 45 of the *North Briton* and his poem "Essay on Woman").

The *Appendix to the Chronicle* devotes twenty of thirty-six pages to a selection of papers illustrating the development of events in Massachusetts. Special prominence is given the refusal of the township of Hatfield to send representatives to the convention held on 22 September, on the grounds that "the measures the town of Boston are pursuing, and proposing to us and the people of this province to unite in, are unconstitutional, illegal and wholly unjustifiable . . . ." The *Register* thus reveals the dilemma of those who originally opposed American taxation but who could not condone the extremism of the American reaction: they welcomed any evidence that suggested such extremism was not a universal phenomenon. The King and the ministry of course preferred a conspiracy theory. The King's speech opening Parliament in November chose to blame ". . . the mischievous designs of those turbulent and seditious persons, who, under false pretenses, have but too successfully deluded numbers of my subjects in America." The whole of this speech is extracted from *State Papers*, since it indicates how seriously the ministry regarded the state of American affairs and the Government's intention to make America the main business of the new session.[4]

3. As discontent with economic conditions grew, working-class violence became a serious problem, and not infrequently Wilkes was confusedly identified as a popular hero. In the ugly shooting affray at Shadwell in London's East End in April, the rioting coal-heavers cried the slogan: "Wilkes and Liberty." *AR*, 1768, p. 224].
4. See extracts for 1769, pp. [52*–[61*.

In America, the quiet which began to take place upon the repeal of the stamp act was again disturbed, and the affairs of that country again fell into confusion. The laws which had been passed[1] last year, for the purpose of raising a revenue in the Colonies by the laying of duties on the importation of glass, paper, and some other commodities from England, and the consequent establishment of Custom-houses in their ports, have been productive of very alarming disturbances in the Colonies, and of consequences highly prejudicial to the commercial interests of this country. It may appear unfortunate, that, after the recent example of the mischiefs that attended the stamp act, and the consequent repeal of it from a conviction of those evils, a measure of a similar tendency should be so suddenly adopted, before the ill humours that had arisen from the former had yet subsided. Much has been said pro and con on this subject, and most of the arguments already used on the repeal of the stamp act have been repeated; this discussion will properly appear in our next volume, when, from the consequences attending this measure, it becomes an object of national and parliamentary consideration.

The first public instance of disgust shewn upon this occasion was at Boston, where, at a meeting of the inhabitants, several resolutions Oct. 27, 1767. were entered into, for the encouragement of manufactures, the promoting of œconomy, and the lessening and restraining the use of foreign superfluities. These resolutions, all of which were highly prejudicial to the commerce of this country, contained a long list of enumerated articles, which it was either determined not to use at all, or in the smallest possible quantities. A subscription was opened at the same time, and a committee appointed for the en-

couragement of their own former manufactures, and the establishment of new ones. Among these, it was resolved to give particular encouragement to the making of paper, glass, and the other commodities that were liable to the payment of the new duties, upon importation. It was also resolved to restrain the expences of funerals, to reduce dress to a degree of primitive simplicity and plainness, and in general not to purchase any commodities from the mother country, that could be procured in any of the Colonies.

These resolutions were adopted, or similar ones entered into, by all the old Colonies on the continent.[2]
Feb. 11, 1768. In some time after, a circular letter was sent by the Assembly of Massachuset's Bay, signed by the Speaker, to all the other Assemblies in North America. The design of this letter was to shew the evil tendency of the late Acts of Parliament, to represent them as unconstitutional, and to propose a common union between the Colonies, in the pursuit of all legal measures to prevent their effect, and a harmony in their applications to Government for a repeal of them. It also expatiated largely on their natural rights as men, and their constitutional ones as English subjects; all of which, it was pretended, were infringed by these laws.

It happened, unfortunately, that a continued course of altercation, and an almost total difference of opinion upon every subject, had prevailed for some years between the Assemblies of Massachuset's Bay and the Governor of that Colony. This altercation was carried on with much asperity; and both sides, on some occasions, seemed more attentive to the keenness of their observations, and the tartness of their replies, than to the utility or propriety of the measures they were pursuing. The severity of these altercations left a bitterness behind, that was far from being

favourable to that happy temper and conciliating disposition, which were now so much to be wished.

A letter which the Governor had received from the Earl of Shelburne, one of the principal Secretaries of State, and which contained very severe animadversions on the conduct of the Assembly, was, in pursuance of the Governor's order, and the intention of writing it, read to that body by the Secretary. This letter caused great heats in the Assembly; and it is said, the strictest decency was not observed in the debates it occasioned, and the observations that were made upon it. In these debates it was said, that the charges made in it must have been founded upon a misrepresentation of facts by the Governor, in his dispatches to the Ministry; and a Committee was appointed to wait on him, to desire a copy of Lord Shelburne's letter, as well as of those which he had wrote himself relative to the Assembly, and to which the charges in that must refer. These copies being refused, the Assembly wrote a letter to the Secretary of State, in which they recite the circumstances of the transaction, and take great pains to vindicate their own conduct at the expence of the Governor, to whose misrepresentation they charge the Minister's ill opinion of it. They also wrote letters to the Lords of the Treasury, and most of the great Officers of State, in which, along with great professions of loyalty, they remonstrated strongly against the operations of the late Acts of Parliament; which they insinuated to be contrary to the Constitution, and totally subversive of their rights and liberties.

The Governor, finding that there was no hopes to mollify the refractory spirit which was so predominant in the Assembly, adjourned it. In the March 4. Speech which he delivered upon this occasion were many strictures on their conduct, particularly in regard to Lord Shelburne's letter; and he complained greatly of some turbulent factious members, who, under false pretences of patriotism, had unhappily acquired too great an influence, as well in the Affembly, as among the people; who facrificed their country to the gratification of their paffions, and to the fupport of an importance which could have no exiftence but in times of trouble and confufion.

In the midft of thefe diftractions in America, a new eftablifhment was made at home, by which a Secretary of State was appointed to[4] the department of the Colonies only. A great deal was hoped from this arrangement. Lord Hillfborough, who appeared firft in that office, wrote a circular letter to the Governqrs of all the Colonies, who had before received the circular letters from the Affembly at Bofton. By this letter his Majefty's diflike to that meafure was expreffed in the ftrongeft terms. It was declared, that he confidered it, as of the moft dangerous and factious tendency; calculated to inflame the minds of the people; to promote an unwarrantable combination; to excite an open oppofition to, and denial of, the authority of Parliament; and to fubvert the true principles of the Conftitution: And that his Majefty expected from the known affection of the refpective Affemblies, that they would defeat this flagitious attempt to difturb the public peace, and treat it with the contempt it deferved, by taking no notice of it.

Another letter, of the April 22. fame date, was wrote to Governor Bernard, in which the fame exceptions to the circular letter are repeated, which is faid to have been a meafure carried through a thin houfe at the end of a feffion, and in which the Affembly departed from that fpirit of prudence, and refpect to the Con-

ftitution, which feemed to have influenced a majority of its members, in a full houfe, and at the beginning of the feffion; from whence his Majefty could not but confider it as a very unfair proceeding, and to have been carried by furprize through the Houfe of Reprefentatives. A requifition was then made, in his Majefty's name, That the new Affembly would refcind the refolution which gave birth to the circular letter, and declare their difapprobation of, and diffent to, fo rafh and hafty a proceeding: That, as his Majefty had the fulleft reliance on the affections of his fubjects in the Maffachufet's Bay, he had the better ground to hope, that the attempts made by a defperate faction to difturb the public tranquillity would be difcountenanced, and that the execution of the meafure recommended would not meet with any difficulty.

This part of the letter June 21. was laid before the new Affembly by the Governor, with a meffage in which he earneftly requefted their compliance; but obferved, that, in cafe of a contrary conduct, he had received his Majefty's inftructions in what manner to act, and muft do his duty. This produced a meffage from the Affembly, in which they defired a copy of the inftructions which the Governor alluded to, as well as of fome letters and papers which he had laid before the Council. The Governor fent a copy of the remainder of Lord Hillfborough's letter, in which the inftructions were contained, to the Affembly, by which he was directed, in cafe of their refufal to comply with his Majefty's reafonable expectation, to diffolve them immediately, and to tranfmit a copy of their proceedings upon it, to be laid before the Parliament.

The Affembly not having given any anfwer to the requifition for about a week, the Governor

fent a meffage to urge them to it; in anfwer to which they applied for a recefs, that they might have an opportunity to confult their conftituents upon the occafion. This being refufed, the queftion was put for refcinding the refolution of the laft houfe, which paffed in the negative by a divifion of ninety-two to feventeen. A letter was then refolved on to Lord Hillfborough, and an anfwer to the meffages from the Governor. In both thefe pieces great pains are taken to juftify the conduct of the laft Affembly, as well as of the prefent; the charges of furprize, and of a thin houfe, are abfolutely denied; and, on the contrary, they fay, that the refolution for the circular letter was paffed in a full feffion, and by a great majority. The legality of that meafure was defended, as it was the inherent right of the fubjects to petition the King, either jointly or feverally, for a redrefs of grievances. In regard to refcinding the refolution it was obferved, that, to fpeak in the language of the common law, it was not now executory, but to all intents and purpofes executed: That the circular letters had been fent, and many of them anfwered; that both have appeared in the public papers; and that they could now as well refcind the letters as the refolves on which they were founded, and that both would be equally fruidlefs. In the letter to the Secretary of State, they made feveral comments, with great freedom, on the nature of the requifition; and alledged that it was unconftitutional, and without a precedent, to command a free Affembly, on pain of its exiftence, to refcind any refolution, much lefs that of a former Houfe. They complained greatly of the bafe and wicked mifreprefentations that muft have been made to his Majefty, to caufe him to confider a meafure perfectly legal and conftitutional, and which only tended to lay the grievances of his subjects before the Throne, as of an ' inflammatory nature, tending to create unwarrantable combinations, and to excite an opposition to the authority of Parliament,' which are the terms in which it is described in the letter. They conclude with professions of the greatest loyalty, and the strongest remonstrances against the late laws. They were in the mean time preparing a petition to the King for the removal of their Governor, in which they laid a number of charges against him, that were urged with great acrimony; but, before the finishing hand could be put to it, the Assembly was dissolved.

The circular letters, which the Secretary of State had wrote to the other Colonies, were attended with as little efficacy as that which was sent to Boston. The different Assemblies wrote answers to that of Massachuset's Bay, which were received by the late Speaker, in which they expressed the highest approbation of their conduct, and a firm resolution to coincide in their measures. Some of them also returned addresses to the Secretary of State, in which they not only justified the measures taken by the Assembly at Boston; but animadverted, with great freedom, on several passages, as well as on the requisition, contained in his letter. In the mean time, most of them entered into resolutions, not to import or purchase any English goods, except what were already ordered for the ensuing fall and such articles of necessity as they could not do without, until the late laws were repealed.

Previous to the dissolution of the Assembly, a great tumult happened at Boston, June 10. in consequence of a seizure made by the Board of Customs, of a sloop belonging to one of the principal merchants of that town. It appears [5] that this sloop was discharged of a cargo of wine, and in part re-

loaded with a quantity of oil, which was however done under pretence of converting her into a store, without any great attention having been paid to the new laws, or to the Custom-house regulations. Upon the seizure, the officers made a signal to the Romney man of war; and her boats were sent manned and armed, who cut away the sloop's fasts, and conveyed her under the protection of that ship. The populace having assembled in great crowds upon this occasion, they pelted the Commissioners of the Customs with stones, broke one of their swords, and treated them in every respect with the greatest outrage; after which, they attacked their houses, broke the windows, and hauled the Collector's boat to the common, where they burnt it to ashes.

The Officers of the Customs, upon these extraordinary acts of outrage, found it necessary, for the security of their lives, to retire aboard the man of war, from whence they removed to Castle William, a fortification on a small island in the harbour, where they resumed the functions of their office. In the mean time, Town-meetings were held, and a remonstrance presented to the Governor, in which the rights they claimed were supported in direct opposition to the Legislature, and an extraordinary requisition made, that he would issue an order for the departure of his Majesty's ship the Romney out of the harbour.

The temper and conduct of the people became every day more licentious. That republican spirit to which this Colony owed its foundation, and the levelling principles in which the inhabitants were nursed, being now operated upon by measures which they regarded as totally subversive of their rights, and inflamed by the arts of some factious and designing men, who had great influence among them, they seemed equally incapable to prescribe the due limits to their pas-

sions, and to preserve a proper decency in the manner in which they expressed them. Their public writers, as well as speakers, were generally very intemperate; and a certain stile and manner was introduced, which seemed peculiar to themselves, and too ridiculous for serious composition. In some of these publications, while they seemed, on one hand, to forget their dependance as Colonies, and to assume the tone of distinct and original States; on the other, they eagerly claimed all the benefits of the English constitution and the highest rights of Englishmen, but did not recollect, that it was that dependance only, which could entitle them to any share of those rights and benefits. A light and irreverent language became the mode, in all matters which related to Government, or even to the Legislature; but when their Provincial Assemblies came to be mentioned, they were no longer known by that appellation, but were upon every occasion distinguished by the title of Parliaments.

A report that their Petition to the King had not been delivered by the Secretary of State, contributed greatly to excite the ferment and ill blood among the people. It was said that the Petition was refused to be received in London, upon an objection that was made, that the Colony Agent was not properly authorised to deliver it, as he had been [6] appointed by the Assembly without the consent of the Governor. The dissolution of the General Assembly increased the disorder; and it may be supposed that a circumstance attending the sloop that was lately seized, which was the property of one of the Representatives of the town of Boston, did not contribute to lessen it.

While things were in this unhappy situation, two regiments were ordered from Ireland to support the Civil government, and several detachments from different parts of the continent rendezvouzed at Halifax for the same purpose. No account of a menace made by the most dangerous and cruel enemy could excite a greater alarm than this intelligence did at Boston, and it was treated in all the language of invasion and conquest. Upon the first rumour of it, a meeting of the inhabitants was immediately summoned at Faneuil-hall, Sept. 12. where they chose one of their late popular Representatives as Moderator. A Committee was then appointed to wait on the Governor, to know what grounds he had for some intimations he had lately given, that some regiments of his Majesty's forces were expected in that town; and at the same time to present a Petition, to desire he would issue precepts to convene a general Assembly with the greatest speed; to both which an immediate answer was required. The Governor answered, that his information about the arrival of the troops was of a private nature, and that he could do nothing as to the calling of another Assembly for this year, until he received his Majesty's instructions, under whose consideration it now was.

A Committee, which had been appointed to consider of the present state of their affairs, gave in their report a long declaration and recital of their rights, and the supposed infractions of them, which had been lately made; and passed several hasty resolutions, particularly in regard to the legality of raising or keeping a standing army among them, without their own consent, which they founded on the Act of the first of King William, which declares it to be contrary to law, to keep an army in the kingdom in time of peace without the consent of Parliament. This report

and the resolutions were unanimously agreed to by the Assembly, and a general resolution passed, which was also founded on a clause in the same law, which recommends the frequent holding of Parliaments, by which a Convention was summoned to meet at Boston. In pursuance of this resolution, the four Members who had represented the town in the late Assembly were now appointed as a Committee to act for it in the Convention; and the Selectmen were ordered to write to all the other towns in the Province, to propose their appointing Committees for the same purpose.

The most extraordinary act of this Town-meeting, was a requisition to the inhabitants, that, as there was a prevailing apprehension in the minds of many of a war with France, they should be accordingly provided with arms, ammunition, and the necessary accoutrements, so as to be properly prepared in case of sudden danger. A day of public prayer and fasting was then appointed, and the meeting dissolved.

The circular letter which the Select-men sent to the other towns in the province, was wrote in the same spirit as the acts and resolutions which it inclosed, and on which it was founded. In this time of general distemper, when ninety-six towns appointed committees to attend the convention, the town of Hatfield refused to concur in this measure; and the spirited and judicious answer which the inhabitants returned to the Select-men at Boston, will be a lasting monument of the prudence and good sense that influenced their conduct. This letter, as well as the other original papers relative to this transaction, our readers will see in the Appendix to the Chronicle.

The first act of the Convention, was a message to the Governor, in which they Sept. 22.

disclaimed all pretence to any authoritative or governmental acts: that they were chosen by the several towns, and came freely and voluntarily, at the earnest desire of the people, to consult and advise such measures as may promote peace and good order in the present alarming situation. They then reiterate the present grievances, complain that they are grossly misrepresented in Great Britain, and press the Governor in the most urgent terms to convoke a General Assembly, as the only means to guard against those alarming dangers that threatened the total destruction of the Colony. The Governor admonished them, as a friend to the Province, and a well-wisher to the individuals of it, to break up their assembly instantly, and to separate before they did any business: That he was willing to believe that the gentlemen who issued the summons for this meeting were not aware of **the nature of the high offence they were committing; and that those who have obeyed them have not considered the penalties they shall incur, if they persist in continuing their session: At present, ignorance of law may excuse what is past; a step farther will take away that plea: That a meeting of the Deputies of the towns is an assembly of the Representatives of the people to all intents and purposes; and that the calling it a Committee of Convention will not alter the nature of the thing.** He added, that if they did not regard this admonition, he must, as Governor, assert the prerogative of the Crown in a more public manner: That they may assure themselves, for he spoke from instruction, the King was determined to maintain his entire Sovereignty over that Province; and whoever should persist in usurping any of the rights of it, would repent of his rashness.

This answer produced another message, wherein they justified their meeting as being only an assemblage of private persons, and desired explanations as to the criminality with which their proceedings were charged. The Governor refused to receive that or any other message from them, as it would be admitting them to be a legal Assembly, which he would not by any means allow. The Convention then appointed a Committee, who drew up a report in terms of great moderation, which was approved of by the Assembly. In this they assign the causes of their meeting, disclaim all pretence to any authority whatsoever, and advise and recommend it to the people to pay the greatest deference to Government, and to wait with patience for the result of his Majesty's wisdom and clemency, for a redress of their grievances. They at the same time declare for themselves, that they will in their several stations yield every possible assistance to the Civil magistrate, for the preservation of peace and order, and the suppression of riots and tumults. The Convention having then prepared a representation of their conduct, and a detail of many of the late transactions, to be transmitted to their Agent in London, Sept. 29. was broke up.

The day the Convention broke up, the fleet from Halifax, consisting of several frigates and sloops of war, and some transports, with two regiments and a detachment of artillery on board, arrived in the harbour. Some difficulties arose at first about quartering the troops, which the Council refused to agree to, as the barracks of Castle William were sufficient to receive them; this was however got over by providing quarters, which were then to be considered as barracks, and the Council upon that footing allowed them barrack provisions. General Gage arrived soon after,[10] as did the two regiments from Ireland. A tolerable harmony has subsisted between the people and the troops; and the town and province have been in general very quiet.

•••

The public writings, which the extraordinary transactions in our colonies have this year produced, are so numerous and diffuse, that in themselves they would form a volume of very considerable bulk; for which reason, it is only in our power to select a few of the most interesting and important of them for our readers.

Copy of the Agreement entered into by the inhabitants of Boston, the capital of the province of Massachusetts-bay.

THE merchants and traders in the town of Boston having taken into consideration the deplorable situation of the trade, and the many difficulties it at present labours under on account of the scarcity of money, which is daily increasing for want of the other remittances to discharge our debts in Great Britain, and the large sums collected by the officers of the customs for duties on goods imported; the heavy taxes levied to discharge the debts contracted by the government in the late war; the embarrassments and restrictions laid on the trade by several late acts of parliament; together with the bad success of our cod fishery this season, and the discouraging prospect of the whale fishery, by which our principal sources of remittance are like to be greatly diminished, and we thereby rendered unable to pay the debts we owe the merchants in Great Britain, and to continue the importation of goods from thence;

We, the subscribers, in order to relieve the trade under those discouragements, to promote industry, frugality, and œconomy, and to discourage luxury, and every kind of extravagance, do promise and engage to and with each other as follows:

First, That we will not send for or import from Great Britain, either upon our own account, or upon commission, this fall, any other goods than what are already ordered for the fall supply.

Secondly, That we will not send for or import any kind of goods or merchandize from Great Britain, either on our own account, or on commissions, or any otherwise, from the 1st of January 1769, to the 1st of January 1770, except salt, coals, fish-hooks and lines, hemp, and duck bar lead and shot, wool-cards and card-wire.

Thirdly, That we will not purchase of any factor, or others, any kind of goods imported from Great Britain, from January 1769, to January 1770.

Fourthly, That we will not import, on our own account, or on commissions, or purchase of any who shall import from any other colony in America, from January 1769, to January 1770, any tea, glass, paper, or other goods commonly imported from Great Britain.

Fifthly, That we will not, from and after the 1st of January 1769, import into this province any tea, paper, glass, or painters colours, until the act imposing duties on those articles shall be repealed.

In witness whereof, we have hereunto set our hands, this first day of August, 1768.

New-York, Sept. 15. The following resolves are agreed to by the tradesmen of this city, reflecting on the salutary measures entered into by the people in Boston and this city, to restrict the importation of goods from Great Britain, until the acts of parliament laying duties on paper, glass, &c. are repealed: and being animated with a spirit of liberty, and thinking it our duty to exert ourselves by all lawful means, to maintain and obtain our just rights and privileges, which we claim under our most excellent constitution as Englishmen, not to be taxed but by our own consent or that of our representatives: and in order to support and strengthen our neighbours the merchants of this city, we the subscribers, uniting in the common cause, do agree to and with each other, as follows:

I. That we will not ourselve purchase or take any goods or merchandize imported from Europe, by any merchant, directly or indirectly contrary to the true intent and meaning of an agreement of the merchants of this city, on the 27th of August last.

II. That we will not ourselves or by any other means, buy any kind of goods from any merchant store-keeper, or retailer, (if any such there be) who shall refuse to join with their brethren in signing the said agreement; but that we will use every lawful means in our power to prevent our acquaintance from dealing with them.

III. That if any merchant, importing from Europe, should import any goods in order to sell them in this province, contrary to the above agreement, that we ourselves will by no means deal with such importers; and as far as we can, by all lawful means, endeavour to discourage the sale of such goods.

V. That we will endeavour to fall upon some expedient to make known such importers or retailers as shall refuse to unite in maintaining and obtaining the liberties of their country.

V. That we, his majesty's most dutiful and loyal subjects, inhabitants of the city of New-York, being filled with love and gratitude to our present most gracious sovereign, and the highest veneration for the British constitution, which we unite to plead as our birth-right, and are always willing to unite to support and maintain, give it as our opinion, and are determined to deem those persons who shall refuse to unite in the common cause, as acting the part of an enemy to the true interest of Great Britain and her colonies, and consequently not deserving the patronage of merchants or mechanics.

New-York, Sept. 5, 1768.

PROCEEDINGS at BOSTON: *From the New-York Gazette of Monday, Sept. 26, 1768.*
Boston, Sept. 19.

At a meeting of the freeholders, and other inhabitants of the town of Boston, legally qualified and warned in public town meeting assembled, at Faneuil-Hall, on Monday the 12th of September, A. D. 1768.

The meeting was opened with prayer by the Rev. Dr. Cooper.

The hon. James Otis, esq; was unanimously chosen moderator.

THE petition of a considerable number of the respectable inhabitants to the select-men, dated the 8th instant, praying that the town might be forthwith legally convened, to enquire of his excellency the governor, the grounds and reasons of sundry declarations made by him, that three regiments may be daily expected, two of them to be quartered in this town, and one at Castle-William; as also to consider of the most wise, constitutional, loyal, and salutary measures to be adopted on such an occasion, was read, whereupon the following vote was passed:

Whereas it has been reported in this town meeting, that his excellency the governor has intimated his apprehensions that one or more regiments of his majesty's troops are daily to be expected here:

Voted, That the hon. Thomas Cushing, esq; Mr. Samuel Adams, Richard Dana, esq; Benj. Kent, esq; and Dr. Joseph Warren, be a committee, to wait upon his excellency, if in town, humbly requesting that he would be pleased to communicate to the town the grounds and assurances he may have thereof.

Upon a motion made and seconded,

Voted, That the following petition be presented to his excellency the governor; and a committee was appointed for that purpose, who were directed humbly to request his excellency to favour the town with an immediate answer.

To his excellency Francis Bernard, esq; governor, &c.

May it please your excellency,

THE inhabitants of the town of Boston legally assembled, taking into consideration the critical state of the public affairs, more especially the present precarious situation of our invaluable rights and privileges, civil and religious, most humbly request that your excellency would be pleased forthwith to issue precepts for a general assembly, to be convened with the utmost speed, in order that such measures may be taken as in their wisdom they may think proper for the preservation of our said rights and privileges.

And your petitioners, as in duty bound, &c.

Upon a motion made and seconded, a committee was appointed to take the state of our public affairs into consideration, and report at the adjournment the measures they apprehend most salutary to be taken in the present emergency.

Adjourned till the next day ten o'clock, A. M.

Tuesday, the 13th Sept. ten o'clock, A. M. met accordingly.

THE committee appointed yesterday to wait upon his excellency with the petition and request of the town, reported from his excellency the following answer in writing:

Gentlemen,

MY apprehensions that some of his majesty's troops are to be expected in Boston, arise from information of a private nature: I have received no public letters, notifying to me the coming of such troops, and requiring quarters for them; whenever I do, I shall communicate them to his majesty's council.

The business of calling another assembly for this year is now before the king, and I can do nothing in it until I receive his majesty's commands. FRA. BERNARD.

The committee appointed to take the state of our public affairs into consideration, reported the following declaration and resolves.

WHEREAS it is the first principle in civil fociety, founded in nature and reafon, that no law of the fociety can be binding on any individual without his confent, given by himfelf in perfon, or by his representative, of his own free election:

And whereas in and by an act the Britifh parliament paffed in the firft year of the reign of king Will and queen Mary, of glorious and bleffed memory, entitled, An declaring the rights and liberties the fubject, and fettling the ceffion of the crown; the preamble of which act is in thefe words, vz ' Whereas the late king James Second, by the affiftance of evil councellors, judges, and min fters, employed by him, did deavor to fubvert and extirpate proteftant religion, and the laws liberties of this kingdom;' it exprefly, among other things, clared, 'That the levying money the ufe of the crown, by preten of prerogative, without grant parliament, for a longer time or other manner than the fame is granted, is illegal:

And whereas in the third year the reign of the fame king Will and queen Mary, their majef were gracioufly pleafed, by th royal charter, to give and grant the inhabitants of this his majef province, all the territory ther defcribed, to be holden in fiee common foccage: and alfo to dain and grant to the faid in bitants certain rights, liberties privileges therein exprefly mention among which, it is granted, eftabl ed, and ordained, that all and ev the fubjects of them, their h and fucceffors, which fhall go te babit within the faid province territory, and every of their child which fhall happen to be born th or on the feas in going thither returning from thence, fhall and enjoy all liberties and immu ties of free and natural fubje within any of the dominions of them, their heirs and fucceffors, es all intents, purpofes, and con-

structions whatever, as if they and every of them were born within the realm of England:

And whereas by the aforefaid act of parliament made in the firft year of the faid king William and queen Mary, all and fingular the premifes contained therein are claimed, demanded, and infifted on, as the undoubted rights and liberties of the fubjects born within the realm:

And whereas the freeholders and other inhabitants of this town, the metropolis of the province in the faid charter mentioned, do hold all the rights and liberties therein contained to be facred and inviolable; at the fame time publicly and folemnly acknowledging their firm and unfhaken allegiance to their alone rightful fovereign king George the third, the lawful fucceffor of the faid king William and queen Mary to the Britifh throne: Therefore,

Refolved, That the faid freeholders and other inhabitants of the town of Bofton, will, at the utmoft peril of their lives and fortunes, take all legal and conftitutional meafures to defend and maintain the perfon, family, crown, and dignity of our faid fovereign lord, George the third; and all and fingular the rights, liberties, privileges, and immunities, granted in the faid royal charter; as well thofe which are declared to be belonging to us as Britifh fubjects by birthright, as all others therein fpecially mentioned.

And whereas by the faid royal charter it is fpecially granted to the great and general court or affembly therein conftituted, to impofe and levy proportionable and reafonable affeffments, rates, and taxes, upon the eftates and perfons of all and every the proprietors and inhabitants of the faid province or territory, for the fervice of the king, in the neceffary defence and fupport of his government of the province, and

the protection and prefervation of his fubjects therein: Therefore,

Voted, As the opinion of this town, that the levying money within this province for the ufe and fervice of the crown, in other manner than the fame is granted by the great and general court or affembly of this province, is in violation of the faid royal charter; and the fame is alfo in violation of the undoubted natural rights of fubjects, declared in the aforefaid act of parliament, freely to give and grant their own money for the fervice of the crown, with their own confent, in perfon, or by reprefentatives of their own free election.

And whereas in the aforefaid act of parliament it is declared, that the raifing or keeping a ftanding army within the kingdom, in time of peace, unlefs it be with the confent of parliament, is againft law; it is the opinion of this town, that the faid declarations are founded in the indefeafible right of the fubjects to be confulted, and to give their free confent, in perfon, or by reprefentatives of their own free election, to the raifing and keeping a ftanding army among them; and the inhabitants of this town, being free fubjects, have the fame right, derived from nature, and confirmed by the Britifh conftitution, as well as the faid royal charter; and therefore the raifing or keeping a ftanding army, without their confent, in perfon, or by reprefentatives of their own free election, would be an infringement of their natural, conftitutional, and charter rights; and the employing fuch arts for the enforcing of laws made without the confent of the people, in perfon, or by their reprefentatives, would be a grievance.

The foregoing report being divers times diftinctly read, and confidered by the town, the queftion was put, Whether the fame fhall be accepted and recorded?

and paſſed unanimouſly in the affirmative.

Upon a motion made and ſeconded, the following vote was unanimouſly paſſed, viz.

WHEREAS by an act of parliament of the firſt of king William and queen Mary, it is declared, that for the redreſs of all grievances, and for amending, ſtrengthening, and preſerving the laws, parliaments ought to be held frequently; and inaſmuch as it is the opinion of this town, that the people labour under many intolerable grievances, which, unleſs ſpeedily redreſſed, threaten the total deſtruction of our invaluable, natural, conſtitutional, and charter rights:

And furthermore, as his excellency the governor has declared himſelf unable, at the requeſt of this town, to call a general court, which is the aſſembly of the ſtates of this province for the redreſs of ſuch grievances:

Voted, That this town will now make choice of a ſuitable number of perſons, to act for them as a committee in convention with ſuch as may be ſent to join them from the ſeveral towns in this province, in order that ſuch meaſures may be conſulted and adviſed, as his majeſty's ſervice, and the peace and ſafety of the ſubjects in the province, may require.

Whereupon the hon. James Otis, eſq. hon. Thomas Cuſhing, eſq. Mr. Samuel Adams, and John Hancock, eſq. were appointed a committee for the ſaid purpoſe; the town hereafter to take into conſideration what recompence ſhall be made them for the ſervice they may perform.

Voted, That the ſelect-men be directed to write to the ſelect-men of the ſeveral towns within this province, informing them of the foregoing vote; and to propoſe that a convention be held, if they ſhall think proper, at Faneuil-hall, in this town, on Thurſday the 22d of September inſtant, at ten o'clock before-noon.

Upon a motion made and ſeconded, the following vote was paſſed by a very great majority, viz.

WHEREAS by an act of parliament of the firſt of king William and queen Mary, it is declared, that the ſubjects, being proteſtants, may have arms for their defence; it is the opinion of this town, that the ſaid declaration is founded in nature, reaſon, and ſound policy, and is well adapted for the neceſſary defence of the community:

And foraſmuch as, by a good and wholeſome law of this province, every liſted ſoldier, and other houſholder (except troopers, who by law are otherwiſe to be provided) ſhall be always provided with a well-fixed firelock, muſket, accoutrements and ammunition, as is in the ſaid law particularly mentioned, to the ſatisfaction of the commiſſion officers of the company; and as there is at this time a prevailing apprehenſion in the minds of many, of an approaching war with France; in order that the inhabitants of this town may be prepared in caſe of ſudden danger: *Voted*, That thoſe of the ſaid inhabitants, who may at preſent be unprovided, be, and hereby are, requeſted duly to obſerve the ſaid law at this time.

The hon. Thomas Cuſhing, eſq. communicated to the town a letter received from a committee of the merchants in the city of New-York, acquainting him with their agreement relative to a non-importation of Britiſh goods:—Whereupon the town, by a vote, expreſſed their higheſt ſatisfaction therein.

The town taking into ſerious conſideration the preſent aſpect of their public affairs, and being of opinion that it greatly behoves a people profeſſing godlineſs, to addreſs the Supreme Ruler of the world, on all occaſions, for that wiſdom which is profitable to direct;

Voted unanimouſly, That the ſelect-men be a committee to wait on the ſeveral miniſters of the goſpel within this town, deſiring that the next Tueſday may be ſet apart as a day of faſting and prayer.

Ordered, That the votes and proceedings of the town in their preſent meeting be publiſhed in the ſeveral news-papers.

The town voted their thanks to the moderator for his good ſervices, and then the meeting was diſſolved.

Atteſt,
W. COOPER, Town-clerk.

_____

The following is a copy of the circular letter, written by the ſelect-men of this town, and directed to the ſelect-men of the ſeveral towns within this province; agreeable to a vote at the meeting on the 13th inſt.

Gentlemen, Boſton, Sept. 14.

YOU are already too well acquainted with the melancholy and very alarming circumſtances to which this province, as well as America in general, is now reduced. Taxes, equally detrimental to the commercial intereſts of the parent country and her colonies, are impoſed upon the people, without their conſent: taxes deſigned for the ſupport of the civil government in the colonies, in a manner clearly unconſtitutional, and contrary to that in which, till of late, government has been ſupported, by the free gift of the people in the American aſſemblies or parliaments; as alſo for the maintenance of a large ſtanding army; not for the defence of the newly-acquired territories, but for the old colonies, and in time of peace. The decent, humble, and truly loyal applications and petitions from the repreſentatives of this province, for the redreſs of theſe heavy and very threatening grievances, have hitherto been ineffectual, being aſſured from authentic intelligence that they have not yet reached the royal ear: the only effect of tranſmitting thefe applications hither-to perceivable, has been a mandate from one of his majefty's fecre-taries of ftate to the governor of this province, to diffolve the general affembly, merely becaufe the late houfe of reprefentatives refufed to refcind a refolution of a former houfe, which implied nothing more than a right in the American fubjects to unite in humble and dutiful petitions to their gracious fovereign, when they found themfelves aggrieved: this is a right naturally inherent in every man, and exprefly recognized at the glorious Revolution as the birth right of an Englifhman.

This diffolution you are fenfible has taken place; the governor has publicly and repeatedly declared that he cannot call another affembly; and the fecretary of ftate for the American department, in one of his letters communicated to the late houfe, has been pleafed to fay, ' proper care will be taken for the fupport of the dignity of government;' the meaning of which is too plain to be mifunderftood.

The concern and perplexity into which thefe things have thrown the people, have been greatly aggravated by a late declaration of his excellency governor Bernard, that one or more regiments may foon be expected in this province.

The defign of thefe troops is every one's apprehenfion; nothing fhort of enforcing by military power the execution of acts of parliament, in the forming of which the colonies have not, and cannot have, any conftitutional influence. This is one of the greateft diftreffes to which a free people can be reduced.

The town which we have the honour to ferve, have taken thefe things at their late meeting into their moft ferious confideration: And as there is in the minds of many a prevailing apprehenfion of an approaching war with France, they have paffed the feveral votes, which we tranfmit to you, defiring that they may be immediately laid before the town whofe prudentials are in your care, at a legal meeting, for their candid and particular attention.

Deprived of the councils of a general affembly in this dark and difficult feafon, the loyal people of this province will, we are perfuaded, immediately perceive the propriety and utility of the propofed committee of convention: and the found and wholefome advice that may be expected from a number of gentlemen chofen by themfelves, and in whom they may repofe the greateft confidence, muft tend to the real fervice of our gracious fovereign, and the welfare of his fubjects in this province, and may happily prevent any fudden and unconnected meafures, which in their prefent anxiety, and even agony of mind, they may be in danger of falling into.

As it is of importance that the convention fhould meet as foon as may be, fo early a day as the 22d of this inftant September has been propofed for that purpofe—and it is hoped the remoteft towns will by that time, or as foon after as conveniently may be, return their refpective committees.

Not doubting but that you are equally concerned with us, and our fellow citizens, for the prefervation of our invaluable rights, and for the general happinefs of our country, and that you are difpofed with equal ardor to exert yourfelves in every conftitutional way for fo glorious a purpofe.

Signed by the felect-men.

The following articles of intelligence from Bofton are taken from the fame paper.

IT is faid that orders for troops to be quartered in this province, are in confequence of letters wrote here on the 19th of March laft.

On Thurfday next there will be a general mufter of the regiment in this town; and, we hear, a critical view of the arms of the foldiers.

Monday in the night the poft contiguous to liberty tree was fawed off; the damage was inconfiderable, but difcovers the evil difpofition of the perpetrators of fuch a bafe action.

[*By private advices we hear, that the perfon who performed the above feat was detected, and flogged by the populace till he confeffed by whom he was fet upon this enterprize.*]

The following fpirited and judicious anfwer, to the circular letter from the felect men of Bofton, is the beft comment upon many of their late tranfactions that has yet appeared; and will be a lafting teftimonial of the good fenfe and moderation that directed the conduct of the inhabitants of Hatfield in New England upon this occafion.
From the *Maffachufets Gazette* of *Thurfday, October 6, 1768.*

At a full meeting of the inhabitants of the town of Hatfield, September 22, 1768.

A Letter from the felect-men of the town of Bofton, together with the votes paffed by the faid town the 12th and 13th inft. was, by the felect-men, communicated to this town, which being read calmly, and fully deliberated and confidered, the queftion was then put by the moderator, Whether this town will chufe any perfon or perfons a committee to meet in convention with others in Bofton, as propofed in the faid letter? and it paffed unanimoufly in the negative. It was then moved and feconded, that the meeting would chufe a committee to prepare an anfwer to the felect-men of Bofton, to be laid before this town for their confideration at the time to which this meeting fhall be adjourned: it paffed unanimoufly in the affirmative. A committee was chofe accordingly, and then the meeting adjourned till to-morrow at five o'clock in the afternoon.

Sept. 23. The inhabitants being affembled agreeable to adjournment, the committee appointed yefterday report, which being repeatedly read and duly confidered, was accepted; and then unanimoufly refolved, that the following anfwer be fent by the felect-men as foon as may be to the felect-men of the town of Bofton:

Gentlemen,

WE have fully confidered your proposal of a convention, and the reafons you are pleafed to affign for it, and hereby take the liberty to exprefs our fentiments.

We are not fenfible that the ftate of America is fo alarming, or the ftate of this province fo materially different from what they were a few months fince, as to render the meafure you propofe either falutary or neceffary. The act of parliament for raifing a revenue, fo much complained of, has been in being and carrying into execution for a confiderable time paft, and proper fteps taken by feveral governments on this continent to obtain redrefs of that grievance; and humble petitions by them ordered to be prefented to his majefty, we truft, have already, or foon will reach the royal ear, be gracioufly received, and favourably anfwered; and the petition from the houfe of reprefentatives of this province the laft year among the reft: if it fhould not, for want of an agent from this province at the court of Great Britain to prefent it, we prefume you very well know, if it be an impolitic and imprudent omiffion, where to lay the blame; and we apprehend that nothing that can or will be done by your propofed convention can or will aid the petition.

And here we beg leave to fay, that we judge that it would be much for the intereft of this province to have an agent at this critical day: a perfon that would have ferved us faithfully, we make no doubt, might have been found;

but the reafons given, and the methods we hear have been taken, to prevent it, are diffatisfactory, and give us much uneafinefs.

We are further informed, that all matters of a public and private nature lying before the laft general court were fully confidered and acted upon, and all then propofed to be done, finifhed before the adjournment, except the impeachment of his majefty's reprefentative, which perhaps might not have been agreed to had they fat longer, or not been afterwards diffolved. We are forry for that circumftance that occafioned fo early a diffolution of the general court; though we muft own that the governor by charter is vefted with that power; yet we wifh, if he had judged it confiftent with his duty to the king, it had been as ufual: however, we hope another will be foon called, or at fartheft on the laft Wednefday in May next,—and that in the mean time the public affairs of the province will not greatly fuffer.

And here we propofe to your confideration, whether the circular letter, which gave fuch umbrage, containing thefe expreffions, or others of the like import, 'that the king and parliament, by the late revenue act, had infringed the rights of the colonies, impofed an inequitable tax, and things yet worfe might be expected from the independence and unlimited appointments of crown officers therein mentioned,' was fo perfectly innocent, and entirely confiftent with that duty and loyalty profeffed by the houfe of reprefentatives the laft year, in their petition to his majefty; and whether the laft houfe might not have complied with his majefty's requifition, with a full faving of all their rights and privileges, and thereby prevented our being deftitute of a general court at this day.

We cannot comprehend what pretence there can be of the propofed convention, unlefs the pro-

bability for a confiderable number of regular troops being fent into this province, and an apprehenfion of their being quartered, part in your town, and part at the caftle.—And here we would obferve, that it was a matter of doubt and uncertainty whether any were coming or not; if otherwife, for what purpofe the king was fending them, whether for your defence in cafe of a French war (as you tell us there is in the minds of many a prevailing apprehenfion of one approaching (and, if we don't mifunderftand your letter, induced them to pafs the votes tranfmitted to us), or whether they are deftined for the protection of the new-acquired territories, is altogether uncertain: that they are to be a ftanding army in time of peace, you give us no evidence; and if your apprehenfions are well grounded, it is not even fuppofable they are intended as fuch—and if your town meant fincerely, we can't fee the need they had of interpofing in military matters, in an unprecedented way requefting their inhabitants to be provided with arms, &c. (a matter till now always fuppofed to belong to another department), efpecially as they muft know fuch a number of troops would be a much better defence in cafe of war than they had heretofore been favoured with: to fuppofe what you furmife they may be intended for, is to miftruft the king's paternal care and goodnefs;—if, by any fudden excurfions or infurrections of fome inconfiderate people, the king has been induced to think them a neceffary check upon you, we hope you will, by your loyalty and quiet behaviour, foon convince his majefty, and the world, they are not longer neceffary for that purpofe, that thereupon they will be withdrawn, and your town and the province faved any farther trouble and expence from that quarter.

We are fenfible the colonies labour under many difficulties, and we greatly fear what the consequences of the disputes with our mother country will prove; however, we are far from thinking the measures you are pursuing have any tendency to deliver the good people of this province, but, on the contrary, immerge them in greater; — after all, we should hope (were it not for your present attempt, attended with a bad complexion) we might soon have deliverance from our present troubles, and things restored as at the first. The governments have, in our opinion, consulted, and are pursuing, the properest methods to obtain redress of their grievances; our duty is to wait with patience the event, unless we are determined to take the alternative. How far passion and disappointment and private resentment may influence any to hurry their neighbours into such mad and desperate measures, we don't know, but pray God prevent. Suffer us to observe, that in our opinion the measures the town of Boston are pursuing, and proposing to us and the people of this province to unite in, are unconstitutional, illegal, and wholly unjustifiable, and what will give the enemies of our constitution the greatest joy, subversive of government, destructive of that peace and good order which is the cement of society, and have a direct tendency to rivet our chains, and deprive us of our rights and privileges, which we the inhabitants of this town desire may be secured to us, and perpetuated to our latest posterity.

Thus we have freely expressed our sentiments, having an equal right with others, though a lesser part of the community, and take this first opportunity to protest against the proposed convention — and hereby declare our loyalty to his present majesty, and fidelity to our country; and that it is our firm resolution, to the utmost of our power, to maintain and defend our rights in every prudent and reasonable way, as far as is consistent with our duty to God and the king.

Attest,
Oliver Partridge, town-clerk.

Boston, Sept. 26.

On Thursday last, the 22d instant, a number of gentlemen, upwards of seventy, from the different parts of this province, assembled at Faneuil-hall in this town: these gentlemen, by the appointment of the several towns to which they belong, to the number of sixty-six towns besides districts, then and there convened, to consult and advise the most effectual measures for promoting the peace and good order of his majesty's subjects in the province, as far as they lawfully might, under the present very dark and threatening aspect of the public affairs. The debates and proceedings are open: their first step was to prepare an humble petition to the governor of the province, praying that his excellency would be pleased to convene the constitutional assembly of the province; and three of their number were appointed to present the same.

The Petition is as follows, viz.

May it please your excellency,

THE committee chosen by the several towns in this province, and now convened in Boston, to consult and advise such measures as may most effectually promote the peace and good order of his majesty's subjects in this government, at this very dark and distressing time, take the earliest opportunity, openly to disclaim all pretence to any authoritative or governmental acts: nevertheless as we freely and voluntarily come from the different parts of the province, at the earnest desire of the inhabitants, and must be supposed to be well acquainted with their prevailing temper, inclination, and sentiments, under the present threatening aspect of our public affairs, we think ourselves indispensably obliged, from a sense of duty to his majesty, to whom we, and the people of this province, bear the firmest allegiance, and from the tenderest concern for the welfare of his subjects, with all due respect to your excellency, to declare our apprehensions of the absolute necessity of a general assembly.

If ever this people needed the direction, the care, and the support of such an assembly, we are humbly of opinion that their present circumstances immediately require it.

Your excellency cannot be insensible of their universal uneasiness, arising from their grievances occasioned by the late acts of parliament for an American revenue: from an authentic information that the dutiful and loyal petition of the late house of representatives has not been allowed to reach the presence of our gracious king: from the dissolution of the late general assembly: from undoubted advice that the enemies of Britain, and the colonies, are still unwearied in the most gross misrepresentations of the people of the province to his majesty's ministers, as being on the eve of a general insurrection; and from the alarming intelligence that the nation by means of such misrepresentations is incensed to a high degree, so that it is generally apprehended that a standing army is immediately to be introduced among the people, contrary, as we apprehend, to the bill of rights— a force represented to be sufficient to overawe and controul the whole civil power of the province; which must render every right and possession dreadfully precarious.

From these weighty considerations, and also that the people may not be thrown into a total despair; that they may have a frelh opportunity, at the next meeting of the parliament, of taking off the impreffion from the mind of the nation, made by fuch mifreprefentations as is before mentioned, and by that means preventing the moft unhappy confequences to the parent country, as well as ourfelves; we beg leave moft earneftly to pray, that your excellency would commiferate his majefty's truly loyal fubjects of this province under their deplorable circumftances, and reftore to them the full poffeffion of their invaluable charter-right to a general affembly, and caufe one to be immediately convened, that the moft effectual meafures may be taken, in the manner preferibed by our happy conftitution, for the redrefs of grievances, for the preventing an unconftitutional encroachment of military power on the civil eftablifhment, for the promoting the profperity of his majefty's government, and the peace, good order, and due fub**miffion of his fubjects in the province, and making the neceffary provifion for the fupport of government, and, finally, for the reftoration of that harmony, union and affection, between the nation and the colonies, which appear to us to be in the utmoft danger of being totally and irrecoverably loft.—As in duty bound, the committee fhall ever pray,**

In the name and behalf of the committee,

Thomas Cufhing, chairman.

His excellency was pleafed to decline receiving the petition; but delivered to the gentlemen the following writing, viz.

Gentlemen,

YOU muft excufe me from receiving a meffage from that affembly which is called a committee of convention; for that would be to admit it to be a legal affembly, which I can by no means allow.'

The faid writing not being figned by the governor, the gentlemen, at the requeft of the committee, declared in writing, under their hands, that his excellency delivered the fame to them, in confequence of their offering to him the petition.

The day following, the chairman acquainted the committee, that he had received of the fecretary of the province a writing figned by the governor, dated yefterday, which was publicly read, and is as follows:

By his excellency FRANCIS BERNARD, efq. captain-general and governor in chief of the province of Maffachufetts-bay, and vice admiral of the fame.

To the gentlemen affembled at Faneuil hall under the name of a committee of convention.

AS I have lately received from his majefty ftrict orders to fupport his conftitutional authority within this government, I cannot fit ftill, and fee fo notorious a violation of it, as the calling an affembly of the people by private perfons only. For a meeting of the deputies of the towns is an affembly of the reprefentatives of the people to all intents and purpofes; and it is not the calling it a committee of convention that will alter the nature of the thing.

I am willing to believe that the gentlemen who fo haftily iffued the fummons for this meeting were not aware of the high nature of the offence they were committing; and they who have obeyed them have not well confidered of the penalties which they will incur if they fhould perfift in continuing their feffion and doing bufinefs therein. At prefent, ignorance of law may excufe what is paft: a ftep farther will take away that plea.

It is therefore my duty to interpofe, at this inftant, before it is too late. I do therefore earneftly admonifh you, that inftantly, and

before you do any bufinefs, you break up this affembly, and feparate yourfelves. I fpeak to you now as a friend to the province, and a well-wifher to the individuals of it.

But if you fhould pay no regard to this admonition, I muft as a governor affert the prerogative of the crown in a more public manner. For affure yourfelves (I fpeak from inftruction), the king is determined to maintain his entire fovereignty over this province, and whoever fhall perfift in ufurping any of the rights of it, will repent of his rafhnefs.

FRA. BERNARD.

Province-Houfe,
Sept. 22. 1768.

On the 24th, five gentlemen were appointed to wait on his excellency governor Bernard with the following meffage:

Meffage to the GOVERNOR.

May it pleafe your excellency,

THE committee from a number of towns in this province, now convened at Faneuil-hall, having received from your excellency a meffage, containing a remonftrance againft our thus meeting, and an admonition to break up and feparate ourfelves inftantly, and before we do any bufinefs, have taken the fame into our ferious and attentive confideration; and we affure your excellency, that though, according to the beft of our abilities, we have confidered the matters that are hinted by your excellency as the foundation of your meffage, yet we are not able to collect fufficient information therefrom to place our prefent meeting and proceedings in the fame light in which they feem to lie in your excellency's mind. We do affure your excellency moft freely, that neither the views of our conftituents in fending us, nor the defign of any of us in this meeting, was to do, propofe, or confent to, any thing oppugnant to, or inconfiftent with, the regular execution of government in this his majesty's province; and that though the letters from the select-men of the town of Boston, to the respective towns from which we came, might first give rise to our being chosen and sent; yet that neither the said letter from the select-men of the town of Boston, nor any votes of the said town accompanying the same, were considered by our respective towns in the choosing, nor by us in our assembling, as the foundation and warrant of our convening. But may it please your excellency, being assured that our constituents, as well as ourselves, have the most loyal and affectionate attachment to the person and government of our rightful sovereign king GEORGE the third, we beg leave to explain to your excellency the real cause and intention of our thus convening.

Your excellency cannot be unacquainted with the many difficulties under which his majesty's subjects on the whole continent of America apprehend themselves to labour, and of the uneasiness which the subjects in this province have repeatedly expressed on the same account. The minds of the people who have sent us are greatly disturbed, that the humble and dutiful petition of their representatives for the removal of those difficulties has not been permitted to reach the royal ear; and they are greatly agitated with the expectation of a standing army being posted among us, and of the full exertion of a military government; alarmed with these apprehensions, and deprived of a house of representatives, their attention is too much taken off from their daily occupations; their morals and industry are in danger of being damaged, and their peaceable behaviour disturbed for want of such persons as they can confide in, to advise them in these matters, and to make application for their redress.

Your excellency will further naturall conceive that those of his majesty's subjects who live remote from Boston, the center of their intelligence, and whose occupations do not admit of much knowledge of public affairs, are subjected to many misrepresentations of their public concerns, and those generally of a most aggravated kind; nor is it in the power of the most knowing persons amongst us to wipe off the pernicious effects of such rumours without the appearance of a public enquiry.

Induced by these motives, and others of the same kind, our constituents thought it no ways inconsistent with good order and regular government, to send committee-men to meet with such committees as might be sent from the several towns in the province, to confer upon these matters, and learn the certainty of those rumours prevailing amongst us, and to consult and advise as far as comes legally within their power to such measures as would have the greatest tendency to preserve the peace and good order among his majesty's subjects, and promote their due submission; and at the same time to consult the most regular and dutiful manner of laying our grievances before our most gracious sovereign, and obtaining a redress of the same. This, we assure your excellency, is the only cause and intention of our thus convening; and we are exceeding sorry it should be viewed by your excellency in an obnoxious light.

Your excellency may be assured, that had our constituents conceived, or did their committee thus convened conceive, this proceeding to be illegal, they had never sent us, nor should we pretend to continue our convention: but as your excellency, in the message with which you have been pleased to favour us, has not been so explicit in pointing out the criminality of our present proceeding as we could have wished, but has left us to our own judgement and understanding, to search it out, we would with all duty to your excellency, as the representative of our rightful sovereign, request of your excellency to point out to us wherein the criminality of our proceedings consists, being assured we cautiously mean to avoid every thing that has the least appearance of usurpation of government in any of its branches, or any of the rights of his majesty's sovereignty, or that is in the least incentive to rebellion, or even a mental disaffection to the government by law established and exercised.

Your excellency will be pleased, in your well-known knowledge of human nature, and the delicacy of British privileges, to be sparing in your frowns on our present proceeding; we being at present inclined to think, till better informed, that if criminality be imputed to us, it will be applied only to our doings, and not to the professed manner and design of our meeting; but if your excellency has a different apprehension of the matter, we entreat an explanation of the same, and assure your excellency we shall deliberately attend to it. Nothing could give us more uneasiness than a suggestion that our proceedings are criminal; not so much from a fear of personal punishment, as from a fixed aversion we have to any thing inconsistent with the dignity of our sovereign, and the happiness of his extended dominion; and we flatter ourselves, that when the real design of this convention is understood, it will prove an argument to evince the entire loyalty of his majesty's subjects in this province, and their disposition to peace and good order.

In the name and behalf of the committee of a number of towns in this province, convened in Boston, Sept. 24, 1768.

Tho. Cushing, Chairman.

These gentlemen reported also in writing, that they had accordingly waited on his excellency, and that he was pleased to say he could not receive the message.

The committees then appointed nine gentlemen of their number, to consider and report the most effectual measures, consistent with the express design of their convening, to promote the peace and good order of his majesty's subjects in the province.

This committee having made their report on the 26th, a letter with a representation of their transactions, and grievances, in which was inclosed a petition to his majesty, to be delivered in person, was forwarded to their agent Denys de Bert, esq. in London, and on the 29th the convention dispersed. At this convention, committees from 96 towns, and eight districts, were present.

An address of the subscribers, members of his majesty's council of the province of the Massachusetts-bay.

To his excellency general Gage, commander in chief of his majesty's forces in America.

SIR,

A General council being held yesterday, gives the distant members of it, together with members in the town and neighbourhood, the pleasure of addressing you. We take the first opportunity of doing it, and, at the same time, of paying our compliments to your excellency.

In this time of public distress, when the general court of the province is in a state of dissolution, when the metropolis is possessed with troops, and surrounded by ships of war, and when more troops are daily expected, it affords a general satisfaction, that your excellency has visited the province, and has now an opportunity of knowing the state of it by your own observation and inquiry.

Your own observation will give you the fullest evidence that the town and province are in a peaceful state. Your own inquiry will satisfy you, that, though there have been disorders in the town of Boston, some of them did not merit notice; and that such as did have been magnified beyond the truth.

Those of the 18th of March, and 10th of June, are said to have occasioned the above-mentioned armament to be ordered hither. The first was trivial, and could not have been noticed to the disadvantage of the town, but by persons inimical to it; especially, as it happened in the evening of a day of recreation: the other was criminal, and the actors in it were guilty of a riot; but we are obliged to say, it had its rise from those persons who are loudest in their complaints about it, and who, by their overcharged representations of it, have been the occasion of so great an armament being ordered hither; we cannot persuade ourselves to believe they have sufficient evidence to support such representations, which have most unjustly brought into question the loyalty of as loyal a people as any in his majesty's dominions.

This misfortune has arisen from the accusation of interested men, whose avarice, having smothered in their breasts every sentiment of humanity towards this province, has impelled them to oppress it to the utmost of their power, and, by the consequence of that oppression essentially to injure Great Britain.

From the candour of your excellency's sentiments, we assure ourselves you will not entertain any apprehension that we mean to justify the disorders and riotous proceedings that have taken place in the town of Boston: we detest them, and have repeatedly and publicly expressed that detestation, and, in council, have advised governor Bernard to order the attorney-general to prosecute the perpetrators of them; but, at the same time, we are obliged to declare, in justice to the town, that the disorders of the 10th of June last, occasioned by a seizure made by the officers of the customs, appear to have originated with those who ordered the seizure to be made. The hour of making the seizure, at or near sun-set, the threats and armed force used in it, the forcibly carrying the vessel away, and all in a manner unprecedented, and calculated to irritate justly the apprehension, that the seizure was accompanied with those extraordinary circumstances, in order to excite a riot, and furnish plausible pretences for requiring troops a day or two after the riot; and, as if in prosecution of the last mentioned purpose, notwithstanding there was not the least insult offered to the commissioners of the customs either in their persons or property, they thought fit to retire, on the pretence of security to themselves, on board the Romney man of war, and afterwards to Castle William; and when there, to keep up the idea of their being still in great hazard, procured the Romney, and several other vessels of war, to be stationed, as if to prevent an attack upon the castle, which they affected to be afraid of.

These proceedings have doubtless taken place, to induce a belief among the officers of the navy and army, as they occasionally came hither, that the commissioners were in danger of being attacked, and procure from those officers representations coincident with their own, that they really were so; but their frequent landing on the main, and making incursions into the country, where it would have been easy to seize them, if any injury had been intended, demonstrates the insincerity of the declarations, that they immured themselves at the castle for safety. This is rather to be accounted for, as being an essential part of the concerted plan for procuring troops to be quartered here, in which they and their co-adjutors have fucceeded to their wifh, but, unhappily, to the mutual detriment and uneafinefs of both countries.

We thought it abfolutely neceffary, and our duty to the town and province require us, to give your excellency this detail, that you might know the fentiments of this people, and that they think themfelves injured, and injured by men to whom they have done no injury. From the juftnefs of your excellency, we affure ourfelves, your mind will not admit the impreffions to their difadvantage from perfons who have done the injury.

Your excellency, in your letter to governor Bernard, of the 11th of September, gave notice, that one of the regiments from Halifax was ordered for the prefent to Caftle William, and the other to the town; but you was pleafed afterwards to order them into the town.

If your excellency, when you know the true ftate of the town, which we can affure you is quite peaceable, fhould think his majefty's fervice does not require thofe regiments to continue in the town, it will be a great eafe and fatisfaction to the inhabitants, if you will pleafe to order them to Caftle William, where commodious barracks are provided for their reception, or to Point Shirley, in the neighbourhood of it, in either of which, or in both, they can be well accommodated.

As to the two regiments expected here from Ireland, it appears from lord Hillsborough, of the 30th of July, they were intended for a different part of North America.

If your excellency fhould think it not inconfiftent with his majefty's fervice, that they fhould be fent to the place of their firft deftination, it will contribute to the eafe and happinefs of the town and province, if they might be ordered thither.

As we are true and faithful fubjects of his majefty, have an affectionate regard for the mother country, and a tender feeling for our own, our duty to each of them makes us wifh, and we earneftly beg your excellency, to make a full inquiry into the diforders above-mentioned, into the caufes of them, and the reprefentations that have been made about them; in doing which, your excellency will eafily difcover who are the perfons, that, from lucrative views, have combined againft the peace of the town and province, fome of whom, it is probable, have difcovered themfelves already by their own letter to your excellency.

In making the inquiry, though many imprudences, and fome criminal proceedings, may be found to have taken place, we are perfuaded, from the candour, generofity, and juftice, which diftinguifh your character, your excellency will not charge the doings of a few, and thofe of an inferior fort, upon the town and province; and, with regard to thefe individuals, if any circumftances fhall appear juftly to extenuate the criminality of their proceedings, your excellency will let them have their effect: and on the fame candour and generofity we can rely, that your excellency's reprefentations of this affair to his majefty's minifters will be fuch as even the criminals themfelves will allow to be juft.

(Signed)
Bofton, October 27.
J. Danforth, &c.

To the foregoing addrefs, the general gave the following anfwer.
Gentlemen,

I return you thanks for the honour you do me in this addrefs, and am greatly obliged to you for the good opinion you are pleafed to conceive of me.

Whatever may have been the particular caufe of the difturbances and riots which have happened in the town of Bofton, thefe riots, and the refolves which were publifhed, have induced his majefty to order four regiments to this town, to protect his loyal fubjects in their perfons and properties, and to affift the civil magiftrate in the execution of the laws.

The difcipline and order which will be preferved among the troops, I truft, will render their ftay in no fhape difrefpectful to his majefty's dutiful fubjects in this town; and that the future behaviour of the people will juftify the beft conftruction of their paft actions, which I flatter myfelf will be fuch as to afford me a fufficient foundation to reprefent to his majefty the propriety of withdrawing moft part of the troops.

(Signed)
Bofton, October 27th.
Thomas Gage.

The two following pieces, taken from Bofton news-papers, are fo uncommonly curious, and bear fuch peculiar marks of originality, in their ftile, manner, and fentiments, that we make no doubt but they will be entertaining to many of our readers.

Bofton, Sept. 5.
By letters from Rhode-ifland we learn, that John Robinfon, efq. one of the commiffioners, after his late elopement, travelled very privately in bye-ways till he got to Newport, where, on Wednefday laft, he made his public entry, as much to the furprize of moft of the inhabitants, as if he had dropped from the clouds. It was even imagined by fome of the credulous and timid, that he had been killed at Bofton, and that the pale and trembling figure prefenting itfelf to view, was indeed but the ghoft of their old friend Jack Robinfon. However, the next morning was found pofted up at the Swing-

bridge, on the Long-wharf, an advertisement to the following purport, viz. 'This is to defire all the true fons of Liberty, and none elfe, to appear under Liberty-tree in Newport, at eight o'clock this evening, to confult what meafures are neceffary te be taken with the —infamous John Robinfon, who had the impudence to make his public appearance in our ftreets yefterday, having, before he made his elopement, boafted among his brother commiffioners, that he could be well fupported in the execution of his office at Rhode-ifland, and be fully protected from the leaft infult.' At the time and place appointed, fome hundreds, not to fay thoufands, affembled, and went in queft of mafter commiffioner to the tavern, where, it was faid, he lodged the night before. But after a very diligent fearch (not by virtue of a writ of affiftance, but by candle-light) of the houfe, outhoufes, bales, barrels, meal-tubs, trunks, boxes, packs and packages, packed and unpacked, and in fhort of every hole and corner fufficient to conceal a ram cat, or a commiffioner, they could find neither. On this, they returned peaceably to their refpective habitations, without the leaft injury to the perfon or property of any man. What is become of mafter Jacky, we cannot (fays our correfpondent) yet learn. Some think he is gone to Virginia, to enquire if they will not give 10.000 l. fterling, for the beatitudes attendant more immediately on the colony where the American board is fixed, as it was given out laft fall that their agent had offered it ; others think he is on his return to Maffachufetts,

Where once more pent in William's caftle,
Be he fhut up as if in Baftile.

Laft night lodged at Dorchefter, John Robinfon, efq. and this morning proceeded to the caftle.
Bofton, Sept. 26.

Peterfham, Sept. 24. On the 19th inftant the fons of Liberty here (after chufing a committee-man to attend the convention at Bofton) appointed the next day to meet and dedicate a tree to the moft amiable goddefs, at 45 minutes paft two o'clock, P. M. Accordingly they met at the time appointed, and having made choice of a beautiful young elm, they cut off 17 ufelefs branches (leaving 92 thereon) and one of them taking hold of the tree uttered the following words : 'O Liberty! thou divine goddefs! may thofe that love thee flourifh as the branches of this tree! but thofe that have thee be cut off and perifh as thefe 17, which we are now about to commit to the flames.' And a pile of condemned fhingles being inftantly fet on fire, the amputated branches, together with the effigies of the 17 ftrong affes, were caft thereon and confumed, while the well-known fong of Liberty was fung; and having fcattered their afhes towards the four winds of heaven, they gave three cheers, and then walked back in proceffion, where a difh of barley coffee was prepared for them : after which the following conftitutional toafts were drunk :

1. The KING.
2. The Queen and Royal Family.
3. May we always be under his Majefty's protection, may he always hear our grievances, and fend us fpeedy relief.
4. The downfall of Tyranny of all kinds.
5. Lord Chatham, Wilkes, and all our Friends at home.
6. The brave Corficans.
7. Thofe who had rather die than fubmit to the iron yoke of Slavery.
8. To the memory of our glorious intrepid Anceftors.
9. The generous Farmer.
10. The famous Ninety-two.
11. The Town of Bofton.
12. James Otis, efq.

13. A fpeedy Repeal of all unconftitutional acts.
The whole was conducted with the greateft decency and order.

* * *

His majefty's moft gracious fpeech to both houfes of parliament, on Tuefday the eighth day of November, 1768.

My lords, and gentlemen,

THE opportunity which the late general election gives me of knowing, from their reprefentatives in parliament, the more immediate fenfe of my people, has made me defirous of meeting you as early as could be, confiftent with your own convenience. The fhortnefs of the laft feffion of the late parliament prevented their profecuting the confideration of thofe great commercial interefts, which had been entered upon in the preceding feffion. You will, I am perfuaded, agree with me in opinion, that your deliberations on thofe very important objects ought to be refumed without lofs of time ; and I truft that they will terminate in fuch meafures, as may be productive of the moft confiderable and effential benefits to this nation.

It would have given me great fatisfaction to have been able to acquaint you, that all the other powers of Europe had been as careful, as I have ever been, to avoid taking any ftep that might endanger the general tranquillity. I have conftantly received, and do ftill receive from them, the ftrongeft affurances of their pacifick difpofitions towards this country. No affurances, however, fhall divert my conftant refolution, ftedfaftly to attend to the general interefts of Europe ; nor fhall any confideration prevail upon me to fuffer any attempt that may be made, derogatory to the honour and dignity of my crown, or injurious to the rights of my people.

At the clofe of the laft parliament, I expreffed my fatisfaction at the appearances which then induced me to believe, that such of my subjects, as had been misled in some part of my dominions, were returning to a just sense of their duty. But it is with equal concern that I have since seen the spirit of faction, which I had hoped was well nigh extinguished, breaking out afresh in some of my colonies in North America; and, in one of them, proceeding even to acts of violence, and of resistance to the execution of the law; the capital town of which colony appears, by late advices, to be in a state of disobedience to all law and government; and has proceeded to measures subversive of the constitution, and attended with circumstances that manifest a disposition to throw off their dependance on Great Britain. On my part, I have pursued every measure that appeared to be necessary for supporting the constitution, and inducing a due obedience to the authority of the legislature. You may rely upon my steady perseverance in these purposes; and I doubt not but that, with your concurrence and support, I shall be able to defeat the mischievous designs of those turbulent and seditious persons, who, under false pretences, have but too successfully deluded numbers of my subjects in America; and whose practices, if suffered to prevail, cannot fail to produce the most fatal consequences to my colonies immediately, and, in the end, to all the dominions of my crown.

Gentlemen of the house of commons,

The proper estimates for the service of the ensuing year I have ordered to be laid before you; fully relying on your readiness to grant me the necessary supplies. Indeed I cannot have a doubt of finding, in this house of commons, the same affectionate attachment to my person and government, as I have always hitherto experienced from my faithful commons.

My lords, and gentlemen,

It is with great satisfaction that I now find myself enabled to rejoice with you upon the relief, which the poorer sort of my people are now enjoying, from the distress which they had so long laboured under from the high price of corn. At the same time that we are bound devoutly to acknowledge, in this instance, the gracious interposition of Providence, it will become us to apply the best precautions that human wisdom can suggest, for guarding against the return of the late calamity. In the choice, however, of proper means for that purpose, you cannot proceed with too great circumspection.

I have nothing further to recommend to you, than that in all your deliberations you keep up a spirit of harmony among yourselves. Whatever differences of opinion may prevail in other points, let it appear, that wherever the interest of your country is immediately concerned, you are all ready to unite. Such an example from you cannot fail of having the best effects upon the temper of my people in every part of my dominions; and can alone produce that general union among ourselves, which will render us properly respected abroad, and happy at home.

Notes, 1768

1. The Townshend Acts; see "Introduction, 1767."

2. The *Register* oversimplifies the matter. The resolutions of the Boston town meeting (actually held on 28 October 1767) called for nonimportation of "foreign superfluities" and the encouragement of domestic manufactures. They were sent to every township in Massachusetts and to all the main towns of the other colonies. However, by no means all of Massachusetts agreed to the program and elsewhere only Connecticut and Rhode Island towns had accepted it by December. Despite the forceful arguments of John Dickinson's *Letters of a Pennsylvania Farmer,* published between December 1767 and February 1768, Philadelphia merchants came to no agreement until March 1769. The disunity among Boston and New York merchants is indicated by the new Boston initiative in March 1768, which was accepted in principle by New York in April, but followed by new formal resolutions from these towns on 1 and 27 August respectively. See *Appendix to the Chronicle,* pp. [235–[237; the dateline on the New York document—15 September—is most likely that of the report of this agreement published in the *Pennsylvania Gazette* for that day.

3. William Petty, Earl of Shelburne (1737–1805), Secretary of State for the Southern Department, July 1766–January 1768, wrote this letter to Bernard on 17 September 1767.

4. Moves to separate colonial, particularly American, affairs from the work of the Secretary of State for the Southern Department had been sporadic since 1757. The post of Secretary of State for the Colonies (its holder often referred to thereafter, till the demise of the office in 1782, as the American Secretary) was created on 20 January 1768; Wills Hill, Earl of Hillsborough (1718–93), who had served twice as President of the Board of Trade, was the first incumbent.

5. The *Liberty* was owned by John Hancock (1737–93), one of the wealthiest Boston merchants and already prominent in local politics. Historians disagree about whether Hancock was a smuggler or the victim of a customs officers' conspiracy. In any event, the considerable popularity he gained as a result of this case helped to make him a leading Massachusetts politician of this era. See D. H. Watson, "Joseph Harrison and the *Liberty* Incident," *William and Mary Quarterly,* 1963, 3rd ser., 20, pp. 585–95.

6. The tensions in Massachusetts politics are reflected by the existence of three representatives for the colony in London. Richard Jackson (1721–68), M.P. for Weymouth, Grenville's secretary in 1764, and something of an expert on American affairs, was agent for the colony. After a series of disputes, Denys De Berdt (c. 1694–1791) was appointed agent for the assembly, while the council retained William Bollan (1710–76).

7. James Otis (1725–83), prominent Boston lawyer and a leading Massachusetts politician, was since 1760 one of the most active opponents of British measures directed at America.

8. Thomas Cushing (1725–88), Speaker of the Massachusetts House of Representatives, 1766–74; Samuel Adams (1722–1803), leading radical; James Otis; and John Hancock.

9. The report printed in the *Appendix to the Chronicle* (p. 246]) gives the number of towns as sixty-six, the figure quoted in the *Boston Evening Post* for 26 September. A manifesto of the convention, published by that journal on 3 October, gives the figure as ninety-six.

10. Thomas Gage (1721–87) served in America from 1751; he was promoted to Major-General in 1761 and was Commander-in-Chief in North America from 1763 to 1772.

Introduction

1769

By the fall of 1768, those who believed that a ministry led by Pitt would restore tranquility and unity to the empire were obliged to face the extent of their illusions. Chatham himself was incapacitated by illness for well over a year. He virtually withdrew from public affairs, and leadership was allowed to fall on his devoted adherent, the young Duke of Grafton.[1] The ministry had been extensively reorganised at the end of 1767 and the beginning of 1768. Lord North[2] was pressed into taking the post of Chancellor of the Exchequer after Townshend's death, and four members of the Duke of Bedford's party were recruited, two into major posts.[3] Finally, Hillsborough became the new Secretary for the Colonies.

Grafton's inexperienced attempt to broaden the base of the administration created unreconcilable disunity.

1. Augustus Henry Fitzroy, 3rd Duke of Grafton (1748–1813).

2. Frederick, Lord North (1732–92), first son of the first Earl of Guildford, not therefore a peer in his own right, so sat in the House of Commons as M.P. for Banbury until he succeeded his father as 2nd Earl of Guildford in 1790.

3. John Russell, 4th Duke of Bedford (1710–61), was the centre of a significant political group which joined the Grenville ministry in 1763 and continued to support Grenville in opposition to Rockingham. In 1768, Granville Levison-Gower, 2nd Earl Gower (1721–1803), became Lord President of the Council, and Thomas Thynne, 3rd Viscount Weymouth (1734–96), became Secretary of State for the Northern Department (in place of Conway—and, later, Secretary of the Southern Department, instead of Shelburne); John Montagu, 4th Earl of Sandwich (1718–92), became Postmaster-General, and Richard Rigby (1722–88), M.P. for Tavistock (1754–88), became Paymaster-General.

Perhaps most significant, the new men in various ways all favoured a harder line toward America. Thus, Grafton found himself, Camden, and Shelburne representing a minority viewpoint in the Cabinet Council, that advocating a relatively conciliatory approach. Indeed, Shelburne opposed most of his colleagues on nearly all major issues, so that the King and Grafton determined to get rid of him. This move aroused Chatham[4] to make a decision: he resigned on 14 October 1768. (Shelburne's resignation followed on 19 October.) Grafton was thus left with the leadership of a ministry in which the majority believed that firm measures were essential to ensuring American obedience to imperial authority.

This attitude was to find strong support in Parliament, which had viewed with the gravest concern the behaviour of Massachusetts. Parliament prepared to debate the Government's American policy in the pre-Christmas session of 1768. On 28 November and 7 December, a large number of selected official papers were laid before the House of Commons to illustrate the defiant attitude of Massachusetts and to outline the administration's counter-measures. On 15 December, the House of Lords adopted eight resolutions, presented by Hillsborough, condemning most of the recent activities of Massachusetts as unconstitutional and illegal.

The Duke of Bedford then proposed an address to the Crown suggesting the immediate punishment of the ringleaders of the recent disorders in Massachusetts by invoking the act of Henry VIII's reign which permitted trial by special commission *in England* for treason committed outside the King's dominions. The House of Commons deferred consideration of the resolutions and Bedford's proposed address until the January session. On 25 January, the House refused to lay before the committee of the whole about to discuss American affairs a petition protesting the Townshend duties signed by the majority of the Massachusetts Council; the next day, it refused to hear a petition from the council's agent[5] against the invocation of the act of Henry VIII. It then debated the Lords' resolutions and address. Powerful opposition voices spoke against the use of the statute of Henry VIII. Grenville

4. Chatham was also outraged by the decision to appoint a new resident governor for Virginia in place of his protegé Sir Jeffrey Amherst, who had held the office since 1759 but had not resided in the colony since 1764.
5. William Bollan (see "Notes, 1768," n. 6.)

condemned the proposal and the Government with equal severity and when the debate was continued on 8 February, several members of the Rockingham group, including Burke, again opposed it with force and eloquence. However, the Lords' resolutions and address were approved 169 to 65 votes[6] and sent to the King on 13 February.

The use of the Henrician statute was doubtless meant only as a threat at this point, but Hillsborough suggested to the Cabinet Council a set of fairly savage measures intended to restore order in America.[7] The King rejected most of them but was prepared to consider a repeal of the Townshend duties (except for that on tea) for any colony which voted permanent funds adequate to pay Crown officials. Actually the net yield of the Townshend duties seemed to be about 25 percent less than the cost of collection, and the political and commercial damage they were causing was demonstrable. Thus, on 19 April, when former governor of Massachusetts Thomas Pownall[8] moved that the House of Commons debate repeal, his motion was accepted.

Grafton however failed to get his Cabinet colleagues to commit themselves to total repeal on 1 May, and Parliament was prorogued on 9 May. Parliament did not meet again until January 1770, and a partial repeal was carried by a new ministry nearly a year after Pownall's motion.

The *Register* again records American affairs as they appeared before Parliament. The historical section consists of eighty-nine pages; about nine are devoted to Parliament's debates in January and February on the American problem, and the Townshend duties and the applicability of the Henrician statute are presented as central issues. The *Register*'s account is a detailed and valuable source for these debates.[9] It reveals particularly

6. *Journal of the House of Commons*, vol. 32, p. 186.

7. Hillsborough's proposals included abrogation of the Massachusetts Charter if the House of Representatives formally denied Parliament's legislative authority, and replacement of the election of the colony's council by Crown appointment. See *The Correspondence of King George III*, ed. Sir John W. Fortescue, 6 vols. (London, 1927–28), vol. 2, pp. 81–85.

8. Thomas Pownall (1722–1805), Governor of Massachusetts, 1757–9; M.P. for Tregony, 1767–74, and Minehead, 1774–80. He opposed the resolution and address of the Lords in the debate of 8 February, but then, and again in April, he strongly defended Parliament's total legislative authority.

9. Other main sources are *Sir Henry Cavendish's Debate of the House of Commons during the Thirteenth Parliament of Great Britain, Com-*

well the concern of the House of Commons for the constitutional issues involved and also the extent to which American policy had been used by Opposition groups to attack the ministry.

Yet America occupies a small portion of the *Register*'s attention in 1769. The outbreak of war between Russia and Turkey, which spread from the borders of Poland to the Crimea, provides material for four of the six chapters in the historical section. Another chapter deals with problems in India and two with matters raised in Parliament. The whole of Chapter VIII and a portion of Chapter IX describe the extraordinary events involving John Wilkes and the Middlesex election. Wilkes was elected as one of two members for the county and then declared unfit to sit, on the grounds that he had published one seditious and three obscene libels. He was expelled from the House of Commons, triumphantly reelected, and expelled three more times, to become a popular hero. When the House finally declared his opponent elected, the constitutionality of these proceedings was hotly debated in and out of Parliament. Significantly, the Freeholders of Middlesex, in their petition to the Crown on 24 May, castigated the "evil counsellors" who were subverting the constitution not only in England but also in America, having ". . . produced to our suffering fellow subjects in that part of the world, grievances and apprehensions similar to those of which we complain at home."[10] Similarly, Wilkes's activities were widely reported in America, were he was pictured as the heroic victim of the same assault upon liberty which the colonials believed to be directed at them.

Despite its length, the *Appendix to the Chronicle* for 1769 contains only one item directly relating to America— undated estimates of shipping and trade between Britain

monly Called the Unreported Parliament . . . , ed. John Wright, 2 vols. (London, 1841); the letter of William Johnson, Agent for Connecticut, to Governor William Pitkin, 9 February 1769, in *Collections of the Massachusetts Historical Society*, 1885, 5th ser., vol. 9, pp. 312–21; and the letter of Charles Garth, Agent for South Carolina, to the South Carolina Committee of Correspondence, 9 February 1769, in *South Carolina Historical and Genealogical Magazine*, 1930, vol. 31, pp. 46–52. The *Register*'s account may be assumed to have been composed some time after the event, since the 1769 volume was late (published 21 July 1770), and in addition, the pagination of the second half of Chapter VIII and the whole of Chapter IX indicates an insert.

10. *AR*, 1769, p. [199.

and the North American colonies.[11] The parliamentary address to the Crown following the debate on 8 February and the King's reply extracted from the *State Papers,* indicate the hard line that would be taken against the colonies.

11. See "Notes, 1769," n. 5.

Proceedings on the American affairs. Resolutions, and address; great debates thereon. Agreement made for five years with the East-India company. Resolution for payment of the debts on the civil lift. Expulsion of Mr. Wilkes; re-elections: final incapacitation.

THE critical state of our colonies, as well from the great importance of the subject, as the particular attention that was paid to it from the throne, was of course considered as the principal object of the present session. The public had long wished, with an anxious solicitude, for this meeting, as they hoped an effectual remedy would be found for the disorders, and an end consequently put to the disturbances in that part of the world. The heavy censures passed in the late speech, upon the conduct of one of the principal North American colonies, could not fail to increase this anxiety and eagerness of expectation, upon the issue of a business in which the whole British empire was deeply interested. Those who imagined that the supreme authority of the legislature ought to be exerted to its utmost extent; who were disgusted with many extravagancies lately committed, and thought that the unexampled licentiousness which appeared in the province of Massachusets Bay, should be curbed with a strong hand, were gratified with the present appearances; which seemed to bespeak measures of vigour and severity. On the other hand, the advocates for America, those who from principle were lovers of constitutional freedom, as well as those who were naturally inclined to moderation, were considerably alarmed, as they thought they per-

ceived a disposition, to urge matters to violent and perhaps dangerous extremities.

A committee of the whole house had been formed early in the session, for the purpose of an enquiry into American affairs. This was a measure that the different parties which divided that assembly were equally desirous of entering into; but as the motives were different upon which they acted, so were the modes of enquiry which they wished to pursue. On one side it was confined to those late transactions, which from their nature, either as seeming to impugn the legislative authority, or from their violation of order, and direct opposition to government, must necessarily induce censure. On the other, it was proposed to take a retrospective view of the conduct of government for several years in colony affairs, and not content with punishing disorders, to trace back to the source, and remove the causes of them.

We have already seen that motions were made and over-ruled, before the Christmas recess, for the laying of papers before the committee; which would not only have led to a discussion of the rights claimed by the colonies, but also to a close enquiry into the conduct of the several governors and other officers of the crown, as well as into the propriety of the orders which at different times had been issued to them from home. As

coercive measures seemed now to be adopted by administration, these enquiries were accordingly opposed by their friends, who probably thought that the dignity of government might suffer from such discussions. An infinite number of other papers relative to America, were however laid before the committee, and a number of resolutions, together with an address upon the same subject, which had originated in the house of lords, were also brought under their consideration. Frequent and long debates arose upon these subjects in both houses; wherein, contrary to the pre-conceived opinion without doors, the superior strength of the ministry was constantly apparent, and they were upon every question supported by a great majority.

During this course of debate and enquiry, a petition in the name of the major part of the council of the province of Massachuset's Bay, signed by Mr. Danforth, as president of the council, was presented to the house. It however appearing, that this petition had not passed in a legal assembly of the council, and that consequently no person could be authorised to sign it as president, it was refused under that title, and was ordered to be brought up, only as a petition from Samuel Danforth, in behalf of the several individual members of the council at whose request it had been signed.

Jan. 25. 1769.

This petition, the design of which was to obtain a repeal of the late revenue acts, conveyed the arguments for that purpose, in terms of the greatest temper and moderation. The charter immunities and privileges of the colonies, and their general rights as English subjects, were enlarged upon, without seeming to call in question the supreme power of the legislature; although it was implied that those rights had been violated, and it was requested that they might be secured in future. The inability of the colony to address the house in their legislative capacity, from the dissolution of the general assembly, was regretted; and a long recital made of the difficulties, hardships, and dangers which their ancestors had experienced, who for the preservation of civil and religious liberty, had made settlements in the most inhospitable forests, and been exposed to the rage of the most savage and cruel enemies; where, from the nature of the climate, and the infertility of the soil, no advantage to their temporal interests was even to be hoped for, and the utmost that could be expected, was only a scanty subsistence in consequence of the most unremitted labour. From these premises it was inferred, that they not only dearly purchased their settlements, but acquired an additional title, besides their common claim as men and as British subjects, to the immunities and privileges which they asserted had been granted to them by charter.

The great and willing services performed by the colonies at their own expence in our wars; the old ones having been all established without any expence to the mother country; the infinite advantages she derives from them; the share they virtually bear in our taxes, by the consumption of our manufactures; their inability to pay the duties, and the ill consequences resulting from the late laws, not only to them but to the mother country, were brought as arguments to solicit their repeal, and to shew the title they held, not only to a security of their rights, but even to favour.

Resolutions, and an address to his majesty upon American affairs, were however passed in the house of lords, and thence transmitted to the commons, by which they became the act of the two houses. By these resolutions, the late acts of the house of representatives of the province of Massachuset's Bay, which tended to call in question, or to import a denial of the authority of the supreme legislature, to make laws to bind the colonies in all cases whatsoever, were declared to be illegal, unconstitutional, and derogatory of the rights of the crown and parliament of Great Britain. The circular letters wrote by the same assembly, to those of the other colonies, requiring them to join in petitions, and stating the late laws to be infringements of the rights of the people in the colonies, were also declared to be proceedings of a most unwarrantable and dangerous nature, calculated to inflame the minds of the people in the other colonies, and tending to create unlawful combinations, repugnant to the laws of Great Britain, and subversive of the constitution. Feb. 8.[2]

The town of Boston was declared to have been for some time past in a state of great disorder and confusion, disturbed by riots and tumults of a dangerous nature, in which the officers of the revenue had been obstructed by violence in the execution of the laws, and their lives endangered: that neither the council of the province, nor the ordinary civil magistrates, had exerted their authority for suppressing the said riots and tumults: that in these circumstances of the province of Massachuset's Bay, and of the town of Boston, the preservation of the public peace, and the due execution of the laws, became impracticable, without the aid of a military force to support and protect the civil magistrate, and the officers of his majesty's revenue. That the declarations, resolutions, and proceedings, in the town-

meetings at Boston, on the 14th of June, and 12th of September, were illegal and unconstitutional, and calculated to excite sedition and insurrection. That the appointment, at the town-meeting on the 12th of September, of a convention to be held in the town of Boston, on the 22d of that month, to consist of deputies from the several towns and districts in the province, and the writing of a letter by the select men, to each of the said towns and districts, for the election of such deputies, were proceedings subversive of government, and evidently manifesting a design in the inhabitants of Boston, to set up a new and unconstitutional authority, independent of the crown. The elections by the several towns and districts, of deputies to sit in the convention, and the meeting of it, were also declared to be daring insults offered to his majesty's authority, and audacious usurpations of the powers of government.

In the address, the greatest satisfaction was expressed at the measures which had been pursued to support the constitution, and to induce in the colony of Massachuset's Bay, a due obedience to the authority of the mother country. The most inviolable resolution was declared, to concur effectually in such farther measures as might be judged necessary to maintain the civil magistrates in a proper execution of the laws; and it was given as matter of opinion, that nothing would so effectually preserve royal authority in that province, as bringing the authors of the late unfortunate disorders to exemplary punishment. Upon this conviction it was earnestly requested, that governor Barnard might be directed to transmit the fullest information he could obtain, of all treasons, or misprision of treason, committed within his government since the 30th of Dec. 1767, together with the names of the persons who were most active in the perpetration of such of-[3]

fences; that his majesty might issue a special commission for enquiring into, hearing, and determining upon the guilt of the offenders within this realm, pursuant to the provisions of a statute made in the 30th year of Henry VIII;[4] in case his majesty, upon governor Barnard's report, should see sufficient ground for such a proceeding.

Notwithstanding the powerful majority by which these resolutions and the address were carried through, no measures were ever opposed with more firmness, nor no subject more ably discussed, than this was through the long course of debate with which it was attended. As both the right and the propriety of American taxation, were brought within this discussion, the arguments under these heads have already been given, on the occasion of laying on, and of the repeal of the stamp duties. New ground was however taken, upon the inutility of the late revenue laws, their inexpediency, the measures pursued by administration for the execution of them, and some parts of the address.

It was said, that the inutility of these laws was so evident, that the ministers did not even pretend to support them upon that ground, but rested their defence upon the expediency of establishing the right of taxation. That this right had been sufficiently established, and the dignity and supreme authority of the legislature properly asserted, by the declaratory act of the 6th of his present majesty, as well as by a multitude of revenue laws passed in the former reigns, and even in this. These laws answered all the good purposes for which the late law is pretended to have been passed, at the same time they excited no alarm, and did not drag after them any part of that long train of evils, of which the late act had already been productive. That with all the consequences of the stamp act before their eyes, a full conviction of which (or at least

a pretence of such a conviction) induced parliament the year before to repeal it, and that tranquility at least had been the consequence of that repeal, wantonly to make another experiment of the same nature, less productive of revenue, but more vexatious in its mode, and more pernicious in its effects, than the former, was, to call it no worse, such a degree of absurdity as could scarcely be equalled. That loaded with all the destructive consequences which could attend the most general and comprehensive tax upon America, these laws in fact only taxed the mother country; and that the laying of duties upon British commodities and manufactures landed in the colonies, was, in effect, granting premiums to excite the industry of the Americans, and to put them upon raising the one, and rivalling us in the other. In these censures the Rockingham and Grenville parties (supposed on this point to be irreconcileable) entirely united. They urged, that admitting the repeal of the stamp-act to have been an improper measure, yet, from the moment of that repeal, the policy of the mother country was altered, though her rights were not abridged. An attempt to tax the colonies, no longer stood upon its antient footing of wisdom and practicability.

That it was now the mode, with those who had been the original cause of all the present disorders in America, to represent the people there as nearly in a state of rebellion, and thus artfully endeavour to make the cause of the ministry the national cause, and to persuade us, that because the people, aggravated by a series of blunders and mismanagements, and emboldened by the weakness and inconsistency of government, have shewn their impatience in the commission of several irregular and very indefensible acts, that they want to throw off the authority of the mother country. That indeed it was too true, that popular prejudices were very dangerously meddled

with, and that therefore all wise governments made great allowances for them, and when there was a necessity of counteracting them, always did it with the greatest art and caution. That the temper of the Americans, in this respect, was well known from the former trial; but what means were used to soften it, or to dispose them more favourably to this experiment? A number of duties were laid on, which derive their consequence only from their odiousness and the mischiefs they have produced; and an army of custom-house officers, who from their novelty, an opinion that the taxes were only created for them, as indeed they could scarcely answer any other purpose, and from many other circumstances, were, if possible, more odious than the duties, were sent to collect them. That this measure, as might have been expected, not having proved sufficient to establish the success of the experiment, another army, still more odious, and much more dangerous, was sent to inforce it. It was said, that some of those who were the framers, or under whose auspices these duties had been laid on, were themselves the zealous supporters, and at the head of that opinion, which totally denied the right in the legislature of any taxation in America; that their names had been held up in the colonies as objects of the highest veneration, and their arguments were made the foundation of whatever was there understood to be constitutional writing or speaking: Was it then to be wondered at, that the Americans, with such authorities to support them in opinions, which were, in the highest degree, flattering to their importance, should, in that warmth of imagination, fly into the greatest extravagancies, upon a direct and immediate violation of what they were taught to consider, as their most undoubted and invaluable rights? or can we be surprized, that such unaccountable contradictions between language and conduct, should produce the unhappy consequences which we now experience.

That part of the address which proposed the bringing of delinquents from the province of Massachusets, to be tried at a tribunal in this kingdom, for crimes supposed to be committed there, met with still greater opposition than the resolves, and underwent many severe animadversions. Such a proceeding was said to be totally contrary to the spirit of our constitution. A man charged with a crime, is, by the laws of England, usually tried in the county in which he is said to have committed the offence, that the circumstances of his crime may be more clearly examined, and that the knowledge which the jurors thereby receive of his general character, and of the credibility of the witnesses, might assist them in pronouncing, with a greater degree of certainty, upon his innocence or guilt. That as the constitution, from a conviction of its utility, has secured this mode of trial to every subject in England, under what colour of justice can he be deprived of it by going to America? Is his life, his fortune, his happiness, or his character, less estimable, in the eye of the law, there than here? or, are we to mete out different portions of justice to British subjects, which are to lessen in degree, in proportion to their distance from the capital. If an American has violated the laws by a crime committed there, let him be tried there for the offence; but let him not be torn above 3000 miles, from his family, his friends, his business, and his connections; from every assistance, countenance, comfort, and counsel, necessary to support a man under such trying and unhappy circumstances, to be tried by a jury who are not, in reality, his peers, who are probably prejudiced, and who may perhaps think themselves, in some degree, interested against him.

It was said, that it would be difficult in the last degree, if not utterly impossible, for the accused person to bring over the necessary evidence for his vindication, tho' he were entirely innocent; that it would require a very affluent fortune to bring from Boston to London all the witnesses who would be indispensably requisite; that many others may be thought essential at the time, who were not so, and who would add equally to the expence, and others overlooked or forgot, who might be of the greatest consequence; that he must also bring reputable persons to testify the general tenor of his conduct and behaviour, though they could, perhaps, give no evidence as to the particular fact with which he was charged. That, on the other side, the witnesses against him, supported by the countenance and protection of government, maintained at the national expence, and sure of a compensation for their loss of time, besides, perhaps, the hopes of future reward and provision, would not only be easily collected, but that it was to be feared too many would think it an eligible employment, and become eager candidates for it.

That in this situation, charged with a crime against the authority of the mother country, the judges who are to determine his fate, are the people against whom he is supposed to have transgressed; those who have constructed the act with which he is charged into a crime, whose passions are heated, and who are at once parties, accusers, and judges. That if he is even acquitted, the consequence will probably be his total ruin, as, independent of the great loss of time that will attend the prosecution, few fortunes will be able to bear the consequent expences; to say nothing of the loss of health, and the numberless vexations and oppressive circumstances that will attend so long a confinement, in a vain struggle between the impotence of weakness, and the coercive exertions of power. Thus, it was said, that the life, fortune, and

character, of every man, who had the misfortune to become obnoxious to the governor of a province, would, in some degree, lie at his disposal; as pretences on which to found a charge could never be wanting, and the sort of evidence necessary to give a colour to the prosecution, might be easily found.

It was represented as a strange measure, upon this occasion, to drag out of the oblivion in which it had so long deservedly lain, and in which it should have continued for ever buried, an obsolete law, which was passed in one of our most cruel and tyrannical reigns, only to answer a temporary and arbitrary purpose. That our constitution was not then, in any degree, defined; that, such as it was, it continually underwent every flagrant violation, which the whim or cruelty of a capricious tyrant was capable of directing; that it would be much to our honour, if many of the public acts of that reign could be totally forgotten; and that it was hoped, that no part of the line of publick conduct then pursued, would be proposed as a model for the present times. It was observed, that we had not a colony existing at the time of passing that law; that they consequently could not be intended by it, and that an attempt now to comprehend them in it, was not more oppressive to them than dangerous to us. But if this address, taken in one view, presented a very disadvantageous idea of the equity and moderation of our government, in another view it reflected no less on the wisdom of the British parliament. They contended that the execution of the project was utterly impossible; nay, that it never was intended to be carried into execution; that therefore it could serve no other purpose, than to furnish matter to the leaders of sedition in the colonies, further to exasperate the populace, without conveying any sort of terror, which might check them in their dangerous practices.

Such were some of the arguments

made ufe of in the courfe of thefe debates, by thofe who did not approve of the late and prefent meafures purfued in regard to our colonies, and who, of courfe, oppofed the refolutions and addrefs in queftion. Many of the moft forcible of thefe arguments were but little, if at all replied to on the other fide; nor was the utility nor expediency of the late revenue laws much defended. The minifters (from whatever caufe) were even unufually cold and languid, in the fupport of the refolutions, and the addrefs which they had propofed for executing the law of Henry VIII; and when they were afked, with a degree of infult, which of them would own himfelf the advifer of that meafure, they feverally declined to adopt it. The ground principally and moft ably taken to juftify the taxes objected to, as well as to fhew the propriety of the meafures now under confideration, was the violent conduct of the Americans; which put government under a neceffity of ufing methods, however difagreeable to itfelf, abfolutely neceffary for the fupport of its dignity, and of the legiflative authority.

It was faid, that the repeal of the ftamp-act, inftead of producing the hoped-for effects of gratitude, for the tender confideration fhewn to their fuppofed diftreffes, and of a due fubmiffion to government, had, on the contrary, operated in fuch a manner on the licentioufnefs of the Americans, that it became highly neceffary to eftablifh fome mark of their dependance on the mother-country. That the late duties, fo much complained of, were, for one of the reafons now objected to them, the fmallnefs of their produce, chofen as fufficient to anfwer that purpofe, at the fame time that they were the leaft oppreffive that could be thought of, were not internal taxes, and that their whole produce was to be applied to the fupport of their own civil eftablifhments. That

the republican principles, and licentious difpofition of the inhabitants of the province of Maffachufets-bay, being operated upon by fome factious and defigning men among them, broke out into acts of the moft daring infolence, and the moft outrageous violence, which fufficiently fhewed the original neceffity of making them fenfible of their dependance on the Britifh legiflature; that by the language held forth, and the writings publifhed among them, they feemed rather to confider themfelves as members of an independent ftate, than as a colony and province belonging to this country.

That from the ill-judged fyftem upon which the government of that province had been originally eftablifhed, the council was appointed by the affembly, and the grand juries are elected by the townfhips; fo that thefe factious men having got a great lead in the affembly, and being themfelves the rulers of the popular phrenzy, guided and directed as they liked the whole civil government; fo that all juftice and order were at an end, wherever their interefts or paffions were concerned. That in thefe circumftances, the populace freed from all legal reftraints, and thofe that fhould have been the fupporters of government, and the confervators of the public peace, fetting themfelves the firft example of contempt to the one, and giving every private encouragement to the breach of the other, proceeded at length to the commiffion of fuch acts, as, if not now deemed downright rebellion, would in other times have been judged and punifhed as fuch; and which, in any conftruction of the term, can be confidered but very little fhort of it. That it was then high time for government to interfere, and effectually to curb diforders, which, if fuffered to proceed any farther, could no longer be confidered by that name: that the example fet by the people of Bofton, and the rafh and daring meafure adopted

by their affembly, of fending circular letters to the other colonies, had already produced a great effect; and if not checked, was likely to fet the whole continent in a flame: that accordingly fome fhips of war and troops were fent to Bofton, who, without bloodfhed, or coming to any violent extremity, reftored order and quiet to that province.

That nothing but the moft fpirited and vigorous refolutions, fupported by a fucceffion of meafures equally firm and vigorous, could bring the colonies to a proper fenfe of their duty, and of their dependence upon the fupreme legiflator. That the fpirit which prevailed in Bofton, was fo totally fubverfive of all order and civil government, and the conduct of the magiftrates had left fo little room for any hope of their properly fulfilling their duty during the continuance of the prefent ferment, that it became abfolutely neceffary to revive and put in execution that law of Henry VIII. by which the king is empowered to appoint a commiffion in England, for the trial there of any of his fubjects guilty of treafon in any part of the world. That unlefs this meafure was adopted, the moft flagrant acts of treafon and rebellion might be openly committed in that province with the greateft impunity, as the civil power was neither difpofed, nor could take cognizance of them. That the perfons who were guilty of thefe crimes, and who had already caufed fo much trouble and confufion, were no objects of compaffion, for any particular circumftances of expence or trouble that might attend this mode of bringing them to juftice, which were only to be confidered as a fmall part of the punifhment due to their crimes: that it was ungenerous to fuppofe, that government would make an improper ufe of this law by the harraffing of innocent perfons; and that there was no reafon to queftion the integrity or the impartiality of our juries. Indeed they obſerved, that it was rather unlikely the act would be executed at all; as they were in hopes that ſuch a ſeaſonable ſhew of ſo much vigour and lenity, would operate to bring the people of the colonies to a ſenſe of their duty, and to a ceſſation from their former ſeditious practices. Such were the arguments and hopes of adminiſtration in propoſing, and of parliament in adopting this ſyſtem. Unfortunately, however, experience has not made good, in any degree, theſe expectations.

. . .

An addreſs of both houſes of parliament, on Monday the 13th of February, 1769.

Moſt gracious ſovereign,

WE your majeſty's moſt dutiful and loyal ſubjects, the lords ſpiritual and temporal, and commons, in parliament aſſembled, return your majeſty our humble thanks, for the communication your majeſty has been graciouſly pleaſed to make to your parliament, of ſeveral papers relative to public tranſactions in your majeſty's province of Maſſachuſets-bay.

We beg leave to expreſs to your majeſty our ſincere ſatisfaction in the meaſures which your majeſty has purſued, for ſupporting the conſtitution, and for inducing a due obedience to the authority of the legiſlature; and to give your majeſty the ſtrongeſt aſſurances, that we will effectually ſtand by and ſupport your majeſty, in ſuch further meaſures as may be found neceſſary to maintain the civil magiſtrates in a due execution of the laws, within your majeſty's province of Maſſachuſets-bay. And, as we conceive that nothing can be more immediately neceſſary, either for the maintenance of your majeſty's authority in the ſaid province, or for guarding your majeſty's ſubjects therein from being further deluded by the arts of wicked and deſigning men, than to proceed in the moſt ſpeedy and effectual manner for bringing to condign puniſhment the chief authors and inſtigators of the late diſorders, we moſt humbly beſeech your majeſty, that you will be graciouſly pleaſed to direct your majeſty's governor of Maſſachuſets-bay to take the moſt effectual methods, for procuring the fulleſt information that can be obtained, touching all treaſons, or miſpriſions of treaſon, committed within his government, ſince the 30th day of December, 1767; and to tranſmit the ſame, together with the names of the perſons who were moſt active in the commiſſion of ſuch offences, to one of your majeſty's principal ſecretaries of ſtate, in order that your majeſty may iſſue a ſpecial commiſſion, for inquiring of, hearing, and determining, the ſaid offences, within this realm, purſuant to the proviſions of the ſtatute of the 35th year of the reign of king Henry VIII, in caſe your majeſty ſhall, upon receiving the ſaid information, ſee ſufficient ground for ſuch a proceeding.

His majeſty's moſt gracious anſwer.

My lords and gentlemen,

The ſincere ſatisfaction you expreſs in the meaſures which I have already taken, and the ſtrong aſſurances you give of ſupporting me in thoſe which may be ſtill neceſſary, to maintain the juſt legiſlative authority, and the due execution of the laws, in my province of Maſſachuſets-bay, give me great pleaſure.—I ſhall not fail to give thoſe orders which you recommend, as the moſt effectual method of bringing the authors of the late unhappy diſorders in that province to condign puniſhment.

. . .

Total amount of Britiſh ſhips and ſeamen employed in the trade between Great Britain and her colonies on the continent of America—of the value of goods exported from Great Britain to theſe colonies—and of their produce exported to Great Britain and elſewhere. [5]

Colonies	Ships	Seamen	Exports from Great Britain.	Exports from the Colonies.
Hudſon's Bay	4	130	£. 16,000	£. 29,340
Labrador				49,050
American Veſſels, 120				
Newfoundland (2000 boats)	380	20,560	273,400	345,000
Canada	34	408	105,000	105,500
Nova Scotia	6	72	26,500	38,000
New England	46	552	395,000	370,000
Rhode Iſland, Connecticut and New Hampſhire	3	36	12,000	114,500
New York	30	330	531,000	526,000
Pennſylvania	35	390	611,000	705,500
Virginia and Maryland	330	3,960	865,000	1,040,000
North Carolina	34	408	18,000	68,350
South Carolina	140	1,680	365,000	395,666
Georgia	24	240	49,000	74,200
St. Auguſtine	2	24	7,000	
Penſacola	10	120	97,000	63,000
	1,078	28,910	3,370,900	3,924,606

Notes, 1769

1. Though the Grafton ministry was internally disunited, it could expect support for a firm line towards America from the Court party, the Bedford group, and, on occasion, Grenville's followers, as well as from a number of independent country gentlemen.

2. The resolutions and address were approved by the Lords on 15 December, and debated by the Commons on 25 January and 8 February, when they were also adopted by the Lower House.

3. Misprision of treason had come to be defined as concealing knowledge of treasonable designs.

4. Actually 35 Henry VIII c. 2.

5. Source unidentified. Figures for 1769 for those of the Thirteen Colonies named in the *Register*'s list are:

	Imports from Great Britain £ Sterling	Exports from Colonies £ Sterling
Massachusetts, Connecticut Rhode Island, and New Hampshire	223,696	550,090
New York	75,931	231,906
Pennsylvania	204,980	410,757
Virginia and Maryland	714,944	991,402
North Carolina and South Carolina	327,084	569,585
Georgia	58,341	96,170

See *Historical Statistics of the United States: Colonial Times to 1957* (Washington, D.C.: U.S. Bureau of the Census, 1960), ser. Z243–55, p. 758. These 1769 figures are, of course, distorted by the effects of nonimportation agreements. However, comparison of the *Register*'s table with figures in *Historical Statistics of the United States*, ser. Z21–34, p. 757, for imports from *England*, produces virtually no correlation for any year from 1764 to 1768, even allowing for estimates of differences created by (a) imports from Britain as opposed to England alone and (b) the use of "official values" for goods, which had not been updated since the 1720s (assuming the *Register*'s source used estimates of real values). Though in 1766 and 1767 the value of New England imports from *England* is roughly equivalent to the *Register*'s figure (i.e., £409,000 and £406,000 respectively), the remaining import values given in the *Register* are very much higher than the official estimates, in the case of Pennsylvania, for example, by nearly 40 percent in 1767, and nearly 50 percent for Virginia and Maryland in the same year.

1770

Introduction

Eighteen days after Parliament began its new session on 9 January 1770, the Duke of Grafton resigned. He had lost the confidence of the King by the end of the previous session, in May 1768, was publicly rebuffed by his political mentor and idol Chatham (who had partially recovered), vilified in the popular press (notably by "Junius"[1]), and isolated in the Cabinet. The King was determined that Grafton's replacement would be Lord North, who accepted the office of First Lord of the Treasury and thus became first minister to the Crown on 29 January.[2]

The House of Commons turned to American affairs on 5 March, and North proposed repeal of the Townshend duties, with the exception of that on tea. North emphasised the damage caused to British commercial interests by the other acts but the necessity for retaining the Tea Act, precisely because its preamble asserted what the

1. A series of letters, published in various journals between 1769 and 1772 and signed "Junius," was the vehicle for savage criticism of the Government and individuals. Scholarly opinion tends to view the pseudonym as that of Sir Philip Francis (1740–1818).
2. North had earned a reputation in financial matters and as a speaker in the Grenville ministry. Chatham offered him an office in 1766 which he accepted without enthusiasm: he was reluctant to accept the Exchequer in 1767. His importance increased during the next two years as he took over leadership of the House of Commons from Conway and was delegated more and more Treasury business by Grafton. The King was resolved that North should succeed Grafton in January 1770, perhaps because the growing strength of the Opposition in the House of Commons made it advisable to have the first minister in the Lower House.

Americans denied, that Parliament had the right to tax trade to raise revenue. North argued that the colonies would likely threaten to extend nonimportation until other trade laws were also repealed and that total repeal would merely encourage this sort of blackmail. He argued further that the existing nonimportation agreements should not be taken in the same light, since they were damaging American prosperity more than they were British. Pownall moved for total repeal, and the ensuing debate heard the full range of arguments against American taxation in general and the retention of the tea duty in particular. Nonetheless, the motion was defeated. There is some evidence to suggest that an attempt was made to repeat the tactic of 1765–1766, and mobilise merchant support, but with less success. Again, fears of a colonial war which would involve the Bourbon powers may have been heightened by the restless French aggression indicated by the annexation of Corsica by France in 1769. A bill to repeal the other duties was brought in on 9 March, accepted without further debate a month later, and passed by the Lords on 11 April. It was signed by the King the next day. Townshend's grand policy, designed to secure an American contribution to the support of the Crown's administration in America, lay in ruins. The North ministry however had no substitute policy toward America to offer.

Even before the partial repeal of the Townshend duties, there were signs that the colonial nonimportation agreements were breaking down. By the summer of 1770, the movement disintegrated in a welter of intercolonial recriminations. North was correct in claiming that nonimportation was damaging American commercial interests more than British. The colonial radicals consequently could no longer rely on general support for the use of the trade issue to unite Americans against the exercise of imperial authority in the colonies. They were forced to rely on a propaganda campaign to focus popular hostility on the British government, which they presented as a ministerial clique using a corrupt and subservient Parliament to subvert the constitution. The radicals' campaign employed real and immediate grievances, in particular, the popular resentment against customs enforcement and British troops. These grievances were connected, since customs officers often used writs of assistance for search and seizure of contraband, and thus aroused bitter opposition (a good deal of customs activity looked like straightforward racketeering), so that enforcement required military support.[3] In New York and Boston, the presence of British troops gave the appearance of a garrison (which in Boston after 1768 to all intents and purposes it was). Political leaders consequently could allege a deliberate and visible threat to liberty. The antagonism of workmen toward off-duty soldiers who took jobs locally at wages much lower than normal was perhaps even more significant.[4] The British soldiers in America were no more "brutal and licentious" than at other times and places, but they created and reacted to intense local hostility. In 1770, this antagonism erupted into bloody clashes.

Early in 1770, New York workers and sailors fought soldiers in a two-day affray at Golden Hill. After a series of incidents involving citizens and soldiers over the previous two weeks, British soldiers were involved in a clash on 5 March which the popular leaders promptly named the Boston Massacre. Apart from the facts that the soldiers fired on a mob, killed three men and fatally wounded two more, the details of this event were obscured in a flood of depositions, affidavits, newspaper reports, and pamphlets which are in conflict and often appear to be describing different events. Paul Revere's famous cartoon showing a platoon of soldiers firing a volley on the order of their officer at a helpless, unarmed crowd of citizens is probably farthest from the truth. The propaganda value of this sort of interpretation nonetheless ensured its dissemination by the American press throughout the colonies. It should be remembered that at the trial of the troops in October and November 1770, the officer and six men were acquitted on the charge of murder (two soldiers were found guilty of manslaughter) and that the soldiers were defended by American counsel

3. The new American Board of Customs Commissioners, set up to enforce the Townshend Acts, certainly intensified action on technicalities to the point where deliberate harassment and corruption were alleged. (See Oliver M. Dickerson, *The Navigation Acts and the American Revolution* (Philadelphia, 1951), pp. 212–19, 224–50. Writs of assistance, requiring local law-enforcement officers to assist customs officers up to and including forcible entry into any private house, had been extended to the colonies in 1696 but had been challenged in law in Massachusetts from 1760 and were universally detested.

4. Richard B. Morris, *Government and Labour in Early America* (New York, 1946), pp. 190–92.

which included John Adams.[5] Immediately after the "massacre," Boston seemed so near open insurrection that Lieutenant-Governor Hutchinson was obliged to order the withdrawal of British troops to Castle William to pacify the mob. By the time of the trial, however, tempers had cooled, nonimportation had collapsed, and the radicals watched their influence disintegrate. Despite the continued radical rhetoric, popular American resistance seemed to have died with the repeal of the Townshend duties.

The *Register*'s historical section deals with these events in parts of two chapters only. Four chapters describe in detail the progress of the war in the East, one is devoted to events in Central Europe and one to French affairs. Chapters VII, VIII, and IX deal with British politics and parliamentary business; the main items include the attempt to resolve the constitutional issues raised by the Middlesex election, the challenge posed by the development of radicalism in the City of London, and political problems in Ireland. Close attention is also given the motion intended to disenfranchise lower officers in the revenue service and the debate over the civil list (these reflect the Opposition to an allegedly sinister increase in the power of the Crown through the use of patronage).[6]

Less than four of the ninety-five pages of the whole historical section describe the partial repeal of the Townshend duties. The Boston Massacre is mentioned merely as a "... late alarming riot" and used as an introduction to the Opposition's assault on the ministry in the summer session over the conduct of American policy. A similar attack in the House of Lords[7] was equally vigorous and as unsuccessful. The *Appendix to the Chronicle* presents two detailed accounts of the Boston Massacre, the first from the *Boston Gazette*, the second from a letter of Captain Preston, the officer involved, to General Gage, his commander-in-chief. A brief account of Preston's trial and acquittal is added.

5. John Adams (1735–1826) was already an acknowledged leader of those who opposed the extension of parliamentary legislation into American affairs on constitutional grounds, but his commitment to the rule of law ensured his determination that the Boston trial should not produce a travesty of justice.

6. A view given its most influential form in Edmund Burke's *Thoughts on the Cause of the Present Discontents*.

7. A series of condemnatory resolutions were proposed by the Duke of Richmond. *AR*, 1770, pp. *94]–[95*; not extracted here.

The Annual Register—1780

Two other items from this section are also extracted. The letter from the Society of the Supporters of the Bill of Rights illustrates the connection between English radicals and the American protest.[8] The account of the activities of the North Carolina Regulator movement in the fall of 1770 is a different type of American news, since the *Register* had previously ignored political and social tensions within the colonies. Thus, no attention was paid to the anti-rent protest in Duchess County, New York, in 1766, nor to the insurrection of the Paxton Boys on the Pennsylvania frontier against the Quaker-dominated assembly's Indian policy in 1764. Frontier grievances against the coastal elite which dominated the colonies' politics exploded in the Carolinas in the late 1760s. In South Carolina, the Regulators demanded the creation of an adequate local government to deal with lawless elements threatening the safety of property of the settlers in the backcountry. In North Carolina, the Regulators rose in armed revolt against corrupt local government, and were broken by forces raised by the governor in 1771. The *Register*'s account of the riot in Hillsborough on 24 and 25 September gives no indication of the Regulators' grievances and appears to be included in the *Appendix to the Chronicle* as an item of curiosity.

8. See "Introduction, 1769."

Nothing had yet been done in the affairs of the colonies; but a petition having been now prefented by the American merchants, fetting forth the great loffes they fuftained, and the fatal effects of the late laws, which, for the purpofe of raifing a revenue in the colonies, had impofed duties upon goods exported from Great Britain thither; the miniftry March 5. thought it proper to bring in a bill, for the repeal of fo much of the late act, paffed in the feventh of his prefent Majefty, as related to the impofing of a duty on paper, painters colours, and glafs ; the tax upon tea, which was laid on by the fame act, being ftill to be continued.

The motives affigned for the bringing in of this bill, were the dangerous combinations which thefe duties had given birth to beyond the Atlantic, and the diffatisfaction they had created at home, among the merchants who traded to the colonies ; which made this matter an object of the moft ferious confideration. It was remarkable, upon this occafion, that the minifter condemned thefe duties in the grofs, and the law by which they were founded, as fo abfurd and prepofterous, that it muft aftonifh every reafonable man, how they could have originated in a Britifh legiflature ; yet, notwithftanding this decifive fentence, propofed a repeal of but a part of

the law, and ftill continued the duty upon tea; left they fhould be thought to give way to the American ideas, and to take away the impofitions, as having been contrary to the rights of the colonies.

On the other fide, it was moved to amend the motion, and that the act, which laid on thefe duties, fhould be totally repealed. To this it was objected, that the colonies, inftead of deferving additional inftances of tendernefs, did not deferve the inftance then fhewn, for their refolutions became more violent than ever; that their affociations, inftead of fupplicating, proceeded to dictate, and grew at laft to fuch a height of temerity, that adminiftration could not, for its own credit, go as far as it might incline, to gratify their expectations; that was the tax under consideration to be wholly abolished, it would not either excite their gratitude or re-establish their tranquility; they would set the abolition to the account, not of the goodness, but of the fears of government, and upon a supposition that we were to be terrified into any concession, they would make fresh demands, and rise in their turbulence, instead of returning to their duty. Experience, fatal experience, has proved this to be their disposition. We repealed the stamp-act to comply with their desires, and what has been the consequence? Has the repeal taught them obedience; has our lenity inspired them with moderation? On the contrary, that very lenity, has encouraged them to insult our authority, to dispute our rights, and to aim at independent government.

Can it then be proper, in such circumstances, while they deny our legal power to tax them, to acquiesce in the argument of illegality, and by the repeal of the whole law, to give up that power? Thus, to betray ourselves out of compliment to them, and through a wish of rendering more than justice to America, resign the controuling supremacy of England.— By no means; the properest time to exert our right of taxation, is, when the right is refused. To temporize is to yield, and the authority of the mother country, if it is now unsupported, will, in reality, be relinquished for ever.

It was said, that there was great stress laid, both within and without doors, upon the advantages of our traffick with America, and that the least interruption of the customary intercourse, was held up in the most terrifying colours to the kingdom; but that there were the best reasons to believe, that the associations not to buy British goods, would speedily destroy themselves; for the Americans, to distress us, would not long persevere in injuring themselves; they are already weary of giving an advanced price for the commodities they are obliged to purchase; and after all the hardships, under which they say their commerce groans, it is still obviously their interest not to commence manufacturers. It was allowed to be true, that our exports to America had fallen very much of late; and that in the year 1768, they exceeded those of 1769, by the prodigious sum of 744,000 l. they amounting in the former to 2,378,000 l. and in the latter, only to 1,634,000 l. but this great disproportion was accounted for, by supposing, that the non-importation which ensued, being then foreseen by the importers, they prepared for it, by laying in a double quantity of goods.

As to the particular duty to be continued upon tea, it was said, that the Americans had no reason to find fault; because when that was laid, another was taken off, which obliged them to pay near a shilling in the pound upon an average, whereas the present only imposes three-pence; therefore as America in this article feels an ease of nine-pence per pound, she cannot properly accuse us of oppression, especially as every session has of late been productive of material advantages to her, either in bounties, free-ports, or other considerable indulgences.

On the other side, many of the general arguments which we have formerly given upon this subject, both as to the right and the expediency of our levying taxes, were again repeated, and the whole proceedings with regard to America were reiterated, and became the subject of the severest animadversion. The minister observed, that the taxes were absurd—How came he to support the administration that imposed them? How came he not to have discovered this absurdity earlier? All the world had been sensible of it, and the repeal of the act had been frequently proposed. That repeal was refused, as they were resolved not to relax in favour of America, whilst America denied the right. Has America acknowledged it? Have they yet departed from their combination? The ministers (said they) condemn the concessions of their predecessors; yet they begin themselves by concession; with this only difference, that theirs is without grace, benignity, or policy; and that they yield after a vexatious struggle. That every reason given for the repeal of a part of this act, must extend, not only with equal, but with greater force to the whole. That the only cause assigned for not repealing the whole, was to preserve the preamble, because it maintains the right of taxing the Americans; an argument totally futile and ridiculous, as there are two positive laws declaratory of that right, and there are many other taxes at this moment existing, in exercise of the right, so that as the mischiefs occasioned by the act in question, have at length been acknowledged by the other side, no absurdity can be more glaring, than their pretence for making only a partial repeal.

That a partial repeal, instead of producing any benefit to the mother-country, will be a real grievance; a certain expence to ourselves, as well as a source of perpetual discontent to the colonies. By continuing the trifling tax upon tea, while we take off the duties upon painters colours, paper and glass, we keep up the whole establishment of the custom-houses in America, with their long hydra-headed trains of dependants, and yet cut off the very channels through which their voracious appetites are to be glutted. In fact, the tea duty will by no means answer the charge of collecting it, and the deficiencies must naturally be made up out of the coffers of this country, so that this wise measure of a partial repeal is to plunder ourselves, while it oppresses our fellow-subjects, and all for the mere purpose of preserva paltry preamble, which is utterly useless and unnecessary.

That Parliament had plighted its faith to the East India company, to remove the duty of 25 per cent. from teas, in order that the company might be enabled to sell them upon terms equally low with the Dutch, whose moderation in price constantly obtained a preference at every market. That the 25 per cent. was indeed taken off accordingly, but what was done with one hand was undone by the other; a fresh duty was laid on the commodity, and laid in such a manner, that it must operate as an absolute prohibition to the sale of their teas through every part of the extensive continent of English America, where they were before in general estimation. That as a proof of this assertion, the teas sent to America in the year 1768, amounted to no less than 132000 l. whereas in 1769, they amounted to no more than 44000 l. and probably this year, they will not exceed a quarter of that sum, as the proceedings here are hourly becoming more and more repugnant to the minds of the colonies, and as agreements have been lately entered into for the absolute disuse of that article. In justice therefore to the East India company, who have so considerable a stake in the national welfare, and pay so liberally to the support of government, the promise made to them ought to be discharged with the most punctual fidelity—that a discontinuance of the 25 per cent. on their teas was not a discharge of that promise; it was only to be discharged by enabling them to sell upon terms as reasonable as the Dutch.

It was added, that as it seemed probable that a rupture between England and her old enemies, was at no great distance, it would be acting wisely in administration, to reconcile our domestic divisions, and to regain the confidence of our colonies, before such an event took place. That at the same time that the act in question was diametri-

cally repugnant to all the principles of commerce, there was not the smallest plea of utility to be urged in its defence; that even upon the principle of a spendthrift, if immediate profit was only to be considered, and all other consequences laid by, it had not that sordid recommendation; its whole produce, in its utmost extent, not exceeding 16000 l. a year, which was no more than sufficient to bear the expences that attended it. Let us then dismiss this pitiful *preamble* tax, and make the repeal total, unless the ministers would convince us, that a provision for their new custom-house instruments beyond the Atlantic, is the only motive for this shameless profusion of the public treasure.

Such were some of the arguments upon this interesting question; and it was remarkable upon this occasion, that several gentlemen in office opposed the motion, even as it originally stood. The reasons given for this conduct were chiefly these; of consistency on the part of parliament, the general obstinacy of the Americans, and the violences committed in different parts of that continent, particularly at Boston. The question for the amendment being put, it was rejected by a considerable majority, the numbers being 204 to 142; the original motion was afterwards carried without a division. [1]

• • •

The state of affairs in America [2] had not yet been entered into. though they had been particularly recommended by the speech from the throne, and seemed to be one of the great objects, which required the utmost attention, and maturest consideration of Parliament. The account which had been received of the late alarming riot in Boston, between the soldiers and town's people, and the consequence that followed, of the two regiments that were stationed in the barracks there, being under a compulsatory necessity of retiring from the town and going to Castle William, without any order from Govern-

ment for so doing, seemed to make this matter so urgent, as not to admit of any delay, before some conclusive measures were taken upon it; and the time pressed the more immediately, as a speedy prorogation was the natural consequence of the season.

The Ministry, however, were very shy and tender upon this head, and seemed to wish rather to trust to a temporizing conduct with the colonies, and the hope of profiting by their disunion or necessity, than to lay open a series of discordant measures, which, however the separate parts might be defended by the immediate plea of expediency at the time, could bear no critical test of enquiry, when compared and examined upon the whole.

However this might have been the principle upon which American affairs were suffered hitherto to lie dormant, notwithstanding the recommendation from the throne, it was by no means satisfactory to those, who had opposed every part of the conduct of administration with regard to America.

A motion was accord- [3] ingly made for an address to the Throne; setting forth the disputes that had arisen among the several governors and commanders, in almost all the colonies, since the appointment of a commander in chief; that the colonies have been for some time, and are still, from this and other causes, in a state of the greatest disorder, and confusion; that the people of America complain of the establishment of an army there, as setting up a military government over the civil; and therefore praying, that all these matters may be reconsidered, and such measures taken, as would replace things there, upon a constitutional footing.

This motion was introduced, by observing, that in the present critical situation of affairs, they were expressly called upon, to enquire how the Ministers here, no less than their Officers there, have man-

May 8.

aged fo unfortunately, as to kindle the prefent flame of diffention between the mother country and her colonies. That in fulfilling this duty, they muft not only confider the matter of fact, but the right of things; not only the turbulence of the Americans, but the caufe of that turbulence; and not only the power of the crown, but the equity with which that power had been exercifed.

This motion had the ufual fate of thofe made by the minority. It did not, however, prevent other fteps upon the fame fubject A fet of refolutions were propofed, by which the whole minifterial fyftem for feveral years paft, with relation to America, was taken into confideration. All the contradictory inftructions to the Governors were canvaffed; and their inconfiftency and ill effects pointed out. Taxes impofed — repealed — impofed again, and repealed again. Affemblies diffolved—called again; and fuffered to fit and proceed to bufinefs, without difavowing or difcountenancing the meafures which had procured the former diffolution. Promifes made to the affemblies, that certain duties fhould be repealed and taxes taken off; which were unwarrantable, of dangerous confequence, and a high breach of privilege; and that it was equally derogatory from the honour of the crown, and the freedom of parliamentary deliberations, to have its faith pledged to the performance of fuch promifes. Troops fent—driven out — violence, and fubmiffion, alternately made ufe of. Treafons charged, adopted by Parliament, not proved, nor attempted to be proved; or if exifting, not attempted to be detected and punifhed; an infult on the dignity of Parliament, and tending to bring either a reflection on its wifdom and juftice, or to encourage treafons, and treafonable practices, by not carrying into execution the meafures recommended by Parliament.

All thefe refolutions, which may be feen in the Votes of the Houfe of Commons, were rejected by a great majority; nor did adminiftration enter much into a difcuffion or refutation of the matter or charges which they contained. The general arguments of the turbulence of the Americans, the difpofition of the colonies to difclaim all dependance on the mother country, the neceffity of fupporting its authority and the dignity of government, and the right of the crown to ftation the troops in any part of the dominions; together with the neceffity of their being employed to fupport the laws, where the people were in little lefs than a ftate of rebellion, were thofe principally made ufe of. There was nothing pleafant in the view of the conduct of American affairs; and adminiftration aimed at getting rid of the difcuffion as foon as poffible, and put a negative on, or poftponed by previous queftions, all thefe refolutions.

. . .

The unhappy Riot at Bofton has been fo varioufly reprefented, and is in itfelf of fo interefting a Nature, that we think it neceffary to lay the different Accounts of it before our Readers. [4]

Bofton, March 12.

ON the evening of Monday, being the 5th current, feveral foldiers of the 29th regiment were feen parading the ftreets with their drawn cutlaffes and bayonets, abufing and wounding numbers of the inhabitants.

" A few minutes after nine o'clock, four youths, named Edward Archbald, William Merchant, Francis Archbald, and John Leech, jun. came down Cornhill together, and feparating at Doctor Loring's corner, the two former, in paffing a narrow alley, where a foldier was brandifhing a broad fword, of an uncommon fize, againft the walls, out of which he ftruck fire plentifully, and a perfon of a mean countenance, armed with a large cudgel, by him, Edward Archbald bid Mr. Merchant take care of the fword, on which the foldier turned round, ftruck Archbald on the arm, and then pufhed at Merchant. Merchant then ftruck the foldier with a fhort ftick, and the other perfon ran to the barrack, and brought with him two foldiers, one armed with a pair of tongs, the other with a fhovel; he with the tongs purfued Archbald back thro' the alley, collared and laid him over the head with the tongs. The noife brought people together, and John Hicks, a young lad, coming up, knocked the foldier down, but let him get up again; and more lads gathering, drove them back to the barrack, where the boys ftood fome time as it were to keep them in. In lefs than a minute ten or twelve foldiers came out, with drawn cutlaffes, clubs, and bayonets, and fet upon the unarmed Boys, who, finding the inequality of their equipment, difperfed. On hearing the noife, one Samuel Atwood came up to fee what was the matter, and met the foldiers aforefaid rufhing down the alley, and afked them if they intended to murder people? they anfwered, Yes, by G—d, root and branch! with that one of them ftruck Mr. Atwood with a club, which was repeated by another, and, being unarmed, he turned to go off, and received a wound on the left fhoulder, which reached the bone. Retreating a few fteps, Mr. Atwood met two officers, and faid, Gentlemen, what is the matter? they anfwered, you'll fee by and by. Immediately after, thefe heroes appeared in the fquare, afking where were the boogers? where were the cowards? thirty or forty perfons, moftly lads, being by this means gathered in King-ftreet, Capt. Prefton, with a party of men with charged bayonets, came from the main-guard, and taking their ftations by the Cuftom-houfe, began to pufh and drive the people off, pricking fome, and threatening others; on which the people grew clamorous, and, it is faid, threw fnow-balls. On this the captain commanded his men to fire, and more snow-balls coming, he again said, d—n you, fire, be the consequence what it will!—One soldier then fired, and a townsman, with a cudgel struck him over the hands with such force that he dropt his firelock, and, rushing forward, aimed a blow at the captain's head, which grazed his hat, and fell pretty heavy upon his arm: however, the soldiers continued the fire, successively, till seven or eight, or, as some say, eleven guns were discharged.

" By this fatal manœuvre, several were laid dead on the spot, and some lay struggling for life; but what shewed a degree of cruelty unknown to British troops, at least since the house of Hanover has directed their operations, was an attempt to fire upon, or stab with their bayonets, the persons who undertook to remove the slain and wounded! At length,

" Mr. Benjamin Leigh, of the Delph Manufactory, came up, and after some conversation with Capt. Preston, relative to his conduct, advised him to draw off his men; with which he complied.

" The dead are Mr. Samuel Gray, killed on the spot, the ball entering his head and beating off a large portion of his skull.

" A mulatto man, named Crispus Attucks, born in Framingham, who was here in order to go for North Carolina, also killed instantly: two balls entering his breast, one of them in special goring the right lobe of the lungs, and a great part of the liver most horribly.

" Mr. James Caldwell, mate of Capt. Morton's vessel, in like manner killed by two balls entering his back.

" Mr. Samuel Maverick, a promising youth of seventeen years of age, son of the widow Maverick, mortally wounded; a ball went through his belly, and was cut out at his back: he died the next morning.

" A lad, named Christopher Monk, about seventeen years of age, apprentice to Mr. Walker, shipwright, wounded; a ball entered his back about four inches above the left kidney, near the spine, and was cut out of the breast on the same side; apprehended he will die.

" A lad, named John Clark, about seventeen years of age, whose parents live at Medford, wounded; a ball entered just below his groin and came out at his hip, on the opposite side; apprehended he will die.

" Mr. Edward Payne, of this town, Merchant, standing at his entry door, received a ball in his arm, which shattered some of the bones.

" Mr. John Green, taylor, coming up Leverett's-lane, received a ball just under his hip, and lodged in the under part of his thigh, which was extracted.

" Mr. Robert Patterson, a seafaring man, wounded; a ball went through his right arm, and he suffered great loss of blood.

" Mr. Patrick Carr, about 30 years of age, who worked with Mr. Field, leather breeches maker, in Queen-street, wounded; a ball entered near his hip and went out at his side.

" A lad named David Parker, an apprentice to Mr. Eddy the wheelwright, wounded; a ball entered his thigh.

" The people were immediately alarmed with the report of this horrid massacre, the bells were set a ringing, and great numbers soon assembled at the place where this tragical scene had been acted; their feelings may be better conceived than expressed; and while some were taking care of the dead and wounded, the rest were in consultation what to do in those dreadful circumstances. But so little intimidated were they, notwithstanding their being within a few yards of the main-guard, and seeing the 29th regiment under arms, and drawn up in King-street, that they kept their station, and appeared, as an officer of rank expressed it, ready to run upon the very muzzles of their muskets. The Lieut. Governor soon came into the Town-house, and there met some of his Majesty's council, and a number of civil magistrates; a considerable body of the people immediately entered the council-chamber, and expressed themselves to his honour with a freedom and warmth becoming the occasion. He used his utmost endeavours to pacify them, requesting that they would let the matter subside for the night, and promising to do all in his power that justice should be done, and the law have its course; men of influence and weight with the people were not wanting on their part to procure their compliance, by representing the horrible consequence of a promiscuous and rash engagement in the night. The inhabitants attended to these suggestions, and the regiment under arms being ordered to their barracks; they separated and returned to their dwellings by one o'clock. At three o'clock Captain Preston was committed to prison, as were the soldiers who fired, a few hours after him.

" Tuesday morning presented a most shocking scene, the blood of our fellow-citizens running like water through King-street, and the Merchants Exchange, the principal spot of the military parade for about 18 months past. Our blood might also be tracked up to the head of Long Lane, and through divers other streets and passages.

" At eleven o'clock the inhabitants met at Faneuil-hall, and after some animated speeches they chose a committee of fifteen respectable gentlemen to wait upon the Lieut. Governor in council, to request of him to issue his orders for the immediate removal of the troops.

The Message was in these words:

" That it is the unanimous opinion of this meeting, that the inhabitants and soldiery can no longer live together in safety; that nothing can rationally be expected to restore the peace of the Town, and prevent further blood and carnage, but the immediate removal of the troops; and that we therefore moſt fervently pray his honour that his power and influence may be exerted for their inſtant removal."

His Honour's Reply.
Gentlemen.

" I am extremely ſorry for the unhappy differences between the inhabitants and troops, and eſpecially for the action of the laſt evening, and I have exerted myſelf upon that occaſion that a due enquiry may be made, and that the law may have its courſe. I have in council conſulted with the commanding officers of the two regiments who are in the town. They have their orders from the General at New-York. It is not in my power to countermand thoſe orders. The council have deſired that the two regiments may be removed to the caſtle. From the particular concern which the 29th regiment has had in your differences, Colonel Dalrymple, who is the commanding Officer of the Troops, has ſignified that that regiment ſhall, without delay, be placed in the barracks at the Caſtle, until he can ſend to the General and receive his further orders concerning both the regiments, and that the mainguard ſhall be removed, and the 14th regiment ſo diſpoſed and laid under ſuch reſtraint, that all occaſion of future diſturbances may be prevented."

The foregoing Reply having been read and fully conſidered—the queſtion was put, Whether the report be ſatisfactory ? Paſſed in the negative (only one diſſentient) out of upwards of 4000 voters.

" It was then moved, that John Hancock, Eſq; Mr. Samuel Adams, Mr. William Molineux, William Phillips, Eſq; Dr. Joſeph Warren, Joſhua Henſhaw, Eſq; and Samuel Pemberton, Eſq; be a Committee to wait on his Honour the Lieutenant Governor, and inform him, that the Reply made to the Vote of the inhabitants is by no means ſatisfactory; and that nothing leſs will

ſatisfy, than a total and immediate removal of all the troops.

" The Committee having waited upon the Lieutenant Governor, his Honour laid before the Board a vote of the town of Boſton, paſſed this afternoon, and then addreſſed the Board as follows :

" *Gentlemen of the Council,*

" I lay before you a vote of the town of Boſton, which I have juſt now received from them, and I now aſk your advice, what you judge neceſſary to be done upon it.

" The Council thereupon expreſſed themſelves to be *unanimouſly* of opinion, " that it was abſolutely neceſſary for his Majeſty's ſervice, the good order of the town, and the peace of the province, that the troops ſhould be immediately removed out of the town of Boſton; with which opinion Colonel Dalrymple gave his word of Honour that he would acquieſce."

Upon the above report, the inhabitants expreſſed the higheſt ſatisfaction; and after meaſures were taken for the ſecurity of the town, the meeting was diſſolved.

A moſt ſolemn proceſſion was made through Boſton at the funeral of the four murdered youths.[5] On this occaſion all the ſhops were ſhut up, all the bells in the town were ordered to toll, as were thoſe in the neighbouring towns, and the bodies that moved from different quarters of the town, met at the fatal place of action, and were carried together through the main ſtreets, followed by the greateſt concourſe of people ever known, all teſtifying the moſt ſenſible grief, to a vault provided for them in the middle of the great burying-ground.

From the time of this fatal tragedy, a military guard of town militia has been conſtantly kept in the Town-houſe and Town-priſon, at which ſome of the moſt reſpectable citizens have done duty as common ſoldiers.

In conſequence of this affair, the inhabitants of Roxburgh petitioned the Lieutenant Governor

Hutchinſon to remove the troops from Boſton; and received for anſwer, *That he had no authority to order the King's troops from any place where they are poſted by his Majeſty's order;* at the ſame time he acquainted them with what had been done with the concurrence of the commanding officer.

Caſe of Captain Thomas Preſton of the 29th Regiment. 6

IT is matter of too great notoriety to need any proofs, that the arrival of his Majeſty's troops in Boſton was extremely obnoxious to its inhabitants. They have ever uſed all means in their power to weaken the regiments, and to bring them into contempt, by promoting and aiding deſertions, and with impunity, even where there has been the cleareſt evidence of the fact, and by groſly and falſely propagating untruths concerning them. On the arrival of the 64th and 65th, their ardour ſeemingly began to abate; it being too extenſive to buy off ſo many; and attempts of that kind rendered too dangerous from the numbers. But the ſame ſpirit revived immediately on its being known that thoſe regiments were ordered for Hallifax, and hath ever ſince their departure been breaking out with greater violence. After their embarkation, one of their Juſtices, thoroughly acquainted with the people and their intentions, on the trial of the 14th regiment, openly and publickly, in the hearing of great numbers of people, and from the ſeat of juſtice, declared, " that the ſoldiers muſt now take care of themſelves, *nor truſt too much to their arms*, for they were but a handful; that the inhabitants carried weapons concealed under their cloaths, and would deſtroy them in a moment *if they pleaſed.*" This, conſidering the malicious temper of the people, was an alarming circumſtance to the ſoldiery. Since which ſeveral diſputes have happened between the towns people and soldiers of both regiments, the former being encouraged thereto by the countenance of even some of the Magistrates, and by the protection of all the party against Government. In general such disputes have been kept too secret from the Officers. On the 2d instant, two of the 29th going through one Gray's rope-walk, the rope-makers insultingly asked them if they would empty a vault. This unfortunately had the desired effect by provoking the soldiers, and from words they went to blows. Both parties suffered in this affray, and finally the soldiers retired to their quarters. The Officers, on the first knowledge of this transaction, took every precaution in their power to prevent any ill consequences. Notwithstanding which, single quarrels could not be prevented; the inhabitants constantly provoking and abusing the soldiery. The insolence, as well as utter hatred of the inhabitants to the troops, increased daily; insomuch, that Monday and Tuesday, the 5th and 6th instant, were privately agreed on for a general engagement; in consequence of which several of the militia came from the country, armed to join their friends, menacing to destroy any who should oppose them. This plan has since been discovered.

On Monday night, about eight o'clock, two soldiers were attacked and beat. But the party of the towns people, in order to carry matters to the utmost length, broke into two Meeting Houses and rang the alarm bells, which I supposed was for fire as usual, but was soon undeceived. About nine some of the guard came to and informed me, the town inhabitants were assembling to attack the troops, and that the bells were ringing as the signal for that purpose, and not for fire, and the beacon intended to be fired to bring in the distant people of the country. This, as I was Captain of the day, occasioned my repairing immediately to the main guard. In my way there I saw the people in great commotion, and heard them use the most cruel and horrid threats against the troops. In a few minutes after I reached the guard, about an hundred people passed it, and went towards the Custom House, where the King's money is lodged. They immediately surrounded the centinel posted there, and with clubs and other weapons threatened to execute their vengeance on him. I was soon informed by a townsman, their intention was to carry off the soldier from his post, and probably murder him. On which I desired him to return for further inteligence; and he soon came back and assured me he heard the mob declare they would murder him. This I feared might be a prelude to their plundering the King's chest, I immediately sent a non-commissioned officer and twelve men to protect both the centinel and the King's money, and very soon followed myself, to prevent (if possible) all disorder; fearing lest the officer and soldiery by the insults and provocations of the rioters should be thrown off their guard and commit some rash act. They soon rushed through the people, and, by charging their bayonets in half circle, kept them at a little distance. Nay, so far was I from intending the death of any person, that I suffered the troops to go to the spot where the unhappy affair took place, without any loading in their pieces, nor did I ever give orders for loading them. This remiss conduct in me perhaps merits censure; yet it is evidence, resulting from the nature of things, which is the best and surest that can be offered, that my intention was not to act offensively, but the contrary part, and that not without compulsion. The mob still increased, and were more outrageous, striking their clubs or bludgeons one against another, and calling out, 'Come on, you Rascals, you 'bloody Backs, you Lobster Scoundrels; fire if you dare, G— damn ' you, fire and be damn'd; we know ' you dare not;' and much more such language was used. At this time I was between the soldiers and the mob, parleying with and endeavouring all in my power to persuade them to retire peaceably; but to no purpose. They advanced to the points of the bayonets, struck some of them, and even the muzzles of the pieces, and seemed to be endeavouring to close with the soldiers. On which some well-behaved persons asked me if the guns were charged; I replied, yes. They then asked me if I intended to order the men to fire; I answered no, by no means; observing to them, that I was advanced before the muzzles of the men's pieces, and must fall a sacrifice if they fired; that the soldiers were upon the half-cock and charged bayonets, and my giving the word fire, on those circumstances, would prove me no officer. While I was thus speaking, one of the soldiers, having received a severe blow with a stick, stepped a little on one side, and instantly fired; on which turning to, and asking him why he fired without orders, I was struck with a club on my arm, which for some time deprived me of the use of it; which blow, had it been placed on my head, most probably would have destroyed me. On this a general attack was made on the men by a great number of heavy clubs, and snowballs being thrown at them, by which all our lives were in imminent danger; some persons at the same time from behind calling out, 'Damn your bloods, why do ' not you fire?' Instantly three or four of the soldiers fired, one after another, and directly after three more in the same confusion and hurry.

The mob then ran away, except three unhappy men who instantly expired, in which number was Mr. Gray, at whose rope-walk the prior quarrel took place; one more is since dead, three others are dangerously, and four slightly wounded. The whole of this melancholy affair was transacted in almost twenty minutes. On my asking the soldiers why they fired without orders, they said they heard the word " Fire," and supposed it came from me. This might be the case, as many of the mob called out, " Fire, fire," but I assured the men that I gave no such order, that my words were, " Don't fire, stop your firing :" In short, it was scarce possible for the soldiers to know who said fire, or don't fire, or stop your firing. On the people's assembling again to take away the dead bodies, the soldiers, supposing them coming to attack them, were making ready to fire again, which I prevented by striking up their firelocks with my hand. Immediately after a townsman came and told me, that 4 or 5000 people were assembled in the next street, and had sworn to take my life with every man's with me; on which I judged it unsafe to remain there any longer, and therefore sent the party and sentry to the Mainguard, and when they arrived there, telling them off into street firings, divided and planted them at each end of the street to secure their rear, momently expecting an attack, as there was a constant cry of the inhabitants, " To arms, to arms—turn out with your guns," and the town drums beating to arms. I ordered my drum to beat to arms, and being soon after joined by the different companies of the 29th regiment, I formed them as the guard into street firings. The 14th regiment also got under arms, but remained at their barracks. I immediately sent a Serjeant with a party to Colonel Dalrymple, the Commanding Officer, to acquaint him with every particular. Several Officers going to join their regiment were knocked down by the mob, one very much wounded, and his sword taken from him. The Lieutenant-Governor, and Colonel Carr, were soon after met at the head of the 29th regiment, and agreed that the regiment should retire to their barracks, and the people to their

houses; but I kept the piquet to strengthen the guard. It was with great difficulty that the Lieutenant-Governor prevailed on the people to be quiet and retire : at last they all went off, excepting about a hundred.

A Council was immediately called, on the breaking up of which, three Justices met, and issued a Warrant to apprehend me and eight Soldiers. On hearing of this procedure, I instantly went to the Sheriff, and surrendered myself, though for the space of four hours I had it in my power to have made my escape, which I most undoubtedly should have attempted, and could easily have executed, had I been the least conscious of any guilt. On the examination before the Justices, two witnesses swore that I gave the men orders to fire; the one testified he was within two feet of me; the other, that I swore at the men for not firing at the first word. Others swore they heard me use the word, fire; but whether do or do not fire, they could not say; others, that they heard the word fire, but could not say if it came from me. The next day they got five or six more to swear I gave the word to fire. So bitter and inveterate are many of the malecontents here, that they are industriously using every method to fish out evidence to prove it was a concerted scheme to murder the inhabitants. Others are infusing the utmost malice and revenge into the minds of the people, who are to be my Jurors, by false publications, Votes of Towns, and all other artifices. That so, from a settled rancour against the Officers and Troops in general, the suddenness of my Trial after the affair, while the people's minds are all greatly inflamed, I am, though perfectly innocent, under most unhappy circumstances, having nothing in reason to expect, but the loss of life in a very ignominious manner, without the interposition of his Majesty's justice and good-

An Account of the Trial of Captain Preston, at Boston, in New-England.

THE Trial began on Wednesday the 24th of October, and was continued from day to day, Sunday excepted, till Tuesday the 30th. The witnesses who were examined on both sides amounted to about 50. The Lawyers for the Crown were Mr. Barne and Mr. Samuel Quincy; for the prisoner, Mr. Auchmuty and Mr. John Adams. Each of them spoke three hours at least. About Monday noon the Judges began their charge. Judge Trowbridge, who spoke first, entered largely into the contradictory accounts given by the witnesses, and declared, that it did not appear to him that the prisoner gave orders to fire; but if the Jury should think otherwise, and find it proved that he did give such orders, the question then would naturally be, What crime is he guilty of ? They surely could not call it murder.—Here he explained the crime of murder in a very distinct manner, and gave it as his opinion, that by law the prisoner was not guilty of murder; observing, that the King had a right to send his troops here; that the Commanding Officer of these troops had a right to place a Centinel at the Customhouse; that the Centinel placed there on the night of the 5th of March was in the King's peace; that he durst not quit his post; that if he was insulted or attacked, the Captain of the Guard had a right to protect him; that the prisoner and his party, who came there for that purpose, were in the King's peace; that while they were at the Customhouse, for the purpose of protecting the centinel, it was plainly proved that they had been assaulted by a great number of people; that the people assembled there were not in the King's peace, but were by law considered as a riotous mob, as they attacked the prisoner and his party with pieces of ice, sticks, and clubs;

and that even one of the witnesses against him confessed he was armed with a Highland broadsword; that the rioters had knocked down one of the soldiers of the party, laid hold of several of their muskets, and that, before the soldiers fired, the cry was, Knock them down! Kill them! Kill them! That all this was sworn to by the witnesses, and if the Jury believed them, the prisoner could not be found guilty of murder. He then proceeded to explain what the law considered as man-slaughter, and observed, as before, that if they gave credit to the witnesses, who testified the assaults made on the prisoner and his party, they could not find him guilty of man-slaughter, and concluded with saying, that if he was guilty of any offence, it could only be excusable homicide; that this was only founded on the supposition of the prisoner's having given orders to fire, for if this was not proved, they must acquit him.

Judge Oliver, who spoke next,[7] began with representing, in a very nervous and pathetic manner, the insults and outrages which he, and the Court, through him, had received on a former occasion (meaning the trial of Richardson) for[8] giving his opinion in a point of law; that, notwithstanding, he was resolved to do his duty to his God, his King, and his country; that he despised both insults and threats, and that he would not forego a moment's peace of conscience for the applause of millions. He agreed in sentiment with the former Judge, that the prisoner was not guilty.

Judge Cushing spoke next, and agreed entirely with the other two, with regard to the prisoner's case.

Judge Lyndex concluded. He spoke a considerable time, and was of the same opinion with the other Judges. Towards the close of his speech he said, " Happy I am to find, that, after such strict examination, the conduct of the prisoner appears in so fair a light; yet I feel myself, at the same time, deeply affected, that this affair turns out so much to the disgrace of every person concerned against him, and so much to the shame of the town in general. " The Jury returned their verdict, *Not Guilty*. He was immediately discharged, and is now in the Castle. Great numbers attended during the whole trial, which was carried on with a solemn decency.

. . .

Genuine Copy of a Letter sent by a Committee of the Supporters of the Bill of Rights to the Honourable the Commons House of Assembly of South Carolina, in Answer to the Letter from the Assembly of South Carolina, concerning a subscription to the Society of Fifteen hundred Pounds Sterling.

To the Hon. Commons House of Assembly of South Carolina.

Gentlemen,

' WE are directed by the Society, Supporters of the Bill of Rights, to transmit to you their thanks, for the very honourable testimony you have at once given of your own sentiments, and of your approbation of their conduct.

' The same spirit of union and mutual assistance, which dictated your vote in our favour, animates this Society. We shall ever consider the rights of all our fellow-subjects throughout the British empire, in England, Scotland, Ireland, and America, as stones of one arch, on which the happiness and security of the whole are founded. Such would have been our principle of action, if the system of despotism, which has been adopted, had been more artfully conducted; and we should as readily have associated in the defence of your rights as our own, had they been separately attacked.

' But providence, has mercifully allotted to depraved hearts, weak understandings: the attack has been made by the same men, at the same time, on both together, and will serve only to draw us closer in one great band of mutual friendship and support.

' Whilst the Norman troops of the first William kept the English in subjection, his English soldiers were employed to secure the obedience of the Normans. This management has been too often repeated now to succeed.

' There was a time when Scotland, though then a separate and divided nation, could avoid the snare, and refused, even under their own Stuarts, to enslave their ancient enemies. The chains, which England and Scotland disdained to forge for each other, England and America shall never consent to furnish.

' Property is the natural right of mankind; the connexion between taxation and representation is its necessary consequence. This connexion is now broken, and taxes are attempted to be levied both in England and America, by men who are not their respective representatives. Our cause is one— our enemies are the same. We trust our constancy and conduct will not differ. Demands, which are made without authority, should be heard without obedience.

' In this, and in every other constitutional struggle on either side of the Atlantic, we wish to be united with you, and are as ready to give as to receive assistance.

' We desire you, gentlemen, to be persuaded, that, under all our domestic grievances and apprehensions, the freedom of America is our particular attention; and these your public act and solemn engagement, afford us a pleasing presage, and confirm our hopes, that, when luxury, misrule, and corruption, shall at length, in spite of all resistance, have destroyed this noble constitution here, our posterity will not, like your gallant ancestors, be driven to an inhospitable shore, but will find a welcome refuge, where they may still enjoy the rights of Englishmen amongst their fellow-subjects, the descendants and brothers of Englishmen.

We are, gentlemen,

With the greatest respect,

Your most obedient servants and affectionate fellow-subjects,

Signed subjects,

John Glynn, Chairman,
Richard Oliver, } Treasurers.
John Trevanion, }
Robert Bernard, }
Joseph Mawbey, } Committee
James Townsend, }
John Sawbridge, }

. . .

Extraordinary Conduct of the Regulators, in the Back Settlements of North Carolina.

From the New-York Gazette.

Newbern, North Carolina, Oct. 5,

ON Wednesday last a special messenger arrived in town from Granville county, to his excellency the governor, with the melancholy account of a violent insurrection, or rather rebellion, having broke out in Orange county, among a set of men who call themselves Regulators, and who for some years past have given infinite disturbance to the civil government of this province, but now have sapped its whole foundation, and brought its courts of justice to their own controul.

These people have for a long time opposed paying all manner of taxes, have entertained the vilest opinion of the gentlemen of the law, and often threatened them with their vengeance. Accordingly, as the Hon. Judge Henderson, and several gentlemen of the law, were returning from Salisbury circuit to Hillsborough, to hold the court there, they were way-laid by a number of them with their rifles; but happily having notice of their hellish design, by taking a contrary rout, eluded their bloody plot. They still gave out their threats of meeting them at Hillsborough, and wreaking their vengeance on them there.

These menaces were treated with contempt, or rather as the violent ravings of a factious and discontented mob, than any settled and fixed resolutions of men of property to commit so daring an insult to the laws of the country, and accordingly the court was opened, and proceeded to business: but on Monday, the second day of the court, a very large number of those people, headed by men of considerable property, appeared in Hillsborough, armed with clubs, whips, loaded at the ends with lead or iron, and many other offensive weapons, and at once beset the court-house. The first object of their revenge was Mr. John Williams, a gentleman of the law, who they assaulted as he was entering the court; him they cruelly abused with many and violent blows with their loaded whips on the head, and different parts of his body, until he by great good fortune made his escape, and took shelter in a neighbouring store. They then entered the court-house, and immediately fixed their attention on Colonel Fanning, as the next object of their merciless cruelty; he for safety had retired to the Judge's seat, as the highest part of the court-house, from which he might make the greatest defence against these blood-thirsty and cruel savages; but vain were all his efforts, for after behaving with the most heroic courage he fell a sacrifice to numbers.

They seized him by the heels, dragged him down the steps, his head striking very violently on every step, carried him to the door, and forcing him out, dragged him on the ground over stones and brickbats, struck him with their whips and clubs, kicked him, and spit and spurned at him, and treated him with every possible mark of contempt and cruelty; till at length, by a violent effort of strength and activity, he rescued himself from their merciless claws, and took shelter in a house; the vultures pursued him there, and gave him a stroke that will probably destroy one of his eyes: in this piteous and grievously maimed condition they left him for a while, retreated to the court-house, knocked down, and very cruelly treated the deputy clerk of the crown, ascended the bench, shook their whips over Judge Henderson, told him his turn was next, ordered him to pursue business, but in the manner they should prescribe, which was, that no lawyers should enter the court-house, no juries but what they should pack, and order new trials in cases where some of them had been cast for their malepractices. They then seized Mr. Hooper, a gentleman of the law, dragged and paraded him through the streets, and treated him with every mark of contempt and insult.

This closed the first day. But the second day presented a scene, if possible, more tragic: immediately on their discovering that the Judge had made his escape from their fury, and refused to submit to the dictate of lawless and desperate men, they marched in a body to Colonel Fanning's house, and on a signal given by their ringleaders, entered the same, destroyed every piece of furniture in it, ript open his beds, broke and threw in the streets every piece of china and glass ware in the house, scattered all his papers and books in the winds, seized all his plate, cash, and proclamation money; entered his cellar, and gorging their stomachs with his liquors, stove and threw in the streets the remainder; being now drunk with rage, liquor, and lawless fury, they took his wearing cloaths, stuck them on a pole, paraded them in triumph through the streets, and to close the scene, pulled down and laid his house in ruins. Hunter and Butler, two of their chiefs, stripping in buff, and beginning the heroic deed.

They then went to a large handsome church bell, that Colonel Fanning, at the expence of 60 or 70l. had made a present of to the church of Hillsborough, and split it to pieces, and were at the point of pulling down the church, but their leaders, thinking it would betray their religious principles, restrained them. Their revenge being not yet satiated on this unhappy gentleman, they again pursued him, again cruelly beat him, and at length with dogs hunted him out of town, and with a cruelty more savage than blood-hounds, stoned him as he fled.

When they had fully glutted their revenge on the lawyers, and particularly Colonel Fanning, to shew their opinion of courts of justice, they took from his chains a negroe that had been executed some time, and placed him at the lawyer's bar, and filled the Judge's seat with human excrement, in derision and contempt of the characters that fill those respectable places.

Notes, 1770

1. The Repeal Act became law on 12 March, as 10 Geo. III c. 17.

2. That is, the internal problems of government and public order, as opposed to the question of the repeal of the Townshend duties.

3. The motion was introduced by Thomas Pownall.

4. This account is taken from the *Boston Gazette and Country Journal* for 12 March.

5. The fifth fatal casualty, Patrick Carr, died on 14 March.

6. Preston's account is from a letter, dated 13 March, written by him to General Gage from the Boston jail, where he and his men were confined after surrendering themselves to city magistrates on 5 March.

7. Peter Oliver (1713–91), a member of an old Massachusetts family, was a judge of the Superior Court of Plymouth County in 1770 and Chief Justice in 1771. By 1774, he was a prominent Loyalist.

8. Ebenezer Richardson, a customs tidesman, had an unpleasant personal reputation and was widely detested. On 22 February, he fired on a gang of youths who claimed he was a customs informer and were stoning his house. One boy was killed, and Richardson narrowly escaped a lynching. His trial finally took place, after several postponements, on 20 April (six weeks after the Boston Massacre). Judge Oliver was abused by the spectators in court when he gave his judicial opinion that Richardson had acted in self-defence. After the jury brought in a verdict of guilty of murder, the judges postponed sentencing. In the ensuing weeks, Oliver was subjected to vitriolic press attacks and many personal threats.

9. Edmund Fanning (1739–1818), a favourite of Governor Tryon and judge of the Superior Court for the Salisbury district, was widely detested for alleged corruption when he was a Register of Deeds for Orange County. He became a Loyalist in 1774 and raised troops to fight on the British side.

Introduction

1771
1772
1773

For the years 1771, 1772, and even 1773, the *Annual Register* is virtually silent on American affairs. In the 1771 volume, a single paragraph in Chapter II of the historical section comments:

> With respect to the colonies it was observed, that the people in most of them had begun to depart from those combinations which were calculated to distress the commerce of this country: the Province of Massachusetts Bay was however still complained of, where, it was said, very unwarrantable practices were still carried on, and the good subjects oppressed by the same lawless violence which had too long prevailed there.[1]

Apart from this, the main descriptive and documentary sections—the *History of Europe, Appendix to the Chronicle,* and *State Papers*—contain almost no references to the American colonies for all three years. Yet the *Register's* coverage of each year's events continued to expand to deal with other matters.[2]

Analysis of the historical section indicates which events the *Register* considered significant. In 1771, two chapters deal with European affairs, one with the progress of the Russo-Turkish War, and one with Germany, Poland, and France; six chapters report British concerns. The clash

1. *AR*, 1771, p. [17.
2. The historical article had 73 pages in 1769, 95 in 1770, 94 in 1771, 105 in 1772, and 108 in 1773. The *Appendix to the Chronicle* and *State Papers* fluctuated quite widely in size beginning in 1765, but the average number of items in the *Appendix* increased by 34 percent, and in the *State Papers*, by 48 percent, for the years 1771–73 inclusive, as against the average for 1765–70 inclusive.

with Spain over the Falkland Islands is described in detail. This conflict had been brewing since 1766 and nearly led to war in 1770, but it was resolved in 1771. The *Register* reports a range of domestic problems raised in Parliament, including a major debate over the powers of the judiciary and of the Crown law officers, and the head-on clash between the City of London and the House of Commons arising from the reporting of parliamentary debates.[3]

The emphasis is reversed in 1772. Six chapters cover European affairs and only two describe British politics. The *Register* foresaw a possible disruption of the European political system and of the balance of power through the partition of Poland, Russian successes against Turkey, the coup d'état in Sweden, and the revolution in Denmark. As for Britain,

> . . . a sullen languor (perhaps in such a government as this not the most desirable of events) began in general to prevail with those who had hitherto opposed, and still disapproved, of the general measure of administration.[4]

Nevertheless, some issues produced extended debate, notably the Government's motion to increase the naval establishment by 25,000 men for the current year, the Royal Marriage Bill (preventing the descendants of George II from marrying without prior consent of the sovereign), and a bill for relieving Dissenting ministers of the necessity of subscribing to the doctrinal parts of the Thirty-nine Articles. At the end of March, the affairs of the East India Company finally came before Parliament, and the attempt to bring in a regulatory bill led instead to the appointment of a committee of enquiry.

In 1773, the *Register*'s historical account continued to concentrate on developments in Europe. Russia's ambitious policy of expansion is seen as finally overreaching itself; the Pugachev revolt and the insurrection of the Don Cossacks and Crim Tartars reveal the weakness of Russia's government, while the "war on the Danube" is recognised "to have been highly ruinous and destructive to Russia." One chapter is devoted to the problems of the Turkish Empire and one to Poland; a brief review of France, Spain, and Italy particularly notes the "final suppression" of the Jesuits. The three chapters covering British politics give exclusive treatment to the Carib prob-

3. See "General Introduction."
4. *AR*, 1772, p. [*81.

lem in St. Vincent (which the Opposition was quick to use to embarrass the Government), the East India Company crisis, and the bill brought in to regulate the company's affairs.

If the *Register* accurately reflects public opinion, the major imperial concern from 1771 to 1773 was the crisis in the affairs of the East India Company. The problem in 1766 was how to deal with the company's expected enormous annual profit of over £2 million; in 1773, it was how to prevent the company from going bankrupt. The cost of administration and war absorbed the expected profits of the dewanni revenue, while earnings from trade diminished. A huge surplus of tea[5] could not be disposed of on the British market because of competition from smuggled Dutch tea, encouraged by the high import duty. Parliament agreed to suspend the duty in 1767 on the guarantee of the company that it would indemnify the Government for the value of the duty lost. Between 1769 and 1772, the cost of the indemnity wiped out the company's profits, and by 1772 the company could not meet its debts of over £1½ million.[6] This credit crisis reverberated throughout the tightly interlocked financial network of the City of London, and because of the large extent of public investments in the company, the Government was seriously worried.

The company's problems were widely blamed on its "imperialism" and the corruption of its servants in India, although both these arguments reveal ignorance of the real situation. Direct intervention by the state was opposed on the grounds that public administration of the company's territories would create a fearsome increase in the Crown's patronage, beyond the control of Parliament. Reform of the company's organisation by legislation might also breach its charter and form a precedent for similar attacks elsewhere.

The issues were hotly debated in Parliament and the company's affairs were investigated by a select as well as a secret committee of the House of Commons. Finally, in 1773, North's government produced three pieces of legislation: the Regulatory Act[7] modified the structure of the company in London and India, thus permitting some state

5. About 15 million lbs. in 1767 and nearly 17 million in 1773.
6. P.R.O. Treasury Papers 1/488. A set of papers here presents in detail the company's assets and liabilities for 1772–73 and graphically reveals the extent of the company's difficulties.
7. 13 Geo. III c. 63.

control; the Relief Act[8] arranged for a series of loans to ease the immediate credit problem; and the Tea Act[9] allowed direct exportation of tea to the American colonies free of duty, in order to offload the surplus at a profit. This legislation was not a solution, but a set of expedients, born out of the struggle in Parliament, to alleviate the company's problems. Abuses in India soon became the target of a crusade led by Burke, and the need for thorough reform and reorganisation was reluctantly recognised.

Between 1766 and 1770, Parliament's concern was diverted from India by events in America. But, in 1772 and 1773, Indian affairs distracted attention from America. Consequently, the open challenge to imperial authority posed by the colonies, led by Massachusetts, seemed particularly serious at the close of 1773. Parliament's inattention, however, and not the realities of American attitudes, gave substance to the contention that America would remain quiescent if unprovoked by inexpedient legislation. Beginning in 1770, a series of incidents[10] indicated that Americans were no longer content to merely assert their right to freedom from taxation by Parliament. They now rejected Parliament's right to legislate American affairs in general, including the regulation of trade. The Tea Act was the focus of American defiance in 1773 because it was thought to be a device for securing a concealed revenue[11] and an attempt to create a British monopoly. Neither was the ministry's motive, but Britain was soon to learn that the problems of empire were not many and separable but one interconnected whole.

8. 13 Geo. III c. 64.
9. 13 Geo. III c. 44.
10. Active opposition to customs enforcement escalated to armed assault and the destruction of revenue vessels; the case of the *Gaspée*, in 1772, received the most notoriety (hence its inclusion in the *Register;* see *AR,* 1774, pp. [45–46]).
11. The imported tea would still pay the 3d. duty.

Introduction

1774

For nearly ten years, Englishmen had tended to regard Massachusetts as the centre of disaffection in British North America. It is thus not surprising that many Englishmen also believed that a decisive action to isolate Massachusetts would teach all the colonies the necessity of obedience. Yet there was ample evidence of the widespread determination in the colonies to resist British legislation and regulation, and it was obvious that there was emerging a significant unanimity of opposition based on intercolonial contacts.

In June 1772, the revenue schooner *Gaspée* was destroyed by a gang of Rhode Islanders, irate at the commander's overzealous antismuggling activities. The crime went entirely unpunished, despite investigation by a royal commission. Amid the protests against the very existence of the commission, the Virginia House of Burgesses decided in March 1773 to set up an intercolonial committee of correspondence to work in liaison with other colonies to defend colonial rights. Every other colony established similar committees between May 1773 and February 1774, thus creating an effective basis for united action.

The value of this technique had already been demonstrated within Massachusetts. Governor Bernard's successor, Thomas Hutchinson, found that the General Court was determined to challenge measures it interpreted to be in violation of charter rights. In October 1772, rumours that judges' salaries were to be paid out of customs duties provided a focus for attack. The General Court was not in session, so the initiative passed to the radical-dominated Boston town meeting, which promptly created a committee of correspondence to secure the support of the rest of Massachusetts. By January 1773, one-third of the colony's townships supported Boston's resolves that successive British governments had systematically violated the constitutional rights of the colony.

This success led the radicals to make a determined bid on 2 June to gain control of the General Court by dramatically producing letters to Britain written by leading officials. Letters written by Hutchinson and Andrew Oliver were represented as encouraging subversion of the colony's constitution and imposition of arbitrary authority from Britain.[1] On 23 June, the assembly voted to petition the Crown to recall Hutchinson and Oliver.

Before this petition was heard,[2] the Boston radicals again demonstrated their growing power. The opposition to the Tea Act became vocal in New York and Philadelphia in October 1773, and in November, mass meetings in Boston demanded that the tea be returned to Britain. On 14 December, Hutchinson refused to give the ships clearance papers without payment of the duty on their cargo, and a well-organised group dressed as Mohawk Indians boarded the ships and dumped 342 chests of tea into Boston harbour. Radicals in Philadelphia and New York were determined to prevent the landing of tea consigned there, and their resolve was strengthened by reports of the Boston Tea Party (probably brought by that indefatigable news-bearer, Paul Revere).

The Cabinet met at the end of January 1774 to discuss appropriate countermeasures but protracted consultations involving the King, General Gage,[3] the Crown law officers, the American Secretary, and Dartmouth's subordinates delayed bringing the problem before Parliament until 7 March. Meanwhile, reports of the disorder in Massachusetts and resistance in other colonies produced

1. See "Notes, 1774," n. 5.
2. The petition was presented to the King on 3 December and referred to the Privy Council, which, on February 1774, dismissed its claims as groundless and its purpose as seditious. *Acts of the Privy Council, Col. Ser. 1766–83*, pp. 387–88.
3. Gage was consulted, as Commander-in-Chief in North America, as to the amount of military force needed to enforce law and order in Massachusetts. He was also asked if he would accept the governorship in place of Hutchinson; he agreed and received his commission on 9 April.

considerable public anger in England. Even those who had consistently sympathised with the American position now condemned what appeared to be outright lawlessness. It was now clear that a significant section of the American popular leadership claimed a form of political independence based on an interpretation of constitutional principle quite incompatible with even the most flexible and liberal British interpretations of imperial relationships.

The North ministry was confident that it could get solid support for legislation which would decisively reassert parliamentary authority and make an example of Massachusetts. The result was the Coercive Acts or, as they were promptly termed in America, the Intolerable Acts. The Boston Port Act in effect closed Boston harbour to commerce until the Crown could be assured that "peace and obedience" had been restored. The Act for Better Regulating the Government of Massachusetts Bay altered the colony's charter of 1691 so that the council was appointed by the Crown, judges were appointed by the governor, jurors were nominated by the sheriffs. Town meetings (other than the annual meeting which elected officers and assemblymen) could be held only with the written permission of the governor. The Act for the Impartial Administration of Justice permitted the governor to send officials accused of capital crimes in the course of their duties for trial in another colony, or Britain. In addition, two further acts were applied. To ensure adequate military presence, the Quartering Act of 1766 was made applicable to all the colonies (with Massachusetts specifically in view).[4] The Quebec Act was of far greater significance. It was designed to solve the problems of the boundaries and government of Canada, matters under review since 1763. The act recognised French civil law and land tenure, granted Roman Catholic toleration, and extended the southwestern Canadian boundary to the Ohio River. Americans regarded the act as a deliberate attempt to hem in New England by a colony responsive to executive control (Quebec had no elected assembly) and inhabited by former enemies alien in cus-

4. 14 Geo. III c. 54, received the royal assent by commission 2 June 1774.

tom, language, and religion. Americans tended to regard the Quebec Act as part of the Coercive Acts.

The ease with which the legislation was passed by Parliament[5] reflected the public anger against America in Britain. Opposition within Parliament was vocal but ineffective. Chatham rejected the role of party leader, Shelburne held together a handful of Chathamites and his own supporters, the Rockingham group (potentially the most significant opposition) was ill-organised, lacked positive direction, and suffered from low morale.[6] Moreover, the powerful alliance of politicians, the City, merchants, and colonial agents, which secured repeal of the Stamp Act in 1766 and of the Townshend duties in 1770, disintegrated. The rise of radicalism in the City of London had alienated Chatham and the Rockinghams.[7] Merchants engaged in trade with North America were alarmed by the threat of another rupture in Atlantic commerce, but their complaints and petitions were useless when addressed to an unsympathetic administration. North decided that political issues were more important than economic issues; the King agreed and had no intention of permitting a change of government. The position of colonial agents in London was weakened by factionalism in their colonies, and some, particularly Franklin,[8] were identified with the specific American challenge to British sovereignty and thus discredited.[9]

The Opposition in Parliament argued strenuously against most aspects of North's American legislation in both Houses but was effective in modifying only the

5. In the House of Commons, the Boston Port bill passed its third reading without a division, the Massachusetts government bill by a majority of 239 to 64, and the administration of justice bill by 127 to 24.
6. Bernard Donaghue, *British Politics and the American Revolution: The Path to War, 1773–75* (London, 1964), ch. 6.
7. Lucy S. Sutherland, *The City of London and the Opposition to Government 1768–1774*, The Creighton Lecture 1958 (London, 1959).
8. Benjamin Franklin (1706–90), internationally renowned as a philosopher and scientist; Postmaster-General of the colonies, 1753–74, and reappointed by the Continental Congress, 1775–76; Pennsylvania delegate to the Congress, 1775–76; one of the committee which drafted the Declaration of Independence. In 1774, Franklin was London agent for Pennsylvania, Georgia, New Jersey, and the Massachusetts Assembly.
9. Jack M. Sosin, *Agents and Merchants; British Colonial Policy and the Origins of the American Revolution 1763–1775* (Lincoln, Neb., 1965), ch. 8.

Quebec Act.[10] That act was also the subject of a protest petition from the City. The Opposition had no demonstrably viable alternative to the Government's policy toward America. The only possible alternative was contained in Burke's famous speech on American taxation, delivered on 19 April in response to a motion of Rose Fuller to repeal the tea duty. Burke argued that an abandonment of any attempt to tax the colonies would restore them to obedience. He upheld the Declaratory Act but argued that it was unwise ever to exercise British sovereignty in full; he thus claimed he had rejected "abstractions" to offer a commonsense view. He believed imperial unity would be assured if Parliament was seen as both a local British and the imperial legislature, to coordinate colonial legislatures, which would retain the privilege of raising local taxes, unless an imperial emergency required Parliament to supervene. Burke thus appealed for an assertion of theoretical supremacy, a practical compromise, and a return to the "antient policy" of confining British colonial legislation to the regulation of commerce.[11]

Burke's speech was widely applauded for its brilliant rhetoric, but his argument did not convince the majority in Parliament.[12] Many were now certain that Americans would not be satisfied with a mere repeal of the tea tax and that they would also reject the Acts of Trade. Moreover, despite Burke's irritated dismissal of "abstractions," his notion of asserting, but not exercising, parliamentary sovereignty ignored the fact that some Americans had already decisively rejected that sovereignty and could be considered in open insurrection. It was impractical for Britain to return to a less centralised and more casual colonial policy, since Americans apparently regarded self-government not as a privilege, but as a right. This position gave little room for compromise and conciliation. Most Englishmen agreed with North when he said "we are now to establish our authority, or give it up

10. Modifications to the boundary clauses were accepted, to allow for some of the claims of Pennsylvania and New York, the latter colony having its interests represented by its agent, Edmund Burke.

11. *Parliamentary History*, vol. 17, 1215–69. Dodsley reprinted the speech as a pamphlet on 10 January 1775; three editions were printed in three weeks.

12. The motion was defeated 182 to 49.

entirely."[13] Dartmouth put it even more starkly: "The question then is, whether these laws are to be submitted to; if the people of America say no, they say in effect that they will no longer be a part of the British Empire."[14]

North's government could therefore claim to be making a stand on an unavoidable issue of principle that had solid public support. The Coercive Acts were specific measures passed on the assumption, however, that Americans would react solely out of self-interest and fear. The North government never credited Americans with an exactly similar belief that the issue was one of principle requiring unity and, if necessary, self-sacrifice. Events were to show this was an unfortunate error of judgement.

Before North presented the issues to Parliament, the Massachusetts Assembly continued its attack on judges who were prepared to receive a royal salary. Chief Justice Oliver remained recalcitrant, and the assembly promptly tried to impeach him. This move was narrowly averted by Hutchinson, who prorogued the House, thus ensuring his own final isolation in the colony's politics. At this point, popular leaders secretly began preparing for armed resistance. Gage arrived in Boston on 17 May to take up the governorship, and news of the Boston Port Act had already galvanised the radicals into fresh action. The Boston Committee of Correspondence circularised other Massachusetts towns, Connecticut, Rhode Island, New York, and Pennsylvania for support in a nonimportation agreement, to last until Boston's rights were restored. The Boston radicals had been working in secret, but the committee was forced into the open on 27 June by a counterattack from moderates and conservatives who feared more damaging reprisals from Britain. Gage's determination to enforce the Coercive Acts, however, mobilised popular pressure behind the radicals, so that the moderates were committed to resistance in order to maintain their political influence.

By the fall of 1774, Massachusetts was in open insurrection, from the British point of view. Gage's attempts to implement the Massachusetts Government Act resulted in

13. From the debate on the Massachusetts government bill, 2 May; *Parliamentary History*, vol. 17, 1316.
14. From a letter to Joseph Reed of Philadelphia, 11 July; *Life and Correspondence of Joseph Reed*, ed. W. B. Reed, 2 vols. (Philadelphia, 1847), vol. 1, pp. 74–76.

the closure of the courts, and his council appointees were publicly declared enemies of the colony. The ban on town meetings led to county meetings, the most significant of which, at Suffolk in September, produced a set of radical resolves condemning the Coercive Acts as unconstitutional; recommending preparation for armed resistance, major economic sanctions against Britain, and nonpayment of taxes until the acts were repealed; and calling on Massachusetts to form a new government. After Gage refused to reconvene the General Court in September, the previously elected delegates met as a provincial congress and prepared for military action.

The other colonies rallied to the support of Massachusetts just as other Massachusetts towns had rallied to support Boston rather than take advantage of her plight or avoid association. The intercolonial committees of correspondence were an important instrument in creating a pattern of resistance throughout most of the colonies by early 1775. The direction and goal of resistance was not yet defined, since few radicals were prepared to argue for outright independence, and the moderates, who feared the repercussions of open revolt within colonial politics and society, hoped for a compromise solution.

Several colonies advocated in the early summer of 1774 a continental congress, to provide an institutional base for colonial unity; delegates from twelve colonies met in Philadelphia in September.[15] Paul Revere brought details of the Suffolk Resolves in the second week of deliberations, and the resolutions were unanimously approved by the delegates on 17 September. The moderates were disturbed by this success and hoped to ensure an accommodation with Britain by supporting Joseph Galloway's[16] plan for a system of government for America which amounted to home rule with what, a century later, would be regarded as dominion status. The plan of union was rejected and the Continental Congress concentrated on drafting resolutions which recommended a stoppage of all trade with Britain until American grievances were rectified,

15. Georgia failed to reach agreement on sending delegates. A late meeting (27 August) in North Carolina delayed attendance of that colony's fifteen delegates until halfway through the Congress.
16. Joseph Galloway (c. 1731–1803), prominent Philadelphia politician, Speaker of the Pennsylvania Assembly, essentially a conservative and ultimately a Loyalist.

listed their grievances, and listed those acts of Parliament since 1763 which had violated their rights. The Congress summarised its position in the document termed the Association on 20 October, and on 21 October, drew up an address to the people of Britain to show that America was the victim of a ministerial conspiracy. On the same day, the Congress produced a memorial justifying its actions to the colonies it represented. On 26 October, it drafted a carefully worded appeal for support to the inhabitants of Quebec, and the Congress concluded its business by adopting a petition to the King. Four days earlier, the delegates had resolved to convene again on 10 May 1775 if American grievances had not been redressed before then.

Official reports about the Congress reached the British government on 13 December (though unofficial correspondence had provided Dartmouth information since September). Despite Opposition protests, North therefore delayed debate on American affairs until January 1775.

The *Annual Register* for 1774 devotes three of the seven chapters in the historical section and a large portion of the *Appendix to the Chronicle* to American matters. The *History of Europe* includes chapters on the end of the Russo-Turkish War, the Pugachev revolt in Russia, German politics, and the accession of Louis XVI and southern European affairs. The last three chapters, thirty-five of the seventy-eight pages, describe British politics. Chapter V briefly analyses the political situation at the beginning of the year, then traces the "discontents and disorders" in America from 1722 to defiance of the Tea Act, and concludes by noting Parliament's concern with the effects of the recent act to preserve the value of gold coin, with the navy estimates, with the high levels of taxation, and with the now annual motion for shorter Parliaments and for "restoring the rights" of the Middlesex electors. Chapter VI begins with the debate on the motion to perpetuate Grenville's act for the settlement of disputed elections and proceeds to describe the March and April debates on America and the passage of the Boston Port Act. Chapter VII describes the debate over Rose Fuller's motion to repeal the tea duty and the passage of the Massachusetts Government Act, the Administration of Justice Act, and the Quebec Act.

The *Register*'s account is mainly full and accurate. The review of American affairs beginning in 1772 condemning the factionalism of colonial politics is overgenerous, since it is an exaggeration to claim that "... the governors of *most* [emphasis added] of the colonies, and the people, were in a continual state of warfare." The *Gaspée* affair may be regarded as "the greatest outrage, which was committed in this state of disorder ... ," though other examples could easily be found (notably the destruction of the naval sloop *Liberty* under similar circumstances at Newport in July 1769, or the attack on customs official John Musket on the Delaware River in November 1771). The *Register* fails, however, to note the alarming colonial reaction to the board of enquiry set up to investigate the *Gaspée* incident.

The *Register*'s coverage of parliamentary debates is again a most useful additional source for the Opposition arguments in the House of Lords, for the debates on the Massachusetts government and administration of justice bills were not officially recorded (on 11 May, even members of the House of Commons were excluded as spectators in the upper chamber). The account of the debates is full and generally impartial, but it is easy to see that the *Register* is highly critical of Government policy and sympathetic to the Rockingham opposition. On the other hand, Burke's speech on American taxation is given a very general précis of less than three hundred words found under a brief review of Opposition arguments for repeal of the tea duty. The entry in the *Chronicle* on this debate notes that "on this occasion Mr. E. Burke distinguished himself in a masterly manner."[17] The *Register* also omits mention of the extension of the Quartering Act, usually considered one of the Coercive Acts.

As usual, the *Register* concludes the British part of the historical section with the end of the summer session of Parliament. Events in America in the summer and fall of 1774 are therefore postponed to the 1775 volume. However, of twenty-two items in the *Appendix to the Chronicle*, thirteen refer to America, and these include the Association of the Continental Congress, the petition of the Congress to the King, its address to the people of Britain, and the address to the inhabitants of Quebec. The *State Papers* gives the usual speeches from the throne and addresses in reply from both Houses of Parliament.

This section includes three other documents (all extracted here). The debate on the Massachusetts govern-

17. *AR*, 1774, p. [111.

ment bill in the House of Lords ended on 11 May, and the bill was passed 92 to 20. Subsequently, ten peers headed by Rockingham signed a dissent embodying their views. Again, on 18 May, having lost the division on the administration of justice bill 43 to 12, eight peers signed a similar dissenting protest. Finally, nine Opposition peers, outraged by the Government's refusal to lay full details of the American despatches before the House at the beginning of the new Parliament on 30 November (see "Introduction, 1775"), signed another formal protest, which on this occasion was written by Burke.

General state of public affairs previous to the meeting of parliament. Ministry. Parties. Discontents in the colonies; increased by various causes. Great heats at Boston, occasioned by the discovery of certain letters. Petition for the removal of the governor and lieutenant-governor. Scheme for the exportation of tea by the East-India company to the colonies, excites a general alarm throughout the continent. Particular causes which operated in rendering that measure more generally obnoxious. Resolutions universally entered into to prevent the landing of the teas. Tumultuous assemblies of the people in different colonies; committees appointed. Three ships laden with tea arrive at Boston; their cargoes thrown into the sea. Similar outrages in some other places; most of the tea ships obliged to return home with their cargoes, and the whole scheme rendered every-where abortive. Parliament meets. King's speech. Gold coin. Debates on the navy establishment, and on various other parts of the supplies. Annual motion for shortening the duration of parliament. Annual motion relative to the Middlesex election.

WHILE the state of public affairs on the continent of Europe wears a doubtful appearance, our own great national concerns unfortunately afford too much matter for serious reflection. The recess of parliament, indeed, was attended with nothing remarkable in affairs merely domestic. In general, a greater quiet seemed to take place in the minds of the people, than at any time since the commencement of the present parliament. The affairs of the East-India company, in the preceding session, had considerably taken off their attention from those objects which were the principal sources of discontent and jealousy. All communities of mankind have a strong disposition to hostility with others, when there is any prospect that the contention will be attended with profit to themselves; and the hopes of lessening their own burdens, whether by the spoils of the East or the West, have as certain an efficacy in quieting the political scruples of the people at large, as ambition, or any other motives, can have with respect to their rulers. A moralist may think that such ideas are held out only to deceive the people, and that, while they are eagerly endeavouring to catch at an imaginary advantage, they are totally blind to the fatal precedent which they establish against themselves.

Other matters concurred to this state of public quiet. Those who had so often petitioned for the dissolution of the present parliament, and many others, who, as little satisfied with some of its proceedings, had notwithstanding, from various causes, refrained from that mode of seeking relief, now consoled themselves with the reflection, that the period of its political existence approached; and were not without hopes, that, as the time grew nearer, when the representatives would be returned to their constituents, and might expect, that their past conduct would become the measure of future support, they would accordingly provide for that event by some popular acts, which, if they did not immediately strike at the root of those measures that were deemed the most obnoxious, would at least have given general satisfaction in other respects. This was the more hoped for, not only as it was consonant to former experience; but that, as the heat and bitterness of contention would have time to wear away, a calmer season of reflection, and a more undisturbed view of things, might, as opposition thought, naturally be expected.

Administration had long carried every thing with so triumphant a sway, that no common event seemed capable of endangering its security. The opinion of their stability was increased even by the nature of the measures which had been adopted: the more unlikely they were to succeed, the more splendid the success of the undertaking appeared. The minds of the people, engaged by a succession of new objects, were no longer quite so powerfully affected by what had so strongly agitated them for some years past. This remission in the spirit of the people at large had given a facility for desertions of several from the opposition to the court, which was liberal in rewarding those seasonable conversions. [1]

There was no very material change in the state of parties, except that general decline of strength in the opposition. The Rockingham party still continued whole and unbroken, and invariably pursued its original line of public conduct. By this means, though constantly overpowered, it notwithstanding continued in some degree formidable. The same differences of opinion or affections, and the same occasional junction in others, still took place between them and that which was attached to the earl of Chatham. We have more than once had occasion to observe, how much this appearance of a want of union blunted the edge, and weakened the force, of opposition.

While affairs were in this dormant state at home, fresh matter unfortunately occurred, for the blowing up into a flame those embers of discontent and discord, which had too long been kept alive in America. The insignificant duty of threepence per pound on tea, which had been left behind singly in the year 1770, when all the other articles enumerated in the same bill for the purpose of raising a revenue had been repealed, was now doomed to be the fatal bone of contention between the mother country and her colonies. We have seen that it was then too truly foretold, by those who struggled hard for the repeal of the whole, and who had always declared against every idea of an internal taxation on America, that the leaving of one duty, and the discharge of the others, could answer no other purpose, than the lessening of that scanty revenue, which was scarcely sufficient, in its full amount, to answer the expence of its collection; that by this means,

instead of profit or benefit, a new charge, to supply the deficiency, would be thrown upon the state at home: while all the other evils, which were then acknowledged as the motives for a partial repeal, would be continued in their utmost extent.

We have already had too many opportunities of recollecting the truth of this prediction, and have already shewn upon different occasions, the severe strictures which have been passed at home, upon the whole system of American government. The consequent discontents and disorders continued to prevail, in a greater or lesser degree, through all the old colonies on the continent. The same spirit pervaded the whole. Even those colonies which depended most upon the mother country for the consumption of their productions, entered into similar associations with the others; and nothing was to be heard of, but resolutions for the encouragement of their own manufactures, the consumption of home products, the discouragement of foreign articles, and the retrenchment of all superfluities. But still these were only symptoms of discontent, which had little effect on the trade to the colonies. That trade, which had somewhat stagnated on the late non-importation agreement, revived again, and even flourished. The article indeed of tea, was by the resolutions of several colonies strictly prohibited; but it still continued to be introduced both from England and other countries, and the duties were paid, though with some small appearance of exterior guard and caution.

In the mean time, the governors of most of the colonies, and the people, were in a continual state of warfare. Assemblies were repeatedly called, and suddenly dissolved. Their time was employed, while fitting, in reiterating grievances, and framing remonstrances. Other matters sprung up, besides the tea duty and the custom-houses, to increase the general discontent.

The late adopted measure, of the governors and judges being paid [2] their salaries by the crown, and thereby, as they were removeable at pleasure, rendered intirely dependent on that, and totally independent of the people, and provincial assemblies, however right or necessary in the present state of affairs, afforded an inexhaustible source of ill-humour and complaint.

The greatest outrage, which was committed in this state of disorder, happened at Providence in Rhode-island, where his Majesty's armed schooner, the Gaspee, having been stationed to prevent the smuggling for which that place was notorious, the vigilance of the officer, who commanded the vessel, so enraged [3] the people, that they boarded her at midnight, to the number June 10th, 1772. of two hundred armed men, and after wounding him, and forcing him and his people to go on shore, concluded this daring exploit by burning the schooner. Though a [4] reward of 500l. together with a pardon, if claimed by an accomplice, was offered by proclamation for the discovering and apprehending any of the persons concerned in this atrocious act, no effectual discovery could be made.

An odd incident happened, which served to revive, with double force, all the ill temper and animosity that had long subsisted between the executive part of government and the people, in the province of Massachuset's bay. This was the accidental discovery, and publication, of a number of confidential letters, which had been written during the course of the unhappy disputes with the mother country, by the then governor and deputy-governor of that colony, to persons in power and office in England. The letters contained a very unfavourable representation of the state of affairs, the temper and disposition of the people, and the views of their leaders, in that province; and tended to shew, not only the ne- [5]

cessity of the most coercive measures; but that even a very considerable change of the constitution, and system of government, was necessary, to secure the obedience of the colony.

These letters indeed were in part confidential and private; but the people of the colony insisted, that they were evidently intended to influence the conduct of government, and must therefore be shewn to such persons as had an interest in preserving their privileges. Upon the death of a gentleman in whose possession these letters then happened, they by some means, which are not known, fell into the hands of the agent for the colony of Massachuset's bay, who immediately transmitted them to the assembly of that province, which was then sitting at Boston. The indignation and animosity which these letters excited on the one side, and the confusion on the other, neither need nor admit of description.

After several violent resolutions in the house of representatives, the letters were presented to the council, under the strictest injunction from the representatives, that the persons, who were to shew them, should not by any means suffer them, even for a moment, out of their own immediate hands. This affront to the governor was adopted by the council; and, upon his requiring to examine the letters that were attributed to him, thereby to be enabled, either to acknowledge them if genuine, or to reprobate them if spurious, that board, under the pretence of this restriction, refused to deliver them into his hands; but sent a committee to open them before him, that he might examine the hand-writing. To this indignity he was obliged to submit, as well as to the mortification of acknowledging the signature.

Such a new source of discord was not wanting in that colony. The house of assembly passed a petition and remonstrance to his Majesty, June 23, 1773.

in which they charged their governor and lieutenant-governor with being betrayers of their trusts, and of the people they governed; of giving private, partial, and false information; declared them enemies to the colony, and prayed for justice against them; and for their speedy removal from their places. So wide was the discontent, and so weak the powers of government in that assembly, that these charges, with many others, were carried through by a majority of 82 to 12.

As we have just observed, the article of tea continued, notwithstanding the strong resolutions of the colonists, to be still imported into America; yet by the advantages which foreigners had in the sale of the low priced teas, as well as the general odium attending the British teas, which, as bearing a parliamentary duty, were considered as instruments of slavery, the East India company was thought to suffer much by the dispute with the colonies.

Thus circumstanced, the minister in the last session, as some apparent consolation to that company, for the strong measures which were then pursued against it by government, brought in a bill, by which they were enabled to export their teas, duty free, to all places whatsoever. In consequence of this measure, the company departed in some degree from its established mode, of disposing of its teas by public sales to the merchants and dealers, and adopted the new system, of becoming its own exporter and factor. Several ships were accordingly freighted with teas for the different colonies by the company, where it also appointed agents for the disposal of that commodity.

The success of this scheme, and any utility to be derived from it, if it did succeed, were at the time much questioned: some active members in that company, and one gentleman of great consideration amongst them, remonstrated against it, as rather calculated for the establish-

ment of the revenue law in America, than as a favour or service to the company. It is true, that they had then about seventeen millions of pounds of tea in their ware-houses; but though this appeared an immense quantity to those who were not versed in the state of the trade, it was said, in reality to be only equal to about two years usual consumption, and it was always intended to have a year's stock in hand.

It appears that the company was not itself quite satisfied as to the utility of this measure, and accordingly consulted some of the most eminent persons in the tea trade upon the subject. By some of the most intelligent of these it was represented, as the wildest scheme that could be imagined, and the most remote from affording the relief which they wanted. That even supposing it attended with all the success of which it was possibly capable, the returns would be too slow and too precarious, to supply in any degree the company's present exigencies in point of cash; that on the other hand, it would be offering the greatest injury to the merchants, who were their established and never failing customers; who purchased their teas at all risks, and paid vast sums of money at stated times independent of them. Certain measures were also proposed, relative to the holding of two public sales within given distances of time, by which the company would not only dispose of all its teas, but would receive, as they supposed, by the first payment, at the end only of five months, no less than 1,200,000l. in cash: a sum so considerable, and to be paid in so short a time, that it would probably enable them to refrain from the fatal loan, which they were negociating with the public. The first measure, being a favourite with government, was adopted, notwithstanding these reasons and proposals.

If such were the opinions formed upon this scheme at home, it was universally considered in the colonies, as calculated merely to circumvent them into a compliance with the revenue law, and thereby open the door to an unlimited taxation. For it was easily seen, that if the tea was once landed and in the custody of the consignees, no associations, nor other measures, would be sufficient to prevent its sale and consumption; and nobody could pretend to imagine, that when taxation was established in one instance, it would restrain itself in others. Besides that all the dealers both legal and clandestine, who as tea is an article of such general consumption in America, were extremely powerful, saw their trade taken at once out of their hands. They supposed that it would all fall into the hands of the company's consignees, to whom they must become in a great measure dependent, if they could hope to trade at all. The East India company by the late regulations was brought intirely under the direction of government. [6] The consignees were of course such as favoured administration, and for that reason the most unpopular people in America. Particularly at Boston, they were of the family [7] and nearest connections of those gentlemen, whose letters as we have observed, had at that time kindled such prodigious heats and animosities among the people. It was at an unlucky time that they thought they saw a monopoly formed in favour of the most obnoxious persons, and that too for the purpose of confirming an odious tax. The same spirit seemed to run like wildfire throughout the colonies, and without any apparent previous concert, it was every where determined, to prevent the landing of the teas at all events.

At the same time, the East India company became so exceedingly odious to the people, that a mere opposition to her interests, abstracted from all other causes, would have embarrassed any measure that was undertaken in her favour. The colonists said, that she was quitting her usual line of conduct, and wantonly becoming the instrument of giving efficacy to a law which they detested: thereby involving them, as they affirmed, in the present dangerous dilemma, either of submission to the establishment of a precedent which they deemed fatal to their liberties, or of bringing matters to a crisis which they dreaded, by adopting the only means that seemed left to prevent its execution.

As the time approached when the arrival of the tea ships for the execution of the new plan was expected, the people assembled at different places in great bodies, and began to take such measures as seemed most effectual to prevent the landing of their cargoes. The tea consignees, who had been appointed by the India company, were obliged in most places (and in some, at the peril of property, if not of life) to relinquish their appointments, and to enter into public engagements not to act in that capacity. Committes were appointed by the people in different towns and provinces, whom they armed with such powers as they supposed themselves enabled to bestow. They were authorized to inspect merchants books; to propose tests, to punish those whom they considered as contumacious, by the dangerous proscription of declaring them enemies to their country, and of assembling the people when they thought necessary. In a word, their powers were as indefinite, as the authority under which they acted.

In the tumultuous assemblies which were frequently held upon this occasion, numberless resolutions were passed, extremely derogatory with respect to the authority of the supreme legislature. Inflammatory hand bills, and other seditious papers were continually published; nor were the conductors of news-papers, nor the writers of various pamphlets, much more guarded in their conduct, or temperate in their manner. Even at Philadelphia, which had been so long celebrated, for the excellency of its police and government, and the temperate manners of its inhabitants, printed papers were dispersed, warning the pilots on the river Deleware, not to conduct any of those tea ships into their harbour; which were only sent out for the purpose of enslaving and poisoning all the Americans; at the same time, giving them plainly to understand it was expected, that they would apply their knowledge of the river, under the colour of their profession, in such a manner, as would effectually secure their country from so imminent a danger. At New York, in a similar publication, those ships are said to be loaden with the fetters which had been forged for them in Great Britain, and every vengeance is denounced against all persons, who dare in any manner contribute to the introduction of those chains. All the colonies seemed to have instantly united in this point.

The town of Boston, which had been so long obnoxious to government, was the scene of the first outrage. Three ships laden with tea, having arrived in that port, the captains were terrified into a concession, that if they were permitted by the consignees, the board of customs, and the Fort of Castle William, they would return with their cargoes to England. These promises could not be fulfilled; the consignees refused to discharge the captains from the obligations under which they were chartered for the delivery of their cargoes; the custom-house refused them a clearance for their return: and the governor to grant them a passport for clearing the fort.

In this state, it was easily seen by the people of the town, that the ships lying so near, the teas would be landed by degrees, notwithstanding any guard they could keep, or measures take to prevent it; and it was as well known, that if they were landed, nothing could prevent their being disposed of, and thereby the purpose of establishing the monopoly and raising a revenue fulfilled. To prevent this dreaded consequence, a number of armed men, under the disguise of Mohawk Indians, boarded the Dec. 18th. 1773. ships, and in a few hours discharged their whole cargoes of tea into the sea, without doing any other damage, or offering any injury to the captains or crews. It was remarkable, that the government, civil power, garrison of Fort William, and armed ships in the harbour, were totally inactive upon this occasion.

Some smaller quantities of tea, met afterwards with a similar fate, at Boston, and a few other places; but in general, the commissioners for the sale of that commodity, having been obliged to relinquish their employment, and no other persons daring to receive the cargoes which were consigned to them, the masters of the tea vessels, from these circumstances, as well as from a knowledge of danger, and the determined resolution of the people, readily complied with the terms which were prescribed, of returning directly to England, without entangling themselves by any entry at the custom-houses. At New York it was indeed landed under the cannon of a man of war. But the government there were obliged to consent to its being locked up from use. In South Carolina some was thrown into the river as at Boston.

Such was the issue of this unfortunate scheme. Some disposition to these disturbances was known pretty early; but as their utmost extent was still unknown, the meeting of parliament was deferred until after the holidays.

• • •

A few days after the question on the Grenville bill was carried, the American dispatches arrived, and[8] brought advice of the outrages committed on board the tea ships at Boston. This intelligence occasioned a message from the throne to both houses, in which they are informed, that in consequence of the unwarrant-March 7. able practices carried on in North-America, and particularly of the violent and outrageous proceedings at the town and port of Boston, with a view of obstructing the commerce of this kingdom, and upon grounds and pretences immediately subversive of its constitution, it was thought fit to lay the whole matter before parliament; fully confiding, as well in their zeal for the maintenance of his Majesty's authority, as in their attachment to the common interest and welfare of all his dominions, that they will not only enable him effectually to take such measures as may be most likely to put an immediate stop to those disorders, but will also take into their most serious consideration, what further regulations and permanent provisions may be necessary to be established, for better securing the execution of the laws, and the just dependence of the colonies upon the crown and parliament of Great Britain.

This message was attended with a great number of papers relating to the late transactions in the colonies, containing copies and extracts of letters from the several governors; from the commander of the forces; from the admiral in Boston harbour; from the consignees of the tea at Boston, to one of the ringleaders of the faction in that town, with votes and resolves of the town of Boston, previous to the landing of the tea, and narratives of the transactions which succeeded that event; a petition from the consignees to the council of Massachusets, praying that their persons and property might be taken under the protection of government, with the refusal of the council to interfere in any manner in the business; a proclamation issued by the governor, to forbid factious meetings of the inhabitants; and the transactions of the Massachusets council, condemning the measure of destroying the tea, and advising legal prosecutions against the perpetrators, none of whom were known, nor was there any possibility of their discovery.

They also contained details from the different governors, of all transactions relative to the teas, which took place in their respective governments, from the first intelligence of their being shipped in England, to the date of their letters; threats and prophetic warnings, which were continually sent to the gentlemen to whom the teas were consigned; copies of certain printed papers, with a great number of fugitive inflammatory pieces, hand bills, alarms, violent resolves of town meetings, illegal proceedings of committees, and extraordinary minutes of council.

As the same spirit pervaded the whole continent, so the same language, sentiment, and manner, prevailed in all these written or printed pieces, whether circulated in the province of Massachusets, or in the other colonies.

The presentment of the papers was accompanied with a comment upon them, and particularly those that related to the transactions at Boston, in which the conduct of the governor was described and applauded, and that of the prevailing faction represented in the most atrocious light. It was said that he had taken every measure which prudence could suggest, or good policy justify, for the security of the East-India company's property, the safety of the consignees, and the preserving of order and quiet in the town. Every civil precaution to prevent the mischiefs that followed had been used in vain. His Majesty's council, the militia, and the corps of cadets, had been all separately applied to, for their assistance in the preservation of the public peace, and the support of the laws; but all without effect, they refused or declined doing their duty. The sheriff read a proclamation to the faction at their town meeting, by which they were commanded to break up their illegal assembly; but the proclamation was treated with the greatest contempt, and the sheriff insulted in the grossest manner.

That he had it undoubtedly in his power, by calling in the affistance of the naval force which was in the harbour, to have prevented the deftruction of the tea; but that as the leading men in Bofton had always made great complaints of the interpofition of the army and navy, and charged all difturbances of every fort to their account, he with great prudence and temperance, determined from the beginning to decline a meafure, which would have been fo irritating to the minds of the people; and might well have hoped, that by this confidence in their conduct, and truft repofed in the civil power, he fhould have calmed their turbulence, and preferved the public tranquillity.

Thus, faid the minifters, the people of Bofton were fairly tried. They were left to their own conduct, and to the exercife of their judgment, and the refult has given the lie to all their former profeffions. They are now without an excufe: and all the powers of government in that province, are found infufficient to prevent the moft violent outrages. The loyal and peaceable people of a mercantile town, (as they affect to be peculiarly confidered,) have given a notable proof to the world of their juftice, moderation, loyalty, and affection for the mother country, by wantonly committing to the waves a valuable commodity, the property of another loyal mercantile body of fubjects; without the pretence of neceffity, even fuppofing that their oppofition to the payment of the duties could juftify fuch a plea; as they had nothing to do but to adhere to their own refolutions, of nonconfumption, effectually to evade the revenue laws.

It was concluded upon the whole, that by an impartial review of the papers now before them it would manifeftly appear, that nothing could be done by either civil, military, or naval officers, to effectuate the re-eftablifhment of tran-

quillity and order in that province, without additional parliamentary powers to give efficacy to their proceedings. That no perfon employed by government, could in any act, however common or legal, fulfil the duties of his office or ftation, without its being immediately exclaimed againft by the licentious, as an infringement of their liberties. That it was the fettled opinion of fome of the wifeft men, both in England and America, and the beft acquainted with the affairs of the colonies, that in their prefent ftate of government, no meafures whatfoever could be purfued, that would in any degree remedy thofe glaring evils, which were every day growing to a more enormous and dangerous height. That parliament, and parliament only, was capable of re-eftablifhing tranquillity among thofe turbulent people, and of bringing order out of confufion. And that it was therefore incumbent on every member, to weigh and confider, with an attention fuitable to the great importance of the fubject, the purport of the papers before them, and totally laying all prejudices afide, to form his opinion upon the meafures moft eligible to be purfued, for fupporting the fupreme legiflative authority, the dignity of parliament, and the great interefts of the British Empire.

This is in fubftance what was urged by miniftry upon the fubject when they prefented the papers. But as things were to be brought to a crifis with the colonies, and very ftrong meafures were refolved upon, it was apprehended, that the merchants would be affected, and make fome oppofition. To prevent this all the public papers were fyftematically filled with writings on this fubject, painting the mifconduct of the colonies in the ftrongeft colours, and in particular urging the impoffibility of the future exiftence of any trade to America, if this flagrant outrage on commerce fhould go unpunifhed.

Thefe with many other endeavours to the fame end were not without an effect. The fpirit raifed againft the Americans became as high and as ftrong as could be defired, both within and without the houfe. In this temper a motion was made for an addrefs to the throne, " to return " thanks for the meffage, and the " gracious communication of the " American papers, with an af- " furance, that they would not " fail to exert every means in " their power, of effectually pro- " viding for objects fo important " to the general welfare, as main- " taining the due execution of the " laws, and fecuring the juft de- " pendence of the colonies upon " the crown and parliament of " Great Britain."

This motion produced a warm debate, or rather difcuffion upon American affairs. For though the leaders in oppofition, difclaimed all intention of impeding the meafures of government in a matter of fuch high importance, until they were at leaft thoroughly explained, and their tendency underftood, and therefore would not move any queftion, or propofe a divifion for the prefent; yet they ftrongly condemned the manner in which hafty, ill-digefted addreffes were paffed, without enquiry or information, and the houfe continually pledged for the performance of acts which were never further thought of. Former fpeeches and addreffes, from the year 1768, to 1770, were called for and read, and fhewn to be exactly of the fame nature and tendency with the prefent. It was then farcaftically afked, in what part of the journals the confequent refolutions were to be found, or what hiftorical record preferved an account of the meafures which were taken to fulfil their intention.

Some of them faid they feared, that if, as heretofore, nothing at all fhould be done, that government would fall into ftill greater contempt; or if to fecure againft this ill effect they should plunge from sloth and neglect into violence and precipitation, government would bring on an universal resistance, which perhaps it might never be able to overcome. That America was allowed on all hands to be extremely distempered. They thought the subject required the most delicate and temperate management. But whatever course of reformation was taken, they were very certain, that no good could possibly arise from it, unless the radical cause of the quarrel was removed, and the minds of the Americans made easy on the business of Taxation. That they ought not only to examine into the behaviour of the Americans who had resisted Government; but into that system of violence which had provoked, and of weakness which had encouraged, their resistance. That the house could never support ministers with reputation or effect, unless they enquired into their conduct; and supported them only as that conduct appeared to have been just and rational. That therefore a strict retrospect into the management of ministers was essentially connected with an enquiry into the state of America. Otherwise weakness and ignorance would be encouraged in the government of an object, which required every exertion of wisdom and vigilance. And that this must inevitably end in the loss of our colonies in spite of all the votes and resolutions of parliament.

They said that a retrospect even for punishment might often be necessary; but that a retrospect to direct their own conduct and to take away the authority of feeble and destructive counsellors, even where no direct guilt was charged, was always their duty and their interest.

On the other hand the ministers strongly dissuaded from all retrospect, as tending only to inflame. The business they said was important and pressing. In the examina-

tion of this great question great points would be canvassed.—Is America any longer to be dependent on this country?—How far is it connected?—In what degree? —In what manner? It might be a great question whether the colonies should not be given up? But if this question shall be decided in the negative, then it would be necessary to examine in what manner their subordination should be preserved, and authority enforced? These points required the most serious investigation; in which, the retrospect recommended, would be unnecessary and perhaps dangerous; as encouraging those whom it was the business of parliament by every means to reduce to obedience.

By the voting this address ministry gained a greater advantage than at first appeared; for they found by the disposition of the house, which was strongly against all retrospect, that they would confine themselves to the mere misbehaviour of the Americans. The violence of the Americans was public and unquestioned, and when the enquiry was confined to that ground, it would be easy to carry any proposition against them. It was of great consequence to the minister, that no part whatsoever of the weakness and disorderly state of so many governments, should be laid to the charge of those who had for some years the entire direction of them in their hands.

As the storm which was gathering against the colonies would probably be directed against Massachuset's Bay, Mr. Bollan, agent for the council of that province, thought it necessary to present to the house, by way of precaution, a petition desiring that he might be permitted to lay before the house the acta regia of queen Elizabeth and her successors, for the security of the Planters, and their descendents, and the perpetual enjoyment of their liberties. These documents he presumed had never been laid before the house, nor had

the colonies ever had an opportunity to ascertain and defend these rights. This petition was received without difficulty, and ordered to lie upon the table.

The minister, after having moved that the King's message of the 7th of March should be read, opened his plan for the restoration of peace, order, justice, and commerce in the Massachuset's Bay. He stated that the opposition to the authority of parliament had always originated in that colony, and that colony had been always instigated to such conduct, by the irregular and seditious proceedings of the town of Boston. That therefore for the purpose of a thorough reformation, it became necessary to begin with that town, which by a late unparalleled outrage had led the way to the destruction of the freedom of commerce in all parts of America. That if a severe and exemplary punishment were not inflicted on this heinous act, Great Britain would be wanting in the protection she owed to her most peaceable and meritorious subjects. That had such an insult been offered to British property in a foreign port, the nation would have been called upon to demand satisfaction for it.

He would therefore propose that the town of Boston should be obliged to pay for the tea which had been destroyed in their port. That the injury was indeed offered by persons unknown and in disguise, but that the town magistracy had taken no notice of it, had never made any search for the offenders, and therefore by a neglect of a manifest duty became accomplices in the guilt. That the fining of communities for their neglect in punishing offences committed within their limits, was justified by several examples. In king Charles II.'s time the city of London was fined when Dr. Lamb was killed by unknown persons. The city of Edinburgh was fined, and otherwise punished for the affair of Captain

Porteous. A part of the revenue of the town of Glasgow had been sequestered until satisfaction was made for the pulling down Mr. Campbell's house. These examples were strong and in point, for such punishments. The case of [9] Boston was far worse. It was not a single act of violence. It was a series of seditious practices of every kind, and carried on for several years.

He was of opinion therefore that it would not be sufficient to punish the town of Boston by obliging her to make a pecuniary satisfaction for the injury, which, by not endeavouring to prevent or punish, she has in fact encouraged; security must be given in future, that trade may be safely carried on, property protected, laws obeyed, and duties regularly paid. Otherwise the punishment of a single illegal act is no reformation. It would be therefore proper to take away from Boston the privilege of a port until his Majesty should be satisfied in these particulars, and publicly declare in council, on a proper certificate of the good behaviour of the town, that he was so satisfied. Until this should happen, the Custom-house officers who were now not safe in Boston, or safe no longer than while they neglected their duty, should be removed to Salem, where they might exercise their functions. By this Boston might certainly suffer. But she ought to suffer; and by this resolution would suffer far less punishment than her delinquencies fully justified. For she was not wholly precluded from all supply. She was by this proposition only to be virtually removed seventeen miles from the sea. The duration of her punishment was entirely in her own power. For when she should discharge this just debt to the E. I. company, which had been contracted by her own violence, and given full assurances of obedience in future to the laws of trade and revenue, there was no

doubt, but that his Majesty, to whom he proposed to leave that power, would again open the port, and exercise that mercy which was agreeable to his royal disposition. Unanimity was strongly recommended. This was a crisis which demanded vigour. He was by no means an enemy to lenient measures. Resolutions of censure and warning will avail nothing. Now is the time to stand out; to defy them with firmness and without fear. A conviction must be produced to America that we are in earnest and will proceed with firmness and vigour. This conviction would be lost if they found us doubting and hesitating. Some friends to British authority may indeed suffer a little. But if with this temporary inconvenience we compare the loss of the country and its due obedience it will bear no comparison. It is said, the Americans will not pay their debts. This they threatened before the repeal of the stamp act. The act was repealed. What was the consequence? They did not pay. This threat, if attended to, must disable parliament equally in all its operations. This act will not require a military power to enforce it. Four or five frigates will be sufficient. But if it should, he would not scruple to use a military force which might act with effect and without blood shed. The other colonies will not take fire at the proper punishment inflicted on those who have disobeyed the laws. They will leave them to suffer their own punishments. If they do combine with them, the consequences of their rebellion belong not to us but to them. We are only answerable that our measures are just and equitable. Let us proceed (said he) with firmness, justice, and resolution, which course, if pursued, will certainly produce that due obedience to the laws of this country, and that security of the trade of this people which I so ardently wish for.

Upon these arguments leave was given to bring in a bill "for the immediate re-" Mar. 14. "moval of the officers concerned "in the collection of the customs "from the town of Boston in the "province of the Massachuset's "Bay in North America, and to "discontinue the landing and dis- "charging, lading and shipping "of goods, wares and merchan- "dize at the said town of Boston "or within the harbour thereof."

In the progress of the bill a motion was made for an amendment, for the purpose of laying a fine on the town of Boston, equivalent to the damage sustained by the East-India company. This fine or satisfaction if they refused to pay, then and not before the penalties of this act were allowed to take place. The proposition was rejected, and this bill, pregnant with so many important consequences, was pushed on with so much vigour and dispatch, that it did not remain long in the house.

At the first introduction it was received with very general applause. The equity of obliging a delinquent town to make satisfaction for the disorders which arose from their factious spirit, and negligent police, was so striking, that many things which might appear exceptionable in the act were overlooked. The cry raised against the Americans, partly the natural effect of their own acts, and partly of the operations of government, was so strong as nearly to overbear the most resolute and determined in the opposition. Several of those who had been most sanguine favourers of the colonies now condemned their behaviour; and applauded the measure, as not only just, but lenient. Others indeed stood firmly on their old ground: but after having delivered their opinions at large in the preliminary debates, when the motion was made for leave to bring in the bill, they did not enter so largely into the matter. They contented themfelves, in that ftage of the bufinefs, with deprecating the bill; predicting the moft fatal confequences from it, and lamenting the fpirit of the houfe, which drove on, or was driven on, to the moft violent meafures, by the mifchiefs produced by injudicious councils; one feeming to render the other neceffary. They declared that they would enter little into a debate which they faw would be fo fruitlefs; and only fpoke to clear themfelves from having any fhare in fuch fatal proceedings.

But in the progrefs of the bill, oppofition feemed to collect itfelf, and to take a more active part. Mr. Bollan, the agent of the council of Maffachufet's bay, prefented a petition, defiring to be heard for the faid council, and in behalf of himfelf and other inhabitants in the town of Bofton. The houfe refufed to receive the petition. It was faid, that the agent of the council was not agent for the corporation, and no agent could be received from a body corporate, except he were appointed by all the neceffary conftituent parts of that body. Befides, the council was fluctuating, and the body by which he was appointed could not be then actually exifting. This vote of rejection was heavily cenfured. The oppofition cried out at the inconfiftency of the houfe, who but a few days ago received a petition from this very man in this very character; and now, only becaufe they chufe to exert their power in acts of injuftice and contradiction, totally refufe to receive any thing from him, as not duly qualified. Were not the reafons equally ftrong againft receiving the firft as the fecond petition? But what, they afferted, made this conduct the more unneceffary and outrageous, was, that at that time the houfe of lords were actually hearing Mr. Bollan on his petition, as a perfon duly qualified, at their bar. Thus, faid they, this houfe is at once in contradiction to the other and to

itfelf. As to the reafons given againft his qualification, they are equally applicable to all American agents; none of whom are appointed as the minifter now requires they fhould be—and thus the houfe cuts off all communication between them and the colonies whom they are affecting by their acts.

On the third reading, another petition was prefented by the lord-mayor in the name of feveral natives and inhabitants of North-America then in London. It was drawn with remarkable ability. They ftated that "the proceedings were repugnant to every principle of law and juftice; and under fuch a precedent no man in America could enjoy a moment's fecurity; for if judgment be immediately to follow an accufation againft the people of America, fupported by perfons notorioufly at enmity with them, the accufed unacquainted with the charge, and from the nature of their fituation utterly incapable of anfwering and defending themfelves, every fence againft falfe accufation will be pulled down. They afferted, that law is executed with as much impartiality in America as in any part of his Majefty's dominions. They appealed, for proof of this, to the fair trial and favourable verdict in the cafe of captain Prefton and his foldiers. That in fuch a cafe the interpofition of parliamentary power was full of danger and without precedent. The perfons committing the injury were unknown. If difcovered, the law ought firft to be tried. If unknown, what rule of juftice can punifh the town for a civil injury committed by perfons not known to belong to them. That the inftances of the cities of London, Edinburgh, and Glafgow, were wholly diffimilar. All thefe towns were regularly heard in their own defence. Their magiftrates were of their own chufing (which is not the cafe of Bofton) and therefore they were more equitably refponfible. But in Bofton the King's governor has the power, and had

been advifed by the council to exert it: if it has been neglected, he alone is anfwerable. They ended by ftrongly infifting on the injuftice of the act, and its tendency to alienate the affections of America from this country; and that the attachment of America cannot long furvive the juftice of Great-Britain.

This petition was received; but [10] as no hearing was defired, no particular proceeding was had upon it. In anfwer to the matter it contained, the minifterial fide contended, that if they were to wait to hear, they might wait for ever, as the town would not acknowledge their authority. That even if they fhould plead their caufe here, this would fpin out the affair into an unmeafureable length; whereas the trade of England called for immediate and effectual protection. They afked whether the houfe doubted the exiftence of the offence, or of their own competence to enquire into and to punifh it. That as to leaving Bofton to the mercy of the crown, it was doing it a favour: for where could mercy be better placed than in its legal depofitory, which was always in the breaft of the crown. On this the debates were long and vehement. The oppofition contended, that this act was not for the purpofe of impofing a fine for an offence: if it had, it would ftill be liable to all the objections ftated in the petition. The option of laying a fine, and proceeding on non-payment to extremities, had been propofed and rejected by the houfe. That the bill ftood therefore fimply as a profcription of one of the greateft trading towns in the Britifh dominions from the ufe of their port, and from all the commerce by which more than 20,000 people obtained their bread. That if this profcription was made determinable on any certain or fpecific act, it might be tolerable. But have we not (faid they) given an extent of power to his Majefty to prevent the port of Bofton from ever being reinftated, if the King fhould think proper? What limit or line is drawn, to define when it may be proper, right, and juft, that the port of Bofton fhould be reinftated? It depends wholly on the pleafure of the King, that is of minifters. Was, this neceffary, either for punifhment of the Boftonians, or for fatisfaction to the Eaft-India company? It could only be made for the purpofe of eftablifhing a precedent of delivering over whole towns and communities to an arbitrary difcretion in the crown. They denied that this was like the cafes in which the mercy of the crown was to take place. That none was at the mercy of the crown, except when the known law, on a fair hearing, condemned to a certain punifhment. But in this cafe where was the law, the hearing, or the fixed punifhment? They afked what precedent there was for depriving a maritime city of its port, and then leaving them to the mercy of the crown, to reftore the port, or not, at pleafure? Precedents had been fhewn of towns that had been fined. They denied that thofe precedents applied to the cafe: and if they had, ftill it was only a fine; the trade of the place went on juft as before. But here, faid they, a fine is laid; the trade is prohibited until it is paid; and when the fine is paid, the city may be as far from recovering her trade as ever. The act provides that the crown muft have fatisfaction, that the laws of trade and revenue fhall be obeyed. There is a fting in this. The act, under pretence of an indemnity to the company, is meant to inforce the fubmiffion to taxes. America will fee this; and the caufe of Bofton will be made the caufe of all the colonies. They are all as guilty as Bofton. Not one has received the tea: fome have deftroyed it, others fent it back. And when Bofton is fingled out as the victim, none there can be fo dull as not to fee, that this election is made to lull them afleep to the confequences of an act, which, on a fubmiffion of one city, muft go, one by one,

to all the reft; until they are fucceffively delivered over to the arbitrary mercy of the crown? That all this violence and precipitation is for the fake of trade, they could never believe; becaufe no complaint was come from any one trader or manufacturer; no not even from the company itfelf, which was the immediate fufferer. On the contrary, they feared this act would prove deftructive of trade, and the origin of very great troubles.

Thefe and many other objections were made, and ftrongly urged againft the bill, and the debate

continued for a long time. However the oppofition did not divide; either chufing not to fhew a difference amongft themfelves, and weak numbers; or, as they faid, not to prevent this act from having the utmoft operation its friends could promife themfelves in bringing America to obedience.

The bill paffed the houfe on the 25th of March, and was carried up to the lords, where it was likewife warmly debated, but. as in the commons, without a divifion. It received the royal affent on the 31ft [11] of March.

Motion preparatory to a repeal of the tea duty laid in 1767. Debate upon the policy of a repeal at this particular time. Negative put on the motion. Bill brought in for the better regulating the government of Maffachufet's bay: debates upon it: petitions againft it: rejected by the houfe: the bill paffed: carried to the lords: proceedings.there: paffes the lords. Bill for the impartial adminiftration of juftice in Maffachufet's Bay: debates: the bill paffes both houfes. Bill for the government of Quebec, brought into the houfe of lords, and paffed: fent to the commons: debates: paffes the commons, but with great amendments. Clofe of the feffion. Speech from the throne.

SEVERAL gentlemen, who had voted for the bill to fhut up the port of Bofton, were neverthelefs of opinion, that fomething of a conciliatory and redreffing nature fhould attend this meafure of feverity, and might give the greater efficacy to it. That parliament, whilft it refented the outrages of the American populace, ought not to be too willing to irritate the fober part of the colonies. That, if they had fatisfaction in the matter of taxes, they would become inftrumental in keeping the inferior and more turbulent in order; and that this facrifice to peace would be at no confiderable expence, as the taxes were of very little value to Great-Britain; but a very heavy burthen on the minds of the Americans, as they confidered the impofitions which they had no fhare in granting, rather as badges of flavery than contributions to government. A motion was accordingly made preparatory to a repeal of the tea duty laid in 1767. The arguments ufed in fupport of the

general propofition, and in oppofition to it, were nearly the fame as thofe which have been ftated in former volumes of the Regifter. But the debate upon the policy of a repeal at this particular time, was long and earneft. The party for the repeal ftrongly urging experience, which they infifted was in their favour. That the attempt to tax America had inflamed, the repeal had quieted, and the new taxes had inflamed it again. That even the partial repeal of fome of the new taxes had produced no fmall degree of tranquillity in America, until the attempt to enforce what remained by the late Eaft India act, had again thrown the empire into confufion. They were of opinion, that this act of condefcenfion would fhew, that parliament meant by their penal acts to punifh diforders in the colonies; but that they regarded alfo their privileges and their quiet. The good effect of their rigour would depend on a tincture of lenity. They were of opinion that this lenitive would render rigour unneceffary. They therefore earneftly preffed the repeal of the obnoxious tea duty that remained, as a very probable method of reftoring tranquillity and obedience. To enforce this they entered into a large field, and the merits and fuccefs of the feveral plans of colony-government for feveral years were laid open and fully difcuffed.

But to thefe arguments it was anfwered, that fuppofing the tea duty fo contemptible an object as was reprefented; which however the minifter denied, yet a repeal at this time would fhew fuch a degree of wavering and inconfiftency as would defeat the good effects of the vigorous plan, which after too long remiffnefs was at length adopted. That parliament ought to fhew that it will relax in none of its juft rights, but enforce them in a practical way. That fhe ought to fhew that fhe is provided with fufficient means of making herfelf obeyed whenever fhe is refifted. If this tax is repealed, what anfwer is to be given when they demand the repeal of the tax on wine? No anfwer, until all is furrendered, even America herfelf. That if the houfe perfifted in the meafures begun, there was no doubt, they faid, of fucceeding, or, to adopt the expreffion ufed, " of becoming *victorious*." And this victory could only be obtained by a firm, confiftent, juft, and manly conduct.

On thefe grounds a negative was put on this motion, which had been propofed fo often in former feffions. The numbers in its favour were alfo much fmaller than upon former occafions. The difpofition to carry things to extremities with America was become very general; and as the repeal of the ftamp-act was much condemned by the minifterial fide, and its authors greatly decried, they repofed the higheft confidence in the fuccefs of meafures of a contrary nature.

The Bofton port bill formed only one part of the coercive plan propofed by the miniftry as the effectual method of bringing her into obedience. Others of a deeper and more extenfive nature were behind, and appeared in due time. Soon after the rejection of this motion a bill was brought in for " the better regulating government in the province of Maffachufet's Bay." The purpofe of this bill was to alter the conftitution of that province as it ftood upon the charter of King William; to take the whole executic power out of the hands of the democratic part, and to veft the nomination of counfellors, judges, and magiftrates of all kinds, including fheriffs, in the crown, and in fome cafes in the King's governor, and all to be removeable at the pleafure of the crown.

In fupport of this bill, the minifter[12] who brought it in alledged, that the diforders in the province of Maffachufet's Bay not only diftracted that province within itfelf, but fet an ill example to all the colonies. An executive power was wanting in the country. The force of the civil power confifts in the *Poffe comitatus*; but the Poffe are the very people who commit the riots. That there was a total defect in the conftitutional power throughout. If the democratic part fhew a contempt of the laws, how is the governor to enforce them? Magiftrates he cannot appoint: He cannot give an order without feven of the council affenting: And let the military be never fo numerous and active, they cannot move in fupport of the civil magiftracy, when no civil magiftrate will call upon them for fupport. It is in vain, faid they, that you make laws and regulations here, when there are none found to execute them in that country. It therefore became abfolutely neceffary to alter the whole frame of the Maffachufet's government, fo far as related to the executive and judicial powers. That the juries were alfo improperly chofen. Some immediate and permanent remedy muft be adopted. The minifter therefore propofed the prefent bill, which he hoped would give ftrength and fpirit to the civil magiftracy, and energy to the executive power.

The oppofition to this bill was much more active and united than upon the Bofton port-act. The minority alledged, that this carried the principle of injuftice much further. That to take away the civil conftitution of a whole people, fecured by a charter, the validity of which was not fo much as queftioned at law, upon mere loofe allegations of delinquencies and defects, was a proceeding of a moft arbitrary and dangerous nature. They faid that this was worfe than the proceedings againft the American and Englifh corporations in the reigns of King Charles and King James the Second, which were however thought the worft acts of thofe arbitrary reigns. There the charge was regularly made; the colonies and corporations called to anfwer; time given; and the rules of juftice, at leaft in appearance, obferved. But here, they faid, there was nothing of the kind, nothing even of the colour of juftice; not one evidence has been examined at the bar, a thing done on the moft trivial regulation affecting any franchife of the fubject. That the pretences for taking away this charter, in order to give ftrength to government, will never anfwer. The miniftry was afked, whether the colonies, which are already regulated nearly in the manner propofed by the bill, were more fubmiffive to our right of taxation than this of Maffachufet's Bay? If not, what is got by this bill, that can be fo very material to the authority of parliament, as to rifk all the credit of parliamentary juftice by fo ftrong and irregular a proceeding? That the part of the act which affected juries was made without fo much as a fingle complaint of abufe pretended. Nay they faid, that the cafe of the late captain Prefton, Mr. Otis, and many others, fhewed with what juftice the juries there acted. They denied that the juries were improperly chofen; that they were appointed by a better method than ours, by a sort of ballot, in which no partiality could take place. That by this new regulation the sheriff is appointed, without any qualification, by the governor, and to hold the office at his pleasure. This is a power, said they, given to the governor, greater than that given by the constitution to the crown itself. And this they insisted was a great abuse, instead of a reformation; and tended to put the lives and properties of the people absolutely into the hands of the governors.

The minority argued, that the disorder lay much deeper than the forms of government. That the people throughout the continent were universally dissatisfied, and that their uneasiness and resistance was no less in the royal governments than in any other. That the remedy could only be in the removal of the cause of the distemper, and in quieting the minds of the people. That the act had a direct contrary tendency; and they feared, instead of giving strength to government, it would destroy the little remains of English authority which was left in the colonies.

April 28. Mr. Bollan, the agent of the Massachuset's council, again made an effort in favour of his province, and attempted to petition for time to receive an answer from the province to the account he had sent of the proceedings against them. But the house refused to receive the petition, by a majority of 95 to 32.

The same natives of America who had petitioned against the Boston port bill, also renewed their endeavours by a petition against this. It was pointed with an uncommon energy and spirit. They petitioned for time until advices should arrive from the colony, stating in strong terms a great variety of objections against the bill, and ending with a most pathetic prayer to the house, " to consider that the restraints which such acts of severity impose, are ever attended

with the most dangerous hatred: In a distress of mind which cannot be described, the petitioners conjure the house, not to convert that zeal and affection which has hitherto united every American hand and heart in the interests of England into passions the most painful and pernicious. Most earnestly they beseech the house, not to attempt reducing them to a state of slavery, which the English principles of liberty they inherit from their mother country will render worse than death. That they will not by passing these bills reduce their countrymen to the most abject state of misery and humiliation; or drive them to the last resource of despair."

This petition from the Americans resident in London, very strongly indicated the effect which this bill would have in the place where it was intended to operate. This petition had leave to lie upon the table, but had no other notice taken of it. The bill passed by a prodigious May 2d. majority, after a debate which lasted with uncommon spirit for many hours.

Equally warm debates attended the bill in the house of Lords. The objections were nearly the same with those made in the house of commons, with particular reflexions upon the greater rapidity with which it was hurried through the house of lords; and the peculiar impropriety in a court of justice, of condemning the colony, and taking away its charter, without any form of process. The lords in opposition cried out against a bill altering the constitution of a colony without having so much as the charter containing the constitution so altered, laid before them. That the bill had also altered the courts and the mode of judicial proceedings in the colony, without an offer of the slightest evidence to prove any one of the inconveniencies, which were stated in general terms in the preamble, as arising from the present mode of trial in the province.

The absolute necessity of a powerful and speedy remedy for the cure of a government, which was nothing but disorder, was, in substance, the principal reason alledged for the omission of enquiry and evidence, and the superseding the ordinary rules of judicial proceeding. Besides, the ministerial lords denied, that the process was of a penal nature; they insisted that it was beneficial and remedial, and a great improvement of their constitution, as it brought it nearer to the English model. This again was denied by the lords of the minority, who said that the taking away of franchises granted by charter had ever been considered as penal, and all proceedings for that purpose conducted criminally. Otherwise, it was said, nothing could be safe in any man's hands, the taking away of which another man might consider as beneficial. That a council holding their places at the pleasure of the crown did not resemble the house of lords; nor approach in any thing to the perfection of the British constitution. The debate on the third reading was long, but May 11th. the division only 20 to 92.

The disposition so prevalent in both houses to strong measures, was highly favourable to the whole ministerial plan for reducing America to obedience. The good reception of the proposal for changing the charter government of Massachusets Bay, encouraged them to propose very soon after another bill, without which, it was said, that the scheme would be entirely defective. In the committee on American papers it was ordered that the chairman should move for leave to bring in " a bill for the impartial ad- " ministration of justice in the " cases of persons questioned for " any acts done by them in the " execution of the laws, or for the " suppression of riots and tumults " in the province of Massachuset's " Bay in New England."

This bill provides, that in case

13

any perfon is indicted in that province for murder, or any other capital offence, and that it fhall appear to the governor that the fact was committed in the exercife or aid of magiftracy in fuppreffing tumults and riots, and that it fhall appear to the governor, that a fair trial cannot be had in the province, he fhall fend the perfon fo indicted, &c. to any other colony, or to Great-Britain, to be tried. The charges on both fides to be borne out of the cuftoms. This act to continue for four years.

The minifter ftated, that this bill was neceffary to the effect of the two former. It was in vain to appoint a magiftracy that would act, if none could be found hardy enough to put their orders in execution. Thefe orders would moft probably be refifted by force; this force would neceffitate force alfo to execute the laws. In this cafe, blood would probably be fpilled. Who would rifk this event, though in the execution of his cleareft duty, if the rioters themfelves, or their abettors, were to fit as his judges? How can any man defend himfelf on the plea of executing of your laws, before thofe perfons who deny your right to make any laws to bind them? He alledged, that fuch an act was not without precedent at home. Where fmuggling was found to be notorioufly countenanced in one county, the trial for offences of that kind has been directed in another. The rebels of Scotland in the year 1746 were tried in England. All particular privileges give way to the public fafety; when that is endangered, even the habeas corpus act, the great palladium of public liberty, has been fufpended. That the act he propofed did not eftablifh a military government, but a civil one, by which the former was greatly improved. They gave to the province a council, magiftrates, and juftices, when in effect they had none before. You do not, faid he, fcreen guilt, you only protect innocence. That

we muft fhew the Americans we will no longer fit quietly under their infults; and that even when roufed, our meafures are not cruel and vindictive, but neceffary and efficacious. This is the laft act he had to propofe in order to perfect the plan. That the reft depended on the vigilance of his majefty's fervants in the execution of their duty; which he affured them fhould not be wanting. That the ufual relief of four regiments for America, had been all ordered to Bofton. That General Gage, in whofe abilities he placed great reliance, was fent as governor and commander in chief. That while proper precautions were taken for the fupport of magiftracy, the fame fpirit was fhewn for the punifhment of offenders; and that profecutions had been ordered againft thofe who were the ringleaders in fedition. That every thing fhould be done firmly, yet legally and prudently, as he had the advantage of being aided by the ableft lawyers. That he made no doubt, that by the fteady execution of the meafures now taken, obedience and the bleffings of *peace* would be reftored. The event, he predicted, would be advantageous and happy to this country.

The minority oppofed this bill with the fame vehemence with which they combated the former. And firft, they denied the foundation of the whole bill, " That it could tend to the procuring of an impartial trial:" For if a party fpirit againft the authority of Great-Britain would condemn an active officer there as a murderer, the fame party fpirit for preferving the authority of Great-Britain, might acquit a murderer here, as a fpirited performer of his duty. There is no abfolute fecurity againft the effect of party fpirit in judicial proceedings, when mens minds are inflamed with public contefts. But before the people there are judged unworthy of the exercife of the rights which the conftitution has

given them, fome abufe ought to be proved. But has, faid they, any proof been given or attempted of fuch an abufe? The cafe of Captain Prefton was recent. This officer and fome foldiers had been indicted at Bofton for murder, for killing fome perfons in the fuppreffion of a riot. This is the very cafe the act fuppofes. How did the trial turn out? He was honourably acquitted. Therefore the bill is not only unfupported, but contradicted by fact. They infifted, that, having no fort of reafon for impeaching the tribunals of America, the real intention was to fet up a military government; and to provide a virtual indemnity for all the murders and other capital outrages which might be committed by that barbarous kind of authority. For they afked, how the relations of a murdered man could poffibly profecute, if they muft come three thoufand miles from their families and occupations to do it? The charges of the witneffes were to be borne out of the cuftoms, but the governor was to judge how much ought to be allowed; and they could not conceive, that any man would voluntarily offer himfelf as a witnefs, when by that means, upon a meer payment of charges, he was to be removed fo far from his native country. Every man of common fenfe would fly from fuch an office. But if the charges of the witneffes were to be borne by government, who was to bear the charges of the profecution, and the expence of fuch voyages, and of the delays in England which might be poffibly for years? For this the act makes no provifion. A poor man, who could eafily carry on fuch a profecution at his door at Bofton, muft give it up when the caufe is removed to Middlefex. They therefore ftrenuoufly maintained, that this was holding out an encouragement for all kinds of lawlefs violence. They denied that the cafes of trials for fmuggling, and of treafon in the last rebellion, did at all apply to the present; because the inconvenience of prosecution or defence was comparatively insignificant on account of the little distance to which the trials were removed. In fine, they denied the necessity of this act, even if no justice were ever to be expected in New England, because the prerogative of the crown might step in, and the governor might always reprieve a person, who should happen to be convicted notoriously against law and reason. They apprehended, that the course of justice being stopped by this act, would give rise to assassinations and dark revenge among individuals; and most probably to open rebellion in the whole body.

The debate on this bill was even more warm than on the former, and the publications of the time quote an old member who is rarely [14] in opposition, as having ended his speech with these remarkable words: " I will now take my " leave of the whole plan—you " will commence your ruin from " this day. I am sorry to say, that " not only the house has fallen " into this error, but the people " approve of the measure. The " people, I am sorry to say it, are " misled. But a short time will " prove the evil tendency of this " bill. If ever there was a na- " tion running headlong to its " ruin, it is this."

The bill passed the house on the sixth of May, and being carried up to the house of peers, occasioned warm debates upon the same principles upon which it was discussed in the house of commons. The Lords of the minority entered on this, as on the former bill, a very strong protest. Neither house was full during the debates on this bill, as the arguments on the two latter bills had been all along very much blended; and the parties had tried their strength by division on the bill for altering the Massachuset's charter. On both

questions, however, the numbers of the minority had all along continued very low and disproportioned. [15]

The session was drawing near to the usual time of recess; and the greatest number of the members, fatigued with a long attendance on the American bills, were retired into the country. In this situation, a bill which has engaged a great deal of the public attention was brought into the house of lords: " The bill for making more ef- " fectual provision for the go- " vernment of the province of " Quebec in North America."

This passed through that house with very little if any observation. But when it came down to the house of commons it met with a very different reception. A disposition immediately appeared in that house to criticise it with unusual severity. The party for ministry seemed to be a little alarmed at this spirit, partly because, from its easy passage through the house of lords, it was not so much expected; but principally, because they apprehended it would create more uneasiness among the people out of doors than any of the former bills. In this case the passions which had been excited by the disorders in America, did not operate in their favour. And as the act had for a part of its objects establishments touching religion, it was far more likely to give occasion for popular complaint. The ministry therefore found it necessary not to carry things with so high an hand as in the preceding bills. They admitted that this bill came down to the house of commons in a very imperfect state; and that they would be open to any reasonable alterations and amendments. This plan might be discussed more at leisure than that for regulating the colony of Massachuset's Bay; in that case it was necessary to shew a degree of vigour and decision, or all government might be lost and all order

confounded. But here they were not so much pressed; for though that government wanted regulation extremely, yet the people were disposed to peace and obedience. A good deal of time was spent in going through this affair; great altercations arose in the committee; many witnesses were examined. Among these were general Carleton, governor of Canada; Mr. Hay, chief justice of that province; Mr. Mazeres, cursitor baron of the Exchequer, late attorney general there, and agent to the English inhabitants of Canada; Dr. Marriot, the King's advocate general in England; Monf. Lolbiniere, a French gentleman of considerable property in Canada. [16]

The principle objects of the Quebec bill were to ascertain the limits of that province, which were extended far beyond what had been settled as such by the King's proclamation of 1763. To form a legislative council for all the affairs of that province, except taxation, which council should be appointed by the crown, the office to be held during pleasure; and his majesty's Canadian Roman catholic subjects were entitled to a place in it. To establish the French laws, and a trial without jury, in civil cases, and the English laws, with a trial by jury, in criminal. To secure to the Roman catholic clergy, except the Regulars, the legal enjoyment of their estates, and of their tythes from all who are of their own religion. These were the chief objects of the act. It was said in favour of them; that the French who were a very great majority of the inhabitants of that country, having been used to live under an absolute government were not anxious for the forms of a free one, which they little understood or valued. That they even abhorred the idea of a popular representation, observing the mischiefs which it introduced in their neighbouring countries. Besides these considerations, it would be unreasonable to have a representative body, out of which all the natives should be excluded; and perhaps dangerous to trust such an instrument in the hands of a people but newly taken into the British empire. They were not yet ripe for English government.

That their landed property had been all granted, and their family settlements made on the ideas of French law. The laws concerning contracts and personal property were nearly the same in France and England. That a trial by juries was strange and disgustful to them. That as to religion, it had been stipulated to allow them perfect freedom in that respect by the treaty of Paris, as far as the laws of England permitted. The penal laws of England with respect to religion, they said, did not extend beyond this kingdom, and though the King's supremacy extended further, a provision was made in the act to oblige the Canadians to be subject to it; and an oath prescribed as a test against such papal claims as might endanger the allegiance of the subjects. That it was against all equity to persecute those people for their religion. And people have not the freedom of religion who have not their own priesthood. And as to the provision for the payment of tythes, it was at best only setting down their clergy where they were found at the conquest. In one respect they were worse, as no person professing the protestant religion was to be subject to them, which would be a great encouragement to conversions. As to the new boundary different from that established by the proclamation, it was said that there were French scattered on several parts beyond the proclamation limits who ought to have provision made for them; and that there was one entire colony at the Illinois.

To this it was replied, that a form of arbitrary government established by act of parliament, for any part of the British dominions,

was a thing new to the history of this kingdom. That it was of a most dangerous example, and wholly unnecessary. For either the then present form, such as it was, might be suffered to remain, meerly as a temporary arrangement, tolerated from the necessity which first gave rise to it, or an assembly might be formed on the principles of the British constitution; in which the natives might have such a share as should be thought convenient. That such an assembly was not impracticable, appeared from the example of Grenada. Why did the ministers chuse to admit the Roman Catholicks of Canada into a legislative council, and deny the propriety of their fitting in a legislative assembly by a free election? Nothing, said they, could induce ministry to embrace that distinction, but the hatred which they have to any such assemblies, and to all the rights of the people at large. Whatever was said of the inclination of the Canadian new subjects, which attached them so closely to arbitrary power, there was nothing in their petition which looked that way. This is an experiment for setting up an arbitrary government in one colony, which may be more patient of it than the rest, in order to extend by degrees that mode of ruling to all the others. As to a jury, it was said, that that mode of trial was commended, and envied to this nation, by the best foreign writers. It might have some circumstances a little aukward at first, like every thing else that is new; but that it was impossible it should be disliked on acquaintance. Why did the bill give it in criminal cases, if it were not an eligible mode of trial? The people could not have an objection to trust their property to the tribunal, to which they had trusted their lives. They argued that the grand security of liberty is the power of having civil actions tried by a jury; as in cases of arbitrary imprisonments, and many other violations of the rights of the subject, the re-

dress has been always sought in these civil actions. They said that the English residing in Canada, and the merchants of Great Britain who trusted their property on a presumption that it was to be protected by English law, think they are deceived to find it to be tried by French customs, and French forms of trial.

On the subject of religion the conflict was very warm. The minority insisted that the capitulation provided for no more than a bare toleration of the Roman Catholic religion; which they were willing they should enjoy in the utmost extent; whereas this is an establishment of it. That the people of Canada had hitherto been happy under that toleration, and looked for nothing further. By this establishment, said they, the Protestant religion enjoys at best no more than a toleration. The popish clergy have a legal parliamentary right to a maintenance; the protestant clergy are left at the king's discretion. Why are not both put at least on an equal footing, and a legal support provided for both?

Further they asked, why the proclamation limits were enlarged, as if it were thought that this arbitrary government could not have too extensive an object. If there be, which they doubted, any spots on which some Canadians are settled, provide, said they, for them; but do not annex to Canada immense territories now desart, but which are the best parts of that continent, and which run on the back of all your antient colonies. That this measure cannot fail to add to their other discontents and apprehensions, as they can attribute the extension given to an arbitrary military government, and to a people alien in origin, laws, and religion, to nothing else but that design, of which they see but too many proofs already, of utterly extinguishing their liberties, and bringing them by the arms of those very people whom they had helped to conquer, into a state of the most abject vassalage.

17

The bill received in the course of these debates many amendments, so as to change it very greatly from the state in which it came down from the House of Lords; but the groundwork remained the same. A motion was made to give at least a jury at the option of the parties; but this proposition was rejected. Another was made to grant them the benefit of the habeas corpus. That also was rejected. Throughout the whole progress of the business, though well fought, the numbers in the minority were uncommonly small. It produced, nevertheless, much greater uneasiness and discontent out of doors than any of the bills for punishing of the old colonies.

This discontent called on the attention of the House of Lords; so that when the bill was returned to them with the amendments, there was a considerable opposition to it, although in some respects less exceptionable than when it had passed their house with so little notice; but, as in all the other questions, so in this, the minority shewed no strength in numbers. 18

The session had now stretched far into the summer. The business of it had been of as much importance as that, perhaps, of any session since the revolution. Great changes had been made in the economy of some of the colonies, which were thought foundations for changes of a like nature in others; and the most sanguine expectations were entertained by the ministry, that when parliament had shewn so determined a resolution, and the advocates for the colonies had appeared so very little able to protect them, the submission throughout America would be immediate; and complete obedience and tranquillity would be secured in future. The triumphs and mutual congratulations of all who supported these measures, within doors and without, were unusually great.

June 22. The speech from the throne at the end of the session expressed similar sentiments.

His Majesty told the parliament, "That he had observed with the utmost satisfaction, the many eminent proofs they had given of their zealous and prudent attention to the public, during the course of this very interesting session of parliament." Then, after mentioning with applause their proceedings relative to the gold coin, he tells them, "That the bill which they had prepared for the government of Quebec, and to which he had then given his assent, was founded on the clearest principles of justice and humanity; and would, he doubted not, have the best effects in quieting the minds and promoting the happiness of his Canadian subjects. That he had long seen with concern a dangerous spirit of resistance to his government and the execution of the laws prevailing in the province of Massachuset's Bay. It proceeded at length to such an extremity, as to render their immediate interposition necessary, and they had accordingly made provision as well for the suppression of the present disorders, as for the prevention of the like in future. The temper and firmness with which they had conducted themselves in this important business; and the general concurrence with which the resolution of maintaining the authority of the laws in every part of his dominions, had been adopted and supported, could not fail of giving the greatest weight to the measures which had been the result of their deliberations. That nothing on his part should be wanting to render them effectual. That he had received the most friendly assurances from the neighbouring powers, which gave him the strongest reason to believe that they had the same pacific dispositions as himself. After thanking the Commons for the supplies, he ended with recommending to both houses to carry into their counties the same affectionate attachment to his person, and the same zeal for the public welfare, which had distinguished all their proceedings in this session of parliament."

APPENDIX to the CHRONICLE.

Letter from the Affembly of Maffa-chufett's Bay *to Lord* Dartmouth.

To LORD DARTMOUTH.
Province of Maffachufett's Bay,
June 29, 1773.

My Lord,

THE re-eftablifhment of the union and harmony that formerly fubfifted between Great Britain and her colonies, is earneftly to be wifhed by the friends of both. As your lordfhip is one of them, the two houfes of the affembly of this province beg leave to addrefs you.

The original caufes of the interruption of that union and harmony may probably be found in the letters fent from hence to adminiftration, and to other gentlemen of influence in parliament, fince the appointment of Sir Francis Bernard to the government of this province; and there is great reafon to apprehend that he, and his coadjutors, originally recommended and laid the plans for the eftablifhing the American revenue, out of which they expected large ftipends and appointments for themfelves, and which, through their inftrumentality, has been the occafion of all the evils that have fince taken place.

When we had humbly addreffed his majefty, and petitioned both houfes of parliament, reprefenting our grievances, and praying for the repeal of the *revenue acts*; the like inftruments, and probably the fame, exerted themfelves to prevent thofe *petitions* being laid before his majefty and the parliament, or to fruftrate the prayer of them. Of this we have juft had fome new and unexpected evidence, from *original letters* of Gov. Hutchinfon and Lieut. Gov. Oliver, in which the former particularly and exprefsly,

by his letter of the 10th of December, 1768, endeavoured, in co-operation with Gov. Bernard, to fruftrate a petition of a number of the council for the repealing thofe acts, and to procure his majefty's cenfure on the petitioners; and the letters of the latter, by the difadvantageous idea conveyed by them of the two houfes of affembly, manifeftly tended to create a prejudice againft any petition, coming from a body of fuch a character; and his letter of the 11th of May, 1768, in particular, mentions the petition of the houfe of reprefentatives to his majefty, and their letters to divers noble lords, with fuch circumftances as had a tendency to defeat the petition, and render the letters of no effect.

It is manifeft, my lord, what practices and arts have been ufed to miflead adminiftration, both in the firft propofal of American revenue acts, and in the continuance of them; but when they had loft their force, and there appeared, under the influence of your lordfhip, a difpofition in parliament to repeal thofe acts, his excellency Gov. Hutchinfon, in his fpeech at the opening of the laft feffion of the general court, was pleafed to throw out new matter for contention and debate, and to call on the two houfes, in fuch a preffing manner, as amounted to little fhort of a challenge, to anfwer him; into fuch a dilemma were they brought by the fpeech, that they were under a neceffity of giving fuch anfwers to it as they did, or having their conduct conftrued into an acquiefcence with the doctrines contained in it, which would have been an implicit acknowledgment, that the province was in a ftate of fubjection, differing very little from flavery. The anfwers were the effects of neceffity, and this neceffity occafioned great

grief to the two houfes.

The people of this province, my lord, are true and faithful fubjects of his majefty, and think themfelv s happy in their connection with Great Britain; they would rejoice at the reftoration of the harmony and good-will that once fubfifted between the parent ftate and them; but it is in vain to expect this happinefs during the continuance of their grievances; and while their *charter rights, one after another, are wrefted from them.* Among thefe rights is the fupporting of the officers of the crown by grants from the affembly; and, in an efpecial manner, the fupporting of the judges in the fame way, on whofe judgment the province is dependent in the moft important cafes of life, liberty, and property. If warrants have not yet been, or if they already have been iffued, we earneftly beg the favour of your lordfhip's interpofition to fupprefs or recall them.

If your lordfhip fhould condefcend to afk, "Whrt are the means of reftoring the harmony fo much defired!" we fhould anfwer in a word, that we are humbly of opinion, if things were brought to the general ftate in which they ftood at the conclufion of the late war, it would reftore the happy harmony which at that time fubfifted.

Your lordfhip's appointment to be principal fecretary of ftate for the American department has given the colonies the higheft fatisfaction: they think it a happy omen, and that it will be productive of American tranquility, confiftent with their rights as Britifh fubjects.

The two houfes humbly hope for your lordfhip's influence to bring about fo happy an event; and in the mean time they can with full confidence rely on your lordfhip, that the *machinations of Sir Francis Bernard,* and other known enemies of the peace of Great Britain and her colonies, will not be fuffered to prevent or delay it.

This letter, which has been agreed

on by *both houses*, is in their name, and by their order, signed and transmitted to your lordship, by,

My Lord,

Your Lordship's most obedient, And very humble servant,

Thomas Flucker, Sec.

The preceding is a true copy of the letter wrote to the Right Hon. the Earl of Dartmouth. (Attested, *Thomas Flucker*, Sec.)

Petition of the American Congress to the King.

To the King's most Excellent Majesty.

Most gracious Sovereign,

WE your majesty's faithful subjects of the colonies of New Hampshire, Massachusett's Bay, Rhode Island and Providence plantations, Connecticut, New York, New Jersey, Pennsylvania, the Counties of Newcastle, Kent and Suffex on Delaware, Maryland, Virginia, North Carolina, and South Carolina, in behalf of ourselves and the inhabitants of *those* colonies, *who have deputed us to represent them in general congress,* by this our humble petition beg leave to lay our grievances before the throne.

A standing army has been kept in these colonies ever since the conclusion of the late war, without the consent of our assemblies; and this army, with a considerable naval armament, has been employed to enforce the collection of taxes.

The authority of the commander in chief, and under him of the brigadiers-general, has in time of peace been rendered supreme in all the civil governments in America.

The commander in chief of all your majesty's forces in North America, has in time of peace been appointed governor of a colony. The charges of usual offices have been greatly increased, and new expensive and oppressive offices have been multiplied.

The judges of admiralty and vice-admiralty courts are impowered to receive their salaries and fees from the effects condemned by themselves; the officers of the customs are impowered to break open and enter houses, without the authority of any civil magistrate founded on legal information.

The judges of courts of common law have been made entirely dependent on one part of the legislature for their salaries, as well as for the duration of their commissions. Counsellors holding their commissions during pleasure, exercise legislative authority.

Humble and reasonable petitions from the representatives of the people have been fruitless.

The agents of the people have been discountenanced, and governors have been instructed to prevent the payment of their salaries: assemblies have been repeatedly and injuriously dissolved: commerce has been burthened with many useless and oppressive restrictions.

By several acts of parliament made in the fourth, fifth, sixth, seventh, and eighth years of your present majesty's reign, duties are imposed on us for the purpose of raising a revenue, and the powers of admiralty and vice-admiralty courts are extended beyond their ancient limits; whereby our property is taken from us without our consent, the trial by jury in many civil cases is abolished, enormous forfeitures are incurred for slight offences; vexatious informers are exempted from paying damages, to which they are justly liable, and oppressive security is required from owners before they are allowed to defend their right.

Both houses of parliament have resolved that colonists may be tried in England for offences alledged to have been committed in America, by virtue of a statute passed in the thirty-fifth year of Henry the VIII, and in consequence thereof, attempts have been made to enforce that statute. A statute was passed in the twelfth year of your majesty's reign, directing that persons charged with committing any offence therein described, in any place out of the realm, may be indicted and tried for the same in any shire or county within the realm; whereby the inhabitants of these colonies may, in sundry cases, by that statute made capital, be deprived of a tryal by their peers of the vicinage.

In the last sessions of parliament an act was passed for blocking up the harbour of Boston; another, empowering the governor of Massachusett's Bay to send persons indicted for murder in that province to another colony, or even to Great Britain for tryal, whereby such offenders may escape legal punishment; a third, for altering the chartered constitution of government in that province; and a fourth, for extending the limits of Quebec, abolishing the English and restoring the French laws, whereby great numbers of British freemen are subjected to the latter, and establishing an absolute government and the Roman Catholic religion throughout those vast regions that border on the westerly and northerly boundaries of the free Protestant English settlements; and a fifth, for the better providing suitable quarters for officers and soldiers in his majesty's service in North America.

To a sovereign " who glories in the name of Briton," the bare recital of these acts must, we presume, justify the loyal subjects who fly to the foot of his throne, and implore his clemency for protection against them. [19]

From this destructive system of colony administration, adopted since the conclusion of the last war, have flowed those distresses, dangers, fears, and jealousies, that overwhelm your majesty's dutiful colonies with affliction; and we defy our most subtle and inveterate enemies to trace the unhappy differences between Great Britain and these colonies from an earlier period, or from other causes than we have assigned. Had they proceeded, on our part, *from a restless levity of temper, unjust impulses of ambition, or artful suggestions of seditious persons,* we should merit the opprobrious terms frequently bestowed on us by those we revere.

But so far from promoting innovations, we have only opposed them; and can be charged with no offence, unless it be one to receive injuries, and be sensible of them.

Had our Creator been pleased to give us existence in a land of slavery, the sense of our condition might have been mitigated by ignorance and habit; but thanks to his adorable goodness, we were born the heirs of freedom, and ever enjoyed our right under the auspices of your royal ancestors, whose family was seated on the British throne to rescue and secure a pious and gallant nation from the popery and despotism of a superstitious and inexorable tyrant.

Your majesty, we are confident, justly rejoices, that your title to the crown is thus founded on the title of your people to liberty; and therefore we doubt not but your royal wisdom must approve the sensibility that teaches your subjects anxiously to guard the blessing they received from *Divine Providence*, and thereby to prove the performance of that compact, which elevated the illustrious house of Brunswick to the imperial dignity it now possesses.

The apprehension of being degraded into a state of servitude, from the pre-eminent rank of English-freemen, while our minds retain the strongest love of liberty, and clearly foresee the miseries preparing for us and our posterity, excites emotions in our breasts, which though we cannot describe, we should not wish to conceal. Feeling as men, and thinking as subjects, in the manner we do, silence would be disloyalty. By giving this faithful information *we do all in our power* to promote the great objects of your royal cares, the tranquility of your government, and the welfare of your people.

Duty to your majesty, and regard for the preservation of ourselves and our posterity, the primary obligations of nature and of society, command us to intreat your royal attention; and as your majesty enjoys the signal distinction of reigning over freemen, we apprehend the language of freemen cannot be displeasing.

Your royal indignation, we hope, will rather fall on those designing and dangerous men, who daringly interposing themselves between your royal person and your faithful subjects, and for several years past incessantly employed to dissolve the bands of society by abusing your majesty's authority, misrepresenting your American subjects, and prosecuting the most desperate and irritating projects of oppression, have at length compelled us, by the force of accumulated injuries, *too severe to be any longer tolerable,* to disturb your majesty's repose by our complaints.

These sentiments are extorted from hearts *that much more willingly* would bleed in your majesty's service; yet so greatly have we been misrepresented, that a necessity has been alledged of taking our property from us without our consent, " to defray the charge of the administration of justice, the support of civil government, and the defence, protection, and security of the colonies." But we beg leave to assure your majesty, that such provision has been, and will be made for defraying the two first articles, as has been, and shall be judged by the legislatures of the several colonies just and suitable to their respective circumstances; and for the defence, protection, and security of the colonies, their militias, if properly regulated, *as they earnestly desire may immediately be done,* would be fully sufficient, at least in times of peace; and, in case of war, your faithful colonists will be ready and willing, as they ever have been, when constitutionally required, to demonstrate their loyalty to your majesty, by exerting their most strenuous efforts in granting supplies and raising forces. Yielding to no British subjects in affectionate attachment to your majesty's person, family, and government, we too dearly prize the privilege of expressing that attachment by those proofs that are honourable to the prince who receives them, and to the people who give them, *ever to resign it to any body of men upon earth.*

Had we been permitted to enjoy in quiet the inheritance left us by our forefathers, we should at this time have been peaceably, chearfully, and usefully employed in recommending ourselves by every testimony of devotion to your majesty, and of veneration to the state from which we derive our origin. But though now exposed to unexpected and unnatural scenes of distress, by a contention with that nation, in whose parental guidance, on all important affairs, we have hitherto with filial reverence constantly trusted, and therefore can derive no instruction in our present unhappy and perplexed circumstances from any former experience; yet we doubt not but the purity of our intention, and the integrity of our conduct, will justify us at that grand tribunal before which all mankind must submit to judgment.

We ask but for peace, liberty, and safety; we wish not a diminution of the prerogative, nor do we solicit the grant of any new right in our favour; your royal authority over us, and our connection with Great Britain, we shall always carefully and zealously endeavour to support and maintain.

Filled with sentiments of duty to your majesty, and of affection to our parent state, deeply impressed by our education, and strongly confirmed by our reason, and anxious to evince the sincerity of these dispositions — We present this petition only to obtain redress of grievances, and relief from fears and jealousies occasioned by the system of statutes, and regulation adopted since the close of the late war, for raising a revenue in America; extending the powers of courts of admiralty; trying persons in Great Britain for offences alledged to be committed in America; affecting the province of Massachusett's Bay, and altering the government, and extending the limits of Quebec—By the abolition of which system, the harmony between Great Britain and these colonies, so necessary to the happiness of both, and so ardently desired by the latter, with the usual intercourses, will be immediately restored.

In the magnanimity and justice of your majesty, and the parliament, we confide for a redress of our other grievances; trusting, that when the causes of our apprehensions are removed, our future conduct will prove us not unworthy of the regard we have been accustomed in our happier days to enjoy. For, appealing to that Being who searches thoroughly the hearts of his creatures, we solemnly profess that *our councils have been influenced by no other motive than a dread of impending destruction.*

Permit us then,

Most Gracious Sovereign,

In the name of all your faithful people in America, with the utmost humility to implore you, for the honour of Almighty God, whose pure religion our enemies are undermining; for the glory, which can be advanced only by rendering your subjects happy, and keeping them united; for the interests of your family, *depending in an adherence to the principle that enthroned it;* for the safety and welfare of your kingdoms and dominions, threatened with almost unavoidable dangers and distresses; that your majesty, as the loving father of your whole people, connected by the same bands of law, loyalty, faith, and blood, though dwelling in various countries, will not suffer the transcendent relation formed by these ties, to be further violated in uncertain expectation of effects, which, if attained, never can compensate *for the calamities through which they must be gained.*

We therefore most earnestly beseech your majesty, that your royal authority and interposition may be used for our relief, and that a gracious answer may be given to this petition.

That your majesty may enjoy every felicity through a long and glorious reign over loyal and happy subjects, and that your descendants may inherit your prosperity and dominions till time shall be no more, is, and always will be our sincere and fervent prayer.

Philadelphia, Nov. 1774.

(Signed)

H. *Middleton,*	W. *Floyd,*
J. *Sullivan,*	H. *Wisner,*
N. *Folsom,*	S. *Boerum,*
T. *Cushing,*	W. *Livingston,*
S. *Adams,*	J. D. *Hart,*
J. *Adams,*	S. *Craine,*
R. *Treatpaine,*	R. *Smith,*
S. *Hopkins,*	G. *Reid,*
S. *Ward,*	M. *Tilghman,*
E. *Biddle,*	T. *Johnson, jun.*
J. *Galloway,*	W. *Paca,*
J. *Dickinson,*	S. *Chare,*
J. *Morton,*	R. H. *Lee,*
T. *Mifflin,*	P. *Henry,*
G. *Ross,*	G. *Washington,*
C. *Humphreys,*	F. *Pendleton,*
C. *Rodney,*	R. *Bland,*
T. *M'Kean,*	B. *Harrison,*
E. *Dyer,*	W. *Hooper,*
R. *Sherman,*	J. *Hews,*
Silas *Deane,*	R. *Caswell,*
P. *Livingston,*	T. *Lynch,*
J. *Alsop,*	C. *Gadsden,*
J. *Low,*	J. *Rutledge,*
J. *Duane,*	E. *Rutledge.*
J. *Jay,*	

To the People of Great Britain, from the Delegates appointed by the several English Colonies of New Hampshire, Massachusett's Bay, Rhode Island, and Providence Plantations, Connecticut, New York, New Jersey, Pennsylvania, the Lower Counties on Delaware, Maryland, Virginia, North Carolina, and South Carolina, *to consider of their Grievances in General Congress, at Philadelphia, September 5th,* 1774.

Friends and Fellow Subjects,

WHEN a nation, led to greatness by the hand of Liberty, and possessed of all the glory that heroism, munificence, and humanity can bestow, descends to the ungrateful task of forging chains for her Friends and Children, and, instead of giving support to Freedom, turns advocate for Slavery and Oppression, there is reason to suspect she has either ceased to be virtuous, or been extremely negligent in the appointment of her Rulers.

In almost every age, in repeated conflicts, in long and bloody wars, as well civil as foreign, against many and powerful nations, against the open assaults of enemies and the more dangerous treachery of friends, have the inhabitants of your island, your great and glorious ancestors, maintained their independence and transmitted the rights of men and the blessings of liberty to you their posterity.

Be not surprised therefore, that we, who are descended from the same common ancestors; that we, whose forefathers participated in all the rights, the liberties and the constitution, you so justly boast, and who have carefully conveyed the same fair inheritance to us, guarantied by the plighted faith of government, and the most solemn compacts with British sovereigns, should refuse to surrender them to men, who found their claims on no principles of reason, and who prosecute them with a design, that, by having our lives and property in their power, they may with the greater facility enslave you.

The cause of America is now the object of universal attention: it has at length become very serious. This unhappy country has not only

20

been oppressed, but abused and misrepresented; and the duty we owe to ourselves and posterity, to your interest, and the general welfare of the British empire, leads us to address you on this very important subject.

Know then, That we consider ourselves, and do insist, that we are, and ought to be, as free as our fellow-subjects in Britain, and that no power on earth has a right to take our property from us without our consent.

That we claim all the benefits secured to the subject by the English constitution, and particularly that inestimable one of trial by jury.

That we hold it essential to English liberty, that no man be condemned unheard, or punished for supposed offences, without having an opportunity of making his defence.

That we think the legislature of Great Britain is not authorised by the constitution to establish a religion fraught with sanguinary and impious tenets, or to erect an arbitrary form of government in any quarter of the globe. These rights, we, as well as you, deem sacred. And yet, sacred as they are, they have, with many others, been repeatedly and flagrantly violated.

Are not the proprietors of the soil of Great Britain lords of their own property? Can it be taken from them without their consent? Will they yield it to the arbitrary disposal of any man, or number of men whatever? — You know they will not.

Why then are the proprietors of the soil of America less lords of their property than you are of yours, or why should they submit it to the disposal of your parliament, or any other parliament, or council in the world, not of their election? Can the intervention of the sea that divides us cause disparity in rights, or can any reason be given, why English subjects, who live three thousand miles from the royal palace, should enjoy less liberty than those who are three hundred miles distant from it?

Reason looks with indignation on such distinctions, and freemen can never perceive their propriety. And yet, however chimerical and unjust such discriminations are, the parliament assert, that they have a right to bind us in all cases without exception, whether we consent or not; that they may take and use our property when and in what manner they please; that we are pensioners on their bounty for all that we possess, and can hold it no longer than they vouchsafe to permit. Such declarations we consider as heresies in English politics, and which can no more operate to deprive us of our property, than the interdicts of the Pope can divest kings of sceptres which the laws of the land and the voice of the people have placed in their hands.

At the conclusion of the late war — a war rendered glorious by the abilities and integrity of a minister, to whose efforts the British empire owes its safety and its fame: at the conclusion of this war, which was succeeded by an inglorious peace, formed under the auspices of a minister of principles and of a family unfriendly to the protestant cause, and inimical to liberty:— we say at this period, and under the influence of that man, a plan for enslaving your fellow-subjects in America was concerted, and has ever since been pertinaciously carrying into execution.

Prior to this æra you were content with drawing from us the wealth produced by our commerce. You restrained our trade in every way that could conduce to your emolument. You exercised unbounded sovereignty over the sea. You named the ports and nations to which alone our merchandize should be carried, and with whom alone we should trade; and, though some of these restrictions were grievous, we nevertheless did not complain; we looked up to you as to our parent state, to which we were bound by the strongest ties: and were happy in being instrumental to your prosperity and your grandeur.

We call upon you yourselves to witness our loyalty and attachment to the common interest of the whole empire: did we not, in the last war, add all the strength of this vast continent to the force which repelled our common enemy? Did we not leave our native shores, and meet disease and death, to promote the success of British arms in foreign climates? Did you not thank us for our zeal, and even reimburse us large sums of money, which, you confessed, we had advanced beyond our proportion and far beyond our abilities? You did.

To what causes, then, are we to attribute the sudden change of treatment, and that system of slavery which was prepared for us at the restoration of peace?

Before we had recovered from the distresses which ever attend war, an attempt was made to drain this country of all its money, by the oppressive stamp-act. Paint, glass, and other commodities, which you would not permit us to purchase of other nations, were taxed; nay, although no wine is made in any country subject to the British state, you prohibited our procuring it of foreigners, without paying a tax, imposed by your parliament, on all we imported. These and many other impositions were laid upon us most unjustly and unconstitutionally, for the express purpose of raising a revenue. — In order to silence complaint, it was, indeed, provided, that this revenue should be expended in America for its protection and defence.—These exactions however can receive no justification from a pretended necessity of protecting and defending us. They are lavishly squandered on court favourites and ministerial dependants, generally avowed enemies to America, and employing themselves, by partial representations, to traduce and embroil the colonies. For the necessary support of government here, we ever were and ever shall be ready to provide. And, whenever the exigencies of the state may require it, we shall, as we have heretofore done, chearfully contribute our full proportion of men and money. To enforce this unconstitutional and unjust scheme of taxation, every fence, that the wisdom of our British ancestors had carefully erected against arbitrary power, has been violently thrown down in America, and the inestimable right of trial by jury taken away in cases that touch both life and property. It was ordained, that, whenever offences should be committed in the colonies against particular acts imposing various duties and restrictions upon trade, the prosecutor might bring his action for the penalties in the courts of admiralty; by which means the subject lost the advantage of being tried by an honest uninfluenced jury of the vicinage, and was subjected to the sad necessity of being judged by a single man, a creature of the crown, and according to the course of a law which exempts the prosecutor from the trouble of proving his accusation, and obliges the defendant either to evince his innocence or to suffer. To give this *new judicatory* the greater importance, and as if with a design to protect false accusers, it is further provided, " that the judge's certificate, of there having been probable causes of seizure and prosecution, shall protect the prosecutor from actions at common law for recovery of damages."

By the course of our law, offences committed in such of the British dominions in which courts are established, and justice duly and regularly administered, are to be there tried by a *jury of the vicinage*. There the offenders and the witnesses are known, and the degree of credibility to be given to their testimony can be ascertained. In all these colonies justice is regularly and impartially admini-

stered; and yet, by the construction of some, and the direction of other acts of parliament, offenders are " to be taken by force, together with all such persons as may be pointed out as witnesses, and carried to England, there to be tried in a distant land, by a *jury of strangers*," and subject to all the disadvantages that result from want of friends, want of witnesses, and want of money!

When the design of raising a revenue from the duties imposed on the importation of tea into America had in a great measure been rendered abortive, by our ceasing to import that commodity, a scheme was concerted by the ministry with the East India company, and an act passed enabling and encouraging them to transport and vend it in the colonies. Aware of the danger of giving success to this insidious manœuvre, and of permitting a precedent of taxation thus to be established among us, various methods were adopted to elude the stroke. The people of Boston, then ruled by a governor, whom as well as his predecessor, Sir Francis Bernard, all America considers as her enemy, were exceedingly embarrassed. The ships which had arrived with the tea were by his management prevented from returning. The duties would have been paid: the cargoes landed and exposed to sale; a governor's influence would have procured and protected many purchasers. While the town was suspended by deliberations on this important subject, the tea was destroyed. Even supposing a trespass had been committed, and the proprietors of the tea entitled to damages,—the courts of law were open, and judges appointed by the crown presided in them.— The East India company however did not think proper to commence any suits, nor did they even demand satisfaction either from individuals or from the community in general. The ministry, it seems, officiously made the case

their own, and the great council of the nation descended to intermeddle with a dispute about private property.—Divers papers, letters, and other unauthenticated *ex parte* evidence were laid before them; neither the persons who destroyed the tea, nor the people of Boston, were called on to answer the complaint. The ministry, incensed by being disappointed in a favourite scheme, were determined to recur from the little arts of finesse, to open force and unmanly violence. The port of Boston was blocked up by a fleet, and an army placed in the town. Their trade was to be suspended, and thousands reduced to the necessity of gaining subsistence from charity, till they should submit to pass under the yoke, and consent to become slaves; by confessing the omnipotence of parliament, and acquiescing in whatever disposition they might think proper to make of their lives and property.

Let justice and humanity cease to be the boast of your nation! Consult your history, examine your records of former transactions, nay turn to the annals of the many arbitrary states and kingdoms that surround you, and shew us a single instance of men being condemned to suffer for imputed crimes *unheard, unquestioned*, and without even the specious *formality of a trial*; and that too by laws made expressly for the purpose, and which had no existence at the time of the fact being committed. If it be difficult to reconcile these proceedings to the genius and temper of your laws and constitution, the task will become more arduous when we call upon our ministerial enemies to justify, not only condemning men untried and by hearsay; but involving the innocent in one common punishment with the guilty, and for the act of thirty or forty, to bring poverty, distress and calamity on thirty thousand souls, and these not your enemies, but your friends, brethren, and fellow-subjects;

It would be some consolation to us, if the catalogue of American oppressions ended here. It gives us pain to be reduced to the necessity of reminding you, that under the confidence reposed in the *faith of government,* pledged in a royal charter from a British sovereign, the fore-fathers of the present inhabitants of the Massachusett's Bay left their former habitations, and established that great, flourishing, and loyal colony. Without incurring or being charged with a forfeiture of their rights, without being heard, without being tried, without law, and without justice, by an act of parliament " their charter is destroyed, their liberties violated, their constitution and form of government changed." And all this upon no better pretence, than because in one of their towns a trespass was committed on some merchandize, said to belong to one of the companies, and because the ministry were of opinion that such high political regulations were necessary to compel due subordination and obedience to their mandates.

Nor are these the only capital grievances under which we labour. We might tell of *dissolute, weak, and wicked governors* having been set over us : of legislatures being suspended for asserting the rights of British subjects, of needy and ignorant dependants on great men, advanced to the seats of justice and to other places of trust and importance ; of hard restrictions on commerce, and a great variety of smaller evils, the recollection of which is almost lost under the weight and pressure of greater and more poignant calamities.

Now mark the progression of the ministerial plan for enslaving us. Well aware that such hardy attempts (to take our property from us — to deprive us of that valuable right of trial by jury—to seize our persons, and carry us for trial to Great Britain — to blockade our ports—to destroy our charters, and change our forms of government) would occasion, and had already occasioned great discontent in all the colonies, which might produce opposition to these measures, an act was passed " to protect, indemnify, and screen from punishment, such as might be guilty even of *murder*, in endeavouring to carry their oppressive edicts into execution ; " and by another act " the dominion of Canada is to be so extended, modelled, and governed," as that by being disunited from us, detached from our interests, by civil as well as religious prejudices, that by their numbers swelling with catholic emigrants from Europe, and by their devotion to administration, so friendly to their religion, they might become formidable to us, and, on occasion, be fit instruments in the hands of power, to reduce the ancient free protestant colonies to the same state of slavery with themselves.

This was evidently the object of the act : and in this view, being extremely dangerous to our liberty and quiet, we cannot forbear complaining of it, as hostile to British America. — Superadded to these considerations, we cannot help deploring the unhappy condition to which it has reduced the many English settlers, who, encouraged by the royal proclamation, promising the enjoyment of all their rights, have purchased estates in that country. They are now the subjects of an arbitrary government, deprived of trial by jury, and when imprisoned cannot claim the benefit of the habeas corpus act, that great bulwark and palladium of English liberty : — nor can we suppress our astonishment, that a British parliament should ever consent to establish in that country a religion that has deluged your island in blood, and dispersed impiety, bigotry, persecution, murder, and rebellion, through every part of the world.

This being a true state of facts, let us beseech you to consider to what end they lead.

Admit that the ministry, by the powers of Great Britain, and the aid of our Roman Catholic neighbours, should be able to carry the point of taxation, and reduce us to a state of perfect humiliation and slavery ; such an enterprize would doubtless make some addition to your national debt, which already presses down your liberties, and fills you with pensioners and placemen. We presume, also, that your commerce will somewhat be diminished : however, suppose you should prove victorious—in what condition will you then be ? What advantages, or what laurels will you reap from such a conquest ?

May not a ministry, with the same armies, enslave you ?—It may be said, you will cease to pay them ; "—but remember the taxes from America, the wealth, and we may add the men, and particularly the Roman Catholics of this vast continent, will then be in the power of your enemies ; nor will you have any reason to expect, that after making slaves of us, many among us should refuse to assist in reducing you to the same abject state.

Do not treat this as chimerical : —Know that in less than half a century, the quit-rents reserved to the crown, from the numberless grants of this vast continent, will pour large streams of wealth into the royal coffers, and if to this be added the power of taxing America at pleasure, the crown will be rendered independent on you for supplies, and will possess more treasure than may be necessary to purchase the remains of liberty in your island.—In a word, take care that you do not fall into the pit that is preparing for us.

We believe there is yet much virtue, much justice, and much public spirit in the English nation.— To that justice we now appeal. You have been told that we are seditious, impatient of government, and desirous of independency, Be assured that these are not facts but calumnies.—Permit us to be as free as yourselves, and we shall ever esteem a union with you to be our greateſt happineſs; we ſhall ever be ready to contribute all in our power to the welfare of the empire—we ſhall conſider your enemies as our enemies, and your intereſt as our own.

But if you are determined that your miniſters ſhall wantonly ſport with the rights of mankind; if neither the voice of juſtice, the dictates of the law, the principles of the conſtitution, nor the ſuggeſtions of humanity can reſtrain your hands from the ſhedding human blood, in ſuch an *impious cauſe*, we muſt then tell you — " That we never will ſubmit to be hewers of wood or drawers of water for any miniſtry or nation in the world."

Place us in the ſame ſituation that we were at the cloſe of the laſt war, and our former harmony will be reſtored.

But leſt the ſame ſupineneſs, and the ſame inattention to our common intereſt, which you have for ſeveral years ſhewn, ſhould continue, we think it prudent to anticipate the conſequences.

By the deſtruction of the trade of Boſton, the miniſtry have endeavoured to influence ſubmiſſion to their meaſures. The like fate may befal us all; we will endeavour therefore to live without trade, and recur for ſubſiſtence to the fertility and bounty of our native ſoil, which will afford us all the neceſſaries and ſome of the conveniencies of life. We have ſuſpended our importation from Great Britain and Ireland; and in leſs than a year's time, unleſs our grievances ſhould be redreſſed, ſhall diſcontinue our exports to thoſe kingdoms and the Weſt Indies.

It is with the utmoſt regret, however, that we find ourſelves compelled, by the over-ruling principles of ſelf-preſervation, to adopt meaſures detrimental in their conſequences to numbers of our fellow-ſubjects in Great Britain and Ireland. But we hope, that the magnanimity and juſtice of the Britiſh nation will furniſh a parliament of ſuch wiſdom, independence,

and public ſpirit, as may ſave the violated rights of the whole empire from the devices of *wicked miniſters*, and *evil counſellors*, whether in or out of office, and thereby reſtore that harmony, friendſhip, and fraternal affection between all the inhabitants of his majeſty's kingdoms and territories, ſo ardently wiſhed for by every true and honeſt American.

The Aſſociation of the American Congreſs.

WE his majeſty's moſt loyal ſubjects, the delegates of the ſeveral colonies of New-Hampſhire, Maſſachuſett's Bay, Rhode-Iſland, Connecticut New-York, New-Jerſey, Pennſylvania, the three lower counties of Newcaſtle, Kent, and Suſſex, on Delaware, Maryland, Virginia, North-Carolina, and South-Carolina, deputed to repreſent them in a continental congreſs, held in the city of Philadelphia, on the fifth day of September, 1774, avowing our allegiance to his majeſty, our affection and regard for our fellow-ſubjects in Great Britain and elſewhere, affected with the deepeſt anxiety, and moſt alarming apprehenſions at thoſe grievances and diſtreſſes, with which his majeſty's American ſubjects are oppreſſed, and having taken under our moſt ſerious deliberation, the ſtate of the whole continent, find, that the preſent unhappy ſituation of our affairs is occaſioned by a ruinous ſyſtem of colony adminiſtration adopted by the Britiſh miniſtry about the year 1763, evidently calculated for inſlaving theſe colonies, and, with them, the Britiſh empire. In proſecution of which ſyſtem, various acts of parliament have been paſſed for raiſing a revenue in America, for depriving the American ſubjects, in many inſtances, of the conſtitutional trial by jury, expoſing their lives to danger, by directing a new and illegal trial beyond the ſeas, for crimes alledged

to have been committed in America; and in proſecution of the ſame ſyſtem, ſeveral late, cruel, and oppreſſive acts have been paſſed reſpecting the town of Boſton and the Maſſachuſett's Bay, and alſo an act for extending the province of Quebec, ſo as to border on the weſtern frontiers of theſe colonies, eſtabliſhing an arbitrary government therein, and diſcouraging the ſettlement of Britiſh ſubjects in that wide extended country; thus by the influence of civil principles and ancient prejudices to diſpoſe the inhabitants to act with hoſtility againſt the free proteſtant colonies, whenever a wicked miniſtry ſhall chuſe ſo to direct them.

To obtain redreſs of theſe grievances, which threaten deſtruction to the lives, liberty, and property of his majeſty's ſubjects in North-America, we are of opinion, that a non-importation, non-conſumption, and non-exportation agreement, faithfully adhered to, will prove the moſt ſpeedy, effectual, and peaceable meaſure: and therefore we do, for ourſelves and the inhabitants of the ſeveral colonies, whom we repreſent, firmly agree and aſſociate under the ſacred ties of virtue, honour, and love of our country, as follows;

Firſt. "That from and after the firſt day of December next, we will not import into Britiſh America, from Great Britain or Ireland, any goods, wares or merchandize whatſoever, or from any other place any ſuch goods, wares or merchandize, as ſhall have been exported from Great Britain or Ireland; nor will we, after that day, import any Eaſt-India tea from any part of the world; nor any molaſſes, ſyrups, paneles, coffee, or piemento, from the Britiſh plantations, or from Dominica; nor wines from Madeira, or the weſtern iſlands: nor foreign indigo.

Second. That we will neither import, nor purchaſe any ſlave imported, after the firſt day of December next; after which time, we will wholly difcontinue the flave trade, and will neither be concerned in it ourfelves, nor will we hire our veffels, nor fell our commodities or manufactures to thofe who are concerned in it.

Third. As a non-confumption agreement, ftrictly adhered to, will be an effectual fecurity for the obfervation of the non-importation, we, as above, folemnly agree and affociate, that, from this day, we will not purchafe or ufe any tea imported on account of the Eaft-India company, or any on which a duty hath been or fhall be paid; and from and after the firft day of March next, we will not purchafe or ufe any Eaft-India tea whatever; nor will we, nor fhall any perfon for or under us, purchafe or ufe any of thofe goods, wares, or merchandize, we have agreed not to import, which we fhall know, or have caufe to fufpect, were imported after the firft day of December, except fuch as come under the rules and directions of the tenth article herein after mentioned.

Fourth. The earneft defire we have, not to injure our fellow-fubjects in Great Britain, Ireland, or the Weft-Indies, induces us to fufpend a non-exportation, until the tenth day of September, 1775; at which time, if the faid acts and parts of acts of the Britifh parliament herein after mentioned are not repealed, we will not directly or indirectly, export any merchandize or commodity whatfoever to Great Britain, Ireland or the Weft-Indies, except rice to Europe.

Fifth. Such as are merchants and ufe the Britifh and Irifh trade, will give orders, as foon as poffible, to their factors, agents and correfpondents, in Great Britain and Ireland, not to fhip any goods to them, on any pretence whatfoever, as they cannot be received in America; and if any merchant, refiding in Great Britain or Ireland, fhall directly or indirectly fhip any goods, wares, or merchandize, for America, in order to break the

faid non-importation agreement, or in any manner contravene the fame, on fuch unworthy conduct being well attefted, it ought to be made public; and, on the fame being fo done, we will not from thenceforth have any commercial connexion with fuch merchant.

Sixth. That fuch as are owners of veffels will give pofitive orders to their captains or mafters, not to receive on board their veffels any goods prohibited by the faid non-importation agreement, on pain of immediate difmiffion from their fervice.

Seventh. We will ufe our utmoft endeavours to improve the breed of fheep and increafe their number to the greateft extent, and to that end, we will kill them as fparing as may be, efpecially thofe of the moft profitable kind; nor will we export any to the Weft-Indies or elfewhere: and thofe of us who are or may become over-ftocked with, or can conveniently fpare any fheep, will difpofe of them to our neighbours, efpecially to the poorer fort, on moderate terms.

Eighth. That we will in our feveral ftations encourage frugality, œconomy, and induftry; and promote agriculture, arts, and the manufactures of this country, efpecially that of wool: and will difcountenance and difcourage every fpecies of extravagance and diffipation, efpecially all horfe-racing, and all kinds of gaming, cockfighting, exhibitions of fhews, plays, and other expenfive diverfions and entertainments. And on the death of any relation or friend, none of us, or any of our families will go into any further mourning drefs, than a black crape or ribbon on the arm or hat for gentlemen, and a black ribbon and necklace for ladies, and we will difcontinue the giving of gloves and fcarfs at funerals.

Ninth. That fuch as are venders of goods or merchandize, will not take advantage of the fcarcity of goods that may be occafioned by this affociation, but will fell the

fame at the rates we have been refpectively accuftomed to do, for twelve months laft paft.—And if any vender of goods or merchandize, fhall fell any fuch goods on higher terms, or fhall in any manner, or by any device whatfoever, violate or depart from this agreement, no perfon ought, nor will any of us deal with any fuch perfon, or his or her factor or agent, at any time thereafter, for any commodity whatever.

Tenth. In cafe any merchant, trader, or other perfons fhall import any goods or merchandize after the firft day of December, and before the firft day of February next, the fame ought forthwith, at the election of the owner, to be either re-fhipped or delivered up to the committee of the county or town wherein they fhall be imported, to be ftored at the rifque of the importer, until the non-importation agreement fhall ceafe, or be fold under the direction of the committee aforefaid; and in the laft mentioned cafe, the owner or owners of fuch goods, fhall be reimbursed (out of the fales) the firft coft and charges; the profit, if any, to be applied towards relieving and employing fuch poor inhabitants of the town of Bofton, as are immediate fufferers by the Bofton port bill; and a particular account of all goods fo returned, ftored, or fold, to be inferted in the public papers; and if any goods or merchandizes fhall be imported after the faid firft day of February, the fame ought forthwith to be fent back again, without breaking any of the packages thereof.

Eleventh. That a committee be chofen in every county, city, and town, by thofe who are qualified to vote for reprefentatives in the legiflature, whofe bufinefs it fhall be attentively to obferve the conduct of all perfons touching this affociation: and when it fhall be made to appear to the fatisfaction of a majority of any fuch committee, that any perfon within the limits of their appointment has violated this association, that such majority do forthwith cause the truth of the case to be published in the Gazette, to the end that all such foes to the rights of British America may be publickly known, and universally contemned as the enemies of American liberty; and thenceforth we respectively will break off all dealings with him or her.

Twelfth. That the committee of correspondence in the respective colonies do frequently inspect the entries of their custom-houses, and inform each other from time to time of the true state thereof, and of every other material circumstance that may occur relative to their association.

Thirteenth. That all manufactures of this country be sold at reasonable prices, so that no undue advantage be taken of a future scarcity of goods.

Fourteenth. And we do further agree and resolve that we will have no trade, commerce, dealings or intercourse whatsoever, with any colony or province, in North-America, which shall not accede to, or which shall hereafter violate this association, but will hold them as unworthy of the rights of freemen, and as inimical to the liberties of their country,

And we do solemnly bind ourselves and our constituents, under the ties aforesaid, to adhere to this association until such parts of the several acts of parliament passed since the close of the last war, as impose or continue duties on tea, wine, molasses, syrups, paneles, coffee, sugar, piemento, indigo, foreign paper, glass, and painters colours, imported into America, and extend the powers of the admiralty courts beyond their ancient limits, deprive the American subject of trial by jury, authorise the judge's certificate to indemnify the prosecutor from damages, that he might otherwise be liable to, from a trial by his peers, require oppressive security from a claimant of ships or goods seized, before he

shall be allowed to defend his property, are repealed.—And until that part of the act of the 12. G. III. ch. 24. intituled, " An act for the better securing his majesty's dock yards, magazines, ships, ammunition, and stores," by which, any persons charged with committing any of the offences therein described, in America, may be tried in any shire or county within the realm, is repealed—And until the four acts passed in the last session of parliament, viz. That for stopping the port and blocking up the harbour of Boston—That for the altering the charter and government of the Massachusett's Bay — And that which is intituled, " An act for the better administration of justice," &c.—And that " For extending the limits of Quebec, &c." are repealed. And we recommend it to the provincial conventions, and to the committees in the respective colonies, to establish such farther regulations as they may think proper, for carrying into execution this association.

The foregoing association being determined upon by the *congress*, was ordered to be subscribed by the several members thereof; and thereupon we have hereunto set our respective names accordingly.

In Congress, Philadelphia, Oct. 20, 1774. Signed, 21

PEYTON RANDOLPH, *President.*

New-Hampshire. John Sullivan, Nat. Folsom.
Massachusett's Bay. Tho. Cushing, Samuel Adams, John Adams, Robert Treat Paine.
Rhode-Island. Stephen Hopkins, Sam. Ward.
Connecticut. Eliphalet Dyer, Roger Sherman, Silas Deane.
New-York. Isaac Low, John Alsop, John Jay, James Duane, William Floyd, Henry Weisner, S. Boerum.
New-Jersey. James Kinsey, William Livingston, Stephen Crane, Richard Smith.
Pensylvania. Joseph Galloway,

John Dickinson, Charles Humphreys, Thomas Mifflin, Edward Biddle, John Morton, George Ross.
Newcastle, &c. Cæsar Rodney, Thomas M'Kean, George Read.
Maryland. Matth. Tilghman, Tho. Johnson, William Paca, Sam. Chase.
Virginia. Richard Henry Lee, Geo. Washington, P. Henry, Jun. Rich. Bland, Benjamin Harrison, Edmund Pendleton.
North-Carolina. William Hooper, Joseph Hawes, R. Caswell.
South-Carolina. Henry Middleton, Thomas Lynch, Christopher Gadsden, John Rutledge, Edward Rutledge.

Address of the General Congress to the Inhabitants of the Province of QUEBEC.

Friends, and Fellow-Subjects,

WE, the delegates of the colonies of New-Hampshire, Massachusett's Bay, Rhode-Island, and Providence Plantations, Connecticut, New-York, New-Jersey, Pennsylvania, the counties of Newcastle, Kent and Sussex on Delaware, Maryland, Virginia, North-Carolina, and South-Carolina, deputed by the inhabitants of the said colonies, to represent them in a general congress at Philadelphia, in the province of Pennsylvania, to consult together of the best methods to obtain redress of our afflicting grievances, having accordingly assembled, and taken into our most serious consideration the state of public affairs on this continent, have thought proper to address your province, as a member therein deeply interested.

When the fortune of war, after a gallant and glorious resistance, had incorporated you with the body of English subjects, we rejoiced in the truly valuable addition, both on our own and your account; expecting, as courage and generosity are naturally united, our brave enemies would become our hearty friends, and that the Divine Being would bless to you the dispensations of his over-ruling providence, by securing to you and your latest posterity the inestimable advantages of a free English constitution of government, which is the privilege of all English subjects to enjoy.

These hopes were confirmed by the King's proclamation, issued in the year 1763, plighting the public faith for your full enjoyment of those advantages.

Little did we imagine that any succeeding ministers would so audaciously and cruelly abuse the royal authority, as to with-hold from you the fruition of the irrevocable rights, to which you were thus justly entitled.

But since we have lived to see the unexpected time, when ministers of this flagitious temper have dared to violate the most sacred compacts and obligations, and as you, educated under another form of government, have artfully been kept from discovering the unspeakable worth of that form you are now undoubtedly entitled to, we esteem it our duty, for the weighty reasons herein after mentioned, to explain to you some of its most important branches.

" In every human society, (says the celebrated Marquis Beccaria)[22] there is an effort continually tending to confer on one part the height of power and happiness, and to reduce the other to the extreme of weakness and misery. The intent of good laws is to oppose this effort, and to diffuse their influence universally and equally."

Rules stimulated by this pernicious " effort," and subjects, animated by the just " intent of opposing good laws against it," have occasioned that vast variety of events, that fill the histories of so many nations. All these histories demonstrate the truth of this simple position, that to live by the will of one man, or set of men, is the production of misery to all men.

On the solid foundation of this principle, Englishmen reared up the fabric of their constitution with such a strength, as for ages to defy time, tyranny, treachery, internal and foreign wars: and as an illustrious author* of your nation, hereafter mentioned, observes, " They gave the people of their colonies the form of their own government, and this government carrying prosperity along with it, they have grown great nations in the forests they were sent to inhabit."[23]

In this form the first grand right is, that of the people having a share in their own government, by their representatives, chosen by themselves, and in consequence of being ruled by laws which they themselves approve, not by edicts of men over whom they have no controul. This is a bulwark surrounding and defending their property, which by their honest cares and labours they have acquired, so that no portions of it can legally be taken from them, but with their own full and free consent, when they in their judgment deem it just and necessary to give them for public services; and precisely direct the easiest, cheapest, and most equal methods, in which they shall be collected.

The influence of this right extends still farther. If money is wanted by rulers, who have in any manner oppressed the people, they may retain it, until their grievances are redressed; and thus peaceably procure relief, without trusting to despised petitions, or disturbing the public tranquillity.

The next great right is that of trial by jury. This provides, that neither life, liberty nor property can be taken from the possessor, until twelve of his unexceptionable countrymen and peers, of his vicinage, who from that neighbourhood may reasonably be supposed to be acquainted with his character, and the characters of the witnesses, upon a fair trial, and full enquiry,

face to face, in open court, before as many of the people as choose to attend, shall pass their sentence upon oath against him; a sentence that cannot injure him, without injuring their own reputation, and probably their interest also; as the question may turn on points that, in some degree, concern the general welfare: and if it does not, their verdict may form a precedent, that, on a similar trial of their own, may militate against them.

Another right relates merely to the liberty of the person. If a subject is seized and imprisoned, though by order of government, he may, by virtue of this right, immediately obtain a writ, termed a Habeas Corpus, from a judge, whose sworn duty it is to grant it, and thereupon procure any illegal restraint, to be quickly enquired into and redressed.

A fourth right is, that of holding lands by the tenure of easy rents, and not by rigorous and oppressive services, frequently forcing the possessors from their families and their business, to perform what ought to be done, in all well regulated states, by men hired for the purpose.

The last right we shall mention, regards the freedom of the press. The importance of this consists, besides the advancement of truth, science and morality, and arts in general, in its diffusion of liberal sentiments on the administration of government, its ready communication of thoughts between subjects, and its consequential promotion of union among them, whereby oppressive officers are shamed or intimidated into more honourable and just modes of conducting affairs.

These are the invaluable rights that form a considerable part of our mild system of government: that sending its equitable energy through all ranks and classes of men, defends the poor from the rich, the weak from the powerful, the industrious from the rapacious, the peaceable from the violent, the tenants from the lords, and all from their superiors.

These are the rights, without which a people cannot be free and happy, and under the protecting and encouraging influence of which, these colonies have hitherto so amazingly flourished and increased. These are the rights a profligate ministry are now striving, by force of arms, to ravish from us, and which we are, with one mind, resolved never to resign but with our lives.

These are the rights you are entitled to, and ought at this moment in perfection to exercise. And what is offered to you by the late act of parliament in their place? Liberty of conscience in your religion? No. God gave it to you; and the temporal powers with which you have been and are connected firmly stipulated for your enjoyment of it. If laws divine and human, could secure it against the despotic capacities of wicked men, it was secured before. Are the French laws in civil cases restored? It seems so. But observe the cautious kindness of the ministers who pretend to be your benefactors. The words of the statute are, that those " laws shall be the rule, until they shall be varied or altered by any ordinances of the governor and council." Is the " certainty and lenity of the criminal law of England, and its benefits and advantages," commended in the said statute, and said to " have been sensibly felt by you," secured to you and your descendants? No. They too are subject to arbitrary " alterations" by the governor and council; and a power is expressly reserved of " appointing such courts of criminal, civil and ecclesiastical jurisdiction, as shall be thought proper." Such is the precarious tenure of mere will, by which you hold your lives and religion.

The crown and its ministers are

impowered, as far as they could be by parliament, to establish even the *inquisition* itself among you. Have you an assembly composed of worthy men, elected by yourselves, and in whom you can confide, to make laws for you, to watch over your welfare, and to direct in what quantity, and in what manner, your money shall be taken from you? No. The power of making laws for you is lodged in the governor and council, all of them dependent upon, and removable at the *pleasure* of a minister.—Besides, another late statute, made without your consent, has subjected you to the impositions of *excise*, the horror of all free states; they wresting your property from you by the most odious of taxes, and laying open to insolent tax-gatherers, houses the scenes of domestic peace and comfort, and called the castles of English subjects in the books of their laws. And in the very act for altering your government, and intended to flatter you, you are not authorised to " assess, levy, or apply any *rates* and taxes, but for the inferior purposes of *making roads*, and erecting and repairing *public buildings*, or for other *local* conveniencies, within your respective towns and districts." Why this degrading distinction? Ought not the property honestly acquired by *Canadians* to be held as sacred as that of *Englishmen*? Have not Canadians sense enough to attend to any other public affairs, than gathering stones from one place and piling them up in another? Unhappy people! who are not only injured, but insulted. Nay more!—With such a superlative contempt of your understanding and spirit has an insolent minister presumed to think of you, our respectable fellow-subjects, according to the information we have received, as firmly to persuade themselves that your gratitude, for the injuries and insults they have recently offered to you, will engage you to take up arms, and render

yourselves the ridicule and detestation of the world, by becoming tools, in their hands, to assist them in taking that freedom from *us*, which they have treacherously denied to *you*; the unavoidable consequence of which attempt, if successful, would be the extinction of all hopes of you or your posterity being ever restored to freedom: for idiotcy itself cannot believe, that, when their drudgery is performed, they will treat you with less cruelty than they have us, who are of the same blood with themselves.

What would your countryman, the immortal *Montesquieu*, have said to such a plan of domination, as has been framed for you? Hear his words, with an intenseness of thought suited to the importance of the subject.—" In a free state, every man, who is supposed a free agent, *ought to be concerned in his own government*; therefore the *legislative* should reside in the whole body of the *people*, or their *representatives*."—" The political liberty of the subject is a *tranquillity of mind*, arising from the opinion each person has of his *safety*. In order to have this liberty, it is requisite the government be so constituted, as that one man need not be *afraid* of another. When the power of *making* laws, and the power of *executing* them, are *united* in the same person, or in the same body of magistrates, *there can be no liberty*; because apprehensions may arise, lest the same *monarch* or *senate* should *enact* tyrannical laws, *to execute* them in a tyrannical manner." [24] [25]

" The power of *judging* should be exercised by persons taken from the *body of the people*, at certain times of the year, and pursuant to a form and manner prescribed by law. *There is no liberty*, if the power of *judging* be not *separated from the legislative* and *executive* powers." [26] [27]

" Military men belong to a profession, which *may be* useful, but is *often* dangerous."—" The en- [28] joyment of liberty, and even its support and preservation, confists in every man's being allowed to speak his thoughts, and lay open his sentiments." [29]

Apply these decisive maxims, sanctified by the authority of a name which all Europe reveres, to your own state. You have a governor, it may be urged, vested with the *executive* powers, or the powers of *administration*. In him, and in your council, is lodged the power of *making laws*. You have *judges*, who are to *decide* every cause affecting your lives, liberty or property. Here is, indeed, an appearance of the several power: being *separated* and *distributed* into *different* hands, for checks one upon another, the only effectual mode ever invented by the wit of men, to promote their freedom and prosperity. But scorning to be illuded by a tinselled outside, and exerting the natural fagacity of Frenchmen, *examine* the specious device, and you will find it, to use an expression of Holy Writ, " a painted sepulchre," for burying your lives, liberty and property.

Your *judges*, and your *legislative council*, as it is called, are *dependent* on your *governor*, and *he* is *dependent* on the servant of the crown in Great Britain. The *legislative*, *executive* and *judging* powers are *all* moved by the nods of a minister. Privileges and immunities last no longer than his smiles. When he frowns, their feeble forms dissolve. Such a treacherous ingenuity has been exerted in drawing up the code lately offered you, that every sentence, beginning with a benevolent pretension, concludes with a destructive power: and the substance of the whole, divested of its smooth words, is—that the crown and its minister shall be as absolute throughout your extended province, as the despots of Asia or Africa. What can protect your property from taxing edicts, and the rapacity of necessitous and cruel masters? your persons from *lettres de tachet*, gaols, dungeons, and oppressive service? your lives and general liberty from arbitrary and unfeeling rulers? We defy you, casting your view upon every side, to discover a single circumstance, promising from any quarter the faintest hope of liberty to you or your posterity, but from an entire adoption into the union of these colonies.

What advice would the truly great man before mentioned, that advocate of freedom and humanity, give you, was he now living, and knew that we, your numerous and powerful neighbours, animated by a just love of our invaded rights, and united by the indissoluble bands of affection and interest, called upon you, by every obligation of regard for yourselves and your children, as we now do, to join us in our righteous contest, to make a common cause with us therein, and take a noble chance for emerging from a humiliating subjection under governors, intendants, and military tyrants, into the firm rank and condition of English freemen, whose custom it is, derived from their ancestors, to make those tremble who dare to think of making them miserable.

Would not this be the purport of his address? " Seize the opportunity presented to you by Providence itself. You have been conquered into liberty, if you act as you ought. This work is not of man. You are a small people, compared to those who with open arms invite you into a fellowship. A moment's reflection should convince you which will be most for your interest and happiness, to have all the rest of North America your unalterable friends, or your inveterate enemies. The injuries of Boston have roused and associated every colony, from Nova-Scotia to Georgia. Your province is the only link wanting to compleat the bright and strong chain of union. Nature has joined your country to theirs. Do you join your political interests. For their own fakes, they never will desert or betray you. Be assured that the happiness of a people inevitably depends on their liberty, and their spirit to assert it. The value and extent of the advantages tendered to you are immense. Heaven grant you may not discover them to be blessings after they have bid you an eternal adieu."

We are too well acquainted with the liberality of sentiment distinguishing your nation, to imagine, that difference of religion will prejudice you against a hearty amity with us. You know, that the transcendent nature of freedom elevates those, who unite in the cause, above all such low-minded infirmities. The Swiss Cantons furnish a memorable proof of this truth. Their union is composed of Catholic and Protestant states, living in the utmost concord and peace with one another, and thereby enabled, ever since they bravely vindicated their freedom, to defy and defeat every tyrant that has invaded them.

Should there be any among you, as there generally are in all societies, who prefer the favours of ministers, and their own interests, to the welfare of their country; the temper of such selfish persons will render them incredibly active in opposing all public-spirited measures, from an expectation of being well rewarded for their sordid industry, by their superiors: but we doubt not you will be upon your guard against such men, and not sacrifice the liberty and happiness of the whole Canadian people and their posterity, to gratify the avarice and ambition of individuals.

We do not ask you, by this address, to commence acts of hostility against the government of our common sovereign. We only invite you to consult your own glory and welfare, and not to suffer yourselves to be inveigled or intimidated by infamous ministers so far, as to become the instruments of their cruelty and despotism, but to unite with us in one social compact, formed on the generous principles of equal liberty, and cemented by such an exchange of beneficial and endearing offices as to render it perpetual. In order to complete this highly desirable union, we submit it to your consideration, whether it may not be expedient for you to meet together in your several towns and districts, and elect deputies, who afterwards meeting in a provincial congress, may chuse delegates, to represent your province in the continental congress to be held at Philadelphia, on the tenth day of May, 1775.

In this present congress, beginning on the 5th of last month, and continued to this day, it has been with universal pleasure, and an unanimous vote, resolved, that we should consider the violation of your rights, by the act for altering the government of your province, as a violation of our own; and that you should be invited to accede to our confederation, which has no other objects than the perfect security of the natural and civil rights of all the constituent members, according to their respective circumstances, and the preservation of a happy and lasting connection with Great-Britain, on the salutary and constitutional principles herein before mentioned. For effecting these purposes, we have addressed an humble and loyal petition to his majesty, praying relief of our grievances; and have associated to stop all importation from Great Britain and Ireland, after the first day of December, and all exportation to those kingdoms and the West Indies, after the tenth day of next September, unless the said grievances are redressed.

That Almighty God may incline your minds to approve our equitable and necessary measures, to add yourselves to us, to put your fate, whenever you suffer injuries which you are determined to oppose, not on the small influence of your single province, but on the consolidated powers of North-America, and may grant to our joint exertions an event as happy as our cause is just, is the fervent prayer of us, your sincere and affectionate friends and fellow-subjects.

By order of the Congress,
HENRY MIDDLETON, president.
Oct. 26, 1774.

Articles of Impeachment of high Crimes and Misdemeanors against Peter Oliver, Esq; Chief Justice of the Superior Court of Judicature, &c. over the province of Massachusett's Bay, by the House of Representatives in General Court assembled, in their own name, and in the name of all the inhabitants of that province, February 24, 1774.

THE principal articles of impeachment were in substance as follows:——" Whereas Peter Oliver, Esq; Chief Justice of the superior Court of Judicature over this province, a Court wholly erected and constituted by the great and general court or assembly by a power granted to the said general court by the clause in the royal charter, well knowing the premises but not regarding the same, with design to subvert the constitution of this province as established by royal charter, and to introduce into the said court a partial, arbitrary, and corrupt administration of justice, declining to take and receive any more of the grants of the general assembly of this province, did, on or about the 10th day of January, 1774, at Boston, take and receive, and resolve for the future to take and receive from his Majesty's ministers and servants, a grant or salary for his services as Chief Justice of the said superior court, against his own knowledge of the said charter, and of the way and manner prescribed therein for the support of his Majesty's government in the province and contrary to uninterrupted, and approved usage and custom since the erecting and constituting of the said court: and the said Peter Oliver, Esq; continues in his said resolution so to do, against the opinion and conduct of the other judges of the said court, each of whom has declared respecting himself his resolution to the contrary. And whereas the unmerited sum of 400l. granted by his Majesty, and annually to be paid to the said Peter Oliver, Esq; for his services as Chief Justice of the said superior court, together with the hopes of its augmentation, if he is still suffered to continue in the said office, cannot fail to have the effect of a continual bribery in his judicial proceedings, and expose him to a violation of his oath. And by his accepting and receiving the said sum he hath betrayed the corruption and baseness of his heart, and the sordid lust of covetousness, in breach of his engagements to rely solely upon the grants of the general assembly, necessarily implied and involved in his accepting the said office.

" And the said Peter Oliver, Esq; did, on the 8th of February instant, cause to be delivered to this house a writing under his own hand, dated Feb. 3, the purport of which was as follows:

" *May it please your Honours,*
In the year 1756, I was appointed as a justice of the superior court, and accepted the office contrary to my own inclination, but by the persuasion of gentlemen who were then members of the general assembly. In this office I have continued for above 17 years; and I hope your honours will excuse me if I say, that I never was yet conscious that I had ever been guilty of any violations of the laws of my country in a judicial capacity, but have always endeavoured to act with that fidelity required in so important a character; and with this sentiment I doubt not of ever consoling my-

self in the approbation of my own mind.

During these 17 years I have annually felt the great inconveniencies of my judicial office, by suffering in my private business, and not having a salary which would any ways support my family, which was large, and I cannot charge myself with any degree of extravagance in the support of it; and I wish I may not have been too parsimonious for the dignity of the province, in my judicial character.

I can with the strictest truth assert, that I have suffered, since I have been upon the bench of the superior court, in the loss of my business, and not having sufficient to maintain my family, from my salaries, above 3000 l. sterling! I have repeatedly thrown myself on former assemblies for relief, but never have obtained any redress: I have repeatedly attempted to resign my office, but have been dissuaded from it, by many respectable gentlemen who encouraged me with hopes of support, but I never received any relief in that way.

When his Majesty of his great goodness and favour granted me a salary (as he did to several others on the continent in my station) it was without any application of mine; and when it was granted, I thought it my incumbent duty, from the respect and gratitude which I owed to his Majesty, from a sense of that fidelity which I owed to my country, by being enabled to discharge the duty of my office in being less embarrassed in my mind whilst in the execution of it, and being more at liberty to qualify myself for the duties of it in vacation time, as also from a principle of justice due to my family and to others: on these accounts, and not from any avaricious views, I was obliged to take his Majesty's grant from the 5th of July, 1772, to the 5th of January, 1774, and have taken the grant of the province only until July.

With respect to my not taking any future grant from his Majesty, permit me to say, that without his Majesty's leave I dare not refuse it, lest I should incur a censure of the best of sovereigns. And as the tenor of the grant is during my residence in the province as chief justice, I receive it as during good behaviour, which in my opinion preserves me from any undue bias in the execution of my office."

The house of representives expressed their resentment at the above writing in very severe terms, charging the said Mr. Oliver with ungratefully, falsely, and maliciously, labouring to lay imputation and scandal on this his Majesty's government, &c. and conclude their articles of impeachment as follows:

"Wherefore this house of representatives, in their own name, and in the name of all the inhabitants of this province, do impeach the said Peter Oliver, Esq; of the high crimes and misdemeanors aforesaid. And they pray that the said Peter Oliver, Esq; Chief Justice of the Superior Court of Judicature, &c. over this whole province, may be put to answer to all and every of the premises; and that such proceedings, examinations, trials, and judgments, may be had and ordered thereon, as may be agreeable to law and justice."

The above articles of impeachment were agreed to; the yeas being 92, the nays 8.

The house having, previous to the carrying up this impeachment, acquainted the governor of their resolution, and desired he would then be in the chair; his excellency was pleased to send them the following message, viz.

"*Gentlemen of the House of Representatives,*

By your message of yesterday you informed me, that you had resolved to impeach Peter Oliver, Esq; Chief Justice of the Superior Court, &c. before the Governor and Council, of high crimes and misdemeanors, and that you had prepared the articles of impeachment; and prayed that I would be in the chair, that you might then have an opportunity of laying them before the Governor and Council.

I know of no species of high crimes and misdemeanors, nor any offence against the law committed within this province, let the rank or condition of the offender be what it may, which is not cognizable by some judicatory or judicatories, and I do not know that the Governor and Council have a concurrent jurisdiction with any judicatory in criminal cases, or any authority to try and determine any species of high crimes and misdemeanours whatsoever.

If I should assume a jurisdiction, and with the council try offenders against the law without authority granted by the charter, or by a law of the province in pursuance of the charter, I should make myself liable to answer before a judicatory which would have cognizance of my offence, and his Majesty's subjects would have just cause to complain of being deprived of a trial by jury, the general claim of Englishmen, except in those cases where the law may have made special provision to the contrary.

Whilst such process as you have attempted to commence shall appear to be unconstitutional, I cannot shew any countenance to it.

Milton, Feb. 26.

T. HUTCHINSON."

The house, upon the consideration of this message, sent up to the Governor and Council the same articles, with an introduction and conclusion in a different form from the other; by no means however retracting their impeachment, or their original address for the removal of the Chief Justice. The introduction was altered as follows:

" Articles of high crimes and

misdemeanors offered and presented to his excellency the governor, and to the honourable his Majesty's council, against Peter Oliver, Esq; Chief Justice, &c. this 1st day of March 1774.

[Here the articles were brought in, *totidem verbis*, as they stood in the impeachment, and the conclusion was as follows, viz.]

All which matters, contained in the foregoing articles, the said house of representatives are ready to verify and prove. They therefore pray in their own name, and in the name of all the inhabitants of this province, that the governor and council would give orders that the said Peter Oliver, Esq; may be notified to make answer to the charges contained in the foregoing articles, and be brought to a hearing and trial thereon; that if he be found guilty thereof, he may, by the governor and council, be forthwith removed from his said office, and some other more worthy be nominated and appointed in his stead."

There were 78 members present in the house, and the division was 71 to 7.

To the Hon. the Commons of Great Britain in Parliament assembled.

The humble Petition of several Natives of North America. (Presented March 25, 1774.)

SHEWETH,

THAT your petitioners, being natives of his majesty's dominions in America, are deeply interested in every proceeding of the house, which touches the life, liberties, or property of any person or persons in the said dominions. That your petitioners conceive themselves and their fellow-subjects intitled to the rights of natural justice, and to the common law of England, as their unalienable birthright. That they apprehend it to be an inviolable rule of natural

justice, that no man shall be condemned unheard; and that, according to law, no person or persons can be judged without being called upon to answer, and being permitted to hear the evidence against them, and to make their defence; and that it is therefore with the deepest sorrow they understand that the house is now about to pass a bill, to punish with unexampled rigour the town of Boston, for a trespass committed by some persons unknown upon the property of the East India company, without the said town's being apprized of any accusation brought against them, or having been permitted to hear the evidence, or to make their defence. That your petitioners conceive such proceedings to be directly repugnant to every principle of law and justice; and that, under such a precedent, no man, or body of men, in America, could enjoy a moment's security; for if judgment be immediately to follow an accusation against the people of America, supported even by persons notoriously at enmity with them; the accused, unacquainted with the charge, and, from the nature of their situation, utterly incapable of answering and defending themselves; every fence against false accusation will be pulled down, justice will no longer be their shield, nor innocence an exemption from punishment. That the law in America ministers redress for any injuries sustained there; and they can most truly affirm, that it is administered in that country with as much impartiality as in any other part of his majesty's dominions. In proof of this, they appeal to an instance of great notoriety, in which, under every circumstance that could exasperate the people, and disturb the course of justice, Captain Preston and his soldiers had a fair trial, and favourable verdict. While the due course of law holds out redress for any injury sustained in America, they apprehend the interposition of

parliamentary power to be full of danger, and without any precedent. If the persons who committed this trespass are known, then the East-India company have their remedy against them at law; if they are unknown, the petitioners cannot comprehend by what rule of justice the town can be punished for a civil injury committed by persons not known to belong to them; and the petitioners conceive, that there is not an instance, even in the most arbitrary times, in which a city was punished by parliamentary authority, without being heard, for a civil offence not committed in their jurisdiction, and without redress having been sought at common law. The cases which they have heard adduced are directly against it. That of the king against the city of London, was for a murder committed within its walls, by its citizens, in open day; but even then, arbitrary as the times were, the trial was public in a court of common law, the party heard, and the law laid down by the judges was, that it was an offence at the common law to suffer such a crime to be committed in a walled town *tempore diurno*, and none of the offenders to be known or indicted. The case of Edinburgh, in which parliament did interpose, was the commission of an atrocious murder within her gates, and aggravated by an overt act of high treason, in executing, against the express will of the crown, the king's laws. It is observable, that these cities had, by charter, the whole executive power within themselves; so that a failure of justice necessarily ensued from the connivance. In both cases, however, full time was allowed them to discharge their duty, and they were heard in their defence; but neither has time been allowed in this case, nor is the accused heard, nor is Boston a walled town, nor was the fact committed within it, nor is the executive power in their hands, as it is in those of London and Edinburgh. On the contrary, the governor himself holds that power, and has been advised by his majesty's counsel to carry it into execution; if it has been neglected, he alone is answerable; if it has been executed, perhaps at this instant, while punishment is inflicting here on those who have not been legally tried, the due course of law is operating there, to the discovery and prosecution of the real offenders. Your petitioners think themselves bound to declare to the house, that they apprehend, a proceeding of excessive rigour and injustice will sink deep in the minds of their countrymen, and tend to alienate their affections from this country; and that the attachment of America cannot survive the justice of Great Britain; and that, if they see a different mode of trial established for them, and for the people of this country; a mode which violates the sacred principles of natural justice, it must be productive of national distrust, and extinguish those filial feelings of respect and affection which have hitherto attached them to the parent State: urged therefore by every motive of affection to both countries, by the most earnest desire, not only to preserve their own rights, and those of their countrymen, but to prevent the dissolution of that love, harmony, and confidence, between the two countries, which was their mutual blessing and support, your petitioners humbly pray, that the said bill may not pass into a law.

Second Petition of several Natives of America.

To the Hon. the Commons of Great Britain in Parliament assembled.

(Presented May 2, 1774.)

SHEWETH,

THAT your petitioners are again constrained to complain to the house of two bills, which, if carried into execution, will be fatal to the rights, liberties, and peace, of all America. Your petitioners have already seen, with equal astonishment and grief, proceedings adopted against them, which, in violation of the first principles of justice and of the laws of the land, inflict the severest punishments, without hearing the accused. Upon the same principle of injustice, a bill is now brought in, which, under the profession of better regulating the government of the Massachusett's Bay, is calculated to deprive a whole province, without any form of trial, of its chartered rights, solemnly secured to it by mutual compact between the crown and the people. Your petitioners are well informed, that a charter so granted, was never before altered, or resumed, but upon a full and fair hearing; that therefore the present proceeding is totally unconstitutional, and sets an example which renders every charter in Great Britain and America utterly insecure. The appointment and removal of the judges, at the pleasure of the governor, with salaries payable by the crown, puts the property, liberty, and life of the subject, depending upon judicial integrity, in his power. Your petitioners perceive a system of judicial tyranny deliberately at this day imposed upon them, which, from the bitter experience of its intolerable injuries, has been abolished in this country. Of the same unexampled and alarming nature is the bill, which, under the title of a more impartial administration of justice in the province of Massachusett's Bay, impowers the governor to withdraw offenders from justice in the said province, holding out to the soldiery an exemption from legal prosecution for murder, and in effect subjecting that colony to military execution. Your Petitioners intreat the house to consider what must be the consequence of sending troops, not really under the controul of the civil power, and unamenable to the law, among a people whom they have been industriously taught, by the incendiary arts of wicked men, to regard as deserving every species of insult and abuse; the insults and injuries of a lawless soldiery are such as no free people can long endure; and your petitioners apprehend, in the consequences of this bill, the horrid outrages of military oppression, followed by the desolation of civil commotions. The dispensing power which this bill intends to give to the governor, advanced as he is already above the law, and not liable to any impeachment from the people he may oppress, must constitute him an absolute tyrant. Your petitioners would be utterly unworthy of the English ancestry, which is their claim and pride, if they did not feel a virtuous indignation at the reproach of disaffection and rebellion, with which they have been cruelly aspersed. They can with confidence say, no imputation was ever less deserved. They appeal to the experience of a century, in which the glory, the honour, the prosperity of England, has been, in their estimation, their own; in which they have not only borne the burthen of provincial wars, but have shared with this country in the dangers and expences of every national war. Their zeal for the service of the crown, and the defence of the general empire, has prompted them, whenever it was required, to vote supplies of men and money, to the utmost exertion of their abilities. The journals of the house will bear witness to their extraordinary zeal and services during the last war, and that but a very short time before it was resolved here to take from them the right of giving and granting their own money. If disturbances have happened in the colonies, they intreat the house to consider the causes which have produced them, among a people hitherto remarkable for their loyalty to the crown, and affection for this kingdom. No history can shew, nor will human native admit of, an instance of general discontent, but from a general sense of oppression. Your petitioners conceived, that when they had acquired property under all the restraints this country thought necessary to impose upon their commerce, trade, and manufactures, that property was sacred and secure; they felt a very material difference between being restrained in the acquisition of property, and holding it, when acquired under those restraints, at the disposal of others. They understand subordination in the one, and slavery in the other. Your petitioners wish they could possibly perceive any difference between the most abject slavery, and such entire subjection to a legislature, in the constitution of which they have not a single voice, nor the least influence, and in which no one is present on their behalf. They regard the giving their property by their own consent alone as the unalienable right of the subject, and the last sacred bulwark of constitutional liberty: if they are wrong in this, they have been misled by the love of liberty which is their dearest birthright; by the most solemn statutes, and the resolves of the house itself, declaratory of the inherent right of the subject; by the authority of all great constitutional writers, and by the uninterrupted practice of Ireland and America, who have ever voted their own supplies to the crown; all which combine to prove that the property of an English subject, being a freeman or a freeholder, cannot be taken from him but by his own consent. To deprive the colonies therefore of this right, is to reduce them to a state of vassalage, leaving them nothing they can call their own, nor capable of any acquisition but for the benefit of others. It is with infinite and inexpressible concern, that your petitioners see in these bills, and in the principles of them, a direct tendency to reduce their countrymen

to the dreadful alternative of being totally enslaved, or compelled into a contest the most shocking and unnatural with a parent state, which has ever been the object of their veneration and their love; they intreat the house to consider, that the restraints which examples of such severity and injustice impose, are ever attended with the most dangerous hatred. In a distress of mind which cannot be described, your petitioners conjure the house, not to convert that zeal and affection, which have hitherto united every American hand and heart in the interests of England, into passions the most painful and pernicious: most earnestly they beseech the house, not to attempt reducing them to a state of slavery, which the English principles of liberty they inherit from their mother country will render worse than death; and therefore humbly pray, that the house will not, by passing these bills, overwhelm them with affliction, and reduce their countrymen to the most abject state of misery and humiliation, or drive them to the last resources of despair.

Authentic Copy of the Address and Petition presented to the King by the Corporation of London, previous to his Majesty's signing the Bill for the better Government of Quebec.

"To the KING's Most Excellent Majesty.

Most Gracious Sovereign!

WE your Majesty's most dutiful and loyal subjects, the Lord Mayor, Aldermen, and Commons, of the city of London, in Common Council assembled, are exceedingly alarmed that a bill has passed your two Houses of Parliament, entitled, "An Act for making more effectual provision for the government of the province of Quebec, in North-America," which

we apprehend to be entirely subversive of the great fundamental principles of the constitution of the British monarchy, as well as of the authority of various solemn acts of the legislature.

"We beg leave to observe, that the English law, and that wonderful effort of human wisdom, the trial by Jury, are not admitted by this bill in any civil cases, and the French law of Canada is imposed on all the inhabitants of that extensive province, by which both the persons and properties of very many of your Majesty's subjects are rendered insecure and precarious.

"We humbly conceive, that this bill, if passed into a law, will be contrary, not only to the compact entered into with the numerous settlers, of the reformed religion, who were invited into the said province under the sacred promise of enjoying the benefit of the laws of your realm of England, but likewise repugnant to your royal proclamation of the 7th of October, 1763, for the speedy settling the said new government.

"That, consistent with the public faith pledged by the said proclamation, your Majesty cannot erect and constitute courts of judicature and public justice for the hearing and determining all cases, as well civil as criminal, within the said province, but as near as may be agreeable to the laws of England; nor can any laws, statutes, or ordinances, for the public peace, welfare, and good government of the said province, be made, constituted, or ordained, but according to the laws of this realm.

"That the Roman-catholic religion, which is known to be idolatrous and bloody, is established by this bill, and no legal provision is made for the free exercise of our reformed faith, nor the security of our protestant fellow-subjects of the church of England in the true worship of Almighty God, according to their consciences.

" That your Majesty's illustrious family was called to the throne of these kingdoms in consequence of the exclusion of the Roman-catholic ancient branch of the Stuart line, under the express stipulation that they should profess the protestant religion, and, according to the oath established by the sanction of parliament in the first year of the reign of our great deliverer, King William the Third, your Majesty at your coronation has solemnly sworn that you would, to the utmost of your power, maintain the laws of God, the true profession of the Gospel, and the protestant reformed religion established by law.

" That, although the term of imprisonment of the subject is limited to three months, the power of fining is left indefinite and unrestrained, by which the total ruin of the party may be effected by an enormous and excessive fine.

" That the whole legislative power of the province is vested in persons to be solely appointed by your Majesty, and removable at your pleasure, which we apprehend to be repugnant to the leading principles of this free constitution, by which alone your Majesty now holds, or legally can hold, the imperial crown of these realms.

" That the said bill was brought into parliament very late in the present session, and after the greater number of the members of the two Houses were retired into the country, so that it cannot fairly be presumed to be the sense of those parts of the legislature.

" Your petitioners, therefore, most humbly supplicate your Majesty, as the guardian of the laws, liberties, and religion, of your people, and as the great bulwark of the protestant faith, that you will not give your royal assent to the said bill.

" And your petitioners, as in duty bound, will ever pray."

Abstract of an Act to discontinue, in such Manner and for such Time as are therein mentioned, the Landing and Discharging, Lading or Shipping, of Goods and Merchandise, at the Town, and within the Harbour, of Boston, *in* Massachusett's Bay, *in* North-America.

THE preamble declares, That as dangerous commotions and insurrections have been fomented and raised in the town of Boston, in the province of Massachusett's-bay, by ill-affected persons, to the subversion of government, and to the utter destruction of the public peace; in which commotions certain valuable cargoes of teas, the property of the East-India company, and on board vessels lying within the bay or harbour of Boston, were seized and destroyed: and as, in the present condition of the town and harbour, the commerce of his Majesty's subjects cannot be safely carried on there, nor the customs duly collected; it is therefore expedient that the officers of his Majesty's customs should be forthwith removed from the said town: and it is therefore enacted, That from and after the first day of June, 1774, it shall not be lawful for any person or persons to lade, or cause to be laden or put, off or from any quay, wharf, or other place, within the town of Boston, or in or upon any part of the shore of the bay, commonly called the harbour of Boston, into any ship, vessel, boat, &c. any goods, wares, or merchandise whatsoever, to be carried into any other country or place whatsoever, or into any other part of the province of the Massachusett's-bay, or to take up, discharge, or cause or procure to be taken up, or discharged, within the town, out of any boat, lighter, ship, &c. any goods, wares, or merchandise whatsoever, to be brought from any other country or place, or any other part of the province of the Massachusett's-bay, upon pain of the forfeiture of the goods and merchandise, and of the boat, ship, or other bottom into which the same shall be put, or out of which the same shall be taken, and of the guns, ammunition, tackle, furniture, and stores, in or belonging to the same : and if any such goods, wares, or merchandise, shall, within the town, or in any the places aforesaid, be laden or taken in from the shore into any barge, or boat, to be carried on board any ship outward bound to any other country, or other part of the province of the Massachusett's-bay, or be laden or taken into such barge, or boat, from or out of any ship coming in from any other country or province, or other part of the province of the Massachusett's-bay, such barge, boat, &c. shall be forfeited.

And it is further enacted, That if any wharfinger, or keeper of any wharf, or their servants, shall take up or land, or knowingly suffer to be taken up, or shall ship off, or suffer to be waterborne, at or from any of their wharfs, &c. any such goods or merchandise; in every such case, all and every such wharfinger, and every person who shall be assisting, or concerned in the shipping or putting on board any boat, or other vessel, for that purpose, or in the unshipping such goods and merchandise, or to whose hands the same shall knowingly come after the loading, shipping, or unshipping thereof, shall forfeit and lose treble the value thereof, to be computed at the highest price which such sort of goods and merchandise shall bear at the place where such offence shall be committed, at the time when the same shall be so committed, together with the vessels and boats, and all the horses, cattle, and carriages, made use of in the shipping, unshipping, landing, or conveyance of any of the goods and merchandise.

It is further enacted, That if any ship or vessel shall be moored or lie at anchor, or be seen hovering within the bay, or within one league from the said bay, it shall and may be lawful for any admiral, chief-commander, &c. of his Majesty's fleet or ships of war, or for any officer of his Majesty's customs, to compel such ship or vessel to depart to some other port, or to such station as the officer shall appoint, and to use such force for that purpose as shall be found necessary: and if such ship or vessel shall not depart, within six hours after notice for that purpose given, such ship or vessel, with all the goods laden on board, and all the guns, tackle, and furniture, shall be forfeited, whether bulk shall have been broken or not.

Provided always, That nothing in this act contained shall extend, or be construed to extend, to any military or other stores for his Majesty's use, or to the ships or vessels whereon the same shall be laden, which shall be commissioned by his Majesty; nor to any fuel or victual brought coastwise from any part of the continent of America, for the necessary use and sustenance of the inhabitants of the town of Boston, provided the vessel wherein the same are to be carried shall be duly furnished with a cocket and let-pass, after having been duly searched by the officers of his majesty's customs at Marble-head, in the port of Salem, in the province of Massachusett's Bay; and that some officer of his majesty's customs be also there put on board the vessel, who is authorised to go on board, and proceed with the vessel, together with persons properly armed, for his defence, to the town or harbour of Boston; nor to any ships or vessels which may happen to be within the harbour of Boston on or before the first day of June, 1774, and may have either laden, or be there with intent to load, or to land or discharge any goods and merchandise, provided the ships and vessels do depart the harbour within fourteen days after the first day of June, 1774.

It is further enacted, That all seizures and forfeitures, inflicted by this Act, shall be made and prosecuted by any admiral or commissioned officer, of his majesty's fleet,

or by the officers of the customs, or by some other person authorised by warrant from the Lord High Treasurer, or the commissioners of his majesty's treasury for the time being, and by no other person; and if any such officer, or other person authorised, shall, directly or indirectly, take or receive any bribe, to connive at such lading or unlading, or shall make or commence any collusive seizure or agreement for that purpose, or shall do any other act, whereby the goods, or merchandise, prohibited, shall be suffered to pass either inwards or outwards, or whereby the forfeitures inflicted by this act may be evaded, every such offender shall forfeit the sum of 500 l. for every such offence, and shall become incapable of any office or employment; and every person who shall give, or promise, any such bribe, or shall contract with any person, so authorised, to commit any such offence, shall forfeit the sum of 50 l.

It is further enacted, That the forfeitures and penalties inflicted by this act shall be prosecuted, and recovered, and be divided and applied, in like manner as other penalties inflicted by any act or acts of parliament, relating to the trade or revenues of the British colonies or plantations in America, are directed to be prosecuted, or recovered, divided, and applied, by two several acts of parliament, the one passed in the fourth year of his present Majesty, (intitled, An Act for granting certain duties in the British colonies and plantations in America; for continuing an Act passed in the Sixth of George the Second, intitled, An Act for the better securing the trade of his Majesty's sugar colonies in America, &c, the other passed in the Eighth year of his present Majesty's reign, (intitled, An Act for the more easy recovery of the penalties and forfeitures inflicted by the acts of parliament relating to the trade of the British colonies and plantations in America.)

It is further enacted, That every

charter party bill of lading, and other contract for consigning, shipping, or carrying any goods and merchandise, to or from the town of Boston, or any part of the bay or harbour, which have been made or entered into, or which shall be made or entered into, so long as this Act shall remain in full force, relating to any ship which shall arrive at the town or harbour, after the first day of June, 1774, shall be, and the same are hereby declared to be, utterly void, to all intents and purposes.

It is further enacted, That, whenever it shall be made to appear to his Majesty, in his Privy-Council, that peace and obedience to the laws shall be so far restored in the town of Boston, that the trade of Great-Britain may safely be carried on there, and his Majesty's customs duly collected, and his Majesty shall adjudge the same to be true, it shall be lawful for his Majesty, by proclamation, or order of Council, to assign and appoint the extent, bounds, and limits, of the port or harbour of Boston, and of every creek or haven within the same, or in the islands within the precinct thereof; and also to appoint such and so many other places and wharfs, within the harbour, creeks, &c. for the landing and shipping of goods, as his Majesty shall judge necessary; and to appoint such and so many officers of the customs as his Majesty shall think fit; after which it shall be lawful for any person to lade, or to discharge and land upon, such wharfs, &c. so appointed within the harbour, and none other, any goods and merchandise.

Provided always, That if any goods or merchandise, shall be laden or discharged upon any other place than the quays, or places, so to be appointed, the same, together with the ships and other vessels employed, and the horses and carriages used to convey the same, and the person or persons concerned therein, or to whose hands the same shall knowingly come, shall suffer all the forfeitures and penalties imposed by this or any other Act on the illegal shipping or landing of goods.

Provided also, That nothing herein contained shall extend, or be construed, to enable his Majesty to appoint such port, wharfs, places, or officers, in Boston, or in the bay or islands, until it shall sufficiently appear to his Majesty that full satisfaction hath been made by or on behalf of the inhabitants of the town of Boston to the company of merchants trading to the East-Indies, for the damage sustained by the company by the destruction of their goods sent to Boston, on board ships as aforesaid; and until it shall be certified to his Majesty, in council, by the governor, or lieutenant-governor, of the province, that reasonable satisfaction hath been made to the officers of the revenue, and others; who suffered by the riots above-mentioned, in the months of November and December, in the year 1773; and in the month of January, in the year 1774.

And it is further enacted, That, if any action or suit shall be commenced, either in Great-Britain or America, against any person or persons, for any thing done in pursuance of this act of parliament, the defendant or defendants, in such action or suit, may plead the general issue, and give the act, and the special matter, in evidence, at any trial, and that the same was done in pursuance of this act: and if it shall appear so to have been done, the jury shall find for the defendant or defendants; and if the plaintiff shall be non-suited, or discontinue his action, after the defendant or defendants shall have appeared; or if judgment shall be given upon any verdict or demurrer, against the plaintiff; the defendant or defendants shall recover treble costs, and have the like remedy for the same, as defendants have in other cases by law.

An Abstract of an Act for the better regulating the Government of the Province of Massachusett's-bay.

THIS act declares, that from and after the 1st of August, 1774, so much of the charter granted by King William to the inhabitants of Massachusett's-bay, which relates to the time and manner of electing Counsellors for that province, shall be revoked and made void, and that from that day the Council for the province shall be composed of such of the inhabitants, or proprietors of lands, within the same, as shall be appointed by his Majesty, with the advice of the Privy-council, agreeable to the practice now used in respect to the appointment of Counsellors in such of his Majesty's other colonies in America, the governors whereof are appointed by commission under the great seal of Great-Britain: Provided, that the number of Counsellors shall not, at any one time, exceed thirty-six, nor be less than twelve.

That the assistants or counsellors shall hold their offices during the pleasure of his Majesty, and enjoy all the privileges at present held by counsellors of the province, under the charter; and shall, upon their admission into the council, take the oaths, &c.

That after the first day of July, 1774, his Majesty's governor, or, in his absence, the lieutenant-governor, may nominate or remove, without the consent of the council, all Judges of the inferior courts of common-pleas, justices of the peace, and other officers to the council or courts of justice belonging.

That, from and after the first day of July, 1774, his Majesty's governor, or, in his absence, the lieutenant-governor, may nominate and appoint the sheriffs without the consent of the council, and remove such sheriffs with such consent, and not otherwise.

That, upon every vacancy of the offices of chief justice and judges of the superior court, the governor, or lieutenant-governor, without the consent of the council, shall have full power to nominate the persons to succeed to the offices, who shall hold their commissions during the pleasure of his Majesty.

That from the first day of Aug. 1774, no meeting shall be called by the select men, or at the request of any number of freeholders of any township, without the leave of the governor, or, in his absence, of the lieutenant-governor, in writing, expressing the special business of the meeting, first had and obtained, except the annual meeting in the months of March or May, for the choice of select men, constables, and other officers, or except for the choice of persons to fill up the offices on the death or removal of any of the persons first elected to such offices, &c.

That from thenceforth, the jurors to serve at the superior courts of judicature, general gaol-delivery, &c. shall be summoned and returned by the sheriff of the respective counties within the said province.

That the constables shall, at the general sessions of the peace, deliver to the justices of the peace a true list of the names and places of abode of all persons within the respective towns for which they serve, qualified to serve upon juries; which justices, or any two of them, at the sessions, shall cause to be delivered a duplicate of the lists, by the clerk of the peace of every county, to the sheriffs, or their deputies, within ten days after such sessions; and cause each of the lists to be fairly entered into a book by the clerk of the peace; and no sheriff shall impannel or return any person or persons to serve upon any grand jury, or petit jury, in any of the courts, that shall not be named or mentioned in such list: and, to prevent a failure of justice, through the neglect of constables to make such returns of persons qualified to ferve on juries, the clerks of the peace of the counties are hereby commanded, twenty days at leaft next before the month of September, yearly, to iffue forth precepts to the conftables of the feveral towns, requiring them to make fuch returns of perfons qualified to ferve upon juries as hereby directed ; and every conftable, failing at any time to make fuch return to the juftices in open court, fhall forfeit the penalty of five pounds Sterling.

That no perfon who fhall ferve as a juror fhall be liable to ferve again as a juror for the fpace of three years, except upon fpecial juries.

That if, by reafon of challenges, or otherwife, there fhall not be a fufficient number of jurors ; then the jury fhall be filled up de talibus circumftantibus, to be returned by the fheriff, unlefs he be a party, or interefted or related to any party or perfon interefted in fuch profecution or action.

That in cafe any perfon, fummoned to ferve upon the grand or petit jury, fhall not ferve according to his fummons, he fhall be fined in any fum not exceeding ten pounds, nor lefs than twenty Shillings Sterling.

The names of the jurors are to be drawn out of a box or glafs, and if any of them are challenged by the parties, other names to fupply their places are to be drawn out under the direction of the fheriff. All perfons applying for fpecial juries are to defray the expences occafioned by the trial ; and if any action be brought againft the fheriff for any thing he fhall do by virtue of this act, he may plead the general iffue, and, if a verdict be found for him, recover treble damages.

An Abftract of an Act for the impartial Adminiftration of Juftice in the Cafes of Perfons queftioned for

any Acts done by them in the Execution of the Law, or for the Suppreffion of Riots, in the Province of the Maffachufett's-bay.

THIS act declares, That if any inquifition, or indictment, fhall be found, or if any appeal fhall be preferred againft any perfon, for murther, or other capital offence, in the province of Maffachufett's-bay, and it fhall appear, by information given upon oath to the governor, or to the lieutenant-governor, that the fact was committed by the perfon againft whom fuch indictment fhall be found, either in the execution of his duty as a magiftrate, for the fuppreffion of riots, or in the fupport of the laws of revenue, or in acting in his duty as an officer of revenue, or in acting under the direction and order of any magiftrate, for the fuppreffion of riots, or for the carrying into effect the laws of revenue, &c. and if it fhall alfo appear, to the fatisfaction of the faid governor, or lieutenant-governor, that an indifferent trial cannot be had within the province, it fhall be lawful for the governor, or lieutenant-governor, to direct, with the advice of the council, that indictment fhall be tried in fome other of the colonies, or in Great-Britain ; and, for that purpofe, to order the perfon againft whom fuch indictment fhall be found to be fent, under fufficient cuftody, to the place appointed for his trial, or to admit fuch perfon to bail, taking a recognizance, from fuch perfon, with fufficient fureties, in fuch fums of money as the governor, or the lieutenant-governor, fhall deem reafonable, for the perfonal appearance of fuch perfon at the place appointed for trial.

And, to prevent a failure of juftice, from the want of evidence on the trial of any fuch indictment, &c. the governor is authorized to bind in recognizances to his Majefty all fuch witneffes as the profecutor, or perfon againft whom fuch

judgment fhall be found, fhall defire to attend the trial of the indictment, for their perfonal appearance, at the time and place of fuch trial, to give evidence : and the governor fhall appoint a reafonable fum to be allowed for the expences of every fuch witnefs.

The witneffes are to be free from all arrefts, during their journey to any trial, and till they return home.

All perfons brought before juftices, &c. accufed of any capital crime, in the execution of their duty, may be admitted to bail, and may poftpone their trials, in order to the matter being heard in another colony.

When the governor directs the trial to be in any other colony, he is to tranfmit the indictment, &c. to the governor of fuch other colony, who is to caufe it to be delivered to the chief juftice, who fhall immediately proceed upon trial ; and if the governor directs the trial to be in Great-Britain, he is to tranfmit the indictment to one of the fecretaries of the ftate, who is to direct it to be filed in the court of King's-Bench ; and if any fuch indictment be accounted bad, from any error, or defect, the fame fhall be quafhed, and a new indictment preferred. This act to take effect on the firft day of June, 1774, and to continue in force during the term of three years.

Abftract of the Bill for the Government of Quebec.

THE act for making more effectual provifion for the government of the province of Quebec, in North-America, extends the province Southward to the banks of the Ohio, Weftward to the banks of the Miffifippi, and Northward to the boundary of the Hudfon's bay company.

By the firft claufe, the proclamation of October 7, 1763, is to be void after the firft of May, 1774.

By the second clause, the Romish clergy are to have the exercise of their religion, subject to the King's supremacy, as established by the first of Queen Elizabeth; and may enjoy and receive their accustomed dues and rights from persons professing the Romish religion; with a proviso that his Majesty shall not be disabled from making such provision for the support and maintenance of a Protestant clergy, as he shall think fit.

By the third clause, all Canadian subjects, except religious orders and communities, are to hold all their properties, &c. as if the proclamation had not been made; and all controversies relative to property and civil rights, are to be determined by the Canada laws now in being, or such as may be hereafter enacted by the governor, lieutenant-governor, and legislative council, as hereafter described, with a proviso that such persons who have a right to alienate goods, lands, or credits, in their life-time, may bequeath them to whom they will at their death; and also is not to extend to lands granted, or that may be granted by his Majesty in common soccage.

By the fourth clause, the criminal law of England is instituted, subject to such amendments as may hereafter be made by the legislative powers hereafter described.

By the fifth clause, after giving the reason a legislative authority is appointed, consisting of persons resident there, not less than seventeen, nor more than twenty-three, to be appointed by his Majesty, with the advice of his Privy-council, under his or their sign manual, to make ordinances for the government of the province, with a prohibition from laying on taxes; and also every ordinance, &c. made, is to be transmitted to his Majesty, and if disallowed by his Majesty, every ordinance, &c. is to cease upon his Majesty's order in council being promulgated at Quebec; provided likewise, that no ordi-

nance touching religion, inflicting any greater punishment than fine, or imprisonment for three months, shall be valid till it receives his Majesty's approbation; and provided also, that no ordinance shall be passed at any meeting of council, except between January 1, and May 1, unless upon some urgent occasion, when every member of council resident at Quebec, or within fifty miles thereof, is to be personally summoned by the governor, or by the lieutenant governor, or commander in chief in his absence, to attend the same.

By the sixth and last clause, his Majesty and successors may erect any courts criminal, civil, and ecclesiastical, within the province of Quebec, by letters patent under the great seal, whenever his Majesty shall judge necessary.

...

The Lords Protest against the Bill for better regulating the Government of the Province of Massachuset's Bay.

Die Mercurij, 11° Maij, 1774.

THE order of the day being read for the third reading of the bill, intituled, " An Act for the better regulating the Government of the Province of the Massachuset's Bay, in New-England;" and for the Lords to be summoned;

The said bill was accordingly read the third time.

Moved, That the bill, with the amendments, do pass.

Which being objected to,

After a long debate,

The question was put thereupon. It was resolved in the affirmative.

Contents	69	} 92
Proxies	23	
Not contents	20	} 20
Proxies	0	

DISSENTIENT,

Because this bill, forming a principal part in a system of punishment and regulation, has been carried through the house without a due regard to those indispensible rules of public proceeding, with-

out the observance of which no regulation can be prudently made; and no punishment justly inflicted. Before it can be pretended, that those rights of the colony of Massachuset's Bay, in the election of counsellors, magistrates, and judges, and in the return of jurors, which they derive from their charter, could with propriety be taken away, the definite legal offence, by which a forfeiture of that charter is incurred, ought to have been clearly stated and fully proved; notice of this adverse proceeding ought to have been given to the parties affected; and they ought to have been heard in their own defence. Such a principle of proceeding would have been inviolably observed in the courts below. It is not technical formality, but substantial justice. When therefore the *magnitude* of such a cause transfers it from the cognizance of the inferior courts, to the high judicature of parliament, the Lords are so far from being authorised to reject this equitable principle, that we are bound to an extraordinary and religious strictness in the observance of it. The subject ought to be indemnified by a more liberal and beneficial justice in parliament, for what he must inevitably suffer by being deprived of many of the *forms* which are wisely established in the courts of ordinary resort for his protection against the dangerous promptitude of arbitrary discretion.

2dly, Because the *necessity* alledged for this precipitate mode of judicial proceeding cannot exist. If the numerous land and marine forces, which are ordered to assemble in Massachuset's Bay, are not sufficient to keep that single colony in any tolerable state of order, until the cause of its charter can be fairly and equally tried, no regulation in this bill, or in any of those hitherto brought into the House, are sufficient for that purpose; and we conceive, that the mere celerity of a decision against the charter of that province, will not reconcile the minds of the people to that mode of government which is to be established upon its ruins.

3dly, Because Lords are not in a situation to determine how far the regulations of which this bill is composed, agree or disagree with those parts of the constitution of the colony that are not altered, with the circumstances of the people, and with the whole detail of their municipal institutions. Neither the charter of the colony nor any account whatsoever of its courts and judicial proceedings, their mode, or the exercise of their present powers, have been produced to the house. The slightest evidence concerning any one of the many inconveniencies, stated in the preamble of the bill to have arisen from the present constitution of the colony judicatures, has not been produced, or even attempted. On the same general allegations of a declamatory preamble, any other right, or all the rights of this or any other public body, may be taken away, and any visionary scheme of government substituted in their place.

4thly, Because we think, that the appointment of all the members of the council, which by this bill is vested in the crown, is not a proper provision for preserving the equilibrium of the colony constitution. The power given to the crown of occasionally increasing or lessening the number of the council on the report of governors, and at the pleasure of ministers, must make these governors and ministers masters of every question in that assembly; and by destroying its freedom of deliberation, will wholly annihilate its use. The intention avowed in this bill, of bringing the council to the platform of other colonies, is not likely to answer its own end; as the colonies, where the council is named by the crown, are not at all better disposed to a submission to the practice of taxing for supply without their consent,

than this of Massachuset's Bay. And no pretence of bringing it to the model of the English constitution can be supported, as none of those American councils have the least resemblance to the House of Peers. So that this new scheme of a council stands upon no sort of foundation, which the proposers of it think proper to acknowledge.

5thly, Because the new constitution of judicature provided by this bill is improper, and incongruous with the plan of the administration of justice in Great Britain. All the judges are to be henceforth nominated (not by the crown) but by the governor; and all (except the judges of the superior court) are to be removable at his pleasure, and expressly without the consent of that very council which has been nominated by the crown.

The appointment of the sheriff is by the will of the governor only, and without requiring in the person appointed any local or other qualification; that sheriff, a magistrate of great importance to the whole administration and execution of all justice, civil and criminal, and who in England is not removable even by the royal authority, during the continuance of the term of his office, is by this bill made changeable by the governor and council, as often, and for such purposes as they shall think expedient.

The governor and council, thus intrusted with powers, with which the British constitution has not trusted his majesty and his privy-council, have the means of returning such a jury in each particular cause, as may best suit with the gratification of their passions and interests. The lives, liberties, and properties of the subject are put into their hands without controul; and the invaluable right of trial by jury is turned into a snare for the people, who have hitherto looked upon it as their main security against the licentiousness of power.

6thly, Because we see in this bill the same scheme of strengthening the authority of the officers and ministers of state, *at the expence of the rights and liberties of the subject*, which was indicated by the inauspicious act for shutting up the harbour of Boston.

By that act, which is immediately connected with this bill, the example was set of a large important city, (containing vast multitudes of people, many of whom must be innocent, and all of whom are unheard) by an arbitrary sentence, deprived of the advantage of that port, upon which all their means of livelihood did immediately depend.

This proscription is not made determinable on the payment of a fine for an offence, or a compensation for an injury; but is to continue until the ministers of the crown shall think fit to advise the king in council to revoke it.

The legal condition of the subject (standing unattainted by conviction, for treason or felony) ought never to depend upon the arbitrary will of any person whatsoever.

This act, unexampled on the records of parliament, has been entered on the journals of this house as voted *nemine dissentiente*, and has been stated in the debate of this day, to have been sent to the colonies, as passed without a division in either house, and therefore as conveying the uncontroverted universal sense of the nation.

The despair of making effectual opposition to an *unjust* measure, has been construed into an approbation of it.

An unfair advantage has been taken on the final question for passing that penal bill, of the absence of those Lords, who had debated it for several hours, and strongly dissented from it on the second reading; that period on which it is most usual to debate the principle of a bill.

If this proceeding were to pass without animadversion, Lords might think themselves obliged to reiterate their debates, at every stage of every bill which they oppose, and to make a formal division whenever they debate.

7thly, Because this bill, and the other proceedings that accompany it, are intended for the support of that unadvised scheme of taxing the colonies, in a manner new, and unsuitable to their situation and constitutional circumstances.

Parliament has asserted the authority of the legislature of this kingdom, supreme and unlimited, over all the members of the British empire.

But the legal extent of this authority furnishes no argument in favour of an unwarrantable use of it. The sense of the nation on the repeal of the stamp act was, *that in equity and sound policy, the taxation of the colonies for the ordinary purposes of supply, ought to be forborn;* and that this kingdom ought to satisfy itself with the advantages to be derived from a flourishing and increasing trade, and with the free grants of the American assemblies; as being far more beneficial, far more easily obtained, less oppressive, and more likely to be lasting, than any revenue to be acquired by parliamentary taxes, accompanied by a total alienation of the affections of those who were to pay them. This principle of repeal was nothing more than a return to the ancient standing policy of this empire. The unhappy departure from it, has led to that course of shifting and contradictory measures, which have since given rise to such continued distractions; by which unadvised plan, new duties have been imposed in the very year after the former had been repealed; these new duties afterwards in part repealed, and in part continued, in contradiction to the principles upon which those repealed were given up; all which, with many weak, injudicious, and precipitate steps taken to enforce a compliance, have kept up that jealousy, which on the repeal of the stamp act was

subsiding; revived dangerous questions, and gradually estranged the affections of the colonies from the mother country, without any object of advantage to either. If the force proposed should have its full effect, that effect we greatly apprehend may not continue longer than whilst the sword is held up. To render the colonies permanently advantageous, they must be satisfied with their condition. That satisfaction we see no chance of restoring, whatever measures may be pursued, except by recurring, in the whole, to the wise and salutary principles on which the stamp act was repealed.

Richmond,	Rockingham,
Portland,	Abergavenny,
Abingdon,	Leinster,
King,	Craven,
Effingham,	Fitzwilliam.
Ponsonby,	

The Lords Protest against the Bill, for the impartial Administration of Justice, in certain specified Cases, in the Province of Massachuset's Bay.

Die Mercurij, 18° *Maij,* 1774.

THE order of the day being read for the third reading of the bill, intituled, " An Act for the impartial Administration of Justice in the Cases of Persons questioned for any Acts done by them in the Execution of the Law; or for the Suppression of Riots and Tumults in the Province of the Massachuset's Bay, in New-England;" and for the Lords to be summoned;

The said bill was accordingly read a third time.

Moved, that the bill do pass; Which being objected to, After a long debate, The question was put, whether this bill shall pass?

It was resolved in the affirmative.

Contents — 43

Not contents — 12

DISSENTIENT,

1st, Because no evidence what-

soever has been laid before the house, tending to prove, that persons acting in support of public authority, and indicted for murder, cannot receive a fair trial within the province, which is the object of this bill. On the contrary, it has appeared, that an officer of the army, charged with murder, has there received a fair and equitable trial, and been acquitted. This fact has happened even since the commencement of the present unhappy dissentions.

2dly, Because, after the proscription of the port of Boston, the disfranchisement of the colony of Massachuset's Bay, and the variety of provisions which have been made in this session for new modelling the whole polity and judicature of that province, this bill is an humiliating confession of the weakness and inefficacy of all the proceedings of parliament. By supposing that it may be impracticable, by any means that the public wisdom could devise, to obtain a fair trial there for any who act under government, the house is made virtually to acknowledge the British government to be universally odious to the whole province. By supposing the case, that such trial may be equally impracticable in every other province of America, parliament does in effect admit that its authority is, or probably may, become hateful to all the colonies. This, we apprehend, is to publish to the world, in terms the most emphatical, the little confidence the supreme legislature reposes in the affection of so large and so important a part of the British empire. If parliament believed that any considerable number of the people in the colonies were willing to act in support of British government, it is evident that we might safely trust the persons so acting to their fellow colonists for a fair trial for acts done in consequence of such support. The bill, therefore, amounts to a declaration that the house knows *no means of retaining the colonies in due obedience, but by an army rendered independent of the ordinary course of law in the place where they are employed.*

3dly, Because we think that a military force, sufficient for governing upon this plan, cannot be maintained without the inevitable ruin of the nation.

Lastly, Because this bill seems to be one of the many experiments towards an introduction of essential innovations into the government of this empire. The virtual indemnity provided by this bill for those who shall be indicted for murders committed under colour of office, can answer no other purpose. We consider that to be an indemnity which renders trial, and consequently punishment impracticable. And trial is impracticable when the very governor, under whose authority acts of violence may be committed, is impowered to send the instruments of that violence to three thousand miles distance from the scene of their offence, the reach of their prosecutor, and the local evidence which may tend to their conviction. The authority given by this bill to compel the transportation from America to Great Britain, of any number of witnesses at the pleasure of the parties prosecuting and prosecuted, without any regard to their age, sex, health, circumstances, business or duties, seems to us so extravagant in its principle, and so impracticable in its execution, as to confirm us further in our opinion of the spirit which animates the whole system of the present American regulations.

Richmond,   Portland,
Fitzwilliam,   Craven,
Ponsonby,   Leinster,
Rockingham,   Manchester.

• • •

Protest of the Lords.
Die Mercurii, 30ᵒ Novembri, 1774.

THE lord chancellor reported his majesty's speech, and the same being read by the clerk,

Moved, that an humble address be presented to his majesty, to return his majesty the thanks of this house for his most gracious speech from the throne.

To declare our abhorrence and detestation of the daring spirit of resistance and disobedience to the laws, which so strongly prevails in the province of the Massachuset's Bay, and of the unwarrantable attempts in that and other provinces of America, to obstruct, by unlawful combinations, the trade of this kingdom.

To return his majesty our humble thanks for having been pleased to communicate to us, that he has taken such measures, and given such orders, as his majesty hath judged most proper and effectual for the protection and security of the commerce of his majesty's subjects, and for carrying into execution the laws, which were passed in the last session of the late parliament, relative to the province of the Massachuset's Bay.

To express our entire satisfaction in his majesty's firm and stedfast resolution to continue to support the supreme authority of the legislature over all the dominions of his crown, and to give his majesty the strongest assurances that we will chearfully co-operate in all such measures, as shall be necessary to maintain the dignity, safety, and welfare of the British empire.

That as this nation cannot be unconcerned in the common interest of Europe, we have the greatest satisfaction in being acquainted with the conclusion of the peace between Russia and the Porte; that we confide in his majesty's endeavours to prevent, as far as possible, the breaking out of fresh disturbances; and from the assurances given to his majesty by other powers, we have the pleasing expectation that nothing is likely to intervene that may interrupt the present happy tranquillity in Europe.

That it is no less our duty than our inclination to proceed with temper and unanimity in our deliberations and resolutions, and to inculcate, by our example, a due reverence for the laws, and a just sense of the excellency of our constitution; and, impressed with the deepest gratitude for the many blessings we have enjoyed during the course of his majesty's reign, to testify with unaffected zeal at this conjuncture our inviolable fidelity to his majesty, and our serious attention to the public welfare.

Then an amendment was proposed to be made to the said motion, by inserting, after the word *throne,* at the end of the first paragraph, these words:

To desire his majesty would be graciously pleased to give direction for an early communication of the accounts which have been received concerning the state of the colonies, that we may not proceed to the consideration of this most critical and important matter, but upon the fullest information; and when we are thus informed, we shall, without delay, apply ourselves with the most earnest and serious zeal, to such measures as shall tend to secure the honour of his majesty's crown, the true dignity of the mother country, and the harmony and happiness of all his majesty's dominions.

Which being objected to,
After long debate,

The question was put, whether these words shall be inserted in the said motion?

It was resolved in the negative.

Contents   —   13 }
Non contents   —   63 }

DISSENTIENT,

Because we cannot agree to commit ourselves with the *careless facility of a common address of compliment,* in expressions, which may lead to measures in the event fatal to the lives, properties, and liberties of a very great part of our fellow subjects.

We conceive that an address upon such objects as are before us, and at such a time as this, must necessarily have a considerable influence upon our future proceedings; and must impress the public with an idea of the general spirit of the measures which we mean to support.

Whatever methods we shall think it adviseable to pursue, either in support of the mere authority of parliament, which seems to be the sole consideration with some, or for reconciling that authority with the peace and satisfaction of the whole empire, which has ever been our constant and invariable object, it will certainly add to the weight and efficacy of our proceedings, if they appear the result of full information, mature deliberation, and temperate enquiry.

No materials for such an enquiry have been laid before us; nor have any such been so much as promised in the speech from the throne, or even in any verbal assurance from ministers.

In this situation we are called upon to make an address, arbitrarily imposing qualities and descriptions upon acts done in the colonies, of the true nature and just extent of which we are as yet in a great measure unapprized; a procedure which appears to us by no means consonant to that purity which we ought ever to preserve in our judicial, and to that caution which ought to guide us in our deliberate capacity.

2. Because this address does, in effect, imply an approbation of the system adopted with regard to the colonies in the last parliament. This unfortunate system, conceived with so little prudence, and pursued with so little temper, consistency, or foresight, we were in hopes, would be at length abandoned, from an experience of the mischiefs which it has produced, in proportion to the time in which it was continued, and the diligence with which it has been pursued; a system which has created the utmost confusion in the colonies, without any rational hope of advantage to the revenue, and with certain de-

triment to the commerce of the mother country. And it affords us a melancholy prospect of the disposition of lords in the present parliament, *when we see the house, under the pressure of so severe and uniform an experience, again ready, without any enquiry, to countenance, if not to adopt, the spirit of the former fatal proceedings.*

But whatever may be the mischievous designs, or the inconsiderate temerity, which leads others to this desperate course, we wish to be known as persons who have ever disapproved of measures so pernicious in their past effects, and their future tendency, and who are not in haste, without enquiry or information, to commit ourselves in declarations which may precipitate our country into all the calamities of a civil war.

Richmond,	Torrington,
Portland,	Ponsonby,
Rockingham,	Wycombe,
Stamford,	Camden.
Stanhope,	

Notes, 1774

1. Many of the new members elected in the 1768 general election had tended to vote with the Opposition. By the beginning of 1774 however, fifteen of them supported the Court party. J. Brooke, *The Chatham Administration* (London and New York, 1956, p. 352.) From among those defectors the loss of able speakers like Charles Cornwall (1735–89) and Lord George Germain (see "Notes, 1776," n. 43) was much regretted by the Rockingham group—though neither had been a consistent Rockingham adherent.

2. In 1772, the Government implemented the aim of the Townshend Act of 1767, as stated in its unrepealed preamble, and applied it to Massachusetts; the governor and judges of the Superior Court were to have their salaries paid by the Crown from the American revenues.

3. Lieutenant William Dudingston.

4. Governor Joseph Wanton (1705–80) offered a reward of £100 on 12 June; the proclamation of the subsequent board of inquiry offered a £500 reward.

5. Thirteen letters were sent by Benjamin Franklin to the Speaker of the Massachusetts Assembly, six were written by Thomas Hutchinson, then Lieutenant-Governor; four by Andrew Oliver, then the colony's Secretary; the remaining three by lesser officials. All the letters were dated between May 1767 and October 1769, and all but one were addressed to Thomas Whately, onetime Secretary to the Treasury but then holding no office. The principals involved and historians later give differing versions of how the letters came into Franklin's possession. The *Register* tends to follow, in part, the explanation given in the *Boston News-Letter* for 28 April 1774.

6. The *Register* reflects the attitude of the Rockingham group, which had opposed North's Regulatory Act of 1773. In fact, the act was very far from bringing the East India Company "... entirely under the direction of government." See, for example, Lucy S. Sutherland, *The East India Company in Eighteenth-Century Politics* (Oxford, 1952), chs. 9, 10.

7. The company approached Hutchinson's sons Thomas and Elisha, as well as the firms of Richard Clarke & Sons, and Benjamin Faneuil, Jr., to act as consignees.

8. The act of 1770 regulating procedure for the decision of disputed elections by Parliament was made permanent in 1774, despite the opposition of the Government.

9. In 1628, an angry London crowd beat to death a Dr. Lambe, an astrologer and quack doctor reported to be the unpopular Duke of Buckingham's personal wizard. Despite direct instructions from the

The Annual Register—1774

King, the City authorities failed to apprehend those responsible; consequently, a heavy fine was imposed and payed in quotas from each of the City companies. (North's memory is therefore at fault—the incident took place in the reign of Charles I, not Charles II.) In 1725, popular reaction to the malt tax in Glasgow led a hostile mob to sack the house of Daniel Campbell, M.P. for Glasgow Burghs, who supported the malt bill. The city was obliged to pay £6080 in compensation. The following year, John Porteous, Captain of the City Guard, who had earlier ordered his men to fire on a hostile crowd, was lynched by an irate Edinburgh mob. The city was fined £2000.

10. Frederick Bull (c. 1714–84), Lord Mayor, 1773–74, and M.P. for the City, 1773–84.

11. 14 Geo. III c. 19.

12. Lord North.

13. The bill received the royal assent 20 May, to become 14 Geo. III c. 45.

14. Rose Fuller (?1708–77), M.P. for Rye and wealthy Jamaican planter, generally voted with the Court party but consistently opposed coercion toward America.

15. The bill received the royal assent 20 May, to become 14 Geo. III c. 39.

16. Guy Carleton (1724–1808), Governor and Commander-in-Chief of Quebec, later (1786) 1st Baron Dorchester. Francis Masères (1731–1824), Attorney-General of Quebec 1766–69. James Marriott (1730?–1803), Advocate-General from 1764, knighted 1778, when made a judge of the Vice-Admiralty Court. William Hey (Hay) (1733–97), Chief Justice of Canada from 1766. The Chevalier Michel Chartier de Lotbinière, whose landholdings were affected by the boundaries to be established by the Quebec Act.

17. Of the four Windward Islands ceded by France to Britain by the Peace of Paris (1763), Grenada alone had a sizable population of French settlers (about 3500). The terms of the surrender of the island, in 1762, and of the peace treaty guaranteed protection of the possessions of those that chose to remain under British rule (many did not). In 1765, those Frenchmen who had been confirmed in possession of their lands and had taken an oath of allegiance were permitted by the governor to vote in elections for the assembly. In 1768, the Privy Council both confirmed their voting rights and permitted French Catholics, without subscribing to the Anglican "test," in limited numbers to sit on the council, be elected to the assembly, act as J.P.s, and have an appointment in the Court of Judicature. However, the English settlers protested these concessions and prevented their full implementation until 1770. In 1779, shortly before Grenada was recaptured by France, Governor George Macartney (1737–1806) felt the whole policy had been a mistake: "It was imagined that such favour might have ensured their gratitude, and that our kindness would have been repaid by the natural returns of Duty and Affection; We however find ourselves cruelly mistaken; They have disappointed every good expectation that was formed of them. . . . They have retained most of the ill qualities of their own nation, without acquiring the good ones of ours, and at the end of seventeen Years, there is scarcely one of the whole adopted race whom government can venture to confide in." P.R.O. CO/101/23, pp. 95–96. See also "Notes, 1779," no. 89.

18. The bill received the royal assent 22 June, to become 14 Geo. III c. 83.

19. The phrase was used by George III in his first speech from the throne, 18 November 1760.

20. For the colonial affiliations of these signatories, compare those of the Association of the American Congress, pp. [217–18], which are grouped by delegation. Two signatories to the petition not among those for the Association are P[hilip] Livingston (New York) and J[ohn] D. Hart (New Jersey). F. Pendleton is a misprint for E[mund] Pendleton.

21. Peyton Randolph (?1721–75). A prominent Virginia politician since the 1750s, he was basically conservative in outlook but achieved a unique position of authority in the Virginia patriot party. Speaker of the House of Burgesses, and Chairman of the Virginia Committee of Correspondence in 1773, he was elected first President of the Continental Congress, resigned the post for reasons of health in October 1774, resumed it in May 1775, but died two weeks later.

22. Marchese Cesare di Beccaria Bonesana (1739–94), *Dei Delitti e delle Pene.* The quotation is taken from a contemporary English translation, *An Essay on Crimes and Punishments, Translated from the Italian, with a Commentary attributed to M. De Voltaire, Translated from the French* (London: J. Almon, 1767), intro. p. 1.

23. Charles de Secondat, Baron de Montesquieu (1689–1755). This and the following quotations from *De L'Esprit des Lois* do not conform precisely to the most popular contemporary English translation, that of Thomas Nugent (2 vols., London, 1752), and therefore may well be taken from the French. A popular edition available at the time was *Oeuvres de Monsieur de Montesquieu, Nouvelle edition, revue, corrigé et considérablement augmenti par l'auteur* (Amsterdam and Leipsig: Arkstée and Merkus, 1757). The quotation is from Livre 19, ch. 27, p. 438, of this edition.

24. Ibid., Livre 11, ch. 6, p. 211.

25. Ibid., p. 208.

26. Ibid., p. 210.

27. Ibid., p. 208.

28. Ibid., Livre 19, ch. 27, p. 437.

29. Ibid., p. 435. It should be noted that the quotations above are taken out of context, some have portions of the original omitted and are juxtaposed out of the original order to give a specific effect. Livre 11, ch. 17, is that part of *De L'Esprit des Lois* in which Montesquieu praises the *English* constitution as that embodying political liberty.

30. Henry Middleton (1717–84), prominent South Carolina politician, conservative in outlook but opposed to British policy from 1770; President of the Continental Congress, 22 October 1774–10 May 1775.

1775

Introduction

During the fall of 1774, the Government was forced to recognise that the policy of coercion, far from ensuring the submission of the colonies, had produced unprecedented resistance. Gage's reports at first convinced Dartmouth that conciliation was the only practical approach, but they convinced the King and most of the Cabinet of precisely the opposite: that failure to show firmness would at once be viewed by the Americans as a surrender to their claims for political autonomy. Therefore, the North ministry put together a new set of measures during the Christmas recess. These provided that Gage's troops be reinforced (and galvanised into decisive action); that the navy in American waters be strengthened; that the colonies have an embargo placed on their trade with foreign nations; and, finally, that Parliament might waive the right of direct taxation if each colony voted a permanent provision to pay for its administration and defence.[1] This combination of a threat of force with a hint of compromise partly reflected divisions in the Cabinet but it also conformed to North's notions of a flexible strategy, not just because it might be successful in America, but because it might broaden his support in Parliament.

On 19 January, the Prime Minister laid a selection of the American papers before the Commons, and Dart-

---

1. Bernard Donaghue, *British Politics and the American Revolution: The Path to War, 1773–75* (London, 1964), pp. 219–26.

mouth presented them to the Lords on the following day. The ensuing debates continued until 27 March. On 20 January, Chatham launched a general attack on the Government's American policy and proposed the withdrawal of troops from Boston as a gesture of goodwill. On 1 February, he proposed a comprehensive plan for a settlement based on conciliation. The plan asserted British sovereignty but denied Britain the power to tax the colonies without their consent. It proposed repeal of most of the legislation objectionable to Americans and the recognition of the Philadelphia Congress. In turn, Chatham expected the Congress to formally recognise parliamentary sovereignty and to grant American revenues, to alleviate the national debt. All the ministers in the Lords except Dartmouth condemned the plan outright, while Camden and the Rockinghams supported it (although the Rockinghams opposed the plan's implicit repeal of the Declaratory Act). The motion was defeated by a majority of two to one. Some historians have condemned Parliament's shortsightedness and praised Chatham's vision, but Chatham virtually ensured the dismissal of his startling proposals by failing (as usual) to prepare the ground.[2] Moreover, it is likely that the moderate leadership in America would have accepted the voluntary taxation clause, and certainly the radicals would have rejected formal recognition of parliamentary sovereignty.

North was now ready to introduce the Government's policy. He first neatly headed off the manufacturing towns' attempt to pressure the Government with petitions for a settlement with America by referring the petitions to a committee separate from the committee of the whole, which was due to consider American affairs. The petitions were thus quietly buried.[3] Then on 2 February, North proposed an address to the Crown which would declare Massachusetts to be in a state of rebellion, abetted by other colonies, and would ask the King to take appropriate action. The Opposition strongly denied that any colony was in rebellion and claimed the disorders were the product of Government policy, but the address was approved by a solid majority. The Opposition tried to

2. Chatham told Rockingham of his intentions only on 31 January and then gave no details.
3. The London petition was presented on 23 January, when the decision to hear them separately was taken; further petitions were presented at intervals, up to 15 March.

have the address recommitted on 6 February and in a long and vigorous debate argued that it would force the Americans to fight. The motion was lost and the address passed the Lords, after a recriminatory debate, the following day. Eighteen Opposition peers then entered a formal protest condemning the address as "amounting to a declaration of war." On 10 February, North secured a motion to bring in a bill restraining the trade of New England with foreign powers and her participation in the fishery. On 13 February, two thousand extra seamen were voted for the year, and Secretary at War Barrington asked for funds for four thousand more soldiers on 15 February.

The final part of the ministry's policy package was introduced on 20 February, when North offered his Conciliation Resolution. It was proposed that if any colony permanently provided the costs of its administration and defence, Britain would forbear to levy taxes, except those for the regulation of trade, and the net profits from those would be credited to the colony. North believed this was a nice compromise, since it offered a concession while implicitly asserting parliamentary sovereignty. The Prime Minister however had made the same mistake as Chatham; he had failed to prepare the ground. Many Government supporters thought the resolution contradicted the coercion policy and thus indicated weakness. Some thought it would humiliate the King, whose views on coercion were well known. The Opposition condemned the resolution as a fraud, and argued that it was an attempt to divide the Americans and blackmail them into recognising parliamentary supremacy. For a while, confusion among the Government's supporters made the Opposition's attack especially dangerous, until Sir Gilbert Elliot rallied Government support with a crisp speech which showed the compatibility of the resolution with the policy as a whole. Actually, North's replies in the debate revealed that the Opposition's criticisms were largely correct. In terms of the American situation, the resolution was more irrelevant than Chatham's motion. However, the motion passed the committee of the whole by 274 to 88 and was adopted without a division when it was reported back.

The New England restraining bill moved inexorably through the Commons despite sustained Opposition attacks. It was debated on 6 and 8 March, passed the Lords after a dire warning from Camden that it would provoke war,[4] and became law on 30 March (15 Geo. III c. 10). North had hinted on 19 February that the act might have to be followed by another directed at the southern colonies, and on 9 March he moved to extend the bill's provisions to New Jersey, Pennsylvania, Maryland, Virginia, and South Carolina. He argued that despatches revealed these colonies to be in rebellious support of the Association of the Philadelphia Congress. New York and North Carolina were excluded because they had failed to support the Association and because there were other vague signs of loyalty. This bill passed its third reading on 5 April and was approved by the Lords on 13 April. It became law as 15 Geo. III c. 18.

The debate over the second bill produced the most significant Opposition statement of the year, Burke's speech on conciliation on 22 March. The speech was prepared with great care, took two and a half hours to deliver, and was received with great applause. Burke refused to consider Parliament's right to tax America, saying: "The question with me is, not whether you have the right to make your people miserable; but whether it is not your interest to make them happy." He quoted impressive (and accurate) statistics to show the value of American trade to Britain. He analysed the special factors which produced a marked spirit of liberty in America and argued that it was necessary as a concession to that spirit to abandon parliamentary taxation of the colonies in favour of a system of grants made by the colonial assemblies. He insisted that there was no evidence that a concession would be followed by demands to repeal the trade laws. Burke proposed thirteen resolutions: the first six outlined the American issues as he saw them; the next five called for repeal of the post-1767 legislation which was obnoxious to the Americans; and the last two called for colonial judges to hold office during good behavior and for reform of the Vice-Admiralty Courts. Burke's speech was suffused by appeals to a concept of empire based on common traditions, interests, and loyalties, rather than on theories of subordination and the restraints of law.

The House of Commons probably agreed with some of Burke's practical points, but it was unconvinced that

---

4. *Parliamentary History*, vol. 18, 436–46. Sandwich ridiculed the notion of Americans actually fighting British regulars and proposed that the act be made permanent. Ibid., 446–47.

changes in the mode of raising colonial revenue would affect the real issue—American refusal to accept Parliament's sovereign legislative power. Burke believed imperial unity was essential, but the Government and its majority did not accept Burke's theories as a basis for unity. For them, the only ultimately reliable and unifying factor was a sovereign British Parliament. They believed the American rebellion had begun a drift toward anarchy which could not be arrested by concessions that obscured parliamentary sovereignty. As for the Americans, in any negotiations on Burke's proposals, they would probably have required major modifications in the trade laws, abolition of the Vice-Admiralty Courts, and a redefinition of Parliament's powers.

Burke's appeal was followed by other attempts at conciliation. David Hartley suggested on 27 March that American revenue could be raised by free grants from the colonial assemblies under letters of requisition from the Crown, approved by Parliament. Hartley's motion was rejected as were four more presented by him later. In a surprisingly direct attack, the Lord Mayor and aldermen of the City of London presented a remonstrance to the King on 10 April which deplored the Government's American policy and asked for the dismissal of the ministry. They received a stinging rebuke for their temerity.

When Parliament reassembled after the Easter recess it drifted through routine business until the end of the session; only two items relating to America emerged. On 15 May, Burke, acting as agent for New York, tried to present a remonstrance which claimed loyalty to the Crown yet supported New England and produced a list of grievances. North promptly opposed reception of the remonstrance by the House, since it defied the Declaratory Act;[5] a similar memorial to the House of Lords was also thrown out. Camden presented a petition from the Protestant settlers in Quebec on 17 May and used it to condemn virtually every aspect of the Quebec Act, whose repeal he then moved. Dartmouth defended the act vigorously and secured the rejection of the motion. Sir George Savile made a similar unsuccessful motion for repeal in the Commons the following day. The session closed on 26 May; three days later news of Lexington and Concord appeared in the London papers.

5. There was, of course, a nice irony in North's invoking the Rockinghams' Declaratory Act against Burke.

The time lag in transatlantic communications was particularly significant in 1775.[6] Events overtook policy, and the policymakers continued to pursue vanished goals in ignorance. Dartmouth wrote to Gage on 27 January to inform him that the Government intended to restore order in Massachusetts, by force if necessary. Dartmouth rejected Gage's view that twenty thousand troops would be required and implicitly criticised Gage's failure to take decisive action. Gage was instructed to arrest the rebel political leaders, prevent the training of militia, and seize local stores of armaments.[7] The latter instruction was however held in London until 27 February and did not reach Gage until 16 April. Gage had long been convinced that decisive action would provoke armed conflict with most of the local population, and he was not prepared to take the responsibility until he received specific orders. Having received them, on the night of 18 April, he ordered an expedition to seize a store of arms and powder at Concord. Messengers from Boston relayed the alarm, and at daybreak on 19 April the British advance guard was met by a small force of "minutemen" at Lexington. Firing broke out which left eight Americans dead and ten wounded.[8] The British force moved on to Concord and after finding nearly all the munitions removed, again exchanged fire with the locals. The British then marched back to Boston, harassed every mile by the local militia. The arrival of a relief force and the inaccuracy of American fire prevented a rout, but the British force nonetheless suffered 273 casualties.[9] By 23 April, Boston was under

6. The irreducible time lag produced by contemporary transportation limitations should not be confused with delays consequent on error or procedure. Nor, as far as government was concerned, should the time lag be assumed to be the same for England to America as for America to England. One estimate suggests that, at the beginning of the eighteenth century, news could reach Massachusetts from an unofficial source in England in forty-five days, while a governor's report from the colony might take an average time of sixty-three days to reach the ministry. I. K. Steele, "Time, Communications and Society: The English Atlantic, 1702," *Journal of American Studies*, 1974, vol. 8, pp. 1–21.

7. *Correspondence of General Thomas Gage with the Secretaries of State and with the War Office and the Treasury, 1763–1775*, Yale Historical Publications, Manuscripts and Edited Texts, xi–xii, ed. C. E. Carter, 2 vols. (New Haven, Conn., 1931–33), vol. 2, pp. 179–81.

8. Despite vast literature on this the first armed engagement of the war, the question of which side fired first remains undecided.

9. Christopher Ward, *The War of the Revolution*, ed. and comp. J. R. Alden, 2 vols. (New York, 1952), vol. 1, p. 50.

siege by several thousand militia, and the civil war had
begun.

The Massachusetts Provincial Congress learned of
North's address, the New England restraining bill, and
the despatch of reinforcements to Gage on 3 April. Like
most of the emerging colonial popular governments, the
Massachusetts congress was split between moderates and
radicals, a split involving attitudes toward both the imperial relationship and toward the colony's own political
and social structure.[10] The congress therefore moved un-
certainly and cautiously, by refusing to commit itself to
raising an army to oppose Gage and by actually adjourning on 15 April. Lexington and Concord showed how far
the congress lagged behind popular sentiment. The
chairman of the Committee of Public Safety, Joseph Warren, provided leadership on 19 April and immediately
after, by producing a circular letter which presented the
situation as a product of ruthless British aggression which
required the creation of a provincial army. He organised
reports, carefully including atrocity stories, to influence
British public opinion. The provincial congress hastily
reassembled on 23 April, made Warren acting president,
and voted to raise an army.[11] Some of the leaders advocated caution, but the assemblies in Rhode Island and
Connecticut at once voted to raise armies (which
amounted to recognition of the unofficial action of their
militia units). Outside New England, news of the fighting
provoked political demonstrations in New York City, and
the western counties in Pennsylvania began raising forces
despite the extreme caution of the colony's leadership.
South Carolina organised for its own defence. The real
impetus for American resistance, however, came from the
Continental Congress.

The Congress reassembled on 10 May and immediately
revealed a deep division between advocates of reconciliation with Britain on the basis of recognition of American
rights and those supporting autonomy for the colonies,
who were beginning to consider complete independence.
The Congress had no planned policy, and thus its actions

10. For a new analysis of political divisions in the colony in this period,
    see S. E. Patterson, *Political Parties in Revolutionary Massachusetts*
    (Madison, Wis., 1973).
11. The colony's other top leaders—the two Adamses, Hancock, and
    Cushing—were about to depart as delegates to the Philadelphia
    Congress.

were largely the product of inner tensions and the pressure of external events.

The Congress began by considering an appeal for help from Massachusetts. But on 18 May, news of the capture of Fort Ticonderoga was received,[12] and the Congress was obliged to endorse that embarrassing aggression. On 25 May, the Congress directed New York to prepare its defences against a possible British attack. The following day, North's Conciliation Resolution was referred to discussion in committee, and on 29 May the Congress approved a letter to the French inhabitants of Quebec designed to secure their support. Another urgent letter from Massachusetts pushed the Congress into authorising that colony to recreate its own legal government and on 14 June, the Congress ordered Maryland, Virginia, and Pennsylvania to raise six companies of riflemen to join the Continental Army. On 15 June, George Washington was appointed commander-in-chief of the army "raised or to be raised"—largely at the instigation of John Adams, who was anxious to secure the commitment of the southern colonies to a united American response to the hostilities begun in New England. The appointment of other general officers became an orgy of political bargaining which continued until 22 June.[13] Congress also voted on that date to raise two million Spanish dollars on bills of credit for American defence. The Congress thus had taken decisive steps toward assuming the powers of a national government.

Events again overtook colonial deliberations. Gage was reinforced with troops, including Major-Generals Howe, Clinton, and Burgoyne, and fresh instructions dated 15 February ordering him to take more decisive action. Gage's effective power was limited to the improvement of Boston's defences by occupying the hills north and south of the town. American military leaders were informed of Gage's intention, and they ordered the seizure of Bunker Hill on the Charlestown peninsula to the south. The American soldiers occupied Breed's Hill instead, and Gage dislodged them after a bloody engagement which cost him 1,054 casualties. Burke wrote to a friend: "Two such victories, as Mrs. B. observes after Pyrrhus, would ruin

12. See "Notes, 1775," n. 76.
13. See "Notes, 1775," n. 87.

General Gage."[14] Bunker Hill (as history has irrevocably named it) was not only a pyrrhic victory for Gage, it convinced Americans that effective resistance against the British army was possible.[15]

The Continental Congress heard of the battle on 22 June. In response, Washington was sent to command the army in Massachusetts on the twenty-third, Schuyler was dispatched to Ticonderoga to prepare an invasion of Canada on the twenty-seventh, and articles of war were adopted on 30 June. The Congress was therefore committed to a war with goals not yet declared. The Declaration of the Causes and Necessity of Taking Up Arms was adopted on 6 July, yet on the eighth another petition to the King (drafted by the conservative John Dickinson) was approved. This petition blamed the ministers for the conflict and prayed for direct royal intervention to end it; the petition was then despatched together with a justificatory appeal to the people of Britain. The moderates still hoped for reconciliation, but Congress intensified the trade embargo, appointed Franklin (who returned from England on 5 May) as postmaster-general of the "United Colonies," and recommended that each colony prepare its military defences. North's Conciliation Resolution was rejected on 13 July, and on 21 July so was a proposal for a confederation of the colonies and another for opening the ports to foreign trade in retaliation against the Restraining Acts.[16] The deep divisions within the Congress delayed a declaration of independence for another year.

News of these events reached Britain in stages during the long summer parliamentary recess. The Government tried to dismiss the first reports of Lexington and Concord (printed in the London newspapers on 29 May) as American propaganda (which to some extent they were), but official despatches received from Gage on 10 June re-

14. Burke to Charles O'Hara, 26 July 1775, in *The Correspondence of Edmund Burke*, ed. Thomas W. Copeland, 9 vols. (Cambridge and Chicago, 1961–70), vol. 3 (ed. G. H. Gutteridge), p. 182. Gage has been much criticised for ordering a frontal assault instead of adopting Clinton's plan to cut off the Americans from the rear by an amphibious operation. There were, however, good military arguments for a direct attack on a hastily prepared position defended by militia, and Gage could not have anticipated from previous experience the qualities of officer leadership and fire discipline shown by the Americans. Howe at the time thought Clinton's plan impractical.
15. See "Notes, 1775," n. 84.
16. See "Notes, 1775," n. 89.

vealed the seriousness of the situation. The Government had believed it could wait until the new session of Parliament in October to respond to the American reaction to North's policy measures. But when the Cabinet met on 15 and 21 June it was forced to recognise that Britain was at war. On hearing of the capture of Ticonderoga and Crown Point on 26 July, the Government decided to raise twenty thousand troops. Barrington doubted that this could be managed, even by sending Hanoverian garrisons to Gibralter and Minorca, thus releasing British soldiers to serve in Ireland, so that troops there could be sent to America. The King and the majority of the Cabinet were however determined to crush the American rebellion by using whatever military force was necessary. Otherwise, they believed they would be acquiescing in the disintegration of the empire.

Parliament met on 26 October, and Rockingham at once challenged the King's speech, which had referred to the American rebellion as aiming at independence; he proposed an amendment to the reply, which blamed the disorders on the ministry's measures and called for a policy review, in the light of full information, to prevent civil war. The amendment was outvoted, and nineteen peers signed a formal protest. A similar amendment in the Commons, introduced by Lord John Cavendish, was also decisively rejected, as was a motion to recommit it the following day. The Opposition then tried to hamstring Barrington's plan for sending troops to America by claiming that the use of Hanoverian troops in any of the dominions of the Crown without consent of Parliament was unconstitutional. This tactic was defeated in the Lords on 1 November and in the Commons on the third. On 10 November, North replaced Dartmouth, as Secretary of State for the Colonies, with Lord George Germain, an energetic politician who strongly supported punitive policies towards America.[17] On the same day, the Opposition in the House of Lords moved to use a petition brought from the Continental Congress by Richard Penn[18] as a basis for conciliation. The motion was inevitably defeated after a vigorous debate.

Burke tried to bring in a bill on 16 November which would have allowed the Continental Congress to arrange

17. See "Notes, 1776," n. 43.
18. See "Notes, 1775," n. 91.

American revenues, while confining Britain to regulating colonial trade. He added many of the propositions in his speech of 22 March, but he accepted an implicit modification of the Declaratory Act, since his bill would formally deny Parliament the right of taxing America.[19] In many ways, the bill offered a more realistic solution to the original imperial problems than Burke's earlier proposals, and it was so recognised by the House.[20] The majority, however, was no longer prepared to think in terms of concessions.

On 21 November, North moved for a bill to replace the Restraining Acts with legislation prohibiting all trade with America, and at the same time giving the Crown commissioners authority to pardon any colony and restore its trade if it submitted to Britain. North also proposed abandoning parliamentary taxation of the colonies if they would offer an alternative method of paying for their administration and defence. The Opposition fought the prohibitory bill in both Houses, terming it an act of war which treated America as a foreign state. Nonetheless, it passed with substantial majorities and became law on 26 December (16 Geo. III c. 5).

The year closed with Britain and America committed to hostilities. The Opposition in Parliament had predicted the slide into war but failed to prevent it, partly because of its own disunity and weak leadership but also because the majority considered Opposition arguments to be unrealistic. The North government had been guilty on occasion of using the American issue for party-political ends, but to the majority the Government's determination to restore imperial unity by force seemed to be the only practical solution.

The *Register* for 1775—a year particularly eventful from the historian's viewpoint—presented a full and detailed account of both Britain's and America's situation. The much delayed date of publication (6 September 1776) permitted the editor to incorporate material on America which would have been available in England only after

19. *Parliamentary History*, vol. 18, 963–78.
20. Burke's motion was defeated 210 to 105. The *Register* notes: "This was the highest proportion in numbers which the opposition had hitherto borne to the majority." *AR*, 1776, p. [109.

the late summer of 1775.[21] The dominance of the American issue in British politics is reflected in the historical section, which doubled in size from 1774—of the 158 pages, 142 are devoted to the Anglo-American crisis. One chapter only deals with European affairs (notably the Spanish-Moroccan war, disturbances in the Austrian Empire, and the aftermath of the recent war in Russia and Turkey).

The first three chapters deal with the period after the summer of 1774, which was not covered in the previous volume. Chapter I describes the disintegration of royal government in Massachusetts, the emergence of the provincial congress, and the growth of resistance in other colonies. There are some errors in dating and in the order of events in the colonies other than Massachusetts, but the account nonetheless reveals sound sources of information. Chapter II reviews the activities of the Continental Congress. There were no public reports of congressional debates, so the *Register*'s account is based on items the Congress published—for this reason, Galloway's plan of union is not mentioned. Chapter III records the pre-Christmas parliamentary session and provides a sound analysis of the decision to call a general election in the fall of 1774. It also reveals North's anxiety in trying to postpone a discussion of American affairs until a fresh policy had been worked out by the Cabinet, and the impotence of the Opposition. The next four chapters cover, in unprecedented detail, parliamentary affairs from January to the summer recess. These chapters are thus an important supplement to other sources of information on these debates. The *Register*, as usual, presents the arguments of each side separately, without reference to the order of speakers, so its narrative tends to obscure the pattern of the debate and give a force to the Opposition which was actually denied it by its disunity and numerical weakness.

21. The editor offers no explanation in the preface for the delay in publication (except to refer to the importance of events "... having delayed us to a much greater length than usual"). The delay may have been the result of the death of John Campbell and a hiatus until Walker King's assistance was arranged. Alternately, it may reflect the heavy pressures of the year on Burke, assuming that he was still preparing the historical section (see "General Introduction.") From this point on, however, the delay in publication increases, until by 1783 it amounts to nineteen months after the May deadline maintained from 1758 to 1767.

However, the high quality of the debates is evidenced throughout.

Chapter VIII details events in America up to mid-summer. The excellent account of Lexington and Concord only omits mention of the role played by the messengers despatched by Joseph Warren on the night of 18 April to warn the locals. It judiciously notes that whether British or American fired the first shot was ". . . a matter of little consequence, in a political view, as things were now too far advanced to leave for a probable hope of any other than such a final issue." The *Register* then accepts however that the evidence pointed to British responsibility. The atrocity stories produced by both sides are rejected as equally unlikely exaggerations. The report of the activities of the Continental Congress again derives from its published statements and therefore gives no hint of internal disunity.

The *Appendix to the Chronicle* for 1775 consists almost entirely of minor news items not connected with the American crisis,[22] together with the list of parliamentary supplies for the year and the ways and means account. The *State Papers* consists of fourteen items, and only one (the Address of the Chief Governor to the Irish Parliament) is not abstracted here. These items include Parliament's address to the Crown of 9 February; the protest of the dissenting peers and the King's reply of 10 February; the speeches from the throne of 26 May and 26 October; and a selection of the more important petitions and addresses from the City of London, the Lord Mayor, aldermen, and London merchants. American papers from the Continental Congress include the Declaration of the Causes and Necessity of Taking Up Arms and the second petition to the King. Franklin's proposals for a colonial confederation are erroneously described as "Articles entered into" and incorrectly dated 20 May 1775.[23]

22. One exception might be the short report (pp. [239–[242] on the extraordinary Sayre case. Stephen Sayre was an American, resident in London, associated with Wilkes and the City radicals; he was Sheriff, 1773–74. On 23 October 1775, Sayre was arrested on a charge of treason, accused of attempting to bribe one Francis Richardson, an Adjutant in the Guards, to assist him in seizing the King and overthrowing the Government. His accuser, Richardson, was himself also an American by birth. Sayre successfully sued the Secretary of State, Lord Rochford, for false arrest. *AR*, 1776, pp. [53–[55.

23. See "Notes, 1775," n. 89.

Of all the volumes since 1765, the *Register* for 1775 seems to show most the influence of Burke, if not his actual hand (the preface is particularly Burkean). But even if this remains a matter of supposition, the historical section, despite its overall impartiality in reporting the parliamentary debates, betrays a consistent Rockingham viewpoint. For example, the opening of Chapter III deplores the failure of the merchants to regard the American situation as critical. This attitude denied the Rockinghams the chance to repeat their politically successful tactical alliance of 1765–1766. Similarly, in Chapter IV, the attention paid to North's device of consigning the petitions from the trading and manufacturing towns to what Burke described as a "Committee of oblivion" reflects the Opposition's anger at being outmanoeuvered.

Again in Chapter III, the use by Wilkes and the radicals of "tests" for parliamentary candidates in the general election of 1774 is given prominence, and the condemnation of the test is in accord with Burke's well-known views on the subject. Burke's major speeches—on American taxation and on conciliation—receive detailed attention, but no more than their importance warrants (in the case of the speech on American taxation, perhaps less). The treatment of events in America, however, shows a fairly consistent underestimation of the gulf between Britain and the colonies. Chapter II is overly optimistic about the residual loyalty of the colonies, specifically in the estimation of their willingness to continue accepting regulation of trade along traditional lines. Chapter VIII shows a reluctance, despite the accurate reporting, to recognise that the Massachusetts Provincial Congress was a revolutionary government effectively in control of the colony. The Americans are seen as enjoying a "unanimity" which was "amazing" and throughout showing "a firm determination of resistance" by methods which could not be approved, but, by implication, were comprehensible in the light of the treatment the Americans had received. To present the case otherwise would have been to admit that reconciliation was impossible and civil war inevitable.

PREFACE.

IT was not without regret that we found the diffentions between this country and its colonies at length ripened into a civil war. The perfon to whofe lot it falls to defcribe the tranfactions of domeftic hoftility, and the fteps which lead to it, has a painful, and generally unthankful office. People can fcarcely judge with temper of fuch an hiftory in a century after the events. It is a perilous fituation when we are to be tried by prefent paffions. Interefted as we are in this conteft in common with all Englifhmen, and affected as we muft be in common with all men of humanity, we have never been tempted to depart from the fteady courfe of impartiality, which we have always obferved, and in which the public has hitherto fupported us. It indeed little becomes us to be dogmatical and decided in our opinions in this matter, when the public, even on this fide of the water, is fo much divided; and when the firft names of the country have differed fo greatly in their fentiments. It is no longer our tafk to defcribe devaftation in Poland, or flaughter on the Danube. The evil is at home.

We are as truly fenfible of the importance as of the delicacy of the fubject. The fenfe of that importance, which is fomething more than was generally apprehended even when the transactions in parliament were passing, has obliged us to a much greater length than usual. We have given every thing as fully as we were enabled to do from any materials we could obtain. However we may have failed in the attempt, neither application nor labour were wanting on our side, nor expence considered on that of the publisher, in endeavouring to render the work worthy of the acceptance of the public.

. . . .

IT happens most unfortunately this year, that our own public affairs not only take the lead among those of Europe, but have in a great degree absorbed all other matter of political speculation. A cessation seems to take place in the animosities and designs of other states. The great disturbers of mankind appear to forget their rapacity and ambition, whilst they contemplate the new and unthought-of spectacle we exhibit to the world, and perhaps eagerly predict the advantages which they may derive from its fatal consequences.

It need scarcely be mentioned, that the unhappy contest in which we are involved with our colonies, is the event which has thus excited the attention of mankind. Those colonies, which were so long our strength and our glory, whose rapid growth and astonishing increase [1] mocked the calculations of politicians, and outstripped the speculations of philosophers; those colonies, which equally excited the apprehensions of our enemies, and the envy of our friends, still attract the eyes of the world, to them and to us, as to a common center; but present a very different appearance of things to observation. Happy will it be, if this general attention is productive of no other sentiment, than the admiration which arises from novelty, or the generous sympathy which feels for the miseries of mankind.

The penal laws, which we saw passed, in the last session of the last parliament, relative to the colony of Massachusett's Bay, and which were intended to operate both as a chastisement for past, and a preventative of future misdemeanors in that province, were unfortunately productive of effects very different from those which the sanguine promoters of those bills had hoped, and which administration had held out to the nation. Other purposes were expected from them besides punishment and prevention. It was expected, that the shutting up of the port of Boston would have been naturally a gratification to the neighbouring towns, from the great benefits which would accrue to them, by the splitting and removing of its commerce; and that this would prove a fruitful source of jealousy and disunion within the province. It was also thought, that the particular punishment of that province would not only operate as an example of terror to the other colonies, but that from the selfishness and malignity incident to mankind, as well as from their common jealousies, they would quietly resign it to its fate, and enjoy with pleasure any benefits they could derive from its misfortunes. Thus it was hoped, that besides their direct operation, these bills would eventually prove a means of dissolving that band of union, which seemed of late too much to prevail amongst the colonies.

The act called the Military Bill, [2] which accompanied these laws, and which was formed to support and encourage the soldiery in beating down all possible resistance to the other acts, it was imagined, would compleat the design, and bring the colonies to a perfect submission. In confidence of the perfection of this plan of terrors, punishments and regulations, and of the large force by sea and land (as it was then thought) which was sent to strengthen the hands of government, administration reposed in the most perfect security; and ended the session in the most triumphant manner, and with the mutual congratulations of all concerned in those acts, which may be well remembered, and which we have described in our last volume.

The event, in all these cases, was however very different. The neighbouring towns disdained every idea of profiting in any degree by the misfortunes of their friends in Boston. The people of the province, instead of being shaken by the coercive means which were used for their subjugation, joined the more firmly together to brave the storm; and seeing that their ancient constitution was destroyed, and that it was determined to deprive them of those rights, which they had ever been taught to revere as sacred, and to deem more valuable than life itself, they determined at all events to preserve them, or to perish in the common ruin. In the same manner, the other colonies, instead of abandoning, clung the closer to their devoted sister as the danger increased; and their affection and sympathy seemed to rise in proportion to her misfortunes and sufferings.

In a word, these bills, (as had been too truly foretold by their opposers at home) instead of answering the purposes for which they were intended, spread a general alarm from one end to the other of the continent, and became the cement of a strict and close union between all the old colonies. They said it was now visible, that charters, grants, and established usages, were no longer a protection or defence; that all rights, immunities, and civil securities, must vanish at the breath of an act of parliament. They were all sensible, that they had been guilty, in a greater or lesser degree, of those unpardonable sins which had drawn down fire upon Boston; they believed, that vengeance, tho' delayed, was not remitted; and that all the mercy, the most favoured or the least culpable could expect, was to be the last that would be devoured.

It may be remembered in the last session, that the minister had announced in the House of Commons, the appointment of General Gage[3] to the government of the province of Massachusett's Bay, and to the command in chief of the army in North-America. As this gentleman had borne several commands with reputation in that part of the world; had lived many years there, and had sufficient opportunities of acquiring a thorough knowledge of the people, and was besides well approved of by them, great hopes were formed of the happy effects which would have resulted from his administration; and it is little to be doubted, if his appointment had been at a happier time, and his government free from the necessity of enforcing measures which were generally odious to the people, but these expectations would have been answered.

The jealousy and ill blood between the governors and governed in the province of Massachusett's Bay, which we have formerly taken notice of, had ever since continued. The House of Representatives had presented a petition and remonstrance to the Governor, early in the spring, for the removal of Peter Oliver, Esq; Chief Justice of the Superior Court of Judicature, from his office; this request not being complied with, they exhibited articles of impeachment against him, of high crimes and misdemeanors, in their own name and that of the province, which they carried up to the Council-board, and gave the governor notice to attend as judge upon the trial. The charge against the Chief Justice was, the betraying of his trust, and of the chartered rights of the province, by accepting a salary from the crown, in consideration of his official services, instead of the customary grant from the House of Representatives. The resolution for carrying up this impeachment was carried by a majority of 92 to 8; from whence some judgment may be formed of the general temper of the province, and their unanimity, even in this strong and extraordinary measure.

The Governor refused to receive the articles, and totally disclaimed all authority in himself and the Council to act as a judicatory, for the trial of any crimes or misdemeanors whatever. The House of Representatives, far from giving up the matter, only changed their mode of attack; and the Governor finding that they would persist in a prosecution under some form or other, and that every new attempt would only serve to involve things in still greater difficulty, or at least to increase the animosity, thought it necessary, at the conclusion of the month of March, to dissolve the Assembly.

Such was the state of things in the province of Massachusett's Bay, when Gen. Gage arrived in his government. The hopes that might have been formed upon a change of administration, and the **May 13th, 1774.** joy that generally attends the coming of a new Governor, were, however, nipped in the bud, by the arrival just before of a ship from London, which brought a copy of the Boston Port Bill; and a Town-Meeting was sitting to consider of it, at the very time he arrived in the harbour. As this fatal news[4] was totally unexpected, the consternation which it caused among all orders of people was inexpressible. The first measure was the holding of the Town-Meeting we have mentioned, at which resolutions were passed, and ordered to be immediately transmitted to the other colonies, inviting them to enter into an agreement to stop all imports and exports to and from Great-Britain and Ireland, and every part of the West-Indies, until the act was repealed, as the only means (they said) that were left for the salvation of North-America and her liberties. They besides expatiated on the impolicy, injustice, inhumanity, and cruelty of the act, and appealed from it to God and the world.

In the mean time, copies of the act were multiplied with incredible expedition, and dispatched to every part of the continent with equal celerity. These had the effect which the poets ascribe to the Fury's torch; they set the countries in a flame through which they passed. At Boston and New-York, the populace had copies of the bill printed upon mourning-paper with a black border, which they cried about the streets under the title of a barbarous, cruel, bloody, and inhuman murder. In other places, great bodies of the people were called together by public advertisement, and the obnoxious law burned with great solemnity.

There was, however, a very surprising mixture of sobriety with this fury; and a degree of moderation was blended with the excess into which the people were hurried.

This extraordinary combustion in

the minds of all ranks of the people did not prevent the Governor's being received with the usual honours at Boston. The new Assembly of the province met of course a few days after, the Council, for the last time, being chosen according to their charter. The Governor [5] at their meeting laid nothing more before them than the common business of the province; but gave them notice of their removal to the town of Salem, on the first of June, in pursuance of the late act of parliament. The Assembly, to evade this measure, were hurrying through the necessary business of the supplies with the greatest expedition, that they might then adjourn themselves to such time as they thought proper; but the Governor having obtained some intelligence of their intention, adjourned them unexpectedly to the 7th of June, then to meet at Salem. Previous to this adjournment, they had presented a petition to the Governor, for appointing a day of general prayer and fasting, which he did not think proper to comply with.

In the mean time, Provincial or Town-meetings were held in every part of the continent; in which, tho' some were much more temperate than others, they all concurred in expressing the greatest disapprobation of the measures which were pursued against Boston, an abhorrence of the new act, and a condemnation of the principles on which it was founded, with a resolution to oppose its effects in every manner, and to support their distressed brethren, who were to be the immediate victims.

The House of Burgesses, of the province of Virginia, appointed the 1st of June, the day on which the Boston Port Bill took place, to be set apart for fasting, prayer, and humiliation, to implore the Divine interposition, to avert the heavy calamity which threatened destruction to their civil rights, with the evils of a civil war; and to give one heart and one mind to the

people, firmly to oppose every injury to the American rights. This example was either followed, or a similar resolution adopted, almost every where, and the 1st of June became a general day of prayer and humiliation throughout the continent.

This measure, however, procured [6] the immediate dissolution of the Assembly of Virginia; but before their separation, an association was entered into and signed by 89 of the members, in which they declared, that an attack made upon one colony, to compel submission to arbitrary taxes, was an attack on all British America, and threatened ruin to the rights of all, unless the united wisdom of the whole was applied in prevention. They therefore recommended to the committee of correspondence, to communicate with the several committees of the other provinces, on the expediency of appointing deputies from the different colonies, to meet annually in General Congress, and to deliberate on those general measures, which the united interests of America might, from time to time, render necessary. They concluded with a declaration, that a tender regard for the interests of their fellow-subjects the merchants and manufacturers of Great-Britain, prevented them from going further at that time.

At Philadelphia, about 300 of the inhabitants immediately met, [7] and appointed a committee to write to the town of Boston. Their letter was temperate, but firm. They acknowledged the difficulty of offering advice upon that sad occasion; wished first to have the sense of the province in general; observed, that all lenient applications for obtaining redress should be tried before recourse was had to extremities; that it might perhaps be right to take the sense of a General Congress, before the desperate measure of putting an entire stop to commerce was adopted; and that it might be right, at any rate, to

reserve that measure as the last resource, when all other means had failed. They observed, that if the making of restitution to the East-India Company for their teas, would put an end to the unhappy controversy, and leave the people of Boston upon their ancient footing of constitutional liberty, it could not admit of a moment's doubt what part they should act; but it was not the value of the tea, it was the indefeasible right of giving and granting their own money, a right from which they could never recede, that was now the matter in consideration.

A Town-meeting was also held [8] at New-York, and a committee of correspondence appointed; but they were as yet, in general, very temperate in their conduct; and Government had a much stronger interest in that colony than in any other. The case was far different [9] at Annapolis in Maryland, where the people of that city, though under a proprietary government, exceeded the other colonies in the violence of their resolutions; one of which was to prevent the carrying on of any suits in the courts of the province, for the debts which were owing from them in Great-Britain. This resolution, however, was neither adopted nor confirmed by the Provincial meeting which was held soon after; nor was it any where carried into practice.

In general, as might have been expected in such great commercial countries, the proposal for shutting up the ports (former resolutions of this kind having been much abused for the private gain of individuals) was received with great seriousness, hesitation, and coldness; and considered as the last desperate resort, when all other means of redress should fail. In other respects, upon the arrival of the news from Boston, moderation was little thought of any where, and the behaviour of the people was nearly similar in all places. At the numberless public meetings which were held upon that occasion, throughout the continent, they passed every resolution, and adopted every measure they could for the present think of, to shew their utmost detestation of the Boston Port bill, and to express their determination of opposing its effects in every possible manner.

In this state of general dissatisfaction, complaint, and opposition, General Gage had the temporary satisfaction of receiving an address of congratulation, signed by 127 gentlemen, merchants and inhabitants of Boston, who were either the best addicted to government, the most moderate, or to whom the present measures seemed the least obnoxious. Besides the compliments customary upon these occasions, a declaration of the strong hopes which they had founded upon the General's public and private character, and a disavowal, as to themselves, of all lawless violences, they lamented, that a discretionary power was not lodged in his hands, to restore trade to its former course, immediately, upon the terms of the late law being fully complied with; and shewed, that as the act stood at present, notwithstanding the most immediate compliance, so much time would be lost, before his favourable account of their conduct could reach the King and Council, and produce the wished-for effect, as would involve them in unspeakable misery, and they feared in total ruin.

A few days after, an address from the Council was presented to the Governor, which contained some very severe reflections on his two immediate predecessors, to whose machinations, both in concert and apart, that body attributed the origin and progress of the disunion between Great-Britain and her colonies, and all the calamities that afflicted that province. They declared, that the people claimed no more than the rights of Englishmen, without diminution or abridgment; and these, as it was the indispensable duty of that board, so it should be their constant endeavour

to maintain, to the utmost of their power, in perfect consistence, however, with the truest loyalty to the crown, the just prerogatives of which they would ever be zealous to support.

This address was rejected by the Governor, who would not suffer the chairman of the committee to proceed any further, when he had read the part which reflected on his predecessors. He afterwards returned an answer to the Council in writing, in which he informed them, that he could not receive an address which contained indecent reflections on his predecessors, who had been tried and honourably acquitted by the Privy Council, and their conduct approved by the King, That he considered the address as an insult upon his Majesty, and the Lords of his Privy Council, and an affront to himself.

The House of Representatives, [10] upon their meeting at Salem, passed a resolution, in which they declared the expediency of a general meeting of committees from the several colonies, and specified the purposes which rendered such meeting necessary. By another, they appointed five gentlemen, of those who had been the most remarkable in opposition, as a committee to represent that province. And by a third, they voted the sum of 500 l, to the said committee, to enable them to discharge the important trust to which they were appointed.

As neither this appointment, nor disposal of the public money, could be at all agreeable to the Governor, he accordingly refused his concurrence to the latter; upon which the assembly passed a resolution, to recommend to the several towns and districts within the province, to raise the said 500 l. by equitable proportions, according to the last provincial tax. A recommendation, which, at present, had all the force of a law.

The Assembly foreseeing that their dissolution was at hand, were determined to give the people a public testimony of their opinions,

and under the title of recommendations to prescribe rules for their conduct, which they knew would be more punctually complied with, than the positive injunctions of laws. They accordingly passed a declaratory resolution, expressive of their sense of the state of public affairs, and of the designs of government, in which they advanced, that they, with the other American colonies, had long been struggling under the heavy hand of power; and that their dutiful petitions for the redress of intolerable grievances had not only been disregarded; but that the design totally to alter the free constitution and civil government in British America, to establish arbitrary governments, and to reduce the inhabitants to slavery, appeared more and more to be fixed and determined. They then recommended in the strongest terms to the inhabitants of the province, totally to renounce the consumption of India teas, and, as far as in them lay, to discontinue the use of all goods imported from the East-Indies and Great-Britain, until the public grievances of America should be radically and totally redressed. And the more fully to carry this essential purpose into effect, it was strongly recommended, that they should give every possible encouragement to the manufactures of America.

Though the committee, that was appointed to conduct this business, endeavoured to carry it on with the greatest privacy, the Governor, notwithstanding, obtained some intelligence of it, and on the very day upon which they made their report, he sent his Secretary to pronounce their immediate dissolution. The Secretary, upon his arrival, finding the door locked, sent the House-messenger to acquaint the Speaker, that he had a message from the Governor, and desired admittance to deliver it. The Speaker, in some time, returned for answer, that he had acquainted the House with the message which he had received, and that their orders were to keep the door faft. Upon this refufal of admittance, the Secretary caufed proclamation to be made, upon the ftairs, of the diffolution of the General Affembly. Such was the iffue of the final conteft between the Governor of Maffachufett's Bay, and the laft Affembly which was holden in that province, upon the principles of its charter.

June 17th.

The day after the diffolution of the Affembly, a moft pathetic, but at the fame time firm and manly addrefs, was prefented from the merchants and freeholders of the town of Salem to the Governor. We cannot forget, that this town was now become the temporary capital of the province, in the place of Bofton; and that the General Affembly, the Courts of Juftice, the Cuftom-Houfe, and, fo far as it could be done by power, the trade of that port were removed thither; fo that they were already in poffeffion of a principal fhare of thofe fpoils, which it was fuppofed would have effectually influenced the conduct of that people, and thereby have bred fuch incurable envy, jealoufy and animofity, between the gainers and fufferers, that the refractory capital finding herfelf abandoned, and being left alone to ruminate upon her forlorn fituation, would foon be reclaimed, and brought to as full a fenfe of her duty, as of her punifhment.

Whether this opinion was founded upon a thorough knowledge of human nature in general, or took its rife from particular inftances, which were extended in fpeculation to the whole, may perhaps, in a certain degree, be determined from the following generous fentiments of the inhabitants of Salem. They fay, " We are deeply afflicted with a fenfe of our public calamities; but the miferies that are now rapidly haftening on our brethren in the capital of the province, greatly excite our commiferation; and we hope your excellency will ufe your endeavours to prevent a further accumulation of evils on that already

forely diftreffed people."——" By fhutting up the port of Bofton, fome imagine that the courfe of trade might be turned hither, and to our benefit; but nature, in the formation of our harbour, forbids our becoming rivals in commerce with that convenient mart. And were it otherwife, we muft be dead to every idea of juftice, loft to all feelings of humanity, could we indulge one thought to feize on wealth, and raife our fortunes on the ruin of our fuffering neighbours."

This whole addrefs is remarkable for the propriety with which it is conducted, and the juftnefs of its fentiments. They treat the governor with the higheft refpect, and hope much from his general character, as well as from his conduct in a former government; they exprefs the ftrongeft attachment to the mother country, the deepeft concern for the prefent unhappy troubles, and the moft fervent wifhes for a fpeedy and happy reconciliation, to obtain which, they are willing to facrifice every thing, compatible with the fafety and dignity of Britifh fubjects.

The general had formed confiderable hopes upon the conduct of the merchants; who he expected would have entered into the fpirit of the late law, and by removing their commerce along with the cuftom-houfe to Salem, have thereby the fooner induced the capital to the compliances which were wifhed by government. In thefe expectations he was difappointed. It is probable, that the merchants thought it fit and neceffary to keep fair with government, and in general difapproved of all violences; but it feems evident, that they did not enter heartily into the new meafures. It feems alfo probable, that he believed the friends of the fyftem of government now adopted, to be ftronger and more numerous than they really were. An experiment was however made, which fet this matter in a clear light. The friends of government

attended a town-meeting at Bofton, and attempted to pafs refolutions for the payment of the tea, and for diffolving the committee of correfpondence; but they found themfelves loft in a prodigious majority; and had no other refource, than the drawing up of a proteft againft the proceedings of that affembly.

In the mean time, rough draughts of the two remaining bills relative to the province of Maffachufett's-Bay, as well as of that for quartering the troops in America, all of which were in agitation in England, at the time that the laft fhips failed from thence, were received in Bofton, and immediately circulated throughout the continent. The knowledge of thefe bills, filled up whatever was wanting before, of violence and indignation in moft of the colonies. Even thofe who were moderate, or feemed wavering, now became fanguine. The idea of fhutting up the ports, became common language, and to be confidered as a matter of neceffity. Nothing was to be heard of, but meetings and refolutions. Liberal contributions for the relief of their diftreffed brethren in Bofton, were every where recommended, and foon reduced into practice. Numberlefs letters were written from towns, diftricts, and provinces, to the people of Bofton, in which, befides every expreffion of fympathy and tendernefs, they were highly flattered for their paft conduct, and ftrongly exhorted to a perfeverance in that virtue, which brought on their fufferings.

The people of America at this time, with refpect to political opinions, might in general be divided into two great claffes. Of thefe, one, was for rufhing headlong into the greateft extremities; they would put an immediate ftop to trade, without waiting till other meafures were tried, or receiving the general fenfe of the colonies upon a fubject of fuch alarming importance; and though they were eager for the holding of a congrefs, they would

11

leave it nothing to do, but to prosecute the violences which they had begun. The other, if less numerous, was not less respectable, and though more moderate, were perhaps equally firm. These were averse to any violent measures being adopted until all other means were ineffectually tried; they wished further applications to be made to Great-Britain; and the grievances they complained of, with the rights which they claimed, to be clearly stated, and properly presented. This, they said, could only be done effectually by a general congress, as in any other manner it might be liable to the objection of being only the act of a few men, or of a particular colony. We, however, acknowledge a third party, which were the friends to the administration in England, or more properly, those who did not totally disapprove of its measures; but their still small voice was so low, that except in a very few particular places, it could scarcely be distinguished.

The more violent, who had not patience to wait for the result of a congress, entered into other measures. An agreement was framed by the committee of correspondence at Boston, which they entitled a solemn league and covenant, wherein the subscribers bound themselves in the most solemn manner, and in the presence of God, to suspend all commercial intercourse with Great-Britain, from the last day of the ensuing month of August, until the Boston Port-Bill, and the other late obnoxious laws were repealed, and the colony of Massachusett's-Bay fully restored to its chartered rights. They also bound themselves in the same manner, not to consume, or to purchase from any other, any goods whatever, which arrived after the specified time, and to break off all commerce, trade, and dealings, with any who did, as well as with the importers of such goods. They renounced in the same manner, all

future intercourse and connection with those who should refuse to subscribe to that covenant, or to bind themselves by some similar agreement, with the dangerous penalty annexed, of having their names published to the world.

The covenant, accompanied with [12] a letter from the committee at Boston, was circulated with the usual activity, and the people, not only in the New England governments, but in the other provinces, entered into this new league with the greatest eagerness. It seems, however, that similar agreements had been entered into about the same time, in various parts of the continent, and without any previous concert with each other, any more than with those at Boston.

General Gage was much alarmed at this proceeding; to which its name, as well as its tendency, might possibly contribute. He accordingly published a June 29th. strong proclamation against it, in which it was stiled an unlawful, hostile, and traiterous combination, contrary to the allegiance due to the king, destructive of the lawful authority of the British parliament, and of the peace, good order, and safety of the community. All persons were warned against incurring the pains and penalties due to such aggravated and dangerous offences, and all magistrates charged to apprehend and secure for trial, such as should have any share in the publishing, subscribing, aiding, or abetting the foregoing, or any similar covenant.

This proclamation had no other effect than to exercise the pens and the judgment of those who were versed in legal knowledge, by endeavouring to shew, that the association did not come within any of the treason-laws, and that the charges made by the governor, were consequently erroneous, unjust, and highly injurious. They said he had assumed a power, which the constitution denied even to the

sovereign, the power of making those things to be treason, which were not considered as such by the laws; that the people had a right to assemble to consider of their common grievances, and to form associations for their general conduct towards the remedy of those grievances; and that the proclamation was equally arbitrary, odious, and illegal.

Measures were now every where taken for the holding of a general congress; and Philadelphia, from the convenience of its situation, as well as its security, was fixed upon as the place, and the beginning of September, the time for meeting. Where an assembly happened to be sitting, as in the case of Massachusett's-Bay, they appointed deputies to represent the province in the congress. But as this happened to be the case in very few instances, the general method was, for the people to elect their usual number of representatives, and these, at a general meeting, chose deputies from among themselves; the number of which, in general, bore some proportion to the extent and importance of the province; two being the least, and seven the greatest number, that represented any colony. But whatever the number of representatives were, each colony had no more than a single vote.

At these county or provincial meetings, a number of resolutions were constantly passed, among which a declaration that the Boston Port-Act was oppressive, unjust, unconstitutional in its principles, and dangerous to the liberties of America, was always among the foremost. At Philadelphia, a petition signed by near 900 freeholders was presented to Mr. Penn, the Governor, intreating him to call a general assembly as soon as possible. This request being refused, the province proceeded to the election July 15th. of deputies, who soon after met at Philadelphia. As the resolutions passed at this meeting, carry more the marks of cool and temperate deliberation, as well as of affection to the mother country, than those of many others, and are at the same time equally firm in the determination of supporting what they thought their rights, we shall be the more particular in our notice of them.

They set out with the strongest professions of duty and allegiance to the sovereign, which could be well devised; and declare their abhorrence of every idea, of an unconstitutional independence on the parent state; upon which account, they say, that they view the late differences between Great-Britain and the colonists, with the deepest distress and anxiety of mind, as fruitless to her, grievous to them, and destructive of the best interests of both. They then, after expressing the most ardent wishes for a restoration of the former harmony, declare that the colonists are entitled to the same rights and liberties within the colonies, that the subjects born in England are within that realm.

They reprobated in the strongest terms the late bills relative to the province of Massachusett's-bay, and declare that they consider their brethren at Boston, as suffering in the common cause of all the colonies. They also declare, the absolute necessity of a congress, to consult together, and to form a general plan of conduct to be observed by all the colonies, for the purposes of procuring relief for their suffering brethren, obtaining redress of their general grievances, preventing future dissentions, firmly establishing their rights, and the restoration of harmony between Great-Britain and her colonies upon a constitutional foundation.

They acknowledge, that a suspension of the commerce of that large trading province with Great-Britain, would greatly distress multitudes of their industrious inhabitants; but declare that they are ready to offer that sacrifice, and a much greater, for the preservation of their liberties; that, however, in regard to the people of Great-Britain, as well as of their own country, and in hopes that their just remonstrances might at length have effect, it was their earnest desire, that the congress should first try the gentle mode of stating their grievances, and making a firm and decent claim of redress. They conclude with warning dealers not to raise the price of their merchandize beyond the usual rates, on account of any resolutions that might be taken with respect to importation; and by a declaration, that, that province would break off all dealing and commercial intercourse whatsoever, with any town, city, or colony on the continent, or with any individuals in them, who should refuse, decline, or neglect to adopt and carry into execution such general plan as should be agreed upon in the congress.

August 1st. At a meeting of the delegates of the several counties of Virginia at Williamsburgh, which lasted for six days, besides professions of allegiance and loyalty, of regard and affection for their fellow-subjects in Great-Britain, equally strongly expressed with those which we have mentioned, and several resolutions in common with the other colonies, they passed others which were peculiar, and considering the state and circumstances of that province, with its immediate dependence on the mother country for the disposal of its only staple commodity, must be considered very deserving of attention, because strongly indicating the true spirit of that people.

Among these, they resolved not to purchase any more slaves from Africa, the West-Indies, or any other place; that their non-importation agreement should take place on the first of the following November; and that if the American grievances were not redressed by the 10th of August 1775, they would export, after that time, no tobacco, nor any other goods whatever, to Great-Britain; and to render this last resolution the more effectual, they strongly recommended the cultivation of such articles of husbandry, instead of tobacco, as might form a proper basis for manufactures of all sorts; and particularly to improve the breed of their sheep, to multiply them, and to kill as few of them as possible. They also resolved to declare those enemies to their country, who should break through the non-importation resolution. The people of Maryland, the other great tobacco colony, were not behindhand with those of Virginia in their determinations; and the two Carolinas, whose existence seemed to depend upon their exportation, were by no means among the least violent.

Thus the Boston Port-Bill and its companions, had even exceeded the prognostications of their most violent opponents. They had raised a flame from one end to the other of the continent of America, and united all the old colonies in one common cause. A similar language was every where held; or if there was any difference in the language, the measures that were adopted were every where directed to the same object. They all agreed in the main points, of holding a congress, of not submitting to the payment of any internal taxes, that were not, as usual, imposed by their own assemblies, and of suspending all commerce with the mother country, until the American grievances in general, and those of Massachusett's-Bay in particular, were fully redressed.

The people, as is always the case, were, from circumstances or temper, more or less violent in different places; but the resolution as to the great object of debate, the point of taxation, was every where the same, and the most moderate, even at New York, seemed determined to endure any evils, rather than submit to that. At Newport, in Rhode Island, the flame burned higher than in some other places; an inflammatory paper was there published, with a motto in capitals " Join or Die ;" in this piece the state of Boston was represented as a siege, and as a direct and hostile invasion of all the colonies; " the generals of despotism," it says, " are now drawing the lines of circumvallation around our bulwarks of liberty, and nothing but unity, resolution, and perseverance can save ourselves and our posterity from what is worse than death,—Slavery."

What rendered this state of affairs the more dangerous, was, that it did not arise from the discontent of a turbulent or oppressed nobility, where, by bringing over a few of the leaders, the rest must follow of course, or persist only to their ruin; nor did it depend upon the resolution or perseverance of a body of merchants and dealers, where every man habitually studious of his immediate interest, would tremble at the thought of those consequences, which might essentially affect it ; and where a few lucrative jobs or contracts, properly applied, would split them into numberless factions; on the contrary, in this instance, the great force of the opposition to government, consisted in the land-holders throughout America. The British lands in that vast continent, are generally portioned out in numberless small freeholds, and afford that mediocrity of condition to the possessors, which is sufficient to raise strong bodies and vigorous minds; but seldom that superabundance, which proves so fatal to both in old and refined countries. The American freeholders at present, are nearly, in point of condition, what the English Yeomen were of old, when they rendered us formidable to all Europe, and our name celebrated throughout the world. The former, from many obvious circumstances, are more enthusiastical lovers of liberty, than even our Yeomen were.

Such a body was too numerous to be bribed, and too bold to be despised without great danger.

In this untoward state of public affairs, General Gage had the consolation to receive a congratulatory address from the Justices of the Peace of Plymouth county, assembled at their general sessions, in which, besides the customary compliments, they expressed great concern at seeing that the inhabitants of some towns, influenced by certain persons, calling themselves committees of correspondence, and encouraged by some, whose business it was as preachers of the Gospel, to inculcate principles of loyalty and obedience to the laws, entering into a league, calculated to increase the displeasure of the sovereign, to exasperate the parent country, and to interrupt the harmony of society. A protest was also passed by several gentlemen of the county of Worcester, against all riotous disorders, and seditious practices. These efforts had however no other effect, than probably to lead the governor as well as administration into an erroneous opinion, as to the strength and number of the friends of government in that province.

Though liberal contributions were raised in the different colonies for the relief of the suffering inhabitants of Boston ; yet it may be easily conceived, that in a town, containing above 20,000 inhabitants, who had always subsisted by commerce, and the several trades and kinds of business subservient to it, and where the maintenance of numberless families depended merely upon locality, that the cutting off of that grand source of their employment and subsistence, must, notwithstanding any temporary reliefs, occasion great and numerous distresses. Even the rich were not exempt from this general calamity, as a very great part of their property consisted in wharfs, warehouses, sheds, and all those numerous erections, which are destined

to the purposes of commerce in a great trading port, and were no longer of any value.

They, however, bore their misfortunes with a wonderful constancy, and met with a general sympathy and tenderness, which much confirmed their resolution. Their neighbours, the merchants and inhabitants of the town and port of Marblehead, who were among those that were to profit the most by their ruin, instead of endeavouring to reap the fruits of their calamity, sent them a generous offer of the use of their stores and wharfs, of attending to the lading and unlading of their goods, and of transacting all the business they should do at their port, without putting them to the smallest expence ; but they at the same time exhorted them to persevere in that patience and resolution, which had ever been their characteristic.

Soon after the General's arrival in his government, two regiments [13] of foot, with a small detachment of the artillery, and some cannon, were landed at Boston, and encamped on the common, which lies within the Peninsula on which the town stands. These troops were by degrees reinforced by the arrival of several regiments from Ireland, New York, Hallifax, and at length from Quebec. It may be easily conceived, that the arrival and station of these troops, was far from being agreeable to the inhabitants; nor was the jealousy in any degree less, in the minds of their neighbours of the surrounding counties. This dissatisfaction was further increased by the placing of a guard at Boston Neck ; (which is the narrow Isthmus that joins the Peninsula to the continent), a measure of which the frequent desertion of the soldiers, was either the cause, or the pretext.

In this state, a trifling circumstance gave the people of Boston a full earnest of the support they might expect from the country in case of extremity, and an opportunity of knowing the general temper of the people. A report had been spread, perhaps industriously, that a regiment posted at the neck, had cut off all communication with the country, in order to starve the town into a compliance with any measures that might be proposed to them. Upon this vague report, a large body of the inhabitants of the county of Worcester immediately assembled, and dispatched two messengers express to Boston, to discover the truth of the intelligence. These envoys informed the town, that if the report had been true, there were several thousand armed men, ready to have marched to their assistance; and told them further, that they were commissioned to acquaint them, that even though they might be disposed to a surrender of their liberties, the people of the country would not think themselves at all included in their act. That by the late acts of the British parliament, and the bills which were pending therein, when the last intelligence was received, their charter was utterly vacated; and that the compact between Great-Britain and the colony being thus dissolved, they were at full liberty to combine together in what manner and form they thought best for mutual security.

Not long after, the governor issued a proclamation August 4th. for the encouragement of piety and virtue, and for the preventing and punishing of vice, prophaneness, and immorality. This proclamation, which was avowedly in imitation of that issued by his majesty upon his accession, seems, like most acts of government about this time, to have been wrong placed, and ill-timed. The people of that province had always been scoffed at, and reproached by their enemies, as well as by those of looser manners, for a pharisaical attention to outward forms, and to the appearances of religious piety and virtue. It is

scarcely worth an observation, that neither proclamations or laws can reach farther than external appearances. But in this proclamation " Hypocrisy" being inserted among the immoralities, against which the people were warned, it seemed as if an act of state were turned into a libel on the people; and this insult exasperated greatly the rage of minds already sufficiently discontented.

Along with the new laws, which did not arrive till the beginning of August, Governor Gage received a list of 36 new counsellors, who in conformity to the new regulations of them, were appointed by the crown, contrary to the method prescribed by the charter, of their being chosen by the representatives in each assembly. Of these gentlemen, about 24 accepted the office, which was a sufficient number to carry on the business of government, until a fresh nomination should arrive for filling up the vacancies.

Matters were now, however, unfortunately tending to that crisis, which was to put an end to all established government in the province. The people in the different counties became every day more outrageous, and every thing bore the semblance of resistance and war; in Berkshire, and Worcester counties in particular, nothing was to be seen or heard of, but the purchasing and providing of arms, the procuring of ammunition, the casting of balls, and all those other preparations, which testify the most immediate danger, and determined resistance. All those, who accepted of offices under the new laws, or prepared to act in conformity with them, were every where declared to be enemies to their country, and threatened with all the consequences due to such a character. The people of Connecticut, looking upon the fate of their neighbouring colony to be only a prelude to their own, even exceeded them in violence.

The new judges were rendered every where incapable of proceeding in their office. Upon opening the courts, the great and petty juries throughout the province, unanimously refused to be sworn, or to act in any manner, under the new judges, and the new laws. The acting otherwise was deemed so heinous, that the clerks of the courts found it necessary to acknowledge their contrition in the public papers, for issuing the warrants by which the juries were summoned to attend, and not only to declare, that let the consequences be what they may, they would not act so again; but that, they had not considered what they were doing, and that if their countrymen should forgive them, they could never forgive themselves for the fault they had committed. At Great Barrington, and some other places, the people assembled in numerous bodies, and filled the court-house and avenues in such a manner, that neither the judges nor their officers could obtain entrance; and upon the sheriff's commanding them to make way for the court; they answered, that they knew no court, nor other establishment, independent of the ancient laws and usages of their country, and to none other would they submit, or give way upon any terms.

The new counsellors were still more unfortunate than the judges. Their houses were surrounded by great bodies of the people, who soon discovered by their countenance and temper, that they had no other alternative than to submit to a renunciation of their offices, or to suffer all the fury of an enraged populace. Most of them submitted to the former condition; some had the fortune to be in Boston, and thereby evaded the danger, while others, with great risque, were pursued and hunted in their escape thither, with threats of destruction to their houses and estates.

The old constitution being taken away by act of parliament, and the new one being rejected by the people, an end was put to all forms of law and government in the province of Massachusett's-Bay, and the people were reduced to that state of anarchy, in which mankind are supposed to have existed in the earliest ages. The degree of order, however, which by the general concurrence of the people, was preserved in this state of anarchy, will for ever excite the astonishment of mankind, and continue among the strongest proofs of the efficacy of long established habits, and of a constant submission to laws. Excepting the general opposition to the new government, and the excesses arising from it, in the outrages offered to particular persons who were upon that account obnoxious to the people, no other very considerable marks appeared of the cessation of law or of government.

In the mean time, General Gage thought it necessary for the safety of the troops, as well as to secure the important post and town of Boston, to fortify the neck of land, which afforded the only communication, except by water, between that town and the continent. This measure, however necessary, could not but increase the jealousy, suspicion, and ill blood, which were already so prevalent; but was soon succeeded by another, that still excited a greater alarm. The season of the year was now arrived for the annual muster of the militia; and the general, having probably some suspicion of their conduct when assembled, or, as they pretended, being urged thereunto by those secret advisers and talebearers, to whose insidious arts, and false information, for a long time past, as well as the present, the Americans attributed all their own calamities, and the troubles that had arisen between both countries; however it was, he seized upon the ammunition and stores, which were lodged in the provincial arsenal at Cambridge, and had them brought to Boston. He also,

at the same time, seized upon the powder which was lodged in the magazines at Charles-Town, and some other places, being partly private property, and partly provincial.

This excited the most violent and universal ferment that had yet been known. The people assembled to the amount of several thousands, and it was with the greatest difficulty, that some of the more moderate and leading gentlemen of the country, were able to restrain them from marching directly to Boston, there to demand a delivery of the powder and stores, and in case of refusal to attack the troops. A false report having been intentionally spread about the same time, and extended to Connecticut, in order probably, to try the temper of that province, that the ships and troops had attacked the town of Boston, and were then firing upon it, when the pretended bearers of the news had come away, several thousands of those people immediately assembled in arms, and marched, with great expedition, a considerable distance, to the relief, as they supposed, of their suffering neighbours, before they were convinced of the mistake.

About this time, the governor's company of cadets, consisting wholly of gentlemen of Boston, and of such, in general, as had always been well affected to government, disbanded themselves, and returned to the general the standard, with which, according to custom, he had presented them upon his arrival. This slight to the governor, and apparent disrelish to the new government, proceeded immediately from his having taken away Mr. Hancock's commission, who was the colonel of that corps. A Colonel Murray of the militia, having accepted a seat in the new council, 34 officers of his regiment resigned their commissions in one day; so general was the spirit which was now gone forth.

The late measure of seizing the powder, as well as the fortifications

which were erecting on Boston-neck, occasioned the holding of an assembly of delegates, from all the towns of the county of Suffolk, of which Boston is the county town and capital. In this assembly a great number of resolutions were passed, some of which militated more strongly with the authority of the new legislature, than any that had yet appeared. They are, however, introduced by a declaration of allegiance; but they also declare it to be their duty, by all lawful means to defend their civil and religious rights and liberties; that the late acts are gross infractions of those rights; and that no obedience is due from that province, to either, or any part of those acts; but that they ought to be rejected as the wicked attempts of an abandoned administration to establish a despotic government. They engaged that the county should support and bear harmless all sheriffs, jurors, and other persons who should suffer prosecution for not acting under the present unconstitutional judges, or carrying into execution any orders of their courts; and resolved, that those who had accepted seats at the council-board, had violated the duty they owed to their country, and that if they did not vacate them within a short limited time, they should be considered as obstinate and incorrigible enemies to their country.

They also past resolutions against the fortifications at Boston-neck; the Quebec bill; for the suspension of commerce; for the encouragement of arts and manufactures; for the holding of a provincial congress; and to pay all due respect and submission to the measures which should be recommended by the Continental Congress. They recommended to the people to perfect themselves in the art of war, and for that purpose, that the militia should appear under arms once every week. That, as it had been reported, that several gentlemen who had rendered themselves conspicuous by contending for the violated rights of their country, were to be apprehended, in case so audacious a measure should be carried into execution, they recommend, that all the officers of so tyrannical a government, should be seized, and kept in safe custody, until the former were restored to their friends and families.

Then followed a recommendation, which in the present state of things amounted to a peremptory command, to the collectors of the taxes, and all other receivers and holders of the public money, not to pay it as usual to the treasurer; but to detain it in their hands, until the civil government of the province was placed on a constitutional foundation; or until it should be otherwise ordered by the Provincial Congress. They, however, declare, that notwithstanding the many insults and oppressions which they most sensibly feel and resent, they are determined to act merely on the defensive, so long as such conduct may be vindicated by reason, and the principles of self-preservation. They conclude by exhorting the people to restrain their resentments, to avoid all riots and disorderly proceedings, as being destructive of all good government; and by a steady, manly, uniform, and persevering opposition, to convince their enemies, that, in a contest so important, in a cause so solemn, *their conduct should be such as to merit the approbation of the wise, and the admiration of the brave and free, of every age, and of every country.*

They then appointed a committee to wait Sept. 9th. upon the governor, with a remonstrance against the fortifying of Boston-neck; in which they declare, that though the loyal people of that county think themselves oppressed by some late acts of the British parliament, and are resolved, by *divine assistance*, never to submit to them, they have no inclination to commence war with his majesty's troops. They impute the present extraordinary ferment in the minds of the people, besides the new for-

tification, to the seizing of the powder, to the planting of cannon on the Neck, and to the insults and abuse offered to passengers by the soldiers, in which, they say, they have been encouraged by some of the officers; and conclude, by declaring, that nothing less than a removal or redress of those grievances, can place the inhabitants of the county in that situation of peace and tranquillity, which every free subject ought to enjoy. In this address they totally disclaimed every wish and idea of independency, and attributed all the present troubles, to misinformation at home, and the sinister designs of particular persons.

To this address General Gage answered, that he had no intention to prevent the free egress and regress of any person to and from the town of Boston; that he would suffer none under his command to injure the person or property of any of his majesty's subjects; but that it was his duty to preserve the peace, and to prevent surprize; and that no use would be made of the cannon, unless their hostile proceedings should render it necessary.

Before public affairs had arrived at their present alarming state, the governor, by the advice of the new council, had issued writs for the holding of a general assembly, which was to meet in the beginning of October; but the events that afterwards took place, and the heat and violence which every where prevailed, together with the resignation of so great a number of the new mandamus counsellors, as deprived the small remainder of all efficacy, made him think it expedient to countermand the writs by a proclamation, and to defer the holding of the assembly to a fitter season. The legality of the proclamation was however called in question, and the elections every where took place without regard to it. The new members accordingly met at Salem, pursuant to the precepts; but having waited a day, without the governor, or any substitute for

him attending, to administer the oaths, and open the session, they voted themselves into a Provincial Congress, to be joined by such others as had been, or should be elected for that purpose; after which, Mr. Hancock, so obnoxious to the governor's party, was chosen chairman, and they adjourned to the town of Concord, about 20 miles from Boston.

Among their earliest proceedings, they appointed a committee to wait upon Oct. 11th. the governor with a remonstrance, in which they apologized for their present meeting by representing, that the distressed and miserable state of the colony, had rendered it indispensably necessary to collect the wisdom of the province by their delegates in that Congress; thereby to concert some adequate remedy to prevent impending ruin, and to provide for the public safety. They then express the grievous apprehensions of the people from the measures now pursuing. They assert, that even the rigour of the Boston port bill is exceeded, by the manner in which it is carried into execution. They complain of the late laws, calculated not only to abridge the people of their rights, but to licence murders; of the number of troops in the capital, which were daily increasing by new accessions drawn from every part of the continent; together with the formidable and hostile preparations in Boston-neck; all tending to endanger the lives, liberties, and properties, not only of the people of Boston, but of the province in general. They conclude by adjuring the general, as he regards his majesty's honour and interest, the dignity and happiness of the empire, and the peace and welfare of the province, to desist immediately from the construction of the fortress at the entrance into Boston, and to restore that pass to its natural state.

The general was involved in some difficulty in giving them an answer, as he could not acknowledge the legality of their assembling. The necessity of the times however prevailed. He expressed great indignation that an idea should be formed, that the lives, liberties, or property of any people, except avowed enemies, should be in danger from English troops. Britain, he said, could never harbour the black design of wantonly destroying or enslaving any people; and notwithstanding the enmity shewn to the troops, by withholding from them almost every necessary for their preservation, they had not yet discovered the resentment which might justly be expected to arise from such hostile treatment. He reminded the Congress, that while they complain of alterations made in their charter by acts of parliament, they are themselves, by their present assembling, subverting that charter, and now acting in direct violation of their own constitution; he therefore warned them of the rocks they were upon, and to defist from such illegal and unconstitutional proceedings.

By this time Boston was become the place of refuge to all those friends of the new government, who thought it necessary to persevere in avowing their sentiments. The commissioners of the customs, with all their officers, had also thought it necessary, towards the conclusion of the preceding month, to abandon their head quarters at Salem, and to remove the apparatus of a custom-house, to a place which an act of parliament had proscribed from all trade. Thus the new acts of parliament on one hand, and the resistance of the people on the other, equally joined to annihilate all appearance of government, legislation, judicial proceedings, and commercial regulations.

Upon the approach of winter, the general had ordered temporary barracks to be erected for the troops, partly, perhaps, for safety, and partly to prevent the disorders and mischiefs, which in the present state and temper of both, must be the unavoidable consequences of their being quartered upon the inhabitants. Such, however, was the dislike to their being provided for in any manner, that the select-men and the committees obliged the workmen to quit their employment, though the money for their labour would have been paid by the crown. The general had as little success in endeavouring to procure carpenters from New-York, so that it was with the greatest difficulty he could get those temporary lodgments erected; and having endeavoured also to procure some winter covering from the latter city, the offer to purchase it was presented to every merchant there, who to a man refused complying with any part of the order, and returned for answer, " that they never would supply any article for the benefit of men who were sent as enemies to their country."

Every thing now tended to increase the mutual apprehension, distrust, and animosity between government and the people. Those of Boston, either were, or pretended to be, under continual terror, from the apprehensions of immediate danger, to their properties, liberties, and even their lives. They were in the hands of an armed force whom they abhorred, and who equally detested them. The soldiers on the other hand, considered themselves in the midst of enemies, and were equally apprehensive of danger from within and without. Each side professed the best intentions in the world for itself, and shewed the greatest suspicion of the other. In this state of doubt and profession, things were rendered still worse, by a measure, which did not seem of sufficient importance in its consequences, to justify its being hazarded at so critical a season. This was the landing of a detachment of sailors by night, from the ships of war in the harbour, who spiked up all the cannon upon one of the principal batteries belonging to the town.

In the mean time the Provincial Congress, notwithstanding the cautions given, and dangers held out by the governor, not only continued their assembly, but their resolutions having acquired, from the disposition and promptitude of the people, all the weight and efficacy of laws, they seemed to have founded in effect something like a new and independent government. Under the style of recommendation and advice, they settled the militia; they regulated the public treasures; and they provided arms. They appointed a day of public thanksgiving, on which, among the other enumerated blessings, a particular acknowledgment was to be made to the Almighty, for the union which so remarkably prevailed in all the colonies.

These and similar measures, induced General Gage to issue a proclamation, Nov. 10th. in which, though the direct terms are avoided, they are charged with proceedings, which are generally understood as nearly tantamount to treason and rebellion. The inhabitants of the province were accordingly, in the king's name, prohibited from complying, in any degree, with the requisitions, recommendations, directions, or resolves of that unlawful assembly.

General Congress held at Philadelphia. Previous instructions to some of the deputies. Acts of the Congress. Approbation of the conduct of the province of Massachusett's-Bay, and of the late resolutions passed by the county of Suffolk. Resolutions. Declaration of rights. Letter to General Gage. Association. Resolution for a future Congress. Petition to the king. Memorial to the people of Great-Britain. Address to the inhabitants of Canada. Address to the colonies. The Congress breaks up.

DURING these transactions in the province of Massachusett's-Bay, the twelve old colonies, including that whole extent of continent which stretches from Nova-Scotia to Georgia, had appointed deputies to attend the General Congress, which was held at Philadelphia, and opened on Monday the 5th of September 1764. Such was the unhappy effect of the measures, pursued, perhaps somewhat too avowedly, and for that reason the less wisely, for reducing America by division, that those twelve colonies, clashing in interests, frequently quarrelling about boundaries and many other subjects, differing in manners, customs, religion, and forms of government, with all the local prejudices, jealousies, and aversions, incident to neighbouring states, were now led to assemble by their delegates in a general diet, and taught to feel their weight and importance in a common union. Whatever may be the event, it was undoubtedly a dangerous experiment to bring matters to this crisis.

Several of the colonies had given instructions to their deputies previous to their meeting in congress. In general, they contained the strongest professions of loyalty and allegiance; of affection for the mother country; of constitutional dependance on her; and of gratitude for benefits already received in that state. They totally disclaimed every idea of independence, or of seeking a separation; acknowledged the prerogatives of the crown, and declared their readiness and willingness to support them with life and fortune, so far as they are warranted by the constitution. The Pensylvanians, in particular, declare that they view the present contests with

the deepest concern; that perpetual love and union, an interchange of good offices, without the least infraction of mutual rights, ought ever to subsist between the mother country and them.

On the other hand, they were unanimous in declaring, that they never would give up those rights and liberties which, as they said, descended to them from their ancestors, and which, they said, they were bound by all laws, human and divine, to transmit whole and pure to their posterity; that they are entitled to all the rights and liberties of British-born subjects; that the power lately assumed by parliament is unjust, and the only cause of all the present uneasiness; and that the late acts respecting the capital and province of Massachusett's-Bay, are unconstitutional, oppressive, and dangerous.

The instructions, however, of the several colonies that pursued that mode, differed considerably from each other. In some great violence appeared. Others were more reasonable. In some nothing was spoken of but their grievances. Others proposed likewise terms on their part to be offered to Great-Britain—Such as an obedience to all the trade laws passed, or to be passed, except such as were specified; and the settling an annual revenue on the crown for public purposes, and disposable by parliament. The deputies however were instructed, that in these and all other points, they were to coincide with the majority of the congress. This majority was to be determined by reckoning the colonies, as having each a vote, without regard to the number of deputies which it should send.

The debates and proceedings of the congress were conducted with the greatest secrecy, nor have any parts of them yet transpired, but those which they thought proper to lay before the public. The number of delegates amounted to fifty-one, who represented the several English colonies of New-Hampshire, Massachusett's-Bay, Rhode-Island, and Providence Plantations, Connecticut, New-York, New-Jersey, Pensylvania, the lower counties on Delaware, Maryland, Virginia, North-Carolina, and South-Carolina. [14]

Sept. 17th. The first public act of the Congress was a declaratory resolution expressive of their disposition with respect to the colony of Massachusett's-Bay, and immediately intended to confirm and encourage that people. In this they expressed, in the most pathetic terms, how deeply they felt the sufferings of their countrymen in that province, under the operation, as they said, of the late unjust, cruel, and oppressive acts of the British parliament; they thoroughly approved of the wisdom and fortitude with which their opposition to these ministerial measures had hitherto been conducted, as well as of the resolutions passed, and measures proposed, by the delegates of the county of Suffolk; and earnestly recommended a perseverance in the same firm and temperate conduct, according to the determinations of that assembly. This was immediately published, and transmitted to that province, accompanied with an unanimous resolution, That contributions from all the colonies for supplying the necessities, and alleviating the distresses of their brethren at Boston, ought to be continued in such manner, and so long, as their occasions may require.

By the subsequent resolutions of the Congress, they not only formally approve of the opposition made by that province to the late acts; but further declare, that if it should be attempted to carry them into execution by force, all America should support it in that opposition.—That if it be found absolutely necessary to remove the people of Boston into the country, all America should contribute towards recompensing them for the injury they might thereby sustain.—They recommend to the inhabitants of Massachusett's-Bay, to submit to a suspension of the administration of justice, as it cannot be procured in a legal manner under the rules of the charter, until the effects of the application of the Congress for a repeal of those acts, by which their charter rights are infringed, is known.—And that every person who shall accept, or act under, any commission or authority, derived from the late act of parliament, changing the form of government, and violating the charter of that province, ought to be held in detestation, and considered as the wicked tool of that despotism, which is preparing to destroy those rights, which God, nature, and compact, hath given to America. They besides recommended to the people of Boston and Massachusett's-Bay, still to conduct themselves peaceably towards the general, and the troops stationed at Boston, so far as it could possibly consist with their immediate safety; but that they should firmly persevere in the defensive line of conduct which they are now pursuing. The latter part of this instruction evidently alluded to and implied an approbation of the late resolutions of the county of Suffolk, relative to the militia, and to the arming of the people in general. The Congress conclude by a resolution, that the transporting, or attempting to transport any person beyond the sea, for the trial of offences committed in America, being against law, will justify, and ought to meet with resistance and reprisal.

These resolutions being passed, the Congress wrote a letter to General Gage, in which, after repeating the complaints which had been

before repeatedly made by the town of Boston, and by the delegates of different counties in the province of Massachusett's-Bay, they declare the determined resolution of the colonies, to unite for the preservation of their common rights, in opposition to the late acts of parliament, under the execution of which the unhappy people of that province are oppressed: that, in consequence of their sentiments upon that subject, the colonies had appointed them the guardians of their rights and liberties, and that they felt the deepest concern, that, whilst they were pursuing every dutiful and peaceable measure to procure a cordial and effectual reconciliation between Great-Britain and the colonies, his excellency should proceed in a manner that bore so hostile an appearance, and which even those oppressive acts did not warrant. They represented the tendency this conduct must have to irritate and force a people, however well disposed to peaceable measures, into hostilities, which might prevent the endeavours of the Congress to restore a good understanding with the parent state, and involve them in the horrors of a civil war. In order to prevent these evils, and the people from being driven to a state of desperation, being fully persuaded of their pacific disposition towards the king's troops, if they could be assured of their own safety, they intreated, that the general would discontinue the fortifications in Boston, prevent any further invasions of private property, restrain the irregularities of the soldiers, and give orders that the communications between the town and country should be open, unmolested, and free.

The Congress also published a declaration of rights, to which, they say, the English colonies of North-America are entitled, by the immutable laws of nature, the principles of the English constitution, and their several charters or compacts. In the first of these are life, liberty, and property, a right to

the disposal of any of which, without their consent, they had never ceded to any sovereign power whatever. That their ancestors, at the time of their migration, were entitled to all the rights, liberties, and immunities, of free and natural born subjects; and that by such emigration, they neither forfeited, surrendered, nor lost, any of those rights. They then state, that the foundation of English liberty, and of all free government, is a right in the people to participate in their legislative council; and proceed to shew, that as the colonists are not, and, from various causes, cannot be represented in the British parliament, they are entitled to a free and exclusive power of legislation in their several provincial legislatures, where their right of representation can alone be preserved, in all cases of taxation and internal policy, subject only to the negative of their sovereign, in such manner as had been heretofore used and accustomed.

In order to qualify the extent of this demand of legislative power in their assemblies, which might seem to leave no means of parliamentary interference for holding the colonies to the mother country, they declare that from the necessity of the case, and a regard to the mutual interest of both countries, they chearfully consent to the operation of such acts of the British parliament, as are, bona fide, restrained to the regulation of their external commerce, for the purpose of securing the commercial advantages of the whole empire to the mother country, and the commercial benefits of its respective members, excluding every idea of taxation, internal or external, for raising a revenue on the subjects in America, without their consent.

They also resolved, that the colonies are entitled to the common law of England, and, more especially, to the great and inestimable privilege of being tried by their peers of the vicinage. That they are entitled to the benefit of such of the English statutes as existed at the time of their colonization, and which they have by experience found to be applicable to their several local and other circumstances. That they are likewise entitled to all the immunities and privileges, granted and confirmed to them by royal charters, or secured by their several codes of provincial laws. That they have a right to assemble peaceably, consider of their grievances, and petition the king for redress; and that all prosecutions, and prohibitory proclamations for so doing, are illegal. That the keeping of a standing army, in times of peace, in any colony, without the consent of its legislature, is contrary to law. That it is essential to the English constitution, that the constituent branches of the legislature should be independent of each other; that, therefore, the exercise of legislative power, by a council appointed during pleasure by the crown, is unconstitutional, and destructive to the freedom of American legislation.

They declared in behalf of themselves and their constituents, that they claimed, and insisted on the foregoing articles, as their indubitable rights and liberties, which could not be legally taken from them, altered, or abridged, by any power whatever, without their own consent, by their representatives in their several provincial legislatures. They then enumerated the parts, or the whole, of eleven acts of parliament, which had been passed in the present reign, and which they declared to be infringements and violations of the rights of the colonists; and that the repeal of them was essentially necessary, in order to restore harmony between Great-Britain and them. Among the acts of parliament thus reprobated, was the Quebec bill, which had already been the cause of so much discussion at home, and which they termed, "An act for establishing the Roman Catholic religion in the province of Quebec, abolishing the equitable system of English laws,

and erecting a tyranny there;" to the great danger, (as they asserted) from so total a dissimilarity of religion, law, and government, of the neighbouring British colonies, by the assistance of whose blood and treasure that country was conquered from France.

After specifying their rights, and enumerating their grievances, they declared, that, to obtain redress of the latter, which threatened destruction to the lives, liberty, and property of the people of North-America, a non-importation, non-consumption, and non-exportation, agreement, would prove the most speedy, effectual, and peaceable measure; they accordingly entered into an association, by which they bound themselves, and of course their constituents, to the strict observance of the following articles.—1st. That after the first day of the following December, they would import no British goods or merchandize whatsoever, nor any East-India tea, from any part of the world; nor any of the products of the British West-India islands; nor wines from Madeira, or the Western islands; nor foreign indigo.—2. That, after that day, they would wholly discontinue the slave-trade, and neither hire vessels, nor sell commodities or manufactures to any concerned in that trade.—3. That from the present date, they will use no tea on which a duty had been or shall be paid; nor after the 1st of March ensuing, any East-India tea whatever, nor any British goods, imported after the 1st of December, except such as come under the rules and directions which we shall see in the 10th article.—4. By this article, the non-exportation agreement is suspended to the 10th of September 1775; after which day, if the acts of parliament which they had before recited are not repealed, all exportation is to cease, except that of rice to Europe.—5. The British merchants are exhorted not to ship any goods in violation of this association, under penalty of their never holding any

commercial intercourse with those that act otherwise.—6. Owners of ships are warned to give such orders to their captains, as will effectually prevent their receiving any of those goods that are prohibited.—7. They agree to improve the breed of sheep, and to increase their number, to the greatest possible extent.—8. This article tends to encourage frugality, œconomy, and industry; to promote agriculture, arts, and manufactures; to discountenance all expensive shows, games, and entertainments; to lessen the expences of funerals; to discontinue the giving of gloves and scarfs, and the wearing of any other mourning than a piece of crape or ribbon.—9. Venders of goods are to sell them at the usual prices, without taking any advantage of the present situation of affairs.—10. This article seems in a certain degree to soften the rigour of the first, and permits a conditional importation for two months longer, at the option of the owner; who, if he will deliver up any goods that he imports before the first of February, to the committee of the place that they arrive at, they are to be sold under their inspection, and the prime cost being returned to the importer, the profits are to be applied to the relief of the sufferers at Boston. All goods that arrive after that day, to be sent back without landing, or breaking any of the packages.—The three following articles relate to the appointing of committees, to prevent any violation of the foregoing, and to publish the names of the violators in the Gazette, as foes to the rights, and enemies to the liberty of British America; they also regulate the sale of domestic manufactures; that they may be disposed of at reasonable prices, and no undue advantages taken of a future scarcity of goods.—By the 14th and last article, any colony or province, which shall not accede to, or which shall hereafter violate the association, is branded as inimical to the liberties of their country, and all dealings or intercourse whatever with such colony is interdicted.

This association was subscribed by all the members of the congress; and the foregoing resolutions were all marked, *nemine contradicente*. They afterwards resolved, that a congress should be held in the same place, on the 10th day of the following May, unless the redress of grievances, which they have desired, should be obtained before that time; and they recommended to all the colonies to chuse deputies, as soon as possible, for that purpose. They also, in their own names, and in the behalf of all those whom they represented, declared their most grateful acknowledgments, to those truly noble, honourable, and patriotic advocates of civil and religious liberty, who had so generously and powerfully, though unsuccessfully, espoused and defended the cause of America, both in and out of parliament.

They then proceeded to frame a petition to his majesty, a memorial to the people of Great-Britain, an address to the colonies in general, and another to the inhabitants of the province of Quebec. The petition to his majesty contained an enumeration of their grievances; among which are the following, viz. The keeping of a standing army in the colonies in time of peace, without the consent of the assemblies; and the employing of that army, and of a naval force, to enforce the payment of taxes. —The authority of the commander in chief, and of the brigadiers general, being rendered supreme in all the civil governments in America.—The commander in chief of the forces, in time of peace, appointed governor of a colony.— The charges of usual offices greatly increased, and new, expensive, and oppressive offices, multiplied. —The judges of the admiralty courts impowered to receive their salaries and fees from the effects condemned by themselves; and the officers of the customs to break

open and enter houses, without the authority of the civil magistrate.— The judges rendered entirely dependent on the crown for their salaries, as well as for the duration of their commissions. Counsellors, who exercise legislative authority, holding their commissions during pleasure.——Humble and reasonable petitions from the representatives of the people fruitless. —The agents of the people discountenanced, and instructions given to prevent the payment of their salaries; assemblies repeatedly and injuriously dissolved; commerce burthened with useless and oppressive restrictions.

They then enumerate the several acts of parliament passed in the present reign for the purpose of raising a revenue in the colonies, and of extending the powers of admiralty and vice-admiralty courts beyond their ancient limits; whereby their property is taken from them without their consent, the trial by jury, in many civil cases abolished, enormous forfeitures incurred for slight offences; vexatious informers are exempted from paying damages, to which they are justly liable, and oppressive security is required from owners before they are allowed to defend their right.

They complain of the parliamentary vote for reviving the statute of the 35th Henry VIIIth, and extending its influence to the colonists; and of the statute of the 12th of his present majesty, whereby the inhabitants of the colonies may, in sundry cases, by that statute made capital, be deprived of a trial by their peers of the vicinage. They then recite the three acts of the preceding session, relative to Boston and the province of Massachusett's-Bay; the Quebec act, and the act for providing quarters for the troops in North-America.

The petition repeatedly contains the strongest expressions of loyalty, of affectionate attachment and duty to the sovereign, of love and ve-

neration for the parent state; they attributed these their sentiments to the liberties they inherited from their ancestors, and the constitution under which they were bred; while the necessity which compelled, was the apology for delivering them. They at the same time promised themselves a favourable reception and hearing from a sovereign, whose illustrious family owed their empire to similar principles.

They declare, that from the destructive system of colony administration, adopted since the conclusion of the last war, have flowed those distresses, dangers, fears and jealousies, which overwhelm the colonies with affliction; and they defy their most subtle and inveterate enemies to trace the unhappy differences between Great-Britain and them from an earlier period, or from other causes than they have assigned. That they ask but for peace, liberty and safety; they wish not for a diminution of the prerogative, nor do they solicit the grant of any new right in their favour; the royal authority over them, and their connection with Great-Britain, they shall always carefully and zealously endeavour to support and maintain. That, "appealing to that Being who searches thoroughly the hearts of his creatures, they solemnly profess, that their councils have been influenced by no other motive than a dread of impending destruction."

They conclude by imploring his majesty, in the name of all America; and a solemn adjuration by all that is sacred and aweful; that, "for the glory, which can be advanced only by rendering his subjects happy, and keeping them united; for the interests of his family, depending in an adherence to the principle that enthroned it; for the safety and welfare of his kingdoms and dominions, threatened with almost unavoidable dangers and distresses; that, as the loving father of his whole people, connected by the same bands of law, loyalty, faith, and blood, though dwelling in various countries, he will not ſuffer the tranſcendent relation formed by theſe ties, to be further violated in uncertain expectation of effects, which, if attained, never can compenſate for the calamities through which they muſt be gained."

This petition was ſubſcribed by all the delegates.

In the memorial to the people of this country, they pay the higheſt praiſe to the noble and generous virtues of their and our common anceſtors; but they do it in a manner, that inſtead of reflecting any comparative honour on the preſent generation in this iſland, rather reproaches us with a ſhameful degeneracy. They afterwards ſay, that born to the ſame rights, liberties, and conſtitution, tranſmitted to them from the ſame anceſtors, guarantied to them by the plighted faith of government, and the moſt ſolemn compacts with Britiſh ſovereigns, it is no wonder they ſhould refuſe to ſurrender them to men, whoſe claims are not founded on any principles of reaſon, " and who proſecute them " with a deſign, that, by having " their lives and property in their " power, they might with the " greater facility enſlave us." They complain of being oppreſſed, abuſed, and miſrepreſented; and ſay, that the duty they owe to themſelves and to their poſterity, to our intereſt, and to the general welfare of the Britiſh empire, leads them to addreſs us on this very important ſubject.

After complaining of grievances in the ſtyle and ſubſtance of the petition, they recall the happy ſtate of the empire on both ſides of the Atlantic, previous to the concluſion of the late war; and ſtate the advantages which we derived, and to which they willingly ſubmitted, from the ſyſtem of colony government then purſued; they ſay, they looked up to us as to their parent ſtate, to which they were bound by the ſtrongeſt ties;

and were happy in being inſtrumental to our proſperity and grandeur. They call upon ourſelves to witneſs their loyalty and attachment to the common intereſts of the whole empire: their efforts in the laſt war: their embarking to meet diſeaſe and death in foreign and inhoſpitable climates, to promote the ſucceſs of our arms; and our own acknowledgments of their zeal, and our even reimburſing them large ſums of money, which we confeſſed they had advanced beyond their proportion, and far beyond their abilities.

They aſk to what cauſes they are to attribute the ſudden change of treatment, and that ſyſtem of ſlavery, which was prepared for them at the reſtoration of peace; they trace the hiſtory of taxation from that time, and aſſert, that thoſe exactions, inſtead of being applied to any uſeful purpoſe, either for this country or that, have been laviſhly ſquandered upon court favourites and miniſterial dependants; that they ever were, and ever ſhall be ready to provide for the neceſſary ſupport of their own government; and, whenever the exigencies of the ſtate may require it, they ſhall, as they have heretofore done, chearfully contribute their full proportion of men and money.

They then proceed to ſtate and examine the meaſures and the ſeveral acts of parliament, which they conſider as hoſtile to America, and ſubverſive of their rights; or, in their words, the progreſſion of the miniſterial plan for enſlaving them. They repreſent the probable conſequences to this country of a perſeverance in that ſcheme, even ſuppoſing it attended with ſucceſs; addition to the national debt; increaſe of taxes; and a diminution of commerce, muſt attend it in the progreſs; and if we are at length victorious, in what condition ſhall we then be? What advantages, or what laurels ſhall we reap from ſuch a conqueſt?

They artfully endeavour to render

theirs a cauſe common to both countries, by ſhewing that ſuch ſucceſs would in the event, be as fatal to the liberties of England as to thoſe of America. They accordingly put the queſtion, May not a miniſter with the ſame armies that ſubdued them enſlave us? If to this it be anſwered, that we will ceaſe to pay thoſe armies, they pretend to ſhew, that America reduced to ſuch a ſituation, would afford abundant reſources both of men and money for the purpoſe; nor ſhould we have any reaſon to expect, that after making ſlaves of them, they ſhould refuſe to aſſiſt in reducing us to the ſame abject ſtate.——In a word (they ſay) " Take care that you do not fall " into the pit that is preparing " for us."

After denying the ſeveral charges, of being ſeditious, impatient of government, and deſirous of independency, all of which they aſſert to be calumnies; they, however, declare that, if we are determined, that our miniſters ſhall wantonly ſport with the rights of mankind; if neither the voice of juſtice, the dictates of the law, the principles of the conſtitution, nor the ſuggeſtions of humanity, can reſtrain our hands from the ſhedding of human blood in ſuch an impious cauſe, they muſt tell us,—— " That they never will ſubmit to be hewers of wood, or drawers of water for any miniſtry or nation in the world."

They afterwards make a propoſal, which it were much to be wiſhed had been more attended to, as it affords at leaſt no unfavourable baſis for negociation.—— " Place us" ſay they, " in the ſame ſituation that we were at the cloſe of the laſt war, and our former harmony will be reſtored."

They conclude this memorial, by expreſſing the deepeſt regret for the reſolutions they were obliged to enter into for the ſuſpenſion of commerce, as a meaſure detrimental to numbers of their fellow-subjects in Great-Britain and Ireland; they account and apologize for this conduct, by the over-ruling principles of self-preservation; by the supineness, and inattention to our common interest, which we had shewn for several years: and by the attempt of the ministry, to influence a submission to their measures by destroying the trade of Boston. "The like fate," they say, "may befall us all; we will endeavour therefore, to live without trade, and recur for subsistance to the fertility and bounty of our native soil, which will afford us all the necessaries and some of the conveniencies of life." They finally rest their hopes of a restoration of that harmony, friendship, and fraternal affection, between all the inhabitants of his majesty's kingdoms and territories, so ardently wished for by every true American, upon the magnanimity and justice of the British nation, in furnishing a parliament of such wisdom, independency, and public spirit, as may save the violated rights of the whole empire from the devices of wicked ministers and evil counsellors, whether in or out of office.

Of all the papers published by the American congress, their address to the French inhabitants of Canada, discovers the most dextrous management, and the most able method of application to the temper and passions of the parties, whom they endeavour to gain.—— They state the right they had, upon their becoming English subjects, to the inestimable benefits of the English constitution; that this right was further confirmed by the royal proclamation in the year 1763, plighting the public faith for their full enjoyment of those advantages. They impute to succeeding ministers an audacious and cruel abuse of the royal authority, in withholding from them the fruition of the irrevocable rights, to which they were thus justly entitled.—That as they have lived to

see the unexpected time, when ministers of this flagitious temper have dared to violate the most sacred compacts and obligations, and as the Canadians, educated under another form of government, have artfully been kept from discovering the unspeakable worth of that, from which they are debarred, the congress think it their duty, for weighty reasons, to explain to them some of its most important branches.

They then quote passages on government from the Marquis Beccaria and their countryman Montesquieu, the latter of whom they artfully adopt as a judge, and an irrefragable authority upon this occasion, and proceed to specify and explain, under several distinct heads, the principal rights to which the people are entitled by the English constitution; and these rights, they truly say, defend the poor from the rich, the weak from the powerful, the industrious from the rapacious, the peaceable from the violent, the tenants from the lords, and all from their superiors.

They state, that without these rights, a people cannot be free and happy; and that under their protecting and encouraging influence, the English colonies had hitherto so amazingly flourished and increased. And, that these are the rights which a profligate ministry are now striving by force of arms to ravish from themselves; and which they are, with one mind, resolved never to resign but with their lives.

They again remind the Canadians that they are entitled to these rights, and ought at this moment to be in the perfect exercise of them. They then ask, what is offered to them by the late act of parliament in their place. And from thence proceed to a severe examination of the Quebec act, in which they attempt to shew, that it does not afford them, and has not left them a civil right or security of any kind, as every thing it

seems to grant, and even the laws they possessed before, are liable to be altered and varied, and new laws or ordinances made, by a governor and council appointed by the crown, and consequently, wholly dependent on, and removeable at the will of a minister in England; so that all the powers of legislation, as well as that of granting and applying the public supplies, and disposing of their own property, being thus totally out of the hands and controul of the people, they are liable to the most abject slavery, and to live under the most despotic government in the universe.

After pretending to point out numberless deformities in that law, and placing them in such points of view, as were sufficient to render it odious to mankind, as well as hideous to the Canadians, they represent, as an insult added to their injuries, the hopes upon which, they said, it had been founded by the minister; he expecting, that through an invincible stupidity in them, and a total inability of comprehending the tendency of a law, which so materially affected their dearest interests, should in the excess of a mistaken gratitude, take up arms, and incur the ridicule and detestation of the world, by becoming willing tools in his hands, to assist in subverting the rights and liberties of the other colonies; without their being capable of seeing, that the unavoidable consequences of such an attempt, if successful, would be the extinction of all hopes to themselves and their posterity of being ever restored to freedom; for idiotcy itself, (say they) "cannot believe, that, when their drudgery is performed, they will treat you with less cruelty than they have us, who are of the same blood with themselves."

They again apply to their passions, and partiality for their countryman, by calling up the venerable Montesquieu, and desiring them to apply those maxims, sanctified by the authority of a name which all Europe reveres, to their own state; they suppose him alive, and consulted by the Canadians as to the part they should act in their present situation. They are told (after expatiating on the subject of freedom and slavery) that they are only a small people, compared with their numerous and powerful neighbours, who with open arms invite them into a fellowship; to seize the opportunity in their favour, which is not the work of man, but presented by Providence itself; that it does not admit of a question, whether it is more for their interest and happiness, to have all the rest of North America their unalterable friends, or their inveterate enemies; that as nature had joined their countries, let them also join their political interests; that they have been conquered into liberty, if they act as they ought; but that their doing otherwise will be attended with irremediable evils.

They endeavour to obviate the jealousies and prejudices which might arise from the difference of their religious principles, by instancing the case of the Swiss cantons; whose union is composed of Catholic and Protestant states; who live in the utmost concord and peace with each other, and have been thereby enabled to defeat all attempts against their liberties. This instance, though perhaps the most apposite that could have been brought for the purpose, would not, however, have born the test of much examination.

They declare, that they do not require them, to commence acts of hostility against the government of their common sovereign; that they only invite them to consult their own glory and welfare, and not to suffer themselves to be inveigled or intimidated by infamous ministers so far, as to become the instruments of their cruelty and despotism. They conclude by informing them, that the congress had with universal pleasure, and by an unanimous vote, resolved,

that they should consider the violation of their rights, by the act for altering the government of that province, as a violation of their own; and that they should be invited to accede to their confederation, which had no other objects than the perfect security of the natural and civil rights of all the constituent members, according to their respective circumstances, and the preservation of a happy and lasting connection with Great-Britain, on the salutary and constitutional principles before mentioned.

In the address to the colonies they inform them, that as in duty and justice bound, they have deliberately, dispassionately, and impartially examined and considered all the measures that led to the present disturbances; the exertions of both the legislative and executive powers of Great-Britain, on the one hand, and the conduct of the colonies on the other. That upon the whole, they find themselves reduced to the disagreeable alternative, of being silent and betraying the innocent, or of speaking out and censuring those they wish to revere. In making their choice of these distressing difficulties, they prefer the course dictated by honesty, and a regard for the welfare of their country.

After stating and examining the several laws that were passed, and the measures pursued with respect to America, from the year 1764, to the present period, they enquire into the motives for the particular hostility carried on against the town of Boston, and province of Massachusett's-Bay, though the behaviour of the people in other colonies, had been in equal opposition to the power assumed by parliament, and yet no step whatever had been taken against any of them by government. This they represent as an artful systematic line of conduct, concealing among others the following designs: 1st. That it was expected, that the province of Massachusett's would be

irritated into some violent action, that might displease the rest of the continent, or that might induce the people of England to approve the meditated vengeance of an imprudent and exasperated ministry. If the unexampled pacific temper of that province should disappoint that part of the plan, it was in that case hoped, that the other colonies would be so far intimidated, as to desert their brethren, suffering in a common cause, and that thus disunited, all might be easily subdued.

After examining the Quebec act, and pretending to assign the motives on which it was founded, they say, that from this detail of facts, as well as from authentic intelligence, it is clear, beyond a doubt, that a resolution is formed, and now is carrying into execution, to extinguish the freedom of the colonies, by subjecting them to a despotic government.

They then proceed to state the importance of the trust which was reposed in them, and the manner in which they have discharged it. Upon this occasion, they say, that though the state of the colonies would certainly justify other measures than those which they have advised; yet they have for weighty reasons given the preference to those which they have adopted. These reasons are, that it is consistent with the character which the colonies have always sustained, to perform, even in the midst of the unnatural distresses and imminent dangers that surround them, every act of loyalty; and therefore they were induced to offer once more to his majesty the petitions of his faithful and oppressed subjects in America.—That from a sense of their tender affection for the people of the kingdom from which they derive their original, they could not forbear to regulate their steps by an expectation of receiving full conviction that the colonists are equally dear to them. That they ardently wish the social band between that body and the colonies may never be diffolved, and that it cannot, until the minds of the former fhall become indifputably hoftile, or their inattention fhall permit thofe who are thus hoftile to perfift in profecuting, with the powers of the realm, the deftructive meafures already operating againft the colonifts; and, in either cafe, fhall reduce the latter to fuch a fituation, that they fhall be compelled to renounce every guard but that of felf-prefervation.—That, notwithftanding the vehemence with which affairs have been impelled, they have not yet reached that fatal point; that they do not incline to accelerate their motion, already alarmingly rapid; and they have chofen a method of oppofition that does not preclude a hearty reconciliation with their fellow citizens on the other fide of the Atlantic.

That, they deeply deplore the urgent neceffity that preffes them to an immediate interruption of commerce, which may prove injurious to their fellow-fubjects in England; but truft they will acquit them of any unkind intentions; by reflecting that they fubject themfelves to fimilar inconveniencies; that they are driven by the hands of violence into unexperienced and unexpected public convulfions, and that they are contending for freedom, fo often contended for by their anceftors.

They conclude by obferving, that the people of England will foon have an opportunity of declaring their fentiments concerning their caufe. " That in their piety, " generofity, and good fenfe, they " repofe high confidence; and can- " not, upon a review of paft events, " be perfuaded that they, the de- " fenders of true religion, and the " affertors of the rights of man- " kind, will take part againft " their affectionate Proteftant bre- " thren in the colonies, in favour " of their open and our own fe- " cret enemies, whofe intrigues, " for feveral years paft, have been " wholly exercifed in fapping the

" foundation of all civil and re- " ligious liberty."

Thefe public acts being paffed, October 26th. the delegates put an end to their feffion, on the 52d day from the opening of the congrefs.

Without examining the truth of their allegations, or pretending to form any opinion upon a fubject, on which the firft names in this country have differed fo widely, it muft be acknowledged, that the petition and addreffes from the congrefs have been executed with uncommon energy, addrefs, and ability; and that confidered abftractedly, with refpect to vigour of mind, ftrength of fentiment, and the language, at leaft of patriotifm, they would not have difgraced any affembly that ever exifted.

State of affairs previous to the diffolution of Parliament. The new Parliament meets. Speech from the throne. Addreffes. Amendments propofed. Debates. Proteft. Apparent irrefolution with refpect to America. Eftimates of fupply formed upon a peace eftablifhment. Reduction in the naval department.

WHILST matters of this magnitude were tranfacting in America, an unexampled fupinenefs with regard to public affairs, prevailed among the great body of the people at home. The Englifh nation, which ufed to feel fo *tremblingly alive*, upon every conteft that arofe between the remoteft powers in Europe, and to intereft itfelf fo much in the iffue, as fcarcely to be with-held from becoming a party where-ever juftice or friendfhip pointed out the way, by a ftrange reverfe of temper, feemed at this time, much more indifferent to matters, in which were involved its own immediate and deareft interefts. Even the great commercial and manufacturing bodies, who muft be the firft to feel, and the laft to lament any finifter events in the colonies, and who are generally remarkable for a quick forefight and provident fagacity in whatever regards their intereft, feemed now to be funk in the fame carelefnefs and inattention with the reft of the people.

Several caufes concurred to produce this apparent indifference. The colony contefts were no longer new. From the year 1765, they had, with but few, and thofe fhort intermiffions, engaged the attention of parliament. Moft of the topics on the fubject were exhaufted, and the vehement paffions which accompanied them had fubfided. The non-importation agreement, (by divifions within the colonies, which, if not caufed, were much forwarded by the conceffions with regard to feveral of the taxes laid in 1767) had broken up, before it had produced any ferious confequences. Moft people therefore flattered themfelves, that as things had appeared fo very frequently at the verge of a rupture, without actually arriving at it, that now, as formerly, fome means would be found for accommodating this difpute. At worft it was conceived, that the Americans would themfelves grow tired. And as an opinion was circulated with fome induftry and fuccefs, that a countenance of refolution, if perfevered in for fome time, would certainly put an end to the conteft, which (it was faid) had been nourifhed wholly by former conceffions, people were in general inclined to leave the trial of the effects of perfeverance and refolution, to a miniftry who valued themfelves on thofe qualities. The court had alfo with great tenacioufnefs adhered to this fyftem for fome years. It frequently got the better, not only of the regular opposition, but of parties in the ministry itself, who were from time to time inclined to relax either from fear, weariness, or change of opinion. All these things had hitherto indisposed the body of the nation from taking part in the sanguine manner they had hitherto done on other subjects, and formerly on this.

From these causes, administration being totally disengaged at home, was at full leisure to prosecute the measures which it had designed against America, or to adopt such new ones, as the opposition there rendered necessary towards carrying the new laws into execution. The times indeed were highly favourable to any purpose, which only required the concurrence of that parliament, and the acquiescence of the people.

Notwithstanding these favourable circumstances on the one side, and that general indifference which prevailed on the other, it was not totally forgotten by either, that the time for a general election was approaching, and that the parliament had but one session more to compleat its allotted term. In some few places, where the popular spirit ran high, tests were already proposed to be signed by their future candidates, previous to their receiving any assurance, or promise of support from the electors. At a meeting of the freeholders of the county of Middlesex, a test was proposed to Mr. Wilkes and Serjeant Glynne,[15] and by them signed, in which they engaged their utmost endeavours to promote bills for shortening the duration of parliaments, for the exclusion of placemen and pensioners from the house of commons; for a more fair and equal representation of the people; for vindicating the injured rights of the freeholders of that county, and through them of all the electors in the kingdom; for procuring a repeal of the four late American acts, viz. That for the province of Quebec, and the three which affected the town of Boston, and

the province of Massachusett's-Bay; besides binding themselves, so far as in them lay, to restore and defend that excellent form of government, which had been modelled and established at the revolution.

Tests, upon much the same principles, were proposed in London and some other places; and it is still the opinion of some of those, who were sanguine in that mode of proceeding, that the apprehension of its becoming general influenced the subsequent conduct of administration to the dissolution of parliament. This opinion, however, seems ill founded. There was no reason then to expect, nor is there now to imagine, that the mode of subscribing to tests would have become general, or even extensive. The influence of administration, in a great number of the boroughs, and in many of the counties, is at all times too well known to be called in question; and the principal and most celebrated leaders in opposition totally disclaimed all tests whatever, as unworthy of themselves, derogatory of their character as senators, and restrictive of their rights as men.

Other more probable causes must be sought, for the measure of dissolving the parliament. The civil list was again become deeply in debt, and the distresses of the lower part of the houshold, from the withholding of their wages, were become so notorious, and so much spoken of, that it seemed disgraceful to the nation, as well as grievous to the sovereign. It was therefore thought, and probably rightly, that it was intended, in the ensuing session, not only to demand a large sum of money for the discharge of the standing debt, but also that a requisition would be made, for such a considerable and certain yearly addition to the civil-list revenues, as would prevent all such mortifying applications for the future.

Though no doubt could be entertained of the good will and compliance of the then parliament, it was, perhaps, not thought prudent, to

load them with so disagreeable a task, at the eve of a general election. Recent experience had shewn, that this was a subject which would excite much general discussion; and that however a majority might, from their zeal to the ease of their sovereign, overlook all the difficulties that could be raised within doors, such a settlement, attended with the payment of a great present balance, and loaded with an entailed irredeemable future incumbrance, would not at all be satisfactory without. People are apt to be out of humour at the parting with their money, and an application for future trust and favour, in such a temper, would seem, at least, ill timed. On the other hand, such a measure would be nothing in the hands of a new parliament, and would be worn out of memory, or become only an historical reference, at the time of their natural demise. The sinister events which have since taken place have, however, hitherto prevented the making of any requisition of this nature.

Another motive may, perhaps, be supposed, for the measure of dissolution. That parliament had already passed the most hostile laws against America; and as they could not, with so good a grace, rescind their own acts, the minister was, in some degree, tied down to a perseverance in the support of those measures on which they were founded; whereas, in a new House of Commons, he would be somewhat at large in chusing or altering his line of conduct, as circumstances varied, and they, if necessary, might throw all the odium of those laws upon their predecessors.

It may also be supposed, that as the issue of the American measures became every day more precarious, it was thought a right measure to have the elections over, before any unfortunate event could change the temper, or irritate the minds of the people. If this should coincide with the time of a general election, there was no doubt but the opposition must carry every thing before it. This, in all likelihood, was the strongest and most prevalent motive to this resolution, though the others might have had their share. And it may be safely concluded, that a saving to the friends of government, by curtailing the time for contest and expence, particularly in the counties, was not at all overlooked upon this occasion. Indeed, the opposition complained that they did not receive fair play; that some places were lost by surprize; and, they said, that those in the secret had infinite advantages, by setting out betimes for the scene of action, and taking the necessary measures to strengthen their interest, before even a suspicion of the design was formed on the other side.

However it was, very unexpectedly, and much to the surprize of the nation in general, (as it had not been a measure much practised of late years, no similar instance having occurred since the year 1746, and even that being an unique in the long reign of George II.) a pro-

September 30th.

clamation was issued for the dissolution of the parliament, and the calling of a new one, the writs for which were made returnable on the 29th day of the following November. Notwithstanding the surprize, and shortness of the time, some of the elections were contested with extraordinary perseverance and ardor.

In London, the popular party carried every thing before them, and returned all the members. Mr. Wilkes was again elected to represent the county of Middlesex, without a shadow of opposition from the court, and Lord Mayor of that city for the ensuing year; and there was no doubt that the court party, grown somewhat wiser by long and bitter experience, would no longer controvert his seat. The dispute, concerning that single seat, had produced to them more troubles, vexation, and disgraces, than the contest with the twelve united colonies of America. It would have been an imprudence, of the grossest

kind, to mix these disputes in the present crisis; and thus, after near fourteen years struggle, it was thought the best way to leave him master of the field.

It was said, by some of those who are curious in attending to such observations, that notwithstanding the surprize, and the shortness of the time, a greater number of the old members were thrown out than was common at general elections. However the fact might be, those who were the best acquainted with men and things, did not augur any change of system from this circumstance. The court, notwithstanding all the ill success of all the measures from which the best success was so confidently expected, seemed firmly resolved to persevere in the same course. It is said, that private advices from America encouraged them to set a light value on the public appearances.

On the meeting of the new parliament, Sir Fletcher Norton was, without opposition, appointed Speaker. In the speech from the throne, the two Houses were informed, that a most daring spirit of resistance and disobedience to the law still unhappily prevailed in the province of Massachuset's Bay, and had, in divers parts of it, broke forth in fresh violences of a very criminal nature; that these proceedings had been countenanced and encouraged in others of the colonies, and unwarrantable attempts made to obstruct the commerce of this kingdom, by unlawful combinations; that such measures had been taken, and such orders given, as were judged most proper and effectual for carrying into execution the laws which were passed in the last session of the late parliament, for the protection and security of commerce, and for restoring and preserving peace, order and good government, in the province of Massachuset's Bay; that they might depend upon a firm and stedfast resolution to withstand every attempt to weaken or impair the

Nov. 30th, 1774.

supreme authority of this legislature over all the dominions of the crown, the maintenance of which was considered as essential to the dignity, the safety, and the welfare of the British empire; his Majesty being assured of receiving their assistance and support while acting upon these principles.

The greatest satisfaction was expressed, at the peace concluded between Russia and the Porte, whereby the general tranquillity of Europe was rendered compleat; and the usual assurance given of every endeavour to preserve that tranquillity, of which there was the greater hope, as other powers gave the strongest assurances of an equally pacific disposition.

No particular supply was demanded; but it was not doubted, that the same affectionate confidence, and the same proofs of zeal and attachment, would be met with in this House of Commons, which had been constantly received from others. The speech concluded, by particularly recommending to both Houses, at this time, to proceed with temper in their deliberations, and with unanimity in their resolutions. To let the people, in every part of the dominions, be taught, by their example, to have a due reverence for the laws, and a just sense of the blessings of our excellent constitution.

An address, in the usual form, having been moved for, an amendment was proposed, on the side of opposition, that his Majesty would be graciously pleased to communicate the whole intelligence he had received from America, to the House, as well as the letters, orders, and instructions upon that business. The proposal for this amendment was productive of some considerable debate, as well as of a division.

The supporters of the original address went, in the first place, upon the old ground, that addresses were no more than general compliments, matters of course at the beginning of every session, which did not preclude any future enquiries; that particular measures were not at that time, in any degree, objects of their consideration: and that American affairs would come in their due order before them, when there would be sufficient time for deliberation, and considering them either separately or in general.

On the other side, it was contended, that though no particular measures were immediately under consideration, yet, the address being drawn up in very general terms, it implied, or even contained, a general approbation of all the late measures pursued with respect to America; that this general judgment could not, nor ought not, to be given without the fullest and clearest information; that a delay in forming such judgment, while the most important concerns both of England and America were hanging upon it, might be fatal to both in its consequences; and that it was a deception to the inexperienced, and an insult to the House, to pretend that their addresses were words without meaning, and to be considered only as echoes to the speech.

This speech, they said, was not merely a compliment. It included a scheme of policy. It included a scheme of unfortunate policy; from whence nothing good had sprung, and from which nothing good could rationally be expected. They had hitherto been grossly deceived, and this expression of good humour and confidence, (for it was that at least, or it was nothing) must belie the genuine feelings of a new parliament, which ought to be cautious in committing itself in the measures of the old, before it had time or means of examining them. They said that this caution would be but decent, even tho' the acts of the former parliament had not left the empire in a flame; but when they met in the midst of the conflagration, it was absolutely incumbent on them to know something of the true nature of the affair, before they took any measures for heaping on new combustible matter. However pretenders to moderation might delude themselves, or attempt to delude others, with an idea of the unoperative nature of an address, they would certainly find their previous approbation pleaded against a subsequent dissent.—and an advantage taken from thence, to infuse an opinion into the nation in general, into Europe, and into America, that parliament had, that day, solemnly adopted all the former proceedings with regard to the colonies. That this opinion would alienate more and more the affections of the colonies from this nation, and therefore it would be necessary to lay a ground for their future system, by an examination into the true nature and effects of the past.

The minister said, that it was not a proper time for entering into any discussion of the affairs of America; he seemed to acknowledge, that a reconciliation was highly desirable, but that as no terms had yet been proposed by America, nor concessions offered, it could not be presumed, that England would make offers of submission; and that as matters were in this state of suspense, he hoped the motion for an amendment would be withdrawn.

Several gentlemen who make a merit of being considered as totally disengaged from all parties and connections, said they would vote for the original address; not that they would in any degree be considered to approve of the late measures against America, or that this vote should be at all supposed an engagement with regard to their future conduct on that subject; but they would do it merely as a matter of business and course, and hold themselves, notwithstanding, entirely at liberty upon all future questions.

In the course of this debate, the conduct of the late parliament underwent much severe animadversion, and the minister was reminded of the mighty effects he had predicted from the late acts against America; they were to humble that whole continent in the dust, without any further trouble, and the punishment of Boston was to strike an universal panic on all the colonies; that refractory town would be totally abandoned; and instead of obtaining relief, a dread of the same fate would prevent even the appearances of pity; that the event has, in every instance, been the direct reverse of the expectations thus held out. The cause of Boston is now become the cause of all America; her sufferings have given her a kind of pre-eminence and supremacy, which she could never otherwise have acquired; and these measures, instead of dividing the colonies, have joined them in a closeness of friendship and union, which perhaps no other means in nature could have done. The great speakers in opposition never distinguished themselves in a more striking manner, than in this day's debate.

The division shewed, that opposition had not gained any great accession of strength by the general election, and also, that the temper of the House at present, with respect to America, was not essentially different from that of the late parliament. The numbers in support of the address, as it originally stood, were 264, and those who voted for the amendment, amounted to 73 only.

The address from the Lords was not less warmly debated than that from the House of Commons. It was couched in very strong terms, and declaratory of their abhorrence and detestation of the daring spirit of resistance and disobedience to the laws, which so strongly prevailed in the province of Massachusett's Bay, and of the unwarrantable attempts in that and other provinces of America, to obstruct, by unlawful combinations, the trade of this kingdom.

A noble Duke, who has long [20] been distinguished by his manly, resolute, and inflexible spirit in opposition, moved an amendment in the following words: " To desire "his Majesty would be graciously pleased to give directions for an early communication of the accounts which have been received concerning the state of the colonies, that we may not proceed to the consideration of this most critical and important matter, but upon the fullest information; and when we are thus informed, we shall, without delay, apply ourselves with the most earnest and serious zeal to such measures as shall tend to secure the honour of his Majesty's crown, the true dignity of the mother country, and the harmony and happiness of all his Majesty's dominions."

The Lords in opposition argued, that they could not agree to commit themselves with the careless facility of a common address of compliment, in expressions, which may lead to measures in the event fatal to the lives, properties, and liberties of a very great part of their fellow-subjects. They considered an address, in the present situation, as necessarily carrying a considerable influence upon their future proceedings, and as impressing the public with certain ideas of the measures which they mean to support; that whatever measures they shall think it adviseable to pursue, it will certainly add greatly to the weight and efficacy of their proceedings, if they appear the result of full information, mature deliberation, and temperate enquiry; that no materials for such an enquiry have been laid before them, nor even so much as promised; that in this situation they are called upon to make an address, arbitrarily imposing qualities and descriptions upon acts done in the colonies, of the true nature and just extent of which they are as yet in a great measure unapprized; a procedure, which, they think, by no means consonant to that purity which they ought ever to preserve in their judicial, and to that caution which ought to guide them in their deliberate capacity.

They besides objected to the address, its implying an approbation of the unfortunate system adopted with regard to the colonies in the last parliament; a system which, they represented, as conceived without prudence, and pursued without temper, consistency, or foresight. After enlarging upon the mischiefs it had produced, without a rational prospect of advantage, they said that it afforded a melancholy prospect of the disposition of Lords in the present parliament, when they see the House, under the pressure of so severe and uniform an experience, again ready, without any enquiry, to countenance, if not to adopt, the spirit of the former fatal proceedings.

To this, besides the general observations on addresses, it was answered by the ministerial side, that the proceedings in America had been such, that if they were not met by something spirited in the language of parliament, immediately at its meeting, the cause would seem to be given up; and this would be a declaration without enquiry, as that proposed in the address; that for their part, nothing was farther from their thoughts, than a concession either expressed or implied; that they hoped this parliament would shew the same regard for its dignity, by which the late parliament had acquired so much honour; and one minister confessed,[21] that he had advised the dissolution, lest popular dissatisfaction, arising from untoward events, should break the chain of those public measures which were necessary to reduce the colonies to due obedience. The sooner the new parliament spoke out upon the subject, the better.

The debate was long and vehement, though the minority was but 13 to 63 on the division. It was rendered memorable by the circumstance of having produced a protest, the first we remember to have heard of upon an address, and that too very strong and pointed. The protest concluded with the following remarkable declaration:

"But whatever may be the mischievous designs, or the inconsiderate temerity, which leads others to this desperate course, we wish to be known as persons who have ever disapproved of measures so pernicious in their past effects, and their future tendency, and who are not in haste, without enquiry or information, to commit ourselves in declarations which may precipitate our country into all the calamities of a civil war."[22]

Notwithstanding the hostile tone of the speech, and the great majority that supported the addresses in both Houses, there appeared the most glaring irresolution on the side of ministry, with respect to American affairs. It seemed as if no plan had yet been formed, nor system adopted upon that subject. The minister appeared less than usual in the House of Commons, and studiously avoided all explanation. Many imagined that he was thwarted and overruled by what in the cant phrase is called the interior cabinet, and did not approve of the violent measures that were there generated. It was even at this time supposed, that he was feeling his own strength, and had some thoughts of making an effort to emancipate himself from those shackles, which rendered him answerable for the acts of others, who were not themselves in any degree responsible.[23]

Other causes might, perhaps with more probability, be assigned for this irresolution. The minister might still have his doubts with respect to the temper of the new parliament. The landed interest, which must first contribute to the support of coercive measures, was not yet prepared to look in the face the direct avowal of a war; and an increase of the land-tax, where there was no incitement of national glory, and even the question of interest sufficiently doubtful, might meet with a general and fatal opposition. The whole weight of the mercantile interest, and of the great manufacturing body of the nation, was also to be apprehended.

However it was, whether it proceeded from irresolution, a want of system, or a difference of opinion in the cabinet, there was a strange suspension of American business previous to the Christmas recess, and the minister seemed evidently to shrink from all contest upon that subject. The national estimates were entirely formed upon a peace establishment. The land-tax was continued at three shillings in the pound; no vote of credit was required; the army remained upon its former footing, and a reduction of 4000 seamen took place, only 16,000 being demanded for the ensuing year.

Upon the last of these articles it was observed on the side of opposition, that there was no reconciling the conduct of administration in a reduction of 4000 seamen with the speech from the throne, which announced the affairs of America to be in a most critical and alarming situation, and seemed to call for the most vigorous and decisive measures. That this had all the appearance of being a ministerial trick; a forming of estimates, in the first instance, which were only designed as wastepaper, and never intended to be adhered to, and afterwards to surprize and drive the house into grants of an improper and burdensome nature; that gentlemen could not face their constituents in the recess, without being able to give them any information, either relative to future burdens, or to what would be necessarily involved in such an enquiry, whether compulsive measures were really intended to be pursued against the Americans; for that to talk of enforcing the acts upon a reduced establishment, either naval or military, was a sort of language fit to be held only to children.

The minister not being then in[24] the House, a noble Lord who sate upon the same bench with him, said, he had authorized him to acacquaint the House, that he had no information whatever to lay before it, nor measures to propose respecting America. Other gentlemen on the same side said, that this was not a proper time for a discussion of American affairs; that when they came before them in a parliamentary way, every gentleman would be at full liberty to declare his sentiments, and support his opinions, when, it was not to be doubted, but the minister would give very good reasons as well for the delay, as for the naval reduction.

An attempt was made in those debates, and supported with pleasantry, to turn the tables upon the gentlemen in opposition, who had for several years been complaining of the greatness of our peace establishment both by sea and land, and now seemed to oppose a reduction as soon as it was attempted by the ministers. But they justified their conduct on the appearance of public affairs, as well as the speech from the throne; they said, an imposition upon the House and the public, by delusive estimates, was not a method of shewing respect to the one, or attention to the other, and the heavy loss and expence that might be incurred in that mode, under the several heads of an increased navy debt, services not provided for, and perhaps a vote of credit, were fully shewn. The strange inconsistency of administration, with respect to American affairs, was severely scrutinized. It was asserted, that the whole was a cheat, in order to delude the people into a war, rendered doubly ruinous and disgraceful by a defective preparation; that the ministers obstinately resolved not to make peace by any reasonable political concession, nor war by any vigorous military arrangement; but by fluctuating between both, deprived the nation of a possibility of deriving benefit from either. Far from saving for the public, this delay of incurring timely charge would certainly aggravate the future expence, as they would assuredly feel in due time. That they were far from desiring war; as little did they relish large peace establishments: but if, against their will, war must be carried on, common sense dictated, that it ought to be carried on with effect; and that if a peace establishment, and even lower than a peace establishment, was sufficient to support a war, this afforded a demonstrative proof, that the peace establishment had been shamefully prodigal.

In answer to this, the minister of[25] the naval department publicly asserted, in the House of Lords, that he knew the low establishment proposed would be fully sufficient for reducing the colonies to obedience. He spoke with the greatest contempt both of the power and the courage of the Americans. He held, that they were not disciplined nor capable of discipline, and that formed of such materials, and so indisposed to action, the numbers of which such boasts had been made, would only add to the facility of their defeat.

Although on these grounds the establishment stood, or seemed to stand as reduced, the ministers did not disclaim any further arrangements of a political nature. By being frequently urged, some explanation was drawn out on that subject in the House of Commons. A gentleman called publicly upon[26] the minister in that House to know, whether he had any information to lay before them, or any measures to propose respecting America, for if he had not, he thought it the duty of parliament to interpose, to call for papers, and to proceed on such information, however defective, as they could obtain. He concluded by totally reprobating the measures adopted by the late parliament, as equally impolitic and impracticable; and said, that they never could be prudently or effectually carried into execution.

The lord at the head of the treasury did not enter much into a justification of the measures of the late parliament. He said the subject would require the utmost diligence and attention, as a matter of the greatest magnitude ever debated within their walls; that he could not entirely acquiesce in the condemnation of measures hastily, which had been taken up and adopted upon such weighty motives; that at the time, it was impossible to foretel precisely how they might answer; but that they should have a fair trial before they were reprobated; and that the wisdom and policy of them could be only finally known in the event. That he had information which he would lay before the House soon after the holidays; and that he would so far adopt the gentleman's ideas who had called upon him, as to propose the appointment of a committee for taking the affairs of America into consideration.

Much altercation arose upon this delay in business of such vast importance as the American; and that the papers and all necessary means of information should be so long retained from the House. Upon these occasions, the ridiculous and distressing situation in which General Gage and his little army stood in Boston; at the same time, in a certain degree, besieging, and themselves besieged, was a subject productive of much animadversion, as well as raillery.

A gentleman in office, and who [27] not long since had become a convert to the principles of administration, just before the recess pulled the mask a little aside, both with respect to the American business, and to the state of the estimates. He said, that any increase of the one, however necessary; or the explanations required on the other, would, in the present season, be highly improper; that such proposals at the eve of an adjournment, could only be intended to embarrass administration; that a compliance with them, would spread such an alarm among the merchants, with respect to their property, as might be productive of the most dangerous consequences; and that they were matters only to be entered upon, when the measures at large, and the means of carrying

them into execution, were brought together, and connected in one view.

Nothing of any consequence was transacted in the House of Lords from the passing of the address, except that a motion was made, and at length carried, for putting an end to that scandalous contention with the Commons, by which, ever since the year 1770, the members of each house were interdicted from the other.

Lord Chatham's motion. Debates. Petitions. London petition withdrawn. Petitions offered from the American agents. Rejected.

THE apprehensions of the ministry, that they would meet with a vigorous opposition from the mercantile interest in the pursuit of their American measures, were not ill founded. During the recess a general alarm was spread, and several meetings of the great bodies of North-American merchants in London and Bristol were held, where those measures by which they were so deeply affected, were fully discussed, their consequences explained, and petitions to parliament prepared and agreed upon in both places. The times were, however, altered, and such an opposition-now, was not productive of the efficacy or danger, which till very lately would have rendered it terrible.

The minister found the opposition reinforced from another quarter, which in other times, and other situations, would have been formidable. The Earl of Chatham, after a long absence, appeared in the House of Lords, to express his utmost dissent and disapprobation to the whole system of American measures. Though his power and influence were from many causes much lessened, his appearance could at no time be wholly without effect.

Jan. 20th. 1775. On the first day of the meeting after the recess, the nobleman at the head of American affairs, having laid the papers belonging to his department before the Lords, Lord Chatham moved an address to his majesty, for recalling the troops from Boston. This motion was ushered in and supported by a long speech, in which he represented this measure as a matter of immediate necessity; an hour now lost in allaying the ferment in America, might produce years of calamity; the present situation of the troops rendered them and the Americans continually liable to events, which would cut off the possibility of a reconciliation; this conciliatory measure, thus well timed; this mark of affection and good-will on our side, will remove all jealousy and apprehension on the other, and instantaneously produce the happiest effects to both. He announced this motion to be introductory to a plan he had formed for a solid, honourable, and lasting settlement between England and America; he now only set his foot upon the threshold of peace.

He severely reprehended administration for eight weeks delay in communicating the American papers, at so very critical a period. He charged them with deluding and deceiving the people of this country in several instances; by general misrepresentations of the colonies; by persuading them that the disputes there were the affair of Boston only, in which the rest were totally unconcerned; and that the appearance of a single regiment there, would restore every thing to quiet. He attributed the sudden dissolution of the parliament, to the same principle of deception. He condemned the whole late series of American laws and measures; said he contended not for indulgence, but justice to America; that if we consulted either our interest or our dignity, the first advances to peace and concord should come from us; that conceffion comes with a better grace, and more falutary effects, from the fuperior power; and warned them of the humiliating difgrace, of repealing thofe acts through neceffity, which they refufed to do from other motives. He is faid to have concluded the fpeech with the following remarkable words, " If the minifters thus perfevere in *mifad-* " *vifing* and *mifleading* the king, I " will not fay that they can alienate " the affections of his fubjects from " his crown, but I will affirm, that " they will make the crown *not* " *worth his wearing.*—I will not " fay that the king is betrayed, " but I will pronounce that—*the* " *kingdom is undone.*"

Whatever difference of opinion in the cabinet might have produced an apparent irrefolution previous to the recefs, it now became evident, that meafures were finally fettled with refpect to America. Though the military and naval ftrength was not increafed, a plan of coercion feemed to be determined on. The language of the lords in adminiftration was high and decifive. They condemned the conduct of the Americans in the ftrongeft and moft unreferved terms; and juftified all the acts of adminiftration, and all the late laws without exception. They infifted, that all conciliating means having proved ineffectual, it was high time for the mother country to affert her authority, or for ever to relinquifh it. If the tafk be difficult now, what muft it be in a few years? Parliament muft be obeyed, or it muft not; if it be obeyed, who fhall refift its determinations? If it be not, it is better at once to give up every claim of authority over America. The fupremacy of the Britifh legiflature cannot be difputed; and the idea of an inactive right, when there is the moft urgent neceffity for its exercife, is abfurd and ridiculous. If we give way on the prefent occafion, from miftaken notions of prefent advantages in trade and commerce, fuch a conceffion will

infallibly defeat its own object; for it is plain, that the navigation act, and all other regulatory acts, which form the great bafis on which thofe advantages reft, and the true interefts of both countries depend, will fall a victim to the interefted and ambitious views of America. In a word, it was declared, that the mother country fhould never relax till America confeffed her fupremacy; and it was avowed to be the minifterial refolution, to enforce obedience by arms.

In this debate it did not appear that the Lords in the minority were fully agreed on the propriety of recalling the troops. Some lords, who were the moft earneft for peace, did not think it at all juft or wife, to leave thofe who had rifqued their lives in favour of the claims of this country, however illfounded, or improperly exercifed, as unprotected victims to the rage of an armed and incenfed populace; and that too, before any previous ftipulations were made for their fafety. They thought that if proper conceffions were made, the troops then at Bofton were not numerous enough to raife an alarm on account of a fuppofed ill faith in keeping them up, and could by no means prevent the reftoration of peace. It was wrong at firft to fend the force; but it might be dangerous to recal it before that was accomplifhed. They however fupported the motion becaufe it looked towards that great object; and becaufe, they faid, they thought any thing better than a perfeverance in hoftility. In argument, it was denied that lenient means had been ineffectually tried with the colonies; and on the contrary infifted, that they had been continually irritated by a feries of abfurd, contradictory, wanton, and oppreffive meafures. That the profcription of Bofton, untried and unheard, whereby 30,000 people were configned to famine and beggary, for the alledged crimes of a few, was an injuftice and cruelty

fcarcely to be paralleled. That, as if it had been done to inflame them to madnefs, and to keep hoftility always in their eyes, an army, merely of irritation, as it evidently could anfwer no other purpofe, was fent amongft them. That unfortunately, paffion, obftinacy, and ill-will, under the direction of inability and ignorance, had been made the principles for governing a free people. That America only wants to have fafety in property, and perfonal liberty; and the defire of independency was falfely charged on her. It was alfo infifted on, that the colonies never denied or queftioned the acts of navigation, except when excited to it by injury.

That the fpecious language, of the fupremacy of the Britifh legiflature, the interefts of Great-Britain, of her authority over the colonies, and other phrafes equally founding, was artfully held out to deceive and delude both parliament and people; they were pompous words, and might fwell the importance of the meaneft mechanic; but they would neither prevent the miferies of a civil war, preferve our commerce, nor reftore our colonies if once loft.

After a pretty long debate, for that houfe, the queftion was rejected by a vaft majority, there appearing upon a divifion, no lefs than 68 who oppofed, to 18 only, who fupported the motion. This divifion was rendered remarkable, by having a prince of the blood, his Royal Highnefs the Duke of Cumberland, for the firft time in the minority. [28]

This decifive victory reftored the confidence of the minifter, and perhaps encouraged him to meafures in the other houfe which he would not otherwife have hazarded. Upon laying the American papers before the Houfe of Commons, a celebrated gentleman in the oppofition, defired they might be informed, whether thefe papers contained all the intelligence the mi- [29]

nifters had received from America. The minifter replied, that he would not undertake to fay they did, as thofe he had brought were extracts, containing only the facts in the original letters; that the writers opinions were not mentioned, it having been frequently found, that the making public the private opinions of people in office, had been attended with bad confequences; therefore his majefty's fervants had determined, for the future, never to mention the private opinion of any perfon.

The gentleman who propofed the queftion faid, that in fome cafes it might be proper to keep a perfon's private opinion fecret; but, in fo critical and alarming an affair as that of the Americans, the opinions of people in power, on the fpot, muft be of great fervice. Their judgments muft operate here as facts; at leaft, facts unconnected with the opinions of thofe who beft knew the fpirit and tendency of each action, would be of little ufe, tending only to miflead: an act of violence is committed—if we know neither the motive to it—to what it is likely to lead—or what force will probably fupport it—how can a true judgment be made of it? As to the opinion concerning the meafures proper to be purfued for quieting thefe troubles; there too the opinion of thofe on the fpot, and poffeffing every means of information, was of the firft importance. That things were gone too far, to think it neceffary to manage the opinions of any man in office in America. The rifque to be run (at fuch a time) is a neceffary confequence of their fituation; and they would be more endangered by the ignorance of parliament concerning their fentiments, than by any fentiments they could deliver. That in 1766 (the year, he faid, of happy reconciliation) every paper, without referve, had been laid before the Houfe, and no man fuffered by it. He therefore was of opinion, that the whole of the information

received from America ought to be laid before the Houfe, and not extracts of particular letters, fuch as fuited the minifter's purpofe.

This propofition not being admitted, the minifter moved, that the papers fhould, on the 26th inftant, be referred to the confideration of a committee of the whole Houfe. They confifted principally of letters between fome of the minifters, and the governors of moft of the colonies; and were tranfmitted in this mutilated ftate to the committee.

The principal trading and manufacturing towns in the kingdom, having waited to regulate their conduct as to American affairs, by that of the merchants of London and Briftol, now accordingly followed the example of thofe two great commercial bodies, and prepared petitions upon that fubject to be prefented to parliament. The petition from the merchants of London, was of courfe the firft delivered, and being prefented by one of the aldermen of that city, who was likewife a member of parliament, he moved, that it fhould be referred to the committee, who were appointed to take into confideration the American papers. **Jan. 23d.**

This feemed to be fo natural, and fo much a matter of courfe, as fcarcely to admit of a controverfy. The minifters had, however, by this time, hit upon a manoeuvre, which, though fuccefsful for the prefent, may not in all feafons be fo happily drawn into practice; but by which, the fhower of petitions was fo effectually thrown off, that they became a matter of fport rather than of concern. It was difcovered, that this matter was to be taken up in a political, not a commercial light. That therefore, as there was little connection between the views of the Houfe, and thofe of the merchants, it would be the higheft abfurdity, that a committee, whofe thoughts were occupied by the firft, fhould be at

all broke in upon or difturbed by the latter. It was accordingly propofed, to appoint a feparate committee for the confideration of the merchants petition, and for that purpofe an amendment was moved, that it fhould be referred to a committee on the 27th, the day fucceeding that on which the committee was to take the American papers into confideration.

It was reprefented, that the committee for the confideration of the American papers was appointed with a view to their coming to fome fpeedy refolution, fuited to the dignity of parliament, and to the prefent ftate of affairs in America; that the reftoration of peace in that country, depended as much upon the immediate application, as upon the vigour of the meafures determined; that the great variety of facts, and mafs of matter, which of courfe muft come under confideration in the committee to which the petition was referred, would be a work of tedious enquiry, and long toil; that fuch a length of enquiry was incompatible with the difpatch neceffary in the bufinefs with which it would be coupled by the motion; that the hands of government would thereby be tied up, and the powers of parliament reftrained from giving that fpeedy relief, which the preffure of public affairs requires; and that the views and objects of the enquiry originating with the American papers, and the petition, being totally diftinct in their nature, the determinations and execution arifing from both muft be different.

On the other fide, adminiftration was very feverely handled. They faid, that it would be fairer and more manly to reject the petition at once, than to endeavour in this manner to defeat it; that the pretence of appointing a committee was a fhameful pitiful evafion; that while to avoid the rejection of a petition which had nothing exceptionable in the matter or the form, they fuffered it into the houfe,

30

they, at the same time, took care it should never be heard; or, what was more insulting to the petitioners, and more disgraceful to parliament, to hear it, after a determination. Is it then true, said they, that in a question concerning the colonies, politics and commerce are separate and independent considerations? But if they are, still the information which the merchants may give in their evidence of matters merely political, may be of advantage to the House. Their correspondencies are of all kinds. They do not scruple to offer to the House all they know of the state of that country, without those fears which it seems affect our officers in America. And as the minister had refused to give them the whole correspondence, this supplemental information became the more necessary. That if there was not sufficient time to enquire into and settle the American business, why was a month lost in dissipation during the Christmas recess, for which the dearest interests of the empire were to be sacrificed, and perhaps its existence as an empire hazarded. That after all, what time would be lost? One day perhaps—One petition contained the merits of the whole—and all the evidence might be examined to that. This, they said, was the course in the year 1766, when an act of reconciliation, which in its nature required more haste, was before the House. Much larger correspondence, and infinitely more evidence, than probably would now appear, was then before them. It did not delay a business which experience had shewn to be beneficial; that therefore, they need not be in such a violent haste, to new coercive measures, which the same experience had shewn, in late instances, to be highly pernicious.

The question being at length put, the motion for the amendment was carried by a majority of more than two to one, the numbers being 197, who voted for the lat-

ter, against 81 who supported the original motion.

A similar fate attended the petitions from Bristol, Glasgow, Norwich, Liverpool, Manchester, Birmingham, Wolverhampton, Dudley, and some other places, all of which were in turn consigned to what the opposition termed the committee of oblivion.

On the day appointed for taking the American papers into consideration, a second, and very strong petition was presented from the merchants of London, in which they argue, that the connection between Great-Britain and America originally was, and ought to be, of a commercial kind; and that the benefits derived therefrom to the mother country are of the same nature; that observing the constant attention which the British legislature had for more than a century given to those valuable objects, they had been taught to admire the regulations by which that connection had been preserved, and those benefits secured, as the most effectual institution which human wisdom could have framed for those salutary purposes; that presuming therefore on that opinion, and supported by that observation, they represent, that the fundamental policy of those laws of which they complain, and the propriety of enforcing, relaxing, or amending them, are questions inseparably united with the commerce between Great-Britain and America; and consequently, that the consideration of the one cannot be entered on, without a full discussion of the other.

They then lament the late decision, by which their petition was referred to a separate committee, and by which, they say, they are absolutely precluded from such a hearing in its support, as could alone procure them that relief, which the importance and present deplorable state of their trade required. They conclude by praying, that they may be heard, by them-

selves or their agents, in support of their former petition, and that no resolution respecting America may be taken by the House, or by any committee thereof, until they shall be fully heard.

It was then moved, that the order for referring the merchants petition to a separate committee should be discharged, and that it should be referred to the committee of the whole House, who were appointed to consider the American papers.

This motion was supported by the gentlemen in the minority, as they contended, on the principles of law, justice, reason, and expediency. The indignity and mockery offered to so great a body as the merchants of London by the late resolution, which with an insidious affectation of civility, received the petition with one hand, and threw it out of the window with the other, was painted in strong colours. It was said, that the matter of that petition, was not merely the business of the merchants, nor even of this kingdom in particular; it was the business of the whole empire, every part of which was concerned in the event; yet this matter of such momentous concern, was referred to a committee, called up, nobody knew why, for the framing of commercial regulations, which were neither wanted, nor applied for; while this committee did not even pretend to have the remotest concern with those great points of commercial policy, which were the objects of the petition. That to compleat this system, and render its wisdom equally conspicuous in all its parts, the committee, to whose consideration those objects were avowedly referred, to which the petition applied, were doomed to grope their way in the dark, without a single ray of information; the probable, and almost inevitable consequence of which, must be the involving us in a most destructive and ruinous civil war.

In further supporting the motion

on the merchants petition, it was observed, that the reason given by those who sent the petition to that committee (which was described by various appellations of mockery and derision), for not referring them to that on American papers, was of a most extraordinary and unheard of nature; it was, that the resolutions of that committee were to be solely on the grounds of policy, and that the commercial examination would delay the measures necessary for the coercion of America. That this was to anticipate and predetermine the future proceedings in a committee, as a reason for keeping information from it; how did they know what measures would be pursued there, and on what principles? Was there any instruction to the committee so to confine itself? Or was it that the ministry had already not only resolved what that committee was to do, but reckoned upon it so much as a certainty, and as a matter so justifiable, that they did not scruple to avow it, and to make it a ground of argument for what the House ought, or ought not to have brought before its committee. This proceeding was represented to be of a most alarming and unprecedented nature. It was further added, that if they meant hostility, the reason they gave for not hearing, was the strongest for it; that as their war must ever be dependent on their finances, and their finances must depend upon their commerce, the true state of that commerce was necessary to be known, especially as colonies and commerce are inseparably connected.

The arguments on the other side were partly personal; partly political. In either way they did not seem to furnish reasons against hearing the merchants; and from the nature of the measure which afterwards was adopted, it did not seem very material whether it passed a month earlier or later. It was said, that interested and factious people had induced the merchants to sign their petitions. That they came too late, and as the merchants had confided so long in parliament, they ought to do so still. That the American trade was destructive, unless the supremacy of parliament, and the rights of sovereignty, were vigorously asserted. That if in this attempt commerce should be suspended, the funds sustain a shock, and the landed property experience a diminution, such evils must be patiently submitted to, and the merchants must forego their interest, for the permanent advantages which they may expect when the Americans are subdued. It was also mentioned, that the merchants might be quieted, by passing a law to compel the several colonies to pay all the debts, which any individuals of those provinces owed here.

All the debates on this subject of the petitions, were attended with an unusual degree of asperity, and even acrimony on the side of opposition. The charges of negligence, incapacity, and inconsistency, were rung in the ears of the minister. The acts of the last parliament were arraigned in the severest terms, and said to be framed on false information, conceived in weakness and ignorance, and executed with negligence. The ministers were told, that a bitter day of reckoning would come, when they would be convicted of such a chain of blunders and neglects, as would inevitably draw vengeance on their heads. A pathetic picture was drawn and deplored, of the miseries of that civil war, which must be incurred through their rashness and blind precipitation. Trade destroyed—The revenue impoverished — The poor starving—Manufactures stagnating —The poor-rate running into the land-tax, and both devouring the estates.

The conduct also of the late parliament was scrutinized without mercy in the course of these debates, and its memory was treated with more than want of respect. A gentleman, who is remarkable for a [31] sarcastic poignancy in his observation, in sketching a short history of that parliament, said, that they began their political life with a violation of the sacred right of election in the case of Middlesex; that they had died in the act or Popery, when they established the Roman Catholic religion in Canada; and that they had left a rebellion in America, as a legacy.

In endeavouring to obviate some of the charges brought against him, the minister attributed the delay before the holidays, in the first place, to the want of necessary information, and in the second, to his having understood from several persons, who had means of being well informed, that a petition was on its way to the throne, from the meeting which the Americans called a continental congress, which was of so conciliatory a nature, as to make way for healing and lenient measures, and for reconciling all matters in an amicable manner. As to other charges upon the American subject, he said, that it was impossible for him to have foreseen the proceedings in America respecting the tea; that the duty had been quietly collected before; that the great quantity of teas in the warehouses of the East-India Company, as appeared by the report of the Secret Committee, made it necessary to do something for the benefit of the Company; that it was to serve them that nine-pence in the pound weight draw-back was allowed; that it was impossible for him to foretell that the Americans would resist at being able to drink their tea at nine-pence in the pound cheaper.

This defence called up a gentleman of great weight in the East- [32] India Company, and who has been long celebrated for his knowledge in its affairs. He said, that he got up merely to speak to a matter of fact; that he could not sit still and hear the noble Lord plume himself on actions which, of all others, were the moſt reprehenſible in this train of political abſurdities; that it was unbecoming to alledge that this dangerous meaſure had been adopted to ſerve the Eaſt-India Company, when it was notorious, that the Company had requeſted the repeal of the three-pence per pound in America, and felt and knew the abſurdity of giving a. draw-back here, and laying a duty there; a meaſure equally a ſolecicifm in commerce and politics. That the Company offered their conſent, that government ſhould retain 6d. in the pound on the exportation, if the 3d. was remitted in America. That the gentleman himſelf, then ſpeaking, had, in his place, requeſted and intreated the noble Lord, to remove the cauſe of diſpute; and that he then foretold to him the conſequence of perſevering in error.

After ſome ſevere reflections, he ſhewed, that the Company had thus preſented the happieſt opportunity which could have offered, for removing with credit the cauſe of difference with America. The ſupporting the authority of parliament was the only cauſe aſſigned by the miniſter himſelf, for retaining the duty on tea; at the ſame time, that he acknowldged it to be as anti-commercial a tax, as any of thoſe which he had repealed upon that principle. Here, then, ſprung the happieſt occaſion of doing right, without interfering on the claims on either ſide. The Eaſt-India Company aſk; their ſituation required the relief. It could not be alledged that it was done at the inſtance of American diſcontent. But the golden bridge was refuſed. New contrivances were ſet on foot to introduce the tea into America. That various intrigues, ſolicitations, and counter-ſolicitations, were uſed to induce the Chairman, and Deputy Chairman of the Company, to undertake this raſh and fooliſh buſineſs; that it had been proteſted againſt, as contrary to

the principles of their monopoly: yet the power of miniſtry prevailed, and they would, notwithſtanding, cover all thoſe facts, which are ready, from their conſequences, to convulſe the whole empire, under a pretence of the pureſt intentions in the world, merely of ſerving the Eaſt-India Company.

Theſe facts were conſidered as incontrovertible, as none of them were denied at that time or afterwards. The queſtion was rejected upon a _Jan. 26th._ diviſion by a very great majority, there appearing in ſupport of the motion, for reſcinding the former reſolution relative to the merchants petition, only 89, to 250 who oppoſed that meaſure.

Though it was then late, a petition was offered from Mr. Bollan, Dr. Franklin, and Mr. Lee, three American agents, ſtating, that they[33] were authorized by the American continental congreſs, to preſent a petition from the congreſs to the King, which petition his Majeſty had referred to that Houſe; that they were enabled to throw great light upon the ſubject, and prayed to be heard at the bar, in ſupport of the ſaid petition. On this a violent debate aroſe, partly on the ſame grounds with the former, partly on different.—The miniſtry alledged that the congreſs was no legal body, and none could be heard in reference to their proceedings, without giving that illegal body ſome degree of countenance; that they could only hear the colonies through their legal aſſemblies, and their agents properly authorized by them, and properly admitted here; that to do otherwiſe, would lead to inextricable confuſion, and deſtroy the whole order of colony government.

To theſe arguments it was anſwered, that regular colony government was in effect deſtroyed already: in ſome places, by act of parliament; in others, by diſſolution of aſſemblies by governors; in ſome, by popular violence. The

queſtion now was, how to reſtore order? That this congreſs, however illegal to other purpoſes, was ſufficiently legal for preſenting a petition.—It was ſigned by the names of all the perſons who compoſed it, and might be received as from individuals. That it was their buſineſs rather to find every plauſible reaſon for receiving petitions, than to invent pretences for rejecting them. That the rejection of petitions was one principal cauſe, if not the moſt powerful cauſe, of the preſent troubles. That this mode of conſtantly rejecting their petitions, and refuſing to hear their agents, would infallibly end in univerſal rebellion; and not unnaturally, as thoſe ſeem to give up the right to government who refuſe to hear the complaints of the ſubject. This petition was rejected upon a diviſion by a majority of 218 to 68.

The London merchants, however, did not ſubmit patiently to the indignity with which they thought themſelves now treated. The ſpirit which had at all times diſtinguiſhed that great commercial body was not loſt; nor was the rank and conſideration, which they ever held in the affairs of this country, forgotten. The day following the rejection of their ſecond petition, being that on which the committee of oblivion was to hold its firſt meeting, and their buſineſs of courſe the firſt to come before it, a gentleman, one of their body, deputed by the committee of merchants, in their name repreſented at the bar of the Houſe, "that merchants revealing at that bar the ſtate of their affairs, was a meaſure which all would wiſh to avoid, unleſs upon ſuch great occaſions as the preſent, where the public weal is evidently at ſtake, when their duty as good ſubjects requires it of them; but when the mode of examination is ſuch as totally precludes them from anſwering the great public object, which in their opinion is clearly the caſe at preſent, they beg [34] leave humbly to fignify, that they wave appearing before the committee which has been appointed; and that the merchants are not under any apprehenfions refpecting their American debts, unlefs the means of remittance fhould be cut off by meafures that may be adopted in Great-Britain."

During this war of the petitions, one had been fent from Birmingham and prefented, entitled, a petition from the inhabitants of that town and neighbourhood, in which they fet forth, that any relaxation in the execution of the laws, refpecting the colonies, would greatly injure the commerce of Birmingham; and ftrongly urging, that the Houfe would exert its utmoft endeavours to fupport the authority of the laws. No other petition or addrefs had then appeared in favour of ftrong meafures againft America; and it was fufpected,[35] that this had been procured by indirect practice, as moft of thofe, who had figned the paper, were perfons no ways concerned in the ftaple manufactures of the place; at leaft, fuch as were, did not export any confiderable quantity to America. Another petition, to a contrary effect, was figned and prefented by thofe, who dealt moft largely in that branch. A leading gentleman in the minority ob-[36] ferved, that the miniftry had frequently reproached the oppofition with unfair methods in procuring thefe petitions; that now, one place having fpoken fuch different languages, they had an opportunity of difcovering the truth of that matter, and of effectually difcouraging fuch matters for the future: he therefore moved, that it fhould be an inftruction to the committee, to enquire into the manner of procuring and figning both petitions; and alfo, how far the perfons, feverally figning them, are concerned in the trade to North-America. The motion, as ufual, was overruled.

In this manner the parties tried their feveral forces in parliament and in the nation, previous to the bringing in the grand meafure, on which the miniftry refted their hope of finally breaking the fpirit which gave them fo much trouble in America. It was evident, that their failure in their former plans had not in the leaft abated the readinefs fhewn by both Houfes of Parliament to adopt any others which adminiftration fhould propofe; and it was confidently believed and afferted, that when the merchants and manufacturers were deprived of all hopes of preventing the operation of force, it would then become their intereft to give all poffible effect to it. They would thus become, by degrees, a principal fupport of that caufe, which they now fo eagerly oppofed. When once every thing was made to depend on war, nothing but the fuccefs of that war could give the trading body any hopes of recovering their debts and renewing their commerce: therefore, not only this opinion, of the efficacy of fuch a mode of proceeding in America, but the hopes of compelling a great body at home to concurrence, made the minifters more and more refolved to go through, and complete the coercive plan they had begun with.

Lord Chatham's conciliatory bill with refpect to America. Debates. The bill rejected. Petition from the Weft-India planters, and the merchants of London, to the Houfe of Commons. Addrefs to the Throne moved for in that Houfe, by the Minifter. Great debates; amendment moved for; rejected; original motion for the addrefs carried by a great majority. Motion for re-committing the addrefs, upon receiving the report from the committee. Debates longer than before. The motion rejected. Conference with the Lords. Petitions from the merchants and planters to the Lords. Debate on a point of order, whether the petitions fhould be received, previous to the making of a motion for filling up the blanks in the addrefs. Motion made. Previous queftion put. Great debates, both with refpect to the previous queftion, and the fubject of the addrefs. Motion for the previous queftion rejected by a great majority; original motion, by which the Lords concurred with the Commons in the addrefs, agreed to. Protefts.

THE noble Earl, who lately[37] made a motion in the Houfe of Lords for the recall of the troops from Bofton, not difcouraged at the great majority by which his motion was rejected, ftill perfevered in the profecution of that conciliatory fcheme with America, which he then in part announced, and to which that motion was only introductory. He accordingly brought into that Houfe the outlines of a bill, which he hoped would anfwer that falutary purpofe, under the title of "A provifional act for fettling the troubles in America, and for afferting the fupreme legiflative authority and fuperintending power of Great-Britain over the colonies."

Feb. 1.

He intreated the affiftance of the Houfe to digeft the crude materials, which, thrown together in the nature of a bill, he now prefumed to lay before them; to bring and reduce the whole to that form, which was fuited to the dignity and importance of the fubject, and to the great ends to which it was ultimately directed. He called on them to exercife their candor, and deprecated the effects of party or prejudice; of factious fpleen, or a blind predilection. He declared himfelf to be actuated by no narrow principle, or perfonal confideration whatever; and faid, that though the propofed bill might be looked upon as a bill of conceffion, it was impoffible but to confefs, at the fame time, that it was a bill of affertion.

This bill caufed a great variety of difcuffions within and without doors. The miniftry found it a propofition of reconciliation by conceffion, which was caufe fufficient (independently of the obnoxious quarter from whence it came) to induce them to reject it; their plan being at that time, tho' a little varied afterwards, to fhew a firm refolution not to give way, in any inftance, whilft the oppofition in America continued. Others faid, that the bill contained a multiplicity of matter. Many of its parts were liable to, and feemed to require much feparate difcuffion: they were fo numerous, and fo various in their nature, that the aggregate mafs appeared too great to be comprized in one draught. As it was in a great meafure conditional, its operation depended, not only on the confent, but the acts of others; and a long time might elapfe before it could be certainly known, whether it was or was not to operate. He laid down, as a condition not to be controverted, and upon which all the benefits of the act depended, a full acknowledgment of the fupremacy of the legiflature, and the fuperintending power of the Britifh parliament. It did not abfolutely decide in words upon the right of taxation, but partly as a matter of grace, and partly, to appearance, as a compromife, declared and enacted, that no tallage, tax, or other charge fhall be levied in America, except by common confent in their provincial affemblies; a manner of conceffion, which feems to imply the right. It afferts, as an undoubted prerogative, the royal right to fend any part of a legal army to any part of its dominions, at all times, and in all feafons, and condemns a paffage in the petition from the continental congrefs, which militates with that right; but, as a falvo, declares, that no military force, however legally raifed and kept, can ever be lawfully employed to violate and deftroy the juft rights of the people; a declaration which, it was faid, would afford little relief to a people

groaning under the preffure of a military government; as whoever held the fword, would decide upon the queftion of law.

This bill legalized the holding of a congrefs in the enfuing month of May, for the double purpofe of duly recognizing the fupreme legiflative authority and fuperintending power of parliament over the colonies, and for making a free grant to the King, his heirs and fucceffors, of a certain and perpetual revenue, fubject to the difpofition of parliament, and applicable to the alleviation of the national debt. Taking it for granted that this free aid would bear an honourable proportion to the great and flourifhing ftate of the colonies, the neceffities of the mother country, and their obligations to her; on thefe conditions, it reftrained the powers of the admiralty courts to their ancient limits, and without repealing, fufpended for a limited time thofe late acts, or parts of acts, which had been complained of in the petition from the continental congrefs. It placed the judges upon the fame footing, as to the holding of their falaries and offices, with thofe in England; and fecured to the colonies all the privileges, franchifes and immunities, granted by their feveral charters and conftitutions.

The noble Lord, at the head of the American department, behaved with great moderation. He faid, that the bill took in fuch a variety of matter, that it was impoffible to pronounce any immediate opinion concerning its propriety; and that as its noble author did not feem to prefs the Houfe to any immediate decifion, but appeared rather defirous that it fhould be maturely and fully confidered, he fuppofed it would be agreeable to him, and he would have no objection to receive it upon that condition, that it fhould lie upon the table till the American papers were firft taken into confideration.

Whether refpect for the framer of the bill, or whatever the motives

were that induced this conceffion, they had no effect on the other Lords in adminiftration, who oppofed it with fo much heat, as to forget that attention which its author, and the importance of the fubject, feemed to demand. It is unufual in parliament to reject, on the firft propofition, any bill for an object allowed to be neceffary; and promifing, however faintly or rudely, any plan for obtaining the end propofed. But the proceeding on this occafion was different. They condemned, without referve, the bill in the whole, and in all its parts; and cenfured the mode of bringing it in, as irregular, unparliamentary, and unprecedented; that it was impoffible to conceive how fuch a mafs of matter, fo important in its nature, fo extenfive in its confequences, and directed to fuch a variety of objects, each of them worthy of a feparate confideration, could be thus brought forward together, and in fuch a manner; that the matter fhould have been laid before the Houfe in feparate proportions, each of which fhould be fingly difcuffed, as leading to one great comprehenfive fyftem.

It was befides contended, that this bill fell in with the ideas of America in almoft every particular, and held out no one fecurity; that fhould we be bafe and daftardly enough to betray the rights of the parliament of Great-Britain, the Americans would only agree to thofe parts of it that fuited their own views, and totally difclaim thofe that were held out as matters of fubmiffion or conceffion. But above all other caufes it was condemned, as not only giving a fanction to the traiterous proceedings of the congrefs already held, but by the appointment of another, to legalize fuch meetings by act of parliament.

It was faid, that the fufpenfion of thofe acts, propofed in the bill, would, to every fubftantial purpofe, amount to an actual repeal; that if the laws for eftablifhing the admiralty courts were repealed, the act of navigation would be of no farther avail, and become only a dead letter. The rebellious temper and hostile disposition of the Americans was much enlarged upon; that they were not disputing about words, but about realities; that though the duty upon tea was the pretence, the restrictions upon their commerce, and the hope of throwing them off, were the real motives of their disobedience; that they had already attacked and taken one of the King's forts, and seized his stores and ammunition, to employ them against himself; that if any thing can constitute rebellion, this must; that this was no time for concession; and that, to concede now, would be to give the point up for ever. It was therefore moved, and strongly supported by all the Lords on that side, that the bill should be rejected in the first instance.

The noble framer defended himself and his bill from the numerous attacks which were made on both, with great spirit and vigour. The indignity which was offered, seemed to renew all the fire of youth; and he retorted the sarcasms, which were levelled upon him from different quarters, with a most pointed severity. If he was charged with hurrying this business in an unusual and irregular manner into parliament, he placed it to the critical necessity of the times; to the wretched inability and incapacity of the ministers, who, though they declared all America to be in rebellion, had not, at this late season, a plan to propose, or a system to pursue, for the adjustment of public affairs; that under such circumstances of emergency on one side, when perhaps a single day might determine the fate of this great empire; and such a shameful negligence, inattention, and want of ability on the other, no alternative remained, but either to abandon the interests of his country, and relinquish his duty, or to pro-

pose such measures as seemed the most capable of restoring peace and quiet. He then called upon the servants of the crown, to declare, whether they had any plan, however deficient, to lay before the House? And that if they had, he would set them an example of candour which they by no means deserved, by instantly withdrawing the present bill.

Though it was evident, that no previous concert had been held with the Lords in opposition, in respect to this bill, and that few of them, perhaps, would have approved of it in all its parts if there had; yet they all felt, as in their own case, the insult offered, and the contempt shewn, by throwing it out in this abrupt and disgraceful manner. The most moderate contended, that both the framer and some of the matter of the bill, deserved a better reception; that they were entitled to a fair hearing and a free discussion; that it would convey to foreigners, as well as natives, very unfavourable ideas of the justice of that House, and of its hostile disposition towards the colonies, if the first propositions that were made, for the restoration of peace and harmony, were to be rejected in so harsh and unprecedented a manner, without even affording them a fair hearing. Conciliatory measures should at least be examined, whether it were found eligible to adopt them or not. The bill was in their hands; they might strike out the objectionable parts; and undoubtedly they would find many which it might be highly useful to retain.

This debate of course called up the whole of the American affairs, which accordingly underwent much discussion. On one side, the dangers of a civil war were shewn, as well with respect to its domestic as foreign consequences, and its miseries strongly painted; our present calamitous situation deplored, and the men and the measures execrated that involved us in such a

labyrinth of evils. On the other, the dangers were in part lessened, and those that were supposed, respecting foreign states, denied; the consequent evils of rebellion were incident to dominion and government; and, in the present instance, sprung entirely from the original traiterous designs, hostile intentions, and rebellious disposition of the Americans. The nature of the subjects, and the state of temper on both sides, produced much warmth, severe altercation, and even personal animadversion.

After a long and most pointed debate, the bill was rejected by a majority of 61 to 32; not being even allowed to lie upon the table. Upon this question his Royal Highness the Duke of Cumberland voted in the minority.

The day after this debate, a petition was presented to the House of Commons, from the planters of the sugar colonies residing in Great Britain, and the merchants of London trading to those colonies. In this petition they set forth, how exceedingly they were alarmed at the association and agreement entered into by the continental congress, in consequence of which all trade between North America and the West Indies were to cease at a given day, unless the acts of parliament therein specified were repealed by that time. They stated, that the British property in the West India islands amounted to upwards of thirty millions sterling; that a further property of many millions was employed in the commerce created by the said islands; a commerce comprehending Africa, the East Indies and Europe; and that the whole profits and produce of those capitals ultimately center in Great-Britain, and add to the national wealth, while the navigation necessary to all its branches, establishes a strength which wealth can neither purchase nor balance.

They shewed, that the sugar plantations in the West-Indies are subject to a greater variety of contingencies than many other species of property, from their necessary dependance on external support; that therefore, should any interruption happen in the general system of their commerce, the great national stock, thus vested and employed, must become precarious and unprofitable; and that the profits arising from the present state of those islands, and that are likely to arise from their future improvement, in a great measure depend on a free and reciprocal intercourse between them and the several provinces of North-America, from whence they are furnished with provisions and other supplies, absolutely necessary for their support and the maintenance of their plantations.

They then proceed to shew, that they could not be supplied from any other markets, and in any degree proportionate to their wants, with those articles of indispensable necessity, which they now derive from the middle colonies of North America; and that if the agreement and association of the congress take full effect, which they firmly believe will happen, unless the former harmony which subsisted between this kingdom and the American colonies, to the infinite advantage of both, be restored, the islands, will be reduced to the utmost distress. This petition, like all the former upon the same subject, was referred to the established petition committee.

The time was at length arrived, when the minister thought proper to open his designs with respect to America. On the day, upon which the West-India petition had been presented, he in a long speech recapitulated the information contained in those American papers which had been referred to the committee; he then proceeded to discriminate the temper, disposition, and degrees of resistance, that prevailed in the several colonies; to point out those where moderation really prevailed; with others,

where, he said, violence was concealed under the mask of duty and submission; and finished the group by naming those which he considered to be in a state of actual rebellion. He asserted, that several arts had been practiced on both sides of the Atlantic, to raise this seditious spirit to its present alarming height. After this charge, he proceeded to draw a comparison between the burdens borne by the people in England, and those in America; in which, allowing his premises and calculations, the disparity appeared about fifty to one; that is, a man in England, ceteris paribus, pays fifty times as much money to the public expence as a man in America.

He then proceeded to lay down the legislative supremacy of parliament; to state the measures adopted by America to resist it, and the almost universal confederacy of the colonies, in that resistance. Here, he said, he laid his foot on the great barrier, which separated, and for the present disunited both countries; and on this ground alone, of resistance and denial, he would raise every argument leading to the motion which he intended to make; and this motion, he explained, would be for an address to the king, and for a conference with the lords that it might be the joint address of both Houses. He then gave a sketch of the measures he intended to pursue, which were, to send a greater force to America; to bring in a temporary act to put a stop to all the foreign trade of the different colonies of New England, particularly to their fishery on the Banks of Newfoundland, till they returned to their duty; at the same time declaring, that whenever they should acknowledge the supreme authority of the British legislature, pay obedience to the laws of this realm, and make a due submission to the king, their real grievances, upon their making proper application, should be redressed.

The minister said, that the other

colonies were not so culpable, and he hoped might yet be brought to a sense of their duty to the mother country by more lenient measures. The question now, he said, lay within a very narrow compass: it was simply whether we should abandon all claims on the colonies, and at once give up all the advantages arising from our sovereignty, and the commerce dependant on it? or whether we should resort to the measures indispensably necessary in such circumstances, and thereby insure both?

The address was to the following purpose. To return thanks for the communication of the American papers, and to declare, that having taken them into most serious consideration, they find that a part of his majesty's subjects in the province of the Massachusett's-Bay, have proceeded so far as to resist the authority of the supreme legislature, and that a rebellion at this time actually exists within the said province; that they see with the utmost concern, that they have been countenanced and encouraged by unlawful combinations and engagements entered into, in several of the other colonies, to the injury and oppression of many of their innocent fellow-subjects resident within the kingdom of Great-Britain and the rest of his Majesty's dominions; that this conduct appears the more inexcusable, when they consider with how much temper his Majesty and the two Houses of Parliament have acted, in support of the laws and constitution of Great-Britain. They declare, that they can never so far desert the trust reposed in them, as to relinquish any part of the sovereign authority over all the dominions, which by law is vested in his Majesty and the two Houses of Parliament; and that the conduct of many persons, in several of the colonies, during the late disturbances, is alone sufficient to convince them how necessary this power is, for the protection of the lives and fortunes of all his

Majefty's fubjects; that they ever have been, and always fhall be, ready to pay attention and regard to any real grievances of any of his Majefty's fubjects, which fhall in a dutiful and conftitutional manner be laid before them; and whenever any of the colonies fhall make a proper application to them, they fhall be ready to afford them every juft and reafonable indulgence; but that, at the fame time, they confider it as their indifpenfable duty, humbly to befeech his Majefty, that he will take the moft effectual meafures to enforce due obedience to the laws and authority of the fupreme legiflature; and they beg leave in the moft folemn manner, to affure his Majefty, that it is their fixed refolution, at the hazard of their lives and properties, to ftand by his Majefty, againft all rebellious attempts, in the maintenance of his juft rights, and thofe of the two Houfes of Parliament.

This addrefs was fo loaded with confequences, the extent of which could not be defined, that it not only called up all the powers of oppofition; but even fome few of the moft moderate, and who in conformity to that habit of temper, had ufually gone with adminiftration, as a fmooth, fafe, and eafy way of travelling, feemed now to feel a kind of chill and horror, at entering upon fo decifive a meafure, and, as they apprehended, fo dangerous in the tendency, and inexplicable in the event.

A gentleman of the firft emi-[39] nence in the law, though not now in office, followed the minifter through the whole detail of his fpeech, and anfwered the different pofitions. He affirmed, that though the premifes might be right, the conclufions were erroneous; that having examined with legal precifion the definitions of treafon, he infifted that the Americans were not in rebellion. That the appearances of riot, diforder, tumult, and fedition, which had been fo faithfully recounted, as they were

not of a nature to imply rebellion directly in themfelves, fo neither did they arife from motives, which render acts of the fame or lefs magnitude truly and properly rebellious. That nothing in the papers have either fuch acts or motives. Whatever the diforders might be, they were created by the conduct of thofe, whofe views were to eftablifh defpotifm; and which were manifeftly directed to reduce America to the moft abject ftate of fervility, as a prelude to the realizing of the fame wicked fyftem in the mother country. He concluded by infifting, that an oppofition to arbitrary meafures was warranted by the conftitution, and eftablifhed by precedent.

The other gentlemen of the minority entered but little into the juridical part of the debate. They contended, that it was a matter of little importance, whether the difturbances which prevailed in all the colonies, might be termed in legal acceptation Rebellions or not. The queftion before the Houfe was, whether it was prudent for Parliament, and at that time, to *declare* them fo. For if Parliament fhould find it neceffary, in the courfe of events, to reconcile by any conceffion, treaty with and conceffion to Rebels, would be highly difhonourable to Parliament. If treaty fhould not take place, their arms would never be the more powerful for diftinguifhing the war by the name of a rebellion. That it would render many in America, if not all, quite defperate; and make them think themfelves contending for their lives, properties, and families, as well as for their political liberty. It was vainly expected (they faid) that this method of choofing out Maffachufett's-Bay as the only feat of rebellion, could ever blind the other colonies to the confequences, or perfuade them to abandon, what they had already made a common caufe in the moft public and folemn manner poffible. That it was well known, no act of

violence had been committed in Maffachufett's-Bay, which was not equalled by fomething of a fimilar, and even fometimes exceeded by acts of a more heinous nature, in every other province. That therefore, the only effect of this violent but partial declaration of rebellion, would be to delude ourfelves into preparations of hoftility, as if againft one province only, when in truth, we had twelve to contend with; and what weakened our preparations would give ftrength to theirs. That the experience of laft year in the partial proceedings againft Bofton, might ferve to teach the Houfe the infufficiency and mifchief of fuch low and contemptible politicks. That inftead of repeating errors in defiance of experience; they ought at laft to open their eyes to their real fituation. The colonies were now compacted into one body. The proceeding of one was become the proceeding of all. Every attempt to difunite them had been found to ftrengthen their union; all feverities, to augment their rage and indignation; that therefore they ought, inftead of menacing other places, railing at Maffachufett's-Bay, and declaring a partial rebellion, to provide in good earneft and the utmoft expedition, for a general war, or general reconciliation with the colonies.

On the other fide, the crown lawyers and minifterial debaters infifted, that fuch Americans as came within certain defcriptions, had been guilty of certain acts, and that ftill perfevered in the fupport and commiffion of thofe acts, were in a ftate of actual rebellion. That thofe, who by open force make a general refiftance to the execution of the laws, are by all writers confidered as guilty of high treafon. That many in England had been tried, convicted, and executed for that offence without any complaint of illegality and injuftice. Were not the acts of as open violence and as much levelled againft the laws in Maffachufett's-Bay, as any of thofe proceedings fo feverely punifhed here? Or is high treafon and rebellion of a different nature in America and England? As to the declaration of parliament, it does not preclude the future mercy of the crown, if the rebels fhould appear to be deferving of it. The very addrefs was itfelf an act of mercy, in warning an ignorant and obftinate people of their danger. That it was not neceffary to punifh univerfally; the punifhment of a few of the worft fort of traitors, fuch as Hancock and his crew, might be fufficient to teach the reft their duty in future. That the boafted union of the colonies would diffolve the moment parliament fhewed itfelf refolved on meafures of vigour and feverity. The whole of their attempt, both in their political confederacy, and their commercial affociations, was founded upon principles of felf-denial, fuffering, and rigour, to which human nature was not equal; and therefore muft prefently fall to the ground. That therefore both juftice and reafon required fuch a declaration of parliament at the prefent in fupport of its authority, which might as well be formally abandoned, as not refolutely afferted. Some gentlemen too (one of them of rank in the army) treated all idea of refiftance[40] by the Americans with the utmoft contempt. They faid, that they were neither foldiers, nor ever could be made fo; being naturally of a pufillanimous difpofition, and utterly incapable of any fort of order or difcipline. That by their lazinefs, uncleanlinefs, or radical defect of conftitution, they were incapable of going through the fervice of a campaign; but would melt away with ficknefs before they could face an enemy. So that a very flight force would be more than fufficient for their complete reduction; and to this purpofe many ludicrous ftories were told greatly to the entertainment of the Houfe,

A gentleman, who had not long[41] before fat at the treafury board, from whence he had been removed for a fpirit not fufficiently fubmiffive, and whofe abilities were as unqueftioned as the fpirit for which he fuffered, moved to leave out all but the preliminary words of the addrefs, and to fubftitute after them the following, " But deploring " that the information which they " (the papers laid before the Houfe) " had afforded, ferved only to " convince the Houfe that the mea- " fures taken by his Majefty's fer- " vants tended rather to widen " than to heal the unhappy dif- " ferences between Great-Britain " and America," and then prayed an alteration in the fame.

Upon a divifion in a very full Houfe, the amendment was rejected by a large majority, there being 304 againft, to 105, who fupported the queftion. The queftion being then put upon the original motion for the addrefs, was carried by nearly the fame majority, the numbers being 296, to 106.

The minority had not yet, however, done with the bufinefs. Upon receiving the report from the American committee a few days after, a noble lord, whofe family have at[42] all times been remarkable for their attachment to the conftitution and liberties of their country, and whofe anceftor had a principal fhare in the revolution, made a motion to recommit the addrefs which had been agreed to in the committee. He fupported his motion with many arguments; faid, that the reconfideration of a meafure which appeared to him and many others to be fraught with the greateft mifchiefs, and which from its nature, was undoubtedly capable of much evil, could not be looked upon as time thrown away, or mifpent. He ftated our domeftic fituation, and that in which we ftood both with refpect to the colonies and to foreign powers; from all which he inferred the impropriety and danger of

a declaration from that houfe, of the exiftence of a rebellion in any part of our dominions; he fhewed the defperate meafures into which it might precipitate the Americans; and the advantage that might be taken of fuch an occafion by our powerful and watchful neighbours, whofe ancient enmity and jealoufy were much increafed, by the glory we had acquired, and the difgrace and lofs they had fuffered in the laft war. His head and his heart, he faid, joined in deprecating the horrors of a civil war; which would be rendered ftill more dreadful by involving in its certain confequences, a foreign one with the combined forces of great and powerful nations. He particularly called the attention of the Houfe to the unequal ballance of our lofs and our gain in the event; in which we might find our revenue deftroyed, our trade annihilated, and our empire itfelf overturned. And what was the prize to be gained, by running all this rifque, and encountering fo much danger? If we were fuccefsful, we might fubdue America; by which we gained nothing; America being, to all wife intents and purpofes, our own already; and much more profitably fo, than it could be in virtue of any conqueft.

This motion introduced the longeft and moft interefting debate that had taken place in the prefent parliament. All the queftions upon American affairs that had been agitated fince the year 1764, and all the arguments they gave rife to, were again, in fome degree, controverted or revived; with the addition of thofe which new matter and a change of circumftance afforded, or the greateft ingenuity could fuggeft. The matter is of fuch importance that we fhall be excufed going over the debates, as they became known to the public; although fomething like repetition in a bufinefs like this is inevitable.

It was acknowledged on all

hands, that the subject was one of the most important that had ever been debated in that House; and the present crisis the most perilous and intricate of any in which this nation had been involved since the revolution. It was contended by those who opposed the motion, that either the legislative power of this kingdom has authority over all its dominions, or it has none over any part of them; it cannot be partial, nor can any one branch of that legislature, by any act or charter whatever, exempt any particular set of his subjects from the authority of the whole; and that which was never exercised was just the same as lost. It was allowed, that for the sake of tranquillity, of our trade and manufactures, it were much to be wished, that lenient measures could be successfully pursued; but it was said, that there were none which could be proposed or adopted, that had not already been repeatedly and ineffectually tried; that the Americans were too ungrateful, too refractory, and too incorrigible, to be won by kindness, or retained by benefits; and that the mildness, lenity, and tenderness, which had been constantly practised by government in all its proceedings with the colonies, and which they insidiously interpreted as the effects of timidity, became thereby, in a great degree, productive of the present fatal consequences.

It was asserted, that the Americans had long been aiming at independency; and that as soon as they thought themselves able, and a pretence occurred, they insolently and openly avowed their eagerness to put the design in execution; that it was our business and duty as Englishmen, at any price and at any hazard, to prevent its completion; to crush the monster in its birth; to bring them back, before it is too late, to a sense of their duty, their condition, and their obligations to us; to a proper re-

membrance, that their present potency, the excess of their greatness and riches, is the consequence of our favour; and that their very existence has been purchased by us at an immense expence of blood and treasure. That the danger was immediate and pressing; and that, regardless of consequences, we must encounter it like men; that every moment's delay increases the evil, and it would be highly criminal to our country, as well as an act of the most consummate baseness and cowardice, by a mean temporizing to shift it off from ourselves, and leave it in all its accumulative bulk and weight, to drop upon the heads of our posterity.

Many of the acts and resolutions of the continental congress, with passages from their petition, and instances from the general proceedings of the Americans, were brought to justify the sentiments, corroborate the assertions, and enforce the arguments that were used upon this occasion. The dangers from foreign powers supporting the Americans was said to be imaginary; besides the most pacific assurances, those, of whom we might be with reason most apprehensive, were too much interested in colony matters, to give any support to a resistance, which might in its example be so ruinous to themselves. It was still contended by several of those who opposed the motion, that an appearance of vigorous measures, with some reinforcement to the troops at Boston, would prove sufficient to quell the disturbances in America, without the drawing of blood, or coming to any of those extremities, which had been so often predicted, and pathetically lamented on the other side. They seemed still to suppose, that the friends of government were much stronger and more numerous, than there is any reason at present to think they really were; and that they were prevented from declaring themselves, partly from the sudden violence of the discontented, and partly from a want of mutual de-

pendance, and knowledge of each others sentiments.

On the other side, the address was stigmatized as cruel, sanguinary and unjust; that supposing some acts to have been committed, which might have borne the construction of rebellion in the strict rigour of the law, it would still have been more humane, more politic, and more becoming the wisdom of the legislature, not to have seen them in that sense; to give passion time to subside, and reason to operate, than by such a rash, hasty, and violent measure, to set, themselves, the example of intemperance, and drive men headlong to defiance and desperation.

It was denied that the Americans had either sought or wished for independency; though it was too much to be feared, from the present complexion of the times, that through our violence and our madness, we should at length urge them to that extremity. It was asked, from whence we can form any judgment of the thoughts and intentions of men, but from their actions and their words? By the first of these, which are indeed the tests of the human disposition, the Americans have given the strongest and most unequivocal demonstrations of their filial piety towards the mother-country; they have fought and bled by our side. In the time of necessity, they did not wait to be chilled by consulting the cold rules of prudence, as the measure of the support and assistance which they were to give us; with liberal hearts, they gave every thing; our journals, in the same instance, bear witness to our own justice, and to their liberality.

Nor are their words less unequivocal than their actions. Even in the midst of the present disturbances; when our ministers have excited innumerable fears and jealousies, and by every provocation screwed their passions up even to madness; yet in this state of distraction, they require no more for the restoration of harmony, than to be placed in the same situation that they were at the close of the last war.

It was said, that waving all questions upon the right of taxation, wise governments had ever paid a respect even to prejudices of a long standing, when they were establish-ed among great bodies of the people; that the Americans had been nursed up in a long series of years, in ideas of certain rights, of which, the electing of their own represen-tatives, and the disposal of their money for the public service only through them, were among the principal. That if this was an er-ror, the crown and parliament were equally faulty with the Americans, having in their whole conduct con-stantly nourished the delusion. That at the time of the repeal of the stamp act, two of the first names of this kingdom, for abili-ty, as well as for legal knowledge, besides many others, utterly de-nied the right of taxation; yet in-stead of any stigma for the holding of those opinions, which are now to be construed into rebellion, the Americans saw, immediately after, one of those great men not only placed at the head of public af-fairs, but the framer of a whole administration, and the other ap-pointed to the highest civil office under the crown, and what is em-phatically called the keeper of the king's conscience. Was it then[43] to be wondered at, that the Ame-ricans, with such authorities on their side, should be tenacious of a right so invaluable in its nature, which has been at all times considered as the distinction between freemen and slaves, which had been confirmed by so long a prescription, and upon which, to this instant, the wisest and honestest men, even in the mother country, are divided in opinion.

It was further urged, that if conquest was determined, the force intended, which the mi-nister rated at about ten thousand men, was totally inadequate to the end. But that waving that point, and supposing we should succeed in conquering the Ameri-cans, the colonies must of course be ruined in the conflict, the vast and profitable trade, which de-pended upon them lost, and as no future means could be devised for their government, without the con-tinual intervention of a large mili-tary force, this nation would ever after be saddled with a very great and certain expence, while the re-sources that should provide for it were wantonly cut off. But if we imagined that the powers of Eu-rope would sit still during this con-test, we must suppose a system of policy now to prevail, or rather an extension of folly, all over Europe, which never before was known in any period of its existence.

It was remarkable in this de-bate, that a gentleman high in of-[44] fice declared, that his ideas upon the subject differed totally from those which in the present debate seemed to be adopted by the noble lord at the head of administration; that he could not give his assent to a measure, at the very thoughts of which his soul shuddered; that he disapproved of the whole system with respect to America; and wish-ed it to be reconsidered in every point of view, lest wrong and op-pression should render resistance justifiable. He observed, that though some persons less respon-sible had uniformly persevered in a style of the most inflexible rigour, that noble person at the head of the finances, had frequently chang-ed his language; and seemed to suffer under great occasional de-pression; that he even declared at times, that he did not mean to tax America; and seeming besides to speak but slightly of the right of taxation, and giving some inti-mation even of consenting to a re-peal of the tea duty, that we were then contending only about words and quiddities, and entering into a ruinous war without an object.

Much ill temper appeared in every part of the House, in the course of both these debates. The ministers were charged with acting uniformly and systematically upon Tory and arbitrary principles, which were subversive of the con-stitution, destructive of the rights of the people, and had thrown the whole empire into a state of con-fusion and distraction. That by a pursuance of these disgraceful and ruinous measures, they had tarn-ished the lustre of the crown, alien-ated the affections of the people, and sunk the nation, from the highest pinnacle of power and glory, to a degree of contempt in the estimation of the rest of Eu-rope, which, only a few years ago, it would have been deemed impos-sible for the accumulated misfor-tunes and disgraces of an age to have accomplished. But that in the true spirit of a Tory admini-stration, they had sacrificed the honour and interest of the nation in all transactions with foreigners, and reserved all the spirit, the pride, the dignity, and the force of government, to be played off against the liberties of the people at home. They were repeatedly told, that a bitter day of retribu-tion would inevitably come, when they must answer to the justice of their country, for the mischiefs they had already done, and for the irretrievable ruin into which they were plunging the nation. In a word, it was said, that the short and simple question before the House, was, whether we should lose our colonies, or give up our mini-sters?

On the other side, all the evils and disturbances in America, were by charge or implication attributed to the opposition. Much was said about faction at home, a republican spirit and principles, and that the Americans were spirited up to their violence and rebellion, by incen-diary writers and speakers in Eng-land. In the course of this violence and heat, a gentleman, having[45] spoken something of Catalines at home, who ought to be dragged forth to public disgrace and punishment, was called to from the other side to point them out; and told, that the imputation was undoubtedly right, but he seemed to misplace it; that if he meant by Catalines, those who were involving their country in all the horrors and miseries of a civil war, they could be easily found; but it would be on that side where he did not wish the search to be made.

After a debate which continued till half an hour past two o'clock in the morning, the question being at length put, the motion for the recommitment of the address was rejected by nearly the former majority, the numbers upon the division being 288 against, to 105, who supported the motion.

Feb. 7th. A conference was held the next day with the lords, at the request of the commons, to propose their joining in the address. In the mean time, a petition from the merchants of London, concerned in the commerce to North America; and another from the West India merchants and planters, were presented to the Marquis of Rockingham, to be laid before the lords by that nobleman, previous to their entering upon American affairs.

Whether the ease with which petitions had been rendered fruitless in the other house, had encouraged a similar disposition to render them equally ineffectual here, we shall not pretend to say, but however it was, or from whatever cause it proceeded, this period seemed particularly fatal to that mode of application for redress.

The lords being returned from the conference, and the president having made the report and read the address, the Marquis of Rockingham stood up to introduce and present the petitions; but the noble Earl at the head of the American department, having risen to speak at the same time, a great dispute arose who should be the first heard. In this state of confusion, the lord[46] keeper, instead of deciding by his own eye or opinion, put the question, whether the lord in administration should be then heard? This proceeding called up a noble Duke[47] on the other side, who insisted, that it was a most slavish position, and unworthy their rank and character, that any lord in that house, should have a preference to any other; and still more so, to render that preference the act of the house, by putting it to the question. The dispute was now brought into the form of a regular debate, in which, on one side, the importance and nature of the subject which the marquis had to propose, was said, independent of any other causes, to entitle it to a preference; and the necessity and justice of their accepting the merchants petitions, and hearing their allegations, before they entered into any resolutions upon American affairs, were strongly urged. It was alledged, that they not only sat there in their legislative, but in their judicial capacity, and were therefore bound by all the ties of justice, as well as of official duty, to obtain every possible light and information upon the subject before them. That the pretence of delay, or loss of time, could not avail in this instance, as there was nothing dependent on the address, which required any sudden resolution. But if there even were, a matter which involved in its consequences, not only the justice of the House, but the interests and safety of the nation, should not be hastily nor unadvisedly decided upon, nor should a mere attention to forms, supposing them to be established or authenticated, be deemed a sufficient cause for cutting off the means of information.

On the other side, the method of stating and proposing the question was justified by some precedents, most of which were brought from the house of commons; and it was contended, that the chairman in either house, had a right, either to decide immediately upon the question, or to state it in such manner, and to propose such party as he pleased; that the proposed mode of proceeding on the petitions, while the other business was before them, was unusual and unparliamentary; and that independent of all other causes, the preference upon this occasion should be given to the noble lord in administration, as a mark of the respect owing to the other branch of the legislature. The question being at length put, the motion was carried without a division.

Upon this decision, the nobleman in whose favour it was carried, made the usual motion, merely for the sake of securing the occupancy of the ground, viz. That the blank which was left open in the address presented by the Commons, should be filled up by the insertion of those words "The Lords Spiritual and Temporal," &c. which were to render that instrument the joint act of both Houses.

The Marquis then acquainted the House with the nature and great importance of the petitions which he had to present; that they were immediately relative to the business under consideration; and were well worthy of arresting any determination of theirs, for at least one day, being certain, that within that short period, information of infinite consequence would be laid before them; perhaps sufficient to alter, or at least to soften the rigour of those measures, which they were now madly, hastily, and blindly proceeding to adopt. That to remove every doubt of their being intended, either to gain time, or to cause delay, he was authorized by the West India merchants to inform them, that if necessitated so to do, they were ready, without counsel or further preparation, instantly to offer evidence to prove, that several of the West-India islands could not be able to subsist after the operation of the proposed address in America. He then said, that as a question was now before the House, which must be first disposed of, before the matter of the petitions could come regularly under their cognizance, and as he still hoped they would be willing to hear the petitioners, as men suffering under the heaviest misfortunes, none of which could be attributed to their own misconduct, he would be under the necessity, as the only means left, of moving the previous question, which would open a door for taking into consideration the general state of the petitioners grievances.

It was further urged, in supporting the motion for the previous question, that the papers which had been laid before them by the ministers, were so manifestly defective, and avowedly curtailed, that no certain information could be derived from them of the real state of the object on which they were going to decide; that in such a situation, they should accept with pleasure that information, which if it had not been voluntarily offered, it would have been their duty to have sought, at any expence, whether of time or otherwise; that if the papers had been even in their original state, without garbling or mutilation, still, there was no species of information relative to the colonies, to which the merchants were not more competent, and less liable to imposition through ignorance, or to impose upon others through prejudice, than the public officers employed by the crown; of which, if there was any doubt before, the erroneous opinions, false ideas, and misrepresentation of facts, upon which the fatal acts of the last parliament were founded, afforded too melancholy an experience. That the express prayer of the petitioners being, that they might be heard before any resolution was taken respecting America, the refusal of

this act of justice, or of even suffering the petitions to be presented, was a proceeding of the most unwarrantable nature, and directly subversive of the most sacred rights of the subject. They summed up their arguments by concluding, that justice in regard to individuals, policy with regard to the public, and decorum with regard to themselves, required that they should admit the petitions; and that a refusal of them was no less than a denial of justice.

On the other side, some of the lords spoke tenderly with respect to the merchants; said they deserved every mark of attention and respect, which was consistent with the interests of the empire at large; that although their grievances were imaginary, their complaints were deserving of indulgence. It was, however, to be hoped, that when they maturely considered that the steps now taking were to prevent the return of such evils in future, they would not only chearfully acquiesce in the wisdom of parliament in the present instance, but be gratefully thankful hereafter; for if the supremacy of the legislature was once given up, their trade, commerce, and every possible advantage accruing from them, would soon be annihilated. It was therefore to be hoped, that the merchants would, on the present occasion, submit to a temporary inconvenience, or even to a short-lived distress, to insure the most permanent and lasting benefits; and manifest that degree of magnanimity, which a sense of their own interests, founded in submission and acquiescence to the wisdom of parliament, must, upon mature consideration and past experience, most certainly suggest.

Thus far, the debate was confined to the subject of the previous question; but with respect to the original motion, it branched out far more extensively. The questions of treason, rebellion, and constructive treasons, were deeply en-

tered into by two great Law Lords, [48] one of whom has long been at the head of one of the first departments in his profession, the chief court of criminal justice; and the other, within a few years, the highest officer under the crown. As these learned Lords differed totally, both in their legal and political opinions and sentiments, a long debate was carried on, with great eagerness, warmth, and ability between them; in which a vast stock of professional, as well as general learning, was displayed on both sides. On the one, the Americans were pronounced to be in absolute rebellion; while a rich, and most fertile imagination, had an opportunity of exerting all its ingenuity, in traversing the almost inextricable mazes of constructive treasons; from whence were drawn such stores of inferences, deductions, conclusions, and distinctions, as were not easily developed or separated, when involved in the splendor of a most powerful eloquence. The learned Lord on the other side, with equal abilities, as full a share of legal knowledge, and an eloquence not inferior to any, stuck close to the letter of the law, and as absolutely denied the charge made upon the Americans. He rested the whole ground of argument upon the statute of the 25 Edward III. and would admit of no species of treason but what was therein described, nor of any constructive treason that was not already clearly established by precedents in the courts, founded upon that basis. It is much to be lamented, that with all the boasted excellency of our constitution, a question of so vast a magnitude, as to include in its consequences the lives, fortunes, and honours of all the subjects of this empire, should still remain involved in such obscurity, as not only to admit of a difference of opinion, but that even the great oracles of the law are bewildered in its darkness.

With respect to the immediate question, it was insisted on the one fide, that we were reduced to the alternative of adopting the most effectual and coercive measures, or of relinquishing for ever all claim of dominion and sovereignty over the colonies; that no medium could possibly be devised, which would exclude the inevitable consequence of either system absolutely prevailing; for that, on the one hand, the supremacy of the British legislature must be compleat, entire, and unconditional; or, on the other, the colonies must be free and independent: that all enquiry about the right or expediency of taxation was now fruitless; taxation was no longer the question; it was only the pretence of American disobedience and resistance; all their acts strike at the superintending power of the legislature; that was their real grievance: and a repeal of any one of those laws which they complained of, would be a renunciation of all sovereignty for ever. That it was an absurdity of the most monstrous kind, to suppose that they had a right distinct from the legislature in any one particular, and not in all; if they had such a right, the defence of it would justify resistance; and to contend that subjects had a right to resist the government, was a doctrine which could not be maintained, on any principles of civil government, reason, experience, or common sense.

As to the petitioners, it was not doubted but they were aggrieved; it might be granted, that all their allegations were well founded, and that they laboured under great and singular distresses; it was as little to be doubted, that the landed gentlemen, the merchants, manufacturers, mechanics, and every order of men in the nation, would all heavily feel, in their several situations, the threatened calamities. But these were circumstances that did not interfere with the motion; they are a part of the evils incident to mankind, which may be deplored but cannot be avoided. The events of war are ever uncertain; its ca-

lamities great, and undefined; we may be defeated; we may lose that sovereignty we are struggling to retain; but these are the inevitable conditions of warfare: nor are they more grievous in the present instance than in others. The question now under consideration is, whether, allowing all the inconveniencies, difficulties, and dangers that are supposed, and taking into full contemplation every possible contingency that human foresight and prudence could suggest, we should relinquish our rights, or resolve, at all events, resolutely to persist in their exertion?

On the other side, the madness of entering into a civil war, merely to cover and support a series of ministerial violence, misconduct, and misrule, with the ruin and destruction that must inevitably attend such unnatural cruelty and injustice, were painted in the strongest colours. The learned Lord, who had asserted the Americans to be in rebellion, was severely reprehended; it was said, that with all his legal knowlege and ability, he had not been able, in any degree, to support the charge, and that such cruel and inflammatory representations, at this alarming crisis, were very unbecoming the gravity and dignity of his situation, and the several high relations he stood in to the state. It was shewn, that as commerce was the source of our wealth and our power, and its destruction, the inevitable consequence of persevering in the present insane and pernicious measures; so we were running headlong into a civil war, and at the same time cutting off, irretrievably, the means which enabled us to support any; the consequence of which, in the natural course of things, must be our falling an open and defenceless prey to the first bold invader. It was also asserted, that every engine had been employed, and every art too successfully essayed, to render the landed interest a party in this ruinous work, and to lead it into the

fatal error of considering itself as distinct from the commercial; as if the latter could sustain any injury which the former must not equally feel. But, it was asked, what rose the value of the lands, but commerce? What supported commerce but the lands?—their interests being as inseparable as the benefits they derived from each other were mutual and reciprocal.

It was asserted, that the violent matter of the dangerous address before them, was highly aggravated by the unusual and violent manner in which it was attempted to be precipitated through the House; that they were not to be allowed the interposition of a moment's time for recollection or deliberation, before they were to be driven headlong into a declaration of civil war. A conference was held with the Commons; an address, which took in subjects of such a nature and magnitude as to strike the mind with dread and horror, presented; all extraneous information, altho' offered, positively refused; all petitions, arbitrarily rejected; and the whole of this most awful business, received, debated, and intended to be concluded in a single day; that no legal grounds were laid, either in argument or in fact, to shew that a rebellion, properly so called, existed in the province of Massachusett's Bay, when the papers of the latest date, and from whence alone they derived their information, were written; that the overt acts, to which the species of treason affirmed in the address ought to be applied, were not established, nor any offenders marked out; but a general mass of the acts of turbulence, said to be done at various times and places, and of various natures, were all thrown together to make out one general constructive treason; nor was there any sort of proof of the continuance of any unlawful force, from whence it could be inferred that a rebellion was at the present time existing.

It was further contended, that the cases of constructive treason had been already so far extended by the judges, and the distinctions upon them were so nice and subtle, that no wise man would wish to increase their number, or to add to their authority; much less ought so high an authority as the two Houses of Parliament, without the clearest evidence of uncontroverted overt-acts, to denounce so cruel a judgment, as a declaration of rebellion, against a great body of the people; a declaration, in every view of it, big with the most horrible and direful consequences; and which, if confirmed by that House, will from that instant authorize every species of rapine, plunder, massacre, and persecution.

This extraordinary debate was attended with some singular circumstances. A great Law Lord, who [49] had been so severe in his charge against the Americans, condemned also, in the most explicit and unreserved terms, (to the great surprize of most of his auditors) the measure of laying on the duties in the year 1767, which he declared to be the most absurd and pernicious that could be devised, and the cause of all our present and impending evils. If this declaration was unexpected, the acknowledgment that followed was still more so. Three great [50] Lords, who were at that time cabinet counsellors, and held the first offices in the state, declared separately in their places, that they had no share in that measure, nor had ever given it any approbation; and two of them condemned it in express terms, while the third, who was still in high office, did not by any means pretend to support it. It seems they were in some way over-ruled. But the manner in which a measure of ministry was carried against the opinion of ministers was not explained.

It cannot be wondered, that such a disclosure relative to a matter, which had already convulsed the whole empire, and was still more

to be dreaded in its future consequences, should excite the most general amazement, mixed with a great share of indignation and regret in particulars. The fatal and over-ruling secret influence, which, as they said, had so long guided and marred all the public affairs of the nation, was accordingly deplored and animadverted upon in different parts of the House.

In the course of the heat, which sprung from much collateral matter that was thrown in upon this occasion, a series of arraignment, justification, assertion, denial, animadversion, and recrimination took place, in which many things passed, that were either new in that House, or extraordinary in their nature. The learned Lord, who had condemned the measure of laying on the American duties in the year 1767, was himself, partly by implication, and in part directly, charged with having a principal share in those secret counsels, which had been stigmatized as the most obnoxious and ruinous to the nation; notwithstanding his repeated declaration, that he had not acted as an efficient cabinet counsellor for several years. These charges were urged and opposed with a degree of asperity, and a harshness of personal altercation, not often heard in that House; with violent threats on the one side, and general defiance on the other.

At length, the previous question being put, according to the noble Marquis's motion, at 40 minutes past one o'clock in the morning, was lost by a prodigious majority, the numbers, including the proxies, being 104, to 29, only, who supported the previous question. The main question being then put, whether to agree with the Commons in the address, by inserting the words necessary to fill up the blank, it was carried in the affirmative, by something near the same majority.

Both the previous question, and the main question, were, however, each of them productive of a separate protest, which were signed by eighteen Lords, who conclude their reasons of dissent in the following words: " Because the means of enforcing the authority of the British legislature, is confided to persons, of whose capacity for that purpose, from abundant experience, we have reason to doubt; and who have hitherto used no effectual means of conciliating or of reducing those who oppose that authority: this appears in the constant failure of all their projects, the insufficiency of all their information, and the disappointment of all the hopes, which they have for several years held out to the public. Parliament has never refused any of their proposals, and yet our affairs have proceeded daily from bad to worse, until we have been brought, step by step, to that state of confusion, and even civil violence, which was the natural result of these desperate measures."

We therefore protest against an address, amounting to a *declaration of war*, which is founded on no proper parliamentary information; which was introduced by refusing to suffer the presentation of petitions against it, (although it be the undoubted right of the subject to present the same); which followed the rejection of every mode of conciliation; which holds out no substantial offer of redress of grievances; and which promises support to those ministers who have inflamed America, and grossly misconducted the affairs of Great-Britain."

Message from the throne for an augmentation of the forces. Bill for restraining the commerce of the New-England colonies, and to prohibit their fishery on the banks of Newfoundland, &c. brought into the House of Commons. Great opposition to the bill. Petition and evidence against it. Petition and evidence from the town of Pool in support of the bill. Petition from the Quakers. Long debates. Motion for an amendment over-ruled. The bill carried through by great majorities. Meets with equal opposition in the House of Lords. Petitions and evidence as before. Great debates. Question for committing the bill, upon the second reading, carried by a great majority. Motion on the third reading for an amendment, to include several other colonies in the restrictions of the bill. The question carried upon a division. The bill passed, and returned with the amendment to the Commons. Protest. Conference; the Commons give reasons for refusing to concur in the amendment; the Lords agree to the rejection. The bill receives the royal assent.

THE answer from the throne to the address, besides the usual thanks, contained an assurance of taking the most speedy and effectual measures, for enforcing due obedience to the laws and authority of the supreme legislature; together with a declaration, that, whenever any of the colonies should make a proper and dutiful application, his Majesty would be ready to concur in affording them every just and reasonable indulgence; and concluded with an earnest wish, that this disposition might have an happy effect on their temper and conduct.

The answer was accompanied with a message from the Throne to the Commons, in which they were informed, that as it was determined, in consequence of the address, to take the most speedy and effectual measures for supporting the just rights of the crown, and the two Houses of Parliament, some augmentation to the forces by sea and land would be necessary for that purpose. This message was referred, as usual, to the committee of supply.

While measures were thus taking to apply a military force to the cure of the disorders in America, other means were thought necessary to come in aid of this expedient. The military force might indeed coerce and punish the disobedient, and effectually support the magistrate in case of insurrection; but how to get the body of magistracy to act, or any sufficient number upon ordinary occasions to engage heartily in their cause, did not appear. The change in the charter of Massachusett's Bay had not produced the desired effect. Even if it should, the inferior magistrates must evidently be taken in the country; sheriffs, constables, select men, grand and petty juries, must be aiding to the higher magistrates, or nothing could be done; and the idea of having troops in every parish would be ridiculous. The coercive plan being therefore still relied on, it was proposed to chuse a punishment so universal, as by the inconveniencies which every man felt, would interest every man in procuring obedience and submission to the late acts of parliament. For this reason the minister moved for leave to bring in a bill to restrain the trade

Feb. 10.

and commerce of the provinces of Massachusett's Bay, and New Hampshire; the colonies of Connecticut and Rhode-Island, and Providence Plantation, in North-America, to Great-Britain, Ireland, and the British islands in the West-Indies; and to prohibit such provinces and colonies from carrying on any fishery on the banks of Newfoundland, or other places therein to be mentioned, under certain conditions, and for a limited time.

He supported the proposed bill (of which he had given some previous intimation) on the following grounds: that as the Americans had refused to trade with this kingdom, it was but just that we should not suffer them to trade with any other nation; that the restraints of the act of navigation, were their charter; and that the several relaxations of that law, were so many acts of grace and favour; all which, when they ceased to be merited by the colonies, it was reasonable and necessary should be recalled by the legislature; that the fisheries on the banks of Newfoundland, as well as all the others in North-America, were the undoubted right of Great-Britain, and she might accordingly dispose of them as she pleased; that as both Houses had declared a rebellion in the province of Massachusett's Bay, it was therefore just to deprive that province of the benefits which it derived from those fisheries.

With respect to the other colonies of New-England included in the bill, he observed, that though there was still a governor and government in the province of New Hampshire, yet government was so weak there, that a quantity of powder had been taken out of one of the King's forts by an armed mob; besides, that from the vicinity of that province to Massachusett's Bay, if it were not included, the purpose of the act would be defeated. Nor was the ill temper of the people of Connecticut found less deserving of their being included in the general punishment, who, upon a report that the soldiery had killed some people in Boston, marched a large body of men into the province of Massachusett's; and though that body returned, on finding the falsity of the report, the temper and disposition they shewed, as well as the general state and conduct of the colony, did not by any means entitle them to favour. The argument of vicinity was also as applicable to the last province as to that of New Hampshire.

The minister having stated the reasons on which he acted, declared, that he would not be averse to such alleviations of the act, as would not prove destructive of its great object; and therefore he would only propose it as temporary, to continue either to the end of the year, or of the next session of parliament;—and he would also propose, that particular persons might be excepted, upon their obtaining certificates from the Governor of the province, in which they resided, of their good behaviour, or upon their subscribing to a test, acknowledging the rights of parliament.

This bill, besides the matter that was peculiar to its own nature, brought up in its course the whole series of American controversy. With regard to this particular measure, the principle of involving the innocent in the punishment of the guilty was alternately combated, with serious argument, pathetic remonstrance, and pointed ridicule. What legislature had ever established a precedent of equal cruelty and injustice, with the condemning of half a million of people to perish with famine, for the supposed crimes of a few unknown persons? Such precedents were only to be sought for in the history of the most savage and barbarous tyrants; but not among the judicial acts of legislators. Why were three other provinces to be punished for a rebellion supposed only in one? or if they were also in rebellion, why were they not declared so? One province was to be deprived of its subsistence, because a rebellion, no body knew where, nor by whom, was, however, said to be lurking in some part of it. A second province was to be punished, because it happened to be next door to rebellion; a third, because it would be doing nothing to let that escape; and a fourth must be starved, because the ministers could not otherwise square their plan. Very bad reasons, they said, had been given for punishing the other New-England colonies; but no reason at all had been assigned for including *Rhode Island* in the common restriction: unless perhaps the mere neighbourhood might be the cause, which was left to be guessed, ministry being silent as to that province. It was said, that in whatever other matters of policy our ministers might be found deficient, they had the most infallible receipt for making rebellions, and the happiest talent in hitting upon measures for the ruin of trade and commerce, and the dismemberment of a great empire, of any set of men that ever conducted the public affairs of any country.

It was said, that the cruelty of the bill exceeded the examples of hostile rigour with avowed enemies; that in all the violence of our most dangerous wars, it was an established rule in the marine service, to spare the coast-fishing craft of our declared enemies; always considering, that we waged war with nations, and not with private men; and that it would be unworthy the character of a great and brave people, and even savage and barbarous, to deprive poor wretches of their means of hard-earned livelihood, and the miserable village inhabitants of the sea-coasts, of their daily food. It was known that the people of New-England subsist much on fish; and that the sale of that commodity supplies them with the means of purchasing flour and several other articles necessary to life; three of the provinces in question not raising wheat for the fourth part of their demand: so that we now inhumanly intend to starve whole provinces, and these our own people, excepting only such, as a Governor may think proper to favour; a paltry pretence of lenity, which will serve only to cover the most scandalous partiality, and give rise to unjust preference, monopoly, and to all kinds of the most shameful and pernicious jobbs. They desired the proposer of the bill to recollect that he had frequently spoken of the multitude of friends he had in all those provinces; and now, by his own measure, he not only confounded the innocent with the guilty, but friends with enemies, and involved his own partizans in one common ruin with the rest.

But this was not only to operate upon supposed rebels, or upon those who had the misfortune of being their neighbours, or who it was imagined either did or might conceal rebellion; but it was also to punish the people of Great-Britain, who were charged with no delinquency, not even of concealment or neighbourhood, and who must lose a very great share of their property which was lying in the proscribed provinces, in consequence of this bill. For, as New-England was not productive of staple commodities, sufficient to pay the great balance which it was always under a necessity of owing in this country, it had no other means of discharging that debt than through the fishery, and the circuitous trade dependent on it: so that to cut off those means was, in fact, to beggar our merchants and manufacturers; and the British legislature was, in its wisdom, going to pass a disabling bill, to prevent the payment of debts to its British subjects.

It was further contended, that the absurdity of the bill was even equal to its cruelty and injustice. That its object was to take away a trade from our colonies, which all who understood its nature knew we could not transfer to ourselves. That God and nature had given the fisheries to them, and not to us; and set limits to our avarice and cruelty, which we could not pass; that when they were once destroyed, we could neither benefit by them ourselves, nor restore them to those, whom we had thus violently and unjustly deprived of the means of subsistence; that distance and local circumstances shut us out in the first instance; and with respect to the other, that the little capital, ves-fels, and implements of fishermen, the majority of whom muft ever be neceffarily poor, could only be kept up by the conftant returns of profit, and when the returns failed, the capital and implements would be loft for ever. That the people muft either perifh, or apply themfelves to other occupations, from which they could not be recalled at will. That we were thus finding cut the means for Providence of punifhing our own cruelty and injuftice; for that thofe fifheries, which were a more inexhauftible, and infinitely more valuable fource of wealth and power than all the mines in the new world, would not only be loft to ourfelves, but would be thrown into the fcale againft us, by falling, in a very great degree, into the hands of our natural rivals and enemies. They obferved alfo, that the fifherman, having no occupation, muft of courfe become a foldier. Thus we provoke a rebellion by the injuftice of one fet of acts, and then recruit the rebellious army by another.

In fupport of the bill, befides the arguments that were originally urged, the charges of injuftice and cruelty were denied; and it was faid, that whatever diftrefs the bill might bring upon the colonies, they could not complain of the legiflature, as they not only deferved it by their difobedience, but had themfelves fet the example. That they had entered into the moft unlawful and daring combinations, as far as in them lay, to ruin our merchants, impoverifh our manufacturers, and to ftarve our Weft-India iflands. That nothing could be more equitable than to prohibit the trade of thofe who had prohibited ours. That if any foreign power had offered us only a fmall part of the infult and injury that we had received from our colonies, the whole nation would have been in a flame to demand fatisfaction, and woe to the minifterr who were flack in obtaining it. Were we then to act the part of bullies with all the reft of mankind, only to be kicked at home by our own people?

The charge of cruelty was faid to be equally ill founded. This was a bill of humanity and mercy, as well as of coercion; it being the only moderate means of bringing the difobedient provinces to a fenfe of their duty, without involving the empire in the horrors of a civil war. They had daringly incurred all the penalties of contumacy and rebellion, and were liable to the fevereft military execution, without any imputation of cruelty. Inftead of thefe dreadful punifhments which they fo juftly merited, they were to be brought to their fenfes without any feverity, only by a reftriction on their trade, which would laft no longer than their contumacy. Thus government would be fupported, without the miferies of war, or the effufion of blood.

As to the charge of involving the innocent with the guilty, friends with foes, the propriety or impropriety, the juftice or injuftice of fuch an act, depended on the neceffity of the meafure. That whenever this was the cafe, the neceffity might be lamented, but could not be helped. That a town of ours, held by rebels or enemies, might contain the beft of our friends, and thofe friends too might be the more numerous part of the inhabitants; but ftill the miferies of a fiege, and poffibly of a famine muft be fubmitted to, or the town never could be recovered.

Never, faid they, was a meafure more truly neceffary than the prefent. The colonies had too long impofed upon and deluded us, by the bugbear of withdrawing their trade, hoping, through the terror of our merchants and manufacturers, to bend the legiflature to a compliance with all their demands, until they had brought their defigns to fuch a ripenefs, as to be able to throw off the mafk, and openly to avow their rebellious purpofes. That this was the third time, within a few years, in which they had thrown the whole commerce of this country into a ftate of the greateft confufion. That both colonies and commerce were better loft than preferved upon fuch terms; that life itfelf could not be worth the keeping in a conftant ftate of uncertainty and fear. Things were now come to a crifis, and the conflict muft be borne. We muft either relinquifh our connections with America, or fix them upon fuch a fure and certain bafis, as would effectually prevent the return of thofe evils.

The minority replied, that the neceffity was pretended, not real. That this meafure, fo far from neceffary, was by no means expedient. That the parallel with foreign nations did not hold. That nothing bound a foreign nation but fear. But is that the bond of internal government, and the foundation of fecurity at home? To revenge injuries in your own domeftic difputes is not the way to prevent their return. The way to lafting peace is to cut off the caufe of thofe difputes, otherwife they will return the moment the terror is over; or perhaps rigour may rather provoke than terrify; and then you fall from bad to worfe. They afked, whether the acts of rigour of the laft feffion had produced any of the effects which were expected from them?

The queftion being called for late at night, the motion for bringing in the bill was carried upon a divifion by a majority of more than three to one, the numbers being 261 to 85 only.

In the further progrefs of the bill, a petition from the merchants and traders of London, who were interefted in the American commerce, was prefented againft it, upon fome of the commercial principles mentioned in the foregoing debate; and particularly on the danger, even to our own fifheries, from fuch prohibition.

A motion being made, that the petitioners fhould be heard by themfelves or their counfel againft the bill, and in fupport of their allegations, it was agreed to; in confequence of which a long train of witnesses, consisting of merchants and captains of ships, who resided in England or North-America, and who had been long versed in the trade and fisheries of both, were examined at the bar of the House, the evidence being conducted by Mr. David Barclay, who was appointed agent to manage this business by the committee of American merchants.[52]

In the course of this evidence, (among a vast quantity of other interesting matter) it appeared, that so long ago as the year 1764, the four provinces of New-England employed, in their several fisheries, no less than 45,880 ton of shipping, and 6002 men; and that the produce of their fisheries in the foreign markets for that year, amounted in sterling money to the sum of 322,220l. 16s.—It also appeared, that the fisheries had increased very much since that time; that the New-England fish was much better than that taken by ships fitted out from Great-Britain; that all the materials used in the fisheries, except salt, and the timber of which the vessels are built, were taken from this country; and that the nett proceeds of the fish were remitted here.

It was also given in evidence, that neither the whale nor the cod fishery could be carried on, to any degree of equal extent and advantage, either from Newfoundland or Great-Britain, as from North-America; that there were several local circumstances, and some natural advantages in favour of the latter, which could neither be counteracted or supplied; that with respect to transferring the fisheries to Nova-Scotia or Quebec, were government even to furnish them with a capital, they had neither vessels nor men; nor could they procure them from any other place than New-England; that in any case, the stopping of one fishery, and the creation of another, must take up much time, and that in the interval the trade would be inevitably lost; and that the people belonging to the American fisheries had such an abhorrence of the military government established at Halifax, and so invincible an aversion to the loose habits and manners of the people, that nothing could induce them to remove thither, even supposing them reduced to the necessity of emigration. It also appeared, that there was nearly a million of money owing from New-England to the city of London only.

They also stated to the House, that the calamities consequent of the bill must fall, in a marked and particular degree, upon people who, from the nature of their occupations, must be innocent; for as the people belonging to the fisheries pass the greater part of the year at sea, they could have no share in the disturbances or crimes which were imputed to others. The case of the inhabitants of Nantucket was particularly hard. This extraordinary people, amounting to between five and six thousand in number, nine tenths of whom are Quakers, inhabit a barren island, fifteen miles long by three broad, the products of which were scarcely capable of maintaining twenty families. From the only harbour which this steril island contains, without natural products of any sort, the inhabitants, by an astonishing industry, keep an 140 vessels in constant employment. Of these, eight are employed in the importation of provisions for the island, and the rest in the whale fishery; which, with an invincible perseverance and courage, they have extended from the frozen regions of the Pole to the coasts of Africa, to the Brazils, and even as far south as the Falkland Islands; some of those fishing voyages continuing for twelve months.

A petition, from the merchants, traders, and principal inhabitants of the town of Poole, in Dorsetshire, was presented, being in avowed opposition to that from London, and in support of the principles of the fishery bill. This petition (which has since been disclaimed and condemned, by another from the town, corporation, and principal inhabitants) set forth, that the restraints upon the colonies would not by any means be injurious to commerce; that the foreign markets might be amply supplied, by extending the Newfoundland fishery from England; that the said fishery already exceeded half a million annually, all which centers in this kindom, whereas the profits of the colony fisheries go elsewhere; that the fishery from the mother country is a constant nursery for seamen for the navy; but that the American seamen are not compellable to serve their country in times of war. They concluded by soliciting, no less for their own immediate advantage than for the universal benefit of their country, such encouragement to the British fishery to Newfoundland, as parliament should think proper.

A merchant of Poole, who had long traded to Newfoundland, was examined in support of the bill. He endeavoured to shew, that if the New-England fishery was stopped, the foreign markets might notwithstanding be sufficiently supplied, and in support of that position asserted, that the fishery might be extended to any degree from Great-Britain, as we had men, money, and ships sufficient for the purpose. He, however, cautiously evaded answering any questions that might lead to conclusions different from those which he wished to establish. Being asked, whether the ships fitted out for the Newfoundland fishery from Great-Britain, were not fitted out at one third more expence than those from North-America? he answered, that he was no judge of that matter; and the question being put, How many men were employed to an hundred ton of shipping, on an average? he had not considered that subject. This evidence did not appear sufficiently satisfactory to overthrow the whole weight of the former testimony.

In other matters, this witness was sufficiently informed. It appeared that about 400 ships, of about 36,000 tons burthen, 2000 fishing shallops, of 20,000 tons burthen, and 20,000 men, were employed in the British Newfoundland fishery. That above 600,000 quintals of fish were taken annually, which upon an average of seven years, were worth 14 s. per quintal, and with the other amounts, consisting of salmon, cod oil, seal oil, and furs, exceeded half a million annually. And that of the 20,000 men, from Great-Britain and Ireland, employed in that fishery, 8000, necessarily continued in Newfoundland all the winter.

A petition was delivered from the Quakers, in behalf of their brethren and others, the inhabitants of Nantucket, in which they stated their innocence, their industry, the utility of their labours both to themselves and the community, the great hazards that attended their occupation, and the uncertainty of their gains; and shewed that if the bill passed into a law, they must in a little time be exposed to all the dreadful miseries of famine. The singular state and circumstances of these people, occasioned some attention to be paid to them. A gentleman on the side of administration said, that on a principle of humanity he would move, that a clause should be added to the bill, to prevent its operation from extending to any whale ships, which sailed before the first of March, and were at that time the property of the people of Nantucket.

On this petition, and indeed in every stage of the bill, the debate rekindled; and at each revival burned more intensely than before. It was attacked upon every ground of policy and government; and with the greatest strength of language and height of colouring. The minority made amends for the smallness of their numbers by their zeal and activity. They contended, that though the avowed object of this bill was the support of the legislative authority of Great-Britain over America, its real tendency was finally to root up and destroy whatever still remained of it; that it seemed calculated to convince the colonies, that there was no one branch of supreme authority, which parliament might not abuse in such a manner, as to render it reasonable to deny, and necessary to resist the whole. That when at first it was thought wisdom to overthrow established privileges, and to combat the prejudices of whole nations, (which however founded, were rendered respectable from their antiquity and extent) by starting up the new claim of taxation, the Americans went no further than to deny our right of internal taxation; having gained the point of urging them to question one right, we soon convinced them, both by argument and practice, that an external tax might be made to answer all the purposes, and to produce all the mischiefs of internal taxation. They then denied our right of taxing for supply. Parliament then proceeded violently to deprive them of their charters, and to change the course of justice and of trials. Then they were pushed to deny the power of internal legislation. But still in the midst of all their violence and all their provocation to it, they never hitherto had formally rejected the power of parliament to bind their trade. But we are now to convince them, that if but a single branch of legislative power is left to this country, we can distort that branch in such a manner, that it shall include all the purposes of an unlimited tyranny.

It was said to be evident, that this bill was intended merely to exasperate the colonies into open and direct rebellion. For though the ministers would be readily acquitted, from having the smallest disposition to military atchievement or glory; yet, as by the absurdity of their conduct, and the oppressiveness of their designs, they had thrown the colonies into a state of disobedience, disorder, and confusion, which it would require the greatest abilities to manage or restore to order, and yet did not come within any legal description of treason, they found themselves bewildered, and utterly incapable of conducting government in so nice and critical a situation. But if they could bring things to the length of rebellion, the course of proceeding, however ruinous and desperate, would be simple and obvious; and it might be hoped, that past error would be forgot, and present inability past unobserved, in the tumult. Upon this principle, and no other, it was said, the bill could answer its purpose; for by cutting off from the Americans all means of acquiring a livelihood, or receiving provisions, no alternative was left but starving or rebellion.

They said that the pretence of relaxing the rigour of this act by powers given to certain governors and the majority of certain councils, was not a corrective but an aggravation of its ill principle. What was it but leaving the subsistance of whole provinces to the arbitrary discretion of those men? That arbitrary power, of less extent, committed to good and tried men would be too great a trust; but the extravagant power of this bill, was to be lodged in the hands of two governors whom the House did not know, (as it was impossible for them to know who might be governors, when the act took place) and to the majority of two councils, every one of whom were equally unknown to them. But if it should even happen, that one or both of these governors and their council should be disposed to mercy, and that the people should submit to the hardest impositions which the very ministers could wish to lay upon them, still the conditions of redemption were clogged with such difficulties, as scarcely left a possibility of its being obtained, until a new law was passed for the repeal of the present. To compleat (as they said) the climax of absurdity, deception and cruelty, in this pretence to clemency and justice, the two whole provinces of Connecticut and Rhode island, were cut off from even those means of redemption, futile as they were; for by this act their governors had no power of relieving them. They must go to the governor and council of another, and it might be rival and adverse province, for their deliverance from this restraint. For this extraordinary provision no reason could be known; but that by the constitution of those provinces, the governors were chosen by the people, instead of being appointed by the crown. Thus the crime for which 200,000 people were to be famished, consisted in the form of government which they received from this country. And it was insisted, that the inevitable operation of this bill must be, to fix so indelible an hatred of this country and its legislature in the minds of the Americans, as would alienate them from us for ever, and render all future plans of reconciliation hopeless.

It was said, that the present parliamentary scheme of preserving its authority by destroying its dominions, was new, and unheard of in the history of civilized nations. That in all other cases of rebellion, the established practice was, to punish the rebels, but to spare the country. In foreign wars the country of an enemy was frequently weakened and wasted, because by so doing the strength of an adverse power was impaired; but the sovereign ought never to forget, that the strength of his country, though a rebellion may for a time exist in it, is still his own strength. Here we have inverted the order of things, and begin by destroying the country and rooting up its commerce in such a manner, as to render it useless to its future possessors. That evil principles were prolific; the Boston Port-Bill begot this New-

England Bill; this will beget a Virginia Bill; and that again will become the progenitor of others; until, one by one, parliament has ruined all its colonies, and rooted up all its commerce; until the statute book becomes nothing but a black and bloody roll of proscriptions; a frightful code of rigour and tyranny; a monstrous digest of acts of penalty, incapacity, and general attainder; and that wherever it is opened, it will present a title for destroying some trade, or ruining some province.

On the other side, the contumacy, rebellious acts, and treasonable designs of the Americans, were brought to answer all objections. They first provoked penalties by their disobedience, and then denied the right of the power which had been put under a necessity of inflicting those penalties. Some gentlemen on that side, acknowledged the harshness of the measure, and said that they adopted it with the greatest reluctance; but they lamented, that the necessity of the times, and the conduct of the Americans, had rendered harsh measures indispensably necessary. A much greater number contended that the bill was in every respect proper and just, and considering the offences of those who were its objects, in a high degree merciful. They contended, that though the New-England provinces did not produce wheat sufficient for their consumption, they had great plenty of Indian corn, and did not want other resources to prevent a real famine; and that though their fisheries were shut up by sea, they did not want fish in their rivers. A few went so far as to regret, that the bill did not convey punishments adequate to the crimes of the Americans; and dreaded that the famine, which had been so strongly prognosticated, and so pathetically lamented, would not take place. They said, that the bill was coercive, and that the coercion which

put the speediest end to the dispute, was the most useful, and in the end the most merciful; that the object of consideration was not, whether the Americans were to be starved or not; but which were the most eligible means of compelling them to submit, and to return to their duty. It was said, that they had no alternative but to starve or to rebel; but they had a much easier and better choice, which was to submit. If they were reduced to hard fare by their obstinacy, it would still be better than they deserved; and if they even perished by famine, it would not be a greater punishment than they merited. In its nature it resembled the connected guilt and punishment of self-murder.

Upon the second reading of the bill, it was carried through by the vast majority of 215 to 61. On the 8th of March it was read the third time, when a motion was made for the insertion of a clause, that nothing in the act should extend to prohibit the importation into any of the said provinces, of fuel, corn, meal, flower, or other victual, brought coastwise from any part of America.

In support of this motion, all the pleas that had been before used on the side of humanity were again brought up, with the addition of such fresh argument, as ingenuity, or the recollection of new matter, could supply. It was particularly urged, that this clause was taken from the Boston Port-Bill of the last year; a bill, which its strongest advocates did not pretend to be distinguished by its lenity or humanity; could there then be a reason for throwing away this year, the small stock of humanity we possessed in the foregoing? or for leaving a proof upon record, that the present parliament exceeded the last in cruelty? It was observed, that administration constantly boasted of the great number of friends which government had in those very provinces; will not their being involved in one common ruin and misery with the rest, oblige them to plunge desperately into one common course of defence? when they find that these are the mercies you extend to your friends, will they not of course become your enemies? Besides, it was said, that the fate of General Gage, and the handful of brave men which he commanded, might probably hang upon this rash and cruel act; when the Americans see that the bloody flag is hoisted out, and all possibility of retreat, and means of accommodation cut off; when they see that you are finally determined, not only upon their ruin but extermination, is it to be supposed that they will not be prompted to the most violent acts; and that they will not exert their present superiority of power, to stave off, if not to prevent the impending destruction.

On the other side it was insisted, that coercion having become absolutely necessary, it was not sufficient we should restrain the trade of the New-England colonies, while they refused to trade with us; they must also feel the weight of our power, and the effects of our resentment, until they became experimentally sensible of the ill-consequences that attended their denial of the authority of parliament; and were brought to a thorough knowledge of their own littleness and insignificance when under our displeasure, or that they dared to enter into any competition with us of power, and that all their former greatness and happiness proceeded from our paternal tenderness and care. This was the only sure and conclusive method, of curing the present, and of preventing future evils of the same nature. And are we to fear, that our friends will be alienated by the punishment of our and their enemies. Is it not more natural, that they should take up arms against those who have been the means of bringing such calamities on them, than against their friends and protectors; who besides will shew

such a respectable force, as to give them full encouragement to appear against their rebellious neighbours; and thus deliver not only the innocent, but consequentially even the guilty themselves.

Some pains were also taken in this debate to remove or lessen the imputations of cruelty and inhumanity which had been so repeatedly thrown upon this bill and its promoters. For this purpose, a gentleman who had held consider-[53] able offices for several years in North-America, declared that the New-England provinces were in fact provision colonies; that they were great grazing settlements; and though they did not apply themselves so much to tillage as others, they, however, besides Indian corn, produced rye and barley in plenty; that though they imported wheat and flower, the first was to be considered as an article of luxury, which they might well do without, and the second was for the purpose of fitting out their ships, of which, as that business would now be at an end, they could have no farther occasion; so that the apprehensions of famine, he said, were groundless. A considerable law officer of the other[54] part of the united kingdom, who had used some very harsh expressions on the subject of famine, which had brought on very severe animadversions from one side, and did not even escape censure on the other, took an opportunity upon this occasion to endeavour to soften them by explanation.

The question being at length put, upon the motion for the additional clause, it was rejected by about the usual majority, the numbers being 188, to 58 only. The bill was then carried.

Nor did the Fishery Bill meet with less opposition in the House of Lords than in that of the Commons. A petition from the London merchants, similar to that which had been laid before the other

House, was presented by the noble Marquis, who had unsuccessfully laboured for the reception of the former petitions, previous to the discussion of the American address. Two of the witnesses were also examined, who had already appeared before the House of Commons, in behalf of the merchants. In their present evidence they took in some new ground, which tended to shew the vast importance and extent of the American commerce.

On the other side, the former witness from Poole, with another from the same place, who had been a captain of a ship, were examined; and the testimony of two officers of rank in the sea service, one of whom held a considerable[55] office in the naval department, and both had served upon the Newfoundland station, was also received. All this evidence was brought to shew, that the British Newfoundland fishery might be extended to such a degree as to supply all the European markets; that if an absolute prohibition took place, so as to exclude the Americans totally and perpetually from the fisheries, it would be of the greatest benefit to this nation; and that upon every principle of policy and commerce, both to strengthen our navy and increase our trade, they should be restricted entirely and perpetually to our own people.

Upon the motion for committing the bill after the second reading, the noble Marquis, who had presented the petition, opposed it with great ability. He examined the general principles of the bill, and the means devised for enforcing it. He afterwards entered, with great knowledge of the subject, into a detail of the American trade in general, and more particularly, into a comparative view of that of New-England at different periods; by this, the vast and rapid growth of that colony appeared truly astonishing; he shewed, that in the year 1704, the whole amount of the exports to the New-England provinces, was only about 70,000 l. annually; that in the year 1754, it had risen to 180,000 l. in the succeeding ten years to about 400,000 l.; and in the last ten years, had nearly doubled that sum. He concluded a speech which took in a great variety of matter, by a general and total disapprobation of all the measures pursued relative to the colonies, since the repeal of the stamp act; and predicted, that an useful and constitutional agreement in sentiments, and a cordial reciprocity of interests, would never take place between them and the mother country, until the same principles were once more recurred to, and similar measures adopted.

A great law lord on the same side said, that he rose with the greatest reluctance, as he was already wearied by the unavailing efforts he had continually made in every part of the American business; that the great and certain majorities in both houses, differing from his opinions, and overbearing with a high and powerful hand the feeble efforts on that side, had almost wearied him into a despair of obtaining any thing in that question, or on that subject, by argument or debate; but that notwithstanding, a sense of his duty to interpose his endeavours towards the vindication of justice, and the service of his country, should outweigh every other consideration. He accordingly entered into the general nature, spirit and character of the bill, shewed its operation and tendency, and examined its fitness, its wisdom, and its justice, with his usual force and clearness.

In this course of legal and political examination, he took particular notice of the nature of the evidence which had been brought before the House in support of the bill. Two inconsiderable men of the town of Poole, contrary to the declared sense of all the merchants of England, were, he said, brought to instruct their lordships in the political system of Great-Britain and America; they were to convince them, that the profits of the commerce of America did not enrich this country; they were to satisfy the legislature, that the utter destruction of American trade would strengthen the navy, and invigorate the marine of England; and the words of these redoubtable politicians were to be taken, that if the New-England fishery was destroyed, we should notwithstanding be able to supply the foreign markets, and that the loss of five or six hundred thousand pounds annually, the value of that fishery, would not only be immediately replaced at home, but prove a great benefit to this country. Such was the importance and magnitude of the subjects which were to be decided upon by such persons; but he hoped they would see the frivolous and contemptible nature of such evidence, and that such narrow and interested minds are totally unfit for such mighty discussions.

The lords on the other side, differed greatly as to the principles on which they supported this bill; though they all united in the main point of its being necessary. Some considered it as a lenient means of bringing the Americans back to their duty; who would have been averse to any strong coercion, and much more to every idea of taxation. A more numerous body, who seemed to comprehend its nature and operation more perfectly, considered it as a bill of firmness and vigour; as a severe, but just and necessary act of retaliation and punishment; they, however, would not by any means that its operation should extend any further, than was necessary to fill up the measure of justice, and to bring the refractory colonies to a full and compleat submission; they accordingly could not bear the idea of considering it in any degree as a *commercial*, and still less, as a *permanent* regulation. Others again, considered it merely as a matter of

trade, abstracted from all ideas of coercion and punishment; as a permanent commercial regulation of great importance, to restrain the trade of the colonies, and thereby to strengthen and increase the commercial interest of this country; these would not listen to any proposition for purchasing the obedience of the Americans, by any time sacrificing an object, from which they expected the most extraordinary benefits. To these last might be added the first lord of the admiralty, with, perhaps, a few more, who considered only its political operation, as a means of increasing our maritime power. All those who wished to render it a permanent regulation, seemed to go beyond the designs of the ministers, at least of those in the House of Commons, who intended this bill merely as coercive.

In the course of this debate much complaint was made of the garbled, defective, and mutilated accounts of American affairs that were laid before them; it was said that public and known facts were withheld from them; that the scraps and extracts of letters which were shewn to them by the ministers, were only partial representations, calculated for particular purposes; that they had all along in this business been misled and misinformed. That the people would at length see how they had been deceived, and how parliament was led blindfolded; that it would be in vain then for the ministers to hope to cover themselves by the present fashionable language, that every thing had been done by parliament, as it would be obvious to the meanest capacity, that from their total want of information, they neither did nor could do any thing but as they were directed.

After long and warm debates, the question was carried by a great majority, the numbers being 104, to 29 who opposed the bill.

On the 21st of March, upon the third reading of the bill, a motion was made for an amendment, that the colonies of New-Jersey, Pensylvania, Maryland, Virginia, and South Carolina, should be included in the same restrictions with the New England provinces. In support of this amendment, it was urged, that by the late accounts which arrived, and letters which were upon their table, it appeared, that the several provinces specified in it, had rendered themselves equally culpable with those of New-England; and that of course they ought to suffer under one common punishment; that at the time the bill originated in the House of Commons, this information was not received; but that now they were in possession of evidence fully sufficient to authorize this amendment; and that without it, the bill would be imperfect, and the punishment partial.

On the other side it was said, that the letters and informations alluded to, were no more in the contemplation of the House, either in its legislative or deliberative capacity, than if they had never existed; they had not even been read in the House; they had never been considered; nor had the accused parties been heard in their own defence; so that one half of the continent of North-America was to be punished, without any trial, proof, or enquiry whatever. That such a mode of proceeding was totally unparliamentary and unprecedented; that it was no less repugnant to the established rules of equity and judicial decision, which always and in every instance, supposed the party accused had been heard, before judgment was pronounced; and, that if such a mode of executive speedy justice were to obtain in that house, it would be productive of the most dangerous and alarming consequences.

The question being put upon the amendment it was carried by 52 to 21; and the prohibitions of the bill consequently extended to the five new provinces. The que-

stion was then put upon the bill, and carried by a majority of 73 to 21; and it was accordingly returned to the Commons with the amendment.

This bill was productive of a protest signed by sixteen lords. Among other severe strictures, they represent it as one of those unhappy inventions, to which parliament is driven by the difficulties that daily multiply upon them, from an obstinate adherence to an unwise system of government. They say, that government which attempts to preserve its authority by destroying the trade of its subjects, and by involving the innocent and guilty in a common ruin, if it acts from a choice of such means, confesses itself unworthy; if from inability to find any other, admits itself wholly incompetent to the end of its institution. They severely censure the attempt made to bribe the nation into an acquiescence in this arbitrary act, by holding out to them as a temptation for that purpose, the spoils of the New-England fishery; this they represent to be a scheme full of weakness and indecency; of indecency, because

it may be suspected that the desire of the confiscation has created the guilt; and of weakness, because it supposes, that whatever is taken from the colonies is of course to be transferred to ourselves. But this protest is particularly distinguished, by the severe censure passed upon a Lord high in office,[57] who, in the late debates, to remove all apprehension of the dangers which might arise from the measures that were in agitation, threw out, most unadvisedly, a charge of general cowardice against the Americans.

The amendment, made by the Lords, caused a disagreement between the title and body of the bill, which would have caused great embarrassment to the officers who were to carry it into execution; and the amendment was accordingly rejected by the Commons. This matter occasioned the holding of a conference, a few days after, between the two Houses, at which, the reasons offered by the Commons, having appeared satisfactory, the Lords agreed in rejecting the amendment; and the bill received the royal assent on the 30th of March.[58]

THE New-England restraining act was so much the principal figure in this important session, that in attending to its progress we passed over other matters of which we are now to take notice.

Feb. 13th. Upon a motion for an addition of 2000 seamen to be employed for the ensuing year, the ministers were reminded of their conduct before Christmas, in deceiving the country gentlemen with the appearances of a reduced peace establishment, and thereby leading them gradually into violent and coercive measures, each of which was supposed to be the last, while they were rendered incapable of seeing at any one point of view, either the extent of the expence in which they were involving their constituents, or of the danger in which they were plunging themselves and the nation. This mode of proceeding was represented as an high insult to the House, and an open mockery of that good faith and confidence, that ought to subsist between the Minister and the Commons; and that the application now for a grant of 2000 seamen, when they knew that five times the number would not be sufficient to carry their designs into execution, was an aggravated repetition of the insult; that this mode of procedure was besides calculated to give a full opening to that ruinous practice of gaming in the funds, whereby those in the secret of affairs had an opportunity of making immense fortunes at the public expence.

The ministers avoided all precise explanation as to future applications for supply: they could not pretend to foretel what events might possibly happen, and could not therefore bind themselves by any specific engagement; but they hoped that this would be the last application of the kind. The insinuation as to the funds was universally disclaimed, and the motion for the augmentation agreed to.

The subject was however brought up, and the same objections made two days after, upon a motion in the committee of supply, for an augmentation of 4,383 men to the land forces. This motion was attended with an explanation of the intended military arrangements, by which it appeared, that the force at Boston would be augmented to about 10,000 men, which was deemed sufficient for enforcing the laws; and that the appointment of a number of additional officers, (a measure which was complained of, as incurring a needless expence) was necessary, as it was intended to carry on the operations against the Americans by detachments.

This mode of carrying on the war, was much condemned on the other side for its cruelty; for the indiscriminate destruction of friends as well as foes, with which it must be attended; and the total ruin of a country which we considered as our own, and which must be the inevitable consequence, if the measure could at all succeed. But it was insisted, that the force, both by sea and land, was totally inadequate to the purpose for which it was ordained; and that the national money was to be squandered away, without a possible return of advantage, or even a probability of its attaining the ends to which it was directed. For, they said, that the use of an insignificant force must infallibly have the effect of encouraging the colonies to that resistance, which it was possible the early appearance of a great fleet and army might awe and check in the beginning. The augmentation was carried without difficulty.

Whilst parties thus pursued their debates with much eagerness and animosity, and nothing but defiance was hurled at America on the part of government, the noble Lord at the head of administration amazed all parties, and seemed for a time almost to dissolve his own, by that famous conciliatory motion with respect to America, which

was then, and has been since, the subject of so much discussion. The motion was for passing the following resolution: — That when the governor, council and assembly, or general court of his Majesty's provinces or colonies, shall propose to make provision, according to their respective conditions, circumstances, and situations, for contributing their proportion to the common defence, such proportion to be raised under the authority of the general court, or general assembly of such province or colony, and disposable by parliament; and shall engage to make provision also for the support of the civil government, and the administration of justice in such province or colony, it will be proper, if such proposal should be approved of by his Majesty in parliament, and for so long as such provision shall be made accordingly, to forbear, in respect of such province or colony, to levy any duties, tax, or assessment, or to impose any further duty, tax, or assessment, except only such duties as it may be expedient to impose for the regulation of commerce; the nett produce of the duties last mentioned, to be carried to the account of such province, colony, or plantation respectively.

The minister introduced this motion by a long speech, in which he endeavoured to shew that it was founded upon the late address, particularly the following passage— " and whenever any of the colonies shall make a proper application to us, we shall be ready to afford them every just and reasonable indulgence;"—he, however, seemed to build more upon the principles by which he was actuated in moving for that address, and the explanations he then made to the House, than upon the literal construction of any part of it. He said, that it was his sense, and he believed it to be the sense of the House, that parliament, in the passing of that address, not only meant to shew the Americans its firm determination in the support of its just rights; but also its tenderness, and conciliatory disposition, upon the making of proper concessions; and that particularly, upon the great object of dispute, the point of taxation, although they could never give up the right, and must always maintain the doctrine that every part of the empire was bound to bear its share of service and burthen in the common defence; yet, as to the *mode* of contribution, if that, and not the question of right, was the bone of contention, if the Americans would propose such means as were most agreeable to themselves, and at the same time would effectually answer the end, parliament would not hesitate a moment to *suspend the exercise* of the right; and that they would concede to the Americans the authority of raising their share of the contribution themselves.

He said, that the address required such a comment as the proposed resolution; an explanation by parliament itself, which would leave no room for doubt, nor opportunity of evasion; that as it held out ideas of peace, it should shew in the most clear, explicit, and definitive terms, what the conditions were upon which it might be obtained. This resolution marked the ground on which negociation might take place; it was explicit, it defined the terms, specified the persons from whom the proposals must come, and to whom they must be made; it pointed out the end and purpose for which the contributions were to be given, and the persons from whom the grant of them was to originate: and it takes away every ground of suspicion as to the application of the revenue to purposes for which the Americans would not grant their money, by its specific appropriation to the public defence.

That this resolution would be an infallible touchstone to try the sincerity of the Americans; if their professions are real, and their opposition only founded upon the principles which they pretend, they must, consistently with those principles, agree with this proposition; but if they are actuated by sinister motives, and have dangerous designs in contemplation, their refusal of these terms will expose them to the world. We shall then be prepared, and know how to act; after having shewn our wisdom, our justice, and our humanity, by giving them an opportunity of redeeming their past faults, and holding out to them fitting terms of accommodation; if they reject them, we shall be justified in taking the most coercive measures, and they must be answerable to God and man for the consequences.

He declared himself of opinion, that no declaration of his, or even of the House itself, could bind to an adherence strictly to any former resolution relative to the submission to be required of the colonies, previous to a relaxation on our side. That the greatest nations, this nation included, had often made the most solemn declarations, and entered into the most religious engagements to adhere unalterably to certain points, which afterwards, when circumstances changed, they departed from without scruple and without blame. He instanced in the late Spanish war, in which we declared, that we should never make peace unless the point of *search* was given up; yet peace was made without giving up the search. In the *grand alliance*, the parties engaged to each other that no prince of the House of Bourbon should sit on the throne of Spain; yet peace was made with a prince of the House of Bourbon fitting on that throne. He cited many other instances of a like dereliction of objects, and displayed great historical knowledge and ability in applying it. He added, that in this instance he was the more ready to give way, because it was found by experience, that besides the displeasure our attempt to tax had caused in the colonies, the result proved very

unproductive in point of revenue, from the want of a local knowledge of the best methods of imposing and collecting the duties.

Upon the first bruit of conciliatory measures being proposed by the minister, it was surmised, that he was either going to resign, and would first make a disavowal of those public measures which had been lately pursued, or that from some strange convulsion in the internal cabinet, the whole political system of government was to be changed; all those members who were within hearing accordingly hastened to the House, with the most eager expectation. Nor was the astonishment less within doors. From some perplexity in its construction, and obscurity in the words, the extent or drift of the motion was not immediately comprehended. The courtiers looked at each other with amazement, and seemed at a loss in what light to consider the minister. That numerous high prerogative party, who always loved a strong government, in whatever hands it might be lodged, and accordingly had, upon principle, ever opposed any relaxation in favour of the colonies, heard the propositions with horror, and considered themselves as abandoned and betrayed. Even some of the old staunch friends of government, who had always gone with every administration, and uniformly pursued the same line of conduct in all changes of men and measures, began now more than to waver. In a word, the treasury benches seemed to totter, and that ministerial phalanx, which had been so long irresistible, ready to break, and to fall into irretrievable disorder.

The opposition to the minister's motion, accordingly originated on his own side. They asserted, that the propositions contained in it, so far from being founded upon, were in direct opposition to every principle and idea of the address; that by adopting it, they must give up every ground they had gone upon in the whole courfe of American meafures; that it was a contradiction to all the acts and declarations of parliament; that even upon the principles of the gentlemen in oppofition, (to whom it was intended as a means of paying court) it could be productive of no good confequence; but upon their own, would be attended with numberlefs bad ones; that the propofal was, in effect, an acknowledgment of fomething really grievous in the idea of taxing America by parliament; that it was therefore a fhameful prevarication, and a mean departure from principle. They finally concluded, that they would make no conceffions to rebels with arms in their hands; and that they would enter into no meafure for a fettlement with the Americans, in which an exprefs and definitive acknowledgment from them, of the fupremacy of parliament, was not a preliminary article. So high was the diffatisfaction on this fide, that a motion was made for the chairman of the committee to quit the chair. The minifter was repeatedly called upon his legs, either to make explanations, or to endeavour to reconcile feeming contradictions.

In this ftate of diforder and confufion, when all government and command feemed at an end, it was found neceffary to change the ground of argument. This tafk fell to the lot of a gentleman of the long robe,[59] who had been for fome years in oppofition, and had lately diftinguifhed himfelf for his zeal in promoting all the meafures for reducing the colonies. This learned gentleman undertook to interpret the fpeech and motion, and to prove that nothing lefs was meant or effected by either than a dereliction of the claims or right of parliament, or a yielding in any degree to the infolence of the Americans; but, on the contrary, a more wife and effectual method of enforcing the rights of the one and repreffing the infolence of the other. As the fpeech of the noble propofer had

feemed chiefly addreffed to the oppofition, this was intended to gain the majority, whofe diffent was of far greater importance. He had the addrefs in a few minutes to hufh the troubled waves to peace.

He foon convinced the malcontents, that the appearances of conceffion, lenity, and tendernefs, which had fo much alarmed them in the motion, were of fuch a nature, that they could not interfere with the moft rigid meafures which they wifhed to enforce. He faid, that the addrefs included two correfpondent lines of conduct, which feemed hitherto to have efcaped their penetration; one of thefe was to reprefs thofe that were in rebellion, and to eftablifh the government and enforce the laws of this country in the colonies; the other, to protect its friends, and thofe that were acting under its authority. They had already taken, and were in a train of taking, the moft decifive meafures for effecting the firft of thefe purpofes; and the motion went no further than to provide for the fecond. What will parliament lofe by accepting this motion? The right? It exprefsly referves it. It is fo effential a part of fovereignty, that parliament, if it would, cannot furrender it. Does it fufpend the profitable exercife of the right? So far from it, that it fhews the firm refolution of parliament to enforce the only effential parts of taxation, by compelling the Americans to provide what we, not they, think juft and reafonable for the fupport of the whole empire, without a compliance with which they cannot hope to make any terms of reconciliation with us. Nothing ought fo much to animate the ardour of the youth of this kingdom to a refolute exertion, as this firm determination of parliament; or encourage the gallant officers and troops who are going abroad to enforce this fpirited propofition, as a certainty that they were not going to fight (as had been often reproachfully urged to them) for trifles, and vain points of honour, but

for a fubftantial revenue. The difpute was at length put upon its proper footing—Revenue, or no revenue.

This explanation had fo good an effect, that the minifter himfelf improved upon the idea, and acknowledged, in the courfe of the debate, that he did not expect his propofitions would be generally received by the Americans, but that he intended by them to feparate the grain from the chaff. If it did no good there, it would do good here; it would unite the people of England by holding out to them a diftinct object of revenue; as it united England, it would difunite America: whatever province came firft to make a dutiful offer, would be kindly and gently treated; and if but one province accepted the offer, the whole confederacy would be broken; and that union, which alone rendered them formidable, would be diffolved.

The gentlemen in oppofition were far from controverting any of the charges that were brought on the other fide againft the motion. They allowed every quality that had been afcribed to it except conciliation, which they utterly denied its poffeffing. If it led to peace, their eagernefs for that wifhed-for object would induce them to receive it, under all the circumftances of contradiction, prevarication, meannefs, and humiliation, with which it was faid, and they acknowledged it to be loaded. But inftead of poffeffing that happy property, which with them would have atoned for all its bad ones, they faid it was infidious, bafe, and treacherous, in the higheft degree; and calculated to render incurable all thofe mifchiefs which it pretended to remedy; that it was founded upon the wretched principles of the Bofton Port bill, and would be productive of fimilar effects; the minifter acknowledged this to be a cheat, as that was, and intended for the fame purpofe, to difunite the Americans; the immediate effect of the former, was to throw all the colonies, from Nova-Scotia to Georgia, into one common mafs of union ; if any further cement was wanting to confolidate that mafs, this fcheme would fupply it moft abundantly.

It was faid, that the mode in which this motion was fupported by adminiftration, was the moft ridiculous that ever was attempted in parliament ; they held it out to one fide of the houfe as a meafure of conceffion ; and to the other, as a ftrong affertion of authority; they were renewing that miferable fyftem of low cunning and folly by which they were governed in the tea-act, which to this country was to be a duty of fupply, and to the Americans, a tax only of regulation. It was obferved, that there was a fudden and total change in the principles upon which the minifters would have us fuppofe that we were entering into a civil war. In the whole courfe of this bufinefs, until the prefent day, they had conftantly denied their having any conteft about an American revenue; they reprefented the whole to be a difpute for obedience to trade laws, and to the general legiflative authority; but now they fuddenly change their language, and think they fhall intereft the nation, confole our manufacturers, and animate our foldiers, by perfuading them that it is not a conteft for empty honour, and merely to fupport the dignity of parliament ; that it has an object in view which ftrikes more immediately on the fenfes, the acquifition of a fubftantial revenue; but this attempt of impofition upon the people will be found as futile as their other deceptions, and the propofed revenue as empty a phantom as the fuppofed honour.

It was faid, that though the mode of collection might admit of fome faving under that head, it could not change the nature of the tax ; the people are as effectually taxed without their confent, by being compelled to the payment of a grofs

fum, as by an aggregate of fmall duties to the fame amount; but with this odious difference, that the former carries all the appearance of a contribution or ranfom levied by an hoftile army in a ftate of avowed warfare. That this fcheme of taxation exceeded in oppreffion any other that the rapacity of mankind had yet devifed. In all other cafes, fome fpecific fum was demanded, and the people might form fome opinion of what they could confider as their own, for the remaining term of the ordinance ; but here they were left totally in the dark, as to the extent of the demand ; it might be fixed at the half, at the whole, or at more than they were worth ; and the fame power that authorized the demand, might render their bodies anfwerable for the deficiency.

The ridiculous circumftances that muft attend this mode of taxation, fuppofing it poffible to be carried into execution, were ftrongly painted. The colonies were to be held in durance by fleets and armies, until they fhould fingly and feparately offer to contribute to a fervice, the nature of which they could not know, in a proportion which they could not guefs, and on a ftandard which they will be fo far from being able to afcertain, that parliament which is to hold it, has not ventured even to hint what they expect. Thus the Houfe is to be converted into an auction-room, the fpeaker to hold the hammer, and the colonies to be held prifoners of war, until they confent to a ranfom, by bidding againft each other and againft themfelves, and until the king and parliament fhall call to ftrike down the hammer, and fay—enough. If the firft offer of an affembly was not deemed fufficient, it was afked what the remedy would be ? The bufinefs muft of courfe go back to America, and the fleets, armies, and durance muft of courfe continue, until further offers were made by another affembly, and thefe were again difcuffed in ano-

ther feffion, and perhaps by another parliament; thus the abfurdity and impracticability of this propofition were equal to its oppreffivenefs. The bufinefs would be in an eternal rotation between Europe and America, and nothing ever be finifhed ; while our diftractions, confufions, and expence would every hour increafe. Upon the whole they concluded, that the Americans would receive thefe infidious propofitions with the greateft indignation ; that as they would fhew them more clearly the neceffity, fo they would confirm them the more ftrongly in their union and oppofition. That revenue from a free people muft be the *confequence* of peace, not the *condition* on which it is to be obtained ; and that if we attempted to invert this order, we fhould have neither peace nor revenue.

Notwithftanding the general diffatisfaction with which this motion was received by the friends of adminiftration, who thought their dignity not a little lowered by it, and believed the effects of conciliation or difunion propofed by it, to be very uncertain, it was thought better not to give a triumph to oppofition by rejecting a propofition made by the minifter. It was thought alfo, that this refolution being fufceptible of a variety of interpretations, as had appeared in the debates, fuch an interpretation might be hereafter adopted, as fhould be moft fuitable to their circumftances. Accordingly, though fome of thofe who in the beginning had openly declared themfelves, and could not recede, voted (on grounds totally adverfe to them) with oppofition, the reft of the numbers went as ufual ; and the queftion was carried on a divifion 274 to 88.

We fhould have obferved before, that upon the 1ft of this month, Mr. Sawbridge, having previoufly obtained a call of the Houfe, repeated his annual motion for fhortening the duration of parliament. The motion was fupported ; but as

60

ufual produced no debate; admi-niftration being totally filent upon the fubject. It was, probably, from the fame certainty of the event, that the majority was not quite fo great as in the preceding year and parliament, the numbers upon a divifion being 195 againft, to 104 who fupported the motion.

Sir George Saville's annual mo-tion relative to the Middlefex elec-tion, was this year taken out of his hands, being yielded with pro-priety to the gentleman who was immediately affected by that deci-fion. Mr. Wilkes, who was now Lord-Mayor, and who reprefented the county of Middlefex in parlia-ment, took up in perfon his own caufe, and two days after the de-bate on the conciliatory motion, moved, " That the refolution of " this Houfe of the 17th of Fe-" bruary 1769," 'that John Wilkes, ' Efq; having been in this feffion ' of parliament expelled this Houfe, ' was, and is, incapable of fitting ' in the prefent parliament,' " be " expunged from the journals of " this Houfe, as being fubverfive of " the rights of the whole body of " electors of this kingdom."

This motion was ably fupported by the lord-mayor, who was alfo well feconded; and a confiderable debate enfued, in which much of the ground we have formerly traced, was again gone over. The queftion was overruled by a majority of 68, which taking in the uncommon ful-nefs of the Houfe upon the prefent occafion, was nearly upon a pro-portional par with that of the pre-ceding year; the numbers now be-ing, in fupport of the motion, 171, to 239, by whom it was rejected.

On the day that the New-Eng-land fithery-bill had paffed the Houfe of Commons, adminiftration were called upon by a gentleman in oppofition, for a copy of a letter written by the noble minifter at the head of the American department, to the lieutenant-governor of New-York, and dated upon the 10th of Dec. 1774; as containing matter

of information worthy the confider-ation and attention of the Houfe. This application the minifters refuf-ed to comply with; who faid they were the fole judges what matter was or was not proper to be laid before the Houfe; that a fpirit of curiofity might prompt people to require the feeing of many papers, which it would be very improper to expofe to public view; and that from the nature of executive government, many matters muft neceffarily be kept fecret. That if they could be proved to have abufed this truft they were refponfible.

This occafioned much cenfure on the audacity of refufing to lay ne-ceffary information before the Houfe, efpecially when particular papers were called for and fpecified; and many reflections were made upon the fhameful tamenefs which fubmitted to fuch daring infolence, and to be led blindfold in matters upon which the fate of the nation and empire immediately depended. A motion was alfo made for an ad-drefs to his majefty, that the paper in queftion might be laid before the Houfe; but it paffed in the nega-tive.

It was then obferved, that a pe-tition and memorial of an extraor-dinary nature, from the affembly of the ifland of Jamaica, to the king in council, was reported to have been received fome confider-able time before, and the minifters being queftioned as to the fact, were alfo afked, whether that was among the fecrets of ftate which was not fit to be communicated to parliament. This omiffion the mi-nifters attributed to inattention, and to their not confidering it as a mat-ter of any great confequence; but they now confented to lay it before the Houfe.

This petition and memorial from the affembly of Jamaica, was drawn up in very ftrong terms. In ex-preffing the moft perfect duty and allegiance to the throne, and the ftrongeft attachment to, and reli-ance on their fellow-fubjects in

Great-Britain, they however ob-ferved, that thefe difpofitions were founded on that moft folid and durable bafis, the continued en-joyment of their perfonal rights, and the fecurity of their property. They recite their conftant good be-haviour, and ftate even their weak-nefs and inability of refiftance, as evidences that they cannot be ac-tuated by factious or dangerous mo-tives; and proceed to fhew, that the moft dreadful calamities to their ifland, and the inevitable deftruc-tion of the fmall fugar colonies, muft be involved in a continuance of the prefent unnatural conteft with the Americans. They after-wards enter into a full, free, and argumentative difcuffion of the late claims of the mother country, and of the rights of the colonies; the former of which they combat, and defend the latter with great force. They abfolutely deny that their an-ceftors, the fettlers or conquerors of the colonies, could receive any rights or privileges from their fel-low-fubjects in England at the time of their emigration; the peers could not communicate their privileges, and the people had no rights, but thofe of which the former were equally poffeffed; but the crown, whofe prerogatives were totally in-dependent of both, for the great purpofes of colonization, commu-nicated to all the colonies, though in different degrees, a liberal fhare of its own royal powers of govern-ment. Thefe powers, as well as their original rights and privileges, have been confirmed to them by every means which can be devifed for affording fecurity to mankind; charters, proclamations, profcrip-tion, compact, protection, and obe-dience. From the foregoing, and other premifes, they infer and de-clare, that the colonifts are not fub-jects to the people of England; and infift on their own rights of legifla-tion. They afterwards fay, that they equally deplore, and behold with amazement, a plan, almoft carried into execution, for reducing the colonies into the most abject state of slavery; and they supplicate the throne, and demand and claim from the sovereign, as the guarantee of their just rights, that no laws shall be forced upon them, injurious to their rights, as colonists, or Englishmen; and that as the common parent of his people, his majesty would become a mediator between his European and American subjects.

About the same time, a petition from the city of Waterford in Ireland was presented to the House, setting forth the fatal consequences that will result to that city in particular, and to the kingdom in general, from a continuance of the present unhappy differences between Great-Britain and the colonies; they state, that in that case, they will be deprived of the only valuable branch of export which they are permitted to carry on with the colonies, that of their linen manufactures; a misfortune which they already begin too sensibly to feel.

The fishery-bill had scarcely cleared the House of Commons, when the minister brought in another, "To restrain the trade and commerce of the colonies of New-Jersey, Pensylvania, Maryland, Virginia, and South-Carolina, to Great-Britain, Ireland, and the British islands in the West-Indies, under certain conditions and limitations." As measures of this nature were now familiar, he only thought it necessary to observe, that as the southern provinces had acceded to the non-importation and non-exportation agreement, as well as the northern, it was conformable to reason and justice that they should equally feel our resentment, and experience the same degree of punishment.

Nothing that could be called a debate arose upon this motion. The strange fluctuation and contradiction that appeared in our public councils, was, however, commented upon on both sides of the House, and lamented on one. It was said, that only a few days before, they

March 9th.

were mocked with conciliatory propositions, and nothing was to be heard but concession and moderation; temptations were to be held out to the better disposed colonies, to induce them to break the confederacy; the wheat was to be separated from the chaff, the elect from the reprobate; but now we are told, that the only way to restore peace and harmony, to reconcile the Americans cordially to our government, and to save our commerce from that destruction which seems almost inevitable, is to lump them all indiscriminately, without distinction of friend or foe, in one common punishment; and to drive the whole continent of America into despair, as a necessary preparative to their being restored to good temper.

During the time that this bill was in agitation, a long series of important evidence in behalf of the West-India merchants and planters, and in support of the petition which they had lately presented, was laid before the House. The celebrated Mr. Glover, the author of Leonidas, appeared as agent and manager for the petitioners upon this occasion. This gentleman conducted the business with great ability, and gained much applause by the eloquence and vast extent of commercial knowledge he displayed, in a very long speech which he delivered at the bar of the House, upon summing up, combining and explaining the different parts of the evidence. In this speech he stated, with uncommon precision, the immense value of the objects that were under consideration; endeavoured to shew, that the spirit which had for some time been so prevalent, both within doors and without, for the extorting of pecuniary contributions from the colonies, was inconsistent with true policy, with a right knowledge of commerce, of their circumstances, or of the benefits we already derived from them; and expatiated most pathetically upon the fatal consequences which he apprehended from

a perseverance in the present measures.

It appeared by this evidence, that the sugar colonies were to be considered as vast manufactories, with this peculiar distinction from others, that they were obliged to raise their own materials; that the cane was the raw material; sugar, melasses, and rum, the manufacture; that the raising of provision was, and must necessarily continue to be a very secondary object; that if necessity should at any time render it otherwise, the manufacture must of course decline, in proportion to the attention paid to the other; but that the scarcity of land in the small islands, the great value of cultivable land, for the purpose of raising the material in all, together with the excessive price of labour, and many insurmountable natural impediments, rendered the raising of any thing near a sufficient stock of provisions utterly impracticable. That the middle colonies of North-America were the great sources of supply to the West-India islands, not only for provision, but for an article equally necessary, which is understood under the term of lumber, and by which is meant every kind of timber and wood that is used in building and the cooperage, excepting only some particular cases, wherein great strength and durability are required, and in which the hard woods peculiar to the tropical regions are preferable. It was also clearly shewn, that no other sources of supply could be opened either in America or in Europe, which, with respect to time, quantity, and many other circumstances, could prevent the dreadful effects of a famine in the sugar islands; an event which would be rendered still the more dreadful, by the vast superiority of the negroes to the white people in number, and the horrible barbarities which must be expected from them, in circumstances of calamity that would destroy all order and distinctions among the most civilized nations.

62

And that if there were even a possibility of averting this fatal event, the islands would notwithstanding be ruined as their great staple commodities of sugar and rum would be useless for want of casks to contain them; and they could not receive staves from any part of Europe, upon such terms as they were able to comply with.

This course of enquiry and evidence has been the means of rendering the vast importance and value of the sugar colonies more generally understood, than they perhaps would otherwise have been, and they are matters which may well exercise the speculations of the present, and the admiration of future ages. It appeared by a very moderate calculation, in which large allowances were made for every possible excess, that the capital in those islands, consisting in cultivated lands, buildings, negroes, and stock of all kinds, did not amount to less than the immense sum of sixty millions sterling. That their exports of late years to Great-Britain run to about 190,000 hogsheads and puncheons of sugar and rum annually; amounting in weight to near 95,000 tons, and in value to about 4,000,000l. exclusive of a great number of smaller articles, and of their very great export to North-America. That their growth was so rapid, and improvement so great, that within a very few years, their export of sugar to this kingdom was increased 40,000 hogsheads annually, amounting to about 800,000l. in value. It seems probable, though it could not be precisely ascertained, that more than one half of that vast capital of 60,000,000l. was either the immediate property, or was owing to persons resident in this country. It also appeared, that the revenue gained above 700,000l. a year upon the direct West-India trade, exclusive of its eventual and circuitous products, and of the African trade. It was fully shewn, that this immense capital and trade,

as well as the African, neither of which could subsist without the other, were from nature and circumstance both totally dependent upon North-America. Such were the stakes which we were now setting at hazard.

March 22d. In a few days after, Mr. Burke made his conciliatory propositions with respect to the colonies. These propositions were contained in a set of resolutions, and were accompanied and elucidated by that celebrated speech, which has been since published, and is in every body's hands.

He observed, that the questions on which they were that day to decide, were, Whether they ought to concede; and what that concession ought to be; and that to enable them to determine both on the one and the other of those great questions with a firm and precise judgment, it was necessary to consider distinctly the true nature, and the peculiar circumstances of the object before them; because after all their struggles, whether they would or not, he insisted, that they must govern America, according to that nature, and to those circumstances; and not according to their own imaginations; not according to abstract ideas of right; nor by any means according to mere general theories of government.

Upon this principle he examined and explained, with the utmost minuteness and accuracy, the internal and external, the natural and accidental circumstances of the colonies; he considered them with respect to situation, resources, extent, numbers, amazing growth of population, rapid increase of commerce, fisheries, and agriculture; from these he shewed their strength and importance; he then enquired into that unconquerable spirit of freedom, by which they are distinguished from all other people now existing in the known world; this violent passion for liberty he traced from the sources of descent, educa-

tion, manners, religious principles, forms of government, and distance from the original mover of government.

From all these circumstances he deduced the line of policy which should be pursued with regard to America. The detail was enriched and illustrated with a number of the most interesting facts, and curious observations, tending to establish the ideas of American government which he had laid down; to shew, that it must be adapted to the feelings, to the established habits and received opinions of the people; and that all schemes of government which had been or should be proposed, without paying a due attention to these matters, would be found ineffectual, dangerous, or ruinous.

We should deem it inexcusable to quit this part of the subject, without laying before our readers the astonishing growth of the colonies within a little more than half a century, and the prodigious share they contributed to our greatness; a matter of the first importance to ourselves; which perhaps cannot in any degree be paralleled in the history of mankind; and which will equally excite the admiration, and exercise the scepticism of future ages. This gentleman, in taking a comparative view of the trade of this country at different periods, made it appear, that the whole exports to North-America, the West-Indies, and Africa, in the year 1704, amounted only in value to 569,930l. That in the year 1772, which was taken upon a medium, as being neither the highest nor the lowest of those which might have been applied to of late, the exports to the same places, (including those from Scotland, which in the year 1704 had no existence) amounted to no less than 6,024,171l. being in the proportion of nearly eleven to one. He also shewed, that the whole export trade of England, including that to the colonies, amounted at the first period of

1704, only to 6,509,000l.—Thus the trade to the colonies alone, was at the latter period, within less than half a million of being equal to what this great commercial nation carried on at the beginning of the present century with the whole world. And stating the whole export commerce of this country at present, at sixteen millions, that to the colonies, which in the first period constituted but one twelfth of the whole, was now very considerably more than one third.

However astonishing this general increase of the whole colonies may appear, the growth of the province of Pensylvania is still more extraordinary. In the year 1704, the whole exports to that colony amounted only to 11,459l. and in 1772, they were risen to 507,909l. being nearly fifty times the original demand; and almost equal to the whole colony export at the first period. [64]

The mover, before he stated his own propositions; examined and controverted the different schemes which had been either proposed, or talked of for the government of America; particularly the idea of governing by force; a method, which being very easy and plausible in theory, and requiring no skill nor ability in the design or comprehension, the gross of mankind are fond of recurring to, in all cases which perplex their understanding. This favourite idea he combated with great force, upon the different grounds of its temporary nature; its uncertainty; its destroying the object in the very endeavour to preserve it; and that we have no sort of experience in favour of force as an instrument in the rule of our colonies. That on the contrary, their growth and their utility have been owing to methods altogether different.

He then laboured to prove, that without enquiring whether it was to be yielded as a matter of right, or granted as a matter of favour, the only method of governing the colonies with safety and advantage, was by admitting them to an *interest in our constitution*; and, by recording that admission in the journals of parliament, to give them as strong an assurance as the nature of the thing would admit, that we mean for ever to adhere to that solemn declaration of systematic indulgence.

In the stating and prosecution of this subject, he disclaimed all discussions of right; the question being to be considered solely as a matter of policy; he was not enquiring whether they had a right to render their people miserable; but whether it was not their interest to render them happy? they were not to take the opinion of a lawyer on what they *might* do; but they were to consult reason, humanity, justice, and true policy, in what they *ought* to do. He likewise disclaimed all manner of new projects whatever; professing to derive the theoretic part of his propositions from the ancient constitutional policy of this kingdom with regard to representation, as that policy has been declared in acts of parliament; and the practical, from plain matters of fact, acknowledged as such in the journals of the House; he would only bring them back to that road which an uniform experience had marked out as the best; and in which they had walked with security, advantage, and honour, until the year 1763; that other methods might be more ingenious; but in constitutional discussions, it was much more safe to attend to experience, and to the practice of their ancestors, than to any speculations however refined or plausible. That those ancestors, who had left them such inestimable legacies, and such living monuments of their wisdom, as that constitution, and those colonies, were the safest guides they could follow in any thing that related to the preservation of either.

He then went into an historical detail of the manner of admitting Ireland, Wales, and the counties palatine of Chester and Durham, into an interest in the constitution: The state of things preceding that admission, and the consequences which followed. He shewed from all these instances, that this interest in the British constitution, was not only the cause of the internal happiness of those countries, but of their union with and obedience to the crown and supreme legislature.

From this experience, the communication to the members of an interest in the constitution, became the great ruling principle of British policy; the mode of applying it being varied according to circumstances. Where the districts could be taken into the constitution, they were united, as in the case of Wales, and the counties palatine. Where that was not the case, the constitution was sent to them, as in Ireland. Similar constitutions, accommodated to their respective circumstances, were given to the colonies; and as long as the spirit of these constitutions was preserved, every thing went on happily. When it was violated, every thing fell into confusion.

His whole plan therefore was to go back to our old policy; and to record it in the journals, as a settled ground of future parliamentary proceedings, in order to guard against the mischiefs of our late inconstancy. He made the doctrine, language, and mode of reasoning, contained in the preambles to former acts of parliament, the models whereby to frame his resolutions; and meant by them to establish the equity and justice of a taxation of America, by *grant*, and not by *imposition*. To mark the *legal competency* of the colony assemblies for the support of their government in peace, and for public aids in time of war. To acknowledge that this legal competency has had *a dutiful and beneficial exercise*; and that experience has shewn the *benefit of their grants*, and the *futility of parliamentary taxation as a method of supply*.

This was the substance of the six first resolutions. To these were added some others relative to the settlement of an independent judicature; for regulating the court of admiralty; and for the repeal of the late coercive acts of parliament. The first resolution upon which the debate began, was as follows.— "That the colonies and plantations of Great-Britain in North-America, confisting of fourteen separate governments, and containing two millions and upwards of free inhabitants, have not had the liberty and privilege of electing and fending any knights and burgesses, or others, to reprefent them in the high court of parliament."

On this motion, and on the whole matter, the debate was long and animated. It was objected, in general, that thefe refolutions abandoned the whole object for which we were contending. That in words indeed they did not give up the right of taxing; but they did fo in effect. The firft refolution, they faid, was artfully worded, as containing in appearance nothing but matters of fact; but if adopted, confequences would follow highly prejudicial to the public good. That the mere truth of a propofition did not of courfe make it neceffary or proper to refolve it. As they had frequently refolved not to admit the unconftitutional claims of the Americans, they could not admit refolutions directly leading to them. They had no affurance, that if they fhould adopt thefe propofitions, the Americans would make any dutiful returns on their fide; and thus the fcheme, purfued through fo many difficulties, of compelling that refractory people to contribute their fair proportion to the expences of the whole empire, would fall to the ground. The Houfe of Lords would not, they faid, permit another plan, fomewhat of the fame kind, fo much as to lie on their table; and the Houfe of Commons had

in this feffion already adopted one, which they judged to be conciliatory upon a ground more confiftent with the fupremacy of parliament. It was afferted, that the American affemblies had made provifion upon former occafions—but this, they faid, was only when preffed by their own immediate danger; and for their own local ufe. But if the difpofitions of the colonies had been as favourable as they were reprefented, ftill it was denied, that the American affemblies ever had a legal power of granting a revenue to the crown. This they infifted to be the privilege of parliament only; and a privilege which could not be communicated to any other body whatfoever. In fupport of this doctrine, they quoted the following claufe from that palladium of the English conftitution, and of the rights and liberties of the fubject, commonly called the Bill, or Declaration of Rights; viz. that "Levying money for, or to the ufe of the crown, *by pretence of prerogative*, without grant of parliament, for a longer time, or in other manner, than the fame is or fhall be granted, is illegal."

This claufe, they infifted, clearly enforced the exclufive right in parliament of taxing every part of the empire. And this right, they faid, was not only prudent, but neceffary. The right of taxation muft be inherent in the fupreme power; and being the moft effential of all others, was the moft neceffary, not only to be referved in theory, but exercifed in practice; or it would, in effect, be loft, and all other powers along with it. This principle was carried fo far, that it was faid any minifter ought to be impeached, who fuffered the grant of any fort of revenue from the colonies to the crown. That fuch a practice in time of war, might poffibly be tolerated from the neceffity of the cafe; but that a revenue in time of peace could not be granted by any of the affemblies, without fub-

verting the conftitution. In the warmth of profecuting this idea, it was afferted, by more than one gentleman on that fide, that the eftablifhment of a parliament in Ireland, did not by any means preclude Great-Britain from taxing that kingdom whenever it was thought neceffary. That, that right had always been maintained, and exercifed too, whenever it was judged expedient; and that the Britifh parliament had no other rule in that exercife, than its own difcretion. That all inferior affemblies in this empire, were only like the corporate towns in England, which had a power, like them, of making bye-laws, for their own municipal government, and nothing more.

On the other fide, it was urged, that the claufe in the declaration of rights, fo much relied on, was calculated merely to reftrain the prerogative, from the raifing of any money within the realm, without the confent of parliament; but that it did not at all reach, nor was intended to interfere, with the taxes levied, or grants paffed by legal affemblies out of the kingdom, for the public fervice. On the contrary, parliament knew at the time of paffing that law, that the Irifh grants were fubfifting, and taxes conftantly levied in confequence of them, without their once thinking, either then or at any other time, of cenfuring the practice, or condemning the mode as unconftitutional. It was alfo faid, that different parliaments at different periods, had not only recognized the right, but gratefully acknowledged the benefit which the public derived from the taxes levied, and the grants paffed by the American affemblies. As to the diftinction taken of a time of war and the neceffity of the cafe— they faid it was frivolous and wholly groundlefs. The power of the fubject in granting, or of the crown in receiving, no way differs in time of war, from the fame powers in time of peace; nor is any diftinction on such a supposition made in the article of the Bill of Rights. They argued therefore, that this article of the Bill of Rights is confined to what it was always thought confined, the prerogative in this kingdom; and bound indeed the crown; but could not, in securing the rights and liberties of the subject in this kingdom, intend to annihilate them every where else. That as the constitution had permitted the Irish parliament and American assemblies to make grants to the crown; and that experience had shewn, that these grants had produced both satisfaction and revenue, it was absurd to risque all in favour of theories of supremacy, unity, sovereign rights, and other names, which hitherto had led to nothing but confusion and beggary on all sides, and would continue to produce the same miserable effects, as long as they were persisted in. That the mover had very wisely avoided these speculative questions, and confined himself to experience; and it would be well if they could persuade themselves to follow that example.

The previous question was moved on the first proposition and carried by 270 to 78.

The ill success that had attended all conciliatory propositions hitherto, excepting those which originated from government, did not deter another gentleman on the [65] same side, (Mr. Hartley) within a very few days after, from making a similar attempt. This was regulated on the conciliatory proposition moved by Lord North. It proposed that a letter of requisition should be sent to the colonies by a secretary of state on a motion from that House, for contribution to the expences of the whole empire. On his plan, the inestimable privilege of judging for themselves of the expediency, fixing the amount, and determining the application of the grants, would still be left in the assemblies. The compulsory threat

March 27th.

would be left out. It removed the objection of a revenue raised without consent of parliament, since this requisition would be made at their express desire.—Other motions followed, not for the repeal, (as in the propositions lately negatived) but the suspension of certain acts for three years.

As this motion bore some resemblance to that rejected in the House of Lords at the beginning of the session, though supported and combated with ability, it is not necessary here to repeat the topics, to which the unhappy state of the times has so often obliged us to recur. The motion was rejected without a division.

During the progress of the second restraining bill, an additional clause was moved for by the minister, whereby the counties of Newcastle, Kent, and Sussex, on Deleware, in North-America, were included in the prohibitions of that bill. This motion was carried without a division; but was productive of some pointed observation on its being unprecedented and unknown in the annals of parliament, and on the injustice and cruelty of condemning people unheard, and even without enquiry. To these charges it was answered in general, that those counties were equally culpable with the other provinces, and that the papers before the House contained sufficient information to justify the insertion of that clause.

Upon the third reading of the bill, considerable debates arose, and a young nobleman of the first rank and [66] greatest hopes was much distinguished, not only by his opposition to the bill, and his total condemnation of the whole series of American measures; but by the very pleasing specimen of modesty and ability which he now exhibited in his first speech. He however delivered his sentiments with great resolution and firmness; declared that he was glad a debate had taken place, as it afforded him an op-

April 5th.

portunity of avowing his political creed, and of making some open profession of his sentiments on so very important, and very serious a national question. That from the fullest conviction of his soul, he disclaimed every idea both of policy and right internally to tax America: he disavowed the whole system. It was commenced in iniquity; pursued in resentment; and could terminate in nothing but blood. And he pledged himself, that under whatsoever shape in futurity it might be revived, by whomsoever produced and supported, it should, from him, meet the most constant, determined, and invariable opposition. He predicted that this bill would immediately bring on a civil war.

From the other side it was answered, that his apprehensions of a civil war were not grounded in any knowledge of the Americans, who would bluster indeed, but never fight, or think of opposing General Gage, with arms; and as to the cruelty of this act, it was to be no longer severe than they were rebellious. The matter having been before amply discussed, the debate was not long, nor the attendance considerable on the part of the minority. The bill passed without difficulty. [67]

During these transactions several petitions were received from manufacturing towns in Great-Britain and Ireland against the coercive acts. Some counter petitions were also received, calling for an enforcement of the laws of Great-Britain as the only means of preserving a trade with the colonies, and asserting that the trade hitherto had suffered none, or an inconsiderable diminution by the combination of the Americans. Much altercation arose on the truth of facts alledged on both sides, as well as on the manner of obtaining the signatures, and the quality of those who signed. The minority insisted, that the most who signed these war petitions (as they called them) were persons of none or a remoter interest in the American trade; but of that description of warm and active party men commonly called Tories. —And they entered into several examinations to prove the truth of the former part of their assertion. This produced many long and hot debates.

Other petitions were presented to the crown and equally disregarded. One from the British settlers in Canada against the Quebec bill, in which they state, that upon the faith of the royal proclamation of the 7th of October 1763, they had settled in that province, purchased houses and lands, and entered so extensively into trade, commerce, and agriculture, that the value of land and the wealth of the inhabitants were thereby more than doubled; and after stating their dutiful behaviour to government, and the peace and amity in which they live with the new subjects, grievously complain, that they find themselves, by the late act of parliament, deprived of the franchises which they inherit from their ancestors, and cut off from the benefit and protection of the English laws; that in their stead they are to be governed by the laws of Canada, to which they are utter strangers; and which they consider to be disgraceful to them as Britons; ruinous to their property, by taking away the invaluable privilege of trials by juries; and destructive to their personal liberty and security, as well by dissolving the habeas corpus act, as by the extraordinary powers which are lodged in the hands of the governor and council.

The Quakers also presented a petition, in which, besides endeavouring to diffuse the influence of that spirit of peace, which is the predominant principle in their religious system, they liberally (without attempting to confine loyalty to their own sect) declare themselves persuaded, that there are not in his majesty's extensive dominions, subjects more loyal, and more zealously attached to his royal person, his family, and government, than in the provinces of America, and amongst all religious denominations.

In this season of public discontent, when all men's minds were agitated on one side or other, the city of London, not discouraged by the fate of all its applications for a number of years past, once April 10th. more approached the throne, with an address, remonstrance, and petition; upon a subject, and in a manner, as little calculated to obtain a favourable reception as any of the preceding. In this remonstrance, they recapitulated the whole catalogue of American grievances; declared their abhorrence of the measures, which had been pursued, and were then pursuing, to the oppression of their fellow-subjects in the colonies; that these measures were big with all the consequences which could alarm a free and commercial people; a deep and perhaps fatal wound to commerce; the ruin of manufactures; the diminution of the revenue, and consequent increase of taxes; the alienation of the colonies; and the blood of his majesty's subjects. But that they looked with less horror at the consequences, than at the purpose of those measures. Not deceived by the specious artifice of calling despotism, dignity; they said, they plainly perceived, that the real purpose was, to establish arbitrary power over all America. They justify the resistance, to which, they say, his majesty's faithful subjects have been driven by these grievances, upon the great principles of the constitution, actuated by which, at the glorious period of the revolution, our ancestors transferred the imperial crown of these realms to the illustrious House of Brunswick. They say, "Your petitioners are persuaded, that these measures originated in the secret advice of "men who are enemies equally to "your majesty's title and to the "liberties of your people. That "your majesty's ministers carry "them into execution by the same "fatal corruption which has enabled them to wound the peace "and violate the constitution of "this country—thus they poison "the fountain of public security, "and render that body which "should be the guardian of liberty, a formidable instrument of "arbitrary power."——"Your "petitioners do therefore most "earnestly beseech your majesty, "to dismiss immediately, and for "ever, from your councils, those "ministers and advisers, as the "first step towards a redress of "those grievances which alarm "and afflict your whole people. "So shall peace and commerce be "restored, and the confidence and "affection of all your majesty's "subjects be the solid supporters "of your throne."

As Mr. Wilkes was now Lord Mayor, he of course attended officially to present this remonstrance, and was cautioned by the Lord in waiting, that his majesty expected he should not speak to him. The following answer was delivered from the throne, "It is with the "utmost astonishment that I find "any of my subjects capable of "encouraging the rebellious disposition which unhappily exists "in some of my colonies in North "America. Having entire confidence in the wisdom of my "parliament, the great council of "the nation, I will steadily pursue those measures which they "have recommended for the support of the constitutional rights "of Great-Britain, and the protection of the commercial interests of my kingdoms." This remonstrance was productive of a particular mark of resentment. In a few days after its being presented, a letter was received by the Lord Mayor from the Lord Chamberlain, in which, as chief magistrate of the city of London, he acquainted him from his majesty, that he would not receive on the throne, any address, remonstrance, or petition, of the Lord Mayor and Aldermen, but in their corporate capacity.

As the American fisheries were now abolished, it became necessary to think of some measures for supplying their place, and particularly to guard against the ruinous consequences of the foreign markets either changing the course of consumption, or falling into the hands of strangers, and those perhaps inimical to this country. The consumption of fish oil, as a substitute for tallow, was now become so extensive, as to render that also an object of great national concern; the city of London alone expending about 300,000 l. annually in that commodity. Whatever present purposes the evidence lately before the House might answer, in shewing that there was a sufficient fund of money, ships, men, and inclination ready, for an immediate transfer of the fisheries, not only without loss, but with great gain and benefit, it soon became evident, that the minister did not chuse to risque matters of such infinite importance upon the veracity of those representations.

It seemed also necessary in the present state of public affairs, that the kingdom of Ireland should be taken more notice of, and some greater consideration paid to her interests, than had been the practice for many years. The question between the colonies and parliament, particularly in the manner in which it had been lately argued, was not calculated to quiet that kingdom. The repose of all the parts still at rest was never more necessary. In the crisis to which matters were now evidently tending, little doubt remained, that even assistance would be requisite from that country; besides, her patience, her sufferings, and her forbearance, were to be held up as a mirrour, and in contrast to the co-

lonies; and though these merits had long passed unregarded, this did not seem a fit season to encourage an opinion, that a similar conduct would never obtain any reward. The nature of the benefit was however to be considered, and nothing could seem better adapted than a donation which would be an advantage instead of a loss to the giver. A share in the first fruits of a spoil, was also a lure of undoubted efficacy for enticing future service. It was not, in itself, very considerable; but it was said it might be considered as a beginning; and small benefits carry weight with those who had not been habituated to great favours.

It was shewn in the course of the late evidence before the House, that the exports from this country to Ireland amounted to 2.400,000l. annually; besides her supporting a large and excellent standing army, at all times ready for our defence; and the immense sums of her ready cash, which her numerous absentees, pensioners, and placemen spend in this country. Yet from oppressive restrictions in trade, some of them highly impolitic and prejudicial to ourselves, that country is cut off from the benefit of her great natural staple commodity, as well as excluded in general from the advantages which she might derive from her admirable situation, and her great number of excellent harbours.

The minister accordingly moved for a committee of the whole House, to consider of the encouragement proper to be given to the fisheries of Great-Britain and Ireland. This attention to Ireland was generally approved of, and after some conversation upon the hardships which that country suffered, it was proposed by some gentlemen who were particularly attached to its interests to extend the motion, by adding the words *trade and commerce*, and thereby affording an opportunity of enquiring particularly into the state of that kingdom, and of granting

such relief and indulgence in those respects, as could be done without prejudice to ourselves. The minister did not object to the reasonableness or expediency of entering upon this subject at a proper time; but said that the proposed amendment would introduce a mass of matter, much too weighty and extensive for present consideration; that he would therefore confine the motion to the immediate object of the fisheries, leaving the other matter at large.

The committee in its progress granted several bounties to the ships of Great-Britain and Ireland, for their encouragement in prosecuting the Newfoundland fishery; and the minister went farther than his original avowal, by two resolutions which he introduced and passed in favour of the latter kingdom. By the first of these it was rendered lawful to export from Ireland, cloathes and accoutrements for such regiments on the Irish establishment as were employed abroad; and by the second, a bounty of five shillings per barrel, was allowed on all flax-seed imported into Ireland. This last resolution was passed to prevent the evils that were apprehended to that country, from the cutting off its great American source of supply in that article. Another resolution was also passed, by which the Irish were allowed to export provisions, hooks, lines, nets, tools and implements, for the purposes of the fishery. Some Gentlemen of Ireland however complained that clauses were insidiously stolen into the act to prevent its operating in any considerable extent, and to prevent the employment of English capitals in that kingdom. The committee, besides, agreed to the granting of bounties for encouraging the whale-fishery, in those seas that were to the southward of the Greenland and Davis's streights fisheries; and upon the same principle took off the duties that were payable upon

April 27th.

the importation of oil, blubber, and bone from Newfoundland, &c. They also took off the duty that was payable on the importation of seal-skins.

May 15th. Towards the close of the session Mr. Burke acquainted the House, that he had received a paper of great importance from the General Assembly of the province of New-York; a province which yielded to no part of his Majesty's dominions in its zeal for the prosperity and unity of the empire, and which had ever contributed, as much as any, in its proportion, to the defence and wealth of the whole. He observed, that it was a complaint, in the form of a remonstrance, of several acts of parliament, some of which, as they affirmed, had established principles, and others had made regulations, subversive of the rights of English subjects. That he did not know whether the House would approve of every opinion contained in that paper; but that as nothing could be more decent and respectful than the whole tenor and language of the remonstrance, a mere mistake in opinion, upon any one point, ought not to prevent their receiving it, and granting redress on such other matters as might be really grievous, and which were not necessarily connected with that erroneous opinion. He represented this direct application from America, and dutiful procedure of New-York, in the present critical juncture, as a most desirable and even fortunate circumstance; and strongly urged, that they never had before them so fair an opportunity of putting an end to the unhappy disputes with the colonies as at present; and he conjured them, in the most earnest manner, not to let it escape, as possibly the like might never again return.

He then moved, That the representation and remonstrance of the General Assembly of the colony of New-York, To the Honourable the Knights, Citizens, and Burgesses, of Great-Britain, in Parliament assembled, be brought up. The minister immediately moved an amendment, which was an indirect though effectual negative upon the motion, by inserting, that the said Assembly claim to themselves rights derogatory to, and inconsistent with, the legislative authority of parliament, as declared by an act of the 6th of his present Majesty, entitled, &c. It was contended in opposition to the motion, that the honour of parliament required, that no paper should be received by that House, which tended to call in question its unlimited authority; that they had already relaxed in very essential points, but they could not hear any thing which tended to call in question their right of taxation; that the declaratory act must be repealed, before such a paper was admitted to be brought up; that the House never received even petitions of that nature; but that here the name of a petition was studiously avoided, lest any thing like an obedience to parliament should be acknowledged.

On the other side it was said, that without regard to any abstract questions upon the authority of parliament, or the rights of individuals, a particular consideration was due, in the present circumstances, to the temperate conduct and exemplary good behaviour of the province of New-York. In the midst of all the violence which overspread the continent, that colony preserved her legislature and government entire; and when every thing seemed elsewhere tending to a civil war, she dutifully submitted her complaints to the justice and clemency of the mother country. That assembly which was now applying to them, in such moderate and respectful terms, for a redress of grievances, was the same, which not long before had been so highly applauded by the minister, for refusing to accede to the association of the general congress. Were the ministers then determined, or did they think

it could answer any useful purpose, to drive every part of America into an equal state of desperation? There were times and seasons when wise men would avoid the discussion of odious questions. There were times in which it was highly prudent to let claims of right, however founded, lie dormant. New-York, it was said, was already in bad odour with her sister colonies from the coolness and temperance of her conduct; with what face can she resist their reproaches, or persevere in that moderation, when it is known that she is treated with a contempt and disregard, which could not perhaps be justified with respect to the most contumacious? When it is known, that so far from obtaining a redress of grievances, her complaints of them will not even be heard? What answer, said they, can be given by the friends of the authority of parliament to those, who shall reproach them with their confidence in its declarations to such as should dutifully apply for redress of grievances? The predictions of those who said it would be vain to look for redress from parliament, are verified. Those who promised better things are disgraced. What resource will New-York have, in such circumstances, but by endeavouring to regain the esteem and confidence of the other colonies to exceed them in violence?

During the debates, the question was repeatedly called for, and being at length put upon the minister's amendment, it was carried upon a division by a majority of 186 to 67; and the question being then put upon the amended motion, it was rejected without a division.

The assembly of New-York had also transmitted a memorial to the Lords, and a petition to the King. The Duke of Manchester brought [68] in the memorial to the Lords, and moved for its being read. This motion brought on much discussion; but which served sufficiently to shew the general temper and complexion with respect to the subject. It was said, that the title of the paper rendered it inadmissible, as the term *memorial* was only applicable to the representations which passed between sovereigns; that the noble mover had not sufficiently explained the contents, and that it might contain some matter not fit to be heard. In the same spirit, some remedies were proposed; that if the noble Duke did not chuse to explain the contents, he might read the paper in his place, as a part of his speech; or if that was thought too troublesome, the clerk might stand by him, and read it for him.

To these objections it was answered, that the lowest commissioned officer in the service had an unquestioned right to present a memorial to his Majesty, in any case of real or supposed grievance; so that the term in question did not at all militate with their dignity; that the noble mover of the question had sufficiently explained the matter, by reading the prayer of the memorial, and shewing that it was for a redress of grievances; that for farther particulars he referred them to the original which he proposed to be read; declining, rendering himself responsible for the fate of the petition, by the explanations which he might give of the contents. The proposed remedies were rejected with indignation, and an end at length put to this altercation by calling the question, when, upon a division, the motion for reading the memorial was rejected by a majority of 20, the numbers being 45 against, to 25, who supported the question. Such was the fate of the applications made by the assembly of New-York for a redress of their supposed grievances. Nothing done in parliament seemed to be better calculated to widen the breach between Great-Britain and the colonies.

The day before this transaction, a petition to the Lords from the British inhabitants of the province of Quebec, was presented to that House by Lord Camden. This petition was founded upon the same principles with that which was lately presented to the throne; and the petitioners, after stating the grievances which they suffered in consequence of the late law, conclude by imploring their Lordships' favourable interposition, as the hereditary guardians of the rights of the people, that the said act may be repealed or amended, and that the petitioners may enjoy their constitutional rights, privileges, and franchises.

Some endeavours were also ineffectually used to prevent the reading of this petition. It was asked by what means it came into the noble Lord's hands? how they could be satisfied that it came really from the persons to whom it was attributed? And the propriety of receiving any petition, which did not come through the hands of the Governor and Council, was called in question. To these it was replied, that the first was a matter of very little consequence; the petition had been for some time in town, and had been refused by every Lord in administration; as to the second, the agent for the province would remove every doubt on that head; and as to the third, it was said to be a new and dangerous doctrine, that petitions for the redress of grievances could only be transmitted through the hands of those, whose interest it might be to suppress them totally, and who from situation were liable to be themselves the authors of those grievances.

The noble Lord who introduced the petition then observed, that upon the fullest examination of the late law, he found it so thoroughly impolitic, pernicious, and incompatible with the religion and constitution of this country, that no amendment, nor any thing short of a total repeal, would be sufficient. He arranged his objections to it under the following heads: viz. The extension of the limits of Quebec—the establishment of Popery there—and the civil despotism in which the inhabitants of that immensely extended province are to be perpetually bound, by being deprived of all share in the legislative power, and subjected in life, freedom, and property, to the arbitrary ordinances of a Governor and Council, appointed by, and dependant upon, the crown.

The noble Lord expatiated upon these different subjects, and having brought a great number of facts and arguments to shew the impolicy, injustice, tyranny, and iniquity of that law, declared, that it deserved to be reprobated by the unanimous voice of parliament, and that if there remained the smallest regard for liberty and the constitution in one part of the House, or for the Protestant religion in the other, they must necessarily concur in their censure. He then proposed a bill, which was read to the House, for the repeal of the late act, and which was not to take effect until the 1st of May, 1776, thereby to afford time for the providing of a proper form of government for that province.

This measure was strongly opposed by administration, and a motion was made by the nobleman who presided at the head of the American department, that the bill should be rejected. They contended on that side, that the French Canadians were rendered exceedingly happy by the late law; in support of which assertion, they produced an address to General Carleton the Governor, upon his arrival in that province, and another to the King, wherein they expressed their thanks and gratitude for being restored to their antient rights and privileges. These, they said, were indubitable proofs how much the people were pleased, and expected to be benefitted by the change, and removed every doubt of the utility of the present system. They represented the British settlers, supposing them to have concurred unanimously in the matter of the petition, to be, comparatively, only a handful of people ; and infifted, that upon no one principle of good policy, juftice, or public faith, near an hundred thoufand peaceable loyal fubjects fhould be rendered unhappy and miferable, merely to gratify the unreafonable requeft of two or three thoufand perfons, who wifhed for what was impracticable, and thought themfelves deprived of what they had in poffeffion.

As much cenfure had been expreffed or implied, both within doors and without, relative to the whole conduct of the bifhops in the Canada tranfactions, as if they had not only neglected, but abandoned the interefts of the Proteftant religion, the reverend Father of that venerable bench now ftood up to juftify the Quebec act, fo far as it related to religious matters ; which he did upon the principles of toleration, the faith of the capitulation, and the terms of the definitive treaty of peace. After long debates, in which much extraneous matter feemed to be purpofely brought in, and a long law conteft, between a learned Lord high in [69] office and the noble framer of the bill, the motion for its rejection was carried upon a divifion, at ten o'clock at night, by the majority of fixty, the numbers being 88, who oppofed, to 28 Lords only, who fupported the bill. The two royal Dukes, and brothers, were in the minority upon this divifion.

About the fame time, another petition from the fame 18th. inhabitants of Quebec, was prefented to the Houfe of Commons by Sir George Saville, in which, befides the matters they had ftated in the two former, they reprefented, that a petition to his Majefty, in the name of all the French inhabitants of that province, and upon which the late law had been avowedly founded, was not fairly obtained, and had neither received the concurrence, nor even been communicated to the people in general; on the contrary, that it had been carried about in a fecret manner, and figned by a few of the nobleffe, advocates, and others who were in their confidence, through the fuggeftions, and under the influence of the clergy; and they affirmed, that the inhabitants in general, the French freeholders, merchants, and traders, were as much alarmed as themfelves, at the introduction of the Canadian laws. They concluded by praying, that the faid act may be repealed or amended, and that they may have the benefit and protection of the Englifh laws, in fo far as relates to perfonal property; and that their liberty may be afcertained, according to their antient conftitutional rights and privileges.

The gentleman who introduced the petition, having exercifed that acutenefs of difquifition, and that livelinefs of imagery, by which among other eminent qualities he is diftinguifhed, in examining and laying open the weak or obnoxious parts of the Quebec act, and throwing a new light even upon thofe which had already undergone the higheft degree of colouring, concluded his fpeech with a motion, for repealing the late act for the better government of the province of Quebec. Though this motion produced fome confiderable debates, the fubject was already fo much exhaufted, that they could not be very interefting ; excepting that the minifter, in the courfe of them, avowed his intention, if it fhould become neceffary, of arming the Canadians againft the other colonies. He, however, declared his firm perfuafion, that the troubles in America would be fettled fpeedily, happily, and without bloodfhed. The motion was rejected upon a divifion by a majority of more than two to one, the numbers being 174 to 86.

The money-bills which received the royal affent, at the clofe of the feffion, were accompanied with a fpeech from the Speaker to his Majefty, ftating the heavinefs of the grants, which nothing but the particular exigencies of the times could juftify in a feafon of profound peace; he, however, gave an affurance, that if the Americans fhould perfift in their refolutions, and the fword muft be drawn, the Commons would do every thing in their power to maintain and fupport the fupremacy of this legiflature. He befides praifed the late law for determining controverted elections, and concluded by expreffing his confidence, that the money now granted would be faithfully applied to the purpofes for which it was appropriated.

In the fpeech from the throne, the moft May 26th. perfect fatisfaction in their conduct, during the courfe of this important feffion, was expreffed. It was faid, that they had maintained, with a firm and fteady refolution, the rights of the crown and the authority of parliament, which fhould ever be confidered as infeparable; that they had protected and promoted the commercial interefts of thefe kingdoms; and they had, at the fame time, given convincing proofs of their readinefs (as far as the conftitution would allow them) to gratify the wifhes, and remove the apprehenfions of the fubjects in America; and a perfuafion was entertained, that the moft falutary effects muft, in the end, refult from meafures formed and conducted on fuch principles. A favourable reprefentation was made of the pacific difpofition of other powers, and the ufual affurance given of endeavouring to fecure the public tranquillity. Much concern was expreffed, that the unhappy difturbances, in fome of the colonies, had occafioned an augmentation of the land-forces, and prevented the intended reduction of the naval eftablifhment from being compleated; and great thanks were returned for the chearfulnefs and public fpirit with which they had granted the fupplies. It concluded with the usual recommendation, to preserve and cultivate, in their several counties, the same regard for public order, and the same discernment of their true interests, which have in these times distinguished the character of his Majesty's faithful and beloved people; and the continuance of which cannot fail to render them happy at home, and respected abroad.

State of affairs in America during the sitting of parliament. Preparations. Ordnance seized in Rhode Island. A fort taken, and powder seized in New Hampshire. Resolutions of the general congress approved of and confirmed in different places — rejected by the assembly of New-York. Proceedings of the new provincial congress in Massachusett's Bay. Detachment sent to seize on some cannon at Salem. Dispute at a draw-bridge. Affair at Lexington and Concord. Loss on both sides. Province rise in arms. Boston invested by great bodies of the militia. Provincial congress address the people of Great-Britain. Measures pursued for the array and support of an army; pay of the officers and soldiers fixed, and rules for its regulation and government published. Capitulation with the inhabitants of Boston not adhered to. Continental congress meet at Philadelphia. Resolutions for the raising of an army, the establishment of a paper currency, and to prevent the British fisheries from being supplied with provisions. Application from the people of New-York to the congress. Crown-Point and Ticonderoga surprized. Generals and troops arrive at Boston. Engagements in the islands near Boston. General congress resolve that the compact between the crown and the province of Massachusett's Bay is dissolved. Erect a general post-office. Proclamation of rebellion by Gen. Gage. Action at Bunker's Hill. Light-house burnt. Consequences of the Quebec act. Declaration of the general congress, in answer to the late proclamation. Address to the inhabitants of Great-Britain——to the people of Ireland. Petition to the king. Georgia accedes to the general confederacy. Gen. Washington appointed commander in chief of all the American forces by the general congress.

DURING these transactions at home, affairs were every day becoming more dangerous in America. Whatever hesitation or doubt might before have operated with the timid, or principles of caution and prudence with the moderate, they were now all removed by the determinations of the general congress. These became immediately the political creed of the colonies, and a perfect compliance with their resolutions was every where determined upon, as soon as the general sense of the people could be obtained. The unanimity which prevailed throughout the continent was amazing. The same language was held by town and provincial meetings, by general assemblies, by judges in their charges, and by grand juries in their presentments; and all their acts tended to the same point. It was a new and wonderful thing to see the inhabitants of rich and great commercial countries, who had acquired a long established habitual relish for the superfluities and luxuries of foreign nations, all at once determined to abandon those captivating allure-ments, and to restrain themselves to bare necessaries. It was scarcely an object of greater admiration, that the merchant should forego the advantages of commerce, the farmer submit to the loss of the sale of his products and the benefits of his industry, and the seaman, with the numberless other persons dependant upon trade, contentedly resign the very means of livelihood, and trust to a precarious subsistence from the public spirit or charity of the opulent. Such however was the spectacle, which America at that time, and still in some degree, exhibited to the world.

Great hopes were however placed on the success of the petition from the continental congress to the throne. Nor was it supposed, that their general application to the people of England would have been unproductive of effect. A still greater reliance was not unreasonably placed upon the effect which the unanimity and determinations of the congress would produce, in influencing publick opinions and measures at home.

These hopes and opinions had

for a time a confiderable effect in reftraining thofe violences which afterwards took place. But however well they might feem to be founded, and however general their operation, the principal leaders, and moft experienced men, did not appear to build much upon them, and accordingly made fome preparation for the worft that might happen. The fouthern colonies began to arm as well as the northern, and to train and exercife their militia; and as foon as advice was received of the proclamation iffued in England to prevent the exportation of arms and ammunition to America, meafures were fpeedily taken to remedy the defect. For this purpofe, and to render themfelves as independent as poffible of foreigners for the fupply of thofe effential articles, mills were erected, and manufactories formed both in Philadelphia and Virginia, for the making of gunpowder, and encouragement given in all the colonies for the fabrication of arms of every fort. Great difficulties however attended thefe beginnings; and the fupply of powder, both from the home manufacture and the importation, was for a long time fcanty and precarious.

The Governor's proclamation againft the provincial congrefs in Maffachufetts Bay, had not the fmalleft effect, either upon the proceedings of that affembly, or the conduct of the people, who paid an implicit obedience to its determinations. As expreffes continually paffed between that body and the general congrefs, no doubt can be entertained, that its meafures were regulated by their opinion. The critical fituation of the capital was an object of much confideration; nor was it eafy to determine in what manner to provide for the fafety of the inhabitants, and to prevent its becoming a fore thorn in the fide of the province, if matters fhould proceed to extremity. From its natural advantages of fituation, with the works thrown up

on the Neck, Bofton was already become a very ftrong hold; and was capable, with little difficulty, of being rendered a place of fuch ftrength, as, under the protection of a navy, would leave but little hope of its being ever reduced. From the fame caufes it was liable to be converted, at the difcretion of the Governor, into a fecure prifon for the inhabitants, who would thereby become hoftages for the conduct of the province at large.

Different propofals were faid to be made to prevent or remedy thefe evils. One was, fimply, to remove the inhabitants; another, to fet a valuation upon their eftates, burn the town, and reimburfe them for their loffes. Both thefe fchemes were found to be clogged with fo many difficulties as rendered them impracticable. Force was the only expedient which could be applied with fuccefs; but they did not as yet feem difpofed to proceed to that extremity. In the mean time, numbers of the principal inhabitants quitted the town, under the real or pretended apprehenfion of immediate violence from the troops, or of being kidnapped and fent to England, to ftand trial for fuppofed offences.

The provincial congrefs, having done all the bufinefs that was thought proper or neceffary for the prefent, diffolved themfelves towards the end of November, having firft appointed another meeting to be held in the enfuing month of February. This ceffation afforded an opportunity to the friends of government, or loyalifts, as they now called themfelves, to fhew themfelves in a few places; to try their ftrength and numbers, and to endeavour to refift the general current. Some affociations for mutual defence were accordingly formed, and a refufal was made, in a few towns, to comply with the refolutions of the provincial congrefs; but the contrary fpirit was fo prevalent, that thofe attempts were foon quelled. The diffentients were overwhelmed by

numbers. All thefe attempts came to nothing.

As foon as an account was received at Rhode Ifland, of the prohibition on the exportation of military ftores from Great-Britain, the people feized upon and removed all the ordnance belonging to the crown in that province, which lay upon fome batteries that defended one of the harbours, and amounted to above forty pieces of cannon of different fizes. A captain of a man of war, having waited upon the governor to enquire into the meaning of this procedure, was informed, with great franknefs, that the people had feized the cannon to prevent their falling into the hands of the king's forces; and that they meant to make ufe of them to defend themfelves againft any power that fhould offer to moleft them. The affembly of that ifland alfo paffed refolutions for the procuring of arms and military ftores, by every means, and from every quarter in which they could be obtained, as well as for training and arming the inhabitants.

The province of New-Hampfhire had hitherto preferved a greater degree of moderation than any other of the New-England governments. As foon, however, as intelligence arrived of the tranfactions at Rhode-Ifland, with a copy of their refolutions, and of the royal proclamation which gave rife to them, a fimilar fpirit operated upon that people. A body of men accordingly affembled in arms, and marched to the attack of a fmall fort, called William and Mary, confiderable only for being the object of the firft movement in the province. This was eafily taken, and fupplied them with a quantity of powder, by which they were enabled to put themfelves into a ftate of defence.

Dec. 14th, 1774.

No other acts of extraordinary violence took place during the winter. A firm determination of refiftance was, however, univerfally spread, and grew the stronger by the arrival of the King's speech, and the addresses of the new parliament; which seemed, in the opinion of the Americans, nearly to cut off all hopes of reconciliation. It is remarkable that all the acts and public declarations, which here were recommended as the means of pacifying, by intimidating that people, constantly produced the contrary effect. The more clearly a determination was shewn to enforce an high authority, the more strenuously the colonists seemed determined to resist it. The assembly of Pensylvania, which met by adjournment towards the close of the year, was the first legal convention which unanimously approved of and ratified all the acts of the general congress, and appointed delegates to represent them in the new congress, which was to be held in the ensuing month of May.

The proceedings were similar in other places, whether transacted by the assemblies, or by provincial conventions of deputies. The convention of Maryland appointed a sum of money for the purchase of arms and ammunition. A provincial convention, which was held at Philadelphia in the latter end of January, passed a number of resolutions for the encouragement of the most necessary manufactures within themselves; among which, salt, gunpowder, saltpetre, and steel, were particularly recommended. They also passed a resolution, in which they declared it to be their most earnest wish and desire to see harmony restored between Great-Britain and the colonies; and that they would exert their utmost endeavours for the attainment of that most desirable object. But that if the humble and loyal petition of the congress to his Majesty should be disregarded, and the British administration, instead of redressing their grievances, should determine by force to effect a submission to the late arbitrary acts of parliament, in such a situation they hold it their indispensable duty to resist such force, and at every hazard to defend the rights and liberties of America.

The assembly of New-York, which met in the beginning of the year, was, however, a single exception to the rest of the continent. In this assembly, after very considerable debates upon the question of acceding to the resolutions of the general congress, it was rejected upon a division; though by a very small majority. They afterwards proceeded to state the public grievances, with an intention of laying them before the king and parliament; a mode of application in which they were much encouraged by the lieutenant-governor, and from which they presaged the happiest effects, flattering themselves, that when all other means had failed of success, they should have the lasting honour of procuring a thorough reconciliation between the mother country and the colonies: a hope, however fruitless, which probably had a great effect in their late determination. It was also said, that this method had been suggested to them from authority in England. They accordingly drew up that petition to the king, memorial to the lords, and representation and remonstrance to the commons, the inefficacy of which we have already seen.

The new provincial congress, which met at Cambridge, in Massachusetts Bay, did not deviate from the line which had been chalked out by their predecessors. Among other resolutions they published one, to inform the people, that from the present disposition of the British ministry and parliament, there was real cause to fear, that the reasonable and just applications of that continent to Great-Britain for peace, liberty, and safety, would not meet with a favourable reception; but, on the contrary, from the large reinforcement of troops expected in that colony, the tenor of intelligence from Great-Britain, and general appearances, they have reason to apprehend, that the sudden destruction of that colony in particular was intended, for refusing, with the other American colonies, tamely to submit to, what they termed, the most ignominious slavery.

They therefore urged, in the strongest terms, the militia in general, and the *minute men* in particular, to spare neither time, pains, nor expence, at so critical a juncture, in perfecting themselves forthwith in military discipline. They passed other resolutions for the providing and making of fire-arms and bayonets; and renewed more strictly the prohibition of their predecessors, against supplying the troops at Boston with any of those necessaries which are peculiarly requisite for the military service; the markets at Boston being still open to the supply of provisions. As we have made use of a term which has hitherto been unknown in military transactions, it may require some explanation. By *minute men* are to be understood a select number of the militia, who undertake to hold themselves, upon all occasions, and at the shortest notice, in readiness for actual service. By their alertness they have since shewn that the name was not misapplied.

A circular letter from the secretary of state for the American department, forbidding, in the king's name, and under pain of his displeasure, the election of deputies for the ensuing general congress, was productive of no manner of effect; the elections every where took place, even in the province of New-York, notwithstanding the late resolution in their assembly.

Things continued very quiet at Boston. To which the injunctions of the different congresses perhaps contributed as much, as the ships of war that crowded the harbour, or the force that was stationed in the town. The calm was however precarious and fallacious on both

Jan. 10, 1775.

70

Feb. 1.

fides. Combuftible matter had been gathered in abundance. More was in preparation, and the leaft fpark was likely to kindle a general conflagration.

Governor Gage having received intelligence that fome brafs cannon were depofited in the town of Salem, fent a detachment of troops under the command of a field officer, on board a tranfport, in order to feize upon and bring them to Bofton. The troops having landed at Marblehead, proceeded to Salem, where they were difappointed as to finding the cannon; but having fome reafon to imagine they had been only removed that morning in confequence of their approach, it induced them to march further into the country in hopes of overtaking them. In this purfuit they arrived at a draw-bridge over a fmall river, where a number of the country people were affembled, and thofe on the oppofite fide had taken up the bridge to prevent their paffage. The commanding officer ordered the bridge to be let down, which the people peremptorily refufed, faying, that it was a private road, and that he had no authority to demand a paffage that way. For to the laft moment the language of peace was preferved, and until the fword was decifively drawn, all refiftance was carried on upon fome legal ground. Upon this refufal, the officer determined to make ufe of a boat, thereby to gain poffeffion of the bridge; but the country people perceiving his intention, feveral of them jumped into the boat with axes, and cut holes thro' her bottom, which occafioned fome fcuffle between them and the foldiers in and about the boat. Things were now tending to extremities, as the commander feemed determined to force his paffage, and the others as refolutely bent to prevent it. In this fituation, a neighbouring clergyman, who had attended the whole tranfaction, remonftrated with the lieutenant-colonel, upon

Feb. 26.

the fatal confequences which would inevitably attend his making ufe of force. And finding that the point of military honour, with refpect to making good his paffage, was the principal object with that gentleman, it being then too late in the evening to profecute his original defign, he prevailed upon the people to let down the bridge, which the troops took poffeffion of; and the colonel having pufhed a detachment a little way into the country, in exercife of the right which he affumed, they immediately after returned, without moleftation, on board the tranfport. Thus ended this firft expedition, without effect, and happily without mifchief. Enough appeared to fhew upon what a flender thread the peace of the empire hung; and that the leaft exertion of the military would certainly bring things to extremities. The people, fince the acts for cafting away their charter, and for protecting the foldiery from any trial in the province, confidered themfelves as put under military government. Every motion of that body became fufpected, and was in their eyes an exertion of the moft odious and moft dreadful tyranny.

This appearance of refiftance feems, on the other fide, to have greatly irritated the military, for from this time they appear to have lived upon worfe terms with the inhabitants of Bofton than they had hitherto done; fome general and wanton infults, as well as particular outrages having been complained of. But the crifis was now faft approaching, in which all leffer evils and calamities were to be loft and forgotten in the contemplation of thofe of a great and ferious nature.

The provincials having collected a confiderable quantity of military ftores at the town of Concord, where the provincial congrefs was alfo held, General Gage thought it expedient to detach the grenadiers and light infantry of the army, under the command of lieutenant-

colonel Smith, and major Pitcairn [71] of the marines, in order to deftroy them. It is faid and believed, that this expedition had another object in view, which was to feize on the perfons of Meffrs. Hancock and Adams, thofe great and obnoxious leaders of the faction which oppofed the new fyftem of government. The detachment, which was fuppofed to confift of about 900 men, embarked in boats at Bofton on the night preceding the 19th of April, and having gone a little way up Charles river, landed at a place called Phipps's Farm, from whence they proceeded with great filence and expedition towards Concord. Several officers on horfeback in the mean time fcoured the roads, and fecured fuch country people as they chanced to meet with at that early time. Notwithftanding thefe precautions, they difcovered, by the firing of guns and the ringing of bells, that the country was alarmed, and the people actually began to affemble in the neighbouring towns and villages before day-light.

Upon their arrival at Lexington, about five in the morning, they found the company of militia, belonging to that town, affembled on a green near the road; upon which an officer in the van called out, *Difperfe, you rebels; throw down your arms, and difperfe:* the foldiers at the fame time running up with loud huzzas, fome fcattering fhots were firft fired, and immediately fucceeded by a general difcharge, by which eight of the militia were killed and feveral wounded,

Thus was the firft blood drawn in this unhappy civil conteft. Great pains were taken on each fide to fhew the other to have been the aggreffor upon this occafion. A matter of little confequence, in a political view, as things were now too far advanced to leave room for a probable hope of any other than fuch a final iffue. It was faid in the Gazette, that the troops were firft fired upon from fome neighbouring houses. There is some obscurity in this business, for it appears, from the general tenor of the evidence, as well of some of our own people who were taken prisoners, as of a great number of the provincials, all whose depositions were regularly taken and attested by proper magistrates, that the firing both at Lexington and Concord was commenced by the troops. Indeed it seems evident, that a single company of militia, standing, as it may be said, under the muzzles of our soldiers guns, would have been sufficient pledges to prevent any outrage from their friends and neighbours in the adjoining houses.

After this execution, the detachment proceeded to Concord, the commanding officer having previously dispatched six companies of light infantry to possess two bridges which lay at some distance beyond the town, probably with a view of preventing any of the stores from being carried off that way; or, if he had orders about the seizure of persons, to prevent the escape of those whom it was his object to secure. A body of militia, who occupied a hill in the way, retired at the approach of the troops, and passed over one of those bridges, which was immediately after taken possession of by the light infantry. The main body having arrived at the town, proceeded to execute their commission, by rendering three pieces of iron cannon unserviceable, destroying some gun and other carriages, and throwing several barrels of flour, gunpowder, and musket ball into the river. In the mean time, the militia which retired from the hill, seeing several fires in the town which they apprehended to be of houses in flames, returned towards the bridge which they had lately passed, and which lay in their way thither. Upon this movement, the light infantry retired on the Concord side of the river, and began to pull up the bridge; but upon the near approach of the militia, (who seemed studiously to

have avoided all appearance of beginning the attack, and made as if they only wanted to pass as common travellers) the soldiers immediately fired, and killed two men. The provincials returned the fire, and a skirmish ensued at the bridge, in which the former seem to have been under some disadvantage, and were forced to retreat, having several men killed and wounded, and a lieutenant and some others taken.

About this time the country rose upon them. The troops were attacked on all quarters; skirmish succeeded upon skirmish; and a continued, though scattering and irregular fire, was supported through the whole of a long and very hot day. In the march back of six miles to Lexington, the troops were exceedingly annoyed, not only by the pursuers, but by the fire from houses, walls, and other coverts, all of which were filled or lined with armed men.

It happened fortunately, that General Gage, apprehensive of the danger of the service, had detached Lord Percy early in the morning[72] with 16 companies of foot, a detachment of marines, and two pieces of cannon, to support Colonel Smith's detachment, and that they were arrived at Lexington, by the time the others had returned from Concord. This circumstance was the more fortunate, as it is reported the first detachment had by that time expended all their ammunition; but if that even had not been the case, it scarcely seems possible that they could have escaped being cut off or taken in the long subsequent retreat of fifteen miles.

This powerful support, especially the cannon, afforded a breathing-time to the first detachment at Lexington, which they already much wanted. The field pieces obliged the provincials to keep their distance. But as soon as the troops resumed their march, the attacks, as the country people became more numerous, grew in proportion more violent, and the danger was con-

tinually augmenting, until they arrived about sun-set at Charlestown; from whence they passed over directly to Boston, under the protection (as the provincials say) of the guns of the Somerset man of war; the troops being entirely spent and worn down, by the excessive fatigues they had undergone. They had marched that day near 35 miles.

The loss was not so great on either side, as the length, irregularity, and variety of the engagement might seem to indicate; which may be attributed to the provincials not being at first powerful in number, and to their being afterwards kept at some distance by the field pieces. The king's troops, as may be expected, were the greater sufferers, having lost in killed, wounded, and prisoners, 273 men, of which 65 were killed, 2 lieutenants, and above 20 private men taken prisoners, and Colonel Smith, with another lieutenant-colonel and several officers, wounded. By the provincial account, which gives the names and places of abode of those who fell on their side, their loss in killed and wounded (including those who fell by the first fire in the morning at Lexington) amounted only to about sixty, of which near two thirds were killed.[73]

By the nearest calculation that can be made, there were from 1800 to 2000 of the best troops in the service (being about half the force that was then stationed at Boston) employed upon this expedition. The event sufficiently shewed how ill informed those were who had so often asserted at home, that a regiment or two could force their way through any part of the continent, and that the very sight of a grenadier's cap, would be sufficient to put an American army to flight.

Upon this occasion, each side charged the other with the most inhuman cruelties. Civil wars produce many such charges; but we have good reason, and some authority for believing, that these accounts, if at all true on either fide, were much exaggerated. On one fide it is certain, that an officer and fome of the foldiers who were wounded and prifoners, gave public teftimonials of the humanity with which they were treated ; and that the provincial commanders fent an offer to General Gage, to admit his furgeons to come and drefs the wounded.

Although on the other fide, the regulars were charged with killing the old, the infirm, the unarmed, and the wounded, without mercy ; with burning feveral houfes, and plundering every thing that came in their way ; we have had too conftant and uniform an experience of the honour of our officers, and the humanity of our foldiers, not to confider this account as equally exaggerated.

This affair immediately called up the whole province in arms ; and though a fufficient number were fpeedily affembled effectually to inveft the king's troops in Bofton, it was with difficulty that the crowds who were haftily marching from different parts, could be prevailed upon to return to their refpective homes. The body of militia which furrounded Bofton, amounted, as it was faid, to above 20,000 men, under the command of the Colonels Ward, Pribble, Heath, Prefcot,[74] and Thomas, who for the prefent acted as generals, and having fixed their head quarters at Cambridge, formed a line of encampment, the right wing of which extended from that town to Roxbury, and the left to Myftick, the diftance between the points being about thirty miles. This line they ftrengthened with artillery. They were fpeedily join-[75] ed by Colonel Putnam, an old and brave provincial officer, who had acquired experience and reputation in the two laft wars. He encamped with a large detachment of Connecticut troops in fuch a pofition, as to be readily able to fupport thofe who were before the town.

In the mean time the provincial congrefs, which was now removed to Watertown, drew up an addrefs to the inhabitants of Great-Britain, in which they ftated the moft material particulars, relative to the late engagement, and took pains to fhew, that hoftilities were firft commenced, and blood drawn, both at Lexington and Concord by the regulars. They complain of the ravages committed by them in their retreat; place much dependence on the honour, wifdom, and valour of Britons, from which they hope their interference in preventing the profecution of meafures, which, they reprefent, as equally ruinous to the mother country and the colonies ; they make great profeffions of loyalty ; but declare, that they will not tamely fubmit to the perfecution and tyranny of a cruel miniftry, and (appealing to Heaven for the juftice of their caufe) that they are determined to die or be free.

The provincial congrefs alfo paffed a vote for the array and fupport of an army ; fixed the pay of the officers and foldiers, and publifhed rules and orders for its regulation and government. To provide for the military expence, they paffed a vote for the iffuing of a confiderable fum in paper currency, which was to be received in all cafes as money, and the faith of the province pledged for its payment. As the term for which they were chofen was to expire on the 30th of May, they gave notice for the election of a new congrefs, to meet on the 31ft of that month at the fame place, and to be continued for fix months, and no longer. They alfo paffed a refolution, that General Gage had, by May 5th. the late transactions, and many other means, utterly difqualified himfelf from ferving that colony as a governor, or in any other capacity, and that therefore no obedience was in future due to him ; but that on the contrary he ought to be confidered and guarded againft, as an unnatural and inveterate enemy to the country.

The affair at Lexington (though fome fuch event muft have been long forefeen and expected) excited the greateft indignation in the other colonies, and they prepared for war with as much eagernefs and difpatch as if an enemy had already appeared at each of their doors. The bravery fhewn by the militia in this their firft effay, and the fuppofed advantages they had obtained over the regulars, were matters of great exultation ; while thofe who fell in the action were regretted with the deepeft concern, and honoured, not only as patriots, but as martyrs, who had died bravely in the caufe of their country. The outrages and cruelties charged upon the king's forces, however unjuftly founded, produced a great effect, and increafed the public fever.

In fome places the magazines were feized, and in New-Jerfey the treafury ; a confiderable fum of money in which was appropriated to the payment of the troops they were raifing. At the fame time, without waiting for any concert or advice, a ftop was almoft every where put to the exportation of provifions ; and in fome places all exportation was ftopt, till the opinion of the general congrefs upon that fubject was known. Lord North's conciliatory plan, or the refolution founded upon it, was totally rejected by the affemblies of Penfylvania and New-Jerfey ; nor was it received any where.

In the mean time, the governor and forces at Bofton, as well as the inhabitants, continued clofely blocked up by land ; and being fhut out from all fupplies of frefh provifions and vegetables, which the neighbouring countries could have afforded by fea, they began to experience thofe inconveniencies which afterwards amounted to real diftrefs. As the inhabitants had now no other refource for their fubfiftance than the king's ftores, the provincials were the more ftrict in preventing all fupplies, hoping that the want of provifions would lay the governor under a necessity of consenting to their departure from the town; or at least that the women and children would be suffered to depart, which was repeatedly applied for. It is probable that the governor considered the inhabitants as necessary hostages for the security of the town, at least, if not of the troops. However it was, he at length entered into a capitulation with the inhabitants, by which, upon condition of delivering up their arms, they were to have free liberty to depart with all their other effects. The inhabitants accordingly delivered up their arms; but to their utter dismay and astonishment, the governor refused to fulfil the conditions on his side. This breach of faith, and the consequences that attended it, were much complained of. Many, however, both then, and at different times after, obtained permission to quit the town; but they were obliged to leave all their effects behind; so that those who had hitherto lived in ease and affluence, were at once reduced to the extremity of indigence and misery. The general congress ranked amongst their bitterest complaints, the sufferings of the inhabitants in this respect. They say that passports were granted or retained in such a manner, that families were broken and the dearest connections separated; part being compelled to quit the town, and part retained against their will. This, by far the most dishonourable to government, we are obliged in fairness to state according to the provincial narrative, no other having appeared to contradict or qualify it. The poor and the helpless were all sent out.

The continental congress having met at the May 10th. time appointed at Philadelphia, soon adopted such measures as confirmed the people in their resolution and conduct. Among their first acts were resolutions for the raising of an army, and the establishment

of a large paper currency for its payment; the " *United Colonies* " (by which appellation they resolved that they should be known and distinguished for the future) being securities for realizing the nominal value of this currency. They also strictly prohibited the supplying of the British fisheries with any kind of provision; and to render this order the more effectual, stopt all exportation to those colonies, islands, and places, which still retained their obedience. This measure, which does not seem to have been expected, or even apprehended at home, occasioned no small distress to the people at Newfoundland, and to all those employed in the fisheries; insomuch that to prevent an absolute famine, several ships were under a necessity of returning light from that station, to carry out cargoes of provisions from Ireland.

The city and province of New-York, notwithstanding their former moderation, seemed, upon receiving an account of the late action, to receive also a plentiful portion of that spirit which operated in the other colonies. A most numerous association was accordingly formed, and a provincial congress elected. But as some regiments from Ireland were expected speedily to arrive there, and that capital, besides, lies open to the sea, its situation became very critical. In these circumstances, a body of Connecticut men arrived in the neighbourhood of that city, avowedly for its protection, and probably also to support the present disposition of the people. Their strength was not, however, sufficient to afford an effectual protection; nor, if it had been greater, would it have availed against an attack by sea. The city accordingly applied, through its delegates, to the continental congress for instructions how to act upon the arrival of the troops. The congress advised them for the present, to act defensively with respect to the troops, so far as it could be done consistently with their own se-

curity;—to suffer them to occupy their barracks, so long as they behaved peaceably and quietly; but not to suffer them to erect any fortification, or in any manner to cut off the communications between the city and country; and if they attempted hostilities, that they should defend themselves, and repel force by force. They also recommended to them to provide for the worst that might happen, by securing places of retreat for the women and children; by removing the arms and ammunition from the magazines; and by keeping a sufficient number of men embodied for the protection of the inhabitants in general. The departure of so many helpless objects from the places of their habitation, was a very affecting spectacle. That once flourishing commercial city was now become almost a desart. It was by its own inhabitants devoted to the flames. It happened, perhaps happily for New-York, that the troops being more wanted at Boston, were not landed there.

In the mean time, several private persons belonging to the back parts of Connecticut, Massachusett's, and New-York, undertook at their own risque, and without any public command or participation, an expedition of the utmost importance, and which not only in its consequences most materially affected the interest and power of government in the colonies; but had brought the question to the critical nicety of a point, and the decision to depend merely upon accident, whether we should have a single possession left in North-America. This was the surprize of Ticonderoga, Crown-Point, and other fortresses, situated upon the great lakes, and commanding the passes between the British colonies and Canada. It seems that some of those who were among the first that formed this design, and had set out with the greatest privacy in its prosecution, met by the way with others, who, without any previous concert, were embarked in the fame project; fo extenfive was that fpirit of enterprize which thefe unhappy contefts called into action. Thefe adventurers, amounting in the whole to about 240 men, under the command of a Colonel Eafton, and a Colonel Ethan Allen, with great perfeverance and addrefs, furprized the fmall garrifons of Ticonderoga and Crown-Point. Thefe fortreffes were taken without the lofs of a man on either fide. They found in the forts a confiderable artillery, amounting, as they faid, to above 200 pieces of cannon, befides fome mortars, howits, and quantities of various ftores, which were to them highly valuable; they alfo took two veffels, which gave them the command of Lake Champlain, and materials ready prepared at Ticonderoga for the building and equipping of others.

May 25th. During thefe transactions the Generals Howe, Burgoyne, and Clinton, arrived at Bofton from England, together with a confiderable number of marines, and draughts from other regiments, to fupply the vacancies there. Thefe were foon followed by feveral regiments from Ireland, fo that the force at Bofton, with refpect to number, the goodnefs of the troops, and the character of the commanders, was become very refpectable; and it was generally believed, that matters could not continue much longer in their then fituation.

Nothing remarkable had yet happened fince the commencement of the blockade, except two fmall engagements which arofe from the attempts of either party to carry off the ftock of fome of thofe fmall iflands, with which the Bay of Bofton is interfperfed, and which afforded the mixed fpectacle of fhips, boats, and men, engaged by land and water. In both thefe fkirmifhes (each of which continued for many hours) the king's troops were foiled, with fome lofs; and in the laft, which happened at Hogg and Noddle's-Iflands, an armed fchooner being left by the tide, the people, after ftanding a fevere fire of fmall arms, and two pieces of artillery from the fhore, were at length obliged to abandon her, and fhe was burnt by the provincials.

Notwithftanding the late reinforcements, and the arrival of generals of the moft active character, the troops continued for fome time very quiet at Bofton. On the other fide, it is probable that an attempt would have been made to ftorm that town, while the people were hot in blood after the affair of Lexington, if a concern for the prefervation of the inhabitants had not prevailed over every other confideration. It muft however be allowed, that from the number of veffels of war, which nearly furrounded the peninfula, as well as the vaft artillery by which it was protected, and the excellency of the troops, that fuch an attempt muft have been attended with great difficulty and danger, and that the deftruction of the town muft have been laid down as an inevitable confequence. There were other matters alfo of confideration. A repulfe to new troops, or the carnage that would even attend fuccefs in fo arduous a conflict, might have been attended with fatal confequences; the people were not only new to war, but they were in a new and ftrange ftate and fituation; they were entering into an untried, unthought of, and unnatural conteft, loaded with the moft fatal confequences, without experience to guide, or precedent to direct them; they had not yet in general renounced all hopes of an accommodation, and thofe who had not, would totally condemn any violence which fhut them out from fo defirable an event; in fuch a wavering ftate of hope, fear, and uncertainty, much caution was to be ufed, as any untoward event, might fuddenly damp the ardour of the people, diffolve their refolutions, and fhake all their confederacies to pieces.

June 8th. In the mean time the continental congrefs refolved, that the compact between the crown and the people of Maffachufett's-Bay, was diffolved, by the violation of the charter of William and Mary; and therefore recommended to the people of that province, to proceed to the eftablifhment of a new government, by electing a governor, affiftants, and houfe of affembly, according to the powers contained in their original charter. They paffed another refolution, that no bill of exchange, draught, or order, of any officer in the army or navy, their agents, or contractors, fhould be received or negociated, or any money fupplied to them by any perfon; and prohibited the fupplying of the army, navy, or fhips employed in the tranfport fervice, with provifions or neceffaries of any kind. They alfo erected a general poft-office at Philadelphia, which extended through all the united colonies; and fome time after, placed Dr. Franklin, who had been difgraced and removed from that office in England, at the head of it. Thus had they, in effect, though only under the name of recommendation and counfel, affumed all the powers of a fupreme government.

About the fame time June 12th. General Gage iffued a proclamation, by which a pardon was offered in the king's name, to all thofe who fhould forthwith lay down their arms, and return to their refpective occupations and peaceable duties, excepting only from the benefit of the pardon, *Samuel Adams* and *John Hancock*, whofe offences were faid to be of too flagitious a nature to admit of any other confideration than that of condign punifhment. All thofe who did not accept of the proffered mercy, or who fhould protect, affift, fupply, conceal, or correfpond with them, to be treated as rebels and traitors. It alfo declared, that as a ftop was put to the due courfe of juftice, martial law fhould take place till the laws were reftored to their due efficacy. It is needless to observe, that this proclamation had as little effect as any of those that preceded it. Hancock was about that time chosen president of the continental congress.

This proclamation was looked upon as the preliminary to immediate action. Accordingly, from that moment both sides held themselves in readiness for it. The post of Charlestown had hitherto been neglected by both the parties. The provincials thought it necessary for them, whether they should chuse to act on the defensive or offensive. They accordingly made the necessary preparations, and sent a body of men thither at night with the greatest privacy, to throw up works upon Bunker's-Hill, an high ground that lies just within the isthmus, or neck of land that joins the peninsula to the continent. This peninsula is very similar to that on which Boston stands, excepting that the isthmus is considerably wider, and that Bunker's-Hill is much higher than any hill in the latter. The towns are only separated by Charles-River, which in that part is only about the breadth of the Thames between London and Southwark; so that Charlestown seemed to hold the same connection with Boston, that the Borough does with that city.

The party that was sent upon this service, carried on their works with such extraordinary order and silence, that though the peninsula was surrounded with ships of war, they were not heard during the night, and used such incredible dispatch in the execution, that they had a small but strong redoubt, considerable entrenchments, and a breast-work, that was in some parts cannon proof, far advanced towards completion by break of day. The sight of the works, was the first notice that alarmed the Lively man of war early in the morning, and her guns called the town, camp, and fleet to behold a sight, which seemed little less than a prodigy.

June 17th.

A heavy and continual fire of cannon, howitzers, and mortars, was from thence carried on upon the works, from the ships, floating batteries, and from the top of Cop's-Hill in Boston. Such a great and incessant roar of artillery, would have been a trial to the firmness of old soldiers, and must undoubtedly have greatly impeded the completion of the works; it is however said, that they bore this severe fire with wonderful firmness, and seemed to go on with their business as if no enemy had been near, nor danger in the service.

About noon, General Gage caused a considerable body of troops to be embarked under the command of Major-General Howe, and Brigadier-General Pigot, to drive the provincials from their works. This detachment consisted of ten companies of grenadiers, as many of light infantry, and the 5th, 38th, 43d, and 52 battalions, with a proper artillery, who were landed and drawn up without opposition, under the fire of the ships of war. The two generals found the enemy so numerous, and in such a posture of defence, that they thought it necessary to send back for a reinforcement before they commenced the attack; they were accordingly joined by some companies of light infantry and grenadiers; by the 47th regiment, and by the first battalion of marines, amounting in the whole, as represented by General Gage's letter, to something more than 2000 men.

The attack was begun by a most severe fire of cannon and howitzers, under which the troops advanced very slowly towards the enemy, and halted several times, to afford an opportunity to the artillery to ruin the works, and to throw the provincials into confusion. Whatever it proceeded from, whether from the number, situation, or countenance of the enemy, or from all together, the king's forces seem to have been unusually staggered in this attack. The provincials threw some men into the houses of

Charlestown, which covered their right flank, by which means, General Pigot, who commanded our left wing, and to whose activity, bravery, and firmness, much of this day's success was owing, was at once engaged with the lines, and with those in the houses. In this conflict, Charlestown, whether by carcasses thrown from the ships, or by the troops, is uncertain, was unfortunately set on fire in several places, and burnt to the ground. The provincials stood this severe and continual fire of small arms and artillery, with a resolution and perseverance, which would not have done discredit to old troops. They did not return a shot, until the king's forces had approached almost to the works, when a most dreadful fire took place, by which a number of our bravest men and officers fell. Some gentlemen, who had served in the most distinguished actions of the last war, declared, that for the time it lasted, it was the hottest engagement they ever knew. It is then no wonder, if under so heavy and destructive a fire, our troops were thrown into some disorder. It is said, that General Howe, was for a few seconds left nearly alone; and it is certain, that most of the officers near his person, were either killed or wounded. His coolness, firmness, and presence of mind on this occasion cannot be too much applauded. It fully answered all the ideas so generally entertained of the courage of his family. It is said, that in this critical moment, General Clinton, who arrived from Boston during the engagement, by a happy manœuvre, rallied the troops almost instantaneously, and brought them again to the charge. However that was, their usual intrepidity now produced its usual effects; they attacked the works with fixed bayonets, and irrestible fury, and forced them in every quarter. Though many of the provincials were destitute of bayonets, and, as they affirm, their ammunition was expended, a number of them fought desperately within the works, and were not drove from them without difficulty. They at length retreated over Charlestown neck, which was enfiladed by the guns of the Glasgow man of war, and of two floating batteries. They suffered but little loss from this formidable artillery, though the dread of it had prevented some regiments who were ordered to support them from fulfilling their duty.

Thus ended the hot and bloody affair of Bunker's-Hill, in which we had more men and officers killed and wounded, in proportion to the number engaged, than in any other action which we can recollect. The whole loss in killed and wounded, amounted to 1054, of whom 226 were killed; of these, 19 were commissioned officers, including a lieutenant-colonel, 2 majors, and 7 captains; 70 other officers were wounded. Among these who were more generally regretted upon this occasion, were Lieutenant-colonel Abercromby, and the brave Major [80] Pitcairne of the marines. The majors Williams and Spendlove, the [81] last of whom died of his wounds some time after the action, had also sealed their lives with such distinguished honour, as to render their loss the more sensibly felt. The event sufficiently shewed the bravery of the king's troops. There was scarcely a single officer who had not some opportunity of signalizing himself; the generals and field officers used the most extraordinary exertions. All these circumstances concur in shewing the hard and dangerous service in which they were engaged. The battle of Quebec, in the late war, with all its glory, and the vastness of the consequences of which it was productive, was not so destructive to our officers, as this affair of a retrenchment cast up in a few hours. It [82] was a matter of grievous reflection, that those brave men, many of whom had nobly contributed their share, when engaged against her natural enemies, to extend the military glory of their country into every quarter of the globe, should now have suffered so severely, in only a prelude to this unhappy civil contest.

The fate of Charlestown was also a matter of melancholy contemplation to the serious and unprejudiced of all parties. It was the first settlement made in the colony, and was considered as the mother of Boston, that town owing its birth and nurture to emigrants from the former. Charlestown was large, handsome, and well built, both in respect to its public and private edifices; it contained about 400 houses, and had the greatest trade of any port in the province except Boston. It is said, that the two ports cleared out a thousand vessels annually for a foreign trade, exclusive of an infinite number of coasters. It is now buried in its ruins. Such is the termination of human labour, industry, and wisdom; and such are the fatal fruits of civil dissentions.

The king's troops took five pieces of cannon out of six, which the provincials brought into the peninsula; and they left about 30 wounded behind them. No other prisoners were taken. Their loss, according to an account published by the provincial congress, was comparatively small, amounting to about 450, killed, wounded, missing, and prisoners. On our side they are confident, that the slaughter was much more considerable; but of this we had no particulars, as the account said, that the provincials buried a great number of their dead during the engagement. This is an extraordinary circumstance. But the loss they lamented most, was that of Dr. Warren, who acting as a major-general, commanded the party upon this occasion, and was killed, fighting bravely at their head, in a little redoubt to the right of the lines. This gentleman, who was rendered conspicuous by his general merit, abilities, and eloquence, had been one of the delegates to the first general, and was at this time president of the provincial congress;

but quitting the peaceable walk of his profession as a physician, and breaking through the endearing ties of family satisfactions, he shewed himself equally calculated for the field, as for public business or private study, and shed his blood gallantly in, what he deemed, the service of his country. They lost some other officers of name, one of whom, a lieutenant-colonel, died of his wounds in the prison at Boston.

Both sides claimed much honour from this action. The regulars, from having, it was said, beaten three times their own number out of a strongly fortified post, and under various other disadvantages. On the other side, they represented the regulars as amounting to 3000 men, and rated their own number only at 1500; and pretended, that this small body not only withstood their attack, and repeatedly repulsed them with great loss, notwithstanding the powerful artillery they had brought with them, but that they had at the same time, and for several hours before, sustained a most intolerable fire, from the ships of war, floating batteries, and fixed battery at Boston, which prevented them from being able in any degree to finish their works. What their exact number was cannot be easily known. It was not probably so large as it was made in the Gazette account; nor so small as in that given by the Americans. However, the provincials were by no [83] means dispirited by the event of this engagement. They had shewn a great degree of activity and skill in the construction of their works; and of constancy, in maintaining them under many disadvantages. They said, that though they had lost a post, they had almost all the effects of the most compleat victory; as they entirely put a stop to the offensive operations of a large army sent to subdue them; and which they continued to blockade in a narrow town. They now exulted, that their actions had thoroughly refuted those aspersions which had been thrown upon them in England, of a deficiency in spirit and resolution.[84]

From this time, the troops kept possession of the peninsula, and fortified Bunker's-Hill and the entrance; so that the force at Boston was now divided into two distinct parts, and had two garrisons to maintain. In one sense, this was useful to the troops, as it enlarged their quarters; they having been before much incommoded by the streightness in which they were confined in Boston, during the excessive heats that always prevail there at that season of the year; but this advantage was counterballanced by the great additional duty which they were now obliged to perform. Their situation was irksome and degrading. They were surrounded and insulted by an enemy whom they had been taught to despise. They were cut off from fresh provisions, and all those refreshments of which they stood in the greatest need, and which the neighbouring countries afforded in the greatest plenty. Thus their wants were continual and aggravating remembrancers of the circumstances of their situation. Bad and salt provisions, with confinement and the heat of the climate, naturally filled the hospitals; and the number of sick and wounded was now said to amount to 1600. Under these circumstances it was rather wonderful that the number was not greater. But few in comparison died.

The provincials, after the action at Bunker's-Hill, immediately threw up works upon another hill opposite to it on their side of Charlestown neck; so that the troops were as closely invested in that peninsula as they had been in Boston. They were also indefatigable in securing the most exposed posts of their lines with strong redoubts covered with artillery, and advanced their works close to the fortifications on Boston neck; where, with equal boldness and address, they burnt an advanced guard house belonging to our people. As the latter were abundantly furnished with all manner of military stores and artillery, they were not sparing in throwing shells, and supporting a great cannonade upon the works of the provincials, which had little other effect than to inure them to that sort of service, and to wear off the dread of those noisy messengers of fate. On the other side, they seem to have been cautious in expending their powder.

A regiment of light cavalry which arrived at Boston from Ireland, and which were never able to set foot beyond that garrison, served only to create new wants, and to increase the incommodities of the people, as well as of the army. The hay which grew upon the islands in the bay, became now an object of necessary attention, as well as the sheep and cattle which they contained; but the provincials having procured a number of whaling-boats, and being masters of the shore and inlets of the bay, were, notwithstanding the vigilance and number of the ships of war and armed vessels, too successful in burning, destroying, or carrying away, those essential articles of supply. These enterprises brought on several skirmishes, and they grew at length so daring, that they burnt the light-house, which was situated on an island at the entrance of the harbour, though a man of war lay within a mile of them at the time; and some carpenters being afterwards sent, under the protection of a small party of marines, to erect a temporary light-house, they killed or carried off the whole detachment.

During these transactions a kind of predatory war commenced, and has since continued, between the ships of war, and the inhabitants on different parts of the coasts. The former being refused the supplies of provisions and necessaries which they wanted for themselves or the army, endeavoured to obtain them by force, and in these attempts were frequently opposed, and sometimes repulsed with loss by the country people. The seizing of ships in conformity to the new laws, or to the commands of the admiral, was also a continual source of animosity and violence, the proprietors naturally hazarding all dangers in the defence, or for the recovery of their property. These contests drew the vengeance of the men of war upon several of the small towns upon the sea coasts, some of which underwent a severe chastisement.

The pernicious consequences of the late Quebec-act, with respect to the very purposes for which it was framed, were now displayed in a degree, which its most sanguine opponents could scarcely have expected. Instead of gaining the French Canadians to the interest of government by that law, the great body of the inhabitants were found as adverse to it, and as much disgusted at its operation, as even the British settlers. General Carleton, the governor of that province, who had placed much confidence in the raising of a considerable army of Canadians, and being enabled to march at their head to the relief of General Gage, (a matter which was so much relied upon at home, that 20,000 stands of arms, and a great quantity of other military stores had been sent out for that purpose) found himself now totally disappointed. The people said, that they were now under the British government; that they could not pretend to understand the causes of the present disputes, nor the justice of the claims on either side; that they did, and would shew themselves dutiful subjects, by a quiet and peaceable demeanor, and due obedience to the government under which they were placed; but that it was totally inconsistent with their state and condition, to interfere, or in any degree to render themselves parties, in the contests that might arise between that government and its ancient subjects. It was in vain that the governor issued a proclamation for assembling the militia, and for the execution of martial law; they said they would defend the province if it was attacked;

but they abfolutely refufed to march out of it, or to commence hoftilities with their neighbours. The governor, as the laft refort, applied to the Bifhop of Quebec, to ufe his fpiritual influence and authority with the people towards difpofing them to the adoption of this favourite meafure, and particularly that he would iffue an epifcopal mandate for that purpofe, to be read by the parifh priefts in the time of divine fervice; but the bifhop excufed himfelf from a compliance with this propofition, by reprefenting, that an epifcopal mandate on fuch a fubject, would be contrary to the canons of the Roman Catholic church. The ecclefiaftics, in the place of this, iffued other letters, which were however pretty generally difregarded. The nobleffe alone, who were chiefly confidered in the Quebec-act, fhewed a zeal againft the Englifh colonifts. But feparated as they were from the great body of the people, they exhibited no formidable degree of ftrength.

Other endeavours which were ufed to involve the colonies in domeftic troubles proved equally abortive. Confiderable pains were taken, by the means of feveral agents who had influence on them, to engage thofe numerous tribes of Indians that ftretch along the backs of the colonies, to caufe a diverfion, by attacking them in thofe weak and tender parts. But neither prefents, nor perfuafions, were capable of producing the defired effect. From whatever chance or fortune it proceeded, thofe favage warriors, who had at other times been fo ready to take up the hatchet without fupport or encouragement, now turned a deaf ear to all propofals of that nature, and declared for a neutrality. They ufed much the fame reafons for this conduct that the Canadians had done; they did not underftand the fubject; were very forry for the prefent unfortunate difputes; but it was not fit nor becoming for them, to take any part in quarrels between Englifhmen, for all of

whom, on both fides of the water, they had the higheft affection. This was an object of too much importance to be overlooked by the congrefs. They accordingly employed proper perfons to cultivate favourable difpofitions in the Indians; and by degrees took fuch meafures as obliged the agents for government to provide for their own fafety. It is faid, that fome of the Indians made propofals to take up arms on their fide; but that they were only requefted to obferve a ftrict neutrality.

General Gage's late proclamation increafed the animofity, indignation, and rage, which were already fo generally prevalent, and brought out a declaration from the general congrefs, **July 6th.** which, in the nature of thofe general appeals that are made to mankind, as well as to heaven, in a declaration of war, fet forth the caufes and neceffity of their taking up arms. Among the long lift of thofe fuppofed caufes, befides the late hoftilities, they ftate the endeavours ufed to inftigate the Canadians and Indians to attack them, and feverely reproach General Gage, for, what they call, perfidy, cruelty, and breach of faith, in breaking the conditions which he had entered into with the inhabitants of Bofton; they are not lefs free in their cenfure of the army, whom they charge with the burning of Charleftown, wantonly and unneceffarily.

In ftating their refources, they reckon upon foreign affiftance as undoubtedly attainable, if neceffary. They, however, afterwards fay, that, left this declaration fhould difquiet the minds of their friends and fellow-fubjects in any part of the empire, they affure them, that they mean not to diffolve that union which has fo long and happily fubfifted between them, and which they fincerely wifh to fee reftored; that neceffity has not yet driven them to that defperate meafure, or induced them to excite any other nation to war againft them; they

have not raifed armies with ambitious defigns of feparating from Great-Britain, and eftablifhing independent ftates; they fight not for glory or for conqueft.—This declaration was read with great, ferious, and even religious folemnity, to the different bodies of the army who were encamped around Bofton, and was received by them with loud acclamations of approbation.

This declaration was followed by an addrefs to the inhabitants of Great-Britain; another to the people of Ireland; and a petition to the king. All thefe writings were drawn up in a very mafterly manner; and are, in refpect to art, addrefs, and execution, equal to any public declarations made by any powers upon the greateft occafions.

The congrefs had in their declaration, without naming it, reprobated the principles of Lord North's conciliatory propofition, which they call an infidious manœuvre adopted by parliament. They, however, afterwards, took the refolution more formally into confideration. It had been communicated to them by direction, or at leaft permiffion from that minifter, in the hand-writing of Sir Grey Cowper, one of the two principal fecretaries of the treafury.[85] In the courfe of a long and argumentative difcuffion, they condemn it, as unreafonable and infidious; that it is unreafonable, becaufe, if they declare they will accede to it, they declare, without refervation, that they will purchafe the favour of parliament, not knowing at the fame time at what price they will pleafe to eftimate their favour; that it is infidious, becaufe individual colonies, having bid, and bidden again, till they find the avidity of the feller too great for all their powers to fatisfy, are then to return into oppofition, divided from their fifter colonies, whom the minifter will have previoufly detached by a grant of eafier terms, or by an artful procraftination of a definitive anfwer. They conclude upon the whole, that the propofition was held up to the world, to deceive it into a belief, that there was nothing in dispute but the *mode* of levying taxes; and that parliament having now been so good as to give up that, the colonies must be unreasonable in the highest degree if they were not perfectly satisfied.

The colony of Georgia at length joined in the general alliance. A provincial congress having assembled in the beginning of the month of July, they speedily agreed to all the resolutions of the two general congresses in their utmost extent, and appointed five delegates to attend the present. As it were to make amends for the delay, they at once entered into all the spirit of the resolutions formed by the other colonies, and adopted similar; and declared, that though their province was not included in any of the oppressive acts lately passed against America, they considered that circumstance as an insult rather than a favour, as being done only with a view to divide them from their American brethren. They also addressed a petition, under the title of an humble address and representation, to his majesty; which, however threadbare the subject had already been worn, was not deficient in a certain freshness of colouring, which gave it the appearance of novelty. From this accession to the confederacy, they henceforward assumed the appellation of the *Thirteen United Colonies*.

In the mean time the general congress, in compliance with the wishes of the people in general, and the particular application of the New-England provinces, appointed George Washington, Esq; [86] a gentleman of affluent fortune in Virginia, and who had acquired considerable military experience in the command of different bodies of the provincials during the last war, to be general and commander in chief of all the American forces. They also appointed Artemus Ward, Charles Lee, Philip Schuyler, and Israel Putnam, Esqrs. to be major-

generals; and Horatio Gates, Esq; [87] adjutant-general. Of these general officers, Lee and Gates were English gentlemen, who had acquired honour in the last war; and who from disgust or principle now joined the Americans. Ward and Putnam were of Massachusett's-Bay, and Schuyler of New-York. The congress also fixed and assigned the pay of both officers and soldiers; the latter of whom were much better provided for than those upon our establishment.

The Generals Washington and Lee arrived at the camp before Boston in the beginning of July. They were treated with the highest honours in every place through which they passed; were escorted by large detachments of volunteers, composed of gentlemen, in the different provinces; and received public addresses from the provincial congresses of New-York and Massachusett's-Bay. The military spirit was now so high and so general, that war and its preparations occupied the hands and the minds of all orders of people throughout the continent. Persons of fortune and family, who were not appointed officers, entered chearfully as private men, and served with alacrity in the ranks. Even many of the younger quakers forgot their passive principles of forbearance and non-resistance, and taking up arms, formed themselves into companies at Philadelphia, and applied with the greatest labour and assiduity to acquire a proficiency in military exercises and discipline. It was said, (but no computation of that sort can be ascertained) that no less than 200,000 men were in arms and training throughout the continent. [88]

The blockade of Boston, was continued with little variety, throughout the year, and during a considerable part of the ensuing. The troops, as well as the remaining inhabitants, suffered much from fevers, fluxes, and the scurvy, which were brought on through confine-

ment, heat of weather, and badness of provisions. Other matters which originated in this season, particularly the proceedings on the side of Canada, being extended in their principal consequences into the ensuing year, will with more propriety find a place in its history.

• • •

The humble Address of the Right Honourable the Lords Spiritual and Temporal, and Commons, in Parliament assembled; presented to his Majesty on Thursday the 9th of February, 1775.

Most Gracious Sovereign,

WE, your Majesty's most dutiful and loyal subjects, the Lords Spiritual and Temporal, and Commons, in parliament assembled, return your majesty our most humble thanks for having been graciously pleased to communicate to us the several papers relating to the present state of the British colonies in America, which, by your majesty's commands, have been laid before us: We have taken them into our most serious consideration; and we find, that a part of your majesty's subjects, in the province of the Massachusett's-Bay, have proceeded so far as to resist the authority of the supreme legislature; that a rebellion at this time actually exists within the said province; and we see, with the utmost concern, that they have been countenanced and encouraged by unlawful combinations and engagements, entered into by your majesty's subjects in several of the other colonies, to the injury and oppression of many of their innocent fellow-subjects, resident within the kingdom of Great-Britain, and the rest of your majesty's dominions: This conduct, on their part, appears to us the more inexcusable, when we consider with how much temper your majesty, and the two houses of parliament, have acted in support of the laws and constitution of Great-Britain.

We can never so far desert the trust reposed in us, as to relinquish any part of the sovereign authority over all your majesty's dominions, which, by law, is vested in your majesty and the two houses of parliament; and the conduct of many persons, in several of the colonies, during the late disturbances, is alone sufficient to convince us how necessary this power is for the protection of the lives and fortunes of your majesty's subjects.

We ever have been, and always shall be, ready to pay attention and regard to any real grievances of any of your majesty's subjects, which shall, in a dutiful and constitutional manner, be laid before us; and, whenever any of the colonies shall make a proper application to us, we shall be ready to afford them every just and reasonable indulgence: At the same time, we consider it as our indispensable duty humbly to beseech your majesty, that you will take the most effectual measures to enforce due obedience to the laws and authority of the supreme legislature; and we beg leave, in the most solemn manner, to assure your majesty, that it is our fixed resolution, at the hazard of our lives and properties, to stand by your majesty against all rebellious attempts in the maintenance of the just rights of your majesty and the two houses of parliament.

His Majesty's most Gracious Answer.

' My Lords and Gentlemen,

' I thank you for this very dutiful and loyal address, and for the affectionate and solemn assurances you give me of your support in maintaining the just rights of my crown, and of the two houses of parliament; and you may depend on my taking the most speedy and effectual measures for inforcing due obedience to the laws, and the authority of the supreme legislature.

' Whenever any of my colonies

shall make a proper and dutiful application, I shall be ready to conclude with you, in affording them every just and reasonable indulgence; and it is my ardent wish, that this disposition may have a happy effect on the temper and conduct of my subjects in America.''

Protest of several of the Lords, on its being resolved in their House, on Tuesday, the 7th of February 1775, to put a main Question, viz. To agree with the Commons in the foregoing Address, sent by them to their Lordships for their concurrence, by filling up the Blank left in it for that Purpose, with the Words, "Lords Spiritual and Temporal;" as likewise another Protest of several of the Lords, on their House's agreeing with the Commons in said Address.

Dissentient,
1st. THE previous question was moved, not to prevent the proceeding in the address, communicated at the conference with the Commons, but in order to present the petitions of the N. American merchants and of the West-India merchants and planters, which petitions the House might reject if frivolous, or postpone if not urgent, as it might seem fit to their wisdom; but to hurry on the business to which these petitions so materially and directly related, the express prayer of which was, that they might be heard before "any resolution may be taken by this right honourable House respecting America;" to refuse so much as to suffer them to be presented, is a proceeding of the most unwarrantable nature, and directly subversive of the most sacred rights of the subject. It is the more particularly exceptionable, as a Lord, in his place, at the express desire of the West-India merchants, informed the House, that if necessitated so to do, they were ready, without

counsel, or farther preparation, instantly to offer evidence to prove, that several islands of the West-Indies could not be able to subsist after the operation of the proposed address in America. Justice, in regard to individuals, policy, with regard to the public, and decorum, with regard to ourselves, required that we should admit this petition to be presented. By refusing it, justice is denied.

2dly. Because the papers laid upon our table by the ministers, are so manifestly defective, and so avowedly curtailed, that we can derive from them nothing like information of the true state of the object on which we are going to act, or of the consequences of the resolutions which we may take. We ought, as we conceive, with gladness, to have accepted that information from the merchants, which, if it had not been voluntarily offered, it was our duty to seek. There is no information concerning the state of our colonies (taken in any point of view) which the merchants are not far more competent to give than governors or officers, who often know far less of the temper and disposition, or may be more disposed to misrepresent it than the merchants. Of this we have a full and melancholy experience, in the mistaken ideas on which the fatal acts of the last parliament were formed.

3dly. Because we are of opinion, that in entering into a war, in which mischief and inconvenience are great and certain (but the utmost extent of which it is impossible to foresee) true policy requires that those who are most likely to be immediately affected should be thoroughly satisfied of the deliberation with which it was undertaken: and we apprehend that the planters, merchants, and manufacturers will not bear their losses and burthens, brought on them by the proposed civil war, the better for our refusing so much as to hear them previous to our engaging in that war; nor will our precipitation in resolving, add much to the success in executing any plan that may be pursued.

We protest therefore against the refusal to suffer such petitions to be presented, and we thus clear ourselves to our country of the disgrace and mischief, which must attend this unconstitutional, indecent and improvident proceeding.

Richmond,	Portland,
Ponsonby,	Camden,
Archer,	Fitzwilliam,
Rockingham,	Scarborough,
Wycombe,	Abergavenny,
Effingham,	Abingdon,
Torrington,	Craven,
Stanhope,	Courtenay,
Cholmondeley,	Tankerville.

Then the main question was put, whether to agree with the Commons in the said address, by inserting the words (*Lords Spiritual and Temporal, and*)

It was resolved in the affirmative.

Contents	87
Not contents	27

Dissentient, 1st. Because the violent matter of this dangerous address was highly aggravated by the violent manner in which it was precipitately hurried through the House. Lords were not allowed the interposition of a moment's time for deliberation, before they were driven headlong into a declaration of civil war. A conference was held with the Commons, an address of this importance presented, all extraneous information, although offered, positively refused; all petitions arbitrarily rejected, and the whole of this most awful business received, debated, and concluded in a single day.

2dly. Because no legal grounds were laid in argument or in fact, to shew that a rebellion, properly so called, did exist in Massachusett's-Bay, when the papers of the latest date, and from whence alone we derive our information, were written. The overt-acts to which the species of treason affirmed in the

address ought to be applied, were not established, nor any offenders marked out: but a general mass of the acts of turbulence, said to be done at various times and places, and of various natures, were all thrown together to make out one general constructive treason. Neither was there any sort of proof of the continuance of any unlawful force, from whence we could infer that a rebellion does now exist. And we are the more cautious of pronouncing any part of his majesty's dominions to be in actual rebellion, because the cases of constructive treason, under that branch of the 25th of Edward the Third, which describes the crime of rebellion, have been already so far extended by the judges, and the distinctions thereupon so nice and subtle, that no prudent man ought to declare any single person in that situation, without the clearest evidence of uncontrovertible overt-acts, to warrant such a declaration. Much less ought so high an authority as both houses of parliament, to denounce so severe a judgment against a considerable part of his majesty's subjects, by which his forces may think themselves justified in commencing a war, without any further order or commission.

3dly. Because we think that several acts of the last parliament, and several late proceedings of administration with regard to the colonies, are *real grievances*, and just causes of complaint; and we cannot, in honour, or in conscience, consent to an address which commends the temper by which proceedings, so very intemperate, have been carried on; nor can we persuade ourselves to authorize violent courses against persons in the colonies who have resisted authority, without, at the same time, redressing the grievances which have given but too much provocation for their behaviour.

4thly. Because we think the loose and general assurances given by the

address, of future redress of grievances, in case of submission, is far from satisfactory, or at all likely to produce their end, whilst the acts complained of continue unrepealed, or unamended, and their authors remain in authority here, because these advisers of all the measures which have brought on the calamities of this empire, will not be trusted whilst they defend as just, necessary, and even indulgent, all the acts complained of as grievances by the Americans; and must, therefore, on their own principles, be bound in future to govern the colonies in the manner which has already produced such fatal effects; and we fear that the refusal of this House, so much as to receive, previous to determination (which is the most offensive mode of rejection) petitions from the unoffending natives of Great-Britain, and the West India islands, affords but a very discouraging prospect of our obtaining hereafter any petitions at all, from those whom we have declared actors in rebellion, or abettors of that crime.

Lastly, Because the means of enforcing the authority of the British legislature, is confided to persons of whose *capacity*, for that purpose, from abundant experience, we have reason to doubt; and who have hitherto used no effectual means of conciliating or of reducing those who oppose that authority: this appears in the constant failure of all their projects, the insufficiency of all their information, and the disappointment of all the hopes, which they have for several years held out to the public. Parliament has never refused any of their proposals, and yet our affairs have proceeded daily from bad to worse, until we have been brought, step by step, to that state of confusion, and even civil violence, which was the natural result of these desperate measures.

We therefore protest against an address amounting to a *declaration of war*, which is founded on no proper parliamentary information; which was introduced by refusing to suffer the presentation of petitions against it, (although it be the undoubted right of the subject to present the same) which followed the rejection of every mode of conciliation; which holds out no substantial offer of redress of grievances; and which promises support to those ministers who have inflamed America, and grosly misconducted the affairs of Great-Britain.

Richmond,	Cholmondeley,
Craven,	Abingdon,
Archer,	Portland,
Abergavenny,	Camden,
Rockingham,	Effingham,
Wycombe,	Stanhope,
Courtenay,	Scarborough,
Torrington,	Fitzwilliam,
Ponsonby,	Tankerville.

Message of his Majesty to the House of Commons, on Friday, the 10th of February, 1775.

" George R.

" HIS Majesty being determined, in consequence of the address of both Houses of Parliament, to take the most speedy and effectual measures for supporting the just rights of his crown, and the two Houses of Parliament, thinks proper to acquaint this House, that some addition to his forces by sea and land will be necessary for that purpose; and doubts not but his faithful Commons, on whose zeal and affection he entirely relies, will enable him to make such augmentation to his forces as the present occasion shall be thought to require.

" G. R."

Petition of the Lord Mayor of the City of London, *&c. presented to the House of Commons, on* Friday, *the 24th of* February, 1775.

To the Honourable the Commons of Great Britain, in Parliament assembled.

The Humble Petition of the Lord Mayor, Aldermen, and Commons of the City of London, *in Common-Council assembled,*

Sheweth,

" THAT although your petitioners bear all due respect to the policy of those acts of parliament, which have antiently preserved Great-Britain a necessary and beneficial commerce with our colonies, yet they are exceedingly alarmed at the consequences that must ensue, if the bill now depending in this honourable house should pass into a law, entitled, " A Bill to restrain the Trade and Commerce of Massachusett's Bay and New Hampshire, and Colonies of Connecticut and Rhode Island, and Providence Plantation in North-America, to Great-Britain, Ireland, and the British Islands in the West-Indies, and to prohibit such provinces and colonies from carrying on any fishery on the banks of Newfoundland, or other places therein to be mentioned, under certain conditions, and for a time to be limited;" the said bill, as your petitioners conceive, being unjustly founded, because it involves the whole in the punishment intended for the supposed offences of a few.

" That it must, in its consequences; overwhelm thousands of his Majesty's loyal and useful subjects with the utmost poverty and distress, inasmuch as they will be thereby deprived of the fisheries, which are the natural means of supporting themselves and families.

" That the extensive commerce between Great-Britain and her colonies will, by this bill, be greatly injured, as a capital source of remittance will be stopt, which will not only disconnect the future commercial intercourse between those colonies and this country, but will eventually render them incapable of paying the large debts already due to the merchants of this city.

" That the utmost confusion will probably ensue from enforcing this bill, if passed into a law, as it cannot be supposed that a great number of men, naturally hardy and brave, will quietly submit to a law which will reduce them almost to famine, they not having within themselves provisions sufficient for their subsistence.

" That it will induce the French to extend their fisheries, and by that means increase the wealth and strength of our rivals in trade, to the great prejudice of this country.

" That your petitioners feel for the many hardships which their fellow subjects in America already labour under, from the execution of several late acts of parliament, evidently partial and oppressive, and which seem to be extended and continued by this bill; inasmuch as it confirms those acts, which in particular cases deprive the American subject of trial by jury, prohibit the Americans from carrying provisions from one colony to another, invite a contraband trade, under military protection, prevent any subject of Great-Britain or Ireland from being part owner of certain American ships or vessels; and vest an undue and dangerous authority in the governor and council of Massachusett's Bay.

" Your petitioners, therefore, humbly pray this honourable house, that the said bill may not pass into a law,"

Articles of Confederation and perpetual Union, entered into by the Delegates of the several Colonies of New-Hampshire, Massachusett's, &c. &c. &c. &c. &c. &c. &c. &c. &c. &c. in General Congress, met at Philadelphia, May 20th, 1775. [89]

ARTICLE I.

THE name of the confederacy shall henceforth be, The United Colonies of North America.

II. The united colonies hereby severally enter into a firm league of friendship with each other, binding on themselves and their posterity, for their common defence against their enemies, for the security of their liberties and properties, the safety of their persons and families, and their mutual and general welfare.

III. That each colony shall enjoy and retain as much as it may think fit of its own present laws, customs, rights, privileges, and peculiar jurisdictions, within its own limits; and may amend its own constitution, as shall seem best to its own assembly or convention.

IV. That for the more convenient management of general interests, delegates shall be elected annually, in each colony, to meet in General Congress, at such time and place as shall be agreed on in the next preceding Congress. Only where particular circumstances do not make a deviation necessary, it is understood to be a rule, that each succeeding Congress is to be held in a different colony, till the whole number be gone through, and so in perpetual rotation; and that accordingly, the next Congress after the present shall be held at Annapolis, in Maryland.

V. That the power and duty of the Congress shall extend to the determing on war and peace, the entering into alliances, the reconciliation with Great-Britain, the settling all disputes between colony and colony, if any should arise, and the planting new colonies where proper. The Congress shall also make such general ordinances thought necessary to the general welfare, of which particular assemblies cannot be competent, viz. those that may relate to our general commerce or general currency, to the establishment of posts, the regulation of our common forces; the Congress shall also have the appointment of all officers civil and military, appertaining to the general confederacy, such as general treasurer, secretary, &c. &c. &c.

VI. All charges of war, and all other general expences to be incurred for the common welfare, shall be defrayed out of a common treasury, which is to be supplied by each colony, in proportion to its number of male polls between 16 and 60 years of age; the taxes for paying that proportion are to be laid and levied by the laws of each colony.

VII. The number of delegates to be elected, and sent to the Congress by each colony, shall be regulated from time to time, by the number of such polls returned; so as that one delegate be allowed for every 5000 polls. And the delegates are to bring with them to every Congress an authenticated return of the number of polls in their respective colonies, which is to be taken for the purposes above mentioned.

VIII. At every meeting of the Congress, one half of the members returned, exclusive of proxies, shall be necessary to make a quorum; and each delegate at the Congress shall have a vote in all cases; and if necessarily absent, shall be allowed to appoint any other delegate from the same colony to be his proxy, who may vote for him.

IX. An executive council shall be appointed by the Congress out of their own body, consisting of 12 persons, of whom in the first appointment, one third, viz. four, shall be for one year, four for two years, and four for three years; and as the said terms expire, the vacancies shall be filled up by appointments for three years, whereby one third of the members will be chosen annually; and each person who has served the same term of three years as counsellor, shall have a respite of three years, before he can be elected again. This council, of whom two-thirds shall be a quorum, in the recess of the Congress, is to execute what shall have been enjoined thereby; to manage the general continental business and interests, to receive applications from foreign countries, to prepare matters for the consideration of the Congress, to fill up, *pro tempore*, continental offices that fall vacant, and to draw on the general treasurer for such monies as may be necessary for general services, and appropriated by the Congress to such services.

X. No colony shall engage in an offensive war with any nation of Indians, without the consent of the Congress or great council above-mentioned, who are first to confider the justice and necessity of such war.

XI. A perpetual alliance, offensive and defensive, is to be entered into, as soon as may be, with the Six Nations; their limits ascertained, and to be secured to them; their lands not to be encroached on, nor any private or colony purchase to be made of them hereafter to be held good, nor any contract for lands to be made, but between the great council of the Indians at Onondega and the general Congress. The boundaries and lands of all the other Indians shall also be ascertained and secured to them in the same manner; and persons appointed to reside among them in proper districts, who shall take care to prevent injustice in the trade with them; and be enabled at our general expence, by occasional small supplies, to relieve their personal wants and distresses; and all purchases from them shall be by the Congress, for the general advantage and benefit of the united colonies.

XII. As all new inftitutions may have imperfections, which only time and experience can difcover, it is agreed that the General Congrefs, from time to time, fhall propofe fuch amendments of this conftitution as may be found neceffary, which being approved by a majority of the colony affemblies, fhall be equally binding with the reft of the articles of this confederation.

XIII. Any and every colony from Great-Britain upon the continent of North-America, not at prefent engaged in our affociation, may, upon application, and joining the faid affociation, be received into the confederation, viz. Quebec, St. John's, Nova-Scotia, Bermudas, and the Eaft and Weft Floridas, and fhall thereupon be entitled to all the advantages of our union, mutual affiftance, and commerce.

Thefe articles fhall be propofed to the feveral provincial conventions or affemblies, to be by them confidered; and, if approved, they are advifed to empower their delegates to agree and ratify the fame in the enfuing Congrefs; after which the union thereby eftablifhed is to continue firm, till the terms of reconciliation propofed in the petition of the laft Congrefs to the King are agreed to; till the acts, fince made, reftraining the American commerce and fisheries, are repealed; till reparation is made for the injury done to Bofton by fhutting up its port; for burning Charlestown, and for the expence of this unjuft war; and till all the British troops are withdrawn from America. On the arrival of thefe events, the colonies are to return to their former connections and friendfhip with Great-Britain; but on failure thereof, this confederation is to be perpetual.

WHEREAS it hath pleafed God to blefs thefe countries with a moft plentiful harveft, whereby much corn and other provifions can be fpared to foreign nations who may want the fame:

Refolved, That after the expiration of fix months, from the 20th of July inftant, being the day appointed by a late act of parliament of Great-Britain, for reftraining the trade of the confederate colonies, all cuftom-houfes therein (if the faid act be not firft repealed) fhall be fhut up, and all the officers of the fame difcharged from the execution of their feveral functions; and all the ports of the faid colonies are hereby declared to be thenceforth open to the fhips of every ftate in Europe that will admit our commerce, and protect it, who may bring in and expofe to fale, free of all duties, their refpective produce and manufactures, and every kind of merchandize, excepting teas, and the merchandize of Great-Britain, Ireland, and the British Weft-India iflands.

Refolved, That we will, to the utmoft of our power, maintain and fupport this freedom of commerce for two years certain after its commencement, any reconciliation between us and Great-Britain notwithftanding, and as much longer beyond that term as the late acts of parliament for reftraining the commerce and fifheries, and difallowing the laws and charters of any of the colonies, fhall continue unrepealed.

Addrefs, &c. of the Lord Mayor of the City of London, *&c. prefented to his Majefty, on* Friday *the 14th of* July, 1775.

To the King's Moft Excellent Majefty.

The humble Addrefs and Petition of the Lord Mayor, Aldermen, and Commons of the City of London, *in Common Council affembled.*

" Moft gracious Sovereign,

YOUR Majefty's moft loyal and dutiful fubjects, the Lord Mayor, Aldermen, and Commons of the city of London, in Com-

mon Council affembled, with all humility beg leave to lay themfelves at your royal feet, humbly imploring your benign attention towards the grievous diftractions of their fellow-fubjects in America.

The characteriftic of the people, Sire, over whom you reign, has ever been equally remarked for their unparalleled loyalty to their fovereign, whilft the principles of the conftitution have been the rule of his government, as well as a firm oppofition whenever their rights have been invaded.

Your American fubjects, Royal Sire, defcended from the fame anceftors with ourfelves, appear equally jealous of the prerogatives of freemen, without which they cannot deem themfelves happy.

Their chearful and unafked-for contributions, as well as willing fervices to the mother country, whilft they remained free from the clog of compulfory laws, will, we are fure, plead powerfully with the humanity of your difpofition, for gracioufly granting them every reafonable opportunity of giving, as freemen, what they feem refolutely determined to refufe under the injunction of laws made independent of their own confent.

The abhorrence we entertain of civil bloodfhed and confufion will, we truft, Sire, if not wholly exculpate us in your royal mind, yet plead powerfully in our favour, for the warmth with which we lament thofe meafures, whofe deftructive principles have driven our American brethren to acts of defperation.

Convinced of the earneft difpofition of the colonifts to remain firm in all duteous obedience to the conftitutional authority of this kingdom, permit us, moft gracious fovereign, to befeech you that thofe operations of force, which at prefent diftract them with the moft dreadful apprehenfions, may be fufpended; and that, uncontrouled by a reftraint incompatible with a free government, they may poffefs an opportunity of tendering fuch terms of accommodation, as, we doubt not, will approve them worthy of a diſtinguiſhed rank among the firmeſt friends of this country."

Signed by order of court,

WILLIAM RIX.

To which addreſs and petition his Majeſty was pleaſed to return the following anſwer:

" I AM always ready to liſten to the dutiful petitions of my ſubjects, and ever happy to comply with their reaſonable requeſts; but, while the conſtitutional authority of this kingdom is openly reſiſted by a part of my American ſubjects, I owe it to the reſt of my people, of whoſe zeal and fidelity I have had ſuch conſtant proofs, to continue and enforce thoſe meaſures by which alone their rights and intereſts can be aſſerted and maintained."

His Majeſty's moſt gracious Speech to both Houſes of Parliament, Friday, May 26, 1775.

" My Lords and Gentlemen,

I Cannot, in juſtice to you, forbear to expreſs my intire ſatisfaction in your conduct, during the courſe of this important ſeſſion.

You have maintained, with a firm and ſteady reſolution, the rights of my crown, and the authority of parliament, which I ſhall ever conſider as inſeparable: you have protected and promoted the commercial intereſts of my kingdoms, and you have, at the ſame time, given convincing proofs of your readineſs (as far as the conſtitution will allow you) to gratify the wiſhes, and remove the apprehenſions, of my ſubjects in America; and I am perſuaded, that the moſt ſalutary effects muſt, in the end, reſult from meaſures formed and conducted on ſuch principles.

The late mark of your affectionate attachment to me, and to the Queen, and the zeal and unanimity which accompanied it, demand my particular thanks.

I have the ſatisfaction to acquaint you, that, as well from the general diſpoſitions of other powers, as from the ſolemn aſſurances which I have received, I have great reaſon to expect the continuance of peace: nothing on my part, conſiſtent with the maintenance of the honour and intereſt of my kingdoms, ſhall be wanting to ſecure the public tranquillity.

Gentlemen of the Houſe of Commons,

It gives me much concern, that the unhappy diſturbances in ſome of my colonies have obliged me to propoſe to you an augmentation of my army, and have prevented me from completing the intended reduction of the eſtabliſhment of my naval forces. I cannot ſufficiently thank you for the chearfulneſs and public ſpirit with which you have granted the ſupplies for the ſeveral ſervices of the current year.

My Lords and Gentlemen,

I have nothing to deſire of you but to uſe your beſt endeavours to preſerve and to cultivate, in your ſeveral counties, the ſame regard for public order, and the ſame diſcernment of their true intereſts, which have in theſe times diſtinguiſhed the character of my faithful and beloved people; and the continuance of which cannot fail to render them happy at home, and reſpected abroad."

Then the Lord Chancellor, by his Majeſty's command, ſaid,

My Lords and Gentlemen,

It is his Majeſty's royal will and pleaſure, that this Parliament be prorogued to Thurſday the twenty-ſeventh day of July next, to be then here held; and this Parliament is accordingly prorogued to Thurſday the 27th day of July next.

A Declaration by the Repreſentatives of the United Colonies of North-America, *now met in General Congreſs at* Philadelphia, *ſetting forth the Cauſes and Neceſſity of their taking up Arms.* [90]

IF it was poſſible for men, who exerciſe their reaſon, to believe that the Divine Author of our exiſtence intended a part of the human race to hold an abſolute property in, and an unbounded power over others, marked out by his infinite goodneſs and wiſdom, as the objects of a legal domination, never rightly reſiſtible, however ſevere and oppreſſive; the inhabitants of theſe colonies might at leaſt require from the Parliament of Great-Britain ſome evidence, that this dreadful authority over them has been granted to that body. But a reverence for our Great Creator, principles of humanity, and the dictates of common ſenſe, muſt convince all thoſe who reflect upon the ſubject, that government was inſtituted to promote the welfare of mankind, and ought to be adminiſtered for the attainment of that end. The legiſlature of Great-Britain, however ſtimulated by an inordinate paſſion for a power not only unjuſtifiable, but which they know to be peculiarly reprobated by the very conſtitution of that kingdom, and deſperate of ſucceſs in any mode of conteſt where regard ſhould be had to truth, law, or right, have at length, deſerting thoſe, attempted to effect their cruel and impolitic purpoſe of enſlaving theſe colonies by violence, and have thereby rendered it neceſſary for us to cloſe with their laſt appeal from reaſon to arms. Yet, however blinded that aſſembly may be, by their intemperate rage for unlimited domination, ſo as to ſlight juſtice and the opinion of mankind, we eſteem ourſelves bound, by obligations of reſpect to the reſt of the world, to make known the juſtice of our cauſe.

Our forefathers, inhabitants of the iſland of Great-Britain, left their native land, to feek on thefe fhores a refidence for civil and religious freedom. At the expence of their blood, at the hazard of their fortunes, without the leaft charge to the country from which they removed, by unceafing labour and an unconquerable fpirit, they effected fettlements in the diftant and inhofpitable wilds of America, then filled with numerous and warlike nations of Barbarians. Societies or governments, vefted with perfect legiflatures, were formed under charters from the crown, and an harmonious intercourfe was eftablifhed between the colonies and the kingdom from which they derived their origin. The mutual benefits of this union became in a fhort time fo extraordinary, as to excite aftonifhment. It is univerfally confeffed, that the amazing increafe of the wealth, ftrength, and navigation of the realm, arofe from this fource; and the minifter, who fo wifely and fuccefsfully directed the meafures of Great-Britain in the late war. publicly declared, that thefe colonies enabled her to triumph over her enemies. —Towards the conclufion of that war, it pleafed our Sovereign to make a change in his counfels.— From that fatal moment the affairs of the Britifh empire began to fall into confufion, and, gradually fliding from the fummit of glorious profperity, to which they had been advanced by the virtues and abilities of one man, are at length diftracted by the convulfions that now fhake it to its deepeft foundations. The new miniftry, finding the brave foes of Britain, though frequently defeated, yet ftill contending, took up the unfortunate idea of granting them a hafty peace, and of then fubduing her faithful friends.

Thefe devoted colonies were judged to be in fuch a ftate, as to prefent victories without bloodfhed, and all the eafy emoluments of ftatutable plunder. The uninterrupted tenor of their peaceable and refpectful behaviour, from the begin-

ning of colonization; their dutiful, zealous, and ufeful fervices during the war, though fo recently and amply acknowledged in the moft honourable manner by his Majefty, by the late King, and by Parliament; could not fave them from the meditated innovations. Parliament was influenced to adopt the pernicious project, and, affuming a new power over them, have, in the courfe of eleven years, given fuch decifive fpecimens of the fpirit and confequences attending this power, as to leave no doubt concerning the effects of acquiefcence under it. They have undertaken to give and grant our money without our confent, though we have ever exercifed an exclufive right to difpofe of our own property. Statutes have been paffed for extending the jurifdiction of courts of Admiralty and Vice-admiralty beyond their ancient limits, for depriving us of the accuftomed and ineftimable privilege of trial by jury, in cafes affecting both life and property; for fufpending the legiflature of one of the colonies; for interdicting all commerce of another; and for altering fundamentally the form of government eftablifhed by charter, and fecured by acts of its own legiflature folemnly confirmed by the crown; for exempting the ' murderers' of colonifts from legal trial, and, in effect, from punifhment; for erecting in a neighbouring province, acquired by the joint arms of Great-Britain and America, a defpotifm dangerous to our very exiftence; and for quartering foldiers upon the colonifts in time of profound peace. It has alfo been refolved in parliament, that colonifts, charged with committing certain offences, fhall be tranfported to England to be tried.

But why fhould we enumerate our injuries in detail? By one ftatute it is declared, that Parliament can ' of right make laws to bind us in all cafes whatever.' What is to defend us againft fo enormous, fo unlimited a power? Not a fingle

man of thofe who affume it is chofen by us, or is fubject to our controul or influence; but, on the contrary, they are all of them exempt from the operation of fuch laws; and an American revenue, if not diverted from the oftenfible purpofes for which it is raifed, would actually lighten their own burdens, in proportion as they increafe ours. We faw the mifery to which fuch defpotifm would reduce us. We for ten years inceffantly and ineffectually befieged the throne as fupplicants; we reafoned, we remonftrated with parliament in the moft mild and decent language. But adminiftration, fenfible that we fhould regard thefe oppreffive meafures as freemen ought to do, fent over fleets and armies to enforce them. The indignation of the Americans was roufed, it is true; but it was the indignation of a virtuous, loyal, and affectionate people. A congrefs of delegates from the united colonies was affembled at Philadelphia, on the 5th day of laft September. We refolved again to offer an humble and dutiful petition to the King, and alfo addreffed our fellow fubjects of Great-Britain. We have purfued every temperate, every refpectful meafure; we have even proceeded to break off our commercial intercourfe with our fellow fubjects, as the laft peaceable admonition, that our attachment to no nation upon earth would fupplant our attachment to liberty. This, we flatter ourfelves, was the ultimate ftep of the controverfy; but fubfequent events have fhewn how vain was this hope of finding moderation in our enemies.

Several threatening expreffions againft the colonies were inferted in his Majefty's fpeech. Our petition, though we were told it was a decent one, that his Majefty had been pleafed to receive it gracioufly, and to promife laying it before his parliament, was huddled into both houfes amongft a bundle of American papers, and there neglected. The Lords and Commons, in their addrefs, in the month of February, said, ' that a rebellion at that time actually existed within the province of Massachusett's-Bay; and that those concerned in it had been countenanced and encouraged by unlawful combinations and engagements, entered into by his Majesty's subjects in several of the other colonies; and therefore they besought his Majesty that he would take the most effectual measures to enforce due obedience to the laws and authority of the supreme legislature.' Soon after the commercial intercourse of whole colonies, with foreign countries and with each other, was cut off by an act of parliament; by another, several of them were intirely prohibited from the fisheries in the seas near their coasts, on which they always depended for their sustenance; and large re-inforcements of ships and troops were immediately sent over to General Gage.

Fruitless were all the intreaties, arguments and eloquence of an illustrious band, of the most distinguished peers and commoners, who nobly and strenuously asserted the justice of our cause, to stay or even to mitigate the heedless fury with which these accumulated and unexampled outrages were hurried on. Equally fruitless was the interference of the city of London, of Bristol, and many other respectable towns, in our favour. Parliament adopted an infidious manœuvre, calculated to divide us, to establish a perpetual auction of taxations, where colony should bid against colony, all of them uninformed what ransom should redeem their lives; and thus to extort from us at the point of the bayonet the unknown sums that should be sufficient to gratify, if possible to gratify, ministerial rapacity, with the miserable indulgence left to us of raising in our own mode the prescribed tribute. What terms more rigid and humiliating could have been dictated by remorseless victors to conquered enemies? In our circumstances, to accept them would be to deserve them.

Soon after the intelligence of these proceedings arrived on this continent, General Gage, who, in the course of the last year had taken possession of the town of Boston, in the province of Massachusett's-Bay, and still occupied it as a garrison, on the 19th day of April, sent out from that place a large detachment of his army, who made an unprovoked assault on the inhabitants of the said province, at the town of Lexington, as appears by the affidavits of a great number of persons, some of whom were officers and soldiers of that detachment; murdered eight of the inhabitants, and wounded many others. From thence the troops proceeded in warlike array to the town of Concord, where they set upon another party of the inhabitants of the same province, killing several and wounding more, until compelled to retreat by the country-people suddenly assembled to repel this cruel aggression. Hostilities thus commenced by the British troops, have been since prosecuted by them without regard to faith or reputation. The inhabitants of Boston being confined within that town by the General, their Governor; and having, in order to procure their dismission, entered into a treaty with him; it was stipulated that the said inhabitants, having deposited their arms with their own magistrates, should have liberty to depart, taking with them their other effects. They accordingly delivered up their arms; but, in open violation of honour, in defiance of the obligation of treaties, which even savage nations esteem sacred, the Governor ordered the arms deposited as aforesaid, that they might be preserved for their owners, to be seized by a body of soldiers; detained the greatest part of the inhabitants in the town, and compelled the few, who were permitted to retire, to leave their most valuable effects behind.

By this perfidy wives are separated from their husbands, children

from their parents, the aged and sick from their relations and friends, who wish to attend and comfort them; and those who have been used to live in plenty, and even elegance, are reduced to deplorable distress.

The General further emulating his Ministerial Masters, by a proclamation bearing date on the 12th day of June, after venting the grossest falshoods and calumnies against the good people of these colonies, proceeds to ' declare them all, either by name or description, to be rebels and traitors, to supersede the course of the common law, and instead thereof to publish and order the use and exercise of the law martial.'—His troops have butchered our countrymen; have wantonly burnt Charlestown, besides a considerable number of houses in other places; our ships and vessels are seized; the necessary supplies of provisions are intercepted; and he is exerting his utmost power to spread destruction and devastation around him.

We have received certain intelligence, that General Carleton, the Governor of Canada, is instigating the people of that province and the Indians to fall upon us; and we have but too much reason to apprehend, that schemes have been formed to exite domestic enemies against us. In brief, a part of these colonies now feels, and all of them are sure of feeling, as far as the vengeance of administration can inflict them, the complicated calamities of fire, sword, and famine. We are reduced to the alternative of chusing an unconditional submission to the tyranny of irritated ministers, or resistance by force. The latter is our choice. We have counted the cost of this contest, and find nothing so dreadful as voluntary slavery. Honour, justice, and humanity forbid us tamely to surrender that freedom which we received from our gallant ancestors, and which our innocent posterity have a right to receive from us. We cannot endure the infamy and guilt of resigning succeeding generations to that wretchedness which inevitably awaits them, if we basely intail hereditary bondage upon them.

Our cause is just: Our union is perfect: Our internal resources are great, and, if necessary, foreign assistance is undoubtedly attainable. We gratefully acknowledge, as signal instances of the divine favour towards us, that his Providence would not permit us to be called into this severe controversy, until we were grown up to our present strength, had been previously exercised in warlike operations, and possessed of the means of defending ourselves. With hearts fortified with these animating reflections, we most solemnly before God and the world declare, that, exerting the utmost energy of those powers which our beneficent Creator hath graciously bestowed upon us, the arms we have been compelled by our enemies to assume, we will, in defiance of every hazard, with unabated firmness and perseverance, employ for the preservation of our liberties, being with one mind resolved to die freemen rather than to live slaves.

Lest this declaration should disquiet the minds of our friends and fellow-subjects in any part of the empire, we assure them, that we mean not to dissolve that union which has so long and so happily subsisted between us, and which we sincerely wish to see restored. Necessity has not yet driven us into that desperate measure, or induced us to excite any other nation to war against them. We have not raised armies, with ambitious designs of separating from Great-Britain, and establishing independent states. We fight not for glory, or for conquest. We exhibit to mankind the remarkable spectacle of people attacked by unprovoked enemies, without any imputation, or even suspicion, of offence. They boast of their privileges and civilization, and yet proffer no milder conditions than servitude or death.

In our own native land, in defence of the freedom that is our birthright, and which we ever enjoyed till the late violation of it; for the protection of our property, acquired solely by the honest industry of our forefathers, and ourselves; against violence actually offered, we have taken up arms. We shall lay them down when hostilities shall cease on the part of the aggressors, and all danger of their being renewed shall be removed, and not before.

With an humble confidence in the mercies of the supreme and impartial judge and ruler of the universe, we most devoutly implore his divine goodness to conduct us happily through this great conflict, to dispose our adversaries to reconciliation on reasonable terms, and thereby to relieve the empire from the calamities of civil war.

By order of the congress,

JOHN HANCOCK, President.

Attested,

CHARLES THOMPSON, Secretary.

Philadelphia, July 6, 1775.

A Second Petition from the General Congress in America, to his Majesty.

THE following is a true copy of the Petition from the General Congress in America, to his Majesty, which we delivered to Lord Dartmouth the first of this month, and to which, his Lordship said, no answer would be given.

Sept. 4, 1775. 91   Richard Penn.
Arthur Lee.

To the King's most excellent Majesty.

Most Gracious Sovereign,

WE your Majesty's faithful subjects of the colonies of New Hampshire, Massachusett's-Bay, Rhode Island, and Providence Plantations, Connecticut, New York, New Jersey, Pennsylvania, the counties of New Castle, Kent and Sussex in Delaware, Maryland, Virginia, North and South Carolina, in behalf of ourselves and the inhabitants of these colonies, who have deputed us to represent them in General Congress, entreat your Majesty's gracious attention to this our humble petition.

The union between our mother-country and these colonies, and the energy of mild and just government, produced benefits so remarkably important, and afforded such assurance of their permanency and increase, that the wonder and envy of other nations were excited, while they beheld Great-Britain rising to a power the most extraordinary the world had ever known. Her rivals observing that there was no probability of this happy connection being broken by civil dissentions, and apprehending its future effects, if left any longer undisturbed, resolved to prevent her receiving so continual and formidable an accession of wealth and strength, by checking the growth of these settlements, from which they were to be derived.

In the prosecution of this attempt, events so unfavourable to the design took place, that every friend to the interest of Great-Britain and these colonies, entertained pleasing and reasonable expectations of seeing an additional force and extension immediately given to the operations of the union hitherto experienced, by an enlargement of the dominions of the crown, and the removal of ancient and warlike enemies to a greater distance.

At the conclusion, therefore, of the late war, the most glorious and advantageous that ever had been carried on by British arms, your loyal colonies, having contributed to its success by such repeated and strenuous exertions as frequently procured them the distinguished approbation of your Majesty, of the late king, and of parliament, doubted not but that they should be permitted, with the rest of the empire, to share in the bleſſings of peace, and the emoluments of victory and conqueſt. While theſe recent and honourable acknowledgments of their merits remained on record in the journals and acts of that auguſt legiſlature, the parliament, undefaced by the imputation, or even the ſuſpicion of any offence, they were alarmed by a *new ſyſtem of ſtatutes* and regulations, adopted for the adminiſtration of the colonies, that filled their minds with the moſt painful fears and jealouſies; and, to their inexpreſſible aſtoniſhment, perceived the dangers of a foreign quarrel quickly ſucceeded by domeſtic dangers, in their judgment of a more dreadful kind.

Nor were their anxieties alleviated by any tendency in this ſyſtem to promote the welfare of the mother-country: for though its effects were more immediately felt by them, yet its influence appeared to be injurious to the commerce and proſperity of Great-Britain.

We ſhall decline the ungrateful taſk of deſcribing the irkſome variety of artifices practiſed by many of your Majeſty's miniſters, the deluſive pretences, fruitleſs terrors, and unavailing ſeverities, which have from time to time been dealt out by them in their attempts to execute this impolitic plan, or of tracing through a ſeries of years paſt the progreſs of the unhappy differences between Great-Britain and theſe colonies, which have flowed from this fatal ſource. Your Majeſty's miniſters perſevering in their meaſures, and proceeding to open hoſtilities for enforcing them, have compelled us to arm in our own defence, and have engaged us in a controverſy ſo peculiarly abhorrent from the affections of your ſtill faithful coloniſts, that when we conſider whom we muſt oppoſe in this conteſt, and if it continues, what may be the conſequence; our own particular misfortunes are accounted by us only as parts of our diſtreſs.

Knowing to what violent reſentments and incurable animoſities civil diſcords are apt to exaſperate and inflame the contending parties, we think ourſelves required by indiſpenſable obligations to Almighty God, to your Majeſty, to our fellow-ſubjects, and ourſelves, immediately to uſe all the means in our power, not incompatible with our ſafety, for ſtopping the further effuſion of blood, and for averting the impending calamities that threaten the Britiſh empire. Thus called upon to addreſs your Majeſty on affairs of ſuch moment to America, and probably to all your dominions, we are earneſtly deſirous of performing this office with the utmoſt deference to your Majeſty; and we therefore pray that your royal magnanimity and benevolence may make the moſt favourable conſtructions of our expreſſions on ſo uncommon an occaſion.

Could we repreſent, in their full force, the ſentiments which agitate the minds of us, your dutiful ſubjects, we are perſuaded your Majeſty would aſcribe any ſeeming deviation from reverence, in our language, and even in our conduct, not to any reprehenſible intention, but to the impoſſibility of reconciling the uſual appearances of reſpect with a juſt attention to our preſervation againſt thoſe artful and cruel enemies, who abuſe your royal confidence and authority for the purpoſe of effecting our deſtruction.

Attached to your Majeſty's perſon, family and government, with all the devotion that principle and affection can inſpire, connected with Great-Britain by the ſtrongeſt ties that can unite ſocieties, and deploring every event that tends in any degree to weaken them, we ſolemnly aſſure your Majeſty that we not only moſt *ardently deſire the former harmony between her* and theſe colonies may be reſtored, but that a *concord may be eſtabliſhed* between them upon ſo firm a baſis as to perpetuate its bleſſings uninter-

rupted by any future diſſentions to ſucceeding generations in both countries; to tranſmit your Majeſty's name to poſterity, adorned with that ſignal and laſting glory that has attended the memory of thoſe illuſtrious perſonages, whoſe virtues and abilities have extricated ſtates from dangerous convulſions, and by ſecuring happineſs to others, have erected the moſt noble and durable monuments to their own fame.

We beg leave further to aſſure your Majeſty, that notwithſtanding the ſufferings of your loyal coloniſts, during the courſe of the preſent controverſy, our breaſts retain too tender a regard for the kingdom from which we derive our origin, to requeſt ſuch a reconciliation, as might in any manner be inconſiſtent with *her dignity or her welfare* Theſe, related as we are to her, honour and duty, as well as inclination, induce us to ſupport and advance; and the apprehenſions that now oppreſs our hearts with unſpeakable grief being once removed, your Majeſty will find your faithful ſubjects, on this continent, ready and willing, at all times, as they have ever been, with their lives and fortunes, to aſſert and maintain the rights and intereſts of your Majeſty and of our mother-country.

We therefore beſeech your Majeſty, that your royal authority and influence may be graciouſly interpoſed, to procure us relief from our afflicting fears and jealouſies, occaſioned by the ſyſtem before mentioned, and to ſettle peace through every part of your dominions; with all humility ſubmitting to your Majeſty's wiſe conſideration, whether it may not be expedient, for facilitating theſe important purpoſes, that your Majeſty be pleaſed to *direct ſome mode* by which the united applications of your faithful coloniſts to the throne, in purſuance of their common councils, may be improved into a happy and permanent reconciliation ; and that in the mean time measures be taken for preventing the further destruction of the lives of your Majesty's subjects, and that such statutes as more immediately distress any of your majesty's colonies be repealed. For by such arrangements as your Majesty's wisdom can form, for collecting the united sense of your American people, we are convinced your Majesty would receive such satisfactory proofs of the disposition of the colonists toward their sovereign and the parent state, that the wished for opportunity would soon be restored to them, of evincing the sincerity of their professions, by every testimony of devotion becoming the most dutiful subjects, and the most affectionate colonists.

That your Majesty may enjoy a long and prosperous reign, and that your descendants may govern the dominions, with honour to themselves and happiness to their subjects, is our sincere and fervent prayer.

JOHN HANCOCK.

Colonies of New Hampshire. John Langdon, Thomas Cushing.

Massachusett's Bay. Samuel Adams, John Adams, Robert Treat Paine.

Rhode Island. Stephen Hopkins, Samuel Ward, Eliphant Dyar.

Connecticut. Roger Sherman, Silas Dean.

New York. Philip Levingston, James Duane, John Alsop, Francis Lewis, John Jay, Robert Levingston, junior, Lewis Morris, Wm. Floyd, Henry Wisner.

New Jersey. William Levingston, John Deharts, Richard Smith.

Pennsylvania. John Dickenson, Benjamin Franklin, George Ross, James Wilson, Charles Wilson, Charles Humphreys, Edward Biddle.

Delaware Counties. Cæsar Rodney, Thomas M'Kean, George Read.

Maryland. Matthew Tilghman, Thomas Johnson, junior, William Pace, Samuel Chase, Thomas Stone.

Virginia. P. Henry, junior, R. Henry Lee, Edmond Pendleton, Benjamin Harrison, Thomas Jefferson.

North Carolina. Wm. Hooper, Joseph Hewes.

South Carolina. Henry Middleton, Thomas Lynch, Christopher Gadsden, J. Rutlege, Edward Rutlege.

• • •

The Address, Memorial, and Petition, of several of the Gentlemen, Merchants, and Traders of the City of London, presented by a Deputation of them to his Majesty, on Wednesday the 11th of October, 1775.

To the King's most Excellent Majesty.

The humble Address, Memorial, and Petition of the Gentlemen, Merchants, and Traders of London.

May it please your Majesty,

WE your Majesty's most dutiful and loyal subjects, the Gentlemen, Merchants, and Traders of London, beg leave to approach your Majesty with unfeigned assurance of affection and attachment to your Majesty's person and government, and to represent, with great humility, our sentiments on the present alarming state of public affairs.

By the operation of divers acts of the British parliament, we behold, with deep affliction, that happy communion of interests and good offices, which had so long subsisted between this country and America, suspended, and an intercourse (which, augmenting, as it grew, the strength and dignity of your Majesty's dominions, hath enabled your Majesty to defeat the natural rivals of your greatness in every quarter of the world) threatened with irretrievable ruin.

We should humbly represent to your Majesty, if they had not been already represented, the deadly wounds which the commerce of this country must feel from these unfortunate measures ; that it has not yet more deeply felt them is owing to temporary and accidental causes which cannot long continue.

But we beg your Majesty to cast an eye on the general property of this land, and to reflect what must be its fate when deprived of our American commerce.

It fills our minds with additional grief to see the blood and treasure of your Majesty's subjects wasted in effecting a fatal separation between the different parts of your Majesty's empire, by a war, uncertain in the event, destructive in its consequences, and the object contended for lost in the contest.

The experience we have had of your Majesty's paternal regard for the welfare and privileges of all your people, and the opinion we entertain of the justice of the British parliament, forbid us to believe, that laws, so repugnant to the policy of former times, would have received their sanction, had the real circumstances and sentiments of the colonies been thoroughly understood, or the true principles of their connection with the mother-country been duly weighed : we are therefore necessarily constrained to impute blame to those by whom your Majesty and the parliament have been designedly misled, or partially informed of those matters, on a full knowledge of which alone, determinations of such importance should have been founded.

We beg leave further to represent to your Majesty, that, in questions of high national concern affecting the dearest interests of a state, speculation and experiment are seldom to be justified : That want of foresight is want of judgment ; and perseverance in measures, which repeated experience hath condemned, ceases to be error.

We might appeal to the history of all countries to shew, that force hath never been employed with success, to change the opinions or convince the minds of freemen; and, from the annals of our own in particular, we learn, that the free and voluntary gifts of the subject have ever exceeded the exactions of the sword.

Restraining, prohibitory, and penal laws have failed to re-establish the public tranquillity; and the present state of this unfortunate dispute affords reason to believe, that, as it commenced without policy, it must be prosecuted by means which the natural and constitutional strength of Great-Britain cannot supply.

In your Majesty's justice we confide for a fair construction of an apprehension we have conceived, that your Majesty hath been advised to take foreign troops into British pay, and to raise and discipline Papists both in Ireland and Canada, for the purpose of enforcing submission to laws which your Majesty's Protestant subjects in America conceive to be destructive of their liberties, and against which they have repeatedly petitioned in vain.

Anxious to vindicate the national honour, we would willingly discredit reports of slaves incited to insurrection, and barbarous nations encouraged to take arms against our American brethren, if they had not prevailed without refutation, and filled the minds of your Majesty's faithful subjects with indignation and horror.

If to these circumstances of peril and distress our fears could suggest any addition, we might justly expect it from the resentment of those powerful enemies, who have ever shewn a readiness to take advantage of our internal commotions, and will joyfully embrace the occasion of avenging that disgrace they sustained, during the late glorious war, from the united arms of Great-Britain and America;—and we should indeed be reduced to despair, but that we are encouraged to look up to your Majesty, the common father of all your people, as the happy instrument in the hands of Divine Providence, which bringeth good out of evil, for restoring to this distracted empire the blessings of mutual confidence, liberty, and peace.

For the speedy effecting of which, we most humbly beseech your Majesty to cause hostilities to cease in your Majesty's colonies in America, and to adopt such mode of reconciling this unhappy controversy as may best promote the interest of commerce and the welfare of all your people.

[Signed by 1171 persons.]

Address of a very numerous Body of the Merchants *and* Traders *of the* City *of* London, *presented by a Deputation of them to his Majesty, on* Saturday *the* 14th *of* October 1775. *Which Address his Majesty was pleased to receive very graciously; and the Gentlemen of the Deputation had the Honour to kiss his Majesty's Hand.*

To the King's most Excellent Majesty.

Most Gracious Sovereign,

WE your Majesty's faithful and loyal subjects, merchants and traders of the city of London, filled with the deepest concern at the unjustifiable proceedings of some of your Majesty's colonies in America, beg leave to approach your royal throne to testify our entire disapprobation and abhorrence of them, with the most solemn assurances that we will support your Majesty with our lives and fortunes, in maintaining the authority of the legislature of this country, which, we conceive, does and ought to extend over and pervade every part of the British dominions.

With regret and indignation we see colonies, which owe their existence, and every blessing that attended their late prosperous situation, to this their parent country, unnaturally regardless of the fostering hand that raised and supported them, and affecting distinctions in their dependence, not founded in law, or in the constitution of Great-Britain.

We are convinced by the experienced clemency of your Majesty's government, that no endeavours will be wanting to induce our deluded fellow-subjects to return to their obedience to that constitution which our ancestors bled to establish, and which has flourished, pure and uninterrupted, under the mild government of the House of Hanover.

May that Being, who governs the universe, so direct your Majesty's councils and measures, that, from the present confusion, order may arise, and peace again be restored.

That your Majesty may long reign over an happy and united people is the earnest prayer of,

May it please your Majesty,
Your Majesty's most faithful and loyal subjects.
[Signed by 941 persons.]

His Majesty's most gracious Speech to both Houses of Parliament, on Thursday, *the* 26th *Day of* October, 1775.

My Lords and Gentlemen,

THE present situation of America, and my constant desire to have your advice, concurrence, and assistance on every important occasion, have determined me to call you thus early together.

Those who have long too successfully laboured to inflame my people in America by gross misrepresentations, and to infuse into their minds a system of opinions repugnant to the true constitution of the colonies, and to their subordinate relation to Great-Britain, now openly avow their revolt, hostility, and rebellion. They have raised troops, and are collecting a naval force; they have seized the public revenue, and assumed to themselves legislative, executive, and judicial powers, which they already exercise, in the most arbitrary manner, over the persons and properties of their fellow-subjects; and although many of these unhappy people may still retain their loyalty, and may be too wise not to see the fatal consequence of this usurpation, and wish to resist it; yet the torrent of violence has been strong enough to compel their acquiescence, till a sufficient force shall appear to support them.

The authors and promoters of this desperate conspiracy have, in the conduct of it, derived great advantage from the difference of our intentions and theirs. They meant only to amuse, by vague expressions of attachment to the Parent-state, and the strongest protestations of loyalty to me, whilst they were preparing for a general revolt. On our part, though it was declared in your last session, that a rebellion existed within the province of the Massachusett's Bay, yet even that province we wished rather to reclaim than to subdue. The resolutions of parliament breathed a spirit of moderation and forbearance; conciliatory propositions accompanied the measures taken to enforce authority; and the coercive acts were adapted to cases of criminal combinations amongst subjects not then in arms. I have acted with the same temper; anxious to prevent, if it had been possible, the effusion of the blood of my subjects, and the calamities which are inseparable from a state of war; still hoping that my people in America would have discerned the traiterous views of their leaders, and have been convinced, that to be a subject of Great-Britain, with all its consequences, is to be the freest member of any civil society in the known world.

The rebellious war now levied is become more general, and is manifestly carried on for the purpose of establishing an independent empire. I need not dwell upon the fatal effects of the success of such a plan. The object is too important, the spirit of the British nation too high, the resources with which God hath blessed her too numerous, to give up so many colonies which she has planted with great industry, nursed with great tenderness, encouraged with many commercial advantages, and protected and defended at much expence of blood and treasure.

It is now become the part of wisdom, and (in its effects) of clemency, to put a speedy end to these disorders by the most decisive exertions. For this purpose, I have increased my naval establishment, and greatly augmented my land-forces; but in such a manner as may be the least burthensome to my kingdoms.

I have also the satisfaction to inform you, that I have received the most friendly offers of foreign assistance; and if I shall make any treaties in consequence thereof, they shall be laid before you. And I have, in testimony of my affection for my people, who can have no cause in which I am not equally interested, sent to the garrisons of Gibraltar and Port Mahon a part of my Electoral troops, in order that a larger number of the established forces of this kingdom may be applied to the maintenance of its authority; and the national militia, planned and regulated with equal regard to the rights, safety, and protection of my crown and people, may give a farther extent and activity to our military operations.

When the unhappy and deluded multitude, against whom this force will be directed, shall become sensible of their error, I shall be ready to receive the misled with tenderness and mercy; and, in order to prevent the inconveniences which may arise from the great distance of their situation, and to remove, as

soon as possible, the calamities which they suffer, I shall give authority to certain persons upon the spot to grant general or particular pardons and indemnities, in such manner, and to such persons, as they shall think fit, and to receive the submission of any province or colony which shall be disposed to return to its allegiance. It may be also proper to authorise the persons so commissioned to restore such province or colony, so returning to its allegiance, to the free exercise of its trade and commerce, and to the same protection and security, as if such province or colony had never revolted.

Gentlemen of the House of Commons,

I have ordered the proper estimates for the ensuing year to be laid before you; and I rely on your affection to me, and your resolution to maintain the just rights of this country, for such supplies as the present circumstances of our affairs require. Among the many unavoidable ill consequences of this rebellion, none affects me more sensibly than the extraordinary burthen which it must create to my faithful subjects.

My Lords and Gentlemen,

I have fully opened to you my views and intentions. The constant employment of my thoughts, and the most earnest wishes of my heart, tend wholly to the safety and happiness of all my people, and to the re-establishment of order and tranquillity through the several parts of my dominions, in a close connection and constitutional dependance. You see the tendency of the present disorders, and I have stated to you the measures which I mean to pursue for suppressing them. Whatever remains to be done, that may farther contribute to this end, I commit to your wisdom. And I am happy to add, that, as well from the assurances I have received, as from the general appearance of affairs in Europe, I fee no probability that the meafures which you may adopt will be interrupted by difputes with any foreign power.

The following Addrefs of the Liverymen of the City of London has been prefented to his Majefty, by Thomas Wellings, *Chairman,* John Spiller, Gabriel Leekey, William Judd, Evan Pugh, Roger Griffin, *and* Thomas Moore, *Efqrs. being introduced by the Lord of his Majefty's Bed-Chamber in waiting; which Addrefs his Majefty was pleafed to receive very gracioufly: and they had the honour to kifs his Majefty's hand.*

To the King's Moft Excellent Majefty.

Moft Gracious Sovereign,

FROM the warmeft fenfe of duty to your Majefty, and love of our country, we, your Majefty's loyal fubjects, liverymen of the city of London, whofe names are hereunto fubfcribed, with the freedom we ever mean to affert as Englifhmen, and with that deference which we owe, as good fubjects, to your Majefty, prefume to approach your royal prefence, and to entreat your attention to the genuine fentiments of a loyal and dutiful people.

It is with the deepeft concern we obferve, that our fellow-fubjects in your Majefty's American colonies are now in open rebellion. A malignant fpirit of refiftance to law and government has gone forth amongft them, which we firmly believe has been excited and encouraged by felfifh men, who hope to derive private emolument from public calamities: from the counfels, the perfuafions, the influence of fuch men, God protect your Majefty. The intereft, the honour, the fovereignty of your kingdom of Great-Britain, are now at ftake: as the guardian of thofe, we truft you will ever affert and preferve them.

In this great work, be affured, Sire, that under your Majefty's direction we will, with the greateft chearfulnefs, exert ourfelves to the utmoft of our abilities, in fupport of thofe laws which are our protection, and of that government which is our blefling.

Whilft we prefume to approach your Majefty, with hopes you will exert the conftitutional power you poffefs, to fubdue fuch of your deluded people as are now acting in open defiance of the laws, permit us, gracious Sire, to implore your clemency towards thofe whofe eyes may be opened to a full conviction of their offences; and who, hereafter, when reafon and reflection fhall prevail over paffion and prejudice, may be reftored to the allegiance which they owe to the mother-country and their fovereign.

That your Majefty and your pofterity may long reign over a people, happy in enjoying thofe bleffings which the acceffion of your anceftors to the throne of thefe kingdoms has hitherto infured to us, is the unfeigned and ardent wifh of your Majefty's moft dutiful, faithful, and devoted fubjects.

[The above addrefs was figned by 1029 liverymen.]

Notes, 1775

1. The population of the American colonies rose from 434,600 in 1715 to 2,554,500 in 1774–75. Merrill Jensen, ed., *English Historical Documents*, vol. 9: *English Colonial Documents to 1776* (London and New York, 1955), pp. 479–80.

2. That is, the extended Quartering Act, 14 Geo. III c. 54.

3. Thomas Gage (1719–87) was appointed Governor of Massachusetts in April 1774; he retained the post of Commander-in-Chief in North America.

4. Gage arrived at Castle William on 13 May, but did not make his formal entry into Boston until 17 May. On 10 May, Captain Shalyer, of the *Harmony*, brought details of the Boston Port Act.

5. Among other provisions, the Massachusetts Government Act abrogated the right under the 1691 charter for the assembly to elect members of the council and required that they be appointed by the Crown, to serve at the royal pleasure.

6. The Virginia House of Burgesses resolved on 24 May to support Boston, and in consequence, the governor ordered a dissolution on 26 May. On 26 May, eighty-nine members met at the Raleigh Tavern in Williamsburg and signed their agreement.

7. The Philadelphia meeting took place on 20 May. The relative moderation of the letter sent to Boston reflects careful planning by a group using the prestige of John Dickinson to avoid an immediate split between the radicals and the conservatives. A later meeting, on 18 June, took a more forthright stand.

8. The first New York meeting was held on 16 May; at this and subsequent meetings, the moderates outmanoeuvered the radicals.

9. The Annapolis meeting was held on 25 May, and it revealed major disagreements between radicals and moderates.

10. Following his instructions, Gage transferred the seat of government from Boston to Salem, where the assembly reconvened on 7 June.

11. This abortive counterattack against the Boston Committee of Correspondence on 27 June was outvoted four to one.

12. The Solemn League and Covenant was actually approved on 6 June.

13. The 43rd and 4th regiments, with a detachment of Royal Marines.

14. The total number of delegates attending the first session of the Continental Congress was fifty-six; forty-five were present at the opening of business on 5 September and latecomers (mainly from New York and North Carolina) arrived as late as 1 October.

15. John Glynn (1722–79), M.P. for Middlesex, 1768–79.

16. The radicals' introduction of a manifesto of political objectives (Wilkes's "Declaration"), intended to commit the candidates, was attempted in the constituencies of Westminster, Middlesex, the City of London, Southwark, Worcester, Cambridge, and Southampton. Radicals contested other seats, but apparently without the use of Wilkes's "Declaration."

17. The 1768 Parliament was due to terminate in March 1775. The King decided on the advantages of a premature dissolution on 24 August (George III to North, 24 August 1774, *The Correspondence of King George III*), ed. Sir John W. Fortescue, 6 vols. (London, 1927–28), vol. 3, p. 1501.

18. During the long wait in the summer for official reports on the American reaction to the Coercive Acts and on the resolves of the Continental Congress, the Government generally evinced confident optimism. Dartmouth received some early warning of the likely direction of events from his private correspondence with Joseph Reed and Hutchinson, and he transmitted similar views. Some evidence suggests that the ministry was receiving reports from a member of the Philadelphia Congress, possibly John Jay of New York. See Merrill Jensen, *The Founding of a Nation: A History of the American Revolution 1763–1776* (New York and London, 1968), p. 571.

19. Fletcher Norton (1716–89), M.P. for Guildford, 1763–82; Attorney-General, 1763–65; Speaker, 1770–80.

20. Charles Lennox, Duke of Richmond (1735–1806); Secretary of State for the Southern Department, May–July 1766; a consistent associate of Rockingham.

21. Henry Howard, Earl of Suffolk (1739–79); Secretary of State for the Northern Department, 1771–79.

22. See *AR*, 1774, pp. [276–[278.

23. Burke developed his fears of the growth of an unconstitutional "influence" in government at length in *Thoughts on the Cause of the Present Discontents* (1770), in which the "cant phrase" "interior cabinet" is used.

24. Francis Seymour Conway (1743–1822), eldest son of the Earl of Hertford and styled Lord Beauchamp until he succeeded his father in 1794; M.P. for Oxford, 1768–94; and a Lord of the Treasury, 1774–80.

25. John Montagu, Earl of Sandwich (1718–92), was appointed First Lord of the Admiralty in January 1771. He held the post until March 1782.

26. Rose Fuller.

27. Charles Wolfran Cornwall (1735–89), M.P. for Winchelsea, 1774–80, and for Rye, 1780–89; a Lord of the Treasury, 1774–80; Speaker, 1780–89.

28. Henry Frederick, Duke of Cumberland and Strathearn (1745–90), fourth son of the late Frederick, Prince of Wales, and brother of George III.

29. Edmund Burke (1729–97), M.P. for Wendover, 1765–74; Bristol, 1774–80; and Malton, 1780–94; private secretary to Rockingham from 1765.

30. George Hayley (d. 1781), M.P. for London, 1774–81.

31. Isaac Barré (1726–1802), M.P. for Chipping Wycombe, 1761–74, and for Calne, 1774–90; served in America in the Seven Years War and maintained his American contacts thereafter; in Parliament, an adherent of Shelburne.

32. George Johnstone (1730–87), M.P. for Appleby, 1774–80; former Governor of West Florida, and a director of the East India Company, 1784–86.

33. Arthur Lee (1740–92), youngest of the four well-known Lee brothers of Stratford, Virginia, was a resident of London from 1768. A lawyer and businessman, he was active in radical politics and was made agent of the Massachusetts Assembly, at the instigation of Samuel Adams, in 1770.

34. Thomas Wooldridge (d.c. 1794), member of the Musicians Company.

35. On 1 February, a petition signed by the mayor and aldermen of Leeds also supported coercion. Both the Birmingham and the Leeds petitions were followed by counterpetitions from both boroughs praying for relief from the effects of the stoppage in the Atlantic trade. A second petition from Nottingham, and petitions from Huddersfield and from Trowbridge, Wiltshire, all supported the Government.

36. Edmund Burke.

37. Chatham.

38. North argued that eight million Britons paid £10 million per annum in taxes, compared with three million Americans who payed only £75,000 p.a. to support the costs of colonial administration. The American figure (ignoring the overestimate for population) is probably too low, since it takes no account of local taxation. A modern estimate suggests that in 1765, Britons paid about 26 shillings per head per annum in taxes and Americans about an average of 1 shilling; both figures would be revised upward, but in the same proportion, for 1775. R. R. Palmer, *Age of the Democratic Revolution: A Political History of Europe and America, 1790–1800*, vol. 1: *The Challenge* (Princeton, N.J., 1959), p. 155. North's ratio should therefore be reduced to about twenty-five to one.

39. John Dunning (1731–83), Solicitor-General, 1768–70; one of Shelburne's group and consistently in opposition from 1768.

40. James Grant (1720–1806), M.P. for Tain Burghs, 1773–80; Colonel of the 55th Foot; he served in America during the last war, when he was known for his contempt for colonial troops. He served as Governor of East Florida, 1763–73, and returned to America, as a Brigadier, in the spring of 1775.

41. Charles James Fox (1749–1806), M.P. for Malmesbury, 1774–80; a Lord of the Treasury, 1773–February 1774. He had begun to demonstrate the qualities of brilliance and instability which earned him a unique political reputation. He was dismissed from the Treasury by North in February 1774; at first he adopted an independent line on American issues but soon became a firm opponent of the Government.

42. Lord John Cavendish (1732–76), fourth son of the Duke of Devonshire; M.P. for York, 1768–84. His great-grandfather was one of the seven signatories of the invitation to William of Orange in 1688.

43. Chatham and Camden.

44. William Joliffe (1745–1802), M.P. for Petersfield, 1768–1802; one of the Lords of Trade, 1772–79, and generally a supporter of North.

45. Sir William Mayne (1722–94), M.P. for Canterbury and Gratton, 1774–80, was challenged to identify his "Catalines" by Thomas Townshend (1733–1800), M.P. for Whitchurch, 1754–83.

46. Henry Bathurst (1714–94), created Lord Apsley 1771; succeeded his father as Lord Bathurst 1775; Lord Chancellor and Keeper of the Great Seal, 1771–78 (and therefore presiding over the House of Lords).

47. Duke of Richmond.

48. Lords Mansfield and Camden. William Murray (1705–93), created Baron Mansfield 1756; Earl of Mansfield, 1776; Lord Chief Justice, 1756–88.

49. Mansfield.

50. That is, Mansfield, then later in the debate, Camden and Shelburne.

51. Governor John Wentworth (1737–1820) was unable to prevent the seizure of Fort William and Mary and the removal of its armaments by four hundred armed men on 14 December 1774.

52. David Barclay (1728–1809), Quaker banker and merchant in the North American trade who was active in trying to promote plans for conciliation through his contacts with Franklin.

53. See "Introduction, 1769," n. 8.

54. Henry Dundas (1742–1811), M.P. for Edinburghshire, 1774–82; Solicitor-General for Scotland, 1766–May 1775; Lord Advocate, 1775–83.

55. Admiral Molyneux Shuldham (c. 1717–98), Governor and Commander-in-Chief, Newfoundland 1772–75; M.P. for Fowey, 1774–84. Sir Hugh Palliser (1723–96), Comptroller of the Navy, 1770–75; M.P. for Scarborough, 1774–79, and for Huntingdon, 1780–84.

56. Camden.

57. Lord Sandwich.

58. 15 Geo. III c. 10.

59. Gilbert Elliot (1722–77), M.P. for Roxburghshire, 1765–77; Keeper of the Signet from 1766; Treasurer of the Navy from March 1770 to his death.

60. John Sawbridge (1732–95), M.P. for Hythe, 1768–74, and for London, 1774–95; Lord Mayor of London, 1775–76. He introduced this motion each year beginning in 1771.

61. Sir George Savile (1726–84), 8th Baronet, M.P. for Yorkshire, 1759–83; a much respected country gentleman long associated with Rockingham.

62. Richard Glover (?1712–85), former M.P. (1761–68) for Weymouth and Melcombe Regis; author of the epic poem *Leonidas*, published in 1737; a merchant with widespread interests.

63. The actual value of the sugar islands to Britain was soon challenged by Adam Smith. Two recent assessments may be found in R. B. Sheridan, "The Wealth of Jamaica in the Eighteenth Century," *Economic History Review*, 1965, vol. 18, pp. 292–311; R. P. Thomas, "The Sugar Colonies of the Old Empire: Profit or Loss for Great Britain," *Economic History Review*, 1968, vol. 21, pp. 30–45; and Sheridan's rejoinder, pp. 46–61. Sheridan estimates the aggregate wealth (personality and realty) of the British West Indies immediately before the revolution to be around £30 million, yielding £2.578 million annual profit, or an 8.4 percent return on investment. Thomas agrees to a wealth figure of around £30 million, but estimates the total income at only £1.45 million, and from that he subtracts the costs of possession and administration and the extra cost to the British consumer of high-priced British West Indian sugar protected by a high tariff. The subtraction leaves a "social return" of only £660,000 per anum, or 2 percent on capital invested. Thomas therefore regards the sugar islands as having been the recipients of a serious misallocation of resources and as being simply unprofitable imperial possessions.

64. Burke informed the House that his trade figures for 1704 were taken from ". . . an original manuscript of Davenant." (Charles Davenant [1656–1714] was Inspector General of Exports and Imports, 1705–14, and author of a number of economic tracts.) Those for 1772 were from ". . . the accounts on your table" (i.e., those prepared from the Inspector General's ledgers).

65. David Hartley (c. 1730–1813), M.P. for Kingston-upon-Hull, 1774–80 and 1782–84; between 1775 and 1779, he made eight motions for conciliation with America.

66. Charles Manners, Marquis of Granby (1754–87), a follower of Chatham.

67. 15 Geo. III c. 18.

68. George Montagu, 4th Duke of Manchester (1737–88); he was consistently in opposition to Government policy toward America from 1770.

69. The Archbishop of Canterbury, Frederick Cornwallis (1713–83), stated that four Anglican clergymen had already been appointed in Canada. Camden and Mansfield took up the last two hours of the debate with lengthy legal arguments.

70. Cadwallader Colden (1688–1776), Lieutenant-Governor of New York from 1761 and a firm Loyalist.

71. Francis Smith (1723–91), Lieutenant-Colonel of the 10th Foot; an undistinguished officer who had been with his regiment since it was sent to America in 1767. John Pitcairn (1722–75), Major in the Royal Marines sent to Gage in 1774.

72. Hugh Percy (1742–1817), styled Earl Percy, eldest son of the Duke of Northumberland; he was Colonel of the 5th Fusiliers and accepted service in America in 1775 with the rank of Brigadier-General.

73. The casualty figures generally agreed are British—73 killed, 174 wounded, 26 missing; American—49 killed, about 40 wounded, 5 missing.

74. Artemus Ward (1727–1800), a senior militia officer in Massachusetts in 1775, was ill on 19 April but took command of the forces surrounding Boston on 20 April. On 19 May, he was commissioned General and Commander-in-Chief of the Massachusetts forces. Jededia Preble (Pribble) (1707–84). William Heath (1737–1814) was a member of the Massachusetts Provincial Congress and of its committee of safety. He was appointed Brigadier-General in Massachusetts in February 1775, and he took command of the forces besieging Boston until Ward's arrival. He was promoted to Major-General in Massachusetts, and commissioned Brigadier-General in the Continental Army in June 1775. William Prescott (1726–1795) was a Colonel in the Massachusetts forces. John Thomas (1724–76), a former militia officer, raised his own regiment in Massachusetts; he was promoted to Lieutenant-General of the Massachusetts forces in May 1775.

75. Israel Putnam (1718–90) was formerly an American provincial officer with wide and colourful experience and dubious military qualities; he was Brigadier-General of Connecticut forces and Major-General in the Continental Army in May 1775.

76. On 3 May, Benedict Arnold (1741–1801), a Connecticut merchant and militia officer, was commissioned Colonel by the Massachusetts Committee of Safety, to lead an expedition against Ticonderoga. The Connecticut assembly had already agreed to despatch a small force for the same purpose. On 7 May, the Connecticut volunteers combined with a group from Massachusetts led by James Easton and John Brown, and with a larger force of Green Mountain Boys, led by Ethan Allen (1738–89), who was active in the fight between New York and New Hampshire over the disputed border area later to become Vermont. Arnold joined Allen on 9 May and, after an abortive attempt to assume overall command, claimed a joint command with Allen in the successful capture of the fort on 10 May. Two days later, Allen's third-in-command, Seth Warner (1743–84), captured Crown Point.

77. William Howe (1729–1814) was a Major-General in 1772 and M.P. for Nottingham, 1758–80. He was originally averse to serving in America, but he accepted his posting in February 1775 and replaced Gage as Commander-in-Chief in effect on October 1775 (formally in April 1776). John Burgoyne (1722–92), Major-General in 1772, M.P. for Preston, 1768–92. Henry Clinton (1730–95), Major-General in 1772, M.P. for Newark, 1774–84; received the local rank of Lieutenant-General in October 1775 and became Howe's second-in-command.

78. Hancock was elected President of the Congress on 24 May 1775.

79. Robert Pigot (1720–96), Lieutenant-Colonel of the 38th Regiment, former M.P. for Wallingford.

80. James Abercromby, former A.D.C. to Amherst in the Seven Years War, Lieutenant-Colonel in 1770; brother of the more distinguished Robert Abercromby.

81. Not identified.

82. At the battle on the Plains of Abraham at Quebec (13 September 1759), British officer losses were 10 killed, 37 wounded. At Bunker Hill, there were 19 killed, 37 wounded. John W. Fortescue, *History of the British Army*, 13 vols. (London, 1899–1930), vol. 2, p. 353; vol. 3, p. 159. Officer losses at Bunker Hill were the heaviest for any battle of the War of Independence.

83. Historical consensus suggests that the Americans numbered about 3,000 perhaps one-third of whom saw no action, and the British forces amounted to around 2,500.

84. In the long run, the effects of this victory may have been counterproductive, since Bunker Hill "... not only elated the Americans ... but encouraged them to a blind and fatal trust in indisciplined troops, which went near to bring ruin to their cause." Fortescue, *History of the British Army*, vol. 3, p. 160.

85. Sir Grey Cooper, Bt. (c. 1726–1801), M.P. for Saltash, 1774–84; Secretary to the Treasury, 1765–82.

86. George Washington (1732–99) had a sound military reputation from his service in the Seven Years War, but his appointment was mostly due to political considerations.

87. Charles Lee (1731–82). Following his retirement from the British Army after the Seven Years War, Lee served in the Polish Army (1767 and 1769), became a landowner in Virginia in 1773, identified himself with the radicals, and actively sought military appointment. Philip Schuyler (1733–1804), a member of the prominent New York family, had seen some service in the Seven Years War. He was an unpopular moderate who, like Washington, owed his commission to political expedience. Horatio Gates (1728–1806) retired from the British Army in 1765 and became a Virginia landowner in 1772; a friend of Washington, he, like Lee, saw personal opportunity in an American military appointment. In June 1775, Congress also appointed eight brigadier-generals, seven of whom were New Englanders.

88. Given the degree of patriotic and military fervour, a figure of 200,000 men in *arms and training* (using the terms in the loosest sense) is barely possible. Congress authorised raising an army of over 20,000 in July, but only 6,000 had enlisted by December. The 17,000 militia besieging Boston expected their term of service to expire at the end of the year (Washington was forced to appeal for 5,000 militia to serve until mid-January 1776). About 10,000 militia were raised in the south by the end of 1775.

89. No Articles of Confederation were adopted at this time. What the *Register* prints here are (1) Franklin's proposals for confederation as submitted to the Congress and (2) his proposals for declaring the colonies independent of the Navigation Acts, both read on 21 July, but neither adopted. Copies of both documents fell into British hands from a ship seized on its way to South Carolina. See *Journals of the Continental Congress 1774–1789*, ed. W. C. Ford, 34 vols. (Washington, D.C., 1904–37), vol. 2, pp. 195–201, esp. p. 195, n. 1; p. 200, n. 1.

90. A first draft of this declaration was produced by a committee and rejected by the Congress on 26 June. On 6 July, another draft was produced, by the collaboration of Thomas Jefferson (1743–1826), Virginia delegate to the Congress 1775–76 and outstanding political intellect of the period, with John Dickinson (1732–1808), Pennsylvania delegate to the Congress 1774–76, leading political writer, who favoured reconciliation with Britain until 1776.

91. Dickinson's petition was carried by Richard Penn (see "Notes, 1776," n. 45) to London, and sent by him and Arthur Lee to Dartmouth on 21 August. They were told the King would give no answer, so they released copies to the London newspapers, which first printed it on 6 September.

1776

Introduction

The *Annual Register* left no doubt at what point in 1776 hopes for imperial reunion based on conciliation ended. On 14 March, the Lords rejected Grafton's proposed proclamation which offered to suspend hostilities if the colonies would submit a petition of rights and grievances to the Crown. The *Register* notes:

> This day will perhaps hereafter be considered as one of the most important in the English History. It deeply fixed a new colour upon our public affairs. It was decisive on this side of the Atlantic, with respect to America; and may possibly hereafter be compared with, and considered as preliminary to that, on which, unhappily, in a few months after, the independence of that continent was declared on the other .... No alternative now seemed to be left between absolute conquest and unconditional submission.[1]

Peace proposals had indeed been considered by the Cabinet since November 1775, but the discussions revealed the administration's disunity. After months of wrangling, North finally proposed a compromise. The two Howe brothers would be joint peace commissioners with the power to offer pardons to Americans who abjured rebellion. The abolition of all revolutionary assemblies and the restoration of royal government, followed by the establishment of American revenues as an alternative to parliamentary taxation, were conditions to precede a

1. *AR*, 1776, pp. [*139–140*].

cessation of hostilities. The Peace Commission was established with these instructions on 3 May 1776.

These proposals hardly improved on those decisively rejected by the Americans in 1775.[2] But North again was following a multiple strategy. He believed an offer of peace, no matter how unrealistic the terms, might divide American opinion; placate Cabinet doves like Dartmouth; persuade public opinion that continuation of the war was not inevitable; and dissuade France from helping the Americans. His strategy was ineffective on all counts.

Parliament reassembled after the Christmas recess, on 25 January, but no significant debate on American affairs took place for nearly a month.[3] On 20 February, Charles James Fox moved for a committee of enquiry into the causes of the British military failure in North America. The motion inaugurated a lengthy debate and was defeated 240 to 104. North presented the treaties with Brunswick and Hesse for the hire of 12,000 and 5,000 mercenaries on 29 February. The opposition attacked the treaties by asserting they were not cost-effective, but lost the motion to refer the treaties to the Committee of Supply 242 to 88. In the Lords, the Duke of Richmond moved for an address to the Crown rejecting the treaties and calling for an immediate end to hostilities in America. The ensuing debate on 5 March was vigorous but, inevitably, the Opposition met defeat.[4] On 10 March, Barrington presented the extraordinary army expenses for 1775. This gave the Opposition an opportunity to make sarcastic comparisons between the army's ignominious retreat to Boston and previous spectacular campaigns which cost far less. On 14 March, Grafton introduced his conciliation address to the Lords, and saw it defeated 91 to 31. During this session, the only debate which caused the Government embarrassment began on 2 May in the Commons over abuses of the licensing system applied to vessels carrying provisions and stores to the army in America. But North secured a vote in the Commons on 9 May to dissolve the resultant committee of enquiry, and on 13

2. They represented, to a large degree, the hard-line position of Germain.
3. The House of Commons was poorly attended for several weeks—indeed, the *Register* refers to "... the very remarkable neglect of attendance which prevailed" until mid-March. *AR*, 1776, p. 140*].
4. *Journal of the House of Lords*, vol. 34, p. 577.

May the Lords agreed to postpone further examination of the question until the next session. Parliament rose for the summer recess on 23 May.

The war which began so badly for Britain in April of 1775 presented an even gloomier picture by Christmas. By September, the ministry accepted that Boston was untenable; Howe was ordered to evacuate his forces to New York, but lack of transports trapped him for the winter. On 4 March 1776, Washington moved artillery to Dorchester Heights overlooking Boston and Howe began evacuating on 17 March, but to Halifax, not to New York. The general dared not commit the army and its accompanying host of noncombatants (including over a thousand Loyalists) in hastily prepared and overcrowded transports, without adequate provisions, to a landing against unknown opposition.

In the fall of 1775, the ministry continued to pursue a piecemeal strategy. Reinforcements were ordered for Carleton's independent command in Quebec in late September, but some were diverted for an expedition against Charleston, headed by Sir Peter Parker and Clinton, scheduled to leave in early November. It was reported that Loyalist support in the southern colonies was sufficient to detach them from the rebellion if a British show of force was made. So when Germain succeeded Dartmouth on 10 November, the situation seemed under control. But on 23 December, the ministry heard that Quebec was under assault from two American armies, led by Montgomery and Arnold; from the newly-arrived Burgoyne that Howe was still in Boston and that the reinforcements for Canada and the Charleston expedition had not departed because of transport difficulties and bad weather.

Germain acted energetically. He despatched a naval emergency relief force with a regiment of troops and three supply ships to Quebec. (It sailed on 22 February.) Howe's plans for an attack up the Hudson followed by a joint assault with Carleton in New England were approved on 5 January, and arrangements were made to provide 16,500 extra troops for Howe and 10,000 for Carleton. These troop numbers committed the Government to hiring 12,500 German mercenaries. More important, the ordinary problems of troop transportation became more complicated in the search for sufficient transports to despatch the troops and their supplies simultaneously, so that the campaign could begin in the spring.[5] The forces finally left England between the first week in April and 7 July, and arrived sporadically between late June and mid-August. Nevertheless, the effort was impressive, and one historian has noted that it was ". . . a logistical effort on the oceans which had no parallel till 1944."[6]

The Americans had captured key points in Canada, including Montreal, by late November, but the siege of Quebec made no headway. On 30 December, an American assault, born of desperation, was repulsed, and American forces were irreparably damaged. Montgomery was killed. Carleton held out against the remnants of the besiegers until reinforcements arrived on 6 May, and then he scattered his demoralised enemy. When Carleton's reinforcement was complete, he and Burgoyne prepared to push down to Lake Champlain, where Arnold had persuaded his regrouped and reinforced troops to hold Ticonderoga and command the lake with a small fleet. From 19 June to the beginning of October, Carleton deliberately constructed a fleet of transports and gunboats from local timber and reassembled three small warships brought overland in sections from the St. Lawrence. On 11 October, this force wiped out Arnold's fleet and retook Crown Point, but Carleton judged it too near winter to continue the offensive, did not attack Ticonderoga, abandoned Crown Point, and returned to Quebec. Carleton saved Canada, but a possible junction with Howe on the upper Hudson was postponed until the following year.

The expedition to Charleston was irrelevant before the troops sailed, and Germain forwarded fresh orders to Clinton in February giving him the option of abandoning the target and joining Howe. By the time the expedition arrived at Cape Fear on 2 May, the counterrebellions of Carolina Loyalists had been crushed, and on 28 June Clinton and Parker made a poorly coordinated and fruitless attack on Charleston. In late July, Clinton sailed north to join Howe and arrived on 1 August.

Howe left Halifax for New York on 11 June, landed on Staten Island on 3 July, and waited for reinforcements,

---

5. See D. Syrett, *Shipping and the American War, 1775–83: A Study of British Transport Organisation* (London, 1970). It was only slowly realised that British troops in America would be quite unable to raise provisions and supplies there, or even from the West Indies, and that everything would have to be brought from Britain.

6. P. Mackesy, *The War for America, 1775–83* (London, 1964), p. 65.

using the time to proclaim the instructions of the Peace Commission. On 22 August, he landed on Long Island and, five days later, drove the Americans from their positions in a series of highly efficient manoeuvres. Howe, however, failed to press the assault, possibly to encourage the rebels to take the peace proposals seriously. Washington therefore was able to withdraw his army across the East River. Clinton led an attack across the river on 15 September, and New York was taken. Then, after another lengthy pause, Howe pushed Washington out of Harlem and forced him to retreat from White Plains on 31 October. The American garrison in Fort Washington surrendered after a crushing assault; the Americans in Fort Lee fled. Cornwallis pushed into New Jersey and, joined by Howe, forced Washington across the Delaware into Pennsylvania by the first week in December. At the same time, Clinton occupied Rhode Island. Washington regrouped his forces (losing Charles Lee, who was captured while moving to join Washington on 13 December) and took Trenton from its Hessian garrison on 26 December. Trenton was quickly retaken by Cornwallis, and Washington retreated to establish winter quarters in Morristown.

The year thus appeared to bring Britain considerable success in military terms. Canada was secured, a major base was acquired in New York, an ice-free harbour for the navy in Rhode Island was obtained, Washington was driven out of lower New York and east New Jersey. The rebels' link with New England was forced into an exterior arc crossing the Hudson forty miles north of New York City. Yet, Howe's army was far from meeting Carleton on the Hudson as originally planned, and Carleton had to begin the next campaign from Quebec instead of Ticonderoga. On no occasion had the American forces been smashed. Moreover, the British navy failed to impose a rigorous blockade, so American coastal trade, and privateering, flourished.[7] The situation may have been partly the result of a conscious policy of leniency to permit success of the Howe Peace Commission; if so, it was a waste of effort and opportunity. Richard Howe sent

7. The navy's problems were considerable. Of fifty-nine warships on the American station in mid-1776, thirty-six were transporting or assisting the army, and fourteen were convoying empty supply ships, leaving only nine for blockade work. P. Mackesy, *The War for America*, p. 100.

an advance proclamation of the peace proposals to the colonies on 20 June; but after the landing on Staten Island, he and his brother ignored the Declaration of Independence and reproclaimed their mission on 14 July, 19 September, and 30 November. The British released General Sullivan, who was captured at Long Island, in an attempt to persuade the Congress to negotiate. But the delegation which met Richard Howe on 11 September demanded recognition of independence as a first step; apart from in the area controlled by British troops the peace proposals were rejected or ignored, since they offered the Americans no acceptable basis for negotiation.

News of events in America reached England with the inevitable time lag. The ministry learned of Howe's evacuation of Boston on 2 May, the failure of the attack on Canada on 3 June, the Declaration of Independence on 12 August, and Howe's victory on Long Island on 10 October. The capture of New York confirmed the views held by the King and Germain that a military victory would be the most rapid road to the end of the rebellion. North was dubious, but when Parliament reconvened on 31 October, the speech from the throne denounced the American leadership for rejecting the proposals for conciliation and announced a planned campaign to capitalise on the success in Canada and New York. The Opposition despaired. In May, Burke wrote, ". . . I can hardly believe, by the Tranquility of everything about me, that we are a people who have just lost an Empire."[8] Even a British military success could scarcely be welcomed because, as Rockingham said in October, ". . . I feared a decisive victory on either side, would create such insolence in the conquering part, as would render anything like an amicable reunion of the empire impracticable."[9] Well-worn tactics were all that remained. In the Commons, Cavendish proposed an amendment to the address in reply to the speech from the throne and demanded an enquiry into ministerial conduct; Rockingham proposed a similar motion in the Lords. Both motions were defeated by substantial majorities though both produced extended debates. Parts of the Government line were absurd: for example, it was

8. Burke to Richard Champion, 30 May 1776, in *The Correspondence of Edmund Burke*, ed. Thomas W. Copeland, 9 vols. (Cambridge and Chicago, 1961–70), vol. 3 (ed. G. H. Gutteridge), p. 268.
9. Rockingham to Burke, 13 October 1776, ibid., p. 296.

alleged that the leadership in the Congress exercised despotism over the people of America. The Opposition however was embarrassed on being reminded in the Lords that it had denied that America sought independence, and now that independence was declared, it should logically support coercion.

Cavendish tried again on 6 November. He produced a copy of Richard Howe's proclamation of 20 June, recently published in the London newspapers (but never brought before Parliament). Cavendish claimed that the offer to revise British legislation offensive to Americans exceeded the commissioners' instructions and derogated from the authority of Parliament. He moved that the House form a committee of the whole to consider a revision, but the motion was defeated after debate. At this point, the Rockingham group, having failed to influence the majority in Parliament, or public opinion, began to absent themselves formally from Parliament when American affairs were discussed. Their absence was a prelude to their "secession" in January 1777.

The events of 1776 were of such significance that the *Register* justified expansion of the historical section to 192 pages ("it trebled in extent the amount of the History in any year of the late war"). The expansion was used to excuse late publication, on 25 September 1777.[10] However, a considerable portion of this volume deals with events in 1775 not covered in the previous volume. Chapter I describes the American invasion of Canada and the abortive assault on Quebec, giving prominence to justifying the invasion and overstressing the support given to the Americans by the French Canadians. That support is viewed as an inevitable result of the Quebec Act, so strongly condemned by the Rockinghams. Chapter II gives a retrospect of the expulsion of Governor Dunmore from Virginia, adds a brief note on the Carolinas, and comments in passing on the excessive optimism over the potential number of Loyalists in the south: "a mistake, and an unfortunate one, which like an epidemical distemper, seems to have spread through all our official departments in America." Nevertheless the failure of the colonies to adopt the Articles of Confederation is explained in terms of a reservoir of residual loyalty to

10. *AR*, 1776, preface, p. iv.

Britain, rather than, for example, of intercolonial suspicions and jealousies.

Chapters III to VI cover the parliamentary proceedings for the pre-Christmas session of 1775 in considerable detail. Particular attention is paid to the American petition brought by Richard Penn and the latter's examination before the House of Lords. These chapters also treat the Opposition motions for amendment to the speech from the throne at the opening of the session in October, the ensuing debates, the Opposition attack on the measure for hiring mercenaries, Burke's November conciliation bill, and the prohibitory bill. The use of eighty-four pages for events from the previous year is explained simply at the end of Chapter VI: Parliament had dealt with "... a multiplicity of matter and business, scarcely ever known before Christmas."

Parliamentary affairs from January to May 1776 are analysed in Chapter VII. The furore over a possible breach of privilege by the Lord Lieutenant of Ireland, Fox's motion for an enquiry into the army's failure in America, the debates in both Houses over the mercenary treaties, the Opposition attack on the size of the army's extraordinary expenses, Grafton's conciliation proposal, the defeat of the Scottish militia bill, and the attempt to force an enquiry into abuses in the licensing of supply ships to America are prominently recorded. These developments are discussed in accurate detail, and the accounts of the debates are particularly full. The Opposition arguments are given their usual particular attention, but it is noticeable that the *Register* mentions only incidentally the point made by Opposition speakers so prominently and consistently in the March debates, namely that American rebellion would eventually provide an opportunity for a Bourbon war of revenge.

Chapter VIII devotes thirty-six pages to the campaigns in America between March and December, mentioning the Declaration of Independence and the negative progress of the Peace Commission. The accounts of the military engagements are full but generally uncritical of the tactics adopted. The reports usually accept the official explanation (where any is given) for Howe's slow advance. The estimate of the damage to New York City in the attempt to fire it on 20 September is exaggerated. That was the work of enthusiasts acting without orders, for Nathaniel Greene's advice to Washington on 5 September to destroy the city before the British took it directly conflicted with the instructions of Congress to preserve the city.[11] The description of the advance through New Jersey does not include Trenton, and thus the chapter closes with the prevailing British viewpoint on the effects of the military successes and the likelihood of an imminent collapse of the rebellion. The final chapter deals with European affairs. It stresses that the American revolt has caused "... an union in a certain degree, either in act or sentiment, of the commercial world against us," and notes the sinister military preparations of France and Spain.

The *Appendix to the Chronicle* contains no material of direct relevance to American issues. The *State Papers* consists of twelve items, all of which are included here. In addition to reprinting the City of London's petition to Parliament and the protest of the dissenting peers against the reply to the speech from the throne, both of October 1775, the *Register* indicates the speaker's closure speech and the speech from the throne terminating the parliamentary session in May 1776. Items about America include Commodore Parker's letter to the governor of New York warning that naval vessels are instructed to treat opposition in the coastal towns as open rebellion; Carleton's instructions on the treatment of American fugitives (intended to illustrate his lenience and humanity); Richard Howe's general letter of 20 June announcing the Peace Commission, together with the order of Congress requiring the publication of the proposals; the resolutions of the Committee of Safety of Savannah to destroy local property and shipping in order to deny them to the British; and the Declaration of Independence. Two items contrast the attitudes of Portugal and Spain toward the American rebels. The *Register* fails to note that Portugal feared an imminent attack from Spain, that the British alliance alone could frustrate that attack, or that British diplomats exerted every possible pressure to get Portugal to publicly condemn assistance to the Americans. In its determination to have the colonies formally united, the *Register* also prints the proposed Articles of Confederation as having been "resolved upon and signed" (see "Notes, 1776," n. 97).

11. *Journals of the Continental Congress 1774–1789*, ed. W. C. Ford, 34 vols. (Washington, D.C., 1904–37), vol. 5, p. 733.

PREFACE.

IT would be a bad return to the continued favours we experience from the Public, if our zeal and induſtry was not proportioned to the importance of the ſubjeᶜts on which we treated, and to their intereſt in them. The tranſaᶜtions of foreign nations, however general or extenſive their conſequences, however connected by intereſt or alliance we might be in them, or however brilliant the matter which they afforded for hiſtory, are not only of a ſecondary but very remote conſideration, when placed in any degree of compariſon with the ſubjeᶜts of which we now treat. Our public affairs are unfortunately at preſent the hiſtory of all that part of the world which affords materials for any. Britains, however deeply, are not alone intereſted in the conſequences. They may extend, not only to the refined, but widely into the more uncultivated parts of the Globe. It therefore behoved us, not to paſs through negligence, omit through hurry, or render obſcure by an ill-timed brevity, any matter which tended to the elucidation of a ſubjeᶜt, in which our Readers are ſo immediately and deeply concerned. The time of publication was with us, and we will believe with them, by no means the principal objeᶜt of attention. We might have saved much labour and time by publishing early, and, of course, more imperfectly.

Our Publisher has liberally seconded our views in affording the expence consequent of so great an extension of the Historical Article. He thinks he cannot do too much to testify his gratitude to the Public, and desires we would observe, that from the abundance of matter which is now necessarily discussed, it trebles in extent the amount of the History in any year of the late war. For ourselves, if we have the happiness to experience a continuance of that approbation with which we have been so long honoured by the Public, it will be an additional spur to our future industry.

Retrospective view of American affairs in the year 1775. Motives which led to the invasion of Canada. Forts of Chamble and St. John taken. Montreal taken. General Carleton retires to Quebec. Armed vessels surrender. Arnold appears before Quebec. Is joined by General Montgomery. The city summoned. Siege. Attempt to take Quebec by escalade. Montgomery killed. Arnold wounded. Rebels retire from before the walls.

AS the hopes of a reconciliation with the mother country, upon the conditions claimed by the Americans, became more faint, so they grew more daring in their designs, and extended their views to the remote consequences, as well as to the immediate conduct of a war. The apparent tendency, and avowed design of the Quebec act, had early drawn their attention and awakened their apprehensions, in relation to the dangers with which they were threatened from that quarter. These apprehensions produced the address to the French inhabitants of Canada, of which we have formerly taken notice.

The success which attended the expedition to the Lakes, with the reduction of Ticonderoga and Crown-Point, in the beginning of the summer 1775, by which, it might be said, that the gates of Canada were thrown open, rendered the affairs of that country more immediately interesting, and encouraged the Congress to a bold measure, which they would not otherwise perhaps have ventured upon. This was no less than the sending of a force for the invasion and reduction of that country.

A measure of so extraordinary a nature required the most serious consideration. The commencing of an offensive war with the sovereign, was a new and perilous undertaking. It seemed totally to change the nature of the ground on which they stood in the present dispute. Opposition to government had hitherto been conducted on the apparent design and avowed principle only, of supporting and defending certain rights and immunities of the people, which were supposed, or pretended, to be unjustly invaded. Opposition, or even resistance, in such a case, supposing the premises to be fairly stated, is thought by many to be entirely consistent with the principles of the British constitution; and this opinion is said to have received the sanction of precedents of the first authority. At any rate, the questions in dispute were of such a nature, that mankind might for ever be divided in opinion, as to the matter of right or wrong, justice or injustice, oppression or good government. But to render themselves at once the aggressors, and not content with vindicating their own real or pretended rights, to fly wantonly in the face of the sovereign, carry war into his dominions, and invade a province to which they could lay no claim, nor pretend no right, seemed such an outrage, as not only overthrew every plea of justifiable resistance, but would militate with the established opinions, principles, and feelings of mankind in general.

On the other hand, the danger was pressing and great. The extraordinary powers placed in the hands of General Carleton, the Governor of Canada, by a late commission, were new, alarming, and evidently pointed out the purposes for which they were granted. By these he was authorized to embody and arm the Canadians, to march them out of the country for the subjugation of the other colonies, and to proceed even to capital punifhments, againft all thofe, and in all places, whom he fhould deem rebels and oppofers of the laws. The ftrong powers of government which he alfo poffeffed within his province, were equal to thofe of the moft arbitrary European monarchs, and had been already felt both by the Englifh and French fubjects. Thus, though the Canadians had hitherto refufed to be embodied, or to march upon any terms out of the province, it was eafily feen, that as foon as the Governor's authority was fupported by the arrival of a body of Englifh forces, they would be obliged implicitly to obey him, as well in that, as all other matters. He had befides, already engaged a confiderable number of the Canada, and other Indians in his fervice, and if his arms once became predominant, the defire of fpoil and blood would bring them in crowds from the remoteft defarts to his affiftance. Befides, they were perfectly acquainted with, and therefore had every thing to dread, from the zeal, the fpirit of enterprize, and the military talents, of that able and refolute officer.

In thefe circumftances, confidering a war not only as inevitable, but as already begun, they deemed it inconfiftent with reafon and policy, to wait to be attacked by a formidable force at their backs, in the very inftant that their utmoft exertions would be requifite, and probably infufficient, for the protection of their capital cities and coafts, againft the refentment of the mighty power whom they had fo grievoufly offended, and with whom they were entering into fo untried and arduous a conteft. They argued, that preventing the known hoftile intentions of an enemy, by forestalling his defigns ere they could be carried into execution, was as much a matter of felf-defence, and lefs cruel, than waiting to be attacked by him under every difadvantage, and when he had arrived at his utmoft force.

There was no natural law, nor convention among mankind, by which a perfon was bound to be a fimple and inactive looker-on, while his enemy was loading a gun for his deftruction; was he to wait till the execution took place, for fear he fhould be deemed an aggreffor? Queftions in cafuiftry, however edifying upon other occafions, have nothing to do in circumftances upon which the fate of nations depend. Were they only to feek a remedy, when the favages had penetrated into their country, and the fury of the flames which confumed their fettlements, were only retarded by the blood of their women and infants?

The Congrefs were alfo fenfible, that they had already gone fuch lengths as could only be juftified by arms. The fword was already drawn, and the appeal made. It was too late now to look back, and to waver would be certain deftruction. If a certain degree of fuccefs did not afford a fanction to their refiftance, and difpofe the court of Great-Britain to an accommodation upon lenient terms, they would not only lofe thofe immunities for which they at prefent contended, but all others would lie at the mercy of a jealous and irritated government. In fuch a ftate, their moderation in the fingle inftance of Canada, they thought, would be a poor plea for compaffion or indulgence.

The knowledge they had of the prefent ftate of affairs, and the temper of the people in Canada, alfo contributed much to encourage them in this enterprize. They knew that the French inhabitants, excepting the noblesse and clergy, were in general as much difcontented at the overthrow of the Englifh laws, and the introduction of the prefent fyftem of government, as even the Britifh fettlers. It feemed therefore probable, that this difcontent, operating with the rooted averfion which they bore to their ancient proud and oppreffive

tyrants, the noblesse, or lords of the manors, and the mortal dread which they entertained of being again reduced to their former ftate of feudal and military vaffalage, would induce them to confider the Provincials rather as friends than invaders, and to embrace fo favourable an opportunity of obtaining a fhare in that freedom for which they were contending. Though they were perfectly unacquainted with the nature of the particular controverfy, and little interefted in it, it feemed to be for freedom, and American freedom, and the name was pleafing. It was in favour of colonies; and Canada was a colony.

The Congrefs accordingly determined not to lofe the prefent favourable opportunity, while the Britifh arms were weak and cooped up in Bofton, for attempting the reduction of that province. The Generals Schuyler and Montgomery, with two regiments of New-York militia, a body of New-England men, and fome others, amounting in the whole to near 2000 men, were appointed to this fervice. A number of bateaux, or flat boats, were built at Ticonderoga and Crown-Point, to convey the forces along Lake Champlain to the river Sorel, which forms the entrance into Canada, and is compofed of the furplus waters of the lakes, which it difcharges into the river St. Lawrence, and would afford a happy communication between both, were it not for fome rapids that obftruct the navigation.

Not above half the forces were yet arrived, when Montgomery, who was at Crown-Point, received fome intelligence which rendered him apprehenfive that a fchooner of confiderable force, with fome other armed veffels, which lay at the fort of St. John's, on the river Sorel, were preparing to enter the lake, and thereby effectually obftruct their paffage. He thereupon, in the latter end of Auguft, proceeded with fuch force as he had to the ifle Aux Noix, which lies in the entrance of the river, and took neceffary meafures to guard againft the paffage of thofe veffels into the lake. Schuyler, who at that time commanded in chief, having alfo arrived from Albany, they publifhed a declaration to encourage the Canadians to join them, and with the fame hope or defign, pufhed on to the fort of St. John, which lies only about a dozen miles from the ifland. The fire from the fort, as well Sept. 6th. as the ftrong appearances of force and refiftance which they obferved, occafioned their landing at a confiderable diftance, in a country compofed of thick woods, deep fwamps, and interfected with creeks and waters. In this fituation they were vigoroufly attacked by a confiderable body of Indians, who did not neglect the advantages which they derived from it; along with which, finding that the fort was well garrifoned and provided, they found it neceffary the next day to return to their former ftation on the ifland, and to defer their operations until the arrival of the artillery and reinforcements which were expected.

Schuyler upon this retreat returned to Albany, to conclude a treaty which he had for fome time been negotiating with the Indians in that quarter, and found himfelf afterwards fo occupied by bufinefs, or broken in upon by illnefs, that the whole weight and danger of the Canada war fell upon Montgomery, a man moft eminently qualified for any military fervice. His firft meafure was to detach thofe Indians who had joined General Carleton from his fervice, and being ftrengthened by the arrival of his reinforcements and artillery, he prepared to lay fiege to the fort of St. John. This fort was garrifoned by the greater part of the 7th and 26th regiments, being nearly all the regular troops then in Canada; and was well provided with ftores, ammunition, and artillery.

The provincial parties were fpread over the adjacent country, and were every where received with open arms by the Canadians, who befides joining them in confiderable numbers, gave them every poffible affiftance, whether in carrying on the fiege, removing their artillery, or fupplying them with provifions and neceffaries. In this ftate of things, the adventurer Ethan Allen, who without any commiffion from the Congrefs, had a principal fhare in the original expedition to the lakes, and the capture of the forts, and who fince, under the title of colonel, feems rather to have acted as a partizan, than as obedient to any regular command, thought to fignalize, and raife himfelf into importance, by furprizing the town of Montreal. This rafh enterprize he undertook at the head of a fmall party of Englifh Provincials and Canadians, without the knowledge of the commander in chief, or the affiftance, which he might have procured, from fome of the other detached parties. The event was fuitable to the temerity of the undertaking. Being met at fome diftance from the town, by the militia, under the command of Englifh officers, and fupported by the few regulars who were in the Sept. 25th. place, he was defeated and taken prifoner, with near forty of his party, the reft who furvived efcaping in the woods. Allen, with his fellow-prifoners, were by General Carleton's orders loaded with irons, and fent in that condition on board a man of war to England, from whence, however, they were in fome time remanded back to America.

The progrefs of Montgomery [2] was for fome time retarded by a want of ammunition fufficient for carrying on a fiege; which of all operations demands the greateft fupply of powder and ball. The fort of St. John's, which commands the entrance into Canada, could not be reduced without a tolerable provifion of that kind. A fortunate event difengaged him from this difficulty. A little fort called *Chamble* lay deeper in the country, and feemed covered by St. John's. It was garrifoned by a fmall detachment of the 7th regiment, and was in no very defenfible condition. To this he turned his firft thoughts, and by pufhing forward a party joined by fome Canadians, he eafily made himfelf mafter of that fort. Here he found confiderable ftores; but the article of greateft confequence to him was the gunpowder, which they were much diftreffed for, and of which they took above 120 barrels. This acquifition facilitated the fiege of St. John's, which had languifhed for want of ammunition.

The garrifon of St. John's, under the command of Major Prefton, [3] amounted to between 6 and 700 men, of which about 500 were regulars, and the reft Canadian volunteers. They endured the difficulties and hardfhips of a very long fiege, augmented by a fcarcity of provifions, with unabating conftancy and refolution. In the mean time, General Carleton was indefatigable in his endeavours to raife a force fufficient for its relief. Attempts had been for fome time made by Colonel M'Lean, for [4] raifing a Scotch regiment, under the title of Royal Highland Emigrants, to be compofed of natives of that country who had lately arrived in America, and who in confequence of the troubles had not obtained fettlements. With thefe and fome Canadians, to the amount of a few hundred men, the Colonel was pofted near the junction of the Sorel with the river St. Lawrence. The General was at Montreal, where, with the greateft difficulty, and by every poffible means, he had got together near a thoufand men, compofed principally of Canadians, with a few regulars, and fome Englifh officers and volunteers. With thefe he intended a junction with M'Lean, and then to have marched directly to the relief of St. John's. But upon his attempting to pass over from the island of Montreal, he was encountered at Longueil by a party of the Provincials, who easily repulsed the Canadians, and put a stop to the whole design. Another party had pushed M'Lean towards the mouth of the Sorel, where the Canadians having received advice of the Governor's defeat, immediately abandoned him to a man, and he was obliged to make the best of his way to Quebec with the emigrants.

In the mean time, Montgomery pushed on the siege of St. John's with great vigour, had advanced his works very near the body of the fort, and was making preparations for a general assault. Nor was there less alacrity shewn in the defence, the spirit as well as the fire of the garrison being equally supported to the last. In this state of things, an account of the success at Longueil, accompanied by the prisoners who were taken, arrived at the camp, upon which Montgomery sent a flag and a letter by one of them to Major Preston, hoping, that as all means of relief were now cut off by the Governor's defeat, he would, by a timely surrender of the fort, prevent that farther effusion of blood, which a fruitless and obstinate defence must necessarily occasion.

The Major endeavoured to obtain a few days time in hopes of being relieved; but this was refused, on account of the lateness and severity of the season; he also endeavoured, in settling the terms of capitulation, to obtain liberty for the garrison to depart for Great Britain, which proved equally fruitless, and they were obliged, after being allowed the honours of war on account of their brave defence, to lay down their arms, and surrender themselves Nov. 3d. prisoners. They were allowed their baggage and effects, the officers to wear their swords,

and their other arms to be preserved for them till the troubles were at an end. In all transactions with our forces, Montgomery writ, spoke, and behaved with that attention, regard, and politeness, to both private men and officers, which might be expected from a man of worth and honour, who found himself involved in an unhappy quarrel with his friends and countrymen. All the prisoners were sent up the Lakes by the way of Ticonderago, to those interior parts of the colonies which were best adapted to provide for their reception and security. The Provincials found a considerable quantity of artillery and useful stores in the place.

Upon M'Lean's retreat to Quebec, the party who had reduced him to that necessity, immediately erected batteries on a point of land at the junction of the Sorel with the river St. Lawrence, in order to prevent the escape down the latter of a number of armed vessels, which General Carleton had at Montreal; they also constructed armed rafts and floating batteries for the same purpose. These measures effectually prevented the passage of General Carleton's armament to Quebec, which were not only foiled in several attempts, but pursued, attacked, and driven from their anchors up the river by the Provincials; so that as General Montgomery approached Montreal immediately after the surrender of St. John's, the Governor's situation, whether in the town or aboard the vessels, became equally critical.

This danger was soon increased by the arrival of General Montgomery at Montreal, where a capitulation was proposed by the principal French and English inhabitants, including a kind of general treaty, which Montgomery refused, as they were in no state of defence to entitle them to a capitulation, and were unable to fulfil the conditions on their part. He,

however, gave them a written answer, in which he declared, That the continental army having a generous disdain of every act of oppression and violence, and having come for the express purpose of giving liberty and security, he, therefore, engaged his honour to maintain, in the peaceable possession of their property of every kind, the individuals and religious communities of the city of Montreal. He engaged for the maintenance of all the inhabitants in the free exercise of their religion; hoped that the civil and religious rights of all the Canadians would be established upon the most permanent footing by a provincial congress; promised that courts of justice should be speedily established upon the most liberal plan, conformable to the British Constitution; and, in general, complied with other articles, so far as they were consistent, and in his power. This security being Nov. 13th. given to the people, his troops took possession of the town.

Nothing could now afford the slightest hope of the preservation of any part of Canada but the lateness of the season. Whether through inability for so great an enterprize, or from difference of opinion, the invasion of that province was not undertaken until the season for military operations was nearly passed. To balance this, there remained but an handful of regular troops in Canada, and the taking of General Carleton, which seemed nearly certain, would have rendered its fate inevitable. Fortune, however, determined otherwise, and at the time that all hopes of the armed vessels being able to get down the river were given up, and that Montgomery was preparing bateaux with light artillery at Montreal to attack them on that side, and force them down upon the batteries, means were successfully taken for conveying the Governor in a dark night, in a boat with muffled paddles, paft the enemies guards and batteries, and he arrived fafely at Quebec, which he found environed with danger from an unexpected quarter. As it was impracticable to fave the fhips, General Prefcot [5] was obliged to enter into a capitulation with the Provincials, by which the whole of the river naval force, confifting of eleven armed veffels, was furrendered into their hands, the General himfelf, with feveral other officers, fome gentlemen in the civil department, Canadian volunteers, and near 120 Englifh foldiers, all of whom had taken refuge on board upon the approach of General Montgomery to Montreal, becoming prifoners of war.

Whilft the Provincials were thus carrying on the war in Upper Canada from the New-York fide, and by the old beaten courfe of the Lakes, an expedition, confiderably diftinguifhed by its novelty, fpirit, enterprize, by the difficulties that oppofed, and the conftancy that fucceeded in its execution, was undertaken directly againft the lower part of the province and the city of Quebec, from the New-England fide, by a route which had hitherto been untried, and confidered as impracticable. This expedition was undertaken by Colonel Arnold, who about the middle of September, at the head of two regiments, confifting of about 1100 men, marched from the camp near Bofton, to Newbury Port, at the mouth of the river Merrimack, where veffels were in readinefs to convey them by fea to the mouth of the river Kennebec, in New Hampfhire; a voyage of about forty leagues.

On the 22d of the fame month they embarked their ftores and troops in 200 batteaux, at Gardiner's Town, on the Kennebec, and proceeded with great difficulty up that river, having a rapid ftream, with a rocky bottom and fhores, continually interrupted by falls and carrying places, with numberlefs other impediments to encounter. In this paffage the batteaux were frequently filled with water, or overfet; in confequence of which a part of their arms, ammunition, and provifions were fometimes loft. At the numerous carrying places, befides the labour of loading and reloading, they were obliged to convey the boats on their fhoulders. The great carrying place was above twelve miles acrofs. That part of the detachment which was not employed in the batteaux, marched along the banks of the river, and the boats and men being difpofed in three divifions, each divifion encamped together every night. Nor was the march by land more eligible than the paffage by water. They had thick woods, deep fwamps, difficult mountains, and precipices, alternately to encounter, and were at times obliged to cut their way for miles together through the thickets. At the carrying places they were obliged to traverfe the fame ground feveral times heavy loaded. From all thefe impediments their progrefs was of courfe very flow, being in general only from four or five to nine or ten miles a day. The conftant fatigue and labour caufed many to fall fick, which added to their difficulties, and provifions grew at length fo fcarce, that fome of the men eat their dogs, and whatever elfe of any kind that could be converted to food.

When they arrived at the head of the Kennebec, they fent back their fick, and one of the Colonels [6] took that opportunity of returning with his divifion, under pretence of the fcarcity of provifions, without the confent or knowledge of the Commander in Chief, who had marched forwards. By this defertion, and the fick that were returned, Arnold's detachment was reduced about one third from its original number. They, however, proceeded with their ufual conftancy; and having croffed the heights of land, as a ridge that extends quite through that continent is called, and from whence the waters on either fide, take courfes directly contrary to thofe on the other, they at length arrived at the head of the river Chandiere, which running through Canada, falls into the river St. Lawrence, near Quebec. Their difficulties now were growing to an end, and they foon approached the inhabited parts of Canada; on the 3d of November, a party which they had pufhed forward returned with provifions, and they foon after came to a houfe, being the firft they had beheld for thirty-one days, having fpent that whole time in traverfing an hideous wildernefs, without ever meeting any thing human.

The Canadians received them here with the fame good-will that Montgomery's corps had experienced in the neighbourhood of Montreal; they fupplied them liberally with provifions and neceffaries, and rendered them every other affiftance in their power. Arnold immediately publifhed an addrefs to the people figned by General Wafhington, of the fame nature with that which had been before iffued by Schuyler and Montgomery. They were invited to join with the other colonies in an indiffoluble union. To range themfelves under the ftandard of general liberty. They were informed, that the armament was fent into the province, not to plunder, but to protect and animate them; that they themfelves were enjoined to act, and to confider themfelves, as in the country of their beft friends; they were requefted, therefore, not to defert their habitations, nor fly from their friends; but to provide them with fuch fupplies as their country afforded; and he pledged himfelf for their fafety and fecurity, as well as for an ample compenfation.

The city of Quebec was at this time in a state of great weakness, as well as internal discontent and disorder. The British merchants and inhabitants had been long much disgusted and dissatisfied. Their opposition to the Quebec Act, and the petitions which they had sent to England upon that subject, had been grievously resented by their own government; and from that period, they had, as the discontented said, not only been slighted and treated with indifference; but even regarded with an apparent eye of distrust and suspicion. They complained, that as the great political object in that country, was to attach the native Canadians inviolably to government, so the French noblesse, and civil officers, became, excepting the British military, the only favourites; and these having soon acquired the manners and affectations of all other courtiers and favourites, passed no occasion to insult the English as malcontents, with the violence of their zeal, and the outrageousness of their loyalty. They represented, that these new courtiers industriously brought up questions upon public affairs, and discourses upon government in their company, and then construed that freedom of opinion, which the native English had derived from nature and habit, as well as from present discontent, as proceeding from real ill design and disaffection. There needs not a stronger proof how little they were trusted or regarded, than that when the troops were sent off to Montreal and the Sorel to oppose the rebels, notwithstanding the very alarming state of public affairs, and that the city, together with the large property which they possessed in it, were left exposed without a garrison; yet their application for leave to be embodied as a militia for its defence, so far from being complied with, was not even, as they affirmed, deemed worthy of an answer. How much of this representation was the mere effect of discontent, we cannot undertake to say. It is certain that great heartburnings and animosities prevailed among the English civil subjects and the military power in that government, which the Quebec Act irritated and inflamed to an high degree.

Neither does it appear that any great reliance could be placed at that time upon the French inhabitants for the defence of the city. Many of them were at least wavering, and some worse. As to other matters, there were no troops of any sort in the place, until M'Lean's handful of new raised emigrants arrived from the Sorel. Some marines which the Governor had sent for to Boston, were refused by a naval council of war, from the lateness of the season, and the danger of the navigation. The militia, however, had been lately embodied by the Lieutenant-Governor.

Such was the state of affairs at Quebec, when Nov. 9th. Arnold and his party appeared at Point Levi, opposite the town. The river was fortunately between them, and the boats secured, otherwise it seems highly probable that they would have become masters of the place in the first surprise and confusion. This defect was indeed remedied in a few days by the alacrity of the Canadians, who supplied them with canoes, and they effected their passage in a dark night, notwithstanding the vigilance of the armed vessels and frigates of war in the river. But the critical moment was now passed. The discontented inhabitants, English and Canadians, as soon as danger pressed, united for their common defence. They became seriously alarmed for the immense property which Quebec contained. They desired to be, and were, embodied and armed. The sailors had landed, and were at the batteries to serve the guns, the defendants were considerably superior in number to the assailants, and Arnold had no artillery. In these circumstances, his only hope must have been the defection of the inhabitants; and disappointed in that, nothing remained practicable for him, but intercepting the roads, and cutting off the supplies, until the arrival of Montgomery. He accordingly paraded for some days on the heights near the town, and sent two flags to summon the inhabitants; but they were fired at, and no message admitted; upon which, he at length drew off his detachment into quarters of refreshment.

In the mean time, Montgomery having found plenty of woollen manufactures, and other articles of wear, at Montreal, took that opportunity of new-cloathing his troops, who had suffered excessively from the severity of the climate, the deepness of the roads, and the want of covering suitable to such circumstances. Notwithstanding the flattering appearance of his successes, the situation of that commander was far from being enviable; and indeed was attended with continual and growing difficulties, that nothing less than his own genius could surmount. The difficulty of conducting and governing an army, composed wholly of new soldiers, and these led directly from their civil occupations to the field, even supposing them raised in old countries, and where subordination is the most perfectly established, will be conceived by those persons who are the least conversant in military affairs. But here the troops were composed of men the most unused, and who from principles, habits, and manner of life, were the most averse to every idea of subordination, of any civilized people in the known world; they were to be trained on through numberless wants and distresses, through strange and desart countries, and when arrived at the scene of action, with arms in their hands, in all the wantonness of military parade and novel power, their wants were to be endured, their appetites restrained, and their licentiousness controuled, for fear of alienating the affections of the Canadians, while every appearance of a harsh or strict military discipline was equally to be avoided, under the dread of their own defection. They were besides only enlisted for a certain short term, according to the usual practice of the colonies; and as the time of their discharge now drew near, there was nothing but the name of their leader, and affection to his person, to keep them longer together.

General Carleton arrived at Quebec about the time that Arnold's detachment had retired from its neighbourhood, and immediately took such measures for its defence, as were suitable to that military character which he had long established. His first act was to oblige all those to quit the town with their families, who refused to take up arms in its defence. The garrison, including all orders who did duty, consisted of about 1500 men, a number, supposing them even the best troops, totally unequal to the defence of such extensive works, if an equal weakness had not prevailed on the side of the besiegers. Of these, it could scarcely be said that any were regulars, M'Lean's corps being newly raised, and the only company of the 7th regiment which had escaped being taken, consisting principally of recruits; the rest were composed of the British and French militia, a few marines, and about 450 seamen, belonging to the King's frigates, and to the merchant ships that wintered in the harbour. These last, habituated to the management of great guns, and to prompt manœuvres, were the real strength of the garrison.

Montgomery, having left some troops in Montreal and the forts, and sent detachments into different parts of the province, to encourage the Canadians, as well as to forward supplies of provisions and necessaries, pushed on with as many men as could be spared from these services, and such artillery as he could procure, to join Arnold. Their march was in winter; through bad roads, in a severe climate; beneath the fall of the first snows, and therefore made under great hardships; which, however, they encountered with equal resolution; and arrived with incredible expedition at Quebec.

Dec. 5th. Upon their arrival before the town, Montgomery wrote a letter to the Governor, magnifying his own strength, stating the weakness of the garrison, shewing the impossibility of relief, and recommending an immediate surrender, to avoid the dreadful consequences which must attend a storm, irritated as, he said, his victorious troops were, at the injurious and cruel treatment which they had in various particulars received at his hands. Though the flag that conveyed this letter, as well as every other was fired at, and all communication absolutely forbidden by the Governor, Montgomery found other means to convey a letter of the same nature; but neither threats nor dangers could produce any effect upon the inflexible firmness of the veteran Governor.

It does not appear that Montgomery's forces were very much superior in number or quality, to those, such as they were, who defended the town. His only prospect of success seemed therefore to be founded upon the impression which the parade of his preparations, and the violence of his attacks might make upon the motley garrison, or if those failed, to weary them out by continual motions and false alarms. He accordingly commenced a bombardment, with five small mortars, which continued for some days, and might have been supposed to have answered the former of those intentions, by throwing the garrison into disorder; but the intrepidity of the Governor, seconded by the bravery, indefatigable industry and perseverance, of the chief officers, as well as the activity of the seamen and marines, prevented the expected effect. We must do justice also to the garrison in general, who nobly followed the example, and supported the bravery of their commanders, and endured the incommodities, wants and distresses, incident to so long a siege, joined to a most grievously severe and unremitted duty, with wonderful constancy and resolution.

In a few days Montgomery opened a six-gun battery at about 700 yards distance from the walls; but his metal was too light to produce any considerable effect. In the mean time, the snow lay deep upon the ground, and the severity of the climate was such, that human nature seemed incapable of withstanding its force in the field.

The hardships and fatigues which the Provincial soldiers underwent, both from the season, and the smallness of their number, seemed incredible, and could only be endured from their enthusiastic adherence to their cause, and through the affection or esteem which they bore to their General. This constancy must however fail, if the evils were increased, or too long continued. The time for which many of the soldiers had engaged was also expired, or expiring; and it could not be answered how soon they might insist upon returning home, nor whether such an event would not totally break up the little army. It is said, that the New-York men were too sensible of the climate, and did not shew the vigour or perseverance of those hardy New-Englanders who had traversed the deserts with Arnold.

In these circumstances, Montgomery thought that something

decisive must be immediately done, or that the benefit of his past successes would, in a great degree, be lost to the cause in which he was engaged, and his own renown, which now shone in great lustre, be dimmed, if not obscured. He knew the Americans would consider Quebec as taken from the instant that they heard of his arrival before it. That the higher their expectations were raised, the more grievous the disappointment would be in case of a failure. Their confidence of success was founded upon the high opinion which they held of his courage and ability; to forfeit that opinion, was the worst of all possible consequences. Yet, to attempt the city by storm, with a garrison equal in number to the assailants, and the great natural strength of the upper town to encounter, which is one of those places that are usually called impregnable, seemed an effort truly desperate. But great minds are seldom good calculators of danger; and if the glory in view be great, do not minutely attend to the difficulties which lie in their way to that object. Indeed, the most illustrious military atchievements, in all ages, have owed their success to a noble contempt of common forms, and common calculations. Fortune, in contempt of the pride of man, ever was, and ever will be, the great arbiter in war. Upon the whole, Montgomery, depending much upon fortune, and not a little upon the nature and disposition of the garrison, determined upon a desperate attempt to carry the place by escalade.

Whilst he was making the necessary preparations for this purpose, it is said that the garrison received intelligence of it by some deserters, and that he perceived, by their motions, that they were not only acquainted with the general design, but with the particular mode of carrying it into execution, which they were accordingly pre-

paring with the utmost vigour and order to oppose. This untoward circumstance, rendered a total change in his original dispositions necessary, and it is not impossible, that this disarrangement had a considerable influence on the succeeding events. However that was, early in the morning, on the last day of the year 1775, and under the cover of a violent snow-storm, he proceeded to this arduous attempt. He had disposed of his little army in four divisions, of which two carried on false attacks against the upper town, whilst himself and Arnold conducted two real against opposite parts of the lower. By this means the alarm was general in both towns, and might have disconcerted the most experienced troops: from the side of the river St. Lawrence, along the fortified front, and round to the Bason, every part seemed equally threatened, if not equally in danger.

About five o'clock, Montgomery, at the head of the New York troops, advanced against the lower town, at Aunce de Mere, under Cape Diamond; but from some difficulties which intervened in his approach, the signal for engaging had been given, and the garrison alarmed, before he could reach the place. He however pressed on in a narrow file, upon a scanty path, with a precipice to the river on one side, and an hanging rock over him; seized and passed the first barrier, and accompanied by a few of his bravest officers and men, marched boldly at the head of the detachment to attack the second. This barricade was much stronger than the first. Several cannon were there planted, loaded with grape shot. From these, as well as from a well-directed and supported fire of musquetry, an end was at once put to the hopes of this enterprizing officer, and to the fortune of his party in Canada. The General himself, with his Aid de Camp, some

other officers, and most of those who were near his person, fell upon the spot. The command devolved upon a Mr. Campbell, who immediately retired without any farther effort. Whether he yielded too easily to the first impression, as the Americans asserted, it is impossible for those who are not perfectly acquainted with all the particulars to determine. [7]

In the mean time, Arnold, with a body of those troops who had originally signalized themselves by the memorable expedition under his command into Canada, supported by some New-York artillery, made their attempt on that part of the town called the Saut at Matelot, and having penetrated through St. Roques, they attacked a small but well defended battery, which they carried with considerable loss, after an hour's sharp engagement. They had likewise the fortune upon this occasion to be left without a commander; for Arnold's leg being shattered by a shot, he was necessarily carried off to the camp. His place was, however, well supplied by the goodness of the officers, and the resolution of the men; who being ignorant of Montgomery's misfortune, were so far from being dispirited by their own, that they pushed on with great vigour, and made themselves masters of another barrier. [8]

The garrison now being recovered from their surprize, and their hands cleared in all other quarters, had time to attend to the situation of Arnold's division, and to perceive the opportunity which was offered of cutting them off. Their situation was such, that in attempting a retreat, they must pass for a considerable way within fifty yards of the walls, exposed to the whole fire of the garrison. To render their fate inevitable, a considerable detachment, with several field pieces, issued through a gate which commanded that passage, and attacked them furiously in the rear, whilst they were already fully occupied in every other part, by the troops which now poured upon them from all quarters. In these desperate circumstances, without a possibility of escape, attacked on all sides, and under every disadvantage of ground as well as number, they obstinately defended themselves for three hours, and at length surrendered prisoners of war.

The prisoners were treated with the greatest humanity by General Carleton; a conduct, which the habitual military severity of his temper, rendered the more honourable. All enmity to Montgomery expired with his life, and respect to his private character prevailed over all other considerations; his dead body received every possible mark of distinction from the victors, and was interred in Quebec with all the military honours due to a brave soldier. It appears by comparing different circumstances previous and subsequent to this engagement, that the rebels, in killed, wounded, and prisoners, did not lose fewer than half their number. A letter from Arnold, written soon after, states their remaining force at only 700 men.

Thus fell Richard Montgomery. He was a gentleman of good family in the kingdom of Ireland, served with reputation in the late war, and fell in the prime of life. The excellency of his qualities and disposition had procured him an uncommon share of private affection, as his abilities had of public esteem; and there was probably no man engaged on the same side, and few on either, whose loss would have been so much regretted both in England and America. He is represented as a real and eager lover of liberty; and having married a lady, and purchased an estate in New York, was from thence induced to consider himself as an American. Thus, say his friends, he was led by principle, to quit the sweets of an easy for-

tune, the enjoyment of a loved and philosophical rural life, with the highest domestic felicity, to take an active share in all the miseries and dangers of the present troubles. He had undoubtedly considerable, and probably great, military abilities; and it remains to be lamented, that a man who seemed so well formed to support the interests and glory of his country against her natural foes, should have perished in an unnatural and most unhappy civil contest. In America, he was revered as a martyr to the cause of human nature, and the liberties of mankind. What was more extraordinary, the most powerful speakers in the British parliament displayed their eloquence in praising his virtues and lamenting his fate. A great orator, and veteran fellow soldier of his in the late war, shed abundance of tears, whilst he expatiated on their fast friendship and participation of service in that season of enterprize and glory. Even the minister, extolled his virtues, whilst he condemned the rebellious cause they were employed in, and the fatal effects which their mistaken application had produced.

The Governor and officers acquired great and deserved honour by this defence, and the behaviour of the raw garrison would have done credit to veterans. It afforded an instance, how far the conduct and example of a few brave and experienced officers might operate, in rendering the rawest and worst formed troops respectable. Indeed, the emulation arising between the different orders of men which composed the garrison, probably converted an apparent weakness into a real strength.

The besiegers immediately quitted their camp, and retired about three miles from the city, where they strengthened their quarters in the best manner they were able, being apprehensive of a pursuit and attack from the garrison. The

latter, however, though now superior in number, were unfit for a service of that nature, and their able Governor, with a degree of wisdom and sobriety equal to his intrepidity and firmness, contented himself with the unexpected advantage and security he had gained, without hazarding the fate of the province, and perhaps of America, in any rash enterprize. The city was now completely out of danger, and the great succours which were expected, could not fail to relieve the whole province

By the death of Montgomery, the command of the American army devolved upon Arnold, whose wound rendered him, for the present, unequal to so arduous a task. Their perseverance was, however, astonishing in their circumstances. They had lost besides their General, (in whom it might be said all their hopes and confidence resided) the best of their officers, and the bravest of their fellows, with a part of their small artillery. The hope of assistance was distant, and at best, the arrival of succours must be slow. It was well known that the Canadians, besides being naturally quick and fickle in their resolutions, were peculiarly disposed to be biassed by success, so that their assistance now grew extremely precarious. The severity of a Canada winter, was also far beyond any thing they were acquainted with, and the snow lay above four feet deep upon a level. In these circumstances, it required no small share of activity, as well as address, to keep them in any manner together. Arnold, who had hitherto displayed uncommon talents in his march into Canada, (which may be compared to the greatest things done in that kind) discovered on this occasion the utmost vigour of a determined mind, and a genius full of resources. Defeated and wounded as he was, he put his troops into such a situation as to keep them still formidable. He dispatched an express to Wooster, who was at Montreal, to bring succours, and to assume the command; but as this could not be done immediately, he bore up with the force he had against the difficulties with which he was surrounded. From that time, the siege was for some months converted into a blockade, and Arnold found means effectually to obstruct the arrival of any supplies of provisions or necessaries in the town.

Virginia. Provincial Congress. Powder removed from the magazine at Williamsburg. Consequences thereof. Assembly convened. Magazine rifled. Lord Dunmore retires on board a ship of war. Various transactions between the Governor and the Assembly. Report from the Committee of Enquiry. Refusal of the Governor to go on shore to pass the bills. Assembly will not attend him on board the Fowey, and put an end to their session. Convention of Delegates held. Means used to arm the province. Declaration to justify their proceedings. Lord Dunmore repulsed in his attempt to destroy the town of Hampton. Proclamation for martial law, and the emancipation of the Negroes. Action near the Great Bridge. Connelly taken prisoner, and his scheme for raising the Indians and the Back Settlers, discovered and frustrated. Town of Norfolk reduced to ashes by Lord Dunmore. Transactions in South and North Carolina. General Gage returns to England. Command of the army at Boston devolves upon General Howe. Continental army before Boston enlist for a new term. Town of Falmouth cannonaded, and nearly destroyed. Law passed by the Assembly of Massachusets Bay, for granting letters of marque and reprisal. Articles of confederation proposed by the Continental Congress. Commercial resolution, suspending in certain cases the prohibition with respect to exportation and importation. Declaration in answer to the royal proclamation of the 23d of August.

DURING these proceedings in Canada, a long course of jealousy, distrust, suspicion, and altercation, between the Governor,[10] and the major part of the governed, in the colony of Virginia, finally terminated in open hostility, and a ruinous, intestinal, and predatory war. These unhappy effects proceeded (as is too frequently the case) from a cause apparently unimportant; but as the heat of controversy nourished the quarrel, so mutual distrust and apprehension supplied the place of an object.

The people of that colony, as we have formerly shewn, had been at least as forward as any other, in all the common acts, of sending Delegates to the General Congress, acceding to its decrees, under whatever form or title they were issued, and in the instituting of committees, and the entering into associations, among themselves. They were also among the freeest in expressing their resolutions, and the readiest in shewing their determination, to support, at all risques and events, what they deemed, or termed, the rights of America. But in other respects, the greatest order and quiet was preserved in the province; and notwithstanding the uneasiness excited by the prorogation or dissolution of their assemblies, and the consequent expiration of their militia laws, (which, in a country where a great majority of the people are in a state of slavery, was a circumstance of the most alarming nature, and which might have been attended with the most fatal consequences) yet with these causes of complaint, the people seemed to pay a more than common degree of attention and personal regard, to the Earl of Dunmore, their Governor.

In this state of things, however, the want of a legal assembly, seeming to give some sanction to the holding of a convention, a Provincial Congress was assembled in the month of March, 1775, who immediately (under the cover of an old law of the year 1738, which they said to be still effective) took measures for arraying the militia; but to supply in some degree those defects in that law, to remedy which, as they pretended, all subsequent ones had been passed, they recommended to each county to raise a volunteer company, for the better defence and protection of the country.

This interference in the militia, probably alarmed the Governor, and seems to have been the cause, that rendered the public magazine belonging to the colony in the capital city of Williamsburg, an object of his apprehension. Ap. 20, 1775. However that was, he soon afterwards employed the Captain of an armed vessel, which lay at a few miles distance in James River, with a detachment of marines, to convey the powder, by night, from the magazine on board his ship.

Though this measure was conducted with great privacy, it was by some means discovered the ensuing morning, when the apparent secrecy, and seeming mysteriousness of the act, increased the consternation and alarm among the inhabitants, who immediately assembled with such arms as they had at hand, with an intention of demanding, or, perhaps, obtaining, restitution of the gun-powder. The Mayor and corporation, however, prevented their proceeding to any extremities, whilst they presented an address to the Governor, stating the injury, reclaiming the powder as a matter of right, and shewing the dangers to which they were peculiarly liable from the insurrection of their slaves; a calamity, which had for some time been particularly apprehended, and which the removal of their only means of defence, would at any time have accelerated.

His Lordship acknowledged, that the gun-powder had been removed by his order; said, that as he had heard of an insurrection in a neighbouring county, and did not think it secure in the magazine, he had it conveyed to a place of perfect security; but gave his word, that whenever an insurrection rendered it necessary, it should be immediately returned. He also said, that it had been removed in the night to prevent giving an alarm; expressed great surprize at the people's assembling in arms; and observed, that he could not think it prudent to put powder into their hands in such a situation.

Whatever satisfaction this answer might have afforded to the magistrates, they prevailed on the people to retire quietly to their houses, without any remarkable outrage, that we can learn, having been committed; indeed it appeared, from depositions afterwards taken by order of the assembly, that the officers of the men of war on that station, and particularly the gentleman who might be supposed to have rendered himself obnoxious by removing the powder, appeared publicly in the streets during the time of the greatest commotion, without their receiving the smallest insult. A report being, however, spread in the evening, that detachments from the men of war were upon their march to the city, the people again took to their arms, and continued all night upon the watch, as if in expectation of an attack from an enemy. They also from this time increased their night patroles, and shewed an evident design to protect the magazine from any further attempts.

The whole value of the powder and arms in the magazine, or any purpose to which they were capable of being converted, either in the hands of friends or enemies, seemed very inadequate to the alarm, suspicion, and disturbance, which this measure excited. The

quantity of powder removed amounted only to fifteen half barrels, containing fifty pounds each, of a very ordinary sort, and the remaining stock left behind in the magazine, to about six of the same kind; neither does it appear that the number of serviceable muskets was sufficient to answer any essential purpose, or even to justify apprehension, and the caution of stripping these of their locks, only marked the suspicion from which it proceeded. A considerable quantity of old arms, and common trading guns, were not meddled with. Upon the whole, this act derived its only importance, from time, manner, and circumstance.

The Governor seems to have been exceedingly irritated at the behaviour of the people in these commotions, and perhaps resented too highly, for such times, their assembling in arms, not only without, but with an evident intention to oppose his authority. In this warmth of temper some threats were thrown out, which upon a cooler reflection would probably have been avoided. Among these, a threat of setting up the royal standard, of enfranchizing the negroes, arming them against their masters, and destroying the city, with other expressions of a similar nature and tendency, not only spread a general alarm throughout the colony, but excited a kind of abhorrence of government, and an incurable suspicion of its designs.

In the mean time, several public meetings were held in different counties, in all of which, the measure of seizing and removing the powder, as well as the Governor's threats, were reprobated in the strongest terms. Some of the gentlemen of Hanover, and other of the neighbouring counties, were not, however, satisfied with simple declarations. They assembled in arms to a considerable number, under the conduct of a Mr. Henry,[11]

who was one of the provincial Delegates to the General Congress, and marched towards Williamsburg, with an avowed design, not only to obtain restitution of the gun-powder, but to take such effectual measures for securing the public treasury, as should prevent its experiencing a similar fate with the magazine. A negociation was, however, entered into with the magistrates, when they had arrived within a few miles of the city, in which it was finally settled, that the Receiver-General of the colony's security, for paying the value of the gun-powder, should be accepted as restitution, and that upon the inhabitants engaging for the future, effectually to guard both the treasury and magazine, the insurgents should return to their habitations.

The alarm of this affair, induced Lady Dunmore, with the Governor's family, to retire on board the Fowey man of war in James River, whilst his Lordship, with the assistance of a detachment of marines, converted his palace into a little garrison, fortified it in the best manner he was able, and surrounded it with artillery. A proclamation from the Governor and Council, in which Henry and his followers were charged with rebellious practices, in extorting the value of the powder from the Receiver-General, and the present commotions were attributed to disaffection in the people, and a desire of changing the established form of government, served only to afford more room for altercation, and to increase the heat and discontent. Several county meetings were held, Henry's conduct vindicated and applauded, and resolutions passed, that at the risque of every thing dear, he and his followers should be indemnified from all suffering, loss, and injury, upon that account. The charge of disaffection was peremptorily denied, and those of changing the form of government, and causing the present troubles, retorted. They insisted, that they wanted nothing but to preserve their ancient constitution, and only opposed innovations, and that all the disturbances sprung from the Governor's late conduct.

As there are times when all circumstances seem to conspire, towards the nourishment and increase of political, as well as natural, disorders, so it appeared now in Virginia, every thing tending to one common center of distrust, jealousy, and discontent. The copies of some letters from the Governor to the Minister of the American department, were by some means procured, and public and severe censures passed upon them, as containing not only unfavourable, but unfair and unjust representations, as well of facts, as of the temper and disposition of the colony. Thus one distrust begot another, until all confidence being totally lost on both sides, every false report that was circulated, was believed on either, and served for its time to keep up the public fever.

In this state of commotion and disorder, upon the arrival of dispatches from England, the General Assembly was suddenly and unexpectedly convened by the Governor. The grand motive for this measure, was to procure their approbation and acceptance of the terms, included in Lord North's conciliatory motion, and the parliamentary resolutions founded thereupon. His Lordship, accordingly in his speech, used his utmost address to carry this favourite point; he stated the favourable disposition of parliament, as well as of government, towards the colonies; the moderation, equity, and tenderness, which induced the present advances towards a happy reconciliation; he dwelt upon the justice of their contributing to the common defence, and bearing an equitable proportion of the public burthens,

June 1st.

observed, that as no specific sum was demanded, they had an opportunity of giving a free scope to their justice and liberality, and that whatever they gave, would be a free gift, in the fullest sense of the terms; that they would thus shew their reverence for parliament, and manifest their duty and attachment to the Sovereign; and the kindness with which it would be taken, that they met, on their side, the favourable disposition shewn on the other, towards bringing the present unhappy disputes to a period. He also took pains to convince them, from the proceedings and resolutions of parliament, that a full redress of all their real grievances, would be the immediate consequence of their compliance.

The first act of the assembly, was the appointment of a committee to enquire into the causes of the late disturbances, and particularly to examine the state of the magazine, that necessary measures might be accordingly taken for its replenishment. Though the magazine was the property of the colony, it was in the custody of the Governor, who appointed a keeper, so that an application to him for admittance was necessary. During an altercation which arose upon this subject, and before the order for admittance was obtained, some people of the town and neighbourhood broke into the magazine, and carried off some of the arms; several members of the House of Burgesses, however, used their personal interest and application in getting as many of them as they could, returned. It appeared by the report of the Committee, that they found most of the remainder of the powder buried in the magazine yard, where it had been deposited by the Governor's orders, and suffered considerable damage from the rain; the depriving the muskets of their locks was also now discovered, as well as the nakedness and insufficiency of the

magazine in all respects. Among other matters which served to irritate the people, was the planting of spring-guns in the magazine, (without giving any public notice of such a mode of security) and some effect they had taken at the time of the late depredations.

Whilst the Governor's speech, with the propositions which it recommended, were yet under the consideration of the assembly, and before their address was determined upon, his lordship, with his lady and family, quitted the palace privately, and suddenly, at night, and retired on board the Fowey man of war, which then lay near York town, on the river of the same name. He left a message for the House of Burgesses, acquainting them, that he thought it prudent to retire to a place of safety, as he was fully persuaded, that both himself and his family were in constant danger of falling sacrifices to the blind and unmeasurable fury of the people; that so far from intending to interrupt their sitting, he hoped they would successfully proceed in the great business before them; that he would render the communication between him and the House as easy and safe as possible; and that he thought it would be more agreeable to them to send some of their members to him as occasion should require, than to have the trouble of moving their whole body to a nearer place. He assured them, that he should attend as usual to the duties of his office, and of his good disposition to restore that harmony which had been so unhappily interrupted.

8th.

This message produced a joint address from the Council and House of Burgesses; declaring their unbelief that any persons in that province, could meditate so horrid and atrocious a crime as his lordship apprehended; lamenting that he had not acquainted them with the ground of his uneasiness before he had adopted this measure, as they would have used all possible means to have removed every cause of his disquietude; they feared that his removal from the seat of government would be a means of increasing the uneasiness which unhappily prevailed among the people; declared that they would chearfully concur in any measure which he should propose for the security of himself and his family; observing how impracticable it would be to carry on the business of the session with any degree of propriety and dispatch, whilst he was at such a distance, and so inconveniently situated. They concluded by intreating his return, with his lady and family, to the palace, which would afford great public satisfaction, and be the likeliest means of quieting the minds of the people.

Lord Dunmore returned a written answer, in which he justified his apprehensions of danger, from the public notoriety of the commotions among the people, as well as of the threats and menaces with which they were attended; besides complaints of the general conduct and disposition of the House of Burgesses, he specified several charges against that body; that they had countenanced the violent and disorderly proceedings of the people, particularly with respect to the magazine, which was forced and rifled in the presence of some of their members; that instead of the commitment of those persons who had been guilty of so daring and heinous an offence, they only endeavoured to procure a restitution of the arms. That the House, or its Committee, had ventured upon a step fraught with the most alarming consequences, in appointing guards, without his approbation or consent, under pretence of protecting the magazine, shewing thereby a design of usurping the executive power, and of subverting the constitution.

He observed, that no means could be effectual for affording the security which they proposed to concur in, but, by reinstating him in the full powers of his office, by opening the courts of justice, and restoring the energy of the laws; by disarming all independent companies, or other bodies of men, raised and acting in defiance of legal authority; by obliging the immediate return of the King's arms and stores; and by, what was not less essential than any other matter, their own example, and their endeavours to remove that general delusion which kept the minds of the people in a continual ferment, and thereby to abolish that malice and spirit of persecution, which now operated so dangerously against all those, who from duty and affection to their King and country, opposed the present measures, and who from principle and conviction differed with the multitude in political opinion. That these were the means to afford the security requisite for all parties; and that, for the accomplishment of those ends, together with the great object and necessary business of the session, he should have no objection to their adjourning to the town of York, where he would meet them, and remain till the business was finished.

He concluded by representing, that unless they had a sincere and active desire of seizing the opportunity which was now offered by parliament, of establishing the freedom of their country upon a fixed and known foundation, and of uniting themselves with their fellow-subjects of Great Britain in one common bond of interest and mutual assistance, his return to Williamsburg would be as fruitless to the people, as it might possibly be dangerous to himself; but that if their proceedings manifested that happy disposition, he would return with the greatest joy, and consider it as the most fortunate event of his life, if they gave him an opportunity to be an instrument of promoting their happiness, and

of being a successful mediator between them and the supreme authority.

The mollifying terms of the conclusion, were by no means equal to the removal of the acrimony excited by those severe charges and implications, which were contained in the foregoing parts of this long message. It accordingly produced a reply of an uncommon length, under the form of an address, which was fraught with all the bitterness of recrimination, as well as with defensive arguments, and an examination of facts. The House had now received the report of its Committee relative to the causes of the late disturbances, backed by the depositions of a number of British merchants, who were resident in different and remote parts of the colony, all whose testimony tended to shew the general tranquillity which prevailed previous to the late affair of the powder, and the Governor's declaration relative to the slaves, the latter of which, so far as it was believed, having particularly irritated the people; that notwithstanding, quiet and order were soon every where restored, and still continued; that there was a general acquiescence every where in the determinations of the General and Provincial Congress; but they all concurred in believing, that the people had no design or wish of an independency on Great Britain; and some, that, on the contrary, they had a most eager desire for such a connection, as it stood before the late acts of parliament; they were unanimous in their opinion, that a redress of the grievances complained of, would establish a perfect tranquillity, and produce a reconciliation with the parent state.

To refute the charges or insinuations of disaffection and disloyalty, the House of Burgesses took a retrospective view of the behaviour of the people, and of several transactions in the colony, for some years back; they stated the happinefs which they derived under the conduct of former Governors, as a ftrong contraft to their prefent fituation ; they attributed that happinefs, particularly in a very late inftance, to the difcountenancing of tale-bearers and malicious informers, to a proper examination of every fubject, and the taking of nothing upon truft ; and, finally, to the tranfmitting home a faithful reprefentation of things in the colony. They ftated their former conduct and behaviour with refpect to his Lordship, and obferved, that changes feldom happened without fome fufficient caufe ; that refpect was not to be obtained by force from a free people ; that nothing was fo likely to infure it, as dignity of character, a candid and exemplary conduct. That they did not mean to infinuate his Lordfhip would, defignedly, mifreprefent facts ; but that it was much to be feared, he too eafily gave credit to defigning perfons, who, to the great injury of the community, poffeffed much too large a fhare of his confidence.

They controverted the facts, and examined, with great feverity, the reprefentations and charges contained in thofe two letters to the Earl of Dartmouth, which we have already taken notice of; thefe they reprefented as exceedingly injurious and unjuft, as founded on mifconception, mifinformation, the height of colouring, the misftating, or the affumption of facts, without evidence. They then proceeded to juftify the fteps which had been taken with regard to the militia ; their fuppofed countenance to the acts done concerning the magazine, and the other matters which firft excited, and afterwards inflamed, the controverfy.

14th. The Houfe of Burgeffes alfo prefented their addrefs in anfwer to the Governor's fpeech, in which they entered into a long difcuffion of the propofition contained in the parliamentary refolution, founded upon Lord North's

conciliatory motion. This they combated upon the fame grounds, and with a variety of arguments of the fame nature, that we have formerly ftated ; and they ultimately declared, that as it only changed the form of oppreffion, without leffening its burthen, they could not clofe with its terms. They obferved, however, that thefe were only offered as the fentiments of an individual part of the whole empire ; and for a final determination, they referred the affair to the General Congrefs, before whom they would lay the papers. To them alfo they referred the difcovery of that proper mode of reprefenting their well-founded grievances, which his Lordfhip affured them, would meet with the attention and regard fo juftly due to them. For themfelves, they made the following declaration : " We have exhaufted every mode of application which our invention could fuggeft, as proper and promifing. We have decently remonftrated with parliament ; they have added new injuries to the old. We have wearied our King with fupplications ; he has not deigned to anfwer us. We have appealed to the native honour and juftice of the Britifh nation ; their efforts in our favour have been hitherto ineffectual."

In this ftate of diftruft and ill humour on both fides, every day afforded new ground for bickering, and every incident frefh room for altercation, fo that there was a continued intercourfe, by addreffes, meffages, and anfwers, between the Houfe of Burgeffes and the Fowey. This was a fingular fituation ; an attempt to govern, without choofing, or finding it fafe, to fet a foot on fhore in the country to be governed.

At length, the neceffary bills having paffed the affembly, and the advanced feafon requiring their attendance in their feveral countries, the Council and Burgeffes jointly intreated the Governor's

prefence, to give his affent to them and finifh the feffion. They obferved, that though the bufinefs had been greatly impeded by his abfence from the feat of government, and they had fubmitted to the inconvenience of repeatedly fending their members twelve miles to attend his Excellency on board a fhip of war, they could not but think it highly improper, and too great a departure from the conftitutional and accuftomed mode of tranfacting their bufinefs, to prefent the bills to him at any other place than the capital.

Lord Dunmore in his anfwer was fomewhat rough. He infifted upon his right of calling them to any place in the colony, where the exigence of affairs might render their attendance neceffary. He further obferved, that as he had not been made acquainted with the whole proceedings of the Affembly, he knew of no bills of importance, which, if he were inclined to rifque his perfon again among the people, they had to prefent to him, nor whether they were fuch as he could affent to if they had.

To obviate thefe objections, though it was an unprecedented act, the Affembly fent the bills, as well as other papers which were afterwards demanded, on board the Fowey, for his infpection. The moft interefting of thofe bills, feemingly to all parties, was that for the payment of the forces, who had lately, under his Lordfhip's command, fuffered confiderably, at the fame time that they had done effential fervice to their country, by their bravery and fuccefs in the late Indian war. This bill was objected to by the Governor, for its impofing a tax upon the importation of flaves, and for fome informality in refpect to the emiffion of paper money. The other bills were approved of.

This produced the final addrefs from the Houfe of Burgeffes, in which they intreated his Excellency, that he would meet them the ensuing day at Williamsburg, to pass the bills that were ready; expressed their hopes, that he could not still entertain any groundless fears of personal danger; but declared, that if it was possible he remained under so strange an influence, they pledged their honours, and every thing sacred, for his security. If nothing could prevail, they requested that he would grant a commission for passing such bills as he approved.

Lord Dunmore persisted in the objections he had made to the bill; said, that the well-grounded cause he had for believing his person not safe at Williamsburg, had increased daily. That he therefore could not meet them, as they requested, at the capital; but that he would be ready to receive the House on the following Monday, at his present residence, for the purpose of giving his assent to such acts as he should approve of.

This answer put an end to all public correspondence and business between the Governor and colony. The transferring the Legislative Council and House of Representatives of a great country on board a man of war, was evidently not to be expected. Their danger in such a situation, if on other accounts it were possible they could put themselves into it, was no less than Lord Dunmore's could be on land. It may, however, be supposed, that the Governor's conduct was operated upon by causes, or influenced by motives, with which we are unacquainted.

Upon receiving the foregoing answer, the Burgesses passed resolutions, in which they declared, that the message requiring them to attend the Governor on board a ship of war, was a high breach of their rights and privileges. That the unreasonable delays thrown into their proceedings, and the evasive answers to their sincere and decent addresses, gave them reason to fear that a dangerous attack was meditated against the unhappy people of that colony, and it was therefore their opinion, that they should prepare for the preservation of their property, and their inestimable rights and liberties. And then, strongly professing loyalty to the King, and amity to the mother country, they broke up their session.

Thus, unhappily, was an end put, for the present, to the English government in the colony of Virginia. A convention of delegates was soon appointed to supply the place of the assembly, who having an unlimited confidence reposed in them by the people, became accordingly possessed of an unlimited power in all public affairs. These immediately took in hand the raising and embodying of an armed force, as well as the providing means for its support, and pursued every other measure which could tend to place the colony in a strong state of defence. Whilst they were pursuing these dangerous steps, they published a declaration in justification of their conduct, tracing the measures that led to the present unhappy state of public affairs, setting forth the cause of their meeting, and shewing the necessity of immediately putting the country in a posture of defence, for the protection of their lives, liberties, and properties. They concluded as the assembly had done, with the strongest professions of faith and loyalty, and declared, that as, on the one hand, they were determined at the peril of the extremest hazards, to maintain their just rights and privileges, so on the other, it was their fixed and unalterable resolution, to disband such forces as were raised for the defence of the colony, whenever their dangers were removed, and America restored to its former state of tranquillity and happiness.

Whether Lord Dunmore expected that any extraordinary advantages might be derived from an insurrection of the slaves, or that he imagined there was a much greater number of people in the colony, who were satisfied with the present system of government, than really was the case, (a mistake, and an unfortunate one, which like an epidemical distemper, seems to have spread through all our official departments in America) upon whatever grounds he proceeded, he determined, though he relinquished his government, not to abandon his hopes, nor entirely to lose sight of the country which he had governed. He accordingly, being joined by those friends of government, who had rendered themselves too obnoxious to the people to continue with safety in the country, as well as by a number of runaway negroes, and supported by the frigates of war which were upon the station, endeavoured to establish such a marine force, as would enable him, by means of the noble rivers, which render the most valuable parts of that rich country accessible by water, to be always at hand, and ready to profit, of any favourable occasion that offered.

Upon this, or some similar system, he by degrees equipped and armed a number of vessels of different kinds and sizes, in one of which he constantly resided, never setting his foot on shore but in a hostile manner; the force thus put together, was, however, calculated only for depredation, and never became equal to any essential service. The former, indeed, was in part a matter of necessity, for as the people on shore would not supply those on board with provisions or necessaries, they must either starve, or provide them by force. The Virginians pretend, that while the depredations were confined to those necessary objects, the respect which they bore to the rank and office of their governor, prevented his meeting with any resistance; but their nature was soon changed into open and avowed hostility. Obnoxious persons, they said, were seized and carried on board the ships;

plantations ravaged and deftroyed; the negroes carried off; houfes burnt, and at length lives loft on both fides. In one of thefe expeditions, his Lordfhip deftroyed a number of iron cannon, and carried off fome others, which he fuppofed were provided for the purpofes of rebellion, though the Virginians affert they were fhip guns. Thefe proceedings occafioned the fending of fome detachments of the new-raifed forces to protect the coafts, and from thence enfued, a fmall, mifchievous, predatory war, incapable of affording honour or benefit, and in which, at length, every drop of water, and every neceffary, was purchafed at the price or the rifque of blood.

During this ftate of hoftility, he procured a few foldiers from different parts, with   Oct. 25th. whofe affiftance, an attempt was made to burn a port-town, in an important fituation, called Hampton. It feems the inhabitants had fome previous fufpicion of the defign, for they had funk boats in the entrance of the harbour, and thrown fuch other obftacles in the way, as rendered the approach of the fhips, and confequently a landing, impracticable on the day in which the attack was commenced. The fhips cut a paffage through the boats in the night, and began to cannonade the town furioufly in the morning; but at this critical period, they were relieved from their apprehenfions and danger, by the arrival of a detachment of rifle and minute men, from Williamfburg, who had marched all night to their affiftance. Thefe, joined with the inhabitants, attacked the fhips fo vigoroufly with their fmall arms, that they were obliged precipitately to quit their ftation, with the lofs of fome men, and of a tender which was taken.

In confequence of this repulfe, a proclamation was iffued by the Governor, dated on board the fhip William,   Nov. 7th. off Norfolk, declaring, that as the civil law was at prefent infufficient to prevent and punifh treafon and traitors, martial law fhould take place, and be executed throughout the colony; and requiring all perfons capable of bearing arms to repair to his Majefty's ftandard, or to be confidered as traitors. He alfo declared all indented fervants, negroes, or others, appertaining to rebels, who were able and willing to bear arms, and who joined his Majefty's forces, to be free.

This meafure of emancipating the negroes, excited lefs furprize, and probably had lefs effect in exciting the defired infurrection, from its being fo long threatened and apprehended, than if it had been more immediate and unexpected. It was, however, received with the greateft horror in all the colonies, and has been feverely condemned elfewhere, as tending to loofen the bands of fociety, to deftroy domeftic fecurity, and encourage the moft barbarous of mankind, to the commiffion of the moft horrible crimes, and the moft inhuman cruelties; that it was confounding the innocent with the guilty, and expofing thofe who were the beft friends to government, to the fame lofs of property, danger, and deftruction, with the moft incorrigible rebels. It was faid to eftablifh a precedent of a moft dangerous nature in the new world, by giving a legal fanction to the arraying and embodying of African negroes, to appear in arms againft white men, and to encounter them upon an equal footing in the field; for however founded diftinctions with refpect to colour may appear, when examined by the tefts of nature, reafon, or philofophy, while things continue in their prefent ftate, while commerce, luxury, and avarice, render flavery a principal object in the political fyftem of every European power that poffeffes dominion in America, the idea of a pre-eminence muft always be cherifhed, and confidered as a ne-ceffary policy. This meafure is perhaps liable to be charged with another political fault, which has attended too many others that have been lately adopted with refpect to America, viz. that of violent irritation, without affording any adequate benefit.

The proclamation, however, with Lord Dunmore's prefence, and the encouragement of the fmall marine force he had with him, produced, for the prefent, fome effect in the town of Norfolk, and the adjoining country, where many of the people were well affected to government. He was accordingly joined by fome hundreds both of blacks and whites, and many others, who did not chufe to take an active part, publicly abjured the Congrefs, with all its acts, and all conventions and committees, whatever. It is probable that Lord Dunmore now hoped, that the facility and good difpofition which he experienced here, would have been fo general, as to enable him to raife a confiderable armed force, and thus, perhaps, without any foreign affiftance, to have the glory of reducing one part of the province by the means of the other.

This pleafing hope was interrupted by intelligence, that a party of the rebels were marching towards them with great expedition. To obftruct their defigns, and protect the well-affected, he took poffeffion of a poft called the Great-Bridge, which lay at fome miles diftance from Norfolk, and was a pafs of great confequence, being the only way by which they could approach to that town. Here he conftructed a fort on the Norfolk fide of the bridge, which he furnifhed well with artillery, and rendered as defenfible as the time would admit. Notwithftanding the loyalty of the people in this quarter, which included two fmall counties, it does not appear that his force was at all confiderable, either as to number or quality; he had indeed about 200 regulars, including the grenadiers of the 14th regiment, and a body called the Norfolk volunteers; the rest were a motley mixture of blacks and whites. The enemy, under the command of a Colonel Woodford,[12] fortified themselves also, within less than cannon shot of our people; they had a narrow causeway in their front, which must be passed to come at their works, so that both parties seemed pretty well secured from surprize.

In this state they continued quiet on both sides for some days, until at length a design was formed, of surprizing the rebels in their entrenchments. This was undertaken before day-[13]light. Capt. Fordyce, at the head of his grenadiers, amounting to about sixty, led the attack. They boldly passed the causeway, and marched up to the entrenchments with fixed bayonets, and with a coolness and intrepidity, which first excited the astonishment, and afterwards the praise of their enemies; for they were not only exposed naked to the fire in front, but enfiladed by another part of the works. The brave Captain, with several of his men, fell; the Lieutenant, with others, were taken, and all the survivors of the grenadier company, whether prisoners or not, were wounded.

Dec. 9th.

The fire of the artillery from the fort, enabled our people to retire without pursuit, as well as to carry off many of their dead and wounded. It will excite no great surprize, that the slaves in this engagement, did more prejudice to our own people, than to the enemy. It has been said, that we were led into this unfortunate affair, through the designed false intelligence of a pretended deserter, who was tutored for the purpose: however that may be, it was grievous, that such uncommon bravery should be squandered to no purpose. Capt. Fordyce was interred with every military honour by the victors, who shewed due respect to his fo-

mer merit, as well as to the gallantry which signalized his last moments. The English prisoners were treated with great kindness; the Americans who had joined the king's standard, with equal rigour.

The King's forces retired from the post at the Great-Bridge the ensuing night, without any other loss than a few pieces of cannon, and some trifling stores which they left behind; and as all hopes in this quarter were now at an end, Lord Dunmore thought it necessary to abandon the town and neighbourhood of Norfolk, and retired again with his people on board the ships, which were considerably increased in number, by those which they found in that port. Many of the well-affected, (or Tories, which was the appellation now given to them throughout America) thought it prudent, with their families, to seek the same asylum, whither they also carried the most portable and valuable of their effects. Thus his Lordship formed a considerable fleet, with respect to the number of vessels and tonnage, and these were also crouded with people; but the ships were without force, and contained mouths without hands fit to navigate them. The rebels took possession of Norfolk, and the fleet moved to a greater distance.

During these transactions a scheme had been in agitation, for raising a considerable force at the back of the colonies, particularly in Virginia and the Carolinas, where it was known there were many well affected to the King's government; it was hoped that some of the Indian nations might be induced to become parties in this design; and that thus united, they not only would make such a diversion, as must greatly alarm and distress the rebels, but that they might penetrate so far towards the coasts, as to form a junction with Lord Dunmore. One Connelly, a native of Pensylvania, an[14] active enterprizing man, who seems

to have been well calculated for such an undertaking, was the framer of this design; and his project being approved by Lord Dunmore, he with great difficulty and danger carried on a negociation with the Ohio Indians, and his friends among the back settlers, upon the subject. This having succeeded to his satisfaction, he returned to Lord Dunmore, who sent him with the necessary credentials to Boston, where he received a commission from General Gage, to act as colonel commandant, with assurances of support and assistance, at the time and in the manner appointed. It was intended, that the garrisons which we had at Detroit, and some other of the remote back forts, with their artillery and ammunition, should be subservient to this design, and the adventurer expected to draw some assistance, at least, of volunteers and officers, from the nearest parts of Canada. He was to grant all commissions to the officers, and to have the supreme direction in every thing of the new forces, and as soon as they were in sufficient condition, he was to penetrate through Virginia in such a manner, as to meet Lord Dunmore, at a given time in the month of April, in the vicinity of Alexandria, upon the river Potowmac, who was to bring such a naval force, and other assistance, as was deemed necessary for the purpose. It was also a part, and not the least comprehensive of this plan, to cut off the communication between the northern and southern colonies.

Thus far, affairs seemed to look well with our adventurer; but on his road through Maryland to the scene of action, and when he was so far advanced that the worst seemed nearly over, the vigilance, or suspicious temper of one of the committees, unfortunately frustrated all his hopes. Being taken up on suspicion, with two of his associates who travelled along with him, his papers betrayed every thing; among these was the general scheme of the design, a letter from Lord Dunmore to one of the Indian chiefs, with such other authentic vouchers, as left nothing to be doubted. The papers were published by the Congress, and the undertakers sent to prison.

As it does not appear that the loyalists were very lenient to those who differed with them in political opinions, during the short time of their superiority in the country adjoining to Norfolk, so now, upon the turn of affairs, the obtaining a plausible shew of justice, under the colour of retaliation, afforded such a favourable opportunity for the practice of severity, and the gratification of private pique, and natural malignity, on the other side, as is never known to be neglected by any party in similar circumstances. For though many had taken shelter on board the ships, a much greater number remained behind, some being willing to hazard some danger, rather than abandon their property; others hoping that their conduct, from its moderation, would bear enquiry; and the majority, from their having no prospect of subsistance if they quitted home, and an expectation that their obscurity would save them from notice. To conclude, such charges of oppression, injustice, and cruelty, were made on both sides, as are usually done in such cases.

In the mean time, the people in the fleet were distressed for provisions and necessaries of every sort, and were cut off from every kind of succour from the shore. This occasioned constant bickering between the armed ships and boats, and the forces that were stationed on the coast, particularly at Norfolk. At length, upon the arrival of the Liverpool man of war from England, a flag was sent on shore, to put the question, whether they would supply his Majesty's ships with provisions, which being an-

swered in the negative, and the ships in the harbour being continually annoyed by the fire of the rebels, from that part of the town which lay next the water, it was determined to dislodge them by destroying it. Previous notice being accordingly given to the inhabitants, that they might remove from the danger, the first day of the new year was signalized by the attack, when a violent cannonade, from the Liverpool frigate, two sloops of war, and the Governor's armed ship the Dunmore, seconded by parties of the sailors and marines, who landed and set fire to the nearest houses, soon produced the desired effect, and the whole town was reduced to ashes.

It appears from a gazette published in the Governor's ship, (who had removed the printing press and materials thither from Norfolk) that it was only intended to destroy that part of the town which was next the water; but that the rebels compleated the destruction, by setting fire to the back and remote streets, which, as the wind was in their favour, would have otherwise been safe from the fury of the flames. It is not, however, easy to prescribe limits to the progress of a fire in such, or indeed in any circumstances. A few of those who landed, as well as of the rebels, were killed and wounded.

Such was the fate of the unfortunate town of Norfolk, the most considerable for commerce in the colony, and so growing and flourishing before these unhappy troubles, that in the two years from 1773 to 1775, the rents of the houses increased from 8000 to 10000 pounds a year. The whole loss is estimated at above 300,000l. However just the cause, or urgent the necessity, which induced this measure, it was undoubtedly a grievous and odious task to a governor, to be himself a principal actor, in burning and destroying the best town in his government. The rebels, after this transaction,

to cut off every resource from the ships, and partly perhaps to punish the well-affected, burnt and destroyed the houses and plantations within reach of the water, and obliged the people to remove, with their cattle, provisions, and portable effects, farther into the country.

Nor was the situation of other governors in America, much more eligible than that of Lord Dunmore. In South-Carolina, Lord [15] William Campbell, having, as they said, entered into a negociation with the Indians, for coming in to the support of government in that province, and having also succeeded in exciting a number of those back settlers, whom we have heretofore seen distinguished in the Carolinas, under the title of Regulators, to espouse the same cause, the discovery of these measures, before they were sufficiently ripe for execution, occasioned such a ferment among the people, that he thought it necessary to retire from Charles-Town on board a ship of war in the river, from whence he returned no more to the seat of his government. In the mean time a Mr. Drayton, who was judge of the [16] superior court, and one of the most leading men in the colony, marched with a strong armed force to the back settlements, where a treaty was concluded between him and the leaders of the Regulators, in which the differences between them were attributed to misinformation, a misunderstanding of each others views and designs, and a tenderness of conscience on the side of the latter, which prevented their signing the associations, or pursuing any measures against government; but as they now engaged, neither by word nor act to impede or contravene such proceedings as should be adopted and pursued by the province in general, nor to give any information, aid, or assistance, to such British troops as should at any time arrive in it, so they were to be entirely free in their conduct otherwise, to enjoy a safe neutrality, and to suffer no molestation, for their not taking an active part in the present troubles.

The government of the province was lodged in a council of safety consisting of 13 persons, with the occasional assistance of a committee of ninety-nine. As they had intelligence that an armament was preparing in England, which was particularly intended against it, no means were left untried for its defence, in disciplining the forces, procuring arms and gun-powder, and particularly in fortifying and securing Charles-Town.

Similar measures were pursued in North-Carolina, (with the difference that Governor Martin was[17] more active and vigorous in his proceedings) but was attended with as little success. The Provincial Congress, Committees, and Governor were in a continued state of the most violent warfare. Upon a number of charges, particularly of fomenting a civil war, and exciting an insurrection among the negroes, he was declared an enemy to America in general, and to that colony in particular, and all persons forbidden from holding any communication with him. These declarations he answered with a proclamation of uncommon length, which the Provincial Congress resolved to be a false, scandalous, scurrilous, malicious, and seditious libel, and ordered to be burnt by the hands of the common hangman.

As the Governor expected by means of the back settlers, as well as of the Scotch inhabitants and highland emigrants, who were numerous in the province, to be able to raise a considerable force, he took pains to fortify and arm his palace at Newbern, that it might answer the double purpose of a garrison and magazine. Before this could be effected, the moving of some cannon excited such a commotion among the people, that he found it necessary to abandon the palace, and retire on board a sloop of war in Cape Fear river. The people upon this occasion, discovered powder, shot, ball, and various military stores and implements, which had been buried in the palace garden and yard; this served to inflame them exceedingly, every man considering it as if it had been a plot against himself in particular.

In other respects, the province had followed the example of their neighbours in South-Carolina, by establishing a council and committees of safety, with other substitutes for a regular and permanent government. They also pursued the same methods of providing for defence, of raising, arming and supporting forces, and of training the militia, and shewed equal vigour and eagerness in all their proceedings. The Provincial Congress published an address to the inhabitants of the British empire, of the same nature with those we have formerly seen to the people of Great-Britain and Ireland, containing the same professions of loyalty and affection, and declaring the same earnest desire of a reconciliation.

General Gage having returned in the beginning of October to England, the command in chief of the army at Boston, devolved upon General Howe, who soon after issued a proclamation, by which, such of the inhabitants as attempted to quit the town without licence, were condemned to military execution, if detected and taken, and if they escaped, to be proceeded against as traitors, by the forfeiture of their effects. By another, such as obtained permission to quit the town, were restrained by severe penalties, from carrying more than a small specified sum of money with them. He also enjoined the signing and entering into an association, by which the remaining inhabitants offered their persons for the defence of the town, and such of them as he approved of, were to be armed, formed into companies, and instructed in military exercises and discipline, the remainder being obliged to pay their quotas in money towards the common defence.

As the limited term, for which the soldiers in the army before Boston had enlisted, was nearly expired, a committee from the General Congress, consisting of several of its most respectable members, were sent thither, to take the necessary measures, in conjunction with Gen. Washington, for keeping it from disbanding. This, however, does not seem to have been a work of any great difficulty, the whole army having re-enlisted for a year certain to come. Of all the difficulties which the Americans met, in their attempts towards the establishment of a military force, nothing affected them so grievously, or was found so hard to be remedied, as the want of gun-powder. For though they used[18] the utmost diligence in the collecting and preparing of nitre, and in all the other parts of the manufacture, the resource from their industry in that respect, must necessarily be slow, and with regard to any considerable effect, distant. Nor had they yet opened that commerce, nor entered into those measures with foreign states, which have since procured them a supply of military articles. Indeed the scarcity of powder was so great, that it is said the troops at Bunker's-Hill, had not a single charge left at the end of that short engagement: and it is also said, that the weakness of the army before Boston in that respect, was at one time so great, that nothing but our ignorance of the circumstance, could have saved them from being dispersed and ruined. They, however, left nothing undone to supply this defect, and among other temporary expedients, had contrived to purchase, without notice or suspicion, all the powder upon the coaft of Africa, and plundered the magazine in the ifland of Bermuda, of above 100 barrels, which was carried off (as it was pretended) without the knowledge of the inhabitants.

In the courfe of the depredation, threat, and hoftility, which continually occurred on the fea-coafts, the town of Falmouth, in the northern part of the province of Maffachufett's-Bay, was doomed to experience Oct. 18th. a fhare of thofe calamities, which were afterwards difpenfed in a greater degree to Norfolk in Virginia. Some particular violence or mifbehaviour, relative to the loading of a maft fhip, drew the indignation of the Admiral upon this place, and occafioned an order for its deftruction. The officer who commanded the fhips upon this occafion, gave two hours previous notice to the inhabitants to provide for their fafety, and this time was further enlarged till the next morning, under the cover of a negociation for delivering up their artillery and fmall arms, at the price of faving the town. This, however, they at length refufed to comply with; but had made ufe of the intermediate time in removing fo many of their effects as they could procure carriages for, or as the darknefs and confufion of the night would admit of.

About 9 o'clock in the morning, a canonade was begun, and continued with little intermiffion through the day. Above 3000 fhot, befides bombs and carcaffes, were thrown into the town, and the failors landed to compleat the deftruction, but were repulfed with the lofs of a few men. The principal part of the town, (which lay next the water) confifting of about 130 dwelling houfes, 278 ftores and warehoufes, with a large new church, a new handfome courthoufe, the old town-houfe, with the public library, were reduced to afhes; about 100 of the worft houfes, being favoured by the fitu-

ation and diftance, efcaped deftruction, though not without damage. Though the fettlements in this quarter were new, being moftly eftablifhed fince the laft war, this fmall town was amazingly thriving, being fituated on a fine harbour, and having a very confiderable trade, fo that it was computed to contain about 600 families, though little more than one third of that number of dwelling-houfes.

The deftruction which fell upon Falmouth, probably accelerated in the affembly of Maffachufett's-Bay, the daring meafure (under the pretence of protecting their coafts) of Nov. 13th. paffing an act, for granting letters of marque and reprifal, and the eftablifhment of courts of admiralty, for the trial and condemnation of Britifh fhips. In this law they declared an intention, of only defending the coafts and navigation of America, extending the power of capture only to fuch fhips as fhould be employed in bringing fupplies to the armies employed againft them.

In the courfe of the fummer, articles of confederation and perpetual union, between the feveral colonies which were already affociated, with liberty of admiffion to thofe of Quebec, St. John's, Nova-Scotia, the two Floridas, and Bermudas, containing rules for their general government in peace and war, both with refpect to foreigners and each other, were drawn up by the General Congrefs, and by them tranfmitted to the different colonies, for the infpection and confideration of their refpective affemblies. If thefe articles met with their approbation, they were to empower their delegates in the enfuing general congrefs, to ratify and confirm them; and from that time, the union which they eftablifhed was to continue firm, until, befides a redrefs of their grievances, reparation was made for the loffes fuftained by Bofton, for the burning of Charles-Town, for the ex-

pences of the war, and until the Britifh troops were withdrawn from America. When thofe events took place, the colonies were to return to their former connections and friendfhip with Great-Britain; but on failure thereof, the confederation to be perpetual.

The people, however, were not yet fufficiently irritated, nor their affections and prejudices fufficiently broken, to accede to a confederacy, which, though conditionally framed and worded, yet led to a total feparation from the mother country. For though they took up arms and oppofed government, ftill, it was, in general, under the hope of obtaining thereby a redrefs of grievances; and that being the nearer and more agreeable object, they would not willingly look to any thing further, efpecially to one fo dreadful as a total feparation. It required a longer time in the contemplation of real or fuppofed injuries, and in fpeculations upon future, together with frefh and conftant fources of irritation, to arrive at that habit of vexation and hatred, which was neceffary to break ties of fo long a ftanding, and to familiarize fo new an idea.

A refolution was alfo paffed by the Congrefs at the appearance of autumn, that as America was bleffed with a moft plentiful harveft, and fhould have a great fuperfluity to fpare for other nations, fo, if the late reftraining laws were not repealed, within fix months from the 20th of July, on which they commenced, the cuftom-houfes fhould be every where fhut up, and their ports from thenceforth be open to every ftate in Europe, (which would admit and protect their commerce) free of all duties, and for every kind of commodity, excepting, only, teas, and the merchandize of Great-Britain, and her dependencies. And the more to encourage foreigners to engage in trade with them, they paffed a refolution, that they would, to the utmoft of their power, maintain and support such freedom of commerce for two years certain after its commencement, notwithstanding any reconciliation with Great-Britain, and as much longer as the present obnoxious laws should continue.—They also, immediately, suspended the non-importation agreement, in favour of all ships that should bring gunpowder, nitre, sulphur, good muskets fitted with bayonets, or brass field pieces, such ships being to be loaded in return with the full value of their cargoes.

Dec. 6th. Towards the close of the year, the General Congress published a declaration, in answer to the royal proclamation for suppressing rebellion and sedition, which was issued at St. James's on the 23d of August. In this piece they combated and denied the charges of forgetting their allegiance, of treason, and rebellion, and took particular notice of the dangerous tendency, and indiscriminate nature of a clause, prohibiting under the severest penalties, the carrying on of any correspondence from England, with any persons in rebellion, or the aiding or abetting of such. But not content with critical observations, they conclude with a declaration in the name of the people of the united colonies, That whatever punishment shall be inflicted upon any persons in the power of their enemies, for favouring, aiding, or abetting, the cause of American liberty, should be retaliated in the same kind and the same degree, upon those in their power, who have favoured, aided, or abetted, or should favour, aid, or abet, the system of ministerial oppression.

State of affairs previous to the meeting of parliament. City public transactions. Letter from New-York. Addresses from the guild of merchants in Dublin, to Lord Effingham, and to the protesting peers. Resolutions of the sheriffs and commons of the city of Dublin. Riot of the sailors at Liverpoole. Petition from the American Congress, presented by Mr. Penn. Addresses. State of parties. Ancient animosities revived. Petitions. Newfoundland. Negociations for foreign troops. Great supplies of provisions sent for the support of the army in Boston. Vast expences of that service. Reports circulated for some time before the opening of the session. Conspiracy. Mr. Sayre sent to the Tower.

ADMINISTRATION was now so closely entwined in the present American system, that there was scarcely a possibility of overthrowing the one, without involving the other in its fall; whilst that system was, itself, so firmly supported, that nothing less than some violent and extraordinary convulsion, seemed even capable of shaking it. Yet, notwithstanding this pledge of security, the ministers could not but feel great uneasiness, at the accounts that were daily received from the colonies during the recess of parliament.

For though opposition were not very strong in number, they were as quick in discovering faults and errors, as they were indefatigable in exposing them, and in tracing effects up through the labyrinth of their causes. In truth, affairs had run so counter in America, and every measure had produced an effect so directly contrary to what was proposed or expected, that it was not easy to set a good face upon the matter, either to the parliament, or to the nation.

It is true that many former ministerial incumbrances, had been rubbed off by the calling of a new parliament; all engagements with the old, all promises and mistakes, being thereby at one dash obliterated. But a new and heavy score had already been run up, in the single session which had elapsed of the present parliament. The restraining bills, passed by this, were to have affixed a seal to all the acts of its predecessors. The general distress arising from a general punishment in the colonies, would,

it was hoped, render the majority, the avengers of government, and the punishers of the incorrigible. The conciliatory resolution, independent of every thing else, in its double capacity of converting and dividing, was supposed well adapted to accomplish all that was wanted. To these, however, was added an army, sufficient, as the sanguine thought, to look America into subjection, without the trouble of a blow. And to crown the whole, a naval force, which would in itself be nearly equal to the purpose.

Each of these must become a subject of animadversion, and it would not be easy in some, to ward against the charges of misinformation, ignorance, misconception, or incapacity, which would assuredly attend them. In particular, the questions respecting the war, must be exceedingly embarrassing. Since extremities were determined upon, why was not a sufficient force sent in time, to run down or prevent all opposition? Why has such a course of irritation and threat been carried on for several years, as to give the people warning of their danger, and time to throw themselves into their present strong state of defence? If it now appears that five times the number are scarcely adequate to the service, How could the minister have been so totally ignorant and misinformed, as to suppose that 10,000 men could subdue America without bloodshed?

These and many other questions would be much easier put than answered. To remedy the mischiefs of paft tardinefs, it was determined to carry on the war with a vigour that fhould aftonifh all Europe, and to employ fuch an army in the enfuing campaign, as never before had entered the new world? This, it was faid, befides the grand object, would be the moft effectual means of filencing clamour, and of preventing troublefome, and now ufelefs, enquiries. When once the people were heartily engaged in a war, they would never wait to recollect, much lefs to animadvert on, the original caufes of difpute; but would in their ufual manner, and from their natural difpofition, carry it on with eagernefs, and if gratified now and then with a brilliant ftroke of fuccefs, care nothing about future burthens or confequences. Thus the public opinion would be fecured; they had already fhewn a decided fuperiority in parliament; and the efforts of the minority, ftruggling with the general opinion, and directed againft the apparent national intereft, would only tend to render them every day more feeble; and deprive them of that popularity, which is the foul of oppofition.

The late engagements in America, had, in a certain degree, affected both the national and military pride of the people. Many of thofe, who had not approved of our late conduct with refpect to the colonies, thought it now too late to look back, or to enquire into paft caufes, that government muft be fupported at any rate, that we muft not hefitate at any expence or danger to preferve our dominions, and that whoever was right in the beginning, the American infolence deferved chaftifement at prefent.

Many caufes concurred to prevent the lofs of the American commerce from being yet generally felt. The prodigious remittances in corn during our fcarcity, which we muft do the Americans the juftice to fay, they with great honefty made in difcharge of their debts,

with the much larger than ufual fums which they were enabled to pay, from the advanced prices of oil, tobacco, and other commodities, all together occafioned a prodigious influx of money.

The failing of the flota from Spain, the armament againft Algiers, and the peace between the Ruffians and Turks, occafioned an unufual demand for goods and manufactures of various forts, from Spain, the North of Europe, and Turky, which keeping up a brifk circulation in trade, bufinefs, and money, all contributed to the fame effect.

The war itfelf, the fupplying of an army and navy with provifions and neceffaries of every fort, at fo prodigious a diftance, gave employment and emolument to an infinite number of people, engaged a vaft quantity of fhipping in the tranfport fervice, which would have been otherwife idle, and caufed fuch a buftle of bufinefs, and circulation of cafh, as checked all obfervation of other deficiencies, and ftifled all attention to future confequences. A golden harveft alfo, was not only opened to the view of contractors, but they had already enjoyed fuch a fhare of the fruits, as was fufficient to excite the moft eager rage for its continuance and renewal. It is fcarcely neceffary to mention the numberlefs dealers and gamefters, in lotteries, ftocks, and other money transactions, who profit by all wars. Thefe contributed to keep up the fpirits of the people, and to animate them to this civil contention.

On the other hand, the great bodies of American, African, and Weft-India merchants, with the Weft-Indian planters, had too long forefeen, and already too deeply experienced, the fatal effects of the prefent unhappy conteft. They accordingly, with a majority of the inhabitants of the great trading cities of London and Briftol, ftill wifhed and ftruggled

to have matters reftored to their ancient ftate, and reprobated all the meafures which led to the prefent crifis. No inconfiderable part of the people in other places, though grown lefs loud in their demands for peace, ftill, however, remained diffatisfied with the prefent meafures. In Ireland, though thofe in office, and the principal nobility and gentry declared againft America, by far the majority of the proteftant inhabitants there, who are ftrenuous and declared whigs, ftrongly leaned to the caufe of the colonies.

It muft, however, be acknowledged, that an unufual apathy with refpect to public affairs, feemed to prevail with the people, in general, of this country; of which a ftronger proof needs not to be given, than that which will probably recur to every body's memory, that the accounts of many of the late military actions, as well as of political proceedings of no lefs importance, were received with as much indifference, and canvaffed with as much coolnefs and unconcern, as if they had happened between two nations with whom we were fcarcely connected. We muft except from all thefe obfervations, the people of North Britain, who, almoft to a man, fo far as they could be defcribed or diftinguifhed under any particular denomination, not only applauded, but proffered life and fortune in fupport of the prefent meafures. The fame approbation was alfo given, and affurances made, though with fomewhat lefs earneftnefs and unanimity, by a great number of towns in England. The recruiting fervice, however, which may be confidered as a kind of political barometer with refpect to the fentiments of the loweft orders in cafes of that nature, went on very heavily for the land and fea fervice, both in England and Ireland, though no encouragement was wanting, nor means left untried, for the making of extraordinary levies.

In this state of things, at a meeting of the citizens of London in Common-hall for the election of their annual officers, the Lord-Mayor laid before them his Majesty's answer to their last remonstrance, together with the subsequent letter from the Lord Chamberlain,* giving notice, that the King would not receive, on the throne, any more of their petitions, except in their corporate capacity. Upon this information, they passed a number of resolutions, in one of which they declared, " That whoever advised his Majesty to declare he would not in future receive on the throne any address, remonstrance, and petition, from the Lord-Mayor, Aldermen, and Livery of London, are enemies to the right of the subject to petition the throne, because such advice is calculated to intercept the complaints of the people to their Sovereign, to prevent a redress of grievances, and alienate the minds of Englishmen from the Hanoverian succession."

They then agreed upon another address, remonstrance, and petition, which at least equalled any of the former, in those sentiments, declarations, and charges, which were considered as most obnoxious. Among those expressions that were the least exceptionable, they desire his Majesty to consider, " what " the situation of his people here " must be, who have nothing now " to expect from America, but " Gazettes of blood, and mutual " lists of their slaughtered fellow- " subjects." In other respects, they passed the severest and harshest censures upon the Grand Council and Representative of the nation, as also upon ministers and secret advisers; and they conclude with a prayer for the dissolution of parliament, and a dismission for ever of the present ministers and advisers.

June 24, 1775.

A resolution was passed at the same time, that this address should not be presented, unless it was received sitting on the throne; and the Sheriffs having accordingly waited on the King to know when he would be pleased to receive it, they were informed, that it would be accepted the next day at the levee, to which one of the Sheriffs replied, that the Livery in Common-Hall had resolved that their address should not be presented, unless it was received on the throne, the King immediately put an end to farther application by the following words: " I am " ever ready to receive addresses " and petitions; but I am the " judge where."

In consequence of this failure with respect to the petition, another Common-Hall was held in a few days, when the proceedings of the Sheriffs, and the King's answer, being reported to them, the latter was ordered to be entered in the city books; after which they resolved, That the King is bound to hear the petitions of his people, it being the undoubted right of the subject to be heard, and not a matter of grace and favour.—That the late answer was a direct denial of the right of that court to have their petitions heard.—That such denial renders the right of petitioning the throne, recognized and established by the Revolution, of no effect.—And that the adviser, directly or indirectly, of the refusal, was equally an enemy to the happiness and security of the King, and to the peace and liberties of the people.

They then ordered that their remonstrance, which was refused to be heard on the throne, should be printed in the public papers, and signed by the Town Clerk; that the Sheriffs, attended by the Remembrancer, should wait on the King, and deliver, in their name,

July 4th.

into his hand, a fair copy of their resolutions, both on Midsummer-day, and the present, signed by the Town Clerk; and that they should be also printed in the public papers.—The resolutions were accordingly presented, and received without any answer.

The Common-Hall then passed an instruction to their representatives in parliament, directing that they should move immediately at the next meeting, for an humble address from the Commons to his Majesty, requesting to know who were the advisers of those fatal measures, which had planted popery and arbitrary power in America, and had plunged us into a most unnatural civil war, to the subversion of the fundamental principles of English liberty, the ruin of our most valuable commerce, and the destruction of his Majesty's subjects; also to know who were the advisers of the present measure of refusing petitions; and then to move for an impeachment of the authors and advisers of all those measures, that by bringing them to public justice, evil counsellors might be removed from before the King, his throne established, the rights of the people vindicated, and the whole empire restored to the enjoyment of peace, liberty, and safety.

Notwithstanding this heat of resentment in the Common-Hall, which, with the refusal on the other side, seemed to cut off all communication, in the way of petition, between the city and the throne, a very moderate and temperate application of that nature, under the title of an humble Address and Petition, was, within a few days after, moved for, and carried by a majority, after considerable debate, in the body corporate, consisting in the court of Lord-Mayor, Aldermen, and Common-Council. In this petition, they deplored the grievous distractions in America, lamented those measures whose de-

15th.

structive principles had driven their brethren there to acts of desperation, and strongly asserted their loyalty and affection, notwithstanding those acts, justifying their conduct upon that love of liberty which actuates all the members of the empire; they applied to the humanity of the Sovereign to heal the miseries of his people; hoped that the former conduct of the Americans, their free gifts and ready service, in both of which they sprung far beyond, not only demand, but expectation, would procure a liberal and favourable construction of their present actions, and plead powerfully for granting them every reasonable opportunity of giving as freemen, what they seemed resolutely determined to refuse, under the injunction of laws made independent of their own consent. They concluded with the most pathetic supplications, that the present operations of force might be suspended; and that the Americans, uncontrouled by a restraint incompatible with a free government, might possess an opportunity of tendering such terms of accommodation, as, they did not doubt, would approve them worthy of a distinguished rank among the firmest friends of this country.

This petition was received upon the throne, and his Majesty said in answer, That he was always ready to listen to the dutiful petitions of his subjects, and ever happy to comply with their reasonable requests; but while the constitutional authority of this kingdom was openly resisted by a part of his American subjects, he owed it to the rest of his people, of whose zeal and fidelity he had such constant proofs, to continue, and enforce, those measures by which alone their rights and interests could be asserted and maintained.

Previous to these city transactions, a letter was received from the Committee of New York, addressed to the Lord-Mayor, Alder-

men, and Common-Council, containing, together with a copy of their association, a recital of most of those grievances and complaints, which we have so often been under a necessity of repeating. In this piece they rejected, and commented with severity upon, the terms included in the minister's conciliatory proposition; they declared the willingness of the colonies, in the ancient form of requisition, and upon suitable emergencies, to contribute to the support of the empire; but they must contribute of their voluntary gift as Englishmen; they testified their fidelity and inviolable loyalty, with their affection to this country; stated the great danger at present, of further irritation with respect to the colonies; declared the unanimity of their citizens in defending their rights at all risques; and trust in the most vigorous exertions of the city of London, towards restoring union, mutual confidence, and peace to the whole empire.

The Earl of Effingham, whose [19] military genius had led him when a youth into the army, and had since prompted him to ripen theory into experience wherever real service was to be found, by acting as a volunteer in the war between the Russians and Turks, had since his return, as a peer in parliament, uniformly opposed the whole system of measures pursued against the Americans, and finding, at length, that the regiment in which he served was intended for the American service, thought it inconsistent with his character, and unbecoming of his dignity, to enforce measures with his sword, which he had so utterly condemned in his legislative capacity. He accordingly wrote a letter of resignation to the Secretary at war, in which having declared the chearfulness with which he would sacrifice life and fortune in support of the safety, honour, and dignity, of his Majesty's crown and person,

he observed, that the same principles which had inspired him with these unalterable sentiments of duty and affection to the King, would not suffer him to be instrumental in depriving any part of his people of those liberties, which form the best security for their fidelity and obedience to his government. He expressed the deepest regret, and greatest mortification, at being obliged to quit a profession which had been that of his ancestors for many ages, to the study and practice of which from childhood his past life had been applied, and his future intentionally dedicated; and that as he waved the advantage which the custom of the service entitled him to, the right of selling what he had bought, he intreated, that he might be allowed to retain his rank in the army, that whenever the envy or ambition of foreign powers should require it, he might be enabled to serve his Majesty and his country in that way, in which of all others he thought himself best calculated to do it with effect.

This nobleman's resignation, or rather the cause from which it proceeded, gave great offence, and the request of retaining his rank in the army, we believe, was not complied with. Some officers had not shewn the satisfaction in going upon that service, which they would have done upon any other. A few, indeed, who could not conquer their repugnance to it had quitted. But the majority thought, that where the superior authorities of King and parliament had decided, it was no part of their military duty to enquire into the justice or policy of the quarrel.

This conduct, however, rendered that nobleman extremely popular among those who held similar opinions in regard to the American measures, and who still composed a numerous body in England and Ireland. This soon appeared in the city, where among the resolutions passed in the Common-

Hall on Midsummer-day, and which were afterwards presented to the King, public thanks were ordered to be given to "the Right Honourable the Earl of Effingham, for having, consistently with the principles of a true Englishman, refused to draw that sword, which has been employed to the honour of his country, against the lives and liberties of his fellow-subjects in America." And soon after, a similar address of thanks, but in still fuller terms, was presented to him from the Guild of Merchants in Dublin.

This last body, who in Dublin form a corporation, presented also an address of thanks to the several Peers, who (as they say) "in support of our constitution, and in opposition to a weak and wicked administration, protested against the American Restraining Bills." This address to the Protesting Lords, (to which was affixed the corporation seal) was sent to each separately, and a separate answer accordingly given, all of which appeared at that time in the public papers.

The Sheriffs and Commons of the city of Dublin, had for some time endeavoured to obtain the concurrence of the Lord-Mayor and board of Aldermen, in a petition to the throne, against the measures pursued with respect to the colonies; but were answered by the latter, upon their first application, that the matter was of the *highest importance*, and therefore *inexpedient*. Upon a subsequent occasion, however, they seem to have concurred in the measure, as a committee of six Aldermen, with as many Commoners, and the Recorder, were appointed to draw up a petition and address; this task, after several weeks preparation or delay, being at length accomplished, the petition was arrested in its further progress, by a negative from the Lord-Mayor and Aldermen.

Upon this disappointment, the Sheriffs and Aug. 28.

Commons prefaced the two following resolutions by a declaration, that "Anxious to preserve our reputations, from the odium that must remain to all posterity on the names of those, who in any wise promote the acts now carrying on in America, and feeling the most poignant grief, as well on account of the injured inhabitants of that continent, as on that of our brave countrymen, sent on the unnatural errand of killing their fellow-subjects, have resolved, That it is the duty of every good citizen to exert his utmost abilities to allay the unhappy disputes that at present disturb the British empire.— That whoever would refuse his consent to a dutiful petition to the King, tending to undeceive his Majesty, and from which it could be hoped that the effusion of one drop of subject blood might be prevented, is not a friend to the British Constitution."—Such was at present the state of political opinion among the merchants, and the principal protestant inhabitants of the city of Dublin.

The inability of purchasing, and providing for, Negroes, which the present disputes had occasioned in our West-India islands, together with the loss of the American market for slaves, and the impediments caused by the proclamations of council against the exportation of arms and ammunition, had, all together, nearly extinguished our African trade. This loss was more particularly felt in the port of Liverpoole, which had possessed a much greater part of that commerce than any other in the kingdom. As the Guinea ships now arrived they were laid up, in an uncertainty of their future disposition, whilst their crews looked in vain for other employment. As other branches of commerce were also slackened in a great degree, and that the crews of the Greenland ships, upon their return in July and the beginning of August, were as usual discharged, the number of seamen out of employ in

that town became very great, and according to some accounts amounted to about 3000.

In this situation, the seamen complained that an attempt was made by the merchants to lower their wages, in consequence of which a violent commotion was excited among them, in which they cut the rigging of some ships to pieces, assaulted some houses, and committed other violences. They, however, dispersed again, and all became quiet; but the seizing a number of them, and sending them to prison, re-kindled the flame with greater violence, so that without any extraordinary bias upon the common course of things in such circumstances, it might well have ended in the destruction of that flourishing town. The sailors immediately assembled, procured not only fire-arms, but cannon, and were proceeding to the destruction of the prison, when its safety was purchased by the enlargement of their companions. But their rage was by this time too high, and they were too much inflamed by liquor, to be appeased by reasonable concessions. They not only proceeded to destroy the houses of obnoxious persons, but they at length marched in a body to demolish the Exchange. This danger was foreseen, or probably announced by themselves, a considerable time before the attempt, so that the Exchange was shut up, barricaded, and well garrisoned by the merchants and townsmen. They, however, made several confused attacks, which continued through the course of a night, and part of Aug. 29th, the ensuing morning; during which, through their drunkenness and disorder, they laid themselves so open to the fire of the defendants, (who were themselves safe under cover) that several of them were killed and wounded. The arrival of a detachment of light-horse, at length put an end to the disorder. It was then apprehended, that this would prove only a prelude to other disorders. But the affair was accidental; and sufficient employment for the seamen was soon found in the King's service.

About this time, Mr. Penn, late Governor, and one of the proprietors of Pensylvania, arrived from thence, with a petition from the General Congress to the King, which he presented through the hands of Lord Dartmouth. During the short time that the fate of this petition hung in suspence, the most sanguine hopes were formed, by those who were earnest for peace, or friends to America, that it would have led to a happy reconciliation; more especially, as it had already transpired, that it contained professions of the greatest loyalty, and was couched in the most moderate and humble terms. But in proportion to the extent of these hopes, was the greatness of the disappointment to those who eagerly wished for so desirable an event, when they found that Mr. Penn was informed by the American minister, that no answer would be given to the petition. The Americans had also laid great stress upon the success of this final application, and are said to have relaxed their operations considerably upon that idea, until they heard the event.

This petition, which was subscribed by all the members of the Congress, teemed with expressions of duty, respect, and loyalty, to the King, and of affection to the parent state. They attribute all the differences and misfortunes which have hitherto taken place, to a pernicious system of government, adopted at the close of the late war, and to the evil designs and conduct of ministers since that time. They declare in one part, That they not only most ardently desire, that the former harmony between the mother country and the colonies may be restored, but that a concord may be established between them upon so firm a basis, as to perpetuate its blessings, un-

interrupted by any future dissentions, to succeeding generations in both countries. And in another, That notwithstanding the sufferings of his Majesty's loyal colonists, during the course of the present controversy, their breasts retain too tender a regard for the kingdom from which they derive their origin, to request such a conciliation, as might in any manner be *inconsistent with her dignity or her welfare*. That, these, related as they are to her, honour and duty, as well as inclination, induce them to support and advance; and the apprehensions, that now oppressed their hearts with unspeakable grief, being once removed, his Majesty will find his faithful subjects on that continent, ready and willing, at all times, as they have ever been, with their *lives and fortunes, to assert and maintain the rights and interests of his Majesty, and of their mother country.*

It may perhaps hereafter be a matter of doubt, when the war and its consequences are much better remembered, than the circumstances that preceded, or the causes that led to it, whether it was possible that such sentiments could really prevail with either of the parties, at the time that so unnatural, and so unhappy a contest took place between them. The particular drift and design of this petition, distinct from its great and general object of a restoration of harmony and peace, will be understood by their own words in the following passage—" With all humility submitting to your Majesty's wise consideration, whether it may not be expedient, for facilitating these important purposes, that your Majesty be pleased to direct some mode by which the united applications of your faithful colonists to the throne, in pursuance of their common-councils, may be improved into a happy and permanent reconciliation; and that in the mean time measures be taken for preventing the further

[20]

destruction of the lives of your Majesty's subjects, and that such statutes as more immediately distress any of your Majesty's colonies be repealed."

Whatever the inward intentions of the parties were, the language was conciliatory, and the request not immoderate. Those who favoured the plan of pacifying by concession, loudly clamoured at the answer of Lord Dartmouth, as calculated to drive the colonies to the last extremities of independence and foreign connection; for this reception, they said, of so dutiful and decent an address, amounted to no less than a renunciation of their allegiance. On the other hand, the friends of the ministry took it in a different point of view. The petition, they allowed, had a decent appearance. But did they formally admit the rights of parliament? Were they not still in arms? and in that situation could their sincerity be relied on? They said, that they only wanted to gain time by a negociation, until they had formed their government, and established their strength in such a manner, as would render all future efforts for their reduction ineffectual. We had already gone far in the expences of a war; we should not now stop short; but reap the benefits to government, which always arise from unsuccessful rebellion. And besides those great objects, of punishing the obnoxious, and providing for our friends, to rivet, without leaving room for a future contest, that unconditional submission upon the Americans, which no treaty or negociation could ever obtain. While on the contrary, if amicable terms were now entered into, all our expence and preparation would be thrown away; we must shrink from the proposals we had made to foreign Princes for hiring their troops, which would degrade us in their eyes, as our tameness in putting up with the insolence of our own people, would in those of all Europe; and all the buſtle we had made would paſs over, without having impreſſed the colonies with a ſenſe of our dignity, or with the terror of our power. Beſides, the nation was prepared by the language of war for the event, and it was not certain that vigorous meaſures, if it ſhould be found neceſſary to reſume them, would be ſo well received as they were in the preſent temper of the nation, whoſe favourable diſpoſition was to be carefully cultivated, and employed in the critical moment.

As the time approached for the meeting of parliament, addreſſes were poured in from different quarters, ſome in violent, others in more temperate language, but all condemning the conduct of the Americans, approving of all the acts of government, and in general, recommending a perſeverance in the ſame ſtrong meaſures, until the colonies were reduced to a thorough obedience, and brought to a full ſenſe both of their errors and duty. In ſeveral of theſe, very intemperate reflections were paſſed upon thoſe gentlemen who had oppoſed adminiſtration in the preſent American meaſures, who were repreſented as factious and deſperate men, and ſtigmatized as being not only encouragers, but in a great degree the authors of the American rebellion. This exceedingly inflamed the leaders of the minority againſt the procurers of thoſe addreſſes; and only ſerved to irritate the ſpirit of oppoſition againſt the miniſters and meaſures which the addreſſes were intended to ſupport.

As all the ancient diſtinctions between Whig and Tory, had of late been unhappily revived, they now appeared in full vigour; and as Mancheſter took the lead in addreſſes, it was ſaid, with great acrimony, that they were the legitimate offspring only of Tory towns, though they ſprung up accidentally from the Tory party in others; while all the odium of encouraging civil war, devaſtation, and bloodſhed, with the atrocious deſign of miſleading government, by giving it partial and falſe ideas of the diſpoſition of the nation in general, was attempted to be thrown upon them. It was ſaid, that diſtraction at home, and diſhonour abroad, were the conſtant effect of the predominance of Tory councils. Theſe reproaches were laughed at on the other ſide, who, ſtrong in the ſanction of authority, turned the tables upon the Whigs, and charged them not only with a cauſeleſs oppoſition, but with diſaffection to government. The writers who more openly attacked the Whigs, as ſuch, and by that name, declared, that they were the perpetual enemies to government. That if they appeared to ſupport it for a time, it was only becauſe they had rendered it ſubſervient to their faction; but that whenever it was put upon an independent and reſpectable bottom, their eternal animoſity againſt it could not be concealed. At this time the preachers, after a long intermiſſion, entered into politics. Some of thoſe diſtinguiſhed by the name of Methodiſts, began to revive the doctrine of paſſive obedience, nearly as it had been aſſerted in the laſt century. By degrees this mode of preaching went higher. On the other hand, ſome clergymen, eſpecially of the Diſſenters, eſpouſed the cauſe of liberty with great fervour.

Thoſe who wiſhed to be conſidered as Whigs, divided amongſt themſelves. They who ſtood with the court, reproached the oppoſition with having abandoned their principles. That true Whigs were the ſtrongeſt ſupporters, not the mean betrayers, of the rights of parliament. That formerly Whigs oppoſed the crown, when it ſet up prerogative in oppoſition to parliament; but modern corrupt and degenerated whiggiſm, maliciouſly and unconſtitutionally oppoſed the crown, becauſe it acted in concurrence with parliament, and in ſupport of its inherent rights. That thoſe whom the oppoſition called Tories (at a time when all toryiſm was loſt in general loyalty, and love of law and liberty) were much more truly deſerving the appellation of Whigs, than they who now proſtituted its name, and diſgraced its principles, by abetting an inſolent and ſlaviſh rebellion, againſt the ſole guardian of freedom and order.

The other party retorted theſe charges with ſcorn. They ſaid, that their adverſaries, the Court Whigs, were ſo fond of their new allies the Tories, that they had perfectly gleaned their opinions and language. They denied toryiſm to exiſt, only becauſe they had become Tories themſelves. They aſſerted, that whiggiſm did not conſiſt in the ſupport of the power of parliament, or of any other power; but of the rights of the people. That as long as parliament protected thoſe rights, ſo long parliament was ſacred. But if parliament ſhould become an inſtrument in invading them, it was no better in any reſpect, and much worſe in ſome, than any other inſtrument of arbitrary power. That the ancient Whigs, like the modern, contended for things, not names. That the Tories are likewiſe now, as well as formerly, true to their principles. They never quarrelled with a parliament of their own party; that is, a parliament ſubſervient to the crown, arbitrary, intolerant, and an enemy to the freedom of mankind. That if parliaments deſtroy the liberty of the ſubject in America, they are overturning its principle every where. They ſaid, that to be burthened by parliament is not law and liberty, as the Tories in the maſk of Whigs have the effrontery to aſſert; but to have the public exigencies judged of, and its contributions aſſeſſed, by a parliament or ſome other aſſembly (the name is immaterial) of its own choice,—

this is law and liberty; and nothing else is so. Such are whig principles; because if they were different, the whig principles could not form a scheme of liberty; but would be just as slavish as any that were ever imputed to the abettors of the rankest despotism.

In this manner, the controversies dividing and subdividing the nation, the public became somewhat less languid towards the meeting of parliament. Petitions met the addresses from various parts of the kingdom; and it was for some time doubtful which way the scale would incline. From the cities of London and Bristol very long representations were presented, dwelling chiefly on the inefficacy of all the late coercive and restrictive measures; the mischiefs which were inevitable to our own trade from the destruction of the American; the advantage which our rival neighbours would derive from our divisions. The danger and shame of employing foreign mercenaries to decide our domestic differences; and the improper manner of carrying on the war by burning of towns, savage invasions, and insurrections of negroes. They state in proof of the disposition of America to reconciliation, the large remittances she had made, the large debts she had voluntarily paid; and particularly the supply of corn from thence, after all export trade from England had ceased; by which means the miseries of actual famine in this country had been prevented. On the whole, they implore the termination of so unfortunate a dispute by pacific methods, and by accommodation, rather than by arms.

The Newfoundland fishery in the present year, did not in any degree answer the expectations which were held out in the preceding session, of the ease with which the great American share of it was immediately transferrible to the people of Great Britain, and the signal advantages which they would from thence derive. For though there was probably some small increase of ships and men both from England and Ireland employed in the fishery, they were not in any manner equal to supplying the deficiency which the late law had occasioned, even supposing that no new obstacles were thrown in their way, and that all other matters had continued in their usual state. But the retaliation, which was practised by the Americans, of cutting off our fisheries from all provisions and supplies from the colonies, (a measure which, however simple and obvious, does not seem to have been apprehended till it was felt) threw the whole business upon the banks and coasts of Newfoundland into the greatest disorder and confusion, and brought distress upon all who were employed by sea or land. To prevent the still more dreadful consequences of famine, a number of ships, instead of being loaded with fish, were necessarily sent off light, to procure flour and provisions wherever they were to be found. Upon the whole, it was computed, that to the value of a full half million sterling was left in the bowels of the deep, and for ever lost to mankind, by the first operation of the Fishery Bill.

Those who were averse to the American measures, considered the calamities which fell on the British fishery as a sort of judgment from heaven, against those who made laws to deprive mankind of the benefits of nature. To the same cause they were ready to attribute a dreadful tempest, the fury of which was chiefly discharged on the shores of Newfoundland. This aweful wreck of nature, was as singular in its circumstances, as fatal in its effects. The sea is said to have risen thirty feet almost instantaneously. Above seven hundred boats with their people perished, and several ships with their crews. Nor was the mischief much less on the land, the waves overpassing all mounds, and sweeping every thing before them. The shores presented a shocking spectacle for some time after, and the fishing nets were hauled up loaded with human bodies.

These circumstances, together with the ill success of the last campaign, and the difficulty of recruiting at home, seemed for a while to cast some damp upon the spirit, which had been raised and kept alive with so much industry for carrying on the American war. But the court was not discouraged. Through all obstacles they proceeded directly to their object. They opened several negociations on the continent of Europe, in order to supply the deficiency at home. The obtaining of such an aid, was upon this occasion a matter of difficulty. The vastness of the distance, and the adventuring to a new world, were terrifying, and rendered the prospect of return doubtful. Germany is now the only country in Europe which is an open market for that sort of traffic. But the sending of its people to such a distance, being liable to be construed as contrary to the constitutions of the empire, might chance to be resented, not only by the head of that body, but perhaps by one of its members. And if the opinions, or likings, of men who were constrained to act merely as machines, were matters at all to be considered, the idea of such a voyage, to an inland people who scarcely knew the sea by report, must have been dreadful and odious in the highest degree.

In these difficulties, a negociation is said to have been entered into with the court of Petersburg for 20,000 Russians. It is believed that this treaty was at one time in considerable forwardness. But the extreme distance of the service, the difficulty of recall, the little probability that many of them would ever return, and, above all, the critical state of public affairs throughout Europe, and particularly in the North, after the moſt ſanguine hopes, prevented its ſucceſs. A long negociation was alſo carried on at the Hague, for the Scotch brigade, which has been for many years in the Dutch ſervice, and always allowed to be recruited from Scotland. No doubt was entertained for a time of ſucceſs in this treaty, and it cauſed great debates in the Aſſembly of the States-General, where the ſimilarity between the preſent ſtruggles of the Americans, and their own original efforts againſt oppreſſion, were deſcribed by ſome of the ſtates in warm colours, and the impropriety of a republic, which had herſelf purchaſed freedom at ſo dear a price, and by ſo long and arduous a ſtruggle, interfering in any manner, in depriving others of their liberties, was placed in the ſtrongeſt point of view, until at length the propoſal was rejected. In Holland, the Engliſh party is always exceedingly powerful. But on this occaſion, thoſe who were the moſt warmly affected to the intereſt of this nation, were ſaid to have been againſt the meaſure of ſending the troops. They declared loudly againſt a war which tended to drive America to the protection of France, as ruinous to the welfare both of England and of Holland; and thought it better by withholding the means of it, to compel the Britiſh miniſtry to pacific courſes. The city of Rotterdam, and ſome other towns, were an exception to this general ſentiment. In the former, the merchants of North Britain have had a long eſtabliſhment and great power, and the opinions prevalent in that part of the united kingdom, muſt have great weight in that commercial city. It is not a pleaſing circumſtance, though perhaps of no conſequence, that is all the countries of Europe, in which public affairs are a ſubject either of writing or converſation, the general voice has

been rather in favour of the Americans. Even Voltaire and Rouſſeau, who never agreed in any thing elſe, are ſaid to hold the ſame opinion upon that ſubject.

Diſappointed in Ruſſia and in Holland, we were thrown back upon Germany, as our only reſource for foreign troops. A ſucceſsful negociation was accordingly opened with the Princes of Heſſe and Brunſwick, and ſome ſmaller ſtates, by which we at length contracted for large bodies of men, the particulars of which we ſhall ſee in their due place. In the mean time, the King thought it neceſſary to ſend five battalions of his electoral troops, to replace the like number of Engliſh, in the important garriſons of Gibraltar and Minorca, thereby to increaſe the force in America with the addition of the latter.

Towards the latter part of the ſeaſon, government went to a vaſt expence, in ſending out proviſions and neceſſaries of all ſorts, for the ſupply and relief of the army in Boſton. As the want of freſh proviſions of every ſort was one of their principal grievances, and had cauſed much ſickneſs amongſt them, the remedy of that evil was an object of principal conſideration. For this purpoſe, much cattle of all kinds were contracted for and ſhipped for America. It is ſaid, that no leſs than 5000 oxen, 14000 of the largeſt and fatteſt ſheep, with a vaſt number of hogs, were purchaſed and ſent out alive. Vegetables of all kinds were alſo bought up in incredible quantities, and new arts were employed in curing them. Ten thouſand butts of ſtrong beer were ſupplied by two brewers.

Five thouſand chaldron of coals [21] were purchaſed in the river, and ſhipped off for Boſton; even the article of faggots was ſent from London. The ſeemingly trifling neceſſaries of vegetables, caſks, and vinegar, amount, in two diſtinct articles, where they are de-

tached from the general comprehenſion of other proviſions, to near 22000l. And though we had but a ſingle regiment of light cavalry at Boſton, the articles of hay, oats, and beans, amounted to nearly as much. The immenſe charge of ſupplying an army at ſuch a diſtance, was now for the firſt time experimentally felt. Beſides the expence of theſe articles we have mentioned, and the charge of flour, corn, and ſalted proviſions, near half a million of money was expended in the purchaſe of coined Spaniſh and Portugal ſpecie, and tranſmitted, for the extraordinary and contingent articles in various branches of military operations, which were confined nearly to a ſingle town. The expence ſwelled in every thing. From the multitude of tranſports employed in the different parts of the ſervice, the price of tonnage was raiſed one-fourth above its uſual rate. As the contracts were very lucrative, the connections of thoſe who had intereſt to obtain them extenſive, and the number of perſons who found employment or benefit by the different ſervices infinite, it is not to be wondered at, that ſuch a concurrence of circumſtances, formed a numerous and zealous party in ſupport of government; and that they ſhould earneſtly wiſh for the continuance of a war, by which they profited ſo much.

It did not ſeem an ill-founded expectation, that theſe liberal ſupplies, beſides reſtoring health and ſpirits to our forces, would have ſilenced the general clamour that had been raiſed, and removed the too juſt complaints that had been made by the army, of the bad and unwholeſome quality of the proviſions with which they had been lately furniſhed. Things, however, turned out very untowardly in this reſpect. Whether it was, that the orders were not iſſued in time, or that delays occurred in the execution, which could neither have been foreſeen or prevented;

however it was, the transports were not ready to proceed on their voyage, until the year was so far advanced as to render it nearly impracticable. By this means they were detained upon our own coasts by contrary winds, or tossed about by tempests, until the greater part of their live cargoes of hogs and sheep, particularly the latter, perished, so that the channel was every where strowed with the floating carcasses of these animals, as they were driven about by the winds and tides. A great part of the vegetables, over fermented and perished.

Nor was the condition of the transports mended when they got clear of our own coasts. They were peculiarly unfortunate as to winds and weather in the mid seas, and as they approached to the place of their destination, the American periodical winds were set in, which blew full in their teeth, and drove them off from the coasts. Thus several of them were blown off to the West-India islands, where they arrived in great distress; others that got entangled with the American coasts, were either taken, or seized in those harbours and creeks where they put in for shelter. The few that arrived at Boston, had beat the seas from three to four months, and being nearly wrecks, their cargoes suffered accordingly. A very inconsiderable portion of the refreshment procured at so vast an expence, and that too in a miserable condition, arrived at the place of its destination.

As the compassion and humanity of this country are always awake to the wretched, and particularly to those who are sufferers in the cause of the public, a subscription was opened towards the latter end of the year, for the relief of the soldiers at Boston, and of the widows and children of those that were slain. This scheme was most liberally supported, and several thousand pounds were subscribed in a little time. A great number, however, withheld their benevolence from this purpose upon principle, who could not have been suspected of doing it upon any other account. Those who considered the measures now pursuing, as unjust and oppressive to America, and ruinous to their country, thought they should participate in the guilt of those crimes, and render themselves answerable for the mischiefs which they foreboded, if they gave encouragement, much less granted rewards, to those who were the immediate actors in carrying them into execution. Many also thought, that such contributions were degrading to the service; but that it was still more derogatory to the honour of a great nation, to admit that any of its servants, much less those who were fighting its battles, should be considered as objects of public charity. Others thought it absurd to add to the vast mass of expences already incurred by the public, and which, if they had been well applied, were, as they said, more than sufficient to have provided the greatest comfort and abundance to the soldiery. Some ships which arrived from Boston, and exhibited the spectacle of maimed and wounded soldiers, with the wives and children of those that were slain, all of whom were in the most extreme degree of misery and wretchedness, did not fail to quicken the humanity of such as were not actuated by the motives we have mentioned. This subscription was, however, considered as a kind of political touchstone, and the degree of attachment to government, was supposed to be measured by the extent of the bounty.

By these and other means, the spirit in favour of the American war was kept up. To discountenance the strong opposition, which it was thought would be made, towards the opening of the session the minds of men were filled with rumours of conspiracies and treasonable correspondences with the rebels in America. The most distinguished noblemen and gentlemen of the minority were directly pointed at. They were charged with having been the incendiaries, who by their dark and wicked practices had kindled up the war. This language sounded in many of the addresses. But the news-papers were industriously filled with it. There it was daily and confidently asserted, that a very great number of letters from the most considerable Peers and members of parliament had been intercepted, and were actually in the hands of government. These they asserted would be laid before the Grand Council of the nation, when the Tower would be speedily filled with persons of rank, and a full harvest of impeachments and punishments succeed. This was carried so far, that it was said a number of the members of both houses, who were described and understood, would not venture to attend their duty in parliament at the meeting.

Such reports, if not perfectly well founded, are cautiously to be encouraged or permitted, as certain inevitable consequences must necessarily follow, which may be productive of much mischief and danger. For when the minds of any people have been long brooding over such subjects, treasons, plots, and conspiracies, will haunt the sleeping and waking dreams of the weak, and exercise the profligate and wicked ingenuity of those, who make use of the public fear and credulity in framing accusations. They may serve even to suggest schemes, which otherwise might not be thought of, to men of an enthusiastic turn and daring character.

At the opening of the session, the report of a conspiracy of a most extraordinary nature, at first alarmed the public fears, though it afterwards became a subject of less serious discussion. It was announced in the Gazette, that a Mr. Sayre, an American born, and then a banker in London, was committed by the Secretary of State to the Tower, for high treason. At first, people connected this account with the former reports; and it was universally supposed, that the treason of Mr. Sayre, consisted in remitting money, and conveying intelligence from parties here to the insurgents in America. When the real story came to be known, it could be scarcely believed, that the offence with which he stood charged, was nothing of this sort. The crime for which he was committed, was a design of seizing the person of his Majesty, at noon-day, in his passage to the House of Peers; of conveying him a prisoner to the Tower, afterwards out of the kingdom, and overturning the whole form of government. The means, indeed, seemed very inadequate to the greatness of the end. An inconsiderable sum of money was to be disposed of in bribing a few Serjeants of the guards, who were also to lay out a part of it in bribing their men, and this handful, in the faces of the great majority of their fellows who were not bribed, were to effect the double and arduous work of seizing the King's person and the Tower at the same time. Nothing seemed prepared for a purpose of this kind; nothing to overcome the military power which would assemble from all parts of the kingdom; to say nothing of the other obvious impediments.

It was said in justification of the commitment on such extraordinary matter, that though there was but one witness to this charge, his testimony was positive. That the folly of a wicked attempt, did not prove that no such attempt could be made. That as the information was officially laid before the Earl of Rochford, (who was then Secretary of State for the southern department) whatever degree of [22] [23]

credit it obtained in his private opinion, he was obliged officially, as the King's person was at all mentioned, and any danger to it implied, to prevent the possibility of such an attempt. It must be admitted, that this justification, supposing the process unexceptionable, seems perfectly good in law; but whether it is equally so in point of policy and discretion, may be doubted. It might have been as advisable, to have examined into the nature of the transaction. and how far it might be supported by further evidence, before so public and decided a step was taken.

In whatever manner the discretion of this proceeding may be thought of, it is certain, that Mr. Sayre was taken in his house, and his papers seized, when being examined before the Secretary of State, and confronted with his accuser, bail was refused for his appearance, and he was committed to close confinement in the Tower. Oct. 23d.

The report of this transaction flew like wild-fire throughout the kingdom, and for a while confirmed all the rumours that had been already spread of treasonable

acts and designs; whilst anxiety for the safety of the King's person, and the indignation and horror excited by so atrocious a design, absorbed all other considerations with respect to public affairs.

In the mean time, the order with respect to Mr. Sayre's confinement, was so strictly complied with, that it was with difficulty, and by particular application, his wife was permitted to see him, while all his other friends were refused that liberty. His confinement, however, lasted only for five days, at the end of which time, an Habeas Corpus being granted for his appearance before the Lord Chief Justice of the King's-Bench, the matter appeared in such a light to that noble Lord, that he not only readily admitted him to bail, but received his own security in the trifling sum of 500l. and that of two sureties in as much, for his appearance to answer for the charge. No prosecution was attempted, and the bail being discharged, he sued Lord Rochford for illegal imprisonment, for which a jury granted him a thousand pounds damages, liable, however, to the future determination on a question of law.

Speech from the throne. Address. Motion for an amendment. Great debates. Amendment rejected, and the original address passed by a great majority. Debates renewed upon receiving the report. Motion for recommitment, withdrawn. Motion for a new amendment, substituted in its place. Amendment rejected, after long debates, and the original address passed. Motion for an amendment to the address in the House of Lords. Great debates. Original address passed. Protest.

SUCH was in general the state of public affairs in England and America, previous to and about the time of the meeting of parliament. In the speech from the throne, after accounting for this early meeting by the situation of America, heavy complaints were made of the misrepresentations of the leaders of sedition in the colo-Oct. 26th, 1775. nies, who having first infused into the minds of the people, a system of opinions repugnant to their true constitutional subordination, had at length commenced hostilities, and usurped the whole powers of government. His Majesty then entered into the difference of the views of those leaders, and of those of the crown and parliament, from whence the former derived their present advantages. The view of the latter was rather to undeceive, than punish. Therefore only small forces were sent, and propositions of a conciliatory nature accompanied the measures taken to enforce authority. The former, whilst they endeavoured to delude with specious professions, had in view nothing but the establishing of an independent empire. That the consequences of the success of each plan were too obvious. The spirit of the British nation was too high, and its resources too numerous, to suffer her tamely to lose what had been acquired with so great toil, nursed with great tenderness, and protected at much expence of blood and treasure. That wisdom, and in the end clemency, required a full exertion of these resources. That the navy had been increased, and the land forces greatly augmented. Foreign succours (though no treaty was then concluded) were held out. The disposition of the Hanover troops in Mahon and Gibraltar was specified. In the end, an assurance of the royal mercy was given, as soon as the deluded multitude should become sensible of their error, and to prevent the inconveniences which might arise from the great distance of their situation, and to remove as soon as possible the calamities which they suffer, authority would be given to certain persons upon the spot, to grant general or particular pardons and indemnities, in such manner, and to such persons, as they should think fit, and to receive the submission of any province or colony which should be disposed to return to its allegiance. It was also observed, that it might be proper to authorise such commissioners, to restore any province or colony, returning to its allegiance, to the free exercise of its trade and commerce, and to the same protection and security as if it had never revolted.

At the conclusion they were informed, that from assurances received, as well as from the general appearances of affairs in Europe, there was no apparent probability that the measures which they might adopt, would be interrupted by disputes w th any foreign power.

The addresses in answer to this speech, which, as usual, were an adoption of the whole, with no other alteration in the terms, but what was necessary to the difference of situation of the makers, produced similar effects with those of the preceding session; long and earnest debates in both houses, and a protest in one. The resemblance was not less perfect in the superior force by which they were carried through.

The minority were little disposed to give way to these addresses in the form in which they were brought in. An amendment to the address in the House of Commons was moved for by Lord John Cavendish, proposing to leave out the whole, except the introductory paragraph, and to substitute in the place a declaration, " That they beheld, with the utmost concern, the disorders and discontents in the colonies, rather increased than diminished by the means that had been used to suppress and allay them; a circumstance alone sufficient to give them just reason to fear, that those means were not originally well considered, or properly adapted to their ends. That, they were satisfied by experience, that the misfortune had, in a great measure, arisen from the want of full and perfect information of the true state and condition of the colonies being laid before parliament; by reason of which, measures injurious and inefficacious had been carried into execution, from whence no salutary end could have been reasonably expected; tending to tarnish the lustre of the British arms, to bring discredit on the wisdom of his Majesty's councils; and to nourish, without hope of end, a most unhappy civil war.

" That, deeply impressed with the melancholy state of public concerns, they would, in the fullest information they could obtain, and with the most mature deliberation they could employ, review the whole of the late proceedings, that they may be enabled to discover, as they will be most willing to apply, the most effectual means of restoring order to the distracted affairs of the British empire, confidence to his Majesty's government, obedience, by a prudent and temperate use of its powers, to the authority of parliament, and satisfaction and happiness to all his people. That, by these means, they trust to avoid any occasion of having recourse to the alarming and dangerous expedient, of calling in foreign forces to the support of his Majesty's authority within his own dominions, and the still more dreadful calamity, of shedding British blood by British arms."

This motion brought on a series of long and most interesting debates, which were conducted with the utmost eagerness, and unceasing energy on both sides, and intermixed with much acrimony and bitterness. In this contest the speech was taken to pieces, and every part of it most severely scrutinized. The ministers were charged with having brought their sovereign into the most disgraceful and unhappy situation of any monarch now living. Their conduct had already wrested the sceptre of America out of his hands. One half of the empire was lost, and the other thrown into a state of anarchy and confusion. After having spread corruption like a deluge through the land, until all public virtue was lost, and the people were inebriated with vice and profligacy, they were then taught, in the paroxysms of their infatuation and madness, to cry out for havoc and war. History could not shew an instance, of such an empire ruined in such a manner. They had lost a greater extent of dominion in the first campaign, of a ruinous civil war, which was intentionally produced by their own acts, than the most celebrated conquerors had ever acquired in so short a space of time.

The speech was said to be composed of a mixture of assumed and false facts, with some general undefined and undisputed axioms, which no body would attempt to controvert. Of the former, that of charging the colonies with aiming at independence, was severely reprehended, as being totally unfounded, being directly contrary to the whole tenor of their conduct, to their most express declarations both by word and by writing, and to what every person of any intelligence knew of their general temper and disposition. But what they never intended, we may drive them to. They will undoubtedly prefer independence to slavery. They will never continue their connection with this country, unless they can be connected with its privileges. The continuance of hostility, with the determined refusal of all security for these privileges, will infallibly bring on separation.

The charge of their making professions of duty, and proposals of reconciliation, only for the insidious purpose of amusing and deceiving, was equally reprobated. It was insisted, that, on the contrary, these had from the beginning, told them honestly, openly, and bravely, without disguise or reserve, and declared to all the world, that they never would submit to be arbitrarily taxed by any body of men whatsoever, in which they were not represented. They did not whisper behind the door, nor mince the matter; they told fairly what they would do, and have done, if they were unhappily urged to the last extremity. And that though the ministers affected not to believe them, it was evident, from the armament which they sent out, that they did; for however incompetent that armament has been to the end, no body could admit a doubt that it was intended

to oppose men in arms, and to compel by force; the incompetence for its purposes proceeding merely from that blind ignorance, and total misconception of American affairs, which had operated upon the ministers in every part of their conduct.

This shameful accusation, they said, was only to cover that wretched conduct, and, if possible, to hide or excuse, the disgrace and failure that had attended all their measures. Was any other part of their policy more commendable, or more successful? Did the cruel and sanguinary laws of the preceding session, answer any of the purposes for which they were proposed? Had they in any degree fulfilled the triumphant predictions, had they kept in countenance the overbearing vaunts of the minister? They have now sunk into the same nothingness with the terrors of that armed force which was to have looked all America into submission. The Americans have faced the one, and they despise the injustice and iniquity of the others.

Yet the ministers cannot pretend that they have entered, or been led, blindfolded into these destructive measures. They have been repeatedly warned, session after session, of the danger in which they were involving themselves, and of the ruin into which they were plunging the nation; the consequences were so truly foretold, the predictions have been so exactly verified, that they seem now rather the effect of some extraordinary inspiration, than of reason founded upon observation, and applied to the nature and relation of things. These warnings they received from those gentlemen in opposition, whom they wish and endeavour to stigmatize, as operated upon only by factious motives, as enemies to their country, and as framers of sedition both here and in America. These are the Cassandra's, who foretold

the destruction which the ministers were bringing upon their country, and who, because they foresaw the danger, are unworthily to be blackened with the imputation of having produced the evils which they foretold.

But the ministers, they said, had other sources of information, and which, in spite of reason and experience, they were still evidently determined to rely upon. These were the false, partial, illiberal representations, of artful, designing, and interested men, who had held public offices in America, and who wanted to increase their own influence, emoluments, and authority, as well as to find the means of gratifying their petty prejudices and resentments, by extending the powers of the crown to the prejudice of the people. Men who became at length so soured by the opposition they met with, and the consequent disappointment in all their schemes, that all their sentiments seem to have been dictated only by malice and revenge.

The disgrace and danger of calling in foreign troops to settle our domestic quarrels, of rendering them the arbiters in a contest with our own people, were strongly insisted upon by the opposition. They said, that this new dignity, of which we were become of late so wonderfully fond, was of a very peculiar nature. That while it was so irritable with respect to our own people, that the mention of an American right or privilege, operated upon it in the most violent degree, it crouched in the most suppliant manner in its commerce with foreigners. It was not difficult to bring examples from history, to shew the danger of calling in foreigners in such circumstances.

The country gentlemen were repeatedly called upon to support the amendment, and not to give their approbation to the dangerous and sanguinary measures proposed in the speech, until they had, at least, confidered the fubject, and had the neceffary information laid before them. They were afked, if they would for ever continue to run blindfolded into every deftructive meafure that was propofed, without once hefitating or reflecting upon the common ruin, in which they were involving themfelves with the nation? Would they ftill follow, without examination or enquiry, thofe leaders who had already deceived and mifled them in every thing, until they had brought us into our prefent moft difaftrous circumftances? Had they yet had time to confider the difficulties attending the fupport of an army of 70,000 men, on the other fide of the Atlantic? Had they calculated how many thoufand tons of fhipping would be neceffary for their conveyance, and for their fupport, or what the expence might amount to, of fupplying them with frefh provifions from Smithfield market, and with vegetables, and all other neceffaries, from London and its neighbourhood? Thefe were matters of ferious confideration. The landtax muft this feffion be rifen to four fhillings, and the moft fanguine imagination can fcarcely hope that it will ever again be lowered, even fuppofing the moft fortunate change of circumftances. Thus are their eftates already mortgaged to one fifth of the value of their clear income; and if this ruinous war is carried on to the extent that is held out, they might expect at its end to find the mortgage doubled.

They were taught to confider, fuppofing, (which was far from being admitted) that we fhould be fuccefsful, how they fhould be repaid the enormous expences which they muft neceffarily incur in profecuting the conflict. They were afked, whether burnt towns, military executions, a total lofs of trade, a change, or annihilation of property, with ruined and depopulated provinces, ftill fmoking under all the calamities of a cruel civil war, would be able to repay fifty, fixty, or a ftill greater number of millions of money, which would probably be loft or expended in the conteft. This firft lofs, great as it might be, was not, however, the worft part of the confequence. Thofe wide and ruined dominions, irritated as the remaining poffeffors ever muft continue, with an immortal abhorrence of our name and nation, could only be kept in fubjugation, by an immenfe ftanding army, and a very confiderable naval force. They demanded whether any gentleman, the leaft informed in the hiftory of mankind, could once imagine, that fuch an eftablifhment would or could be fupported by fuch a people. America, in its priftine ftate of vigour and felicity, when it gloried in the Englifh conftitution, was itfelf a living and unparalleled proof of its excellence, and pointed it out as an honour to human nature and fociety, muft, even in that ftate, have funk beneath the burthen. How will it be then when fhe is thus fallen and debilitated, and when fhe confiders every man employed in that fervice by fea and land, as rivetting on her chains, as her fworn and implacable enemy?

The fleet and army of England, and as fhe has not men fufficient, hofts of foreign mercenaries muft be hired, and compofe her ftanding peace eftablifhment. The confequences of fo enormous an additional power thrown into the hands of the crown, are too obvious to require any comment, and too melancholy to be dwelt upon with pleafure. The Englifh conftitution will inevitably perifh in the fame grave, into which our pride and injuftice had a little before precipitated the liberties of America.

If fuch are the confequences of the moft perfect fuccefs which the minifters can wifh for, by the compleat reduction of the colonies, they afked, in what fituation fhall we be if we fail in the attempt? The moft violent advocates for war, do not even pretend to any certainty of fuccefs. That queftion is acknowledged by all to be problematical; and are the confequences in that event to be totally overlooked? Should we unfortunately be foiled and difgraced in a ruinous conteft with our own people, in a war attended with circumftances of expence, before unheard of in the hiftory of mankind, and unfuppofed in the calculations of politicians; fhould our fleets and armies be wafted and ruined, our treafures exhaufted, our expenditure and taxes increafed, in an inverfe proportion to our lofs of power, dominion, and commerce, whilft a newly-acquired debt was overwhelming the old, and our ancient friends and fellow-fubjects were become our rivals and competitors in every thing that was left, if the poffibility of thefe unhappy events is admitted, is not the prefent a proper time to view them in their utmoft extent, and to ufe every poffible means to prevent their taking place? Is not the fituation in which fuch circumftances would place us with refpect to the reft of Europe, an object of confideration?

Surely no fubjects were ever difcuffed in any affembly, which called more ftrongly for the fulleft and cleareft information, the moft mature deliberation, and for higher wifdom in determining.

Upon the whole, it was contended by oppofition, that either adminiftration had been moft grofsly impofed upon themfelves in every thing relative to the colonies, or had intentionally deceived and mifled parliament, by the fuppreffion of true information, and the advancement of falfe, in order thereby to lead the nation piecemeal, and by ftated progreffes into a war, until they were fo far involved, that there could not be a possibility of receding. From these premises they inferred, that whether our calamities proceeded from their ignorance and incapacity, or from a traiterous defign of impofition, in either cafe, they were no longer fit to be trufted in any public affairs, much lefs with thofe, which they had already involved in fuch ruin, it being totally immaterial in this refpect, what motives influenced their conduct, or from what caufes their faults proceeded.

On the other fide, the veracity of the fpeech in all its parts, was warmly contended for. In particular, the charge againft the Americans of feeking independence, was moft ftrenuoufly fupported. In proof, it was afked, whether the Congrefs had not feized all the powers of government? Whether they had not raifed armies, and taken meafures for paying, cloathing, and fubfifting them? Have they not iffued bills to a great amount upon continental credit? Are they not forming a marine? Are they not waging war in all its forms againft this country, at the very inftant that they hypocritically pretend to owe a conftitutional obedience to her? Are thefe acts of fovereignty and independence, or are they only the dutiful and loyal applications of fubjects for obtaining a redrefs of grievances? It was infifted, that their words correfponded with their actions; that in the intercepted letters and papers, as well as the public writings and declarations of feveral of their leaders, they boaft of the labour and fuccefs with which they are new modelling their government, and talk of their new empire as already eftablifhed. Can any one after this pretend to queftion the tendency of their views?

It was afked, what even the language they held out for the deception of this country amounted to? The Congrefs have declared in general terms that they did not aim at independency. But if we examine their particular claims, and compare them with this general affertion, we fhall find, that the dependence which they would acknowledge, will virtually amount to little more than a nominal obedience to whoever fits on the throne, and very nearly a renunciation of the jurifdiction of the British legiflature.

As to conciliation, every hope of that fort, was faid, to be now at an end. Parliament had already tried every experiment to reclaim the incorrigible difpofition of the Americans, endeavouring, if poffible, to avoid bringing matters to the utmoft extremity. But what has fhe gained by this conduct? her lenity, her reluctance to punifh, was conftrued into weaknefs and fear, and the time which fhe facrificed to forbearance and moderation, was feduloufly applied by the Americans to preparation and war. If the matter in difpute were merely a contention for a revenue, it might be prudent to fufpend that claim till a more favourable feafon; parliament, though fhe could not give up the right of taxation, had already obviated the objections that were made to the exercife of it, by permitting the Americans to tax themfelves; but what return have they made to this indulgence? they have given a new proof of their difobedience and contempt; for though they knew any reafonable fum would be accepted, they would not gratify this country fo far as to contribute a fingle fhilling towards the common exigencies of the ftate.

In a word, it was infifted, that the queftion was no longer confined to any particular exercife of the authority of Great Britain, but extended to the very being of the fovereignty itfelf. That in this ftate, an accommodation was impracticable; and any advance towards it on our fide, except in the line laid down in the fpeech, and accompanied with fuch a military force as would command obedience, would be pernicious as well as difgraceful. It was acknowledged, that it were much to be wifhed, that affairs were now precifely in the fame fituation, that they had been in the year 1763; but matters had taken fuch a turn, and things were fo totally changed fince that time, that it was in vain now to look back; and as to a repeal of the great body of American laws which had been paffed within that period, fuch a meafure would be a virtual furrender of America, to all ufeful or beneficial intents and purpofes whatfoever.

As to any retrofpect into the caufes of thefe troubles, or the manner in which we had been brought into the prefent unhappy fituation, it was not apprehended that fuch an enquiry could anfwer any ufeful purpofe. The prefent object was to remedy, not to inveftigate the evil. It was believed, that no miniftry fince the time of the ftamp act had been entirely free from blame upon the fubject; that probably the fault did not fo much lie in any particular meafures, as in that variable and fluctuating conduct, which had fo remarkably prevailed with refpect to America; that the nature of our government, however, had rendered fuch a conduct in fome degree unavoidable; but the great weight of blame was thrown upon thofe, who not fatisfied with expreffing their difapprobation of particular meafures, had argued both within and without doors, againft the authority of the fupreme legiflature itfelf; and who, from an excefs of zeal in fupport of America, and an apprehenfion that the colonies might be ruled with too heavy a hand, feemed too much to forget the interefts of the mother country.

As to the expediency of adopting the meafures propofed in the fpeech, it was faid, that it did not admit of a queftion. We were now in a fituation, which did not afford a possibility of receding, without shame, ruin, and disgrace. The contest was empire. We must either support and establish our sovereignty, or give up America for ever. The eyes of all Europe were upon them. The future fate of the British Empire, and of ages yet unborn, would depend upon their firmness or indecision. A strong picture was drawn, of the consequences that would attend America's becoming an independent empire; of her interference with us, in our trade, and in our dearest interests, in every quarter of the globe. It was acknowledged, that the reduction of America would be attended with great and numerous difficulties. That it was a contest of the most serious nature; and however successful we might be, that the consequences must be severely felt by the nation. But however aweful the situation, it was the first duty of a great national assembly, not to despair of the republic; and where the interests of a great people were at stake, difficulties must be encountered and overcome, not submitted to.

The difficulties were not, however, greater than we had often surmounted. Let us recollect the strength, the numerous resources, and above all, the high and invincible spirit of the British nation, which, when rouzed, knows no opposition, but rises in proportion to the magnitude of the difficulty and danger. Let us recollect the great, extensive, and successful wars, which this country carried on before America was known; or that late period when we defended this very people from the attacks of the most powerful and warlike nation in Europe; when our armies gave law, and our fleets rode triumphant on every coast. Shall we then be told, that this people of yesterday, whose greatness is the work of our own hands, can resist the powerful efforts of this nation.

As to the danger apprehended from foreign powers, they said, that we were never more unembarrassed in that respect than at present; but that however, it were ridiculous to suppose, that we were to court the approbation; and wait the consent of every state in Europe, before we durst venture to quell or to punish, a commotion or rebellion among our own people. They concluded, that war was at all times an evil, but in many instances, as in this, an inevitable one; that in such cases, regret or complaint could answer no purpose; we were plunged in, and must depend upon our native resources and bravery to carry us through as successfully as they had already so often done upon other occasions.

Amongst the matter brought forth by the replies to some of the foregoing positions, the conciliatory proposition of the preceding session, became of course a subject of discussion. The opposition contended, that taxation, as it had been originally, was still the object of contention; that it was not in any degree changed by what was falsely and ridiculously called the conciliatory proposition; the Americans denied the right and resisted the power of taxation, as unconstitutional; an insidious proposal is held out, solely with regard to the temporary manner of exercising that right; a proposal which, far from giving it up, had been supported as the strongest and most effectual exercise of it, and which was evidently calculated, only to produce dissentions amongst the colonies, without satisfaction to that country, or relief to this. No change is made in the claim, or in the cause of dispute. They reject that also; and the question is still in its original state, without the least change in respect to its nature or essence. They therefore insisted, that it was not fact, that the Americans when constitutionally called upon, had ever refused to contribute a just proportion to the defence of the empire.

The question of rebellion was also agitated; and it was asserted, that the taking up of arms in the defence of just rights, did not, according to the spirit of the British constitution, come within that comprehension. It was also asserted with great confidence, that notwithstanding the mischiefs the Americans had suffered, and the great losses they had sustained, they would still readily lay down their arms, and return with the greatest good-will and emulation to their duty, if candid and unequivocal measures were taken for re-instating them in their former rights. But that this must be done speedily, before the evils had taken too wide an extent, and the animosity and irritation arising from them, had gone beyond a certain pitch.

The boasted lenity of parliament was much rallied. It was asked, whether the Boston port bill, by which, without trial or condemnation, a number of people were stripped of their commercial property, and even deprived of the benefit of their real estates, was an instance of it? Was it to be found in the fishery bill, by which large countries were cut off from the use of the elements, and deprived of the provision which nature had allotted for their sustenance? Or was taking away the charter, and all the rights of a people, without trial or forfeiture, the measure of lenity from which such applause was now sought? Was the indemnity held out to military power lenity. Was it lenity to free soldiers from a trial in the country, where the murders with which they should stand charged, when acting in support of civil and revenue officers, were committed, and forcing their accusers to come to England at the pleasure of a governor.

In the course of these long and warm debates, all the old questions, on the right of taxation, on virtual representation, on the dignity of parliament, the supremacy of the legislature, and on the abfolute neceffity, that a fupreme and uncontroulable power, muft be fomewhere lodged in all governments, were again canvaffed; and the old ground, which had been fo often traced, was fo embellifhed, either by a frefhnefs of colouring, or by changing the pofition, or fituation of the objects, as to give it in feveral parts the appearance of novelty.

The gentleman who had fe-[24] conded the motion for the addrefs, and who had himfelf been a governor of one of the fouthern colonies, having hazarded fomething like a propofal, for encouraging the negroes in that part of America to rife againft their mafters, and for fending fome regiments to fupport and encourage them, in carrying the defign into execution, was moft feverely reprehended from the other fide, and the fcheme totally reprobated, as being too black, horrid, and wicked, to be heard of, much lefs adopted by any civilized people.

Thefe long debates were put an end to, at about half an hour paft four o'clock in the morning, by a divifion upon the latter motion; when the amendment was rejected by a majority of 278, againft 108. The original queftion being then put, the motion for the addrefs was carried without a divifion.

Though the fatiguing bufinefs they had gone through, and the latenefs of their breaking up, would have well excufed the recefs of a day, the forms of the houfe in this inftance prevented it, as they were obliged, that afternoon, to receive the report upon the addrefs, from the committee. This circumftance afforded an opportunity for renewing all the preceding debates, and for bringing up fuch fubjects, as had either been paffed over, or but flightly touched upon before.

To explain this matter it will be neceffary to obferve, that the part of the fpeech which mentioned as a favour the fending of Hanove-

rian troops to Gibraltar and Minorca, as well as the correfponding part of the addrefs, which acknowledged and returned thanks for it in that fenfe, had, befides the party in declared oppofition, given difguft to feveral of thofe gentlemen, who call themfelves independent; a diftinction, which is well known, to include a numerous and powerful body in that houfe. The gentlemen under that appellation, who had long been diftinguifhed in the late reigns for the fteadinefs of their oppofition to court meafures, have for feveral years paft taken the contrary fide, and been as remarkable, from an uniform fupport of adminiftration, in almoft all cafes. In American affairs particularly, they have always been among the foremoft, in propofing or fupporting the moft coercive meafures.

It is fo well known, as fcarcely to require mention, that an averfion to continental connections, with fomething bordering upon an antipathy, to the employing of foreign troops in any cafe whatfoever, had formerly been one of the moft diftinguifhed tenets, in the political creed of the party which we have defcribed; and whatever revolutions other parts of their doctrine may fince have undergone, this article feems to have been preferved tolerably pure and inviolate. Upon this occafion, however, it fhewed its efficacy; for fome of thefe gentlemen were fo diffatisfied, that though they warmly approved of all the other parts of the addrefs, they, upon that account only, went away without giving their votes. Others who continued in the houfe would not, however, give their votes, until they had received what they underftood to be an affurance, that full fatisfaction would be afterwards given upon that fubject.

In this, however, they found themfelves totally difappointed, no difpofition at all of the fort appearing in the minifter. Whether they

confidered themfelves as deceived or not, with refpect to the implied condition on which many of them had fupported the addrefs in the preceding debate, it is probable, that they thought themfelves much flighted in not having a greater deference paid to their opinion and principles, and it is not to be doubted, that the meafure itfelf appeared to them as exceedingly illegal and dangerous. By this means, when the report came to be received, the minifter found, to his furprife, the addrefs unexpectedly attacked and oppofed from all quarters; thofe who excepted only to that particular part, being thrown into one common mafs of oppofition, with thofe who equally condemned it in all its principles.

It was infifted upon in the moft peremptory terms, that the meafure was illegal and unconftitutional in the higheft degree; that it was directly repugnant to, and fubverfive of the principles, of the bill of rights; that it would eftablifh a precedent of a moft alarming and dangerous tendency, as it recognized a right in the crown to introduce foreigners into the Britifh dominions, and to raife armies without the confent of parliament; that it was ftill rendered the more alarming, and required the more immediate reprobation, from its being wanton and unneceffary in point of policy, and from its being fo ftrenuoufly defended by the minifters, both of which afforded too much room for apprehenfion; that its oftenfible purpofes covered others of a very different nature.

On the fide of adminiftration, the exceptionable claufe in the addrefs was defended, as being only a compliment; as returning thanks only for the good intentions from which it originated, without including any approbation of the meafure itfelf; that decency abfolutely required the firft, though they fhould hereafter condemn the other. The measure itself was vindicated on the plea of necessity, on the ill consequences that might have proceeded from delay; on the ground of precedent, particularly that of the Dutch troops in the year 1745; its being thoroughly legal and constitutional, was also strongly contended for; and the crown lawyers endeavoured to restrain the construction of the bill of rights, by shewing that its operation extended no farther than this island.

In the mean time, the minister was repeatedly called upon from different parts of the house, and by many of his old and warm friends, as well as by the real opposition, to give an assurance, that if the address were permitted to pass in its present form, he would, on some future day to be appointed, bring the legality of the measure under the consideration of the house. The minister was, however, at that time absolutely inflexible on that point. He perhaps considered this peevishness in his own party, as deserving rather of reprehension than indulgence. No direct answer could be obtained from him; and at length, when it could be no longer shifted off, he said with an apparent indifference, that the military estimates would soon be laid before the house, which he supposed would afford a fitter opportunity for the discussion of the subject than the present.

However it was, many of the country gentlemen, who usually fell in with the court, did not consider this steadiness as well timed. A motion was made by one of them, and seconded by another, for re-committing the address. The debates which now arose became so general, as by degrees to take in the whole round of American business. Nothing was left untouched. In the course of them it was repeatedly thrown out both by friends and adversaries, that the Hanoverian business was not a

measure of the minister's own; and hints were given that it had been dictated by the same overruling influence, which had often before been charged in other matters, with obliging him to act contrary to his disposition and opinion. Upon this imputation of secret influence, he avowed the measure, and acknowledged he was one of those who advised it; declared that he thought it perfectly justifiable, and was satisfied that it was defensible on every principle both of law and of the constitution.

It being found that the general motion for re-commitment, had a good deal divided the country gentlemen, many of whom had already voted for the address, and were still, as well as those who had not, zealous supporters of its general principles, the gentleman who made, was prevailed upon to withdraw his motion, and another was framed which was confined to the particular ground of objection, that the obnoxious passage should be expunged, and the following words inserted in its place, " we will immediately take into consideration the measure of introducing foreign troops into any part of the dominions of the crown of Great Britain, without the previous consent of parliament." This motion again united the country gentlemen, with those who were averse to the address at large.

The minister at length feeling the affair more serious than he could have apprehended, and dreading to come to a division until the country gentlemen were recalled to their standard, with great address, converted to immediate use, a hint which was thrown out on purpose by one of the law officers. He all at once changed his ground, quitted the high and peremptory tone of authority, said, that though he had advised the measure as believing it right, and though he still continued to think so, yet as other gentlemen, for whom he had ever held the highest

deference, seemed to be of another opinion, he had no objection that the question should be brought in a regular and parliamentary manner before the house, when he would chearfully abide by their determination; and if it was their general sense, that the measure was illegal, or unconstitutional, he should rest the defence on the ground of necessity only, and then its advisers might receive the protection, as was always practised in such cases, of an act of indemnity.

This concession set every thing to rights. The country gentlemen being now satisfied, returned to their usual temper and disposition, and the opposition was again reduced to what was properly so called. In this state of things, the question being put 27th about one o'clock in the morning, the amendment was rejected, and the address in its original state accordingly passed upon a division, by a majority of 176, to 72.

Among several peculiar circumstances which attended the debates of both these days, was the total defection of Gen. Conway from administration upon the first, who after expressing the utmost detestation of that official principle, that persons holding places must implicitly support government in all cases whatsoever, and however contrary to their opinion, he then condemned in the most decisive terms the American war, which he declared to be cruel, unnecessary, and unnatural; calling it in plain terms a butchery of his fellow-subjects, and to which his conscience forbade him to give an assent. He reprobated every idea of conquering America, upon all the grounds of justice, expediency, and practicability. He declared in the most unreserved terms against the right of taxation; and wished to see the declaratory law repealed, though it had been passed under his own auspices when in administration, and though on abstract legal principles he thought it right, and at the time of passing it proper and necessary, rather than it should be employed to colour designs, the most opposite to the intentions publicly declared of those who supported it in parliament; and particularly opposite to the fullest declaration of his own at the time of his moving it.

He, as well as several other gentlemen, repeatedly called upon the minister, to give them some information of the state of affairs in America, that they might know with certainty upon what ground they stood, and were likely hereafter to stand, before they passed a bloody address, which would be a standing record against them, and which, notwithstanding the profusion of sophistical arguments that were now used to palm it upon them, by endeavouring to explain away its substance, and to represent it only as froth and compliment, would not only be found a curb upon, but must in a great degree influence their conduct throughout the session, notwithstanding any information they might hereafter obtain. Some of the country gentlemen likewise, said they had gone with the minister in the preceding session, upon a supposition that he had given them authentic information with regard to America; but now finding by the event that they had been totally deceived, it became absolutely necessary to have a full and clear state of affairs laid before them, prior to their entering into any business upon the subject.

This matter pressed very hard upon, and was extremely vexatious to administration. The accounts from America were at that time far from favourable. It was even doubtful whether we had any thing left there. The giving of any particular information, with the power which the minister now possessed in the house, was indeed easily staved off. But too much was already publicly known from other sources, not to render it difficult to account for the failure of success in many instances, and to guard against the censure which of course attended it. One gentleman in administration acknowledged that there had been mismanagement somewhere; but whether by the parliament, in not granting a sufficient force; by the ministry, in an improper application of the force granted; or by the officers who commanded, in not carrying the designs which were formed into execution, he would not determine. He however seemed to lean upon the latter, by talking of a parliamentary enquiry. He also made an apology for administration, upon the ground of the peculiar situation of a minister in this country, who, notwithstanding any sagacity or prescience he might be endued with, must wait for the opinion of the people, before he could attempt to carry any great design into execution; and that if government had demanded a force of 40 or 50,000 men in the preceding session, parliament, perhaps, might not have granted them. [26]

Another gentleman in high power and office, though not properly a member of administration, acknowledged there were faults somewhere; but afterwards confined them, by saying he did not know whether they were in the sea, or the land department. Some of those who were particularly attached to the minister, charged him, notwithstanding, with want of vigour in the American business; but consoled him with the assurance that it was not yet too late, and recommended an immediate adoption of the most coercive measures. They also condemned severely the inactivity of the preceding campaign; but left the blame at large as to the objects. [27]

The minister pledged himself to proceed with vigour and activity. Acknowledged that he had been deceived in events; but that he had adapted his measures last session to the then state of affairs, not imagining that all America would have armed in the cause. Administration, he said, proceeded upon the information they had received; if other gentlemen were in possession of better, why did they not communicate it? Observed, that if we suffered by the war, America would suffer much more. A great force should be sent out, accompanied with offers of mercy, upon a proper submission. It could not be supposed, that America, without money, without trade, without resources, would continue to prefer a ruinous war with Great Britain, to the blessings of peace, and a happy dependence upon her. He professed, that there were no intentions to oppress America; but on the contrary, to establish the most mild, just, and equitable government there.

The question upon the address, was scarcely less warmly agitated in the house of lords than in that of the commons. As soon as it had been moved for and seconded, the Marquis of Rockingham, after taking a retrospective view of the conduct of different administrations for some years with respect to America, and tracing a long series of what he considered as weak, contradictory, and oppressive measures, through the various stages of their unhappy consequences, unto their final termination in the present upshot of calamity, then proceeded to examine different parts of the speech, which he condemned in the most pointed terms, contending that the measures which

were recommended from the throne, and which it was proposed they should now give a sanction to by an address, bore the most portentous aspect to the British empire, and were big with the most ruinous and fatal consequences. His lordship concluded his speech by moving for an amendment to the address, similar to that which we have reprefented in the other houfe.

The prefent debate was rendered particularly remarkable, by the fudden and unexpected defection of* a noble duke, who had been for fome years at the head of adminiftration, had refigned of his own accord, at a critical period; but who had gone with government ever fince, and was at this time in high office. The line which he immediately took, was ftill more alarming to adminiftration than the act of defection. Befides a decifive condemnation of all their acts for fome time paft with refpect to America, as well as of the meafures now held out by the fpeech, he declared that he had been deceived and mifled upon that fubject; that by the withholding of information, and the mifreprefentation of facts, he had been induced to lend his countenance to meafures which he never approved; among thofe, was that in particular of coercing America by force of arms; an idea the moft diftant from his mind and opinion; but which he was blindly led to give a fupport to from his total ignorance of the true ftate and difpofition of the colonies, and the firm perfwafion held out that matters would never come to an extremity of that nature, that an *appearance* of coercion was all that was requifite to eftablifh a reconciliation, and that the ftronger government appeared, and the better it was fupported, the fooner all difputes would be amicably adjufted.

He declared, that nothing lefs than a total repeal of all the American laws which had been paffed fince the year 1763, could now reftore peace and happinefs, or prevent the moft deftructive and fatal confequences; confequences which could not even be thought of, without feeling the utmoft degree of grief and horror; that nothing could have brought him out in the prefent ill ftate of his health, but the fulleft conviction of his being

right, a knowledge of the critical fituation of his country, and a fenfe of what he owed to his duty and to his confcience; that thefe operated fo ftrongly upon him, that no ftate of indifpofition, if he were even obliged to come in a litter, fhould prevent his attending to exprefs his utmoft difapprobation of the meafures which were now purfuing, as well as of thofe which he underftood from the lords in office, it was intended ftill to purfue. He concluded by a declaration, that if his neareft relations, or deareft friends, were to be affected by this queftion, or that the lofs of fortune, and of every other thing which he moft efteemed, was to be the certain confequence of his prefent conduct, yet the ftrong conviction and compulfion, operating at once upon his mind and confcience, would not permit him to hefitate upon the part which he fhould take.

Such an explicit condemnation of their paft conduct and prefent views, and coming from fuch an authority, feemed at firft view as alarming to adminiftration as it was to the houfe. No body could yet tell, nor even guefs, where the defection might end. It was, however, productive of lefs effect than could have been expected, and confequently attended with none of the danger that was probably apprehended. A right reverend Prelate of great eloquence and ability, who in the preceding feffion, had both fpoken and voted for coercive meafures, took the fame part, and accounted for the change in his fentiments and conduct, upon the fame principles that the noble duke had done—mifinformation, deception, a total failure of all the promifes, and difappointment in all the hopes, held out by adminiftration; but above all, the ruinous confequences of the conteft, and the now evident impracticability of coercion.

A noble lord in adminiftration, and who continued firmly in its [29]

fupport, alfo acknowledged that he with his brethren in office had been greatly deceived, and thereby mifled in their conduct, with refpect to American affairs; from whence it proceeded, that the meafures taken were by no means proportioned to the nature and extent of the fervices which they were expected to perform. All thefe acknowledgements from fo many quarters of the want of real information, or charges of being mifled by falfe, afforded a ftrong ground of argument to the oppofition in fupport of the amendment to the addrefs, which was calculated to gain time for a thorough inveftigation of thefe matters, to prevent their being plunged blindly into all the horrors of a civil war, and from pledging themfelves to fupport the fanguinary meafures propofed in the fpeech, before they were capable of forming any judgment upon their neceffity or expediency. This ground they accordingly difpofed of to the beft advantage, and maintained ftrongly; and though the noble lord we have laft mentioned, attributed thofe miftakes to unforefeen events, and afterwards endeavoured to explain away the entire force of what he had faid, the impreffion it had made, concurring with fo many other teftimonies, was not eafily removed.

The arguments againft the addrefs, and confequently in fupport of the amendment, were neceffarily upon the fame ground in general with thofe in the other houfe—The great hazard of our failing in the attempt to reduce America by force, the little value it would be of if we fucceeded, when conquered, and the total inability of Great Britain to retain, for any length of time, fuch a fpecies of dominion, together with the ruinous confequences that muft attend on, what was called, fo wild and abfurd an attempt, were ftrongly urged, and placed in different points of view; whilft the innumerable advantages we must immediately forego in such a contest, were contrasted with the substantial benefits we should continue to reap from a state of tranquillity, reciprocal good temper, and mutual confidence. A few, who held the highest notions of the supremacy of the legislature, yet condemned in the strongest terms, as an act of absolute insanity, every idea of a war, or of attempting to reduce the Americans to obedience by mere coercion. A young nobleman, who within a few days after obtained a considerable place at court, and who had been remarkable in the preceding session for his violence against the Americans, now distinguished himself by his condemnation in the most pointed terms of the ministry, charging them with having failed in their promises and information, of being misled themselves, or purposely misleading others, and therefore not to be trusted or supported with safety; he had not, however, changed his sentiments with respect to America, but considered matters as totally changed there, through their want of timely vigour, and the season for coercion being now passed. Upon that account therefore, and a total want of dependence on the future conduct of such men, he was for closing with the noble duke's proposal, of repealing all the laws since the year 1763, as the only means now left for restoring the public tranquility.

It was not easy for the lords in administration to ward off all the attacks which were made upon them from such different quarters. The failure and disappointment in many instances in America, were attributed to a number of events, which no sagacity could have foreseen, nor prudence prevented. Such was the defection of New York, which had been overawed, and compelled into measures by the Connecticut insurgents, which the people there would never other-

wise have adopted. Such was the general union of the colonies, particularly of the southern with the northern; a fact of so extraordinary a nature, as must stagger the faith of posterity, and which seems subversive of every principle founded upon reason and experience, and of every inference derived from a knowledge of mankind. It was acknowledged, that administration, had been mistaken and deceived in many particulars; but such must ever be the case, when the source of information lies at so great a distance; they communicated with men, and as such they were liable to err; if they had been to regulate their conduct by mere matters of fact, mistakes would have been scarcely excusable; but from the nature of this business, they were obliged to proceed upon a kind of information, which related more to opinion than to facts, being the temper and disposition of the several colonies; all they could do in this case, was to apply to those who had the best opportunity of being thoroughly informed on the subject; whatever success might attend this method, it was not in the power of humanity to have done better.

It was, however, still to be hoped, that when a sufficient force was sent out to emancipate the friends of government, the well disposed, and the peaceable, and this force accompanied with terms of grace to those who had violated the laws, that the colonies would soon return to their duty, without waiting to experience those calamities, or urging the mother country to those measures of devastation and ruin, which had been so strongly depictured, and so pathetically lamented, on the other side. But however that might be, we were now in a situation which admitted but of one choice of measures. We must either reduce the colonies to submission, or for ever relinquish all power and dominion over them, and all advantage from north America.

A noble lord at the head of a very great department, upon which the power and security of this country principally depend, acknowledged, that a species of deception had been necessarily practised in the preceding session, particularly in respect to the navy, by concealing the extent of the real force which would be necessary for the American service, from an apprehension, that such a demand would have excited a great opposition, and thereby have impeded, if not totally frustrated, the prosecution of those measures which government intended with regard to America. This systematic species of deception, was severely animadverted upon by the lords in opposition, who represented it as a most contemptuous treatment of that house, as misleading parliament and the nation, and trepanning them into a war; and was, they said, an imposition of such a nature as no body could have ventured upon, much less avowed, without the most absolute certainty of impunity for any conduct.

In this debate a noble duke *, who has long been distinguished by his firmness and perseverance in opposition, after some very severe observations upon the conduct of administration, as well as strictures upon the speech ,and the address, took notice, that the public papers had held out threats against some of the members of both houses, in order to stifle the freedom of debate; that he understood he was one of the persons singled out, and meant to be honoured upon this occasion. He now called upon his threatners and accusers; if any such were present, (he would not pretend to say there were) he defied them; he scorned their menaces, and invited them to make good their charges. He did not suppose, he said, that any noble lords in administration would encourage or use such base, futile, and scandalous means to intimidate the members in either house of parliament from doing their duty, even though they had supposed, that so shameful and unjustifiable a scheme could have produced the desired effect.

The noble lord who seconded[32] the address, having spoken with great freedom of a desperate faction, and incendiaries at home, to whom he attributed the rebellion in America, and a similar language being held by some others, who charged all opposition to the measures of administration, to factious and ambitious motives, the matter was most spiritedly taken up by another noble duke, not less distinguished on the same side,[33] than the former whom we have just mentioned. He solemnly declared, that while-ever he sate in that house, he would not endure such language, nor suffer such unconstitutional attempts to check and destroy all freedom of debate, to pass without the severest reprehension which he was capable of bestowing. He called upon the lords who had made those accusations, if they had any grounds to justify them, to bring them forward, or else to confess that they had no authority for what they said or insinuated. If they were silent, the house must conclude they had none, and as such could not permit them to interrupt that freedom and decorum of debate, for which they had at all times been so justly distinguished.

As the point of accusation was relinquished, as well by the silence upon this occasion, as by some specific disavowals in the course of the debates, a noble earl on the[34] same side, said he might now congratulate the public, upon the ministry having pronounced the funeral oration of their addresses. He said, that from the language of those addresses, and the various threats which had been industriously circulated, he came to town with some apprehensions, not for himself, but left the zeal of some friend, for the violated rights of

his suffering fellow-subjects, should have led him into any unguarded expressions, and thereby have enabled some dark designing lawyer, to stab the public freedom through the indiscretion of an individual. He said he did not blame the addressers, who had thus unjustly aspersed the characters of those whose aim was, by steady, just, and temperate counsels, to save this deluded country from destruction. They had been deceived, and were deceived by those very ministers, who being now called upon, explicitly avow, without shame or remorse, that they have no evidence to support their accusation.

The manner of obtaining the addresses, also became a matter of discussion, from its being insisted upon by one side, that they were to be considered as the full voice and sense of the nation, which conveyed through them the fullest approbation of the present measures, and the most perfect confidence in administration. This called up a noble lord in opposition,[35] who spoke from his own knowledge, of the surreptitious manner in which an address was obtained, and presented in the name of one of our principal trading and manufacturing cities; that it had been drawn up, and shamefully smuggled through by the mere agents, and known creatures of administration, without any previous notice to the citizens; that nine tenths of those who had signed it, did not know a single syllable of its contents; that with all the influence, and all the unfair means which were used, only 117 subscribers could be procured; but that when a counter address was proposed, which militated with every part of the former, and conveyed truth to the foot of the throne, it was carried fairly and openly through all the usual forms, and signed by considerably more than three times the number.

After long debates, the question upon the amendment being put

about 11 o'clock at night, it was rejected upon a division by a majority of 40, the numbers being 69, to 29, the original motion for the address was then carried by a majority of 76 (including 10 proxies) to 33 who opposed the question. Two bishops were in the minority on this division.

The address was productive of a protest signed by nineteen lords, in which they combat the civil war, as unjust and impolitic in its principles, dangerous in its contingent, and fatal in its final consequences. After condemning the injustice and imprudence of our conduct, in rejecting the American petitions and applications for a reconciliation, with the indecency and folly of affecting to disbelieve their loyalty, when they express it in the warmest professions, and expatiating upon the known and the probable evils of the contest, they describe the absurdity of refusing to give credit to the declarations of our fellow-subjects, and blindly confiding in the insidious professions of the natural enemies of this country, thereby, it is to be dreaded, preparing an easy prey for those who prudently sit quiet, beholding British forces, which, if united, might carry terror into the heart of their dominions, destroying each other. Thus, every event, which-ever way it turns, is a victory to them. Our very hospitals furnish them with daily triumphs; the greater, as they are certain, without any risque to them of men or money.

They censured the calling in of foreign forces to decide domestic quarrels, as disgraceful and dangerous; and reprobated in the strongest terms the late measure of employing the Hanoverians, at the mere pleasure of the ministers, by which they appear to be considered as a part of the British military establishment, to take a rotation of garrison duties through these dominions. They sum up and conclude the protest by declaring, "we cannot therefore consent to an address, which may deceive his majesty and the public, into a belief of the confidence of this house in the present ministers, who have deceived parliament, disgraced the nation, lost the colonies, and involved us in a civil war against our clearest interests; and upon the most unjustifiable grounds, wantonly spilling the blood of thousands of our fellow-subjects."

. . .

A debate arose about the same time, on laying the army estimates for the ensuing year before the house, the opposition pressing very closely for information, as to the number, condition, and situation of the troops now in America, whilst the ministers, as usual in this business, refused the satisfaction required. This occasioned a motion, That there be laid before the house an account of the last returns of the number of effective men, in the several regiments and corps in his Majesty's service, serving in North America, together with a state of the sick and wounded; distinguishing the several places where the said troops are stationed.

Nov. 1st.

This motion was opposed as being unsupported by precedent; and that the calling for the returns of an army in time of war, by a resolution of the house, would establish one highly inconvenient and dangerous. That the return of an army, includes the most accurate and authentic account of every particular relative to it. Could it be proper or safe to publish such a state, to furnish such information, while the enemy was in the field? while he was in a state to convert such intelligence to the highest advantage? No ministers could pretend to carry on the public business, if any gentleman had a right to demand and obtain such information. If ministers act badly, they should be turned out of their places; and not to ruin the public service, and

destroy all confidence in them while in office, by calling for improper accounts.

On the other side it was asserted, that a precedent was so far from being wanting, that it was to be found just at hand, and no longer ago than the affair of the Caribs at St. Vincent's. That information was now indispensably necessary, as it was acknowledged that the officers of the crown had hitherto been deceived themselves, and deceived parliament, for want of it. That the pretence of danger, from the enemy's becoming master of our secrets, was too ridiculous to deserve a serious answer. Could any body be weak enough to imagine, that the returns of three months standing from America, and received from this by Washington three months hence, could afford him any information relative to the army at Boston? He has them every day under his eye. But it is not from the enemy, they said, but from parliament, that the true state of the troops is to be withheld.

How can we pretend to judge of the propriety or sufficiency of the estimates for future service, of the number of new forces which we should vote for, without knowing the state of those which we have already? But, said they, was the fair truth to be laid before the house, the demands of ministers would be found inconsistent with the facts they produced. This was the case last session; they kept back all information, and imposed on the house, in order to get the cry of the people before the extent of the evil was known. The question being then put, was rejected upon a division, by a majority of 170, to 63, who supported the motion.

A motion was then made from the Admiralty in the Committee of Supply, that 28,000 seamen, including 6,665 marines, should be voted for the service of the ensuing year. This was accompa-

7th.

nied with a general outline of the services to which the navy should be applied; particularly, that the fleet on the North-American station should amount to seventy-eight sail. One of the first and most distinguished of our naval commanders opposed this motion, as the force, he said, was much too great for a peace establishment, and totally inadequate to a war. He shewed, that the number of ships designed for the American service, would demand so great a proportion of the complement of seamen proposed, that our coasts at home must be left naked and defenceless, in a season of such imminent peril and danger, or that our West-India islands, and all other distant services, must be wholly abandoned. He also arraigned, in the most unequivocal terms, the present government and conduct of our naval affairs, which he represented to be such, as not only merited much reprehension, but an immediate change of system, to prevent the most dangerous consequences. [37]

Administration defended itself upon the circumstances of the time which required a great fleet in America; while the state of affairs in Europe did not call for the same exertion at home. The professions of the neighbouring courts were pacific and friendly; and what was of more weight than professions, their armaments were not unusual or considerable. It was not fitting to alarm them by unnecessary preparations, which would justify them in arming on their side; and thus, by an injudicious shew of apprehension, we might be brought into real danger, and certain expence. That the guard-ships were so many, so well appointed, and on a short notice could be so well manned, as to be much superior to what any other power could bring against us. This would keep us in a respectable situation, without overstraining our national resources.

A few days after, a gen- [38]

tleman in opposition made a motion for an address to his Majesty, that the commissioners appointed to act in America, for the purposes held out in the speech, should be authorized to receive proposals for conciliation, from any general convention, congress, or other collective body, that should be found to convey the sentiments of one or more of the continental colonies, suspending all enquiry into the legal or illegal forms under which such colony or colonies may be disposed to treat; " as the most effectual means to prevent the effusion of blood, and to reconcile the honour and permanent interest of Great Britain with the requisitions of his Majesty's American subjects."

The gentleman introduced his motion with a speech, in which he shewed from a number of authorities both in the ancient and modern part of our history, that it was not only customary with the crown to treat with conventions of the people, which were assembled without any of the legal forms ; but that such assemblies, in the name and under the authority of the people, had several times disposed of the crown itself, a right which our Kings fully acknowledged, by most thankfully receiving it at their hands.

From these and various other precedents he argued and inferred, that it was no diminution of dignity in the crown or parliament to treat with the American conventions, under whatever forms or denominations they were held. And in further support of his position, brought the remarkable instance of the most powerful and arbitrary monarch in Europe, Lewis the XIVth, who did not disdain to enter into and conclude a treaty, negociated by two Marshals of France, with a contemptible handful of rebellious Cevennois, and their leader, the son of a baker,[39] whose name is perpetuated to posterity, by being subscribed to the same instrument which bears the signature of the haughty Lewis.

The motion was seconded, but produced little or no debate. It was said, in general, that peace was much to be wished for; but that the entering into any treaty with the Congress, would be an acknowledgement of its being a legal assembly, which must, of course, determine the whole question of dispute in favour of America. For if that meeting was legal, our whole conduct must have been a course of injustice. That it was more consonant with the dignity of parliament to find some other method; that by waiting a little, such an opportunity might offer; and that, at worst, it would be time enough to apply to this as the last resort. The question being put, it passed in the negative without a division.

8th. On the following day, the[40] minister in the war department laid the estimates of the land-service for the ensuing year before the Committee of Supply. These estimates exceeded two millions, including the staff, the difference between the English and Irish establishment in the pay of the latter, the pay of the five Hanoverian battalions, near 100,000l. levy-money, and the extraordinary unprovided expences of the ordnance in the preceding year, which, notwithstanding the limited sphere of service, amounted to .223,655l. His Lordship shewed, that the whole force appointed for the land-service, abroad and at home, would amount to about 55,000 men, of which upwards of 25,000 would be employed in America. He acknowledged, that though this was the general arrangement, he was sorry to say it was only on paper, for that scarcely any of the corps were completed to their full complement. He said, that no means had been untried to remedy this defect. That the bounty had been raised, and the standard lowered ; attempts had been made to enlist Irish Roman Catholics, and to incorporate foreigners singly into the British regiments ; but all failed of the expected effect, and the recruiting service still went on very slowly. He endeavoured to obviate the popular observation which had been so often repeated, and he knew would be now renewed, that the difficulty, or rather impracticability of procuring men, proceeded from the abhorrence, with which the people in general regarded the present odious civil war. He mentioned several causes for this slackness, but rested chiefly on the flourishing state of our manufactures, (notwithstanding the predictions of opposition) which, whilst it brought a temporary distress on the service, was a proof of the real strength of the kingdom, and its ability fully to support this or any war.

He also threw out, without pretending, however, to any absolute authority, that every idea of taxing America, was now entirely given up ; and that the only remaining consideration, was to secure the constitutional dependency of that country. That this could only be effected by such a conduct, as shewed the most determined resolution of maintaining our constitutional rights, and that for this purpose, it was intended to send out such an armament, as would be sufficient to enforce them, if America should still persist in her disobedience. That this armament would be attended with commissioners, who should be furnished with powers to accommodate matters ; and that a great military officer, who stood high in the esteem both of his sovereign and the nation, was intended to be the first commissioner.

Some of the country gentlemen, as well as the opposition in general, were much dissatisfied at not being able to obtain any information from the minister, relative to his intended operations, whether with respect to the measures for bringing about an accommodation, or for the prosecution of the war. The former said, they voted with him for the militia and the augmentation of the navy, in a firm persuasion, and understanding it as a matter of course, that before the remaining supplies were granted, he would have laid his plan before the house. That if they had not thought so, they would not have given their support to measures, which it seemed now they were not to be acquainted with. That it looked as if it were meant that they should vote the estimates first, and hear the reasons afterwards; or in other words, that the house should begin with a division, and end with a debate. They said, that in looking for information, they did not mean a few scraps of garbled and mutilated papers; but that verbal and official information, which they thought it the ministers duty to impart to parliament. That it was particularly necessary they should receive information as to the persons who were to be appointed as Commissioners in America, and the nature and extent of their commission, that parliament might be enabled to judge, whether they were men fit to be entrusted with so important a negociation, and whether the terms they carried out, were consistent with the dignity of Great Britain to offer, and the interest of the Americans to receive.

One of the country gentlemen was so earnest in this desire of information, and so picqued at finding no disposition in the minister to give the satisfaction which he required, that he attempted to break up the committee without its coming to any resolution, by moving, " that the Chairman should quit the chair," which was seconded by another gentleman under the same description.

Though the minister did not think it prudent, or was not prepared to give any direct or explicit answer, he, however, thought it necessary to do something to keep that party in temper. He said, that the commission to be sent, would be in conformity to the intimation given from the throne; that the gentlemen need not make themselves uneasy, under the apprehension that any treaty of concession would be agreed to without the consent of parliament; but that it would be necessary to know upon what grounds the Americans would treat, before the powers sufficient to ratify what the Commissioners might think expedient, were derived from parliament. When the terms that America was willing to submit to, were in a state proper to be laid before the house, that, in his opinion, would be the proper time to take the sense of parliament on previous communications, and leave it to judge of the alternative, whether the offers of America could be accepted with honour, or whether we ought to reduce them to a state of obedience, however difficult or hazardous the undertaking.

In the further prosecution of the subject, the opposition insisted, that the estimates were under-rated in such a degree, as to afford no clue whereby to form any judgment of the extent of the expences. That the proposed force of 25,000 men, was totally inadequate to the purposes of absolute coercion. This was supported by the opinion of a great general officer, who had [41] long been in administration, and who declared it in the most unreserved terms; the other military gentlemen present were called upon to declare their dissent, if they thought otherwise; but they all continued silent. The mixt system of war and conciliation was represented as highly improper. The measure adopted, whether of peace or war, should be clear, simple, and decided, not involved in doubt, perplexity, and darkness. If war was resolved, and it was determined to compel America to submission, let the means of coercion be such, as will, to a moral certainty, insure success. The force employed must be able to command terms, or it does nothing. If, on the contrary, peace is really wished for, and terms of conciliation are to be proposed, your prepositions ought to be so clear as to be obvious to every common understanding, and so simple as to baffle the powers of chicanery.

On the other side it was said, that the force proposed, when its operations were directed to specific services, and supported by a formidable fleet, would be fully sufficient for the purpose, and such as all America could not withstand; nor was it probable, that they would enter into so arduous a contest, when terms were held out to them at the very instant, which would fully preserve their rights. The idea of simple war, or simple concession, was strongly controverted. It was said, that a conquest over our own subjects, was neither sought nor desired. That it was our interest, as it was our wish, to reclaim, not to destroy or enslave. That in the present state of things in America, this desirable object could only be obtained by such an armament as would command respect, strike an awe into the factious, and enforce a submission to the conciliatory terms which we proposed, if coercion became absolutely necessary. And that either to withdraw the force we already had there, or to leave it exposed to the insults and danger of a greater on the side of the rebels, would not only be in the highest degree disgraceful to ourselves, but would, in its consequences, be equally ruinous to both countries.

A gentleman in office, but who [42] has for several years been considered as possessing much more real than ostensible power, departed totally from these temperate ideas of conduct which the minister professed, and on which he valued himself. He was of opinion, that all attempts of conciliation would be fruitlefs: obferved, that at any rate, a number of terms were to be made, and fecurities given, before conciliation could be obtained. That terms of force were the meafures chalked out by his Majefty in the fpeech; attended, however, with conditions of conciliation, and gracious offers of forgivenefs and protection. On this foundation, the prefent vote on the eftimates was propofed; but if premature explanations were defired; if the gentlemen, who had pledged themfelves to fupport thofe meafures, had altered their minds, or had withdrawn their confidence from the King's fervants, he faw no poffible way to remedy matters but by a change of adminiftration. He, however, animadverted feverely on the cowardice of declining the conteft, almoft in the very outfet, after their having gone fuch lengths in bringing matters to that crifis.

This being confidered as the language of authority, was alfo underftood, both by the country gentlemen and oppofition, as fully tantamount to a declaration for war. The latter did not let it pafs without obfervation and ftricture. They faid, it was treating parliament with every poffible degree of difrefpect. Meafures are concerted in the cabinet; the King is made by the minifters to exprefs the general intentions which they had there determined upon; the Houfe of Commons is defired to fupport thofe meafures, by voting an enormous war eftablifhment; and when queftions are afked, and explanations are defired, even by the very friends of adminiftration, the gentlemen who call for a plan are very laconically referred to the King's fpeech. The fpeech holds out generals, and refers you to particulars; when thefe particulars are called for, the fpeech is quoted, as the true ftandard of information.

After long debates, the queftion being put upon the firft of the refolutions in the eftimate, was carried upon a divifion by the ufual majority, the numbers being 227, to 73 who oppofed the refolution. The other refolutions were agreed to of courfe.

IT was not difficult to forefee, that the late unexpected conduct of the Duke of Grafton would occafion, at leaft, one remove among the great offices of ftate. It was, however, accompanied with fome which were not publicly thought of. Whether the unhappy ftate of American affairs had difgufted the Earl of Dartmouth with the office of conducting them, or that government imagined a more aufтere and inflexible character, with their natural concomitant a determinate conduct, were neceffary to reftore peace and order, however it was, that nobleman Nov. 10th. now quitted the American fecretaryfhip, and received the privy feal which had been held by the Duke of Grafton.

The arduous tafk of conducting the American department was repofed on Lord George Sackeville Germaine. The principal attachment of that noble Lord had been to Mr. Grenville. After Mr. Grenville's death, indeed, he continued for fome time firm on his former ground; and did not join in that defection from the minority which immediately followed that event. But he began at length to flacken in oppofition. He fell in with adminiftration in the proceedings againft the Eaft-India Company in 1773; and took a full and decided part in all the coercive meafures which had been purfued againft the Americans, during the prefent troubles. His connections with Mr. Grenville probably made him fupport with more zeal and fteadinefs the higheft claims of parliamentary authority; and as he was generally efteemed a man of bufinefs, and an able debater, he was fought for at a time, when the extraordinary powers in the fame line, upon the other fide, feemed, notwithftanding the fuperiority of numbers, not a little to diftrefs adminiftration. It will not be conceived, that this appointment ftrengthened the hope or increased the satisfaction of those who held the opinion, that conciliatory measures could only bring the present troubles to a speedy and happy conclusion.

At the same time, the Earl of Rochford having retired from public business, was succeeded as Secretary of State for the Southern department by Lord Weymouth, who had continued out of employment since his resignation on the affair of Falkland island. And a few days after, Lord Lyttelton, who had been distinguished at the opening of the session by the severity of his strictures upon administration, was called to the Privy Council, and appointed Chief Justice in Eyre beyond Trent. Lord Pelham was also appointed to the great wardrobe, and Lord Ashburnham, Keeper of the Stole. [44]

The affair of the petition from the Congress, which Mr. Penn had lately presented to his Majesty, had frequently been brought [45] up in both houses by the opposition, both as affording a ground of conciliation, and a subject of reproach to the ministers, for their total neglect of that and all other applications of the same nature. A copy of the petition being, however, laid before the Lords among other papers on the 7th of November, a noble Duke in oppo- [46] sition observed, that he saw Mr. Penn below the bar, and he moved, that he might be examined, in order to establish the authenticity of the petition, before they entered into any debates upon its contents, thereby to obviate the doubts which might otherwise probably arise upon that head, and be the means of interrupting their proceedings.

As the Lords in administration were well aware, that the views of the noble mover and his friends, went farther than the authenticity of the petition, and extended to the laying before the house all the information, with respect to America, which they could draw from a person so thoroughly master of the subject as Mr. Penn, and not being at all disposed that such matters should now be brought forward, they used every means to prevent or defeat the examination. They objected to the motion on the subject of order; on its informality; on its want of precedent; being contrary to their established mode of proceeding; that the bringing in of extraneous matter by surprize, and breaking in upon their most serious and important deliberations, by suddenly calling their attention off to the examination of witnesses, and to new subjects of discussion, would be destructive of that order and gravity which had always distinguished their proceedings.

They also contended, that this measure would establish a most pernicious precedent, as it would necessarily follow, that every petition, from whatever quarter of the globe, must be accompanied by the evidence to establish its authenticity. They observed, that improper questions might be asked, and such answers drawn from Mr. Penn, as might tend to prejudice him with respect to his private fortune and affairs in America; that his evidence might have the same effect with respect to others, who were also friends to government in America, and who by a public exposure of their private conduct in its favour, would be liable to personal danger, and ruin to their fortunes. They also insisted, that as the evidence, let it turn out as it may, would be only *ex parte*, the house could not found any resolution upon it; nor could it be presumed, that the single testimony of an individual, however respectable the character may be, could at all influence their conduct or opinion, in questions of such great national and political import. To prevent, however, every pretence for the enquiry, they offered to admit the authenticity of the petition without any proof.

On the other side, they said, that the objections as to order were so trifling, as to be unworthy of their time and attention; that the proposed examination was, however, fully supportable upon that ground, as well as in point of precedent. They offered to tie themselves down as to the questions to be put, and that the Lords, who opposed the measure, should object to any which they did not approve. And they lamented, in the most pathetic terms, the disposition which they saw in the house, to shut out every species of information relative to America, to continue to the last in darkness, and to rush headlong themselves, and plunge the nation along with them, into inevitable ruin and destruction. That this was the more surprizing, and the more lamentable, as the fatal consequences which had already proceeded from a similar conduct, were so sensibly felt at this very instant, as to convulse the empire through all its parts.

The motion being rejected upon a division, by a majority of 56 to to 22, the noble mover, who is distinguished for his perseverance, made another, That Mr. Penn should be examined at the bar on the next day. Though the examination of a witness in this form, unconnected with any other matter, could not be refused, yet so disagreeable was every enquiry of this nature, that a further debate arose upon it; but it was at length reluctantly agreed to, that he should be examined on the 10th. [10th.] Several curious particulars relative to much controverted subjects, came out upon the examination of this gentleman. He was personally acquainted with almost all the members of the Congress, had been Governor of the colony, and resided in the city, in which they assembled and held their deliberations, and had every opportunity, from office, family connection, locality of property, and an extensive acquaintance, to obtain the fullest information of the state of affairs in America, as well as of the temper and disposition of the people. It was also evident, that his discernment was equal to the forming a just estimate of things; and there could scarcely be a suspicion of partiality, in favour of any measure which could tend to American independency, as the great fortune of his family, if not wholly lost, must be much impaired by such an event, and their great powers and prerogatives certainly subverted.

Among the remarkable parts of his testimony, (which we must recollect, consisted only of answers to such specific questions as were proposed) was an absolute negative to the supposition or charge, that any designs of independency had been formed by the Congress. He declared, that the members composing that body had been fairly elected; that they were men of character, capable of conveying the sense of America; and that they had actually conveyed the sense of their constituents. That the different provinces would be governed by their decisions in all events. That the war was levied and carried on by the colonists, merely in defence of what they thought their liberties. That the spirit of resistance was general, and they believed themselves able to defend their liberties against the arms of Great Britain.

That the colony of Pensylvania contained about 60,000 men able to carry arms. That of these, 20,000 had voluntarily enrolled themselves to serve without pay, and were armed and embodied before the Governor's departure. Being questioned as to the nature of that volunteer force, he said, that it included the men of best fortune and character in the province, and that it was generally composed of men who were possessed of property, either landed

or otherwise. That an additional body of 4,500 minute men had since been raised in the province, who were to be paid when called out on service. That they had the means and materials of casting iron cannon in great plenty. That they cast brass cannon in Philadelphia. And that they made small arms in great abundance and perfection.

That the colonies had been dissatisfied with the reception of their former petitions; but that they had founded great hopes upon the success of that which he brought over; that it was stiled the *Olive Branch*; and that he had been congratulated by his friends upon his being the bearer of it. That it was greatly to be feared, that if conciliatory measures were not speedily pursued, they would form connections with foreign powers; and that if such connections were once formed, it would be found a matter of great difficulty to dissolve them. Being asked, " whether the people of the different provinces were now in a state of freedom?" he said, that they thought themselves so; whether, " the most opulent inhabitants would not prefer freedom under this country to what they now enjoy?" he answered, that they would prefer it to any other state of freedom; and that notwithstanding their determination to support the measures of the Congress, they wished for a reconciliation with this country. He denied its being an object of the Congress to throw off the regulations of their trade; and acknowledged, that the most thinking men in Philadelphia were of opinion, that a refusal of the present petition would be a bar to all reconcilement.

The other parts of the evidence related to the Stamp Act, the repeal, and the declaratory law. This gentleman was in America at that period, and declared that the first had occasioned great discontent, uneasiness, and distress;

that the repeal had given such abundant joy; that its anniversary was celebrated as a day of mirth and festivity. That the Americans were satisfied with their condition, notwithstanding the Declaratory Act; and that if Great Britain had left things in the state they then were, the Americans would have remained content. The questions relative to the degree of subordination acknowledged by the colonies, having been multiplied and closely urged by a noble Lord high in office, the witness declared, that he believed the colonies are inclined to acknowledge the imperial authority of Great Britain, but not in taxation.

It was observed, with some severity of animadversion, as a singular circumstance in the present situation of affairs, what appeared upon this examination, that neither the Secretary of State who received the petition, nor any other minister or person in authority, had, since the arrival of the witness in England, proposed a single question to him, or desired the smallest information relative to the state of affairs in America, or to the disposition or temper of the people. This circumstance was used to give countenance to the charge so often repeated by the opposition, that a system had been chalked out for administration, which they were obliged blindly to pursue, and to act in it merely as machines, without being at liberty to form an opinion as to justice, eligibility, or consequence.

After the examination was finished, the Duke of Richmond, who had been its proposer, made a motion, That the petition from the Continental Congress to the King, was ground for a conciliation of the unhappy differences at present subsisting between Great Britain and America. The motion was well introduced, and ably supported by the noble mover and his friends. They stated the necessity of an immediate reconciliation in every point of view, whether with with respect to ourselves, the colonies, or our situation in respect to foreign powers. That nothing but carnage, desolation, an augmentation of expence, with a decrease of revenue, a weakness and debility growing in proportion to the urgent necessity which would call for strength and exertion, with all the cruel and grievous calamities inseparable from civil discord, would be the fruits obtained by a pertinacious pursuit of the war.

They represented the unsurmountable difficulties which would occur, if an absolute conquest of America was intended; the natural strength of that continent, composed alternately of strong inclosures, thick forests, and deep swamps, and every where intersected with vast rivers. The immense difficulty and expence, if not utter impracticability, of supplying such an army as would be adequate to the purpose, with subsistence from England, and the little prospect, if the obstinacy or perseverance of the Americans continued, of providing it on the spot. The advantages which the latter would derive from their being at home, and from having their subsistence at hand; from their perfect knowledge of the country, whereby every strong ground, pass, and defile, would be to them a fortress, and every forest afford a secure retreat. That the overrunning of a province, the seizing, plundering, or destroying several of their towns, though ruinous to them, would afford no essential advantage to us, even confining the consideration merely to the immediate object of the war, in the attainment of general conquest. Our dominion would extend no farther than the immediate operation of our arms, and would cease with it. The instant we marched to subdue another province, that which we quitted, would become at least as hostile as that which we entered.

To a strong picture of difficulties, dangers, and disgrace, they contrasted the numberless blessings of peace, and shewed the happy opportunity which the petition afforded of averting the numerous, and some of them fatal evils, which had been described. They said, that if this opportunity were now lost, it could never be regained. That providence seemed with a peculiar kindness to put it in their way to rescue their country from ruin, without warring directly with their passions or prejudices, as they might now descend, without disgrace, or without wounding their pride, from those high stilts of authority and dignity on which they were unhappily mounted, and which rendered them blind to its interest and security.

They observed, that as the idea of laying taxes on America, for the purpose of raising a revenue, had been, in their discourses at least, repeatedly given up by the ministers, the question of conciliation was much less complex, than when that doctrine had been maintained, both in principle, and in its most extensive consequences. That the great object now of discussion, was what Great Britain claimed, and what America was willing to accede to. The great remaining claim of the former, appears to be no more than what it ever was, a general supreme and controuling power over the colonies, with respect to their external government, and the regulation of their trade and commerce. That these rights were established and secured by the great body of American laws passed before the year 1763, and by the act of navigation. That as the Americans were ready and willing to return to their former obedience, and to stand in the same subordinate relation to the legislature, which they had done previous to the year 1763, the only remaining object of contention, was the laws passed since that period.

In this state of things, they contended, that the petition offered the fairest ground of conciliation. They expressly declare, that they desire no concession derogatory to the honour of the mother country. The delegates of the people of America beseech his Majesty to recall his troops; which could only be considered as a prayer for a suspension of arms. All they desire as a preliminary, is the repeal of sundry acts; by which was to be understood, those that deprived them of their fisheries, trade, and charters. The repeal of the laws passed since 1763, was not now mentioned, nor would it at any time have been insisted on. A revision of those laws, with a repeal of the grievous and burdensome parts of them, would be right and necessary; and would be as consistent both with our interest and justice, as it would be conducive to the satisfaction and ease of the Americans. They, like all others in similar circumstances, carry their claims much farther in the heat and litigation of contest, under the immediate pressure of great grievances, and the apprehension of greater, than they would in a cooler temper, and happier situation. Let us only shew a disposition to concede, and to redress their grievances, and concession will come faster from them than the warmest imagination can conceive. Meet them on the ground of conciliation, which they now propose, and you may afterwards prescribe your own terms.

On the other side, it was said, that it was impossible to recognize the petition on which the present motion was founded, without relinquishing in that act the sovereignty of the British parliament. That treating with an unlawful assembly, who at the very instant declared themselves to be in a state of open resistance and hostility, would be, to all intents and purposes, legalizing their proceedings, and acknowledging them the constitutional representatives of an independent sovereign state. If they were subjects, they could not affemble or deliberate, but in a mode, and for the purposes prescribed by the constitution. If they were not, it would be in the highest degree ridiculous to treat with them in a capacity which they disclaimed.

It was denied, that the ideas of laying on duties in America, for the purpose of raising a revenue, were totally laid aside; if the Americans, like dutiful and affectionate subjects, had met us in our kind proposition, of levying an equitable revenue on themselves in such manner as they liked best, there would be no occasion for realizing such ideas; some respectable persons, also, in administration as well as out, might question the immediate practice in point of expediency; but a thought of relinquishing the right was never entertained. But supposing, for a moment, that such a concession were made, it would not surely be inferred, that because Great Britain had given up the exercise of supreme dominion in one particular mode, she had also given it up in every other. The Americans deny the right of controul, in the most effectual manner, for they declare against the exercise of it, in every instance wherein it militates with their interests, or with their traiterous views and rebellious designs. They refuse obedience to the declaratory law, the act for quartering soldiers, the law for establishing vice-admiralty courts, and, in a word, to every law which they do not like, and then tell us, with a most consummate effrontery, that they acknowledge our undoubted right of legislative controul, but will not permit us to exercise that right.

It was insisted by some Lords, who were more warm than the generality, that the petition was an insidious and traiterous attempt to impose upon the King and parliament; that while the authors held out smooth language and false professions for that purpose, they were at the very instant, in their appeals to the people of Great Britain and Ireland, abusing the parliament, denying its authority, and endeavouring to involve the whole empire in rebellion and bloodshed, by inviting their fellow-subjects in these kingdoms, to make one common cause with them in opposition to law and government. That no alternative remained with these worst of rebels, who not content with the enjoyment of their own crimes wanted to render them general, but the most speedy and effectual measures for their subjugation and punishment. These also, which were only few, endeavoured to lessen the weight of the evidence which had been now laid before them, by charging it with partiality and prejudice.

The question being at length put, between ten and eleven o'clock at night, after very considerable debates, the motion was rejected upon a division, by a majority of 86, including 26 proxies, to 33, including 6 proxies.

About the same time, the minister in the House of Commons, after shewing, in the Committee of Supply, the necessity of reducing America to obedience, and remarking on the great expence that must necessarily attend that measure, took an opportunity of convincing the landed gentlemen, of the propriety and expediency of applying to them for their support upon so great and important a national occasion, at a time, he acknowledged, when the other resources of the state were incompetent to the purpose. He accordingly moved, that the land-tax for the year 1776, be four shillings in the pound. 13th.

This motion occasioned a variety of debates and conversations. Some of the opposition congratulated the country gentlemen upon the four shillings, as the happy and enviable first fruits of their darling coercive American measures; whilst they, at the same time, endeavoured to shew by calculations on the state of the funds and expenditure, that it would be a perpetual mortgage on their estates, which no change of circumstance, or even favourable turn of fortune, could ever wear off; for that, let affairs now be ever so speedily accommodated, nothing less than a land tax at that rate would be sufficient for our future peace establishment.

The principal leaders of opposition did not interfere much upon this occasion. Some gentlemen said, that as the services were voted, the army and navy must not be starved, and as the supplies must be raised in some manner, they would vote for this tax, as less prejudicial than any other that could be thought of. One of them, however, could not forbear commenting on this method of voting money, for services not known to the house, or on which, at least, they had no substantial controul, as it furnished ministers with opportunities of applying it to purposes which were in the last degree ruinous and fatal to the constitution. 47

Some of the country gentlemen were out of sorts about the Indemnity Bill, an object which they seemed to consider, as the only one relative to the constitution that demanded attention. This bill had lain dormant since the first reading, without any notice whatever being taken of it, and they considered it so seriously, as partly to make its being brought forward, a condition of their agreeing to the land-tax. Several others of them were, however, much dissatisfied, upon a subject of more substantial, if not constitutional import. Many gentlemen had supported government in all the coercive measures which it had pursued against America, with a view, and in a firm hope and persuasion, that the great revenue to be drawn from that part of the world, would in a proportional degree have lessened their own burthens. Upon this principle, they would have advanced money, as in a law-suit, while the object in view was capable of repaying them with great interest, besides an advantageous and ample compensation for the risque; but they were not yet keen enough, as litigators too frequently are, to pursue the contest to ruin, (when they found the object unproductive) merely for the sake of the sport which it afforded. They accordingly finding, by the language held since the opening of the session by the ministers, that the idea of taxation was generally given up, either as inexpedient, or as totally impracticable, now declared, that if the original object of dispute was abandoned, they could not think of expending any more money in a contest, which, besides being unproductive of benefit, was attended with evils that could only be palliated upon that principle; and that therefore they would oppose the noble Lord's motion for an increase of the land-tax.

The minister thought it expedient to satisfy both parties, of these, sometimes troublesome, but always useful, friends. This was easily done with the first, by informing them, that their favourite bill was in perfect safety and good condition, and would be immediately brought forward. As to the second, he assured them, that the idea of taxation, and of levying a productive revenue from America, was never abandoned; and that when any thing of that sort dropped from the ministers, they intended no more, than that it was abandoned for the present; that is, that the dispute at present was of a much higher nature than it had been originally, and that taxation was but a matter of secondary consideration, when the supremacy and legislative authority of this country was at stake. That he would have them therefore perfectly understand, that whatever general terms the ministers might at any time make use of, taxation neither is, nor ever was, out of their view. As a further proof of his sincerity upon this subject he declared, that there was no means by which the legislative authority and commercial controul of this country over the colonies could be insured, but by combining them with taxation.

This explanation gave full content, and after a mixed debate, which lasted till ten o'clock, the question being put upon an amendment which had been early moved, That the land-tax should be three shillings instead of four, it passed in the negative upon a division, by a majority of 182 to 47; the original motion then passed of course.

15th.
In two days after, the house being in a committee upon the Militia Bill, a motion was made for an amendment, by inserting words to the following purpose in the preamble, That the said power of assembling and embodying the militia, shall not extend beyond the continuance of the present rebellion. This motion brought on some warm and considerable debates. The opposition said, that if the ministers opposed this motion, it would convince them beyond a doubt, that the suspicions they had formed with respect to this bill were too well founded, which were, that it was brought in merely as a colourable pretext to arm the crown with a power hitherto unknown to the constitution.

They argued, that the bill, from the very frame of it, was taken up on a temporary idea, and directed to temporary purposes, which would cease to be objects of policy, the instant that the civil war was terminated. That the avowed object and principle of the bill, was to afford a greater scope to our military operations in America, by making such a provision for internal defence and security, as might enable us to employ the standing regular forces upon that service.

That however necessary it might be in cases of real and great emergency, to arm the crown, pro tempore, with extraordinary powers for certain purposes of safety, it was always, not only in the spirit, but practice of our government, to recall those powers, as soon as the purposes were answered, or the motives ceased, for which they were granted. And that it could not be pretended, that any fair or constitutional motive would remain after the conclusion of the present troubles, for continuing this power in the crown, as it was already enabled by the old law, to call out the militia in all other cases of real emergency. And they insisted, that the very point meant to be covertly carried by this bill, was what no king of England, even the most despotic, had ever been able to gain; that it was a power at all times retained, and till now, most jealously watched and guarded by the people; and that, on this was grounded the leading contest between Charles the First and his parliament, long before that assembly had been charged with any factious views, or had entertained any idea of the troubles which afterwards took place.

On the other side, great encomiums were made on the popular and constitutional defence of a militia, and much wonder expressed, that a measure which tended so particularly to the security of the people, and the rendering standing armies unnecessary, should be opposed by those, who pretended a more than ordinary zeal in the care and protection of their liberties. That the apprehended dangers which it was supposed would arise from the powers granted by the bill. and upon which such powers of colouring had been bestowed to render them frightful and hideous, were purely visionary, and mere creatures of the imagination. That no ill use could be made of the power, without the concurrence of the people themfelves; for though the Prince might affemble the militia, they muft be paid by parliament. That prefuming parliament fhould become a party in betraying its own rights and thofe of the people, was fuppofing a cafe which could not exift, or if it did, which no human prudence or forefight could poffibly guard againft; for fuch a confpiracy of the executive and legiflative powers of the ftate, fuppofed not an abufe, but an actual fubverfion and diffolution of government. That all reafoning on fuch an hypothefis was abfurd; who could the people truft, if they could not truft themfelves? if they were feized with fuch a madnefs as to make a furrender of their rights and liberties, no power under heaven could prevent them.

This anfwer feems perfectly fatisfactory with regard to the general power of the crown over the militia; but it does not appear of equal force to remove the main objection, and which ftruck directly at the principle of the bill, viz. the rendering a law perpetual, which was framed only for an immediate and temporary purpofe, without any apparent motive, or fufficient caufe for fo doing. This was by no means fatisfactorily anfwered, it being only evafively faid, that if the law was a good one, it fhould always ftand, and if otherwife, fhould not pafs at all. This would prove too much; as it would be a reafon againft all temporary bills.

The queftion being put on the amendment, it was rejected on a divifion in the committee, by a majority of 140 to 55. Another amendment was then propofed, "That the militia fhould not be called out of their refpective counties, unlefs in cafe of actual invafion." This likewife paffed in the negative. A claufe was then propofed, to impower his Majefty to affemble the parliament in fourteen days, whenever the prefent act, in the event of a war or rebellion in any part of the dominions of the Britifh crown, fhould be called into operation. This claufe was agreed to without a divifion.

15th. Several motions were made on the fame day by the Duke of Grafton, which produced confiderable debates in the other houfe. The firft of thefe was to lay before the houfe, an account of the number of forces ferving in America, previous to the commencement of hoftilities, with their feveral ftations and diftributions, in order to lay a ground-work for fuch advice as that houfe, impelled by a fenfe of duty, might think fit to fubmit to his Majefty's confideration. The fecond, for a ftate of the army now in America, according to the lateft returns. The third, for laying before them the plans that had been adopted for providing winter quarters for thofe troops; with an account of the number of forces in the provincial army, according to the beft eftimate that could be obtained. The fourth, that an eftimate of the forces now in Great Britain and Ireland fhould be laid before them. And the fifth, that an eftimate of the military force neceffary to be fent againft America, with an account of the number of artillery, fhould alfo be laid before the houfe.

In fupport of thefe motions, the fame ground was taken, which had been repeatedly trodden in both houfes fince the opening of the feffion, upon the fame fubject. Some new obfervations were however added. It was faid, that they had heard oblique cenfures thrown out upon the commanders both by fea and land. What were they to do, amidft fuch a chaos of charges, denials, blunders, miftakes, imputed negligence, and incapacity? Were they ftill to wander in darknefs and uncertainty; to grope their way without a ray of light, or the fmalleft information for their direction? They profeffed, that they did not want cabinet, but parliamentary information; they did not want to know the detail, nor the different means intended to give their meafures fuccefs; they do not defire to fee eftimates, with any view of comparing them with the returns; nor do they mean to enter into any enquiry, with an intention of having the wrong information, by which minifters have confeffed themfelves deceived and mifled, traced to its fource. They only wanted to know that general ftate of things, and thofe facts, which by warning them of the difficulties they had to encounter, would point out the beft means of obviating or furmounting them; and that this could not be fo well effected in any other manner, as by learning a true ftate of the force preparing againft us, and comparing it with our own abilities and immediate refources. That there were precedents in favour of fuch motions; and the enemy was fo fituated as to come readily at the account of what was fo anxioufly concealed from parliament.

On the other fide, the enquiries propofed, with thofe which they were fuppofed to lead to, were faid to be unprecedented, highly improper and dangerous. That it was contrary to every rule of office, as well as every maxim of war and common fenfe, to furnifh our enemies with fuch intelligence, as might be the means of either availing themfelves of our weaknefs, or refifting our power. That the rebel leaders themfelves could not wifh for any thing more in their favour, than a difclofure of the plans of our military operations, and an exact ftate of our ftrength or weaknefs. That fecrecy, whether with refpect to deliberation or action, was the effence and life of war, upon which its fuccefs muft for ever in a great degree depend. It was afferted, that the meafures determined here, were much fooner known in the rebel camp, than in the King's army. And it was infifted, that the precedent to be established by a compliance with these motions, of the legislative forcing itself, and breaking in upon the executive power, would be more dangerous even than the other consequences, as it must of course, if brought into practice, totally obstruct the measures of government, and render it impracticable to conduct the public affairs.

The debate, as usual, wandered from the main subject, and took in several branches of the American business. Much warmth appeared, and some severe personal animadversion took place, upon different occasions which occurred in the course of the debates. The question being at length put upon each of the motions separately, that only, for an estimate of the forces now in Great Britain and Ireland, was agreed to. The rest were rejected without a division.

The opposition were not so dejected by their multiplied defeats in both houses of parliament, as to abandon all hopes of a reconciliation; they daily endeavoured to shew it necessary in the attempt, and practicable in the execution.

16th. On the day succeeding the Duke of Grafton's motions, Mr. Burke, notwithstanding the ill success of his conciliatory propositions in the preceding year, brought in a bill to answer the same purposes in the present.

The business was introduced by a petition upon the present American differences, from the considerable cloathing towns and neighbourhood of Westbury, Warminster, and Trowbridge, in the county of Wilts. This petition was intended to counteract a late address which had been procured in the same part of the country, and to prevent, as the petitioners say, the dreadful effects which might arise, from similar misrepresentations being conveyed to parliament. But what brought it directly home to Mr. Burke's object of conciliation, was the earnest manner in which they deprecated the horrors of a civil war, and conjured the house, by every thing solemn, sacred, or dear, to adopt such lenient measures, as might restore that affectionate intercourse between this country and the colonies, which, they said, could alone prevent those calamities that they most pathetically lamented or described. He therefore wished (after observing that the manufacturing part of the petitioners were all men who carried on business as principals upon their own account, and that, he was authorized to say, were possessed of more than half a million of English property,) that the prayer of the petition should be considered as an exordium to the business which he was going to propose.

The motion was, " That leave be given to bring in a bill for composing the present troubles, and for quieting the minds of his Majesty's subjects in America." Its object was to procure conciliation and peace by concession; and that great charter from the crown to the people, passed in the 35th year of Edward the First, and known by the name of *Statutum de tallagio non concedendo*, was its avowed model.

The framer introduced his bill with a speech, which he supported for upwards of three hours with great ability, and which seemed to vie with the magnitude of the subject, in the amazing compass of British and American matter which it included. He complained of the difficulties under which moderate men, who advised lenient and healing measures, lay, in times of civil commotion; that their moderation was imputed to a want of zeal, and their fears for the public safety to a want of spirit; but that on the present unhappy occasion, these were increased in an unusual degree, as every thing that was proposed on the side of lenity, was unfairly construed, and industriously represented, as intended to give a countenance to rebellion; and that such arts had been practised, and menaces thrown out, as would, if they had not been opposed with a great share of firmness by the friends to the peace of their country, have put an end to all freedom of debate, and indeed to all public deliberation whatever.

He observed, that there were three plans afloat for putting an end to the present troubles. The first, simple war, in order to a perfect conquest. The second, a mixture of war and treaty. And the third, peace grounded on concession. In the investigation of these he observed, that the first branched into two parts; the one direct by conquest, the other indirect by distress. He then examined the means which had been laid before them, for carrying on the ensuing campaign upon the former principle, and found many reasons to shew that they were insufficient for the purpose. As for the predatory, or war by distress, he placed its nature and consequences in various points of view, and endeavoured to satisfy his hearers, that it was calculated to produce the highest degree of irritation and animosity, but never had, nor never could, induce any one people to become subjects to the government of another. That it was a kind of war adapted to distress an independent people; but not to coerce disobedient subjects.

He concluded the subject of conquest by observing, that as there appeared no probability of success in the detail of any of the arrangements that were proposed, neither was there any authority to give them a sanction; not one military or naval officer having given an opinion in their favour, and several of the first, in both departments, having decided directly against them. Thus, as no man of military experience would vouch for the sufficiency of the force, neither would any one in the commissariate answer for its subsistence from the moment that it left the sea coast; so that its subsistence and its operation were confessedly incompatible.

He next examined the mixed system of war and treaty, and exposed, with his usual acuteness and disquisition, its numberless defects, ruinous procrastination, and final inconclusiveness. He ridiculed the absurdity of sending out pardons to people who neither applied for, nor would accept of them; as if nothing but an amnesty were wanting to restore peace in America; and as if the great objects of dispute were totally lost and forgotten. He also condemned in the strongest terms the arbitrary powers which were to be vested in the commissioners, of granting general or particular pardons, in such manner, and to such persons only, as they should think proper; without any established line for the government of their conduct on the one side, or known measure of obedience for the attainment of security on the other.

Having endeavoured to establish the inefficacy and ruinous consequences of both these systems, he proceeded to an explanation of his own, founded upon the idea of *concession previous to treaty*. He stated the necessity of concession; that its necessity being admitted, it should be immediately adopted, and appear a mere act of *their own free grace*. That this measure, besides preventing the destructive consequences attending the protraction incident to negociation, would sustain their own dignity much better, and have infinitely more efficacy in conciliating the colonies, than any concession upon treaty. That the first ground of treaty must be confidence. That all confidence in government, on the side of the Americans, had been destroyed through the measures pursued for the last ten years. That this confidence could only be restored by the interposition of parliament; by its coming in as an

aid and security for government, and laying out some firm ground as a foundation for conclusive and final peace.

He observed, that as taxation had been the origin of the present differences, an arrangement of that question, either by enforcement or concession, was a preliminary indispensably essential to peace. He entered largely into that subject; considered it under both heads, and said, that the impracticability of the former was now acknowledged by the ministers themselves. He observed, that parliament was not the representative, but the sovereign of America. That sovereignty was not in its nature an idea of abstract unity; but was capable of great complexity and infinite modifications, according to the temper of those who are to be governed, and to the circumstances of things; which being infinitely diversified, government ought to be adapted to them, and to conform itself to their nature, instead of vainly endeavouring to force that to a contrary bias. That though taxation was inherent in the supreme power of society, taken as an aggregate, it did not follow that it must reside in any particular power in that society. Thus, in the society of England, the King is the sovereign; but the power of the purse is not in his hands; yet this does not derogate from his authority in those things, in which the constitution has attributed power to him.

Having pressed the necessity of giving up the point of taxation to the utmost, he, however, expressed his regret, at our being obliged to surrender any (even that most odious and scarcely ever to be exercised) part of legislative authority; but this, he said, was the natural and inevitable consequence of injudicious exertions of power. That people who quarrel unreasonably among themselves, and will not reconcile their differences in due season, must submit to the

consequences incident to the situation in which they have involved themselves. That there was no dishonour in any kind of amicable adjustment of domestic quarrels; that he would rather yield an hundred points, when they were Englishmen that gave and received, than a single point to a foreign nation; and we were in such circumstances as would oblige us to yield either to one or the other.

He then stated the reasons which induced him to make the statute de tallagio, 35 Ed. I. the pattern for his bill. For this purpose he shewed the similarity of the ancient disputes that arose between the kings and the people of England on the subject of taxation, to those now subsisting between the parliament and the natives of America; that the claim of sovereignty was the same in both instances, and the evils which were effectually removed by the statute de tallagio, corresponded exactly with those which the present bill was intended to remedy. That they had happily a precedent of the first authority to afford a clue for their conduct. For however the question of right was, our kings were formerly in the practice of levying taxes upon the people by their own authority; that they justified this practice upon the very same principles, and with the same arguments, which are now used to support the right of parliament in taxing the Americans. They contended that the crown, being charged with the public defence, must be furnished also with the means of providing for it. That it would be absurd to commit a trust into the hands of one person, and to leave the power of executing it to depend upon the will of another. They therefore maintained the king's indefeasible right to tax the people, and that it was a power so essential to sovereignty, as to be inseparable from the crown. But notwithstanding the force of these arguments, and the allurements of the claim, one of the greatest and wisest of our monarchs, by an express and positive act, cut off from the sovereign power this right of taxing.

That statute, he observed, has been the foundation of the unity and happiness of England from that time; that it was absolutely *silent about the right*, and confined itself to giving satisfaction in future; that it laid down no general principles which might tend to affect the royal prerogative in other particulars; and that in all human probability, the preservation of the other branches of the prerogative, was owing to the clear and absolute surrender of that. He shewed that statute confisted of three principal parts; viz. a renunciation of taxing.—a repeal of all laws which had been made upon a contrary principle,—and a general pardon. He then shewed the conformity of his own bill to the spirit of that act, supposing Great Britain to stand in the place of the sovereign, and America in that of the subject; and that though the circumstances were not in every respect parallel, they were sufficiently so to justify his following an example, that gave satisfaction and security on the subject of *taxes*, and left all other rights and powers whatsoever, exactly upon the bottom on which they had stood before that arrangement had taken place.

From the account we have seen of the model, it will not be difficult to form some judgment of the construction of the copy. The great object of the bill was a renunciation of the exercise of taxation, without at all interfering in the question of right. It preserved the power of levying duties for the regulation of commerce, but the money so raised, was to be at the disposal of the several general assemblies. The crown was empowered, when necessary, to convene general meetings of deputies from the several colonies, and their acts were to be binding upon all. The duty act of the year 1767, with the late coercive and penal laws, were to be repealed. And a general amnesty was granted, upon the Americans laying down their arms within a given time. All future revenues, were to be free aids from the subjects there, as well as here.

The principal objections made to the bill were, that it conceded too much for us, and not near enough to satisfy the Americans. That their claims reached, not only to the declaratory act, and to all the others passed since 1763, but included in their sweep all the revenue laws from the act of trade down to the present time. They complain of all laws laying duties for the express purpose of revenue, and the bill goes no farther back than the year 1767; but to render the remedy real and efficient, it should be carried back to the year 1672. The Americans likewise complain of the admiralty jurisdiction, which, though it has undergone some change in its form, is as old as the act of navigation; this bill, which means to redress their grievances, and recover their confidence, should give them satisfaction on that, and every other head of grievance or complaint, or it did nothing.

As the bill did not reach far enough to answer its purposes on the one hand, so they said it gave up rights on the other, which had never been called in question till the present disputes began. For the vesting all duties which should be collected under any future laws for the regulation of commerce in the disposal of the assemblies, as if they had been levied immediately under their authority, was an acknowledgement, and establishing it as a principle, that parliament never had any right to the disposal of such revenues, and amounted in fact, to a virtual repeal of all the statutes from the act of trade downwards, in which any such specific appropriations had been made.

They also contended, that as a plan of accommodation had been already chalked out in the speech from the throne, it would be indecent and disrespectful to majesty, and withdrawing the confidence of parliament from those ministers who advised the measure, to adopt any other plan of conciliation, until that was either first disposed of, or that administration had declined the undertaking. A great part of the house were as usual of opinion, that nothing less than coercion, in its full extent, could answer any useful purpose, and said, that the greater disposition Great Britain shewed towards conciliation, the more obstinate, rebellious, and insolent, America would become.

The bill was ably supported, and the debates long and interesting. Most of the leaders and able speakers in opposition having taken a distinguished part in them. They were also powerfully opposed, and the most celebrated orators on both sides, were said, to have merited on that day, a more than common share of applause. The previous question, which had been early moved for, being at length put, was carried upon a division, at near four o'clock in the morning, by a majority of just two to one, the numbers being 210, to 105 who supported the motion. This was the highest proportion in numbers which the opposition had hitherto borne to the majority.

20th. In a few days after, the minister brought in the famous Prohibitory bill, totally interdicting all trade and intercourse with the thirteen united colonies. All property of Americans whether of ships or goods, on the high seas or in harbour, are declared forfeited to the captors, being the officers and crews of his majesty's ships of war; and several clauses of the bill were inserted to facilitate and to lessen the expence of the condemnation of prizes, and the recovery of prize money. This bill, besides its primary object, repealed the Boston Port, with the fishery, and restraining acts, their provisions in some instances being deemed insufficient in the present state of warfare, and their operation in others, being liable to interfere with that of the intended law. It also enabled the crown to appoint commissioners, who besides the power of simply granting pardons to individuals, were authorized to enquire into general and particular grievances, and empowered to determine, whether any part, or the whole of a colony, were returned to that state of obedience, which might entitle them to be received within the king's peace and protection, in which case, upon a declaration from the commissioners, the restrictions in the present bill were to cease in their favour.

The fire of opposition was rekindled by this bill, and it was encountered with great vigour in both houses. Is this, said they, the conciliatory proposition by which the house and the nation have been flattered. Are we to find peace in a cruel, indiscriminate, and perpetual declaration of war, against all the people in our own colonies? they said, that it was cutting off at the root all hopes of future accommodation; that it drove England and America to the fatal extremity, of absolute conquest on the one side, or absolute independency on the other. That it was as formal an act of abdication as could be penned, of our government over the colonies. That it would precipitate the Americans headlong into the arms of some foreign power; that it would compell them of necessity, to convert their merchant ships into privateers, whereby our West India islands would be totally ruined, and our foreign commerce in general suffer greater injury, than in any war in which we had ever been in-

volved. That our present wise and happy councils were not satisfied with the loss of America; but they must throw Africa and the West Indies after it, and hazard the security of every remaining part of the empire, in whatever quarter of the globe it was situated.

The supposed absurdity, and contradictory nature of the bill were ridiculed. It begins, said they, with a declaration of war, and a confiscation of the effects of 13 colonies, and after 35 of the most violent, cruel, and impolitic clauses, it concludes with some fallacious nugatory provisions, rather talking about, than proposing the attainment of peace. Can it be seriously said or expected, that offers of pardon will satisfy men who acknowledge no crime, and who are conscious, not of *doing* but of *suffering* wrong? Or will the prospect of exemption from commercial seizures, without the redress of any grievance, disarm those who have deliberately refused all commerce until their grievances shall be redressed. It was also contended, that as the Americans would inevitably open their ports to foreigners in consequence of this bill, so it would of course involve the ministers in that evil, which, notwithstanding their domestic sanguinary disposition, they of all others dreaded the most; it would involve them in a foreign war, which they had so repeatedly sacrificed the national honour to avoid.

It was said in support of the bill, that the Americans were already in a state of warfare with us, and while that war continued, it must necessarily be carried on by sea and land, and conducted in every manner and respect, as it would have been against alien enemies. That the nature, situation, and distance of that continent, rendered the operations by sea indispensable, as those by land, without that auxiliary, if not insufficient, would at least prove dilatory,

and the attainment of their object distant. That the stronger, more urgent, and immediate, the coercion was, the fewer would be the mischiefs, the less the expence, and the sooner would peace and order be restored. That an ill-judged appearance of lenity, by staying, or rendering languid, the hand of coercion, would be cruelty in the extremest degree, and prove equally ruinous to England and America.

That whatever real or apparent hardships or severities were contained in the bill, they were unavoidable in the present state of things, and it was in the power of the Americans, either collectively or individually, to prevent their operation. That the commissioners went out with the sword in one hand, and terms of conciliation in the other. America had the choice. Every colony had it in its power to take the benefit of the latter. It had only to acknowledge the legislative supremacy of Great Britain, or if unwilling to accede to such a general declaration, to contribute of its own accord towards the support of government, and thereby, as one of the parts of the empire, entitle itself to the protection of the whole, and the work was done, no severity or hardship would be known by that colony.

As to the losses which our merchants and the West India islands might sustain, these, if real, could only be lamented among the many other evils incident to war. But these evils, they said, were purely imaginary, and only held out to distress government, and impede its operations, by alarming the minds of the people, and exciting a domestic ferment. Would any one venture to assert, that America, destitute of resources, without a ship of war in her possession, and all her ports and docks open to our fleets, could encounter the naval power of Great Britain, or that the latter was not sufficient to protect our islands and commerce from loss and insult? With respect to foreign powers, their dispositions were said to be friendly towards us; but were it otherwise, none of them who held possessions in America, could be so blind to their own interest and security, as to encourage or support the rebellion of colonies; much less to suffer the establishment of an independent state in the new world.

The bringing in of this bill was attended with an unusual circumstance. Mr. Fox moved an amendment, to leave out the whole title and body of the bill, excepting only the parts, which related to the repeal of the Boston Port, the fishery, and the restraining acts. This motion occasioned very warm debates, and much animadversion, which continued till after midnight, when the question being put, the amendment was rejected upon a division, by a majority of 192 to 64 only.

The bill was not less debated on the 1st of December, when it was brought up for the second reading. In this stage, it was moved to commit it for the 5th, upon which several gentlemen requested the minister to postpone it for a few days, as the West India merchants and planters had advertised for a meeting of their body, upon that subject, on the 6th, thereby to give them an opportunity of laying any evidence or information they should think necessary before the house. This, though asked as a favour, was also represented as a matter of fairness and justice, where property was in any degree concerned, much more when so immense a share of it was at stake as in the present instance. The request, however, not being complied with, it was moved to amend the former motion, by putting off the commitment of the bill to the 12th. This amendment was lost upon a division, of 207 to 55; and the main question being put, after some further debate, was carried.

On the 5th, it again caused much debate. Several gentlemen, who wished to vote for the conciliatory part, but not for any other, complained that in its present form, it was an heterogeneous irreconcilable mixture of war and conciliation; that this mixture of hostility and conciliation in the same bill, must be intended, either to confound the attention by the variety of the objects, and divert it from observing the incongruity of the various parts, or to preclude debate, by carrying on the subject-matter of two bills in one. Lord Folkestone therefore moved, that the bill might be divided into two separate ones, that each might be separately considered and debated.

On the other hand it was supported by arguing, that nothing was so natural as what had been called so contradictory; war or peace in the same proposition. That they were the proper alternative in all such contests; war or resistance; peace or submission. What would the opposition have said if no powers of peace had been left? Though the motion was rejected by a majority of 76 to 34, the debates were continued in the committee, and carried on to the ensuing day, with great warmth and severity of observation. Another motion was made, that the chairman should leave the chair, in order to give time to the West India merchants to prepare and present their petition, which was overruled by a majority of 126 to 34. Other motions were made and received a negative without a division. Some amendments were however proposed and adopted. The clause for vesting the property of the seizures in the captors, was strongly combated. It was said that it would be a disgrace to the honour of the navy, which would be degraded by it into the rank of pirates; that it would taint the principles and corrupt the hearts of our brave seamen, who would thereby acquire habits of cruelty,

of piracy, and of robbery, with respect to their fellow-subjects, which could never be worn off; that it would extinguish in their breasts, all patriotism, all national pride and glory, and all generous ardour against our natural enemies, and substitute in their place a base indiscriminate spirit of rapine, which would equally affect friends and foes.

The extraordinary discretionary powers granted to the commissioners were much condemned, and said to be of such a nature, as should not be entrusted to any set of men in a free government; that they were vested in the sovereign upon certain occasions, but his ministers were considered as responsible for the due exercise of them; so that this bill granted a despotic and uncontroulable power to the commissioners, which the crown itself did not possess. One gentleman observed, that as this bill answered all the purposes, which the most sanguine and violent of the Americans could wish, in order to oblige their people to coalesce as one man in shaking off our government, its title should be altered and fitted to its purpose, and then it would be entitled, " A bill for carrying more effectually into execution the resolves of the Congress."

Upon receiving the report from the committee on the 8th, the petition from the West India merchants was read, and counsel heard in its support, after which it was moved, to postpone the further consideration of the report until the 23d, of the following January. This was supported upon the thinness of the house, most of the country gentlemen having quitted town. It was said, to offend against every rule of decency, to be equally disgraceful to parliament, and injurious to the nation, to hurry on national business of the greatest magnitude and importance, at such a season, and in so shameful and unprecedented a manner.

To these and numberless other strictures it was replied, that early notice had been given of the intention of the bill; that a fortnight had elapsed between the motion for bringing it in and the second reading, which was the time for debating the principle of a bill; that as it pursued the ideas thrown out in the speech from the throne, in the most exact conformity, it could consequently contain nothing novel; and that no matter or circumstance could possibly arise during the recess of parliament, which could alter their sentiments with respect to America, except its submission, in which event the bill would cease to operate. The whole of the American business was this day as fully debated, and as eagerly discussed, as if this had been the first time of its coming before them. The question being at length put, the motion for postponing the report was rejected.

A motion being then made by Mr. Burke, that Mr. Delancey, a [48] gentleman of great consideration at New York, and now obliged to come to England on account of his dissent from the proceedings of the Congress, should attend the house, it was rejected. Upon which, with a design to expose the neglect of all evidence, and refusal of information, which now prevailed, the following motion was made, " that it is necessary and proper to come to a resolution, that evidence relative to the state of America, the temper of the people there, and the probable operations of an act now depending, is unnecessary to this house; this house being already sufficiently acquainted with those matters."

On the 11th, previous to the third reading of the Prohibitory Bill, a motion was made by governor Johnston, that no evidence had been laid before the house of the delinquency of the province of Georgia, which was notwithstanding included in the same common punishment with the other colonies. This motion also tended to shew, the absurdity of proceeding without information, and the injustice of condemning without proof. Though this motion passed in the negative it occasioned a warm debate, in which the ministers were hard put to support the charge of delinquency.

As the minority now declared that they saw, that all attempts to withstand the force which was carrying the bill through, were utterly futile, and that the country gentlemen had (as they said) shamefully deserted their duty, and abandoned the public business, most of them grew weary of so fruitless a contest, and the house was thinly attended on that side, at the time of passing the bill. An attempt was however made to lessen the rigour of forfeitures, with respect to the trade between our West India islands and the continent of America, the ships in which were liable to confiscation, before they could possibly know that they had incurred any penalty, or that any such law was in existence. Another was also made, to defer the last reading till after the holidays; but they both proved equally fruitless, and the bill was passed upon a division, by a majority of 112 to 16 only.

We must now recur to several transactions which passed during the progress of this bill. We have already seen that several fruitless attempts had been made by opposition, to obtain information as to the state of the forces in North America, as well as of the expences hitherto incurred on the different parts of that service, so far as they could be made out. Notwithstanding the constant disappointment that attended these enquiries, Mr. Fox moved, to lay before the house, an account of the expences of the staff, hospitals, extraordinaries, and all military contingencies whatsoever, of the army in America, Nov. 22d. from August 1773, to August 1775, inclusive. He said that he had drawn up the motion in those words, in order that it might comprehend and lay open an astonishing scene of ministerial delusion to the house. That it would bring the staff, which had been artfully held back, into the full glare of day; it would shew that the expence of ordnance in the year 1775, had exceeded that in any of the duke of Marlborough's glorious campaigns; and it would give sufficient ground for prediction, that it would in the present year be considerably greater, than in any of the most victorious ones of the last war, when we were engaged in a contest, either directly or indirectly, with almost all the great powers in Europe, and retained a military force of 338,000 men in actual pay; it would shew how they were imposed upon in all other estimates as well as in that of the ordnance, in which the minister had the temerity to incur a debt of 240,000l. though every branch of the military service had been amply provided for by his own acknowledgement, and according to his own arrangements.

The ministers paid little attention to the reasons urged in support of this enquiry. They said, that some of the accounts were on the table, and they would all be regularly laid there, in their proper season; that they appertained to different heads of service or provision, and came properly under examination, when those several heads were to be considered; that it was unusual, irregular, and troublesome, to demand such accounts, when there was no question or business before the house to authorize such demands; and that however administration might be disposed to comply with such a requisition, it was not in their power to do it, as several of the accounts were not yet received.

This refusal, and the indifference with which it was accompanied, brought on some severe strictures. It was infisted, that the motion was strictly parliamentary; that it could convey no secret to the enemy; that no instance could be produced of the refusal of such information, except in cases where the want of the necessary materials rendered the compliance impossible; that this was obviated by the mover, who required no accounts nor information but what were in their custody or power. That their sitting any longer there was a mere farce, and could answer no purpose of their institution, if accounts of that nature could be refused. The question passed in the negative without a division.

On the same day the militia bill was read the third time, when a rider was proposed by Sir George Saville, and received, by which its duration was limited to seven years. The bill was then passed.

The third reading of the indemnity bill, brought 24th. on a very warm and animated debate. A motion was made for leaving out of the preamble those words, "doubts having been entertained of the legality of the measure;" and to insert in their place the following amendment, "that the measure of sending the Hanoverian troops to the garrisons of Gibraltar and Minorca was not warranted by law, and was against the spirit of the constitution." It was contended in support of the motion, that the bill in its present state carried an absurdity glaring on its very face; its body contained an indemnity for an offence, while the preamble declared that none had been committed; that it was an insult upon the house to propose the remittal of a punishment, and to make it acknowledge at the same time that none had been incurred; the mockery, they said, was too gross to be endured. That however dangerous the measure of introducing foreign troops was, the

precedent to be established by the bill was infinitely more so, as it was obtaining the sanction of parliament for that violation of the laws, and dangerous infraction of the constitution. That the minister came before the house in a situation, no other had ever ventured; he first violated the laws of his country, and then had the effrontery to come to parliament, not to claim its indulgence, but to make it testify, that what he had done was perfectly right and unexceptionable.

It can scarcely pass observation, that the minister found himself frequently obliged to vary his ground in the course of this business. In its beginning, to prevent the defection of the court part of the country gentlemen, after an appearance of firmness which bordered upon obstinacy, he suddenly seemed to conform to their ideas, in agreeing to the bringing in of the indemnity bill. When the great point of the address was gained, he seemed totally to forget the matter, and did not wish to be reminded of it. Their importunity at length growing troublesome, and many great points still remaining to be obtained, he seemed to coincide in their opinion, and accordingly brought in the bill; but took care to construct it in such a manner, as that it should answer purposes extremely differing from those which they intended. Since that time, he had continually varied his tone, from firmness to concession, and from concession to firmness, in proportion to the objects he had in view, and to the apparent complexion and present temper of the house. Having now nearly carried all the great points of the session through, and most of the country gentlemen being absent, he returned to his original doctrine, from which he would not recede in the smallest degree, and declared, that as far as his vote went, he would not suffer the alteration of a tittle in

the bill;—he wanted no indemnity, and let those who were in love with the measure, take the bill as it was, or not at all. However innocent the motives were, it certainly afforded matter of uneasiness to the friends of government, and to those who were the most remote from party views and prejudices, to see the court so eager at this critical time, to establish a precedent for the introduction of foreign troops without the consent of parliament, and so anxious, to prevent any thing like a censure which might in future be a clog to such a measure.

The amendment was rejected upon a division, by a majority of 130 to 58; and the bill accordingly passed in its original state.

In pursuance of the instructions from the city of 27th. London to its representatives, Mr. Alderman Oliver made a motion for an address to his majesty, to impart to the house, the original authors and advisers of several of the late measures (which were passed into laws, and were now specified), relative to America, before those measures were proposed in parliament. This business was undertaken without the approbation of, or any concert with, opposition in general, who disliked it upon many accounts, particularly, as being ineffective in its nature, very unparliamentary in its form and spirit, as not being founded upon any fact, and as offering a justification to ministers, by taking away their responsibility, and supposing their obnoxious measures to be the acts of other, or of unknown, persons. The minister turned it into ridicule, with much wit and spirit; and the opposition, in order to get rid of it without a flat negative, called for the order of the day, and failing in that, they moved the previous question; but the ministers being determined that the motion should not pass without reprobation, prevented that escape by a majority of 156 to 16; and the main question being then put, the motion was rejected upon a division, by a majority of 163 to 10 only. 50

The discouragement arising from the disappointment which he experienced in the preceding session, was not sufficient to deter Mr. Hartley from a similar

Dec. 7th.

attempt in the present, with a view of bringing about a reconciliation between Great Britain and her colonies. His plan of accommodation, which, in its ground and principle was much the same with his former, was principally formed on the general language of administration and that of the Congress, which, he was of opinion, did not so much disagree as was commonly imagined; the former growing every day more apparently indifferent about taxation, and the latter admitting a general superintendency in parliament.

The object of his propositions, were, first, an address to his majesty for a suspension of hostilities; a bill to enable the province of Massachusets bay to elect an assembly and council, according to their late charter; a test bill, establishing a right of trial by jury in all criminal cases, to all slaves in north America, for annulling all laws in any province repugnant thereto, and to be registered by the respective assemblies of all the colonies. Upon a compliance with this test of obedience, the operation of the two following bills was to commence, viz. a bill for a permanent reconciliation, by repealing all the laws since the year 1763, and thereby placing the colonies in the exact situation in which they stood at that time; and a general indemnity bill. The whole was concluded with a motion for an address to the throne, that when quiet was restored, it might be proper to send letters of requisition, as usual, to the several colonies, for such supplies as were

necessary for government and defence. This proposition seems to have been carried on nearly as little in concert with the generality of the opposition as the former.

The ministers treated these conciliatory propositions with some degree of inattention and indifference. They said, in general, that the main subject of these motions had been already frequently and fully discussed; that until the plan proposed from the throne was tried, and its effects known, it was nugatory, and wasting the time of the house, to break in upon them with fresh proposals; that the sense of a great majority of the house had been frequently declared against the principles of these resolutions; that they held out no security, and were accompanied with no solemn sanction, that if they were acceded to on our part, they would be accepted by the Americans; that the claim of taxation virtually included the claim of sovereignty, it being impossible to relinquish the one without surrendering the other; and that the idea of obtaining a productive revenue from America had never been abandoned.

The debate was of course short, and the question being put upon the first resolution, it was rejected upon a division by a majority of 113 to 21; the other resolutions received a negative without a division.

The Indemnity Bill, after all the trouble it had given to the minister and to the country gentlemen in the House of Commons, was thrown out by the Lords. It was opposed in that house by the Marquis of Rockingham, who condemned it in very strong terms, upon the direct variance between the preamble and the enacting clauses; he said, that the holding out of an indemnity, while it asserted that the persons indemnified were guilty of no offence, would render it a disgrace to our laws and legislation; and that it besides,

under that colour of indemnity, gave a sanction to a glaring violation both of the law and constitution, in placing foreign troops in our garrisons. As the Lords in administration agreed with the noble Marquis upon the point of impropriety or absurdity in its structure, and did not think an indemnity at all necessary, they readily coincided in rejecting the bill, so that it was thrown out without either defence or division.

The Prohibitory Bill met with great opposition in the House of Lords, almost every part of it undergoing a specific discussion. Upon the motion for 15th. its commitment after the second reading, the debates were long, able, and animated; and some very warm and pointed personal altercation and animadversion took place. The Lords in opposition combated the bill upon every ground of policy, justice, and expediency. On the former they observed, that by considering the Americans as a foreign nation, and declaring war on them in that character, this bill drew the line of separation, chalked out the way, and prepared their minds, for that independency which they were charged with affecting; that the English on both sides of the ocean, were now to be taught by act of parliament, to consider themselves as separate and distinct nations; as nations susceptible of general hostility, and proper parties for mutual declarations of war, and treaties of peace. That by the promiscuous and indiscriminate rapine of the property of friends and foes, authorized by the bill, it must compleat what yet remained to be compleated, of union in North America against the authority of parliament; and that the friends of government in that country, whose numbers and power have been so much boasted of by administration, will now plainly see, that parliament is much more inclined to distress, than able or willing to protect.

Its impolicy and injustice with respect to the West Indies, was represented to be still more glaring. Here it inflicts a much more certain and severe punishment upon a people not even suspected of crime or offence, than it is capable of extending to the most refractory of the Americans. An act of the British parliament, is called in as a supplementary aid, and an extension of the authority of the Congress, in that measure, which of all others adopted by that body, was the most reprehensible and unjustifiable on their side, and the most pernicious to us, the cutting off their usual supplies of provisions and necessaries from those unhappy islands. The measure of confiscating those vessels, which, to avoid all breach of the laws, and all illicit commerce, were laid up by the owners in their own docks and harbours, there waiting to be brought into use upon a return of peace and better times, was equally reprobated.

But of all the parts of this law, none was treated with so much severity in that house, or excited such apparent indignation, as that clause, by which all those who were taken on board the American vessels, were indiscriminately compelled, without distinction of persons, to serve as common sailors in our ships of war. This clause was marked with every possible stigma, and was described by the Lords in their protest, as " a refinement in tyranny," which, " in a sentence worse than death, obliges the unhappy men who shall be made captives in this predatory war, to bear arms against their families, kindred, friends and country; and after being plundered themselves, to become accomplices in plundering their brethren." The injustice and cruelty of this clause, they said, was still heightened, by rendering the unhappy persons who were thus compelled, subject to the articles of war, and liable to be shot for desertion. They pathetically represented the miseries to which persons in this melancholy situation, particularly those of the better sort, would be subject, from the insolence and outrage of those with whom they were obliged to serve, who being themselves destitute of liberal principles and education, would still continue to consider and treat them as rebels; nor did they consider it as the smallest part of the calamity, that they would be frequently obliged to be lookers on, when the spoils of their honest industry, and the natural support of their sober families, was squandered in riot and debauchery, by those profligate comrades, with whom they were at the same time obliged to live, and to serve. Upon the whole, this situation, was said, to be the last degree of wretchedness and indignity, to which human nature could be subjected; and that a cruelty, unknown to the most savage nations, was thus to be practised by Englishmen on Englishmen. They insisted, that no man could be despoiled of his goods as a foreign enemy, and at the same time obliged to serve the state as a citizen, upon any principle of law or right, known among civilized nations. That such a compulsion upon prisoners as the present, is unknown in any case of war or rebellion; and the only examples of the sort that can be produced, must be found among pirates;—the outlaws and enemies of human society.

To these and many other charges against the nature and principles of the bill, the cruelty, the daring rebellion, and the ultimate treasonable views of the Americans, were brought in justification. They were not even content with rebellion simply, they had commenced an offensive war against us, and invaded our dominions with numerous armies. The principle of the bill was, to make a naval war upon America; and as in such cases it would be impossible to make distinctions in favour of the innocent, the bill was framed according to the general ideas of carrying on war against a foreign enemy, where it is always taken for granted, that every individual is concerned in and abetting every act of public hostility. That nothing could be more right or expedient, than the encouragement given to that most useful and deserving body of our people, the seamen, by vesting in them the effects which they should take from the enemy; that it would induce them to act with double vigour, and be at the same time a means of manning the navy; and that it had been practised in the two last wars, when its good effects were too well and too generally known to require any illustration. That this bill was indispensably necessary, as no existing law had foreseen, or provided for the case, of carrying on a sea war against rebels.

As to the cruelty and injustice so much complained of, in compelling the crews of the American vessels to serve in the navy, these charges were so far from being acknowledged, that this measure was said to be an act of grace and favour to them; instead of confining them in a close prison during the continuance of the war, which must be the case if they were considered as alien enemies, or punishing them as traitors, if considered as rebels, they were immediately rated upon the King's books, and put upon the same footing with a great body of his most useful and faithful subjects; suffering no inconvenience but that which they were always liable to, of being pressed into his Majesty's service; as to the supposed violation of their principles, which was so much lamented, their pay and emoluments were said to be a full compensation for all scruples and delicacies of that nature.

The supposed mischiefs arising to our West-India islands, were said to be greatly aggravated; but at any rate, as well as the losses which the well-disposed in North America might sustain, were to be considered as a part of those unavoidable evils which are incident to war. A great law Lord [51] declared, in the further progress of the bill, that we were not now to consider the questions of original right or wrong, justice or injustice ; we were engaged in a war, and we must use our utmost efforts to obtain the ends proposed by it ; we must fight or be pursued ; and the justice of the cause must give way to our present situation. To this he applied the laconic speech of a brave Scotch officer in the service of Gustavus Adolphus, who, pointing to the enemy, said to his men, " See you those, lads; kill them, or they will kill you."

After long debates, which were ably supported till near eleven at night, the question for commitment being put, was carried upon a division, by a majority of 78, including 30 proxies, to 19, including seven proxies.

In this state of the bill, a protest of uncommon length, and still greater energy, was entered against it, in which several of its parts underwent the severest scrutiny, and the season of carrying a bill through, so unprecedented in its nature, and important in its consequences, at a time when, they say, most of the independent members of both houses were called away by their domestic affairs, and when few but those in the immediate pay of the court, and attending on their employments, remained in town, was particularly condemned.

In three days after, upon going into a committee on the bill, the Duke of Manchester moved for deferring the commitment till after the holidays. He founded his motion, besides the importance and novelty of the bill, upon the reports which were then arrived of our losses in Canada. The motion was supported by the Marquis of

Rockingham, upon the farther ground, of the alarm which the bill had excited among the trading and commercial part of the nation. The motion passed in the negative without a division.

The noble Duke then offered to present a petition from the merchants of Bristol, stating the ruinous consequences of the bill, to themselves in particular, as well as to the mercantile interest in general. But as the order of the day had been already moved for, it was said, that the petition could not now be received. Some clauses in favour of the British traders, and of the West-India islands, were, however, proposed by the Lords in administration, and received by the committee, which, it was supposed, would in some degree remedy the grievances stated in the petition.

On the third reading of the bill, an amendment, 20th. in favour of the merchants, to one of the clauses, was proposed by the Marquis of Rockingham, intending to prolong the commencement of the operation of the bill, from the 1st of January to the 1st of March, and thereby to preserve from confiscation the property of those merchants, who under the faith of parliament in the two restrictive laws, had loaded vessels with lumber in North America for the West-India islands. This was opposed on two grounds ; first, that it was contrary to established practice, to oppose any particular clause in a bill at the third reading, the objection must go to the whole, and not to any particular part ; and secondly, that the delay required in the operation, would overthrow the principle of the bill, and render it totally inefficacious. The motion was lost without a division, and the bill passed of course.

The bill being returned on the next day to the Commons, the amendments were agreed to, after [52] an ineffectual attempt to defer the

consideration of them for six months. Thus was a recess at length obtained, after pushing forward a multiplicity of matter and business, scarcely ever known before Christmas.

Petition from the colony of Nova Scotia. Resolutions passed, but no bill brought in. Motion and debates relative to a message sent to the parliament of Ireland. Motion for an enquiry into the causes of the ill success in North America. Great debates. German treaties laid before the House of Commons, and produce long debates. Duke of Richmond's motion for an address relative to the German treaties. Great debates. Motion rejected. Protest. Considerable debates in the Committee of Supply. Motion for extraordinary expences carried by a great majority. Duke of Grafton's motion for an address relative to the colonies. Debates. Motion rejected. Progress of the bill for a militia in Scotland. Bill at length rejected. Enquiry into licences granted to ships bound to North America. Speech from the throne.

THE rapidity with which a continued succession of business was carried through, and the earnestness with which matters of great concern were agitated before the recess of parliament, occasioned our passing over a petition from the assembly of Nova Scotia, which was presented to each House at the opening of the session. It was sent from that assembly in consequence of Lord North's conciliatory proposition; and was intended, by those who promoted it in that colony, as a pattern and precedent for the rest. It was a separate proposal, and in that light coincided with the general policy, which dictated the conciliatory proposition. It seemed to propose some revenue originating in the colonies, and to be enacted by parliament; and though the probable amount would be inconsiderable, yet the establishment of the doctrine being at that time of more consideration, than the amount of the revenue immediately to be obtained, the petition was more favourably received by administration; and on the very first day of the session, when the Speaker laid it before the House of Commons, a short day was appointed for taking it into consideration, though not without some animadversion on the part of opposition, who treated the whole as one of those mean contrivances, by which ministry, as they said, were in the practice of mocking the credulity and implicit confidence of parliament; and they predicted, that it would come to the end which was to be expected from its futility, and the impracticable nature of the scheme which it was intended to execute.

The mode of granting a revenue proposed by this assembly, was the payment of some specific duty per cent. upon the importation of all foreign commodities, bay salt only excepted, by which means the amount of the revenue would at all times bear a due relation and proportion to the opulence and consumption of the province. It was intended, that the rate of this duty should in the first instance be fixed by parliament, and afterwards be perpetual and unchangeable, excepting only, that at certain stated times it was to undergo such regulation, as would preserve the comparative value of money and commodities in its original state.

When the proposition came to be debated in the committee, the objections which had been only hinted the first day, were more largely and strongly enforced. Against those the ministers contended, that the faith of the house and nation obliged them to give effect to a plan laid before them in consequence of their own resolution, to which the offer was substantially agreeable. That the smallness of the revenue offered could be no objection; that if it was a poor provision, it came from a poor province; but it would grow with the circumstances of the country; and under this plan we should find an advantage from the prosperity of our colonies very different from our former experience, when we found only an increase of insolence, and not of support and supply, from their increase of strength. That the fidelity of parliament to its engagements, and the moderation of its demands, would engage the other colonies to submission, and would disabuse them with regard to the violent prejudices instilled into them by their factious leaders. That more favourable times and good management would improve this moderate beginning into a beneficial revenue.

On the other hand, the minority treated it with the greatest scorn. They said it was a thing not fit to be seriously debated. That if the ministers had bound the public faith to this absurd and ridiculous project, it was a great aggravation of their offence so to trifle with the national honour. That the old revenue which they were to give up, every part of which (except the tea tax) had been quietly paid in all the colonies, was of more value than the new duties which were proposed to be granted; and this was the sort of relief to the public burthens sought by our war, and by the conciliatory proposition which was framed to end it. They said, that the principle of the tea tax continued to haunt them in every thing they did; for as that tax drew back a duty which ought to be paid here, in order to impose a smaller duty in America, this was exactly of the same nature, but of a much wider, and of a more mischievous extent, as it laid eight per cent. not on one article, but on all the certificate goods sent from England, from which, to facilitate the trade to the colonies, we had drawn back all the duties payable at home. These, and very many other objections, drew the debates into length in the committee; but the ministry, though evidently embarrassed, were resolved to carry resolutions conformable to the petition.

Many causes concurred to lessen the effect of this petition from Nova Scotia. That province had cost government immense sums of money, without its growth or value in any degree corresponding with the expence. It was still unequal to the support of its own civil government, the expence of which was annually granted by parliament; so that the offer of a revenue in such circumstances, however laudable the motives and intention, carried in some degree a ludicrous appearance. As it was also under the influence of a military power, its acts could not be supposed to carry any great weight as an example, with those colonies who abhorred such an appearance, and whose present troubles arose from a defence of their civil immunities and constitution.

The petition besides contained a long catalogue of grievances, the redress of which was as earnestly pressed, though in more supplicant language, as a similar redress had been by the other provinces, and seemed in some degree to be considered as conditional and necessary, towards the establishment of a permanent connexion, and for retaining the affection and obedience of the people. The assembly also pressed most earnestly, that when at any time future exigencies should require further supplies, the requisition should be made in the usual manner formerly practised, whereby they might have an opportunity of shewing their duty and attachment, their sense of the cause for which it was made, and by that means, and that only, of rendering the sovereign acquainted with the true sense of his people in that distant part of his dominions. So that upon the whole, excepting the profession of submission to the supreme legislature, which had only of late been a question any where, and the proposal of a duty, which seemed little more than a commercial regulation, this petition did not contain any thing essentially different from the former applications of other colonies.

Nov. 23d. Resolutions to the following purpose were however proposed by the minister, and passed in a committee, as foundations for an intended bill; viz. That the proposal of a poundage duty, ad valorem, upon all commodities imported, (bay salt excepted) not being the produce of the British dominions in Europe or America, to be disposed of by parliament, should be accepted, and the duty fixed at 8 s. per cent. upon all such commodities. That as soon as the necessary acts for that purpose were passed by the assembly of Nova Scotia, and had received the royal approbation, all other taxes and duties in that province should cease and be discontinued, and no others laid on, while those acts continued in force, excepting only such duties as were found necessary for the regulation of commerce, the nett produce of which were to be carried to the account of the province. And to admit an importation into that province of wines, oranges, lemons, currants, and raisins, directly from the place of their growth and produce.

This relaxation of the Act of Navigation, though not very considerable, was intended to shew the favourable disposition of parliament towards this province, which had set so laudable an example of obedience; and seemed to hold out to the colonies in general, an enlargement of commerce, as a compensation for their acceding to the conciliatory resolution. Indeed much attention was paid to this petition, as forming a model for future taxation, and proving, what had been denied, that the system of the conciliatory proposition was not impracticable. Serious hopes were entertained of its effect until it had passed the committee. But it seemed as if the pacific system, in which this was considered as a leading part,

was about that time laid aside. Whatever the cause might have been, to the surprize of many, the whole matter was suffered to die away; no bill was brought in, and the petition was heard no more of after the holidays.

• • •

20th. In a few days after Mr. Fox made a motion, That it be referred to a committee to enquire into the causes of the ill success of his Majesty's arms in North America, as also, into the causes of the defection of the people of the province of Quebec. This gentleman introduced and supported his motion with his usual great ability. He declined, he said, for the present, to enter into any recapitulation of the causes of the unhappy dispute with America. He should not develope that system, from whence the measures now carrying on were supposed to originate. He should forbear to animadvert upon a system, that in its principles, complexion, and every constituent part, gave the fullest and most unequivocal proofs, that its ultimate design was the total destruction of the constitution of this free form of government. These were assertions that might be disputed. He wished to draw their attention to certain well-known, indisputable, uncontrovertible facts. Upon the same principle he declined entering into any of the questions of right or claims on either side. He did not mean to controvert the expediency, practicability, nor a single ministerial ground, on which the present measures respecting America were taken up, pursued, or defended. He would even, for argument sake allow for the present, that administration had acted perfectly right. But all these matters being admitted in their favour, and the ground cleared in all other respects, he would examine, from the time that coercive measures had been adopted, the means that had been used for giving them effect.

He intended to commence his proposed enquiry at the time, when the minister, in the month of February, 1774, proposed to the house certain resolutions, as a ground of complaint, which he followed with the Boston Port Bill. This he fixed as the æra, when coercive measures were undeniably determined upon. He grounded his motion on the clear and positive assertion, and repeatedly acknowledged fact, that there had been mismanagement, misconduct, incapacity, or neglect, somewhere; and supported its propriety and necessity, upon the simple alternative, that these faults, and their consequent evils, must be imputed either to our ministers at home, or to our military commanders abroad; either the former had planned measures which were impracticable, or if practicable, had not afforded them the necessary support, or else the latter had failed in carrying them into execution, and were incapable of doing their duty; in either case, it was fit to know where the fault lay; or if it was shared between them, it was absolutely necessary, before it was too late, and the nation fell a victim to misconduct and incapacity, that the house should be fully informed on the subject, and enabled to remedy the evil, by being rendered sensible, that the one were as unfit to deliberate and determine, as the other to perform or carry into execution.

He hoped, that as he had made such concessions, in dropping all other subjects of dispute, in order to simplify the immediate question, and lay its objects nakedly, and abstracted from all other matter before them, as he had drawn a line between, and intended totally to separate measures from men, that no independent gentleman would refuse to concur in the enquiry. Indeed, he did not see upon what principle any gentleman in that character could oppose it; and insisted, that if the ministers were not conscious of being culpable in the highest degree, they would rejoice at such an opportunity of vindicating their conduct to the public, and of letting them see, that our present national disgraces and misfortunes, and the misapplication of that support which they had so liberally given, were not owing to their ignorance, incapacity, or want of integrity. Public justice demanded such an enquiry. The individuals on whom the obloquy rested, were entitled to be heard in their own defence. To withhold the information necessary to their justification, would be an insult to the nation, as well as an act of private injustice. None but the guilty could wish to evade it. None of our commanders by sea or land, could be sure of preserving their honour for a single moment; if they were to be buried under public disgrace, in order to hide, protect, or palliate, the ignorance, blunders, and incapacity of others.

He entered into a short but comprehensive detail of the measures which had hitherto been pursued in supporting the plan of coercion, in which he drew in the most glowing colours, and placed in the strongest lights, such representations of what, he stiled, folly in the cabinet, ignorance in office, inability in framing, and misconduct in executing, with such a shameful and servile acquiescence in parliament, as, he said, had never before disgraced the councils of this, or perhaps any other country. Upon the whole, he was exceedingly pointed and severe upon the ministers, and little less so, with respect to the body which he was addressing.

Administration seemed exceedingly embarrassed in this debate, and as little united as in the former. The weight of defence, or of evading the enquiry, fell principally upon the gentlemen in inferior and less responsible office; the minister himself not rising until the close of the debate. A noble Lord, under the description we have mentioned, moved the previous question early in the debate, which did not, however, lessen its extent, or shorten its duration. The topics used in the speech from the throne, furnished the principal arguments against the motion. The court party admitted that little had been done, great losses had been sustained, and errors apparently of no small magnitude committed. But the fault lay, where the punishment would finally fall, not in the ministers, but in the rebels. The Americans had taken an unworthy and base advantage of the clemency, and desire of conciliation, by which Great Britain was actuated; whilst we, unwilling to proceed to the rigours of punishment, were proposing terms of mutual advantage, and endeavouring to establish a lasting harmony, they were strengthening themselves in rebellion, and making every preparation for war. Thus was a season for effectual coercion unfortunately lost; but in a manner that will ever do honour to our national character, and convince all mankind of the lenity, forbearance, and temperate justice of our government; whilst it equally shews the incorrigible turpitude of our rebellious colonists.

Others said, that as affairs in America were totally changed, so was likewise, and with propriety, the conduct of government. Till the sword was drawn, conciliatory measures were pursued; as soon as that event took place, we adopted the most effectual means of coercion, which would be steadily persevered in till the end was accomplished. That it was unfair, to state objections against the conduct of administration in the early stages of this business, which were only applicable to a state of hostility and open rebellion; that what was wisdom in the former situation, would be treachery or madness in the latter. And that government was already taking the most effectual and decisive measures, to remedy those very evils which were the proposed objects of censure.

It was besides said, that if such an enquiry were at all necessary, this was not the proper season. It should be deferred till the end of the war, when there would be leisure and opportunity for such an investigation. Several of those who were the objects of enquiry, or whose testimony would be necessary, were not in the kingdom; they were now fulfilling their duty in America; strenuously endeavouring to remedy all evils, to remove all causes of complaint, and to atone for past errors, if any had been committed. It was also contended, that as a change of measures had been announced from the throne, it would be highly disrespectful and improper to enter into such an examination, untill those measures were tried and the event known.

Several, however, on the same side, joined the minority in severely censuring the conduct hitherto pursued; but congratulated themselves on the present change of system, and the happy consequences which they expected from so vigorous a scheme of coercion. The previous question being at length put, at near three in the morning, the motion was rejected upon a division, by a majority of 240, to 104.

The treaties lately entered into between his Majesty, the Landgrave of Hesse-Cassel, the Duke of Brunswick, and the hereditary Prince of Hesse-Cassel, for the hiring of different bodies of their troops for the American service, amounting in the whole to about 17000 men, having been laid before the house, and a motion being made by Feb. 29th. the minister for referring them to the Committee of Supply, this matter became a subject of very considerable debate.

The measure in general of procuring foreign troops was supported, on the necessity of reducing América, and the total impracticability, which had already been fully experienced, of raising by any means, and in any degree, a sufficient number of levies within these kingdoms for that purpose. It was, however, further contended, that if such forces could have been raised at home, and even to the amount supposed necessary in point of number, it could not be expected, that raw and undisciplined troops, who had never seen any service, and who were not yet hardened to any change of food, climate, or habits of life, could answer the purpose so well, as tried experienced veterans, whose constitutional habits were already formed, as well as their military. To these was added, the great loss which the withdrawing so many hands from husbandry and manufactures would be to the nation. And it was also remembered, that the expence in that case would not end with the war; but that the nation would be saddled with the heavy and lasting incumbrance, of the half-pay establishment of near thirty battalions. So that in every point of view, whether considered with respect to general policy, or national expediency, the present treaties would be found equally prudent and necessary.

It then only remained to be considered, whether these treaties were conducted with all the judgment, and managed with all the frugality, that the nature of the case would admit. With respect to this point, if the necessity was admitted, which it was presumed no body would attempt to controvert, it would of course be acknowledged, that the troops must be obtained at any price, and upon any terms, which did not exceed in extent or value the urgency of the demand. This, however, they said, was not the case, and the terms were so far from being proportioned to the

necessity, that they were substantially the same with those of former treaties, by which we obtained troops for purposes of infinitely less national importance than the present. But, even supposing that the case had been otherwise, and that the present terms had not been so advantageous as those upon some former occasions, but bore some relation to the necessity; still, they insisted, that the measure would have been highly prudent and œconomical, and that, considering merely the point of expence, it would be found that the foreign troops were obtained much cheaper than home levies, supposing they could be procured as usual. They closed these arguments by observing, that this measure was no matter of surprize or novelty, as we had at all times been under a necessity of employing foreigners in our wars.

On the other side, this measure was reprobated in all its parts. The necessity absolutely denied. We forced on, said they, a civil war most wantonly, and this was one of the first of its alarming and ruinous consequences. Great Britain, they said, was now disgraced in the eyes of all Europe, to answer purposes apparently of her power and dominion, but in reality of her subjection and servitude. She was to be impoverished, and what was still perhaps worse, she was compelled to degrade herself, by applying in the most mortifying and humiliating manner to the petty Princes of Germany for succours against her own subjects, and submitting to indignities never before prescribed to a crowned head, presiding over so great and powerful a nation. In support of these positions, they took the treaties to pieces, and pointed out, as objectionable, the following parts;— That the troops were to enter into pay before they began to march; a thing never known before. That levy-money was to be paid at the rate of near 7l. 10s. a man. That, not satisfied with this extortion, those princes were also to be subsidized. That they had the modesty to insist on a double subsidy. That the subsidy is in one instance to be continued for two years, and for one year in another, after the troops have returned to their respective countries. And that a body of 12000 foreigners are to be introduced into the British dominions, under no controul of either King or parliament; for the express words of the treaty are, " that this body of troops" (being the Hessians) " shall remain under the command of their General, to whom his most serene Highness has entrusted the command."

The debates were long and warm, and were of course productive of a very late night. The bad terms upon which these forces were obtained was much laboured by the opposition, and they entered into various calculations to shew, that besides the extraordinary expences in the point of exportation, every thousand Germans, upon this system, would cost the nation more than 1500 of its own levies. A point merely speculative was also much agitated, the ministers endeavouring to render the present great expences more eligible, by representing that they would not be lasting, and that this German addition to the forces already voted, would be fully sufficient for the subjugation of the Americans, and the bringing of the war to a final and happy conclusion in the ensuing campaign. It was, indeed, held out, that this great force would in all likelihood have little more to do, than to shew itself and return. A great body of the very best soldiery in Europe; inspired only with military maxims and ideas, too well disciplined to be disorderly and cruel, and too martial to be kept back by any false lenity, could not fail of bringing matters to a speedy conclusion. This measure would prove to be true economy as well as true po-

licy. If a little more levy-money was paid than for British, the men we had were trained, not raw troops; and as for the continuance of the payment for some time after the war, this was but reasonable, as the Landgrave, and the other Princes, could not have their troops returned to them as soon as we might accept the submission of the rebels.

In answer to this it was confidently asserted on the side of opposition, that neither the present, nor any other force we were able to send out, would be equal to an absolute conquest of America, either in one, or in two campaigns, and that this was only the beginning, even without the interference of any foreign power, of the most ruinous and fatal war we were ever engaged in. The question upon the minister's motion being put after two o'clock, it was carried upon a division, by a majority of 242, to 88.

This matter was again much agitated on March 4th. receiving the report from the Committee of Enquiry; several objections were made to different parts of the treaties, and several explanations demanded relative to others, which were either said to be obscure in themselves, or to leave some essential matter unprovided for. The first resolution of the committee being carried, the following motion was then made by Colonel Barré, and agreed to, " That an humble address be presented to his Majesty, to humbly desire him to use his interest, that the German troops in British pay, now or hereafter, may be cloathed with the manufactures of this country."

Nor was the affair of the 5th. German treaties less agitated in the House of Lords, where the Duke of Richmond moved for an address, of considerable length, to his Majesty, which, besides several pointed observations relative to the treaties in particular, took

in a comprehensive view of the situation of American affairs in general, and the probable consequences of a perseverance in the present measures, all tending to give weight and efficacy to a request, that his Majesty would be graciously pleased to countermand the march of the troops of Hesse, Hanau, and Brunswick; and likewise give directions for an immediate suspension of hostilities in America, in order to lay a foundation for a happy and permanent reconciliation between the divided parts of this distracted empire.

The noble mover took a most comprehensive view of the subject. He entered into an historical detail of the several treaties which had been concluded with the Landgrave's of Hesse from the year 1702 to the present, and shewed, that in every succeeding treaty from the first they had risen in their demands, and established every fresh extortion as a precedent not to be departed from in the future. That the present treaty, however, outstripped all others, not only in point of imposition, but of the unaccountable and unprecedented conditions which it included. As to the first, he shewed from various laborious and accurate calculations, that the use of 17,300 mercenaries for the present year, would not, taking in all contingencies, cost the nation less than one million and a half sterling; an expence, he maintained, not to be paralleled in the history of mankind, for the service of an equal number of men.

These matters, however serious in the present miserable state of our finances, and the enormous weight of public burthens we groan under, were not, he said, what pressed most forcibly on his mind. It was the tenor of the treaties, the ambiguous terms in which they were conceived, and the dangerous precedents they established or slid into, that principally called forth his attention, and gave rife to his fears. He obferved, he faid, with grief, and the beft founded jealoufy, that an overruling influence had for fome years paft pervaded our councils; that this influence had been exercifed in effecting meafures of a moft dangerous and dark complexion; that it fometimes made its approaches by ftealth, at other times rendered itfelf vifible in open day, and proceeded to acts of violence. Hanoverians had been brought into the Britifh dominions without the confent of parliament. An attempt had been made to place Ireland in the hands of foreigners. And if any doubt remained of the tendency of thofe meafures, it was removed by thefe treaties, which afforded the moft ample matter for great and ferious alarm.

He obferved, that though the treaties expreffed the contrary in words, they were not in reality founded upon any found principle of alliance or reciprocal fupport. They contained a mere mercenary Smithfield bargain, for the price of a certain number of hirelings, who were bought and fold like fo many beafts for flaughter. There was no common intereft which mutually bound the parties; and if there were, both our conduct, and that of thofe Princes, was the moft fingular ever known. They were to be fubfidized. They were to have levy-money. They were to have a double fubfidy. Their corps were to be kept up compleat. They were to be paid till the troops returned to their refpective countries; and the fubfidies were to be continued after the fervice.

Yet in this downright mercenary bargain of fale and purchafe, we were bound, that if any of thofe Princes were attacked, or fhould wantonly begin, or provoke an attack, for the engagement was left general and unconditional, we fhould affift them with our utmoft force. Thus, we were not only to pay double for the affiftance of a

few thoufands of foreign mercenaries, but we were befides bound in the moft folemn engagements to fupport the quarrels and interefts of their mafters; a kind of contract, which might, not improbably, involve us in a continental war.

He then reminded the Lords who had fupported the late peace of Paris, of the language which they, and all others on the fame fide, held towards the clofe of the late war. A noble Earl, who then prefided at the head of public affairs, and a late Duke, who con-[54] cluded that treaty, with all their friends and partizans, difclaimed in words and in writing, both within doors and without, all continental connections of whatever nature; and all employment of foreigners, whatever the fervice or neceffity. They admitted themfelves, that the enemy were at our feet, and the conqueft of the Spanifh fettlements in a manner certain, yet they fubmitted to a peace certainly inadequate, on no other ground but our inability to raife taxes; they faid, that the national debt was too enormous, to accept, even this advantage, at any price; that we were already ruined by fuccefs; and that even to profecute certain conqueft, would be the height of political phrenzy. He afked, what extraordinary change of circumftances had fince taken place, that now-renders a doubtful, and in any cafe ruinous civil war, a war equally incapable of fame and advantage, to be not only thought eligible, but to be profecuted with a degree of eagernefs, with an acrimony and malignity, unknown upon any other occafion? How comes the reprobated policy of employing foreign forces to be now revived? Will the paying off feven millions of the national debt in thirteen years peace, juftify this change of fyftem, when the extraordinary expences of the enfuing campaign will amount to a greater fum? Or

will it hereafter be credited, that they are the fame men who held thofe doctrines, who reduced them into practice, who broke off all continental connections, and who furrendered the fruits of a moft glorious and fuccefsful war, to obtain a tranfient and inadequate peace, who are the framers of all the prefent meafures?

That claufe in the 9th article of the Heffian treaty, which provides that the crown fhall employ thofe troops as it thinks proper by land in Europe, was much commented on by the noble mover, and other lords on the fame fide, and reprefented as bearing a moft dark and dangerous complexion. It was afked, what country in Europe, except thefe kingdoms, they could be employed in? what military operations were intended for them here? Were fuch meafures propofed, as it was forefeen would render a foreign force neceffary in this country? And was a civil war here alfo intended, to round the prefent fyftem?

All the American queftions were of courfe brought up in the further fupport of the motion, and all the old ground of the injuftice, inexpediency, impracticability, the ruinous effects, and fatal tendency of the war, again gone over. It was alfo ftrongly urged, that as the Americans had hitherto abftained from applying for affiftance to foreign powers, and had ventured to commit themfelves fingly in this arduous conteft, rather than have recourfe to fo odious and dangerous a refuge, it was the height of political folly and madnefs in us, to induce them to depart from that temperate ground, by fetting them an example of fo fatal a tendency. For it cannot be doubted, if this dangerous meafure is carried into execution, that they will immediately retaliate, and think themfelves fully juftified by the example, in forming alliances with foreign powers, and hiring foreign forces, (if they do not procure them upon terms more advantageous to themselves and ruinous to us,) to oppose those mercenaries whom we send for their destruction. Nor is it any more to be doubted, that other powers in Europe, of a very different cast and order, from those of Hesse, Brunswick, and Hanau, will consider themselves, to be fully as well entitled to interfere in our domestic quarrels. And thus, whilst in the rage and madness of civil contention, the strength and flower of the nation is exhausted on the other side of the Atlantic, we shall lie open and defenceless to the attacks of our most formidable and vindictive enemies.

It was contended, that these, and numberless other evils which were stated, would be prevented or remedied, by a compliance with the motion; and that parliament would thereby have time and opportunity to propose such conditions as the ultimatum of its demands, as it would be fitting for Great Britain to offer, and for America, as a great constituent part of the empire, to accept.

The ministers defended the treaties upon the same ground in general, on which they had been supported in the house of commons. The principal stress was laid upon the strong plea of necessity, which covered the measure at large. As to particular objections, they contended, that upon the whole, the terms were more reasonable than could have been expected. That the suddenness of the requisition, the known necessity from which it proceeded, together with the novelty, distance, length of sea voyage, and other disagreeable circumstances particularly attending this service, would have warranted much higher demands. That the treaties were framed in conformity to established usage and precedent. That the undertaking the defence of the German states from whom we hired troops, could not be supposed to operate towards bringing on a war in Germany; that the pompous high sounding phrases of alliance, were mere sounds, a form of words which conveyed no meaning, and which consequently could not be supposed, or intended, to be binding. That the supposed articles of expence were overrated in the calculations held out by the noble duke; but supposing it otherwise, and that they had even been still greater, the necessity which induced the measure, would of course have compelled our acquiescence in the terms. That if the war was finished in one campaign, an event which there was every reason to expect, or even in two, the terms would be found not only reasonable, but highly favourable on our side. It was indeed acknowledged, that if the war was prolonged to a more distant period, they must from their nature become disadvantageous; but this was so totally improbable as not to merit consideration.

On the whole what were they to do? Were they to sit still, and to suffer an independent hostile empire to arise out of an unprovoked rebellion? Were they tamely to suffer the trade of the American colonies, the object of so much care, attention, and expence, of so many laws and so many wars, to be given away to foreigners, merely from a scruple of employing foreign forces, to preserve to ourselves the benefits so truly our own and so dearly purchased? If we have nothing to complain of because British blood is shed in a British quarrel, what can the Americans reasonably object to it? They in effect, by refusing to contribute to its support, deny themselves to be a part of the British empire, and therefore making themselves foreigners, they cannot complain that foreigners are employed against them. They said, that we had nothing to fear from their retaliating upon us. That the other powers who have colonies in America, know too well the danger and mischief of a rebellion on the present principles, to give it any sort of countenance. That princes indeed are governed more by policy than equity; but in this instance their policy is our security. But if they should be, contrary to all appearance and probability, willing to countenance this rebellion from a desire of partaking in an open trade, and lowering the importance of this country, the terrible consequences which would arise from such an event, leave no room for deliberation; but require that we should crush this infant rebellion with every force of every kind before foreigners can take advantage of it.

It was observable in this, and some late debates, that as melancholy pictures were drawn of the situation to which this country would be reduced by the loss of the colonies, in order therefrom to induce the most vigorous coercion, as had heretofore, in the earlier stages of this business, been exhibited by the opposition, for the very different purpose, of preventing those coercive measures, which they apprehended, or said, would lead to the present unhappy crisis.

The debates were long and interesting, and contained a great deal of curious, though much of it was extraneous matter. Among other subjects which lay out of the direct line of debate, the cruelty and impolicy with which the war was carried on in America, by ruining the country, and burning commercial and defenceless towns, was much insisted on by the opposition. The recent destruction of Norfolk in Virginia, which, they said, was principally inhabited by people violently attached to the king's government, with the new and particular circumstance of its being transacted under the governor's orders, was commented upon with the greatest severity, and reprobated in the strongest terms.

His royal highness the duke of Cumberland, took an active part upon this occasion in support of the motion; declaring his entire disapprobation of the conduct of the ministers, and of the present American system. He also pathetically lamented, that " Brunswickers, who once, to their great honour, were employed in the defence of the liberties of the subject, should now be sent to subjugate his liberties, in another part of this vast empire." The motion was rejected by the usual majority, the numbers upon a division being 100, including 21 proxies, to 32, including 3 proxies, who supported the question. It was, however, attended with an unusual protest, which only reciting the terms of the proposed address, concluded with the signatures of the respective protesting peers to a silent dissent.

The secretary at war gave notice about this time, that he would move, at a short specified day, for a supply, to the amount of 845,165l. towards defraying the extraordinary expences of the land forces, and other services incurred, between the 9th of March 1775, and 31st of January 1776. This vast demand for extraordinaries, incurred in so short a time, and in so confined and inefficacious a service, rouzed all the vigour, and wakened all the fire of opposition; which seemed upon this occasion to blaze out in such a manner, as for a time to dazzle and confound administration.

They examined the journals to shew, that neither the glorious campaign of 1704, which saved the German empire, and broke and ruined that military force which had been for half a century the scourge and terror of Europe, nor that of 1760, which gave us the vast continent of North America, had in any degree equalled in expence, the shameful campaign of Boston in 1775. They endeavoured to prove by various calculations, that the maintenance of 8,509, wretched, disgraced, and half-starved forces in Boston, had not

cost the nation much less, in a period short of a year, than an hundred pounds each man. They called upon the ministers to answer, and examined the state of national finance to enquire, in what manner we were capable of supporting in the present and future campaigns, 50,000 men in America at a proportional expence, exclusive of the naval, ordnance, and other charges, of our standing expences, and of the hazard of a foreign war.

All the powers of eloquence were displayed, in describing in the most glowing colours, the successes and glories of queen Anne's, and of the last war. The names of Godolphin and Pitt were reechoed; whilst all the force of wit and ridicule was exhausted, in contrasting the situation and circumstances of those seasons, with the present. Blenheim and Schellenburgh, were opposed to Lexington and Bunkers Hill; and to compleat the group, the river Mystic was for once placed in the[55] same view with the Danube.

The ministers seemed for a considerable time nearly overwhelmed by the torrent. But finding its vehemence rather to increase than lessen, they at length rested for support upon the strong sanction of parliament. They said, that they had acted in this business from the beginning, not only with the concurrence, but the approbation of parliament; that they had not sought it, nor taken it up wantonly; they had found it; it was a legacy left by their predecessors, and of which they found parliament in possession. That whenever that body should think it necessary to alter its conduct or opinions; to abandon, or to modify the present measures, they would readily give up their own opinions, and acquiesce in either; but whilst they found themselves in possession of the full confidence and approbation of a great majority of that house, they never would desert the trust reposed in them, but would conti-

nue to fulfil their duty at all events. And that there only were two simple questions arising on this matter, whether the money had been properly applied? and whether the measures that induced the expenditure were necessary? that the first would in due time be authenticated by the proper vouchers, and parliament had already repeatedly given its sanction to the second. That, as to the inglorious appearance of the campaign, they said that it had the same origin with all the rest of our misfortunes, too good an opinion of the Americans. That it was never believed, that they could be wicked enough to unite with the Massachusets Bay in rebellion, nor consequently able to shut up his majesty's forces in Boston, and prevent the supply which the abundance of that country yielded. That now our eyes are opened; and the measures taken in consequence, must open the way to abundance; and it was then to be hoped, that it would not be necessary to send all their provision from Europe. At present indeed it was unhappily necessary; and whatever the expence might be, they could not justify themselves in starving either the army or the cause. That the vigour and generosity of this session would give repose and œconomy to the next.

On the second day's debate, when the motion was [11th.] regularly made, after a very warm discussion, the question was carried on a division by a majority of 180, to 57. It was, however, scarcely less debated on the following day, upon receiving the report from the committee.

That vast and invincible majority, which had hitherto overruled every proposal of the same nature, was not sufficient to deter the duke of Grafton from still trying, whether an attempt towards a reconciliation with the colonies might not be received in some new form, or in some manner rendered palatable. He accordingly mov-
[14th.] ed for an address, that in

order to prevent the further effusion of blood, and to manifest how desirous the king and parliament are to restore peace to all the dominions of the crown, and how earnestly they wish to redress any real grievances of his majesty's subjects, a proclamation might be issued, declaring, that if the colonies, within a reasonable time before or after the arrival of the troops destined for America, shall present a petition to the commander in chief, or to the commissioners to be appointed under the late act; setting forth in such petition, which is to be transmitted to his majesty, what they consider to be their just rights and real grievances; that in such case, his majesty will consent to a suspension of arms; and that he has authority from his parliament to assure them, that their petition shall be received, considered, and answered.

The great object of this motion, seems to have been to remedy the defects of the late prohibitory, or capture act; which, as the opposition had all along contended, held out a delusive shew of peace, without furnishing any means, or containing any powers, by which that object could possibly be attained. Besides the general arguments which the subject afforded, the noble mover specified two particular circumstances, which rendered a compliance with the motion, or the adoption of some equivalent substitute, at this time absolutely necessary. The first of these was the new doctrine of *unconditional submission* on the side of America, which had been held out in the other house by the noble lord at the head of the American department;—The second, was the intelligence, which the noble duke had himself received, that two French gentlemen had some time before gone to North America, where they had held a conference with Gen. Washington at his camp, and were by him referred to the Continental Congress, to

which they immediately repaired. To prevent or remedy the ill effects which a knowlege of the former, and the consequent opinion that it was the established political doctrine of Great Britain, must necessarily produce upon the Americans, and the extremities to which it would naturally drive them, he inferred the necessity of some specific declaration from parliament, the laying of some ground open for accommodation, and throwing so much light upon it, as would enable them in some degree to judge, what conditions we were willing to grant, or what concession to accept; and would at least relieve them from the horrors, and disarm them of the rage, which the bare idea of unconditional submission must necessarily excite. The latter circumstance, not only shewed the immediate danger of the interference of foreigners in our civil contention; but what was still more alarming, gave too much reason to apprehend, that the interference was already commenced, and that from a most dangerous, and naturally hostile quarter.

This day will perhaps hereafter be considered as one of the most important in the English History. It deeply fixed a new colour, upon our public affairs. It was decisive, on this side of the Atlantic, with respect to America; and may possibly hereafter be compared with, and considered as preliminary to that, on which, unhappily, in a few months after, the independence of that continent, was declared on the other. Administration now, and their numerous friends, totally changed their stile and language upon that subject. All modifications were laid aside; all former opinions and declarations done away; conciliation, they said, was little less than impracticable; and that if any thing could be added to the difficulties of such a scheme, it would be by concession. The tone of the house

of lords was much higher than that of the house of commons had ever been, although the language was grown much more firm and determined there also than it had been at the beginning of the session. No alternative now seemed to be left between absolute conquest and unconditional submission.

The debates were long and various, and notwithstanding the beaten ground which was travelled over, would at another season have been interesting. Most of the considerable speakers on both sides took a large share in them. Much altercation and contradiction took place, between several lords who were of the cabinet in the years 1767, and 1769, relative to the American measures which were at those times adopted. Much pointed and direct animadversion took place between two great law lords, one of whom has long been out of office. The question being put [56] after 11 o'clock at night, the motion was rejected by a majority of 91, including 20 proxies, to 31, including three proxies.

• • •

It may be necessary to take some notice of an affair, which about this time made a great noise in the city, occasioned much discontent amongst the merchants, and was at length, though without effect, brought into both houses of parliament. A clause in the late prohibitory act, which enabled the admiralty to grant licences to vessels for conveying stores and provisions to the forces upon the American service, had been made use of to countenance a trade in individuals who were favoured, by which, it was said, that a monopoly was formed, and the American trade was transferred from the ancient merchants, and known traders, to a few obscure persons of no account or condition; and an illicit commerce established under the sanction of that bill, which was utterly subversive of one of its principal apparent objects.

It appears that thefe licences were very loofely compofed, and very carelefsly granted; that the commiffioners of the cuftoms did not chufe to interfere much in the bufinefs; that though the licences were recalled and fome alterations made in them, this meafure produced little effect; and that even, when the noife grew loud, and fomething like a parliamentary enquiry was announced or begun, though fome of the goods were unfhipped, yet in general the fcheme fucceeded; the fhips which had cleared out for Bofton, only altering the deftination of their voyage, and taking a new clearance for Halifax and Canada, with liberty to go to any other port in America. It appeared in evidence before the houfe of commons, that by thefe and other means, a greater quantity of all manner of goods calculated for the North American market, had been fhipped within a few weeks, than was done in any of the ufual feafons of exportation.

A great clamour was raifed in the city. It was faid that it was exceedingly grievous to the great body of American merchants, who had already fuffered fo feverely in confequence of thefe troubles, and who in obedience to the late act of parliament, were at this very time finking under the incumbrance of a vaft quantity of goods, which they had purchafed for that, and for which they could find no other market, to fee the trade, which for a number of years they had conducted with the greateft reputation and fairnefs, fmuggled out of their hands, by a fet of nominal merchants and unknown adventurers. The injury was rendered ftill the more grievous, by being committed under the colour of law, and under the licence of authority.

The firft public notice that was taken of this bufinefs was in the houfe of lords, where the earl of Effingham, a little before the re-

cefs at eafter, made a motion which was agreed to, that lifts of thofe fhips and of their cargoes, as well as the licences which were granted by the admiralty, fhould be laid before the houfe.

We fuppofe, that the holidays, together with the dutchefs of Kingfton's trial, prevented the matter from being more immediately purfued in that houfe. However that was, it was taken up in the houfe of commons by the lord[57] May 2d. mayor, who moved for a committee to enquire into the whole tranfaction. Adminiftration feemed very fore and very angry upon this occafion; and, as the oppofition faid, ufed every poffible means to baffle or defeat the enquiry. They faid it proceeded from ill temper and malignity, and was only intended to embarrafs and diftrefs government; and foretold truly, that it would come to nothing. Some faid that the matters complained of were too trifling for notice, and were only intended for the eafe, benefit, and comfort of the troops; others went fo far as to infift, that the act was not violated, and that provifions and ftores included every thing that could adminifter to the wants or luxuries of man or woman. The minifter, however, at length acknowledged, that the powers given in the act had been mifunderftood, and the licenfes abufed; but that as thefe matters were already rectified, and a ftop put to the mifchief, their lofing time at this late feafon in fuch an enquiry could anfwer no purpofe. He afterwards practifed a manœuvre, which he knew would effectually check its progrefs, by agreeing in part with the motion, but changing the mode of enquiry, from an open or felect committee up ftairs, to a committee of the whole houfe within doors.

8th. In this committee, feveral witneffes were examined, and among other matter that appeared it came out, that one of thofe

nominal merchants, and a principal actor in this bufinefs, who had freighted five large fhips with the moft valuable commodities, was fo totally unqualified for fuch an undertaking, that he hawked about a letter in the city, from a very confiderable officer belonging to the treafury, in order to obtain goods upon that credit. It was faid by the oppofition, that fome of the principal witneffes were fent purpofely out of the way; that the papers which the houfe demanded, and which were abfolutely neceffary for the purpofes of the enquiry, were defignedly held back at fome of the public offices; they were therefore defirous to poftpone it for a few days, until the proper information could be obtained, and accordingly moved the queftion of adjournment at three feveral times, but were conftantly overpowered by a majority. At length, after being kept up till five o'clock in the morning, the minifter diffolved the committee (without its coming to any refolution whatever) by the previous queftion, "That the chairman do now leave the chair," which was carried by a majority of 105 to 31.

On the 13th the earl of Effingham revived the matter in the houfe of lords, by moving that the neceffary papers fhould be laid before the houfe, in order to profecute the enquiry in the enfuing feffion. This brought on very warm debates, and fome farther extraordinary matter, than what had appeared in the other houfe, was laid before the lords. The nicenefs of fituation at length prevailed, and the minifters confented to the motion.

The bufinefs being all carried through, and a vote of credit obtained for a million to anfwer any intermediate fervice, an end was May 23d. at length put to the feffion. The fpeech from the throne contained nothing very ftriking. The ufual fatisfaction in their conduct was expreffed.

Information was given, that no alteration had taken place in the state of foreign affairs, and that the assurances received of the disposition of the several European powers, promised a continuance of the general tranquillity. A regret was expressed for the extraordinary supplies which it had been necessary to demand; and thanks given to the commons for the readiness and dispatch with which they were granted; as well as an acknowledgment, that they had shewn an equal regard to the exigencies of the service, and the ease of the people, in the manner of raising them. A proper frugality was promised. It was observed, that they were engaged in a great national cause, the prosecution of which must be attended with many difficulties, and much expence; but when they consider that the essential rights and interests of the whole empire are deeply concerned in the issue of it, and can have no safety or security but in that constitutional subordination for which they are contending, it affords a conviction that they will not think any price too high for such objects. A hope was still entertained, that his rebellious subjects would be awakened to a sense of their errors, and by a voluntary return to their duty, justify the restoration of harmony; but if a due submission, should not be obtained from such motives and dispositions on their part, it was trusted, that it should be effectuated by a full exertion of the great force with which they had entrusted his majesty.

disabled the ships of war from preventing the mischief. The loss of most of the coal ships was particularly felt, as fuel could not be procured, and the climate rendered that article indispensable. The wretched inhabitants were in a state still more deplorable. Detained against their will, cut off from all intercourse with their friends, exposed to all the consequences of that contempt and aversion with which a great part of them were regarded by the soldiery, and at the same time in want of almost every necessary of life. Calamitous however as that situation was, it served as a sort of refuge to those, who were either zealous in favour of the king's government, or so dissatisfied with the new state of things, that they could no longer live with comfort, some of them hardly with safety, in their own homes.

It was even feared, that the military stores would fail, and salt provisions at length grew scarce. The troops at Bunker's Hill underwent great hardships, being obliged to lie in tents all the winter, under the driving snows, and exposed to the almost intolerably cutting winds of the climate in that season, which, with the strict and constant duty occasioned by the strength and vicinity of the enemy, rendered that service exceedingly severe both to the private men and officers. Various attempts were made, to remedy, or to lessen some of the wants which now prevailed in the army. That of firing, which was the most immediately and intolerably pressing, was in some measure relieved by the destruction of houses.

The attempts made to procure provisions were not attended with any great success. Some vessels which were sent to Barbadoes, obtained, through the assistance of the governor, and before the matter was fully known, a quantity so moderate, that it would not at other times have been more taken

Distresses of the army at Boston during the winter. New batteries opened, and the town bombarded. Embarkation. Gen. Howe departs with the army to Halifax. Siege of Quebec raised. Rebels repulsed at Three Rivers. Montreal, Chamblee, and St. John's retaken; all Canada recovered. Regulators and Emigrants totally defeated and dispersed in North Carolina. Hopkins strips the Bahama Islands of stores and artillery. Lord Dunmore abandons the coasts of Virginia; Fugitives dispersed. Sir Peter Parker's squadron, with Lord Cornwallis and troops, arrive at Cape Fear, where they meet Gen. Clinton; proceed to Charlestown. Attack on Sullivan's Island. Circular letter from the Congress for the establishment of new governments in the colonies. Declaration of Independency. Lord, and Gen. Howe appointed Commissioners for restoring Peace in the Colonies. Gen. Howe, with the army, land at Staten Island. Circular Letter, sent by Lord Howe to the Continent, and published by the Congress. Letter to Gen. Washington, refused. Conference between Adjutant Gen. Paterson, and Gen. Washington. Plots at New York, and Albany. Army landed at Long Island. Americans defeated with great loss. Retire silently from their Camp, and quit the Island. Gen. Sullivan sent upon parole with a message from Lord Howe to the Congress. Fruitless conference between his Lordship and a Committee of the Congress. Descent on York Island; City of New York taken; set on fire, and a great part burnt. Army pass through the dangerous navigation called Hell Gate; land at Frogs Neck; Skirmish at the White Plains. Forts Washington and Lee taken, and the whole of York Island reduced. Jerseys overrun. Rhode Island reduced.

THE delays and misfortunes which the transports and victuallers from England and Ireland had experienced, reduced our forces at Boston to great distress. To their distress was added the mortification of seeing several vessels which were laden with the necessaries and comforts of life, taken in the very entrance of the harbour; whilst different circumstances of tide, wind, or situation, notice of than any common occurrence in trade; but being now cut off from their usual resources, and having, as they said, a famine staring them in the face, with 80,000 Blacks, and 20,000 Whites to feed, and no sufficient stock in hand, nor no certain supply in prospect, the measure was deemed so dangerous, that it occasioned a direct address from the assembly to the king, including, along with the detail of their own melancholy situation, strong complaints against the conduct of the governor.

A detachment of marines, with an armed ship and some transports, were sent to Savanna in Georgia, with a view, as it would seem by the event, of obtaining cargoes of rice and other provisions, whether by force or otherwise. The militia, however, took to their arms, and would not permit the marines to land, nor the ships to hold any correspondence with the shore. In the course of the debate which arose upon this occasion, some officers belonging to the colony were seized and detained on board the ships, and their release being refused with a high hand, and other circumstances of aggravation occurring on both sides, some batteries were speedily erected by the militia on the banks of the river, and an engagement with cannon and small arms took place, in which some blood was spilt, and seven loaded vessels belonging to the colony, which the commanders of the king's armed vessels, seemingly by collusion with the Captains or owners, had got possession of, and whose cargoes would effectually have answered their purpose, were designedly burnt in the conflict.

In this state of things on our side, the provincials before Boston, were well covered, and well supplied in their lines. They expected with the most earnest solicitude the setting in of the frost, which usually takes place there about Christmas, and generally covers the harbour, and all the adjoining rivers and creeks, with a surface of solid ice. They founded great hopes upon this, as upon a most powerful auxiliary, by whose aid they not only extended their views to the recovery of the town, but to the seizure or destruction of the fleet, as well as of the land forces.

In these they were disappointed. The winter was uncommonly mild, and the frosts had none of the effects they expected. The expectation, however, probably influenced their operations, and occasioned their continuing more quiet than they otherwise would have done. The arrival of a copy of the king's speech, with an account of the fate of the petition from the continental congress, is said to have excited the greatest degree of rage and indignation amongst them; as a proof of which, the former was publicly burnt in the camp; and they are said upon this occasion to have changed their colours, from a plain red ground, which they had hitherto used, to a flag with thirteen stripes, as a symbol of the number and union of the colonies. [59]

In the mean time, the arrival by degrees of several of those scattered vessels which had sailed from these kingdoms with provisions and necessaries, alleviated in a considerable degree the distresses of the forces at Boston; and though the winter was not severe enough to answer all the purposes of their enemies, the climate prevailed so far, as to render both parties fond of their quarters; to check the spirit of enterprize, and to prevent the effusion of blood; so that for two or three months, an unexampled quiet prevailed on both sides.

During this state of things, the American cruizers and privateers, though yet poor and contemptible, being for the greater part no better than whale boats, grew daily more numerous, and successful against the transports and storeships; and among a multitude of other prizes, had the fortune of taking one, which gave a new colour to their military operations. This was an ordnance ship from Woolwich, which had unfortunately separated from her convoy, and being herself of no force, was taken without defence by a small privateer. This vessel contained, besides a large mortar upon a new construction, several pieces of fine brass cannon, a large quantity of small arms and ammunition, with all manner of tools, utensils, and machines, necessary for camps and artillery, in the greatest abundance. The loss of this ship was much resented in England, and occasioned some very severe animadversion upon the admiralty, both within doors and without, for hazarding a cargo of such value and importance in a defenceless vessel.

The tranquillity at Boston, was in the beginning of March unexpectedly broken in upon, by some sudden and unexpected movements on the side of the rebels. It is said, that as soon as the Congress had received intelligence of the prohibitory act, and of the hiring of foreign troops, they immediately dispatched instructions to Gen. Washington, totally to change the mode of carrying on the war, and to bring affairs at Boston to the speediest decision that was possible, in order that the army might be disengaged, and at liberty to oppose the new dangers with which they were threatened.

However this was, a battery was opened near the water side, at a place called Phipp's Farm, on the night of the 2d of March, from whence a severe cannonade and bombardment was carried on against the town, and repeated on the ensuing nights. Whilst the attention of the army was occupied by the firing of houses and other mischiefs incident to this new attack, they beheld with inexpressible surprize, on the morning of the 5th, some confiderable works appear on the other side of the town, upon the heigths of Dorchester Point, which had been erected in the preceding night, and from whence a 24 pound, and a bomb battery, were soon after opened. Some of our officers have acknowledged, that the expedition with which these works were thrown up, with their sudden and unexpected appearance, recalled to their minds those wonderful stories of enchantment and invisible agency, which are so frequent in the Eastern Romances.

The situation of the army was now very critical. The new works, along with those others which it was evident would now be speedily constructed on some of the neighbouring hills, would command the town, a considerable part of the harbour, of the beach, from whence an embarkation must take place in the event of a retreat, and render the communication between the troops in the works at Boston Neck, and the main body, difficult and dangerous.

In these circumstances no alternative remained, but to abandon the town, or dislodge the enemy and destroy the new works. Gen. Howe, with his usual spirit and resolution, adopted the latter, and took the necessary measures for the embarkation on that very evening of five regiments, with the light infantry and grenadiers, upon a service, which the whole army must of course have been ultimately engaged in. This design was frustrated by the intervention of a dreadful storm at night, which rendered the embarkation impracticable, and thereby probably prevented the loss of a great number of brave men, if not of the whole army.

It is not, however, to be wondered at, that with a high sense of the British military honour, as well as of his own, the general should hazard much, rather than submit to the indignity of abandoning the town. He commanded a force, which he knew had been considered and represented here, as sufficient to look down all opposition in America; and which, in reality, with respect to the number of regiments, if not of men, the excellency of the troops, the character of the Officers, and the powerful artillery which they possessed, would have been deemed respectable in any country, and dangerous by any enemy. With such troops, to give up that town which had been the original cause of the war, and the constant object of contention since its commencement, to a raw and despised militia, seemed, exclusive of all other ill consequences, a disgrace not to be borne. But these brave men had, by a variety of events, and perhaps it will be thought, through original error and misconduct in the arrangement of the war, been reduced to such circumstances, and hedged in, in such a manner, that no means were left for an exertion of their force and courage, that were not subject to the greatest danger, without affording a prospect of success.

Fortune prevented this perilous trial in the first instance. On the day that succeeded the tempest, the design was reassumed; but upon a nearer inspection it was discovered, that a new work had been thrown up, which was stronger than any of the former, and that the whole were now so completely fortified, that all hope of forcing them was at an end. It became clear also, that Boston was not a situation very happily chosen for the improvement of any advantage which might be obtained towards the reduction of the colonies.

Nothing now remained but to abandon the town, and to convey the troops, artillery, and stores, on board the ships. Nor was this last resort free from difficulty and danger. The enemy, however, continued quiet in their works, and made not the smallest attempt to obstruct the embarkation, or even to molest the rear. It is said, and, though it was positively denied by the ministers in both houses, seems to be generally believed, that some kind of convention or agreement, whether verbal, or only understood by secondary means, was established between the commanders in chief on each side, and that the abstaining from hostility on the one, was the condition of saving the town on the other. In proof of this it is affirmed, that conbustibles were ready laid for firing the town, and that the selectmen were permitted to go out, and to hold a conference with Gen. Washington upon the subject.

Notwithstanding this security, the embarkation could not be regulated in such a manner, though ten days were spent in carrying it into execution, as to prevent some degree of precipitation, disorder, and loss. It resembled more the emigration of a nation, than the breaking up of a camp. 1500 of the inhabitants, whose attachment to the royal cause had rendered them obnoxious to their countrymen, incumbered the transports with their families and effects. The Officers had laid out their money in furniture, and such other conveniencies, as were necessary to render their situation tolerable; no purchasers could be procured for these effects; and it would have been cruelty in the extreme to many of them, to have been under a necessity of leaving their whole substance behind. The soldiers were embarrassed by their continual duty, and all carriages and labour that could be procured in the town, were of course monopolized by the emigrant inhabitants. Every person had some private concern, which was sufficient to occupy his time and thoughts. The sick, wounded, women, and children, called for every care and attention, and of course increased the embarrassment and distress. It will not be difficult to suppose some part of the confusion incident to such circumstances.

The General's situation was truly pitiable. But he bore it with great fortitude; and conducted the whole with admirable temper. Some discontents appeared, which were to be endured and allayed. Scarcity of provisions, and ill success, always breed discontent in camps. This was in some measure the case at present. The General having received no advices from England since the preceding month of October, they considered themselves in a great measure as abandoned, and left to extricate themselves as they might out of the unfortunate situation in which they had been involved. Discontents are exceedingly fruitful; one generating a number of others in a very small space of time. Mutual jealousies prevailed between the army and navy; each attributing to the other, the cause of some part of that uneasiness which itself felt. The intended voyage to Halifax, was subject to circumstances of a very alarming nature. The coast, at all times dangerous, was dreadfully so at this tempestuous equinoctial season, and the multitude of ships, which amounted to about 150, increased the difficulty and apprehension. As the high northeast winds now prevailed, they were also liable to be blown off to the West Indies, without a stock of provisions in any degree sufficient to subsist them in such a passage. And, to render matters still more irksome, they were going to a sterile miserable country, which was incapable of affording those reliefs which they so much wanted. It could not pass the observation, and was highly vexatious to the military, that all this dangerous voyage, if completed, was directly so much out of their way, They were going to the northern extremity of the continent, when their business lay in the southern, or at least about the center.

The necessity of the situation left no choice of measures, and regret

March 17. 1776. was useless. As the rear embarked, Gen. Washington marched into the town, with drums beating, colours flying, and in all the triumph of victory. He was received by the remaining inhabitants, and acknowledged by the refugees, who now recovered their ancient possessions, with every mark of respect and gratitude, that could possibly be shewn to a deliverer. The assembly of the province were not less zealous in their public acknowledgements. His answer was proper, moderate, and becoming his situation. The king's forces were under a necessity of leaving a considerable quantity of artillery and some stores behind. The cannon upon Bunker's Hill, and at Boston Neck, could not be carried off. Attempts were made to render them unserviceable; but the hurry which then prevailed, prevented their having any great effect. Some mortars and pieces of cannon which were thrown into the water, were afterwards weighed up by the town's people.

Thus was the long contested town of Boston at length given up, the colony of Massachusett's Bay, for the present, freed from war, and left at liberty to adopt every measure which could tend to its future strength and security. It was above a week before the weather permitted the fleet to get entirely clear of the harbour and road; but they had ample amends made them in the passage, the voyage to Halifax being shorter and happier than could have been hoped for. Several ships of war were left behind to protect the vessels which should arrive from England; in which, however, they were not perfectly successful, the great extent of the Bay, with its numerous islands and creeks, and the number of small ports that surround it, affording such opportunities to the provincial armed boats, and small privateers, that they took a number of these ships,

which were still in ignorance that the town had changed masters.

As several movements made by the rebels, and particularly their taking stations on the neighbouring islands, indicated a design of attacking Castle William, the possession of which would be the means of locking up the ships of war in the harbour, and of rendering all future attempts upon the town by sea impracticable, General Howe thought it necessary to blow up and demolish the fortifications on that island before his departure.

General Washington was now in possession of the capital of Massachusett's Bay; but being ignorant of the destination of the fleet, and apprehensive of an attempt upon New York, he detached several regiments for the protection of that city, on the very day upon which he took possession of Boston. The royal army were not, however, at that time, in circumstances that admitted of their undertaking any expedition. They did not exceed, it is said, nine thousand healthy and effective men, and were in other respects by no means sufficiently provided.

The estates and effects of those emigrants who had accompanied Gen. How to Halifax, were ordered to be sold, and the produce applied to the public service. Some who ventured to stay behind, though they knew themselves to be obnoxious to the present government, were brought to trial, as public enemies, and betrayers of their country; and the estates of such as were found guilty, were confiscated in the same manner. But nothing occupied so much at present the minds of the people of Boston, or had so much attention paid to it by the province in general, as the putting of that town in such a state of defence, as might prevent a repetition of those evils which it had lately undergone. For this purpose, the greatest diligence was used in fortifying the town and harbour; some foreign engineers were procured to superintend the works, and every inhabitant dedicated two days in the week to their construction. Great doubts may, however, be entertained, whether Boston can be rendered tenable against an army, though these works may preserve it from insult.

During these transactions at Boston, the blockade of Quebec, was continued under great difficulties by Arnold. Reinforcements arrived slowly, and the Canadians, who are not by any means remarkable for constancy, were disheartened and wavering. It seems, as if the Congress was unequal in conduct, as well as resources, to the management of so many operations at the same time. The succours that were sent, suffered incredible hardships in their march; which they endured with that fortitude which had hitherto distinguished the Provincials in this war. On the other hand, General Carleton guarded, with his usual vigilance, against every effort of fraud, force, and surprize; but as all supplies were cut off from the country, the inhabitants and garrison experienced many distresses.

As the season approached, in which supplies from England were inevitable, the Americans grew more active in their operations. They again renewed the siege, and erected batteries, and made several attempts by fire-ships, and otherwise, to burn the vessels in the harbour. They failed in these attempts, though some of them were very boldly conducted; and their troops were at one time drawn up, and scaling ladders, with every other preparation, in readiness for storming the town, during the confusion which they expected the fire would have produced. Though they had not all the success they wished, they however burnt a great part of the suburbs, and the remaining houses being pulled down to prevent the spreading of the conflagration, afforded a most seasonable relief of fuel to the town, which had for some time been exceedingly distressed through the want of that necessary. During this state of things, a party of Canadians which had been embodied

Mar. 25th. by Mr. Beaujeu, with [60] a design of raising the siege, were encountered on their march, and easily dispersed by a detachment of the rebels.

This small success was not long sufficient to support the spirits of the provincials. Having failed in all their attempts with shells, fire-ships, and red hot balls, to cause a conflagration in the city, their hope of taking it by storm ceased, whilst that of succeeding by a regular siege was daily lessened; indeed their artillery was far enough from being equal to any great service. Although considerable reinforcements arrived in the remote parts of the province, the various impediments of bad roads, bad weather, and the want of necessaries suitable to the service, prevented their being able to join them. In the state of despondency consequent of these circumstances, that scourge and terror of the western continent and of its numerous nations, the small pox, broke out, and made its usual cruel ravages amongst them. Nor was the immediate effect with respect to life or health the worst consequence of the calamity; for that disorder being considered as the American plague, and regarded with all the horror incident to that name, the dread of infection broke in upon every other consideration, and rendered it difficult, if not impracticable, to sustain discipline, or preserve order.

In this situation, the provincial accounts inform us, that they intended to raise the siege before the arrival of the succours from England, and that Gen. Wooster, who [61] at that time held the command, with some other of the principal officers, had already gone to Montreal to make some preparations necessary for the facilitating of that purpose. If such a design was formed, it was prevented from being carried successfully into execution, by the zeal and activity of the officers and crews of the Isis man of war, and of two frigates, which were the first that had sailed from England with succours, and who with great labour, conduct, and resolution, having forced their way through the ice, arrived at Quebec before the passage was deemed practicable. The unexpected sight of the ships, threw the besiegers into the greatest consternation, which was not lessened by the immediate effect, of their cutting off all communication between their forces on the different sides of the river.

General Carleton was too well versed in military affairs, to lose any time in seizing the advantages which the present situation afforded. A small detachment of land forces which arrived in the ships of war, together with their marines, being landed with the utmost expedition, and joined to the garrison, the

May 6th. Governor immediately marched out at their head to attack the rebel camp. There he found every thing in the utmost confusion; they had not even covered themselves with an intrenchment, and having already begun a retreat, upon the appearance of our troops they fled on all sides, abandoning their artillery, military stores, scaling ladders, and other matters of incumbrance. The flight was so precipitate as scarcely to admit of any execution; nor were the King's forces in any condition for a pursuit, if prudence could even have justified the measure. Some of the sick became prisoners. During this transaction, our smaller ships of war made their way up the river with such expedition and success, that they took several small vessels belonging to the enemy, and retook the Gaspee sloop of war, which they had seized in the beginning of the preceding winter.

Thus was the mixed siege and blockade of Quebec raised, after a continuance of about five months. And thus was Canada preserved by a fortitude and constancy, which must ever be remembered with honour to the Governor and garrison. From this time, the provincials experienced a continued series of losses and misfortunes in that province. The Governor shewed he was worthy of his success, by an act which immediately succeeded it, and which does great honour to his humanity. A number of the sick and wounded provincials lay scattered about and hid in the neighbouring woods and villages, where they were in the greatest danger of perishing under the complicated pressure of want, fear, and disease. To prevent this melancholy consequence, he issued a proclamation, commanding the proper officers to find out these unhappy persons, and to afford them all necessary relief and assistance at the public expence; whilst, to render the benefit complete, and to prevent obstinacy or apprehension from marring its effect, he assured them, that as soon as they were recovered, they should have free liberty to return to their respective provinces.

Towards the end of May, several regiments from Ireland, one from England, another from General Howe, together with the Brunswick troops, arrived successively in Canada; so that the whole force in that province, when completed, was estimated at about 13,000 men. The general rendezvouz was at Three Rivers, which lies half way between Quebec and Montreal; and at the computed distance of about ninety miles from each. This place lies on the north side of the St. Lawrence, and takes its name from the vicinity of one of the branches of a large river, whose waters are discharged thro' three mouths into that great reservoir.

The provincials continued their retreat till they arrived in the borders of the river Sorel, which falls into the St. Lawrence at the distance of about 140 miles from Quebec, where they joined some of those reinforcements that had not been able to proceed farther to their assistance; but the whole were now sunk in spirit, and debilitated in act. To complete their misfortunes, the small-pox had spread through all their quarters.

These discouraging circumstances were not sufficient to damp the spirit of enterprize in their leaders. A very daring, and not ill laid plan, was formed for the surprize of the King's forces at the Three Rivers; which, if it had been attended with all the success it was capable of, might have been ranked among the most considerable military atchievements of that nature.

The British and Brunswick forces were at this time much separated. A considerable body were stationed at Three Rivers, under the command of Brigadier General Frazer. Another, under that of [62] Brigadier General Nesbit, lay near them on board the transports. A greater than either, along with the Generals Carleton, Burgoyne, Philips, and the German General, Reidesel, were in several divisions [63] by land and water, on the way from Quebec. The distance from Sorel was about fifty miles, and several armed vessels, and transports full of troops, which had got higher up than Three Rivers, lay full in the way.

In the face of all these difficulties, a body of above 2000 men, under the command of a Major General Thompson, embarked at [64] Sorel in fifty boats, and coasting the south side of what is called the Lake of St. Peter, where the St. Lawrence spreads to a great extent, arrived at Nicolet, from whence they fell down the river by night, and passed to the other side, with an intention of surprizing the forces under General Frazer. Three Rivers is rather to be considered as a long village, than a regular town; and the design was, that it should be attacked, a little before break of day, and, at the same instant, by a strong detachment at each end, while two smaller were drawn up in readiness to cover or support them. If the success should have proved complete, the design was extended to the destruction of all those vessels which lay near the shore.

The concurrent circumstances necessary to give effect to this design were too numerous, to afford any strong confidence of success. It was one of those bold undertakings which might have been productive of great advantage; but which was of too perilous a nature for any thing less than the most desperate situation of affairs to justify. They missed their time by about an hour, which, though they passed the armed ships without observation, occasioned their being discovered, and the alarm given at their landing. They afterwards got into bad grounds, and were involved in many other difficulties, which threw them into disorder and confusion. In this state, they found General Frazer's corps in preparation to receive them, having landed several light six pounders, which were played upon them with great effect. While they were thus engaged in front, Brigadier Nesbit, whose transports lay higher up the river, landed his forces full in their way back. June 8th.

Nothing was left but a retreat, the accomplishment of which was more to be wished for than hoped. Nesbit's corps kept the river side to prevent their escape to the boats, while Frazer's, in pursuit, galled them severely with their light artillery. Between both, they were driven for some miles through a deep swamp, which they traversed with inconceivable toil, exposed to constant danger, and enduring every degree of distress. The British troops at length grew tired of the pursuit, and the woods afforded them a wished-for shelter. The first and second in command, with about 200 others, were taken prisoners. It will be easily conceived that our loss was trifling.

This was the last appearance of vigour shewn by the provincials in Canada. The whole army having joined at Three Rivers, pushed forwards by land and water with great expedition. When the 14th. fleet arrived at Sorel, they found the enemy had abandoned that place some hours before, dismantled the batteries which they had erected to defend the entrance into that river, and had carried off their artillery and stores. A strong column was here landed under the command of General Burgoyne, with orders to advance along the Sorel to St. John's, while the remainder of the fleet and army sailed up the river to Longueil, the place of passage from the island of Montreal to La Prairie on the continent. Here they discovered that the rebels had abandoned the city and island of Montreal on the preceding evening, and that if the wind had been favourable, they might have met at this place. The army was immediately landed on the continent, and marching by La Prairie, crossed the peninsula formed by the St. Lawrence and the Sorel, in order to join General Burgoyne at St. John's, where they expected a stand, and a strong resistance would have been made.

That General pursued his march along the Sorel without intermission; but with that caution necessary in a country not wholly cleared of the enemy, and where their last and most desperate efforts were to be expected. He arrived at St. John's on the evening of the 18th, where he found the buildings in flames, and nearly every thing destroyed that could not be carried off. The provincials acted in the same manner at Chamblee, and burned such vessels as they were not able to drag up the rapids in their way to Lake Champlain, where they immediately embarked for Crown Point. Though their flight was precipitate, they sustained no loss, and a General Sullivan, who [65] commanded in the retreat, received public thanks for the prudence with which he conducted it, by which he saved their ruined army, at a time, they say, when it was encumbered with a vast multitude of sick, most of whom were ill of the small-pox.

Thus was an end happily put to the war in Canada. The pleasure of which was, however, considerably checked, by the restraint which was now laid upon the further operation of the army in that quarter. For as the enemy were masters of Lake Champlain, it was impossible for the forces to proceed to the southward, until such a number of vessels were constructed or obtained, as would afford a superiority, and enable them to traverse that lake with safety. The doing this, was a work of labour and time; for though six armed vessels were sent from England for that purpose, the falls of Chamblee rendered the means of conveying them to the lake highly difficult, and a matter which required much ingenuity and industry. A vast number of other vessels were also necessarily to be constructed both for conveyance and protection.

The necessity under which we have seen Governor Martin obliged to seek refuge on board a ship of war in Cape Fear river, did not damp his ardour in the public service, nor restrain his attempts to reduce the province of North Carolina to obedience. His confidence of success was increased, by the knowledge he had, that a squadron of men of war with seven regiments, under the conduct of Sir Peter Parker and Lord Cornwallis, [66] were to depart from Ireland on an expedition to the southern provinces in the beginning of the year, and that North Carolina was their first, if not principal object. He also knew that General Clinton, with a small detachment, was on his way from Boston to meet them at Cape Fear.

The connection he had formed with a body of desperate people, lately considered as rebels to the King's government, now equally enemies to the provincial establishment, whom we have frequently had occasion to take notice of under the name of Regulators, as well as with the Highland emigrants, seemed to insure the reduction of the insurgents, even independent of the expected force. That colony was deemed the weakest in America, except Georgia; and the two parties we have mentioned were numerous, active, daring, and the former were at this time, as well as the latter, zealously attached to the royal cause. The Highlanders were considered as naturally warlike, and the Regulators, from situation, habits, and manner of living, to be much bolder, hardier, and better marksmen, than those who had been bred to other courses, and in more civilized parts of the country.

The Governor sent several commissions to these people for the raising and commanding of regiments, and granted another to a Mr. [67] M'Donald to act as their General. He also sent them a proclamation, commanding all persons, on their allegiance, to repair to the royal standard, which was erected by General M'Donald about the middle of February.

Upon the first advice of their assembling at a place called Cross Creek, Brigadier General Moore [68] immediately marched at the head of the provincial regiment which he commanded, with such militia as he could suddenly collect, and some pieces of cannon, within a few miles of them, and took possession of an important post called Rockfish Bridge, which, as he was much inferior in strength, he immediately intrenched and rendered

defensible. He had not been many days in this position, where he was receiving and expecting succours, when General M'Do-
nald approached at the head of his army, and sent a letter to Moore, inclosing the Governor's proclamation, and recommending to him and his party to join the King's standard by a given hour the next day, or that he must be under a necessity of considering them as enemies.

As Moore knew that the provincial forces were marching from all quarters, he protracted the negociation, in hopes that the Tory army, as they called it, might have been surrounded. In his final answer he declared, that he and his officers considered themselves as engaged in a cause the most glorious and honourable in the world, the defence of the liberties of mankind; he reminded the emigrants of the ungrateful return they made to the kind reception they met in the colony; and the General, with some of his officers, of an oath they had taken a little before, and upon which they were permitted to come into the country, that they only came to see their friends and relations, without any concern whatever in public affairs. In return to the proclamation, he sent them the test proposed by the Congress, with a proffer, that if they subscribed it, and laid down their arms, they should be received as friends; but if they refused to comply, they must expect consequences similar to those which they had held out to his people.

In the mean time, M'Donald perceived the danger he was in of being enclosed, and abruptly quitting his ground, endeavoured, with considerable dexterity, by forced marches, the unexpected passing of rivers, and the greatest celerity of movement, to disengage himself. It seems, the great and immediate object in view with this party, was to bring Governor Martin, with Lord William Camp-

Feb. 15th.

bell, and General Clinton, who had by this time joined them, into the interior country, which they judged would be a means of uniting all the back settlers of the southern colonies in the royal cause, of bringing forward the Indians, and of encouraging the well affected to shew themselves in all places.

The provincial parties were, however, so close in the pursuit, and so alert in cutting the country, and seizing the passes, that M'Donald at length found himself under a necessity of engaging a Colonel Caswell, who, with about a thousand militia and minute men, had taken possession of a place called Moore's Creek Bridge, where they had thrown up an intrenchment. The royalists were by all accounts much superior in number, having been rated from 3000 to 1500, which last number, M'Donald, after the action, acknowledged them to be. The emigrants began the attack with great fury; but M'Cleod, the second in command, and a few more of their bravest officers and men being killed at the first onset, they suddenly lost all spirit, fled with the utmost precipitation, and, as the provincials say, deserted their General, who was taken prisoner, as were nearly all their leaders, and the rest totally broken and dispersed.

This victory was a matter of great exultation and triumph to the Carolinians. They had shewn that their province was not so weak as was imagined; for though their force actually in the engagement was not considerable, they had raised 10,000 men in about ten days. But what was still more flattering, and, perhaps, not of less real importance, they had encountered Europeans (who were supposed to hold them in the most sovereign contempt, both as men and as soldiers) in the field, and defeated them with an inferior force. If the zeal of these people could have been kept dormant until the

[69]

[70]

Feb. 27th.

arrival of the force from Ireland, it seems more than probable that the southern colonies would have considerably felt the impression of such an insurrection. But now, their force and spirits were so entirely broken, their leaders being sent to different prisons, and the rest stripped of their arms, and watched with all the eyes of distrust, that no future effort could be reasonably expected from them. Perhaps too great a dependence was laid on their power and prowess, while those of the opposite side were measured with a scale equally deceitful. It is, however, extremely difficult to regulate or restrain the caprice or violence of those leaders who assume authority in such seasons.

A squadron of five frigates were sent out by the Congress early in the year, under the command of one Hopkins, who sailed with them to the Bahama islands; where they stripped that of Providence, which is the principal, of a considerable quantity of artillery and stores; but were disappointed in the powder, which they most wanted, through the prudence of the Governor, who sent 150 barrels of it away in a small vessel, the night before they landed. They brought off the Governor, and some other public officers, as prisoners; and after taking several prizes in their return, fell in at length with the Glasgow frigate of war, accompanied with a tender, the latter of which they took, and the former escaped with difficulty after a very sharp engagement.

Lord Dunmore, with his fleet of fugitives, continued on the coasts and in the rivers of Virginia for a great part of the year; and as every place was now strictly guarded, these unhappy people, who had put themselves under his protection, underwent great distresses. The heat of the weather, the badness and scarcity of water and provisions, with the closeness

[71]

March 3d.

and filth of the small vessels in which they were crowded, by degrees produced that malignant and infectious distemper, which is known by the name of the Jail or Pestilential Fever. This dreadful disorder made great havock among them, but particularly affected the negroes, most of whom it swept away. After various adventures, in which they were driven from place to place, and from island to island, by the Virginians, several of the vessels were driven on shore in a gale of wind, and the wretched fugitives became captives to their own countrymen. At length, every place being shut against, and hostile to the remainder, and neither water or provisions to be obtained, even at the expence of blood, it was found necessary, towards the beginning of August, to burn the smaller and least valuable vessels, and to send the remainder, amounting to between 40 and 50 sail, with the exiles, to seek shelter and retreat in Florida, Bermudas, and the West-Indies. In this manner ended the hopes entertained by the employment of the negroes to suppress the rebellion in the southern colonies. This measure, rather invidious than powerful, tended infinitely to inflame the discontents in those colonies, without adding any thing to the strength of the royal arms. The unhappy creatures who engaged in it, are said to have perished almost to a man.

It had for some time past been the fortune of the fleets, transports, and victuallers, which had been sent to America, to meet with such exceedingly bad weather on their passage, such delays, and so many untoward circumstances of different sorts, as in a great degree frustrated the end of their destination. Sir Peter Parker's squadron, which sailed from Portsmouth at the close of the year, from an unexpected delay in Ireland, and bad weather afterwards, did not arrive at Cape Fear till the beginning of

May, where they were detained by various causes till the end of the month. There they found General Clinton, who had already been at New-York, and from thence proceeded to Virginia, where he had seen Lord Dunmore, and finding that no service could be effected at either place with his small force, came thither to wait for them.

The season of the year was much against the operations of the troops at this time in the southern colonies, the excessive heat having rendered them sickly even at Cape Fear, notwithstanding the plenty of refreshments they procured, and the little labour they had upon their hands. Something, however, must be done, and Charlestown, the capital of South Carolina, was within the line of Sir Peter Parker and Lord Cornwallis's instructions. They had but little knowledge of General Howe's situation; the only information that General Clinton received of his evacuating Boston, being from the American newspapers. And it happened unluckily, that a vessel, which General Howe had dispatched from Halifax with orders for their proceeding to the northward, met with such delays in her passage, that she did not arrive at Cape Fear till after their departure.

The fleet anchored off Charlestown Bar in the beginning of June. They were joined before they proceeded to action by the Experiment man of war; and the naval force then consisted of the Commodore Sir Peter Parker's ship, the Bristol, of 50 guns; the Experiment, of the same force; the Active, Solebay, Acteon, and Syren frigates, of 28 guns each; the Sphynx of 20, a hired armed ship of 22, a small sloop of war, an armed schooner, and the Thunder bomb-ketch. The passing of the bar was a matter of time, difficulty, and danger, especially to the two large ships, which, notwithstanding the taking out of their guns, and the using of every other

means to lighten them as much as possible, both touched the ground and stuck several times.

The land forces were commanded by General Clinton, Lord Cornwallis, and Brigadier General Vaughan. It was remarkable, that[72] at the time General Clinton sailed from Boston, General Lee, at the head of a strong detachment from the army before that place, immediately set out to secure New-York from the attempt which it was supposed the former would have made upon that city. Having succeeded in that object, General Clinton could not but be surprized at his arrival in Virginia, to find Lee in possession, and in the same state of preparation, in which he had left him at New-York. Upon his departure for Cape Fear, Lee again traversed the continent with the utmost expedition to secure North-Carolina. And at length, upon the further progress of the fleet and army to the southward, Lee again proceeded with equal celerity to the defence of Charlestown.

The first object of our forces, after passing the bar, was the attack of a fort which had been lately erected, though not made altogether complete, upon the southwest point of Sullivan's island. This fort commanded the passage to Charlestown, which lay farther west, at about six miles distance; and notwithstanding the lateness of its construction, was with propriety considered as the key of that harbour. It is said to have been represented to our commanders as in even a more imperfect state than it was found in; but if the description had been otherwise, it is not probable they would have expected that a raw militia could have been able, for any length of time, to have supported the great weight of fire from our ships, even excluding the co-operation of the land forces.

The troops were landed on Long Island, which lies nearer, and to the eastward of Sullivan's; being separated only by some shoals, and a creek called the Breach, which are deemed passable at low water, the ford being represented to our officers as only eighteen inches in depth in that state. The Carolinians had posted some forces with a few pieces of cannon near the north-eastern extremity of Sullivan's Island, at the distance of near two miles from the fort, where they threw up works to prevent the passage of the royal army over the breach. General Lee was encamped with a considerable body of forces on the continent, at the back and to the northward of the island, with which he held a communication open by a bridge of boats, and could by that means, at any time, march the whole, or any part of his force, to support that post which was opposed to our passage from Long Island. The latter is a naked burning sand, where the troops suffered greatly from their exposure to the intense heat of the sun. Both the fleet and army were greatly distressed through the badness of the water; that which is found upon the sea coasts of South Carolina being every where brackish. Nor were they in a much better condition, with respect either to the quantity or quality of provisions.

Notwithstanding the dispatch which these inconveniences rendered necessary, such delays occurred in carrying the design into execution, that it was near the end of the month before the attack upon Sullivan's Island took place; a season which was applied by the enemy with great assiduity to the completion of their works. Every thing being at length settled between the commanders by sea and land, the Thunder bomb, covered by the armed ship, took her station in the morning, and began the attack, by throwing shells at the fort as the fleet advanced. About eleven o'clock, the Bristol, Experiment, Active, and Solebay, brought up directly against the fort,

June 28th.

and began a most furious and incessant cannonade. The Sphynx, Acteon, and Syren, were ordered to the westward, to take their station between the end of the island and Charlestown, partly thereby to enfilade the works of the fort, partly, if possible, to cut off the communication between the island and the continent, which would, of course, cut off the retreat of the garrison, as well as all succours from the latter; and partly to prevent any attempts that might be made by fire-ships, or otherwise, to interrupt the grand attack. This part of the design was rendered unfortunate by the strange unskilfulness of the pilot, who entangled the frigates in the shoals called the Middle Grounds, where they all stuck fast; and though two of them were in some time with damage and difficulty got off, it was then too late, and they were besides in no condition, to execute the intended service. The Acteon could not be got off, and was burnt by the officers and crew the next morning, to prevent her materials and stores from becoming a prey to the enemy.

Whilst the continued thunder from the ships seemed sufficient to shake the firmness of the bravest enemy, and daunt the courage of the most veteran soldier, the return made by the fort, could not fail of calling for the respect, as well as of highly incommoding the brave seamen of Britain. In the midst of that dreadful roar of artillery, they stuck with the greatest constancy and firmness to their guns; fired deliberately and slowly, and took a cool and effective aim. The ships suffered accordingly; they were torn almost to pieces, and the slaughter was dreadful. Never did British valour shine more conspicuous, nor never did our marine, in an engagement of the same nature with any foreign enemy, experience so rude an encounter. The springs of the Bristol's cable being cut by the shot, she lay for some

time exposed in such a manner to the enemy's fire, as to be most dreadfully raked. The brave Captain Morris, after receiving a [73] number of wounds, which would have sufficiently justified a gallant man in retiring from his station, still with a noble obstinacy disdained to quit his duty, until his arm being at length shot off, he was carried away in a condition which did not afford a possibility of recovery. It is said, that the quarter deck of the Bristol was at one time cleared of every person but the Commodore, who stood alone, a spectacle of intrepidity and firmness, which have seldom been equalled, never exceeded. The others on that deck were either killed, or carried down to have their wounds dressed. Nor did Captain Scott, of the Experiment, [74] miss his share of the danger or glory, who, besides the loss of an arm, received so many other wounds that his life was at first despaired of.

The fire from the British ships was not thrown away; though it did not produce all the effect which was hoped and expected. But the fortifications were much firmer than they had been thought, and their lowness preserved them in a great degree from the weight of our shot. They were composed of palm-trees and earth, and the merlons were of an unusual thickness. The guns were at one time so long silenced, that it was thought the fort had been abandoned. It seems extraordinary, that a detachment of the land forces were not in readiness on board the transports or boats, to profit of such an occasion. But these are only a part of the circumstances relative to this engagement which have never been sufficiently cleared up. The praise bestowed upon the garrison for the constancy and bravery of their defence, by the Americans in general, as well as by General Lee, shew that they neither abandoned their guns, nor were changed;

however they might be, and undoubtedly were reinforced. It appears, by their accounts, that the silence of the fort proceeded from the expenditure of all their powder, and their waiting for a supply from the continent; which, probably, did not arrive the sooner, from the necessity of its being conveyed through the line of fire from the men of war.

During this long, hot, and obstinate conflict, the seamen looked frequently and impatiently to the eastward, still expecting to see the land forces advance from Long Island, drive the rebels from their intrenchment, and march up to second the attack upon the fort. In these hopes they were grievously disappointed. Such various accounts have been given of the cause of this inaction of the land forces, that it is difficult to form any decided opinion upon the subject. The Gazette, from whence a satisfactory solution of all difficulties might be expected, is so totally defective and dissatisfactory, that it seems to have laid a foundation for every other error and contradiction relative to this business. That account says, that the King's forces were stopped by an impracticable depth of water, where they expected to have passed nearly dry-shod. To suppose that the Generals, and the officers under their command, should have been nineteen days in that small island, without ever examining, until the very instant of action, the nature of the only passage, by which they could render service to their friends and fellows, fulfil the purpose of their landing, and answer the ends for which they were embarked in the expedition, would seem a great defect in military prudence and circumspection. But there might be reasons for concealing a true state of the affair. Until that state appears, it would be unjust to lay any imputation on the officers concerned in so critical a service. The only rational solution of the fact,

must, for the present, be drawn from the different American accounts. From these it is to be inferred, that the post which the rebels possessed at the end of Sullivan's island, was in so strong a state of defence, the approaches on our side so disadvantageous, and Lee's force in such preparation and capability of crushing us in the conflict, that General Clinton would have run the most manifest and inexcusable risque, of the ruin, if not total loss, of his forces, if he had ventured upon an attack. To this it may be added, that it was only upon a near approach, that our people acquired any certain knowledge of the force of the enemy.

The action continued, until the darkness of the night compelled that cessation, which the eagerness of the assailants, worn down as they were with fatigue, and weakened with loss, was still unwilling to accept. Sir Peter Parker, after every effort of which a brave man is capable, finding that all hope of success was at an end, and the tide of ebb nearly spent, between nine and ten o'clock in the evening, withdrew his shattered vessels from the scene of action, after an engagement which had been supported with uncommon courage and vigour for above ten hours. The Bristol had 111, and the Experiment 79, men killed and wounded; and both ships had received so much damage, that the provincials conceived strong hopes, that they could never be got over the bar. The frigates, though not less emulous in the performance of their duty, being less pointed at than the great ships, did not suffer a proportional loss. The bomb vessel did not do all the service upon this occasion which was expected; whether it was from overcharging, in consequence of having originally taken too great a distance, which has been said, or whether it proceeded from some fault in the construction, which seems more probable; however, it was, the beds of the mortars were in some time so loosened and shattered as to become utterly unserviceable.

Colonel Moultrie, who commanded in the fort, received great and deserved applause from his countrymen, for the courage and conduct by which he was so much distinguished in its defence. The garrison also received a great share of praise, and a serjeant was publicly distinguished by a present of a sword from the President of the colony, for a particular act of great bravery.

During these transactions, the Congress took an opportunity of feeling the general pulse of the people, and of preparing them for the declaration of independency which was to follow, by a kind of circular manifesto to the several colonies, stating the causes which rendered it, as they said, necessary, that all authority under the crown should be totally suppressed, and all the powers of government taken respectively into their own hands. In support of this position, they instanced the Prohibitory Act, by which they were excluded from the protection of the crown; the rejection of their petition for redress of grievances and reconciliation; and the intended exertion of all the force of Great-Britain, aided by foreign mercenaries, for their destruction. They concluded with a recommendation to those colonies, whose government was not already sufficient, to proceed to the establishment of such a form, as was necessary to the preservation of internal peace, and suited to the present exigency of their affairs, for the defence of their lives, liberties, and properties, against the hostile invasions, and cruel depredations of their enemies.

Pensylvania and Maryland were the only colonies, that in part opposed the establishment of a new government, and the declaration of independency. A majority in the assembly of the former, though eager for a redress of grievances, regarded with horror every idea of a total separation from the parent state. But though they knew that great numbers in the province held similar sentiments, they were also sensible, that the more violent formed a very numerous and powerful body; that they had already taken fire at their hesitation, and considered them rather as secret enemies, than luke-warm friends. Their situation was besides difficult. If they broke the union of the colonies, and thereby forfeited the assistance and protection of the others, they had no certainty of obtaining a redress of those grievances, nor the security of those rights, for which they were as willing to contend in their own way as the most violent; but were not yet willing to give up all hope, nor to break off all possibility of accommodation. Thus critically circumstanced, they declared, that the question of independence was a matter of too great importance for them to decide finally upon, and that they would therefore refer it to their constituents, together with the arguments which had been used on both sides of the question.

It was manifestly a step from which it would not be easy to retreat. On one hand, the separation from Great-Britain, even if it could be finally accomplished, must be attended with many evident inconveniences. The protection of the great parent state, and the utility of the power of a common sovereign to balance so many separate, and, possibly, discordant commonwealths, besides many political and many commercial advantages derived from the old union, must appear in a clear light to every sober and discerning person. On the other hand, it was said, that their liberty was their first good, without which all the other advantages would be of no value. That if they were to submit to a great standing army, composed of foreigners as well as English, composed in part even of their own slaves, and of savages, what terms were they to hope for? The moment their arms were laid down, they must be at the mercy of their enemy. For what end did they take up these arms? If it was to secure their liberty, to lay them down without that security, would be to own, that their first resistance was causeless rebellion; and the pardon offered, was the only satisfaction for the present, or security for the future, they were given to expect. Did they resist power only to obtain a pardon? were they so absurd originally, or are they so cowardly now? If then their object is refused to all their entreaties by Great-Britain; if she abandons them to plunder without redemption, except on unconditional submission, how is the object of their resistance to be obtained? By war only. But as long as they acknowledge the claims of the crown of Great-Britain, so long will their councils and their generals be destitute of all civil and military authority. The war they carry on must of course be irregular, feeble, and without the smallest prospect of success. Orders will be given, which none will be obliged to obey; and conspiracies and mutinies will be formed, which none will have a just power to punish or repress. Neither will any foreign power give them any support against the hostile combination of Great-Britain, and so many foreign powers as she has called to her assistance, so long as they hold themselves to be subjects. We do not break the connexion (said they); it is already broke and dissolved by an act of parliament; and thus abandoned, all laws human and divine not only permit, but demand of us, to provide every internal and external means for our own preservation.

In these sentiments, by a reference to the people, the matter was brought to a fair trial of strength between the two parties; when it was carried by great majorities, that the delegates should agree to the determination of the Congress. This decision, however, occasioned much dissension in the province, and has founded a considerable party in opposition to the present government.

In Maryland, the delegates were instructed by a majority of seven counties to four, to oppose the question of independency in the Congress; which they accordingly did; and having given their votes, withdrew totally from that assembly. But the horror of being secluded and abandoned, together with the reproaches of the others, and perhaps the dread of their resentment, soon gave a new turn to the conduct, if not to the disposition of that province. The delegates were again instructed to return to the Congress, and to act there, as they thought best for the interest of their country. This completed the union of the colonies in that measure.

The fatal day at length arrived, which, (however the final consequences may be) must be deeply regretted by every true friend to this empire, when [76] thirteen English colonies in America, declared themselves free and independent states, abjured all allegiance to the British crown, and renounced all political connection with this country. Such are the unhappy consequences of civil contention. Such the effects that may proceed from too great a jealousy of power on the one side, or an ill-timed doubt of obedience on the other. The declaration has been seen by every body; it contains a long catalogue of grievances, with not fewer invectives; and is not more temperate in stile or composition, than it is in act. July 4th.

There were three principal objects proposed in the conduct of the British forces in the present campaign. The first was the relief of Quebec, and the redemption of Canada, which also included the subsequent invasion of the back parts of the colonies by the way of the lakes. The second was the making a strong impression on the southern colonies, which it was hoped would at least have succeeded so far as to the recovery of one of them. The third was the grand expedition against the city and province of New-York.

Of the two collateral parts of this plan we have already seen the event, so far as the first was yet capable of being carried into execution. On the third, the greatest hopes of success were not unjustly founded. Much the better part of the province of New-York is inclosed in islands, which being long[77] and narrow, were exposed on all sides to the hostility of our fleets, and to the descents of our troops, with every advantage in their favour, whilst they continued in a state of enmity. When reduced, the protection of the ships of war would be as effectual in their preservation, as their hostility had been in their reduction. The central situation of this province afforded great advantages. The war could be carried on with equal facility either in Connecticut, and the continent of New-York on the eastern side, or in New Jersey, and from thence to Pensylvania on the western; or it may be transferred to and from either at pleasure. So that this position enabled the British commander to prescribe the scene of action, and to quit it when he liked; while, if the army was withdrawn from the field, he might, by the means of the great north river, and the different channels between the islands and the main land, with his ships and detachments harrass and ruin the adjoining countries; at the same time that the rebels, however powerful, could make no attempt on the islands, that would not be attended with the greatest disadvantages, and liable to the most imminent danger. Another great object in view from this situation was, that if General Carleton could pene-

trate to Hudson's, or the great north river, General Howe might thereby totally cut off all communication between the northern and southern provinces. To crown these advantages, Long Island, which is very fertile in wheat and all other corn, and abounded with herds and flocks, was deemed almost equal in itself to the maintenance of an army. The inhabitants were also supposed to be in general well affected to the royal cause.

The attainment of these great objects, and the conduct of the grand armament which was necessary to the purpose, were committed to Admiral Lord Howe, and his brother the General; men who stood high in the opinion and confidence of the nation, as well from their own merit and services, as from the military character and bravery of the family. To this service was allotted a very powerful army, consisting, besides the national forces, of about 13,000 Hessians and Waldeckers. The whole force, if the different parts of which it was composed could have been united in the beginning of the campaign, it was supposed, would have amounted to about 35,000 men. It will be easily conceived by those acquainted with military affairs, that all calculations of this nature, though founded upon the best official information, will far exceed, even at a much nearer distance than America, the real effective number that can ever be brought to action. This force, when united, was, however, truly formidable, and such as no part of the new world had ever seen before. Nor was it, perhaps, ever exceeded by any army in Europe of an equal number, whether considered, with respect to the excellency of the troops, the abundant provision of all manner of military stores and warlike materials, or the goodness and number of artillery of all sorts with which it was provided. It was besides supported

by a very numerous fleet, particularly well adapted to the nature of the service. Besides their military powers, the General and Admiral were appointed the commissioners under the late act of parliament, for restoring peace to the colonies, and for granting pardon to such as should deserve the royal mercy.

The situation of the army at Halifax, and the long stay of above two months which it was obliged to make there, still waiting the arrival of some of the reinforcements from England to enable it to go upon service, was neither pleasing to the General, nor comfortable to the men. The country was in no situation to afford them a sufficient supply of provisions or necessaries; nor was the place even capable of providing quarters on shore for the private men, who were obliged to continue on board the ships during the whole of their stay. As the summer advanced, the General grew impatient at the delay, and was probably further urged by the scarcity of provisions. He accordingly, without waiting for his brother, or the expected reinforcements, departed, with Admiral Shuldham, and the fleet and army, from Halifax, about the 10th of June, and near the end of the month, arrived at Sandy Hook, a point of land that stands at the entrance into that confluence of sounds, roads, creeks, and bays, which are formed by New-York, Staten, and Long, islands, the continent on either side, with the North and Rareton rivers.

On their passage, they were joined by six transports with Highland troops on board, who were separated from several of their companions in the voyage. It appeared soon after, that some of the missing ships, with about 450 soldiers, and several officers, were taken by the American cruizers. The General found every approachable part of the island of New-York strongly fortified, defended by a numerous artillery, and guarded by little lefs than an army. The extent of Long Ifland did not admit of its being fo ftrongly fortified, or fo well guarded; it was, however, in a powerful ftate of defence; had an encampment of confiderable force on the end of the ifland near New-York, and feveral works thrown up on the moft acceffible parts of the coaft, as well as at the ftrongeft internal paffes.

Staten Ifland, being of lefs value and confequence, was lefs attended to. The General July 3d. landed on the ifland without oppofition, to the great joy of thofe of the inhabitans who had fuffered for their loyalty; and the troops being cantoned in the villages, received plenty of thofe refrefhments which they fo much wanted. He was met by Governor Trion, with feveral well-affected gentlemen who had taken refuge with him on board a fhip, at Sandy Hook, who gave him a full account of the ftate and difpofition of the province, as well as of the ftrength of the enemy. He had the fatisfaction of being joined by about fixty perfons from New Jerfey, who came to take arms in the royal caufe, and about 200 of the militia of the ifland were embodied for the fame purpofe, which afforded the pleafing profpect, that when the army was in force to march into the country and protect the royalifts, fuch numbers would join it, as would contribute not a little to bring the prefent troubles to a fpeedy conclufion.

Lord Howe arrived at Halifax about a fortnight after his brother's departure, from whence he proceeded to Staten Ifland, where he arrived before the middle of July. His firft act was to fend July 14th. afhore, by a flag, a circular letter to the feveral late Governors of the colonies, acquainting them with his civil and military powers, and defiring that they would publifh, as generally as poffible, for the information of the people, a declaration which ac-

companied the letter. In this piece he informed the public of the powers with which his brother and he were endued under the late act of parliament, of granting general or particular pardons to all thofe, who, in the tumult and difafter of the times, might have deviated from their juft allegiance, and who were willing, by a fpeedy return to their duty, to reap the benefits of the royal favour, and of declaring any colony, province, county, town, port, diftrict, or place, to be at the peace of his Majefty; in which cafe, the penal provifions of that law would ceafe in their favour. It alfo promifed, that a due confideration fhould be had to the fervices of all perfons who contributed to the reftoration of the public tranquillity.

Thefe papers being immediately forwarded by General Wafhington to the Congrefs, were as fpeedily publifhed by them in all the newspapers, with a preface or comment of their own, in the form of a refolution; that the publication was in order that the people of the united ftates might be informed of what nature are the commiffioners, and what the terms, with the expectation of which the court of Great-Britain had endeavoured to amufe and difarm them; and that the few who ftill remained fufpended by a hope founded either in the juftice or moderation of that court, might now at length be convinced, that the valour alone of their country, is to fave its liberties.

At and about the fame time, different flags were fent afhore by Lord Howe, accompanied by fome of his officers, with a letter directed to George Wafhington, Efq; which that General refufed to receive, as not being addreffed with the title, and in the form, due to the rank which he held under the United States. The Congrefs highly applauded the dignity of this conduct, in a public refolution paffed for the purpofe; by which they directed, for the future, that

none of their commanders fhould receive any letter or meffage from the enemy, but fuch as fhould be directed to them in the character which they refpectively fuftained.

At length, Adjutant-General Paterfon was fent 20th, [78] to New-York by General Howe, with a letter addreffed to George Wafhington, &c. &c. &c. That General received him with great politenefs, and the ufual ceremony of blindfolding, in paffing through the fortifications, was difpenfed with in his favour. The Adjutant regretted, in the name of his principals, the difficulties which had arifen with refpect to addreffing the letters; declared their high efteem for his perfon and character, and that they did not mean to derogate from the refpect due to his rank; and that it was hoped the et cetera's would remove the impediments to their correfpondence. The General replied, that a letter directed to any perfon in a public character fhould have fome defcription or indication of it, otherwife it would appear a mere private letter; that it was true the et cetera's implied every thing; but they alfo implied any thing; and that he fhould abfolutely decline any letter directed to him as a private perfon, when it related to his public ftation.

A long conference enfued on the fubject of prifoners, and the complaints which were made on both fides, particularly by the Congrefs, relative to the treatment they received. The adjutant having obferved, that the commiffioners were armed with great powers; that they would derive the greateft pleafure from effecting an accommodation; and that himfelf wifhed to have that vifit confidered as making the firft advance towards that defirable object: he received for anfwer, among other things, that, by what had appeared, their powers were only to grant pardons; that thofe who had committed no fault wanted no pardon; and that they themfelves were only defending what they deemed their indisputable right. The adjutant was received by General Washington in great military state, and the utmost politeness was observed on both sides.

Some small time previous to the arrival of the fleet and army, plots in favour of the royal cause were discovered in New York and Albany, which were productive of much trouble. Some few executions took place, great numbers were confined, and many, abandoning their houses under the operation of their fears, were pursued as outlaws, and enemies to their country. The estates of those unfortunate people, against whom there were proofs, were seized. In the mean time, new forms of government were established in all those colonies, which deemed the former insufficient for their present situation, and the others made the alterations necessary to adapt their old forms to the new system. The declaration of independence was also published in all the colonies, and every where received and accompanied with the greatest public testimonials of joy. This confidence and boldness in the midst of so untried and dangerous a struggle, and at the eve of so formidable an invasion, shewed either great presumption, a knowledge of internal strength, or a certainty of foreign support, which appeared alarming.

The first division of Hessians, with the British troops by whom they were accompanied, sailed directly from England to Halifax, as Lord Howe had done, being still ignorant of the general's departure from that place. By this means the month of August was considerably advanced before their arrival at New York, and it was of course some days longer before any expedition of importance could be undertaken by the commissioners. In the mean time they were joined by Sir Peter Parker and General Clinton, with the squadron and forces from South-Carolina, as well as by some regiments from Florida and the West Indies.

All the forces being now arrived, except about one half of the Hessians, who, though on their way, were not speedily expected, an attempt upon Long Island was resolved upon, as being more practicable, and therefore better fitted for the first essay than New York, as affording a greater scope for the display to advantage of military skill and experience, and as abounding with those supplies which so great a body of men as were now assembled by sea and land necessarily demanded.

The necessary measures being taken by Aug. 22. the fleet for covering the descent, the army was landed without opposition near Utrecht and Gravesend, on the south-west end of the island, and not far from the narrows where it approaches closest to Staten Island. General utnam was at that time with a strong force encamped at Brookland, or Brooklyn, at a few miles distance, on the north coast, where his works covered the breadth of a small peninsula, having what is called the East river, which separated him from New York, on his left; a marsh, which extended to Gowan's Cove, on his right; with the bay and Governor's Island to his back. The armies were separated by a range of hills covered with wood, which intersect the country from east to west, and are, in that part, called the heights of Guana. The direct road to the enemy lay through a village called Flat Bush, where the hills commenced, and near which was one of the most important passes. As the army advanced, the north coast was to the left, the south to the right, and Flat Bush was nearly in the center between both. The island in that part is kept narrow by Jamaica bay, on the right, but soon widens. General Putnam had detached a considerable part of his army to occupy the woody hills, and possess the passes; and if the commanders upon this service had been skilful and vigilant, they could not have been easily passed.

Lord Cornwallis pushed on immediately with the reserve, and some other troops, to Flat Bush, where finding the enemy in possession of the pass, he complied with his orders in making no attempt upon it. When the whole army was landed, the Hessians, under General Heister, composed the center at Flat Bush; Major General Grant commanded the left [79] wing, which extended to the coast; and the principal army, containing much the greater part of the British forces, under the command of General Clinton, Earl Percy, and Lord Cornwallis, turned short to the right, and approached the opposite coast at Flat Land.

Every thing being prepared for forcing the hills, and advancing towards the enemy's lines, General Clinton, at the head of the van of the army, consisting of the light infantry, grenadiers, light horse, reserve under Lord Cornwallis, and other corps, with fourteen field pieces, began, as soon as it was dark on the night of the 26th, to move from Flat Land, and passing through the part of the country called the New Lots, arrived upon the road which crosses the hills from Bedford to Jamaica, where turning to the left towards the former of these places, they seized a pass of the utmost importance, which through some unaccountable and fatal neglect of the enemy's generals, was left unguarded. The main body, under Lord Percy, with ten field pieces, followed the van at a moderate distance, and the way being thus happily open, the whole army passed the hills without noise or impediment, and descended by the town of Bedford into the level country which lay between them and Putnam's lines.

The engagement was begun early in the morning by the Hessians at Flat Bush, and by General Grant on the coast, and a warm cannonade, with a brisk fire of small arms, was eagerly supported on both sides for some hours. In the mean time, the ships made several motions on the left, and attacked a battery on Red Hook, not only to distract the right of the enemy, who were engaged with General Grant, but to call off their attention totally from the left and rear, where all their danger lay. Those who opposed the Hessians in the left and center, were the first apprized of the march of the British army, and of their own danger. They accordingly retreated in large bodies, and in tolerable order, with their artillery, in order to recover their camp, but soon found themselves intercepted by the King's troops, who furiously attacked, and drove them back into the woods. There they again met the Hessians, and were alternately chased and intercepted by the light infantry and dragoons. In these desperate circumstances, some of their regiments, overpowered and outnumbered as they were, forced their way to the lines, through all the difficulties and dangers that opposed and surrounded them, Others, perhaps not less brave, perished in the attempt. Some kept the woods and escaped; others, less fortunate, were lost under the same protection. The nature of the country, and variety of the ground, occasioned a continuance and extension of small engagements, pursuits, and slaughter, which lasted for many hours.

Never was any body of men more effectually entrapped: their right, which was engaged with General Grant on the coast, were so late in their knowledge of what was passing, that they were intercepted in their retreat by some of of the British troops, who, besides turning the hills, and their left, had in that morning traversed the whole extent of country in their rear. Such of these as did not chuse to take to the woods, which were the greater number, were obliged to throw themselves into the marsh at Gowan's Cove, which we have already taken notice of, where many were drowned, and others perished more miserably in the mud: a considerable number, however, made their escape this way to the lines, though they were thinned in every part of the course by the fire of the pursuers.

Their loss was represented as exceeding 3000 men, including about 1000 who were taken prisoners. Almost a whole regiment from Maryland, consisting altogether of young men of the best families in the country, was cut to pieces. Undoubtedly their loss must have been great, though they do not acknowledge any such number in their accounts. This action, however, broke their spirits exceedingly. They not only lost a number of their best and bravest men, but the survivors lost that hope of success, and confidence in their own prowess, which are so essential to victory. New soldiers, in the fulness of spirits, and pride of bodily strength, can scarcely conceive any advantage over them, which the old can derive from discipline and a knowledge of their business. And if they are well commanded, and skilfully led to action in this temper, so that their opponents are deprived of an opportunity of turning these advantages to account, they will do wonderful execution: for not being yet capable of thoroughly comprehending danger, nor having known by experience the pain and vexation of wounds, they are often more daring, adventurous, and violent than veterans. But if, as in the present instance, they find courage and strength totally useless; that when they are making the greatest, and, as they think, most effectual efforts, they find them all thrown away, and that they are surrounded, overpowered, and destroyed, by means [80] which they cannot understand, they withdraw all due confidence from those things on which they had before placed too much, and ascribe an irresistible power to military skill and discipline which they do not really possess. Thus they abandon their natural strength, and it will be some time before they have confidence enough in their new knowledge to call it effectually into action.

Great errors seem to have been committed on the side of the provincial commanders. They say, that a body of not more than four or five thousand men was surrounded by the whole force of the British army. They endeavour to palliate their misconduct in getting into that situation by representing, that they had no idea that more than about that number of British troops were landed on the island. It does appear as if no more had landed in the first embarkation; but either from a change or concealment of plan, very great bodies were afterwards embarked and passed. The provincials too, as usual with men in misfortunes, hinted treachery in some of those who were employed to discover the motions of their enemy, and to guard the passes, by the occupying of which [81] they had been surrounded.

Nothing could exceed the spirit and alacrity shewn by all the different corps of which the British army was composed in this action. The ardour of the soldiers was so great, that it was with difficulty the generals could call them off from attacking the enemy's lines, in the eagerness of their pursuit after the fugitives. Nor is it improbable, in that temper, that they would have carried every thing before them. It may be supposed, that the emulation between the foreign troops and the British did not lessen the desire of being distinguished on either side in this their first action. Too much praise cannot be given to the ability which planned this enterprize, nor to the promptness and exactitude with which the several generals carried their respective parts of it into execution.

Three of the enemy's commanders, viz. Major General Sullivan, with the Brigadiers General Lord Sterling and Udell, and ten other[82] field officers, were among the prisoners. The loss on the side of the British and Hessians was very trifling, being under 350 in killed and wounded; of which the former did not compose one fifth. An officer with a few men were taken prisoners. The victorious army encamped in the front of the enemy's works on that evening, and on the 28th, at 27th. night, broke ground in form at 600 yards distance from a redoubt which covered the enemy's left.

General Washington passed over from New York during the engagement, and is said to have burst into a poignant exclamation of grief, when he beheld the inextricable destruction in which some of his best troops were involved. Nothing was now left, but to preserve the remainder of the army on Long Island. He knew that the superior power of the royal artillery would soon silence their batteries, and that if their lines were forced, which, in their present depression of spirits, and comparative weakness in number as well as discipline, there was little hope of preventing, they must all be killed or taken. If he attempted to strengthen them by reinforcements from New York, he hazarded the loss of that island, which was already menaced on every side, and kept in continual alarm and apprehension by the fleet. A danger not less than any other was still to be considered; the men of war only waited for a fair wind to enter and take possession of the East river, which would have totally cut off all communication between the islands. In this situation, no hope remained but in a retreat; a matter of no small difficulty and danger, under the eye of so vigilant an enemy, and with so powerful an army, flushed with success, close to their works. This arduous task was, however, undertaken, and carried into execution with great ability by General Washington. In the night of the 29th, their troops were withdrawn from the camp and their different works, and with their baggage, stores, and part of their artillery, were conveyed to the water-side, embarked, and passed over a long ferry to New York, with such wonderful silence and order, that our army did not perceive the least motion, and were surprised in the morning at finding the lines abandoned, and seeing the last of the rear guard (or, as they say, a party which had returned to carry off some stores that were left behind) in their boats, and out of danger. Those who are best acquainted with the difficulty, embarrassment, noise, and tumult, which attend even by day, and no enemy at hand, a movement of this nature with several thousand men, will be the first to acknowledge, that this retreat should hold a high place among military transactions.

Soon after the retreat from Long Island, General Sullivan was sent upon parole with a message from Lord Howe to the Congress. In this he stated, that though he could not at present treat with that assembly as such, yet he was very desirous of having a conference with some of their members, whom he would consider for the present only as private gentlemen, and would himself meet them at such place as they should appoint. He said, that he had, in conjunction with the General, full powers to compromise the dispute between Great-Britain and America, upon terms advantageous to both, the obtaining of which had detained him near two months, and prevented his arrival before the declaration of independency took place. That he wished a compact might be settled at this time, when no decisive blow was struck, and neither party could say they were compelled to enter into the agreement. That if the Congress were disposed to treat, many things which they had not yet asked, might and ought to be granted to them; and that if upon the conference any probable ground of an accommodation appeared, the authority of Congress must be afterwards acknowledged, or the compact could not be complete.

The Congress returned for answer, that being the representatives of the Free and Independent States of America, they could not with propriety send any of their members to confer with him in their private characters; but that, ever desirous of establishing peace on reasonable terms, they would send a committee of their body to know whether he had any authority to treat with persons authorized by Congress for that purpose, in behalf of America, and what that authority was, and to hear such propositions as he should think fit to make respecting the same.

Dr. Franklin, Mr. Adams, and Mr. Rutledge, being appointed as[83] a committee upon this occasion, waited accordingly upon Lord Howe in Staten Island. The committee sum up the account of this conference, which they laid before the Congress, in the following words: " Upon the whole, it did not appear to your committee, that his lordship's commission contained any other authority of importance than what is contained in the act of Parliament, viz. That of granting pardons, with such exceptions as the commissioners shall think proper to make, and of declaring America, or any part of it, to be in the King's peace upon submission. For, as to the power of enquiring into the state of America, which his lordship mentioned to us, and of conferring and consulting with any persons the commissioners might think proper, and representing the result of such converfations to the miniftry, who (provided the colonies would fubject themfelves) might, after all, or might not, at their pleafure, make any alterations in the former inftructions to governors, or propofe in Parliament any amendment of the acts complained of, we apprehended any expectation from the effect of fuch a power would have been too uncertain and precarious to be relied on by America, had fhe ftill continued in her ftate of dependance."

In this manner the hopes of negociation by the commiffioners ended. They endeavoured to make amends for their failure in their civil capacity by the vigour of their military operations. The royal army being now divided from the ifland of New York only by the Eaft river, were impatient to pafs that narrow boundary. They pofted themfelves along the coaft wherever they could fee or front the enemy, and erected batteries to anfwer, if not to filence theirs. A fleet, confifting of confiderably more than 300 fail, including tranfports, covered the face of the waters, while the fhips of war, hovering round the ifland, threatened deftruction to every part, and were continually engaged with one or other of the batteries by which it was furrounded. The fmall iflands between the oppofite fhores were perpetual objects of conteft, until, by dint of a well-ferved artillery, the aid of the fhips, and the intrepidity of the troops, they fecured thofe which were moft neceffary for their future operations. Thus, an almoft conftant cannonade was kept up for many days, and the troops who had fo lately efcaped from the moft imminent danger, had little time to quiet their apprehenfions.

Every thing being at length prepared for a defcent, feveral movements were made by the fhips of war in the North River, in order to draw the attention of the enemy to that fide of the ifland. Other parts feemed equally threatened, and increafed the uncertainty of the real object of attack. The feizure of the ifland of Montrefor, near Hell Gate, and erecting a battery on it to filence one which the provincials had at Horen's Hook, feemed to indicate a defign of landing in that part, which was near the center of New York Ifland.

Whilft the rebels were in this ftate of expectation and uncertainty, the firft divifion of the army, under the command of General Clinton, with Earl Cornwallis, Major General Vaughan, Brigadier General Leflie, and the Heffian Colonel Donop, embarked at the head of Newtown bay, which runs pretty deep into Long Ifland, and where they were out of all view of the enemy. Being covered by five fhips of war upon their entrance into the river, they proceeded to Kepp's bay, about three miles north of New York, where being lefs expected than in fome other places, the preparation for defence was not fo great. The works, however, were not inconfiderable, nor deftitute of troops, but the fire from the fhips was fo inceffant, and fo well conducted, that they were foon abandoned, and the army landed without oppofition.

Sept. 15.

The enemy immediately abandoned the city of New York, with their other pofts on that part of the ifland, and retired towards the north end, where their principal ftrength lay. They were obliged to leave their artillery, which was confiderable, and their military ftores (of which, except powder, there was plenty) behind. They fuftained fome lofs in flain, and a greater in prifoners, as well in the retreat, as in the fubfequent fkirmifhes which took place during the day. The fore remembrance of their late lofs was ftrongly vifible in every part of their conduct, and their own accounts acknowledged, that feveral of the regiments behaved ill.

A brigade of the Britifh army having taken poffeffion of New York, the reft encamped not far from the center of the ifland, with the right at Horen's Hook, on the Eaft river, and the left at the North river, near Bloomingdale; thus occupying the extent of the ifland from fhore to fhore, which, though about 16 miles in length, is not much above one in breadth. The enemy were very ftrong in the north of the ifland, where they had great works erected; particularly at Kingfbridge, by which their communication with the continent of New York was kept open, where the works were fo confiderable on both fides of the paffage, that in their prefent ftate of force they feemed to defy all attempts on either. Their neareft encampment was on the heights of Harlem, at the diftance of about a mile and a half. M'Gowan's pafs, and the ftrong grounds called Morris's heights, lay between them and Kingfbridge, and were defenfible againft a very fuperior force. In this fituation of both armies, frequent fkirmifhes of courfe happened, and it was found by degrees that their late apprehenfions began to wear away.

General Howe had not been many days in poffeffion of New York, when fome incendiaries, who probably had ftayed behind and concealed themfelves for that purpofe, being determined, if poffible, to prevent its being of any benefit to the conqueror, prepared combuftibles with great art and ingenuity, and taking the advantage of dry weather and a brifk wind, fet fire to the city about midnight, in feveral places at the fame time. Thus, near a third of that beautiful city was reduced to afhes, and nothing lefs than the courage and activity of the troops, as well as of the failors who were difpatched from the fleet, could have preferved any

20th.

part of the remainder. Many of the wretches who were, as it is said, concerned in this atrocious bufinefs, being detected, experienced a fummary juftice, and were precipitated by the fury of the foldiers into thofe flames which they had themfelves kindled.

The general perceiving that no attempt could be made on the enemy upon the fide of New York, which would not be attended with great danger, without affording any equal profpect of fuccefs, determined at length upon a plan of operation, which would either oblige them to quit their prefent ftrong fituation, or render their perfeverance in holding it extremely dangerous. For this purpose, Oct. 12. the greater part of the army being embarked in flat boats and other fmall craft proper for the fervice, paffed fuccefsfully through the dangerous navigation of Hell Gate, which forms a communication between the Eaft river and the Sound, and landed on Frog's Neck, near the [85] town of Weft Chefter, which lies on that part of the continent belonging to New York, upon the fide of Connecticut.

Earl Percy, with two brigades of Britifh troops, and one of Heffian, continued in the lines near Harlem to cover New-York. Though this movement was highly judicious in the prefent exact ftate of things, it feems as if it would have been extremely dangerous if General Wafhington had commanded a veteran army on whofe performance he could rely, and that the corps under Lord Percy would in that cafe have been in great danger. It is, however, to be obferved, that the powerful fleet which furrounded that narrow ifland, would have afforded fhelter and protection in almoft any fituation to which they could have been reduced. This fleet was of infinite fervice in all the operations of the campaign. In this the inferiority of the provincials was moft felt, being totally deftitute of any force of that nature.

The army was detained for fome days at Frog's Neck, waiting for the arrival of the provifions and ftores, and of a reinforcement which was drawn from Staten Ifland. They then proceeded through Pelham's Manor to New Rochelle, which lies on the coaft of the Sound, as that channel is called, which feparates the continent from Long Ifland. At this place they were joined by the greater part of a regiment of light horfe from Ireland, one of the tranfports having been taken in the paffage. They were alfo joined by the fecond divifion of Heffians under General Knyphaufen, with a regiment of Waldeckers, both of which had [86] arrived at New-York fince the departure of the army from thence.

The firft object of this expedition was to cut off the communications between Wafhington and the eaftern colonies; and then, if this meafure did not bring him to an engagement, to enclofe him on all fides in his faftneffes on the north end of York Ifland. The King's troops were now mafters of the lower road to Connecticut and Bofton; but to gain the upper, it was neceffary to advance to the high grounds called the White Plains; a rough, ftony, and mountainous tract; which, however, is only part of the afcent, to a country ftill higher, rougher, and more difficult. Upon the departure of the army to the higher country, it was deemed neceffary to leave the fecond divifion of Heffians, with the Waldeck regiment, at New Rochelle, as well to preferve the communications, as to fecure the fupplies of provifions and neceffaries that were to arrive at that port. Indeed the army was now fo powerful, that it was enabled to fupport every fervice.

General Wafhington was not inattentive to the danger of his fituation. He faw, that if he continued where he was, he would at length be compelled to commit the whole fortune of the war, and the fafety of all the colonies to the hazard of a general engagement; a decifion, of which he had every caufe to apprehend the event, and in which a defeat would be final, as there could fcarcely be a poffibility of retreat. His army likewife, which had been difheartened by their late misfortunes, was then much reduced by ficknefs, which the feverity of the fervices, indifferent quarters, infufficient cloathing, the want of falt and other neceffaries, joined to a flovenlinefs generally prevalent in America, had rendered general, and very fatal in his camp.

A grand movement was accordingly made, by which the army was formed into a line of fmall, detached, and entrenched camps, which occupied every height and ftrong ground from Valentine's Hill, not far from Kingfbridge, on the right, to the White Plains, and the upper road to Connecticut, on the left. In this pofition they faced the whole line of march of the King's troops at a moderate diftance, the deep river Brunx covering their front, and the North river at fome diftance in their rear, whilft the open ground to the laft afforded a fecure paffage for their ftores and baggage to the upper country. A garrifon was left for the protection of Fort Wafhington, the lines of Harlem and Kingfbridge.

In this fituation of the enemy, General Howe thought it neceffary to proceed with great circumfpection. The progrefs was flow, the march of the army clofe, the encampments compact, and well guarded with artillery, and the moft foldier-like caution ufed in every refpect. This did not reftrain the enemy from fending parties over the Brunx to impede their march, which occafioned feveral fkirmifhes, in which the royal army were generally fuccefsful. Upon the approach of the army to the White Plains, the enemy quitted their detached camps along the Brunx, and joining their left, took a strong ground of encampment before the British on the former.

Every thing being prepared for bringing the enemy 28th. to action, the army marched early in the morning in two columns towards the White Plains, the left being commanded by General Heister. Before noon, all the enemies advanced parties being drove back to their works by the light infantry and Heffian Chaffeurs, the army formed, with the right upon the road from Mamoroneck, at about a mile's distance from their center, and the left to the Brunx, at about the same distance from the right flank of their entrenchments.

A body of the enemy poffeffed an advantageous ground, that was feparated from their right flank by the Brunx, and which alfo by its windings, covered that corps in front from the left of our army. As this poft would have been of great confequence in attacking that flank of the entrenchments, Brigadier General Leflie, with the fecond brigade of British troops, the Heffian grenadiers under Colonel Donop, and a battalion of that corps, were ordered to diflodge the enemy. Previous to their attack, Colonel Ralle, who commanded a bri-[87] gade of Heffians on the left, had paffed the Brunx, and gained a poft, which enabled him to annoy the enemies flank, while they were engaged with the other forces in front.

Though the paffage of the river was difficult, it was performed with the greateft fpirit, and the 28th, and 35th regiments, being the firft that paffed, formed with the greateft fteadinefs, under the enemies fire on the oppofite fide; they then afcended a fteep hill, in defiance of all oppofition, and rufhing on the enemy, foon routed, and drove them from their works. No lefs alacrity was fhewn by the other troops in fupporting thefe two regiments. The gaining of this important poft took up a confiderable time, which was prolonged by the enemy's ftill fupporting a broken and fcattered engagement, in defence of the adjoining walls and hedges. In the evening, the Heffian grenadiers were ordered forward upon the heights within cannon fhot of the entrenchments, the 2d brigade of British formed in their rear, and the two Heffian brigades, on the left of the fecond. The right and center of the army did not remove from the ground upon which they had formed. In that pofition the whole army lay upon their arms during the night, with a full intention, and in the higheft expectation, of attacking the enemy's camp next morning.

It was perceived in the morning that the enemy had drawn back their encampment in the night, and had greatly ftrengthened their lines by additional works. Upon this account the attack was deferred, and it was thought neceffary to wait for the arrival of the 4th brigade, and of two battalion of the 6th, which had been left with Lord Percy at New York. Upon the arrival of thefe troops, the neceffary difpofitions were made in the evening, for attacking the enemy early on the laft of October; but an extreme wet night and morning prevented this defign from being carried into execution.

In the mean time, General Wafhington had not the fmalleft intention of venturing an engagement, whilft there was a poffibility of its being avoided. He knew that delay was in fome fort victory to him. That fmall actions, which could not in the leaft affect the public fafety, would more effectually train his men to fervice, and inure them to danger, than a general action, which might in one day decide their own, and the fate of America. It muft be acknowledged, that in the courfe of this campaign, and more particularly in this part of it, he fully performed the part of no mean commander.

The American accounts fay, that upon our covering four or five batteries with a powerful artillery, preparatory to an attack, together with the General's knowledge that by turning his camp, the British might become poffeffed of hills at his back which totally commanded it, he found it neceffary to change his pofition. He accordingly quitted his camp on the night of the 1ft of November, and took higher ground towards the North Caftle diftrict, having firft fet fire to the town or village of White Plains, as well as to all the houfes and forage near the lines. The British army on the next day took poffeffion of their entrenchment.

General Howe feeing that the enemy could not be enticed to an engagement, and that the nature of the country did not admit of their being forced to it, determined not to lofe time in a fruitlefs purfuit, and to take this opportunity of driving them out of their ftrong holds in York Ifland; an operation which their army could not now poffibly prevent. For this purpofe, General Knyphaufen croffed the country from New Rochelle, and having taken poffeffion of King's Bridge without oppofition, entered York Ifland, and took his ftation to the north of Fort Wafhington, to which the enemy had retired at his approach.

Fort Wafhington lay on the weft fide of New York Ifland, not far from King's Bridge, near Jeffery's Hook, and almoft facing Fort Lee on the Jerfey fide, from which it was feparated by the North River. This work, though not contemptible, was not fufficient to refift heavy artillery; and it was by no means of a fufficient extent for any other purpofe than the ftrengthening of lines. But the fituation was extremely ftrong, and the approaches difficult.

The army having Nov. 13th. returned flowly by the

North River, encamped on the heighths of Fordham, at a moderate distance from King's-Bridge, with that river on its right, and the Brunx on the left. Every thing being prepared for attacking the Fort, and the commander, Colonel Magaw, refusing a summons to surrender, and declaring he would defend it to the last extremity, a general assault was determined upon, as saving the time that would be lost in regular approaches. The garrison consisted of near 3000 men, and the strong grounds round the Fort were covered with lines and works. Four attacks were made at the same time. The first, on the north side, was conducted by General Knyphausen, at the head of two columns of Hessians and Waldeckers. The second, on the east, was led on by Brigadier General Mathew, at the head of the 1st and 2d battalions of light infantry, and two battalions of guards, supported by Lord Cornwallis with the 1st and 2d battalions of grenadiers, and the 33d regiment. These forces crossed the East River in flat boats, and as the enemies works there extended the breadth of the island, redoubts and batteries were erected on the opposite shore, as well to cover the landing of the troops, as to annoy those works which were near the water. The third attack, which was principally intended as a feint to distract the enemy, was conducted by Lt. Colonel Sterling, with the 42d regiment, who passed the East River lower down, between the 2d and 4th attacks. The last attack was made by Lord Percy, with the corps which he commanded on the south of the island. All the attacks were supported with a numerous, powerful, and well served artillery.

The Hessians under Gen. Knyphausen had a thick wood to pass, where the enemy were very advantageously posted, and a warm engagement was continued for a considerable time, in which the for-

88

16th.

90

mer were much exposed, and behaved with great firmness and bravery. In the mean time the light infantry landed, and were exposed both before and after to a very brisk and continual fire from the enemy, who were themselves covered by the rocks and trees among which they were posted. The former, however, with their usual alertness and activity, extricated themselves by clambering up a very steep and rough mountain, when they soon dispersed the enemy, and made way for the landing of the rest of the troops without opposition. During these transactions, Lord Percy having carried an advanced work on his side, Col. Sterling was ordered to attempt a landing, and two battalions of the 2d brigade to support him. This service was effected by the Colonel with great bravery. He advanced his boats through a very heavy fire, which they bore with the greatest firmness and perseverance, and forcing his way up a steep height, gained the summit, and took 170 prisoners, notwithstanding a bold and good defence made by the enemy.

In the mean time Colonel Ralle, who led the right column of General Knyphausen's attack, having forced the enemy, after a considerable opposition, from their strong posts in his line, pushed forward to their works, and lodged his column within an hundred yards of the fort; and being soon after joined by the General with the left column, who had at length overcome the impediments which he met with in the wood, the garrison surrendered prisoners of war. The loss on either side was not in any degree proportioned to the warmth, length, and variety of the action. The quantity of gunpowder found in the Fort was utterly inadequate to the purpose of almost the shortest defence. How so large a body was left with so poor a provision, is extremely unaccountable. But the narrative of all these transactions is hitherto very imperfect.

89

Upon this acquisition, a strong body of forces under the command of Lord Cornwallis was passed over the North River, in order to take Fort Lee, and make a further impression in the Jerseys. The garrison of 2000 men, had a narrow escape, by abandoning the Fort just before his lordship's arrival, leaving their artillery, stores, tents, and every thing behind. Our troops afterwards overrun the greater part of both the Jerseys without opposition, the enemy flying every where before them; and at length extended their winter cantonments from New Brunswick to the Delaware. If they had any means of passing that river upon their first arrival in its neighbourhood, there seems little doubt, considering the consternation and dismay which then prevailed among the enemy, that they might easily have become masters of the city of Philadelphia; but the former, very prudently, either destroyed the boats, or removed them out of the way.

During these successes in the Jerseys, Gen. Clinton, with two brigades of British, and two of Hessian troops, with a squadron of ships of war under the command of Sir Peter Parker, were sent to make an attempt upon Rhode Island. In this enterprize they succeeded beyond expectation. The rebels having abandoned the island at their approach, they took possession of it without the loss of a man; at the same time that they blocked up Hopkins's squadron, which was in the harbour of Providence, on the adjoining Continent. The squadron and troops continued here during the winter, where they had better quarters than any other of the king's forces. Hitherto the royal army had succeeded in every object since their landing at Staten Island. The Provincial army, besides the loss by sword, by captivity, and by desertion, began to dwindle to very small numbers, from the nature of their military

18th.

Dec. 8th.

engagement. They were only enlisted for a year; and the colonists, who were but little used to any restraint, very ill brooked, even so long an absence from their families. At the expiration of the term, but few were prevailed upon to continue in service. Every thing seemed to promise a decisive event in favour of the royal arms, and a submission of some of the principal colonies was hourly expected.

General conduct of European powers with respect to the American troubles. France. Military preparations. Count de St. Germain placed at the head of the war department. Musquetaires reduced. Mr. Necker placed at the head of the Finances. Spain. Extraordinary military preparations. Dispute with Portugal. Improvements. Discoveries in the Southern Ocean. New Academy. Vienna. Torture abolished. Toleration enlarged. Bohemia peasants on the royal demesnes freed from their former state of villainage. Attempt to open a trade with the East Indies. Russia. Endeavours to people the uncultivated parts of the Empire. Grand Duchess dies. Grand Duke marries the Princess of Wirtemberg. Porte. Bassora taken by the Persians. Northern kingdoms. Holland.

WHILST our own affairs have opened so extensive a field of business and action, the rest of Europe has happily preserved its tranquillity, and affords few objects of historical discussion. Indeed it seems as if the transactions we have described, had occasioned a kind of pause in the active politicks of other states. The unhappy contention in which we are engaged, is of such general importance in its progress, and may be so widely extensive in its consequences, that every commercial state finds itself interested in the one, and its speculation strongly excited by the other. Political enthusiasts, like all others, overlook all obstacles to the establishment of their favourite system, and all impediments in the way to that point, which they have fixed upon as the summit of attainment. Such a schemer as Alberoni, would now[91] see a prospect opened for a total change in the political system of Europe, and a new arrangement of power and commerce in both the worlds. However the race of projectors may become extinct in other sciences, they are immortal in the affairs of nations. In them Alberoni's are never wanting.

It is not then to be wondered at, that the political attention of some of the great European states should be strongly attracted by objects, in which Great Britain and her colonies should only have an interest; or that the consciousness of a power, which would enable them to convert all favourable circumstances to the greatest advantage, should dispose them to look forward to possible consequences. It is as little a matter of surprize, that other states, whose views are more limited, should endeavour to profit of the present conjuncture.

No alliance, no ties of political friendship founded upon mutual interest and safety, and no other can subsist between states, are capable of resisting the allurements of commerce, with its concomitants wealth and power, when these, even approach in value, to that of the bands which cemented the union. If such be their influence upon the closest alliance, upon those who are bound by many common motives of connection and friendship, what must it be upon natural enemies; upon jealous and suspicious rivals; upon those who dread, or who have experienced our power; or even such as only envied our greatness? Without the attainment of those benefits to themselves, the simply withdrawing them from an envied or dreaded power, and thereby lessening its importance and the apprehension it excited, would be an object of the first consideration.

France and Spain have opened their ports, with the greatest apparent friendship to the Americans, and treat them in every respect as an independent people. The remonstrances of the British ministers have availed but little. They already have a taste of the sweets of that commerce which we had so long secluded from the rest of the world; and which would have still preserved our greatness if we had lost all other. They now begin to know by experience the extent of those advantages, which before were only objects of an uncertain speculation, and whose real value was not well understood by ourselves. Not content with reaping the benefits of the American commerce, by keeping barely within the pale of a verbal neutrality, they go farther; they solicit, and afford the means for its continuance. The American privateers have been openly received, protected, and cherished, and the rich prizes they have taken from the British merchants, rather publicly sold in the French ports, both in Europe and the colonies. Artillery and military stores of all kinds have been likewise sent; whether really bought with their own money, or supplied gratis, is uncertain. At this the British ministers find themselves obliged, sometimes, to remonstrate, sometimes to wink. French engineers and officers have also joined the Americans, in numbers not before known upon any occasion of foreign or volunteer service. It signifies little to enquire, whether this has been practised by permission, or suffered by connivance.

Two evils attend this unhappy civil contention, which at the same time that they distinguish it from other wars, render it more dangerous and grievous than any. The one is, that by the advantages which it lays open, either immediately, or in prospect, to other nations, it causes an union in a certain degree, either in act or sentiment, of the commercial world against us; holding out a temptation to mankind to become our enemies. The other is, the weakness which it induces with respect to foreign powers. Our dominions are not only severed at that critical juncture, when it is too evident that a strict union of the whole would be particularly necessary; but a new enemy springs up in the separated part, which from the extraordinary vigour of exertion, proceeding from the novelty of the situation, the danger attending it, and the bitterness of domestic enmity, acquires an efficacy and force, far beyond what it contributed, or knew it possessed, when in unity, and only forming a subordinate share of general defence. Thus we have been obliged to be the tame spectators of a conduct, which in another season would have been deemed insufferable, and to submit to a degree of injury and insult which we never before experienced, or, at least, which was never offered with impunity.

Neither was neighbourhood, long alliance, the power of proclamations, or the vigilance of our Ambassador, sufficient to restrain the Dutch from sharing in those advantages which were now offered. In a word, all the nations who possess colonies in America, were eager to partake of the new and unexpected commerce which was now opened; and all, excepting the Portuguese, who, much against their inclination, have been restrained through our influence at that Court, still continue most sedulously to profit of the opportunity. This disposition has, by degrees, appeared pretty general in other European states.

It must indeed be acknowledged, that this commerce, whilst confined merely to the European colonies in the New World, may be justified upon some very reasonable grounds. The French, Dutch, and Danish islands in the West-Indies, as well as our own, had at all times been supplied by North-America with various commodities, some of which, such as provisions and lumber, were even essential to their existence. Nor were all the Spanish colonies, notwithstanding their extent of continent, wholly free from this necessity. It could not then be expected, that these States, from any regard to our private quarrels, or attention to our acts of parliament, should suffer their islands to be starved, or their staple commodities lost. Nor could the ruin which they saw coming upon our own West India islands, and palliated chiefly by captures from the Americans, be the smallest inducement to their submitting to a similar mischief.

However, from this invasion of the American trade by foreigners one advantage is derived, if not to the commerce and navigation, yet to the manufactures of England; that these nations not having yet got into the way of providing a proper assortment for the American market. they resort hither for supply. This is felt in all the manufacturing towns; and the Ministry owe much of their quiet, during the present contention, to that source.

It is probable that Europe is much indebted, for the continuance of its tranquillity, to the pacific disposition of the French monarch, which is supposed with difficulty to have restrained the activity or restlessness of a close ally and powerful neighbour, as well as the ardor of the princes of the blood, the nobility, and the nation in general, who are thought to be eagerly disposed to a war. Indeed, from whatever cause it proceeds, the American party is so strong in France, that it seems nearly to include the whole nation, except the ruling part of the Court. However that may be, the present disposition of that Court is favourable to the happiness of mankind, and, in the present state of affairs, particularly fortunate to Great-Britain.

The military preparations, however, in France, particularly on the sea-coasts, and the naval armaments, have been so considerable, that no explanation which could be given of the motives, was sufficient for a time to allay the alarm and apprehension which they excited. It was said, that as the seas were covered with English fleets and American cruizers, and not only an actual war carried on, but such armies sent to the New World as had never before appeared there, it became necessary for France to arm in such a manner, as would effectually secure her colonies, and protect her commerce: That her engagements with Spain, and the disputes between that power and Portugal, rendered it besides necessary, that she should be in such a state of preparation, as in case of a rupture would enable her to fulfil them: And that it was very extraordinary, that those who, besides being themselves in the highest possible state of warlike preparation, had also sent hosts of armed foreigners into the New World, should make objections to their neighbours putting themselves in a proper state of security. Whatever satisfaction these answers afforded, no better could be obtained; and it is very probable, that a greater reliance was placed upon a knowledge of the temper of the French Ministers, and of the cabals which prevailed in the Court, than upon any assurances they could have given. All together were not sufficient to prevent alarm, or totally to remove apprehension.

...

Petition of the City of London, presented, separately, to both Houses of Parliament, with only the necessary Variation in the Title, &c. at the Opening of the Second Session of the Fourteenth Parliament of Great-Britain.

The humble Petition of the Lord Mayor, Aldermen, and Commons of the City of London, in Common Council assembled.

Sheweth,

THAT this court having taken into its most serious consideration the present distressed situation of our fellow-subjects in America, are exceedingly alarmed for the consequences of those coercive measures, which are pursuing against them—measures that must (notwithstanding the great uncertainty of their success) eventually be productive of new and more burthensome taxes, the increase of an enormous national debt; and finally, we fear the loss of the most valuable branch of our commerce, on which the existence of an infinite number of industrious manufacturers and mechanics entirely depends.

That his Majesty having been graciously pleased, in answer to a late humble and dutiful address and petition to the throne, praying a cessation of hostilities with America for the purpose of obtaining time, and thereby giving an opportunity for a happy and lasting reconciliation with his Majesty's American colonies, to declare, that *he should abide by the sense of his parliament,* this court conceived it to be their indispensable duty, thus early in the session, in the most respectful manner to apply to this Right Hon. House, that it will be pleased to adopt such measures for the healing of the present unhappy disputes between the mother country and the colonies, as may be speedy, permanent, and honourable.

Protest of several of the Lords against their House's Address, in answer to the King's Speech, at the opening of the foresaid Session of Parliament.

Dissentient.

1st. BECAUSE we cannot, as Englishmen, as Christians, or as men of common humanity, consent to the prosecution of a cruel civil war, so little supported by justice, and so very fatal in its necessary consequences, as that which is now waging against our brethren and fellow-subjects in America. We have beheld with sorrow and indignation, session after session, and notwithstanding repeated warnings of the danger, attempts made to deprive some millions of British subjects of their trade, their laws, their constitution, their mutual intercourse, and of the very food which God has given them for their subsistence. We have beheld endeavours used to enforce these impolitic severities at the point of the bayonet. We have, on the other hand, beheld so large a part of the empire, united in one common cause, really sacrificing with chearfulness their lives and fortunes, and preferring all the horrors of a war raging in the very heart of their country, to ignominious ease. We have beheld this part of his Majesty's subjects, thus irritated to resistance, and so successful in it, still making professions (in which we think it neither wise nor decent to affect a disbelief) of the utmost loyalty to his Majesty; and unwearied with continued repulses, repeatedly petitioning for conciliation, upon such terms only as shall be consistent with the dignity and welfare of the Mother Country. When we consider these things, we cannot look upon our fellow-subjects in America in any other light than that of freemen driven to resistance by acts of oppression and violence.

2dly. Because this unnatural war, thus commenced in oppres-

sion, and in the most erroneous policy, must, if persevered in, be finally ruinous in its effects. The commerce of Great Britain with America was great and increasing, the profits immense, the advantages, as a nursery of seamen, and as an inexhaustible magazine of naval stores, infinite; and the continuance of that commerce, particularly in times of war, when most wanted to support our fleets and revenues, not precarious, as all foreign trade must be, but depending solely on ourselves. These valuable resources, which enabled us to face the united efforts of the House of Bourbon, are actually lost to Great Britain, and irretrievably lost, unless redeemed by immediate and effectual pacification.

3dly. Because Great Britain, deprived of so valuable a part of its resources, and not animated, either with motives of self-defence, or with those prospects of advantage and glory which have hitherto supported this nation in all its foreign wars, may possibly find itself unable to supply the means of carrying on a civil war, at such a vast distance, in a country so peculiarly circumstanced, and under the complicated difficulties which necessarily attend it. Still less would we be able to preserve by mere force that vast continent, and that growing multitude of resolute freemen who inhabit it; even if that, or any country, was worth governing against the inclination of all its inhabitants. But we fear, that while we are making these fruitless efforts, refusing to give credit to the declarations of our fellow-subjects, and blindly confiding in the insidious professions of the natural enemies of this country, we are preparing an easy prey for those who prudently sit quiet, beholding British forces, which, if united, might be in a condition, from their valour, numbers, and discipline, to carry terror into the very heart of their kingdoms, destroying each other. Every event, which ever way it turns, is a victory to them. Our very hospitals furnish them with daily triumphs, the greater as they are certain, without any risque to them of men or money.

4thly. Because we conceive the calling in foreign forces to decide domestic quarrels, to be a measure both disgraceful and dangerous; and that the advice which Ministers have dared to give to his Majesty, which they have avowed and carried into execution, of sending to the garrisons of Gibraltar and Port Mahon, the dominions of the crown of Great Britain, a part of his electoral troops, without any previous consent, recommendation or authority of parliament, is unconstitutional. That Hanoverian troops should, at the mere pleasure of the ministers, be considered as a part of the British military establishment, and take a rotation of garrison duties, through these dominions, is, in practice and precedent, of the highest danger to the safety and liberties of this kingdom, and tends wholly to invalidate the wise and salutary declaration of the grand fundamental law of our glorious deliverer King William, which has bound together the rights of the subject, and the succession of the crown.

5thly. Because the ministers, who are to be intrusted with the management of this war, have proved themselves unequal to the task, and in every degree unworthy of public trust. Parliament has given them every assistance they asked; no unforeseen accidents have stood in their way; no storms have disabled or delayed their operations; no foreign power hath, as yet, interfered; but notwithstanding these advantages, by their ignorance, negligence, and want of conduct, our arms have been disgraced; upwards of ten thousand of the flower of our army, with an immense artillery, under four Generals of reputation, and backed with a great naval force, have been miserably blockaded in one sea port town; and after repeated and obstinate battles, in which such numbers of our bravest men have fallen, the British forces have not been able to penetrate one mile into the country which they were sent to subdue; important fortresses are seized, the Governors are driven from their provinces, and it is doubtful, whether at this moment we are in possession of a single town in all North America. Whether we consider its extent, or its commerce, England has lost half its empire in one campaign. Nor can we impute the misconduct of ministers to mere inability, nor to their ignorance of the state of America, upon which they attempt to justify themselves; for while some members of administration confess they were deceived as to the strength and condition of the provinces, we have from others received official information, that the insufficiency of the navy was concealed from parliament, and part of administration, from a fear of not receiving support from its members. We cannot, therefore, consent to an address, which may deceive his Majesty and the Public into a belief of the confidence of this House in the present ministers, who have disgraced parliament, deceived the nation, lost the colonies, and involved us in a civil war against our clearest interests; and upon the most unjustifiable grounds, wantonly spilling the blood of thousands of our fellow-subjects.

TORRINGTON
FITZ WILLIAM
ARCHER
THANET
CHOLMONDELEY
KING
PORTLAND
STAMFORD
PONSONBY
ABINGDON
MANCHESTER
DEVONSHIRE
CHEDWORTH

BOYLE
CRAVEN
SCARBOROUGH
EFFINGHAM
ROCKINGHAM
RICHMOND.

Letter from Commodore Sir Henry [92] Parker, to W. Tryon, Esq; Governor of New York, and by His Excellency communicated to the Mayor of New York.

Phœnix, at New York, Dec. 18.

SIR,

BEING ordered by my instructions from Vice-Admiral [93] Graves, Commander in Chief of his Majesty's ships and vessels in North America, publicly to signify to all towns accessible to his Majesty's ships, that, in case any violences shall hereafter be offered to any of the officers of the crown, or other peaceably-disposed subjects of his Majesty; or if any bodies of men shall be raised and armed in the said towns, or any military works erected, otherwise than by order of his Majesty, or those acting under his authority; or if any attempts shall be made to seize or destroy any public magazines of arms, ammunition, or other stores; in all or either of those cases, it will be my duty to treat the said towns as in open rebellion against the King.

I am to request that your Excellency will be pleased to let the above instructions be publicly made known in the town of New York, at the same time you will assure them, that I shall be happy in granting the town every protection in the power of his Majesty's ships under my command.

I am, Sir,
Your most obedient
and most humble servant,
H. PARKER.

Proclamation by General Carleton for the Relief of the fugitive Provincials, after they had been driven from before Quebec.

WHEREAS I am informed, that many of his Majesty's deluded subjects, of the neighbouring provinces, labouring under wounds and divers disorders, are dispersed in the adjacent woods and parishes, and in great danger of perishing for want of proper assistance; all captains and other officers of militia are hereby commanded to make diligent search for all such distressed persons, and afford them all necessary relief, and convey them to the General Hospital, where proper care shall be taken of them: all reasonable expences which may be incurred in complying with this order shall be repaid by the Receiver-General.

And, lest a consciousness of past offences should deter such miserable wretches from receiving that assistance which their distressed situation may require, I hereby make known to them, that as soon as their health is restored, they shall have free liberty to return to their respective provinces.

Given under my hand and seal of arms, at the Castle of St. Lewis, in the city of Quebec, this 10th day of May, 1776.
GUY CARLETON.

Substance of the Speech made by Sir Fletcher Norton, Speaker of the House of Commons, to his Majesty, previous to that, by which his Majesty, on the 23d of May, put an End to the Second Session of the Fourteenth Parliament of Great-Britain.

THE Speaker observed, "that, since the commencement of the present session, several wise, salutary, and necessary laws had been enacted, particularly the law for prohibiting all trade and commerce with America, the law for the more speedy and effectual manning of his Majesty's navy, and the law for establishing a national militia: he observed, that his faithful Commons, with equal assiduity and attention, performed their duty, in the course of a very long and severe session: that the business of America engrossed the greatest part of their time, and that nothing had been left undone, on their part, to bring that matter to a speedy and happy conclusion: that the measures, necessary to effect so desirable an end, had brought on a very heavy expence: that nothing had been wanting on the part of his faithful Commons in order to strengthen the hands of government, for they had voted the most full and ample supplies: that, convinced of the justice and necessity of securing the subordinate dependence of America, they had chearfully co-operated in every proposition for securing the duty of his Majesty's subjects in that country, and their obedience to the legislative power of Great Britain: that his faithful Commons, whatever measures may have been taken for the security of both, by a proper exertion of the strength of this country, did not wish for conquest, but were desirous of peace and conciliation. And, on the whole, trusting to his Majesty's parental attention to the interests of every part of the empire, they had a full reliance on his Majesty's wisdom and goodness, that the present disputes with America would be happily terminated; and would be established on so firm a basis, and put on so permanent a footing, as to prevent a return of the same evil in times to come."

The King's most gracious Speech to both Houses of Parliament, on Thursday the 23d of May, when His Majesty put an End to the foresaid Session of Parliament.

My Lords and Gentlemen,

THE conclusion of the public business, and the advanced season of the year, make it proper for me to give you some recess; but I cannot put an end to this session without assuring you, that the fresh instances of your affectionate attachment to me, and of your steady attention and adherence to the true interests of your country, which you have shewn through the whole course of your important deliberations, afford me the highest satisfaction.

No alteration has happened in the state of foreign affairs since your meeting; and it is with pleasure I inform you, that the assurances which I have received of the dispositions of the several powers in Europe, promise a continuance of the general tranquillity.

Gentlemen of the H. of Commons,

It is with real regret and concern that I find myself under the necessity of asking of my faithful Commons any extraordinary supplies: I thank you for the readiness and dispatch with which they have been granted; and they are the more acceptable to me, as you have shewn, in the manner of raising them, an equal regard to the exigencies of the service, and the ease of my people: and you may be assured, that the confidence you repose in me shall be used with proper frugality, and applied only to the purposes for which it was intended.

My Lords and Gentlemen,

We are engaged in a great national cause, the prosecution of which must inevitably be attended with many difficulties and much expence: but when we consider, that the essential rights and interests of the whole empire are deeply concerned in the issue of it, and can have no safety or security but in that constitutional subordination for which we are contending, I am convinced that you will not think any price too high for the preservation of such objects.

I will still entertain a hope, that my rebellious subjects may be awakened to a sense of their errors, and that, by a voluntary return to their duty, they will justify me in bringing about the favourite wish of my heart, the restoration of harmony, and the re-establishment of order and happiness in every part of my dominions. But, if a due submission should not be obtained from such motives and such dispositions on their part, I trust that I shall be able, under the blessing of Providence, to effectuate it by a full exertion of the great force with which you have intrusted me.

Circular Letter written by Lord Howe, to the Governors of the American Provinces, on his Arrival on the Coast of Massachuset's Bay, and an inclosed Declaration addressed to the Inhabitants; with the Resolutions and Proceedings of the Continental Congress relative to both.

The Circular Letter.

Eagle, off the Coast of the Province of Massachuset's Bay, June 20, 1776.

SIR,

BEING appointed Commander in Chief of the ships and vessels of his Majesty's fleet employed in North America, and having the honour to be by his Majesty constituted one of his Commissioners for restoring peace to his colonies, and for granting pardons to such of his subjects therein, as shall be duly solicitous to benefit by that effect of his gracious indulgence; I take the earliest opportunity to inform you of my arrival on the American coast, where my first object will be an early meeting with General Howe, whom his Majesty hath been pleased to join with me in the said commission.

In the mean time, I have judged it expedient to issue the inclosed declaration, in order that all persons may have immediate information of his Majesty's most gracious intentions: and I desire you will be pleased forthwith to cause the said declaration to be promulgated, in such manner, and in such places within the province of as will render the same of the most public notoriety.

Assured of being favoured with your assistance in every measure for the speedy and effectual restoration of the public tranquillity, I am to request you will communicate, from time to time, such information as you may think will facilitate the attainment of that important object in the province over which you preside. I have the honour to be, with great respect and consideration, Sir, your most obedient humble servant,

HOWE.

The Declaration.

By Richard Viscount Howe, of the kingdom of Ireland, one of the King's Commissioners for restoring peace to his Majesty's colonies and plantations in North America, &c.

WHEREAS by an act passed in the last session of parliament, to prohibit all trade and intercourse with the colonies of New Hampshire, Massachuset's Bay, Rhode Island, Connecticut, New York, New Jersey, Pennsylvania, the three lower counties on Delaware, Maryland, Virginia, North Carolina, South Carolina, and Georgia, and for other purposes therein mentioned, it is enacted, that " it shall and may be lawful to and for any person or persons appointed and authorised by his Majesty, to grant a pardon or pardons to any number or description of persons, by proclamation in his Majesty's name, to declare any colony or province, colonies or provinces, or any county, town, port, district, or place, in any colony or province, to be at the peace of his Majesty;" and that " from and after the issuing of any such proclamation in any of the aforesaid colonies or provinces, or if his Majesty shall be graciously pleased to signify the same by his royal proclamation, then, from and after the issuing of such proclamation," the said " act, with respect to such colony or province, colonies or provinces, county, town, port, district, or place, shall cease, determine, and be utterly void." And whereas the King, desirous to deliver all his subjects from the calamities of war, and other oppressions which they now undergo; and to restore the said colonies to his protection and peace, as soon as the constitutional authority of government therein may be replaced, hath been graciously pleased, by letters-patent under the great seal, dated the 6th day of May, in the sixteenth year of his Majesty's reign, to nominate and appoint me, Richard Viscount Howe, of the kingdom of Ireland, and William Howe, Esq; General of his forces in North America, and each of us, jointly and severally, to be his Majesty's Commissioner and Commissioners for granting his free and general pardons to all those, who in the tumult and disorder of the times, may have deviated from their just allegiance, and who are willing, by a speedy return to their duty, to reap the benefits of the royal favour: and also for declaring in his Majesty's name, any colony, province, county, town, port, district or place, to be at the peace of his Majesty; I do therefore hereby declare, That due consideration shall be had to the meritorious services of all persons who shall aid and assist in restoring the public tranquillity in the said colonies, or in any part or parts thereof: that pardons shall be granted, dutiful representations received, and every suitable encouragement given for promoting such measures as shall be conducive to the establishment of legal government and peace, in pursuance of his Majesty's most gracious purposes aforesaid.

Given on board his Majesty's ship the Eagle, off the coasts of the province of Massachuset's Bay, the 20th of June, 1776.

HOWE.

The Resolution of the Congress.

In Congress, July 19.
RESOLVED, That a copy of the circular letters, and of the declaration they inclosed from Lord Howe to Mr. Franklin, Mr. Penn, Mr. Eden, Lord Dunmore, Mr. Martin, and Sir James Wright, late Governors, sent to Amboy by a flag, and forwarded to Congress by General Washington, be published in the several gazettes, that the good people of these United States may be informed of what *nature* are the commissions, and what the *terms*, with the expectation of which the insidious court of Great Britain has endeavoured to amuse and disarm them ; and that the few who still remain suspended by a hope founded either in the justice or moderation of their late King, may now at length be convinced that the valour alone of their country is to save its liberties.

Extract from the Journals.
(Signed)   CHA. THOMSON, Sec.

Lord Howe and General Howe issued a second declaration, on the 19th of September ; and a third, on the 30th of November following, the substance of which the reader will find in the Chronicle.

Singular Resolutions agreed to, some Time about the Middle of the present Year, in the Council of Safety, at Savannah, in Georgia, to destroy their Houses and Shipping, rather than let them fall into the Hands of their Enemies.

In the COUNCIL of SAFETY.

For the safety of the Province, and the good of the United Colonies, it is unanimously resolved,

THAT the houses in the town of Savannah, and the hamlets thereto belonging, together with the shipping now in our port, the property, or appertaining to the friends of America, who have associated and appeared, or who shall appear in the present alarm to defend the same, and also the houses of widows and orphans, and none others, be forthwith appraised.

Resolved, That it be considered, as a defection from the cause of America, and a desertion of property, in such persons. who have and shall leave the town of Savannah, or the hamlets thereto belonging, during the present alarm; and such persons shall be precluded from any support or countenance towards obtaining an indemnification.

Resolved, That it be incumbent upon the friends of America in this province to defend the metropolis, as long as the same shall be tenable.

Resolved, That rather than the same shall be held and occupied by our enemies, or the shipping now in the port of Savannah taken and employed by them, that the same shall be burnt and destroyed.

Resolved, That orders shall be issued to the commanding officer, directing him to have the foregoing resolution put in execution.

A true Copy from the Minutes,
ED. LANGWORTH, Sec. 94

The two following Papers seem to exhibit the Extremes of Zeal and Indifference, with which the Powers of Europe regard the present Quarrel between Great Britain, and her North-American Colonies ; and, therefore, cannot but be entertaining to the Reader.

Decree of his Most Faithful Majesty the King of Portugal, dated the 4th of July, 1776.

WHEREAS we have lately been informed, that the British Colonies of North America have, by an act of the Congress held on the 5th of May last past, not only declared themselves entirely free from all subjection to the crown of Great Britain, but were moreover actually employed in forming and enacting laws by their own private authority, in opposition to the lawful rights of our brother, friend, and ally, the King of Great Britain: and whereas so pernicious an example ought to engage every Prince, even those it interests the least, not to abet, favour, or assist, by any means, directly or indirectly, such subjects united in such direct and open rebellion against their natural sovereign : it is our pleasure, and we do hereby ordain, that no ship, with lading or without, coming from any of the ports of the aforesaid British America, shall be allowed any intercourse with, or entrance into any of the ports of these our kingdoms, or of the dominions thereunto belonging ; but that, on the contrary, they shall be forced away immediately on their arrival, without succour of any kind whatever : and that as to the masters of vessels who have hitherto been suffered to enter (there not appearing reason for their being excluded) it shall be notified to them, that within the precise term of eight days, to be counted successively, they shall quit the said ports with their vessels, which shall first be searched, in order to discover if they have gun-powder on board, or any other of those warlike stores, the export of which was prohibited to them by our Royal Decree of the 21st of October last, directed to the officers of our arsenal and exportation duties : and that if any such stores or ammunition shall be found put on board by stealth, the said vessels, as a capture from declared rebels, shall be confiscated for the use of carrying on the public buildings ; and so be it understood by the Council of our Finances, which shall order printed copies of this our Decree to be taken off, and fixed up in all the public places of the city of Lisbon, and in all the ports of this kingdom, and that of Algarve, that it may come to the knowledge of all, and that no one may plead ignorance.

Palace of the Aejuda, fourth of June, one thousand seven hundred and seventy-six.

With the royal signature.

Substance of a Letter, dated at St. Ildefonso, the 7th of October, written by the Marquis De Grimaldi, to the Governor of Bilboa, relative to an American Corsair, which had taken five English Ships, and had been detained thereupon at said Port, at the Request of the English Vice-Consul; with the Proceedings of the Governor, in consequence thereof.[95]

" THAT having received advice from the Governor of Bilboa, respecting the detention of an American ship, named the Hawke, Captain John Lee, and the several attestations of the persons concerned, which had been laid before his Majesty, he had been pleased to declare, "That in consequence of the amity subsisting between his Catholic Majesty and the King of Great-Britain, he should maintain a perfect neutrality during the present war; that he should not give any aid to the Colonists; but should not deny their being admitted into any ports of his dominions, while they conformed to the laws of the country."

In consequence of the above letter, the Governor set at liberty the American vessel, delivered her back her papers, and supplied her with such provisions, water, &c. (care being taken that no prohibited goods should be sent on board) as should enable her to proceed on her voyage.

Reasons assigned by the Continental Congress, for the North-American Colonies and Provinces withdrawing their Allegiance to the King of Great-Britain.

In CONGRESS, July 4, 1776.

A DECLARATION *by the* REPRESENTATIVES *of the* UNITED STATES *of* AMERICA, *in* GENERAL CONGRESS *assembled.*

WHEN in the course of human events it becomes necessary for one people to dissolve the political bands which have connected them with another, and to assume among the powers of the earth the separate and equal station to which the laws of nature and of Nature's God intitle them, a decent respect to the opinions of mankind requires that they should declare the causes which impel them to the separation.

'We hold these truths to be self-evident; that all men are created equal; that they are endowed by their Creator with certain unalienable rights; that among these are life, liberty, and the pursuit of happiness. That to secure these rights, governments are instituted among men, deriving their just powers from the consent of the governed; and, whenever any form of government becomes destructive of these ends, it is the right of the people to alter or abolish it, and to institute a new government, laying its foundation on such principles, and organizing its powers in such form, as to them shall seem most likely to effect their safety and happiness. Prudence indeed will dictate that governments long established should not be changed for light and transient causes; and accordingly all experience hath shewn, that mankind are more disposed to suffer, while evils are sufferable, than to right themselves by abolishing the forms to which they are accustomed; but, when a long train of abuses and usurpations, pursuing invariably the same object, evinces a design to reduce them under absolute despotism, it is their right, it is their duty, to throw off such government, and

to provide new guards for their future security. Such has been the patient sufferance of these colonies, and such is now the necessity which constrains them to alter their former systems of government. The history of the present —— of —— ——, is a history of repeated injuries and usurpations, all having in direct object the establishment of an absolute tyranny over these States. To prove this, let facts be submitted to a candid world.[96]

He has refused his assent to laws, the most wholesome and necessary for the public good.

He has forbidden his governors to pass laws of immediate and pressing importance, unless suspended in their operation till his assent should be obtained; and, when so suspended, he has utterly neglected to attend them.

He has refused to pass other laws for the accommodation of large districts of people, unless those people would relinquish the rights of representation in the legislature; a right inestimable to them, and formidable to tyrants only.

He has called together legislative bodies at places unusual, uncomfortable, and distant from the depository of their public records, for the sole purpose of fatiguing them into compliance with his measures.

He has dissolved Representatives Houses repeatedly, for opposing, with manly firmness, his invasions on the rights of the people.

He has refused, for a long time after such dissolution, to cause others to be erected; whereby the legislative powers, incapable of annihilation, have returned to the people at large for their exercise; the State remaining in the mean time exposed to all the dangers of invasion from without, and convulsions within.

He has endeavoured to prevent the population of these States; for that purpose obstructing the laws for naturalization of foreigners, refusing to pass others to encourage their migrations hither, and raising the conditions of new appropriations of lands.

He has obstructed the administration of justice, by refusing his assent to laws for establishing judiciary powers.

He has made judges dependent on his will alone, for the tenure of their offices, and the amount and payment of their salaries.

He has erected a multitude of new offices, and sent hither swarms of officers to harrass our people, and eat out their subsistence.

He has kept among us in times of peace standing armies, without the consent of our legislatures.

He has affected to render the military independent of, and superior to, the civil power.

He has combined with others to subject us to a jurisdiction foreign to our constitution, and unacknowledged by our laws, giving his assent to their pretended acts of legislation:

For quartering large bodies of armed troops among us:

For protecting them, by a mock trial, from punishment for any murders which they should commit on the inhabitants of these States:

For cutting off our trade with all parts of the world:

For imposing taxes on us without our consent:

For depriving us, in many cases, of the benefit of trial by jury:

For transporting us beyond seas to be tried for pretended offences:

For abolishing the free system of English laws in a neighbouring province, establishing therein an arbitrary government, and enlarging its boundaries, so as to render it at once an example and fit instrument for introducing the same absolute rule into these colonies:

For taking away our charters, abolishing our most valuable laws, and altering fundamentally the forms of our governments:

For suspending our own legislatures, and declaring themselves invested with power to legislate for us in all cases whatsoever.

He has abdicated government here, by declaring us out of his protection, and waging war against us.

He has plundered our seas, ravaged our coasts, burnt our towns, and destroyed the lives of our people.

He is, at this time, transporting large armies of foreign mercenaries, to complete the works of death, desolation, and tyranny, already begun with circumstances of cruelty and perfidy scarcely paralleled in the most barbarous ages, and totally unworthy the Head of a civilized nation.

He has constrained our fellow-citizens, taken captive on the high seas, to bear arms against their country, to become the executioners of their friends and brethren, or to fall themselves by their hands.

He has excited domestic insurrections amongst us, and has endeavoured to bring on the inhabitants of our frontiers the merciless Indian savages, whose known rule of warfare is an undistinguished destruction of all ages, sexes, and conditions.

In every stage of these oppressions we have petitioned for redress, in the most humble terms; our repeated petitions have been answered only by repeated injury. —A prince, whose character is thus marked by every act which may define a tyrant, is unfit to be the ruler of a free people.

Nor have we been wanting in attention to our British brethren. We have warned them, from time to time, of attempts, by their legislature, to extend an unwarrantable jurisdiction over us; we have reminded them of the circumstances of our emigration and settlement here; we have appealed to their native justice and magnanimity; and we have conjured them by the ties of our common kindred, to disavow these usurpations, which would inevitably interrupt our connections and correspondence. They too have been deaf to the voice of justice and consanguinity. We must therefore acquiesce in the necessity which denounces our separation, and hold them, as we hold the rest of mankind, enemies in war, in peace friends.

We, therefore, the Representatives of the United States of America, in General Congress assembled, appealing to the Supreme Judge of the world for the rectitude of our intentions, do, in the name, and by the authority of the good people of these Colonies, solemnly publish and declare, that these United Colonies are, and of right ought to be, FREE AND INDEPENDENT STATES, and that they are absolved from all allegiance to the British crown, and that all political connection between them and the state of Great-Britain is, and ought to be, totally dissolved; and that, as free and independent States, they have full power to levy war, conclude peace, contract alliances, establish commerce, and to do all other acts and things which independent States may of right do. And for the support of this declaration, with a firm reliance on the protection of Divine Providence, we mutually pledge to each other our lives, our fortunes, and our sacred honour.

Signed by order, and in behalf of the Congress,

JOHN HANCOCK, President.

Attest, CHARLES THOMSON, Secretary.

Articles of Confederation and perpetual Union between the States of New-Hampshire, Massachuset's-Bay, Rhode-Island, Connecticut, New-York, Pensylvania, the Counties of Newcastle, Kent, and Suffex, on Delaware-River, Maryland, Virginia, North-Carolina, South-Carolina, Georgia.

N. B. Thefe articles of Confederation, after having been long weighed and difcuffed, line by line, in the Congrefs, were at length refolved upon and figned by all the Delegates, the 4th of October, 1776, at Philadelphia, fuch as they are here fet forth; and in confequence were immediately fent to the other States to be confirmed by them. 97

ARTICLE I.

THE Thirteen States above mentioned, confederate themfelves under the title of The UNITED STATES of AMERICA.

II.

They contract, each in their own name, by the prefent conftitution, a reciprocal treaty of alliance and friendfhip for their common defence, for the maintenance of their liberties, and for their general and mutual advantage; obliging themfelves to affift each other againft all violence that may threaten all, or any one of them, and to repel in common all the attacks that may be levelled againft all or any one of them, on account of religion, fovereignty, commerce, or under any other pretext whatfoever.

III.

Each State referves to themfelves alone the exclufive right of regulating their internal government, and of framing laws in all matters that are not included in the articles of the prefent Confederation, and which cannot any way prejudice the fame.

IV.

No State in particular fhall either fend or receive embaffies, begin any negociations, contract any engagements, form any alliances, conclude any treaties with any king, prince, or power whatfo-ever, without the confent of the United States, affembled in General Congrefs.

No perfon, invefted with any poft whatever under the authority of the United States, or of any of them, whether he has appointments belonging to his employment, or whether it be a commiffion purely confidential, fhall be allowed to accept any prefents, gratuities, emoluments, nor any offices or titles of any kind whatever, from any kings, princes, or foreign powers.

And the General Affembly of the United States, nor any State in particular, fhall not confer any title of nobility.

V.

Two, nor feveral of the faid States, fhall not have power to form alliances or confederations, nor conclude any private treaty among themfelves, without the confent of the United States affembled in General Congrefs, and without the aim and duration of that private convention be exactly fpecified in the confent.

VI.

No State fhall lay on any impofts, nor eftablifh any duties whatever, the effect of which might alter directly, or indirectly, the claufes of the treaties to be concluded hereafter by the Affembly of the United States with any kings, princes, or power whatfoever.

VII.

There fhall not be kept by any of the faid States in particular, any veffels or fhips of war above the number judged neceffary by the Affembly of the United States, for the defence of that State and its commerce; and there fhall not be kept on foot in time of peace by any of the faid States, any troops above the number determined by the Affembly of the United States, to guard the ftrong places or forts neceffary for the defence of that State; but each State fhall always keep up a well-difciplined militia, fufficiently armed and equipped, and fhall be careful to procure, and keep in conftant readinefs, in the public magazines, a fufficient number of field pieces and tents, with a proper quantity of ammunition and implements of war.

VIII.

When any of the faid States fhall raife troops for the common defence, all the officers of the rank of colonel, and under, fhall be appointed by the legiflative body of the State that fhall have raifed the troops, or in fuch manner as that State fhall have judged proper to regulate the nominations; and when any vacancy happens in thefe pofts, they fhall be filled up by the faid State.

IX.

All the expences of war, and all other difburfements, that fhall be made for the common defence or the general weal, and that fhall be ordered by the Affembly of the United States, fhall be paid out of the funds of a common treafury.

That common treafury fhall be formed by the contribution of each of the aforefaid States, in proportion to the number of inhabitants of every age, fex, or quality, except the Indians exempt from taxes in each State; and in order to fix the quota of the contribution, every three years the inhabitants fhall be numbered, in which enumeration the number of white people fhall be diftinguifhed; and that enumeration fhall be fent to the Affembly of the United States.

The taxes appropriated to pay this quota, fhall be laid and levied in the extent of each State by the authority and orders of its legiflative body, within the time fixed by the Assembly of the United States.

X.

Each of the said States shall submit to the decisions of the Assembly of the United States, in all matters or questions referred to that Assembly by the present act of Confederation.

XI.

No State shall engage in war without the consent of the United States assembled in Congress, except in case of actual invasion of some enemy, or from a certain knowledge of a resolution taken by some Indian nation to attack them, and in that case only, in which the danger is too urgent to allow them time to consult the other States.

No particular State shall give any commission to vessels, or other ships of war, nor any letters of marque or reprisal, till after a declaration of war made by the Assembly of the United States; and even in that case they shall be granted only against the kingdom or the power, or against the subjects of the kingdom, or of the power against which war shall have been so declared; and shall conform, respecting these objects, to the regulations made by the Assembly of the United States.

XII.

In order to watch over the general interest of the United States, and direct the general affairs, there shall be nominated every year according to the form settled by the legislative body of each state, a certain number of delegates, who shall sit at Philadelphia until the General Assembly of the United States shall have ordered otherwise; and the first Monday in November of each year, shall be the æra fixed for their meeting.

Each of the above mentioned States shall preserve the right and power to recall, at any time whatever of the year, their delegates, or any one of them, and to send others in the room of them for the remainder of the year, ; and each of the said States shall maintain their delegates during the time of the General Assembly, and also during the time they shall be members of the Council of State, of which mention shall be made hereafter.

XIII.

Each State shall have a vote for the decision of questions in the General Assembly.

XIV.

The General Assembly of the United States, shall alone and exclusively have the right and power to decide of peace and war, except in the case mentioned in article XI. —to establish rules for judging in all cases the legitimacy of the prizes taken by sea or land, and to determine the manner in which the prizes taken by the land or sea forces, in the service of the United States, shall be divided or employed;—to grant letters of marque or reprisal in time of peace; — to appoint tribunals to take cognizance of piracies, and all other capital crimes committed on the high seas;—to establish tribunals to receive appeals, and judge finally in all cases of prizes; —to send and receive ambassadors; —to negociate and conclude treaties or alliances;—to decide all differences actually subsisting, and that may arise hereafter between two or several of the aforementioned States, about limits, jurisdiction, or any other cause whatsoever; —to coin money, and fix its value and standard; — to fix the weights and measures throughout the whole extent of the United States;—to regulate commerce, and treat of all affairs with the Indians who are not members of any of the States; —to establish and regulate the posts from one State to another, in the whole extent of the United States, and to receive on the letters and packets sent by post, the necessary tax to defray the expence of that establishment;—to appoint the general officers of the land forces in the service of the United States;—to give commissions to the other officers of the said troops, who shall have been appointed by virtue of article VIII;—to appoint all the officers of marine in the service of the United States; — to frame all the ordinances necessary for the government and discipline of the said land and sea forces; and to direct their operations.

The General Assembly of the United States shall be authorized to appoint a Council of State, and such committees and civil officers as they shall judge necessary for guiding and dispatching the general affairs, under their authority, whilst they remain sitting; and after their separation, under the authority of the Council of State. —They shall chuse for president one of their members, and for secretary the person whom they shall judge fit for that place; and they may adjourn at what time of the year, and to what place in the United States they shall think proper.—They shall have the right and power to determine and fix the sums necessary to be raised, and the disbursements necessary to be made;—to borrow money, and to create bills on the credit of the United States;—to build and fit out fleets;—to determine the number of troops to be raised or kept in pay;—and to require of each of the aforesaid States, to compose the army, a contingent proportioned to the number of its white inhabitants.——These requisitions of the General Assembly shall be binding, and in consequence the legislative body of each State shall nominate the particular officers, levy the men, arm and equip them properly; and these officers and soldiers, thus armed and equipped, shall proceed to the place, and within the time fixed by the General Assembly.

But if the General Assembly, from some particular circumstances, should think proper to exempt one or several of the States from raising troops, or to demand of them less than their contingent, and should on the contrary judge it convenient that one or several others should raise more than their contingent; the number extraordinary demanded shall be raised, provided with officers, armed and equipped in the same manner as the contingent, unless the legislative body of that, or of those of the States to whom the requisition shall have been made, should deem it dangerous for themselves to be drained of that number extraordinary, and in that case they shall furnish no more than what they think compatible with their safety; and the officers and soldiers so raised and equipped, shall go to the place, and within the time fixed by the General Assembly.

The General Assembly shall never engage in any war, nor grant letters of marque or reprisal in time of peace, nor contract any treaties of alliance or other conventions, except to make peace, nor coin money or regulate its value, nor determine or fix the sums necessary to be raised, or the disbursements necessary to be made for the defence or advantage of the United States, or of some of them, nor create bills, nor borrow money on the credit of the United States, nor dispose of any sums of money, nor resolve on the number of ships of war to be built or purchased, or on the number of troops to be raised for land or sea service, nor appoint a commander or chief of the land or sea forces, but by the united consent of nine of the States: and no question on any point whatsoever, except for adjourning from one day to another, shall be decided but by a majority of the United States.

No delegate shall be chosen for more than three years out of six.

No person invested with any employment whatever in the extent of the United States, and receiving, by virtue of that employment, either by himself, or through the hands of any other for him, any salaries, wages, or emoluments whatever, shall be chosen a delegate.

The General Assembly shall publish every month a journal of their sessions, except what shall relate to treaties, alliances, or military operations, when it shall appear to them that these matters ought to be kept secret. The opinions *pro* and *con* of the delegates of each State, shall be entered in the journals as often as any one of the delegates shall require it; and there shall be delivered to the delegates of each State, on their demand, or even to any one of the delegates of each State, at his particular requisition, a copy of the journal, except of the parts above mentioned, to be carried to the legislative body of his respective State.

XV.

The Council of State shall be composed of one delegate of each of the States, nominated annually by the other delegates of his respective State; and the case where these electors might not be able to agree, that delegate shall be nominated by the General Assembly.

The Council of State shall be authorised to receive and open all the letters addressed to the United States, and answer them; but shall not contract any engagements binding to the United States.—They shall correspond with the legislative bodies of each State, and with all persons employed under the authority of the United States, or of some of the particular legislative bodies.---They shall address themselves to these legislative bodies, or to the officers to whom each state shall have entrusted the executive power, for aid and assistance of every kind, as occasion shall require.---They shall give instructions to the generals, and direct the military operations by land or by sea; but without making any alterations in the objects or expeditions determined by the General Assembly, unless a change of circumstances intervening and coming to their knowledge since the breaking up of the Assembly, should render a change of measures indispensably necessary. They shall be careful of the defence and preservation of the fortresses or fortified ports.—They shall procure information of the situation and designs of the enemy.---They shall put in execution the measures and plans that shall have been resolved by the General Assembly, by virtue of the powers with which they are invested by the present confederation.---They shall draw upon the treasurers for the sums, the destination of which shall have been settled by the General Assembly, and for the payment of the contracts which they may have made by virtue of the powers that are granted to them.---They shall inspect and reprove, they shall even suspend all officers civil or military acting under the authority of the United States. --- In the case of death or suspension of any officer whose nomination belongs to the General Assembly, they may replace him by what person they think proper until the next Assembly.---They may publish and disperse authentic accounts of the military operations.---They may convene the General Assembly for a nearer term than that to which they had adjourned when they separated, if any important and unexpected event should require it for the welfare or benefit of the United States, or of some of them.---They shall prepare the matters that are to be submitted to the inspection of the General Assembly, and lay before them at the next sitting all the letters or advices by them received, and shall render an exact account of all that they have done in the interim.---

They shall take for their secretary a person fit for that employment, who before he enters on his function shall take an oath of secrecy and fidelity.---The presence of seven members of the Council will empower them to act.---In case of the death of one of their members, the Council shall give notice of it to the colleagues of the deceased, that they may chuse one of themselves to replace him in the Council until the holding of the next general meeting; and in case there should be but one of his colleagues living, the same notice shall be given to him, that he may come and take his seat untill the next sitting.

XVI.

In case that Canada should be willing to accede to the present confederation, and come into all the measures of the United States, it shall be admitted into the union, and participate in all its benefits. But no other colony shall be admitted without the consent of nine of the States.

The above articles shall be proposed to the legislative bodies of all the United States, to be examined by them; and if they approve of them, they are desired to authorise their delegates to ratify them in the General Assembly; after which all the articles which constitute the present confederation, shall be inviolably observed by all and every of the United States, and the union shall be established for ever.

There shall not be made hereafter any alteration in these articles, nor in any of them, unless that the alteration be previously determined in the General Assembly, and confirmed afterwards by the legislative bodies of each of the United States.

Resolved and signed at Philadelphia, in Congress, the 4th of October, 1776.

Notes, 1776

1. Richard Montgomery (1738–75). Formerly a British officer who served in the Seven Years War, he settled in New York in 1773, was elected to the colony's provincial congress in May 1775, and was appointed Brigadier-General in the Continental Army in June.

2. Allen was returned to America in June 1776, was paroled in New York, but was later imprisoned for breaking parole. He was exchanged for a British officer in May 1778, rewarded with a colonelcy in the Continental Army, and returned to intrigue and guerrilla warfare designed to secure independent status for Vermont.

3. Charles Preston, Major in the 26th. Regiment.

4. Allan Maclean (1725–84). An officer of considerable military experience—some in America—he was commissioned in June 1775 as Lieutenant-Colonel in command of a corps of Highlanders to be raised from clansmen who settled in Canada after the previous war.

5. Richard Prescott (1725–88), Colonel of the 7th Foot with local rank of Brigadier-General from November 1775. He was exchanged in September 1776 and recaptured in July 1777 in a raid designed to secure the exchange of General Charles Lee. Prescott's arrogance earned him the detestation of Americans, and his second capture, the ridicule of the British press. He served in America throughout the war and was promoted to Lieutenant-General in 1782.

6. Roger Enos (1729–1808), Lieutenant-Colonel of the 2nd Connecticut Regiment, court-martialed but acquitted for this defection.

7. Colonel Donald Campbell, not further identified.

8. Arnold was succeeded by Daniel Morgan (1736–1802), veteran frontier fighter and Captain of one of the two Virginia rifle companies founded in 1775. His subordinates persuaded him *not* to attempt the second barrier until reinforced; the delay proved fatal.

9. Estimated figures are British—5 killed, 18 wounded, out of 1,800; Americans—60 killed or wounded, 426 captured, out of about 800.

10. John Murray, 4th Earl of Dunmore (1732–1809), Governor of Virginia from 1770.

11. Patrick Henry (1736–99), leading Virginia radical, opposed by more moderate elements who ensured that he was superceded in the military operations against Dunmore. Nevertheless, Henry was elected first Revolutionary Governor of Virginia, in June 1776.

12. William Woodford (1734–80), Colonel of the Virginia 3rd Regiment, later Brigadier-General; captured at Charleston in 1780.

13. Not identified.

14. John Connolly (c. 1750–?), an agent of Dunmore from 1774; imprisoned after his capture in 1775, until exchanged in 1780; recaptured in 1781 after a second abortive Loyalist conspiracy.

15. William Campbell (c. 1732–78), fourth son of the Duke of Argyll, Governor of Nova Scotia, 1766–73, and of South Carolina, 1773–76.

16. William Henry Drayton (1742–79) was at first opposed to radical politics in South Carolina, but after 1772 he became a prominent popular leader in the revolutionary movement in the colony. His mission to the backcountry was generally unsuccessful, since the frontier elements saw their real oppressors as the coastal elite rather than the British.

17. Josiah Martin (1737–86), Governor of North Carolina, 1771–75.

18. See O. W. Stephenson, "The Supply of Gunpowder in 1776," *American Historical Review*, 1925–26, vol. 30, pp. 271–81.

19. Thomas Howard, 3rd Earl of Effingham (1747–91). He resigned his commission in April; the letter was published in the press in September.

20. See *AR*, 1775, *State Papers*, pp. 272]–276], and n. 91, below.

21. A chaldron was a variable dry measure of coal usually reckoned to be 28¼ hundredweight at London Docks, and 53 hundredweight in Newcastle, or 3164 lbs. and 5936 lbs. respectively.

22. Stephen Sayre (1736–1818); see "Introduction, 1775," n. 22, and *AR*, 1775, pp. [239–[243.

23. William Henry Nassau de Zulestein, 4th Earl of Rochford (1717–81); Secretary of State for the Northern Department, 1768–75.

24. William Henry Lyttleton (1724–1808), Governor of South Carolina, 1755–60, and of Jamaica, 1760–66; M.P. for Bewdley, 1774–90, and a consistent supporter of North.

25. Thomas Powys (1743–1800), M.P. for Northants, 1774–97; an independent who became increasingly critical of North over the war, and by 1780, an ally of the Rockinghams.

26. Charles Cornwall.

27. Richard Rigby (1722–88); see "Introduction, 1769," n. 3. Now an active supporter of North, he advocated ruthless coercion of the Americans.

28. John Hinchcliffe (?–1794), Bishop of Peterborough, 1769–94.

29. Earl Gower; see "Introduction, 1769," n. 3.

30. Thomas Lyttleton (1744–79), succeeded his father as 2nd. Baron in 1773, appointed Chief Justice in Eyre North of the Trent, November 1775.

31. Sandwich.

32. John Ward, 2nd Viscount Dudley and Ward (1725–88), a steady North supporter.

33. Duke of Manchester.

34. Earl of Shelburne.

35. William Craven, 6th Baron Craven (1738–91).

36. In 1769, the Black Caribs (actually descendants of castaway slaves) on St. Vincent began resisting British West Indian planters' attempts to acquire their lands. In 1772, Lord Hillsborough ordered a military

The Annual Register—1776

expedition to enforce their submission, but the troops suffered serious losses from disease. Opposition in the House of Commons castigated the Government for aggression against innocent natives, and demanded an enquiry. On 11 December 1773, North acceded to the Opposition demand to lay all papers relating to the expedition before the House; debates continued in the next session, until 15 February 1773. One of the leading anti-Government speakers was Germain. See *Parliamentary History*, vol. 17, 568–75.

37. Augustus Keppel (1725–86), second son of the Earl of Albemarle, M.P. for New Windsor, 1761–80; Vice-Admiral, 1770. A bitter opponent of the American war and loosely attached to the Rockingham group, he nevertheless accepted command of the Channel Fleet in 1778.

38. Temple Simon Luttrell (?1738–1803), M.P. for Milborne Port, 1775–80.

39. Jean Cavalier (1681–1740), leader of the Protestant revolt in the Cevennes in 1702; ultimately fled to England and was made Lieutenant-Governor of Jersey in 1738.

40. William Wildman, 2nd Viscount Barrington (1717–93), Secretary at War, 1755–61, 1765–78.

41. General Conway.

42. Charles Jenkinson (1729–1808), M.P. for Hastings, 1774–80, and Saltash, 1780–86. A consistent supporter of Government, he held minor office for years, was a close confidant of North, and was widely assumed to have great influence with the King. Burke believed him to be the centre of the "secret influence" over the Crown and suggested his movements should be under surveillance. (*The Correspondence of Edmund Burke*, vol. 3, pp. 89–90). From his appointment as Secretary at War in December 1778 to North's resignation in 1782, Jenkinson was the King's closest confidential advisor.

43. George Sackville, later Germain (1716–85), third son of the Duke of Dorset, M.P. for East Grinstead, 1768–82. Sackville's potentially brilliant career in the army was cut short in 1759, when he was dismissed for failing to obey a crucial order at the battle of Minden. At a subsequent court-martial (called at his own request), he was declared "unfit to serve his Majesty in any military capacity whatsoever." He was accused of cowardice and publicly despised, yet Sackville worked his way back into politics after George III's succession, adopted the name Germain, reestablished his personal reputation by a duel in 1770, and after a period in opposition, became a firm supporter of the Government in its coercive policy toward America.

44. Viscount Weymouth, see "Introduction, 1769," n. 3. Thomas Pelham Clinton (1742–95), second son of the Duke of Newcastle; John Ashburnham, 2nd Earl Ashburnham (1725–1812).

45. See *AR*, 1775, pp. 262]–266], and notes 90 and 91, below. Richard Penn (1736–1811) was the grandson of William Penn, and Lieutenant-Governor of Pennsylvania, 1771–73.

46. Duke of Richmond.

47. Sir George Savile.

48. Oliver Delancey (1718–85), a member of one of the wealthiest and most powerful New York families, was by this point committed to a Loyalist position.

49. Richard Oliver (1735–84), M.P. for the City of London, 1770–80; Alderman, 1770–78. He was imprisoned in the Tower for arresting a parliamentary messenger during the 1771 battle over the reporting of debates. He was closely associated with Wilkes, but soon came to oppose the latter in City politics.

50. The minority vote is usually given as twelve. See for example, Sir Lewis Namier and J. Brooke, *The History of Parliament: The House of Commons 1754–90* (HMSO, 1964), vol. 3, p. 225.

51. Lord Mansfield.

52. The prohibitory bill received the royal assent on 22 December, to become 16 Geo. III c. 5.

53. Robert Nugent, Viscount Clare (1709–88), created 1st Earl Nugent July 1776; Joint Vice-Treasurer of Ireland, 1768–82.

54. John Stuart, 3rd Earl of Bute (1713–92), first minister, 1762–63. Bedford was Bute's plenipotentiary in the negotiations leading to the Treaty of Paris, 1763.

55. The Mystic River lies on the northeast side of the Charlestown peninsula opposite Boston.

56. Mansfield and Camden.

57. Elizabeth Chudleigh (1720–88) was secretly married to Augustus John Hervey, brother of the Earl of Bristol, and later, after a successful suit (through perjury) in an ecclesiastical court for jactitation of marriage against Hervey, was remarried to Evelyn Pierrepoint, Duke of Kingston. The Duke's nephew instituted a charge of bigamy against her after his uncle's death. The ensuing trial before the House of Lords was one of the most spectacular of the century. When found guilty, the lady claimed privilege of peerage and was therefore discharged without punishment.

58. John Sawbridge.

59. Various flags had already been used by the Americans; that adopted by Washington on assuming command of the Continental Army at Cambridge in July 1775 was thirteen alternating red and white stripes with the crosses of St. Andrew and St. George in the upper corner. The "Stars and Stripes" (thirteen alternating red and white stripes, and thirteen stars on a blue ground) was created by the Flag Resolution of the Continental Congress on 14 June 1777.

60. Not identified.

61. David Wooster (1711–77), veteran American militia officer of the Seven Years War, appointed Major-General of Connecticut troops in April 1775, and Brigadier-General in the Continental Army in June; recalled by Congress in June 1776 from command of the Canada expedition on grounds of incompetence.

62. Simon Fraser (1729–77), Lieutenant-Colonel of the Fraser Highlanders, promoted to Brigadier on 8 June 1776 after his successful defence of Trois-Rivières. Fraser was killed at Saratoga the following year.

63. William Phillips (?1731–81), an officer in the Royal Engineers with a distinguished record, was promoted to Colonel in 1772 and given the local rank of Major-General when posted to America in May 1779. Fredrich Adolphus, Baron Riedesel (1738–1800), a Hessian officer serving the Duke of Brunswick; appointed commander of the first body of Brunswickers sent to America under the agreements made by North in 1775.

64. William Thompson (1736–81), Colonel of the Pennsylvania Rifle Regiment in 1775, appointed Brigadier-General in the Continental Army, March 1776.

65. John Sullivan (1740–95), New Hampshire delegate to the Continental Congress, 1774–75 and 1780–81; appointed Brigadier-General in the Continental Army, June 1775.

66. Sir Peter Parker (1712–1811), Rear Admiral, 1777, 1st Baronet, 1782. Charles Cornwallis (1738–1805), 2nd Earl Cornwallis, 1st Marquis, 1793.

67. Donald MacDonald (1712–85?).

68. James Moore (1737–77), North Carolina radical, commander of the 1st North Carolina Continentals from September 1775, Brigadier-General in the Continental Army from March 1776.

69. Richard Caswell (1729–89), prominent North Carolina politician, delegate for that colony to the Continental Congress, 1774–76; Colonel of the North Carolina Partisan Rangers; and Governor, 1776–80.

70. Not identified.

71. Esek Hopkins (1718–1802), Rhode Island privateer in the Seven Years War, was appointed Commander-in-Chief of the Continental Navy (eight vessels), December 1775. His failure to sink the British frigate *Glasgow* in the early hours of the morning of 6 April off Block Island, New York, was the first demonstration of an incompetence which led to Hopkins's dismissal in January 1778.

72. John Vaughn (?1731–95), commanded a regiment in America during and after the Seven Years War and was promoted to Brigadier-General in January 1776; M.P. for Berwick-upon-Tweed, 1774–95, knighted, 1792.

73. John Morris, Captain in 1775.

74. Alexander Scott, Captain in 1776.

75. William Moultrie (1730–1805), South Carolina militia officer appointed Colonel of the 2nd South Carolina Regiment in June 1775 and Brigadier-General in the Continental Army in 1777.

76. The vote on the independence resolution was taken on 2 July. Jefferson's draft of the declaration was modified over the next two days, and on the evening of 4 July, Congress ordered it to be authenticated and printed. On 19 July, the document was formally entitled the "Declaration of Independence . . .," and the engrossed copy was presented for signature on 2 August.

77. Richard Howe, 4th Viscount Howe (1726–99), Rear Admiral, 1770; Vice-Admiral, 1775; Commander-in-Chief of the American station, 1776–78; M.P. for Dartmouth, 1757–82; joint peace commissioner with his brother William. He resigned his command in 1778 after the appointment of the Earl of Carlisle's peace commission.

78. James Paterson, Adjutant-General of British Forces in America, 1776–78; returned with local rank of Brigadier-General in 1779.

79. Leopold Philip von Heister (1707–77), Commander-in-Chief of the Hessians in America, was recalled in 1777 after the defeat at Trenton. James Grant; see "Notes, 1775," n. 40. Grant was a Brigadier in 1776, though he may have held the local rank of Major-General.

80. There is a wide disparity between contemporary British and American estimates of the American losses. A conservative estimate indicates that approximately 300 were killed and 1,200 taken prisoner. D. S.

Freeman, *George Washington*, 7 vols. (New York, 1948–57), vol. 4, p. 157 n., 162, 167 n. Howe's figure was 3,300 casualties, Washington's, 800.

81. In addition to wholly inadequate intelligence, the Americans suffered from Greene's replacement by Sullivan, who did not know the terrain, and Sullivan's supersession by Putnam, who was simply incompetent. The British and German attack, by contrast, was executed with textbook efficiency.

82. William Alexander (1726–83) was an unsuccessful claimant to the earldom of Stirling but known in America as Lord Stirling. A prominent member of the New Jersey political elite, he was appointed Colonel of the 1st New Jersey Regiment in 1775 and Brigadier-General in the Continental Army in March 1776. Udell, not identified.

83. Edward Rutledge (1749–1800), prominent South Carolina politician, delegate to the Continental Congress, 1774–76, and one of the last to be converted to voting for independence.

84. Alexander Leslie (?1740–94), Lieutenant-Colonel of the 64th Regiment in Halifax in 1775, transferred to Boston and promoted to Brigadier-General for the New York campaign. Carl Emil von Donop (1740–77), Colonel commanding the Hessian grenadiers.

85. More properly Throg's Neck (named after John Throgmorton, a seventeenth-century settler).

86. Wilhelm, Baron von Knyphausen (1716–1800), second-in-command of the Hessians under Heister.

87. Johann Gottlieb Rall (?1720–76), Hessian Colonel.

88. Not identified.

89. Edward Mathew (1729–1805), Brigadier-General in 1776, commanding the brigade of Guards.

90. Thomas Stirling (1733–1808), Lieutenant-Colonel, commanding the 42nd Regiment.

91. Cardinal Guilio Alberoni (1664–1752), Spanish First Minister, 1715–19; responsible for an adventurous foreign policy which cost Spain heavily, hence his banishment in 1719.

92. The commander of the *Phoenix* (a forty-four-gun frigate) was Hyde Parker (1739–1807), a Captain from July 1763, knighted in 1779, promoted to Admiral in 1793. He may have been appointed Commodore for his duties off New York and up the Hudson, 1775–76.

93. Samuel Graves (1713–87), Admiral, 1770; Commander-in-Chief, North American station, 1774–76.

94. Edward Langworth(y) (c. 1738–1802), Georgia delegate to the Continental Congress, 1777–79.

95. Jeronimo, Marquis de Grimaldi (1720–86), Spanish Foreign Minister, 1763–71.

96. The words omitted are, of course, "King of Great Britain."

97. The resolution for a declaration of independence moved in Congress on 7 June included a clause for a "plan of confederation." A committee was appointed to draft a plan on 11 June and produced it on 12 July; detailed consideration led to a second version being placed before Congress on 20 August. The version printed here is a paraphrase of that of 20 August. The Articles of Confederation were not signed and transmitted to the individual states on 4 October, nor at any point in 1776, but were finally sent for ratification on 15 November 1777.

1777

Introduction

North's government could point in triumph to the military successes achieved by the close of 1776 and speak complacently of its apparent dominance of Parliament only by remaining ignorant of, or simply ignoring, the situation. The moment for crushing the rebellion by militarily defeating the Continental Army had passed. Victory now required conquest of America and that, even if it was possible, as Germain himself put it in a moment of weakness, "would be of no utility,"[1] because imperial unity could not be maintained indefinitely by force of arms. Moreover, the Government's apparently invincible parliamentary majority masked the internal dissensions which riddled the administration and the Cabinet's deteriorating relationship with the military and naval commanders.

North's refusal or inability to exercise positive leadership in the Cabinet permitted its internal divisions to grow. Sandwich tried to disguise the appalling weakness of the navy until he could repair its strength. He fended off Germain's criticisms with difficulty and began to doubt North's support. Attorney-General Thurlow enjoyed the growing confidence of the King and sought higher office. Dartmouth and Barrington had no confidence in

---

1. The remark was made after news of the Saratoga surrender became public. *Last Journal of Horace Walpole, 1771–83*, ed. Dr. Doran, 2 vols. (London 1859), vol. 2, p. 169.

the war policy, and were anxious to resign. Weymouth and Gower were considering a reshuffle to produce a ministry without North. The first minister himself was prone to fits of depression and, between 24 February and the end of March 1777, was seriously ill from a riding accident. He sporadically talked of resignation. He was dissuaded by the King, who promised him unfailing support[2] while continuing to communicate directly with individual members of the Cabinet and to intervene forcefully within the departments of state.

Germain's personal direction of the war increasingly brought him into conflict with the commanders. He became dissatisfied with Howe because of the general's inactivity after taking New York, and he became irritated with Howe's demands for the needs of the next campaign. Germain thus began to favour openly the views of Cornwallis and Burgoyne and indulged his personal animosity toward Carleton to force the latter to resign. Admiral Howe's growing demands for more ships were embarrassing, and Germain became incensed by the lenience practised by the Howe brothers in their attempt to forward the success of the Peace Commission.[3] Campaign planning for 1777 clearly revealed these tensions.

Just as 1776 began with panic that resulted from inadequate planning, so 1777 was characterised by a profusion of plans. On 30 November 1776, Howe proposed to hold Washington in Jersey, secure New York and Rhode Island, attack Boston and push an army up the Hudson to meet the advance expected from Carleton, then take Philadelphia and move into the south. This ambitious scheme required 15,000 extra men. On 21 December, Howe proposed instead to hold New York and Rhode Island, send 3,000 troops up the Hudson to meet Carleton, and make Philadelphia the main target. Germain was horrified by the cost of the first plan, so on 3 March he approved the second. He earlier agreed to permit Bur-

2. The King's generous loan of £20,000 in September 1777, to assist North out of his chronic personal financial difficulties, may have left North with a sense of obligation which did not permit him to resign as long as the King insisted his services were required.

3. The Howes made a further proclamation, on 15 March 1777, offering pardons on the simple condition of laying down arms. Germain insisted this offer should have an early termination date, which was finally set as 2 May.

goyne to lead the long-discussed thrust out of Canada which would cut off New England, and he informed Carleton of Howe's reduced assistance on the Hudson. Before receiving Germain's approval, Howe sent (on 20 January) a third plan—to attack Philadelphia by sea and leave the remainder of his force under Clinton, to hold New York and Rhode Island, with the possibility of using 3,000 Loyalists on the Hudson. Howe was prompt to inform Carleton that substantial support from New York was now unavailable. Germain received this plan on 8 May, and ten days later he wrote urging Howe to finish in Pennsylvania as expeditiously as possible and move to help Burgoyne. This despatch was delayed and did not reach Howe until 16 August, by which time he was en route to Philadelphia.

In the light of these developments, contemporaries and historians have tried to fix the blame for the subsequent disaster at Saratoga. In any judgement of the issue, it should be remembered that Germain and the Cabinet simultaneously approved Burgoyne's planned advance down the Hudson to Albany and Howe's proposal to take Philadelphia with no material assistance to Burgoyne. Burgoyne was never informed that Howe would *not* assist him, but neither did he insist at any time during the planning that such assistance was essential to his advance. Burgoyne recognised the difficulties involved in forcing his way south to Albany, but he almost certainly minimised them at this stage. Howe made it clear that he could give no real help from New York to the northern army and assumed this was understood by Germain and Burgoyne.

Howe began operations in June with 18,000 men. Washington's army was reduced to a core of about 1,000 regulars through the expiration of enlistments and through desertion, but it was rebuilt to about 9,000 by May. The Americans were ensured an adequate supply of weapons, powder, and equipment by captures, trade with the French and Dutch, and secret aid from France. Howe spent a month manoeuvring to trap Washington into a battle and, having failed, on 23 July embarked 15,000 troops for a seaborne invasion of Pennsylvania. He arrived at Delaware Bay on 29 July and, against the advice of the naval officer who had reconnoitered the area, decided to effect a landing in Chesapeake Bay, where contrary winds delayed the disembarkation until 25 August.[4] Washington was astonished by Howe's behaviour but moved to meet him at Brandywine Creek, where on 11 September the Americans were repulsed, but allowed to retreat and re-group. Howe entered Philadelphia on 26 September and held off Washington's counterattack at Germantown on 4 October. Between 6 October and 21 November, combined naval-military operations cleared, at some cost, the Americans out of the forts on the Delaware River. An indecisive action at Whitemarsh at the end of the first week in December ended with Washington's withdrawal to winter quarters in Valley Forge and Howe and Cornwallis's retirement to more comfortable quarters in Philadelphia.

The capture of Philadelphia was a small achievement because the Americans had no notion that its fate would materially affect the war.[5] Howe had again failed to destroy the enemy in the field, and he doubted Germain would ever give him the reinforcements he considered necessary for victory, so he offered his resignation on 22 October. Two weeks earlier, disaster had overtaken Burgoyne.

Carleton followed Germain's instructions to assist Burgoyne's campaign but resigned in disgust at the way he himself had been treated. Burgoyne began his advance with an army of 9,500 men on 20 June and drove the Americans out of Ticonderoga on 5 July, dispersing the rearguard after a clash at Hubbardton two days later. Burgoyne then chose a more difficult route to the Hudson—via Skenesborough and Fort Edward—arguing that it was the direction of the enemy's retreat and that his advance would force the abandonment of Fort Edward, which was reached on 29 July. Schuyler delayed the advance with every possible obstruction and Burgoyne ran dangerously short of supplies. He despatched a foraging expedition into the Connecticut Valley on 6 August, but it was routed at Bennington on 16 August by a militia

---

4. Howe was not misled by faulty naval intelligence; he made an error of judgement and had bad luck with the weather. W. H. Moomaw, "The Denouement of General Howe's Campaign of 1777," *English Historical Review*, 1964, vol. 79, no. 3, pp. 498–512.

5. The Congress moved to Lancaster on 18 September and York on 30 September.

force under Stark. Three days later, Schuyler was replaced by Gates, who was reinforced by Lincoln, Arnold, and Morgan and a body of New England militia, who cut the British line of communication with Canada. A secondary British force despatched from Oswego under St. Leger wiped out a militia unit at Oriskany on 6 August, but it was baulked at Fort Stanwix and, after being deserted by its Indian allies, retreated to Montreal.

Burgoyne wrote to Germain on 20 August that he would obey his instructions (which he interpreted as being inflexible) to march on Albany. He then crossed the Hudson toward Saratoga. On 19 September, his advance forces met Gates at Freeman's Farm and held their position, although with heavy losses. It is possible Burgoyne could have forced Gates to retreat if he had followed this engagement with a major assault, but he learnt that Clinton had launched a diversionary attack up the Hudson so he dug in and waited. Clinton took Verplancks on 5 October and Fort Montgomery three days later, then sent Vaughan up the river with 2,000 men to Albany; in the event he could go no further than Esopus, forty-five miles short of his objective. Burgoyne was now nearly surrounded by forces twice the size of his own and his desperate attempt to break out on 7 October failed, in the process he lost 600 men and was left in an untenable position. On 13 October, Burgoyne was advised by his officers to surrender. He argued with Gates over the terms but finally capitulated on 17 October. The convention agreed to by Gates and Burgoyne permitted the British army to return to England provided it would not serve again in America. The Congress was outraged at such lenient terms, and Howe sought to circumvent them, so the convention was never implemented and most of the soldiers were ultimately held as prisoners of war. Burgoyne returned to England to participate in a longer battle in Parliament and in the press over who was to blame.

Parliament resumed on 21 January 1777. The Rockinghams had discussed various tactics during the recess and finally resolved to formally "secede." They abandoned the resolution in April, but for nearly three months the Opposition was materially weakened. On 6 February, the House of Commons passed without division an act authorising the licensing of privateers against the Americans. On the same day, Germain introduced a bill to suspend habeas corpus in cases of high treason in America or on the high seas, or of piracy. The bill was savagely attacked by the Opposition (minus the Rockinghams) and was not well supported, so the Government was forced to accept a weakening amendment to secure its passage. The Government received a further setback in April, when the King asked for a vote of funds to meet his outstanding debts and for an increase in the civil list. The Opposition naturally attacked the second part of the bill as an attempt to increase Crown patronage, but lost the division only by 109 to 137. Speaker Sir Fletcher Norton took an unusual step by commenting on the generosity of the sum voted. Fox promptly introduced a cleverly worded amendment which could be taken as an implied criticism of the Crown and, to the King's chagrin, secured a majority. There was little opportunity for further embarrassment of the administration until 22 April, when proposals made by George Johnstone brought a new internal crisis in the affairs of the East India Company before the House. Poor attendance at the debate and the absence of most of the leading members of the Government reduced the value of Opposition attack, and of the smaller government majority when the motion was rejected 90 to 67. On 30 May, a sick but still fiery Chatham moved to address the Crown, recommending the repeal of legislation since 1763 which the Americans regarded as grievances. He believed it was the simplest way to end a civil war about to give the Bourbon powers an opportunity to ruin Britain. Government spokesmen argued that independence was the American goal, that concessions were irrelevant, and that the danger from France and Spain was imaginary. As far as conciliation was concerned, they were right, but Chatham lived just long enough to see France declare war in March of the following year. His motion, however, and a similar one proposed in the Commons were unsuccessful,[6] and Parliament rose on 6 June for the summer recess.

The Government and the country waited for news from America throughout the summer, but news was slow to arrive. Reports of success at Ticonderoga arrived in late August, followed by two months of silence. The Government was anxious not to face Parliament until it had information to rebut Opposition assaults, therefore the

6. Chatham's motion was defeated 99 to 28. In the Commons, the motion did not go to a division.

new session was postponed from 18 September until 30 October and again to 20 November (Parliament actually met on 18 November). By 28 October, there were rumours of St. Leger's retreat, and on 1 November reports of Burgoyne's increasing difficulties were in the press. The following day, news of Howe's victory at Brandywine produced public rejoicing.

The Rockinghams were planning strategy throughout this period and argued with other Opposition groups over how they could win public support. Even before the news of Brandywine, Burke gloomily noted, "The greatest number have a sort of an heavy lumpish acquiescence in Government, without much respect or esteem for those that compose it. I really cannot avoid making some very unpleasant prognostics from this disposition of the people."[7] As for the independent country gentlemen in Parliament: "They no longer criticise, as all disengaged people in the world will, on the acts of Government; but they are silent under every evil and cover up every ministerial blunder and misfortune with the officious zeal of men, who think they have a party of their own to support in power."[8] The Rockinghams finally decided to await events and to take opportunities as they arose, though Fox, among others, had hoped for a more positive strategy.

When Parliament resumed, the Opposition had basically agreed only to oppose. They quickly adopted the concerted tactic of demanding sight of official papers in order to force an enquiry into Government policy. The amendments to the address in response to the speech from the throne were bitterly critical, and Chatham added a lengthy attack in the Lords. An opportunity more favourable for the Opposition developed on 26 November in the debate following presentation of the navy estimates. The statement of Britain's available naval strength given in the Lords by Sandwich was challenged in the Commons by Opposition speakers as a deliberate fabrication.[9] They successfully moved that the reports of the naval commanders be produced. The Opposition kept up the pressure,

7. Burke to Fox, 8 October 1777, in *The Correspondence of Edmund Burke*, ed. Thomas W. Copeland, 9 vols. (Cambridge and Chicago, 1961–70), vol. 3 (ed. G. H. Gutteridge), pp. 381–82.

8. Ibid., p. 383.

9. See "Notes, 1778," n. 14.

and though Germain fended off the persistent attacks, the Government faltered as its confidence was eroded by rumours of disaster in America. On 1 December, Fox moved for a parliamentary enquiry into the state of the nation—North agreed—and Fox also asked that a full range of papers which would reveal the progress and cost of the war be laid before the House. To this North strongly objected, and despite news that the Lords had just agreed to a similar motion, the Fox motion lost 178 to 89.[10] Then on 3 December, Germain was obliged to admit in a response to a challenge from Barré that Burgoyne had surrendered. Fox promptly castigated Germain's "obstinate, wilful ignorance and incapacity," but lost his motion to produce Burgoyne's instructions.[11]

The Opposition was now in full cry, but the Government, despite its despondency, was far from losing control. On 4 December, the Committee of Supply's report of the ordnance costs for the coming year resulted in an Opposition assault, which North neatly deflected. On the following day, David Hartley's resolutions for ending the war on the grounds of its expense and ruinous results were rejected without division. At the same time, Chatham's motions in the Lords for copies of Burgoyne's instructions and those relating to the use of the Indians lost 40 to 19. Wilkes proposed on 10 December to repeal the Declaratory Act, but his proposal naturally received no support from the Rockinghams and lost 160 to 10.[12] The Opposition's last chance came on 11 December, when the Government proposed to adjourn until 20 January but despite its lengthy attempt to delay the recess and keep up the pressure, the Opposition lost in both Houses.

The *Register*'s publication was continually delayed, and the volume for 1777 was not available until November 1778. This permitted a full account of the military operations up to the year's end, with a wealth of detail. The historical section grew to 188 pages, and the editor continued to use size as an excuse for delay: ". . . the quantity of matter, independent of any merit in the arrangement or composition, may account, if it does not atone, for the lateness of our publication this year."[13]

10. *Parliamentary History*, vol. 19, 512–32.
11. Ibid., 532–42.
12. Ibid., 542–49, 549–59, 485–511, 559–72.
13. *AR*, 1777, preface, p. iv.

Chapter I reviews Carleton's advance from Canada, his retreat from Ticonderoga, and Washington's successful counterattack in New Jersey at the close of 1776. The American propaganda allegations of British atrocities are noted, and the account implies that there was some substance to the accusations against the Hessians. Their behaviour may have alienated ". . . a malcontent people who . . . were still to be reclaimed, not destroyed." The psychological value of Trenton to the Americans is appreciated, and an accurate summary of the basic problems of war in America is added. Chapters II and III report domestic affairs in the second half of 1776; comment on additions to the peerage; note changes in the persons responsible for the education of the Prince of Wales and his brother; comment on the lamentable effects of the war on British shipping and on the West Indies; cite a clash between the City and the navy over impressment; and relate the villainies of an arsonist who attempted to destroy the royal dockyards. The debates over the replies to the King's speech opening the new session are given close attention, as are those consequent on Cavendish's motion to revise the legislation objectionable to the colonies. The merits of the first Rockingham secession are critically examined, and the attempt to force an enquiry into the state of the navy concludes the retrospect of the previous year.

Chapter IV is entirely devoted to the extensive debates over Germain's bill to suspend habeas corpus in treason cases. Chapter V is almost wholly taken up with the debates over the King's requirement for an increase in the civil list and concludes with the failure of Grafton's conciliation motion. Chapter VI covers parliamentary business dealt with between May and the closure in June. It concentrates on Fox's motion supporting the speaker's remarks on the civil list issue and includes a lengthy analysis of the East India Company crisis and Chatham's reconciliation motion.

Howe's 1777 campaign is described in twenty-eight pages of accurate detail in Chapter VII, which concludes perceptively, "Yet with all this tide of success, all the fruit derived from our victories at the close of the campaign, amounted to no more than simply a good winter lodging for our army in the city of Philadelphia." Chapter VIII follows Burgoyne's campaign as far as Fort Edward (revealing a sound knowledge of the alternative routes open to him from Ticonderoga). Chapter IX devotes twenty-one pages to the disintegration of Burgoyne's advance and the surrender at Saratoga, but postpones judgement "upon the general plan or system of this campaign" beyond commenting that the lack of cooperation between Burgoyne and Howe is "... not to be easily accounted for." The final chapter reviews events in Europe perfunctorily in eleven pages.

The *Appendix to the Chronicle* contains sixteen items, including an account of the trial of the dockyard arsonist. It is unrelated to American matters, except for a transcript of the petition from the City of London protesting the bill suspending habeas corpus, and an exchange of letters between Richard Howe and Benjamin Franklin deriving from the former's role as peace commissioner. The *State Papers* is composed of twenty-five items, and the following are included here: the speech from the throne at the opening of Parliament in October 1776; the address in reply from the House of Lords, and the protest of the dissentient Lords; the complaint of the British ambassador to the Netherlands over Dutch assistance to the Americans, and the Dutch reply; Howe's open letter of 20 June 1776 announcing the terms of the Peace Commission and the resolution of the Congress ordering its publication; the second and third proclamations of the Peace Commission, together with a copy of a pardon and the American oath of allegiance, plus Washington's proclamation requiring those who had accepted pardons either to surrender them or go over to the enemy; and the Saratoga articles of surrender.

PREFACE.

HAVING now arrived at the conclusion of our Twentieth Volume, we should have been disposed to have celebrated this year as a sort of jubilee, and season of self-congratulation, if the awful aspect of the times had not forbidden every emotion bordering upon levity, and afforded matter of the most serious consideration and reflection to every member of the community. No circumstance of time, nor state of affairs, can, however, repress our gratitude, or restrain our acknowledgements to the Publick, for that continued favour, which, as it has during so many years, constantly increased with our labours, so it has alone enabled us to encounter the arduous task of appearing annually before them in so many successive publications, upon each of which, their former esteem, and future approbation, were, of course, in some degree hazarded.

The importance and magnitude of our historical business have unhappily risen to nearly the highest pitch at which they seem capable of arriving. We relate events, in which every member of this wide and divided empire is deeply interested; in which many thousands are immediately and personally concerned; and wherein its best blood is too copiously shed. The incidents are numberless, and the parties concerned in every incident numerous. It is not easy to steer a safe course of history, through the rage of civil contest, and amidst the animosity and malignity of contending factions. Under these circumstances, we are obliged to as much caution as will not be injurious to truth. And whilst publick affairs continue of such extent and importance, and that materials of all kinds both political and military grow upon us in the manner they do at present, we shall be much more solicitous to fulfil our duty, and preserve our reputation with the Publick, by a due attention to the matter which we lay before them, than at all concerned as to the inconfequential circumstance of a later or earlier publication.

Our Publisher has made an obfervation to us, which he fays efcapes moft readers, who have not fome acquaintance with what is technically termed the bufinefs of the prefs. He fays, that the Hiftorical Article is at prefent fwelled to fuch an extent, that if it were printed feparately, and in the common mode of publication, it would fill a volume of nearly the fame fize, with that in which it is now included; whilft from the circumftance of clofe printing, and its being confidered only as a comparatively fmall part of a diffufe and large work, the dimenfions which it would acquire in its natural growth, are not perceived in its prefent contracted ftate. Under this confideration, the quantity of matter, independent of any merit in the arrangement or compofition, may account, if it does not atone, for the latenefs of our publication this year.

Retrospective view of American affairs in the year 1776. Preparation in Canada for the armament on Lake Champlain. State of the American force. Engagement near the iffe Valicour. Arnold retires; purfuit; overtaken; burns his veffels. Crown Point deftroyed and abandoned. General Carleton lands there with the army. Motives for not attacking Ticonderoga. General Carleton returns with the army to Canada. Situation of affairs to the foutbward. General Lee taken. Perfeverance of the Congrefs. Meafures for renewing their armies. Lands allotted for ferving during the war. Money borrowed. Addrefs to the people. Petitions from the inhabitants of New York, and from thofe of Queen's county in Long Ifland, to the Commiffioners. Critical ftate of Philadelphia. Congrefs retire to Baltimore. Divifions in Penfylvania. Defertions. Surprize at Trenton. Lord Cornwallis returns to the Jerfeys. Prevented from attacking the enemy at Trenton by impediments of fituation. General Washington quits his camp, and attacks Colonel Mawhood, near Princetown. Lord Cornwallis returns from the Delaware to Brunfwick. Americans over-run the Jerfeys. Britifh and Auxiliary forces keep poffeffion of Brunfwick and Amboy, during the remainder of the winter. Indian war. Articles of confederation and perpetual union between the thirteen revolted Colonies.

THE efforts to remove thofe obftacles that had reftrained the progrefs of the Britifh arms on the fide of Canada, in the fummer of 1776, were equal to the importance of the objects in view, and the greatnefs of the difficulties which were to be furmounted. The weight and execution of the naval equipment, fell of courfe upon the officers and men of that department, whofe ability, zeal, and perfeverance in the performance, can never be too much applauded. The tafk was indeed arduous. A fleet of above thirty fighting veffels, of different kinds and fizes, all furnifhed with cannon, was to be little lefs than created; for though a few of the largeft were reconftructions, the advantage derived from thence depended more upon the ufe of materials which the country did not afford, than upon any faving as to time, or leffening of labour. When to this is added, the tranfporting over land, and afterwards dragging up the rapids of St. Therefe and St. John's, 30 longboats, a number of flat boats of confiderable burthen, a gondola, weighing 30 tons, with above 400 battoes, the whole prefented a complexity of labour and difficulty, which feemed fufficient to appal even the fpirit of Britifh feamen. However it muft be allowed that the labour did not fall folely on them. The foldiers had their part; and what is to be lamented, the peafants and farmers of Canada were taken from their ploughs, and compelled by power to bear a fhare in toils, from whence they could derive no honour or advantage.

Though the equipment was compleated in about three months, the nature of the fervice, as well as the eagernefs of the commanders and army, required, if it had been poffible, a ftill greater difpatch. The winter was faft approaching, two inland feas to be paffed, the unknown force of the enemy on each to be fubdued, and the ftrong pofts of Crown Point and Ticonderoga, defended and fupported by an army, to be encountered fword in hand. To add to thefe impediments, the communication between the Lakes Champlain and George, did not admit the paffage of thofe veffels of force, which, after being successful on the one, might be equally wanted on the other. And if all those difficulties were surmounted, and Lake George passed, there still remained a long and dangerous march through intricate forests, extensive morasses, and an uncleared country, still in a state of nature, before they could reach Albany, which was the first post to the southward that could afford them rest and accommodation.

The spirit of the commanders rose in proportion to the difficulties which were to be encountered. The objects in view were great, the glory to be acquired tempting, and the desire of their attainment seemed to lessen or remove obstacles, which to a cold or lukewarm speculation would have appeared insuperable. If the Lakes could be recovered, and Albany possessed, before the severity of the winter set in, the northern army would hold a principal share in the honour of bringing the war to a speedy conclusion. It was conceived that they could then pour destruction at will, into the heart either of the middle or the northern colonies, each of which would be exposed to them in its most tender and defenceless part. Whilst the possession of Hudson's river would establish and secure their communication with General Howe, it would equally sever and disconnect the southern and northern provinces, leaving thereby the latter to sink under the joint weight of both armies, or to accept of such terms as they could obtain, without the participation of the others. Nor could General Washington attempt to hold any post in New York or the Jerseys, with such a superiority of force as already oppressed him in front, and General Carleton's army at his back. The successes of their fellows on the side of New York, increased the impatience, and excited the jealousy of this army, every one apprehending that the

war would be brought to an end, before he could have an opportunity of sharing in the honour of that happy event.

With all this ardour, and the most unremitting industry, it was not until the month of October, that the fleet was in a condition to seek the enemy on Lake Champlain. The force was very considerable with respect to the place and service, extraordinary in regard to the little time spent in its formation, and such as, a very few ages ago, would have been deemed formidable even upon the European seas. The ship Inflexible, which may be considered as Admiral, had been re-constructed at St. John's, from whence she sailed in 28 days after laying her keel, and mounted 18 twelve pounders. One schooner mounted 14, and another 12, six pounders. A flat-bottomed radeau carried six 24, and six 12 pounders, besides howitzers; and a gondola, 7 nine pounders. Twenty smaller vessels, under the denomination of gunboats, carried brass field pieces from 9 to 24 pounders, or were armed with howitzers. Some long boats were furnished in the same manner. About an equal number of large boats acted as tenders. Those we have taken notice of, were all intended for, or appertaining to battle; we omit the vast number destined for the transportation of the army, with its stores, artillery, baggage and provisions.

The armament was conducted by Captain Pringle, and the fleet navigated by above 700 prime[1] seamen, of whom 200 were volunteers from the transports, who after having rivalled those belonging to the ships of war in all the toil of preparation, now boldly and freely partook with them in the danger of the expedition. The guns were served by detachments of men and officers belonging to the corps of artillery. In a word, no equipment of the sort was ever better

appointed, or more amply furnished with every kind of provision necessary for the intended service.

The enemy's force was in no degree equal, either with respect to the goodness of the vessels, the number of guns, furniture of war, or weight of metal. Sensible, though they were, of the necessity of preserving the dominion of the Lakes, and aided in that design by the original force in their hands, with a great advantage in point of time for its increase, their intentions in that respect were counteracted by many essential, and some irremediable deficiencies. They wanted timber, artillery, ship-builders, and all the materials necessary for such an equipment. Carpenters, and all others concerned in the business of shipping, were fully engaged at the sea ports in the construction and fitting out of privateers, whilst the remoteness, and difficulty of communication, rendered the supply of bulky materials extremely tedious. When we consider the difficulties on their part, we think it not just to deny the Americans the praise, of having combated, and in part overcome them, with an assiduity, perseverance, and spirit, which did not in the least fall short of what had been employed against them. For their fleet amounted to 15 vessels of different kinds, consisting of two schooners, one sloop, one cutter, three gallies, and eight gondolas. The principal schooner mounted 12 six and four pounders. They were commanded by Benedict Arnold, who was now to support upon a new element, that renown which he had acquired on land in the Canada expedition.

General Carleton was too full of zeal, and too anxious for the event, not to head the British armament, and having proceeded up the Lake, discovered the enemy's fleet drawn up with great judgment, being very advantageously posted,

Oct. 11. 1776.

and forming a strong line, to defend the passage between the island of Valicour and the western main. Indeed they had at the beginning placed themselves with so much skill behind the island, that an accident only discovered their position. The King's squadron, without this seasonable discovery, would have left them behind; an event, which if it had happened, might have been attended with the most serious consequences. It is said, that the unexpected sight of a three masted ship of such force, upon the Lake, threw the enemy into the utmost, and most visible consternation. It does not seem, however, probable, that a matter of such public notoriety in Canada, should have been so long with-held from them.

A warm action ensued, and was vigorously supported on both sides for some hours; but the wind being unfavourable, so that the ship Inflexible, and some other vessels of force could not be worked up to the enemy, the weight of the action fell upon the schooner Carleton and the gun-boats, which they sustained with the greatest firmness, such extraordinary efforts of resolution being displayed both by men and officers, as merited and received the highest applause from their commanders. It is to be presumed, that when so much praise was due and given to the conduct and valour of a superior force on our side, the enemy must not have acted their part amiss.

The detachment belonging to the corps of artillery, were highly distinguished, and did most essential service in the gun-boats. But the same impediments still continuing, which prevented their being seconded by the other vessels, Captain Pringle, with the approbation of the General, thought it necessary for the present, to withdraw those that were engaged from the action. At the approach of night, he brought the whole fleet to anchor in a line, and as near as possible to the enemy, in order to prevent their retreat.

In this engagement the best schooner belonging to the enemy was burnt, and a gondola carrying three or four guns sunk, from whence we may form some reasonable conjecture of the execution done upon their other vessels. Being now fully sensible of their inferiority, they took the opportunity which the darkness of the night afforded, of endeavouring to escape from their present imminent danger, hoping to obtain shelter and protection at Crown Point. Arnold concerted and executed this design with ability, and fortune seemed at first so favourable to his purpose, that they were out of sight by the next morning. The chace being, however, continued without intermission both on that and the succeeding day, the wind, and other circumstances peculiar to the navigation of the Lake, which had been at first in favour of the Americans, became at length otherwise, so that they were overtaken and brought to action a few leagues short of Crown Point, about noon on the 13th.

A very warm engagement ensued, and continued about two hours, during which those vessels that were most a head, pushed on with the utmost speed, and passing Crown Point, escaped to Ticonderoga; but two gallies and five gondolas which remained with Arnold made a desperate resistance. During this action, the Washington galley, with Waterburg, a Brigadier General, and the second in command, on board, struck, and [2] was taken. Arnold, at length, finding it was impossible to withstand the superiority of force, skill, and weight of metal, with which he was overborne, and finding himself but ill seconded by the Captains of some of his vessels, determined that his people should not become prisoners, nor the vessels a prey to the enemy. He executed this design with equal resolution and dexterity, and run the Congress galley, in which himself was, with the five gondolas, on shore in such a manner, as to land his men safely and blow up the vessels, in spite of every effort that was used to prevent both.

Loss and defeat were so far from producing their usual effect with respect to Arnold, that his conduct in this command raised his character still higher than it was before with his countrymen. They said that he not only acted the part of a brave soldier, but that he also amply filled that of an able naval commander. That the most experienced seaman could not have found a greater variety of resources, by the dexterity of manœuvre, evolution, and the most advantageous choice of situation, to compensate for the want of force, than he did; that when his vessels were torn almost to pieces, he retreated with the same resolution that he fought, and by the happiest and most critical judgment, prevented his people and them from falling into the hands of the enemy. But they chiefly gloried in the dangerous attention he paid to a nice point of honour, in keeping his flag flying, and not quitting his galley till she was in flames, lest the enemy should have boarded and struck it.

Thus was Lake Champlain recovered, and the enemy's force nearly destroyed, a galley, and three small vessels being all that escaped to Ticonderoga. The enemy, upon the rout of their fleet, having set fire to the houses, and destroyed every thing which they could not carry off, at Crown Point, evacuated that place, and retired to their main body at Ticonderoga. Gen. Carleton took possession of the ruins, where he was soon joined by the army. As he continued there till towards the end of the month, and, besides several reconnoitring parties, pushed on at one time strong detachments on both sides of the Lake, who approached within a small distance of Ticonderoga, at the same time that vessels appeared within cannon shot of the works, to examine the nature of the channel, and found its depth, little doubt can be entertained that he had it in contemplation to attempt that place. The strength of the works, the difficulty of approach, the countenance of the enemy, and the ignorance of their number, with other cogent reasons, prevented this design from taking place.

It was evident that this post could not be forced in its present state, without a very considerable loss of blood, whilst the benefit arising from success would be comparatively nothing. The season was now too far advanced to think of passing Lake George, and of exposing the army to the perils of a winter campaign, in the inhospitable, and impracticable wilds to the southward. As Ticonderoga could not be kept during the winter, the most that could be expected from success, would be the reduction of works, more indebted to nature than to art for their strength, and perhaps the taking of some cannon; whilst the former would be restored, and the latter replaced by the enemy, before the army could interrupt their proceedings in the ensuing summer. But if the defence should be obstinate, although the army were in the end successful, it would probably thereby be so much weakened, that all prospect of advantage in the future campaign would, in a great measure, be annihilated. The difficulty, perhaps impossibility, of keeping open the communication with Canada, and subsisting the army during the winter was obvious. General Carleton therefore reimbarked the army without making any attempt, and returning to Canada, cantoned them for the winter in the best manner the country afforded.

It is fit that we should now turn our attention to the important transactions in the South. We saw towards the conclusion of the last campaign, that Lord Cornwallis had not only overrun the Jerseys, but that the Delaware was the only apparent obstacle, which seemed capable of retarding the progress of his army, in the reduction of Philadelphia and the adjoining provinces. The American army was indeed no more. It is said that the greatest number which remained embodied did not exceed 2500 or 3000 men. This was all that remained of an army, which at the opening of the campaign amounted, as it is said, to at least twenty-five thousand. There are some who represent it as having been at that time much stronger. The term of their engagement being expired, which, along with the obligation of duty, discharged all apprehension of disgrace, there was no keeping together, at the heel of a ruinous campaign, troops broken and dispirited, equally unaccustomed to subordination, and to a long absence from their countries and families. Those small bodies, who from personal attachment, local circumstances, or a superior perseverance and bravery, still continued with the Generals Washington and Lee, were too inconsiderable in force, to demand much attention on the one side, or to inspire confidence on the other; whilst the support to be derived from new levies, not yet formed, was too remote and precarious, to afford much present consolation to the Americans.

Dec. 13th. In this critical situation of their affairs, the capture of Gen. Lee seemed to render them still more hopeless. That officer, at the head of all the men which he could collect or keep together, being on his march to join General Washington, who had assembled the Pensylvania militia to secure the banks of the Delaware, was, from the distance of the British cantonments, betrayed into a fatal security, by which, in crossing the upper part of New Jersey from the North river, he fixed his quarters, and lay carelessly guarded, at some distance from the main body. The operation of zeal, or desire of reward in an inhabitant, having communicated this situation to Col. Harcourt, who commanded the [3] light horse, and had then made a desultory excursion at the head of a small detachment to observe the motions of that body, he conducted his measures with such address and activity, and they were so well seconded by the boldness and rapidity of motion which distinguish that corps, that the guard was evaded, the centries seized without noise, the quarters forced, and Lee carried off, though all that part of the country was in his favour, and that several guarded posts, and armed patrols, lay in the way.

The making of a single officer prisoner, in other circumstances would have been a matter of little moment; but in the present state of the raw American forces, where a general deficiency of military skill prevailed, and the inexperience of the officers was even a greater grievance than the lack of discipline in the soldiers, the loss of a commander, whose spirit of enterprize was directed by great knowledge acquired in his profession acquired by actual service, was of the utmost importance, and the more distressing, as there was little room to hope it could be soon supplied.

The rejoicing in Great Britain on this occasion was equal at least to the dejection of the Americans. It was conjectured, that some personal animosities between this General and several officers in the army, as well as persons of power at court, contributed not a little to the triumph and exultation of that time.

The capture of Gen. Lee was also attended with a circumstance, which has since been productive of much inconvenience to both sides, and of much calamity to individuals. A cartel, or something of that nature, had some time before been established for the exchange of prisoners between the Generals Howe and Washington, which had hitherto been carried into execution, so far as time and other circumstances would admit. As Lee was particularly obnoxious to government, it was said, and is supposed, that Gen. Howe was tied down by his instructions from parting with him upon any terms, if the fortune of war should throw him into his power. Gen. Washington not having at this time any prisoner of equal rank with Lee, proposed to exchange six field officers for him, the number being intended to balance that desparity; or if this was not accepted, he required that he should be treated and considered suitably to his station, according to the practice established among polished nations, and the precedent already set by the Americans in regard to the British officers in their hands, until an opportunity offered for a direct and equal exchange.

To this it was answered, that as Mr. Lee was a deserter from his Majesty's service, he was not to be considered as a prisoner of war, that he did not at all come within the conditions of the cartel, nor could he receive any of its benefits. This brought on a fruitless discussion, whether Gen. Lee, who had resigned his half pay at the beginning of the troubles, could be considered as a deserter, or whether he could with justice be excluded from the general benefits of a cartel, in which no particular exception of person had been made; the affirmative in both these positions being treated by Washington with the utmost indignation.

In the mean time Lee was con-fined in the closest manner, being watched and guarded with all that strictness and jealousy, which a state criminal of the first magnitude could have experienced in the most dangerous political conjuncture. This conduct not only suspended the operation of the cartel, but induced retaliation on the other side, and Colonel Campbell, who had hitherto enjoyed every degree of liberty consistent with his condition, and had been treated with great humanity by the people of Boston, was now thrown into a dungeon, and treated with a rigour equal to the indulgence he had before experienced. Those officers who were prisoners in the southern colonies, though not treated with equal rigour, were, however, abridged of their parole liberty, and deprived of other comforts and satisfactions, which had hitherto rendered their condition uncommonly easy. It was at the same time declared, that their future treatment should in every degree be regulated by that which Gen. Lee experienced, and that their persons should be answerable, in the utmost extent, for any violence that was offered to him.

This was not the only instance in which the Congress manifested a firm and undaunted resolution. In the midst of the dangers with which they were environed, far from giving way to any thing like unconditional submission, they made no overtures towards any kind of accommodation. On the other side none were made to them. They prepared to renew the war, and to repair their shattered forces with all diligence. They were now convinced of the inefficacy of temporary armies, engaged only for a short term, and calculated merely to repel a sudden invasion, when opposed to the constant war of a powerful enemy, and the incessant efforts of regular forces, It could never be hoped, with new men thus changed every year, to make any effectual stand against veteran troops, and their present critical situation afforded too alarming an experience, of the fatal consequences which might attend that period of utter imbecility, between the extinction of the old army, and the establishment of the new. To guard against this evil in future, which could not be remedied for the present, they issued orders about the middle of September, for the levying of 88 battalions, the soldiers being bound by the terms of enlistment to serve during the continuance of the war.

The number of battalions which each colony was by this ordinance appointed to raise and support, may be considered as a pretty exact political scale of their comparative strength, framed by those who were interested in its correctness, and well acquainted with their respective circumstances. Massachusett's Bay and Virginia were the highest on this scale, being to furnish 15 battalions each; Pensylvania came next, and was rated at twelve; North Carolina 9, Connecticut and Maryland 8 each, New York, and the Jerseys, the latter considered as one government, were, in consequence of their present situation, set no higher than 4 battalions each.

The liberality of the Congress in its encouragement to the troops, was proportioned to the necessity of speedily compleating the new army. Besides a bounty of twenty dollars to each soldier at the time of enlisting, lands were to be allotted at the end of the war to the survivors, and to the representatives of all who were slain in action, in different stated proportions, from 500 acres, the allotment of a Colonel, to 150, which was that of an Ensign; the private men, and non-commissioned officers, were to have 100 acres each. As a bar to the thoughtlessness and prodigality incident to soldiers, and to prevent the most worthless and undeserving from obtaining for trifles, those rewards due to the brave for their blood and services, all these lands were rendered unalienable during the war, no assignment or transfer being to be admitted at its conclusion.

The Congress had before, as an encouragement to their forces by sea and land, decreed that all officers, soldiers, and seamen, who were or might be disabled in action, should receive, during life, one half of the monthly pay to which they were entitled by their rank in the service, at the time of meeting with the misfortune. Notwithstanding these encouragements, it seems, as if the condition of serving during the indefinite term of the continuance of the war, was not generally agreeable, to a people so little accustomed to any kind of subordination or restraint; so that in the month of November, the Congress found it necessary to admit of another mode of enlistment for the term of three years, the soldiers under this compact receiving the same bounty in money with the others, but being cut out from any allotment of lands.

With all these encouragements given by the Congress, the business of recruiting went on, however, but heavily; and it must not be imagined, that the army actually raised, did at any time bear any proportion in effective men to that which was voted.

The holding out a promise of lands as an inducement to fill up their armies, was probably intended to counteract the effect of a similar measure which had some time before been adopted on the side of the crown, large grants of vacant lands, to be distributed at the close of the troubles, having been promised in its name to the Highland emigrants, and some other new troops raised in America, as a reward for their expected zeal and loyalty in the reduction of the rebellious colonies. A measure which tended more to increase and excite the animosity of the people, than any other perhaps which could have been proposed in the present circumstances. For they universally considered the term vacant, as signifying forfeited, which being an effect of the treason laws yet unknown in America, excited the greater horror; the people being well aware from the experience of other countries, that if the sweets of forfeiture were once tasted, it would be equally happy and unusual, if any other limits, than those which nature had assigned to their possessions, could restrain its operation.

The annual supplies raised in the different colonies by their respective assemblies, being insufficient to provide for the extraordinary expences of so large an army, together with the other numerous contingencies, inseparable from such a war, the Congress found it necessary to negociate a loan to answer these purposes. They accordingly passed a resolution to borrow five millions of dollars, at an interest of four per cent. the faith of the united states being pledged to the lenders for the payment both of principal and interest.

As the situation of their affairs became extremely critical, and the preservation of Philadelphia to all appearance hopeless, at the time that Lord Cornwallis had overrun the Jerseys, and that the British forces had taken possession of the towns and posts on the Delaware, the Congress published an address Dec. 10th. to the people in general, but more particularly to those of Pensylvania and the adjacent states. The general objects of this piece, were to awaken the attention of the people, remove their despondency, renew their hopes and spirits, and confirm their intentions of supporting the war, by shewing that no other means were left for the preservation of those rights and liberties for which they originally contended. But it was particularly and immediately intended to forward the completion of the new army, and to call out the inhabitants of the neighbouring countries to the defence of Philadelphia.

For these purposes they enumerated the causes of the troubles, the supposed grievances they had endured, the late oppressive laws which had been passed against them, dwelt much upon the contempt with which all their petitions and applications for redress had been treated; and to shew that no alternative but war, or a tame resignation of all that could be dear to mankind remained, they asserted, that even the boasted Commissioners for giving peace to America had not offered, nor did yet offer, any terms but pardon on absolute submission. From this detail and these premises they deduced the necessity of the act of independency, asserting, that it would have been impossible for them to have defended their rights against so powerful an aggressor, aided by large armies of foreign mercenaries, or to have obtained that assistance from other states which was absolutely necessary to their preservation, whilst they acknowledged the sovereignty, and confessed themselves the subjects of that power, against which they had taken up arms, and were engaged in so cruel a war.

They boasted of the success that had in general attended their cause and exertions, contending that the present state of weakness and danger, did not proceed from any capital loss, defeat, or from any defect of valour in their troops, but merely from the expiration of the term of those short enlistments, which had in the beginning been adopted from an attention to the ease of the people. They assured them that foreign states had already rendered them essential services, and had given the most positive assurances of further aid.

And they excited the indignation and animofity of the people, by expatiating upon the unrelenting, cruel, and inhuman manner, in which, they faid, the war was carried on, not only by the auxiliaries, but even by the British forces themselves.

Complaints of this kind held a diftinguished place in all the American publications of that time. Some of them indeed contained nothing elfe, but details of rapes, rapine, cruelty and murder. Though thefe accounts were undoubtedly highly exaggerated, it is, however, to be apprehended, that too much room was afforded for complaints of that nature. The odium began with the Heffians, and has fince ftuck clofely to them, though the British troops were far from efcaping a share of the imputation. The former, naturally fierce and cruel, ignorant of any rights but thofe of defpotifm, and of any manners, but thofe eftablished within the narrow precinct of their own government, were incapable of forming any diftinction between ravaging and deftroying an enemy's country, where no prefent benefit was intended but plunder, nor no future advantage expected but that of weakening the foe, and the reducing of a malecontent people, (who, though in a ftate of rebellion, were ftill to be reclaimed, not deftroyed) to a due fenfe of obedience to their lawful fovereign.

It has been faid, that in order to reconcile them to fo new and ftrange an adventure, fome idea had been held out to them in Germany, that they should obtain large portions of the lands which they were to conquer in America, and that this notion, however abfurd, made them at firft confider the ancient poffeffors as their natural enemies; but that when they found their error, they confidered the moveable plunder of the country, not only as a matter of right, but an inadequate recompence for undertaking fuch a voyage, and engaging in fuch a war.

Military rapine may be eafily accounted for without any recourfe to fuch a deception. It had been obferved from the beginning, that the moft mortal antipathy fubfifted between the Americans and Heffians. The former, contending themfelves for freedom, and filled with the higheft notions of the natural rights of mankind, regarded with equal contempt and abhorrence, a people, whom they confidered as the moft fordid of all mercenary flaves, in thus refigning all their faculties to the will of a petty defpot, and becoming the ready inftruments of a cruel tyranny. They reproached them with the higheft poffible degree of moral turpitude, in thus engaging in a domeftic quarrel, in which they had neither intereft or concern, and quitting their homes in the old world to butcher a people in the new, from whom they never had received the fmalleft injury; but who, on the contrary, had for a century paft afforded an hofpitable afylum to their harraffed and oppreffed countrymen, who had fled in multitudes to efcape from a tyranny, fimilar to that under which thefe were now acting, and to enjoy the bleffings of a liberty moft generoufly held out to them, of which thefe mercenaries would impioufly bereave the German as well as Englifh Americans.

Such fentiments, and fuch reproaches, did not fail to increafe their natural ferocity and rapacioufnefs; and it is faid that they continued in a courfe of plunder, until they at length became fo encumbered and loaded with fpoil, and fo anxious for its prefervation, that it grew to be a great impediment to their military operations.

However difagreeable this conduct was, and contrary to the nature of the British commanders, it was an evil not eafily to be remedied. They could not venture to hazard the fuccefs of the war, in fo diftant a fituation, and fuch precarious and critical circumftances, by quarreling with auxiliaries, who were nearly as numerous and powerful as their own forces. Allowances were neceffarily to be made for a difference of manners, opinions, and even ideas of military rules and fervice. Without opening any general ground of diflike or quarrel, it required all the conftancy, and all that admirable equanimity of temper which diftinguish General Howe's character, to reftrain the operation of thofe picques, jealoufies, and animofities, the effects of national pride, emulation, and a difference of manners, which no wifdom could prevent from fpringing up in the two armies.

It was fcarcely poffible that the devaftation and diforders practifed by the Heffians, should not operate in fome degree in their example upon the British troops. It would have been difficult to have punished enormities on the one fide, which were practifed without referve or apprehenfion on the other. Every fuccefsful deviation from order and difcipline in war, is certainly and fpeedily followed by others ftill greater. No relaxation can take place in either without the moft ruinous confequences. The foldier, who at firft fhrinks at trifling exceffes, will in a little time, if they pafs without queftion, proceed, without hefitation, to the greateft enormities.

From hence fprung the clamour raifed in America of the defolation which was fpread through the Jerfeys, and which by taking in friends and moderate men, as well as enemies, did great injury to the royal caufe, uniting the latter more firmly, and urging to activity, or detaching, many of the former. Nor could the effect be confined to the immediate fufferers; the exaggerated details which were published of thefe enormities, ferving to imbitter the minds of men exceedingly through all the colonies. These accounts being also transmitted to Europe, seemed in some degree to affect our national character; in France particularly, where the people in general, through the whole course of this contest, have been strongly American, they were readily received and willingly credited. Among other enormities which received the censure of our neighbours in that country, the destruction of the public library at Trenton, and of the college and library at Princetown, together with a celebrated orrery made by Rittenhouse, [5] said to be the best and finest in the world, were brought as charges of a Gothic barbarity, which waged war even with literature and the sciences.

In about a month after the taking of New York, the inhabitants of that city and island, presented a petition to Lord and General Howe, the commissioners for restoring peace to the colonies, signed by Daniel Horsemanden, Oliver De [6] Lancy, and 946 others, declaring their allegiance, and their acknowledgment of the *Constitutional Supremacy* of Great-Britain over the colonies; and praying, that in pursuance of the former declarations issued by the Commissioners, that city and county might be restored to his Majesty's peace and protection.

This petition to the Commissioners was followed by another to the same purpose, from the freeholders and inhabitants of Queen's County in Long Island. It was observed of these petitions, that the acknowledgment of the Constitutional Supremacy in one, and of the Constitutional Authority, of Great-Britain in the other, were very guardedly expressed, all mention of parliament being omitted, and the great question of unconditional submission left totally at large. It is also remarkable, that though the inhabitants of York Island and Queen's County, besides raising a considerable body of

troops for the King's service, and establishing a strong militia for the common defence, had given every other testimony of their loyalty which could be expected or wished, yet these petitions were not attended to, nor were they restored to those rights which they expected in consequence of the declarations, as well as of the late law for the appointment of Commissioners.

The critical situation of Philadelphia, which a night or two's frost would have laid open to the British forces, obliged the Congress, about the close of the year, to consult their own safety by retiring to Baltimore, in Maryland. In this state of external danger, the dissentions which sprung up among themselves were not less alarming to the Americans. We have formerly shewn that the declaration of independency had met with a strong opposition in Philadelphia, not only from those who were called or considered as Tories, but from many, who in all other matters had been among the most forward in opposing the claims of the crown and parliament. The carrying of the question by a great majority throughout the province, was far from lessening the bitterness of those who opposed it, amongst whom were most of the Quakers, a great and powerful body in that colony; so that the discontented in this business, forgetting in the present their ancient animosity, with all its operating causes, coalesced with the Tories or loyalists, whom they had formerly persecuted, and considered as betrayers, and inveterate enemies of their country, thus composing all together a very formidable party.

In consequence of this dissention, and of the ill success of the rebellious arms during the greater part of the campaign, which disposed many to look to their safety, a Mr. Galloway, the family of Allens, [7] with other leading men, either in Pensylvania or the Jerseys, some of whom had been members of the

Congress, fled to the Commissioners at New York, to claim the benefits of the general pardon which had been offered; expecting, as matters then stood, to return speedily home in triumph. These were, however, much less troublesome and dangerous to the Americans, than those who kept their ground, who were so numerous and powerful, that upon the approach of the British forces to the Delaware, they prevented the order for fortifying the city of Philadelphia from being carried into execution. This eccentric and alarming movement in the seat of life and action, obliged General Washington, weak as he was, to detach three regiments, under the command of Lord Stirling, effectually to quell the opposition of that party, and to give efficacy to the measure of fortifying the city. This decisive conduct answered all its purposes, except that of fortifying the city, a design which seems to have been abandoned as not practicable, or not necessary at that time.

As the season grew too severe to keep the field, and the frosts were not yet sufficiently set in for the passage of the Delaware, it became necessary towards the middle of December to put the British and auxiliary forces under cover. They were accordingly thrown into great cantonments, forming an extensive chain from Brunswick on the Rariton to the Delaware, occupying not only the towns, posts, and villages, which came within a liberal description of that line, but those also on the banks of the Delaware for several miles, so that the latter composed a front at the end of the line, which looked over to Pensylvania.

Things were now in such a situation, that there seemed to be as little probability of interrupting the designs, or endangering the security on the one side, as of renewing the spirit, or retrieving the weakness, on the other. In this state of affairs, a bold and spirited enterprize, which shewed more of brilliancy than real effect in its first appearance, became capable in its consequences of changing in a great measure the whole fortune of the the war. Such extraordinary effects do small events produce, in that last and most uncertain of human decisions.

Colonel Rall, a brave and experienced officer, was stationed with a brigade of Hessians, consisting of three battalions, with a few British light-horse, and 50 chaffeurs, amounting in the whole to 14 or 1500 men, at Trenton, upon the Delaware, being the highest post which the royal army occupied upon that river. Colonel Donop, with another brigade, lay at Bordentown, a few miles lower down the river; and at Burlington, still lower, and within twenty miles of Philadelphia, a third body was posted. The corps at Trenton, as well as the others, partly from the knowledge they had of the weakness of the enemy, and partly from the contempt in which they held him, considered themselves in as perfect a state of security, as if they had been upon garrison duty in their own country, in a time of the profoundest peace. It is said, and seems probable, that this supposed security, increased that licence and laxity of discipline, of which we have before taken notice, and produced an inattention to the possibility of a surprize, which no success or situation can justify in the vicinity of an enemy, however weak or contemptible.

These circumstances, if they really existed, seem not to have escaped the vigilance of General Washington. But, exclusive of these, he fully saw and comprehended the danger to which Philadelphia and the whole province would be inevitably exposed, as soon as the Delaware was thoroughly covered with ice, if the enemy, by retaining possession of the opposite shore, were at hand to profit

of that circumstance, whilst he was utterly incapable of opposing them in the field.

To ward off this danger, he with equal boldness and ability formed a design to prevent the enemy, by beating up their quarters; intending to remedy the deficiency of force by the manner of applying it; by bringing it nearly to a point; and by attacking unexpectedly and separately those bodies which he could not venture to encounter if united. If the design succeeded only in part, it might, however, induce the enemy to contract their cantonments, and to quit the vicinity of the river, when they found it was not a sufficient barrier to cover their quarters from insult and danger; thus obtaining that security for Philadelphia, which, at present, was the principal object of his attention.

For this purpose, General Washington took the necessary measures for assembling his forces (which consisted mostly of drafts from the militia of Pensylvania and Virginia) in three divisions, each of which was to arrive at its appointed station on the Delaware, as soon after dark, and with as little noise, as possible, on the night of Christmas day. Two of these divisions were under the command of the Generals Erwing and Cadwallader, the first of which was to pass the river at Trenton Ferry, about a mile below the town, and the other still lower towards Bordentown. The principal body was commanded by Mr. Washington in person, assisted by the Generals Sullivan and Green, and consisted of about 2500 men, provided with a train of 20 small brass field pieces.

With this body he arrived at M'Kenky's Ferry, about nine miles above Trenton, at the time appointed, hoping to be able to pass the division and artillery over by midnight, and that it would then be no difficulty to reach that place long before daylight, and

effectually to surprize Rall's brigade. The river was, however, so incumbered with ice, that it was with great difficulty the boats could make their way through, which, with the extreme severity of the weather, retarded their passage so much, that it was near four o'clock before it was compleated. They were still equally delayed and incommoded in the march by a violent storm of snow and hail, which rendered the way so slippery, that it was with difficulty they reached the place of destination by eight o'clock.

The detachment had been formed in two divisions immediately upon passing the river, one of which, turning to the right, took the lower road to Trenton, whilst the other, with General Washington, proceeded along the upper, or Pennington road. Notwithstanding the delays they met, and the advanced state of daylight, the Hessians had no knowledge of their approach, until an advanced post, at some distance from the town, was attacked by the upper division, the lower, about the same time, driving in the outguards on their side. The regiment of Rall, having been detached to support the picket which was first attacked, was thrown into disorder by the retreat of that party, and obliged to rejoin the main body. Colonel Rall now bravely charged the enemy, but being soon mortally wounded, the troops were thrown into disorder after a short engagement, and driven from their artillery, which consisted only of six battalion brass field pieces. Thus overpowered, and nearly surrounded, after an ineffectual attempt to retreat to Princetown, the three regiments of Rall, Lossberg, and Knyphausen, found themselves under the unfortunate necessity of surrendering prisoners of war.

As the road along the river-side to Bordentown led from that part of Trenton most remote from the enemy, the light horse, chaffeurs, a considerable number of the private men, with some few officers, made their escape that way. It is also said, that a number of the Hessians who had been out marauding in the country, and accordingly absent from their duty that morning, found the same refuge, whilst their crime was covered under the common misfortune.

The loss of the Hessians in killed and wounded was very inconsiderable, not exceeding 30 or 40 at the most; that on the other side was too trifling to be mentioned; the whole number of prisoners amounted to 918. Thus was one part of General Washington's project crowned with success; but the two others failed in the execution, the quantity of ice being so great, that the divisions under Erwing and Cadwallader, found the river, where they directed their attempts, impassable. If this had not been the case, and that the first, in pursuance of his instructions, had been able to have possessed the bridge over Trenton Creek, not one of those who made their way to Bordentown could have escaped. But if the design had taken effect in all its parts, and the three divisions had joined after the affair at Trenton, it seems probable that they would have swept all the posts on the river before them.

As things were, General Washington could not proceed any further in the prosecution of his design. The force he had with him was far from being able even to maintain its ground at Trenton, there being a strong body of light infantry within a few miles at Princetown, which by the junction of Donop's brigade, or other bodies from the nearest cantonments, would have soon overwhelmed his little army. He accordingly repassed the Delaware the same evening, carrying with him the prisoners, who, with their artillery and colours, afforded a day of new and joyful triumph at Philadelphia.

This small success wonderfully raised the spirits of the Americans. It is an odd, but a general disposition in mankind, to be much more afraid of those whom they do not know, than of those with whom they are acquainted. Difference of dress, of arms (though less useful), of complexion, beard, colour of the hair or eyes, with the general manner, air, and countenance, have at different times had surprising effects upon brave, disciplined, and experienced armies. The Hessians had hitherto been very terrible to the Americans; and the taking of a whole brigade of them prisoners, seemed so incredible, that at the very time they were marching into Philadelphia, people were contending in different parts of the town, that the whole story was a fiction, and indeed that it could not be true. The charm was now, however, dissolved, and the Hessians were no longer terrible. In the mean time General Washington was reinforced by several regiments from Virginia and Maryland, as well as with several new bodies of the Pensylvania militia, who, with those of that province already under his command, were much distinguished in the hard service of the ensuing winter campaign.

The surprize at Trenton did not excite less amazement in the British and auxiliary quarters, than it did joy in those of the Americans. Blame was loosely scattered every where. That three old established regiments, of a people who make war their profession, should lay down their arms to a ragged and undisciplined militia, and that with scarcely any loss on either side, seemed an event of so extraordinary a nature, that it gave full scope to the operation of conjecture, suspicion, censure, and malignity, as different tempers were differently affected.

The General was blamed for laying so extensive a chain of cantonments; Rall was condemned for marching out of the town to meet the enemy; and the character of the Hessians, in general, did not rise in the opinion of their allies.

As to the first, the General had foreseen the objection, but he depended upon the weakness of the enemy, the good disposition of the inhabitants, the considerable force which was stationed in the advanced posts, and was besides influenced by a desire to cover and protect the county of Monmouth, where a great number of the people were well affected to the royal cause. It may be added, that perhaps no line of cantonment or posts can be contrived so compact and secure, as not to admit the possibility of an impression in some one part, by a force much inferior to the aggregate power of the defensive.

With respect to Colonel Rall, if the charge against him was well founded, his misconduct sprung from an error, which was generally prevalent among the officers and men both of the British and Hessian forces. The fact is, that from the successes of the preceding campaign, and the vast superiority which they perceived in themselves in every action, they had held the Americans in too great contempt both as men and as soldiers; and were too apt to attribute those advantages to some extraordinary personal virtue and excellence, which were in reality derived from the concurrence of a number of other, and very different causes; from military skill, experience, and discipline; from the superior excellence of their small arms, artillery, and of all other engines, furniture, and supplies, necessary for war; and still more particularly, to a better supply, and a more dexterous and effective use of bayonets, which gave them a great superiority over the Americans, who were poorly furnished with this kind of arms, and were by no means expert in the use of them.

The alarm now spread, induced the British and auxiliary troops immediately to assemble, and General Grant, with the forces at Brunswick and that quarter, to advance speedily to Princetown; whilst Lord Cornwallis, who had gone to New York in his way to England, found it necessary to defer his voyage, and return post to the defence of the Jerseys. They were not now without an enemy to encounter, for General Washington, encouraged by the reinforcements he had received, had again passed the Delaware, and was with his whole force at Trenton.

Lord Cornwallis marched immediately to attack the enemy, whom he found Jan. 2, 1777. in a strong position, formed at the back of Trenton Creek, being in possession of the bridge and other passages, which were well covered with artillery. After several skirmishes in the approach, a cannonade ensued on both sides, which continued until night. A brigade of the British troops lay that night at Maidenhead, six miles from Trenton, and another upon its march from Brunswick, consisting of the 17th, the 40th, and 55th regiments, under the command of Lieutenant Colonel Mawhood, were [10] at Princetown, about the same distance beyond Maidenhead.

In this situation on both sides, General Washington, who was far from intending to risque a battle, having taken the necessary precaution of keeping up the fires, and every other appearance of still occupying his camp, and leaving small parties to go the rounds, and guard the bridge and the fords, withdrew the rest of his forces in the dead of night, and with the most profound silence. They marched with such expedition towards Princetown, that though they took a large circuit by Allenstown, partly to get clear of the Trenton, or Assumpink Creek, and partly to avoid the brigade which lay at Maidenhead, their van fell in at sunrise the next morning with Colonel Mawhood, who had just begun his march. That officer not having the smallest idea of their force, the fogginess of the morning, or circumstances of the ground, preventing him from seeing its extent, considered it only as the attempt of some flying party to interrupt his march, and having easily dispersed those by whom he was first attacked, pushed forwards without further apprehension. But in a little time, he not only found that the 17th regiment which he led, was attacked on all sides by a superior force, but that it was also separated and cut off from the rest of the brigade, whilst he discovered, by the continued distant firing, that the 55th, which immediately followed, was not in better circumstances.

In this trying and dangerous situation, the brave commander, and his equally brave regiment, have gained immortal honour. After a violent conflict, and the greatest repeated exertions of courage and discipline, they at length, by dint of bayonet, forced their way through the thickest ranks of the enemy, and pursued their march to Maidenhead undisturbed. The 55th regiment was little less pressed, and finding it impossible to continue its march, with great resolution made good its retreat, and returned by the way of Hillsborough to Brunswick. The 40th regiment, which was still at Princetown when the action began, suffered less than the others, and retired by another road to the same place. The enemy acknowledged that nothing could exceed the gallant behaviour of the corps under Mawhood.

Though the number killed, considering the nature and warmth of the engagements, was not so considerable as might have been expected; yet, upon the whole, the three regiments suffered severely; their loss in prisoners amounting to about 200; the killed and wounded were much fewer. The Americans had many more killed, among whom were some brave officers, particularly a General Mercer, belonging to Virginia, who was much esteemed and lamented. [11]

It cannot escape the observation of any person who has attended to the circumstances of this war, that the number slain on the side of the Americans, has in general greatly exceeded that in the royal army. Though every defect in military skill, experience, judgment, conduct, and mechanical habit, will in some degree account for this circumstance, yet perhaps it may be more particularly attributed to the imperfect loading of their pieces in the hurry of action, than to any other cause; a defect, of all others, the most fatal; the most difficult to be remedied in a new army; and to which even veterans are not sufficiently attentive. To this may also be added the various make of their small arms, which being procured, as chance or opportunity favoured them, from remote and different quarters, were equally different in size and bore, which rendered their being fitted with ball upon any general scale impracticable.

This active and unexpected movement, with its spirited consequences, immediately recalled Lord Cornwallis from the Delaware, who was, not without reason, alarmed for the safety of the troops and magazines at Brunswick. The Americans, still avoiding a general action, and satisfied with their present advantages, crossed the Millstone river, without any further attempt. In a few days, however, they overrun East Jersey as well as the West, spreading themselves over the Raritan; even into Essex county, where, by seizing Newark, Elizabeth Town, and Woodbridge, they became masters of the coast opposite to Staten Island. Their principal posts were taken and strengthened with so much judgment, that it was not practicable to diflodge them. The royal army retained only the two pofts of Brunfwick and Amboy, the one fituated a few miles up the Rariton, the other on a point of land at its mouth, and both holding an open communication with New York by fea.

Thus by a few well concerted and fpirited actions, was Philadelphia faved, Penfylvania freed from danger, the Jerfeys nearly recovered, and a victorious and far fuperior army, reduced to act upon the defenfive, and for feveral months reftrained within very narrow and inconvenient limits. Thefe actions, and the fudden recovery from the loweft ftate of weaknefs and diftrefs, to become a formidable enemy in the field, raifed the character of General Wafhington, as a commander, very high both in Europe and America; and with his preceding and fubfequent conduct, ferve all together, to give a fanction to that appellation, which is now pretty generally applied to him, of the American Fabius.

Nor was this change of affairs to be attributed to any error in the Britifh Generals, or fault in the troops which they commanded; but depended entirely upon the happy application of a number of powerful and concurring circumftances, which were far beyond their reach or controul. Though many of thefe were forefeen and pointed out, by thofe who from the beginning, either oppofed in public, or regretted in private, this war, and that others are now obvious to every body, it may not, however, be amifs to fpecify fome of thofe caufes which clogged it with particular difficulties.

Among the principal of thefe may be confidered the vaft extent of that continent, with its unufual diftribution into great tracts of cultivated and favage territory; the long extent of fea coaft in front, and the boundlefs waftes at the back of the inhabited countries,

affording refource or fhelter in all circumftances; the numberlefs inacceffible pofts, and ftrong natural barriers, formed by the various combinations of woods, mountains, rivers, lakes, and marfhes. All thefe properties and circumftances, with others appertaining to the climates and feafons, may be faid to fight the battles of the inhabitants of fuch countries in a defenfive war. To thefe may be added others lefs local. The unexpected union, and unknown ftrength of the colonies; the judicious application of that ftrength, by fuiting the defence to the nature, genius, and ability, of the people, as well as to the natural advantages of the country, thereby rendering it a war of pofts, furprizes, and fkirmifhes, inftead of a war of battles. To all thefe may be added, the people's not being bridled by ftrong cities, nor fettered by luxury to thofe which were otherwife, fo that the reduction of a capital had no effect upon the reft of the province, and the army could retain no more territory than what it occupied, which was again loft as foon as it departed to another quarter.

During the remaining winter, and the whole of the fpring, the army under Lord Cornwallis continued much ftraitened at Brunfwick and Amboy, the troops undergoing, with the greateft perfeverance and refolution, the hardfhips of a moft fevere and unremitting duty, whilft their ranks were thinned by a continued feries of fkirmifhes, which were productive of no real advantage on either fide, other than that of inuring the Americans to military fervice. In a word, every load of forage which was procured, and every article of provifion, which did not come from New York, was fought or purchafed at the price of blood.

The confequences of the late military outrages in the Jerfeys were feverely felt in the prefent change of circumftances. As foon as for-

tune turned, and the means were in their power, the fufferers of all parties, the well difpofed to the royal caufe, as well as the neutrals and wavering, now rofe as a man to revenge their perfonal injuries and particular oppreffions, and being goaded by a keener fpur, than any which a public caufe, or general motive, could have excited, became its bittereft and moft determined enemies. Thus the whole country, with too few exceptions, became hoftile; thofe who were incapable of arms, acting as fpies, and keeping a continual watch for thofe who bore them; fo that the fmalleft motion could not be made, without its being expofed and difcovered, before it could produce its intended effect. Such were the untoward events, that in the winter damped the hopes of a victorious army, and nipped the laurels of a foregoing profperous campaign.

We have formerly had occafion to fhew, the bad fuccefs which invariably attended the repeated attempts that had been made, of calling off the attention and force of the fouthern colonies from the fupport of the general alliance to their own immediate defence, by involving them effectually in civil war and domeftic contention, either through the means of the well affected in general, the Regulators and Highland emigrants in the Carolinas, or of the Negroes in Virginia. We have alfo taken fome fmall notice, of the charges made by the infurgents in fome of thefe provinces againft their governors, of endeavouring to bring the favages down to further thofe defigns.

The failure in thefe attempts, was not fufficient to damp the zeal of the Britifh agents among the Indian nations, nor to render them hopelefs of ftill performing fome effential fervice, by engaging thefe people to make a diverfion, and to attack the fouthern colonies in their back and defencelefs parts. The Indians, ever light in act and faith, greedy of prefents, and eager for fpoil, were not difficultly induced, by a proper application of the one, and the hope of the other, concurring with their own natural difpofition, to forget the treaties which they had lately confirmed or renewed with the colonifts, and to engage in the defign.

It was held out to them, that a Britifh army was to land in Weft Florida, and after penetrating through the Creek, Chickefaw, and Cherokee countries, and being joined by the warriors of thofe nations, they were jointly to invade the Carolinas and Virginia, whilft another formidable force by fea and land, was to make a powerful impreffion on the coafts. Circular letters to the fame import, were fent by Mr. Stuart, the[12] principal agent for Indian affairs, to the inhabitants of the back fettlements, requiring all the well-affected, as well as all thofe, who were willing to preferve themfelves and their families from the inevitable calamities and deftruction of an Indian war, to be in readinefs to repair to the royal ftandard, as foon as it was erected in the Cherokee country, and to bring with them their horfes, cattle, and provifions, for all of which they were promifed payment. They were likewife required, for their prefent fecurity, and future diftinction from the King's enemies, to fubfcribe immediately to a written paper, declaratory of their allegiance.

The fcheme was fo plaufible, and carried fuch a probability of fuccefs, that it feemed to have had a very extenfive operation upon the difpofition of the Indians, and to have prepared them in a great meafure for a general confederacy againft the colonies. Even the fix nations, who had before agreed to the obfervance of a ftrict neutrality, now committed feveral fmall acts of hoftility, which were afterwards difowned by their elders and chiefs. The Creek Indians,

more violent, began the fouthern war with all their ufual barbarity, until finding that the expected fuccours did not arrive, they, with a forefight uncommon among Indians, ftopped fuddenly fhort, and repenting of what they had done, were, in the prefent ftate of affairs, eafily excufed; and being afterwards applied to for affiftance by the Cherokees, returned for anfwer, that they, the latter, had plucked the thorn out of their foot, and were welcome to keep it.

But the Cherokees fell upon the adjoining colonies with determined fury, carrying, for a part of the fummer, ruin and defolation wherever they came, fcalping and flaughtering the people, and totally deftroying their fettlements. They were foon, however, checked, and feverely experienced, that things were much altered, fince the time of their former warfare upon the fame ground, and that the martial fpirit now prevalent in the colonies, was extended to their remoteft frontiers. They were not only repulfed or defeated in every action, by the neighbouring militia of Virginia and the Carolinas, but purfued into their own country, where their towns were demolifhed, their corn deftroyed, and their warriors thinned in repeated engagements, until the nation was nearly exterminated, and the wretched furvivors were obliged to fubmit to any terms prefcribed by the victors; whilft the neighbouring nations of Indians were filent and paffive fpectators of their calamities.

Nor was this Indian war more fortunate, with refpect to its effect on the well-affected in thofe quarters; who are not only faid, to a man, to have expreffed the utmoft averfion to the authors, and abhorrence of the cruelty of that meafure, but that fome of the chief leaders of the tories, avowed a recantation of their former principles, merely upon that account.

It was in the midft of the buftle

and danger of the war, and when the fcale of Fortune feemed to hang heavily againft them, by the defeat on Long Ifland, and the reduction of New York, at a time when a great and invincible force by fea and land, carried difmay and conqueft wherever it directed its courfe, that all the members of the Congrefs ventured[13] to fign that remarkable treaty of perpetual compact and union between the thirteen revolted colonies, which lays down an invariable fyftem of rules or laws, for their government in all public cafes with refpect to each other in peace or war, and is alfo extended to their commerce with foreign ftates. This piece, which may be confidered as a moft dangerous fupplement to the declaration of independency, was publifhed under the title of articles of confederation and perpetual union between the thirteen fpecified ftates, and has fince received, as the neceffary forms would permit, the feparate ratification of each colony. Such was in general the ftate of affairs in America at the clofe of the year 1776.

Oct. 4.

THE interval that elapsed during the recess of parliament, was not much checkered with such domestic events as could greatly excite the attention of the public. As war seemed now as inevitable as it was fully provided for, the narrow alternative which was lodged in the hands of the Commissioners affording little room for other expectation, the attention of the nation was suspended for the present, and people only looked forward 'to the consequences of that event. Those who approved of hostility, saw their desires now gratified to the utmost, and those who differed with them in opinion found it useless to repine. Thus, all former subjects of debate and discussion being swallowed up in the final decision, public affairs seemed to be scarcely thought of, and a degree of stillness prevailed among the people, perhaps unequalled in any country or age, during the rage of a foreign or domestic warfare.

War is seldom unpopular in this country; and this war was attended with some circumstances which seldom have accompanied any other. The high language of authority, dignity and supremacy, which had filled the mouths of many for some years, fed the vanity of those who could not easily define, or who perhaps had never fully considered, the extent of the terms, or of the consequences which they were capable of producing; and the flattering idea of lessening the national burthens, by an American revenue, whilst it was fitted to the comprehension of the meanest capacity, was not less effective in its operation upon those of a superior class and order. To the powerful principles of national pride and avarice, was added a laudable disposition to support those national rights which were supposed to be invaded, and a proper indignation and resentment to that ingratitude and insolence which were charged upon the Americans, and to which only the present troubles were attributed by those, who were most active in fomenting the principles of hostility, which at that time prevailed, far more than they had done at the beginning of this contest.

In such circumstances, it is not to be wondered at, if a majority of the people gave at least a kind of tacit approbation to the war; but as it was not attended with national antipathy or rivalship, established enmity, or even a present competition for glory, they did not feel themselves so much interested in its success, or altogether so anxious about its consequences, as they would in those of another nature. On the other hand, that great body of the people, who had at all times reprobated the measures which led to the present troubles, and who considered them as not less dangerous to the constitution, than ruinous to the power and glory of the nation, could not be supposed sanguine in their wishes for a success, which they deemed liable to more fatal consequences than any loss or defeat. The great distance of the seat of war, also rendered its effects less interesting. For distance produces in some degree the effect of time with respect to sensibility; and the slaughter, cruelties, and calamities, which would wring the heart if they happened in the next county, are slightly felt at three or four thousand miles distance. The distance also prevented all apprehension of immediate danger; the expences of the contest were not yet sensibly felt; and the bulk of mankind never think of remote consequences.

From these, and other causes, a general, and perhaps blameable, carelessness and indifference prevailed throughout the nation. Nor was it easily roused from this drowsy apathy, which like all other habits was confirmed by time. For when at length, the American cruizers, not only scoured the Atlantic ocean, but spreading their depredations through the European seas, brought alarm and hostility home to our doors; when the destruction which befell the homeward bound richly laden West India fleets, poured equal ruin upon the planters in the islands and the merchants at home; when an account of the failure of some capital house in the city, was almost the news of every morning; even in that state of public loss and private distress, an unusual phlegm prevailed, and the same tranquil countenance and careless unconcern was preserved, by those who had not yet partaken of the calamity. A circumstance which is not sufficiently accounted for, even from the vast numbers who thought themselves officially, or by connection bound, to give a countenance to the war as a favourite court measure, nor the still greater of those who profited by its continuance.

In this state of public affairs and disposition at large, administration had acquired such an appearance of stability, as seemed to render them, for some considerable time to come, superior to the frowns of fortune. Supported by an irresistible majority in parliament, they were already armed with every power which they were capable of desiring or wishing for the establishment of their American system;

whilft, as the nation was now too deeply engaged in their meafures to be capable of retracting, it would be found equally difficult to commit the profecution of them to any other hands. Thus the power which produced the meafures, was infured during their continuance. All apprehenfion from the oppofition of an ill united minority had been long worn off; and it feemed now rather neceffary to give a colour and fanction to their proceedings, by recording the vaft fuperiority which decided every queftion in their favour, than as at all capable of counteracting, or even impeding their defigns.

* * *

Such was in general the ftate of [14] public affairs, during the recefs, and for fome time after the meeting of parliament. The fpeech from the throne Oct. 31ft. feemed to breath in-1776. dignation and refentment. It would have afforded much fatisfaction that the troubles which had fo long diftracted the colonies had been at an end; and that the unhappy people, recovered from their delufion, had delivered themfelves from the oppreffion of their leaders, and returned to their duty; but fo daring and defperate (it was faid) was the fpirit of thofe leaders, whofe object had always been dominion and power, that they had openly renounced all allegiance to the crown, and all political connection with this country; that they had rejected, with circumftances of indignity and infult, the means of conciliation held out to them under the authority of the royal commiffion; and had prefumed to fet up their rebellious confederacies for independent ftates. Much mifchief was forefeen from the growth of this rebellion, if it was fuffered to take root, not only with refpect to the fafety of the loyal colonies, and to the commerce of thefe kingdoms, but to the general fyftem of Europe.

One great advantage would, however, be derived, from the object of the rebels being openly avowed, and clearly underftood; it would produce unanimity at home, founded on a general conviction of the juftice and neceffity of our meafures.

The two houfes were informed of the recovery of Canada, and of the fucceffes on the fide of New York, which, notwithftanding the unavoidable delays that retarded the commencement of the operations, were of fuch importance, as to afford the ftrongeft hopes of the moft decifive good confequences; but that, notwithftanding this fair profpect, another campaign muft, at all events, be prepared for.

Amicable affurances were ftill received from other courts; endeavours were ufed to conciliate the differences between Spain and Portugal; and though a continuance of the general tranquillity was hoped, it was, however, thought expedient, in the prefent fituation of affairs, that we fhould be in a refpectable ftate of defence at home. The great confequent expence was regretted; but no doubt was entertained, that the importance of the objects under confideration, would procure a chearful grant of the neceffary fupplies.

It declared, that his Majefty could have no other object in this arduous conteft than the true interefts of all his fubjects; and it afferted, that no people ever enjoyed more happinefs, or lived under a milder government, than the revolted provinces; that their boafted improvements in every art, their numbers, their wealth, their ftrength by fea and land, were irrefragable proofs of it. The fpeech concluded with a declaration, that his Majefty's defire was to reftore to them the bleffings of law and liberty, equally enjoyed by every Britifh fubject, which they had fatally and defpe-

rately exchanged for all the calamities of war, and the arbitrary tyranny of their chiefs.

The addreffes were framed in the ufual manner, and, according to the practice of late years, produced great debates, and propofed amendments, of a clear contrary nature, in both houfes. That of the Commons, befides confirming, repeating and adopting, all the pofitions in the fpeech, attributes the circumftances of infult and indignity, which accompanied the rejection, by the American leaders, of the means of reconciliation gracioufly held out to them by his Majefty, to their refentment of his firm and conftant adherence to the maintenance of the conftitutional rights of parliament, divefted of every poffible view of any feparate interefts of the crown; and expreffes the ftrongeft fentiments of gratitude for that attachment to the parliamentary authority of Great Britain, which had thus provoked the infolence of the chiefs of the rebellion.

Lord John Cavendifh moved an amendment, which was of greater length than the original addrefs. [15] In this piece, (which included a comprehenfive view of the minifterial conduct with refpect to America,) after a declaration of the moft earneft zeal for his Majefty's true intereft, and the real glory of his reign, and the deepeft concern, at beholding the minds of a very large, and lately loyal and affectionate part of his people, entirely alienated from his government; it was inferred, that fuch an event, as the difaffection and revolt of a whole people, could not have taken place, without fome confiderable errors in the conduct obferved towards them.

Thefe errors were imputed, to the want of fufficient information being laid before parliament, and to the repofing of too great a degree of confidence in Minifters; who, though by duty obliged, and by office enabled, to study and to know the temper and disposition of his Majesty's American subjects, and to pursue the most salutary measures, had totally failed in all. To this misplaced confidence, and want of parliamentary information, was attributed, the pursuit of schemes formed for the reduction and chastisement of a supposed inconsiderable party of factious men, and which had driven thirteen large provinces to despair. That every Act of Parliament which had been proposed as a means of procuring peace and submission, had become a new cause of hostility and revolt; until we are almost inextricably involved in a bloody and expensive civil war; which, besides exhausting at present the strength of all his Majesty's dominions, exposing our allies to the designs of their and our enemies, and leaving this kingdom in a most perilous situation, threatens, in its issue, the most deplorable calamities to the whole British race.

It lamented, that in consequence of the credit given to the representation of Ministers, no hearing had been afforded to the reiterated complaints and petitions of the colonies, nor any ground laid for removing the original cause of those unhappy differences, which took their rise from questions relative to parliamentary proceedings, and can be settled only by parliamentary authority. That, by this fatal omission, the Commissioners nominated for the apparent purpose of making peace, were furnished with no legal powers, but that of giving or with-holding pardons at their pleasure, and that for relaxing the severities of a single penal Act of Parliament; leaving the whole foundation of this unhappy controversy just as it stood in the beginning.

It represented in strong colours, the fatal consequences of not sending out the Commissioners for seven months after the time, that

their speedy departure had been announced by the speech from the throne; by which neglect, it says, the inhabitants of the colonies, apprized that they were put out of the protection of government, and seeing no means provided for their entering into it, were furnished with reasons but too colourable for breaking off their dependency on the crown of this kingdom.

It gave an assurance, that the House, by removing their confidence from those who had in so many instances grossly abused it, would endeavour to restore to parliament the confidence of all the people. To answer this end, it was proposed to make enquiries into the grievances of the colonies, into the conduct of Ministers with regard to them, the causes, that the commerce of this kingdom had been left exposed to the reprisals of the colonies, at the very time when their seamen and fishermen, being indiscriminately prohibited from the peaceful exercise of their occupations, and declared open enemies, must have been expected, with a certain assurance, to betake themselves to plunder, and to wreak their revenge on the commerce of Great Britain.

It observed, that a wise, moderate, and provident use of the late advantages gained in arms, might be productive of happy effects: and gave an assurance, that nothing should be wanting on their part, to enable his Majesty to take full advantage of any disposition to reconciliation, which might be the consequence of the miseries of war, by laying down real permanent grounds of connection between Great Britain and her colonies, on principles of liberty and terms of mutual advantage.

It concluded with the following declaration, which contained high and liberal sentiments. "We should look with the utmost shame and horror, on any events that should tend to break the spirit of any large part of the British na-

tion: to bow them to an abject unconditional submission to any power whatsoever; to annihilate their liberties, and to subdue them to servile principles and passive habits, by the mere force of foreign mercenary arms; because, amidst the excesses and abuses which have happened, we must respect the spirit and principles operating in these commotions. Our wish is to regulate, not to destroy them; for though differing in some circumstances, those very principles evidently bear so exact an analogy with those which support the most valuable part of our own constitution, that it is impossible, with any appearance of justice, to think of wholly extirpating them by the sword, in any part of his Majesty's dominions, without admitting consequences, and establishing precedents, the most dangerous to the liberties of this kingdom."

A similar amendment to the address of the Lords was moved for by the Marquis of Rockingham, and both were supported with great force and animation, and the debates in both Houses, long, various, and interesting. In these, the speech from the throne, which was considered merely as the act of the Minister, was taken to pieces without ceremony, and treated in all its parts with unusual asperity.

It was asked, where those mighty leaders were found, whom the Americans obeyed so implicitly, and who governed them with so despotic a rule? They had no grandees amongst them;—their soil is not productive of nobility. No people upon earth, in an equal state of improvement, with so great an extent of country, so diffusive a commerce with mankind, and in possession of so large a share of substantial personal property, were so nearly in a state of equality. There were not many large, and there were no over-grown fortunes among them. Mr. Hancock, was a plain merchant, of fair character, and confiderable fubftance in Bofton; he poffeffed no fuper-eminence over his brethren, nor authority over the people, till the prefent troubles called him into both. Mr. Wafhington poffeffed fuch a landed eftate, as feveral very private gentlemen in every county in England poffefs, which enables them to exhibit fuch a degree of hofpitality, as procures them refpect and regard in their own diftricts, without their being heard of or known beyond thofe limits. Others, who now figure in the field or the Congrefs, were, and would have continued, ftill more obfcure. By what magic is it then, that thofe people, who are reprefented as violent republicans, as levellers in principle, who are faid to abhor all thofe diftinctions which cuftom and authority have eftablifhed in other parts of the world, fhould all at once have changed their nature, and, what is perhaps ftill more extraordinary, have fubdued their prejudices, fo as to refign all their faculties of thinking, and powers of acting, to a few unknown defpots?

The anfwer, they faid, was obvious, and was merely this, that the affertion was falfe; and that it was at the fame time fo palpably abfurd, as not to merit a ferious refutation. The Americans had been driven by oppreffion to a vindication of their rights; and, at length, by our invincible perfeverance, in the madnefs and injuftice of our conduct, to a defence of them by arms. In this fituation, driven together by common danger and calamity, and compelled to the laft refource of which human nature is capable, they were under the fame neceffity, which all people (even favages, in their original ftate of nature and equality) ever have been, and muft ever continue to be, in fimilar circumftances, of creating leaders, to conduct their public affairs, and to command their armies. Thefe

leaders, can have no other powers than what the people think fitting and neceffary to intruft them with. Their reprefentatives in the Provincial affemblies, are elected annually; the general Congrefs expires with the year. At that period, all power returns again to the people at large, who again delegate it in fuch proportions, and to fuch perfons, as they think proper. Thus, thofe fuppofed tyrants, who are reprefented as trampling equally upon all laws, and upon the necks of the people, as governing them with rods of fcorpions, and practifing upon them a defpotifm, fcarcely known in the oldeft eftablifhed tyrannies, are no other, than their own public officers and fervants, appointed at their will, and removeable at their pleafure. With what face then has the Minifter approached Parliament, or ventured to infult Majefty, with fo unqualified and fhamelefs an impofition.

In the fame fpirit, faid they, of impofing upon, and with the additional defign of irritating the nation, it is advanced, that the Americans have rejected, with circumftances of indignity and infult, the means of conciliation held out to them under the commiffion. This falfehood, they faid, was engrafted upon a fimilar one of the preceding feffion, by which it was held out, that terms of accommodation would be referred to the confideration of parliament. Though this was neither defigned nor effected, yet to nourifh the delufion of the people, a folitary claufe was thrown into the capture act, empowering the crown to appoint Commiffioners to grant pardons; a matter to which it was as fully competent, without, as with an Act of Parliament. Thus, the boafted means of conciliation, which the Americans had fo ungratefully and contumacioufly rejected, were nothing more than a naked offer of pardon, upon terms, the very idea of which are

abhorrent to the nature of every fubject of this free government. The Minifters well knew that they would never voluntarily accept the terms of unconditional fubmiffion, and they intentionally drove them, though they dare neither avow the defign nor the motives, to the only remaining alternative of refiftance, and its fcarcely avoidable confequence, the declaration of independence. To prevent, however, the poffibility of any change of difpofition, the effect of any alleviating circumftances, and to render them totally enraged and defperate, the commiffion, fuch as it was, and the Commiffioners, were detained for feveral months, until the whole fyftem of irritation and punifhment of the penal laws, including (what they called) the indifcriminate injuftice and cruelty of the Capture Act, by which they [16] were declared enemies, put out of the protection of the law, and their property held out as a common fpoil, had full time and fcope for their operation. Nor could any fubmiffion, however general and unconditional, mitigate their calamities, as there were no perfons upon the fpot, who had authority to receive it if offered, nor to relax or fufpend the feverity of the laws in favour of thofe who returned to their duty. Yet now the nation are to be ftill mifled, and farther inflamed, by holding out an idea, that equitable and gracious means of conciliation had been propofed to the Americans, and by them rejected with the moft unparalleled fcorn and infolence.

The pofition in the fpeech, that no people ever enjoyed greater happinefs, or lived under a milder government, than the revolted colonies, in fupport of which their improvement in arts, their number, their wealth, and their ftrength by fea and land, were brought in proof, was faid to imply a virtual and moft juft cenfure on the conduct of adminiftration. Upon what principle of wifdom or policy was such a people forced into rebellion? This power and greatness, which composed a part of our own, and which was not to be equalled in the history of colonization by any other people, owed its growth to the just and equal system of the English laws and constitution, and to the blessings of a mild and equitable government. Why was this admirable system of wisdom and equity, which produced such noble, nay wonderful effects, departed from? The speech holds out, that the present measures are intended to restore the blessings of law and liberty to America. Why were those blessings interrupted? Will their being offered at the point of the bayonet increase their value? Why was the fair fabrick which had been the work of so many ages destroyed; in order to re-establish that by the sword, which prudence and good government, had already seemed to fix for ever?

The amicable and pacific sentiments attributed to other powers, at the time that all Europe was armed in such a manner, as bespoke the most immediate design or apprehension of hostility, was equally animadverted on, and represented as a part of that principle of deception and imposition, which, as they affirmed, run through the whole. In this instance, the Minister's actions gave the most direct and unqualified contradiction to his words. At the very time, that he was holding out this delusive appearance of security to parliament, the whole nation was alarmed and thrown into confusion, and its commerce ruined, by the unexpected issue of press warrants, together with the unusual circumstances of rigour and violence with which they were carried into execution. Here his conduct is open and undisguised, and removes at once that veil of deception which involves his declarations.

The expectation of unanimity from the present situation of affairs, was treated as a matter of unbecoming levity, as well as of disrespect to those to whom it was directed. Was ever any thing more truly ridiculous, (said the Opposition) than the calling for unanimity in measures, because those measures had been uniformly productive of all the mischiefs which had been foreseen and predicted? As we have uniformly opposed, said they, the whole train of these destructive measures, in explaining the motives of our conduct, we have as constantly stated their natural consequences, which amounted to an exact prediction of all those evils that have ensued. No prophecies were ever more accurately fulfilled. And now, when the empire is severed, America for ever lost, when distraction prevails at home, and ruin surrounds us without, the Minister, with a degree of facetiousness and humour, which might obtain credit in another place, and upon other occasions, takes it for granted, that we shall now be unanimous, in the support of that ruinous system, and the prosecution of those destructive measures, which have already brought on all our calamities.

It was insisted, that nothing could save this country, from still more fatal consequences than those which it had already experienced, but an immediate recal of the armies from America, a repeal of all the penal and obnoxious laws against that people, and a full restoration of their charters and rights. That these measures, operating upon the established habits, and upon the natural affection of the Americans, might still prove the means of reuniting the severed parts of the empire. But that if irritation, a bitterness proceeding from the losses they have sustained, and the cruelties they suffered, with a relish for the novel sweetness of power and command, and a knowledge of their strength, should operate so far on the side of the Americans, as to render this consummation (which of all others was the most devoutly to be wished) impracticable, if such was found to be our unhappy situation, nothing in that case was left to be done, upon any principle of sound reason and right policy, but immediately to acknowledge their independence, and by concluding a commercial and federal treaty of union with them, again to collect together such small part as could yet be retained of those glorious advantages, which in the high career of our pride, injustice and madness, we had scattered abroad.

It availed nothing now, they said, to reflect upon what we were, or what we had lost; we must conform ourselves with prudence to our present situation, or get into a worse. Unwise conduct, and evil counsels, generally brought on their own punishment. We must now submit, however disagreeable to our feeling, to that chastisement which we have too justly merited. The more we struggle, and the longer we persist in the obstinacy of error, the greater shall we find the measure of our punishment; nor will it in a little time be circumscribed within any rule of proportion.

They strongly asserted, that a war with the whole House of Bourbon, in conjunction with our late friends and fellow subjects the Americans, must be the inevitable, and not distant, consequence of a perseverance in our present measures. Our ally, Portugal, whom we were bound by every tie to protect, was already menaced with immediate danger. If we even submitted to the degradation in the eyes of all Europe, of sacrificing our ally, our faith, and our interest, to present apprehension of danger, that would afford no permanent security, as the present conduct of France and Spain, the nature of their preparations, and the support which they already afforded the Americans, sufficiently shewed the part which they would take in our unhappy civil contention.

Were we now then in a condition, when we found ourselves unable, with all the assistance we could derive from our mercenary auxiliaries, only to reduce our own revolted subjects, to encounter the whole force of the House of Bourbon, united with that of the Americans? Our national defence by sea and land lay now in America, and in a great measure at the mercy of those two powers. Was this then a season, with an accumulating debt, a decreasing revenue, an exhausture of our resources, with divided councils, and a distracted people at the verge of political despair, to engage in so arduous a contest? In so dire and calamitous a situation, a speedy reconciliation, upon any terms, with the colonies, was the only means left of political salvation. Grievous and painful though the loss of America would be, it was not, however, the upshot of calamity. The question of the Americans being our friends, or being in confirmed enmity, and in compact with our natural enemies, went perhaps to that of our existence as a state.

Upon these and many other grounds, they reprobated the proposed addresses in both houses, which they charged with subscribing to the ill-founded panegyricks which the Ministers had composed upon themselves in the speech, with involving the nation in a continuance of the same ruinous measures which had occasioned all its calamities, and with giving a parliamentary sanction to a number of misrepresentations and fallacies, calculated merely to amuse, deceive, mislead, or inflame the people. Whilst they contended, that the amendments would afford that time and opportunity to parliament, which their duty, a proper regard to their own dignity, and the alarming state of public affairs,

all equally demanded, for enquiring diligently into the state of the nation, tracing the sources of our present calamities, and for considering and devising all possible means of averting the innumerable dangers with which we were surrounded.

On the other side, the speech was defended in all its parts; its veracity, prudence, justice, and magnanimity, being equally supported and applauded. It was affirmed to be replete with the strongest marks of sound policy and royal wisdom, as well as with indubitable proofs of the greatest paternal regard and tenderness, for the prosperity, happiness, and freedom, of all the subjects of this empire, however remote or separated. The amendment to the address was opposed, as bringing matters forward, which, for the present, formed no part of the business before parliament. If Ministers had neglected their duty; if they suffered themselves to be deceived; or if they misled parliament; these, or any of them, might be proper objects of enquiry at a suitable and convenient season. But this was neither the time, nor could those matters be the proper subject of the present address. The only question now before them, that was worthy of debate, was very simple in its nature, comprizable in a small compass, and easily decided. It was only, whether we chose to resign all the benefits which we derived from our colonies, all those fruits, to which our vast expenditure of blood and treasure in their nurture and defence, gave us a most legal and equitable right, and by truckling to the defiance and insult hurled at us by the Americans, cut off at once the sources of our power and opulence, and submit of consequence to a degradation from that rank which we now hold in the political system of mankind, or whether, by a full exertion of our power, whilst yet in strength and

vigour, we preserve all those advantages, assert our ancient glory, restore the supreme and indivisible authority of the British legislature, and bring our ungrateful and rebellious subjects to a due sense of their duty and dependence.

These, said they, are the great objects under the consideration of parliament. The declaration of independency has done away all other questions on the American subject. Taxation, legal rights, charters, and acts of navigation, are now no more. That whirlpool has swallowed them all within its vortex. It was only through the strength derived from her colonies, that this nation was enabled to hold a first place among the greatest powers in Europe. Take them away, and she sinks into nothing. Her very existence, as an independent nation, will be at stake. It is only now then to be determined, whether, without an effort, we shall submit ingloriously to inevitable ruin, or whether, by a vigorous exertion, we retain our usual power and splendor.

It was not, however, doubted, that, even independently of motives of interest and safety, the unparalleled baseness and ingratitude of the Americans, with the daring insolency of their conduct, would rouse the British spirit in such a manner, that it would take speedy and effectual measures for their chastisement. But, notwithstanding that the atrociousness of their crimes would nearly justify any severity of punishment, it was still wished, that when brought to a proper knowledge of their duty and condition, they should be treated with lenity; far from the insinuation held out in the amendment, of reducing them to a servile or abject submission.

Some of the young Lords were severe upon the factious spirit which prevailed here, as well as in America; attributing it to the former, that the latter had been brought into action. And it was infisted, that as the opposition had hitherto avowedly formed their conduct, upon an opinion, that the Americans had never designed, or even aimed at independency, and had reprobated every idea of that nature, with an abhorrence equal to that shewn on their side, they were now bound, in conformity with their own words and principles, to support, with the utmost vigour, those measures which were necessary for their reduction. That this was the ground of unanimity held out in the speech, and which had been treated with such ridicule and asperity, though no conclusion could be fairer drawn, whilst it was supposed they acted upon any line of consistency. That their unanimity now in support of government, was the smallest reparation which they could make to the nation, for the countenance they had unhappily given, and the share they consequently held in fomenting the present disturbances. And that it was to be hoped, they would now, by candidly confessing their error, convince the world they were only mistaken, and not intentionally wrong.

The ideas of despondency, which were held out on the other side, were said to be as chimerical, as the alarming representation of public affairs, to which they belonged, was unfounded. The happy success which had already attended our arms in America, afforded sufficient room for the strongest hopes, that the troubles there would be speedily terminated. That they would probably prove a source of happiness on all sides, as they would afford an opportunity for fixing the government of the colonies on a permanent basis, and finally settling all those questions which had hitherto been the cause of debate. That nothing was wanting to bring affairs to this wished-for crisis, but unanimity here, and vigour in America. That the ensuing campaign, supposing every obstacle which could take place, would undoubt-

edly be conclusive in its effect. And that in this state of things it could not be conceived, how any friend to the interests of this country, could wish to weaken the hands of government, or hesitate a moment in agreeing to the address, when the measures to which it was intended to give a sanction, were the only means to save the British empire from certain ruin and destruction.

The appearances of danger from foreign powers, were in part denied; in part palliated. It was said, that the strongest assurances of amity continued to be received from France; that the differences between Spain and Portugal were likely to be accommodated; and that our arming, induced other powers also to arm, from motives merely of prudence and caution. They also recurred to the old doctrine, that it being directly contrary to the interest, it could not be supposed consonant to the desire of France or Spain, that any powerful independent state should be established in America. Such an event must interfere with their commercial interests in both worlds; the idea of independence might become contagious, and spread to their own colonies; and they might be immediately endangered by the power and ambition of a new and rising state. If any sinister designs were, however, lurking, they had not escaped, they said, the penetrating eyes of our Ministers, who, by their present spirited preparation, had put it out of the power of any insidious rival, or enemy, to take us by surprize, or to convert the situation of our affairs to their advantage. A conduct replete with such wisdom, that it merited the warmest approbation, instead of captious enquiries, and a disposition to draw unfavourable conclusions.

The Minister took some pains in the House of Commons, to reconcile the apparent contradiction which had been alledged, between

the assurances of amity held out in the speech, and the present sudden armament. He avowed the passage and the measure by acknowledging his advice to both; and asserted, that the one was strictly true, and both perfectly consistent. It was not deemed prudent to rely so far upon any assurances, as to be off our guard; and as other powers were arming, it was determined we should be prepared for all events.

Such was the state of warfare between the two parties. The numbers in favour of ministry continued nearly as usual; but it was observed, that the spirit of the debate on their side visibly slackened. The addresses were not defended with the accustomed animation in either house. The great and almost uniform successes of the campaign, having produced no effect whatever towards a pacification, had somewhat damped the expectations which had been generally formed from a system of coercion. The armament in our ports announced more apprehensions from foreign powers, than were removed by the declarations, or the arguments, of the Ministers on the subject. A great and growing expence was foreseen. It was admitted, that the reduction of America was no longer to be considered as the work of a campaign.

On the other hand, though the advantages obtained in America had not produced all the effect that was expected by sanguine expectants, yet it appeared absurd to desert the pursuit of a great object in the very midst of victory. Besides, the declaration of independency seemed a great bar to accommodation. Without doors, it produced the full effect proposed by the speech, by adding greatly to the alienation of the people at large from the Americans, their cause, and their pretensions. Ministry certainly derived from thence no small degree of strength throughout the nation.

The question upon the amendment being put in the House of Commons, the motion was rejected by a majority of 242, to 87, being almost three to one. The main question being then brought forward, the original address was carried in nearly the same proportion, the numbers being 232, to 83.

The majority in the House of Lords was, as usual, still greater, the amendment being rejected by 91 Lords, including nine proxies, to 26 Lords only, who supported the motion upon a division. The proposed amendment was entered at full length as a protest, and signed by fourteen Peers.

Debates upon a proclamation issued in America by the Commissioners. Motion for a revisal of the American laws by Lord John Cavendish. Motion rejected by a great majority. Secession. Arguments urged for and against the propriety of a partial secession. 45,000 seamen voted. Debate on naval affairs. Supplies for the naval and the land service. Recess.

IN a few days after the presenting of the addresses, a declaration from Lord Howe and his brother, which had been issued in America soon after the taking of New York, addressed to the people at large of that continent, and calculated to induce separate bodies of them, independently of the Congress, to negociate with the Commissioners upon terms of conciliation, made its first appearance here in one of the common papers of the morning. It was remarked, that although the usual Gazette had been published the evening before, and an extraordinary one, giving an account of the taking of New York, on the preceding day, neither of these had taken any notice of this public instrument.

In this proclamation the Commissioners acquaint the Americans, with his Majesty's being graciously pleased to direct a revision of such of his royal instructions, as may be construed to lay an improper restraint upon the freedom of legislation in any of his colonies, and to concur in the revisal of all such acts, by which his subjects there may think themselves aggrieved. **Nov. 6th.** This piece being brought into the house by Lord John Cavendish, he seemed to consider it as a news-paper forgery, and, in that light, a most daring imposition upon the public; supposing, that if it had been authentic, its first public appearance must have been either on their own journals or in the Gazette. He therefore called upon the Ministers, to be satisfied as to the authenticity of the paper.

The Ministers acknowledged that such a proclamation had been published, and that they did not doubt but the paper now read was a true copy of it. The noble proposer expressed his astonishment both at the contents of the declaration, and the accidental manner in which a matter of that moment and nature came to the knowledge of the House. He observed, that in the whole course of the American business, the Ministers had treated parliament with a degree of indignity, and marks of contempt, which were not only before unknown, but which no credulity could have believed possible, whilst the shadow or name of the constitution remained, and the relative situation of Ministers in this country was remembered. They were, he said, in every instance treated merely as cyphers, excepting when they were used as the instruments in some odious work. When their name was wanted in such cases, they were called on, by way of requisition, to give a sanction to acts which rendered them abhorred by their fellow-subjects in every part of the empire. When these measures, through their own enormity,

failed in the execution, the odium was left to rest upon the head of parliament, whilst the crown and its ministers, assuming a moderation and lenity, which they find necessary, when experience has taught them the impracticability, and, perhaps, danger, of the design, become all at once the ostensible mediators between them and the people, undertaking to restrain their violence, or to rectify their injustice, and thus obtain the merit of whatever degree of grace it is then found proper to mete out, holding them still in the singular situation of being reprobated for all unpopular acts, and being neither thanked or considered for those which are kind or favourable.

Thus, in the present instance, Commissioners are sent out with an intention of carrying a certain act of parliament into execution, armed at the same time with certain parliamentary powers for restoring peace; these powers, having been narrowed to the Minister's taste, extend no farther than to the receiving of submissions, and the granting pardons. These, as might well be expected, are found utterly ineffective. When, lo! to their astonishment, as well as that of all others, parliament discover, by chance, through the medium of a common news-paper, that they are to undertake a revision of all those laws of their own making, by which they had aggrieved the Americans.

Yet, however disagreeable this treatment was to himself, and must be to every person who regarded the dignity of that House, or who reflected, that the constitution could subsist no longer, than while the different parts of the legislature were kept in due poize and proper balance, with respect to each other, as well as to the people at large, his Lordship said, that notwithstanding, he felt a dawn of joy break in upon his mind at the bare mention of reconciliation, whatever colour the measures might wear that led to so desireable an event. The great object of restoring peace and unity to this distracted empire, outweighed so far with him all other present considerations, that he not only would overlook punctilios upon that account, but even such matters of real import, as would upon any other occasion call all his powers into action.

Without any further observation then on the engagements entered into by the Ministers for parliament, he thought it highly necessary to embrace the opportunity of their being seized with so happy a disposition, and to give them all possible weight and assistance towards carrying it into effect, and bringing the present troubles to a speedy and happy termination. The sanction of parliament, he said, to their propositions, was absolutely necessary for this purpose. For the Ministers themselves were not less convinced than every other person, that they could not hold out any proposals to the Americans, however equitable in appearance, or even candid in fact, which the latter would not suspect of covering some treachery, and of being insidiously intended, by deceiving or dividing them, to deprive them by circumvention and fraud of those liberties, which they found force insufficient to destroy. In such circumstances of distrust, all attempts at negociation must be fruitless. The sanction of parliament will then come in happily to afford that confidence, without which no treaty can ever produce an amicable conclusion; so that if the Ministers are really serious and honest in their proposals, and are not playing that part which the Americans always charge and suspect them with, they will, instead of opposing, chearfully accept of that aid and support, which can alone give effect to this measure.

On these grounds his Lordship moved, that the House should resolve itself into a committee, to consider of the revisal of all acts of parliament, by which his Majesty's subjects in America think themselves aggrieved.

The Ministers denied, that there was any thing novel, any thing that bore the appearance of leading, or that carried any design of dictating to parliament, in the promise held out by the Commissioners. On the contrary, as it was founded on the great principle which had pervaded the conduct of administration from the beginning, so it was the language of parliament at the very outset. The great object of both, was the restoration of peace in America. The address of both Houses in February 1775, the bills which followed that address, the act of parliament under which the Commissioners acted, and their declaration, which is now held up as an object of offence, all tended to the same point. The parliament had delegated the authority now exercised, specifically in the act, and generally by the address. The leading object of the address, was a recommendation to his Majesty to hear and enquire into grievances, to transmit an account of them home, and to engage, on the part of the legislature, that where grievances really existed, they should be redressed. The proclamation goes no farther. Even without these sanctions, the King, as the head and mouth, both of the nation and legislature, would have been warranted in such an engagement, as a motive of encouragement, and ground of reconciliation. Should it be said, that no redress of grievances would be afforded? or that the King could not venture to engage for the other parts of the legislature in an act of justice, lest it should be construed into a violation of their rights?

The charges against the Ministers of endeavouring to keep this transaction secret, and of hiding their conduct from the knowledge and inspection of parliament, were said to be equally groundless. Could any intended or possible privacy be supposed, with respect to a public proclamation, which was posted for the inspection of all mankind upon the walls and houses of New York? The idea was absurd. The Ministers did not indeed think it of sufficient moment to be laid before parliament. It was as yet no treaty nor part of a treaty, it was barely a preliminary which might possibly lead to one. Had a negociation been even commenced, it would have been equally absurd and improper to communicate it to parliament during its progress, unless it was suspended at some point, upon which the intervention of parliament became necessary. Thus the negociation between Mr. Pitt and M. de Bussy [17] was not published during its pendency.

The motion was opposed upon many grounds. It was said, that it would discredit the Commissioners, and throw unexpected difficulties in the way of a negociation, which was probably already begun, and perhaps considerably advanced. It was now in their hands, in the common, natural, and regular course of business; why then undo whatever has been done, and disgrace the Commissioners, by taking it from them, without some sufficient motive? If it should be said, that the motion would not detract from the powers of the Commissioners, but, on the contrary, increase them; though the assertion is not admitted, yet other objections equally conclusive would lie against the measure even upon that ground. By giving them the sanction proposed by the motion, it would evidently appear, that they were not before armed with parliamentary powers sufficient to fulfil the professed objects of their commission; a circumstance which must naturally excite the jealousy of the Americans, and fill them with the most alarming doubts, as to their real views, and the true object of their mission. Besides, why should parliament run before the Commissioners in their concessions? Who knows but that the Americans would be satisfied with far less than we should here accord to them? By this premature bounty, we might defeat the endeavours of the Commissioners to obtain the most advantageous terms for the crown, the parliament, and the trading interest of this kingdom.

That to revise or repeal laws, under the idea of redressing the grievances of a people, who totally denied the authority of those laws, and who consequently could not be aggrieved by them, would be an absurdity of so superlative a degree, as could not fail exciting the ridicule of mankind. The Americans have declared themselves independent; what avails it to deliberate upon the concessions, which we are willing, or it is fitting for us to make, until we know whether any concession will bring them back to an acknowledgment of our authority? Shall we admit of their independency, by treating with them as sovereign states? or shall we subject ourselves to their contempt and derision, by debating upon the degree of authority which we shall exercise over those, who totally deny our right and power to exercise any?

In a word, said they, the question of independency must first be settled as a preliminary, before any treaty can be entered into, or any concession made. Let them give that up, and acknowledge our legislative authority, and then we shall willingly, and with propriety, form legislative regulations for their future ease and government. But whilst they persist in their claim of independency, and hurl defiance at us as sovereign states, no treaty can be thought of, and concessions would be as futile, as ridiculous and disgraceful. Upon the whole it was finally declared, that until the spirit of in-

dependency was effectually subdued, it would be idle to enter upon any revisions, or to pass any resolutions, as means of conciliation; and that the sword must be first taken out of the hands of the governing part of America, before that purpose could be accomplished. That the Congress did not at present govern America; but held it enthralled under the most cruel tyranny. That from our late successes, and the difference between the troops which composed the armies on either side, there was little room to doubt, that this arbitrary power would soon be dissolved, when the great body of the people, finding themselves emancipated from the cruel yoke of their leaders, and the charm by which they had been blindfolded and misled, being now at an end, they will return to their duty with as much rapidity, as they had before entered into the revolt. Then will be the time to think of legislative regulations for their future government, and to talk of lenity, forbearance, and even concession; at present, such ideas and such language are fruitless, if not worse.

The explanations given to reconcile the declaration of the Commissioners with the rights of parliament, and the respect due to that body, were by no means satisfactory to the other side. They first denied the fact on which the arguments of ministry were founded; namely " that the " promise of concurring in the " revisal of laws was a matter of " negociation." It was a power given previous to any treaty, either in progress, or even in commencement; and the refusal to do what was so promised, would, instead of forwarding, prevent any transaction of the kind. They laughed at the idea, of the Americans being satisfied with asking less than we should voluntarily grant, and the danger of our outdoing their demands by our con-

cessions. They said it was an evident mockery. The crown had promised in this proclamation something which without parliament it could not perform.

They insisted, that neither the address of 1775, nor any of the documents mentioned, came in any degree up to the matter in question. They extended no farther than to the receiving of complaints of grievances, and referring them to the consideration of parliament, that it might judge of their validity, and prescribe a remedy if necessary. But the promise in the declaration, if not a piece of hypocrisy held out merely to deceive and trepan the Americans, can mean nothing less, than an engagement on the side of the crown for the future conduct of parliament. Nay it goes farther, it engages that parliament shall act directly contrary to its own opinion, sentiments, and conduct, in a matter, on which it has repeatedly declared and confirmed them; for as the crown cannot possibly have any share in the revisal of laws, though it has on their being passed or repealed, the engagement can mean nothing else than the repeal of those acts, though all the world knows, that the house has constantly rejected every overture of that nature, with the highest disdain, and most determined perseverance.

Nor was the slight and contempt shewn to parliament less in any part of the American business. Though they granted the most unbounded supplies without account or enquiry, and lavished their constituents money with a profusion unknown in any other period, yet were they kept totally in the dark in all matters necessary for their knowledge, and only shewn at certain times so much light, as was sufficient to mislead them for some particular purpose. Thus, nothing is to be heard from ministers within these walls, but the heroic language of subjugation, unconditional submission, and a war of conquest. America is to be subdued; charters are to be modified or annihilated at pleasure; and an effective revenue is to be obtained, sufficient to render our own burthens quite easy. Whilst parliament is thus amused, and these doctrines secure an irresistible party, and the bulk of the people on this side of the water, the most moderate measures and fascinating promises are held out by the same ministers on the other side, and nothing is to be heard in America, but peace, conciliation, and parental tenderness. If a stragling fact finds its way into the house by the aid of a news-paper, we are at one time told that its notoriety rendered a communication of it unnecessary, as by only stepping to New York, any body might have read it there upon the walls of the burning houses; and at another, we are gravely informed, that as Mr. Pitt did not communicate some private conversation which passed between him and M. de Bussy, it would not be fitting to intrust parliament with the secrets contained in a public proclamation.

But nothing was so totally reprobated by opposition, or gave rise to so much asperity in the debate, as the doctrine of entering into no treaty or negociation with the Americans, until they had rescinded the declaration of independency. This was, they said, a doctrine founded in cruelty, and crying out for blood. It was telling them in express terms, that they must either surrender their arms, all the rights of freemen, and submit to any slavery which it was thought proper to impose on them, (for unconditional submission could mean nothing else,) or they must prepare to endure the utmost extremities of war, and to fight it out to the last man.

They asked upon what precedent this horrid doctrine was founded. Philip the IId of Spain, who was, in his day, considered as the most gloomy, cruel, and despotic tyrant in Christendom, when he was in the same circumstances with the Netherlanders, whom he had also forced to a declaration of independency, accommodated, notwithstanding, the extravagance of his pride, and the bitterness of his resentment, to a wiser, as well as more humane policy. He condescended to treat with those daring rebels, who by declaring themselves sovereign and independent, had thrown off all allegiance to him; he, by public edict, admitted their ships to enter his ports, and to depart in safety; he made proposals to these new states; and he finally and positively declared, that he would redress all their grievances. Our own histories, as well as those of other nations, both antient and modern, abound with such instances. What code of history or policy, then, have our ministers made the rule of their present conduct?

But, they said, that the Americans had been systematically and designedly driven to the present extremity. All the measures pursued for a succession of years, tended uniformly to that point. And finally, the commission for peace was kept back for seven months, until all possibility of its producing any effect was at an end, and the Americans, as had been well foreseen, were driven to their last resource of independency. All the bloodshed and devastation that has since taken, and that will hereafter take place, it was said, would lie at the door of the authors of that delay. This it was that laid the noble city of New York in ashes, that covered the plains with slaughter and desolation, and steeped the bayonets of foreign mercenaries in British blood.

And now having succeeded in urging them to desperation, to the uttermost degree of resistance, and to the last resort of independency, they bring these inevitable consequences of their own measures, as arguments to prove, that nothing but force, the violence of armies, and the extremities of war, can bring them to a reasonable and proper way of thinking and acting; that the sword is the only mode of reasoning with Americans; conquest the only means of rendering them free and happy; and Hessians and Highlanders the most skilful logicians, for enlightening their minds, and convincing their understanding.

Upon the whole they concluded, that if the house refused to concur in the proposed motion, it would afford a full conviction to the Americans, that the proposals held out by the Commissioners were indeed insidious and treacherous; that no reliance could for the future be placed, nor conditions of any sort safely entered into with government, as the latent pretence of a parliamentary negative, would always afford a sanction to the most shameful breach of contract and faith; and that all the world would thereby see with horror, that the different parts of the British government, had united in an odious confederacy, for the detestable purposes of destroying and exterminating, instead of governing their colonies.

The question being at length put, was rejected upon a division by a majority of 109, to 47 only who supported the motion.

From this time a great number of the minority, particularly of the Rockingham party, began to relax in their attendance upon parliament in either house; or rather to withdraw themselves wholly and avowedly upon all questions which related to America, and only to attend upon such matters of private bills or bufinefs, in which they had fome particular concern or intereft. This conduct was fo marked, that fome of the principal leaders of oppofition, after attending the Houfe of Commons in the morning upon private bufinefs, as foon as a public queftion was introduced, took a formal leave of the Speaker, and immediately withdrew. Though by this means a clear field was left to the minifters, and the vaft articles of fupply were carried without a debate; yet thefe filent votes, in the granting and difpofal of fuch immenfe fums of the national treafure, was by no means fo pleafant a circumftance, as might at firft fight be imagined; the trouble of being obliged to liften to the arguments of a minority, which was not fufficiently numerous to throw any real impediment in the way of bufinefs, and of undergoing occafionally the fatigue of a late evening, being abundantly compenfated by that fanction, which a decided majority afforded upon every queftion to their meafures. Whilft the paffing of fuch refolutions without debate or enquiry, feemed in fome degree to leave them open for future difcuffion.

This meafure of a fort of partial fecefsion, was juftified upon feveral grounds. They faid, that in the prefent ftate of things, all oppofition to the meafures of government, particularly with refpect to American affairs, was not only vain and fruitlefs, but from the overbearing and refiftlefs force, which fupported the minifters in every queftion, it became worfe; it became frivolous and contemptible. That it was too degrading to themfelves to be the continual inftruments of oppofing the ineffective weapons of reafon and argument, to the deaf infolence of an irrefiftable force, which had long fince determined upon its conduct, without the fmalleft regard to either.

That there was no fuch thing as faving a people againft their will. And that they had for a fuccefsion of years, repeatedly apprized and warned the nation, of the dangers attending thofe ruinous meafures which it was purfuing; and of the fatal precipice that muft terminate that mad career, in which they were blindly and defperately driven.

They faid, that by various arts, by fuccefsfully playing with their paffions, through the falfe ideas of domination and intereft which were held out to allure and deceive them, together with the infinite numbers who were interefted in the continuance of our public calamities, and the unbounded influence of the crown, which of late pervaded, almoft, every recefs, the people, who in the beginning were rather difinclined to thefe meafures, inftead of benefiting by counfel or taking heed by warning, had unhappily, in a very great degree, adopted the opinions and prejudices intended by thofe who were interefted in their delufion. That now, every meafure propofed, and every violence declared againft America, is confidered as a matter of courfe, to be in favour and fupport of Great Britain, whilft every attempt at curing or allaying our unhappy civil ferment, is ftigmatized as the offspring of faction, and as a traitorous dereliction of the rights and authority of the parent ftate. That good and bad fuccefs are equally urged and admitted as motives for a perfeverance in thofe meafures, which have already plunged the empire in civil war, diftraction, and ruin. That in fuch a ftate of affairs, and during the prevalence of fuch difpofitions, all ftruggles to oppofe, would rather inflame than leffen the diftemper of the public counfels. That as it was not the part of a wife man to ftrive with impoffibilities, fo neither was it

confiftent for thofe, who regarded their honeft fame beyond all other things, excepting their principles and honour, to draw upon themfelves the odium of their fellow citizens, by ineffectual efforts to ferve them. That they would therefore, preferving their principles ftill unfhaken, referve their activity for rational endeavours, when the prefent delirium might be fo far allayed, either with the people or with their minifters, as to afford fome room for its operating with advantage.

This example was not, however, followed, nor the conduct approved of, by feveral members of the oppofition. They even loudly blamed this proceeding. They queftioned, whether any member could, confiftently with his duty, withdraw himfelf individually from the bufinefs of parliament, merely from an opinion that he would be outvoted, and that his attendance would therefore be ufelefs. They acknowledged, that a fecefsion, collectively in a body, had not only the fanction of precedent, but might be practifed with great advantage, and be productive of much benefit in fuch cafes as the prefent. But for this purpofe, they faid, it muft be attended with the following circumftances. In the firft place, it muft be general, including the whole minority againft the meafure that provoked the fecefsion; and in the next, that it fhould not be a filent act; but that the motives for the fecefsion fhould be proclaimed, either by a remonftrance on the journals, or a public addrefs to the people. Under thefe circumftances, they faid, that fecefsion was not only juftifiable but laudable, and in cafes of imminent danger to the conftitution, might operate as a call to the nation, and awaken the people to a fenfe of their fituation.

The other and greater part of the minority denied, that any rule, but every man's prudence and opinion of his duty, could be prescribed on such an occasion. That though minority was a term used in ordinary speech; minorities were not corporate bodies, nor bound to act as such; nor could any precedents be of avail in matters of that nature. They had no way of compelling *unanimity*; and nothing but unanimity could make them act in the manner prescribed. The greater number could not decide. If a difference of opinion appeared, men must stand on their character, and their reasons for their conduct.

On this, as on many former occasions, the opposition discovered great dissension, and much personal and party dislike to each other; to the great strengthening of ministry; who though divided also amongst themselves, yet being involved in one official system, and supported by the crown, did not suffer so much by their discord. In this situation, a few of the minority rather increased their efforts.

* * *

Bill for granting letters of marque and reprisal, passed, with a small amendment in the title, by the Lords. Bill for securing persons charged with high treason, brought in by the Minister. Great debates upon the second reading. Question of commitment carried by a great majority. Amendment passed in the committee. Second amendment rejected. Debates renewed on receiving the report. Petition from the city of London against the bill. Amendment moved and agreed to. Second proposed clause of amendment rejected. Great debates on the third reading. Clause proposed by way of rider, is received with an amendment. Question upon the third reading carried upon a division. The bill passes the Lords without any amendment.

A Bill for enabling the Admiralty, to grant commissions, or letters of marque and reprisal, as they are usually called, to the owners or captains of private merchant ships, authorizing them to take and make prize of all vessels with their effects, belonging to any of the inhabitants of the thirteen specified revolted American colonies, was passed, without debate or opposition, in the House of Commons, soon after the recess. It did not cost much more trouble to the Lords, with whom it only underwent the trifling alteration, of inserting the words letters of *permission*, in the place of letters of *marque*, the latter being thought only applicable to reprisals on a foreign enemy.

Feb. 6. 1777.

On the same day, the Minister moved in the House of Commons, for leave to bring in a bill, to enable his Majesty to secure and detain, persons charged with, or suspected of, the crime of high treason committed in America, or on the high seas, or the crime of piracy. He prefaced the motion by observing, that during the present war in America, many prisoners had been made; who were in the actual commission of the crime of high treason; that there were others guilty of that crime, who might be taken, but who for want of sufficient evidence, could not at present be securely confined. That it had been customary in cases of rebellion, or danger of invasion from without, to enable the crown to seize suspected persons. That he would not, however, be thought to hint at any present necessity of entrusting Ministers with such a power in general; the times were happily different from those which called for such exertions in their utmost extent; neither rebellion at home, nor foreign war, were at present to be apprehended. For these reasons, it was not meant to ask the full power, usually obtained in former cases of rebellion. But as the law stood at present, it was not possible for government, officially, to apprehend the most suspected person. Another circumstance which required an immediate remedy was, that the crown had at present no means of confining rebel prisoners, or those taken in the crime of piracy on the high seas, but in the common gaols; a measure not only inconvenient but impracticable. In the present state of affairs it was absolutely necessary, that the crown should be enabled to confine prisoners under those descriptions, and to provide for their security, in the same manner that was practised with respect to other prisoners of war, until circumstances might make it adviseable to proceed criminally against them. Such, he said, were the purposes of the bill.

The bill was accordingly brought in and read on the ensuing day, and a motion made, that it should be read the second time on the 10th, which was the following Monday. It now appeared, that the enacting clause, rendered all persons taken in the act of high treason, committed in any of the colonies, or on the high seas, or in the act of piracy, or who are or shall be charged with or suspected of any of those crimes, liable to be committed to any common gaol, or to any other special place of confinement, appointed for that purpose under his Majesty's sign manual, within any part of his dominions, there to be detained in safe custody, without bail, mainprize, or trial, during the continuance of the law, with a provision, however, enabling a certain number of the Privy Council to grant an order, for admitting such persons to bail or trial.

Of the few minority members who were present, a gentleman of [20] the first eminence in his profession, and who, a few years since, filled the second law office under the crown with the greatest reputation, expressed the utmost astonishment, that a matter of such magnitude and importance, a bill that struck directly at that great palladium of the British constitution, and only security to the rights and liberties of the people, the habeas corpus law, should be brought in without proper notice, at a season when the House was so badly attended, and an attempt made to precipitate its passage in so extraordinary a manner, as to propose the second reading within three or four days of its being first heard of. He said, besides the defect in point of notice, it had been brought in unfairly; as it was totally different from what the Minister had announced it to be on the preceding day. Nor was it less discordant in its own parts, neither the title nor the preamble affording any idea of the extraordinary matter contained in the enacting clauses. That he was equally shocked and alarmed, to see a bill which was to suspend all the functions of the constitution, brought in under such circumstances, and attempted to be smuggled through a thin house under false colours, before the nation could be apprized of its danger, or their constituents have the smallest notice, that they were going to surrender the foundation of all their other rights, and the peculiar characteristic of the British liberty and government. Mr. Dunning, who made these exceptions, seeing the House then going to divide upon the question for the second reading, which he knew would be carried, moved to have the bill printed, which, being agreed to, prevented the division.

The alarm excited by this bill, recalled a few of those gentlemen who had of late absented themselves from the House. The debates became long, animated, and highly interesting, and were not unfrequently intermixed with the severest animadversion.

The opposition in the first place contended, that, upon the Minister's own premises, the bill was entirely needless; for as we were neither involved in a rebellion at home, nor engaged in a war without, there could be no legitimate reason for investing the crown with so dangerous a power. Even a foreign war, of whatever magnitude, could not justify such a measure, unless there were some valid reasons for supposing, that an invasion would be encouraged and supported by some powerful internal faction. It was a measure only to be adopted in cases of the greatest emergency, when the constitution and liberties of the people were at stake, and every thing must be hazarded for their preservation. Dictatorial power, was an edged tool not to be played with. The crown had already swelled so far in power and influence, beyond those limits which were assigned to it at the revolution, as to afford too much room for serious reflection, to every serious man and lover of his country. In this situation of things, there could be neither reason nor prudence, in lifting it up at once beyond all law and restraint. The war against the Americans was, perhaps unfortunately for this country, popular; a circumstance which removed every colour of pretence for a measure of this nature. And the power of drawing out the militia without the concurrence of parliament, together with the immense force by sea and land, and the unbounded supplies of money, with which the Ministers were entrusted, were fully sufficient for the strength and security, for all the fair and honest purposes of government.

With respect to its effect on America, they said, that its operation would render the present unhappy animosities between the English of these islands and that continent implacable, and not only cut off the hope, but the possibility of any future reconciliation; that under the colour of retaliation, it would excite, or afford, an opportunity for the exercise of the greatest personal injuries, and the most horrible cruelties, on both sides.

That its present injustice was as glaring, as its future effect would be cruel and unhappy. For that letting the question lie dormant, though they by no means gave it up, as to the justice or propriety of considering or treating as pirates, those Americans who were taken in arms, or carrying on war against our commerce upon the high seas, it was capable of reaching persons of so different a character, that all mankind must agree in condemning its injustice. This bill, they said, would, or might, be extended to others, besides those who made or intended reprisals; it might, for any thing that appeared, be extended to the captain and crew of the peaceable merchantman, who unable to live by any other means than those to which they were bred, are conveying a cargo of the commodities of their native country to a market. These under other laws might possibly be considered as smugglers; but it will remain for this to punish them as pirates.

This bill, they said, was not, however, calculated for the meridian of America; its operation was intended much nearer home. The Ministers, daring, headlong, violent, and arbitrary, as they were, had not yet courage to take off the mask, and openly to strike the fatal blow which they intended. They were still afraid, without the pretext of foreign or domestic war, to avow their designs in the face of day, by a total suspension of the habeas corpus law. How do they act in this nicety of situation?

They patch the lion's hide with the fox's skin, and endeavour to supply the deficiency of courage with cunning. They bring in surreptitiously, under a false title, and introduce, under a delusive preamble, a dark, perplexed, ambiguous, and insidious bill, which holds out sufficient ostensible matter to keep Englishmen agape, with tales of high seas, Americans, and piracies, whilst they are, in the mean time, cutting through their liberties, and stabbing the constitution of their country to the vitals.

In the same view of deception, said they, upon this first trial of their strength in so new and dangerous a measure, they limit the duration of the bill to one year, as an experiment; but who does not see, that the same fatal influence, which will now grant a dictatorial power without the colour of a necessary motive, will render it permanent without the trouble of a pretext. In the mean time, the public are to be hoodwinked and deluded under the false covering of a law to punish the rebellious Americans, a matter about which they are so perfectly indifferent, that very few of them will even take the trouble of reading the bill, at the same time that it will draw every subject of this country, residing either in the East or the West Indies, in the unoffending provinces of America, on the coasts of Africa, and all that immense body of the people who in any manner use the seas, within its perilous vortex. Nor will those be safer, who for health, business, or pleasure, cross the channel between Dover and Calais, nor the multitudes who continually pass and repass between England and Ireland. A fishing party, who go out for pleasure in the summer, will be put out of the protection of the laws, and in fact proscribed, as soon as they have passed low water mark.

Nor let the midland Englishman, who never saw the sea, triumph in his security. He may soon experience, to his cost, how far the dexterity and ingenuity of the crown lawyers may extend the yielding texture of this ambiguous bill to his enthralment. The wide circuit of the human mind is not more various and extensive than the suspicious nature of man, nor more fertile than the principle of revenge and ambition, which leads to private ill and public oppression. This secure and unoffending Englishman may find himself suddenly seized, carried off without warning from his family, transported to the Highlands of Scotland, the rock of Gibraltar, the burning coasts of Africa, the most pestilential and loathsome dungeon in the putrid marshes of Bengal, or to any other part of this wide extended empire, in which it is thought fitting to institute prisons by the sign manual. There he may continue to languish during the term of this bill, without a possibility of legal succour, and cut off from the advice and assistance of his nearest friends. When the act expires, indeed, if it is not renewed, and that the unhappy sufferer has still preserved life, through the horrors of captivity, and the stench of his dungeon, he may again return to his native country. He may then, perhaps, be tempted to enquire what he was confined and banished for; the answer is ready, " for treason:" as he is conscious of his innocence, he will endeavour to throw himself upon the laws of his country for justice, and challenge his accusers to the proof, and to make good their charge; but the ministerial agent, by whom he was kidnapped, will laugh in his face, and tell him there was no charge against him, but he was suspected; and, producing this act of parliament, it will be an effectual plea in bar of every remedy he can seek.

Such are the terrors, and the real dangers, said they, which this bill will hold out to every subject of this realm. For as a bare suspicion of treason will be sufficient for all the dreadful consequences that are mentioned, no rank or order of men can be exempt from them. The first subjects, and most eminent citizens, may become victims to the immediate jealousy, rancour, or arbitrary caprice, of the presiding ministers. Their deputies, in their several gradations, down to the lowest understrapper in office, will take in the other classes of mankind. Neither distance nor obscurity will be a protection. There is no man so unknown, or place so remote, in which some private enemy may not disturb his repose, or where some busy, ignorant, or profligate magistrate, may not conceive his duty concerned, feel his vanity tickled, or, perhaps, find a gratification of the most infamous passions, in the indulgence of an unfounded, or the prosecution of a pretended, suspicion. Poverty and obscurity, which usually afforded shelter to the humble and the weak in the tempests of states, will only render the doom of the unhappy culprit irrevocable. No body needs to be informed, that hundreds of unfortunate men linger out their miserable lives in the state prisons of arbitrary countries, merely because they are forgotten, though the system of government under which they originally suffered no longer exists, and those acts for which they were then punished, might now perhaps be deemed meritorious.

This bill besides creates a new order of punishments, unknown before in our penal laws, and endues the crown with powers which it could not obtain by a total suspension of the habeas corpus law, and which it did not possess before its formation. A power of banishment to any part of the globe, attended with circumstances which include the most bloody species of proscription, may be expected in a little time to form one of the standing prerogatives of the crown.

They said it would be idle and absurd to oppose such a bill upon legal grounds, or to bring it to any test of legal enquiry; for where there was neither reason nor justice, there could be no law. Law supposes a rule, prescribes a duty, respecting either the public or individuals; it points out the transgression, defines the offence, annexes the punishment, and specially provides and directs all the intermediate step between the charge and conviction; but more particularly the measure and quantity of the punishment. Now if this bill is examined, it will be found deficient in every one of these requisites. No crime is described; no enquiry into innocence or criminality takes place. The punishment is inflicted in the first instance, and examination is to follow. Suspicion supplies the place of evidence. Any man may be suspected; but his guilt or innocence are entirely out of the question; his punishment is to continue, and no enquiry to be made into either during the existence of the present bill. Such is this thing, which is to be called a law; which enacts punishments without examination or trial; combines their duration with its own existence; and cuts off all possible means of redress.

They said, that this bill served as a kind of key, or index, to the designs which ministers had for some years been manifestly forming, the objects of which they rendered visible from time to time, as opportunity served, as circumstances proved favourable, as influence increased, and power strengthened. A gentleman, equally celebrated for his wit and his eloquence, compared it to the first [21] scene of the last act of a play, when some important transaction or circumstance, affecting the principal personages in the drama, is revealed to the audience, which besides unravelling those mysteries contained in the former acts, opens at once the whole extent of the author's plot, or design, and leads directly to the catastrophe. This plan, they said, had been long observable to those who took the trouble of marking and comparing the different parts that appeared, and preserving the connection between them; and however covertly hid, or artfully held back out of sight, had been systematically adopted, and steadily pursued; it was nothing less than robbing America of her franchises, as a previous step to the introduction of the same system of government into this country.

Such were the colours, in which the nature, tendency, and design, of this bill were described by the opposition. On the other side it was said that nothing less than a malignity of disposition, which led to the most groundless and unwarrantable suspicions, a perverse and captious temper, disposed to quarrel, without distinction, with all the measures of government, and a determination to impede all its acts, however salutary or necessary, or else the most factious and dangerous motives, could have given birth to the suggestion, that this bill meant or intended any thing farther, than what it fairly imported, a power to apprehend, commit, and imprison, persons actually guilty of treasonable offences committed in America, on the high seas, or of the crime of piracy. That it was not less absurd and preposterous than malignant, to suppose it was framed intentionally to reach or overtake persons guilty, or presumed to be guilty, of offences committed within the realm. That if government suspected any part or body of the people at home, of a disposition which tended to acts of that dangerous nature supposed by the bill, their application would have been fair, open, and direct; they would have accompanied the request with their motives for making it; they would have come to parliament, and desired a suspension of the Habeas Corpus Act, in so many words, stating at the same time, what should ever accompany such a requisition, the ground of necessity upon which it was made. No parliament ever refused to comply with such a request in such circumstances; much less could such a refusal be apprehended at the present time, if administration be really in possession of that overruling influence, and dangerous power, which have been magnified into such terrific forms by the opposition.

The present bill, they said, was framed upon the most wise, humane, and equitable principles. It was calculated more to prevent mischief, than to inflict punishment, much less to establish persecution. The innocent man had nothing to fear; but it was equally consistent with right policy and humanity, to hold out terrors to the guilty. And whatever harsh epithets had been applied by the other side to the bill, or to its framers, that government must ever be considered as the wisest, most humane, and most equitable, which directs its attention to devise means for the prevention of crimes, instead of endeavouring to deter men from a violation of the laws by rigorous and sanguinary punishments.

But supposing the bill should have the operation that was attributed to it within the realm, what colourable objection could lie to it even upon that ground? It would still create no new power, however it might declare an old one. Several acts are declared by the statutes to be high treason. Others come within the class of constructive treasons, which are not explicitly defined by any statute; many of which are however established by precedents, and the judgment of the courts. If it should then appear that any persons in this country had unlawfully corresponded with the rebels in America, had supplied them with money, arms, implements of war, or intelligence, it is very possible that such acts might bring them within some of those descriptions of high treason, which are laid down by the statutes, or founded upon them. In such case, there is no treason constructed by this bill; it only enables the crown to secure the persons of such dangerous offenders, with greater expedition and effect, than it could have done in the common course of legal proceedings. Will this then be considered as a rational ground of objection to the bill? Or will it be contended, that a man's residence within the kingdom, affords him an impunity for all acts of treason he may chuse to commit? If there were any such men in this country, it would be a sufficient motive, exclusive of any other, for passing the bill. But they still asserted, that this country contained no such description of men; that treason and rebellion were properly and peculiarly the native growth of America; and that the bill could only operate on its proper objects.

The Ministers urged, in the strongest terms, the necessity there was for strengthening the hands of government at this critical period. They said it would be impossible to carry on public business, without delegating powers to the crown upon extraordinary occasions, which would not be proper, because they would not be wanted, in ordinary cases. Parliament were the proper judges, when, and to whom, to entrust such extraordinary powers. If necessity was a good ground for granting them, that necessity most apparently and incontrovertibly existed at present. The present situation of affairs rendered it necessary for government to call for

every assistance, which it was in the power of parliament to delegate or create. If parliament had not a confidence in the ministers, it was in vain for them to endeavour to conduct the public business. If it had a proper confidence in the crown and its ministers, it was in the last degree of absurdity to mix it with idle fears and ill-founded suspicions.

They concluded, that the whole weight of the objections made to the entrusting of the crown with the power demanded, depended upon the supposition of its being applied to evil and dangerous purposes. That this conclusion was unfair and unfounded; equally false in reason and argument. It It would be as logical, and more consonant to reason and experience, to suppose that this power would be only used with the strictest propriety. Parliament was the great constitutional check on all power. If the powers delegated at present, should in any degree be abused, that will hereafter afford a most proper subject of parliamentary enquiry, and its vengeance will hang over those offenders who dared to violate their trust. But sure it is an extraordinary mode of reasoning, to argue against the use, from the possible abuse of the bill.

Notwithstanding the vigour of opposition, the division upon the question of Feb. 10th. commitment, after the second reading, sufficiently exposed its weakness in point of number; the bill being committed for the following Thursday, by a majority of 195 to 43.

Upon the day appointed, a gentleman in office informed the committee, that having observed in the late debate, that the special power of appointing places of confinement, under the sign manual, in any part of his Majesty's dominions, had been much urged in argument, and created apprehensions, that persons taken into custody within the realm, were liable

to be sent beyond sea, to distant places of confinement; and that his Majesty's servants having no such idea in contemplation, and though they were convinced the clause in its present state did not admit of that interpretation, were, however, willing to give every reasonable satisfaction to those who thought otherwise, and would therefore obviate and remove the doubts which arose upon that construction. That he understood this was the only solid ground of objection which could be taken against the bill, and that, in order to render the bill palatable, and unobjectionable to all parties, he would move, that the words " in any part of his Majesty's dominions," should be left out, and that the words " within the realm," should be inserted in their place.

This concession was far from satisfying the opposition. They said, that the power of indiscriminate banishment, however hideous, was only a matter of secondary consideration; that the power of apprehending and confining the person of the subject, upon bare suspicion, without a pretext of any legal cause, was the great object of alarm and danger, and what could alone afford life and activity to the other. They contended, that a line should be drawn between the innocent and the guilty; that the degree of probability attending the suspicion, and the degree of guilt, upon which the suspicion was founded, should be defined so clearly, that the innocent might know when they were in a state of security, and by what error or trespass it might be forfeited; and that a mode of redress should be provided, in cases where the powers granted by the bill were manifestly or grossly abused. And that upon every idea of justice and equity, a distinction should be made, even with respect to the Americans, between those persons who were in actual arms, and such as only submitted to the respective governments in which they resided, and to an authority which they were unable to resist.

But, in the name of goodness, said they, if the intentions of the ministers are as pure and as innocent as they profess, why do they refuse to confine the operation of this bill to its proper object? Why extend it to Great-Britain? If such powers are necessary in America, let them be created; but let their direction be fixed. If they are wanted in this country, what are they mincing the matter for, and making a secret of it to parliament? Let them, in their own manner, make the demand in so many words; let them, by their own rule of conduct, state the necessity for so doing; and when this is done, to the satisfaction of parliament, let them obtain the power in the most ample and comprehensive manner they can desire. But to disclaim the intention of seeking the power, and at the same time endeavour by specious and delusive pretences to obtain it, carried such an appearance of duplicity, imposition, and contempt of that assembly, as was not to be paralleled in any former transaction between ministers and parliament.

The ministers still insisted upon the purity of their intention; that the present amendment removed all manner of ambiguity from the bill, and must afford satisfaction to any thing less than a fixed determination to find fault in all events, and to oppose indiscriminately in all cases. The title of the bill, its preamble, and the occasion of bringing it in, all served to fix its locality, and as explanations of its true import and design. These would effectually prevent or clear up any possible misconstruction of the enacting clauses.

A gentleman in opposition, said [23] he would put administration to a test, as to the sincerity of their professions, and the innocency of intention in the bill. If these were real, they could have no objection to the amendment he was going to propose, which only tended to limit the operation of the bill to its avowed objects. He accordingly moved for a clause of amendment, to specify that the offence for which any person was apprehended, on suspicion or otherwise, " within the kingdom," must have been stated, to be committed within the kingdom, and not elsewhere.

In the mean time, a gentleman of considerable rank in judicial [24] proceedings, though not one of those who are immediately considered as the crown lawyers, dissented totally from the opinion held out by his brethren in office. He acknowledged, that the bill was manifestly at variance with the title and preamble; that the first held out only a power to the crown of apprehending and committing, upon grounds of suspicion, such persons as are described in the preamble, who have been, or may be, brought into this kingdom; but the enacting part, not only gives that power, but it grants a general power, of taking all persons up without any specification of crime whatever. That it was absurd to say, that the locality of the crime was marked out by the bill. Where was the redress provided? There was no redress, but by an application to the privy council, who were now to be invested with the powers belonging to the courts of common law. But the mischief would be done, in the first instance, previous to any such application, and the Habeas Corpus Act, would be in fact suspended, to all its intents and purposes, within the realm, for crimes not pretended to have been committed within it. He was therefore clearly of opinion, that it was better to suspend the Habeas Corpus at once; because in that case, every man would know what he had to depend on, and every good subject would acquiesce in a power, created for the public benefit.

So unexpected a difference of opinion, in such a quarter, and so powerful a confirmation of the objections laid by their antagonists, coming from such an authority, could not fail to surprize, if not to stagger the ministers, and must, at another season, have proved fatal to the bill. The critical situation of public affairs, and the necessity of strengthening government, were, however, brought to the support of the measure in this exigency, and the last proposed clause of the amendment was rejected upon a [25] division, by a majority of five to one, the numbers being 125, to 25 only, who supported the motion.

This defeat did not prevent the debate from being renewed with equal if not greater vigour on the following day, when Feb. 14th. the report was received by the house from the committee. A petition strongly opposing the bill, was also received from the city of London on the same day. They concluded this petition with a declaration, That measures so violent and unconstitutional; so subversive of the sacred and fundamental rights of the people, and subjecting them to the most cruel subjection and bondage, would, in the judgment of the petitioners, be introductive of every species of mischief and confusion; and thereby precipitate the impending ruin of this country.

In this debate, a gentleman in opposition moved for a clause of [26] amendment, That nothing should be deemed piracy within the true meaning and legal construction of the act, but acts of felony committed on the ships or goods of the subject on the high seas. This amendment was the more particularly contended for, as by some of the former statutes of piracy, the trading or corresponding with pirates was ordained to be felony without the benefit of clergy; and it was apprehended, that persons who had innocently traded with the Americans, might, by construction of law, and coupling their meaning with the present bill, have been subjected to the penalties of these statutes. The statute 9 George I. chap. 24. was accordingly called for and read, to shew that the ground of jealousy was fairly stated, and the inference clearly made out.[27]

The first appearance of a disposition to relax in any degree with respect to the bill, or to assent to the justice of any objections that were made to it, was upon this occasion shewn by the minister. He disclaimed for himself, and for the framers and supporters of the bill in general every intention of wrong, oppression, and injustice, and the smallest design of extending its operation beyond its avowed objects, and therefore agreed to the amendment with the utmost chearfulness, hoping thereby to remove every possible ground of jealousy.

This success, and the appearance of flexibility which attended it, encouraged the framer of the amendment to propose another of still more general importance, tending to remove the great objects of alarm and contention; the general power of commitment, and the operation of the bill in this country. For this purpose he moved, That no person shall be secured or detained, under, or by virtue of this act, for high treason, or suspicion of high treason, unless such person shall be charged to have been locally resident in his Majesty's said colonies and plantations in North America, at the time he shall be charged with, or suspected of committing high treason.

Besides such of those arguments which we have already stated, as applied particularly to the subject of the motion, it was further supported on the following grounds. That the power of general commitment had a most dark and dangerous aspect. That as the bill stood at present, every man in the kingdom was liable to be deprived of his liberty under the pretence of treason committed in America, although he had never been out of his own county or parish. That it was absurd and preposterous to continue the bill under its present title, which related to America only, when by construction of law it was meant to include Great Britain. That in reason and fact, a person never out of England, could not be guilty of high treason committed in America; if not, but that it is supposed he may be guilty of that crime in this country, why not hold that language in the bill, and add to the title, the words " or in Great-Britain?" And they contended, that the ministers could not do less in conformity with their own professions, if they were really sincere in them, than to grant the security required, by a compliance with the present motion.

On the other side, several cases were quoted, in which, by construction of law, charges of treason laid to be committed in one place, though they were afterwards proved to be committed in another, were notwithstanding admitted as valid; and they contended, that though an offence might be committed here, by a person who had never been out of the kingdom, yet its operation in America, would constitute one complete offence. The fact might not be criminal, in the first instance, and might become criminal afterwards from its consequences, and yet, by a fair and justifiable construction of law, be deemed one compleat act. They concluded, that the proposed clause would destroy one of the main purposes of the bill; and that it would not afford any protection to the innocent, although it might effectually screen the guilty. The motion was accordingly rejected upon a division, by a majority of 49 to 14.

Though all the grounds of argument seemed exhausted on both sides, in the long and frequent contention which attended this bill in every part of its progress, and that the spirit of the disputants might, by this time, have been well deemed in the same situation, yet the vigour of the combatants seemed to grow with the toil, and the third reading, produced one of the longest, most interesting, and most animated debates, that has been known.

Feb. 17th.

Mr. Dunning, who first laid open the principle and tendency of the bill, and had since been indefatigable, both in his general opposition, and his endeavours to disarm it of some of those powers which he considered as the most dangerous, not discouraged by the rejection of Mr. Powys's last clause of amendment on the second reading, proposed another, nearly similar, to be added to the bill by way of rider. He introduced the amendment with a speech fraught with legal and professional knowledge, in which, with his usual ability, he went through and examined the whole course of controversy on both sides, and having combated the arguments which had been used in support of the bill, and pointed out the evil consequences to be apprehended in its present state, moved an additional clause to the following purport : Provided also, and be it hereby declared, that nothing herein contained is intended, or shall be construed, to extend to the case of any other prisoner, or prisoners, than such, as have been in some one of the colonies before-mentioned, or on the high seas, at the time or times of the offence or offences, wherewith he or they shall be charged.[28]

A gentleman, who sat not far from the Minister on the treasury bench, agreed to receive the clause in part, if the mover would admit an amendment of his own to be interwoven with, and added to it; viz. that the words, "In some one of the colonies, or on the high seas," should be left out, and the words, "Out of the realm," inserted in their room; and that the following words, "Or of which they shall be suspected," should be added to, and conclude the original clause.

If this amendment did not afford all that was wished, the acceptance of the clause, even in its present form, was, however, an object of great consequence with the minority, who now considered the bill as having nearly lost two of its most dangerous fangs; the last, though not entirely drawn, being now tolerably blunted. But this concession was far from being pleasing to that part of the majority, who had at all times been eager in the pursuit of the most violent measures against America, and who were also supposed, to be much disposed to the support or establishment of a strong government at home.

Whilst some of the gentlemen under this description were reprobating the clause, and contending that the bill, even in its original state, did not convey all the powers, with which it was necessary to arm the crown in the present situation of affairs, they discovered, to their unspeakable astonishment, that the minister had totally changed his tone upon that subject. He now exculpated himself in particular, and administration in general, from every intention of establishing any unconstitutional precedents, or of seeking or wishing any powers to be entrusted either to the crown or to themselves, which were capable of being employed to bad or oppressive purposes; disavowed all design of extending the operation of the bill beyond its open and avowed objects; said it was intended for America, not for

Great Britain; that as he would ask for no power that was not wanted, so he would scorn to receive it by any covert means; and whilst he expressed his concern for the jealousy excited by any ambiguity that appeared in the bill, hoped that the present amended clause would afford full satisfaction to the gentlemen on the other side of the house, and that the law would now meet with the approbation of all parties.

This unexpected conduct caused great dissatisfaction on his own side. Those who had been the avowed supporters of the bill, thought themselves particularly ill treated. They were engaged in a very unpopular, and what might have turned out a very odious business, and after they had worked through it with unusual toil, and encountered no small share of obloquy by the way, they were deserted at the very instant of completion, and that in such a manner, as seemed calculated merely to disgrace the whole measure, to confirm all the charges and surmises of their adversaries, and to fix all the odium upon them.

It was, however, observed before, that the court parties were far from being united; that administration did not draw kindly together; that the crown lawyers did not agree; these circumstances occasioned the humorous observation of a gentleman in the[29] minority, that administration were as much at variance, as the title, preamble, and body of the bill.

Though the amended clause was much opposed in debate, it was, however, at length received without a division. The minority could not now conceal their joy and triumph. A gentleman eminent for his eloquence and abilities,[30] felicitated the house and the nation, on the escape they had from, at least a temporary state of tyranny, and which was per-

haps intended, in good time, to have been rendered perpetual. He congratulated the minority, who notwithstanding their weakness in number, had accomplished that happy event, by their correction of so reprehensible and dangerous a bill; though a minority, the ministers were not only convinced, but ashamed, and had accepted of their alteration. The noble Lord at the head of affairs, he said, was obliged to the minority alone, for digesting, altering, and correcting his bill; neither he nor the nation, owed any obligation to his numerous friends the majority, who were ready to swallow it, with all its original crudities, errors, injustice, and cruelty.

Their gaining this favourite point, did not prevent their still continuing to combat, though more faintly, the principle of the bill, and carrying their opposition, after a long and late debate, to a division upon the question of the third reading, which was carried against them by a majority of 112 to 35. The main question being then put, that the bill do pass, it was carried without a division.

The bill passed the Lords without debate or amendment; the minority peers having so generally absented themselves from that house, that the Earl of Abingdon found himself alone in entering a protest against it.[31]

• • •

State of affairs at New-York previous to the opening of the campaign. Loyal provincials embodied, and placed under the command of Governor Tryon. Expedition to Peek's Kill. To Danbury, under General Tryon. Magazines destroyed. General Wooster killed. Vessels and provisions destroyed at Sagg Harbour, by a detachment from Connecticut under Colonel Meigs. Advantages derived by General Washington, from the detention of the army at New-York through the want of tents. Different schemes suggested for conducting the operations of the campaign, all tending to one object. General Sir William Howe takes the field; fails in his attempts to bring Washington to an action; retires to Amboy. Turns suddenly and advances upon the enemy. Skirmishes. Americans under Lord Sterling defeated. Washington regains his strong camp. Royal army pass over to Staten-Island. Alarm excited by the preparations for the grand expedition. General Prescot carried off from Rhode-Island. Rate of interest upon the public loan, advanced by the Congress. Monuments decreed for the Generals Warren and Mercer. Fleet and army depart from Sandy Hook. Force embarked on the expedition. Congress and Washington alarmed by the loss of Ticonderoga. Fleet arrives at the River Elk, after a tedious voyage, and difficult passage up Chesapeak Bay. Army lands at Elk Ferry. Declaration issued by the General. Washington returns to the defence of Philadelphia. Advances to the Brandywine, and to Red-Clay Creek. Various movements on both sides. Action at the Brandywine. General Knyphausen makes an attack at Chad's Ford. Lord Cornwallis marches round to the forks of the Brandywine, where he passes, in order to attack the enemy's right. Defeats General Sullivan. Pursues his advantages until stopped by night. General Knyphausen passes at Chad's Ford. Enemy, every where defeated. Loss on both sides. Reflections on the action. Victory not decisive. Foreign officers in the American service. Motions of the armies. Engagement prevented by a great fall of rain. Major-General Grey, surprizes and defeats a party of Americans under General Wayne. Royal army passes the Schuylkill, and advances to German-Town. Lord Cornwallis takes possession of Philadelphia. Some of the principal inhabitants sent prisoners to Virginia, upon the approach of the army. Attack on the new batteries at Philadelphia. Delaware frigate taken. Works constructed by the Americans to render the passage of the Delaware impracticable. Successful expedition to Billing's Fort, and a passage made through the lower barrier. Royal army surprized and attacked by the Americans at German-Town. Americans repulsed with loss and pursued. Brigadier-General Agnew, and Colonel Bird killed. Army removes to Philadelphia. Unsuccessful attack upon the enemy's works on the Delaware. Hessians repulsed with great loss at Red Bank. Colonel Donop killed. Augusta man of war and Merlin sloop destroyed. New and effectual measures taken for forcing the enemy's works. Mud Island, and Red Bank, abandoned, and taken with their artillery and stores. Americans burn their gallies and other shipping. Passage of the Delaware opened to Philadelphia. General Sir William Howe, finding all his efforts to bring Washington to a general action fruitless, returns with the army to Philadelphia. Americans hut their camp at Valley Forge for the winter.

WE have already shewn the state and situation of the armies in America during the winter and greater part of the spring. As the season opened, and enlarged the field of enterprize, our commanders did not neglect seizing those advantages which nature and their naval superiority presented, in a country deeply intersected by navigable rivers, and continually laid open in other parts by the numberless inlets and channels, which the peculiar construction of the islands and coasts, admit in their junction with the ocean and those rivers.

In the mean time a considerable body of provincial troops was formed under the auspices of General Sir William Howe, which by degrees amounted to several thousand men, and which under that denomination included, not only American, but British and Irish refugees from the different parts of the continent. This corps was entirely officered, either by those gentlemen, who for their attachment to the royal cause had been obliged to abandon their respective provinces, or by those who lived under that protection in the New-York islands. The new troops were placed for the temporary time of their service, upon the same footing as to pay, subsistence, and clothing, with the established national bodies of the royal army, with the further advantage to the private men and non-commissioned officers, that they were entitled to considerable allotments of vacant lands at the end of the troubles. This measure, besides its utility in point of strength, afforded some present provision to those, who having lost every thing in this unhappy contest, were now thrown upon the crown, as their only refuge, for support; whilst on the other side, instead of their being an heavy and unprofitable burden to the crown, they were placed in a condition which enabled them to become active and useful instruments in effecting its purposes. At the same time, this acquisition of strength, derived from, and growing in the country, carried a most flattering appearance, and seemed to indicate resources for the prosecution of the war in the very theatre of action.

As all new forces must of course be much fitter for defence, than for active service in the field, so it added much to the apparent utility of this measure, that the royal provincials could immediately be disposed of to the greatest advantage, in the protection and defence of New-York and the adjacent islands, supplying thereby the place of veteran troops, and affording a free scope to the distant operations of the grand army. To render this defensive system for the islands more complete, Governor Tryon, who already in his civil capacity commanded the militia, and who had taken the utmost pains in its establishment, was now placed by the commander in chief at the head of the new corps, under the title and rank of Major-General of the provincials, whereby he was enabled effectually to combine and bring into action the joint force of these separate bodies.

The great natural strength of the country, the vicinity of the North River, with its convenience in respect to the seat of war, had induced the Americans, during the winter, to erect mills and establish their principal magazines, in that rough and mountainous tract called the Manor of Courtland. Thus it became their grand repository, and trusting in the security of this natural citadel, neither industry was lacking, nor expence spared, in abundantly providing it with immense supplies of provisions, forage, and stores, of all sorts. A place, otherwise of no importance, called Peek's Kill, which lies about fifty miles up the North River from New-York, served as a kind of port to Courtland Manor, by which it both received provisions, and dispensed supplies.

Sir William Howe was well aware of these circumstances in general, and was as well convinced of the decisive consequences which must ensue from the cutting off those resources, which the enemy had with such infinite labour and expence accumulated for the support and prosecution of the war.

A general attempt upon Courtland Manor, would not only be dangerous, from the strength of the country, and impracticability of the ground; but must from its own nature be rendered abortive; as the length, the parade, and the manner of the preparation, would afford the Americans time and warning to assemble their whole force in that quarter; where, if we still persisted in our design, we must fight under every possible disadvantage, and a moral certainty of great loss; and if they did not chuse, even upon these terms, to hazard an engagement with us, they would have sufficient time to remove their magazines, before we could bring the point to any decision.

Peek's Kill, was, however, within reach, and the General determined to profit of that circumstance. Colonel Bird, with a detachment of about 500 men, under the conduct of a frigate of war, and other armed vessels, was sent on board some transports up the North River for that service. The enemy upon the approach of the British armament, finding, or thinking themselves, unequal to the defence of the place, and being convinced, that there was no possible time to remove any thing but their arms and bodies, set fire to the barracks and principal storehouses, and then retired to a strong pass at about two miles distance, which commanded the entrance into the mountains, and covered a road which led to some of the mills and other deposits. The British troops upon their landing, perceiving that they could not have time or opportunity to bring off the provisions or other articles, completed the conflagration. All the magazines were destroyed. The troops re-embarked when the service was performed, and the armament, after destroying several small craft laden with provisions, returned.

^{replaced:} Mar. 23d. 1777. [32]

This service, however, was far from filling up the outline of the General's design. The magazines at Peek's Kill were not of the importance and magnitude which he had been led to expect, and something, if possible, must still be done, to weaken the enemy by cutting off their resources. He obtained intelligence, that the Americans had deposited large quantities of stores and provisions in the town or village of Danbury, and other places in the borders of Connecticut, which lay contiguous to Courtland Manor. An expedition was accordingly undertaken for the destruction of these deposits, the charge of which, as an introduction to his new military command, was committed to Governor Tryon, who was assisted by those active and able officers, Brigadier-General Agnew, and Sir William Erskine. The expedition was said to be undertaken on a plan of General Tryon, who had flattered himself with finding a junction of many provincials in that quarter as soon as he should appear with the troops. [33]

The detachment appointed to this service consisted of about 2000 men, who being passed through the Sound, under the convoy of a proper naval armament, were landed near Norwalk in Connecticut, about 20 miles to the southward of Danbury. As the country was in no state of preparation, nor under any apprehension of the design, the troops advanced without interruption, and arrived at Danbury the following day. They now perceived that the country was rising to intercept their return, and as no carriages could be procured, if it had been otherwise, to bring off the stores and provisions, they immediately proceeded to the destruction of the magazine. In the execution of this prompt service, the town was unavoidably burnt.

The detachment returned on the 27th by the way of Ridgefield. In

^{replaced:} April 25th.

the mean time the Generals Wooster, Arnold, and Silliman, having[34] haftily arrived from different quarters, and collected fuch militia as were within their reach, endeavoured by every poffible means to interrupt their march, until a greater force could arrive to fupport them with effect in the defign of cutting off their retreat. The firft of thefe officers hang upon the rear of the detachment, whilft Arnold, by croffing the country gained their front, in order to difpute their paffage through Ridgefield. Nor could the excellent order and formidable appearance of the Britifh forces, who had large covering parties well furnifhed with field pieces on their flanks and rear, nor the tumultuary manner in which a militia not very numerous were got together, prevent the Americans, upon every advantage of ground, from making bold attempts to interrupt the progrefs of the King's army. In one of thefe fkirmifhes, Wooster, an experienced provincial officer, who had ferved with fome reputation in the two former wars, at an age approaching clofely to feventy, and in the active exertion of a valour, which favoured more of rafhnefs, than of the temperance and difcretion of that time of life, was mortally wounded, and died with the fame refolution that he had lived.

The royal forces had only got quit of Wooster, when they found themfelves engaged with Arnold, who had got poffeffion of Ridgefield, and with lefs than an hour's advantage of time, had already thrown up fome fort of an entrenchment to cover his front. The courage and difcipline of the Britifh troops, would have triumphed over an enemy more equal in force and condition. The village was forced, and the Americans drove back on all fides. The action was fharp, and Arnold difplayed his ufual intrepidity. His horfe having been fhot within a few yards of our foremoft ranks, he fuddenly disengaged himfelf, and drawing out a piftol, fhot the foldier dead who was running up to transfix him with his bayonet.

General Tryon lay that night at Ridgefield, and renewed his march on the morning of the 28th. The enemy having been reinforced with troops and cannon, the army was exceedingly harraffed during this day's march. Every advantageous poft was feized and difputed, whilft hovering parties on the flanks and rear, continually endeavoured to difturb the order of march, and to profit of every difficulty of ground. The army at length gained, in good time, the Hill of Compo, within cannon fhot of the fhips. It was then evening, and their ammunition exhaufted, although it is reported, that they had been fupplied with fixty rounds a man at their outfet upon the expedition. The forces immediately formed upon the high ground, where the enemy feemed more determined and refolute in their attack than they had been hitherto. In this fituation, the General ordered the troops to advance, and to charge with their bayonets. This order was executed with fuch impetuofity, that the enemy were totally broken, and every thing being prepared at the fhore for their reception, the troops were reimbarked without further moleftation.

Large quantities of corn, flour, and falt provifions, a great number of tents, with various military ftores and neceffaries, were deftroyed in the courfe of this expedition. The lofs of men on the royal fide, was, as ufual, much lefs confiderable than could have been expected; the whole, in killed, wounded, and miffing, amounting to 172, of whom more than two-thirds were wounded. The general lofs under all thefe heads on the American fide was more than double, and the number of the flain about four to one. On the Britifh fide no officer was killed. On theirs, befides General Wooster, they loft three colonels, and a Dr. Atwater, a gentleman[35] of confideration in that country. The number of officers that happened to be in the country, and to affemble upon the occafion, was out of all proportion to that of the private men; whilft the raw and undifciplined ftate of the militia, together with their weaknefs in point of number, obliged the former, as well as thofe volunteer gentlemen who joined them, to uncommon exertions, and to expofe themfelves in an extraordinary degree. Thefe circumftances may account for the number of men of rank, in their fervice, who fell on that fide.

Upon the whole, the effect of this expedition did not probably anfwer the expectation upon which it was founded. The actual public ftores at Danbury and other places, were far inferior to what they had been fuppofed or reprefented; and though much mifchief was done, it may appear doubtful, whether the lofs fuftained on the one fide, was equivalent to the rifque encountered on the other. Events, however, are not to be confidered as tefts of conduct, and it muft ever be one of the firft objects with a great General, to render the force of the enemy inefficacious by cutting off their refources.

It was perhaps in return for this expedition that the Connecticut men not long after paid a vifit to Long-Ifland. Having received intelligence that commiffaries had for fome time been employed on the eaft end of Long-Ifland, in procuring forage, grain, and other neceffaries for the Britifh forces, and that thefe articles were depofited for embarkation at a little port called Sagg Harbour; the diftance of that place from New-York, and the weaknefs of the protection, which confifted only in a company of foot, and an armed fchooner of twelve guns, afforded encouragement for a defign to fruftrate that fcheme of fupplying the wants of the army. The principal difficulty and danger lay in the passing and repassing of the Sound, which was continually traversed by the British cruizers.

Colonel Meigs, an enterprizing [36] officer, who had attended Arnold in the expedition to Quebec, and had been taken prisoner in the attempt to storm that city, conducted this enterprize. Having passed his detachment in whale-boats through the Sound, and landed on the north branch of the island, where it is intersected by a bay that runs in far from the east end, it seems by the account, which is not in that part very clear, as if they had carried their boats over that arm of the land. They, however, embarked again on the bay, which he crossed with 130 men, and landed on the south branch of the island, within four miles of Sagg Harbour. They arrived at the place before day, and notwithstanding the resistance they met with from the guard and the crews of the vessels, and the vigorous efforts of the schooner, which kept up a continued fire of round and grape shot at 150 yards distance, they fully completed their design; having burnt a dozen brigs and sloops which lay at the wharf, and entirely destroyed every thing on the shore. They brought off with them about 90 prisoners, consisting of the officer who commanded with his men, the commissaries, and most of the masters and crews of the small vessels which they destroyed. A circumstance which renders this expedition particularly curious, if a fact, is asserted by the Americans. They say, that the party returned to Guildford, in Connecticut, in 25 hours from the time of their departure, having during that space, not only effectually completed the design of their expedition, but having traversed no less, by land and by water, than 90 miles. A degree of expedition, which requires some credu-

May 23d.

lity to be admitted; and from whence, if the fact is established, it would appear that Meigs possesses no inconsiderable portion of that spirit which operated in the Canada expedition.

The season for action was now advanced; but from some improvidence or inattention unaccounted for, at home, the army was restrained from taking the field through the want of tents and field equipage. Lord Cornwallis, however, made shift with the old tents, to encamp the forces at Brunswick on the hills that commanded the Rariton, and along the communications upon that river to Amboy; the example being followed at the latter place by General Vaughan.

This delay was of the utmost importance to the Americans. The winter campaign had been principally carried on by detachments of the militia, the greater part of whom returned home when the time of their service was expired. Others, more generous, more patient of toil, or more sanguine in the common cause, outstayed the allotted time, merely from a consideration of the weakness of the army, and the ruin which must attend their departure before it was reinforced. In the mean time, the business of recruiting under an engagement of serving during the war, or even for three years, went on but slowly. The term of service was contrary to the genius and habits of the people, and the different provinces found the greatest difficulty in raising any thing near the stipulated proportion of troops which had been allotted for each by the congress. In this extremity, the making of draughts from the militia, was looked to in several as the dernier resort. Such an act of force, however, upon those who were contending for liberty on the most enlarged plans, and who considered all the rights of freemen as sacred, was irksome and dangerous. Every method was tried to avoid having recourse

to this disagreeable measure and final resource. In some of the colonies the enlisting of apprentices, and of Irish indented servants was permitted, contrary to former resolutions and decrees, with a promise of indemnification to their masters. As a farther check upon the increase of the force in the Jerseys, the New England provinces, which abounded with men, were taken up with their domestic concerns. An invasion was expected on the side of Canada; Hudson's River and Rhode-Island afforded continual room for apprehension; nor did an expedition against Boston appear at all improbable; especially, as the great number of British prizes which were brought into that port, had, besides rendering it an object of the first importance, renewed, and even increased, if possible, the detestation and abhorrence with which that people had been long regarded.

In such circumstances, the advantages of an early campaign, and the benefit which the enemy derived from the delay, are obvious. The fine weather brought reinforcements from all quarters to the Jerseys. Those who shuddered at a winter's campaign, grew bold in summer; and the certainty of a future winter, had no greater effect than distant evils usually have. Upon this increase of strength, towards the latter end of May, General Washington quitted his former position in the neighbourhood of Morris-Town, and advancing within a few miles of Brunswick, took possession of the strong country along Middle Brook.

Upon this single movement, hung a great part of the future events of the war in the Jerseys. Washington turned that advantageous situation, to every account of which it was capable. His camp, winding along the course of the hills, was strongly entrenched, fortified, and well covered with artillery; nor was it better secured by its immediate natural or artificial defences, than by the difficulties of approach which the ground in front threw in the way of an enemy. In this situation he commanded a view of the British encampment on the hills of Brunswick, and of much of the intermediate country towards that place and Amboy.

The great object of the campaign on the side of New-York seems to have been, that Sir William Howe should have penetrated through the Jerseys to the Delaware, driving Washington before him, so as to clear those provinces entirely of the enemy, at the same time, reducing the inhabitants to so effectual a state of subjection, as to establish a safe and open communication between that city and the army. If in the prosecution of this design the enemy hazarded a battle, nothing was more wished, nor could any great doubt be entertained of success; or if they constantly retired, which was more to be expected, the consequences in regard to the general objects would be nearly the same, and the army having, by the reduction of the Jerseys, left every thing safe in its rear, and secured the passage of the Delaware, would of course become masters of Philadelphia, which from its situation was incapable of any effectual defence, and could only be protected by Washington, at the certain expence and hazard of a battle.

In this manner several conceived and reasoned on the operations in Jersey. Others were clearly of opinion, that the bringing of Washington to a decisive action upon terms of any tolerable equality with regard to ground, in such a country, and against his inclinations, was a thing impracticable. That if he could not be brought to such an action in such a manner, so as wholly to drive him out of the Jerseys, the attempt to pass a river like the Delaware, full of armed vessels in its stream, strong forts in its islands, great obstructions in its channels, with an enemy in front, and leaving a strong army on their rear, would be a very unadvised enterprize; and the failure in it would be the total and immediate ruin of the royal cause in America.

On the other hand, if the obstacles in the Jerseys were found so great, that they could not be overcome without much loss of time and expence of blood, it was thought adviseable, in those circumstances, to profit of the powerful naval force, and the infinite number of transports and vessels of all sorts which lay at New York; to combine this powerful auxiliary (which had hitherto produced such signal advantages, in every instance where it could be brought into action) with the land force, and by conveying the army by sea to the place of its destination, to elude all those difficulties, by which the passage through the Jerseys might be clogged. In this alternative, the object was still the same, the means of attaining it being only changed. Philadelphia was the immediate point in view. If that object was properly chosen, and the general opinion at that time pointed it out as the most eligible, the passage by sea seemed the most secure of its effect, though unquestionably the slowest in the operation. The Delaware, or the great Bay of Chesapeak, opened the way into the heart of the richest and best of the central colonies, and led either directly, or by crossing a country of no great extent, to the possession of that place. That point gained, Philadelphia was to become the place of arms, and center of action, whilst every part of the three hostile and flourishing Provinces of Pennsylvania, Virginia, and Maryland, would, from their deep bays and navigable rivers, be exposed to the combined powerful action, and continual operation of the land and marine force. However, before this plan was adopted, as we shall see, measures were taken in the Jerseys, if possible, to bring Washington to an action.

The operations in the southern or central provinces, however efficacious or extensive, did not, by any means, include all the great objects of the campaign. Something was of course to be expected on the side of Canada, where a very considerable army had been collected, and by the success of the last campaign on the lakes, had a way opened for it to penetrate into the back parts of the New-England and New-York provinces. The command in this expedition was committed to General Burgoyne, who was reported to be author of the plan. The great body was to be seconded by a lesser expedition from the upper part of Canada, by the way of Oswego to the Mohawk River. This scheme was eagerly adopted by the ministers, who founded the greatest hopes upon its success. All the advantages that had ever been expected from the complete possession of Hudson's River, the establishment of a communication between the two armies, the cutting off all intercourse between the Northern and Southern Colonies, with the consequent opportunity of crushing the former, detached and cut off from all assistance, it was now hoped would have been realized. The greater hopes were conceived of it, from the opinion entertained of the effect of the savages on the minds of the Americans. It was known, that the provincials in general were in great dread of them from their cruel and desolating manner of making war. These were therefore collected at great expence, and with much labour, from all parts of the continent. In a word, this expedition seemed to become the favourite object of the present year.

The tents and field equipage, with a body of Anspach troops, and a number of British and German recruits, having at length arrived at New-York by the beginning of June, the General, Sir

William Howe, paſſed over to the Jerſeys, and took the field about the middle of that month. The enemy were now in a ſtrong ſtate of defence. Waſhington's army, beſides the advantages it derived from the inacceſſible poſts which it occupied, was become more confiderable as to number and force. Several bodies of the New-England troops, under the Generals Gates, Parſons, and Arnold, advanced to [37] the borders of the North River, where they were ready to paſs over to the Jerſeys, whenever opportunity invited their action, or the neceſſity of their friends demanded their aſſiſtance. At the ſame time, the Jerſey militia aſſembled from every quarter with the greateſt alacrity, ſo that in every poſition it took, and motion it made, the army was watched and environed by enemies.

The General left nothing untried that could provoke Waſhington to an engagement, nor no meaſure uneſſayed that could induce him to quit his poſition. He puſhed on detachments; and made movements, as if he intended to paſs him, and advance to the Delaware. This manœuvre proving ineffectual, he advanced in the front of his lines, where he continued for four days, exploring the approaches to his camp, and accurately examining the ſituation of his poſts, hoping that ſome weak or unguarded part might be found, upon which an attack could be ventured with a probability of ſucceſs, or that, in the nearneſs of the armies, chance, inadvertence, impatience, or error, might occaſion ſome movement, or be productive of ſome circumſtance, which would open the way to a general engagement. All theſe hopes were fruſtrated. Waſhington knew the full value of his ſituation. As he had too much temper to be provoked or ſurprized, into a dereliction of his advantages, ſo he had too much penetration to loſe them by circumvention or ſleight. And

he had too long profited of that rule of conduct from which he had not once hitherto deviated during the courſe of the troubles, of never committing the fortune of America to the hazard of a ſingle action, to depart from it upon this occaſion, when it was not even demanded by any urgent neceſſity.

Sir William Howe did not yet ſeem to have abandoned his deſign, of enticing Waſhington to quit his faſtneſſes. He ſuddenly retreated, and June 19th. not without ſome apparent marks of precipitation, from his poſition in the front of the enemy, and withdrawing his troops from Brunſwick, returned with the whole army towards Amboy. If the General's deſign was what we have ſuppoſed, this movement produced all the immediate effect which he could have expected. The army was eagerly purſued by ſeveral large bodies of the American regular forces as well as of the Jerſey militia, under the command of the Generals Maxwel, Lord Sterling, and Conway; the latter of [38] whom was a Colonel of the Iriſh Brigade, and one of that numerous train of officers in the French ſervice, who had taken an active part againſt Great Britain in this unhappy civil war.

Such trifling advantages as the beſt regulated retreat muſt afford to the purſuers, and ſome exceſſes committed, perhaps with a view to the general deſign, by the retiring ſoldiers, ſerved to increaſe the ardour, and inflame the paſſions of the Americans. The meaſures which the General immediately adopted at Amboy completed the deluſion. The bridge which was intended for the Delaware, was thrown over the channel which ſeparates the Continent from Staten Iſland. The heavy baggage, and all the incumbrances of the army, were paſſed over. Some of the troops followed, and every thing was in immediate preparation for the paſſage of the reſt of

the army. By theſe judicious meaſures, if the immediate deſign failed of effect, every thing was forwarded as much as it could be for the intended embarkation; a meaſure of which the Americans had as yet no knowledge.

Every thing concurred, along with the vanity natural to mankind, in inducing the Americans to believe, that this retreat was not only real, but that it proceeded from a knowledge of their ſuperiority, and a dread of their power: Even Waſhington himſelf, with all his caution and penetration, was ſo far impoſed upon by this feint, that he quitted his ſecure poſts upon the Hills, and advanced to a place called Quibble town, to be the nearer at hand for the protection or ſupport of his advanced parties.

The Britiſh General loſt no time in endeavouring to profit of thoſe 26th. circumſtances. He immediately marched the army back by different routs, and with great expedition, from Amboy. He had three objects in view. To cut off ſome of the principal advanced parties; to come up with, and bring the enemy to an engagement in the neighbourhood of Quibbletown; or, if this deſign, through the celerity of the enemy, failed in the effect, it was intended that Lord Cornwallis, who, with his column, was to take a conſiderable circuit to the right, ſhould, by turning the enemy's left, take poſſeſſion of ſome paſſes in the mountains, which, by their ſituation and command of ground, would have reduced them to a neceſſity of abandoning that ſtrong camp, which had hitherto afforded them ſo advantageous a ſecurity.

Lord Cornwallis having diſperſed the ſmaller advanced parties of the enemy, fell in at length with Lord Sterling, who with about 3000 men, ſtrongly poſted in a woody country, and well covered by artillery judiciouſly diſpoſed, not only lay full in his way, but ſhewed

a determination to difpute his paffage with vigour and firmnefs.
The ardour excited upon this occafion by an emulation between
the Britifh and Heffian troops was
confpicuous and irrefiftible. All
obftacles gave way to their impetuofity in prefling forward, to try
who fhould obtain the honour of
firft coming to a clofe engagement
with the enemy. The party of
Americans firft attacked, unable
to withftand the fhock, were foon
routed on all fides, having fuftained, befides no inconfiderable
lofs in men, that of three pieces of
brafs ordnance, which were taken
by the Britifh Guards, and the
Heffian grenadiers. The purfuit
was continued as far as Weftfield,
but the woods, and the intenfe
heat of the weather, prevented its
effect.

In the mean time, Gen. Wafhington foon perceived, and as
fpeedily remedied his error, by
withdrawing his army from the
plains, and again recovering his
ftrong camp on the hills. At the
fame time, penetrating into Lord
Cornwallis's further defign, he fecured thofe paffes in the mountains,
the poffeffion of which by the Britifh troops, would have expofed
him to the neceffity of a critical
change of pofition, which could
not have been executed without
danger.

Thus was this, apparently, well
concerted fcheme of bringing the
enemy to an action, or at leaft
of withdrawing them from their
ftrong holds, rendered abortive, by
the caution and prudence of Gen.
Wafhington. Sir William Howe
was now convinced, that he was
too firmly attached to his defenfive
plan of conducting the war, to be
induced by any means, other than
by fome very clear and decided advantage, to hazard a general engagement. Nothing then remained
to be done in the Jerfeys. To advance to the Delaware, through a
country entirely hoftile, and with
fuch a force in his rear, appeared

to the Britifh commanders no better than madnefs. All delay was
therefore not only fruitlefs, but a
wafte of that time and feafon,
which might be employed to great
advantage elfewhere. The General accordingly returned with the
army to Amboy, on the fecond day
from its departure on the expedition, and paffed it over on the next
to Staten Ifland, from whence the
embarkation was intended to take
place.

The preparations for this grand
expedition excited a general alarm
throughout the Continent. Bofton,
the North River, the Delaware,
Chefapeak-Bay, and even Charles-
Town, were alternately held to be
its objects. General Wafhington,
in purfuance of the intelligence
which he continually received from
New-York, and the other Iflands,
was conftantly difpatching expreffes
to put thofe places upon their
guard, againft which, from immediate information, he fuppofed for
the time the ftorm to be directed.
It was one of the manifeft advantages of proceeding by fea, that it
was impoffible for Wafhington directly to know where the ftorm
would fall. He muft therefore
keep his pofition; and the King's
army muft neceffarily make a confiderable progrefs towards its object, before he could be in a condition to refift them; and fuch a progrefs would not leave him that
choice of pofts, by which hitherto
he had avoided a general action.

During the ceffation procured by
preparation on the one fide, and
apprehenfion on the other, a fpirited adventure on the fide of
Rhode Ifland, not only retaliated
the furprize of Gen. Lee, but
feemed to procure an indemnification for his perfon. Col. Barton, a Provincial, with feveral
other officers and volunteers, paffed
by night from Provi-
dence to Rhode Ifland, July 10th.
and though they had a long paffage by water, they eluded the
watchfulnefs of the fhips of war

and guard boats which furrounded
the ifland, and conducted their enterprize with fuch filence, boldnefs, and dexterity, that they furprized Gen. Prefcot, who commanded in chief, in his quarters,
and brought him and his Aid-de-
Camp, through all thofe perils,
fafe to the Continent. This little
adventure produced much exultation on the one fide, and more regret than it feemed to deferve on
the other, from the influence which
it muft neceffarily have on the deftination of Gen. Lee. It was,
however, particularly galling and
grievous to Gen. Prefcot, who not
long before had carried matters to
fuch a length, as to fet a price
upon Arnold, and offer a reward
for taking his perfon, as if he had
been a common out-law or robber;
an infult which Arnold immediately returned, by fetting an inferior price upon the General's perfon.

Some time previous to thefe
tranfactions, the Congrefs had
found it neceffary to advance the
rate of intereft upon the large loan
which they propofed for the fervice and upon the credit of the
united Provinces, from four, which
was firft offered, to fix per cent.
As a teftimony of public gratitude,
and a future incitement to, what
they confidered or held out, as
virtue and patriotifm, they ordered, that a monument fhould be
erected at Bofton, in honour of
Major General Warren, who commanded and fell in the engagement at Bunker's Hill, and another in Virginia, in honour of
Brigadier General Mercer, who
was flain in the action near Prince
Town; the refolution conveying
in a very few words, the higheft
eulogium on the character and merits of the deceafed. They likewife decreed, that the eldeft fon of
the former of thefe gentlemen, and
the youngeft fon of the latter,
fhould be educated at the expence
of the United States. As Mercer
had a good landed eftate, the pro-

priety of adopting his youngeſt ſon as the child of the public is obvious.

Notwithſtanding the preparations that had already been made for the embarkation, and the aſſiſtance afforded by the crews of near 300 veſſels, yet ſuch are the unavoidable delays incident to ſuch operations when at all extenſive, that it was not until the 23d of July that the fleet and army were able to depart from Sandy Hook. In order more effectually to perplex and deceive the enemy, the General ordered ſome tranſports, with a ſhip cut down to act as a floating battery, up the North River, a little before the embarkation was completed; a feint which ſucceeded ſo far as to induce Waſhington to detach a conſiderable body of his army acroſs that river.

The force that embarked upon the expedition conſiſted of 36 Britiſh and Heſſian battalions, including the light infantry and grenadiers, with a powerful artillery, a New-York corps called the Queen's Rangers, and a regiment of light horſe. Seventeen battalions, with a regiment of light horſe, and the remainder of the new Provincial corps, were left for the protection of New-York and the adjoining iſlands. Rhode Iſland was occupied by ſeven battalions. So much was the active force of the army reſtrained, by the poſſeſſion, which it was, however, indiſpenſably neceſſary to hold, of theſe important poſts. It is ſaid, that the General intended to have taken a greater force with him upon the expedition; but that upon the repreſentations of Gen. Clinton, who was to command in his abſence, of the danger to which the iſlands would be expoſed, from the extenſiveneſs of their coaſts, and the great number of poſts that were neceſſarily to be maintained, he acknowledged the force of theſe arguments by relanding ſeveral regiments.

Whilſt both Gen. Waſhington and the Congreſs were ſufficiently engaged, by their attention to the movements, and apprehenſion of the deſigns, of the powerful fleet and army which was conducted by the brother Generals and Commiſſioners, the rapid progreſs of General Burgoyne on the ſide of the Lakes, and the unaccountable conduct of their own commanders in abandoning Ticonderoga; were events ſo alarming and unexpected, that they could not fail to perplex their counſels, and conſiderably to impede their defenſive preparations in other parts. The Congreſs behaved with firmneſs in this exigency. They immediately iſſued orders for a recal to head quarters, and an enquiry into the conduct of the general officers who had abandoned Ticonderoga; they directed Waſhington to appoint other commanders; and they likewiſe directed him to ſummon ſuch numbers of the militia from the eaſtern and central provinces for the northern ſervice, as he ſhould deem ſufficient for reſtraining the progreſs of the enemy.

The voyage was far from being favourable to the fleet and army, engaged on the expedition. It coſt them a week to gain the Capes of Delaware. The information which the commanders received there, of the meaſures taken by the enemy for rendering the navigation of that river impracticable, afforded ſo little encouragement to the proſecution of their deſign by that way, that it was given up, and a paſſage by Cheſapeak Bay, to that part of Maryland which lies to the Eaſt of that vaſt inlet, and not at a very great diſtance to the South-Weſt of Philadelphia, was adopted in its place, as preſenting fewer obſtacles to their operations. The winds were ſo contrary in this part of the voyage, that the middle of Auguſt was turned before they entered Cheſapeak Bay; a circumſtance highly inconvenient and irkſome in that hot ſeaſon of the year, with ſo great a number of men and horſes crowded and cooped up in the veſſels; but which muſt have been attended with the moſt fatal conſequences, if the foreſight of the commanders had not guarded againſt every event by the unbounded proviſion they had made for the voyage, as a failure in any one article, even that of water, would have been probably irremediable.

The winds fortunately proved fair in the Bay, ſo that the fleet gained the mouth of the River Elk near its extremity, in ſafety, through a moſt intricate and dangerous navigation for ſuch a multitude of veſſels, in which the Admiral performed the different parts of a commander, inferior officer, and pilot, with his uſual ability and perſeverance. Having proceeded up the Elk as far as it was capable of admitting their paſſage, the army was at length relieved from its long and tireſome confinement on board the tranſports, being landed without any oppoſition at Elk Ferry, in a degree of health and condition which could ſcarcely have been expected, on the 25th of Auguſt. Whilſt one part of the army advanced to the head of Elk, the other continued at the landing place, to protect and forward the artillery, ſtores, and neceſſary proviſions, the General not permitting the troops to be much incumbered with baggage; indeed the ſcarcity of carriage rendered even a great abridgment in the article of tents neceſſary.

In the mean time, Gen. Waſhington, with the army from the Jerſeys, had returned to the defence of Philadelphia, and upon advice of the deſcent at Elk, advanced to the Brandywine Creek, or River, which, croſſing the country about half way to that city, falls into the Delaware. Their force, including the militia, amounted to 15,000 men, which was probably about the number, making the neceſſary allowance for poſts and communications, that the royal army could bring into action.

Sir William Howe, in order to quiet and conciliate the minds of the people in Penfylvania, the Delaware Counties, and the adjacent parts of Maryland, and to prevent a total defertion and defolation of the country in the front of the army, publifhed a declaration, in which he promifed, that the ftricteft regularity, good order and difcipline, fhould be obferved by the army, and the moft perfect fecurity and effectual protection afforded to all his Majefty's peaceable and well difpofed fubjects; extending at the fame time this fecurity and protection to fuch perfons, who not having been guilty of affuming legiflative or judicial authority, might otherwife have acted illegally in fubordinate ftations, upon the provifion of their immediate return to their habitations, and peaceable demeanor for the future. He alfo offered a free and general pardon to all officers and foldiers in arms, who fhould furrender themfelves to the royal army.

It was not till the 3d of September, that the army was enabled to quit the head of Elk, and purfue its courfe towards Philadelphia. In the mean time, the enemy had advanced from the Brandywine, and taken poft on Red Clay Creek, from whence they pufhed detachments forward, to occupy difficult pofts in the woods, and to interrupt, by continual fkirmifhes, the line of march. As the country was difficult, woody, and not well known, and that the genius of the enemy lay to profit of fuch circumftances, the General advanced flowly, and with extraordinary caution. He was from neceffity, as well as difpofition, fparing of his troops. Recruits were brought from a prodigious diftance, and procured with difficulty even at the fource. Every man killed, wounded, or taken, was to him an irreparable lofs, and fo far as it went, an incurable weakening of the army, for the prefent year at leaft. On the other hand, the enemy

were at home. Every lofs they fuffered was not only immediately repaired, but the military ability of the furvivors was increafed by every deftruction of their fellows.

This caution could not, however, prevent fome fkirmifhes, in which the royal forces were almoft always victorious. It does not appear that the Americans made all the ufe that might be expected of the advantages which the country afforded for harraffing and impeding the progrefs of the Britifh army. After feveral movements on both fides, the enemy retired beyond the Brandywine, where they took poffeffion of the heights, and covered the fords, with an evident intention of difputing the paffage of that river.

In this fituation the Britifh army, at day break, advanced in two columns towards the enemy. The right, under the command of Gen. Knyphaufen, marched directly to Chad's Ford, which lay in the center of the enemy's line, where they expected, and were prepared for the principal attack; their right and left covering other lefs practicable fords and paffages for fome miles on either hand. A heavy cannonade commenced on both fides about ten o'clock, which was well fupported during the day, whilft the General, to amufe and deceive the enemy, made repeated difpofitions for forcing the Ford, the paffage of the River feeming to be his immediate and determined object. To impede or fruftrate this defign, they had paffed feveral detachments to the other fide, who, after a courfe of fkirmifhes, fometimes advancing, and at others obliged to retire, were at length finally, with an eager purfuit, driven over the River. Thus the noife and femblance of a battle was held up, and the expectation kept continually alive to the moft immediate and decifive confequences.

Whilft the attention of the Americans was thus fully occupied in

the neighbourhood of Chad's Ford, and that they fuppofed the whole royal force was in their front, Lord Cornwallis, at the head of the fecond column, took a long circuitous march to the left, until he gained the Forks of the Brandywine, where the divifion of the river rendered it of courfe more practicable. By this very judicious movement, his Lordfhip paffed both branches of the river at Trimbles' and at Jeffery's Ford, without oppofition or difficulty, about two o'clock in the afternoon, and then turning fhort down the river, took the road to Dilworth, in order to fall upon the enemy's right.

General Wafhington having, however, received intelligence of this movement about noon, endeavoured, as well as he could, to provide againft its effect, by detaching General Sullivan, with all the force he could venture to withdraw from the main body, to oppofe Lord Cornwallis. Sullivan, fhewed a confiderable fhare of judgment and ability in the execution of this commiffion. He took a very ftrong pofition on the commanding grounds above Birmingham church, with his left extending towards the Brandywine, his artillery advantageoufly difpofed, and both flanks covered with very thick woods.

As this difpofition obliged Lord Cornwallis to form a line of battle, it was about four o'clock before the action began. Neither the good difpofition of the enemy, the advantages of fituation, nor a heavy and well fupported fire of fmall arms and artillery, were at all fufficient to reftrain the impetuofity of the Britifh and Heffian troops. The light infantry, chaffeurs, grenadiers, and guards, rufhing on through all obftacles and dangers, drove the enemy, in fpite of all their efforts, though not without a fpirited oppofition, from their pofts, and purfued them pellmell into the woods on their rear. In the mean time, a part of the enemy's right, which had not been broken, took a second strong position in a wood on the same side, from whence, after some considerable resistance, they were dislodged and pursued by detachments from the second line.

Several bodies of the troops that were first engaged, got so deeply entangled in the woods through the eagerness of pursuit, that they were not able to rejoin the army before night. In the mean time, as the main and collected body continued advancing, they came upon a corps of the enemy which had not yet been engaged, and which had taken possession of a strong post, to cover the retreat of the defeated wing of their army. A very warm engagement now ensued, and this post was so vigorously defended, that it was some time after dark before it could be forced. The darkness, the uncertainty of the ground, of General Knyphausen's situation, together with the extreme fatigue which the troops had undergone, in a long march and severe action, which had scarcely admitted of the smallest respite during the whole course of the day, all concurred in preventing the army from pursuing its advantages any farther.

General Knyphausen, after successfully amusing the enemy all day with the apprehension of an attack which he did not intend, made his passage good in the evening, when he found that they were already deeply engaged on the right. He carried the entrenchment, and took the battery and cannon, which defended and covered Chad's Ford. At this instant, the approach of some of the British troops, who had been entangled in, and had penetrated through the woods, threw the enemy into such a consternation, that an immediate retreat, or rather flight, took place in all parts. The lateness and darkness of the evening, prevented a pursuit here, as it had done on the right.

A few hours more daylight, would have been undoubtedly productive of a total and ruinous defeat to the Americans.

A part of their troops, among whom were particularly numbered some of the Virginia regiments, and the whole corps of artillery, behaved exceedingly well in some of the actions of this day, exhibiting a degree of order, firmness, and resolution, and preserving such a countenance in extremely sharp service, as would not have discredited veterans. Some other bodies of their troops behaved very badly. Their loss was very considerable, which probably was the cause that it was not particularly specified in their own accounts. In the Gazette it was computed, at about 300 killed, 600 wounded, and near 400 taken prisoners. They also lost ten small field pieces, and a howitzer, of which all, but one, were brass.

The loss in the royal army was not in proportion, being something under five hundred, of which [40] the slain did not amount to one fifth. The officers suffered considerably, especially in wounded, though no one of higher rank than a captain was killed. The enemy retreated first to Chester, and on the next day to Philadelphia. The victorious army lay that night on the field of battle.

Washington, so far as we can judge at this distance, seems to have been more out-generalled in this action, than any other since the beginning of the war. This conclusion is not, however, to be considered as established; as we are sensible that it may well be questioned, from the premises even before us. The defence of such a length of river, intersected with fords, and some at remote distances, was undoubtedly impracticable. If it be asked then why the attempt was made, it may be answered, that his great object was to harrass, and to interrupt the progress of the royal army to Philadelphia, by

every possible means, which did not involve his own in the risque of a general engagement; that even a superior loss of men, was not to be considered by him, to whom perhaps it was necessary to learn, even by a dangerous experiment, the improvement and state of his own troops. His choice of a post on the Brandywine, in preference to those more defensible that were nearer to Philadelphia, has been censured; but how far this choice was altogether in his power does not fully appear. And, however deficient he was in point of intelligence, with respect to Lord Cornwallis's movement, he shewed great ability in his endeavours to remedy that negligence, by the prompt and judicious measures which he took to cover his right. Whatever the merits or demerits were on this side of the question, it must be acknowledged, that the movements of the royal army were judicious and masterly.

The present unhappy contest was so interesting to foreigners, and rendered America so conspicuous a theatre of action, that it drew bold and enterprizing spirits, from different parts of Europe, either merely in search of glory and rank, or to acquire military experience and improvement. Among the numerous instances of this nature which might be given, a few are necessary, and will be sufficient. The Marquis de la Fayette, a [41] young French nobleman, of the first rank, and of large fortune, was so carried away by this enthusiasm, as to purchase and freight a ship with military stores (in which he embarked with several of his friends) for the service of the Americans; he bore a command, and was wounded in this action. The Baron St. Ovary, another French volunteer, for whose release the Congress shewed a particular attention, was soon after made a prisoner. De Coudry, a French General, was about this time drowned in the Schuylkill, through his eagerness to come in time into action. Roche de Fermoy, was a member of the council of war, who had signed the resolution for abandoning Ticonderoga. Pulawski, a noble Pole, commanded a detachment of American light-horse in the action of the Brandywine. Count Grabouskie, another Polish nobleman, was about the same time killed on the North River, exhibiting great intrepidity on the British side, and bestowing his last breath in encomiums on the undaunted courage displayed by the partners of his danger, and witnesses of his fall. [42]

It is to be observed, that in the battle of the Brandywine, the rebel forces were met in the open field, and with no very great advantage of situation. A victory was clearly obtained over them; but it was not of that final and decisive kind which the publick had expected as the certain consequence of such a meeting. People rarely consider how much trivial and accidental circumstances render all things of this kind extremely uncertain, even with any superiority of troops, or goodness of generalship.

Notwithstanding the victory of the King's troops, and the precipitate flight of the enemy, the royal army proceeded with caution and circumspection; and it did not seem unnecessary; for the rebels were not disheartened; and Mr. Washington exerted himself with ability and diligence to repair his defeat. The army was posted in the neighbourhood of Concord and Ashetown, whilst a detachment was sent to seize on Wilmington, which was made a receptacle for the sick and wounded. Upon a movement towards Goshen, the General received intelligence upon his march, that the enemy had quitted Philadelphia, and were advanced upon the Lancaster road, a few miles above that place. Upon this advice, he took such effectual measures for bringing them to an immediate engagement, that nothing

but the event which followed could have frustrated his design. An excessive fall of rain, which overtook both armies upon their march, and which continued without intermission for 24 hours, rendered both parties equally and totally incapable of action.

In the course of a number of movements on both sides which took place for some days after, and in which every measure was ineffectually used, to involve the enemy in similar circumstances to those which they had so lately and with such loss escaped, intelligence having been received, that General Wayne, with 1500 men, was [43] lying in the woods upon some scheme of enterprize, in the rear, and at no great distance from the left wing of the army, Major-General Grey was detached at night, with two regiments, 20th. [44] and a body of light infantry, to surprize that corps. That General conducted the enterprize with equal ability and success; and, perhaps, in emulation of a remarkable action of the late war in Germany, took effectual measures that a single shot should not be fired in the course of the expedition, and that the execution should only be done by the point of the bayonet. In the prosecution of this design, the enemy's out posts and pickets were completely surprized and forced without noise, about one in the morning, and the troops being guided by the light of their fires, rushed in upon the encampment, where a severe and silent execution took place; about 300 being killed or wounded upon the spot, and a number of prisoners taken; the remainder escaping by the darkness of the night, and some prudent dispositions made by the officer who commanded the Americans, with the loss of the greater part of their baggage, arms, and stores. The victors, in this brisk action, lost only a captain of light infantry and three private men, with about the same number wounded.

The General finding that the enemy could not by any means be brought to action, and that they were evidently abandoning even the protection of the capital, rather than hazard that final decision, made such movements and took such positions as gave him the command of the Schuylkill, and enabled him, at length, to pass the army over that river without opposition. There being nothing now to impede his progress, the army Sept. 26th. advanced to Germantown, and Lord Cornwallis, on the next morning, took possession of Philadelphia. Thus was the rich and flourishing city of Philadelphia, the capital late of the most rising colony, and attended with the most singular circumstances, that history can give any example of, and the seat of that general congress of delegates, who dispensed laws and government to the continent of North America, reduced without opposition, and consequently without damage.

This circumstance was more fortunate than had been expected. For it was generally apprehended, and had been even spoken of by themselves as a settled and fixed determination, to destroy the city, whenever it was found that it could be no longer protected, rather than suffer it to become a place of arms, and the center of operation to the British fleets and armies. A number of the Quakers, and some other of the principal inhabitants of Philadelphia, to the amount of more than twenty, who had been justly considered as strongly attached to the royal cause, and violently inimical to the present ruling powers, had been taken into custody upon the immediate danger of an invasion. These gentlemen positively refused to give any security in writing, or even verbal attestation, of attachment, submission, or allegiance, to the present government, or of not holding a correspondence with those whom they represented as enemies. They even refused to confine themfelves to their refpective dwelling-houfes, and boldly appealing to the laws for redrefs and fecurity to their perfons, ftrongly reproached thofe, who under the pretence of afferting and protecting the liberties of the fubject, had involved the whole continent in civil war and contention, and who thus, at the fame time, in the moft arbitrary and tyrannical manner, deprived him of his perfonal liberty, and of every fecurity which he derived from the laws. They were anfwered, that the laws themfelves, and all other confiderations muft give way to the public fafety, in cafes of great and imminent danger; that there was no new nor particular hardfhip in the prefent meafure, which was juftified by the practice of all ftates in fimilar circumftances; that in England, in its higheft ftate of freedom, and under its happieft governments, the Habeas Corpus law was fufpended in cafes of internal commotion, or the apprehenfion of foreign invafion; that there, fufpicion only was a fufficient ground for fecuring the perfon of the fubject, without regard to rank, quality, or to any fecurity he might propofe to give for his peaceable demeanour; but that their fituation was much more favourable to themfelves, if their incorrigible obftinacy, their dangerous defigns againft the ftate, and their mortal enmity to the government, had not precluded them from its benefit; they were not retained in prifon merely upon fufpicion, however ftrong and well founded that was, and however juftifiable the meafure would be upon that ground only; it was immediately in their power to return in the moft unreftrained liberty to their habitations, only by complying with that very moderate teft of their principles and conduct which was required, and fhewing that obedience to government, and good difpofition to the ftate, which every member of fociety owed to the community to

which he belonged, as a return for the protection which he received. But that as they denied all allegiance to the ftate, they of courfe difclaimed its protection, and forfeited all the privileges of citizenfhip; whilft by refufing every fecurity for their peaceable demeanour, they could only be confidered as its moft dangerous and determined enemies. As thefe gentlemen were unconquerable in their refolution not to fubmit to the propofed teft, they were all fent off to Staunton, in Virginia, as a place of fecurity, upon the approach of the royal army.

As foon as Lord Howe had received intelligence of the fuccefs at the Brandywine, and the determined progrefs of the army to Philadelphia, he took the moft fpeedy and effectual meafures for conducting the fleet and tranfports round to the Delaware, not only to be at hand to concur in the active operations of the campaign, but to fupply the army with thofe provifions, ftores, and neceffaries, which he knew, muft by that time have been indifpenfably neceffary. The voyage was intricate, tedious, and dangerous; and nothing lefs than the fuperior fkill and ability which was exerted, in the conduct and management of fo great a number of fhips, could have prevented the lofs from being confiderable. As the paffage to Philadelphia was yet impracticable, the fleet drew up and anchored along the weftern or Penfylvania fhore, from Reedy Ifland to Newcaftle.

When the Britifh troops had taken poffeffion of Philadelphia, their firft object was the erecting of batteries to command the river, as well to prevent the intercourfe of the American veffels between their upper and lower pofts, as to protect the city from any infult by water. The neceffity of this meafure became obvious, almoft, as foon as it was determined upon. The very day after the arrival of

the forces, the American frigate Delaware, of 32 guns, anchored within 500 yards of the unfinifhed batteries, and being feconded by another frigate, with fome fmaller veffels, they commenced, and fupported for fome hours, a very heavy cannonade, both upon the batteries and the town. They did not, however, difplay the judgment, which their knowledge of the river might be fuppofed to afford. Upon the falling of the tide the Delaware grounded fo effectually that fhe could not be got off, which being foon perceived by the grenadiers, they brought their battalion field pieces to play upon her with fo true a direction and excellent effect, that the Delaware being obliged to ftrike her colours, was boarded and taken by an officer and detachment of that corps. Brigadier-General Cleveland immediately profited of[45] the effect of the battalion guns, by directing the whole fire of the batteries to the other veffels, which were compelled to retire, with the lofs of a fchooner which was driven afhore.

The Americans had at vaft expence, and with wonderful labour and induftry, conftructed great and numerous works, to render the paffage of the Delaware up to Philadelphia impracticable. In the profecution of this defign, they had erected works and batteries upon a flat, low, marfhy ifland, or rather a bank of mud and fand, which had been accumulated in the Delaware near the junction of the Schuylkill, and which from its nature was called Mud, but from thefe defences, Fort-Ifland. On the oppofite fhore of New Jerfey, at a place called Red-Bank, they had alfo conftructed a fort or redoubt, well covered with heavy artillery. In the deep navigable channel, between, or under the cover of thefe batteries, they had funk feveral ranges of frames or machines, to which, from a refemblance in the conftruction, they had given the appellation of chevaux de frize, being composed of transverse beams, firmly united, pointing in various directions, and strongly headed with iron. These were of such a weight and strength, and sunk in such a depth of water, as rendered them equally difficult to be weighed or cut through, and destructive to any ship which had the misfortune of striking against them. No attempt for raising them, or for opening the channel in any manner, could, however, be made, until the command of the shores on both sides was fully obtained.

About three miles lower down the river, they had sunk other ranges of these machines, and were constructing for their protection some considerable and extensive works, which, though not yet finished, were in such forwardness as to be provided with artillery, and to command their object, at a place on the Jersey side called Billing's Point. These works and machines were further supported by several gallies mounting heavy cannon, together with two floating batteries, a number of armed vessels and small craft of various kinds, and some fire ships. In a word, the Delaware seemed to teem with every defensive preparation, which could render the hostile operations and movements of a fleet, in the confined and uncertain navigation of a river, extremely dangerous.

Upon the representation of Captain Hammond, of the Roe-[46] buck, who with some other ships of war had arrived in the Delaware before Lord Howe, the General detached two regiments, consisting of three battalions, under Colonel Stirling,[47] to dislodge the enemy from Billingsfort. The detachment having crossed the river from Chester, where the ships lay, performed the service effectually without loss or opposition. Oct. 1st. The enemy, without waiting to be attacked, as soon as they heard of their approach, im-

mediately spiked their artillery, set fire to the barracks, and abandoned the place with the greatest precipitation. The detachment waited to destroy, or to render unserviceable, those parts of the works which fronted the river. This success, with the spirit and perseverance exhibited by the officers and crews of the ships under his command, enabled Captain Hammond, through great difficulties, and a vigorous opposition from the marine force of the enemy, to carry the principal object of the expedition into effect, by cutting away and weighing up so much of the chevaux-de-frize, as opened a narrow and difficult passage for ships through this lower barrier.

Upon the return of the detachment from Jersey, another regiment was sent to meet them at Chester, in order that they might altogether form a sufficient escort for a large convoy of provisions to the camp. The army still lay at German-Town, a very long and confiderable village, about half a dozen miles from Philadelphia, and which, stretching on both sides of the great road to the northward, forms a continued street of two miles in length. The line of encampment crossed German-Town at right angles about the center, the left wing extending on the west from the town to the Schuylkill. That wing was covered in front, by the mounted and dismounted German chasseurs; a battalion of light infantry, and the Queen's American rangers, were in the front of the right; and the 40th regiment, with another battalion of light infantry, were posted at the head of the village. Lord Cornwallis lay at Philadelphia, with four battalions of grenadiers; and we have already seen, that three regiments had been detached on the side of Chester.

The enemy were encamped at Skippach Creek, about 16 miles from German-Town. They had received some reinforcements, and

they were not ignorant that the royal army was weakened by the detachments it had made to Philadelphia and Chester. These circumstances induced an enterprize, little expected, and seemingly as little suited, to the general caution, and to the supposed genius and disposition of Washington. Instead of shunning, as usual, every thing that might lead to an action, the American army quitted its strong post at Skippach Creek at six in the evening, and marched all night to surprize and attack the royal army in its camp at German-Town.

At three o'clock in the morning, their approach was 4th. discovered by the patroles, and the army was immediately called to arms. They began their attack upon the 40th regiment, and the battalion of light infantry by which it was accompanied. These corps, after a vigorous resistance, being at length overpowered by numbers, were pressed and pursued into the village. In this exigence, a measure upon which much of the future fortune of the day depended, was instantly and happily adopted by Lieutenant-Colonel Musgrave,[48] who threw himself with six companies of the 40th regiment into a large and strong stone house, which lay full in the front of the enemy.

By this measure they were checked in their forward hope and design of gaining complete and immediate possession of that long town; which among other great and obvious advantages, would have enabled them effectually to separate the right and left wings of the royal army. The Colonel and his brave party, surrounded by a whole brigade, and attacked on every side with great resolution, defended the house with the most undaunted courage; and though the enemy at length brought cannon up to the assault, he still maintained his post with equal intrepidity, pouring a dreadful and unceasing fire through the windows, until affairs had taken such a turn as afforded him relief.

This was accomplished by Major-General Grey, who bringing the front of a great part of the left wing by a timely movement to the village, led on three battalions of the 3d brigade, who attacked the enemy with vigour, and were as bravely supported and seconded, by Brigadier-General Agnew, at the head of the 4th brigade. The engagement was now for some time very warm; but the enemy being attacked on the opposite side of the village by two regiments of the right wing, were thrown into total disorder, and driven out of the town with considerable slaughter.

In the mean time, the light infantry and pickets of the right wing, supported by the 4th, and seconded by the 49th regiment, were warmly engaged with the enemy's left; but General Grey, after forcing their troops in the village, having passed it, and bringing the left wing forward, they immediately retired on all sides. The enemy was pursued for some miles; but the country being woody, strong, and enclosed, the pursuit was attended with so little effect, that they carried their cannon clear off. Lord Cornwallis arrived with a squadron of light-horse from Philadelphia, towards the close of the engagement, and joined in the pursuit; whilst three battalions of grenadiers from the same place, who had run themselves out of breath in the ardour of succouring their fellows, were too late to come in for any share of the action.

It appears that the morning was exceedingly foggy, to which the Americans (who had considerable success in the beginning of the action) attribute their not improving the advantages they at first gained, in the manner which they would otherwise have done. For they were not only, as they assert, through this circumstance, prevented from observing the true situation of the enemy, by which the latter had time to recover from the effect of the first impression they had made on them; but the different bodies of their own army were kept in ignorance of each others movements and success, and were consequently incapable of acting in concert. It is even said, that some of their parties, in the thickness of the fog, had poured their fire upon each other under a blind mistake on both sides of being engaged with the enemy. Washington paid great compliments to the right wing for its good behaviour, of which he had been a witness, but he left the conduct of the left, at least, doubtful, by saying that he had not yet received sufficient information to found any opinion on.

The loss of the royal army in this action, including the wounded and a few prisoners, rather exceeded that at the Brandywine, the whole amounting to 535; but the proportion of slain was still smaller than in that engagement, and scarcely exceeded 70. In this number were unhappily some very brave and distinguished officers; particularly Brigadier-General Agnew, and Lieutenant-Colonel Bird. The number of officers wounded was considerable. The American loss was estimated in the Gazette, at between 200 and 300 slain, 600 wounded, and above 400 prisoners. Among the slain was General Nash, and several other officers of all ranks; 54 officers were taken prisoners. In this action the Americans acted upon the offensive; and though repulsed with loss, shewed themselves a formidable adversary; capable of charging with resolution, and retreating with good order. The hope therefore entertained from the effect of any fair action with them as decisive and likely to put a speedy termination to the war, was exceedingly abated.

The taking of Philadelphia was not attended with all the advantages expected from that conquest.

The rebel army, however straitned, still kept the field; and until the Delaware could be cleared, it was obvious, that the army could not support itself in that town for the winter. Therefore, as the whole effect of the campaign depended upon that operation, about a fortnight after the battle, the King's army removed from German-Town to Philadelphia, as being a more convenient situation for the reduction of Mud, or Fort Island, and for co-operating with the naval force in opening the navigation of the river. The enemy had returned after the action at German-Town, to their old camp at Skippach Creek, where they still continued.

Measures being concerted between the General and Admiral for removing the obstructions of the river, the former ordered batteries to be erected on the western shore, or Pensylvania side, in hopes of assisting in dislodging the enemy from Mud Island, the difficulty of access to which, was found to render its reduction a much more tedious and difficult operation than had been expected. He also detached a strong body of Hessians across the river at Cooper's Ferry, opposite the town, who were to march down and force the redoubt of Red Bank, whilst the ships, and the batteries on the other side, were to carry on their attacks against Mud Island and the enemy's marine force. The Hessian detachment was led by Colonel Donop, (who had gained great reputation in various actions of this war) and consisted, besides light infantry and chasseurs, of three battalions of grenadiers, and the regiment of Mirbach. The American force at Red Bank was estimated at about 800 men.

Though nothing could exceed the good dispositions made for these several attacks, nor the exertions of vigour and courage displayed both by the land and naval force on their different elements, yet

49

this enterprize not only failed of success, but was in every respect unfortunate. Colonel Donop attacked the Oct. 22d. enemy's entrenchments with the utmost gallantry, and after a very sharp action, succeeded in carrying an extensive out-work; but he found the enemy better covered in the body of the redoubt, and the defence more vigorous than he expected. The brave Colonel was there mortally wounded and taken prisoner. Several of his best officers were killed or disabled, and the Hessians, after a desperate engagement, were repulsed with great loss. Colonel Mingerode, the next [50] in command, being likewise dangerously wounded, the detachment was brought off by Lieutenant-Colonel Linsing, having suffered [51] much in the approach to and retreat from the assault, by the fire of the enemy's gallies and floating batteries. The loss of the Hessians, whether as to private men or officers, was never particularly authenticated; it was, however, known to be very considerable: probably not less than four or five hundred men.

The men of war and frigates destined for the attack, having made their way with difficulty through the lower barrier, took every possible disposition that the nature and situation of the river would admit for the destruction of the upper works and defences, where they commenced their assault at the same time that Colonel Donop was engaged at Red Bank. Fortune was not more favourable here than ashore. The ships could not bring their fire to bear with any great effect upon the works. The extraordinary obstructions with which the enemy had interrupted the free course of the river, had even affected its bed, and wrought some alteration in its known and natural channel. By this means, the Augusta man of war, and Merlin sloop, were grounded so fast at some distance from the chevaux-de-

frize, that there was no possibility of getting them off. In this situation, though the skill and courage of the officers and crews of the several vessels, prevented the effect of four fire ships which the enemy had sent to destroy the Augusta, she unfortunately took fire in the engagement, which placed the others under a necessity of retiring with the utmost expedition, to get beyond the effect of the explosion. In these urgent and difficult circumstances, the Merlin was hastily evacuated, and laid in a train of destruction, and the greater part of the officers and crew of the Augusta saved; but the second Lieutenant, Chaplain, and Gunner, with no inconsiderable number of the common men, unhappily perished.

The ill success of this enterprize, by no means damped the resolution of the commanders, in prosecution of the absolutely necessary work of opening the navigation of the Delaware. New ground was taken, new measures adopted, and every preparation made that could insure success to the design. Nor were the enemy idle on their side. They well understood the great consequence it was of to them to keep the naval force separated from the army, and to render the communication between them tedious and difficult. They accordingly left nothing undone to strengthen their defences.

The officers and seamen of the fleet were incessantly employed in conveying heavy artillery, provisions and stores, up the river, by a difficult channel on the west side, to a small morassy island, where they erected batteries, which greatly incommoded the enemy's works on Mud Island. Every Nov. 15th. thing being prepared for an attack, the Isis, and Somerset, men of war, passed up the east channel, in order to attack the enemy's works in front; several frigates drew up against a fort newly erected on the Jersey side, near

Manto Creek, which was so situated as to flank the men of war in their station; and two armed vessels, mounted with 24 pounders, successfully made their way through the narrow channel on the western side at the back of Hogg Island; a matter of the greatest importance with respect to the success of the attack, as these two vessels, in concert with the batteries newly erected in Province Island, enfiladed the principal works which the enemy had erected on Mud Island.

A heavy fire was supported on both sides. At length, the vigorous attack made by the Isis in front, and by the two armed vessels and the batteries in other quarters, so overpowered the enemy in the fort and works on Mud Island, that towards evening their artillery was entirely silenced. And they perceiving that measures were taking for forcing their works on the following morning, and being also sensible that, in the present state of things, they were not defensible, they set fire to every thing that was capable of receiving it, and abandoned the place in the night.

The loss of the enemy in men was said to be very considerable; that of the fleet, was more trifling than could have been supposed. Their artillery and some stores were taken at Mud Island. In two days after, Lord Cornwallis passed over with a detachment from Chester to Billing's Fort, where he was joined by a body of forces just arrived from New York. They proceeded all together to Red Bank, which the enemy abandoned at their approach, leaving their artillery with a considerable quantity of cannon ball and stores behind them. The works were demolished.

The enemy's shipping having now lost all protection on either side of the river, several of their gallies and other armed vessels took the advantage of a favourable night, to pass the batteries of Philadelphia, and escape to places of security farther up. The discovery of this transaction occasioned the sending an officer with a party of seamen to man the Delaware frigate lately taken, and lying at Philadelphia, and the taking of such other measures, as rendered the escaping of the remainder impracticable. Thus environed, the crews abandoned and set fire to their vessels, which were all consumed to the amount of seventeen of different sorts, including the two floating batteries, and fireships. With all these advantages, the season of the year, and other impediments, rendered the clearing of the river, in any considerable degree, impracticable; so that the making or discovering of such a channel, as might admit the passage of transports and vessels of easy burden with provisions and necessaries for the use of the army at Philadelphia, was all that could be obtained at present.

General Washington being reinforced by 4000 men from the northern army, advanced within 14 miles of Philadelphia, to a place called White Marsh, where he encamped in a very strong position, with his right to the Wissahichon Creek, and the front partly covered by Sandy Run. As this movement seemed to indicate a disposition to adventure, General Howe was not without hopes, that the late reinforcement would encourage them to hazard a battle for the recovery of Philadelphia. If such was their intention, he was determined that they should not cool in it, for want of an opportunity of bringing it into action; or if they still adhered to their usual system of caution and defence, it was still reasonably to be hoped that upon a close inspection of their situation, some part of their camp would be found so vulnerable as to admit of a successful impression.

Upon these grounds the General marched the army from Philadelphia on the 4th of December at night, and took post on Chesnut Hill, in the front of the enemy's right on the next morning. Finding that their right afforded no opening for an attack, he changed his ground before day on the 7th, and took a new position opposite to their center and left. Some skirmishes happened, in which the enemy were constantly defeated, and their flying parties pursued home almost to their works. The General, at length, after continuing above three days constantly in their sight, advancing within a mile of their lines, and examining their works with the closest attention, finding that nothing could provoke or entice them to action, and that their camp was in every part inaccessible, gave up the prosecution of a design which was evidently fruitless. The army also suffered greatly from the severity of the weather, both officers and soldiers being totally destitute of tents and field equipage.

The General accordingly began his march to Philadelphia on the afternoon of the 8th, in full view of the enemy, without being pursued, or in the smallest degree incommoded on his return. As the season was now too far advanced, to admit of any other attention than what related to the accommodation of the army, a grand detachment was sent out to procure forage for the winter, which was successfully performed. In the mean time, Washington removed his camp from White Marsh to Valley Forge, upon the Schuylkill, about 15 or 16 miles from Philadelphia, in a very strong, and consequently secure position. Nothing could afford a stronger proof, to whoever considers the nature and disposition of those people, of the unbounded influence on the minds both of his officers and men which that General possessed, than his being able, not only to keep them together, but to submit to the incommmodities and distresses incident to living in a hutted camp, during the severe winter of that climate, and where all his supplies of provision and stores must come from a great distance, at much expence and no small hazard. It was also a proof with many others, of the general strong disposition of America, to suffer all things rather than submit to force.

Such was the issue of the campaign upon the Delaware. A campaign which affords much room for the most serious reflection. The British arms were crowned with the most brilliant success. Two very considerable victories were obtained. In all lesser actions, bating the affair at Red Bank, they were equally triumphant. Yet with all this tide of success, all the fruit derived from our victories at the close of the campaign, amounted to no more than simply a good winter lodging for our army in the city of Philadelphia; whilst the troops possessed no more of the adjacent country than what they immediately commanded with their arms. It was still more discouraging, that the enemy had given repeated proofs, that however he might engage them when he thought it to his advantage, it was impossible for the royal army to bring him to action against his consent. This gave occasion to much uneasiness in England; where the news of the first successes had caused the greatest exultation, which was now succeeded with very gloomy reflections on the peculiar and fatal circumstances, which, from the nature of the country, and other co-operating causes, had distinguished this war, from all others in which we had ever been concerned; and in which victory and defeat were nearly productive of the same consequences.

Canada. Conduct of the northern expedition committed to General Burgoyne. Preparations made by General Carleton. Line of conduct pursued by him upon the new arrangement. Different opinions upon the utility and propriety of employing the Savages. State of the force under the command of General Burgoyne. Canadians obliged to contribute largely to the service. Expedition under Colonel St. Leger. War feast, and speech to the Indians at the river Bouquet. Manifesto. Royal army invest Ticonderoga and Mount Independence. Council of war held, and the forts abandoned by the Americans. Boom and bridge cut through. Pursuit by land and water. American gallies and batteaux destroyed near Skenesborough Water-falls. Americans set fire to, and abandon their works. Rear of the Americans overtaken by General Frazer near Hubberton. Colonel Francis defeated and killed. General St. Clair, with the remains of his army, take to the woods; and arrive at length at Fort Edward. Enemy bravely repulsed by Colonel Hill, and the 9th regiment, who are obliged to engage under a vast superiority of force. Americans set fire to, and abandon Fort Anne. Extraordinary difficulties encountered by the royal army in the march to Fort Edward. American Army retires to Saratoga.

WE now turn from exemplifying victory without equivalent advantage in one quarter, to behold the most mischievous consequences of defeat in another. The war upon the side of Canada and the lakes was committed to the charge of Lieutenant-General Burgoyne; an officer whose ability was unquestioned, and whose spirit of enterprize, and thirst for military glory, however rivalled, could not possibly be exceeded.

This appointment, however palliated or justified, by the propriety or supposed necessity of the Governor's constant residence in his province, could not fail of being sensibly felt, and could scarcely be supposed not to give umbrage, to General Carleton, to whose abilities, and resolution, this nation in general acknowledged, and the world attributed, the preservation of Canada. It was said, that his powers had been diminished in proportion to the greatness of his services. His military command extended before to every part of America, whither he might find it fitting to conduct the army under his direction. It was now suddenly restrained to the narrow limits of his own province. He had, said his friends, in the preceding campaign, not only driven the enemy out of Canada, but a great naval armament had been formed, the enemy's force on Lake Champlain destroyed, and Crown Point recovered, under his authority. The lateness of the season only, prevented him from attacking Ticonderoga, and immediately prosecuting the war to the southward. He had, during the winter, exerted his usual industry, and applied his military skill and judgment, in the forwarding of every preparation, which might conduce to the success of the design in the ensuing campaign. At the opening of the communication with England, instead of the reinforcement which he had required and expected for the completion of his purpose, he received an arrangement totally new, which as it had been framed without any reference to his judgment, or attention to his approbation, left nothing to his discretion or opinion in the execution. Two expeditions were to be formed, in each of which, the number and nature of the troops to be employed, the particular service of each corps, with its subdivisions, and the smallest detachment to be made from it, had been minutely and precisely specified by the Minister. He was not even consulted as to the number or nature of the troops which were to remain in his hands for the defence or security of Ca-

nada. In a word, the army which he had lately commanded was taken out of his, and placed in other hands, and officers who lately acted under his direction, were by a detraction from his authority, virtually placed in independent commands; for their instructions to put themselves under the orders of Sir William Howe, seemed little more than a mockery, as that General had informed Sir Guy Carleton, that the concerted operations of the campaign on his side, would lead him to such a distance, as to render any communication of that nature impracticable.

That the Governor felt and understood this arrangement and these appointments in the manner we have related from the complaints of his friends in England, seems evident from the immediate resignation of his government which then took place; but as the notification, the appointment of another, and the passage of his successor from Europe, were all works of time, he was still, however ungrateful the task, obliged to continue in the exercise of his office, during a longer period than that of which we are treating.

Under these circumstances, and in this trying and difficult situation, he endeavoured to shew that resentment could not warp him from his duty, and he applied himself with the same diligence and energy, to forward by every possible means, and to support in all its parts the expedition, as if the arrangement was entirely his own. This conduct, however praiseworthy, was not less necessary, from the peculiar nature of the service which was to be performed; a service exceedingly complicated in the arrangement, uncommonly numerous in the parts; and many unusual in practice. It will not be difficult to conceive, how effectually negligence, dislike, obstinacy, or even a colourable and rational difference of opinion in some difputable points, might frustrate all the hopes founded upon such a system.

Nothing of this sort intervened, to damp the spirit or to defeat the success of the expedition. The preparations were carried on with vigour.

We have before taken notice, that the ministers, and more particularly the noble Lord at the head of the American department, were not only particularly interested in the event, but had founded the most sanguine hopes upon the success of this expedition. Nothing was accordingly left undone on their side, which, in proportion to the number of regular troops that could be spared for that particular service, might conduce to give efficacy to their operations. Besides, Canada it was hoped would supply a warlike though undisciplined militia, well calculated for, and acquainted with, the peculiar nature of the service and country.

To strengthen and increase this irregular, but necessary aid, arms and accoutrements were amply provided, to supply those numerous loyalists, who were expected to join the royal army as soon as it approached or penetrated the frontiers of the adjacent provinces. As a powerful artillery is considered to be the great and effective arm in an American war, where a numerous and undisciplined enemy is to be continually attacked in difficult posts, and driven out of woods and fastnesses, so this part of the service was particularly attended to, and the brass train that was sent out upon this expedition, was perhaps the finest, and probably the most excellently supplied as to officers and private men, that had ever been allotted to second the operations of any army, which did not far exceed the present in number. [52]

Besides these forces, several nations of savages had been induced to come into the field. This measure was defended upon the supposed necessity of the case; as if from their character it was presumed they could not lie still, and if not engaged in the King's service, would have joined the Americans. Whatever advantages were hoped from them, General Carleton did not in the preceding year make much use of them; but civilly dismissed them at the close of the campaign, on a promise of their appearing in the next if required. There has been a good deal of discussion, which we want materials to settle, how far he approved of their employment at all. The friends of ministry said, that he had recommended and forwarded the measure. Others said, that partly from humanity, partly from his forming a just estimate of their services, and knowing by experience the extent of their powers and ability in war, he was unwilling to use them, knowing that they were capricious, inconstant, and intractable. That as their ideas of war and of courage were totally different from those of civilized nations, so, notwithstanding their ferocity of character, and the incredible specimens of passive valour which they sometimes exhibited in cases adapted to their own opinions, they not only abhorred, but dreaded, whatever is considered as fair and generous service among Europeans, wherein the contending parties bravely seek and are included in one common danger, trusting only for success to their superior skill and courage. That their object and design in all wars, was not to fight, but to murder; not to conquer, but to destroy. In a word, that their service was uncertain, their rapacity insatiate, their faith ever doubtful, and their action cruel and barbarous.

Whatever his reasons were for not employing them in a more early and effectual manner, if it were in his power to do it, as early and effectually as was imagined, this conduct was far from being generally approved of at home. Those who were particularly warm in their zeal against the colonies, began somewhat to forget their natural humanity in their anger. They insisted, that every appearance of lenience in such circumstances was actual cruelty in the effect, by acting as an incentive to disobedience, and increasing the objects of punishment. That on the contrary, partial severity was general mercy; as timely exertions of justice, and strict inflictions of punishment, were at all times the sure means of preventing crimes. That the only method of speedily crushing the rebellion, was to render the situation of the actors in it so intolerable, that a cessation from danger, and the blessings of repose, should become the only objects of their contemplation and hope. That the means were but little to be attended to, when they led to the accomplishment of so great and happy a purpose, as the destruction of rebellion, and the restoration of order and legal government. And that in all convulsions of states, the innocent were too frequently involved in the calamities which were intended or wished to be confined entirely to the guilty; but such was the lot and condition of mankind, and this evil, however deplored, could not in numberless instances be avoided or prevented. This doctrine was supported by the avowed friends of government, whether out of office, or in the subordinate departments of the state; it was also generally supposed to be consonant to the opinions of the ministers, and that General Carleton's scruples or niceties upon this point were by no means acceptable. [53]

However this was, in the present arrangement, the aid of the savages was considered as a principal member of that force which was destined to the prosecution of the northern war, and the Governor of Canada was accordingly enjoined to use his utmost weight and influence, in bringing the Indian nations forward in support of the expedition. His zeal was as active in fulfilling this duty, as it was in every other which appertained to the present service. Nor was his success disproportioned to his zeal. Whether it proceeded from the Governor's influence with the Indians, their avidity to seize the presents which were now liberally distributed amongst them, from their own innate thirst for war and plunder, or more probably, from the joint operation of all these causes, their remote as well as near nations poured forth their warriors in such abundance, that he became at length apprehensive, that their numbers might render them an incumbrance rather than an aid to the army.

The regular force allotted to the expedition conducted by General Burgoyne, consisting of British and German troops, amounted to 7173 men, exclusive of the artillery corps. Of these, the German corps (consisting mostly of Brunswickers) amounted to 3217. The force required by that General in the proposals which he laid before the Minister, consisted of 8000 regulars, rank and file, besides the artillery, a corps of watermen, 2000 Canadians, including hatchetmen, and other workmen, with a thousand, or more, savages. We have no certain information what numbers of these auxiliaries were in actual service upon the expedition.

Canada was largely rated, and its inhabitants must have sensibly felt the proportion which they were allotted to contribute towards this service. In the proposals laid before the Minister, besides the militia and various species of workmen supposed necessary to be immediately attached to the army, and to accompany it on the expedition, chains of their militia, patroles, and posts, were expected to occupy the woods in the frontiers on the rear of the army, partly to intercept the communication between the enemy and the ill affected

in Canada, partly to prevent desertion and to procure intelligence, and for various other duties necessary towards keeping the country in quiet. Another great call upon them was for workmen to complete the fortifications at Sorel, St. John's, Chamblee and Isle au Noix, which it was supposed would amount to 2000 men. A still greater call upon the Canadians, and the more grievous, as it was at their seed-sowing season, was for the transport of all the provisions, artillery-stores, and baggage of the army, from the different repositories to the water, and afterwards at the carrying places, besides the corvees for making the roads. It was estimated that this service would for some time before, and at the opening of the campaign, require no less than 2000 men, besides a very large proportion of horses and carts.

General Burgoyne was seconded by able and excellent officers. Of these, Major-General Philips of the artillery, who had gained such distinguished renown by his conduct in that service during the late war in Germany, deserves to be particularly mentioned. He was likewise assisted by the Brigadier-Generals, Frazer, Powel, and Hamilton, all distinguished officers, [54] with the Brunswick Major-General Baron Reidesel, and Brigadier-General Speeht. The army was, in every respect, in the best condition that could possibly be expected or wished, the troops being in the highest spirits, admirably disciplined, and uncommonly healthy.

The detachment on the expedition to the Mohawk River under Colonel St. Leger, did not probably exceed seven or eight hundred [55] men, consisting of 200 drawn from the 8th and 34th regiments, a regiment of New-Yorkers, lately raised by, and under the command of, Sir John Johnson, being mostly [56] emigrants from his own country adjoining to the intended scene of action, with some Hanau chasseurs,

a company of Canadians, and another of newly raised rangers. These were joined by a strong body of savages, in part conducted, or if it may be termed officered, by a number of British and Americans. The regular force left in Canada, including the Highland emigrants under that denomination, amounted to about 3700 men.

The army being at length arrived and encamped at the River Bouquet, on the west side of Lake Champlain, and at no very great distance to the northward of Crown Point, General Burgoyne, there met the Indians in congress, and afterwards, in compliance with the customs of those people, gave them a war feast. The speech which he made to the savages upon this occasion has been published. It was calculated, in those powerful strains of elocution by which that gentleman is distinguished, to excite their ardour in the common cause, and at the same time to repress their barbarity. For this purpose he took pains in explaining to them the distinction, between a war carried on against a common enemy, in which the whole country and people were hostile, and the present, in which good and faithful subjects were largely, and of necessity, intermixed with rebels and traitors. Upon this principle he laid down several injunctions for the government of their conduct, particularly, that they should only kill those who were opposed to them in arms; that old men, women, children, and prisoners, should be held sacred from the knife or hatchet, even in the heat of actual conflict; that they should only scalp those whom they had slain in fair opposition; but that under no pretence, subtlety, or colour of prevarication, they should scalp the wounded, or even dying; much less kill persons in that condition, by way of evading the injunction. And they were promised a compensation for prisoners, but

June 21. 1777.

informed that they should be called to account for scalps. These endeavours did in some measure mitigate, but were not of force wholly to restrain their ferocity; of which some unhappy instances afterwards appeared.

The General soon after dispersed a manifesto, calculated to spread terror among the contumacious, and particularly to revive in their minds every latent impression of fear derived from knowledge or information of the cruel operations of the savages, whose numbers were accordingly magnified, and their eagerness to be let loose to their prey, described with uncommon energy. The force of that great power, which was now spread by sea and land, to embrace or to crush every part of America, was displayed in full, lofty, and expressive language. The rebellion, with its effects, and the conduct of the present governors and governments, were charged with the highest colouring, and exhibited a most hideous picture, of unparalleled injustice, cruelty, persecution and tyranny. Encouragement and employment were assured to those, who with a disposition and ability suited to the purpose, should actually assist in redeeming their country from slavery, and in the re-establishment of legal government. Protection and security, clogged with conditions, restricted by circumstances, and rather imperfectly or inexplicitly expressed, were held out to the peaceable and industrious, who continued in their habitations. And all the calamities and outrages of war, arrayed in their most terrific forms, were denounced against those who persevered in their hostility.

The army having made a short stay at Crown Point, for the establishment of magazines, an hospital, and other necessary services, proceeded, in concert with the naval armament, to invest Ticonderoga, which was the first object of their destination. Although the rash and ill conducted attempt made upon that place in the year 1758, with the consequent repulse and heavy loss sustained by the British army, rendered it at that time an object of general attention, it may not at this distance of time be wholly unnecessary to take some notice of its situation, as well as of its state of defence.

Ticonderoga lies on the western shore, and only a few miles to the northward from the commencement of that narrow inlet, by which the water from Lake George is conveyed to Lake Champlain. Crown Point lies about a dozen miles farther north at the extremity of that inlet. The first of these places is situated on an angle of land, which is surrounded on three sides by water, and that covered by rocks. A great part of the fourth side was covered by a deep morass, and where that fails, the old French lines still continued as a defence on the north-west quarter. The Americans strengthened these lines with additional works and a blockhouse. They had other posts with works and blockhouses, on the left, towards Lake George. To the right of the French lines they had also two new blockhouses with other works.

On the eastern shore of the inlet, and opposite to Ticonderoga, the Americans had taken still more pains in fortifying a high circular hill to which they gave the name of Mount Independence. On the summit of this, which is Tableland, they had erected a star fort, enclosing a large square of barracks, well fortified and supplied with artillery. The foot of the mountain, which on the west side projected into the water, was strongly entrenched to its edge, and the entrenchment well lined with heavy artillery. A battery about half way up the mount, sustained and covered these lower works.

The Americans, with their usual industry, had joined these two posts by a bridge of communication thrown over the inlet. This was, like many other of their performances, a great and most laborious work. The bridge was supported on 22 sunken piers of very large timber, placed at nearly equal distances; the spaces between these were filled with separate floats, each about fifty feet long and twelve feet wide, strongly fastened together with chains and rivets, and as effectually attached to the sunken pillars. On the Lake Champlain side of the bridge, it was defended by a boom composed of very large pieces of timber, fastened together by rivetted bolts and double chains, made of iron an inch and half square. Thus not only a communication was maintained between these two posts, but all access by water from the northern side was totally cut off. [57]

It is to be observed, that as the inlet immediately after passing Ticonderoga, assumes a new form, suddenly widening to a considerable breadth, and becoming navigable to vessels of burden, so from thence it also holds the name of Champlain, although it is not yet properly a part of the lake. On the other hand, the southern gut from Lake George, besides being narrow, is also rendered unnavigable by shallows and falls; but on its arrival at Ticonderoga, it is joined by a great body of water on the eastern side, called, in this part, South River, but higher up towards its source, before the junction of the elder branch with the younger, which runs from South Bay, it is known under the appellation of Wood Creek. The confluence of these waters at Ticonderoga, forms a small bay to the southward of the bridge of communication, and the point of land formed by their junction, is composed of a mountain called Sugar Hill. [58]

Notwithstanding the apparent strength of Ticonderoga from what we have hitherto seen, it is entirely overlooked, and its works effectually commanded by Sugar Hill. This circumstance occasioned a consultation among the Americans as to the fortifying of that Mount; but their works were already far too extensive for their powers of defence, and would require ten or twelve thousand men to be effectually manned. It was likewise hoped, that the difficulty of access to the Sugar Mount, and the savage inequality of its surface, would prevent the enemy from attempting to profit of its situation.

It would be exceedingly difficult from the information before us, to form any authentic estimate of the number of Americans that were in the actual defence of these two posts. It appears by the commander in chief, General St. Clair's exculpatory [59] letter to the congress, as well as by the resolutions of the council of war, which accompanies it, that his whole force, including 900 militia, who were to quit him in a few days, was only about 3000 men; that these were ill equipped, and worse armed; particularly in the article of bayonets, an arm so essential in the defence of lines, that they had not one to ten of their number. This account would seem not only satisfactory but conclusive, if it had not been contradicted by others. In a detail of the transactions of the campaign, transmitted by the war office of Massachusetts Bay to the American deputies in France, and for the conveyance of which a light ship was sent out on purpose, they state St. Clair's force at near 5000 men well equipped and armed. It is, however, to [60] be observed, that they talk with great bitterness of that General's conduct, as he had done in his first letter to congress, with respect to the behaviour of two of their regiments: It may also be supposed, that in a statement of their affairs intended to operate upon the sentiments and conduct of a court, from which they already received essential benefits, and looked forward to much greater, they would rather increase the weight of blame upon an unfortunate officer, than detract from the public opinion of their own conduct and power, by attributing weakness to their councils, or inefficacy to their arms.

As the royal army approached to the object of its destination, it advanced with equal caution and order, on both sides of the lake, the naval force keeping its station in the centre, until the one had begun to enclose the enemy on the land side, and the frigates and gun-boats cast anchor just out of cannon shot from their works. Upon the near approach of the right wing on the Ticonderoga side, upon the 2d of July, the Americans immediately abandoned and set fire to their works, block-houses, and saw-mills, towards Lake George, and without sally, interruption, or the smallest motion of diversion, permitted Major General Phillips to take possession of the very advantageous post of Mount Hope, which besides commanding their lines in a great and dangerous degree, totally cut off their communication with that lake. The same supineness and total want of vigour appeared in every thing on their side, except in the keeping up of an ineffectual roar of cannon, which was so much contemned on the other as not to be once returned.

In the mean while, the royal army proceeded with such expedition in the construction of its works, the bringing up of artillery, stores and provisions, and the establishment of its posts and communications, that by the 5th, matters were so far advanced, as to require little more time for compleatly investing the posts on both sides of the lake. Sugar Hill was also examined, and the advantages it presented were so important, though attended with infinite labour and difficulty, from the necessity of making a road to its top through very rough ground, and constructing a level there for a battery, that this arduous task was undertaken, and already far advanced towards its completion, through the spirit, judgment, and active industry of General Phillips.

In these circumstances, a hasty council was on that day held by the American Generals, to which their principal went, as he informs us, already predetermined as to his conduct. It was represented, that their whole effective numbers were not sufficient to man one half of the works; that as the whole must consequently be upon constant duty, it would be impossible for them to sustain the fatigue for any length of time; and that as the enemy's batteries were ready to open, and the place would be completely invested on all sides within 24 hours, nothing could save the troops, but an immediate evacuation of both posts. This determination was unanimously agreed to by the council, and the place was accordingly evacuated on that night.

However justly this representation of their condition and circumstances was founded, and however necessary the determination of the council was in the present state of their affairs, one apparently capital error on the side of the commanders, must strike every common observer. If their force was not sufficient for the defence of the works, why did they not form this resolution in time? Why did they not withdraw the troops, artillery, and stores, and demolish the works before the arrival of the enemy? Why did they wait to be nearly surrounded, until their retreat was more ruinous than a surrender under any conditions that could be proposed, and little less destructive in the event, than if the works had been carried by storm?

These are questions that time and better information alone can answer, if ever they should clearly answer, in favour of the American Generals.

The baggage of the army, with such artillery, stores, and provisions, as the necessity of the time would permit, were embarked with a strong detachment on board above 200 batteaux, and dispatched, under convoy of five armed gallies, up the south river, in their way to Skenesborough. The main army took its route by the way of Castletown, to reach the same place by land.

July 6th. The first light of the morning had no sooner discovered the flight of the enemy, than their main body was eagerly pursued by Brigadier General Frazer, at the head of his brigade, consisting of the light troops, grenadiers, and some other corps. Major General Reidesel was also ordered to join in the pursuit by land, with the greater part of the Brunswick troops, either to support the Brigadier, or to act separately, as occasion might require, or circumstances direct. The enemy left a prodigious artillery behind them, which with those taken or destroyed in the armed vessels at Skenesborough, amounted to no less than 128 pieces, of all sorts, serviceable and unserviceable. They also left some military stores of different sorts, and no inconsiderable stock of provisions in the forts.

General Burgoyne conducted the pursuit by water in person. That brigde and those works, which the Americans had laboured hard for ten months to render impenetrable, were cut through in less time by the British seamen and artificers, than it would have cost them to have described their structure. In a word, they did their business with such speed and effect, that not only the gun boats, but the Royal George and Inflexible frigates, had passed through the bridge by nine o'clock in the morning. Several regiments embarked on board the vessels, and the pursuit up the river was supported with such vigour, that by three o'clock in the afternoon, the foremost brigade of the gun-boats, was closely engaged with the enemies gallies near Skenesborough Falls. In the mean time, three regiments which had been landed at South Bay, ascended and passed a mountain with great expedition, in order to attack the enemy's works at the falls, and thereby cut off their retreat. But their speedy flight prevented the execution of that design. Upon the approach of the frigates, the gallies, which were already overborne by the gun-boats, lost all spirit; two of them were accordingly taken, and three blown up. The rebels now giving way to their despair, set fire to their works, stockaded fort, mills, and batteaux, after which they escaped as well as they could up the Wood Creek. This stroke seemed to complete the ruin of their ill-fated army, for the batteaux were deeply loaded, besides their baggage, with ammunition, stores, and provisions; so that they were now left naked in the woods, destitute of provision, and without any other means of defence, than what they derived from the arms in their hands.

Confusion and dismay, equally attended their main body on the left. The soldiers had lost all respect for, and confidence in their commanders. It would be fruitless to expect resolution, where no order nor command could be maintained.

Brigadier Frazer continued and supported the chace through the vehement heat of a burning day, with his usual activity and vigour. Having received intelligence that the enemy's rear were at no great distance, and were commanded by Colonel Francis,[61] one of their best and bravest officers, his troops lay that night on their arms. He came up

7th. with the enemy, at five in the morning, whom he found strongly posted, with great advantage of ground, and a still greater superiority in point of number. As he expected every moment to be joined by General Reidesel, and was apprehensive that the enemy might escape if he delayed, he did not hesitate to begin the attack. The advantages which they possessed in ground and number, and perhaps more than both, the goodness of their commander, induced them to make a better stand than might have been expected from their condition in other respects.

As Frazer's corps was not supported near so soon as had been expected, the engagement was long; and though the light infantry and granadiers gave several striking proofs of their superiority, affairs were still undecided and critical. The arrival of the Germans was at length decisive. The enemy fled on all sides, leaving their brave commander, with many other officers, and above 200 private men, dead on the field. About the same number, besides a Colonel, seven Captains, and ten Subalterns were taken prisoners. Above 600 were supposed to be wounded, many of whom perished miserably in the woods. The principal loss on the side of the royal army, was that of Major Grant, a brave officer, who was killed. St. Clair, with the van of the American army, was at this time at Castletown, about six miles farther on. Upon the account of this disaster, and of the more fatal ſtroke at Skeneſborough, and under the apprehenſion of being intercepted at Fort Anne, he ſtruck on to the woods on his left, probably uncertain whether he ſhould direct his courſe towards the New England provinces and the upper part of the Connecticut, or to Fort Edward.

During theſe advantages on the left, Colonel Hill was detach-[62] ed with the 9th regiment from Skeneſborough towards Fort Anne, in order to intercept the fugirives who fled along the Wood Creek, whilſt another part of the army was employed in carrying batteaux over the falls, in order to facilitate their movement to diſlodge the enemy from that poſt. In that expedition, the Colonel was attacked by a body of the enemy, conſiſting, as he conceived, of ſix times the number of his detachment, who finding all their efforts in front ineffectual to force the judicious poſition which he had taken, attempted to ſurround the regiment. This alarming attempt, put him under a neceſſity of changing his ground in the heat of action. Nothing leſs than the moſt perfect diſcipline, ſupported by the cooleſt intrepidity, could have enabled the regiment to execute ſo critical a movement in the face of the enemy, and in ſuch circumſtances. It was however performed with ſuch ſteadineſs and effect, that the enemy, after an attack of three hours, were ſo totally repulſed, and with ſuch loſs, that after ſetting fire to Fort Anne, they fled with the utmoſt precipitation towards Fort Edward, [63] upon the Hudſon's river.

The loſs of the royal army, in all this ſervice, and in ſo many different engagements, ſome of which were warm, and ſeemed liable to loſs, was very ſmall. The whole in killed and wounded, not much exceeding two hundred men.

Such was the rapid torrent of ſucceſs, which ſwept every thing away before the northern army in its outſet. It is not to be wondered at, if both officers and private men were highly elated with their fortune, and deemed that and their proweſs to be irreſiſtible; if they regarded their enemy with the greateſt contempt, conſidered their own toils to be nearly at an end, Albany to be already in their hands; and the reduction of the northern provinces to be rather a matter of ſome time, than an arduous taſk full of difficulty and danger.

At home, the joy and exultation was extreme; not only at court, but with all thoſe who hoped or wiſhed the unqualified ſubjugation, and unconditional ſubmiſſion of the colonies. The loſs in reputation was greater to the Americans, and capable of more fatal conſequences, than even that of ground, of poſts, of artillery, or of men. All the contemptuous and moſt degrading charges which had been made by their enemies, of their wanting the reſolution and abilities of men, even in the defence of whatever was dear to them, were now repeated and believed. Thoſe who ſtill regarded them as men, and who had not yet loſt all affection to them as brethren; who alſo retained hopes that a happy reconciliation upon conſtitutional principles, without ſacrificing the dignity or the juſt authority of government on the one ſide, or a dereliction of the rights of freemen on the other, was not even now impoſſible, notwithſtanding their favourable diſpoſitions in general, could not help feeling upon this occaſion, that the Americans ſunk not a little in their eſtimation. It was not difficult to diffuſe an opinion, that the war in effect was over; and that any further reſiſtance, would ſerve only to render the terms of their ſubmiſſion the worſe. Such were ſome of the immediate effects of the loſs of thoſe grand keys of North America, Ticonderoga and the lakes.

General Burgoyne continued for ſome days, with the army partly at Skeneſborough, and partly ſpread in the adjoining country. They were under the neceſſity of waiting for the arrival of tents, baggage, and proviſions. In the mean time, no labour was ſpared in opening roads by the way of Fort Anne, for advancing againſt the enemy. Equal induſtry was uſed in clearing the Wood Creek from the obſtacles of fallen trees, ſunken ſtones, and other impediments which had been laid in the way by the enemy, in order to open a paſſage for batteaux, for the conveyance of artillery, ſtores, proviſions, and camp equipage. Nor was leſs diligence uſed at Ticonderoga, in the carrying of gun-boats, proviſion veſſels, and batteaux, over land into Lake George. Theſe were all laborious works, but the ſpirit of the army was at that time ſuperior to toil or danger,

General Schuyler was at Fort Edward upon the Hudſon's river, where he was endeavouring to collect the militia, and had been joined by St. Clair, with the wretched remains of his army, who had taken a round about march of ſeven days through the woods, in which, from the exceeding badneſs of the weather, with the want of covering, proviſions, and all manner of neceſſaries, they had ſuffered the moſt extreme miſery. Many others of the fugitives had alſo arrived; but ſo totally broken down, that they were nearly as deſtitute of arms, ammunition, and all the materials of war, as they were of vigour, hope, and ſpirit, to uſe them with effect.

Although the direct diſtance from Fort Anne, where the batteaux navigation on Wood Creek determined, or even from Skeneſborough to Fort Edward, was no greater, than what in England would be conſidered as a moderate ride of exerciſe, yet ſuch is the favage face and impracticable nature of the country, and fuch were the artificial difficulties which the induftry of the enemy had thrown in the way, that the progrefs of the army thither, was a work of much preparation, time, and labour. It will fcarcely be believed in after times, and may now be received with difficulty in any other part of the world, that it coft an active and fpirited army, without an enemy in force to impede its progrefs, not many fewer days in paffing from one part to another of a country, than the diftance, in a direct line, would have meafured miles. Yet fuch, however extraordinary, is the fact. Befides that the country was a wildernefs in almoft every part of the paffage, the enemy had cut large timber trees in fuch a manner, on both fides of the road, as to fall acrofs and lengthways, with their branches interwoven; fo that the troops had feveral layers of thefe frequently to remove, in places where they could not poffibly take any other direction. The face of the country war likewife fo broken with creeks and marfhes, that in that fhort fpace, they had no lefs than forty bridges to conftruct, befides others to repair; and one of thefe was of log work, over a morafs two miles in extent. All thefe toils and difficulties were encountered and overcome by the troops with their ufual fpirit and alacrity. The enemy were too weak, too much difpirited, and probably too much afraid of the Indians, to add very materially to thefe difficulties. Some fkirmifhing and firing there was, however, on every day's march, in which, as ufual, they conftantly came off lofers.

It is true, that General Burgoyne might have adopted another route to Hudfon's river, by which moft of thefe particular difficulties would have been avoided. By returning down the South river to Ticonderoga, he might again have embarked the army on Lake George, and proceeded to the fort which takes its name, and lies at its head, from whence there is a waggon road to Fort Edward. To this it was objected, and probably with reafon, that a retrograde motion in the height of victory, would tend greatly to abate that panic with which the enemy were confounded and overwhelmed; that it would even cool the ardour, and check the animation of the troops, to call them off from the profecution of their fuccefs, to a cold and fpiritlefs voyage; and that their expedition would undoubtedly be checked by the refiftance and delay which they muft expect at Fort George; whereas when the garrifon perceived that the army was marching in a direction, which was likely to cut off their retreat, they would undoubtedly confult their fafety in time, by abandoning the poft.

The enemy abandoned Fort Edward, and retired to Saratoga, at the approach of the royal army, which, from the impediments we have feen in the march, was not until the end of July. The enthufiafm of the army, as well as of the General, upon their arrival on the Hudfon's river, which had been fo long the object of their hopes and wifhes, may be better conceived than defcribed. As the enemy, by previoufly abandoning Fort George, and burning their veffels, had left the lake entirely open, a great embarkation of provifions, ftores, and neceffaries, was already arrived at that poft from Ticonderoga. The army was accordingly fully and immediately employed, in tranfporting thefe articles, with artillery, batteaux, and fuch other matters as they judged neceffary for the profecution of their future meafures, from Fort George to Hudfon's river.

General terror excited by the loss of Ticonderoga, and the expected progress of the savages. New England governments notwithstanding shew no appearance of submission. Arnold sent with a reinforcement to the northern army. Ill effects produced by the cruelties of the Indians. Difficulties experienced by the royal army in the neighbourhood of Fort Edward, and in the conveyance of provisions and stores from Lake George. Movement made down the North River, and a bridge of rafts thrown over near Saratoga, in order to facilitate the operations of Colonel St. Leger. Expedition to surprize the magazines at Bennington, under the conduct of Colonel Baum. Colonel Breyman ordered forward to support the expedition. Baum defeated and taken prisoner; Breyman also defeated. Ill consequences. Fort Stanwix obstinately defended against Colonel St. Leger. General Harkimer attempts to relieve the fort with a body of militia, who are mostly cut to pieces. Cruelty, and ill conduct of the savages; grow sullen and intractable; oblige Colonel St. Leger to raise the siege with precipitation and loss. Villainy of their behaviour on the retreat. Siege raised before the arrival of Arnold and his detachment to the relief of the fort. General Gates takes the command of the American army. General Burgoyne with the royal army pass the North River at Saratoga, and advance to attack the enemy near Still Water. Difference of opinion upon that measure, as well as the motives which led to its being adopted. Severe and heavy action on the nineteenth of September. Both armies fortify their camps. Unfortunate action on the seventh of October. Camp stormed. Death of General Frazer, Colonel Breyman, and Sir James Clarke. Distressed situation of the royal army. Masterly movement made, and an entire new position taken in the night. New engagement eagerly sought, but refused on the next day by the enemy. Retreat to Saratoga. Previous desertion of the Indians and others. Royal army reduced to the utmost streights. Nearly surrounded on all sides. Cut off from all means of subsistence, and possibility of retreat. Councils of war. Convention concluded with General Gates. Terms of the convention. State of the army. Successful expedition by Sir Henry Clinton and General Vaughan up the North River. Several forts taken; Esopus and other places destroyed. Colonel Campbell, with the Majors Sill and Grant, and Count Graboushie, a Polish nobleman, killed in this expedition. Some observations on the campaign.

NOTHING could exceed the astonishment and terror, which the loss of Ticonderoga, and its immediate consequences, spread throughout the New England provinces. The General's manifesto, in which he displayed the powers and numbers of the savages, added perhaps to the effect. It was remarkable, however, that in the midst of all these disasters, and consequent terrors, no sort of disposition to submit appeared in any quarter.

The New England governments in particular, though most immediately menaced, did not sink under their apprehension of the common danger. They, as well as the congress, acted with vigour and firmness in their efforts to repel the enemy. Arnold, whom we have lately seen at the engagement at Danbury, was immediately sent to the reinforcement of the northern army, who carried with him a train of artillery which he received from Washington. On his arrival he drew the American troops back from Saratoga to Still Water, a central situation between that place, and the mouth of the Mohawk river, where it falls into Hudson's. This movement, was to be the nearer at hand to check the progress of

Colonel St. Leger, who was now advancing upon the former of these rivers. His forces were daily increased through the outrages of the savages, who, notwithstanding the regulations and endeavours of General Burgoyne, were too prone to the exercise of their usual cruelties, to be effectually restrained by any means. The friends of the royal cause, as well as its enemies, were equally victims to their indiscriminate rage. Among other instances of this nature, the murder of Miss M'Crea, which happened some small time after, struck every breast with horror. Every circumstance of this horrid transaction served to render it more calamitous and afflicting. The young lady is represented to have been in all the innocence of youth, and bloom of beauty. Her father was said to be deeply interested in the royal cause; and to wind up the catastrophe of this odious tragedy, she was to have been married to a British officer on the very day that she was massacred. [64]

Occasion was thence taken to exasperate the people, and to blacken the royal party and army. People were too apt to jumble promiscuously, and to place in one point of view, the cruelties of these barbarians, and the cause in which they were exerted. They equally execrated both. Whilst they abhorred and detested that army, which submitted to accept of such an aid, they loudly condemned and reprobated that government, which could call such auxiliaries into a civil contest; thereby endeavouring, as they said, not to subdue but to exterminate, a people whom they affected to consider, and pretended to reclaim as subjects. General Gates, in the course of these transactions, was not wanting by several publications to aggravate and inflame the picture of these excesses; and with no small effect.

By this means, the advantages expected from the terror excited by these savage auxiliaries were not only counteracted; but this terror rather, it may be thought, produced a directly contrary effect. The inhabitants of the open and frontier countries had no choice of acting; they had no means of security left, but by abandoning their habitations, and taking up arms. Every man saw the necessity of becoming a temporary soldier, not only for his own security, but for the protection and defence of those connections which are dearer than life itself. Thus an army was poured forth by the woods, mountains, and marshes, which in this part were thickly sown with plantations and villages. The Americans recalled their courage; and when their regular army seemed to be entirely wasted, the spirit of the country produced a much greater and more formidable force.

In the mean time, the army under General Burgoyne, in the neighbourhood of Fort Edward, began to experience those difficulties, which increased as it farther advanced, until they at length became insurmountable. From the 30th of July, to the 15th of August, the army was continually employed, and every possible measure used, for the bringing forward of batteaux, provisions and ammunition, from Fort George to the first navigable part of Hudson's River, a distance of about 18 miles. The toil was excessive in this service, and the effect in no degree equivalent to the expence of labour and time. The roads were in some parts steep, and in others required great repairs. Of the horses which had been supplied by contract in Canada, through the various delays and accidents attending so long and intricate a combination of passage by land and carriage by water, not more than one third were yet arrived. The industry of the General had been able to collect no more than 50 teams of oxen, in all the country

through which he had marched, or this in which he at present sojourned. These resources were totally inadequate to the purposes of supplying the army with provisions for its current consumption, and to the establishment at the same time of such a magazine as would enable it to prosecute the further operations of the campaign. Exceeding heavy rains added to all these difficulties; and the impediments to the service were so various and stubborn, that after the utmost exertions for fifteen successive days, there was not above four days provision in store, nor above ten batteaux in the Hudson's River.

In these embarrassing and distressing circumstances, the General received intelligence, that Colonel St. Leger had arrived before, and was conducting his operations against Fort Stanwix. He instantly and justly conceived, that a rapid movement forward at this critical juncture would be of the utmost importance. If the enemy proceeded up the Mohawk, and that St. Leger succeeded, he would be liable to get between two fires; or at any rate, General Burgoyne's army would get between him and Albany, so that he must either stand an action, or by passing the Hudson's River, endeavour to secure a retreat higher up to the New-England provinces. If, on the other hand, he abandoned Fort Stanwix to its fate, and fell back to Albany, the Mohawk country would of course be entirely laid open, the junction with St. Leger established, and the combined army at liberty and leisure to prescribe and chuse its future line of operation.

The propriety of the movement was evident; but the difficulty lay, and great indeed it was, in finding means to carry the design into execution. To maintain such a communication with Fort George during the whole time of so extensive a movement, as would afford a daily supply of provision to an

army, whilst its distance was continually increasing, and its course liable to frequent variation, was obviously impracticable. The army was too weak to afford a chain of posts for such an extent; continual escorts for every separate supply would be a still greater drain; and in either case, the enemy had a body of militia within a night's march, at White Creek, sufficient to break the line of communication.

Some other source of supply was therefore to be sought, or the design to be dropped, and the prospect of advantage which it presented totally relinquished. The enemy received large supplies of live cattle from the New-England provinces, which passing the upper part of the Connecticut river, took the route of Manchester, Arlington, and other parts of the New Hampshire grants, a tract of land disputed between that province and New York, until they were at length deposited at Bennington, from whence they were conveyed as occasion required to the rebel army. Bennington lies between the forks of the Hosick River, before their obtaining that name, and without being touched by either, and not 20 miles to the eastward of Hudson's; a place so obscure, and so incapable from situation of being otherwise, that nothing but the present troubles could have called it into notice. It was however at this time, besides being a store for cattle, a deposit for large quantities of corn and other necessaries; and what rendered it an object of particular attention to the royal army, a large number of wheel carriages, of which they were in particular want, were also laid up there. This place was guarded by a body of militia, which underwent such frequent changes that its number was necessarily uncertain.

The General saw that the possession of this deposit, would at once remove all the impediments that restrained the operations of the army, and enable him to proceed directly in the prosecution of his design. He accordingly laid a scheme to surprize the place, and entrusted the execution of it to the German Lieutenant-Colonel Baum,[65] who had been already selected, and was then preparing to conduct an expedition tending to similar purposes, towards the borders of the Connecticut River.

The force allotted to this service amounted to about 500 men, consisting of about 200 of Reidesel's dismounted German dragoons, Captain Frazer's marksmen, the Canada volunteers, a party of provincials who were perfectly acquainted with the country, and about a hundred Indians; the corps carried with them two light pieces of artillery.

In order to facilitate this operation, and to be ready to take advantage of its success, the army moved up the east shore of Hudson's River, where it encamped nearly opposite to Saratoga, having at the same time thrown a bridge of rafts over, by which the advanced corps were passed to that place. At the same time Lieutenant-Colonel Breyman's corps,[66] consisting of the Brunswick grenadiers, light infantry, and chasseurs, were posted at Batten Kill, in order if necessary to support Baum.

The latter in his march fell in with a party of the enemy who were escorting some cattle and provisions, both of which he took with little difficulty and sent back to the camp. The same fatal impediment which retarded all the operations of the army, viz. the want of horses and carriages, concurred with the badness of the roads in rendering Baum's advance so tedious, that the enemy were well informed of his design, and had time to prepare for his reception. Upon his approach to the place, having received intelligence that the enemy were too strong to be attacked by his present force with

any prospect of success, he took a tolerable good post near Santcoick Mills, on the nearer branch of what becomes afterwards the Hosick River, which is there called Walloon Creek, and at about four miles distance from Bennington; dispatching at the same time an express to the General with an account of his situation.

Colonel Breyman was accordingly dispatched from Batten Kill to reinforce Baum. That evil fortune now began to appear, which for some time after continued to sweep every thing before it. Breyman was so overlayed by bad weather, so sunk and embarrassed in bad roads, and met with such delays from the weakness and tiring of horses, and the difficulty of passing the artillery carriages, through a country scarcely practicable at any time, and now rendered much worse by the continual rain, that he was from eight in the morning of the 15th of August, to four in the afternoon of the following day, notwithstanding every possible exertion of men and officers, in getting forward about twenty-four miles.

A General Starke, who com-[67] manded the militia at Bennington, determined not to wait for the junction of the two parties, advanced in Aug. 16th. the morning, whilst Breyman was yet struggling with the difficulties of his march, to attack Baum in his post, which he had entrenched, and rendered as defensible as time and its nature would permit. The loyal provincials who were along with him, were so eager in their hopes to find what they wished to be real, that when the enemy were surrounding his post on all sides, they for some time persuaded him, that they were bodies of armed friends who were coming to his assistance. The colonel soon discovered their error, and made a brave defence. His small works being at length carried on every side, and his two pieces of cannon taken,

most of the Indians, with several of the provincials, Canadians, and British marksmen, escaped in the woods. The German dragoons still kept together, and when their ammunition was expended, were bravely led by their Colonel to charge with their swords. They were soon overwhelmed, and the survivors, among whom was their wounded Colonel, were made prisoners.

Breyman, who had the hard fortune not to receive the smallest information of this engagement, arrived near the same ground about four in the afternoon, where instead of meeting his friends, he found his detachment attacked on all sides by the enemy. Notwithstanding the severe fatigue they had undergone, his troops behaved with great vigour and resolution, and drove the Americans in the beginning from two or three different hills on which they had posts. They were however at length overpowered, and their ammunition being unfortunately expended, although each soldier had brought out forty rounds in his pouch, they were obliged with great reluctance to abandon the two pieces of artillery they had brought with them, and to retreat in the best manner they could; a circumstance to which the lateness of the evening was very favourable.

The loss of men sustained by[68] these two engagements could not be less than five or six hundred, of whom, however, the greater part were prisoners. But this was not the only or the greatest loss. The reputation and courage which it afforded to the militia, to find that they were able to defeat regular forces; that neither Englishmen nor Germans were invincible, nor invulnerable to their impression; and the hope and confidence excited by the artillery, and other trophies of victory, were of much greater consequence. This was the first turn which fortune had taken in favour of the Americans in the northern war, since some time before the death of Montgomery; misfortune had succeeded misfortune, and defeat had trod upon the heel of defeat, since that period. This was the first instance in the present campaign, in which she seemed even wavering, much less that she for a moment quitted the royal standard. The exultation was accordingly great on the one side; nor could the other avoid feeling some damp to that eagerness of hope, and receiving some check to that assured confidence of success, which an unmixed series of fortunate events must naturally excite.

St. Leger's attempt upon Fort Stanwix, (now named by the Americans Fort Schuyler) was soon after its commencement favoured by a success so signal, as would in other cases, and a more fortunate season, have been decisive as to the fate of a stronger and much more important fortress. General[69] Harkimer, a leading man of that country, was marching at the head of eight or nine hundred of the Tryon county militia, with a convoy of provisions, to the relief of the fort. St. Leger, well aware of the danger of being attacked in his trenches, and of withstanding the whole weight of the garrison in some particular and probably weak point at the same instant, and equally well understanding the kind of service for which the Indians were peculiarly calculated, judiciously detached Sir John Johnson, with some regulars, the whole or part of his own regiment, and the savages, to lie in ambush in the woods, and intercept the enemy upon their march.

It should seem by the conduct of the militia and their leader, that they were not only totally ignorant of all military duties, but that they had even never heard by report of the nature of an Indian war, or of that peculiar service in the woods, to which from its nature and situation their country was at all times

liable. Without examination of their ground, without a reconnoitring, or flanking party, they plunged blindly into the trap that was laid for their destruction. Being thrown into sudden and inevitable disorder, by a near and heavy fire on almost all sides, it was completed by the Indians, who instantly pursuing their fire, rushed in upon their broken ranks, and made a most dreadful slaughter amongst them with their spears and hatchets. Notwithstanding their want of conduct, the militia shewed no want of courage in their deplorable situation. In the midst of such extreme danger, and so bloody an execution, rendered still more terrible by the horrid appearance and demeanour of the principal actors, they recollected themselves so far as to recover an advantageous ground, which enabled them after to maintain a sort of running fight, by which about one third of their number was preserved.

Aug. 6th.

The loss was supposed to be on their side about 400 killed, and[70] half that number prisoners. It was thought of the greater consequence, as almost all those who were considered as the principal leaders and instigators of rebellion in that country were now destroyed. The triumph and exultation were accordingly great, and all opposition from the militia in that country, was supposed to be at an end. The circumstance of old neighbourhood and personal knowledge between many of the parties, in the present rage and animosity of faction, could by no means be favourable to the extension of mercy; even supposing that it might have been otherwise practised with prudence and safety, at a time when the power of the Indians was rather prevalent, and that their rage was implacable. For according to their computation and ideas of loss, the savages had purchased this victory exceeding dearly; 33 of their number having been slain, and 20 wounded,

among whom were several of their principal leaders, and of their most distinguished and favourite warriors. This loss accordingly rendered them so discontented, intractable, and ferocious, that the service was greatly affected by their ill disposition. The unhappy prisoners were however its first objects; most of whom they inhumanly butchered in cold blood. The New-Yorkers, rangers, and other troops, were not without loss in this action.

On the day, and probably during the time of this engagement, the garrison, having received intelligence of the approach of their friends, endeavoured to make a diversion in their favour, by a vigorous and well-conducted sally, under the direction of Colonel Willet, their second in command.[71] Willet conducted his business with ability and spirit. He did considerable mischief in the camp, brought off some trophies, no inconsiderable spoil, some of which consisted in articles that were greatly wanted, a few prisoners, and returned with little or no loss. He afterwards undertook, in company with another officer, a much more perilous expedition. They passed by night through the besiegers works, and in contempt of the danger and cruelty of the savages, made their way for 50 miles through pathless woods and unexplored morasses, in order to raise the country, and bring relief to the fort. Such an action demands the praise even of an enemy.

Colonel St. Leger left no means untried to profit of his victory by intimidating the garrison. He sent verbal and written messages, stating their hopeless situation, the utter destruction of their friends, the impossibility of their obtaining relief, as General Burgoyne, after destroying every thing in his way, was now at Albany receiving the submission of all the adjoining countries, and by prodigiously magnifying his own force. He represented, that in this state of things, if, through an incorrigible obstinacy, they should continue a hopeless and fruitless defence, they would, according to the practice of the most civilized nations, be cut off from all conditions, and every hope of mercy. But he particularly dwelt upon the pains he had taken in softening the rage of the Indians for their late loss, and obtaining from them security, that in case of an immediate surrender of the fort, every man of the garrison should be spared; whilst on the other hand they declared with the most bitter execrations, that if they met with any further resistance, they would not only massacre the garrison, but that every man, woman and child in the Mohawk country would necessarily, and however against his will, fall sacrifices to the fury of the savages. This point he said he pressed entirely on the score of humanity; he promised on his part, in case of an immediate surrender, every attention which a humane and generous enemy could give.

The Governor, Colonel Gansevort, behaved with great firmness.[72] He replied, that he had been entrusted with the charge of that garrison by the United States of America; that he would defend the trust committed to his care at every hazard, and to the utmost extremity; and that he neither thought himself accountable for, nor should he at all concern himself about any consequences that attended the discharge of his duty. It was shrewdly remarked in the fort, that half the pains would not have been taken, to display the force immediately without, or the success at a distance, if they bore any proportion at all to the magnitude in which they were represented.

The British commander was much disappointed in the state of the fort. It was stronger, in better condition, and much better defended than he expected. After great labour in his approaches, he found his artillery deficient, being insufficient in weight to make any considerable impression. The only remedy was to bring his approaches so near that they must take effect; which he set about with the greatest diligence. In the mean time, the Indians continued sullen and intractable. Their late losses might have been cured by certain advantages; but the misfortune was, they had yet got no plunder, and their prospect of getting any seemed to grow every day fainter. It is the peculiar characteristic of that people, to exhibit in certain instances degrees of courage and perseverance which shock reason and credibility, and to betray in others the greatest irresolution and timidity; with a total want of that constancy which might enable them for any length of time to struggle with difficulty.

Whilst the commander was carrying on his operations with the utmost industry, the Indians received a flying report that Arnold was coming with a thousand men to relieve the fort. The commander endeavoured to hearten them, by promising to lead them himself, to bring all his best troops into action, and by carrying their leaders out to mark a field of battle, and the flattery of consulting them upon the intended plan of operation. Whilst he was thus endeavouring to soothe their temper, and to revive their flagging spirits, other scouts arrived with intelligence, probably contrived in part by themselves, which first doubled, and afterwards trebled the number of the enemy, with the comfortable addition, that Burgoyne's army was entirely cut to pieces. The Colonel returned to camp, and called a council of their chiefs, hoping that by the influence which Sir John Johnson, and the superintendants Claus and Butler had[73] over them, they might still be induced to make a stand. He was disappointed. A part of the Indians decamped whilst the council was sitting, and the remainder threatened peremptorily to abandon him if he did not immediately retreat.

Aug. 22d. The retreat was of course precipitate; or it was rather, in plain terms, a flight, attended with disagreeable circumstances. The tents, with most of the artillery and stores, fell into the hands of the garrison. It appears by the Colonel's own account, that he was as apprehensive of danger from the fury of his savage allies, as he could from the resentment of his declared American enemies. It also appears from the same authority, that the Messasages, a nation of savages to the west, plundered several of the boats belonging to the army. By the American accounts, which are in part confirmed by others, it is said that they robbed the officers of their baggage, and of every other article to which they took any liking; and the army in general of their provisions. They also say, that at a few miles distance from the camp, they first stripped of their arms, and afterwards murdered with their own bayonets, all those British, German, and American soldiers, who from an inability to keep up, fear, or any other cause, were separated from the main body.

The state of the fact with respect to the intended relief of the fort is, that Arnold had advanced by the way of Half Moon up the Mohawk River with 2000 men for that purpose; and that for the greater expedition, he had quitted the main body, and arrived by forced marches through the woods, with a detachment of 900 at the fort, on the 24th in the evening, two days after the siege had been raised. So that upon the whole, the intractableness of the Indians, with their watchful apprehension of danger, probably saved them from a chastisement, which would not have been tenderly administered.

Nothing could have been more untoward in the prefent fituation of affairs, than the unfortunate iffue of this expedition. The Americans reprefented this and the affair at Bennington as great and glorious victories. Nothing could exceed their exultation and confidence. Ganfevort and Willet, with General Starke and Colonel Warner, who had commanded at Bennington, were ranked amongft thofe who were confidered as the faviours of their country. The northern militia began now to look high, and to forget all diftinctions between themfelves and regular troops. As this confidence, opinion and pride increafed, the apprehenfion of General Burgoyne's army of courfe declined, until it foon came to be talked of with indifference and contempt, and even its fortune to be publicly prognofticated. In the mean time, General Gates, on whofe conduct and ability it appears the Americans had placed much reliance, arrived to take the command of the army; an event which gave a new fpur to their exertion, and afforded an additional fupport to their hopes. The arrival of Gates enabled Arnold, who ftill held the next place in every thing to the commander in chief, and between whom it appears the moft perfect harmony prevailed, to fet out on that expedition to Fort Stanwix, which has been juft related.

During this time, General Burgoyne continued in his camp on the eaftern fhore of the Hudfon's River, nearly oppofite to Saratoga, where he ufed the moft unremitting induftry and perfeverance, in bringing ftores and provifions forward from Fort George. As a fwell of the water occafioned by great rains had carried away his bridge of rafts, he threw another, of boats, over the river at the fame place. Having at length by good management obtained and brought forward about thirty days provifion, with other neceffary ftores,

he took a refolution of paffing the Hudfon's River with the army, which he accordingly carried into execution towards the middle of September, and encamped on the heights and in the plain of Saratoga, the enemy being then in the neighbourhood of Still Water.

Though this meafure of paffing the Hudfon's River, has not only been a fubject of much difcuffion at home, but alfo of parliamentary enquiry; yet as it ftill lies open, without any decifion on its merits, and that the General's inftructions are not publicly known, nor perhaps all his motives thoroughly underftood, we fhall not prefume to form any opinion upon the queftion. It will be fufficient to obferve, that in his letter to the American Minifter he fays, That he thinks it a duty of juftice to take upon himfelf the meafure of having paffed the Hudfon's River, in order to force a paffage to Albany. And that he did not think himfelf authorized to call any men into council, when the peremptory tenor of his orders, and the feafon of the year, admitted of no alternative. He alfo gives, in a fubfequent part of the fame letter, the following ftate of his reafoning, at a time when the army was in very critical and hazardous circumftances. " The expedition I com-" manded was evidently meant as " firft to be *hazarded*. Circum-" ftances might require it fhould " be *devoted*; a critical junction of " Mr. Gates's force with Mr. " Wafhington might poffibly de-" cide the fate of the war; the " failure of my junction with Sir " Harry Clinton, or the lofs of " my retreat to Canada, could " only be a partial misfortune." [74] Whether his retreat was at this period quite practicable, even if his orders had not been to advance at all hazards, is uncertain.

Such it feems were the principles of the General's conduct in fome of the fucceeding events. As the army advanced along the river to-

wards the enemy, they found the country very impracticable, being covered with thick woods, and a continual repair of bridges neceffary. Being at length Sept. 19th. arrived in the front of the enemy, fome woods only of no great extent intervening, the General put himfelf at the head of the British line which compofed the right wing. That wing was covered by General Frazer and Colonel Breyman, with the grenadiers, and light infantry of the army, who kept along fome high grounds which commanded its right flank, being themfelves covered by the Indians, provincials, and Canadians, in the front and flanks. The left wing and artillery, under the Majors General Phillips and Reidefel, kept along the great road and meadows by the river fide.

The enemy, being incapable from the nature of the country of perceiving the different combinations of the march, iffued from their camp in great force, with a defign of turning the right wing, and taking the British line on the flank. Being unexpectedly checked in this defign, by the ftrong pofition of General Frazer, they immediately countermarched, and the fame particularity of country which had occafioned their miftake, now operating as effectually to prevent the difcovery, and confequently the taking any advantage of their fubfequent movement, they directed their principal effort to the left of the fame wing.

The British troops were not a little furprized, at the boldnefs with which they began the attack, and the vigour and obftinacy with which it was fuftained, from three o'clock in the afternoon, till after funfet. Arnold led on the enemy, and fought danger with an eagernefs and intrepidity, which though much in his character, was at no time more eminently diftinguifhed. The enemy were, however, continually fupplied with frefh troops, whilft the weight of the action lay principally for a long time upon the 20th, the 21st, and 62d regiments. It will be needless to say, that they behaved with their usual firmness and gallantry, though it may not be totally superfluous to observe, that the greater part of these three regiments, were engaged for near four hours without intermission.

Most of the other corps of the army, bore also a good share in the business of the day. The 24th regiment, which belonged to Frazer's brigade, with the grenadiers and a part of the light infantry, were for some time brought into action, and charged with their usual spirit and bravery. Breyman's riflemen, and some other parts of his corps, also did good service; but these troops only acted partially and occasionally, as the heights on which they had been originally posted, were of too great importance to be totally evacuated.

Major General Phillips upon first hearing the firing, made his way with Major Williams and a [75] part of the artillery through a very difficult part of the wood, and from that time rendered most essential service. It seems as if in one instance his presence of mind had nearly saved the army, when, in the most critical point of time, he restored the action by leading up the 20th regiment, the enemy having then obtained a great superiority of fire. Though every part of the artillery performed, almost, wonders, the brave Captain Jones (who was unfortunately, though gloriously, killed) with his brigade, were particularly distinguished. Major-General Reidesel also exerted himself to bring up a part of the left wing, and arrived in time to charge the enemy with bravery and effect. Just as the light closed, the enemy retired; and left the royal army masters of the field of battle. The darkness equally prevented pursuit and prisoners.

Upon the whole, the royal army gained nothing but honour by this arduous struggle and hard-fought battle. They had now grappled with such an enemy as they had never before encountered in America; and such as they were too apt to imagine it could not produce. The flattering ideas that the Americans could only fight under the covert of walls, hedges, or entrenchments, and were incapable of sustaining a fair and open conflict in the field, were now at an end. This opinion had also been in some measure shaken in the south. Here they met with a foe who seemed as eager for action, as careless of danger, and as indifferent with respect to ground or cover as themselves; and after a hard and close contest of four hours, hand to hand, when darkness put an end to the engagement, the royal forces but barely kept the field, and the Americans only returned to their camp.

We lost many brave men in this action, and it was not much matter of comfort that the Americans had lost a greater number. The army lay all night on their arms in the field of battle, and in the morning took a position nearly within cannon shot of the enemy's camp, fortifying their right wing, and extending their left so as to cover those meadows through which the river runs, and where their batteaux and hospitals were placed. The 47th regiment, with that of Hesse Hanau, and a corps of provincials, were encamped in the meadows as an additional security. The enemy's right was incapable of approach, and their left was too strongly fortified to be insulted.

The zeal and alacrity of the Indians began from this time to slacken. Though the General complains in his dispatches of the ill effects of their desertion, he does not specify the particular time of their abandoning the army. This close and dangerous service was by no means suited to their disposition, and the prospects of plunder were narrowed to nothing. Fidelity and honour were principles for which they had no terms, and of which they could frame no ideas. Some letters had lately passed between Gates and General Burgoyne, in which bitter reproaches relative to the barbarities committed by the savages were thrown out by the one, and those charges were in general denied, and in part palliated on the other. The savages likewise received some check on account of the murder of Miss M'Crea. Upon some or all of these accounts they deserted the army in the season of its danger and distress, when their aid would have been most particularly useful; and afforded a second instance within a short time of the little reliance that should be placed on such auxiliaries.

A great desertion also prevailed amongst the Canadians and British provincials, nor does it seem as if the fidelity or services of those who remained were much depended on or esteemed. General Burgoyne had from the beginning, nor did it entirely forsake him to this time, a firm hope of being powerfully succoured if wanted, or at any rate of being met and joined at Albany, by a strong force from the army at New-York. He now received with great difficulty a letter in cypher from Sir Harry Clinton, informing him of his intention to make a diversion on the North River, by attacking Fort Montgomery, and some other fortresses which the rebels had erected in the highlands, in order to guard the passage up that river to Albany. Though this diversion fell far short of the aid which the General expected, he, however, hoped that it might afford essential service by obliging Gates to divide his army. He accordingly returned the messenger, and afterwards dispatched two officers in disguise, and other confidential persons, all separately and by different routes, to acquaint Clinton with his exact state, situation, and condition; to press him urgently to the immediate profecu-tion of his defign; and to inform him, that he was enabled in point of provifion, and fixed in his deter-mination, to hold his prefent pofi-tion, in the hope of favourable events, until the 12th of the fol-lowing month.

In the mean time every means were ufed for fortifying the camp, and ftrong redoubts were erected for the protection of the magazines and hofpitals, not only to guard againft any fudden attack, but for their fecurity in any future move-mentwhich the army might make in order to turn the enemy's flank. The ftricteft watch on the motions of the enemy, and attention on every quarter to their own fecurity, became every day more indifpenfi-ble, as Gates's army was conti-nually increafing in force by the acceffion of freth bodies of the mi-litia.

The fpirit of exertion and enter-prize which was now raifed in the New-England provinces, was be-come too general, and too much animated by fuccefs, to be eafily withftood at once in all the different points of its direction. Whilft Ge-neral Burgoyne was fully engaged with Gates and Arnold, and found himfelf immediately involved in circumftances sufficiently perplex-ing, all his difficulties were in-creafed, and his fituation was ren-dered much more critical and pre-carious, by an unexpected enter-prize of the militia from the upper parts of New Hampfhire and the head of the Connecticut, totally to cut off all means of communication with Canada, by recovering the forts of Ticonderoga and Mount Independence, and becoming again mafters, at leaft, of Lake George.

The expedition was under the direction of General Lincoln, and the immediate execution was com-mitted to the Colonels Brown,[76] Johnfton, and Woodbury, with de-detachments of about 500 men each. They conducted their ope-rations with fuch fecrecy and ad-drefs, that they effect-ually furprized all the Sept. 17th. out pofts between the landing place at the north end of Lake George, and the body of the fortrefs of Ticonderoga. Mount Defiance, Mount Hope, the French lines, and a block-houfe, with 200 bat-teaux, an armed floop, and feve-ral gun-boats, were almoft inftant-ly taken. Four companies of foot, with nearly an equal number of Canadians, and many of the offi-cers and crews of the veffels, were made prifoners; whilft they afforded freedom to a number of their own people, who were con-fined in fome of the works they had taken. In this heat of fuc-cefs, they brought the cannon out of the armed veffel they had ta-ken, and after repeated fummons to Brigadier Powel who command-ed, and who gallantly rejected all their propofals, they for four days made reiterated attacks up-on the works at Ticonderoga and Mount Independence; until find-ing that they were repulfed in every affault, and totally unequal to the fervice, they at length abandoned the defign.

In the beginning of October, General Burgoyne thought it ex-pedient, from the uncertainty of his fituation, to leffen the foldiers rations of provifion; a measure, which however difagreeable to an army, was now fubmitted to with a chearfulnefs which merited the higheft regards, and did the great-eft honour to the troops. Things continued in this ftate until the 7th of October, when there being no appearance or intelligence of the expected co-operation, and the time limited for the ftay of the army in its prefent camp within four or five days of being expired, it was judged advifeable to make a movement to the enemy's left, not only to difcover whether there were any poffible means of forcing a paffage, fhould it be neceffary to advance, or of diflodging them for the convenience of retreat, but alfo to cover a forage of the army, which was exceedingly dif-treffed by the prefent fcarcity.

A detachment of 1500 regular troops, with 2 twelve-pounders, 2 howitzers, and 6 fix-pounders, were ordered to move, being com-manded by the General in per-fon, who was feconded by thofe ex-cellent officers the Majors General Phillips and Reidefel, with Briga-dier General Frazer. No equal number of men was ever better commanded, and it would have been difficult indeed, to have matched the men with any equal number. The guard of the camp upon the high grounds, was com-mitted to the Brigadiers General Hamilton and Speight; that of[77] the redoubts and the plain near the river, to Brigadier Goll. The force of the enemy immediately in the front of the lines, was fo much fuperior, that it was not thought fafe to augment the de-tachment beyond the number we have ftated.

The troops were formed within three quarters of a mile of the enemy's left, and the irregulars were pufhed on through bye ways to appear as a check on their rear. But the further intended opera-tions of the detachment were pre-vented, by a very fudden and moft rapid attack of the enemy upon the Britifh grenadiers, who were pofted to fupport the left wing of the line. Major Ackland,[78] at the head of the grenadiers, fuf-tained this fierce attack with great refolution; but the numbers of the enemy enabling them, in a few minutes, to extend the attack a-long the whole front of the Ger-mans, who were pofted immediate-ly on the right of the grenadiers, it became impracticable to move any part of that body, for the purpofe of forming a fecond line to fupport the flank, where the great weight of the fire ftill fell.

The right was ftill unengaged; but it was foon perceived that the enemy were marching a ftrong body round their flank, in order to cut off their retreat. To oppose this bold and dangerous attempt, the light infantry, with a part of the 24th regiment, which were joined with them at that post, were thrown into a second line, in order to cover the retreat of the troops into camp.

Whilst this motion was yet in process, the enemy pushed a fresh and strong reinforcement to decide the action on the left, which being totally overpowered by so great a superiority, was compelled by dint of force to give way; upon which, the light infantry and 24th regiment were obliged, by a very quick movement, to endeavour to save that wing from being totally ruined. It was in this movement, that the brave Brigadier General Frazer was mortally wounded. An officer whose loss would have been severely felt, and his place with difficulty supplied, in a corps of the most accomplished officers.

The situation of the detachment was now exceedingly critical; but the danger to which the lines were exposed was still more alarming and serious. Phillips and Reidesel were ordered to cover the retreat, and those troops which were nearest, or most disengaged, returned as fast as they could for their defence. The troops in general retreated in good order, though very hard pressed. They were obliged to abandon six pieces of cannon; the horses not only being destroyed, but most of the brave artillery men, who had, as usual, under the conduct of Major Williams, displayed the utmost skill and ability in their profession, along with the most undaunted resolution, being either killed or dangerously wounded.

The enemy pursued their success with great eagerness. The troops had scarcely entered the camp, when the Americans stormed it in different parts with uncommon fierceness; rushing to the lines through a severe fire of grape shot and small arms, with the utmost fury. Arnold led on the attack with his usual impetuosity, against a part of the entrenchments into which the light infantry under Lord Balcarres, with a part of the line, had thrown themselves by order. He there met with a brave and obstinate resistance. The action continued very warm for some time, each side seeming to vie with the other in ardour and perseverance. In this critical moment of glory and danger, Arnold was grievously wounded, just as he was forcing his way into, or had already entered the works. This could not fail to damp his party, who after long and repeated efforts were finally repulsed.

Affairs were not so fortunate in another quarter. Colonel Breyman, who commanded the German reserve, being killed, the entrenchments defended by that corps were carried sword in hand, and they were totally routed with the loss of their baggage, tents, and artillery. This misfortune was not retrieved, although orders for the recovery of the post were dispatched by the General; and his relation of the transaction seems to imply some blame to those who failed in the execution. By this means the enemy gained a dangerous opening on our right and rear. The night only put an end to the engagement.

It would seem that nothing could now exceed the distress and calamity of the army. They bore it with that excellency of temper, and that unconquerable firmness and resolution, which are natural to, and were worthy of British soldiers. It was evidently impossible to continue in their present situation, without submitting to a certainty of destruction on the ensuing day. A total change of position was accordingly undertaken, and as it seems to have been conceived with great judgment, was carried into execution during the night, with a degree of coolness, silence, order, and intrepidity, which has seldom been equalled, and will certainly be never exceeded. It was not the movement of a wing or a part; it was a general remove of the whole army, of the camp and artillery, from its late ground, to the heights above the hospital; thus, by an entire change of front, to reduce the enemy to the necessity of forming an entire new disposition. All this was accomplished in the darkness, and under the doubt and apprehension of such a night, so fatally ushered in, and accompanied throughout with circumstances of such uncommon peril; as were sufficient to disturb the best formed mind, and to shake the firmest resolution, without loss; and what was still more, without disorder.

Many brave men fell on this unfortunate day. The officers suffered exceedingly. Several who had been grievously wounded in the late action, and who disdained an absence from any danger in which their fellows were involved, were again wounded in this. Among those of greater note, or who were distinguished by higher rank, who fell, besides General Frazer and Colonel Breyman, whom we have mentioned, Sir James Clarke, [79] Aid de Camp to General Burgoyne, was mortally wounded and taken prisoner. Major Williams of the artillery, and Major Ackland of the grenadiers, were also taken, the latter being wounded. Upon the whole, the lists of killed and wounded, though avowedly imperfect, and not including the Germans, were long and melancholy.

On the next day, the army, being sensible that Oct. 8th. nothing less than a successful and decisive action could extricate them from their present difficulties, continued without effect, during its course; to offer battle repeatedly in their new position, to the enemy.

They were preparing with great coolness, the carrying of measures into execution, which were less dangerous, though not less effectual, than the attack of a brave and desperate enemy, in strong and fortified ground. A continued succession of skirmishes were, however, carried on, and these did not pass without loss on both sides.

In the mean time, the British General discovered, that the enemy had pushed a strong body forward to turn his right, which if effected, he would have been completely enclosed on every side. Nothing was left to prevent this fatal consequence, but an immediate retreat to Saratoga. The army accordingly began to move at nine o'clock at night; and tho' the movement was within musket shot of the enemy, and the army encumbered in the retreat with all its baggage, it was made without loss. A heavy rain which fell that night, and continued on the ensuing day, though it impeded the progress of the army, and increased the difficulties of the march, served at the same time to retard, and in a great measure to prevent the pursuit of the enemy. In this unhappy necessity, the hospital with the sick and wounded, was of course, and must have been inevitably, abandoned. In this instance, as well as in every other which occurred in the course of these transactions, General Gates behaved with an attention and humanity, to all those whom the fortune of war had thrown into his hands, which does honour to his character.

On the side of the Americans,[80] the loss in killed and wounded was great; and it is supposed exceeded that of the British. They, however, lost no officer of note; but the Generals Lincoln and Arnold were both dangerously wounded.

From the impediments in the march which we have mentioned, the army did not pass the fords of the Fish Kill Creek, which lies a little to the northward of Saratoga, until the 10th in the morning. They found a body of the enemy already arrived, and throwing up entrenchments on the heights before them, who retired at their approach over a ford of the Hudson's river, and there joined a greater force, which was stationed to prevent the passage of the army. No hope now remained but that of effecting a retreat, at least as far as Fort George, on the way to Canada. For this purpose, a detachment of artificers under a strong escort, was sent forward to repair the bridges, and open the road to Fort Edward. But they were not long departed from the camp, when the sudden appearance of the enemy in great force, on the opposite heights, with their apparent preparation to pass the Fish Kill, and bring on an immediate engagement, rendered it necessary to recal the 47th regiment, and Frazer's marksmen, who, with Mackoy's provincials, composed the escort. The workmen had only commenced the repair of the first bridge, when they were abandoned by their provincial guard, who ran away, and left them to shift for themselves, only upon a very slight attack of an inconsiderable party of the enemy. All the force of discipline, and all the stubbornness derived from its most confirmed habits, were now necessary to support even the appearance of resolution.

The farther shore of the Hudson's river, was now lined with detachments of the enemy, and the batteaux loaded with provisions and necessaries, which had attended the motions of the army up the river, since its departure from the neighbourhood of Still Water, were exposed, notwithstanding any protection which could possibly be afforded, to the continual fire and attacks of these detachments. Many boats were taken, some retaken, and a number of men lost in the skirmishes, upon these occasions. At length it was found that the provisions could only be preserved by landing and bringing them up the hill to the camp; a labour which was accomplished under a heavy fire with difficulty and loss.

In these deplorable circumstances, councils of war were held, to consider of the possibility of a further retreat. The only measure that carried even the appearance of practicability, hard, difficult, and dangerous as it was, was by a night march to gain Fort Edward, the troops carrying their provisions upon their backs. The impossibility of repairing the roads and bridges, and of conveying in their present situation the artillery and carriages, were too evident to admit of a question. It was proposed to force the fords at or near Fort Edward.

Whilst preparations were making for carrying this forlorn and desperate resolve into execution, intelligence was received, that the enemy had already with great foresight, provided for every possible measure that could be adopted for an escape, and that this final resort was accordingly cut off. Besides, being strongly entrenched opposite to the fords which it was intended to pass, they had a camp in force, and provided with artillery, on the high and strong grounds, between Fort Edward and Fort George; whilst their parties were every where spread along the opposite shore of the river, to watch or intercept the motions of the army, and on their own, the enemy's posts were so close, that they could scarcely make the smallest movement without discovery.

Nothing could be more deplorably calamitous, than the state and situation of the army. Worn down by a series of hard toil, incessant effort, and stubborn action; abandoned in their utmost necessity and distress by the Indians; weakened by the desertion, or disappointed and discouraged by the timidity and inefficacy of the Canadians and Provincials; and the regular troops reduced by repeated and heavy losses, of many of their best men and most distinguished officers, to the number of only 3,500 effective fighting men, of whom not quite 2,000 were British. In these circumstances, and in this state of weakness, without a possibility of retreat, and their provision just exhausted, they were invested by an army of four times their own number, whose position extended three parts in four of a circle round them; who refused to fight from a knowledge of their condition; and who from the nature of the ground could not be attacked in any part.

In this helpless condition, obliged to lie constantly on their arms, whilst a continued cannonade pervaded all the camp, and even rifle and grape shot fell in every part of the lines, the British troops retained their constancy, temper, and fortitude, in a wonderful and almost unparalleled manner. As true courage submits with great difficulty to despair, they still flattered themselves with the hope of succour from their friends on the New York side, or, perhaps with not less fervent wishes, of an attack from the enemy; thereby to quit all scores at once, and either to have an opportunity of dying gallantly, or extricating themselves with honour. In the mean time, the enemy's force was continually increased by the pouring in of the militia from all parts, who were all eager to partake of the glory, the spoil, or the pleasure of beholding the degradation of those whom they had so long dreaded, and whom they unhappily considered as their most implacable enemies.

At length, no succour appearing, and no rational ground of hope of any kind remaining, an exact account of the provisions was taken on the evening of the 13th of October, when it was found that the whole stock in hand, would afford no more than three days bare subsistence for the army. A council was immediately called; and the General thinking it right and just, in a matter so momentous to individuals, as well as the whole, to obtain the general opinion and suffrage of the army, so far as it could with propriety be collected, invited, besides the Generals and field officers, all the Captains commanding corps or divisions, to assist at the council. The result was, an unanimous determination to open a treaty and enter into a convention with General Gates.

Gates shewed no marks of arrogance, nor betrayed no signs of being carried away by the present extraordinary torrent of success. The terms were moderate, considering the ruined state and irretrievable circumstances of the army; and that it was already in effect at the enemy's mercy, being equally incapable of subsisting where it was, and of making its way to a better situation. The principal difficulty related to a point of military honour, in which the British Generals and troops were peremptory, and Gates far from being stiff.

The principal articles of the convention, exclusive of those which related to the provision and accommodation of the army, in its way to Boston, and during its stay at that place, were, That the army should march out of the camp with all the honours of war, and its camp artillery, to a fixed place where they were to deposit their arms: To be allowed a free embarkation and passage to Europe from Boston, upon condition of their not serving again in America, during the present war; the army not to be separated, particularly the men from the officers; roll-calling, and other duties of regularity to be ad-

Oct. 17th.

mitted; the officers to be admitted on parole, and to wear their side arms; all private property to be sacred, and the public delivered upon honour; no baggage to be searched or molested; all persons of whatever country, appertaining to, or following the camp, to be fully comprehended in the terms of capitulation; and the Canadians to be returned to their own country, liable to its conditions.

General Gates fulfilled all the conditions, so far as he was, or could be concerned in them, with the utmost punctuality and honour. His humanity and politeness, in every part of this business, have been much celebrated; without a single detraction, so far as we have heard, from the most favourable accounts that have been given of his conduct. This was the more praise-worthy, as some late, as well as former circumstances, had highly enraged the American militia; the army in its last movements, whether from military necessity, or the vexation and ill-temper incident to their situation, or the joint operation of both, having burnt and destroyed many houses, and some of them buildings of great value. The extraordinary and severe execution which now took place upon the North River, would also have afforded too much colour for a different mode of conduct. It is even said, and we do not find that it has been contradicted, that this General paid so nice and delicate an attention to the British military honour, and to the character and feelings of those brave troops, who now experienced so deplorable a reverse of fortune, that he kept his army close within their lines, and did not suffer an American soldier to be a witness to the degrading spectacle of piling their arms.

The Americans state the whole number who laid down their arms, including Canadians, Provincials, volunteers, regulars, and irregulars, of all sorts, at 5752 men. In this number is undoubtedly included, though not specified, all the artificers, labourers, and followers of the camp. They also state the number of sick and wounded left in the hospitals at the retreat from the camp near Still Water, to 528 men, and the loss besides in the army, in killed, wounded, taken, or deserted, from the 6th of July downwards, to 2,933; the total amount of these numbers being 9,213 men. By another account, the number is carried above ten thousand. They also got a fine train of brass artillery, amounting to 35 pieces of different sorts and sizes.

During these unfortunate transactions, Lieutenant General Sir Henry Clinton, conducted his expedition up the North River with great success. He had embarked about 3000 men for that service, accompanied by a suitable naval force, consisting of ships of war, armed gallies, and smaller vessels, under the conduct of Commodore Hotham. Their first object was[81] the reduction of the forts Montgomery and Clinton, which tho' of considerable strength, being at that time in a very unguarded state, it was determined to attempt by a coup de main. They were situated on either side of a creek, which descended from the mountains to the North River, and their communication preserved by a bridge. Several necessary motions being made to mask the real design, the troops were landed in two divisions, at such a distance from their object, as occasioned a considerable and difficult march through the mountains; which was however calculated and conducted with such precision, that the two detachments arrived on the opposite sides of the creek, and began their separate attack on the forts, Oct. 6th. at nearly the same time. The surprize and terror of the garrisons was increased by the appearance of the ships of war, and the arrival and near fire of the gallies,

which approached so close as to strike the walls with their oars. The assault on both sides of the creek was exceedingly vigorous, and the impetuosity of the troops so great, that notwithstanding a very considerable defence, both the forts were carried by storm. As the soldiers were much irritated, as well by the fatigue they had undergone, and the opposition they met, as by the loss of some brave and favourite officers, the slaughter of the enemy was considerable.

Upon the loss of the forts, the rebels set fire to two fine new frigates, and to some other vessels, which with their artillery and stores were all consumed. Another fort called Constitution, was in a day or two after, upon the approach of the combined land and naval force, precipitately set on fire and abandoned. General Tryon also, at the head of a detachment, destroyed a new and thriving settlement called Continental Village, which contained barracks for 1500 men, with considerable stores. The artillery taken in the three forts, amounted to 67 pieces of different sizes. A large quantity of artillery and other stores, with ammunition, and provisions, were also taken. A large boom and chain, the making of which was supposed to have cost 70,000 l. and the construction of which was considered as an extraordinary proof of American labour, industry, and skill, was in part destroyed, and in part carried away. Upon the whole, the American loss in value, was probably greater than upon any other occasion since the commencement of the war. Their strength and attention were drawn away to the northward, and other things must have been neglected, whilst they applied both to the principal object. Our loss in killed and wounded was not great as to number, but some distinguished and much lamented officers fell. Of these, be-

sides Lieutenant Colonel Campbell, who commanded the attack on Fort Montgomery, Major Sill, was from the general esteem he had acquired through his many excellent qualities, universally regretted. Major Grant of the New[82] York volunteers, and Count Graboufki, a Polish nobleman, and Aid de Camp to General Clinton, were also slain in the assault on these forts.

The expedition did not end with this success. Sir James Wallace,[83] with a flying squadron of light frigates, and General Vaughan, with a considerable detachment of troops, continued, for several days, their excursion up the river, carrying terror and destruction wherever they went. At the very time that General Burgoyne was receiving the most favourable conditions for himself and a ruined army, the fine village or town of Esopus, at no very great distance, was reduced to ashes, and not a house left standing. The extraordinary devastation which attended every part of this expedition, of the necessity of which we are not judges, was productive of a pathetic but severe letter, from General Gates, then in the height of victory, to General Vaughan.

On the approach of Gates, the troops and vessels retired to New York, having dismantled the forts, and for a time at least, having left the river defenceless. But that enterprize, though conducted with spirit and ability, was of little moment in the general account.

Such was the unfortunate issue of the northern campaign: The event of an expedition which was undertaken with the most confident hopes, and for some time pursued with very flattering appearances of success. It was supposed the principal means for the immediate reduction of the colonies; but it has only served, in conjunction with other operations, which in the first instance have succeeded better, to demonstrate the difficulties attending the fub-jugation of a numerous people at a great diftance, in an extenfive country marked with ftrong lines, and abounding in ftrong natural defences, if the refources of war are not exceedingly deficient, and that the fpirit of the people is in any degree proportioned to their fituation. It may now, whatever it was in the beginning, be a matter of doubt, whether any fuperiority of power, of wealth, and of difcipline, will be found to over-ballance fuch difficulties.

It would not be eafy at prefent, as many things neceffary to be known have not yet been fully explained, and improper, as the whole is ftill a fubject of public inveftigation, to attempt forming any judgment upon the general plan or fyftem of this campaign. The general conduct of the war this year has already undergone much cenfure; and undoubtedly, the fending of the grand army at fuch a diftance to the fouthward, whilft the inferior was left ftruggling with infurmountable difficulties in the north, when it would feem that their junction or co-operation, would have rendered them greatly fuperior to any force which could have been poffibly brought to oppofe their progrefs, feems, in this view of things, not to be eafily accounted for. It is, however, a fubject, upon which no conclufive opinion can yet be formed.

FRIDAY, February 7, Lord North prefented the bill to enable his majefty to fecure and detain perfons charged with, or fufpected of high-treafon in North America, or on the feas for piracy, which was read the firft time. On Friday the 14th, the bill was read a fecond time, and ftrongly oppofed.

During the debate, it was announced to the houfe, that the fheriffs of London and Middlefex, attended by the city remembrancer, were in waiting, with a petition to the houfe, againft the faid bill's being paffed; the fheriffs were accordingly ordered in, when they prefented the following petition from the city of London againft the American high-treafon bill, which was ordered to lie on the table till the third reading of the faid bill.

To the honourable the Commons of Great-Britain in parliament affembled.
The humble Petition of the Lord Mayor, Aldermen, and Commons, of the city of London, in Common Council affembled.

SHEWETH,
' THAT your petitioners have feen a bill depending in this honourable houfe, to impower his majefty to fecure and detain perfons charged with, or fufpected of, the crime of high-treafon committed in North America, or on the high feas, or the crime of piracy.
' That, if the faid bill fhould pafs into a law, your petitioners are apprehenfive it will create the greateft uneafinefs in the minds of many of his majefty's good fubjects, and tend to excite the moft alarming difturbances: all perfons indifcriminately being liable, upon the ground of fufpicion alone, without any oath made, and without convening the parties, or hearing what they can alledge in their own juftification, to be committed to a remote prifon in any corner of the realm, there to remain without bail or mainprize.
' That the Habeas Corpus act, which is the great fecurity of the liberties of the people, will be fufpended.
' That your petitioners are deeply affected with what they conceive will be the dangerous confequences of fuch a law, as from little motives of refentment, and various other inducements, there may be perfons competent to commit who may be tempted to exercife that power in its utmoft latitude and extent.
' That meafures fo violent and unconftitutional; fo fubverfive of the facred and fundamental rights of the people, and fubjecting them to the moft cruel oppreffion and bondage, will, in the judgment of your petitioners, be introductive of every fpecies of mifchief and confufion, and thereby precipitate the impending ruin of this country.
' Your petitioners therefore earneftly befeech this honourable houfe, That the faid bill may not pafs into a law, or at leaft to take fuch care as in their wifdom may feem meet, to prevent it from being extended in its operation or conftruction to any of his majefty's fubjects refident in thefe kingdoms.'

Monday, Feb. 17, at the third reading of this bill, a warm debate enfued, and, the queftion being put, the numbers for the bill paffing were 112, againft it, 35.

Dr. Price's *Account of the Progress of the National Debt, from* 1739 *to* 1775.

	Principal.	Interest.
	£.	£.
AMOUNT of the principal and interest of the national debt before the war which began in 1740	46,382,650	1,903,961
Amount in 1749 immediately after the war	78,166,906	2,765,608
Increased by the war	31,784,256	861,757
Diminished by the peace from 1748 to 1755	3,089,641	111,590
Amount at the commencement of the last war	75,077,264	2,654,018
Amount at the end of the war in 1763	146,582,844	4,840,811
Increased by the last war	71,505,580	2,186,803
Diminished by the peace, in 12 years, from 1763 to 1775	10,639,793	400,000
Amount at Midsummer, 1775	135,943,051	4,440,811

. . .

Genuine Correspondence between Lord Howe *and Dr.* Franklin.

AS the subject of the following *authentic letters*, the time when they were written, and the rank and reputation of the writers, render them of much importance to the public, we cannot doubt of their being acceptable to the generality of our readers.

Eagle, June 20, 1776.

" I cannot, my worthy friend, permit the letters and parcels which I have sent you, in the state I received them, to be landed, without adding a word upon the subject of the injurious extremities in which our unhappy disputes have engaged us.

" You will learn the nature of my mission from the official dispatches which I have recommended to be forwarded by the same conveyance. Retaining all the earnestness I ever expressed, to see our differences accommodated, I shall conceive, if I meet with the disposition in the colonies which I was once taught to expect, the most flattering hopes of proving serviceable, in the objects of the king's paternal solicitude, by promoting the establishment of lasting peace and union with the colonies. But if the deep-rooted prejudices of America, and the necessity of preventing her trade from passing into foreign channels, must keep us still a divided people, I shall, from every private, as well as public motive, most heartily lament that it is not the moment wherein those great objects of my ambition are to be attained ; and that I am to be longer deprived of an opportunity to assure you personally of the regard with which I am,

" Your sincere and faithful
Humble servant,
HOWE.

" P. S. I was disappointed of the opportunity I expected for sending this letter at the time it was dated, and have been ever since prevented by calms and contrary winds, from getting here to inform General Howe of the commission with which I have the satisfaction to be charged, and of his being joined in it.
Off Sandy Hook, 12 July,
Superscribed
To Benjamin Franklin,
Esq. Philadelphia."

" *Philadelphia, July* 30, 1776.

" I Received safe the letters your lordship so kindly forwarded to me, and beg you to accept my thanks.

" The official dispatches to which you refer me, contain nothing more than what we had seen in the act of parliament, viz. offers of pardon upon submission ; which I was sorry to find, as it must give your lordship pain to be sent so far on so hopeless a business.

" Directing pardons to be offered to the colonies who are the very parties injured, expresses indeed that opinion of our ignorance, baseness and insensibility, which your uninformed and proud nation has long been pleased to entertain of us ; but it can have no other effect than that of encreasing our resentment. It is impossible we should think of submission to a government that has, with the most wanton barbarity and cruelty, burnt our defenceless towns, in the midst of winter ; excited the savages to massacre peaceful farmers, and our slaves to murder their masters ; and is even now bringing foreign mercenaries to deluge our settlements with blood. These atrocious injuries have extinguished every spark of affection for that parent country we once held so dear : but were it possible for us to forget and forgive them, it is not possible for you, I mean the British nation, to forgive the people you have so heavily injured : you can never confide again in those as fellow-subjects, and permit them to enjoy equal freedom, to whom, you know, you have given such just causes of lasting enmity ; and this must impel you, if we are again under your government, to endeavour the breaking our spirit by the severest tyranny, and obstructing, by every means in your power, our growing strength and prosperity.

" But your lordship mentions, ' the king's paternal solicitude for promoting the establishment of lasting peace and union with the colonies.' If by peace is here meant a peace to be entered into by distinct states, now at war, and his majesty has given your lordship power to treat with us, of such peace, I may venture to say, though without authority, that I think a treaty for that purpose not quite impracticable, before we enter into foreign alliances : but I am persuaded you have no such powers. Your nation, though (by punishing those American governors who have fomented the discord, rebuilding our burnt towns, and repairing, as far as poſſible, the miſchiefs done us) ſhe might recover a great ſhare of our regard, and the greateſt ſhare of our growing commerce, with all the advantages of that additional ſtrength, to be derived from a friendſhip with us; yet I know too well her abounding pride, and deficient wiſdom, to believe ſhe will ever take ſuch ſalutary meaſures. Her fondneſs for conqueſt, as a warlike nation; her luſt of dominion, as an ambitious one; and her thirſt for a gainful monopoly, as a commercial one, (none of them legitimate cauſes of war) will all join to hide from her eyes every view of her true intereſt, and will continually goad her on, in theſe ruinous diſtant expeditions, ſo deſtructive both of lives and of treaſure, that they muſt prove as pernicious to her in the end, as the Croiſades formerly were to moſt of the nations in Europe.

" I have not vanity, my lord, to think of intimidating, by thus predicting the effects of this war; for I know it will in England have the fate of all my former predictions, not to be believed, till the event ſhall verify it.

" Long did I endeavour, with unfeigned and unwearied zeal, to preſerve from breaking that fine and noble china vaſe, the Britiſh empire; for I know, that being once broken, the ſeparate parts could not retain even their ſhares of the ſtrength and value that exiſted in the whole; and that a perfect re-union of theſe parts could ſcarce ever be hoped for. Your lordſhip may poſſibly remember the tears of joy that wet my cheek, when at your good ſiſter's in London, you once gave me expectations that a reconciliation might ſoon take place. I had the misfortune to find theſe expectations diſappointed, and to be treated as the cauſe of the miſchief. I was labouring to pre-

vent. My conſolation under that groundleſs and malevolent treatment was, that I retained the friendſhip of many wiſe and good men in that country, and among the reſt, ſome ſhare in the regard of Lord Howe.

" The well-founded eſteem, and permit me to ſay, affection which I ſhall always have for your lordſhip, make it painful for me to ſee you engaged in conducting a war, the great ground of which, as deſcribed in your letter, ' is the neceſſity of preventing the American trade from paſſing into foreign channels: to me it ſeems that neither the obtaining nor retaining any trade, how valuable ſoever, is an object for which men may juſtly ſpill each others blood: that the true and ſure means of extending and ſecuring commerce, are the goodneſs and cheapneſs of commodities; and that the profits of no trade can ever be equal to the expence of compelling it, and holding it by fleets and armies. I conſider this war againſt us, therefore, as both *unjuſt* and *unwiſe*; and I am perſuaded that cool and diſpaſſionate poſterity will condemn to infamy thoſe who adviſed it; and that even ſucceſs will not ſave from ſome degree of diſhonour thoſe who have voluntarily engaged to conduct it.

" I know your great motive in coming hither, was the hope of being inſtrumental in a reconciliation; and believe, that when you find that to be impoſſible, on any terms given you to propoſe, you will relinquiſh ſo odious a command, and return to a more honourable private ſtation.

" With the greateſt and moſt ſincere reſpect, I have the honour to be, my lord, your lordſhip's moſt obedient, humble ſervant,   B. FRANKLIN."
Directed
To the Right Hon. Lord Viſcount Howe.
* * *

His Majeſty's moſt gracious Speech to both Houſes of Parliament, on Thurſday the 31ſt Day of October, 1776.

My Lords and Gentlemen,

NOTHING could have afforded me ſo much ſatisfaction as to have been able to inform you, at the opening of this ſeſſion, that the troubles, which have ſo long diſtracted my colonies in North America, were at an end; and that my unhappy people, recovered from their deluſion, had delivered themſelves from the oppreſſion of their leaders, and returned to their duty: but ſo daring and deſperate is the ſpirit of thoſe leaders, whoſe object has always been dominion and power, that they have now openly renounced all allegiance to the crown, and all political connection with this country: they have rejected, with circumſtances of indignity and inſult, the means of conciliation held out to them under the authority of our commiſſion; and have preſumed to ſet up their rebellious confederacies for independent ſtates. If their treaſon be ſuffered to take root, much miſchief muſt grow from it, to the ſafety of my loyal colonies, to the commerce of my kingdoms, and indeed to the preſent ſyſtem of all Europe. One great advantage, however, will be derived from the object of the rebels being openly avowed, and clearly underſtood; we ſhall have unanimity at home, founded in the general conviction of the juſtice and neceſſity of our meaſures.

I am happy to inform you, that, by the bleſſing of Divine Providence on the good conduct and valour of my officers and forces by ſea and land, and on the zeal and bravery of the auxiliary troops in my ſervice, Canada is recovered; and although, from unavoidable delays, the operations at New York could not begin before the month of Auguſt, the ſucceſs in that province has been ſo important as to give the strongest hopes of the most decisive good consequences: but, notwithstanding this fair prospect, we must, at all events, prepare for another campaign.

I continue to receive assurances of amity from the several courts of Europe; and am using my utmost endeavours to conciliate unhappy differences between two neighbouring powers; and I still hope, that all misunderstandings may be removed, and Europe continue to enjoy the inestimable blessings of peace: I think nevertheless that, in the present situation of affairs, it is expedient that we should be in a respectable state of defence at home.

Gentlemen of the House of Commons,

I will order the estimates for the ensuing year to be laid before you. It is matter of real concern to me, that the important considerations which I have stated to you must necessarily be followed by great expence: I doubt not, however, but that my faithful commons will readily and chearfully grant me such supplies, as the maintenance of the honour of my crown, the vindication of the just rights of parliament, and the publick welfare, shall be found to require.

My Lords and Gentlemen,

In this arduous contest I can have no other object but to promote the true interests of all my subjects. No people ever enjoyed more happiness, or lived under a milder government, than those now revolted provinces: the improvements in every art, of which they boast, declare it: their numbers, their wealth, their strength by sea and land, which they think sufficient to enable them to make head against the whole power of the the mother country, are irrefragable proofs of it. My desire is to restore to them the blessings of law and liberty, equally enjoyed by every British subject, which they have fatally and desperately ex-

changed for all the calamities of war, and the arbitrary tyranny of their chiefs.

The humble Address of the Lords Spiritual and Temporal in Parliament assembled.

Most gracious Sovereign,

WE, your majesty's most dutiful and loyal subjects, the lords spiritual and temporal, in parliament assembled, beg leave to return your majesty our humble thanks for your most gracious speech from the throne.

It is with the truest satisfaction we congratulate your majesty on the success of your arms in the province of New York, the recovery of Canada, and the fair prospect of decisive good consequences, which, under the blessing of Divine Providence, is now opened by the firmness of your majesty's councils, the valour and good conduct of your majesty's officers and forces by sea and land, and by the zeal and bravery of the auxiliary troops in your majesty's service.

We beg leave to assure your majesty, that nothing would have given us equal happiness to the having been informed by your majesty, at the opening of this session, that the troubles, which have so long distracted North America, had been at an end; that your majesty's unhappy people in those provinces had recovered from their delusion, and, awakened by a due sense of their misfortunes and misdoings, had delivered themselves from the oppression of their leaders, and were returned to their duty. While we lament that your majesty's humane and merciful intentions have been frustrated by the neglect shewn to the means of conciliation, notified under the authority of your majesty's royal commission, we feel the strongest indignation at the insolent manner in which they were rejected; and we want words to express our abhorrence of the desperate spirit of those overbearing men, who with

an insatiable thirst of power and dominion, which has uniformly actuated all their proceedings, have now renounced allegiance to the crown, and all political connection with Great Britain; and, with an arrogance equal to the enormity of the attempt, left a doubt of their real designs should remain on the breast of any person whatever, have set up their rebellious confederacies for independent states. We are fully aware of the mischief which would accrue from the success of this treason, to your majesty's loyal colonies, to the commerce of this nation, and, more remotely indeed but not less certainly, to the system of Europe, and to every state upon the continent of Europe possessed of distant colonies.

We reflect with pleasure on the solid advantage which will be derived from the object of the rebels being openly avowed and clearly understood, the unanimity which will prevail at home, founded in a conviction of the justice and necessity of your majesty's measures. Inspired with the same zeal for the cause of our country which animates the kingdom at large, we will steadily support your majesty in the vindication of the honour of your crown, and the just rights of parliament, and will chearfully concur in making the necessary provisions for those great purposes.

The assurances of amity, which your majesty continues to receive from the several courts of Europe, afford us great satisfaction; we entertain the most grateful sense of the endeavours, which your majesty is exerting to conciliate unhappy differences between two neighbouring powers; and we trust that, by your majesty's auspicious endeavours, these misunderstandings will be removed, and Europe continue to enjoy the inestimable blessings of peace. Permit us, Sir, at the same time to return your majesty our dutiful thanks for your provident attention in guarding against any events which may arise out of the present situation of affairs, by keeping us in a respectable state of defence at home.

With hearts full of duty and gratitude, we acknowledge the happiness, which, under your majesty's mild government, is extended to every part of the British empire; of which the late flourishing state of the revolted provinces, their numbers, their wealth, their strength by sea and land, which they think sufficient to enable them to make head against the whole power of the mother country, shew that they have abundantly participated. And we earnestly hope, that your majesty's paternal object of restoring your distracted colonies to the happy condition from which, by their own misconduct, they are wretchedly fallen, will be speedily attained.

Protest of the Lords.

Die Jovis, 31° Oct. 1776.

UPON the motion for the above address an amendment was moved by the Marquis of Rockingham, and seconded by the Duke of Manchester, which produced a long debate; when the question being put, the house divided,

Contents - - 26
Non-contents 82 ⎱ 91
Proxies - - 9 ⎰

The question was next put on the address, and carried in the affirmative.

Dissentient,

For the reasons contained in the amendment proposed and rejected, viz.

" To assure his majesty, that animated with the most earnest and sincere zeal for his true interest, and the real glory of his reign, we behold with inexpressible concern, the minds of a very large, and lately loyal and affectionate part of his people, entirely alienated from his government. Nor can we conceive, that such an event as the disaffection and revolt of a whole people, could have taken place without some considerable errors, in the conduct observed towards them.

" These erroneous measures we conceive are to be imputed to a want of sufficient information being laid before parliament; and to too large a degree of confidence being reposed in those ministers, who from their duty were obliged, and from their official situation were best enabled to know the temper and disposition of his majesty's American subjects; and were, therefore, presumed most capable of pointing out such measures as might produce the most salutary effect. Hence the schemes which were formed for the reduction and chastisement of a supposed inconsiderable party of factious men, have driven thirteen large provinces to despair! Every act which has been proposed as a means of procuring peace and submission, has become a new cause of war and revolt; and we now find ourselves almost inextricably involved in a bloody and expensive civil war, which besides exhausting, at present, the strength of his majesty's dominions, exposing our allies to the designs of their, and our enemies, and leaving this kingdom in a most perilous situation, threatens in its issue, the most deplorable calamities, to the whole British race.

" We cannot avoid lamenting, that in consequence of the credit afforded to the representations of ministers, no hearing has been given to the reiterated complaints and petitions of the colonies: neither has any ground been laid, for removing the original cause of these unhappy differences, which took their rise from questions relative to parliamentary proceedings, and can be settled *only* by parliamentary authority. By this fatal omission, the commissioners nominated for the apparent purpose of making peace, were furnished with no legal power, but those of giving or withholding pardons at their pleasure; and of relaxing the severities of a single penal act of parliament, leaving the whole foundation of this unhappy controversy as it stood at the beginning.

" To represent to his majesty, that in addition to this neglect, when, in the beginning of the last session, his majesty, in his gracious speech to both houses of parliament, had declared his resolution of sending out commissioners for the purposes therein expressed, as speedily as possible; no such commissioners were sent, until nearly seven months afterwards; and until the nation was alarmed by the evacuation of the only town, then held for his majesty, in the thirteen united colonies. By this delay, acts of the most critical nature, the effect of which must as much depend upon the power of immediately relaxing them on submission, as in enforcing them upon disobedience, had only an operation to inflame and exasperate. But if any colony, town, or place, had been induced to submit by the operation of the terrors of those acts, there were none in the place, of power sufficient to restore the people so submitting to the common right of subjection. The inhabitants of the colonies, apprized that they were put out of the protection of government, and seeing no means provided for their entering into it, were furnished with reasons but too colourable, for breaking off their dependency on the crown of this kingdom.

" To assure his majesty, that removing our confidence from those who in so many instances have grosly abused it, we shall endeavour to restore to parliament, the confidence of all his people.

" To this end, it may be adviseable to make a more minute enquiry into the grievances of the colonies, as well as into the conduct of ministers, with regard to them. We may think it proper, particularly, to enquire how it has happened, that the commerce of this kingdom has been left exposed to the reprisals of the colonies, at the very time that their seamen and fishermen being indiscriminately prohibited from the peaceable exercise of their occupations, and declared open enemies, must be expected, with a certain assurance, to betake themselves to plunder, and to wreak their revenge on the commerce of Great Britain.

" That we understand, that amidst the many disasters and disgraces which have attended on his majesty's arms in many parts of America, an advantage has been gained by his majesty's British and foreign mercenary forces, in the province of New York. That if a wise, moderate and prudent use be made of this advantage, it is not improbable, that happy effects may result from that use. And we assure his majesty, that nothing shall be wanting on our part to enable his majesty to take full advantage of any dispositions to reconciliation, which may be the consequence of the miseries of war, by laying down, on our part, real permanent grounds of connection between Great Britain and the colonies, on principles of liberty and terms of mutual advantage.

" That whilst we lament this effusion of English blood, (which we hope has not been greater or other than necessity required and honour justified) we should most heartily congratulate his majesty, on any event leading to the great desirable end of settling a peace, which might promise to last, by the restoration of the ancient affection which has happily subsisted between this kingdom and its colonies; any other would necessarily require, even in case of a total conquest, an army to maintain, ruinous to the finances, and incompatible with the freedom of his ma-

jesty's people. We should look with the utmost shame and horror, on any events, of what nature soever, that should tend to break the spirit of any large part of the British nation, to bow them to an abject unconditional submission to any power whatsoever, to annihilate their liberties, and to subdue them to servile principles, and passive habits, by the mere force of mercenary arms. Because, amidst the excesses and abuses which have happened, we must respect the spirit and principles operating in these commotions; our wish is to regulate, not to destroy them. For though differing in some circumstances, those very principles evidently bear so exact an analogy with those which support the most valuable part of our own constitution, that it is impossible, with any appearance of justice, to think of wholly extirpating them by the sword in any part of his majesty's dominions, without admitting consequences, and establishing precedents the most dangerous to the liberties of this kingdom.

Richmond,	Craven,
Devonshire,	Fitzwilliam,
Portland,	Abingdon,
Manchester,	De Ferrars,
Rockingham,	Effingham,
Scarborough,	Abergavenny,
King,	Ponfonby."

The humble Address of the House of Commons to the King.

Most gracious Sovereign,

WE, your majesty's most dutiful and loyal subjects, the commons of Great Britain in parliament assembled, beg leave to return your majesty the humble thanks of this house, for your most gracious speech from the throne.

While we lament the continuance of the troubles which have so long distracted your majesty's colonies in North America, and of the calamities and oppressions which our unhappy fellow subjects are still

suffering under the arbitrary tyranny of their leaders; we cannot forbear to express our detestation and abhorrence of the audacious and desperate spirit of ambition, which has at last carried those leaders so far, as to make them openly renounce all allegiance to the crown, and all political connexion with this country, and in direct terms to presume to set up their rebellious confederacies for independent states.

We consider their rejection of the gracious and condescending means of reconciliation, held out to them, under the authority of your majesty's commission, as a fresh and convincing proof that the object of these men has always been power and dominion; but we can impute the circumstances of indignity and insult accompanying this proceeding to no other motive than a resentment of your majesty's firm and constant adherence to the maintenance of the constitutional rights of parliament, divested of every possible view of any separate interests of the crown: and we beg leave to assure your majesty, that the same attachment of your majesty to the parliamentary authority of Great Britain, which hath provoked the insolence of the chiefs of this rebellion, cannot but operate, as it ought to do, in fixing your majesty still deeper, if possible, in the affections of a British house of commons.

With reverence and gratitude to Divine Providence, permit us to express our unfeigned joy, and to offer our sincere congratulations to your majesty, on the success which has attended the good conduct and valour of your majesty's officers and forces both by sea and land, and the zeal and bravery of the auxiliary troops in your service, in the recovery of Canada; and in the important operations in the province of New York, which give the strongest hopes of the most decisive good consequences.

It is with much satisfaction we learn, that your majesty continues to receive assurances of amity from the several courts of Europe: and we thankfully acknowledge your majesty's goodness and paternal concern for the happiness of your people, in your constant attention to preserve the general tranquillity; and it is our most earnest wish that, by your majesty's interposition, all misunderstandings and differences between two neighbouring powers may be happily reconciled, and Europe still enjoy the blessings of peace.

Your faithful commons consider it as a duty which they owe to your majesty, and to those they represent, to grant your majesty such supplies as the weighty considerations, which your majesty has been pleased to state to us, shall be found to require; and we have a well-grounded confidence, that, at this time, when the object of the rebels is openly avowed and clearly understood, the general conviction of the justice and necessity of your majesty's measures must unite all ranks of your faithful subjects in supporting your majesty with one mind and heart in the great national cause in which you are engaged.

Translation of a Memorial presented by Sir Joseph Yorke to the States General, on the 21st of February 1777.[84]

SINCE the commencement of the unnatural rebellion, which has broke out in the English colonies against the legal constitution of the mother country, the undersigned ambassador extra-ordinary and plenipotentiary of the King of Great Britain, has had frequent occasions to address himself to your high mightinesses, in the name of his master, to engage them by all motives of national interest, of good neighbourhood, of friendship, and finally of treaties, to put a stop to the clandestine commerce which is carried on between their subjects and the rebels. If the measures which your high mightinesses have thought proper to take had been as efficacious as your assurances have been amicable, the undersigned would not now have been under the disagreeable necessity of bringing to the cognizance of your high mightinesses, facts of the most serious nature.

The king hath hitherto borne, with unexampled patience, the irregular conduct of your subjects in their interested commerce at St. Eustatia, as also in America. His majesty has always flattered himself, that in giving time to your high mightinesses to examine to the bottom this conduct, so irregular and so insufferable, they would have taken measures necessary to repress the abuse, to restrain their subjects within bounds, and to make them respect the rights and friendship of Great Britain.

The complaints which I have orders to make to their high mightinesses, are founded upon authentic documents annexed to this memorial, where their high mightinesses will see with astonishment, and I doubt not at the same time with displeasure, that their new governor, Mr. Van Graaf, after having permitted an illicit commerce at St. Eustatia, hath passed his forgetfulness of his duty to the point of conniving at the Americans in their hostile equipments, and the permitting the seizure of an English vessel, by an American pirate, within cannon shot of that island. And in aggravation to the affront given to the English nation, and to all the powers of Europe, to return from the fortress of his government the salute of a rebel flag. In return to the amicable representations made by the president of the neighbouring island of St. Christopher, on these facts of notoriety, M. Van Graaf has answered in a manner the most vague and unsatisfactory, refusing to enter at all into the subject, or into an explanation of the matter with a member of his majesty's council of St. Christopher's, dispatched by the president for that purpose to St. Eustatia.

After exhibiting the documents annexed, nothing remains with me but to add, that the king who had read them, not with less surprize than indignation, hath ordered me to expressly demand of your high mightinesses, a formal disavowal of the salute by Fort Orange, at St. Eustatia, to the rebel ship, the dismission and immediate recall of Governor Van Graaf, and to declare further, on the part of his majesty, that until that satisfaction is given, they are not to expect that his majesty will suffer himself to be amused by mere assurances, or that he will delay one instant to take such measures as he shall think due to the interests and dignity of his crown.

(Signed)   Jos. YORKE.
Given at the Hague, Feb. 21, 1777.

Memorial delivered by Order of the States General, to the Court of Great Britain, in answer to the above Memorial, by the Envoy extraordinary and Plenipotentiary of their High Mightinesses.

SIRE,

IT is with the most profound respect, that the under-signed envoy extraordinary and plenipotentiary of their high mightinesses, in consequence of the orders which he hath received, hath the honour to represent to your majesty, that the memorial which your ambassador hath presented to their high mightinesses on the 21st of last month, has touched them very sensibly; that they find themselves obliged to make complaint of the reproaches which are contained in it, as if their high mightinesses were to be suspected of a will and intention of amusing your majesty by amicable assurances, which they have falfified by their acts; alfo of the menacing tone which reigns in that memorial, and appears to their high mightineffes too highly ftrained, beyond that which is the accorded and accuftomed manner, and that ought to take place between two fovereign and independent powers, and efpecially between two neighbouring powers, which have been, of fo many years continuance, united by the ties of good harmony and mutual friendfhip.

Their high mightineffes truft that on all occafions, and particularly in refpect to the unfortunate troubles of your majefty's colonies in America, they have held a conduct towards your majefty, which has been expected from a good neighbour, and a friendly and affectionate power.

Their high mightineffes, Sire, hold your majefty's friendfhip in the higheft eftimation, and wifh to do every thing in their power (as far as the honour and dignity of their ftate will permit them to go) to cultivate it ftill more and more; but they cannot at the fame time fo far reftrain themfelves, as to difguife the very poignant fenfation, with which that memorial hath impreffed them.

It is alone from the motive of demonftrating to your majefty every poffible regard, and to prove that their high mightineffes will not neglect any thing, which may ferve to inveftigate properly the truth of the facts, from whence the complaints made to them feem to have arifen, that they have refolved to inftitute an enquiry in a manner the moft fummary, and cut off all trainings of delay.

To this end their high mightineffes, paffing by the ordinary and ufual form in like cafes, requiring a report in writing from their officers and others employed in their colonies, have already difpatched their orders to the commandant of St. Euftatia, to render himfelf within the republic without delay,

and as foon as poffible, to give the neceffary information of all that has paffed within the ifland of St. Euftatia, and that which hath come to his knowledge relative to the American colonies and their veffels, during the period of his command, and to lay his conduct, touching that matter, before the eyes of their high mightineffes.

The under-figned is charged by his orders to bring the information of this refolution to your majefty, as alfo that their high mightineffes make no difficulty of difavowing, in the moft exprefs manner, every act or mark of honour which may have been given by their officers, or by any of their fervants, to the veffels of your majefty's colonies of North-America, or that they may give hereafter, fo far as thofe acts or marks of honour may be of fuch a nature, as that any can conclude from them that it is intended thereby, in the leaft degree, to recognize the independence of thofe colonies.

The under-figned is alfo further charged to inform your majefty, that their high mightineffes have, in confequence, given their orders to their governors and councils in the Weft-Indies, and have enjoined them afrefh, in the ftrongeft terms, to obferve exactly the placards and orders againft the exportation of military ftores to the American colonies of your majefty, and to fee them executed moft rigoroufly.

(Signed)   WELDEREN.
Date London, March 26, 1777.

A Circular Letter of Lord Howe, *to the Governors of the* American *Provinces.*

Eagle, off the Coaft of the Province of Maffachufett's-bay, June 20, 1776.

SIR,

BEING appointed commander in chief of the fhips and vef-

fels of his majefty's fleet employed in North America, and having the honour to be by his majefty conftituted one of his commiffioners for reftoring peace to his colonies, and for granting pardons to fuch of his fubjects therein, as fhall be duly folicitous to benefit by that effect of his gracious indulgence; I take the earlieft opportunity to inform you of my arrival on the American coaft, where my firft object will be an early meeting with General Howe, whom his majefty hath been pleafed to join with me in the faid commiffion.

In the mean time, I have judged it expedient to iffue the inclofed declaration, in order that all perfons may have immediate information of his majefty's moft gracious intentions: and I defire you will be pleafed forthwith to caufe the faid declaration to be promulgated, in fuch manner, and in fuch places within the province of   as will render the fame of the moft public notoriety.

Affured of being favoured with your affiftance in every meafure for the fpeedy and effectual reftoration of the public tranquillity, I am to requeft you will communicate, from time to time, fuch information as you may think will facilitate the attainment of that important object in the province over which you prefide. I have the honour to be, with great refpect and confideration, Sir, your moft obedient humble fervant,   HOWE.

Firft Declaration.

By Richard Vifcount Howe, of the Kingdom of Ireland, one of the King's Commiffioners for reftoring Peace to his Majefty's colonies and plantations in North America, &c.

DECLARATION.

WHEREAS by an act paffed in the laft feffion of parliament, to prohibit all trade and intercourfe with the colonies of New Hampfhire, Maffachufett's-bay, Rhode

Island, Connecticut, New York, New Jersey, Pennsylvania, the three lower counties on Delaware, Maryland, Virginia, North Carolina, South Carolina, and Georgia, and for other purposes therein mentioned, it is enacted, that " it shall and may be lawful to and for any person or persons appointed and authorised by his majesty, to grant a pardon or pardons to any number or description of persons, by proclamation in his majesty's name, to declare any colony or province, colonies or provinces, or any county, town, port, district, or place, in any colony or province, to be at the peace of his majesty;" and that " from and after the issuing of any such proclamation in any of the aforesaid colonies or provinces, or if his majesty shall be graciously pleased to signify the same by his royal proclamation, then, from and after the issuing of such proclamation, the said " act, with respect to such colony or province, colonies or provinces, county, town, port, district, or place, shall cease, determine, and be utterly void." And whereas the king, desirous to deliver all his subjects from the calamities of war, and other oppressions which they now undergo; and to restore the said colonies to his protection and peace, as soon as the constitutional authority of government therein may be replaced, hath been graciously pleased, by letters patent under the great seal, dated the 6th day of May, in the sixteenth year of his majesty's reign, to nominate and appoint me, Richard Viscount Howe, of the kingdom of Ireland, and William Howe, Esq; general of his forces in North America, and each of us, jointly and severally, to be his majesty's commissioner and commissioners for granting his free and general pardons to all those, who in the tumult and disorder of the times, may have deviated from their just allegiance, and who are willing, by a speedy return to their duty, to reap the benefits of the royal

favour: and also for declaring, in his majesty's name, any colony, province, county, town, port, district or place, to be at the peace of his majesty; I do therefore hereby declare, That due consideration shall be had to the meritorious services of all persons who shall aid and assist in restoring the public tranquillity in the said colonies, or in any part or parts thereof: that pardons shall be granted, dutiful representations received, and every suitable encouragement given for promoting such measures as shall be conducive to the establishment of legal government and peace, in pursuance of his majesty's most gracious purposes aforesaid.

Given on board his majesty's ship the Eagle, off the coasts of the province of Massachusett's-bay, the 20th of June, 1776.

HOWE.

Resolution of the Congress upon the above Declaration.

In Congress, July 19.
RESOLVED, That a copy of the circular letters, and of the declaration they inclosed from Lord Howe to Mr. Franklin, Mr. Penn, Mr. Eden, Lord Dunmore, Mr. Martin, and Sir James Wright, late Governors, sent to Amboy by a flag, and forwarded to Congress by Gen. Washington, be published in the several Gazettes, that the good people of these United States may be informed of what *nature* are the commissioners, and what the *terms*, with the expectation of which the insidious court of Great Britain has endeavoured to amuse and disarm them; and that the few who still remain suspended by a hope founded either in the justice or moderation of their late king may now at length be convinced that the valour alone of their country is to save its liberties.

Extract from the Journals.
(Signed)
CHARLES THOMSON, Sec.

A Second Declaration of the American Commissioners.

By Richard Viscount Howe, of the Kingdom of Ireland, and William Howe, Esq; General of his Majesty's Forces in America, the King's Commissioners for restoring Peace to his Majesty's Colonies and Plantations in North America, &c.

DECLARATION.

ALTHOUGH the Congress, whom the misguided Americans suffer to direct their opposition to a re-establishment of the constitutional government of these provinces, have disavowed every purpose of reconciliation not consonant with their extravagant and inadmissible claim of independency, the king's commissioners think fit to declare, that they are equally desirous to confer with his majesty's well-affected subjects upon the means of restoring the public tranquillity, and establishing a permanent union with every colony as a part of the British empire.

The king being most graciously pleased to direct a revision of such of his royal instructions as may be construed to lay an improper restraint upon the freedom of legislation in any of his colonies, and to concur in the revisal of all acts by which his subjects there may think themselves aggrieved, it is recommended to the inhabitants at large to reflect seriously upon their present condition, and to judge for themselves, whether it be more consistent with their honour and happiness to offer up their lives as a sacrifice to the unjust and precarious cause in which they are engaged, or to return to their allegiance, accept the blessings of peace, and be secured in a free enjoyment of their liberty and properties upon the true principles of the constitution.

Given at New-York, the 19th day of September, 1776.

HOWE.

W. HOWE.

By command of their excellencies,

HENRY STRACHEY.

Third Declaration.

By Richard Viscount Howe, of the Kingdom of Ireland, and William Howe, Esq; General of his Majesty's Forces in America, the King's Commissioners for restoring Peace to his Majesty's Colonies and Plantations in North-America, &c.

PROCLAMATION.

WHEREAS by our declarations of the 20th of June and 19th of September last, in pursuance of his majesty's most gracious intentions towards his subjects in the colonies or provinces of New Hampshire, Massachusett's-bay, Rhode-Island, Connecticut, New-York, New Jersey, Pennsylvania, the three Lower Counties on Dalaware, Maryland, Virginia, North-Carolina, South-Carolina, and Georgia, all persons speedily returning to their just allegiance were promised a free and general pardon, and were invited to accept, not only the blessings of peace, but a secure enjoyment of their liberties and properties, upon the true principles of the constitution: And whereas, notwithstanding the said declarations, and the example of many who have availed themselves of the assurances therein made, several bodies of armed men, in open contempt of his majesty's proffered clemency, do still continue their opposition to the establishment of legal government and peace; and divers other ill disposed persons, pursuing their own ambitious purposes in the exercise of a lawless influence and power, are using fresh endeavours, by various arts and misrepresentations, to alienate the confidence and affection of his majesty's subjects; to defeat every plan of reconciliation, and to prolong the unnatural war between Great Britain and her colonies: Now, in order to the more effectual accomplishment of his majesty's most gracious intentions, and the speedy restoration of the public tranquillity; and duly considering the expediency of limiting the time within which such pardon as aforesaid shall be granted, and of specifying the terms upon which only the same shall and may be obtained, We do in his majesty's name, and by virtue of the powers committed to us, hereby charge and command all persons whatsoever, who are assembled together in arms against his majesty's government, to disband themselves and return to their dwelling, there to remain in a peaceable and quiet manner: And we also charge and command all such other persons as are assembled together under the name of General or Provincial Congresses, committees, conventions, or other associations, by whatever name or names known and distinguished, or who, under the colour of any authority from any such Congress, committee, convention, and other association, take upon them to issue or execute any orders for levying money, raising troops, fitting out armed ships and vessels, imprisoning, or otherwise molesting his majesty's subjects, to desist and cease from all such treasonable actings and doings, and to relinquish all such usurped power and authority, so that peace may be restored, a speedy remission of past offences quiet the apprehensions of the guilty, and all the inhabitants of the said colonies be enabled to reap the benefit of his majesty's paternal goodness in the preservation of their property, the restoration of their commerce, and the security of their most valuable rights, under the just and moderate authority of the crown and parliament of Great Britain: And we do hereby declare, and make known to all men, that every person, who within sixty days from the day of the date hereof shall appear before the governor, or lieutenant-governor, or commander in chief, in any of his majesty's colonies or provinces aforesaid, or before the general or commanding officer of his majesty's forces in America, or any other officer in his majesty's service having the command of any detachment or parties of his majesty's forces there, or before the admiral or commander in chief of his majesty's fleets, or any other officer commanding any of his majesty's ships of war, or any armed vessel in his majesty's service, within any of the ports, havens, creeks, or upon the coasts of America, and shall claim the benefit of this proclamation, and at the same time testify his obedience to the laws, by subscribing a declaration in the words following: " *I, A. B. do promise and declare, that I will remain in a peaceable obedience to his majesty, and will not take up arms, nor encourage others to take up arms, in opposition to his authority;*" shall and may obtain a full and free pardon of all treasons and misprisions of treasons, by him heretofore committed or done, and of all forfeitures, attainders, and penalties for the same; and upon producing to us, or to either of us, a certificate of such his appearance and declaration, shall and may have and receive such pardon made and passed to him in due form.

Given at New York this thirtieth day of November, 1776.

HOWE.

W. HOWE.

By command of their excellencies,

HENRY STRACHEY.

Copy of the free Pardon granted by his Majesty's Commissioners, to such Persons as claimed the Benefit of the above Declarations.

(L. S.) Howe.

GEORGE the Third, by the Grace of God of Great Britain,

France, and Ireland, king, defender of the faith, and so forth, to all men to whom these presents shall come, greeting; know ye, that we, of our especial grace, certain knowledge, and mere motion, and out of the zeal and affection which we have and bear to our subjects, have pardoned, remised, and released, and by these presents do pardon, remise, and release, to A. B. merchant of the town of _____ in the province of _____ otherwise called _____ or by whatsoever other name or firname, dignity, office, or place, the said A. B. shall be reputed, called, or named, all and singular treasons, as well high treasons as petit treasons, rebellions, insurrections, and conspiracies, against us, our crown and dignity, and also all manner of misprisions of treason, or other misprisions by him the said A. B. at any time heretofore had, done or perpetrated, whether the said A. B. of the premises, or any of them, should have been indicted, appealed, sued and adjudged, outlawed, convicted, condemned, or attainted or not. We also pardon, remise, and release by these presents, to the aforesaid A. B. all and singular judgments, pains of death, punishments, and issues and profits of all domains, manors, lands, tenements, and other hereditaments, of him the said A. B. on occasion of the premises, or any of them, by him the said A. B. forfeited or lost, and to us, by reason of the premises, due, belonging, or appertaining.

Given at New York, this _____ day of December, 1776.
By command of his excellency,
HENRY STRACHEY.

American Oath of Allegiance.

In CONGRESS, *October* 21, 1776.
RESOLVED, That every officer who holds or shall hereafter hold a commission, or office from Congress, shall subscribe the following declaration, and take the following oath, viz.

"I _____, do acknowledge the thirteen united states of America, namely, New-Hampshire, Massachusett's-Bay, Rhode-Island, Connecticut, New-York, New-Jersey, Pennsylvania, Delaware, Maryland, Virginia, North-Carolina, South-Carolina, and Georgia, *to be free, independent, and sovereign states*; and declare that the people thereof have no allegiance or obedience to George the third, King of Great Britain; and I renounce, refuse, and abjure any allegiance or obedience to him. And I do swear, that I will, to the utmost of my power, support, maintain, and defend the said united states against the said king George the third, and his heirs and successors, and his and their abettors, assistants and adherents; and will serve the said united states in the office of _____, which I now hold, and in any other office which I may hereafter hold, by their appointment, or under their authority, with fidelity and honour, and according to the best of my skill and understanding.
So help me God.
By order of Congress,
JOHN HANCOCK, President.

Proclamation by his Excellency George Washington, *Esq; General and Commander in Chief of all the Forces of the United States of* America.

WHEREAS several persons, inhabitants of the united states of America, influenced by inimical motives, intimidated by the threats of the enemy, or deluded by a proclamation issued the 30th of November last, by Lord and General Howe, stiled the king's commissioners for granting pardons, &c. (now at open war, and invading these states) have been so lost to the interest and welfare of their country, as to repair to the enemy, sign a declaration of fidelity, and in some instances have been compelled to take the oaths of allegiance, and engaged not to take up arms, or encourage others so to do, against the King of Great Britain. And whereas it has become necessary to distinguish between the friends of America and those of Great Britain, inhabitants of these States; and that every man who receives protection from, and as a subject of, any State (not being conscientiously scrupulous against bearing arms) should stand ready to defend the same against hostile invasion; I do, therefore, in behalf of the United States, by virtue of the powers committed to me by Congress, hereby strictly command and require every person, having subscribed such declaration, taken such oaths, and accepted such protection and certificate, to repair to head quarters, or to the quarters of the nearest general officer of the Continental army, or militia, (until further provision can be made by civil authority) and there deliver up such protection, certificate and passports, and take the oath of allegiance to the United States of America: Nevertheless hereby granting full liberty to all such as prefer the interest and protection of Great Britain to the freedom and happiness of their country, forthwith to withdraw themselves and families within the enemy's lines. And I do hereby declare, that all and every person who may neglect or refuse to comply with this order, within thirty days from the date hereof, will be deemed adherents to the King of Great Britain, and treated as common enemies to these American states.

Given at Head Quarters, Morris Town.
By his excellency's command,
ROBERT H. HARRISON, Sec. 86

Papers relating to the Capitulation of Lieutenant General Burgoyne's Army at Saratoga.

No. I.

October 13, 1777.

LIEUT.-GEN. Burgoyne is desirous of sending a field-officer with a message to Major-General Gates, upon a matter of high moment to both armies. He requests to be informed at what hour General Gates will receive him to-morrow morning.

Major-General Gates.

ANSWER.

MAJ.-GEN. Gates will receive a field-officer from Lieutenant-General Burgoyne at the advanced post of the army of the United States, at ten o'clock to-morrow morning, from whence he will be conducted to head quarters.

Camp at Saratoga, 9 o'clock,
P. M. October 13, 1777.
Lieutenant-General Burgoyne.

No. II.

Major Kingston *delivered the following Message to Major-General Gates,* October 14, 1777. [87]

AFTER having fought you twice, Lieutenant-General Burgoyne has waited some days, in his present position, determined to try a third conflict against any force you could bring to attack him.

He is apprised of the superiority of your numbers, and the disposition of your troops to impede his supplies, and render his retreat a scene of carnage on both sides. In this situation he is impelled by humanity, and thinks himself justified by established principles and precedents of state, and of war, to spare the lives of brave men upon honourable terms: should Major-General Gates be inclined to treat upon that idea, General Burgoyne would propose a cessation of arms during the time necessary to communicate the preliminary terms by which, in any extremity, he and his army mean to abide.

No. III.

Major-General Gates's *Proposals, together with Lieutenant-General* Burgoyne's *Answers.*

I. GENERAL Burgoyne's army being exceedingly reduced by repeated defeats, by desertion, sickness, &c. their provisions exhausted, their military horses, tents, and baggage taken or destroyed, their retreat cut off, and their camp invested, they can only be allowed to surrender prisoners of war.

Answer. Lieut.-General Burgoyne's army, however reduced, will never admit that their retreat is cut off, while they have arms in their hands.

II. The officers and soldiers may keep the baggage belonging to them. The generals of the United States never permit individuals to be pillaged.

III. The troops under his Excellency General Burgoyne will be conducted by the most convenient route to New-England, marching by easy marches, and sufficiently provided for by the way.

Answer. This article is answered by General Burgoyne's first proposal, which is here annexed.

IV. The officers will be admitted on parole; may wear their side arms, and will be treated with the liberality customary in Europe, so long as they, by proper behaviour, continue to deserve it; but those who are apprehended having broke their parole, as some British officers have done, must expect to be close confined.

Answer. There being no officer in this army under, or capable of being under, the description of breaking parole, this article needs no answer.

V. All public stores, artillery, arms, ammunition, carriages, horses, &c. &c. must be delivered to commissaries appointed to receive them.

Answer. All public stores may be delivered, arms excepted.

VI. These terms being agreed to, and signed, the troops under his

Excellency Gen. Burgoyne's command, may be drawn up in their encampments, where they will be ordered to ground their arms, and may thereupon be marched to the river-side, to be passed over in their way towards Bennington.

Answer. This article inadmissible in any extremity. Sooner than this army will consent to ground their arms in their encampment, they will rush on the enemy, determined to take no quarter.

VII. A cessation of arms to continue till sun-set, to receive General Burgoyne's answer.

(Signed) *Horatio Gates.*
Camp at Saratoga, Oct. 14, 1777.

No. IV.

MAJOR Kingston met the Adjutant-General of Major-General Gates's army, October the 14th, at sun-set, and delivered the following message:

If General Gates does not mean to recede from the 6th article, the treaty ends at once.

The army will, to a man, proceed to any act of desperation, rather than submit to that article.

The cessation of arms ends this evening.

No. V.

Lieutenant-General Burgoyne's *Proposals, together with Major-General* Gates's *Answers.*

THE annexed answers being given to Major-General Gates's proposals, it remains for Lieutenant-General Burgoyne, and the army under his command, to state the following preliminary articles on their part.

I. The troops to march out of their camp with the honours of war, and the artillery of the intrenchments, which will be left as hereafter may be regulated.

I. The troops to march out of their camp with the honours of war, and the artillery of the intrenchments, to the verge of the river where the old fort stood, where their arms and artillery must be left.

II. A free paſſage to be granted to this army to Great-Britain, upon condition of not ſerving again in North-America during the preſent conteſt; and a proper port to be aſſigned for the entry of tranſports to receive the troops whenever General Howe ſhall ſo order.

II. Agreed to for the port of Boſton.

III. Should any cartel take place, by which this army or any part of it may be exchanged, the foregoing article to be void, as far as ſuch exchange ſhall be made.

III. Agreed.

IV. All officers to retain their carriages, bat-horſes, and other cattle; and no baggage to be moleſted or ſearched, the lieutenant-general giving his honour that there are no public ſtores ſecreted therein. Major-General Gates will of courſe take the neceſſary meaſures for the ſecurity of this article.

IV. Agreed.

V. Upon the march the officers are not to be ſeparated from their men; and in quarters the officers ſhall be lodged according to rank; and are not to be hindered from aſſembling their men for roll-calling, and other neceſſary purpoſes of regularity.

V. Agreed to, as far as circumſtances will admit.

VI. There are various corps in this army compoſed of ſailors, batteau-men, artificers, drivers, independent companies, and followers of the army; and it is expected that thoſe perſons, of whatever country, ſhall be included in the fulleſt ſenſe, and utmoſt extent of the above articles, and comprehended in every reſpect as Britiſh ſubjects.

VI. Agreed to in the fulleſt extent.

VII. All Canadians, and perſons belonging to the eſtabliſhment in Canada, to be permitted to return there.

VII. Agreed.

VIII. Paſſports to be immediately granted for three officers, not exceeding the rank of captain, who ſhall be appointed by General Burgoyne to carry diſpatches to Sir William Howe, Sir Guy Carleton, and to Great-Britain by the way of New-York, and the public faith to be engaged that theſe diſpatches are not to be opened.

VIII. Agreed.

IX. The foregoing articles are to be conſidered only as preliminaries for framing a treaty, in the courſe of which others may ariſe to be conſidered by both parties; for which purpoſe it is propoſed that two officers of each army ſhall meet and report their deliberations to their reſpective generals.

IX. This capitulation to be finiſhed by two o'clock this day, and the troops march from their encampment at five, and be in readineſs to move towards Boſton tomorrow morning.

X. Lieutenant-General Burgoyne will ſend his deputy adjutant-general to receive Major-General Gates's anſwer to-morrow morning at ten o'clock.

X. Complied with.

(Signed) *Horatio Gates.*
Saratoga, Oct. 15, 1777.

No. VI.

THE eight firſt preliminary articles of Lieutenant-General Burgoyne's propoſals, and the 2d, 3d, and 4th of thoſe of Major-General Gates of yeſterday, being agreed to, the foundation of the propoſed treaty is out of diſpute; but the ſeveral ſubordinate articles and regulations neceſſarily ſpringing from theſe preliminaries, and requiring explanation and preciſion between the parties, before a definitive treaty can be ſafely executed, a longer time than that mentioned by General Gates in his anſwer to the 9th article becomes indiſpenſably neceſſary. Lieutenant-General Burgoyne is willing to appoint two officers immediately to meet two others from Major-General Gates, to propound, diſcuſs, and ſettle thoſe ſubordinate articles, in order that the treaty, in due form, may be executed as ſoon as poſſible.

(Signed) *John Burgoyne.*
Camp at Saratoga, Oct. 15, 1777.

Major Kingſton has authority to ſettle the place for a meeting of the officers propoſed.

Settled by Major Kingſton on the ground where Mr. Schuyler's houſe ſtood.

No. VII.

IN the courſe of the night, Lieutenant-General Burgoyne has received intelligence that a conſiderable force has been detached from the army under the command of Major-General Gates during the courſe of the negotiations of the treaty depending between them. Lieutenant-General Burgoyne conceives this, if true, to be not only a violation of the ceſſation of arms, but ſubverſive of the principles on which the treaty originated, viz. a great ſuperiority of numbers in General Gates's army. Lieutenant-General Burgoyne therefore requires that two officers on his part be permitted to ſee that the ſtrength of the forces now oppoſed to him is ſuch as will convince him that no ſuch detachments have been made; and that the ſame principle of ſuperiority on which the treaty firſt began ſtill exiſts.

16th October.

No. VIII.

Articles of Convention between Lieutenant-General Burgoyne and Major-General Gates.

I.

THE troops under Lieutenant-General Burgoyne to march out of their camp with the honours of war, and the artillery of the intrenchments, to the verge of the river where the old fort ſtood, where the arms and artillery are to be left: the arms to be piled by word of command from their own officers.

II. A free paſſage to be granted the army under Lieutenant-General Burgoyne to Great-Britain, on condition of not ferving again in North-America during the prefent conteft ; and the port of Bofton is affigned for the entry of tranfports to receive the troops whenever General Howe fhall fo order.

III. Should any cartel take place, by which the army under General Burgoyne, or any part of it, may be exchanged, the foregoing article to be void, as far as fuch exchange fhall be made.

IV. The army under Lieutenant-General Burgoyne to march to Maffachufetts Bay, by the eafieft, moft expeditious and convenient route ; and to be quartered in, near, or as convenient as poffible to Bofton, that the march of the troops may not be delayed when tranfports arrive to receive them.

V. The troops to be fupplied on their march, and during their being in quarters, with provifions, by Major-General Gates's orders, at the fame rate of rations as the troops of his own army ; and, if poffible, the officers horfes and cattle are to be fupplied with forage at the ufual rates.

VI. All officers to retain their carriages, bat-horfes, and other cattle ; and no baggage to be molefted or fearched, Lieutenant-General Burgoyne giving his honour that there are no public ftores fecreted therein. Major-General Gates will of courfe take the neceffary meafures for a due perform-. ance of this article. Should any carriages be wanted during the march, for the tranfportation of officers baggage, they are, if poffible, to be fupplied by the country at the ufual rates.

VII. Upon the march, and during the time the army fhall remain in quarters in the Maffachufetts Bay, the officers are not, as far as circumftances will admit, to be feparated from their men. The officers are to be quartered according to their rank, and are not to be hindered from affembling their men for roll-callings, and other neceffary purpofes of regularity.

VIII. All corps whatever of General Burgoyne's army, whether compofed of failors, batteau-men, artificers, drivers, independent companies, and followers of the army, of whatever country, fhall be included in the fulleft fenfe and utmoft extent of the above articles, and comprehended in every refpeft as Britifh fubjects.

IX. All Canadians, and perfons belonging to the Canadian eftablifhment, confifting of failors, batteau-men, artificers, drivers, independent companies, and many other followers of the army, who come under no particular defcription, are to be permitted to return there : they are to be conducted immediately, by the fhorteft route, to the firft Britifh poft on Lake George, are to be fupplied with provifions in the fame manner as the other troops, and are to be bound by the fame condition of not ferving during the prefent conteft in North-America.

X. Paffports to be immediately granted for three officers, not exceeding the rank of captains, who fhall be appointed by Lieutenant-General Burgoyne to carry difpatches to Sir William Howe, Sir Guy Carleton, and to Great-Britain by the way of New York ; and Major-General Gates engages the public faith that thefe difpatches fhall not be opened. Thefe officers are to fet out immediately after receiving their difpatches, and are to travel the fhorteft route, and in the moft expeditious manner.

XI. During the ftay of the troops in the Maffachufetts Bay, the officers are to be admitted on parole, and are to be permitted to wear their fide-arms.

XII. Should the army under Lieutenant General Burgoyne find it neceffary to fend for their cloathing and other baggage from Canada, they are to be permitted to do it in the moft .... manner, and the neceffary paffports granted for that purpofe.

XIII. Thefe articles are to be mutually figned and exchanged tomorrow morning at nine o'clock ; and the troops under Lieutenant-General Burgoyne are to march out of their intrenchments at three o'clock in the afternoon.

Horatio Gates, Maj. Gen.
Camp at Saratoga,
Oct. 16, 1777.
(True Copy.)

To prevent any doubts that might arife from Lieutenant-General Burgoyne's name not being mentioned in the above treaty, Major-General Gates hereby declares that he is underftood to be comprehended in it as fully as if his name had been fpecifically mentioned.

Horatio Gates.

Notes, 1777

1. Captain Thomas Pringle, Rear Admiral, 1794, Vice-Admiral, 1801.

2. Brigadier-General David Waterbury (1722–1801) of Connecticut.

3. William Harcourt (1743–1830), later, 3rd Earl Harcourt, Commander of the 16th Light Dragoons.

4. John Campbell (1753–84), probably captured when Fort Chambly was taken in October 1775.

5. David Rittenhouse (1732–96), the celebrated American astronomer.

6. Daniel Horsmanden (1694–1778), Chief Justice of New York.

7. Galloway (see "Introduction, 1774," n. 16) was Pennsylvania delegate to the Congress in 1774; he became a firm Loyalist by 1775 and worked closely with Howe after the occupation of Philadelphia.

8. James Ewing (1736–1806), Pennsylvania militia officer. John Cadwalader (1742–86), Pennsylvania militia Colonel, refused appointment as Brigadier-General in the Continental Army in February 1777 to serve at the same rank in the militia.

9. Nathaniel Greene (1742–86), youngest of the brigadier-generals appointed by Congress in 1775; replaced, because of illness, as Commander on Long Island in August 1776. He established a considerable military reputation by the end of the war.

10. Charles Mawhood (?1732–80), Lieutenant-Colonel of the 17th Regiment.

11. Hugh Mercer (?1725–77), Scots emigrant who fought in the Pennsylvania Regiment during the Seven Years War. Commissioned Colonel of the 3rd Virginia Regiment in February 1776, he was appointed Brigadier-General in the Continental Army in June.

12. John Stuart (c. 1708–79), Superintendant of Indian Affairs for the Southern District from 1762 to 1775, when his arrest was ordered by the South Carolina Assembly for his efforts to raise the Indians on behalf of the British.

13. See "Notes, 1776," n. 97.

14. See "Introduction, 1777."

15. Cavendish's amendment, and that of Rockingham in the Lords, was apparently composed by Burke. The *Correspondence of Edmund Burke*, vol. 3, p. 299, n. 1.

16. That is, the Prohibitory Act of November, 1775.

17. William Pitt, then Secretary of State for the Southern Department, accepted exploratory negotiations by France for ending the Seven Years War in 1761; the French envoy was Francois de Bussy (1699–?1780).

18. 17 Geo. III c. 7.

19. Germain (i.e., not North).

20. John Dunning.

21. Charles Fox.

22. Sir Grey Cooper.

23. This speech appears to be that made by Thomas Powys on 14 February, when the bill was reported back to the House. *Parliamentary History*, vol. 19, 22.

24. John Morton (?1714–80), M.P. for Wigan, 1775–80; Chief Justice of Chester from 1762; Attorney-General to the Queen from 1770.

25. The amendment referred to here was proposed by George Dempster (1732–1818). M.P. for Perth Burghs, 1769–90, to limit the objects of the bill to "the better protection of the inhabitants of Great Britain." *Parliamentary History*, vol. 19, 17.

26. Thomas Powys.

27. "An Act to oblige all persons, being Papists, in that Part of Great Britain called Scotland, and all persons in Great Britain refusing or neglecting to take the Oaths appointed for the security of His Majesty's Person and Government, by several acts herein mentioned, to register their names and real estates." The act refers to persons refusing the oath yet enjoying the protection and benefit of government while ". . . contriving, stirring up and supporting . . . Rebellions, Insurrections and Conspiracies."

28. Charles Cornwall.

29. Probably John Dunning. The remark as quoted here does not appear in any of the other records of the debate, but Dunning is reported as speaking in a similar vein on 17 February.

30. Charles Fox.

31. 17 Geo. III c. 9.

32. Lieutenant-Colonel John Bird of the 15th Regiment.

33. Brigadier-General James Agnew, Colonel of the 44th Regiment. William Erskine (1728–95) had a distinguished record from the Seven Years War and was posted to America with the local rank of Brigadier-General in 1776.

34. Gold Selleck Silliman (1732–90), Brigadier-General of the Connecticut militia.

35. Not identified.

36. Return Jonathan Meigs (1740–1823), Lieutenant-Colonel of Sherburne's Regiment (one of the sixteen Additional Continental Regiments). The Congress awarded him a sword of honour for this expedition.

37. Samuel Parsons (1737–89), Colonel of the 6th Regiment, promoted to Brigadier-General in August 1776.

38. William Maxwell (1733–97), veteran of the Seven Years War, appointed Brigadier-General in October 1776. Thomas Conway (c. 1735–1800?), an Irishman raised in France, Colonel in the French army by 1772, permitted to serve in America in 1776 (with the rank of Brigadier-General from May 1777), and, later, centre of intrigues against Washington.

39. William Barton (1748–1831), Major of Stanton's Rhode Island State Troops; voted a sword of honour for this exploit and promoted to Lieutenant-Colonel in November 1777.

40. Fortescue gives British casualties as 577. John W. Fortescue, *History of the British Army*, 13 vols. (London, 1899–1930), vol. 3, p. 216.

41. Marie Joseph du Motier, Marquis de Lafayette (1757–1834), was a wealthy, aristocratic junior officer in the French army who sought service in America in a spirit of romantic adventure and, at nineteen, was commissioned Major-General without specific command in the Continental Army in July 1777.

42. Major Bernde St. Ouary was recaptured in January 1778. Philippe Charles Tronson du Coudray (1738–77), French artillery officer who brought a group of officers, men, and guns to America in May 1777 on the promise that he would be appointed Major-General of Ordnance. The friction created by this appointment had become a serious problem when he was accidentally drowned in September 1777. Mathias Alexis Roche de Fermoy (fl. 1760–77), a French officer appointed Brigadier-General in the Continental Army in November 1776, had a reputation for incompetence and ambition. Casimir Pulaski (c. 1748–79), Polish officer of dragoons and emigré in Paris. He arrived in America in July 1777 and was appointed to command of the Continental Cavalry in September. Grabouski(e), Polish Count, volunteer A.D.C. to Clinton, killed in 1777.

43. Anthony Wayne (1745–94), Pennsylvania officer promoted to Brigadier-General in February 1777, later achieved a considerable reputation.

44. Charles Grey (1729–1807), posted to America in 1776 with the local rank of Major-General. His highly effective surprise attack at Paoli was promptly described by the Americans as an inhumanly executed massacre and became one of the propaganda myths of the war.

45. Brigadier-General Samuel Cleaveland of the artillery; not otherwise identified.

46. Andrew Snape Hamond (1738–1828), promoted to Captain in 1770, ordered to blockade Chesapeake and Delaware bays from 1775, and knighted for his services in 1778; later a Baronet, Governor of Nova Scotia, and Comptroller of the Navy.

47. Thomas Stirling.

48. Thomas Musgrave (1737–1812), Lieutenant-Colonel of the 40th Regiment.

49. Fortescue gives British losses as 537 killed and wounded, 14 captured; American losses, 673, with 400 taken prisoner. Fortescue, *History of the British Army*, vol. 3, pp. 220–21.

50. Lieutenant-Colonel Friedrich Ludwig von Minnigerode (d. 16 October 1779).

51. Not identified.

52. Burgoyne began the campaign with forty-two field pieces and ninety-six cannon in the flotilla.

53. Germain wrote to Burgoyne on 23 August 1776: "I hope every precaution has been taken to secure the Indians to our interest. The Congress is exerting all their interest to debauch them from you . . . The dread of the people of New England etc. have of a war with the savages proves the expediency of our holding that scourge over them. The Indians report that had General Carleton permitted them to act last year, Canada would not have been in the hands of the rebels." Quoted in Alan Valentine, *Lord George Germain* (Oxford, 1962), p. 187.

54. Powel, not identified.? Sir Robert Hamilton, Colonel of the 40th Regiment, later Lieutenant-General.

55. Barry St. Leger (1737–89), a veteran of the Seven Years War, Lieutenant-Colonel promoted to Brigadier-General for this expedition.

56. Sir John Johnson (1742–1830), son of Sir William Johnson, Superintendant of Indian Affairs for the Northern District. A Loyalist, he had broken his parole to escape to Canada, where he was commissioned Lieutenant-Colonel to raise a regiment of New York Loyalists.

57. These defences may have been planned in 1776 by John Trumbull (1756–1843), who later became the best-known American artist of the era. They were constructed under the supervision of Polish adventurer Thaddeus Kosciuszko (1746–1817), who had been commissioned Colonel of Engineers in October 1776 and posted to Gates's command.

58. Usually called by historians Mount Defiance, after the fort eventually created on it, but termed the Sugar Loaf by successive defenders of Ticonderoga from 1758.

59. Arthur St. Clair (1737–1818), formerly an officer in the Royal American Regiment, appointed Colonel of the 2nd Pennsylvania Battalion in January 1776, Brigadier-General in August, and Major-General to replace Gates in February 1777. Congress recalled him in disgrace, but a court-martial held at his request cleared him on all charges.

60. Historians have not agreed on the size of the American force; figures quoted vary from 2,500 to 5,000.

61. Turbott Francis (1740–97) commanded a Massachusetts regiment. The officer commanding this rearguard was Seth Warner. Robert Grant, Major in the 24th Regiment, not otherwise identified.

62. Lieutenant-Colonel commanding the 9th Regiment, not otherwise identified.

63. One version suggests the Americans withdrew on hearing Indian war cries, which they took to herald the arrival of reinforcements from Burgoyne; the noise was found to have been made by a lone officer who had advanced ahead of his Indian scouting party.

64. The facts of Jane McCrea's murder are forever lost in the propaganda produced around this classic atrocity story, which almost certainly encouraged recruitment into the New England militia in the following weeks.

65. Lieutenant-Colonel Friedrick Baum, Commander of the Brunswick Dragoons.

66. Lieutenant-Colonel Heinrich Breymann, Commander of the Advance Corps of the Brunswick Division.

67. John Stark (1728–1822), veteran frontier ranger of the Seven Years War, Colonel of the 1st New Hampshire Regiment. His refusal to accept orders from Major-General Benjamin Lincoln (see n. 76, below) resulted in his accidental presence at Bennington, to Baum's misfortune.

68. Anglo-German losses are usually quoted as 207 killed and 700 taken prisoner.

69. Nicholas Herkimer (1728–77), Brigadier-General of New York militia.

70. The figure of 400 dead is that given by St. Leger to Burgoyne; a likelier estimate is about 200. See Howard Swiggett, *War Out of Niagara: Walter Butler and the Tory Rangers* (New York, 1933), p. 87.

71. Marinus Willett (1740–1830) served in a New York regiment in the Seven Years War, became a prominent New York radical by 1775, and was appointed Lieutenant-Colonel of the 3rd New York Regiment in 1776. He was awarded a sword of honour by Congress for the Fort Stanwyx exploit.

72. Peter Gansevoort (1749–1812), Colonel of the 3rd New York Regiment in 1776 and Commandant at Fort Stanwyx.

73. John Butler (1728–96), and Daniel Claus acted as deputies for Guy Johnson, Superintendant of Indian Affairs for the Northern District after 1774, during Johnson's absence in England and New York, 1775–78.

74. Burgoyne's report was published in the *London Gazette* for 16 December. The interpretation he puts on his instructions here shows remarkable ingenuity but scant regard for the facts. For this letter, see E. B. de Fonblanque, *Political and Military Episodes in the Latter Half of the Eighteenth Century, Derived from the Life and Correspondence of the Right Honourable John Burgoyne* (London, 1876), pp. 290–93.

75. Major Griffith Williams, second-in-command to Phillips in Burgoyne's artillery.

76. Benjamin Lincoln (1733–1820), originally a Massachusetts militia commander; appointed, on Washington's recommendation, Major-General in the Continental Army, February 1777; commanded the New England militia at Saratoga. Colonel John Brown, Commander of a Connecticut regiment; Colonel Francis Johnston, Commander of the 5th Pennsylvania Regiment; ?Colonel Benjamin Ruggles Woodbridge, commanded a Massachusetts militia regiment.

77. Speight (misspelling for Specht), Brigadier-General in the Brunswick contingent, not otherwise identified. Brigadier-General von Gall, Colonel of a Hesse-Hanau regiment.

78. John Dyke Acland (1746–78), M.P. for Callington from 1774 to his death, and so vigorous a supporter of coercion toward America that he first tried to raise a regiment to fight there, then bought a major's commission in the 20th Regiment, and joined Burgoyne in 1776. His wife, Lady Harriet (1730–1815), daughter of the Earl of Ilchester, accompanied her husband on the campaign and, after his wounding and capture at Saratoga, crossed the American lines under a flag of truce to nurse him.

79. Not James, but Sir Francis Carr Clerke (1748–77), 7th Baronet and Captain in the 3rd Foot Guards.

80. On the contrary, the British suffered about 600 casualties and the Americans, 150.

81. William Hotham (1736–1813), Commodore on the American station, 1776–80, promoted to Vice-Admiral in 1790, and created Baron Hotham in the Irish peerage in 1797.

82. Campbell and Sill, not identified; Alexander Grant, Major in the New York volunteers.

83. James Wallace (1731–1803), knighted February 1777, Captain in 1771, and promoted to Rear-Admiral in 1794.

84. Sir Joseph Yorke (1724–92), British Ambassador at the Hague, 1761–80; created Baron Dover 1788.

85. Henry Strachey (1736–1810), M.P. for Bishops Castle, 1774–78, and for Saltash, 1778–80; created 1st Baronet 1801; appointed Secretary to the Howe Peace Commission.

86. Robert Hanson Harrison, one of Washington's aides from October 1775.

87. Burgoyne's Adjutant-General, not otherwise identified.

1778

Introduction

The nature of Britain's struggle with America changed in 1778. In March, the war with France which the Opposition predicted for so long became an imminent reality, yet Britain's basic failure to prepare to resume the struggle with her most formidable enemy meant a reappraisal of strategic objectives in the light of available resources and a reconsideration of the whole policy of forcing America back into the empire.

France was preparing for war to recoup her losses even before the Seven Years War ended, and she watched Britain's developing conflict with the Thirteen Colonies closely. From late 1775, France surreptitiously sent supplies to America through the enterprising agent, Caron de Beaumarchais. America and France were cautious about entering a formal alliance; America because it would close the door on a reconciliation with Britain, France because she would be economically and militarily unready for a premature conflict with Britain. The liaison developed over the next three years. The Continental Congress sent Silas Deane to Paris in March 1776, and in September resolved to seek to negotiate a treaty. Deane was joined by Franklin and Arthur Lee, and they were authorised to make commercial concessions in return for an alliance. France sought to involve Spain, but caution in Madrid postponed Spanish participation. France also had no intention of tying herself to America if the colonies could not successfully resist British military power. Saratoga was therefore decisive, since America demonstrated a capacity for successful military resistance, and Britain might now seek an accommodation with the colonies and end the debilitating struggle. Consequently, the French-American negotiations proceeded rapidly after December 1777; treaties of commerce and amity were signed on 6 February 1778.[1] British agents reported details of the negotiations to London as they progressed, so the ministry was fully apprised before the French ambassador informed North officially on 13 March.

Britain might have been informed but she was not prepared. North's refusal, endorsed by the King, to face the political repercussions of financing the restoration of Britain's naval strength—a restoration consistently urged by Sandwich—had left the nation gravely weakened. A successful war against France depended on an ability to blockade the French fleets in Europe, attack her overseas colonies, and wreck her maritime commerce. A continued war in America simultaneously required control of the Atlantic. Yet Sandwich claimed that the ships available in England were barely sufficient to guard home waters; blockade was impossible, and the ships in America would have to supplement the home fleet and provide detachments for any expedition. So control of the Atlantic was perforce abandoned at the outset. Moreover, Britain could not adopt the basic arrangement used in the two previous wars with France, that of securing an ally to commit France to a land war in Europe, for Britain's inept foreign policy since 1761 had left her friendless.

Strategic logic dictated the abandonment of America, but though the King may have recognised the purely military imperative, he felt it was outweighed by unacceptable political consequences. The loss of America, it was thought, would severely damage the commercial empire on which Britain's prosperity and power were seen to be based. The loss would instantly reduce Britain's standing among the powers of Europe and blemish her national and monarchical honour. Such a decision would be a confession of failure which would require the replacement of North's compliant ministry with one composed of

1. S. F. Bemis, *The Diplomacy of the American Revolution* (Edinburgh and London, 1957), pp. 58–69; C. R. Ritcheson, *British Politics and the American Revolution* (Norman, Okla., 1954), pp. 233–41. For the text of both treaties see *Treaties and Other International Acts of the United States of America*, ed. D. H. Miller, 8 vols., (Washington, D.C., 1931–48), vol. 2, pp. 3–29, 35–41.

Opposition men whom the King regarded as personal enemies. A compromise was therefore inevitable. Negotiations would be reopened with America, to seek a settlement short of recognition of independence. Britain would withdraw her forces to fundamentally secure bases in North America, from which raids on the American coast could be made, and reserve her strength for a naval war with France.

Germain's instructions show the development of this thinking. On 7 March, he instructed Clinton, the new commander-in-chief in America, to concentrate on raiding the coast of New England from Halifax and New York, holding or evacuating Philadelphia as circumstances warranted. On 21 March, a week after official notification of the Franco-American treaty, fresh orders were despatched. Philadelphia was to be evacuated at once, New York also if peace negotiations failed or if the Americans attacked. Clinton was to despatch an expedition to establish a base in Georgia and release troops for a combined operation against St. Lucia in the French West Indies. Rhode Island was to be held if possible, but the new British headquarters would be in Halifax, Nova Scotia. These objectives would have been realistic if Britain had the naval power to control the Atlantic and interdict the Caribbean to a French fleet. That power was lacking.

The North ministry was badly shaken by the Saratoga disaster and faced the prospect of a Bourbon war with dismay. Yet when Parliament resumed after the Christmas recess, no clear policy emerged in the face of the inevitable Opposition assault. The Opposition had also failed to use the recess constructively and its deep divisions were exposed; the Rockinghams began to move toward recognition of American independence, while Chatham became more adamant than ever on the need to retain America within the empire.

On 20 January, Fox demanded that the House see the papers for the Saratoga campaign. North conceded that the House had this right in general but he refused to comply in this instance. The Opposition then attacked the spate of private subscriptions for raising troops, which rumours of a French war precipitated , and thus appeared to demonstrate a lack of patriotism. On 2 February, both Houses finally went into a committee of the whole to consider the state of the nation. Richmond in the Lords and Fox in the Commons both lost motions to send no more troops to America by substantial margins (although the division in the Commons—259 to 165—seemingly indicated a significant growth of Opposition support). On 4 February, the private subscription levies were attacked again; on the sixth, Burke theatrically denounced the use of Indians as allies; and on the eleventh, Fox demanded full information on British forces in America (claiming that the war had cost 20,000 British lives to date, an exaggeration of 1,600 percent). These motions were lost and the Opposition was forced to face the galling fact that, weak as North's ministry was, the Opposition was weaker.

Moreover, North now had a semblance of a policy. The Cabinet agreed on 11 February to renounce Britain's right of taxation in return for an American defence contribution, and to send a new peace commission. The commission was the brainchild of Lord Suffolk's intriguing, ambitious under-secretary of state, William Eden, and was to be composed of Gower's son-in-law, the Earl of Carlisle, George Johnstone,[2] and Eden himself, together with the commanders-in-chief. Each was to have broad powers of concession, short of granting independence.[3] North introduced this policy package to Parliament on 19 February, staggering the independent country gentlemen and leaving the Opposition—which could scarcely oppose conciliation—to criticise details and to vainly demand parliamentary control of appointments to the commission. Fox tried to introduce a more promising line of attack by defying the Government to deny that a Franco-American treaty now existed.[4] North, who knew on 2 February that the agreement was on the point of being signed, continued to prevaricate.

North had tried hard to resign after the news of Saratoga, but the King would not allow it so that, beset with doubts and anxieties, he was obliged to soldier on. The two conciliation bills emerged from committee much altered, but they passed their third reading in the Commons on 2 March without difficulty and became law by

2. Richard Jackson (see "Introduction, 1765") had originally been proposed but he refused the post.
3. For the formation of the Carlisle Peace Commission, see Ritcheson, *British Politics and the American Revolution*, pp. 258–66; for its negotiating terms, ibid., pp. 268–70.
4. See "Notes, 1778," n. 57.

the middle of the month. North indeed apparently lost interest in the Peace Commission, possibly because secret contacts with the American envoys in Paris indicated no settlement was likely without prior recognition of American independence, and perhaps because he was absorbed in preparing a budget to secure new taxes to pay the escalating war costs.

Fresh problems emerged. The Rockinghams had persistently pressed to reduce the Crown's influence over legislature, in particular, the "secret influence" exercised in awarding offices of profit and government favours. Diminishing such influence through a programme of "economical reform" developed as a major item in the Opposition's line of attack. An attempt to impose a 25 percent tax on placeholders' salaries was defeated on 2 March by a tiny margin of 147 to 141—a clear sign that the independent country gentlemen were becoming restive. Sir Philip Jennings Clerke's bill to exclude contractors from the House of Commons was accepted on 13 April and 1 May, and was defeated on its third reading by a slender margin, 113 to 109. Simultaneously, the Government was faced with growing unrest in Ireland, where trade was seriously affected by the American war. After a long delay, North proposed trade concessions on 7 April, and on the twentieth, under pressure submitted a bill allowing direct Irish exports to the colonies. The Rockinghams supported Irish relief, despite a flood of petitions against the measure from British manufacturers. The issue still was far from settled.

News of the Franco-American treaty could not be withheld indefinitely. Weymouth was informed officially by the French ambassador on 13 March; the British ambassador was recalled at once; and North told the Commons. The long awaited war against the French was about to open.[5] Barrington had already asked to resign as Secretary at War.[6] Lord Amherst was appointed commander-in-chief in Britain with a seat in the Cabinet, and Admiral Keppel (he was related to both the Duke of Richmond and

5. The French began seizing British vessels in the Channel in mid-March, and British reprisals followed. Keppel sailed on 12 June, to attack the French fleet; war was not, however, formally declared until 16 July.

6. Barrington's resignation was accepted on 16 December and he was replaced by Charles Jenkinson.

Charles Fox and had been long hostile to the Government) was appointed to command the Home Fleet.

Both the Government and the Opposition revised their tactics when faced with the crisis. North sought to strengthen the ministry by making overtures to the Opposition; but vague proposals to bring Chatham into the Government were abortive, and North then had to settle rivalries within the Cabinet. This process lasted until the beginning of June, when Thurlow was promoted to Lord Chancellor and Wedderburn took over as attorney-general. The Rockinghams finally decided to call for recognition of American independence, and on 23 March Richmond announced the new party line in the Lords when he made an unsuccessful motion to withdraw British forces from America. Chatham, seriously ill but outraged by what he viewed as a betrayal, made a dramatic appearance on 7 April for the Lords Committee on the State of the Nation. He condemned outright the abandonment of America, collapsed during the debate, and died on 11 May.

Chatham's death did not remove the divisions within the Opposition. Shelburne assumed leadership over Chatham's followers, and he had an equal record of hostility toward recognising American independence and a personal reputation for duplicity, which ensured that the Rockinghams would suspect his smallest manoeuver. The Opposition assault against the Government continued specifically over the Saratoga debacle and the nation's preparedness for war with France. On 19 March, Fox moved to condemn the ministry's American policy, but despite a long and hard debate, the motion was defeated overwhelmingly. On 13 May, Burgoyne arrived home and, despite Government attempts to prevent a public review of his conduct, took his seat in the Commons and prepared to defend himself by attacking Germain.[7] On 26 May, Robert Vyner, an independent who supported the war but was disillusioned by Government policy, moved for an enquiry and he gave Burgoyne an opportunity to blame his failure on inflexible ministerial orders. Vyner lost his motion but Wedderburn also lost when he tried to

7. Burgoyne was released on parole by Washington so that he might return to justify his action publicly; the Government refused him a court-martial and arranged an army enquiry *in camera*.

have Burgoyne disqualified from sitting while he was a prisoner of war. During the remainder of the year, the Government tried to muzzle Burgoyne and also to get him to return to America, but failed in both endeavours. The problem soon worsened: William Howe returned to Britain on 2 July and with his brother, who soon after resigned his command, looked for an enquiry to justify their conduct in America. The ministry managed to postpone that move until the following year.

The new appointments were not entirely tractable. Keppel complained vociferously about the state of the Channel Fleet, in fear that he would be blamed for any lack of success. Actually, the critical naval situation became generally acknowledged. Reinforcements for the West Indies and America were essential, yet could not be sent without weakening the Channel Fleet, which Keppel, in an excess of caution, insisted must be increased, to guard against a French invasion. As a result, no squadron was sent to the Mediterranean to block the Toulon Fleet, and its escape induced a protracted period of intense anxiety in Britain and delayed the despatch of a squadron under Admiral Byron to America. Keppel sailed on 13 June and returned in haste on the twenty-seventh, when he feared he might meet a superior French fleet. He sailed again on 9 July and fought an ineffective action off Ushant on 27 July, but between the end of August and the end of October, he failed to catch the French again. Keppel's failure to destroy the French in June was soon to become the centre of a major controversy.

Clinton arrived at Philadelphia to supersede Howe on 8 May, and the following day received Germain's instructions of 21 March. He did not detach forces for the expedition to St. Lucia right away and decided that his transports were insufficient to evacuate all of his army and its stores. Accordingly, he sent off the stores and his Loyalist adherents by sea and on 18 June began marching the army to New York. Washington followed the twelve-mile column and finally attacked. The British repulsed Charles Lee's inept attack at Monmouth Courthouse and the British troops eventually arrived in New York without further problems. The Continental Army survived the dreadful privations of winter in Valley Forge and received three months drilling from the new inspector general, Von Steuben. Washington himself emerged unscathed from an attempt to replace him as commander-in-chief known as the Conway Cabal. The American leadership now anticipated great things from the French alliance.

The French fleet under d'Estaing arrived off the American coast on 8 July, found Philadelphia evacuated, and proceeded to blockade New York. Finding it impossible to press their attack over the bar at Sandy Hook on 22 July, the French joined the Americans and launched a combined land and sea operation against Rhode Island, Sullivan leading an American army to invest Newport. Lord Howe then took the British fleet out to force d'Estaing to fight but a gale on 13 August scattered both fleets. After an indecisive action on the thirteenth, Howe retreated to New York and d'Estaing to Boston. In the absence of French support, Sullivan was obliged to retreat, complaining bitterly about the value of French help. Clinton then executed his orders to mount a series of coastal raids. Grey inflicted much damage at Bedford on 6 September and Martha's Vineyard on the eighth, then foraging parties up the Hudson clashed with American forces at Tappan and Pound Ridge on 28 September.

After months of bickering and intrigue, the Carlisle Peace Commission arrived in America on 5 June—to learn that Philadelphia was to be evacuated, for the commissioners had never been told of the new military orders. Eden was enraged because the commission could scarcely now pretend to negotiate from a position of strength. News of the pending evacuation, added to the discovery that Congress had approved the treaty with France, revealed the Government's indifference to the commissioners' role and left the commissioners with no hope of success.[8] They nevertheless informed Congress of their powers and terms of settlement, and left on 18 June for New York. There they received a reply. Congress offered to negotiate a treaty of friendship and commerce if and when George III recognised American independence and withdrew British forces. On 9 July therefore the commission appealed directly to the American people, but also made a second approach to Congress. D'Estaing, however, had brought the new French minister to Philadelphia, and from this point, the commission was ignored, then ridiculed, for George Johnstone privately attempted to communicate with Henry Laurens, president of the Con-

---

8. Ritcheson, *British Politics and the American Revolution*, p. 273.

gress, and clumsily endeavoured to bribe Joseph Reed and Robert Morris to pressure the opening of negotiations. The despised and rejected commission issued a general proclamation on 3 October appealing to the state legislatures to make peace on the terms proposed to Congress and threatening a much harsher war if the states refused, it then returned to England.[9]

The conciliation part of the Government's policy failed (perhaps as expected) but military planning brought limited successes. The naval force under Admiral Barrington spent the summer struggling to defend the British sugar islands and failed to prevent a French capture of Dominica on 7 September, but Clinton finally despatched the West Indies expeditionary force and on 13 December a combined operation captured St. Lucia. On 10 October, Clinton received instructions from Germain reemphasising the need for an attack on the southern states. Lieutenant-Colonel Archibald Campbell, with three thousand men, was ordered to Georgia to link up with General Prevost from St. Augustine and on 29 December the campaign in the south began with the capture of Savannah.

In retrospect, it is easy to see how 1778 was a turning point. The entry of France reduced the American war to a single theatre of operations in a rapidly developing global conflict. North's pathetic attempts to resign were frustrated by the King, but now the ministry was showing not just its internal dissensions but signs of eventual disintegration as well. The Rockinghams, in contrast, were emerging as a remotely conceivable alternative government— and they had accepted the necessity of recognising American independence. The pattern of British politics also changed as new issues, Ireland and economical reform, permitted the Opposition a broader base and the possibility of wider support for its attacks on the Government.

The *Annual Register* for 1778 was not published until December 1779 and the preface ceased making apologies for the delay, though it does refer to "the extraordinary bulk of our History." The historical section expands to 236 pages (the largest so far) despite, as the editor remarks, ". . . our utmost endeavours (both for our own sake and

9. Johnstone had left after the embarrassing disclosure of his attempted private negotiations; Eden and Carlisle returned on 27 November.

that of our Readers) to compress it within more moderate limits." An examination of the text, however, suggests these efforts might have been better directed if brevity was a major criterion, for events are described in exceptional detail. The military campaign in America was a much slighter affair in 1779 than in the previous year but it still receives 29 pages of coverage, not including the invasion of Georgia or the capture of St. Lucia, which occurred in December, nor the naval manoeuverings which culminated in the indecisive fight off Ushant in July. Seven chapters, a total of 176 pages, are devoted to parliamentary affairs, which take up the bulk of the historical section. Indeed, the year saw a large number of important debates but they are reported at unusual length and with remarkable fidelity.

The historical section consists of ten chapters. Chapters I and II deal with European affairs, concentrating on the origins and development of the War of the Bavarian Succession. Chapters III and IV cover the parliamentary debates of the pre-Christmas session of 1777, and emphasise the Opposition's concentration on the demand that official papers be produced. Chapter V is entirely devoted to the issues raised by the subscriptions for new troop levies. Chapter VI covers the debates from 27 January to 6 February. Chapter VII describes the development of North's conciliation programme. Chapters VIII and IX deal with the reaction to the Franco-American treaty, the Opposition's use of Burgoyne, the emergence of the Irish problem, the attempt to exclude contractors from Parliament, the Rockinghams' public avowal of the need to recognise independence, Chatham's last speech, and the increasing tempo of the Opposition's attack on the state of the navy. At several points, the *Register*'s reporting of debates provides more detail than is found in any other contemporary source. Chapter X is a lengthy account of affairs in America, neatly indicating the futility of the Carlisle Peace Commission and providing an exact account of the retreat to New York, the battle of Monmouth Courthouse, and the defence of Rhode Island. The *Register* pointedly stresses the patriotic ardour produced by fighting the traditional enemy, the French, in implicit contrast to the unpopular fight against the Americans.

The historical section is larger and so are the *Appendix to the Chronicle* and the *State Papers*. The *Appendix* has nineteen items covering a broad range of interest. The details of the extravagant entertainment organised for General Howe prior to his departure, and papers illustrating the formal establishment of the Franco-American alliance (these being the only items relating to America) are extracted here. The *State Papers* has twenty-four items, including the usual speeches from the throne, addresses from Parliament and petitions, and the manifestos of Frederick II and Maria Theresa concerning the Bavarian succession issue. The royal speeches and addresses from Parliament; the Lords' protest of 7 December 1778 against the Carlisle Peace Commission's proclamation of 3 October (discussed in *AR*, 1779, pp. 82]–[83); the petitions from the City of London of 13 March for an end to the American war; a 16 December petition from the West India merchants to the same purpose; the official instructions to the Peace Commission and its proclamation of 3 October; the original instructions to the American diplomatic emissaries sent to Europe; the formal rejection of the Government's two conciliation acts by the Pennsylvania Assembly; papers illustrating the exchanges between the Peace Commission and Congress; and the text of the Franco-American treaty signed on 6 February are all extracted here.

THE Hiftory of the year 1778, is more confined in its nature than that of many others. It is more properly the Hiftory of the Britifh Nation, however feparated, or into whatever divifions unhappily thrown, than that of the world in general, or of Europe in particular. If it is therefore lefs interefting to Foreigners, it is proportionally the more fo to Englifhmen. It records matters in which they are all concerned. No man, nor no ftation, can be free from their confequences. No common apathy can afford an indifferent fpectator. We are exhibited upon the grand theatre of action, to perform a part equally conspicuous and perilous, and the world is still in a gaze for the event.

Although it be a year which has not afforded those great and signal actions, which throw a fascinating splendour over the face of History, it has abounded with business of less lustre, but of the most important nature, in a degree, perhaps, unequalled, in our annals. Our attention to domestic matters, has not, however, prevented our paying a due regard to that war, which was commenced with such tremendous appearances in Germany, and so speedily and happily concluded. The extraordinary bulk of our History, notwithstanding our utmost endeavours (both for our own sake and that of our Readers) to compress it within more moderate limits, will, we hope, afford an unquestionable testimony to the Public, that neither our zeal, nor our industry, are slackened by their favour.

* * *

State of Affairs previous to the Meeting of Parliament. Consequences of the American War with respect to Commerce. Conduct of France. Stability of Administration equally secured by good or bad success. Sanguine hopes raised by General Burgoyne's success at Ticonderoga, checked by subsequent accounts. Speech from the Throne. Addresses. Amendments moved in both Houses. Great Debates. Protest.

NO equal space of time for several years past, afforded so little domestic matter worthy of observation, as that part of the year 1777, which elapsed during the recess of parliament. Neither the town nor the country presented any new object of party contention. The American war, and many of its consequences, were now scarcely objects of curiosity, much less of surprize; and being in the habit of deriving no benefit from our colonies, and of considering them only in a state of enmity and hostility, it seemed as if their total loss would be no longer a matter of much wonder or concern; but that rather on the contrary, that event would be felt, as a cessation from war, expence and trouble, usually is felt in other cases.

The loss and ruin brought upon numbers of individuals, by this fatal quarrel between the mother country and her colonies, was little thought of, excepting by the sufferers, and had, as yet, produced no apparent change in the face of public affairs. For although our foreign commerce, was by this time, considerably embarrassed, and loaded with extraordinary charges; although it was already reduced in some of its parts, and in others, such as the African branch, nearly annihilated; it had not yet received those strokes, or at least they were not yet so sensibly felt, which have since shaken the mercantile interest of this country to a degree which it had not often before experienced.

Indeed that commerce, which had so long equally excited the envy of other nations, and the admiration of mankind, was so immense in its extent, and involved such a multitude of great and material objects in its embrace, that it was not to be shaken by any usual convulsion of nature, nor to be endangered by any common accident of fortune. It accordingly bore many severe shocks, and sustained losses of a prodigious magnitude, before they were capable of apparently affecting its general system.

We have formerly shewn that the American war, from its peculiar nature, and the greatness of the expence, with which it was conducted and supplied, had produced a new species of commerce, which, however ruinous in its ultimate effects, had for the present a flattering appearance. For this substitute, including all the traffick appertaining to or consequent of the war, as well as the commercial speculations which arose by licenced exception or evasion of the several restraining acts of parliament, afforded employment, like a great and legitimate commerce, to an infinite number of persons, and quantity of shipping, yielding at least equal benefits to the gross of those who were concerned; and far greater emoluments, devoid of risque, or even of the employment of much capital, to the principals, than the profits of any real or open trade could possibly admit.

Thus, however frail its establishment, and necessarily short its duration, a new, powerful, and numerous connection was formed, totally distinct from the great, ancient, mercantile interest; and thus, although our Gazettes teemed with bankruptcies, generally doubling and trebling in number, whatever had been usually known, in the same time, in this country, yet the gainers, or the candidates for gain in the new adventures, were so numerous, and presented such an appearance of ease, affluence, and content, that the plaintive but feeble voice of the unfortunate was little attended to; and the chearfulness which the splendour and happiness of the former spread all around, prevented any gloomy reflections from arising in the minds of those who had as yet no sensible feeling of the public calamity.

It is true, that the coasts of Great Britain and Ireland were insulted by the American privateers, in a manner which our hardiest enemies had never ventured in our most arduous contentions with foreigners. Thus were the inmost and most domestic recesses of our trade rendered insecure; and a convoy for the protection of the linen ships from Dublin and Newry, was now for the first time seen. The Thames also presented the unusual and melancholy spectacle, of numbers of foreign ships, particularly French, taking in cargoes of English commodities for various parts of Europe, the property of our own merchants, who were thus reduced to seek that protection under the colours of other nations, which the British flag used to afford to all the world.

Against this must be set, that his Majesty's ships took a prodigious number of American vessels, both on their own coasts and in the West Indies. The perseverance with which the Americans supplied the objects for these captures, by continually building new ships, and seeking new adventures, seemed almost incredible. At a time when the whole of a trade, carried on under such discouraging circumstances, seemed to be extinguished, the Gazettes teemed again with the account of new captures; which, though for the greater part, they were not of much value singly, yet furnished, at times, some very rich prizes; and, in the aggregate, were of a vast amount. They probably much overballanced the losses which we sustained from their privateers. But it was, to a thinking mind, melancholy, that we had a computation of that kind to make.

The conduct of France during this whole year, in every thing that regarded England and America, was so slightly covered, and so little qualified, that it seemed to leave no room for any doubt, (excepting with those who were determined to place so implicit a faith in words, as to admit of no other species of evidence) as to the part which she would finally take in the contest. As she was not yet, however, in sufficient preparation for proceeding to the utmost extremities, nor her negociations with the Americans advanced to an absolute determination, she occasionally relaxed in certain points, when she found herself so closely pressed by the British ministers, that an obstinate perseverance would precipitate matters to that conclusion, which she wished for some time longer to defer.

Thus, when a bold American adventurer, one Cunningham, had taken and carried into Dunkirk, with a privateer fitted out at that port, the English packet from Holland, and sent the mail to the American ministers at Paris, it then seemed necessary in some degree to discountenance so flagrant a violation of good neighbourhood, as well as of the standing treaties between the two nations, and even of the particular marine laws and regulations established in France, in regard to her conduct with the people of other countries. Cunningham, and his crew, were accordingly committed for some short time to prison. Yet this appearance of satisfaction was done away by the circumstances which attended it. For Cunningham's imprisonment was represented to the Americans, as proceeding merely from some informality in his commission, and irregularity in his proceedings, which had brought him to, if not within, the verge of piracy, and which were too glaring to be entirely passed over without notice. And he was, with his crew, not only speedily released from their mock confinement, but he was permitted to purchase, fit out, and arm, a much stronger vessel, and better sailer than the former, avowedly to infest as before the British commerce.

It was in the same line of policy, that when the French Newfoundland fishery would have been totally intercepted and destroyed in case of an immediate rupture, and that the capture of their seamen would have been more ruinous and irreparable, than the loss even of the ships and cargoes, Lord Stormont obtained, in that critical situation, an order from the ministers, that all the American privateers, with their prizes, should immediately depart the kingdom. Yet, satisfactory as this compliance, and conclusive as this order appeared, it was combated with

[1]

[2]

such ingenuity, and such expedients practised to defeat its effects, that it was not complied with in a single instance throughout the kingdom. It, however, answered the purpose for which it was intended, by gaining time, and opening a subject of tedious and indecisive controversy, until the French ships were safe in their respective ports.

It would seem, that Monsr. de Sartine, the French Minister of the marine, and great advocate for the American cause, was determined, that whatever charges of duplicity might be brought against his country, they should not rest personally with himself. For this Minister, upon some reports which tended to discourage the commerce with the Americans, as if the court would not protect its subjects in conveying the products of that continent in their vessels, which would accordingly become legal prizes to the English if taken, assured the several chambers of commerce by a public instrument, and in direct contravention of all our navigation laws, that the King was determined to afford the fullest protection to their commerce, and would reclaim all ships that were taken under that pretext.

July 4th, 1777.

Upon the whole, whatever evasion or duplicity might have appeared in the language or professions of France, her conduct was so unequivocal in the course of this business, that the only matter of surprize would be, if it could be thought possible that she imposed upon any people by the one, or that they could mistake her designs in the other. It indeed required no great sagacity to discover, that she had now acquired so thorough a relish for the sweets of the American commerce, that nothing less than the most irresistible necessity, could induce her to forego the possession of what she had obtained, and the vast hopes with which she flattered herself in future. But as

yet she waited the event of the American campaign, and the completion of her naval equipments, (which were carried on with the greatest diligence and in the most public manner at Brest and Toulon,) before she risqued any decisive step.

No change of any sort, whether by death, removal, or internal arrangement, had taken place in administration during the recess. Every day of the American war rivetted the ministers faster in their seats. Good and bad success produced the same effect in that respect. In the former instance, who could be deemed so fitting to conclude the business, as those by whom it was framed, and so far happily conducted? In the other, who could be found hardy enough to undertake the completion of a ruinous system, which, besides its failure already in the execution, was originally, and in its nature, clogged with infinite difficulty and danger? Thus situated, and supported by an uncontrollable force in parliament, it seemed that nothing could disturb their repose, until the present American system was in some manner disposed of.

General Burgoyne's success at Ticonderoga, with the total discomfiture and ruin which every where attended the Americans in their precipitate flight on the borders of Lake George, excited the greatest triumph on the side of administration; and whilst it wonderfully elevated the spirits, was considered nearly as crowning the hopes of all those who had supported or approved of the war. We have already seen that the northern expedition was looked upon as the favourite child of government. The operations on the side of the Jerseys and Philadelphia were evidently considered in a very secondary point of view. As the noble Lord who conducted the American affairs had all the applause of this measure, which was considered entirely as his own, it is not to be

wondered at, that both himself and his brethren in office should be deeply interested in the event, and value themselves highly on the appearance of success.

The subsequent dispatches from General Burgoyne did not long support the hopes which were founded on the first successes. The unexpected difficulties and delays which the army experienced in advancing a few miles from Skenesborough to the southward, were, however, counterballanced in opinion by its arrival on the Hudson's River, the retreat of the enemy from Fort Edward, their abandoning Fort George and the Lake, by which a free passage was opened from Ticonderoga, and St. Leger's success in defeating and ruining the Tryon county militia near Fort Stanwix.

All the former and present sanguine expectations which had been formed, were, however, in a great measure overthrown by the advices which were received some time previous to the meeting of parliament; an event which was probably this year held back, in the full confidence of its being ushered in with the particulars of some great and decisive success. Those which came to hand, after a tedious season of expectation, bore a very different complexion. The insuperable difficulties that necessarily suspended the operations of an army in such a country, and under such circumstances, were now practically discovered. The double defeat of Baum and Breyman, by a supposed broken and ruined militia, in an attempt to remove or to lessen some of those difficulties, was still more dispiriting; and was not in any degree cured by the hope which the General expressed, of support and assistance from the co-operation of Sir William Howe's army; both as it marked a despondency of success from his own force, and that the ministers knew the impossibility of his receiving any support from

Oct. 31st.

that quarter. But, as if it had been to crown the climax of ill news and ill fortune, the same dispatches were accompanied with others from Sir Guy Carleton, which brought an account of the failure of the expedition to Fort Stanwix, the bold and unexpected attack of the rebels on the side of Ticonderoga, and of a still more unexpected and extraordinary event, in a short sketch of the desperate and doubtful action which was fought on the 19th of September between General Burgoyne and Arnold; which, naked as it was of circumstances, seemed to shew the latter to be the assailant, by the mention of his retiring to his camp when the darkness had put an end to the combat.

Although the knowledge of these events seemed to open a view to some of the succeeding misfortunes, and even afforded room to presage a part of those unparalleled calamities which befell the northern army, it was still hoped, by those who were most sanguine in their expectations, that General Burgoyne, being so near Albany, could not fail of making his way good to that place; and that being then securely lodged, he would have an opportunity of concerting with Sir Henry Clinton, the means, either separately or jointly, of distressing the northern colonies; or if the season and other circumstances did not encourage that design, they might decide upon the propriety of maintaining the post at Albany during the winter, or of advancing to New York if more eligible. In the worse case that could happen, they entertained no doubt of effecting his retreat back to Canada. Others were apprehensive of some of the fatal consequences that ensued.

Such was in general the state of affairs, so far as they were known, and of public opinion, at the meeting of parliament. The accounts from Sir William Howe went no farther than the successful landing of the army at the head of Elk;

his preparation for advancing towards Philadelphia; with the situation and apparent design of the enemy to impede his progress.

Nov. 20th. 1777. The speech from the throne expressed great satisfaction, in having recourse to the wisdom and support of parliament in this conjuncture, when the continuance of the rebellion in America demanded their most serious attention. The powers with which parliament had entrusted the crown for the suppression of the revolt, were declared to have been faithfully exerted; and a just confidence was expressed, that the courage and conduct of the officers, with the spirit and intrepidity of the forces, would be attended with important success; but under a persuasion that both houses would see the necessity of preparing for such further operations, as the contingencies of the war, and the obstinacy of the rebels might render expedient, his Majesty was, for that purpose, pursuing the proper measures for keeping the land forces complete to their present establishment; and if he should have occasion to increase them, by contracting any new engagements, a reliance was placed on their zeal and public spirit to enable him to make them good.

Although repeated assurances were received of the pacific disposition of foreign powers, yet as the armaments in the ports of France and Spain were continued, it was thought adviseable to make a considerable augmentation to our naval force; it being equally determined not to disturb the peace of Europe on the one hand, and to be a faithful guardian of the honour of the crown on the other.

The Commons were informed, that the various services which had been mentioned, would unavoidably require large supplies; and a profession was made, that nothing could relieve the royal mind from the concern which it felt for the

heavy charge they must bring on the people, but a conviction of their being necessary for the welfare and essential interests of these kingdoms.

The speech concluded, with a resolution of steadily pursuing the measures in which they were engaged for the re-establishment of that constitutional subordination, which his Majesty was determined to maintain through the several parts of his dominions; accompanied with a profession of being watchful for an opportunity of putting a stop to the effusion of the blood of his subjects; a renewal or continuance of the former hope, that the deluded and unhappy multitude would return to their allegiance, upon a recollection of the blessings of their former government, and a comparison with the miseries of their present situation; and a declaration, that the restoration of peace, order, and confidence to his American colonies, would be considered by his Majesty as the greatest happiness of his life, and the greatest glory of his reign.

The addresses were so exactly in the present established style and form, and in such perfect unison with the speech, that any particular notice of them would be needless. All the measures which it held out, whether in act or design, were applauded; its positions confirmed; and an unlimited concurrence agreed. The ministers received their usual portion of praise in that share assigned to the prudence and wisdom of our public counsels; and the firmness, dignity, humanity, and paternal tenderness expressed in the speech, were highly extolled.

The address in the House of Commons was moved for by Lord Hyde, and supported, besides a panegyric on the matter and nature of the speech, by stating the necessity which originally induced the war, and which still operated with equal, if not greater force, for its continuance, until the great purpose for which it was undertaken was attained, by bringing the Americans to a proper sense of their condition and duty, and replacing the colonies in their due state of dependance on government, and subordination to the supreme legislature. It was said, that notwithstanding the news-paper abuse thrown upon our commanders, the fullest confidence was to be placed, and the strongest hopes of success formed, on their zeal, ability, prudence and spirit; that the superior excellency and intrepidity of our troops was acknowledged by all the world; and that with such commanders and forces by sea and land, unrivalled as they were by any other country, no doubt could be entertained, that the contest would be brought to a happy, and not very distant conclusion. But that this happy consummation could only be attained by affording the most perfect confidence, and the fullest support to government; whilst any illiberality of thinking, or narrowness of acting in either respect, must necessarily have the worst effect on the operation of all the measures which tended to a final settlement. And that it was evident, as well from his Majesty's most gracious declaration, as from the humanity and general prudence of government, that an immediate stop would be put to the effusion of blood, as soon as the conduct of the misled multitude in America, whether from the success of our arms, or from a due sense of their own past and present condition, should render it consistent with the honour, the dignity, and the interest of the nation, to adopt measures of lenity, and to restore that tranquillity and happiness to all the people, which are the natural consequences of subordination, order, and a reverence for the laws.

A young member, who seconded the motion for the address, felt himself so fully satisfied in the wisdom and rectitude of the government-

ing powers, and had such conviction of the utility of their measures, that he could not refrain from being lost in astonishment, if it should be found that any man, who was a native of this country, and bred up in due allegiance to the throne, could, under any impulse of faction, venture to stand up in that house, and so far to abet the American rebels, as to express a sentiment contrary to the spirit of the measures which were adopted by government, and which were now so graciously communicated to parliament. He also insisted, that the nation was never so flourishing as at present; that trade and manufactures, instead of declining, had increased and thriven, during the contest with America; and that some excess in luxury, the usual concomitant of increasing riches, and effect of opulence, was the only circumstance of our condition which could afford room for regret or apprehension to the most austere, or the most desponding. He concluded, that those, if any, who held a difference of opinion upon those subjects, must be under the immediate influence and domination of the most perverse and factious spirit.

The conclusions involved in this declaration or opinion had no effect in deterring the Marquis of Granby, from immediately avowing those very principles and that conduct which had been so loudly condemned. This young nobleman, who from his first coming into parliament, had uniformly opposed the whole system of American measures, introduced his motion for an amendment to the proposed address, by stating and lamenting, in a concise manner, but pathetic terms, the ruinous and melancholy effects which the present unnatural war had produced both in England and America; representing and enforcing at the same time the still more fatal consequences which must necessarily

ensue from its continuance. He declared, with great humanity, that he felt himself nearly equally interested in all the calamities which it had or would spread among the English on either side of the Atlantic; that it made but little difference, in point of effect, on which side the expence of blood or treasure seemed more particularly to lie; it was on either, a lessening of the common stock, an exhausture of the common strength, and a further dissolution of that union, the restoration of which could only again render us happy, as well as great.

Under these persuasions he felt the most ardent desire for grasping at the present moment of time, and having the happiness even to lay the groundwork of an accommodation. He observed, that all the force, all the powers, all the foreign and domestic resources of this country, had for three years been ineffectually exerted, in order to obtain peace with that continent at the point of the sword. That allowing, as he most willingly did, under the fullest conviction, and with the greatest satisfaction, all the merit that was attributed to our commanders, and all the intrepidity to our troops, it was now evident, from those very circumstances, that there must have been either some egregious misconduct in the plan and management of the war, or that it was attended with such inherent and insurmountable difficulties as it would be a folly to contend with any longer. In either case, the effect was the same; for if the failure even proceeded from the inability of those who were entrusted with the conduct of our public affairs, we were not now in a condition to engage in a new experiment, under any change or ability of guidance.

As we had then so full an experience of the impracticability of coercion, it was time to abandon so ruinous a project, and apply to gentler methods for attaining an object, which was so essential to our well being, that our dearest interests, our greatness, and perhaps even our existence, were entwined in its substance. He would therefore recommend it to the ministers to forge bonds of amity for the minds, instead of chains for the bodies of the Americans, and flattering himself that the present moment of uncertainty, with respect to the success of our arms, would be a right and most proper season for giving an unasked and unequivocal mark of cordiality and kindness, he would move an amendment to the address; the substance of the amendment being—" To " request of his Majesty to adopt " some measures for accommodat- " ing the differences with Ame- " rica; and recommending a ces- " sation of all hostilities, as ne- " cessary for the effectuating of so " desireable a purpose; with an " assurance, that the Commons " were determined to co-operate " with him in every measure that " could contribute to the re-esta- " blishment of peace, and the " drawing such lines as should " afford sufficient security to the " terms of pacification."

The motion for the amendment was seconded by Lord John Cavendish, and supported in general by the opposition upon the following grounds: That three years war, at an immense expence, with 55,000 land forces, and a hundred ships of war, had only left us in nearly the same situation that we begun. We had lost Boston, and we gained New York. The loss of one army was too much to be apprehended; its escape indeed, in any manner, and with any loss, was the utmost that could be hoped. If the other army should even succeed against Philadelphia, what prospect would that afford of bettering our affairs? On the contrary, was there not every reason to apprehend, that such a separation of our forces would be attended with the most alarming

consequences, and even endanger the loss of the whole.

Every hope of obtaining a revenue from America had been long over; the country gentlemen were called upon, to know if any one of them would still avow the entertaining of so frantic an idea. Yet in that blind pursuit, the offspring, they said, of folly, ignorance, obstinacy, and injustice, we had already squandered above fifteen millions of money, which was finally sunk, and every shilling of it for ever lost to the nation. If peace were at this moment concluded, they said, without contradiction, that by the time we had brought home and disbanded our forces, got rid of our German connections, with all the other incumbrances, incident to, or consequent of the war, we should have increased the national debt above thirty millions more than it had been at the commencement of the troubles; which would then far exceed all calculations that had ever been made relative to the ability of the nation, and the degree of burthen which it was capable of supporting.

They observed, that the speech did not in any degree look towards peace. Untaught by experience and loss, it shewed an obstinate determination to persevere to the last in the same fatal measures, which had already sunk us to our present state of humiliation, misfortune, and disgrace; that, in a word, it led to an eternity of war; or to such a continuance of it as was only to receive a period, from our not having a shilling left to support it longer. That fresh hopes of success were continually held out from the throne, and the coming year has constantly been announced, as that which should conclude our misfortunes, and fix a period to our insanity. The seasons are not more constant in their succession, than the renewal of expectation, and the failure of success in every year. Will then, said they, no unremitted succession of

failures in hopes and promises, no repetition of disappointment, nor series of calamity, prove sufficient to restore us to our reason, or to awaken us to a sense of our condition?

The boasted sentiments of humanity which had been so highly extolled, were said to be very becoming, so far as they went, from a Prince to his people; but unfortunately, they were openly and palpably contradicted, as well by every part of the conduct of the ministers in other matters, as by the requisitions made in the speech itself. They were to judge of their intentions by other tests, than by the particular professions which they held out at certain seasons for the attainment of certain purposes; these sentiments were said to come under that description, and that, in fact, they were intended merely to renew the deception which had been so successfully practised two years before, when both the nation and parliament were amused with the hopes then held out, of proposing a rational scheme for an accommodation with the colonies; instead of which, they found themselves laughed at several months after, when the ministers had obtained all they wanted under that colour, by the mockery of sending commissioners out to offer pardons to the Americans.

It was said, that the language held out, of the prosperity of the nation, was, exclusive of its being totally unfounded, little less than a mockery of its distress. The rise of interest, the fall of stocks, and of real estates in their value at market, were political barometers of such a nature as left no room to doubt of their accuracy. If other proofs were wanting, our Gazettes, however defective in other respects, presented long memorials, the authenticity of which would not be doubted, of private calamity arising from public misfortune and distress. Nor were the causes incompetent to the effects. The loss of our vast

American import and export commerce, was in itself such a detraction of national opulence and strength, as must have severely and visibly affected the œconomy of the greatest and wealthiest state that ever existed. But when to this is added the consequent ruin brought upon our West-India islands and trade; the near annihilation of our African, Mediterranean, and Levant commerce, with the ruin in a great degree of our fisheries, the absurdity of supposing that we are thriving under such circumstances, is so obvious as not to merit an answer. We are now in the state of substantial traders suffering great losses in a bad season, who are still enabled to support for a time their former port and appearance, from the property and credit which they had established in better times.

It was asked, whether the destruction of our home trade, by the swarms of American privateers which had during the Summer infested and insulted our coasts; the terror into which the metropolis of Ireland had been thrown, and the fortifying for the first time in all our wars of its harbour; with the consignment to foreigners of the freight of our native commodities, from the incompetency of the British flag to the protection of its own commerce; whether these circumstances were to be adduced merely as evidences of national strength and prosperity, or whether the credit of them was to be applied to the general wisdom of our counsels, and to the particular ability with which the war was conducted? If such are already the consequences of an American contest with our revolted colonies only, what are we to expect when an European war is brought home to our doors by the junction of the whole House of Bourbon with those colonies, whom we now seem incapable of contending with to effect singly? This fatal event, said they, has been long foreseen and repeatedly foretold by the opposition, as the certain result of the folly, injustice, and violence of our counsels, and the infatuated blindness and obstinacy of government. These predictions had been the constant jest of the Ministers, whose ill timed and ill fated ridicule, was confirmed by those standing majorities, who have uniformly supported them in their most ruinous measures; but if there were any deficiency of other confirmations, the verity of these predictions is now established by the speech before us; nor will the unwillingness with which the acknowledgement is made, nor the necessity by which it is extorted, lessen the validity of that testimony.

The House was repeatedly called upon, and exhorted in the most urgent terms, to reflect seriously upon the present critical state of public affairs; that they were involved at this moment in such a situation of difficulty and danger, as they had never before experienced; that it therefore behoved them to act with the greatest circumspection, and by the prudence and wisdom of their present conduct to atone for past errors, and to afford a remedy to their consequent evils, so far as they were yet capable of being cured. And they were warned, not by a blind and precipitate vote, without a single ray of information on public affairs for their guidance, to pass an address, which, besides an approbation of all their past conduct, would afford a sanction to the Ministers for a perseverance in the same destructive measures which had involved us in the present most unhappy situation.

Upon the whole it was said, that they were now, in the language which had been so often used on the other side, to pass, or not to pass the Rubicon; they were to cast the die, in their present resolution, which was to determine war or peace, safety or destruction. They were not only to vote war or peace with America, but war or peace with the House of Bourbon. The address, and the amendment, afforded either alternative. A gentleman whose powers of eloquence, have been universally celebrated, supplicated the House in the most pathetic terms, to seize the present happy moment for attempting an accommodation, when neither elated with insolent victory, nor debased with abject defeat; we could with honour to ourselves make such proposals to our colonists, as they could without dishonour accept. [6]

On the other side the Minister said, that he supposed there was not a second opinion in the nation with respect to peace, nor a wish that did not tend to its accomplishment; that no man in or out of the House wished more fervently for that happy event than he did himself; that the only difference of opinion which could arise, was on the means of attaining that wished-for object; but that the proper moment for chalking out the lines of an accommodation was not yet arrived: that happy moment could only be found in the season of victory; the attempt would be as futile, as it would be productive of ridicule, disgrace and contempt, at any other. He seemed tacitly to give up the idea of taxation, by not considering it as a bar in the way of accommodation; and objected to a cessation of arms, as it would seem a direct admission of the American claim of independency; but he said that the Commissioners were enabled to grant a cessation whenever they deemed it expedient, and that such overtures were made or accepted on the other side, as afforded any fair ground for opening a negociation.

To remove the visible impression which had been made by the language and opinion of a foreign war held out by the opposition, he said, that from the information he had been able to collect, there was no reason to apprehend such an event. France and Spain held out the language of friendship, and he believed they were sincere. As it was not their interest now to quarrel with us, he could not believe that it was their intention. The present contest exhibited a new and very doubtful case. For if America should grow into a separate empire, it must of course cause such a revolution in the political system of the world, that a bare apprehension of the unknown consequences which might proceed from so untried a state of public affairs, would be sufficient to stagger the resolution of our most determined or enterprizing enemies. It was, however, acknowledged, that strong remonstrances on our side had been necessary to obtain explanation or redress, at times that the language or conduct of France had appeared unintelligible or equivocal; and that, as only a limited confidence could with prudence be placed on any promises whatever in the political intercourse of nations, and that the two powers in question had thought proper to keep up great armaments in their respective ports, he had deemed it prudent to put this country in an equal state of defence, and thereby to guard against the possibility of a surprize.

It was further advanced on the same side, that, independent of arms, there was every reason for hoping that the troubles in America would be brought to a happy conclusion; that the great bounties [7] which the Congress offered to soldiers, was an irrefragable proof of the difficulty which they experienced in endeavouring to recruit their forces; that the hardships which the people actually suffered at present under the despotism of their tyrants, compared with that mild and happy government which they had withdrawn themselves from, and under which they had risen to such a degree of power and greatness, had already nearly

brought them to a sense of their error, and would soon make them sick of rebellion. That the proposed amendment, if carried, would only tend to revive and keep up that wild spirit of independence, by which the people had so long been hurried away from the right use or application of their reason; and that they could not therefore but consider themselves as enemies to their country, were they not to stamp a direct negative upon the amendment.

Some others went so far as to insist, that the contest now, was not whether America should be dependent on the British legislature; but whether Great Britain or America should be independent? Both, they said, could not exist in that state together. For such were the sources of wealth and power in that vast continent, from its extent, its products, its seas, its rivers, its unparalleled growth in population, and above all, its inexhaustible fund of naval treasures, that this small island, which had hitherto supported its greatness by commerce and naval superiority, would be so cramped in its own peculiar resources, and overlayed upon its proper and natural element, that it must in a few years sink to nothing, and perhaps be reduced to that most degrading and calamitous of all possible situations, the becoming a vassal to her own rebellious colonies, if they were once permitted to establish their independence, and of course their power.

These gentlemen laughed at the idea of a cessation of arms, which they represented as the most absurd that could possibly be conceived. How said they, is it to be obtained? Is a herald to be sent to the rebel camp with the proposition? If they refuse to comply with it, how are we to act? Must our troops lie upon their arms, and suffer themselves to be beaten and their throats cut, only to give the world a specimen of their forbear-

ance, and shew that their passive is equal to their active valour? The Congress have already refused to negociate or treat with our Commissioners upon any terms, without a previous and absolute acknowledgement of their independency. This indeed would cut off at one stroke all the matters in contest; but then it would leave nothing behind to treat about.

As the opposition entered into a rigorous scrutiny of the conduct of administration with respect to American measures in general, as well as to what related more particularly to the prosecution of the war, the debate was of course trained from its original ground; so that the immediate subject of the speech, the address or the amendment, seemed to be in some degree forgotten or abandoned, during the eagerness of charge, and the severity of censure on the one side, or the solicitude of personal defence, and the vexation of recurring to a justification of past measures on the other.

In this course of stricture and censure, in which a more than common degree of acuteness and asperity were displayed, a gentleman highly celebrated for his ability, and not less distinguished by his constant opposition to the Ministers, than by the severity with which he scrutinizes their measures, laid a double portion of that general blame and reproach which, he said, was due for our present calamitous situation, to the share of the noble Lord who presides at the head of the American department. To his administration he principally attributed, besides the most ruinous measures, and disgraceful consequences of the war, the final loss of our colonies. To him he also attributed the inhuman measure of employing the savages, not, he said, to subdue, but to exterminate, a people whom we still pretended to call our subjects; a measure, which he described, as a warfare against human nature, with- [8]

out its being capable of producing any real military advantage; and calculated merely for the destruction of the weak or the peaceable, for the murder of old men, women and children.

It required no less than the acknowledged ability of the noble Minister, to withstand the torrent of wit and eloquence, in which these charges and censures were involved, and in some degree to deaden the effect of that brilliance of colouring with which the picture was charged. He entered into a defence of several parts of his conduct in the American war, in a speech much longer than was usual from him; and as to the particular charge of employing the Indians, he asserted that it was a matter of necessity on the part of government; for that the Americans had before tampered with them, and had strained every nerve to induce them to take an active part against the royal cause; so that in this measure, which had been described in such colours of horror, and reprobated with such warmth of indignation, we only successfully copied the example which had been set, though it failed in the execution, by the immaculate and infallible Congress.

The whole weight of debate on that side, fell upon the Ministers themselves, or upon a very few official men. The country gentlemen were unusually blank. They saw not only an end to all their hopes of obtaining a revenue from America, but they found themselves saddled with the burthen of a war, which in point of expence, proportional to the service or force employed, was infinitely more ruinous than any other in which the nation had ever been involved, without even a remote prospect of its being brought by any means to a conclusion. For the hope of attaining that end by arms was now pretty well done away, whilst the unalterable determination of government to continue the war was

evident; so that the only resort left for its accomplishment, must have been by a direct and total renunciation of all their former professions and principles.

This was a degree of practical philosophy which could scarcely be expected. That party however, thinking it right to persevere, at least until the fate of the campaign should become more explicit, sacrificed to its opinion of consistency, by giving their silent votes, but nothing more than their silent votes to the Minister. The motion for the amendment was accordingly rejected by a majority, which was at least, nothing inferior to what had been usual upon such occasions, the numbers being 243, to 86 who supported the amendment to the address. The debate was renewed in the House on the ensuing day upon bringing up the report from the committee, and a motion made for recommitting the address. The report was however received, and the address confirmed, on a division at 11 o'clock, by a still greater majority than before.

The address in the House of Lords was moved for by Earl Percy, who had lately succeeded to that Barony by the death of his mother the Dutchess of Northumberland, and the motion was seconded by the young Earl of Chesterfield. An amendment was moved by the Earl of Chatham, which accorded in matter and design with that proposed in the other House, a cessation of hostilities being recommended as preparatory to the opening of a treaty for the restoration of peace in America, and the final settlement of the tranquility of those invaluable provinces, by a removal of the unhappy causes of this ruinous civil war, and by a just and adequate security against a return of the like calamities in times to come. With an assurance, that the Lords would chearfully co-operate, in such explicit and most solemn declarations and pro-

visions of fundamental and irrevocable laws, as might be judged necessary for ascertaining and fixing for ever the respective rights of Great Britain and her colonies.

The noble Earl introduced and supported his amendment with a speech of considerable length, which, notwithstanding the pressure of years and infirmities, afforded no equivocal testimony of that commanding eloquence, which had once been so renowned; and of those great abilities, which shone with such lustre in the days of the prosperity and glory of his country. He, however, experienced, upon this, as upon several succeeding occasions, a change of condition, which to a man of his high and unconquered spirit, who still saw fresh in recollection the time, when the fortune of Europe seemed to hang upon his voice, and that he appeared the great arbiter of peace or war to mankind, could not fail of being exceedingly mortifying and grievous. His friends observed that it was a melancholy proof, that no powers of eloquence or ability can attain their object, nor extent of merit or services preserve a due weight or regard, any longer than they are connected with and supported by power; and they remarked, that it seemed to become fashionable, if not a rule of conduct, with the Court Lords, not only to treat his speeches and propositions with an affected indifference, which seemed to border too nearly upon contempt, but to thwart, and endeavour to overbear him on smaller matters, in a manner, which in other places, would have probably been considered, at least, as captious and petulant.

The noble Earl found great fault, both as to matter and manner, with the speech from the throne. He said, it had been customary on similar occasions, not to lead parliament, but to be guided by it; it had been usual to ask the advice of that House, the hereditary Great Council of the nation, not to dictate to it. But the present speech, said he, tells of measures already agreed upon, and very cavalierly desires your concurrence. It indeed talks of wisdom and support; and it counts on the certainty of events yet in the womb of time; but in point of plan and design it is peremptory and dictatorial. This he insisted, was treating them in the most contemptuous manner; it was a language not fit to be endured, and for which the Ministers who advised it deserved the severest reprehension. It was besides the language of an ill founded confidence, supported only by a succession of disappointments, disgraces, and defeats. It required them to place an unlimited confidence in those, who had hitherto misguided, deceived, and misled them; and to grant, not what they might be satisfied was necessary, but what the Ministers might think so; troops, fleets, treaties, and subsidies, not yet revealed. If they should agree to the proposed address, they should stand pledged for all these, whatever their extent; they could not retreat; whatever they might be, they must stand bound to the consequences.

In stating his arguments for the amendment, he asserted some facts, and predicted the same consequences, which were foreseen in the House of Commons. He declared, that the House of Bourbon would break with us; that he knew their intentions to be hostile; and that the present, was the only time, in which parliament or the nation would have it in their power to treat with America. That France and Spain had done a great deal; but they had declined to do all that America desired. That America was at that time in an ill humour; and might then be detached from her connections with those powers, if reasonable terms of accommodation were held

out to her; but if not, the opportunity would be lost; an opportunity, which he foretold, we should never again have. And describing the war with its consequences, in that strong and comprehensive language, by which he was so particularly distinguished, after declaring that the plans of the Ministers were founded in destruction and disgrace, he said further, " It is, my Lords, a ruinous and destructive war; it is full of danger; it teems with disgrace, and must end in ruin."

The motion for the amendment was supported by nearly all the eloquence and ability on that side of the House; most of the distinguished speakers having taken so full and active a share in the debate, as to render it exceedingly interesting. As the immediate danger of a foreign war, and our inability to support it whilst we continued involved in our unhappy domestic contest, was one of the strongest new grounds of argument taken by the opposition, in support of all other and former motives for an accommodation, the noble Lord at the head of the Admiralty, to obviate any effect founded upon that apprehension, drew a most flattering representation of our then state of naval force and preparation. That Minister is said to have declared, that we had at that instant a naval force in readiness for immediate service, superior to any thing which the whole House of Bourbon could then oppose to it; that we were so forward in point of preparation, as to insure to a certainty a continuance of that superiority; that he should be wanting in the discharge of his duty if it were otherwise; and that happy in giving the present information, he wished it to be generally known, that we had nothing to dread from France and Spain, but should be at full liberty to prosecute this war, to a fair, honourable, and happy issue.

The noble Lord who moved the amendment, had also dwelt long, and with much severity of animadversion, not only on the war and on its consequences, but on the mode of carrying it on, by which he said all remains of brotherly love towards us, must be eradicated from the bosoms of our countrymen in America. That the tomohawk and the scalping knife, were disgraceful weapons for enforcing British authority. That the calling on the savages, whose way of making war is to murder women and children, and to burn their prisoners of war alive by slow fires, and then to eat their flesh, was a scandalous proceeding in a civilized and Christian nation. A noble Duke long celebrated in opposition, after calling on the right reverend Bench, to assist in the Christian purpose of stopping the effusion of Christian Protestant blood, reminded them that their temporal concerns were only a secondary object of their sitting there; that their first duty was, by example, mildness, and persuasion, to soften the public deliberations; and particularly in cases which so materially affect the object of all religion, as the morality of actions; and were of such extent as that now under deliberation. That it became a mere jest, to retire from that House when a poor criminal was at their bar, because they could not bring themselves to vote in a case of blood, and yet to advise the most sanguinary measures, in which the lives of thousands were involved.

To all this the Ministry answered, that a state of war was as little desired by them as by the Lords in opposition; but that when they were at war, they must use the instruments of war. Much declamation they said had been poured out; and much artifice used to soften us into a false tenderness, by dwelling on the use of the scalping knife and tomohawk; but that the musquet and the bay-

¹⁰

onet were far more terrible weapons. If the savages destroyed more than they were wished to destroy, and that women and children fell (contrary to the wishes and endeavours of those who employed the savages) in the common havock, they alone were to be blamed, who by their unprovoked rebellion first brought on the necessity of arms, and then by tampering with the savages, had thought to set the example from which they suffered. That it was not, however, of importance, who first set the example of the employment of that people. They were found in the country, and whoever made war there, must have them for friends or enemies. That they had been used in the late war between the French and English indiscriminately, as each could obtain their assistance, both having equally endeavoured at it. That the very terror of their mode of making war, renders them the most eligible instrument for speedily extinguishing the rebellion, as it would operate more powerfully on the minds of those who were at a distance and yet untouched; and since war cannot be made without bloodshed, it ought to be considered as merciful rather than cruel; as it tended to shorten the calamities of that dreadful state—and one of the Ministers concluded with [11] saying, that he thought the measure perfectly just and wise; and that the administration would be highly censurable, if, entrusted as they were, with the suppression of so unnatural a rebellion, they had not used all the means which God and nature had put into their hands.

The whole of these arguments, but particularly the last expression, rekindled the flame of Lord Chatham's eloquence; and he had been seldom known so brilliant as in the severe animadversions he made on the hypothesis of the noble Lord, that the indiscriminate slaughter of men, women and children, and the torturing and devouring of captives, were the means of war furnished by God and nature; which notions, he said, standing so near the throne, must pollute the ear of Majesty.

In this manner, and with vehement altercations, the whole conduct and principle of the war, and of the opposition to it, was torn to pieces. The question being at length put towards eleven at night, the amendment was rejected by a majority of 97, including 13 proxies, to 28 Lords who supported the motion. The main question on the address being then put, was carried without a division. A short protest was entered by the Duke of Richmond and Earl of Effingham, which contained their dissent only in these words——" Because this address is a repetition of, or rather an improvement on, the fulsome adulation offered, and the blind engagements entered into on former occasions by this House, relative to this unhappy civil war."

Parliamentary enquiries into the state of public affairs, adopted by the Opposition in both Houses. Motion for 60,000 seamen. Animadversions on the state of the navy. Debates on the motion for a new bill, to continue the powers granted by the former, for the suspension in certain cases of the Habeas Corpus Law. Progress of the bill. Debates on the motion for four shillings in the pound, land tax. Motion by Mr. Fox for an enquiry into the state of the nation. Subsequent motions. Motion for certain papers, after long debates rejected upon a division. Circumstances attending the disclosure of the unhappy event at Saratoga. Debates upon the magnitude of the sum granted in the committee of supply for the ordnance service. Motion by Colonel Barre for papers, rejected. Mr. Hartley's motions relative to the American war, rejected. Motion by Mr. Wilkes for the repeal of the declaratory law, rejected upon a division. Great debates upon the motion of adjournment. Amendment moved by Mr. Burke. Original motion carried upon a division by a great majority. Transactions in the House of Lords, similar to those of the Commons. Duke of Richmond's motion for an enquiry into the state of the nation, agreed to. Lord Chatham's motion for the orders and instructions to General Burgoyne, after considerable debates, rejected upon a division. Debates upon a second motion by the same noble Lord, relative to the employment of the savages in the American war. Motion rejected on a division. Debates upon the question of adjournment. Motion carried upon a division.

FROM this time to the recess, and indeed during the greater part of the session, enquiry into the conduct of public affairs, whether particular or general, became the great object of opposition in both Houses. Neither the highly pleasing representation of the state of our Navy, both in point of immediate effect, and forwardness of preparation for future service, which had been laid before the Lords, nor the further confirmation of that state, which was given by the board of Admiralty in the House of Commons, were in any degree capable of curing the infidelity of those, who either, from what they stated as direct information, or for other reasons, held a strong and determined opinion, that the navy was shamefully and dangerously deficient in both respects.

Indeed that favourable representation produced effects, very different from what were probably wished or expected: for instead of removing doubt, or silencing enquiry, it increased the one, and added a spur to the other. At the same time it involved the Admiralty in a kind of dilemma, which it was not easy to get clear of.

For if our navy was in that powerful and flourishing state which had been described, it was not easy to assign any colourable reason for concealment; and to oppose with a good grace enquiries, tending to the establishment and promulgation of a fact, which it was our interest that all mankind should be acquainted with; and which would hold out the only effectual bar to restrain the designs of our enemies, if they intended to profit of our intestine troubles.

The unhappy news which arrived from America, opened also an ample field for enquiry, as well with respect to the plans and scheme of the war framed at home, as to the conduct and means which were used for their accomplishment abroad. It seemed necessary to know, whether the failure of success lay with the design or the execution; or if with neither, but proceeding merely from such inherent obstacles as it was impossible to surmount, to devise the speediest measures, with the least possible loss or dishonour, for withdrawing from so unfortunate and ruinous a pursuit.

Nov. 26th. Upon a motion in the committee of supply, that 60,000 seamen should be voted for the sea service of the ensuing year, 1778, as the Commissioner of the Admiralty who[12] made the motion, was, in pursuance of a call upon him for that purpose, entering into some detail of the disposition and state of the navy, so far as related to the ships upon service abroad, and in commission at home, the first law officer of the crown in that House,[13] excited some surprize, by objecting to his proceeding in that official explanation of matters appertaining to his own department, and immediately relative to the question before them, although it had been freely entered into as soon as it was proposed by the Lord of the Admiralty, and who seemed naturally to be the competent judge of its propriety. The learned gentleman contended, that the disclosure of particular strength or weakness which such a detail must afford to our enemies, would be equally improper and pernicious; that if any hostile intentions were entertained, it would be in fact, pointing out and instructing them, where and in what manner to direct their operations; that secrecy was the very life and spirit of all military enterprize; that the disclosure of such secrets to enemies, would be an act of the most unparalleled insanity; and that the honourable gentleman must undoubtedly have mistaken the nature of the question, when he indicated a disposition to an official compliance.

Such a check upon information, from so unexpected a quarter, and to which the matter seemed so entirely foreign, brought out much severe observation on the other side, and gradually extended the debate to a great variety of matter. They said, that to refuse official information relative to the state and strength of the navy, at a time that so vast a demand was made upon them for its support, was a procedure contrary to the known rules and usages of parliament; that they had a right to know, as well what they were voting for, as what they were voting; and that they trusted, however compliant the House had been upon every matter relative to the American war, they would not endure such a refusal without proper animadversion.

They said that the French were well acquainted both with the state and distribution of our naval force; but that foreigners, whether hostile or friendly, were no objects of concealment with the Ministers; they were not so totally ignorant of themselves, and of the nothingness of their counsels in respect to other nations, not to know that they were incapable of producing any secrets, which could be worth the smallest purchase to an enemy. It was parliament, and parliament only, that the wretched policy, the concealments and secrets of the Ministers reached to. If they could withhold all means of information from the representatives of the people, and from the hereditary guardians of the nation, and thus lead them in the dark, from one scene of public error, delusion, and imposition to another, as they had hitherto successfully practised from the commencement of the American contest, their designs were accomplished, and they arrived at the summit of all their wishes. Their system of secrecy went no further. It might be retailed in foreign and domestic gazettes, without giving them the smallest uneasiness, provided that it were withheld from parliament, or that a majority would accept the terms *official information*, and *secrets of government*, as a bar to every species of information and enquiry, and a plea for the most obstinate blindness, and unpardonable ignorance.

They concluded, that there could not be a stronger evidence of the bad condition of the navy, and of the misapplication of the vast and unusual sums of money, which had of late years been granted for its support and increase, than that dread which the Ministers constantly shewed, of all enquiry into its real state. If it had been in that which they pretended, they would have been as eager to particularize and display its strength, as they are now studious to keep every thing relative to it in darkness. And with great reason, said they, for besides the honour which it would do to themselves as Ministers, and the love and gratitude with which it would inspire their country; it would afford the best security which they could possibly obtain, for the good faith and pacific conduct of the House of Bourbon. They would then have no occasion to tremble at the thoughts of a war, nor to degrade under that apprehension, as they have done for several years, the Majesty of this country, by crouching to every insult, indignity, and real injury, offered by foreign nations.

On the other side, some gentlemen did not think that such enquiries were parliamentary. Others did not recollect that details of the fort had been usually entered into upon similar occasions. Those who particularly defended the Admiralty said, that they wished for nothing more than to lay open a true state of the navy, in every particular, to the whole world. That its formidable condition would strike terror in foreign nations; it would put domestick faction to shame, and give real comfort to every well wisher to his country. But if it once came to be a practice to lay these matters before the public when it was thought expedient to make a display of our strength, there may be times, when a prudent concealment, would be argued as a proof of weakness. It was in contemplation of such future occasions, and as a general principle of policy, and not from a consciousness of any present defect, that the state of the navy was wished to be held back from parliamentary inspection. The Commissioners of the Admiralty, however, being very closely pressed, at length consented to enter into the detail under certain modifications.

A statement of the navy being accordingly given, several of its parts were controverted, and some said to be in a great degree unfounded. The assertion of the first Lord in the other House, and which was confirmed by his colleagues in this, that we had 35 ships of the line for home defence, fully manned, and fit for immediate service, besides seven more, which only wanted such a number of their complement of men, as might be supplied with the greatest ease and expedition, was contradicted in the most express and unqualified terms. Indeed that [14] assertion had the fortune to experience the same fate in the other House; and it was strongly insisted upon in both, from what was said to be undoubted information, that our whole force in condition for immediate service on the home defence, did not at most exceed 20 sail of the line.

These strong charges on the one side, were combated by assertions equally strong on the other. It was insisted by the Commissioners, that the British navy had never been in a more respectable or flourishing state than at present; and that whether it was considered with relation to immediate service, or preparation for future, it was in either respect, far superior to the united maritime force of the House of Bourbon.

Some few of the opposition objected to the motion for 60,000 seamen, merely as tending to the support of a war, the principle and object of which they detested, and which they said could never be brought to a conclusion, under the inability with which it was conducted. Others objected to the enormity of the supply, at a time when we were at peace with all the world, excepting only the trouble we had in chastising a few of those ragged mobs in our own colonies, who had so long been the objects of our contempt and ridicule. They observed, that when the famous French armament was destroyed at La Hogue, we employed, but little more than half the number of seamen which was now required. That, in the glorious year 1759, the naval establishment did not exceed by a single man the number which was now demanded; and the whole expence, including naval ordnance, stores, and a large debt of a million, amounted only to 5,200,000l. though the peace establishment for the year 1778, will exceed five millions. And that if France could thus ruin us by an insupportable expence under the name and delusive appearance of peace, any state of war would be preferable to such a condition.

As a conviction of the necessity of a strong naval protection was much superior on all sides, to any confidence reposed in the good disposition which the Ministers attributed to foreign powers, the resolution for 60,000 seamen was accordingly agreed to in the committee without any division.

Upon receiving the report next day from the committee, those gentlemen who had more particularly and directly attacked the Admiralty Board on the score of its conduct, having now obtained some fresh information as to facts, renewed their charges with a degree of vehemence, which brought on much heat and personal asperity on both sides. The report being however received and passed without a division, Mr. Luttrel, [15] in order to support his charges, moved that the last weekly returns received at the Admiralty, from the commanders in chief at the home ports and stations, should be laid before the House. This was at first opposed, on the old ground of affording improper intelligence to our enemies; but it being perceivable, that the sense of the House, with which the Minister also coincided, seemed to lean to the other side, the Lords of the Admiralty at length acquiesced, and the motion was agreed to.

The bill of the preceding session for the suspension in certain cases of the Habeas Corpus law being now near expiring, the Attorney General, premising that the same cause still continued, namely the rebellion in America, which had at first rendered that measure necessary, moved for leave to bring in a bill to renew the powers of the former during a certain limited term.

26th.

This revival of an act which they had originally deemed so obnoxious, renewed the activity of some of the gentlemen in opposition, who contended that it was first necessary to know what effect the former bill had produced, before they consented to a renewal of its powers. Upon this ground Mr. Baker moved for and carried [16] an address, requiring a correct return and full description of all the prisoners, with an account of the prisons, whether in Great Britain or America, in which they were confined, together with copies of their several commitments, an account of the bail offered for their enlargement, and all other proceedings whatever of the privy council, in consequence of the powers vested in them by the late bill, to be laid before the House. This motion was afterwards amended and enlarged by the same gentleman, so as to include all persons who had been taken up for high treason, from the day after the battle of Lexington, being the 18th of April, 1775, to the date of the late act.

The new ground taken on that side, in the different debates that arose during the progress of the bill, was, that as the past act had produced no manner of effect, and of course could have remedied no evil, it was evidently useless in the first instance, and consequently unnecessary by a renewal in the second; that the tampering wantonly with a matter of so much consequence to the people, as the suspension of any part of a law, the full operation of which was their only security for life and liberty, and that without any plea of necessity, or even room now left for the pretence of utility, was a proceeding of a most dangerous nature.

With respect to the operation of the bill on the American prisoners of war, the conduct of administration was said to be in the highest degree inconsistent. Our Generals on the other side of the Atlantic have established a public cartel, such as is agreed to with an alien enemy, for the exchange of prisoners with the colonists. In Europe, the conduct is totally reversed. His Majesty's Minister at the court of France, when a proposal is made to him by the American delegates there, to lessen the miseries of war, on this, as well as the other side of the Atlantic, by the establishment of a similar cartel, answers them in lofty terms, that he receives no applications from rebels, excepting they come to implore for mercy. The answer was undoubtedly spirited, and becoming the representative of a great nation; but where is the consistency on the side of the ministers?

On the other side it was argued, that the same causes still continued, which had rendered the original bill necessary. That the matter should be considered in a much more favourable light than that in which it was represented. The bill was instituted, not so much to punish, as to prevent rebellion. Nothing could more clearly shew the excellency of its design and effect, than the very reasons which were brought to prove its being unnecessary, from the little scope that had been afforded for its operation. If scarcely any persons had suffered confinement or inconveniency from the powers which it lodged in the crown, it only shewed that those crimes had not been committed, to the prevention of which they were directed. That there was no room to doubt, but the terrors held out by the former bill, had awed numbers of disaffected people into obedience and fidelity, and thereby shut the door against domestic rebellion; that as it had thus in its past operation prevented the commission of numberless crimes, and the hard but necessary exercise of justice in their consequent punishments, there was no reason to doubt but it would produce the same happy effects in its future; and that it was the characteristic of good government to provide in the first instance for the prevention, not the punishment of crimes.

This avowal of suspending the liberty of the subject, and administering terror, like Prior's physick, " *by way of prevention,*" [17] rouzed all the spirit and ability of one of the most distinguished leaders of opposition in that house. He [18] observed, that the same arguments might hold good to eternity, and the suspension of the Habeas Corpus law be continued upon that ground to the end of time; that if that mode of reasoning should prevail in the house, the fence of liberty might be cut down, and Britons be at once deprived of their most valuable privileges; the same cause for which the bill is passed in this session, will hold equally good in the next, and in every other. The land-tax, said he, was introduced as a temporary revenue, and through that means granted by the House; the army was at first voted for one year only; but now your army is a standing army; your land-tax is a standing revenue to maintain this standing army; and this suspension may be considered, like them, as a standing measure of government, and thus consequently become an eternal suspension and destruction of the Habeas Corpus law.

The ministers denied the conclusions drawn by this gentleman to be in any degree fairly deducible from the premises, and totally disclaimed, on their own side, any designs inimical to the liberties of the people, or intention of continuing the suspension of the Habeas Corpus Act, any longer than the particular circumstances of the times rendered the measure necessary, and that its utility continued evident.

Notwithstanding the opposition in point of argument which this bill encountered, it was carried through without a division until the last reading, which happened on the 4th of December, when it was passed by a majority of 116 to 60. [19]

28th. On a motion in the Committee of Ways and Means, for granting a land-tax of four shillings in the pound, it was observed, on the side of opposition, that in all this disposal of the public money, not a single country gentleman had risen to speak of peace, or to complain of the war. That their supineness, or their acquiescence, deserved the severest reprehension. If they were asleep to the distresses of their country, they ought to be awakened; if they were ignorant, they ought to be informed; or if they were merely indolent, they should be rouzed. In pursuing this train of observation, the gentleman entered [20] into some detail of the hitherto nearly unparalleled expences of the war, and of the still greater, which they were to provide for in the ensuing year. In contrast to these effects of the war, he enquired into the state of expectation with which it was attended. Were we to be relieved by conquest from this burden of taxation? By no means, there is no conquest aimed at; our administrators say, that the drawing of a revenue from the colonies by that means is not the object of the contest, and they acknowledge that if it were, the Americans would not be able to bring any revenue into our exchequer. Thus, said he, we are irrecoverably ruining ourselves, merely upon a punctilio of honour, only to have it to say that we exceeded the Americans in obstinacy, and that in an absurd and unjust contest, commenced and forced into being by ourselves, we nobly persevered in violence and injustice, until, at the expence of absolute destruction to both parties, we may have the glory of compelling our colonies to acknowledge the wisdom, policy, and equity of our proceedings.

This attack called up two gentlemen, who are more particularly, or avowedly, attached to the court, than others of that party. [21] They entered upon the old question of the right of taxation; said, we were contending for a right, which, if relinquished in the manner that was proposed and wished on the other side, would terminate in the loss of America, and the consequent ruin of this country. That a right established, and not exercised, was in fact no right. And that, as we were heavily taxed ourselves, it was but reasonable, that when we had compelled the colonies to return to their duty, they should contribute in common with the rest of their fellow subjects to the support of that government, of whose protection they were to be equally partakers. That if we were now tamely to give them up to their own madness, we should do them the greatest of all injuries; we should deprive them of the benefit of the best constitution in the world. A tame dereliction of the rights of that constitution, would destroy the best hold we had upon their affections, and justly forfeit all their confidence.

The second of these gentlemen charged the whole American war, with all its consequences and misfortunes, to the opposition made to government in this country, both within doors and without; and then recurring to his ground of debate, and borrowing the ideas and phraseology of a great law Lord in the other House, said, that the question now was, whether the Americans should kill us, or we kill them; so that we were acting entirely at present upon the defensive.

A gentleman on the other side, [22] after observing that he considered what had fallen from the two last speakers as the sentiments of their party, said, he would, upon their own ground, propose two questions as a test to administration, and a

third to those who were considered as their principal supporters in the present measures, viz. Would any minister stand up in his place, and venture to fix a time for the termination of the present contest, that is, when the right now so warmly contended for will be established? Will any minister say, that upon a supposition of the greatest success on our part, and the most thorough reconciliation or submission on the other, we are to expect a revenue from America? If then, said he, neither a period is pretended to be fixed to the present waste of blood and waste of treasure; and though it could, if no revenue, either to replace the immense sums we have already spent, or the more enormous expence which we are likely to incur, I wish to know from any of those, who with an unlimited attachment to every court measure, choose to call themselves country gentlemen, how they can justify, even on their own ground, to themselves, or to their constituents, the persisting in measures, which do not promise the attainment of a single object for which they ostensibly give them their support.

A gentleman who represents the [23] most extensive landed property, and the most numerous body of freeholders, under any collective description in the kingdom, after placing, with his usual refinement, the offensive motives to the war in several ludicrous points of view, and adding to those already avowed, that it was persevered in merely to gain the confidence of the Americans, and that we were to beat them only to secure their affections; farther observed, that there had been more money already expended in this ruinous pursuit, from the conclusion of which the smallest benefit was not even expected, than would serve to have purchased, inclosed, cleared, manured, cultivated, sown, and planted, all the waste lands in Britain;—more than would have converted all the heaths, hills, and wastes in the kingdom into gardens. Such he said were the motives, and such the effects of this war; and such the ground upon which they were called to grant the present supply.

These disputes gave rise to an enquiry into the state of the nation. It was said, that it was in vain to waste time in general declamation upon a subject which could only be determined by an exact deduction of particulars. The great question of the propriety of carrying on this American war, could only be settled by a view of the experience we have had; and a calculation of the means which remain to the nation for the attainment of this favourite object. On Dec. 2d. these grounds Mr. Fox having moved for a committee of the whole house to consider of the state of the nation, gave a short sketch of the matters which he proposed to lay before them as the principal objects of their consideration, under the following heads;—1st, The expences of the war, and the resources which the nation possessed, to raise the supplies necessary for its continuance;—2dly, The loss of men from that war;—3dly, The situation of trade, both with respect to America and the foreign markets;—4thly, The present situation of the war; the hopes that might be rightly entertained from its continuance; the conduct and measures of the present administration; the means of obtaining a lasting peace; and our present situation with regard to foreign powers;—5thly, What progress the commissioners had made, in consequence of the powers with which they were entrusted, for the purpose of bringing about a peace between Great Britain and her colonies.

Under these general heads, he observed, that many other enquiries would arise, and it would be the business of the committee to follow every path that tended to lead to a thorough investigation and discovery of the state of the nation. If it should appear, said he, that the nation is in a bad state, and that the late and present measures of administration had reduced us to an extremity of danger, which he was afraid they certainly had, a new system must be introduced, and a new set of ministers appointed; but if, on the contrary, the nation should be found in a flourishing state, and the present measures likely to prove successful, the present system should by all means be continued, and the present ministers remain in power; for he was convinced that none but the present ministers, would prosecute the present system.

The minister agreed to the motion with great appearance of cordiality, and said he would do every thing in his power to second the design of the mover, and to promote the great end which he had in view. That nothing could render him more happy, than an opportunity of convincing the House, that the nation was in a much more flourishing state, than many of the other side either actually did, or affected to believe it. He, however, reserved to himself the right of withholding any such papers from the House, as it might be inconvenient, dangerous, or prejudicial to government to expose.

Mr. Fox followed his motion with several others—For, An account of all the troops foreign and domestic, that had been employed since the year 1774;—Lists of all the ships of war that had been employed in that time, and of those that had been lost, taken, or destroyed, with exact returns of the men that had been killed or taken prisoners.—The last general returns of all the hospitals in North America;—Copies of the last returns of the troops in Great Britain, Ireland, North America, and the West Indies;—With lists of the ships of war employed as convoys to protect the trade of this country.—And in order to afford time for procuring the papers, lists, and accounts required, as well as for their being separately examined, and their matter duly weighed by the members, he proposed that the meeting of the committee should be fixed for the 2d of February.

All these motions having passed without opposition, he moved for an address to lay before them copies of all such papers as related to any steps taken for the fulfilling of that clause of the prohibitory act of the 16th of his present Majesty, by which persons appointed and authorized by him, for certain purposes therein specified, were empowered, under certain conditions, to declare any colony, province, district, port, or place, to be at the peace of his Majesty; and also, for returns of those colonies, or places, which had, in conformity with their compliance to the proposed conditions, and pursuant to the powers of the said act, been declared to be at the King's peace.

This motion put an end to the acquiescence of the Minister, who opposed it strongly, upon the ground that the producing and exposing of any papers relating to a negociation during its existence, would be a proceeding not only contrary to all established forms and practice, but totally subversive of the business in hand, and probably attended with the greatest prejudice to the cause in general. He declared himself ready and willing to grant every reasonable information in his power; but he also declared, that he neither could nor would consent to make discoveries, which would not be less inconsistent with all sound wisdom and true policy, than prejudicial to government, and contrary to the real interests of this country.

This refusal called up all the powers of debate on both sides.

It was further urged in opposition to the motion, that negociations with rebels in arms, could not be entered into with the people at large, but must be privately conducted with select bodies of men, perhaps with individuals; and the greatest secrecy observed in the whole transaction, as any discovery might draw the vengeance of those who held different principles, upon such particular bodies or individuals. But that, in truth, they did not know that any negociation had been entered into. It was impossible that any treaty of conciliation could be opened with rebels in arms standing up for independence. The very act would be an acknowledgement of their independence.

These reasons were very lightly treated on the other side: The only injury, they said, which could possibly arise from the motion, and indeed the only that was apprehended, was to the ministers themselves, by a disclosure of their conduct to parliament. The Americans were thoroughly informed on the spot, and in the first instance, of every particular relative to the subject. They were not themselves seeking to pry into secrets of state, or to discover the private intelligence, which government, by political means, might receive from particular persons. The motion went only to public transactions, with public persons or bodies of people, in their public capacity. No others could be enabled to give efficacy to any negociation or treaty.

It was, they said, merely a parliamentary enquiry into the result of a parliamentary act. The commission to Lord and Sir William Howe was the consequence of an act which originated with them; and it was not only a propriety, but a duty, to examine into those transactions which had followed their appointment. Some parts of the subject were already publickly known, and disclosed so much of

the matter as was sufficient to shew that the enquiry was not only proper, but necessary. It appears by these, said they, that neither New York, Long Island, Staten Island, or any other territory we have gained possession of in America, have as yet been restored to the King's peace. It is also known, that Governor Tryon has written to General Sir William Howe, one of the commissioners, for the purpose of restoring New York to that security and benefit; but that the General returned for answer, that it was not in his power to do any thing in the business, without the concurrence of the noble Lord who presided in the American department. This was accordingly a matter which came of course within the care and investigation of the committee; they were to enquire how far the measures pursued by the ministers at home, and by the commissioners abroad, tended to fulfil the intentions of the House; and whether any part of the failure in effect lay with the one or the other.

Whilst the debate, notwithstanding the frequent calls for the question on the side of the majority, was yet kept up in full heat and vigour, and that the first law officer of the crown was in the midst of a speech, wherein he was with the greatest ability stating the ill policy which it would be in the ministers, and the danger with which it would be attended to the state, to disclose information of such importance at this critical period of time, intelligence was received from the other house, that the same motion had been made by the Duke of Grafton, and was agreed to by the Lords in administration.

Nothing could exceed the embarrassment into which the ministers were thrown upon this unexpected intelligence. Nor did the opposition miss the opportunity of improving it. Wit, ridicule, and the most pointed observation, be-

ing alternately applied to support the advantage which it afforded. The Minister was rallied on the awkwardness of his situation, and the strange dilemma in which he was involved, of either recording by a resolution of the House, that the Commons of England were not worthy of being entrusted with secrets which were freely communicated to the Lords, or of being under a necessity to intreat a large part of those numerous friends and supporters, who had so long carried him triumphantly through all opposition, to abandon their colours upon this occasion, and unwillingly to leave their leader to undergo the disgrace of voting in a cabinet minority. The Minister was humourously advised, as the only means of extricating himself from that dilemma, and as affording the only salvo in his power for the indignity offered to that house, to impeach those ministers, who in defiance of that wisdom and sound policy, which he had just laid down as the motives for his refusal, had dared to betray the King's secrets to the House of Lords; a measure of justice, in which the opposition assured him of their most hearty support.

But they entered with more seriousness and severity into the contemptuousness of the treatment, and said, that to grant a motion for papers to be laid before one house, and refuse it to another, was such an indignity as it was hoped no British house of commons would ever submit to. The majority were called upon to consider the manner in which they were treated; they were held unworthy to be trusted with a secret; they were told it would be fatal to trust them; and yet this mighty secret was thrown upon an open table in another place, from whence the news-papers would entrust all those with it, in whatever quarter of the world, who were only capable of reading English. Was this a treatment, they said, for free men, and the representatives of free men to bear? They are not to be trusted; they must not know secrets; their superiors might search into the state of the nation, but they were either too insignificant to be consulted, or too dangerous to be trusted. They were desired to reflect on the importance of the situation in which they were placed; on their responsibility to that great body of free and independent electors, to whom they owed their political existence; and to bear in mind the regard due to their own honour, whether as men, or as members of a British parliament.

The Minister felt himself so goaded on all sides, and the attacks were rendered so extremely vexatious by the diversity of manner with which they were conducted, that he could not refrain from growing warm, and seemed for a short time to be surprized out of his usual good humour. He said, that whatever effect the present anecdote might have upon the House at large, he should, for his own part, adhere to his former opinion. He could not indeed bring himself to believe, that an unauthenticated anecdote could possibly produce any change in their sentiments. He reprobated in terms of great asperity, and condemned as exceedingly disorderly, the introducing of any thing that passed in the other House, with a view of influencing the determinations of that. What the other had done, or might do, was nothing, he said, to them. The House of Commons were not to be guided in their deliberations by any extrinsic consideration whatever; much less by the act or conduct of any other body. If they should submit to any influence or direction of that sort, it would be, indeed, a dereliction of their importance and dignity. But they never had, and he trusted they never would. He concluded, that the King's servants in the other

house were certainly entrusted with the secrets of government, and were competent judges for themselves, of what ought, and what ought not to be disclosed. That he also, having the same right of judging for himself, held his first opinion, that the motion was of an extent which neither wisdom nor sound policy could agree with; and that it was dangerous and unprecedented to give such papers to the public as were now demanded, pending a negociation.

The debate, as usual, wandered over a great part of the American affairs; but the ground, however wide in extent, had been already so frequently traversed, that it could not afford much novelty. A federal commercial union was talked of by some as the only hope now left with regard to America. Others still thought, that an accommodation was not yet impossible. That if proposals really amicable, accompanied by equally good dispositions, were made; and that these were supported by that unfeigned sincerity, that fairness of design and openness of conduct, which can alone restore confidence, and which would even in some degree regain affection, the Americans might still be induced to coalesce with this country in such a degree of union, as, along with securing all their own rights, might preserve to her a monopoly of their trade; the only advantage which in justice or wisdom, they insisted, that Great Britain should ever have sought from her colonies. But to the want of those dispositions, of that sincerity, fairness, and openness, they attributed the failure in every scheme of accommodation which had been hitherto adopted.

A renewal of the severe censures, which the mover of the present motion had in a late debate passed upon the conduct of the noble Lord at the head of the American department, and which now seemed to be directed with new fer-

vour, called that Minister again to enter into some defence or justification of his measures. In the warmth incident to such a situation, the noble Minister was led or surprized into an acknowledgement, that notwithstanding the great power and vast resources of this country, the bravery of our fleets and armies, and the ability of our officers, he began to despair of the practicability of reducing the Americans to obedience by force of arms, if they should continue to preserve their union entire.

He also acknowledged, that he had great reason to doubt the validity of much of the information which he had received from that quarter; but insisted, that his measures would be found perfectly justifiable, when candidly compared with the information on which they were founded; and that it would appear, they must necessarily have been crowned with success if that had been true. He, notwithstanding these acknowledgements, persisted in his opinion, as to the propriety of continuing the war, and of the most decisive exertion in its prosecution; reprobated the idea of a federal union with rebels; declared America to be nearly ruined, and suffering under every species of human misery and calamity; and, building much upon the disunion of the several colonies, as well as of the people in each, and on the accounts, which, though not sufficiently authenticated, he had reason to believe to be true, of the great successes of Sir William Howe, he still entertained an expectation, that if means were devised to prevent the secret assistance which they received from some of the European powers, the Americans might still be compelled to return to their duty.

This unexpected acknowledgement of matters which had been so often urged on the other side, to shew the impolicy of the contest in its origin, with the hopelessness of success, and the ruinous consequences of the pursuit, coming from such a quarter, seemed at once a dereliction of all the strong ground of argument, and to afford the most incontrovertible evidence of the wisdom and necessity of bringing the troubles to that speedy conclusion, which was so much contended for on the other side.

In taking this ground, the opposition animadverted on the supposed incongruity of several parts of his lordship's speech and conclusions. He acknowledges, said they, the impracticability of subduing the colonies if they continue united; he does not pretend that he is certain that they are not united; and yet he urges the prosecution of the war, although, upon his own state of the question, there is not the smallest hope of success. They insisted, that it was not yet too late for an accommodation, founded upon clear, permanent, and constitutional principles, which, though not affording all the advantages we enjoyed, before they were scattered by our folly and injustice, would still be of the greatest utility to this country. But that if the ministers persisted any longer in their system of devastation and carnage, and placed their trust of subduing minds and affections in the tomohawk and scalping knife, there could be no doubt but the temper and minds of the Americans would become so soured and alienated, by repeated cruelties and renewed losses, that they would never after listen to any terms of accommodation, nor agree to hold any political relation whatever with this country. One of the noble Lord's grounds of hope (such hope as it was) consisted in keeping from them the clandestine aid of foreign powers. What reason had they to think that such aid would not be continued, increased, and avowed? The ministers would, however, act now, they said, as they had done in many former parts of the American business. They first predicted

events and then pursued such a line of conduct, as of necessity verified their predictions. Thus they asserted, that independency was the sole and original aim of the colonies; but finding that the people were exceedingly backward in applying to that last and fatal resort, they adopted such effectual measures of violence and injustice, as drove them headlong into independence. They now assert that the Americans will not listen to any terms of accommodation; and they will accordingly pursue the same effectual measures, until they have driven them so fast into the arms of France, that it will not be in their power, if they were even so disposed, ever to look back, much less to return, to their ancient political connections with this country.

The question being at length put, it soon appeared that the Minister had not adopted that part of the alternative which had been proposed to him on the other side, of voting in a minority; and Mr. Fox's motion, for laying those papers before the Commons, which had been granted to the Lords, was, in a manner which in other seasons would have been deemed incredible, rejected upon a division, by a majority of 178 to 89.

Dec. 3d. The succeeding day was marked by the disclosure of the melancholy catastrophe of General Burgoyne's expedition, and the unhappy fate of the brave but unfortunate northern army at Saratoga. A disclosure, which excited no less consternation, grief, and astonishment in both houses, than it did of dismay on the side of the ministers. The noble Lord at the head of the American department, being called upon by a gentleman in opposition for the purport of the dispatches which were received from Canada, was the unwilling relater of that melancholy event, in the House of Commons.

This of course brought out, with fresh fervour, and additional asperity, all the censures and charges that ever had been, or that could be, passed or made, whether relative to the principle or policy of the contest, the conduct of the war, or the general incapacity of the ministers. After condemning and rebrobating the latter in terms of the utmost severity, the opposition applied the most pathetic expressions which our language affords, to deplore the fate of the gallant General and his brave army, who, they said, after surmounting toils, dangers, and difficulties, which should have crowned them with lasting glory and honour, and shewing themselves superior to every thing, excepting only the injustice of the cause in which they were engaged, and the inherent fatality of that ill-starred direction under which they acted, were so overwhelmed in the joint operation of these concurring causes, as not only to be plunged into irretrievable ruin, but also, what had never before happened to such men, nor could ever again be the reward of such actions, they were finally sunk into disgrace.

They condemned the whole plan and design of the expedition in the most unqualified terms. Said, that it was an absurd, an inconsistent, and an impracticable scheme, unworthy of a British minister, and which the Chief of a tribe of savages would have been ashamed to acknowledge. They reminded the American Minister that they were not judging from events, but how often and earnestly they had warned him of the fatal consequences of his favourite plan. When they had truly foretold the event, they were only laughed at, and told they were speaking in prophecy; was he yet satisfied of the truth of their predictions?

Ignorance, they said, had stamped every step taken during the expedition; but it was the ignorance of the Minister, not of the General; a minister who would venture, fitting in his closet, to direct, not only the general operations, but all the particular movements, of a war carried on in the interior deserts of America, and at a distance of three thousand miles. A junction between Howe and Burgoyne was the object of this expedition; a measure which might be effected without difficulty by sea in less than a month; but the Minister chooses it should be performed by land; and what means does he use for the accomplishment of this purpose? Why truly, said they, as it was necessary for the armies to meet, it might have been reasonably imagined, that the northern army would have advanced to the southward, or the southern to the northward; or if it were intended that they should meet any where about the center, that they would both have set out in those directions about the same time; but the Minister despising such simple and natural means of effecting a junction, dispatches one army from New York still farther south, and sends the other to follow it from Canada in the same direction; so that if they both continued their course till doomsday, it would be impossible for them to meet.

But the noble Lord, they said, was the implicit slave of report, and the continual dupe to the false informations of men, who were interested in his deception; men who profited of the common calamities of England and America. Thus, on one day we had only a trifling mob to quell; nine tenths of the people were not only zealously but violently attached to government; and yet, most strange to tell, this vast majority of the people, as if loyalty had deprived them of all the powers and properties of men, suffered themselves to be fleeced and driven like sheep, by that ragged handful of their own rabble. The next day, when we were to ransack Europe for troops, and exhaust Great Britain to maintain them, the Americans were suddenly become numerous and powerful. The delusion was then become highly contagious; and they were to be brought to their senses by nothing short of the exertion of the whole strength of this country. Again, we were told that the Americans were all cowards; a grenadier's cap was sufficient to throw whole provinces into panics; it seemed, however, odd enough, that 55,000 men, with an immense naval force, should be sent to reduce poltrons. Will the Minister now venture to say, that the gallant army at Saratoga, with a noble artillery, and conducted by officers of the most distinguished merit, were compelled to the disgrace of resigning their arms and their liberty, by a wretched contemptible rabble, without spirit or discipline? But such, they said, was the misrepresentation and falsehood, which, partly intended to impose upon the nation, and partly operating upon the wretched folly, credulity, and incapacity of the ministers themselves, had already led to the loss of America, and to our present state of calamity and disgrace; and which, under the fostering influence of that perverse blindness and obstinacy, which have been so long the bane, and at the same time the only distinction of our public counsels, would terminate in the final destruction of this country.

The time and occasion did not serve for bold words or lofty language on the side of administration. The ministers, indeed, were sufficiently humbled. The noble Lord at the head of affairs, acknowledged that he was unfortunate. He, at the same time, justified his intentions; and declared that he was and would be ready, whenever the general voice of the House desired it, to enter into an explanation of his conduct, and a defence of his measures. He also declared, that no man from the beginning had wished more earnestly for peace than he had done himself, nor would do more to obtain it now; and that if the laying down of his place and his honours could accomplish that wished for purpose, he would gladly resign them all. He said, that he had been dragged to his place againg his will; but that however disagreeable it might be, whilst he continued in possession, he would support it to the best of his power. He concluded by observing, (the House being then in a committee of supply) that whatever their future determination as to peace or war might be, it was necessary they should grant the supplies which were now demanded; as, if even a cessation of arms should take place, the expences must still continue, until the armies were brought home and discharged or reduced.

The American Minister declared, that he was ready to submit his conduct in planning the late expedition to the judgement of the House. If it appeared impotent, weak, and ruinous, let the censure of the House fall upon him. He was ready to abide it, as every Minister who had the welfare of his country at heart, should at all times, he said, be ready to have his conduct scrutinized by his country. But having also said something, of wishing that the House would not be over hasty in condemnation, that they would suspend their judgment on the conduct both of the General and of the Minister relative to this unhappy event; hoping that the conduct of both would appear free from guilt; these expressions, or some others of the same nature, being considered as tending to criminate, or insinuate blame on the General, were highly resented on the other side, and contributed not a little to that severity of censure which he experienced on this day.

On the following day several motions for papers and accounts, deemed necessary for the information of the future committee into the state of the nation, were made by Colonel Barre, and agreed to by the House. These took in an account of all the grants for the payment of national and foreign troops from the 29th of Sept. 1774: —of the officers appointed to collect the stamp duties in America: —of the recruits raised in Great Britain and Ireland,—and of the persons appointed to act in the Commissariate of America; all within the time first given.

Upon receiving the report from the committee of sup-ply, that 682,816l. should be [4th.] granted for the ordinaries and extraordinaries of the office of ordnance in the ensuing year; the magnitude of the sum rouzed the opposition into action, and occasioned a motion by Sir P. Jennings Clerke, to recommit the [25] report. In the speech made by that gentleman in support of his motion, he charged the perseverance of the Ministers in their present mad and destructive system, to the most unworthy of all motives, the mere covetuousness of retaining their places; for as they knew, he said, that they were so exceedingly odious to the Americans, that they never would enter into any treaty, much less conclude a peace with them, so the greediness for their present emoluments, superseding all other considerations, induced them to persist in war to the final destruction of their country. To avert this supposed danger, he made a ludicrous proposal, That as in a promotion of Admirals, old Captains, of less supposed capacity than others, were promoted but not employed, and vulgarly called Admirals of the Yellow Flag, being admitted to the pay of the rank—so, that a similar establishment should be made for Ministers, who should be allowed to continue the pay and name, whilst men, more fit, should execute the employment.

The enormity of the sum proposed for the ordnance service, (though since much increased) occasioned, however, much serious animadversion. The opposition said that it exceeded the ordinaries and extraordinaries of the ordnance in the year 1759, by no less than 140,000l. that glorious year which saw us at the zenith of our power and glory, when we had 250,000 men in arms, and that the thunder of our artillery by sea and land, was heard with terror and effect in every quarter of the globe; when we made war in Europe, Asia, Africa, the West Indies and North America. Yet in the year for which this vast sum is demanded, we employ but 89,000 men, and these engaged only in a petty contest with our own people. They asked if such glaring impositions on the publick were fit to be endured; and in what manner the representatives could face their constituent after submitting to them.

On this subject they were particularly pressed by Mr. Burke, who for some time receiving no answer, and the speaker proceeding to put the question, declared he would not suffer the question to be put, until some explanation was given. He looked upon order as contemptible, when instead of forwarding, it stood in opposition to the substance of their duty. That here was a comparative expence, which, stated against the comparative service, was at first view utterly unaccountable. He called strongly on the gentlemen of the Board of Ordnance for an answer. At length, the gentlemen of that board who were present, said that they were not judges of the service. They had punctually executed the orders which they had received, and that the utmost œconomy prevailed in their several departments. One gentleman attributed much of the extraordi-[26]nary expence to the extreme and peculiar hostility of the country in which the train was acting; which was so bitter, beyond the example of other wars, that supplying nothing whatever towards the service, the number of articles to be sent from hence became prodigious. Another said that the [27] charge was much increased, by the artillery acting in different bodies on distinct and remote services. He also said, that the foreign troops in British pay in the late war found their own ammunition, which being provided for in their respective contracts, lessened the official estimates of the ordnance expence prodigiously. This ground was accordingly taken by the Minister who contended, that though we employed 250,000 men in that year, the British forces, for whom the estimates were made, constituted only an inconsiderable part of that number. But as he was not prepared for the question, and had neither compared the estimates, nor provided the necessary documents, the matter of fact was left to be ascertained on another day, and the report of the committee of supply was agreed to without a division.

On the ensuing day, Colonel Barre having moved, That copies or extracts of all letters relating to reinforcements, of the ships, the mariners, or the land forces, received by the Secretaries of State from General Gage, Lord Howe, General Howe, and General Carleton, from the 5th of July, 1775, should be laid before the House; the American Minister objected to it, from his not being sufficiently aware of its consequences. He said it extended to a period before his introduction into office. It contained the intelligence of several years, and he confessed he was so unprepared, that he could not suddenly answer on the propriety of submitting them to the House. But he promised, that the purport of those papers should be laid before them on the day of general enquiry. After fome confiderable debate, the motion was rejected by the previous queftion without a divifion.

Mr. Hartley then made feveral motions, which he intended to be paffed as refolutions of the Houfe, upon the following grounds, That the farther profecution of the American war muft be attended with an enormous expence:—That the expences of another campaign, added to thofe already incurred, would probably amount to between 30 and 40 millions fterling, which muft create an alarming increafe of the principal and intereft of the national debt; and muft require many additional heavy and burthenfome taxes, land-taxes, as well as others, upon the Britifh fubjects to defray:——That the further profecution of this war, muft be deftructive of the navigation, commerce, riches, and refources of this country, as well as of the lives of his Majefty's fubjects; and that it will leave us in an exhaufted ftate, with our land and fea forces at the diftance of 3000 miles, open to the infult or attack of any fecret or infidious enemy;—and, that it is unbecoming the wifdom and prudence of parliament, to proceed any farther in the fupport of this fruitlefs, expenfive, and deftructive war; more efpecially, without any fpecific terms of accommodation being declared.

Mr. Hartley had prepared eftimates to fupport the pofitions laid down in his motions, if the Houfe would enter into the enquiry; and, if the refolutions were agreed to, he propofed to follow them with an addrefs to his Majefty, being the fame, or fimilar to, that which he had laid before the Houfe in the preceding feffion, recommending an immediate ceffation of hoftilities, with fuch other meafures as appeared to that gentleman, to be the moft effectual towards bringing about a final accommodation.

The Minifter made light of the matter. He faid the motions were out of time and improper. They were only fitting for the cognizance of a committee, not of a Houfe. Every body muft acknowledge, and he himfelf among the foremoft; the truth of the firft refolution, that the profecution of the war muft be attended with enormous expence; but he thought it impoffible for the Houfe to decide on the fecond, before the day of general enquiry, when having all the matter in any degree relative to the fubject before them, they would be able to determine upon it with propriety. As the oppofition did not enter much into the bufinefs, the debate was languid; and foon wandered from the immediate queftion to converfations or bickerings upon different parts of the general fubject. The motions were all feparately rejected without a divifion.

Dec. 10th. On the laft day of the fitting of parliament previous to the Chriftmas recefs; Mr. Wilkes moved for a repeal of the declaratory law of the year 1766, as introductory to feveral other motions which he intended, if the firft paffed, for the repeal of all the laws obnoxious to the Americans which had been paffed fince the year 1763. He faid that the repeal of thefe laws was required as a *fine qua non* by the Americans; and that in particular, they had reprobated that declaratory act as a fountain from whence every evil had flowed. The previous queftion was immediately moved by a noble Lord on the Treafury Bench, and feconded[28] by the Minifter, who alfo entered into fome confiderable difcuffion of the fubject of the motion. Although a debate of fome length enfued, the oppofition in general, were more taken up, with a defence of the ground and principle on which the declaratory law had been founded, againft the attacks made upon it by the mover and a

few others; and in ftating the particular fituation of affairs, which, they infifted, had at that time rendered it not only a wife, but an abfolutely neceffary meafure, than in fupporting the motion, although they would now readily give up that bill, or any bill, as an opening to conciliation. They faid, that the great teft of the goodnefs or badnefs of a law, namely its good or ill effect, had decided on that act. That America had never complained of it until it was made an hoftile ufe of, and in that cafe, the beft acts might become a caufe of offence. That things were now on a new bottom. Other things befides the repeal or the making of acts muft be done. The previous queftion being put, was carried on a divifion by a majority of 160 to 12.[29]

As the firft object of government in all parliaments, namely, the obtaining of money, was now pretty well attained, near nine millions fterling having been already granted in fupplies, during only about fixteen days actual fitting upon bufinefs, and that the Minifters were by this time, as heartily fick of enquiry, as they were fufficiently fore with cenfure; it was determined to procure a fufficient breathing time, in order to anfwer the different purpofes, of a recovery from paft fatigue, a relief from prefent toil, and due preparation for the future hard fervice which was expected, by an early and long recefs for the holidays. Another object of no fmall importance, which it is fuppofed the court had at that time in contemplation, and which would have been fully fufficient in itfelf for the adoption of this meafure, will be explained in the next chapter.

As foon, accordingly, as Mr. Wilkes's motion was difpofed of, the noble Lord who had moved the previous queftion, moved alfo for an adjournment to the 20th of January, and fupported his motion on the following grounds; that the supplies, at present neceffary, were voted; the ufual bufinefs before the Chriftmas recefs was gone through, that nothing farther could be done until the event of the campaign in America was known; that if it were even otherwife, the Houfe was never attended at that feafon; that no new events were likely to happen, which could render the advice or affiftance of parliament neceffary within that time; that however eager fome perfons were to expatiate on, or to enhance, the misfortune of the Canada expedition, nothing could be done in that bufinefs, until the arriva' of information, and of the neceffary documents from America; and, that as a general enquiry was appointed, it was equally fair and neceffary to allow the fervants of the crown time for preparation.

On the other fide, the propofal for fo early and long a recefs was reprobated in the ftrongeft terms. They faid, that an adjournment of fix weeks in fo critical and dangerous a fituation of public affairs, when all the collective powers and wifdom of parliament might be neceffary for the immediate prefervation of the nation, would be a moft rafh and hazardous proceeding. That, taken in all its circumftances, it was unprecedented in all the records of parliament. That, in a feafon of the greateft public danger we ever experienced; involved in the moft lamentable fpecies of all wars, a civil war; attended, as that was, with circumftances of expence, lofs, ruin, and difgrace before unheard of; and at the eve of a rupture with the whole united Houfe of Bourbon; for parliament to be affembled fo late as the 20th of November, and to propofe a long adjournment of more than fix weeks on the 10th of December, was a meafure of fo extraordinary and dangerous a nature, that they could not refrain,

they faid, from being loft in aftonifhment, how any perfon that was honoured with the royal confidence, could dare to abufe it with fuch an advice. But daring and abfurd as the meafure was, it was attended with one circumftance, which, they faid, muft afford the greateft pleafure to every real friend to his country. It portended the falling of the curtain, and the exit of thofe weak, obftinate, and improvident Minifters, who had driven us into our prefent diftrefsful fituation. They are no longer able, faid they, to face their adverfaries in parliament. They fly from public obfervation and enquiry, and brood over their approaching difgrace in a kind of political defpair; they tremble too late for confequences, which they have neither the ability to provide againft, nor the fortitude to meet.

The Minifter contended, that the arguments offered againft the motion had proved nothing. The campaign was already terminated, and they could form no conclufions relative to it till they knew the event. France did not moleft us, nor did he believe that either France or Spain had any intention of the fort; but whether they had or not, we were prepared for the worft that could happen; and fhould advance our preparation as much, or more, during the recefs, than if the parliament were fitting. He therefore infifted, that Mr. Burke's propofed amendment to the motion, of fubftituting the words " this day fennight," for the " 20th of January," would only retard the bufinefs of the ftate, without anfwering any ufeful purpofe. If, upon a full enquiry after the recefs, meafures of a confequential nature fhould become neceffary, the committee for an enquiry into the ftate of the nation, which was not to meet until the 2d of February, would afford the proper, and the only proper time, to debate and

deliberate on them. He hoped the campaign had produced events, which would enable us to prepare and enforce terms of conciliation with the colonies, on true conftitutional grounds with refpect to both. That it would be abfurd to propofe American plans, which muft in the nature of things depend upon the ftate of America, when we could at beft pretend to a very partial knowledge of it. The events of the campaign would be known at the time propofed for their meeting; and then, when the whole of the military operations, and of the intended meafures, could come fully and properly together before them, he would move the Houfe to confider of the conceffions which it might be proper for them to lay down as the bafis of a treaty; and he yet trufted, that their endeavours would prove effectual in bringing about a permanent peace, and a lafting union between both countries.

The leaders of oppofition, ridiculed the idea of the prefent Minifters becoming negociators for peace and conciliation with the Americans, as the greateft of all poffible abfurdities. The colonies, they faid, had been fo often abufed, deceived, and trifled with by them, and fo thoroughly underftood the principles which were the fpring of all their actions, that they never would liften to any terms of peace, however flattering, which made their way to them through fo obnoxious a channel. No negociation could poffibly fucceed in their hands. Every body, faid they, knows, that the Americans openly charge, (whether truly or falfely was not the queftion) all the lofs and calamity which has befallen both countries, to their incapacity, malignity, and obftinacy. Exclufive of the refentment arifing from the mifery which they have endured through their means, can any man in the cool poffeffion of his reafon fuppose, that they will enter into any measures of friendship, or system of union with men whom they suspect, detest, and despise. They insisted, that the House of Bourbon were hostile; that they only waited for the full consummation of that favourable crisis, by the expectation of which they had for a long time regulated all their conduct; that, in the wretched struggle with our own people, we had lost Portugal, alienated Holland, and had not a single ally left upon the face of the earth, excepting, that the petty mercenary states of Germany, who hired out the blood of their subjects, were by some depravation of language and ideas, to be considered as allies. What season then, said they, could be so fitting for enquiry and deliberation, or at what time could procrastination prove more pernicious than the present, when one army is annihilated, another, little less than besieged, and our hereditary and natural enemy negociating a treaty with our colonies, by which, if once concluded, America will be irrecoverably lost to this country.

The question being at length put, about 10 at night, the motion of adjournment was carried upon a division by a majority of 155 to 68.

During these transactions in the House of Commons, the business in that of the Lords, abstracted from the supplies, was conducted upon the same ground, and in general with the same effect. The Duke of Richmond had moved for an enquiry into the state of the nation, on the same day that Mr. Fox had made his motion in the House of Commons. The enquiry was also fixed to the same date in both; and the subsequent motions for papers and information made by his grace, corresponded with those in the other House, and were agreed to in the same manner.

On the 5th of December, the Earl of Chatham moved, that copies of all orders and instructions to General Burgoyne, relative to the northern expedition, should be laid before the House. The noble Earl introduced his motion with a speech of considerable length, in which he dissected and reprobated several parts of that from the throne without reserve or ceremony; and taking a large sweep into public measures, he seemed to summon all the powers of his eloquence, and all his natural vehemence, to the direct censure of the Ministers, and the most unqualified condemnation of their conduct. Among other causes, to which, in this course, he attributed the unhappy change which had taken place in our public affairs, he particularly reprobated, in terms of the greatest bitterness, a court system, which he said, had been introduced and persevered in for the last fifteen years, of loosening and breaking all connection; destroying all faith and confidence; and extinguishing all principle, in different orders of the community. A few men, he said, had got an ascendency, where no man should have a personal ascendency; by having the executive powers of the state at their command, they had been furnished with the means of creating divisions, and familiarizing treachery. Thus were obscure and unknown men; men totally unacquainted with public business; pliable, not capable men; and the dregs, or renegades of parties, brought into the highest and most responsible stations; and by such men, was this once glorious empire reduced to its present state of danger and disgrace. Then rising into his usual force of expression: the spirit of delusion, he said, had gone forth.—The Ministers had imposed on the people. —Parliament had been induced to sanctify the imposition.—False lights had been held out to the country gentlemen.—They had been se-

duced into the support of a most destructive war under the impression, that the land tax would have been diminished by the means of an American revenue. But the visionary phantome thus conjured up for the basest of all purposes, that of deception, was now about to vanish.

The debate was long, animated, and well supported on both sides. The Ministers, though plainly somewhat depressed, defended themselves with resolution. They said they knew nothing of the private influence that had been talked of. That it was a topic taken up or laid down by men as it suited their views. That they never had imposed on the people or on parliament; but communicated such information as was true, provided it was safe. That they had never laid any thing false before them; but be the event what it would, they never would repent the vigorous steps they had taken for asserting the rights of parliament, and the dignity of their country. The question being at length put, the motion was rejected on a division by a majority of 40 to 19.

The noble Earl then immediately moved for an address, to lay before them copies of all the orders or treaties relative to the employment of the savages, acting in conjunction with the British troops against the inhabitants of the British colonies in North America, with a copy of the instructions given by General Burgoyne to Colonel St. Leger.

As no measure had ever been marked with a greater severity of language, or had excited stronger appearances of disgust and horror, than that, to which the motion related, the Ministers were accordingly very tender upon the subject, and could ill disguise the indignation and resentment which they felt, at its being so frequently and vexatiously brought within observation. And as the noble framer of the present motion, had been among the foremost in his censures on the subject, and that the bitterness of his late speech was not yet worn off; the matter was taken up with great warmth. The same arguments used to defend it in the House of Commons were relied upon in the Lords. The Ministry strongly asserted the justice and the propriety of the measure, on principle and on example. As Lord Chatham had asserted that when he was Minister, he had always declined to make use of so odious an instrument in the last war, though a foreign one, this assertion was flatly contradicted by the King's servants, who said they were able to lay before the House proof from the records of office, of his having given orders to treat with the savages for their assistance. Appeals were made to the noble Lord who then commanded in [30] America, and had taken his instructions from Mr. Pitt, at that time Secretary of State, whether he had not such in his army, and whether he was not authorised to use them. The Lords of the minority contended, that the case of a foreign war, where the affections of the people are no object, made a difference; and that the French had made use of the same instrument to a much greater degree, which might justify retaliation. The debate was attended with an unusual degree of charge, denial, personality, and acrimony; in which course of painful altercation, a noble Earl, who [31] had lately possessed a principal government in America, both took, and endured no inconsiderable share. The motion was at length thrown out by the previous question, about 11 o'clock at night, the majority being nearly the same as in the foregoing division.

Dec. 11th. The motion of adjournment, was scarcely less agitated in the House of Lords, than in that of the Commons. In the warmth of debate, a noble Lord high in office, having thrown out somewhat, which, [32] though apparently spoken in general terms, was understood as more particularly directed to the Earl of Chatham, and was interpreted as an assertion, "that no advice or opinion from Lords on that side would be received at the throne," this language was highly resented and severely reprehended by a noble Duke and Earl in opposition, who declared [33] it, besides being exceedingly presumptuous, to be no less unparliamentary and unconstitutional. The Sovereign, they said, had an undoubted right to chuse his servants; but in this moderate and popular government, he was likewise bound to chuse with wisdom; to consult the interests of the public, and in many situations even their likings, with respect to those Ministers, to whom he was entrusted to commit the direction and conduct of their dearest and most important concerns. And for any person, however high in office or situation, to venture to forerun the prerogative, to limit the royal discretion and right of action, by pretending to predict who should or should not be employed or consulted, and thus to proscribe wisdom, honesty, and ability from the public service, if they only happened to be exerted in opposition to ministerial measures, was equally indecent and injurious with respect to the crown, and dangerous to the rights of the people. In fact, it was no less, they said, than imputing sentiments to the Sovereign unbecoming his station, and directly repugnant to the duties prescribed to him by the constitution. After long debates, the motion of adjournment was carried upon a division, by a majority of 47 to 17.

Subscription for the American prisoners. State of public affairs. Scheme for raising a body of troops to supply the loss at Saratoga. Difficulties attending that measure. Subscriptions for raising new levies. Manchester and Liverpoole raise regiments. Failure of the attempt in the corporations of London and Bristol. Large private subscriptions in both cities. Several regiments raised in Scotland, and independent companies in Wales. Great debates in both Houses on the measure of raising forces without the knowledge or consent of parliament; and on the question of legality with respect to private contributions or benevolences. Motion in the committee of supply for cloathing the new forces, after long debates, carried upon a division. Earl of Abingdon's motion for summoning the judges on the question, overruled. His other motions for passing a censure on the measure, after long debates rejected upon a division.

GREAT complaints were about this time circulated, that the American prisoners in this country, who amounted to several hundreds, were treated with a degree of rigour which fell little short of cruelty. These rumours extended even to France; and occasioned the American deputies in that country, after an unsuccessful attempt to establish a cartel with the British Minister at Paris, to transmit a letter, couched in strong terms of complaint, to the first Lord of the Treasury upon the subject. This letter contained a particular charge, which, though we think not to be true in the manner stated, we are sorry not to have seen publicly refuted, viz. that a number of these unhappy people, were now in a state of bondage, on the coasts of Africa, and in the East Indies, who had been compelled to submit to that condition, under the menaces of an immediate and ignominious death. We have some reason to suppose that this charge related more particularly to some of those prisoners who had been taken in Canada, and who being partly terrified by threats, and partly unable to withstand the miseries of their confinement, which were aggravated for the purpose, entered as soldiers into our service, merely as a means of facilitating their escape. Several of these being taken in the act of desertion, and being liable to death by our military laws, which could afford no provision for the force or terror under which they had acted, possibly might have obtained their forfeit lives, on condition of their being sent to garrison some of our forts on the coast of Africa, or of their entering for life into the service of the East India company.

As to the prisoners who were kept in England, their penury and distress was undoubtedly great, and was much increased by the fraud and cruelty of those who were entrusted with the government and supply of their prisons. For these persons, who indeed never had any orders for ill treatment of the prisoners, or countenance in it, having however, not been overlooked with the utmost vigilance, besides their peculiar prejudices and natural cruelty, considered their offices only as lucrative jobs, which were created merely for their emolument. Whether there was not some exaggeration, as usually there is, in these accounts, it is certain, that though the subsistence allowed them by government, would indeed have been sufficient, if honestly administered, to have sustained human nature, in respect to the mere article of food, yet the want of clothes, firing, and bedding, with all the other various articles, which custom or nature render conducive to health and comfort, became particularly insupportable in the extremity of the winter. In consequence of complaints made

by the prisoners, the matter was very humanely taken up in the House of Peers by Lord Abingdon, who moved for accounts relative to their treatment; and soon after, a liberal subscription was carried on in London and other parts with the enlarged spirit which distinguishes this nation, and with only a slight opposition in the beginning, as being officiously supposed a measure not pleasing to Ministry. This subscription, co-operating with a stricter attention on the part of government, provided a sufficient remedy for the evil.

The loss of the northern army with respect to all future service in the American war, seemed a fatal check to that favourite system of conquest and unconditional submission, which had been so long and so stedfastly persevered in by the court. Nor were other matters relative to the war, much more favourable to the scheme of coercion. The successes on the side of Pensylvania, though many and considerable, and what in other cases would have been followed by more decisive effects, by no means answered the hopes that were formed on that expedition; nor did the present state of affairs there, indicate any such future advantage, as might countervail the loss in the other. The resources in Germany were nearly exhausted. Men were not only procured with difficulty, but one of the great powers, actually refused a passage through a skirt of his dominions, to a body of those which were already in the British service. Although this difficulty was evaded, at the expence of a long circuitous march, and much loss of time; it became however evident, from that and other circumstances, that the utmost which could be expected in future from that country, would be to recruit the German forces already in America.

Under these disagreeable circumstances with respect to Ame-

rica, the aspect of affairs was becoming every day more louring and dangerous in Europe. Indeed the conduct of the House of Bourbon had been long so unequivocal, that nothing less than that sort of blindness, in which the mind is too liable to be involved by the eagerness of a favourite pursuit, could have permitted the possibility even of a doubt, as to their present views, and ultimate designs. Yet notwithstanding all these difficulties, losses, and dangers, the system of conquest, or of compelling the Americans by force to a return of their duty, was so strongly supported, and so firmly adhered to, that it seems to have been still determined, in spite of loss and misfortune, to persevere in it to the last, and that even if it should be thought expedient to offer terms of peace, on which point there seemed to be some difference among the Ministers, yet all agreed, that whatever terms might be held out with the one hand, should be enforced with the sword by the other.

For the support of this determination, a measure of no small difficulty became, however, indispensably necessary. This was to establish such a body of new troops at home, as would not only supply the place of Burgoyne's army, but also help to fill up the wide chasms, which death, wounds, sickness and desertion, had made in the remaining force in America, by sending out full and complete regiments, to replace those who had suffered most in the war. For the sending any more of the old battalions from England or Ireland, without the leaving of some corps in their place, equal at least to them in point of number, was a measure which would have met with a violent opposition in both kingdoms. Nor can it possibly be supposed that the Ministers, however they found it necessary to disguise or conceal their sentiments, could be free from apprehension that the time was approaching, when our home force would be necessary for our home defence.

But although the necessity of raising a considerable body of new troops, was, on this ground of policy, sufficiently evident, the means of accomplishing that purpose were by no means so obvious. The late misfortune, and the little apparent room for hope which now remained of bettering our condition by force, afforded no encouragement for an application to parliament on the subject. It was evident indeed, that the Ministers, by the hastiness and length of the prorogation, and by some feeling expressions which dropped from one of them, chose at that time as little parliamentary conversation about America as possible; nor did they wish to renew it, until they should be able to afford better prospects of their strength and means of prosecuting the war, than at that time appeared.

In these circumstances, it was thought fitting to hazard an experiment on the zeal of those persons and parties, who had all along shewn the greatest eagerness in the prosecution of the American war; an experiment which would afford them also an opportunity of testifying their particular attachment and loyalty to the crown beyond the measure of parliamentary supply. By this means it was hoped that such a body of troops might be raised, without any previous application to parliament, and with the flattering appearance of saving expence in the first instance to the public, as would answer the desired purpose.

These expectations were not altogether ill founded. But as the measure carried an unconstitutional appearance, and might be made liable to the charge of interfering with the rights of parliament; and of violating some of those restrictions which it had been found

necessary to lay on the prerogative; besides the motives just now assigned; some considerable management was necessary as to the time and manner of making the experiment. For if it had been attempted during the actual sitting of parliament, it would not only have the whole weight of opposition to encounter whilst it was yet in embryo, and whilst the uncertainty of success would prevent its being supported with any spirit; but it could not be foreseen, how far their example and arguments might, in a matter of a new and doubtful nature, have extended beyond their own pale. Upon these accounts it was supposed, that the Minister thought it prudent, not only to make the experiment during the recess, but to render that longer than usual, in order to afford time for discovering its operation and effect before it underwent any discussion; being well satisfied, that when a business was once accomplished, any objections that were then made to the propriety or principle of the measure would be of little avail.

Some men of rank and influence, who had either adopted the measure from a conviction of its expedience and propriety, or who, upon advice, had engaged in its support and furtherance, used means in those places where their interest lay, both to found the disposition of the people, and to give it that direction which was necessary for the purpose. The towns of Manchester and Liverpoole, whether of their own motion, or through application, were the leaders in this business, which they engaged in with the greatest fervour, and immediately sent an offer to court to raise each a regiment of a thousand men. In other places, public meetings of towns, counties, and great corporate bodies, were encouraged, at which resolutions were proposed for the general levying of men for the service.

The setting of such an example by the city of London, would have been upon this occasion a matter of the greatest importance; not only from the ample support which that great body would have administered, if it had entered heartily into the measure; but from the countenance which it would have afforded to the ministers, the approbation it would have implied of their past, and the sanction it would have given to their future measures, together with the general effect which its conduct would have had upon the nation at large. Nor did the distance, coolness, frequent bickerings, and variance, which had for several years taken place between the court and the city, by any means exclude this idea. Several of the popular leaders in that body had, from various causes, lost much of their former weight and influence. Patronage and influence had also shifted hands much in the city since the commencement of the troubles. The great commercial orders for the foreign markets, which used to render the inferior citizens in a great measure dependent upon the capital wholesale dealers, and long established mercantile houses, were either now no more, or they were come into the possession of the contractors for carrying on the war, a vast and lucrative commerce, or centered in the monopoly lately set up under colour of licences. Thus all business being in the hands of people necessarily devoted to government, the elections went of course that way; and though the acclamations of the electors at all times, and the show of hands generally, announced a great majority in favour of the popular candidates, yet when it came to that serious point, where the elector's vote was to become a standing record, and to rise in judgment against him, if it went contrary to the will of his employer, it was not to be so much depended upon as in former times, when the employment of tradesmen was more at large.

To confirm and fecure their power, a numerous fociety was formed under the influence of the leaders of the court party, who were by themfelves denominated the affociated Livery, but were generally called the White Hart Affociation, from the tavern at which their principals held their great meetings, and which might be confidered as the head quarters of the party. This party grew exceedingly numerous and powerful; and great numbers of thofe who had at firft entered into the fociety merely for convenience, became at length partizans in the caufe, through the vexation which they continually fuffered, from the conftant reproach of their former fellows in public conduct and opinion, who now ftigmatized them as bafe deferters from the caufe of liberty, and betrayers of thofe rights of the city which they were fworn to maintain, and of that independency which they were bound by every tie to defend to the utmoft.

This affociation accordingly, had for fome time taken an avowed and active part in the city elections. For by advertifing in the public papers thofe candidates whom they were determined to fupport, thefe notices became in effect mandates to that great part of the livery, who were in fome degree within the reach or influence of their leaders, or who, from moderation of temper, prudence, or timidity, did not chufe to expofe themfelves to the enmity of fo numerous and powerful a party and fuch a compact collective body, acting under order, in ftrict union and concert, and enabled to bear any expence, by a large common ftock purfe, proved a ballance and more than a ballance to the popular focieties, which, from their difunion and other caufes, daily wafted away, and at length feem to have quite expired. The chief magiftrate of the city be-

longed alfo to this fociety, and was clofely connected in dealing with government.

Notwithftanding thefe favourable circumftances, the bufinefs was conducted with caution and addrefs. The chief magiftrate was faid to have received both inftruction and encouragement, in a place and fituation where they could not fail to have operated with uncommon efficacy. As a prelude to the opening of the bufinefs to the corporation, the Affociators advertifed for a public meeting on the fubject, where they expected to a certainty, that the appearance would have been fo numerous and refpectable in fupport of the meafure, and the affent fo univerfal in its favour, that they fhould then carry it to the greateft extent they wifhed, without difficulty, and perhaps without oppofition, in the Common Council. To their aftonifhment, however, they found themfelves deferted upon this occafion by the greater part of thofe, who had hitherto regularly obeyed all their mandates with refpect to election to city offices. Such was the effect of the original averfenefs from the American war, and fuch the difguft towards miniftry on the late unfavourable events, that the meeting was not only badly attended, but many of thofe who appeared prefented fuch captious faces, and the countenances in general were fo little promifing, that the leaders did not think it fafe to hazard the name, and in that all the influence and power of the party, by the propofal of any queftion, and the affembly broke up as it met, without entering upon any bufinefs whatever.

This difappointment was not capable of reftraining the induftry or checking the zeal of the chief magiftrate. He had newly refufed to call a court, when he fuppofed the bufinefs would have been contrary to his own liking, and that of his party, although a requifition in

writing, figned by the four reprefentatives of London in parliament, as well as by feveral other of the moft eminent citizens, had been prefented for the purpofe. And though he knew that this act had been productive of the moft unqualified cenfure, as being at leaft an unufual ftretch of his authority, yet fuperfeding all appearance of inconfiftency, by what he confidered as the urgent exigency of the public, he fuddenly called a court on this bufinefs.

The original intention was faid to be, that the city of London fhould raife and maintain a body of 5,000 men, to ferve for three years, or during the continuance of the war. But whether it was from the late failure at the Affociation, or whatever other caufe, no fpecification of number was included in the Jan. 16th, motion now made for 1778. the purpofe; it being only propofed, that a bounty fhould be granted by the city for the raifing of men for the land and fea fervice.

A full loofe was now given to thofe refentments which the popular party had for fome time been hoarding; and the debates became exceedingly warm. It was contended, in fupport of the motion, that in the prefent perilous fituation in which we ftood with refpect to our natural enemies, it became an abfolute and indifpenfable obligation on that great city to give the moft public teftimonial of its duty, affection, and loyalty; that the fame motives equally concurred, with the additional fpur of intereft joined to the defire of fecurity, in their affording every affiftance in their power, towards exterminating the feeds of rebellion on the other fide of the Atlantic, and reducing our colonies to fubmiffion and order; that the late lofs we had fuftained could only be replaced by the moft vigorous exertions; that every man fhould contribute to the public de-

36

fence, in times of public danger; and that the city of London had ever stood forth as an example to the rest of the nation in perilous seasons, and had always been distinguished with honour for her spirit and exertion in the most critical situations of danger.

On the other side it was answered, that it would be the greatest and most ridiculous of absurdities, for the city now to countenance and support coercive measures, after having so repeatedly, and even recently, reprobated this unhappy and destructive civil war in all its parts, and recommended conciliation in the strongest terms, in all those numerous addresses which they had presented to the throne on the subject. That the city had already suffered most essentially in her commercial concerns, by those fatal measures which had plunged us in our present unhappy situation; that it was evident to every unprejudiced person, that national ruin must be the inevitable consequence of their continuance. That undoubtedly London had ever been distinguished by her loyalty, her free support of government, and her magnanimous exertions in all cases of national emergency; but these instances were in cases, wherein wise measures had involved us in just wars, for the maintenance of the national interest and honour; the same disposition and principles which operated on her conduct in those particulars, equally forbade her support of unjust, oppressive, and tyrannical measures; more especially when they terminated in a cruel civil war, the destruction of our own people, and tended directly to the ruin of this late flourishing empire. In conclusion, they summed up the arguments in such a manner, as to bring their principal force within two points of view, in each of which the condemnation of the motion was included; first, as a measure tending to revive and inflame the embers of a war, unjust in itself, and ruinous to this country; and secondly, as being contradictory and absurd upon the face of their own former proceedings.

The motion was supported by a majority of eleven to nine in the court of Aldermen; but thrown out by so great a majority of the Common Council, that while the lowest calculation held it at three to one, it was estimated by the highest at 180 to 30. Upon this complete victory, a resolution was moved and passed, which condemned in strong terms the giving any countenance to, or being in any manner instrumental in the further continuance of the present ruinous and destructive war. Notice was at the same time given, that an address, petition, and remonstrance, should be moved for at the next court, praying, " that his Majesty would offer such terms to our American brethren, as would put a stop to the present calamitous war." During the agitation of the original question, the chief magistrate was handled with unprecedented severity, under the double charge, which was made in the most flat and unqualified terms, of his having been closetted for the exertion of his public interest and official authority in this business, and of his being also under the mean influence of self-interest, in the view of procuring a contract for the supply of the new forces with certain articles which were manufactured or prepared in his own calling. Nor was the general reprehension of the court less when the business was over, for the glaring partiality, as they said, of his conduct, the shortness of notice, and informality with which they were convened, and the dangerous attempt to carry a question of such importance by surprize. These matters were pushed so seriously, that a formal and public enquiry into the authority by which he had been guided, was not only mentioned, but the proposal with some difficulty evaded.

Such was the ill success that attended this attempt in the city of London.

Upon this defeat the disappointed party said, that the deficiency of loyalty in the corporation should not damp its spirit in individuals; and that at a time when subscriptions were publicly opened and quickly filled for American rebels, it was surely the least that could be done by the well-affected and friends to royalty, to subscribe liberally to the support of King and government. A subscription was accordingly opened, and a committee appointed at the London Tavern to conduct the business; and as it took its rise among monied men, and that the leaders and principal proposers were necessarily liberal in their contributions, above 20,000l. was soon subscribed. As the advertisements which they published in the papers upon this occasion, became a subject of much discussion and censure both within doors and without, we shall transcribe the passage which gave such particular offence; viz. " At a meeting of " several merchants and others, " friends to their King and coun- " try, in order to support the " constitutional authority of Great " Britain over her rebellious colo- " nies in America; it was unani- " mously resolved and agreed, " that a voluntary subscription be " opened for the above purpose; " and that the money arising " therefrom be applied, under the " direction of a committee of the " subscribers, in raising men for " his Majesty's service, in such " manner as his Majesty in his " wisdom shall think fit."

A similar attempt was made in Bristol to induce the corporation to raise a body of men. The event was also similar. The design failed with respect to the corporate body; but a number of names to large sums of money appeared in a private subscription, which rivalled in the amount that at London. But whether it proceeded from the difcuffion which this manner of raifing or granting money underwent in parliament, or from whatever caufe, we do not find that either of thefe fubfcriptions were productive of any great effect. Neither did the intended meafure fucceed better in the counties. A ftrong government intereft was foiled in Norfolk; and the attempt produced a petition of uncommon force and energy from the freeholders of the county to parliament againft the American war. Nor was the attempt of a noble Lord in Warwickfhire more fuccefsful. Sub-[37] fcriptions were indeed opened, in different places, by thofe who were, or who would be thought, particularly attached to government.

In Scotland it was thought proper to give encouragement to the raifing of new regiments; a meafure which was adopted there with the greateft avidity. The cities of Edinburgh and Glafgow fubfcribed liberally; raifed a regiment of a thoufand men each; and were indulged, like Manchefter and Liverpoole, with the nomination of officers. Several individuals undertook and performed the raifing of regiments in the Highlands. The conditions were generally the fame, and very advantageous both to the raifers and to the officers. Several independent companies, amounting to fomething about a regiment in point of number, were raifed in Wales; but the battalions, excepting thofe of Manchefter and Liverpoole, were all formed in Scotland.

The minifters had thoroughly fhaken off their panic during the recefs. The raifing of the new forces not only enabled them again to fupport the American fyftem, which fcarcely before feemed tenable; but it afforded no contemptible teftimony, and which in argument was eafily advanced to a proof, that their conduct received the full approbation of the people, and that the general fenfe of the nation went with them in their meafures. Thus they were enabled to meet parliament with confidence; and, under fo efficacious a fupport as the public voice and approbation, to brave all enquiries into paft conduct, as well as into the prefent ftate or condition of the nation.

Indeed the facility with which thefe enquiries were agreed to in the hour of tribulation and difmay, it is probable, was now fufficiently regretted. But it was hoped, that the fpirit which was now raifed, and the parliamentary modes of defeating the objects of all enquiry, would take away all effect of the advantage which they had fuffered the oppofition to obtain over them.

Notwithftanding this fmooth ftate of affairs at home, the minifters were far from being at eafe. Majorities and acts of parliament, though poffeffing wonderful efficacy in their proper place, were neither capable of reclaiming our revolted colonies, nor of preventing the defigns of our foreign enemies. It has fince appeared from the moft indubitable evidence, that adminiftration had for fome time been in poffeffion of information from the Britifh Minifter at Paris, not only of the negociation for a commercial treaty between that court and the Americans, but alfo of another private and confidential treaty, which was conducted with the moft profound fecrecy, and fraught with matter of the moft dangerous nature to this country. How this knowledge is to be reconciled with the public meafures then purfued, we have no bufinefs to examine.

The firft bufinefs that was taken up by the oppofition in both houfes, was the meafure of raifing the new levies during the recefs. Sir P. J. Clerke obferved in the Houfe of Commons, that he had

Jan. 22d, 1778.

promifed feveral of his neighbours in the country to make an enquiry into the bufinefs. That the people had been told, that the American war was the war of parliament; and that they were therefore exceedingly alarmed, to hear that a large body of forces had been raifed during the recefs, not only without the knowledge or advice of parliament, but without the fmalleft intimation having been given by the Minifter before the adjournment, that any fuch fcheme was even in contemplation. That, on the contrary, they had heard the noble Lord had informed the Houfe, that he fhould have a conciliatory propofition to lay before them at their next meeting, which he hoped would prove highly advantageous to this country. But that inftead of a peace, he faid, the noble Lord had produced an army; and what was ftill worfe, an army raifed under the aufpices of perfons who had never been noted for loyalty to their Sovereign, or attachment to the conftitution. The grand object of his enquiry, he faid, was to know in what hands the fword was entrufted; for however neceffary it might be to raife troops for this or any other war, it was abfolutely incumbent on them to take care that the fword was placed in fafe hands; and that it might not be turned againft themfelves.

He accordingly moved for an addrefs, that an account of the number of troops ordered to be raifed during the late adjournment, with a fpecification of the different corps, the names of the officers appointed to their command, and alfo the names of all the officers appointed to ferve in each rank in the different corps, with the time of their former fervice and rank in the army, fhould be laid before them.

The motion being agreed to, the Minifter took that opportunity of declaring the happinefs he felt in being able to inform the Houfe, that the original purposes of the adjournment had not only been answered by the active exertions which had been used in the several departments of the public service, but that the voluntary unsolicited efforts of several loyal subjects had likewise contributed to that effect. That a subscription had lately been set on foot in several parts of the kingdom, which not only intimated the most valid indications of truly patriotic zeal, but which also afforded the most flattering testimony of the public satisfaction in the conduct of administration. That it was no small comfort and encouragement, to persons entrusted with the management of public affairs, to find that the general opinion entertained of their conduct and measures, was not to be influenced by contingencies, nor to give way to those unexpected and unlucky accidents of fortune, which no sagacity could foresee, nor human wisdom provide against; and that it must afford a pleasure peculiarly grateful to every true Englishman, to see the spirit and fortitude of the people rise with their difficulties, and in the present state of public emergency, to shine out in so particularly conspicuous a manner.

This self congratulation, and approbation of the measure by the Minister, drew out its absolute condemnation from the opposition, who charged it with being equally unconstitutional, illegal, extravagant, and dangerous. They asked why parliament was not informed of the design? Why so long a recess was made, at a time that so important and so dangerous a measure, as the raising of an army within the kingdom, was in contemplation? They said, that if the raising of one regiment, in so unconstitutional a manner, was to be maintained or justified, the same arguments would reach to twenty, fifty, or to any given number. If this doctrine was admitted, what fence or protection could the laws or the constitution afford against arbitrary power? The friends and promoters of that system, in order to establish their favourite mode of government, would have nothing more to do, than, in the absence of parliament, under the colour of loyalty, or pretence of danger, to promote subscriptions for the raising of troops; and when these were once embodied and armed, would their arguments, their silent votes, or their resolutions, within them walls, or any act of theirs without, prevent, even for a moment, the subversion of the constitution? With respect to the purposes for the effecting of which those troops were raised, and the supposed necessity arising from the general state of public affairs, as well as from the unhappy war with our colonies, they said, that either parliament had no right at all to interfere in such matters, or they were the best and only proper judges, both of the purposes and the necessity. They concluded by warning the Ministers with great bitterness, that although the essence of the constitution was lost, it behoved them still to preserve at least the forms of it; and not to venture, under the subterfuge of a long adjournment, contrived by themselves for the purpose, to exercise the great constitutional, and indivisible power of parliament, that of granting money. For, they insisted, that the present measure was virtually no less; the Ministers had incurred the actual expenditure, and bound the faith of parliament in the first instance, and then they call upon the Commons, as a matter of course, to provide for that expenditure.

The Minister defended the measure on several grounds; on that of necessity; on the impracticability of communicating, what was not known to the Ministers themselves at the time of adjournment; and lastly, he insisted, that the measure was in itself perfectly innocent, with respect both to constitution and law. The necessity, he presumed, would not be disputed; the arguments used, and the positions laid down every day on the other side, went to the establishment as an undoubted fact, that the present force in America was not adequate to its purpose. If then the colonies should obstinately persist in rejecting all reasonable terms of accommodation, the right policy, the œconomy, and the wisdom, of using the most vigorous exertions to bring the contest to a speedy conclusion, and to render the ensuing campaign decisive, was so obvious, that it must surely flash conviction on all parties and orders of men. He said it was not in the power of administration before the recess, to bring the matter as a measure before parliament, because, in fact, except in a very few instances, they were totally ignorant of what afterwards happened. Offers, indeed, had been made; but how far the spirit would have extended; or in what instances it might have been thought proper to receive or reject such offers, were matters at that time unknown. And, as to the charges thrown out with so much vehemence and acrimony, of illegality, breach of the constitution, and contempt of parliament, he denied that they were in any degree founded. The American war, he said, was a constitutional and a popular war; it was particularly a parliamentary war; what then could be more constitutional, than the offers made by the people, and accepted of by the crown? The right and authority of the supreme legislature was denied; arms had been taken up by our rebellious subjects in America, in maintenance of that denial; a numerous, and very loyal part of the people at home, had expressed their abhorrence of so unnatural a rebellion; and, in proof of the sincerity of their sentiments, offered their persons and their purses in support of the constitutional rights of their country. Was so laudable an action, ever before marked with such reproach and condemnation.

The House being in a committee of supply on the 4th of February, a motion was made by the Secretary at War, that the sum of 286,632l. 14s. 6d. should be granted for cloathing the new forces, for the current year; this motion occasioned a renewal of the debate, which was supported with great vigour on both sides. We shall, however, without distinction of time or place, bring together in one point of view, the most material arguments which were offered at different times in either House, upon a subject which was so much, and so warmly agitated in both.

We have already seen the ground taken by the Minister in defence of the measure. In the further prosecution of the question, the point of legality was principally supported on the ground of precedent, drawn from the time of the rebellion in the year 1745, and the beginning of the late war. In the former of these æras, several of the nobility and gentry raised regiments at their own expence; and subscriptions were not only opened and received, but persons went about from house to house to collect money for the common defence; in which case, though no absolute force was used, it was well understood, that a refusal to contribute, however unwilling any individual might be, or however ill it might suit, with the real, though secret state of his circumstances, would subject him to be marked as disaffected, and render his future situation in that neighbourhood disagreeable and uneasy. In the latter instance, ten new regiments had been raised by the crown; and the city of London had subscribed a large sum of money (which example was followed by other corporations and public bodies) for the raising of men for the public service. The first of these measures, they said, having been cavilled at by the disaffected of that time, and also by others, who though well disposed to government, yet either doubted its being constitutional, or directly questioned its legality; the late Lord Chancellor Hardwicke, whose principles with respect to the constitution, and to the rights and security of the subject, can never be called in doubt, publicly undertook, with his usual ability, its support and defence, and, whilst he asserted its legality and propriety, reprehended the censure thrown upon it in strong and decisive terms. And with respect to the second, so far from its being then objected to; Mr. Secretary Pitt, wrote a most florid letter to the corporation of London, full of acknowledgements, in the King's name, for their zeal and immediate service, as well as for the laudable example which they had set to others.[38]

A great law Lord, at the head of his profession, said, that although the Bill of Rights declared, that to keep a standing army within the kingdom in time of peace, was contrary to law; yet that provision in the declaration of rights, could by no means apply to the present question, when we were not only in a state of war, but engaged in a war of a most important and eventful nature. One of the law officers in the House of Commons, said, that the Bill of Rights law spoke for itself, and was conditional; and that the Mutiny Act, was regulating, not restrictive: that if it was not, it would be the most dangerous law that ever was enacted; for it must be construed so as entirely to tie up the King's hands, from using proper means for the defence or preservation of the kingdom; let the exigencies of the times, or the necessities of the state, be what they may. His second, in that House, also contended, that con-[39][40][41]tributions, really and purely voluntary, were legal in the strictest sense of the word. Some other gentlemen of the same profession in that House, and who were usually on the same side, considered the measure as illegal; but said, that as the rebellion ought to be quelled by any means whatever, the means in this instance must be justified by the necessity, and they would therefore vote for the supply.

Another great law Lord, in the other House, said, that the King, by his prerogative, was empowered to levy men and raise an army. When men were raised, the new levies were reported to parliament; whose duty it then was, if they judged the measure right and necessary, to provide for their subsistence; or otherwise, if they disapproved of the measure, to pass their censure on it by giving a negative to the supply, which was in effect a resolution for disbanding the troops. With respect to the argument so much urged and insisted on, that parliament ought to be consulted as to the raising of men, previous to new levies of any kind; he said, that long experience had shewn the impolicy of such a custom, and therefore it was never practised. The King in raising an army, as in making a subsidiary treaty, never applied to parliament till after each was effected; and it had for ages been deemed a sufficient security to the constitution, that parliament had it in its power to disband the one, or to set aside the other, by passing its negative upon either. The noble Lord said it was a fact well known, that every man might give the King money; it was equally well known, that every man might either leave or give the King land; it had been often done, and no person ever dreamed of its being illegal. That there could not be a greater misrepresentation than in comparing the present subscriptions to benevolences: the donations so nominat-[42]

ed in antient times, though called free-gifts, were notoriously the contrary; men were, when a commission for public benevolences to the crown was issued, compelled to contribute, and if they refused, or withheld their proportion, they lost their liberty, and were sent to prison. Let it be considered what the purpose was of the present subscriptions; it was generously and laudably to assist the King with levy money; a matter often practised, and always essentially serviceable to the state. The nation could not possibly be injured. The public subscriptions went to furnish additional levy money, to make the bounties larger than government usually gave, and by that means to quicken and render more easy the filling of the old corps, and the completing of the army. Supposing even that more men were raised than the number allotted by parliament, what would the consequence be? Nothing more, than that the crown must apply to them for subsistence money to maintain those extra troops. It would then be in the power of either House to negative the new levies, by refusing the supply, who must of course be disbanded. In this final upshot of things, the new recruits would have to return home, with the money in their pockets which they had received from the bounty of the subscribers; and these latter, who could be the only losers, would sacrifice so much money as a testimony of their loyalty and zeal. But what mischief or loss could the nation thereby suffer? Or what injury could the liberties of the subject, or the privileges of parliament sustain, by any part of the transaction.

It was said, that the unqualified censure and reproach, which was thrown upon the places and countries where the levies were made, and upon the men of whom they were composed, were equally unjust and ungenerous. What happy

spot of our island could be shewn, which, in the long course of our dissentions and civil wars, had not undergone the censure, or suffered under the taint of rebellion? Was it then equitable or reasonable to stigmatize every district or country, which had ever produced a rebel, or a band of rebels? Were the sins of the fathers to rain down for ever upon the heads of their descendants through all generations? Or what was still, if possible, more absurd and unjust, were those whose ancestors had been entirely innocent, or even perhaps meritorious, to undergo the same common curse and punishment, only because they had the misfortune of being born in the same country, and breathing the same air? A part of the people in question, had by their eminent services in the last war, sufficiently atoned for any faults or crimes imputable to their ancestors, and freely washed out with their blood, any stigma which the conduct of the latter could be supposed to leave on their country.

On the other side it was said, that those precedents which had been quoted, did not in any degree come up to the question, or in any manner justify the present measure. In times of great public danger, and circumstances of uncommon exigency, what at other periods would not only be imprudent but illegal, might become warrantable. The tyrant's plea, state necessity, had occasionally given a sanction to many measures which were not strictly justifiable with regard to the constitution. On this ground, and on no other, the raising of regiments, and other acts in the service of government, during the immediate danger of the last rebellion, either were, or could be excused. In the year 1745, besides being involved in a dangerous foreign war, a most inveterate rebellion was raised within the kingdom, which went to the direct subversion of the constitu-

tion, and the total overthrow of all our civil and religious rights. Rebellion then stalked with giant strides towards the capital; and was approaching fast to the gates of the palace. In such a moment of imminent danger, when all law, government, property, and personal security were at stake, every other consideration and matter must necessarily give way, to self preservation and immediate defence. The situation, which threw us back into a temporary state of nature, superseded all other considerations. It was then undoubtedly right to provide for the public safety, by the best means which the nature of the case would admit; and when both the laws and the constitution were at stake, it would be ridiculous to hesitate at a temporary violation of them for their defence.—But how, said they, did that case resemble this of America, where the time did not press; where the enemy was three thousand miles off; and where we had still a vast fleet and army, both victorious? This is not a measure taken from necessity to be referred to a parliament not then sitting—but a parliament actually sitting is prorogued for the purpose of carrying the measure into execution.

The latter instances, they said, were still more remote in all their parts from the present question. The new regiments which were raised in the beginning of the late war, had the virtual sanction of parliament. A standing act, called an act of credit, had been passed in favour of his late Majesty, by which the sanction of parliament was granted in certain predicaments, to all the operations of the crown. (This position was, however, controverted; and the act of credit was said to be of a later date, than the raising of the forces.) But without any such sanction, the addresses of both Houses, upon the subject of the war, and of the national defence, [43] or even the vicinity, and alarming preparation of the enemy, would have sufficiently justified the measure.

As to the subscriptions raised by the city of London and other public bodies during the late war, they were said to have been disposed of in the most constitutional manner; they were not applied to raise or maintain an army independent of parliament, but to further the public service, by granting premiums to recruits for the filling up of the old regiments, and to seamen, or able landmen, for manning the navy. But in the present instance, 15,000 men are raised, or appointed to be raised, during the fitting, and without the consent or knowledge of parliament; whilst a self-created body of men at the London Tavern, venture to propose themselves as a substitute for parliament, and to assume its most essential property, and inalienable right and authority, that of granting money, which is to be disposed of without its controul, either to the maintenance of this new army, or to any other purpose which the wisdom of the crown, or in reality its Ministers, might deem fitting.

A great law Lord, who had [44] some years ago filled the first civil office under the crown with high and universal applause, reprobated the measure in all its parts, as well as much of the doctrine which was now advanced by his professional opponents in its support. He pronounced the measure of raising troops, without the consent, and during the fitting of parliament, to be absolutely illegal, unconstitutional, and a high violation of the fundamental privileges of parliament. That, to judge of the necessities of the state, in point of measures offensive or defensive, and to make provision accordingly, was of the very essence of parliament; and that to take any measure therefore, while the parliament was in being, and of course in an active, and not passive state, without previous information, consultation, and advice, was an act little short of superseding its authority, and stripping it of its rights. And that the committees at the London Tavern and at Bristol, had acted a daringly illegal, and truly alarming part; they had assumed a legislative power, and had acted in that capacity, in which, according to the spirit of the constitution, and the express meaning of the Bill of Rights, parliament only were empowered to act. He concluded by declaring, that both the measure, and the arguments which were brought in support of it by the two learned Lords in high office, tended to no less in their consequences, than the utter subversion of the constitution.

A lawyer of the first eminence [45] in his profession, and who had also been, some years before, one of the first law officers of the crown in the other House, entered more deeply into the question of legality, with respect to the raising of men; after a most curious and learned investigation of the law, commencing with it as it stood before the custom of raising or keeping mercenary soldiers in time of peace had been practised, and brought down to the introduction of the mutiny act, he drew from thence a positive deduction, that there was not the colour of support, afforded either by the common or statute law, nor even by the acts of usurped prerogative, to the doctrine of making levies without the consent, and during the fitting of parliament.

Others quoted the standing preamble to the annual Mutiny Act, which expressly declares, that the King shall not raise an army within the kingdom in time of peace. They asked, if the offensive measures carried on by government at its own discretion, in endeavouring to quell a rebellion at 3,000 miles distance, could be considered as endangering the internal security of this country in such a degree, as could warrant so flagrant a violation of the constitution and laws? They observed that standing armies had been the constant engines of tyranny, by which the civil rights and liberties of the people had been destroyed in every state in Europe. And that the principal argument used on the other side, namely, " that there could be no danger in the raising of an army by the crown, as parliament must be applied to for its payment," was not only overthrown by the very act which it was brought to defend, but that that position shewed the enormity and danger of the act in the strongest colours; for the army is not only raised, but the example is set, and reduced to practice, how money may be provided for the support of that army, without the concurrence or controul of parliament.

Nor did the question of benevolences and free gifts, undergo less discussion, nor their being again brought into practice, incur less censure, than the doctrine of raising forces without the participation of parliament. They were declared to have been illegal at all times, and in all the stages of the constitution. Benevolences, they said, were first introduced in the turbulent, distracted, and bloody times of Edward the fourth. They were among the numberless deplorable consequences of our unhappy civil wars of that period; and had been constantly and uniformly condemned by all our great legal and constitutional authorities. They had been suppressed by two acts of parliament. And even in the arbitrary reign of James the first, when he attempted to procure benevolences in a manner exactly similar to the present, by sending his confidential servants to different parts of the kingdom to raise spontaneous and voluntary subscriptions; although the measure was unaccompanied with any circumstance of force whatever, yet Mr. St. John, who was esteemed the best constitutional lawyer in the kingdom, and who became afterwards Lord Chief Justice, opposed those subscriptions with the greatest vehemence, and declared, (along with other still stronger expressions) that the attempt to get money for the King's use in that way, was a breach of his Majesty's coronation oath; and that it was no less than an abetting of perjury, in all those who subscribed. And although Mr. St. John was prosecuted in the Star Chamber, he was acquitted; and the most arbitrary and tyrannous court that ever existed, has thereby left a judgment on record, that resistance to such subscriptions, by any means, or in any language, is not reprehensible.

They said, that every gift to the crown for public purposes, was an aid, and had been early and wisely marked out, as a breach of the privileges of parliament. The evident spirit of the constitution at all times, and independent of any particular laws, which were only passed to cure some immediate violation of it, was, that the crown should receive no supplies whatever, but through the medium of parliament; for that would be to make the crown independent of parliament, and of course to render parliament an useless burthen to the nation. Money is power; money produces armies; and the liberties of all countries must fall before armies.

The Bill of Rights declares, " That the levying of money for, or to the use of the crown, by pretence of prerogative without grant of parliament, or for a longer time, or in any other manner, than the same is or shall be granted, is illegal." If it cannot be denied, that to levy money is to raise it, it must be equally acknowledged, that the measure under consideration, has consisted in the raising of money to the use of the crown without grant of parliament; and

that for the worst and most dangerous of all possible purposes, the raising of an armed force independent of parliament.

To shew that they had not introduced novel doctrines upon the subject, and as an instance, that the concurrence of parliament had at all times been deemed necessary to render even voluntary benevolences legal, they quoted the statute of the 13th of Charles the Second, by which, they said, it appeared, that notwithstanding the madness of joy with which a great part of the nation was seized at the restoration, and the consequent disposition to make almost any concessions to the crown, together with the inevitable distresses which that Prince laboured under, in consequence of his long banishment and penury; yet the parliament of that time, although too tender to lay any additional burthens upon the people, would not suffer the precedent to be established, of his pressing wants being supplied, by any aid or benevolence from the wealthy and well disposed part of his subjects, without the authority of an express and positive law for the purpose. They accordingly passed the law in question, by which the term for the receiving of benevolences, to be purely voluntary, was not only limited to a moderate period; but the folly, prodigality, and vanity of individuals, was guarded against, by a strict limitation of the sums of money which they were allowed to bestow upon the crown; no Commoner being permitted to exceed 200l. nor Peer to exceed 400l. in his benevolence.

They observed, that the present measure overthrew the only colourable argument which had ever been brought, to justify the conduct of parliament in endeavouring to tax the colonies, and thereby bringing on the present nefarious war, with all the fatal consequences which are still to attend or succeed their final loss.

It had been held out, " That if the colonies, now that they were grown powerful and opulent, gave free grants to the crown, as they had hitherto customarily done upon requisition, the crown might become independent on parliament for supplies." This, they said, became the constant cry of Ministers to amuse and to deceive the people; and the cloak to hide their worst designs. The unparalleled self denial, and patriotism of the crown, in thus rejecting a proffered tyranny, became also, under their immediate direction or influence, not only the constant theme of praise with the whole tribe of ministerial writers; but the standing doctrine, and the unceasing source of flattery in the pulpit, with all those prudent and numerous labourers in the vineyard, who did not wish to sow their seed in a barren or ungrateful soil. And the terrifying apprehension of danger arising from the foregoing ministerial position, was continually held out as a scarecrow to parliament, until they were at length driven into those toils of absurdity in which they resolved, That the American legal assemblies should not give and grant their own money, lest they should render the crown independent of parliament, but that they themselves would give and grant the American money, without its real owners having any share at all in its disposition. And shall we now, said they, suffer the same measure to be adopted and carried into execution at home, and under our noses, by private persons, the prevention of which in legislative bodies, was the pretext for involving us in that unnatural and savage war by which we have lost America.

In the House of Commons, the manner of raising the new forces, was no less condemned in point of political œconomy, with respect to expence; inefficacy in point of purpose; and injustice to the old standing corps of the army; than in what related to the laws and the constitution. They insisted, that upon every principle of œconomy, and every idea of military judgment; the augmentation, if at all necessary, should have been effected, by filling up the old regiments to their full war complement, which was the method practised in the last, as well as in others of our former wars. By that means, an equally numerous, and a much more effectual addition in point of service, would have been made to the army. Every military man, said they, will acknowledge the extreme difficulty in the act, as well as the great length of time that is necessary, to the forming of a body of men, who are all entirely raw, and all equally unacquainted with arms, to military habits, discipline, and a necessary adroitness in their evolutions and mechanical exercises. Whereas if a third, or even an equal number of the same men, are incorporated with the steady veterans of an old regiment, they become soldiers insensibly; and the discipline of the one, being supported by the bodily strength and vigour of the other, they will form a joint body nearly invincible.

They proceeded to examine what real benefit the public would derive from the so much boasted generosity of the subscribers and raisers of regiments. They estimated the expence of raising a thousand new levies, at about 5000l. and for so much money, supposing the subscriptions to be real and voluntary gifts, and that those men were applied to the filling up of old battalions; they allowed, that the public would be obliged to, and really benefited by the generosity or patriotism of the subscribers. But instead of this œconomical, wise, and established practice, on the side of the public, and this disinterested generosity, on that of the individual, what is the real state of the case? The public receives with one hand from a contractor, under the name of a free-gift for the raising of men, a very small portion of what it is giving to him with the other in a contract; and to complete this curious bubble, the thousand men are formed into a new regiment for the benefit of the raisers; who, if they chuse to sell the commissions, will receive three or four times as much ready money for them, as the amount of the whole expence in raising the men; and for this imaginary present of 5000l. the public must pay at least 30,000l. which is the lowest estimate at which the full and half-pay of the officers can be rated. Thus, if the 16 regiments, now raising, or in contemplation, can be completed, the whole extent of the supposed gratuities to the public will amount to 80,000l. for which the nation is to pay, at the lowest computation, no less than 480,000l. Such, said they, are the disinterested benefits offered to the nation by contractors, addressers, and schemers; such the political wisdom, and prudent œconomy of our Ministers; and such the attention they pay to alleviate those distresses, which they have themselves brought upon a ruined and unhappy people.

Nor was the injury and injustice offered by this measure to the army, and the prejudice to the service in general, less, they said, than the imposition upon the public, and the danger which it held out to the constitution. Rank and promotion were given in a new and unprecedented manner. New and unknown men, or only known by their having obtained commissions in those new regiments, which were suddenly raised and as suddenly broken at the tail of the late war, were now brought forwards from their obscurity, to jump at once over the heads and to take the lead of those brave officers, who had served with the most distinguished reputation in both wars, and who were at this instant shedding their blood, or sacrificing their constitutions, in the desart forests, or under the burning suns of America. Gentlemen had been appointed to the command of regiments, who were never in the service before, to the great injury and discouragement of all the officers of the army. If it was necessary or determined, they said, to raise new regiments, they should in justice have been offered to the oldest Lieutenant Colonels in the service; who would not only have gladly embraced the offer upon the present terms; but who would individually, if such a bargain had been fitting for government, have advanced considerable sums of money for the purchase of the opportunity. And, as to the recruiting service for the old regiments in the usual manner, it was not only entirely annihilated by this measure, but the extraordinary premiums now given, must necessarily cause an extraordinary desertion from the established corps.

They said, that persecution was as opposite to their principles as injustice. They did not wish to visit the crimes of the fathers upon the children. They had given the clearest proofs of the contrary disposition; and persons in the minority, had not only been consenting, but even been forward and active in the restoration of deserving men, who had by their good service expiated the crime of former rebellions. As little could they be suspected of meaning to proscribe particular countries for being fertile in rebellion. But it was impossible to avoid suspecting the motives to the subscriptions, or the purposes for which the new levies were raised; when it was seen that the contributors to the former were chiefly contractors, would-be contractors, jobbers, and other such like vermin of the state, who gave a penny to the public purse with a view of robbing it of a pound, and that the latter, with a marked and singular care and predilection,

46

were entirely the offspring of places, which had at all times been notorious for their Jacobite principles, and which had produced many of those who were deeply and principally concerned in the last rebellion. That such sudden and unaccountable professions or appearances of loyalty from such persons, could not fail of exciting doubt and jealousy in any case; and afforded great room for believing in the present, that they had rather changed their object, and abandoned in a fit of despair, that man in whose cause they had formerly been so active, than that they had by any means relinquished those high, prerogative, and arbitrary principles, which had so peculiarly attached them to him and his family. But when it was also considered that these very men, were the principal addressers for enslaving three millions of their fellow-subjects in America, are still the advocates for continuing all the calamities and horrors of the present cruel and unnatural war, and are now the first to take up arms in this country, and the only persons entrusted with them, common sense will tell us, that there is something more than loyalty or attachment to the House of Hanover in this conduct on their side; and that upon the whole, it is full time for every person who loves his country, and reveres its constitution as established at the revolution, to be seriously alarmed for both.

Some few in both Houses, carried the charge of partiality in the court, and the danger of placing the sword in improper hands, which was coupled along with it, to a still greater length. They said, that although they had no prejudices with respect to persons being born on one or the other side of a hill or a river, yet when so manifest a predilection was shewn to certain particular districts, as to confine the raising of a whole army (and in so extraordinary a

manner) entirely within them, to the utter exclusion of the rest of the nation; and when it was also considered, that those people, so favoured and selected, were themselves tainted with the most incorrigible prejudices, and the most violent animosity, to the country, the constitution, or to both, it was impossible not to be alarmed at the consequences. They said, that there were many gentlemen of the best and noblest families in England, who had dedicated their lives with the most distinguished zeal and spirit to the military service of their country; and who having fought our foreign battles, with great glory to themselves, and advantage to the nation, and being also deeply interested in the preservation of the state, were not only the proper persons to be entrusted with its defence, but were also entitled to such rewards as attended that distinction. It was upon this ground, that a noble Earl who had moved for the opinion of the judges on the question of the new levies in the House of Lords, declared in his place, that if the legality of the measure was established, he also would raise a regiment, not for the purpose of its going to America, but that of remaining in England, to assist in protecting our liberties.

The expedient of redeeming public credit by an application to private benevolence, and of supporting the boasted dignity and authority of government, by sending about a begging box for the benefit of the treasury, were thrown into various shades of ridicule, in which the produce of the subscriptions to the regiments, and the state of subscription to the loans and rates of the publick funds were set in opposition, and the incompetency of the one to the support of the other exposed in many ludicrous points of view.

The question being at length put in the committee of supply, upon the Secretary at war's mo-

tion, that 286,632l. 14s. 6d. should be granted for cloathing the new forces, it was carried upon a division, by a majority of 223 to 130. The having any division upon a question of supply, and its being opposed by so considerable a minority, were two unusual circumstances which attended this motion. The debate was warmly renewed on the next day, being the 5th of February, upon receiving the report from the committee, but the question was again carried. We do not remember any business which created so much heat in parliament.

This business was introduced in the House of Lords by the Earl of Abingdon, who having given previous notice soon after the recess, moved, on the 27th of January, " That a day be fixed for summoning the judges to attend this House, in order to take their opinions upon the present mode of raising troops, without the authority of parliament." The attendance of the judges was, however, overruled by the majority, and the motion withdrawn by the noble Earl. It was principally contended on one side, that the judges were only called upon to attend, when they were to give their opinions on matters of mere law, relative to questions previously framed, and arising from facts already proved to the satisfaction of the House; that the motion of any single Peer for their attendance was nugatory; and that a convention of the judges in their judicial capacity, could only be obtained by an order of the House at large.

In answer to this doctrine, it was urged in vain by the Lords in opposition, That during the sitting of parliament, the judges were, as appeared by their journals, daily attendants upon that House; that there were writs always issued previous to every new parliament, requiring their attendance; that their proper place was on the Wool Sacks; that they formed in some

47

meafure a part of the Houfe; and that according to its rules and orders they were always fuppofed to be prefent. They contended farther, that although, on account of their other important avocations, the conftant attendance of the judges was excufed, and their prefence was only expected when they were fpecially fummoned; yet, they infifted, that a motion for their attendance, by any noble Lord in his place, was a motion granted as a matter of courfe, comprized within the ftanding order of the Houfe; and that it was contrary to parliamentary cuftoms to refufe it. This was infifted upon fo pofitively by the Duke of Richmond, that he called upon the Lords on the other fide, to produce a fingle precedent of fuch a refufal. It was however thought more eligible to eftablifh a precedent, than to put the judges to the tafk of a legal decifion on the meafure in queftion.

The confideration of the queftion on which it had been propofed to have taken the opinion of the judges, having been laid over to the 4th of February, the bufinefs was on that day refumed by the Earl of Abingdon, who made the two following motions, " Refolved, that it be the opinion of this Houfe, that the giving or granting of money, as private aids, or benevolences, without the fanction of parliament, for the purpofe of raifing armies for his Majefty's fervice, is againft the fpirit of the conftitution, and the letter of the law." And, " Refolved, that it be the opinion of this Houfe, that the obtaining of money by fubfcription, and under the direction of a committee of the fubfcribers, to be applied in raifing of men for his Majefty's fervice, in fuch manner as his Majefty fhall think fit, is not only unconftitutional and illegal, but a direct infringement of the rights, and an abfolute breach of the privileges of parliament."

The debates were long and warm, and exceedingly interefting, from the great difplay of legal and conftitutional knowledge which was exhibited ; an amendment was moved early in the debate, by a noble Lord who was then high in office, but who is fince dead, and [48] which went not only to the total overthrow of the original refolutions, but to the eftablifhment of the very principle which they were intended to condemn. The intended amendment was, that after the words, " Refolved, that it is the opinion of this Houfe," the following fhould immediately fucceed, " that voluntary fubfcriptions of money, to be applied towards completing the troops which his Majefty has ordered at this time to be levied for the public fervice, are contributions for legal purpofes, made in a warrantable manner, and highly meritorious."

This amendment being productive of much animadverfion, and condemned as unfair and unufual by the other fide, and not feeming to be approved of by fome Lords on the fame, was withdrawn ; and the queftion being at length put, the original refolutions were rejected by a majority of juft three to one, the numbers being 90 to 30 who fupported the motion upon a divifion.

Various motions preparatory to the enquiry into the ftate of the nation. Duke of Grafton's motion for papers rejected. Mr. Fox and Colonel Barre's motions alfo rejected. Complaints on the refufal of papers, and of the defectivenefs of thofe which were prefented. Avowed motives of the oppofition in the enquiry. Mr. Fox opens the enquiry in the grand committee of the Commons. Refolution moved and rejected. Mr. Burke's motions relative to the employment of the favages. Rejected after long debates. Mr. Fox's motions in the committee, relative to the ftate of the forces in America from the commencement of the war, and the loffes fuftained on that fervice, rejected, after much debate. Debate on the appointment of a Chairman, on opening the committee of the Lords. Lord Scarfdale voted to the chair on a divifion. Debates on the Duke of Richmond's motion againft fending any part of the old eftablifhed home military force on diftant fervice. Motion rejected. Merchants give evidence at the bar, of the great loffes fuftained by commerce in the courfe of the war. Counter evidence, intended to fhew the national advantages derived from the war. Several refolutions moved by the Duke of Richmond, founded on the facts ftated in the evidence of the Merchants. Refolutions fet afide, after much debate, by the previous queftion.

THE critical fituation of affairs, both foreign and domeftic, naturally directed the public attention to the opening of the committee on the ftate of the nation ; whilft hope and anxiety were kept equally awake to the refult of that enquiry. As the time approached, frequent motions were made by the leaders of oppofition in both Houfes, for the various fpecies of information which they deemed neceffary, towards elucidating the different fubjects which they propofed as objects of future difcuffion, and the fupport of thofe points which they wifhed to eftablifh.

In fome inftances thefe motions were complied with, and in others rejected. We have already touched upon the circumftances which tended to a change of difpofition in the Minifters upon this fubject. A motion made by the Duke of Grafton on the 27th of January, fell within the latter predicament. This motion was for " a copy of the answer sent to the **Commissioners** for restoring peace to his **Majesty's** colonies in America, in consequence of their letter to Lord George Germaine, dated the 30th of November 1776, excepting such part of said answer as **might affect the safety of any individual.**" It was opposed by the Ministers on the same general grounds which were taken by those in the House of Commons previous to the recess, for the refusal of **all papers that might tend to the disclosure of any negociation between the Commissioners and the Americans,** pending the supposed existence of such negociation. An uncertain limitation of time, but capable of including the duration of the powers granted to the Commissioners.

On the other side a new ground of argument was afforded, from the letter which produced the answer in question being already before the House; so that the one seemed a necessary appendage to the other. It also appeared by the letter in hand, that the Commissioners were not only doubtful as to the extent of their own powers; but that they were in a still greater state of uncertainty, with respect to the propriety of exercising those which they knew they possessed; and that upon these accounts they had stated their difficulties, and written to administration for instructions.

Upon this ground the opposition contended, that the conduct of the Ministers in the instructions which they then gave, must have consequently determined the event of the subsequent measures pursued by the Commissioners. If that conduct, said they, was wise, prudent, and expedient, as we suppose it was, they can have no reasonable objection to submit it, any more than the motives upon which they acted, to the consideration of the House; but if this is refused, it will then certainly be equally fair in argument and consonant with reason to presume, that be-

ing conscious of their own misconduct, and afraid of its being exposed, they avail themselves of their present influence to screen it from the knowledge of the public.

To this, and much more, which was advanced on that side, the inexpediency of disclosure, was the **conclusive reply,** and afforded an inexpugnable line of defence on the other. The Lords in office, however, at the same time, totally disclaiming all desire or intention of with-holding any information which could with propriety be communicated; and asserting, that the paper in question, if it had been produced, would not have answered any of the purposes for which it was so eagerly demanded. Indeed the noble Lords seemed to be strangers in so extraordinary a degree to the paper now demanded, and to vary so much in their ideas of its nature and contents, that this singular circumstance afforded an opportunity for a charge which was strongly urged on the other side, that no such paper either did now or ever exist; that no answer or instructions had been sent to the Commissioners; but that in this, as in other cases of the greatest national importance, the public business had been totally neglected. After considerable debates, the motion was rejected without a division.

A motion made on the same day in the other House by Mr. Fox, met with a similar fate, being disposed of by the previous question without a division. That motion was in part, upon the same ground with one made in the other House, by the Earl of Chatham before the recess, being a requisition of copies of the instructions given to General Burgoyne, together with such parts of Sir William Howe's instructions, as tended to any co-operation with the northern army. It was opposed upon the ground of impropriety and unfairness with respect to the absent General, who

should in justice be present to explain and defend his conduct, whenever any such enquiry was instituted. The Ministers had no objection, they said, to any scrutiny that related merely to themselves; but in this business, besides the justice due to the absent, they were themselves particularly affected in point of delicacy; for they found that many gentlemen understood a passage in the General's letter, as acknowledging in some degree, fault or error on one side or other, and as seeming to bring the matter to an issue, whether it lay with himself or with the Ministers; so that in these peculiar circumstances, it was impossible for them to agree to any enquiry into the subject, until he was present.

On the other side, the opposition distinguished between general enquiry, and particular charge or accusation; the motion, they said, neither led to or supposed any charge or accusation, either against the General, or against the Ministers; it only required the knowledge of instructions, which the House must at some time be in possession of, and which was at present particularly necessary for the directing of its judgment, in the forming a true estimate of the progress and state of the American war, and being thereby enabled to determine upon the most prudent and feasible measures for the restoration of the public tranquility. And that the inspection of these instructions could no more preclude a future enquiry into the conduct, than it could establish the justification of any of the parties concerned. However these matters might be, the motion was thought ill timed; and the refusal of Ministry to lay these papers before the House was generally justified.

This motion being disposed of in the manner we have mentioned; Colonel Barré moved, that " copies of all letters and extracts of letters, which had passed between

General Gage, Lord Howe, Sir William Howe, and General Carleton, from the 1st of July 1775, to the 27th of January 1778," should be laid before the House. Colonel Barré made also two other motions on the 29th of January, requiring accounts of the state of the artillery, &c. in store in America, at the commencement of the year 1774, and of the quantity since shipped for that continent. The two first of these motions were supported on the certainty, that transactions so long passed could have no effect on any present operations. The last was particularly grounded on the vast charge of the artillery beyond the example of any former war. The first and last were both however overruled on the same principle, the dread of giving information to the enemy.

The complaints made in both Houses by the opposition for the rejection of papers were not greater than those which they continually repeated, of the failure of delivery with respect to those already ordered, and the exceeding defectiveness, erroneousness, and unsatisfactoriness of those which were presented; and which they stated, as being totally ncompetent to the purposes for which they had been ordered; and, as shewing rather a mockery of the authority of parliament, than a due compliance with its resolutions.

The Ministers replied, that when gentlemen moved for papers, they frequently did not see or consider the extent to which their motions went. That contracts for cloathing, victualling, and supplying the troops with rum, porter, and the various other articles necessary for the service, together with the treasury minutes relative to all such contracts for four entire years, had been demanded. That these were so exceedingly voluminous, that it required more time than the Ministers themselves could have apprehended to obey the order of parliament. That they did not wish to evade the enquiry; it was their sincere desire to comply, as strictly as possible, with the orders of parliament. But that they neither did, nor should, consider themselves responsible for any incorrectness that might appear in the accounts. They denied that any information was designedly withheld. No doubt could be entertained, but that the different offices presented such materials as they were possessed of, so far as they had been included in the orders which they received. It might happen in some cases, that the accounts which were demanded had not been received. In others, perhaps, the original motions had not been directed to the proper offices. But these were not matters that lay with them.

The complaints on the other side, however, continued to the last; nor did they acknowledge that the cause was ever entirely remedied. Some accounts they said were deficient, others imperfect, and some totally omitted. Responsibility was shifted one moment, and official knowledge the next. Those, who under the immediate authority of parliament, endeavoured to procure information for its guidance, in matters of the greatest national importance, were wearied and baffled by chicane and evasion. It was not this, or it was not that person's business to give information; or the papers did not belong to this or to that office, was the satisfaction they received; and thus they were left to grope their way through a chaos of uncertainty and error. It was the business of Ministers, they said, and would have been their practice, if they had relied on the rectitude of their conduct, or the wisdom of their measures, to have procured, without giving any trouble to the other side, every species of information that could be wanted, in order to their own exculpation, and thereby to establish a perpetual record of their innocence and ability.

Before we enter into any detail of the subject, it may not be entirely unnecessary to take a short view of the avowed motives of the opposition in this enquiry; including also, the objects which they wished to establish thereby, and the conclusions to draw therefrom. The grand motive of the whole enquiry was the establishment as an incontrovertible fact, of, not only the expediency, but the absolute necessity of bringing the American war to the speediest possible conclusion. — Of restoring harmony upon a broad, and consequently equitable bottom between the mother country and her colonies.— And the establishment of a permanent union at any rate, but still upon the best terms which the present unhappy situation of affairs would admit of between them.

To obtain this end it was necessary, they said, to combat and overthrow those doctrines which had been so long held out by the Ministers, so constantly supported and adopted by those vast majorities which were seen in two parliaments, and to an invincible perseverance in which, the contest, war, and all their consequences to both countries were attributed by the opposition. But as these doctrines had hitherto been impregnable to all arguments founded on probability, the natural reason of things, historical evidence, or analogy, and unshaken by all speculations into future evils or dangers; it was now thought necessary to try them by the strong tests of established facts and recent experience, founded on, and immediately rising from their own principles.

Upon this ground of proceeding it was necessary in the first instance, in order to obviate delay and trouble in the progress, to establish certain leading facts as simple and incontrovertible positions; such as, that the war had lasted for a certain specified time; that a certain force by sea and land had been employed in its prosecution; that it was attended with a certain stated expence of money and of lives, and that our utmost efforts in a three years war, had not produced any material advantage. From a few established facts of this nature, and all founded upon the documents before them, various deductions and .conclusions were to be drawn, and various questions of political confideration arising from the whole, were to be stated, examined, and to become objects of parliamentary enquiry, deliberation, and decision.

Thus, if our utmost efforts in a three years war had produced no material change of circumstances in our favour, it became an object of the utmost moment to weigh the consequences on all hands, which might probably attend our further perseverance in the contest. On this point, several questions of the greatest magnitude and importance, would naturally and necessarily arise. The first would be, whether our resources, in any probability or hope of success, were equal to the longer continuance of so great an exhausture of blood and treasure? If this appeared in the affirmative, the next consideration would be, whether the object was equivalent to the expence, loss, and risque of the pursuit? The question of practicability must form another object of consideration; and if it appeared, that our utmost exertion of force had already failed of effect, when the enemy was much weaker, and more incapable in every respect than at present; it would remain to be shewn, upon what ground of reason or probability our hope of future success was founded. These matters being discussed, the probability of a foreign war afforded the next great question; and on this part of the subject the opposition contended, that the danger of our becoming victims to

the malice and ambition of our natural enemies, in the state of debility and exhausture brought on by our civil contest, when our principal military force was at a distance of three thousand miles, and such measures perhaps taken by the enemy, as would render its return to our defence exceedingly doubtful, if not impracticable, presented a state and situation of public affairs, the most tremendous that this country, in its greatest perils, had ever encountered. This great branch of the subject led naturally to an enquiry into the state of our military home defence, both by land and by sea, including with these kingdoms, that also of our Mediterranean garrisons; and the defectiveness which appeared upon this enquiry, afforded room for the subsequent resolutions which were moved for, to prevent the farther lessening of our domestic force, by sending any more of the old troops to America.

Feb. 2d. Mr. Fox opened the enquiry in the grand committee of the House of Commons, with his usual ability, energy, and perspicuity, in a speech which continued for about two hours. Although, in the ample explanation which he gave of the motives and proposed ends of the enquiry, he took a comprehensive retrospective view of the conduct of American affairs, from the adoption of those measures which he supposed led directly to the ensuing troubles, to the actual commencement of hostilities, and the prosecution and events of the war; yet he observed, that the particular matter which he should refer on that day to their decision, would only compose a small part of the business, which, he hoped, would thoroughly engage the farther consideration of the committee. He requested of the House, not to mix the matter in hand with any thing that had passed before, but to go plainly and directly to the business; to consider, with the attention and

temper which the great importance of the subject required, the actual state of their country, and in what manner Great Britain might be extricated from the critical situation in which she then stood. He wished, in considering the subject, that all gentlemen would at least agree so far with him, as to divest themselves of all former opinions, of all favourite ideas, and of all those prejudices which might have been contracted in the course of past debate, and strengthened by the warmth of altercation; that they would take up their opinions anew, as they arose naturally from the subject of enquiry, or were founded on fair deductions from the information before them; neither considering themselves as friends or enemies to America, nor regarding that country as an object either of love or hatred; but considering it merely as a part, and a very considerable part of the British empire.

The method he should lay down, he said, as the most likely to bring men to a right understanding in respect to the present state of the nation, and to point out the conduct which it would be our interest in future to pursue, would be simple, concise, and, he hoped, equally clear and conclusive; he would state certain incontrovertible facts from the papers before them, and draw the fair, if not inevitable conclusions arising from those facts. Thus, with respect to the army, he would state, that in the four years, commencing with 1774, and ending with 1777, an army, consisting in each year of a certain number of thousands of men, had been employed in America, and that certain military operations had been performed by that army; he would shew that army to have been much stronger and more numerous within that period, and the enemy to have been much weaker and more incapable of war, than both are at present; he should in the next place state the impoffibility of increafing that army. The hopeleffnefs of fuccefs with an inferior force, after the repeated and continued failure with one much greater; and then he would fhew the enormous expence which had been already incurred, its rapid increafe, and the inability of the nation to its fupport.

The refources in men and money thus failing, it was a natural conclufion, and could not in fairnefs to the minifters but be fuppofed, that there muft be fome fort of negociation in hand towards an endeavour of accommodating matters; and in this part of the bufinefs, he faid, it could not be too much lamented, that his motion for the papers relative to that fubject had been rejected; for as the committee would thereby have difcovered, and become competent judges of the nature of thofe impediments that had hitherto prevented fuch negociations from producing their proper effect, they would of courfe be enabled to provide fuch adequate remedies, as would effectually remove every obftruction to the reftoration of the public tranquillity.

As prefatory to the retrofpective view which he took of thofe meafures that led to the prefent ftate of affairs, he laid it down as an incontrovertible axiom, That it was impoffible for any country to fall within fo few years from the high pitch of power and glory which we had done, without fome radical error in its government. After ftating the agreement with the Eaft-India company as the immediate fource of all the fubfequent troubles, he obferved that the minifters upon that occafion fell into a moft capital error; by looking through the wrong end of the perfpective, they miftook a great object for a little one; they took thirteen colonies for one; and the whole continent of America for the fingle province of Maffachufet's Bay. They forgot that a

southern colony, Virginia, was no lefs jealous of its rights, nor warm in their affertion, than Maffachufet's; and they forgot that common danger would unite them all. Through this fatal error, of not being aware of the weight of that oppofition which they were to encounter, their means were totally difproportionate to the end which they propofed; and it will not be queftioned as an undoubted maxim in politicks, that every attempt to eftablifh power, or to crufh infurrection, with means inadequate to the end, will only ferve to increafe oppofition in the one cafe, and to eftablifh, inftead of fuppreffing rebellion in the other.

Yet, totally blind to thefe confequences, the meafures which the minifters purfued againft the town of Bofton, and colony of Maffachufets, were of fuch a nature as neceffarily compelled the other twelve colonies to become hoftile in their own defence, and to enter into a common band of union with that town and colony. He infifted that parliament would not **have paffed the irritating and hoftile laws of the year 1774, if it had not been for the defective and partial information laid before them by the minifters; but that, on the contrary, if they had been acquainted with the real nature, with the true ftate and extent of the oppofition in America, they would have adopted the moft healing and conciliating, inftead of the moft irritating and violent meafures.** In treating of the caufes which led to the final determined oppofition and ftrict union of the colonies, he particularly reprobated the bill for the bringing of Americans for trial to England, and the Quebec Act. The former, he faid, without entering into the queftion of its juftice or injuftice, fhould, fince it had been adopted as a meafure of policy, have been fupported upon the fame ground, by a force equal to the terrors which it announced, and to the alarm which it inevit-

ably excited. But as the act excited indignation at our injuftice as well as terror, fo the infufficiency of the army, by which it was to be enforced, only excited the derifion of the Americans without leffening their refentment. It taught them to contemn the power of this country, as much as they abhorred its injuftice.

The Quebec Act, he faid, united all parties in America. The moft moderate, or thofe who were fuppofed the beft affected to the Britifh government, could fcarcely after that fay a word in favour of the intentions of the legiflature. They faw a form of government eftablifhed, which the violent held out as the model of that which was to be extended over the whole continent. It afforded an unanfwerable argument, that the intentions of Great Britain were hoftile and vindictive in the extreme; and that they had no refource left but in felf-defence. The moderate party, if any fuch were ftill left, were ftruck dumb. Thus, the framers of the Quebec Act, he faid, whoever they were, became in fact the great and effective friends of the violent party in America. If they had not thus feafonably interpofed, there would have been a chance of America's being divided; or at leaft the degrees of refiftance would have been different in the colonies. But this made them all not only more firmly united, but equally zealous and animated; equally determined to go all lengths rather than fubmit.

He then ftated the impolicy of rejecting the very dutiful and affectionate petition from New York; and the unhappy confequences that refulted from that rejection. Yet notwithftanding all thefe acts and circumftances of irritation, violence, and malignity; notwithftanding the bitternefs and animofity arifing from the blood firft drawn at Lexington, and afterwards more profufely fhed at

Bunker's Hill; America, he said, still seemed unwilling to have recourse to those fatal extremities, which to the loss and ruin of this country she has since unhappily adopted. She once more applied, but it was for the last time, to the equity and wisdom of government, for peace, security, and a renewal of amity. The petition which the Congress presented through Mr. Penn to the throne, was, all circumstances considered, couched in terms of uncommon moderation, as well as of the greatest respect; and, besides disclaiming every idea of that independency with which they had been charged in the preceding session, contained the strongest professions of duty, as well as the warmest of affection. Every body knows the fate of that petition, and that it was not even deemed worthy of an answer. The consequences of that rejection will probably be too long felt and remembered.

He then combated the position laid down by the ministers, and upon which they justified the rejection of that petition, namely, that the Americans were not sincere in their professions or proposals; and that they only held them out to gain time for preparation, and to deceive their own people, whilst the scheme of independence was already fixed and determined upon by them. In reviewing the operations of the war, the principal conclusion he wished to draw was, that from the inefficacy of the great force already employed, and the little advantage that had been derived from the very considerable successes which had upon several occasions attended our arms, it was now evident to a demonstration, that from some inherent and insuperable obstacles, the scheme of coercion was absolutely impracticable; and that negociation now afforded the only hope of bringing the contest to any termination, that would not prove ruinous, if not fatal to this country.

Having established (as he conceived) this position, Mr. Fox proceeded to clear the way for his immediate motion, by an enquiry into the state of our home defence; in which he made it appear from the papers before them, that at this time, when we were in immediate danger of encountering the whole force of the house of Bourbon united with that of America, the army in England and Ireland, including the garrisons of Gibraltar and Minorca, had been so exceedingly reduced and weakened by the continual drain for the war, as to fall several thousand men short of that peace establishment, which had been deemed necessary for our protection in seasons of the greatest tranquillity.

Upon this ground, and upon the idea which he stated and supported, that no force which we were now capable of sending to America, could render the army there so powerful as it had been at the commencement of the preceding campaign, which however produced no effect, that could in any degree justify the hope or expectation of complete conquest, he moved, as a resolution of the committee, for an address to his Majesty, that no part of the old established national forces in these kingdoms, or in the garrisons of Gibraltar or Minorca, should be sent to America.

To the infinite surprize of every body without doors, who had seen so full a house drawn down to attend the result of an enquiry of so much expectation, no debate whatever ensued, nor was the smallest reply made to the speech or the motion. In this singular situation, the question being called for, the motion was rejected upon a division, by a majority of 259, to 165 by whom it was supported. So large a minority appearing in support of the question, seemed to indicate that more discussion ought to have been employed. By that appearance also, occasion was given

to the sanguine on one side to hope, that it presaged some considerable change in the disposition and conduct of parliament. Such was the event of the first day's enquiry into the state of the nation in the house of commons.

Feb. 6th. In a few days after Mr. Burke moved for an address to lay before the house, copies of all papers that had passed between any of his Majesty's ministers and the Generals of his armies in America, or any persons acting for government in Indian affairs, relative to the military employment of the Indians of America, in the present civil war, from the first of March, 1774, to the first day of January, 1778.

He supported the motion with his usual ability, in a speech of great length, (near three hours and a half) which excited so much applause, that many gave it a preference to any other he had ever spoken. Indeed this applause was carried to such a pitch, that while one gentleman, in his place, wished it to be printed, and affixed to all the church-doors which contained the proclamation for a general fast, a member of great distinction and in high office congratulated the ministers upon admitting no strangers on that day into the gallery, as the indignation of the people might have been excited against them to a degree, that would have endangered their safety. No very particular account of this speech has appeared. The abstract in the public prints was nearly the following.

Mr. Burke observed, that one of the grand objects of the enquiry into the state of the nation, was the condition and quality of the troops employed in America. That an account of the king's *regular* forces, and those of his *European* allies, were already before them. That hitherto no account had appeared of his *irregular* forces, particularly those of his *Savage* allies; although great de-

49

pendance had been placed upon them, and they had been obtained at a very great expence. That it was necessary to examine into this point; because an extension of their mode of making war had lately been strenuously recommended. The prevailing idea was, that, in the next campaign, the plans hitherto pursued were to be abandoned; and a war of distress and intimidation was to take place of a war of conquest, which was now found to be impracticable.

He said that this mode of war had already been tried upon a large scale, and that the success which had hitherto attended it would afford the best evidence how far it might be proper to extend it to all our troops, and to all our operations. That if it did not promise to be very decisive as a plan merely military, it could be attended with no collateral advantages, whether considered with respect to our reputation as a civilized people, or to our policy, in regard to the means of reconciling the minds of the colonies to his Majesty's government.

He then stated what the nature of a war, in which Indians were the actors against a civilized people, was; and observed, that the fault of employing them did not consist in their being of one colour or another; in their using one kind of weapon or another; but in their way of making war; which was so horrible, that it not only shocked the manners of all civilized nations, but far exceeded the ferocity of any other barbarians that have been recorded either by ancient or modern history. He observed, that the Indians in North America had but two principal objects in their wars; the one was the indulgence of their native cruelty, by the destruction, or, if possible, the extermination of their enemies; the other, which always depended on the former, was the glory of acquiring the greatest number of human scalps, which were hung up and preserved with the greatest care in their huts, as perpetual trophies of victory, conquest, and personal prowess. As they had neither pecuniary emoluments, nor those honorary titles or distinctions, which are so flattering in civilized nations, to bestow, the rewards of danger and warfare consisted in human scalps, in human flesh, and the gratifications arising from torturing, mangling, roasting alive by slow fires, and frequently even devouring their captives. Such were the rewards of Indian warriors, and such the horrors of an Indian war.

He then proceeded to shew, that the employment of the Savages in the wars between the French and the English, did not in any degree come up to the measure in question, nor did it stand on the same principles. When those nations first made settlements in North America, the Indian tribes were, comparatively, numerous and powerful states; the new settlers were accordingly under an inevitable necessity, not only of cultivating their friendship, and forming alliances with them, but of admitting them as parties in their contests and wars with each other; the affairs of both nations were so inextricably entangled with those of the people who had sold or given them lands, and admitted them to a share of their country, that they could not be separated; their contracts on both sides created a mutual interest; and while the Savages retained any degree of their original power, they could not be indifferent to the disputes that arose among their new neighbours.

But the case was now totally altered. The English colonies were the only Europeans in North America; and the Savages were so entirely reduced in number and power, that there was no occasion for holding any political connection with them as nations. They were now only formidable from their cruelty; and to employ them was merely to be cruel ourselves in their persons: and thus, without even the lure of any essential service, to become chargeable with all the odious and impotent barbarities, which they would inevitably commit, whenever they were called into action.

Mr. Burke then proceeded to examine the arguments or apologies that had been used by the ministers in either house, in defence or alleviation of the measure. These he arranged under three heads, the first and principal of which was contained in the assertion, "That if his Majesty had not employed them the rebels would." To this he answered, that no proof whatever had been given of the Americans having attempted an offensive alliance with any one tribe of savage Indians. Whereas the imperfect papers already before the house demonstrated, that the King's ministers had negociated and obtained such alliances from one end of the continent of America to the other. That the Americans had actually made a treaty on the footing of neutrality with the famous Five Nations, which the ministers had bribed them to violate, and to act offensively against the colonies. That no attempt had been made in a single instance on the part of the King's ministers to procure a neutrality; and, that if the fact had been (what he denied it to be) that the Americans had actually employed those Savages, yet the difference of employing them against armed and trained soldiers, embodied and encamped, and employing them against the unarmed and defenceless men, women and children, of a country, widely dispersed in their habitations, was manifest; and left those who attempted so inhuman and unequal a retaliation without a possibility of excuse.

The other heads of defence were, "That great care had been taken to prevent that indiscriminate murder of men, women, and children, which was customary with the savages;" and "that they were always accompanied by disciplined troops to prevent their irregularities." On these he observed, that if the fact had been true, the service of the Savages would have been a jest; their employment could have answered no purpose; their only effective use confisted in that cruelty which was to be restrained; but he shewed, that it was so utterly impossible for any care or humanity to prevent or even restrain their enormities, that the very attempt was ridiculous: in proof of which, both the present and former wars afforded numerous instances; and it particularly appeared both in General Burgoyne's and Col. St. Leger's expeditions, that although no pains were neglected to check their barbarity, they indiscriminately murdered men, women, and children; friends and foes, without distinction; and that even the slaughter fell mostly upon those who were best affected to the King's government, and who, upon that account, had been lately disarmed by the Provincials. The murder of Miss M'Rea on the morning of her intended marriage with an officer of the King's troops, and the massacre in cold blood of the prisoners who had been taken in the engagement with Gen. Harkemer, only needed to be mentioned to excite horror, and at the same time to shew the impracticability of restraining the barbarities of the Savages.

With respect to the latter of the foregoing positions, (that the Savages had always been accompanied with regular troops) Mr. Burke gave it a direct contradiction. He shewed that whole nations of Savages had been bribed to take up the hatchet, without a single regular officer or soldier amongst them. This had been particularly the case of the Cherokees, who were bribed and betrayed into war,

under the promise of being assisted by a large regular force; they had accordingly invaded Carolina in their usual manner, but for want of the promised support, were nearly exterminated; and the remains of that people now lived in a state of servitude to the Carolinians.

He stated the monstrous expence, as well as the inefficacy, of that kind of ally; and the unfortunate consequences that had attended their employment. That one Indian soldier cost as much as five of the best regular or irregular European troops. That the expence of these Indians had not been less than 150,000l. and yet there never had been more than seven or eight hundred of them in the field, and that only for a very short time. So that it appeared as if our ministers thought, that inhumanity and murder could not be purchased at too dear a rate. He shewed that this ally was not less faithless, than inefficacious and cruel. That on the least appearance of ill success, they not only abandoned their friends, but frequently turned their arms upon them. And he attributed the fatal catastrophe at Saratoga to the cruelties exercised by these barbarians, which obliged all mankind, without regard to party, or to political principles, and in despite of military indisposition, to become soldiers, and to unite as one man in the common defence. Thus was the spectacle exhibited of a resistless army springing up in the woods and deserts.

He also passed some severe strictures on the endeavours in two of the southern colonies, to excite an insurrection of the negro slaves against their masters. He insisted that the proclamation for that purpose was directly contrary to the common and statute law of this country, as well as to the general law of nations. He stated in strong colours the nature of an insurrection of negroes; the horrible conse-

quences that might ensue from constituting 100,000 fierce barbarian slaves, to be both the judges and executioners of their masters; and appealed to all those who were acquainted either with the West India Islands or the Southern Colonies, as to the murders, rapes, and horrid enormities of every kind, which had ever been acknowledged to be the principal objects in the contemplation, of all negroes who had meditated an insurrection. The vigour and care of the white inhabitants in Virginia and Maryland, had providentially kept down the insurrection of the negroes. But if they had succeeded, he asked what means were proposed for governing those negroes, when they had reduced the province to their obedience, and made themselves masters of the houses, goods, wives, and daughters, of their murdered lords? Another war must be made with them, and another massacre ensue; adding confusion to confusion, and destruction to destruction.

The result of his speech was, that our national honour had been deeply wounded, and our character as a people debased in the estimation of foreigners, by those shameful, savage and servile, alliances, and their barbarous consequences. That instead of any military effect of value, they had only led to defeat, ruin, and disgrace; serving to embitter the minds of all men, and to unite and arm all the Colonies against us. That the ineffective attempt upon the negroes, was the grand cause of that greater aversion and resentment, which appeared in the Southern, than in many of the Central and Northern Colonies; of their being the first to abjure the King; and of the declaration made by Virginia, that if the rest should submit, they would notwithstanding hold out singly to the last extremity; for what security could they receive, that if they admitted an English governor, he would not raise their negroes on them, whenever he thought it good to construe any occasional disturbances into a rebellion, and to adopt martial law as a system of government.

He concluded, that the only remedy for the alienation of affections, and the distrust and terror of our government, which had been brought on by these inhuman measures, was for parliament to enquire seriously and strictly into them; and by the most marked and public disapprobation, to convince the world that they had no share in practices, which were not more disgraceful to a great and civilized nation, than they were contrary to all true policy, and repugnant to all the feelings of humanity. For that it was not in human nature for any people to place a confidence in those, to whom they attributed such unparalleled sufferings and miseries; and the colonies would never be brought to believe, that those who were capable of carrying on a war in so cruel and dishonourable a manner, could be depended on for a sound, equitable, and cordial peace; much less that they could be safely entrusted with power and dominion.

The ministers could scarcely have any new ground to take in this debate, and accordingly applied their force principally to support those assertions or arguments, which had been stated and combated, by Mr. Burke. They insisted, that every thing that had been advanced relative to a neutrality on the side of the Indians, was delusive, and utterly impracticable in fact. That the disposition of the Indians, and the applications made to them by the Colonies, afforded a clear and indisputable proposition, that no other alternative was left, but that of either employing them ourselves, or submitting to the consequences of their enmity. That the operations of a war in America must necessarily be combined with the nature of the country, still more than half a wilderness, as well as with the nature and disposition of the native inhabitants of that wilderness; insomuch, that no war ever was, nor still can be carried on in that country, in which the Indians will not inevitably mix. And that supposing their assistance had been rejected on both sides, they would notwithstanding have become a destructive party in the war, by scalping and murdering each indiscriminately, wherever they found themselves superior in force. Thus, they contended, that the employment of the Indians was a matter of absolute necessity, and by no means a measure of choice or inclination.

They said, that no proposals of neutrality had ever been made to the Indians by any of the contending parties in America, whether French, English, or Americans, excepting only when the proposing party had failed in its endeavours to procure their assistance, and would thereby prevent their operation on the opposite side. That this had been particularly the case of the Congress with respect to that neutrality which had been so much boasted as an instance of moderation and humanity. That the Indians had at all times been a principal object of American policy, with every European nation that held possessions on that continent. That Indian treaties had been entered into in the last war, and those people employed successfully against our French and Christian neighbours, without the measure exciting any part of that outcry and complaint which is now so industriously raised. That those treaties had been renewed, confirmed, and continued, down to the present time; that it was well known that superintendants were constantly employed at a great expence by government, to create and preserve alliances with the Indian nations; and that parliament gave every session the fullest sanction to this policy, in approving of and recognizing those alliances and treaties, by granting specific sums of money to the disposal of those superintendants, for the purpose of being laid out in presents, and distributed among the leading warriors and chiefs of the Indian nations.

The minister remarked on the observation that had been made, of danger arising from strangers being admitted to hear the debate; he said, that he also was very glad of that circumstance of an empty gallery, but that it proceeded from a very different cause; for he would have been apprehensive that if the public had been acquainted with the unfounded charges and aspersions brought by gentlemen on the other side, to traduce the honour and character of their country, it might, indeed, have raised their indignation and resentment to a very dangerous degree. He also entered into some defence of the measure of emancipating the negroes in Virginia, and encouraging them to join the royal army. He said the proclamation did not call on them to murder their masters, as had been stated in the debate; it only called upon them to take up arms in defence of their sovereign. He acknowledged the employment of the savages to be a bad, but stated it as an unavoidable measure; and combated the charges of cruelty by recriminating upon the Americans, who, he said, hung up their own people by dozens, for no other crime than their supplying our camp with provisions.

After a warm debate of seven hours, Mr. Burke's motion was rejected upon a division, by a majority of 223, to 137 who supported the question. That gentleman, notwithstanding, followed his first motion by several others—For copies of all treaties and conventions with the Indians of North America, and all messages, speeches, and symbols, sent by any persons acting in his Majesty's service, or under their orders, from the 1st of March, 1774.—For an account of all money, arms, ammunition, stores, and the quantity, kind, and value of goods given to any of the said Indians, or consigned to any person for them, on account of his Majesty, or any person employed in his or the public service.—For an account of the numbers, nations, and names of chiefs, of the American Indians, who have been in arms against the colonies of North America, since the 1st of March, 1774; as also of those who have acted in his Majesty's armies, with their state and numbers, as by the last returns, and where employed.—For an account of the number of negroes of Virginia who have repaired to his Majesty's standard, from the 1st of March, 1774, and the corps which they formed or were embodied in, together with the names of the officers commanding the said corps, and serving therein; as also their number and condition, as by the last return.—And lastly, For copies of all orders given, and information received, relating to the raising negroes for his Majesty's service, in North and South Carolina. All these motions were separately negatived.

Feb. 11th. In a few days after, the House being in a committee on the state of the nation, Mr. Fox stated a number of facts relative to the war in America, which were founded on conclusions drawn from the papers before them. As the accounts given in relative to the armies in America, were extremely deficient, in those heads of information, from whence any knowledge could be derived of the specific loss of men sustained in the war, and that those in particular which related to the state of the foreign troops, presented little more than a blank in that respect, the Duke of Richmond and Mr. Fox, who conducted the enquiry in both houses, adopted the same

simple method for remedying that defect, and thereby establishing the point of fact. For this purpose, having established from the documents before them, the exact number of effective men which were in America, in the year 1774, and previous to the commencement of hostilities, which they shewed to be 6,864, they added to that amount the number of reinforcements and recruits, whether native or foreign, which had been sent from Great-Britain, Ireland, or Germany, during the intermediate time; and these aggregates being cast into one round sum, and compared with the number of effective men, which from the last returns appeared to be still left on that continent, the difference, amounting to something about twenty thousand, was stated as the exact loss of men sustained in the war to the latest date, whether by desertion, slain in battle, dead through disease, or otherwise incapacitated for service, by wounds, captivity, or sickness.

Mr. Fox having opened the ground which he was to take, with his usual perspicuity, explained the nature of a succession of twelve motions which he intended to make, and of the points which they went to establish. He would shew, to the satisfaction of the committee, that we had lost 20,000 men by the war, and that the expence of treasure had already amounted to full twenty-five millions. He would then appeal to the judgment of the committee, considering, that we had gained nothing by this fatal contest hitherto, and that instead of the undisciplined rabble we were first engaged with, we were now to contend with a powerful, numerous, and well-disciplined enemy, whether it was not full time for them to reflect in the most serious manner, on the very critical and alarming situation of public affairs. To consider, whether our resources of men and money were equal to the difficult and ha-

zardous task of conquest; or if that should appear, on due examination, to be totally impracticable, whether it was not incumbent on parliament, immediately to devise some means for putting an end to our public calamities, and to endeavour to avert those imminent dangers with which we are on every side threatened. That in every consideration of this mad, improvident, and destructive war, they should bear constantly in mind, that besides our having suffered such disgraces in its progress as this country never before experienced, all those thousands of lives and millions of money, had not only been thrown away to no manner of purpose, but that on the contrary, that vast expence of blood and treasure had rendered conciliation infinitely more difficult, and consequently our situation as a nation infinitely worse, than if the sword had never been drawn, a shilling spent, or a life lost.

He then proposed his leading motion as a foundation for the succeeding, and as an incontrovertible fact arising from the evidence before them, viz. "Resolved, that it appears to this committee, that in the year 1774, the whole of the land-forces serving in North America, did not amount to more than 6,864 effective men, officers included."

The Secretary of War said, that however they might have been founded in point of fact, he could not have avoided disapproving of the resolutions, as being highly improper and ill timed; but that when he also knew, that some of the principal of them were totally unfounded in fact, he could have no difficulty in giving them a direct negative. The honourable mover had stated as a fact, that 20,000 men had been already lost in this war; this, he contended, to be a gross error, for he could demonstrate by returns which he had in his hands, that the whole number slain in three years war did not exceed 1200. He did not mean to[50] include in that number those who died natural deaths, who deserted, were made prisoners, or who had been rendered unfit for service by wounds or sickness; but only such as had been slain in battle. And that if this erroneous statement of the loss of men was to go out into the world under the sanction of parliament, it would not only establish false, but very pernicious ideas, with respect to the state, nature, conduct, and consequences of the war.

The minister declared the propositions to be reprehensible and impolitic in the highest degree; and was amazed, that while our affairs were represented to be in the most critical and alarming situation, how the author of that assertion could, with any colour of reason, propose that the state of our armies should be exposed to our enemies, during the actual state and existence of a war, which, according to the language held on that side, was every day expected to be extended in a still more dangerous degree; but that if he had even approved of the purport of the motion, it was impossible he could agree to it, until the prodigious difference in calculation, which appeared to be no less than sixteen to one, between the honourable mover, and the noble lord at the head of the war office, from whom also the whole information upon the subject was derived, could be in some manner settled. That he would therefore recommend to Mr. Fox to withdraw his motion, until this great difference in point of calculation was settled, when it would be time enough to consider the merits of the question; but that if this was not agreed to, he must be under a necessity of endeavouring to set it by, by moving to report some progress.

To this it was replied, that the mover had not supposed or stated, that 20,000 men had been actually slain outright in battle; he had only shewn and stated from the documents before them, that the deficiency of the force sent to America, exclusive of what was raised in the country, amounted at the date of the latest returns to that number. That however some parts of the question might be interesting to humanity, it availed but little to the public, and nothing at all to the service, what proportions of that twenty thousand had been killed upon the spot in action, died of their wounds, perished by disease or fatigue, deserted to the enemy, or who lived to present a maimed and mutilated spectacle of human nature at home, condemned to drag out a life of misery, and to exist a dead burthen and constant expence to their country.

That it was not the fault of opposition if false or imperfect accounts had been laid before parliament; they had taken great pains to prevent or to remedy those defects. But that if the noble Lord sent in papers of a different complexion, from those which he relied on for his own private use and information, it was no wonder that there should be mistakes in the calculations, and that those mistakes should also be exactly such as the noble Lord pleased. But they insisted that there could be no mistake to affect the question in its principal and material point. The state of the effective force sent out, and of that which still remained, could not be controverted; and the difference was the undoubted loss sustained in the war. The noble Lord's calculation of the number actually slain, they said, might be easily overthrown, but it was no part of the present business.

In answer to the noble Lord at the head of the treasury, they observed, that an enquiry into the state of the war, and consequently of the army, was the principal object of the committee. That it would be a farce to talk of enquiring into the state of the nation, and to omit those great objects, which in fact included every thing that could be worth their enquiry. That if enquiry was not made during the war, it could never be made to any purpose; it would be too late when the die was cast, the contest concluded, and our fate, perhaps for ever, decided; and that at any rate, if the men who now opposed it succeeded, and still continued in office, they could easily evade all enquiry into their conduct when the subject was no longer interesting. That the establishment of such a doctrine would amount to no less in effect, than a public remission of all crimes and treasons committed by men in office against the state during the continuance of a war; for that iniquitous Ministers would have nothing more to do for their security in the utmost state of turpitude, than to prolong a war, to the detriment and ruin of their country, until the indignation of the people was exhausted, and that their crimes were at length obliterated from the public memory. They concluded by asserting, that the Minister's pretence or argument for opposing the motion, on the danger of exposing the state of our forces to the enemy, was not more frivolous in point of argument, than it was repugnant to practice, and unsupported by precedent; and that their journals abounded with instances, of parliamentary enquiries into the state of our fleets and armies, the conduct of commanders, and the causes of miscarriage, public loss, or disgrace, being instituted in the midst of the heat, violence, and danger, of our most arduous wars.

The debate was well supported; most of the principal members of the opposition having taken a considerable share in the question. As the Minister had announced to the House previous to the speaker's quitting the chair, that he should on the following Tuesday, the 17th, lay before them a plan of conciliation with America; this notice occasioned much conversation, and some animadversion, distinct from the main subject. The opposition declared, that if the noble Lord's intended plan of conciliation, was fair and open, founded in justice, good faith, and right policy, and warranted by the principles of the constitution, it should meet with the most hearty and unreserved concurrence on their side of the House. But they had too much cause for fearing that it would not answer that description; for they could scarcely be persuaded, (unless the ideas of cruelty and meanness were inseperable,) that the same men who had rejected the most humble petitions and dutiful remonstrances with haughtiness and contempt, could ever consent to hold out any plan that was fairly meant to secure those rights, which they had so long endeavoured to annihilate by the sword.

A young gentleman of great fortune, and of still greater expectations, whose father had first laid or adopted the scheme of American taxation, and who had himself hitherto given some support to the war, upon the same principle, and in the common hope which operated upon so many, of obtaining an effective revenue from the colonies, after explaining the motives for his present conduct in voting with the opposition, which were not founded upon any departure from his former principles and opinions, but entirely owing to the unhappy measures pursued by government, which had now reduced those to be merely matters of speculation; he then reprobated with an extraordinary degree of severity the whole conduct of administration, whether with respect to the American business in general, or to the war in particular,

In the course of a very able speech, he deplored the disgrace brought, not upon our arms, but on our counsels, by the ill-fated, rash, and undigested expedition from Canada. He lamented the want of protection to our commerce, the consequent weight of insurance on our merchants, and the declining state of public credit. He hoped a day of retribution would come, when Ministers would be called to a severe account for the disgrace and infamy which they had brought upon their country, by involving it in a war which they were incapable of conducting, and deceiving the nation into an immense expence and great loss, by holding out promises of a revenue which their inability had obliged them to abandon. He sincerely wished that the noble Lord's plan of conciliation might succeed; but he had every reason in the world, he said, to apprehend it would not. A previous confidence between the parties, was the very life and basis of all negociation and treaty. The noble Lord himself would not venture to say, that any such source of accommodation subsisted between Ministers and the ruling powers in America. Nobody was ignorant, he said, that every possible occasion had been given by the present administration, to fix in the breasts of the people of America and their leaders, the most rooted hatred and inveterate rancour. Under such singular circumstances of disappointment and disgrace on one side, and such provocations on the other, he would appeal to the candour of those whose dispositions might lead them to the highest point of expectation, whether there was the most distant prospect of any success from a treaty, which was to be conducted on the part of Great Britain, by men who were universally execrated from one end of the continent of North America to the other.—Men, he said, whose best and sincerest intentions would be only interpreted as lures to ensnare and betray. Under the full influence of these persuasions, he could not but fear, that whatever the noble Lord's intentions might be, his plan would be rejected by America, which would only furnish Ministers with an apology for trying the experiment of one more fatal and disgraceful campaign; after which he would venture to predict, that all further attempts to subdue, or hopes to treat with America would be at an end, and that country irretrievably lost for ever to this.

The Minister refrained from taking any notice of the asperities that had dropped from this gentleman, and only gave a general answer to his opinions, along with those which had been thrown out by others, relative to his proposed scheme of conciliation. He said, that as he never meant to negociate away the rights of this country, to procure himself any temporary convenience; so he never wished to encroach on those of America. His own private opinion never varied; but if his proposition should not meet with the approbation of the majority in that House, or that it should undergo any alteration, in either event he would gladly acquiesce. As to the particular favourable disposition of America towards inviduals or parties in that or the other House, he said, that by every thing that had yet appeared, all men and all parties seemed equally obnoxious to them; and whenever propositions came to be made, he was inclined to believe, that the object of the colonies would not be by whom they were made, but whether they were such as answered their expectations. For his own part, he was ready and willing to resign the disagreeable task to whoever was thought better qualified, and was contented to accept of it. He wished as sincerely for pacification as any one person in either House; and so the end was obtained, it was a matter of no consequence to him by whom, or in what manner it was accomplished.

Mr. Fox had thrown out in his

speech, that he had been informed it was intended to send out other Generals, and that upon that ground, great expectations were formed on the success of the ensuing campaign. For himself, he said he expected, that whoever should succeed to the present gentlemen in command, would meet with the exact fate of their predecessors; they would be one day charged with indolence, inactivity, and want of spirit; with a designed procrastination of the war, from motives of lucre and private interest; and on the next, with quixotism, knight errantry, and disobedience to instructions. He then gave ample testimony to the bravery and good conduct of the Generals; contended, that they did not miscarry through want of skill in their profession, or from any neglect of their duty, but merely from their being employed on a service, in which it was impossible for them to succeed; and that if Ministers shewed any trace of wisdom throughout their whole conduct, it was in their choice of officers; although they now basely insinuated, that it was only in the choice of Generals that they had been deceived; and that it was to their fault alone, that all the miscarriages in the prosecution of the American measures were to be imputed. No reply was made to these observations.

Mr. Fox's first motion was at length set aside about 11 at night, by another, for the Chairman's [52] leaving the chair, and reporting some progress, which was carried upon a division by a majority of 263 to 149. He then, notwithstanding the advice of the Ministers, as in the first instance, to withdraw his other propositions, determined to take the sense of the House upon each singly, and they all accordingly received a separate negative without a division.

During this warfare in the House of Commons upon various parts of the general enquiry into the state of the nation, that great and important subject was not less agitated in the House of Lords, where it was conducted with unusual temper and ability, together with a perseverance scarcely to be paralleled, by the Duke of Richmond; who was also exceedingly well supported by nearly all the principal characters of opposition among the Lords. Nor was there less address shewn in one House than the other, in the manner of frustrating the principal objects of enquiry.

A debate on the choice of a chairman, upon the opening of the general committee on the 2d of February, being a matter in itself of little or no consequence, afforded an early indication of the temper which was likely to prevail with the majority in the course of the business. The noble Duke who moved for the committee, had nominated the Duke of Portland [53] as Chairman, which was immediately opposed on the other side by the nomination of Lord Scarsdale. [54] It was said in support of the latter, that it was a rule of that House for one person always to take the chair in such cases; that the noble Lord in question had frequently presided in it with the greatest propriety and dignity; and that it would imply a tacit disapprobation of his conduct, to appoint a new Chairman while the former was present. It was further said, that as the business of the committee was likely to be arduous, it would require all the known industry and experience of the noble Lord to be conducted with propriety.

The Duke of Richmond replied, that he had no particular reason for naming the noble Duke, but that his character and abilities entitled him to every mark of honour and attention which they could bestow; that it had been always usual for the person who moved for a committee of the whole House to be complimented with the nomination of a Chairman, as a matter of course; and that although it was otherwise a matter of no consequence, he wished his nomination in this instance to be adhered to, as it would appear some sort of insult to the noble Duke if it were set aside. He concluded with observing, that it appeared an ill omen with respect to the important business before them, that they should not enter upon it with that cordiality and amicable union of sentiment, with which he had hoped to find them inspired; declared that no solid objection had been offered to the noble Duke's taking the chair; and lamented so early a manifestation of party spirit.

It was farther contended on the same side, that there was no order or resolution of the House which entitled one Lord to be Chairman more than another; but that, in strict duty, each of them ought to discharge the office in his turn; so that if any one Lord had taken more than his share of the duty, it should be an argument why he should be relieved from it both then and in future; and that it was a jest to talk that any particular degree of experience or knowledge of business was necessary to its discharge, as there was not a member of either House who was not fully competent to the duty.

On the other side it was still insisted, that the Chairman who had been once appointed in a committee of the whole House, was after, when present, considered as perpetual Chairman; and that such being the uniform rule, those who attempted to depart from it, and not those who adhered to it, were to be charged with manifesting a spirit of party. The matter being put to the question, the Duke of Richmond's nomination was rejected upon a division, by a majority of 58 to 33, and Lord Scarsdale accordingly took the chair.

Although the Duke of Richmond took a wide range through the extensive subjects of their deliberation, he confined the immediate business of the day to the state of our home military defence, and having with great pains and labour drawn clear calculations from a multitude of perplexed and undigested accounts, he endeavoured to convince the committee of its great deficiency, considered merely as a *Peace Establishment*. He then stated the great and immediate probability of a foreign war, which was also acknowledged and confirmed by the speech from the throne; and from thence drew the impolicy and danger of rendering our home defence, deficient as it already was, still weaker, by any further drains for foreign service.

Upon this ground he made the following motion as the foundation of an address: " Resolved, that " this committee, taking into " consideration the continuance " of the armaments in the ports " of France and Spain, of which " his Majesty was pleased to in- " form parliament in a speech " from the throne at the opening " of this session ; and also taking " into consideration that a very " great part of our naval and " land forces are on the other side " of the atlantic ocean, and there- " fore not applicable to the de- " fence of this kingdom upon any " emergency ; and that the forces " in Great Britain, Ireland, Gib- " raltar and Minorca, are at this " time less in number by 5673 " men, than the establishment has " been in times of tranquillity and " peace ; is of opinion, that no " part of the old corps, which " are left in Great Britain, Ire- " land, Gibraltar or Minorca, can " be spared for any distant ser- " vice, without leaving this king- " dom and its immediate depen- " dencies in a most perilous, weak, " and defenceless condition, there- " by inviting a foreign war, and " exposing the nation to insult " and calamity."

The motion was principally op-posed by the Lords in administration upon the following grounds. The impolicy in exposing to rival powers the weakness of our home defence. The impropriety of parliament interfering in any manner to restrain the crown in the exercise of its inherent prerogative, that of raising, directing, and employing of the military force of the kingdom; and that to restrain or regulate that exercise, would be in fact to suspend it. That the defence of this kingdom did not depend on its army. The navy was our great and sure bulwark of defence. Our fleets had ever been irresistible ; and our navy was never in a more respectable condition than at present. It was, in its present state of preparation, the great pledge for our internal security, and for the pacific conduct of our neighbours. The passage in the King's speech had been totally wrested from its purpose ; and the inference drawn from it was unfounded and unjustifiable. The nature and extent of the dependance which should be placed on the disposition or professions of foreign courts, varied with circumstances ; and it would be highly unwise in the course of political events to rely solely on assurances. That predictions of the same nature with the present, relative to the conduct and designs of foreign powers, had been frequently repeated for some years, but were not yet in any instance justified by experience. But that in any case, supposing the worst that could possibly happen, and that all that was held out on the other side should be realized ; surely it would be exceedingly imprudent to invite a war, by acquainting our foreign rivals in power and greatness, that we were either unprepared or unable to meet an enemy. They concluded, that the resolution would amount to a public acknowledgment of our inability to reduce the Americans ; and consequently to the renunciation of all our

rights, and to the establishment of their independence.

The Lords in opposition ridiculed the ideas of secrecy affected on the other side ; which they also represented as an insult on the understanding of that House. Could they themselves imagine, that any person in or out of it, with the most common share of understanding and information, could swallow such an absurdity, as that our foreign enemies were ignorant of the state of our land forces, and of our home defence. The detail of the names and numbers of the several corps, and the places of their distribution, is constantly in print. The estimates are annually and publicly laid before parliament The accounts from which the resolution is drawn are now before parliament. Not a single solid objection, they said, had been made to the noble Duke's motion ; his facts were unanswered, and thereby established ; no man had ventured to contradict or controvert them. All they have advanced, exclusive of the shameful pretence of deceiving our enemies, by concealing our weakness in one instance, and making a false display of our strength in another, amounts to no more, said they, than that we should now, in the instant of greatest danger which this country ever experienced, repose a thorough confidence in the vigilance and ability of those ministers for our future preservation, who by a long series of error and misconduct, and a failure, through inability, of all their measures, have at length brought our affairs to the present perilous crisis. In the course of the debate, a war with France was repeatedly declared to be inevitable ; a noble Duke predicted with confidence that it would take place before three months were elapsed ; he said, that to prevent a junction between France, Spain, and America, we should make peace with the latter at all events ; and exclaimed with eagernefs, " Peace with America, and war with all the world."

The queftion being at length put, the Duke of Richmond's notion was rejected upon a divifion by a majority of 93 to 31.

The committee on the ftate of the nation being refumed on the 6th, feveral eminent merchants were brought by the Duke of Richmond to be examined at the bar, whofe evidence went to eftablifh the great loffes which our commerce had fuftained by the war. The examinations were long and interefting; no pains were omitted by the Lords on either fide of the Houfe in their enquiries; nor were thofe on the minifterial fide deficient in point of ftricture and crofs examination. Upon the whole, the evidence was unufually clear and accurate.

To leffen or weaken the effects which might be produced by this enquiry into the ftate of our commercial loffes by the war, the noble Lord at the head of the Admiralty thought it fitting in three days after to bring counter-evidence before the committee, in order to fhew the advantages which it had afforded. His Lordfhip obferved, that as the noble Duke had brought witneffes to prove the loffes fuftained by the commerce of this country, it was neceffary, as well for their information, as to prevent an *ex parte* evidence from going abroad into the world, to fhew how far the loffes fuftained by Great Britain had been compenfated for, whether by the prizes taken from our rebellious colonies, or by the opening of new branches of commerce. He then moved, that the witneffes whom he had brought for the purpofe fhould be examined at the bar.

This was objected to by the Duke of Richmond as informal. He faid, he could not eafily difcern for what purpofe this evidence was to be produced. For to form a juft eftimate of the effect of this war on our commerce, the trade loft muft be fet againft the captures made; and though they fhould prove equal, (which he believed would not be ferioufly afferted) all the captures made from our trade by the Americans would be fo much clear lofs. But whatever it might turn out, he faid, he would by no means endeavour to preclude his Lordfhip from bringing what evidences he pleafed relative to this enquiry at a proper time; that his own lay open to his crofs-examination, and he had it in his power to controvert every thing they advanced; but that to take up another matter before the former was difpofed of, was unparliamentary; and was befides, not dealing with that candour and opennefs which might be expected. He then appealed to their lordfhips, whether in every ftage of the enquiry he had not previoufly acquainted them with the fubftance of his intended motions; only wifhing and hoping that every noble Lord would have been influenced by the fame motives which actuated himfelf, namely, an earneft defire to come at every degree of information, which might open any way for attempting to relieve or alleviate the prefent very great diftreffes of this country.

To this it was anfwered by a great law Lord, that the fubjects[55] on which the committee was to hear evidence were blended; loffes had been proved, and eftimates made to the difadvantage of Great Britain; and as the evidences now to be examined intended to prove, that thofe eftimates were not fo confiderable as they had been ftated, it was certainly quite regular to proceed on that examination. This opinion was, however, controverted; and after a confiderable debate, the motion for examining the witneffes was carried upon a divifion by a majority of 66 to 25.

The noble Earl's witneffes amounted only to three; the firft of whom, being a proctor belonging to the court of Admiralty, was brought forward to teftify the number of American prizes which had been condemned in his court. The fecond, was a confiderable adventurer in a whale fifhery, which had been difcovered and profecuted with great advantage in the fouthern American feas, as well as on the coafts of Africa, by the Britifh colonies, before the commencement of the troubles; but which had only of late been attempted from this country, on its dropping out of the hands of the Americans, and in confequence of the fcarcity and high price of oil, through the general failure in our fifheries. The third, was an old captain in the Newfoundland cod and whale fifheries.

It appeared from the evidence of the fecond, that the fouthern fifheries were capable in time, and under the bleffings of tranquillity, (more efpecially if they could be retained as a monopoly) of becoming exceedingly profitable. The fperma ceti whale, which abounds in thofe feas, is reprefented as being by far the moft valuable of his fpecies. He ftated that fifteen veffels of about 170 tons each, had been employed in that fifhery the preceding year; but it was drawn out upon his crofs-examination, that the returns in product that year, (which was however deemed very fuccefsful) run upon an average only between forty and fifty tons to each veffel. It was at the fame time known, although we believe not directly fpecified by this witnefs, that the very oil which was the product of this fifhery, as well as thofe of all others, were now rifen to about double their ufual price. He alfo acknowledged, that they were under a neceffity of employing four American harpooners in each veffel, as the Britifh feamen were not yet capable of executing that capital part of the bufinefs.

It did not feem that the third witnefs eftablifhed any thing very material. He only stated what was evident to every body, that as we had now a monopoly of the Newfoundland fishery by the exclusion of the Americans, so, if we were capable of prosecuting it to the utmost extent, the whole profits, which they formerly shared with us, would, in that case, center entirely in our own hands. But he was obliged to acknowledge, that the present scarcity of seamen prevented in a very great degree our profiting of that circumstance; and upon being closely pressed, he seemed uncertain, whether, laying by all consideration of the European markets, we should even be able to supply our West-India islands from that fishery, if the pressing of seamen was continued in its present rigour by the Admiralty. He acknowledged that we were obliged to employ American harpooners in the Newfoundland whale fishery.

On the 11th of February, the committee being resumed, the Duke of Richmond recapitulated the evidences which he had brought before them, preparatory to a set of motions which he had to make, being, he said, only resolutions of plain matters of fact, arising from the evidence before them, and which would be grounds for their lordships further deliberation.

His Grace accordingly stated his resolutions to the following effect: That in the course of trade, a very considerable ballance was always due from the merchants in North America to the merchants of Great Britain, towards the discharge of which remittances were made in goods to a great amount, since the commencement of the present troubles, and whilst the trade between this kingdom and the colonies was suffered to remain open.—That since the passing of the several acts for prohibiting the fisheries of the colonies in North America, their mutual intercourse with each other, all trade and commerce between them and this kingdom, and for making prize of their ships, and distributing their value, as if they were the effects of our enemies, amongst the seamen of his Majesty's navy, the number of vessels belonging to Great Britain and Ireland, taken by ships of war and privateers belonging to the said colonies, amount to 733.—That, of that number, it appears that 47 have been released, and 127 retaken; but that the loss on the latter, for salvage, interest on the value of the cargo, and loss of a market, must have been very considerable.—That the loss of the remaining 559 vessels, which have been carried into port, appears, from the examination of merchants, to amount at least to 2,600,000l.—That of 200 ships annually employed in the African trade, before the commencement of the present civil war, whose value, upon an average, was about 9,000l. each, there are not now forty ships employed in that trade, whereby there is a diminution in this branch of commerce of 160 ships, which at 9,000l. each, amount to a loss of 1,440,000l. per annum.—That the price of insurance to the West Indies and North America, is increased from two, and two and a half, to five per cent. with convoy; but without convoy, and unarmed, the said insurance has been made at fifteen per cent. But generally ships in such circumstances cannot be insured at all.—That the price of seamen's wages is raised from one pound ten shillings, to three pounds five shillings per month.—That the price of pot-ash is increased from eight shillings to three pounds ten shillings per hundred weight.—That the price of sperma-ceti oil has increased from thirty-five pounds to seventy pounds per ton.—That the price of tar is raised from seven and eight shillings, to thirty shillings per barrel.—That the price of sugars, and all commodities from the West Indies, and divers sorts of naval stores from North America, is greatly enhanced.—That it appears to this committee, that the present diminution of the African trade, the interruption of the American trade to the West Indies, and the captures made of the West-India ships, have greatly distressed the British colonies in the West Indies.—That the numbers of American privateers, of which authentic accounts have been received, amount to 173; and that they carried 2556 guns, and at least 13,840 seamen, reckoning 80 men in each ship.—And that, of the above privateers, 34 have been taken, which carried 3,217 men, which is more than 94 men to each vessel.

The noble Lord at the head of the Admiralty declared, that every day's experience served to confirm him in his original opinion, that the enquiry into the state of the nation was pregnant with the most ruinous consequences, and could not be productive of the smallest benefit. That it only went to publish to the world those things which in prudence and policy should be concealed. That no war could be conducted without difficulty, embarrassment, and loss; but that it was a new system of policy to let enemies into the secret of national difficulty or imbecility. But he also contended that the American commerce had suffered more than ours by the war; that upon the whole, we had in that respect been gainers in the contest; and that upon a fair examination a considerable ballance would be found in our favour.

In support of this position, he controverted the evidence given by the merchants; said that their estimates in point of value were rated too high; and their lists of ships taken by the enemy erroneous. That if some branches of commerce failed, (which ever was and will be the case with all nations, whether in peace or in war) others of greater value were established.

Upon this ground, he estimated the benefits to be derived from the southern fishery, and even its present value, at a very high rate; and the American share of the Newfoundland fishery, which was calculated in its duplicate state of a prize to us, and a loss to them, was appreciated in the same manner. The noble Lord stated the number of American prizes which had been taken at 904, which estimated, he said, at the very moderate valuation of 2,000l. each ship and cargo upon an average, would amount to 1,808,000l. to which, if the value of the fisheries was added, it would appear that this country was not benefited less already by the war than 2,200,000l. besides that every shilling of that money was a total loss to our rebellious colonies. He concluded, that these facts totally overthrew the Duke's resolutions in point of establishing an estimate of national loss; and that although nobody wished more for an end to the war than he did, yet its continuance was in many respects advantageous to this country, and would be still more so.

On the other side the Lords were earnestly called upon to consider, that the questions which they were to decide upon, were facts already established before them, and to which, without a total violence to reason and propriety, they could not refuse their assent. That so far the ground was cleared for their further deliberations, and opened a view in one great national department, how far the further prosecution of the war would be consistent with sound policy, and with the public welfare. And the supposed danger of affording information to our enemies, relative to facts which were already of public notoriety, met with that degree of ridicule with which the subject had of late been not unfrequently treated.

The noble Duke who was the proposer of the motions observed, that as they did not mix with any other matter, the noble Earl's detail did not in any degree interfere with them, and could not with any colour of propriety or reason be brought to set them aside. He observed with exceeding severity, that the dangers with which we were surrounded, and the calamities in which this country was overwhelmed, could no longer excite surprize or wonder, when a minister at the head of the marine, that most capital department of the state, and upon which its power and preservation entirely depended, should betray such shameful and total ignorance of trade and commerce, as to lay down as an incontrovertible position, that, because the great number of ships we had lost in the war might be ballanced by another number of vessels taken from the Americans, the nation, upon the whole, consequently sustained no loss. He asked, whether any other Lord present could be persuaded, that the commerce of this country was not affected by the loss of 773 vessels, estimated in value at considerably above two millions of money, which had been taken from our merchants, because an equal value in prizes (supposing the fact to be true, which was, however, by no means admitted) had been taken from the Americans, and distributed among the seamen of the royal navy. The case was still the more deplorable, he said, as the value of all those cargoes, if we had not been at war with the Americans, would, in the circuitous course of trade, have centered in Great Britain.

Some difficulty arose as to the mode of disposing of the question. For the nature of the facts stated in the resolutions scarcely admitted of a direct negative, and the putting of the previous question is not customarily practised in committees. To solve this difficulty a noble Lord high in office moved, that the chairman should quit the chair, on which the committee divided, when the motion was carried by a majority of 80 to 32 Lords. The House being thus resumed, the Duke of Richmond moved his string of resolutions, when the previous question was put upon each separately, and carried.

56

Petition from the county of Norfolk. Lord North's conciliatory propositions. Two bills brought in thereon. Effect of the Minister's speech. Conduct of the minority with respect to his conciliatory scheme. Mr. Fox states his information of the conclusion of a treaty between France and the American deputies; calls upon the Minister for an explanation on that subject. Progress of the bills. Mr. Serjeant Adair's motion for the appointment of commissioners, after much debate, rejected. Mr. Powys's motion to admit a clause for the repeal of the Massachusets Charter Act, rejected on a division. Motion by Mr. Powys for the repeal of the American Tea Act, and by Mr. Burke for extending the provisions of the Declaratory Bill to the West Indies; both agreed to. Conciliatory bills pass the Commons. New house-tax. Mr. Gilbert moves for a tax of one-fourth upon salaries, annuities, pensions, fees, and perquisites of offices under the crown. Motion carried upon a division; but rejected the following day, on receiving the report from the Committee, by a small majority. Mr. Fox's motion in the Committee of Enquiry, relative to the state of the royal navy, after much debate, set aside by the previous question. Mr. J. Luttrell's motion for an instruction enabling the American commissioners to promise the removal of any minister or ministers, who they should discover to be so obnoxious to the colonies, as thereby to prevent the restoration of tranquillity, rejected upon a division. Letter from General Gates to the Earl of Thanet read by the Marquis of Rockingham. Motion by the Duke of Richmond, that the letter should lie on the table, after some debate, rejected. Duke of Richmond's motions relative to the state of the forces in America, after much debate, set aside by the previous question. State and amount of the expences incurred by the war in America, set forth by the Duke of Richmond; who proposes a number of resolutions founded thereon, which are all set aside as before. Motion for the attendance of the Surveyor of the navy, made by the Duke of Bolton, and rejected upon a division. Several subsequent motions made by the same nobleman, and tending to an enquiry into the state of the navy, after considerable debates rejected. American conciliatory bills passed by the Lords. Enquiry into the conduct of the transport service by the Earl of Effingham, whose resolutions thereon are rejected.

A Petition of uncommon energy, signed by 5,400 inhabitants of the county of Norfolk, including the city of Norwich, was presented and read to the Commons on the morning of the day that the Minister was to lay open his conciliatory plan with America. In this piece, a comprehensive view was taken of the conduct of public affairs, and the effect of public measures, both at home and abroad. Among others, the measure of raising men and money by free gifts and contributions for the service of the crown, a purpose for which, they say, they were called upon themselves, in a manner equally alarming, by persons of great power and rank in his Majesty's service, receives the most explicit marks of their disapprobation. The piece abounds with strong expressions.—" A misrepresentation of our unhappy " situation would be a mockery of " our distress. An empire is lost. " A great continent in arms is to " be conquered or abandoned." After a melancholy representation of public affairs, they trust, " that " the House of Commons, whose " duty calls, and whose competence and constitution enables " them to come to the bottom of " those evils, will seriously enquire into the causes of our present calamitous situation, for " we greatly fear that we, with " the rest of your constituents, " have been hitherto greatly deceived and deluded, with regard to the nature, the cause, " and the importance of the American troubles, as well as concerning the means of quieting " them, both legal and coercive; " else, we should not have the " misfortune of seeing acts of parliament made, only to be sent " back to be repealed; armies " sent out to enforce them, only " to be returned to us as prisoners " under capitulation; and, to " speak with the filial confidence " of free subjects, we plainly declare ourselves unwilling to " commit any more of our national glory to attaint, and the " persons of more of our countrymen to foreign hardships and " perils, without any common " human security, that they shall " not, by the same errors, be " exposed to the same calamities " and disgraces, which many of " those have fallen into who have " already been sent forth. Without wise councils at home, we " cannot have empire or reputation abroad."

The noble Lord at the head of affairs, however little satisfied he might be with the censures passed or implied in this petition upon public conduct and measures, could find nothing in it to militate with any propositions that tended to a conciliation with America. He introduced his conciliatory propositions with a recital of his creed in all American matters. In that he asserted, that peace had at all times been his governing principle. That with that object in view, his conduct had been uniform, and his measures consistent; but that events had been in general exceedingly untoward. That he had always known, that American taxation could never produce a beneficial revenue; that there were many sorts of taxes which could not at all be laid on that country; and of those that could, few would prove worth the charge of collection. That although the Stamp Act was the most judicious that could be chosen for that pur-

Feb. 17th.

pose; yet, notwithstanding the high rate at which that duty had been formerly estimated, he had not believed its produce would have been a very considerable object.

That he, accordingly, had never proposed any tax on the Americans; he found them already taxed when he unfortunately came into administration. That as his principle of policy was to have as little discussion on these subjects as possible, and to keep the affairs of America out of parliament; so, as he had not laid, he did not think it adviseable for him to repeal the tea tax; nor did he look out for any particular means of enforcing it. That the measure of enabling the East-India company to send teas on their own account to America, with a drawback of the whole duty here, was a regulation of such a nature, being a relief instead of an oppression, that it was impossible he should suppose it could have excited a single complaint amongst the Americans, much less to be productive of the consequences that followed. These he attributed in part to the disaffected, and in part to those who were concerned in a contraband trade, who represented it to the populace as a monopoly; so that the people were excited to tumult upon a principle totally distinct from every idea of taxation.

With respect to the coercive acts, he said they were called forth by, and appeared necessary in, the distemper of the time; but that in the event they had produced effects which he never intended, nor could possibly have expected. That immediately upon the discovery of that failure, he proposed, before the sword was drawn, a conciliatory proposition. His Lordship said he thought at the time, and still continued to think, the terms of that proposition would form the happiest, most equitable, and most lasting bond of union between Great Britain and her colonies. But, that by a variety of discussions, a proposition that was ori-

ginally clear and simple in itself, was made to appear so obscure, as to go damned to America; so that the Congress conceived, or took occasion to represent it as a scheme for sowing divisions, and introducing taxation among them in a worse mode than the former, and they accordingly rejected it.

He complained that the events of war in America had turned out very differently from his expectations, and from what he had a right to expect; and that the great and well appointed force sent out, and amply provided for by government, had produced a very disproportioned effect hitherto. That he could not but confess himself exceedingly disappointed at this failure of effect in our military force. He did not mean at that time to condemn, or even to call into question, the conduct of any of our commanders, but he had been disappointed. That Sir William Howe had been in the late actions, and in the whole course of the campaign, not only in the goodness of troops, and in all manner of supplies, but in point of numbers too, much superior to the American army which opposed him in the field. That General Burgoyne, who was at length overpowered by numbers, had been in numbers, until the affair at Bennington, near twice as strong as the army under General Gates. Considering all these things, the events had been very contrary to his expectation. But to these events, and not to those expectations, he must make his plan conform.

As the foundation of his conciliatory scheme, he proposed the bringing in two bills under the following heads: " A bill for declaring the intentions of the parliament of Great Britain, concerning the exercise of the right of imposing taxes within his Majesty's colonies, provinces, and plantations in North America." And, " A bill to enable his Majesty to appoint commissioners, with sufficient powers to treat, consult, and

agree upon the means of quieting the disorders now subsisting in certain of the colonies, plantations, and provinces of North America."

The noble Lord observed, that it was intended to appoint five commissioners, and to endow them with very extensive powers. They should be enabled to treat with the Congress by name, as if it were a legal body, and so far to give it authenticity, as to suppose its acts and concessions binding on all America. To treat with any of the provincial assemblies upon their present constitution, and with any individuals in their present civil capacities or military commands, with General Washington, or any other officer. That they should have a power to order a suspension of arms. To suspend the operation of all laws. And to grant all sorts of pardons, immunities, and rewards. That they should have a power of restoring all the colonies, or any of them, to the form of its ancient constitution, as it stood before the troubles; and in any of those where the King nominated the governors, council, judges, and other magistrates, to nominate such at their discretion, until his further pleasure was known.

That as the deficiency of powers in the former commissioners had been objected to, so the Congress had raised a difficulty, on pretence of the non-admission of their title to be independent states. To remove that difficulty, should the Americans now claim their independence on the outset, he would not insist on their renouncing it, until the treaty had received its final ratification by the King and parliament of Great Britain. That the commissioners should be instructed to negociate for some reasonable and moderate contribution towards the common defence of the empire when re-united; but to take away all pretence for not terminating this unhappy difference, the contribution was not to be insisted on as a *sine qua non* of the treaty; but that if the Americans should refuse so reasonable and equitable a proposition, they were not to complain, if hereafter they were not to look for support from that part of the empire to whose expence they had refused to contribute.

He observed it might be asked, if his sentiments had been always such with respect to taxation and peace as he had now stated them to be, why he had not made this proposition at an earlier period? To this he answered, his opinion had ever been, that the moment of victory was the proper season for offering terms of concession. And with an eye to several reflections which had of late been thrown upon him by the tory party, and hoping perhaps to obviate some part of that greater weight of censure which he now apprehended from that quarter, he declared, that, for his part, he never had made a promise which he did not perform, or receive any information which he did not communicate. That he only kept back the names of those who had given him information, and which it would have been unfaithful and inhuman to divulge. That, he promised a great army should be sent out, and a great army had accordingly been sent out, to the amount of 60,000 men and upwards; that he had promised a great fleet should be employed, and a great fleet had been employed, and is still employed; he promised that they should be provided with every kind of supply, and they had been so most amply and liberally, and might continue to be so for years to come. And, that the House had all along been in full possession of the whole subject, so that if they were deceived, they had deceived themselves.

The Minister concluded a long, able, and eloquent speech, which kept him full two hours up, by saying, that on the whole his concessions were from reason and propriety, not from necessity; and

that we were in a condition to carry on the war much longer. We might raise many more men, and had many more men ready to send; the navy was never in greater strength, the revenue but little sunk, and a few days would shew that he should raise the funds for the current year at a moderate rate. But he submitted the whole, with regard to the propriety of his past and present conduct to the judgment of the House.

A dull melancholy silence for some time succeeded to this speech. It had been heard with profound attention, but without a single mark of approbation to any part, from any description of men, or any particular man in the House. Astonishment, dejection, and fear, overclouded the whole assembly. Although the Minister had declared, that the sentiments he expressed that day, had been those which he always entertained; it is certain, that few or none had understood him in that manner; and he had been represented to the nation at large, as the person in it the most tenacious of those parliamentary rights which he now proposed to resign, and the most remote from the submissions which he now proposed to make. It was generally therefore concluded, that something more extraordinary and alarming had happened than yet appeared, which was of force to produce such an apparent change in measures, principles, and arguments.

It was thought by many at that time, that if the opposition had then pressed him, and joined with the warm party which had hitherto supported the Minister, but which was now disgusted and mortified in the highest degree, the bills would have been lost. But, in fact, they took such a hearty part with the Minister, only endeavouring to make such alterations in, or additions to the bills, as might increase their eligibility, or extend their effect, that no appearance of party remained; and some of his complain-

ing friends vexatiously congratulated him on his new allies. These new allies, however, though they supported his measures, shewed no mercy to his conduct.

Mr. Fox complimented the Minister on his conversion, and congratulated his own party on the acquisition of so potent an auxiliary. He was glad to find that his propositions did not materially differ from those which had been laid before them by his friend Mr. Burke three years before; and reminded the House, that although they were then rejected by the Minister, three years war had convinced him of their utility. He observed that the noble Lord was so perfect a proselyte, that the very same arguments which had at that time been so ineffectually used by the minority, and in nearly the same words, were now adopted by his Lordship. He ironically applauded his resolution in relinquishing the right of taxation, from the high satisfaction which it must afford to several country gentlemen, who had placed so firm a reliance on his former declarations. Nor was he less pleased with the power to be given to the commissioners for restoring the charter of Massachusets, as that was a proof of his Lordship's wisdom in framing the act by which it was destroyed. For, to do, and to undo, to destroy and to restore, were not only the singular prerogative, and high felicity of power, but they were also the most exalted acts of wisdom.

He wished that this concession had been made more early, and upon principles more respectful to parliament. To tell them, that if they were deceived, they had deceived themselves, was neither kind nor civil to an assembly, which, for so many years, had relied upon him with the most unreserved confidence. That all public bodies, like the House of Commons, must give a large confidence to persons in office; and their only method of preventing the abuse of that confidence, was to punish those who misinformed them concerning the state of their affairs, or who had conducted them with negligence, ignorance, or incapacity.

The noble Lord's defence of measures, if he could have established a real defence, would have done the highest honour to his logical abilities, as it would have been no less than a justification of the most unjustifiable measures that had ever disgraced any minister, or ruined any country. But his whole arguments might be collected into one point, and all his excuses into one apology, when the whole would be comprized, and fully expressed, in the simple word ignorance! a palpable and total ignorance of every part of the subject.—He hoped, and he was disappointed.—He expected a great deal, and found little to answer his expectations. — He thought America would have submitted to his laws, and they resisted them.—He thought they would have submitted to his armies, and they beat them with inferior numbers.—He made conciliatory propositions, and he thought they would succeed, but they were rejected.—He appointed commissioners to make peace, and he thought they had powers, but he found they could not make peace, and nobody believed they had any powers.

He, however, said, that as the present propositions were much more clear and satisfactory than the former, for necessity had at length compelled the noble Lord to speak plain, they should accordingly receive his support, and he supposed that of all his friends on the same side of the House. Undoubtedly, said he, they would have given full satisfaction, and have prevented all the loss, ruin, and calamity, which England and America have since experienced, if they had been offered in time. But if the concession should be found ample enough, and then

found to come too late, what punishment will be sufficient for those ministers who adjourned parliament, in order to make a proposition of concession, and then neglected to do it, until France had concluded a treaty with the Independent States of America, acknowledging them as such? He did not speak from surmize, he said; he had it from authority which he could not question, that the treaty he mentioned had been signed in Paris ten days before,[57] counting from that instant. He therefore wished the ministry would give the House satisfaction on that very interesting point; for he feared that it would be found, that their present apparently pacific and equitable disposition, with that proposition which seemed the result of it, owed their existence to the previous knowledge of the conclusion of a treaty, which must, from its nature, render that proposition as useless to the peace, as it was humiliating to the dignity of Great Britain.

Others of the opposition said, that they would vote for the proposition, as they would for any thing that looked even towards, or that could in any possible event tend to a reconciliation; but they declared at the same time, that they had not the smallest hope of its producing any good effect. For they did not think it to be in nature, and consequently not possible, that the Americans, after having been driven to the final extremity and last refuge of mankind against oppression, should now, when they had successfully established their independency by arms, again commit those rights and immunities, which they have just redeemed at so dear a price, to the custody of those very men, who have convulsed the empire in all its parts, through the unnatural violence of the efforts which they used for their destruction; nor that any art could induce them to receive the olive branch from those hands,

which were so deeply polluted, and still reeking with the blood of their country.

Some of the country gentlemen, who had all along supported the ministry in general, and who were supposed particularly attached to this minister, being much piqued at that expression of his, that "they had not been misled or deceived," rose in great warmth and asserted, they said, with indignation, that they had been grosly deceived and misled by the uniform language of government for three years past;[58] and one gentleman went so far as to say, that he should feel for the humiliating blush of his sovereign, when he gave his assent to the proposed bills. On the declaration of a great law officer, that a security[59] for the congress debts, and a reestablishment of the credit of their paper currency, would be one of the objects of the commission, and one of the principal inducements held out to that body to return to its allegiance, another gentleman,[60] zealously attached to the court declared, that he would much more readily consent to give currency to forged India bonds, and counterfeit bank notes, than to paper which had been fabricated to carry on rebellion against the King and parliament of Great Britain. In general that party declared, that as the point of taxation, which could be the only rational ground of the war, was now given up, peace should be procured by any means, and in the speediest manner. Nor did the Minister escape being asked, as taxation had not at any time been his object, what were the real motives of the war? and whether he had sported away thirty thousand lives, with thirty millions of money, and in that amusement put not only the unity, but the existence of the empire to the hazard, merely to try the mettle of the Americans, and to discover what spirit they would shew in the defence of every thing that was dear to them.

Such things muft be borne in fuch fituations. The Minifter being clofely preffed on different hands for fome explanation relative to the treaty faid to have been concluded between France and America, at length declared, that he had no authority upon which to pronounce abfolutely with refpect to that event; that a report had for fome time prevailed, that fuch a treaty was in agitation; that its conclufion was not only poffible, but perhaps too probable;—that, however, as it had not yet been authenticated by the Ambaffador, the prefumption lay that it had not taken place. This brought out an exclamation from a gentleman in [61] oppofition, that when the nation was at a very large expence, in fupporting diplomatique eftablifhments, and reprefentatives of majefty, in the different courts of Europe, it was in the higheft degree fhameful, and not a little alarming, that in a matter of fuch momentous concern, the intelligence of a private gentleman fhould be more early, or more authentic, than that of the Minifter of Great Britain.

In the progrefs of the bills Mr. Serjeant Adair moved, Feb. 23d, [62] that it be an inftruction to the committee of the bill for appointing commiffioners, that they have power to make provifion for nominating the commiffioners by the bill. He faid, that this was no infringement on the prerogative of the crown; it was no matter that lay within its ordinary federal capacity; it was a commiffion appointed by parliament, in order to treat about the rights of parliament itfelf, the fufpending its laws, and the furrender of its rights, or of what it had always confidered or claimed as fuch; that for the Houfe to give blindly fuch a power out of its hands, to be exercifed at the mere pleafure of the crown, and by perfons to them utterly unknown, was in effect a complete furrender of

the whole conftitution of this country into the hands of the King. That, he therefore thought himfelf bound to refift this moft unconftitutional meafure by every means in his power; that as to any difficulties which might be fuppofed in the execution of this mode of appointment, they had been all completely got over in the Eaft-India bill, where, with fuch fufficient facility, parliament had nominated commiffioners for a matter of mere executive government, and one in which no parliamentary rights or powers were at all concerned. That he hoped, as himfelf and the other gentlemen of the late minority had given, and would continue to give, fo clear a fupport to the conciliatory meafures of th Minifter, late as they were adopted, he alfo hoped the Minifter, on his part, would likewife act a fair and candid part with them, and not take them in for a dangerous extenfion of prerogative, whilft they were joining him in an attempt to reftore peace to the country.

The learned gentlemen on the other fide contended, that a compliance with the motion would be taking the executive power out of the hands of the crown. That to hold out to the world at this time, that parliament entertained any jealoufy of the crown, would tend greatly to counteract, inftead of in any degree promoting the good effects, that were intended by the bill; and might alfo, in the prefent critical juncture of affairs, be attended with very pernicious confequences otherwife. That it would be a violent act, after having empowered and directed the crown to carry on the war, and after having authorized the crown to make peace, if it could have been effected by the fubmiffion of America, for the legiflature on a fudden to hold their hand and fay, the crown fhall not negociate for peace. That there was no inftance of parliament taking fuch an appointment into their own hands, ex-

cepting once in the reign of Richard the Second, and that act was repealed a few years after with reproach, as an ufurpation of the rights of the crown. That the progrefs of fuch a bufinefs in the Houfe would be attended with the groffeft inconveniences; the confequent difcuffion of names and of individuals would be odious in the higheft degree; and as it was impoffible that 550 perfons fhould ever agree in fuch a nomination, the hiftory of their diffentions would accompany the commiffion to America. But if it were true, as it was every day faid on the other fide to be, that the minifters could command a majority, then the nomination would of courfe lie in the crown without its avowal; and parliament would thereby be precluded from its natural controul upon minifters, of calling them to account for mifadvifing the crown in the appointment, however future circumftances might render fuch an interference neceffary.

They further faid, that the powers intended to be given by the commiffion, could not be fafely executed by any other perfons than thofe appointed by the crown. That the crown had been entrufted with the appointment of commiffioners to treat upon the union of the two kingdoms, who had power to fufpend the acts of parliament which prevented a free trading intercourfe between both, during the progrefs of the treaty; and that they had been ordered to keep the whole tranfactions fecret, which order they had inviolably obferved. They concluded, that nothing could give a proper weight and fupport to the prefent commiffion, but the perfect confidence which parliament fhewed that they repofed in government.

The motion was, notwithftanding, fupported with great fpirit by fome of the principal fpeakers in the oppofition. They faid, that the prefent was a queftion merely of men.—That the meafure was already decided upon, which was to give a full power to difpofe of all the legiflative acts, and all the legiflative powers of parliament, fo far as they concerned America. That there never had been fuch a truft delegated to men, and that therefore nothing was ever more important than the proper choice of them. That if minifters had hitherto fhewn, in any one inftance, that they had formed a right judgment on men, they would admit that they ought to be entrufted with the nomination of men upon this occafion. Exclufive of honefty, which, they faid, they would enter into no difcuffion of with the minifters, the ground of confidence in men was founded on two things; namely, that they were incapable of deceiving others, and were alike incapable of being deceived themfelves. That the minifters had been repeatedly and publicly charged in that houfe, by thofe who had all along fupported their meafures, with having deceived them; and that their only juftification had been, that they were themfelves deceived in every particular relating to America. Now, take it, faid they, which way you pleafe, whether they were deceivers, as their friends affert, or deceived, as themfelves alledge, they are not fit on either ground to be trufted. They, who had judged fo ill of the men they had credited, in all their information concerning America, would not judge better in the choice of thofe whom they nominated to get rid of the fatal confequences of that ill information. They faid, that the conftant defence made by the minifters, with regard to the ill fuccefs of their army in America, was the incapacity, error, or neglect, of the generals they had themfelves appointed; that although they did not believe that to have been the real caufe, yet on their own confeffion, they had made a wrong judgment of the perfons they had employed; and if they were fo un-

happy in the choice of generals, what reafon was there to fuppofe they would prove more fortunate in the choice of negotiators?

They further contended, that nothing could fo effectually defeat the purpofe of the commiffion, as the leaft thought that parliament repofed any confidence in the prefent fervants of the crown. That this would be a perpetual fource of diftruft, jealoufy and animofity to the Americans. That nobody could pretend, nor could they themfelves venture to affert, that this miniftry, or any perfons of their appointment, could have any title to the confidence of America. The minifters were all the declared and eftablifhed enemies of America, and were only brought to a late and abject fubmiffion, by a failure of their utmoft efforts to opprefs them by force. If thefe have the appointment of commiffioners, they will neceffarily be men of their own ftamp, character, and complexion: perfons who would be much more folicitous to fcreen their employers than to ferve their country; and who from nature, education, and habits, are much better qualified to irritate than to appeafe America. An high officer of the ftate, faid they, who has been the author of all the violent and coercive meafures againft the colonies, will, in virtue of his office, have the nomination of the commiffioners. Suppofe, faid they, the Americans fhould lay down as an indifpenfible preliminary to an accommodation, the removal or punifhment of this minifter, would any body pretend that the perfons nominated by him could be confidered as impartial commiffioners, or fitting perfons to difcharge the great truft repofed in them by the ftate and parliament of Great-Britain? But they were aftonifhed, they faid, at the infolence of minifters, who, when they fhould be wrapped in fackcloth and afhes, for the defolation and ruin which they had brought

upon their country, were prefumptuoufly making demands of unlimited confidence, and calling to have the few remaining powers which had been left to parliament furrendered into their hands.

They concluded with laying it down as an axiom, that no good could proceed from any negociation whatever, in which the prefent minifters had any fhare or concern. They obferved, that the prefent momentous affair was not too little to be undertaken by parliament itfelf; that if parliamentary rights muft be negociated upon, it was fitting to be done by a committee of the two houfes of parliament. That in order to fettle India affairs, a committee of the houfe had fat in Leadenhall-ftreet; they might as well fit in America; if the diftance was greater, fo was the magnitude and importance of the object. But they faid, the fcheme and drift of the whole was evident. The minifters intended to pay their court, and to obliterate their crimes, by increafing the prerogative in the fame proportion that they leffened the empire. And thus the prefent war, which was pretended to be made for the double purpofe of preventing the crown from obtaining a revenue from America independent of parliament, and afferting the power of the houfe of commons to tax all the Britifh dominions, would at length terminate in a furrender of the right of taxation, and of all other parliamentary rights, whether of advice or controul, which interfered in any degree with the power of the crown.

The motion was rejected without any divifion being demanded by the oppofition. The minifters took no fhare in the debate, and the oppofition feemed unwilling to throw any impediment in the way of the bills, when the only hope, fmall as it was, which they placed on their fuccefs, depended on the difpatch with which they were expedited through parliament, and afterwards forwarded to America.

Upon the difpofal of this motion, another was made by Mr. Powis, That it fhould be an inftruction to the committee on the conciliatory bills, to receive a claufe for the repeal of the Maffachufetts charter act. This motion drew out much mixed converfation upon American affairs; official men feemed not now to be fo much pinned to opinion as ufual; and fome other gentlemen, who had not generally made any great difplay of their fentiments, were now rather more communicative upon the fubject. Upon the whole, it would have appeared at this moment that a great majority of the houfe had at all times execrated the American war; but that many had been led individually in the crowd from one ftep to another, without looking much farther before them, and ftill expecting the laft to be conclufive, until the American declaration of independence aftonifhed them with a new, awful, and unexpected fituation of public affairs. This alarming appearance of things feemed to leave no other alternative, than the fitting down fupinely with the lofs of the colonies, or the greateft national union, and the moft vigorous exertions for their reduction. The failure in arms exhibited another fcene equally novel and unexpected, and feemed at this time pretty generally to excite a kind of melancholy wifh, that many of thofe extremities had been avoided, which it was not now in the power either of fortune or wifdom entirely to remedy.

Several of the minifter's friends, however, ftrongly condemned his prefent conciliatory meafures; and indeed the only rubs the bills met with in their paffage was from his own fide. Some of thefe infifted upon the exercife as well as the right of taxation in their utmoft extent; and even went fo far as to affert, that it was a right fo inherent in parliament, and fo effentially woven into the conftitution, that no refignation of it could

be valid. Others, who were more numerous, lamented the degradation which the bills would bring upon the government, the counfels, and the dignity of this country. They infifted, that our refources were not only great, but inexhauftible; and that nothing but a fpirited and vigorous exertion of our powers was wanting for the accomplifhment of much greater matters than the fubjugation of America. They bitterly lamented that pufillanimity in our counfels, which, after fo great an expence of blood and treafure, could fubmit not only to give up all the objects of the conteft, but meanly enter into a public treaty with armed rebels, and thereby virtually acknowledge and eftablifh that independence which they claimed. They faid, that while it would ferve greatly to excite the courage of the rebels, and increafe their infolence in the higheft degree, it would on the other hand greatly difpirit our own troops, totally diffolve all that confidence and hope, which the loyal or well-difpofed Americans had repofed in our faith or our power, and would befides render us contemptible in the eyes of all European ftates. To crown this climax of ill confequences, they predicted that the bills would not produce the end propofed.

To this the oppofition faid, that although they totally differed with thofe gentlemen in all their other pofitions, they very nearly agreed with them in their prediction. They had great apprehenfions, that from the latenefs of adopting the meafure, it would not produce that happy effect, which they themfelves fo much wifhed, and which they were certain a great majority of the nation, deriving conviction from feelings which were much more forcible than any logical deductions, began now moft ardently to pant after. They acknowledged, that the chances in point of calculation were infinitely

againft the fuccefs of the meafure; but ftill there was a chance; and the object of a peace with America was of fo tempting a nature, including not only the happinefs but the prefervation of this country, that the fmalleft chance againft whatever fuperiority of odds, was not to be given up at any price. It was upon this account, they faid, that they overlooked many things which they difapproved of in the bills, as they would not in any manner impede or delay the bufinefs, where fuch a prize was at ftake.

Mr. Powis's motion occafioned a long mixture of converfation and debate, which was continued till half paft twelve at night. Some gentlemen, even in office, wifhed to extend it to the total repeal of all the American obnoxious laws. Indeed it was agreed on all fides, that upon the principle of conciliation, this muft be a meafure of neceffity; and the minifter himfelf, in opening his propofitions, had declared his willingnefs to give up all the obnoxious American laws, from the 10th of February, 1763. The only difference of opinion now upon the fubject was the time of carrying the meafure into execution; that is, whether it fhould be preliminary to, or a confequence of the treaty. Although the minifter gave no fpecific opinion upon the fubject, and, indeed mixed but little in the debates fince the introduction of the bufinefs, yet as thofe confidential perfons, who are at all times fuppofed to be in the fecret of affairs, took the latter part of the alternative, and that, notwithftanding the prefent conciliatory temper of the houfe, the motion was at length rejected by a majority of 181 to 108; no doubt can be entertained that his fentiments were on the fame fide of the queftion.

The bills underwent great alterations in their progrefs both through the houfe and the committee. Whether it proceeded from a change of opinion, or from whatever other cause, the powers to be entrusted with the commissioners were much narrowed from what had been at first held out by the minister. The opposition complained that parliament had divested itself effectually of those powers; but instead of their being communicated to those persons who were to negociate a treaty at so great a distance, where immediate conclusions might be absolutely necessary, a circumstance which alone afforded the ostensible motive for their being demanded or granted, they were reserved at home in the hands of the ministers, to be hereafter detailed as they thought proper. This was easily accomplished by the means of the crown lawyers, under the colour of making those powers agree with instructions, whose nature and purpose were totally unknown to all persons excepting themselves and the ministers. Some of the opposition complained greatly of this conduct, which they said was totally subversive of the great principle of the bill, viz. That commissioners upon the spot would be better able to determine what was immediately fitting to be done, than parliament or any other body could, at the distance of three thousand miles; but the expunging from the bill of those discretionary powers which were intended for the commissioners, rendered it, they said, with respect to its avowed purpose, little more than a piece of waste paper: so that as it then stood, its real effect could be only to vest in the ministers a suspending power out of parliament, under the form and colour of instructions to commissioners, instead of the open and usual mode of carrying it by bill through both houses. The danger of the precedent, in this view of the business, and the competence of those who were to be entrusted with such a power, afforded sufficient ground for animadversion; but the eager hope of attaining the great point in view, subdued all other considerations, and prevented any great degree of opposition.

Some members of the opposition were the means of considerably extending the effect of the bills with respect to their original purpose.

25th. Mr. Powis having moved, That it be an instruction to the committee, to receive a clause for the repeal of the American tea-act, passed in the year 1767, it was agreed to. And Mr Burke, having on the same day moved, that the provisions of the bill should be extended to the West-Indies, his motion was likewise agreed to.

The title of the bill relative to taxation was also totally altered from its original state. It was foreseen that the words " for declaring the intentions of the parliament of Great Britain concerning the exercise of the right of imposing taxes," would be exceedingly offensive to the Americans, as being declaratory of the right, and merely a suspension of the exercise. The new title, under which it was passed, being in more general terms, it was hoped would have given satisfaction, and was as follows: " For removing all doubts and apprehensions concerning taxation by the parliament of Great-Britain, in any of the colonies, provinces and plantations in North-America and the West Indies, and for repealing so much of an act made in the seventh year of the reign of his present Majesty, as imposes a duty on tea imported from Great-Britain into any colony or plantation in America, or relates thereto."

Although the third reading of the bills brought out a considerable share of mixed debate and conversation, yet they were both passed without a division. **March 2d.** [63]

The minister found it necessary to lay a new tax on houses, and another upon wines, in order to secure the interest of six millions which he was obliged to borrow for the services of the ensuing year. This occasioned some **9th.** debate in the committee of supply, the house-tax being considered, by the gentlemen in opposition, as being not only a land-tax in effect, but as being also exceedingly disproportionate and oppressive, and falling particularly heavy upon the inhabitants of London and Westminster, who already paid so vast a proportion to the land-tax, and whose burdens, including with that, poor-rates, window-tax, watch, lights, pavement, and other imposts, amounted in several parishes to more than eight shillings in the pound. Whilst, to render it still more grievous, it frequently happened that those who were the least able to bear them, bore the heaviest burthens.

The question being however agreed to, Mr. Gilbert, having [64] some days before given notice to the house of his intention, after lamenting the negligence and prodigality with which the national business was conducted, and stating the necessity of appointing a committee to enquire into the expenditure of the public money, more particularly into the exorbitancy of contracts and the abuses of office, then moved, That the better to enable his Majesty to vindicate the honour and dignity of his crown and dominions, in the present exigency of affairs, there be granted one fourth part of the nett annual income upon the salaries, fees, and perquisites of all offices under the crown, excepting only those held by the Speaker of the House of Commons, the Chancellor, or Commissioners of the Great Seal, the Judges, Ministers to foreign parts, Commissioners, Officers in the army and navy, and all those which do not produce a clear yearly income of two hundred pounds to their possessors; the tax also extending to all annuities, pensions, stipends, or other yearly pensions issuing out of the Exchequer, or any branch of the revenues; and was to commence from the 25th of March, 1778, and to continue for one year, and during the continuance of the American war.

Such was the temper which at that immediate time happened to be prevalent, or rather, such was the effect arising from the general diffatisfaction excited by the untoward appearance of public affairs, that this motion, which was made by a gentleman in office, and closely connected with one branch of ministry, to the aftonifhment of every body, and to the exceeding alarm of administration, was carried by a majority of 100 to 82 in the committee. And although the ministers fummoned all their forces from all quarters within reach on the enfuing day, in order to oppofe the motion on receiving the report from the committee; and those who had interest with all their strength, it was rejected only by a majority of fix, the numbers upon a division being 147, to 141 who fupported the question. Nor would it have been loft if the opposition had been at all unanimous in its fupport. For fome of their principals confidered it as a measure which would have been exceedingly diftreffing to individuals, without any adequate public advantage. For men in office frequently had no other fupport but their income, and had been long ufed to live up to its full extent; and thofe who had interest with government would be repaid from the public purfe (frequently with advantage) what they had feemed to contribute towards it; and the only real contribution would arife from thofe, who being deftitute of intereft, were the leaft capable of bearing the tax.

On the following day, the 11th. committee into the state of the nation being refumed, the state of the navy was the fubject introduced by Mr. Fox, who after clearing and laying out his ground with his ufual ability, and feveral introductory motions, propofed the following as the refult of the whole, "Refolved, that the prefent state of the royal navy, for the defence of Great-Britain and Ireland, is inadequate to the very dangerous crifis of public affairs."

Mr. T. Luttrell took a principal fhare in this debate, and apologifed for the length of time which his courfe of inveftigation muft neceffarily take up, from the double confideration, that moft of the naval papers which had, after fo much trouble, been at length laid before them, were ordered by the Houfe in confequence of motions made by himfelf, and that he was bound, now that the means were in his hands, of maintaining and making good thofe reiterated charges which, in the two preceding, as well as the prefent feffion, he had brought againft the minifters of the admiralty department. In this courfe of inveftigation and calculation, which took up about three hours, he particularly ftated, that the public had paid about double the fum for the ordinaries and extraordinaries of the navy during the laft eight years, which the eftimates of the fame fervices had amounted to in the eight years which commenced with the year 1755, and ended with 1762, a period which included the whole of the late war.

The motion was well fupported, all the principal fpeakers of the opposition taking an active fhare in the debate. A great naval commander, in whom the nation repofed the greateft hope and confidence in cafe of foreign danger, took the fame fide; although he was then under appointment to the command of the grand fleet which was intended for our home defence. On the other fide, the question, in point of debate, was only oppofed by the admiralty and treasury benches. It was at length got rid of by the previous question, without a division.

On the following day the Minifters were not a little furprized at an unexpected motion made by Mr. James Luttrell, for an addrefs [65] to his Majefty, that he would be gracioufly pleafed to inftruct the Commiffioners, whom he might name, for the purpofes of carrying into execution the prefent American bills, that in cafe they fhould find, that the continuance in office of any public Minifter, or Minifters of the crown of Great Britain, fhould be found to imprefs fuch jealoufies or miftruft in one or more of the revolted colonies, as might tend materially to obftruct the happy work of peace and fincere reconciliation between Great Britain and her colonies; that the faid Commiffioners might be enabled to promife, in his Majefty's name, the earlieft removal of fuch Minifter or Minifters from his councils.

This motion was highly refented by the Minifters, and not lefs warmly fupported by a great part of the opposition. Others, however, on that fide differed in opinion, and although they acknowledged, that there was but little room to hope for conciliation or peace with America under the aufpices of the prefent Minifters, yet they confidered the propofed meafure as too humiliating and degrading to this country; and thought, that if it fhould be found neceffary (as they conceived it was) to change Minifters, it ought to be done previoufly, and not to be the confequence of a treaty with the Americans. The motion was at length rejected upon a division by a majority of 150 to 55.

Whilft various matters were thus continually agitated by the Commons, the Lords did not feem to be much more at eafe in their Houfe. For what with the enquiry into the state of the nation, the occafional objects of difcuffion of which the prefent times were fo productive, and the ufual ftationary bufinefs, few days paffed without affording fomething interefting. A finguiar letter had been written by General

Gates, foon after the convention of Saratoga, to the Earl of Thanet,[66] with whom it appears that General had formerly lived in habits of great intimacy and friendfhip. This letter, which was forwarded to the noble Earl through the medium of General Burgoyne, was, excepting a fhort obfervation on the feverity of General Lee's confinement, and a fhorter remembrance to two common friends, entirely upon public bufinefs.

The conquering General, after a fhort view of the fate of the northern Britifh army, haftens to declare, that " born and educated in England; he cannot help feeling for the misfortunes brought upon his native country, by the wickednefs of that adminiftration, who began, and had continued this moft unjuft, impolitic, cruel and unnatural war." He ftates, that the difmemberment of the empire, the lofs of commerce, of power and confequence amongft the nations, with the downfal of public credit, are but the beginning of thofe evils, which muft inevitably be followed by a thoufand more, unlefs timely prevented by fome lenient hand, fome great ftate phyfician, with the firmnefs, integrity and abilities of a Chatham, joined to the wifdom, virtue and juftice of a Camden. Such a man, he fays, aided and fupported by perfons as independent in their fortunes as unfullied in their honour, and who never bowed their heads to Baal, might yet fave the finking ftate.

But that great objeet he contended could only be obtained by a confirmation of that independency, which the people of that continent were determined only to part with along with their lives. Such a Minifter, he faid, would do as all other wife ftatefmen had done before him. He would be true to the welfare and intereft of his country; " and, by refcinding the refolutions paffed to fupport that fyftem which no power on earth can eftablifh, he will endeavour to preferve fo much of the empire in profperity and honour, as the circumftances of the times, and the mal-adminiftration of thofe who ruled before him, have left to his government."

" The united ftates of America," he faid, " are willing to be the friends, but never will fubmit to be the flaves of the parent country. They are by confanguinity, by commerce, by language, and by the affeetion which naturally fprings from thefe, more attached to England than any other country under the fun. Therefore, fpurn not the bleffing which yet remains. Inftantly withdraw your fleets and armies; cultivate the friendfhip and commerce of America. Thus, and thus only, can England hope to be great and happy. Seek that in a commercial alliance; feek it ere it be too late, for there only you muft expeet to find it."

He concluded with the following declaration : " thefe, my Lord, are the undifguifed fentiments of a man that rejoices not in the blood fhed in this fatal conteft ; of a man who glories in the name of an Englifhman, and wifhes to fee peace and friendfhip between Great Britain and America, fixed upon the firmeft foundation."

The noble Earl who had received the letter was fo much indifpofed with a cold; that, on the 16th of February, when he introduced it, he was only able barely to inform the Houfe who it came from, its purport, and to defire it might be read by the clerk. This was oppofed by the court Lords, who held that it would be exceedingly improper for that Houfe to enter into any correfpondence with a rebel officer or General, or to frame any refolution upon his information ; and that the letter might alfo contain matter which it would be highly unfitting for their Lordfhips to hear. As it could not however be controverted, that the noble Earl would have had a right to read the letter as a part of his fpeech, if he had been in health fo to do, the objeetions were accordingly removed by the Marquis of Rockingham's undertaking that office for him.

The Duke of Richmond then moved that the letter fhould lie on the table, which brought on a very confiderable debate ; it being contended on one fide, that the authority which it came from, a rebel General in arms againft his Sovereign, would have been in itfelf a fufficient ground for the rejeetion of the motion. But that it was befides only a private letter from one gentleman to another, and containing merely the opinions of an individual. Were the Congrefs bound to abide by any propofitions held out by General Gates, or to ratify his conclufions ? It was beneath their own dignity to make a private correfpondence, if it had not been even encumbered with thofe particular circumftances which rendered it totally inadmiffible, in any degree the fubjeet of their deliberations. But what in faet did this letter hold out ? The very terms vaguely mentioned in it, were fuch as their Lordfhips had repeatedly reprobated, when propofed to them by fome of their own body, and placed in a much more agreeable drefs and form. It contained an infinuation, that America was determined to preferve her independency. Was General Gates's word a fufficient authority to the King's fervants for acceding to that pofition ? Were they to withdraw the army and the fleet, and to throw the nation at the feet of America, merely upon his advice or affertion ? That part of it which confifted in an inveetive againft the prefent adminiftration, they fuppofed would rather draw the contempt than the attention of the Houfe. Thofe who were fond of inveetives againft Minifters, might frequently have an opportunity of hearing them much more forcibly and elegantly expressed, by noble Lords within these walls than by Mr. Gates.

On the other side it was contended, that General Gates, from his situation, rendered exceedingly conspicuous by his late success, was a person of great weight and importance in America; that the only means of obtaining the sense of the people in that country, was by hearing the sentiments of such men; that the circumstance of his being an Englishman, and the consideration of that affection, which, if he had not even declared it, every body must judge from his own feelings, that he still inevitably retained for his native country, ought to afford the greater weight to his opinions; that it would have been happy indeed if such information had been hitherto properly regarded, instead of the delusive and fatal representation of things, which had been transmitted by prejudiced or interested Governors, and other official persons, by which Ministers had repeatedly acknowledged themselves to have been missed, and through whose means, the nation had been evidently deluded into that ruinous war, which has brought on all our present calamities. That the motion was attended with a peculiar propriety at present, from the notice given by the Minister in the other House, of his intention to lay a plan of pacification with America speedily before parliament; a measure which must render every species of information necessary; and why not read Mr. Gates's letter here, when Commissioners were to be sent with powers to treat with him personally in America? They said that the springs of government had been hitherto polluted, because the channels of intelligence had been stopped; that Ministers had not only shut their own eyes constantly to the light of truth, but had uniformly endeavoured to render it equally invisible to parliament; and, that to reject the motion,

would be to shew a determination of still pursuing that ruinous system, which had already produced such fatal effects, of shutting their ears to information, and continuing wilfully and perversely in error.

The motion being rejected without a division, the committee of enquiry into the state of the nation was resumed, when the Duke of Richmond opened the business of the day by observing that he had several resolutions to propose, which were intended to establish the state of the army, and the number of effective men serving in America, in the different years of 1774, 1775, 1776, & 1777, with the services and events of each campaign, as they appeared from the papers which were referred to the consideration of the committee. Having then stated the necessity of the committee's coming to some result upon the matters that appeared before them, as the name or pretence of an enquiry would otherwise become an absolute mockery; he moved his first resolution, viz. "that it appears to this committee, so far as they are informed from the returns referred to them, that the greatest number of regular land forces serving in North America, in 1774, did not exceed 6884 men, including officers."

The Lords in administration opposed the motion upon the ground of impropriety and inexpedience. It would be needless, they said, to repeat the arguments which they had used in a late debate, as they applied in every instance to the present occasion. The circumstances corresponded so exactly in both cases, that there could be no doubt, that the same motives which then induced their Lordships to reject those resolutions which originated in the same quarter, would operate equally with respect to the present. If the noble Duke persisted in his motion, they would be under a necessity therefore of moving that the Chairman should quit the chair,

in order to make way for the previous question.

This concise method of preventing the establishment of facts, and frustrating the ends of the enquiry, was reprehended with great warmth and vehemence by some of the Lords on the other side. They said, that if Ministers were thus enabled and determined, to get rid of every proposition founded on undeniable facts which appeared in the enquiry, merely by a brief rejection, and without any reasons assigned, it would be better at once to put an end to an investigation, from which so much good had been augured, and by which the nation had been so long amused. That it would be acting a much more manly part, for the Ministers to avow their sentiments openly, and to break up the committee, than thus insidiously to deceive the public, by holding out an opinion that they countenanced the enquiry, and at the same time using such underhand measures as effectually checked its progress, and rendered it totally useless and nugatory. And that the only idea which they had hitherto held out, for the committee's not coming to resolutions of fact, "lest it should afford a knowledge of our real condition to our enemies," was so replete with absurdity, that it would appear a libel upon any body of men, who were only furnished with the most moderate share of common intelligence, to suppose it could have the smallest influence upon their conduct. But that even that argument, wretched as it was, could not apply in the present instance; for resolutions of facts, by being merely proposed, exposed all that could be known to the world, as effectually under the previous question, or a negative, as under an affirmative vote. The effect therefore of their refusing to concur, would not be the preventing of truth from being known; but making it known, that they had a dislike to declaring the truth.

A great law Lord, who has been long out of office, declared, that [67] it had been at all times the usage of parliament to form resolutions on matters of fact, which resolutions were considered as the data from which the conclusions were to be drawn; and finally to be the ground of the measures meant to be proposed, in consequence of such information. He said, he was free to declare, that the present mode of putting a negative on every resolution proposed, was in fact pretending to give information, but refusing the use of that information. For when every fact was established, the whole enquiry at an end, and the grand conclusions relative to future measures came to be made, where were the facts to be found on which the House was to proceed? They were indeed to be found in the Journals, but under the infliction of a negative by the previous question, which in so many words imported, that as it had not been necessary or proper to resolve the facts, it must of course be unnecessary and improper to agree to the conclusions. This argument, he said, was obvious and incontrovertible. It would in fact amount to a premature dissolution of the committee; and if administration were determined to adhere in the future progress of the enquiry to that conduct they had hitherto observed, he thought it much better to dissolve it at once; much more candid to stop its mouth, than by a mere outside shew of an enquiry, to amuse the people without doors with high expectations, when it was finally resolved, by those who led majorities within, that no one benefit or advantage whatever should be derived from it. He concluded, that from the conduct of the Ministers, he had long apprehended with concern that this would have been the fate of the committee; but that as soon as he was informed that the Minister in the other House had pro-

posed introducing a plan for peace, (which was the sole object of the committee) pending the enquiry, his doubts were changed to a certainty, and he saw at once through the whole scheme of the manœuvre. He saw that a substitute was adopted in the place of the enquiry, to prevent a clamour without doors; and that under the cover of this contrivance, the committee would meet with a violent and immature death from the hands of the Minister and his mutes.

The severity of manner as well as of language, with which these and other strictures were passed, could not fail to draw out some explanation from the other side. The Lords in administration declared, that they could not see the utility or the necessity of the committee's coming to any resolution at present; nor did they think, in fact, that it was their business so to do; that they were to proceed regularly with the enquiry, and after having gone through it progressively, and adverted to every distinct object of it, were to form some general conclusion deduced from, and grounded upon the result of the whole investigation. A great law Lord, in the first office of the [68] state, agreed, that it was always customary for committees to agree to resolutions of fact; but he endeavoured to weaken the force of that concession by asserting, that the conclusions intended to be deduced from those facts ought to be opened to the committee, previous to their entering into any resolution upon the subject; and, that as the noble Duke's intentions, in that respect, were, as yet, altogether a secret to the committee, although, so far as he could guess, they were probably of the same nature with some inadmissible propositions, that had been lately heard of in favour of America, he would accordingly vote for the Chairman's leaving the chair.

The question being at length put, for Lord Scarsdale to leave the

chair, it was carried in the affirmative by a majority of forty; the numbers being 66 to 26. The committee being thus dissolved for the present, the Duke of Richmond made his original motion, which he followed with eleven others upon the ground we have already stated, all of which were separately rejected by the previous question without a division.

The committee being again resumed on the 19th of February, the Duke of Richmond proposed their entering into an investigation of the expences which the American war had cost the nation; and in order to obviate that dread and aversion which he knew was prevalent, with respect to the intricate and tiresome nature of accounts, he had already, himself, with exceeding labour and perseverance, gone through all the operose work of calculation. Thus, infinite quantities of matter, detail, and calculation, being compressed under their respective heads, and comprized in a comparatively small compass of space, became, without any great degree of trouble or fatigue, manageable subjects of comment and enquiry.

The noble Duke having stated the causes which rendered their being well informed on this part of the subject of the war particularly necessary, proceeded to state the extraordinary expences arising from the war, of each of the four last years separately, and the whole being ascertained, as nearly as it could yet be possibly done, amounted to the gross sum of 23,894,792 l. He then shewed, from the example of the last war, as well as by various calculations, that if the great work of peace was to be now accomplished in the speediest possible manner, there would remain behind a farther tail of expence, which, at the most moderate computation, would amount to at least nine millions. So that the public expence attending the American contest, however speedily and happily it might now be brought to a conclusion, and independent of all other contingent losses, would, at the lowest calculation, amount to near thirty-three millions sterling.

To establish these facts, he framed a string of resolutions, founded upon the accounts before them, declaring the several heads of service, and the amount of the total extra expence in each year. He hoped, that as the resolutions of fact which he was about to propose, would essentially further the project for peace, which they knew was speedily to come within their Lordships consideration, and as they would also serve to open the eyes of the public, and convince the people at large of the necessity of putting an immediate end to the war, that they would meet with no opposition ; much less that they should not experience the fate of the several others which he had moved in the course of the enquiry. He then concluded by moving his leading or preliminary resolution.

The Lords in administration did not attempt to controvert the calculations, but concisely declared, that the resolutions were highly inexpedient, unparliamentary, and incapable of answering any useful purpose. That they could by no means agree to the doctrine, that the mere matter of resolutions being founded in fact, could be any sufficient cause for their being agreed to. There were many truths that might be easily ascertained, which it would be exceedingly improper to declare, or to give a parliamentary sanction to. That it was equally inexpedient and foolish to expose the national weakness and infirmities. And, that instead of promoting the purpose held out by the noble Duke, the publishing of facts declarative of weakness, would produce a directly contrary effect, and render any plan of peace that could be proposed, infinitely more hazardous and difficult. That if

they had foreseen the purposes to which it had been intended to direct the committee, they would have opposed its formation originally in the most open and direct manner. They threw out some hints towards its dissolution, and concluded with moving that the Chairman should leave the chair.

The Duke of Richmond replied, that our weakness was already perfectly known to every body but ourselves, and had been so long before the commencement of the committee ; but if any doubt could remain on that head, the resolutions themselves, recorded upon the Journals, and from thence communicated to the public, under full information that their authenticity as facts could not be questioned, even by the persons who had given them a negative, annihilated all pretence of concealing our present dangerous and defenceless state, either from our enemies, or from the people of this country. It would therefore, he said, be much more consonant with that haughty and explicit tone affected by Ministers, to declare, that the motive which induced them to put a negative upon such matters of undoubted fact was, that those facts contained the most full and unequivocal proofs of their misconduct ; that they informed the nation, that its present alarming and ruinous situation was brought upon it by a set of Ministers, who had wantonly plunged it into an unjust and unnatural war ; who had spilt its best blood, and already wasted twenty-four millions of its treasure ; and who at length, after persisting in those weak and wicked measures for more than three years, and after refusing so much as to hear of any terms, but such as would have reduced the colonies to absolute slavery, were now preparing to sue for peace, and to make the most humiliating concessions.

The question being put upon the motion for quitting the chair, it was carried upon a division by a

majority of 66 to 28. The Duke of Richmond then moved his several resolutions, which were all separately set aside by the previous question.

Previous to the division, that nobleman had taken notice, that he had gone through as many heads of the public enquiry, as came properly within his knowledge, habits of life, or mode of application ; that he hoped some other Lords would take up the business where he ended ; and that particularly, those papers on the table, relative to the navy, would be taken into due consideration, by those Lords who were properly masters of the subject. In this he evidently pointed to a noble Duke and Earl, who being themselves [69] high in the naval service, had for some time, by the solicitude of their enquiries into its state and condition, given no small occasion to call forth the ability of the noble Lord who presided in that department. This part of the enquiry was accordingly taken up and pursued by the Duke of Bolton, who was particularly and professionally seconded by the Earl of Bristol.

On the 25th of February, the Duke of Bolton moved that the Surveyor of the navy should attend the House. This was personally opposed by the noble Lord at the head of the navy, who insisted that the giving any further information on the subject was both unnecessary and inexpedient. He had ever held but one opinion, he said, in that respect, which was, that it would be highly imprudent, even in its present very flourishing state, to divulge its condition. On the other side it was contended, that the motion was in direct conformity with the order of the House, which had long since directed an enquiry into the state of the navy, and that all information relative to the subject should be communicated to the committee ; without which, indeed, the name or pretence of an enquiry, would appear too ridiculous for the place and subject.

The debate of course brought out much animadversion with respect to that great and flourishing state of the navy, which had been so triumphantly held out, and so frequently repeated, since the opening of the session. Nor was this unmixed with declarations of apprehension and concern, at now discovering (as they expressed it) in this season of danger, that those representations were totally unfounded, and the flattering hopes raised upon them of course illusive. The noble Lord at the head of that department, still, however, supported, with unabated firmness, the validity of his former position, and insisted, that the navy was never in a greater or more flourishing state than at present; but something having, seemingly, slipped from him, probably owing to the warmth of altercation, as if it were a maxim of policy with all states, not only to keep their naval affairs a profound secret, but to give exaggerated representations of their maritime force, and to state ships upon paper which were not actually fit for service; these expressions, or something tantamount to them, did not by any means serve to lessen the severity of observation on the other side.

Two precedents were also brought by a noble Lord, one from the Journals of the Lords, and the other from the Commons, shewing, that in the year 1707, a similar enquiry to the present having been then instituted, notwithstanding the dangerous and widely extended war in which we were involved, and notwithstanding that Prince George of Denmark was then at the head of the admiralty, yet without any regard to those considerations, or to that necessity of secrecy now dwelt upon; an account was laid before both Houses, of the quantity and value of the naval stores in all the yards, and many other matters of equal importance

and delicacy to the full, as the objects of the present enquiry, were then fully and publicly discussed. This brought out an observation, that if the present motion was rejected, it would be a proof that they treated the present first Lord of the admiralty with greater respect, than their ancestors had done the husband of the Queen of England upon a similar occasion. The motion was however rejected, by a majority of 23 to 11 Lords.

The committee being again resumed on the 2d of March, the Duke of Bolton opened the business with a speech, tending to point out from the papers before them, much mismanagement in the conduct of naval affairs. He dwelt particularly upon the great mercantile losses we had sustained; which he attributed principally, to the refusal, or misemployment of convoys, and to the want of judgment in stationing our ships and frigates of war.

He entered into the neglects and errors with relation to a proper defence of the West Indies. He then took a wide range through the whole circuit of naval affairs, in which he displayed much professional skill and ability, and concluded a long speech with several motions for resolutions, tending principally to shew the state of our fleet serving in America under [70] Lord Howe, with respect both to ships of war and frigates; their original complement of men, with the loss they had sustained in the war; with the state, number, and condition of the line of battle ships for home defence, and of the frigates for home service.

The noble Earl, whose conduct had been the subject of censure in [71] this speech, after correcting some errors in point of fact or calculation, which, he said, the noble mover had fallen into, entered into a discourse of no small length in order to do justice to the merits of his own administration of naval affairs. In this detail, he repeated

some assertions, which had long before been the subject of much animadversion, relative to the deplorable and most ruinous state in which he had found the navy at his coming into office. In the conclusion, he entered into a defence or justification of his conduct relative to the losses sustained by commerce. He acknowledged that trade had suffered; but said it was an inconvenience which could not have been prevented. It was a consequence of the mode of carrying on the war in America. Frigates were absolutely necessary for that service; and if we had possessed a sufficient number of them, to have also supplied the stations which the noble Duke had alluded to, there could not be a doubt that our commerce would have been better protected. To weaken, however, the idea of the damage sustained by commerce, he denied that the rapid decline of the African trade had proceeded from the war. That branch of commerce, he said, had been overdone; the trade had been on the decrease for several years before the troubles with America commenced, and must have been by this time nearly on its present state if they had never taken place. Other matters of charge or censure he excused, by saying the best had been done, that the particular circumstances would admit. But if it had been otherwise, and the facts were just as the noble Duke had stated them, still he could not be liable to any censure; he acted only ministerially; the measures were deliberated and resolved upon elsewhere; and if he did his duty in executing the orders he received, he was by no means responsible for the consequences.

The matter was agitated for some time with great bitterness by the Lords on the other side. They could not, they said, repress their grief and indignation at the deplorable state of our navy, which was not only clearly proved by the noble Duke who conducted the enquiry, but, to their aftonifhment, fubftantially acknowledged by the great officer who prefided in that department, notwithftanding his endeavours to palliate and qualify facts, and to evade the conclufions which they evidently led to. They reminded him and his colleagues in office, of the high founding language and boaftings which they had held through the feffion. When themfelves had complained of the weaknefs of our internal military defence, and of its infufficiency for the protection of this ifland, they were anfwered that it was a matter of little confequence; that our navy was our great national bulwark; it was that we were to depend upon in the day of trial; it was invincible, and fuperior to any thing our natural enemies could bring againft us. " We are able " to cope with the whole united " force of the Houfe of Bourbon." —" The more France and Spain " know of our navy, the better; " a thorough knowledge of its " ftate is the beft means of fe- " curing us againft the defigns of " our enemies." Such was the current language of minifters. But what, faid they, do we hear on this day? That all our apprehenfions were well founded; and that all thofe boaftings were the offspring of fallacy and deceit. This was not a bare affirmation without proof; the noble Earl, they faid, who prefides in the counfels of this country, had juft told the Houfe fo in as many words. He did not put a negative on the refolutions for their not being founded on truth, but merely becaufe they would be an avowal of our naval weaknefs.

The court party, without admitting, or much controverting thefe pofitions, ftood firm on their old ground of the danger and impolicy of exhibiting fuch details, whether true or falfe, to public infpection. The refolutions were at length re-jected upon a divifion, by a majority of 64 to 26.

The American conciliatory bills were carried through the Lords without a divifion; being introduced and read on the 3d of March; read the fecond time on the 5th, and paffed on the 9th. They were, however, reprobated in the whole or in part, by a few individuals, who confidered them as exhibiting fuch marks of humiliation and difgrace, as the moft unhappy periods in the hiftory of this country had never before equalled. Some of the oppofition confidered them as highly difgraceful to this country, as well as incapable of producing the wifhed-for effect. The laft propofition feemed to have been the general opinion of that party.

The Earl of Abingdon, although he would not obftruct the bills by an oppofition in the Houfe, entered his fingle diffent in a proteft againft them. The Duke of Grafton, on the fecond reading of the bills, informed the Houfe that he had received information which he could not queftion, that a treaty had been actually figned between the court of France and the American deputies. He faid that his noble kinfman had put the queftion [72] in the other Houfe to the Minifter, from whom he was able only to procure an evafive anfwer. That fome clear explanation of a matter in itfelf of fo important a nature, and which was at that time fo immediately critical, was abfolutely neceffary, previous to their entering into any difcuffion of bills, whofe effect muft entirely depend upon the fact which was to be explained. That, if the information was true, it was abfurd to infult parliament with the appearance of reconciliation, when it was no longer practicable. If minifters knew the fact, they were culpable in the higheft degree, in concealing intelligence of fo important a nature from parliament, and leading it, under the cover of that concealment, into meafures of futility and public difhonour. Or, if they pleaded ignorance, their conduct was ftill, if poffible, more reprehenfible, and their incapacity more glaring, in being entirely deficient in that fpecies of information which it was the firft duty of their ftations to procure. He called loudly for an anfwer as to the point of fact, and defired it might be remembered, that it was on the 5th of March he put that queftion to the King's minifters.

A noble Lord, the nature of [73] whofe high office afforded him every opportunity of information in all public matters, faid, he had indeed heard of fuch a treaty from out-door report, and alfo that the queftion had been put and fully anfwered in the other Houfe; but he affured their lordfhips, in the moft precife terms, that he knew not of any fuch treaty as had been mentioned, having been figned, or entered into, between the court of France and the deputies of the congrefs. He hoped it would likewife be remembered, that it was on the 5th of March when he declared in his place, that he knew nothing of any fuch treaty, nor had received any authentic information of its being either in exiftence or contemplation.

The committee of enquiry being refumed on the 12th of March, the bufinefs was opened and conducted by the Earl of Effingham, who having previoufly obtained an order for papers and the attendance of witneffes, obferved, that the profufion which prevailed in the different departments of the ftate, and the wafte and mifapplication of the public treafure, which more particularly attended every thing relative to the prefent unhappy and unfortunate war, were become fo notorious and enormous, as to demand their moft ferious attention and immediate interference. That this muft have been of courfe a principal object of their enquiry into the ftate of the nation; but that in the prefent unhappy feafon, when the nation was already groaning under the weight of new and accumulating burthens, when the fources of taxation were already exhaufted in fuch a degree, that the whole time and invention of the Minifter feemed unequal to the difcovery of new fubjects for it; when he was already obliged to borrow money for the fervice of the current year, at a higher premium than had been given in the courfe of the laft war, and far beyond the legal rate of intereft; and when we were at the eve of a foreign war of fuch extent and danger, as would render the ftricteft œconomy neceffary to our immediate prefervation, under all thefe circumftances, it became doubly incumbent on their lordfhips, both as an obligation of public and private duty, to look carefully into the expenditure of the public money, and by correcting the profligacy of minifters and public officers, to apply a fpeedy and effectual remedy to this crying and ruinous grievance.

The bufinefs of the prefent day, his Lordfhip obferved, went no farther than to the novel conduct, and its confequences, of the Treafury Board, in departing from its proper line of bufinefs, and taking into its hands the unprecedented management of the tranfport fervice. But this was introductory to that thorough inveftigation, which he intended, of the public accounts in general. He acknowledged, ironically, that the whole of the expenditure which was to be the object of their immediate enquiry, amounted only to about 600,000l. which, to thofe who were in the practice of voting or paffing millions, without care or examination, might appear too trifling a matter to become a fubject of their ferious confideration. But when he had made it appear, as he would, that the lofs to the public in this comparatively fmall expenditure, amounted to no lefs than one fourth

of the whole fum; when it was recollected, that the detection in this inftance afforded full room for a prefumption, that the fame wafte prevailed in the difpofal and management of thofe immenfe fums which were annually raifed upon the people; he trufted, however trifling or unworthy of their attention the lofs of 150,000l. in one article of expenditure might appear, their lordfhips would fee the propriety of fupporting him in the commencement of an enquiry, which tended to a general reformation, in a matter of fuch vaft importance, and fuch univerfal concern, as the expenditure of the public treafure.

It appeared (contrary as they ftated to the general courfe of official bufinefs) that the treafury going out of its proper department, and entering upon a tafk to which it feemed totally incompetent, took the whole bufinefs of the tranfport fervice into its own poffeffion. That inftead of adhering to the practice of the navy-board, which was in continual exercife under their eyes, of publicly advertifing for propofals, and without any regard to the price at which it then and ftill procured freight, they entered into a private bargain with a Mr. Atkinfon, in confequence of[74] which they had for a long time paid twelve fhillings and fixpence a ton on an infinite quantity of freight, befides allowing him two and a half per cent. for his commiffion or agency. And that inftead of employing a proper officer from the king's yards, as a check upon this agent, to meafure the fhips, and afcertain their condition, thefe matters were left entirely to himfelf, who informed the Lords that he employed a furveyor for that purpofe.

Both the noble Earl, and the other Lords who fupported the enquiry, ftigmatized the whole tranfaction with Atkinfon in the moft direct terms, as a jobb of the moft difgraceful and fhameful nature.

They faid, it carried about it all its proper and characteriftical marks. It was a moft beneficial contract, made in the dark, with a noted and highly-favoured contractor. The Treafury-board entered into a bufinefs with which they had no concern and were totally unacquainted, merely, to all appearance, upon that, and no other account. They had departed, in making the bargain, from all the fair and open rules of conduct, which had been laid down and eftablifhed by the navy-board in the execution of the fame fervice. And all their boafted merit in at length lowering the price of freight fixpence in the ton, and cutting off one per cent. from their agent's commiffion, proceeded from a motive which had no relation to public good or œconomy. Their favourite contractor had, from the multitude of his beneficial bargains, brought himfelf and them within the notice of parliament. They were obliged, upon that account, after it had undergone a parliamentary difcuffion, to fubmit the ftate and nature of his well-known rumcontract to the infpection and decifion of feveral capital and intelligent merchants; and thefe gentlemen, who were pitched upon by themfelves, reprobated the whole tranfaction in the moft decifive terms. Under thefe circumftances they thought it neceffary to curtail a part of the glaring exorbitances of the prefent contract, (which we find to be then done without any difficulty) and to make fome apparent fhew of reftoring the tranfport bufinefs to the navy board; an offer which was, however, managed in fuch a manner, that its producing a refufal was well underftood.

The noble Lord at the head of the navy undertook the defence of the treafury, which he performed with his ufual ability. It was ftated on that fide, that the fervice was new, and the neceffity irrefiftable. It was the firft time that fuch an army had ever been maintained at such a distance. The troops must be fed at all events. Every thing depended on the promptness of the supply. And notwithstanding the great exertions used for that purpose, the letters from the commander in chief were frequent, urgent, and complaining. An infinite quantity of shipping was to be procured, and must be obtained on any terms. The greatness of the demand necessarily raised the price. The cause of the Treasury's being obliged to pay higher for freight than the navy-board, was explained by Atkinson's evidence. It appeared by that, that from essential differences in the two services, the owners of shipping preferred that of the naval department, at a lower price, and that paid in navy-bills, which were liable to a considerable discount, to the Treasury service, at an advanced price, and ready money payment.

No doubt, it was said, could be entertained, that every possible œconomy was practised by the Treasury. They undertook this troublesome business meerly to save expence by the appointment of new officers. They struck sixpence off the freight as soon as it could be done; and they even reduced the agent's commission one per cent. But they did not chuse that an army of Englishmen and friendly foreigners should be starved in a hostile land, whilst they were haggling about freight. So that instead of a vote of censure, they deserved the public thanks of their country for their zeal and alacrity in this business. They concluded, that although they did not question the veracity of the facts, or the exactness of the estimates contained in the noble Earl's resolutions, they must oppose them and all other resolutions upon matters of fact.

It was accordingly moved, that the chairman should quit the chair, which was carried upon a division by a majority of 39 to 18. Lord Effingham then proposed the string

of resolutions which he intended for the establishment of his facts; which being all set aside by the previous question, without a division, he then moved his concluding resolution, intended as a censure upon the conduct of the Treasury, and stating therefrom a loss to the public, to a very great amount. The House divided upon this question, which was rejected, by a majority of 35 to 17.

Motion by Mr. Grenville rejected. French Declaration. Royal Message. Great Debates on the Address. Amendment moved by Mr. Baker. Amendment rejected; and the original Address at length carried on a division. Great debates on the Message and Address in the House of Lords. Amendment moved by the Duke of Manchester. Rejected, and the original Address carried, as before, on a division. Great debates on Mr. Fox's motions relative to the failure of the Canada expedition. Rejected on a division. Counter motion, carried in the Committee, but not reported. Col. Barré's motion for a Committee to inspect the public accounts, agreed to, under certain modifications. Petition from Newcastle. Motion by Mr. Wilkes, relative to private aids, or loans to the crown, rejected on a division. Opposition to the House-tax bill. Several amendments, moved and rejected, on separate divisions. Committee appointed to consider of the trade of Ireland. Resolutions passed, and bills brought in, on that subject. Sir William Meredith's motion for a repeal of the declaratory act, laid by. Bill brought in and passed, to enable his Majesty to make a suitable provision for the younger part of the Royal family, as well as for the Duke of Gloucester's children. Motion by Sir P. J. Clerke for bringing in the contractor's bill, carried on a division. Great opposition formed to the Irish bills. Contractor's bill read the first time; and the motion for its being read the second, carried upon a division. Second reading of the contractor's bill, Lost upon the question of commitment, by a majority of two only. Great debate on the message for a vote of credit. Debate on the second reading of the Irish bills. Sir Cecil Wray's motion rejected. Bills committed. Proceedings in the House of Commons on the death of the Earl of Chatham.

THE time at length arrived when France was to throw off the mask entirely with respect to America, and to realize all those predictions, which had been so long held out, and so frequently repeated by the minority, and which had, till lately, afforded a constant topic of ridicule to ministers and majorities. It had been repeatedly said, that the House of Bourbon would not support the Americans on the double account, that it would be teaching an evil lesson against themselves, and which might be too soon practised, to their own colonies, and that the establishment of an independent state and rising empire in the new world, would be dangerous to their future interests both in Europe and America. A doctrine which, considered meerly as a subject for speculative controversy, might undoubtedly afford room for some discussion, if, directly contrary to the disposition and practice of the rest of mankind, they looked more to future and remote contingencies, than to the greatest present advantages, and to the gratification of the most urgent and powerful passions.

Mar. 16th. On the day previous to the laying of the declaration from France before both Houses, the minister gave notice to the Commons, that he should have occasion on the following to present a message from the Throne to that House. Mr. Grenville replied, that he believed the subject of the message was already anticipated by the House; and, in order that gentlemen might be truly, as well as fully informed, in a matter of so great importance, before they tied themselves down to any particular measures by an answer, he would move for an address, " to lay before the House, " copies of all communications " from his Majesty's ambassador " at the court of France, or the " French ambassador at this court, " touching any treaty of alliance, " confederacy, or commerce, en- " tered into between that court " and the revolted colonies in " North America."

The minister directly moved the previous question, giving as a reason, that the exposure of the papers demanded, would be a most unpardonable and pernicious act of treachery, to those, who at the greatest risque, had communicated secret intelligence to government. Mr. Grenville offered to prevent an effect which he abhorred, by inserting the words " or extracts," after, copies, in the motion; but the minister insisted that no amendment could be received after the previous question had been moved. This conduct was, however, reprobated with so much indignation on the other side, and represented as an act of quibbling and chicane, so unworthy of, and unfitting for that place, that the minister withdrew his motion, and the amendment was received. The previous question being then again moved, the minister carried it upon a division by a majority of 231 to 146.

On the following day, 17th. the Royal message, accompanied by the French declaration, signed, on the 13th, by M. de Noailles, the ambassador from that court, were presented to the Commons by the minister. The former, after mentioning the matter of fact, with respect to the notification, acquainted them, that in consequence of that offensive communication, his Majesty had

sent orders to his ambassador to withdraw from the court of France. Then stating the justice and good faith of his Majesty's conduct towards foreign powers, and the sincerity of his wishes to preserve the tranquillity of Europe, he trusts, that he shall not stand responsible for the disturbance of that tranquillity, if he should find himself called upon to resent so unprovoked and so unjust an aggression on the honour of his crown, and the essential interests of his kingdoms, contrary to the most solemn assurances, subversive of the law of nations, and injurious to the rights of every sovereign power in Europe. It concluded with a declaration, that, " his Majesty, relying, with the firmest confidence on the zealous and affectionate support of his faithful people, is determined to be prepared to exert, if it shall become necessary, all the force and resources of his kingdoms; which he trusts will be found adequate to repel every insult and attack, and to maintain and uphold the power and reputation of this country."

The French declaration seems to state the actual independence of the Americans, as it was declared by them on the 4th of July, 1776, as a justification for consolidating, by a formal convention, the connection begun to be established between the two nations, and the signing a treaty of friendship and commerce, intended to serve as a foundation for their mutual good correspondence. Under an insulting parade of cultivating the good understanding between France and Great-Britain, the knowledge of this transaction is said to be communicated, accompanied with a declaration, that the contracting parties have paid great attention, not to stipulate any exclusive advantages in favour of France; and that the United States have reserved the liberty of treating with every nation whatever, upon the same footing of equality and reciprocity.

It is taken for granted, that the new proofs now given of a constant and sincere disposition for peace, will produce similar effects on our side; and that his Britannic Majesty, animated by similar sentiments, will equally avoid every thing that might alter the good harmony subsisting between the two crowns; and that he will particularly take effectual measures to prevent the commerce between France and America from being interrupted, and to cause all general commercial usages, as well as the particular rules subsisting between France and England, to be observed. It concludes with an intimation, that the French King, being determined to protect effectually the lawful commerce of his subjects, and to maintain the dignity of his flag, had, in consequence, taken eventual measures for these purposes, in concert with the United States of North America.

The minister moved an address to the Throne, which, besides echoing back and confirming the principal positions in the message, declares the highest indignation and greatest resentment at the unjust and unprovoked conduct of France, which, in another part, it calls " that restless and dangerous spirit of ambition and aggrandizement, which has so often invaded the rights and threatened the liberties of Europe." It concludes with the strongest assurances of the most zealous assistance and support; and a declaration of the firmest confidence, that, in every demonstration of loyalty to his Majesty, and of love to their country, his faithful subjects would vie with each other; and that no considerations would divert or deter them from standing forth in the public defence, and from sustaining, with a steady perseverance, any extraordinary burthens and expences, which should be found necessary for enabling his Majesty to vindicate the honour of his crown, and to protect the just rights and essential interests of these kingdoms.

Mr. Baker moved, that an amendment, to the following purport, should be inserted after the words, " assurances of support," in the address, viz. " hoping and trusting that his Majesty will be graciously pleased to remove from his counsels those ministers, in whose conduct, from experience of the pernicious effects of their past measures, his people can place no confidence in the present momentous situation of public affairs. Sir George Yonge warmly seconded [76] the amendment, and was himself as warmly supported. The principal ground of argument was, the folly and danger of committing the conduct of the most arduous war, in which this country was ever involved, to those men, who had already shewn themselves totally unequal to its government in the most profound quiet and peace; whose pernicious counsels and measures had converted that season of happiness and prosperity into all the horrors and mischiefs of a most unnatural, cruel, and destructive civil war; whose ignorance and incapacity in the management of that war of their own creation, joined to that incorrigible obstinacy, which, disdaining all counsel, and rejecting all warning, were at length the unhappy means, of for ever severing the British empire, and of finally plunging this nation in all its present danger and calamity.

But they dwelt principally upon the present glaring and criminal instance (as they termed it) of incapacity or negligence, in not being able, in a time of profound peace, and when intelligence was so procurable as to be obtained by a private gentleman, to discover the designs or transactions of the court of France, until they were put in actual force and open avowal against us. Or if they were acquainted with these circumstances, they were still more criminally culpable, they said, in having taken no single measure to guard against so momentous an event, nor made the smallest provision for the protection either of these kingdoms or of our foreign possessions, which were every where, whether in the East or West Indies, the Mediterranean, or at home, left defenceless, and open to insult and danger. Is then the fate of Great-Britain, they cried, in this critical season of danger, to be committed to the hands of such men? Is the disgrace, ruin, and discomfiture, which attended their three years war, singly with America, the motive for entrusting them now with the conduct of a war against the whole house of Bourbon, closely united with those very Americans? It was in vain, they said, to talk of calling forth the spirit of the nation, by men who had lost all confidence with the people. They were universally and justly considered as an administration composed of imbecility and deceit; no honest and disinterested man would venture to entrust them with his property; and it was no detraction to their character to say, that they were not more detested at home, than they were the contempt and derision of all foreigners.

They concluded, that the knowledge which the French, as well as the rest of Europe had, of the wretched weakness and instability of our counsels, and of the precipitate absurdity, and continued misconduct of our Ministers, was the cause, which, after long rendering us a bye-word, and mockery among the nations, had encouraged the House of Bourbon to offer us the present insult. That, in fact, if the Ministers had been pensioners to France, they could not have promoted the interests of that country more effectually than they had actually done. That in these circumstances, it would be in vain to offer any support to his Majesty, without informing him at the same time of the incapacity of those to whom he had entrusted the management of the public affairs. That as it would be impossible, after such repeated instances of folly, neglect, and incapacity, for the nation to repose any confidence in his present Ministers, so their removal could alone realize any offers of support, and revive the drooping spirit of the people. That single measure, they said, would strike more terror into the enemies of this country, than all the warlike preparations which we were capable of making, under the present notorious imbecility of our counsels and measures.

In answer to this, the Minister declared his fixed and unalterable resolution, that in the present situation of public affairs, he would keep his place at all events. He said, that the interest of the empire, no less than his own pride and sense of honour, now rendered his continuance in office absolutely necessary. It would be a disgrace, which he was determined not to incur, to abandon the helm, while the ship of state was tossed about in a storm, until he had brought her safely into port. He could see but little foundation for the present public alarm; the fall of the stocks, he said, was merely [77] the effect of that sudden panic, which was the usual concomitant of a beginning war. The apparent backwardness to fill the present loan, he, however, attributed rather to the greatness of the national debt, than to the mere approach of a war. Great Britain had always been so punctual in the payment of the interest due to her creditors, that she could never want money for the public service. The dread of an invasion, he said, was a mere bugbear; and if it should take place, the nation would have but little reason to be apprehensive for the consequences. Our navy never was, at the commencement of a war, in so flourishing a condition as at present; the new levies were nearly compleated; and that the public might be rendered entirely eafy on the fubject of invafion, his Majefty intended to recur to that conftitutional fource of defence, which was fo great a favourite with the other fide of the Houfe, by drawing out and embodying the militia. He concluded, that the infult offered by France was of the moft difgraceful nature; that as he knew the honour of the nation was dear to every gentleman in that Houfe, fo he trufted there was not a man in it who would not rifque his life and fortune to wipe off the ftain it had received; and that confequently, no one would refufe to agree to an addrefs, which only went to affure the King, that he fhould find in his faithful Commons, every fupport neceffary to maintain the honour of his people, and the dignity of his crown.

Several of the moft refpectable members of the oppofition, as well as fome gentlemen who were not of that party, confidered an immediate acknowledgement of the independency of the Americans, as not only the wifeft, but the only meafure now to be adopted, which could extricate us, without ftill greater loffes, and with any tolerable profpect of future advantage from our antient colonies, out of our prefent danger and difficulties. Their independence, was not only already eftablifhed, but had obtained fuch time to fix and fettle upon its foundations, that it appeared now too firm to be fhaken by our utmoft efforts, even fuppofing it were left, without any foreign fupport, merely to that of its own inherent ftrength. But, in that fituation, to form any hope of our being equal to its overthrow, under the acknowledgement and fupport of the Houfe of Bourbon, was, they faid, an idea only fit to be entertained by bedlamites; and any attempt of the fort, could be only confidered as the laft act of political defpair, infatuation, and phrenzy.

On the other hand, by fubmitting prudently to that neceffity in which we have been involved by our own perverfenefs and folly, and acknowledging in time that independency of the colonies, which we muft otherwife be at length compelled, under the moft ruinous circumftances, to acknowledge; we fhall immediately, and in the firft inftance, prevent the double war with the Houfe of Bourbon and America. We fhall thereby prevent thofe mutual connections, friendfhips, habitudes of life, communication of fentiments, manners, and language, which muft otherwife be the inevitable confequence of fuch a participation in a common courfe of danger and warfare, and under fuch a ftate of apparent obligation on one fide. By this means, faid they, America will be emancipated from all connection with France, excepting merely what is included in the dead letter of a treaty of commerce, and what may depend upon the payment of a public debt, which, in this cafe, fhe would not be long in difcharging; but which, a continuation of the war would every day increafe, and of courfe, not only bind her more clofely to the Houfe of Bourbon, but if it became enormous would even abridge her freedom of acting. In this cafe alfo, the open commerce which America would carry on with all the world, would neceffarily leffen her connection with, and weaken her dependence on France. But what would ftill, they faid, be of greater importance than any thing yet mentioned, the refentments of America would grow cool; the fenfe of thofe injuries and fufferings which fhe experienced at our hands, would daily weaken; commerce would neceffarily renew our former intercourfe; friendfhips and affections would again be revived; their children would again come here for their education; and religion, language, fimilarity of laws, cuftoms, and manners,

would all have their influence, in rendering us as nearly one people, as it was ftill poffible. And thus, faid they, we fhould derive greater advantages from the predilection and affection of America, in giving us a preference in point of commerce, and fupporting us with a filial regard, as a friendly and faithful ally, in any emergency of diftrefs or danger, than we could draw from that continent, under any circumftance of conqueft, or condition of flavery; fuppofing the poffibility of our accomplifhing the one, and inflicting the other.

It was, however, contended by thofe who held the oppofite opinion, that nothing could be a more complete difgrace to the nation, than to furrender its juft and natural fuperiority to the deceitful and infolent interpofition of France. That the hopes arifing from the fuppofed new alliance with the independent ftates of America, were wild and vifionary. That thofe who would refufe the very liberal offers that were now to be made, were determined enemies to their own people in America, as well as to this country. That it would be bafe and cruel to expofe thofe, who had rifqued all things in the fupport of Government, to the infolence and fury of the rebellious party; and the more fo, as the well affected was by far the more numerous divifion of that people.

The queftion being at length put, at half paft two in the morning, the amendment was rejected, and the original addrefs accordingly carried upon a divifion, by a majority of 263 to 113.

The French notification, accompanied with the royal meffage, were on the fame day prefented to the Lords by Lord Weymouth, who alfo moved for an addrefs fimilar to that propofed to the Commons. The cenfures paffed upon that conduct of public affairs which had brought on the prefent crifis, were, on this occafion, and fome others that followed, delivered in a much higher tone, and in more express and unqualified terms, than those which were produced by the same, or similar subjects in the other House.

The Duke of Manchester was the first to declare, that however great the provocation given by France might be, he must notwithstanding totally oppose the address, if the approaching war was to be conducted by the same men who were the authors of all our present calamities. Men, he said, in whose hands nothing could succeed; and in whom it would be madness to confide. He reminded the House of the frequent admonitions and warnings Ministers had received from the Lords on that side; and in which almost every progressive step towards national ruin, even to the very important business of the present day, had been truly and exactly foretold. They received, he said, continual communications of such facts and circumstances, as seemed sufficient to open the eyes of the most obstinate and incredulous; but in spite of facts and circumstances, they unhappily got majorities to support them against the strongest convictions of probability and common sense. And now have brought us to the melancholy dilemma of not being in a state to preserve peace, or to prosecute a war.

The noble Duke then moved the following amendment, to be inserted immediately after the word "support" in the address, viz. "whenever his Majesty shall, from a regard to the honour of his crown, and the safety of his people, remove from his councils those persons, under whose administration, no plan, civil or military, has been successful; and the colonies, so valuable a part of the empire, have been lost to the nation, and driven into connections with the court of France; and whose longer continuance in power, we are bound to represent to his Majesty, may highly endanger the safety of his crown, and of the remaining part of his dominions."

Some secret and invisible power, which they represented as having for several years guided all the state movements, and as being the real and efficient cause of all the national misfortunes and calamities, became an object of loud animadversion with some of the Lords. They said that this invisible power was the crying evil, and the great grievance to be provided against. That this unconstitutional subserviency, which indeed could only be established, through the shameful and base servility of Ministers, had been the fatal source of all the evils which had poured in upon this country during the present reign. That, whoever resisted this secret, concealed impulse, however able or fitting to serve the state, was proscribed; whilst those who paid the desired obedience to it, however weak, ignorant, or incapable, were immediately patronized, promoted, and required no other qualification, to rise to the possession of the first and most responsible offices.

The noble Minister who moved the address, said, he would not for the present enter into any exculpation of himself, or of his brethren in office; he would reserve a formal defence for a formal accusation. He could not however avoid observing, that an unproved accusation of Ministers, and a condemnation of their conduct untried and unheard, was as unfair and unjust, as it was contrary to all propriety with respect to time, place, and occasion. This was not, however, the principal ground upon which he must oppose the amendment; but for its being clogged with a condition which implied, that what was right and necessary in itself should not be pursued, unless something else were granted. At a time when the very being of the kingdom seemed to stand on a precarious basis, and that his Majesty requested their united assistance to support that along with his own dignity, it carried a most ungenerous appearance to tack compulsatory conditions, as the price of a necessary service. If the address met their sentiments, let it receive their sanction as the necessary consequence of its propriety and expedience; but let not unreasonable concessions be made the measure of duty. And if Ministers were found incapable or guilty upon a proper examination, an application then to the throne, unmixed with any foreign matter, would, undoubtedly, meet with proper attention. As to the secret influence talked of, the King's Ministers knew of none. They had done their duty upon their own opinions. If these opinions were erroneous and honest, they would be pardoned; if just and well founded, they would meet support and applause. If their conduct was faulty, they would deserve punishment; and they were ready couragiously to support their own conduct in their own persons, and to abide the just sense of the House, without skulking behind the throne or parliament, or exculpating themselves upon the idea of any secret influence whatever.

The very few Lords on the same side who entered into any part of the debate, said, they opposed the amendment as unprecedented and indecent. That it would be little less than offering a direct insult to the Sovereign; and that it would be equally injurious and unjust to his servants, to condemn them by a hasty and rash censure, before they were heard in their own defence. That the failure of their plans was by no means a proof of inability or misconduct; it might have proceeded from numberless circumstances with which they were yet unacquainted; and as no wisdom or ability could command success, its failure consequently could not, without farther evidence, imply any room for censure.

On the other side it was contended. that there was not a more proper, or truly parliamentary method of foliciting a redrefs of grievances, than by propofing that redrefs as the term of compliance to a requeft. It was the ftrong ground and foundation of all thofe checks which parliament held upon the crown. Without that there could be no fuch checks, and parliaments would be ufelefs. The condition to be annexed to the addrefs, was therefore perfectly in order, and in full conformity with parliamentary ufage. But if it had been otherwife, when the ftate was acknowledged to be fhaken to its foundations, and its very exiftence at ftake, forms were too ridiculous to be thought of. Such a fituation of public affairs, prefented the feafon for creating of new precedents fuitable to the occafion, inftead of being fuperftitioufly bound by thofe which were obfolete and ufelefs. The propofed condition was entwined with the national welfare; it was founded on matter of fact, and of public notoriety; it was not only a proper anfwer to, but it was demanded by the meffage from the crown; that meffage requires affiftance and fupport, and this points out the only certain ground by which they can be obtained. The objection made to a condemnation without trial, a noble Earl humoufly obferved to be unfounded; the Mi-[78] nifters, he faid, had been long,—too long tried; and were now under the condemnation of all the difinterefted part of the nation.

Several of the Lords on that fide, objected greatly to the paffionate and inflammatory expreffions ufed in the meffage, and which were echoed back in the addrefs. They were no lefs than tantamount, they faid, to a declaration of war. Was the nation in condition, or its military force in a ftate of preparation to abide the confequences? There was no call for any violence or intemperance of language. There was not an angry expreffion in the French refcript. The matter of fact, they faid, fhould have been ftated plainly to parliament for their deliberations, and they might well have declared in return, their determination to fupport upon all occafions, both the dignity of the crown and the interefts of the nation, without entangling themfelves with any fpecific refolution or promife, and without the fmalleft occafion for any inflammatory language on either fide. They faid, that however grievous the meafure taken by France might be, and in fact was, yet that war was by no means an inevitable, or even neceffary confequence of the prefent declaration. We had ourfelves ufed a fimilar conduct on former occafions, with refpect both to France and Spain, without its being productive of any immediate war with either. And, however we might lament the occafion and its confequences, reprobate the conduct which expofed us to them, or vainly and paffionately exclaim againft the perfidioufnefs of the act, it was in reality one of thofe meafures of political advantage, which no rival nation, under a wife and active government, could have overlooked or neglected. In thefe circumftances then, there feemed no neceffity for entering into a war; if, without injury to the honour of Great Britain, war could be avoided it ought.

It behoved us firft to confider what the object of the war was, and our ability of attaining that object; and in the next place moft ferioufly to reflect, upon the poffible confequences of our failing in the attempt. The only object of a prefent war with France muft be the recovery of America; an object which every man in his fenfes muft now fee to be totally unattainable. What then, faid they, is to be done? The anfwer is fhort, and the ftrait line of conduct before you. Cancel your inflammatory votes, and your menacing declarations. Annihilate that ridiculous conciliatory fyftem, which feems to have been calculated only to render parliament a fubject of mockery and derifion. And, inftead of fending out Commiffioners to be laughed at, to return as they went, and to render our public counfels ftill more contemptible, arm them with powers to acknowledge the independency of the Americans, if they infift upon it, and to conclude the moft advantageous treaty of peace and commerce with them, that can now be obtained. But at any rate, let your conduct with regard to France be what it may, eftablifh peace with America. The point of honour, muft in this cafe give way to neceffity. The attempting impoffibilities can only render our ruin inevitable. It is impoffible to recal what we have wantonly thrown away. By thefe means we fhall obtain fecurity. We fhall be extricated from our immediate dangers and difficulties. We fhall gain breathing time, which in our prefent fituation is a matter of the firft importance. And we muft truft to time, fortune, and future wifdom, to remedy fome of thofe evils, and to reftore fome of thofe advantages, which our violence have produced, or our folly fquandered.

The oppofition were not, however, unanimous in their opinion, with regard to admitting the independence of America. It was held and firmly fupported, as the only means of faving the nation, by the Marquis of Rockingham and the Duke of Richmond, and feemed to be entertained by moft, or all, of thofe Lords who compofe that party. But the Earls of Chatham, Temple, and Shel-[79] burne, with fome other Lords whofe fentiments were generally in unifon with theirs, could not bear the idea of a feparation from America, nor confequently of its independence. This they confidered as the greatest of all possible political and national evils, and as including the utter degradation and final ruin of this country. The evil, (though not to the utmost extent it was described) was acknowledged on the other side; but the possibility of preventing it was the matter in question.

The question being at length put upon the Duke of Manchester's amendment, it was rejected upon a division by a majority of 100, including 16 proxies, to 36, including two proxies, who supported the question. The main question being afterwards put on the original address, it was carried by a proportional majority, though the numbers were smaller on both sides.

Among the singularities of that day's debate, a noble Earl, in the warmth excited by the subject declared, that the nation was betrayed, and that nothing less than treachery could account for those measures which led to its present situation. The fatal effects of a supposed system of corruption, which was said to be at this time generally prevalent, became a subject also of much animadversion, in the course of which the conduct of a majority in the other House underwent such strictures, as were probably never before heard within those walls.

The committee on the state of the nation March 19th. being resumed in the House of Commons, the subject of the late expedition from Canada was taken up by Mr. Fox; who having first caused the papers relative to that measure to be read, proceeded to state the grounds of his intended motions. His principal object was to shew that the measure was originally absurd and impracticable in the design; and that the failure of effect being accordingly inevitable, all the subsequent losses and misfortunes were to be directly charged to the noble Lord at the head of the American department,

and not to the officers who were entrusted with the execution. He accordingly proposed three resolutions tending to establish the following points, that the plan of the expedition was impolitic, unwise, and incapable of producing any good effect; that the provision made for it was inadequate to the object; and that General Burgoyne had acted agreeably to the tenor of his instructions. From these, he said, he deduced a fourth resolution, which he reserved, and which was intended to pass the censure of the House, upon the noble Lord who was the ostensible author of the expedition.

This business brought on the longest debate that had taken place during the course of the session; and called forth little less than the whole ability on both sides of the House. The framer of the motion was thought in his introductory speech, to have even transcended his customary style of exertion, and his friends by no means lost any ground in their support. On the other side, the ground of impropriety in bringing on the business during the absence of those generals, who until the contrary was established, must be considered as principal parties in the charge, was again taken. That there had been a fault, and a great one, somewhere, was universally allowed. A whole army had been lost. The nature and fortune of the war thereby totally changed. A new, and most dangerous foreign war was the immediate consequence; the loss of America, and even more, might possibly be the final. The causes that led to such a series of fatal consequences, they said, required undoubtedly the strictest investigation; and the fault, wherever it lay, might demand even more than censure. But the general acknowledgement of a fault or crime, could by no means imply the Minister to be the guilty per-

son; nor could the enquiry be properly conducted, nor the charge fixed as justice directed, until all the parties were present, and all the evidence.

The direct charges made against the American Minister by the opposition, however, necessarily called forth some direct defence; and no pains were omitted to shew, that the northern expedition was, in the first place, a wise and necessary measure; that it was capable of success, and the design evidently practicable; and that the noble Secretary in whose department it lay, had omitted nothing which could be done by an attentive Minister to insure its success. They also endeavoured much to controvert a point insisted on by the opposition, that General Burgoyne's orders were peremptory with respect to his advancing to Albany. They said, that however peremptory the letter of instructions might appear, a discretionary latitude of conduct, to be regulated by circumstances and events, was always necessarily implied and understood. This, with much more upon the subject, will, however, properly appear, in the relation of the long discussion which this business underwent in the ensuing session of parliament.

The question being at length put, the first resolution was rejected upon a division, by the great majority of 164 to 44. The event of this division was resented by the mover, Mr. Fox, with an unusual degree of warmth, and an appearance of the highest indignation. He not only declared that he would not propose another motion; but taking the resolution of censure out of his pocket, tore it in pieces, and immediately quitted the House.

The conquering party were not, however, satisfied with this victory. They were determined in the present warmth of success to pursue the advantage, and to render it complete by a vote of negative approbation. A great law officer accordingly moved, that it [81] does not appear to this committee, that the failure of the expedition to Canada arose from any neglect in the Secretary of State for the colonies. Although this motion was carried in the committee, yet as the chief argument of the majority turned upon the injustice of any decision in the absence of the parties, a decision in favour of the party present did not appear very equitable; it was thought, on consideration among themselves, that it would be more expedient not to proceed upon it; therefore, the resolution was not reported to the House, by which it was rendered in effect a non-entity.

As the charge of a boundless profusion in the public expenditure, had afforded a constant theme for animadversion to the opposition in both Houses during the session, Col. Barre, who had frequently taken up, and commented with severity upon detached parts of the subject, at length determined to render the whole an object of parliamentary enquiry. In a comprehensive view which he took of various parts of the subject, the conduct of ministers and contractors, with the exorbitant profits supposed to be gained on contracts and agencies, underwent no small share of censure and animadversion. He concluded an able speech, some parts of which threw the minister into an unusual degree of warmth, and even betrayed him into some irregularity in point of order, and with respect to interruption, by moving for a "com-
Mar. 30th. "mittee to inspect
" the public accounts with respect
" to expenditure, and to report
" their opinion thereon to the
" House."

Several of the gentlemen in office opposed the motion as unnecessary, from a conviction, they said, that the treasury had acted with the utmost prudence and œconomy in the disposal of the public money. They said, that if any undue profits had in some particular instances been obtained by contractors, the treasury would oblige them to refund such sums, as soon as the accounts could be examined, and the necessary enquiries made. They also said that this was not a fit season for a committee of accounts; the House was not in a proper disposition, nor the nation in a proper temper, for such a discussion; it would only afford fresh matter for the calumnious spirit of the times to prey upon; and might be productive of great mischief, by disseminating ill-founded charges, and exciting causeless jealousies and suspicions among the people.

Amendments and modifications were proposed on the same side, particularly by leaving the words, " to report their opinion thereon," out of the motion, and by referring the matter to a select committee. These points were agreed to, and 21 gentlemen were accordingly chosen by ballot as a select committee, although the gentleman who framed the original motion, said he would rather withdraw it, than to join in deceiving the public by hanging out hopes of redress, when it was evident from the train in which the business was now proposed to be placed, that nothing useful could be effected.

On the same day, a petition of uncommon rigour against the Ministers was presented from the town and county of Newcastle upon Tyne. In this piece, after a long enumeration of grievances and evils, particularly those appertaining to the civil war, they call upon parliament, that its wisdom and attention may be " seriously en-
" gaged to investigate, and effec-
" tually root out, the cause of
" these evils; and to establish the
" peace and happiness of society,
" by humbly addressing his Ma-
" jesty to remove from his pre-
" sence and counsels for ever those
" men, who from motives of inte-
" rest, or vindictive ambition, may
" have destroyed this peace, in-
" terrupted this happiness, and
" forfeited the confidence of the
" people; and to prevent succeed-
" ing delinquents from being mis-
" led by the flattering hopes of
" impunity, we pray, that legal
" but rigorous and exemplary pu-
" nishments may be impartially
" inflicted upon any who are found
" to have betrayed the just rights,
" and sacrificed the welfare, of
" their country; that such effec-
" tual check may be given to vice
" and corruption, and such coun-
" tenance and encouragement to
" public virtue, as may unite a
" free and generous people upon
" the solid basis of loyalty and mu-
" tual affection."

A motion made by
April 2d. Mr. Wilkes for bringing in a bill " more effectually to
" prevent the dangerous and un-
" constitutional practice of giving,
" or granting money to the crown,
" as a private aid, loan, benevo-
" lence, or subscription, for pub-
" lic purposes, without the consent
" of parliament," was, after a
" short debate, rejected upon a
division, by a majority of 71, to
40.

On the same day the Minister gave notice, that he would on the following move for some allowance to be made to the subscribers on the present loan, in order to make up the loss sustained by them, in consequence of the change which had taken place in public affairs since the time of their subscription, and which had materially affected the marketable value of the funds. He said this proposal was equitable and just, as the event in question had taken place before their first payment was made. And, that if the subscribers were to be the sufferers, it would be out of the power of any Minister to raise a loan upon any future occasion, however critical.

This proposal was however reprobated in such unreserved terms by the opposition, that, although it was afterwards talked of, the Minister never thought fitting to bring it forward. They said they were astonished at the noble lord's temerity, and his consequent contempt of parliament; it was, indeed, beyond endurance. So barefaced a proposition had never been made in that House; and if it were received it would establish a precedent, of a more dangerous nature, than even any of those hitherto furnished, for the practice of future Ministers. With such a precedent, all ideas of loans and of contracts would become ridiculous. Did not the noble lord tell the House, with his usual confidence and tone of authority, the great advantage he had allowed the subscribers in this very loan; and had he the face now to come, and propose to take a sum of money out of the national purse, in order to supply any deficiency of intended and expected profit which might fall to the lot of those friends, to whom, as marks of favour, of private and parliamentary kindness, he had already parcelled out that loan in such shares as were due to their respective merits? Suppose, said they, that these subscribers had (as has frequently been the case) made six or eight per cent. upon their money, would they come to the treasury, or to that bar, to acknowledge that their gains were exorbitant, and that they were come to refund the extraordinary profits?

The house-tax bill was either combated in the whole, or controverted in its parts, by some in the opposition, in every part of its progress through the House of Commons. They said it was particularly injurious, unjust, and oppressive, from its being unequally and partially allotted, as near nine-tenths of its burthens were to be borne by the metropolis, and the county of Middlesex. That it carried more the appearance of a bill of punishment on the citizens of London, for their daring to oppose the American war, than a fair,

equal, and proportionate tax on property. And, they said it was a most grievous and melancholy consideration, that those who, within and without that House, had either personally opposed or execrated all the measures that tended to that fatal event, should, in themselves and their posterity, have their properties taxed, and their inheritances perpetually mortgaged, to supply the immense sums lavished in schemes of folly, cruelty, and injustice, which they equally lamented and detested.

Failing in their opposition to the general principle of the bill, they used the most strenuous efforts in the committee on the second of April, for lessening its effect with respect to the poorer orders of the people. Upon this principle they first moved, that houses of 10l. a-year, and under, should not be rated to the tax. This question, after considerable debate, being lost on a division, by a majority of 69 to 51; they then moved, that houses of 7l. a-year, and under, should be exempted. Upon this being rejected on a division, they descended through different gradations of rents, down to five pounds one shilling; having brought every question to a division, and lost every one. The bill was passed on the 6th.

The distresses of Ireland had long been an object of regret, even with many of those who had no particular interest in that country. Without entering into the causes from which these originated, it will be sufficient to observe, that they had grown to their present alarming and deplorable state, under the unhappy consequences of the American war; so that the country became unequal to the support of that great establishment, with which it had (perhaps too inconsiderately) encumbered itself, when the flourishing state of all other parts of the British empire, had diffused a considerable degree of prosperity even thither.

• • •

April 6th. On the day previous to this business, Sir [82] William Meredith had moved for a repeal of the declaratory act of the year 1766, as preparatory to that of the other obnoxious American laws; the whole measure being in his opinion absolutely necessary before the departure of the commissioners, to afford any prospect of success to their negociation. The motion was opposed by Mr. Burke, who spoke much at length on the question, and with much applause from the greater part on both sides of the House. The tendency of his speech was to prove that the act, as an abstract proposition of law, was wise at the time it was made. That it produced great advantage at that time, to the measures for healing the differences with America; and that it produced no ill effect. That the House had already formally renounced the obnoxious power in question, which was supposed to be involved in that act; and that therefore this repeal, would be only for parliament to give itself the lie, for no manner of purpose. The motion was gently rejected without a division, by a motion for its being adjourned for two months.

• • •

The arrival of General Bur- [83] goyne from America, with some peculiar circumstances accompanying or consequent of that event, served, all together, to cause a revival of the business relative to the northern expedition, and seemed to indicate such an accession of new matter of investigation, as might possibly keep parliament together longer than had been expected. That once favourite General, soon discovered, upon his return, that he was no longer an object of court favour, or of ministerial countenance. He was, in the first instance, refused admission to the royal presence, and from thence experienced all those marks of being in disgrace, which are so well understood, and so quickly perceived, by the retainers and followers of courts.

Under these circumstances of disgrace and interdiction, a court of enquiry was appointed; but the general officers reported, that, in his then situation, as a prisoner on parole to the Congress, under the convention—they could not take cognizance of his conduct. This spirited officer then demanded a court martial—which on the same grounds was refused. He then declared himself under a necessity of throwing himself upon parliament, for a public enquiry into his conduct. The business was not, however, taken up, as he expected, by any side of the House at his first appearance. Possibly the lateness of the season, and the fear of the determination of a ministerial majority, might deter the opposition from any steps to that purpose. Mr. Vyner,[84] however, removed any difficulty that occurred on either side, by May 26th. moving for a committee of the whole House, to consider of the state and condition of the army which surrendered themselves prisoners, on convention, at Saratoga, in America; and also by what means Lieutenant General Burgoyne, who commanded that army, and was included in that convention, was released, and is now in England.

The motion was seconded by Mr. Wilkes, and an amendment moved by Mr. Fox, for the insertion of the following words, immediately after the word "consider" "of the transactions of the northern army under Lieutenant General Burgoyne, and"—. The motion and amendment afforded that opportunity to the General which he was seeking for, of explaining the nature and state of his situation, and the particular circumstances of that persecution, as he termed it, under which, he described himself, as most injuriously suffering.

He accordingly vindicated his own conduct, and the honour of the brave army which he commanded, with great ability, in a long and eloquent speech. As the general discussion of the subject was passed over to the ensuing session, and will of course become an object of our future recital, we shall for the present only take notice of such peculiar matter relative to the immediate business, as will serve to explain the ground of debate, or as could not be related with propriety hereafter.

The General seconded the motion and the amendment, as tending to that general enquiry into his conduct, which could alone vindicate his character and honour, from the aspersions of ministerial writers, and all the other means which had been used, as well during his absence, as since his arrival, to injure both. He entered into a justification of his conduct with respect to the cruelties charged to the savages, and a vindication of his regular forces, from the inhumanities attributed to them. He insisted that he had not exceeded his orders, and that they were positive and peremptory. That the House had been designedly misled to his prejudice in the former enquiry upon this subject, by laying before them his original plan for the Canada expedition, and leaving them in the opinion that all its parts had been punctually complied with; although the Minister who laid it before them, knew the contrary to be the fact, and that some of its most material clauses had been erased. He observed that the papers which had been laid before them, were in some respects deficient, and in others superfluous. Among the latter he particularly complained of the exposure of a private and confidential letter, which could[85] answer no public purpose, and at the same time evidently tended to his personal prejudice. And among the former, the withholding of several others, which were not in the same predicament, some of which would have removed the ill impression and effect caused by that letter, and others would have afforded explanations of several material parts of his conduct, and rendered a long train of correspondence which was laid before them unnecessary. But he complained still more of the disclosure of a paper of the most secret nature, containing his thoughts upon the manner of conducting the war from the side of Canada. Upon this part of the subject he exclaimed with great energy, "what officer will venture hereafter to give his opinion upon measures or men when called upon by a Minister, if his confidence, his reasonings, and his preferences, are to be thus invidiously exposed, to create jealousies and differences among his fellow officers, and at last to put an imposition upon the world, and make him responsible for the plan as well as the execution of a hazardous campaign."

After stating and refuting a number of calumnies, which, from interested or malevolent purposes, had been industriously propagated against him, he said, that under such circumstances of the greatest injury to the reputation of one of their members, together with that of his character having already been brought into question before them, and his direct assertion, that the information which the House had then gone upon was incomplete and fallacious, he knew not what description of men could justly refuse, to him personally, a new and full enquiry.

He put it strongly to the feelings of his auditors, and to make it individually their own case, the situation of an injured and persecuted man, debarred, by an interdiction, from the possibility of vindicating himself to his Sovereign, and put by, if not inevitably precluded from the judgment of a military tribunal, if thus, disgraced at court, and cut off from resource in the line of his profession, he should also at last, in his final appeal to the justice and equity of his country, find himself disappointed in the only possible means of justification that remained, by the refusal of a parliamentary investigation of a measure of state, with which the rectitude or criminality of his conduct was inseparably blended. After applying this matter particularly and forcibly to his brother officers in parliament, as a common cause of the profession, from the discouragement and injury which the service must suffer under the establishment of such a precedent, and various other considerations applied to different parts of the House, he wound up the whole of that part of the subject, by declaring, that he waved an appeal to private sentiments, and desired the motion to be considered as a call upon the public duty of the House; and he required and demanded, in his place, as a representative of the nation, a full and impartial enquiry into the causes of the miscarriage of the northern army in an expedition from Canada.

The American Minister declared his concern for the exposure of the private letter, which he attributed to accident, or official mistake. As to the General's not having access to his Sovereign, he said there were various precedents for the refusal, until his conduct had undergone a military enquiry, which could not yet be done. And concluded, that as military men were the natural and proper judges of the subject, he could not see the propriety of any interference by parliament in the business. Other gentlemen in office, besides confirming that opinion, held parliament as totally incompetent to any decision on the question. And one of the law officers said, they had one enquiry already, which afforded sufficient information to form an opinion, and nothing [86] more could be done for the present.

The question being at length put on Mr. Fox's amendment, it was rejected on a division, by a majority of 144 to 95. And, the main question, after some unusual warmth of altercation, was set by at a late hour by the previous question, which was carried without a division.

Although the Ministers did not seem much disposed on this day to enter into any particular discussion with the General, yet, if any such measures were intended to be kept, they were fully done away by the part which he took in an ensuing debate; when it also seemed that they were not unprepared for the event.

This was in consequence 28th. of a motion made by Mr. Hartley, for an address to prevent the prorogation of parliament, and that they should continue sitting for the purpose of assisting and forwarding the measures already taken for the restoration of peace in America; and that they might be in readiness, in the present critical situation and prospect of public affairs, to provide for every important event at the earliest notice. In a warm speech which General Burgoyne made in support of the motion, he advanced matters and opinions which could not fail of being exceedingly grating to the Ministers, and which were resented accordingly. Particularly, his describing them, as totally insufficient and unable to support the weight of public affairs in the present critical and dangerous emergency.

To the general knowledge of this incapability, he attributed the diffidence, despondency, and consternation, which were evident among a great part of the people; and a still more fatal symptom, he said, that torpid indifference to our impending fate, which prevailed among a yet greater number. After stating the general pa-

nic that might result from this general state of temper and opinion, he said, "the salvation of the country depends upon the confidence of the people in some part of government." He then proceeded to censure without reserve, the whole public conduct pursued since the delivery of the French rescript; particularly in whatever related to offence, defence, and the total neglect of all means to inspirit the nation. In a course of striking military observations, illustrated by late and popular historical examples, he used the following, "it will be difficult for those who are most conversant in history, and accurate in observation, to point out examples, where, after an alarm, the spirits of men have revived by inaction. He knew of no great exertions, where the governing counsels have shewn apprehension and terror, and consequent confusion at the outset."

The drift of the speech was to shew the necessity of complying with the motion, in order, besides other great objects, that the presence of parliament, might restore the confidence, and renew the spirit of the nation; and he said, that if the King's Ministers should take the lead in opposition to the motion, and use their influence for its rejection, he should hold them to be the opposers of national spirit, opposers of public virtue, and opposers of the most efficacious means to save their country.

Although, in the course of his speech, he had disclaimed all hostility, it was notwithstanding understood and resented as a declaration of war; and accordingly brought out a bitter reply, mixed with much personality, from a gentleman high in office; and not [87] less noted for freedom of speech, than for his other eminent qualities. After stating his reasons against the motion, upon the same grounds which we have seen taken at the Christmas recess, he particularly applied himself to the last speaker, who, he said, being a prisoner, was in fact dead to all civil, as well as military purposes, and, as such, had no right to speak, much less to vote in that House. He then threw some degree of ridicule, in his state of it, upon the General's application or wish for a trial. The honourable gentleman, he said, knew, when he desired a trial, that he could not be tried; he was upon parole; he was, as a prisoner under that parole, not at liberty to do any act in his personal capacity. —Suppose, for instance, he should be tried and found guilty, who could punish him? No one certainly. A prisoner is always bound to his first engagement, and amenable to the stipulations of those who have prescribed the terms. To talk therefore of trial, without the power to punish, was a farce; the power to try, implied the power to punish; or such a power meant nothing.

One of the law officers of the crown took up the same ground of[88] argument, and made it an object of serious and real discussion. In a speech, fraught with general knowledge and ancient learning, and in which the doubts and arguments were too methodically arranged, to admit any doubt of their preparation for the purpose, he endeavoured to establish from the example of Regulus, in the Roman history, and other precedents, that the General (the convention of Saratoga being now broken) was merely in the state of a common prisoner of war; and that, consequently, he was not sui juris, but the immediate property of another power. From whence he insisted, with the fullest appearance of conviction to himself, that the General, under his present obligations, was totally incapable of exercising any civil office, incompetent to any civil function, and incapable of bearing arms in this country.

The General expressed the utmost indignation at this attempt to overthrow all his rights, as a man, a citizen, and a soldier. He urged, that the convention was not broken. That the Congress, from some ill-founded jealousy in respect to some circumstances of his own conduct, and still more, from their doubt of the faith of administration, had only suspended the execution of it on their side, until it had received a formal ratification from government. That he was bound to no condition by the convention, excepting the single one, of not serving in America; not by his parole, but that of returning, on due notice being given, on the demand of the Congress. He stated an instance from the last war, of a noble Lord then present, who[89] was taken prisoner at St. Cas, and whose parole situation came directly home to the point in question. But it seemed as if fortune had foreseen and provided, for this new impediment which was to be created, in order to a further limitation of the right of sitting in parliament. For it appeared, that the idea of restraining him by his parole, from giving any vote against America in parliament, had been adopted by some of the leaders there; but that it had not only been rejected with disdain, but that it had been further said, they wished him to attend his duty in parliament, from a certainty, that his intimate knowledge of the state of affairs on both sides, would induce him, by every means in his power, to accelerate, what, they declared, they so much wished for, a peace, upon proper terms. In the debate, it was pressed upon the whole, as arising from the maxims and practice of warfare established among civilized nations, that the General, was not only at full liberty to serve against any other enemy, but that, if he had defeated or destroyed an American fleet or army, in any other of the three quarters of the world, it cou'd not by any construction be interpreted as a breach of his parole.

The Speaker put an end to all cavil upon the subject, by deciding the question in favour of General Burgoyne, and the learned law-officer appeared to acquiesce in his opinion. But the principal leaders of the opposition did not let the matter pass off so easily. They warmly resented the illiberal treatment, as they termed it, offered to the General, in his present circumstances of accumulated misfortune. And, upon this occasion, the researches of the learned law officer, in the fabulous legends of barbarous antiquity, and his fixing upon the very questionable story of Regulus in the first punic war (an æra when it lay in the option of the victors, whether to massacre, sell, or to keep as slaves, their prisoners) as a precedent for the present times; and thereby, not only to overthrow the modern laws of warfare, but to render it the test of a British senator's holding his seat in parliament, underwent no small share of animadversion and ridicule.

Mr. Hartley's motion was at length rejected on a division, by a majority of 105 to 53. This did not prevent Sir James Lowther, on[90] the day before the recess, from moving for an address, that parliament might be continued sitting by adjournments, until a happy termination of the present public exigencies. His motion, however, met with a similar fate to the former.

During this constant state of warfare in one House, public affairs were not less warmly agitated in the other. On the 23d of March a motion was made by the Duke of Richmond for an address, " That all the ships of war and land forces be immediately withdrawn from the ports and territories of the thirteen revolted provinces, and disposed of in such manner as should seem best calculated for the defence of the remaining parts of the empire, in the difficult situation in which we are unfortunately placed; humbly befeeching his Majefty, to take into his particular confideration the condition of England and Ireland to repel a foreign invafion; and imploring him to take the moft fpeedy and effectual meafures for providing for the fecurity of thefe kingdoms."

This motion brought on a very warm and interefting debate; in which, the chief leaders of oppofition entered into a large field of difcuffion, and cenfure. The minifters and their friends were not equally active in the debate. It was principally oppofed by the Firft Lord of the Admiralty, who, without much controverting the propriety or neceffity of the propofed meafure, founded his oppofition to the motion on the ground of fecrecy, expedience, and policy, with refpect to the mode of carrying it into execution; which fhould not be fubject to the expofure incident to a parliamentary difcuffion. He accordingly moved the previous queftion; which was at length carried upon a divifion, by a majority of 56 to 28.

An acknowledgment made by the noble Lord, to whofe department the information particularly belonged, of an unhappy confequence of the American conteft, which had been long forefeen, and frequently urged by the oppofition in both Houfes, and which had hitherto been treated by the minifters, rather as a fubject of ridicule, than of ferious confideration, was a circumftance in this debate which could not pafs unnoticed. The noble Lord at the head of the admiralty, attributed the fcarcity of feamen (to which the prefent infufficiency of the navy could only be charged, as he faid there were fhips enough ready for fea), merely to the want of thofe American failors, who had contributed to man our fleets in former wars. Thefe the noble Lord eftimated at 18,000; and obferved, that if we confidered that thofe men were now employed againft us, it made a real

difference of 36,000 feamen.—A fatal confequence, indeed, of our unhappy civil war; and yet fo obvious, that the latenefs of the difcovery fcarcely excites lefs furprize than regret.

Several motions made by the Earl of Effingham, on the laft of March, relative to naval affairs, were the means of introducing a very long and interefting debate, in which the noble mover, with the Dukes of Bolton and Richmond, took the principal fhare on one fide, and the noble Lord at the head of the department in queftion, found fufficient occafion for the full exertion of all his faculties, on the other. The motions went,—To, An account of the ftate of the fhips in his Majefty's navy, in the latter end of the year 1770.—Of the ordinary eftimates of the navy from 1770, to 1778, inclufive.—Of the number of fhips broke up and fold, with the old ftores fold, and an account of what both fold for, all within that term—An account of the buildings, rebuildings, and repairs of fhips and veffels, over and above thofe charged in the wear and tear, of the year 1777.—And concluded with fome accounts relative to ftoppages.

The objects of the enquiry were, in the firft place, to afcertain the real ftate of the navy; a knowledge of which, at this critical feafon, the Lords on that fide reprefented, as being not only of the higheft importance, but as being abfolutely neceffary with refpect to the public fafety; more efpecially, as they infifted, and endeavoured to demonftrate from public facts and confequences, that parliament had hitherto been intentionally mifled, in all the official information which had been laid before them on that fubject. The fecond was to detect and remedy thofe malverfations of office, neglect of its great and principal duty, and profufion of the public money, which had been fo long and fo frequently charged to

the account of that department. It feemed alfo to be a part of the drift of the enquiry, to overthrow that pofition which they had heard fo often repeated, of the ruinous condition of the navy when it was placed in the hands of its prefent conductors, and of its wonderful growth and profperity under their nurture.

The noble Earl fupported his refolutions with no moderate fhare of abilities, in a fpeech replete with information, and including fuch a feries of naval facts, as fufficiently fhewed, the induftry with which he had obtained a thorough knowledge of his fubject. He concluded, by ftrenuoufly recommending to the Firft Lord of the Admiralty, on his own account, and as the beft means of fhewing, that he was not liable to any part of that heavy cenfure which he had thrown out againft the board in general, to confent to the motions; or if they implied any thing, which, in the noble Lord's own opinion, could tend to afford any improper information to our foreign enemies, that he would propofe fuch modifications or alteration of them, as fhould prevent that effect; but not to let an opinion go abroad into the world, that all the charges which had been laid now or at other times upon that ground had been fo well founded, that he could not venture to ftand the teft of an enquiry.

The noble Lord at the head of that department wifhed with great fervour, that the committee of enquiry had never been inftituted; and afferted his full conviction, that the matters which had already come out in the courfe of its fitting, particularly with refpect to the navy, had been extremely prejudicial to the interefts of this country. He accordingly recurred to that beaten but ftrong ground, (which had already repelled fo many affaults) of political fecrecy, and the danger of difclofure. It may well be believed, that no pains were omitted, nor provocation spared by his noble affailants, to induce him to quit this ground of advantage; but the noble Lord, with all the caution and temper of a veteran and experienced general, could neither be tempted nor provoked to abandon it.

After much feverity of animadverfion the queftion being at length put on the firft refolution, it was rejected on a divifion, by a majority of 50 to 20. The fecond and fifth were agreed to; but the third and fourth were negatived feparately without a divifion.

This was the laft act of the grand committee of the nation in the Houfe of Lords. The Duke of Richmond, who had moved that committee, thought it neceffary on the 7th of April, to clofe the enquiry. Though, he faid, he had failed by the prevalence of that power he wifhed to correct, in feveral of thofe objects for which he propofed the committee, he attributed feveral public and important benefits to it. He faid, that an afcertainment of the ftate of the army, of the ftate of the navy, of the general expenditure in confequence of the American war, and a particular inveftigation of a part of that expenditure, were the refult of their enquiries: and he firmly believed, that it was owing merely to the committee, that the minifters had been fo far brought to their fenfes, as to fet about fomething like an attempt, towards an accommodation with the Americans. He faid, the enquiry was highly neceffary, from the circumftantial recital of the moft interefting information which it had produced; and that as it had been of fingular advantage to the nation, he was exceedingly happy to find that it had met with the univerfal approbation of all ranks of people.

It alfo afforded him great pleafure, that the conduct of it had been approved of by their Lordfhips, who had in no one inftance

expreffed their diflike of the manner of agitating the various queftions which had been introduced, either by other Lords, or by himfelf; the only objection made to either, amounting not to a denial of the refolutions of fact offered to their confideration, (which had been on all fides acknowledged to be truifms) but merely to an argument of the inexpediency of paffing fuch refolutions at that particular period of time. He then ftated his reafons for clofing the enquiry; and after having taken, with his ufual ability, a general review of the whole bufinefs, he fhewed the motives for winding it up by the addrefs to the throne which he was going to propofe.

He accordingly moved for an addrefs of great length, containing an abftract of the various fpecies of information which had been obtained by the enquiry, the fum of the different refolutions which had been founded on that information, and propofed to the committee, and fome general refults arifing from the whole. Among thefe were the following:—The defective ftate of the navy; being neither in any degree anfwerable to the affurances repeatedly given by the Firft Lord of that department, to the vaft fums granted for its ufe, nor competent to the fervices which it may very fhortly be called to fulfil.—The increafe of debt incurred by the war; the intereft of which, being equal to a land-tax of three fhillings in the pound, and added to our former burthens, will, they fear, under the circumftances of a diminifhed trade, render it difficult for this country to fupport the national faith.—That, by an enquiry into fome parts of this enormous expenditure it appears, that the mode of contracting and engaging for the transports and fupplies of the army has been unufual and prodigal, and fuch as affords ground for fufpicion of corrupt management.—The truly alarming ftate of public cre-

dit, proceeding, along with the enormity of the national debt, from the want of confidence in minifters, who have juftly forfeited the good opinion of the nation. And this want of confidence evident, from the low ftate of the public funds; and ftill more, from the difcredit of the new loan, which now fells confiderably under par, although the terms given this year for fix millions, when we have yet had no foreign war whatever, are higher than thofe which were given for twelve millions in 1761, which was the 7th year of a war with the houfe of Bourbon.—And, that from the melancholy ftate of facts which they have recited, they fee it impoffible to carry on the prefent fyftem of reducing America by force of arms.

After much implied and expreffed cenfure and condemnation of public meafures, an avowed opinion, that nothing lefs than a mifreprefentation of American affairs, could have induced the Crown and Parliament to the profecution of fo fatal a war, and an advice for the recal of the fleets and armies from the revolted colonies, and the effectuating of a reconciliation with them, the intended addrefs concludes as follows, " That " we think it our duty, on offering " to his Majefty this unhappy, but " true reprefentation of the ftate " of his dominions, to exprefs our " indignation at the conduct of " his Minifters, who have caufed " it; who, by abufing his confi- " dence, have tarnifhed the luftre " of his crown; who, by their " unfortunate counfels have dif- " membered his empire, wafted " the public treafures, funk his " public credit, impaired the com- " merce of his kingdoms, dif- " graced his arms, and weakened " his naval power, the pride and " bulwark of this nation; whilft " by delaying to reconcile the dif- " ference which they had excited " amongft his people, they have " fuffered fuch an alliance to take

" place, between the former fub-
" jects, and the antient rivals of
" Great-Britain, and have neither
" taken meafures to prevent, nor
" formed alliances to counteract
" fo fatal an union."

" That in this calamitous,
" although they truft not de-
" fperate fituation of public af-
" fairs, they repofe their ultimate
" hope in his Majefty's paternal
" goodnefs. That they have no
" doubt, that he will look back to
" the principles, both political and
" conftitutional, which gave rife
" to the Revolution, from whence
" we have derived the happinefs
" of being governed by princes of
" his illuftrious houfe. That he
" will reflect on the examples of
" his predeceffors from that au-
" fpicious period, during which
" the profperity, the opulence, the
" power, the territory, and the
" renown of his throne and nation
" have flourifhed and increafed
" beyond all example. That he
" will particularly call to mind
" the circumftances of his acceffion
" to the crown, when he took pof-
" feffion of an inheritance fo full
" of glory, and of the truft of
" preferving it in all its luftre.
" That deeply affected with thefe
" confiderations, he will be gra-
" cioufly pleafed to put an end to
" a fyftem, too well underftood
" in its nature, and too forely felt
" in its effects, which by the arts
" of wicked men has prevailed in
" his court and adminiftration,
" and which, if fuffered to con-
" tinue, will complete the mife-
" ries which have begun; and
" leave nothing in this country
" which can do honour to his go-
" vernment, or make the name of
" an Englifhman a matter of that
" pride and diftinction, in which
" his Majefty and his fubjects had
" fo much reafon to glory in for-
" mer happy times."

It was in the great debate upon
this addrefs, that the Earl of Chatham was feized with that fainting
fit in the midft of the Lords, which,
notwithstanding fome appearances
of recovery, was the unhappy prelude to his death. The noble
Duke who had moved the addrefs,
upon that melancholy incident,
propofed to adjourn the bufinefs to
the following day, which was immediately complied with. The
debate was accordingly renewed on
the next day, but was, by a divifion
in the oppofition, confined to themfelves; for, as the Earl of Chatham had on the preceding, ftrongly
protefted againft any meafure that
tended to the difmemberment of
the empire, and to the acknowledgement of the independence of
America, to the fame ground was
taken up and fupported on this by
the Earl of Shelburne. They were
forry to differ from thofe whom
they otherwife fo greatly refpected.
But the independency of America
they confidered as an end to the
dignity of this crown, and to all
the future poffible importance of
this kingdom: Who will dare,
faid Lord Chatham, to difinherit
the Prince of Wales and the Bifhop
of Ofnaburg? They were willing
to encounter all dangers, and to
rifque all confequences, fooner
than fubmit to that fatal propofition; and hoping, that this country was ftill poffeffed of refources
in men and money, not only equal
to a perfeverance in the ftruggle,
but to the attainment of a final
triumph over all our enemies, and
to that of the grand object, the recovery of America, to whofe liberties they never were enemies, but
ever wifhed to place them upon a
fure and permanent bafis.

On the other hand, the Duke of
Richmond, and moft of the other
Lords of the oppofition, who compofe the body of the Whiggs, or
what is called the Rockingham
party, declared their grief and horror, at the difmemberment of the
empire, and the confequent ruin
brought upon this country, to be
as great, as that of any perfons
within or without that Houfe.
They were as ready as any others,
to trace the caufes, and to join in
punifhing the authors of the meafures, which led to this fatal calamity. As they were as deeply concerned in the event, fo they would
go as great lengths, at the hazard
of life and fortune, on any fair
ground of hope, and rational profpect of fuccefs, for the reftoration
of the empire to its former ftate
of power, glory, and felicity. But
thefe declarations on any fide, were
now, they faid, words without
meaning or effect. The mifchief
was done. America was already
loft. Her independence was eftablifhed as firmly as that of other
ftates. We had fufficient caufe for
regret; but our lamentation on
that fubject was of no more avail,
than it would for the lofs of Nor-
mandy or France. If we had been
infpired with a fpirit of conqueft,
before our means and our ftrength
were exhaufted in, what they called, this frantic and wicked war, it
might have been directed to much
more feafible objects, from their
being much nearer home, as well
as from the general union of the
empire, than the conqueft of America. They concluded, that the
attempting of impoffibilities, and
the braving of danger without the
means of oppofing it, were equally
repugnant to wifdom, and to the
real character of courage. And
that the only part now left for
wifdom and prudence to act, was
to look to the prefervation and improvement of the remaining parts
of the empire; which could only
be done, by an immediate peace
with America, and a return of
friendfhip with our late fellow-
fubjects. That the grand object
of the policy of this kingdom, in
its prefent circumftances, was to
prevent America from growing into
habits of connection with France;
and if a refufal of the acknowledgement of an independence,
which we know to exift, and are
unable to deftroy, ftood in the way
of a reconciliation, they could not
come into that refufal. —In the

previous debate, the Duke of Richmond frequently and strongly pressed the Earl of Chatham (though with the greatest deference), to specify the means that he had, for making the Americans renounce the independence of which they were in possession. That great man candidly confessed, that he, for his part, was unable to point out the means; but he believed that they existed. The Duke of Richmond said, that if he could not, no man could; and that it was not in his power to change his opinion on the noble Lord's authority, unsupported by any reasons, but a recital of the calamities which must attend a state of things, which they both knew to be already decided.

The question being at length put, the motion for the address was rejected on a division, by a majority of 50 to 33. A noble Earl,[92] could not refrain from expressing some considerable share of resentment upon this division. He said, that "These dead majorities would "be the ruin of the nation. Let "the question be what it will, "though the salvation of this "country depend upon it, if it "be moved by certain persons, it "is sure of a negative." He then said to the other Lords on the same side, that they had been told by Ministers, it was the only way in which his Majesty would receive their counsel; but there were other modes, he said, by which they had a right to give their counsel, however it might be received. And, he proposed, that the Minority should wait upon his Majesty, in a body, with the address; it contained information, he said, worthy of the royal ear; it was not for him to forejudge the effect. Although the proposal seemed in part to be agreed to, and only deferred for further consideration; yet the measure was not carried into execution.

The following short protest was, however, entered, and signed by twenty Lords. "Because we think

"the rejection of the proposed ad- "dress at this time, may appear "to indicate in this House, a de- "sire of continuing that plan of "ignorance, concealment, deceit, "and delusion, by which the So- "vereign and his people have al- "ready been brought into so "many and so great calamities. "We hold it absolutely necessary "that both Sovereign and people "should be undeceived, and that "they should distinctly and au- "thentically be made acquainted "with the state of their affairs, "which is faithfully represented "in this proposed address, at a "time when our existence as a "nation may depend upon our "conceiving a just idea of our "real situation, and upon our "wisdom in making a proper use "of it."

• • •

On the same day, the Earl of Derby moved for an address, tend-[93] ing to an enquiry into the difficulties which obstructed the faithful performance of the convention signed at Saratoga; which he founded, as well on a regard to the public faith, as to the gallant men, who were now suffering as prisoners in America, through a failure in fulfilling the terms of that capitulation. The noble Minister who was present, declared his total ignorance of the subject, and objected to the motion on account of the lateness of the season, and the nearness of the prorogation, which was to take place on the following day; a circumstance which rendered the enquiry utterly impracticable. As the noble Earl would not, however, withdraw his motion, it was, after some debate, disposed of by the previous question, without a division.

This avowal of immediate prorogation called up the Duke of Bolton, who after stating the danger and difficulty of the times, and the alarming state of these kingdoms, under the immediate threat and apprehensions of an invasion, without any proper means of de-

fence in their hands, or wisdom in our public councils, to adopt such measures, as would direct their operations to effect, if there were, closed a speech of considerable length, by moving an address, for deferring the prorogation of parliament until the present very dangerous crisis might be happily terminated.

The debate was long and interesting, and the motion was supported by most of the principal Lords of the opposition; but as it was necessarily on the same ground with that which we have stated upon the same subject in the House of Commons, our entering into any particular detail of it is thereby rendered unnecessary. The navy was again brought into question, and the First Lord of that department again put upon some justification or defence of naval affairs or measures; in the course of which he also again found occasion to complain of misrepresentation, even with respect to words or matters that were charged to him in the last debate; and was put to an absolute denial or contradiction of matters, which the professional Lords on the other side positively insisted to be incontrovertible and authenticated facts. The motion was rejected, upon a division, by a majority of 42 to 20.

Particular thanks were returned in the speech from the throne, for the zeal shewn June 3d. in supporting the honour of the crown, and for their attention to the real interests of the subjects, in the wise, just, and humane laws, which had been the result of their deliberations. His Majesty's desire to preserve the tranquillity of Europe had been uniform and sincere; he reflected with great satisfaction, that he had made the faith of treaties and the law of nations the rule of his conduct; let that power by whom this tranquillity should be disturbed, answer to their subjects and to the world for all the fatal consequences of war.

The vigour and firmness of Parliament had enabled his Majesty to provide for such events and emergencies as might happen; and he trusted, that the experienced valour and discipline of the fleets and armies, with the loyal and united ardour of the nation, armed and animated in defence of every thing that is dear to them, would be able, under the protection of Divine Providence, to defeat all the enterprizes which the enemies of the crown might presume to undertake, and convince them how dangerous it was to provoke the spirit and strength of Great-Britain. The Commons were thanked for the chearfulness with which they had granted the large and ample supplies for the service of the year, as well as for their care in raising them in a manner the most effectual and the least burthensome; and the warmest acknowledgments were due, for the provision made for the more honourable support of the Royal Family.

Thus was brought to a conclusion, this long, tedious, and exceedingly laborious session of Parliament. A session, in which a greater number of the most interesting and important public questions were agitated, although not generally decided upon, than any other, perhaps, within the space of a century past. And which also afforded more frequent room for expectation and hope to the people, with respect to the conduct of public affairs, than any that we remember.

State of the hostile armies in Philadelphia and its neighbourhood during the winter. Hard condition of the brave army under the convention of Saratoga. Suspension of the treaty by the congress, until a ratification is obtained from the court of Great-Britain. Predatory expeditions from Philadelphia and Rhode Island. Draught of the Conciliatory Bills published in America. Effect produced by it on both sides. Conduct, and resolutions of the Congress. Simeon Dean arrives with the French treaties. Sir Henry Clinton arrives to take the command of the army at Philadelphia, in the room of General Sir William Howe, who returns to England. Arrival of the Commissioners for restoring peace, &c. Letter to the Congress. Secretary to the Commissioners refused a passport. Answer returned by the Congress to the Commissioners. Further particulars relative to the proposed negociation. Evacuation of Philadelphia. Difficulties encountered by the British army in their march across the Jersies. General Washington crosses the Delaware. Battle near Monmouth. Gen. Lee, tried by a court martial, and suspended. British army pass over to Sandy Hook Island, and are conveyed by the fleet to New York. Toulon squadron arrive on the coast of America. Appear before Sandy Hook, where they cast anchor. Alarm, and preparations at Sandy Hook and New York. Departure of the French fleet. Arrival of reinforcements to Lord Howe. French fleet appear before Rhode Island. Defensive preparations by General Sir Robert Pigot. Invasion of that island meditated by the Americans, to second the operations of the French. Lord Howe sails to the relief of Rhode Island. D'Estaing, quits the harbour and puts to sea, to meet the British squadron. Fleets separated, at the point of engaging, by a violent storm. Captain Rayner, in the Isis, bravely engages a French man of war of 74 guns. D'Estaing returns to Rhode Island, and proceeds from thence to Boston. Is pursued by Lord Howe. Gen. Sullivan lands in Rhode Island. Invests the British posts. American army greatly disconcerted by D'Estaing's departure. Sullivan retreats, and at length totally quits the island. Lord Howe, finding D'Estaing's squadron so strongly secured in Nantasket Road, as to render an attack impracticable, returns from Boston.

FROM this war of words and opinions in the old world, we are led to a war of deeds and arms in the new. The one, notwithstanding the supposed summary decisiveness of its nature, being little more conclusive than the other. The hostile armies at Philadelphia and Valley Forge, passed the severity of the winter, within a few miles of each other, in great quiet. The assailants, however, contrary to the general course and circumstance of war, had the advantage of a capital city, and that a fine one, for their quarters; whilst the native army was under a necessity of enduring all the extremity of the season, under a hutted camp in the open field. Notwithstanding this great advantage in point of ease and convenience, the lines and redoubts with which it was found necessary to cover the city of Philadelphia, did not permit the British or auxiliary forces to rust in their military habits, or to grow languid in the exercise of their military duties. Upon the whole, the army was well supplied and healthy.

In the mean time, the gallant and unfortunate army, that had been under a necessity of submitting to the terms of the convention at Saratoga, met with great and unexpected delays and difficulties in respect to their return to Europe, and underwent many grievous vexations, in that station which had been allotted for their reception in the neighbourhood of Boston. The former of these, however, opened the great ground of grievance, as the succeeding could not otherwise have been of any considerable duration. Notwithstanding the enmity which unhappily prevails between the now disjoined parts of the British nation, it affords us no satisfaction in treating this subject, that truth and justice compel us, strongly to condemn the conduct of the Congress; who seem, upon this occasion, to have departed widely from that system of fairness, equity, and good faith, so essential to new States, and which had hitherto appeared, in a considerable degree, to have been the guide of their actions.

It seems to have been rather unlucky, at least in point of time, that a requisition for some deviation from the terms of the convention, had been made by the British commanders. This was for the embarkation of the convention troops, either at the Sound, near New York, or at Rhode Island, instead of Boston, which was the place appointed for their departure to Europe. And in consequence of the expectation entertained, that this proposal would have been complied with, the transports for the conveyance of the troops were assembled at Rhode Island. The Congress, however, not only refused to comply with the requisition, but made it a ground of a pretended suspicion, that the measure was proposed, merely to afford an opportunity to the convention troops to join their fellows, with an intention then of making some pretence for evading or breaking the terms of the capitulation, and continuing to act in America, to the great detriment and danger of the common cause. To strengthen this colour of suspicion, they pretended, that the 26 transports which were provided at Rhode Island, were insufficient for the conveyance of above 5,600 men, in a winter voyage, to Europe; and, that in the present state of things, with respect to provisions, both in the British fleet and army, it was scarcely possible that they could have been victualled for so long a voyage, and so great a number, in so short a time.

In the mean time, great complaints having been made, by the British officers near Boston, of the badness of the quarters with which they had been provided, and which they represented, as being neither conformable to their expectation, rank, or to the terms of the capi-

tulation, the sense and construction of some strong expostulation which was made by General Burgoyne, in a letter of complaint upon the subject, was wrested by the Congress to a direct declaration, that the convention had been broken on their part, by a violation of its conditions. This they represented as a matter of the most serious and alarming nature; which indicated a full intention in the British General and army, to consider the convention as dissolved, by this supposed violation of it which was charged on their side, as soon as they got without the limits of their power; and a declaration of the sort now made, under the present circumstances of that army, would appear, they said, no small public justification of their future conduct, in acting as if they were in no degree bound, when at large, by a capitulation, which they had formally disavowed under restraint.

Some paltry resolutions which were passed, as to the soldiers not having faithfully delivered up all their accoutrements, were of so shameful a nature, as to be highly disgraceful to the Congress; and seemed strongly to indicate, that they were ready to grasp at any pretence, however weak or futile, by which they could evade the terms of the convention, without incurring the charge of a direct breach of public faith.

It was in vain that the General explained the intention, as well as the construction of that passage in his letter, which went no farther than to a well-founded complaint, and a demand of redress pursuant to the terms of the convention. It was to as little purpose that his officers, in order to remove this new difficulty, respectively signed their parole, which they had hitherto refused doing, until they could obtain redress in the article of quarters, and which was not at any time granted. The General even offered to pledge himself, that notwithstanding the injurious

suspicion entertained of his own honour and that of his officers, they would still join with him in signing any writing or instrument that might be thought necessary, for strengthening, confirming, or renewing, the validity of the convention.

But the Congress were inexorable. It was easily seen, that the measure which they had adopted was not so lightly taken as to be easily given up; and that explanations and securities could produce no effect on their determination. Jan. 8, 1778. They had passed a resolution from which they never receded, that the embarkation of Gen. Burgoyne and his army should be suspended, until a distinct and explicit ratification of the convention at Saratoga should be properly notified by the court of Great-Britain to Congress. Although the treaties between France and America were not at that time concluded, it does not seem impossible, that the councils of that court had some considerable operation upon the conduct of the Congress in this extraordinary transaction. Perhaps being so closely pressed as they were, by a part only of the King's forces, then in actual possession of the most considerable of their cities, for magnitude, wealth, and commanding situation, they thought, that suffering those convention troops to be sent to Europe, from whence they might be easily replaced, would entirely turn against them the scale of war; and therefore, they chose to sacrifice their reputation, by an act never excusable, rather than their Being at this critical hour.

Some successful predatory expeditions into the Jersies, and on the Delaware, with the surprize of a party of the enemy (who suffered no inconsiderable loss in men) on the Pensilvania side, by Lieutenant-Colonel Abercrombie, were the only military operations which distinguished the remaining admi-

94

niftration of General Sir William Howe in the command of the army. The lofs of the Americans in thefe expeditions, and in fome others, which were undertaken from Rhode Ifland towards the end of May, was exceedingly great, both with refpect to public and private property. Ships, boats, houfes, places of worfhip, ftores of all forts, and of whatever nature, whether public or private; in a word, every thing ufeful to man that was liable to the action of fire, was in fome places confumed by it. The officers, however, attributed fome of the enormities, with refpect to the burning of private houfes, to the licence and rage of the foldiers, and declared them to be entirely contrary to their intentions and orders.

The Americans, as ufual, made the fevereft charges of cruelty, many of which we hope to be unfounded, againft the troops employed in thefe expeditions. Particularly the denial of quarter, and the flaughtering men in cold blood, feveral of whom, they faid, neither had arms in their hands, nor were in any military capacity. They alfo complained, (on the Rhode Ifland fide, where the charges were ftronger made) as a lefs cruel, though not more defenfible act of injuftice, the carrying off the peaceable inhabitants of the country, and detaining them as prifoners of war, until they fhould at fome time or other be exchanged, for an equal number of foldiers taken on their fide in arms. And although it was replied to this complaint, that as by their laws, every inhabitant from 16 to 60, was liable to be called upon to take up arms, and was therefore to be confidered and treated at all times as a foldier, whether he was found in actual fervice or not, we can by no means think the reafoning included in this anfwer fatisfactory or conclufive. Upon the whole, even if the treaty between France and America, had not unhappily rendered all hope of fuccefs from the prefent conciliatory fyftem hopelefs, thefe predatory and irritating expeditions would have appeared peculiarly ill timed and unlucky. Though ftrongly and warmly recommended by many here as the moft effectual mode of war, we fcarcely remember an inftance in which they have not been more mifchievous than ufeful to the grand objects, either of reducing, or of reconciling the colonies.

During thefe tranfactions, neither the Congrefs, nor General Wafhington, omitted any means or preparation for a vigorous campaign; whilft both, in their public acts, boldly held out to the people the hope of its being the laft, and of their driving the Britifh forces entirely out of America. The General, having now proved the fubmiffion and patience of his army in their long winter encampment, ftruck off all the fuperabundant baggage both of men and officers, to the clofeft line of neceffity, and ventured upon every other reform, which could render them agile in fervice, and effective in action. He alfo tried the influence of his own name and character, by a public letter to the farmers of the Middle Colonies, to requeft their providing and fattening cattle for the fervice of the army in the enfuing campaign. The Congrefs, among their other attentions to the war, iffued a refolution, ftrongly urging the young gentlemen of the different colonies, to raife a body of light cavalry, to ferve at their own expence, during the campaign; offering them fuch allurements and honorary diftinctions in the fervice, as were calculated to reconcile that order of men, to the reftraints and duties of a military life, in the fimple rank and character of private volunteers.

A rough draught of the conciliatory bills, as they appeared on the firft reading in the Houfe of Commons, was received at New York by Governor Tryon, about the middle of April, who ufed all means to circulate them among the people at large of the revolted colonies.

This unexpected meafure of Miniftry in England, excited equal aftonifhment and indignation in our own army, who thought that nothing could exceed the degradation which they felt in fuch a conceffion. The nature and circumftances of the war, and the long courfe of injuries and loffes which had been offered and received, had by this time rendered every individual a partizan in the conteft. They had been taught to think, that nothing lefs than abfolute conqueft on their fide, or the moft unconditional fubmiffion on the other, could bring it to a conclufion. They blufhed at the recollection, and thought their perfonal honour wounded in the recantation which was now to be made, of all that high language and treatment, which they had been accuftomed to hold or to offer to rebels. The difappointment was the greater, as thefe papers were the fubftitute to a reinforcement of 20,000 men, which they had expected. If fuch were the feelings of the Britifh army, it may not be eafy to defcribe thofe of the numerous body of American refugees, whofe paffions being irritated to the higheft degree, thought they beheld all their public and private hopes, as well as the gratification of their perfonal refentments, cut off at one blow. The bills were not, however, to produce the effect that was expected or apprehended; and, unhappily, an end was not yet to be put to the calamities of war..

The mode of circulating thefe papers, was confidered, or reprefented, by the Americans, as an infidious attempt to divide the people; and the Congrefs, to fhew their contempt of it, ordered them to be immediately publifhed in their Gazettes. General Washington, in answer to Governor Tryon, who had sent him several copies of the draughts, with a request that they might be circulated among the officers and men of his army, enclosed in his letter to him a printed news-paper, in which they had been inserted by the order of the Congress; accompanied by the printed resolutions of that body upon the subject. And Governor Turnbull, upon a similar letter [95] and application, observed, that propositions of peace were usually made from the supreme authority of one contending power to the similar authority of the other; and that the present, was the first instance within his recollection, in which they had ever been addressed to the people at large of the opposite power, as an overture of reconciliation. He proceeded with the following words, "There was a day when even this step, from our then acknowledged parent state, might have been accepted with joy and gratitude; but that day, sir, is past irrevocably. The repeated rejection of our sincere, and sufficiently humble petitions; the commencement of hostilities; the inhumanity which has marked the prosecution of the war on your part in its several stages; the insolence which displays itself on every petty advantage; the cruelties which have been exercised on those unhappy men, whom the fortune of war has thrown into your hands; all these are insuperable bars to the very idea of concluding a peace with Great Britain, on any other conditions, than the most absolute perfect independence." He concluded his letter with the following observation upon the restoration of union by a lasting and honourable peace, which he declared to be the ardent wish of every honest American, viz. "The British nation may then, perhaps, find us as affectionate and valuable friends as we now are determined and fatal enemies, and will derive from that friendship more solid and real advantage than the most sanguine can expect from conquest."

The result of the deliberations, and of several resolutions upon the subject by the Congress, April 22d. was a declaration, that any man, or body of men, who should presume to make any separate or partial convention or agreement with Commissioners under the crown of Great Britain, should be considered and treated as enemies to the United States. That the United States, could not with propriety hold any conference or treaty with any Commissioners on the part of Great Britain, unless they should, as a preliminary thereto, either withdraw their fleets and armies, or else, in positive and express terms, acknowledge the independence of the said states. And, inasmuch as it appeared to be the design of their enemies, to lull them into a fatal security, they called upon the several states, to use the most strenuous exertions, to have their respective quotas of troops in the field as soon as possible; and that all their militia might be held in readiness to act as occasion should require. All the resolutions upon this subject were unanimously agreed to.

In a few days after, May 2d. Simeon Deane arrived [96] express from Paris, at York Town, where the Congress had sat since the loss of Philadelphia, with those fatal instruments, which seemed to stamp a seal upon the separation of America from England. He had been conveyed from France in a Royal frigate of 28 guns, appointed for the purpose, and brought with him, for ratification by the Congress, copies of the two treaties, of alliance, and of commerce, which had been concluded between France and the United States. The last of these was the first that had been executed, being signed on the 30th of January; the treaty of alliance was dated the 6th of February. Deane also brought an account of many other matters which were highly pleasing, as well as what related to the history of the negociation, and of its conclusion:

The joy and exultation of the Americans upon this occasion, could only be rivalled by their public demonstrations of them. The Congress immediately published a Gazette, which, besides a summary of the general information they had received, exhibited some of the most flattering articles of the treaties, with their own comments upon them, to the people; in which the extraordinary equity, generosity, and unparalleled honour, (as they described it) of the French King, were extolled in the highest degree. In this piece, they seemed to count upon Spain as being already a virtual party to the alliance, and to consider the naval force of both nations as united in their cause. They also built much upon the friendship of other great powers, and boasted of the favourable disposition of Europe in general to America.

About the same time, Gen. 8th. Sir Henry Clinton arrived to take the command of the army at Philadelphia, in the room of Sir William Howe; who returned to England, to the great regret of both officers and soldiery in general. In the beginning of June, the three Commissioners from England, being the Earl of Carlisle, Mr. Eden, and Governor Johnstone, (with whom were joined in [97] the commission, the Commander in Chief, Sir Henry Clinton) arrived in the Delaware.

The Commissioners im- June 9th. mediately dispatched a letter, with the late acts of parliament, a copy of their commission, and other papers, to the President of the Congress; but their Secretary, Dr. Ferguson, who was in- [98] tended to convey the papers, and to act as an agent for conducting the negociation upon the spot with the Congress, being refused a pass-port for that purpose, they were obliged to forward them by common means.

The Commissioners proposed, even at this outset, several con-cessions and arrangements, which, at an earlier period, would have restored peace and felicity to the whole empire. They offered to consent to an immediate cessation of hostilities by sea and land.—To restore a free intercourse, and to renew the common benefits of naturalization through the several parts of the empire.—To extend every freedom to trade, that the respective interests on both sides could require.—To agree, that no military force should be kept up in the different states of North America, without the consent of the General Congress, or of the particular assemblies.—To concur in measures calculated to discharge the debts of America, and to raise the credit and value of the paper circulation. — To perpetuate the common union, by a reciprocal deputation of an agent or agents, from the different states, who should have the privilege of a seat and voice in the parliament of Great Britain; or, if sent from Britain, in that case to have a seat and voice in the assemblies of the dif-ferent states to which they might be deputed respectively, in order to attend to the several interests of those by whom they were deputed.—And, in short, to establish the power of the respective legislatures in each particular state, to settle its revenue, its civil and military establishment, and to exercise a perfect freedom of legislation and internal government; so that the British states throughout North America, acting with Great Bri-tain in peace and war, under one common Sovereign, might have the irrevocable enjoyment of every privilege, that was short of a total separation of interest, or consistent with that union of force, on which the safety of the common religion and liberty depends.

Although these papers produced very considerable debates, which were renewed on different days, from the 11th to the 17th of June, in the Congress, yet the answer which they then returned, through the medium of their President, Henry Laurens, was sufficiently[99] brief, however conclusive. They observed to the Commissioners, that the acts of the British parliament, the commission from their Sove-reign, and their letter, supposed the people of those states to be subjects of the crown of Great Britain, and were founded on the idea of dependence, which was totally inadmissible. They in-formed them, that they were in-clined to peace, notwithstanding the unjust claims from which the war originated, and the savage manner in which it had been con-ducted. They would therefore be ready to enter upon the considera-tion of a treaty of peace and com-merce, not inconsistent with trea-ties already subsisting, when the King of Great Britain should de-monstrate a sincere disposition for that purpose. But, the only solid proof of that disposition would be, an explicit acknowledgement of the independence of those states, or the withdrawing of his fleets and armies.

Such were the conditions, which an unhappy concurrence of events induced on the one side, and which the operation of the same causes rendered inadmissible on the other. The Congress, at the same time, issued an unanimous approbation of Gen. Washington's conduct in re-fusing a passport to Dr. Ferguson.

Although the Congress, as a body, did not enter into any liti-gation with the Commissioners upon the general subject of their mission, yet some of their members, parti-[100]cularly Mr. Drayton, one of the delegates for South-Carolina, and others, perhaps, not officially con-nected with them, entered the lists of controversy in the public pa-pers, with no small degree of acri-mony. For, as the Commissioners seemed to carry along with them an idea, which at the time of their appointment, was endeavoured with great care to be established in Eng-land, viz. " that the bulk of the Americans were well affected to the British government, and that the greater part of the remainder were only held in a state of delusion by the Congress," they accordingly, upon this failure of negociation with that body, directed their fu-ture publications, in the manner of appeals to the people at large; seeming, thereby, to realize in some degree, the charge so repeat-edly made on the other side, that their only object was, under the insidious appearance of concilia-tion, to excite either a separation amongst the colonies, or the peo-ple to tumults against their respec-tive governments. And, as the Congress not only permitted, but affected to forward, the publica-tion of all matters upon the sub-ject, so, the writers we have men-tioned, undertook to obviate the effect, which those issued by the Commissioners might have upon the people at large.

The strongest argument which they held out upon this occasion to the people was, that they had al-ready concluded a solemn treaty with France, on the footing of, and for the establishment of their independency. That if they now treated with the Commissioners upon the ground of dependence, they should at once break their faith with France, forfeit their cre-dit with all foreign nations, be considered as a faithless and infa-mous people, and for evermore be cut off from even the hope of fo-reign succour or resource. At the same time they would be thrown to-tally on the mercy of those, who had already pursued every measure of fraud, force, cruelty, and de-ceit for their destruction; as neither the King, the Ministers, nor the Parliament of England, would be under a necessity of ratifying any one condition which they agreed upon with the Commissioners. Or if they even found it necessary to ratify them for present purposes, it would be only to call a new parliament to undo the whole. Nothing, they said, could be trusted to an enemy whom they had already found so faithless, and so obstinately persevering in malice and cruelty. The fraudulent intention of the proposed negociation, they said, was strongly evinced, by the Commissioners holding out conditions which went far beyond their avowed powers; being neither warranted by the commission, nor by the acts of parliament which they presented.

If any strong hope of success in the negociation had remained, the evacuation of Philadelphia, and the consequent retreat of the army to the northward, just at the arrival of the Commissioners, would have completely frustrated them. Commissioners accompanying a retreating army, which was in the act of abandoning the principal advantage of two years war, could not promise themselves a great superiority in any treaty; and the more advantageous the offers which they should make in such circumstances, the more their concessions would be considered as proofs of weakness, not of good-will. This measure was carried into execution on the 18th of June, and the whole British army passed the Delaware on the same day, without interruption or danger, under the excellent dispositions made by the Admiral, Lord Howe, for the purpose.

Washington, having penetrated into the intention of abandoning Philadelphia, had already sent General Maxwell with his brigade to[101] reinforce the Jersey militia, in order to throw every possible obstruction in the way of the British army, so that by impeding their progress, he might himself be enabled to bring up his force in such time, as to profit of those opportunities, which, it was well to be supposed, so long a march through so dangerous a country would have afforded, of attacking them with great advantage. This detached corps and the militia, did not, however, effect any thing more of importance than the breaking down of the bridges; the great superiority of the British force, having obliged them to abandon the strong pass at Mount Holly, without venturing an opposition.

The British army, notwithstanding, encountered much toil, difficulty, and numberless impediments in their march. They were encumbered with an enormous baggage, including provisions; the number of loaded horses and wheel-carriages being so great, as to cover an extent of twelve miles, in the narrow line of march, which the nature of the country and roads afforded. This incumbrance, so far at least as related to the provision, proceeded, however, from the foresight and wisdom of the General, Sir Henry Clinton; who being well aware, that the hostility of the country would cut off every source of subsistence from the troops, which was not within their own immediate comprehension, and being also uncertain as to the delays and obstructions which might occur on his march, was too prudent to put the fate of a whole army in any degree of hazard, for the trouble or difficulty that attended the conveyance of a certain and sufficient supply. The heat of the weather, which was then excessive, with the closeness of the narrow roads through the woods, and the constant labour of renewing or repairing bridges, in a country every where intersected with creeks and marshy brooks, were, all together, severely felt by the army.

From all these causes, its progress was exceedingly slow; and nothing less than these could have accounted, for its spending so many days in traversing so narrow a country. When the army had advanced to Allen's Town, it became a matter of consideration with the General, whether to keep the direct course towards Staten Island, across the Rariton, or whether, by taking the road to his right, and drawing towards the sea-coast, he should push on to Sandy Hook. He knew that the Generals Washington and Lee, with the whole continental force on that side, had already passed the Delaware; and he had heard, that General Gates, with the northern army, was advancing to join them on the Rariton. The difficulty of passing the Rariton, and the circumstances with which it might have been attended, under his incumbrances, in the face of an enemy, with other concurring causes, determined him to the right-hand course, as much the more eligible.

On the other hand, General Washington, who had crossed the Delaware far above Philadelphia, at Coryel's Ferry, attributed, with his usual foresight and caution, the slow movements of the British army, to a design of decoying him into the low country, when, by a rapid movement on the right, they might gain possession of the strong grounds above him, and so enclosing his army to the river, force him to a general engagement under every disadvantage. Under this persuasion, in which it is possible his sagacity deceived him, as the peculiar circumstances of the British army rendered it totally incapable of any such rapid movements as he apprehended, the slowness on the one side retarded the motions on the other. It is, however, likewise probable, that Washington reserved himself entire for the passage of the Rariton; which he concluded would have been their course, and which he knew would have afforded him great advantage in an attack.

But when he discovered that the British army had departed from its expected line of direction, and was bending its way on the other side towards the sea-coast, he immediately changed his system, and sent several detachments of chosen troops, under the general conduct of the Marquis de Fayette, to harrass the army in its march, himself following, at a suitable distance, with the whole force. As affairs grew more critical upon the near approach of the van of one army to the rear of the other, General Lee was dispatched with two brigades, to reinforce, and to take the command of the advanced corps; which, by Washington's account, amounted then to about 5000 men, although from the several detachments which he specifies, it would seem to have been stronger.

Sir Henry Clinton, on the march to a place called Freehold, judging from the number of the enemy's light troops which hovered on his rear, that their main body was at no great distance, judiciously determined to free that part of the army, from the incumbrance and impediment of the baggage, which he accordingly placed under the conduct of General Knyphausen, who led the first column of the army. The other, which covered the line of march, being now disengaged and free for action, formed a body of troops which could not easily be equalled, and was under the immediate command of the General. It was composed of the 3d, 4th, and 5th brigades of British, two battalions of British, and the Hessian grenadiers, a battalion of light infantry, the guards, and the 16th regiment of light dragoons.

June 28th. On the morning after this arrangement, General Knyphausen, with the first division and the carriages, began at the break of day to move, directing their march towards Middletown, which lay ten or twelve miles on their way, in a high and strong country. The second divi-

sion, under the Commander in Chief, continued for some hours on their ground in the neighbourhood of Freehold, both to cover the line of march, and to afford time for the chain of carriages to get clear on their way.

Having begun to march about eight o'clock, some parties of the enemy which appeared in the woods on their left flank, were engaged and dispersed by the light troops; but as the rear-guard descended from the heights above Freehold, into a valley about three miles in length, and one in breadth, several columns of the enemy appeared, likewise descending into the plain, who about ten o'clock began to cannonade the rear. The General at the same instant received intelligence, that the enemy were discovered marching in force on both his flanks. He was immediately struck, that an attack on the baggage was their principal object; and as the carriages were then entangled in defiles which continued for some miles, it seemed a matter of no small difficulty to obviate the danger.

In this critical situation, the General, with great quickness and presence of mind judged, that a vigorous attack, and severe pressure, upon that body of the enemy which harrassed his rear, would recall the detachments on his flanks to its assistance, and seemed to be the only probable means of saving the convoy. For although he had good information, that General Washington was at hand with his whole army, which he heard was estimated at 20,000 men; yet, as he knew that his main body was separated from that corps which attacked Lord Cornwallis, in the rear, by two considerable defiles, he was not apprehensive that he could pass a greater body of troops through them, during the execution of the measure which he intended, than what the force along with him was well able to oppose; whilst on the other hand, even with

that division of the army, Washington's situation would not be a little critical, if he should chance to come upon him, when he was struggling in his passage through the defiles.

Guarding, however, against every possible result of the measure, and to be in preparation for the event of a general engagement, he recalled a brigade of the British Infantry, and the 17th regiment of light dragoons, from Knyphausen's division, and left direction for them to take a position which would effectually cover his right flank, being the side on which he was most jealous of the design of the enemy. In the mean time, the Queen's light dragoons, had with their usual spirit attacked and routed the enemy's cavalry, under the Marquis de Fayette, and drove them back in confusion on their own infantry. The General then made dispositions to attack the enemy in the plain; but before he could advance, they fell unexpectedly back, and took a strong position on the heights above Monmouth Court-House.

The heat of the weather was in that season always intense; but upon that particular day was so excessive, as to be seldom equalled, even in the sultry summers of that continent; so that the troops were already greatly fatigued. The situation of the army, however, rendered the most vigorous exertion necessary. The British grenadiers, with their left to the village of Freehold, and the guards on their right, began the attack with such spirit, that the enemy soon gave way. But their second line preserved a better countenance; and resisted a fierce and eager attack with great obstinacy. They were, however, at length, completely routed; but in this exigency, with a very unusual degree of recollection, as well as resolution, took a third position with so much judgment, that their front was covered by a marshy hollow, which scarcely admitted the practicability of an attack by that way.

Sir Henry Clinton brought up part of the second-line, and made some other dispositions to attack the enemy in this post, and the light Infantry and Rangers, had already turned their left for that purpose; but the army in general, was now so overpowered by heat and fatigue, that upon consideration, he thought it better not to press the affair any farther. He was also by this time confident, that the purpose which had induced him to the attack was gained, in the preservation of the convoy. A bold attempt of the enemy, to cut off the retreat of the light Infantry, rendered some new movements, notwithstanding the excessive toil of the day, still necessary. The army at length returned to that position, from whence they had first driven the enemy, after their quitting the plain.

The General's opinion with respect to the design on the baggage, was justified in the event; and the propriety of his subsequent conduct in attacking the enemy on that principle confirmed. Two brigades of the enemy's light troops had passed the army, one on each flank, in that view, and had actually made the attempt; but by the good dispositions made by the commanders, the firmness of the 40th regiment, and the ready service of the light Horse, they were repulsed at the first onset, and the engagement in the plain then commencing, were immediately recalled.

Sir Henry Clinton having now fully attained his object, for the Generals Knyphausen and Grant,[102] with the first division and baggage, were arrived at Nut Swamp, near Middletown, could have no inducement for continuing in his present situation. The troops had already gained sufficient honour, in forcing successively, from two strong positions, a corps of the enemy, which, he was informed, amounted to near 12,000 men; and the merit of the

service was much enhanced, by the unequalled circumstances of heat and fatigue under which it was performed. The enemy were much superior in force to the division immediately under his command; and if the equality had been even nearer, it would still seem imprudent to have hazarded an engagement, at such a distance from the rest of his army, in a country, not only entirely hostile, but which from its nature, must have been ruinous to strangers under any circumstance of defeat. And as the heat of the weather rendered marching by day intolerable, so the moon-light added much to the eligibility of the night for that purpose. Upon some or all of these accounts, the troops having reposed till ten o'clock, the army was again put in motion, and they marched forward to join their fellows.

Such was the detail of the action at Freehold, or Monmouth, as it is otherwise called, as given on our side. The loss, in slain, was not considerable in point of number, but rendered grievous by that of the brave Colonel Monckton. That[103] gallant officer, who had frequently encountered death in all its forms, had the fortune of being more than once grievously wounded, both in the last war, and the present; and after the hair-breadth escape of a recovery, when left among the dead on the field, was only reserved to be killed on this day, at the head of the second battalion of Grenadiers. This day and action were also rendered remarkable by the singular circumstance, unparalleled in the history of the New World, of 59 soldiers perishing! without receiving a wound, merely through the excessive heat and fatigue. Several of the Americans also, inured as they were to the climate, died through the same cause.

The Americans claim great honour to that part of their troops which had an opportunity of being engaged in this action. They likewise claim, though without any ap-

parent ground, the advantage as the affair now stands; but pretend that they should have gained a complete and decisive victory, if it had not been for the misconduct and disobedience of orders of General Lee. That officer, had some time before, by an exchange, obtained a release from his long confinement at New York; and we have already seen, was appointed to take the command of those different bodies of troops, which had been detached to harrass the British army, and to impede its march.

It appears from General Washington's account of the matter, that he being well informed, that if the British army once gained the high and strong country near Middletown, no attempt could afterwards be made upon them, with the smallest prospect of success, he accordingly determined to fall upon their rear immediately upon their departure from the strong grounds in the neighbourhood of Freehold, on which they had encamped during the night of the 27th. He communicated this intention to General Lee, with orders to make his dispositions for the attack, and to keep the troops lying upon their arms in constant preparation; which he also practised himself in the main body.

Washington having received an express at five in the morning, that the British army had begun their march, immediately dispatched an order to Lee to attack them; acquainting him at the same time, that he was marching directly to his support, and that for the greater expedition, he should cause his men to disincumber themselves of that part of their baggage, which (it appears from hence) they carried upon their backs. To his great surprize and mortification, however, when he had marched above five miles, he met the whole advanced corps retreating, which they informed him was by General Lee's orders, without their making the smallest opposition, excepting the single fire of one detachment, to repulse the British light Horse.

The General found the rear of the retreating corps hard pressed by the enemy ; but, by forming them anew, under the brave and spirited exertions of their officers, (as he says) he soon checked the advance of the British forces ; and, having by this means gained time to plant some batteries of cannon, and to bring up fresh forces, the engagement hung in an equal poize. In this situation, (he continues) the enemy finding themselves warmly opposed in front, made an attempt to turn his left flank ; but were bravely repulsed and driven back by some detached parties of Infantry. A similar attempt on the right, was repelled by General Green ; who afterwards, in conjunction with General Wayne, took such positions, and kept up so severe and well directed a fire, as compelled the British forces to retire behind that defile, where the first stand had been made in the beginning of the action.

In that situation, in which their flanks were secured by thick woods and morasses, and their front only assailable through a narrow defile, he notwithstanding made dispositions (he says) for attacking them ; but the darkness came on so fast, as not to afford time for their surmounting the impediments in their way. The main body, however, lay all night upon their arms on the place of action, as the detached parties did in the several positions which they had been ordered to take, under a full determination of attacking the British army when the day appeared ; but they retreated in such profound silence in the night, that the most advanced posts, and those very near them, knew nothing of their departure until morning.

Washington represents the number of British buried by the Americans, to be about four times greater, than the loss acknowledged by our Gazette ; and his own, as much under that state. He says, they carried off their wounded, excepting four officers, and about forty soldiers. He gives high and unusual praise, and expresses himself under the greatest obligation to the zeal, bravery, and conduct of his officers ; and says, the behaviour of the troops in general, after they had recovered from the surprize, occasioned by the retreat of the advanced corps, was such as could not be surpassed. The public acknowledgements of the Congress, were very flattering to the army, but particularly so to the General and to his officers ; in which they affected to consider this action as a battle, and the result as a great and important victory, obtained over the grand British army, under the immediate command of their General.

Washington took care to inform the Congress, that the nature of the country rendered any further pursuit of the British army fruitless ; and all attempts to disturb their embarkation at Sandy Hook, equally impracticable and dangerous. He accordingly detached only some light troops to observe and attend their motions, and drew off the main body of the army to the borders of the North River. The Americans lost some officers of name in this action ; particularly a Colonel Bonner of Pensylvania, and a Major Dickenson of Virginia, both of whom were much regretted. [104]

It appears that General Washington used some very harsh and severe expressions, in the face of the army, to General Lee, upon meeting him, on the retreat of his corps, from the place of action ; amounting to a direct charge of a disobedience of orders, want of conduct, or want of courage. This produced two passionate letters from Lee, (who was likewise put under arrest) with an answer from Washington, all written on the day or night of the action. A court martial was instantly demanded, and as instantly ordered ; and so speedily carried into execution, as to be opened at Brunswick on the 4th of July. The charges laid against Lee were, first, disobedience of orders, in not attacking the enemy on the 28th of June, agreeable to repeated instructions. For misbehaviour before the enemy on the same day, by making an unnecessary, disorderly, and shameful retreat. And lastly, for disrespect to the Commander in chief, by the two letters we have mentioned. The result of the Court, after a trial which lasted to the 12th of August, was the finding General Lee guilty of the first charge. The finding him in part guilty of the second, " Of misbehaviour before the enemy, by making an unnecessary, and, in some few instances, a disorderly retreat." They also found him guilty of disrespect to the Commander in chief ; and sentenced him, to be suspended from any command in the armies of the United States, for the term of twelve months. It is impossible [105] for us to enter into the merits of this sentence ; in which party might have had a great share. When a dispute had been carried to so great an height, between an officer on whom the Americans reposed their chief confidence, and one subordinate and less popular, it is not difficult to divine where the blame will be laid.

In the mean time, the British army arrived at the high lands of Navesink, in the neighbourhood of Sandy Hook, on the last of June ; at which latter place, the fleet from the Delaware, under Lord Howe, after being detained in that river by calms, had most fortunately arrived on the preceding day. It had happened in the preceding winter, that the peninsula of Sandy Hook, had been cut off from the continent, and converted to an absolute island, by a violent breach of the sea ; a circumstance then of little moment, but which might now have been attended with the moſt fatal conſequences. By the happy arrival of the fleet, at the inſtant when its aſſiſtance was ſo critically neceſſary, the ability of the noble commander, and the extraordinary efforts of the ſeamen, this impediment was ſpeedily removed; a bridge of boats being completed with ſuch expedition, that the whole army was paſſed over this new channel on the 5th of July; and were afterwards conveyed with eaſe to New York; neither army nor navy yet knowing the circumſtances of danger and ruin in which they had been ſo nearly involved.

For an unexpected enemy had now arrived on the coaſt of North America, who was to give a new, and a ſtrange turn to the circumſtances of the war. On the ſecond day after the conveyance of the army from Sandy Hook, Lord Howe received intelligence by his cruizers, that D'Eſtaing's fleet had [106] been ſeen on the coaſt of Virginia, on the very day that the army had paſſed the bridge at Sandy Hook If D'Eſtaing had met the tranſports, either in the Delaware, or on the paſſage from thence, loaded and encumbered as they were, and convoyed only by two ſhips of the line, with a number of frigates, the conſequence with reſpect to the fleet is obvious. But it may not ſo immediately appear, that the fate of the army was ſo intimately combined with that of the fleet, that the deſtruction of the one, would have been the inevitable loſs of the other. For as the army could not then, by any poſſible means, have proſecuted its way to New York; and would have been encloſed on one ſide by the American army, and on the other by the French fleet, cut off from all ſupply of proviſion, and deſtitute of every reſource, a repetition of the Saratoga cataſtrophe, muſt have been the certain conſequence.

Although this fatal event was prevented by the bad weather, and unexpected impediments which D'Eſtaing met with on his voyage; yet, if he had directed his courſe directly to New York, inſtead of the Cheſapeak or Delaware; things could ſcarcely have been better; as he would then have come upon the fleet and army, when they were entangled, either with the laying or paſſing of the bridge at Sandy Hook. In either circumſtance deſtruction would have been inevitable; and would have been of an amount and magnitude, with reſpect both to the marine and land ſervice, and the conſequences hanging upon it, which, perhaps, has not been equalled of late ages. But D'Eſtaing's great object was the ſurpriſe of the fleet in the Delaware, and the conſequent encloſure of the army at Philadelphia; fortunately the winds and weather fruſtrated his deſign. Upon the whole, it may not be eaſy to point out a more ſignal or providential deliverance.

The danger, though leſſened, was not, however, immediately removed; and it ſtill required the moſt conſummate ability and fortitude, to render the kindneſs of fortune effective. On the 4th day after the account was received of his arrival on the coaſt, and ſubſequent advice of his having anchored at the Delaware being alſo received, D'Eſtaing appeared ſuddenly, and rather unexpectedly, in ſight of the July 11. Britiſh fleet at Sandy Hook. His force was great, and in good condition, conſiſting of twelve ſhips of the line, and three frigates of ſuperior ſize. Among the former, were ſeveral ſhips of great force and weight of metal; one carrying 90, another 80, and ſix carrying 74 guns each; and the ſquadron was ſaid to have no leſs than eleven thouſand men on board. On the other ſide, the Britiſh fleet under Lord Howe, conſiſted of ſix ſixty-four gun ſhips, three of fifty, and two of forty guns, with ſome fri-

gates and ſloops. Moſt of the former had been long on ſervice, were accordingly in bad condition, and were alſo wretchedly manned. If any thing, however, could remedy ſuch eſſential defects, it might have been hoped for, from the ſuperior abilities of their Commander, and the excellency of his Officers.

They had, however, the advantage of being in poſſeſſion of that port or harbour which is formed by Sandy Hook; the entrance of which is covered by a bar, and from whence the inlet paſſes to New York. The expected, and avowed object of D'Eſtaing, was to force that paſſage, and to attack the Engliſh ſquadron in the harbour. Notwithſtanding the utmoſt exertions of preparation made by Lord Howe, that the time could poſſibly admit; yet, from contrary winds, and other unavoidable incidents, the ſhips were not completely arrived in their reſpective ſituations of defence, nor had there been time to choſe thoſe ſituations with the judgment which was afterwards exerciſed, when D'Eſtaing appeared without the Hook. Under theſe circumſtances, which, with reſpect to the effect, might be conſidered, in ſome degree, as affording the advantages of a ſurpriſe, if he had puſhed on directly to paſs the bar and force the paſſage, it would ſeem, that neither the advantage of ſituation, nor any eminence of ability or virtue on the other ſide, could be capable of counteracting the vaſt ſuperiority of his force. The conflict would have been undoubtedly dreadful; and perhaps, in that reſpect, might have exceeded any thing known in naval hiſtory; but the greateſt portion of human ſpirit, muſt require ſome adequate degree of ſtrength, to render its exertions effective.

A diverſity of opinion ſeems to prevail, on the practicability of the great ſhips of the French fleet paſſing in force through the ſtrait, and over the bar. Some are of opinion that it might have been attempted with prudence. If fo, it may be confidered as a happinefs on all fides, that D'Eftaing was not poffeffed of that fpirit of enterprize which would have been equal to fo arduous an attempt; that the terror of the Britifh flag was yet in no degree weakened; and that the name of the noble Commander who oppofed him, added fome weight to that effect. D'Eftaing accordingly caft anchor on the Jerfey fide, about four miles without the Hook, and in the vicinity of the fmall town of Shrewfbury.

The fpirit that was difplayed on this occafion, not only in the fleet and army, but through every order and denomination of feamen, was never exceeded, and will not often be equalled. A thoufand volunteers were immediately difpatched from the transports to the fleet. The remainder of the crews, could not reftrain their indignation at being left behind, and fought every poffible means, by hiding in the boats or otherwife, to efcape on board the men of war; fo that the agents could fcarcely keep by force a fufficient number of hands for the watch of their refpective fhips. The mafters and mates of the merchantmen and traders at New York, folicited employment with the greateft earneftnefs; and took their ftations at the guns with the common failors. Others hazarded every thing, by putting to fea in light veffels, to watch the motions of the enemy, and perform other neceffary fervices. One in particular, with a noble difintereftednefs and gallantry, which may be compared with any thing known in hiftory, offered to convert his veffel (in which his whole hope and fortune lay) into a firefhip, to be conducted by himfelf; and fpurned with difdain every propofal of indemnification or reward.

It will afford no furprife, that this fpirit fhould fhine out in the army with equal luftre; and that the light infantry and grenadiers, who had fcarcely recovered the fatigue of a moft toilfome and dangerous march, and with many of the Officers wounds ftill green and fore, fhould, notwithftanding, contend with fuch eagernefs, to ferve on board the men of war as marines, that the point of honour was obliged to be decided by lots. In a word, the public fpirit, zeal, bravery, and magnanimity, difplayed upon this occafion, would have ftamped a character upon a nation that before had none; and is an honour even to this country. It muft, however, be acknowledged, that the popularity of the noble Commander, and the confidence founded on his great qualities, contributed not a little to thefe exertions.

The French fleet continued at anchor in the pofition we have mentioned, and taking in water and provifions, for eleven days. It may be well fuppofed, that as D'Eftaing did not profit of the firft opportunity that offered, that any attempt made by him, after the exertions on the other fide had taken their full effect, and the judicious defenfive difpofitions made by the Britifh Admiral were completed, would have been not only ineffectual, but probably (notwithftanding the fuperiority of his force) ruinous. Neither the confidence arifing from D'Eftaing's hefitation, or from their own courage, was, however, any allay to the mixed paffions of grief and indignation which now agitated the Britifh feamen. They endured the mortification, for the firft time, of feeing a Britifh fleet blocked up and infulted in their own harbour, and the French flag flying triumphant without; and this was ftill more deeply embittered and aggravated, by beholding every day, veffels under Englifh colours (who had ftill been ignorant of the lofs of their ufual protection), captured under their eyes by the enemy. They looked out every hour with the utmoft anxiety, and in the moft eager expectation, for the arrival of Byron's fquadron.

D'Eftaing's fleet at length appeared under way; and as the wind was favour- July 22. able, and the fpring tides at the higheft (the water rifing that afternoon thirty feet on the bar) it was expected that he intended to carry his long delayed menace into execution; and that that day would have afforded one of the hotteft and moft defperate engagements that had ever been fought, during the long enmity and rivalfhip that had fubfifted between the two nations. Every thing was at ftake on the Britifh fide. If the naval force was deftroyed, (and nothing lefs than deftruction or victory could have ended the conflict) the vaft fleets of tranfports and victuallers, with the army, muft all have fallen along with it. D'Eftaing, however, thought the attempt too dangerous; and fhaping his courfe another way, was in a few hours out of fight.

Nothing was ever more critical than this commander's ftay at Sandy Hook; and few things could be more fortunate in the prefent circumftances, than his departure at the exact period that he did. For if the whole, or any part, of Admiral Byron's fleet had [107] arrived during his ftay, confidering the ruined ftate in which it reached the coafts of America, there could fcarcely have been a hope, of its not falling, almoft, a defencelefs prey into his hands. That unfortunate fquadron is faid to have been, in many refpects, badly equipped and provided. In this ftate they had the fortune of meeting unufually bad weather for the feafon; and being feparated in different ftorms, and lingering through a tedious paffage, arrived, fcattered, broken, fickly, difmafted, or otherwife damaged, in various degrees of diftrefs, upon different and remote parts of the coast of America. Between the departure of D'Estaing on the 22d and the 30th of July, the Renown, of 50 guns, from the West Indies, the Raisonable and Centurion of 64 and 50, from Hallifax, and the Cornwall, (one of Admiral Byron's squadron) of 74 guns, all arrived singly at Sandy Hook. The joy arising from this reinforcement, could scarcely be superior to that excited by a sense of the imminent danger which they had so fortunately escaped. It seemed no less an instance of good fortune, that the Cornwall was in better condition than most of the other ships of that squadron.

This failure of the excellently laid scheme, which had been concerted by the French ministry with the American deputies at Paris, for the surprize and capture of the British fleet and army, whether on the Delaware or its borders, necessarily called for new counsels and measures. Rhode Island was the object now fixed upon, as that which would admit the mutual operation of the new allies by land and sea. This was the motive of D'Estaing's departure from Sandy Hook; and for this purpose, General Sullivan assembled a body of troops in the neighbourhood of Providence, for an invasion of the island, on its north end, from the continent; whilst D'Estaing, was to enter the harbour of Newport, near its southern extremity, and after destroying the shipping, by a powerful assault on the works facing the sea, to place the British forces between two fires.

The French fleet either blocked up or entered the several inlets, between which Rhode Island, and its adjoining lesser islands, are enclosed, and which form a communication more or less navigable in the different branches, between the open sea and the back continent, on the 29th of July. The main body cast anchor without

Brenton's Ledge, about five miles from Newport; two of their line of battle ships ran up the Naraganset passage, and anchored off the north end of the island of Conanicut, where they were shut up several days from rejoining the fleet by contrary winds; while some of their frigates, entering the Seconnet passage, occasioned the blowing up of the King Fisher sloop and two armed gallies, which could not otherwise avoid falling into the hands of the enemy.

Major General Sir Robert Pigot, who commanded the British[108] forces, took every measure in the power of a brave and experienced officer, that could tend to a vigorous and most obstinate defence. The troops, artillery, and cattle, were immediately conveyed from the island of Conanicut; the troops at the out posts in Rhode Island, were in constant readiness, at the first signal, to join the main body; the works to the sea were strengthened by every possible means, and the seamen belonging to the vessels that were destroyed, as well as those that could be spared from others, were called to their favourite occupation of serving the artillery. The transports (which must otherwise have fallen into the enemies hands) were sunk in different parts of those channels and passages, which might have afforded them an opportunity of attacking the works with advantage. The royal frigates were removed as far from danger as possible; but as their loss or destruction must be inevitable in the prosecution of the enemy's design, they were dismantled of their artillery and stores, and the necessary measures taken for securing the latter part of the alternative.

Two opposite bays, in the inlets on the eastern and western sides of the island, compress it so much, as to form a kind of Isthmus, by which the southern end, that spreads into the ocean, is connected with the main body.

The town of Newport lies just within this peninsula, at the opening of the Isthmus, on the western side of the island, and facing the island of Conanicut; the space between both forming a bay, which includes, or forms the harbour. The inlet to the harbour from the sea, called the Middle Channel, is narrow, and enclosed by Brenton's Point, and the opposite point of Conanicut, which form the southern extremities of both islands. A bar of high grounds, which crosses the Isthmus from channel to channel above Newport, was strongly covered with lines, redoubts, and artillery; so that the Peninsula might be considered as a garrison, distinct from the rest of the island; and under the protection of a superior naval force, might in a great measure defy any attempts from the northern side, supposing that an enemy had made good its landing in such circumstances. But the enemy being masters by sea, rendered the task of defence, under the apprehension of an attack on both sides at the same time, exceedingly arduous. The commander had however, just before, received a reinforcement of five battalions; the troops were in excellent condition and spirit; and the body of seamen, both with respect to labour and danger, were no small addition to their means of resistance.

The force destined against them by land, was not so considerable as their information had led them to apprehend. The business on that side seems to have been committed mostly, if not entirely, to the northern colonies, who were those immediately concerned in the event. General Sullivan, is however said to have assembled about 10,000 men; of whom, at least half, were composed of volunteers from New England and Connecticut. As the operations of the French fleet, were regulated by those of the army on land, they continued inactive, until Sullivan was in condition to pass over from the continent to the north end of the island. On the 8th of August, finding that measure in forwardness, and the wind being favourable, they entered the harbour under an easy sail, cannonading the batteries and town as they passed, and receiving their fire, without any material effect on either side. They anchored above the town, between Goat Island and Conanicut, but nearer to the latter, on which both the French and Americans had parties for some days past.

As soon as the determination of the enemy to enter the harbour became apparent, the commanders found themselves under the grievous necessity of burning the Orpheus, Lark, Juno, and Cerberus frigates; as they were soon after of sinking the Flora and Falcon. [109]

As soon as Lord Howe received advice of the danger of Rhode Island, he determined to attempt every thing, which resolution, under the direction of reason and judgment, could undertake for its preservation. His squadron, notwithstanding the late reinforcements, was still, with respect to effective force, and weight of metal, so far inferior to the enemy, that to hazard an engagement, without some collateral advantage to counteract so great a superiority, would seem a degree of rashness inconsistent with his character. In point of number, he was indeed superior to the French, his squadron now consisting of one 74, seven 64, and five 50 gun ships, besides several frigates; but the great deficiency in other respects, appears from the bare recital of the rates. Every thing in such a situation was, however, to be tried, and he was determined that nothing should be left undone. The account indeed he received of the separated state of the French fleet, some of them involved in the channels, and the bulk lying without, afforded some room for a hope, that he might bring on an engagement upon more equal terms than could have been otherwise expected.

But notwithstanding the utmost possible expedition, he met with such unavoidable delays, that he was not able to reach Rhode Island, until the day after the French fleet had entered that harbour. Aug. 9th. From the situation in which the enemy now lay, he was enabled to communicate directly with General Pigot; the result of which was, that under the present circumstances, the affording him any essential relief was impracticable.

A sudden change of wind to the north-east, afforded an equal change of circumstances, and on the following day, the French Admiral stood out to sea with the whole fleet, those in the Naraganset Passage, as well as the port. Lord Howe, justly deeming the weather-gage too great an advantage to be added to the superior force of the enemy, contended for that object with all the skill and judgment incident to an able and experienced seaman. On the other hand, D'Estaing, notwithstanding his superiority, was as eager to preserve this advantage, as his adversary to obtain it. This contest of seamanship prevented an engagement 11th. on that day; but the wind on the following still continuing adverse to the design of the British Admiral, he determined to make the best of the present circumstances, and to engage the enemy; forming the line in such a manner as to be joined by three fire ships, which were under the tow of as many frigates. A strong gale of wind, which afterwards increased to a violent tempest, and continued for near 48 hours, not only put by the engagement by separating the fleets, for the present, but scattered them in such a manner, and caused so much damage on both sides, as rendered an engagement for some time impracticable.

The French suffered greatly in this tempest, two of their capital ships being dismasted, and others much damaged. Some untoward situations, and unusual circumstances, were produced by this conflict of the elements. The Languedoc of 90 guns, D'Estaing's own ship, had lost all her masts, and was met in that condition on the evening of the 13th, by the Renown of 50 guns, Capt. Dawson, [110] who attacked her with such fury, as well as judgment and advantage, that no doubt could have been entertained of the event, if the daylight had continued. But the darkness of the night, and freshness of the gale, whose violence was not yet quite allayed, compelled Capt. Dawson to cease from his attack, after he had poured several broadsides close into her, and had, besides other apparent damage, shot away her rudder. He, however, lay to, as closely as possible, for the night, intending to renew the attack in the morning, and considering her as little less than a certain prize. The appearance of six French men of war, by whom he was chaced at day light, and who were possibly led that way by the firing, put an end to Dawson's hopes, and relieved the French Admiral from this very urgent distress.

Upon the same evening, and about the same hour, the Preston, likewise of 50 guns, Commodore Hotham, fell in with the Tonnant, a French 80 gun ship, with only her main-mast standing. The Commodore attacked her with the same spirit and effect, with which Captain Dawson had engaged the Languedoc. The circumstances were likewise similar in every respect. The night obliged him to draw off, with the same intention of renewing the engagement, and under the same certainty of success; whilst the appearance of a part of the French fleet in the morning, frustrated both.

The circumstances of advantage afforded by the tempest, were not, however, entirely confined to one side. It held out one on the other, which was productive of one of the most gallant and brilliant naval actions, of this, or of any war. The Isis of 50 guns, Capt. Raynor, Aug. 16th, [111] was eagerly chaced and engaged by a French 74 gun flag-ship, supposed to be the Zèle, though other accounts say the Cesar. The Frenchman was much the better sailer, and the circumstances of the ships with respect to the tempest were the same, they having both entirely escaped the effects of its fury. In this very unequal contest, in which the greatest resolution and skill, would seem incapable of supplying the deficiency of force on the one side, a close and desperate engagement was maintained with the greatest obstinacy on both, for an hour and a half, and within pistol shot distance. At the end of that time, the Isis had obtained so manifest a superiority in the action, that the French ship was glad to put before the wind, and call in the aid of all her sails, to escape from so determined an enemy. The Isis had suffered so much in her masts and rigging as to be incapable of attempting a pursuit.

It is not easy to determine whether to admire more, the gallantry exhibited in this singular action, or the modesty of the brave commander in his account of it. This was indeed so extreme, that his Admiral was obliged in some degree to supply the defect, by acquainting the Admiralty, that the honour of the day was not more owing to the resolution of the Captain, or the intrepidity of his officers and crew, than to the professional skill and ability of the former. The loss of men was considerable on the French side,

and M. de Bougainville, the cele-[112] brated and philosophic navigator, who was their commander, is said to have lost an arm in the action. The loss in the Isis was very moderate. The high honour which [113] the young Duke of Ancaster acquired as a volunteer in this action, only serves to embitter the loss which his country has since sustained, by the premature death of a nobleman, who so early distinguished himself in her service, and from whom she had so much to expect.

Although the British squadron suffered much less in the storm than the French, yet their damage was so considerable, as unavoidably to cost some time at Sandy Hook or New York, in proportion to their wants, whether only to refit, or to repair. The French fleet returned to Rhode Island on the 20th, where they anchored without the harbour, and sailed from thence on the 22d for Boston, in order to repair their shattered ships. Lord Howe, having got his ships in condition with an expedition that surprized every body, pursued them with the greatest eagerness, hoping to overtake them by the way.

In the mean time, General Sullivan had landed on the north end of Long Island, by the way of Howland's Ferry, on the 9th of August, being the day that D'Estaing went out of the harbour to meet Lord Howe. The extreme badness of the weather, impeded for some days the bringing forward of his stores and artillery, and of course retarded the progress of his army. On the 17th, however, they broke ground on Honeyman's Hill, near the British works, and began to construct batteries, and to form lines of approach; the British forces being no less active, in throwing up new works, and constructing new batteries, to counteract theirs. We have already observed, that General Pigot was under no great

apprehension of an attack in front; the general object of apprehension was the concurrent assault of D'Estaing on the town and works to the water; but the great point of danger was his landing a body of troops in the southern peninsula, which would have laid the garrison open in the rear, whilst they were desperately engaged on the front and flank in defence of their works.

The critical and most timely appearance of Lord Howe with the British squadron, happily obviated this apprehension and danger in the first instance; and D'Estaing's consequent departure, or flight to Boston, removed them entirely. His sailing out of the harbour to engage Lord Howe, does not seem by any means to have been a judicious measure. The nature of the port, the narrowness of the passage from the sea, with the means of defence afforded by the island of Conanicut, which was occupied by himself and his allies, held out, all together, so strong a security to his fleet, that scarcely any naval superiority, which, however, did not exist, could have justified any attempt upon it. In this state, it would seem, that he should first have secured his object, which appears to have been much within his reach, before he put out to sea, either to engage, or to seek for Lord Howe. But vanity seems here to have had some share in his determination. The glory of vanquishing a British squadron, and of obtaining a triumph over a commander of great name, and of a country which so seldom afforded such laurels, was a temptation not to be resisted by D'Estaing.

Yet, after all the ill consequences of this vain and ruinous pursuit, if he had entered the harbour, and co-operated with the Americans, in conformity with their most earnest solicitations, when he anchored the second time before Rhode Island, it would seem that the state of the garrison would have been extremely perilous, and that he had a fair prospect of retrieving, by a stroke of no small importance, the failure of success in his grand object. Such a successful co-operation would likewise have had a wonderful effect in conciliating the minds of his new allies, and in giving them an idea, which they were not very apt to entertain, of the vigour and efficacy of French councils and arms. It may indeed be objected, and truly, that his two dismasted ships could not have been repaired, nor, perhaps, the rest of his squadron refitted, at Rhode Island; but as they might have continued there in perfect security for any length of time, if he had succeeded in his object, this objection does not appear to be of sufficient weight for its being abandoned.

The American army in Rhode Island, and the people of the Northern Colonies in general, complained loudly of this conduct. They said, that they had been led into an expedition, of prodigious expence, labour, trouble, and danger, under the assurance, of the most effective co-operation of the French fleet. That, under this sanction, they had committed their lives and liberties on the invasion of an island, where, without a naval protection, they were likely to be enclosed like wild beasts in a toil; and that in this situation, they were first deserted, for a vain and fruitless pursuit, and then totally abandoned, at the very time that they had brought the business on their side to the point of completion.

Under these discontents and apprehensions, Sullivan was deserted by the New England and Connecticut volunteers, who composed the better half of his army; and by this means, if we credit the American accounts, his numbers were so much reduced, as to be inferior, in point of force,

to the garrison. In these circumstances, and under the immediate apprehension of his retreat being cut off, Sullivan extricated himself with a degree of prudence and ability, which would have done honour to an older General; nor would the behaviour of his troops have disgraced more veteran soldiers.

Having begun to send off his heavy artillery and baggage on the 26th of August, he retreated from his lines on the 29th; and though he was most vigorously pursued, and repeatedly attacked in every quarter wherever an opening was made, by the British forces, yet he took his measures so well, and had chosen his posts so judiciously, that although much honour was claimed and deserved on both sides, he gained the north end of the island without sustaining any considerable loss. Being there, from the nature of the ground, and the situation of his posts, in a state of security, he passed his army over by the way of Bristol and Hoyland ferries, on the night of the 30th, without interruption, to the continent. Nor was his good fortune inferior to his conduct, as Sir Henry Clinton arrived just after with such a force from New York, as would have left no doubt of the fate of his forces, if they had still continued on the island.

On the same day that Sullivan abandoned Rhode Island, Lord Howe entered the bay of Boston, where, to his great mortification, he found that D'Estaing was arrived before him. This was, however, increased, when upon a close inspection he discovered, that he was so effectually covered in Nantasket Road, by the batteries erected, and the measures of defence taken, by the Americans and French, on the adjacent points and islands, that an attack upon him, with any prospect of success, was utterly impracticable.

Thus, with great honour to

himself, and advantage to his country, did that great naval commander, bring the campaign with his powerful adversary to a conclusion. With an inferiority of force, which held out mere preservation as the summit of hope, he, by a continued and rapid succession of the greatest possible exertions, masterly manoeuvres, and wise measures, having first counteracted, and at length defeated, all the views and attempts of his enemy, obliged him to fly for refuge to those new allies whom he came to protect, and insulted him under that protection. Leaving him in a condition at parting, which rendered him incapable of any further service in those seas for the remainder of the year.

• • •

[114]

Particulars of the Mischianza, *exhibited in* America *at the Departure of General* Howe.

Copy of a Letter from an Officer at Philadelphia *to his Correspondent in* London.

Philadelphia, May 23, 1778.

FOR the first time in my life I write to you with unwillingness. The ship that carries home Sir William Howe will convey this letter to you; and not even the pleasure of conversing with my friend can secure me from the general dejection I see around me, or remove the share I must take in the universal regret and disappointment which his approaching departure hath spread throughout the whole army. We see him taken from us at a time when we most stand in need of so skilful and popular a commander; when the experience of three years, and the knowledge he hath acquired of the country and people, have added to the confidence we always placed in his conduct and abilities. You know he was ever a favourite with the military; but the affection and attachment which all ranks of officers in this army bear him can only be known by those who have at this time seen them in their effects. I do not believe there is upon record an instance of a Commander in Chief having so universally endeared himself to those under his command; or of one who received such signal and flattering proofs of their love. That our sentiments might be the more universally and unequivocally known, it was resolved amongst us, that we should give him as splendid an entertainment as the shortness of the time, and our present situation, would allow us. For the expences, the whole army would have most chearfully contributed; but it was requisite to draw the line somewhere, and twenty-two field-officers joined in a subscription adequate to the plan they meant to adopt. I know your curiosity will be raised on this occasion; I shall therefore give you as particular an account of our *Mischianza* as I have been able to collect. From the name you will perceive that it was made up of a variety of entertainments. Four of the gentlemen subscribers were appointed managers—Sir John Wrottesley, Col. O'Hara, Major Gardiner, and Montresor, the chief engineer. On the tickets of admission, which they gave out for Monday the 18th, was engraved, in a shield, a view of the sea, with the setting sun, and on a wreath, the words *Luceo discedens, aucto splendore resurgam.* At top was the General's crest, with *vive vale!* All round the shield ran a vignette, and various military trophies filled up the ground. A grand regatta began the entertainment. It consisted of three divisions. In the first was the Ferret galley, having on board several General Officers, and a number of Ladies. In the centre was the Hussar galley, with Sir William and Lord Howe, Sir Henry Clinton, the officers of their suite, and some Ladies. The Cornwallis galley brought up the rear, having on board General Knyp-

haufen and his suite, three British Generals, and a party of Ladies. On each quarter of these gallies, and forming their division, were five flat boats, lined with green cloth, and filled with Ladies and Gentlemen. In front of the whole were three flat boats, with a band of music in each—Six barges rowed about each flank, to keep off the swarm of boats that covered the river from side to side. The gallies were dressed out in a variety of colours and streamers, and in each flat boat was displayed the flag of its own division. In the stream opposite the centre of the city, the Fanny armed ship, magnificently decorated, was placed at anchor, and at some distance a-head lay his Majesty's ship Roebuck, with the Admiral's flag hoisted at the foretop mast-head. The transport ships, extending in a line the whole length of the town, appeared with colours flying, and crouded with spectators, as were also the openings of the several wharfs on shore, exhibiting the most picturesque and enlivening scene the eye could desire. The rendezvous was at Knight's Wharf, at the northern extremity of the city. By half after four the whole company were embarked, and the signal being made by the Vigilant's manning ship, the three divisions rowed slowly down, preserving their proper intervals, and keeping time to the music that led the fleet. Arrived between the Fanny and the Market Wharf, a signal was made from one of the boats a-head, and the whole lay upon their oars, while the music played *God save the King*, and three cheers given from the vessels were returned from the multitude on shore. By this time the flood-tide became too rapid for the gallies to advance; they were therefore quitted, and the company disposed of in the different barges. This alteration broke in upon the order of procession, but was necessary to give sufficient time for displaying the entertainment that was prepared on shore.

The landing place was at the Old Fort, a little to the southward of the town, fronting the building prepared for the reception of the company, about 400 yards from the water by a gentle ascent. As soon as the General's barge was seen to push for the shore, a salute of 17 guns was fired from the Roebuck, and, after some interval, by the same number from the Vigilant. The company, as they disembarked, arranged themselves into a line of procession, and advanced through an avenue formed by two files of grenadiers, and a line of light-horse supporting each file. This avenue led to a square lawn of 150 yards on each side, lined with troops and properly prepared for the exhibition of a tilt and tournament, according to the customs and ordinances of ancient chivalry. We proceeded through the centre of the square. The music, consisting of all the bands of the army, moved in front. The Managers, with favours of blue and white ribbands in their breasts, followed next in order. The General, Admiral, and the rest of the company succeeded promiscuously.

In front appeared the building, bounding the view through a vista formed by two triumphal arches, erected at proper intervals in a line with the landing place. Two pavilions, with rows of benches, rising one above the other, and serving as the advanced wings of the first triumphal arch, received the Ladies, while the Gentlemen ranged themselves in convenient order on each side. On the front seat of each pavilion were placed seven of the principal young Ladies of the country, dressed in Turkish habits, and wearing in their turbans the favours with which they meant to reward the several Knights who were to contend in their honour. These arrangements were scarce made when the sound of trumpets was heard at a distance; and a band of Knights, dressed in ancient habits of white and red silk, and mounted on grey horses, richly caparisoned in trappings of the same colours, entered the lists, attended by their Esquires on foot, in suitable apparel, in the following order:—Four trumpeters, properly habited, their trumpets decorated with small pendent banners—A herald in his robes of ceremony; on his tunic was the device of his band, two roses intertwined, with the motto, *We droop when separated.*

Lord Cathcart, superbly mounted on a managed horse, appeared as chief of these Knights; two young black slaves, with sashes and drawers of blue and white silk, wearing large silver clasps round their necks and arms, their breasts and shoulders bare, held his stirrups. On his right hand walked Capt. Hazard, and on his left Capt. Brownlow, his two Esquires, one bearing his lance, the other his shield.

His device was Cupid riding on a Lion, the Motto, *Surmounted by Love.* His Lordship appeared in honour of Miss Auchmuty.

Then came in order the Knights of his band, each attended by his Squire, bearing his lance and shield.

1st Knight, Hon. Capt. Cathcart, in honour of Miss N. White. —Squire, Capt. Peters. Device, a heart and sword; Motto, *Love and Honour.*

2d Knight, Lieut. Bygrove, in honour of Miss Craig——Squire, Lieut. Nichols. — Device, Cupid tracing a Circle; Motto, *Without end.*

3d Knight, Capt. André, in honour of Miss P. Chew.—Squire, Lieut. André—Device, two Gamecocks fighting; Motto, *No Rival.*

4th Knight, Capt. Horneck, in honour of Miss N. Redman.—Squire, Lieut. Talbot.—Device, a burning Heart; Motto, *Absence cannot extinguish.*

5th Knight, Capt. Matthews, in honour of Miss Lond——Squire, Lieut. Hamilton.—Device, a winged Heart; Motto, *Each Fair by Turn.*

6th Knight, Lieut. Sloper, in honour of Miss M. Shippen.—— Squire, Lieut. Brown.—Device, a Heart and Sword; Motto, *Honour and the Fair.*

After they had made the circuit of the square, and saluted the Ladies as they passed before the pavilions, they ranged themselves in a line with that in which were the Ladies of their Device; and their Herald (Mr. Beaumont), advancing into the centre of the square, after a flourish of trumpets, proclaimed the following challenge:

" The Knights of the Blended Rose, by me their Herald, proclaim and assert that the Ladies of the Blended Rose excel in wit, beauty, and every accomplishment, those of the *whole world*; and should any Knight or Knights be so hardy as to dispute or deny it, they are ready to enter the lists with them, and maintain their assertions by deeds of arms, according to the laws of ancient chivalry."

At the third repetition of the challenge the sound of trumpets was heard from the opposite side of the square; and another Herald, with four Trumpeters, dressed in black and orange, galloped into the lists. He was met by the Herald of the Blended Rose, and after a short parley they both advanced in front of the pavilions, when the Black Herald (Lieut. More) ordered his trumpets to sound, and then proclaimed defiance to the challenge in the following words:

" The Knights of the Burning Mountain present themselves here, not to contest by words, but to disprove by deeds, the vain-glorious assertions of the Knights of the Blended Rose, and enter these lists to maintain, that the Ladies of the Burning Mountain are not excelled in beauty, virtue, or accomplishments, by any in the universe."

He then returned to the part of the barrier through which he had entered; and shortly after the Black Knights, attended by their Squires, rode into the lists in the following order:

Four Trumpeters preceding the Herald, on whose tunic was represented a mountain, sending forth flames.—Motto, *I burn for ever.*

Captain Watson, of the guards, as Chief, dressed in a magnificent suit of black and orange silk, and mounted on a black managed horse, with trappings of the same colours with his own dress, appeared in honour of Miss Franks. He was attended in the same manner as Lord Cathcart. Capt. Scot bore his lance and Lieut. Lyttleton his shield. The Device, a Heart, with a Wreath of Flowers; Motto, *Love and Glory.*

1st Knight, Lieut. Underwood, in honour of Miss S. Shippen.— Squire, Ensign Haverkam.—Device, a Pelican feeding her young; Motto, *For those I love.*

2d Knight, Lieut. Winyard, in honour of Miss P. Shippen.—— Squire, Capt. Boscawen.—Device, a Bay-leaf; Motto, *Unchangeable.*

3d Knight, Lieut. Delaval, in honour of Miss B. Bond.—Squire, Capt. Thorne.—Device, a Heart, aimed at by several arrows, and struck by one; Motto, *One only pierces me.*

4th Knight, Monsieur Montluissant, (Lieut. of the Hessian Chasseurs) in honour of Miss B. Redman.—Squire, Capt. Campbell.— Device, a Sun-flower turning towards the Sun; Motto, *Je vise à vous.*

5th Knight, Lieut. Hobbart, in honour of Miss S. Chew.—Squire, Lieut. Briscoe.——Device, Cupid piercing a Coat of Mail with his Arrow; Motto, *Proof to all but Love.*

6th Knight, Brigade-Major Tarlton, in honour of Miss W. Smith. —Squire, Ensign Heart.—Device, a Light Dragoon; Motto, *Swift, vigilant, and bold.*

After they had rode round the lists, and made their obeisance to the Ladies, they drew up fronting the White Knights; and the Chief of these having thrown down his gauntlet, the Chief of the Black

Knights directed his Esquire to take it up. The Knights then received their lances from their Esquires, fixed their shields on their left arms, and making a general salute to each other, by a very graceful movement of their lances, turned round to take their career, and, encountering in full gallop, shivered their spears. In the second and third encounter they discharged their pistols. In the fourth they fought with their swords. At length the two Chiefs, spurring forward into the centre, engaged furiously in single combat, till the Marshal of the Field (Major Gwyne) rushed in between the Chiefs, and declared that the Fair Damsels of the Blended Rose and Burning Mountain were perfectly satisfied with the proofs of love, and the signal feats of valour, given by their respective Knights; and commanded them, as they prized the future favours of their Mistresses, that they would instantly desist from further combat. Obedience being paid by the Chiefs to this order, they joined their respective bands. The White Knights and their attendants filed off to the left, the Black Knights to the right; and, after passing each other at the lower side of the quadrangle, moved up alternately, till they approached the pavilions of the Ladies, when they gave a general salute.

A passage being now opened between the two pavilions, the Knights, preceded by their Squires and the bands of music, rode through the first triumphal arch, and arranged themselves to the right and left. This arch was erected in honour of Lord Howe. It presented two fronts, in the Tuscan order; the pediment was adorned with various naval trophies, and at top was the figure of Neptune, with a trident in his right hand. In a niche, on each side, stood a Sailor with a drawn cutlass. Three Plumes of Feathers were placed on the summit of each wing, and in the entablature was this in-

scription: *Laus illi debetur, et alme gratia major.* The interval between the two arches was an avenue 300 feet long, and 34 broad. It was lined on each side with a file of troops; and the colours of all the army, planted at proper distances, had a beautiful effect in diversifying the scene. Between these colours the Knights and Squires took their stations. The Bands continued to play several pieces of martial music. The company moved forward in procession, with the Ladies in the Turkish habits in front; as these passed, they were saluted by their Knights, who then dismounted and joined them: and in this order we were all conducted into a garden that fronted the house, through the second triumphal arch, dedicated to the General. This arch was also built in the Tuscan order. On the interior part of the pediment was painted a Plume of Feathers, and various military trophies. At top stood the figure of Fame, and in the entablature this device,—*I, bone, quo virtus tua te vocet; I pede fausto.* On the right hand pillar was placed a bombshell, and on the left a flaming heart. The front next the house was adorned with preparations for a fire-work. From the garden we ascended a flight of steps, covered with carpets, which led into a spacious hall; the pannels, painted in imitation of Sienna marble, enclosing festoons of white marble: the surbase, and all below, was black. In this hall, and in the adjoining apartments, were prepared tea, lemonade, and other cooling liquors, to which the company seated themselves; during which time the Knights came in, and on the knee received their favours from their respective Ladies. One of these rooms was afterwards appropriated for the use of the Pharaoh table; as you entered it you saw, on a pannel over the chimney, a Cornucopia, exuberantly filled with flowers of the richest colours; over the door, as you went out, another presented it-

self, shrunk, reversed, and emptied.

From these apartments we were conducted up to a ball-room, decorated in a light elegant stile of painting. The ground was a pale blue, pannelled with a small gold bead, and in the interior filled with dropping festoons of flowers in their natural colours. Below the surbase the ground was of rose-pink, with drapery festooned in blue. These decorations were heightened by 85 mirrors, decked with rose-pink silk ribbands, and artificial flowers; and in the intermediate spaces were 34 branches with wax-lights, ornamented in a similar manner.

On the same floor were four drawing-rooms, with side boards of refreshments, decorated and lighted in the same stile and taste as the ball-room. The ball was opened by the Knights and their Ladies; and the dances continued till ten o'clock, when the windows were thrown open, and a magnificent bouquet of rockets began the fireworks. These were planned by Capt. Montresor, the chief engineer, and consisted of twenty different exhibitions, displayed under his direction with the happiest success, and in the highest stile of beauty. Towards the conclusion, the interior part of the triumphal arch was illuminated amidst an uninterrupted flight of rockets and bursting of baloons. The military trophies on each side assumed a variety of transparent colours. The shell and flaming heart on the wings sent forth Chinese fountains, succeeded by fire-pots. Fame appeared at top, spangled with stars, and from her trumpet blowing the following device in letters of light, *Tes Lauriers font immortels.*—A saucer of rockets, bursting from the pediment, concluded the *feu d'artifice.*

At twelve supper was announced, and large folding doors, hitherto artfully concealed, being suddenly thrown open, discovered a magnificent saloon of 210 feet by 40, and 22 feet in height, with three alcoves on each fide, which ferved for fide-boards. The cieling was the fegment of a circle, and the fides were painted of a light ftraw-colour, with vine leaves and feftoon flowers, fome in a bright, fome in a darkifh green. Fifty-fix large pier-glaffes, ornamented with green filk artificial flowers and ribbands; 100 branches with three lights in each, trimmed in the fame manner as the mirrours; 18 luftres, each with 24 lights, fufpended from the cieling, and ornamented as the branches; 300 wax-tapers, difpofed along the fupper tables; 430 covers, 1200 difhes; 24 black flaves, in oriental dreffes, with filver collars and bracelets, ranged in two lines, and bending to the ground as the General and Admiral approached the faloon: all thefe, forming together the moft brilliant affemblage of gay objects, and appearing at once as we entered by an eafy defcent, exhibited a *coup d'oeil* beyond defcription magnificent.

Towards the end of fupper, the Herald of the Blended Rofe, in his habit of ceremony, attended by his trumpets, entered the faloon, and proclaimed the King's health, the Queen, and Royal Family, the Army and Navy, with their refpective Commanders, the Knights and their Ladies, the Ladies in general: each of thefe toafts was followed by a flourifh of mufic. After fupper we returned to the ball-room, and continued to dance till four o'clock.

Such, my dear friend, is the defcription, though a very faint one of the moft fplendid entertainment, I believe, ever given by an army to their General. But what muft be moft grateful to Sir W. Howe, is the fpirit and motives from which it was given. He goes from this place to-morrow; but, as I underftand he means to ftay a day or two with his brother on board the Eagle at Billingfport, I fhall not feal this letter till I fee him depart from Philadelphia.

Sunday 24th. I am juft returned

from conducting our beloved General to the water-fide, and have feen him receive a more flattering teftimony of the love and attachment of his army, than all the pomp and fplendor of the *Mifchianza* could convey to him. I have feen the moft gallant of our officers, and thofe whom I leaft fufpected of giving fuch inftances of their affection, fhed tears while they bid him farewel. The gallant and affectionate General of the Heffians, Knyphaufen, was fo moved, that he could not finifh a compliment he began to pay him in his own name and that of his Officers who attended him. Sir Henry Clinton attended him to the wharf, where Lord Howe received him into his barge, and they are both gone down to Billingfport. On my return, I faw nothing but dejected countenances.

Adieu, &c.

An Account of the Ceremony obferved at the firft Audience given to Monfieur Gerard, *Minifter Plenipotentiary from the* French *King to the* Rebel Colonies, *by their General* Congrefs; *a Copy and Tranflation of the* French *King's Letter to them, his Minifter's Speech in Congrefs, with their Reply by the Prefident.*

Philadelphia, Auguft 11.

LAST Thurfday being the day appointed by Congrefs for the audience of the Sieur Gerard, Minifter Plenipotentiary from his moft Chriftian Majefty, that Minifter received audience accordingly. In purfuance of the ceremonial eftablifhed by Congrefs, the Hon. Richard Henry Lee, Efq. one of the delegates from Virginia, and the Hon. Samuel Adams, Efq. one of the delegates from Maffachufett's-bay, in a coach and fix, provided by Congrefs, waited upon the Minifter at his houfe. In a few minutes the Minifter and the two delegates entered the coach,

Mr. Lee placing himfelf at the Minifter's left hand on the back feat, Mr. Adams occupying the front feat; the Minifter's chariot being behind received his fecretary. The carriages being arrived at the ftate-houfe in this city, the two members of Congrefs, placing themfelves at the minifter's left hand, a little before one o'clock, introduced him to his chair in the Congrefs-chamber; the Prefident and Congrefs fitting —the Minifter being feated, he gave his credentials into the hands of his Secretary, who advanced and delivered them to the Prefident. The Secretary of Congrefs then read and tranflated them; which being done, Mr. Lee announced the Minifter to the Prefident and Congrefs; at this time the Prefident, the Congrefs and the Minifter rofe together: he bowed to the Prefident and the Congrefs; they bowed to him: whereupon the whole feated themfelves. In a moment, the Minifter rofe and made a fpeech to Congrefs, they fitting. The fpeech being finifhed, the Minifter fat down, and, giving a copy of his fpeech to his Secretary, he prefented it to the Prefident. The Prefident and the Congrefs then rofe, and the Prefident pronounced their anfwer to the fpeech, the Minifter ftanding. The anfwer being ended, the whole were again feated, and, the Prefident giving a copy of the anfwer to the Secretary of Congrefs, he prefented it to the Minifter. The Prefident, the Congrefs, and Minifter, then again rofe together: the Minifter bowed to the Prefident, who returned the falute, and then to the Congrefs, who alfo bowed in return: and, the Minifter having bowed to the Prefident and received his bow, he withdrew, and was attended home in the fame manner in which he had been conducted to the audience.

Within the bar of the Houfe, the Congrefs formed a femicircle on each fide of the Prefident and the Minifter: the Prefident fitting at one extremity of the circle, at a table upon a platform elevated two fteps,——the Minifter fitting at the oppofite extremity of the circle in an arm-chair upon the fame level with the Congrefs. The door of the Congrefs-chamber being thrown open, below the bar, about 200 gentlemen were admitted to the audience, among whom were the Vice-prefident of the fupreme executive Council of Pennfylvania, the fupreme executive Council, the Speaker, and members of the Houfe of Affembly, feveral foreigners of diftinction, and officers of the army.

The audience being over, the Congrefs and the Minifter, at a proper hour, repaired to an entertainment by Congrefs given to the Minifter; at which were prefent by invitation feveral foreigners of diftinction and gentlemen of public character. The entertainment was conducted with a decorum fuited to the occafion, and gave perfect fatisfaction to the whole company.

In Congrefs, Aug. 6, 1778.

According to order the honourable the Sieur Gerard being introduced to an audience by the two members for that purpofe appointed, and being feated in his chair, his Secretary delivered to the Prefident a letter from his moft Chriftian Majefty, which was read in the words following:

Very dear great friends and allies,

THE treaties which we have figned with you, in confequence of the propofals your Commiffioners made to us in your behalf, are a certain affurance of our affection for the United States in general and for each of them in particular, as well as of the intereft we take, and conftantly fhall take, in their happinefs and profperity. It is to convince you more particularly of this, that we have nominated the Sieur Gerard,

Secretary of our Council of State, to refide among you in the quality of our Minifter Plenipotentiary; he is the better acquainted with our fentiments toward you, and the more capable of teftifying the fame to you, as he was entrufted on our part to negociate with your Commiffioners, and figned with them the treaties which cement our union. We pray you to give full credit to all he fhall communicate to you from us, more efpecially when he fhall affure you of our affection and conftant friendfhip for you. We pray God, very dear great friends and allies, to have you in his holy keeping. Your good friend and ally.

Signed,

LOUIS.

Verfailles, March 28, 1778.
(Under-figned) GRAVIER de VERGENNES.

(Directed)
To our very dear great Friends the Prefident and Members of the General Congrefs of North America.

The Minifter was then announced to the Prefident and the Houfe, whereupon he arofe and addreffed Congrefs in the fpeech, which, when he had finifhed, his Secretary delivered the fame in writing to the Prefident as follows:

Gentlemen,

THE connection formed by the King, my mafter, with the United States of America, is fo agreeable to him, that he could no longer delay fending me to refide among you for the purpofe of cementing it. It will give his Majefty great fatisfaction to learn that the fentiments, which have fhone forth on this occafion, juftify that confidence with which he hath been infpired by the zeal and character of the Commiffioners of the United States in France, the wifdom and fortitude which have directed the refolutions of Congrefs, and the courage and perfeverance of the people they reprefent; a confidence

which you know, gentlemen, has been the bafis of that truly amicable and difinterefted fyftem, on which he hath treated with the United States.

It is not his Majefty's fault that the engagements he hath entered into did not eftablifh your independence and repofe without the further effufion of blood, and without aggravating the calamities of mankind, whofe happinefs it is his higheft ambition to promote and fecure. But, fince the hoftile meafures and defigns of the common enemy have given to engagements purely eventual an immediate, pofitive, permanent, and indiffoluble force, it is the opinion of the King my mafter, that the allies fhould turn their whole attention to fulfil thofe engagements in the manner moft ufeful to the common caufe, and beft calculated to obtain that peace which is the object of the alliance.

It is upon this principle his Majefty hath haftened to fend you a powerful affiftance, which you owe only to his friendfhip, to the fincere regard he has for every thing which relates to the advantage of the United States, and to his defire of contributing with efficacy to eftablifh your repofe and profperity upon an honourable and folid foundation. And further it is his expectation that the principles, which may be adopted by the refpective governments, will tend to ftrengthen thofe bonds of union, which have originated in the mutual intereft of the two nations.

The principal object of my inftructions is to connect the interefts of France with thofe of the United States. I flatter myfelf, gentlemen, that my paft conduct in the affairs which concern them hath already convinced you of the determination I feel to endeavour to obey my inftructions in fuch manner as to deferve the confidence of Congrefs, the friendfhip of its members, and the esteem of the citizens of America.

GERARD.

To which the President was pleased to return the following Answer:

SIR,

THE treaties between his most Christian Majesty and the United States of America so fully demonstrate his wisdom and magnanimity, as to command the reverence of all nations. The virtuous citizens of America in particular can never forget his beneficent attention to their violated rights; nor cease to acknowledge the hand of a gracious providence in raising them up so powerful and illustrious a friend. It is the hope and opinion of Congress, that the confidence his Majesty reposes in the firmness of these states will receive additional strength from every day's experience.

This assembly are convinced, Sir, that, had it rested solely with the most Christian King, not only the independence of these states would have been universally acknowledged, but their tranquillity fully established. We lament that lust of domination, which gave birth to the present war, and hath prolonged and extended the miseries of mankind. We ardently wish to sheathe the sword and spare the farther effusion of blood; but we are determined, by every means in our power, to fulfil those eventual engagements which have acquired positive and permanent force from the hostile designs and measures of the common enemy.

Congress have reason to believe, that the assistance so wisely and generously sent will bring Great Britain to a sense of justice and moderation, promote the common interests of France and America, and secure peace and tranquillity on the most firm and honourable foundation. Neither can it be doubted, that those, who administer the powers of government within the several states of this union, will cement that connection with the subjects of France, the beneficial effects of which have already been so sensibly felt.

Sir, from the experience we have had of your exertions to promote the true interests of our country as well as your own, it is with the highest satisfaction Congress receive, as the first Minister from his most Christian Majesty, a gentleman, whose past conduct affords a happy presage, that he will merit the confidence of this body, the friendship of its members, and the esteem of the citizens of America.

HEN. LAURENS, Pres.

In Congress,
August 6, 1778.

The Secretary of Congress then delivered to the Minister a copy of the foregoing reply, signed as above; whereupon the Minister withdrew, and was conducted home in the manner in which he was brought to the House.

Extract from the minutes.

CHARLES THOMSON, Sec.

• • •

His Majesty's most gracious Speech to both Houses of Parliament, on Thursday the 20th Day of November, 1777.

My Lords and Gentlemen,

IT is a great satisfaction to me, that I can have recourse to the wisdom and support of my parliament, in this conjuncture, when the continuance of the rebellion in North America demands our most serious attention. The powers, which you have intrusted me with for the suppression of this revolt, have been faithfully exerted; and I have a just confidence, that the conduct and courage of my officers, and the spirit and intrepidity of my forces, both by sea and land, will, under the blessing of divine providence, be attended with important success: but as I am persuaded, that you will see the necessity of preparing for such further operations, as the contingencies of the war, and the obstinacy of the rebels may render expedient, I am, for that purpose, pursuing the proper measures for keeping my land forces compleat to their present establishment; and if I should have occasion to increase them, by contracting any new engagements, I rely on your zeal and publick spirit to enable me to make them good.

I receive repeated assurances from foreign powers of their pacifick dispositions. My own cannot be doubted: but, at this time, when the armaments in the ports of France and Spain continue, I have thought it advisable to make a considerable augmentation to my naval force, as well to keep my kingdoms in a respectable state of security, as to provide an adequate protection for the extensive commerce of my subjects; and as, on the one hand, I am determined that the peace of Europe shall not be disturbed by me, so, on the other, I will always be a faithful guardian of the honour of the crown of Great Britain.

Gentlemen of the House of Commons,

I have ordered the estimates for the ensuing year to be laid before you. The various services which I have mentioned to you will unavoidably require large supplies: and nothing could relieve my mind from the concern which I feel for the heavy charge which they must bring on my faithful people, but the perfect conviction that they are necessary for the welfare and the essential interests of my kingdoms.

My Lords and Gentlemen,

I will steadily pursue the measures in which we are engaged for the re-establishment of that constitutional subordination, which, with the blessing of God, I will maintain through the several parts of my dominions: but I shall ever be watchful for an opportunity of putting a ftop to the effufion of the blood of my fubjects, and the calamities which are infeparable from a ftate of war. And I ftill hope, that the deluded and unhappy multitude will return to their allegiance; and that the remembrance of what they once enjoyed, the regret for what they have loft, and the feelings of what they now fuffer under the arbitrary tyranny of their leaders, will rekindle in their hearts a fpirit of loyalty to their Sovereign, and of attachment to their mother country; and that they will enable me, with the concurrence and fupport of my parliament, to accomplifh, what I fhall confider as the greateft happinefs of my life, and the greateft glory of my reign, the reftoration of peace, order and confidence to my American colonies.

The humble Addrefs of the Lords Spiritual and Temporal in Parliament affembled.

Moft gracious Sovereign,

WE, your Majefty's moft dutiful and loyal fubjects, the Lords Spiritual and Temporal, in parliament affembled, beg leave to return your Majefty our humble thanks for your moft gracious fpeech from the throne.

Permit us, Sir, to offer our congratulations to your Majefty on the increafe of your domeftic happinefs by the birth of another Princefs, and the recovery of your royal confort; who is moft highly endeared to this nation, as well by her Majefty's eminent and amiable virtues, as by every new pledge of fecurity to our religious and civil liberties.

We are duly fenfible of your Majefty's goodnefs in recurring to the advice and fupport of your parliament in the prefent conjuncture, when the rebellion in North America ftill continues; and we

return your Majefty our unfeigned thanks for having communicated to us the juft confidence which your Majefty repofes in the zeal, intrepidity, and exertions of your Majefty's officers and forces both by fea and land : but at the fame time that we entertain a well-founded hope of the important fucceffes, which, under the bleffing of providence, may be expected, we cannot but applaud your Majefty's unwearied vigilance and wifdom in recommending to us to prepare, at all events, for fuch further operations as the contingencies of the war and the obftinacy of the rebels may render expedient : we are therefore gratefully fenfible of your Majefty's confideration in purfuing the meafures neceffary to keep your land forces complete to the prefent eftablifhment; and we owe it both to your Majefty and to ourfelves to fay, that we fhall chearfully concur in enabling your Majefty to make good fuch new engagements with foreign powers, for the augmentation of the auxiliary troops, as the weighty motives your Majefty has ftated to us may induce you to contract.

It is with great fatisfaction we learn that your Majefty receives repeated affurances from foreign powers of their pacific difpofitions; and with hearts full of gratitude and admiration, we acknowledge your Majefty's humane, fteady, and dignified conduct, which is equally well calculated to demonftrate to the world, your Majefty's wifh to preferve the general tranquillity of Europe, and your determination to maintain the honour of the crown, the fecurity of thefe kingdoms, and the commercial interefts of your fubjects.

We thankfully receive your Majefty's declaration of perfeverance in the meafures now purfuing, for the re-eftablifhment of a juft and conftitutional fubordination through the feveral parts of your Majefty's dominions; and we beg

leave to affure your Majefty, that we participate the defire which at the fame time animates your royal breaft, to fee a proper opportunity for putting an end to the effufion of blood, and the various calamities infeparable from a ftate of war.

The conftant tenor of your Majefty's reign has fhewn, that your whole attention is employed for the fafety and happinefs of all your people; and whenever our unhappy fellow-fubjects in North America fhall duly return to their allegiance, we fhall readily concur in every wife and falutary meafure which can contribute to reftore confidence and order, and fix the mutual welfare of Great Britain and her colonies on the moft folid and permanent foundations.

PROTEST *of the* LORDS.

Die Jovis, 20° *Nov.* 1778.

UPON the motion for the above addrefs, the following amendment was moved by the Earl of Chatham, " That this Houfe does moft humbly advife and fupplicate his Majefty, to be pleafed to caufe the moft fpeedy and effectual meafures to be taken for reftoring peace in America, and that no time may be loft, in propofing an immediate ceffation of hoftilities there, in order to the opening a treaty for the final fettlement of the tranquillity of thofe invaluable provinces, by a removal of the unhappy caufes of this ruinous civil war, and by a juft and adequate fecurity againft a return of the like calamities in times to come. And this Houfe defires to offer the moft dutiful affurance to his Majefty, that they will in due time cheerfully co-operate with the magnanimity and tender goodnefs of his Majefty, for the prefervation of his people, by fuch explicit and moft folemn declarations and provifions of fundamental and irrevocable laws, as may be judged neceffary for afcertaining and fixing for ever the refpective rights of Great Britain and her colonies."

When the queftion being put, the Houfe divided. Contents 28. Non-contents 84.

The queftion was then put on the addrefs, and carried in the affirmative.

" Diffentient,

" Becaufe this addrefs is a repetition of, or rather an improvement on, the fulfome adulation offered, and of the blind engagements entered into on former occafions by this Houfe, relative to this unhappy civil war."

EFFINGHAM.
RICHMOND.

The humble Addrefs of the Houfe of Commons to the King.

Moft gracious Sovereign,

WE, your Majefty's moft dutiful and loyal fubjects, the Commons of Great Britain in parliament affembled, beg leave to return your Majefty the humble thanks of this Houfe, for your moft gracious fpeech from the throne.

Deeply interefted in every event which tends to increafe your Majefty's domeftic felicity, and impreffed with the livelieft fentiments of duty and attachment to the Queen; we beg leave to offer to your Majefty our congratulations on the birth of another Princefs, and on her Majefty's happy recovery.

We affure your Majefty, that we take a fincere part in the confidence which your Majefty expreffes, that the conduct and courage of your officers, and the fpirit and intrepidity of your forces both by fea and land, will, under the divine providence, be attended with important fuccefs. But at the fame time we entirely concur with your Majefty in thinking,

that it is neceffary to prepare for fuch further operations as future events, and the contingencies of the war, may render expedient. And we learn with much fatisfaction, that your Majefty is for that purpofe purfuing the proper meafures for keeping your land forces compleat to their prefent eftablifhment. And whenever your Majefty fhall be pleafed to communicate to us any new engagements, which you may have entered into for increafing your military force, we will take the fame into our confideration. And we truft your Majefty will not be difappointed in the gracious fentiments which you entertain of the zeal and public fpirit of your faithful Commons.

We are truly fenfible, that your Majefty's conftant care for the welfare of your people, and your generous concern for the happinefs of mankind, difpofe your Majefty to defire, that the peace of Europe may not be difturbed: but we acknowledge with equal gratitude your Majefty's attention to the fecurity of your kingdoms, and the protection of the extenfive commerce of your fubjects, in having made a confiderable augmentation to your naval force, on which the reputation and importance of this nation muft ever principally depend. And we hear with the higheft fatisfaction, and rely with perfect confidence on your royal declaration, that your Majefty will always be the faithful guardian of the honour of the Britifh crown.

We beg leave to affure your Majefty, that we will without delay enter into the confideration of the fupplies for the enfuing year; and that we will chearfully and effectually provide for all fuch expences as fhall be found neceffary for the welfare and effential interefts of thefe kingdoms, and for the vigorous profecution of the meafures in which we are engaged, for the re-eftablifhment of that conftitutional fubordination, which

we truft, with the bleffing of God, your Majefty will be able to maintain through the feveral parts of your dominions.

We acknowledge with equal gratitude and admiration your Majefty's paternal declaration, that you will be ever watchful for an opportunity of putting a ftop to the effufion of the blood of your fubjects, and the calamities of war.

Permit us to affure your Majefty, that we cannot but ftill entertain a hope, that the difcernment of their true interefts, the remembrance of the bleffings they once enjoyed, and the fenfe of their prefent fufferings under the arbitrary tyranny of their leaders, will induce the deluded and unhappy multitude to return to their allegiance, and will reanimate their hearts with a fpirit of loyalty to their Sovereign, and of attachment to their mother country.

The gracious and condefcending manner in which your Majefty expreffes your defire, that you may be enabled to reftore peace, order, and confidence, to your American colonies, cannot fail of endearing your Majefty to the hearts of all your fubjects: and we affure your Majefty, that when this great work can be accomplifhed, and fettled on the true principles of the conftitution, your Majefty may depend on the moft zealous concurrence and fupport of your faithful Commons.

On Tuesday the 17th day of March, the following Meffage was fent to both Houfes of Parliament from the King.

GEORGE R.

HIS Majefty, having been informed, by order of the French King, that a treaty of amity and commerce has been figned between the court of France, and certain perfons employed by his Majefty's revolted fubjects in North America, has judged it neceffary to direct, that a copy of the declaration, delivered by the French ambassador to Lord Viscount Weymouth, be laid before the House of Commons; and at the same time to acquaint them, that his Majesty has thought proper, in consequence of this offensive communication on the part of the court of France, to send orders to his ambassador to withdraw from that court.

His Majesty is persuaded, that the justice and good faith of his conduct towards foreign powers, and the sincerity of his wishes to preserve the tranquillity of Europe, will be acknowledged by all the world; and his Majesty trusts, that he shall not stand responsible for the disturbance of that tranquillity, if he should find himself called upon to resent so unprovoked and so unjust an aggression on the honour of his crown, and the essential interests of his kingdoms, contrary to the most solemn assurances, subversive of the law of nations, and injurious to the rights of every sovereign power in Europe. His Majesty, relying with the firmest confidence on the zealous and affectionate support of his faithful people, is determined to be prepared to exert, if it shall become necessary, all the force and resources of his kingdoms; which he trusts will be found adequate to repel every insult and attack, and to maintain and uphold the power and reputation of this country.

G. R.

The Declaration mentioned in the Message was as follows.

' THE under-signed Ambassador of his Most Christian Majesty has received express orders to make the following declaration to the court of London:

' The United States of North-America, who are in full possession of independence, as pronounced by them on the 4th of July, 1776, having proposed to the King to consolidate, by a formal convention, the connection begun to be established between the two nations, the respective Plenipotentiaries have signed a treaty of friendship and commerce, designed to serve as a foundation for their mutual good correspondence.

' His Majesty, being determined to cultivate the good understanding subsisting between France and Great Britain, by every means compatible with his dignity, and the good of his subjects, thinks it necessary to make his proceeding known to the court of London, and to declare at the same time, that the contracting parties have paid great attention not to stipulate any exclusive advantages in favour of the French nation; and that the United States have reserved the liberty of treating with every nation whatever, upon the same footing of equality and reciprocity.

' In making this communication to the court of London, the King is firmly persuaded it will find new proofs of his Majesty's constant and sincere disposition for peace; and that his Britannic Majesty, animated by the same sentiments, will equally avoid every thing that may alter their good harmony; and that he will particularly take effectual measures to prevent the commerce between his Majesty's subjects and the United States of North-America from being interrupted, and to cause all the usages received between commercial nations to be, in this respect, observed, and all those rules which can be said to subsist between the two crowns of France and Great Britain.

' In this just confidence, the undersigned Ambassador thinks it superfluous to acquaint the British Minister, that, the King his master being determined to protect effectually the lawful commerce of his subjects, and to maintain the dignity of his flag, his Majesty has, in consequence, taken eventual measures in concert with the United States of North-America.

Signed,

Le M. De Noailles.'

London, March 13, 1778.

Humble Address of the Lords Spiritual and Temporal in Parliament assembled.

Most gracious Sovereign,

WE, your Majesty's most dutiful and loyal subjects, the Lords Spiritual and Temporal, in parliament assembled, return our humble thanks to your Majesty for the communication of the paper presented to the Lord Viscount Weymouth by the order of the French King, and for acquainting us, that in consequence of this offensive declaration, your Majesty has thought proper to order your Ambassador to withdraw from the court of France. And we beg leave to assure your Majesty, that it is with the utmost difficulty we can restrain the strongest expressions of the resentment and indignation which we feel for this unjust and unprovoked aggression on the honour of your Majesty's crown, and the essential interests of your kingdoms, contrary to the law of nations, and injurious to the rights and possessions of every sovereign power in Europe.

The good faith and uprightness of your Majesty's conduct towards foreign powers, and the sincerity of your intentions to preserve the general tranquillity, must be acknowledged by all the world; and your Majesty cannot be considered as responsible for the disturbance of this tranquillity, if you should find yourself called upon to resist the enterprises of that restless and dangerous spirit of ambition and aggrandisement, which has so often invaded the rights and threatened the liberties of Europe.

We should be wanting in our duty to your Majesty and to ourfelves, if we did not give your Majefty the ftrongeft affurances of our moft zealous affiftance and fupport. Every fentiment of loyalty to your Majefty, and of love to our country, will animate us to ftand forth in the public defence, and to promote every meafure that fhall be found neceffary for enabling your Majefty to vindicate the honour of your crown, and to protect the juft rights and effential interefts of thefe kingdoms.

An addrefs in the fame terms, was prefented by the Commons.

PROTEST of the LORDS.

Die Lunæ, Dec. 7, 1778.

Moved,

THAT an humble addrefs be prefented his Majefty, to exprefs to his Majefty the difpleafure of this Houfe at a certain manifefto and proclamation, dated the third day of October, 1778, and publifhed in America under the hands and feals of the Earl of Carlifle, Sir Henry Clinton, Knight of the Bath, and William Eden, Efq. Commiffioners for reftoring peace to the colonies, and counterfigned by Adam Ferguson, Efq. Secretary to the commiffion ; the faid manifefto containing a declaration of the following tenour:

' If there be any perfons, who, divefted of miftaken refentments, and uninfluenced by felfifh interefts, really think it is for the benefit of the colonies to feparate themfelves from Great Britain, and that fo feparated they will find a conftitution more mild, more free, and better calculated for their profperity, than that which they heretofore enjoyed, and which we are empowered and difpofed to renew and improve ; with fuch perfons we will not difpute a pofition which feems to be fufficiently contradicted by the experience they have had. But we think it right to leave

them fully aware of the change which the maintaining fuch a pofition muft make in the whole nature and future conduct of this war, more efpecially when to this pofition is added the pretended alliance with the court of France. The policy, as well as the benevolence of Great Britain, have thus far checked the extremes of war, when they tended to diftrefs a people, ftill confidered as our fellowfubjects, and to defolate a country, fhortly to become again a fource of mutual advantage ; but, when that country profeffes the unnatural defign, not only of eftranging herfelf from us, but of mortgaging herfelf, and her refources, to our enemies, the whole conteft is changed, and the queftion is, how far Great Britain may, by every means in her power, deftroy or render ufelefs a connection contrived for her ruin, and for the aggrandifement of France. Under fuch circumftances, the laws of felf-prefervation muft direct the conduct of Great Britain ; and, if the Britifh colonies are to become an acceffion to France, will direct her to render that acceffion of as little avail as poffible to her enemies.'

To acquaint his Majefty with the fenfe of this Houfe, that the faid Commiffioners had no authority whatfoever, under the act of parliament in virtue of which they were appointed by his Majefty, to make the faid declaration, or to make any declaration to the fame, or to the like purport ; nor can this Houfe be eafily brought to believe that the faid Commiffioners derived any fuch authority from his Majefty's inftructions.

Humbly to befeech his Majefty, that fo much of the faid manifefto as contains the faid declaration be forthwith publicly difavowed by his Majefty, as containing matter inconfiftent with the humanity and generous courage which, at all times, have diftinguifhed the Britifh nation, fubverfive of the max-

ims which have been eftablifhed among chriftian and civilifed communities, derogatory to the dignity of the crown of this realm, tending to debafe the fpirit and fubvert the difcipline of his Majefty's armies, and to expofe his Majefty's innocent fubjects, in all parts of his dominions, to cruel and ruinous retaliations.

Which being objected to, after long debate, the queftion was put thereon,

It was refolved in the negative.

Contents	34	} 37
Proxies	3	
Non-contents	55	} 71
Proxies	16	

Diffentient,

1ft. Becaufe the public law of nations, in affirmance of the dictates of nature and the precepts of revealed religion, forbids us to refort to the extremes of war upon our own opinion of their expediency, or in any cafe to carry on war for the purpofe of defolation. We know that the rights of war are odious, and, inftead of being extended upon loofe conftructions and fpeculations of danger, ought to be bound up and limited by all the reftraints of the moft rigorous conftruction. We are fhocked to fee the firft law of nature, felf-prefervation, perverted and abufed into a principle deftructive of all other laws ; and a rule laid down, by which our own fafety is rendered incompatible with the profperity of mankind. Thofe objects of war, which cannot be compaffed by fair and honourable hoftility, ought not to be compaffed at all. An end that has no means, but fuch as are unlawful, is an unlawful end. The manifefto exprefsly founds the change it announces from a qualified and mitigated war to a war of extremity and defolation, on the certainty that the provinces muft be independent, and muft become an acceffion to the ftrength of an enemy. In the midft of the calamities, by which our loss of empire has been preceded and accompanied; in the midst of our apprehensions for the farther calamities which impend over us, it is a matter of fresh grief and accumulated shame to see, from a commission under the great seal of this kingdom, a declaration for desolating a vast continent, solely because we had not the wisdom to retain, or the power to subdue it.

2dly. Because the avowal of a deliberate purpose of violating the law of nations must give an alarm to every state in Europe. All commonwealths have a concern in that law, and are its natural avengers. At this time, surrounded by enemies and destitute of all allies, it is not necessary to sharpen and embitter the hostility of declared foes, or to provoke the enmity of neutral states. We trust that by the natural strength of this kingdom we are secured from a foreign conquest, but no nation is secured from the invasion and incursions of enemies. And it seems to us to the height of frenzy, as well as wickedness, to expose this country to cruel depredations, and other outrages too shocking to mention (but which are all contained in the idea of the extremes of war and desolation) by establishing a false, shameful, and pernicious maxim, that, where we have no interest to preserve, we are called upon by necessity to destroy. This kingdom has long enjoyed a profound internal peace, and has flourished above all others in the arts and enjoyments of that happy state. It has been the admiration of the world for its cultivation and its plenty; for the comforts of the poor, the splendor of the rich, and the content and prosperity of all. This situation of safety may be attributed to the greatness of our power. It is more becoming, and more true, that we ought to attribute that safety, and the power which procured it, to the ancient justice, honour, huma-

nity, and generosity of this kingdom, which brought down the blessing of providence on a people who made their prosperity a benefit to the world, and interested all nations in their fortune, whose example of mildness and benignity at once humanised others, and rendered itself inviolable. In departing from those solid principles, and vainly trusting to the fragility of human force, and to the efficacy of arms, rendered impotent by their perversion, we lay down principles, and furnish examples of the most atrocious barbarity. We are to dread that all our power, peace, and opulence, should vanish like a dream, and that the cruelties which we think safe to exercise, because their immediate object is remote, may be brought to the coasts, perhaps to the bosom of this kingdom.

3dly. Because, if the explanation given in debate be expressive of the true sense of the article in the manifesto, such explanation ought to be made, and by as high authority as that under which the exceptionable article was originally published. The natural and obvious sense indicates, that the extremes of war had hitherto been checked: that his Majesty's Generals had hitherto forborne (upon principles of benignity and policy) to desolate the country: but that the whole nature, and future conduct of the war, must be changed, in order to render the American accession of as little avail to France as possible. This, in our apprehensions, conveys a menace of carrying the war to extremes, and to desolation; or it means nothing. And, as some speeches in the House (however palliated) and as some acts of singular cruelty, and perfectly conformable to the apparent ideas in the manifesto, have lately been exercised, it becomes the more necessary, for the honour and safety of this nation, that this explanation should be made. As it is refused, we have only to

clear ourselves to our consciences, to our country, to our neighbours, and to every individual who may suffer in consequence of this atrocious menace, of all part in the guilt, or in the evils that may become its punishment. And we chuse to draw ourselves out, and to distinguish ourselves to posterity, as not being the first to renew, to approve, or to tolerate the return of that ferocity and barbarism in war, which a beneficent religion, enlightened manners, and true military honour, had for a long time banished from the Christian world.

Camden,	Rockingham,
Abingdon,	Tankerville,
Fitzwilliam,	Ponsonby,
Fortescue,	Derby,
Grafton,	Manchester,
Craven,	Portland,
J. St. Asaph,	Beaulieu,
Richmond,	Harcourt,
Bolton,	Effingham,
Radnor,	Wycombe,
Egremont,	Scarborough,
Abergavenny,	Cholmondeley,
Coventry,	Devonshire,
De Ferrars,	Foley,
Ferrars,	Spencer.
Stanhope,	

• • •

Commons of the City of London, *in Common Council assembled. (Presented March* 13, 1778.)

Most gracious Sovereign,

WE your Majesty's most dutiful and loyal subjects, the Lord Mayor, Aldermen, and Commons of the city of London, in common council assembled, attached to your Majesty's royal house by principle, to your person by the truest affection, and to the honour and prosperity of your government by every interest, which can be dear to the heart of man; in this present deplorable state of the affairs of this once great and flourishing country, with most profound humility implore leave to lay ourselves at your Majesty's feet, to reprefent to your Majefty the fentiments and wifhes of a faithful and afflicted people.

When this civil war was firft threatened, your loyal city of London, in concurrence with the fenfe of many other refpectable public bodies of your kingdom, and many of the wifeft and beft of your fubjects, did moft humbly deprecate this evil, forboding but too truly the charges, calamities, and difgraces of which it has been hitherto productive, and the greater to which it is ftill likely to fubject this kingdom.

Your faithful people, on that occafion, had the misfortune to receive from your Majefty an anfwer more fuitable to the imperfect manner in which (they fear) they expreffed fentiments full of duty, than to your Majefty's own moft gracious difpofition, their inviolable reverence to their Sovereign, and their unfhaken zeal for his true glory. They retired in a mournful and refpectful filence, patiently awaiting the difpofition of providence, and the return of your Majefty's favour and countenance, whenever experience fhould fully difclofe, in its true light, the well-founded nature of their apprehenfions, and the fatal tendency of thofe counfels by which the nation has been mifled.

For mifled and deceived your Majefty, and many of your fubjects, have been. No pains have been omitted to hide from both the true nature of the bufinefs in which we are engaged; no arts have been left untried to ftimulate the paffions of your fubjects in this kingdom; and we are confident that infinitely more fkill and attention have been ufed to engage us in this war, than have been employed to conduct it to honour or advantage, if honour or advantage could be obtained by any conduct in fuch a war. We have been induftrioufly taught to fufpect the profeffions and to defpife the refiftance of our brethren, (Eng-

lifhmen like ourfelves) whom we had no fort of reafon to think deficient in the fincerity and courage which have ever diftinguifhed that name and race. Their inclinations have been mifreprefented, their natural faculties depreciated, their refources mifcalculated, their feelings infulted, until fury and defpair fupplied whatever might be defective in force. We have feen a whole army, the flower of the trained military ftrength of Great Britain and her allies, famifhing in the wildernefs of America, laying down their arms, and owing their immediate refcue from death to thofe very men whom the murders and rapines of the favages (unhappily employed) had forced from hufbandmen into foldiers, and who had been painted in fuch colours of contempt as to take away all confolation from our calamity.

We have feen another army, equally brave, and equally well commanded, for two years in an almoft continued courfe of victory, by which they have only wafted their own numbers, without decreafing the ftrength of the refifting power, without leading to any fort of fubmiffion, or bringing to your Majefty's obedience even the fmalleft and weakeft of thirteen revolted provinces. The union of thofe provinces amongft themfelves, and their animofity to your Majefty's adminiftration, have only been increafed by the injudicious methods taken to break the one, and to fubdue the other. Fleets and armies are maintained in numbers almoft equal, and at an expence comparatively far fuperior, to whatever has been employed in the moft glorious and fuccefsful ftruggles of this country againft a combination of the moft ancient and formidable monarchies of Europe. A few inconfiderable detached iflands, and one deferted town on the continent, where your Majefty's combined army has a perilous and infecure footing, are the

only fruits of an expence exceeding twenty millions, of ninety-three fhips of war, and fixty thoufand of the beft foldiers which could be procured either at home or abroad, and appointed for that fpecial fervice. Your Majefty's forces, both by fea and land, have (we are told) done all that could be expected from the moft accomplifhed difcipline, and the moft determined courage; and yet the total defeat of fome of thefe forces, and the ineffectual victories of others, have almoft equally confpired to the deftruction of your power, and the difmemberment of your empire. We fhould be unpardonably negligent of our duty to your Majefty, to ourfelves, and to our country, if we did not thus folemnly exprefs our feelings upon this dreadful and decifive proof of the madnefs with which this attempt was originally made, and which, faithfully following it thro' every ftep of its progrefs, and every meafure for its execution, has completed, by uniform mifconduct, the mifchiefs which were commenced in total ignorance. We are convinced that not the delufions of artful and defigning men, (which, like every thing falfe, cannot be permanent,) but the general fenfe of the whole American people is fet and determined againft the plans of coercion, civil and military, which have been hitherto employed againft them; a whole, united, and irritated people cannot be conquered. If the force now employed cannot do it, no force within our abilities will do it.

The wealth of this nation is great, and our difpofition would be to pour it out with the moft unreferved and chearful liberality, for the fupport of the honour and dignity of your crown: but domeftic peace and domeftic œconomy are the only means of fupplying expence for war abroad: in this conteft our refources are exhaufted, whilft thofe of our rivals are spared, and we are, every year of the continuance of this war, altering the balance of our public strength and riches in their favour.

We think ourselves bound, most dread sovereign, to express our fears and apprehensions to your Majesty, that at a time when your Majesty's gracious speech from the throne has hinted, and your vast naval preparations in a style much more explicit announce to us and the world, the critical state in which we stand with regard to the great neighbouring powers, we have not the comfort to learn, from that speech, from any assurance of your Majesty's servants, or even from common fame, that any alliance whatever has been made with the other great states of Europe, in order to cover us from the complicated perils so manifestly imminent over this nation. We have as little reason to be certain that alliances of the most dangerous kind are not formed against us.

In this state of anxious doubt and danger, we have recourse to the clemency and wisdom of your Majesty; the tender parent and vigilant guardian of your people, that you will graciously take such measures as may restore internal peace, and (as far as the miserable circumstances into which the late destructive courses have brought us will permit) reunite the British nation, in some happy, honourable, and permanent conjunction; lest the colonies, exasperated by rigours of continued war, should become totally alienated from their parent country; lest every remaining spark of their affection should be extinguished in habits of mutual slaughter and rapine; and lest in some evil hour, they who have hitherto been the great support of the British strength, should become the most formidable and lasting accession to the constant enemies of the power and prosperity of your kingdoms.

We humbly hope and trust, that your Majesty will give all due efficacy to the concessions (we wish those concessions may not have come too late) which have been proposed in parliament; and we have that undoubted reliance on the magnanimity of your Majesty's enlarged and kingly affections, that we are under no apprehensions of your Majesty being biassed by private partiality to any set of men, in a case where the good, where the very being of your people is at stake; and with an humble confidence we implore and supplicate your Majesty, that nothing may stand in the way of those arrangements, in your councils and executive offices, which may best forward the great, necessary, and blessed work of peace, and which may tend to rescue your affairs from unwise and improvident management, and which may obtain, improve, and secure the returning confidence of all your people. In such measures and such arrangements, and for such an end, your citizens of London will never fail to give your Majesty their most affectionate and steady support.

To which his Majesty was graciously pleased to answer,

" I can never think that the zeal of my subjects, the resources of my kingdoms, and the bravery of my fleets and armies, can have been unwisely and improvidently exerted, when the object was to maintain the constitutional subordination which ought to prevail through the several parts of my dominions, and is essential to the prosperity of the whole: but I have always lamented the calamities inseparable from a state of war; and shall most earnestly give all the efficacy in my power to those measures which the legislature has adopted for the purpose of restoring, by some happy, honourable, and permanent conciliation, the blessings of peace, commerce, affection, and confidence between the mother country and the colonies."

• • •

Copy of the Petition of the West India Planters and Merchants, presented to the King, Dec. 16, 1778.

To the King's most excellent Majesty.

The humble Address and Petition of the Planters and Proprietors in your Majesty's Sugar Colonies, and of the Merchants trading to, and connected with the said Colonies, whose Names are hereunto subscribed, in behalf of themselves and others interested therein.

Most gracious Sovereign,

"WE your Majesty's most dutiful and loyal subjects, the planters and proprietors in your Majesty's sugar colonies, and the merchants trading to, and connected with the said colonies, whose names are hereunto subscribed, in behalf of ourselves and others interested therein, humbly approach your royal presence, with all assurances of fidelity to your person and government; and, with the utmost humility, represent to your Majesty:

That, on the commencement of the unhappy divisions between this kingdom and the colonies in North America, your petitioners, impressed with a proper sense of duty to your Majesty, and of the circumstances of their situation, did represent to your Majesty's ministers their apprehensions of the dangers and distresses to which the sugar islands were necessarily exposed.

That the fatal consequences, thus apprehended by your petitioners, have been in a great measure unhappily experienced during the three last years, by a general scarcity of provisions in all the islands, in some of them nearly approaching to famine, and by a want of almost every article essential to the culture of their plantations; so that their estates and property have

been confiderably impaired in value, and continue expofed to further diminution; whilft their effects
have been captured on the high
feas to a very great amount.

That, although your petitioners
had early and anxioufly reprefented
to your Majefty's minifters the neceffity of an adequate protection for
the iflands, they have now to lament, from the lofs of Dominica,
and the imminent danger of the
other iflands, that the frequent applications which they have made
for protection have not had their
defired effect.

That your petitioners are now
in the moft anxious ftate of fuf-
pence, from the delay of the fuccours fent from New-York to the
Leeward Iflands, which have been
fo unfeasonably afforded, as to
leave all thofe iflands expofed to
the further hoftile attempts of the
enemy. And, though the affurances of protection, given to your
petitioners by one of your Majefty's minifters, in fome meafure
tend to remove their immediate
apprehenfions, yet they appear too
general and precarious, to quiet
their minds, as to the future fafety
of the Leeward Iflands;—whilft
the important ifland of Jamaica
has been almoft left to its own efforts; which, from the comparatively fmall number of white inhabitants, are become particularly
fevere, and, joined to the fufpenfion of culture, neceffarily confequent on military duty, muft, in
time, prove ruinous: a naval force
being the firft and principal fecurity of the iflands in general.

Labouring under the weight of
thefe calamities, your petitioners
cannot avoid further humbly expreffing to your Majefty their melancholy apprehenfions, left the
defolating fyftem which appears to
them to have lately been denounced by your Majefty's Commiffioners,
in North-America, may be productive of confequences to your petitioners, at prefent not fully forefeen, nor fufficiently attended to,
by your Majefty's fervants.

Your petitioners would wifh,
Sire, to fupprefs thofe emotions,
which the calamities of war, thus
aggravated by indifcriminate and
unbounded defolation, muft naturally create in their minds; and,
confining themfelves to the immediate object of their own prefervation, they humbly fubmit to
your Majefty's wifdom, that the
late declaration of your Majefty's
Commiffioners, if carried into effect, may provoke the fevereft retaliation from an irritated people,
intimately acquainted with the fituation of the iflands, their weak
and acceffible parts: and that the
ravages, which may be committed, even by a fmall force, may
be fufficient to reduce any ifland
to fo wafte a condition, as not to
admit of its being reftored to its
former ftate, without an enormous
expence and the labour of years.

Moft gracious Sovereign,
We feel ourfelves indifpenfably called upon to lay this reprefentation before your Majefty, the
conftitutional guardian of the property of all your fubjects: that we
may not appear to have neglected
our duty, by omitting to apprize
your Majefty of thefe important
and melancholy truths.

Thus circumftanced, we reft our
prefent fecurity on your Majefty's
parental care of the interefts of
your fubjects at large, for a fufficient protection againft the dangers that threaten the property of
your petitioners, in the Weft-India
iflands: and we humbly pray, your
Majefty will be gracioufly pleafed
to take into your royal confideration the unavoidable refult of thefe
calamities, which we apprehend
muft extend themfelves to your
Majefty's revenue, to your maritime power, and to the manufactures, commerce, and wealth of
your fubjects in general.

. . .

*Copy of the Commiffion granted by
his Majefty to the Right Hon. Frederick Earl of Carlifle, the Right
Hon. Richard Lord Vifcount Howe,
Sir William Howe, William
Eden, Efq. and George Johnftone, Efq. for the quieting and
extinguifhing of divers Jealoufies
and Apprehenfions of Danger in the
Americans.*

George the Third, by the grace of
God, of Great Britain, France,
and Ireland, King, Defender of
the Faith, &c.
To our trufty and right well beloved Coufin and Counfellor Frederick Earl of Carlifle, Knight
of the moft ancient Order of the
Thiftle; our right trufty and
well beloved Coufin and Counfellor, Richard Lord Vifcount
Howe, of our kingdom of Ireland; our trufty and well beloved Sir William Howe, Knight
of the moft Honourable Order
of the Bath, Lieutenant-General of our forces, General and
Commander in Chief of all and
fingular our forces employed, or
to be employed, within our Colonies in North America, lying
upon the Atlantic Ocean, from
Nova Scotia on the North to
Weft Florida on the South, both
inclufive; William Eden, Efq.
one of our Commiffioners for
Trade and Plantations; and
George Johnftone, Efq. Captain
in our royal navy.

Greeting:
WHEREAS, in and by our
commiffion and letters patent under our Great Seal of Great
Britain, bearing date on or about
the 6th day of May, in the 16th
year of our reign, we did, out of an
earneft defire to deliver all our fubjects and every part of the dominions belonging to our crown from
the calamities of war, and to reftore them to our protection and
peace, nominate and appoint our
right trufty and well beloved coufin and counfellor Richard Lord

Viscount Howe, of our kingdom of Ireland, and our trusty and well beloved William Howe, Esq. now Sir William Howe, Knight of of the Bath, Lieutenant-General of our forces in North America only, and each of them jointly and severely, to be our Commissioner and Commissioners on that behalf, to so perform and execute all the powers and authorities in and by the said commission and letters patent entrusted and committed to them, and each of them, according to the tenor of such letters patent, and of such further instructions as they should from time to time receive under our signet or sign manual, to have, hold, execute, and enjoy the said office and place, offices and places of our Commissioner and Commissioners as therein mentioned, with all rights, members, and appurtenances thereunto belonging, together with all and singular the powers and authorities thereby granted unto them, the said Lord Viscount Howe, and General Sir William Howe, and each of them, for and during our will and pleasure, and no longer, in such manner and form, as in and by our said recited commission and letters patent, relation being thereunto had, may, among divers other things therein contained, more fully, and at large appear. And whereas for the quieting and extinguishing of divers jealousies and apprehensions of danger to their liberties and rights, which have alarmed many of our subjects in the Colonies, Provinces, and Plantations of New-Hampshire, Massachusetts Bay, Rhode-Island, Connecticut, New-York, New-Jersey, Pennsylvania, with the three Lower Counties on Delaware, Maryland, Virginia, North-Carolina, South-Carolina, and Georgia, and for a fuller manifestation of our just and gracious purposes, and those of our parliament, to maintain and secure all our subjects in the clear and perfect enjoyment of their liberties, and rights, it is in and by a certain act made and passed in this present sessions of parliament, intitled, " An Act to enable his Majesty to appoint Commissioners, with sufficient powers to treat, consult, and agree upon the means of quieting the disorders now subsisting in certain of the Colonies, Plantations, and Provinces in North America," among other things enacted, that it shall and may be lawful for his Majesty, from time to time, by letters patent under the Great Seal of Great Britain, to authorize and empower five able and sufficient persons, or any three of them, to do and perform such acts and things, and to use and execute such authorities and powers as in the said act are for that purpose mentioned, provided, and created. And whereas we are earnestly desirous to carry into full and perfect execution the several just and gracious purposes abovementioned : Now know ye, that we have revoked and determined, and by these presents do revoke and determine our said recited commission and letters patent, and all and every power, authority, clause, article, and thing therein contained. And further know ye, that we, reposing especial trust and confidence in your wisdom, loyalty, diligence and circumspection in the management of the affairs to be hereby committed to your charge, have nominated and appointed, constituted and assigned, and by these presents we do nominate, appoint, constitute and assign you, the said Frederick Earl of Carlisle, Richard Viscount Howe, Sir William Howe, William Howe, William Eden, and George Johnstone, or any three of you, to be our Commissioners in that behalf, to use and exercise all and every the powers and authorities hereby entrusted and committed to you, the said Frederick Earl of Carlisle, Richard Viscount Howe, Sir William Howe, William Eden, George Johnstone, or any three of you, and to so perform and execute all other matters and things hereby enjoined and committed to your care, during our will and pleasure, and no longer, according to the tenor of these our letters patent, and of such further instructions as you shall from time to time receive under our signet or sign manual. And it is our royal will and pleasure, and we do hereby authorise, empower, and require you, the said Frederick Earl of Carlisle, Richard Viscount Howe, Sir William Howe, William Eden, George Johnstone, or any three of you, to treat, consult and agree with such body or bodies politic and corporate, or with such assembly or assemblies of men, or with such person or persons as you, the said Frederick Earl of Carlisle, Richard Viscount Howe, Sir William Howe, William Eden, George Johnstone, or any three of you shall think meet and sufficient for that purpose, of and concerning any grievances, or complaints of grievances, existing, or supposed to exist, in the government of any of the Colonies, Provinces or Plantations abovementioned respectively, or in the laws and statutes of this realm, respecting them or any of them, or of and concerning any aids or contributions to be furnished by any of the said Colonies, Provinces, or Plantations respectively, for the common defence of this realm, and the dominions thereunto belonging; and of and concerning any other regulations, provisions, matters and things, necessary or convenient for the honour of us and our parliament, and for the common good of all our subjects. And it is our further will and pleasure, That every regulation, provision, matter, or thing, which shall have been agreed upon between you, the said Frederick Earl of Carlisle, Richard Viscount Howe, Sir William Howe, William Eden, George Johnstone, or any three of you, and such persons or bodies politic as aforesaid, whom you or any three of you have judged meet and sufficient to enter into such agreement, shall be fully and distinctly set forth in writing, and authenticated by the hands and seals of you or any three of you on one side, and by such seals and other signature on the other as the occasion may require, and as may be suitable to the character and authority of the body politic or other person so agreeing; and such instruments so authenticated shall be by you or any three of you transmitted to one of our principal Secretaries of State, in order to be laid before our parliament for the further and more perfect ratification thereof; and until such ratification, no such regulation, provision, matter or thing, shall have any other force or effect, or be carried further into execution than is hereafter mentioned. And we do hereby further authorise and empower you, the said Frederick Earl of Carlisle, Richard Viscount Howe, Sir William Howe, William Eden, and George Johnstone, or any three of you, from time to time, as you or any three of you shall judge convenient, to order and proclaim a cessation of hostilities on the part of our forces by sea or land, for such time, and under such conditions, restrictions, or other qualifications, as in your discretions shall be thought requisite, and such order and proclamation to revoke and annul in the same manner and form.—And it is our further will and pleasure, and we do hereby require and command all our officers and ministers, civil and military, and all other our loving subjects whatsoever, to observe and obey all such proclamations respectively. And we do hereby, in further pursuance of the said act of parliament, and of the provisions therein contained, authorise and empower you the said Frederick Earl of Carlisle,

Richard Viscount Howe, Sir William Howe, William Eden, and George Johnstone, or any three of you, by proclamation under your respective hands and seals, from time to time, as you shall see convenient, to suspend the operation and effect of a certain act of parliament, made and passed in the 16th year of our reign, for prohibiting all trade and intercourse with certain Colonies and Plantations therein named, and for the other purposes therein also mentioned, or any of the provisions or restrictions therein contained, and therein to specify at what time and places respectively, and with what exceptions and restrictions, and under what passes and clearances, in lieu of those heretofore directed by any act or acts of parliament for regulating the trade of the Colonies and Plantations, the said suspension shall take effect, and the said suspension and proclamation in the same manner and form to annul and revoke. And we do hereby further authorise and empower you, the said Frederick Earl of Carlisle, Richard Viscount Howe, Sir William Howe, William Eden and George Johnstone, or any three of you, from time to time, as you shall judge convenient, to suspend in any places, and for any time during the continuance of the said first recited act, the operation and effect of any act or acts of parliament which have passed since the 10th day of February, 1763, and which relate to any of our Colonies, Provinces, or Plantations abovementioned in North America, so far as the same relate to them, or any of them, or the operation and effect of any clause, or any provision or other matter in such acts contained, so far as such clauses, provisions, or matters, relate to any of the said Colonies, Provinces, or Plantations. And we do hereby further authorize and impower you, the said Frederick Earl of Carlisle, Richard Viscount Howe, Sir Wil-

liam Howe, William Eden, and George Johnstone, or any three of you, to grant a pardon, or pardons, to any number or description of persons within the said Colonies, Provinces, or Plantations. And we do hereby further authorize and empower you, the said Frederick Earl of Carlisle, Richard Viscount Howe, Sir William Howe, William Eden, and George Johnstone, or any three of you, in any of our Colonies, Provinces, and Plantations aforesaid respectively, wherein we have usually heretofore nominated and appointed a Governor, to nominate and appoint, from time to time, by any instrument under your hands and seals, or the hands and seals of any three of you, a proper person, to be the Governor and Commander in Chief in and for such Colony, Province, or Plantation respectively, to have, hold, and exercise the said office of Governor and Commander in Chief in and for such Colony, Province, or Plantation respectively, with all such powers and authorities any Governor of such Province, heretofore appointed by us, might or could have exercised, in as full and ample manner and form as if such Governor and Commander in Chief had been nominated and appointed by our letters patent heretofore granted for appointing any such Governor and Commander in Chief. Whereas, by certain letters patent under our great seal, bearing date on the 29th day of April, in the sixteenth year of our reign, we have constituted and appointed you, the said Sir William Howe, to be General and Commander in Chief of all and singular our forces employed, or to be employed, within our Colonies of North America, lying upon the Atlantic ocean, from Nova-Scotia on the North, to West-Florida on the South, both inclusive, to have, hold, exercise, and enjoy the said office during our will and pleasure; and in case you, the said Sir William Howe, should, by death, or any other manner, be disabled from exercising the said command, it was our will and pleasure, therein expressed, that the same, with all authorities, rights, and privileges, contained in that our said commission, should devolve upon the person who should be next in rank to the said Sir William Howe. And whereas our trusty and well beloved Sir Henry Clinton, Knight of the most honourable Order of the Bath, Lieutenant-General of our forces, and General of our forces in our army in America only, now actually bears our commission, and is next in rank to you, the said Sir William Howe: know it it is our will and pleasure, and we do hereby order and appoint, that whenever the said command in the said letters patent mentioned shall, in pursuance thereof, devolve upon the said Sir Henry Clinton, all and every the powers and authorities hereby entrusted and committed to you the said Sir William Howe, shall forthwith cease and determine, and the said powers and authorities, and every of them, shall from thenceforth be entrusted and committed, and are hereby entrusted and committed, to the said Sir Henry Clinton, to use and exercise the same powers and authorities, and to perform and execute all other the matters and things as aforesaid, in as full and ample extent and form, and no other, as you, the said Sir William Howe, are hereby authorised to use and exercise, do, perform, and execute the same. And we do hereby require and command all our officers, civil and military, and all other our loving subjects whatsoever, to be aiding and assisting unto you, the said Frederick Earl of Carlisle, Richard Viscount Howe, Sir William Howe, William Eden, and George Johnstone, in the execution of this our commission, and of the powers and authorities therein contained. Provided always, and we do hereby

declare and ordain, that the several offices, powers, and authorities hereby granted, shall cease, determine, and become utterly null and void, on the 1st day of June, which shall be in the year of our Lord 1779, although we shall not otherwise in the mean time have revoked and determined the same. In witness whereof, we have caused these our letters to be made patent. Witness ourself, at Westminster, the 13th day of April, in the 18th year of our reign.

By the King himself.
YORK.

Manifesto and Proclamation by his Majesty's American Commissioners.

HAVING amply and repeatedly made known to the Congress, and having also proclaimed to the inhabitants of North America in general, the benevolent overtures of Great Britain towards a re-union and coalition with her colonies, we do not think it consistent either with the duty we owe to our country, or with a just regard to the characters we bear, to persist in holding out offers which in our estimation required only to be known to be most gratefully accepted; and we have accordingly, excepting only the commander in chief, who will be detained by military duties, resolved to return to England a few weeks after the date of this manifesto and proclamation.

Previous however to this decisive step, we are led by a just anxiety for the great objects of our mission, to enlarge on some points which may not have been sufficiently understood, to recapitulate to our fellow-subjects the blessings which we are empowered to confer, and to warn them of the continued evils to which they are at present blindly and obstinately exposing themselves.

To the members of the congress

then we again declare that we are ready to concur in all satisfactory and just arrangements for securing to them and their respective constituents the re-establishment of peace, with the exemption from any imposition of taxes by the parliament of Great Britain, and the irrevocable enjoyment of every privilege consistent with that union of interests and force on which our mutual prosperity, and the safety of our common religion and liberties depend. We again assert that the members of the congress were not authorised by their constituents, either to reject our offers without the previous consideration and consent of the several assemblies and conventions, their constituents, or to refer us to pretended foreign treaties, which they know were delusively framed in the first instance, and which have never yet been ratified by the people of this continent. And we once more remind the members of the congress, that they are responsible to their countrymen, to the world, and to God, for the continuance of this war, and for all the miseries with which it must be attended.

To the general assemblies and conventions of the different colonies, plantations, and provinces abovementioned, we now separately make the offers which we originally transmitted to the congress; and we hereby call upon and urge them to meet expressly for the purpose of considering whether every motive, political as well as moral, should not decide their resolution to embrace the occasion of cementing a free and firm coalition with Great Britain. It has not been, nor is it our wish, to seek the objects which we are commissioned to pursue by fomenting popular divisions and partial cabals; we think such conduct would be ill suited to the generous nature of the offers made, and unbecoming the dignity of the king and the state which make them. But it is both our wish and our duty to encourage and support any men or bodies of men, in their return of loyalty to our sovereign, and affection to our fellow-subjects.

To all others, free inhabitants of this once happy empire, we also address ourselves. Such of them as are actually in arms, of whatsoever rank or description, will do well to recollect, that the grievances, whether real or supposed, which led them into this rebellion, have been for ever removed, and that the just occasion is arrived for their returning to the class of peaceful citizens. But if the honours of a military life are become their object, let them seek those honours under the banners of their rightful sovereign, and in fighting the battles of the united British empire, against our late mutual and natural enemies.

To those whose profession it is to exercise the functions of religion on this continent, it cannot surely be unknown, that the sovereign power with which the congress is endeavouring to connect them, has ever been averse to toleration, and inveterately opposed to the interest and freedom of the places of worship which they serve; and that Great Britain, from whom they are for the present separated, must, both from the principles of her constitution and of protestantism, be at all times the best guardian of religious liberty, and most disposed to promote and extend it.

To all those who can estimate the blessings of peace and its influence over agriculture, arts, and commerce, who can feel a due anxiety for the education and establishment of their children, or who can place a just value on domestic security, we think it sufficient to observe, that they are made by their leaders to continue involved in all the calamities of war, without having either a just object to pursue, or a subsisting grievance which may not instantly be redressed.

But if there be any persons who, divested of mistaken resentments,

and uninfluenced by selfish interests, really think that it is for the benefit of the colonies to separate themselves from Great Britain, and that so separated they will find a constitution more mild, more free, and better calculated for their prosperity than that which they heretofore enjoyed, and which we are impowered and disposed to renew and improve; with such persons we will not dispute a position which seems to be sufficiently contradicted by the experience they have had. But we think it right to leave them fully aware of the change, which the maintaining of such a position must make in the whole nature and future conduct of this war, more especially when to this position is added the pretended alliance with the court of France. "The policy as well as the benevolence of Great Britain have thus far checked the extremes of war when they tended to distress a people still considered as our fellow-subjects, and to desolate a country shortly to become again a source of mutual advantage; but when that country professes the unnatural design not only of estranging herself from us, but of mortgaging herself and her resources to our enemies, the whole contest is changed; and the question is, how far Great Britain may, by every means in her power, destroy or render useless a connection contrived for her ruin, and for the aggrandizement of France. Under such circumstances the laws of self-preservation must direct the conduct of Great Britain, and if the British colonies are to become an accession to France, will direct her to render that accession of as little avail as possible to her enemy."

If however there are any who think that notwithstanding these reasonings the independence of the colonies will in the result be acknowledged by Great Britain, to them we answer, without reserve, that we neither possess nor expect powers for that purpose; and that

if Great Britain could ever have sunk so low as to adopt such a measure, we should not have thought ourselves compellable to be the instruments in making a concession which would, in our opinion, be calamitous to the colonies, for whom it was made, and disgraceful, as well as calamitous to the country from which it is required. And we think proper to declare, that in this spirit and sentiment we have regularly written from the continent to Great Britain.

It will now become the colonies in general to call to mind their own solemn appeals to heaven in the beginning of this contest, that they took arms only for the redress of grievances, and that it would be their wish, as well as their interest, to remain for ever connected with Great Britain. We again ask them, whether all their grievances, real or supposed, have not been amply and fully redressed; and we insist that the offers we have made leave nothing to be wished in point either of immediate liberty or permanent security; if those offers are now rejected, we withdraw from the exercise of a commission with which we have in vain been honoured; the same liberality will no longer be due from Great Britain, nor can it either in justice or policy be expected from her.

In fine, and for the fuller manifestation as well of the disposition we bear, as of the gracious and generous purposes of the commission under which we act, we hereby declare, that whereas his majesty, in pursuance of an act, made and passed in the last session of parliament, intituled, "An act to enable his majesty to appoint commissioners with sufficient powers to treat, consult, and agree upon the means of quieting the disorders now subsisting in certain of the colonies, plantations, and provinces in North America," having been pleased to authorise and impower us to grant a pardon or pardons to any number or description of persons within the colonies, plantations, and provinces of New Hampfhire, Maffachufett's Bay, Rhode Ifland, Connecticut, New York, New Jerfey, Pennfylvania, the three lower counties on Delaware, Maryland, Virginia, North Carolina, South Carolina and Georgia. And whereas the good effects of the faid authorities and powers towards the people at large, would have long fince taken place, if a due ufe had been made of our firft communications and overtures; and have thus far been fruftrated only by the precipitate refolution of the members of the congrefs not to treat with us, and by their declining to confult with their conftituents, we now, in making our appeal to thofe conftituents, and to the free inhabitants of this continent in general, have determined to give them what in our opinion fhould have been the firft object of thofe who appeared to have taken the management of their interefts, and adopt this mode of carrying the faid authorities and powers into execution. We accordingly hereby grant and proclaim a pardon or pardons of all, and all manner of treafons or mifprifions of treafons. by any perfon or perfons, or by any number or defcription of perfons within the faid colonies, plantations or provinces, counfelled, commanded, acted, or done, on or before the date of this manifefto and proclamation.

And we further declare and proclaim, that if any perfon or perfons, or any number or defcription of perfons within the faid colonies, plantations and provinces, now actually ferving either in a military or civil capacity in this rebellion, fhall, at any time during the continuance of this manifefto and proclamation, withdraw himfelf or themfelves from fuch civil or military fervice, and fhall continue thenceforth peaceably as a good and faithful fubject or fubjects to his Majefty to demean himfelf or themfelves, fuch perfon or perfons, or fuch number and defcription of

perfons, fhall become, and be fully entitled to, and hereby obtain, all the benefits of the pardon or pardons hereby granted; excepting only from the faid pardon or pardons every perfon, and every number or defcription of perfons, who, after the date of this manifefto and proclamation, fhall, under the pretext of authority, as judges, jurymen, minifters, or officers of civil juftice, be inftrumental in executing and putting to death any of his Majefty's fubjects within the faid colonies, plantations and provinces.

And we think proper further to declare, that nothing herein contained is meant, or fhall be conftrued, to fet at liberty any perfon or perfons now being prifoner or prifoners, or who during the continuance of this rebellion fhall become a prifoner or prifoners.

And we offer to the colonies at large, or feparately, a general or feparate peace, with the revival of their ancient government, fecured againft any future infringements, and protected for ever from taxation by Great Britain. And with refpect to fuch further regulations, whether civil, military, or commercial, as they may wifh to be framed and eftablifhed, we promife all the concurrence and affiftance that his majefty's commiffion authorifes and enables us to give.

And we further declare that this manifefto and proclamation fhall continue and be in force FORTY DAYS from the date hereof; that is to fay, from the third day of October to the eleventh day of November, both inclufive.

And in order that the whole contents of this manifefto and proclamation may be more fully known, we fhall direct copies thereof, both in the Englifh and German language, to be tranfmitted by flags of truce to the congrefs, the general affemblies or conventions of the colonies, plantations and provinces, and to feveral perfons both in civil and military capacities within the

faid colonies, plantations and provinces. And for the further fecurity in times to come of the feveral perfons, or numbers or defcriptions of perfons, who are or may be the objects of this manifefto and proclamation, we have fet our hands and feals to thirteen copies thereof, and have tranfmitted the fame to the thirteen colonies, plantations and provinces abovementioned, and we are willing to hope that the whole of this manifefto and proclamation will be fairly and freely publifhed and circulated for the immediate, general, and moft ferious confideration and benefit of all his majefty's fubjects on this continent. And we earneftly exhort all perfons who by this inftrument forthwith receive the benefit of the king's pardon, at the fame time that they entertain a becoming fenfe of thofe lenient and affectionate meafures whereby they are now freed from many grievous charges which might have rifen in judgment, or have been brought in queftion againft them, to make a wife improvement of the fituation in which this manifefto and proclamation places them, and not only to recollect that a perfeverance in the prefent rebellion, or any adherence to the treafonable connexion attempted to be framed with a foreign power, will, after the prefent grace extended, be confidered as crimes of the moft aggravated kind; but to vie with each other in eager and cordial endeavours to fecure their own peace, and promote and eftablifh the profperity of their countrymen, and the general weal of the empire.

And purfuant to his majefty's commiffion we hereby require all officers civil and military, and all others his majefty's loving fubjects whatfoever, to be aiding and affifting unto us in the execution of this our manifefto and proclamation, and of all the matters herein contained.

Given at New York, this third day of October, 1778.

CARLISLE   (L. S.)
H. CLINTON   (L. S.)
Wm. EDEN   (L. S.)

By their Excellency's Command,
ADAM FERGUSON, Secretary.

The following is an authentic Copy of the Instructions given by Congress to the American Plenipotentiaries sent to the several Courts of Europe.

In CONGRESS, Dec. 30, 1776.

Resolved,

THAT commissioners be sent to the courts of Vienna, France, Spain, Prussia, and the Grand Duke of Tuscany.

That the several Commissioners of the United States be instructed to assure the respective courts, that notwithstanding the artful and insidious endeavours of the court of Great Britain to represent the congress and inhabitants of these states to the European powers, as having a disposition again to submit to the sovereignty of the crown of Great Britain, it is their determination, at all events, to maintain their independence.

That the commissioners be respectively directed to use every means in their power, to procure the assistance of the emperor of Germany, and of their most Christian, Catholic, and Prussian Majesties, for preventing Russian, German, and other foreign troops, from being sent to North America for hostile purposes against the United States, and for obtaining a recall of those already sent.

That his most christian majesty be induced, if possible, to assist the United States in the present war with Great Britain, by attacking the Electorate of Hanover, or any part of the dominions of Great Britain in Europe, the East or West Indies.

That the Commissioners be further empowered to stipulate with the court of France, that all the trade between the United States, and the West India Islands, shall be carried on by vessels either belonging to the subjects of his most christian majesty or these states, each having liberty to carry on such trade.

That the commissioners be likewise instructed to assure his most christian majesty, that should his forces be employed, in conjunction with the united states, to exclude his Britannic majesty from any share in the cod fishery of America, by reducing the islands of Newfoundland and Cape Breton; and that ships of war be furnished, when required, by the united states to reduce Nova Scotia, the fishery shall be enjoyed equally, and in common, by the subjects of his most christian majesty, provided the province of Nova Scotia, island of Cape Breton, and the remaining part of Newfoundland, be annexed to the territory and government of the united states.

That should the proposals, made as above, be insufficient to produce the proposed declaration of war, and the commissioners are convinced that it cannot otherwise be accomplished, they must assure his most christian majesty, that such of the British West India islands, as in the course of the war shall be reduced by the united force of France and these states, shall be yielded an absolute property to his most christian majesty. The united states engage, on timely notice, to furnish at the expence of the said states, and deliver at some convenient port or ports, in the said states, provisions for carrying an expedition against the said islands, to the amount of two millions of dollars, and six frigates, mounting not less than twenty-four guns each, manned and fitted for sea; and to render any other assistance which may be in their power, as becomes good allies.

That the commissioners for the courts of France and Spain consult together, and prepare a treaty of commerce and alliance, as nearly as may be, similar to the first proposed to the court of France, and not inconsistent therewith, nor disagreeable to his most christian majesty, to be proposed to the court of Spain; adding thereto,

That if his catholic majesty will join with the united states in a war with Great Britain, they will assist in reducing to the possession of Spain, the town and harbour of Pensacola, provided the citizens and inhabitants of the united states shall have the free and uninterrupted navigation of the Mississippi and the use of the harbour of Pensacola; and will, provided it shall be true that his Portuguese majesty has insultingly expelled the vessels of these states from his ports, or has confiscated such vessels, declare war against the said king, if that measure shall be agreeable to, and supported by the courts of France and Spain.

That the commissioners for the court of Berlin consult with the commissioners at the court of France, and prepare such treaty or treaties of friendship and commerce to be proposed to the king of Prussia, as shall not be disagreeable to their most christian and catholic majesties.

Extract of the Minutes,
CHARLES THOMPSON,
Secretary of the Congress.

By Order of the Congress,

JOHN HANCOCK, President.

In General Assembly of Pensylvania, May 25, 1778.

The house resumed the consideration of the resolves respecting the draughts of the two bills proposed in the British parliament, and, after considerable debates thereupon, they were unanimously adopted as follows, viz.

THE house having taken into consideration the speech of Lord North, in the British house of commons, on the 19th of February last, and the two bills ordered to be brought in by him, &c. in consequence thereof; the one intituled, " A bill for declaring the intentions of the parliament of Great Britain, concerning the exercise of the right of imposing taxes within his majesty's colonies, provinces, and plantations in North America;" the other intituled, " A Bill to enable his majesty to appoint commissioners, with sufficient power to treat, consult, and agree upon the means of quieting the disorders now subsisting in certain of the colonies, plantations, and provinces in North America;" together with the proceedings of congress thereupon on the 22d day of April last, as published in the Pennsylvania Gazette of the 24th day of the same month; and having maturely considered the same, came to the following resolutions; to wit,

1. Resolved unanimously, That the delegates or deputies of the united states of America, in congress assembled, are invested with exclusive authority to treat with the king of Great Britain, or commissioners by him duly appointed, respecting a peace between the two countries.

2. Resolved unanimously, That any man, or body of men, who shall presume to make any separate or partial convention, or agreement with the king of Great Britain, or with any commissioner or commissioners under the crown of Great Britain, ought to be considered and treated as open and avowed enemies of the united states of America.

3. Resolved unanimously, That this house highly approved of the declaration of congress, " That these united states cannot, with propriety, hold any conference or treaty with any commissioners on the part of Great Britain, unless they shall, as a preliminary thereto, either withdraw their fleets and armies, or else in positive and express terms acknowledge the independence of the said states."

4. Resolved unanimously, That the congress have no power, authority, or right, to do any act, matter, or thing whatsoever, that may have a tendency to yield up or abridge the sovereignty and independence of this state without its consent previously obtained.

5. Resolved unanimously, That this house will maintain, support, and defend the sovereignty and independence of this state with their lives and fortunes.

6. Resolved unanimously, That it be recommended to the supreme executive council of this state, forthwith to order the militia to hold themselves in readiness to act as occasion may require.

Extract from the minutes,
JOHN MORRIS, jun.
Clerk of the General Assembly.

In CONGRESS.
June 13, 1778.

AN express arrived with a letter of the 11th, from General Washington, which was read, and a packet in which it was inclosed, together with other papers, a letter signed ' Carlisle, William Eden, G. Johnstone,' dated ' Philadelphia, June 9, 1778,' and directed ' to his excellency, Henry Laurens, the president, and other members of the congress;' which letter was read to the words, ' insidious interposition of a power, which has from the first settlement of these colonies been actuated with enmity to us both; and notwithstanding the pretended date or form of the French offers,' inclusive; whereupon the reading was interrupted, and a motion was made not to proceed farther, because of the offensive language against his most christian majesty. Debates arising thereon,

Ordered, that the consideration of the motion be postponed, and congress adjourned till ten o'clock on Monday June 16.

Congress resumed the consideration of the motion respecting the letter from the commissioners of the king of Great Britain, which being postponed.

A motion was made, ' That the letter from the commissioners of the king of Great Britain lie on the table.' Passed in the negative.

On the motion—Resolved,' That the letter and the papers accompanying it be read.' Whereupon a letter of the 9th, and one dated June, 1778, both signed, ' Carlisle, William Eden, G. Johnstone,' and a paper indorsed, ' Copy of the commission for restoring peace, &c. to the Earl of Carlisle, Lord Viscount Howe, Sir William Howe, or in his absence Sir Henry Clinton, William Eden, and George Johnstone,' were read, and also three acts of the British parliament, one intituled, ' An act for repealing an act passed in the 14th year of his present Majesty's reign, intituled, an act for the better regulating the government of the province of Massachusett's-bay, in New-England,' the other two the same as the bills already published. The letters are as follow:

To his excellency Henry Laurens, the President, and other Members of Congress.

Gentlemen, With an earnest desire to stop the further effusion of blood and the calamities of war, we communicate to you, with the least possible delay after our arrival in this city, a copy of the commission with which his Majesty is pleased to honour us, as also the acts of parliament on which it is founded; and at the same time that we assure you of our most earnest desire to re-establish, on the basis of equal freedom and mutual safety, the tranquillity of this once happy empire, you will observe, that we are vested with powers equal to the purpose, and such as are even unprecedented in the annals of our history.

In the present state of our affairs, though fraught with subjects of mutual regret, all parties may draw some degree of consolation, and even an auspicious hope from the recollection that cordial reconciliation and affection have, in our own and other empires, succeeded to the contentions and temporary divisions not less violent than those we now experience.

We wish not to recall subjects which are now no longer in controversy, and will reserve to a proper time of discussion both the hopes of mutual benefit, and the consideration of evils that may naturally contribute to determine your resolutions as well as our own on this important occasion.

The acts of parliament which we transmit to you, having passed with singular unanimity, will sufficiently evince the disposition of Great Britain, and shew that the terms of agreement, in contemplation with his majesty and with his parliament, are such as come up to every wish that North America, either in the hour of temperate deliberation, or of the utmost apprehension of danger to liberty, has expressed.

More effectually to demonstrate our good intentions, we think proper to declare, even in this our first communication, that we are disposed to concur in every satisfactory and just arrangement towards the following among other purposes:

'To consent to a cessation of hostilities, both by sea and land. To restore free intercourse, to revive mutual affection, and restore the common benefits of naturalisation through the several parts of this empire. To extend every freedom to trade that our respective interests can require. To agree that no military force shall be kept up in the different states of North America, without the consent of the general congress, or particular assemblies. To concur in measures calculated to discharge the debts of America, and raise the value and credit of the paper circulation.

'To perpetuate our union, by a reciprocal deputation of an agent or agents from the different states, who shall have the privilege of a seat and voice in the parliament of Great Britain; or, if sent from Britain, to have in that case a seat and voice in the assemblies of the different states to which they may be deputed respectively, in order to attend to the several interests of those by whom they are deputed.

'In short, to establish the power of the respective legislatures in each particular state, to settle its revenue, its civil and military establishment, and to exercise a perfect freedom of legislation and internal government, so that the British states throughout North America, acting with us in peace and war, under our common sovereign, may have the irrevocable enjoyment of every privilege that is short of a total separation of interest, or consistent with that union of force, on which the safety of our common religion and liberty depends.

'In our anxiety for preserving those sacred and essential interests, we cannot help taking notice of the insidious interposition of a power, which has from the first settlement of these colonies been actuated with enmity to us both. And notwithstanding the pretended date, or present form, of the French offers to America, yet it is notorious, that these were made in consequence of the plans of accommodation previously concerted in Great Britain, and with a view to prevent our reconciliation, and to prolong this destructive war.

'But we trust that the inhabitants of North-America, connected with us by the nearest ties of consanguinity, speaking the same language, interested in the preservation of similar institutions, remembering the former happy intercourse of good offices, and forgetting recent animosities, will shrink from the thought of becoming an accession of force to our late mutual enemy, and will prefer a firm, free, and perpetual coalition with the parent state to an insincere and unnatural foreign alliance.

'This dispatch will be delivered to you by Dr. Ferguson, the secretary to his majesty's commission; and, for further explanation and discussion of every subject of difference, we desire to meet with you either collectively or by deputation, at New-York, Philadelphia, York-Town, or such other place as you may propose. We think it right, however, to apprize you, that his majesty's instructions, as well as our own desire, to remove from the immediate seat of war, in the active operations of which we cannot take any part, may induce us speedily to remove to New-York; but the commander in chief of his majesty's land-forces, who is joined with us in this commission, will, if it should become eligible, either concur with us in a suspension of hostilities, or will furnish all necessary passports and safe conduct, to facilitate our meeting, and we shall of course expect the same of you.

'If after the time that may be necessary to consider of this communication, and transmit your answer, the horrors and devastations of war should continue, we call God and the world to witness, that the evils which must follow are not to be imputed to Great Britain; and we cannot without the most real sorrow anticipate the prospect of calamities which we feel the most ardent desire to prevent. We are, with perfect respect, Gentlemen, your most obedient and most humble servants,

Carlisle, W. Eden, G. Johnstone.

To his Excellency Henry Laurens, President, and other Members of Congress.

Gentlemen, The dispatch inclosed with this, was carried this morning to the nearest post of General Washington's army by Dr. Ferguson, Secretary to his Majesty's commission for restoring peace, &c. but he, not finding a passport, has returned to this place. In order to avoid every unnecessary delay, we now again send it by the ordinary conveyance of your military posts; as soon as the passport arrives, Dr. Ferguson shall wait upon you according to our first arrangement. We are, with perfect respect, gentlemen, your most obedient and most humble servants,

Carlisle, W. Eden, G. Johnstone.

Ordered, that they be referred to a committee of five.

Eodem Die, P. M. The committee to whom were referred the letters and papers from the Earl of Carlisle, &c. Commissioners from the King of Great Britain, reported the draft of a letter, which was read.

Resolved, that the consideration thereof be postponed till to-morrow.

June 17th, 1778. Congress resumed the consideration of the draft of the letter, in answer to the letter and papers received from the Earl of Carlisle, &c. Commissioners from the King of Great Britain, which was unanimously agreed to, and is as follows:

To their Excellencies the Right Hon. the Earl of Carlisle, William Eden, and George Johnstone, Esqrs. Commissioners from his Britannic Majesty, Philadelphia.

I have received the letter from your Excellencies of the 9th instant, with the inclosures, and laid them before Congress. Nothing but an earnest desire to spare the farther effusion of human blood could have induced them to read a paper, containing expressions so disrespectful to his Most Christian Majesty, the good and great ally of these states, or to consider propositions so derogatory to the honour of an independent nation.

' The acts of the British parliament, the commission from your Sovereign, and your letter, suppose the people of these states to be subjects of the crown of Great Britain, and are founded on an idea of dependence, which is utterly inadmissible.

' I am further directed to inform your Excellencies, that Congress are inclined to peace, notwithstanding the unjust claims from which this war originated, and the savage manner in which it hath been conducted; they will therefore be contented to enter upon a consideration of a treaty of peace and commerce, not inconsistent with treaties already subsisting, when the King of Great Britain shall demonstrate a sincere disposition for that purpose. The only solid proof of this disposition will be an explicit acknowledgement of the independence of these states, or the withdrawing his fleets and armies. I have the honour to be, your Excellencies most obedient and humble servant,

HENRY LAURENS, President.
York-Town, July 17, 1778.

Resolved unanimously, that Congress approve the conduct of General Washington, in refusing a passport to Dr. Ferguson. Published by order of Congress.

CHARLES THOMSON, Sec.

In CONGRESS, June 17, 1778.

Whereas many letters, addressed to individuals of these United States, have been lately received from England, through the conveyance of the enemy, and some of them which have been under the inspection of members of Congress, are found to contain ideas insidiously calculated to divide and delude the good people of these states:

Resolved, that it be, and is hereby earnestly recommended to the legislative and executive authorities of the several states, to exercise the utmost care and vigilance, and take the most effectual measures to put a stop to so dangerous and criminal a correspondence.

Resolved, that the Commander in Chief, and the Commander in each and every military department

be, and he and they are hereby directed to carry the measures recommended in the above resolution into the most effectual execution.

Extract from the minutes.
CHARLES THOMPSON, Sec.

Private Letter from Governor Johnstone to Henry Laurens, Esq.

Philadelphia, June 10, 1778.
Dear Sir,

I beg to transfer to my friend Doctor Ferguson the private civilities which my friends Mr. Manning and Mr. Oswald request in my behalf. He is a man of the utmost probity, and of the highest esteem in the republic of letters.

If you should follow the example of Britain in the hour of her insolence, and send us back without a hearing, I shall hope from private friendship that I may be permitted to see the country, and the worthy characters she has exhibited to the world, upon making the request, in any way you may point out. I am, with great regard, dear Sir, your most obedient and most humble servant,

GEORGE JOHNSTONE.

To his Excellency,
HENRY LAURENCE, Congress.

ANSWER.

York-Town, June 14, 1778.
Dear Sir,

Yesterday I was honoured with your favour of the 10th, and thank you for the transmission of those from my dear and worthy friends Mr. Oswald and Mr. Manning. Had Dr. Ferguson been the bearer of these papers, I should have shewn that gentleman every degree of respect and attention that times and circumstances admit of.

It is, Sir, for Great Britain to determine, whether her Commissioners shall return unheard by the Representatives of these United States, or revive a friendship with the citizens at large, and remain among us as long as they please.

You are undoubtedly acquainted with the only terms, upon which Congress can treat for accomplishing this good end; terms from which, although writing in a private character, I may venture to assert with great assurance, they never will recede, even admitting the continuance of hostile attempts; and that, from the rage of war, the good people of these states shall be driven to commence a treaty westward of yonder mountain. And permit me to add, Sir, on my humble opinion, the true interest of Great Britain, in the present advance of our contest, will be found in confirming our independence.

Congress in no hour have been haughty; but to suppose, that their minds are less firm in the present, than they were, when destitute of all foreign aid, even without expectation of an alliance; when, upon a day of general public fasting and humiliation, in their house of worship, and in the presence of God, they resolved 'to hold no conference or treaty with any Commissioners on the part of Great Britain, unless they shall, as a preliminary thereto, either withdraw their fleets and armies, or in positive and express terms acknowledge the independence of these states,' would be irrational.

At a proper time, Sir, I shall think myself highly honoured by a personal attention, and by contributing to render every part of these states agreeable to you; but, until the basis of mutual confidence shall be established, I believe, Sir, neither former private friendship, nor any other consideration, can influence Congress to consent, that even Governor Johnstone, a gentlemen who has been so deservedly esteemed in America, shall see the country. I have but one voice, and that shall be against it. But let me instruct you, my dear Sir; do not hence conclude that I am deficient in affection to my old friends, through whose kindness I have obtained the honour of the present correspondence, or that I

am not, with very great personal respect and esteem, Sir,

Your most obedient
And most humble servant,
HENRY LAURENS.

The Hon. Governor JOHN-STONE, Esq. Philadelphia.

Treaty of Alliance, Eventual and Defensive, between his most Christian Majesty Louis *the Sixteenth, King of France and* Navarre, *and the Thirteen United States of* America, *concluded at* Paris, *6th February,* 1778.

THE Most Christian King, and the United States of North-America, to wit, New-Hampshire, Massachusett's-Bay, Rhode island, Connecticut, New Jersey, Pennsylvania, Delaware, Maryland, Virginia, North Carolina, South-Carolina, and Georgia, having this day concluded a treaty of amity and commerce, for the reciprocal advantage of their subjects and citizens, have thought it necessary to take into consideration the means of strengthening those engagements, and of rendering them useful to the safety and tranquillity of the two parties; particularly in case Great Britain, in resentment of that connection, and of the good correspondence which is the object of the said treaty, should break the peace with France, either by direct hostilities, or by hindering her commerce and navigation, in a manner contrary to the rights of nations, and the peace subsisting between the two crowns.—And his Majesty and the said United States having resolved in that case to join their councils and efforts against the enterprizes of their common enemy—

The respective Plenipotentiaries, impowered to concert the clauses and conditions proper to fulfil the said intentions, have, after the most mature deliberation, concluded and

determined on the following articles.

Art. I. If war should break out between France and Great Britain, during the continuance of the present war between the United States and England, his Majesty and the said United States shall make it a common cause, and aid each other mutually with their good offices, their councils, and their forces, according to the exigency of conjunctures, as becomes good and faithful allies.

Art. II. The essential and direct end of the present defensive alliance is, to maintain effectually the liberty, sovereignty, and independence, absolute and unlimited, of the said United States, as well in matters of government as of commerce.

Art. III. The two contracting parties shall each on its own part, and in the manner it may judge most proper, make all the efforts in its power against their common enemy, in order to attain the end proposed.

Art. IV. The contracting parties agree, that in case either of them should form a particular enterprize in which the concurrence of the other may be desired, the party whose concurrence is desired, shall readily and with good faith join to act in concert for that purpose, as far as circumstances and its own particular situation will permit; and in that case, they shall regulate by a particular convention the quantity and kind of succour to be furnished, and the time and manner of its being brought into action, as well as the advantages which are to be its compensation.

Art. V. If the United States should think fit to attempt the reduction of the British power, remaining in the Northern parts of America, or the islands of Bermudas, those countries or islands, in case of success, shall be confederated with, or dependent upon, the said United States.

Art. VI. The Most Christian King renounces for ever the possession of the islands of Bermudas, as well as of any part of the continent of America, which before the treaty of Paris, in 1763, or in virtue of that treaty, were acknowledged to belong to the crown of Great Britain, or to the United States, heretofore called British Colonies, or which are at this time, or have lately been, under the power of the King and crown of Great Britain.

Art. VII. If his Most Christian Majesty shall think proper to attack any of the islands situated in the Gulph of Mexico, or near that Gulph, which are at present under the power of Great Britain, all the said isles, in case of success, shall appertain to the crown of France.

Art. VIII. Neither of the two parties shall conclude either truce or peace with Great Britain, without the formal consent of the other first obtained; and they mutually engage not to lay down their arms, until the independence of the United States shall have been formally or tacitly assured by the treaty or treaties that shall terminate the war.

Art. IX. The contracting parties declare, that, being resolved to fulfil, each on its own part, the clauses and conditions of the present treaty of alliance, according to its own power and circumstances, there shall be no after-claims of compensation, on one side or the other, whatever may be the event of the war.

Art. X. The Most Christian King and the United States agree, to invite or admit other powers, who may have received injuries from England, to make a common cause with them, and to accede to the present alliance, under such conditions as shall be freely agreed to, and settled between all the parties.

Art. XI. The two parties guarantee mutually from the present time, and for ever, against all other powers, to wit—The United States to his Most Christian Majesty the present possessions of the crown of France in America, as well as those which it may acquire by the future treaty of peace; and his Most Christian Majesty guarantees on his part to the United States, their liberty, sovereignty, and independence, absolute and unlimited, as well in matters of government as commerce, and also their possessions, and the additions or conquests that their confederation may obtain during the war, from any of the dominions now or heretofore possessed by Great Britain in North America; conformable to the fifth and sixth articles above written, the whole as their possessions shall be fixed and assured to the said States, at the moment of the cessation of their present war with England.

Art. XII. In order to fix more precisely the sense and application of the preceding article, the contracting parties declare, that in case of a rupture between France and England, the reciprocal guarantee declared in the said article shall have its full force and effect the moment such war shall break out; and if such rupture shall not take place, the mutual obligations of the said guarantees shall not commence until the moment of the cessation of the present war between the United States and England, shall have ascertained their possessions.

Art. XIII. The present treaty shall be ratified on both sides, and the ratifications shall be exchanged in the space of six months, or sooner if possible

In faith whereof the respective Plenipotentiaries, to wit, on the part of the Most Christian King, Conrad Alexander Gerard, Royal Syndic of the city of Strasbourg, and Secretary of his Majesty's Council of State—And on the part of the United States, Benjamin Franklin, deputy to the General Congress, from the State of Pensylvania, and President of the convention of said State; Silas Deane, heretofore deputy from the State of Connecticut; and Arthur Lee, Counsellor at Law, have signed the above articles both in the French and English languages; declaring nevertheless, that the present treaty was originally composed and concluded in the French language, and they have hereunto affixed their seals.

Done at Paris, the sixth day of February, one thousand seven hundred and seventy-eight.

(L. S.)　C. A. GERARD,
(L. S.)　B. FRANKLIN,
(L. S.)　SILAS DEANE,
(L. S.)　ARTHUR LEE.

119

Notes, 1778

1. Gustavus Conyngham (1747–1819), the notorious "Dunkirk Pirate."

2. David Murray, Viscount Stormont (1727–96), Ambassador to Paris, 1772–78; Secretary of State for the Northern Department, 1779–82.

3. Antoine Raymond de Sartine, Comte d'Alby (1729–1801), Minister of Marine from 1774.

4. Thomas Villiers (1753–1824), eldest son of the Earl of Clarendon, styled Lord Hyde until he succeeded his father in 1786; M.P. for Christchurch, 1774–80.

5. Sir Gilbert Elliot (1751–1814), M.P. for Roxburghshire, 1777–84; son of the previous holder of the seat (see "Notes, 1775," n. 59).

6. Edmund Burke.

7. Congress had increased its enlistment bounty to $20 and one hundred acres of land for those who volunteered for the duration of the war. In 1777, some states were offering additional bounties of $33.30, while Massachusetts doubled this in an effort to compete for available men. The state bounties inevitably reduced enlistment in the Continental Army and encouraged desertion for "bounty jumping."

8. Charles Fox.

9. Philip Stanhope, 5th Earl of Chesterfield (1755–1815).

10. Duke of Richmond.

11. Lord Suffolk.

12. John Buller (1721–86), M.P. for East Looe, 1747–86; Lord of the Admiralty, 1765–80; generally acting as spokesman for the Admiralty in the Commons, 1771–80.

13. Edward Thurlow (1731–1806), M.P. for Tamworth, 1765–1806, created Baron Thurlow of Ashfield 1778; Solicitor-General, 1770–71; Attorney-General, 1771–78; Lord Chancellor, 1778–April 1783 and December 1783–June 1792.

14. The Navy List Book for May 1777 gives 35 ships of the line in full commission in home waters (P.R.O., Adm/8/53). However, Sandwich's memorandum to North of 8 December 1777 admitted, "I fear that France and Spain united have at least an equal number in Europe in commission, and I believe they have many more ready to receive men." He went on to say that almost the whole of the French force was in Europe, while the bulk of the Spanish fleet was abroad, already able to "collect a formidable fleet at the Havana without detaching any from Europe." This left Britain vulnerable in the West Indies, North America, the East Indies, and the Mediterranean, where the enemy could despatch vessels the moment war broke out. Sandwich then argues: "Will our 42 ships

supply the necessary detachments to answer this purpose, and to leave us superior at home to anything the House of Bourbon can bring against us in Europe after their detachment is made? Certainly not." He concludes by recommending that the 7 ships short of seamen be commissioned immediately and a further 7 made ready. *The Private Papers of John, Earl of Sandwich, First Lord of the Admiralty, 1771–1782*, ed. G. R. Barnes and J. H. Owen, 4 vols. (London: Naval Records Society, 1932–38), vol. 1, pp. 333–34. Though Sandwich's statement of available warships is therefore technically correct, the impression his remarks made in the debate in the House of Lords is deliberately misleading.

15. Temple Simon Luttrell.

16. William Baker (1743–1824), M.P. for Aldborough, 1777–80, was attached to the Rockingham group.

17. As Doctors give physic by way of prevention
MATT alive and in health of his TOMB-STONE took care
For delays are unsafe, and his pious intention
May haply be never fulfill'd by his Heir.
Matthew Prior (1664–1721), *My Own Monument*, lines 1–4.

18. Burke.

19. To become 18 Geo. III c. 1.

20. Isaac Barré.

21. Robert Henley Ongley (c. 1721–85), created Baron Ongley in the Irish peerage 1776; M.P. for Bedfordshire, 1761–80. Sir Herbert Macworth (1737–91), created Baronet 1776; M.P. for Cardiff Burghs, 1766–90.

22. Fox.

23. Sir George Savile.

24. Barré.

25. Phillip Jennings (1722–88), added Clarke to his name on succeeding to his uncle's estates in 1774; created Baronet 1774; M.P. for Totnes, 1768–88; consistently opposed the American war from November 1777.

26. Benjamin Langlois (1727–1802), M.P. for St. Germans, 1768–80; Clerk of Deliveries at the Ordnance.

27. Sir Charles Frederick (1709–85), M.P. for Queenborough, 1754–84; Surveyor-General at the Ordnance.

28. Lord Beauchamp.

29. *Parliamentary History*, vol. 19, 589, gives the vote as 160 to 12.

30. Jeffrey Amherst (1717–97), created Baron Amherst 1776; Commander-in-Chief in America, 1758–63.

31. The Earl of Dunmore.

32. Lord Suffolk.

33. The Duke of Richmond and the Earl of Shelburne.

34. Willoughby Bertie, 4th Earl of Abingdon (1740–99).

35. Prussia refused passage across her territory to troops of Anspach-Bayreuth.

36. John Sawbridge, George Hayley, Richard Oliver, and Frederick Bull.

37. George Greville, 2nd Earl of Warwick (1746–1816). Walpole (*Last Journals of Horace Walpole, 1771–83*, ed. Dr. Doran, 2 vols. [London, 1859], vol. 2, p. 179) claims Warwick was "discouraged by the jealousy of Lord Hertford" (Francis Seymour Conway, 1st Earl of Hertford [1718–94], Lord Lieutenant of Warwickshire).

38. Philip Yorke, 1st Earl of Hardwicke (1690–1764); Lord Chancellor, 1737–56.

39. Lord Bathurst.

40. Edward Thurlow.

41. Alexander Wedderburn (1733–1805), M.P. for Okehampton, 1774–78; Solicitor-General, 1771–78; Attorney-General, 1778–80; created Baron Loughborough 1795.

42. Mansfield.

43. Lord Effingham argued that in 1756 ten regiments were raised without Parliament's consent, but this had in effect been sanctioned by "a Standing Act, called an Act of Credit." However, ". . . so far from the concurrence of parliament being unnecessary on these occasions, that there was an act of parliament, made in the 2nd session of the 2nd parliament of Charles II, whereby it was expressly declared, that their coincidence was necessary to the existence of such a measure." *Parliamentary History*, vol. 19, 634–35. This account of the debate gives no indication of a challenge on the date of the "Act of Credit."

44. Mansfield.

45. Camden.

46. Offers were made to raise regiments in Scotland, and from Manchester and Liverpool. In the debate on 22 January, Fox is reported to have said that "Scotland and Manchester were so accustomed to disgrace, that it is no wonder if they pocketed instances of dishonour and sat down contented with infamy." *Parliamentary History*, vol. 19, 621.

47. Lord Abingdon.

48. Lord Suffolk (died 6 March 1779).

49. Both *Parliamentary History* (vol. 19, 707) and Walpole (*Last Journals*, vol. 2, p. 194) attribute these remarks to George Johnstone, who had held no office since the end of his governorship of West Florida in 1767.

50. Barrington's figure was calculated from the official returns made by the commanding officers (c.f. *AR*, 1781, p. 264]).

51. George Grenville (1753–1813), son of George Grenville (see "Notes 1775," n. 13), M.P. for Buckinghamshire, 1774–79; an independent who opposed the war from 1778, though until 1779 a supporter of parliamentary sovereignty over America.

52. William Putleney (1729–1805), M.P. for Shrewsbury, 1775–1805, chaired this committee of the whole.

53. William Henry Cavendish-Bentinck, 3rd Duke of Portland (1738–1809).

54. Nathaniel Curzon, 1st Baron Scarsdale (1726–1804), who had chaired the committee of the whole on 2 February.

55. Lord Bathurst?

56. Suffolk?

57. The treaties of amity and commerce between France and the United States were signed in France on 6 February. Walpole, in *Last Journals*, vol. 2, p. 207, states that his cousin Thomas (1727–1803), M.P. for King's Lynn, 1768–84, who had learned of the treaties through his French contacts, gave him the news. Together they decided to inform Fox, but only immediately before the debate, since they distrusted Burke and Rockingham.

The Annual Register—1778

58. George Grenville.

59. Not identified.

60. Not identified.

61. Not identified.

62. James Adair (?1743–98), M.P. for Cockermouth, 1775–80); Serjeant-at-Law, 1774, Recorder of Lincoln, 1779–89.

63. To become 18 Geo. III c. 12 and 13.

64. Thomas Gilbert (?1719–98), M.P. for Lichfield, 1768–94, Comptroller of the Great Wardrobe, 1763–82.

65. James Luttrell (c. 1751–88), M.P. for Stockbridge, 1775–84; brother of Temple Simon Luttrell.

66. Sackville Tufton, 8th Earl of Thanet (1733–86).

67. Camden.

68. Bathurst.

69. Harry Paulet (Powlett), 6th Duke of Bolton (1719–94), Admiral of the Fleet, 1770; Governor of the Isle of Wight, 1766–80. Augustus John Harvey, 3rd Earl of Bristol (1724–99), Rear-Admiral, 1775; Vice-Admiral, 1778.

70. Earl of Effingham.

71. George, Prince of Denmark (1653–1708), consort of Queen Anne, made Lord High Admiral in 1702.

72. Fox. Both were descended from illegitimate offspring of Charles II. *Parliamentary History*, vol. 19, 834, reports Grafton's referring to Fox as his "honourable kinsman" not, as here, "noble kinsman." As the second son of Henry Fox, created Baron Holland of Foxley in 1763, Charles James had no title of peerage.

73. Lord Weymouth (See "Introduction, 1769," n. 3). Weymouth transferred to the Southern Department in November 1775 and was Secretary for both departments, March–October 1779.

74. A partner in the firm Muir, Son and Atkinson, with which the Treasury had contracted in February 1776 to hire vessels for shipping provisions to the army in America. Atkinson offered to accept any commission the Treasury thought reasonable when it was decided to reduce the rate from $2\frac{1}{2}$ percent in June 1777. This generous indifference may have been not entirely unconnected with the fact that the firm was running its own cargoes to America in ships hired as Treasury victuallers. The case is illustrative of the complex problem of organising supplies for the army and of the division of responsibility between the Treasury and the Navy Board. See D. Syrett, *Shipping and the American War, 1775–83: A Study of British Transport Organisation* (London, 1970), esp. pp. 130–36.

75. Emanuel Marie Louis, Marquis de Noailles (1743–1822), Ambassador to London from May 1776.

76. Sir George Yonge (1733–1812), 5th Baronet, M.P. for Honiton, 1763–96; an opponent of the war.

77. In the Commons debate on 22 January, Burke pointed out that 3 percent consols stood at $71\frac{1}{4}$ on a fund of £5 million, while in 1760, the fifth year of the Seven Years War, they stood at 79 on a fund of £23 million. *Parliamentary History*, vol. 19, 617.

78. Not identified.

79. Richard Temple, Earl Temple (1711–79), a politician whose prominence was greatest in the previous two decades, when he had an uneasy relationship with Chatham (his brother-in-law).

80. Abingdon.

81. Wedderburn.

82. Sir William Meredith (?1725–90), 3rd Baronet, M.P. for Liverpool, 1761–80.

83. Burgoyne landed at Portsmouth on 13 May.

84. Robert Vyner (1717–99), M.P. for Lincoln, 1774–84.

85. Burgoyne's letter to Germain of 1 January 1777 in which, among other matters, he mentioned his approach to the King for a new command and the hope that Germain would support his application. Burgoyne claimed that he thought publication of this letter would lead the public to believe he had sought to supplant Carleton.

86. Thurlow.

87. Richard Rigby; his bluntness of speech and virulence in debate were famous.

88. Wedderburn.

89. Lord Frederick Cavendish (1729–1803), third son of the Duke of Devonshire; M.P. for Derby, 1754–80. He followed a military career and served in the expedition to St. Cas in September 1758, when he was captured.

90. Sir James Lowther (1736–1802), 5th Baronet, M.P. for Cumberland, 1774–84, who became an opponent of the Government's American policy in 1775.

91. George Augustus Frederick, Prince of Wales (1762–1830); Frederick Augustus (1763–1827), elected Bishop of Osnaburg 1764, created Duke of York 1784.

92. Lord Abingdon.

93. Edward Smith Stanley, 12th Earl of Derby (1752–1834).

94. Robert Abercromby (1740–1827), Lieutenant-Colonel of the 37th Regiment, later distinguished himself in India, where he was promoted to Major-General in 1790 and knighted.

95. Jonathan Trumbull (1710–85), Governor of Connecticut since 1769. Elected to the office (under the provisions of the colony's charter), he was the only governor in the Thirteen Colonies in 1775 to lead the revolutionary movement in his province. His organisation of supplies for Washington's army was regarded as a particularly serious problem by British commanders.

96. Simeon Dean, brother of Silas Deane, the American envoy sent to France in 1776 (see n. 119, below).

97. Frederick Howard, 5th Earl of Carlisle (1748–1825); William Eden (1744–1804), M.P. for New Woodstock, 1774–84; George Johnstone.

98. Adam Ferguson (1723–1816), celebrated Professor of Philosophy at the University of Edinburgh.

99. Henry Laurens (1724–92), wealthy Charleston merchant active in South Carolina politics, Vice-President of the state in 1776; delegate to the Continental Congress in 1777, and President, November 1777–December 1778.

100. William Henry Drayton (see "Notes, 1776," n. 16), South Carolina delegate to the Congress, 1778–79.

101. William Maxwell had been sent to Mount Holly across the Delaware from Philadelphia, and another unit to Chad's Ford to warn of any British attempt to leave by Head of Elk.

102. James Grant (see "Notes, 1775," n. 40).

103. Henry Monckton (1740–78), fourth son of the 1st Viscount Galway and brother of Robert Monckton, Wolfe's second-in-command at Quebec in 1759, Lieutenant-Colonel of the 45th Regiment, commander of the 2nd Battalion of the Grenadiers at Monmouth. One contemporary account puts British losses at 112 dead and 174 wounded, and quotes a Trenton newspaper which puts American losses at 600 killed and wounded. B. Uhlendorf, ed., *Revolution in America: Confidential Letters and Journals, 1776–84, of Adjutant General Major Baurmeister of the Hessian Forces* (New Brunswick, N.J., 1957), p. 187.

104. Not identified.

105. Lee did not serve again. After receiving an offensive letter from him regarding his possible permanent suspension, the Congress felt obliged to make reality of rumour and on 10 January 1780 dismissed him from the army.

106. Jean-Baptiste-Charles-Henri-Hector, Comte d'Estaing (1729–94), Vice-Admiral from 1777.

107. John Byron (1723–86), promoted to Vice-Admiral in January 1778 and appointed successor to Lord Howe. He reached Sandy Hook on 30 July.

108. Robert Pigot (see "Notes, 1775," n. 79), was promoted to Major-General in August 1777.

109. The frigates were destroyed on 5 August as the result of a reconnaissance up the eastern and middle channels by a squadron of four French vessels commanded by Admiral Pierre André de Suffren de St. Tropez (1729–88).

110. George Dawson, Captain in 1777, Acting Captain of the *Renown*.

111. John Raynor, Captain in 1775.

112. Louis Antoine de Bougainville (1729–1811) served under Montcalm in the Seven Years War and transferred from the army to the navy in 1763. His voyage of exploration to the Pacific, which was completed as a circumnavigation of the world, 1767–69, earned him an international reputation; hence, "philosophic" refers less to his temperament than to his scientific interests.

113. Robert Bertie, 4th Duke of Ancaster (1756–79).

114. The famous farewell party given in Howe's honour on 18 May 1778, organised by his staff officers for a total of 750 guests. The staff officers paid 3,313 guineas and "the great English shop of Coffin and Anderson took in £12000 sterling for silk goods and other fine materials, which shows how much money was lavished on this affair and how elegantly the ladies were dressed." *Revolution in America: Confidential Letters and Journals of Major Baurmeister*, pp. 177–78. I have not thought it necessary to attempt to identify all the individuals named in the letter.

115. Conrad Alexandre Gerard (1729–90?), first French minister to the United States, from July 1778.

116. Richard Henry Lee (1732–94), eldest of the four brothers, had played a leading role in Virginia politics since the 1760s, was a delegate to the Congress, 1774–80, and played a key role in the adoption of the independence resolution.

117. Charles Gravier, Comte de Vergennes (1717–87), French Foreign Minister from 1774.

118. Not further identified.

119. Silas Deane (1737–89), Connecticut delegate to the Continental Congress 1774–76 and appointed first agent to France to secure supplies and assistance for the American cause. Ambitious and unscrupulous, he was accused of using his position for personal profit and he early became involved with the British espionage agents Edward Bancroft and Paul Wentworth, though to what extent he was duped is a matter of controversy.

1779

Introduction

The military planning of 1778 was, within its limits, successful but the Government had begun to realise the implications of the nation's naval weakness—particularly in view of the expected entry of Spain into the war. The strategy for the recovery of America shifted both because of the necessity to defend the whole empire from a Bourbon onslaught, and the experience of American operations. Germain's instructions to Clinton on 23 January 1779 were aimed at driving Washington's army into the Highlands between the Hudson and Connecticut rivers in order to allow creeping pacification of the middle colonies, while coastal raids from New England and the Chesapeake kept the American forces pinned down. Clinton was to be reinforced by units from England and from Grant's returning West Indies expedition, and supported by the navy throughout. The plans were based on the following assumptions: that a majority of Americans in the middle colonies were basically Loyalists waiting for some guarantee of safety before returning to the imperial fold;[1] that British naval supremacy would permit America and the West Indies to be regarded as a single, interconnected western Atlantic theatre of war; and that close cooperation between military and naval commanders would ensure flexible efficiency. On all counts the Government miscalculated.

1. A notion fostered by the returning peace commissioners and emigré Loyalists like Joseph Galloway.

News of the 1778 successes did not reach England until February 1779, but the southern campaign rolled forward. Prevost joined Campbell and Augusta was taken on 27 January. The American defending force in Georgia had proved quite ineffective and Robert Howe, its commander, was replaced by Benjamin Lincoln, who was promptly defeated at Briar Creek on 3 March. In response to Lincoln's advance into Georgia, Prevost invaded South Carolina and reached Charleston on 10 May but after a series of scattered engagements, he retreated to Savannah. The ensuing stalemate continued through the heat of the summer. Governor Rutledge of South Carolina called for aid from d'Estaing and on 23 September began a siege of Savannah. His protracted preparations resulted in such a delay that d'Estaing feared being caught by the British fleet. He thus insisted on a premature assault on the British defences on 9 October; the attack was bloodily repulsed, and the siege terminated on 20 October. Georgia was to remain safely in British hands for the next four years and Americans again had reason to complain about the practical value of the French alliance.

Meanwhile, the raiding policy was put into effect. General Mathew led a force in a successful attack on Virginia, beginning on 5 May, and inflicted serious damage. On 28 May, Clinton ordered an expedition up the Hudson; it took Stony Point, Verplancks Point, and Fort Lafayette, preparatory to taking West Point, the American fort controlling the gateway to the Highlands. But on 16 July, Anthony Wayne led a courageous midnight counterattack and retook Stony Point, though Robert Howe (transferred from the south) failed to recapture Fort Lafayette. Wayne's success encouraged Henry Lee to attack Paulus Hook on 19 August but he could not follow up his initial victory and was obliged to withdraw rapidly after inflicting heavy losses and taking a number of prisoners. On 3 July, a British raid against Connecticut damaged and looted New Haven and Newark but Clinton decided to evacuate Rhode Island to concentrate his forces against the unknown threat from d'Estaing's fleet. Serious dissension between the commander-in-chief and the new commanding admiral, Marriot Arbuthnot, reduced the effectiveness of British operations and so depressed Clinton that he asked to resign. The raiding policy generally achieved its objectives, but it predictably aroused popular American anger and stiffened resistance.

Three years of patient negotiation by Vergennes came to fruition in April, when, by the Treaty of Aranjuez, Spain entered the conflict (actually declaring war on Britain on 16 June). Spain aimed to regain Gibraltar and Minorca and exclude Britain from the Gulf of Mexico. She had little desire to see an independent America acting as a dangerous example to her own colonies, and had designs on the Mississippi and plans for penetrating into the North American interior. Though Spain began by besieging Gibraltar and threatening Minorca the addition of the Spanish to the French fleets automatically clinched Bourbon naval supremacy in all theatres. In the West Indies (where a Spanish attack could eventually be expected) Admiral Byron was impotent to prevent the reinforcement of the French fleet and was unable to prevent the loss of St. Vincent in June and Grenada in July. A successful raid on Omoa in the Gulf of Honduras was small gain compared to the loss of West Florida in October. As Britain lost control of the Caribbean and was confined to a defensive role, d'Estaing's fleet was free to menace any part of the theatre; he was thus able to immobilise Clinton in New York and prevented him from sending forces by sea to enlarge the gains of the southern campaign. Actually, Clinton had received orders in the summer to mount a major expedition against the Carolinas but he could not begin the operation until he received definite news of d'Estaing's abandonment of the siege of Savannah. He and Cornwallis sailed for Charleston on 26 December.

The western Atlantic did not receive essential naval reinforcements because Britain faced the prospect of a Franco-Spanish invasion in the summer of 1779. She thus sacrificed the ocean to guard the Channel. The junction of the French and Spanish fleets on 23 July precipitated a crisis and the Channel Fleet waited off the Scilly Isles to prevent an attack on England or Ireland and to protect the East and West India convoys. The attempt at interception was a complete failure; the enemy fleet stood off Plymouth on 15 August and a near-panic ensued. The danger however was exaggerated; although a French army was waiting in Brittany, the combined fleet was running short of provisions and it had to destroy the British Channel Fleet before it could establish a successful beachhead. For seventeen days, weather and mistakes prevented an engagement and on 4 September the combined fleet was ordered back to port.[2]

Naval matters dominated the opening of the first parliamentary session of 1779 because Keppel's failure at Ushant the previous July eventually produced a public furore and became a party-political issue. In October 1778, Keppel's second-in-command, Admiral Palliser, was accused in the press of disobedience which prevented a decisive outcome at Ushant. Palliser demanded a written exoneration from Keppel, which was, naturally, not forthcoming, so he published his own defence. The Rockinghams rushed to support Keppel, Sandwich and the Government supported Palliser. Though Sandwich refused the Earl of Bristol's demand for an enquiry in November, in December, the Opposition were enraged to hear that Keppel was to be court-martialled.[3]

The court-martial began on 7 January, and on 11 February Keppel was exonerated of the charges—to public rejoicing and street violence in London.[4] The Opposition promptly demanded Palliser's dismissal but was outmanoeuvred when Palliser resigned his naval offices and it was decided that he should be given a court-martial.[5] The Opposition then switched their attack to the Admiralty and particularly to Sandwich. On 23 February, Fox asked for the papers relating to the movements of the French fleet and on 3 March moved to condemn Sandwich for giving Keppel an inadequate fleet. Fox lost the division 204 to 170. Then on 8 March, he launched a general attack on Government policy based on the state of the navy. The Opposition's support weakened however and Fox's motion lost 246 to 174. Dunning moved to debate the powers of the Admiralty to order a court-martial but lost 228 to 135. On 23 April, the Earl of Bristol's motion in the Lords to

2. For a detailed analysis of the invasion scare, see A. Temple Patterson, *The Other Armada: The Franco-Spanish Attempt to Invade Britain in 1779* (Manchester, 1960).

3. Rockingham's comment to Burke was: "What diabolical villainy." *The Correspondence of Edmund Burke*, ed. Thomas W. Copeland, 9 vols. (Cambridge and Chicago, 1961–70), vol. 4 (ed. John A. Woods), p. 31.

4. Partisan support of the two admirals also severely damaged naval morale for an indefinite period.

5. Palliser was acquitted but not entirely exonerated on 5 May.

dismiss Sandwich also lost, 78 to 39. Public interest in the Keppel affair waned and further attacks by Fox using this issue failed because the majority of M.P.s were no longer prepared to support a faction fight in a time of national danger. The danger was the invasion crisis, which engendered panic and an outburst of patriotic sentiment. Here again the Rockinghams were out of tune with popular sentiment, for they chose to criticise the volunteer regiments raised by private subscription.[6]

The Opposition's concentration on the Keppel affair tended to divert its attention from other major political issues but the Government still faced several serious problems in 1779. Ireland was dissatisfied with the concessions of 1778 and reacted by creating nonimportation associations. More serious, the failure of the Irish government to set up a militia resulted in the formation of volunteer associations directed by prominent Protestants, with an implicit threat to use them to force measures from Britain to alleviate Irish distress. During the spring, North stalled endlessly in the face of English merchant protests against concessions to Ireland, despite Opposition pressure. The effects of the trade boycott and perhaps a fear that Ireland might go the way of America, as the Opposition warned, finally pushed North into preparing legislation in November.

The Government also faced an alarming increase of strength in the movement for economical reform, which now had wide popular support. The emergence of the Yorkshire Movement under Christopher Wyvill set a pattern and county associations began to apply external pressure on Parliament. On 29 November, Wyvill produced the Yorkshire programme: to reduce "influence," protect the rights of voters, increase the number of county M.P.s, circularise the county to petition Parliament for the reduction of placeholders, and reform the Civil List. Rockingham uneasily supported the movement in his home county. He saw the advantages of a popular base in the county and of the petitioning movement, but he did not

6. Rockingham believed that because the previous session's militia bill had been passed without the clause permitting the militia to double in size, the new regiments were illegal. Burke thought they would become a kind of "... Test of particular attachments; and would be used to create influences in the Country...." Burke to Rockingham, 8 August 1779, *The Correspondence of Edmund Burke*, vol. 4, p. 113.

approve any attempt to reform representation in Parliament. On 7 December, Richmond in the Lords moved to reform the Civil List (the motion lost 77 to 36), and on 15 December Burke in the Commons produced a scheme to eliminate fifty placeholders at a saving of £200,000 per annum. Wyvill agreed to an alliance with the Rockinghams but was determined to prevent their domination of the movement. At the county meeting on 30 December, the committee set up to supervise the petition embodying the movement's aims deliberately excluded peers and M.P.s. The Rockinghams continued to believe that they were using the movement but actually they had been reduced to a peripheral influence.

These issues diminished the Opposition's interest in the war and their only sustained assault against the Government took place after the Easter recess. They had forced the formation of a committee of enquiry into the conduct of the war on 29 March; the committee sat from 22 April to 30 June and gave the Opposition several opportunities for attack. However, the Opposition failed in its attempt to force a review of the actions of Clinton's second-in-command, Cornwallis, on 29 April although North eventually conceded a parliamentary examination of Cornwallis. On 11 June, Sir William Meredith futilely moved for peace with America—the House did not divide—and the Opposition failed to postpone prorogation until after the committee produced its report. Finally, Cavendish moved to concentrate the nation's energies on the Bourbon war and lost 156 to 80 on 3 July.

The Opposition had failed to erode the Government's majority but the stresses of the year shook North's nerve. He anxiously tried to resign while making abortive efforts to induce some of the Opposition leaders to enter the ministry—at the beginning of the year feelers were put out to Fox and in December to Shelburne. The ministry, so long riddled with dissension, began to fall apart in the fall of 1779. Suffolk died in March; North's desire to replace him with Hillsborough was strongly opposed by Wedderburn and Eden, so the post simply remained unfilled. In October, Gower resigned over the treatment of Ireland, and he was shortly followed by Weymouth. North was finally prodded into action; he persuaded Lord Stormont to leave his diplomatic post in Paris and take the Northern Department. Bathurst replaced Gower as Lord

President and the rest of the Cabinet accepted Hillsborough as Southern Secretary.

North knew that the King's determination was the real factor holding the ministry together, but he did not know that the King was now checking on him through private correspondence with Charles Jenkinson and John Robinson. The King's obstinacy prevented North removing Germain, who had become a liability, because George III was not anxious to lose a minister still committed to the American war. A government drawn from the Opposition was unthinkable, particularly after the December negotiation:

> Nothing less will satisfy them than a total Change of Measures and Men; to obtain their Support I must deliver up my Person, my Principles, and my Dominions into their hands; I must also abandon every Old, Illustrious, and faithful servant I have to be treated as their resentment or their mercy may incline them.[7]

The delay in the *Annual Register*'s publication continued to grow, and the volume for 1779 was published on 13 January 1781. The editor blamed the delay on the amount of material generated by reporting the war.[8] The historical section was reduced in size from the high point of 1778 to 214 pages. The ten chapters are entirely devoted to the war and parliamentary affairs, with no reference to events in Europe. Chapter I begins with a review of the British raids on the American coast in the fall of 1778 and proceeds to give an account of the frontier war on the "dark and bloody ground" of the Ohio Valley, the region up to the Great Lakes and the backcountry of Pennsylvania and New York. The *Register*'s description of the Wyoming Valley massacre appears to be taken entirely from American sources, which painted the Tory-Indian allies in the blackest colour. The account of George Rogers Clark's activities is generally accurate, as is that of William Butler's raid on Joseph Brant's base, although it fails to mention that Butler's attack was in reprisal for Brant's raid on German Flats in September 1778. The *Register* is quick to condemn the involvement of the Indians and in its account implicitly supports the line taken by Burke

---

7. *The Correspondence of King George III*, ed. Sir John W. Fortescue, 6 vols. (London, 1927–28), p. 520.

8. *AR*, 1779, preface, p. vii.

that the use of the savages in the war is a disgrace to a
civilised nation. The description of Clark's successes concludes with some satisfaction that the Indians were given
a taste of their own medicine. Yet the *Register* explains
fairly the Wyoming Valley massacre as a product of intercolonial tension over the area and a direct result of inten-
sification of local hostilities which made the national
conflict here truly a civil war.

Chapter II follows the activities of the Carlisle Peace
Commission to their futile conclusion, mentions Lafayette's childish challenge to Carlisle, and ends with
Campbell's expedition to Georgia, the capture of Savannah, and the junction with Prevost. Chapter III traces the
naval war in the Americas in 1778 from the French capture of Dominica in September to the British seizure of St.
Lucia in December. Chapter IV deals with the movements
of the Channel Fleet in the summer of 1778, culminating
in the engagement off Ushant in July, and concludes with
a careful defence of the "prudent and temperate conduct"
of Keppel. Chapter V covers the pre-Christmas parliamentary session of 1778, and pays particular attention to the
Opposition's protest against the peace commissioners'
proclamation of 3 October and the development of the
Keppel affair up to the calling of the court-martial.

Parliamentary affairs from January 1779 to the summer
recess are treated in detail in the next three chapters.
Keppel's trial and the aftermath, Sir Philip Jennings
Clerke's second failure to pass a bill excluding contractors
and the debates on the Irish problem are dealt with in
Chapter VI. Chapters VII and VIII cover the progress of
the Opposition assault on the Admiralty and Sandwich,
the Government's conduct of the war, its failure to solve
the Irish problem, and the battle over the militia bill.
Chapter VII also includes an account of the April debate
on the affairs of the East India Company and problems in
Madras.

The final two chapters return to the progress of the war.
Chapter IX begins with a brief review of the extension of
the war to India in the late summer of 1778,[9] and pro-
ceeds to describe the operations of Prevost and Lincoln in
South Carolina and Georgia, the British raids to the
Chesapeake, up the Hudson, and on the New England

9. See "Introduction, 1780."

coast. Chapter X reviews the naval operations in the West Indies, concentrating on the loss of Grenada and the failure to recover the island, and concludes with the abortive Franco-American siege of Savannah.

The *Appendix to the Chronicle* and *State Papers* are again substantial; the *Appendix* contains nineteen items, the *State Papers*, no less than thirty-nine. The following extracts from the *Appendix to the Chronicle* are included here: Burgoyne's public justificatory letter; copies of his correspondence with the Secretary at War, which he also chose to publish; the official report of the famous fight between the American, John Paul Jones, and his British naval rivals off Scarborough in September; and Lafayette's silly challenge to Carlisle, and the latter's reply. Extracts from the *State Papers* include: the speech from the throne at the opening of the 1778 pre-Christmas session and the addresses in reply of both Houses of Parliament; the Lord's protest against the peace commissioners' notorious proclamation of 3 October 1778; the King's message to Parliament announcing the outbreak of the war with Spain, and the protest from the dissenting Lords to the address in reply; a translation of the French manifesto justifying the declaration of war against Britain and Britain's reply; two documents illustrating the growing tension with Holland, here specifically referring to the help given by the Dutch to John Paul Jones; the text of the Franco-American treaty of friendship and commerce; and the manifesto of Congress of 30 October 1778 in reply to the last proclamation of the Peace Commission.

THE Year of which we treat, presented the moſt aweful appearance of public affairs, which this country had perhaps beheld for many ages. All ancient ſyſtems of policy, relative to any ſcheme of equality or balance of power, ſeemed forgotten in Europe. Friends and allies were no more with reſpect to us. On the contrary, whether it proceeded from our fault, or whether it was merely our misfortune, mankind seemed to wait, with an aspect which at best bespoke indifference, for the event of that ruin which was expected to burst upon us. every year of this period, so full of trouble both abroad and at home, has produced so much matter, that the business of one has run in upon the other. The Reader will thus account for the delay which has annually increased. Perhaps we ought rather to apologize for bringing out the matter so crudely, as we are obliged to do, to keep tolerably within time, than for a delay rendered necessary by the magnitude of our task. Happy shall we deem the hour, when, recurring from the horrors of war to the pleasant ways of peace, we shall have the pleasure of announcing to the Public, the glad tidings of returning tranquillity.

It has happened fortunately, that the expected evil and danger, were less dreadful in the encounter, than in the distant appearance. The great combination of the House of Bourbon with the American Colonies, was far from producing all those effects which were undoubtedly expected. If our own successes were not great, and rather negative than direct in their nature, our loſſes, however conſiderable, were ſtill leſs than might have been apprehended. It affords no ſmall room both for ſatisfaction and hope, that no diminution of national glory has taken place, through any failure of native valour in our Seamen and Soldiers. They have ſupported in all caſes, and under whatever circumſtances of diſadvantage, their antient character.

Retroſpective view of American affairs in the year 1778. *Expedition to Bedford, Fair Haven ; and to Martha's Vineyard. Admiral Montague diſpoſſeſſes the French of the iſlands of St. Pierre; and Miquelon. Lord Cornwallis, and Gen Knyphauſen, advance into the enemy's country, on both ſides of the North River. Surprize of Baylor's light horſe. Succeſs of the expedition to Egg Harbour. Surprize of Pulaſki's legion. Cruel depredations by Butler, Brandt, and the ſavages, on the back frontiers. Deſtruction of the new ſettlement at Wyoming, attended with circumſtances of ſingular cruelty and barbarity. Col. Clarke's expedition from Virginia, for the reduction of the Canadian towns and ſettlements in the Illinois country. Conſequences of Clarke's ſucceſs Expedition from Schoharie to the Upper Suſquehanna. Deſtruction of the Unadilla and Anaquago ſettlements.*

WE have ſeen in our laſt volume, that the effectual protection which the French ſquadron received from their new allies, at Boſton, had entirely fruſtrated Lord Howe's deſign of attacking D'Eſtaing in that road or harbour. Upon this failure of hope with reſpect to his primary object, the noble Admiral immediately returned to the ſuccour of Rhode Iſland, which, we have alſo ſeen, had been inveſted, and vigorouſly attacked, by General Sullivan. And finding that

Sept. 8th, 1778.

iſland already freed from danger, he proceeded to New York, where, in conſequence of what is underſtood by a previous leave of abſence, he reſigned the command of the fleet into the hands of Admiral Gambier, and returned to England.

Sir Henry Clinton, who had embarked with 4,000 men for the relief of Rhode iſland, had two other material objects in view, in one or both of which he might probably have ſucceeded, if he had not been detained by contrary winds a few hours beyond his time, or that Sullivan had not been attentive to the danger to which he was exposed, when he found himself finally abandoned by the French fleet, and in consequence deserted by the New England volunteers, who composed the better part of his force. One of these was to cut off Sullivan's retreat to the continent ; and the other, which might have been either adopted as principal, or pursued as a secondary object, was to attack the Americans in their head quarters and principal place of arms at Providence ; the destruction, or effectual dismantling of which, would have removed an eye-sore, and constant source of apprehension, at least, from the immediate vicinity of Rhode Island.

Sullivan's timely retreat having frustrated these designs, Sir Henry Clinton, on his return to New York, dispatched Major General Grey, with the fleet of transports and troops, under the convoy of Captain Fanshawe, of the Carysfort frigate,[1] upon an expedition to the eastward. The first object of this expedition was to exterminate some nests of small privateers, which abounded in the rivers and creeks adjoining to Buzzards Bay, in that part of New England called the Plymouth Colony ; which from their vicinity to Rhode Island and the Sound, greatly infested the trade of New York, as well as the adjacent coasts of Long Island ; whilst the nearness of their retreats, with the smallness of their vessels, and the shallowness of their creeks, secured them in a great measure from all pursuit.

This service was performed with great effect by the detachment under the command of the Major General. Between six in the evening, when the troops were landed, and twelve, on the following day, the work was completely done ; destroying in their course about seventy sail of shipping, besides a great number Sept. 5th.

of small craft. The detachment likewise burnt or destroyed in the same manner, the magazines, wharfs, stores, warehouses, rope walks, and vessels on the stocks, both on the Bedford and Fair Haven sides of the Acushnet river.

The transports and troops proceeded from Fair Haven to the island called Martha's Vineyard ; the inhabitants of which, like those of Nantucket, were once celebrated for their enterprize, skill, and great success in the fisheries. This island, being, however, the reverse of Nantucket in point of fertility, afforded a considerable and most desirable contribution, consisting of 10,000 sheep, and 300 oxen, for the public service at New York.

In the mean time, Admiral Montague,[2] who commanded on the Newfoundland station, no sooner received intelligence that D'Estaing had commenced hostilities on the coasts of North America, than, in consequence of provisional orders with which he had been furnished for the purpose, he dispatched Commodore Evans,[3] with the Romney and some frigates, together with a detachment of marines and artillery, to seize on the small islands of St. Pierre and Miquelon, which had been allotted to France by the last treaty of peace, for the purpose of curing and drying their fish, and serving as a store-house and shelter for the vessels employed in their fishery.

As France had been particularly restricted by the late treaty from fortifying those islands, and equally tied down from any increase of a small limited number of troops in them, which were only adapted to the support of the civil government, and not to any purposes of defence, against whatever might deserve the name of enemy, this service was accordingly performed without difficulty. A capitulation was granted, in consequence of which the Governor, with the inhabitants, and the garrison, a-

mounting in the whole to about 2,000, were transmitted to France ; all the accommodations of habitation, trade, and fishery were destroyed ; and the islands thrown back into their original state.

Upon the return of the troops from the Bedford expedition, and with the contributions raised at Martha's Vineyard, Gen. Sir Henry Clinton determined upon another to Egg Harbour, on the Jersey coast, where the enemy had a number of privateers and prizes, and what was still more interesting, some very considerable salt works. To draw away their attention from the objects of this expedition, and in order also to procure forage and fresh provisions for the army, Lord Cornwallis advanced into Jersey with a strong body of troops, where he took a position between Newbridge, on the Hackinsack, to his left, and the North river, to his right. At the same time, Lieut. Gen. Knyphausen, advancing with another division of the army on the West Chester side, took a parallel position, his left reaching to the North River, near Wepperham, and his right extending to the Brunx.

It would not be easy to conceive any situation more favourable for the carrying on of military operations with advantage. The two divisions being only separated by the North River, could, by the means of their flat boats, unite their whole force on either side of it within twenty-four hours ; whilst, by the command of the Channel, which their marine afforded all the way up to the Highlands, Washington's forces, which were likewise separated in the same manner, but much more dispersed, could not have been assembled in less than ten days. And even then, if he should quit his strong ground in the Highlands, in order to pass over to the relief of the Jerseys, he must have subjected himself to hazard the consequences of a general action, in a country, which from its nature, would have been very unfavourable to him in such an event. By this means, the provinces of New York and the Jerseys were in a great measure laid open to the army; the necessary supplies of forage and provisions were plentifully obtained; and an opportunity was afforded to the well affected of coming in for protection or service. Such was one, among the numberless advantages, which our naval command of the seas and rivers afforded in the course of this war.

Baylor's regiment of light horse, which had been lately raised in Virginia, and was generally called Mrs. Washington's regiment, became a victim upon this occasion,[4] to the design of Lord Cornwallis, with the immediate address, and prompt execution of Major General Grey. This regiment having been detached with some militia to watch and interrupt the foragers, their vicinity to the North River, in the villages of Old and New Taapan, where they lay, with other circumstances of situation, and perhaps more than any, their unsoldierly security, and carelessness with respect to guards and posts, induced Lord Cornwallis to form a plan for their surprize in the night. In pursuit of this design, whilst Gen. Grey, with the light infantry, and some other troops, advanced by Sept. 27th. night on the left, to surprize the enemy on that side, a detachment was made from Knyphausen's corps, on the right, consisting of the 71st regiment under Col. Campbell, and an American[5] light corps, called the Queen's Rangers, who having passed the North River, intended to have enclosed them so effectually, that being placed between two fires, few or none of them could escape.

Some deserters from the column on the right, prevented the completion of the scheme. These having at the most critical moment, rouzed the militia who lay in New Taapan, from their trance of security, afforded a clear opportunity for their escape, before the column could come up. But the Major General conducted his division, with so profound a silence, and such excellency of order, that they not only cut off a serjeant's patrole of twelve men, without any noise, but completely surrounded the village of Old Taapan without any discovery, and surprized Baylor's horse, asleep and naked, in the barns where they lay. A severe execution took place, and the regiment was entirely ruined.

Capt. Ferguson of the 70th regiment, with about 300 land forces,[6] were detached on the expedition to Little Egg Harbour, on the Jersey coast, under the convoy of Capt Colins of the Zebra, with two[7] other frigates, besides some light armed vessels and gallies, which, from their capacity of running into shallow water, were particularly adapted to the nature of the intended service.

The convoy arrived at the place of its destination about the beginning of October; but as the wind and other circumstances retarded the passage of the ships over a bar which lay in their way, and that every thing in such an enterprize depended upon expedition, the troops were crowded, as circumstances would admit, into the gallies and small craft, which were lightened, by taking out every thing that was not essentially necessary to the immediate service. It seems, that the enemy having received some intelligence of the design against them, had suddenly sent out to sea, such of their privateers as were in any degree of readiness, in order thereby to evade the impending danger. The larger of their remaining vessels, consisting mostly of prizes, were, for their greater security, hauled up the river Mullicus as far as they could go, to a place called Chesnut Neck, which lay about 20 miles from the mouth of the river.

Their smaller privateers, and craft of different sorts, were carried still farther up into the country.

The detachment, with the lighter armed vessels, proceeded, through a most difficult passage, to Chesnut Neck; being obliged to work their way at random through numberless shoals, without the aid of a pilot, or any knowledge of the channels. Having successfully overcome these difficulties, they discovered on their arrival, an appearance of resistance which they could scarcely have expected; one battery shewing itself close to the water side, and another, with a breast work manned, to cover it on an adjoining eminence. But upon a nearer approach it was discovered, that these works were totally destitute of artillery; and the troops being landed under a well directed cannonade from the gallies and gun boats, the neighbouring militia, who had undertaken their defence with small arms, soon found the task beyond their ability, and were, with little difficulty, and without any loss, obliged to abandon them and disperse.

The detachment found ten vessels at this place; which were of a considerable size, and mostly British prizes. Although these were in general valuable, yet the difficulty of the navigation, and the danger of delay, rendered the carrying them off impracticable; they were accordingly fired and destroyed. And as the trade of New York had suffered greatly from their depredations, the commanders determined to root out this nest of privateers as effectually as possible. Under this determination, they destroyed the settlements, storehouses and works of every sort.

The good will of the officers and troops would have led them to complete the business, by proceeding up the river, and destroying the remainder of the enemy's shipping, in their last retreat, at the Forks, if the difficulties had not appeared too discouraging, and the danger too imminent to be prudently encountered. The delays which they met with in their return, owing to the ftranding of fome of the veffels, afforded an opportunity to the troops of making fome fuccefsful excurfions into the neighbouring country. In thefe they deftroyed fome confiderable falt works, as well as the houfes and fettlements of feveral perfons, who had either been confpicuous by their activity in the rebellion, charged with oppreffion and cruelty to the well affected, or who had been concerned in the fitting out of privateers ; a fpecies of fervice, however, more calculated to gratify refentments on one fide, and to excite them on the other, than to produce any effential end with regard to the iffue of the war.

When the troops had rejoined the fquadron, a delay occafioned by contrary winds in Egg Harbour, afforded an opportunity to enterprizing officers for the performance of new fervice, and that of a more active and fpirited nature, than what they had already executed. A French captain, with fome private men, who had deferted from Pulafki's legion, gave fuch an account of the carelefs manner in which three troops of horfe, and as many companies of infantry, all belonging to that corps, were cantoned, at only a few miles diftance, that the commanding officers by fea and land, judged it a fufficient ground for undertaking an expedition to furprize and beat up their quarters. The advantage of conveying the troops by water to within a fmall diftance of their deftination, together with the information given by the deferters of an unguarded bridge, which lay a little on their fide of the fcene of action, the poffeffion of which would ferve in cafe of neceffity, effectually to cover the retreat back to their veffels, added much to the apparent eligibility of the defign.

The deferters fpoke truth in this inftance, and the fuccefs was accordingly anfwerable to the expectation. 250 men were embarked, who after rowing ten miles, were landed long before day-light, within a mile of the bridge and defile we have mentioned ; thefe being feized without difcovery, and a proper guard left to fecure the poffeffion, the reft of the detachment pufhed forward, and fo completely furprized Pulafki's light infantry in the houfes where they lay, as nearly to cut them to pieces without refiftance. The victors numbered above fifty dead bodies. Several officers, and among them, the Baron de Bofe, a lieutenant colonel, with a captain, and an adjutant, perifhed in this flaughter. Capt. Ferguson obferves in his report, that it being a night attack, little quarter could be given, fo that only five prifoners were taken. Though fome attempt was made by Pulafki's horfe, and the remains of his infantry, to harrafs the detachment on their retreat, the good countenance which they kept, and the poffeffion of the bridge, rendered it totally ineffectual. [8]

Civil wars are unhappily diftinguifhed from all others, by a degree of rancour in their profecution, which does not exift in the hoftilities of diftinct nations, and abfolute ftrangers. They are of courfe fruitful in circumftances grievous to humanity. In fuch cafes, the moft trifling occafions, the moft vague and abfurd rumours, will irritate the multitude in all armies, to acts of great rigour and cruelty. An account given by the deferters, that Pulafki had iffued public orders, forbidding his corps to grant any quarter to the Britifh troops, afforded a new edge to the fury of the foldiers, and fhut up their bofoms againft every feeling of pity or remorfe. This tale, totally unfupported, as it fhould feem, by any former, concurrent, or fubfequent circumftance, might well be attributed to the malice of the deferters ; and perhaps on all fuch occafions, it were better not to credit too haftily, thofe reports which urge to acts of unufual feverity, by charging a like intention to the enemy.

This and the former expedition afforded an opportunity for a renewal of thofe complaints, which the Americans had fo loudly and repeatedly made, of the inhumanities and cruelties exercifed by fome corps of the Britifh troops, as well as by their auxiliaries. A number of real or fuppofed facts, were now particularly fupplied by the furprize of Baylor's regiment, which was reprefented as a cold-blood maffacre of naked men, furprized in their fleep ; and who, from a reliance on the laws of war and cuftoms of nations, being in full expectation of quarter when they made no refiftance, would not leffen or hazard that fecurity, by even an attempt to lay hold of their arms, or the fmalleft motion of defence. The depofitions of [9] feveral of the foldiers who had been left as dead, or who had otherwife unaccountably efcaped, were taken upon oath, authenticated in the ufual forms, and publifhed by authority. Some of the witneffes who appeared upon this occafion, afforded fuch extraordinary inftances of the tenacioufnefs of human nature, in fome particular cafes and circumftances, with refpect to life, that a recital of the facts as they are ftated, may poffibly be confidered by fome as a matter of phyfical curiofity. Of about a dozen wounded foldiers who appeared to give their evidence, three had received in a regular gradation, from nine to eleven ftabs each, of bayonets, in the breaft and trunk of the body, befides feveral wounds in other parts. Two others had received, the one five, and the other fix, ftabs in the body. It will undoubtedly excite the admiration of whoever confiders the nature of the weapon, and the force which it derives, as well from the weight of the musket to which it is fixed, as from the manner in which it is used, and the strength of the operator, that these men were not only able to give their testimony at a considerable distance of time, but that no doubt seems then to have been entertained of their recovery.

Although some tribes of the Indians, particularly of those commonly called the Six Nations, had sent congratulations to General Gates on his success at Saratoga, and seemed to enjoy great satisfaction in that event, and that others took different opportunities of expressing similar sentiments, yet the presents which they continually received from England, the industry of the British agents, and the influence of the great number of American refugees which had taken shelter amongst them, all operating in conjunction upon their own native and unconquerable passion for rapine, soon led them to contradict in act, their sentiments or professions upon that occasion. The success which attended the small expeditions undertaken by individuals of different tribes, under the guidance of the refugees, who knew where to lead them directly to spoil, and how to bring them off without danger, soon spread the contagion of havock through the adjoining nations, so that, in a little time, destruction raged very generally through the new settlements, on the back of the northern and middle Colonies.

Colonel Butler, whose name we have seen, as an Indian agent and commander, in the wars on the side of Canada, and who had great influence with some of the northern nations of that people, together with one Brandt, an half Indian by blood, a man of desperate courage, but, as it is said by the Americans, ferocious and cruel beyond example, were the principal leaders in these expeditions. The vast extent of the frontiers, the scattered and remote situation of the settlements, the nature of the combined enemy, which seemed to coalese in one point of action, all the properties of British, American, and savage warfare, together with the exact knowledge which the refugees possessed of every object of their enterprize, and the immediate intelligence which they received from their friends on the spot, afforded them such advantages in these expeditions, that the wretched settlers, found all personal resistance as ineffectual, as public protection was impracticable. To complete their calamity, submission could procure no mercy, nor was age, sex, or condition, in too many instances, capable of allaying the fury of their enemy.

In this course of havock, the destruction of the fine, new, and flourishing settlement of Wyoming, was particularly calamitous to the Americans. That district, situated on the eastern branch of the Susquehanna, in a most beautiful country, and delightful climate, although claimed by, and in the natural order of things seeming properly to appertain to Pensylvania, was notwithstanding, since the last war, settled and cultivated with great ardour, by a numerous swarm from the populous hive of Connecticut. This measure was, however, so much opposed and resented by Pensylvania, and so obstinately supported by its antagonist, that after much altercation, it became at length the foundation of an actual war between the two Colonies, in which they engaged with such earnestness, that it was not even terminated by the contest with the mother country, until the danger grew so near and so imminent on both sides, as of necessity to supersede for the present all other considerations. Their respective charters, and the grants of land under them, interfered strangely with each other. It may be presumed, that the crown in those days did not take much trouble in settling the geography of boundless wastes, which afforded no immediate value, and whose future cultivation, or any disputes about their limits, appeared to be matters of so remote and uncertain a speculation, as to excite no great degree of present attention.

The colony of Connecticut obtained by their grant, all the lands westward, within their proper degrees of latitude to the South Seas, which were not already occupied by other powers. New York, and New Jersey, were then within that exception, being both foreign, and they stretched directly across, in the way of that grant. Pensylvania was afterwards granted to its proprietors, lying on the farther side, and in a parallel line, with these two provinces. The Connecticut men acknowledged the validity of the exception with respect to New York and Jersey; but insisted, that their right emerged on the western boundary of those provinces, in the course of the supposed line, and could not in any degree be affected by a later grant made to Pensylvania. A claim, which if established, would narrow the limits of the last province to a degree, which would most materially affect its power and interests; and which lying open, as it still does, may possibly be productive of very material consequences with respect to the future state of America.

The settlement of Wyoming consisted of eight townships, each containing a square of five miles, beautifully situated on both sides of the Susquehanna. In such a country, situation, and climate as we have described; and blest with a soil luxuriantly fertile; where every man possessed an abundance, which was, however, the fruit of moderate labour and industry;

where no man was very rich, nor very great; the inhabitants exhibited upon the whole, such a picture of primeval happiness, as has feldom been equalled; and fuch, indeed, as humanity in its prefent ftate feems fcarcely capable of exceeding.

The fettlement increafed and throve accordingly. And notwithstanding its infant ftate, and the oppofition they met from Philadelphia, population was already become fo vigorous amongft them, that they had fent a thoufand men to ferve in the Continental army. Yet, with this exceffive drain from the cultivation of a new Colony, there farms were ftill fo loaded with plentiful crops of every kind, and their paftures fo abundantly covered with cattle, that their fupplies to the army in thofe refpects, were at leaft in full proportion to that which they afforded in men. Nor had they been deficient in providing againft thofe dangers, to which, from their remote fituation, they were particularly expofed; and had accordingly conftructed for that purpofe no lefs than four forts, which feemed, at leaft, fully fufficient to cover the fettlement from the irruptions of the favages.

But neither the happinefs of climate, the fertility of foil, nor the remotenefs of fituation, could prevent the evils of party and political difcord from fpringing up amongft them. It might indeed appear from the fupply of men which they had fent to the army, that only one political principle pervaded the fettlement; a fupply fo ill fuited to the ftate and ftrength of an infant colony, that it feems difficult whether to admire more, the excefs of zeal from which it proceeded, or the total want of prudence, policy, and wifdom, under which it was directed. But notwithstanding this appearance, they had no inconfiderable mixture of loyalifts

among themfelves, and the two parties were actuated by fentiments of the moft violent animofity. Nor were thefe animofities confined to particular families or places, or marked by any line of diftinction; but creeping within the roofs, and to the hearths and boards where they were leaft expected, ferved, as it afterwards fatally appeared, equally to poifon the fources of domeftic fecurity and happinefs, and to cancel the laws of nature and humanity.

It would feem extraordinary, if fuch inftances had not occurred upon other occafions, that this devoted people had frequent and timely warnings of the danger to which they were expofed by fending all their beft men to fo great a diftance, without their taking any timely meafures for their recall, or even of procuring a fubftitute of defence or protection. Their quiet had been interrupted by the favages, joined with marauding parties of their own countrymen, in the preceding year; and it was only by a vigorous oppofition, in a courfe of fuccefsful fkirmifhes, that they had been driven off or difperfed. Several of thofe whom they called Tories, and others who had not before been fufpected, had at that time and fince abandoned the fettlement, and along with a perfect, and confequently dangerous knowledge of all the particulars of their fituation and circumftances, were well known to have carried along with them fuch a ftock of private refentment, from the abafement and infults they had fuffered from the prevailing party, as could not fail to give a direction to the fury, and even a new edge to the cruelty, of their favage and inveterate enemies.

A fort of public act which had taken place in the fettlement fince the laft invafion, was preceded with, and productive of circumftances, which afforded caufe for the greateft alarm, and for every

poffible defenfive precaution. An unufual number of ftrangers had, under various pretences, and the fanction of that univerfal hofpitality which once fo much diftinguifhed America from the old world, come into the Colony, where their behaviour became fo fufpicious, that they were at length taken up and examined, when fuch evidence appeared againft feveral of them, of their acting in direct concert with the enemy, on a fcheme for the deftruction of the fettlements, that about twenty were fent off under a ftrong guard to Connecticut, in order to be there imprifoned and tried for their lives. The remainder of thefe ftrange Tories, againft whom no fufficient evidence could be procured, were only expelled. It was foon well known, that this meafure of fending their fellows to Connecticut, had excited the rage of thofe called Tories, in general, whether in arms on the frontiers, or otherwife, in the moft extreme degree; and that all the threats which had ever been denounced againft this people, were now renewed with aggravated vengeance.

As the time approached for the final cataftrophe, the Indians practifed a more refined diffimulation, if not greater treachery, than had been cuftomary with them. For feveral weeks previous to the intended attack, they repeatedly fent fmall parties to the fettlement, charged with the ftrongeft profeffions of friendfhip, declarations, of the fulleft defire and intention to preferve the peace inviolate on their fide, and requefts, that the fame favourable and pacific difpofition might be entertained and cultivated on the other. Thefe parties, befides lulling the people in their prefent deceitful fecurity, anfwered the purpofes, of communicating with their friends, and of obferving the immediate ftate of affairs in the Colony. Some alarm, or fenfe of their danger, began, however, to spread among the people, and letters were sent to General Washington, and to others in authority, representing their situation, and demanding immediate assistance. As the time more nearly approached, some small parties of the enemy, more impatient than the rest, or more eager and covetous to come in for the first fruits of the spoil, made sudden irruptions into the settlement, and committed several robberies and murders; in the course of which, whether through ignorance, or whether from a total contempt of all ties and obligations, they massacred the unhappy wife and five children of one of those men, who had been sent for trial, in their own cause, to Connecticut.

At length, in the beginning of July, 1778, the enemy appeared suddenly, but in full force, on the Susquehanna. They were led by Butler, that distinguished partizan, whose name we have already mentioned; who was assisted by most of those leaders, who, like him, had rendered themselves terrible in the present frontier war. Their force was estimated at about 1,600 men, of whom, something less than one fourth were Indians, led by their own chiefs; the others, were disguised and painted in such a manner, as not to be distinguished from the savages, excepting only their officers, who being dressed in regimentals carried the appearance of regulars. One of the smaller forts, which was mostly garrisoned by those called Tories, was by them given up, or as it was said betrayed. Another was taken by storm, where, although they massacred the men in the most inhuman manner, they spared the women and children.

It seems odd enough, if not singular, that another Colonel Butler, and said to be a near relation to the invader, should chance to have the defence of Wyoming, ei-[11]

ther committed to his charge, or by some means fall to his lot. This man, with nearly the whole force of the settlement, was stationed in the principal fort, called Kingston; whither also, the women, children, and defenceless of all sorts, as the only place of common refuge, crowded for shelter and protection. It would seem, from his situation and force in that place, that he might there have waited, and successfully resisted, all the attempts of the enemy. But this man was so wretchedly weak, that he suffered himself to be enticed by his namesake and kinsman, to abandon the advantage and security afforded by his fortress, and to devote those under his charge to certain destruction, by exposing them naked to so severe an enemy. Under the colour of holding a parley for the conclusion of a treaty, he was led into an agreement, that upon the enemy withdrawing their force, he should march out to hold a conference with them in the open field, and that at so great a distance from the fort, as shut out every possibility of the protection which it otherwise afforded. To render this measure still more unaccountable, he, at the same time, shewed so great a distrust of the enemy, and seemed so thoroughly apprehensive of their designs, that he marched 400 men well armed, being nearly the whole strength of his garrison, to guard his person to the place of parley.

Upon his arrival there, he was greatly surprized at finding nobody to treat with; but not being willing to return without finishing his business, he advanced towards the foot of the neighbouring mountains, still hoping that he might hear or see something of those he wanted. As the country began to grow dark and woody, a flag at length appeared, at a considerable distance among the bushes, the holders of which seemed so much afraid of treachery and danger

from his side, that they retired as he advanced; whilst he, endeavouring to remove this ill impression, still pursued the flag.

This commander of a garrison did not once perceive his danger, until his party was thoroughly enclosed, and he was suddenly awakened from his dream, by finding it attacked at once on every side. His behaviour in this wretched situation, could scarcely have been expected from the conduct which led him into it. He and his party, notwithstanding those circumstances of surprize and danger which might have disconcerted the most veteran troops, fought with resolution and bravery; and kept up so continual and heavy a fire for three quarters of an hour, that they seemed to gain a marked superiority over their numerous enemy.

In this critical moment of danger, some sudden impulse of fear, or premeditated treachery in a soldier, which induced him to cry out aloud that the colonel had ordered a retreat, determined at once the fate of the party, and possibly that of the final author of their ruin. In the state of confusion that ensued, the enemy breaking in on all sides without obstruction, commenced an unresisted slaughter. Considering the great superiority of numbers on the side of the victors, the fleetness of the savages, and the fierceness of the whole, together with the manner in which the vanquished had been originally surrounded, it affords no small room for astonishment, that the commander of the garrison, with about seventy of his party, should have been able to effect their escape, and to make their way good to a small fort on the other side of the river.

The conquerors immediately invested Fort Kingston, and to cheer the drooping spirits of the weak remaining garrison, sent in for their contemplation, the bloody scalps of 200 of their late relations, friends, and comrades. Colonel Dennison, the present[12] commander of the fort, seeing the impossibility of any effectual defence, not having force sufficient even to man the works for one effort, went with a flag to Butler, to know what terms he would grant on a surrender; to this application of weakness and misery, Butler, with all the phlegm of a real savage, answered in two short words, " the hatchet." In these dreadful circumstances, the unfortunate governor having defended his fort, until most of the garrison were killed or disabled, was at length compelled to surrender at discretion. Some of the unhappy persons in the fort were carried away alive; but the barbarous conquerors, to save the trouble of murder in detail, shut up the greater part promiscuously in the houses and barracks, which having then set on fire, they enjoyed the savage pleasure of beholding the whole consumed in one general blaze.

They then proceeded to the only remaining fort, called Wilkesborough, which, in hopes of obtaining mercy, was surrendered without resistance, or without even demanding any conditions. Here the tragedy was renewed with aggravated horrors. They found here about seventy of that sort of militia, who are engaged by the different provinces, merely for the guard and defence of their respective frontiers, and who are not called to any other service. With these, as objects of particular enmity, the slaughter was begun; and they were butchered with every possible circumstance of the most deliberate, wanton, and savage cruelty. The remainder of the men, with the women and children, not demanding so much particular attention, were shut up as before in the houses, which being set on fire, they perished all together in the flames.

A general scene of devastation was now spread through all the townships. Fire, sword, and the other different instruments of destruction alternately triumphed. The corn fields were set on fire, and the standing corn, now almost ready for the sickle, burnt as it grew. The houses, furniture, valuables of every kind, together with all those improvements which owed their rise to the persevering toil, and patient industry of man, were as completely destroyed, as their nature, or the industry of the spoilers would admit. The settlements of the Tories alone, generally escaped, and appeared as islands in the midst of the surrounding ruin. It has been often observed, that the practice and habit of cruelty with respect to any particular object, begets a facility in its execution, and a disposition to its commission, with regard to all others. Thus, these merciless ravagers, when the main objects of their cruelty were exhausted, seemed to direct their animosity to every part of living nature; and, as if it were a relaxation or amusement, cut out the tongues of the horses and cattle, leaving them still alive only to prolong their agonies.

The following are a few of the more singular or detached circumstances of barbarity, which are related as parts of this massacre. A Captain Bedlock, who had been[13] taken prisoner, being stripped naked, had his body stuck full of sharp pine splinters, and then a heap of knots of the same wood being piled round him, the whole was set on fire, and his two companions, the Captains Ranson and Durgee, thrown alive into the[14] flames. It is said, that the returned Tories, who had at different times abandoned the settlement in order to join in those savage expeditions, were the most distinguished for their cruelty. Among these, one, whose mother had married a second husband, butchered with

his own hands, both her, his father-in-law, his own sisters, and their infant children. Another, who, during his absence, had sent home several threats against the life of his father, now not only realized them in person, but was himself, with his own hands, the exterminator of his whole family; mother, brothers, and sisters, mingled their blood in one common carnage, with that of the ancient husband and father.

However painful the task of reciting such horrible barbarities, (many of the worst circumstances of which are spared) it may not be totally useless, if they serve to produce a dislike of that promptitude of entering into wars, which is but too natural to people, as well as to princes, when they see the consequences, which their passion, often for trivial and contemptible objects, so frequently produce; and by which they are led gradually, not only to great crimes and great misfortunes, but even to a total change and degradation of their nature.

It is necessary to observe with respect to the destruction of Wyoming, that as no narrative of the exploits of the leaders in that transaction, whether by authority or otherwise, has as yet appeared in this country, we can only rely, for the authenticity of the facts which we have stated, upon the accounts[15] published by the Americans. As these have already been long exposed to the view of all Europe, without their yet producing a single contradiction, any natural, but improper partiality, which might be a temptation to induce us, either to draw a veil over the whole, or to suppress any of the parts of that transaction, would therefore of course, be as fruitless in the effect, as disgraceful in the design. Happy should we deem it, for the honour of humanity, that the whole account was demonstrated to be a fable. The event has already shewn, the impolitic nature of these proceedings, which have only served to fix a bitter and lasting resentment in the minds of the colonists.

The sufferings of the refugees, consisting mostly of women and children, (the broken parts, and scattered relicks of families, who had escaped to the woods during the different scenes of this devastation) were little less deplorable, than those of their friends who had perished in the ruins of their houses. Dispersed and wandering in the forests, as chance and fear directed their steps, without any mutual knowledge or communication, without provision or covering, they had a long tract of deserts to traverse, without guide or direction. They accordingly suffered every degree of distress. Several women were delivered alone in the woods, at a great distance from every possibility of relief. If these, through vigour of mind, or strength of constitution, escaped, undoubtedly others, in similar, and in different circumstances, perished.

Although the fate of Wyoming, and the lamentations of the survivors, had served alternately to freeze every breast with horror, and to melt it with compassion; yet the various objects and exigencies of the war rendered the Americans incapable for the present, of executing that vengeance on their savage enemy, which was, however, fully intended at a proper season. Some small expeditions were, indeed, undertaken, which, from the difficulties attending them, and the spirit of enterprize under which they were conducted, were not destitute of merit, and consequently, are not unworthy of observation, in the narrative of a campaign not distinguished by any activity in the great and splendid operations of war.

Of this sort was an expedition undertaken in the course of the summer from Virginia, under the conduct of a Col. Clarke, with a [16] small party of between two and three hundred men. It cannot but appear astonishing to those, who have been generally used to contemplate military operations, only as they are circumscribed within the narrow confines of European countries, that the object of this enterprize was at so vast a distance, as that the party in their way, were obliged to traverse no less than about 1200 miles, of a boundless, uncultivated, and uninhabited waste, through which they were under a necessity of conveying, every necessary for subsistence, and every equipment for action. It is, however, to be observed, that their conveyance, for much the greater part of the way, was by water.

Their object was the reduction of those French settlements, which had been planted by the Canadians on the upper Missisippi, in that fine and fertile region, as it is described, which taking its name from a noted nation of Indians, is called the Illinois country. It appears, that much of the mischief which had fallen upon the southern and middle colonies from the incursions of the savages, had been attributed to the activity of the governor of those settlements; who, since the com- [17] mencement of the troubles, acting as an agent for government, and paying large rewards for scalps, had besides been indefatigable in his continual endeavours of exciting the Ohio and Missisippi Indians, to undertake expeditions against the back settlements. This conduct was the motive to the present distant expedition.

The party after a long course down the Monongahela, and what might be considered in point of extent, as a voyage, on the Ohio, arrived at length at the great falls of the latter, within about 60 miles of its mouth, where they hid their beats, and bent their course by land to the northward. In this stage of the expedition, after consuming all the provisions which they had been able to carry on their backs, they endured a hard march of two days without any sustenance. We may therefore well credit their assertion, that when they arrived in this hungry state, about midnight, at the town of Kaskaskias, they were unanimously determined to take it or to perish in the attempt.

This town contained about 250 houses, and was sufficiently fortified to have withstood a much stronger enemy; but as the imagined security which the people derived from their remoteness, forbid all ideas of danger, it of course superseded all precaution against a surprize. This was accordingly as complete as possible. The town and fort were taken, without noise or opposition, before the people were well awake; and the inhabitants were so effectually secured, that not so much as a single person escaped to alarm the neighbouring settlements. The governor, Philip Rocheblave, who [18] was considered as so inimical to the Americans, was sent to Virginia, with all the written instructions which he had received from Quebec, Detroit, and Michillimackinack, for setting on and paying the Indians. The inhabitants were compelled to take an oath of allegiance to the United States; and the fort became the principal citadel and head quarters of the victors.

A small detachment which was pushed forward from this place on horseback, surprized and took with as little difficulty, three other French towns, which lay from fifteen to about seventy miles farther up the Missisippi. In all, the inhabitants seemed to have transferred their allegiance with great facility; nor were those dispersed in the country behind-hand with them; who, without waiting for any operation of force or necessity, flocked in by hundreds to take the new oath.

The situation of this small party, in the heart of the Indian country, at the back of some of their most cruel and hostile tribes, in the track of many others, and more or less in the way of all, was converted to peculiar advantage, by the extraordinary activity, and unwearied spirit of their commander. He directed and timed his attacks with such judgment, and executed them with such silence and dispatch, that the savages, at length, found their own mode of war effectually turned upon them. Surprized in their inmost retreats, and most sequestered recesses, at those times and seasons, when they were scarcely less indisposed for action, than unprepared for defence, they experienced in their own huts and families, that unexpected slaughter and destruction, which they had so frequently carried home to others. Thus feeling in the most sensible manner, those calamities which they were only wont to administer, they grew cautious and timid; and the continual danger to which their families were exposed, damped, for a while, the ardour of the warriors in undertaking expeditions. In the mean time, the Americans in the back settlements, not only hearing of Clarke's successes, but immediately feeling their benefit, began to shake off their terror, and even seemed by degrees to partake of his spirit and enterprize. [19]

An expedition, in some degree of the same nature, was also undertaken, from the remote and upper parts of Pensylvania in the month of October, under the conduct of a Col. Butler; the present [20] being, however, as much directed against several considerable settlements belonging to those people whom they called Tories (and who, from the violence of their past hostilities, had become particularly obnoxious), as against the Indians, with whom they seem to have been intermixed as one people. This party, which consisted of a Pensylvania regiment, covered by riflemen and rangers, took its departure from Schobarie; and having gained the head of the Delaware, marched down that river for two days; from whence, turning off to the right, they struck across the mountains to the Sesquehanna, which was the scene of action.

Without entering into a detail of particulars, it will be sufficient to observe, that they totally burnt and destroyed, both the Indian castles or villages in that quarter, and the other settlements. But that, notwithstanding the utmost address and precaution were practised for the purpose of a complete surprize, the inhabitants, both Tories and Indians, had the fortune to escape; a deliverance of no small moment in their situation; as the vengeance for Wyoming, where they bore a distinguished part, would undoubtedly have fallen heavy upon them. The destruction was extended for several miles on both sides of the Susquehanna; in the course of which, the fruits of a plentiful harvest, together with the only saw-mill and grist-mill in that whole country, shared an equal fate with the houses and every other article useful or necessary to man.

The difficulties, distresses, and dangers, which the party encountered in this expedition, were peculiar to that part of the world; and required no small share of that patient fortitude, and hardiness of body and mind, which can scarcely be acquired without long habitude, under certain marked circumstances of situation, by any considerable number of men. Notwithstanding the occasional assistance which they derived from their pack-horses, they were under a necessity of carrying six days provisions on their backs; and thus loaded, continually to wade through rivers and creeks of such a depth and magnitude, that they would scarcely appear passable, without any incumbrance, to men unused to such service. In these circumstances, after the toil of a hard march, and in some situations not venturing to make fires for fear of discovery, they were obliged to endure, without cover, the chilling nights and heavy rains peculiar to that climate and season; whilst their arms were rendered useless, at those times when they were most liable to the sudden attack of an enraged and cruel enemy, whose principal effort lay in that sort of surprize. These were, however, only small matters, when compared with the danger which awaited their return, and which they hardly escaped. This was the sudden rising of the great rivers in their way, occasioned by the continual rains, whilst they were still in the enemy's country, (who were very strong in that quarter) their provisions nearly expended, and every moment affording fresh room for apprehension, that their return would become totally impracticable. A strenuous and bold exertion, to which fortune was, at least, negatively favourable, prevented the fatal consequences of that event. [21]

In this manner, the savage part of the war was carried on in America with mutual boldness and perseverance; and waste and cruelty inflicted and retorted, with infinite variety of scenes of horror and disgust.

Review of conciliatory measures pursued by the commissioners for restoring peace in America. Attempt to open and smooth the way to a negociation by private communications and correspondence, fails in the effect, and is highly resented by the Congress. Resolutions by that body against holding any Communication or intercourse with one of the commissioners. Gentleman in question, declines acting any longer in the commission, and publishes a declaration in answer to the Congress. Declaration from the remaining commissioners in answer to that body. Final manifesto and proclamation by the commissioners. Cautionary measures recommended by the Congress to the people; followed by a counter manifesto, threatening retaliation. Singular letter from the Marquis de la Fayette, to the Earl of Carlisle. American expedition for the reduction of the British settlements in the country of the Natches, on the borders of the Missisippi. Expedition from New-York, under the conduct of Commodore Parker and Colonel Campbell, for the reduction of the province of Georgia. Landing made good, and the rebels defeated. Town of Savannah taken, and the province in general reduced. Major-General Prevost arrives from the southward; takes the town and fort of Sunbury, and assumes the principal command.

IT affords no small degree of pleasing relaxation, to return from all the rage of war, and all the horrid ferocity of savages, and once more to tread in the pleasing paths of civil life. We have indeed beheld the first in its most shocking and degraded form. Stripped of all that "pomp, pride, "and circumstance," which serve so strongly to fascinate the imagination, and divested of that glare of glory, which throws a shade over its deformities, the ghastly carcass has not only been exposed in all its nakedness, but polluted and distained by the bloody hands of barbarians. From so horrid a scene, we naturally turn with pleasure, to trace the tranquil mazes of negociation, and to review the acts and conduct of men in the most refined state of society.

We briefly stated in our last volume, the insuperable difficulties which the Congress had thrown in the way of that conciliatory system, with which the Commissioners had been charged from England to America; and that an acknowledgment of independency, or the total withdrawing of the military force, were the peremptory and only conditions held out by the former, upon which they would admit the opening of any negociation. One of the gentlemen who was appointed in the commission, having served [22] in the navy, on the American coast, and afterwards been governor of a province there, had formed considerable connexions, and an extensive acquaintance in that country; and he now hoped that these circumstances might be of essential service, by using them as means to facilitate the attainment of the great object in view. This seemed the more feasible, as his parliamentary conduct since that time, had been in such direct opposition to all those measures, which were deemed hostile or oppressive with regard to the Colonies, that it could scarcely fail of greatly increasing, instead of diminishing, any influence which he might then have acquired. Under these circumstances he deemed it reasonable to conclude, that the direct applications of friendship, under the covert and freedom of a private correspondence, together with the sanction of personal esteem and opinion, might operate more happily in smoothing or removing those difficulties which stood in the way of an accommodation, than the stiff, tedious, and formal proceedings of public negociation. He was besides well aware, as indeed it was publicly avowed, that the Commissioners laboured under the capital impediment, of the Americans, with whom they were to treat, placing no manner of confidence in the faith or equity of the authority under which they acted; but that on the contrary their distrust of administration had grown so long, and was become so rivetted and confirmed, that they suspected every proposal that was made, as held out only to circumvent; and as the mere offspring of duplicity and treachery. To remove this ill impression, would have been evidently an object of the utmost importance towards the opening of a negociation, and the hope of entering into a treaty. But if the accomplishment of this appeared to be an impracticability, it did not seem a very unreasonable expectation, that the character which this gentleman had acquired in his political capacity, of being an avowed friend to the rights and constitutional liberties of America, further strengthened and confirmed by the known principles of the opposition in general, with whom he had so long acted in parliament, might produce that necessary degree of confidence in a private, which unhappily could not be obtained in a public negociation.

Under some of these, and perhaps other ideas, he endeavoured to commence or renew a private correspondence with several members of the Congress, and other persons of consideration. Thus in fact, endeavouring to establish a double system of negociation; the one, ostensible, with the Congress at large; the other, unseen and private, with individuals whose influence might not only facilitate, but even in some degree direct, the proceedings of the former. Some of these letters, which have been published, seem rather of an unusual cast, considering the peculiar circumstances and situation of the writer. While, as a common friend to both countries, he pathetically lamented their mutual calamities, he seemed no way sparing in his censure of the conduct and measures on the side of government which led to the present troubles; nor did he any more support the justice of the original claims set up by the mother country, than he did the prudence or policy of endeavouring to enforce them. Upon the whole, he used a freedom with the authority under which he acted, not customary with those entrusted with delegated power, and afforded such a degree of approbation to the conduct of the Americans in the past resistance which they had made to it, as is seldom granted by negociators to their opponents. But it was perhaps not ill fitted to confirm that character of neutrality, which might have helped him to insinuate himself into the minds of the Americans.

However right the principles might be, upon which this insinuating scheme of conciliation was adopted, its effects were rather untoward; and the Congress affected to consider it in a very different point of view, from that in which it had been wished or intended to be placed. The first instance of this disposition that appeared, was in a resolution passed by the Congress, about a week after their first communication with the Commissioners. In this, after stating simply as a fact, and without any particular direction, that many letters addressed to individuals of the United States, had been lately received through the conveyance of the enemy; and that some of these were found to contain ideas, insidiously calculated to divide and delude the people; they, therefore, earnestly recommended to the governments of the respective states, and strictly directed the commander in chief, and other officers, to take the most effectual measures for putting a stop to so dangerous and criminal a correspondence.

This was followed by a resolution in the beginning of July, that all letters of a public nature, received by any members of Con-

gress, from the agents, or other subjects of the King of Great-Britain, should be laid before that body. It need scarcely be doubted, that the contents of these objects of enquiry were already well known, but this measure afforded a sanction to the disclosure of private and confidential correspondence, which was indeed necessary to lessen its odium, and at the same time held out authorized ground to the Congress, whereon to found their intended superstructure. Several letters being accordingly laid before them, a passage in one, from Governor Johnstone to General Joseph Reed, and in another, from that gentleman to Mr. Morris, together with an account given by General Reed, of a verbal message or proposal delivered to him by a lady, afforded an opportunity to Congress for entering into those violent measures, by which they interdicted all intercourse and correspondence with Mr. Johnstone.

The first of these exceptionable passages, went no farther than a sort of general proposition, that the man who could be instrumental in restoring harmony between both countries, would deserve more from all the parties concerned in or affected by the quarrel and reconciliation, "than ever yet was bestowed on human kind."—The second, in the letter to Mr. Morris, was more particular. After a complimentary declaration, of believing the men who conducted the affairs of America incapable of being influenced by improper motives, it, however, proceeds upon the subject of the negociation in the following terms:—" But in " all such transactions there is " risque; and I think that who- " ever ventures should be secured, " at the same time that honour " and emolument should naturally " follow the fortune of those who " have steered the vessel in the " storm, and brought her safely " to port. I think that Washington " and the President have a right

" to every favour that grateful " nations can bestow, if they could " once more unite our interests, " and spare the miseries and de- " vastations of war."

But the transaction in which the lady was concerned, afforded the principal ground for that indignation and resentment expressed by the Congress. This matter, as stated by General Reed, went to a proposal of engaging the interest of that gentleman in promoting the object of the commission, viz. a reunion between the two countries, in which event, he should receive an acknowledgment from government of ten thousand pounds sterling; together with any office in his Majesty's gift in the colonies. To which, Mr. Reed, finding (as he says) that an answer was expected, replied, that, " he was " not worth purchasing; but such " as he was, the King of Great- " Britain was not rich enough to " do it."

Aug. 11th. 1778. The Congress issued a declaration, including three resolutions, upon the subject, which they sent by a flag to the British Commissioners at New-York. The declaratory part contained a recital at length of those passages in the letters which we have taken notice of, together with the particulars of the conversation which had passed between Mrs. Ferguson, the lady in question, and General Reed. By the resolutions they determine, That the contents of the said paragraphs, and the particulars in Reed's declaration, cannot but be considered as direct attempts to corrupt and bribe the Congress of the United States of America. That, as they feel, so they ought to demonstrate, the highest and most pointed indignation against such daring and atrocious attempts to corrupt their integrity.—And, " That it is incompatible with " the honour of Congress to hold " any manner of correspondence " or intercourse with the said

"George Johnstone, Esq; espe-
"cially, to negociate with him
"upon affairs, in which the cause
"of liberty and virtue is inte-
"rested."

These proceedings drew out an exceedingly angry and vehement declaration from the gentleman in question; in which, whatever sufficient cause he had for indignation and resentment, the immediate operations of passion were, perhaps, rather too apparent. Those persons, and that body, which were lately held up as examples of virtue and patriotism to all mankind, and whose names seemed to be equalled with the most celebrated in antiquity; were now, not only found to be destitute of every virtue under heaven; but were directly charged with being the betrayers and destroyers of their country; with acting directly contrary to the sense and opinion of the people in general, and of sacrificing their dearest interests to the most unworthy and base motives; and with deluding their unhappy constituents, and leading them blindfold to irretrievable ruin. After charging the Congress with forgetting every principle of virtue and liberty, it creates no surprize that he declares himself indifferent as to their good opinion; nor that their resolution was so far from being a matter of offence to him, that he rather considered it as a mark of distinction.

With respect to the facts or charges stated by the Congress, they are neither absolutely denied, nor acknowledged, by Mr. Johnstone in this piece; he consequently does not enter into any justification of his own conduct; but declares a reservation to himself of the liberty, if he should think proper, of publishing before he left America, such a justification, against the aspersions thrown on his character. He also seems indirectly to deny the charge, by attributing the resolutions to the malice and treachery of the Congress, who intended them only for the purposes of inflaming their wretched constituents to endure all the calamities of war, and as a means for continuing their delusion, thereby to frustrate all the good effects intended by the commission for the restoration of tranquillity. But to defeat their purposes in this respect, he declared, that he should for the future decline acting as a commissioner, or taking the smallest share in any business, whether of negociation or other, in which the Congress should be any way concerned. It may not be unnecessary here to observe, that this gentleman afterwards absolutely disowned the particular transaction with Mr. Reed.

The tone of this publication, accorded but badly with the high and flattering elogiums, which this gentleman had so lately bestowed on the Americans, in those very letters which were the subject of the present contest. In one of these, to Mr. Dana, is the follow-[26] ing remarkable passage:—"If you "follow the example of Britain in "the hour of her pride, insolence, "and madness, and refuse to hear "us, I still expect, since I am "here, to have the privilege of "coming among you, and seeing "the country; as there are many "men, whose virtues I admire "above Greek and Roman names, "that I should be glad to tell my "children about." The same request, in equivalent terms, appears in a letter to Mr. Laurens, the president; and in that to General Reed, among other not dissimilar expressions are the following,— "Your pen and your sword have "both been used with glory and ad"vantage in vindicating the rights "of mankind, and of that com"munity of which you was a "part. Such a conduct, as the "first and superior of all human "duties, must ever command my "warmest friendship and vene"ration."

This piece from the Congress also drew out a declaration in answer from the other Commissioners, viz. Lord Carlisle, Sir Henry Clinton, and Mr. Eden; which [27] went to a total and solemn disavowal, so far as related to the present subject, of their having had any knowledge, directly or indirectly, of those matters specified by the Congress. They, however, took care at the same time to guard effectually against any inference that might from thence be drawn, of their implying any assent to the construction put upon private correspondence by the Congress; or of their intimating thereby a belief, that any person could have been authorized to hold the conversation stated by that body. With respect to the charges and resolutions, so far as they related merely to their late brother commissioner, they did not think it necessary, they said, to enter into any explanation of the conduct of a gentleman, whose abilities and integrity did not require their vindication. They however gave a testimony from their own knowledge to the liberality of his general sentiments, and the fair and equitable principles upon which he had wished to restore the harmony, and to establish the union between the Mother Country and the Colonies, on terms mutually beneficial.

But the great objects of this declaration, as well as of that issued by Governor Johnstone, and of other former and subsequent publications, were to defeat the effect of the French treaties, to controvert the authority of the Congress, with respect to its acceptance or confirmation of them, and to render the conduct of that body suspicious or odious to the people. For these purposes, having first laid it down as an incontrovertible fact, that an alliance with France was totally contrary to the interests of America, and must in its effects prove utterly subversive, both of her civil and religious rights, they then proceeded to demonstrate, that she was not bound in honour, nor tied down by any principle of public faith, to adhere to those treaties. In support of this doctrine, they endeavoured to establish as proof, that the French concessions owed their origin entirely to the conciliatory propositions of Great Britain. For that being well aware of the returning union, felicity and strength, which the lenient conduct of the crown and parliament would immediately introduce throughout the British Empire, the court of Versailles, merely with a view of prolonging the troubles, and of rendering the Colonies instruments to Gallic ambition and perfidy, suddenly complied with those conditions, and signed those treaties, which she had before constantly and disdainfully rejected.

They then proceeded to examine the validity of that sanction which those treaties were supposed to derive, from the confirmation which they had since received in America; and endeavoured much to establish as a general doctrine and opinion, that the Congress had far exceeded their powers, both in that respect, and in their laying down unreasonable and inadmissible preliminaries, as an insuperable bar to their own proposed negociation, and to defeat, without hearing or deliberation, all the amicable purposes of their mission. They insisted, that the Congress were not authorized or warranted, by their own immediate constitution, to take such decisive measures, and finally to pronounce upon questions of such infinite and lasting importance, without recurring to the general sense of the people, and receiving the opinion and instructions of their constituents, after a full and open discussion of the different subjects in their respective assemblies.

Upon this ground, they pointed all their artillery directly against the Congress; whom they charged with betraying the trust reposed in them by their constituents, with acting contrary to the general sense of the people, and with sacrificing their interests and safety to their own ambitious views and interested designs. Indeed, however strange it may appear, there seems no doubt, that notwithstanding the repeated trials which the long continued, various, and extensive operations of the war had seemed to afford, of the disposition of the people in so many Colonies, the Commissioners themselves were fully persuaded, that a vast majority of them were firmly attached to the British government, and totally adverse to the rebellion. It is, however, to be considered, that all the information they could receive on the subject, was through the medium of men, whose minds were violently heated, by their sufferings, their losses, their hopes, their loyalty, and undoubtedly in many instances, by their private and party animosities.

The Congress, and those who wrote in their defence, and apparently with authority, controverted these positions, the inferences drawn from them, and the facts they were founded on. They first attacked the position which would naturally operate with most force upon the minds and opinions of men, viz. that the conclusion of the French treaties was entirely owing to the conciliatory propositions held out by the British parliament. This they asserted to be contradicted by facts and dates; and this point was strongly urged by the American popular writers, particularly Mr. Drayton, and the author of a celebrated publication, entitled, from the signature, *Common Sense*,[28] who with great industry pointed out to the public, the defectiveness, incoherence, or contradic-

tion of the evidence. But not satisfied with apparently gaining this point, they undertook to prove the direct reverse of the proposition, and pretended to shew, that the British concessions, instead of being the cause, were the immediate effect, of the French negociation and treaties. It was shrewdly observed in one of these publications, that the Commissioners, who now totally denied that the Congress had any power or authority to conclude the French treaties, had themselves proposed to enter into a treaty with that very body; and that the uncommon chagrin and disappointment which they openly avowed upon meeting with a refusal, was a sufficient testimony, how fully they were satisfied of its competence to that purpose.

In refuting what they asserted as errors of fact on the part of the Commissioners, some of these writers did not scruple to avail themselves of the same instrument, and asserted things which were not true, or which are at least highly improbable. Particularly, that to bribe the acquiescence of France in the ruin of America, that power was offered a cession of some considerable part of our East India possessions, and the same privileges and advantages on the Coast of Africa, which were enjoyed by the subjects of England.

Although the Commissioners did not expect that the facts or arguments stated in their declarations, would produce any serviceable effect in the conduct of the Congress, it was still hoped, that they would have operated powerfully upon the people at large. This source of hope being also at length exhausted, and the Commissioners convinced by experience, that the design of detaching any particular province, or large collective body of the people, so far from the general union as to enter into a private or separate negociation, was as fruitless, as the attempt of opening a treaty with the Congress in the name of the whole, had already proved ineffectual, determined totally to change their mode of conduct, and to denounce hostility and destruction, in their most terrific forms, to those who had rejected conciliation and friendship. The operations of terror might possibly produce those effects, which the smooth language of peace was found incapable of attaining: or, if the loss of America was inevitable, it was determined to render it of as little value to its present and future possessors as possible.

The partizans of the predatory scheme in England, from whom this idea seems to be taken, asserted, that the nature of the country exposed it more to the ravage of such a war as was intended or threatened, than perhaps any other upon the face of the globe. Its vast line of sea coast was indefencible by any possible means, against the efforts of a superior marine, accompanied by such a moderate land force, as would be necessary for the purposes of a desultory and exterminating war; and those numberless navigable creeks and rivers, which had in happier days conveyed commerce to every door, and spread plenty, independence, and industry, thro' every cottage, now afforded equal means and facility, for the carrying of sudden and inevitable destruction, home to the most sequestered fire-side. The impracticability of evading the dangers arising from situation was farther increased, by that mode of living in small, open, scattered towns and villages, which the nature and original circumstances of the country had prescribed to the inhabitants.

The Commissioners Oct. 3d. accordingly issued and 1778. published that signal valedictory manifesto and proclamation, which has since been an object of so much discussion at home and abroad;

and which has afforded a subject, that was no less agitated in both Houses of the British Parliament, than in the American Congress.

In that piece, they entered into a long recapitulation of facts and arguments which had been generally stated in former declarations, relative to the French treaties, the conduct and views of the Congress, their criminal obstinacy in rejecting all proposals of accommodation, and their total incompetency, whether with respect to the conclusion of treaties on the one hand, or to their rejection on the other. With an enumeration of their own repeated endeavours for the restoration of tranquillity and happiness to the people, and a review of the great advantages, held out by the equitable and conciliatory propositions which they had made, they announce their intention of speedily returning to England, as, under the circumstances of treatment and rejection which they had experienced, their longer stay in America would be as inconsistent with their own dignity, as with that of the authority which they represented. They, however, held out during the remainder of their stay, the same favourable conditions, and should still retain the same conciliatory disposition and sentiments, which they had hitherto proposed or manifested.

The Commissioners then thought it necessary to inform and warn the people, of the total and material change which was to take place, in the whole nature and future conduct of the war, if they should still persevere in their obstinacy; more especially, as that was founded upon the pretended alliance with France. Upon this subject they expressed themselves as follows: "The policy, as well "as the benevolence of Great "Britain, had hitherto checked "the extremes of war, when "they tended to distress a people, "still considered as fellow-sub-

"jects, and to desolate a coun- "try, shortly to become again a "source of mutual advantage; "but when that country professes "the unnatual design, not only "of estranging herself from us, "but of mortgaging herself and "her resources to our enemies, "the whole contest is changed; "and the question is, how far "Great Britain may, by every "means in her power, destroy or "render useless, a connection "contrived for her ruin, and for "the aggrandizement of France.

"Under such circumstances, "the laws of self-preservation "must direct the conduct of "Great Britain; and, if the "British Colonies are to become "an accession to France, will di- "rect her to render that accef- "sion of as little avail as possi- "ble to her enemy"

The first act of the Con- gress in consequence of this 10th. manifesto, was a cautionary declaration or notice to the public, stating, that as there was every reason to expect, that their unnatural enemies, despairing of being able to enslave and subdue them by open force, would, as the last effort, ravage, burn, and destroy every city and town on that continent, which they could come at; they therefore strongly recommended to all those people, who lived in places exposed to their ravages, immediately to build huts, at the distance of at least thirty miles from their present habitations, whither they were to convey their wives, children, cattle, and effects, with all who were incapable of bearing arms, on the first alarm of the enemy.

So far, the policy of the measure was prudent and justifiable; but the following clause of this public instrument, however coloured by a display of humanity, confined merely to terms, towards its conclusion, or even covered under the pretence of being intended only to operate in terrorem, can scarcely escape condemnation, as being exceedingly reprehensible and unjust in its principle. The resolution is couched in the following words, viz. "That immediately when the "enemy begin to burn or destroy "any town, it be recommended "to the people of these states, to "set fire, to ravage, burn and "destroy, the houses and properties of all Tories, and enemies to the freedom and independence of America, and secure the persons of such, so as "to prevent them from assisting "the enemy, always taking care, "not to treat them or their families with any wanton cruelties, "as we do not wish, in this particular, to copy after our enemies, or their German, negro, "and copper-coloured allies."

This was followed, in about[29] three weeks, by a counter manifesto on the part of the Congress, filled with bitterness and acrimony. In this they boast, that since they could not prevent, they strove, at least, to alleviate the calamities of war; had studied to spare those who were in arms against them, and to lighten the chains of captivity. In contrast to this portrait of their own conduct, they drew a hideous picture of those enormities which they attributed to the other side. They charge their enemy with having laid waste the open country, burned the defenceless villages, and having butchered the citizens of America. That their prisons had been the slaughter-houses of her soldiers, their ships of her seamen, and, that the severest injuries had been aggravated by the grossest insults. That, foiled in their vain attempt to subjugate the unconquerable spirit of freedom, they had meanly assailed the representatives of America with bribes, with deceit, and with the servility of adulation.

As a specimen of the spirit which inspired this piece, and the acrimony with which it abounds,

we shall give the following passage in their own language—"They "have made a mock of humanity, "by the wanton destruction of "men: they have made a mock "of religion, by impious appeals "to God, whilst in the violation "of his sacred commands: they "have made a mock even of "reason itself, by endeavouring "to prove, that the liberty and "happiness of America could "safely be entrusted to those who "have sold their own, unawed "by the sense of virtue, or of "shame."

They conclude the piece with the following threat of retaliation. "But since their incorrigible dispositions cannot be touched by "kindness and compassion, it becomes our duty by other means "to vindicate the rights of humanity."

"We, therefore, the Congress "of the United States of America, do solemnly declare and "proclaim, that if our enemies "presume to execute their threats, "or persist in their present career "of barbarity, we will take such "exemplary vengeance as shall "deter others from a like conduct. We appeal to that God "who searcheth the hearts of men, "for the rectitude of our intentions. And in his holy presence we declare, that as we are "not moved by any light and "hasty suggestions of anger or revenge, so through every possible change of fortune, we will "adhere to this our determination."[30]

Thus, unhappily, did the second commission for the restoration of peace in America, prove as futile in the event as the former. Although it would be too much to affirm, that any proposal made by the commissioners, or any circumstances attending their mission, could have been productive of the desired effect, after the conclusion of the French treaties; it would however seem, that nothing could

have been more untoward in point of time, and more subversive of the purposes of their commission, than the sudden retreat from Philadelphia, which took place almost at the instant of its being opened. However necessary this measure might have been considered in a military view, the disgrace of a retreat, and the loss of a province, were undoubtedly omens very inauspicious to the opening of a negociation. It has been publicly said, (however strange it must appear) that one of the commissioners, at least, was totally unacquainted, even at the time of their arrival, that this measure was not only intended, but that the orders for its execution actually accompanied their mission.[31]

As if Fortune had designed, that this commission should have been distinguished in every part of its existence from all others, it was also attended with the singular circumstance, of a letter from the Marquis De la Fayette, (whose military conduct had placed him very high in the opinion of the Americans, as well as in their service) to the Earl of Carlisle, challenging that nobleman, as first commissioner, to the field, there to answer in his own person, and in single combat, for some harshness of reflection upon the conduct of the French court and nation, which had appeared in those public acts or instruments, that he and his brethren had issued in their political capacity. It is almost needless to observe, that such proposal, which could only be excused by national levity, or the heat and inexperience of youth, was rejected by the noble Lord to whom it was addressed, with the slight that it deserved.

Whilst New York, the Jersies, Pennsylvania, and the borders of Connecticut had hitherto endured all the calamities of war, it fortuned, that the northern and southern, as well as the more interior colonies, enjoyed no inconsiderable degree of general tranquillity. The early transactions in the neighbourhood of Boston, the attempt on Charlestown, Lord Dunmore's adventures in Virginia, with the subjugation of the Tories in North and South Carolina, being the principal exceptions to this observation. The continual petty hostilities carried on between the inhabitants of the two neighbouring weak colonies of Georgia and East Florida, served, however, to keep the rumour of war alive to the southward; and an expedition undertaken in the spring of this year by a party of Americans, conveyed its effects to the Mississippi, and afforded no small cause of alarm, to the whole new colony of West Florida, which had hitherto been totally clear of the general tumult.

The expedition was, however, confined in its present effect to its immediate object, which only extended to the reduction of the British settlements in that country which had formerly belonged to a distinguished Indian nation called Natches; who many years before had fallen victims to European policy, the whole people having been perfidiously exterminated by the French. These settlements were under the government, and considered as a part of West Florida; but being too remote for protection, if it could even have been afforded, the inhabitants preserved their property by surrendering without resistance to a Captain Willing, who commanded the[32] American party, and who, although they were surprized and totally in his power, granted them every condition which they required, for their present and future security. It seems by the account, as if this party had fallen down the Mississippi by water; but from what place is not specified. It is probable, and seems in some degree confirmed by subsequent events, that the objects of this expedition were not confined merely to the reduction of the country in question, but were extended to the establishment of an intimate correspondence with the Spaniards at New Orleans, and to further views upon West Florida.

The state and circumstances of the war, as well as of the forces under his command, together with the winter season, which restrained, if it did not entirely shut up enterprize, in the northern and central colonies, afforded an opportunity to General Sir Henry Clinton, towards the close of the year, to direct his views to the southward. The recovery of the province of Georgia, although in itself neither great nor powerful, was in various respects a matter of the utmost importance. Its products were indeed considerable, and rendered more so, by their being greatly wanted. In particular, nothing could be more essential to the support of a fleet and army at so great a distance from their principal sources of supply, than its staple commodity, rice, which was now dedicated to the service of our enemies, whether in Europe or America. The possession of this province would also, by presenting a new barrier to the enemy, relieve East Florida from those constant alarms, incursions, and dangers, to which it had been so long exposed. And the two Florida's, with this, would all together form such an aggregate establishment of strength at the southern extremity of the continent, as could not fail greatly to influence the future operations and fortune of the war.

Important as these objects were, this acquisition held out one still greater. The southern colonies produced those commodities which were most wanted and most valuable in the European markets. France took off a prodigious quantity of their staple products; and the quiet and security which they had hitherto enjoyed, admitted so vigorous a cultivation, that their export trade seemed little otherwise affected by the war, than what it suffered from the British cruizers. Thus, in effect, the continental credit in Europe was principally upheld by the southern colonies; and they became the medium through which they received those supplies, that were not only indispensibly necessary to the support of the war, but even to the conducting of the common business and affairs of life. The recovery of Georgia, would not only put an end to that quiet and security upon which so much depended, but would open so wide a door into South Carolina, as could never be effectually closed whilst it was held by a vigorous enemy; at the same time, that the vicinity of Charlestown would constantly expose it to his enterprize, and that the fate of the whole colony inevitably hung upon that of the capital.

All these important consequences, and perhaps others, were fully comprehended by the General; and the time and season serving, he entrusted the conduct of the expedition in the land department, so far as it was undertaken from New York, to Colonel Campbell, a[33] brave and able officer, whose misfortune of being taken with a part of his regiment on their passage to America, as well as his subsequent sufferings under a long confinement near Boston, we have formerly seen. The force appointed to act under this gentleman's command, consisted of the 71st regiment of foot, two battalions of Hessians, four of provincials, and a detachment of the royal artillery.

The transports, with this force, sailed from Sandy Hook, on the 27th of November 1778; being escorted by a small squadron of ships of war, under the command of Commodore Hyde Parker. In the mean time, instructions had been communicated to Major General Prevost, who commanded the[34] troops in East Florida, to collect all the force that could possibly be spared, from the mere neceſſary defence of the fort and garriſon of St. Auguſtine, and to ſecond the views of the expedition, by a vigorous invaſion of the province of Georgia on that ſide, and by even endeavouring to penetrate ſo far, as to be able to co-operate immediately with Colonel Campbell, in his intended attack on the capital town of Savannah.

It does not ſeem from any thing that appears, that the Americans were aware of the object of this enterprize; or, perhaps, the greatneſs of the diſtance, prevented their being able to take any meaſure for defeating its effect. The fleet arrived at the iſland of Tybee, near Dec. 23d. the mouth of the river Savannah, in ſomething under a month. On the following day, the Commodore, with the greater part of the tranſports, got over the bar, and anchored in the river, within the Light Houſe of Tybee; but, from ſome unavoidable circumſtances of delay, it was not until the 27th that they were there joined by the reſt of the fleet. The commanders being totally ignorant of the force of the enemy, and of the ſtate of defence which they were to encounter, ſeized this opportunity of delay, in endeavouring to procure intelligence. For this purpoſe, a company of light infantry, with a naval officer and ſailors, were diſpatched, in two flat boats, up one of the creeks, and had the fortune of ſeizing and bringing off two men, who afforded the moſt ſatisfactory information. The commanders were now acquainted, that the batteries which had been conſtructed for the defence of the river, had been ſo much neglected, as to be grown out of repair and condition; and, that there were very few troops in the town, but that re-inforcements were daily expected. They alſo gave ſuch exact information, of the ſituation of two row gallies, which had been armed for the defence of

the river, as afforded means after for cutting off their retreat, by any of thoſe numerous creeks which interſect that country.

Upon this intelligence, the commanders determined to loſe no time in the proſecution of their enterprize. Colonel Campbell had already ſeized the opportunity afforded by the delay, in making a new and advantageous arrangement with reſpect to part of his force. He had formed two corps of light infantry, which were drawn from the provincial battalions, and attached one of theſe to Sir James Baird's light company, of the 71ſt (Highlanders), and the other to Captain Cameron's company, of the ſame regiment.[35] A meaſure excellently calculated, to transfuſe the ſpirit, vigour, and confidence of veteran troops, equally inured to danger and to victory, to thoſe who being yet raw, were diffident of their own powers, from mere ignorance of their effect.

Every thing being in due preparation, the Vigilant led the way up the river, on the 28th, being attended by the Greenwich and Keppel armed veſſels, and followed by the tranſports, who formed three diviſions, in the order eſtabliſhed by the commanders for deſcent. At the ſame time the Comet bomb-galley was ſent up the ſouth channel, to prevent the enemy's row-gallies from eſcaping by the inland navigations. On finding that the battery on a place called Salters Iſland, was totally deſerted by the enemy, the armed veſſels puſhed forward towards the intended landing place; but a number of the tranſports had grounded on the Flats by the way, which neceſſarily retarded for ſome time the landing. The activity and judgment of Captain Stanhope[36] of the navy, who acted as a volunteer in this ſervice, obviated this difficulty, as far as its nature would admit. Having undertaken the command of the flat boats, he embarked the whole firſt diviſion of

the troops with ſuch celerity, that he joined the Vigilant with very little loſs of time, after ſhe had taken that ſtation which the ſhallowneſs of the water would admit, at about random cannon ſhot diſtance from the landing place. It was, however, then dark; and the enemy's fires ſhewing that they had taken poſt, and intended defence, the landing was deferred until morning.

The deſtined landing place was a poſt of great importance; exceedingly difficult of acceſs; and which was accordingly capable of being eaſily put in ſuch a ſtate of defence, as might have effectually reſiſted a vaſt ſuperiority of force. But it was the firſt practicable landing place on the Savannah river, the whole country between it and Tybee being a continued tract of deep marſh, interſected by the extenſive creeks of St. Auguſtine and Tybee, beſides a number of other cuts of deep water, which were impaſſable by troops at any time of the tide.

The firſt diviſion of the troops, conſiſting of all the light infantry of the army, the New York volunteers, and the firſt battalion of the 71ſt regiment, under the conduct of Lieutenant Colonel Maitland, were landed at break of day.[37] From the landing-place, a narrow cauſeway of ſix hundred yards in length, with a ditch on each ſide, led through a rice ſwamp to one Gerridoe's houſe, which ſtood upon a kind of blunt and abrupt promontory, called in ſea language a bluff, riſing conſiderably above the level of the rice-ſwamp. The light infantry under Captain Cameron, being firſt landed, formed directly, and puſhed forward along the cauſeway. As they approached the poſt they meant to attack, they received a ſmart fire of muſquetry, from a ſmall party of about fifty rebels, to whom its defence had been committed. But the troops, incenſed at the loſs of their Captain, who had fallen by that fire, afforded them no time for charging again, so that they were almost instantly dispersed in the woods.

Thus, after so much time as the enemy had for preparation, so weak or confused were their counsels, that a most difficult landing place was secured to the army, and an open way gained to their capital, at no greater expence than the loss of one brave officer, with about half a dozen private men killed or wounded. Colonel Campbell, having taken a view of the country from Gerridoe's farm, discovered the rebel army, under Major General Robert Howe, drawn up about half a[38] mile east of the town of Savannah, with several pieces of cannon in their front. He was prompted by this sight, the apprehension of their retiring unmolested and whole, and the length of service, which that early hour of the day promised to afford, to push forward with the troops already landed, and to expect the remainder as they could come up.

The commander in chief accordingly, having left a detachment to guard the landing-place, advanced directly towards the enemy. When the army had passed a cross road, which intersected the great one leading to the town, the division of the Wissenbach regiment was left to take post at that place, both in order to cover the rear, and to preserve the communication with the landing place. The troops then advanced along the great road in the utmost security; a thick impenetrable wooded swamp covered the left of the line of march, and the light troops and flankers effectually scoured the cultivated plantations on the right. From whatever caution or delay it happened, the troops did not reach the open country before three o'clock, at which time they halted within about a thousand yards of the enemy. The enemy were in appearance, and fancied themselves exceedingly strongly posted; and would in reality have been found so, had the British commander made the attack exactly in the manner they wished, and to which they had vainly directed all their views and expectation. They were yet to be instructed in one of the most obvious maxims of warfare, that the very causes which induced them to wish the attack to be made in a particular quarter, would, almost to a certainty, produce a contrary effect, and direct its operation elsewhere.

They were formed in two divisions on either side of the great road. Half their regular forces, consisting of two regiments of Carolina troops, under the command[39] of Colonel Eugee, extended from the road, on their left, to a wooded swamp on their right; which was covered by houses defended with rifle-men. The other division of their regular troops, consisting of part of three Georgia battalions, under Colonel Elbert, with the[40] road to their right, were covered on the left by rice swamps; being further strengthened by the fort of Savannah Bluff behind their left, which would have operated in attack as a second flank. The town of Savannah, encompassed with the remains of an old line of entrenchment, covered their rear. One piece of cannon was planted at the extremity of their line on the right, one on the left, and two pieces occupied the traverse, across the great road, in the center of their line. About 100 paces in front of this traverse, at a critical spot between two swamps, a trench was cut across the road, and about 100 yards in front of the trench, a marshy rivulet run almost parallel the whole extent of their front; and to render the passage still more difficult, they had destroyed the bridge which led over this brook.

Col. Campbell soon discovered, by the countenance, as well as the movements of the enemy, that they equally wished and expected that he should attack them on the left; and he accordingly omitted no means that could serve to cherish that opinion, and continue its delusion. For that purpose he ordered the 1st battalion of the 71st to draw off and form on the right of the road, and then marching up to the rear of the light infantry, that corps was drawn off still more to the right, thereby increasing the jealousy of the enemy for their left, and impressing a full idea, that he was in the act of extending his front to that quarter. The happiest effect of this manoeuvre, however, was, that the light infantry had thereby got into a hollow ground, by which they were totally covered from the view of the enemy.

Fortune, the great friend to enterprize in war, and whose favours no prudent officer will ever deny, had thrown a negro into the hands of the commander, whose intelligence he turned to the happiest account. This man knew a private path through the wooded swamp on the enemy's right, through which he promised to lead the troops without observation or difficulty. To profit the more effectually of this discovery, it happened that the hollow way into which the light infantry had now fallen, continued winding all round the rear of the army until it joined the morass and wood in question. Sir James Baird was accordingly directed to pursue the course of the valley with the light infantry, until he arrived at the path pointed out by his guide, by which he would be enabled to turn the enemy's right flank, and by a moderate circuit to fall in upon the rear of that wing. The New-York volunteers, under Colonel Turnbull,[41] were ordered to support the light infantry.

During the course of this movement, the artillery were formed in a field on the left of the road, and concealed from the enemy by a swell of ground in front, up which it was intended to run them, as soon as the signal was made for action. From that commanding ground, they could either bear advantageously upon the right of the rebel line, or cannonade any body of troops in flank, which they might detach into the wood to retard the progress of the light infantry. An Hessian regiment was formed upon the left of the artillery.

During all this time, totally blind to their danger, the enemy continued to amuse themselves with their cannon, although a single fire was not returned : a circumstance, which, along with the stillness and immobility of the British troops, might have reasonably excited apprehension, distrust, and watchfulness. At length, Colonel Campbell, convinced that the light infantry had got effectually round upon their rear, suddenly brought forward the cannon, and commanded the line to move briskly on to the enemy. The well-directed fire of the artillery, the rapid advance of the 71st regiment, and the forward countenance of the Hessians, so overpowered the enemy, that they instantly fell into confusion, and dispersed.

In the mean time, the light infantry having arrived at the new barracks, which were full in the way they were making to the rear of the enemy, fell in unexpectedly with a body of the militia of Georgia, who were there stationed with artillery; to guard the great road from Ogeeche ; these were soon routed, with the loss of their cannon, and as Sir James Baird was in full pursuit of the fugitives, in his way to fall upon the main body, the terrified and scattered troops of the Carolina and Georgia brigades, came running across the plain full in his front. Nothing could exceed the confusion and rout that now ensued, when the light infantry, with the rapidity peculiar to that corps, threw themselves in headlong upon the flanks of a flying enemy, already sufficiently broken and confused.

No victory was ever more complete. 38 commissioned officers, 415 non-commissioned and privates, 48 pieces of cannon, 23 mortars, the fort with its ammunition and stores, the shipping in the river, a large quantity of provisions, with the capital of Georgia, were all in the possession of the conquerors before dark. Neither the glory of the victory, nor the military renown arising from the judicious measures, and admirable manoeuvres which led to it, could reflect more honour upon the commander in chief, than every other part of his conduct. His triumph was neither disdained by an unnecessary effusion of blood, nor degraded by present or subsequent cruelty. The moderation, clemency, and humanity of all his conduct, will be considered still the more praise-worthy, when it is recollected, that he was under the immediate impression of such peculiar circumstances of irritation and resentment, as had not been experienced by any other British officer, who had borne command during the American war.

The loss of the Americans in slain was very small, considering the nature of the complete rout they had undergone. Only about fourscore men fell in the action and pursuit, and about thirty more perished in their attempts to escape through the swamp. The conduct of their commanders requires no observation. Every body will see they knew nothing of their business. Although the fugitives fled, and consequently led the pursuit, through the town of Savannah, and that many of the inhabitants were then in the streets, yet, such was the excellent discipline observed, that in that heat of blood, not a single person suffered, who had not arms in his hands, and who was not besides in the act either of flight or resistance. The commander having received some information, that the setting of the capital on fire, in case of its loss, had been once a matter in contemplation with the enemy, took effectual measures to guard against that design, if still intended. No place in similar circumstances, ever suffered so little by depredation, as the town of Savannah did upon this occasion even taking into the account, that committed by their own negroes during the darkness of the approaching night. A strong circumstantial testimony, that those enormities, so frequently attributed to the licence of the soldiers, should with much more justice be charged to the indefensible conduct of their superiors ; whether by a previous relaxation of discipline, an immediate participation in the guilt, or a no less culpable sufferance of the enormity.

Through the activity and prompt union of the commanders in chief by land and sea, and the spirit and diligence of their officers, General Howe, with the broken remains of his army, was not only compelled to retreat into South-Carolina, but notwithstanding many impediments in their way, and some wants not easily remedied, particularly horses for their artillery, they, within less than a fortnight, had recovered the whole province of Georgia (excepting only the town of Sunbury) to the British government. In that time they had restored tranquillity every where, afforded protection to all who remained in or returned to their houses, established such posts as secured the whole line of frontier on the side of South-Carolina, and formed the well-affected, who came in with their rifles and horses, into a corps of light dragoons.

In the mean time, Major-General Prevost found no small difficulty in bringing together, from their scattered and remote cantonments, the small parties with which he was to make an impression on the side of Florida. The getting forward

42

his artillery, stores, and provisions, as the enemy were masters of the navigation in general, both along the coasts, and on the greater waters inland, was no less difficult. In these operations, the troops underwent unusual hardships and distresses, which they bore with the most exemplary fortitude and temper; both officers and soldiers having been reduced to live for several days solely upon oysters, and enduring at the same time the greatest heat and fatigue, without complaint, despondency, or murmur. The major-general having at length brought forward a few pieces of artillery, suddenly surrounded the town and fort of Sunbury, on the frontiers of Georgia. The garrison, consisting of about 200 men, made some shew of defence, and gave the commander the trouble of opening trenches. But although they were supported by some armed vessels and gallies, yet all hope of relief being now totally cut off by the reduction of the rest of the province, they found it necessary to surrender at discretion. This happened just at the time, when Colonel Campbell, after the settlement of the interior country, had returned to Savannah, and was preparing to set out on an expedition for the reduction of Sunbury. The command devolved of course to General Prevost on his arrival at Savannah.

and much more dangerous war, without any mitigation of the old; we behold her engaged with her antient rival and hereditary enemy; with one of the most mighty and most warlike powers in Europe, rendered still more dangerous by his vicinity; and in this double warfare with old friends and old enemies, not only bereaved of her natural strength, but a great part of it turned against her, she is left alone to endure the unequal combat, abandoned by all mankind, and without even the pretence of a friend, or the name of an ally in the world.

Such was the unfortunate situation, such the calamitous picture, which Great Britain exhibited in the year 1778. So aweful a crisis; so perilous a state of public affairs; demanded those supreme degrees of wisdom in counsel, and of efficacy in action, which are so seldom united with each other, and which are still more rarely united with true patriotism. If such situations are sometimes blest with the extraordinary good fortune, of calling forth great talents from inertness or obscurity, it much more frequently happens that they produce a totally contrary effect. For the vastness of the occasion is too liable to dazzle, to bewilder, and to confound, that useful mediocrity of talents and abilities, which, however, unequal to the situation, is exceedingly well calculated for the common conduct and purposes of mankind.

However it was, or from whatever causes it proceeded, whether from a fluctuation or discordance of opinions, disagreement in temper and views among the ministers, whether from the want of any previous or established system, or that the flattering ideas of some partial or general accommodation, still interfered with and counteracted all other modes of proceeding, so it was, that some appearance of irresolution and indecision, which at that critical period prevailed in the counsels and measures of Great

State of public affairs during the recess of parliament. Address and petition from the city of London. Militia embodied. Camps formed. Admiral Keppel appointed to the command of the grand fleet for the home service. Peculiar situation of that commander. Fleet sails from St. Hellens. Licorne, French frigate, stopt and detained. Blameable conduct of the Captain, in firing unexpectedly into the America man of war. Desperate engagement between the Aretbusa, and the Belle Poule, frigates. French schooner, bravely taken by the Alert cutter. Another French frigate falls in with the fleet; and is, with the Licorne and schooner, brought to England. Fleet returns to Portsmouth for a reinforcement. Rewards and bounty of the French king, to the officers and crew of the Belle Poule. Admiral Keppel sails again from Portsmouth. Falls in with the French fleet under the count d'Orvilliers; and after a chace of five days, brings them at length to action. Account of the engagement on the 27th of July. View of those circumstances which were supposed to have prevented that action from being decisive. French Fleet escape in the night, and return to Brest. Prudent and temperate conduct observed by the admiral. Returns to Plymouth to refit. Proceeds again to sea, but cannot meet the French fleet.

FROM these scenes of distant hostility, it is time we should direct our attention nearer home, and take a view of those immediate measures pursued by Great Britain, to extricate herself from the difficulties of that new, singular, and perilous situation, in which she had so unfortunately been involved. A situation, indeed, more singular and perilous, could scarcely be traced in history.

Weakened and distracted by a domestic contest, which equally consumed her strength and resources; in which victory was attended with consequences, that were always of equivocal advantage, and defeats produced the whole of their natural effects; while the balance of fortune in that single contest was yet so doubtful, that the inability of reducing her revolted colonies, was held out as an ostensible and sufficient cause for considering and treating them as independent and sovereign states; in the midst of this critical struggle, we see Great Britain suddenly involved in a new

Britain, was so palpable, as neither to escape the observations of friends or of enemies. Notwithstanding repeated causes of alarm, we seemed to be taken by surprise. The language of the court, as soon as it could collect itself, was sufficiently firm; and seemed inspired by a spirit of vigour suited to an occasion which called for efforts of an extraordinary kind. It was rather even the tone of indignation and vengeance, than mere constancy and resolution. But this spirit very soon evaporated; and nothing was talked of in a war of conquest and vengeance but self-defence.

The enemies of ministry were loud on this occasion. They said, that by this timid plan, neither suited to the emergency, nor to the language held upon it, the opportunity was lost, by some sudden, great, and signal blow, of reviving our antient name and character; and of inspiring that reverence to our national vigour and military prowess, which it was so necessary for us to maintain and establish with other nations, whether friendly or inimical, at the outset of such a war.

It was supposed, that a double scheme of partial accommodation, the one part avowed, and the other secret, and founded upon systems directly opposite, was about that period prevalent, and had no small share in influencing the conduct of public affairs. The first part of this scheme was founded on the idea of detaching America, through the intervention of the Commissioners, from the alliance with France. Nothing could possibly have been more essential to the interests, the reputation, and to the grandeur of Great Britain, than the success of this measure. France would then have been left to encounter all her force alone, which, if properly directed, she was yet by no means capable of enduring.

The event of that part of the scheme we have already seen. The second, was that of detaching France from America; and consequently leaving the latter exposed to that resentment, which in the other instance, would have been directed against the first. Although this part of the scheme, even supposing it capable of success, could not stand in any degree of real comparative value with the former, yet it held out certain flattering ideas, which might even render it, in some degree, a favourite. For the dereliction of America by France, would have left the former open, and now totally hopeless, to that complete and final subjugation, or unconditional submission, which had so long been the great object of court and ministers. But this scheme seemed from the beginning hopeless, though it for a while entertained the imaginations of many. Great Britain had no bribe of sufficient magnitude to purchase from France this dereliction of her object. If such could have been offered, and offered with effect, it must have been before the conclusion of the treaty: but the treaty was concluded.

Every part of the conduct of France from the commencement of the American troubles, either tended directly, or but ill disguised her design, to bring matters to the present crisis. To the period of that treaty, however, her policy lay open to the influence of circumstances, and her conduct was, and undoubtedly would have been in any case, governed by them. But when once she had taken the decided and dangerous part, of publicly avowing her sentiments and views, and of openly binding herself in the face of the world to the performance and support of those treaties which she had concluded with the Americans, it was then not only evident that she had gone too far to recede, but that she had also chosen her ground, and determined and was fully disposed and determined

to abide the consequences. So that every hope founded upon her change of system; seemed little better than visionary.

There were some strong indications, that a third, and more comprehensive scheme of pacification than either of the foregoing, was at one time in agitation. This was no less, than the conclusion of an immediate peace and alliance with the Colonies, under the acknowledgment of that independence, which it was laid down as a principle, they had already virtually and irretrievably obtained, and thereby cutting off at one stroke, every cause of war, and of dispute with America. In that case, if a plan of prudence, not very glorious, had been pursued, there was an end of the quarrel both with America and France. If the reduction and punishment of France was the object, the war against her might be pursued with undissipated force. On the very day of the delivery of the French rescript, a paper to that purpose, written by an old and strong advocate for the American war, was delivered at the doors of the two Houses.

If this scheme ever had any substantial being in the ministry, it was, however, but of short duration; and was so far from being brought forward, or any more heard of in that quarter, that when propositions of a similar nature, were soon after made by the opposition in both Houses of Parliament, and strongly supported, on the ground both of expedience and necessity, they were violently opposed, and accordingly over-ruled (as we have formerly seen) by the ministers.

To some such variety of opinions, with respect to the means of accommodation, the grand questions of peace and war, and the mode of prosecuting the latter may probably be attributed those appearances of fluctuation, and indecision, which, at that period, were fo ftrongly and repeatedly charged, as the characteriftic marks of our counfels and measures. And to fuch caufes muft be attributed, the reception of the report, of a reproach faid to be thrown out by the French minifter, at the moment of his departure from London, viz. "That the Britifh counfels " were fo totally undetermined and " indecifive, in every matter, whe- " ther of public or private concern, " that he never could get a pofi- " tive anfwer from the minifters, " upon any bufinefs, whether of " fmall, or of the higheft import- " ance."

March 13th, 1778. On the very day that the French re-fcript had been de-livered to the Secretary of State, an addrefs and petition from the City of London, praying for the adoption of fuch meafures as would moft forward the reftoration of in-ternal peace, tend to refcue pub-lic affairs from unwife and im-provident management, and ob-tain, improve, and fecure, the re-turning confidence of the people, was prefented to his Majefty. This piece, which was of unufual length, and a mafterly compofition in point of writing, contained, in the moft qualified language, and the moft guarded and refpectful terms, a feries of the fevereft ob-fervations and cenfures, on (what they termed) thofe fatal counfels, and that conduct of public affairs, and meafures, which equally mif-leading and deceiving the Prince and the people, led to the prefent dangerous and unhappy crifis. Along with a recapitulation of the loffes, misfortunes, and dif-graces of the war, with a ftriking picture of the various calamities and miferies, which they attri-bute to that public conduct they fo ftrongly condemn, they by no means forget to take notice, how repeatedly they had deprecated, and how truly foreboded, in their former applications to the throne, (and in concurrence with the fenfe

of many other refpectable public bodies, and of many of the wifeft and beft of his Majefty's fubjects) the prefent evils and dangers, as well as thofe greater to which the nation is ftill liable, as the inevi-table confequences of the mea-fures which were purfued; neither did they pafs without notice the inefficacy of their former applica-tions, and the anfwers which had been given to their addreffes and remonftrances upon public affairs.

Among other political obferva-tions, all implying or charging neglect or mifconduct on the fide of government, they particularly noticed in the prefent inftance, that there was no appearance of our having formed any alliance with any of the other great powers of Europe, in order to cover us from the complicated perils fo ma-nifeftly imminent over this nation, at a time when there was but too much reafon to apprehend, that alliances of the moft dangerous kind were formed againft us.

The anfwer, which was longer than ufual, feemed alfo to indicate a greater attention, both to the fubject of the addrefs, and to the body whofe act it was, than had been always manifefted upon fimilar occafions. It comprehended in fubftance, that, although it could not be allowed, that the force and refources of the ftate, had been un-wifely and improvidently exerted, when the object was the main-tenance of that conftitutional fub-ordination which ought to prevail through its feveral parts; yet, the calamities infeparable from a ftate of war had been conftantly la-mented; and, an affurance was given, that his Majefty would moft earneftly give all the efficacy in his power, to thofe meafures which the legiflature had adopted, for the purpofe of reftoring, by a happy and permanent conciliation, all the bleffings and advantages of peace.

Whatever hopes or motives ope-rated towards a temporizing con-

duct on the fide of England, it was foon perceivable, that no fimi-lar caufes influenced that of France. No fooner was the account con-veyed with unufual difpatch to that court, of the immediate effects, which the delivery of the refcript from their minifter feemed to have produced in London, than orders March 18th. were inftantly iffued for the feizure of all thofe Britifh veffels, which were found in any of the French ports. This example was followed by a fimilar order in Great Britain. But thefe meafures produced no great effect on the one fide or the other, as there were few fhips in the ports of either.

The order for the feizure of the Britifh veffels, was in three days followed by another meafure ftill more decifive, and which feemed as if it were intended by France, to affix fuch a feal to her late de-claration, as would not only con-vince her new allies of her fince-rity, but put it out of her own power to retract from her engage-ments with them. This was the public audience and reception given to the three American deputies, Dr. Franklyn, Silas Deane, and Arthur Lee, as ambaffadors from the United States, by the French monarch. The deputies were introduced by M. de Vergen- 21ft nes, and received by the King, with the ufual formalities and ce-remonials, which the etiquette of courts has eftablifhed on the intro-duction of minifters from fovereign ftates. A great and ftriking event as any which has been known in the latter ages. Nothing could be defired more mortifying to the Crown of 43 Great Britain

Certain appearances were, how-ever, ftill to be preferved by France as well as by England; and the King's ordinance, affording new and extraordinary advantages to the captors of prizes, as an encourage-ment and fpur to the vigour of the marine fervice, although it was figned on the 28th of March, was kept dormant, without publication or effect, until the beginning of July.

To complete the defensive plan, which was declared to be only preliminary to one more effectual, to be taken up in due time, in England the militia were immediately called out and embodied, upon the rising of parliament; and being joined by the regular forces, the numbers of the one being apportioned in some degree to that of the other, camps were formed at Winchester, Salisbury, St. Edmund'sbury in Suffolk, Warley Common in Essex, and Coxheath in Kent. But the eyes and the confidence of the nation, were turned as usual, towards that naval force, which had so long been the object of its pride and hope.

This hope and confidence were still farther increased, by the appointment of a distinguished, and exceedingly popular admiral, in [44] the highest esteem with his own profession, as well as the public, to the command of, what was called, the grand fleet at Portsmouth. It happened, however, most unhappily, that at this critical season of national danger, our navy was not altogether capable of supporting the expectations which were formed. Some time elapsed before any considerable force could be got together. [45]

* * *

Speech from the throne. Amendment moved to the address in the House of Commons. Great Debates. Amendment rejected upon a division. Opposition to the address in general, in the House of Lords, but no amendment proposed. Address carried upon a division. Motion to address the Crown, in the House of Commons, for a disavowal of certain passages in the late manifesto issued by the Commissioners at New York. The motion, after long debates, rejected upon a division. Similar motion by the Marquis of Rockingham, likewise causes much debate, and is rejected upon a division. Protest. Circumstances, which tended to the rendering the late action at Brest, a subject of parliamentary discussion. Admiral Keppel, being called upon, gives some account of that business in the House of Commons. Answered by Sir Hugh Palliser. Reply. Court martial ordered for the trial of Admiral Keppel. Conduct of the admiralty censured and supported: Question, relative to the discretionary powers of that board, much agitated. Bill brought in and passed, for the holding of the trial of Admiral Keppel on shore, (in consideration of his ill state of health) instead of its being held board a ship, as before prescribed by the law. Recess.

MANY circumstances contributed to render the meeting of parliament, at the opening of the session on which we are now to enter, an object of peculiar expectation to the public. The close of the first campaign of a war with France, opened a wide field for discussion, as well as speculation. The principal officers who had held commands in America, were now returned to their seats in parliament. The Commissioners appointed under an act of the last session to settle the disturbances in America, were likewise returned. And altho' the unfortunate event

Nov. 26th. 1778.

of the propositions was well known, much information, with regard to the military, as well as to the civil affairs of that country, was expected from the ability and stations of the gentlemen who were joined in the commission. An opinion of certain differences between the commissioners and commanders, excited the curiosity of all men; people being ever sure to look on with a peculiar interest, when the importance of public questions is enlivened by a mixture of personal anecdote.

The speech from the throne was replete with complaints, of the unexampled and unprovoked hostility of the court of France. With regard to the events of the war, it was short and inexplicit. Grounding the hopes of success on future exertions, on the state of preparation, and on the spirit of the people, more than on the actions of the campaign; which were alluded to with a coldness, that might easily be construed into censure. Notice was, however, taken of the protection afforded to commerce, and of the large reprisals made upon the injurious aggressors.

The professions of neutral powers were represented as friendly; but their armaments suspicious—The failure of the conciliatory measures, was regretted—The necessity of active exertions by sea and land, pointed out by the situation of affairs, was urged in general terms, without specifying any plan of operations—With regard to the American war, a total silence was observed.

The address of the House of Commons, with the usual professions of attachment and support, repeated, in nearly the same expressions, the sentiments contained in the speech. The opposition moved to substitute, in the place of part of the address, the following amendment—" To assure his Majesty, that with the truest zeal for the honour of the crown, and the warmest affection for his Majesty's person and family, the House was ready to give the most ample support to such measures as might be thought necessary for the defence of these kingdoms, or for frustrating the designs of that restless power, which has so often disturbed the peace of Europe; but that they thought it one of their most important duties, in the present melancholy posture of affairs, to enquire by what fatal councils, and unhappy systems of policy, this country had been reduced from that splendid situation, which in the early part of his Majesty's reign, made her the envy of all Europe, to such a dangerous state, as that which had of late called forth our utmost exertions, without any adequate benefit."

It was contended on the side of opposition, that if the unanimity, so strongly recommended by the proposers of the address, was indeed an infallible resource in the ruin of public affairs, the ministers, it must be owned, had used every means to induce the people to concur in its necessity. But, they said, that the utility of a general concurrence in any measure, depended entirely upon the wisdom of the measure in question. That the approbation of measures must be either retrospective, or prospective. With regard to the first, no plans already executed, could be affected by any subsequent difference of opinion. With regard to the latter, as no plan for the conduct of the war was announced in the speech, or even hinted at by ministers, to agree to unanimity upon an object not yet proposed, was perfectly absurd. Then what was to induce the House to unanimity, but the recommendation of a set of men, who were known to agree with each other in no one article, of disposition, principle, council, or action? Unanimity, they said, was a plausible and specious word, but the thing could hardly ever exist; because the wise and the ignorant would always differ; and if it ever should take place, infinite mischief would ensue, as that could only happen through the prevalence of obstinacy, which is the natural and constant companion of folly. That, in the present instance, it would serve only to give sanction to the past, and energy to the future blunders of administration; and to commit the fate of the nation in a new and still more dangerous war to the inability of the same men, who had in so wretched, and so ruinous a manner conducted the old. That, to concur in an address, which conveyed any idea of the slightest satisfaction in the present ministers,

instead of producing vigour in our own exertions, or terror in our enemies, would only serve to fill Englishmen with despair, and Frenchmen with joy and confidence, at seeing that the deliberative government was as abject as the executive was contemptible, and that the incapacity of the one, could only be equalled by the servility of the other.

Considering the speech from the throne, merely as the words of the minister, it was insisted, that it advanced an absolute falsehood. For the speech asserted, that our arms had not been attended with the success, which the justice of our cause, and the vigour of our exertions, seemed to promise. But they insisted, that the success was far greater than could have been expected, considering the inferiority of our fleets, and the shameful tardiness of our preparations. That, taking in these circumstances, our escaping in any manner from ruin or disgrace, might well be accounted as a very high degree of good fortune; and indeed, as far exceeding all rational expectation. And that consequently, " the speech not only asserted a falsehood, but that it also threw a false, unjust, and illiberal slander, on the commanders in the service of the crown; loading them with a censure which ought to fall on the ministers alone."

They further urged, that the speech included no less than a direct libel upon parliament, in calling the late measures which had been taken to pacify America, the plans of parliament. That the arrival of the commissioners at Philadelphia, without any knowledge of the intention to evacuate that city, had saddled them from the beginning with the distrust which was held of their immediate employers, and had taken away that appearance of openness, and that opinion of confidence and authority, which form the necessary foundation of every treaty and

every pacification. It was asked, whether the glaring absurdity of that conduct was the plan of parliament? Or was parliament called together every winter for no other purpose, than to relieve the ministers from the yearly burthen of disgrace, which was the certain result of all their measures?

The conciliatory propositions themselves were arraigned, as being at once, humiliating to England, and unsatisfactory to America. But, it was asserted, that notwithstanding its defects and absurdity, the adoption of that scheme could not be said to be wholly useless —For it had cut up by the roots, every fallacious argument, by which ministers had beguiled the nation into the fatal American war, by the universal surrender of all its objects.

With regard to the system to be recommended in the conduct of the war, opposition seemed to hold no second opinion, and to call out, as with one voice—Attack France—France, said they, entered into alliance with America from motives of interest. When she finds herself vigorously attacked, and feels the heavy impressions of war, with all their consequences and distresses, in her own dominions, she will grow weary of the prospect of remote and uncertain advantages, and abandon an ally from whom she receives nothing but a participation of war and calamity. —On the other hand, they said, the spirit of America is sustained by the powerful incentives, both of liberty and self-preservation. Every effort we make to subdue that spirit, drives our colonies still more into the arms of France; who, in the mean time, feels no inconvenience from the protection she affords. And consequently, every drop of English blood which we shed in America, serves only to cement an alliance, fatal to the power and happiness of the British empire.

On the other side, the friends of

administration seemed rather to follow the example of the speech, by declining to enter into a discussion of the policy of the American war: either, because it was not thought prudent to avow the determination they had made in their own minds, or that they chose to leave themselves open, to embrace whatever system of conduct, the necessity of affairs might hereafter require. But upon the past conduct of the war, and the preparation and distribution of the armaments employed in the summer, they entered into a detailed justification.

They said, that if the fleet under Admiral Byron, had been sent out earlier than it was, an opportunity would have been given to the fleet under M. d'Estaing, to have joined that at Brest; and thereby, that France would have obtained a superiority in the Channel. That such a conduct would have left us in a state of weakness at home, of which it would be impossible that the enemy should not take advantage. That, by maintaining the superiority in the channel, we prevented France from making our own seas, the scene of her exertions; and in a manner obliged her to detach and divide her forces. And, what nation would not, if she could, keep the seat of war at a distance from her own territories?

It was likewise contended, that the evacuation of Philadelphia, was a measure dictated by the soundest principles of policy. For, they said, that on the accession of France to this war, the defence of our own islands, and the attacking hers, became an object, though not, as the opposition would have it, an exclusive object. That this of necessity drew off a considerable body of our troops; and the grand army being thus weakened, it had been judged necessary to diminish the extent of our line, in order to unite and compact our forces. That, it was too well known to require argument or proof, that

the operation of a closely united force was far more efficacious, serving at once to impress terror, and to overpower resistance, than if it had been weakened by extension and distance. That, to garrison every town on the continent of America, was an undertaking for which no army could suffice; and that an attempt of the sort, was certainly not the method, by which any man could hope to crush the present rebellion. It being therefore necessary to compact the forces, into one body, the only question was, when one or the other must be adopted, whether New York or Pensylvania should be abandoned? And, said they, what reason could be assigned for collecting the whole army into Philadelphia? The situation is not near so central with regard to the colonies as New York; nor is it near so convenient in other respects, whether with regard to the co-operation of the fleet, the receiving of supplies, or to the general operations of the war.

These arguments must be allowed to be satisfactory with regard to the measure in question. But the opposers of administration were too acute, not to turn them to their own advantage. They accordingly asserted, that the justification of the individual measure, was the full condemnation of the whole system from which it arose. That the advocates of the America war, had themselves now fully demonstrated the impossibility of success. For they had shewn, that every advance which the army could make in America, reduced it to this alternative, either, by retaining the acquisition to divide and debilitate its own strength, or else to stand exposed to the disgrace and mortification, by treading back their own steps, to shew the inutility of all their labours. That no man could dream of conquering a continent, by sitting down in a single town. That, therefore, while the nation

persisted in carrying on an offensive war in America, whether our army advanced, whether it retreated, or whether it stood still, the effect would be the same; a fruitless, hopeless, expensive, and cruel, because unnecessary, war.

Although the ministers were observed to decline entering into a subject, which had already been so often, and so thoroughly debated, and upon which their adversaries always shewed a desire to press them, there arose from a new and unexpected quarter, an advocate for the continuation of the system of coercion. One of the gentlemen employed in the late commission to America, whether the information he received in that country induced him to confide in the operation of force, or whether a nearer view of the object, mixed with a sense of disappointment at the failure of one plan of pacification, had animated him with the hopes of conquest, in a long speech, here and there interspersed with some expressions of diffidence, strongly urged the continuance of an offensive war with America. [46]

He said his view had always been, that force should accompany concession, and that the Americans should see in this country, a manly determined spirit of perseverance: that thereby they might be moved to consider well, between the evils of war in a dubious contest, and the immediate advantages of peace upon honourable and advantageous terms. He said, it was necessary to confirm the minds of your friends, as well as to terrify your enemies; that he believed two thirds of the people of America, fully desired to return to their ancient connection with Great Britain; that nothing but a surrounding army, and the diffidence they had in the support of government, prevented that spirit from breaking out into acts of hostility with the Congress. And, that therefore, the failure of the conciliatory plans, was to be imputed to the sudden retreat of the army from Philadelphia, and not to the weakness of the English interest there.

Notwithstanding the general tendency of that gentleman's speech in favour of the views of administration, he declared, that he did not imagine the present ministers were able to draw forth the resources which England afforded, or to apply them with ability sufficient, to compass so important an object as the reduction of the disobedient provinces. But on the other hand, he was afraid, that those who were likely to succeed them, although they might be possessed of greater capacity, and more of the public confidence, were too desirous of surrendering all the objects of the contest, without any struggle, at all equal to the antient reputation of England. That, he acknowledged the situation to be extremely perilous, and the danger great; but that on such occasions, the noble qualities of the human mind, perseverance, fortitude, and the love of our country, shine in their greatest lustre.

After a very long and vehement debate, the House at length divided, about half past two in the morning, when the amendment was rejected by a majority of 226, to a 107.

The address in the House of Lords, was necessarily supported upon much the same ground with that of the House of Commons. The numerous public and private virtues of the sovereign were largely expatiated upon, in order to place in the strongest point of view, the obstinacy, ingratitude, and baseness, of his rebellious subjects in America; whilst the royal good faith with respect to foreign nations, and his Majesty's religious adherence to treaties, were no less strongly contrasted with the perfidious conduct of France. The usual arguments were used for unanimity, and perseverance in the American war; for the first, from the national danger; for the second, from the loss of honour and safety which must be sustained in abandoning that great continent to France.

On the other side, the lords in opposition proposed no amendment to the address; but condemning it entirely in all its parts, (as they did the matter of the speech itself) would put an absolute negative on the whole. Here too the topics were in general similar to those used in the other House. Enquiry, they said, full and complete enquiry, into the conduct of the war, and into the real state of public affairs, was now the proper and immediate object of parliament. This was no season for sending the voice of adulation to the throne. It was now a matter of necessity, that the eyes of the Sovereign should be opened to the real state of his affairs; and it would be dishonest to himself, as well as treason to the state, to conceal any part of the dangers of his situation. The arguments used for promoting the address, appeared to them to be cogent arguments for enquiry. The loss of our honour, the danger of the nation, the discontents in every part of the British dominions, and the dissentions in the navy and army, originating in the ill conduct of government, called for discussion and remedy. They did, and could only originate, from a weak and a wicked system of government. A system founded upon false principles, upheld by obstinacy, folly, and error, if not by malice; and inevitably tending by its own nature to ruin and destruction. This system, they said, must be totally effaced; new men and new measures must be adopted, before any success can be rationally expected in war, or security or honour in peace.

The lords in administration could not refrain from expressing their astonishment at the new and extraordinary measure, of attempting to reject the whole of the address to the throne, without a substitution of any other in its room. An amendment, they said, of any of the parts, might have been expected; or if it had even extended to an alteration of the whole, both as to matter and purpose, it would not have excited surprize; but the attempt to put a direct and unqualified negative upon the whole address, without offering or intending any other in its room, was a measure, probably unequalled in the history of parliament. It was fitting, they said, to examine, what degree of consequence the import of this unconditional negative would amount to. His Majesty comes to parliament to seek the aid of his people, for repelling and defeating the perfidious and dangerous designs of France, openly leagued with our own rebellious subjects, for the subversion of his state and government. What answer does the proposed negative make to this requisition. It will substantially declare to all Europe, that we are determined to afford him neither aid nor support against his treacherous enemies; and that his dominions are to lie at the mercy of France.

The grounds of the contest between this country and America, were now, they said, totally shifted; it was no longer a question, as formerly, whether that continent was worth the risque and expence of recovering, as a part of the British dominions; but the question now was, whether we should sink without resistance, under the joint force of France and America, and submit to whatever terms they were pleased to dictate, or whether we should endeavour, by the most vigorous exertions, at once to punish our traiterous and perfidious foes, and by dissolving their unnatural conjunction, to restore the former unity, power, and splendour of the empire. For as affairs now stood, it was impossible, they said, to separate France and America, even in idea, as to any purpose or consequence of the war; and thus, every concession made to the latter, would either afford a direct and substantial aid, or convey a base submission to France.

It was by no means a fair inference, they said, that because from adverse accidents, and circumstances not foreseen or provided against, we had not yet met with that degree of success, which our exertions afforded reason for expecting, all coercion was therefore impracticable, America irretrievably lost, and this country incapable of longer supporting the war. The real facts would be found in the direct reverse of these propositions. America was yet far from being invulnerable; the resources of this country were still great; and her spirit was in no degree broken. They said also, that it was equally illiberal and unjust, to charge those accidents and misfortunes, to which all military events are subject, to the want of judgment or ability, in the design or conduct of the war.

Upon this part of the subject, they entered (as the ministers had done in the House of Commons) into some detail, and some defence, of past measures and conduct. The first Lord of the Admiralty directly denied the fact, as to that fallen, and almost annihilated state of the navy, which had been so strongly urged by a noble lord (in his professional line) [47] on the other side. He acknowledged, that we had been much too slow both in our naval and military preparations; but this tardiness he attributed, partly to the nature of our government, partly to a mistaken lenity, and partly, to the affording a greater degree of credit to the assurances of other powers, than the event shewed they were entitled to.

The lords, on that side, said, that they had no objection to enquiries, provided that they were properly founded, specifically directed, and brought on in a proper season. But they likewise observed, that enquiries into the conduct of men in high stations, were matters of a serious nature; and as they necessarily implied some foundation for censure, should not be lightly taken up, nor wantonly played with. They concluded, that the speech imported no more, than a communication to parliament of the danger of the kingdom from the perfidy of France; the address went no further, than a general declaration to support his Majesty in a war against France; a direct and unqualified negative to the whole, would not only amount to a refusal of that support, but would likewise include a submission to all the machinations, claims, or injuries, to be framed or offered by that insidious power. Could it then be a question with that House, whether they should assure his Majesty of their ready support under the present alarming circumstances? If a war with America, should be involved in a resistance to the perfidious and insolent demands of France, that was not imputable either to the ministers, to parliament, or to the nation at large. The war was just; and it was now become a matter of absolute necessity.

To this the lords in opposition replied, that refusing to address conveyed no negative to the support of any system of war or politicks. But it conveyed, what they meant it should convey, their fullest determination, not to give the smallest degree of credit or support to the present Ministers, of whose incapacity for the conduct of any system, they were already (as they said) convinced, by the most conclusive and the most melancholy experience.

The address was carried upon a division, by a majority of 67 lords, who supported the motion, to 35, who proposed a total negative to the whole.

A copy of the late valedictory manifesto and proclamation issued by the Commissioners in New-York, having appeared in one of the public papers soon after the meeting of parliament, some of those passages in that piece, which we have already had occasion to take notice of, drew the attention of the opposition in both Houses, and induced the Marquis of Rockingham in the one, and Mr. Coke, [48] member for Norfolk, in the other, to move for authentic copies of the original instrument, as a foundation for an enquiry into the subject.

Dec. 4th. A copy of the proclamation of the 3d of October being accordingly laid before the House of Commons, Mr. Coke moved for an address to his Majesty, expressing the displeasure of parliament at certain passages of the manifesto, which, being pointed out as particularly exceptionable, were recited in the body of the proposed address; and declaring it, to be the sense of the House, that the Commissioners had no authority whatsoever, under the act of parliament, in virtue of which they had received their appointment, to hold out any such declaration: nor could that House be easily brought to believe, that they had derived any such authority from his Majesty's instructions. That those Commissioners were sent only to make peace, and not to declare the mode of making war; even if the mode itself had been less contradictory to the whole purpose of their appointment.

It was therefore requested, " that " so much of the manifesto as " contained the said declaration, " be forthwith publickly disa- " vowed by his Majesty, as con- " taining matter, inconsistent with " the humanity and generous

" courage, which, in all times,
" have diftinguifhed the Britifh
" nation; fubverfive of the max-
" ims which have been eftablifhed
" among chriftian and civilized
" communities; derogatory to the
" dignity of the crown of this
" realm; tending to debafe the
" fpirit, and to fubvert the dif-
" cipline of his Majefty's armies;
" and to expofe his innocent fub-
" jects, in all parts of his domi-
" nions, to cruel and ruinous re-
" taliations."

The motion was ftrongly fupported by the oppofition in general, as well as by the mover, upon
the ground of good policy and
felf-prefervation, as well as on
the principles of humanity, civilization, and religion. They faid,
that if we intended to fet the example, of overthrowing all the
rules and compacts, which civilization and chriftianity had eftablifhed among mankind, for leffening the horrors and alleviating
the calamities of war, by the introduction of a new and cruel
fyftem of hoftility, it was abfolutely neceffary, that we fhould
be armed at all points, and every
where prepared, to abide the iffue,
and to repel the confequences.
They afked, if this was the cafe at
prefent?

They ftated, that the northern
coafts of England, and all thofe
of Scotland, were expofed to the
ravages of the moft contemptible
enemy. That the kingdom of
Ireland, was on every fide open
and defencelefs. That fingle
American privateers had already fuccefsfully landed on our
coafts; and that even the houfes
of our nobility had not efcaped
their depredations. Thefe were[49]
armed with all the powers neceffary for carrying the " extremes
of war and defolation" into the
fevereft degree of execution; but
even thefe freebooters, who are
of an order generally confidered as being in a great meafure
lawlefs in war, felt themfelves

bound by thofe compacts eftablifhed between nations, and refpected
thofe laws and rights of humanity,
which this once great and civilized nation, not only intends to
violate, but threatens, by the
mouth of her commiffioners, fo
far as in her lies, totally to annihilate. They, however, found
themfelves happy, they faid, in
having an opportunity of declaring to their country and to pofterity, that they had no fhare in
bringing forward the calamities,
which an avowal of the inhuman
and barbarous principles of the
manifefto muft draw upon the
nation.

This war, they faid, had been
infidioufly and conftantly called by
Minifters the war of Parliament;
but was parliament to be loaded
with the obloquy of conducting it
in a manner, which could only fit
the ideas of a Cherokee or Onon-
dago favage. Parliament had held
forth the mild terms of peace;
but furely it muft be equally falfe
and unjuft, and confidered as a
libel of the bittereft nature, to
charge it with calling to its affiftance the tomohawk and fcalping-
knife, as inftruments of reconciliation; or of threatening death
and defolation to the innocent
multitude in America, if they did
not perform impoffibilities. For
fuch, they faid, were the conditions, annexed to the threats held
out to them. The multitude, if
they would efcape the extremes of
war, were immediately to abandon
home, country, property, all the
natural connections, and all the
commodities of life, and emigrate
from the remoteft parts, through
roads which they would not be
allowed to pafs, and countries
which they would not be permitted to enter, until, in de-
fpite of thefe infuperable bars,
they had arrived at New York,
(where they could find neither
room nor entertainment) there to
accept conditions of peace from
Commiffioners, who were them-

felves actually enduring fome of the
evils of war, being fhut up within the limits of a garrifon, beyond which they durft not fhew
their faces.

An officer, of high family, rank[50]
and diftinction, who had lately returned from America, expreffed
his condemnation of the meafure
in queftion, as well as of the Minifters, with whom he charged it
to originate, in terms of unufual
vehemence. He faid he could
not bear with an even temper the
indignity offered to his profeffion,
by an attempt to convert foldiers
into butchers, affaffins, and incendiaries: He liked honeft open
war againft his enemy; but he
could not endure the abominable
idea, of fheathing his fword in
the bowels of age or innocence;
ftill lefs would he tarnifh the luftre
of the Britifh name by acts of barbarity, in obedience to the mandates, or in fulfilling the defigns,
of the moft infamous adminiftration that ever difgraced a free
country. As a Britifh fenator,
and ftill more particularly, as the
reprefentative of a great manufacturing, trading, and maritime
county, which was peculiarly expofed to the retaliation of an
enemy, he fhould think he ill difcharged his duty, if he did not,
with his utmoft power oppofe a
fyftem, which would not be more
difgraceful than ruinous in its effects; a fyftem, which would invite all the renagadoes of France
and America, to ravage our coafts,
burn our towns, and deftroy our
manufactures; and which would
juftify them in every act of enormity and cruelty, even to the but-
chering in cold blood of our helplefs women and children.

It was pretty generally, and
ftrongly afferted on that fide, that
no peace could ever be derived
from the prefent Minifters. That
they had already poifoned and
polluted all the fources of conciliation. And that, as they had
long fince forfeited all confidence

and opinion with the world, fo there feemed to be a common union of mankind, in fhutting them out from all negociation, treaty, or connection.

On the other fide, the Minifters, and their immediate friends, expreffed the utmoft aftonifhment, at the forced and unnatural conftruction which was put upon the words of the declaration, and the unaccountable manner in which its plain fenfe was attempted to be perverted They declared, that they had never feen a more innocent, humane, fober, confcientious, piece of writing in their lives. They confidered it merely, as a fenfible well-meaning addrefs to the Americans, warning them of the dangers which they muft neceffarily incur by an obftinate perfeverance in their rebellion, and particularly in their unnatural connection with France. That they were not to expect that lenity in future, which they had hitherto experienced during the courfe of the war, while we ftill confidered them as fellow-fubjects, whom we wifhed to reclaim by the moft fingular mildnefs, clemency and indulgence. That nothing more could be fairly inferred from thofe words which were tortured into fo unaccountable a meaning, than that America, in confequence of its leaguing with our inveterate enemy, fhould no longer be treated as a Britifh country, but as a part of the dominions belonging to France; as the Americans, were by their alliance become French, it could afford no caufe of furprize or complaint that they fhould be confidered and treated as Frenchmen.

The Minifters denied in exprefs terms, their intention of introducing or encouraging any new fpecies of war in America, which fhould differ from the general practice in Europe; and declared that they reprobated with as much detefation, as thofe gentlemen

who feemed fo much alarmed, every idea of hoftility that militated againft humanity, or which went to the fubverfion of thofe laws of civilization, that had been calculated to fmooth the rugged face of war. Wanton cruelty, they faid, could neither be patronized by the crown, nor encouraged by any Briton: No Britifh Minifter would dare to fend fuch orders to a Britifh army; nor no Britifh army ever would, or ought, in any cafe, to obey them, in the commiffion of acts of wanton barbarity. But they would not admit, that the burning of a warehoufe converted into a battery, or the deftruction of houfes or towns, that were become repofitories of military ftores, or ufed as places of arms, could at all come within the defcription of cruelty or barbarity. Such acts had been always practifed by the moft civilized nations in Europe; and every thing that could be attempted with a profpect of fuccefs, in order to diftrefs an enemy, and to difable him from injuring his adverfary, had at all times been held juftifiable by the laws of war, and had been confirmed by the practice of all nations. Even at home, did not the laws of England allow us in cafe of invafion to wafte and deftroy our own country, wherever the enemy directed his progrefs, in order to prevent his obtaining provifion or forage? and can a doubt then be entertained, as to the juftice or right of exercifing the fame authority, in deftroying the country of our open and avowed enemy?

On the other fide it was infifted, that as there was no miftaking the words, fo there was no poffibility of explaining away the obvious fenfe of the declaration. The Commiffioners had declared, that the mode of war was to be totally changed; that it was now to be conducted with a degree of rigour and horror before unknown; " they had hitherto refrained

from the extremes of war and the defolation of the country:" the change denounced could be no other, than the carrying of thefe to their utmoft extent. It could not be pretended, with any face or appearance of truth, that the rigours of hoftility had not hitherto been carried on our fide to the utmoft limits, which the laws and rights of war authorize among civilized nations. We had even already acquired an ill name throughout Europe, under the imputation of having exceeded thofe limits. If we had hitherto forbore nothing that the practice and rights of war could authorife, the plan now to be profecuted muft go directly to cancel thofe rights. The laws of war were laws of limitation; for war was conftantly to be limited by neceffity, and its calamities and ravages were to be meafured and bound in upon that principle. But the extremes of war, and the defolation of countries, went beyond all limitations; and as no neceffity could warrant them, they could neither be juftified or excufed, upon any ground of reafon or argument. They fuppofed a cafe, to fhew the line between the extremes and limitations of war. It would, for example, be right and defenfible, becaufe it would be neceffary, to deftroy any fort, garrifon, or town, which afforded immediate ftrength to the enemy, and enabled him to annoy you in the purfuit of your object; it would be proper to burn any houfe from which the enemy fired on you; the neceffity juftifies the meafure; but in would not be lawful, right, or pardonable, to burn any houfe or town becaufe it might happen, at fome future time, to afford fhelter or ftrength to the enemy. They concluded that although the extremes of war, and defolation, were well-founding words, they were dreadful in their meaning and effect; and went to no lefs than the murther of man, woman, and child, the deftruction of countries, and the final annihilation of humanity, or they meant nothing. Nor would the confequences be lefs fatal to thofe who introduced fo odious and inhuman a fyftem, than to the people againft whom its effect was directed; as all mankind would naturally combine againft a nation, which throwing away every fhadow of principle, would venture to recal into the world, all the forgotten cruelties of barbarous ages, and all the horrors of uncivilzed war.

While the oppofition were thus contending, that the words of the declaration clearly contained that certain and precife meaning which they affigned to them, and that the Minifters as ftrongly denied their bearing or conveying any fuch fignification, juftified the Commiffioners, as well as themfelves, from the imputation of holding or avowing fo horrid a doctrine, and reprobated, in terms no lefs ftrong than thofe ufed by their antagonifts, the principle upon which it would have been founded, the debate fuddenly took a new turn, from a circumftance, which was probably as little expected on the one fide as the other.

This was an open acknowledgment, by the only Commiffioner [51] who had yet returned from America, that every charge made by the oppofition againft the proclamation, were fully founded in point of fact, both as to principle and doctrine; at the fame time that he defended and juftified the meafure as well as the principle in all their parts, upon the ground of found policy and neceffity. He faid the proclamation certainly did mean a war of defolation; it meant nothing elfe; it could mean nothing elfe; but the meafure was right and neceffa-

ry; regretted he was not on the fpot to give his fanction; and after a violent condemnation of the Congrefs, declared that no mercy, ought to be fhewn to them; and that if the infernals * could be employed againft them, he fhould approve of the meafure.

This avowal of a doctrine and fact, which the Minifters and their friends had fo totally difclaimed and denied, and confirmation of an interpretation, which they had fo pofitively charged to the virulence of party, and the ingenious malice of their adverfaries, could not but produce fome little embarraffment. It was impoffible to fupport a principle which they had fo recently and fo totally reprobated. They accordingly abandoned both that, and the gentleman by whom it was avowed and juftified to the mercy of the oppofition, without the fmalleft interference in behalf of either.

Both the generals who had returned from the American fervice, voted for the addrefs, and condemned the fuppofed cruelty charged to the proclamation. But this debate was particularly diftinguifhed, by the unexpected and direct attack made upon the American Minifter, by the late commander in chief upon that continent. That general, after feeming to attribute the attacks made upon his reputation and character, to the lenity which he had practifed in the profecution of the war, and obferving, that if thefe did not originate from Minifters, they, at leaft, were not difcouraged or contradicted by them, although they had thofe means of information in their hands, which fully fhewed their injuftice and falfehood, entered into a detail of various matters of complaint, which he laid againft the noble lord at the head of the American depart-

ment, relative to his conduct with refpect to himfelf, and to the command with which he was entrufted in America. To thefe he charged his refignation of that command, and ftrongly urged, (as did likewife his noble brother) that a parliamentary enquiry fhould be inftituted, in order that the conduct both of the commanders and the minifter fhould be fully examined, juftice done on all fides, and the nation acquainted with the true caufe of that failure of fuccefs, which it had hitherto experienced. He concluded his fpeech with a free declaration of his own private opinion, amounting to no lefs in import, than that neither a happy reftoration of peace, nor a fuccefsful profecution of the war, could ever be hoped for, while the conduct of American affairs, was continued in the hands of the prefent noble fecretary for that department.

The noble Minifter feemed aftonifhed at this unexpected attack, and entered into a vindication of his conduct with refpect to the general, fo far as his memory could admit upon fo fudden an occafion; totally difclaiming all intention of injury, and all defign of neglect. As to the conduct of the war, if it had not been as fuccefsful as might have been wifhed, it was not only doing him an injuftice to fuppofe him the caufe of our mifcarriages, but it was fuppofing him of much more confequence than he really was, by attributing to him the fole management of the war; he was only an humble fervant of the crown; and if he had not the greateft abilities to recommend him, he had, however, thus much to offer with truth and confidence in his defence, that he had ever acted fince his coming into office, according to the very beft of his judgment. He had no wifh, he faid, to prevent any enquiry, that might be neceffary to refcue the character of any gentleman from obloquy; and he trufted,

---

* A fort of machines ufed for the deftruction of towns in the wars with France towards the clofe of the laft century.

that if ever a parliamentary enquiry should take place into his own conduct, he should be so well prepared to meet it, that his honour and character should come off in triumph.

The question being put, after long debates, the motion for the proposed address was rejected upon a division, by a majority of 209, to 122.

The Marquis of Rockingham, in a speech which lasted upwards of an hour and a half, introduced and supported his motion, with a great display of knowledge and ability. That nobleman, and the lords on his side, called upon in the most pressing terms, and particularly applied themselves, to the reverend bench of bishops, to exert that charity, humanity and abhorrence of blood and cruelty, which were the leading tenets, and distinguishing characteristics of Christianity, upon a subject, which not only came directly within their cognizance, but in which they seemed bound by their character, to take an unequivocal and decided part. They observed, that all the avowed original motives and objects of the war, were now done away or abandoned, and its nature and principle totally changed. That right reverend body, had hitherto supported the measures of government in the contest with America, under the firm hope and persuasion, founded upon the faith and repeated assurances of Ministers, that the recovery of our colonies was not only practicable, but easily to be attained. So far, the motive of the war might possibly be honourable, and its object fair; the questions of fact, or of policy, did not absolutely lie with them. But they were now informed by an authority which they could not question, that of those very Ministers declared to all the world in their manifesto, that a new system of policy was adopted; and the nature of the contest totally chang-

7th.

ed. That America was relinquished, and the advantages of a connection with our colonies abandoned. And a new species of war was denounced, tending merely and avowedly to revenge, slaughter, and universal destruction.

It could not be even supposed, that they would afford their countenance to so odious, so barbarous a system. They were called upon to exert in their legislative character, the peculiar and most exalted principles of Christianity, in preventing the wanton effusion of human blood, and the destruction of mankind. It could not be imagined, that their natural disposition, would not tend equally with their religious principles, and their professional duty, to the condemnation of all measures of blood, and the utter detestation of all new and cruel aggravations of the horrors of war. Their interference was required in preventing the destruction and sparing the blood, not only of men or of Christians, but of Englishmen, and of Protestants like themselves; and of crushing in the outset an abominable system of warfare, which would, in its progress and consequences, bring ruin and desolation home to their flocks and their doors.

It happened fortunately, they said, that the legal powers, with which they had been invested by the constitution for such pious purposes, would be found in the present instance, fully equal to the duty and emergency. They were the Moderators ordained by the wisdom of the constitution, to check the rage, restrain the passions, and controul the violence, of mere temporal men. Their simple votes upon this occasion, would at once fully express their detestation of the inhuman system in question, and, joined with those of the temporal lords who held the same principle, fully cure its effects. And thus they would afford a new and striking evidence to the

world, of the sanctity of their order, the wisdom of its legislative institution, and the unsullied purity of their profession.

On the ground of retaliation, besides the danger and mischief to Great Britain and Ireland, the irretrievable destruction, which the full, and undoubted, adoption of that system by France and America, would bring upon our West India islands, was strongly urged. And they argued, that from the nature of the sugar plantations and works, and the great capital necessarily lodged in them, the desolation caused by a single privateer upon that system, could scarcely be recovered in an age.

But they particularly reprobated, and indeed their powers of argument, and utmost acumen of censure, seemed principally directed, (as well in the debate, as in the succeeding protest) against those new political principles or maxims, which they charged to the manifesto, viz. That " what we have no interest in preserving, we are called upon by necessity to destroy," and that, " motives of self-preservation, not growing out of any state of circumstances, now in actual existence, but founded upon a policy directed to future uncertain events, should be supposed to authorize or justify, a present general desolation." These principles, they said, would afford a full justification of all the cruelty and destruction of mankind, recorded of the most bloody tyrants, and of the most barbarous nations. They would justify Herod in the murther of the Innocents. Upon this ground, they stated the following causes of dissent in the protest.—viz. " Be-" cause the public law of nations, " in affirmance of the dictates of " nature, and the precepts of re-" vealed religion, forbids us to " resort to the extremes of war, " upon our own opinion of their " *expediency*; or *in any case* to " carry on war for the purpose of

" desolation. We know that the
" rights of war are odious, and
" instead of being extended upon
" loose constructions, and specu-
" lations of danger, ought to be
" bound up and limited by all
" the restraints of the most ri-
" gorous construction. We are
" shocked to see the first law of
" nature, self-preservation, per-
" verted and abused into a prin-
" ciple destructive of all other
" laws; and, a rule laid down,
" by which our own safety is ren-
" dered incompatible with the
" prosperity of mankind. Those
" objects of war, which cannot
" be compassed by fair and ho-
" nourable hostility, ought not
" to be compassed at all. " *An*
" *end that has no means, but such*
" *as are unlawful, is an unlawful*
" *end.*"

The Lords on that side concluded by observing, that no great
force of argument seemed necessary for the condemnation of so
shameful a public instrument, which
springing from a commission under
the great seal of the kingdom,
would otherwise become a standing
record, and monument of national
disgrace; which went to the indiscriminate massacre and extermination of a numerous and widely
extended people, two thirds of
whom, were said by its framers,
to be our warm friends, and inviolably attached to our government. That such a public disavowal was absolutely necessary,
lest it should appear in Europe,
that a British parliament had given
its sanction to the revival of that
ferocity and barbarism in war,
which a beneficent religion, enlightened manners, and true military honour, had so long banished
from the christian world.

On the other hand, the lords in
administration, or office, who were
those only, that took any part on
that side in the debate, totally denied (as the ministers had done in
the House of Commons) the interpretation put upon the words,
and the construction upon the
meaning of the manifesto, by the
opposition. At the same time
they utterly disclaimed, and reprobated even in stronger terms,
the bloody principles which were
charged to, or supposed to dictate
the manifesto. But this charge
they attributed solely, to a disposition for decrying, however unjustly, all the measures of government, and a desire of creating unfounded alarms and uneasinesses
among the people. To obviate
this design, and to prevent the
effects which the strong representations and colouring used on the
other side might produce in the
House, they entered pretty deeply
into a critical disquisition of the
words, and what they described to
be the fair construction of the proclamation, as well as into a justification of the meaning and intention, and a vindication of the conduct and character of the commissioners. They concluded by
hoping, that the lords would not
suffer themselves to be led away,
by a studious and laboured appeal
to their feelings and passions, and
a forced and unnatural misconstruction and misinterpretation of plain
and obvious language, into the
passing of a hasty and unjust censure, not only upon the measures of
government, but upon a noble lord
and gentleman, who were absent in
the service of their country, and
consequently incapable of vindicating themselves.

On this occasion, the new Lord [52]
Chancellor had an opportunity of
displaying in that House, those
abilities which had been so conspicuous in another. A great law
lord, who has been long out of office, and a right reverend prelate, [53]
who is scarcely less distinguished,
by his opposition to many of the
measures of administration, than by
his eloquence, were no less conspicuous on the other side, in their
support of the motion, and in their
unqualified condemnation of the
terms, principle, and spirit of the
proclamation. Both these noble
lords took occasion to reprobate,
in strong terms, the circumstances
attending the destruction of several parts of America, particularly
of the settlement of Wyoming, and
the cruelties exercised by Col.
Butler.

The question being at length
put, the motion for an address of
censure was over-ruled upon a division, by a majority of 71, including proxies, to 37.

Thirty-one names appeared to
the protest, which, if compared
with the number of the minority
on the division, was above the
usual proportion. That protest
was penned with uncommon ability.

. . .

Debates arising on questions of supply, previous to the recess. Augmentation of 14,000 men, to the land service. Trial at Portsmouth. Admiral Keppel, honourably acquitted. Receives the thanks of both Houses. Vice-admiral of the blue resigns his employments, and vacates his seat in the House of Commons. Memorial, signed by twelve admirals, presented. Great discontents in the navy. Resolution of censure moved by Mr. Fox, on the conduct of the admiralty. Motion, after long debates, rejected upon a division. Second motion, of a similar nature, by Mr. Fox, rejected upon a division. Two great naval commanders, declare against acting under the present system. Resignation of naval officers. Sir P. J. Clerke, brings in a bill against the contractors; first question carried upon a division; but the bill rejected upon another. Bill in favour of Dissenters brought in and passed. Affairs of Ireland. Various attempts and proposals for affording commercial relief to that country, prove at length ineffectual.

ALTHOUGH the great questions of supply had been carried through by the ministers, previous to the recess, without any marked opposition, yet they were productive, as has been usually the case of late, of much discussion, enquiry, and observation, relative to the specific services to which they were to be applied, and the nature and amount of the respective demands. The mode of conducting the war was a general ground of objection with the opposition, who contended, that our force by sea and land should be directed against the foreign settlements, or home possessions of our natural enemy, instead of being wasted and spent in fruitless and hopeless exertions on the continent of America.

That party insisted much on what they considered as the ruinous policy, of persevering in the vain attempt of subjugating America by force, supported as it now was by a formidable and dangerous alliance, when we were already taught by a dear bought experience, which had at least afforded conviction to all the rest of mankind, that it was extremely doubtful whether we were capable of executing the task, even if America stood single-handed. Our only rational mode of conduct, and ground of hope, now was, (they said) to press our natural foe, with such vigour and force, as [54]

would compel him to renounce his American system; and then to renew, upon fair and equitable terms, such a communion of interests with that people, as our past injustice and madness would still afford room for obtaining. But no hope of this sort (they said) could ever be entertained upon any rational principle, while we exhausted our force, and squandered our treasure in America. On the contrary, victory and defeat, in that fatal war, produced similar consequences to ourselves, and equally furthered the views of the common enemy. And every year of its continuance, went to establish the ruin of both countries; nor would it require a long succession of such years, to render our own destruction inevitable, whatever might become of America.

On the other hand the ministers contended, that America was reduced to the lowest state of weakness; that her armies were annihilated; that she had already contracted a debt of fifty millions in the prosecution of the war; that her credit was so totally sunk, that the congress bills were sold for one fortieth of their nominal value; that her people were starving, and in want of all the necessaries of life; and that in this state of distress, when they were enduring all the most pressing calamities of war, and every degree of domestic

misery, they were also suffering the most intolerable political oppressions, from the tyranny of their usurped powers of government. That a very great majority of the people abominated the French alliance, and execrated the congress on that account; that the latter had exceeded and abused their powers in that instance; and that the political and hostile connection with France had not been constitutionally ratified; that is, it had not yet received that species of assent, which was fundamentally, and essentially necessary, to constitute a real and binding compact on the people of America.

They asked, whether such a state of things, when opposed by the blessings of peace, and these accompanied with constitutional freedom and security, did not afford the most probable causes, and the best founded reasons for expecting, that the colonies, either separately or conjunctly, would co-operate in measures for removing their public and private distresses; for getting rid of their oppressions, and dissolving such a system of usurpation and tyranny? The probabilities were so strong in our favour, they said, as to amount to little less than actual proofs; and to stop short, and slacken our exertions, at the very moment that so fair a prospect was opened, would be such a degree of political absurdity and madness, as no people had ever before exhibited.

As to withdrawing the troops, or changing the object and direction of the war, it would amount to no less, they said, than a dereliction of America for ever. Nor would the evil be confined to the loss or independence of the revolted colonies merely. Canada, Nova Scotia, Newfoundland, Rhode Island, New York, and the Florida's, must follow of course. Our West India islands could not stay long behind, nor could they afford any benefit while they remained in our hands. And yet, dreadful as these consequences seem, even in idea, the absolute loss to ourselves, would not be the worst part of the evil. But all these vast acquisitions; these unequalled sources of naval dominion, wealth and power, would be thrown into the balance against us. They would become additions to the power and strength of our natural and mortal enemy.

The opposition answered, that it was to prevent those fatal consequences, and to avoid that dreadful state of public affairs, now too faithfully described, that they had constantly opposed the measures which led to the loss of America, and endeavoured at all times to heal the differences with our colonies. But the event, which they so much dreaded, and endeavoured to prevent, had already taken place. America was lost. It was to little purpose to waste time in cavilling about the term independence. She was independent in fact, whether we allowed it or not; nor was it in our power to render her otherwise. Were we then to persevere to the last in our folly, and acting the part of a mad and desperate gamester, to throw away the remainder of our fortune, in a fit of vexation for the loss of that which we had already squandered?

They said, that the same delusive picture of American affairs which was now presented, had with some occasional alterations in the colouring, been exhibited at the opening of every session since the beginning of the troubles. The object was, however, at all times the same. It being merely intended to lead the nation, from year to year, still farther on in error and ruin. The Americans had been alternately represented as cowards, as beggars, as an undisciplined mob, as being not only without arms, and all military provision, but being destitute even of the common means of existence, and in that last state of wretched-

ness, exceedingly well disposed to cut each others throats. And as if there were no bounds supposed to our credulity, nor limits intended to our wonder, they are represented as being in general loyal subjects, and firmly attached to the government of this country; and we are informed, that the many are not only most unaccountably kept in bondage by the few, but that they are compelled to take arms in their hands, and totally contrary to their inclination and will, to fight the battles of a vagrant congress, and of a handful of factious leaders, whom they equally hate and despise, against us, whom they regard and consider as their best friends,

To these representations, they opposed a view of the prodigious force by sea and land, supported at an expence of treasure unknown in any former warfare, which had been so long and so ineffectually employed for the reduction of such a country, defended by such wretched soldiers, and acting under such a feeble and odious government. A force and a treasure, they said, which, under a wise and able direction, might have aspired, and not unsuccessfully, to the subversion of some one, among many, of the oldest and best established states in the universe. And yet, those soldiers, and that government, have successfully resisted this mighty force by sea and land; and have, for a succession of years, and through a variety of hard and bloody conflicts, baffled the utmost efforts, of one of the best provided, best disciplined, and bravest armies that ever existed.[55]

• • •

The noble brothers who lately commanded on the American service, had omitted no occasion during the course of the session, of pressing in the strongest terms, for an enquiry into the conduct of the war, so far particularly, as they were themselves immediately concerned. They supported this urgency of application, and the pro-

priety of the measure, upon the different grounds, of public utility, and of particular justice. They stated it to be a matter of great national importance, that the real causes of our failure, hitherto, of success, might be thoroughly known and understood; as a proper application of that knowledge, could only afford any rational hope of greater advantage in the further prosecution of the war. It was likewise a satisfaction due to the people, for the heavy losses they had sustained, and the immense expences they were at, to let them see the true state of their affairs; as it would be a farther assurance and encouragement to them to discover, that the causes were removed, which had hitherto disappointed their expectations. With respect to themselves, their endeavours to serve their country, had been productive of such a torrent of invective, and unceasing obloquy, as had not perhaps been equalled in any former period; although ministers themselves were silent, and had not ventured to bring any charge against any part of their conduct, they had full reason to believe, and the world held the same opinion, that this abuse proceeded wholly from their hireling emissaries, and pensioned writers. Their conduct had likewise been publicly arraigned in that House, by persons either in office, or who were at least known to be in the confidence and favour of ministers; whilst the latter, thoroughly sensible as they were of the injustice of the censure, and with the full means of their justification in possession, used not the smallest effort for that purpose. On these grounds, they were under a necessity, they said, of demanding a parliamentary enquiry: that if any blame was due in the conduct of the American war, it might be applied to its proper object; and if they were totally clear from it, as they trusted, they might thereby obtain justice, in the vindication of their honour and character.

On the other hand, the ministers, among other causes, objected to the enquiry, as being totally needless. Government had laid no charge against the noble brothers; and on the contrary, several parts of their conduct had met its approbation. As to the abuse or charges contained in newspapers or pamphlets, any more than the opinions held, or censures thrown out by individuals, whether within or without doors, they could not surely be considered of sufficient moment, to authorise the bringing out of an enquiry, which must necessarily break in so prodigiously upon the time and attention of the house, and that in a session, when there was already so much business of importance before them, and so much more still in expectation, or at least within the line of probable contingency. As to themselves, whatever their private opinions in certain matters might be, they had no share in any attacks that were made upon the characters of the noble brothers without doors, nor arraignments of their conduct within. Of these matters they were totally innocent.

Altho' the ministers did not approve of the enquiry, they, however, acquiesced in the motions for laying the American papers before the House; which were accordingly brought forward in great abundance, and continued on the table during a great part of the session. In these were included the whole correspondence between the ministers, and the commanders on the main service in America, from about the time of Sir William Howe's arrival at Boston, in the year 1775, to his return from Philadelphia, in 1778; together with a great number of accounts, returns, and other papers, tending to shew the state, number, effective strength, and condition of the army, at different periods of the intermediate time; their real movements and operations; as well as the different plans of action which had been proposed,

discussed; or concerted, by the ministers and generals.

General Burgoyne was no less importunate in this session, than he had been ever since his return, for an enquiry into his own conduct, and into all matters relative to the Canada expedition. We have already seen, that his particular situation under the convention of Saratoga, had been laid down as an insuperable obstacle to his gratification in that respect; and it may be conceived from obvious causes, that his complaints and applications were now full as little attended to as those of the other commanders. The northern expedition, was, however, so connected in its consequences with the operations of the grand army, and they so materially affected the event and general fortune of the war, that it was not easy to separate matters so blended in any course of enquiry; and this difficulty was increased by the circumstance, that Sir William Howe had been specifically arraigned both within doors and without, for undertaking the southern expedition, at the time that he should have waited to facilitate and support the operations of the other army on the north river. General Burgoyne accordingly seized this opportunity of bringing forward his own business, as necessarily belonging to and inseparable from the rest; so that the House was in possession of the whole correspondence of the three commanders, and of all the documents relative to the different services.

April 29th. Although the House had gone so far as to form itself into a committee for enquiring into the conduct of the American war; had made a previous application to the House of Lords for the attendance of Earl Cornwallis, as an evidence, and had listened for two hours, with the greatest attention, to the very clear and able narrative of his conduct, delivered in the plain eloquence of a soldier by Sir William Howe;

yet, the noble lord at the head of affairs, who had all along expressed the utmost disapprobation of the enquiry, was still determined to quash it. It was said in general, that there had been no necessity, nor even occasion at any time for the enquiry; but that if there had, that necessity or occasion was now fully removed, as well by the able explanation of his conduct given by the honourable general, as by the papers before them. That almost every part of the correspondence went to shew, the utmost satisfaction of government, and its warmest approbation with respect to the services of the two noble commanders; that the personal declarations of the ministers shewed that they still retained the same sentiments; and that a doubt could not be entertained in the committee on the subject. That without regard to occasion, the commanders had hitherto been indulged in bringing forward every thing they proposed, merely to satisfy their delicacy; but that end being attained, it would be absurd to pursue the subject any farther; there was neither charge nor accuser; and it would be merely combating a shadow.

But they went farther, and contended, that if matters had been different, and that an accusation had been really laid against the officers, that House was totally incompetent to any inquiry into, or any decision upon military matters. Military charges and accusations, must be enquired into, tried, and decided upon, in their own proper courts; and no where else. It would be in the highest degree absurd to suppose, that gentlemen sitting in that House, should pretend to judge of the proper distribution of a large military force; of the movements of columns, the evolutions of brigades, or the good or bad dispositions made in a field of battle. The minister seemed to think, that the conduct of ministers was the latent object of the enquiry, with a view of injuring them by a side wind; of trying them in an oblique and indirect manner; if that was the object, he desired it might be declared; that the accuser should stand forth, avow his charge, and compel them to answer. When that was avowed, ministers would know the accuser and the accusation; and they would know in what manner to make their defence. If that was not the object, a further pursuit of the enquiry would be futile and needless.

With a view to the incompetency of the House in military matters, upon Sir William Howe's motion for the examination of Earl Cornwallis, the question was put to him, " upon what points he " meant to interrogate the noble " lord;" to which the general replied, " to the general conduct of " the American war; to military " points generally and particular-" ly." These words were eagerly seized by the minister, who working them up with the original into the form of an amendment, under that colour nearly framed a new motion, which he knew carried its own rejection along with it. The words of the motion in that state were—" That Lord Corn-" wallis be called in and examined " relative to general and particu-" lar military points, touching " the general conduct of the Ame-" rican war."

There was scarcely any thing during the session that drew out such severity of censure, and even of reproach, as this manœuvre, or, as it was termed, trick, in debate, now did. It was said, that so shameless and palpable an evasion of inquiry and truth, and so barefaced an acknowledgment of guilt, had never been ventured upon by any other minister, nor could not have been endured at any other period. The degraded situation of the noble lord, which reduced him to the necessity of adopting so shameful a measure, in order to

screen his associates, and the open acknowledgment which it included, that he durst not venture to trust, even his own standing majority with their guilt, was expressed in those terms of pity, which convey the forest ideas of contempt and ridicule.

It was contended, that the two objects were so closely united, that there was not a possibility, in the present enquiry, of separating the conduct of the ministers, and of the military commanders. No opinion could be formed with respect to the former, without knowing how far their plans were or were not practicable; nor of the latter, without knowing and measuring the means which had been put into their hands. And from whom was this information to be sought or obtained, but from those officers who had served, on the spot, and who being employed in endeavouring to carry those plans into execution, were thoroughly acquainted with the sufficiency or deficiency of the means, as well as with the nature and extent of the impediments which were opposed to them? Several questions would come before the committee, which were merely political and deliberative; and these could only be decided upon, by taking the opinion of professional men on the spot; men who knew the country, were informed of the nature of the resistance expected to be made, and the real motives which gave, or did not give a preference to the measures pursued, before others which might be proposed. To stop such information, therefore, by a vote of that House, was, in fact, the converting parliament into a screen, for preventing an enquiry into the conduct of administration; for if the commander had acted right, it necessarily followed, that the measures of policy were dictated by weakness and ignorance, as they were now attempted to be covered by the most shameful and criminal evasion and imposition.

The point of order was strongly insisted on, and this was said to be the first instance in the annals of parliament, in which the reference of any order of the House to a committee, was clogged with any amendment or condition whatever in that committee The order of the House was specific, for the attendance on that day, and the examination of Lord Cornwallis; and the amendment imported a negative to that order, and accordingly went to a substantial contradiction of it. Thus was the dignity of the House of Commons sacrificed, and their orders treated with a contempt, which would reduce them in all future times to the condition of waste paper, merely to save ministers from that punishment, which they had so justly merited, and which the ruin they had brought upon their country so loudly called for. It was lamented, that any man, or set of men, should possess so baneful an influence, and apply it to so deplorable a purpose, as to induce them in such a manner to a surrender of their own inherent privileges; and thus to establish a precedent, which must go to the banishment of all order and relegation from their future proceedings, and to the introduction of anarchy and confusion.

A general officer, who had acquired great reputation in the late war in Germany, who was even then near the top of his profession, in point of rank, and who had since filled, with no small degree of eminence, one of the highest civil departments of the state, called upon the ministers to declare, whether they denied the competence of the House to institute or proceed upon such an enquiry? He dared them to the assertion; and protested, that during thirty years he had sat in parliament, he never saw so gross an attempt to violate the inherent and constitutional privileges of that House; whether with respect to the breach of order, or to what was of infinitely greater importance, the denying that House to have a right of inquisitorial jurisdiction over every department of the state, every establishment, whether civil, military, or criminal.

The minister's amendment was, however, carried upon a division, though by a smaller majority than might perhaps have been expected in so full a house, the numbers being 189 to 155.

The debate was again renewed on the main question, whether the motion so amended should pass, when the question being called for, it was rejected, although by a smaller majority than on the preceding division, the numbers being 180 to 158. A gentleman of the opposition then moved, in the terms of [57] the original order of the House, That Lord Cornwallis be called in, " and examined respecting the " subject matter of the papers re- " ferred to said committee." This motion was negatived without a division. And thus the enquiry seemed to have been laid to sleep for ever. The committee was not, however, dissolved; for although a motion for that purpose had been proposed early in the debate by a noble lord in office, it had been withdrawn at the minister's desire, who preferred this scheme of management which we have seen. In strictness, the committee was open to receive any testimony tending to the elucidation of the papers before them, excepting that testimony related to military matters; and the whole subject of those papers was military.

The opposition were, however, determined not to let this state of things rest in absolute quiet; and to try how far the House could, upon recollection, and in its proper form, submit to such an apparent contempt and rejection of its authority, by a committee, a creature of its own making, and furnished only with confined and temporary powers, directed to a particular object, and revocable at pleasure.

May 3d. The business was accordingly introduced a few days after, by a recital of the transactions which had passed in the committee, and a renewal of the motion for the examination of Lord Cornwallis, and the whole matter of complaint and redress supported with great vigour.

The minister and his friends had taken but little notice of the charges with respect to the point of order, which had been so strongly urged by the other side in the committee; and he now apparently left room open for an apology on that ground, by an acknowledgment that he was not fully prepared on that subject. He, however, said, that he considered committees of the whole House, and the House itself, as nearly analogous, and their powers co-extensive; so that in reality, the difference between the orders of one, and the resolutions of the other, was merely in terms, as they substantially imported the same thing. They were, on questions of importance, equally well attended; and the difference, in his apprehension, was little more, than whether the speaker was in the chair, or whether one of the members presided for the time in his place.

On the question of competency he was now remarkably tender, and did not at all push that matter as he had done in the committee. He began to perceive that such a principle once laid down might go to great lengths, and such as might prove highly inconvenient to ministers themselves. But with respect to the impropriety of examining witnesses on military questions, he was diffuse; and seemed to lay all his strength to that point. He observed, that as the evidence must be *ex parte*, it could never be deemed, by any rule of reason, sanction of precedent, or consistency with the regular proceedings of judicature, sufficiently full and conclusive, either for acquittal or censure. It might

furnish a good ground for belief or persuasion; but from the nature of the evidence, as well as the manner in which it would be delivered, no man in that House, or without, could lay any other stress upon it, or give it any higher degree of credit, than merely what *ex parte* evidence was entitled to in the first instance, and what testimony, not delivered upon oath, was intitled to in the second. And that, therefore, neither the censure nor acquittal of the honourable general, by a vote of that House, would be capable of changing, in a single instance, the opinions already formed upon that subject.

He had accordingly always held, and still retained his opinion, that enquiries into the conduct of military men, were exceedingly improper in that House. When such occasions occurred, military courts were provided by the constitution for the purpose. He considered a court-martial as the only tribunal, where the party accused could procure substantial reparation for his injured honour, and where, on the other hand, in case of failure or neglect, the justice of the nation could be legally and constitutionally satisfied.

He also observed, that if under the appearance of an enquiry into the conduct of military officers, it was intended to bring charges of neglect or incapacity against ministers, he could not but consider it as an exceedingly unfair mode of proceeding. No man had yet avowed that design. And yet he could not see, what other motives there could be, for urging the present enquiry farther. The House had undoubtedly an inquisitorial power to enquire into and censure the conduct of ministers; but he trusted their conduct was not to be decided upon by the evidence of military men; much less when that evidence was professedly given on military measures, which they had neither planned nor executed. If, however, any specific accusation was brought against ministers, as one of his Majesty's confidential servants, he was ready to have witnesses instantly called to the bar, provided the matter on which they were to be examined was previously stated, and was such as directly and specifically pointed to any one particular measure of administration.

On the other side, it was laid down as a clear and indisputable rule of proceeding in that House, that a committee was always bound by the order of reference made to it; otherwise, there would be two contradictory powers and clashing jurisdictions in the same body; a doctrine too absurd and monstrous to be heard or endured. A great part of their business was transacted by committees, particularly by committees of the whole House; if, therefore, it should be adopted as parliamentary law, that what the House entertained in one instance and referred to a committee, was so far controulable by that committee, as that the latter had an option to disobey the order of reference, all business would be at an end; and as often as circumstances afforded a pretence, the proceedings of that House would be involved in endless confusion, and in contests with itself. The House was therefore called upon, and requested seriously to reflect and consider, the fatal consequences that would necessarily ensue, if it did not preserve a proper controul over its several constituent parts.— The question they were to decide upon was short and plain, but it included much matter:—It was simply this; Shall the House controul and direct a committee appointed by itself, or shall they controul and direct the House?

The ground of propriety, with respect to military enquiries in that House, was not only abundantly supported, but covered with a superfluity both of arguments and of precedents. The debate, however, hung yet in suspence, when the

unexpected part taken by a gentleman high in office, and closely [58] connected with a strong and powerful party, suddenly turned the ballance. That gentleman declared, that although it was with infinite reluctance that he differed in opinion with the two noble lords in administration, yet he could not avoid thinking the conduct of the committee, even at the time, very extraordinary. He had, however, some doubts upon the subject, which occasioned his going away, without speaking or voting, on that night. But these doubts were now totally removed For as he considered certain words (which he recited) that had fallen from the American minister in the present debate, as a direct charge and accusation against the commander in chief, he should think it an act of the greatest cruelty and injustice if the present motion was not passed, in order to afford an opportunity for his vindication and defence.

These words operated like a charm. Nothing would afterwards be listened to from the other side. The minister attempted several times to speak, but in vain. A complete revolution was effected; and the enquiry, which a few days before had been rejected by a majority, was now resumed, with an appearance of almost generally unanimity. The committee was accordingly revived a May 6th. few days after, and the examination of the officers commenced by that of Earl Cornwallis.

It would be equally beyond our purpose, and our limits, to enter into any particular detail of this enquiry. It was taken up with much general expectation, and it might, perhaps, be said hope. The public were in the highest degree impatient for it. Those who had conceived that the total reduction of America ought to have been but the business of one easy campaign, were eager to see the fault fixed upon those generals,

whose mismanagement had rendered the war not only so tedious and so expensive, but at present almost hopeless. Others, wished to fix the fault on the original ill policy of the undertaking, rendered additionally ruinous by the weakness and contradiction of the councils by which it had been conducted. But as the enquiry might be, as in reality it was, drawn out to a very great length, it soon became evident, that those who originally opposed any enquiry at all; and only had given way, because they were unable to resist the torrent, would prevent it from producing any effect; and this it was not difficult to do, as it was in their power to draw the examination of witnesses into an infinite length; and the attention of all being fatigued by such a pursuit, attendance would naturally relax along with it; and the business would languish, and expire of itself.

The officers who were examined were the following, who were also called in the order that we state them, viz. Earl Cornwallis, Major-General Grey, Sir Andrew Snape Hammond, Major Montresor, chief engineer, and Sir George Osborne, [59] a member of the House. Their testimony, taken together, went to the establishment of the following points of fact, or of opinion.—— That the force sent to America was at no time equal to the subjugation of the country—That this proceeded in a great measure from the general enmity and hostility of the people, who were almost unanimous in their aversion to the government of Great-Britain; and also from the nature of the country, which was the most difficult and impracticable with respect to military operations that could possibly be conceived—That these circumstances of country and people, rendered the services of reconnoitring, of obtaining intelligence, of acquiring any previous knowledge that could be depended on, of the state of the roads, and the nature of the ground which they were to traverse, along with the essential object of procuring provisions and forage, exceedingly difficult, and in some respects impracticable — That this latter circumstance rendered it impossible for the army to carry on its operations at any distance from the fleet ; at least, without the full possession, on both its sides, of some navigable river — And that its operations were much retarded, and frequently endangered, by being generally constrained through the circumstances of roads and country, to march only in a single column.

It also went to the establishment of the following particular points, in direct contradiction to several charges which had been made against the conduct of the commander in chief, viz. That the rebel lines and redoubts at Brooklyn, in Long-Island, on the 27th of August 1776, were in such a state of strength and defence, that any immediate attack upon them, without waiting to make proper approaches, and without the artillery, scaling ladders, axes, and other articles necessary to the service, would have been scarcely less than an act of desperate rashness. —That Lord Cornwallis's halting at Brunswick, when in pursuit of the enemy, in the same year, was necessary, as well with respect to the condition of the troops in point of fatigue and provision, as to their number, and the posts which it was first necessary to occupy, in order to preserve their communication ; and that his passing the Delaware, and advancing to Philadelphia, when he afterwards arrived at Trenton, was utterly impracticable, from the total want of boats, and of all other means for that purpose.—That the going by sea to Philadelphia, was the most eligible, if not the only method, which could have been adopted, for the reduction of Pensylvania, and that the Chesapeak was a more eligible passage than the De-laware.—That from the strength of the highlands, and other circumstances, the attempt of going up the North River towards Albany, while Washington was at hand with a strong army, to profit of all the advantages which it must afford, would have been difficult, dangerous, and probably found impracticable in the event. —And that the drawing of General Washington and his army, near 300 miles from the North River, to the defence of Pensylvania, was the most effectual diversion that could have been made in favour of the northern army ; and at the same time held out the greatest probability, that the desire of protecting Philadelphia, would have induced him to hazard a general action ; an event so long and so ardently coveted, as the only means which could tend to bring the war to a speedy conclusion, and which every other measure had been found incapable of producing.

General Howe had endeavoured, in his narrative, as well as in the different speeches which were drawn from him on the subject, to establish as an indisputable fact, and demonstrably to prove from the correspondence before them, that he had constantly stated to the American minister, the great difficulty and impracticable nature of the war ; and the utter impossibility of subjugating that continent with the force under his command. That he had accordingly accompanied the plans for the operations of the campaign of 1777, with a requisition, in one instance, of a reinforcement of 20,000, and in another of 15,000 men, strongly stating and arguing, that nothing less could effectually answer the purpose of bringing the war to a speedy conclusion. That on the other hand, the minister did not seem to credit, that the difficulties were so great as they were represented, nor that so great an additional force as was demanded could be necessary ; and placed much of his dependance in the firm persuasion, that the well-affected in Pensylvania were so numerous, that the general would be able to raise such a force there, as would be sufficient for the future defence and protection of the province, when the army departed to finish the remaining service. That accordingly, he had promised, only about half the force stated in the second number : that not a fifth of the force, even so promised, was at length sent ; and that reinforcement, when it did come, arrived too late to answer any of the original purposes of the campaign.— He likewise stated, and supported by the same authority, that so far from any concert or co-operation being proposed or intended between him and the northern army, that that expedition had never even been casually mentioned, in any of the discussions relative to the plans of the future campaign, which had passed between him and the minister. That the first knowledge he had of that design, and which induced him to write a letter to Sir Guy Carleton upon the subject, was merely from public report. And, that the first intimation he received from the minister, that the smallest degree of support would be expected from him in favour of that expedition, was by a letter which he received in the middle of August, in the Chesapeak, when his measures were already taken in pursuance of that plan which he had previously settled with the noble secretary, and when it would have been too late for him in any case to have receded. But even that letter expressed no more than a confident hope, that he should be returned soon enough back from the southward, to concur in the further operations of the northern army.

It will be easily seen, that nothing could possibly have been more galling or vexatious to the ministers, than some part of this narrative, and of the preceding evidence. Particularly that part of the former, which stated the general's communication of the impracticability of the American war ; or at least the insufficiency of the force appointed to that service for the accomplishment of its purpose, at a time that the ministers held out a language and hopes so directly contrary to the parliament and people of England. The charge of general disaffection among the Americans, which was laid by the general, as well as the other officers, although more guarded perhaps in terms and specification, was likewise an exceeding tender subject with the ministers. The opposition too never omitted any occasion of reminding them, that from the beginning of the troubles, they had been constantly represented by them, as being the acts merely of a faction in America, who had by a sort of surprize possessed themselves of the civil and military powers of that country ; but that the great bulk, or at least a large majority of the people, were firmly attached to the government of Great-Britain. Indeed if that representation was an error, it seems pretty clearly, that the ministers were no less involved in it themselves, than the public. At any rate it was a very favourite opinion ; and nothing could be more grating than this testimony, which went directly to its subversion.

For these and other causes, it was thought necessary to call in question the validity of this evidence, and nothing could so well answer that purpose, as the opposing to it another body of the same nature ; for as no decisive victory was to be gained, nor defeat feared in such a contest, the issue must unavoidably be, the leaving the question of fact in doubt and uncertainty ; and no more was wanted.

It was accordingly proposed, towards, what seem- **13th.**

ed, the close of the examination, that other witnesses should be called in and examined, relative to several matters which were stated in the present evidence. In support of this proceeding it was advanced, that *ex parte* evidence had been received, relative to matters of fact and opinion, to military manœuvres, to the propriety of plans, and to the execution of them ; and that this had been principally directed to the laying of implied or direct charges against the conduct of ministers, particularly of the noble lord at the head of the American department. That it was therefore necessary, fair, and equitable, that witnesses should be brought on the other side, and evidence received relative to those points, and to set aside those charges. The noble minister himself disclaimed the idea of becoming an accuser ; (with which he was charged) but as he was attacked, and charged with being the cause of the miscarriage of the American war, it was necessary he should defend himself ; and the facts which he should state, the witnesses he should bring to support them, and the arguments which he might use, would all tend to that point merely, and not to the accusation of any man. He, however, declared, that his main object in calling witnesses, was to rescue the brave, loyal, and meritorious sufferers in America, from the unjust general imputation or censure thrown on them by the present evidence, particularly that passage which says, that the Americans were " almost unanimous" in their resistance against the claims of this country.

On the other side, the opposition condemned, as extremely unfair and irregular, the proposing to bring forward at the tail of an enquiry, without any previous notice, and when the evidence brought forward by the honourable general, in his own vindication, was nearly closed, new witnesses,

to stir up matter, and perhaps charges, of which he could have no knowledge, and for which he consequently could have made no provision in the examination of his own. That it was a new procedure, and such as would not be endured any where, to draw out the whole of any man's evidence, to examine where its strength or weakness lay, and without an avowal of the smallest intention to controvert any part of it, then suddenly to attempt to conjure up witnesses before unknown and unheard of, and each having before him the part to which he chose to be called, thereby endeavour to overthrow the whole of the former testimony. They likewise spoke in terms of some indignation, to the design of bringing up American refugees, pensioners, and custom-house officers, to impeach and set aside the evidence of military men of high rank, and of great professional knowledge. And, what, said they, is the point which these men are called principally to prove ? why, that the Americans, (that is, themselves) whose places pensions, and existence, depend upon their attachment, are exceedingly well disposed to acknowledge and support the rights and claims of this country over the colonies.

That party, however, in conformity with their professions of wishing for, and furthering, full and general enquiry into public matters, at length acquiesced in the motion, and orders were issued, besides General Robertson, for the attendance of General Jones, Col. Dixon, and Major Stanton ; as also, for John Maxwell, Joseph Galloway, Andrew Allen, John Paterson, Theodore Morris, and Enoch Story, Esqrs. 60

The exceedingly severe and virulent censure and reproach, repeatedly thrown upon General Burgoyne, by some persons high in office, produced at length an effect, which was as little intended as expected, by the authors of the cause from whence it proceeded. The harshness and frequency of the reproach, which was not always guarded or chaste, seemed by degrees to awaken men of all descriptions and parties into some particular consideration, of those very peculiar and unhappy circumstances of situation, under which that officer was compelled to submit to such reproach, without a possibility of vindicating in any manner his character and honour. At length, all sides of the House, seemed at once to feel for and commiserate the unhappy situation of that general.

An occasion for calling forth this disposition presented, itself. Sir William Howe having closed his evidence, and the time being yet open for bringing forward the counter evidence, there was a chasm of some days in the business of the Committee. General Burgoyne seized the opportunity, and while a sense of the recent charge and reproach was still fresh in every mind, he threw himself on the justice, and claimed the protection of the House, conjuring them, that they would afford him an opportunity, by entering upon his defence, to redeem his honour and character from that unwarranted censure, so publicly and licentiously bestowed upon both. He stated, that the argument of the impropriety of military enquiries in the House could not apply to him, even if they had any weight in themselves, as he had frequently applied for a court martial, and had as often been refused it.

He was supported by gentlemen on both sides of the House; and the American minister himself gave into it, and said, that such strong accusations had been recently laid against him, that he was entitled in justice to be heard in his defence. This was readily agreed to, and the next day but one, fixed for his entering upon it.

May 20th.

The officers examined upon this business were Sir Guy Carleton, then Governor of Quebec; Earl of Balcarras; Captain Money, acting Quarter Master General; Earl of Harrington; Major Forbes; Captain Bloomfield, of the artillery; and Lieutenant Colonel Kingston, Adjutant General; all of whom,[61] excepting the first, were present during the whole campaign; and eminent partakers in all the unparalleled difficulties, distresses, and dangers of the northern expedition.

The evidence was unusually clear, plain, accurate, and direct to its matter. It went uniformly to place the character of the suffering and unfortunate general in a very high point of view, whether considered as a man, a soldier, or the leader of an army in the most trying and perilous service. That he possessed the confidence and affection of his army in so extraordinary a degree, that no loss or misfortune could shake the one, nor distress or affliction weaken the other. It established an instance, so far as it could be conclusive, (and a close cross-examination was not able to weaken it) perhaps unequalled in military history; that during so long and continued a scene of unceasing fatigue, hardship, danger, and distress, finally ending in general ruin, and captivity, not a single voice was heard through the army, to upbraid, censure, or blame their general; and that at length, when all their courage and efforts were found ineffectual, and every hope totally cut off, they were still willing to perish along with him. It may, however, be a question of rivalship in honour, what share of the praise arising from this exemplary conduct should be attributed to the general, and what, to the admirable temper, discipline and virtue of his troops?

This evidence, went also, so far as from its nature it was capable

of doing, to the direct overthrow or removal, of every charge or censure, which had been thrown out, or insinuated, against the conduct of the commander; leaving, however, the question of opinion necessarily open, whether his orders for proceeding to Albany were peremptory or conditional; and perhaps leaving likewise some doubts behind, with respect both to the design and to the mode of conducting the expedition, under Colonel Baume, to Bennington. In other matters it seems conclusive; and particularly detects two falsehoods, at the beginning of this enquiry in full credit and vigour; the one, that General Phillips, at the time of the convention, offered to force his way, with a specified part of the army, from Saratoga, back to Ticonderago; the other, that the late gallant General Fraxer, had expressed the utmost disapprobation to the measure of passing the Hudson's river.

The witnesses were generally of opinion, from what they saw and heard of the temper and language of the troops, that nothing less than the passing of that river, and advancing to fight the enemy, could have satisfied the army; or preserved the general's character with it; and that even, after all the misfortunes that happened, it was still universally considered as a matter of necessity which he could not have avoided; or which if he had, that it would have been such a failure, as he never could have forgiven to himself, nor been able to justify to his country. Their testimony went likewise fully and decisively to the subversion of that injurious slander, which it was once a fashion with some persons high in rank and office here to throw out, relative to a supposed natural deficiency of spirit which they attributed to the Americans. Fully masters and judges of the subject, and possessing sentiments more liberal and generous, these officers fcorned to depreciate the character of an enemy, from any refentment for his fair hoftility ; and declared freely, that the Americans fhewed a refolution, perfeverance, and even obftinacy in action, which rendered them by no means unworthy of a conteft with the brave troops to whom they were oppofed. Written evidence, was alfo produced, and fupported, that the number of the rebel army, at the time of the furrender, amounted to 19,000 men, of which thirteen or fourteen thoufand were men actually carrying mufquets.

The examination of General Burgoyne's witneffes being clofed, the American minifter opened the counter evidence, which was brought to oppofe that given in favour of Lord and Sir William Howe. The only witneffes, which it was thought expedient or neceffary to examine on that fide, of thofe whofe names we have ftated, were Major General Robertfon, Deputy Governor of New York ; and Mr. Jofeph Galloway. None of the officers, ordered to attend, except the general abovementioned were called upon. Mr. Galloway had been an American lawyer, and a member of the firft Congrefs ; and was one of thofe that had come over to Sir William Howe at the time when the rebel caufe feemed nearly ruined, by his great fucceffes at New York, and Long Ifland, towards the clofe of the year 1776, and when that violent contention of parties, broke out at Philadelphia, which we have formerly taken notice of. The general had immediately afforded a liberal provifion for this laft witnefs, (from whofe fervices he expected fome confiderable advantages, in which, however, he declared himfelf difappointed) and afterwards advanced him to lucrative, as well as flattering civil employments.

The general tendency of this evidence was to overthrow, invalidate, or weaken, the teftimony already given in favour of the commanders. And the points which it principally laboured to eftablifh for that purpofe, and for the vindication of the minifters, were the following. The vaft majority, who from principle and difpofition, were zealoufly attached to the government of this country, and confequently enemies to the conduct and tyranny of the ruling powers ; this was rated by the firft witnefs at two thirds, and by the fecond at four fifths, of the whole people on that continent. That if a proper ufe had been made of this favourable difpofition of the multitude, it might have been directed to fuch effential purpofes, as would have brought the war to a fpeedy and happy conclufion. That the force fent out from this country was fully competent to the attainment of its object, by the total reduction of the rebellion, and the confequent recovery of the colonies. That the country of America was not in its nature particularly ftrong, much lefs impracticable, with refpect to military operations. That the face of a country being covered with wood, afforded no impediment to the march of an army, in as many columns as they pleafed. That the Britifh troops poffeffed a greater fuperiority over the Americans, in their own favourite mode of bufhfighting, and the detached fervice in woods, than in any other whatever. That armies might carry nineteen days provifion on their backs, and confequently need not be deterred from the undertaking of expeditions, through the want of thofe means of conveyance which are now deemed indifpenfible. That the rebel force, both with refpect to number, and to effective ftrength, was, at the moft interefting periods, if not always, much inferior to what was reprefented. And, to a general condemnation of the fouthern expedition ; along with an endeavour to fhew, the great advantages which would have refulted in that campaign, if Sir William Howe had taken poffeffion of the north river, and directed his operations towards Albany.

Several other more direct charges or accufations were brought againft the military conduct of the brother commanders, which were chiefly undertaken by Mr. Galloway. Particularly with refpect to the going round by the Chefapeak, inftead of up the Delaware, on the fouthern expedition ; the want of fufficient difpatch and vigour in the purfuit of the rebels from Brunfwick acrofs the Jerfies, in the year 1776, to which their efcape was attributed ; the not cutting off Wafhington at Trenton, before he could crofs the river, which was contended to be practicable ; and the not paffing the Delaware, and proceeding to Philadelphia at that time, which, it was afferted, would have put an end to the war ; along with a number of other matters tending to the fame purpofe.

On this the oppofition from time to time remarked, that the greater part of thefe gentlemen's teftimony was founded upon private opinion, hearfay knowledge, intelligence from abfent or unknown perfons, and ftrong affertions of facts, unfupported by any collateral evidence. It was alfo remarked by them, that the only officer produced, had been very little, if at all, out of our garrifons, fince the commencement of the war, and was therefore little qualified, either to give fatisfactory information relative to the difpofition of a people with whom he was fo little converfant, or to give critical opinion on military meafures which he had never feen. As to the witnefs of a civil defcription, they faid it was fingular, that, although bred a lawyer, and habituated to bufinefs, he could fcarcely be brought to recollect the fmalleft part of his own conduct in the moft trying, fignal, and poffibly dangerous fituation of his life, and the moft conspicuous sphere of action to which he had ever been exalted, when a member of the congress; and yet, that the same man, a total stranger to the profession, and only flying for refuge to the British army, should all at once acquire an accuracy with respect to military details, and the complicated business of a camp, which could scarcely be expected from a quarter-master-general, and as suddenly become possessed, along with the minutiæ, of that nice discernment and critical judgment, in the general conduct, and all the great operations of war, which the oldest and most experienced commanders do not often pretend to.

The examination of these two witnesses was spun out, by the intervention of business, and other means, to the end of June. In the mean time, as it was uncertain what farther evidence might be called on that side, and the session being so near a conclusion, Sir William Howe requested, that, in consequence of the attack made upon his character in the evidence of Mr. Galloway, a day might be appointed, on which he should be permitted to bring witnesses, in order to controvert and disprove those charges. This was refused by the ministers, and did not seem to be approved of by the House, who had got tired of the business, and besides saw no possibility of bringing it to a conclusion, during the short remainder of the session. The former said that the general had already met with every indulgence he could reasonably expect; but that the calling in of new witnesses, at that time, could not be admitted; that he however had it still in his power to cross-examine Mr. Galloway as much as he pleased.

This was far from affording any satisfaction to the other side, who complained loudly, that after the attacks made upon the general's character, the refusing to hear evidence in his vindication, was no less than a denial of justice. They were, however, obliged to submit to what they could not remedy. The committee was resumed on the 29th of June; but an advantage being taken of some little delay, (which he stated not to be above a quarter of an hour) in Sir William Howe's not being immediately present for the cross examination of the witness, the committee was suddenly dissolved, without coming to a single resolution upon any part of the business.

. . .

We are now to turn our attention to the other side of the globe; and to relate the effects of this war in the place of its origin. The reduction of Georgia by the royal forces, soon afforded sufficient cause of alarm, and matter for trouble, to the two Carolina's. The Loyalists, or in American language the Tories, in the back parts of North Carolina, conceiving hope and courage from that event, were speedily in motion. We have formerly seen, that these people were numerous in the back of the southern colonies, particularly in those we have now mentioned; and although the loss and defeat which they had sustained under their leader Macdonald, in the beginning of the troubles, with other disappointments and losses of less magnitude, had considerably broken their spirit, and obliged those who were least venturous, or who were most attached to their families and settlements, to an apparent submission to the conditions prescribed by the victors, yet neither submissions nor conventions were sufficient to restrain the effects of that invincible aversion which they bore to their present governors and governments, nor to prevent their watching with the most eager attention for any new opportunity that might offer for their again having recourse to arms, and endeavouring to shake off so grievous a yoke.

The most hardy and desperate of these people, had long been in the condition of outlaws, and had attached themselves to the Indians, and others of their own description, in the incursions on the frontiers. The nature and remoteness of the country, afforded them an opportunity of keeping up a free intercourse with their old friends, neighbours, and fellow sufferers in the same cause, who still continuing at home, had apparently submitted to the present government. This circumstance necessarily served to nourish and strengthen that disposition and spirit which we have described. From these circumstances, and from the cast of mind and of manners acquired by their constant intercourse, whether as friends or as enemies, with the savages, they were ever ready to take up arms; and many of those, who continued in the occupation of their farms, and assumed the character of living peaceably at home, occasionally joined the parties which were openly in arms on the frontiers, and bore a share in all the devastation they committed.

About 700 of these people accordingly assembled in arms, in the back part of North Carolina. It does not seem probable that their hopes could have extended to the bringing about of a revolution in that province by any force of their own; and the distance, with other circumstances, afforded no well founded expectation, that they could have received any timely support for its accomplishment. Their alertness and zeal were, however, stimulated into action by the accounts of General Prevost's success. But their usual ill fortune still stuck by them; and before they were able to do any thing of moment, they were attacked and entirely defeated by some of the nearest militia, having lost near half their number, in killed, wounded, or taken. About 300 of the remainder, however, found means to make their way good in a body to the back part of Georgia; from whence having proceeded to the neareft Britifh pofts, they by degrees joined the royal army. It appears that the loyal party, even in this quarter where it was ftrongeft, (being in a great meafure compofed of emigrants from North Britain,) was infinitely inferior to the ill-affected; and that without the great and continual affiftance of the royal army, the well-affected inhabitants, in no part of America, were in a condition to make head againft the rebels.

South Carolina was the great and immediate object of hope and fear. Its great diftance from the main army, and fcene of action, together with the difficulties of the way, rendered relief flow; and there were other fufficient circumftances to make it uncertain. Money is juftly confidered as the great finew of war; and its want, neceffarily cramped all the military operations of the Americans; the defect, however, increafing, in proportion to the diftance of the fervice, and the confequent increafe of the expence. Thofe who are accuftomed to the aid of boundlefs refources, are apt to conceive no other impediment, than what may arife from the counter operations of the enemy. But a people fcarce of money, new in government, and confequently deftitute of thofe fources and eftablifhments, which the induftry and policy of ages have been accumulating or forming in antient ftates, experience other more infuperable difficulties than marching or fighting in their military operations. Under a due confideration of thefe circumftances, of the mighty force, immenfe wealth, and unbounded fupply of that great power with which they were contending, together with the vaft extent, the remote fervices, and complicated nature of a war, carried on equally by fea and by land, on every fide and on every

quarter, but ftill blazing up more fiercely and ftrongly in the very center of life and action, it muft ever excite the aftonifhment of mankind, and perhaps be hereafter confidered as an inexplicable paradox, by what means the new American Colonies could have been able, for fo long a time, to have fuftained, in any manner, fuch a contention.

Although a detachment of Britifh troops under Colonel Campbell, had penetrated as far up the river as Augufta, which lies 130 miles higher than the town of Savannah, yet the length and difficulty of the communication, and the danger to which it was expofed from the vicinity of the enemy in South Carolina, the river being the only boundary between the two provinces, induced General Prevoft, in fome time after, to recal that party, and to contract his pofts in fuch a manner, that Hudfon's Ferry, at 24 miles diftance, was the upper extremity of that chain which he formed along the frontier from the capital.

In the mean time, General Lincoln, with a reinforcement of continental troops, had arrived for the protection of South Carolina, and was pofted at Purryfburgh, on the north fide of the river, and about 20 miles above the town of Savannah; a circumftance to which probably may be attributed the meafure adopted by General Prevoft, of collecting his force within a clofer compafs. A body of the provincial troops, and militia of the Carolina's and of Georgia, amounting to about 2000 men, were higher up the river, under the command of a General Afhe;[62] and upon the retreat of the detachment from Augufta, were ordered by Lincoln to leave their baggage behind, and paffing the river into Georgia, to take poft in a very ftrong fituation on Briar Creek; intending thereby to cover the upper part of the country,

where the difaffected to the royal caufe, had, on the departure of the Britifh troops, again affumed their wonted fuperiority.

Lieutenant Colonel Prevoft, who[63] was pofted at Hudfon's Ferry, about 13 miles lower down the river, formed a defign of furprizing Afhe in his ftrong poft; a meafure which did not feem very practicable, as Briar's Creek, which covered his front, was for feveral miles too deep to be forded; the Savannah, and a deep morafs covered his left, and he had 200 horfe to guard his right. The defign being ripened for execution, General Prevoft made fuch difpofitions and movements on the borders of the river, between Savannah and Ebenezer, as were fufficient to attract and take up the attention of General Lincoln, during its profecution. The colonel in the mean time, having divided his force into two parts, advanced one, with two pieces of cannon, towards Briar Creek, with an apparent view of attacking the enemy, where they were invulnerable, in front. The other divifion of his force, confifting of the fecond battalion of the 71ft regiment, three companies of grenadiers, fome light infantry and horfe, amounting in the whole to about 900 men, he led himfelf a circuitous march of about 50 miles, in order to get round, or to crofs Briar Creek, and thereby turning the right, to fall unexpectedly upon the rear of the enemy.

The fuccefs of the enterprize was infured by the injudicious conduct of the American General, Afhe, who, in the moment of peril, had detached his light horfe upon fome unprofitable expedition, and thereby laid himfelf open to furprize, and left the only weak part of his camp expofed and uncovered. The furprize was accordingly as complete March 3d. as could have been 1779. wifhed. The Americans were furprized in open day light, and received the firſt notice of danger, from the havock which the Britiſh troops made in their camp. Whole regiments fled without firing a ſhot, and numbers without even attempting to lay hold of their arms. The deep marſh, and the river, which ſhould have afforded ſecurity, became now the inſtruments of their deſtruction. Blinded by their flight and terror, many were ſwallowed up by the one and drowned in the other. Several of the officers, with a regiment of North Carolina men, took bravely, however, to their arms, and gained ſome honour by an ineffectual defence.

The rebels loſt ſeven pieces of cannon, almoſt all their arms, their ammunition, and what baggage they had been under a neceſſity of bringing with them. About 150 men were killed, and 200 taken ; among whom was Brigadier General Elbert, the ſecond in command, and one of their beſt officers, beſides ſome others of note. The number loſt in the Savannah and the ſwamp is not known ; and the loſs on the ſide of the victors was ſo trifling as not to deſerve mention. By this[64] defeat, the province was again cleared of the enemy ; and although the general did not think it prudent to advance his poſts far upwards, yet thoſe which he retained were freed from inſults, his communications were opened with the back country, the loyaliſts both in Carolina and Georgia, were encouraged to join the army, and his force being collected, was ready to act upon any immediate ſervice which might offer.

Such continued, pretty nearly, the ſituation of the two ſmall hoſtile armies until the latter end of April. Separated by a river, which neither of them could venture to paſs in the face of the other, they were both ſecure in their poſts, and each covered his reſpective province. A movement

at that time made by General Lincoln, preſented, however, a new face of affairs, and opened a way for conſequences, which he evidently did not apprehend, and which he undoubtedly would not have hazarded if he had. In order to protect either a meeting, or an election, of delegates for the province of Georgia, which was appointed to be held at Auguſta in the beginning of May, he quitted his ſituation on the lower part of the river, which effectually enabled him to ſecure Charles Town, as well as to cover the province in general, and marched with the beſt part of his army towards that place. Indeed it did not appear eaſy to ſuppoſe, that this meaſure was liable to any dangerous conſequences. The freſhes were then out, which ſeemed to render the river in itſelf a ſufficient rampart ; but the deep ſwamps on the other ſide ſeemed utterly impaſſable ; or if theſe could even be evaded, the general appearance of the flat flooded country along the coaſt, every where interſected with rivers and creeks, ſeemed to forbid all military operations at that ſeaſon on that ſide. But Lincoln did not truſt entirely to natural difficulties ; he beſides left, under the the conduct of General Moultrie, a body eſtimated at about 1500 men, and compoſed chiefly of the provincial militia, to guard the paſſes of the river and ſwamps.

This movement inſpired General Prevoſt with an idea of attempting to penetrate into Carolina. He conſidered, that offenſive operations were neceſſary to ſupport and increaſe the reputation of the Britiſh arms in that quarter ; that his force was already conſiderably increaſed by the acceſſion of loyaliſts from that province as well as Georgia, from whence there was reaſon to hope, that his appearance in the country might induce great bodies of the well-affected to declare in his favour ; and, in any caſe, it

would be the ſure means of obliging Lincoln to abandon his deſign, and would at the ſame time afford an opportunity of procuring a plentiful ſupply of proviſions, which he wanted.

Under the influence of theſe conſiderations, he paſſed the river in different parts near the end of April, with a force, which, ſo far as can be gathered, may be eſtimated at about 3,000 men. Moultrie's militia were ſtruck with ſuch a panic, at ſeeing the Britiſh troops traverſing a country, and emerging from ſwamps which they deemed impaſſable, that they made but a weak reſiſtance in defending the ſeveral ſtrong paſſes which might have effectually checked their progreſs ; and at length, as the country became more practicable, gave way on all ſides, and retired toward Charles Town.

The facility with which the army had triumphed over the extraordinary natural impediments of the country, together with the feeble reſiſtance of the enemy, ſerved to extend the views of the general to objects of greater moment, than thoſe which had operated in engaging him to undertake the expedition. The loyaliſts, in the eagerneſs of their hopes and wiſhes, which no failure or diſappointment could ever ſlacken or damp, failed not to improve this diſpoſition, which was ſo favourable to them. They aſſured the general, as a matter of undoubted certainty, that Charles Town would ſurrender without reſiſtance, at his firſt appearance. The object was ſo important, and the temptation ſo great, that inclination and duty muſt have been equally urgent to its acquiſition. Nor did it ſeem well in the power of a commander, in a matter of ſo much conſequence to the ſtate, to have ſlighted the information of thoſe, who had the beſt means of knowing both the ſtate of the place and the diſpoſition of the people ; it would be no eaſy matter afterwards to ſhew that it deferved no credit, and that the defign was utterly impracticable. General Prevoft, notwithftanding, did not think it fitting entirely to rely upon his own opinion, and therefore called all the field officers of his army to confultation upon the fubject, who unanimoufly concurred in their advice for his advancing directly to Charles Town. The conduct of General Lincoln ferved greatly to ftrengthen this opinion, who was fo pofitively perfuaded, that General Prevoft intended nothing more than to forage the country, that it was not until fome days after the Britifh forces had paffed the river, that he could be induced to return to the defence of the capital. But when he was at length convinced of the real danger of that city, he immediately detached a body of infantry, mounted on horfeback, for the greater expedition, to its defence, and collecting the militia of the upper country, returned with his whole force, to act as circumftances might offer for its relief.

In this fituation of things, the Britifh army were fome days march a-head of Lincoln in the way to Charles Town, and Moultrie's Militia, and Polafki's Legion, retiring from one creek and river to another towards that place, as they were preffed by the former. So many bridges and paffes could not be gained without fome fkirmifhes, but the refiftance was ftill fo weak, that they were attended with no circumftances of any confequence; it is however to be obferved, that as the families and effects of Moultrie's Militia lay pretty generally in the line of march, thefe confiderations touched them fo clofely, that his force fuffered a continual diminution from the outfet, which befides the weaknefs it produced in leffening his numbers, ferved neceffarily to difhearten thofe who remained.

May 11th. At length the Britifh army arrived at Afhley River, which they paffed, a few miles above Charles Town, and advancing along the Neck formed by the two rivers of Afhley and Cooper, took poft within little more than cannon fhot from the works of that city. A continued fucceffion of fkirmifhes took place on that day and the enfuing night, which, though neceffarily attended with lofs on both fides, were of no farther confequence to either. On the following morning, the general fummoned the town to furrender, and held out very flattering conditions to induce them to a compliance. The negociation continued during the day, and a propofal was made by the city for a neutrality for their province during the continuance of the war. This being rejected on the one fide, as the favourable conditions propofed by the general were on the other, the negociation was broken off in the evening, and every preparation made by the inhabitants and garrifon, for vigoroufly repelling a general affault which was expected to take place in the night.

But General Prevoft, finding himfelf totally difappointed in every hope that had been held out to him relative to Charles Town, had other objects of ferious confideration now before him. He found that no offers he could make were fufficient to induce the enemy to a furrender, and that their countenance fhewed the fulleft determination of defence; that their lines were defended by a numerous artillery, and flanked by their armed fhipping and gallies; and that Gen. Lincoln, with a force, at leaft equal, if not fuperior to his own, was faft approaching. On his own fide, he had neither battering artillery, nor a naval force to cooperate with his land forces; which were two articles fo indifpenfably neceffary for carrying the place, that their want feemed an infuperable bar to every hope of fuccefs. And if he were repulfed with any confiderable lofs, which was much to be apprehended, his fituation, involved as he was, in a labyrinth of rivers and creeks, furrounded on all fides by a fuperior enemy, and his retreat continually impeded by fwamps and difficult paffes, feemed fcarcely to admit of a hope, that any part of his fmall army could have been preferved.

Under thefe confiderations, he prudently decamped on that very night, and having previoufly taken care to leave a proper guard for the fecurity of the pafs at Afhley-Ferry, he had by morning returned to the fouth fide of that river without interruption, or the knowledge or fmalleft fufpicion of the enemy, who had been the whole time ftanding to their arms, under the momentary apprehenfion of a furious attack. From thence the army paffed to the iflands of St. James and St. John, which lie to the fouthward of Charles Town Harbour, and from their cultivation and fertility afforded good quarters and plenty of provifions for the troops. Thefe begin that almoft continued fucceffion, and fometimes labyrinth of iflands, into which, the fea with its numerous inlets, and the frequent rivers and creeks, have divided that low flat country, which extends along the coaft from Charles Town to Savannah; the channels by which they are interfected, or feparated from the continent, being in fome places very narrow and inconfiderable, are in others fo great, as to afford excellent harbours or roads for fhipping.

In thefe iflands, the army impatiently expected thofe fupplies of ammunition and neceffaries from New York, which they exceedingly wanted. The firft fhips which had been difpatched with thefe fupplies had the ill fortune, of being either taken, deftroyed, or driven back by the enemy. The arrival of two frigates of war, at length removed the diftreffes of the troops, and enabled the army to return to the fouthward.

The object now with the general

was to take and hold poffeffion of the ifland of Port Royal; a meafure which held out many prefent and future advantages, among which it was not the leaft, that it would afford good quarters and an eligible fituation to the troops, during the intenfe heats and the very unhealthy feafon, which were then either prevailing or approaching. By this means alfo, he would hold a fure footing in South Carolina, from which it was not in the power of the enemy to move him, until the long expected and wifhed for reinforcements arrived, which might enable him to proceed effectually in the reduction of that colony. In the mean time, no pofition could be better chofen for covering Georgia on that fide; the excellent harbour of Port Royal, was the beft ftation in that quarter for the royal fhipping, and its vicinity to the town of Savannah, with the open communication between both places, ferved all together to render it a poft of great importance.

While the greater part of the army were engaged in the operations of moving from one ifland to another, and of eftablifhing the different pofts which it was thought neceffary to occupy during the fickly feafon, General Lincoln thought it a proper opportunity to attack Lieutenant Colonel Maitland, who was ftrongly pofted at the pafs of Stoney Ferry, which feems to be on the inlet between the continent and the ifland of St. John. The Colonel's force confifted of the firft battalion of the 71ft, and one Heffian, together with the Carolina refugees; the two battalions being fo weak and reduced, that his whole number is faid to have amounted only to about 800 men. The poft, however, befides its natural advantages, was well covered with redoubts, an abbatis, and artillery. On the other fide, the American force is reprefented as amounting to 5,000 men, and eight pieces of cannon.

June 20th. They made the attack with great fpirit,

and fupported it for about an hour; but were received with fuch a countenance, and fuch coolnefs and firmnefs, and fo much galled by the fire of an armed flat, which covered the left flank of the poft, that they were then obliged to retire with confiderable lofs. The affailants attribute their retreat to the ftrength of the redoubts, which their light field pieces were totally incapable of making any impreffion on, and to a ftrong reinforcement, which arrived from the ifland of St. John, during the action, to the fupport of the poft. The royal forces loft fome officers as well as men; and above a hundred of both were wounded. The Americans loft fome officers of name; and it cannot be doubted, that their lofs in general was confiderably greater. The army met[65] with no obftruction in its movement to Port Royal; and the feafon put an end to all operations on either fide in that quarter.

In the beginning of May, Sir Henry Clinton concerted with Sir George Collier, who now commanded the marine at New York,[66] an expedition to the Chefapeak, and a defcent upon Virginia, as meafures, which more than any other that could be undertaken, would contribute to the embarraffment and diftrefs of the enemy.

A fufficient naval and land force for the intended purpofes, was accordingly difpatched from New York, under the conduct of Sir Geo. Collier, and Maj. Gen. Mathew. The fleet having fuccefsfully paffed between the Capes of Virginia, the Raifonable man of war, with fome armed tenders, were left in Hampton Road, to block up that port, and to intercept the navigation of the River James; whilft Sir George Collier, having fhifted his pendant to a frigate, proceeded with the fmaller fhips of war and tranfports up Elizabeth River. The town of Portfmouth being their immediate object, and the fleet delayed by fome

circumftances of wind or tide in its paffage, the general and troops, impatient of delay, and apprehenfive that the enemy might have time either to ftrengthen their works or receive fuccours, were landed at May 10th. fome diftance, and marched directly towards that place.

The town was open and defencelefs, but the paffage to it by water was covered by Fort Nelfon, which had been conftructed at about half a mile's diftance for that purpofe. But the garrifon of the fort, knowing that no fuccour was at hand, and that the fort was incapable of any effectual defence, to avoid being furrounded and made prifoners, abandoned it at the approach of the army, who of courfe took poffeffion both of that and the town. The town, or remains, of Norfolk, on the oppofite fide of the river, fell likewife into their hands. Upon the approach of the fleet and army, the enemy burned feveral of the veffels in thefe ports, among which were two large French fhips, loaded with a thoufand hogfheads of tobacco; the celerity of the invaders having, however, checked the deftruction pretty early, feveral others were faved and fell accordingly into their hands.

The general pufhed on detachments to take poffeffion of two ftrong pofts feveral miles in front, which from the nature of the country, ferved to cover the approaches to his camp from any fudden attempt of the enemy. In the mean time, the British guards having marched eighteen miles by night to the town of Suffolk, on the Nanfemond river, arrived there at day-break. They found the place had been haftily abandoned at their approach; and they immediately proceeded to the deftruction of a very large magazine of provifions, together with the veffels and naval ftores which they found there. A fimilar deftruction was carried on at Kempe's landing, Shepherd's, Gofport, Tanner's creek, and other places in that quarter; nor were the frigates and armed veffels lefs active or fuccefsful in their fervice, on the rivers, and in the near parts of the bay.

Within a fortnight, that the fleet and army continued upon the coaft, the lofs fuftained by the Americans was prodigious. Several thoufand barrels of pork, with other provifions in proportion, which had been prepared for Wafhington's army, and a great quantity of ftores, were deftroyed at Suffolk and Shepherd's. In other places thefe articles were brought off. Above 130 fhips and veffels of all forts, were deftroyed or taken. Of thefe, 17 prizes were brought away; among thofe deftroyed or taken, were fome privateers, and veffels of force. All thofe upon the ftocks were burned; a confiderable quantity of naval ftores brought off; and every thing relative to the building or fitting of fhips, that was not conveniently portable, deftroyed.

The commanders received from the loyalifts, according to their ufual cuftom, fuch flattering accounts and pofitive affurances, of the general difpofition of the people of that colony to return to the obedience of their fovereign, and their impatience to fee the royal ftandard erected amongft them, that Sir George Collier could not avoid reprefenting the matter in his letter to Sir Henry Clinton, in the full view in which it appeared to himfelf. If it was not, however, thought fitting to adopt the meafure in its full extent, he ftrongly urged the great advantages which would accrue from fending them fuch reinforcements, as would enable them to hold a footing in the country, by converting Portfmouth into a place of arms, and rendering it thereby a fure afylum for fhipping; purpofes, which from its fituation, it feemed well calculated for anfwering, and which would have totally deftroyed the trade of the Chefapeak. On the

other hand, it was a place removed from fuccour, and in a manner furrounded with the greateft forces of the enemy. It is evident that Sir Henry Clinton faw thefe matters in a very different light, from that in which they were viewed by Sir George Collier. He fent an order for their immediate return. The fleet and army, with their prizes and booty, (having firft demolifhed Fort Nelfon, and fet fire to the ftore-houfes and all the other buildings in the dock-yard at Gofport), arrived fafe at New York before the expiration of the month.

An expedition which General Sir Henry Clinton was upon the point of undertaking up the North River, probably contributed to the more fpeedy recall of the forces from the Virginia adventure. The enemy had for fome time been engaged, and at great labour and expence, in conftructing very ftrong works, at the two important pofts of Verplanks Neck, and Stoney Point, in the Highlands. Thefe pofts, which are on nearly oppofite points of land, the firft being on the Eaft, and the other on the Weft fide of the North river, were of the utmoft importance for keeping the communication open between the Eaftern and Weftern colonies, the great pafs called King's Ferry lying directly between them. As thefe works were nearly completed, but not yet defenfible, the general thought it the proper feafon to avail himfelf of the induftry of the enemy, and to reap the fruits of their toil. Wafhington, who lay with his army at Middle Brook in Jerfey, was at too great a diftance to interrupt the execution of the defign; nor could his efforts at any rate have extended to the eaftern fide of the river. We have already had occafion to fee the prodigious advantage, which the naval command of that great river and boundary afforded to an army, in any fingle or double fcheme of operation on either fide.

The troops deftined for this fervice, under the command of Major General Vaughan, were only newly embarked, when they were joined by the force returned from the Chefapeak, and proceeded all together up the North River; the naval department being under the conduct of Sir George Collier. On the following morning, General Vaughan, with the greater part of the army, landed on the Eaft fide of the river, about eight miles fhort of Verplanks; whilft the remainder, under the conduct of General Pattifon, and accompanied by Sir Henry Clinton, advancing farther up, landed within three miles of Stoney Point. Upon the appearance of the fhips, the enemy immediately abandoned their works; but took care to fet fire to a large block-houfe. Upon the approach of the troops to take poffeffion of Stoney Point; they, however, made fome fhew of refiftance, by drawing up on the hills; but they did not venture to abide the conflict.

The Americans had finifhed a fmall, but ftrong and complete work, on the oppofite fide of the river, which they called Fort la Fayette; this was defended by four pieces of artillery, and a fmall garrifon of between 70 and 80 men. But this little redoubt, though ftrong in itfelf, was effectually commanded by Stoney Point, which lies at about a thoufand yards diftance on the oppofite fhore; and it being exceedingly difficult of approach from its own fide, at leaft for the conveyance of artillery, the attack was accordingly intended from the other. For this purpofe, General Pattifon with infinite fatigue and labour, and the moft indefatigable perfeverance during the night, overcame the difficulties of dragging the heavy artillery from a very bad landing place up a fteep precipice, to the top of the hill; and his exertions and arrangements

(May 30th.)

were so effectual and judicious, that by five on the following morning, he had opened a battery of cannon, and another of mortars, on the summit of the difficult rocks of Stoney Point, which poured a storm of fire over on Fort la Fayette.

The attack was supported by Sir George Collier, who advanced [67] with the gallies and gun-boats within reach of the fort. The cannonade was continued on all sides during the day; and as soon as it was dark, Sir George ordered two of the gallies to pass the fort, and anchor above it, in order to prevent the escape of the garrison by water. In the mean time, General Vaughan with his division, having made a long circuit through the hills, was at length arrived, and had closely invested the fort on the land side. The garrison seeing that all possibility of escape was now cut off, and that their fire was totally overpowered and lost in the magnitude of that which they received, surrendered their little fortress on the following morning, and themselves prisoners of war, without any other stipulation than that of humane treatment. The boldness of their defence certainly merited some praise, although we do not know that it was paid on either side.

The general gave immediate direction for finishing and completing the works of both posts, and for putting Stoney Point in particular, in the strongest state of defence. And for their better support and protection, as well as with a view to the further operations of the campaign, encamped his army at Philipsburg, something about half way down the river to New York Island; which he likewise rendered a post of some importance, by throwing up works, in order for the establishment and preservation of a free communication in future. By the loss of these posts, the rebels in the Jerseys were under a necessity of making a detour of above ninety miles through the mountains, to communicate with the countries East of Hudson's River.

The state of the hostile armies on both sides with respect to actual force, together with the want of money, and the paucity of military provision on one, necessarily limited the views of the opposite commanders, and prevented their undertaking any decisive or extensive operations. They were each in a strong state of defence, and neither had such a superiority of force, as could compel his adversary to relinquish the advantages of his situation. Washington was besides in expectation of foreign aid; and it would have been little consistent with his usual character of caution and judgment, to have run the hazard by any previous attempt, or hasty measure, of weakening his natural strength in such a degree, as might render him incapable of profiting by the assistance of his ally, and the American arms and force, of course contemptible in his eyes. The campaign was accordingly languid, and its operations confined to the surprise of posts, and to desultory excursions; to the last of which, the Americans were now, as at all times, exceedingly exposed, and upon no footing of equality with their enemy.

The numberless small cruizers, whale-boats, and other craft of that nature, from the Connecticut coasts, which infested the sound, lying between that colony and Long Island, were so watchful and constant in their depredations, and their situation afforded them such opportunities, that they had nearly destroyed the trade to and from New York on that side, to the very great discommodity and distress of that city, as well as of the fleet and army. Upon this account, General Sir Henry Clinton, and Sir George Collier, determined on a course of desultory invasions along that coast, with a view of curing the evil, by cutting off the means of depredation in the destruction of their piratical craft, and so far as it could be done, of their other vessels and materials for building.

Governor Tryon, who was likewise a general officer, was appointed to the conduct of the land service in this expedition; his force amounted to about 2,600 men, and he was seconded by Brigadier General Garth, an officer of distinguished merit and activity. [68] The fleet having arrived at Newhaven, the forces were landed, and took possession of that town, and of a battery that covered the harbour, without any great loss, although they met with every impediment in their power, and no small share of irregular resistance from the inhabitants and neighbouring militia. The fort, and every thing for naval or military purposes, were destroyed. The town was spared, although first doomed to destruction, owing to some measures observed by the militia, in not molesting the troops on their retreat.

July 5th.

The fleet departed from Newhaven to Fairfield, where the troops were again landed, and again opposed. Here the town was set on fire, and every thing of value consumed. The same measure was repeated in the subsequent and concluding expedition to Norwalk; where the militia being more numerous, and the resistance greater, than in the former places, both that town and the small one of Greenfield, were totally destroyed. The loss sustained by the Americans in this last act of the expedition was very great. Besides that of their houses, and effects, a considerable number of ships, either finished or on the stocks, with a still greater of whale boats and small craft, with stores and merchandise to a large amount, were all destroyed.

Whether it was, that this course of destruction was contrary to the intention and approbation of Sir Henry Clinton, or from whatever other cause it proceeded, it was suddenly stopped in its career, by an order from that general for the immediate return of the troops. The loss sustained by the royal forces was very trifling, considering the opposition they met with; the whole number, in slain, wounded, and missing, being under 150, of which, not above a seventh were killed on the spot.

The fires and destruction which marked this expedition, were attributed to different causes. Partly to the resentment excited by the rebels, in their firing from the tops and windows of their houses; partly to the zeal of the loyal American refugees, who were implacable in the resentment which they bore to their countrymen on the opposite side, and who from that spirit, along with their intimate knowledge of the country, were particularly necessary in these enterprises; and, as it was said, in some instances to military necessity, the burning of the houses serving to mask the retreat of the troops. Major General Tryon, however, justified the measure, in his letter to the General, upon the fair principles of policy; and said, he should be very sorry, if it was thought less reconcileable with humanity, than with the love of his country, duty to the king, and the law of arms, to which America had been led to make the awful appeal. That the usurpers had professedly placed their hopes of severing the empire, in avoiding decisive actions, upon the waste of the British treasure, and the escape of their own property, during the protracting of the war. That their power was supported by the general dread of their tyranny, and the arts practised to inspire a credulous multitude with a presumptuous confidence in the forbearance of the royal forces. And, that he wished to detect this delusion, and, if possible, without injury to the loyalists.

Whatever force or justice there might be in these arguments, the measure of burning and destroying the country seemed an improper accompanyment to an address of invitation which was circulated among the inhabitants, urging them to return to their duty and allegiance. Mr. Tryon, however, regrets in his letter, the burning of their places of worship; but justly observes, the great difficulty of assigning any fixed limits to a conflagration, where the buildings are close, and the houses composed of such very combustible materials as boards and shingles. This expedition afforded abundant matter, for the renewal and increase of that loud clamour, which the Americans had so long raised, and so widely extended, relative to the cruel, and unheard-of manner, in which, they pretended, that the war was conducted on the royal side. Nor did it seem to produce any great effect with respect to its immediate object, of checking the depredations of the American cruizers; for so bold and numerous were they, that in a very few days after, two of the royal sloops of war were taken by them.

The surprise of Verplanks and Stoney Point, drew Washington and his army from the Jerseys, to the high, strong, and mountainous country, above those posts, and on both sides of the North river. General Sir Henry Clinton's object was, to draw him down, if possible, from these fastnesses into the flat country, and thereby to bring on a general engagement in that sort of ground, which would have been adapted to the exertion of those peculiar advantages, and that decided superiority, which the royal army possessed. This was among the motives which led to the Connecticut expedition; and others of less note, were undertaken upon the same principle. It was, however, a matter of no small difficulty to lead Washington into such an error; nor could any

art in the laying or covering of the design, afford more than a very doubtful prospect of its success.

Whilst the hostile armies were thus watching each other's motions with the most unremitted attention, an enterprise of spirit, and eclat, was undertaken on the American side, and successfully carried into execution by General Wayne. As no industry had been wanting in compleating or repairing the works at Stoney Point, which the length of possession would admit of, that post was now in a very strong state of defence; and was garrisoned by the 17th regiment of foot, the grenadier companies of the 71st, a company of loyal Americans, and some artillery; the whole being under the command of Lieutenant Colonel Johnson. The garrison in the opposite post at Verplanks Neck, was under the conduct of Lieutenant Colonel Webster; and was at least equal in force to that at Stoney Point.

General Wayne was appointed to the difficult task of surprising and reducing Stoney Point; for which he was provided with a strong detachment of the most active infantry in the American army. These troops having set out from Sandy Reach about noon, had a march of about fourteen miles to surmount, over high mountains, through deep morasses, difficult defiles, and roads exceedingly bad and narrow, so that they could only move in single files during the greatest part of the way. About eight o'clock in the evening, the van arrived within a mile and a half of their object, where they halted, and the troops were formed into two columns, as fast as they came up. While they were in this position, Wayne, with most of his principal officers, went to reconnoitre the works, and to observe the situation of the garrison.

It was something not unworthy of observation, that the bayonet,

(margin notes: 69, 13th., 70, 71, 72, July 15th.)

which had been so often fatally employed against the Americans in similar cases, was the only weapon which they used in this attack. It was near midnight before the two columns approached the place; that on the right, consisting of Febiger and Meig's regiments, was led by General Wayne; the [73] van, consisting of 150 picked men, led by the most adventurous officers, and commanded by Lieutenant Colonel Fleury, advanced to [74] the attack, with unloaded muskets and fixed bayonets; they being preceded by an avant-guard, consisting of an officer of the most distinguished courage, accompanied by twenty of the most desperate private men, who, among other offices, were particularly intended to remove the abbatis, and other obstructions, which lay in the way of the succeeding troops. The column on the left, was led by a similar chosen van, with unloaded muskets and fixed bayonets, under the command of a Major Steward; [75] and that was also preceded by a similar forlorn hope. The general issued the most pointed orders to both columns, (which they seem strictly to have adhered to) not to fire a shot on any account, but to place their whole reliance on the bayonet.

The two attacks seem to have been directed to opposite points of the works; whilst a detachment under a Major Murfree engaged [76] the attention of the garrison, by a feint in their front. They found the approaches more difficult, than even their knowledge of the place had induced them to expect; the works being covered by a deep morass, and which at this time was also overflowed by the tide. The Americans say, that neither the deep morass, the formidable and double rows of abbatis, or the strong works in front and flank, could damp the ardour of their troops; who, in the face of a most incessant and tremendous fire of musquetry, and of cannon

loaded with grape shot, forced their way at the point of the bayonet through every obstacle, until the van of each column met in the center of the works, where they arrived at nearly the same instant.

General Wayne was wounded in the head by a musket ball, as he passed the last abbatis; but was gallantly supported, and helped through the works, by his two brave Aid de Camps, Fishbourn and Archer, to whom he acknow- [77] ledged the utmost gratitude in his public letter. Colonel Fleury, who we may perceive by his name to be a French officer, had the honour of striking the British standard with his own hand. Major Steward, and several other officers, received great praise; as did in particular the two Lieutenants, Gibbons and Knox, one of [78] whom led the forlorn hope on the right, as the other did on the left; and who had both the fortune to escape unhurt, although the first lost seventeen men out of twenty in the attack.

There is scarcely any thing in the transactions of war, which affords more room for surprize, and seems less to be accounted for, than the prodigious disparity between the numbers slain in those different actions, which seem otherwise similar, or greatly to correspond, in their principal circumstances, nature and magnitude. Nothing could well be supposed, from its nature and circumstances more bloody, in proportion to the numbers engaged, than this action; and yet the loss on both sides was exceedingly moderate. The fate of Captain Tew of the 17th regiment, who fell in [79] this action, being rather singular and unfortunate, was accordingly regretted. He had been left for dead on the field in the last war; and perhaps no other officer in Europe had survived so great a number of wounds, as he had received in the course of his service. Promotion had been long promised

and expected; but through the want of any particular interest to support that claim, which his long services, merit, and particular sufferings, seemed, indeed, to render unnecessary, he finished his military career at the head only of a company.

Nothing could exceed the triumph of the Americans, upon the success of this enterprize, and the vigour and spirit with which it was conducted. It must, indeed, be acknowledged, that, considered in all its parts and difficulties, it would have done honour to the most veteran soldiers. Washington, the Congress, the General Assembly, and the Supreme Executive Council of Pensylvania, seemed emulous in their acknowledgments, and in the praises which they bestowed upon General Wayne, his officers, and troops. In these they particularly applaud the humanity and clemency shewn to the vanquished, when, (they say) by the laws of war, and stimulated by resentment from the remembrance of a former massacre, they would have been justified in putting the whole garrison to the sword. Nor were real or honorary rewards to the officers forgotten. The total number of prisoners amounted to 543, and the slain of the garrison, according to the American account, to 63; which taken together do not differ very widely from the imperfect return sent in a hurry by Colonel Johnson; taking it for granted, (as was undoubtedly the case) that those whom he reckons as missing, are included in either [80] part of the calculation. The trophies, artillery and stores, were not, in respect to the nature and extent of the post, inconsiderable. [81]

As soon as Stoney Point was taken, the artillery was directly turned against Verplanks, and a furious cannonade ensued, which necessarily obliged the shipping at the latter place to cut their cables, and fall down the river. The news of this difafter, and of Webfter's fituation, who alfo expected an immediate attack on the land fide, no fooner reached Sir Henry Clinton, than he took the moft fpeedy meafures for the immediate relief of the one poft, and the recovery of the other. The whole Britifh land and naval force was accordingly in motion. The general, with the main army, advanced to Dobb's Ferry; the cavalry, with a detachment of light infantry, pufhed forwards to the banks of the Croton river, in order to awe the enemy on that fide, in their attempts by land againft Verplanks; and Sir George Collier, with the frigates, armed veffels, and tranfports of the fleet, having Brigadier General Sterling, with three[82] regiments on board, proceeded up the river.

But however great the importance or value of Stoney Point, Wafhington was by no means difpofed to hazard a general engagement on its account; more efpecially in a fituation, where the command of the river would afford fuch decifive advantages to his enemy in the difpofition, and fudden movement of their troops, whether with refpect to the immediate point of action, or to the feizing of the paffes, and cutting off the retreat of his army, as might probably be attended with the moft fatal confequences. He informs the Congrefs in his letter, that it had been previoufly determined in council not to attempt keeping that poft, and that nothing more was originally intended, than the deftruction of the works, and the bringing off the artillery and ftores. Sir Henry Clinton regained the poft, after it had been three days in the poffeffion of the enemy, and placed a ftrong garrifon in it.

A few repetitions of fuch fuccefs, would have rendered the Americans fo daring and adventurous, that the advanced pofts on the royal fide, muft have been kept in a conftant ftate of alarm

and danger. But Fortune was not always in the fame humour; nor could they often find officers or men, who were capable of acting with fuch vigour and fpirit, as thofe who had fucceeded in the ftorm of Stoney Point. On the very night that Brigadier Sterling had taken poffeffion of that poft, an enterprize fufficiently daring in the defign, and extremely well conducted in the outfet, but which failed wretchedly in the execution, was undertaken againft Paulus Hook, which lies almoft oppofite to the city of New York on the Jerfey fide. It feems that the ftrength of the poft, had induced fuch a remiffnefs on the fide of the garrifon, that the enemy completely furprized the place at three o'clock in the morning, and carried a blockhoufe and two redoubts almoft without any refiftance. In that critical moment of exigency, Major Sutherland, the commander,[83] threw himfelf haftily, with forty Heffians, into another redoubt, from which they kept fo warm and inceffant a fire, that the Americans fcandaloufly deferted their new pofts, with as much expedition, and as little difficulty, as they had been attained; thus, by a retreat as difgraceful, as the attempt had been apparently bold and well conducted, they abandoned a conqueft already evidently in their hands, without having had courage even to fpike the artillery, or to fet fire to the barracks. The commandant had the fortune to redeem his character, by the gallantry with which he retrieved the confequences of his negligence.

But at the heel of thefe tranfactions, intelligence of an alarming nature was received from the eaftward, which fuddenly called Sir George Collier, with the greater part of his naval force, away from New York. This neceffity originated from an expedition undertaken in the fummer from Hallifax by Colonel Macleane, with a[84] view of eftablifhing a ftrong poft

on the river Penobfcot, in the eaftern confines of New England, where that colony borders on Nova Scotia, and amidft thofe new and weak fettlements, which the Maffachufetts people have eftablifhed in that quarter fince the laft war, and formed into a county under the name of Lincoln. The force with which he arrived in the Penobfcot about the middle of June, confifted of a detachment of 450 rank and file of the 74th regiment, and 200 of the 82d; which were convoyed by three floops of war. Here Colonel Macleane began to conftruct a fort, in a fituation perfectly well chofen for annoying the enemy.

This tranfaction occafioned an unufual alarm at Bofton, and the moft vigorous meafures were adopted by that government to prevent its completion. Orders were immediately given for an expedition to the Penobfcot; and in order to fecure armed veffels and tranfports, as well as failors, an embargo of forty days was laid on all their fhipping. As a further encouragement, the ftate gave up its fhare in all prizes that were taken to the captors. A very confiderable naval armament, (for fo new a ftate) under the conduct of Commodore Saltonftall, was accordingly fitted out with extraordinary expedition; and a body of troops embarked under the conduct of a General Lovel.[85]

On the other fide, the works of the new fort, notwithftanding that the utmoft diligence was ufed in their conftruction, were yet fo far from being finifhed, as to afford but very imperfect means of defence, againft any great fuperiority of force. Colonel Macleane had, however, the fortune to receive intelligence of the armament preparing at Bofton, a few days before its arrival; upon which, he immediately changed his plan of operation; and inftead of proceeding farther in the conftruction of works, which there could be no time for completing, applied himself with the greatest assiduity, to the putting of the post in the best present state of defence, which its situation, and the shortness of the notice could admit. In this, as in every thing else, he received the most cordial and efficacious support and assistance from the officers and crews of the three royal frigates in the river, who committed themselves with the greatest chearfulness to abide the fate of the garrison.

July 25th. At length, the hostile and dreaded fleet, to the amount of 37 sail, appeared in sight; and soon after, their armed vessels began to cannonade the ships of war, and a battery of four twelve pounders, which had been thrown up on the bank of the river for their protection. It appears, that the works of the fort were commenced about the middle of a small peninsula, the western point of which run pretty deeply into the river; and the whole, so far as we can judge, forming a sort of hook, within which was included a little bay or harbour, wherein the frigates were stationed. The commander had the precaution to intrench the isthmus or neck, which joined the peninsula to the continent, by which he was secured on the back. The weak side of the peninsula lay to the harbour, the entrance to which was, as we have seen, defended by the frigates, and the four gun battery; and the opposite side, seems not to have admitted of a landing. From this situation, the only feasible means the enemy possessed for approaching the fort, was by effecting a landing on the west point; and even there, the ground was naturally so strong and difficult, as to afford no small room for hope to the commander, that he should be able to protract their operations for some considerable time, which was the great object he had in view, as holding out the prospect of expected relief.

The fire of the enemy was so well returned, that their ships found it necessary to retire; upon which their fleet anchored off the west end of the peninsula. They renewed the attack upon the shipping on the following day; but being again repulsed as before, they seemed, for the present, to give up all hope of succeeding on that side. They made several attempts to land, both on the first night, and after, in which they were also constantly repulsed by the piquets, who were advantageously posted on the point for their reception. To the great surprize, however, and disappointment of the commander and garrison, they made good their landing under a violent cannonade, on the morning of the 28th, and obliged the piquets to retire to the fort.

The attention of the commander, his officers and garrison, were now necessarily confined to the strengthening and defence of their works; operations in which they were equally indefatigable and successful. On the third day after their landing, the 30th, the enemy opened a battery at about 750 yards distance; and in a few days after, another somewhat nearer; but although the cannonade from both was very brisk and well supported, the works were carried on in the fort with the same spirit and industry as before. Thus the besieged exhibited the singular phænomenon, of acquiring a daily accession of internal strength and security, under the immediate assaults of the enemy.

In the mean time, the Americans having erected a battery on an island at the entrance of the harbour, the frigates and shipping thought it necessary, upon a consultation between the land and naval force, to retire farther within the bay or creek; and having also landed guns to cover their own battery, the commander was thereby enabled to withdraw the four

twelve pounders for the defence of the fort. For about a fortnight the cannonade was supported with great spirit on both sides; at the end of which time, the commander received intelligence from a deserter, that a general storm was fixed upon, it being intended to attack the ships and the fort at the same instant. Upon this information, he immediately threw up a small work, covered with light artillery, at about 150 yards distance, in the front of the fort; thus adding a further security and cover to the body of the place.

Whilst the commanders, garrison, and seamen were in impatient expectation of the attack, and without the smallest apprehension as to the event, an unusual quiet being observed on the enemy's Aug. 14th. side, very early in the morning, it induced a closer inspection, in consequence of which it was soon, to their inexpressible astonishment, discovered, that the rebels had totally abandoned their camp and works in the night, and had re-embarked both their forces and artillery. Nor were they left long in the dark as to the cause of this mysterious event; for while they were endeavouring to profit in some degree of the confusion which they saw in the enemy's fleet, Sir George Collier, with his squadron, appeared full to their view in the river.

That commander had sailed from Sandy Hook, in the Raisonable man of war, on the 3d of August, and arrived in the Penobscot, accompanied by the Greyhound, Blonde, Virginia, Camilla, and Galatea frigates. The Americans at first seemed to make some shew of intended resistance, by drawing up in a cresent across the river, as if they determined to dispute the passage. But their resolution soon failed, and a most ignominious flight took place. Perhaps they intended no more by that shew of resistance than to afford time for the transports to make some way up the river, and to gain thereby an opportunity of landing the troops. However that was, a general chace, and unresisted destruction took place; in both of which the three sloops of war, which had been so long cooped up with the garrison, now took an eager part. The fugitives themselves, finding there was no possibility of escape, shortened the business, by setting fire to, and blowing up their own vessels. No destruction could be more complete, for nothing escaped. One frigate of 20 guns, and another of 18, were, however, taken.

Few single towns have ever experienced such a blow to their marine, as Boston now suffered. The Warren, a fine new frigate, of 32 eighteen and twelve pounders, with five others, from 20 to 24 guns, one of 16, and one of 18, were all blown up. Six armed brigs or sloops, from 14 to 16 guns each, with one of 12, met the same fate. The whole number of armed vessels, destroyed or taken, including two, which the squadron took on their passage, amounting to nineteen. A force, little, if at all inferior, whether with respect to ships or guns, to the navy royal of England, for several years after the accession of Queen Elizabeth.

Twenty-four sail of transports were likewise destroyed, and some provision vessels taken. As nothing could be more despicable than the conduct of Saltonstall, so no man could be more execrated than he was by his countrymen. It is even said, that the indignation and rage of the land forces rose so high upon the common disgrace which they were obliged to share in, that they could not refrain from coming to blows with the seamen, in the course of their subsequent return by land. It must, however, be acknowledged, that the Americans were not able to cope with the royal squadron, in an open and regular sea-fight, and that the superior force and weight

of metal of the Raisonable, afforded sufficient cause of terror to frigates. But the passes, windings, and shallows of the river, might have served much to lessen that superiority; and at any rate, excepting the effusion of blood, the most desperate resistance could not have been attended with more fatal consequences than their ignominious flight.

. . .

The alarm excited in the British West India Islands by the superiority of the enemy was not long lived; for D'Estaing's operations[86] were destined to another quarter; nor could he probably have atchieved any thing farther there if it had been otherwise. The footing which the British forces had gained in Georgia and South Carolina, was highly distressing in its present effect, and still more alarming with respect to its probable consequences, to the Americans. The scene of action was so remote from the center of force, and the seat of council, that the war there was in a great degree beyond their reach; and the British marine force, afforded such decisive advantages to the operations of their troops, in countries every where bordered by the sea, and chequered by inland navigations, as could scarcely be counteracted with effect, by any moderate superiority at land.

America had as yet received no very essential service, with respect to the direct operations of the war, from any co-operation of the French arms. The attempt on Rhode Island, in conjunction with D'Estaing, was productive of expence, danger, and loss, without the smallest benefit. Nor did the conduct of that commander afford much of more satisfaction, than the expedition itself did of advantage. On the other hand, the mischief and danger to the southern provinces, had taken place during the height of the connection; and was perhaps scarcely compensated for by the recovery of

Philadelphia; even throwing that event into the scale, as an indirect consequence of the French alliance; and supposing that the British forces would not otherwise have abandoned that capital. It could not besides but be very galling to the Americans, that the protection, equipment, and supply, afforded to the French fleet at Boston, should produce no better effect, than that immediate desertion of their coasts, which exposed them to the southern invasion. Upon the whole, their new alliance had not as yet produced those high advantages, which were undoubtedly held out in the warmth of speculation; nor even that proportion of them, which might have been reasonably expected, as well from a consideration of the motives which led to the connection, as of the general state of affairs, and the means and power of the ally.

Under some of these considerations, or the impression of all, the French court determined now to afford some essential aid to their new allies, by directing D'Estaing's whole force to their assistance; or probably it was a part of the original plan of the campaign, that as soon as he had acquired that effective superiority in the West Indies, which they were resolved to endow him with, he should proceed to the execution of the latter measure. That commander, accordingly, having first waited to see the French homeward bound West India trade clear of danger, proceeded, with about 22 ships of the line, and something less than half the number of large and heavy-metal frigates, in all the pride of a conqueror, to sweep the coasts of North America. His first object, which was expected to be accomplished with little difficulty, was the destruction, of the small force under General Prevost, and consequently freeing the southern colonies from all their present alarm and danger. The second, was of greater importance, and likely to be attended with much greater difficulty and danger ; and that was, a defign to attack, in conjunction with General Washington, the British force at New York, by fea and land at the fame time; and thus, by the reduction of that ifland and its dependencies, along with the confequent ruin of the oppofite fleet and army, to bring the war on that continent to a final conclufion.

Through the fudden and unexpected apearance of the French fleet on the coafts of South Carolina and Georgia, the Experiment man of war, of fifty guns, and three royal frigates, being totally unapprehenfive of danger, and upon feparate fervices, had the misfortune of falling in with them, and thereby adding to their triumph and number. The firft, under the command of Sir James Wallace, was on her paffage from[87] New York to the Savannah with fupplies : and although fhe had been already difmafted in a violent ftorm, fhe made a gallant and defperate defence againft an irrefiftible fuperiority of force, in the view of the hoftile fleet,

General Prevoft was at this time at the town of Savannah ; but the better, if not the greater part of his force, was ftill on the ifland of Port Royal, in South Carolina, where we have already feen it took poft after the retreat from Charles Town. As the enemy were mafters by fea, that corps had no other means of joining the main body, but by the numerous inland navigations which interfect that country. The intercepting of an exprefs by the Americans, who conveyed orders to Colonel Maitland from the general, for fpeedily joining him with the whole effective body under his command, delayed the meafure fo long, that the enemy had time to feize the principal communications before it could take effect. This rendered the junction of that corps with the garrifon, upon

which only any hope of defending the Savannah could be founded, a matter of great doubt, difficulty, and danger. The addrefs of Colonel Maitland, the zeal of his troops, with the diftinguifhed fervices of Lieutenant Goldefbrough[88] of the navy, were happily found fuperior to all thefe obftacles.

As D'Eftaing was obliged to communicate with the government at Charles Town, relative to the movements of General Lincoln, who was to act in concert with him in the intended reduction of Georgia, this probably induced fome delay with refpect to his own operations ; fo that although he alrived on the coaft about the firft of September, it was more than a week after, before, the whole fleet, amounting to above 40 fail, anchored off the Sept. 9th bar of Tybee, at the mouth of the river Savannah. For the three or four fucceeding days, the French were taken up in paffing their troops, in fmall American veffels, through the Offabaw inlet, and landing them at Beaulieu, about 13 miles frow the town of Savannah ; at the fame time that their frigates were occupied in taking poffeffion of the lower river, and of the different inlets ; approaching as near to the town and lines, as the circumftances of water or defence would admit.

On the 15th the French, with Polafki's American light horfe, appeared fo near the Britifh lines, as to fkirmifh with the piquets, and as the force under General Prevoft did not admit of his having any other object in view than the mere defence of the town, his pofts were contracted within the cover of the artillery on the works. On the following day. M. D'Eftaing fent in a haughty fummons to the general, to furrender the place to the arms of his moft Chriftian Majefty. He vaunted in high language, that he commanded the fame troops, a detachment of whom had recently taken the Hof-

pital Hill in Granada by ftorm ; notwithftanding that its natural and artificial ftrength was fo great, that it was deemed impregnable by its defenders. He held out the circumftances of that tranfaction as a leffon of caution, to fhew the futility, and the very great danger, with the force which the general had in his hands, and fuch works as he had to defend, if he ventured to refift the ardour of thofe conquering troops :—Lord Macartney had the good fortune to efcape the firft tranfports of[89] their rage—He could not himfelf reftrain their pillage. General Prevoft was therefore warned, in rather commanding terms, that he fhould be perfonally refponfible, for all the unhappy or fatal confequences, which might be the refult of his obftinacy, in venturing a fruitlefs refiftance againft a force, with which he was totally incapable of contending.

Colonel Maitland's divifion had not yet joined the garrifon ; nor was there any intelligence of their fituation, nor knowledge of their ability to perform the junction. In thefe circumftances, although General Prevoft and his officers were determined, even with the force in their hands, to defend the place to the utmoft extremity, yet it was thought prudent and neceffary to gain all the time that was poffible; and this the more efpecially, as the lines were ftill in a very imperfect ftate of defence, and there had not been time to convey the artillery from the fhipping, for the protection, fuch as they were, of the works. The commander had the addrefs to carry this point. Meffages paffed backwards and forwards; and at length, a truce for 24 hours was agreed upon, to afford time for deliberation.

During this interval, the fortunate arrival of Colonel Maitland, with the troops from Port Royal, prefented a new face of affairs, and furnifhed a frefh ftock of ftrength and fpirits to the defence. An answer was accordingly returned, that they were unanimously determined to defend themselves to the last man. Nothing could prevent the sailors (who had been all drawn from the ships to construct and man the batteries) from expressing their usual ardour, by giving three loud cheers, upon firing the signal gun for the re-commencement of hostilities.

On the day after delivering the summons, Count D'Estaing was joined by General Lincoln, as he had been before by Polaski. The allies took separate but adjoining camps; and each began immediately to carry on their approaches as in a regular siege. Their joint or separate force cannot be very exactly ascertained. The French are said to have landed, from first to last, about 4800 regular troops, besides some hundreds of mulattoes and free negroes, whom they had brought from the West Indies. Lincoln's force was continually increasing; it was supposed not much to exceed 1500 men, at the time of his junction with D'Estaing; but was afterwards estimated from 3000, to 3500 men.

No account has been given of the number of the garrison; but it would seem, from the exceeding weakness of the battalions, and an examination of various relative circumstances, that taking in all descriptions of men, provincial troops, loyalists, under whatever denomination, and sailors, that the whole could not exceed 3000 men. [90]

The spirit, vigour of exertion, and perseverance in toil, which were exhibited in carrying on the defensive works, at least equalled, if not exceeded, any thing of the sort we have read or heard of. From the general to the private centinel, from the commanders of the royal frigates to the common seamen, every man without distinction was employed in the hardest labour, and chearfully underwent his share of the toil. At the time that the general received the French summons, the lines were not only weak and imperfect, but were not protected by above eight or ten pieces of cannon; and at the conclusion of the siege or blockade, the works (by the aid of the ship guns, and the unceasing exertion used in landing and bringing them forward) were covered with a numerous artillery, amounting to near 100 pieces. Nor was the labour or exertion greater than the judgment used in their direction. In this respect, Captain Moncrieffe, the engineer, [91] equally excited the admiration of friends and of enemies. The British forces indeed owed much to his skill and ability; and were accordingly unanimous in their acknowledgments of his services; while the French officers declared, that his works and batteries sprung up every night upon them like champignons. He gained great honour, and merited more substantial rewards.

The enemy were by no means idle in their endeavours to interrupt the works; but their efforts were ineffectual. In the mean time, they spared no industry in carrying on their own; and in about a week after the summons had pushed a sap to 24th. within 300 yards of the abbatis, to the left of the British center. Although the state of General Prevost's force, rendered him exceedingly sparing of his men, yet in the few conflicts which took place, the enemy were constantly and considerably losers. About midnight, between the 3d and the 4th of October, the enemy began a heavy bombardment; and at day-light, they opened a vehement cannonade, with 37 pieces of heavy artillery, and nine mortars, from their land batteries, and 16 cannon from the water. This cannonade was continued, with more or less activity, for five days. Its effect fell mostly upon the town; where, besides the destruction of houses; women, children and negroes were the only sufferers. All others were in the works; and these continually acquired additional strength, instead of sustaining any essential damage, during the violence of this cannonade.

In this distress of the women and children, which was still increased by the throwing in of carcasses, which set some houses [92] on fire, the general wrote a letter to D'Estaing, requiring permission, that they should be sent aboard ships down the river, and placed under the protection of a French man of war, in which state they were to continue until the business should be finally decided. At the same time acquainting him, that his own wife and family, should be among the first to profit of the indulgence. After a delay of three hours, during which the time was filled up by the discharge of cannon and shells, the request was not only refused, but the refusal was conveyed in unusual and insulting language, in a letter signed both by Lincoln and D'Estaing. The attempts made afterwards by the French officers, to charge this harsh and cruel refusal, as well as the mode of it, to the brutality of the American general, are by no means sufficient to exculpate D'Estaing, from his full share in the transaction, and in the disgrace belonging to it; however it may serve to shew their consciousness that the act was indefensible.

Whatever D'Estaing's merits may be as a naval commander, he seems to have committed two capital errors in this adventure by land. The first was, his not immediately attacking the British lines in their original weakness, and before General Prevost was joined by Colonel Maitland. The reasons that may be used against this measure are obvious, and may be answered with little difficulty.—The second was, that as he did lose so much time in carrying on regular approaches againft field works, he fhould have ftill continued to proceed by fap, until he had fo far obviated the defences of the enemy, that his troops might engage them upon fomething approaching to equal terms in the final aſſault. If to this it be oppoſed, that his fleet of heavy capital ſhips was expoſed to great riſque and danger, by lying fo long without ſhelter, upon an inhoſpital coaſt, which could not afford any, and in a moſt critical feaſon of the year; it may well be anſwered, that this very circumſtance afforded the ſtrongeſt motive for immediately attacking his enemy; and confequently could afford no reaſonable cauſe for delaying that attack, whilſt the defenfive ſtrength on the other fide was daily increaſing.

Whatever motives operated upon the French commander in the firſt inftance, it feems as if his temper or patience failed him, in waiting the flow refult of fap in the fecond. It is poſſible, that his approaches had already coſt him more time than he expected; that the refiſtance was alſo much greater; that, as his batteries produced very little effect upon the Britiſh works, he was diſappointed in that refpect likewiſe; and that he finally placed too great a confidence in the fuperiority of his force, and the goodneſs of his troops.

However that was, after a very heavy cannonade and bombardment for feveral hours, the allies attacked the Britiſh lines, Oct. 9th. with their utmoſt force, and with great fury, a little before day-light. The firing began on the left of the Britiſh lines, but foon after became general. As it was ſtill too dark to perceive the movements of the enemy, and uncertain where their principal attacks would take place, no change was made in the diſpoſition of the Britiſh troops; but each command waited coolly in its poſt, prepared for, and expecting, whatever could happen.

The nature of the ground on both flanks of the lines, was fo favourable to the approaches of the enemy, that the defect could not be remedied by all the ſkill and endeavours of the engineer. Thus an attack was to be expected, towards either or both of the points. A fwampy hollow way on the right, might bring the enemy under cover to within a very fmall diſtance of fome of the principal works; on the left, the approach was not fo well covered; but the ground being firm and clear, feemed better calculated for the operation of regular troops, or at leaſt more inviting to them, than that on the other fide. The French being likewiſe encamped on that fide, it was expected that they would direct their whole force to that point; and that the attack on the other, if really undertaken, would be left to the Americans.

The grand attack was, however, directed to the right, whither, D'Eſtaing in perſon led the flower of both armies, and was accompanied by all the principal officers of each. They advanced in three columns, under cover of the hollow we have mentioned; but it feems, that through the darkneſs, they took a greater circuit, and got deeper in the bog, than they needed or intended to have done; a circumſtance, which befides a loſs of critical time, could fcarcely fail of producing fome difarrangement or diſorder. The attack was, however, made with great ſpirit, and fupported with an extraordinary degree of obſtinate perſeverance. A redoubt on the Ebenezar road, was the ſcene of much action, loſs and gallantry. It was obſtinately defended by Captain Taws;[93] the enemy planted two ſtand of colours on it; the parapet was covered with their dead; at length the brave captain fell, gallantly fighting in his redoubt; his fword being plunged, at the inſtant of death, in the body of the third enemy whom he had

ſlain with his own hand. His place was inſtantly and equally ſupplied by Captain Wickham;[94] who, with better fortune, diſplayed acts of the moſt ſignal valour.

While the conflict was ſtill dubious and bloody, particularly at that redoubt, the ſkill and defign which operated in the conſtruction of the new works, were diſplayed with great advantage. Three batteries which were occupied by feamen, took the enemy in almoſt every direction; and made ſuch havock in their ranks, as caufed fome little diſorder, or at leaſt occafioned a pauſe in their violence. At that critical moment of decifion, a body of grenadiers and marines advanced ſuddenly from the lines, and charged the enemy with fuch rapidity and fury, throwing themſelves headlong into the ditches and works amongſt them, that in an inſtant, the redoubt, and a battery to its right, were totally cleared of them. The victors did not purſue their advantage with leſs vigour than they had gained it. The enemy were broken, routed, and driven in the greateſt diſorder and confufion, through the abbatis into the fwamp. The whole was performed with fuch rapidity, that three companies of the moſt active troops in the army, who were ordered to ſuſtain the grenadiers, could not, with all their celerity, come in for any ſhare of the honour.

Although it was then day, yet the fog and the ſmoke together caufed fo great a darkneſs, that the general could form no accurate judgment, either as to the condition or the diſpoſitions of the enemy; and as a conſtant firing was ſtill heard in different parts of the lines, theſe circumſtances, all together, prevented his venturing to purſue the enemy, in their flight and confuſion acroſs the moraſs. They were, however, every where repulſed; but as that was done elſewhere with leſs difficulty, fo their lofs was proportionally fmaller. As the day cleared, the works and ditches near the Ebenezar redoubt, prefented fuch a fpectacle of killed and wounded, as fome of the officers and foldiers faid, had only been equalled at Bunker's hill. At ten o'clock, the enemy requefted a truce, with leave to bury the dead, and carry off the wounded; the firft was granted; but a reftriction laid in point of diftance as to the reft.

The lofs of the enemy, in killed and wounded, was, by the loweft calculations, eftimated from a thoufand to twelve hundred men. The French acknowledged 44 officers, and about 700 private men, on their fide only. The amount of the American lofs was not acknowledged. It was faid, that nothing[95] but mutual reproach, and the moft violent animofity, now took place between the new allies. Each accufed the other with bad conduct or bad performance, and being the author of his own particular lofs or difgrace. It was even faid, that the troops on both fides were with difficulty reftrained from proceeding to extremities; and that the French and American commanders and principal officers, were as little fatisfied with each other as the private men. It was likewife fuppofed, that a ftrong previous jealoufy had fubfifted on the American fide, from D'Eftaing's fummoning the place to furrender to the arms of the French King only.

However thefe things might be, nothing was thought of after by either party, but the means of getting away, with the greateft poffible fpeed and fafety. But it was neceffary to mafk this purpofe, by ftill fupporting the appearance of a blockade. The removal of the French heavy artillery, baggage, fick, and wounded, was particularly a work of time, labour, and difficulty. Great civilities now paffed between the French camp and the Britifh lines; and numberlefs apologies were offered, for

the refufal with refpect to the women and children. They were now preffed to place themfelves in the fituation which they had then requefted; and a particular fhip of war and commander were named, for the reception of Mrs. Prevoft, her children, and company. The anfwer was blunt and foldierly; that what had been once refufed, and that in terms of infult, could not in any circumftance be deemed worth the acceptance.

The celebrated Polifh Count Polafki, whofe name has been fo often mentioned in the American war, was mortally wounded in this action. M. D'Eftaing himfelf was forely wounded in two places. Major-General de Fontange, with[96] fome other French officers of diftinction, were likewife wounded. The lofs on the Britifh fide was inconceivably fmall. Too much could not be faid in praife of every order of men who compofed the defence of the Savannah. The loyalifts of both the Carolinas were diftinguifhed; nor fhould it be forgotten, that the captains and failors of the tranfports took their ftation in the batteries, with the fame alacrity as their brethren in the royal fervice.

In fomething more than a week, Oct. 18th. upon the clearing up of a fog, it was difcovered, that the French and Americans had abandoned their camps in the preceding night. Some purfuit was made, but it was foon found, that they had broken down all the bridges behind them, and purfued their refpective routes with the greateft celerity. It was computed, that the French did not lofe lefs, in every way, than 1500 men on this adventure. Their commander found his fleet, as much out of heart and condition, and nearly as fickly as his army. He accordingly totally abandoned the coaft of America, about the 1ft of November, and proceeded with the greater part of his fleet directly to France; the reft having returned

to the Weft Indies. Such was the beginning and ending of M. D'Eftaing's American campaign; and, fuch the iffue of the great defigns he had formed, and the mighty hopes he had conceived.

* * *

Extract of a Letter from Lieutenant-General Burgoyne to his Conftituents, upon his late Refignation; with the Correfpondence between him and the Secretaries of War, relative to his return to America.

ON the 9th of October, 1779, Lieut. Gen. Burgoyne refigned the command of the Queen's regiment of light dragoons, the government of fort William, and his appointment on the American ftaff. As this refignation appears to have been occafioned by circumftances of a very extraordinary and fingular nature, we have thought it proper, in a work of this kind, to lay before the public the correfpondence at large which paffed between him and the Secretaries of War, together with fuch parts of his letter to his conftituents, as tend to explain more fully the motives of his conduct on that occafion.—After briefly ftating his political fituation previous to his being firft fent to America, and the fteps by which the command of the troops deftined to make a junction with Sir William Howe naturally devolved to him, the General proceeds in the following manner:

"With thofe claims, Gentlemen, to the countenance and goodwill at leaft of government, I proceed to relate the treatment I received.

I had expreffed, in my private letter from Albany to the Secretary of State, my " confi- " dence in the juftice of the King " and his councils to fupport the " general they had thought pro- " per to appoint to as arduous an " undertaking and under as pofi- " tive a direction as a cabinet

" ever framed." I had in the same letter given an opinion of the enemy's troops, upon near inspection of their numbers, appointment and discipline.

Furnished with these materials, and supported by the fidelity with which I had acted, it was not thought expedient I should have access to the King. What other facts might have been cleared up by my interview, and were wished not to be cleared up, the Secretary of State* only can inform the world. Direct means of effecting my exclusion from the King's presence were not practicable; for the case was unprecedented. The pretext adopted was as follows:

It was suggested that an enquiry should be made by a board of general officers into the causes of the miscarriage of the northern expedition; and a court *etiquette* was invented, the foundation of which in reason or precedent I am not acquainted with, *viz.* that the persons whose conduct was so put in question, should not appear at Court pending the enquiry. No difficulty of the competency of such a court was then spoke of, or perhaps thought of, by any but the dark designers of my ruin; the measure therefore could neither affect his Majesty nor his Court with any idea of farther hardship than the delay of a few days to my appearing in his presence.

This arrangement had been prepared by the Secretary of State, in the interval between the notice of my arrival at Portsmouth, which he received in the evening, and my visit to him in Pall-mall, which was before noon the next day.

It will naturally be supposed that the state in which I stood was the first subject of conversation;

on the contrary, I was received with much apparent kindness; explanations passed, but they were friendly; I was heard attentively, through a report of all the transactions subsequent to the Convention of Saratoga; and I was led by degrees, and without suspicion of insidiousness, to the most confidential communication, on my part, of facts, observations, and opinions, respecting very important objects.

If the measure of denying me access to the King had been undecided before, this conversation was of a nature to produce a decision; for it opened truths respecting the dispositions of the people of America, and the state of things there, very different from the ideas which (it is now known, from the line taken by the Secretary of State in the late enquiry) were prevalent in the governing councils of this kingdom.

It was not till after the matter of my communication was exhausted, that the Secretary of State drew from his pocket an order, that I should prepare myself for an enquiry: at which I expressed my fullest satisfaction, till he followed the order with the information of the *etiquette* I before mentioned, that I was not to appear at court.

Having pitched upon this expedient for no other end than to exclude me from the presence of my Sovereign, he could hardly be in pain about the event. If the general officers appointed for a Board of Enquiry, should coincide with the notion that my parole was of such a nature as to bar their proceedings, this would put off my access to the King to a very long day: but if the general officers should not enter into these ideas, he had a resource left. He could

not be unapprized, that such a court was held by high authorities in the law to be illegal; and if I was not to see the King until an illegal or questionable court should make a valid report, I was never likely to enjoy that honour. Either way I was not to have the benefit of an enquiry; but he was to have the advantage of the *pretence* of one, in order to shut the door of St. James's against me. This has been made apparent beyond all possibility of doubt, by every part of his subsequent conduct: but at that time, though I saw a disgrace was intended me, I was not able to estimate the full extent of it.

Thus prevented in my intended appeal to the King, and as I have fatal reason to believe, the King's ear secured against me, attempts were not unthought of to deprive me of a voice in parliament. A great law officer of the crown made, *in the form of* legal doubts, a long and methodical argument against my competence to any civil duty or function: but it was not found so easy to exclude me from your service, as it had been to deprive me of countenance at court; and ministers only shewed by that abortive attempt, what their motives were, in those attempts in which they had been more successful.

Though the late time of the session, and the absence of Sir William Howe and Sir Guy Carleton, who were supposed to be parties, furnished plausible arguments for postponing a parliamentary enquiry in the summer of 1778, it was evident the temper of the House of Commons was inclined to adopt it at the ensuing meeting.

In the beginning of June, I received the conditional order annexed. [No. 1.] Though it bears the King's name, it was avowedly a letter of the cabinet; and there remained no longer a doubt in my mind, that my ruin was made a

---

* Whenever *the Secretary of State* is mentioned in these papers, the person to be understood is the Secretary for the American department, Lord George Germain.

measure of state. Few adepts in the science of oppression could have formed a design better fitted to its end; and it was likely to be successful, whatever part I should take. If I went—my character was lost irretrievably—the falsehoods and aspersions that have since been refuted in the face of those who propagated them, were already gone forth: the numbers of my army, and of that opposed to me, were already grossly mistated; contradictory charges of sloth and precipitancy, as the temper of men at the moment seemed inclined to either, were supported with uniform perseverance:—my friends were stated to be my accusers; and even my integrity, with regard to pecuniary trusts, was glanced at.

If I stayed, the King's order (as it was fallaciously called) was a specious topic; and it was not difficult to foresee, that it would be put into the hands of gentlemen that well knew how to make the utmost of it by art and opportunity. My answer [No. 2.] drew from the cabinet their second letter [No. 3.]; and I give them the satisfaction of knowing, that I felt all they could wish I should feel from the repetition of their severity. I saw in it at once a doubt of my veracity respecting my health, and the most contemptuous disregard of all other principles upon which I had claimed a right of staying in this country. ——Fundamental principles, I thought them, of justice and generosity due from all governments to those who serve them zealously, and in some governments held doubly due to such as in their zeal have been unfortunate.

It must be observed, that the ministry kept a profound silence, both to myself and the public, respecting the ratification of the convention. The same silence they maintained even in parliament long after its meeting. They were perfectly apprised, that the enemy had some time before made the want of that ratification the ground of their refusing to give effect to the part of the treaty which was favourable to the troops. They knew also, that one of the principal objects of my return to England was to negociate in behalf of that deserving body of soldiers and subjects. Their desire of my delivering myself into captivity, at such a time, and under such circumstances, justified something more than a suspicion, that in my absence it was intended either to lay to my charge some breach of faith with the enemy; or to renounce the treaty from the beginning, and by my surrender, to transfer the act from the nation to my person. These are the only two cases which I believe can be produced from the history of nations, wherein an officer, who had made a convention with an enemy, had been delivered up to them. The ratification of the treaty afterwards is no proof that such intentions did not then exist.

I will make no farther observations, Gentlemen, upon this first correspondence between the War-office and me; nor should I have troubled you with these, but that great pains are taken to divert the attention of the public from the pretended order, to my behaviour since the receipt of it. I in no wise seek to evade the public judgment upon any thing I have done: but I claim from the impartial and the candid, a consideration of the pretended order itself, in its principal parts, viz. the ground upon which it is founded; the novel species of cruelty which it supposes within the power of the crown; and lastly, the exercise of such doctrine by men who were parties, and against the man whom they were called upon by their station and their honour to confront.

Nothing farther passed during the recess of parliament: I availed myself of a discretionary power, as I had a right to do, and I made it no secret, that had a direct order been sent me, I should have laid all my commissions at his Majesty's feet.

During the last session of parliament, an inquiry was instituted. The detail of the attempts made by the ministry to defeat it, is too notorious to be necessary upon this occasion. They at last contrived that it should be left imperfect: but in spight of every management, it had answered my purpose so far, as to fix upon record a body of evidence, that I would not exchange for all that power could bestow. It is a justification of misfortune by the voice of honour. It is there apparent, what the army under my command, who felt most and saw best, thought of my actions.—The affections of my gallant comrades, unshaken in every trial, labour, famine, captivity, or death, enable me to despise the rancour of a cabal and all its consequences.

The most important purpose of my return to England having been answered by this vindication, I thought the sacrifice of my commissions, the fruits of the greatest part of my life, not to be necessary. I knew by experience what I had to apprehend in point of health from an American winter; but I scorned to plead it. Conscious of my integrity, I abandoned my public accounts to the rigorous scrutiny of office; and I took occasion publicly to declare, that should it still be thought expedient to deliver me back to the enemy, and a positive order should be sent me for that purpose, I should, as far as in me lay, obey it.

I do not believe any man who knows me doubted the sincerity of that intention. I am persuaded, the framers of the letter of the 24th September were particularly convinced of it. The man who embarked in the situation I did, in the year 1776, could hardly be supposed to want fortitude to undertake an American voyage, in the situation in which I made the declaration. An order, therefore, which I could have obeyed without committing my honour, would not have effected my ruin. Time and circumstances furnished more secure expedients; which I shall now open.

Occasions were taken to visit my offences upon my friends. Examples respecting my nearest connections need not be pointed out, when I am addressing myself to any part of the county of Lancaster. But the principle extended far more wide; and did not the apprehension of farther hurting the men I love restrain me, I could produce instances of hardship in the distribution of military preferments, that no impartial persons will impute to any other cause than the kindness and friendship of the parties to me.

These instances of persecution, it is well known, affected me deeply. There were others yet more irritating.

In the course of the summer, the apprehensions before entertained of an invasion, by the declaration of government, became a certainty. Hardly a British subject could be found so low, so feeble, or even so profligate, as to be exempted from service; while uncommon premiums were raised by begging, and distributed to volunteers, the gaols, and even the feet of the gallows, were resorted to for other recruits.

In this declared dilemma, I know government were not strangers to my intention of fighting my own regiment as colonel; or, should its destination not admit the honour of meeting the enemy in that capacity, of offering myself as a volunteer in the ranks of any corps that might be more fortunately situated.

These several feelings, and many others incident to an oppressed man, were doubtless duly considered; for at the crisis when they could operate most forcibly, it was thought proper most to insult me; at the crisis when the King's servants openly announced, that not a ship or a soldier could be spared from our internal defence, a sentence of banishment was sent me; and even that not in an order, but a reprimand; —a submission to ignominy was required of me; for to put me wholly out of a capacity to draw my sword at such a moment, was virtually, in point of disgrace, to break it over my head. My enemies might have spared superfluous provocations. This alone would have sufficed to prove their sagacity, and to effect their purpose. Let it not be supposed they want knowledge of the human heart. There are among them, who can discern its recesses, and have the skill and the triumph to make a soldier's honour and sensibility the instruments of his own destruction.

I could no longer brook the treatment I received. My letter of the 9th of October to the Secretary at War, [No. 5.] contains my general sentiments.''

Correspondence with Lord Barrington.

[No. 1]
War-Office, June 5. 1778.
S I R,
The King, judging your presence material to the troops detained prisoners in New England, under the convention of Saratoga; and finding in a letter of yours to Sir William Howe, dated April 9, 1778, '' that you trust a short time '' at Bath will enable you to re- '' turn to America*,'' his Ma-

jesty is pleased to order that you shall repair to Boston, as soon as you have tried the Bath waters, in the manner you propose.
I have the honour to be,
Your most obedient,
humble servant,
BARRINGTON.
Lieut. Gen. Burgoyne,
Hertford-street.

[No. 2.]
June 22, 1778.
My Lord,
I have considered the letter I had the honour to receive from your lordship on the 5th instant, with the attention and respect due to an intimation of the King's pleasure. I have now to request your lordship to lay before his Majesty a few particulars of my situation; and to offer to his royal consideration, with all humility on my part, such of my complaints as admit of representation.

My letter to Sir William Howe, referred to in your lordship's letter, was writ in the fulness of zeal to renew my service in arms the ensuing campaign. The satisfaction of succeeding in that application, would have tended to my recovery, or for a time might have prevented my feeling an ill. Deprived of so animating a support, and visited by new and unexpected anxieties, I have now recourse only, as far as the mind is concerned, to a clear conscience, perhaps a more tardy, but, I trust, as efficacious an assistance.

The present season of the year, always favourable to me, gives me the appearance, and indeed, in some degree the sensation of health. But much care is still wanting to

---

* Paragraph of the letter from Lieutenant General Burgoyne to Sir William Howe, which was made the foundation of the above conditional order.
'' I need not expatiate upon the satisfaction I should feel at being put again in a
'' situation to serve under you, as soon as my health will enable me.—I trust that a
'' very short time at Bath will effect that purpose.
'' I have only to add, my trust that you will continue to me the friendship and
'' confidence with which you have always honoured me, and that you will write
'' to me at full by the first opportunity, how I can be employed to serve your views.
'' I have the honour to be, &c.''

restore me to my former state. The remedies prescribed me are repose, regimen of diet, and repeated visits to Bath: my intention, in consequence, was to remain some time in the country, to repair to Bath for a short time next month, and to return thither for a much longer space in the more proper season, the autumn. But whatever may be the benefit of all or any part of this plan, I am persuaded, that to expose my constitution to the next American winter, is in probability to doom me to the grave.

That I should not hesitate at such an alternative, in circumstances of exigency, I am confident the King will admit, when in his grace he shall recollect how often, at his Majesty's call in this war, I have relinquished private duties and affection, more impulsive upon the heart than any we owe to existence. The purposes intimated for my present attendance in America, would, I fear, be very different from services.

The army I commanded, credulous in my favour, and attached to me by the series of conflicts and misfortunes we have in common sustained, would not find material consolation from my return in disgrace; and their disappointment could not but be enhanced by such an indication, that government either thought it inexpedient to ratify the convention of Saratoga, or despaired of a ratification effectuating the redemption of that army; for they would not conceive it possible, had the return of the troops been in view, that any person would have advised the King to what then might have appeared so harsh an act as sending an infirm, calumniated, unheard complainant, across the Atlantic, merely to inspect their embarkation.

Your lordship will perceive the parts of this letter which apply to the council of the throne, from whence I am to suppose the order I have received originated, and in your justice and generosity you will

guard me, my lord, from any supposable presumption of expostulating with the King in person. But I apply to the same qualities in your lordship's mind, for pointing out to his Majesty, independently of his council, other letters, among those transmitted to the Secretary of State, alledging other reasons, and those more prevalent than the attention to health, for my return to England; and permit me, my lord, to add that every one of them receives tenfold weight from what has happened lately, for my continuance in England. The special reason upon which I chiefly rest at present, my lord, is a vindication of my honour.

Until that by full and proper trial is cleared to my Sovereign and to my country, I confess I should feel a removal from hence, though enforced by the term duty, the severest sentence of exile ever imposed; and when the time and circumstances of such removal are farther considered, that Britain is threatened with invasion, and that after an enemy has set my arm at liberty, I am forbid a share in her defence by the council of my own Sovereign.—After these considerations, can I, my lord, be deemed offensive if I venture to declare that so marked a combination of displeasure and hard treatment, would be more than I should be able, or perhaps ought to bear?

My cause, my lord, thus committed to your office and character, I have only to add my reliance that you will do it justice, and the respect with which I have the honour to be, &c. &c. &c.

Lord Barrington.

[No. 3.]
War-Office, June 27, 1778:
S I R,

I took the first opportunity of laying before the King your letter to me, dated the 22d instant. His Majesty continues to think your presence with the troops taken at Saratoga, and still detained pri-

soners in New England, of so much importance to them, that he has commanded me to acquaint you it is his pleasure, that you return to them as soon as you can, without any risk of material injury to your health.

I have the honour to be,
Sir,
Your most obedient,
humble servant,
BARRINGTON.

Lieut. Gen. Burgoyne.

Correspondence with Mr. Jenkinson.

[No. 4.]
War-Office, Sept. 24, 1779.
S I R,

I am commanded by the King to acquaint you, that your not returning to America, and joining the troops, prisoners under the convention of Saratoga, is considered as a neglect of duty, and disobedience of orders transmitted to you by the Secretary at War, in his letter 5th of June, 1778.

I have the honour to be,
&c. &c. &c.
(Signed) C. JENKINSON.

Lieut. Gen. Burgoyne.

[No. 5.]
Hertford-Street, Oct. 9, 1779.
S I R,

I received your letter acquainting me, " that my not returning " to America, and joining the " troops, prisoners under the con- " vention of Saratoga, is consi- " dered as a neglect of duty, and " disobedience of orders transmit- " ted to me, by the Secretary at " War, in his letter of 5th June, " 1778."

During a service of more than thirty years, I have been taught, by the rewards of two successive Sovereigns, to believe, that my military conduct was held deserving of more favourable terms than those which are applied to it in the above recital. I have received from his present Majesty in particular, repeated and conspicuous testimonies of diftinction and good opinion : and I fhould have been the moft ungrateful of men, if I had not felt, and uniformly endeavoured to mark the warmeft and moft dutiful attachment to his perfon, together with a punctilious perfeverance in the execution of all his lawful commands.

Under this fenfe of my paft fituation, your letter, ftated to be written by the King's command, cannot but affect me moft painfully.

The time in which I am charged with neglect of duty, has been employed to vindicate my own honour, the honour of the Britifh troops, and of thofe of his Majefty's allies, under my late command, from the moft bafe and barbarous afperfions, that ever were forged againft innocent men, by malignity fupported by power.

In regard to the fecond charge, I muft firft obferve that there were two letters from the late Secretary at War, upon the fubject of my return to America ; and though you only ftate that of the 5th of June, I conclude it is not meant, that the other of the 27th fhould be fuppreffed, as it is explanatory of the former.

The fignification of the King's pleafure therein contained being clearly conditional, and the condition depending upon my own judgment ; I am unable to conceive by what poffible conftruction it can be confidered as difobedience, that I have not fulfilled an optional condition ; and I am ready and defirous to meet the judgment of a proper tribunal upon that, as upon every other part of my conduct.

In the mean time, Sir, I am not told who it is that confiders my taking advantage of my parole for the purpofes I have done, as a neglect of duty, and breach of orders, and has fo reprefented it to his Majefty. But in this ftate of ignorance concerning my enemies, I muft fay, as well from duty to my Sovereign, as from juftice to myfelf, that they who have abufed

the confidence of their gracious mafter, by fuch a grofs mifreprefentation, merit, and I truft will meet with more of his difpleafure, than they wickedly have drawn upon me.

The punifhment implied in the order referred to, you will obferve, Sir, is unufual as well as cruel. Whether the Minifters of the crown, can legally order a Britifh fubject into captivity either at home or abroad without trial ; or whether they can compel an officer by virtue of his general military obedience, to deliver himfelf to the prifon of the enemy, without any requifition on their part, is (to fay nothing ftronger of it) matter of ferious doubt. On pretence of military obedience, I am ordered to the only part of the world in which I can do no military fervice. An enemy's prifon is not the King's garrifon, nor is any thing to be done or fuffered there, any part of an officer's duty ; fo far from it that it implies a direct incapacity for any military function. What are the military orders I am to give to men who have no arms to fight, and no liberty to march ? Or by what rule is my not being in the hands of rebels, underftood to be a neglect of duty to my Sovereign ? Sir, the thing is too evident ; thofe who calumniate my conduct on this account are defirous not of ferving the King, but of infulting me, and of eftablifhing new, dangerous, unmilitary and unconftitutional powers in themfelves.

While a precedent is eftablifhing in my particular cafe, I requeft it may moreover be remembered that I am deprived of a court martial upon my conduct in America, becaufe I am not fuppofed to be amenable to the juftice of the kingdom : and the King is told I have difobeyed his orders, in the very fame breath that I am ftated not to be accountable to him : by this doctrine it feems fuppofed, that I am not capable of receiving orders

for the purpofes of public juftice or public fervice, but am perfectly fubject to all fuch as have a tendency to my own deftruction.

But it has been fuggefted when no military duty could be devifed as a ground for this order that I might be returned to captivity in a fort of civil capacity. To comfort my fellow prifoners by a participation of their fufferings, and to act as a commiffary to negotiate for them. Could any fufferings of mine alleviate the fmalleft of theirs, I fhould willingly fubmit to any thing the malice of the prefent Minifters could inflict upon me. But it is equally injurious to truth and to their honour and humanity, to fuppofe that my perfecution could make any part of their confolation. What confolation could they derive from my junction to the common captivity, only to tell them that not a name among them is to be found in the numerous lift of late promotions ? And that the negociations to be undertaken in their favour, are to be conducted by the man who is notoriously profcribed by the power in the name of which he is to negotiate ? Who alone of all the officers who have come from America, has been denied all accefs to the King ? Cruelly as I and my fellow fufferers are treated ; I can fcarce bring myfelf to wifh, that they who provide fuch comfort for others, fhould receive it in a fimilar fituation themfelves.

I am forry finally to obferve, that the treatment I have experienced, however contradictory in the reafons affigned for the feveral parts of it, is perfectly uniform in the principle. They who would not fuffer me to approach the King's prefence to vindicate myfelf before him ; who have held that I cannot have a court martial to vindicate myfelf to my profeffion ; and who have done all they could do, to prevent me from vindicating myfelf to my country by a parliamentary enquiry ; are now very fyftematically defirous of burying my innocence and their own guilt, in the prifons of the enemy, and of removing, in my perfon, to the other fide of the Atlantic Ocean, the means of renewing parliamentary proceedings which they have reafon to dread.

Thofe extraordinary attempts to opprefs in my perfon the rights of all fubjects, and to pervert every idea of military obedience, by directing it, not to the fervice of the public, but the ruin of officers, juftified me to my own confcience, in the part I took under the conditional order, referred to in your letter. I found the fame inward juftification in requiring, in the moft public manner, at the clofe of the late feffion of parliament, a clear, peremptory order, in cafe the Minifters perfevered in their intention of refurrendering me to the enemy.

I have received no order ; had an order been fent to me framed in any manner that I could have acted upon it confiftently with the exiftence of character ; I might have made a proteft againft the precedent ; I might have enquired of you, Sir, by what probable means in the prefent pofture of affairs it was to be executed. But in deference to the King's name, as a military fervant, I meant fubmiffion. Your letter, Sir, inftead of an order for my future conduct, is an unjuft reproach of my paft ; for which I humbly implore of his Majefty, and firmly demand of his councils, trial by a court martial. Should that be refufed or procraftinated upon the principle formerly adopted, " that in my pre-" fent fituation no judicature can " have cognizance of my actions;" I can then confider the purport of your letter, Sir, in no other light than that of a difmiffion, a difmiffion as conclufive as any you could have worded in form, and perhaps more poignant. To eat the bread of the crown, however faithfully earned, under a fentence,

without appeal, in the name of the King, of neglect of duty and difobedience of orders, is incompatible with my conception of honour ; an interdiction from my country ; a banifhment to the only part of the world in which I am difabled from ferving that country at the moment of her fate ; and when every other arm, even to the weakeft, is preffed to her defence; thefe circumftances give a critical barbarity to the intentions of the King's advifers, that an Englifh foldier cannot fupport. Therefore, Sir, I find myfelf compelled, if not allowed an early trial, or by the King's grace, upon this reprefentation, reftored to a capacity of fervice, through your official channel to requeft his Majefty, to accept of my refignation of my appointment upon the American ftaff, of the Queen's regiment of light dragoons, and of the government of Fort William, humbly defiring only to referve my rank as lieutenant general in the army, to to render me the more clearly amenable to a court martial hereafter, and to enable me to fulfil my perfonal faith, fhould I be required by the enemy fo to do.

I have the honour to be,
&c.

*The Right Hon. Charles Jenkinfon,
Secretary at War.*

[No. 6.]
War-Office, Oct. 15, 1779.
SIR,

I have received your letter of the 9th inftant, wherein, after ftating your reafons for objecting to the feveral fteps that have been taken with relation to the orders given for your return to North America, you add, that " if you are not al-" lowed an early trial, or if by his " Majefty's grace, upon the repre-" fentations contained in the faid " letter, you are not reftored to " a capacity of fervice, it is your " requeft to his Majefty, that he " will be pleafed to accept your " refignation of your appointment

" to the American ftaff, of the " Queen's regiment of light dra-" goons, and of the government " of Fort William ; humbly de-" firing only to referve your rank " of lieutenant-general in the ar-" my, to render you more clearly " amenable to courts martial here-" after, and to enable you to fulfil " your perfonal faith, fhould you " be required by the enemy fo to " do."

Having laid your letter before the King, I am commanded to acquaint you, that for the reafons fubmitted to his Majefty by the Board of General Officers, in their report, dated the 23d May, 1778, (which reafons fubfift in the fame force now as they did at that time) his Majefty does not think proper that any part of your conduct fhould be brought before a military tribunal, fo long as you fhall continue engaged to re-deliver yourfelf into the power of Congrefs upon their demand, and due notice being given by them. Nor does his Majefty think proper, in confequence of the reprefentations contained in your faid letter, to reftore you, circumftanced as you are, to a capacity of fervice. Neither of thefe requefts can therefore be granted.

I have it farther in command from the King to acquaint you, that his Majefty confiders your letter to me as a proof of your determination to perfevere in not obeying his orders, fignified to you in the Secretary at War's letter of the 5th of June, 1778 : and for this reafon, his Majefty is pleafed to accept your refignation of the command of the Queen's regiment of light dragoons, of the government of Fort William, and of your appointment on the American ftaff, allowing you only to referve the rank of lieutenant-general in the army, for the purpofes you have ftated.

Lord Barrington's letter of the 27th of June is confidered as explanatory of the orders given in his

letter of the 5th of that month.
I have the honour to be,
&c.
(Signed) C. JENKINSON.
Lieut. Gen. Burgoyne.

[No. 7.]
Hertford-Street, Oct. 17, 1779.
SIR,
I received your letter of the 15th instant, informing me, that his Majesty had been pleased to accept my resignation of my military employments, and that I am refused a court martial upon that disobedience, for my perseverance in which, you tell me my resignation is accepted.

I must persist in denying, that I have received any other order, than an order subject to my own discretion.

I must persist in my claim to a court martial.

I apprehend, that if I am not subject to a trial for breach of orders, it implies that I am not subject to the orders themselves.

I do not admit that I cannot legally have a court martial, circumstanced as I am: but those who advise his Majesty, assert it, and they are answerable for this contradiction between their reasoning and their conduct.

The report of the general officers, I humbly conceive, is erroneous. And the subsequent appointment of other gentlemen, exactly in my circumstances (with great merit on their part to entitle them to any distinction) to military employments, subject to orders, and accountable for the breach of them, is one of the reasons for my conceiving, that the King's advisers do not differ from me in opinion, that the general officers were mistaken.

Thinking it probable, Sir, that this letter may close the correspondence between us, I conclude with the sentiments I have never deviated from in any part of it; and I request you to assure his Majesty, with all humility on my part, that

though I have reason to complain heavily of his Majesty's Ministers, my mind is deeply impressed, as it ever has been, with a sense of duty, respect, and affection to his royal person.

I have the honour to be,
&c.
The Right Hon. Charles Jenkinson, Secretary at War.

[No. 8.]
War-Office, Oct. 22, 1779.
SIR,
I have the honour to acknowledge the receipt of your letter, dated the 17th instant, and to acquaint you, that I took the first opportunity of laying it before the King.

I have the honour to be,
Sir,
Your most obedient,
humble servant,
C. JENKINSON.
Lieut. Gen. Burgoyne,
&c. &c. &c.

———————————

Admiralty-Office, Oct. 12, 1779.

A Letter from Captain Pearson, of his Majesty's ship Serapis, to Mr. Stephens, of which the following is a Copy, was yesterday received at this Office:

Pallas, French Frigate, in Congress Service. Texel, Oct. 6, 1779.

SIR,
YOU will be pleased to inform the Lords Commissioners of the Admiralty, that on the 23d ult. being close in with Scarborough, about eleven o'clock, a boat came on board with a letter from the bailiffs of that corporation, giving information of a flying squadron of the enemy's ships being on the coast, and of a part of the said squadron having been seen from thence the day before, standing to the southward. As soon as I received this intelligence, I made the signal for the convoy to bear down under my lee, and repeated it with two guns; notwithstanding which,

the van of the convoy kept their wind, with all sail stretching out to the southward from under Flamborough Head, till between twelve and one, when the headmost of them got sight of the enemy's ships, which were then in chace of them; they then tacked, and made the best of their way under the shore for Scarborough, &c. letting fly their top-gallant sheets, and firing guns; upon which I made all the sail I could to windward, to get between the enemy's ships and the convoy, which I soon effected. At one o'clock we got sight of the enemy's ships from the mast-head, and about four we made them plain from the deck to be three large ships and a brig; upon which I made the Countess of Scarborough's signal to join me, she being in shore with the convoy: at the same time I made the signal for the convoy to make the best of their way, and repeated the signal with two guns: I then brought to, to let the Countess of Scarborough come up, and cleared ship for action. At half past five the Countess of Scarborough joined me, the enemy's ships then bearing down upon us, with a light breeze at S. S. W. at six tacked, and laid our head in shore, in order to keep our ground the better between the enemy's ships and the convoy; soon after which we perceived the ships bearing down upon us to be a two-decked ship and two frigates, but from their keeping end on upon us, on bearing down, we could not discern what colours they were under; at about twenty minutes past seven, the largest ship of the three brought to, on our larboard bow, within musquet shot: I hailed him, and asked what ship it was; they answered in English, the Princess Royal; I then asked where they belonged to; they answered evasively; on which I told them, if they did not answer directly, I would fire into them; they then answered with a shot, which was instantly returned with a broadside; and after exchanging two or three broadsides, he backed his topsails, and dropped upon our quarter within pistol-shot, then filled again, put his helm a weather, and run us on board upon our weather quarter, and attempted to board us, but being repulsed, he sheered off; upon which I backed our top-sails, in order to get square with him again, which, as soon as he observed, he then filled, put his helm a-weather, and laid us athwart hawse; his mizen shrouds took our jib boom, which hung him for some time, till it at last gave way, and we dropt alongside of each other, head and stern, when the fluke of our spare anchor hooking his quarter, we became so close fore and aft, that the muzzles of our guns touched each others sides. In this position we engaged from half past eight till half past ten; during which time, from the great quantity and variety of combustible matters which they threw in upon our decks, chains, and in short into every part of the ship, we were on fire no less than ten or twelve times in different parts of the ship, and it was with the greatest difficulty and exertion imaginable at times that we were able to get it extinguished. At the same time the largest of the two frigates kept sailing round us the whole action, and raking us fore and aft, by which means she killed or wounded almost every man on the quarter and main decks.

About half past nine, either from a hand grenade being thrown in at one of our lower deck ports, or from some other accident, a cartridge of powder was set on fire, the flames of which running from cartridge to cartridge all the way aft, blew up the whole of the people and officers that were quartered abaft the main-mast; from which unfortunate circumstance all those guns were rendered useless for the remainder of the action, and I

fear the greatest part of the people will lose their lives. At ten o'clock they called for quarters from the ship alongside, and said they had struck: hearing this, I called upon the captain to know if they had struck, or if he asked for quarters; but no answer being made, after repeating my words two or three times, I called for the boarders, and ordered them to board, which they did; but the moment they were on board her, they discovered a superior number lying under cover with pikes in their hands ready to receive them; on which our people retreated instantly into our own ship, and returned to their guns again till past ten, when the frigate coming across our stern, and pouring her broadside into us again, without our being able to bring a gun to bear on her, I found it vain, and in short, impracticable, from the situation we were in, to stand out any longer with the least prospect of success; I therefore struck, (our main mast at the same time went by the board.) The first lieutenant and myself were immediately escorted into the ship alongside, when we found her to be an American ship of war, called the Bon Homme Richard, of 40 guns and 375 men, commanded by Captain Paul Jones; [99] the other frigate which engaged us, to be the Alliance, of 40 guns, and 300 men; and the third frigate which engaged and took the Countess of Scarborough, after two hours action, to be the Pallas, a French frigate of 32 guns, and 275 men; the Vengeance, an armed brig of 12 guns, and 70 men; all in Congress service, and under the command of Paul Jones. They were fitted out and sailed from Port l'Orient the latter end of July, and came north about; they have on board 300 English prisoners, which they have taken in different vessels in their way round, since they left France, and have ransomed some others. On my going on board the Bon Homme

Richard, I found her in the greatest distress; her quarters and counter on the lower deck entirely drove in, and the whole of her lower deck guns dismounted; she was also on fire in two places, and six or seven feet water in her hold, which kept increasing upon them all night and the next day, till they were obliged to quit her, and she sunk, with a great number of her wounded people on board her. She had 306 men killed and wounded in the action; our loss in the Serapis was also very great. My officers and people in general behaved well, and I should be very remiss in my attention to their merit were I to omit recommending the remains of them to their lordships favour. I must at the same time beg leave to inform their lordships, that Captain Piercy, in [100] the Countess of Scarborough, was not in the least remiss in his duty, he having given me every assistance in his power, and as much as could be expected from such a ship, in engaging the attention of the Pallas, a frigate of 32 guns, during the whole action.

I am extremely sorry for the misfortune that has happened, that of losing his Majesty's ship I had the honour to command; but, at the same time, I flatter myself with the hopes, that their lordships will be convinced that she has not been given away; but, on the contrary, that every exertion has been used to defend her; and that two essential pieces of service to our country have arisen from it; the one in wholly oversetting the cruize, and intentions of this flying squadron; the other in rescuing the whole of a valuable convoy from falling into the hands of the enemy, which must have been the case had I acted any otherwise than I did. We have been driving about in the North Sea ever since the action, endeavouring to make to any port we possibly could, but have not been able to get into any place till to-day we arrived in the Texel.

Herewith I inclose you the moft exact lift of the killed and wounded I have as yet been able to procure, from my people being difperfed amongft the different fhips, and having been refufed permiffion to mufter them : there are, I find, many more, both killed and wounded, than appears on the inclofed lift, but their names as yet I find impoffible to afcertain ; as foon as I poffibly can, fhall give their lordfhips a full account of the whole.

I am, Sir,
Your moft obedient,
and moft humble fervant,
R. Pearson.

P. S. I am refufed permiffion to wait on Sir Jofeph Yorke, and even to go on fhore.

Abftract of the lift of killed and wounded.
Killed 49.—Wounded 68.

* * *

Copy of the Challenge fent by the Marquis de la Fayette, to the Earl of Carlifle, and the Earl's Anfwer.

To the Earl of Carlifle.

I DID not imagine, my Lord, that I ever fhould have had any transactions but with your generals, and expected not the honour of feeing them but at the head of the armies which they refpectively command. Your letter of the 26th of Auguft to the Congrefs of the United States, and the terms of infult refpecting my country, to which you have figned your name, is the fole caufe of my having any thing now to fettle with your Lordfhip. I deign not to refute the afperfion, but I defire to punifh it. It is from you, as chief of the commiffion, that I demand a reparation as public as hath been the offence, and which muft give the *lie* to the expreffion you have ufed. I fhould not have delayed this demand fo long, if your letter had reached me fooner ;

obliged to be abfent a few days, I hope to find your anfwer at my return. M. Gimot, a French officer, will fettle on my part the time and place of our meeting, to fuit your Lordfhip's conveniency. I doubt not but, for the honour of his countryman, General Clinton will attend you to the field.

As to me, my Lord, it is indifferent who attends you, provided that, to the glory of being a Frenchman, I join that of proving to a gentleman of your country, that no one dares to infult mine with impunity.

(Signed)
La Fayette.

To the Marquis De la Fayette.

SIR,
I HAVE received your letter [101] tranfmitted to me from M. Gimot, and I confefs I find it difficult to return a ferious anfwer to its contents. The only one that can be expected from me as the King's Commiffioner, and which you ought to have known, is, that I do, and ever fhall, confider myfelf folely refponfible to my Country and King, and not to any individual, for my public conduct and language. As for any opinion or expreffions contained in any publications iffued under the commiffion in which I have the honour to be named, unlefs they are retracted in public, you may be affured I fhall never, in any change of fituation, be difpofed to give an account of them, much lefs recal them in private.

The injury alluded to in the correfpondence of the King's Commiffioners to the Congrefs, I muft remind you, is not of a private nature ; and I conceive all national difputes will be beft decided by the meeting of Admiral Byron and Count d'Eftaign.

(Signed)
Carlisle.
New York, October 11, 1778.

* * *

His Majefty's moft gracious Speech to both Houfes of Parliament, November 25th, 1778.

My Lords, and Gentlemen,

I Have called you together in a conjuncture which demands your moft ferious attention.

In a time of profound peace, without pretence of provocation or colour of complaint, the court of France hath not forborne to difturb the public tranquillity, in violation of the faith of treaties, and the general rights of fovereigns, at firft by the clandeftine fupply of arms and other aids to my revolted fubjects in North America, afterwards by avowing openly their fupport, and entering into formal engagements with the leaders of the rebellion, and at length by committing open hoftilities and depredations on my faithful fubjects, and by an actual invafion of my dominions in America and the Weft Indies.

It is, I truft, unneceffary for me to affure you, that the fame care and concern for the happinefs of my people, which induced me to endeavour to prevent the calamities of war, will make me defirous to fee a reftoration of the bleffings of peace, whenever it can be effected with perfect honour, and with fecurity to the rights of this country.

In the mean time, I have not neglected to take the proper and neceffary meafures for difappointing the malignant defigns of our enemies, and, alfo for making general reprifals ; and although my efforts have not been attended with all the fuccefs, which the juftice of our caufe and the vigour of our exertions feemed to promife, yet the extenfive commerce of my fubjects has been protected in moft of its branches, and large reprifals have been made upon the injurious aggreffors, by the vigilance of my fleets, and by the active and enterprizing fpirit of my people.

The great armaments of other powers, however friendly and sincere their professions, however just and honourable their purposes, must necessarily engage our attention.

It would have afforded me very great satisfaction to have informed you, that the conciliatory measures, planned by the wisdom and temper of parliament, had taken the desired effect, and brought the troubles in North America to a happy conclusion.

In this situation of affairs, the national honour and security call so loudly upon us for the most active exertions, that I cannot doubt of your heartiest concurrence and support. From the vigour of your councils, and the conduct and intrepidity of my officers and forces by sea and land, I hope, under the blessing of God, to derive the means of vindicating and maintaining the honour of my crown, and the interests of my people, against all our enemies.

Gentlemen of the House of Commons,

I will order the proper estimates for the service of the ensuing year to be laid before you; and when you consider the importance of the objects for which we are contending, you will, I doubt not, grant me such supplies as you shall judge necessary for the public service, and adequate to the present emergency.

My Lords and Gentlemen,

I have, according to the powers vested in me for that purpose, called forth the militia, to assist in the interior defence of this country; and I have, with the greatest and truest satisfaction, been myself a witness of that public spirit, that steady ardour, and that love of their country, which animate and unite all ranks of my faithful subjects, and which cannot fail of making us safe at home, and respected abroad.

The humble Address of the Lords Spiritual and Temporal in Parliament assembled.

Most Gracious Sovereign,

WE, your Majesty's most dutiful and loyal subjects, the Lords Spiritual and Temporal, in Parliament assembled, beg leave to return your Majesty our humble thanks for your most gracious speech from the throne.

We have the strongest sense of the importance of those objects which render the present conjuncture worthy of the most serious attention.

The disturbance of the public tranquillity by the court of France, without pretence of provocation or colour of complaint, the clandestine assistance, the avowed support, the formal engagements which, at different periods, that court has not thought it inconsistent with its honour, to afford to your Majesty's revolted subjects in North America, and to conclude with the leaders of rebellion, excite in our breasts a just abhorrence of the violation of every public principle which such a conduct manifests, and a determination to concur in every measure, which may enable your Majesty to resent with effect, the hostilities committed on your faithful subjects, and the actual invasion of your Majesty's dominions in America and the West Indies.

We beg leave to express our grateful sense of the tender concern for the happiness of your people, which has uniformly induced your Majesty to endeavour to prevent the calamities of war, and will make your Majesty desirous to see the return of peace, whenever it can be effected with perfect honour and security to the rights of this country.

At the same time we return your Majesty our dutiful thanks for your great care in taking the proper and necessary measures for disappointing the malignant designs of our enemies, and also for making general reprisals, and for the protection which has been derived from the vigilance of your Majesty's fleets to our extensive commerce, in most of its branches, while that of the enemy has materially suffered by the active and enterprizing spirit of our fellow-subjects: And we hope, although your Majesty's efforts have not hitherto been attended with all the success, which the justice of our cause and the vigour of our exertions seemed to promise, that consequences more adequate to both may result from the animated execution of firm and active councils, which the time requires, and with which the spirited perseverance of the British nation has so often surmounted the greatest difficulties.

It is with concern we learn, that the conciliatory measures of parliament have not yet had the good effect with your Majesty's revolted subjects, which was due to the wisdom and temper with which they were planned.

In this situation of affairs, fully sensible that the national honour and security loudly calls for the most active exertions, we will strenuously concur in supporting your Majesty, that, under the blessing of God, means may be derived from the conduct and intrepidity of your Majesty's officers and forces, by sea and land, and the yet undaunted spirit of the nation, to vindicate and maintain the honour of the crown, and the interest of the people of Great Britain.

We return your Majesty our cordial acknowledgments for having called forth the militia, to assist in the interior defence of this country; and it is with joy and exultation we hear the gracious testimony your Majesty is pleased to bear to the public spirit, the steady ardour, and love of their country, which animate that national force, and unite all ranks of your Majesty's faithful subjects in giving signal proofs, to all the world, of a loyalty and zeal which must render us safe at home and respected abroad.

His Majesty's Answer.

My Lords,

I thank you for this loyal and dutiful address: The zeal you shew for my honour and support, and the firmness and vigour you manifest in the present conjuncture, cannot fail to produce the best effects; it must add confidence to my people, and encourage animated efforts to withstand, oppose, and subdue, every hostile attack upon the honour and interests of my kingdoms.

The humble Address of the House of Commons to the King.

Most Gracious Sovereign,

WE, your Majesty's most dutiful and loyal subjects, the Commons of Great Britain in parliament assembled, beg leave to return your Majesty the thanks of this House, for your most gracious speech from the throne.

We acknowledge with the utmost gratitude your Majesty's paternal regard for the happiness of your people, in your earnest and uniform endeavours to preserve the public tranquillity, and the good faith and uprightness of your Majesty's conduct to all foreign powers: And we assure your Majesty, that we have seen with concern and indignation, that tranquillity disturbed by the court of France, without the least pretence of provocation, or colour of complaint; and we have, with the warmest emotion of resentment, marked the progress of their malignant designs against this country, first by a clandestine aid and supply of arms to your Majesty's revolted subjects in North America; afterwards, in violation of the faith of treaties, and contrary to the rights

and common interest of every sovereign state in Europe possessed of colonies and dependencies, by entering into and avowing formal engagements with the leaders of the rebellion; and, at length, by committing open hostilities and depredations, and by actually invading part of your Majesty's dominions in America and the West Indies.

We cannot but feel concern and regret, that the measures taken by your Majesty, for disappointing these hostile and malignant designs, have not been attended with all the success which the justice of the cause, and the vigour of the exertions, seemed to promise; yet, we have at the same time seen with great satisfaction, the extensive commerce of your Majesty's subjects protected in most of its branches, and large reprisals made on the injurious aggressors, by the vigilance of your Majesty's fleets, and the active spirit of the nation.

It would have given your faithful Commons the truest happiness, to have received the communication from your Majesty, that the just and humane purposes of your Majesty and your Parliament, for quieting the minds of your revolted subjects, had taken the desired effect, and had brought the troubles in North America to a happy conclusion.

Your faithful Commons do most heartily concur with your Majesty, in the just approbation you have been pleased to express of the public spirit which has so conspicuously animated all ranks of your Majesty's faithful subjects, to stand forth, at this time of danger, in the service of the militia, who, by their discipline and steady perseverance in their duty, have enabled your Majesty to avail yourself of that constitutional force for the defence of this country.

Your Majesty may rely on the hearty and zealous concurrence and assistance of your faithful

Commons, in enabling your Majesty to make the most active and vigorous exertions by sea and land, for vindicating and establishing the national honour and security; and we beg leave to declare our stedfast resolution, and renew our solemn assurances to your Majesty, that this House, convinced of the importance of the objects for which we are contending, and impelled by every motive of duty and interest that can animate the hearts of Britons, will effectually assist your Majesty in the prosecution of the present just and necessary war; and that we will, to the utmost of our power, support your Majesty against all your enemies.

PROTESTS of the LORDS.

Die Lunæ, Decem. 7mo.

Moved,

THAT an humble address be presented to his Majesty, to express to his Majesty the displeasure of this House, at a certain manifesto and proclamation, dated the third day of October, 1778, and published in America under the hands and seals of the Earl of Carlisle, Sir Henry Clinton, Knt. of the Bath, and William Eden, Esq; commissioners for restoring peace to the colonies, and countersigned by Adam Ferguson, Esq; secretary to the commission; the said manifesto containing a declaration of the following tenour:

" If there be any persons, who, divested of mistaken resentments, and uninfluenced by selfish interests, really think it is for the benefit of the colonies, to separate themselves from Great Britain, and that so separated they will find a constitution more mild, more free, and better calculated for their prosperity, than that which they heretofore enjoyed, and which we are empowered and disposed to renew and improve; with such persons we will not dispute a position, which seems to be sufficiently contradicted by the experience they have had. But we think it right to leave them fully aware of the change which the maintaining such a position must make in the whole nature and future conduct of this war, more especially when to this position is added the pretended alliance with the court of France. The policy, as well as the benevolence of Great Britain, have thus far checked the extremes of war, when they tended to distress a people, still considered as our fellow-subjects, and to desolate a country, shortly to become again a source of mutual advantage: but when that country professes the unnatural design, not only of estranging herself from us, but of mortgaging herself, and her resources, to our enemies, the whole contest is changed, and the question is, how far Great Britain may, by every means in her power, destroy or render useless a connection contrived for her ruin, and for the aggrandisement of France. Under such circumstances, the laws of self-preservation must direct the conduct of Great Britain; and if the British colonies are to become an accession to France, will direct her to render that accession of as little avail as possible to her enemies."

To acquaint his Majesty with the sense of this House, that the said commissioners had no authority whatsoever, under the act of parliament, in virtue of which they were appointed by his Majesty, to make the said declaration, or to make any declaration to the same, or to the like purport, nor can this House be easily brought to believe that the said commissioners derived any such authority from his Majesty's instructions.

Humbly to beseech his Majesty, that so much of the said manifesto as contains the said declaration, be publicly disavowed by his Majesty, as containing matter inconsistent with the humanity and generous courage which, at all times,

have distinguished the British nation, subversive of the maxims which have been established among Christian and civilized communities, derogatory to the dignity of the crown of this realm, tending to debase the spirit, and subvert the discipline of his Majesty's armies, and to expose his Majesty's innocent subjects, in all parts of his dominions, to cruel and ruinous retaliations.

After a long debate, the question was put, and carried in the negative. Contents 37. Non-contents 71, including proxies.

Dissentient,

1st. Because the public law of nations, in affirmance of the dictates of nature, and the precepts of revealed religion, forbids us to resort to the extremes of war upon our own opinion of their expediency, or in any case to carry on war for the purpose of desolation. We know that the rights of war are odious, and instead of being extended upon loose constructions and speculations of danger, ought to be bound up and limited by all the restraints of the most rigorous construction. We are shocked to see the first law of nature, self-preservation, perverted and abused into a principle destructive of all other laws; and a rule laid down, by which our own safety is rendered incompatible with the prosperity of mankind. Those objects of war, which cannot be compassed by fair and honourable hostility, ought not to be compassed at all. An end that has no means, but such as are unlawful, is an unlawful end. The manifesto expressly founds the change it announces from a qualified and mitigated war, to a war of extremity and desolation, on a certainty that the provinces must be independent, and must become an accession to the strength of an enemy. In the midst of the calamities, by which our loss of empire has been preceded and accompanied; in the midst of our

apprehensions for the farther calamities which impend over us, it is a matter of fresh grief and accumulated shame, to see from a commission under the great seal of this kingdom, a declaration for desolating a vast continent, solely because we had not the wisdom to retain, or the power to subdue it.

2dly. Because the avowal of a deliberate purpose of violating the law of nations must give an alarm to every state in Europe. All commonwealths have a concern in that law, and are its natural avengers. At this time, surrounded by enemies, and destitute of all allies, it is not necessary to sharpen and embitter the hostility of declared foes, or to provoke the enmity of neutral states. We trust that by the natural strength of this kingdom, we are secured from a foreign conquest, but no nation is secured from the invasion and incursions of enemies. And it seems to us the height of frenzy, as well as wickedness, to expose this country to cruel depredations, and other outrages too shocking to mention (but which are all contained in the idea of the extremes of war and desolation) by establishing a false, shameful, and pernicious maxim, that where we have no interest to preserve, we are called upon by necessity to destroy. This kingdom has long enjoyed a profound internal peace, and has flourished above all others in the arts and enjoyments of that happy state. It has been the admiration of the world for its cultivation and its plenty: for the comforts of the poor, the splendor of the rich, and the content and prosperity of all. This situation of safety may be attributed to the greatness of our power. It is more becoming, and more true, that we ought to attribute that safety, and the power which procured it, to the ancient justice, honour, humanity, and generosity of this kingdom, which brought down the blessing of Providence on a people who made their prosperity a benefit to the world, and interested all nations in their fortune, whose example of mildness and benignity at once humanized others, and rendered itself inviolable. In departing from those solid principles, and vainly trusting to the fragility of human force, and to the efficacy of arms, rendered impotent by their perversion, we lay down principles, and furnish examples of the most atrocious barbarity. We are to dread that all our power, peace, and opulence should vanish like a dream, and that the cruelties which we think safe to exercise, because their immediate object is remote, be brought to the coasts, perhaps to the bosom of this kingdom.

3dly. Because, if the explanation given in debate, be expressive of the true sense of the article in the manifesto, such explanation ought to be made, and by as high authority as that under which the exceptionable article was originally published. The natural and obvious sense indicates, that the extremes of war had hitherto been checked; that his Majesty's generals had hitherto forborne (upon principles of benignity and policy) to desolate the country; but that the whole nature, and future conduct of the war must be changed, in order to render the American accession of as little avail to France as possible. This, in our apprehension, conveys a menace of carrying the war to extremes and to desolation; or it means nothing. And as some speeches in the House (however palliated) and as some acts of singular cruelty, and perfectly conformable to the apparent ideas in the manifesto, have lately been exercised, it becomes the more necessary, for the honour and safety of this nation, that this explanation should be made. As it is refused, we have only to clear ourselves to our consciences, to our country, to our neighbours, and to every individual who may

suffer in consequence of this atrocious menace, of all part in the guilt, or in the evils that may become its punishment. And we chuse to draw ourselves out, and to distinguish ourselves to posterity, as not being the first to renew, to approve, or to tolerate, the return of that ferocity and barbarism in war, which a beneficent religion, and enlightened manners, and true military honour, had for a long time banished from the Christian world.

Camden,	Rockingham,
Abingdon,	Tankerville,
Fitzwilliam,	Ponsonby,
Fortescue,	Derby,
Grafton,	Manchester,
Craven,	Portland,
J. St. Asaph,	Beaulieu,
Richmond,	Harcourt,
Bolton,	Effingham,
Radnor,	Wycombe,
Egremont,	Scarborough,
Abergavenny,	Cholmondeley,
Coventry,	Devonshire,
De Ferrars,	Foley,
Ferrers,	Spencer,
Stanhope,	

. . .

June 17th the following Message was sent by the King to both Houses of Parliament.

GEORGE R.

THE ambassador of the King of Spain having delivered a paper to Lord Viscount Weymouth, and signified that he has received orders from his court, immediately to withdraw from this country; his Majesty has judged it necessary to direct a copy of that paper to be laid before both Houses of parliament, as a matter of the highest importance to the crown and people; and his Majesty acquaints them at the same time that he has found himself obliged, in consequence of this hostile declaration, to recall his ambassador from Madrid.

His Majesty declares, in the most solemn manner, that his desire to preserve and to cultivate

peace and friendly intercourse with the court of Spain, has been uniform and sincere; and that his conduct towards that power has been guided by no other motives or principles than those of good faith, honour, and justice; and his Majesty sees with the greater surprise the pretences on which this declaration is grounded, as some of the grievances enumerated in that paper have never come to the knowledge of his Majesty, either by representation on the part of the Catholick King, or by intelligence from any other quarter; and in all those cases where applications have been received, the matter of complaint has been treated with the utmost attention, and put into a course of enquiry and redress.

His Majesty has the firmest confidence, that his parliament will, with that zeal and public spirit, which he has so often experienced, support his Majesty in his resolution, to exert all the power, and all the resources of the nation, to resist and repel any hostile attempts of the court of Spain; and that, by the blessing of God, on the rectitude of his intentions, and the equity of his cause, his Majesty will be able to withstand and defeat the unjust and dangerous enterprises of his enemies, against the honour of his crown, and the commerce, the rights, and the common interests of all his subjects.

The humble Address of the Right Honourable the Lords Spiritual and Temporal, in Parliament assembled.

" Most gracious Sovereign,

WE, your Majesty's most dutiful and loyal subjects, the Lords Spiritual and Temporal, in parliament assembled, beg leave to return your Majesty our humble thanks for your most gracious message, and communication of the paper delivered to Lord Viscount Weymouth by the ambassador of the King of Spain, which we cannot but consider as a matter of the highest importance to your Majesty's crown and people ; and for acquainting us, that in consequence of this hostile declaration, your Majesty had found yourself obliged to give orders to your ambassador to withdraw from that court.

We beg leave to assure your Majesty, that among the many proofs we have received of your Majesty's constant care and concern for the safety and happiness of your people, your Majesty's declaration of your sincere desire to preserve and to cultivate peace and friendly intercourse with the court of Spain, cannot fail to inspire us with the highest sentiments of gratitude and attachment ; and that, animated by your Majesty's example, we will, with unshaken fidelity and resolution, and with our lives and fortunes, stand by and support your Majesty against all the hostile designs and attempts of your enemies against the honour of your crown, and the rights and common interests of all your Majesty's subjects."

Upon the motion for the above address, an amendment was proposed by adding the following words :

" That in a moment so critical as that which now presents itself to the consideration of parliament, the most awful this country has ever experienced, it would be deceiving his Majesty, and the nation, if at the same time that we lament the fatal effect of those councils, which, by dividing and wasting the force of the empire, by civil wars, incited our natural enemies to take advantage of our weak and distracted condition ; were we not to represent to his Majesty, that the only means of resisting the powerful combination that now threatens this country,

will be by a total change of that system that has involved us in our present difficulties in America, in Ireland, and at home ; by such means, attended with prudent œconomy and a due exertion of the forces of a free and united people, we trust that his Majesty, with the assistance of Divine Providence, will be able to withstand all his enemies, and to restore Great Britain to its former respected and happy situation."

The question being put, that those words stand part of the address, it was carried in the negative. Contents 32. Non-contents 57.

Dissentient,

Because the amendment proposed, recommending to his Majesty a change of system in the principles and conduct of the war, appears to us to be warranted by every consideration which prudence and experience can suggest, and to be called for by the extreme magnitude of the dangers which surround us. The formal surrender of all right to tax North America, proposed by the very same Ministers, who at the expence of *fifty thousand* lives, and *thirty millions* of money, had for three years successively attempted to establish this claim, necessarily proves, either that those principles of legislation which they had thus asserted and thus abandoned were unjust in themselves, or that the whole power of Great Britain under their conduct was unable to effectuate a reasonable dependency of its own colonies. A dilemma dishonourable to them and ruinous to us ; and which, whatever side is taken, proves them wholly undeserving of the future confidence of a Sovereign and a people whose implicit trust in them (the largest which ever was reposed by any King or any nation) they have abused in a manner of which the records of parliament and the calamities of the nation are but too faithful witnesses.

If the whole force of Great Britain and Ireland, aided by the most lavish grants, assisted by thirty thousand Germans, unobstructed for a long time by any foreign power, has failed in three campaigns against the unprepared provinces of North America ; we should hold ourselves equally unworthy of all trust, if we were willing to confide in those abilities which have totally failed in the single contest with the colonies, for rescuing us from the united and fresh efforts of France and Spain, in addition to the successful resistance of North America.

In such a situation, a change of system appeared to us to be our indispensable duty to advise. We have considered such a change as the only means of procuring that union of councils, that voluntary effort of every individual in the empire which is necessary to be called forth in this hour of danger. We have readily concurred in a sincere offer of our lives and fortunes in support of his Majesty against the attacks of his enemies. Those valuable pledges, both of what is our own personally, and of what belongs to our fellow citizens (which ought to be, and are no less dear to us), give us a full right to claim and demand some better security for their being employed with judgment and effect, for the purposes for which we offer them, than can be derived from the opinion, in which all mankind concur, of the total want of capacity of his Majesty's Ministers.

We have avoided recommending any specific measures, in order not to embarrass government in a moment of such difficulty : but we have no scruple in declaring, that whatever may be the future conduct of Great Britain with respect to America, the collecting our force at a proper time to resist and to annoy our natural rivals and ancient enemies, seems to us beyond a doubt to be proper and expedient.

2dly. We think this advice the more seasonable, because we know the obstinate attachment of the Ministers to that unfortunate system, from the fatal predilection to which they have suffered the safety of the state to be endangered, and the naval strength of our powerful, jealous, and natural rivals to grow under their eyes, without the least attempt at interruption, until it had arrived at its present alarming magnitude, insidious combination, and hostile direction.

3dly. This plan appears to us strongly enforced, by the melancholy condition in which the misconduct and criminal neglects of the Ministers have placed us.— Our best resources wasted and consumed; the British empire rent asunder; a combination of the most powerful nations formed against us, with a naval superiority both in number of ships and alacrity of preparation; and this country now, for the first time, left entirely exposed, without the aid of a single ally. We should think ourselves partakers in the offences of the Ministers, and accessaries to our own destruction, if we neglected any possible means of securing a proper application of all the force we have left, from a blind confidence in persons, on whose account no nation in Europe will have any confidence in us. A manly disposition in parliament to apply the national wisdom to the cure of the national distempers, would restore our credit and reputation abroad, and induce foreign nations to court that alliance which they now fly from; would invigorate our exertions at home; and call forth the full operation of that British spirit which has so often, under the direction of wise counsel and a protecting Providence, proved superior to numbers; but which can have no existence but from a wellfounded opinion, that it is to be exerted under Ministers and commanders who possess the esteem and affection of the people.

We have in vain called for some plan on which to build better hopes, or for some reason for adhering to the present system.

We have in vain requested to know what have been the circumstances of the mediation, what are the grievances complained of by the Spanish court, in order that we may weigh the justice of that war in which we are going to engage, on which foundation alone we can rely for the protection of Providence.

We have urged the necessity of the great council of the nation continuing to sit, that his Majesty may not be deprived of the advice of parliament in such a difficult crisis.

All these representations have been met with a sullen and unsatisfactory silence; which gives us but too much reason to conclude, that Ministers mean to persevere in that unhappy course, which has been the cause of all our misfortunes.

After doing our utmost to awaken the House to a better sense of things, we take this method of clearing ourselves of the consequences which must result from the continuance of such measures.

Richmond,	Manchester,
Abergavenny,	Effingham,
Derby,	Ferrers,
De Ferrars,	King,
Harcourt,	Portland,
Rockingham,	Radnor,
Scarborough,	Coventry,
Ponsonby,	Hereford,
Devonshire,	Foley.
Egremont,	

...

A MANIFESTO *published at Paris, displaying the Motives and Conduct of his Most Christian Majesty towards* England.

TRANSLATION.

WHEN the Sovereign Disposer of events called his Majesty to the throne, France enjoyed the most profound peace.

The first concern of his Majesty was to signify to all the powers of Europe, his sincere desire, that the blessings of peace might be perpetuated to his kingdom. This gracious disposition of his Majesty was generally applauded; the King of England in particular testified his satisfaction, and gave his Majesty the most expressive assurances of sincere friendship. Such a reciprocity of sentiment justified his Majesty in believing, that the Court of London was at last disposed to adopt a mode of conduct more equitable and friendly, than that which had been adopted since the conclusion of the peace of 1763, and that a final stop would be put to those various acts of tyranny, which his subjects had in every quarter of the globe experienced on the part of England, from the æra above mentioned. His Majesty persuaded himself that he could still place the greater reliance on the King of England's protestations, as the primordial seed of the American revolution began to unfold itself in a manner highly alarming to the interest of Great Britain.

But, the Court of London, vainly imputing that to fear or feebleness, which was only the natural effect of his Majesty's pacific disposition, strictly adhered to her customary system, and continued every harrassing act of violence against the commerce and the navigation of his Majesty's subjects. His Majesty represented these outrages to the King of England with the utmost candour, and judging of his sentiments by his own, his Majesty had the greatest confidence, that the grievances would be no sooner made known to the King of England, than he would redress them. Nay, further, his Majesty being thoroughly acquainted with the embarrassment which the affairs of North America had occasioned the Court of London, charitably forbore to increase that embarrassment, by not infifting too haftily on thofe reparation of injuries, which the Englifh Minifters had never ceafed to promife, nor ever failed to evade.

Such was the pofition of affairs between the two Courts, when the meafures of the Court of London compelled the Englifh colonifts to have recourfe to arms to preferve their rights, their privileges, and their liberty. The whole world knows the æra when this brilliant event fhone forth ; the multiplied and unfuccefsful efforts made by the Americans to be reinftated in the bofom of their mother country ; the difdainful manner in which they were fpurned by England ; and finally, the act of independence, which was at length, and could not but have been the neceffary refult of this treatment.

The war in which the United States of North America found themfelves involved, with regard to England, neceffarily compelled them to explore the means of forming connections with the other powers of Europe, and of opening a direct commerce with them. His Majefty would have neglected the moft effential interefts of his kingdom, were he to have refufed the Americans admiffion into his ports, or that participation of commercial advantages which is enjoyed by every other nation.

This conduct, fo much the refult of juftice and of wifdom, was adopted by far the greater part of the commercial ftates of Europe ; yet it gave occafion to the Court of London, to prefer her reprefentations, and give vent to all the bitternefs of complaint. She imagined, no doubt, that fhe had but to employ her ufual ftyle of haughtinefs and ambition, to obtain of France an unbounded deference to her will. But, to the moft unreafonable propofitions, and the moft intemperate meafures, his Majefty oppofed nothing but the calmnefs of juftice, and the moderation of reafon, His Ma-

jefty gave the King of England plainly to underftand, that he neither was, nor did he pretend to be, a judge of the difputes with his colonies ; much lefs would it become his Majefty to avenge his quarrel : that in confequence his Majefty was under no obligation to treat the Americans as rebels ; to exclude them from his ports, and to prohibit them from all commercial intercourfe with his fubjects. Notwithftanding, his Majefty was very ready to fhackle, as much as depended on him, the exportation of arms and military ftores ; and gave the moft pofitive affurance, not only that he would not protect this fpecies of commerce, but that he would alfo allow England free permiffion to ftop thofe of his fubjects who fhould be detected in carrying on fuch illicit traffic, obferving only the faith of treaties, and the laws and the ufages of the fea. His Majefty went ftill further : he was fcrupuloufly exact in obferving every commercial ftipulation in the treaty of Utrecht, although it was daily violated by the Court of London, and England, at the very time, had refufed to ratify it in all its parts. As a confequence of the amicable part thus taken by his Majefty, he interdicted the American privateers from arming in his ports ; he would neither fuffer them to fell their prizes, nor to remain one moment longer in the ports of France, than was confiftent with the ftipulations of the above treaty. His Majefty ftrictly enjoined his fubjects not to purchafe fuch prizes ; and in cafe of difobedience they were threatened with confifcation. Thefe acts, on the part of his Majefty, had the defired effect. But all thefe acts, diftinguifhed as well by their condefcenfion, as by their ftrict adherence to the fpirit and letter of a treaty, which his Majefty, (had he been fo difpofed) might have confidered as nonexifting ; all thefe acts were far

from fatisfying the Court of London. That Court affected to confider his Majefty as refponfible for all tranfgreffions, although the King of England, notwithftanding a folemn act of parliament, could not himfelf prevent his own merchants from furnifhing the North American colonies with merchandize and even military ftores.

It is eafy to conceive how the refufal of yielding to the affuming demands, and arbitrary pretenfions of England, would mortify the felf-fufficiency of that Power, and revive its ancient animofity to France. She was the more irritated from her having begun to experience fome checks in America, which prognofticated to her the irrevocable feparation of her colonies ; and from forefeeing the inevitable calamities and loffes following fuch a feparation ; and obferving France profiting by that commerce, which fhe, with an inconfiderate hand, had thrown away, and adopting every means to render her flag refpectable.

Thefe are the combined caufes which have increafed the defpair of the Court of London, and have led her to cover the feas with her privateers, furnifhed with letters of marque conceived in the moft offenfive terms ; to violate without fcruple the faith of treaties, to harrafs, under the moft frivolous and abfurd pretences, the trade and navigation of his Majefty's fubjects ; to affume to herfelf a tyrannical empire of the fea ; to prefcribe unknown and inadmiffible laws and regulations ; to infult on many occafions his Majefty's flag ; in fhort, to infringe on his territories, as well in Europe as in America, in the moft marked and characteriftic ftyle of infult.

If his Majefty had been lefs attentive to the facred rights of humanity ; if he had been more prodigal of the blood of his fubjects : in fhort, if, inftead of following the benevolent impulfe of his nature, he had fought to avenge wounded honour, he could not have hesitated a moment to make use of reprisals, and to repel those insults which had been offered to his dignity, by the force of his arms. But his Majesty stifled even his just resentments. He was desirous that the measure of his goodness might overflow, because he still retained such an opinion of his enemies, as to expect, they would yield that to moderation and amicable adjustment on his part, which their own interests required of them.

It was these considerations which moved his Majesty to detail the whole of his complaints to the Court of London. This detail was accompanied with the most serious representations, his Majesty being desirous that the King of England should not be left in any uncertainty, as to his Majesty's actual determination to maintain his own dignity inviolate; to protect the rights and interests of his subjects; and to render his flag respectable. But the Court of London affected to observe an offensive silence on every grievance represented by his Majesty's Ambassador; and when it was determined to vouchsafe an answer, it was an easy matter to deny the best authenticated facts; to advance principles contrary to the law of nations, to positive treaties, to marine usage; and to encourage judgments without justice, and confiscations without mercy, not leaving the injured even the means of appeal. At the same time that the Court of London put the moderation and forbearance of the King to the severest trial, in the ports of England there were preparations making and armaments equipping, which could not have America for their object; the design was too determinate to be mistaken. His Majesty, therefore, found it indispensable to make such dispositions on his part, as might be sufficient to prevent the evil designs of his enemy, at the same time provide against depredations and insults similar to those committed in 1755.

In this state of things his Majesty, who had hitherto rejected the overtures of the United States of North America, (and that in contradiction to his most pressing interests) now perceived that he had not a moment to lose in concluding a treaty with them. Their independence had been declared and established; England herself had in some sort recognized that independence, by permitting the existence of acts which carried every implication of sovereignty. Had it been the intention of his Majesty to deceive England, and to adopt measures for the purpose of covering the deception, he might have drawn the veil of secrefy over his engagements with his now allies; but the principles of justice, which have ever directed his Majesty, and his sincere desire of preserving peace, were decisive inducements for him to pursue a conduct more generous and noble: his Majesty conceived it a duty which he owed to himself, to notify to the King of England the alliance he had formed with the United States. Nothing could be more simple or less offensive than the Rescript delivered by his Majesty's Ambassador to the British Minister. But the Council of St. James's were not of this opinion; and the King of England, after having first broken the peace, by recalling his Ambassador, announced to his Parliament the Declaration of his Majesty, as an *act* of hostility, as a formal and premeditated aggression. It would be insulting credulity to suppose it can be believed, that his Majesty's recognition of the independence of the Thirteen United States of America, should of itself have so irritated the King of England; that Prince, without doubt, is well acquainted with all those instances of the kind which not only the British annals, but his own reign, can furnish. His resentment is founded on another principle. The French treaty defeated and rendered useless the plan formed at London for the sudden and precarious coalition that was about to be formed with America, and it baffled those secret projects adopted by his Britannic Majesty for that purpose. The real cause of that extreme animosity which the King of England has manifested, and which he has communicated to his Parliament, was the not being able to regain America, and turn her arms against France.

A conduct thus extraordinary, taught his Majesty what he had to expect from the Court of London; and, even had there remained a possibility of doubt, the immense preparations carrying on in the different ports of England with redoubled vigour, would have cleared up the doubt. Measures so manifestly directed against France, had the effect of imposing a law on his Majesty; he put himself in a condition to repel force by force; it was with this view that he hastened the equipment of his armaments, and that he dispatched a squadron to America under the command of Compte d'Estaing.

It is notorious that the armaments of France were in a condition to act offensively, long before those of England were prepared. It was in his Majesty's power to have made a sudden and a most sensible impression on England. The King was avowedly engaged in the enterprize, and his plans were on the point of being carried into execution, when the bare whisper of peace stayed his hand, and suspended their execution. His Catholic Majesty imparted to the King the desire of the Court of London to avail herself of the mediation of Spain on the subject of conciliation. But his Catholic Majesty would not engage to act as mediator without a previous assurance of his good offices being unequivocally accepted, in a case where he interposed without being made acquainted with the principal objects, which were to serve as the basis of the negociation.

The King received the overture with a satisfaction proportioned to the wish he had uniformly expressed for the continuance of peace. Notwithstanding the King of Spain had professed it to be a matter of perfect indifference to him, whether his mediation was accepted or not ; and that notwithstanding the overtures he made, he left the King, his nephew, entirely at liberty to act as he thought proper ; yet his Majesty not only consented to the mediation, but he immediately countermanded the sailing of the Brest fleet, and he agreed to communicate his conditions of peace the moment that England should express, in positive terms, a desire of reconciliation, in which the United States of North America were to be comprehended, France by no means entertaining an idea of abandoning them : there could not surely be any thing more conformable to the ostensible wishes of the Court of London, than this proposal. His Catholic Majesty lost not a moment to discuss the business with the King of England and his Minister ; but it was quickly discovered by the Court of Madrid, that the English Ministers were not sincere in their overtures for peace. The British Minister talked expressly of his Majesty withdrawing the Rescript which had been delivered by his Ambassador on the 13th of March, 1778, as a preliminary and absolutely necessary step to reconciliation. Such an answer was injurious to Spain as well as to France ; and it developed the hostile intentions of England, in the clearest point of view. Both monarchs viewed each other with amazement ; and altho' his Majesty (always animated with the love of peace) left the Catholic

King to act as he thought most prudent with respect to continuing his mediation, yet he judged it expedient to command his Chargé des Affaires at London, to observe a profound silence on the subject.

The hope of peace continued, however, to flatter the disposition of his Majesty, until the fleets commanded by the Admirals Keppel and Byron sailed out of port. Then it was, that the veil of deception which had served to cover the real intentions of the Court of London, was rent asunder. It was no longer possible to place confidence in her insidious professions, nor could the aggressive design of England be any longer doubted. The face of things being thus changed, his Majesty found himself obliged to make an alteration in those measures he had previously adopted, for the security of his possessions, and to preserve the commerce of his subjects. The event will very soon demonstrate his Majesty's foresight to have been just. The world can witness in what manner his Majesty's frigate the *Belle Poule* was attacked by an English frigate, within view of the coast of France, nor is it less notorious that two other frigates, and a smaller vessel, were surprised and carried into the ports of England. The departure of the fleet under Compte d'Orvilliers became absolutely necessary, to frustrate the designs of the enemies of his Majesty's Crown, and to revenge the insults his flag had received. Providence disposed the triumph in favour of his Majesty's arms : Compte d'Orvilliers, after being attacked by the English, forced them to retreat with considerable damage.

Since that period hostilities have been continued without any declaration of war. The Court of London has not declared it, because she would be wanting in reasons to justify her conduct. Nor has she

being the aggressor, after three of his Majesty's vessels had been captured by the English fleet ; and she felt that she would have ample cause to blush, when the execution of those orders she had sent clandestinely to India should have opened the eyes of all Europe to the degree of reliance which can be placed in her pacific professions, and should have enabled every power in it to determine, to which of the two powers, France or England, the term of *perfidious* most properly applies, an epithet which the English Minister loses no opportunity of bestowing upon France.

As to the King, if he has deferred notifying to the world the multiplied injuries he has sustained from the Court of London ; if he has delayed demonstrating the absolute necessity of his having recourse to arms ; such a procrastination on the part of his Majesty, has been owing to a fond hope that the English Minister would at last recollect himself, and, that either justice, or the more critical situation into which he has plunged his country, would have prevailed on him to change his conduct.

This hope appeared to have been the better founded, as the English Minister was continually dispatching his emissaries to sound his Majesty's dispositions, at the very time the King of Spain was negociating with him for peace. His Majesty, so far from belying those sentiments which he had always expressed, listened with eagerness to the advice of the King his uncle ; and, to convince that Prince of his persevering sincerity, his Majesty entrusted him, without reserve, with those very moderate conditions, on which his Majesty would most gladly have laid down his arms.

The Catholic King communicated to the Court of London the assurances he had received from his Majesty, and he urged that Court to perfect the reconciliation which she had long so earnestly affected to desire. But the English Minister, although constantly feigning a desire of peace, never returned an ingenuous answer to the King of Spain, but was perpetually insulting his Catholic Majesty, with a tender of inadmissible propositions, quite foreign to the object of dispute.

It was now clear from the most indisputable evidence, that England did not wish for peace, and that she negociated for no other purpose but to gain time to make the necessary preparations for war. The King of Spain was perfectly sensible of this truth; nor was he less sensible how much his own dignity was concerned; yet his heart anticipated the calamities of war, and he forgot his own wrongs in his anxious wish for peace. He even suggested a new plan of a cessation of arms for a term of years. This plan was perfectly agreeable to his Majesty, on condition that the United States of America should be comprised in the proposal, and that during the truce, they should be treated as independent. To render it more easy for the King of England to subscribe to this essential stipulation, his Majesty consented that he should either treat immediately with Congress, or thro' the mediation of the King of Spain.

In consequence of these overtures, his Catholic Majesty dispatched his plan to the Court of London. Besides the time limited for the suspension of hostilities (during which the United States were to be considered as independent _de facto_) his Catholic Majesty took it on himself to propose, relative to America, that each party should have the possession of what they occupied at the time of signing the treaty of suspension, guaranteed to them. Such infinite pains did the King of Spain take to stop the effusion of human blood!

There is not a doubt but that these conditions must appear, to every well-judging person, such as would have been accepted; they were, however, formally rejected by the Court of London, nor has that Court shewn any disposition to peace, unless on the absurd condition that his Majesty should abandon the Americans, and leave them to themselves.

After this afflicting declaration, the continuation of the war is become inevitable; and therefore his Majesty has invited the Catholic King to join him in virtue of their reciprocal engagements, to avenge their respective injuries, and to put an end to that tyrannical empire which England has usurped and pretends to maintain upon the ocean.

This succinct exposure of the political views, and the progressive series of events which have occasioned the present rupture between the Courts of Versailles and London, will enable all Europe to draw a parallel between the conduct of his Majesty, and that of the King of England; to render justice to the purity and directness of intention, which during the whole of the dispute has characterised his Majesty; and finally, all Europe will be enabled by this publication to judge, which of the two Sovereigns is the real author of the war which afflicts their kingdoms; and which of the two potentates will be answerable at the tribunal of Heaven, for that train of calamities occasioned by the war!

Paris, 1779.
Published by authority.

The JUSTIFYING MEMORIAL * of the King of Great Britain, in Answer to the EXPOSITION, &c. of the Court of France.

THE ambition of a power, ever a foe to public tranquility, hath at length obliged the King of Great Britain to employ the strength which God and his people have confided to him, in a just and lawful war.—It is in vain that France endeavours to justify, or rather disguise, in the eyes of Europe, by her last Manifesto, the politics which seem to be dictated by pride and cunning, but which cannot be reconciled with the truth of facts, and the rights of nations. That equity, moderation, and love of peace, which have always regulated the steps of the King, now engage him to submit the conduct of himself and his enemies, to the judgment of a free and respectable tribunal, which will pronounce, without fear or flattery, the decree of Europe to the present age, and to posterity. This tribunal, composed of the understanding and disinterested men of all nations, will never regard professions; and it is from the actions of Princes, that they ought to judge of the motives of their conduct, and the sentiments of their hearts.

When the King ascended the throne, he enjoyed the success of his arms in the four quarters of the world! His moderation re-established public tranquility, at the same time that he supported with firmness the glory of his crown, and procured the most solid advantages to his people. Experience had taught him how bitter and afflicting even the fruits of victory are; and how much wars, whether happy or unsuccessful, exhaust a people without aggrandizing their Princes. His actions proved to the world, that he knew the value of peace, and it was at least to be presumed, that that reason which had enlightened him to discern the inevitable calamities of war, and the dangerous vanity of conquest, inspired him with the sincere and unshaken resolution of maintaining the public repose, of which

_____

* Although this Memorial has not been formally avowed, its authenticity is not doubted.

he was himself the author and guarantee. These principles were the foundations of that conduct which his Majesty held invariably for the fifteen years which followed the peace concluded at Paris in 1763; that happy æra of quiet and happiness, will be preserved for a long time, by the recollection, perhaps the regret, of the European nations. The instructions of the King to all his Ambassadors, were impressed with the marks of his character and maxims.

He recommended it to them, as the most important part of their duty, to listen, with the most scrupulous attention, to the complaints and representations of the powers, his neighbours or allies; to stifle in the beginning, all grounds of quarrel that might embitter or alienate the minds of men; to turn aside the scourge of war, by every expedient compatible with the dignity of the Sovereign of a respectable nation; and to inspire all people with a just confidence on the political system of a Court which detested war, without fearing it; which employed no other means than those of reason and sincerity, and which had no other object, but the general tranquillity. In the midst of this calm, the first sparks of discord were kindled in America. The intrigues of a few bold and criminal leaders, who abused the credulous simplicity of their countrymen, insensibly seduced the greatest part of the English Colonies to raise the standard of revolt against the Mother Country, to which they were indebted for their existence and their happiness. The Court of Versailles easily forgot the faith of treaties, the duties of allies, and the right of Sovereigns, to endeavour to profit of circumstances, which appeared favourable to its ambitious designs. It did not blush to debase its dignity, by the secret connections it formed with rebellious subjects; and after having exhausted all the shameful resources of perfidy and dissimulation, it dared to avow, in the face of Europe (full of indignation at its conduct) the solemn treaty which the Ministers of the Most Christian King had signed with the dark agents of the English Colonies, who founded their pretended independence on nothing but the daringness of their revolt. The offensive Declaration which the Marquis de Noailles was ordered to make to the Court of London, on the 13th of March, in the last year, authorized his Majesty to repel, by force of arms, the unheard-of insult that was offered to the honour of his crown; and the King remembered, on that important occasion, what he owed his subjects and himself. The same spirit of imposture and ambition continued to reign in the councils of France.—Spain, who has, more than once, repented having neglected her true interests, to follow blindly the destructive projects of the elder branch of the House of Bourbon, was engaged to change the part of mediator, for that of enemy of Great Britain. The calamities of war are multiplied, but the Court of Versailles hath, hitherto, nothing to boast of the success of its military operations; and Europe knows well how to rate those naval victories, which exist no where but in the Gazettes and Manifestos of pretended conquerors.

Since war and peace impose on nations duties entirely different, and even opposite, it is indispensably necessary to distinguish, in reasoning as well as in conduct, the two conditions: but in the last Manifesto, published by France, these two conditions are perpetually confounded: she pretends to justify her conduct in making the best, by turns, nay, almost at the same time, of those rights which an enemy only is permitted to claim, and of those maxims which regulate the obligations and procedure of national friendship. The finesse of the Court of Versailles, in blending incessantly two suppositions, which have no connection, is the natural consequence of a false and treacherous policy, which cannot bear the light of the day. The sentiments and conduct of the King have nothing to fear from the most severe scrutiny; but, on the contrary, invites it to distinguish clearly what his enemies have confounded with so much artifice. Justice alone can speak, without fear, the language of reason and truth.

The full justification of his Majesty, and the indelible condemnation of France, may be reduced to the proof of two simple, and almost self-evident principles.—First, That a profound, permanent, and, on the part of England, a sincere and true peace, subsisted between the two nations, when France formed connections with the revolted Colonies, secret at first, but afterwards public and avowed.—Second, That according to the best acknowledged maxims, of the rights of nations, and even according to the tenor of treaties actually subsisting between the two crowns, these connections might be regarded as an infraction of the peace; and the public avowal of these connections was equivalent to a declaration of war on the part of the Most Christian King.—This is, perhaps, the first time that a respectable nation had an occasion to prove two truths, so incontestible, the memory of which is already acknowledged by every disinterested and unprejudiced person.

"When Providence called the King to the throne, France enjoyed a most profound peace." These are the expressions of the last Manifesto of the Court of Versailles, which easily remembers the solemn assurances of a sincere friendship, and the most pacific disposition which it received from his Britannic Majesty, and which were often renewed by the intervention of Ambassadors to the two Courts, during four years, until the fatal and decifive moment of the Declaration of the Marquis de Noailles. The queftion then, is to prove, that during this happy time of general tranquillity, England concealed a fecret war under the appearance of peace; and that her unjuft and arbitrary procedure was carried to fuch a pitch, as to render lawful, on the part of France, the boldeft fteps, which are permiffable only in a declared enemy. To attain this object, griefs clearly articulated and folidly eftablifhed, fhould be produced before the tribunal of Europe. This great tribunal will require formal, and, perhaps, repeated proofs of the injury, of the complaint, of a refufal of competent fatisfaction, and of a proteftation of the injured party, that it held itfelf highly offended by fuch refufal, and that it fhould look upon itfelf hereafter as releafed from the duties of friendfhip, and the bonds of treaties, Thofe nations which refpect the fanctity of oaths, and the advantages of peace are the floweft to catch hold of opportunities which feem to difcharge them from a facred and folemn obligation; and it is but with trembling that they dare to renounce the friendfhip of powers, from which they have long borne injuftice and infult.

But the Court of Verfailles hath been either ignorant of thefe wife and falutary principles, or it hath defpifed them; and, inftead of fixing the foundations of a juft and legitimate war, it hath contented itfelf to fpread through every page of its Manifefto, general and vague complaints, expreffed with exaggerations in a metaphorical ftyle.—It goes above threefcore years back to accufe England of her want of care to ratify fome commercial regulations, fome articles of the treaty of Utrecht. It prefumes to reproach the King's minifters with ufing the language of haughtinefs and ambition, without condefcending to the duty of proving imputations as unlikely as they are odious. The free fuppofitions of the ambition, and infincerity of the court of London, are confeffedly healed up, as if they feared to be difcriminated; the pretended infults which the commerce, the flag, and the territories of France, have undergone, are infinuated in a very obfcure manner, and at laft there efcapes an avowal of the engagement which the moft Chriftian King had already made with Spain, " to avenge their refpective wrongs, and put bounds to the tyrannical empire which England had ufurped, and pretended to maintain over every fea."

It is difficult to encounter phantoms, or to anfwer clofely and precifely to the language of declamation. The juft confidence of the King, would doubtlefs defire to fubmit to the ftricteft examination, thofe vague complaints, thofe pretended wrongs, upon which the court of Verfailles has fo prudently avoided to explain itfelf, with that clearnefs and particularity which alone could fupport its reafons, and excufe its conduct. During a fifteen years peace, the interefts of two powerful, and perhaps jealous nations, which approached in fo many places in the old and new world, would inevibly furnifh fubjects of complaint and difcuffion, which a reciprocal moderation, would always know how to fettle, but which are but too eafily fharpened and impoifoned by the real hatred, or affected fufpicions, of a fecret and ambitious enemy: and the troubles of America were but too apt to multiply the hopes, the pretexts, and the unjuft pretenfions of France. Neverthelefs, fuch has been the ever uniform, and ever peaceable conduct of the King and his minifters, that it hath often filenced his enemies; and if it may be permitted to difcover the true fenfe of thefe indefinite and equivocal accufations, whofe ftudied obfcurity betrays the features to fhame and artifice—if it may be permitted of contefted objects which have no exiftence, it may be affirmed with the boldnefs of truth, that feveral of thefe pretended injuries, are announced for the firft time, in a declaration of war, without having been propofed to the court of London, at a time when they might have been confidered with the ferious and favourable attention of friendfhip. In refpect to thofe complaints which the ambaffadors of his moft Chriftian Majefty have communicated from time to time to the King's minifters, it would be eafy to give, or rather to repeat fatisfactory anfwers, which would demonftrate, to the eyes of France herfelf, the King's moderation, his love of juftice, and the fincerity of his difpofition to preferve the general tranquillity of Europe. Thofe complaints, which the court of Verfailles may difpenfe with recollecting, were very rarely founded in truth and reafon; and it was moft generally found that thofe perfons in Europe, America, or on the feas, from whom an ill-founded and fufpected intelligence was derived, had not been afraid to abufe the confidence of France, the better to ferve her fecret intentions.

If fome facts, which France enhanced as the ground of her complaints, were built on a lefs brittle foundation, the King's minifters cleared them without delay, by a moft clear and entire juftification of the motives and rights of their Sovereign, who might punifh a contraband trade on his coaft, without wounding the public repofe; and to whom the law of nations gave a lawful right to feize all veffels which carried arms or warlike ftores to his enemies, or rebellious fubjects. The courts of juftice were always open to individuals of all nations, and thofe muft be very ignorant of the Britifh conftitution, who fuppofe that the royal authority was capable to shut out the means of an appeal. In the vast and extended theatre of the operations of a naval war, the most active vigilance, and the most steady authority, are unable to discover or suppress every disorder; but every time that the court of Versailles was able to establish the truth of any real injuries that its subjects had sustained, without the knowledge or approbation of the King, his Majesty gave the most speedy and effectual orders to stop an abuse, which injured his own dignity, as well as the interest of his neighbours, who had been involved in the calamities of war. The object and importance of this war will suffice to shew all Europe, on what principles the political proceedings of England ought to be regulated. Is it likely, that whilst England employed her forces to bring the revolted colonies of America back to their duty, she should have chosen that moment to irritate the most respectable powers of Europe, by the injustice and violence of her conduct? Equity hath always governed the sentiments and conduct of the King; but on this important occasion, his very prudence is a warrant for his sincerity and moderation.

But to establish clearly the pacific system that subsists between the two nations, nothing more is wanting than to appeal to the very testimony of the court of Versailles. At the very time in which it doth not blush to place all these pretended infractions of the public peace, which would have engaged a Prince less sparing of his subjects blood, to make, without hesitation, reprisals, and to repel insult by force of arms, the minister of the most Christian King spoke the language of confidence and friendship. Instead of denouncing any design of vengeance, with that haughty tone, which at least spares injustice from the reproaches of perfidy and dissimulation, the court of Versailles concealed the most treacherous conduct under the smoothest professions. But those very professions serve, at present, to belie its declaration, and to call to mind those sentiments which ought to have regulated its conduct. If the court of Versailles is unwilling to be accused of a dissimulation unworthy of its grandeur, it will be forced to acknowledge, that till the moment that it dictated to the Marquis de Noailles, that declaration, which has been received as the signal of war, it did not know any grounds of complaint, sufficiently real or important, to authorize a violation of the obligations of peace, and the faith of treaties, to which it had sworn in the face of heaven and earth; and to disengage from that amity, to which, to the last moment, it had repeated the most solemn and lively assurances.

When an adversary is incapable of justifying his violence in the public opinion, or even in his own eyes, by the injuries which he pretends to have received, he has recourse to the chimerical danger to which his patience might have been exposed; and in the place of facts, of which he is totally unprovided, he endeavours to substitute a vain picture, which hath existence only in his own imagination, perhaps his own heart. The minister of the most Christian King, who seems to have felt the weakness of the means they were forced to employ, yet made impotent efforts to support those means, by the most odious and unaccountable suspicions. " The court of London made preparations in its ports, and armaments, which could not have America for their object. Their intention was, consequently, too well determined for the King to mistake them, and from thence it became their duty to make such dispositions, as were capable of preventing the evil designs of his enemy, &c.— In this state of affairs, the King found he had not a moment to lose." This is the language of France; now we will shew that of truth.

During the disputes which had arisen between Great Britain and her colonies, the court of Versailles applied itself, with the most lively and determined ardor, to the augmentation of her marine. The King did not " pretend to reign as a tyrant of the seas," but knows that, at all times, maritime forces have constituted the glory and safety of his dominions; and that they have often protected the liberty of Europe, against the ambitious state, which hath so long laboured to subdue it.

A sense of his dignity, and a just knowledge of his duty and his interest, engaged his Majesty to watch, with an attentive eye, over the proceedings of France, whose dangerous policy, without a motive, and without an enemy, precipitated the building and arming of ships in all her ports; and which employed a considerable part of her revenues in the expence of those military preparations, the necessity or object of which it was impossible to declare. In that conjuncture the King could not avoid following the counsel of his prudence, and the example of his neighbours. The successive augmentation of their marine served as a rule for his; and without wounding the respect that he owed to friendly powers, his Majesty declared publicly to his parliament, that England should be in a respectable state of defence. The naval force which he had so carefully strengthened, was designed only to maintain the general tranquility of Europe; and whilst the dictates of his own conscience disposed the King to give credit to the professions of the court of Versailles, he prepared to have nothing to fear from the perfidious designs of its ambition. France now dares to suppose that the King, " instead of confining himself within the limits of a lawful defence, gave himself up to a hope of conquest, and that the reconciliation of Great Britain with her colonies, announced, on her part, a fixed project of re-allying them with her crown, to arm them against France." Since, then, that the court of Versailles cannot excuse its procedure, but in favour of a supposition destitute of truth and likelihood, the King hath a right to call upon that court, in the face of Europe, to produce a proof of an assertion as odious as bold; and to develope those public operations, or secret intrigues, that can authorise the suspicions of France, that Great Britain, after a long and painful dispute, offered peace to her subjects, with no other design than to undertake a fresh war against a respectable power, with which she had preserved all the appearances of friendship.

After having faithfully exposed the frivolous motives, and pretended wrongs of France, we can reflect, with a certainty, justified by reason and by fact, on the first proposition, so simple and so important—That a peace subsisted between the two nations, and that France was bound by every obligation of friendship and treaty with the King, who had never failed in his legitimate engagement.

The first article of the treaty signed at Paris, the 10th of February 1763, between his Britannic, most Christian, Catholic, and most Faithful Majesties, confirms, in the most precise and solemn manner, the obligations which natural justice imposes on all nations which are in mutual friendship; but these obligations are specified and stipulated in that treaty by expressions as lively as they are just.—— After having comprised, in a general form, all the states and subjects of the high contracting powers, they declared their resolution, " not only never to permit any hostilities by land or sea, but even to procure recipro-

cally, on every occasion, all that can contribute to their mutual glory, interest, and advantages, without giving any succour or protection, directly or indirectly, to those who would do any prejudice to one or other of the high contracting parties." Such was the sacred engagement which France contracted with Great Britain; and it cannot be disguised, that such a promise ought to bind with greater strength and energy against the domestic rebels, than the foreign enemies of the two crowns. The revolt of the Americans put the fidelity of the court of Versailles to a proof; and notwithstanding the frequent examples that Europe hath already seen of its little regard to the faith of treaties, its conduct in these circumstances astonished and enraged every nation which was not blindly devoted to the interests, and even to the caprices of France. If France had intended to fulfil her duty, it was impossible for her to have mistaken it; the spirit as well as the letter of the treaty of Paris, imposed on her an obligation to bar their ports against the American vessels; to forbid her subjects to have any commerce with that rebellious people; and not to afford either succour or protection to the domestic enemies of a crown with which she had sworn a sincere and inviolable friendship. But experience had too well enlightened the King in regard to the political system of his antient adversaries, to suffer him to hope that they would conform exactly to those just and reasonable principles, which would have assured a general tranquility.

As soon as the revolted colonies had compleated their criminal enterprize, by an open declaration of their pretended independence, they thought to form secret connections with the powers who were the least favourable to the interests of their mother country; and to draw from Europe those military

aids, without which it would have been impossible for them to have supported the war they had undertaken. Their agents endeavoured to penetrate into, and settle in the different states of Europe; but it was only in France that they found an asylum, hopes, and assistance. It was beneath the King's dignity to enquire after the æra, or the nature of the correspondence that they had with the ministers of the court of Versailles, and of which the public effects were soon visible in the general liberty, or rather unbounded licence of an illegitimate commerce. It is well known that the vigilance of the laws cannot always prevent artful illicit traders, who appear under a thousand different forms, and whose avidity for gain makes them brave every danger, and elude every precaution: but the conduct of the French merchants, who furnished America not only with useful and necessary merchandize, but even with saltpetre, gun-powder, ammunition, arms, and artillery, loudly declared that they were assured not only of impunity, but even of the protection and favour of the ministers of the court of Versailles.

An enterprize so vain and so difficult, as that of hiding from the eyes of Great Britain, and of all Europe, the proceedings of a commercial company, associated for furnishing the Americans with whatever could nourish and maintain the fire of a revolt, was not attempted. The informed public named the chief of the enterprize, whose house was established at Paris; his correspondents at Dunkirk, Nantz, and Bourdeaux, were equally known. The immense magazines which they formed, and which they replenished every day, were laden in ships that they built or bought, and they scarcely dissembled their objects, or the place of their destination. These vessels commonly took false clearances for the French islands in America, but the commodities which composed their cargo were sufficient, before the time of their sailing, to discover the fraud and the artifice. These suspicions were quickly confirmed by the course they held; and at the end of a few weeks, it was not surprising to hear they had fallen into the hands of the King's officers cruizing in the American seas, who took them even within sight of the coasts of the revolted colonies. This vigilance was but too well justified by the conduct of those who had the luck or cunning to escape it; since they approached America only to deliver the rebels the arms and ammunition which they had taken on board for their service The only marks of these facts, which could be considered only as manifest breaches of the faith of treaties, multiplied continually, and the diligence of the King's ambassador to communicate his complaints and proofs to the court of Versailles, did not leave him the shameful and humiliating resource of appearing ignorant of what was carried on, and daily repeated in the very heart of the country. He pointed out the names, number, and quality of the ships, that the commercial agents of America had fitted out in the ports of France, to carry to the rebel arms, warlike stores, and even French officers, who had engaged in the service of the revolted colonies. The dates, places and persons were always specified, with a precision that afforded the ministers of his most Christian Majesty the greatest facility of being assured of these reports, and of stopping in time the progress of their illicit armaments. Amongst a croud of examples, which accuse the court of Versailles of want of attention to fulfil the conditions of peace, or rather its constant attention to nourish fear and discord, it is impossible to enumerate them all; it is very difficult to select the most striking objects. Nine large ships, fitted out and freighted by the Sieur de Beaumarchais, and his partners, in the month of January, 1777, are not confounded with the Amphitrite, who carried about the same time a great quantity of ammunition, and thirty French officers, who passed with impunity into the service of the rebels. Every month, almost every day, furnished new subjects of complaint; and a short memorial that Viscount Stormont, the King's ambassador, communicated to the Count de Vergennes, in the month of November, in same year, will give a just, but very imperfect idea of the wrongs which Britain had so often sustained — " There is a sixty gun ship at Rochfort, and an East India ship, pierced for sixty guns, at L'Orient. These two ships are destined for the service of the rebels. They are laden with different merchandize, and freighted by Messrs. Chaumont, Holken, and Sebatier. ——The ship L'Heureux, sailed from Marseilles the 26th of September, under another name: she goes streight to New Hampshire, though it is pretended she is bound to the French islands. They have been permitted to take on board three thousand musquets, and 25000 pounds of sulphur, a merchandise as necessary to the Americans as useless to the islands. This ship is commanded by M. Lundi, a French officer of distinction, formerly lieutenant to M. de Bouganville.—L'Hippopotame, belonging to the Sieur Beaumarchais, will have on board four thousand musquets, and many warlike stores for the use of the rebels. —There are about fifty French ships laden with ammunition for the use of the rebels, preparing to sail to North America. They will go from Nantz, L'Orient, St. Malo, Havre, Bourdeaux, Bayonne, and other different ports.—These are the names of some of the persons principally interested; M. Chaumont, M. Menton, and his partners, &c. &c.

In this kingdom, where the will of the Prince meets with no obstacle, succours, so considerable, so public, so long supported; in fine, so necessary to maintain the war in America, shew clearly enough the most secret intentions of the most Christian King's ministers. But they still carried further their forgetfulness, or contempt of the most solemn engagements, and it was not without their permission that an underhand and dangerous war issued from the ports of France, under the deceitful mask of peace, and the pretended flag of the American colonies. The favourable reception that their agents found with the ministers of the court of Versailles, quickly encouraged them to form and execute the audacious project of establishing a place of arms in the country, which had served them for an asylum. They had brought with them, or knew how to fabricate letters of marque, in the name of the American Congress, who had the impudence to usurp all the rights of sovereignty. The partnership, whose interested views easily embarked in all their designs, fitted out ships that they had either built or purchased. They armed them to cruize in the European seas, nay, even on the coasts of Great Britain. To save appearances, the captains of these corsairs hoisted the pretended American flag, but their crews were always composed of a great number of Frenchmen, who entered, with impunity, under the very eyes of their governors and the officers of the maritime provinces. A numerous swarm of these corsairs, animated by a spirit of rapine, sailed from the ports of France, and after cruising in the British seas, re-entered, or took shelter in the same ports. Thither they brought their prizes, and under a rude, weak artifice, which they sometimes vouchsafed to employ, the prizes were fold publicly and commodioufly enough, in the fight of the royal officers, always difpofed to protect the commerce of thofe traders, who violated the laws, to conform to the French miniftry. The corfairs enriched themfelves with the fpoils of the King's fubjects; and after having profited of full liberty to repair their loffes, provide for their wants, and procure all warlike ftores, gunpowder, cannon, and rigging, which might ferve for new enterprizes, they departed freely from the fame ports, to make new cruizes. The hiftory of the Reprifal privateer may be cited from a crowd of examples, to fet the unjuft, but fcarcely artificial, conduct of the court of Verfailles in a clear light. This fhip, which had brought Mr. Franklin, agent of the revolted colonies, to Europe, was received, with two prizes fhe had taken in her paffage. She remained in the port of Nantz, as long as fhe thought convenient; put twice to fea to plunder the King's fubjects, and came quietly into L'Orient with the new prizes fhe had made.

Notwithftanding the ftrongeft reprefentation of the King's ambaffador; notwithftanding the moft folemn affurances of the French minifters, the captain of that corfair was permitted to ftay at L'Orient as long as it was neceffary to refit his fhip, to provide fixty barrels of gunpowder, and to receive as many French feamen, as chofe to engage with him. Furnifhed with thefe reinforcements, the Reprifal failed a third time from the ports of their new allies, and prefently formed a little fquadron of pirates, by the concerted junction of the Lexington and the Dolphin, two privateers; the firft of which had already carried more than one prize into the river of Bourdeaux; and the other, fitted out at Nantz, and manned entirely by Frenchmen, had nothing American, but the commander. Thefe three fhips, which fo publicly enjoyed the protection of the court of Verfailles, in a fhort time afterwards took fifteen Britifh fhips, the greateft part of which were brought into the ports of France, and fecretly fold.—Such facts, which it would be eafy to multiply, ftand inftead of reafonings and reproaches. The faith of treaties cannot avoid being called upon, on this occafion; and it is not neceffary to fhew that an allied, or even a neutral power, can ever permit war, without violating peace. The principle of the law of nations, will, doubtlefs, refufe to the ambaffador of the moft refpectable power that privilege of arming privateers, which the court of Verfailles granted under-hand, in the very bofom of France, to the agents of rebels. In the French iflands, the public tranquility was violated in a manner yet more audacious; and notwithftanding the change of the governor, the ports of Martinico ferved always as a fhelter to corfairs who cruized under American colours, but manned by Frenchmen. Mr. Bangham, agent for the rebels, who enjoyed the favour and confidence of two fucceffive governors of Martinico, directed the arming of thofe privateers, and the public fale of their prizes. Two merchant fhips, the Lancafhire Hero, and the Irifh Gambier, which were taken by the Revenge, affures, that out of her crew, confifting of 125 men, there were but two Americans; and that the owner, who at the fame time was proprietor of eleven other privateers, acknowledged himfelf to be an inhabitant of Martinico, where he was looked upon as the favourite, and the fecret agent of the governor himfelf.

In the midft of all thefe acts of hoftility, (which it is impoffible to call by any other name) the court of Verfailles continued always to fpeak the language of peace and amity, and its minifters exhaufted all the fources of artifice and diffimulation, to lull the juft complaints of Great Britain, to deceive her juft fufpicions, and to ftop the effects of her juft refentment. From the firft æra of the American troubles, to the moment of a declaration of war by the Marquis de Noailles, the minifters of the moft Chriftian King never ceafed to renew the ftrongeft and moft expreffive proteftations of their pacific difpofitions; and however the common conduct of the court of Verfailles was adapted to infpire a juft doubt, yet his Majefty's juft heart furnifhed him with powerful motives to believe that France had at length adopted a fyftem of moderation and peace, which would perpetuate the folid and reciprocal happinefs of the two nations. The minifters of the court of Verfailles endeavoured to excufe the arrival and refidence of the rebel agent, by the ftrongeft affurances, that he found only a fimple afylum in France, without either diftinction or encouragement.

The freedom of commerce, and the thirft of gain, ferve fometimes as pretexts to cover the illegitimate defigns of the fubjects of France; and at a time when they vainly alledged the impotence of the laws to prevent abufes, which neighbouring ftates know fo well how to fupprefs, they condemned, with every appearance of fincerity, the tranfportation of arms and ammunition, which fhe permitted with impunity, for the fervice of the rebels. To the firft reprefentation of the King's ambaffador upon the fubject of the privateers, which were fitted out in the ports of France under American colours, the minifters of his moft Chriftian Majefty replied, with expreffions of furprife and indignation, and by a pofitive declaration, that attempts, fo contrary to the faith of treaties, and the public tranquility, fhould never be fuffered. The train of events, of which a fmall number hath been fhewn, foon manifefted the inconftancy, or rather the falfehood of the court of Verfailles; and the King's ambaffador was ordered to reprefent to the French minifters the ferious, but inevitable confequences of their policy. He fulfilled his commiffion with all the confideration due to a refpectable power, the prefervation of whofe friendfhip was defired, but with a friendfhip worthy of a Sovereign, and a nation little accuftomed to do, or to fuffer injuftice. The court of Verfailles was called upon to explain its conduct, and its intention, without delay or evafion; and the King propofed to it the alternative of peace or war.—France chofe peace in order to wound her enemy more furely and fecretly, without having any thing to dread from her juftice. She feverely condemned thofe fuccours and thofe armaments, that the principles of public equity would not permit her to juftify. She declared to the King's ambaffador, that fhe was refolved to banifh the American corfairs immediately from all the ports of France, never to return again; and that fhe would take, in future, the moft rigorous precautions to prevent the fale of prizes taken from the fubjects of Great Britain. The orders given to that effect aftonifhed the partizans of the rebels, and feemed to check the progrefs of the evil; but fubjects of complaint fprung up again daily; and the manner in which thefe orders were firft eluded, then violated, and at length entirely forgotten, by the merchants, privateers, may, even by the royal officers, were not excufable by the proteftations of friendfhip, with which the court of Verfailles accompanied thofe infractions of peace, until the very moment that the treaty of alliance, which it had figned with the agents of the revolted American colonies, was announced by the French ambaffador in London.

If a foreign enemy, acknowledged by all the powers of Europe, had conquered the King's American dominions, and if France had confirmed by a folemn treaty, an act of violence, that had plundered in the midft of a profound peace, a refpectable neighbour, of whom fhe ftiled herfelf the friend and ally, all Europe would ftand up againft the injuftice of a conduct which fhamefully violated all that is moft facred among men. The firft difcovery, the uninterrupted poffeffion of two hundred years, and the confent of all nations, were fufficient to afcertain the rights of Great Britain over the lands of North America, and its fovereignty over the people that had fettled there with the permiffion, and under the government of the King's predeceffors. If even this people had dared to fhake off the yoke of authority, or rather of the laws, if they had ufurped the provinces and prerogatives of their Sovereign; and if they had fought the alliance of ftrangers to fupport their pretended independence; thofe ftrangers could not accept their alliance, ratify their ufurpations, and acknowledge their independence, without fuppofing that *revolt* hath more extenfive rights than thofe of *war*; and without granting to rebellious fubjects a lawful title to conqueft, which they could not have made but in contempt of both law and juftice. The fecret enemies of peace, of Great Britain, and perhaps of France herfelf, had neverthelefs the criminal dexterity to perfuade his moft Chriftian Majefty, that he could, without violating the faith of treaties, publicly declare, that he received the revolted fubjects of a King, his neighbour and ally, into the number of his allies. The profeffions of friendfhip which accompanied that declaration, which the Marquis de Noailles was ordered to make to the court of London, only ferve to aggravate the injury by the infult; and it was referved for France to boaft of pacific difpofitions in the very inftant that her ambition inftigated her to execute and avow an act of perfidy, unexampled in the hiftory of nations. Yet, fuch as the court of Verfailles dares allow itfelf to ufe. "Yet it would be wrong to believe that the acknowledgment that the King has made of the independence of the Thirteen United States of North America, is what has enraged the King of England: that Prince is, without doubt, not ignorant of all the examples of the like kind that the Britifh annals, even of his own reign, do furnifh."—But thefe pretended examples do not exift.—The King never acknowledged the independence of a people, who had fhaken off the yoke of their lawful Prince; it is doubtlefs very afflicting that the minifters of his moft Chriftian Majefty, have cheated the piety of their Sovereign, to cover, with fo refpectable a name, affertions without any foundation or likelihood, which are contradicted by the memory of all Europe.

At the commencement of the difputes which arofe between Great Britain and her colonies, the court of Verfailles declared, that it did not pretend to be a judge of the quarrel, and its ignorance of the principles of the Britifh conftitution, as well as the privileges and obligations of the colonies, ought to have engaged it to perfift always in fuch a wife and modeft declaration, that would have fpared it the fhame of tranfcribing the manifeftos of the American Congrefs, and of pronouncing now, "That the proceedings of the court of London had compelled its antient colonies to have recourfe to arms for the maintenance of their rights, their privileges, and their liberty." Thefe vain pretenfions have been already refuted in the moft convincing manner, and the rights of Great Britain over that revolted people, her benefactions, and her long patience, have been already proved by reafon and by facts. It is fufficient here to remark, that France cannot take any advantage of the injustice with right, and in fact is the object of dispute. And the King's dignity will not permit him to accept of those proposals, which, from the very beginning of a negociation, grants all that can satisfy the ambition of the rebellious Americans, whilst they exact from his Majesty, without any stipulation in his favour, that he should desist, for a long or indefinite term, from his most lawful pretensions. It is true, the court of Versailles vouchsafed to consent, that the court of London might treat with the Congress, either directly, or by the intervention of the King of Spain. His Majesty, certainly, will not so much demean himself as to complain of that insolence, which seems to grant him, as a favour, the permission of treating directly with his rebellious subjects. But if the Americans themselves are not blinded by passion and prejudice, they will see clearly in the conduct of France, that their new allies will soon become their tyrants, and that that pretended independence, purchased at the price of so much misery and blood, will be soon subjected to the despotic will of a foreign court.

If France could verify that eagerness which she attributes to the court of London, to seek the mediation of Spain, a like eagerness would serve to prove the King's just confidence in the goodness of his cause, and his esteem for a generous nation which hath always despised fraud and perfidy. But the court of London was obliged to own, that the mediation was offered to it by the ministers of the Catholic King, and it claims no other merit, than that of having shown, on all occasions, a lively and sincere inclination to deliver its subjects, nay even its enemies from the scourge of war. The conduct of the court of Madrid, during that negociation, soon shewed the King that a mediator,

who forgets his own dearest interests, to give himself up to the ambition, or resentment of a foreign power, must be incapable of proposing a safe or honourable accommodation. Experience confirmed these suspicions; the unjust and inadmissible scheme just mentioned, was the sole fruit of this mediation. In the same instant that the ministers of the Catholic King offered, with the most disinterested professions, his capital, his good offices, his guaranty, to facilitate the conclusion of the treaty, they suffered to appear from the bottom of obscurity new subjects for discussing, particularly relative to Spain, but upon which they always refused to explain themselves. His Majesty's refusal to accede to the *ultimatum* of the court of Madrid, was accompanied with all convenient precautions and respect: and unless that court will arrogate to itself a right to dictate conditions of peace to an independent and respectable neighbour, there was nothing passed in that conjuncture, which ought to have altered the harmony of the two crowns. But the offensive measures of Spain, which she could never cloath with the fairest appearances of equity, will soon show that she had already taken her resolutions; had been instigated by the French ministry, who had only retarded the declaration of the court of Madrid, from the hope of giving a mortal blow to the honour and interest of Great Britain under the mask of friendship.

Such are the unjust and ambitious enemies, who have despised the faith of treaties, to violate the public tranquility, and against whom the King now defends the rights of his crown and people. The event is yet in the hands of the Almighty; but his Majesty, who relies upon the divine protection, with a firm but humble assurance, is persuaded that the wishes of Europe will support the justice of his cause, and applaud

the success of his arms, which have no other object than to establish the repose of nations on a solid and unshaken basis.

But France herself appears to feel the weakness, the danger, and the indecency of these pretensions; when, in the declaration of the Marquis de Noailles, as well as in her last manifesto, she quits her hold on the right of independence: she is content to maintain, that the revolted colonies enjoy *in fact*, that independence they have bestowed on themselves; that even England herself, in some sort acknowledges it, in suffering acts of sovereignty to subsist; and that therefore France, without any violence of peace, might conclude a treaty of friendship and commerce with the United States of North America. —Let us see in what manner Great Britain had acknowledged that independence, equally imaginary in right, as in fact. Two years had not yet elapsed from the day in which the rebels declared their criminal resolution of shaking off the yoke of their mother country; and that time had been occupied by the events of a bloody and obstinate war. Success had hung in suspence, but the King's army, which possessed the most important maritime towns, continued always to menace the interior provinces. The English flag reigned over all the American seas, and the re-establishment of a lawful dependence, was fixed as the indispensable condition of the peace which Great Britain offered to her revolted subjects, whose rights, privileges, nay even whose prejudices she respected. The court of Versailles, which announced, with so much openness and simplicity, the treaty signed with the pretended States of America, which it found in an independent situation, had alone contributed, by its clandestine succours, to foment the fire of revolt; and it was the dread of peace that engaged France to employ the rumour of that alliance, as the most effectual means to inflame the minds of the people, who began already to open their eyes upon the unfortunate consequences of the revolt, the tyranny of their new leaders, and the paternal disposition of their lawful Sovereign.

Under such circumstances it is impossible, without insulting in too gross a manner both truth and reason, to deny that the declaration of the Marquis of Noailles, of the 13th of March, 1778, ought to be received as a true declaration of war on the part of the most Christian King; and the assurances "that he had taken eventual measures, in concert with the United States of America, to maintain a freedom of commerce," which had so often excited the just complaints of Great Britain, authorised the King, from that moment, to rank France in the number of his enemies. The court of Versailles could not avoid acknowledging that the King of England, after having "recalled his ambassador, denounced to his parliament the measures taken by his Majesty, as an act of hostility, as a formal and premeditated aggression." Such was, indeed, the declaration which both honour and justice demanded from the King, and which he communicated, without delay, to the ministers of the different courts of Europe, to justify before-hand the effects of a lawful resentment. From thence it is useless to seek for orders, that were sent to the East-Indies, to remark the precise day when the fleets of England or France quitted their respective ports, or to scrutinize into the circumstances of the action with the *Belle Poule*, and the taking two other frigates, which were actually carried off in fight of the very coast of France. Hence the reproach made to the King of having so long suspended a formal declaration of war, vanishes of itself. These declarations are only the measures that nations have reciprocally agreed on, to avoid

treachery and surprise; but the ceremonies which announce the terrible exchange of peace for war, the heralds declarations and manifestos are not always necessary, are not always alike. The declaration of the Marquis de Noailles was a signal of the public infraction of the peace. The King directly proclaimed to all nations that he accepted the war which France offered; the last proceedings of his Majesty were rather the offspring of his prudence, than his justice, and Europe may now judge if the court of London wanted means to "justify a declaration of war, and if she did not dare to accuse France, publicly, of being the aggressor."

• • •

Resolutions of their High Mightinesses, *relating to Paul Jones's Squadron and Prizes, delivered to the* English *Ambassador at the* Hague, *on the 25th of October,* 1779.

THAT their High Mightinesses being informed that three frigates had lately arrived at the Texel, namely, two French and one called an American, commanded by Paul Jones, bringing with them two prizes taken by them in the open sea, and called the Serapis and the Countess of Scarborough, described in the ambassador's memorial. That their High Mightinesses having for a century past strictly observed the following maxim, and notified the same by placards, viz. that they will in no respect whatever pretend to judge of the legality or illegality of the actions of those who have on the open sea taken any vessels which do not belong to this country, and bring them into any of the ports of this Republic; that they only open their ports to them to give them shelter from storms or other disasters; and that they oblige them to put to sea again with their prizes without unloading or disposing of their cargoes, but letting them remain exactly as

when they arrived. That their High Mightinesses will not examine whether the prizes taken by the three frigates in question belong to the French or the Americans, or whether they are legal or illegal prizes, but leave all that to be determined by the proper judges, and will oblige them to put to sea, that they may be liable to be retaken, and by that means brought before the proper judge, particularly as his Excellency the Ambassador must own he would have no less a right to reclaim the above-mentioned ships, if they had been private property, than as they have been King's ships; therefore their High Mightinesses are not authorised to pass judgment either upon these prizes, or the person of Paul Jones; that as to what regards acts of humanity, their High Mightinesses have already made appear how ready they are to shew them towards the wounded on board of the vessels, and that they have given orders accordingly. That an extract of the present resolution shall be given to Sir Joseph Yorke by the Agent Vander Burch de Spierinxhock.

At the same time it was resolved, that word should be sent to the Admiralty of Amsterdam that their High Mightinesses approve their proceedings, and adhere to their placard of the 3d of November, 1756, by which it is forbid to meddle with any prizes, or to open their cargoes, so as by that means to free them from being retaken, &c. That this is strictly to be observed with regard to the Serapis and Countess of Scarborough. Their High Mightinesses authorise the said Admiralty to order matters so that these five ships do put to sea as soon as possible, and that they take care they are not furnished with any warlike or naval stores but what are absolutely necessary to carry them safe to the first foreign port they can come at, in order that all suspicion of their being fitted out here may drop.

Memorial prefented by Sir Joseph Yorke, *his Majefty's Ambaffador at the* Hague, *to their* High Mightineffes, *requefting the delivering up the Serapis and Countefs of Scarborough, taken by* Paul Jones.

High and Mighty Lords,

IN thanking your High Mightineffes for the orders which your humanity dictated relative to the wounded men on board the two King's fhips the Serapis and Countefs of Scarborough, I cannot but comply with the ftrict orders of his Majefty, by renewing in the ftrongeft and moft prefling manner his requeft that thefe fhips and their crews may be ftopped, and delivered up, which the pirate Paul Jones of Scotland, who is a rebel fubject, and a criminal of the State, has taken.

The fentiments of equity and juftice which your High Mightineffes poffefs, leave me no room to doubt but that, upon mature deliberation upon all the circumftances of this affair, you will acknowledge the reafonablenefs of this requeft, founded both on the moft folemn treaties now fubfifting between Great Britain and the United Provinces, and the rights and cuftoms of nations in friendfhip and alliance.

The ftipulation of the treaty of Breda of the 10th of July 1667, (Old Stile) confirmed particularly in that of 1716, and all the later ones, are too clear and inconteftible in that refpect for the full force of them not to be felt.

The King would think he derogated from his own dignity, as well as that of your High Mightineffes, was he to enter into the particulars of a cafe fo notorious as that in queftion, or to fet before the eyes of the ancient friends and allies of his crown analogous examples of other Princes and States ; but will only remark, that all the placards even of your High Mightineffes require that all the captains of foreign armed veffels fhall, upon their arrival, prefent their letters of marque or commiffion, and authorifes, according to the cuftom of Admiralties, to treat all thofe as pirates whofe letters are found to be illegal for want of being granted by a fovereign power.

The quality of Paul Jones, and all the circumftances of the affair, are too notorious for your High Mightineffes to be ignorant of them. The eyes of all Europe are fixed upon your refolution ; your High Mightineffes know too well the value of good faith not to give an example of it in this effential rencontre. The fmalleft deviation from fo facred a rule, by weakening the friendfhip of neighbours, may produce ferious confequences.

The King has always gloried in cultivating the friendfhip of your High Mightineffes ; his Majefty conftantly perfifts in the fame fentiments ; but the Englifh nation does not think that it any ways has deferved its fellow-citizens to be imprifoned in the ports of the Republic by a man of no character, a fubject of the fame country, and who enjoys that liberty which they are deprived of.

It is for thefe and many other ftrong reafons, which cannot efcape the wifdom and penetration of your High Mightineffes, that the underwritten hopes to receive a fpeedy and favourable anfwer conformable to the juft expectations of the King his mafter and the Britifh nation.

(Signed)
JOSEPH YORKE."
Done at the Hague, Oct. 29, 1779.

The anfwer which their High Mightineffes caufed to be given to the above memorial was in brief ; " That they will in no refpect take upon them to judge of the legality or illegality or thofe who have on the open fea taken any veffels which do not belong to their country ; that they only open their ports to give them fhelter from ftorms or other difafters ; and that they oblige them to go to fea again with their prizes without fuffering them to unload or difpofe of any part jof their cargoes, that they may be liable to be re-taken in the fame ftate they were taken ; but do not think themfelves authorized to pafs judgment upon thofe prizes, or the perfon of Paul Jones, &c."

• • •

Treaty of Friendfhip and Commerce between the French King *and the* United States *of* North America.

THE Moft Chriftian King, and the Thirteen United States of North America, viz. New - Hampfhire, Maffachufets-Bay, Rhode-Ifland, Connecticut, New-York, New-Jerfey, Pennfylvania, the Counties of Newcaftle, Kent, and Suffex on the Delaware, Maryland, Virginia, North and South Carolina, and Georgia, defirous of eftablifhing, in an equitable and permanent manner, the rules which ought to be obferved, relative to the correfpondence and commerce, which the two parties wifh to eftablifh between their refpective ftates, dominions and fubjects ; his moft Chriftian Majefty and the faid United States have thought proper, and as moft conducive to this end, to found their arrangements on the bafis of the moft perfect equality and reciprocal advantage, taking care to avoid difagreeable preferences, the fources of altercation, embarraffment, and difcontent ; to leave to each party the liberty, refpecting commerce and navigation, of making fuch interior regulations as fhall fuit themfelves ; to found their commercial advantages as well on reciprocal intereft, as on the laws of mutual agreement ; and thus to preferve to both parties the liberty of dividing, each according to his will, the fame advantages with other nations. In this idea, and to accomplish these views, his said Majesty, having nominated and appointed, as his plenipotentiary, M. Conrad Alexander Gerard, royal Syndic of the city of Strasburgh, Secretary of his Majesty's Council of State ; and the United States having, on their part, invested with full powers Meff. Benjamin Franklin, Deputy of the General Congress of the State of Pennsylvania, and president of the assembly of the said state ; Silas Deane, formerly Deputy of the State of Connecticut ; and Arthur Lee, Counsellor at Law : the said plenipotentiaries respectively, after having exchanged their credentials, and upon mature deliberation, have concluded and agreed to the following articles :

Art. I. A firm, inviolable, and universal peace, and a true and sincere friendship, shall subsist between the most Christian King, his heirs and successors, and the United States of America, as well as between his most Christian Majesty's subjects, and those of the said states ; as also between the people, islands, cities, and places, under the government of his Christian Majesty, and the said United States ; and between the people and inhabitants of all classes, without any exception to persons or places. The conditions mentioned in the present treaty, shall be perpetual and permanent between the most Christian King, his heirs and successors, and the said United States.

Art. II. The most Christian King and the United States mutually engage, not to grant any particular favour to other nations, respecting commerce and navigation, which shall not be immediately made known to the other party ; and such nation shall enjoy that favour gratuitously, if the concession is such, or in granting the same compensation, if the concession is conditional.

Art. III. The subjects of the most Christian King shall not pay, in the ports, harbours, roads, countries, islands, cities, and places of the United States, any greater duties or imposts, of what nature soever they may be, or by whatever name they may be called, than such as the most favoured nation shall pay ; and they shall enjoy all the rights, liberties, privileges, immunities, and exemptions, in point of trade, navigation, and commerce, whether in passing from one port of the said States to another, or in going thither, or in returning from or going to any part of the world whatever, as the said nations may or shall enjoy.

Art. IV. The subjects, people, and inhabitants of the said United States, or each of them, shall not pay, in the ports, harbours, roads, islands, cities, and places, within the dominions of his most Christian Majesty in Europe, any greater duties or imposts, of what nature soever they may be, or by whatever name they may be called, than the most favourite nation are or shall be bound to pay ; and they shall enjoy all the rights, liberties, privileges, immunities, and exemptions, in point of trade, navigation, and commerce, whether in passing from one port to another of the said dominions of the most Christian King in Europe, or in going thither, or in returning from or going to any part of the world whatever, as the said nations shall or may enjoy.

Art. V. In the above exemption is particularly comprized the imposition of one hundred pence per ton, established in France upon foreign ships ; excepting when the ships of the United States shall load with French merchandizes in one port of France for another in the same kingdom ; in which case the said ships of the said United States shall discharge the usual rights, so long as the most favourite nations shall be obliged to do

the same ; nevertheless, the said United States, or any of them, shall be at liberty to establish, whenever they shall think proper, a right equivalent to that in question, in the same case as it is established in the ports of his most Christian Majesty.

Art. VI. The most Christian King shall use all the means in his power to protect and defend all the ships and effects belonging to the subjects, people, and inhabitants of the said United States, and of each of them, which shall be in his ports, harbours, or roads, or in the seas near his territories, countries, isles, cities, and places ; and shall use every effort to recover and restore to the lawful proprietors, their agents or order, all the ships and effects which shall be taken within his jurisdiction ; and his most Christian Majesty's ships of war, or other convoys, failing under his authority, shall take, on every occasion, under their protection the ships belonging to the subjects, people, and inhabitants of the said United States, or any of them, which shall keep the same course and make the same route, and defend the said ships, so long as they shall keep the same course and make the same route, against every attack, force, or violence, in the same manner as they are bound to defend and protect the ships belonging to the subjects of his most Christian Majesty.

Art. VII. In like manner the said United States, and their ships of war sailing under their authority, shall protect and defend, agreeable to the contents of the preceding article, all the ships an effects belonging to the most Christian King, and shall use all their efforts to recover and restore the said ships and effects, which shall be taken within the extent of the jurisdiction of the said United States, or either of them.

Art. VIII. The most Christian King will employ his endeavours and mediation with the King or

Emperor of Morocco or Fez, with the Regencies of Algier, Tunis, and Tripoli, or any of them, as well as with every other Prince, State, or Powers, of the Barbary coaſt in Africa, and with the ſubjects of the ſaid King, Emperor, States and Powers, and each of them, to ſecure, as fully and effectually as poſſible, to the advantage, convenience, and ſecurity, of the ſaid United States, and each of them, as alſo their ſubjects, people, and inhabitants, their ſhips and effects, againſt violence, inſult, attack, or depredation, on the part of the ſaid Barbary Princes and States, or their ſubjects.

Art. IX. The ſubjects, inhabitants, merchants, commanders of ſhips, maſters, and ſeamen, of the ſtates, provinces, and dominions of the two parties, ſhall reciprocally refrain from and avoid fiſhing in any of the places poſſeſſed, or which ſhall be poſſeſſed, by the other party. The ſubjects of his moſt Chriſtian Majeſty ſhall not fiſh in the harbours, bays, creeks, roads, and places, which the ſaid United States poſſeſs, or ſhall hereafter poſſeſs ; and in the ſame manner the ſubjects, people, and inhabitants, of the ſaid United States, ſhall not fiſh in the harbours, bays, creeks, roads, coaſts, and places, which his moſt Chriſtian Majeſty actually poſſeſſes, or ſhall hereafter poſſeſs ; and if any ſhip or veſſel ſhall be ſurprized fiſhing, in violation of the preſent treaty, the ſame ſhip or veſſel, and its cargo, ſhall, upon clear proof, be confiſcated. Provided, the excluſion ſtipulated in the preſent article ſhall ſtand good only ſo long as the King and the United States ſhall not ſuffer it to be enjoyed by any other nation whatever.

Art. X. The United States, their citizens and inhabitants, ſhall never diſturb the ſubjects of the moſt Chriſtian King in the enjoyment and exerciſe of the right of fiſhing on the banks of Newfoundland,

any more than in the unlimited and excluſive enjoyment they poſſeſs on that part of the coaſts of that iſland, as ſpecified in the treaty of Utrecht, nor in the rights relative to all and each of the iſles which belong to his moſt Chriſtian Majeſty ; the whole conformable to the true ſenſe of the treaties of Utrecht and Paris.

Art. XI. The ſubjects and inhabitants of the ſaid United States, or any of them, ſhall not be conſidered as foreigners in France, and conſequently ſhall be exempt from the right of eſcheatage, or any other ſuch like right, under any name whatever ; they may, by will, donation, or otherwiſe, diſpoſe of their goods, moveables, and fixtures, in favour of whom they ſhall pleaſe ; and their heirs, ſubjects of the ſaid United States, reſident in France or elſewhere, ſhall ſucceed to them, ab inteſtat, without being obliged to obtain letters of naturalization, and without being expoſed to any moleſtation or hindrance, under pretence of any rights or prerogatives of provinces, cities, or private perſons ; and the ſaid heirs, either by particular title, or ab inteſtat, ſhall be exempt from all right of detraction, or other right of that kind, provided that ſuch or the like local rights are not eſtabliſhed by the ſaid United States, or any of them. The ſubjects of the moſt Chriſtian King ſhall enjoy, on their ſide, in all the dominions of the ſaid States, an entire and perfect reciprocation, with reſpect to the ſtipulations included in the preſent article.

But it is at the ſame time agreed, that the contents of this article ſhall not affect the laws made in France againſt emigrations, or ſuch as may be made hereafter, ſuch being left in their full force and vigour ; the United States, on their ſide, or any of them, ſhall be free to make ſuch laws, reſpecting that matter, as they ſhall judge proper.

Art. XII. The merchant ſhips of both parties, which ſhall be bound

to any port, belonging to a power then an enemy of the other ally, and of which the voyage, or nature of its cargo, ſhall give juſt ſuſpicions, ſhall be bound to produce, either on the high ſeas, or in ports and harbours, not only their paſſports, but alſo certificates, which ſhall expreſsly ſtate, that their cargoes are not of prohibited and contraband wares.

Art. XIII. If the contents of the ſaid certificates lead to a diſcovery, that the ſhip carries prohibited and contraband merchandizes, conſigned to an enemy's port, it ſhall not be permitted to open the hatches of the ſaid ſhip, nor any caſe, cheſt, trunk, bale, caſk, or other caſes, contained therein, or to diſplace or remove the leaſt part of the merchandize, whether the ſhip belongs to the moſt Chriſtian King, or to the inhabitants of the United States, until the cargo has been landed in the preſence of the officers of the Admiralty, and an inventory taken of them ; but they ſhall not be permitted to ſell, exchange, or diſpoſe of the ſhips or cargoes, in any manner whatever, until a fair and legal enquiry has been made, the contraband declared, and the Court of Admiralty ſhall have pronounced the confiſcation by judgment, nevertheleſs without prejudice of ſhips or cargoes, which, by virtue of this treaty, ſhould be conſidered as free. It ſhall not be permitted to retain merchandizes, under pretence that they were found among contraband goods, and ſtill leſs to confiſcate them as legal prizes. In caſe where a part only, and not the whole of the cargo, conſiſts of contraband articles, and that the commander of the ſhip conſents to deliver up to the captor what ſhall be diſcovered, then the captain, who ſhall have made the prize, after having received thoſe articles, ſhall immediately releaſe the ſhip, and in no manner prevent it from purſuing its voyage ; but in caſe that the whole of the contraband articles cannot be all taken into the veſſel of the captor, then the captain of such veſſel shall remain maſter of his prize, notwithstanding the offer to give up the contraband goods, and conduct the ship into the nearest port, conformably to what is above ſpecified.

Art. XIV. It is agreed, on the contrary, that every thing that shall be found embarked by the reſpective ſubjects, in ships belonging to the enemies of the other party, or their ſubjects, shall be confiſcated, without regard to their being prohibited or not, in the same manner as if they belonged to the enemy; excepting, however, such effects and merchandizes as had been put on board the said ships before the declaration of war, or even after the said declaration, if they were ignorant of it at the time of loading; ſo that the merchandizes of the ſubjects of both parties, whether they be found among contraband goods or otherwiſe, which, as hath been juſt mentioned, shall have been put on board a ship, belonging to the enemy, before the war, or even after the said declaration, when unknown to them, shall not be, in any manner, ſubject to confiſcation, but shall be faithfully and truly reſtored, without delay, to the owners who shall claim them; it muſt, however, be underſtood, that it will not be permitted to carry contraband goods into an enemy's ports. The two contracting parties agree, that after the expiration of two months, from the declaration of war, their reſpective ſubjects, from what part of the world ſoever they shall come, shall not be permitted to plead ignorance of the queſtion in this article.

Art. XV. And in order the more effectually to ſecure the ſubjects of the two contracting parties from receiving any prejudice from the ships of war or privateers of either party, orders shall be given to all captains of ships of his moſt Chriſtian Majeſty and the said United States, and to all their ſubjects, to avoid offering insult or doing damage to the ships of either party; and whoever shall act contrary to theſe orders, shall be punished for it, and shall bebound and obliged perſonally, in their own effects, to repair all such damages and loſſes.

Art. XVI. All ships and merchandizes of what nature ſoever, which shall be taken out of the hands of pirates on the high ſeas, shall be conducted into ſome port of the two States, and shall be committed to the care of the officers of the said port, in order that they may be entirely reſtored to the right owner, as ſoon as such property shall be fully and clearly proved.

Art. XVII. The ships of war of his moſt Chriſtian Majeſty, and thoſe of the United States, as well as privateers fitted out by their ſubjects, shall be at full liberty to conduct where they pleaſe such prizes as they shall take from the enemy, without being amenable to the juriſdiction of their admirals or admiralty, or any other power; and the said veſſels, or prizes, entering into the harbours or ports of his moſt Chriſtian Majeſty, or thoſe of the said United States, shall be neither ſtopped nor ſeized, nor shall the officers of such places enquire into the validity of the said prizes, but shall be permitted to depart freely and at full liberty, to such places as directed in the commiſſions, which the captains of the said ships shall be obliged to produce. And, on the contrary, they shall neither give ſecurity nor retreat, in their ports or harbours, to any prizes made on the ſubjects of his Majeſty, or the said United States; and, if such shall be found to enter their ports, through ſtorms or dangers of the sea, they shall be obliged to depart as ſoon as poſſible.

Art. XVIII. Should a ship, belonging to either of the two States, or their ſubjects, run aground, be wrecked, or ſuffer other damages, upon the coaſts belonging to one of the two parties, they shall give all friendly aid and aſſiſtance to such as are in danger, and take every method to ſecure their ſafe paſſage, and return to their own country.

Art. XIX. When the ſubjects and inhabitants of one of the two parties with their ships, whether men of war, privateers, or merchantmen, shall be forced by foul weather, by the purſuits of pirates or enemies, or by any other urgent neceſſity, to ſeek shelter and refuge, to run into and enter ſome river, bay, road, or port, belonging to one of the two parties, they shall be received and treated with humanity and kindneſs, and shall enjoy all the friendship, protection, and aſſiſtance, and shall be permitted to procure refreshments, proviſions, and every thing neceſſary for their ſubſiſtence, for the repairing of their ships, and to enable them to purſue their voyage, paying a reaſonable price for every thing; and they shall not be detained in any manner, nor prevented quitting the said ports or roads, but shall be permitted to depart at pleaſure, without any obſtacle or impediment.

Art. XX. In order the better to promote the commerce of the two parties, it is agreed, that in caſe a war should commence between the two said nations, ſix months shall be allowed, after the declaration of war, to the merchants living in their towns and cities, to collect and tranſport their merchandize; and, if any part of them shall be ſtolen or damaged, during the time above preſcribed, by either of the two parties, their people or ſubjects shall be obliged to make full and perfect ſatiſfaction for the ſame.

Art. XXI. No ſubject of the moſt Chriſtian King shall take a commiſſion, or letters of marque, to arm any ship or veſſel, to act as a privateer againſt the said United

States, or any one of them, or against their subjects, people or inhabitants, or against their property, or that of the inhabitants of any of them, from any Prince whatever, with whom the said United States shall be at war. In like manner, no citizen, subject, or inhabitant of the said United States, or any of them, shall demand or accept any commission, or letters of marque, to arm any ships or vessels, to act against the subjects of his most Christian Majesty, or any of them, or their property, from any Prince or State whatever, with whom his said Majesty may be at war ; and if any of the two nations shall take such commissions, or letters of marque, they shall be punished as pirates.

Art. XXII. No foreign privateer, not belonging to some subject of his most Christian majesty, or to a citizen of the said United States, which shall have a commission from any Prince or power at war with one of the two nations, shall be permitted to arm their ships in the ports of one of the two parties, nor to sell their prizes, nor to clear their ships, in any manner whatever, of their merchandizes, or any part of their cargo ; they shall not even be permitted to purchase any other provisions, than such as are necessary to carry them to the nearest port of the Prince or State, of whom they hold their commission.

Art. XXIII. All and each of the subjects of the most Christian King, as well as the citizens, people, and inhabitants, of the said United States, shall be permitted to work their vessels, in full liberty and security, without any exception being made thereto, on account of the proprietors of Merchandizes on board the said vessels coming from any port whatever, and destined for some place belonging to a power actually an enemy, or which may become such, of his Most Christian Majesty or the United

States. It shall be equally permitted to the subjects and inhabitants above-mentioned, to navigate their ships and merchandizes, and to frequent, with the same liberty and security, the places, ports, and havens, of the powers, enemies to the two contracting parties, or one of them, without opposition or molestation, and to trade with them, not only directly from ports of the enemy to any neutral port, but also from one port of the enemy to another of the same, whether under the jurisdiction of one or more ; and it is stipulated by the present treaty, that all free vessels shall equally enjoy the liberty of trade, and that every thing shall be judged free which is found on board the ships belonging to the subjects of one of the contracting parties, even though the cargo, or part of it, should belong to the enemies of one of them ; excepting always, however, all contraband goods. It is equally agreed, that the same liberty shall extend to persons on board such free ships, even though they shall be enemies to one of the two contracting parties, and shall not be taken from the said ships, unless in arms, and actually in the enemy's service.

Art. XXIV. This free navigation and commerce is extended to all sorts of merchandizes, excepting only such as shall be deemed contraband or prohibited, and under such denomination are comprehended arms, cannons, bombs, with their fusees and other apurtenances, bullets, powder, matches, piques, swords, lances, darts, halberds, mortars, petards, grenades, saltpetre, fusils, balls, bucklers, casques, cuirasses, coats of mail, and other arms of that kind, proper for the defence of soldiers ; gun-locks, shoulder-belts, horses and their trappings, and all other instruments of war whatever. The following merchandizes are not to be considered as contraband or prohibited, viz. all sorts of cloths,

and other woollen stuffs, linen, silk, cotton, or other such matters ; all sorts of clothes, with the materials of which they are usually made ; gold and silver either in specie or otherwise, pewter, iron, latten, copper, brass, coals, and even wheat and barley, and all other sorts of grain and roots ; tobacco and all sorts of spices, salted and dried provisions, dried fish, cheese and butter, beer, oil, wine, sugar, and all kinds, of salt, and, in general, all kinds of provision necessary for the nourishment of man, and for the support of life ; also all sorts of cotton, hemp, linen, pitch, tar, cords, cables, sails, canvas for sails, anchors, parts of anchors, masts, planks, timber and wood of all kinds, and all other things proper for the building and repairing of ships, and other matters whatsoever, which are not in the form of warlike instruments for sea or land, shall not be reputed contraband, much less such as are already prepared for other uses. All the articles above-mentioned are to be comprised among the free articles of merchandize, as well as all the other merchandizes and effects, which are not comprised and particularly named in the list of contraband merchandizes ; so that they may be transported and conducted in the freest manner, by the subjects of the two contracting parties, into any of the enemy's ports ; excepting however, that such places are not actually besieged, blocked up or invested.

Art. XXV. In order to remove and prevent dissentions and quarrels on either side, it is agreed, that in case one of the two parties shall find themselves engaged in a war, the ships and vessels belonging to the subjects or people of the other ally, shall be provided with marine passports, which shall express the name, property, and burden of the ship, as well as the name and place of abode of the master and commander of the said ship, in order that it may from thence appear that the same ship really and truly belongs to the subjects of one of the two contracting parties. These passports are to be annually renewed, in case the ship returns home in the space of one year. It is also agreed, that the above mentioned ships, in case they shall be laden, are to be provided not only with passports, but also with certificates, containing the particulars of the cargo, the place from whence the ship came, and a declaration of what contraband goods are on board; which certificate is to be made in the accustomed form, by the officers of the place from whence the ship sailed; and if it be judged necessary or prudent, to express in the said passports the persons to whom the merchandize belongs, it must be freely complied with.

Art. XXVI. In case any ships of the subjects and inhabitants of one of the two contracting parties should approach the coast of the other, without any intention to enter the port, or, after having entered it, without any intention to unload their cargo, or break bulk, they shall conduct themselves, in that respect, according to the general rules prescribed, or to be prescribed, relative to that matter.

Art. XXVII. When any vessel, belonging to the said subjects, people, and inhabitants, of one of the two parties, shall meet, while sailing along the coast or on the open sea, a ship of war or privateer, belonging to the other, the said ship of war or privateer, in order to avoid disorder, shall bring such vessel too, and send her boat with two or three on board her, to whom the master or commander of the merchantman shall produce his passport, and prove the property of the vessel; and as soon as such passport shall be produced, the master shall be at liberty to pursue his voyage, without being molested, or in any other manner driven or forced to alter his intended course.

Art. XXVIII. It is agreed, that when the merchandizes shall be put on board ships or vessels of one of the two contracting parties, they shall not be subject to be examined again, all such examination and search being to be made before loading, and the prohibited goods being to be stopped and seized on shore, before they could be embarked, unless there are strong suspicions or proofs of fraudulent practices. So that no subject of his Most Christian Majesty, or of the United States, can be stopped or molested for that cause by any kind of embargo; but such subjects of the State, who shall presume to vend or sell such merchandizes as are prohibited, shall be duly punished for such infraction of the treaty.

Art. XXIX. The two contracting parties mutually grant each other the right of maintaining, in their respective ports, Consuls, Vice-Consuls, Agents, and Commissaries, whose business shall be regulated by a particular convention.

Art. XXX. In order further to forward and facilitate the commerce between the subjects of the United States and France, the Most Christian King will allow them in Europe one or more free ports, to which they may bring and sell all the commodities and merchandizes of the Thirteen United States. His Majesty will also grant to the subjects of the said States, the free ports, which have been, and are open, in the French Islands of America; all which free ports the said subjects of the United States shall enjoy, conformably to the regulations which determine that matter.

Art. XXXI. The present treaty shall be ratified by both parties, and the ratifications exchanged, within the space of six months, or sooner if may be. In witness of which, the respective Plenipotentiaries have signed the above articles, both in the French and English language, nevertheless declaring, that the present treaty was originally digested and settled in the French language, to which they have affixed their hands and seals.

Given at Paris the sixth day of the month of February, one thousand seven hundred and seventy-eight.

C. A. GERARD.
B. FRANKLIN.
SILAS DEANE.
ARTHUR LEE.

By the Congress of the United States of America.

MANIFESTO.

THESE United States having been driven to hostilities by the oppressive and tyrannous measures of Great Britain; having been compelled to commit the essential rights of man to the decision of arms; and having been at length forced to shake off a yoke which had grown too burthensome to bear, they declared themselves free and independent.

Confiding in the justice of their cause, confiding in Him who disposes of human events, although weak and unprovided, they set the power of their enemies at defiance.

In this confidence they have continued, through the various fortune of three bloody campaigns, unawed by the powers, unsubdued by the barbarity of their foes. Their virtuous citizens have borne, without repining, the loss of many things which made life desirable. Their brave troops have patiently endured the hardships and dangers of a situation, fruitful in both beyond example.

The Congress considering themselves bound to love their enemies, as children of that Being who is equally the Father of all, and desirous, since they could not prevent, at least to alleviate the calamities of war, have studied to spare those who were in arms against them, and to lighten the chains of captivity.

The conduct of those serving under the King of Great Britain hath, with some few exceptions, been diametrically opposite. They have laid waste the open country, burned the defenceless villages, and butchered the citizens of America. Their prisons have been the slaughter-houses of her soldiers, their ships of her seamen, and the severest injuries have been aggravated by the grossest insults.

Foiled in their vain attempt to subjugate the unconquerable spirit of freedom, they have meanly assailed the Representatives of America with bribes, with deceit, and the servility of adulation. They have made a mock of humanity, by the wanton destruction of men: they have made a mock of religion, by impious appeals to God, whilst in the violation of his sacred commands: they have made a mock even of reason itself, by endeavouring to prove, that the liberty and happiness of America could safely be entrusted to those who have *sold their own*, unawed by the sense of virtue, or of shame.

Treated with the contempt which such conduct deserved, they have applied to individuals; they have solicited them to break the bonds of allegiance, and imbue their souls with the blackest of crimes: but fearing that none could be found through these United States, equal to the wickedness of their purpose, to influence weak minds, they have threatened more wide devastation.

While the shadow of hope remained, that our enemies could be taught by our example to respect those laws which are held sacred among civilized nations, and to comply with the dictates of a religion which they pretend in common with us to believe and revere, they have been left to the influence of that religion, and that example. But since their incorrigible dispositions cannot be touched by kindness and compassion, it becomes our duty by other means to vindicate the rights of humanity.

We, therefore, the Congress of the United States of America, DO SOLEMNLY DECLARE AND PROCLAIM, That if our enemies presume to execute their threats, or persist in their present career of barbarity, we will take such exemplary vengeance as shall deter others from a like conduct. We appeal to that God who searcheth the hearts of men, for the rectitude of our intentions. And in his holy presence we declare, That as we are not moved by any light and hasty suggestions of anger or revenge, so through every possible change of fortune we will adhere to this our determination.

Done in Congress, by unanimous consent, the thirtieth day of October, one thousand seven hundred, and seventy-eight.

Attest,

CHARLES THOMSON, Sec.

Notes, 1779

1. Robert Fanshaw, Captain in 1768.

2. George Montagu (1750–1829), served under his father, Admiral John Montagu, from 1771 to 1776 and was flag captain to his father on the Newfoundland station 1777–79; promoted to Rear-Admiral in 1794, Vice-Admiral, 1795, and Admiral, 1801.

3. ?Henry Francis Evans (d. 1781), Captain in 1778.

4. The 3rd Regiment of Continental Light Dragoons, commanded by Colonel George Baylor (1752–84), and nicknamed "Mrs. Washington's Guards."

5. Archibald Campbell (1739–91), Colonel of the 71st Regiment, promoted to Major-General in 1782; captured in 1776, he had resumed his command on being released in May 1778.

6. Patrick Ferguson (1744–80), celebrated for the invention of the first breechloading rifle used in the British army; achieved a reputation as commander of a ranger corps using this weapon.

7. John Collins (d. 1794), Captain in 1778.

8. Not identified.

9. Grey, of course, repeated his success of September 1777 at Paoli by exactly the same methods at Tappan and became for the second time the villain of an atrocity story.

10. John Butler (see "Notes, 1777," n. 73). Joseph Brant (1742–1807), Mohawk war leader and protegé of the late Sir William Johnson, Superintendant of Indian Affairs for the Northern District. He led the Indians on St. Leger's expedition and was highly regarded by British commanders for his activities in organising Indian raids on the New York border. It is now established that he was not responsible for the Wyoming Valley massacre.

11. Zebulon Butler (1731–95), leader of the Connecticut settlers in the Wyoming Valley, born in Ipswich, Massachusetts, and no relation to John, born in New London, Connecticut.

12. Nathan Denison (c. 1740–1809), Colonel of Connecticut militia and a settler in the Wyoming Valley.

13. Not identified.

14. Robert Durkee and Samuel Ransom, captains of two companies of volunteers from the valley who joined the Continental Army in 1776; not otherwise identified.

15. The *Annual Register*'s version of the Wyoming Valley massacre looks like a classic piece of American propaganda and should be compared with those in Howard Swiggett, *War Out of Niagara: Walter Butler and* the Tory Rangers (New York, 1933); Christopher Ward, The War of the Revolution, ed. and comp. J. R. Alden, 2 vols. (New York, 1952), . . . , vol. 2; William L. Stone, Border Wars of the American Revolution, 2 vols. (N.Y. 1900 ed.), vol. 1. In these accounts (based on the same sources), John Butler's force of Iroquois Indians and Tories advanced against Zebulon Butler's small body of militia, which retreated to Forty Fort. The garrison made the mistake of trying a sortie and was wiped out by John Butler's much larger force, which gave no quarter. No attack under a spurious flag of truce appears to have taken place, and Denison surrendered the fort on specific terms which included protection of the lives and property of settlers. The accounts differ in detail but agree that the Indians became uncontrollable and the settlers fled in panic, many dying in the wilderness as they tried to escape. Those tortured and killed appear to be men "taken in arms" but John Butler seems to have made efforts to prevent this.

16. George Rogers Clark (1752–1818) had already established a reputation as an explorer. His plan for the capture of the French settlements in Illinois (a subgovernment of British Canada) was approved by the State of Virginia, not the Continental Congress.

17. Lieutenant-Governor Henry Hamilton (d. 1796), Commandant at Detroit, 1775–79, had considerable success in securing the allegiance of the Indians, though his reputation for offering rewards for scalps may well be exaggerated.

18. Philippe François Rastel, Sieur de Rocheblave, formerly in the French army in Canada, since 1763 in the British service, Commandant at Fort Gage, Kaskaskia.

19. Hamilton recaptured Vincennes in December 1778, but after a remarkable march in dreadful conditions, in February 1779 Clark retook the fort and sent Hamilton back to Virginia a prisoner. Clark retained control of Illinois and continued to organise border warfare in the northwest and the Ohio Valley.

20. Amid a plethora of Butlers, this is William Butler (d. 1789), one of five brothers, the others being Richard (1743–91), Thomas (1754–1805), Percival (1760–1821), and Edward (d. 1803), from Pennsylvania. All served as officers in the Continental Army, none were any relation of John Butler ("Notes, 1777," n. 73), his son Walter (?1752–81), or Zebulon Butler (n. 11, above).

21. In the chapter heading, these raids are correctly described as "The Destruction of Unadilla and Anaquago settlements," though the names do not appear in the text. Butler's expedition was made in response to Joseph Brant's raid on German Flats in September 1778, which was launched from his base at Unadilla. Brant's retaliation for the destruction of his fortified points around Unadilla was to unite his Indians with a ranger force led by Walter Butler (see n. 20, above) and annihilate the settlements in Cherry Valley in November 1778. The following year, Washington felt able to detach sufficient troops to stabilise the frontier and despatched an expedition under Major-General John Sullivan in May 1779. By November, this expedition destroyed the Iroquois settlements and their agriculture but not their capacity for border warfare, nor did it deal with Walter Butler or Joseph Brant. Frontier fighting continued unabated until the end of the war. See AR, 1780, pp. [*209–[*21.

22. George Johnstone.

23. Joseph Reed (1741–85), President of the second Pennsylvania Provincial Congress in 1775, military secretary to Washington and Adjutant-General with the rank of Colonel in March 1776. Though highly valued by Washington, he resigned from the army in January 1777, but continued to act as the Commander-in-Chief's A.D.C. He had been elected as one of Pennsylvania's delegates to the Continental Congress in 1778 and in this capacity exposed Johnston's attempted bribery.

24. Robert Morris (1734–1806), leading Philadelphia merchant and politician, a Pennsylvania delegate to the Continental Congress, 1766–78, and President of the Pennsylvania Assembly in 1776. His complex business dealings and official connections with Silas Deane's mission in France attracted criticism and attack in 1779.

25. Mrs. Katherine Ferguson, Adam Ferguson's wife. William Eden's wife, Eleanor, also accompanied the entourage of the Peace Commission, despite her advanced pregnancy.

26. Francis Dana (1743–1811) spent some time between 1774 and 1776 in England endeavouring to test support in public opinion for the American position and had returned convinced of the impossibility of reconciliation. He was a member of the Massachusetts Council, 1776–80, and Massachusetts delegate to the Continental Congress, 1777–78. In 1777, he was a member of the committee which examined the proposals of the Howe Peace Commission.

27. The Peace Commission was to include the Commander-in-Chief in America. Clinton had been appointed to succeed William Howe in February 1778.

28. That is, Thomas Paine (1737–1809). His pamphlet directed against the Peace Commission was published in October 1778 as number VI of the sixteen he wrote as a series entitled *The American Crisis*.

29. No resolution of this kind is recorded in the journal of the Congress. Walpole notes that in response to the commission's threats: "The Americans did actually, in a fine manifesto, declare they would take similar steps," (*Last Journals of Horace Walpole, 1771–83*, ed. Dr. Doran, 2 vols. [London, 1859], vol. 2, p. 301), but this could refer to the last paragraph of the manifesto mentioned in n. 30, below.

30. This manifesto was approved on 30 October. *Journals of the Continental Congress 1774–1789*, ed. W. C. Ford, 34 vols. (Washington, D.C., 1904–37), vol. 7, pp. 1080–82.

31. None of the commissioners seem to have known of the orders for the evacuation. Eden was particularly incensed at the deception practised on him by the Cabinet. See C. R. Ritcheson, *British Politics and the American Revolution* (Norman, Okla., 1954), p. 273.

32. Not identified.

33. Archibald Campbell.

34. Augustine Prevost (1723–86), British officer of Swiss origin who had served in America in the Seven Years War and was Colonel commanding the forces in East Florida from 1776. Appointed to command the British troops already in the south in December 1778, he was promoted to the local rank of Major-General in February 1779.

35. Sir James Baird, Grenadier Captain commanding a light infantry company; Cameron, not identified.

36. ?John Stanhope (d. 1800), Captain in 1779.

37. John Maitland (1732–79), eighth surviving son of the Earl of Lauderdale, M.P. for Haddington Burghs, 1774–79. Formerly a captain in the Marines, he was appointed Lieutenant-Colonel commanding the 1st Battalion of the 71st Regiment in October 1778.

38. Robert Howe (1732–86), Colonel of the 2nd North Carolina Regiment in 1775; promoted to Brigadier-General in the Continental Army in 1776 and to Major-General in 1777; commanded the Southern Department until replaced by Lincoln in September 1778, when he became commanding officer in Georgia.

39. Isaac Huger (1743–97), one of five brothers, four of whom served in either the South Carolina militia or the Continental Army. The fifth and eldest, Daniel, was later a delegate to the Continental Congress. Isaac commanded forces against the Cherokee in 1760 and was made Colonel of the 5th South Carolina Continental Regiment in September 1778 and promoted to Brigadier-General in January 1779. The name is pronounced "ew-gee."

40. Samuel Elbert (1743–88), formerly a wealthy merchant, became Colonel of the 2nd Georgia Regiment in 1776 and captured Fort Oglethorpe earlier in 1778.

41. George Turnbull, Loyalist commanding a battalion in De Lancey's New York Volunteer Regiment.

42. Howe was court-martialled for his role in the loss of Savannah, but he was acquitted of all charges. Public hostility in the south caused Washington to transfer him to the northern theatre in April 1779.

43. Horace Walpole's comment was more sarcastic: "Dr. Franklin was received at Versailles in form on the 17th, as Ambassador for the United States of America. This triumph had never been exceeded but by the capture of Francis I by the Constable of Bourbon, which, perhaps, was inferior to Franklin's as the latter was a private man, and triumphed by his own ambition over the King of Great Britain." *Last Journals*, vol. 2, pp. 223–24.

44. Admiral Keppel was nominated to command the Channel Fleet in 1776 and the appointment was approved by the Cabinet on 22 March 1778.

45. The *Annual Register* at this point notes the unprepared state of the fleet at Portsmouth and Keppel's reaction to the situation facing him. The chapter goes on to describe the events leading up to the indecisive battle of Ushant and the public criticism which followed it.

46. George Johnstone.

47. The Earl of Bristol.

48. Thomas William Coke (1754–82), M.P. for Norfolk, 1776–84; voted consistently with the Opposition against North.

49. On 27–28 April 1778, John Paul Jones (see n. 99, below) raided Whitehaven in Cumberland and made an unsuccessful attempt to kidnap the Earl of Selkirk.

50. Thomas Stanley (?1758–79), M.P. for Lancashire, 1776–79, second son of Lord Strange. He was a Major in the 79th Regiment in 1777.

51. Johnstone.

52. Thurlow replaced Bathurst on 8 June 1778, having been created Baron Thurlow of Ashfield.

53. Camden and the Bishop of Peterborough.

54. Chapter VI begins with the parliamentary session commencing 20 January 1779.

55. The chapter continues with Keppel's court-martial and the Opposition attack on the Admiralty.

56. General Conway (see "Notes, 1766," n. 15).

57. Isaac Barré.

58. Richard Rigby.

59. John Montresor (1736–99), an officer in the engineers, who served in America in the previous war and was appointed Chief Engineer in America in 1775. His services were scarcely utilised, and after falling foul of Clinton, he returned to Britain in 1778. Sir George Osborn (1742–1818), 4th Baronet, M.P. for Penryn 1774–80, Horsham 1780–84; entered the army in 1750 and reached the rank of Colonel in 1777; promoted to Major-General in 1779.

60. James Robertson (?1720–88), Governor of New York, 1779–81. Major-General Daniel Jones served in New York from its capture, commanded in the absence of General Pigot. Dixon, Stanton, and Maxwell, not identified. Joseph Galloway (see "Notes, 1777," n. 7). Andrew Allen, son of William Allen, Chief Justice of Pennsylvania; joined Howe after Trenton. John Patterson, a New York Loyalist. Theodore Morris, not identified. Enoch Story, former Inspector of Prohibited Goods in Philadelphia.

61. Alexander Lindsay, 6th Earl of Balcarres (1752–1825), served under Burgoyne and was held prisoner after the Saratoga surrender, until released in 1779. John Money (1752–1817), Captain serving with Burgoyne at Saratoga. Charles Stanhope, Earl of Harrington (1753–1829), M.P. for Thetford, 1774–76, and Burgoyne's A.D.C. at Saratoga. Forbes, not identified. Bloomfield, not identified. Kingston (see "Notes, 1777", n. 87).

62. John Ashe (c. 1720–81), North Carolina politician appointed Brigadier-General of North Carolina militia in 1776; he was censured by a court of enquiry after Briar Creek and retired from military duty.

63. Marc Prevost, younger brother of Major-General Augustine Prevost.

64. Five killed and eleven wounded.

65. Ward gives the losses as: British 26 killed, 103 wounded; Americans: 146 killed and wounded, 155 missing. *The War of the Revolution*, vol. 2, p. 686.

66. Sir George Collier (1738–95), Captain in 1762, knighted in 1775, and in temporary command of the British fleet in America on the recall of Rear-Admiral James Gambier (1723–89), who in turn temporarily assumed overall command during the absence first of Lord Howe, later of Admiral Byron.

67. A confusion: Brigadier-General James Paterson (see "Notes, 1776," n. 78) commanded three infantry battalions in this advance; James Pattison (1724–1805) was Brigadier-General of artillery assisting Paterson's force.

68. George Garth (d. 1819), Colonel in the Guards with the local rank of Brigadier-General in 1779.

69. "My reason for putting a stop to that general officer's further progress at present was that, as Mr. Washington seemed to be determined not to stir from his position and all the militia of the country were assembling in arms, a further prosecution of these desultory descents was likely now to be attended with a greater loss of men than the impression they might make on the enemy would probably compensate. And, indeed, I could not but view with concern the very afflicting damage they had been already productive of to private property, it never having been my intention to extend the destruction to houses of individuals, much less to those of public worship." *The American Rebellion: Sir Henry Clinton's Narrative of the Campaigns, 1775–82, with an Appendix of Original Documents*, ed. W. B. Willcox (New Haven, Conn., 1954), p. 131. Tryon reported that the British losses in the various attacks totalled 20 killed, 95 wounded, and 32 missing. Ibid., p. 415 n.

70. Tryon to Clinton (New York), 20 July 1779, Ibid., p. 414.

71. Henry Johnson (1748–1835), Lieutenant-Colonel of the 17th Regiment.

72. James Webster (?1743–81), Lieutenant-Colonel commanding the 33rd Regiment. His force consisted of the 33rd, Robinson's Loyal American Regiment, and part of Ferguson's ranger corps.

73. Christian Febiger (1746–96), Danish immigrant with a military background, Lieutenant-Colonel of the 2nd Virginia Regiment; commanded the 1st Regiment in Wayne's Brigade at Stony Point.

74. François Louis Teissedre de Fleury, one of the French volunteers in the Continental Army, already distinguished for his courage; voted a silver medal by the Congress for his exploits at Stony Point.

75. Major John Stewart, commanded a battalion in the 2nd Regiment of Wayne's Brigade; like Fleury, awarded a silver medal.

76. Major Hardy Murfree (1752–1809) commanded North Carolina troops in the 4th Regiment of Wayne's Brigade.

77. Not identified.

78. Not identified.

79. Not further identified.

80. Johnson reported 20 killed, 74 wounded, 88 missing, and 472 prisoners.

81. Wayne asked Washington to divide the money equivalent of the value of the materiel captured among the troops; on appraisal the value was $180,655.

82. Thomas Stirling.

83. ?William Sutherland, formerly Clinton's A.D.C.

84. See "Notes, 1776," n. 4.

85. Dudley Saltonstall (1738–96), formerly a privateer, since 1775 senior Captain under Esek Hopkins in the new Continental Navy. He was exonerated in the enquiry which had dismissed his chief (see "Notes, 1776," n. 71) but was himself dismissed for his failure at Penobscot. Solomon Lovell, Brigadier-General in the Massachusetts militia. Paul Revere commanded the artillery in the expedition.

86. D'Estaing had taken St. Vincent on 16 June and Grenada on 4 July. Byron attempted to retake Grenada on 6 July with a fleet inferior to d'Estaing's but the latter's withdrawal prevented a decisive British success.

The Annual Register—1779

87. General Garth was captured with the *Experiment*.

88. ?Thomas Goldsborough, promoted to Commander in 1780, Captain in 1787.

89. George Macartney (1737–1806), Governor of the Southern Caribee Islands, 1775–79, 1st Baron Macartney, 1776 (see "Notes, 1774," n. 17). Considering Governor Macartney defended Hospital Hill with 166 regulars and less than 400 militia against an assault of 2,000 French regulars, it was hardly regarded as impregnable by either attackers or defenders. The French were enraged by the British decision to fight in the first place, and d'Estaing was infuriated by Macartney's refusal to submit to an unconditional surrender. As a result, he permitted the pillage of the British quarters—Macartney was the main victim. Macartney to Germain, 5 July 1779, British Museum Add. Mss. 38718.

90. Clinton states that the British garrison ". . . including the armed inhabitants and sailors did not consist of more than four thousand of which not above twenty-four hundred were regimented troops." *The American Rebellion*, p. 150.

91. James Moncrieff (1744–93), Captain in the engineers who laid the foundation of a reputation for outstanding competence at Savannah.

92. Mortar shells, perforated and filled with incendiary substances.

93. Not identified.

94. Not identified.

95. Prevost's report suggests between 1,000 and 1,200 French and American casualties. Several sources give the figure of 637 French casualties.

96. Vicomte de Fontanges (1740–1822), Major-General commanding d'Estaing's troops.

97. Richard Pearson (1731–1806), Post-Captain in 1793; served in Canada, 1776–78; appointed to command the *Serapis* in March 1778. He was honourably acquitted by the court-martial which reviewed his capture by John Paul Jones, and was knighted in 1780.

98. Philip Stephens (1723–1809), Secretary to the Admiralty, 1763–95, M.P. for Sandwich, 1768–1806.

99. John Paul Jones (1747–92), a Scots merchant seaman who migrated to America in 1773 and through the influence of Joseph Hewes (1730–99), North Carolina delegate to the Continental Congress, was commissioned Lieutenant in the Continental Navy in 1775. From 1776, he was famous as a successful cruiser-raider in British waters (see n. 49, above), and in August 1779 the French government gave him command of an ex-East Indiaman, which he renamed, in honour of Franklin's *Poor Richard's Almanack*, the *Bonhomme Richard*. Jones abandoned his vessel at sea due to the damage it sustained in the fight with the *Serapis* and escaped to Holland.

100. Thomas Piercy (d. 1793), commanded the *Countess of Scarborough*; promoted to the rank of Captain in 1780.

101. Jean-Joseph Sourbader de Gimat, Lafayette's A.D.C. with the rank of Major; from February 1781 commanded a light infantry regiment.

Introduction

1780

In terms of significant developments, 1780 provides interest on every front. On the surface, the war in America seemed to move steadily in Britain's favour and supplies were successfully brought to besieged Gibraltar. The Caribbean however remained an area of alarm and uncertainty, and conflict in India became serious. Even more worrying was the alliance of the northern powers in the League of Armed Neutrality which threatened Britain's ability to interdict the shipping of strategic goods by neutrals to the enemy. Thus, Britain declared war on Holland in anticipation of Holland's adherence to the League. At home, economical reform appeared to be at flood tide. Irish affairs were again in crisis, London was submerged for a week in the chaos and fury of the Gordon Riots, and North called a general election in the vain hope of improving the Government's position in Parliament. At the end of the year, the Opposition was more disunited than ever, yet, wrote Horace Walpole, ". . . the Government that had precipitated us into all these calamities and had achieved nothing, was more popular."[1]

The economical reform movement began the year with vigorous advances. On 21 January, the Yorkshire County Committee prepared a plan of association advocating shorter parliaments and a reform of representation. The committee proposed that votes at the next general elec-

1. *Last Journals of Horace Walpole, 1771–83*, ed. Dr. Doran, 2 vols. (London, 1859), p. 438.

tion be denied any candidate who refused to declare in favour of this programme. Sound organisation through corresponding committees and increasing public enthusiasm resulted in sixteen county meetings in January and petitions from seven major cities. The Rockinghams were displeased with the parliamentary reform aspects of the movement but cooperated with the petitioning groups; Fox actually tried to capitalise on the popular mood without overcommitting himself to a specific programme. On 11 March, Wyvill produced much more radical proposals, including annual parliaments, one hundred new M.P.s for underrepresented areas, and tests for parliamentary candidates. Rockingham did his best to minimise these radical tendencies at the Yorkshire meeting of 28 March but succeeded only in getting an agreement for three-year parliaments. Not only were the Rockinghams unhappy with the direction the movement was taking, they also faced a breach with Shelburne and the Chathamites, who were apparently willing to accept major reforms of Parliament.

On 8 February Sir George Savile presented the Yorkshire petition to Parliament, on the eleventh Burke produced his detailed proposals for economical reform, and on 23 February Burke embodied these in his establishment bill. North prepared for a protracted battle to defend a list of offices against abolition. The American Secretaryship was retained on the list after the debate on 8 March by only 7 votes and the Board of Trade was voted away by 207 to 199 on 13 March. The core of the economical reform programme, i.e., the reforms of the Royal Household and the Civil List, failed to carry on 20 March and was rejected 211 to 158, as a growing number of independents became uneasy at the restrictions imposed on the King. Dunning's famous motion—"that the influence of the Crown has increased, is increasing and ought to be diminished"—was carried, through careful mobilisation of support, on 6 April (233 to 215). A second motion avowing the competency of the House to reform the Civil List or any part of the public expenditure was also carried without a division. On 10 April, Dunning carried two further resolutions for reform of the Civil List and the Household but lost one to exclude thirteen placeholders. On 24 April, he failed in an attempt to keep Parliament sitting until the petitions were acted upon. The high point of the reform movement had been reached on 6 April, when Burke's bill was killed in committee: Dunning's motions were not put into execution, for the Opposition's newfound supporters recoiled from the implications of the reform programme.[2]

The Government had weathered the reform movement, but the Irish situation showed signs of continuing instability. Ireland had been allowed to trade directly with the colonies by an act passed in February, but the Irish grew bitter over North's procrastination and in March eighteen counties petitioned to repeal Poyning's Law. On 19 April, Grattan ominously moved that only the Irish parliament at Dublin could legislate for Ireland. Burke, who angered his British constituents by supporting Irish trade concessions, is alleged to have written "will no one stop this madman, Grattan."[3]

In the weeks that followed, a reduced pressure for reform could also be attributed to the serious divisions revealed in the ranks of the Opposition. Fox supported Sawbridge's motion for shorter parliaments on 8 May, but Burke opposed it, and on 3 June, Richmond moved for a staggering combination of annual parliaments and universal suffrage, indicating that he agreed with Shelburne's view that the Rockinghams were too conservative. Not only therefore were the Shelburne and Rockingham groups at odds, but Fox and Richmond began defecting from the orthodox Rockingham line.

In the midst of these disagreements, the worst urban disturbances in Britain in the century erupted. Between 2 and 9 June London was engulfed in the Gordon Riots. In protest against the Catholic Relief Act of 1778, the Protestant Association was formed in February 1779 and the mentally unstable Lord George Gordon became its leader after more reputable figures withdrew. A large crowd, ostensibly determined to force Parliament to hear a petition for repeal of the Relief Act, rapidly degenerated into a mob, which first attacked many public figures and their London houses, then turned to violence and looting, which reached a peak on 7 June. The City authorities panicked and failed to take adequate measures, and the

---

2. Frank O'Gorman, *The Rise of Party in England: The Rockingham Whigs 1760–82* (London, 1975), pp. 416–20.

3. *The Correspondence of Edmund Burke*, ed. Thomas W. Copeland, 9 vols. (Cambridge and Chicago, 1961–70), vol. 4 (ed. John A. Woods), p. 231.

rioting was not suppressed until the Government finally decided to call in troops. Gordon was sent to the Tower pending trial for treason, while 192 rioters were tried and 25 executed.[4] The riots had two party-political effects: their threat to order produced a reflexive reaction of support for Government, and they deepened the rift between the two wings of the Opposition. Shelburne's connections with the Protestant Association and his behaviour during the riots led Rockingham to suspect him of complicity;[5] Rockingham supported the use of military power as Shelburne opposed it,[6] and in addition, Shelburne advocated lenient treatment for those arrested. These attitudes exacerbated a quarrel based on Shelburne's reputation for duplicity and his growing contempt for Rockingham's conservatism—a view which Fox and Richmond began to share.

North survived the crisis, and at the end of June thought it opportune to sound out Rockingham on terms for a coalition. Rockingham responded by demanding recognition of American independence, the dismissal of Sandwich and Germain, and the appointment of Fox and Richmond to the two Secretaryships of State. The King regarded the terms as outrageous and negotiations ended on 7 July. North then decided to dissolve Parliament one year before its date of expiry and to hold a general election. He assumed the time was favourable because of optimistic news from America, visible divisions among the Opposition, a diminution in pressure from Ireland, and pro-Government feeling after the Gordon Riots. The Treasury calculated that there would likely be an improvement in Government strength, and secret preparations were made to outmanoeuver the Opposition by holding a snap election in September. The Government seriously miscalculated, for it emerged with a net loss of five or six votes.[7] The new Parliament met on 31 October,

4. *Last Journals of Horace Walpole*, p. 424.
5. J. Norris, *Shelburne and Reform* (London, 1963), pp. 132–33. As for Shelburne's behavior during the riots: "Probably he intended no more than to take advantage of the Ministry's desperate situation." Ibid. p. 134.
6. Over 11,000 troops were finally concentrated on or near the capital, and some of the Opposition voiced the conventional fears of abuse of excess military power by the Crown. The King apologised for the use of the troops in his speech to the House of Lords on 19 April.
7. I. R. Christie, *The End of North's Ministry 1780–82* (London, 1958), pp. 3–163.

won an embarrassing struggle over the election of the new speaker (Charles Cornwall), carried the address to the Crown supporting the American war on 6 November by 212 to 130 and the navy estimates on 4 December (two days before adjournment) by an even larger majority. Poor attendance and news of British successes in America had weakened support for the Opposition.

The war plans for 1780 were a compromise between the pressure for decisive measures from the King and Germain and the caution and doubts of Sandwich and Amherst. The Channel Fleet was to remain at strength to guard Britain's coasts and commerce; the West Indies were to be reinforced by a few ships from North America and England and troops from Clinton; Rodney was to relieve Gibraltar and then detach more ships for the Caribbean; while America was to be reconquered piecemeal by the plan of 1779. These plans were erratically modified in the face of naval weakness, the movements of the French and Spanish fleets, and the extension of hostilities to Holland. Rodney drove off a Spanish fleet and resupplied Gibraltar on 16 January, then took five ships to the West Indies. In early February, the Government learnt that France was sending a powerful fleet under the Comte de Guichen to the West Indies. In March, it heard that a squadron under Ternay, with a large body of troops under Rochambeau, was probably destined for America. In May, the Spanish Cadiz fleet left for the Caribbean, while British naval reinforcements were delayed by bad weather. Rodney fought an inconclusive action with Guichen off Martinique on 17 April and prevented the French recapture of St. Lucia in May. The onset of the hurricane season relieved the Bourbon threat to Jamaica, and the ill-concerted British attacks on Nicaragua and the Mosquito Coast disintegrated as a result of incompetence and disease.

Though the American war had become a sideshow for Britain, 1780 ironically seemed to show a steady record of British success. On 13 April, Clinton and Arbuthnot opened the siege of Charleston, Lincoln's expected line of retreat up the Cooper River was cut by the destruction of an American force at Monck's Corner by Banastre Tarleton's Legion and Patrick Ferguson's Rangers. Lincoln proposed to evacuate Charleston on 20 April to save his army, but the city authorities demanded protection. A British bombardment on 9–10 May suddenly reversed the city's defiance and Lincoln surrendered on the twelfth. The capture of the city and of 5,500 American troops was the most serious blow the Americans had suffered in the war up to that time. On 18 May, Clinton moved to end American resistance in South Carolina, Tarleton massacred an American force at Waxhaws,[8] and other units advanced to take Fort Ninety-Six and pacify the area east of Augusta. Clinton was dubious about setting up civilian government immediately (under his powers as a peace commissioner), but on 4 June he decreed that South Carolinians should be ready to serve in the defence of restored royal government and that rebels remaining under arms would be outlawed. The following day, he sailed for New York leaving Cornwallis with 4,000 men to hold the south.

Washington and the Continental Army had survived another winter, but by the spring of 1780, the Americans were suffering from disgracefully inadequate provisions and supplies and from delays in pay, which even when issued was affected by the rapid currency depreciation resulting from the collapse of congressional credit. Morale was poor and two Connecticut regiments mutinied in May. Rumours of these developments led Clinton to believe raids against Washington's forces in New Jersey might start the breakup of the Continental Army. Accordingly, on 7 June, Knyphausen was sent to Elizabethtown to penetrate the area and win over the disaffected American soldiery. But Clinton was badly misinformed about the supposedly declining American morale; Knyphausen was held off by militia at Connecticut Farms and forced back by Greene at Springfield. Clinton finally extricated him on 23 June. By this time, Clinton had other problems, for on 11 June, Ternay's fleet had arrived at Newport and disembarked Rochambeau's army of 5,000 French regulars. Arbuthnot was reinforced by a squadron sent from England under Graves, and he blockaded Rhode Island; but the lack of cooperation between Arbuthnot and Clinton degenerated into increasingly acrimonious exchanges which paralysed any effective action against the French and Americans. Each commander blamed the other (Clinton threatened to resign if Arbuthnot was not recalled); Germain decided there was ". . . a total want of communi-

---

8. Tarleton's reputation for ruthlessness now aroused both fear and anger in the south; he was nicknamed "Bloody Ban."

cation and confidence between the Commanders and . . . both might have done better."[9]

In the south, Cornwallis found that South Carolina was far from being pacified, and had actually erupted into a bitter civil war, which spread to North Carolina and was characterised by savage guerrilla fighting between Tory-Loyalists and Patriots. An American relief force of regulars under the adventurer Johann de Kalb failed to reach Charleston, and in July Washington ordered Horatio Gates to supersede de Kalb and direct resistance in the Carolinas. On 16 August, however, Cornwallis and Rawdon,[10] with a force half the size of Gates's, routed the Americans at Camden and drove them in a headlong retreat.[11] However, the British jubilation was short-lived. After Camden, Cornwallis tried to consolidate his position in North Carolina, using Tarleton and Ferguson in a series of strikes against local forces in September, but Ferguson was killed and his force massacred by hastily gathered militia at Kings Mountain on 7 October. The loss of Ferguson was a serious blow, and worse still, guerrilla forces under capable and effective leaders, like Thomas Sumpter, Andrew Pickens, and Francis Marion, ruthlessly harried Loyalists and menaced British movements. The American regulars were also involved—Washington appointed Greene to recreate the Continental Army in the south, assisted by Von Steuben and supported by "Light Horse Harry" Lee's Legion. Greene took over on 2 December and fortunately found Daniel Morgan available for service, so divided the American forces on 19 December to threaten two areas of South Carolina. Cornwallis in response prepared to start the New Year by defeating the American forces piecemeal.

One of the most dramatic and, in its immediate outcome, tragic events of the war occurred in 1780. Benedict Arnold had become embittered by his treatment by Congress and in May 1779 opened secret negotiations with Clinton with a view to defecting. A year later, he offered to surrender West Point, key fortress to the Highlands, to

9. *Sandwich Papers*, vol. 3, p. 258.
10. The future Marquis of Hastings and Governor-General of India laid the foundation of his military reputation in this campaign.
11. Gates himself led the rout, allegedly reaching Hillsborough on 18 May, having covered the 180 miles from Camden in two and a half days.

which he had recently been appointed commander, in return for £20,000 and a British army command. Clinton basically agreed to these terms but final negotiations were delayed through communications difficulties until August. A final secret meeting between Arnold and Major John André, Clinton's adjutant-general and chief of intelligence, on 21 September resulted in the capture of André, who was attempting to return to the British lines in disguise. André was tried and executed as a spy, despite pleas from many leading British officers. Arnold meanwhile coolly escaped and, though he had not been able to give up West Point, was commissioned a brigadier-general in the British army, compensated for his financial losses, and ordered to raise a Loyalist legion.[12]

The second half of the year saw increasing difficulties for Britain outside America. France, from the beginning of hostilities, had been considering recovering the position in India she had lost at the end of the Seven Years War, but was frustrated in trying to take advantage of the East India Company's weakness and vulnerable military situation because of the naval control established by Admiral Hughes's squadron in 1779. The East India Company was now involved in a double war with the Mahratta Confederacy and with Mysore. In June 1780, Hyder Ali, sultan of Mysore, invaded the Carnatic with a powerful army; there were no doubts France would at once take advantage of the situation and her navy would moreover be able to use Dutch bases at the Cape of Good Hope and Ceylon to establish command of the eastern seas.

The French use of Dutch bases became possible because of Britain's rupture with the Netherlands over the question of neutral trading rights. International law regarding the carriage of goods by a neutral to the ports of a belligerent power was confused and in the process of change. The basic British concern was to prevent the shipment of Baltic naval stores to France and Spain in neutral vessels, and Britain interpreted maritime law to permit her to do so. France, on the other hand, offered inducements to neutrals to carry naval stores for her on

12. The most detailed account of this drama may be found in Carl Van Doren, *Secret History of the American Revolution: An Account of the Conspiracies of Benedict Arnold and Numerous Others Drawn from the Secret Service Papers of the British Headquarters in North America Now for the First Time Examined and Made Public* (New York, 1941).

the principle of "free ships, free goods." The situation changed significantly in April 1780, when Russia proposed that the neutral maritime powers should combine to protect their shipping against any belligerents. The immediate adherence of Russia, Sweden, and Denmark to the League of Armed Neutrality was merely an embarrassing irritation for Britain. If however the Netherlands acceded to the league, the situation would be serious. The large Dutch mercantile marine could run naval stores to the Bourbon powers, protected by a naval combination defending neutral rights, and Britain would be forced to abandon hope of reducing the strength of the Franco-Spanish navy.[13]

Despite the Anglo-Dutch commercial treaty of 1674 and the mutual defence pact of 1678, both still in force, relations between Britain and the Netherlands steadily deteriorated after 1778. The Dutch sustained the French West Indies, traded with Americans, assisted American privateers (notably John Paul Jones), and ran naval stores to France in Dutch convoys, deaf all the while to British protests. In 1779, a British squadron stopped and searched a Dutch convoy in the Channel, and in April 1780 Britain suspended the commercial treaty. By November, Britain had to prevent the Dutch from joining the League—but on an issue which would not automatically enlist the support of the League. An excellent excuse emerged on 3 September, when the former president of the Congress and then American commissioner to the United Provinces, Henry Laurens, was captured at sea. Among his papers were documents indicating a proposed treaty between the city of Amsterdam and Congress. Britain demanded on 10 November that this "secret treaty" be formally disavowed and the Amsterdam signatories punished. She received no satisfactory reply and so declared war on the Dutch on 20 December. The Netherlands had resolved to join the League in November, but the British government correctly judged that the League would not protect the Dutch on an issue that did not

13. Prussia and Austria joined the league in 1781, Portugal in 1782, and the Kingdom of the Two Sicilies in 1783. The combined naval strength of these powers was no real threat to Britain, but the existence of the league left Britain diplomatically isolated and forced her to review her policy on neutral rights and prize law. S. F. Bemis, *The Diplomacy of the American Revolution* (Edinburgh and London, 1957), pp. 162–63.

involve neutral rights.[14] Britain's decision to go to war against another maritime power was questionable. Britain could now harry Dutch commerce, pick off Dutch colonies and naval bases; but she also faced increased enemy naval strength in her home waters, and risked a French occupation of the Dutch naval bases for new attacks overseas.

The *Annual Register* for 1780 was published in January 1782, and the whole preface is used to excuse the delay, stressing the familiar explanation of an "accession of business" which ". . . has arrived at a magnitude before unknown."[15] The historical section is only 2 pages shorter than in 1778, and only 19 of 345 pages are devoted to events in America. The first four chapters are a retrospect of the second half of 1779. Chapter I notes the end of the Bavarian succession dispute and Russo-Turkish tensions, then turns to the opening of the war with Spain and the summer invasion scare. Chapter II comments in detail on Spain's publicly declared reasons for entering the war, then traces the growth of protest in Ireland and the outbreak of anti-Catholic riots in Scotland, and concludes with a note on the ministerial changes made in November. Chapters III and IV cover the pre-Christmas parliamentary session. Chapter III treats the debates following the speech from the throne, Chapter IV the debates over concessions to Ireland and the Opposition's pursuit of economical reform.

The next four chapters report in detail parliamentary affairs from January to July 1780, especially the progress of the county movement and economical reform, with particular attention paid to the roles of Burke and Dunning. The *Register*'s coverage clearly indicates that the Opposition chose to concentrate on this issue, to the virtual exclusion of all others, in its hope to bring down

14. For the development of the quarrel with the Netherlands and the involvement of the league, see Bemis, *The Diplomacy of the American Revolution*, pp. 113–71; for an analysis of Russia's role in creating the league, see I. de Madariaga, *Britain, Russia and the Armed Neutrality of 1780: Sir James Harris's Mission to St. Petersburg During the American Revolution* (London, 1962), esp. pp. 140–94.

15. *AR*, 1780, p. vi. The preface refers to the original delay arising from "long and dangerous illness" and the difficulty of ". . . speedily recovering any considerable portion of lost time" under normal circumstances, while the increase of material ensured that ". . . the original difficulty was not only rendered insurmountable, but the evil of itself became of necessity greater."

the North government. The end of Chapter VIII describes the Gordon Riots and their aftermath and accurately concludes:

> The riot, in the close, threw a general damp upon all endeavours whatever for reformation, however unconnected with its particular object. Popular fury seemed, for that time at least, the greatest of all possible evils. And administration then gathered, and has since preserved, no small degree of power, from a tumult which appeared to threaten the subversion of all government.[16]

The progress of the war is reviewed only in the final two chapters. Chapter IX recounts Rodney's relief of Gibraltar, reports the stoppage of the Dutch convoy, and provides an excellent summary of Britain's attitude toward the creation of the League of Armed Neutrality. The second half of Chapter IX follows the war in America from the summer to the fall of 1779, notes the loss of West Florida and the British attack on Honduras and the Mosquito Coast, and concludes with an account of the American expedition under Sullivan intended to destroy the power of the Six Nations and pacify the frontier. Chapter X begins with the British evacuation of Rhode Island and then devotes eighteen pages to the campaign in the south, from the fall of Charleston to Gates's defeat at Camden and Rodney's unsuccessful attempts to inflict a decisive defeat on Guichen in the West Indies. The treatment of the war in the Carolinas does not describe the spread of guerrilla war in the fall of 1780, but it does note the superficial pacification established by Clinton and extended by Cornwallis. The *Register* closes its account with Tarleton's defeat of Sumpter at Fishing Creek in August. The chapter concludes with an account of Cornwallis's successes (doubtless with the advantages of hindsight in view of the delay in publication) and remarks that "... it has been the singular feature of that war, that victory, on the British side, has been unproductive of its proper and customary efforts."

The *Register*'s historical account of 1780 concentrates on domestic affairs unconnected with the war, so only a small section of Chapter II, i.e., that dealing with the summer invasion scare, and those portions of Chapters VIII and X covering the war in America, are extracted

16. *AR*, 1780, p. 200*].

here. The *Appendix to the Chronicle* contains eighteen items, but apart from four referring to Anglo-French ship-to-ship duels, none are directly concerned with the war. The *State Papers* was expanded to seventy-four pages to accommodate thirty-nine items, and it contains a good deal of relevant material. Extracted here are the incriminating documents captured with Henry Laurens (the Lee-de Neufville draft is described as "a treaty of Amity and Commerce between the Republic of Holland and the United States of America") and the British demand of 10 November for disavowal;[17] papers describing the André affair; and Benedict Arnold's justificatory message explaining his defection.

17. Other items showing the development of the rupture with the Netherlands can be found in pages 342], [345, 374], [375, 376], [379, and 380]; the formation of the League of Armed Neutrality and reactions to it are illustrated by papers printed on pages 346], [347, [349, 350], 352], [353, 354], and [355.

In England, besides all other or former real or supposed causes of dissatisfaction, the long continuance, contrary to the expectations held out, of the American war, and its hopelessness of ultimate success in the minds of many, began now to affect the feelings of the people, so generally and powerfully, as to open a source of discontent, which, by degrees, seemed to grow wider, than any other of which they had hitherto complained. Many of those who had been amongst the foremost in supporting, and the warmest in approving, the measures which led to that issue, and the principle on which they were founded, were now among the loudest in lamenting the consequence of the war, and the most eager for its being brought to a speedy conclusion. No change, they said, had taken place in their original principle or opinion; but they were compelled to conform their sentiments, and to submit, to the present necessity of the times. The weakness of the counsels and measures, under which the American disputes and contest had been suffered to linger for so many years, had, they said, totally changed the state and nature of things. If we have lost, said they, the advantages which she afforded, by our folly, let our wisdom now immediately cut away those fatal incumbrances which are left behind; those incumbrances which clog and impede all our motions, and render all our exertions against the common enemy ineffective. Let the evils follow the benefits. It must be the extreme of madness to retain one without the other.

Such was now the language held by no small number of those, who had formerly supported or approved of the American measures, and by the whole of those who had constantly opposed or condemned them. They also uniformly coincided in another general opinion; which was, by no means to shrink from the war with the house of Bourbon. Holding a firm confidence, that if America was in any manner detached from the quarrel, or even rendered so far ineffective as not to be considered as a principal object, and our whole force, under the guidance of wise counsels, and the ability of those great commanders, which all the world knew we possessed, was directed against our natural enemies in their most vulnerable parts, they would not only be soon sickened of the part which they had taken in our domestic contest; but that we might also make such reprizals on them, as would afford no inconsiderable compensation for the losses we had suffered.

The danger held out of an invasion, and the proclamation ordering [1] provisions to be made against it, were severely criticized by opposition; as tending more to alarm the people than to secure the country;

as weak and indefinite in its directions, and only calculated to draw out a few miserable subscriptions, which might lay a claim of merit for individuals, but could never be a substantial aid to government. It was only indeed a little trick, to confound an attachment to ministers with a regard to the safety of the country.

On the other hand it was contended, that to caution without alarming was a thing impossible. That future directions, when occasions arose, would render the proclamation more explicit. That the whole intent was to make the people alert, and to call forth the general exertion. And as for subscription, if it should shew a confidence in administration, it was a confidence deserved, and would be repaid in the honour and safety of the nation.

The measure was not without effect. Large sums were raised in several counties, and applied to the levying of independent corps or companies. About 20,000l. was subscribed in the city of Westminster, although some considerable parishes refused to concur in the measure. Some of the inhabitants also of that city associated, and were formed into distinct bodies, armed and officered, with a view of being so far trained in military discipline and exercise, as would enable them to act with effect, under the immediate necessity of common defence. In some counties, however, the measure was rejected; and in others it was not proposed. In one, where a considerable subscription was made, the money was transmitted to the disposal of the Marine Society; as a more useful and constitutional application than to the raising of land forces.

In London, the proposal brought out another for a strong petition to the throne, as a previous measure, requiring the dismission of incapable ministers and evil counsellors, and the employment of men in whom the nation could place a confidence, and who might be capable of retrieving its affairs. The final consequence was, that the first proposal, after much discussion, was rejected, and the petition then laid by. In the trading cities and towns, the money was applied to the manning of the navy; by which means, the various bounties to seamen, accumulated in some places, particularly Liverpool, to a height before unheard of. The East India company behaved with a magnificence, suited to its greatness, and to the apparent prosperity of its affairs. Besides a considerable bounty for the raising of 6000 men for the naval service, it made a liberal offer to the crown, which was accepted, of building and furnishing three seventy-four gun ships, as an addition to the royal navy.

The measures of home defence met with similar animadversion. The vast military force which was kept for our internal defence, a purpose to which, they said, the minister had avowedly in parliament sacrificed all other considerations, and particularly hazarded the preservation of our West India Islands, was said to be so injudiciously disposed, as to be rendered incompetent to its only design. Towns of the greatest commercial consequence, and garrisons which defended the most valuable inlets and harbours, were left in a state of nakedness. The defenceless state in which even the great securities to our strength, Portsmouth and Plymouth, were afterwards reported to be, and the consequent danger to which they were supposed to be exposed, upon the approach of the enemy, served much to corroborate these assertions and opinions; and even afforded a degree of strength to others of a similar nature.

All these and many more topics were agitated, and they were agitated with the greater effect, from the junction of the French and Spanish fleets in the channel.[2] The sending the fleets out to America and the East Indies, under the decided superiority of the enemy in our own seas, was much condemned.—Events, which usually decide the publick on political measures, and the inefficiency of those mighty fleets, have at length answered all these criticisms.

The proclamation which had been issued by the commissioners upon their departure from America, together with some ministerial declarations in parliament, had occasioned a very general persuasion, that as no further lenity or forbearance was to be practised with respect to the refractory colonies, (a mistaken tenderness, to which many were apt to attribute the spinning out of the contest for so many years) so the war would have been carried on in the ensuing campaign, with a degree of vigour and activity hitherto unknown. At the same time, the declaration made by the American minister in parliament, that a vast majority of the people on that continent were zealously attached to the interests and government of Great Britain, and that even the remainder were either tired out and heartily sick of the war, or torn to pieces by factions and dissensions among themselves, spread an opinion no less general, that the defence on the one side would be proportionally as weak and ineffective, as the coercion on the other would be powerful and conclusive.

In proportion to the sanguine expectations thus raised, was the disappointment and concern which prevailed towards the close of the year, as the failure of success or inactivity in the American campaign, and the loss and danger in the West Indies, came by degrees to be known. The people were wearied out by the tediousness and length of that war, and disgusted by the continued repetition of hopes and disappointments which they had so long experienced.

In this state of danger from without, and of discontent within, the ministers seemed as little united among themselves, as any class or part of the people who were committed to their government. At the same time, the several parties which formed the opposition seemed to be drawing closer together, and to act with more apparent union and concert than hitherto they had done. At no time do we remember the confidence of the people in government so low, as it appears to have been at that period.

...

It appears from various circumstances, that the Spanish governors and commanders in America and the West Indies, had been acquainted with the intended rupture between Spain and England, long before the declaration presented by their minister to the court of London, on the 16th of June, 1779. It would even seem, that they were informed of the precise time, or very near it, at which that event would take place; for it is asserted, that war was declared in the island of Porto Rico, in a few days after the delivery of that rescript in London; and it is certain, that English vessels were carried into the Havanna as prizes, before any intelligence of that measure could have been possibly received in America. Plans were accordingly laid, and preparations made to the time, which afforded advantage in the commencement of hostilities.

But in no instance was the effect of this pre intelligence so ruinous, as in the loss which it occasioned of the British settlements on the Missisippi, along with the capture of the troops destined to their protection. We have heretofore shewn, that the settlements in that part of Louisiana, being yet too weak for a particular government, were annexed to that of West Florida; which was, however, too distant, to afford any effectual protection. We have also seen that in the preceding year, a party of Americans visited that country, and received a temporary submission from the inhabitants, which they did not stay to maintain. That American expedition, and the defenceless state of the settlements, which it had rendered apparent, were undoubtedly the causes, that some troops had since been sent for their protection.

Don Bernardo de Galvez, the [3] Spanish Governor of Louisiana, having collected the whole force of his Province at New Orleans, first publicly declared the independency of America by beat of drum, and then set out on this expedition. He had previously concerted his measures so well in securing the communications, that Major General Campbell, who [4] commanded at Pensacola, did not receive the smallest information of the danger of the western part of the province, or even that hostility was intended, until the design was nearly effected. With similar address, and profiting of the security which prevailed on our side, he had, by surprize and stratagem, taken a royal sloop of war, which was stationed on Lake Pontchartrain, and was equally successful in seizing several vessels on the lakes and rivers, laden with provisions and necessaries for the British detachment, and one, containing some troops of the regiment of Waldeck.

Aug. 19th, 1779.

Such lucky circumstances, were not necessary to insure success to his enterprize. The whole military force, British and German, stationed for the protection of the country, did not amount to five hundred men; and these had no other cover against a superior enemy, but a newly constructed fort, or more properly Field Redoubt, which they had hastily thrown up, at a place called Baton Rouge. In this place, however, Lieutenant Colonel Dickson, of the 16th [5] regiment, stood a siege of nine days; and when the opening of a battery of heavy artillery had rendered all farther defence impracticable, he obtained conditions very honourable to the garrison, and highly favourable to the inhabitants. The troops, from the nature of their situation, were necessarily obliged to surrender prisoners of war; and it is to be remembered, highly to the honour of the Spanish governor and commander, Don Bernardo de Galvez, that upon this, as well as upon a later occasion of the same unfortunate nature, nothing could exceed the good faith with which he observed the prescribed conditions, nor the humanity, and kindness, with which he treated his prisoners.

The languid nature of the campaign on the side of New York, enabled the Americans, in the beginning and progress of the autumn, to take a heavy vengeance on the Indians, for the cruelties and enormities which they had so long practised on the frontiers. So formidable was this enemy now grown, through the accession of strength and discipline which it derived from the refugees and white adventurers, that a small army, with a train of artillery, under the conduct of General Sullivan, assisted by some other officers of name, were destined to this service. The famous confederacy of the five or of the six nations, as it has been differently called; that confederacy which exhibited the rude outlines of a republic, in the moft hidden defarts of America, was the object of the prefent expedition.

Thefe nations lying at the backs of the northern and middle colonies, amidft the great lakes, rivers, and impenetrable forefts, which feparate them from Canada, had long been renowned for the courage, fidelity, and conftancy, with which they had adhered to the Englifh in their wars with the French; and had even affifted them frequently againft different nations of their own countrymen. In the beginning of the prefent conteft, they had concluded a treaty with the Americans, by which they bound themfelves to obferve a ftrict neutrality during the progrefs of the ftruggle. The Americans faid, that they offered at that time to take up the hatchet againft the Englifh, but that they had rejected the offer upon principle; only requiring of them to adhere ftrictly to the neutrality.

The power of prefents, with the influence of Sir William Johnfon, and fome others who had intereft among them, operating upon their own natural propenfities, foon led them to depart from this pacific line of conduct, and they took a diftinguifhed part in that cruel and deftructive war, which, we have more than once feen, was carried on againft the back fettlement. The Oneida Indians, were the only nation of the confederacy, who had adhered to the neutrality; or at leaft, who were not known to have taken any direct part againft the Americans. They were accordingly deftined to efcape the intended general deftruction. For the principle of this war was extermination; fo far as that can be carried into execution againft an enemy, who feldom can be caught or found, except when, from motives of advantage, he choofes to ftay, or to reveal himfelf. They were of opinion that

nothing lefs, than driving them totally and far from their prefent poffeffions, could ever afford any permanent profpect of fecurity and quiet, to their numerous infant fettlements; which they knew, under thefe circumftances, would foon become the great fources of wealth and ftrength to their refpective ftates.

The Indians marched boldly towards the frontiers of their country to meet the invaders. They were headed by Butler, Brandt, Guy Johnfon, and Macdonald;[6] and, befides affembling all their own tribes and allies, were joined by fome hundreds of refugees, or, as the Americans call them, Tories. They poffeffed themfelves of a difficult pafs in the woods, between Chemung and Newtown, in the vicinity of the Teaoga River; where they conftructed a ftrong breaft-work, made of large logs, of above half a mile in extent; from whence other works, of lefs ftrength, reached a mile and a half, to the top of a mountain in their rear, where a fecond breaft-work was formed.

A warm attack and defence took place, and was continued for two hours; in which Sullivan found that he had full occafion for his artillery to make any effectual impreffion on the breaft-work. The rout of the confederates was accelerated and completed, through the movements that were made by the generals Poor and Clinton, for turning their flanks,[7] and thereby cutting off their retreat. The victory was fo compleat that they never attempted to make another ftand during the fubfequent defolation of their country.

Aug. 29th.
1779.

This action only opened the way to the commencement of Sullivan's expedition; and there was a difficulty ftill remained, which was capable of rendering it in a great meafure ineffective. To render the fervice in any confiderable

degree effectual, it was neceffary that the army fhould be out a month, at leaft, in a country totally unknown, and where no fupplies of any fort could be hoped for; but with all Sullivan's induftry, and the aids of his employers, the diftance, roads, and other circumftances, rendered it impracticable to provide provifion for more than half the time; nor, if there had been more, were packhorfes to be found for its conveyance; although to lighten the carriage, the cattle which they were to live upon were driven along with the army. The fpirit of the foldiers, the hearty zeal of the officers, with an animating fpeech from their general, removed all impediment to the defign: the propofal of fhort allowance was received with the loudeft fhouts of approbation; and the ration for 24 hours was fixed, with univerfal confent, at half a pound of flour, and as much frefh beef; the reduction going even to the falt.

This expedition was worthy of note, as it difcovered a greater degree of policy, and rather an higher ftate of improvement, among thofe Indian nations, than had been expected, even by thofe who had lived near, and almoft in the midft of them. Sullivan difcovered, to his furprize, that no guides could be procured who knew any thing at all of the country; and that the only means he had of finding his way to the Indian towns, were thofe which betray a wild beaft in his den, the track of the inhabitant; which was a much more difficult clue in the former cafe than the latter, as the laft of an Indian file always fmooths and covers over with leaves, the tracks made by his fellows and himfelf; fo that it requires much experience, as well as patience and induftry, to be able to develope and trace them.

The degree of culture about the Indian towns was confiderably higher than could be fuppofed from former obfervations and opinions relative to the cuftoms and manners of thefe people. The beauty of their fituation, in many inftances indicating choice and defign, together with the fize, the conftruction, and the neatnefs of their houfes, were the firft great objects of admiration in this new country. Sullivan fays, in feveral places, that the houfes were not only large, but elegant; and frequently mentions their being huilt of frame-work. The fize of their corn fields excited his wonder, as well as the high degree of cultivation which they fhewed. Some idea may be formed of both, from the quantity of corn the Americans deftroyed in this expedition; which they eftimate at 160,000 bufhels.

But the number of fruit trees which they found and deftroyed, with the fize and antiquity of their orchards, afford an object of much greater admiration; as thefe circumftances not only fhew that cultivation was not of a late date among thefe people, but tend likewife to overthiow that opinion fo generally received, that the Indians are incapable of looking to futurity in their conduct, and confequently totally improvident with refpect to pofterity. Perhaps other inftances of this nature, and in a ftill higher degree, may yet be found, in more remote or hidden parts of America; and perhaps it may be difcovered, that man, in what is called his favage ftate, like beavers, and fome other animals, becomes more favage, carelefs, and improvident, in proportion as he finds that his views are broken, and his fecurity leffened, by the near approach of the civilized part of his own fpecies. Sullivan informs us, that they cut down 1500 fruit trees in one orchard; and takes notice in different places, without the fmalleft obfervation on the fact, that many of the trees carried the appearances of great age. Neither the paft

enormities or cruelties of the Indians, the policy of the motives, the juftice of the refeatment, or even the fuppofed neceffity of the act, can prevent the pain arifing to a fenfible mind, from fuch a havock and deftruction of the labours and hopes of mankind; it is not impoffible, that the very improvidence imputed to the proprietors, renders the blight which thus fell upon the fruits of their poor induftry the more afflicting.

The work of defolation was completed within the piefcribed time, and no more; there not being a day to fpare. In that time, the Americans had deftroyed forty Indian towns; of which, Chinefee, the largeft, contained 128 houfes; but the others bore no proportion as to fize It feems by a paffage in Sullivan's letter, as if they had already began to caft a wiftful eye towards the cultivation of that fine, and, until now, unexplored country. Sullivan gained great public applaufe by this expedition, and received teftimonials of the fulleft approbation and warmeft affection from his officers and army; but he purchafed thefe gratifications at the expence of a ruined conftitution, which has fince reftrained him from all active fervice.

• • •

Rhode Ifland evacuated. Defign againft New York fruftrated by D'Eftaing's failure at Savannah. Expedition againft Charles Town. Sir Henry Clinton lands with the army in South Carolina; takes poffeffion of the iflands of John and James; paffes Afhley River to Charles Town Neck; fiege of that city. Admiral Arbuthnot paffes the Bar with difficulty. American and French marine forces abandon their ftation, and retire to the town, where moft of the former are funk to bar a paffage. The admiral paffes the heavy fire of the fort on Sullivan's Ifland and takes poffeffion of the harbour. General Lincoln fummoned without effect. State of the defences on Charles Town Neck. Colonel Tarleton cuts off a party of the rebels. Col. Webfter paffes Cooper River with a detachment, by which the city is clofely invefted. Lord Cornwallis takes the command on that fide. Siege preffed with great vigour. Admiral Arbuthnot takes Mount Pleafant, and reduces Fort Moultrie. Tarleton defeats and deftroys the rebel cavalry. Capitulation of Charles Town. Garrifon, artillery, frigates, &c. Rebels again defeated by Tarleton, at Waxaw. Regulations by Sir Henry Clinton for the fecurity of the province. Departure for New York. Earl Cornwallis reduces the whole colony. Unexpected danger to which the feverity of the winter had expofed New York; Gallant defence made by Capt. Cornwallis, againft a French fuperior naval force. Three naval actions between Sir George Rodney, and M. de Guichen, productive of no decifive confequences. Infurrections of the loyalifts in North Carolina quelled. Baron de Kalbe marches into that province with a continental force. Is followed by Gen. Gates, who takes the chief command. State of affairs in the two Carolina's. Battle of Camden. Complete victory gained by Lord Cornwallis. Sumpter routed by Tarleton.

THE appearance and continuance of D'Eftaing on the coaft of North America, in the autumn of the year 1779, neceffarily fufpended all active operations on the fide of New York; where none but defenfive meafures could be thought of, under the well-founded apprehenfion of a formidable attack by fea and land, which had been evidently concerted between that commander and General Wafhington. The latter had collected a ftronge force for that purpofe in the Highlands, to which the northern colonies had largely contributed, hoping to end the war by one decisive stroke; and being in poffeffion of the North River, the cloud feemed ready to break upon the iflands, as foon as the French fleet fhould appear in fight; an event that did not feem to be far diftant, as it was expected on both fides by the new allies, that the taking of the Savannah could be little more than the work of a day; and that the fuccefs would not only infpire confidence, but even afford means, for the attainment of the grand object.

Under thefe apparent circumftances of danger, it was found advifeable, befides adopting every other means of a vigorous defence againft a greatly fuperior force, to withdraw the garrifon and marine from Rhode Ifland, and to fuffer that place to fall again into the hands of the Americans

But the defeat of D'Eftaing, and ftill more the lofs of time, which attended his ill conducte enterprize, having totally fruftrated the views of the enemy, ferved equally to extend thofe of General Sir Henry Clinton, and of Admiral Arbuthnot, to active [8] and effective fervice, by an expedition to the fouthern coloni s. Wafhington's army was already in a great meafure broken up. The auxiliaries had returned home; the term of enliftment of a great number of the continental foldiers was expired; and the filling up of the regiments, by waiting for recruits from their refpective ftates, muft necefarily be a work of confiderable time.

South Carolina was the immediate and great object of enterprize. Befides the numerous benefits to be immediately derived from the poffeffion of that province of opulence and ftaple product, and the unfpeakable lofs which it would occafion to the enemy, its fituation rendered it ftill more valuable, from the fecurity which it would not only

afford to Georgia, but in a very confiderable degree, to all that fouthern point of the continent which ftretches beyond it.

Sir Henry Clinton's land force being now whole and concentrated by the evacuation of Rhode Ifland, it afforded means as well as incitement to enterprize. The army was likewife in excellent condition; the reinforcements from England had not been impaired by any fervice; and it was abundantly provided with artillery, and with all the other engines, furniture, and provifion of war. Nor was the naval force lefs competent to its purpofe; there being nothing then in the American feas, which could even venture to look at it. On the other hand, the diftance of South Carolina, from the center of force and action, cut it off from all means of prompt fupport in any cafe; while the prefent ftate of the American army, along with many circumftances in the fituation of their public affairs, rendered the profpect of any timely or effectual relief extremely faint.

Although every thing had been for fome time prepared for the expedition, and the troops even embarked, yet through the defect of any certain intelligence, as to the departure of D'Eftaing from the coaft of North America, it was not until within a few days of the clofe of the year, Dec. 26th. that the fleet and convoy proceeded from New York. The voyage from thence to the Savannah, (where they did not arrive until the end of January) was very unprofperous. Befides its extreme tedioufnefs, the fea was fo rough, and the weather fo tempeftuous, that great mifchief was done among the tranfports and victuallers. Several were loft; others difperfed and damaged; a few were taken by the Americans; an ordinance fhip went down, with all her ftores;

and almoft all the horfes, whether of draught or appertaining to the cavalry, were loft.

From Savannah, the fleet and army proceeded before the middle of February, to the Inlet or harbour of North Edifto, on the coaft of South Carolina, where the army was landed without oppofition or difficulty; and took poffeffion with equal facility, firft of John's Ifland, and next, that of James, which ftretches to the fouth of Charles Town Harbour. We have already had occafion, in our account of Gen. Prevoft's expedition, to take fome notice of the geography and nature of this flat and infulated country. The army afterwards, by throwing a bridge over the Wappoo cut, extended its pofts on the mainland, to the banks of Afhley River, between which and Cooper's River, Charles Town ftands; the approach to it being called the Neck.

The general is not explicit in his information, as to the nature of the difficulties, or rather wants, which were the caufe of detaining the army in this pofition, until near the end of March; he feeming to confider thefe circumftances, as matters already well underftood by the Secretary of State. We only learn, that a train of heavy artillery fupplied by the large fhips of the fleet, with a body of failors, under the conduct of Capt. Elphinftone of [9] the navy, were of fingular fervice in the profecution of the fiege; and that the general found it neceffary to draw a reinforcement from Georgia, which joined him without any other interruption, than the natural difficulties of the country (which were not fmall) during a toilfome march of twelve days.

The paffage of Afhley River was effected with great March 29, 1780.
facility, thro' the aid of the naval officers and feamen, with their boats

and armed gallies; and the army, with its artillery and stores, was landed without opposition on Charles Town Neck. On the night of the 1st of April, they broke ground within 800 yards of the enemy's works; and in a week, their guns were mounted in battery.

In the mean time, Admiral Arbuthnot had not been deficient in his endeavours for the passing of Charles Town Bar, in order effectually to second the operations of the army. For this purpose he shifted his flag from the Europa of the line, to the Roe Buck of 44 guns, which, with the Renown and Romulus, were lightened of their guns, provisions and water, the lighter frigates being capable of passing the bar without that preparation. Yet so difficult was the task in any state, that they lay in that situation, exposed on an open coast, in the Winter season, to the danger of the seas, and to the insults of the enemy, for above a fortnight, before a proper opportunity offered. The bar was, however, then passed (on the 20th of March) without loss; and the entrance of the harbour gained without difficulty.

The enemy had a considerable marine force in the harbour, which might have been expected to contribute more to the defence of the town and passage than it actually did. This consisted of an American ship, built since the troubles, and pierced for 60 guns, but mounting only 44; of seven frigates of the same country, from 32 to 16 guns; with a French frigate of 26 guns, and a polacre of eighteen. These at first, upon the admiral's getting over the bar, shewed a disposition to dispute the passage up the river; and accordingly, they were moored with some armed gallies, at a narrow pass, between Sullivan's Island and the middle ground, in a position which would have enabled them to rake his squadron on its approach to Fort Moultrie.

This appearance of resolution, however, gave way to more timid, and it should seem, less wise council. For abandoning every idea of resistance, and leaving the fort to its own fortune, they retired to Charles-Town; where most of the ships, with a number of merchant vessels, being fitted with chevaux de frize on their decks, were sunk [10] to obstruct the channel of the river between the town and Shutes-Folly; thus converting a living active force into an inert machine. This obstacle removed, and the success of the attack on the land side depending almost entirely on the joint operation of the fleet, the admiral took a favourable opportunity of wind and water, to pass the heavy batteries of Fort Moultrie, on Sullivan's Island; so much celebrated for the obstinate and successful defence, which, we have heretofore seen, it made, against the long, fierce and bloody attack, of Admiral Sir Peter Parker.

The passage was effected, under a severe April 9th. and impetuous fire, with less loss of lives than could have been well expected; the number of seamen killed and wounded being under thirty. The fleet, however, suffered in other respects from the fire of the enemy; and a transport, with some naval stores, was of necessity abandoned, and burnt. But the great object was now gained; they were in possession of the harbour, and took such effectual measures for blocking up or securing the various inlets, that the town was little less than completely invested. As the enemy had placed their principle trust in the defence of the passage up the river, and thereby keeping the harbour free, and their back secure, nothing could be more terrible to them than this situation of the fleet; whereby their defences were greatly multiplied, their attention diverted from the land side, and their means of relief, and even of escape, considerably streightened.

In this state of things, the batteries ready to be opened; the commanders by sea and land, sent a joint summons to General Lincoln, who commanded in Charles-Town; holding out the fatal consequences of a cannonade and storm, stating the present, as the only favourable opportunity for preserving the lives and property of the inhabitants, and warning the commander that he should be responsible for all those calamities which might be the fruits of his obstinacy. Lincoln answered, that the same duty and inclination which had prevented him from abandoning Charles-Town, during sixty days knowledge of their hostile intentions, operated now with equal force, in prompting him to defend it to the last extremity.

The defences of Charles-Town, on the neck, were for their nature and standing, very considerable. They consisted of a chain of redoubts, lines, and batteries, extending from one river to the other; and covered with an artillery of eighty cannon and mortars. In the front of either flank, the works were covered by swamps, originating from the opposite rivers, and tending towards the center; through which they were connected by a canal passing from one to the other. Between these outward impediments and the works, were two strong rows of abbatis, the trees being buried slanting in the earth, so that their heads facing outwards, formed a kind of fraize-work against the assailants; and these were farther secured, by a ditch double picketted. In the center, where the natural defences were unequal to those on the flanks, a horn-work of masonry had been constructed, as well to remedy that defect, as to cover the principal gate; and this during the siege had been closed in such a manner as to render it a kind of citadel, or independent fort.

The siege was carried on with great vigour; the batteries were soon perceived to acquire a superiority over those of the enemy; and the works were pushed forward with unremitted industry. Soon after the middle of April, the second parallel was completed; the approaches to it secured: and it was carried within 450 yards of the main works of the besieged. Major Moncrieffe, who had gained so much honour in the defence of the Savannah, acquired no less applause, from the very superior and masterly manner in which he conducted the offensive operations of the present siege.

The town had kept its communication open with the country, on the farther side of Cooper's river, for some time after it had been invested on other sides by the fleet and army; and some bodies of militia cavalry and infantry began to assemble on the higher parts of that river, who being in possession of the bridges, might at least have become troublesome to the foraging parties, if not capable of disturbing the operations of the army. The general, as soon as his situation would permit, detached 1400 men under Lieutenant-colonel Webster, in order to strike at this corps which the enemy were endeavouring to form in the field, to break in upon their remaining communications, and to seize the principal passes of the country. On this expedition Lieutenant-colonel Tarleton, at the head of a corps of cavalry, and seconded by Major Ferguson's light infantry and marksmen, afforded a striking specimen of that active gallantry, and of those peculiar military talents, which have since so highly distinguished his character. With a very inferior force, he surprized, defeated, and almost totally cut off the rebel party; and having thereby gained possession of Big-

19th.

gin's Bridge on the Cooper River, opened the way to Colonel Webster to advance nearly to the head of the Wandoo River, and to occupy the passes in such a manner, as to shut Charles-Town up entirely.

As the arrival of a large reinforcement from New York, enabled the general considerably to strengthen the corps under Webster, so the importance of the situation, induced Earl Cornwallis to take the command on that side of Cooper's River. Under the conduct of this nobleman, Tarleton attacked, defeated and ruined, another body of cavalry, which the enemy had with infinite difficulty collected together.

In the mean time, the besiegers had completed their third parallel, which they carried close to the rebel canal; and by a sap pushed to the dam which supplied it with water on the 'right, they had drained it in several parts to the bottom. On the other hand, the admiral, who had constantly pressed and distressed the enemy, in every part within his reach, having taken the fort at mount Pleasant, acquired from its vicinity, and the information of the deserters which it encouraged, a full knowledge of the state of the garrison and defences of Fort Moultrie, in Sullivan's Island. In pursuance of this information, and determined not to weaken the operations of the army, he landed a body of seamen and marines, in order to storm the place by land, while the ships battered it in every possible direction. In these circumstances, the garrison, (amounting to something more than 200 men) seeing the imminent danger to which they were exposed, and sensible of the impossibility of relief, were glad, by a capitulation, to surrender themselves prisoners of war.

May 7th.

Thus enclosed on every side, and driven to its last defences, the

general wishing to preserve Charles Town from destruction, and to prevent that effusion of human blood, which must be the inevitable consequence of a storm, opened a correspondence on the following day with Lincoln, for the purpose of a surrender. But the conditions demanded by that commander being deemed higher, than his present circumstances and situation entitled him to, they were rejected and hostilities renewed. The batteries on the third parallel were then opened, and so great a superiority of fire obtained, that the besiegers were enabled under it to gain the counterscarp of the out-work which flanked the canal; which they likewise passed; and then pushed on their works directly towards the ditch of the place.

The objections to the late conditions required by Gen. Lincoln, went principally to some stipulations in favour of the citizens and militia; but the present state of danger having brought those people to acquiesce in their being relinquished, as the price of security, that commander accordingly proposed to surrender upon the terms which were then offered. The British commanders, besides their averseness to the cruel extremity of a storm, were not disposed to press to unconditional submission, an enemy whom they wished to conciliate by clemency. They granted now the same conditions which they had before offered; and the capitulation was accordingly signed.

May 11th.

The garrison were allowed some of the honours of war; but they were not to uncase their colours, nor their drums to beat a British march. The continental troops and seamen were to keep their baggage, and to remain prisoners of war until they were exchanged. The militia were to be permitted to return to their respective homes, as prisoners on parole; and while they adhered to their parole, were not to be molested by the British troops in person or property. The citizens of all sorts to be considered as prisoners on parole; and to hold their property on the same terms with the militia. The officers of the army and navy, to retain their servants, swords, pistols, and their baggage, unsearched. Horses were refused, as to carrying them out of Charles Town; but they were allowed to dispose of them in the town.

Seven general officers, ten continental regiments, and three battalions of artillery, became prisoners upon this occasion. The whole number of men in arms who were taken, including town and country militia, and French, amounted to 5611, exclusive of near a thousand seamen. The number of rank and file, which appear on this list, bear no proportion to the clouds of commission and non-commission officers, which exceed nine hundred. The thinness of the continental regiments accounts partly for this circumstance; it appearing from Lincoln's return to congress, that the whole number of men of every sort included in so many regiments and battalions, at the time of the surrender, did not amount to quite 2500. He boasts in that[12] letter, that he lost only twenty men by desertion, in six weeks before the surrender.

As the siege was not productive of sallies or desperate assaults, which were in a considerable degree prevented by situation, and the nature of the works, the loss of men was not great on either side, and was not very unequally shared. A prodigious artillery was taken; amounting, of every sort, and including those in the forts and ships, to considerably more than 400 pieces. Of these, 311 were found in Charles Town only. Three stout rebel frigates, one French, and a polacre of 16[13] guns, of the same nation, which escaped the operation of being sunk to bar the river, fell likewise into the hands of the victors.

The Carolinians complained greatly of their not being properly assisted by their neighbours, particularly the Virginians, in this long and arduous struggle. If the complaint is at all founded, it can only relate to the not sending of reinforcements to the garrison before the city was closely invested: for the southern colonies possessed no force, which was in any degree equal to the raising, or even to the much incommoding of the siege. Nor does it seem that the augmentation of the garrison would have answered any effectual purpose.[14] At the commencement of the siege, an American lieutenant-colonel, of the name of Hamilton Ballendine, having the fortune of[15] being detected in his attempt to pass to the English camp at night, with draughts of the town and works, immediately suffered the unpitied death of a traitor.

The most rapid and brilliant success now attended every exertion of the British arms; Lord Cornwallis, on his march up the north side of the great Santee river, having received intelligence that the remaining force of the rebels were collected near the borders of north Carolina, dispatched Colonel Tarleton, with the cavalry, and a new corps of light infantry, called the Legion, mounted on horseback, in order to rout and disperse that body, before it could receive any addition of force from the neighbouring colonies.

The enemy being at so great a distance, as not to apprehend almost the possibility of any near danger, had considered other circumstances of convenience more, than the means of securing a good retreat, in their choice of situation. No such negligence could pass unpunished, under any circumstance of distance, with such an enemy as they had now to encounter. Colonel Tarleton, upon this occasion, exceeded even his own usual celerity; and having marched 105 miles in 54 hours, presented himself suddenly and unexpectedly, at a place called Waxaw, before an astonished and dispirited enemy. They, however, positively rejected the conditions which were offered them, of surrendering upon the same terms with the garrison of Charles Town. The attack was highly spirited; the defence, notwithstanding the cover of a wood, faint; and the ruin complete. Above 100 were killed on the spot; about 150 so badly wounded as to be unable to travel, and about 50 brought away prisoners. Their colours, baggage, with the remains of the artillery of the southern army, fell into the hands of the victors. The loss on their side, though the rebels were superior in number, was very trifling.

May 29th.

After this success, there was nothing to resist the arms of Lord Cornwallis; and the reduction of that extensive colony of South Carolina, was deemed so complete, at the time of Sir Henry Clinton's departure, on returning to his government of New York, that he informs the American minister in his letter, that there were few men in the province, who were not either prisoners to, or in arms with the British forces; and he cannot restrain his exultation at the number of the inhabitants who came in from every quarter, to testify their allegiance, and to offer their services, in arms, in support of his Majesty's government; and who, in many instances, had brought as prisoners their former oppressors or leaders.

June 5th.

That commander accordingly, in settling the affairs and government of the province, adopted a scheme of obliging it to contribute largely to its own defence; and even to look forward, in present exertion, to future security, by taking an active share in the suppression of the rebellion on its borders. In this view, he seemed to admit of no neutrals; but that every man, who did not avow himself an enemy to the British government, should take an active part in its support. On this principle, all persons were expected to be in readiness with their arms at a moment's warning; those who had families, to form a militia for

Notwithstanding the tranquil appearances of things in South Carolina, at the time of Sir Henry Clinton's departure from thence, it soon became obvious, that many of the inhabitants were so little satisfied with the present government, that they endeavoured to dispose of their property upon such terms as they could obtain, and totally to abandon the province. This conduct became so frequent and glaring, that Lord Cornwallis found it necessary towards the end of July to issue a proclamation, strictly forbidding all sales and transfers of property, including even negroes, without a licence first obtained from the commandant of Charles Town; and likewise forbidding all masters of vessels, from carrying any persons whatever, whether black or white, out of the colony, without a written passport from the same officer.

In the mean time, Lord Cornwallis, who extended his views to the reduction of North Carolina, had kept up a constant correspondence with the loyalists in that colony, who eagerly urged him to the prosecution of his design. But besides that the heat of the Summer was so excessive, that it would have rendered action exceedingly destructive to the troops, he likewise found, that no army could be subsisted in that country, until the harvest was over. Upon these accounts, he earnestly pressed the friends of the British government in North Ca-

rolina, to keep themselves quiet, and free from all suspicion, though in readiness, until the proper season arrived. But the usual impatience of those people, operated upon by the vigilant jealousy of that government, or, as they said, by its oppression and cruelty, rendered them incapable of profiting of such salutary counsel. Insurrections accordingly took place, which being conducted without order or caution, as well as premature, were easily suppressed. A Col. Bryan, however, with about[16] 800 half armed men, escaped into South Carolina, where they joined the royal forces.

During the necessary continuance of the commander in chief at Charles Town, in regulating the government and affairs of the province, the part of the army destined to active service, was advanced towards the frontiers, under the conduct of Lord Rawdon, who[17] fixed his head quarters at the town of Camden. The advantageous situation of that place on the great river Santee, which afforded an easy communication with several, and remote, parts of the country, together with other inviting and favourable circumstances, induced Earl Cornwallis to make it not only a place of arms, but a general store-house or repository, for the supply of the army in its intended operations. He accordingly used the utmost dispatch in conveying thither from Charles Town, rum, salt, arms, ammunition, and various stores, which, from the distance, and excessive heat of the weather, proved a work of infinite labour and difficulty. That noble commander likewise spared no pains in arming and embodying the militia of the province, and in raising new military corps under well affected leaders.

But during these transactions, a great change took place in the aspect of affairs in North-Carolina.

For besides the suppression of the loyalists, who were treated with little mercy, Major-General the Baron de Kalbe, a German officer[18] in the American service, arrived in that province with 2000 continental troops; and was followed by some bodies of militia from Virginia. The government of the colony were likewise indefatigable in their exertions and preparations, at least for defence, if not for conquest. Troops were raised; the militia every where drawn out; and Rutherford, Caswell, Sumpter, and other leaders,[19] advanced to the frontiers at the head of different bodies of them. Skirmishes took place on all sides, and were attended with various fortune; and the enemy became so dangerous, that Lord Rawdon found it necessary to contract his posts.

It soon appeared, that the submission of many of the South-Carolinians was merely compulsory, and that no conditions or consequences could bind or deter them from pursuing the bent of their inclinations, whenever the opportunity offered. As the enemy increased in strength, and approached nearer, numbers of those who had submitted to the British government, and others who were on parole, abandoned, or hazarded all things, in order to join them. A Colonel Lisle, who had exchanged[20] his parole for a certificate of being a good subject, carried off a whole battalion of militia, which had been raised by another gentleman for Lord Cornwallis, to join Sumpter. Another battalion, who were appointed to conduct about 100 sick of the 71st regiment in boats down the Pedee to George-Town, seized their own officers, and carried them, with the sick men, all prisoners to the enemy.

General Gates was now arrived in North-Carolina, to take the command of the new southern army; and the time was fast approaching, when his high military reputation was to be staked in an arduous contest with the fortune of Earl Cornwallis. In the second week of August, that nobleman having received intelligence at Charles-Town, that Gates was advancing with his army towards Lynche's Creek, that Sumpter was endeavouring to cut off the communications between that city and the army, that the whole country between the Pedee and the Black River had revolted, and that Lord Rawdon was collecting his whole force at Camden, he immediately set off for that place.

He found on his arrival no small difficulties to encounter. Gates was advancing, and at hand, with a very decided superiority of force. His army was not estimated at less than five or six thousand men ; it was likewise supposed to be very well appointed : whilst the name and character of the commander, increased the idea of its force. On the other hand, Lord Cornwallis's regular force, was so much reduced by sickness and casualties, as not much to exceed 1400 fighting men, or rank and file, with four or five hundred militia, and North Carolina refugees. The position of Camden, however advantageous or convenient in other respects, was a bad one to receive an attack. He could indeed have made good his retreat to Charles-Town with those troops that were able to march ; but in that case, he must have left about 800 sick, with a vast quantity of valuable stores, to fall into the hands of the enemy. He likewise foresaw, that excepting Charles-Town and the Savannah, a retreat would be attended with the loss of the two whole provinces of South-Carolina and Georgia.

In these circumstances, the noble commander determined, neither to retreat, nor wait to be attacked in a bad position. He knew that Charles-Town was so well garrisoned and provided, that

it could not be exposed to any danger, from whatever might befal him. That his troops were excellent, admirably officered, and well found and provided in all respects. And that the loss of his sick, of his magazines, the abandonment of the country, and the desertion of his friends, all of which would be the inevitable consequences of a retreat, were almost the heaviest evils which could befal him in any fortune. In his own words, there was "little to lose by a defeat, and much to gain by a victory."

The intelligence which he received, that General Gates had encamped in a bad situation, at Rugley's, about 13 miles from Camden, undoubtedly served to confirm Lord Cornwallis in his determination. He accordingly marched from Camden about 10 o'clock at night, with a full intention of surprizing Gates at Rugley's ; and making his dispositions in such a manner, as that his best troops and greatest force should be directed against the continental regiments ; laying little stress on the militia, if these were sufficiently provided against.

Aug. 15th.

It was almost singular, that at the very hour and moment, at which Lord Cornwallis set out from Camden to surprize Gates, that general should set out from Rugley's in order to surprize him. For although he does not acknowledge the fact in point of design, and even pretends, that his night movement was made with a view of seizing an advantageous position some miles short of Camden ; his order of march, the disposition of his army, with the hour of setting out, and other circumstances, will leave but little room to entertain a doubt of his real object. These leading features will remind some of our readers of a celebrated action in the late war ; in which the Prussian monarch, environed with danger, and sur-

rounded on all sides by armies of enemies, some of which were singly superior to his own, surprized and defeated Laudohn on a night march, when that able general intended to conclude the war by completing the circle, and by surprizing him in a manner which must have been final in its effects. [21]

In the present instance, the light troops and advanced corps on both sides, necessarily fell in with, and encountered each other in the dark, so that the surprize was mutual. In this blind encounter, however, the American light troops being driven back precipitately on their van, occasioned some considerable disorder in that part, if not in their center, which probably was never entirely recovered. Lord Cornwallis repressed the firing early, and immediately formed ; he found that the enemy were in bad ground, and he would not hazard in the dark, the advantages which their situation would afford him in the light ; at the same time that he took such measures as effectually prevented their taking any other. For the ground occupied by both armies, being narrowed and pressed in upon on either hand by deep swamps, afforded great advantages to the weaker in making the attack, and by preventing the stronger from extending their lines, deprived them in a great measure, of those which they should have derived from their superiority in number.

A movement made by the Americans on the left by day-light, indicating some change of disposition or order, does not seem to have been a very judicious measure, in the face of, and so near to, such a commander, and such an army. Lord Cornwallis saw the advantage, and instantly seized it ; Col. Webster, who commanded the right wing, directly charging the enemy's left, with the light infantry, supported by the 23d and 33d regiments. The action soon became general, and was supported near an hour, with wonderful refolution, and the moft determined obftinacy. The firing was quick and heavy on both fides; and intermixed with fharp and well-fupported contefts at the point of the bayonet. The morning being ftill and hazy, the fmoke hung over and involved both armies in fuch a cloud, that it was difficult to fee or to eftimate the ftate of deftruction on either fide. The Britifh troops, however, evidently preffed forward; and at the period we have mentioned, the Americans were thrown into confufion, began to give way on all fides, and a total and general rout foon enfued.

We learn from the American accounts, that the whole body of their militia, (which conftituted much the greater part of their force) excepting only one North-Carolina regiment, gave way and run, at the very firft fire; and that all the efforts of the general himfelf, and of the other commanders, were incapable of bringing them afterwards ever to rally, or to make a fingle ftand; fo that gaining the woods as faft as poffible, they totally difperfed. But the continental regular troops, and the fingle North Carolina regiment of militia, vindicated their own and the national character. They even ftood that laft and fore teft of the goodnefs of troops, the pufh of the bayonet, with great conftancy and firmnefs.

The Britifh commander fhewed his ufual valour and military fkill. And the officers and troops, in their refpective ftations, anfwered his warmeft expectations. But though all are entitled to our applaufe, yet Lord Rawdon, with the two Lieutenant-Colonels Webfter and Tarleton, could not avoid being particularly diftinguifhed.

The victory was complete. The broken and fcattered enemy were purfued as far as Hanging-Rock, above twenty miles from the field

of battle. All their artillery, amounting to feven or eight brafs field pieces, with 2000 ftand of arms, their military waggons, and feveral trophies, were taken. Lord Cornwallis eftimates the flain at eight or nine hundred and fays about a thoufand prifoners were taken. The General, Baron de Kalbe, who was fecond in command, was mortally wounded, and taken. That officer fpent his laft breath in dictating a letter, expreffive of the warmeft affection for the Americans, containing the higheft encomiums on the valour of the continental troops, of which he had been fo recent a witnefs, and declaring the fatisfaction which he then felt in having been a partaker of their fortune, and having fallen in their caufe.

The American Brigadier-General Gregory, was among the [22] flain, and Rutherford was wounded and taken. Although fome brave officers fell, and feveral were wounded, on the Britifh fide, yet the lofs which the army fuftained was upon the whole comparatively fmall. It amounted, including eleven miffing, only to 324, in which number the flain bore a very moderate proportion.

Upon the whole, Gates feems to have been much outgeneralled. He was, however, confoled in his misfortune, (which has fince occafioned his retreat from the fervice) by the approbation of his conduct and fervices, which was publicly beftowed by fome of the affemblies.

General Sumpter had for fome time been very fuccefsful in cutting off or intercepting the Britifh parties and convoys, and lay now with about a thoufand men, and a number of prifoners and waggons which he had lately taken, at the Catawba fords; apparently fecured by diftance, as well as the difficulties of the country. Lord Cornwallis confidered it a matter of great importance to his future operations, to give a decifive blow

to this body, before he purfued his fuccefs by advancing into North-Carolina. He accordingly detached Colonel Tarleton, with the light infantry and cavalry of the legion, amounting to about 350, upon this fervice. The advantages to be derived from woody, ftrong, and difficult countries, are much counterbalanced by the opportunities which they afford of furprize. The brave and active officer employed upon this occafion, by forced marches, judicious meafures, and excellent intelligence, furprized Sumpter fo completely at noon-day, that his men, lying totally carelefs and at eafe, were moftly cut off from their arms. The victory was accordingly nothing more than a flaughter and rout. About 150 were killed on the fpot, about 300, with two pieces of cannon, taken, and a number of prifoners and waggons retaken.

Thefe fplendid fuccefses laid the fouthern colonies open, to all the effects of that fpirit of enterprize which diftinguifhes Earl Cornwallis, and which he communicates to all who act under his command In any other war than the American, they would have been decifive of the fate of thofe colonies. But it has been the fingular fortune of that war, that victory, on the Britifh fide, has been unproductive of its proper and cuftomary effects.

• • •

Papers which were communicated by Sir Jofeph Yorke, by exprefs Orders from the King his Mafter, to his Serene Highnefs the Prince Stadtholder, and which were taken out of Mr. Laurens's Trunk.

THE following are the outlines of a treaty of commerce, which, agreeably to the orders and inftructions of Mr. Engelbert Francis Van Berkel, [23] Counfellor and Penfionary of the city of Amfterdam, directed to me, John de Neufville, citizen of[24] the said city of Amsterdam, I have examined, weighed, and regulated with William Lee, Esq;[25] commissioner from the Congress, as a treaty of commerce, destined to be or as might be concluded hereafter, between their High Mightinesses the States-General of the Seven United Provinces of Holland, and the United States of North America.

Done at Aix-la-Chapelle, the 4th of September, 1778.

Signed, JOHN DE NEUFVILLE.

I hereby certify that the above is a true copy.

Signed, SAMUEL W. STOKTON.[26]

No. I. *Treaty of Amity and Commerce between the Republic of Holland and the United States of America.*

THE preamble recites, that the said contracting states of Holland and America, wishing to establish a treaty of commerce, have resolved to fix it on the basis of a perfect equality, and the reciprocal utility arising from the equitable laws of a free trade; provided that the contracting parties shall be at liberty to admit, as they think good, other nations to partake of the advantages arising from the said trade. Actuated by the above equitable principles, the forementioned contracting parties have agreed on the following articles:

Art. I. There shall be a permanent, unalterable, and universal peace and amity, established between their High Mightinesses of the Seven Provinces of Holland, and the United States of North America; as well as between their respective subjects, islands, towns, and territories, situate under the jurisdiction of the respective states above mentioned, and their inhabitants, without any distinction whatsoever of persons or sexes.

II. The subjects of the United Provinces of Holland shall be liable only to such duties as are paid by the natives and inhabitants of North America, in all the countries, ports, islands, and towns belonging to the said states; and shall enjoy the rights, liberties, privileges, immunities, and exemptions in their trade and navigation, common to the said natives and inhabitants, when the subjects of Holland shall have occasion to pass from one American state to another, as well as when bound from thence to any part of the world.

III. The privileges, &c. granted by the foregoing article to the States of Holland, are, by the present, confirmed to the inhabitants of North America.

IV. The respective subjects of the contracting parties, as well as the inhabitants of the countries, islands, or towns belonging to the said parties, shall be at liberty, without producing a written permission, private or public pass, to travel by land or water or in whatever manner they think best, through the kingdoms, territories, provinces, &c. or dominions whatever, of either of the confederated states, to have their free egress and regress, to remain in the said places, and during the whole time be at liberty to purchase every thing necessary to their own subsistence and use: they shall also be treated with every mark of reciprocal friendship and favour. Provided nevertheless, that in every circumstance they demean themselves in perfect conformity with the laws, statutes, and ordinances of those said kingdoms, towns, &c. where they may sojourn; treating each other with mutual friendship, and keeping up among themselves the most perfect harmony, by means of a constant correspondence.

V. The subjects of the contracting powers, and the inhabitants of all places belonging to the said powers, shall be at liberty to carry their ships and goods (such as are not forbidden by the law of the respective states) into all ports, places, &c. belonging to the said powers, and to tarry, without any limitation of time: to hire whole houses, or in part: to buy and purchase from the manufacturer or retailer, either in the public markets, fairs, &c. all sorts of goods and merchandize not forbidden by any particular law: to open warehouses for the sale of goods and effects imported from other parts: nor shall they be at any time forced against their consent, to bring the said goods and wares to the markets and fairs; provided, nevertheless, that they do not dispose of them by retail or elsewhere: they shall not however, be liable to any tax or duties, on this or any other account, except those only which are to be paid for their ships or goods, according to the laws and customs of the respective states, and at the rate stipulated by the present treaty. Moreover, they shall be entirely at liberty to depart, without the least hindrance, (this extends also to their wives, children, and such servants who may be desirous to follow their master) and to take with them all goods bought or imported at any time; and for such places as they may think proper, by land, or sea, or rivers, or lakes; all privileges, laws, concessions, immunities, &c. to the contrary notwithstanding.

VI. In regard to religious worship, the most unbounded liberty shall be granted to the subjects of the said confederate states, for themselves and families. They shall not be compelled to frequent the churches, &c. but shall have full liberty to perform divine service, after their own manner, without any molestation in either church or chapel, or private houses *(apertis foribus)*. It is farther provided, that any subject of one of the contracting powers dying, in any place belonging to the other, shall be interred in decent and convenient places, allotted for that purpose, and, in fine, that no insult shall, at any time, or in any manner whatever, be offered to the dead or interred bodies.

VII. It is farther agreed and settled, that in all duties, imposts, taxes, &c. laid on goods, persons, merchandize, &c. of each and every subject of the contracting powers, under any denomination whatsoever, the said subjects, inhabitants, &c. shall enjoy equal privileges, franchises, immunities, either in the courts of justice, and in every matter of trade, commerce, or any other case, and shall be treated with the same favour and distinction hitherto granted, or hereafter to be granted to any foreign nation whatsoever.

VIII. Their High Mightinesses, the States General of the Seven United Provinces, shall use the most efficacious means in their power, to protect the ships and goods belonging to any of the United States of America, they private or public property, when in the ports, roads, or seas adjoining the said islands, &c. belonging to their said High Mightinesses, and to use all their endeavours to bring about a restitution to be made to the owners, or their agents, of all vessels and goods captured within their jurisdiction; and the ships of war belonging to their said High Mightinesses shall take under their protection, and convoy the ships belonging to the said American States, or any of the subjects or inhabitants thereof, following the same course, and defend the said ship as long as they sail in company, against all attacks, violence, or oppression, in like manner as they are in duty bound to defend the ships of their High Mightinesses the Seven United Provinces of Holland,

IX. By this article, the same obligation is laid on the American States, in favour of the shipping, &c. belonging to those of Holland.

X. Their High Mightinesses the States of Holland shall interpose, and employ their good offices in favour of the said American States, their subjects and inhabitants, with the Emperor of Morocco, the Regencies of Algiers, Tunis, and Tripoli, and all along the coast of Barbary and Africa, and with the subjects of the said powers, that the ships, &c. of the said American States, be as much as possible, and to the best advantage, protected against the violences, insults, depredations, &c. of the abovesaid princes and subjects on the coast of Barbary and Africa.

XI. It shall be permitted and granted to each and every subject and inhabitant of the contracting powers, to leave, bequeath, or dispose of, in case of sickness, or at their death, all effects, goods, merchandises, ready money, &c. being their property, at or before their decease, in any town, island, &c. belonging to the respective contracting powers, in favour of such person or persons, as they may think proper. Moreover, whether the said subjects should die after having made such wills, or intestate, their lawful heirs, executors, or administrators, dwelling in any part of the possessions of the contracting powers, or aliens coming from other countries, shall be at liberty, without hindrance or delay, to claim, and take possession of, all such goods and effects, conformably to the respective laws of each country. Nor shall their right be disputed, under pretence of any prerogative, peculiar to any seperate province, or person whatsoever. Provided, nevertheless, that the claim to the effects of a person who died intestate, be supported by such proofs as the laws of either of the contracting powers have provided in such cases; all laws, statutes, edicts, *droits d'Au-*

bine, &c. to the contrary notwithstanding.

XII. The effects and property of the subjects of either of the contracting powers, dying in any town, island, &c. belonging to the other, shall be sequestered for the use of the lawful heirs and successors of the deceased. The council, or public minister of the nation, to which the person thus dying belonged, shall take an inventory of all such goods, effects, papers, writings, and books of accounts of the deceased. The said inventory to be delivered into the hands of three merchants of known and approved integrity, who shall be nominated for the purpose of acting as trustees to the heirs, executors, &c. or creditors of the deceased: nor shall any court of judicature interfere, unless the said heirs, &c. should require it in the due course of law.

XIII. The respective subjects of the contracting parties, shall be at liberty to choose for themselves advocates, attornies, notaries, solicitors, and agents; to this end, that such advocates, &c. shall, by the judges of the courts aforesaid, be called in, if the said judges should, by the parties, be required so to do.

XIV. The merchants, commanders, or owners of ships, sailors of every denomination, ships or vessels, effects, and goods in general, belonging to either party, or any of its subjects or inhabitants, shall, at no time, for any private or public purpose, by virtue of any edict whatsoever, be taken, or detained in the countries, ports, islands, &c. belonging to either of the contracting parties, to be employed in the service, to forward military expeditions, or any other purpose; and much less for the private use of any one, by violence, or other means made use of to molest or insult the said subjects. It is farther strictly forbidden to the said subjects on both sides, not to take away, violently, the property of each other ; but, the consent of the proprietor once obtained, they shall be at liberty to purchase, paying ready money for the same. This article, however, is not to be understood as extending to such cases, where the seizure shall be made, or the embargo laid by the authority of the legislative power for debts incurred, or crimes committed, which shall be tried by the due course of law.

XV. It is farther provided and agreed, that all merchants, commanders of ships, and other subjects belonging to their High Mightinesses the States of the Seven United Provinces, shall regulate their private affairs by themselves, or by such agents as they may chuse, in all and every place within the jurisdiction of the United States of America : nor shall they be compelled to employ, or pay any interpreter or broker, but such as they think fit to appoint. Moreover, in the lading, or unlading of ships, the masters shall not be obliged to employ persons appointed for that purpose, by public authority ; but shall be at full liberty to do it themselves, or call in the assistance of any one they shall chuse, without being liable to pay any fee or retribution to any body else. Neither shall they be compelled to land any particular merchandize, to put them on board other ships, to take others on board their own, without their free consent ; or to remain laden longer than they shall think proper. The subjects and inhabitants of the United States of America, shall fully enjoy the same privileges in all the dominions of the States of Holland.

XVI. In case any dispute or controversy should arise between the master of a ship and his crew, belonging to one of the two nations, and then in any port within the dominions of the other, concerning the payment of wages, or

any other matter to be determined by the civil law, the magistrate of such port, or place, shall only require the defendant to deliver to the plaintiff, a declaration under his hand, and witnessed by the said magistrate ; by which the said defendant shall bind himself to appear, and answer the complaint laid against him, before a competent judge in his own country. This being done, the said crew shall not be permitted to leave the ship, or prevent the master from following his course. The merchants of either nation shall be authorised to keep their books in what language and manner they may think best, without the least hindrance or molestation. But, in case it should be necessary, in order to settle a point of law, for them to produce their books, they shall bring them into court for examination ; in such a manner, however, that neither the judge, nor any one else, whatsoever, shall be permitted to peruse any article in the said books, but such as may be absolutely necessary to ascertain the authenticity and regularity of the said books. Nor shall any one, under any pretence whatever, presume to force the said books and writings from the owners, or detain them ; cases of bankruptcy alone excepted.

XVII. The ships of either nation, bound to the respective ports, shall, upon a just cause of being suspected, either in regard to their destination or their cargoes, be obliged to produce, either at sea, in the roads, or ports, not only their passports, but also certificates, witnessing that the goods they have on board are not prohibited by the respective laws.

XVIII. If, upon such certificates being produced, the examining party should discover that some of the goods mentioned in the bills of lading are prohibited by this treaty, or bound to some port belonging to the enemy ; in

such case it shall not be lawful to break into any part of the ship, or force any trunk, boxes, barrels, &c. nor even to displace any part of the cargoes (whether such ship belongs to Holland or America) to come at the said goods, which are not in any ways to be searched until they are landed in presence of some officers of the Admiralty-court, who shall enter a verbal process about them. Nor shall it be permitted to sell, exchange, or adulterate the said goods in any wise, till the law shall have taken its course, and the matter be determined by the sentence of the respective Admiralty-courts, pronouncing them seizable : the ship and other parts of the cargo not prohibited by the treaty, shall not be detained, under the pretence of part of the lading being condemned, and much less confiscated as lawful prizes. But, in case part of the cargo should consist of the said prohibited goods, and the master of the ship shall consent to deliver them up immediately, then the captor, having taken out of the said ship the prohibited goods, shall permit the master to continue his course to the place of his destination : yet, if all the prohibited goods could not be taken on board the captor, the latter shall, notwithstanding the master's free tender of the said goods, bring the former into the nearest port, where it shall be produced in manner aforesaid.

XIX. It is agreed on the contrary, that all effects, &c. of any subject of either state, found on any ship taken from an enemy, such effects, &c. though they be not prohibited by any article of this treaty, shall be considered as lawful prize, and be disposed of as if they belonged to the enemy : (except only in case the war should not have been proclaimed, or not come to the knowledge of the proprietors of the said effects, &c.) which, in such cases only, shall not be liable to be confiscated, but be immediately returned to the owners without any delay, upon their making good their claim: provided, neverthelefs, that the faid goods are not of the kind which are prohibited; nor will it be lawful to fhip them afterwards, for any of the enemy's ports: the two contracting parties agreeing, moreover, that fix months, from the date of a declaration of war, will be confidered as a fufficient notice to the fubjects of either State, whatever quarter of the world they may come from.

XX In order to provide farther for the fafety of the fubjects on both fides, that neither of the parties may be annoyed by the armed fhips or privateers belonging to the other, during the courfe of a war, particular injunctions fhall be laid upon the commanders of fhips and privateers, &c. &c. to the refpective fubjects of the contracting powers, not to vex or offer any moleftation to any one of them; and, in cafe of failure herein, the offending party fhall be punifhed, and compelled to make good the damage, their perfons and fortunes anfwering for the fame.

XXI. All fhips and effects retaken from privateers or pirates, fhall be carried into fome of the ports belonging to either State, and returned to the owners, upon their giving fatisfactory proofs of their right to the faid recaptures.

XXII. It fhall be lawful for all commanders of fhips of war, privateers, &c to carry off freely all fhips and effects taken from the enemy, without being fubject to pay any duty or duties to the Admiralty or other courts; nor fhall fuch prizes be liable to be detained or feized upon in any of the ports of the refpective States: the fearching officers fhall not be permitted to vifit or fearch the faid prizes: the captors whereof will

be at liberty to put back to fea, and convoy the prizes wherever they are directed to be carried; as fpecified in the orders given to the commanders of fuch fhips, privateers, &c. which they fhall be obliged to produce. But all the ports of both States fhall be fhut againft all prizes made on the fubjects of either: and in cafe fuch prizes and captors fhould be driven to fome of the faid ports, by ftrefs of weather, every means fhall be employed to haften their departure.

XXIII. In cafe any fhips, boats, &c. fhould be wrecked or otherwife damaged on the coafts of either of the contracting States, all aid and affiftance fhall be given to the diftreffed crews, to whom paffes and free conduct fhall be granted for their return into their own country.

XXIV. If a fhip or fhips, either of war, or employed for the purpofe of trading, by one of the States, fhould, by ftrefs of weather, imminent danger from pirates, enemies, &c. be compelled to take fhelter in any ports, rivers, bays, &c. belonging to the other, they fhall be treated with all humanity, friendfhip, and moft cordial protection. Leave fhall be granted them to take in provifions and refrefhments at a reafonable rate, and to purchafe whatever they may ftand in need of, either for themfelves or for the purpofe of repairing the damage they may have fuffered, and alfo for the continuation of their voyage. No obftacle whatever fhall be laid in their way to ftop or detain them in any of the faid ports, &c. whence they fhall be at liberty to fail, whenever they may think fit.

XXV. In order to put commerce in the moft flourifhing ftate, it is agreed, that, in cafe a war fhould at any time break out between the contracting parties, fix months fhall be allowed to the refpective fubjects for them to re-

tire with their families and property, to whatever place they may judge proper; alfo to be at liberty, during the above fpace of time, to fell or otherwife difpofe of their goods and chattles, without the leaft hindrance or moleftation. But, above all, it is provided, that the faid fubjects fhall not be detained, by arreftment or feizure. On the contrary, during the aforefaid fix months, the refpective States, and their fubjects, or inhabitants, fhall have good and fpeedy juftice done to them; fo that, during the faid time, they may recover their goods and effects, whether they be in the public funds, or in private hands. And if any part thereof fhould happen to be embezzled, or that any infult or wrong fhould have been offered to the fubjects, &c. of either State, the offending party fhall give the immediate and convenient fatisfaction for fuch embezzlement, wrong, or infult.

XXVI. The fubjects, &c. of either State fhall abftain from requiring or accepting any commiffions or letters of marque from any power then at war with either of faid States, fo as to command armed fhips againft either, and to their determent; and if any individual, belonging to either, fhould fail herein, he fhall be dealt with as being guilty of piracy.

XXVII. It fhall not be lawful for any privateer, not belonging to either of the contracting parties, which might be furnifhed with commiffions, or letters of marque from any power, in actual enemity with either of them, to fit out their fhips in any port belonging to the faid States, therein fell their prizes, or make in any wife an exchange of their faid fhips, merchandize, goods, or effects, being the whole or part of the cargo contained in the aforefaid captures. Nor fhall the faid commanders be permitted to take in provifions, but juft as much as will enable them to reach a port, nearest to the dominion of their employers.

XXVIII. Subjects and inhabitants of both the contracting parties shall be at liberty to navigate their ships (without any distinction of owners, to whom the cargo or cargoes may belong) from all ports whatever belonging to the powers, that then are, or afterwards may be in amity with either of the aforementioned States; as also to trade in their way to or from such places, ports, and towns belonging to the enemies of either party, whether the said place be within the jurisdiction of one or more powers. It is also hereby stipulated, that the freedom of shipping will be extended to the cargoes belonging to the respective subjects or inhabitants of the said States, though the whole, or part of the said cargo should be the enemy's property. This privilege is also to be construed as extending to all persons whatever, on board the said ships (the military in the enemy's service only excepted) as well as contraband goods.

XXXIX. This article contains a large enumeration of the goods prohibited to be carried to the enemy, which comprehends all manner of warlike stores. It gives also an account of such goods as may be lawfully exported, namely cloathing and other manufactured goods of wool, cloth, silks, &c. &c. the matters employed in manufacturing the same; gold and silver either coined or in bullion, all sorts of metals, corn, and seeds, spices, tobacco, meat, salt or smoaked, and every kind of eatables; in fine, ship timber, sails, canvas, and every effect whatever not fashioned in the shape of any tool or warlike instrument usually employed in war, either by sea or land: all the aforesaid goods and wares, shall at no time be looked upon as contraband, and may be carried by the subjects and inhabitants of the

confederate States, even to places belonging to the enemy then at war with either party, excepting only such towns and places, which might happen to be besieged, surrounded or blocked up at the time of shipping off, for their use, the said wares and goods.

XXX. In order to prevent all dissention and difficulty which might arise between the subjects of either State, in case one of them should go to war with some other power or powers, the shipping, &c. belonging to the other party, shall be provided with letters or passes, specifying the name, cargo, and burthen of the ship, together with the captain or master's name, and the place of his residence: that thus it may appear that the ship, &c. belongs truly to the said subjects and inhabitants. The said pass to be worded as shall be mentioned at the end of this present treaty.

These letters, or passes, shall be renewed every year, if the bearers should return to the same port within that time. It is farther agreed, that besides the aforesaid passes certificates shall be given, mentioning every part of the cargoes, the respective places from and to which such ships may be bound. The said certificates to be drawn up in the usual form, before the officers of the place from whence the said ships are to sail; and the said officers shall be at liberty to mention, by name, if they think it expedient, the owners of the cargo or cargoes.

XXXI. The commanders or owners of ships belonging to the contracting parties, entering into any of the roads of either of the said States, who may not think proper to enter into port; or, when entered, will not chuse to unload either the whole or part of their cargo, shall not be compelled to declare in what it consists, unless a well grounded suspicion should arise, on some evident circumstances, of their being laden

for the enemy, or carrying from one of the confederate States, to the other, any prohibited goods; in which case, such commanders, owners, or inhabitants, shall be obliged to shew their passports and certificates, drawn up in the manner hereafter mentioned.

XXXII. When the ships, belonging to either State, sailing coastways, or otherways, shall be met by the ships of war, privateers, &c. of the other party, in order to prevent mischief, the latter shall keep out of the reach of the guns, though it will be lawful for them to send their boats to board the abovesaid merchantmen, not suffering above two or three men at a time to get on board to them. The master, or commander of the said ships, shall present his passports, conformably to the tenor hereafter recited After which, the said ship, or merchantman, shall be at full liberty to continue its voyage, without being searched, chased, or obliged to alter its course, or otherwise molested, under any pretence whatsoever.

XXXIII. It is farther agreed, that all goods and effects whatever, being once put on board of a ship, or ships, belonging to either of the contracting parties, shall not be liable to a second visit, or search, after having undergone that which must precede the lading of such ships; as all prohibited goods must be stopped on the very spot, before they are suffered to be carried on board the ships belonging to either party: the same not being liable to any other kind of embargo for the aforesaid cause. And the subjects of either state, where such effects shall, or should have been seized upon, shall be punished for importing the same, according to the manner provided by the laws, customs, and ordinances of his own native country.

XXXIV. The contracting parties mutually agree, that they shall be at liberty to have their respective consuls, vice-consuls, commissaries, and other agents, appointed by, and for each party. Their functions and officers shall be regulated by a particular convention, whenever either of the contracting powers shall think proper to appoint such officers.

Here follows the form of the passport and certificate, the intention and purport of which, are sufficiently explained in the XXXth article of this treaty.

No. II. *Copy of a Letter to his Excellency* B. Franklin, *Esq. at* Paris.

SIR,

AS your Excellency and the Right Honourable Congress will certainly be already completely informed of my interview, at Aix-la-Chapelle, with Mr. William Lee, about a twelvemonth ago, in the presence of Mr. William Stockton; and as he is shortly to arrive himself, I have made no difficulty, and it gives me even much satisfaction, to expose unto him some trifling alterations, of no great consequence, which are thought necessary to be made in the plan of the treaty of commerce, which is now to be looked over afresh.

The differences consist only in suppressing, in the *sixth* article, all that is mentioned there concerning *religion*; and, in fact, it is absolutely not proper, that any mention thereof should be made between *two republics*, the constitutions and fundamental laws of which plead aloud for a perfect liberty of conscience.

The tenth article, concerning the Barbarian powers, is binding on both sides, in case the same should take place any time hereafter.

The other suppressions which are thought necessary in the articles VIII, XXII, and XXVII, are for the greatest part established to prevent objections. For this reason, the latter part of the *eighth* article has been suppressed, where it is said, *and their ships of war, or convoys, sailing under authority,* &c.

It has likewise been thought proper to suppress the latter part of the XXIId article, which begins with these words, *on the contrary no asylum or refuge shall be granted,* &c.

The XXIIth article at present stands thus: *It shall not be lawful for any privateer, holding any commissions or letters of marque, from any prince or power, in war with any of the high contracting parties, to fit out their ships in the ports belonging to either of the contracting parties, nor therein to sell their prizes, nor to exchange in any other manner whatever, the ships, goods, and merchandizes, being either the whole, or part of the cargo, contained in the said captures.*

These are the measures that have been taken to establish the basis of this treaty; and from a particular regard for the right honourable congress, having by us a copy of the treaty, such as it was drawn up at first, and such as it stands at present, we thought it our duty to inform your excellency of the state in which this important affair is at present, and which we shall always be ready to forward with the same zeal with which it has been begun.

Mr. Stockton will likewise inform your Excellency of some other affairs, which stand in need of some explanations.

Wishing that the union of the *Twenty States* may soon be established upon a permanent footing, we remain, with the most perfect consideration and esteem,

Your Excellency's
most humble and
most obedient servants,
JOHN DE NEUFVILLE and SON.
Amsterdam, July 28, 1779.

P. S. Mr. Stockton will be so kind, and he is very well informed, to give your Excellency and the right honourable Congress all the information necessary with regard to the plan proposed by *Colonel Dircks.*

No. III. *A Letter from Mr.* J. W. Stokton, *to the Rev. Dr.* Witherspoon, *Member of Congress, dated* Amsterdam, April 14, 1779.

SIR,

UNDER the persuasion that you would not be displeased with me, I have taken the liberty of writing several letters to you, since the month of May last, having, since that time, at the requisition of W. Lee, Esq. executed the functions of secretary to the American commission, at the courts of Vienna and Berlin, and I am at present on the point of returning to America with the first convoy. I send this letter to Mr. Adams, who is set out, a few weeks ago, from paris for Nantz, where he proposes to embark on board the frigate 'l Alliance, which, it is thought, will be ready in a few days to sail for Boston.

I should certainly have taken my passage on board the said frigate with him, if it had been possible to convey my effects, which are still here on shore, soon enough to Nantz. I must, therefore, now wait for another favourable opportunity, and I beg the favour of you to acquaint my brother thereof, having lately written to him, to that effect, by the preceding opportunity of a vessel. I have endeavoured, as much as possible, to acquire a thorough knowledge of the true and exact state of political affairs here, considering the interest America has therein; and I flatter myself to have the best informations in that respect.

As a member of the congress, you will certainly have seen, before now, the plan of a treaty of amity and commerce, as destined to be concluded hereafter between the States of Holland and the United States of North America, several copies thereof having been sent to America some time ago. That plan was signed on the 4th of September last, on the part of the city of Amsterdam, by John de Neufville, Esq. properly deputed for that purpose by the pensionary and burgomasters of the said city, and by W. Lee, Esq. commissioner from the Congress, to whom the propositions for the said treaty were made through the channel of the said Mr. de Neufville: but as the character of that gentleman will probably be unknown to you, I think it proper to mention here, that he is one of the principal merchants of Amsterdam. He has manifested much zeal for the true interest of his country, of which he seems to have the most just ideas; and he has often declared to me, that it is much nearer related to the commercial interests of America and France, than to that of Great Britain. The conduct of this merchant, arising from that principle, and besides that, from a principle still more prevalent, namely, that of promoting the success of the efforts for the liberty of each country, will, I hope, always be uniform, and will prove favourable to the cause of America. Consequently, I make no doubt, that the commercial people of America will give him the preference in their future connections, as a Dutch merchant and their friend. This merchant has likewise engaged himself, by his signature to the said plan, being properly authorised to that effect by the regency of Amsterdam, that as long as America shall not act contrary to the interest of the States of Holland, the city of Amsterdam will never adopt any measure that may tend to oppose the interest of America; but will, on the contrary, use all its influence upon the States of the Seven United Provinces of Holland, to effect the desired connection. I need not mention to you the great importance of the city of Amsterdam, in the political affairs of the States-General: you are too well acquainted with the history and state of all countries, to make this necessary. But the less informed politicians will be astonished to learn, that Amsterdam pays two thirds of the quota part of Holland, and that the Province of Holland alone bears two-thirds of the charges of all the Seven United Provinces. The regency of this city has hitherto remained faithful and constant in their engagements, and will, if I am not mistaken, always continue the same, and persist therein invariably.

The patriotic party in Holland has had much trouble to thwart the designs of the prince of Orange, or, to say the same thing in another manner, of the English party.

The court of Great Britain has a great influence upon the deliberations of this country, through the channel of the prince of Orange, who is a relation to the king of Great Britain, and who is supposed to have the same views as the former, with regard to the liberties of the people.

He has some of the less considerable provinces so much in his interest, that this, above all, dares not, as yet, refuse his demands; and consequently the deputies of these provinces have reserved their consent, and divers resolutions, which the province of Holland would otherwise have taken long ago, to the advantage of America: but, unfortunately for us, in this moment, the unanimity of the States is necessary in most of their resolutions.

The spirited conduct which France has lately adopted, in declaring that she would seize all Dutch ships trading with Great Britain, excepting those of Amsterdam and Haerlem, soon brought back the cities of Rotterdam, Dort, and others. These, fearing to send their vessels to sea, and perceiving that the people began to murmur, were obliged to accede to the resolution, by which the deputies of all the other cities of the province of Holland had consented to grant convoys to their vessels, without even excepting those articles of commerce, for which England had continually seized the Dutch ships, ever since the beginning of the war with France.

Such is the actual state of affairs here; and every politician is at present impatient to know what Spain intends to do, which has some time since made very considerable preparations for war.

The post for France is upon its departure; I must, therefore, conclude this letter. I find in the English newspapers, that your sermon on the day of a general fast, has undergone a fifth edition in London. I beg the favour of you to assure your family of my respects, and to acquaint my friends that I am very well, and that I intend to return soon to America. ——I remain, with much respect and esteem Sir,

Your most faithful friend, and humble servant,

(Signed)   J. W. STOKTON.
To the Rev. Mr. Witherspoon, D.D.

No. IV. *A Letter from Colonel Dircks, to the Hon. Henry Laurens, Esq.* [30]

Philadelphia, Dec. 13, 1779.

SIR,

THE remembrance of your Excellency's kind reception, and the friendship which I experienced from you, at the time of my departure for Holland, about a twelve-month ago, engages me, in hearing that your Excellency is upon departing for my country, to form the best wishes for your success. I am sorry, that I am come too late to town, which deprives me of the happiness of having an interview with your Excellency, respecting the affairs of Holland.

I have been in Holland only with a view of uniting the two countries for their reciprocal happiness; and I have succeeded as well as the different circumstances would permit.

I beg the favour that you will be pleased to take charge of the herein inclosed letters for my worthy friends and countrymen, the Barons Van der Capellen, from whom, and their friends, I flatter myself that your Excellency will soon learn, that by my conduct, I have gained several hearts, which are now nobly and zealously inclined for the affairs and the cause of the Americans. I wish that this beginning may in the course of time produce many happy events for the mutual advantage of both countries.

I take the liberty of joining here a list of the names of those, who are altogether the worthy friends of America. I pray God to conduct your Excellency, and to grant you the most perfect success. This is the sincere wish of my heart.

I remain with the greatest consideration and esteem. Sir,

Your Excellency's
    most obedient and
        most humble servant,
(Signed)   J. G. DIRCKS.

List of Names.

Henry Hooft Danielsz, ancient burgomaster of Amsterdam.

Daniel Hooft Danielsz, secretary to the regency of Amsterdam.

Van Berkel, counsellor and pensionary of the city of Amsterdam.

John de Neufville and sons, one of the principal commercial houses of Amsterdam.

N. B. The last can inform your Excellency of all the commercial houses, which are our friends.

The burgomaster Hooft Danielsz can inform your Excellency which are the gentlemen of the regency, in the interest of America.

And the Barons Van der Capellen can inform you of those who are our friends in all the Seven Provinces.

To his Excellency Henry Laurens, Esq.

No. V. *Copy of a Letter from Mr. A. Gillon to John Rutledge,* [31] *Esq. Governor and Commander in Chief of South Carolina, dated Amsterdam, the 1st of March, 1780.*

SIR,

I HAD the pleasure of writing to you the 31st of December last, and I send you at present copies of what I wrote. Mr. Izard [32] meeting with many difficulties, which prevented his departure, and the ice hindering all vessels from failing from hence, I had no opportunity of giving you any advice of my latest negociations here. This letter will be delivered to your Excellency by Mr. George Nixon: he will communicate to [33] you a copy thereof by the first opportunity, as soon as he arrives at St. Eustatia.

I shall likewise send you a copy of the correspondence between Mr. Chamont and a gentleman whom I engaged here to write to him on the subject of the two ships built here; by which you will see, that it was never seriously intended to sell the said ships to me.

Mr. Franklin has never returned me an answer. I thought that the arrival of Mr. Adams at Paris was a good opportunity to revive this affair. I consequently wrote to him, as well as to Mr. Izard, and Mr. A. Lee, that they [34] should address themselves to Monsieur de Sartine, and to the Count de Vergennes, ministers at Versailles, to endeavour to obtain the said vessels, by offering to pay the prime cost, or to take them by appraisement of four impartial persons, to be chosen here by the two parties; especially as I had already removed here all difficulties, having succours promised to me from high authority, and as I could fit them out either as Dutch property for Eustatia, or as American property for any other port. But the answers I received last night from these gentlemen, obliged me to give up the flattering hopes of sending you two of the finest vessels in the world, of one hundred and eighty-six feet keel, fit to carry twenty-eight thirty-six pounders upon one deck. And though they drew too much water for our bar, they would certainly not have tarded to take some vessels which would have answered our purpose. Not that I fear that these gentlemen will not do all in their power to assist me in this affair, and some others; but they foresee that this request, in case it should be granted, might perhaps involve me in other difficulties.

There are several vessels in the ports of France which would fully answer our purposes; but the difficulties which I have already experienced, fully convince me that I shall not obtain any succours. It is for this reason that I have resolved this morning to employ all your money in purchasing bar-iron, nails, cordage, sail-cloth, cables, anchors, ships-stores, and other things necessary to pilots, carpenters, gunners, and coopers; chirurgical instruments and medicines, iron hoops, and all that I thought necessary for three frigates, excepting guns, powder, and military implements, which I am as yet uncertain whether they may be embarked. I intend to buy the most essential articles double what is necessary for these vessels; and likewise double the quantity of the small articles; and in case I should have any money remaining, I intend to employ it in purchasing woollen cloth, linen, shoes, stockings and hats for our troops, and to send all these effects, as soon as possible, by different vessels, to St. Eustatia, from whence you may draw them, by your orders, whenever you shall think it convenient. It will, perhaps, be necessary to insure here the articles which appear to be destined for large ships, in case they should happen to be taken by the English, as well as the cables and anchors.

Messrs. Nicholas, and Jacob Van Staphorst, merchants here,[35] will do the business, and they have promised me a credit of thirty thousand florins (very likely I shall be able to get more from them, on my own credit) until you come yourself, as I now desire you to do, which sum, with Mr. Screipreifer's loan and your[36] own money, will make up a handsome sum, to accomplish the said views, and save the State some loss on the plan proposed by your Excellency to procure it a good marine. Pardon me, if I speak my sentiments at present, on what may be done.

If the State persists in the resolution of having a good marine, the three frigates ought to be built at Philadelphia, Boston and Portsmouth, in New Hampshire. The opposition I have met with in *France proves clearly to me, that they never had an intention that America should have a marine;* otherwise they would certainly have sold the ten ships which were here lying empty, since that would not have diminished their strength, which they made a plea of last spring, when I proposed to them a plan, by which *Georgia would have been delivered* by last May; but even then, they *refused* to let us have *one ship.*

Captain Yoyner has done every thing in his power with respect to your affairs, and he will return to St. Eustatia by the first good opportunity, as will all the other officers. I will follow him immediately: may I, on that account, desire your Excellency to send Captain Yoyner's orders, that he

may find them at St. Eustatia, under cover to Mr. Anson, and the governor of that place, or to whom you please. I shall have great pleasure to find myself equally honoured with your orders, and to know how the goods ought to be shipped there. I think, with your permission, that if two or three continental frigates were sent here to take them, that would be a more certain method; but I cannot know it till after I am arrived there, and I shall place them in the warehouses of good merchants.

I have not been honoured with a single line from our government since the 31st of January, 1779, so that I am at present obliged to act without orders, not doubting that you and my country will readily give me credit for acting to the best of my judgment for your interests, and that you and they will approve of my conduct, since that approbation is the only recompence to which I have looked in all that I have been able to effect by my feeble endeavours. Please God! I should have been able to have done more, if the courage of your pretended friends had not been greater than that of your real ones. I am very certain I should have been with you a long time before this with an ample succour; but I have the consolation to reflect, that I have done as much as any person sent from America has been able to effect in Europe, to obtain credit for a state (South Carolina) which was considered at the time I negociated the loan, as entirely in the possession of the enemy.

I have had many interviews with the lenders; and the brokers in those affairs would have procured me, *in six weeks, a million of florins, at five per cent. interest, for ten or fifteen years,* if the powers with which I was invested had been authorized by our government, and to their satisfaction. However, I have made them promise, that if the *guarantee of Con-*

gress, for which I now write to your Excellency, shall arrive whilst I remain here, *they will advance the said million on that security,* until the full powers and guarants, such as I inclose, which are of their own composition, and translated by their notary, shall come over. I now send you the Dutch original and the translation, for your approbation, and the Dutch original and an English translation of the guarantee of Congress. If I were at this moment in possession of such papers, I could get *four millions of florins,* which makes about *three millions of Carolina currency at five per cent.* payable in fifteen years, viz. *nothing* for the first *ten years,* but *one million every year* afterwards, until the whole was paid. The interest payable every year. The broker's commission, or premium as they call it here, is from one to two per cent. on the capital at the time of your receiving it; one per cent. the merchant's commission, for negociating the business, and one half per cent. on the annual interest, and one per cent. commission on the reimbursement of the capital; which together, would carry the interest to about five and a quarter per cent. a year.

The objections which they make against my present full power is, that it is therein specified, for three frigates, and that there is a complication in saying, that I may negociate any indeterminate sum, instead of naming the fixed sum. This want of specific precision affects them to that degree, that I cannot give them any satisfaction.

Your Excellency is at present informed, upon what condition the sum in question may be procured, in case the State should be in want thereof. If the last should be the case, and if the conditions are approved of, it would be best to send a fit person here with such full powers and guarantee, in sending two or three copies after him : or elfe to fend the faid documents to Meffrs. Nicholas and Jacob Van Staphorft, merchants here, or to fome other good, folid Dutch houfe here, with your orders how the faid money is to be employed here. But as the faid Meffrs. Van Staphorft have laid the foundation of this affair, I leave it to the judgment of your Excellency, whether it would not be beft to intruft them with the execution thereof. I have had dealings with them for above ten years, and am informed that they are generally looked upon as a very folid Dutch houfe, of a good capital, and known integrity.

I have an opportunity of knowing what is doing here, and I have received from perfons of refpectable authority the intelligence fpecified in the paper annexed, The *Dutch* have defigned thefe *nine months* to have a perfon here, authorifed by *Congrefs* ; not that they would receive him as a *public minifter* ; but they are very anxious to have the moft accurate information : and fuch a perfon might have laid the foundation of a treaty with us, until affairs fhall be come to greater maturity : he might alfo have been able to get money here. The objection againft the actual loan of money for the Congrefs here is, that it does not proceed directly from America ; and to ufe the language of the Old Dutchman, it is to be franchifed.

I am perfuaded, that if the Prefident Laurens arrives here foon, he will find a reafonable and ample fum. I have taken the liberty of acquainting the noble Continental Congrefs on what terms. I am fure of being able to borrow here a fufficient fum at about five and quarter, or five and a half per cent. including all expences.

I am in hopes of receiving foon advices from you : if not, I fhall continue as mentioned above, and do as well as I can, making all the difpatch in my power to return

home. I could have wifhed that my fate had been to remain in America, efpecially as I fhould have willingly fupported all fatigues, and, with a good heart, braved all dangers, in preference to the plan of begging, which the neceffity, occafioned by frequent deceptions, has forced me to adopt.

I moft fincerely wifh you health and happinefs, and remain with due refpect, Sir,

Your Excellency's
most obedient and
most humble fervant,
(Signed)   A. GILLON.
P. S. Mr. Beaumarchais will [37] not yet pay any thing, nor furnifh any account.
His Excellency John Rutledge, Efq. Governor and Commander in Chief of South Carolina.

Two letters were alfo communicated, written by J. D. Van Der Capellan to Mr. Laurens, [38] but as they only contain the fentiments of a private individual, we have not thought it neceffary to infert them.

Memorial prefented to the States-General on the 10th inftant, by Sir Joseph Yorke, his Majefty's Ambaffador at the Hague, concerning the five Papers found amongft thofe of Mr. Laurens, late Prefident of the Congrefs.

High and Mighty Lords,

THE King, my mafter, has through the whole courfe of his reign, fhewed the moft fincere defire for preferving the union, which has fubfifted upwards of an age, between his Crown and the Republic. This union is founded on the durable bafis of a reciprocal intereft, and as it has greatly contributed to the welfare of both nations, the natural enemy of both the one and the other is ufing his utmoft policy to deftroy it ; and for fome time paft his endeavours have been but too

fuccefsful, being fupported by a faction that aims at domineering over the republic, and which is at all times ready to facrifice the general intereft to their own private views.

The king has beheld, with equal regret and furprife, the fmall effect which his repeated claims for the ftipulated fuccours, and the reprefentations of his ambaffador, on the daily violation of the moft folemn engagements, have produced.

His Majefty's moderation has induced him to attribute this conduct of your High Mightineffes to the intrigues of a prevailing faction ; and he would ftill perfuade himfelf, that your juftice and difcernment will determine you to fulfil your engagements towards him, and to prove by your whole conduct, that you are refolved vigoroufly to adhere to the fyftem formed by the wifdom of your anceftors, which is the only one that can fecure the fafety and glory of the republic.

The anfwer which your High Mightineffes return to this declaration, which the underfigned makes by the exprefs order of his Court, will be confidered as the touchftone of your intentions and fentiments refpecting the King.

For a long time paft the King has had innumerable indications of the dangerous defigns of an unruly cabal ; but the papers of Mr. Laurens, who ftyles himfelf Prefident of the pretended Congrefs, furnifhes the difcovery of a plot, unexampled in all the annals of the republic. It appears by thefe papers, that the Gentlemen of Amfterdam have been engaged in a clandeftine correfpondence with the American rebels, from the month of Auguft 1778, and that inftructions and full powers had been given by them for the conclufion of a treaty of indifputable amity with thofe rebels, who are the fubjects of a fovereign to whom the republic is united by the clofeft engagements. The authors of this plot do not even attempt to **deny** it, but on the contrary vainly endeavour to justify their conduct.

In these circumstances, his Majesty relying on the equity of your High Mightinesses, demands a formal disavowal of such irregular conduct, which is no less contrary to your most sacred engagements, than to the fundamental laws of the constitution of Batavia. The King demands equally a prompt satisfaction, proportioned to the offence, and an exemplary punishment on the pensioner Van Berkel, and his accomplices, as disturbers of the public peace, and violaters of the law of nations.

His Majesty persuades himself, that the answer of your High Mightinesses will be speedy and satisfactory in all respects; but should the contrary happen,—if your High Mightinesses should refuse so just a demand, or endeavour to elude it by silence, which will be regarded as a refusal; then the King cannot but consider the republic itself as approving of those outrages which they refuse to disavow, and to punish; and after such conduct, his Majesty will find himself under the necessity of taking those measures which the preservation of his own dignity and the essential interests of his people demand.

Given at the Hague,
Nov. 10, 1780.
(Signed)   JOSEPH YORKE.

• • •

Proceedings of a Board of General Officers, held by order of General Washington, *Commander in Chief of the Army of the United States of* America, *respecting Major* John Andrè, *Adjutant General of the* [39] British *Army*, September 29, 1780.

Published at Philadelphia, *by order of Congress.*

Extracts of Letters from General Washington *to the President of Congress.*

Robinson's House in the High Lands, Sept. 29. 1780.

SIR,

I Have the honour to inform the Congress, that I arrived here yesterday about twelve o'clock, on my return from Hartford. Some hours previous to my arrival, Major-general Arnold went from his quarters, which were at this place, and, as it was supposed, over the river to the garrison at West-point, whither I proceeded myself, in order to visit the post. I found General Arnold had not been there during the day, and on my return to his quarters, he was still absent. In the mean time, a packet had arrived from Lieutenant-colonel Jameson, announcing the capture [40] of John Anderson, who was endeavouring to go to New-York with several interesting and important papers, all in the handwriting of General Arnold. This was accompanied with a letter from the prisoner, avowing himself to be Major John Andrè, Adjutant-general to the British army, relating the manner of his capture, and endeavouring to shew that he did not come under the description of a spy. From these several circumstances, and information that the general seemed to be thrown into some degree of agitation, on receiving a letter a little time before he went from his quarters, I was led to conclude immediately, that he had heard of Major Andrè's captivity, and that he would, if possible, escape to the enemy; and accordingly took such measures as appeared most probable to apprehend him; but he had embarked in a barge, and proceeded down the river, under a flag, to the Vulture ship of war, which lay at some miles below Stoney and Verplank's Point. He wrote me a letter after he got on board. Major Andrè was not arrived yet; but I hope he is secure, and that he will be here to-day. I have been, and am taking precautions, which I trust will prove effectual to prevent the important consequences which this conduct on the part of General Arnold, was intended to produce. I do not know the party that took Major Andrè, but it is said it consisted only of a few militia, who acted in such a manner on the occasion, as does them the highest honour, and proves them to be men of great virtue. As soon as I know their names, I shall take pleasure in transmitting them to Congress.

Paramus, Oct. 7, 1780.

SIR,

I have the honour to inclose to Congress a copy of the proceedings of a board of general officers in the cause of Major Andrè, Adjutant-general to the British army. This officer was executed in pursuance of the sentence of the board, on Monday the 2d instant, at twelve o'clock, at our late camp at Tappan. Besides the proceedings, I transmit copies of sundry letters respecting the matter, which are all that passed on the subject, not including the proceedings.

I have now the pleasure to communicate the names of the three persons who captured Major Andrè, and who refused to release him, notwithstanding the most earnest importunities, and assurances of a liberal reward on his part. Their names are, John Paulding, David Williams, and Isaac Vanwert. [41]

Proceedings of a Board of General Officers, held by order of his Excellency Gen. Washington, Commander in Chief of the Army of the United States of America, *respecting Major* Andrè, *Adjutant-general of the* British *Army*, September 29, 1780, *at* Tappan, *in the State of* New York.

PRESENT.

Major - general Green, President; Major - general Lord Stirling, Major - general St. Clair,

Major-general the Marquis de la Fayette, Major-general Howe, Major-general the Baron de Steuben, Brigadier-general Parsons, Brigadier-general Clinton, Brigadier-general Knox, Brigadier-general Glover, Brigadier-general Patterson, Brigadier-general Hand, Brigadier-general Huntington, Brigadier-general Starke, John Laurence, Judge-advocate-general. [42]

Major André, Adjutant-general to the British army, was brought before the board, and the following letter from General Washington to the board, dated head-quarters, Tappan, September 29, 1780, was laid before them, and read:

Gentlemen,

Major André, Adjutant-general to the British army, will be brought before you for your examination. He came within our lines in the night, on an interview with Major-general Arnold, and in an assumed character, and was taken within our lines, in a disguised habit, with a pass under a feigned name, and with the inclosed papers concealed upon him. After a careful examination, you will be pleased, as speedily as possible, to report a precise state of his case, together with your opinion of the light in which he ought to be considered, and the punishment that ought to be inflicted. The Judge-advocate will attend to assist in the examination, who has sundry other papers relative to this matter, which he will lay before the board.

I have the honour to be,
Gentlemen,
your most obedient,
and humble servant,
G. WASHINGTON.

The Board of General Officers convened at Tappan.

The names of the officers composing the board were read to Major André, and on his being asked whether he confessed the matters contained in the letters from his Excellency General Washington to the board, or denied them, he said, in addition to his letter to General Washington, dated Salem, the 24th of September, 1780, which was read to the board, and acknowledged by Major André, to have been written by him, which letter is as follows:

Salem, 24th Sept. 1780.

SIR,

WHAT I have as yet said concerning myself was in the justifiable attempt to be extricated; I am too little accustomed to duplicity to have succeeded.

I beg your excellency will be persuaded, that no alteration in the temper of my mind, or apprehension for my safety, induces me to take the step of addressing you; but that it is to secure myself from an imputation of having assumed a mean character for treacherous purposes, or self-interest: a conduct incompatible with the principles that actuated me, as well as with my condition in life.

It is to vindicate my fame that I speak, and not to solicit security.

The person in your possession is Major John André, Adjutant-general to the British army.

The influence of one commander in the army of his adversary is an advantage taken in war. A correspondence for this purpose I held, as confidential (in the present instance) with his Excellency Sir Henry Clinton.

To favour it, I agreed to meet upon ground not within posts of either army, a person who was to give me intelligence: I came up in the Vulture man of war for this effect, and was fetched by the boat from the shore to the beach: being there, I was told, that the approach of day would prevent my return, and that I must be concealed until the next night. I was in my regimentals, and had fairly risqued my person.

Against my stipulation, my intention, and without my knowledge before hand, I was conducted within one of your posts. Your excellency may conceive my sensation on this occasion, and will imagine how much more I must have been affected, by a refusal to re-conduct me back the next night as I had been brought. Thus become a prisoner, I had to concert my escape. I quitted my uniform, and was passed another way in the night, without the American posts, to neutral ground; and being informed I was beyond all armed parties, and left to press for New-York, I was taken at Tarry-town, by some volunteers.

Thus, as I have had the honour to relate, was I betrayed (being Adjutant-general of the British army) into the vile condition of an enemy within your posts.

Having avowed myself a British officer, I have nothing to reveal but what relates to myself, which is true on the honour of an officer, and a gentleman.

The request I have made to your excellency, and I am conscious that I address myself well, is, that in any rigour policy may dictate, a decency of conduct towards me may mark, that though unfortunate, I am branded with nothing dishonourable; as no motive could be mine, but the service of my king, and as I was involuntarily an impostor.

Another request is, that I may be permitted to write an open letter to Sir Henry Clinton, and another to a friend for cloaths and linen.

I take the liberty to mention the condition of some gentlemen at Charles-town, who being either on parole, or under protection, were engaged in a conspiracy against us. Though their situation is not similar, they are objects who may be sent in exchange for me, or are persons whom the treatment I receive might affect.

It is no less, Sir, in a confidence in the generosity of your mind, than on account of your superior station, that I have chosen to importune you with this letter. I have the honour to be, with the greatest respect, Sir, your excellency's most obedient,

and most humble servant,

JOHN ANDRE, Adj. Gen.

His Excellency Gen. Washington, &c.

He then said, that he came on shore from the Vulture sloop of war, in the night of the twenty-first of September inst. somewhere under the Haverstraw Mountain: that the boat he came on shore in carried no flag, and that he had on a surtout coat over his regimentals, and that he wore his surtout coat when he was taken:—That he met General Arnold on the shore, and had an interview with him there. He also said, that when he left the Vulture sloop of war, it was understood he was to return that night; but it was then doubted: and if he could not return he was promised to be concealed on shore in a place of safety, until the next night, when he was to return in the same manner he came on shore; and when the next day came, he was solicitous to get back, and made enquiries in the course of the day, how he should return, when he was informed he could not return that way, and he must take the route he did afterwards. He also said, that the first notice he had of his being within any of our posts, was, being challenged by the sentry, which was the first night he was on the shore. He also said, that the evening of the twenty-second of September instant, he passed King's Ferry, between our posts of Stoney and Verplank's Points, in the dress he is at present in, and which he said was not his regimentals; and which dress he procured after he landed from the Vulture, and when he was within our post; and that he was proceeding to New York, but was taken on his way at Tarrytown, as he mentioned in his letter, on Saturday the 23d of September instant, about nine o'clock in the morning.

The following papers were laid before the board, and shewn to Major André, who confessed to the board, that they were found on him when he was taken; and said they were concealed in his boot, except the pass:——

A pass from General Arnold to *John Anderson*, which *name* Major André *acknowledged he assumed.*

Artillery orders, September 5, 1780.

Estimate of the force at West-Point and its dependencies, September, 1780.

Estimate of men to man the works at West-point, &c.

Return of ordnance at West-point, September, 1780.

Remarks on works at West-point.

Copy of a state of matters laid before a council of war, by his Excellency General Washington, held the 6th of September, 1780.

A letter signed *John Anderson*, dated September 7, 1780, to Colonel Sheldon *, was also laid before the board, and shewn to Major André, which he *acknowledged* to have been written by *him*, and is as follows:

New York, Sept. 7, 1780.

SIR,

I AM told *my name* is made known to you, and that I may hope your indulgence in permitting me to meet a friend near your out-posts. I will endeavour to obtain permission to go out with a flag which will be sent to Dobb's Ferry, on Monday next, the 11th, at 12 o'clock, when I shall be happy to meet Mr. G—— †. Should I not be allowed to go, the officer who is to command the escort, between whom and myself no distinction need be made, can speak on the affair.

Let me entreat you, Sir, to favour a matter so interesting to the parties concerned, and which is of so private a nature, that the public on neither side can be injured by it.

I shall be happy, on my part, in doing any act of kindness to you, in a family or property concern of a similar nature.

I trust I shall not be detained, but should any old grudge be a cause for it, I should rather risk that, than neglect the business in question, or assume a mysterious character to carry on an innocent affair; and, as friends have advised, get your lines by stealth. I am, Sir, with all regard,

Your most obedient, humble servant,

JOHN ANDERSON.

Colonel Sheldon.

Major André observed, that this letter could be of no force in the case in question, as it was written in New York, when he was under the orders of General Clinton, but that it tended to prove, that it was not his intentions to come within our lines.

The board having interrogated Major André, about his conception of his coming on shore under

* Lest it should be supposed that Colonel Sheldon, to whom the above letter is addressed, was privy to the plot carrying on by General Arnold, it is to be observed, that the letter was found among Arnold's papers, and had been transmitted by Colonel Sheldon, who, it appears from a letter on the 9th of September to Arnold, which inclosed it, had never heard of John Anderson before. Arnold, in his answer on the 10th, acknowledged he had not communicated it to him, though he had informed him, that he expected a person would come from New York, for the purpose of bringing him intelligence.

† It appears by the same letter that Arnold had written to Mr. Anderson, under the signature of Gustavus. His words are, " I was obliged to write with great caution to him, my letter was signed Gustavus, to prevent any discovery, in case it fell into the hands of the enemy."

the fanction of a flag, he faid, "that it was impoffible for him to fuppofe he came on fhore under that fanction; and added, that if he came on fhore under that fanction, he certainly might have returned under it."

Major Andrè having acknowledged the preceding facts, and being afked whether he had any thing to fay refpecting them, anfwered, he left them to operate with the board.

The examination of Major Andrè being concluded, he was remanded into cuftody.

The following letters were laid before the board and read :—Benedict Arnold's letter to Gen. Wafhington, dated September 25, 1780. Colonel Robinfon's letter to General Wafhington, dated September 25, 1780, and General Clinton's letter, dated the 26th of September, 1780, (inclofing a letter of the fame date from Benedict Arnold) to General Wafhington.

On board the Vulture, Sept. 25, 1780.

S I R,

THE heart which is confcious of its own rectitude, cannot attempt to palliate a ftep which the world may cenfure as wrong. I have ever acted from a principle of love to my country, fince the commencement of the prefent unhappy conteft between Great Britain and her Colonies; the fame principle of love to my country actuates my prefent conduct, however it may appear inconfiftent to the world, who very feldom judge right of any man's actions.

I have no favour to afk for myfelf. I have too often experienced the ingratitude of my country to attempt it; but from the known humanity of your excellency, I am induced to afk your protection for Mrs. Arnold, from every infult and injury that a miftaken vengeance of my country may expofe her to. It ought to fall only on me: fhe is as good and as innocent as an angel, and is incapa-

ble of doing wrong. I beg fhe may be permitted to return to her friends in Philadelphia, or to come to me, as fhe may chufe. From your excellency I have no fears on her account, but fhe may fuffer from the miftaken fury of the country.

I have to requeft that the inclofed letter may be delivered to Mrs. Arnold, and fhe permitted to write to me.

I have alfo to afk that my cloaths and baggage, which are of little confequence, may be fent to me; if required, their value fhall be paid in money. I have the honour to be, with great regard and efteem, your excellency's moft obedient fervant,

B. ARNOLD."
His Excellency Gen. Wafhington.

N. B. In juftice to the gentlemen of my family, Colonel Warwick, and Major Franks, I think myfelf in honour bound to declare, that they, as well as Jofhua Smith, Efq; (who I know is fufpected)[43] are totally ignorant of any tranfactions of mine, that they had reafon to believe were injurious to the public.

Vulture, off Sinfink, Sep. 25, 1780.

S I R,

I AM this moment informed, that Major Andrè, Adjutant-general of his majefty's army in America, is detained as a prifoner by the army under your command. It is therefore incumbent on me to inform you of the manner of his falling into your hands: he went up with a flag, at the requeft of General Arnold, on public bufinefs with him, and had his permit to return by land to New York. Upon thefe circumftances, Major Andrè cannot be detained by you, without the greateft violation of flags, and contrary to the cuftom and ufage of all nations; and as I imagine you will fee this in the fame manner as I do, I muft defire you will order him to be fet at liberty, and allowed to return immediately. Every ftep Major

Andrè took, was by the advice and direction of General Arnold, even that of taking a feigned name, and of courfe not liable to cenfure for it.

I am, Sir, not forgetting our former acquaintance, your very humble fervant,

BEV. ROBINSON.
Col. Roy. Americ.[44]
His Excellency Gen. Wafhington.

New York, Sept. 26, 1780.

S I R,

BEING informed that the king's Adjutant-general in America has been ftopt, under Major-general Arnold's paffports, and is detained a prifoner in your excellency's army, I have the honour to inform you, Sir, that I permitted Major Andrè to go to Major-general Arnold, at the particular requeft of that general officer. You will perceive, Sir, by the enclofed paper, that a flag of truce was fent to receive Major Andrè, and paffports granted for his return. I therefore cannot have a doubt but your excellency will immediately direct, that this officer has permiffion to return to my orders at New York.

I have the honour to be, your excellency's moft obedient, and moft humble fervant,

H. CLINTON.
His Excellency Gen. Wafhington.

New York, Sept. 26, 1780.

S I R,

IN anfwer to your excellency's meffage, refpecting your Adjutant-general, Major Andrrè, and delivering my ideas of the reafon why he is detained, being under my paffports, I have the honour to inform you, that I apprehend a few hours muft return Major Andrè to your Excellency's orders, as that officer is affuredly under the protection of a flag of truce, fent by me to him, for the purpofe of a converfation, which I requefted to hold with him relating to myfelf, and which I wifhed to communicate, through that officer, to your excellency.

I commanded at the time at West-point, and had an undoubted right to send my flag of truce for Major Andrè, who came to me under that protection; and having held my conversation with him, I delivered him confidential papers in my own hand writing, to deliver to your excellency. Thinking it much properer he should return by land, I directed him to make use of the feigned name of John Anderson, under which he had by my direction come on shore, and gave him my passports to go to the White Plains, on his way to New-York.——This officer cannot, therefore, fail of being immediately sent to New-York, as he was invited to a conversation with me, for which I sent him a flag of truce, and finally gave him passports for his safe return to your excellency; all which I had then a right to do, being in the actual service of America, under the orders of General Washington, and commanding-general at West-point, and its dependencies.

I have the honour to be your excellency's most obedient, and very humble servant,

B. ARNOLD.

His Excellency Sir Henry Clinton.

The Board having considered the letter from his Excellency General Washington respecting Major Andrè, Adjutant-general to the British army, the confession of Major Andrè, and the papers produced to them, report to his Excellency the Commander in Chief, the following facts, which appear to them relative to Major Andrè:

First, That he came on shore from the Vulture sloop of war, in the night of the 21st of September instant, on an interview with General Arnold, in a private and secret manner.

Secondly, That he changed his dress within our lines; and under a feigned name, and in a disguised habit, passed our works at Stoney and Verplank's points, the evening of the 22d of September instant, and was taken the morning of the 23d of September instant, at Tarry-town, in a disguised habit, he being then on his way for New-York; and when taken, he had in his possession several papers, which contained intelligence for the enemy.

The Board having maturely considered these facts, do also report to his Excellency General Washington, that Major Andrè, Adjutant general to the British army, ought to be considered as a *spy* from the enemy, and that, agreeable to the law and usage of nations, it is their opinion, he ought to suffer death.

Nathaniel Green, major-general, president; Stirling, major-general; La Fayette, major-general; Ar. St. Clair, major-general; R. Howe, major-general; Steuben, major-general; Samuel H. Parsons, brigadier-general; James Clinton, brigadier-general; Henry Knox, brigadier-general artillery; John Glover, brigadier-general; John Patterson, brigadier-general; Edward Hand, brigadier-general; J. Huntington, brigadier-general; John Starke, brigadier-general; John Laurence, judge-advocate-general.

APPENDIX.

Copy of a Letter from Major Andrè, *Adjutant-general, to Sir Henry Clinton, K. B. &c. &c.*

Tappan, Sept. 29, 1780.

SIR,

YOUR excellency is doubtless already apprised of the manner in which I was taken, and possibly of the serious light in which my conduct is considered, and the rigorous determination that is impending.

Under these circumstances, I have obtained General Washington's permission to send you this letter, the object of which is, to remove from your breast any suspicion that I could imagine I was bound by your excellency's orders to expose myself to what has happened. The events of coming within an enemy's posts, and of changing my dress, which led me to my present situation, were contrary to my own intentions, as they were to your orders; and the circuitous route which I took to return, was imposed, (perhaps unavoidably) without alternative, upon me.

I am perfectly tranquil in mind, and prepared for any fate to which an honest zeal for my king's service may have devoted me.

In addressing myself to your excellency on this occasion, the force of all my obligations to you, and of the attachment and gratitude I bear you, recurs to me. With all the warmth of my heart, I give you thanks for your excellency's profuse kindness to me! and I send you the most earnest wishes for your welfare, which a faithful, affectionate, and respectful attendant can frame.

I have a mother and three sisters, to whom the value of my commission would be an object, as the loss of Grenada has much affected their income. It is needless to be more explicit on this subject; I am persuaded of your excellency's goodness.

I receive the greatest attention from his excellency General Washington, and from every person under whose charge I happen to be placed.

I have the honour to be, with the most respectful attachment, your excellency's most obedient, and most humble servant,

JOHN ANDRE, Adjutant-gen.

(Addressed)

His Excellency Sir Henry Clinton, K. B. &c. &c. &c.

Copy of a Letter from his Excellency General Washington, *to his Excellency Sir* Henry Clinton.

Head Quarters, Sept. 30, 1780.

SIR,

IN answer to your excellency's letter of the 26th instant, which I had the honour to receive, I am to inform you, that Major Andrè was taken under such circumstances, as would have justified the most summary proceedings against him. I determined, however, to refer his case to the examination and decision of a board of general officers, who have reported, on his free and voluntary confession and letters, " That he came on shore from the Vulture sloop of war, in the night of the 21st of September," &c. &c. as in the report of the board of general officers.

From these proceedings it is evident, Major André was employed in the execution of measures very foreign to the objects of flags of truce, and such as they were never meant to authorize or countenance in the most distant degree ; and this gentleman confessed, with the greatest candour, in the course of his examination, " That it was impossible for him to suppose, he came on shore under the sanction of a flag."

I have the honour to be your excellency's most obedient, and most humble servant,

G. WASHINGTON.
(Addressed)
His Excellency Sir Henry Clinton.

In this letter, Major André's, of the 29th of September, to Sir Henry Clinton, was transmitted.

New-York, Sept. 26, 1780.

SIR,

PERSUADED that you are inclined rather to promote than prevent the civilities and acts of humanity, which the rules of war permit between civilized nations, I find no difficulty in representing to you, that several letters and messages sent from hence, have been disregarded, are unanswered, and the flags of truce that carried them detained. As I ever had treated all flags of truce with civility and respect, I have a right to hope, that you will order my complaint to be immediately redressed.

Major André, who visited an officer commanding in a district at his own desire, and acted in every circumstance agreeable to his direction, I find is detained a prisoner : my friendship for him leads me to fear, he may suffer some inconvenience for want of necessaries ; I wish to be allowed to send him a few, and shall take it as a favour if you will be pleased to permit his servant to deliver them. In Sir Henry Clinton's absence, it becomes a part of my duty to make this representation and request.

I am, Sir, your Excellency's most obedient humble servant,

JAMES ROBERTSON, Lieut. Gen.[45]

His Excellency Gen Washington.

Tappan, Sept. 30, 1780.

SIR,

I HAVE just received your letter of the 26th. Any delay which may have attended your flags has proceeded from accident, and the peculiar circumstances of the occasion, not from any intentional neglect, or violation. The letter that admitted of an answer, has received one as early as it could be given with propriety, transmitted by a flag this morning. As to messages, I am uninformed of any that have been sent.

The necessaries for Major André will be delivered to him, agreeable to your request.

I am, Sir, your most obedient humble servant,

G. WASHINGTON.

His Excellency Lieut. Gen. Robertson, New-York.

New-York, Sept. 30, 1780.

SIR,

FROM your excellency's letter of this date, I am persuaded the Board of General Officers, to whom you referred the case of Major André, cannot have been rightly informed of all the circumstances on which a judgment ought to be formed. I think it of the highest moment to humanity, that your excellency should be perfectly apprized of the state of this matter, before you proceed to put that judgment in execution.

For this reason, I shall send his Excellency Lieutenant-general Robertson, and two other gentlemen, to give you a true state of facts, and to declare to you my sentiments and resolutions. They will set out to-morrow as early as the wind and tide will permit, and wait near Dobb's-ferry for your permission and safe conduct, to meet your Excellency, or such persons as you may appoint, to converse with them on this subject.

I have the honour to be your Excellency's most obedient and humble servant,

H. CLINTON.

P. S. The Hon. Andrew Elliot, Esq ; Lieutenant - governor, and the Hon. William Smith, Chief Justice of this province, will attend[46] his Excellency Lieutenant-general Robertson.
H. C.
His Excellency Gen. Washington.

Lieutenant - general Robertson, Mr. Elliot, and Mr. Smith, came up in a flag vessel to Dobb's-ferry, agreeable to the above letter. The two last were not suffered to land. General Robertson was permitted to come on shore, and was met by Major-general Greene, who verbally reported, that General Robertson mentioned to him in substance what is contained in his letter of the 2d of October, to General Washington.

New-York, Oct. 1, 1780.

SIR,

I TAKE this opportunity to inform your Excellency, that I consider myself no longer acting under the commission of Congress : their last to me being among my papers at West-Point, you, Sir, will make such use of it as you think proper.

At the fame time I beg leave to affure your Excellency, that my attachment to the true intereſt of my country is invariable, and that I am actuated by the fame principle which has ever been the governing rule of my conduct in this unhappy conteſt.

I have the honour to be, very reſpectfully, your Excellency's moſt obedient humble ſervant,

B. ARNOLD.

His Excellency Gen. Waſhington.

Greyhound Schooner, Flag of Truce, Dobb's-Ferry, Oct. 2, 1780.

SIR,

A NOTE I have from General Greene, leaves me in doubt if his memory had ſerved him to relate to you, with exactneſs, the ſubſtance of the converſation that had paſſed between him and myſelf, on the ſubject of Major Andrè: in an affair of ſo much conſequence to my friend, to the two armies, and humanity, I would leave no poſſibility of miſunderſtanding, and therefore take the liberty to put in writing the ſubſtance of what I ſaid to General Greene.

I offered to prove, by the evidence of Colonel Robinſon, and the officers of the Vulture, that Major Andrè went on ſhore at General Arnold's deſire, in a boat ſent for him with a flag of truce; that he not only came aſhore with the knowledge and under the protection of the general who commanded in the diſtrict, but that he took no ſtep while on ſhore, but by the direction of General Arnold, as will appear by the incloſed letter from him to your Excellency. Under theſe circumſtances, I could not, and hoped you would not, conſider Major Andrè as a ſpy, for any improper phraſe in his letter to you.

The facts he relates correſpond with the evidence I offer; but he admits a concluſion that does not follow. The change of cloaths

and name was ordered by General Arnold, under whoſe directions he neceſſarily was while within his command.

As General Greene and I did not agree in opinion, I wiſhed, that diſintereſted gentlemen of knowledge of the law of war and nations might be aſked their opinion on the ſubject, and mentioned Monſieur Knyphauſen and General Rochambault.

I related, that a Captain Robinſon had been delivered to Sir Henry Clinton as a ſpy, and undoubtedly was ſuch; but that it being ſignified to him, that you were deſirous that the man ſhould be exchanged, he had ordered him to be exchanged.

I wiſhed that an intercourſe of ſuch civilities, as the rules of war admit of, might take off many of its horrors. I admitted that Major Andrè had a great ſhare of Sir Henry Clinton's eſteem, and that he would be infinitely obliged by his liberation; and that, if he was permitted to return with me, I would engage to have any perſon you would be pleaſed to name, ſet at liberty.

I added, that Sir Henry Clinton had never put to death any perſon for a breach of the rules of war, though he had, and now has, many in his power. Under the preſent circumſtances, much good may ariſe from humanity, much ill from the want of it. If that could give any weight, I beg leave to add, that your favourable treatment of Major Andrè, will be a favour I ſhould ever be intent to return to any you hold dear.

My memory does not retain, with the exactneſs I could wiſh, the words of the letter which General Greene ſhewed me from Major Andrè to your Excellency. For Sir Henry Clinton's ſatisfaction; I beg you will order a copy of it to be ſent to me at New-York.

I have the honour to be your Excellency's moſt obedient and

moſt humble ſervant,

JAMES ROBERTSON.

His Excellency Gen. Waſhington.

New-York, Oct. 1, 1780.

SIR,

THE polite attention ſhewn by your Excellency and the gentlemen of your family to Mrs. Arnold, when in diſtreſs, demands my grateful acknowledgment and thanks, which I beg leave to preſent.

From your Excellency's letter to Sir Henry Clinton, I find a Board of General Officers have given it as their opinion, that Major Andrè comes under the deſcription of a ſpy: my good opinion of the candour and juſtice of thoſe gentlemen leads me to believe, that if they had been made fully acquainted with every circumſtance reſpecting Major Andrè, they would by no means have conſidered him in the light of a ſpy, or even of a priſoner. In juſtice to him, I think it my duty to declare, that he came from on board the Vulture at my particular requeſt, by a flag ſent on purpoſe for him by Joſhua Smith, Eſq; who had permiſſion to go to Dobb's ferry to carry letters, and for other purpoſes not mentioned, and to return. This was done as a blind to the ſpy-boats. Mr. Smith at the ſame time had my private directions to go on board the Vulture, and bring on ſhore Colonel Robinſon, or Mr. John Anderſon, which was the name I had requeſted Major Andrè to aſſume: at the ſame time I deſired Mr. Smith to inform him, that he ſhould have my protection, and a ſafe paſſport to return in the ſame boat as ſoon as our buſineſs was completed. As ſeveral accidents intervened to prevent his being ſent on board, I gave him my paſſport to return by land. Major Andrè came on ſhore in his uniform (without diſguiſe) which, with much reluctance, at my particular and preſſing inſtance, he exchanged for another coat. I furnished him with a horse and saddle, and pointed out the route by which he was to return: and as commanding officer in the department, I had an undoubted right to transact all these matters, which, if wrong, Major André ought by no means to suffer for them.

But if, after this just and candid representation of Major André's case, the Board of General Officers adhere to their former opinion, I shall suppose it dictated by passion and resentment; and if that gentleman should suffer the severity of their sentence, I should think myself bound by every tie of duty and honour, to retaliate on such unhappy persons of your army as may fall within my power, that the respect due to flags, and to the law of nations, may be better understood and observed.

I have farther to observe, that forty of the principal inhabitants of South Carolina have justly forfeited their lives, which have hitherto been spared by the clemency of his Excellency Sir Henry Clinton, who cannot in justice extend his mercy to them any longer, if Major André suffers; which, in all probability, will open a scene of blood, at which humanity will revolt.

Suffer me to entreat your Excellency, for your own, and the honour of humanity, and the love you have of justice, that you suffer not an unjust sentence to touch the life of Major André.

But if this warning should be disregarded, and he suffer, I call heaven and earth to witness, that your Excellency will be justly answerable for the torrent of blood that may be spilt in consequence.

I have the honour to be, with due respect, your Excellency's most obedient and very humble servant,

B. ARNOLD.

His Excellency Gen. Washington.

Tappan, Oct. 1, 1780.

SIR,

BUOYED above the terror of death, by the consciousness of a life devoted to honourable pursuits, and stained with no action that can give me remorse, I trust that the request I make to your Excellency at this serious period, and which is to soften my last moments, will not be rejected.

Sympathy towards a soldier will surely induce your Excellency and a military tribunal to adapt the mode of my death to the feelings of a man of honour.

Let me hope, Sir, that if aught in my character impresses you with esteem towards me, if aught in my misfortunes marks me as the victim of policy, and not of resentment, I shall experience the operation of these feelings in your breast, by being informed that I am not to die on a gibbet.

I have the honour to be your Excellency's most obedient, and most humble servant,

JOHN ANDRE,
Adj. Gen. to the British Army.

The time which elapsed between the capture of Major André, which was the 23d of September, and his execution, which did not take place till twelve o'clock on the 2d of October; the mode of trying him; his letter to Sir Henry Clinton, K.B. on the 29th of September, in which he said, " I receive the greatest attention from his Excellency General Washington, and from every person under whose charge I happen to be placed;" not to mention many other acknowledgments which he made of the good treatment he received; must evince, that the proceedings against him were not guided by passion or resentment. The practice and usage of war were against his request, and made the indulgence he solicited, circumstanced as he was, inadmissible.

Published by order of Congress,

CHARLES THOMSON.

General Arnold's *Address to the Inhabitants of America, after having abandoned the Service of the Congress.*

New-York, Oct. 7, 1780.

I SHOULD forfeit, even in my own opinion, the place I have so long held in your's, if I could be indifferent to your approbation, and silent on the motives which have induced me to join the king's arms.

A very few words, however, shall suffice upon a subject so personal; for to the thousands who suffer under the tyranny of the usurpers in the revolted provinces, as well as to the great multitude who have long wished for its subversion, this instance of my conduct can want no vindication; and as to the class of men who are criminally protracting the war from sinister views at the expence of the public interest, I prefer their enmity to their applause. I am, therefore, only concerned in this address to explain myself to such of my countrymen, as want abilities or opportunities to detect the artifices by which they are duped.

Having fought by your side when the love of our country animated our arms, I shall expect, from your justice and candour, what your deceivers, with more art and less honesty, will find it inconsistent with their own views to admit.

When I quitted domestic happiness for the perils of the field, I conceived the rights of my country in danger, and that duty and honour called me to her defence. A redress of grievances was my only object and aim; however, I acquiesced in a step which I thought precipitate, the declaration of independence: to justify this measure, many plausible reasons were urged, which could no longer exist, when Great Britain, with the open arms of a parent, offered to embrace us as children, and grant the wished-for redress.

And now that her worst enemies are in her own bosom, I should change my principles, if I conspired with their designs; yourselves being judges, was the war the less just, because fellow-subjects were considered as our foe? You have felt the torture in which we have raised our arms against a brother. God incline the guilty protectors of these unnatural dissensions to resign their ambition, and cease from their delusions, in compassion to kindred blood!

I anticipate your question, Was not the war a defensive one, until the French joined in the combination? I answer, that I thought so. You will add, Was it not afterwards necessary, till the separation of the British empire was complete? By no means; in contending for the welfare of my country, I am free to declare my opinion, that this end attained, all strife should have ceased.

I lamented, therefore, the impolicy, tyranny, and injustice, which, with a sovereign contempt of the people of America, studiously neglected to take their collective sentiments of the British proposals of peace, and to negociate, under a suspension of arms; for an adjustment of differences; I lamented it as a dangerous sacrifice of the great interests of this country, to the partial views of a proud, ancient, and crafty foe. I had my suspicions of some imperfections in the councils, on proposals prior to the parliamentary commission of 1778; but having then less to do in the cabinet than the field (I will not pronounce peremptorily, as some may, and perhaps justly, that Congress have veiled them from the public eye) I continued to be guided in the negligent confidence of a soldier. But the whole world saw, and all America confessed, that the overtures of the second commission exceeded our wishes and expectations; and if there was any suspicion of the national liberality, it arose from its excess.

Do any believe we were at that time really entangled by an alliance with France? Unfortunate deception! they have been duped by a virtuous credulity, in the incautious moments of intemperate passion, to give up their felicity to serve a nation wanting both the will and power to protect us, and aiming at the destruction both of the mother country and the provinces. In the plainness of common sense, for I pretend to no casuistry, did the pretended treaty with the court of Versailles, amount to more than an overture to America? Certainly not, because no authority had been given by the people to conclude it, nor to this very hour have they authorised its ratification. The articles of confederation remain still unsigned.

In the firm persuasion, therefore, that the private judgment of an individual citizen of this country is as free from all conventional restraints, since as before the insidious offers of France, I preferred those from Great-Britain; thinking it infinitely wiser and safer to cast my confidence upon her justice and generosity, than to trust a monarchy too feeble to establish your independency, so perilous to her distant dominions; the enemy of the Protestant faith, and fraudulently avowing an affection for the liberties of mankind, while she holds her native sons in vassalage and chains.

I affect no disguise, and therefore frankly declare, that in these principles I had determined to retain my arms and command for an opportunity to surrender them to Great Britain; and in concerting the measures for a purpose, in my opinion, as grateful as it would have been beneficial to my country, I was only solicitous to accomplish an event of decisive importance, and to prevent, as much as possible, in the execution of it, the effusion of blood.

With the highest satisfaction I bear testimony to my old fellow-soldiers and citizens, that I find solid ground to rely upon the clemency of our sovereign, and abundant conviction that it is the generous intention of Great Britain not only to leave the rights and privileges of the colonies unimpaired, together with their perpetual exemption from taxation, but to superadd such farther benefits as may consist with the common prosperity of the empire. In short, I fought for much less than the parent country is as willing to grant to her colonies as they can be to receive or enjoy.

Some may think I continued in the struggle of these unhappy days too long, and others that I quitted it too soon.—To the first I reply, that I did not see with their eyes, nor perhaps had so favourable a situation to look from, and that to our common master I am willing to stand or fall. In behalf of the candid among the latter, some of whom I believe serve blindly but honestly—in the bands I have left, I pray God to give them all the lights requisite to their own safety before it is too late; and with respect to that herd of censurers, whose enmity to me originates in their hatred to the principles by which I am now led to devote my life to the re-union of the British empire, as the best and only means to dry up the streams of misery that have deluged this country, they may be assured, that, conscious of the rectitude of my intentions, I shall treat their malice and calumnies with contempt and neglect.

B. Arnold.

Notes, 1780

1. The invasion threat of 1779 produced a number of offers for the raising of new regular regiments of volunteer units, similar to the movement of 1778. An act regularising the formation of volunteer corps was passed in June, and fourteen new regiments of regulars were approved by November. To prevent enemy seizure of horses and wagons for transportation and cattle for food, it was proposed that livestock be driven inland from the coastal districts on notice of invasion. A proclamation explaining these arrangements was issued on 9 July. See A. Temple Patterson, *The Other Armada: The Franco-Spanish Attempt to Invade Britain in 1779* (Manchester, 1960), ch. 6.

2. The fleets combined on 23 July.

3. Bernardo de Galvez (1746–86) was appointed Governor of Louisiana in 1776 and was active before Spain's declaration of war in providing supplies to the Americans and suppressing illegal British trade to his province.

4. John Campbell (d. 1806) served in America after 1776 and was promoted to Major-General in February 1779, having been sent to command British forces in West Florida.

5. Alexander Dickson, not further identified.

6. Both John Butler (see "Notes, 1777," n. 73) and his son Walter were at Newtown; Guy Johnson was not. John McDonnell, a Loyalist, participated in earlier raids with Joseph Brant.

7. Enoch Poor (1736–80), New Hampshire officer appointed Brigadier-General in the Continental Army in 1777. James Clinton (1733–1812), New York officer appointed Brigadier-General in the Continental Army in August 1776.

8. Marriot Arbuthnot (?1711–94), Naval Commissioner at Halifax, 1775–78; promoted to Admiral in 1778; appointed Commander-in-Chief on the North American station in the same year.

9. George Keith Elphinstone (1746–1823), Lieutenant in 1770, commanded the frigate *Perseus*, 1776–80; later, Vice-Admiral, Commander of the Channel Fleet in 1803, and 1st Viscount Keith in 1814.

10. Usually a device of wooden stakes designed to act as a portable obstruction to cavalry. A marine version (sometimes attributed to the inventive genius of Benjamin Franklin) was formed of iron spikes set in a wooden framework and sunk in shallow water.

11. Banastre Tarleton (1754–1833) volunteered for service in America in 1775 and in 1778 was made Lieutenant-Colonel of the British Legion (originally three troops of dragoons and an infantry unit not on the regular establishment, wearing a distinctive green uniform).

The Annual Register—1780

12. The Board of War reported on 21 August that 245 American officers and 2,326 noncommissioned officers and privates were captured. *Journals of the Continental Congress, 1774–1789*, ed. W. C. Ford, 34 vols. (Washington, D.C., 1904–37), vol. 17, p. 743.

13. A three-masted vessel without topmasts.

14. In view of their own conduct, the Carolinas had few grounds for reproaching Virginia. The South Carolina militia showed a general reluctance to mobilise, and Charleston's fortifications had to be repaired by slaves. The garrison was eventually reinforced by 700 North Carolina and 750 Virginia Continentals despatched by Washington. They arrived on 3 March and 6 April respectively. Lincoln could have evacuated his army on the still open northward side on 19 April. However, he was bitterly opposed by Lieutenant-Governor Christopher Gadsden and members of the council, one of whom threatened that the inhabitants of the city would destroy the army's river transports and open the gates to the British if the garrison abandoned them. Christopher Ward, *The War of the Revolution*, ed. and comp. J. R. Alden, 2 vols. (New York, 1952), vol. 2, p. 702.

15. Not identified.

16. Morgan Bryan, Colonel of the North Carolina Provincial Regiment (Loyalist).

17. Francis Rawdon-Hasting (1754–1826), son of the Earl of Moira and styled Lord Rawdon, 1762–83; had served in America since 1774, acting as A.D.C. to Clinton and Adjutant-General, 1778–79; held the rank of Lieutenant-Colonel under Cornwallis in South Carolina.

18. Johann Kalb (1721–80), a German who had served in the French army since 1743 and reached the rank of Brigadier-General in 1776. He toured America in 1768 to report to the French government on the degree of American disaffection, and returned with Lafayette in 1777. Calling himself Baron de Kalb, he was eventually appointed Major-General in the Continental Army in 1777. The relief force for Charleston was his first command.

19. Griffith Rutherford (?1731–c.1800), Brigadier-General of North Carolina militia. Richard Caswell (see "Notes, 1776," n. 69). Thomas Sumpter (1734–1832) fought as a ranger captain against the Cherokee in 1762 and against the British in the southern campaign of 1778, after which he retired with the rank of Colonel. However, when Tarleton's Legion burnt his plantation, he organised partisan resistance in South Carolina and was promoted to Brigadier-General in 1780. Amongst the "other leaders," was Francis Marion (c. 1732–95), about to begin his career as the most effective partisan organiser and guerrilla leader in the war.

20. Not identified.

21. The battle of Liegnitz, 15 August 1760.

22. Isaac Gregory, Brigadier-General in the North Carolina militia; he was wounded but not killed at Camden.

23. Not further identified.

24. "... an adventurous and none too respectable businessman of Amsterdam." S. F. Bemis, *The Diplomacy of the American Revolution* (Edinburgh and London, 1957), p. 158.

25. William Lee (1739–95), elder brother of Arthur Lee, appointed commercial agent of the Congress in Paris in 1777. Frustrated in his attempts to secure recognition of the United States by Prussia and Austria, he turned to intrigue in Holland.

26. Not identified.

27. Richard Stockton (1730–81), New Jersey delegate to the Continental Congress in 1776, was captured by the British and exchanged in 1777, but his health was shattered and he lived in retirement until his death. As a Trustee of Princeton College he was associated with Witherspoon, whom he visited in 1766 in an attempt to persuade him to accept the presidency of the college.

28. John Witherspoon (1723–94), Scots clergyman who became President of the College of New Jersey, Princeton, in 1768; New Jersey delegate to the Continental Congress, 1776–82.

29. John Adams, who was appointed to succeed Silas Deane as Commissioner to France in November 1777. The French government delayed his departure, and he did not arrive in Boston until 2 August.

30. Lieutenant-Colonel Joan Dircks, a Dutch officer in American service who had been on leave of absence in Holland.

31. Alexander Gillon (1741–94), South Carolina merchant and politician, active from 1775 in importing munitions for the Congress; was in France and Holland, 1779–81, to secure ships and naval stores.

32. Ralph Izard (1742–1804), South Carolinian who lived in London, 1771–76. He migrated to Paris and in May 1777 he was named Commissioner to Tuscany. Since, like other states, Tuscany refused to recognise the United States, he remained in Paris to intrigue with the Lees against Franklin. He was recalled in June 1779.

33. Not identified.

34. Arthur Lee.

35. Not further identified.

36. Not identified.

37. Pierre Augustin Caron de Beaumarchais (1732–99), enterprising French agent who had organised shipments of munitions and supplies from France to America since 1776. After Silas Deane's recall (see "Notes, 1778," n. 119), Congress refused to acknowledge Beaumarchais's claims for payment. This decision was reversed in January 1779 but payment was not made until 1835.

38. Joan Derek van der Capellen tot den Poll, a member of the provincial assembly of Overyssel, suggested by letter that an American loan might be raised in Amsterdam.

39. John André (1751–80) served in America after 1774 and was appointed Clinton's Adjutant-General. As head of Clinton's intelligence service, he corresponded with Benedict Arnold after Arnold approached the British in May 1779 with his plan to defect, and again in May 1780, when Arnold offered to surrender West Point.

40. Commanding officer of American troops in North Castle.

41. Volunteer New York militiamen.

42. Members of the court-martial board not hitherto identified in other contexts: Henry Knox (1750–1806), Connecticut officer serving in the Continental Artillery, appointed Brigadier-General in December 1776; John Glover (1732–97), Massachusetts officer, appointed Brigadier-

General in June 1777; John Paterson (1744–1808), Massachusetts officer, appointed Brigadier-General in February 1777; Edward Hand (1744–1802), Pennsylvania officer, appointed Brigadier-General in April 1777; Jedediah Huntington (1743–1818), Connecticut officer, appointed Brigadier-General in May 1777; John Laurence (1750–1810), New York officer, appointed Judge Advocate General in April 1777.

43. Arnold refers to the group of officers, including his aides, which acted as a general's staff and were traditionally called his "family." Richard Varick (1753–1831), a friend of Arnold and his A.D.C. from August 1780. Though cleared of complicity in Arnold's treason, he could obtain no military employment until Washington appointed him as a confidential secretary in May 1781. David Franks, formerly a Loyalist in Canada, joined Arnold in 1776 and was a Major and A.D.C. to Arnold from May 1778. Acquitted of complicity, he was later sent to Europe on diplomatic errands by the Congress. Joshua Hett Smith (1737–1818), brother of the Chief Justice of New York, William Smith, but not a Loyalist. He acted first as Robert Howe's head of intelligence, then Arnold's. In the latter capacity, he organised André's visit to Arnold and his return but was entirely unaware of the real reasons for the meeting. Though acquitted of complicity, he was imprisoned by New York State as a suspected Loyalist, dramatically escaped in 1781, fled to England, and returned to America in 1801.

44. Beverley Robinson (1721–92), Loyalist Colonel of the Loyal American Regiment and leading espionage agent in New York; his home was used for the meeting between André and Arnold.

45. Returned from England to resume his governorship of New York.

46. Andrew Elliot, not further identified. William Smith (1728–93), celebrated lawyer and historian, brother of Joshua Smith.

47. Jean Baptiste Donatien de Vimeur, Comte de Rochambeau (1725–1807), distinguished French soldier, appointed Lieutenant-General commanding the French forces sent to America in 1780.

Introduction

1781

During the first months of 1781, Britain, France, and America were questioning how long their national finances could support the war. France's endemic fiscal instability rapidly approached a crisis, American congressional credit collapsed and the depreciation of continental currency was causing serious unrest. The drain on Britain's resources was probably less severe than many contemporaries believed, but it was bad enough. Britain's military and naval strength was now indisputably stretched beyond its limits and the overextension continually risked disaster.

As the war encompassed a new enemy, Holland, and spread to the East, Britain faced overwhelming difficulties in recruiting for the army, organising transports, and juggling naval resources to meet each shift in the disposition of the enemy fleets. The original plans for 1781 envisaged a successful defence of the British West Indies, relief of Gibraltar, an expedition to seize the Cape of Good Hope and guard the route to India, and reinforcements to permit Clinton to expand his successful campaign in the south. However, these plans were constantly modified as news of enemy moves arrived. The caution which immobilised a large part of the navy in defending the Channel was abandoned in late March and much of the home fleet was used in the relief of Gibraltar. The navy, however, could not prevent a French expedition from beating its British counterpart to the Cape of Good Hope nor France sending a powerful fleet under de Grasse to the Caribbean, with the option to operate on the American coast. Rodney was reinforced in the West Indies at the beginning of the year, but the assistance he needed to give him superiority over de Grasse was delayed by the slow return of the home fleet from Gibraltar. Rodney took St. Eustatius at the end of January but could not prevent de Grasse from capturing Tobago in June and sailing for America on 5 August. On the same day, the specially formed North Sea squadron won a narrow victory over the Dutch off the Dogger Bank. The bulk of the home fleet was diverted to protect British commerce from a combined France-Spanish fleet from the beginning of July into the early Fall. In the summer of 1781, the ministry in London could only hope that the British naval forces in the western Atlantic would be sufficient, and that they would operate decisively to frustrate French naval support for Washington and Rochambeau. The Government learned just how vain that hope had been on 25 November with the news of Cornwallis's surrender on 18 October.

In January 1781, Cornwallis, reinforced by troops under Leslie originally sent to the Chesapeake, was certain that he could now destroy the separated commands of Greene and Morgan. Tarleton, despatched after Morgan, engaged him at Cowpens on 16 January and was badly beaten; this reverse surprised Cornwallis and weakened his overall position. Greene refused to be brought to battle and began a rapid withdrawal across the North Carolina rivers until the British in pursuit slowed to a halt and reversed into a tactical retreat. By March, Greene's strengthened and regrouped forces resumed the initiative and on 15 March met Cornwallis at Guilford Courthouse. A courageous British attack against considerably superior numbers drove the Americans from the field but Cornwallis dared not pursue them and he could not remain in North Carolina with an army short of supplies and harried by local militia. He therefore resolved to push forward to Wilmington and from there link up with a British force which had established itself in Virginia.

As soon as he was certain of Cornwallis's intentions, Greene, undismayed by his recent defeat, struck straight into South Carolina. There the new commander, Lord Rawdon, was contending with serious guerrilla activity but on 25 April he defeated Greene at Hobkirk's Hill. Rawdon knew, however, that he could not risk his army indefinitely in the field and though he prevented Greene taking Ninety-Six on 20 June, he lost Augusta and several British-held posts. Rawdon then called in his outlying units and retired to hold firm in Charleston and Savannah. Rawdon himself then returned to England a sick man and handed over his command to Alexander Stuart. The dogged Greene advanced on Charleston in August but was defeated by Stuart in a vicious fight at Eutaw Springs on 8 September after American discipline briefly disintegrated. But the British had again failed to destroy the enemy so the army, weakened by losses, could only retreat to Charleston. Greene had achieved the distinction of losing every major battle in the campaign while gaining his strategic objective of forcing the British to abandon all of the Carolinas save the bases held in 1780.

In the north, the year began badly for the Americans. The winter of 1780–1781 was worse than that of the previous two years for the Continental Army. Shortages of every kind of supplies produced dreadful hardships and the anger amongst the troops over delayed pay and depreciated currency finally exploded into serious disorder.[1] Six regiments of the Pennsylvania Line mutinied on 2 January, and three New Jersey regiments followed suit on the twentieth. The first case was settled by a congressional committee and the second by firm suppression, but the confidence of American leaders was shaken. Washington also regarded the military situation as discouraging. He could see no way of dislodging the British from New York and feared he would be unable to help Greene and prevent the expansion of British success in the south. Moreover, in December 1780 Clinton sent an expedition under Arnold to begin raids in Virginia, where Arnold devastated Richmond on 4 January and secured a base at Portsmouth. Washington, alarmed at the threat to his home state, sent a small force under Lafayette to Virginia

1. Washington wrote in his circular letter to the New England states on 5 January: "The aggravated calamities and distresses that have resulted, from the total want of pay for nearly twelve months, for want of clothing, at a severe season, and not infrequently the want of provisions, are beyond description. The circumstances will now point out what ought to be done...." J. C. Fitzpatrick, *The Writings of George Washington*, vol. 21, p. 62.

The Annual Register—1781

but the whole strategic situation could be improved only if control of the American coastline could be secured by French naval power.[2]

The French did manage to get a squadron out of Newport on 22 January, but with little effect. While Arbuthnot was repairing storm damage, however, the French fleet escaped southward on 8 March. But Arbuthnot's timely pursuit ended in an action on 16 March off the Chesapeake Capes which left the British ships damaged but still in support of Arnold in Chesapeake Bay. Superseded by General Philips on 26 March, Arnold was sent on a series of successfully destructive raids. Philips died of fever on 10 May, and ten days later Cornwallis arrived from Wilmington. He was reinforced by extra troops from Clinton, who was nonetheless furious at Cornwallis's move to Virginia.[3] On the same day Cornwallis joined Arnold, Washington sent Anthony Wayne to join Lafayette and reduce the British threat. Wayne arrived on 10 June and for nearly a month followed Lafayette's tactic of avoiding a major confrontation with the British army until finally he was convinced that Cornwallis should be pushed into a fight. Cornwallis obliged at Green Spring on 6 July but Wayne extricated himself from what proved to be a British trap. Cornwallis had beaten off Wayne but he had not destroyed the American combined force, and though he continued to drive raids led by Tarleton and Simcoe deep into the state, he now began to dig in on the Yorktown peninsula.

2. In his letter of 30 January to the younger John Laurens, Washington wrote: "How loud are our calls from every quarter for a decisive Naval superiority, and how might the enemy be crushed if we had it!" Ibid., p. 162.

3. Clinton later noted: "Wherefore, having by my written instructions to Lord Cornwallis *clearly and positively directed His Lordship to regard the security of Charleston as a primary object, and not to make any offensive move that should be likely to endanger it,* and it being an incontestable fact that his move into Virginia exposed that port to the most imminent danger,... His Lordship *disobeyed my orders and acted contrary to his duty in doing so."* The American Rebellion: Sir Henry Clinton's Narrative of the Campaigns, 1775–82, with an Appendix of Original Documents, ed. W. B. Willcox (New Haven, Conn., 1954), pp. 288–89. From late in 1780, Cornwallis was communicating directly with Germain and, encouraged by the latter, had begun to act as if he had an independent command. Clinton resigned himself to the move to Virginia: "But what is done cannot be altered. And as your Lordship has thought proper to make this decision, I shall most gladly avail myself of your very able assistance in carrying on such operations as you shall judge best in Virginia." Clinton to Cornwallis, 29 May 1781; The American Rebellion, p. 524.

His decision resulted from a series of conflicting orders from Clinton. Washington had held a conference with Rochambeau at Wethersfield, Connecticut, on 21–22 May. There he learned of the despatch of de Grasse's fleet and discussed the possibility of its cooperating in combined operations, possibly against New York, though Rochambeau preferred an attack against the British in Virginia. Clinton learned of these plans through letters captured in early June but was uncertain whether to believe them. He first instructed Cornwallis to find a good defensive position on the Virginia coast, continue raiding, and send three thousand men back to New York. Cornwallis reluctantly agreed to this reduction of his force after he defeated Wayne. On 8 and again on 11 June, Clinton, now convinced that Washington and Rochambeau were about to attack New York, ordered Cornwallis to send him directly as many men as he could spare. By 11 July, Clinton knew the Americans and French had abandoned the notion of attacking New York, so he ordered Cornwallis to retain his whole force and to occupy Yorktown as a base. Cornwallis moved to do so on 4 August.

On 13 August, Washington learned that de Grasse was prepared to head for the Chesapeake to cooperate with the land forces until the start of the hurricane season in October. Washington left 2,500 men to guard the Highlands and hopefully to immobilise Clinton, and he and Rochambeau marched south. De Grasse had left the West Indies on 5 August and arrived at Chesapeake Bay on 26 August. Hood chased after him five days later and arrived on the American coast on 28 August—but he went on to New York, where he joined the fleet commanded by Admiral Graves.[4] Neither Hood nor Graves realised what a devastating threat de Grasse posed, but on learning that the French squadron had left Newport, they sailed south to catch it, only to meet de Grasse's considerably superior fleet on 5 September.[5] After a brief engagement, Graves watched the French hold an advantageous position for a

4. Arbuthnot turned over his command to Graves when the latter's squadron arrived on 4 July, and returned at once to England. The Admiralty had already decided to send Digby to take over as Commander-in-Chief on the American station.
5. The combined fleet of Graves and Hood numbered nineteen ships of the line and one of fifty guns; de Grasse detached three ships of the line and one fifty-gun to cover the disembarkation of troops in Chesapeake Bay, while meeting Graves with twenty-four of the line.

week and then on 13 September left for New York; this left Cornwallis cut off by sea and land.

Cornwallis was besieged by a combined Franco-American force exceeding 18,000 men, but on 29 September he received a message from Clinton informing him that Admiral Digby's squadron had arrived from England and that the enlarged British fleet would mount a relief expedition. However, the enemy bombardment began on 9 October, two redoubts fell on the fourteenth, a sortie against the enemy artillery failed two days later, and a desperate attempt to evacuate troops across the York River was defeated by bad weather. With his ammunition exhausted and his defences breached at several points, Cornwallis decided to surrender on 17 October and terms were negotiated the next day; the British prisoners were escorted to camps in Virginia and Maryland. Clinton's relief force arrived eight days later, but the catastrophe was irredeemable.

When Parliament reconvened on 23 January 1781, the Opposition was resolved to concentrate on economical reform as the issue most likely to attract the forty or so independent votes necessary to ensure a defeat for the North government, although the Opposition planned to take every opportunity to embarrass the ministry. The relative quiet in Ireland and official optimism about the southern campaign in America suggested that these issues were poor targets and the vote which passed the army extraordinaries by 180 to 57 on 24 January was discouraging. The Government was then pressed to justify the war with the Netherlands (announced on 25 January), but it could scarcely reply to Burke's demands for proof that the war was necessary by giving the real reason, i.e., that it was to prevent the Dutch being aided by the League of Armed Neutrality. The address in reply to the speech from the throne was therefore passed with a smaller majority, 180 to 101.

On 15 February, Burke reintroduced his bill for reform of the Royal Household. North, anxious to avoid demonstrating a possible Government weakness, fought a delaying action until the twenty-fourth, when he felt he could risk a division. The bill was then defeated 233 to 190. The Opposition then broadened its attack: Fox tried to force an enquiry into the Government's financial competence on 8 March. But by the twenty-first, North's budget was accepted; the bills for the exclusion of contractors and the disenfranchisement of revenue officers were thrown out; an attempt to force an enquiry into the Admiralty was defeated on 22 March; and on the twenty-sixth the Government decisively won the motion at the end of the major debate on its financial conduct, 209 to 163. The Opposition now realised that economical reform had lost support both in Parliament and in the country at large. Savile's attempt to move for a committee to review a petition against the influence of the Crown lost on 8 May 212 to 135, and North promptly used the victory to move two bills to improve the Government's finances.

The Opposition was thus forced to use the American war again as the key issue. As early as 20 January, the ministry had received Rawdon's report of the previous October warning that Loyalist support in the south was minimal. The ministry ignored that report and the accumulating evidence of the worsening situation which continued to arrive until the end of April. Burke failed to get approval for a committee of enquiry into the seizure of Dutch property in St. Eustatius on 14 May and not surprisingly, Hartley's bill to give the Crown powers to end the American conflict lost on 30 May by 106 to 72. Then Fox, armed with the published details of the deteriorating British position in the south, competently attacked the Government on 12 June. His attack was poorly answered by Germain, yet his motion for a committee of the whole to consider the war still lost 172 to 99. The Opposition also fared badly when the serious problems of the East India Company were discussed on 23 and 24 June.

Through the summer recess, North planned to secure enough support for the ministry to coast through the short pre-Christmas session. At the same time, the Rockinghams were in despair, and Burke wrote: "I am sure if there be not a very signal Change in the National Temper this people cannot be saved."[6] The first news of the disaster at Yorktown arrived from France on 25 November. It stunned the Government—North is characteristically supposed to have said, "Oh God. It is all over." But the news also took the Opposition by surprise, for the Rockinghams and Shelburne's followers were wholly unreconciled on the issue of American independence and

6. Burke to the Duke of Portland, 12 November 1781. *The Correspondence of Edmund Burke*, ed. Thomas W. Copeland, 9 vols. (Cambridge and Chicago, 1961–70), vol. 4 (ed. John A. Woods), p. 382.

were not ready to exploit the situation in unity. When Parliament reconvened on 27 November, the Opposition lost the vote on the address by 218 to 129. After hurried attempts to rally the ranks on the twenty-seventh and twenty-eighth, the Opposition could only try to force the Government to admit that the address committed the nation to continuing the war in America. On 12 December, however, Sir James Lowther moved to end the war and lost 220 to 179; the vote indicated that the Government was losing some of its supporters. In his reply, North carefully avoided stating what the war's objectives were now supposed to be but he was already envisaging how to concede independence. North survived with a respectable majority in Parliament but his ministry was entering the last stages of disintegration. Government supporters who had shown signs of restiveness during the year were making it clear that they had no confidence in Germain and Sandwich, while within the Cabinet, a revolt was threatened if Germain was not dismissed. The coming year was to bring many changes.

The *Annual Register* for 1781 was published one year late, in May 1783, and the editor did not bother to trouble its readers with "... any detail of the unavoidable and unfortunate interruptions" which caused the delay. The preface regards the account of the year's military events as "... no very imperfect transcript of the art of modern war in all its forms," and indeed the historical section devotes 126 pages[7] out of 202 to them, while three chapters cover parliamentary affairs in faithful detail.

Chapter I briefly reviews European affairs in 1780 and comments on the activities of the navy in home waters in the summer of that year; the next three chapters cover military and naval events in America and the West Indies. Chapter II follows Clinton's return to New York, the raids into New Jersey, and the arrival of Ternay and Rochambeau; it goes on to trace the long and inconclusive duel between Rodney and Guichen in the Caribbean. The *Register* pays tribute to the new wave of patriotism aroused among Americans by the loss of Charleston, but its case is spoiled by the assertion that the congressional appeals to the states to fulfil their requisition quotas for

7. That is, Chapters II to VII inclusive and seven pages of Chapter I, though this includes forty-eight pages covering events of 1780 not recorded in the volume for that year.

the support of the Continental Army were a device ". . . to encourage and to profit of the rising spirit"—instead of a desperate attempt to overcome increasing apathy. Chapter III begins with a description of the effects of the hurricane which devastated the Lesser Antilles in the fall of 1780 and then provides a generally very accurate account of Arnold's defection and André's fate. Again, the *Register* cannot resist praising American patriotism. Actually, though Arnold's example was not widely emulated, the low but steady rate of Americans deserting to the British forces continued.

Cornwallis's campaign in the Carolinas from Kings Mountain to the march to Wilmington is covered in Chapter IV. The account in general is excellent; two exceptions are the serious underestimation of Tarleton's losses at Cowpens, and the mistaken attribution of the slaughter of Pyle's Loyalists to Tarleton and not to "Light Horse Harry" Lee. The chapter, however, is full of perceptive comment. The *Register* sardonically notes the tendency in Britain to regard any British victory as decisive. It points out the consistently unreliable intelligence received by Cornwallis, and stresses, with reference to Guilford Courthouse, that *no* British losses could be regarded as light, since none could be replaced. The account concludes that British successes in strategic terms had been valueless, since "Victory . . . was productive of all the consequences of defeat." Chapter V begins by noting the failure of the states to pay their quotas, the collapse of continental currency, and the resultant effects on the Continental Army. After dealing with the mutinies, the narrative follows Arnold's raids in Virginia and the manoeuvers of the fleets, and it describes at length Greene's campaign against Rawdon. The *Register* notes that the scattered British forces in the south were unable either to control the area or to destroy the enemy in the field but approves Cornwallis's decision to march to Virginia as the product of "an enterprising and determined mind." No reference is made to Clinton's disapproval. Chapter VI is entirely devoted to the war in the Caribbean, beginning with the loss of Pensacola and concluding with Rodney's return to England and de Grasse's departure for the Chesapeake pursued by Hood. The end of the ill-fated British campaign in the south is recounted in Chapter VII. The only major error in the *Register*'s analysis is the assumption that the letters captured from Washington's couriers in early June were deliberately intended to mislead Clinton. The conclusion assumes Yorktown will end the American war and portentiously speculates ". . . of the political state of the whole human race" that "Undoubtedly a new scene is opened."

The remaining three chapters deal with affairs in Parliament. Chapter VIII reviews the progress of domestic matters from the summer recess of 1780, the capture of Henry Laurens, and the breach with the Netherlands, then covers the pre-Christmas session of 1780. Chapter IX details the debates in January, from those on the Dutch war to those on the East India Company. The last chapter devotes sixty-five pages to the slow failure of economical reform, with appropriate references to the debates on the East India Company's problems and Fox's motion for a committee of the whole to consider the American war. Only that portion of Chapter VII that deals with American affairs is extracted here.

The *Appendix to the Chronicle* includes twenty-four items. Those concerning the American war include reports of two ship-to-ship actions; extracts of two letters referring to pacification measures in America which had been captured by the French and published in Holland; a letter suggesting how Benedict Arnold used the money he received as compensation for his defection; one of the letters captured from Washington's courier in June; and a particularly interesting letter by John Adams containing references to American secret agents in London and an italicised passage advocating harsh penalties for crypto-Loyalists in America. The official reports of the state of the British forces in America and the West Indies for 1779, details of losses from 1774 to 1780, embarkation returns of forces sent to America and the West Indies for 1778 to 1780, and totals of men raised in the British Army between 1774 and 1780 are also extracted here. The *State Papers* also contains twenty-four items, including speeches from the throne and parliamentary addresses in reply; the official announcement of war with the Netherlands and the protest of the peers dissenting against the address in reply, and documents indicating the reaction of the League of Armed Neutrality to the Anglo-Dutch war and a Russian offer of mediation. A November 1781 petition from the City of London against the continuance of the American war and a petition from Henry Laurens to the House of Commons praying for release from his imprisonment in the Tower are also extracted here.

T H E year of which we treat was fo abundant in military event, that if all other memorials of the fame nature were loft, it might afford no very imperfect tranfcript of the art of modern war in all its forms, whether by fea or by land. Though we are not aftonifhed by the appearance of fuch immenfe armies as have fo often defolated the old world, nor by thofe actions which have in a day decided the fate of nations and empires, we fee as vaft though lefs concentrated, operations of war, conducted upon its moft fcientific principles. When taken in a general view, the combination of its detached parts forms a great whole, whether confidered with refpect to action or confequence. We fee the war rage, nearly at the fame time, in the countries on both fides of the North River, on the Chefapeak, in South Carolina, the Floridas, North Carolina, Virginia, the Weft Indies, the American the Weft Indian feas. Through this arrangement, in part fortuitious and in part the effect of defign, we are prefented with a number of the beft conducted and fevereft actions recorded in hiftory. We behold, in an unhappy contention between Englifhmen, the greateft exertions of military fkill, a valour which can never be exceeded, and all the perfection of difcipline exhibited on the one fide, and oppofed on the other by an unconquerable refolution and perfeverance, infpired and fupported by the enthufiafm of liberty.

If the foldier finds abundant matter of entertainment and obfervation in the recital of thefe events, the ftatefman and philofopher will not find lefs room for ferious contemplation in the caufes and confequences of the contention. They have led to the eftablifhment of a new epocha in the hiftory of mankind; they have opened the way to new fyftems of policy; and to new arrangements of power and of commerce. To the whole Britifh nation, however difperfed in the old or in the new world, every part of the hiftory of this contention, in all its circumftances and confequences, muft at all times be in the higheft degree interefting.

It would be trefpaffing too far on the indulgence of the public, to trouble them with any detail of the unavoidable and unfortunate interruptions which have occafioned the delay of our prefent publication. We confole ourfelves in the hope, that thofe caufes will not appear in any degree to have operated with refpect to the attention which we have have paid to a faithful difcharge of our duty in the conduct of the Hiftory. The happy return of the public tranquility will, by leffening our labours, enable us to recover our former ftation in point of publication.

P.... .... view of affairs in America and the Weft Indies, in the year .... State of the hoftile armies on the fide of New York, previous to, ... at the arrival, of General Sir Henry Clinton from the reduction of Charles Town. Short campaign in the Jerfies. Connecticut farms. Springfield. Unexpected effect produced by the reduction of Charles Town, ... and exciting the fpirit of union and refiftance in America. Great .... founded on the expected co-operation of a French fleet and ar.... .... of New York, and the final expulfion of the Britifh forces from that continent. Marquis de la Fayette arrives from France. .... Terns, and the Count de Rochambeau, arrive with a French .... or a body of land forces, and are put into poffeffion of the for.... .... harbour of Rhode-Ifland. Admiral Arbuthnot blocks up .... Difpofitions made by Sir Henry Clinton for attack.... .... auxiliaries. Gen. Wafhington paffes the North River, ... attempting New York. Expedition to Rhode Ifland .... experienced by Don Bernard de Galvez, in his .... Befieges and takes the fort at Mobille. Great .... force fent out from Spain, in order to join M. de Guichen in the Weft Indies. Junction of the hoftile fleets, notwithftanding the efforts of Admiral Sir George Rodney, to intercept the Spanifh fquadron and convoy. Sicknefs and mortality in the Spanifh fleet and army, with fome other caufes, preferve the Britifh iflands from the imminent danger to which they were apparently expofed by the great fuperiority of the enemy. Thefe caufes operate ftill farther in their confequences; which affect the whole face and nature of the war in the new world, and entirely fruftrate the grand views formed by France and America, for the remainder of the campaign. Spanifh fleet and army proceed to the Havannah; and M. de Guichen returns from St. Domingo, with a convoy, to Europe. Great preparations made by the Americans for effectually co-operating with the French forces on the arrival of M. de Guichen. Wafhington's army increafed, for that purpofe, to 20,000 men. Invafion of Canada intended, and preparatory proclamations iffued by the Marquis de la Fayette. Caufes which prevented M. de Guichen from proceeding to North America. Sir George Rodney arrives, with a fquadron, at New York.

THE hoftile armies on the fide of New York were fo nearly poized, both with refpect to offenfive force and defenfive ftrength, that their mutual fituation, and comparative circumftances, afforded no great opportunity of exertion or enterprize to General Sir Henry Clinton, upon his return from the taking of Charles Town. The advantages however, derived from the poffeffion of the iflands, their vicinity to the continent, the quick and filent movements of a great number of frigates, and other fmaller armed veffels calculated for the purpofe, and mafter of all the channels and intercourfes, as well as of the adjoining fea, together with the unexampled length of ill connected posts which were to be guarded by the Americans, afforded, almost, continual opportunities, of hasty descent and successful surprize, by which much blood was spilt, and mischief done, without producing any effect, or at least any good one, with respect to the main objects, and great purposes of the war.

This kind of service, except where the object was more considerable than ordinary, was left entirely to the Refugees; who having arms in their hands, nothing else to do, little other provision, and being edged on by the most implacable animosity against their countrymen, eagerly embraced every adventure, which afforded any hope of profit, or what was perhaps still sweeter, of revenge. They were now grown so numerous, that they were strangely permitted to set up a sort of a distinct government in New York, under the conduct of a jurisdiction of their own creation, which they called the Honourable Board of Associated Loyalists. This Board, [1] it is said, was authorized from home; but this is hardly credible; and having a common stock, and their infant excursions at sea, having proved extremely successful, they became every day more numerous and powerful, and possessed something like a fleet, of small privateers and cruizers. Their enterprizes were bold, well conducted, and frequently successful; in which their intimate knowledge of the adjoining coasts, creeks, and villages, afforded them great advantages. But their want of any effectual discipline or government, along with their peculiar, and frequently, personal animosity, leading them to excesses; whilst the summary retribution on the other side, falling into the hands of those, who were either smarting under their own immediate losses, or acting under the impulse of grief and revenge, for the destruc-

tion or slaughter of their friends and relations, and who were likewise actuated by no less strong political prejudices, than their adversaries, the feelings of humanity were suspended, and mercy at an end on both sides. Thus the adjoining coasts of the continent, and particularly the maritime, and nearer part of the Jersies, became scenes of waste and havock; and this predatory war tended neither to subjugation or reconcilement.

A few days previous to the arrival of Sir Henry Clinton, the Generals Knyphausen, Robertson, and Tryon, with a view of attacking some of Washington's advanced posts, passed over by night, with five or six thousand men, from Staten Island, to Elizabeth Town in New Jersey.

June 6th. 1780.
On the following morning, they advanced a few miles to a settlement called the Connecticut Farms, from its having been planted and settled a few years ago, by some inhabitants of that Province. In their march, they were boldly and continually fired at, wherever the ground, or cover of any kind admitted of their approach, by scattering parties of the neighbouring militia. The burning of that new and thriving settlement, (although it did not contain many houses) and of the presbyterian church, together with the unfortunate death of the clergyman's wife, who sitting with [2] her children and family, was shot dead, through the window, in one of her own rooms, afforded new ground of clamour to the Americans, and served not a little, to increase that aversion to the British government and name, which had already taken too deep a root.

It was said on our side, and with superior probability, that this unfortunate lady was killed, without design, by a random shot; but the contrary was strongly urged by the Americans. Her husband's being particularly obnoxious at New York, from the active part

which he had taken, in the support of the American cause, was brought as a corroborating circumstance; and a piteous letter written by himself, and published, could leave no occasion for a farther testimony, with those who were but too much disposed to listen to evidence so correspondent to their own opinions. It is certain, that no degree of good government and discipline in armies, can prevent the nature of particular individuals, from breaking forth into acts of enormity, when those opportunities offer, in which their crimes may escape detection; especially under the ill habits acquired in the outrage and malice of a civil war.

From thence the army marched towards Springfield, being, as before, continually annoyed on their march by the militia; but now with greater effect, as they continually grew more numerous; they found the American General, Maxwell, at the head of the Jersey brigade, and reinforced by all the militia which in a few hours could be collected, well posted at that place. Whether it proceeded from Maxwell's good countenance and position, or from whatever other cause, so it was, that the army halted; and continued on the same ground until night, without advancing. The Americans, however, though inferior in strength, did not permit them by any means to hold their post in quiet; and a very considerable and continual firing, without coming at any time to close action, was kept up during the day. The report in the British line was, that they only waited for the coming up of the waggons and necessaries which were in the rear.

Whatever the cause was, the design of attacking Springfield was given up, and the army returned to Elizabeth Town in the night. They were pursued by the enemy, as soon as day rose, all the way to that place; and they were [3] now grown fo eager and confident, as boldly to attack the 22d regiment, which was pofted at fome fmall diftance in the front of the line. That regiment being ordered to fall back on their approach, was purfued with great rapidity by the enemy, who conconfidered it as the rear-guard of a retiring army, whofe van, they fuppofed, was then paffing over to Staten Ifland. The reception they met, and the appearances they difcovered, foon convinced them of their error, and they retired with precipitation.

It is not eafy to account, for the inaction in the firft inftance at Springfield, any more than for the fubfequent retreat. Undoubtedly, fo much refolution on the part of the Americans, was not expected ; and it appears from fubfequent circumftances, that although no direct attack had been made, the afternoon of that day was bufy and warm. It was faid, that intelligence had been received, of Wafhington's having detached a brigade from Morris-town for the fupport of Maxwell ; that the appearances at his head quarters indicated a determination of making that fupport effectual ; that Maxwell had already been reinforced by fome neighbouring regiments ; and that the country was every where in motion. The expedition itfelf had probably its origin from fome of thofe delufive reprefentations, which had fo often led to mifchievous or unreputable purfuits, concerning either the favourable difpofition of the country to the royal caufe, or the fuppofed weak and contemptible ftate of the American forces.

It was reported at New York, that the Heffian General Knyphaufen, was ftrongly of opinion, and eagerly difpofed, to attack the poft at Springfield ; but that he had been over-ruled by another commander ; and this report received fo much credit, that it was made the foundation of fome ill-

natured pafquinades upon the fubject. However thefe things might be, the Jerfey militia and brigade, with whatever other corps were concerned on the occafion, received public acknowledgments and high praife from Wafhington, for their behaviour in that day's fervice.

The arrival of Sir Henry Clin-[4] ton, which happened immediately after, made no change in the fituation of the royal forces, who ftill maintained their poft at Elizabeth Town. That commander, on the contrary, determined to improve on the original defign, and to afford them an opportunity of acting with effect. For this purpofe, troops were embarked at New York, and fuch movements took place among the fhipping, and fuch preparations were made, as indicated an immediate expedition up the North River. This produced the defired effect in alarming Wafhington ; who being exceedingly apprehenfive for the fafety of Weft Point, and other ftrong holds in the Highlands, immediately marched with the greater part of his army, to fecure thofe, to him, invaluable pofts.

June 23d. This point being gained, the forces at Elizabeth Town, again advanced on their former track towards Springfield. Whatever the original defign might have been, the general's views feemed now to have been extended, to the getting poffeffion, during the abfence of Wafhington with his main force, of the ftrong country of Moriffania, which had fo often afforded a fecure retreat, and an inexpugnable camp, to that commander. At any rate, if it was not found convenient to retain pofts at fuch a diftance, the deftruction of his ftores, magazines, and defences in the mountains, would have been no inconfiderable object.

On the part of the Americans, General Greene, with Stark's and

the Jerfey brigades, fupported by the neighbouring militia, were left to guard thofe difficult hills and defiles, which conftitute the ftrength of the country. Springfield lay at their feet ; and led directly to fome of the principal paffes. The royal troops advanced with rapidity to this place ; where they found the bridge, which led to the village, occupied by a fmall party of about 170 men, under the conduct of a Col. Angel. That officer, turn-[5] ing all the advantages afforded by his fituation (which were many) to the beft account, defended his poft with great gallantry. With that handful of men, he obftinately maintained the bridge, againft a prodigious fuperiority of force, and the moft fpirited attacks, for a quarter of an hour. Finding himfelf at length overpowered, and no relief appearing, he ftill found means to carry off the remainder of his detachment, and even to fave the wounded ; nearly one fourth of his whole number being by that time killed or difabled. The Britifh troops fuffered more in this trifling affair than could have been expected.

Greene lay, at that time, at Short Hills, about a mile above Springfield. But his troops were fo divided in guarding their refpective pofts, and the attack fo unexpected and fudden, that he could not make any detachment, in time, and fufficient for the fupport of Angel, without hazarding the fecurity of the much more important poft which he himfelf occupied. Whether it proceeded from indignation and refentment, at the refiftance and lofs which the troops unexpectedly met at the bridge, or from whatever other caufe it was, Springfield experienced the fame fate with the connecticut farms ; the whole village, excepting four houfes, were reduced to afhes.

This conflagration clofed the enterprize. The ftrength of

Greene's situation, the difficulties of the approach, an ignorance, probably of the state of his immediate force, (which, at that time, amounted only to about a thousand men) and perhaps, the bold defence made at the bridge, all concurred, in preventing the British officers from attempting the pass at Short Hills. It is likewise probable, that the day was considered as being too far advanced, to admit of their proving properly of any advantage which they might obtain; and that it was deemed too great a hazard, to involve the army during the night in the fastnesses of a dangerous country; and surrounded on every side by enemies, whose force, position, and distance, were all equally unknown. The troops were besides without cover or necessaries; and the keeping of a communication open with Elizabeth Town, might have been not less impracticable than dangerous.

Under some or all of these impressions, the royal army made a second retreat from Springfield, and returned on that evening to Elizabeth Town; they being pursued with great spirit, and redoubled animosity, by the country militia, who were highly enraged at the conflagration which they had just beheld; but a strong and well conducted rear-guard, rendered their efforts in a great measure ineffective. The royal forces passed over on the same night to Staten Island; while Washington continued to be amused for some days longer, with the appearances of an expedition up the North River, which probably had not been at all intended.

Thus ended the short campaign in the Jersies. These ineffective attempts, by a force which would once have been deemed capable of sweeping the whole continent before it, sufficiently manifested, that the practical habits of service and danger, without any thing near absolute perfection in discipline, will place all troops nearly upon an equality. It was now evident, that the British forces had an enemy, little less respectable in the field than themselves to encounter; and that any difference which yet remained in their favour would be daily lessened. In a word, it was now obvious, that all that superiority in arms, which produced such effects at the beginning of the contest, was, in a great measure, at an end; and that the events of the war must in the future depend upon fortune, and upon the abilities of the respective commanders.

Such were the unwelcome truths, which if not now first discovered, were at least now fully established. Washington shewed no small degree of exultation in his public orders, upon the great improvement in discipline of the troops and militia, with the happy effects which it hath produced, and the greater which he still hoped. But he did not augur greater benefits from the perfection or courage of the troops, than from that unequalled ardour, which, he said, at present animated all orders of the people.

The matter of fact was, that the loss of Charles Town produced a direct contrary effect to that which might have been naturally expected. For instead of depressing and sinking the minds of the people, to seek for security by any means, and to sue for peace upon any terms, the loss being now come home to every man's feelings, and the danger to his door, they were at once awakened to a vigour of exertion, scarcely to be expected in their circumstances; and which had hardly appeared in the same degree, since the first, or at most, the second year of the contest. For in the intermediate time, the first heat of passion being over, men who were not actively concerned, were fond of recurring to their wonted ease, and soon resumed their usual habits of life; and the din of war being faintly heard at a distance, they were contented to contribute to its support by opening their purses, without much tormenting their minds in the contemplation of an odious subject. And as the bitterness of contention was allayed, and the traces of past grievance or injury faded on the memory, so the spirit of enterprize had proportionally slackened; particularly in those colonies where it was not kept alive by immediate hostility.

Many concurring causes and circumstances served to increase and support that spirit which now appeared among the Americans. The very loss of Charles Town, became a ground of hope, and an incitement to vigour, from the wide separation which it had caused in the British forces, and the consequent incapacity of their divided armies to support each other. But the expectation of a strong naval and military force from France, by the aid of which, they hoped to retaliate on New York for the loss of Charles Town, and even to clear the continent entirely of the British forces, could not but have had a much greater effect.

In the mean time, their principal leaders, as well as the Congress, omitted no means to encourage and to profit of the rising spirit, and to cherish in the people the most sanguine hopes. Letters were written by the committee of that body, which were strengthened and enforced by those from the commander in chief, General Reed, and some other popular commanders, to the different executive governments, to the people at large, and to particular colonies, stimulating them by every motive to the speedy furnishing their respective quotas. The disgrace of appearing contemptible in the eyes of their great ally, and the mischief and ruin which must be the consequence, of their being incapable to benefit of his intentions in their favour, were strongly urged. And the people were passionately called upon, not to suffer the curse of another campaign to rest upon America! The eyes of all Europe were upon them; and their future independence, fortune, and happiness, as they said, depended upon their present exertion. [6]

These remonstrances produced a considerable effect upon the different governments, and seemed to operate no less upon individuals. Many arts were used to keep up the spirit. Large subscriptions were made by private persons for giving energy to the public service. The ladies in Philadelphia first set the example to their own sex, and were distinguished by the sums, which they gave themselves, and procured from their male acquaintance, to be applied as gratuities, in particular instances, and as a general augmentation to the pay of the private soldiers of the army. The example was soon followed, in their own, and in other provinces.

It could scarcely be expected, in the midst of all the confusion and danger, of an uncommonly destructive war, raging no less in the bowels, than in the extremities of a country, that arts, or learning, those happy concomitants of ease and security, should at all be thought of, or almost remembered. It is to the honour of the Americans, that it was under this pressure of circumstances, and amidst all the anxiety of the present season, that the council and assembly of Massachusetts Bay, sitting at Boston, in the beginning of the month of May, established, by a public law, a new and learned society, to be entitled, " The American Academy of Arts and " Sciences." The act, after enumerating several particular objects of their pursuits, adds, " and, in " fine, to cultivate every art and " science, which might tend to

" advance the interest, honour, " dignity, and happiness, of a " free, independent, and virtuous " people." In the same spirit at Philadelphia, after a pompous celebration of the anniversary of American independance, on the 4th of July, the Congress, accompanied by the French minister, with all the officers of the state, attended a commencement for the conferring of degrees in the university of that city. In the public charge delivered by the provost upon that occasion to the students, he gave the reins to a warm imagination, and wandered far in the paths of speculation; painting the rising glories of America in arts and letters, as well as in commerce and arms.

Notwithstanding the apparent penury and misfortune of the times, a bank was instituted, during the present summer, in Philadelphia; and the scheme was so well supported by the principal men of the province, that the allotted capital, of 300,000l Pensylvania currency, to be paid in hard money, was subscribed in a few days. The public service was, however, the principal, if not the only object of this bank. They were to receive the congress money, that is to say, the amount of the taxes, and the supplies remitted by the other colonies; and they were, on the other hand, to answer the public demands, and particularly to furnish the supplies for the army, in the most prompt and efficacious manner; and for the procuring of sufficient resources of cash, they were enabled to pass notes, and to borrow money at 6 per cent. interest. To turn, however, this bank to any considerable advantage, a much greater stability in government, and a much greater care in their finances, is undoubtedly necessary.

Previous to the arrival of the French succours, the Marquis de la Fayette, who had been so much distinguished by the early part

which he took in the American cause, long before his court had thrown by the mask, or even, perhaps, determined on the part which she has since taken, returned from France. His early engagement, and great zeal and activity in the American service, in which he held an high rank, caused him to be received with distinction by Washington, and on his going to Philadelphia, he conveyed a letter, full of the most flattering encomiums, from that commander to the Congress. The result was, a public complimentary resolution of welcome from that body, highly applauding his zeal, and no less acknowledging his eminent services. [7]

To the further encouragement of the Americans, M. de Ternay at length arrived at Rhode Island from France, with a squadron of seven sail of the line, five frigates, and two armed vessels. His own ship, Le Duc de Bourgogne, carried 84 guns, and 1200 men; two others were seventy-fours; and four, carried 64 guns each. He likewise convoyed a fleet of transports, with five old French regiments, and a battalion of artillery, amounting in the whole to about 6,000 men, under the conduct of lieutenant-general the Count de Rochambeau. [8]

July 11th.

The French auxiliaries were received by Major General Heath; who, for the security both of the troops and squadron, against any attempts from New York, put them in possession of the numerous forts and batteries of that island; which, with the diligence and industry peculiar to their country in that respect, they soon put in a high state of defence. In a few days after their arrival, they were attended by a committee, from the general assembly of that state, with an address of congratulation to the Count de Rochambeau, in which they expressed the most grateful sense of the generous and [9] magnanimous aid afforded to the United States, by their illustrious friend and ally, the French monarch; and said they looked forward, with warm hope and expectation, to the end of a campaign, which, through that aid, might prove the happy means of restoring the public tranquility. They concluded, with an assurance of every exertion in the power of the state, for the supply of the French forces with all manner of refreshments and necessaries, and for rendering the service, as happy and agreeable, as it was honourable, to all ranks of the army.

Rochambeau declared in his answer, that he only brought over the vanguard of a much greater force which was destined for their aid; and that he was ordered by the king, his master, to assure them, that his whole power should be exerted for their support. The French troops, he said, were under the strictest discipline; and, acting under the orders of General Washington, would live with the Americans as brethren. He returned their compliments by an assurance, that, as brethren, not only his own life, but the lives of all those under his command, were entirely devoted to their service.

In the mean time Washington, in order to cement the union between both nations, and to prevent those jealousies which were too much to be apprehended on both sides, issued a requisition, in public orders, to the American officers, soliciting, and strongly recommending to them, the wearing of black and white cockades, (the ground being of the first colour, and the relief of the other) as a compliment to, and a symbol of friendship and affection for their generous and magnanimous allies.

It was, indeed, highly grievous, not only to native Englishmen, but to those Americans, who, though equally determined upon liberty and independence with the most violent, yet still looked with-

fully forward, to the renewal of ancient amity, and friendly connections, though upon equal terms, with the mother country, to perceive, not only the influence which France was gaining in the counsels of America, but the progress likewise which she was continually making, in the opinion, and, it is to be feared, in the affections of the people.

Admiral Arbuthnot had only four sail of the line at New York: so that instead of being able to cope with the French squadron, he was under an expectation of being himself attacked in that harbour. This state of things, was, however, soon July 13. changed, by the arrival of Admiral Graves with six sail of the line, from England. The British commanders, having now a decided superiority of force, lost no time, after the newly arrived ships had repaired or supplied the consequences of the voyage, in proceeding to Rhode Island, intending, after taking a near view of the situation of the enemy, to act as circumstances might invite or admit, whether with respect to a direct attack, or to the government of their future operations.

They soon discovered, that the French were in such force, and had already put the fortifications in such condition, that an attack by sea was impracticable. In the mean time, Sir Henry Clinton meditated a joint attack by sea and land; a measure, which it would seem, that the admiral did not approve of; or at least, that he did not heartily concur in. After some delay, occasioned by his not being furnished in time with transports, the general, at length, embarked 6000 of his best troops, with which he proceeded as far as Huntington Bay in Long Island. Some unfortunate disagreement began at this time to appear, and continued long after to prevail, between the commanders in chief by sea and land. Their

dispatches teemed with ambiguity and jealousy, which became more glaring by time. Dislike, was rather more than hesitated; and blame, on one side at least, was more than once implied, if not directly laid. In fine, it soon became evident, that they were little disposed to mutual confidence or concert; and that the strained correspondence between them, was rather the irksome result of necessity, than the spontaneous effect of choice or inclination. Under these untoward circumstances, the troops were re-landed at White-Stone. [10]

In the mean time, Washington, who was strictly attentive to all that was passing, hoped to profit of Sir Henry Clinton's absence with so great a body of the troops, by some rapid motions, suddenly crossed the North River, at the head of 12,000 men, and marched directly towards King's Bridge, with an apparent intention of attacking New York. The failure of the expedition to Rhode Island, and consequent detention of the troops, necessarily frustrated his design.

It does not appear probable, in the present view of things, that the expedition to Rhode Island, even supposing the most chearful co-operation of the fleet and army, could have been attended with any success or benefit, sufficient to counterbalance the danger to which it was unquestionably liable. Besides the natural advantages of situation which that island possesses, and the strength of its forts and batteries, the New England provinces were in readiness to pour in their whole force to the support of the French. They were now impelled to action by other motives than those which usually operated; for they burned with eagerness to have so early, and, what they deemed, so happy an opportunity, of impressing their allies with a high sense of their power and valour. Accordingly, upon the firft bruit of the defign, above 10,000 of their militia and fix-months-men, were fuddenly in arms, and advanced towards Providence; and it is not to be doubted, but that number would have been far more confiderable, if it had been actually carried into execution. With thefe direct impediments in the way of the defign, it will not be fuppofed that New York, thus ftripped of its beft troops, and of the protection of the fleet, could have been exempt from danger, under the vigorous attack intended by Wafhington.

We have feen in our laft volume, the early fuccefs which had attended Don Bernard de Galvez, the Spanifh governor of Louifiana, in his unexpected expedition againft the Britifh fettlements and forces on the Miffifippi. The fuccefs of that enterprize, with a knowledge of the weaknefs which the number of prifoners he had taken, neceffarily induced in the defenfive force of the province, could not fail to extend his views farther; but ftill thinking himfelf too weak for the defigned purpofe, he concerted a plan of operation, with the governor of the Havanna, towards the latter end of the year 1779, in purfuance of which he was to be reinforced and fupported, by a confiderable embarkation from that place, early in the prefent year.

The appointed time being arrived, and De Galvez fuppofing that the expected force from the Havanna was of courfe on its way, and being himfelf impatient of delay, he embarked all the force he was able to raife in his government at New Orleans, and proceeded, under the convoy of fome fmall frigates and other armed veffels, on his expedition, expecting to be followed or met by the force from the Havanna. Jan. 14. 1780.

The delays, difficulties, and dangers, which they encountered on the paffage to Mobille, would appear almoft incredible to thofe who confidered only the diftance, without taking into the account, the ftormy difpofition of the climate at that feafon, the dangerous nature of that unhofpitable coaft, and the numberlefs fhoals which embarrafs, and nearly choke up the mouths of its vaft rivers. After a continued ftruggle with adverfe weather, and the various other impediments we have mentioned, for near a month, the better part of the fleet were driven a-fhore, and feveral of the veffels at length totally wrecked, in the bay of Mobille. By this misfortune, the commander had the mortification of feeing all reafonable hope of fuccefs apparently fruftrated; 800 of his men being caft away on a naked beach, with the lofs of the greater part of their cloaths, arms, and neceffaries of every fort.

The Spaniards bore their misfortunes with that patience, which has at all times been a characteriftic of their nation. Inftead of fhrinking under the difficulties and difcouragements they had experienced, they endeavoured, fo far as it could be done, to convert their lofs into a benefit; breaking up their wrecked veffels, and framing their timber and plank into ladders, and other machines, neceffary for an efcalade; as they had fuftained too great a lofs of artillery and other materials, to attempt a formal fiege. Thofe who had preferved their arms, were obliged to divide them, in fuch a manner as would render them moft ufeful, with thofe who had none; and thofe who ftill remained unarmed, undertook the laborious fervice of the army.

It happened very unfortunately on the fide of the Englifh, who were befides far from ftrong, that an account of the Spanifh fhipwreck was received at Penfacola, with the additional falfehoods, that 700 of their people had perifhed, and that the expedition was entirely laid afide.

The Spanifh commander had no reafon to repent his perfeverence. He was ftrengthened by the arrival of four armed veffels from the Havanna, with a part of the regiment of Navarre on board. Although thefe brought an account, that the principal embarkation was ftill retarded, yet the arrival of fo many fhips and frefh men, with the artillery, ftores, and various neceffaries which they were capable of fupplying, fuddenly caufed a new face of affairs, and afforded a renovation of vigour and life to every thing. The former troops were fpeedily re-embarked, and after a further encounter of other ftorms, difficulties, and dangers, the whole were landed within three leagues of Mobille. Feb. 25.

Mr. Durnford, a captain of engineers, and lieutenant-governor of Weft Florida, commanded the poor garrifon, which was to defend the fort, or caftle (as the Spaniards call it) of Mobille. This confifted of 97 regulars of the 60th regiment; of 16 loyal Marylanders, 3 artillery men, 60 feamen, 54 inhabitants, and 51 armed negroes, which, with two furgeons and a labourer, amounted to 284, of all forts. The enemy attacked the fort by fea and land; and began to open ground on the 9th of March.[11]

On the 12th of March the Spaniards opened their battery, confifting of eight 18, and one 24 pounder. Their fire feems to have had fome confiderable effect, on the embrafures and parapets of the two faces which they attacked; and two of the garrifon guns being difmounted, they at fun-fet hung out a white flag. The capitulation was not, however, figned, until the 14th in the morning, when the fort was given up, and the garrifon furrendered prifoners of war.

This furrender, which appeared

inevitable, was however attended with circumstances which rendered it exceedingly vexatious. For Major General Campbel had marched from Penfacola, with (as the Spaniards fay) 1100 regular forces, and fome artillery, for its relief; and was befides accompanied by fome Talapuche Indians; a people, who being exceffively ferocious and cruel, and the inveterate and mortal enemies of the Spaniards, are by them regarded with a very peculiar dread and horror. The van of Campbell's force was arrived within fight of the Spanifh camp, at the very inftant that the fort was furrendered: and they accordingly ufed the utmoft expedition in taking poffeffion of, and covering themfelves with the works, under the ftrong apprehenfion of an immediate attack. De Galvez boafted, that the Britifh forces in the field and garrifon were fuperior in numbers to his own; and did not fcruple openly to declare, that, with the fmalleft activity and vivacity in their works, the latter might have made good the defence, until the arrival of the fuccour.

It feems upon the whole face of the affair, as it appears at prefent, that the lieutenant-governor had not, from the beginning, the fmalleft idea of any attempt being made for the relief of the place; and that he accordingly, from the firft appearance of the enemy, confidered its lofs as a matter of courfe and inevitable neceffity. The regular force was certainly fuch, as to give little encouragement to a very vigorous defence. Thus the province of Weft Florida, with a weak and divided force, was reduced piecemeal, without its being able any where to make that effectual refiftance, which might have been expected, if it had been concentered in fome one good point of defence.

France had defigns for the earlier part of the campaign in the Weft Indies, in which the co-operation of Spain would be neceffary. She concerted another with the Americans, which was to take place, on their fide, in the latter; and both together went to the direct annihilation (and with a very fufficiently apparent force for the purpofe) of the Britifh power, in both parts of the New world. The fuccefs of the fcheme was founded upon many ftrong grounds of hope and expectation; but like all complex machines, it was liable to be diforderd in the whole, by the failure only of fome of its parts. It was expected, that the great fuperiority of the combined fleets would have enabled them, without much lofs or damage, entirely to crufh the Britifh naval force in the Weft Indies; that, with the great land force, which it was fuppofed would be in their hands, the reduction of Jamaica would not be an object of much difficulty or delay; that fome or all of the fmaller iflands would follow of courfe; but that, without fpending too much time upon leffer matters, M. de Guichen fhould proceed with his[12] whole force to the coafts of North America, where, being joined by Ternay's frefh fhips, and Rochambeau's frefh troops, they fhould, in concert with Wafhington, attack New York by fea and land. As the Americans would ftrain every nerve on the occafion, no doubt of fuccefs in that part of the defign could be entertained; and the reduction of Lord Cornwallis's forces, with the driving of the Britifh finally from the continent, were confidered only as matters of courfe.

It was undoubtedly in confequence, and for the rounding and completion of this fcheme, that preparations were made by the Americans for a winter expedition to Canada, the conduct of which was to be committed to the Marquis de la Fayette. That officer publifhed accordingly a prepara-tory memorial addreffed to the French Canadians, and calling upon them by all the antient ties of allegiance, blood, religion, and country, as well as by the natural and fervent defire of recovering their own freedom, to be in preparation to affift, join, and fupport him upon his arrival; but holding out all the feverities of war, and all the terrors of military execution, to thofe, if any fuch there could be, who blindly perverfe to their own interefts, and forgetful of all thofe ties and duties, fhould in any manner oppofe the arms, or impede the generous defigns of their deliverers. The failure, with refpect to the great objects of the defign, occafioned the laying by for the prefent of this detached part.

It is not to be wondered at, that the near contemplation of fuch vaft objects, and the flattering light in which they appeared, fhould wonderfully elevate the fpirits of the Americans, and greatly invigorate their meafures and counfels. Wafhington's army was accordingly recruited and filled up with fuch diligence, that it was faid to exceed 20,000 men; and the northern provinces were in readinefs to fend their militia, and every denomination of military, to take fhare, along with him and their French allies, in the final overthrow of New York. Nor was it even apprehended, that the failure of the preliminary parts of the plan in the Weft Indies, could at all have affected the main object with refpect to North America.

But it was impoffible that any judgment formed at a diftance, could interfere with M. de Guichen's knowledge of the ftate and condition of his own force. Befides the ficklinefs of his people, he was fenfible that his fhips had fuffered fo much by long fervice in the Weft Indies, as well as in the feveral engagements, that they were not by any means in a condition to encounter, either the roughnefs of the fervice or of the climate, which they muft neceffarily undergo in the North American campaign. This knowledge, and the determination founded upon it, were, however, ftrictly referved to himfelf, or to thofe in his immediate confidence. And when he took a great convoy from the French iflands under his protection, it was ftill thought or expected on all hands, that as foon as he had feen them fo far on their way as to be out of danger, he would then proceed to the coaft of America, for the accomplifhment of the projected enterprize. But that commander proceeded directly to Europe with his fleet and convoy; and the bad ftate of his fhips, when he arrived at Cadiz, fufficiently juftified his conduct.

Nothing was ever more galling to the Americans than this difappointment. It is even faid, that Wafhington himfelf, could not entirely preferve that command of countenance, and equanimity of temper, by both of which he is fo much diftinguifhed. All the views of France and America, with refpect to to the campaign, were now finally fhut up; and the force fent by the former to Rhode Ifland, with a view of general co-operation, was now reduced to act only upon the defenfive as a garrifon. Undoubtedly, Great Britain had a wonderful efcape from the dangers of the prefent campaign; and the ifland of Jamaica has experienced a fingular fortune in the various hair-breadth rifques, which fhe has encountered during the war. Through all this courfe of tranfaction, the Admirals Arbuthnot and Graves, kept the French fquadron as clofely blockaded at Rhode Ifland, as the advantage derived from the occafional fhelter of fome neighbouring iflands could afford, and the uncertainty of the winds and feas would admit.

In the mean time, Sir George Rodney being aware of the origi-[13]

nal defign againft New York; and apprehenfive that both the Britifh land and naval force would be entirely overwhelmed by the vaft fuperiority of the enemy, as foon as he had received certain intelligence of the departure of M. de Guichen from Cape Francois, immediately failed himfelf, with eleven capital fhips, and four frigates, to their fuppofed affiftance and relief. Although he found, foon after his arrival at New York, that this effort of zeal for the public fervice, which had arifen from the fpur of the occafion, might have been difpenfed with; yet he difcovered in the end, that he had no caufe to regret the trouble which he had taken; as it proved the fortunate means of faving the fquadron under his immediate command, from the unknown but dreadful calamity, which was to take place in the Weft Indies. Sept. 14.

* * *

Whilft the Weft India iflands[14] were doubly fuffering, under all the evils of war, and under fome of the greateft calamities of nature, the continent of North America enjoyed fome tolerable refpite from the one, and had pretty well efcaped the other. Admiral Arbuthnot ftill continued his ftation about Gardner's Bay and Block ifland, to watch the motions of M. de Ternay; whilft the induftry of the French was quickened, in completing the fortifications, and increafing the defences of the harbour, at Rhode Ifland, from an apprehenfion of the great fuperiority of naval force, which the arrival of Sir George Rodney had thrown into the fcale on the Britifh fide.

Whether it proceeded from a knowledge that the fortifications at Rhode Ifland were now in fuch ftrength on the land fide, as to bid defiance to any force which Sir Henry Clinton could with fafety draw from New York, whether the harbour was fo well fortified as not to admit the approach of the

fleet, or whether the feafon was fo far advanced, that it would not be prudent to expofe the fhips to the dangerous uncertainty of the weather, we do not know; but however it was, no attempt was made to derive any advantage from the prefent naval fuperiority. The critics upon military affairs, with whom New York, nearly from its firft coming into our hands, peculiarly abounded, were as bitter in their cenfures, and reviled the commanders with as little mercy and decency upon this occafion, as they had both themfelves and their predeceffors upon many others.

During this apparent calm, and a fort of tacit ceffation of hoftility, produced only by the peculiar fituation and circumftances of the parties on both fides, a fcheme of the utmoft importance was in agitation, calculated, if it could have taken effect in its full extent, totally to change the face of affairs in America, and to bring the war to a fpeedy, if not immediate conclufion.

Every reader is fufficiently acquainted with the figure which the American General, Arnold, made, during the whole courfe of the war. In peaceful occupations he was not fo happy. Retired from the army, on account of the wound he received in the caufe of America, and which endeared him to that whole continent, he foon loft the affections of his countrymen, which he had purchafed at fo dear a rate. His conduct in the government of Philadelphia, to which he had been appointed upon the retreat of the Britifh army, was of fuch a nature, or fo reprefented by his enemies, as drew upon him, not only the odium of the inhabitants of that city, but of the province in general. He was charged with oppreffion, extortion, with exorbitant and enormous charges upon the public in his accounts, and with applying the public money and property to his own private ufe. Many of the particulars appear in the publications of the time.

He appealed from the judgment of the commiffioners who had been appointed to infpect his accounts (and who had rejected above half the amount of his demands) to the Congrefs; and they appointed a committee, of their own body, to examine and fettle the bufinefs. The committee not only confirmed the report of the commiffioners, but were of opinion, that they had allowed him more than he had any right to expect or demand. Mr. Arnold fhewed himfelf highly irritated by this determination; and uttered invectives againft the Congrefs, not lefs violent than thofe that he had before thrown out againft the commiffioners.

He was, however, foon obliged to abide the judgment of a court-martial, upon the various charges of malverfation in office, exhibited againft him by the executive government of Philadelphia, as well on the grounds we have mentioned, as on fome others. This court found his conduct (in general terms) highly reprehenfible, and ordered that he fhould be reprimanded by General Wafhington. This fentence gave no fatisfaction to the accufers. They faid, that the confideration of General Arnold's former fervices had rendered his judges too favourable. On the other fide, the party accufed attacked them as giving a general cenfure, becaufe they were refolved to find him guilty, and yet could fix on nothing fpecific.

He who had held fo large a fhare of popularity, could not but feverely feel, that lofs of public opinion and private efteem which he now experienced. He was not of a difpofition to be filent in fuch circumftances. He complained loudly; and made as little fcruple of charging his countrymen in general with ingratitude, as their governors of injuftice.

A calm, however, on all fides, feemed to have fucceeded to thefe violent ftorms. His favour with Gen. Wafhington feems to have continued; and he was foon after his reprimand taken again into actual fervice in the principal army, in a fituation of confiderable [15] rank and truft. In the temper of mind defcribed, and in that fituation, he carried on a negociation with Sir Henry Clinton for the purpofe of returning to his allegiance, and of delivering up the poft and part of the army which he commanded to that General. How the ice was firft broken, the negociation conducted, or how long it had been in agitation, are matters which do not appear, and are of little confequence. Its failure was marked by the unhappy fate of Major André, adjutant-general of the Britifh army; a rifing young officer of great hope, and of no common merit.

This was the gentleman employed, at leaft, in the completion of the meafures taken in concert with Gen. Arnold. Objects of vaft importance, will neceffarily occafion a deviation from all general rules, if not from the principles of action. That now in view, was the moft momentous that could well be offered. It held out, along with the conclufion of a doubtful and dangerous war, no lefs than the final fubjugation, without condition or treaty, of the revolted American Colonies. It is not then to be wondered at, that the near apparent grafp of fo great a prize, fhould banifh all leffer confiderations; and prove fuch a fpur to enterprize, as no rifque, danger, or poffible confequences, could be capable of counteracting. André, who by his open bravery, high ideas of candour, and difdain of duplicity, was not fo fit for an employment, which along with great mechanical boldnefs, required a proportionable degree of diffimulation and circumfpection, yet poffeffed other qualities, which

feemed fully to counterbalance that deficiency. His fidelity and honour were fixed and unalterable; and thefe were qualities not much to be expected in thofe, who in other refpects might feem much fitter for the purpofe. Befides, his place, character, and the confidence of the commander in chief, which he was known fully to poffefs, afforded a weight to his negociation, the want of which in meaner agents would have been attended with many difficulties.

The failure of the French fleet with refpect to the attack on New York, having overthrown all the fchemes of active operation on the fide of the Americans for the prefent feafon, Wafhington ftationed his army (which was now confiderably reduced in number and ftrength) in the ftrong holds of the Highlands, on both fides of the North River, for the winter; where its fituation, befides fecurity, afforded an opportunity of watching the motions of the Britifh forces, and of repreffing the incurfions from New York. In this arrangement of the American forces, the ftrong and very important poft of Weft Point, with its neighbouring dependencies, and a wing, or very confiderable divifion of the army, were entrufted to the cuftody and conduct of Major-General Arnold.

Wafhington's abfence in Connecticut, was probably deemed a favourable opportunity for the final completion of a negociation, which it is evident had for fome time been in hand. The Vulture floop of war had been previoufly ftationed in the North River, at fuch a diftance from Arnold's pofts, as, without exciting fufpicion, would, however, ferve for carrying on the neceffary communication. It appears likewife that a written correfpondence, by other means, and through other channels, had been carried on, between Arnold and Major André, at New York, under the borrowed names of Guftavus and Anderfon.

The outlines of the project were, that Arnold should make such a disposition of the wing of the army under his command, as would enable Sir Henry Clinton completely to surprize their strong posts and batteries, and throw the troops so entirely into his hands, that they must inevitably either lay down their arms, or be cut to pieces on the spot. Besides the immediate possession of those strong holds, thus cheaply obtained, and the cutting off so great a part of the enemy's best force, without loss or difficulty, the consequences would have reached much farther; for the remainder of Washington's army, would then have been laid open in such a manner, to the joint exertion of the British forces by land and water, that nothing less than slaughter, rout, dispersion, and final ruin, could have been the result with respect to the Americans. Such a stroke could not have been recovered. Independent of the loss of the artillery, magazines, and stores, such a destruction of their whole disciplined force, and of most, if not all of their best officers, must have been immediately fatal.

The necessary arrangements being made, Major André was landed at night from the sloop of war, without the American posts, where he found Arnold waiting for him [16] on the shore. The latter conveyed him into camp; where he continued with him, during that night and the following day. In that time it was very unfortunately found necessary to change the British uniform of his regiment, which he had hitherto worn under a surtout coat, for some common dress. From some alarm, apprehensions, or causes, which do not appear, Arnold could not fulfil his promise to Andre, of sending him back, by the same way that he came, in order to get on board the Vulture. On the contrary,[17] he was conveyed the second night,

Sept. 21.

through a remote part of the camp, and then left to pursue a journey of some length, and alone, to New York. He was, however, furnished with a horse, and with passports from Arnold; and being now quite clear of the different guards and posts of the camp, all of which he had passed under the name of Anderson, he could not but think himself in tolerable safety.

But fortune was not in so favourable a mood. In passing through a place called Tarry Town, on the following day, he was stopt by three young volunteers or militia men, who do not seem to have been upon any particular service or duty. His passport seemed at first to produce its intended effect; and after a perusal, they suffered him to proceed without farther trouble. But he had not passed many yards, when one of them, upon a little recollection, was so forcibly struck, by the impression of some particularity, which he conceived he had perceived in the stranger's manner or countenance, that he peremptorily insisted with his companions, upon their examining him more strictly. This recollection was decisive and fatal. Andre was not used to, nor prepared for such encounters. Or, as he said himself in his letter to Washington, " I was too little versed in de- " ception, to practise it with any " degree or hope of success." He offered the captors a considerable purse of gold, and a very valuable watch, for letting him pass; and it would appear from the American accounts, and indeed seems confirmed by the very high praises which they bestowed, upon the virtue and patriotism, as they called it, of three simple young men, in the humblest walks of life, who nobly disdained, besides the immediate temptation, the very fascinating offers of permanent provision, and even of future promotion, which were

made them, on condition of their conveying and accompanying the major to New York.

Upon André's first examination, he still supported the name and supposed character of Anderson, a real or imaginary inhabitant of New York; and though the papers that were found in his boot, subjected him to instant execution, in the usual summary way practised with spies, yet he nobly chose to encounter that immediate danger, and ignominious fate, rather than let any thing come out which could involve Arnold, until he had time to provide tor his safety. The papers were all in Arnold's hand-writing, and contained exact returns, of the state of the forces, ordnance, and defences, at West Point, and its dependencies, with the artillery orders, critical remarks on the works, an estimate of the number of men that were ordinarily on duty to man them, and a copy of some very interesting matters, which had been lately laid before a council of war by the commander in chief.

Several circumstances attending this transaction were highly fortunate to Arnold. Particularly the delay occasioned by its happening at a distance from the camp; as well as through the indecision, which so new and extraordinary a case, that seemed beyond their reach and authority, necessarily produced in those inferior officers or country magistrates, by whom André was first examined.

General Washington returned from Connecticut, about noon on the 25th; André having been then full 48 hours in custody, without any knowledge of the transaction having yet reached the camp. At Arnold's quarters, the general was informed that he had been out for some hours, and was supposed to be gone to West Point, whither he accordingly went, and discovered to his surprize that he had not been there that day; this was, however, increased upon his return, when he found that he was still absent from quarters. But every thing now was upon the point of being cleared up. A packet arrived, with an account of the capture of John Anderson, and enclosing the papers which were found upon him; accompanied likewise, with a letter from the prisoner himself to the general. He was now also informed, that Arnold had received a letter, which threw him into some visible degree of agitation, just before his departure from quarters in the morning. Washington immediately issued orders, to prevent, if possible, his escape; but it was then too late; for Arnold, upon the discovery of his danger, without even waiting to secure or destroy his papers, had abandoned every thing; and proceeding down the river, under the cover of a flag, was then safe on board the Vulture ship of war.

The vindication of his honour, and not the preservation of his life, was the great object with André, in his letter to Washington; in which he avowed his name and character. The imputation of treachery, and the dread of being considered in the base condition of a spy, were worse to him than death. He accordingly laboured to shew, that he did not properly come within that description; that he had held a correspondence with a person under the orders of his general; that his intentions went no farther, than the meeting of that person on neutral ground, for the purpose of intelligence; but that he was circumvented or betrayed, within the American posts; and that being then in fact a prisoner, he was obliged to submit to such measures as were concerted for his escape, by quitting his uniform; and thus was forced into the condition of an enemy in disguise. His only solicitation was, that to whatever

rigour policy might devote him, a decency of treatment might be observed, which would mark, that though unfortunate, he was branded with nothing dishonourable, and that he was involuntarily an impostor.—In a word, his enemies acknowledged, that the letter was conceived, in terms of dignity without insolence, and of apology without meanness.

Washington had immediate measures to take, in order to protect his camp and works from the unknown, but possible consequences of General Arnold's desertion; nor could he be entirely free from apprehension, that the treachery had spread farther than he was yet aware of. It soon appeared, however, that he had no party in the army to support his design; and that if he had any confidents or associates, they were few in number, and men of no great consequence. But though the design was defeated, the idea was alarming in point of precedent; and the contagion of example was still to be dreaded.

Arnold wrote a letter to Washington, from on board the Vulture, on the very day of his escape. In this, he does not enter much into any defence or explanation of his conduct, but seems to rest satisfied in an internal consciousness of rectitude. He declares, that the love of his country, which had been the ruling principle with him through the whole contest, had operated equally upon him in his present conduct, however inconsistent it might appear to the world, who, (he observes) very seldom judge right of any man's actions.—But the great object and design of his letter, was to interest Washington's humanity in the protection of Mrs. Arnold, from the mistaken vengeance of his country; that, he said, ought to fall only upon himself; for she (he exclaimed in the language of passion) " is as

good and as innocent as an angel, and is incapable of doing wrong."

On the same day, Col. Robinson, who was likewise on board [18] the Vulture, and seems so far to have accompanied André on this enterprize, sent a letter to Washington, reclaiming him on the following grounds, viz. That he had gone under the protection of a flag, upon public business with Gen. Arnold, and at his particular request; that he likewise had his licence and passports for returning to New York; that every step he had taken, and even that of assuming a feigned name, had been under the direction of Arnold, which of course freed him from any censure in the transaction; and that, under these circumstances, his farther detention, would be a gross violation of the sanction due to flags, and contrary to the established military customs and usages of all nations.

The following day brought a letter from Sir Henry Clinton, reclaiming André upon the same grounds, of a flag, passports, his own permission, and Arnold's request. It likewise contained an inclosure from Arnold to Sir Henry, stating the circumstances, as he wished them to be understood; assuming to himself the whole guidance and direction of André's conduct, and consequently, as being only responsible for those parts of it that appeared most unfavourable in his present situation; and strongly asserting his own right at that time, as acting in the American service, and being commanding general of West Point and its dependencies, to send his flag of truce for André, to afford him protection by his passports and otherwise, and to return him, by such way, and in such manner, as should, to himself, appear most convenient or proper.

In the mean time, Washington had appointed a board of fourteen general officers, of whom were the two foreign majors general, the Marquis de la Fayette, and the Baron de Steuben, with the assistance of Laurence, the judge advocate general, to examine into, and to report, a precise state of André's case; to determine what light he was to be considered in, and to what punishment he was liable.

This excellent young man, disdaining all subterfuge and evasion, and only studying, by the magnanimity which he should now display, and the intrepidity with which he would encounter the expected sentence, to throw such a lustre over his character, as might prevent the smallest shade of that imputation which he so much dreaded, voluntarily confessed more than he was asked; and sought not to palliate any thing that related to himself, whilst he concealed with the most guarded and scrupulous nicety, whatever might involve others. He acknowledged—that the boat in which he came on shore carried no flag;—that he wore a surtout coat ver his regimentals;—that although it was understood when he left the Vulture, that he should return that night, it was afterwards doubted; but that he was promised to be concealed on shore, in a place of safety, until the following night, when he was to return by the same way that he came. He likewise acknowledged his change of dress in the camp; with all or most of the other circumstances which we have aleady stated; as well, as that Arnold's papers were found concealed in his boot; and that a letter from New York, signed John Anderson, was his own hand writing. Being interrogated by the board with respect to his conception of coming on shore under the sanction of a flag, he with a noble frankness said, that it was impossible for him to suppose he had come on shore under that sanction; adding,

that if he had, he certainly might have returned under it.

The board were exceedingly struck with his candour and magnanimity; and sufficiently shewed how much they felt for his situation. Besides every possible mark of indulgence, and the utmost attention and politeness, they treated him with so scrupulous a delicacy, as to desire at the opening of the examination, that he would not answer any interrogatory whatever, which could at all embarrass his own feelings. André, was himself, deeply sensible of the liberality of their behaviour, particularly in this last instance; and declared to a gentleman, (who we'll suppose to be an American officer) that he flattered himself he had never been illiberal; but that if there were any remains of prejudice in his mind, his present experience must obliterate them.

The board did not examine a single witness; but founded their report merely upon his own confession. In that, after a recital of a few of the principal facts, particularly his passing, under a feigned name, and in a disguised habit, their works at Stoney, and Verplanks Points, on the evening of the 22d, they then declare, that Major André, adjutant general to the British army, ought to be considered as a spy from the enemy; and, that agreeable to the law and usage of nations, it is their opinion, he ought to suffer death.

Washington wrote a short answer to Sir Henry Clinton, on the day after the sentence, in which he stated, that although Major André had been taken under such circumstances, as would have justified the most summary proceedings against him, he had, however, determined to refer his case to the examination and decision of a board of general officers, whose report, founded on his free and voluntary confession and letters, was enclosed. That

from these proceedings it was evident, that Major André was employed in the execution of measures very foreign to the objects of flags of truce, and such as they were never meant, in the most distant degree, to authorize or countenance; and that gentleman himself, had with the greatest candour confessed, it was impossible for him to suppose, that he came on shore under the sanction of a flag.

This drew another letter from Sir Henry Clinton; who, under a presumption, that the board of general officers could not have been rightly informed of all the circumstances on which their judgment ought to be founded, proposed to send Lieut. Gen. Robertson, the governor, of New York, and two other gentlemen, as well to give his excellency a true state of facts, as to explain and declare to him his own sentiments and resolutions upon the subject. The gentlemen were to be at Dobb's Ferry on the following morning, to wait for Gen. Washington's permission and safe conduct, and to meet himself, or whoever else he should appoint, in order to converse upon the subject. He particularly urged it, as a matter of the highest moment to humanity, that the general should fully understand the whole state of the business, before he proceeded to carry the judgment of the board into execution.

Gen. Greene, the president of the late board, was appointed to meet Robertson; but his companions, Mr. Elliot, the lieutenant governor, and Mr. Smith, the chief justice of the province, were not permitted to come on shore. Gen. Robertson used his utmost ingenuity in this conference, upon the grounds which we have already seen, to shew, that André did not come within the character and description of a spy; dwelling particularly on his going ashore under the sanction of a

Sept. 29.

[19]

flag ; and that being then in Arnold's power, and in effect a prisoner, he was not accountable for his subsequent actions, which were all compulsory

As Greene was far from admitting either his facts or conclusions, Mr. Robertson wished, that in an affair so interesting to humanity, and of so much consequence to both armies, as well as to his friend, who was so immediately concerned, the opinions of disinterested gentlemen, who were versed in the laws of war and nations, might be taken on the subject ; and he proposed Gen Knyphausen, and the French General Rochambeau, as proper persons to whom the business might be referred.

Humanity was the last string touched ; but on which more hope seemed to be rested than any other. He said, he wished an intercourse of such civilities between the contending parties, as might lessen the horrors of war ; quoted instances of Sir Henry Clinton's merciful disposition, and said that he had never put any person to death for a breach of the laws of war, although he now had, as well as at former times many labouring under that predicament in his power. He held out, that Major André possessed a great share of the general's esteem ; and that he would be infinitely obliged for his liberation ; and he offered, if the former was admitted to return with him to New York, to engage, that any person whatever who was named, should be set at liberty in return. He observed, that under the present circumstances, much good might arise from humanity, and much evil from the want of it.

Previous to this meeting, Arnold had written a second letter to Gen. Washington : which contained a declaration, that he considered himself no longer as acting under the Congress ; and that

his commission, which lay among his papers at West Point, might be disposed of as he thought proper. In this, as in the former, he took no small pains to convince that commander, of the sincerity, as well as of the invariable nature, of his attachment to to the true interests of his country.

Gen. Robertson presented now also, a long letter from him, tending to the exculpation of Major André, by rendering himself the author of every part of his conduct ; and particularly insisting, on his coming from the Vulture, under a flag which he had sent for the purpose. After a long statement and representation of circumstances, he declared, that if the board of generals, should notwithstanding adhere to their former opinion, he should suppose it dictated by passion and resentment ; and if that gentleman should suffer the severity of their sentence, he should think himself bound by every tie of duty and honour, to retaliate on such unhappy persons of their army as might fall within his power, so that the respect due to flags, and to the law of nations, might be better understood and observed.—He also observed, that forty of the principal inhabitants of South Carolina had justly forfeited their lives, which had hitherto been only spared through the clemency of Sir Henry Clinton ; but who could no longer, in justice, extend his mercy to them, if Major André suffered ; an event, which would probably open a scene of bloodshed, at which humanity must revolt.— He abjured Washington, by his own honour, and for that of humanity, as well as from his love of justice, not to suffer an unjust sentence to touch the life of André. But if that warning should be disregarded, and André notwithstanding suffer, he called heaven and earth to witness, that he alone would be justly answerable

for the torrents of blood that might be spilt in consequence.

It may well be doubted, whether any thing at that time could have encreased the danger of the unhappy predicament in which André already stood ; and Gen. Arnold's interposition must have been well intended ; but letters from him, in the then state of things, it was evident could be of little service.

The succeeding day Oct. 2d. was to close the tragedy. André was superior to the terrors of death ; but that disgraceful mode of dying, which the usage of war had annexed to his unhappy situation, was, to him, infinitely dreadful. He equally wished to die like a soldier, and that, so far as it was possible, every trace and memorial of the cause which led to his fall might be erased. He had accordingly written a pathetic letter, fraught with all the feelings of a man of sentiment and honour, to Washington, imploring a mitigation in that respect. How far a relaxation of the rigid maxims and usages of war might upon this occasion with propriety have been indulged, is a question that involves too many considerations, for us to enter into. But as it was not deemed fitting to grant the request, it was thought humane to evade giving a direct answer. He encountered his fate with a composure, dignity and fortitude, which equally excited the admiration, and melted the hearts of all the spectators.

The sympathy which André excited in the American army, is perhaps unexampled, under any similar circumstances. It was said, that the whole board of general officers shed tears, at the time of drawing up and signing the report ; and that even Washington's eyes were not dry, upon hearing the circumstances of his death. His first request to that commander, of being treated with the distinction due to his rank and character, without regard to his then apparent condition, was, in every instance, excepting only what related to the mere manner of dying, most fully complied with. All those about him, or that he ever saw, treated him with the most marked attention, with the greatest tenderness, and the most scrupulous delicacy. The account of him given by Col. Hamilton aid de camp to Washington,[20] seems rather the elegant eulogium of a warm friend, than the narrative of an enemy, describing the consequences of an attempt which he could not but abhor, and which in its success, would have gone to the destruction of himself, his party, and friends.

This sacrifice, which, in their situation, it is probable the Americans thought absolutely necessary, concluded this unfortunate transaction. Washington transmitted Mrs. Arnold to her husband at New York; who found himself obliged to acknowledge in one of his letters, the protection and kindness which she had received from that commander, as well as the obligations she was under to the gentlemen of his family. He likewise sent him his cloaths and baggage, which Arnold had written for. But with respect to all other matters, his letters were passed over without the smallest notice.

The failure of Arnold's grand project, the unhappy event of which it was productive, (and which deeply affected the whole British army) with the other peculiar circumstances in which he was involved, seemed to render it indispensably necessary, that he should either perform such signal service, as would serve to spread a lustre upon his present situation, or at least take such irreconcileable measures with respect to his old friends, as should convince his new, that he left no room

open for a future retreat. He was made a brigadier general in the British army in America; and it was hoped, that with the aid of the Loyalists, and the discontented of all sorts, under the allurements of British pay and promotion, he could raise a considerable body of forces, to act under his own separate command. If this could be compassed, he might again appear with eclat in the field, justify his defection by success, and by splendid action, dispel the clouds which hung upon his character.

His first public measure, was the issuing an address directed to the inhabitants of America.—In[21] this piece, he takes a review of his own former conduct, assigns the motives on which it was founded, and then justifies his present, by declaring those which had induced him to join the king's arms. He had first encountered the dangers of the field, upon a conception, that the rights of his country were in danger, and that duty and honour called him to her defence. A redress of grievances, was his only object. He however acquiesced in the declaration of independence, although he thought it precipitate. But the many plausible reasons which were urged to justify that measure could no longer exist, when Great Britain, with the open arms of a parent, offered to embrace them as children, and to grant the wished for redress. From the refusal of those proposals, and the pretended French alliance, which was made the ground of that refusal, all his ideas and opinions, with respect to the justice and policy of the war, were totally changed; and he from thence became a confirmed loyalist.

He throws a vast weight of censure upon the Congress, their leaders at large, and that class of undefined men, who are said to be criminally protracting the war,

from sinister views, at the expence of the public interest. He talks of the thousands, who are suffering under the tyranny of the usurpers in the revolted provinces. He repeats many of the arguments which had been used by the late commissioners in America, and by the writers at that time on the British side, to shew the impolicy, tyranny, and injustice, which, along with a sovereign contempt of the people, had operated on the ruling powers, in studiously neglecting to take their collective sentiments on the British proposals of peace; and likewise to shew, that the treaty with France was not then by any means binding. He equally attacks France, and condemns the alliance; laments that the great interests of that country were dangerously sacrificed, to the partial views of a proud, antient, and crafty foe; calls her offer insidious; regards her as too feeble to establish their independency; charges her with being the enemy of the protestant faith; and with fraudulently avowing an affection for the liberties of mankind, while she holds her native sons in vassalage and slavery.

He seems to think that a great multitude, if not the body of the people, hold the same sentiments with respect to public affairs, which he had himself now avowed; and to account for his having so long acted directly contrary to this avowal, he openly acknowledges, that in those principles, he had only retained his arms and command for such an opportunity as he thought fitting for surrendering them to Great Britain; and that, (according to his own explanation) " in concerting the measures for " a purpose, in his opinion, as " grateful as it would have been " beneficial for his country, he " was only solicitous to accom- " plish an event of decisive im- " portance, and to prevent, as " much as possible, in the exe-

" cution of it, the effusion of " blood."

This was followed in about a fortnight, by a proclamation, inscribed *to the officers and soldiers of the continental army, who have the real interests of their country at heart, and who are determined to be no longer the tools and dupes of Congress, or of France.*

Under a persuasion, that the principles he had so lately avowed, animated the greatest part of the continent, he rejoiced in the opportunity he now had, of inviting those whom he addressed, to join his majesty's arms. He was authorized to raise a corps of cavalry and infantry, who with respect to pay, cloathing, and subsistance, were to be upon the same footing, with the other troops in the British service. As an allurement to the private men, they were to receive a bounty of three guineas each, besides payment, at the full value, for horses, arms, and accoutrements; and as he had the appointment of the officers, he should with infinite satisfaction embrace the opportunity of advancing men whose valour he had witnessed. It was, however, expected, that they should either bring in or recruit in a reasonable time, a certain number of men in proportion to their rank.

Great as these encouragements, he said, must appear, to those who had suffered every distress, of want of pay, hunger, and nakedness, from the neglect, contempt, and corruption of Congress, they were nothing to the motives which, he expected, would influence their brave and generous minds. He wished to lead a chosen band of Americans, to the attainment of peace, liberty and safety, and with them to share in the glory of rescuing their native country from the grasping hand of France, as well as from the ambitious and interested views of a desperate party among themselves, who had already brought the colonies to the very brink of destruction. Could they now want evidence, that the funds of their country were either exhausted, or that the managers had applied them to their own private uses? And, in either case, could they any longer continue in their service with honour or advantage? The tyranny of their rulers, had robbed them of their property, imprisoned their persons, drags them to the field of battle, and is daily deluging their country with their blood.

He asked, what America was now, but a land of widows, orphans, and beggars? Even their last stake, religion, he represented to be in such danger, as to have no other security, than what depended upon the exertions of the parent country for their deliverance. In proof, or illustration of this, he asserted a fact upon his own knowledge; viz. That he had lately seen their mean and profligate Congress at mass, for the soul of a Roman Catholic in purgatory, and participating in the rites of a church, against whose anti-christian corruptions, their pious ancestors would have witnessed with their blood.

On this the writers in the American papers remarked, that no other man in America, had ever paid so marked an attention to, or ever entered into such close habits of intimacy and apparent friendship with the French agents, consuls, and residents in that country, as he had uniformly done. That his fine house at Philadelphia was not only at all times devoted to their service, but that he had maintained Monf. Gerard, with his whole family and suite, for several weeks in it, in the most sumptuous manner, until the Congress were able to provide one proper for his reception. And that his constant magnificence and expence, in concerts, balls and entertainments, for the Gallican strangers, were in a stile far superior to any thing of the sort before known in that part of the world; so that the French themselves considered him, as one of the warmest friends to their country on the whole continent. How far this is true, we are totally unable to determine. According to our custom, we fairly state the representations on both sides; and laying facts together, we do our best to enable the reader, to judge of the true condition of America, and the value of our expectations from the state of parties there.

The only public notice taken of Arnold's defection, on the side of America, was a proclamation issued by the executive power of the state in Pensylvania, wherein his name was placed at the head of a list of ten supposed traitors, and of whom five were no higher than the rank of yeomen; who were all summoned to surrender by a given day, in order to abide trial for the treasons wherewith they were charged; or, in case of failure, to be subjected to all the pains penalties, and forfeitures, of high treason.

However disappointed by the failure of Gen. Arnold's original design, and of his subsequent proclamations, hopes were still entertained of the dissentions and distresses which prevailed in the revolted provinces; and which these proclamations appear by no means to have exaggerated. The depreciation of their paper currency was arrived at its ultimate pitch, and it produced all its natural consequences. Some of the earlier emissions of that currency, fell infinitely below their nominal value: that is, one hundred silver dollars, produced as much value at market, as eight or ten thousand paper ones. And even the later emissions, or those which were most valued, had fallen at the rate of forty to one. At the same time, that the circumstances of the war, had raised the price of all foreign commodities, and of many of the most essential articles, to the most enormous pitch. Without supposing very much of mal-administration, we must suppose such a depreciation the inevitable consequence of vast paper emissions, without an adequate money fund to give them strength, and currency. [23]

This particularly affected, and was indeed exceedingly ruinous to the American officers; for although the soldiers were ill clad, and otherwise greatly distressed, they were, however, on the whole, well supplied with provisions. But many, if not most of the officers, had been under a necessity of mortgaging their small estates, to the utmost which they could raise upon them, in order to support the enormous expences of the service. These grievances they had long and repeatedly remonstrated upon, both to the Congress, and to the governments of their respective states; nor were the complaints confined to subalterns, but proceeded equally from the field and general officers. After long waiting, with most astonishing patience, the issue of hopes and promises which were never realized, it was at length so much exhausted, and their wants became so urgent, that a great number of the officers were upon the point of throwing up their commissions, and said they must preserve themselves from utter ruin, by returning to the care and management of their estates and private affairs. That they had hitherto freely spent their blood, and dedicated their lives, to the defence of their country; but that it would be most unreasonable to expect, that they alone, of all the members of the community, should be likewise destined to the sacrifice of their whole private fortunes for its service.

It may then be well considered as a singular circumstance, in this state of great discontent, and of no less real grievance, that such vast offers held out to them, should not have produced some very considerable effect in the American army. And yet, the matter of fact is, that the example of a man of the highest military fame among them, so far from being the means of bringing over, even any small body or detachment of troops, does not seem to be fairly chargeable with the desertion of a single soldier, much less of an officer. It may not be easy to trace many instances in history, of an ill paid, and every respect ill provided army, however veteran in service, and elated by former success, and however knit together by many bands of union here wanting, which could have been proof to such a trial and temptation. [24]

War in South Carolina. State of affairs after the battle of Camden. Inaction caused by the sickly season. Sequestration of estates. Col. Ferguson defeated and killed on the King's Mountain. Gen. Sumpter routed by Col. Tarleton. Brig. Gen. Leslie sent on an expedition from New-York to the Chesapeak. Proceeds to Charles Town, and joins Lord Cornwallis. Gen. Greene arrives in North Carolina, and takes the command of the Southern American army. Colonel Tarleton dispatched to oppose General Morgan, who advances on the side of Ninety-six. Tarleton defeated with great loss. Unfortunate consequences of the destruction of the light troops under Ferguson and Tarleton. Lord Cornwallis enters North Carolina by the upper roads. Leaves Lord Rawdon with a considerable force at Camden, to restrain the commotions in South Carolina. Vigorous, but ineffectual pursuit of Morgan. Destruction of the baggage in the British army. Admirable temper of the troops. Masterly movements by Lord Cornwallis for passing the Catawba. General Williamson killed, and his party routed. Militia surprised and routed by Tarleton. Rapid pursuit of Morgan, who notwithstanding passes the Yadkin, and secures the boats on the other side. British army march to Salisbury; from whence Lord Cornwallis proceeds with the utmost expedition to seize the fords on the river Dan, and thereby cut Greene off from Virginia. Succeeds in gaining the fords. Rapid pursuit of the American army. Their escape, by unexpectedly passing the Roanoke. Extraordinary exertions and hardships of the British army. Proceeds to Hillsborough. Expedition from Charles-Town to Cape Fear River. Wilmington taken, and made a place of arms and supply. Gen. Greene, being reinforced, returns from Virginia; and the British army marches to Allemance Creek. Skirmish between Tarleton's corps, and Lee's Legion. Greene falls back to the Reedy Fork. Strange defect of intelligence, experienced by the British general in North Carolina. American army being farther reinforced, Gen. Greene again advances. Movements on both sides, preparatory to the battle of Guildford. Account of that severe and well-fought action. British officers killed and wounded. Col. Webster dies of his wounds. Gen. Greene retires to the Iron Works on Troublesome Creek. Lord Cornwallis obliged to march to the Deep River, through the want of provisions and forage. Necessities and distresses of the army, oblige Lord Cornwallis to proceed to Wilmington for supplies. Unusual consequences of victory.

DURING these transactions on the side of New York, the excessive heats, and great unhealthiness of the season in South Carolina, had laid an unsuperable restraint upon the arms and activity of Lord Cornwallis, for no small time after the battle of Camden. In the mean time he issued a proclamation for se-

Sept. 16th. 1780. queftrating the eftates of thofe perfons within the province, who were either actually in arms with the enemy, who had abandoned their plantations with a view of joining or fupporting them, or who, by an open avowal of rebellious principles, and other criminal acts, fhould manifeft a defperate perfeverance in oppofing the re-eftablifhment of his majefty's government. To give effect to this purpofe, he appointed a commiffioner to take poffeffion of fuch eftates and property, the annual product of which, excepting the part allotted for the maintenance of the families of thofe defaulters and abfentees, was to be applied to the public fervice, in contributing to defray the expences of the war.

During this fickly feafon, by which the army, notwithftanding its ceffation from toil, was much affected, Lord Cornwallis had difpatched Col. Ferguson, with his own corps of light infantry, and a body of militia, likewife of his training, which was attached to it, to make incurfions on the borders of North Carolina. If no great matter was expected from this expedition, yet, as he was neither incumbered with baggage or artillery, and that his troops were particularly diftinguifhed by their activity and alertnefs; as little danger feemed to be hazarded in the experiment with a broken and difpirited enemy; and misfortune was farther guarded againft by the inftructions given to the commander, immediately to return upon the apprehenfion of any fuperior force; though in fact, none fuch was reafonably to be expected. There were feveral fufficient motives for this expedition. For befides, that the nature of that fort of troops, requires their being kept in almoft continual motion and action, it feemed neceffary to keep the war alive in fome degree upon the frontier; as well to check the confidence of the enemy, as to prevent the fpirits of the loyalifts in that province (where there were many more of the defcription than in any other) from finking under the unavoidable delay and flow movement of the army.

Ferguson was tempted to ftay longer in the mountainous country which partly borders on, and partly forms a part of, Tryon county in North Carolina, than was abfolutely neceffary, under the hope of cutting off a Col. Clarke, who was [25] returning with his detachment from an expedition into Georgia; and was the more encouraged in this delay, from his not having an idea, that there was any force in the country at all able to look him in the face. A numerous, fierce and unexpected enemy, however, fuddenly fprung up in the depth of the deferts. The fcattered inhabitants of the mountains affembled without noife or warning, under the conduct of fix or feven of their militia colonels, to the number of 1600, daring, well mounted, and excellent horfemen.

Col. Ferguson had already received orders from Lord Cornwallis for his return, and was on his way to pafs the Catawba for that purpofe. But difcovering as he croffed the King's mountain, that he was eagerly purfued by a thick cloud of cavalry, he took the beft pofition for receiving them which time and the place would admit of; and which happened to be by no means a bad one. But his men being neither covered by horfe nor artillery, and being likewife difmayed, and aftonifhed, at finding themfelves fo unexpectedly furrounded and attacked on every fide by this cavalry, were not at all capable of withftanding the impetuofity of their charge. A total rout enfued. The colonel, with 150 of his men were killed upon the fpot; about the fame number were wounded; and the prifoners, including the latter, exceeded 800. The Americans fay they took 1500 ftand of arms; and ftate Ferguson's force at 1400 [26] men.

The fall of this officer, who poffeffed very diftinguifhed talents as a partizan, and in the conduct of irregular warfare, was independently even of his detachment, no fmall lofs to the fervice. He was perhaps the beft markfman living; and probably brought the art of rifle fhooting to its higheft point of perfection. He even invented a gun of that kind upon a new conftruction, which was faid to have far exceeded in facility and execution any thing of the fort before known; and he is faid to have greatly outdone even the American Indians, in the adroitnefs and quicknefs of firing and loading, and in the certainty of hitting the mark, lying upon the back, or belly, and every other poffible pofition of the body. It is not certain, that thefe improvements produced all the effect in real fervice, which had been expected, from thofe aftonifhing fpecimens of them that were difplayed in England. Humanity cannot, however, but wifh that this barbarous mode of hoftility, was by univerfal confent, banifhed from the warfare of all nations. [27] It has been reported, that Gen. Wafhington owed his life at the battle of Germantown to this gentleman's total ignorance of his perfon; as he had him fufficiently within reach and view during that action for the purpofe. [28]

This was the firft reverfe of fortune which Earl Cornwallis had experienced in his military career; but fhe feemed now to take vengeance for the delay; for the ftate of his force, and the nature of the war confidered, few things could have been more peculiarly unlucky in the prefent juncture. It was, however, in fome degree apparently recompenced, by the fevere blow which Sumpter, not long after, received from Col. Tarleton.

Gen. Sumpter having raised about a thousand men, advanced towards Ninety-Six, with a view of attacking some of the posts in that neighbourhood, if not the place itself. Tarleton was then at such a distance, as afforded no room for apprehension of him, until, at least, some considerable part of the business was effected; but his motions were so sudden and unexpected, and he passed the Wateree, and the Broad River with such rapidity, that he had nearly surprized his too secure enemy on the South banks of the Ennoree, before he had the smallest apprehension of his danger. This being, however, prevented, by the lucky information of a deserter, Sumpter had barely time to pass that river with the utmost precipitation; but could not save his rear-guard from being cut to pieces.

He continued his flight to the River Tyger, and was pursued by Tarleton, with the cavalry of his legion, and the 63d regiment mounted on horseback, with the utmost rapidity; the infantry of the legion, with the artillery, consisting of a single three pounder, being several miles behind. Sumpter perceiving the danger of attempting to cross the Tyger, with an enemy, flushed with success, close upon his rear, and having also received intelligence that Tarleton had come forward without his infantry, he took a strong position at a place called Black-Stocks, a little short of the river, and confiding in his own superiority of number, determined to stand his attack. This Tarleton did not then intend; for he only wanted to interrupt the flight of the enemy, and keep them in play, until he was joined by the rear; but the eager coming up of the 63d, and their being instantly attacked as they threw themselves from their horses, obliged him, at no small hazard, to put all at the issue, and to fall on directly

with his cavalry. Notwithstanding the cover of some log houses, and the natural advantages of the place, the enemy were driven from their strong post, and forced to pass the river in the utmost disorder.

The Americans lost about 120 men, killed, wounded, or taken.[29] Three of their colonels were among the slain. and Sumpter himself was dangerously wounded. They were certainly fortunate in bringing on the action before the arrival of the rear, as the whole party must otherwise have been inevitably cut off. Of the British troops above fifty were killed or wounded; among the former were some promising and gallant young officers. Tarleton pursued the blow, as soon as he had provided for the wounded; and crossing the river, did not quit the pursuit until he had entirely dispersed Sumpter's corps.

It has perhaps produced no small effect on the fortune of the American war, that every considerable success obtained in its progress, has been eagerly considered at home as decisive and final, at least with respect to that quarter or part of the continent where the advantage was gained, if not to the whole. Nor has repeated experience of the mischief of such confidence, been able to prevent its revival when any new occasion was offered.

The victory at Camden seems to have been considered, even in America, as decisive with respect to the southern colonies; and no obstacle seems to have been understood in Lord Cornwallis's way from thence to the Chesapeak. North Carolina was only considered as the road to Virginia; the determined resistance, and the opposition in every instance of the inhabitants, do not appear to have been any more thought of, than the unconquerable disaffection of those in South Carolina. It must have been under these persuasions,

that the commander in chief at New York, dispatched Brig. Gen. Leslie, with a corps of near 3000 choice troops, about the middle of October to the Chesapeak, in order to co-operate with Lord Cornwallis's operations in Virginia. It was likewise farther in view, that Leslie, with the aid of the marine by which he was convoyed, might, by taking proper stations towards the head of the Chesapeak, or in the vast rivers which fall into it, traverse any succours which were sent from the northern army to the southward. But in all cases, he was to act entirely according to the orders which he should receive from Lord Cornwallis.

The troops were landed at Portsmouth, and other neighbouring places in Virginia, where they found some tobacco and stores; but the vessels which were seized in the harbours and rivers, were the most valuable part of the booty. This was, however, by no means an object to compensate for the delay, which the expedition in the Chesapeak, instead of proceeding directly to Charles-Town, necessarily occasioned to the operations of the southern army.

Lord Cornwallis being at too great a distance to profit of any operations upon the Chesapeak, and it being impossible to form a junction with Leslie's corps by that way, as soon as he had received advice from Sir Henry Clinton of the circumstances, immediately dispatched instructions to the fleet and troops, to proceed without delay to Charles-Town; where they arrived about the middle of December, and Leslie found orders in waiting, that he should immediately march with about 1500 of his men to join the army; the remainder, it seems, being deemed necessary, for the security of the capital, and the support of the communications.

Towards the close of the year,

whilst Lord Cornwallis was making every preparation for a vigorous irruption into North Carolina, Gen. Greene was sent from the northern army by Washington, to take the command of the southern; Gates being now entirely retired; but, as we have heretofore observed, not only without any mark of censure, but with an honourable testimonial of his zeal and services from the assembly of Virginia. Greene stands so high with the Americans as an officer, that he holds the next place to Washington in their military estimation; and, what does not always happen in such cases, is at the same time the great favourite of that commander. He brought no troops from the northern army; depending upon the resources of the southern colonies for their own defence; but was accompanied by Col. Morgan, a brave and distinguished partizan, who had commanded those riflemen in the northern war, that besides being fatal to many brave officers, became so terrible to the Indians under Gen. Burgoyne, and were so far superior to them in their own way, that, to use his own expressive words, they could not be brought within the sound of a rifle shot.

Early in the new year of 1781, Lord Cornwallis advanced with the army towards the borders, keeping his course between the Broad, and the Catawba rivers, until he arrived at a water, called Turney Creek, which falls into the former. Greene had by this time assembled his principal force in Mecklenburg county, North Carolina. In order to impede the progress of the royal army, which he was yet in no condition to encounter in the field, he thought it necessary to make a diversion on their left; and for that purpose, an attack was made upon the important, and now far from weak post of Ninety-Six; while to favour and support the diversion,

Morgan advanced, with about 500 regular troops (mostly belonging to Virginia) and some hundreds of militia, with a detachment of one hundred cavalry, under Col. Washington, upon the Pacolet [30] river.

Tarleton was already on that side, with the legion, consisting of about 300 cavalry, and as many infantry, with the first battalion of the 71st, which was now annexed to it, and one three pounder; and being joined by the 7th regiment, which was marching with another three pounder to the relief of Ninety-Six, he received instructions from the commander in chief, to strike a blow, if possible, at Gen. Morgan; but at all events, to oblige him to pass the Broad River, and thereby prevent all future embarrassment on that side. Morgan retreated, and Tarleton pursued; a state of things, which naturally increases confidence and ardour on the one side, and generally depresses them on the other. Morgan at length found his enemy so close upon him, that he could not pass the Broad River, especially as the waters were exceedingly out, without exposing his troops to greater danger, than he thought he should hazard by an encounter. He accordingly, without hesitation, determined at once upon the part which he should take; and choosing his ground, boldly prepared for battle.

Tarleton came up with his enemy at eight in the morning, and nothing could appear more inviting than the prospect before him. They were drawn up on the edge of an open wood without defences; and though their numbers might have been somewhat superior to his own, the quality of the troops was so different as not to admit a doubt of success; which was still farther confirmed by his great superiority in cavalry; so that every thing seemed to in- Jan. 18th. 1781. [31]

dicate a most complete victory. His line of attack was composed of the 7th regiment, with the foot of the legion, and the corps of light infantry annexed to it; a troop of cavalry covered each flank. The first battalion of the 71st, and the remainder of the cavalry, formed a second line.

Morgan shewed uncommon ability and judgment in the disposition of his force. Seven hundred militia, on whom he placed no great confidence, were exposed to open view, as we have seen, in the first line, on the edge of the wood; but the second, composed of the continental and Virginia troops, was out of sight in the wood; where they were drawn up in excellent order, and prepared for all events.

The militia were little capable of sustaining the impetuosity of their assailants; and were soon broken, routed, and scattered on all sides. It is not to be wondered at, that those troops who had been so long used to carry every thing before them, almost without resistance, now meeting with the usual facility, should at once conclude the day to be their own, and pursue the fugitives with the utmost rapidity. In the mean time, the second line having opened on the right and left in the wood, as well to lead the victors on, as to afford a clear passage for the fugitives, as soon as the former were far enough advanced, poured in a close and deadly fire on both sides, which took the most fatal effect. The ground was, in an instant, covered with the killed and wounded; and those brave troops who had been so long inured to conquer, were, by this severe and unthought of check, thrown into irremediable disorder and confusion.

A total defeat was the immediate consequence. The 7th regiment lost their colours; and the brave men of the royal artillery, who attended the two pieces of cannon, with the characteristic intrepidity and magnanimity of their corps, scorning either to abandon or surrender their guns, were cut to pieces by them. The loss every way, in killed, wounded, and prisoners, exceeded 400 men.[32] Tarleton, in the midst of defeat, exhibited a trait of his character and spirit. When all was lost, he notwithstanding rallied a part of his routed cavalry, who were still ashamed to abandon an officer who had so often led them to victory; with these he unexpectedly charged and repulsed Washington's horse; and had the fortune of retaking the baggage, the slender guard in whose custody it was left being cut to pieces. This, however, from the impossibility of carrying it off, he was obliged mostly to destroy.

This blow, coming so closely upon that at the King's Mountain, produced effects worse than could have been feared from such partial disasters. Indeed they seemed seriously to have influenced all the subsequent operations of the war, and deeply affected its general fortune. The loss of the light troops, especially of the cavalry, could scarcely be repaired; and the nature of the war, rendered this sort of force one of its most effectual arms.

It was the more grievous to Lord Cornwallis, from its being one of those unexpected events, which as it could neither be foreseen nor apprehended, no wisdom could possibly provide against. Most of the troops that were now defeated, had been much distinguished, and constantly successful. It is not even clear that there was any disparity in point of number; and if there had, from long and confirmed experience, it could not have been a matter of much consideration. Nor was it even to be supposed, that Morgan would in any possible circumstance have ventured an engagement; for Greene had already, upon the advance of Lord Cornwallis, abandoned Mecklenburgh county, and retired to the eastern side of the Pedee; which increased the distance so much, that his retreat, under the consequences of an action, seemed extremely hazardous.

The plan adopted by Lord Cornwallis for the winter campaign, was to advance to North Carolina, by the upper, instead of the lower roads, or in other words, to make his way on the western side, instead of keeping the central course through both provinces. Among other motives for this choice, was the hope of cutting Morgan off, or if that failed, at any rate to drive him entirely out of South Carolina, and thereby to relieve Ninety-six, and all that side, from trouble and danger while he pushed forward. Another motive not less cogent for taking the upper road was, that it kept nearer the heads of the rivers, and accordingly led to the fords, which generally lie above their forks; whereas the great rivers were at that season, nearly, if not entirely impassable below the forks, which was the course that the lower road took.

The objects in view with Lord Cornwallis were, by rapid marches, to get between Gen. Greene and Virginia, and by cutting off his reinforcements from that country, either reduce him to a necessity of fighting with his present force, or of giving up the cause altogether, by abandoning North Carolina with precipitation and disgrace. In either case, as he had no doubt of success in the former an opportunity would be afforded, and encouragement given to the loyalists, to fulfil their promises of a general rising, in order to assist in the re-establishment of the British government. In this flattering state of things, government being established, and the province competent to the maintenance of its own internal security, it would likewise prove the means of securing the tranquility of South Carolina. And thus every thing being secured behind, he might then well look forward, with the warmest hopes, and with every prospect of advantage, to the prosecution of his intended operations in Virginia, Maryland, and even still farther northward.

Lord Cornwallis was not less attentive to the security of South Carolina during his absence, than he was to the providing for the active operations of the army under his own immediate command. For this purpose, besides the stationary force at Charles-Town, he left a considerable body of troops under the conduct of Lord Rawdon; whose central situation at Camden, was equally calculated to repress the insurgents within the province, and to maintain the frontiers. A measure indeed that greatly lessened his active force, already too much weakened by the late losses; but which the situation of affairs rendered indispensibly necessary. For Green's situation, hanging with his force upon the eastern banks of the Pedee, whose waters covered him from all near danger, would have afforded him such a command of a great part of the southern frontier, when the main army had pushed on to the northward, as would have endangered, at least, all the eastern side of the province, without such a check as was now provided. And to this was to be added, that South Carolina itself was still torn to pieces by internal commotions, which indeed seemed rather to increase than to lessen with loss and defeat; and that, as Sumpter, Marion, and their[33] other leaders, had now made it a rule to mount all their adherents, and to act entirely on horseback; it became a matter of no small difficulty, either to repress or to punish their irruptions.

Lord Cornwallis, with his usual alertness, immediately dispatched a part of the army, unincumbered with baggage, in the hope of intercepting Morgan, or at least of recovering the prisoners; while he staid behind a day with the remainder, for the purpose of collecting the remains of Tarleton's corps. Nothing could exceed the exertions made by the pursuing troops; but such was the celerity of the enemy, and such the difficulties they encountered, from violent and continual rains, and the consequent swelling of the numberless creeks in their way, that all their efforts were fruitless; and Morgan had gained the upper fords on the Catawba, before they could possibly reach them.

Upon the failure of intercepting Morgan, the army was assembled on the 25th of January, at Ramfoure's Mills, on the south fork of the Catawba. And as the loss of the light troops could only be remedied by the general activity of the whole army, Lord Cornwallis spent two days in the destruction of all the superfluous baggage, and of every thing whatever, which could retard the celerity of the troops, and which was not absolutely necessary to their existence or action. Upon this principle, all the waggons, excepting those loaded with hospital stores, salt, or ammunition, and four empty ones, reserved for the sick or wounded, were destroyed. The temper with which they submitted not only to this, but to a number of other unusual trials and hardships, does infinite honour to every part of that army. They beheld the destruction of their most valuable, and even much of their most necessary baggage; they beheld their spirituous liquor staved, at a season when it would be most wanted, and upon the entrance of a service, which cut off every prospect and hope of a future supply; and the moderate pittance of flower, which they were able to procure and to carry along with them, was their only certain resource for subsist-

ance; yet these difficulties and evils, new and strange as they were, were submitted to with the most general and chearful acquiescence. It seemed indeed the less irksome, as the example was set by the commander in chief himself with the utmost rigour. It was a new phenomenon in a modern army, to behold the general's quarters incapable of affording a glass of wine, or of any kind of strong liquor, and his table as destitute of any thing orderly or comfortable, and even of furniture, as the common soldier's.

The north fork of the Catawba, had been rendered impassable for several days by the rains; and all the fords for more than forty miles above the fork, were besides vigilantly guarded by detachments of the enemy; composed not only of Morgan's corps, but of the militia of the two neighbouring counties of Rowen and Mecklenburg, (both of which were peculiarly inimical to the royal cause) under the conduct of a General Davidson. Lord [34] Cornwallis approached the river by short marches during its height, and by several movements and feints, which indicated a design of forcing his way at different fords before they were yet passable, endeavoured to divide and distract the attention of the enemy. In the mean time, he spared no pains to procure all possible information, as well of the river, and of the country on the other side, as of the state and condition of the enemy. His plan being settled, and the waters somewhat fallen, he detached Colonel Webster, [35] with a part of the army, and all the remaining baggage, to a ford called Beattie's, which lies six miles higher up the river, than another principal ford, which is known by the name of M'Cowen's. General Davidson, was supposed to be posted with 500 militia at Beattie's; and Webster had instructions to make every possible demonstration, as well by canon-

nading as by manœuvres, of his determination to force a passage at that ford.

While Webster was gone upon this service, Lord Cornwallis with the remainder of the army, consisting of the brigade of guards, the regiment of Bose, the 23d, 200 cavalry, and two three pounders, began his march Feb. 1st. about one in the morning, to a private ford, about a mile from M'Cowen's, which was the real object of attempt. The morning being very dark and rainy, and part of their way being thro' a wood where there was no road, the artillery were so embarrassed in a swamp, that the line of march was pushed on to the ford without them; where the head of the column arrived just at the opening of the day. The general soon perceived by the number of fires on the other side, that the ford was much better guarded, and the opposition would consequently be greater than he expected. This rendered the delay of the artillery the more vexatious. But as he knew that the rain then falling would soon render the river impassable, and had before received intelligence, that Greene was on full march from the Pedee, with his whole force, to join Morgan, he saw that something must necessarily be hazarded at the present, to avoid greater future difficulties; and being likewise full of confidence in the zeal and gallantry of Brig. General O'Hara, and of the [36] brigade of guards under his command which formed the head of the column, he determined on the attempt; and directly ordered them to march on through the river, and to prevent confusion, charged them not to fire, until they had gained the opposite bank.

The guards, and their commander, fully justified the high opinion which Lord Cornwallis had entertained of them. The terrors and difficulties of an untried river, upwards of five hundred yards wide, with a strong current, a rocky bottom, water up to the middle, and exposed through the whole passage, to the deliberate aim, and continual fire of the enemy, were equally incapable of making any impression on their cool and determined valour, and of, in any degree, affecting the excellency of their discipline. The light infantry of the guards, being the first that were landed, instantly formed, and in a few minutes killed or dispersed every thing that appeared before them. Gen. Davidson, who unexpectedly, and for himself unfortunately, had arrived at this post, with 300 militia on the preceding evening, was, with some other officers, found among the slain. Colonel Hall [37] of the guards, was the only officer who fell on the British side; and though a good many private men were wounded, yet the loss in every respect would appear incredibly small to those, who are not accustomed to consider the prodigious difference between real and estimated danger, in many parts of military action.

In the mean time, the rear of the column being come up, and the whole passed with the utmost expedition over the river, Colonel Tarleton was dispatched with the cavalry, supported by the 23d regiment, in pursuit of the fugitives, and likewise to scour and examine the country. Having received intelligence from the prisoners, that three or four hundred of the militia, were to assemble that day at a place about ten miles distant, he eagerly seized that opportunity, as well of avenging, as of effacing the memory of the late disaster. He therefore, immediately quitting the infantry, proceeded thither at the head of the cavalry with the utmost expedition; his arrival being so sudden and unexpected, that a complete surprize, great execution, and total dispersion, were almost the instantaneous consequences. This severe stroke, a-

long with the preceding defeat at the ford, had such an effect upon the militia, who had hitherto only heard of the rigours and dangers of war, that they not only immediately abandoned all their posts on the river, but were so totally cowed and dispirited, that they did not once after, in any manner, make the smallest attempt to interrupt the progress of the army in its march to the Yadkin, although its course lay (to use Lord Cornwallis's own words) through one of the most rebellious tracts in America.

Though the enemy had abandoned Beattie's Ford, yet the continual fall of rain, and swelling of the river, had rendered the passage both tedious and difficult to Colonel Webster. It was, however, at length accomplished towards the evening; and he was enabled to join the commander in chief, in some time after dark, at about six miles distance from the ford.

Intelligence being received, that Morgan had commenced a forced march in the afternoon, which it was afterwards found that he had continued through the night, to the northward, towards Salisbury, the desire of retaliating on that commander, was so strong with the army, that they pursued him in the morning with the utmost spirit and vigour; hoping, notwithstanding the distance he had gained, by dint of exertion, still to overtake or intercept him while he was entangled among the rivers. But the difficulties of bad roads, bad weather, and swelled creeks, which they had to surmount, were so great and so numerous, that it could not possibly be done, with the effect that was wished. Morgan had arrived at the trading fort on the Yadkin, in the night between the second and third of February, and during the remainder of that, and in the course of the following day, had passed the body of his infantry, with the cavalry, and most of

the waggons over the river; so that when the guards, by a course of the most strenuous exertions, had come up in the evening, they could only rout and disperse his rear, and take the few remaining waggons.

Morgan having secured the boats on the other side, and the ford through which he had passed his waggons and cavalry being now rendered impassable by the sudden rise of the river, Lord Cornwallis determined to march to the upper fords, which, as we before observed, are generally passable; but he was under a necessity of making some short delay by the way at Salisbury, for the procuring of a hasty and scanty supply of provisions. In the mean time he received intelligence, that Morgan had quitted the banks of the Yadkin, and that Greene was marching with the utmost dispatch to form a junction with him at Guildford. The British commander knowing that Greene had not yet received his reinforcements from Virginia, nor even had time to collect the North Carolina militia, was sensible, that he would by all possible means avoid an engagement in the latter, and of course endeavour to make his way into the other where his support lay. To counteract this design was therefore his great object; and he accordingly endeavoured with the utmost diligence, and every degree of exertion, to get before him to the river Dan; for that river, and the Roanoke into which it falls, form the boundary between the two provinces; and by seizing the upper fords on the first, he hoped to reduce Greene to a necessity either of fighting, or of abandoning his communication with, and all hope of succour from Virginia; while, in the latter case, he would run no small risque of being inextricably enclosed and hemmed in, between the great rivers on the west, the sea on the east, and the forces under the Lords Cornwallis and Rawdon, on the north and south.

It was now a trial of dispatch between both, armies which should first gain the northern frontier. The British succeeded, and cut Greene off from the upper fords ; and Lord Cornwallis being assured, that the lower were impracticable, and that the country could not afford any number of boats, at all sufficient for the passage of Greene's army, thought he could not now escape without a decisive blow, and accordingly pursued him with the utmost expedition. This was, however, impeded by great and numerous difficulties. The intelligence to be obtained, was not only extremely defective, but seems to have been intendedly delusive ; the want of light troops was 'now feverely felt ; and the enemy by their abundance of them, were enabled to break down all the bridges in the line of march, and to throw numberless other impediments in the way of the army. Upon their arrival at Boyd's Ferry, they discovered to their inexpressible grief and vexation, that all their toil and exertions had been vain, and that all their hopes were frustrated. The enemy had been furnished with boats sufficient, (in direct contradiction to all the intelligence received by the British general) to convey their whole army and baggage, on the preceding day and night, over the river.

Nothing ever exceeded, except the vigour and perseverance with which they were encountered and surmounted, the hardships, and difficulties, which the army endured in this long course of march, from Salisbury to the Dan, and then in the pursuit of Greene to Boyd's Ferry. Their wants and distresses were not less than their toils and fatigues. They traversed a country, which was alternately a wild and inhospitable forest, or inhabited by a people, who were at least

Feb. 15th.

highly adverse, however they might venture, or not, to be hostile. When to these we add all the possible incommodities, incident to bad roads, heavy rains, want of cover, and the continual wading through numberless deep creeks and rivers in the depth of winter, we shall still form only very faint and inadequate ideas of the sufferings which they endured.

The army being in no condition to venture the invasion of so powerful a province as Virginia, in the present circumstances, and North Carolina being in a state of the utmost disorder and confusion, Lord Cornwallis, after giving the troops a day's rest, led them by easy marches to Hillsborough, were he erected the royal standard, and issued a proclamation, inviting all loyal subjects to repair to it, and to take an active part in assisting him to restore order and constitutional government to the colony.

During these transactions, Colonel Balfour, who commanded at Charles-Town, equipped a small force for an expedition to Cape Fear River, not only to co-operate with Lord Cornwallis by a diversion on that side, and by gaining possession of Wilmington, but likewise to make that way a conveyance for the furnishing his army with those necessary supplies, which, in the present state of the war, could scarcely be done in any other manner. Major Craig, with about 300 land forces, was dispatched upon this service towards the latter end of January ; and the men were convoyed and supported by Capt. Barclay, in the Blonde frigate, with the Otter and Delight floops of war ; the marine force and the troops, being equally partakers in the fortune of the enterprize.

Capt. Barclay landed all the marines, in order to supply the weakness of the land force, about nine miles short of Wilmington ; the inhabitants sent a deputation

[38]

[39]

[40]

to propose terms, which were not listened to ; and the town being abandoned by its defensive force, consisting of about 150 men, was taken without resistance. The inhabitants delivered up their arms, were admitted to parole, and secured in their property. The British commanders being informed, that several vessels loaded with provisions, amunition, and the effects of those who were in arms, as well as of some Spaniards and French, who had lately settled at Cape Fear, had escaped up the north-east branch of that river, pursued them both by land and water ; four or five were accordingly taken, and some others burnt by the enemy. The batteries being closed in, and the works repaired or completed, Wilmington was made a post of some sort of strength, and continued for some little time to be of importance.

Lord Cornwallis being informed, that a considerable number of loyalists inhabited the country between the Haw and the Deep, rivers, he dispatched Col. Tarleton with the cavalry, and a small body of infantry, to prevent any interruption in their assembling or moving. But it happened most unluckily, that a part of the enemy's light troops had entered the country on one side, at the very time that the British detachment entered it on another ; and that they fell in with a body of about 200 of these people, who under the conduct of a Colonel Pyle, [41] were on their way to join the royal army at Hillsborough. These unfortunate royalists, who had notice of Tarleton's approach, mistaking the enemy for his detachment, and not being yet apprehensive of the wiles and circumvention of war, suffered themselves, without the smallest effort, to be enclosed and surrounded ; when, without resistance, and it is said, crying out for quarter, a number of them were most inhumanly put to the sword ! [42]

In the mean time, Lord Cornwallis having received intelligence, that Greene being reinforced in Virginia had repassed the Dan, he thought it necessary to collect his force by recalling Tarleton; and forage and provisions growing scarce in the neighbourhood of Hillsborough, and the position being too distant to afford countenance and protection to the well affected upon the advance of the enemy, he thought it expedient to make a movement to the Haw River, which he passed, and encamped near Allemance Creek; having pushed Tarleton a few miles forward towards the Deep River, with the cavalry, the light company of the guards, and 150 of Webster's brigade. Greene's light troops soon made their appearance; upon which Tarleton received orders to move forward, and, with proper precaution, to make what discovery he could of the motions and designs of the enemy,

March 2d. Tarleton had not advanced far when he fell in with a considerable corps of the enemy, whom he instantly attacked, and soon routed; but being ignorant of their force, how they were supported, and grown circumspect from experience, he with great prudence restrained his ardour, and desisted from the pursuit. He soon learned from the prisoners, that those he had defeated were the corps called Lee's legion, with three or four hundred Back Mountain men, and some militia, under a Colonel Preston. [43] He likewise discovered through the same intelligence, that Greene, with a part of his army, was at no great distance.

It appeared afterwards, though it does not seem to have been then known to the British general, that Greene had yet only received a part of the reinforcements he expected; and that a more considerable body were then on their way to join him from Virginia. This induced him to fall suddenly back to Thompson's House, near Boyd's Ford, on the Reedy Fork. It is remarkable, and deserving of particular notice, that although this part of the country, where the army now was, was considered and distinguished, as being peculiarly and zealously attached to the British cause and interest; and yet, that Lord Cornwallis should have had occasion pathetically to complain, that his situation was amongst timid friends, and adjoining to inveterate rebels; and, that between them, he had been totally destitute of information; by which means, he lost a very favourable opportunity of attacking the rebel army.

Though Greene had thus fallen back with his main body, he left his light troops and militia to forage and occupy the country in the front of the British army; and those, in defiance of repeated examples, which might well have served to keep them constantly alert and upon their guard, seeming totally to forget the sort of enemy, to whose eyes and observation they were exposed, were dispersed, and posted carelessly at several plantations, consulting only their convenience, and the facility of subsistance. This situation induced Lord Cornwallis to put the army suddenly in motion; with a view, not only of beating up their quarters, and driving them in upon the army, but of attacking Greene himself, if any fair opportunity should offer. He completely succeeded in the first part of his design; and at Weitzell's Mill, on the Reedy Fork, where they ventured to make a stand, the Back Mountain men, and some Virginia militia, suffered considerably; and the second part only failed, through Greene's making a timely and precipitate retreat over the Haw River.

The vicinity of the fords on the Dan, which lay in the rear of the enemy, and the extreme difficulty of subsisting the army, in the intermediate exhausted country, rendered it in vain for the British general to pursue them over the Haw, under any hope of being able to force them to action. He thought therefore, the most eligible course which he could in the present state of things pursue, was, by effectually covering their country, to afford the friends of the royal cause time and encouragement to assemble, and to join the army; keeping an eye at the same time to Cape Fear River; the communication with which it would soon become indispensibly necessary to open, through the grievous distresses of the army, which were now become nearly insupportable, under the want of supplies of every species. He was, however, determined to fight the enemy in the mean time, if their army at all approached, under a full conviction, that nothing less than a clear and decided superiority in arms, could answer the great purpose and end of their exceedingly toilsome and arduous winter campaign, which was to draw forth into action, the supposed numerous loyalists who inhabited that province.

In pursuance of this plan, the army encamped, on the 13th of March, at the Quaker Meetinghouse, within the forks of the Deep River. On the following day, Lord Cornwallis was informed, that General Butler, with a [44] body of North Carolina militia, together with the unexpected reinforcements from Virginia, had all joined Greene; this was accompanied with a very exaggerated representantion of his force, which was stated at no less than nine or ten thousand men; an intelligence, which was considerably nearer the truth, that he was in full march to attack the British army. On the same evening he received authentic intelligence, that Greene had advanced to Guildford, which was only about twelve miles from the British camp.

Lord Cornwallis being now pretty well perfuaded that the enemy intended to venture an engagement, thought it neceffary to fend the waggons and baggage, under a ftronger efcort than he could well fpare, to Bell's Mill, which was confiderably lower down on the Deep River, in the heart of the well-affected country; and on the following morning, at day-break, he March 15. marched with the remainder of the army, either to meet the enemy on the way, or to attack them in their encampment. About four miles from Guildford, the advanced guard, under Col. Tarleton, fell in with Col. Lee's legion, and thofe other light troops whom they had before engaged. Thefe Tarleton again attacked and routed; and the army continuing its march, foon difcovered the enemy drawn up in order of battle, upon a rifing ground, about a mile and a half from Guildford courthoufe. The light troops who had been defeated, having been feveral days entirely detached from Greene's army, the prifoners now taken could give no manner of account, of the order, numbers, or difpofition of the enemy; and the country people, who were examined as to the nature of the ground, whether from ftupidity or defign, were fo exceedingly inaccurate, if not uninteligible in their defcriptions, as to afford very little fatisfaction upon the fubject. Indeed the difficulty of procuring intelligence, and the little reliance to be placed upon that which was obtained, feem to be among the diftinguifhing features of the war in this province.

Under thefe embarraffing circumftances, the Britifh General was obliged to adopt his difpofitions and meafures, principally, to the apparent face of the country and difpofition of the enemy. The country in general prefented a wildernefs, covered with tall woods which were rendered intricate by fhrubs and thick underbrufh; but which was interfperfed here and there, by a few fcattered plantations and cleared fields. In the fpace immediately between the head of the column and the enemy, was a confiderable plantation, one large field of which, was on the left hand of the line of March, and two others, with a wood, of about two hundred yards broad, lying between them, was on the right of it; and beyond thefe fields, the wood continued for feveral miles to the right. In the front, beyond the plantation, was another wood, of about a mile in depth; and its back opened into an extenfive fpace of cleared ground which furrounded Guildford courthoufe. The woods on the right and-left, were reported to be impracticable for cannon; the enemy's firft line appeared drawn up on the fkirts of that in the front.

The wood on the right, appearing to be fomewhat more open than its oppofite, induced Lord Cornwallis to direct his attack againft the enemy's left wing; and the artillery were brought up the road to cannonade their center, whilft he was making his difpofitions in the following order. On the right, the Heffian regiment of Bofe, with the 71ft Britifh, were led by Major-general Leflie, and fupported by the firft battalion of guards. On the left, the 23d and 33d regiments, were led by Col. Webfter, and fupported by the grenadiers, and the fecond battalion of guards, under the conduct of Brigadier-General O'Hara. The German yagers, with the light infantry of the guards, remained in the wood, on the left of the guns; and the cavalry, under Col. Tarleton, were drawn up in the road, in readinefs to act as circumftances might require.

Gen. Greene's army was drawn up in three lines; the front line, which was only in fight, was compofed of the two North Carolina brigades of militia, under their own Generals Butler and Eaton. The fecond line, drawn up at a proper diftance in the wood, was compofed of two brigades of Virginia militia, commanded by the Generals Stephens and Lawfon. But the hope and main ftrength of the army, was placed in the third line, which confifted of two brigades of Virginia and Maryland continental (or regular) troops, under the conduct of Gen. Huger and Col. Williams. Col. Wafhington, with his dragoons, a detachment of continental light infantry, and Lynch's regiment of riflemen, formed a feparate corps to cover the right flank; and Col. Lee, with his legion, a detachment of light infantry, and Campbell's riflemen, were appointed to cover the left. [45]

It is probable that Greene's whole force did not fall much, if any thing, fhort of 6000 men; [46] and it feems as probable, from the long fervice they had gone through, and the confequent thinnefs of the battalions, as well as from other preceding and fubfequent circumftances, that Lord Cornwallis's forces could fcarcely exceed a third of that number. The accounts [47] publifhed at the time on either fide, being always calculated to make certain impreffions, and to anfwer immediate purpofes, can never afford a clue to accurate eftimate in fuch cafes. The fimilarity between Greene's difpofitions on this day, and thofe which had lately fucceeded fo well with Morgan, cannot fail of ftriking every one who attentively confiders both; the refemblance will likewife appear in fome parts of the action, as well as in the plan or defign.

The action began about half an hour paft one o'clock in the afternoon; when Major General Leflie found himfelf fo much out-flanked by the enemy's left, that he was obliged to bring the firft battalion of guards forward into the line, to the right of the regiment of Bofe;

after which he was not long in defeating every thing that yet appeared before him. At the same time, Col. Webster, who advanced with equal vigour on Leslie's left, was no less successful in his front ; but finding that the 33d was exposed to a very heavy fire from the enemy's right wing, he suddenly and judiciously changed his front to the left, aed being supported by the yagers, and light infantry of the guards, attacked and routed them on that side ; while the grenadiers, and second battalion of guards, moved forward to occupy the ground in the center, which he had just quitted.

All the infantry being now in the line, Col. Tarleton was directed to keep his cavalry entire and compact, and not to charge by any means without orders, excepting only, the most evident necessity of protecting some corps from defeat or ruin. In fact, notwithstanding this beginning success, all the severity and danger of the action was yet to come. For, although the North Carolina militia, in the first line, had shamefully abandoned their post, and ran away, without at all standing the conflict ; the Virginia militia, in the second line, were by no means influenced by their example ; they, on the contrary,[48] stood their ground for a considerable time, and fought with great resolution ; and when they were at length broken, and driven back upon the continental troops in the third line, the battle then became only the more arduous and doubtful. It was indeed an action of almost infinite diversity. The excessive thickness of the woods, had rendered the bayonet in a great measure useless ; had enabled the enemy, however broken, to rally, to fight in detachment, and to make repeated and obstinate stands ; it had necessarily and entirely broken the order of battle ; and separated and disjoined the British corps, who could know no more of each other, than what they

gathered from the greatness, the continuance, or the course of the firing, in different quarters. Thus the battle degenerated into a number of irregular, but hard-fought and bloody skirmishes.

On the right, the first battalion of guards, with the regiment of Bose, after they imagined that they had nearly carried every thing before them, were warmly engaged in front, flank and rear, not only with such parts of the routed or broken enemy who had again rallied, but with a part of the extremity of their left wing, which, through the closeness of the wood, had been passed, unbroken and unobserved. A similar firing was continued on the left, where Webster's corps was engaged. In the mean time, the 71st regiment, with the grenadiers, and the second battalion of guards, which were in the center, being uncertain what was passing on either hand, but hearing the fire advance on the left, continued to move on along the road through the wood, being accompanied by the artillery, which kept pace with them, and followed by the cavalry. The guards first gained the cleared ground, near Guildford Court-house, where they found a corps of continental infantry, formed in the open field on the left of the road.

Though the enemy were much superior in number, the second battalion of guards, glowing with impatience to signalize themselves, instantly attacked, and routed them with such effect, as to take their cannon ; but pursuing them with too much ardour into the wood, they were suddenly thrown into confusion by a very heavy and unexpected fire ; and being instantly charged by Col. Washington, at the head of his regiment of dragoons, the disorder was irretrievable, and they were driven back, and pursued into the field, with the loss of the two 6 pounders which they had just taken. The fortune of the day, at this instant,

seemed only to hang by a single hair. The critical bringing up, of two 3 pounders, and their well-timed and well-directed fire, under the conduct of Lieutenant Macleod of the artillery, served[49] to repulse, or at least to keep at bay, the cavalry for the present, and afforded some leisure for breathing and recovery to the guards. In the mean time, the grenadiers, with the 71st regiment, whose passage had been impeded by some deep ravines they fell in with on their way, began to appear, coming out of the wood on the right ; which as it could not fail to damp the enemy, served equally to inspirit the royal troops, and to facilitate the endeavours of Brig. Gen. O'Hara ; who, notwithstanding his being forely wounded, was using the most spirited and successful exertions in rallying the guards. They accordingly, being now confirmed and supported by the coming up of the grenadiers, returned to the charge with fresh ardour ; and to render the affair decisive, the 23d regiment arrived at that instant from the left, and Tarleton came sweeping on with his cavalry. Such a conjunction of favourable circumstances could not but produce their effect. The enemy were attacked on all sides ; defeated ; and not only lost the two first 6 pounders, which they had so lately recovered, but two others, being the whole artillery which they had brought into the field.

About the same time, the 33d regiment, and the light infantry of the guards, after long action, and overcoming many difficulties, had entirely routed the corps which were opposed to them on the left ; so that the action being now entirely ended on that side, the 23d and 71st regiments, with part of the cavalry, were dispatched in pursuit of the flying enemy. In the mean time a heavy firing was still continued in the woods on the right, where the first battalion of guards, and the regiment of Bose, had their hands fully engaged with the militia, in a fort of action which was entirely suited to the habits and genius of the latter. The appearance of the cavalry, and the spirited attack made by Tarleton, contributed much to extricate those regiments, and to occasion the dispersion of the militia in the woods.

Thus ended the very sharp, hard-fought, and exceedingly diversified action at Guildford. An action, in which the persevering valour, and admirable discipline of the British troops, were most eminenlty distinguished. Nothing less, indeed, than an unlimited portion of the one, and an unequalled perfection in the other, could have triumphed against so great a superiority of force, and such insuperable difficulties of ground. Lord Cornwallis declared, in public orders, that he should ever consider it as the greatest honour of his life, to have been placed at the head of so gallant an army; and the merit was so general, that every corps, and almost every officer above the rank of a subaltern, received his public thanks and acknowledgments for their particular and distinguished services. Among these, we must not forget the brave Hessian regiment of Bose, and their gallant commander, Major de Buy.[50]

No public acknowledgment could be made (nor would it have been adequate if there could) of the noble commander's own merits; which, if possible, were more highly distinguished on this day, than in the most brilliant of his former actions. Notwithstanding an exceeding bad state of health, he seemed to be every where present; and afforded support and relief to every corps that was hard pressed. It was then no wonder, that two horses were shot under him; but it may well be deemed such, that he escaped himself unhurt.

On the other side it must be acknowledged, that several of the American corps disputed the day with great constancy; and that they rallied, returned to the charge, and stood several severe shocks, with a perseverance and courage, which would have done honour to veteran troops. The rebel cavalry very much distinguished themselves. It would likewise seem, that Greene shewed no common share of ability, in the drawing up of his army, the choice of his ground, and such a disposition of his force, as was suited both to its nature and theirs. Nor does any want of generalship appear in the course and conduct of the action. The exceeding bad behaviour of the first line, both with respect to effect and example, was sufficient to have introduced disorder and dismay in any army; and could not but greatly influence the fortune of the day.

The loss on the British side, in any comparative estimate, drawn from the length, circumstances, and severity of the action, would appear very moderate; but if considered, either with respect to the number of the army, its ability to bear the loss, or the intrinsic value of the brave men who fell or were disabled, it was great indeed. In the whole it exceeded 500 men; of whom, though scarcely[51] a fifth were killed on the spot, many died afterwards of their wounds; and, undoubtedly, a much greater number were disabled from all future service. At any rate, the army was deprived of about one-fourth in number (and that by no means the least effective) of its present force. The guards lost Col. Stuart, with the Captains, Schutz, Maynard, and Goodricke, besides subalterns.[52] Col. Webster, a brave, experienced, and distinguished officer, who commanded the brigade on the left, died of his wounds, to the no small loss of the service, and the very great regret of the gene-

ral as well as the army. The Brigadier-Generals O'Hara and Howard, as well as Col. Tarleton,[53] and several other officers, were wounded.

The Americans gave no fair state of their loss; which would have been alone a sufficient reason for concluding it to be very considerable. They only published an account of the killed and wounded of the continental troops, who formed but a small part of their army. It was said, that all the[54] houses for many miles round were filled with their wounded. The action was spread through so wide an extent of country, and that so thickly wooded, that the victors could form no estimate of the slain. But whatever that might be, their principal loss consisted in the desertion of that part of the militia who were within any reach of home; for they, according to established custom, seized the opportunity of being dispersed in the woods by an action, to make the best of their way, without once looking back. Gen. Greene bestowed great praises upon the bravery of the Virginia militia, and of the light troops under Lee and Washington, as well as of the Virginia and Maryland regulars. In a very modest letter to the President of the Congress, he satisfies himself with attributing the British success to the superiority of their discipline.

Greene retreated with the continental forces, and such part as could yet be collected of the Virginia militia, to the Reedy-Fork River, which he passed; and says himself, that he halted on the other side of the ford, which was only three or four miles from the last scene of action, until he was joined by the stragglers; but by Lord Cornwallis's account, we are to understand, that he did not stop until he arrived at the iron works on Troublesome Creek, 18 miles from the field of battle. Indeed Greene himself dates his letter, on the following day, from those very iron works; but estimates the distance at little more than half what we have stated. Without entering at all into the question, it is sufficient to observe, that however the Americans were routed, the royal forces were in no condition to maintain a pursuit. Besides that the troops were worn down by the excessive fatigue of a considerable march in the first instance, without baiting, and that immediately succeeded by so long and so toilsome an action, their numerous wounded, who were scattered over an extensive space of country, required the must immediate attention; but to render the impediments to a pursuit utterly insurmountable, the enemy were greatly superior in cavalry, as well as in every species of light troops.

Such was the penury and miserable state of the country, that the troops were without bread for two days that they contined at Guildford; nor could even forage be procured at a nearer distance than nine miles. And though this victory was gained at the entrance of the country in which the loyalists were supposed to he numerous, it does not appear, that it was capable of inducing any body of that people, deserving of name or consideration, to join the royal army. Under these circumstances, Lord Cornwallis moved with the army to Bell's Mill, on the Deep River; whither the baggage had been sent before the action; and was obliged to leave 70 of the worst of the wounded behind, at the New-Garden, Quaker Meeting-house, with proper assistance and accommodation, but of necessity in the power of the enemy.

18th. A march of two days brought the army to Bell's Mill, where they continued two more, as well to afford rest to the troops, as to procure some scanty supply of provisions. The necessities of the army in general, and the distresses of the sick and wounded, left the marching towards Wilmington, in order to obtain those supplies and accommodations which were indispensibly necessary to both, no longer a matter of choice. They accordingly moved, by such easy marches as suited the ease and convenience of the wounded, towards Cross-Creek, upon the north-west branch of the Cape Fear River; being the same, which in its origin, and long after, is known by the name of the Haw. On the way, Lord Cornwallis issued a proclamation, and used every other possible means, as well to conciliate the enemies, and to encourage aad call forth the friends of the royal cause, to the taking an active part in its support. It does not, however, appear, that his endeavours upon this occasion were attended, even after a very splendid victory, with any greater effect, than they had hitherto been, in the course of his long peregrination through different parts of that province.

Such was the strange and untoward nature of this unhappy war, that victory now, as we have already seen in more than one other instance, was productive of all the consequences of defeat. The news of this victory in England, for a while, produced the usual effects upon the minds of the people in general. A very little time and reflection gave rise to other thoughts; and a series of victories caused, for the first time, the beginning of a general despair. The fact was, that while the British army astonished both the old and the new world, by the greatness of its exertions and the rapidity of its marches, it had never advanced any nearer even to the conquest of North Carolina. And such was the hard fate of the victors, who had gained so much glory at Guildford, as, in the first place, to abandon a part of their wounded; and, in the second, to make a circuitous retreat of 200 miles, before they could find shelter or rest. [55]

Lord Cornwallis had been taught to expect, from all the information which he received, that Cross-Creek lay in so plentiful a country, that it would be an exceedingly proper place for affording some days repose and refreshment to his troops. But, to his great disappointment, he found, upon his arrival, that this intelligence was of the usual value, and that neither provisions nor forage were to be procured. This was rendered the more grievous, upon also discovering, that the windings of the river rendered the navigation so tedious, that the troops could not benefit of that mode of conveyance. At length, the arrival of the army in the neighbourhood of Wilmington, on the 7th of April, put an end, for the present, to the unceasing toils, and unspeakable hardships, which they had undergone during the three past months.

Expedition to Virginia under General Arnold. State of grievances which led to the mutiny in the American army. Pensylvania line, after a scuffle with their officers, march off from the camp, and chuse a serjeant to be their leader. Message, and flag of truce, produce no satisfactory answer from the insurgents, who proceed first to Middle-Brook, and then to Prince-Town. Measures used by Sir Henry Clinton to profit of this defection. He passes over to Staten-Island, and sends agents to make advantageous proposals to the mutineers. Proposals for an accommodation, founded on a redress of grievances, made by Gen. Reed, and favourably received by the insurgents; who march from Prince-Town to Trenton upon the Delaware, and deliver up the agents from Sir Henry Clinton. Grievances redressed, and matters finally settled by a committee of the congress. Ravages made by Arnold in Virginia, draw the attention of the French, as well as the Americans, to that country. Gen Washington dispatches the Marquis de la Fayette with forces to its relief. Expedition to the Chesapeak, concerted by M. de Ternay, and the Count Rochambeau, at Rhode Island, for the same purpose, and to cut off Gen. Arnold's retreat. Admirals Arbuthnot and Graves encounter the French fleet, and overthrow all their designs in the Chesapeak. Lord Cornwallis's departure to Wilmington, enables General Greene to direct his operations to South Carolina. Situation of Lord Rawdon at Camden. American army appears before that place. Greene attacked in his camp, and defeated. General revolt in the interior country of South Carolina. Difficulties of Lord Rawdon's situation, notwithstanding his victory. Obliged to abandon Camden, and retire to Nelson's Ferry, where he passes the Santee. British posts taken, and general hostility of the province. Great havock made by the General's Phillips and Arnold in Virginia. Extreme difficulties of Lord Cornwallis's situation at Wilmington. Undertakes a long march to Virginia; arrives at Petersburgh, and receives an account of Gen. Phillip's death. Arrival of three regiments from Ireland at Charles-Town, enables Lord Rawdon to march to the relief of Ninety-Six. Gen. Greene, having failed in his attempt to take the fort by storm, raises the siege, upon the approach of the British army, and is vigorously, but ineffectually pursued. Works at Ninety-six destroyed, and the place abandoned. Lord Rawdon marches to the Congarees; is disappointed in the expected junction of Col. Stuart, and narrowly escapes being surrounded by the enemy, who had intercepted the intelligence of Stuart's failure. He forces his way through Congaree creek, and is joined by Col. Stuart at Orangeburgh. Gen. Greene advances to attack the British army, but retires again in the night. Campaign closes, and situation of the hostile forces during the sickly season. Incredible hardships sustained, and difficulties surmounted, by the British troops in the two Carolinas.

DURING these transactions in the Carolinas, Mr. Arnold, who acted as brigadier-general in the British service, was dispatched by Sir Henry Clinton to make a diversion in Virginia; and perhaps likewise under an expectation, that his former name and character would have drawn large bodies of those, who were represented as having a disposition to return to their allegiance, to his standard. His force, upon this expedition, consisted of the Edinburgh regiment, under Lieutenant-Colonel Dundas, estimated at 600 men; of a mixed American corps, composed of horse and foot, called the Queen's Ranger's, of about the same number, under the command of Col. Simcoe; of Col. Robinson's provincials, and of a small corps of 200 men, which Arnold himself had been able to raise at New York; the whole force amounting to near 1700 men. This expedition being conducted and supported, by such a naval force as was suited to the nature of the service, enabled Gen. Arnold, who arrived in the Chesapeak at the opening of the new year, to do infinite mischief on the rivers, and along the coasts of Virginia.

In the mean time, the Americans had many internal as well as external difficulties and dangers to encounter. We have already taken notice of the well-founded complaints, and the great discontents which prevailed in the American army. These in a great measure proceeded from the slowness of several of the states, in furnishing their respective quotas, whether of men, money, provisions, or cloathing, for the supply of the army. This evil was the more intolerable, from the hopelessness of redress; as the nature of their government did not admit of any coercive power, equal to its remedy. But though this was in a great measure beyond the reach of congress, they did not escape much censure with respect to matters which fell immediately within their power as well as cognizance.

Their ignorance in finance, and their many errors in the whole œconomy of the war, were often animadverted on with great severity by their warmest partizans. It is not indeed easy to conceive, how a body annually elected, continually changing in almost all its parts, and drawn from countries remote from the seat and center of business, could avoid falling into many. The annual election secured the fidelity of the deputies; but it necessarily detracted something from the uniformity and system of public business. The fall of the currency was a grievous blow to the Americans, which perhaps no ability could perfectly prevent or remedy. From hence

56

the grievances and diftreffes of the army equalled, if not exceeded, their complaints and difcontents; and occafioned the refignation of many of their beft officers, as well as the defertion of fome faithful foldiers, who thereby gave up the whole of their long-due arrears, and whom nothing elfe could have induced to abandon their colours. To render their condition the more grievous, while the troops were little lefs than literally naked, it was faid, that cloathing for 5000 men had been purchafed and paid for in France long before; and that through fome unaccountable fupinenefs, another large quantity had lain at Cape Francois for above eighteen months. But the moft intolerable grievance to the foldiery, was an act of real injuftice, as well as a violation of the public faith! for through the failure of feveral of the ftates in not fending their allotted fupply of new troops, many of the foldiers were compelled to ferve far beyond the term of their enliftment, without being able to obtain any fatisfaction, with refpect to their arrears, or even any hope of a difcharge.

Under all thefe circumftances, the mutiny which took place in Wafhington's army, at the opening of the new year, is much lefs a matter of furprize, than its not having happened earlier, being more general, and much more ruinous in its confequences.

The Penfylvania line, which was hutted at Morris-Town, in the Jerfies, unable longer to fupprefs their difcontents, turned out to the number of about 1300 men, Jan, 1, 1781. declaring that they would not ferve any longer, unlefs their grievances were redreffed; particularly with refpect to their pay, cloathing, and provifions, the two firft of which they had not received at all, and there were great deficiencies in the account of the laft. The intervention of the officers occafi-

oned a riot, in which one of them was killed, and four wounded; [57] fome of the mutineers were likewife wounded. They then collected the artillery, ftores, provifions, and waggons, appertaining to their divifion, with all of which they marched in good order out of camp. As they paffed Gen. Wayne's quarters, he fent to requeft of them to defift, and to remonftrate with them on the fatal confequences which muft attend their proceeding any farther. His reprefentations produced no effect; they continued their march until evening, and then chofe an advantageous piece of ground for their encampment, with the fame caution as if they had been in an enemy's country. They likewife elected officers from their own body; and appointed a ferjeant-major, who had been a deferter from the Britifh army, to be their commander, with the rank and title of Major-General; on the [58] following day they marched to Middle-Brook, and on the third to Prince-Town. A meffage was fent to them on the fecond day from camp, defiring to know their intentions; but this they refufed to receive. A flag of truce was afterwards fent; but no general or fatisfactory anfwer could be obtained; fome faid, that they had ferved three years againft their inclination, and would ferve no longer; whilft others made a full redrefs of their grievances, the price of return.

As foon as Sir Henry Clinton had received intelligence of this defection in the army of the enemy, he left no means untried that could turn it to advantage; and indeed it feemed to lead to confequences of no fmall importance. Three Americans went as agents to the infurgents; and were empowered to make the following propofals to them from the commander in chief, viz. To be taken under the protection of the Britifh government; to have a free par-

don for all paft offences; to have the pay due to them from Congrefs faithfully paid, without any expectation of military fervice in return, although it would be received if voluntarily offered; and the only conditions required on their fide, were to lay down their arms, and return to their allegiance. It was alfo recommended to them, to move behind the South River; and an affurance was given, that a body of Britifh troops fhould be in readinefs for their protection, whenever they defired it. The inability of congrefs to fatisfy their juft demands, and the feverity with which they would be treated if they returned to their former fervitude, were points to be ftrongly urged by the agents; and the infurgents were required to fend perfons to Amboy to meet others who would be appointed by the general, in order to difcufs and fettle the treaty, and bring matters to a final conclufion.

In the mean time, the commander in chief, notwithftanding the feverity of the feafon, paffed over to Staten Ifland, with a large body of troops, where they were cantoned in fuch a manner, as to be in readinefs for moving at the fhorteft notice; while fuch meafures were taken in the naval department, as were neceffary for their immediate paffing over to the continent, whenever circumftances might require their acting. This was as much as Sir Henry Clinton could yet venture to do. If he had attempted more, it would have been liable to have overthrown every hope in the onfet. If he had paffed over to the continent, befides exciting a general alarm, it would have been the probable means of throwing the mutineers directly back into the arms of the enemy. The meafures purfued, were thofe only which with fafety and prudence could be ventured upon, until the temper and defigns of the infurgents were farther known; the revolt was properly encouraged, an asylum, with other advantages, were held out, and it was easily seen that greater would be granted. Various other messages and proposals, but much to the same effect or tendency with the former, were afterwards sent; though the Jersey militia had grown so watchful both of the coasts and the interior roads, that the communication became extremely difficult.

After several days stay at Prince-Town, the mutineers, instead of returning towards the British boundaries, as was on our side proposed and hoped, gave an unerring indication of the unfavourableness of their disposition, by advancing to Trenton,
Jan. 9. on the Delaware; a distance which cut off every idea of connection or of their at all acceding to Sir Henry Clinton's proposals; and a measure which held out a most fatal omen to two of his unfortunate emissaries, who were still in their hands. For, previous to their departure from Prince-Town, a printed paper of proposals for an accommodation, signed by General Reed, the president of the executive council of state in Pensylvania, was circulated among the insurgents; and on the day after their arrival at Trenton, an answer, in general very favourable, but requiring some auxiliary conditions, (and those not unreasonable) was returned, with the approbation of the whole by the board of serjeants, who formed their grand committee, or council; and as an earnest of their conciliatory disposition, or, as they said, to remove every doubt of suspicion and jealousy, they delivered up the two unhappy emissaries from New York, who were [59] accordingly hanged without ceremony.

A committee of the congress, of which Gen. Sullivan and Dr. Witherspoon were members, was at [60] length sent to treat with them at Trenton, and the matters in dif-ference were finally settled towards the end of the month. Besides a total oblivion with respect to the past conduct of the mutineers, the matters with respect to pay, cloathing, provisions, and arrears, were adjusted to their satisfaction; and, however grievous it was to the committee, and weakening to the service, they were obliged to consent to the discharge of those, who had duly served out the term of their enlistment. A similar disturbance in the New Jersey line, which was stationed on the same side of the North River, was accommodated in the same manner; but in much less time, and with less trouble. [61]

It was not a little remarkable, that Washington, who was encamped on the New York side of the river, did not make the smallest movement on account of these disorders; nor does it appear that he took any part at all in the transactions or measures that ensued. It seemed either as if he could not rely upon the temper of the troops under his own immediate command, or as if he considered the claims of the insurgents to be well founded, and admitted their wrongs as a justification of their irregularities. Perhaps, upon the whole, he was not sorry that the congress, as well as the governments of the several states, should have been in some degree rouzed and enlivened by such a spur. [62]

Nothing could afford a more striking instance of the general unfavourable disposition of the Americans, with respect to the British government, than the conduct of the insurgents upon this occasion; who, smarting under their wrongs, in that heat of temper which could alone produce and support their violences, and surrounded by the dangers to which they had rendered themselves liable, yet, not only rejected the security and favourable offers held out to them by Sir Henry Clinton, but, as an indelible mark of their irreconcileable enmity, delivered up to destruction the unhappy men who had acted as his agents.

The ravages made by Arnold in Virginia, drew the attention of the [63] Americans, as well as of the French at Rhode Island, particularly to that quarter. The former were now attacked, in their most sensible, as well as most vulnerable part. The haovck made in that country, went directly to the destruction of the very sources of the war, and to the annihilation of all their hopes of independency. With a numerous and warlike people; with considerable resources, more perhaps than any province in America, that country, from its peculiar situation, and from the modes of building, planting, and living, adopted by the inhabitants, is more open and exposed than any other, and, unless protected by a considerable army, is exceedingly weak in every point of defence. In a word, it must in its present state, lie at the mercy, in all its most valuable parts, of whatever enemy is master of the bay of Chesapeak, and consequently of the rivers.

This circumstance was so well understood, that those who censured the conduct of the British commanders, and the plan of the war, had frequently made it one of their principal grounds of attack, that they had not more early adopted operations of a similar nature. They pretended, that a powerful army was kept idle and useless at New York, whilst a right application of a proper part of that force to the southward, would have brought the war to a speedy and happy conclusion. They went so far back in their strictures, as to the time of Lord Cornwallis's being left to prosecute the war in South Carolina, when, they say, that he was not only left in too weak a state to prosecute it with effect and decision, but that he was particularly stripped of the beft and moft active part of the forces; of that part which was peculiarly fuited to the nature of the war and of the country, and which, if not totally ufe-lefs, could not all be wanted, in that quiet and defenfive kind of fervice which prevailed at New-York. They likewife faid, that the expedition under Gen. Leflie fhould have taken place much earlier, and that the force fhould have been three times greater than it really was; by which means, as they pretend, Greene would not only have been prevented from pafling to the fouthward, but, if Lord Cornwallis had the force which he ought in the Carolinas, nothing could prevent his junction with Leflie in the heart of Virginia, and the reduction of all the fouthern colonies, muft have been the immediate and inevitable confequence. They even carried their ftrictures to the prefent expedition under Arnold; which, they faid, fhould have been committed to Gen. Philips, with a force adequate to the greatnefs and importance of the object; a meafure, according to them, which would in a very confiderable degree have compenfated for fome of the former errors and neglects.

To this it has been anfwered, that the commander in chief could not have known, when he returned with part of the army from Charles-Town, that the campaign would have been inactive on the fide of New York; and that the meafures which he immediately purfued on his arrival, fufficiently indicated an intention of rendering it otherwife. The arrival of the French at Rhode Ifland, the expectation of the great force under Guichen, and the plan laid between them and the Americans, of putting an end to the war, by a decifive blow upon himfelf at New York, could not but greatly have affected all his meafures, and neceffarily reftrained his operations. The numerous and extenfive pofts of New York and its dependent iflands, required nothing lefs than an army for the mere purpofe of defence.

Time and events have fhewn, that thefe divided operations which were long called for by feveral military critics, when at length they were adopted, were far from making good the plaufible arguments on which they were undertaken.

The diftreffes and danger of Virginia obliged Wafhington, notwithftanding his weaknefs, to detach 2000 of his beft troops, under the command of the Marquis de la Fayette, to the relief of that, his native country. The French at Rhode Ifland thought an opportunity now offered of atoning for their paft inactivity, by a moft effential fervice to their allies, in cutting off the retreat of Arnold and his party from the Chefapeak; an event, in which the taking him prifoner would not, perhaps, have been the leaft pleafing part of the fervice. Befides fome late increafe to their naval force, they were the farther encouraged to this enterprize, by the misfortune which the Britifh fquadron had newly fuftained, in a dreadful tempeft. In this calamity, the Culloden, a fine new fhip of 74 guns, was totally loft; the Bedford, of the fame force, was difmafted and much damaged; and the America had been feparated, and driven fo far to fea, that her fituation, and even exiftence, were for fome time matters of uncertainty.

But previous to the intended expedition, in which 2000 land forces were to bear a part, the French difpatched a fhip of the line, with fome frigates, to the Chefapeak, with a view as well of furprizing the fmall marine force in that bay, as of difcovering the exact ftate of affairs in Virginia. This fmall fquadron, befides greatly alarming Arnold, who was returned from an expedition up the river James to his principal poft at Portfmouth, had the fortune to fall in with and take the Romulus man of war of 44 guns, which was totally unfufpicious of danger.

The Bedford's mafts being fpeedily replaced by thofe of the Culloden, which had been fortunately faved from the wreck, the Britifh fleet, under the Admirals Arbuthnot and Graves, was much fooner in a condition to oppofe the defigns of the enemy, than they had by any means apprehended. Count Rochambeau, having embarked with the land forces, the French fleet, under M. de Ternay, failed from Rhode Ifland on the 8th of March, and were intercepted off Cape Henry on the 16th, by the Englifh, who had departed two days later from Gardner's Bay. The oppofite fleets were well poifed in point of ftrength; the fuperiority of a few guns on the fide of the Englifh, being more than counterbalanced by the much greater number of men on the other. The line was compofed of eight fhips on each fide, including the Romulus of 40 guns in the one, and the Adamant of fifty in the other.

A partial engagement took place, in which nearly the whole weight of the action fell upon the Robuft, Europe, and the Prudent. The coming up of the fhips in the center, at length relieved the van, who had been expofed to the whole of the enemy's fire. The French line being then foon broken, they gave way, and began to form a new one at fome diftance. The admiral endeavoured to purfue his advantage, by preffing upon the enemy, and renewing the action; but the three fhips which were firft engaged had fuffered fo much in their rigging, that two of them were become fo abfolutely unmanageable, as to be taken in tow, and even the third was too much difabled, in any degree to fuftain a purfuit. Thefe circumftances prevented the Admiral from being able to render the action decifive. The enemy, without an abfolute flight, had by their manœuvres gained a distance of three or four leagues in the forming of their line; and as they were determined not to come to close action, it was now out of his power to force them to it.

He, however, obtained, in part, the essential benefits and the demonstrations of victory. He cut the enemy off from the Chesapeak, who were accordingly obliged to return without landing their troops, and without effecting any one of the purposes of the expedition; and they were reduced to submit to the hard necessity and very grievous mortification of seeing the whole plan of the Virginia campaign disconcerted, and all the sanguine hopes and wishes of their allies frustrated.

Such was Arnold's escape from, probably, the most imminent danger in which he had ever been involved. The loss of men was but trifling on the British side, and was almost entirely confined to the three ships which were first engaged; thirty only were slain, and about seventy wounded. This, like every other naval action in the war, underwent much criticism. It appears that the weather was very squally and unfavourable; and, besides other, perhaps, more cogent reasons, it has or may be advanced, in favour of the admiral, that there are few circumstances, in which it is not exceedingly difficult to force an enemy to close and decisive action at sea, who is absolutely determined to use all possible means for evading that result; and that all vigorous attempts for the purpose, must be liable to the risque of engaging under some disadvantage.

The fleet was detained, by the badness of the weather, for some time in the Chesapeak; which necessarily delayed its pursuit of the enemy. During that interval, a convoy arrived from New York, with Major-Gen. Philips, and about *March 25.*

2000 choice troops on board. The long durance which that distinguished officer, with his fellows of the convention army, had undergone, having been happily terminated, by a new cartel, which had been some months before concluded, he was now appointed to take the chief command in Virginia.

The departure of Lord Cornwallis to Wilmington, having left South Carolina open, Gen. Greene did not neglect the opportunity of directing his views to that province. An experiment upon an untried enemy, was satisfactory in the design, and afforded room for hope in the execution; at the worst, he could not reasonably apprehend falling into rougher hands, than those which he had so recently encountered. But it was also, in reality, that vulnerable part, to which a judicious commander must necessarily have directed his operations. He had, however, still, a vigilant enemy to encounter, from whom no advantage could be cheaply purchased.

The communications were so entirely cut off, that Lord Rawdon had no manner of knowledge of the movements of the British army after the battle of Guildford; much less could he have the most distant idea, of the hard necessity which compelled Lord Cornwallis to fly from the arms of victory, abandon the line of operation, and by a most difficult march of 200 miles, retire out of the way to Wilmington. He could not therefore but be astonished at receiving intelligence, that Greene, whom he looked upon as ruined, or at least as having fled to Virginia, was in full march to South Carolina, with a view of attacking him at Camden. He was likewise informed, about the same time, that Col. Lee had crossed the Pedee, and joined Marion on the Black Creek, or river, with an apparent view of entering

the province on the eastern border. Lord Rawdon judiciously conceived, that this movement was only a feint, subservient to the principal design; intending thereby, to induce him to a division of his small force, and to draw him away from Camden, whilst Greene should in the mean time, by forced marches through a deserted country, from whence no intelligence of his approach could be received, surprize that weakened post in his absence. From this right conception of the design, the measure produced a directly contrary effect to that which was intended; for instead of Lord Rawdon's going himself or detaching, to resist the diversion on that side, it occasioned his immediately recalling Lieut. Col. Watson, who had been long employed with a considerable detachment, for the protection of the eastern frontier. [64]

In the mean time, the doubtful reports which had before reached him were now confirmed, and he received clear information of Greene's approach; and though he was totally ignorant of his force, yet being equally in the dark with respect to Lord Cornwallis's situation, and having no particular instructions for his guidance, he thought it his duty, at all events, to maintain his post. In these circumstances it was highly vexatious, that although some of the militia shewed great zeal and fidelity, in coming from considerable distances to offer their services, yet the scanty state of provisions prevented him from being able to benefit of their assistance, excepting only those, whose particular situation exposed them to suffer from the enemy, and who were, on that account, received within the post.

At length, General Greene appeared in full view. The paucity of troops, and the extensiveness of the posts which they had to defend, were sufficient motives with the British *April 19th.*

commander, for not rifquing the lofs of men, by any attempt to harrafs the enemy in their approach. The fame caufes had obliged him to abandon the ferry on the Wateree, although the South Carolina regiment was on its way to join him from Ninety-Six, and that was its direct courfe. He had however taken his meafures fo well, as to fecure the paffage of that regiment, upon its arrival, three days after. In thefe circumftances, he received a letter from Colonel Balfour at Charles-Town, acquainting him of Lord Cornwallis's fituation; and likewife fignifying to him, that the commander in chief, being fully fenfible of the danger to which he would be expofed in his prefent pofition, wifhed that he might abandon Camden, and retire for fecurity, within the cover of the great River Santee. The neceffity of the meafure was, upon this information, fufficiently obvious; but the accomplifhment of it, was not now within his power.

The efforts made by the enemy to examine the Britifh works, and particularly an attempt to deftroy their mill, neceffarily brought on fome fkirmifhes. By the prifoners taken in thefe excurfions, Lord Rawdon had the fatisfaction to learn, that General Greene's army was not by any means fo numerous as he had apprehended; but that confiderable reinforcements were daily expected. To balance this, he received the unfavourable intelligence, that Marion had taken fuch a pofition, as rendered it impracticable for Col. Watfon to join him, whofe arrival he had till then impatiently expected.

In this ftate of things, it feemed, that fome immediate and decifive effort was become little lefs than abfolutely neceffary, in order to evade much greater, and not far diftant, evil and danger. Greene himfelf had the fortune to make an opening for the operation of this neceffity, in a manner which

was, in appearance, far from being confiftent with his ufual conduct. With a view of a general affault upon the Britifh pofts, he had fent off his artillery and baggage, a day's march in the rear of the army; but foon after he abandoned that refolution, and detached all his militia to bring back the artillery. Such irrefolution, or indecifion of mind, can never be difplayed under the eye of a vigilant enemy, without great, if not certain danger.

Lord Rawdon's intelligence was tardy; but he inftantly perceived the importance of the occafion, and determined as inftantly, if poffible, to feize it. By arming the muficians, drummers, and every being in the army that was able to carry a firelock, he muftered above nine hundred for the field, including fixty dragoons. With this force, and two fix pounders, he April 25th. boldly marched to attack the affailing enemy in their camp, in open daylight, at 10 o'clock in the morning; committing the redoubts, and every thing at Camden to the cuftody of the militia, and of a few fick foldiers. The enemy were pofted about two miles in front of the Britifh lines, upon a very ftrong and difficult pofition, called Hobkirk's Hill. By filing clofe to the fwamps on their right, the Britifh column got into the woods unperceived; and by taking an extenfive circuit, came down on the enemy's left flank; thus depriving them of the principal advantage of their fituation. They were fo fortunate, and the enemy fo fhamefully remifs and inattentive, that they were not in all this courfe difcovered, until the flank companies of the volunteers of Ireland, which led the column, fuddenly poured in upon their pickets. Thefe, though fupported, were almoft inftantly driven in, and purfued to their camp. Although the enemy were in much vifible confufion, yet they

formed with expedition, and received the Britifh column bravely. As if it had been in fome meafure to countervail the difadvantages incident to their furprize, they were cheered, early in the action, by the arrival of three fix pounders; a circumftance, which fhowers of grape-fhot foon announced to the Britifh troops. The attack on that fide was led with great fpirit by Lieut. Col. Campbell,[65] at the head of the 63d, and of the king's American regiment: but the extent of the enemy's line, foon obliged the commander in chief to pufh forward the volunteers of Ireland from the referve. The three corps pufhed the enemy with fuch refolution, that they drove them to the fummit of the hill; and having made room for the reft of the troops to come into action, their rout was then quickly decided. They purfued them about three miles; but the enemy's cavalry being fuperior to the Britifh, their dragoons could not rifque much; and Lord Rawdon, duly confidering his inferiority in number, would not fuffer the infantry to break their order, for any benefit that might be expected from the purfuit of the fugitives.

During the purfuit, a part of the enemy's cavalry, under Colonel Wafhington, whether by defign, or through ignorance of the ftate of the action, came round to the rear, and exacted paroles from feveral of the Britifh officers who lay wounded on the field; they likewife carried off feveral wounded men. The enemy's killed and wounded were fcattered over fuch an extend of ground, that their lofs could not be afcertained; Lord Rawdon thinks the eftimate would be low if it were rated at five hundred; Greene's account makes it too low to be credited.[66] Above an hundred prifoners were taken; befides that a number of their men, finding their retreat cut off, went into Camden, and claimed protection, under the pretence of being deserters. The enemy's canon escaped by great fortune. Being run down a steep hill, among some thick brush wood, they were easily passed without notice, in the warmth of the pursuit, by the British troops; and before their return they were carried clean off by Washington's cavalry.

This defeat was attributed by Gen. Greene to the misconduct of a part of the Maryland regiment. This may be true. But it is plain that his army was surprized. The American discipline, after so much experience, is far from perfect. There have been but few indeed of their commanders, who have not smarted severely under that negligence which laid them open to surprises. It must, however be acknowledged, that the facility with which Greene rallied and formed his troops under the circumstances of their surprize, and the vigorous efforts which he made to retrieve the disaster, sufficiently shewed him to be a brave and able officer in action.

The loss on the British side, however moderate in other respects was much greater than they could afford, and exceeded one-fourth of their whole number. It amounted in killed, wounded and missing, to 258. Of these, only 38 were slain; but the wounded were equally a detraction from immediate strength; and in the present circumstances a very heavy incumbrance. Only one officer fell; but twelve were wounded, and most of them were discharged upon parole. The spirit and judgment shewn by the young commander of the British forces, deserves great commendation. He was most gallantly seconded by his officers and troops.

Most of these actions would in other wars be considered but as skirmishes of little account, and scarcely worthy of a detailed narrative. But these small actions are as capable as any of displaying military conduct. The operations of war being spread over that vast continent, by the new plan that was adopted, it is by such skirmishes that the fate of America must be necessarily decided. They are therefore as important as battles in which an hundred thousand men are drawn up on each side.

Greene retired behind the farther branch of a creek about fourteen miles from Camden, where he took post in order to collect his scattered forces. Whatever credit was obtained by the British forces in this action, like most of the other victories obtained in Carolina, it produced no effect correspondent to its brilliancy. It produced rather the contrary. The first fruit of Lord Rawdon's victory over the enemy in his front, was the general revolt of the whole interior country at his back; so that the difficulties of his situation, instead of being removed or lessened by success, were increased to such degree, as seemed to render them insurmountable. He was sensible of the necessity of his retiring within the Santee; but Lee and Marion were by this time full in his way; and whilst they would have retarded his march in the front, his rear would have been exposed to Greene's pursuits; so that the measure for the present, however highly necessary, appeared impracticable; at least, without suffering the loss and disgrace, of abandoning his stores at Camden, as well as his wounded. On the other hand, Greene was now too distant for a sudden attack; nor could he at all be come at, but by a circuitous march to turn the head of the creek by which he was covered, and that would carry the troops so far out of the way, as to leave Camden open to his attack, without the possibility of their prevention. We have already seen, that Lord Rawdon's force was far too weak, to afford such a detachment as would be equal to the attack on Greene, and at the same time to retain such a strength behind as would be sufficient for the defence of Camden. In this state of difficulty, environed on all sides by enemies, he saw that he would be able to make his post good, against any force that could yet be brought to attack it; and he judged it to be far more prudent and safe to wait with patience for a reinforcement, than to risque the consequences of another line of conduct.

May 7th. At length, he was joined by Col. Watson, after a long, circuitous, exceedingly difficult, and no less dangerous march; in the course of which he had been obliged to pass the Santee twice; the first time going down almost to its mouth for that purpose, and then marching up again nearly to the confluence of the Congarees with that river, in order to repass it. All things considered, this march has been exceeded by few operations of that nature. The detachment was much reduced in point of number, and a small post called Fort Watson, situated at Wright's Bluff, where they deposited their baggage, had been taken by the enemy.

On the day of the arrival of this reinforcement, intelligence was received, that the enemy in the rear had invested, and opened batteries against the post, at Motte's house; which was situated near the junction of the Congaree with the Santee. The relief of this post, as well as the causes which before operated, all concurred in determining Lord Rawdon to make a retreat to Nelson's Ferry upon the Santee, which was sixty miles from Camden, and not a great deal lower than the post at Motte's house; a measure which, besides the relief of that place, and the cover of that great river, would throw the flat and open country, which spreads between it, the Combahee, and the sea-coast, of course including Charles Town, entirely into his hands. But before he put this design in execution, he wished to draw some present advantage from the additional strength which he now possessed; and which would be a means of facilitating his intended movements, by the security which it would afford to his rear.

On his side, Gen. Greene was not idle, nor inattentive to the game he was to play: he had quitted his former ground, and crossing the Wateree, took a new position at the back of Twenty-five-mile Creek. On the very night of the day, upon which Watson's detachment had joined Lord Rawdon, that active commander crossed the Wateree at Camden Ferry, with a view of turning Greene's flank, and attacking the rear of his army; that being the most, or only vulnerable part, the ground in his front being particularly very strong. It does no small honour to Greene's penetration, that as soon as he received intelligence of the reinforcement, (which was in a very short time after its arrival) he immediately foresaw, and considered as inevitable the consequence; and in this opinion, without waiting for farther information, suddenly abandoned his post, some hours before the British troops had passed Camden Ferry, and continued his retreat with the utmost expedition.

Lord Rawdon received this intelligence by the way, but he notwithstanding pursued him with the utmost eagerness and rapidity; and at length found him strongly posted at the back of a water called Sawney's Creek. Upon the strictest examination of his situation in that post, he, to his great disappointment and vexation, found it in every point so strong, that if success could be purchased, it must be at such an expence, as would cripple his force with respect to all future enterprize; whilst the

means of retreat were so fully possessed by the enemy, that the advantages of victory, could not in any degree compensate for the loss with which it must be attended. The creek runs far into the country, and if he attempted to get round it, the enemy, by quitting his station, could still evade all his attempts; and thus much time (which at that juncture was to him of the utmost importance) would have been unprofitably wasted. Under these considerations Lord Rawdon returned to Camden; after having in vain endeavoured to draw the enemy into action by an affectation of concealing his retreat.

9th. On the following day, he published to the troops and to the militia, the design of abandoning Camden; offering to such of the latter as chose to accompany the army, all possible assistance. The night was spent in destroying the works, and in sending off, under a strong escort, the baggage. The remainder of the troops continued at Camden, until the following day was pretty far advanced, in order to recover the march. The most valuable part of the stores were brought off, and the rest destroyed. The mill, prison, and some other buildings, were burnt; and Greene says the town was little better than a heap of ruins. The sick and wounded, who were in too bad a state to bear a removal, were of necessity left behind; and the American prisoners were left to accompany them as an exchange. The army brought off, not only the militia who had been attached to them at Camden; but the well affected, who were afraid to fall into the power of the enemy, whether in that neighbourhood or on the way, were likewise, with their families negroes, and moveable effects, taken equally under protection. Thus incumbered, the only attempt made by the enemy, was with some parties of mounted mi-

litia to harrass the rear; but one of these being circumvented into an ambuscade, their chastisement prevented all farther disturbance on the march.

On the night of the 13th the army began to pass the river at Nelson's Ferry, and by the following evening, every thing was safely landed on the other side. The first intelligence Lord Rawdon received on passing the Santee, was the unwelcome news, that the post at Motte's house, after a gallant defence, had already fallen into the hands of the enemy. This was a heavy stroke, as that place had been made a deposit for all the provisions that were intended for the supply of Camden. Things were, however, worse, than he yet knew, for the strong post at Orangeburgh was already taken, and Fort Granby not long after. Thus the British force in the province was exceedingly weakened, by the number of brave officers and soldiers who fell into the hands of the enemy, through this sudden and unexpected attack upon their detached posts in every part of the country.

Lord Rawdon was met at Nelson's by Col. Balfour, the commandant of Charles-Town; who came hither to represent to him, and to consult upon, the state and circumstances of that city, as well as of the province in general. He stated, that the revolt was universal that from the little room there had been to apprehend so serious and alarming a turn of affairs, the old works of Charles-Town had been in part levelled, to make way for new ones which were not yet constructed; that he had full conviction of the disaffection, in general, of the inhabitants; and that, under these circumstances, his garrison was inadequate to its defence, against any force of consequence that might attempt that city.

The conclusions drawn from a full consideration of this untoward state of affairs were, that if any misfortune happened to the corps under Lord Rawdon, the probable consequence would be, the total loss of the province, including the capital; but that, although the highest degree of prudence and caution were upon that account indispensably necessary, yet, as he was just joined by Major M'Arthur, with about 300 foot and[68] eighty dragoons, he conceived he might, without hazarding too much, endeavour to check the operations of the enemy on the Congaree.

A singular instance now occurred, of the general, if not universal disaffection of the country. For five days after Lord Rawdon had passed the Santee, not a single person of any sort whatever, whether with intelligence, or upon any other account, came near the army; although he had advanced directly from Nelson's Ferry, that night and the following day's march into the country, to a certain point, where the roads from Nelson's and M'Cord's Ferry meet. Nor could the emissaries and spies which he detached on all hands procure him any true intelligence, as to the situation of the enemy, or the state of the country. A number, however, of reports, which were, contradictory in other respects, seemed to concur in one point, which was, that Greene had passed the Congaree River, and was pressing down the Orangeburgh road with a strong force. This intelligence was of too great moment to be slighted; and not only obliged the British commander to relinquish his design of advancing to the Congaree, but laid him under a necessity of falling back to the Entaws, and afterwards of moving to Monk's Corner, for the protection of Charles-Town, and of the rich intervening country.

As the dereliction of the Upper Country, left the post at Ninety-Six entirely exposed to the enemy, Lord Rawdon was under great anxiety for the safety of that garrison. The objects now at stake were, however, too great to be hazarded, for the purpose of protecting that place, or even of extricating the troops; but if no such restraint had been laid upon his activity, it still would have been a question of great doubt, whether, in the present state of things, the design would have been practicable. For besides the growing force of the enemy, and their possession of the posts on all hands, there were no magazines, no deposits of provisions of any kind, for the support of the army on the way; and to trust to the uncertain gleanings of a wasted and hostile country on a march, surrounded on every side by swarms of light troops, and of militia on horseback, with an enemy much superior in number still to encounter, would have been hazardous in the extreme. Thus circumstanced, he dispatched several messengers by different routes; and to guard as much as possible against mischance, applied to Col. Balfour to send others from Charles Town, with instructions to Lieut.[69] Col. Cruger, who commanded at Ninety-Six, to abandon that place, and to remove with the garrison, as speedily as possible, to Augusta, upon the Savannah, which was the nearest post of Georgia.

So bad was the intelligence, and so difficult to be obtained, that it was not until after the arrival of the troops at Monk's Corner, that Lord Rawdon discovered, that it was not Gen. Greene, but Sumpter, who had taken possession of Orangeburgh; the former being then occupied in taking a British post at the Congarees. While the troops were employed in covering the districts from which Charles-Town drew its supplies of provision, Lord Rawdon was preparing for more active service, by unceasing efforts for the augmentation of his cavalry; an arm of force, indispensably necessary for the prosecution of a war in the southern colonies; but that country, which abounded so much in horses, had been so stripped of them by the disaffected, and by the plundering parties of the enemy, that this was now become a measure of no small difficulty.

In the mean time, the Generals Philips and Arnold, carried every thing before them in Virginia; and successively defeated all those bodies of militia which could be suddenly brought together, and were hardy enough to venture the encounter; whilst their best troops were fighting the battles of others in the Carolinas. The long navigation of James River, and of its numerous dependent rivers, branches, and creeks, laid the country open to them, on either hand, as well as to its interior and central parts, for a great extent. At Petersburgh, on its southern branch, otherwise called the Appomatox River, they destroyed four thousand hogsheads of tobacco; being the principal part of the whole annual remittance of the country for France, which had been collected at that place. The damage done by the destruction of shipping and vessels of every sort, both in the rivers and on the stocks, of ship-yards, docks, and all their dependencies, of public buildings, barracks, and warehouses, of timber, stores, flour, and every species of provisions, was prodigious, and indeed seemed almost incredible, after so long a state of war and trouble, and so much particular ravage, as that quarter had already undergone. It however, afforded a melancholy testimonial, of the former prosperity of a country, which had still so much left to lose.

The enemy's marine strength in the river, having, we presume, retired as far as the depth of water would admit, at length drew up in a state of defence, about four miles above a place called Ofborne's, on the fouth, or Appomatox Branch. Gen. Arnold fent a flag to treat with the commander about the furrender of his fleet, which the other refufed to liften to, declaring he would defend it to the laft. Arnold April 27th having ordered up fome artillery, advanced them to the bank of the river, within an hundred yards of a ftate fhip of 20 guns; his troops being not only expofed to her fire, but to that of another of 26 guns, of a ftate brigantine, of 14, befides a number of other fhips and veffels, more or lefs armed; at the fame time that a party of militia kept up a heavy fire of mufquetry from the oppofite fide of the river. The defence was by no means anfwerable, either to this formidable appearance, or to the feemingly refolute anfwer of the commander. The fire of the artillery from the fhore took place fo effectually, that it foon drove the militia from the oppofite fide, and compelled the fhips, not long after, to ftrike their colours. The want of boats, together with the height of the wind, prevented Arnold from being able to take poffeffion of the fhips, until the feamen had not only made their efcape, but had fcuttled and fet fire to feveral of the veffels. Two fhips, and ten leffer veffels, loaded with tobacco, cordage, flour, and other articles, fell, however, into his hands. Four fhips, five brigantines, and a number of fmall veffels, were burnt and funk. The whole quantity of tobacco taken or deftroyed in this fleet, exceeded 2000 hogfheads.

The troops then advanced up the Fork, until they arrived at Manchefter, which lies on the north branch, or properly the main river, and is, including the windings, at leaft 150 miles from its mouth, where it falls into the Chefapeak. There they deftroyed 1200 hogfheads of tobacco; the Marquis de la Fayette with his army, who had arrived at Richmond, on the oppofite fide, the preceding day, being fpectators of the conflagration, which they probably could not, or at leaft did not, attempt to prevent, The army, on their return, made great havock at Warwick; where, along with the fhips on the ftocks and in the river, a large range of rope walks were deftroyed; and a magazine of flour, with a number of warehoufes containing tobacco and other commodities, of tan-houfes, full of hides and bark, were, along with feveral fine mills, all confumed in one general conflagration. The army then returned to the fhipping, (which feem not to have afcended fo far as the Fork) and the whole fell down towards the mouth of the river.

The war was now parcelled out in a ftrange manner, and the Britifh force broken into fmall divifions, and placed in fuch diftant fituations, as to be little capable of concert and mutual fupport. We have feen that it raged pretty equally in South Carolina, North Carolina, and Virginia; while the force feems every where to be fufficient for deftroying confiderable tracts of country, and accumulating a great deal of fpoil, but wholly inadequate to the main purpofe; and incapable of bringing matters to any decifive conclufion. Thus numbers of brave men were continually loft without any equivalent effect; and the veteran battalions were worn down and confumed, by incredible but fruitlefs exertions of valour, and by a feries of the moft brilliant fucceffes, which produced no permanent advantage.

The fituation of Lord Cornwallis at Wilmington was exceedingly difficult and grievous. His force was by this time reduced very low; and probably did not greatly exceed a thoufand effective men. He was informed of the unfortunate turn which affairs had taken in South Carolina; and notwithftanding his reliance on the ability and gallantry of Lord Rawdon, he had too much room for apprehenfion that they would become ftill more critical. The attempt to return to his relief, through fuch vaft tracts of an exhaufted, hoftile, or defart country, would have been attended with infuperable difficulties. The Pedee was full in his way, and was impaffable in the face of an enemy; fo that, befides the impracticability of procuring fubfiftence for his troops in fuch a length of march, he would run the hazard of being hemmed in by Greene, in fuch a manner among the great rivers, that mere neceffity and diftrefs might at length compel them to the difgrace of laying down their arms.

He might indeed have waited at Wilmington, for tranfports to proceed by fea to Charles-Town. But this would have been a meafure fo little reputable, and in the end productive of fo little advantage, that nothing lefs than the moft extreme neceffity, could induce him to fubmit to it. Along with its other ill confequences, much time would be loft, and the cavalry would have been of neceffity facrificed. It would befides totally change the nature of the war; reduce it to be merely defenfive; and feem no lefs than a dereliction of its hope and fortune. All the flattering ideas of the reduction of the fouthern colonies, and even of a co-operation in Virginia, would have been no more.

Under thefe embarraffing circumftances, and environed with the moft perplexing difficulties, he formed the bold and vigorous refolution of marching to Virginia, and endeavouring a junction with General Philips. This meafure, in a fituation which afforded only a choice of difficulties and dangers, was undoubtedly the beft that could have been adopted;

but yet was a resolution of such a nature, as could have been only conceived or entertained by an enterprizing, and determined mind. It was indeed a perilous adventure. The distance was great, the means of subsistence uncertain, and the difficulties and hazards were sufficient to appall the boldest. The troops had already experienced the miseries of traversing an inhospitable and impracticable country, above 800 miles in different directions: and they were now to encounter a new march of 300 more, in much worse circumstances, and under much more unfavourable auspices, than at the outset. Notwithstanding the supplies which they had received at Wilmington, they were still so destitute of necessaries, that, in the noble commander's own words, his cavalry wanted every thing, and his infantry every thing but shoes. Neither, says he, are in any condition to move, and yet they must march to-morrow! He had already himself a sore experience, as he pathetically observed, of the miseries of marching several hundreds of miles through a country, chiefly hostile, frequently desart, which did not afford one active or useful friend, where no intelligence was to be obtained, and where no communication could be established.

The situation of affairs was, however, so urgent, as to admit of no hesitation or delay; for if Greene should return from South Carolina, the junction with Philips would be impracticable; and Lord Cornwallis was in no condition to maintain the war where he was. To guard against the worst that might happen, he dispatched instructions to Col. Balfour, to send transports and provisions to Wilmington, in order that they might be in readiness to receive the troops in case of misfortune. Having thus provided for every possible contingency, he began his march on the 25th of April, and arrived at Petersburgh, in Virginia, in something less than a month.

He there received the unwelcome news, of the loss of Major Gen. Philips; who, to the great detriment of the service, had died of a fever a little before his arrival. That gentleman had been distinguished in early life, by the full approbation which his ability in the conduct of the artillery had received from that great commander, the Prince Ferdinand of Brunswick, on different occasions [70] of the late war in Germany; a commendation which he justified in every part of his subsequent conduct, but particularly in the unequalled toils, duties, and dangers, of the northern war under General Burgoyne.

The command had devolved immediately May 13th. upon General Arnold, on Philips's death; and Sir Henry Clinton was sending General Robertson, the Governor of New York, to assume it, when he received the account of Lord Cornwallis's arrival, which rendered the measure unnecessary. He likewise dispatched a reinforcement of from 1500 to 2000 men, to the Chesapeak, in order to support the war with vigour in Virginia. In this central province, all the scattered operations of active hostility began at length to converge into a point. The plot thickened apace; and here the grand catastrophe of the American war, began at length to open to the fatigued attention of the world. The Marquis de la Fayette, with a very inferior force, kept on the north side of James's River; and with a degree of prudence and caution, which does not always suit the military vivacity of his country and time of life, acted so entirely on the defensive, and at the same time made so judicious a choice of posts, and shewed such vigour and design in his movements, as prevented any advantage being taken of his weakness.

He had been in long and anxious expectation of being joined by General Wayne, with the Pensylvania line; and hoped that junction would have been soon followed by the arrival of Gen. Greene from South Carolina.

Upon the falling down of the British forces towards the mouth of the river, with a view of collecting contributions at Williamsburg, and in the adjoining country, De la Fayette shewed no small activity in counteracting their design; and upon their sudden return up James River, and landing at Brandon, on the south side, he immediately conceived their object to be the forming of a junction with Lord Cornwallis, of whose marching through North Carolina, he had received some faint intelligence. He accordingly made a rapid movement, in order to get before them to Petersburgh, where the advantages of situation would in some considerable degree have compensated for the want of force, and would have rendered the junction troublesome, if not difficult. In this design he was foiled, through the vigilance and foresight of the British commanders; and the last act of Gen. Philips, was the taking possession of Petersburgh, four days only before his death. It does not appear that the Virginia militia displayed any great exertion at this time; and those who joined Fayette, [71] being mostly without arms, could be of little use to him who had not the means of supplying them.

During these transactions, the important post at Ninety-Six, in South Carolina, was closely invested, and held to be in the most imminent danger. It seemed ominous (but such was the hostile state of the country) that none of the messengers, which Lord Rawdon and Colonel Balfour had dispatched to Col. Cruger, with orders for abandoning that place, had been able to reach him. The fort was, however, in a better state of defence than had been expected. The works were completed and strong; and the garrison amounted to near 400 regular troops, besides militia. In these circumstances, Greene found himself obliged to sit down before it in form, on the 22d of May; the garrison made a gallant defence, and the failure of provisions afforded the principal cause of apprehension.

The fortunate arrival of three regiments from June 3d. Ireland, under the conduct of Col. Gould, afforded an opportunity [72] for the relief of this garrison which would otherwise have been desperate. For though they were destined to join Lord Cornwallis, the good disposition and promptness of the commander to concur in the immediate defence of the province, as a more urgent service than any other in view, prevented those difficulties which must otherwise have arisen. These circumstances suddenly changed the face of affairs, and enabled Lord Rawdon to undertake the relief of Ninety-Six.

Augusta had also been for some time besieged; and the whole province of Georgia was deemed to be in such imminent danger, that Lord Rawdon found himself under a necessity, even in that state of weakness which preceded the arrival of the troops from Ireland, to part with the king's American regiment, and to commit it to the hazard of passing in such small craft as were at hand, and without convoy, from Charles-Town, in order to reinforce Sir James Wright at the town of Savannah. Thus the business of the war seemed every where to multiply in proportion to the means and provision that were provided from all quarters for its support.

Lord Rawdon marched from Charles-Town, with something more than 1700 foot, and 150 horse, for the relief of Ninety-Six, in four days after the arrival of the troops from Ireland. He was joined on the way by Col. Doyle, [73] with the troops which he had left at Monk's Corner; and he pressed his march with all the rapidity which the excessive heat of the weather would permit. To prevent the enemy's detachments on the Congaree, and other parts on the eastern side, from reinforcing Greene, while he was pushing forwards, he deviated from the course which he otherwise would have taken, and keeping considerably more to the right, passed the little Saluda, near its junction with the greater river of that name. [74] This route, however, enabled a Colonel Middleton, who was on his way from the Congaree, with about 300 cavalry and mounted militia, to endeavour to harrass his rear, and particularly to obstruct the parties which were necessarily engaged in collecting cattle for the support of the army. After giving some trouble of this nature, Middleton being trained into a well laid ambush, was spiritedly charged by Major Coffin, [75] at the head of the royal cavalry, and his party was so completely routed and dispersed, as never again to appear during the march.

Lord Rawdon received intelligence on his march of the loss of Augusta; that the forces employed in the reduction of that place had joined Greene; and that the latter was determined, rather than give up his point at Ninety-Six, to stand an action. But that commander did not think himself in condition to hazard the encounter of so formidable a foe from without, while his hands were fully occupied by the exertions of an enemy within, who had from the beginning given constant proofs of their determined courage and resolution; and still much less, could his force admit of such a division, as would enable him, with any prospect of success, to encounter Lord Rawdon on his way, and at the same time to leave such a strength behind, as would be necessary for guarding the works, and overaweing the garrison. He was likewise disappointed by Sumpter, to whom he had sent instructions to join him with all the force that could be collected on the side of the Congaree, with a view, as he says, himself, of fighting the British army on its way; but whether it proceeded from some slowness in his movements, or from unavoidable delay, the junction was not effected in time, and the route taken by Lord Rawdon for the purpose, rendered it afterwards impracticable.

But exclusive of these causes, he was not now to learn, the great superiority of his enemy, in all field or general engagements. Nor in fact, was his force very considerable in respect even to number, and it was still much less so in point of estimation. His continental, or regular troops, formed but a diminutive part of the whole; and the others, whatever service they might be of in their own way, were of very little in regular action. On the other hand, he knew that the troops that were marching against him, were fresh, excellent, and that those who were newly arrived were particularly full of ardour for an opportunity to signalize themselves.

He however saw, that something must necessarily be attempted; and that even the running of some risque, which would not be too decisive in its worst consequences, could scarcely, in the present circumstances, be construed into imprudence. He had already pushed his sap very close to the principal redoubt of the fort at Ninety-Six, and had nearly completed a subterraneous passage into the ditch; but his artillery had failed in their effect, and the works of the fort had yet suffered little. The nearness of Lord Rawdon left no time for proceeding farther by regular approach ; and as he could not venture an engagement, he muft either abandon the place fhamefully without an attempt, or hazard a premature affault.

June 19th. Gen. Greene determined upon the latter. The attack was made before day ; and the Americans who were appointed to ftorm the redoubt difplayed an undaunted courage. The garrifon received them with equal gallantry. Scarcely an officer or private man who entered the ditch, but was either killed or wounded ; and yet, though the impracticability of the attempt foon became as obvious to all as its danger, no one betrayed by a fingle movement, the fmalleft indication of quitting his ground. The commander feeing fo many brave men fruitlefsly fall, and that fortune or chance, which fo often befriend bold enterprize, fhewed no difpofition at all of acting in their favour, put an end to the combat, before it became more ruinous, by calling off the remainder foon after day light.

As Greene fcarcely lefs than expected what now really happened, he had accordingly provided for the event. All the heavy baggage and incumbrances of the camp, had been previoufly difpatched acrofs the Saluda ; whither, upon this repulfe, he alfo immediately retired with his whole force. Though the Americans loft fome valuable officers, and not a few private men, in this attack, yet the number actually flain (as frequently happens in fuch cafes) was much below what might have been expected. Nothing could [76] exceed the conduct and firmnefs of the governor and garrifon, whether in the affault, or during every previous part of the fiege.

Lord Rawdon arrived at Ninety-Six on the 21ft of June ; and having received intelligence that Greene had halted in a ftrong pofition behind Rufh River, at about 16 miles diftance, and that he was likewife ftill incumbered with fome waggons and baggage, that active commander put his fatigued troops again in motion, and croffed the Saluda on the following night in his purfuit ; every kind of baggage, even the men's packs, being left behind at Ninety-Six. Greene was, however, fo well acquainted now with the character of his enemy, and fo well guarded againft furprize, that the British troops had fcarcely paffed the Saluda, when he moved with the utmoft expedition from Bufh River. Lord Rawdon purfued him with the utmoft rapidity ; and arrived at the fords of the Ennoree, forty miles from Ninety-Six, within two hours of the time that Greene's army had paffed them. The troops were fo fpent with fatigue, and overcome by the heat, that it was impoffible to do more ; but Greene was fo apprehenfive of his enemies, that he continued his retreat, or rather flight, without ceafing, until he had paffed both the Tyger and the Broad Rivers.

The British commander found it neceffary to abandon the poft of Ninety-Six ; but as he would not omit any mark of attention to the loyalifts of that country, much lefs have it imagined that they were abandoned, he ordered that the principals fhould be convened, and propofals made to them—That if they would keep together, and undertake the defence of the diftrict againft their own difaffected inhabitants, a fmall party fhould be left to keep them in countenance, with the farther encouragement, that detachments from the Congarees fhould at all times be fent to their fupport, equivalent to any force which Greene might difpatch to invade their territory : and that on the other hand, care fhould be taken to provide for the removal of fuch families as fhould prefer to be fixed upon the abandoned plantations, within the new frontier, which was now intended to be eftablifhed.—The refult was, that the loyalifts determined, for the fecurity and prefervation of their families, to bring them away under the protection of the army ; with the farther view, when they were fettled within the affigned limits, that the men fhould be embodied, in order to make incurfions into the difaffected fettlements.

As Lord Rawdon's impatience to profecute the bufinefs of the campaign, would not admit of his waiting for this determination, he left Colonel Cruger behind, with much the greater part of his force, for the purpofe of carrying it into execution ; while he marched himfelf, with 800 infantry, and fixty horfe, for the Congarees.

He had previoufly written, when on his way to Ninety-Six, to Col. Balfour, ftating the expediency of fending a ftrong corps from Charles-Town to Orangeburgh, as a provifion againft any fimilar event that might poffibly happen. Upon Balfour's application to Colonel Gould, he immediately granted a battalion of his corps for that purpofe ; and Lord Rawdon, before his departure from Ninety-Six, had, in confequence, received advice from the commandant of Charles-Town, not only of Gould's compliance, but that the 3d regiment was under orders to arrive at Orangeburgh by a fpecified day, and there to wait his inftructions ; and, as if it were to remove every poffibility of doubt, he received a fucceeding letter from Col. Stuart, who [77] commanded that regiment, with information, that he was already confiderably advanced on his way to Orangeburgh. This information, and a full confidence in the expected fupport, were the grounds upon which Lord Rawdon founded his immediate plan of operation ; and were particularly the caufe of his leaving fo great a part of his force behind, and advancing with rather an unequal corps to the Congarees In the same persuasion, he dispatched a number of messengers by different routes, to meet Colonel Stuart at Orangeburgh, and appointing their junction at the Congarees on the 3d of July.

Through some error or misapprehension, which has not been explained, Colonel Stuart was not only stopped on his march by orders from Charles-Town, but was so far recalled, that he fell back to Dorchester, on his return to that place. It may be observed, that the expectation and apprehension of a French fleet and army on the coast, in order to co-operate with Greene, and to put a final end to the war in that quarter by the reduction of Charles-Town, had a great influence on the operations of this campaign, and on the conduct and movements of the commanders on both sides; it may not therefore be unreasonable to suppose, that this apprehension, perhaps revived by some new report, occasioned the recal of Col. Stuart. But however that may be, it certainly was a measure which, under other circumstances, might have proved fatal in the event to Lord Rawdon; and which was attended with no small danger even in the present instance.

Greene had early information of the state of force in which the British commander marched from Ninety-Six; and had the fortune likewise to intercept a letter from Colonel Stuart, signifying the change that had been made in his instructions, and the consequent impossibility of meeting him at the time and place appointed. These circumstances led him to the design of surrounding Lord Rawdon so effectually that he could not extricate himself, while he continued lingering in the vain expectation of a reinforcement which was not to arrive.

Lord Rawdon by forced marches, in order to surprize a body of militia, of which he had received some intelligence, arrived at the Congarees two days before the appointed time; a rapidity of movement, which probably had no small effect upon the issue of Greene's scheme. He soon discovered that the enemy's light troops were in the neighbourhood, and took the necessary precautions on that account; but his cavalry, regardless of express orders to the contrary, went out by themselves to forage on the morning of the very day upon which Col. Stuart was expected. They were soon surrounded by Lee's legion, and two officers, with forty dragoons, and their horses, were all taken without a blow. This, which in other circumstances would not have been much thought of, was in the present a most grievous stroke; and more particularly so, as the means of procuring intelligence in this crisis of so much danger, was thereby cut off almost entirely. This loss, with the unexpected assemblage of the enemy, which had already been discovered in the neighbourhood, and the unexpected failure on Stuart's side, happily laid open at once to Lord Rawdon, all the danger of his own situation. He accordingly determined instantly to begin his march towards Orangeburgh; and to meet or find Stuart wherever he was.

His route lay across Congaree Creek, at about three miles distance; a broad piece of water, in most parts deep, and enclosed by difficult banks. Colonel Lee, who had been appointed to the guard of this passage, having destroyed the bridge, and felled trees to render the fords impracticable, had then posted himself behind the creek, with a considerable body of cavalry, and some infantry of his legion. The intense heat of the sun about noon, which

July 1st.

seemed almost to disable every sort of motion, and in every species of animal, had thrown the Americans off their guard; and the unexpected arrival of the British forces in that critical period, served much to facilitate the passage. After the exchange of only a few ineffectual shots, a body of infantry were thrown over, who having dispersed the enemy without trouble, the troops soon cleared the fords, and passed them without interruption.

Lord Rawdon was joined on the day after his arrival at Orangeburgh, by Col. Stuart, with his own regiment; but was greatly disappointed at finding that he was unaccompanied by a body of cavalry, which had been promised and which were so particularly wanted. At the same time advice was received, that Greene had passed the Congaree, and was in full march to attack the British army. That commander, having missed, what he little less than considered as a certain prey, had collected all the force which the country afforded, and seemed determined, before they were farther strengthened, to try his fortune in the field. He accordingly led his army within four miles of the British camp; and in the evening, at the head of his cavalry, closely reconnoitred their position. As their situation had but little of strength in it, excepting that the winding of the river, which lay in their rear, would in some measure remedy the total want of cavalry, by serving as a cover to their flanks, and reducing the enemy to a direct attack, Lord Rawdon flattered himself, that Greene's superiority of numbers, would in the morning have tempted him to the trial.

July 10th.

While the British forces were impatient for that wished event, their disposition and countenance had produced a directly contrary effect. For Greene had abandoned his camp, and retired with such expedition in the night, and his movement was so long and effectually covered by his numerous light troops, that he had secured his passage back across the Congaree, before Lord Rawdon had received notice of his retreat. —An unsuccessful attempt made by Sumpter, Lee, and Marion, upon the 19th regiment at Monk's Corner, along with this retreat of Greene, closed the campaign in South Carolina; the intemperateness of the climate, for a season, overcoming the violence of man. Greene being joined by Marion and the rest, took post on the high hills of Santee, to the eastward of that river. The Santee, the Congaree, and the Edisto, were the established boundaries on the British side.

It is impossible to do justice to the spirit, patience, and invincible fortitude, displayed by the commanders, officers, and soldiers, during these dreadful campaigns in the two Carolinas. They had not only to contend with men, and these by no means deficient in bravery and enterprize, but they encountered and surmounted difficulties and fatigues from the climate and country, which would appear insuperable in theory, and almost incredible in the relation. They displayed military, and, we may add, moral virtues, far above all praise. During renewed successions of forced marches, under the rage of a burning sun, and in a climate, at that season, peculiarly inimical to man, they were frequently, when sinking under the most excessive fatigue, not only destitute of every comfort, but almost of every necessary, which seems essential to his existence. During the greater part of the time, they were totally destitute of bread, and the country afforded no vegetables for a substitute. Salt at length failed; and their only resources were water, and the wild cattle which they

found in the woods. Above fifty men, in this last expedition, sunk under the vigour of their exertions, and perished through mere fatigue. We must not, however, confine the praise entirely to the British troops, as a detachment of Hessians, which had been lent upon this occasion by General de Bose, deservedly come in for their[78] proper share. The same justice requires, that the Americans should not be deprived of their share of this fatal glory. They had the same difficulties to encounter, joined to a fortune in the field generally adverse. Yet, on the whole, the campaign terminated in their favour. General Greene having recovered the far greater part of Georgia, and of the two Carolinas.

It is a melancholy consideration, that such talents, bravery, and military virtue, should have been exercised in vain. This inauspicious war, was the only one, in which they would not have produced their proper effect.

. . .

Lord Cornwallis's progress in Virginia. Passes the River James, and the South Anna. Parties detached to scour the interior country. Arms and stores destroyed. Army falls back towards the sea. Rear attacked on the march to Williamsburg. Action previous to passing the River James. Lord Cornwallis fortifies the posts of York Town, and Gloucester Point. Transactions on the side of New York. Junction of the American army under General Washington, and the French forces under the Count de Rochambeau, on the White Plains. Appearances of an attack on New York, Staten Island, and Sandy Hook. Combined army suddenly march to the Delaware, which they pass at Trenton, and continuing their course through Philadelphia, arrived at the head of Elk. Expedition, under the conduct of Gen. Arnold, to New London. Desperate defence made at Fort Griswold, which is taken by storm, with considerable loss. New London burnt. Great loss sustained by the Americans, in the destruction of naval stores and merchandize. Sir Samuel Hood arrives off the Chesapeak; and not meeting the squadron from New York, proceeds to Sandy Hook. M. de Barras sails from Rhode Island to join the Count de Grasse. Admiral Graves departs from New York. M. de Grasse arrives from the West Indies in the Chesapeak. Engagement between the British and French fleets. Lord Cornwallis's army closely blocked up on the side of the Chesapeak. The combined army are conveyed by water from Baltimore, and join the Marquis de la Fayette's forces at Williamsburg. Posts at York and Gloucester closely invested. Siege regularly formed, and trenches opened by the enemy. Resolution of a council of war at New York, to use every exertion of the fleet and army for the succour of the forces in Virginia. Unavoidable delay in refitting the fleet. Sir Henry Clinton embarks, with 7000 land forces, on board the men of war. Defences of York Town ruined, and the batteries silenced, by the superior weight of the enemy's artillery. Take two redoubts, and complete their second parallel. Successful sally. The post being no longer tenable, Lord Cornwallis attempts to pass the troops over to Gloucester Point in the night, but the design is frustrated by a sudden storm. He is obliged to enter into a capitulation with Gen. Washington. Conditions. The British fleet and army arrive off the Chesapeak, five days after the surrender.

WE are now to pursue the course of events and action, from the West Indies to the coasts of North America. Lord Cornwallis, upon taking the command in Virginia, found the enemy in no condition to oppose him with any degree of effect; and the people being at his mercy in that open country, numbers came in daily, both to his own immediate army, and to the corps which he placed under the conduct of Gen. Leslie at Portsmouth, in order to give in their paroles, and to receive protections. He first advanced from Petersburgh, on the Appomatox, to the River James, which he passed at Westover, and thence marching through Hanover county, crossed the South Anna, or Pamonky River; the Marquis de la Fayette constantly following his motions, but at a guarded distance, in every part of his progress.

From the South Anna, he dispatched the Colonels Tarleton and Simcoe, with separate detachments, to scour the interior country. As they penetrated into the inmost recesses, which had hitherto been free from spoil, they were enabled to do great mischief to the Americans. Besides destroying several thousand stand of arms which were under repair, with large quantities of gunpowder, salt, harness, and other matters, which were either designed for, or capable of being applied to military services, they were very near falling upon the Baron de Steuben, who with 800 men was posted at a place called the Point of Fork; and who with difficulty saved his rear from being cut off.

Upon the return of these detachments, Lord Cornwallis fell back with the army to Richmond, on the River James; and afterwards, moving still nearer to the sea, passed the Chickahominy, and towards the latter end of June arrived at Williamsburgh, the capital of Virginia, which lies something about mid-way between the great rivers of York and James. In the course of the march, besides articles similar to those which we have already specified, above 2000 hogsheads of tobacco, with some brass, and a great number of iron ordnance, were destroyed; and a few of the most valuable of the former, with a quantity of shot

and shells, brought off. On their approach to Williamsburgh, Simcoe's corps, which brought up the rear, were pursued, and warmly attacked by a superior force of the enemy; but after a brisk action, the assailants were repulsed; each side boasting the greater loss sustained by the other, as well as the superiority of its force.

The Marquis de la Fayette being now strongly reinforced by the arrival of General Waine, with the Pensylvania succours, and still farther by the junction of the Baron de Steuben's troops, as well as of such militia as Virginia herself was by this time able to arm and assemble, the enemy were become so powerful, as to restrain all distant operations on the British side and even to render the collective movements of the army a matter of guarded caution. Lord Cornwallis was now likewise to look to the ultimate object of the campaign, which was the establishment of a strong post and place of arms, that by embracing some good harbour, or commanding one of the great navigable rivers should equally facilitate the future operations by sea and land. We have formerly seen, that in one of the earliest expeditions to the Chesapeak, Portsmouth had been strongly recommended, and unwillingly quitted by the commanders then that on service, as a post eminently calculated for maintaining by land a kind of warfare, at once defensive on their part, and extremely distressing to the province, and the same time for affording such a station to the British fleets and cruizers, as would render them entirely masters of that great bay. A measure which, it was expected, would annihilate its foreign and domestic commerce, in a great measure cut off the communication between the surrounding provinces, and lay them open to continual descent and invasion, in their most unguarded parts. All ideas at that

time, of the utility of such a post, were indeed founded on the confidence of a constant naval superiority for its protection, as well as of its being defensible by a moderate force on the land side.

This measure of establishing a permanent post, in a good situation for naval enterprize, in Virginia, had for some time become a very favourite object with the ministers at home: and seems, from thence, to have been at length adopted by Sir Henry Clinton. It is however to be observed, that the victory at Guildford, Gen. Arnold's uninterupted progress, together with the reinforcements which had, this year, been sent from Europe to New York, had excited a full expectation at home, that the present campaign would have been decisive with respect to the subjugation of the more southern colonies. It was accordingly urged, that the war in Virginia should be prosecuted with every possible degree of exertion, as well for the purpose of securing the Carolinas, as with a view to the intrinsic value and importance of that province.

It does not seem, that the commander in chief in New York and Lord Cornwallis, entirely coincided in opinion, with respect to the mode of conducting the war in Virginia. The former, under an expectation of being himself attacked by the combined forces of America and France, wished to recall a considerable part of the troops for the security of New York, and only to leave such a number on that service, as would be necessary for the maintenance of such a post as we have mentioned. On the other hand, Lord Cornwallis, who formed his judgment on the spot, seems to have been of opinion, that nothing less than an offensive war could answer any effectual purpose in Virginia; and that a considerable army would be necessary for that end; as an insufficient force, however fuccefsful in the beginning, would, in his judgment, at length, be overborne. He likewife held, that the reduction of that province was effential, both to the fubjugation, and the retention of the Carolinas. But as his whole force, without any reduction, was utterly unequal to that purpofe, and that he likewife feems to have placed no great truft in the advantages to be derived from the eftablifhment of the propofed poft, it became evident that he felt his fituation very uneafy and difagreeable, not only with regard to the difficulties which he forefaw in the fervice, but with refpect to the weight of refponfibility to which he would be liable.

He therefore wifhed much to return to his command in South Carolina, where the illnefs of Lord Rawdon rendered his prefence highly neceffary. This, however, could not be complied with; the commander in chief probably thinking it too hazardous to quit New York himfelf in the prefent ftate of affairs, and perhaps judging, that the fervice in Virginia would require all the abilities of the prefent commander.

Upon a perfonal examination of Portfmouth, with a view to the intended poft, Lord Cornwallis found it totally incompetent to the purpofe; for befides the fituation being exceedingly unhealthy, and that it would require little lefs than an army for its defence, it was incapable of receiving fhips of the line, whofe protection, if neceffary, and a fecure ftation at all times, were the principal objects of the defign. Point Comfort, which had likewife been propofed, was found no lefs incapable or defective; and the pofts of York Town, on the river of the fame name, with Gloucefter Point, cn the oppofite fide, afforded the only remaining choice. Thefe, however, required the whole force which Lord Cornwallis poffeffed

to render them effective; and Sir Henry Clinton upon that information, at length relinquifhed the defign of recalling any part of the troops. The uncertainty, however, upon this point, feems to have confiderably delayed the conftruction of the works for the defence of thofe pofts.

The hot and fickly feafon, which was now for a time to reftrain all military operations on both fides, occafioned Lord Cornwallis's departure from Williamfburgh, with a view of paffing the River James, in order to examine the fituation of Portfmouth, Hampton, and thofe other places on that fide, which had been held out as capable of being converted into the intended fortified poft. The army, upon this movement, having encamped in an open field near James Town, but under the cover of their fhipping, preparatory to their paffing the river, the American commanders were now grown fo confident, that the Marquis de la Fayette immediately pufhed forward the Generals Wayne and Muhlenburgh, with the light troops [79] and van, while he followed himfelf with the remainder of the army, in order to take fome advantage of their fituation, or to interrupt their defign.

Lord Cornwallis received intelligence that the enemy were approaching about noon; and about four o'clock, they attacked his outpofts, in confiderable force, and with no fmall warmth. As he was perfuaded that they would not venture a ferious, attack, excepting under the impreffion that only a rear guard were left on that fide of the river, he accordingly ufed all means that might encourage that opinion of his weaknefs. The ftratagem feems to have taken, for about fun-fet, a body of troops, with artillery, began to form in his front; upon which he immediately ordered the army to advance in two lines upon the enemy. The

July 6th.

attack was begun with great fpirit by the firft line; and there being nothing but militia oppofed to the light infantry on the right, the action was foon over on that fide. But Col. Dundafs's bridgade on the left, confifting of the 43d, 76th, and 80th regiments, meeting the Penfylvania line, with a detachment of De la Fayette's continentals, and two fix pounders, under the conduct of General Wayne, a fhort, but very warm action enfued; in which, however, the Americans were repulfed, and obliged to abandon their cannon. The darknefs prevented any purfuit, and the Britifh army paffed the river in the night. [80]

The Americans reprefent the ardour of their troops to be fo high that it could not be reftrained by their commanders. This circumftance, while it flattered national vanity, ferved another purpofe. It alone could juftify coming to a clofe engagement with fuch a difparity of force. They likewife, to remove the impreffion of the repulfe they had received, attributed the hafty paffage of the river in the night, to the dread entertained of their united force, the reft of the army they fay, being coming up with the utmoft expedition to fupport the van, and on the next day to renew the action. De la Fayette gives great praife to the American commanders, as well as to the officers and troops in general which were engaged. [81]

The Britifh general, finding no place upon examination, on the fouth fide of the river, which could anfwer the purpofe propofed by a permanent poft, and having received Sir Henry Clinton's confent for retaining his whole force, on the grounds which we have already feen, returned with the army, in Auguft, to that peninfula which lies between the great rivers of James and York, and compofes one of the richeft and moft beautiful parts of Virginia. York

Town lies on the river of that name, on the narroweſt part of the peninſula, where it is about five miles over ; Glouceſter Point, is on the north, and oppoſite ſide; and projects ſo far into the river, that the diſtance between both is not much above a mile. They entirely command the navigation of the river, which is ſo deep at this place, as to admit ſhips of great ſize and burthen. Lord Cornwallis applied with the utmoſt diligence and induſtry to fortify theſe poſts, and to render them equally reſpectable by land, and to the water; his force amounting, in the whole, to ſomething about 7000 excellent troops

During theſe tranſactions, Waſhington was playing a game of great addreſs on the ſide of New York. The marauding parties from that city and its dependencies, had long been exceedingly diligent and ſucceſsful in intercepting the American poſts and diſpatches, by which means ſome uſeful knowledge was undoubtedly obtained, with reſpect to their internal affairs, as many of theſe letters were written by their principal commanders, by men in high office, and officers of all ranks in the army. Theſe were publiſhed with great parade and triumph in the New York and Britiſh public papers, as proofs of the poverty, weakneſs, and diſunion, which prevailed among the Americans; and if the originals did not go all the lengths that were wiſhed, it was even ſuppoſed that a little was ſometimes added, to fill up the meaſure. It will be eaſily ſuppoſed, that nothing could be more diſtreſſing to individuals, and perhaps in ſome inſtances prejudicial, than this open expoſure of their moſt confidential communications, upon ſtate and government affairs, The publication of their own private affairs and family ſecrets, would have been alone ſufficiently grievous. 82

It would ſeem, although deſtitute of any poſitive proof, that theſe mortifications ſuggeſted to General Waſhington the idea of turning the tables on the Britiſh commanders; and deriving public advantage from this ſource of public and private vexation and prejudice. He wrote letters to the ſouthern commanders and others, informing them of his total inability to extricate or relieve Virginia, by any other poſſible means, than by a direct attack. in concert with the French troops, upon New York. He held out the difficulties of this enterprize, and ſhewed his doubts of its ſucceſs ; but ſeemed to adopt it merely from the neceſſity of the meaſure, and as the laſt reſort for the preſervation of Virginia. He likewiſe ſtated, that in the late conference which he had held with the Count de Rochambeau, it was abſolutely determined upon ; and that it had ſince received a farther confirmation, from the approbation of the deſign which had been communicated by the French naval commander, who had not been preſent at the conference.

If any thing could raiſe a ſuſpicion of the integrity of theſe letters, it was their being more clear, full, and explicit, than ſeemed abſolutely neceſſary, and their containing matters of a more nice and delicate nature, than it might be ſuppoſed ſo prudent and cautious a commander, would have truſted to a conveyance which experience had already ſhewn to be extremely hazardous. Theſe letters were intercepted, as were others of the ſame nature, and which it is now evident were calculated for the ſame purpoſe, from the French commanders to the French reſident at Philadelphia. 83

It will not be ſuppoſed but that theſe letters, with the farther confirmation which they received from the ſubſequent movements and preparations made by the French and

American armies, muſt have greatly influenced the conduct of the commander in chief at New York; particularly with reſpect to his deſire of recalling a conſiderable part of the troops from Virginia ; as likewiſe in preventing his forming any ſuſpicion of the real deſigns of the enemy.

The French forces under the Count de Rochambeau, being on their way from Rhode Iſland, Gen. Waſhington, in the beginning of July, broke up his camp at New Windſor, and paſſed the North River to meet them. Their junction took place at the White Plains, on the eaſtern, or New England ſide of the river; and to carry on the deception in view, the combined armies encamped at Philipſburg, in a ſituation to overawe King's-Bridge and the adjoining poſts, and even to alarm the iſland of New York. In the remainder of that month, and during the greater part of the following, they continued to beat up, and alarm, the Britiſh outpoſts, on all ſides. A body of 5000 French and Americans took poſt near King's-Bridge in the night, where they continued for 48 hours, with every demonſtration of an intended attack.

In the mean time the two commanders, accompanied by the principal officers of both armies, and attended by the engineers, reconnoitred the iſland of New York cloſely on both ſides from the oppoſite ſhores ; and to render appearances the more ſerious, took plans of all the works under the fire of their batteries. Whilſt a report of the expected daily arrival of the Count de Graſſe was 84 ſeduouſly propagated; and to give it full confirmation, when they had received advice from that commander of the time at which he hoped to arrive at the Cheſapeak, the French troops advanced towards Sandy Hook, and the coaſts oppoſite Staten Iſland, with an apparent view of ſeconding the operations of the fleet, in forcing the one, and seizing upon the other. This deception was carried so far, as to the establishment of a battery near the mouth of the Rariton, and just within the Hook.

After these deceptions had been successfully practised, and New York with its dependencies kept in a continued state of alarm for about six weeks, Washington suddenly passed Aug. 19th. the Croton, and soon afterwards the North River; when he took such a position, as seemed still to indicate that Staten Island was the immediate object. The curtain was now, however, to be drawn up, and every thing being in readiness, the combined army marched directly across the Jersies for Trenton upon the Delaware; this movement being considered at New York only as a feint, until they had already passed that river. It does not however appear, that the force at New York was sufficient to enable Sir Henry Clinton to interrupt their march with any considerable effect; at least, without perhaps risking too much. The allied armies marched through Philadelphia on the 3d and 4th of September; where such courtesies as might be expected, were exchanged between the French commanders and the Congress. From thence they marched to the head of the river Elk, at the bottom of the Chesapeak. There they found all the transports and craft that could be collected, in readiness to facilitate their progress to Virginia; but these could be in no degree adequate to the purpose, after the continued destruction which the American commerce in that bay had so long undergone.

As some consolation for the imminent danger which threatened the British power in Virginia, and some return for the deceptions so successfully practiced by the enemy, their departure from the confines of New York was speedily followed by a successful expedition to Connecticut which was attended with no small loss and ruin to the Americans. The trading town of New London, on the River Thames, was the object of this enterprize; and its conduct, with a sufficient land and marine force, was committed to General Arnold, who was himself a native of that province.

The embarkation having passed over from the Long Island shore in the night, the troops were land-Sept. 6th. ed in two detachments, on each side of the harbour, in the morning; that on the Groten side being commanded by Lieutenant Colonel Eyre, and[85] that on the New London side by the General. Mr. Arnold met with no great trouble on this side; Fort Trumbull, and a redoubt, which were intended to cover the harbour and town, being taken without much difficulty or loss, and the place in itself being entirely defenceless.

But affairs on the other side were more serious. Fort Griswold, which the eager and encouraging zeal of the loyalists had represented as very incomplete in its works, and destitute of any thing like a garrison, was on the contrary found to be very strong, and no less well defended. The general, under the impression of the information he had received, and from the opportunity which the fort afforded to the enemy's ships of escaping up the river, had directed Colonel Eyre to attack the fort directly, and carry it by a coup de main. But upon his obtaining a good view of it in the neighbourhood of New London, he immediately perceived the deception, and that the fort was in a much more formidable state than it had been represented; upon which he dispatched an officer to countermand the orders for an attack.

The officer was too late, and the attack already commenced. The fort was indeed formidable, the defence answerable, and it required all the valour and impetuosity of the two brave regiments which were engaged, to surmount the difficulties and dangers of the encounter. The attack, notwithstanding the little time for observation or counsel, was very judiciously conducted. The work was a square, with flanks; and the troops advancing on three sides at once, succeeded in making a lodgment in the ditch; they then, under the cover of a very heavy and constant fire upon the works, effected a second lodgment upon the fraizing, which was a work of the greatest difficulty, as besides the obstinacy of the defence, the height was so considerable, that the soldiers could only ascend by mutual help from each others shoulders, and those who first ascended, had still to silence a nine pounder, which enfiladed the very spot on which they stood. The troops at length made their way good with fixed bayonets through the embrasures, notwithstanding the fierce defence made by the garrison, who now, changing their weapons, fought desperately hand to hand with long spears.

The 40th and 54th regiments, purchased the honour, great as it was, which they gained in storming this place. Colonel Eyre was wounded in the attack, and the command taken by Major Montgomery, who being killed with a spear, as he gallantly entered the works, was succeeded by Major Bromfield, who had the fortune[86] of completing the reduction of the fort. Two commissioned officers, and 46 men, were killed on the spot, besides eight missing, whose fate may scarcely be considered as doubtful; eight commissioned officers, some of whom died, with 135 non-commissioned and privates, were wounded. The loss of the garrison was proportioned to the obstinacy of their defence. Col. Ladyard, the commander, with[87] moft of his officers, and 85 private men, lay dead in the fort; of 60 who were difabled, much the greater part were mortally wounded; about 70 were made prifoners.

The taking of Fort Grifwold, did not prevent 16 of the American fhips from making their efcape up the river; about a dozen others were burnt. The lofs which the Americans fuftained in the deftruction of this place was prodigious. The quantities of naval ftores, of European manufactures, of Eaft-India, and of Weft-India commodities, are reprefented to have been fo immenfe, as almoft to exceed belief. Every thing, on the town fide of the river, was deftroyed by fire. Nothing was carried off, excepting fuch fmall articles of fpoil as afforded no trouble in the conveyance. The burning of the town, was faid to be contrary to intention and orders, and was attributed to the great quantity of gun powder lodged in the ftore houfes. The bufinefs was fo haftily conducted, that the barracks and a confiderable magazine of gun powder at Fort Grifwold, efcaped that deftruction which involved every thing on the other fide of the river. This is not accounted for, but muft undoubtedly have proceeded from a knowledge of fome movements making by the enemy in the adjoining country.

In the mean time, Sir Samuel Hood had arrived from the Weft-Indies off the Chefapeak, on the 25th of Auguft, with 14 fail of the line, fome frigates, and a fire fhip, where he expected to have met Admiral Graves with the fquadron from New York; but being difappointed, he firft difpatched a frigate with intelligence of his arrival to that commander, and afterwards followed himfelf, with the fquadron, to Sandy Hook, where he arrived on the 28th of the month. We have already feen, that through fome [88]

misfortune, Sir George Rodney's difpatches had not arrived in time at New York, to give any information of Sir Samuel Hood's deftination to the Chefapeak, which, independent of any other caufe, muft have fruftrated the defign of a junction off that bay; and we have likewife feen, that Mr Graves's fquadron had received fo much damage by bad weather in a cruize off Bofton, as rendered fome of the fhips incapable of prefent fervice.

On the very day of Sir Samuel Hood's arrival at Sandy Hook, the commanders at New York received intelligence, that M. de Barras, who fucceeded Ternay in the command at Rhode Ifland, had failed three days before with his fquadron to the fouthward. The hope of intercepting this fquadron before it could join De Graffe, would undoubtedly have been an additional fpur, if fuch had been wanted to Admiral Graves's diligence, in getting fuch fhips as were in readinefs, with the utmoft expedition over the bar. It was, however, the 31ft before this could be done, when bringing five fhips of the line, and a fifty, with him from New York, he took the command of the fleet, and proceeded to the fouthward.

All the prefent operations of the combined enemy, were the refult of a long concerted and well digefted plan; but there happened an extraordinary coincidence in their feveral movements by fea and land, which did not come within the reach of calculation. We have already feen that M. de Barras, had failed from Rhode Ifland on the 25th of Auguft; in three days after, on the 28th, De Graffe arrived with his fleet from the Weft-Indies at the Chefapeak; and within an hour after the French and American armies had reached the head of Elk, they received an exprefs from that commander, with the welcome account of his arrival and fituation. This will appear the more remarkable, if we con- [89][90]

fider the original diftance of the parties, as well from the fcene of action as from each other, and the various accidents, difficulties, and delays, to which they were all liable. M. de Barras did not, however, arrive in the Chefapeak, for near a fortnight after De Graffe; as he took a wide circuitous courfe by the Bermuda Iflands, from the apprehenfion of being intercepted by the Britifh fleet. This caution, which would have been otherwife commendable, was in the prefent inftance abfolutely neceffary; as that officer had in his care ten tranfports, which conveyed from Rhode Ifland the heavy ordnance and other materials indifpenfably neceffary for the fiege of York Town; and upon which the whole hope and fortune of the enterprize depended.

Upon the Count de Graffe's arrival in the Chefapeak, after blocking up York River, he took poffeffion of the River James, which he occupied with his armed veffels and cruizers to a confiderable diftance, as well to prevent any attempt which Lord Cornwallis might make of retreating to the Carolinas, as to cover the boats of the fleet, which were to convey the Marquis de St. Simon, with 3300 land forces from the Weft Indies, 18 leagues up the river, to form a junction with the Marquis de la Fayette. [91]

Admiral Graves received no intelligence of the French fleet, nor they of his approach, until they were difcovered betimes in the morning, lying at anchor, to the number of 24 fail of the line, off Lynnhaven Bay, being juft within Cape Henry, and confequently the mouth of the Chefapeak. The enemy, who were evidently thrown into fome diforder at the unexpected appearance of the Britifh fleet, immediately flipped their cables, and turning out from the anchorage ground, M. de Graffe threw out a fignal for the fhips feverally [Sept. 5th.]

to form the line as they could come up, without any regard to their particular or specified stations.

The British fleet amounted only to nineteen sail of the line, so that the enemy had a superiority, in so moderate a number, of five line of battle ships. Through the delays occasioned by the various manœuvres on both sides, the action did not commence till four o'clock; and then was entirely partial, only the van, and a part of the British center, being able to come near enough to engage with effect. It was evident that M. de Graffe did not wish a close action. He wanted to gain his point in keeping possession of the Chesapeak, and to save his ships, for that and all its correspondent purposes, as much as possible. The 'sence of 1500 of his seamen, who were then employed in conveying M. de St. Simon's troops up the River James, confirmed him in this disposition. Admiral Drake, with the rear division, which, in consequence of the last tack, was now become the van of the British fleet, treated the French van so roughly, that to avoid being entirely ruined, they were obliged to bear away, while M. de Graffe, with the center, edged up, but studiously keeping a considerable distance, in order to cover their retreat. Thus the weight of the action fell principally upon the British van, the center coming in for a more moderate share, and seven sail of the line never being able to get within a proper gun-shot distance of the enemy. From these circumstances, Admiral Drake's division could not but suffer severely

The nearness of the shores, with the danger of the great shoal called the middle ground, probably operated, along with the approaching night, at least upon the British commanders, in putting an end to the engagement about sunset. The slain on board the British

fleet amounted to 90, and the wounded to 230. The Shrewsbury and Intrepid bore more than a proportional share of this loss. Capt. Robinson of the former lost a leg, and Captain Molloy of the Intrepid gained great honour, by the gallantry with which he succoured and covered the Shrewsbury, when overborne and surrounded by the enemy.

Admiral Graves used all measures to keep up the line during the night, with a full determination of renewing the action in the morning. But he discovered that several ships of the van, and the Montague of the center, had suffered so much in their masts, that they were in no condition for renewing the action until they were secured. The Terrible was so leaky, as to keep all her pumps going, and the Ajax, which had likewise long partaken of the evils incident to the West Indian climate and navigation, was in little better condition. These circumstances, in the present state of things, were evils which could only be lamented and endured.

The hostile fleets continued for five successive days, partly repairing their damages, and partly manoeuvring, in sight of each other. The French generally maintained the wind, and consequently had it frequently in their power to engage the British fleet, which they, however, declined, notwithstanding their superiority. M. de Graffe's object, besides securing the Chesapeak, was to cover the arrival of M. de Barras, with the squadron and convoy from Rhode Island. That point being gained, (which was in fact signing the doom of Lord Cornwallis's army) the French fleet returned to the Chesapeak, where they anchored in such a manner, just within Cape Henry, and from thence to the middle ground, as entirely to block up the passage. It happened unluckily, that the two British frigates, the Rich-

mond and Iris, which had been sent to cut away the French buoys at the anchorage ground, were upon this occasion intercepted and taken. In the mean time, a fresh gale, and a head sea, had so much increased the damage and danger of the Terrible that a council of war found it necessary to evacuate and then burn her. After which it was determined to return to New York, in order to refit the ships with the utmost expedition; where the fleet accordingly arrived on the 20th of September. This action, like most other of the naval engagements which we have seen in this war, underwent its full share of criticism and censure.

We have seen that the combined French and American army had arrived at the head of the Elk, where they were too scantily supplied with shipping for their passage down the bay. The light troops of both armies were those only which could be embarked, and the compliment of this easy mode of conveyance seemed to be principally paid to the strangers, while Washington, with the bulk of both armies, pursued their march to Baltimore and Annapolis in Maryland. But the French becoming now entirely masters of the bay, the transports brought by Barras, with the frigates and light vessels of the fleet, were all dispatched to convey the army from Annapolis, which accordingly arrived at Williamsburg before the end of the month; Washington, with some of the principal commanders, having already, by travelling post, joined De la Fayette.

Thus was the brave but ill-fated army under lord Cornwallis by degrees enclosed and surrounded, being shut up by a prodigious naval force on the one side, and an army of above 8000 French, of about as many continental troops, and 5000 militia, on the others; and with no other cover than recent earthen works, haftily thrown up, to oppofe fo great a force, aided by a powerful train of heavy artillery. The French troops employed upon this fervice whether confidered with refpeЄt to officers or private men, feemed to be picked out and chofen as the flower of their armies.

In the three laft days of September, the combined armies clofely invefted Lord Cornwallis in York Town; the French extending from the river above the town to a morafs in the center, where they were met by the Americans, who occupied the oppofite fide from the river to that fpot. It was remarkable that Wafhington in his general orders ftrongly recommended to the Americans, and even charged them, to ufe and depend upon the bayonet, as their beft and moft effential weapon, in cafe they fhould be encountered on the march from Williamfburg; affuring them, that they would thereby effeЄtually cure the vanity of the Britifh troops, who attributed to themfelves fo decided a fuperiority in that fort of clofe and trying combat. Nor did he omit any means to excite that honourable emulation between the allied troops which appeared fo confpicuoufly in the fubfequent operations.

The Britifh general found it neceffary to contraЄt his pofts and defences, which having been extended for the purpofe of commanding the Peninfula, were, in the prefent circumftances, too remote and expofed to be maintained. They were of courfe feized by the enemy as they were abandoned. The poft at Gloucefter Point, on the oppofite fide of the river, which was occupied by Tarleton, with the cavalry, and fome infantry, amounting to about 600 men, was at the fame time clofely invefted by the Duke de Lauzun with his legion, and a body of Virginia militia under General Wieden; but the aЄtive [94]

operations on that fide went no farther than a warm fkirmifh on the firft day in driving in the out pofts.

The trenches were opened by both armies in the night between the 6th and 7th of OЄtober; their attacks were carried on with great vigour; and their batteries were covered with little lefs than an hundred pieces of heavy ordnance. The new loofe works would have been little capable of withftanding fuch a weight of fire, if they had even been completed; but they were fo far from that ftate, that the Britifh troops were not lefs employed in their conftruЄtion under the fire of the enemy than they were in their defence. In a few days, moft of their guns were accordingly filenced their defences in many places ruined, and the enemy's fhells reached even the fhips in the harbour, where the Charon of 44 guns with fome of the tranfports were burnt.

The Britifh fleet, on its return to New York, was joined by the Prudent man of war, with feveral frigates from the Weft Indies; and in a few days after its arrival, was farther reinforced by Rear-admiral Digby, with three fhips of the line from England; but the junction of the Rhode Ifland fquadron, had given fo decided a fuperiority to M. de Graffe, that nothing lefs than the moft defperate circumftances, or that almoft irrefiftible motive which aЄtually fubfifted, could have juftified any attempt towards another encounter.

The defire of extricating Lord Cornwallis and his army, however, prevailed over all confiderations of danger and lofs, and the Britifh naval commanders ufed all poffible expedition in refitting and equipping the fleet at New York. This, however, though unavoidably neceffary, took up more time than could have been afforded at this junЄture. The delay feemed indeed to be in fome degree compenfated, by the arrival of the [95]

Prince William and Torbay men of war from Jamaica. In the mean time a council of war compofed of all the flag and general officers, being held, it was determined that every poffible exertion fhould be ufed both by the fleet and army, to form a junЄtion with the fquadron and army in Virginia. It was however the 19th of OЄtober, before the fleet could get clear over the bar; Sir Henry Clinton with about 7000 of his beft forces, having embarked on board the fhips of war. The fleet now amounted to 25 fhips of the line, two fifties, and eight frigates; and notwithftanding the great fuperiority of force which the enemy ftill retained, the fpirit which operated both upon the common men and officers was fo high that whatever doubts might be formed with refpeЄt to the final point of fuccefs, none could be entertained, but that the expeЄted naval aЄtion would ftand foremoft, among the moft obftinate and the moft bloody, that had yet been known. It was, indeed, a defperate caft, and the fleet and army were both ftaked upon the fortune of one.

During thefe tranfaЄtions on the fide of New York, the united armies which were employed in the fiege of York-Town, fenfible of the efforts that would be made for its relief, and unwilling to ftake all their hopes on the iffue of a naval engagement, ufed the utmoft exertions in the profecution of their works, and fhewed no lefs refolution in their attacks than vivacity in the fire of their batteries. On the night of the 11th of OЄtober, they began their fecond parallel within 300 yards of the works of the place, being within juft half the diftance of the firft, and carried it on with unremitting induftry.

Nothing lefs than the certain hope and expeЄtation of relief, could have induced Lord Cornwallis to attempt the defence of a poft, which he deemed fo incapable of refifting the force oppofed to it, as that which he now occupied. He would otherwife have attempted a retreat, however difficult, or he would even have hazarded an encounter in the open field, and trufting to the gallantry of his troops, leave the reft to the decifion of fortune. Thi hope was farther confirmed by a letter from the commander in chief at New York, dated on the 24th of September, which informed him, that the relief would fail from thence about the 5th of October. Thus circumftanced, Lord Cornwallis could not think himfelf juftified in abandoning his poft; and in rifquing the confequences of thofe defperate meafures, which muft then of neceffity be adopted. On the other hand it happ ned moft unfortunately, that the delay which occurred in refitting and equipping the fleet, rendered it impoffible for Sir Henry Clinton to fulfil his intention.

Two redoubts which were advanced about 300 yards on the Britifh left had greatly incommoded the enemy, and ftill continued to impede their progrefs. It was determined to attack thefe at the fame time at dark, on the evening of the 14th To balance the honour, as well as the duty, between both nations, the attack on one was committed to the Americans, and of the other to the French. Col. Hamilton, Wafhington's aid de camp, commanded the American detachment; which marched to the affault with unloaded arms; paffed the abbatis and palifades without waiting to remove them; and attacking the works on all fides at once, carried the redoubt with the utmoft rapidity. Young Laurens gained[96] great credit upon this occafion. and perfonally took the commanding officer prifoner. The lofs was very moderate on both fides; and Hamilton, in his report to the Marquis de la Fayette, boafts (with what juftice will be decided

for themfelves, by thofe who have attended to the tranfactions of the war) that the foldiery under his command, incapable, as he expreffes himfelf, of imitating examples of barbarity and forgetting recent provocations, fpared every man that ceafed to refift.

The French were equally fuccefsful on their fide, but their lofs was more confiderable; amounting, by their own acknowledgement, to about an hundred in killed and wounded. The emulation between the two nations, appeared in their labour, as well as in action; and the two redoubts were included in the fecond parrallel by daylight.[97]

The taking of thefe two redoubts may be faid to decide the fate of the army. Lord Cornwallis in a letter which he wrote on the following day to Sir Henry Clinton, confiders their fituation as being fo defperate, that he could not recommend to the fleet and army to run any great rifque in endeavouring to fave them. Indeed nothing could be more hopelefs; for, as he fays himfelf in the fame letter, they dared not to fhew a gun to the enemy's old batteries, and they expected that their new ones would be opened on the following morning.

The British commander, however left nothing untried which could procraftinate, if it was impoffible to prevent, the final iffue, which was not more dreaded than expected Being fenfible that his works could not ftand many hours after the opening of the batteries of the fecond parallel, he did every thing that was poffible to interrupt that work, opening new embrazures for g ns, and keeping up a conftant fire with all his howitzers and fmall mortars.

The troops had been fo much weakened by ficknefs, as well as by the fire of the enemy, that the general would not venture any confiderable numbe in the making of fallies, and the enemy had fo

well fecured their flanks, and proceeded in all their operations with fo much regularity and caution, that nothing lefs than a ftron and well fupported attack could produce any effect. The prefent emergency was however, fo critical, that a little before daybreak on the morning of the 16th, he ordered a fortie of about 350 men under the conduct of Lieut. Col. Abercrombie to attack two[98] batteries which appeared to be in the greateft forwardnefs, and to fpike the guns. A detachment of guards with the 80th company of grenadiers, under the command of Lieut. Col. Leake, was appointed to one of thefe, and another of light infantry, under Major Armftrong, to the other battery. Both attacks were made with an impetuofity which could not be refifted. The redoubts that covered both batteries were forced, eleven pieces of cannon fpiked, and the French troops, who had the guard of that part of the entrenchment fuffered confiderably.[99]

Though the vigour and gallantry difplayed in this brifk and fuccefsful action, did the greateft honour to the officers and troops that were engaged, yet it produced no effential fervice. The cannon, which were haftily fpiked, were foon again rendered fit for fervice; and the induftry of the enemy was fo great, that, before dark, the whole parallel and the batteries feemed nearly completed. At the fame time, the works were fo ruined, and the batteries fo overpowered, that there was no part of the whole front attacked, in which the befieged could fhow a fingle gun; and their fhells, which were the laft fource of defence, were nearly expended.

In thefe unfortunate circumftances, Lord Cornwallis had no other choice left but to prepare for a furrender on the following day, or to endeavour to efcape with the greateft part of the troops. He determined upon attempting the latter, under the confideration, that though it fhould prove unfuccefsful in its immediate object, it might at leaft delay the enemy in the profecution of farther enterprizes. The adverfe current of fortune gave a contrary effect to a defign well calculated to delay the fate of Lord Cornwallis's army.

Boats were prepared, under other pretexts, to be in readinefs for receiving the troops at ten at night. in order to pafs them over to Gloucefter Point. The arrangements were made with the utmoft fecrecy; and the intention was, to abandon the baggage, and to leave a detachment behind, in order to capitulate for the town's people, and for the fick and wounded; Lord Cornwallis having already prepared a letter upon the fubject, which was to be delivered to General Wafhington upon his departure.

The firft embarkation, confifting of the light infantry, the guards, and a part of the 23d regiment had arrived at Gloucefter Point, and the greater part of the troops were already landed, when, at that critical moment of hope, apprehenfion, and danger, fortune proved adverfe, and the weather, which was then moderate and calm, inftantly changed to a moft violent ftorm of wind and rain. The boats, with the remaining troops were all driven down the river, and the defign of paffing was not only entirely fruftrated, but the abfence of the boats rendered it impoffible to bring back the troops from Gloucefter. Thus weakened and divided, the army, by this untoward accident, was involved in a ftate of the moft imminent danger.

To increafe the anxiety and peril of this ftate of things, the enemies batteries were opened, with great force and effect, at daybreak; and the paffage at Gloucefter point was now much expofed to their fire. The boats, however, happily returned; and the

troops were brought back without much lofs in the courfe of the forenoon.

But things were now drawing to that crifis, which could no longer be averted. The works were every where finking under the weight of the enemy's artillery; and Lord Cornwallis himfelf could not but concur in opinion, with the engineer and principal officers, that they were already affailable in many places, and that a continuance of the fame fire, only for a few hours longer, would reduce them to fuch a condition, that it would then become defperate to attempt their defence. While **they were expofed to fo heavy a fire from the enemy, they could not return a gun, and only about 100 cohorn fhells remained.** The[100] troops were not only diminifhed **by lofs and by ficknefs, but the ftrength and fpirits of thofe in the works were exhaufted and worn down by conftant watching, and unremitting fatigue. And while they were to be attacked and overborne on all fides by land, the French fhips, in the mouth of York River, feemed prepared to fecond and complete the general ftorm, by water.**

In fuch circumftances it would have been cruelty in the extreme to have facrificed fuch gallant, and in every refpect deferving troops. to a point of honour, which the improved ftate of civilization has wifely exploded, that of ftanding an affault, which could not in the nature of things but prove fuccefsful. Lord Cornwallis accordingly wrote a letter to Gen. Wafhington on the fame day, the 17th propofing a ceffation of arms for 24 hours, and that commiffioners might be appointed on both fides for fettling the terms of capitulation.

The pofts of York and Gloucefter were furrendered on the 19th of October. The troops, with the fame honours which had been granted to the garrifon of Charles-

'Town, were of neceffity obliged to become prifoners of war. They were compofed of British and German regiments, the light infantry, detachments from the guards, and Tarleton's cavalry. They amounted to between five and fix thoufand men; but fuch was the number of fick and wounded, that there were only 3,800 of all forts, capable of bearing arms, in both pofts, on the day of furrender. Fifteen hundred feamen underwent the fate of the garrifon. The officers and foldiers[101] retained their baggage and effects; but all property taken in the country, if vifible, was liable to be reclaimed. The Guadaloupe frigate of 24 guns with a number of tranfports, were furrendered to the conquerors; and about 20 tranfports had been funk or burnt during the fiege. they obtained a numerous artillery of various forts, but not of weight fufficient for their late purpofe of defence in a fiege.

Lord Cornwallis ftrove in vain to obtain better conditions; particularly that the British and German troops might be returned to their refpective countries, as prifoners on parole, on condition of not ferving against France or America until they were exchanged. Some favourable conditions which he wifhed to obtain in behalf of the inhabitants of York-Town, and other Americans, who were under the protection, as they had fhared the fortune, of the British army, were likewife refufed, upon the footing of their being civil matters, which did not come within the authority of the military commanders. To extricate thofe Americans who would have been expofed to imminent danger, he, however, made it a condition, that the Bonetta floop, which was to convey his difpatches to New York, fhould pafs without fearch or examination, he being only anfwerable that the number of perfons fhe conveyed fhould be accounted for as prisoners of war upon exchange. With a retrospective eye to the breach of conditions which the late convention army had so sorely experienced, Lord Cornwallis took care to have it stipulated, that no article of the present capitulation should be violated, under any pretence of making reprisals.

The general himself, with all civil and military officers, excepting those of the latter who were necessarily left behind for the protection and government of the soldiers, were at liberty to go upon parole, either to England or New-York; and the troops, divided as much as possible into regiments, were to be retained within the three governments of Virginia, Pensylvania, or Maryland. Lord Cornwallis observes, in his public letter, that the treatment which he and the army had received in general from the enemy since the surrender, had been perfectly good and proper; but he speaks in warm terms of the kindness and attention shewn to them by the French officers in particular; "their delicate sensibility," he says, "of our situation, their generous and pressing offers of money, both public and private, to any amount, has really gone beyond what I can possibly describe, and will, I hope, make an impression on the breast of every British officer, whenever the fortune of war should put any of them into our power."

Such actions and conduct cast abroad a pleasing shade, which serves to soften the horrors of war, and to hide and alleviate its calamities.

The land forces became prisoners to America; but the seamen, with the ships and furniture, were assigned to M. de Grasse, as a compliment to, and return for, the French naval power and assistance. It was remarkable, that the commissioner appointed by the Americans to settle the terms, and who himself drew up the articles of a capitulation, by which a British army become prisoners to his country, was Col. Laurens, son of that Mr. Laurens, late president of the Congress, who was then, and had been for a considerable time, a close prisoner in the Tower of London. The Viscount de Noailles was the commissioner appointed on the side of France, to act in conjunction with Colonel Laurens.

Such was the very hard fate of the remains of that conquering and gallant army, which had been so highly distinguished in the southern war! We shall say nothing of the share which their noble commander bore in the common misfortune, as he lives in an age which knows how to distinguish the want of success from the want of merit. Neither himself nor his army forfeited any part of their former character. Their position was in many respects a very bad one, and probably would have continued so in any state of fortification; but in its present, it was no more than an entrenched camp and subject to be enfiladed in different parts; while their new half-formed works, were much less capable of withstanding the powerful artillery of the enemy, than they would themselves of opposing their vast superiority of force in the open field. It was pitched upon in one of those unfavourable conjunctures which allow of no good expedient, and where inconveniences must be balanced rather than advantages sought. The troops made the best amends for the difficulties of their situation, by the patience with which they endured an unremitting duty and the greatest fatigues, as well as by the firmness and intrepidity with which they stood a fire of shot and shells, which has seldom been exceeded in magnitude. The French expended 16000 shot and shells in the siege, 3000 of the latter being of the first dimensions; and the fire of the Americans was not less.

The British fleet and army arrived off the Chesapeak on the 24th of October, being five days after the surrender of York-Town. They soon received the unwelcome tidings; but as they were only reports, they waited some days, until the misfortune was fully authenticated. The French fleet, satisfied with their present success, made no manner of movement; and the only object of the expedition being now lost, the British commanders necessarily returned to New York.

Such was the issue of the Virginian war. The loss of Lord Cornwallis's army was too heavy a blow to be soon or easily recovered. It was evident, that it must entirely change the nature of the war on the side of Great Britain; and that it could no longer be carried on extensively by land, at least to any considerable extent. Indeed the surrender at York-Town may be considered as the closing scene of the whole continental war in America. There are few periods in history more capable of rouzing attention and exciting reflections; whether we consider the original policy, and the discussions which ensued; its various events, and sudden changes of fortune; on one side the magnitude of the preparations, and distance of operation from the seat of power, and on the other, the difficulties, pertinacy, and final success of the resistance; or whether we consider the effect this revolution may in future operate on the political state of the whole human race, we shall in every respect find it extraordinary. Undoubtedly a new scene is opened.

. . .

It does not frequently happen, that the incidents which befal individuals, should produce any great effect upon the political conduct or situation of states, and still less upon the general state of public affairs: The capture of Mr. Laurens, late president of the Congress, on his passage from America, was however one of those singular instances, in which the political situation of no small part of Europe seemed considerably affected by the fortune of a single man. It was the occasion, if not the cause, of the precipitate rupture between Great Britain and Holland, and of that friendship and alliance which had for so many years bound together those neighbouring maritime and Protestant powers. That which had been considered as the second maritime power, and more than once boldly supported her claim to the empire of the sea, which had so long participated in the interests and glory of England, was now added to a combination, avowedly formed to reduce, if not entirely to anihilate her naval power.

Mr. Laurens being bound from Philadelphia, in a Congress packet, on an embassy to Holland, was taken in the beginning of September on the banks of Newfoundland, by the Vestal frigate, commanded by Captain Keppel. The[102] package which contained his papers had been thrown overboard, but its bulk preventing it from suddenly sinking, it was saved by the boldness and dexterity of a British seaman, and most of the papers recovered from the effects of the water.

Upon his arrival in England, he was committed as a state prisoner, and upon a charge
Oct. 6th. of high treason, to the Tower of London, under a warrant or order signed by the three secretaries of state. He is said, upon his examination before the ministers, to have claimed the privilege of his situation, in cautiously declining to answer any questions whose tendency he could not immediately perceive, so that little other information was obtained from him than an acknow-

ledgment of his name and of his late condition as president of the Congress.

But this defect was abundantly supplied by his papers. The most important, however of these, and which produced the subsequent effect, were the papers relating to an eventual treaty of amity and commerce between America and[103] Holland, which had been in agitation for more than two years past, and to which Mr. Laurens was furnished with power, to put the finishing hand. Among these was a draught of the treaty, which was, however, only to take effect, when the independence of America should be acknowledged by Great Britain, or confirmed at a peace. The negociators on the side of Holland, were M. Van Berkel, pensionary and counsellor to the city of Amsterdam, (an office of great weight and power) with other members of the regency, assisted by some great commercial houses of that city. It does not appear, that the states general were at all consulted upon, or concerned in the transaction; so that it was more properly a provisional treaty with the states of that city, or at most with the province of Holland, than with the united provinces at large. But Amsterdam depended upon her own weight and influence, including that of the province in which she bears so supreme a sway, together with the public advantages to be derived from the treaty, as fully competent to the purpose of obtaining its ratification, when the proper season arrived; and it seems that the Americans considered this security as fully sufficient.

We have formerly shewn, that the Dutch in general, even at the very commencement of the troubles, much disapproved of the harsh measures, which were then in contemplation or pursuit with respect to America. Many, if not most of these, were at that time well affected to Great Britain,

and lamented upon her own account, as well as that of the Protestant and maritime interests in general, the dangerous tendency, as they held it, of that conduct which she had now adopted; but they likewise, at the same time, felt greatly for the calamities which were falling, or likely to fall upon the British Americans; and could not but deeply sympathize with a people, whose situation bore so near a resemblance to what once had been their own. It was much more upon these principles, than upon any that were inimical to Great Britain, that the Scotch regiments were refused in[104] the beginning of the contest.

But these feelings being continually irritated by the aggravations of the war, what at first seemed to be only a friendly concern or blame for doing-wrong, by degrees degenerated into a settled dislike; and those under its influence, continually fell in with and strengthened the French party, who were acting upon principles directly opposite to those which had originally operated with themselves. Other causes concurred in the same effect. A harsh remonstrance from the court of London, which was represented as holding a domineering and arbitrary language, unfitting to be offered to sovereign and independent states, instead of intimidation, excited nothing but resentment. Some jealousy of the views of the stadholder, fomented by the French faction, had for some time been gaining great ground; and it being supposed that he would be supported in these by the court of London, that circumstance served not a little to loosen the bonds of union between both nations.

The recent circumstances of examining and bringing in the Dutch convoy under Count Byland, in[105] the begining of the year, and the royal proclamation issued in London on the 17th of April, in consequence of the failure of the states general, in not furnishing the succours stipulated by treaty to Great Britain, are fresh in every memory, and were stated in our last volume.

Thus circumstances of irritation and jealousy, were continually accumulating on both sides, until the present event brought things to their ultimate point of decision. Sir Joseph Yorke immediately pressed the business in strong memorials to the states general, and after stating the clandestine correspondence which, it now appeared from Mr. Laurens's papers, the states of Amsterdam had long carried on with the American rebels, and the instructions and powers, which they had given, for entering into a treaty with those rebels, although they were the natural subjects of a sovereign to whom the republic was joined by the strictest ties of friendship, he then demanded, in the name of the king his master, not only a formal disavowal of so irregular a conduct, but also insisted on speedy satisfaction, adequate to the offences, and the punishment of the Pensionary Van Berkel and his accomplices, as disturbers of the public peace, and violaters of the rights of nations.

An immediate answer not being given, the British ambassador continued to press the matter closely several conferences, and at length in a second memorial. The states general then informed Sir Joseph Yorke, by a message, that his memorial had been taken *ad referendum* by the deputies of the respective provinces, according to the received order and constitution of government; and that they would endeavour to frame an answer to it, as soon as the nature of their government would admit. This not being at all deemed satisfactory by the court of London, Sir Joseph Yorke received orders to withdraw from the Hague; and that step was followed, before the close of the year, by

Dec. 20th. a declaration of hostilities against Holland.

The new speaker was exceedingly well received, upon his introduction to the throne, at the

Nov. 1. head of the house, on the following day. The speech to both houses, which immediately succeeded the ceremonial of receiving the speaker, seemed to hold out a motive, without its being directly assigned, for the late dissolution, by declaring more than ordinary satisfaction in meeting parliament, at a time, when the late elections afforded an opportunity of receiving the most certain information of the disposition and wishes of the people, to which his majesty was always inclined to pay the utmost attention and regard. The other objects of the speech were, to state, in a full point of view, the arduous situation of public affairs; the formidable nature, the injustice, and the dangerous views, of that vast combination of force, which was formed against us in support of the American rebellion. The whole force and faculties of the French and Spanish monarchies were drawn forth, and exerted to the utmost, the undisguised object of the confederacy being to gratify a boundless ambition, by destroying the commerce, and giving a fatal blow to the power of Great Britain. It was acknowledged, that the force granted by the last parliament, along with the divine blessing on the bravery of our fleets and armies, had happily succeeded in withstanding the formidable attempts of our enemies, and in frustrating the great expectations which they had formed. The signal successes which had attended the progress of the British arms in Georgia and Carolina, were held out to view; and were said to be gained, with so much honour to the conduct and courage of the officers, and to the valour and intrepidity of the troops, as equalled their highest character in any age, and, it was trusted, would have important consequences in bring-

[106] ing the war to a happy conclusion. But though the accomplishment of that great end was most earnestly desired, they would undoubtedly agree in opinion, that they could only secure safe and honourable terms of peace by such powerful and respectable preparations, as should convince our enemies, that we would not submit to receive the law from any powers whatsoever, and that we are united in a firm resolution to decline no difficulty or hazard in the defence of our country, and for the preservation of our essential interests. The commons were informed, that his majesty saw and felt, with concern, that the various services of the war must, unavoidably, be attended with great and heavy expences; but they were desired to grant such supplies only, as their own security, and the exigency of affairs should be found to require.

The forms of the house of commons happened, upon this occasion, to prevent the speech from being considered or read until the

Nov. 6th. following Tuesday; when an address, adding the usual reassertion of all the propositions contained in the speech, and such compliments as the events of the day suggested, was moved for by Mr. De Grey, [107] and seconded by Sir Richard Sutton. An amendment was moved by Mr. Grenville, and seconded by Col. Fitzpatrick, proposing to [108] leave out the whole address, excepting the complimentary part, and to substitute in the place of the subsequent clauses these words, that, "In this arduous conjuncture we are determined to unite our efforts for the defence of this our country; and we beg leave to assure your majesty, that we will decline no difficulty or hazard in preserving the essential interests of this kingdom."

As the old question, of supporting or abandoning the American war, necessarily held a principal part in the prefent debate, we fhall only attend to the new matter introduced, or the new ground of argument taken, on either fide. It was advanced, in fupport of the addrefs, that our affairs in America were in a much better train, and much more profperous fituation, than they had been at any time fince the convention of Saratoga: that the fplendid fuccefs of Lord Cornwallis in the fouthern colonies, had enhanced the reputation of the Britifh arms, and had in the higheft degree intimidated our enemies. That Carolina was entirely reduced to the obedience of our arms, and the numerous friends of Great Britain in that country, were no longer afraid to avow their fentiments. That it was no longer a queftion of allegiance and independency between us and our colonies; but the queftion now was, whether we fhould relinquifh thofe valuable provinces to the houfe of Bourbon? No lover of his country could hefitate a moment, in oppofing to the laft fuch an acceffion of ftrength to our natural enemy; and no friend of America could wifh that we fhould refign her to the yoke of an arbitrary fovereign.

Nothing, they faid, could be a greater miftake, or more improperly held out, than the language continually ufed on the other fide, that the war was at prefent carried on for the purpofe of conquering America. The fact was directly otherwife. The war was now carried on to protect our numerous American friends from the tyranny and oppreffion of the congrefs. This was a purpofe which neither juftice, humanity, gratitude, or even a regard to our own interefts, would permit us to abandon. It would not now be infifted that America could be recovered by conqueft; but it was well to be hoped, that America was ftill to be regained by this country. The juft and liberal offers made by Great Britain to America, had

produced very great and general effects upon the minds of the people; and it was not to be doubted that more than half the Americans, when freed from their oppreffors, would appear to have been friends to the Britifh government. This then was no feafon for the language of defpondency; our late fignal fuccefles, operating upon this difpofition of the people, muft produce the happieft effects; and, that as we have now feen and corrected our own errors, fo the prevalence of reafon over paffion will operate equally with the Americans, and prevent their being far behind us; efpecially as occafion muft continually be given, for contrafting the happinefs which they enjoyed under our mild government with the tyranny of their prefent rulers, and of feeling more and more their odious and difgraceful dependence on France.

They then contended, that our fituation precluded every profpect of honourable peace, but through the medium of victory; that the profecution of the war with the utmoft energy, until it might be terminated on better and more honourable grounds than at prefent, was effential to the political exiftence of Great Britain; and, in a word, that we muft humble France through the fides of America. That if we even fubmitted to the humiliating and difgraceful meafure of acknowledging the independency of America, ftill, that fatal conceffion which would expofe us to the probable lofs of all our tranfmarine poffeffions and fink the political confequence of this kingdom to nothing in the fcale of Europe, would not accelerate the work of peace, however fervently that happy event was to be defired. America was a new ftate; fhe muft maintain or eftablifh her public character; and fhe was bound by every tie of policy, as well as honour, not to defert her allies, or to leave them ex-

pofed to our collected efforts, in a war undertaken for her advantage. But if it were otherwife, fhe was now too clofely connected with, and too much dependent on France, to have it in her power to enter into a feparate treaty with Great Britain.

Our fituation was undoubtedly difficult and perilous; but, if our native courage did not do it, we might learn from the example of other wife and powerful nations, never to defpond in any circumftances; but to expect the happy effects of fortitude even in the moft adverfe fituations. Nor, in truth, was the heterogeneous confederacy formed againft us, although undoubtedly in a very high degree powerful, by any means fo tremendous and alarming as was reprefented and imagined. Befides the principles of difunion, and many others faults common to all confederacies, this was compofed of powers, which, in the nature of things, were the moft unlikely, if not utterly incapable, of coalefcing, for any continuance, with cordiality, that ever were, or that poffibly could be brought together. The Spaniards had the ftrongeft natural averfion, cherifhed by the accumulated prejudices of all ages, both to the people and country of France. And could it be fuppofed or believed, that the Proteftant republicans of North America, who were more zealoufly attached to their religious and political principles than perhaps any other civilized people, and who were fighting againft their parent country and their own blood for *liberty*, fhould enter into a cordial friendfhip and lafting bands of union with a Roman Catholic and defpotic power, which having enflaved its own people, would not afford the word *liberty* a place in its dictionaries. We fhould then ftrike at the whole confederacy, and not at this part or that feparately, until the vigour of our efforts, operating upon its own principles of diffolution, had fhaken the whole fabric to pieces.

On the other fide it was obferved, that there was every year a new reafon for continuing the American war; firft, it was neceffary to fend troops to deliver the men of property and confequence on that continent from the tyranny of the mob; afterwards to deliver the lower ranks from the oppreffion of the upper, and particularly of the congrefs; and now we are called upon to deliver both from the thraldom in which they were held by France. Such were the vain and empty delufions by which, year after year, the nation had been led through all the calamity, lofs, danger, and difgrace, of this ruinous war. The infatuation of the minifters was now evidently as ftrong, for its continuance, as it had been in the beginning; and they feemed to think the parliament and nation to be as blind and as infatuated as they were themfelves. The laft parliament had, like other the moft abandoned finners, in its dying agonies, confeffed the caufe of its corruption and profligacy; this day would afford a demonftration, when the fatal and corrupt influence then acknowledged, had extended to the prefent. Whatever effect minifterial arts had heretofore produced on the opinions and difpofition of the people, the general cry now was, " Peace with America, and " war, vigorous war, with our " natural enemies;" it remained to be feen, whether the minifters had influence enough in that houfe, to enable them ftill to carry on the American war, to the entire ruin, and contrary to the exprefs fenfe of the nation.

But we are told that our American affairs are now in a much more flourifhng and profperous condition than they have been at any time fince the affair at Saratoga; and that the fplendid victory obtained at Camden, is to decide the fate of that continent. This, faid they has been the conftant language, at every gleam of fuccefs, ever fince the commencement of the war. It is indeed true, that our fucceffes in that time have been fplendid and numerous, and that our officers and troops have upon various occafions obtained great honour; but how far have we, upon the whole, been gainers by thefe advantages? Bofton, was, in the beginning, exchanged for New York. The reduction of that capital, the victory at Long Ifland, that at the Brandy Wine, and the taking of Philadelphia, (the feat of congrefs, and the capital of America) were all, in their refpective day, objects of the greateft triumph, and each held out as leading to fucceffes ftill more fplendid, which muft neceffarily decide the fate of that continent. There will not be the face of a rebel feen in all North America, was the conftant language of thofe times. It would be unneceffary to particularize the real confequences of thefe fucceffes; or to make any comment upon the abandoning of Philadelphia, or the danger which attended the retreat. Another fource of confidence is offered to us in the exchange of Rhode Ifland, the very beft winter harbour in all North America, for CharlesTown, the capital of South Carolina. Let thofe expert in fuch calculations determine on which fide the balance lies. But the glorious victory at Camden is now to make up for every thing, and to revive all our former moft fanguine hopes and illufions. But if we found our judgment on analogy or experience, are we not rather to confider it as the forerunner of fome fatal difafter? What could be more fplendid or flattering than the fuccefs at Ticonderago? Yet that was followed by the lofs of the whole army. Have we lefs reafon now, than we had at that time, to expect fuch a reverfe of fortune as then happened? The [110] confequence of our fuccefs at Charles-Town, was the laying Lord Cornwallis under a neceffity of putting all to the hazard, by encountering a great fuperiority of force at Camden. The merit and honour of that action lie entirely with the general and his army; but what are we to fay to, or to expect from thofe conductors of the war, who laid him under that dangerous neceffity, which renders his victory a miracle? Or if fuch confequences are the natural and inevitable refult of our fucceffes on that continent, with what hope, or to what end, is the war continued?

They obferved farther, that a calamitous circumftance attending that action afforded a direct proof, that the majority of the Americans (as had been fo frequently and confidently afferted by the minifters) were not friendly to this country; but, on the contrary, that they were almoft univerfally attached to the caufe of congrefs. For no fooner had General Gates appeared among the Carolinians, than thofe very men flocked to his ftandard, who had taken the oaths to our government carrying with them the arms that were put into their hands by our general; a circumftance which reduced him to the unhappy neceffity of putting fuch of them as were taken to death. But the very fame neceffity which obliged the general, contrary to his difpofition, to recur to acts of terror, excluded any reliance in the affection of that people againft whom they were neceffary.

It was acknowledged, that great advantages might be derived from the late fuccefs obtained by the good conduct and gallantry of Lord Cornwallis and his army. It might be made the foundation of an honourable and happy peace. Let minifters, faid the oppofition, feize and improve the advantage, and they will deserve and receive the thanks and applause of their country. But have they given us the smallest hopes of such a disposition? On the contrary, said they, does not the speech itself, and does not the proposed address, which is its echo, prove to the conviction of this house, that they are determined to pursue the war to the utmost? They dare not give it up. They must at all events carry it on. And its unpopularity, and that only, is the tenure by which they hold their places. To that object therefore were all others sacrificed. It was upon that account that raw new-raised regiments, under inexperienced officers, were sent to perish, not in detail, but by whole columns, on the West India service, whilst the veterans, who were proof to all climates and seasons, were kept in America.

It would seem to have been rather pleasantly than seriously said, on the other side, that Great Britain standing singly, and without an ally, in the war, had great advantages over the powerful confederacy which was formed against her. If the doctrine had been true, this nation must undoubtedly at present be the most flourishing in the universe, for she is probably the only one in that predicament. It seems, however, to have been seriously advanced, by the subsequent allusions to the league of Cambray, and to the confederacy against Lewis XIV.[111] neither of which can in any degree apply in the present instance. It was common danger, distress, and a participation of interests, that chiefly endeared nations, as well as individuals, to one another; and this tie, for the present, united the French and Americans in the closest friendship. But if we held out to America a separate interest, and that accompanied with such security, as should remove all ideas of a common danger, it was consistent with experience, and the usual course of things, to expect that we might dissolve the friendship, and have an opportunity of successfully treating with her. Indeed, without ascribing to the Americans any unusual degree either of gratitude or perfidy, and considering them merely as men; whose conduct, like that of all others, would naturally be governed by a mixture of both reason and passion, it was fairly to be presumed, that by such a course, and by abstaining from offensive hostilities against them, they might still be detached from the cause of the house of Bourbon.

What would be the consequence, they asked, of withdrawing the troops from America? American independence undoubtedly. Would this be a means of obtaining peace? —it cannot be denied. Could the troops subdue America, if they stayed there? —it is not even hoped. Can the American war be given up without her being independent?—— certainly not. Can peace be obtained upon any other terms than American independence?—the ministers know it cannot. If these things are so, (and they cannot be controverted) the ministers are wasting the blood and treasure of this country without an object.

They totally denied, that our affairs in America were now in a better situation than they had been at any time since the convention of Saratoga; and insisted that we were now, in all respects, in infinitely worse circumstances: but without wasting time, they said, in considering the comparative value of posts, or the relative strength of armies, are we not more than forty millions worse, through the mere expences of the war, than we were at that period? and has not the failure of our commerce, and the exhausture of our resources, been in a still greater proportion?

Every military man, they said, had known, from the time of the affair of Trenton, that all attempts to subdue America were so many fruitless prostitutions of blood and treasure, for that the matter was altogether impracticable. Is it then wise or prudent, said they, for this house to pledge itself precipitately by an address to the farther support and continuance of that ruinous and impracticable war? Let us on the contrary assure his majesty, and declare to all the world, that though we will not longer pursue a measure of folly and ruin, we shall afford every possible support to his arms, when directed against their proper object, the house of Bourbon. Let that house deservedly feel every exertion of our force, and every effect of our resentment. So far the amendment went, and no farther ought they to bind themselves.

Some miscellaneous matter was drawn in, particularly by Mr. Fox and Col. Fitzpatrick, who animadverted greatly on several circumstances relative to the late dissolution, as well as to the general election. The former observed, that the speech began with assuring them that his majesty wished to know the sense of his people, and the same paragraph contained the greatest mockery and insult upon the people, by telling them that he hoped to receive the information he wished for, through the medium of the late elections. Were those elections, said he, free? Was the dissolution previously announced, or the time of it properly chosen? He hoped to God these circumstances would become the object of an enquiry in that house, and that it might be known which of the king's servants, it was, who had dared to advise his majesty to dissolve his parliament, at that particular time that the dissolution took place; at a time when most gentlemen were taken by surprize. Indeed, for himself, he knew the minifters too well, to be furprized if it had taken place in the midft of the harveft, or at whatever moment was the moft prejudicial to the people, or the moft unfavourable to the freedom of election. As it was, it took place when the majority of that houfe, efpecially of thofe who had uniformly oppofed and reprobated the mad and deftructive meafures of minifters, were in camp, and at confiderable diftance from the places they reprefented; fo that the minifters, inftead of confulting the wifhes of the people, and inftead of rendering the event as little injurious as poffible to the internal peace and quiet of the kingdom, had taken pains to render the diffolution of parliament as great and calamitous an evil as could have happened.

He particularly condemned the miniftry for the unconftitutional ufe, they had made of the army. The military, he faid, was a force at all times inimical to liberty, and therefore it behoved every Englifhman to watch the army with a jealous eye. A few months fince, perhaps, the delicate fituation of affairs made it wifer to ac-[112]quiefce in a queftionable meafure, than to hazard the appearance of countenancing the infurrection, by calling in queftion the means ufed to fupprefs it; but now the occafion was over, conftitutional confiderations muft take their turn. He then proceeded to reprehend the minifters in the moft pointed terms, for having dared to fend orders to officers in all the towns of the kingdom, as well in thofe where there had not been the fmalleft pronenefs to tumult, as in thofe where it had entirely fubfided, and that quiet was perfectly reftored, giving them power to act at difcretion, without the authority of the civil magiftrate. Thefe orders, he faid, had not been recalled, till almoft every election was over: and he reprefented it as an alarming violence to the conftitution, and a meafure which called loudly for parliamentary enquiry.

He likewife arraigned the minifters in terms of the utmoft feverity, for the infult which, he faid, had been offered to the navy, and the prejudice done to that fervice by the late appointment of Sir Hugh Pallifer to the government of Greenwich hofpital. A fubject upon which he feemed to exhauft all his powers of cenfure.

The original addrefs was at length carried upon a divifion, by a majority of 212, to 130 who fupported the amendment.

The addrefs in the houfe of lords was moved for, on the day that the fpeech from the throne was delivered by the Earl of Weftmoreland. An amendment was[113] moved by the Marquifs of Carmarthen, which, like that in the[114] houfe of commons, went to the omiffion of the greater part of the addrefs. The debate was neither long nor interefting; and the original addrefs was carried upon a divifion, by a majority of 68 to 23. It was obferved as a fingularity upon this occafion, and was afterwards commented upon in more places than one, that the moderation and virtue of not taking advantage of the opportunity afforded by the late riots, to unite the arms of an enraged populace with thofe of the military, and apply both to the overthrow of the conftitution of this country, and the deftruction of the liberties and rights of the people, according to the example a few years fince fet by the prince in a northern kingdom, were grounds of great acknowledgment and thanks to[115] the fovereign.

• • •

An Account of the Action betwixt the Savage Sloop of War of 16 Guns, Capt. Stirling, and the Congrefs, an American Frigate of 20 Guns, Capt. Geddis; from a Letter of Capt. Stirling's to Rear-Admiral Graves.[116]

Lancafter, Sept. 23, 1781.

SIR,

IT is with the moft poignant grief I acquaint your excellency of the capture of his majefty's floop Savage, late under my command, the particulars of which I have the honour to tranfmit. Early in the morning of the 6th inft. 10 leagues eaft of Charles Town, we efpied a fhip bearing down on us, who when about four miles diftant, hauled her wind to the eaftward, fhewing, by her appearance, fhe was an American cruizer; her force could not be fo eafily diftinguifhed: I therefore gave way to the pleafing idea that fhe was a privateer, carrying 20 nine-pounders, whom I had intelligence was cruizing off here, and inftantly refolved either to bring her to action, or oblige her to quit the coaft; for which purpofe we gave chafe, but were prevented continuing it long, by her edging down, feemingly determined to engage us. Confcious of her fuperiority in failing and force, this manœuvre coincided with my wifhes. I caufed the favage to lay by, till we perceived on her nearer approach, fhe was far fuperior to what we imagined, and that it was neceffary to attempt making our efcape, without fome fortunate fhot, in the courfe of a running fight (which we faw inevitable,) admitted our taking advantages, and bringing on a more equal conflict. At half paft ten fhe began firing her bow chafers, and at eleven, being clofe on our quarter, the action commenced with mufquetry, which, after a good deal of execution, was followed by a heavy cannonade on both fides. In an hour's time I had the mortification to fee our braces and bowlings fhot away, and not a rope left to trim the fail with, notwithftanding every precaution had been taken; however, our fire was fo conftant and well directed, that the enemy did not see our situation, but kept along side of us, till accident obliged him to drop astern. The Savage was now almost a wreck; her sails, rigging, and yards, so much cut, that it was with the utmost difficulty we could alter our position time enough to avoid being raked, the enemy lying directly athwart our stern for some minutes. This was the only intermission of great guns, but musquetry and pistols still did execution, and continued till they opened again, which was not till both ships were almost on board each other, when the battle became more furious than before. Our quarter-deck and forecastle were soon now nearly cleared, scarce a man belonging to either not being killed or wounded, with three guns on our main deck rendered useless. In this situation, we fought near an hour, with only five six-pounders, the fire from each ship's guns scorching the men who opposed them, shot and other implements of war thrown by hand doing execution; when our mizen mast being shot away by the board; our mainmast tottering, with only three shrouds standing ; the ship on fire dangerously; only 40 men on duty to oppose the foe, who was attempting to board us in three places; no succour in sight, or possibility of making further resistance ; I was necessitated, at a quarter before three, P. M. to surrender to the Congress, a private ship of war, belonging to Philadelphia, who carried 215 men, and mounted 20 twelve-pounders on her main deck, and four sixes above, fourteen of which were fought on one side. She lost during the action eleven men, and had near thirty wounded, several of them mortally ; her masts, her sails, and rigging, were so much damaged, that she was obliged to return to port, which

partly answered my wishes prior to the action, as great part of the Carolina trade was daily expected on the coast, and this privateer we saw sailed remarkably fast. Three days were employed putting her in a condition to make sail, and five for the Savage, who was exceedingly shattered. Indeed it is astonishing more damage was not done, as the weather was fine, the water remarkably smooth, and the ships never thirty yards asunder.

The courage, intrepidity, and good behaviour of the officers and ship's company I had the honour to command, deserve the highest commendations, and my warmest thanks.

Lieutenant Shiels distinguished himself by his gallantry, activity, and attention ; as did Mr. Gyam the gunner. Mr. Wightman, the master, fell early in the action, by[117] which I lost the assistance of a good officer. The inferior officers behaved well in their respective stations ; and the men fought with a cool, determined valour, that will ever redound to their credit. I cannot conclude without observing, that Captain Geddis and the officers of the Congress, after fighting us bravely, treated us when prisoners with great humanity. Inclosed is a return of the killed and wounded. I have the honour to be, &c. &c.

CHARLES STERLING.

His Excellency Rear-Adm. Graves.

A list of the officers and men killed and wounded on board his majesty's sloop Savage, Sept. 6. 1781.

Killed, master and 7 seamen : wounded, captain, lieutenant, 3 midshipmen, 21 seamen : total 34.

CHARLES STERLING.

Extract of a Letter from Vice-Admiral Arbuthnot, to Mr. Stephens, dated Bedford, off Sandy Hook, July 4, 1781.

I HAD the honour to mention, in my letter of this date, my intention of reporting some particular circumstances respecting the capture of the Atalanta ; they are communicated in the inclosed paper.

The Atalanta, with a gallantry that does her captain the highest honour, maintained the action some time after the Trepassey struck, until she was a wreck, in which state she was carried to Halifax.

The behaviour of Lieutenant[118] Samuel Arden, of the Atalanta, was brilliant beyond expression : he lost his right arm in the fight, and, the instant it was drest, resumed his station on deck, where he remained until she struck, notwithstanding his weakness and loss of blood.

I doubt not, these matters will be thought entitled to their lordships consideration.

Report of Mr. Philip Windsor, late[119] *Master of his Majesty's Sloop the* Trepassey, *in Hallifax Harbour, June* 11, 1781, *viz.*

ON Sunday the 27th of May, 1781, being on a cruize with the Atalanta sloop, by order from the commanding officer at St. John's, Newfoundland, in lat. 41. long. 61. W. saw a sail at three P. M. S. E. distant 4 leagues ; we bore up, and came within one league ; finding her a large ship, supposed her a two decker, and night coming on we hauled our wind, and sailed in sight of her all night. About twelve at noon the next day, it being almost calm, and the strange ship about half a mile to leeward, she hoisted Rebel colours, and gave the Atalanta and us a broadside, we being then very nigh to each other ; we then bore up close alongside of her, the Atalanta on the starboard, and the Trepassey on the larboard quarter, and began to engage. About an hour after the action began, Captain Smith, of the Trepassey, was killed; upon which I[120] sent to Lieutenant King to acquaint him thereof, in order to his resuming the command, and engaged the enemy in the same position for two hours and a half longer, and at last struck the colours, in obedience to the orders he sent me by Mr. Samuel Pitts,[121] a midshipman of the ship: we lost five seamen killed and ten wounded in the action, which ended at half past three P. M. The Atalanta continued to engage some time, and then struck also.

The rebel frigate proved to be the Alliance.

Captain Edwards of the Atalanta,[122] and his lieutenant, and also lieutenant King of the Trepassey, are carried away as prisoners, and myself was left in charge of the two ships companies put on board of the Trepassey by Mr. Berry,[123] Captain of the Alliance, who for that purpose disabled and turned the Trepassey into a cartel brig; and have brought her in here, with directions to send the cartel to Boston, as Rebel property.

Being thus left in charge of these people, I think it my duty to acquaint you thereof, as commanding officers requesting to be disposed of in such manner as you shall direct; and being ready to answer to any court-martial for my share and proportion in the defence and loss of his majesty's said sloop.

(Signed)
PHILIP WINDSOR, Master of the Trepassey.

N. B. The Atalanta sloop had 16 guns and 125 men: the Trepassey sloop 14 guns and 80 men.

Extract of a Letter from Lord Geo. Germain, *to the Commissioners appointed to restore Peace to* America, *dated* Whitehall, *March* 7, 1781‡.

"I HAVE received your dispatches of the 2d of January, together with the letter from Sir Henry Clinton of the 21st of the same month, and have had the honour to lay them before his majesty. The proclamation of 29th December, which came inclosed with your dispatches, will, I hope, produce those good effects which you expect from it, and which, by its being so well-timed, gives every reason to hope for. It will be a great satisfaction to me to present the king with an address from any one of the revolted provinces, begging your interceffion for pardon, and its being restored to the privilege of British subjects. The narrow limits within which you have circumscribed your exceptions and the generality of assurances given by you of re-establishing the former constitutions, were, I doubt not, very judicious, necessary, and convenient: but as there are many things in the constitution of some of those colonies, and indeed in all of them, in which the people wished to see some alterations; and there being others, which it is the common interest of both countries to change, you must be very careful lest either your actions or proclamations should preclude a thorough investigation of those objects, or prevent the possibility of introducing, in their constitution, such alterations as the people may chuse to grant or solicit.

Extract of a Letter from William Knox, *Esq; Secretary to Lord* Geo. Germain, *to* James Simpson, *Esq; dated* Whitehall, *March* 7, 1781.[124]

"HOPE you will be as good as your word, and write to me as soon as you can reach New-York. When I consider, from the deplorable condition of the rebellious forces, and our great superiority, that the inhabitants of the revolted provinces will probably solicit for a negociation, and perhaps such a request may come from Congress itself, I wish you to be present; for knowing your perfect acquaintance with the dispositions of the inhabitants to republican principles, and their utter aversion to monarchy, it may be in your power to prevent the commissioners making any concession that may tend to keep up those principles amongst the inhabitants, and to see that no alteration be made in their constitutions, as it is intended to establish amongst them distinctions of rank, and new model their government, by that of Great Britain. This method would certainly be more advantageous to the people, as it would bind them more firmly to this country, and be the means of preventing calamities similar to those they now experience."

Copy of a Letter written by Mr. Meyrick *to General* Arnold.[125]

"THE following copy of a letter, written by Mr. Meyrick, one of the army agents in London, to General Arnold, was found in the packet, which was intercepted in its passage to New-York:—

Parliament-street, 30th *Jan.* 1781.
"SIR,
"I have received the honour of your different letters, inclosing bills of exchange upon

---

‡ This letter, and the one following, were taken by the French in the packet for North America, and were afterwards published in the Amsterdam Gazette.

Harley and Drummond, (bankers to the court) to the amount of 5000l. sterling, of the receipt of which I regularly gave you notice. On the day they were paid, I placed the sum in the funds in compliance with your intimation; and as the time was extremely favourable, I flatter myself with the pleasure of meeting your approbation, and that you will be pleased with the manner in which I have disposed of it.

As it is probable that some orders may arrive from you, directing the disposal of your money in some different way from that in which I have employed it, I thought it best not to shut up entirely, as a long time might elapse before I received from you the necessary powers for transferring the capital, in case I had purchased the stock in your name; mean while the dividends could not have been received for your use.—The method I have adopted is commonly practised in similar cases, and I can immediately alter it in whatever manner you think proper, as soon as you will do me the honour to give me notice of your sentiments by a letter. The account is as follows:

Bought by Meff. Samuel and William Scholey, Stock Brokers, for Major-General Arnold, 7000l. sterling in the new annuities, at 72¼ per cent. in the manner following:

	£.	s.	d.
Under the name of Major-Gen. Benedict Arnold, 100l. sterling stock, at 72¼ per cent. in the new consolidated annuities, at 4 per cent. and 6,900l. sterling in the same fund, under the name of James Meyrick, Esq;	4,987	10	0
Commission to the Brokers	8	15	0
Letter of attorney for receiving the dividends	0	1	6
	£.4,996	6	6

There then remains of the 5,003l. three pounds thirteen shillings and six-pence.

Thus by this method, if I receive any instructions from you for employing your money in a different manner, I can sell out the 6,900l. and dispose of your money agreeable to your directions before this letter reaches you; and if it is your wish that it should remain in the funds, it can be placed under your name, by my transferring the 6,900l. and joining it to your 100l. The reason of my purchasing the latter sum in your name was, that you might have an account open. The letter of attorney, here enclosed, enables me also to receive the dividends for the whole 7,000l. after I have transferred, if it is your wish that I should do it. I hope that I have now explained every thing sufficiently, and I can assure you, I have acted with greater care in this transaction than if it had been for myself.

I have the honour to be,
Sir,
Your most obedient
and most humble servant,
JAMES MEYRICK."

THE following letter from [126] his Excellency Gen. Washington was intercepted with many others, and published in the New-York Gazette for April 4th, 1781.

General Washington, *on Public Service.*

To the Honourable Benjamin Harrison, *Esq; Speaker of the House of Delegates,* Richmond, Virginia.

Head Quarters, New Windsor, March 27, 1781.

DEAR SIR,

On my return from Newport, I found your favour of the 16th of February, with its inclosures, at Head Quarters. I exceedingly regret that I could not have the pleasure of seeing you, not only from personal motives, but because I could have entered upon the subject of your mission, in a much more free and full manner than is proper to be committed to paper.

I very early saw the difficulties and dangers to which the southern states would be exposed for resources of cloathing, arms, and ammunition, and recommended magazines to be established, as ample as their circumstances would admit. It is true, they are not so full of men as the northern states; but they ought for that reason to have been more assiduous in raising a permanent force, to have been always ready, because they cannot draw a head of men together, as suddenly as their exigencies may require. That policy has unhappily not been pursued either here or there, and we are now suffering from the remnant of a British army what they could not, in the beginning, accomplish with their forces at the highest. As your requisitions go to men, arms, ammunition and cloathing, I shall give you a short detail of our situation and prospects, as to the first, and of our supplies and expectations as to the three last.

Men. By the expiration of the times of service of the old troops, by the discharge of the levies engaged for the campaign only—and by the unfortunate dissolution of the Pennsylvanian line, I was left, previous to the march of the detachment under the command of the Marquis de la Fayette, with a garrison barely sufficient for the security of West Point—and two regiments in Jersey to support the communication between the Delaware and North River. The York troops I had been obliged to send up for the security of the frontiers of that state. Weak however as we were, I determined to attempt the dislodgment of Arnold in conjunction with the French fleet and army, and made the detachment to which I have alluded.

In my late tour to the eastward, I found the accounts I had received of the progress of recruiting in those states, had been much exaggerated—and I fear we shall, in the end, be obliged again to take a great proportion of their quotas in levies for the campaign, instead of soldiers for three years, or for the war. The regiments of New-York having been reduced to two, they have but few men to raise. Jersey depends upon voluntary enlistments upon a contracted bounty, and I cannot therefore promise myself much success from the mode. The Pennsylvania line you know is ordered to compose part of the southern army. General Wayne is so sanguine as to suppose he will soon be able to move on with 1000 or 1200 men, but I fancy he rather over rates the matter.

You will readily perceive, from the foregoing state, that there is little probability of adding to the force already ordered to the southward. For should the battalions from New Hampshire to New-Jersey inclusive be compleated (a thing not to be expected) we shall, after the necessary detachments for the frontiers and other purposes are made, have an army barely sufficient to keep the enemy in check in New-York. Except this is done, they will have nothing to hinder them from throwing further reinforcements to the southward; and to be obliged to follow by land every detachment of their army, which they always make by sea, will only end in a fruitless dissipation of what may now be called the northern army. You may be assured that the most powerful diversion that can be made in favour of the southern states, will be a respectable force in the neighbourhood of New-York. I have hitherto been speaking of our own resources. Should a reinforcement arrive to the French fleet and army, the face of matters may be entirely changed.

Arms. I do not find that we can, at any rate, have more than 2000 stand of arms to spare, perhaps not so many; for should the battalions which are to compose this army be compleat, or nearly so, they will take all that are in repair or repairable. The 2000 stand came in the alliance from France, and I kept them apart for an exigency.

Ammunition. Our stock of ammunition, though competent to the defensive, is, by a late estimate of the commanding officer of artillery, vastly short of an offensive operation of any consequence. Should circumstances put it in our power to attempt such an one, we must depend upon the private magazines of the states, and upon our allies.—On the contrary, should the defensive plan be determined upon, what ammunition can be spared will be undoubtedly sent to the southward.

Cloathing. Of cloathing we are in a manner exhausted. We have not enough for the few recruits which may be expected, and except that which has been so long looked for and talked of from France should arrive, the troops must next winter go naked, unless their states can supply them.

From the foregoing representation, you will perceive that the proportion of the continental army, already allotted to southern service, is as much as, from present appearances, can be spared for that purpose, and that a supply of arms, ammunition, or cloathing of any consequence must depend, in a great measure, upon future purchases or importation.

Nothing which is within the compass of my power shall be wanting to give support to the southern states; but you may readily conceive how irksome a thing it must be to me to be called upon for assistance, when I have not the means of affording it.

I am, with the greatest regard,
Dear Sir,
Your most obedient
and humble servant,
G. WASHINGTON.
Hon. Benj. Harrison, Esq.

THE following letter from Mr. Adams, ambassador from the American Congress at Amsterdam, to Thomas Cushing, Lieutenant Governor of Massachusets, was found on board the prize Brigantine Cabot, and carried into St. Christopher's.

Amsterdam, Dec. 15, 1780.

DEAR CUSHING,

I writ to you on the 2d instant by way of France, under cover, to Congress; but our friend Heartwell, who delivered me your dispatches, going out by way of St. [127]

Euftatia, may get this letter to you sooner than the other. You will have heard of the unfortunate capture of poor Laurens, with his papers, and the British ambaffador's memorial to the States General in confequence thereof. What it may produce is yet doubtful, though the general opinion here is, that it will be nothing alarming. Sir Jofeph Yorke has prefented a fecond memorial, but you may depend upon it the ftates will not be bullied into any thing. It is thought that England will not at this conjuncture widen the breach with the Republic; but, even if they fhould, it will do us no harm for them to have more enemies to contend with. A rafh ftep taken by them at this time, when all the powers of Europe are jealous of them, and favourably inclined to American independence, may prove their entire ruin. Our independence is confidered here as eftablifhed. The emprefs of Ruffia has already, in effect, taken a decided part in our favour, and other European nations are well inclined to fupport our caufe.

In this city we have many powerful friends, who, as well as all Europe, difdain the pride of the British miniftry, which is not lefs confpicuous in the memorials prefented to their High Mightineffes, than it was in the anfwer returned to the petition of Congrefs. Pride, indeed, feems to be indemial to that nation; but I think it wont be long before we fee its downfall.

I proteft I fee no ground for your gloomy apprehenfions. You talk of the difficulty of recruiting the army, the depreciation of Congrefs notes, the complaints of public creditors, and the flood of counterfeit money among you, &c. Thefe doubts and fears are really provoking, and the fource of them only in your own irrefolute breaft. Can you expect to gain your point, or accomplifh any thing great, without the common incidents of war? Compare yourfelves with other countries, and fee their exertions for things of much lefs moment. England, for example, at the beginning of this war, was a hundred and thirty millions in debt, and yet the British miniftry, meerly to gratify their pride, involved their country in an expence of twenty millions per ann. more.

This caufes a depreciation of their money, and complaints among their creditors, who have quite as much reafon as yours, moft of them having already funk forty per cent. of their capital. Shall we then, who have our all at ftake talk of burthens, and the perplexities of a paper medium.

Different nations have different modes of raifing money for the public expenditure, which is ufually done according to the genius of the people, and the form of their government. Moft of thofe in Europe have occafionally been driven to the ufe of paper money, or making public fecurities ferve the purpofes of a medium in trade; and the English have gone more extenfively into this expedient than other nations: but I believe none have ever made ufe of it with lefs inconvenience, or given their creditors lefs caufe of complaint than the ftates of America have done heretofore. But when almoft every public department among you is filled, as I am informed, with men of rapacious principles, who facrifice the common weal to their private emolument, who encourage gambling, voluptuoufnefs, and every vice, what good can be expected from the wifeft inftitutions? I wifh thefe good gentlemen, whom you mention, would exert themfelves in their feveral profeffions to ftop thofe growing enormities which are the fource of all the calamities of the country, and which fooner or later, if not ftopt, muft end in its deftruction.

Our money matters are in a good way, which I writ to you fully upon in my laft. You muft have patience till they can be accomplifhed, and in the mean time do the beft you can. Many here, who know the country, laugh at your complaints, and fay that a few duties and excifes, judicioufly laid throughout the continent, would pay the whole army expences without being felt. I advife to reftraining the confumption of foreign fuperfluities, and introducing fumptuary laws; though it may be policy, for the encouragement of foldiers, to indulge them in a livery as fplendid as may be convenient.

I am forry to fee you fo anxious for an accommodation, and wifh you had fhewn how it could be done. Are you aware of the revolutions that will unavoidably take place? New arrangements made, and the ftates new modelled, the better to ferve the purpofes of defpotifm; the captors of British property obliged to difgorge; a debt of four millions fterling to be paid the British merchants to fettle old fcores; your fifhery reftrained and put under new regulations; forfeited eftates returned to their former owners; a door opened for innumerable lawfuits for illegal payments; the property of the whole continent fet afloat; and, after all, are you fure our *great ally* would confent to it? In truth, I can fee nothing fhort of independence that can fettle it without the remedy being more fatal than the difeafe.

It is true, I believe, what you fuggeft, that Lord North fhewed a difpofition to give up the conteft, *but was diverted from it, not unlikely, by the reprefentation of the Americans in London, who, in con-*

junction with their coadjutors in America, have been thorns to us indeed on both sides the water ; but I think their career might have been stopt on your side, if the executive officers had not been too timid in a point which I so strenuously recommended at first, namely, to fine, imprison, and hang all inimical to the cause, without favour or affection. I foresaw the evil that would arise from that quarter, and wished to have timely stopt it. I would have hanged my own brother if he had took a part with our enemy in this contest.

I believe there never was an instance of such delusion as those people are under to sacrifice their country, their interest, and their best connections to side with a people who neither reward or thank them ; and I have good authority to say, that a great proportion of them have nothing to live upon but their loyalty. One would think that this alone, if it was known and believed, would be enough to prevent others from falling into the same snare. *Heartwell*, who has been some time incognito in London, will give you much useful information ; he will tell you the talk we have had about a stipend for ——, which would be money well laid out. Those who exert themselves so much in our cause ought to be rewarded, as we are most essentially served by it ; but profound secrecy must be observed.

I shall write to the governor, wherein I shall be more explicit upon some matters which I have writ to Congress upon, and which he probably will communicate, which makes it unnecessary to add any more to you at present.

I am your affectionate friend, &c.
(Copy)   JOHN ADAMS.

• • •

Navy Office, Jan. 23, 1781.

An Account of all the Men raised for his Majesty's Navy, Marines included, from the 29th of September, 1774, to the 29th of September, 1780, distinguishing each Year.

	Years.		No. raised.
From 29th September	1774	——	345
	1775	——	4734
	1776	——	21564
	1777	——	37458
	1778	——	41847
	1779	——	41832
To September —	1780	——	28210
			————
			175990

Navy Office, Jan. 23, 1781.

An Account of all the Number of the Men who have died in actual Service in his Majesty's Navy since the first Day of January, 1776, distinguishing (as far as may be) those who have been killed by the enemy ; and also of the Number of such Men as have deserted the said Service in the same Period, as far as the several Accounts can be made up, distinguishing each Year.

Years.	Died.	Killed by the enemy.	Total killed & died.	Number deserted.
1776 —	1679	105	1784	5321
1777 —	3247	40	3287	7685
1778 —	4801	254	5055	9919
1779 —	4726	551	5277	11541
1780 —	4092	293	4385	7603
Total	18545	1243	19788	42069

War Office, 23d *January,* 1781.

State of his majesty's British regular land forces, officers included, in North America and the West Indies, as they were at the end of the year 1779.

		Commission'd	Staff	Non-Commission'd	Rank and file	Total, Officers included.	Privates wanting to complete.
N. Amer.	Under Sir Henry Clinton, by monthly returns of Dec. 1. 1779 —	591	83	1402	17077	19153	3648
	Under Gen. Haldimand, by monthly returns of Dec. 1, 1779 —	114	32	230	3009	3385	831
	Under the Convention, by monthly return of August 1, 1779 —	134	26	258	1228	1646	2532
W. Indies	By monthly return of Dec. 1, 1779	276	66	712	6076	7130	4238

War Office, January 23d, 1781.

Account of the men lost and disabled in his majesty's British land forces, including two battalions of marines serving on shore, by death, captivity, desertion, wounds or sickness, in North America and the West Indies, from Nov. 1st, 1774, to the date of the last return.

		Dead	Total prisoners*	Deserted	Discharged
1774	North America, under Generals Gage and Haldimand,	30	000	47	16
	West Indies ———————	39	000	4	20
1775	N. America, under Gens. Haldimand, Gage, and Howe,	781	000	115	249
	West Indies ———————	121	000	48	148
1776	N. America, under Sir William Howe, — —	869	744	192	619
	under Sir Guy Carleton — —	200	48	68	36
	West-Indies ———————	86	000	80	38
1777	N. America. under Sir William Howe ———	1202	1274	282	490
	under Sir Guy Carleton ———	81	162	20	29
	under General Burgoyne ———	‡ 220 ‡	484	487	5
	West-Indies ———————	303	000	105	40
1778	N. America, under Sir William Howe ———	1311	641	628	1281
	under Sir Guy Carleton ———	117	146	32	87
	under the Convention of Saratoga ‡,	61 ‡	381	546	83
	West-Indies ———————	236	000	104	71
1779	N. America, under Sir Henry Clinton — —	1154	1020	263	444
	under General Haldimand — —	42	165	27	87
	under the Convention — —	8	259	176	000
	West-Indies ———————	1054	000	122	34
1780	N. America, under Sir Henry Clinton, — —		No return.		
	under General Haldimand — —	58	166	38	30
	under the Convention — —	3	256	172	000
	West-Indies ———————	2036	000	145	178

Embarka-

---

* The War Office have not the means of ascertaining the number of men lost by captivity, having no account of what the whole number of prisoners taken in any one year

War Office, January 23d, 1781.

Embarkation returns of all the British corps and recruits, which have been sent from Great Britain or Ireland, to any part of North-America or the West-Indies, in 1778, 1779, 1780.

Years	Regiments	Commiss. Officers						Staff Officers					Non commiss. Officers, dr. & fifes			Private Men	Total strength, Officers included	Total, Officers included, embarked each year
		Colonels	Lieut Colonels	Majors	Captains	1st Lieutenants	2d Lts or Ens.	Chaplains	Adjutants	Quar. masters	Surgeons	Mates	Serjants	Corporals	Drums & fifes			
1778	70th	0	1	1	6	10	6	0	1	1	1	1	29	27	22	435	591	
	74th	0	1	0	4	18	8	1	0	0	1	1	50	49	22	884	1040	
	82d 6 co.	1	0	1	4	14	2	0	1	1	1	1	29	30	14	568	667	3774
	Recruits	0	0	0	0	00	0	0	0	0	0	0	00	00	00	1476	1476	
1779	76th	0	1	1	8	20	8	0	1	1	1	2	49	50	22	898	1002	
	79th	0	0	1	6	21	7	0	1	1	1	2	48	50	22	957	1117	
	80th	0	0	2	6	19	7	0	1	1	1	2	50	50	22	863	1024	
	82d 4 co.	0	0	1	1	7	5	0	0	0	0	1	20	22	8	350	414	6871
	88th	1	1	1	7	9	6	0	1	1	1	1	30	40	21	710	831	
	89th	1	0	1	4	8	6	0	1	1	1	1	29	33	22	650	758	
	Recruits	0	0	0	0	00	0	0	1	0	0	0	00	00	00	1665	1665	
1780	1st, 1st bat	0	1	1	8	11	7	0	1	1	1	1	30	40	22	666	790	
	13th	0	1	1	6	11	8	0	1	1	1	1	30	40	22	668	791	
	69th	0	1	1	7	11	6	0	1	1	1	1	29	39	21	644	763	
	85th	0	1	2	7	10	5	0	1	1	1	1	25	35	18	586	693	
	86th	1	1	1	6	9	8	0	1	1	1	1	30	37	22	592	711	
	87th	0	1	2	6	11	6	0	1	1	1	1	26	36	22	612	726	
	90th	1	0	2	7	8	7	0	1	1	1	1	27	35	22	599	712	10237
	91st	1	1	1	5	6	7	0	1	1	0	1	26	39	22	568	679	
	92d	0	1	2	7	8	8	0	1	1	1	1	29	40	22	642	763	
	93d	1	1	1	8	7	5	0	1	1	1	1	26	34	21	480	588	
	94th	1	0	1	6	9	7	0	1	1	1	1	26	26	22	563	665	
	99th 9 co.	0	0	1	6	6	8	•	1	1	1	1	27	36	20	603	711	
	Recruits	0	0	0	0	00	0	0	0	0	0	0	00	00	00	1645	1645	
	Total	8	13	25	125	231	139	1	19	19	19	19	665	787	432	18374	20882	20882

may be, or of the prisoners that may have been exchanged in the course of it. They only know what the number of prisoners are at the time that the return is made.

§ The monthly returns not assigning the reason for which soldiers are discharged, the War Office cannot, agreeable to the directions of the order of the House of Commons, distinguish those men who are lost or disabled by wounds or sickness; the whole number discharged are therefore stated, in which those dismissed for misbehaviour, claimed as apprentices, claimed by other corps, draughted from one regiment to another, or discharged for a variety of causes, besides that of inability to serve longer, are included.

‡ ‡ ‡ ‡ The prisoners of the army under these heads, are such as were taken by the enemy previous to the Convention of Saratoga. The men comprehended in the Convention have never been allowed to be prisoners of war; their casualties by death and desertion, and the numbers discharged, are regularly given. The effectives detained in America, contrary to the Convention, are as follow :

	British privates.
By return of November 17, 1777 ——	2883
Ditto 1, 1778 ——	1838
August 1, 1779 ——	1228
Ditto 1, 1780 ——	796

War-Office, January 23d, 1781.

Account of all the men raised in Great Britain and Ireland, for his majesty's land forces on the British establishment, militia and fencible men in North Britain not included, from 29th Sept. 1774, to 29th Sept. 1780.

To 29th September 1775	——	3575
1776	——	11063
1777	——	6882
1778	——	23978
1779	——	16154
To 29th September 1780	——	15233
Total — — — — —		76885

Adjourned to Monday 29th.

• • •

To the King's most excellent Majesty.

The humble Address, Remonstrance, and Petition, of the Lord-mayor, Aldermen, and Livery, of the City of London, in Common-Hall, assembled.

May it please your Majesty,

IMPRESSED with an awful sense of the dangers which surround us, feeling for ourselves and our posterity, anxious for the glory of a country hitherto as much renowned for the virtues of justice and humanity, as for the splendour of its arms, we approach your throne with sentiments becoming citizens at so alarming an hour ; at the same time with that respect which is due to the monarch of a free people, and a prince of the illustrious house of Brunswick, to which we feel ourselves in a peculiar manner attached by all the ties of gratitude and affection.

It is with inexpressible concern that we have heard your Majesty declare in your speech, to both houses of parliament, your intention of persevering in a system of measures which has proved so disastrous to this country. Such a declaration calls for the voice of a free and injured people. We feel the respect due to majesty :

But in this critical and awful moment, to flatter is to betray. Your majesty's ministers have, by false assertions and fallacious suggestions, deluded your majesty and the nation into the present unnatural and unfortunate war. The consequences of this delusion have been, that the trade of this country has suffered irreparable losses, and is threatened with final extinction.

The manufactures in many valuable branches are declining, and their supply of materials rendered precarious, by the inferiority of your majesty's fleet to that of the enemy in almost every part of the globe.

The landed property throughout the kingdom has been depreciated to the most alarming degree.

The property of your Majesty's subjects vested in the public funds, has lost above one third of its value.

Private credit has been almost wholly annihilated by the enormous interest given in the public loans, superior to that which is allowed by law in any private contract. Such of our brethren in America as were deluded by the promises of your majesty's ministers, and the proclamations of your generals to join your majesty's standard, have been surrendered by your majesty's armies to the mercy of their victorious countrymen.

Your majesty's fleets have lost their wonted superiority,

Your armies have been captured,

Your dominions have been lost,

And your majesty's faithful subjects have been loaded with a burthen of taxes, which, even, if our victories had been as splendid as our defeats have been disgraceful, if our accession of dominion had been as fortunate as the dismemberment of the empire has been crushing and disastrous, could not in itself be considered but as a great and grievous calamity.

We do, therefore, most humbly and earnestly implore your majesty to take all these circumstances into your royal consideration, and to compare the present situation of your dominions with that uncommon state of prosperity to which the wisdom of your royal ancestors, the spirit and bravery of the British people, and the favour of Divine Providence, which attends upon principles of justice and humanity, had once raised this happy country, the pride and envy of all the civilized world !

We beseech your majesty no longer to continue in a delusion from which the nation has awakened ; and that your majesty will be graciously pleased to relinquish entirely, and for ever, the plan of reducing our brethren in America to obedience by force ; a plan which the fatal experience of past losses has convinced us cannot be prosecuted without manifest and imminent danger to all your majesty's remaining possessions in the western world.

We wish to declare to your majesty, to Europe, to America itself, our abhorrence of the continuation of this unnatural and unfortunate war, which can tend to no other purpose than that of alienating and rendering irrecoverable the confidence of our American brethren, with whom we still hope to live upon the terms of intercourse and friendship, so necessary to the commercial prosperity of this kingdom. We do, therefore, farther humbly implore your majesty, that your majesty will be graciously pleased to dismiss from your presence and councils all the advisers, both public and secret, of the measures we lament, as a pledge to the world of your majesty's fixed determination to abandon a system incompatible with the interest of your crown, and the happiness of your people.

Signed, by order,

WILLIAM RIX. [128]

Petition of Henry Laurens, *Esq; to the House of Commons.*

To the Right Hon. Charles Wolfran Cornwall, *Speaker, and the Hon. the House of Commons.*

THE representation and prayer of Henry Laurens, a native of South Carolina, some time recognized by the British Commissioners in America by the style of his Excellency Henry Laurens, President of Congress, now a close prisoner in the Tower of London ;

Most respectfully sheweth, That your representer for many years, at the peril of his life and fortune, evidently laboured to preserve and strengthen the ancient friendship between Great Britain and the colonies, and that in no instance he ever excited on either side the dissensions which separated them.

That the commencement of the present war was a subject of great grief to him, inasmuch as he foresaw and foretold, in letters now extant, the distresses which both countries experience at this day.

That in the rise and progress of the war, he extended every act of kindness in his power to persons called Loyalists and Quietists, as well as to British prisoners of war, very ample proofs of which he can produce.

That he was captured on the American coast, first landed upon American ground, where he saw exchanges of British and American prisoners in a course of negociation ; and that such exchanges and enlargements upon parole are mutually and daily practised in America.

That he was committed to the Tower on the 6th of October, 1780, being then dangerously ill, that in the mean time he has, in many respects, particularly by being deprived (with very little exception) of the visits and consultations of his children and other relations and friends, suffered under a degree of rigour almost, if not altogether, unexampled in modern British history.

That from long confinement, and the want of proper exercise, and other obvious causes, his bodily health is greatly impaired, and that he is now in a languishing state : And,

Therefore you representer humbly prays your Honours will condescend to take his case into consideration ; and, under proper conditions and restrictions, grant him enlargement, or such other relief as to the wisdom and benignity of your Honours shall seem fitting.

HENRY LAURENS.

Tower of London,
Dec. 1, 1781.§

Notes, 1781

1. Clinton notes: "Toward the close of this year I received a letter from His Majesty's Secretary of State for American Affairs, with the King's commands to employ the zeal of his faithful refugee subjects within the British lines in annoying the seacoasts of the revolted provinces and destroying their trade." *The American Rebellion: Sir Henry Clinton's Narrative of the Campaigns, 1775–82, with an Appendix of Original Documents*, ed. W. B. Willcox (New Haven, Conn., 1954), p. 237. Germain's instructions were dated 21 April 1780, and Clinton's reply was sent on 23 January 1781. Ibid., p. 192, n. 9. The board included a number of prominent Loyalists and its President was William Franklin (1731–1813), former royal Governor of New Jersey and Benjamin Franklin's son. Clinton disliked the board from its inception and was seriously embarrassed in 1782 by its connivance at the hanging of an American prisoner as an act of vengeance.

2. Hannah Caldwell, wife of James Caldwell (1734–81), pastor of the First Presbyterian Church at Elizabethtown. Caldwell actively supported the American cause after 1776, served as Chaplain and, for a period, Assistant Commissary General to New Jersey forces, and used his church as an army hospital. He moved his family for safety to Connecticut Farms after his church was burned by Tories in 1780.

3. Maxwell had already survived a court-martial for misconduct and resigned after the Springfield action.

4. Knyphausen began the Springfield raid on reports of disaffection in Washington's army and strong Loyalist sympathy in the locality. *Revolution in America: Confidential Letters and Journals, 1776–84, of Adjutant General Major Baurmeister of the Hessian Forces* (New Brunswick, N.J., 1957), p. 353. These reports were rapidly found to be untrue and in addition, ". . . the more we advanced the more it was realised that Washington was always ready to reduce further our still remaining advantage." Ibid., p. 354. Knyphausen therefore withdrew to Elizabethtown as a matter of common sense.

5. Israel Angell (1740–1832), Colonel of the 2nd Rhode Island Infantry.

6. The Continental Army lacked pay, provisions, and materiel and was dangerously under strength; the states failed to meet their quotas and were prevaricating, dilatory, or indifferent. The Congress ordered sharp letters sent "to each of the United States from New Hampshire to Maryland" on 15 June 1781, and to the states from New Hampshire to South Carolina on 17 June; required explicit weekly reports on progress in meeting requisitions from each governor after 21 June; backed this up by distributing on 23 June a letter from Washington indicating the grave state of the army; and on 24 June, issued another circular letter warning that meeting the requisitions "... is become essential not only to the operations of this campaign but to the very existence of the army." *Journals of the Continental Congress 1774–1789*, ed. W. C. Ford, 34 vols. (Washington, D.C., 1904–37), vol. 17, pp. 515–16, 525, 539–40, 551, 576–77.

7. The Congress passed the complimentary resolution on 16 May.

8. Charles Louis d'Arsac, Chevalier de Ternay (1722–80) retired from the French navy after distinguished service in the Seven Years War but rejoined in 1779 and commanded the fleet which transported Rochambeau's expeditionary force to America. He died of fever five months after reaching Newport.

9. See "Notes, 1775," n. 74. Heath was promoted to Major-General in August 1776 and served with a conspicuous lack of distinction after that date.

10. Clinton's open breach with Arbuthnot and the latter's obstructive behaviour are well revealed in *The American Rebellion*, esp. ch. 14.

11. Andrew Durnford, not further identified.

12. Luc Urbain de Bouexic, Comte de Guichen (1712–90), Rear-Admiral in 1778.

13. Sir George Bridges Rodney (1719–92), created Baronet in 1764, Baron Rodney in 1782, Admiral in 1778, Commander-in-Chief in the West Indies, 1779–82.

14. The first part of Chapter III deals with the devastation caused in the West Indies by the hurricane of 10–12 October 1780.

15. Arnold was appointed Commander of West Point on 8 August 1779.

16. André was met by Arnold's aide, Joshua Smith, who escorted him to Robinson's house, where Arnold was waiting. See "Notes, 1780," n. 43, 44.

17. André could not return to the *Vulture* because Colonel James Livingston (1747–1832), Commander of the garrisons in the area of King's Ferry, bombarded the vessel from the shore and forced her to retreat downstream.

18. See "Notes, 1780," n. 44.

19. Friedrich Wilhelm Augustus, Baron von Steuben (1730–94), served in the Prussian army until 1763 and volunteered for service in America while in Paris in 1777. In May 1778, he was appointed Inspector General of the Continental Army with the rank of Major-General; he was responsible for the training and reorganisation of the American forces from 1778 to 1780.

20. Alexander Hamilton (1757–1804), future Secretary of the Treasury in Washington's cabinet; became A.D.C. to the Commander-in-Chief in March 1777; resigned that post after an altercation in 1781.

21. Arnold's "address" was published on 11 October 1780. The text is printed in full in Isaac N. Arnold, *The Life of Benedict Arnold: His Patriotism and His Treason* (Chicago, 1880), pp. 330–32.

22. Arnold had small success in raising his legion. After twelve months, he had recruited only 212 men, nearly 700 less than required. L. Montross, *Rag, Tag and Bobtail: The Story of the Continental Army, 1775–1783* (New York, 1952), p. 390.

23. State paper currency collapsed in 1779 and continental paper in

May 1781. Wholesale prices reveal the degree of inflation. An estimated index based on Philadelphia prices, using a base of 1850–59 = 100, shows the following rise:

1775	78
1776	108
1777	329.6
1778	598.1
1779	7,969.1
1780	10,544.1

Figures from *Historical Statistics of the United States: Colonial Times to 1957* (Washington, D.C.: U.S. Bureau of the Census, 1960), ser. Z 336, p. 772. Partly through the reorganisation of Robert Morris, the Superintendant of Finances, in May 1781, and later through the easing of the strains imposed by the war, prices fell—on this table, to 5,085.8 in 1781 and to 139.6 in 1782. Currency was not truly stabilised until Hamilton's policies were adopted under Washington's administration.

24. While it is true that Arnold's defection did not create a trend, overall the *Register*'s admiration for American patriotism ignores the facts. William Howe's attempts to encourage desertion from the Continental Army and reenlistment in the British forces certainly produced results, as Washington himself admitted—*The Writings of George Washington from the Original Manuscript Sources 1745–1799*, ed. J. C. Fitzpatrick, 39 vols. (Washington, D.C., 1931–44), vol. 8, p. 8. Joseph Galloway's figures of 1,134 soldier and 354 sailor turncoats in the winter of 1777–78 may well be exaggerated, but other evidence suggests the total was not negligible. See, for example, *The Diary of Frederick Mackenzie, Giving a Daily Narration of His Military Service as an Officer of the Regiment of Royal Welsh Fusiliers during the Years 1775–81*, 2 vols. (Cambridge, Mass., 1930), vol. 1, p. 64. It is likely that the majority of defectors were recent immigrants.

25. Elijah Clarke (1733–99), Colonel in the Georgia militia.

26. The *Register*'s account fails to point out that the majority of the dead and wounded were shot down after Ferguson's successor as commanding officer surrendered. Kings Mountain was therefore as much a massacre as Paoli.

27. Military conservatism, not a sense of humanity, prevented wider use of Ferguson's weapon. The .560 calibre, 7-groove rifle was patented in December 1776. The breach was exposed by one turn of a screw-plug attached to the trigger-guard and permitted a fire rate of four shots a minute.

28. "As I was within that distance at which in the quickest firing I have seldom missed a sheet of paper and could have lodged a half a dozen balls in or about him before he was out of my reach I had only to determine but it was not pleasant to fire at the back of an unoffending individual who was acquitting himself very coolly of his duty so I let him alone." From an MS letter dated 31 January 1778, in the possession of Edinburgh University Library; I am indebted to the organisers of the 1776 Exhibition, National Maritime Museum, Greenwich, for sight of this letter.

29. There appears no justification for this figure; most authorities accept the American report of 3 dead and 5 wounded. Tarleton, with about 270 men, forced Sumpter, with about 1,000, to turn and fight; his dispersal of

Sumpter's force was something of a pyrrhic victory, so much so that the Americans claimed the encounter as a British defeat.

30. William Washington (1752–1810), a distant relative of George Washington, Lieutenant-Colonel commanding a mixed body of Virginia cavalry.

31. 17 January.

32. Fortescue gives double this number, and 800 should be regarded as a lower limit; the Americans had 12 killed and 60 wounded. John W. Fortescue, *History of the British Army*, 13 vols. (London, 1899–1930), vol. 3, p. 363.

33. See "Notes, 1780," n. 19. Marion became a serious threat to Cornwallis in the fall of 1780, and his ability to defy pursuit in the difficult terrain of the Carolinas earned him the nickname "Swamp Fox."

34. William Lee Davidson (1746–81), Colonel of North Carolina militia, promoted to Brigadier-General in 1780.

35. See "Notes, 1779," n. 72.

36. Charles O'Hara (?1740–1802), Lieutenant-Colonel in the Coldstream Guards, promoted to command the Guards Brigade under Cornwallis.

37. Not identified.

38. Nisbet Balfour (1743–1832), Lieutenant-Colonel of the 23rd Regiment, appointed Commandant at Charleston by Cornwallis on the latter's departure for the campaign in August 1780.

39. James Craig (1748–1812), promoted to Major in the 82nd Regiment for distinguished service under Burgoyne in 1777; commanded four companies of his regiment in the south from December 1780.

40. Sir James Barclay (1750–93), 7th Baronet; Lieutenant, 1777; Captain, 1783.

41. John Pyle, who had mobilised a body of Loyalists in response to Cornwallis's proclamation.

42. The *Register* appears to make the same mistake as the unfortunate Loyalists, who were wiped out not by Tarleton's Legion but by that of the American, "Light Horse Harry" Lee, whose uniform was similar. Lee used the similarity to spring an audacious trap and, though he denied it, to slaughter the Loyalist contingent. Henry Lee, *Memoirs of the War in the Southern Department of the United States*, rev. ed. (New York, 1869), pp. 256–58. It has not been possible to determine the *Register*'s source for this account and hence to establish whether or not blaming Tarleton was deliberate American propaganda.

43. Colonel William Preston, commanding a Virginia rifle unit.

44. John Butler, Brigadier-General of North Carolina militia (and no relation to the Pennsylvania or New York Butlers).

45. Pinketham Eaton, Brigadier-General of North Carolina militia; Edward Stevens (1745–1820) and Robert Lawson (formerly Colonel of the 4th Regiment), Brigadier-Generals of the Virginia militia; Isaac Huger (see "Notes, 1779," n. 39); Otho Williams (1749–94), Adjutant-General to Greene, enjoyed a considerable reputation for his successes in the campaign up to this point; Lynch's Regiment was a militia unit raised by Charles Lynch (1736–96), reputed originator of "lynch-law" for his punishment of Tory Loyalists, but it was at this point part of Colonel

Washington's Legion; Henry Lee (1756–1818), whose marriage to his cousin united both branches of the Virginia Lees, Lieutenant-Colonel commanding the legion raised in October 1780; William Campbell (1745–81), commanded a unit of partisan riflemen from October 1780.

46. Lee claimed American forces were 1,670 regulars and 2,779 militia. *Memoirs of the War in the Southern Department*, p. 281.

47. The generally accepted figure is 1,900.

48. Lee stated that, to prevent a repetition of their flight at Camden, the Virginia militia had a line of men posted behind them with orders to shoot any who attempted to run. *Memoirs of the War in the Southern Department*, p. 277.

49. Not identified.

50. Johann Christian du Puy, Hessian officer.

51. Fortescue gives 93 killed and 439 wounded. *History of the British Army*, vol. 3, p. 374.

52. None further identified.

53. Lieutenant-Colonel John Howard of the Guards, promoted to Brigadier-General in 1781.

54. Lee indicated the American regulars lost 326 killed, wounded, and missing, and the militia had 94 casualties. *Memoirs of the War in the Southern Department*, pp. 283, 285.

55. Clinton later commented that in the whole campaign Cornwallis "... accomplished no other purpose but having exposed, by an unnecessary retreat to Wilmington, the two valuable colonies behind him to be overrun and conquered by that very army which he boasts to have completely routed but a week or two before." *The American Rebellion*, p. 271.

56. Thomas Dundas (1750–94), Lieutenant-Colonel of the 80th Regiment; John Simcoe (1752–1806), Lieutenant-Colonel, from 1797 Commander of the Queen's Rangers, the Loyalist regiment originally raised by Robert Rogers; Colonel Beverley Robinson's Loyal American Rangers. Clinton's confidence in Arnold is measured by his instructions that the latter should invariably consult Dundas and Simcoe before "... undertaking any operation of consequence." *The American Rebellion*, pp. 482–83.

57. Captain Adam Bettin was killed; two other officers can be identified as wounded.

58. John Williams was elected President of the Board of Serjeants, William Bowzar, Secretary.

59. John Mason, who was involved in several Loyalist conspiracies, and his guide James Ogden.

60. In addition to Sullivan and Witherspoon, the congressional committee also contained John Mathews (1744–1802) of South Carolina, Theodorick Bland (1742–90) of Virginia, and Samuel Atlee. Joseph Reed was the chief negotiator, assisted by James Potter, Brigadier-General of the Pennsylvania militia and member of the council.

61. About two hundred troops of the New Jersey Brigade mutinied on 20 January.

62. Washington actually prepared to go to Princeton on 4 January but decided he would arrive too late to influence events, and in any case his first priority should be preventing the spread of the mutiny. Carl Van Doren, *Mutiny in January: The Story of a Crisis in the Continental Army Now for the First Time Fully Told from Many Hitherto Unknown or Neglected Sources, Both American and British* (New York, 1943), p. 66.

63. Arnold burned tobacco warehouses at Richmond and Simcoe attacked and dispersed some militia at Charles City.

64. John Watson (1748–1826), Lieutenant-Colonel of the 3rd Foot Guards, commanding a volunteer unit at this point.

65. Not identified.

66. Greene reported 18 killed and 248 wounded.

67. The collapse of the 1st Maryland Regiment (acknowledged to be one of the best units in the Continental Army) was held to be the cause of the American defeat, by the court-martial which condemned its Colonel, John Gunby. Military critics have tended to blame Greene's tactics.

68. Archibald McArthur, Major in the 71st Regiment.

69. John Harris Cruger (1738–1807), member of the powerful family with branches and interests in both New York and Bristol; commanded the 1st Battalion of the Loyalist regiment raised by Oliver de Lancey (his father-in-law).

70. Ferdinand, Duke of Brunswick (1721–92), Commander-in-Chief of the forces of Britain and Prussia in Europe during the Seven Years War. He achieved one of the finest military reputations of the age and in 1778 Secretary at War Barrington suggested to George III that Ferdinand be offered the post of Commander-in-Chief in England to meet the French menace, since no British general approached his competence.

71. They made a respectable defence of Petersburg.

72. Paston Gould (d. 1783), promoted to Colonel in 1777, given local rank of first Brigadier and then Major-General as senior officer commanding in the south until November 1781.

73. John Doyle (?1750–1834), Brigade-Major to Cornwallis, later served with distinction in the Revolutionary and Napoleonic wars; created Baronet in 1805 and General of the Army in 1829.

74. Not identified.

75. John Coffin (1756–1838), a member of the prominent Massachusetts family, volunteered for service in the British army in 1775; served in Loyalist units and raised a cavalry unit in Georgia when transferred to the south in 1779.

76. Lee stated that the Americans had 185 casualties. *Memoirs of the War in the Southern Department*, p. 377. British losses were 27 dead and 58 wounded.

77. John Stuart (1759–1815), son of the Superintendant of Indian Affairs for the Southern District; he was commissioned in the 3rd Foot Guards while in England in 1778.

78. Carl von Bose, Brigadier-General in the Hessian forces.

79. John Peter Gabriel Muhlenberg (1746–1807), Lutheran pastor in Virginia before the war, raised the 8th Virginia Regiment in 1776 and was commissioned Brigadier-General in the Continental Army in 1777; he was succeeded by Von Steuben in 1780 as Chief Commander in the south.

80. If Cornwallis had attacked an hour earlier, he could have forced a serious defeat on Lafayette and Wayne; he simply delayed springing his trap too long.

81. The comment does less than justice to Lafayette and Wayne. The former committed less than a third of his forces to support the latter and could have extricated the bulk of his army without difficulty. Wayne, on realising that he had been drawn into an engagement with the whole of Cornwallis's army, promptly attacked and stopped the British advance until darkness permitted a retreat.

82. On 4 April, Rivington's *Gazette* in New York published one letter and an extract from another captured from Washington's couriers. The first, dated 27 March, to Benjamin Harrison, Speaker of the Virginia House of Delegates, gave a detailed, accurate and therefore gloomy view of the state of the American army, and promised a diversion against New York. The second, dated 28 March, to Lund Washington, George Washington's relative and estate manager at Mount Vernon, included a paragraph (the published extract) candidly commenting on the inadequacy of French naval support. Both items were published verbatim with nothing ". . . added, to fill up the measure." See n. 126, below.

83. Details of the plan concocted by Washington and Rochambeau at Wethersfield, Connecticut, on 21–22 May, were contained in a letter from Washington to Lafayette which was intercepted on 3 June. The British were confused by the explicit revelations in the letter and by Washington's immediate attempts to minimise their importance, and speculated whether the despatch was a deliberate ruse. It was not, and the Americans faced serious difficulties as a result of its discovery. Equally important was the capture of Rochambeau's letter to the French minister at Philadelphia, which contained an extract of the instructions of the French war minister. Failure to decipher this letter correctly may have decisively affected Clinton's strategy. See D. S. Freeman, *George Washington*, 7 vols. (New York, 1948–57), vol. 5, pp. 91–92; W. B. Wilcox, "Rhode Island in British Strategy, 1780–1781," *Journal of Modern History*, 1945, vol. 17, pt. 4, pp. 304–31, esp. pp. 322–24.

84. Francois Joseph Paul, Comte de Grasse (1722–88), fought under d'Estaing in the West Indies and in March 1781 was promoted to Rear-Admiral to command the fleet sent to the Caribbean with orders to assist Rochambeau and Washington at his discretion.

85. Edmund Eyre, Lieutenant-Colonel of the 54th Regiment.

86. William Montgomery, Major in the 44th Regiment (apparently killed by a Negro) and Stephen Bromfield, Major in the 40th Regiment.

87. Lieutenant-Colonel William Ledgard of the Connecticut militia.

88. Samuel Hood (1724–1816), created Baronet in 1778 (later Baron Hood, 1782, Viscount, 1796); Rear-Admiral in 1780, second-in-command to Rodney in the West Indies.

89. The details of the naval operations referred to are covered in Chapter VI, *AR*, 1781, pp. [98–[118.

90. Louis, Comte de Barras-Saint Laurent (1719–92), Vice-Admiral commanding the French squadron at Newport; promoted to Lieutenant-General of the Navy, 1783.

91. Claude-Ann, Marquis de Saint-Simon Montblern (1742–98), commanding the French army sent with de Grasse.

92. Francis Samuel Drake (d. 1789), Rear-Admiral in 1780, created Baronet in 1782.

93. Anthony James Pye Molloy, Captain in 1778. Mark Robinson, Lieutenant, Captain in 1790, Rear-Admiral, 1808, Vice-Admiral, 1812.

94. Armand-Louis, Marquis de Gontaut, styled Duc de Lauzun (1747–93), Brigadier-General commanding a foreign volunteer legion of marines. George Weedon (1730–93), Brigadier-General in the Continental Army from February 1777, placed on the inactive list in 1779; organised resistance against the British operations in Virginia in 1780–81 and returned to a militia command for the Yorktown campaign.

95. Robert Digby (1732–1814), Rear-Admiral in 1774; sent to replace Graves as Commander-in-Chief on the American station in 1781, but arrived to find the fleet about to sail for the Chesapeake and postponed taking up his command.

96. John Laurens (1754–1782), son of Henry Laurens, Lieutenant-Colonel and A.D.C. to Washington in 1779, active in the southern campaigns until sent in 1781 to France to assist Franklin in securing more supplies; returned in time to serve in the siege of Yorktown.

97. In the assault on Redoubt 10, Hamilton's losses were 9 killed and 25 wounded; among the French, 15 were killed and 77 wounded at Redoubt 9. In the two redoubts, 73 British and Hessians were captured. The reports do not permit clear estimates of British and Hessian casualties.

98. Robert Abercromby.

99. Not further identified.

100. A small mortar.

101. The total size of Cornwallis's forces is a matter of estimation. The nominal strength on 15 September, excluding seamen, was 8,885; 7,241 prisoners (including camp followers) were taken under the surrender on 20 September, 840 seamen were surrendered separately to de Grasse and 250 Americans were sent off in the *Bonetta*. It is likely that the figure of 840 sailors does not represent the total of naval personnel, which could have been 1,500. Captured material included 214 guns and 7,320 small arms. D. S. Freeman, *George Washington*, vol. 5, pp. 513–16.

102. George Augustus Keppel (d. 1782), Captain in 1782.

103. Actually the draft of the wholly unofficial and unapproved agreement between Lee and de Neufville of 1778. See *AR*, 1780, pp. 356]–[365.

104. The Dutch army included, among other foreign units, a Scottish Brigade (originally recruited in 1570 in Scotland, but now with only officers of Scots origin). North negotiated the hire of the Brigade in 1775, but the Estates General hedged the deal with so many restrictions (including a ban on service outside Europe) that it fell through. Van der Capellen of Overyssel openly opposed the loan of the Brigade because of his support for America.

105. In 1779, a Dutch merchant fleet bound for French and Spanish ports, with some cargoes of naval stores and convoyed by Admiral Bylandt, was captured by a British squadron. The contraband cargoes and ships were declared forfeit by the Prize Courts.

106. Charles Cornwall, elected Speaker on 31 October 1780, acted until his death in 1789.

107. Thomas de Grey (1748–1818), M.P. for Tamworth, 1774–80, for Lostwithiel, 1780–May 1781; one of the Lords of Trade, 1777–81; Under-Secretary for the American Department, 1778–September 1780 (succeeded his father as Viscount Walsingham, May 1781). Sir Richard Sutton (1723–1802), created Baronet in 1772; M.P. for Sandwich, 1780–84; a Lord of the Treasury, 1780–82.

108. Richard Fitzpatrick (1748–1813), younger son of the Earl of Upper Ossory; M.P. for Tavistock, 1774–1807; Lieutenant-Colonel in the 1st Foot Guards; served in America, 1777–78; Secretary at War, 1783.

109. The reference is to the struggle for parliamentary reform by the reduction of sinecures and political pensions by which, the Opposition claimed, Government maintained a corrupt majority.

110. The *Register*'s version of Fox's remarks makes them more prophetic than they may actually have been—compare *Parliamentary History*, vol. 21, 833–34.

111. The alliance organised by Pope Julian II against Venice in 1508 and the Grand Alliance of Britain, Holland, and Austria in 1701.

112. The *Register* refers to the Gordon Riots, 2–9 June 1780, and the measures taken to suppress them. *AR*, 1780, pp. 190]–200], 254]–[287.

113. John Fane, 9th Earl of Westmoreland (1759–1841), succeeded his father in 1774; later a friend of the Younger Pitt and Lord-Lieutenant of Ireland, 1790–95.

114. Francis Godolphin Osborne (1751–99), styled Marquis of Carmarthen, only surviving son of the 4th Duke of Leeds, whom he succeeded in 1789. Called to the House of Lords as Lord Osborne of Kiveton in 1776, he approved of the American war but from 1779 supported economical reform; dismissed from the Lord-Lieutenancy of the East Riding of Yorkshire in 1780, he went into active opposition.

115. In 1772, Gustavus III of Sweden executed a coup d'état which restored the powers of the monarchy.

116. George Geddes, not otherwise identified. Charles Stirling, Lientenant, 1778; Captain, 1783; Rear-Admiral, 1805; Vice-Admiral, 1810.

117. Daniel Shiels, Lieutenant, 1778; Gyam and Wightman, not further identified.

118. Samuel Arden, Lieutenant, 1780; Captain, 1783; promoted for his behaviour in this action.

119. Not identified.

120. James Smyth, Lieutenant, 1778; King, not identified.

121. Not identified.

122. Sampson Edwards, Captain in 1781; Rear-Admiral, 1801; Vice-Admiral, 1809; Admiral, 1814.

123. John Barry (1745–1803), Captain in the Continental Navy from 1776.

124. William Knox (1732–1810), formerly agent for Georgia but dismissed for his defence of the Stamp Act, Under-Secretary in the American Department, 1770–82. James Simpson, British Attorney-General in South Carolina.

125. Not identified.

126. Compared with the duplicate printed in J. C. Fitzpatrick, *The Writings of George Washington*, vol. 21, pp. 380–83 this version of the letter shows very minor changes. Paragraph headings ("Men," "Arms," etc.) are added; there are two changes in paragraph punctuation; and paragraph 4, line 12, reads ". . . but few Infantry" in the duplicate.

127. Not identified.

128. William Rix (c. 1734–1801), Town Clerk of London, 1775–1801.

Introduction

1782

North may have believed at the end of 1781 that it was "all over," and indeed for him it soon was, for his ministry collapsed in the spring of 1782—but the war was far from ended. British garrisons were still besieged in Gibraltar and Minorca; British forces were desperately fighting to retain their hold in India; the West Indies were threatened again; and there remained the problem of what to do in America, where the British army was now holding defensive positions in Charleston, Savannah, and New York. If peace were sought, what price would have to be paid? Could this price be made acceptable to the King, to Parliament, and to the nation?

The beginning of the new year presented the same old problems—the most obvious, the overstretch of naval resources. At the end of 1781, the French decided to strike at the West Indies and at India. On 10 December, they sent out a fleet under Guichen which was to separate into a squadron for each theatre. Britain was virtually unable to collect a force to oppose this fleet, and Admiral Kempenfelt's much inferior force captured only a few transports. To cover the threat, Rodney was sent to the Caribbean with twelve ships and Bickerton to India with three. However, a French expedition from Martinique had already recaptured St. Eustatius in November 1781 and de Grasse, returning from the Chesapeake, took St. Kitts, despite the arrival of Hood on 25 January.[1] Hood could

1. Hood successfully stood off a French attack, but either through the treachery or culpable stupidity of the island's planters, the French land forces were able to force the surrender of the British garrison.

not prevent the loss of Nevis and Montserrat or the capture of Dutch Guiana. However, Rodney's arrival on 25 February at last gave Britain naval superiority in the Caribbean because Guichen was delayed by storm damage and had not joined de Grasse. On 9 April, Rodney began a running fight with the French off Dominica, to prevent de Grasse from combining with the Spanish fleet for an attack on Jamaica. Two days later, off the Iles des Saintes, the French fleet was defeated in the greatest naval victory of the war, though the enemy was not destroyed and results were confined to securing Jamaica.[2]

Three weeks before Rodney fought the battle of the Saints, a new ministry took power in England. The collapse of North's government had taken three months, beginning with the revolt of Dundas and Rigby, who demanded Germain's dismissal. The American Secretary was prepared to go—particularly after the Cabinet on 23 December accepted the appointment of his old enemy Carleton to replace Clinton. Germain however wanted to be compensated with a peerage, and the King wanted to replace him with someone equally committed to continuing the American war. George III was to be disappointed (no one else believed America would not have to be abandoned),[3] but Germain got his peerage, though he suffered the humiliation of having Lord Carmarthen twice move that acceptance of a peer who had been court-martialled was derogatory to the dignity of the House. With Germain gone, the Opposition attacks centred on Sandwich. On 24 January, Fox moved for an enquiry into the state of the navy and lost his motion, after a postponement until 7 February, by only 236 to 217. Such a close defeat in a full House encouraged the Opposition to press forward. On 22 February, Conway moved to end the American war and lost by one vote (194 to 193). The debate was continued on the twenty-seventh, and the same motion finally passed, 234 to 215. North won a division on 8 March by 10 votes and a no-confidence motion on the fifteenth by 9 votes,

2. Controversy still exists over Rodney's tactics, particularly the decision to break the enemy line, instead of parallelling it in orthodox fashion, and whether he could have followed up the French defeat more effectively.

3. Germain was succeeded by Welbore Ellis, who served until the Rockingham ministry abolished the office of American Secretary; colonial affairs were thereafter the responsibility of the Home Secretary.

but he recognised his tenure of power was ended and resigned on 20 March.

The King had already been advised by North to approach the Opposition, but he had first turned yet again to Gower. This move was futile, and the King now faced what he resented and feared most, a government composed of men he detested and who would impose terms he would find intolerable. Thurlow was entrusted on 10 March with discussing with Rockingham the creation of a "broad-bottom" ministry. Rockingham fulfilled the King's worst fears, by demanding as minimum conditions the adoption of Opposition policies on everything from American independence to economical reform. The King then turned to Shelburne, who declined the offer on 21 March because he knew he had insufficient support. Finally, the King negotiated for a Rockingham ministry containing Shelburne, who he now believed would act as a counterbalance to Rockingham's intransigence.

This arrangement was agreed to on 25 March, and the disposition of offices in the new ministry revealed how much Rockingham had conceded. Rockingham himself took the Treasury, Lord John Cavendish became Chancellor of the Exchequer, while Shelburne and Fox, in a reformed system, became Home and Foreign secretary respectively. Thurlow remained as Lord Chancellor; Grafton became Lord Privy Seal; Camden, Lord President of the Council; Conway, Commander-in-Chief and Keppel, First Lord of the Admiralty. Richmond took over the Ordnance, Dunning became Chancellor of the Duchy of Lancaster, and Burke accepted the non-Cabinet office of Paymaster-General. The Rockinghams thus held six posts in the Cabinet, while Shelburne and his followers held four.[4] Shelburne was then given every mark of royal favour and in response became an ardent advocate of the royal prerogative, an attitude that was widely ridiculed in the next few weeks. The King had extricated himself well from what looked, from his point of view, like a desperate situation, by maintaining the divisions in the Opposition in the new government. He then weakened the administration's cohesion still further by allowing Shelburne an

4. J. Cannon, *The Fox-North Coalition: Crisis of the Constitution, 1782–84* (Cambridge, 1969), pp. 2–5. Conway's position is seen here as uncommitted.

equal share with Rockingham in the disposal of patronage, a move certain to create trouble.[5]

The new government was divided over most issues, except economical reform, and in addition to the situation in America faced trouble in Ireland and with the East India Company.[6] Parliament recessed from 27 March to 8 April and when it resumed sitting was presented with the economical reform programme. Bills for the expulsion of contractors from Parliament, the disenfranchisement of revenue officials, and a watered-down version of Burke's establishment bill were passed without much difficulty. The young William Pitt's attempt to extend the programme to reform of representation however was defeated on 9 May by 161 to 141. Trouble in Ireland, where the Volunteers were demanding legislative independence, was temporarily headed off when Parliament resolved to repeal the act of 1720 which confirmed Poyning's Law. The crisis in the affairs of the East India Company had been brewing for several years. North's legislation of 1773 had solved none of the problems. The governor-general, Warren Hastings, was involved in a savage and damaging feud with the council, the governor of Madras had been deposed and imprisoned by his council, and the war against the Mahrattas and Hyder Ali had wrecked the company's finances. The company's affairs therefore again became the subject of enquiry by both a parliamentary select and a secret committee. The committees tended to blame Warren Hastings and so Burke, who adopted Indian affairs as the field for a new moral crusade, supported demands for Hastings's recall: Shelburne however supported Hastings, and the resultant split in the Government left the issue in deadlock for another year.

The fortunes of war in India fluctuated alarmingly. Hyder Ali's destruction of Colonel Baillie's force in September 1780 encouraged the French to try at least to restore the position they had lost in 1763; they decided therefore to reinforce Admiral Suffren's squadron by despatching a force under de Bussy. Through 1781, Britain

5. George III to Thurlow, *The Correspondence of King George III*, ed. Sir John Fortescue, 6 vols. (London, 1927–28), no. 3632, pp. 443–44.

6. The ministry also recalled Rodney for an enquiry into the seizure of property in St. Eustatius, but when news of the victory at the Saints reached London on 18 May, it became impracticable to arraign the national hero.

could spare no more than a small reinforcement of three ships, and Sir Eyre Coote was left, with an army of 1600 regulars, to prevent Hyder Ali from annihilating British power in the Carnatic. Even more than in America, success for British land forces depended on naval control of the coast. Only when the French fleet returned to Mauritius in February 1781, was Coote able to advance, and then in a campaign of extraordinary skill he defeated Hyder Ali's huge army at Porto Novo on 1 July [7] and held him off through the summer and fall. By November it had become essential to deny the French use of Dutch bases. The British thus seized Negapatam and, in January 1782, Trincomalee in Ceylon, the best harbour in the eastern Indian Ocean, was captured. However, Suffren returned in February, fought off Admiral Hughes's squadron, and landed 3,000 troops at Porto Novo. Hyder Ali promptly began a new offensive, which was barely contained by British forces. When Trincomalee was recaptured by Suffren in August, the British position in south India appeared desperate and was only marginally improved by the arrival of Bickerton's squadron and the death of Hyder Ali in December.

America continued to be a problem. When the new government took office, Clinton and Washington faced a stalemate, since neither could take the initiative without naval support, and that had been withdrawn in the fall of 1781. The activities of the Board of Associated Loyalists and the problem of Captain Asgill, who was arbitrarily selected by the Americans to be executed in reprisal for a Loyalist lynching of an American officer, worried Clinton particularly.[8] The new government confirmed its decision to appoint Carleton commander-in-chief and instructed him to evacuate the British forces from New York, Charleston, and Savannah, with authority to arrange a capitulation if he was opposed, and to despatch part of his evacuated forces to the West Indies. The Rockinghams planned to end the war, but they had not thought in terms of practicalities. There were not enough transports available to handle the huge evacuation, and the abandonment

---

7. Fortescue estimates the British and Sepoy forces to be about 7,500 men, and Hyder Ali's about 80,000, one-third of whom were trained and disciplined troops. John W. Fortescue, *History of the British Army*, 13 vols. (London, 1899–1930), vol. 3, pp. 450, 454.

8. See "Notes, 1781," n. 1 and "Notes, 1783," n. 32.

of New York left no satisfactory army base for West Indian operations so the most Carleton could manage in 1782 was the evacuation of Savannah in July. Carleton hoped to negotiate some sort of reunion between Britain and America, but he learned in August that the Government was prepared to concede independence to secure a quick peace, so he offered his resignation in disgust.

Peace negotiations began in April[9] with Shelburne as Home and Colonial Secretary dealing with America and Fox as Foreign Secretary dealing with France and Spain. Each sent his own representative to Paris. Shelburne made the peculiar choice of Richard Oswald, a seventy-seven-year-old Scots merchant in the American trade,[10] and Fox chose Thomas Grenville, brother of Lord Temple. Both ministers shared the fundamental British goal of preserving the empire without significant losses to the Bourbon powers, if necessary by continuing the war against France and Spain. Both also agreed that America must be detached from her allies and prevented from becoming a French satellite, but they differed on how this should be done and on the nature of a future relationship between Britain and the United States. The problems inevitably created by the presence of two separate envoys and the basic differences of view of their chiefs were exacerbated by Shelburne's tendency toward secrecy and his refusal to consult or inform his Cabinet colleagues on his diplomatic activities.

Oswald arrived in Paris on 14 April and asked Franklin for a separate Ango-American treaty.[11] Franklin re-

9. Detailed accounts of the negotiations may be compared in Richard B. Morris, *The Peacemakers, the Great Powers and American Independence* (New York, 1965); V. T. Harlow, *The Founding of the Second British Empire 1763–1793*, vol. 1: *Discovery and Revolution* (London, 1952), esp. chs. 6, 7; S. F. Bemis, *Diplomacy of the American Revolution*, (Edinburgh and London, 1957), esp. chs. 14–18 inclusive. Differing views on Shelburne's role may be found by comparing Harlow, *The Founding of the Second British Empire*, pp. 406–07; J. Cannon, *The Fox-North Coalition*, pp. 36–37; and J. Norris, *Shelburne and Reform* (London, 1963), pp. 357–63.

10. Oswald was without diplomatic experience; he was alarmingly indiscreet and seemed continually prepared to offer concessions before the Americans asked for them. Not surprisingly, the subtle and unscrupulous Franklin, after overcoming his initial amazement, insisted that Oswald remain as chief negotiator for the American treaty.

11. Franklin was joined by John Jay and John Adams at the end of October and in November by Henry Laurens, who was released from the Tower in December 1781 and later exchanged for Cornwallis.

sponded by suggesting that Britain cede Nova Scotia and Canada to the United States by way of reparation for the war. Vergennes, meanwhile, insisted on a general peace treaty, since he was confident France's gains would increase with a few more months of war. Shelburne privately rejected the suggestion to cede Canada but his Cabinet agreed to open general negotiations and Thomas Grenville was sent to France. The division between Fox and Shelburne became crucial at this point. Fox believed an immediate and unconditional offer of independence would bring America out of the war and detach her from France, but Shelburne wanted to use the offer of independence as a lever to persuade America into a new relationship with Britain. At the least, Shelburne desired a close commercial nexus, and he saw the offer as a bargaining counter with France against British war losses. Fox persuaded the Cabinet to endorse the unconditional offer of independence on 23 May but Shelburne simply ignored this decision in his instructions to Oswald. Fox then demanded the Cabinet reaffirm its earlier decision, and when on 26 and 30 May it did not, he announced that he would resign.

At this moment the political configuration changed, for on 1 July, the Marquis of Rockingham died. His followers agreed to offer the leadership to the Duke of Portland but the King was determined to choose Shelburne and few men were prepared to dispute the King's right to choose his first minister. None was willing to accept Fox's argument that the choice should lie with the Cabinet.[12] Fox resigned on 4 July and after a Rockingham party meeting on the seventh Cavendish, who had previously indicated he wished to go, also resigned from the Cabinet. Twelve lesser officeholders (including Burke) also quit. Shelburne replaced Fox with Lord Grantham, an experienced diplomat but a political nonentity; William Pitt became Chancellor of the Exchequer and Thomas Townshend took over as Home Secretary when Shelburne went to the Treasury. The new government was not strong, and Shelburne did not improve his position by lying about Fox's resignation and weakly prevaricating when given the lie in the Lords by Richmond and Keppel. A significant

12. Fox's suggestion was, of course, revolutionary and most men felt that to subject the King to a "tyranny of party" was a truly unconstitutional course.

number of Rockinghams followed Fox into the Opposition, and Shelburne began to believe that his best chance of survival was to attract North's support along with the solid bloc of adherents who followed North into exile.

The peace negotiations continued throughout the summer recess. Shelburne alone directed them, though Thomas Grenville was replaced by the acute and highly experienced Alleyn Fitzherbert as envoy to France. Vergennes had not yet committed France to any formal proposals, for he was still banking on an accumulation of French successes. France entered the war to recoup her losses in the Seven Years War, specifically hoping for gains in India and for a large share of the Newfoundland fishery.[13] Spain on the other hand was not at all ready to negotiate, for she was determined to regain Gibraltar (the siege of which was now well into its third year) and to expel the British from the littoral of the Gulf of Mexico. Neither France nor Spain had a particular interest in seeing America independent. Spain, especially, feared the effects an example of successful rebellion might have in her own empire.

The American peace commissioners, particularly John Jay, had become suspicious of Spanish interests in the Mississippi and of the apparent intention of the French to divide the Newfoundland fishery exclusively between France and Britain. They also correctly suspected that France was prolonging the war for her own ends. Accordingly, America was disposed toward a separate treaty, despite her formal promises to France. The commissioners also knew that Britain had begun a determined effort to persuade France to agree to a peace settlement.

The stumbling blocks to a separate Anglo-American treaty, however, were Franklin's deep suspicion of Shelburne's notions of a new Anglo-American nexus and his insistence on an unequivocal recognition of American independence as a preliminary to negotiations. On 10 July, Franklin offered a double set of draft proposals. The "necessary" British concessions were to be recognition of full independence, the settlement of the boundaries of the thirteen states, confinement of Canada to her pre-1774

---

13. Apart from its considerable commercial value, the Newfoundland fishery was prized as a "nursery of seamen," invaluable for recruitment into the navy in time of war.

limits, and a share of the Newfoundland fishery. The "advisable" concessions suggested by Franklin were indemnification of Americans for war losses, admission of British war guilt, the cession of Canada, and reciprocal commercial advantages for the ships of both states in each other's ports. But before these proposals could be discussed, Franklin demanded proof of Shelburne's intention to recognise independence without conditions. Shelburne was caught between his willingness to compromise on his original policy intentions (he was now prepared to settle for merely preventing America becoming a French satellite), and his promises to the King and public statements in Parliament. On 27 July, the Cabinet agreed to acknowledge independence in the first article of the treaty, but it insisted on amnesty and indemnification for the Loyalists and the repayment of debts owed to British merchants. By 29 August, the Cabinet was prepared to offer recognition of independence before the treaty providing acceptance of the first four articles was agreed, but the American commissioners, alarmed by signs of Bourbon ambitions at American expense, offered a compromise. They suggested their point would be met if Oswald's commission was reworded to refer to the American delegation as representing "The Thirteen United States of America." The Cabinet agreed on 19 September.

On 5 October the Americans presented the draft preliminaries to Oswald. The draft included Franklin's four "necessary" articles; the boundary clause was amended to leave Britain West Florida but it deprived Canada of the Great Lakes and the southern Ontario region. The draft further proposed a reciprocal freedom of navigation and commerce in each other's territories. These points themselves were not entirely acceptable and the negotiations became deadlocked anyway over treatment of the Loyalists and over debts to British merchants. Shelburne was desperate to secure the treaty before Parliament reconvened on 26 November,[14] so he despatched Henry Strachey, joint under-secretary in the Home Office, to assist the too-pliant Oswald. The Americans were as anxious as Shelburne for peace, since their relations with

14. The resumption of the session was eventually postponed until 5 December.

France had deteriorated badly during the summer, but they were immovable on the Loyalist issue.[15] Final negotiations produced a minimal compromise. The Americans conceded their liability to pay all debts contracted before 1775 and enlarged the boundaries of Canada; in return, they received concessions on the Newfoundland fishery. On the question of the Loyalists, the Americans promised only to "recommend" that the individual states treat Loyalists generously. These preliminaries were signed on 30 November.

When Parliament met again on 5 December, Shelburne was already in trouble, for Richmond and Keppel had made clear to the Cabinet their outrage over the concessions offered in the peace negotiations and their anxiety to intensify the war against the Bourbons. The speech from the throne announced, inter alia, that peace preliminaries were agreed with America, and the address in reply was passed without a division. North ably defended the record of his ministry in the debate, while Fox attacked the Government and explained the reasons for his resignation. The real difficulties for Shelburne began in the Lords, where Stormont condemned the Government for granting American independence without conditions. Shelburne denied Stormont's allegations and insisted that the treaty with America was contingent upon a peace with France. Fox seized this opportunity and demanded an explanation in the Commons the next day. There, Conway, Townshend, and Pitt each argued, to Shelburne's vast embarrassment, that independence was indeed unconditional. The King, who had heard of only Pitt's reply, tried to persuade him to announce that he had made a mistake. Pitt refused, Conway supported him, and Shelburne was reduced to refusing to answer questions. Fox thought he could continue to exploit the issue but overreached himself on 18 December by demanding the clause in the peace preliminaries relating to independence be laid before the House. He lost the motion 219 to 46. There was no doubt however that Shelburne's ministry was falling apart and the first minister now hoped for salvation through an alliance with North. North led his followers to ensure

---

15. Their instructions from Congress gave the American envoys no latitude. Britain hoped to settle the Loyalists as a new colony in the Ohio Valley, a move unlikely to recommend itself to the Americans under any circumstances.

Fox's decisive defeat on 18 December but he was deeply concerned over the fate of the Loyalists and suspected that Shelburne had abandoned them. In any event, North was biding his time for a return on his own terms.

Meanwhile, negotiations with the European powers reached a crucial stage. In the spring and summer, France and Spain delayed negotiations in the hope of new war gains. The Netherlands, which had gained nothing and lost everything, demanded restoration of all its losses and recognition of new maritime laws to protect neutrals. France, when pressed in July, talked of major concessions in the fishery, in the West Indies, West Africa, and India. However, Shelburne in private discussions with Vergennes's agent, Rayneval, in September stressed that if France remained intransigent in her exorbitant demands, his ministry would fall and be replaced by one driven by public opinion to a war *à l'outrance* with France. Accordingly, on 6 October, France and Spain presented their terms. France required the revocation of the article of the Treaty of Utrecht which forbade the fortification of Dunkirk (a point of honour rather than practicality); France also wanted St. Lucia and Dominica in the West Indies, and Senegal and Goree in West Africa. Other demands included a restoration of her position in India to what it was in 1754, and a share of the Newfoundland fishery. Spain demanded the cession of Gibraltar and Minorca, East and West Florida, and the Bahamas; the expulsion of the British from the Gulf of Mexico; and a share of the fishery.

Britain regarded the Spanish claims as ludicrous—the September assault on Gibraltar had failed and Spain's military and naval position was weakening steadily. Vergennes, who knew that an Anglo-American treaty was almost agreed and that France was approaching bankruptcy, feared that the negotiations would collapse because of Spanish obstinacy over Gibraltar. So on 20 November, Rayneval was again sent to London. Shelburne and the King were prepared to cede Gibraltar in return for a substantial gain in the West Indies and suggested that France might offer Dominica and Martinique, in turn to be compensated by Spain. Vergennes was thus left with either having France pay for Gibraltar or risking the fall of the Shelburne ministry and prolongation of the war. On 28 November, Spain agreed to the proposed deal over Gibraltar, but by 2 December the news was leaked in London and a violent public reaction, reflected in the attitude of the hawks in the Cabinet, frightened Shelburne into changing the terms. The British proposed on 11 December that Britain retain Gibraltar, cede East and West Florida and Minorca to Spain, and submit British trade in Honduras to regulation. Spain accepted those terms on 15 December.

By this time, the negotiations with France approached conclusion. Britain, in the absence of news from India, was prepared only to confine territorial concessions there to a small area around two French factories; in the West Indies, she was prepared to cede Tobago but required the return of Dominica; in West Africa, France was to have Senegal, but the gum trade was to be shared by both powers. France made particularly strenuous efforts over the fishery and Britain finally conceded French rights to the western coast of Newfoundland and the islets of St. Pierre and Miquelon. Finalising these negotiations continued through December and into the next year. Negotiations with the Netherlands did not advance at all, since the Dutch refused to abate their demands and Britain saw no reason to make concessions beyond agreeing to a truce.

The struggle with America was over. The war had ended and the inevitability of recognising American independence was implicitly, if not overtly, recognised by a House of Commons vote on 27 February. Burke voiced the view of those who had opposed the war throughout when he wrote to Franklin the following day:

> I congratulate you, as the friend of America, I trust, as not the enemy of England, I am sure, as the friend of mankind, on the resolution of the house of commons, carried by a majority of nineteen at two o'clock this morning, in a very full house. It was the declaration of two hundred and thirty four; I think it was the opinion of the whole. I trust it will lead to a speedy peace between the two branches of the English nation, perhaps to a general peace; and that our happiness may be an introduction to that of the world at large.[16]

The reaction of George III was naturally rather different. He was initially outraged by Parliament's decision to end the American war, and when it became obvious that North's ministry was at an end, he thought of abdica-

---

16. *The Correspondence of Edward Burke*, ed. Thomas W. Copeland, 9 vols. (Cambridge and Chicago, 1961–70), vol. 4 (ed. John A. Woods), p. 419.

tion.[17] The King slowly reconciled himself with great reluctance to recognition of American independence: "... I certainly disclaim thinking myself answerable for any evils that may arise from the adoption of this measure, as necessity not conviction has made me subscribe to it."[18] For some time he believed the formality of granting independence was an important factor in bargaining for peace terms:

> ... common sense tells me that if unconditional Independence is granted we cannot ever expect any understanding with America, for then we have given up the whole and have nothing to give for what we want from thence. Independence is certainly an unpleasant gift at best, but then it must be for such conditions of Peace as may justify it.[19]

By the end of 1782, the American preliminaries were signed, but the King's humiliations still rankled when settling details of terms with the Bourbon powers:

> ... I think peace so essential, and that the dreadful resolution of the 27th of February last of the House of Commons has so entirely removed the real cause of the war to the utter shame of that branch of the Legislature, that it would be madness not to conclude peace on the best possible terms we can obtain.[20]

A month earlier, in a letter to Shelburne, the King bitterly suggested that the "dismemberment of America from this Empire" might even be a blessing in disguise for "... knavery seems to be so much the striking feature of its inhabitants that it may not in the end be an evil that they become aliens to this Kingdom."[21] The speech from the throne on 5 December, however, reflecting of course the views of Shelburne, proclaimed a more statesmanlike optimism:

> Religion—language—interest—affections, may, and I hope will yet prove a bond of permanent union between the two countries; to this end, neither attention nor disposition shall be wanting on my part.[22]

17. Bonamy Dobrée, ed., *The Letters of King George III* (London, 1935), p. 154, no. 13.
18. *The Correspondence of King George III*, ed. Sir John W. Fortescue, 6 vols. (London, 1927–28), vol. 6, p. 157, no. 3984.
19. Ibid., p. 81, no. 3841.
20. Dobrée, ed., *The Letters of King George III*, p. 162, no. 21.
21. *The Correspondence of King George III*, p. 154, no. 3978.
22. *AR*, 1783, p. 312].

The *Annual Register* for 1782 clearly recognised the significance of the events it had recorded in the preceding years. The war with America, the editor writes:

> ... has already overturned those favourite systems of policy and commerce, both in the old and in the new world, which the wisdom of the ages, and the power of the greatest nations, had in vain endeavoured to render permanent; and it seems to have laid the seeds of still greater revolutions in the history and mutual relations of mankind.[23]

This volume was published in November 1784 and the preface is an extended, faintly defiant, defence against the "repeated complaints which have been made relative to the delay...." The historical section reaches the greatest length for the whole period, totalling 244 pages. Four full chapters (95 pages) are devoted to events in India. Chapter I retrospectively surveys the East India Company's involvement in war with the Mahrattas and Hyder Ali and Chapter IV concludes with the capture of Trincomalee in January 1782. Chapter V traces the naval war in 1781 in European waters, including details of the siege of Gibraltar, the investment of Minorca, and the battle with the Dutch off the Dogger Bank and concludes with the escape of the French squadrons from Brest in December.

The next three chapters follow parliamentary affairs during the session beginning in November 1781 and recessing in July 1782. Chapter VI reports the Opposition's attack on the speech from the throne which implied that the American war would be continued despite Yorktown; Thomas Pitt's attempt on 30 November to prevent the voting of supplies until the ministry agreed to a change of policy; Burke's attempt to obtain an enquiry into Rodney's looting of St. Eustatius; Sir James Lowther's motion to end the American war; and Burke's bill to improve arrangements for an exchange of prisoners of war. Chapter VII covers the debates from January to March 1782, following Fox's attack on Sandwich and the extensive debates over the conduct of the Admiralty; the Hayne case;[24] the defeat by one vote of Conway's motion on 21 February to end the American war and his victory on the twenty-seventh; the failure of Lord John Cavendish by 10 votes on 8 March to secure assent to resolutions blaming the ministry for the nation's misfortunes; and the failure

23. *AR*, 1783, p. iii.
24. See "Notes, 1782," nn. 14, 15.

of the no-confidence motion of the fifteenth by only 9 votes; the chapter concludes with an account of North's resignation on 20 March. Chapter VIII records the formation of the Rockingham administration, outlines its policies, and describes legislation for Ireland and measures for economical reform. That chapter concludes with the formation of Shelburne's ministry after Rockingham's death and the resignation of Fox and Cavendish. The *Register*'s account gives little indication of the complex negotiations underlying the formation of the Rockingham and Shelburne ministries, or to the constitutional points at issue. However, six pages are devoted to the arguments in both Houses over Fox's resignation, and these arguments provide a good indication of Shelburne's discomfiture.

The last two chapters return to the progress of the war. Chapter IX picks up the last stages of the campaign in South Carolina in 1781 with an account of the battle of Eutaw Springs (which incidentally omits any mention of the collapse of discipline in Greene's army which cost him the victory). The chapter then describes in detail the progress of the naval war in the Caribbean, cataloging the melancholy record of British losses to the French until the triumph at the Saints in April 1782. Chapter X describes the surrender of Minorca and the defence of Gibraltar until its relief by Howe in October.

The historical section in this volume maintains the *Register*'s reputation for detailed and accurate reporting, but it is decidedly partial to the Rockingham position on most issues. The bitingly sarcastic opening to Chapter VI is followed by a paragraph blaming the weakness of the Opposition on the Government's use of patronage and hence the need to rescue the nation from "the effects of a false system of politics" by ensuring "the vigour and independence of Parliament." The dilemma of the ministry after Yorktown is described in terms of its relationship with the Court: "to abandon the war, was at once inevitably to forfeit the support of that secret influence, of which they had too long experienced the effects to be ignorant of its power."[25] The *Register* clearly supports the line taken by Fox in the attack on the speech from the throne in November 1781 as it does the motion, couched in "terms most cool and temperate," of 12 December for "obliging

25. *AR*, 1782, p. [127.

the crown to put an end to an attempt at once ruinous and impracticable" to continue the American war (a view shared at that point by only 179 of 399 voting in the division). Most of Burke's interventions in the debates are noted in detail, occasionally out of proportion to their significance. For example, 3½ columns are devoted to his bill intended to improve the arrangements for the exchange of prisoners of war. In contrast, Pitt's proposal for parliamentary reform, and the lengthy debate which followed, receives half a column.[26] In general, however, the arguments in the debates are faithfully reproduced and North in particular is treated with meticulous fairness.

The *Appendix to the Chronicle* is again of considerable length, containing twenty-one items in forty-nine pages. Most of these are official reports describing the capitulation of America, the siege of Gibraltar, and naval actions. Extracted here, by way of interest, is a letter from Lord George Gordon to Shelburne querying Carleton's announcement that recognition of American independence would precede a general treaty. The *State Papers* is shorter, with sixteen items in twenty-five pages. Extracted here are the Commons address resolving against the continuance of the American war and the King's reply; Carleton's letter to Washington of 7 May covering the official papers from the Rockingham ministry announcing arrangements for the imminent end of hostilities; the congressional resolution of 4 October resolving to make no separate peace with Britain (the resolution resulted from French pressure, relations between the two states having deteriorated during the summer of 1782); a letter dating from 1778 from a French officer serving in the Continental Army to the French minister of war containing several generally unflattering observations regarding the Americans and indicating that Britain might easily subdue the revolution; and, finally, the preliminary articles of peace between Britain and the Bourbon powers signed on 3 January 1783.

26. *AR*, 1782, p. [181.

State of parties at the meeting of parliament. Debates on the speech from the throne. Addresses moved in both Houses, and amendments proposed and rejected. Debate resumed on the report of the address from the Committee. Motion for granting a supply to his Majesty opposed by Mr. T. Pitt, and after a warm debate carried, on a division, in the affirmative. Mr. Burke's motion for a committee of the whole House to inquire into the confiscation and sale of the effects and merchandize taken on the island of St. Eustatius, rejected. Motion by Mr. Hussey for adding 10,000 seamen to the number moved for by government for the service of the year 1782. Sir James Lowther's motion for putting an end to the American war rejected, after a long debate, by a majority of only 41. Debate on the army estimates. Conversation relative to the exchange of prisoners with America. Debate on the motion for adjournment. Petition from Mr. Laurens, presented by Mr. Burke. Recess.

DURING the recess of parliament no material change had taken place, either in the general temper of the nation, or in the political state of the contending parties. A total indifference to the desperate situation of affairs, or at least to the means of retrieving them, seems to have marked, at this time, the character of the people, beyond any former period of our history. The unsuccessful operations of the campaign, a circumstance which in former times had shaken the stability of the most popular administrations, scarcely raised a murmur against the present. The retreat of the Channel fleet recurred with the regularity of an annual review, and was regarded with as much unconcern. Our commerce was intercepted, the coasts of Great Britain and Ireland threatened and insulted; the ancient boast and security of this kingdom, the dominion of the sea, was seen in danger of being transferred to our enemies, without its exciting any other feeling than what the imminence of danger at the time produced. Our very successes had unfortunately been confined against a power whose interests had hitherto been considered as in some measure involving our own; and the [1] inconsiderate joy with which these triumphs over on ancient ally and a weak and unprovided enemy

were received by the people, afforded matter of no small concern to those who revered the old and approved maxims of English policy.

In such a state of things, it cannot be wondered that the enormous weight of influence which ministers derived from the ordinary and established power of the crown, the patronage of immense military establishments, and the annual expenditure of upwards of 20 millions of the public money*, should overpower the unaided and dispirited efforts of those who wished to rouze the nation to a sense of its real situation. The only hope, therefore, that remained of rescuing it from the effects of a false system of politics, under which its ruin seemed no longer problematical, was from the vigour and independence of parliament.

It was evident, from the numbers which divided on the side of opposition during the first session of the new parliament, that, notwithstanding the advantage the court-party had derived from a sudden dissolution, the strength of the minister had declined in the House of Commons. The calamitous event of the campaign in Virginia, the news of which arrived in England but a few days before their second meeting, was [2] likely to increase this defection, and threatened him with conse-

quences not less fatal to his power at home than it was decisive on the object in dispute abroad.

The contest in America had hitherto operated as an insuperable obstacle to the free exercise of parliamentary deliberation and control. The patient acquiescence of so large a majority in both houses, under the repeated disgraces, in which the pursuance of that object had involved the country, could be attributed to no other cause than the necessity they found themselves under of supporting the minister at all events, or of abandoning a favourite war, connected in some measure with their political prejudices, and in which their passions had been artfully and successfully inflamed. But the event, alluded to above, having cut up from the root all hope of subjugating the revolted colonies, in the minds even of the most sanguine adherers to that system, it was not to be expected they would so readily overlook the errors, or connive at the misconduct of those under whose mismanagement they had reaped nothing but mortification and disgrace.

What effect an event of such magnitude would produce in the councils of government, was looked for with an uncommon degree of anxious expectation. The ground on which ministers stood, was known to be extremely slippery and dangerous. The prosecution of the American war was generally understood to be the tenure by which they held their offices from the court. To abandon the war, was at once inevitably to forfeit the support of that secret influence, of which they had too long experienced the effects to be ignorant of its power. To venture to look that power in the face, to bring a full exposure of the state of affairs before the public, and to stand on their own merits, was an experiment which more fortunate ministers might

* The supplies voted for the year 1781 amounted to 25,380,324*l.* 10*s.* 8¾*d.*

have thought too hazardous to be lightly rifked.

It was this view of affairs which appears to have directed admini-ftration in the firft ftep that was neceffary to be taken at the open-ing of the feffions, on the 27th day of November, 1781. The fpeech from the throne continued to hold the fame determined lan-guage with which both houfes had been laft difmiffed. The con-tinuance of the war was afcribed to that reftlefs ambition which firft excited our enemies to com-mence it; and his Majefty was made to declare, that he fhould not anfwer the truft committed to the fovereign of a free people, nor make a fuitable return to his fub-jects for their conftant, zealous, and affectionate attachment to his perfon, family, and government, if he confented to facrifice either to his own defire of peace, or to their temporary eafe and relief, thofe effential rights and perma-nent interefts, upon the mainte-nance and prefervation of which the future ftrength and fecurity of the country muft ever principally depend. The loffes in America were neither diffembled nor pal-liated, but ftated as the ground for calling for the firm concur-rence and fupport of parliament, and a more vigorous, animated, and united exertion of the facul-ties and refources of the nation. This, with the mention of the fafe and profperous arrival of our numerous commercial fleets, the favourable appearance of affairs in the Eaft Indies, and a ftrong re-commendation to parliament to refume their enquiries into the ftate and condition of our domi-nions in that country, formed the fubftance of the King's fpeech.

In the Houfe of Commons, the motion for an addrefs, framed on the ufual form, produced on the part of oppofition a warm and ani-mated debate, which continued till two in the morning. The alarming declaration, contained in the fpeech from the throne, of the intentions of government to continue the profecution of the American war to the laft extre-mity; the infidious attempt to pledge the Houfe, by the propofed addrefs, to the unqualified fupport of a determination fo frantic and defperate, in the fpite of feven years dear-bought experience, and in the teeth of national bankruptcy and ruin; the audacity of holding fuch language at the very inftant when the calamitous effects of the mifconduct of minifters called for penitence and humiliation, were topics urged by Mr. Fox with great eloquence and ability, and followed by a fevere reprehenfion of the principles of the war, of the delufions by which parliament had been led on, year after year, to fupport it, and of the grofs and criminal mifmanagement that ap-peared in every branch of admi-niftration, and particularly in the marine department. To the neg-ligence and incapacity of the mi-nifter at the head of that board, he afcribed the lofs of the army under Lord Cornwallis. That minifter, he faid, had declared in another affembly, that a firft lord of the admiralty who fhould fail in having a fleet equal to the com-bined naval force of the houfe of Bourbon, would be unworthy of his fituation, and deferve to be dragged to condign punifhment. The cafe, he contended, was now before them. The inferiority of the Britifh fleet, in every quarter of the globe, he endea-voured to prove from the events of the campaign; and he conjured the Houfe not to delay that juftice which the noble earl had called down on his guilt. After appeal-ing to the cool and difpaffionate fenfe of the Houfe upon the utter impracticability of reducing the colonies by force, of which they had now had full experience, and calling particularly on the mem-ber who at that time held the office of paymafter-general, and[3]

who had declared on a former oc-cafion, "*that if the capture of Charles-Town produced no decifive confequeuces, he fhould grow weary of the American war,*" to join him in obliging adminiftration to put an end to it, he concluded a fpeech of great length, with moving, [that after the firft paragraph of the addrefs, the following words fhould be fubftituted in the place of the fubfequent claufes: "And we "will, without delay, apply our-"felves with united hearts to pro-"pofe and adjuft fuch councils "as may in this crifis excite the "efforts, point the arms, and by "a total change of fyftem, com-"mand the confidence of all his "Majefty's fubjects."

The impreffion which this fpeech feemed to make on the Houfe, and the filence of thofe who had formerly been the moft forward, on all occafions, to juf-tify the principles and the policy of the American war, called up the minifter early in the debate. He defended, with his ufual dex-terity and addrefs, the grounds of the conteft between Great Britain and her colonies. It did not, he faid, originate, as had been falfely reprefented, in any defign of mi-nifters to aggrandize the power or increafe the influence of the crown: had that been their ob-ject, they had thrown away and rejected the opportunity. It was not the prerogative of the crown, but the claims of parliament, that America had refifted. It was, therefore, to preferve the fupre-macy of parliament, and to main-tain its juft rights and privileges, that they had engaged in the war, and forborne the offer of ad-vancing one branch of the legif-lature to the dominion of Ame-rica, independent of the other two. With refpect to the conti-nuance of the war, the queftion, he afferted, was in no fhape be-fore the Houfe; and that there-fore no gentleman voting for the addrefs, would, as the neceffary refult of fuch a proceeding, pledge himfelf to affent either to any fpecific mode of operations, or to the fupport of a war at all againft the colonifts.

Though this explication of the addrefs was alfo fupported by the third fecretary of ftate, and by the right honourable member who had been fo particularly alluded to in the debate, it was ftill contended on the part of oppofition, that whatever fenfe his Majefty's fervants might, for the prefent, find it convenient to put upon it, the language was too infidious and delufive for the Houfe to adopt; and on a divifion there appeared for the amendment 129; againft it 218.

The attack which had been made, during the courfe of the debate, on the conduct of the firft lord of the admiralty, drew from one of the members of that board [4] a reply in his defence. He afferted, that the crippled ftate in which the noble lord had found the navy, and which had been owing to the parfimonious œconomy of Lord Hawke's admini- [5] ftration, was the caufe of its prefent weaknefs, if fuch a fact really exifted. This, however, he pofitively denied, and endeavoured to prove that it was even ftronger than its boafted ftate in 1759. He afferted, that the firft fleet fent out by Lord Sandwich, was fuperior to that of the enemy; that the nature of the war had rendered it impracticable to meet them in all places with that advantage: but, that even if it fhould be found we were unable to match them in force and numbers, the fault did not lie with the board of admiralty; it being a truth demonftrable from our naval hiftory, that whenever the French directed their whole attention to the improvement and increafe of their marine, they had always rendered it fuperior to that of Great Britain. Thefe pofitions were feverally denied by Admiral

Keppel; but being irrelevant to the queftion before the Houfe, they underwent no further difcuffion for the prefent.

An amendment to the fame effect with that moved in the Houfe of Commons, and expreffed in nearly the fame words, was moved in the Upper Houfe, and rejected by a majority of 75 (including 10 proxies) to 31. The debate alfo turned upon the fame general topics; but it was remarked, that the language of the two fecretaries [6] of ftate in that affembly was much more explicit and unequivocal with refpect to the intentions of government to profecute the war in America, than what the minifters in the other Houfe had ventured to maintain. This circumftance occafioned a fecond debate in the Houfe of Commons, upon receiving the report of the addrefs, on the following day, in which the queftion of the pledge, fuppofed to be conveyed by the addrefs to fupport that war, underwent another very able difcuffion.

On the fide of oppofition it was argued, that the prefent alarming crifis of affairs called, in a particular manner, for the moft explicit and intelligible language from parliament. That from the open and unqualified declaration of his Majefty's fervants in another place, the intentions of government could no longer remain a matter of doubt; and therefore, if the addrefs was not meant to convey to the king an engagement on their part to fupport him in thofe defigns, that it was hypocritical and delufive. That from the dark and ambiguous expreffions of the minifter in that Houfe, in the former debate, and his total filence in the prefent, fome doubts might be entertained refpecting his real private fentiments; but that whatever thofe might be, the meaning of the addrefs could only be collected from the terms in which it was expreffed; that thefe were

intelligible to the loweft capacity; and that it would be highly improper that the honour and reputation of the Houfe fhould be committed in the intrigues of a divided cabinet.

The defence of the addrefs, in its original form, was undertaken by Mr. Dundas, the Lord Advocate for Scotland. He began his [7] argument with obferving, that the news of a late great and national misfortune had not arrived unexpected by him, but that the impreffion it had left on his mind, had induced him to examine, with the moft fcrupulous jealoufy, the fpeech from the throne, fearing to find in it fome expreffion, an approbation of which might in any fort pledge him to a particular line of conduct in that Houfe: that, on the moft minute examination, he had not found any fuch expreffions in it; that its language was firm and manly, calculated to fhew the world that no difafter, however great, could deprefs the fpirit or fink the courage of the nation: but that ftill its language was general; that confequently the addrefs, which, as ufual, was couched in the fame terms, muft be general, and could not be underftood as preclufive of any future vote or parliamentary proceeding whatever. This, he faid, was the fenfe in which thofe who propofed and thofe who voted for the addrefs, underftood it; and he ridiculed the attempt that was made by others, who pretended that they only could conftrue it to force upon them a meaning which they utterly difavowed. Much of the intricacy which had involved the prefent queftion, he conceived, had arifen from the loofe and indefinite ufe of the term, "American war." If by an American war was meant a continental war in America, conducted on the fame military principles on which it had hitherto been carried on, it was with great reafon the Houfe had been cautioned againft pledging themselves for the support of it. But he could discover no such design either in the speech or in the address. But if the retention and defence of such places as were still left in our possession in America was to be called an American war, and under that denomination to be reprobated, he did not think the House yet ripe for such a decision. These, however, were matters totally unconnected with the question before the House; and whenever they came to be debated, which in a short time would undoubtedly be the case, every member, as well those who voted for as against the address, would be at full liberty to deliver their sentiments upon them.

With respect to the diversity of opinions which, it had been insinuated, prevailed amongst the members of the cabinet upon the subject of the future conduct of the war, he should declare his opinion with freedom and boldness, that the minister who, to preserve his situation, could submit to concur in measures which he disapproved, was highly criminal. It would not be admitted as any exculpation of such a minister, to say, he had been over-ruled in the cabinet. " That the King could " do no wrong," was a sacred maxim of the constitution, necessary for the personal safety of the sovereign, and for the free deliberation of parliament; but this maxim implied, that whatever was wrong in the administration of the state, was to be ascribed to his ministers; and that they, jointly and severally, were responsible to the public.

In answer to the arguments that had been drawn from a supposed ambiguity in the language of ministers, it might be asked, he said, what purpose could such a delusion (if any delusion is intended) answer? The cheat would be soon detected; it would scarcely last a week: a question would necessarily soon come before parlia-

ment, which would oblige ministers to speak out fully and explicitly. Being called on to explain to what he alluded, he said, that when ministers called on the House to vote a substitution of forces to replace the 7000 men lost with Lord Cornwallis, they must meet the question fully.

In answer to these arguments, it was again urged, that the intention with which an individual member of parliament might propose to confine his own assent to a general proposition, could be no measure for the proceedings of the House. That the sense and meaning of a written production arose from the words and phrases in which it was expressed. That though the words " American war," were studiously avoided, yet, from the language of former speeches and addresses, and from the whole tenor of the present, it was obviously the prosecution of that war his Majesty called on them to support. That the learned lord had deserted the proper ground of debate when he said so much about the *mode* of conducting the war. The *object* and *end* of it were the material consideration to be spoken to. The argument drawn from the shortness of the time which the delusion presumed could possibly operate, drew on the minister some severe and pointed animadversions from Mr. Burke. Such delusions, he said, the minister dealt in; they were the daily traffic of his invention. A week! he had often held out delusion for half that time; for a day only; nay, for a single hour. He had practised delusions upon the House, which died away before the debate was ended, only to serve the immediate purpose for which they had been contrived.

Among the miscellaneous matter which was introduced into this debate, the same gentleman called the attention of the House to what he conceived to be the most shocking and disgraceful proceeding

that had ever stained the British name: this was the 10th article of the capitulation of Lord Cornwallis, by which the royalists who had joined the British army, were left to the mercy of the civil power in America. By fire and sword, he said, we had forced the Americans to join the king's troops; and those very men who had been fighting with us to quell rebellion, were to suffer an ignominious death for having themselves been rebels. He painted, in the strongest colours, the headlands of the Chesapeak exhibiting the parched quarters of the king's friends; and asked, if it was not a glorious sight to meet the eyes of a prince of the royal blood on his [8] first arrival in America! After a most eloquent and successful application to the feelings of the House on this subject, he begged leave to mention another circumstance that had occurred in the same business, in which a serious mind, without being extremely addicted to superstition, might think it was the special hand of Providence. The Colonel Laurens who had drawn up the articles of capitulation, and in whose custody Lord Cornwallis was at that time a prisoner in America, was the son of Mr Laurens, late president of Congress, who had been committed a close prisoner to the Tower of London, of which Lord Cornwallis was himself the governor; and had thus become a prisoner to the son of his own prisoner.

Amongst the speeches most distinguished in this debate, that of Mr. Wm. Pitt was received with [9] singular marks of applause from every side of the House. At length the question being put, there appeared for bringing up the report 131; against it 54.

• • •

On the day appointed for voting the army supplies (the question alluded to by the Lord Advocate of Scotland, when, he said, ministers Dec. 12th.

would be under the neceffity of coming to fome explicit declaration with refpect to the continuance of the American war) the Houfe was early and uncommonly crowded. The difficulty with which it was forefeen the minifter would be brought to difclofe the intentions of government, and the dexterity he had already fhewn in evading the queftions with which he had been preffed on that fubject, induced the oppofition to bring forward a motion, which, though it fhould fail in its intended effect of forcing from him any binding declaration, might at leaft ferve to difcover the number of thofe in the Houfe, who, without refpect to their general political fentiments, agreed in opinion with them upon the profecution of the war.

As the object of this meafure was to form a coalition from all parties, for the fole purpofe of obliging the crown to put an end to an attempt at once ruinous and impracticable, the motion was drawn without any criminatory retrofpect, in terms the moft cool and temperate. It was " to de- " clare, that the war carried on " in the colonies and plantations " of North America, had been " ineffectual to the purpofes for " which it had been undertaken, " of affording protection to his " Majefty's loyal fubjects there, " and of defeating the hoftile in- " tentions of our confederated " enemies."—And fecondly, " That it was the opinion of " the Houfe, that all farther at- " tempts to reduce the Americans " to obedience by force, would " be ineffectual and injurious to " the true interefts of this country, " by weakening her powers to " refift her ancient and confe- " derated enemies."

The motion was made by Sir James Lowther, and feconded by Mr. Powis in a long and eloquent fpeech, in which the various topics that had been urged in the repeated difcuffions this matter had undergone, were placed in many new and ftriking points of view. As foon as he fat down, Lord North arofe, imagining, he faid, that the Houfe were in immediate expectation of hearing his opinion, and fenfible that the fooner it was given, they would be able with the greater facility and precifion to form a proper judgment on the two propofitions that had been offered to their confideration.

To the motions, he faid, he had great and weighty objections; but before he ftated them to the Houfe, he felt himfelf bound, efpecially after what had paffed on another occafion, to fpeak much more explicitly than what was his ufual cuftom, and indeed, than was wife and politic for a man in a high and refponfible office to do, concerning the future mode of profecuting the war. He then declared, that his Majefty's fervants had come to a determination, that the mode of profecuting hoftilities internally on the continent of America, fhould no longer be followed; but that the form of the war fhould undergo a total change. This declaration, he faid, he fhould not have thought himfelf warranted in duty to make, had not the eftimate of the army, then on the table, declared nearly as much. By thofe eftimates the Houfe would fee that government had not provided itfelf with the means of carrying on the war in the manner it had hitherto been conducted; and, therefore, the Houfe could not require a furer pledge of the future intentions of adminiftration.

Having made this declaration, his lordfhip ftated the objections to which he conceived the motion before the Houfe was liable. He infifted on its impolicy, as it pointed out to the enemy what was to be the future fyftem of the war, and confequently directed them where to prepare for defence, or to plan their attacks with the greateft advantage. He objected to the loofe and general terms in which it was expreffed: a circumftance which he thought alone fufficient to induce the Houfe to reject it. It called on them to refolve againft *all future attempts* to reduce the Americans by force. Were the motion to pafs, though the American privateers fhould infult our coafts, or cut our merchantmen out of harbour, no Englifh officer would venture to attack or oppofe them. Was New York and its dependencies, was Charles Town and Halifax to be evacuated? Defended they could not be, if the motion fhould pafs; at leaft, added the noble lord, if *I* had brought forward fuch a motion, and given it a lefs extenfive explanation, I fhould have been accufed without mercy of fhufflings, twiftings, and evafions, in order to delude the Houfe. Was it intended then that we fhould withdraw our armies and our fhips, give up to them all our ports, open to them all the feas, and fuffer them to give what affiftance they pleafed to the ancient enemies of this country? Was it not known they were bound by treaty to aid the French and Spaniards in the conqueft of the Weft India iflands? And could it be doubted that this would be the firft effect of our totally abandoning the war in America? If it was imagined that fuch a proceeding might facilitate the return of peace, he muft again beg leave to be of a totally different opinion. He could not conceive that the moft effectual way to render an adverfary tractable, and make him reafonable with refpect to terms of peace, would be to declare we would fight him no more.

Thefe were the principal objections made by Lord North; in which he was fupported by Mr. Welbore Ellis and Lord George [10] Germaine. The latter having declared that he regarded the motion as amounting to a resolution to abandon the American war altogether, said, he should make no scruple in assuring the House, that if parliament acceded to it, he should immediately retire; for be the consequence what it might, he would not hold his place on the condition of signing any instrumeut tending to establish the independence of America. Several of the country gentlemen declared themselves satisfied with the assurances given by ministers, considering them as tantamount to the proposition before the House, unless those propositions were designed to go a length which they thought neither constitutional, prudent, safe, nor honourable.

In support of the question, it was contended, that the first objection stated by the noble lord, scarcely deserves a serious answer. That to suppose a resolution to abandon the American war, would in any degree discover to the enemy against what part of their extensive dominions, vulnerable in a thousand places, the next blow would be aimed, was absurd and ridiculous. It would rather tend to produce a contrary effect; at present, they were sure of meeting us, and that to the greatest advantage, on the continent of North America; whereas the measure now recommended, by setting our arms at perfect liberty, would increase the apprehensions, embarrass the councils, and distract the operations of the enemy.

The objection drawn from the latitude of the terms in which the motion was expressed, was said to be equally ill-founded. The most general terms had been adopted, in order to prevent the House, as much as possible, from interfering with the executive branch of government. It was the object of the war government was called on to relinquish: it was all further attempts to reduce the colonies

to obedience by force, that parliament was desired to reprobate. The general conduct of the war against Spain, Holland, and France, united with America, was still left where the constitution had placed it, in the hands of the King; and it was only designed to convey to the crown the opinion that House entertained of the fatal effects of continuing to prosecute the American contest, as one of the primary objects of the war.

As to the effect which the measure proposed would have in accelerating or retarding an honourable accommodation, it was argued, that the particular situation in which the colonists stood, made it necessary for them to avoid, in common prudence, the danger of exciting the jealousy of their allies, by making to Great Britain the first overtures of reconciliation. That the first advances towards it must therefore be made by us; and that nothing would so effectually engage America to meet us, as freeing her from all apprehensions for her own security.

With respect to the assurances given by ministers, which appeared to have so much weight with several members of the House, it was asked to what they amounted, even if they could be depended on, such as they were?—It had been said, that the mode of the war was to be totally changed; that it was not to be conducted on the same plan and on the same scale as before.

A war then it was obvious there was still to be; and Gen. Burgoyne said he was ready, as a professional man, to join issue with those on the opposite side of the House on this single point, Whether the language of the ministers, coupled with their avowed intention of keeping New York and other posts on the continent of America, did not evince an obstinate adherence in the King's councils to offensive war? The

great, if not the only purpose of keeping places of arms upon an enemy's coast, and especially upon a continent, must, he said, be for offensive operations. But even if the consequence should not be granted, the maintenance of posts upon any other principle, would prove not only a most improvident and preposterous mode of war, but equally ruinous with the present.

At two o'clock in the morning the House divided on the question for the order of the day, when there appearing ayes, 220; noes, 179,—the original question was consequently lost.

The number of those who had usually supported the minister, but who voted against him on the present occasion, were supposed to have amounted nearly to twenty. Though this defection was not in itself of sufficient magnitude to be attended with any immediate bad effect to the existence of administration, yet other symptoms appeared, which seemed to threaten it with the most fatal consequences. The total want of union and concert in the cabinet, the great diversity of opinion which prevailed among the servants of the crown, and which they were no longer able to conceal, occasioned among all descriptions of people a very just and universal alarm. Those who had hitherto acted with government from a coincidence of opinion, either found themselves at a loss where to fix in the general wreck of principle, or chose rather to risk a change of system, than expose the country to the inevitable ruin which must have followed the divided and fluctuating state of its councils. Others, who looked only at the fortune of ministers, foresaw with great quickness the weakness those divisions would necessarily occasion, and the dangerous advantage this would give to active and powerful opponents. But what seems to have principally contributed to deftroy that implicit confidence which the House had been in the habit for fo long a courfe of years of repofing in the minifter, was the doubtful and undecided manner in which he was, perhaps, under the neceffity of expreffing himfelf upon the important queftions now under difcuffion. The minds of men being by this means, as it were, fet afloat, every one was in fome fort obliged to think for himfelf; and the great advantage attending ftrong and decided meafures was loft, which impofe on the fenfe of mankind, and often gain fupport and applaufe without examination.

It was alfo remarked in this debate, that the members who, tho' joined to the great body of the Whigs, were fuppofed to act more immediately in concurrence with the Earl of Shelburne, expreffed themfelves upon the fubject of the continuance of the war in America with great caution and referve. The queftion of Independence having alfo unavoidably arifen in the courfe of the day, Mr. Dunning declared it to be his opinion, that the perfon who fhould propofe an avowal of it in favour of America, would be guilty of a crime little fhort of high treafon.

The late hour to which the debate on the 12th had been protracted, made it neceffary to defer proceeding on the bufinefs of the army eftimates till the following Friday, when Dec. 14th. the fubject of the American war underwent, for the fourth time fince the beginning of the feffion, a long and vehement difcuffion. The arguments that had been made ufe of on former occafions were again chiefly recurred to; the infecurity and infufficiency of the affurances given by minifters were urged, not without a mixture of perfonal afperity and invective, on the ground of former delufions, of notorious difunion in the councils, and contra-

dictory language among the members of adminiftration. On the fide of the latter, the debate was but weakly fupported; and the firft lord of the treafury, though called on, in a manner not lefs unufual than unbecoming to the dignity of government, by members poffeffing high offices under the crown, to ftate the differences which fubfifted in the cabinet to the Houfe, contented himfelf with repeating his former declarations.

A divifion again took place, on a motion that the chairman fhould quit the chair, and report a progrefs; which was negatived by 166 to 84; after which the feveral motions made by the fecretary at war were carried without debate.

Dec. 17th. Mr. Burke gave notice of his intentions to move, foon after the expiration of the recefs, for leave to bring in a bill to regulate the mode of exchanging prifoners with America. The law as it then ftood, he faid, was not only unjuft and oppreffive in its principle, but liable to the moft enormous abufes. Its operation, inftead of being directed by the nature of the offences it was intended to affect, was confined to diftinctions purely geographical. Thus it depended, not on the imputed criminality of a prifoner, but on the place where he was taken, or the place to which he was conveyed, whether he fhould be confidered as a traitor, a pirate, or a prifoner of war. Among the abufes which had arifen from the exercife of the power given to government by the act alluded to, he adverted particularly to the fituation of Mr. Laurens and Lieut. Gen. Burgoyne. With refpect to the former, he reprehended with great feverity the cruelty, the injuftice, and the impolicy of the treatment that diftinguifhed perfon had met with. He meant at the proper time to contend, that he was entitled to his freedom on parole, as

a prifoner of war; but whether the Houfe fhould coincide with him in that opinion or not, the enexampled rigour and feverity of his confinement admitted of no excufe. He had called the attention of the Houfe to this very ferious bufinefs at the beginning of the feffion, and had propofed that the lieutenant of the Tower fhould be examined on the fubject at the bar of the Houfe. But from fome appearance of difinclination in government to this ftep, and the fear of injuring, by any hafty proceeding, the perfon whofe fituation he wifhed to relieve, and partly from a perfuafion that minifters would themfelves be defirous of preventing any further difcuffion by redreffing the grievance complained of,—he had declined making any motion on the fubject.

The cafe of Lieut. Gen. Burgoyne was not lefs cruel and oppreffive, his exchange having been prevented by a manœuvre that was likely to doom him to perpetual captivity. A party of the Americans having been cut off by a detachment of British troops, joined by a large party of Indians, the commander, in order to fave the lives of his prifoners from the barbarity of his allies, was obliged to connive at their efcape, having however firft ftipulated with one of the American generals, that the men thus fuffered to efcape, fhould be accounted for in the next exchange. This ftipulation Congrefs had refufed to ratify; and accordingly thefe men (who from the name of the poft where they were taken, were called *Cedar-men*) though generally claimed, had always been tacitly allowed to be fet afide in the fubfequent cartels. But when the American commiffioners had agreed to accept of 1040 prifoners, in exchange for Lieut. Gen. Burgoyne, minifters had for the firft time infifted on their taking the *Cedar-men* as a part of that number; and the Americans being equally determined in refusing them, his exchange, under such circumstances, became a matter of absolute impossibility.

As a farther proof of the partial and oppressive conduct of government towards the lieutenant-general, Mr. Burke informed the House that he had received a letter from Dr. Franklin, inclosing a resolution of Congress, by which he was empowered to treat with the British ministry for the purpose of exchanging General Burgoyne for Mr. Laurens. This negociation Dr. Franklin had requested Mr. Burke to undertake; and he had accordingly made the proper official applications; but hitherto without effect.

In the conversation which afterwards took place on this subject, the charge of Mr. Laurens's having been treated with any unusual rigour was positively denied. In proof of this assertion, a letter was read from the lieutenant-governor of the Tower, dated November 1780, in which he acquaints one of the secretaries of state, that he had waited on Mr. Laurens for the express purpose of satisfying himself with respect to the treatment he had received, and that he learned from his own mouth, that he had met with every civility and kindness that he could possibly hope for. A member also[11] got up and declared, that the lieutenant-governor had again visited his prisoner, within the last three days, and that he had not heard there was the smallest ground of complaint.

Between these contradictory assertions the matter remained suspended till the day of the adjournment of the House, when Mr. Burke brought up a *representation and prayer*, addressed to the House of Commons by Mr. Laurens himself; which was, on a motion, laid on the table. It was remarkable that this petition * was written by Mr. Laurens himself with a black lead pencil;

he having, as is supposed, refused to accept of some indulgences that had been lately offered him, and among the rest, that of pen and ink, the use of which had been during the greatest part of his confinement strictly forbidden him.

It may not be improper in this place to add, that the admission of Mr. Laurens to bail, and the exchange of General Burgoyne, which soon after took place, together with the subsequent alterations in the political government of the country, made it unnecessary for Mr. Burke to proceed with his intended bill of regulation.

In the House of Lords, the ordinary business of government was suffered to proceed without any opposition till the day appointed for passing Dec. 19th. the malt and land-tax bills, when the Marquis of Rockingham moved, that the third reading of the bills should be deferred till the first Wednesday after the recess.

He prefaced this motion by declaring, that a recent public calamity, the retreat of the fleet under Admiral Kempenfeldt, had[12] brought him down that day to the House; that he came without consultation with any person whatever, and with the expectation that he should probably not meet with a single peer who could unite in opinion with him; but that he was neither to be deterred from the faithful discharge of his duty by superiority of numbers, nor disheartened by the thin attendance of his friends.

He then entered into a concise but comprehensive detail of the state of the nation, and urged from thence the necessity of coming to some immediate and decisive measures for saving what remained of the empire from the irretrievable ruin towards which it was rapidly verging. If the difficulties under which the country laboured had arisen from the

ordinary vicissitudes of fortune, he knew, he said, that the pride, the spirit, the perseverance, the unconquerable resolution of Englishmen would still be able to surmount them; but whilst he traced them to their real cause, to the existence of a ruinous system of politics which had blasted the vigour and energy of the country, had driven every man of honour and ability from the service of the crown, and was founded on a principle of weakness and disunion for its basis, he confessed that he felt himself overwhelmed with despair.

After a speech of considerable length, which was delivered with an unusual exertion of voice and a flow of genuine eloquence, he concluded with calling on the noble lords present to join him in delaying for a few days the granting of the proposed supplies, in order that in a fuller assembly, and after a more mature deliberation, they might be better able to judge how far it was prudent to entrust any longer the expenditure of the public money to persons whose gross misconduct was every day the cause of accumulating fresh misfortunes on the country.

The objections made to the proposition of the Marquis, were founded on the mischiefs that would arise from any delay in granting the current supplies of the year, and were nearly the same with those that had been urged before on the like occasion in the other House. The question, as amended, being put, was carried in the negative, and the bills passed without a division.

• • •

The same day the Duke of[13] Richmond brought forward in the House of Lords, a motion of which he had given previous notice, relative to the execution of Colonel Isaac Haynes, an officer[14] in the service of Congress. The fact, as stated by the noble duke, on the authority of letters transmitted to him from America by a person to whom he was an entire stranger, was as follows:—

On the morning of the 26th of July 1781, Colonel Haynes, at that time a prisoner in Charles-Town, was informed by letter from the town-major, " that a " council of general officers would " assemble the next day at ten " o'clock to try him." In the evening, the same day, he received another letter from the same officer, acquainting him, " That in- " stead of a council of general " officers, a court of inquiry " would sit at the hour before " mentioned, for the purpose of " determining under what point " of view he ought to be con- " sidered." In the same letter it was added, " That pen, ink, and " paper, would immediately be " allowed him; and that any " person he chose to appoint " might attend him as counsel." On Sunday the 29th, a memorandum was delivered to him by the adjutant, informing him, " That in consequence of the " court of inquiry held the day " before on his account, Lord " Rawdon and the commandant, " Lieutenant-colonel Balfour, had " resolved upon his execution on " the Tuesday following, for " having been found under arms, " and employed in raising a re- " giment to oppose the British " government, though he had be- " come a subject, and had ac- " cepted the protection of that " government after the reduction " of Charles-Town."

In consequence of this intimation, Colonel Haynes addressed himself to the two commanders in a letter, in which he states that he had been drawn by surprise into a procedure tending to judgment, without knowing it to be such; that when he appeared before the court of inquiry, he did not imagine it was for any other purpose than to determine whether he ought to be looked on as a

British subject or an American, in order, on that decision, to ground the future proceedings; that the counsel he had named had not been found; that he had neglected to summon any witnesses, and by that means had been deprived of the ability of making a legal defence, which he could easily have done, founded both in law and fact, if he had imagined the trial he was then upon was to be final. He therefore desires a regular trial; and if that be not granted, he intreats a respite of the sentence of execution. This application, aided by the solicitations of Governor Bull, and other inhabitants of Charles-Town, procured a respite of eight-and-forty hours; but with this condition, that if General Green made any application whatsoever in his favour, he should that moment be led to execution. On the day appointed, Colonel Haynes was executed.

Such was the state of the fact. The illegality, the barbarity, and the impolicy of the proceeding, were strongly and powerfully urged by the Duke of Richmond. He read to the House an extract from a proclamation of General Green's, in which this execution was represented as a cruel and unjustifiable murder, and a severe retaliation threatened on the persons of British officers; and he called on the House to institute an immediate and effectual inquiry, as the only means of securing their own officers from the danger which hung over them, and of rescuing the British nation from the opprobrious charges of cruelty and barbarity under which it was labouring, in the opinion of all the states of Europe.

The Duke concluded with moving an address to his Majesty, that directions might be given for laying before the House the several papers therein specified, relative to the execution of Col. Haynes. This motion was strongly opposed

by Lord Walsingham, Lord Stormont, and the Chancellor. It was argued, that his Majesty's ministers having declared that they had received no information whatever relative to the facts alluded to, it was beneath the dignity and gravity of the House to proceed to a solemn inquiry on such vague and uncertain surmises as those contained in the letters produced by the noble duke; that it was still less candid and less equitable to attempt, on such slight grounds, to call in question the characters of brave, deserving, and absent officers.

But allowing the facts as stated to be true, and fully authenticated, to the satisfaction of the House, it was contended by the two last-mentioned lords (by the former on the ground of modern practice, and by the latter on that of ancient authority) that Colonel Haynes having been taken in arms after admission to his parole, was liable to be hanged up *instanter*, without any other form of trial than what was necessary to identify the person.[15] The Earl of Huntingdon also ac-[16] quainted the House, that he had authority from Earl Cornwallis to declare, that this had been the practice in several instances under his command in North America.

This doctrine was denied on both grounds with equal confidence, by the Earls of Shelburne and Effingham. It was asserted by the former, from circumstances within his own recollection, that the practice in the last war had been totally different. A great degree of ignominy, perhaps a stricter confinement, was the consequence of such an action: the persons guilty of it were shunned by gentlemen; but it had never before entered into the mind of a commander to hang them.

In answer to the written authority produced by the learned lord, it was remarked by the

Earl of Effingham, that the quotation he had brought from Grotius related to spies, and not to prisoners who had broken their parole. That this was the case could not be disputed, since Grotius could never have heard of a prisoner on parole; it was a modern civility of a very late date, and even not yet prevailing in all countries. In reply to this observation, it was argued by the chancellor, that all the reasoning used by the great author he had quoted in the case of spies, applied *a fortiori* to that of persons who had broke their parole.

At length the question being put, and the House having divided, there appeared for the address 25; against it 73.

The appointment of Mr. Welbore Ellis to the office of secretary of state for the plantation department, vacant by the resignation of Lord Viscount Sackville, and of Lieutenant General Sir Guy Carleton, to succeed the commander in chief of the forces in North America, having occasioned a general alarm amongst those who were persuaded that there still existed a secret and obstinate attachment in the court to the prosecution of the war against the colonies, it was resolved to make another attempt in the House of Commons, to bind up the hands of the executive government by a strong and explicit declaration of the opinion of parliament. With this view, General Conway moved, that an address should be presented to his Majesty, to implore his Majesty to listen to the advice of his commons, that the war in America might no longer be pursued, for the impracticable purpose of reducing the inhabitants of that country to obedience by force; and to express their hopes that his Majesty's desire to restore the public tranquillity might be forwarded, and made effectual, by a happy reconciliation with the revolted colonies.

Feb. 22d.[17]

The debate on this motion lasted till two o'clock in the morning. All the arguments used on former occasions were recurred to on both sides the House; the ministers continued to hold the same vague and undetermined language as before; and, on the division, there appeared for the address, 193; against it, 194.

The event of this division was considered by opposition as a complete victory over the minister on the subject of the American war; and as a majority of the absent members were supposed to coincide in opinion with the former, it was resolved to bring the question before the House again the first opportunity. Accordingly, on the 27th, General Conway moved a resolution, the same in substance with that which had been lost before the holidays, and only altered in the mode of expression, in compliance with the orders of the House.

Feb. 27th.

He introduced his motion by a most eloquent and animated speech, in which he combated all the objections that had been urged on former occasions by the other side of the House.

It had been asserted, that it was unconstitutional for that House to interfere with its advice in matters which specially belong to the executive branch of government. This position he positively condemned, both as repugnant to the spirit of the constitution, and totally unsupported by fact. He proved, from a regular series of precedents, down from the reign of Edward the Third to the accession of his present Majesty, that parliament had always been in the practice of interposing, with its advice, in matters of peace and war, of treaties and alliances, and even in the marriages of the royal family. Such interference had indeed sometimes been reprehended from the throne, as an improper intermeddling in state-

affairs; but parliament, and particularly that House, had generally made its voice to be heard with authority and effect.

Another objection that had been made to the motion, was its being vague, and obscurely worded. That it nearly concerned the dignity of the House, that its orders should be strictly and punctually obeyed; and therefore, it was requisite they should be expressed in the most clear and intelligible manner. It had likewise been asserted, that it could not yet be decidedly collected, from any of the propositions that had been submitted to the House, whether all hostilities in America, on our side, were to cease; or, if war was still to exist, what kind of military operations were intended to be allowed.

In answer to these remarks, General Conway observed, that the words he had adopted in the present motion, " offensive war," were, to military persons, at least, sufficiently descriptive of the species of hostilities to which the motion was designed to put an end. The war was to be strictly defensive, and none other; such a war as General Elliot was then waging in Gibraltar; such a war as General Murray had lately carried on in Fort St. Philip. The necessity of tying up the hands of government thus closely, was evident, from the ingenuity they had shewn in eluding every attempt that had been made to bind them, by some explicit declaration of their own. As soon as it was perceived that the war was in bad odour in the House, and that it was necessary to quiet the alarm which the speech from the throne had excited, they were brought, with some difficulty, to intimate that hostilities should not be carried on to the *same extent* as formerly. This not being deemed satisfactory, it was declared that there should be no *internal continental war*. The apprehensions[18] of the public being rather increased than diminished by these extorted and ambiguous declarations, recourse was next had to a *war of posts*. It is allowed on all hands, say they, that we should keep what we still possess; and certainly no one would object to the changing of our situation, if another should be thought more advantageous, or more tenable. When it was urged that a war of this kind would subject us to all the expence and all the risk of offensive operations, a new and curious device was recurred to, that of a *French war in America*; the invention, as it seemed, of the newly appointed secretary of state. The Americans, that gentlemen had said, with a sort of triumph, are fed, clothed, and paid by France; they are led on by French officers; the French and the American armies are incorporated in one; it was not mere locality that should give a name to a war. France had formerly been fought, with success, in Germany; and he saw no solid objection to fighting her now in America. The folly and madness of such an attempt, General Conway argued, would instantly appear, from what had already happened. France, with 5000 troops, which did not cost her more than 40l. per man a year, was carrying on the war against us, and even with success, who paid for 73,000, at 100l. a man expence in the year.

There was, he said, a fifth kind of war, which rumour had bruited to be in the contemplation of government, a war, at the very mention of which nature shuddered; he meant an *Indian war*. A new officer, under the title of Inspector of Indian affairs, had, he was assured, been lately appointed; he could not acquaint the House for what purpose, but in times like the present, he could hardly think it was meant as a sinecure. This circumstance,

added to a declaration he had heard from one of his Majesty's servants in the former debate,[19] " that we must make the Americans feel the calamities of war, " in order to make them wish for " peace," had, he must confess, given him the most serious and dreadful apprehensions.

He, lastly, cautioned the House against the fallacy of an argument that had been urged with great confidence from the other side: Look, say they, at the army estimates, and you will find unquestionable security, that government does not mean to carry on offensive war in America. General Conway reminded the House, that though 73,000 men were voted and paid for we had never above half that number in actual service. Government had, therefore, only to complete the regiments, and they would have more men in America than ever they had before.

The motion was seconded by Lord Viscount Althorpe, and opposed by Lord North, in a long and able reply. He objected to it as unnecessary, after the assurances that had been given by government; a dangerous, on account of the information it conveyed to our enemies; as impolitic, because it entirely took away from the executive government the use of its discretion; as tending to retard rather than to advance the attainment of peace, the great object in view by both sides of the House. He therefore could only consider the motion as a party measure, and, in that light, he thought it not less exceptionable. If, said he, the House suspects the sincerity of the servants of the crown, if they have any doubts of their ability or integrity, it is not by such a motion as the present that they ought to express their sentiments; they ought to address the crown to remove those ministers in whom they could not place confidence, and to appoint others in whom they could[20]

confide. A minister, he said, ought no longer to continue a minister after he was suspected by that House. He should be like Cæsar's wife, not only free from guilt, but even from suspicion. If, indeed, the House should shew that they had withdrawn their confidence from him, it would be his duty, without waiting for an address for his removal, to wait upon his Sovereign, and, delivering up the seals of his office, say to him, " Sir, I have long served you " with dilligence, with zeal, and " with fidelity, but success has " not crowned my endeavours; " your parliament have withdrawn from me their confidence; all my declarations to them are suspected; therefore, " Sir, let me resign to you those " employments, which I ought " not to keep longer than I can " be serviceable to your Majesty " and your subjects."

Lord North was followed by the Attorney-General, who observed,[21] that there were many more obstacles to be removed, in order to treat of peace with the Americans, than the House seemed to be aware of. At that moment, several acts of parliament were in existence, which would prove insuperable bars to such an attempt. He therefore should recommend, as the first necessary step, a truce; during the continuance of which, the enmity, occasioned by the violence of the contest, might subside; and each party, being at leisure to consult their real interests, might accede to terms of peace, which, having undergone a slow and temperate discussion, might prove more honourable and advantageous, as well as more likely to secure a permanent union, than those resulting from sudden overtures and sudden acquiescence. He declared his intentions of bringing in a bill, with the permission of the House, for these purposes; and he should therefore move, " that the pre-

" sent debate be adjourned until " Wednesday, the thirteenth of " the enfuing month of March."

Several other members took a part in the debate, which again continued till near two o'clock, when, though the propofition of the Attorney was fuppofed to have brought over a few irrefolute votes to the fide of the minifter, there appeared for the adjournment only 215; againft it, 234, exclufive of the two tellers on each fide. The number of thofe who were prefent at the beginning of the debate, but had paired off in the courfe of the evening, were faid to have amounted to 14. The original queftion, and an addrefs to the King, formed upon the refolution, were then carried without a divifion, and the addrefs was ordered to be prefented by the whole Houfe.

On the Monday following, his Majefty's anfwer was reported to the Houfe; in which he affures them, " that in purfuance of their " advice, he fhould take fuch " meafures as fhould appear to " him to be moft conducive to " the reftoration of harmony " between Great Britain and the " revolted colonies; and that his " efforts fhould be directed, in the " moft effectual manner, againft " our European enemies, till fuch " a peace could be obtained as " fhould confift with the intereft " and permanent welfare of his " kingdoms."

The thanks of the Houfe being unanimoufly voted to the King for his gracious anfwer, General Conway rofe again, and, after expreffing his concern at having been reduced to the neceffity of trefpaffing fo frequently of late on the patience of the Houfe, moved another refolution, to the following effect: " that the Houfe " would confider as enemies to " his Majefty and the country, " all thofe who fhould advife, or " by any means attempt, the fur- " ther profecution of offenfive

" war on the continent of North " America, for the purpofe of " reducing the revolted colonies " to obedience by force."

The neceffity of this meafure, in order to fecure and render permanent to the nation the beneficial confequences of their former refolution, had arifen, he faid, from two circumftances. The firft was, that minifters had declared, that though they fhould think themfelves bound to comply with the fenfe of the majority of that Houfe, yet they ftill retained their former fentiments refpecting the want of wifdom and policy in the meafures recommended. The unwilling obedience of perfons, who could bring themfelves to act in direct oppofition to their own judgment, he thought could not be too ftrongly fecured. The anfwer they had advifed his Majefty to return to the addrefs of that Houfe, was another circumftance, affording juft ground of jealoufy and diftruft. In that anfwer, all reference to the profecution of offenfive war was cautioufly avoided; the Houfe was informed, in general terms, that he fhould take fuch meafures as might appear to him moft conducive to the reftoration of peace; but the Houfe had no reafon to fuppofe but that a more vigorous profecution of the war might be deemed one of thefe conducive meafures. The motion, after a feeble oppofition from government, was at length fuffered to pafs, without a divifion.

Thefe refolutions were received by the public with general demonftrations of joy; in the midft of which, the rare fortune of the right honourable gentleman who took the lead in this bufinefs, was much envied and admired, in having thus, a fecond time, given peace to America, and happily put a ftop to the alarming progrefs of thofe dreadful calamities which he had before, but unfortunately in vain, fhewn the way to prevent.

March 6th. Whilft thefe great and important queftions were agitating in the Commons Houfe, the conduct of government, with refpect to the late campaign in North America, underwent a ftrict and fevere fcrutiny in a committee of the lords. After feveral intermediate debates, which chiefly turned on the propriety of producing certain papers and documents from the public offices, the bufinefs was at length brought to a conclufion, on a motion by the Duke of Chandos, " that it was the opinion of [22] " the committee, that the imme- " diate caufe of the capture of the " army under Earl Cornwallis, in " Virginia, appeared to be the " want of a fufficient naval force " to cover and protect the fame." This motion was negatived, by a majority of 72 to 37.

The manly and public-fpirited language held by the minifter in the debate of the 27th of February, had raifed a general expectation that the lofs of the queftion on that day, and the fubfequent meafures of the 4th of March, would have been followed by his immediate refignation. It can fcarcely be doubted, from the daily mortifications to which his continuance in office expofed him, and the extreme improbability of his being able to regain the ground he had loft, but that this would have been the cafe, had he not been induced by other caufes to act contrary both to his principle and inclination. The crifis was doubtlefs, in the utmoft degree, alarming to the court. Had a mere perfonal change of minifters been the point at iffue, it is probable that little ceremony would have been ufed in gratifying the wifhes of parliament. But it was well underftood, that a complete revolution in the internal policy of government would be the inevitable confequence of their removal: a revolution not lefs important in its effects, nor lefs dreaded by the court, than any other which the nation had before experienced.

It was therefore very generally supposed, that the noble lord at the head of the treasury was prevailed on to continue in a situation that was neither honourable to himself nor without injury to the country, till every means were tried of averting what was considered as the most dreadful of evils. The obscure language which he held, when pressed on that ground in the House of Commons, afforded a strong presumption of the truth of this supposition. He declared, at different times, that he kept his post from a principle of gratitude, and not from inclination; that he remained in his employment to prevent confusion; that he should quit it as soon as he could retire with honour; but that particular circumstances stood in the way at present, which he could not farther explain. It was to no purpose, that the indecency of his clinging to office, under the circumstances in which he then stood, and after the declaration he had himself made, was, day after day, urged by opposition with an unusual degree of acrimony; he contented himself with retorting on his adversaries their indecent impatience to get possession of his employments; and with defending himself on the latter part of the charge, by saying, that though parliament had interfered by its advice, and had taken a stronger measure than he thought necessary for securing obedience to it, yet it did not appear, from any vote or resolution they had yet passed, that the House had totally withdrawn its confidence from the present administration.

March 8th. To bring the matter to this issue, the following resolutions were moved by Lord John Cavendish, and seconded by Mr. Powys:

" That it appears to this " House, that since the year 1775, " upwards of one hundred mil- " lions of money have been ex- " pended on the army and na- " vy in a fruitless war:

" That it appears to this " House, that during the above " period, we have lost the thir- " teen colonies of America, " which anciently belonged to " the crown of Great Britain " (except the posts of New York, " Charles-Town, and Savannah) " the newly acquired colony of " Florida, many of our valuable " West India and other islands, " and those that remain are in " the most imminent danger:

" That it appears to this " House, that Great Britain is at " present engaged in an expen- " five war with America, France, " Spain, and Holland, without " a single ally:

" That it appears to this " House, that the chief cause of " all these misfortunes, has been " the want of foresight and abi- " lity in his Majesty's ministers."

The debate, as far as related to the merits of the question, lay within a small compass. In support of the conclusion drawn in the last resolution (for the facts contained in the three first were admitted on all sides) it was argued, in the first place, that a long and uninterrupted series of misfortune and disgrace was in itself a sufficient proof of misconduct; and secondly, that the separate measures of administration were so strongly marked with weakness and folly, as to carry their own condemnation on the face of them. On the other side, it was contended, that misfortune could not be allowed to infer misconduct; and that even granting this, those who planned measures were not solely responsible for them. The fault might be in the execution; and therefore, it would ill become the justice of the House to proceed to a partial censure,

without any previous hearing or enquiry.

This ground, however, appeared so weak, even to the friends of administration, that it was almost entirely deserted, except by the ministers themselves; and the question was taken up with great art and ingenuity on other topics. It was said, that the motion being intended to operate as a vote for the removal of the present ministry, the House would do well, before it adopted so serious a measure, to take a view of the principles and opinions of those who most probably would be their successors. It was asked, if the House was ready to vote the independence of America? If it was prepared to new-model the constitution, to alter the duration of parliaments, and the rights of election? Would it be willing to give up its exclusive privilege of framing money-bills? or was it curious to see the effects of those latent powers which a noble earl had, in the course of his reading, discovered to exist in the House of Peers? Would it consent to a [23] violation of the national faith with the crown, by adopting a celebrated bill of reform in the civil list of expenditure?

It was then demanded, whether that harmony and concord subsisted amongst the new candidates for power, the want of which had been so often and so vehemently urged against the present administration? How would the inflexible spirit of a noble earl, who [24] had pledged his word in the other House, that he would under no circumstances consent to the independence of the colonies, be brought to bend to the opinion of those who seemed so ready to acknowledge it? The same noble person had declared, that he should always wish to see the King his own minister: a doctrine of no trifling political importance, and yet, which would sound very heretical in the ears of most of his friends on the opposite side of the House. With respect to the different sects of political reformers, they were equally numerous, and more at variance with each other than those of religion.

These topics were urged with great eloquence and ability by Mr. Adam and the Lord Advocate [25] of Scotland; the latter of whom called particularly on the member for Westminster to declare, whe-[26] ther, in case he should find himself, when minister, in a minority, he would pay that deference to the opinion of the House which he had so loudly called for from the noble lord? or whether he would not appeal to his other parliament out of doors, and tell them they were betrayed by their representatives? It nearly concerned the House, he said, to have these various matters well and thoroughly understood, before they proceeded to discharge the present ministers from their offices, and threw the whole government of the country into the hands of their opponents.

In defence of his principles and conduct against this personal attack, Mr. Fox observed, that there was a material difference between a private member appealing to his constituents, or to the nation at large, whose agent he was in parliament, and a servant of the crown holding an office at the will of the King, attempting to appeal to them, in that capacity, against parliament. The former he should still contend was in the true spirit of the constitution; the latter, he should as explicitly condemn as subversive of the whole order of it.

The debate lasted till past two o'clock in the morning, when the House divided on the order of the day, which had been moved by the secretary at war, and which was carried by a majority of 10. [27]

• • •

Retrospective view of affairs in North America and the West-Indies, in the year 1781. South Carolina. Battle at the Eutaw Springs. Col. Stuart, with the British forces, retires to Charles Town. Island of St. Eustatius surprized and taken by the Marquis de Bouille. Dutch settlements of Demerary and Essequibo recovered by France. Marquis de Bouille invades the Island of St. Christopher's, with 8,000 men, in the beginning of the year 1782, and is supported by the Count de Grasse, with a great fleet. Gen. Fraser and the Governor, with the few troops on the island, retire to Brimstone Hill. Gallant attempts made by Admiral Sir Samuel Hood, with a very inferior force, to save the island: draws the enemy out to sea, and then seizes the anchorage ground in Basseterre Road, which they had just quitted. French fleet repeatedly attack the English squadron, and are repulsed with loss. Works on Brimstone Hill, in no degree answerable to the strength of the situation. Gallant defence made by the garrison. All the attempts made by the Admiral, and by Gen. Prescot, for the relief of the place, prove ineffectual. The works and buildings on the top of the hill being almost entirely destroyed, Gen. Fraser and Gov. Shirley are obliged to capitulate, and obtain conditions highly honourable to the garrison, and advantageous to the island. English squadron slip their cables, and return to Barbadoes. Nevis and Montserrat follow the fortune of St. Christopher's. Formidable preparations by France and Spain for the invasion of Jamaica. Admiral Sir George Rodney arrives with a strong reinforcement from England, and takes the command of the fleet. Fails in his design of intercepting the French convoy from Brest. Puts into St. Lucia to refit, and to watch the motions of the enemy. Objects, and respective force, of the commanders on both sides. Perilous state of the English affairs in the West-Indies. M. de Grasse proceeds with his fleet and a great convoy from Fort-Royal, in order to form a junction with the French and Spanish forces at Hispaniola. Is immediately pursued by Sir George Rodney. Partial engagement between the French fleet and the van of the English, on the 9th of April. Great sea-fight on the 12th, which lasts from sun-rise to sun-set. Gallantry displayed on both sides. French fleet entirely routed. The Count de Grasse taken in the Ville de Paris. Four other ships of the line taken, and one sunk. Various particulars of the action.

Cesar, one of the French prizes, blown up on the night of the battle. Admiral Sir Samuel Hood detached with a squadron, in pursuit of the enemy. Takes two French ships of the line and two frigates in the Mona passage. Sir George Rodney proceeds with the Count de Grasse and the prizes to Jamaica. Consequences of the late victory. Honours to the successful commanders. Lord Rodney returns to England, and is succeeded by Admiral Pigot. Inactivity of the opposite armies in North America, confirmed by the resolutions of parliament, and by the subsequent negociations for peace.

THE natural boundaries which served in some degree to restrain hostility, and to throw South Carolina into two great allotments, which were respectively held by the Royal and the American forces, could no longer produce their effect than while equal strength or mutual weakness prevented the operation of either party. The calm which attended and succeeded the new partition arrangement made by Lord Rawdon a little before his departure from that province, accordingly lasted no longer than until General Greene had received such reinforcements from without, and had used such internal means in forming and disciplining the state troops and militia of the two Carolinas, as he supposed would enable him to act with effect. As soon as these ends were attained, he marched with his forces from the high hills of Santee, in order to pass the Congaree River, and to attack Col. Stewart who com- [28] manded the British forces then in the field.

That officer was posted at a Col. Thompson's, near M'Cord's Ferry, on the Congaree; his troops were sickly, bread was scarce, and a supply of provision was then on its way to join him. Upon this movement of the enemy he judged it necessary for the security of his convoy, and probably other reasons, to fall back about forty miles to a place called the Eutaw Springs, which lie about sixty miles north of Charles Town. Greene, however, still pursued his design of attacking him, to which he was now farther stimulated by understanding that Col. Stewart intended to establish a strong and permanent post at the Eutaws (for which the place was admirably qualified) to serve as a rampart on that side, to a new and more contracted line of frontier. The former had passed the river at Howel's Ferry; and upon coming to this determination, he sent back his baggage and stores to that place, and pursuing his march until he arrived within seven miles of the Eutaws, encamped in the evening at a plantation called Bardwell; from whence he proceeded early the next morning to attack the royal forces.

General Greene's order of battle seems to have been rather peculiar: an observation by no means intended to arraign his judgment. His first line consisted only of two battalions of South Carolina, and two battalions of North Carolina militia; whilst his great strength was placed in the second, which was composed of three brigades of Continental troops, including two battalions of Virginians, two of Marylanders, and three of North Carolinians. Col. Lee, with his legion, covered one flank, and Henderson, with the state troops of South Carolina, the other. Col. Washington, with his cavalry, and the state troops of Delaware, under a captain, formed a [29] corps de reserve. Brig.-Gen. Marion commanded the first line; and Sumner the North Carolina [30] troops. No certain estimate can be formed of the amount of the American forces. The English accounts state them at about 4000. [31] Greene himself gives no clue; but loosely observes, that they were much inferior to the enemy in number; and in his published letter, seems studiously to represent the battalions in general as being "very small." The first line advanced with two three-pounders, and the second with two six-pounders.

Sept. 8th, 1781. In the morning march, Colonel Washington, with the troops that covered the flanks, formed an advanced guard, and about four miles from the Eutaws fell in with Major Coffin, with a detached party of horse and light infantry, who, after some firing, fell back to the British main body; which, by the American accounts, was drawn up to receive them, between two and three miles in the front of their camp. The action commenced at nine in the morning, and lasted four hours without intermission. As the battle was fought in the woods, and the conflict obstinately maintained on both sides, it was subject to much vicissitude; so that different wings and parties on each were victors, and vanquished by turns; chance and accidental conjunction frequently varying the fortune of the fight. It is impossible to reconcile the English and American accounts, they differ so totally in almost every part of the relation. Both sides claimed the victory, and both had some ground for the claim; both sides held out the highest praises to their officers and men for the eminent services which they performed, and the extraordinary valour they displayed; and the praise was undoubtedly, in the highest degree, merited on both. The contradictions which appear on the opposite accounts are not to be entirely attributed to designed misrepresentation on either side. The nature of the ground contracted the sphere of observation within a very narrow compass; and report is seldom to be relied on as the basis of truth. The consequences must therefore be considered as the best explanation of the action.

It admits of no doubt that the conflict was exceedingly severe, and abounded with instances of the highest gallantry on both sides. The Americans were now inured to arms and danger; and the provincial militia, who alone led on the attack in the first line, not only fought with all the spirit, but with all the perseverance of old and well-tried soldiers. The bayonet, which had so long been dreadful to the Americans, seems now to have become their favourite weapon. General Greene particularly attributes the victory (which he claims as indisputable) to the fierce and irresistible attack of the Virginia and Maryland troops, who, he says, rushed on through a hot cannonade and a shower of bullets to charge the enemy with the bayonet.

It would seem upon the whole, though not acknowledged on our side, that the royal troops were driven back, through a continued series of hard fighting, and with the loss of two pieces of cannon, as far as their camp. That there, as brave and experienced soldiers, still possessing their judgment and faculties in the height of tumult and the extremity of danger, they at once perceived, and as instantly seized, the advantages which the strong ground they were then on afforded. A large and strong brick-house, of three stories, with its adjoining offices and inclosures, was immediately occupied by a large party; another lodged themselves in an almost impenetrable coppice of rugged underwood, called in that country Black Jack; while a third took possession of a palisadoed garden. Thus covered in front, their flanks were well secured by a deep ravine, and other difficulties of ground.

Here then the engagement was renewed with fresh vigour, and with greater severity than before. The Americans brought up the two pieces of cannon they had taken, along with their own six-pounders, to attack the brick-house; while Col. Washington, with the greatest gallantry, made repeated attempts to storm the coppice. All their efforts on both sides were ineffectual. The fire from the one was too severe to be long endured; and Washington was wounded and taken prisoner, in his last attack upon the coppice. The Americans, after a sore loss, were obliged to retreat; for having, in the eagerness of attack, pushed their guns too close to the brick house, their artillery-men and officers were not only destroyed, but the fire was so intolerable, that they could neither bring off the cannon nor the wounded which were within its command. Gen. Greene acknowledges, that he found it necessary, in order to spare the effusion of blood, to draw his troops out of reach of the English fire; but his subsequent retreat of seven miles to his camp at Bardwell's, he attributes entirely to the want of water; a want (if real) undoubtedly of such a nature, as could not but be severely felt through the course of so long a march, so hot a day, and so severe an action. [32]

These circumstances afforded fair ground to the British commander whereon to rest his claim of victory. But others were not equally concurrent; and his situation and force did not admit that the consequences of the action should support the claim with effect. It was certainly a great and most gallant recovery; such as is not often equalled in similar circumstances; and in which the officers and troops had a higher claim to honour than the most complete victory might have afforded in other instances. Greene boasts that he took 500 prisoners (including in that number 70 wounded, whom, he says, the royal forces left behind them on their retreat the following day); that he left a strong picquet on the field of battle; that he collected all his wounded, excepting those who lay under the fire of the brick-house; that early on the following morning he detached Lee and Marion on the way to Charles Town, as well to prevent succours from thence as to embarrass the retreat of the main body while he pursued them; and, that the fugitives from the field of battle had spread such an alarm, that the English burnt their stores at Dorchester, and abandoned their post at Fair Lawn. He acknowledges the loss of two pieces of cannon, but says he brought off one of theirs.

We are left as much in the dark as to the numbers on the royal side, as. we are with respect to the American. Col. Stewart seems apprehensive, as well as Greene, that it might be imagined from the various corps stated to be under his command, that his force was considerably greater than it really was. It may well be supposed, that from the climate, as well as from other causes, they were respectively very thin. Letters from Charles Town, at the time, loosely stated Stewart's force at about 2000.

The loss on the American side, in killed and wounded, by their own account, amounted to between five and six hundred. That [33] of officers, which could not be concealed, was very considerable. One lieutenant-colonel, one major, six captains, and eight other commissioned officers, were killed. Five lieutenant-colonels, thirteen captains, and twenty-five lieutenants, were wounded. On our side, only three commissioned officers were killed on the spot, but several died of their wounds. The whole number of men slain is rated only at eighty-five; the wounded at 351, of which sixteen were commissioned officers; and the missing at 257; of these were ten commissioned officers, fifteen serjeants, and eight drummers. We mention these little particulars, as they serve in some sort to show the diversity and various fortune of the action. No notice is taken in Col. Stewart's account or return of fifteen commissioned officers, who Greene particularly specifies to have been admitted to their paroles on the field of battle. As this return was dated before the retreat from the Eutaws, it could not include the seventy wounded, who were said to have been left behind on that occasion. These, though it was made a matter of boast, could only have been left behind, from their wounds being in too bad a state to admit of a removal. Colonel Stewart was himself wounded, and is said to have been taken prisoner, and afterwards retaken. Every royal officer, who had the smallest command, even to that of a company, had an opportunity of distinguishing himself in some marked degree, which, in more fortunate seasons, and circumstances of less general exertion, would have been deemed an object of public note and applause.

The royal forces decamped on the following evening. Greene pretends that they staved a quantity of rum, and destroyed many stores, through the want of carriages; but what seems utterly improbable, he farther advances, that above 1000 small arms were found, which they had broken and hidden in the Eutaw Springs. In the mean ime, Major M'Arthur was dispatched with so strong a detachment from Charles Town to meet the returning forces, that Marion and Lee could not hazard the smallest attempt to interrupt his purpose; and Greene's pursuit as far as Harrison's Swamp, was probably a mere matter of parade, without the smallest hope of being at all able to disturb the retreat. From that time, the country in the vicinity of Charles Town, and of the neighbouring great rivers, became the scene of a small, cruel, and desultory war, in which, except the design of straitening the capital and its garrison on the one side, provisions, plunder, and the gratification of mutual animosity, were the only objects.

. . .

Copy of a letter from the Right Hon. Lord George Gordon to the Right[34] *Hon. the Earl of Shelburne.*

LORD George Gordon presents his compliments to the Earl of Shelburne, and begs his lordship will do him the favour to inform him whether his Majesty's present cabinet approve of the declaration made in the letter, said to be written by Sir Guy Carleton and Admiral Digby to General Washington : " That his Majesty, in order to remove all obstacles to that peace which he so ardently wishes to restore, has commanded his ministers to direct Mr. Grenville, that the independency of the Thirteen Provinces should be proposed by him, in the first instance, instead of making it a condition of a general treaty ?"

Lord George would not have asked this question to satisfy any private curiosity ; but he thinks it his duty to the King to acquaint Lord Shelburne, as prime minister, that great bodies of the people in the united kingdom of Scotland, are daily pressing Lord George, in the strongest terms, and in the most affectionate expressions, to write his sentiments to them on the present state of public affairs in the united kingdoms ; and Lord George finds, among other serious matters, that the late latter, said to be written by his Majesty's commissioners at New York, not being publicly authenticated in the London Gazette, alarms the suspicions of those who ardently wish for peace with their brethren, that that letter is a forgery, and that peace with America is not intended : and on the other hand, not being contradicted by the King's present servants, it causes the greatest anguish and disgust to those who have conscientiously approved and supported the American war.

The people of Scotland are much distracted and disturbed with this apparent misunderstanding in the cabinet of the united kingdoms, thinking the honour of the united kingdoms is trifled with ; and they are anxious in the highest degree, to receive some information that they may depend upon in so affecting a concern as the independency of America is to their own national, particular, and immediate interest : Lord George therefore hopes Lord Shelburne will condescend to inform him whether the proposal of independency, in the letter said to be written by the King's commissioners, is, or is not, a measure to be adhered to by his Majesty's present administration ?

Lord George has the honour to assure Lord Shelburne, that he wishes he could understand and approve of the measures of the King's counsellors, that he, and those who act with him, might have an opportunity of demonstrating the uprightness and loyalty of their proceedings and intentions, and of exerting themselves, according to their vocations, to the uttermost of their power, in support of good government, the true interest of the people, the honour and happiness of the King's Majesty and his posterity, and the true public liberty, safety, and peace of the three kingdoms of Scotland, England, and Ireland.

Welbeck-street, Oct. 16. 1782.

. . .

Address of the House of Commons to his Majesty, against the further Prosecution of the American War; with his Majesty's most gracious Answer.

RESOLVED, Wedn. Feb. 27, in the House of Commons, " That an humble address be presented to his Majesty, most humbly to represent to his Majesty that the further prosecution of offensive war on the continent of North America, for the purpose of reducing the revolted colonies to obedience by force, will be the means of weakening the efforts of this country against her European enemies, tends, under the present circumstances, dangerously to increase the mutual enmity so fatal to the interests both of Great Britain and America, and, by preventing an happy reconciliation with that country, to frustrate the earnest desire graciously expressed by his Majesty to restore the blessings of public tranquillity."

Resolved, " That the said address be presented to his Majesty by the whole House."

Ordered, " That such members of this House as are of his Majesty's most honourable privy council, do humbly know his Majesty's pleasure when he will be attended by this House."

March 4. *His Majesty was graciously pleased to return the following Answer to the above-mentioned Address of the House.*

" Gentlemen of the House of Commons,

" THERE are no objects nearer to my heart than the ease, happiness, and prosperity of my people.

" You may be assured that, in pursuance to your advice, I shall take such measures as shall appear to me to be most conducive to the restoration of harmony between Great Britain and the revolted colonies, so essential to the prosperity of both; and that my efforts shall be directed in the most effectual manner against our European enemies, till such peace can be obtained as shall consist with the interests and permanent welfare of my kingdoms."

Besides the address of the House of Commons, the following were also presented to his Majesty; at the same time praying for a speedy conclusion of the American war:—

The address, remonstrance, and petition of the county of Middlesex, presented by John Wilkes and George Byng, Esqrs.

Ditto of Surry, by Admiral Keppel and Sir Joseph Mawbey, Bart.

Ditto of London, by the Right Hon. the Lord Mayor;

Ditto of Westminster, by the Hon. Charles James Fox;

Ditto of Southwark, by N. Polhill, Esq. and Sir Richard Hotham, Bart. 35

An Address of Thanks to his Majesty by the House of Commons for the foregoing most gracious Answer to their Address.

IT was resolved *nemine contra dicente,*

" That an humble address be presented to his Majesty, to return his Majesty the thanks of this House for his most gracious answer to their address, presented to his Majesty on Friday last, and for the assurances his Majesty has been pleased to give of his intention, in the pursuance of the advice of this House, to take such measures as shall appear most conducive to the restoration of harmony between Great Britain and the revolted colonies; and that his efforts shall be directed, in the most effectual manner, against our European enemies, until such peace can be obtained as shall consist with the permanent welfare and prosperity of his kingdom; this House being convinced nothing can, in the present circumstances of this country, so essentially promote those great objects of his Majesty's paternal care for his people, as the measures which his most faithful commons have most humbly and earnestly recommended to his Majesty."

The same being read, was ordered to be delivered to his Majesty by the privy counsellors members of the House.

• • •

A Letter from Sir Guy Carleton to his Excellency General Washington; the General's Answer, and Resolution of Congress thereupon.

Philadelphia, June, 1.
Extract of a Letter from his Excellency General Washington, to Congress, dated Head Quarters, 36
May 10, 1782.

" JUST as I am closing these dispatches, a letter from Sir Guy Carleton is handed me, covering sundry printed papers, a copy of which, with the papers, I have now the honour to enclose to your excellency, together with a copy of my answer to him; and I flatter myself my conduct herein will be agreeable to the wishes of Congress."

Head-Quarters, New-York,
SIR, *May 7, 1782.*
HAVING been appointed by his Majesty to the command of the forces on the Atlantic Ocean, and joined with Admiral Digby in the commission of peace, I find it proper in this manner to apprize your excellency of my arrival at New York.

The occasion, Sir, seems to render this communication proper, but the circumstances of the present time render it also indispensable, as I find it just to transmit herewith to your excellency certain papers, from the perusal of which your excellency will perceive what dispositions prevail in the government and people of England towards those of America, and what further effects are likely to follow. If the like pacific dispositions should prevail in this country, both my inclination and duty will lead me to meet it with the most zealous concurrence. In all events, Sir, it is with me to declare, that, if war must prevail, I shall endeavour to render its miseries as light to the people of this continent as the circumstances of such a condition will possibly permit.

I am much concerned to find that private and unauthorised persons have on both sides given way to those passions which ought to have received the strongest and most effectual controul, and which have begot acts of retaliation, which, without proper prevention, may have an extent equally calamitous and dishonourable to both parties, though, as it should seem, more extensively pernicious to the natives and settlers of this country.

How much soever, Sir, we may differ in other respects, upon this one point we must perfectly concur, being alike interested to preserve the name of Englishmen from reproach, and individuals from experiencing such unnecessary evils as can have no effect upon a general decision. Every proper measure which may tend to prevent these criminal excesses in individuals, I shall be ever ready to embrace; and as an advantage on my part, I have, as the first act of my command, enlarged Mr. Livingston, and have written to his father upon the subject of such excesses as have passed in New Jersey, desiring his concurrence in such measures as, even under the conditions of war, the common interests of humanity require.

I am further to acquaint you, Sir, that it was my intention to have sent this day a similar letter of compliment to Congress, but am informed it is previously necessary to obtain a passport from your excellency, which I therefore hope to receive, if you have no objection for the passage of Mr. Morgan to Philadelphia, for the[37] above purpose.

I have the honour to be, &c.
(Signed)
GUY CARLETON.

His Excellency Gen. Washington.

Head Quarters, May 10, 1782.
Sir,
I HAD the honour last evening to receive your excellency's letter of the 7th, with the several papers enclosed.

Ever since the commencement of this unnatural war, my conduct has borne invariable testimony against those inhuman excesses which in too many instances have marked its various progress.

With respect to a late transaction, to which I presume your excellency alludes, I have already expressed my fixed resolution : a resolution formed on the most mature deliberation, and from which I shall not recede.

I have to inform your excellency, that your request of a passport for Mr. Morgan to go to Philadelphia, will be conveyed to Congress by the earliest opportunity ; and you may rest assured that I will embrace the first moment to communicate to you their determination thereon.

Many inconveniences and disorders having arisen from an improper admission of flags at various[38]

posts of the two armies, which have given rise to complaints on both sides. To prevent abuses in future, and for the convenience of communication, I have concluded to receive all flags from within your lines at the post of Dobb's Ferry, and nowhere else, so long as the head quarters of the two armies remain as at present

I have the honour to be, &c.
G. WASHINGTON.
His Excellency Sir Guy Carleton.

By the United States in Congress, assembled May 14, 1782.

THE letter of the 10th, from the commander in chief, being read, inclosing a copy of a letter to him from Sir Guy Carleton, dated head-quarters, New York, May 2, 1782,

Resolved, That the commander in chief be, and hereby is directed to refuse the request of Sir Guy Carleton, of a passport for Mr. Morgan, to bring dispatches to Philadelphia.

Published by order of the Congress.

CHA. THOMPSON, Sec.

RESOLUTION OF CONGRESS.

By the United States in Congress, assembled October 4, 1782.

WHEREAS by the articles of confederation and perpetual union, the sole and exclusive right of making peace is vested in the United States in Congress assembled ; and by the treaty of alliance between his Most Christian Majesty and these United States, it is declared, that neither of the contracting parties shall conclude peace nor truce with Great Britain, without the consent of the other ; and the ministers plenipotentiaries of these United States in Europe, are vested with full power and authority, in their behalf, and in concert with their allies, to negociate and

conclude a general peace: nevertheless, it appears, the British court still flatters itself with the vain hope of prevailing on the United States to agree to some terms of dependence on Great Britain, at least to a separate peace ; and there is reason to believe that commissioners may be sent to America to offer propositions of that nature to the United States, or that secret emissaries may be employed to delude and deceive : In order to extinguish ill founded hopes, to frustrate insidious attempts, and to manifest to the whole world the purity of the intentions, and the fixed unalterable determination of the United States,

Resolved unanimously, That Congress are sincerely desirous of an honourable and permanent peace: that as the only means of obtaining it, they will inviolably adhere to the treaty of alliance with his Most Christian Majesty, and conclude neither a separate peace nor truce with Great Britain ; that they will prosecute the war with vigour until, by the blessing of God on the united arms, a peace shall be happily accomplished ; by which, the full and absolute sovereignty and independence of these United States having been duly assured, their rights and interests, as well as those of their allies, shall be effectually provided for and secured.

That Congress will not enter into the discussion of any overtures for pacification, but in confidence and in concert with his Most Christian Majesty.

That to guard against the secret artifices and machinations of the enemy, it be, and hereby is recommended to the respective States, to be vigilant and active in detecting and seizing all British emissaries and spies, that they may be brought to condign punishment : that it be enjoined on all officers of departments charged with persons coming from the enemy under the protection of flags of truce, to take special care that such persons do not abuse their privileges, but be restrained from all intercourse with the country and inhabitants, which is not necessary for transacting the public business on which they may be sent: and lastly, it is recommended to the several States, that no subject of his Britannic Majesty, coming directly or indirectly from any part of the British dominions, be admitted into any of the United States during the war.

CHA. THOMPSON, Sec.

A FRENCH STATE PAPER.

A Letter from Monsieur du Portail, a French Officer in the service of America, to Monseigneur Le Comte de St. Germain, Secretary of State for the War Department in France, dated at Washington's Camp at White Marsh, twelve miles from Philadelphia. [39]

Nov. 12, 1778.

Monseigneur,

I HAVE had the honour of giving you an account of the battles of Brandywine and German-Town, and of sending you the plans, with that of Philadelphia and its environs, within five leagues, to enable you to judge of the situation of General Howe. I hope you have received them. Till now General Howe has not taken the two forts on the river, which hinder vessels coming up to the city, and deprive him of all communication with them, but by the little passage which I have marked on the map, and from which we can easily cut him off this winter, when we have received a reinforcement of victorious troops from the north. We reckon on striking a stroke on the other side of Schuylkil. There are already troops in the Jerseys on the left-hand bank of the Delaware. On this plan, General Howe will be obliged to remain in Philadelphia, and run a great risk of dying by hunger; but, in truth, we do not hope for so much. He will surely take the forts, if he attacks them well, and then he will have a communication with his fleet. You see, Monseigneur, that for people that have been beat twice, we are in no very bad posture; we owe this to the English having but little cavalry, so that they were incapable of pursuing their victory: we owe it yet more to the woods and obstacles of every sort, with which this country is defended.

In the mean time it is natural enough, after the experience of this campaign, to ask this question, Will the Americans succeed in making themselves free or not? In France, without doubt, they can only judge by what is past; they will hold the affirmative. As for us, who have been witnesses of the whole, it is another affair. To make short of the matter, it is not the good conduct of the Americans that enabled them to make a campaign on the whole sufficiently fortunate. It is the fault of the English. It was an enormous fault of the British government to require General Burgoyne to traverse more than 200 leagues of a country replete with difficulties, almost desert, and of consequence, very useless to take, and that only to join Generals Howe and Clinton in the middle of the country. This project might appear very magnificent in the cabinet of London; but to those who know the country it was highly defective.

This judgment on my part is not after the event. You may remember, perhaps, Monseigneur, that I was in very good humour with the English for opposing to us only ten thousand men here, and that I greatly hoped General Burgoyne would not arrive here till the field could no longer be kept; that his army would be half destroyed by hunger, misery, and desertion, together with daily losses suffered from our militia, scattered through the woods, who fighting thus in a manner peculiar to themselves, the event has been more happy than I could have even hoped.

If the English, instead of making so many diversions, which have been all too much at the expence of the principal action, had opposed General Washington with twenty thousand men, I do not very well know what would have become of us. As for us, in doubling our army, we should have nearly redoubled his force, and we should have nearly tripled our own embarrassment. Thus much for the plan of this campaign.

If we examine next the conduct of General Howe, we shall see that he has not done even what he had in his power to do. As I had the honour to write to you after the battle of Brandywine, "If the English had followed up their advantages that day, Washington's army would have been spoken of no more." Since that time, likewise, General Howe has, in all his operations, exhibited such slowness and timidity, as on every turn to prove the object of my astonishment. But we must recollect, they may send another general, and then we shall not find ourselves so fortunately circumstanced. As for the rest, the events which depend on the ability of generals not being to be foreseen, we cannot count on them in our speculations on the future.

Having then a reference only to the number of troops, I think I may assert, if the English can have here thirty thousand effective troops, they must reduce this country.

A second thing which must hasten this reduction, and even of itself nearly effect it, is the want of warlike stores. They want almost every thing. Another object is, they are in want of both linen and woollen cloths, leather, cordage, falt, fpirituous liquors, fugars, &c. Thefe laft articles are more important than at firft might be imagined. Before the war, the Americans, though defpifing luxury, had in abundance every thing that is neceffary to an eafy and agreeable life. To have no great matters to do; to pafs the greateft part of their time in fmoking or drinking fpirituous liquors or tea, was the tafte of thefe countries. It is then very little with their inclinations that they find themfelves transformed at a ftroke into a warlike people, and reduced to the neceffity of leading a hard and frugal life. So much do they in general deteft the war, that it is eafy to fee, if their wants are but increafed to a certain point, they would prefer the yoke of the Englifh to a liberty which cofts them the comforts of life.

This language aftonifhes you, Monfeigneur; but in truth, fuch is the people. They are foft without refort, without vigour, without paffion, for a caufe which they fuftain only, becaufe it is natural to them to follow the movement with which they have been impreffed. "There is an hundred times more enthufiafm for this revolution in a coffee-houfe at Paris than in all the colonies united."

It is neceffary therefore for France, if fhe wifhes to fupport this revolution, to furnifh the people with every neceffary, nor fuffer them to fuftain any confiderable want. It will coft France a great fum, even fome millions; but fhe will be amply repaid by the annihilation of the marine power of England, which, having no longer any colonies, can in a little time have no marine. Commerce will of confequence pafs over to France, which can in that cafe have no rival among the powers of Europe.

Some perfons have pretended that France has no intereft in feeing the Englifh colonies form a free ftate, and that we might thereby run the hazard of lofing our own colonies; but whoever knows this country, fees that it will be fome ages before they could fend forth a fquadron to make conquefts, and long before that the iealoufies which one province entertains of another (the appearances of which are already difcernible) will have divided them into different ftates, none of which will be to be feared. I may be afked, whether France had not better make a treaty with the United States, and fend twelve or fifteen thoufand men hither, to effect more readily this revolution? This would be the moft effectual method of fpoiling all. This people, though at war with the Englifh, hate the French more than them: we prove this every day; and notwithftanding every thing that France has done, or can do for them, they will prefer a reconciliation with their ancient brethren. Should they for the moment confent to the coming of the French troops, their natural antipathy would foon fhew itfelf, and produce the moft fatal quarrels.

There is yet another object to examine. May not France, forced to make open war on England, feek to poffefs herfelf of Canada, in concert with Congrefs?

After the obfervations in the preceding article, it appears that Congrefs would utterly reject fuch an arrangement. They would not feek freedom in the neighbourhood of the French, for they would not expect to retain it long. If they muft needs be dependent, they had rather be fo on England.

If France does not declare war againft England, fhe muft by every means that policy can fuggeft, prevent the Englifh from having more than from twenty-five to thirty thoufand men here at moft. The American ftates will not have more this campaign. General Wafhington has never had more than 15,000, General Gates 10,000 men, and General Putnam from 5 to 6,000. Perhaps they would not be able to augment the whole by one quarter in cafe of neceffity.

You have here, perhaps, Monfeigneur, more than you have afked of me; but forgive me thefe differtations, through a defire of fulfilling, at leaft, your intentions, and of rendering my abode here, if poffible, ufeful to my country.

I am,
with the moft perfect refpect, &c.
(Signed)
DU PORTAIL.

To Monfeigneur the Count de St. Germain, Minifter of war at the court of France.

• • •

Authentic Copies of the Preliminary Articles of Peace, between his Britannic Majefty and the Moft Chriftian King, his Moft Catholic Majefty, and the United States of America. Signed at Verfailles, the 20th of January, 1783.

Tranflation of the Preliminary Articles of Peace, between his Britannic Majefty and the Moft Chriftian King. Signed at Verfailles the 20th of January, 1783.

IN THE NAME OF THE MOST HOLY TRINITY.

THE King of Great Britain and the Moft Chriftian King, equally animated with a defire of putting an end to the calamities of a deftructive war, and of re-eftablifhing union and good underftanding between them, as neceffary for the good of mankind in general as for that of their refpective kingdoms, ftates, and fubjects, have named for this purpofe, viz. on the part of his Britannic Majefty, Mr. Alleyne Fitz-Herbert, minifter plenipotentiary of his faid Majefty the King of Great Britain; and on the part of his Moft Chriftian Majefty, Charles

Gravier, Comte de Vergennes, counsellor in all his councils, commander of his orders, counsellor of state, minister and secretary of state, and of the commands and finances of his said Majesty for the department of foreign affairs; who, after having duly communicated to each other their full powers in good form, have agreed on the following Preliminary Articles:

Article I. As soon as the preliminaries shall be signed and ratified, sincere friendship shall be re-established between his Britannic Majesty and his Most Christian Majesty, their kingdoms, states, and subjects by sea and by land, in all parts of the world. Orders shall be sent to the armies and squadrons, as well as to the subjects of the two powers, to stop all hostilities, and to live in the most perfect union, forgetting what is passed, of which their sovereigns give them the order and example. And, for the execution of this article, sea-passes shall be given on each side for the ships which shall be dispatched to carry the news of it to the possessions of the said powers.

Art. II. His Majesty the King of Great Britain shall preserve in full right the island of Newfoundland, and the adjacent islands, in the same manner as the whole was ceded to him by the thirteenth article of the treaty of Utrecht, save the exceptions which shall be stipulated by the fifth article of the present treaty.

Art. III. His Most Christian Majesty, in order to prevent quarrels which have hitherto arisen between the two nations of England and France, renounces the right of fishing, which belongs to him by virtue of the said article of the treaty of Utrecht, from Cape Bonavista to Cape St. John, situated on the eastern coast of Newfoundland, in about 50 degrees of north latitude; whereby the French fishery shall commence at the said Cape St. John, shall go round by the north, and, going down the western coast of the island of Newfoundland, shall have for boundary the place called Cape Raye, situated in 47 degrees 50 minutes latitude.

Art. IV. The French fishermen shall enjoy the fishery assigned them by the foregoing article, as they have a right to enjoy it by virtue of the treaty of Utrecht.

Art. V. His Britannic Majesty will cede in full right to his Most Christian Majesty the islands of St Pierre and Miquelon.

Art. VI. With regard to the right of fishing in the Gulf of St. Laurence, the French shall continue to enjoy it conformably to the fifth article of the treaty of Paris.

Art. VII. The King of Great Britain shall restore to France the island of St. Lucia, and shall cede and guarantee to her that of Tobago.

Art. VIII. The Most Christian King shall restore to Great Britain the islands of Grenada and the Grenadines, St. Vincent, Dominica, St. Christopher, Nevis, and Montserrat; and the fortresses of those islands conquered by the arms of Great Britain and by those of France, shall be restored in the same condition in which they were when the conquest of them was made, provided that the term of eighteen months, to be computed from the time of the ratification of the definitive treaty, shall be granted to the respective subjects of the crowns of Great Britain and France, who may have settled in the said islands, and in other places which shall be restored by the definitive treaty, to sell their estates, recover their debts, and to transport their effects and retire without being restrained, on account of their religion, or any other whatever, except in cases of debt or of criminal prosecutions.

Art. IX. The King of Great Britain shall cede and guarantee in full right to his Most Christian Majesty the river of Senegal and its dependencies, with the forts of St. Louis, Podor, Galam, Arguin, and Portendu. His Britannic Majesty shall restore, likewise, the island of Gorée, which shall be given up in the condition in which it was when the British arms took possession of it.

Art. X. The Most Christian King shall, on his side, guarantee to his Majesty the King of Great Britain the possession of Fort James and of the river Gambia.

Art XI. In order to prevent all discussions in that part of the world, the two courts shall agree, either by the definitive treaty, or by a separate act, upon the boundaries to be fixed to their respective possessions. The gum trade shall be carried on in future as the English and French nations carried it on before the year 1755.

Art. XII. In regard to the rest of the coasts of Africa, the subjects of both powers shall continue to frequent them, according to the custom which has prevailed hitherto.

Art. XIII. The King of Great Britain shall restore to his Most Christian Majesty all the establishments which belonged to him at the commencement of the present war on the coast of Orissa, and in Bengal, with liberty to surround Chandernagore with a ditch for draining the waters; and his Britannic Majesty engages to take such measures as may be in his power for securing to the subjects of France in that part of India, as also on the coast of Orissa, Coromandel, and Malabar, a safe, free, and independent trade, such as was carried on by the late French East India Company, whether it be carried on by them as individuals or as a company.

Art. XIV. Pondicherry, as well as Karical, shall likewise be restored, and guaranteed to France; and his Britannic Majesty shall procure, to serve as a dependency round Pondicherry, the two districts of Valanour and Bahour; and as a dependency round Karical, the four contiguous magans.

Art. XV. France shall again enter into possession of Mahé, and of the comptoir at Surat; and the French shall carry on commerce in this part of India conformably to the principles laid down in the thirteenth article of this treaty.

Art. XVI. In case France has allies in India, they shall be invited, as well as those of Great Britain, to accede to the present pacification; and for that purpose a term of four months, to be computed from the day on which the proposal shall be made to them, shall be allowed them to make their decision; and in case of refusal on their part, their Britannic and Most Christian Majesties agree not to give them any assistance, directly or indirectly, against the British or French possessions, or against the ancient possessions of their respective allies; and their said Majesties shall offer them their good offices towards a mutual accommodation.

Art. XVII. The King of Great Britain, desirous of giving his Most Christian Majesty a sincere proof of reconciliation and friendship, and of contributing to the solidity of the peace which is on the point of being re-established, will consent to the abrogation and suppression of all the articles relative to Dunkirk, from the treaty of peace concluded at Utrecht in 1713, inclusively, to this time.

Art. XVIII. By the definitive treaty, all those which have existed till now between the two high contracting parties, and which shall not have been derogated from either by the said treaty, or by the present preliminary treaty, shall be renewed and confirmed; and the two courts shall name commissioners to inquire into the state of commerce between the two nations, in order to agree upon new arrangements of trade, on the footing of reciprocity and mutual convenience. — The said two courts shall together amicably fix a competent term for the duration of that business.

Art. XIX. All the countries and territories which may have been, or which may be, conquered in any part of the world whatsoever, by the arms of his Britannic Majesty, or by those of his Most Christian Majesty, and which are not included in the present articles, shall be restored without difficulty, and without requiring compensation.

Art. XX. As it is necessary to assign a fixed epoch for the restitutions and the evacuations to be made by each of the high contracting parties, it is agreed, that the King of Great Britain shall cause to be evacuated the islands of St. Pierre and Miquelon, three months after the ratification of the definitive treaty, or sooner if it can be done; St. Lucia in the West Indies, and Goree in Africa, three months after the ratification of the definite treaty, or sooner, if it can be done. The King of Great Britain shall, in like manner, at the end of three months after the ratification of the definitive treaty, or sooner, if it can be done, enter again into possession of the islands of Grenada, the Grenadines, St. Vincent, Dominica, St. Christopher, Nevis, and Montserrat.

France shall be put into possession of the towns and comptoirs which are restored to her in the East Indies, and of the territories which are procured for her, to serve as dependencies round Pondicherry, and round Karical, six months after the ratification of the definitive treaty, or sooner, if it can be done.

France shall, at the end of the same term of six months, restore the towns and territories which her arms may have taken from the English or their allies in the East Indies.

In consequence whereof, the necessary orders shall be sent by each of the high contracting parties, with reciprocal passports for the ships which shall carry them, immediately after the ratification of the definitive treaty.

Art. XXI. The prisoners made respectively by the arms of his Britannic Majesty and his Most Christian Majesty, by land and by sea, shall be restored reciprocally, and *bonâ fide*, immediately after the ratification of the definitive treaty, without ransom, and on paying the debts they may have contracted during their captivity; and each crown shall respectively reimburse the sums which shall have been advanced for the subsistence and maintenance of their prisoners, by the sovereign of the country where they shall have been detained, according to the receipts and attested accounts, and other authentic titles which shall be produced on each side.

Art. XXII. In order to prevent all causes of complaint and dispute which may arise on account of prizes which may be made at sea after the signing of these preliminary articles, it is reciprocally agreed, that the vessels and effects which may be taken in the Channel and the North Seas, after the space of twelve days, to be computed from the ratification of the present preliminary articles, shall be restored on each side. That the term shall be one month from the Channel and North Seas, as far as the Canary Islands, inclusively, whether in the ocean or the Mediterranean. Two months from the said Canary Islands, as far as the equinoctial line or equator; and lastly, five months in all other parts of the world, without any exception or any other more particular description of time and place.

Art. XXIII. The ratification of the present preliminary articles shall be expedited in good and due form, and exchanged in the space of one month, or fooner, if it can be done, to be computed from the day of the fignature of the prefent articles.

In witnefs whereof, we, the underwritten minifters plenipotentiary of his Britannic Majefty and of his Moft Chriftian Majefty, by virtue of our refpective full powers, have figned the prefent preliminary articles, and have caufed the feal of our arms to be put thereto.

Done at Verfailles, the 20th day of January, 1783.

(L. S.)

ALLEYNE FITZ HERBERT. [40]

(L. S.)

GRAVIER de VERGENNES.

————

Tranflation of the Preliminary Articles of Peace between his Britannic Majefty and the Moft Catholic King. Signed at Verfailles the 20th of January, 1783.

IN THE NAME OF THE MOST HOLY TRINITY.

THE King of Great Britain and the King of Spain, equally animated with a defire of putting an end to the calamities of a deftructive war, and of re-eftablifhing union and good underftanding between them, as neceffary for the good of mankind in general as for that of their refpective kingdoms, ftates, and fubjects, have named for this purpofe, viz. on the part of his Majefty the King of Great Britain, Mr. Alleyne Fitz-Herbert, minifter plenipotentiary of his faid Majefty; and on the part of his Majefty the King of Spain, Don Peter Paul Abarea de Bolea Ximines d'Urnea, &c. Count of Aranda and Caftel Florido Marquis of Torres, of Villanan and Rupit, Vifcount of Rueda and Yoch, Baron of the Baronies of Gavin, Sietano, Clamofa, Enipol, Trazmoz, La Mata de Caftil, Viego, Antillon, La Almolda, Cortes, Jorva, St. Genis, Robovillet; Oreau, and St. Colome de Farnes, Lord of the Tenance, and Honour of Alcalaten, the Valley of Rodellar, the caftles and towns of Maella, Mefones, Tiurana, de Villaplana, Taradell, and Viladran, &c. Rico Hombre in Arragon, by birth, grandee of Spain of the firft clafs, knight of the order of the Golden Fleece, and of tnat of the Holy Ghoft, gentleman of the King's bed-chamber in emploiment, captain-general of his armies, and his ambaffador to his Moft Chriftian Majefty, who, after having duly communicated to each other their full powers in good form, have agreed on the following preliminary articles:

Article I. As foon as the preliminaries fhall be figned and ratified, fincere friendfhip fhall be eftablifhed between his Britannic Majefty and his Catholic Majefty, their kingdoms, ftates, and fubjects, by fea and by land, in all parts of the world. Orders fhall be fent to the armies and fquadrons, as well as to the fubjects of the two powers, to ftop all hoftilities, and to live in the moft perfect union, forgetting what has paffed, of which their fovereigns give them the order and example; and for the execution of this article, fea-paffes fhall be given on each fide for the fhips which fhall be difpatched to carry the news of it to the poffeffions of the faid powers.

Art. II. His Catholic Majefty fhall keep the ifland of Minorca.

Art. III. His Britannic Majefty fhall cede to his Catholic Majefty Eaft Florida; and his Catholic Majefty fhall keep Weft Florida, provided that the term of eighteen months, to be computed from the time of the ratification of the definitive treaty, fhall be granted to fubjects of his Britannic Majefty who are fettled as well in the ifland of Minorca as in the two Floridas, to fell their eftates, recover their debts, and to tranfport their effects, as well as their perfons, without being reftrained on account of their religion, or under any other pretence whatfoever, except that of debts and criminal profecutions; and his Britannic Majefty fhall have power to caufe all the effects that may belong to him in Eaft Florida, whether artillery or others, to be carried away.

Art. IV. His Catholic Majefty fhall not for the future fuffer the fubjects of his Britannic Majefty, or their workmen, to be difturbed or molefted, under any pretence whatfoever, in their occupation of cutting, loading, and carrving away logwood, in a diftrict of which the boundaries fhall be fixed; and for this purpofe they may build without hindrance, and occupy without interruption, the houfes and magazines neceffary for them, for their families, and for their effects, in a place to be agreed upon, either in the definitive treaty, or within fix months after the exchange of the ratifications; and his faid Catholic Majefty affures to them, by this article, the entire enjoyment of what is above ftipulated, provided that thefe ftipulations fhall not be confidered as derogatory in any refpect from the rights of his fovereignty.

Art. V. His Catholic Majefty fhall reftore to Great Britain the iflands of Providence and the Bahamas, without exception, in the fame condition in which they were when they were conquered by the arms of the King of Spain.

Art. VI. All the countries and territories which may have been, or may be conquered in any part of the world whatfoever, by the arms of his Britannic Majefty, or by thofe of his Catholic Majefty, and which are not included in our prefent articles, fhall be reftored without difficulty, and without requiring compenfations.

Art. VII. By the definitive treaty, all those which have existed till now between the two high contracting parties, and which shall not be derogated from either by the said treaty, or by the present preliminary treaty, shall be renewed and confirmed; and the two courts shall name commissioners to enquire into the state of the commerce between the two nations, in order to agree upon new arrangements of trade, on the footing of reciprocity and mutual convenience; and the two said courts shall together, amicably fix a competent term for the duration of that business.

Art. VIII. As it is necessary to assign a fixed epoch for the restitutions and evacuations to be made by each of the high contracting parties, it is agreed, That the King of Great Britain shall cause East Florida to be evacuated, three months after the ratification of the definitive treaty, or sooner, if it can be done.

The King of Great Britain shall likewise enter again into possession of the Bahama Islands, without exception, in the space of three months after the ratification of the definitive treaty.

In consequence whereof, the necessary orders shall be sent by each of the high contracting parties, with reciprocal passports for the ships, which shall carry them immediately after the ratification of the definitive treaty.

Art. IX. The prisoners made respectively by the arms of his Britannic Majesty and his Catholic Majesty, by sea and by land, shall immediately after the ratification of the definitive treaty, be reciprocally and *bona fide* restored without ransom, and on paying the debts they may have contracted during their captivity; and each crown shall respectively reimburse the sums which shall have been advanced for the subsistence and maintenance of their prisoners by the sovereign of the country where they shall have been detained, according to the receipts and attested accounts, and other authentic titles which shall be produced on each side.

Art. X. In order to prevent all causes of complaint and dispute which may arise on account of prizes which may be made at sea after the signing of these preliminary articles, it is reciprocally agreed that the ships and effects which may be taken in the Channel or in the North Seas, after the space of twelve days, to be computed from the ratification of the present preliminary articles, shall be restored on each side.

That the term shall be one month from the Channel and the North Seas, as far as the Canary Islands inclusively, whether in the ocean or in the Mediterranean; two months from the said Canary Islands, as far as the equinoctial line or equator; and lastly, five months in all parts of the world without exception, or other more description of time and place.

Art. XI. The ratifications of the present preliminary articles shall be expedited in good and due form, and exchanged in the space of one month, or sooner if it can be done, to be computed from the day of the signature of the present articles.

In witness whereof, we the under-written ministers plenipotentiary of his Britannic Majesty and of his Catholic Majesty, by virtue of our respective powers, have agreed upon and signed these preliminary articles, and have caused the seal of our arms to be put thereto.

Done at Versailles the 20th day of January, 1783.

ALLEYNE FITZHERBERT, (L. S.)
LE COMTE D'ARANDA. (L. S.) [41]

Articles agreed upon by and between Richard Oswald, Esq. the Commissioner of his Britannic Majesty for treating of Peace with the [42] *Commissioners of the United States of America, on Behalf of his said Majesty, on the one part—and John Adams, Benjamin Franklin, John Jay, and Henry Laurens, four of the Commissioners of the said States, for treating of Peace with the Commissioner of his said Majesty on their Behalf, on the other part; to be inserted in and to constitute the Treaty of Peace proposed to be concluded between the Crown of Great Britain and the said United States, but which Treaty is not to be concluded until Terms of a Peace shall be agreed upon between Great Britain and France; and his Britannic Majesty shall be ready to conclude such treaty accordingly.* [43]

WHEREAS reciprocal advantages and mutual convenience are found by experience to form the only permanent foundation of peace and friendship between states, it is agreed to form the articles of the proposed treaty on such principles of liberal equity and reciprocity, as that partial advantages, those seeds of discord being excluded, such a beneficial and satisfactory intercourse between the two countries may be established as to promise and secure to both perpetual peace and harmony.

Art. I. His Britannic Majesty acknowledges the said United States, viz. New Hampshire, Massachusets Bay, Rhode Island, and Providence Plantations, Connecticut, New York, New Jersey, Pennsylvania, Delaware, Maryland, Virginia, North Carolina, South Carolina, and Georgia, to be Free, Sovereign, and Independent States; that he treats with them as such; and for himself, his heirs, and successors, relinquishes all claim to the government, propriety, and territorial rights of the same, and every part thereof; and that all disputes which might arise in future on the subject of the boundaries of the said United States, may be prevented, it is hereby agreed and declared that the following are and shall be their boundaries, viz.

Art. II. From the north-west angle of Nova Scotia, viz. that angle which is formed by a line drawn due north from the source of St. Croix River to the Highlands: along the said islands, which divide those rivers that empty themselves into the River St. Lawrence from those which fall into the Atlantic Ocean, to the north-westermost head of Connecticut River, thence down along the middle of that river to the forty-fifth degree of north latitude; from thence by a line due west on said latitude, until it strikes the River Iroquois or Cataraquy; thence along the middle of said river into Lake Ontario, thro' the middle of said lake, until it strikes the communication by water between that lake and Lake Erie; thence along the middle of said communication into Lake Erie, through the middle of said lake until it arrives at the water communication between that lake and Lake Huron; thence along the middle of said water communication into the Lake Huron; thence through the middle of said lake to the water communication between that lake and Lake Superior; thence through Lake Superior, northward of the Isles Royal and Phelipeaux, to the Long Lake; thence through the middle of said Long Lake, and the water communication between it and the Lake of the Woods, to the said Lake of the Woods; thence through the said lake to the most north-western point thereof, and from thence on a due west course to the River Mississippi; thence by a line to be drawn along the middle of the said River Mississippi. until it shall intersect the northermost part of the thirty-first degree of north latitude. South, by a line to be drawn due east from the determination of the line last mentioned, in the latitude of thirty-one degrees north of the

equator, to the middle of the River Apalachicola, or Catahouche; thence along the middle thereof to its junction with the Flint River; thence straight to the head of St. Mary's River; and thence down along the middle of St. Mary's River to the Atlantic Ocean. East, by a line to be drawn along the middle of the River St. Croix, from its mouth in the Bay of Fundy to its source, and from its source directly north to the aforesaid highlands, which divide the rivers that fall into the Atlantic Ocean from those which fall into the River St. Lawrence; comprehending all islands within twenty leagues of any part of the shores of the United States, and lying between lines to be drawn due east from the points where the aforesaid boundaries, between Nova Scotia on the one part, and East Florida on the other, shall respectively touch the Bay of Fundy and the Atlantic Ocean; excepting such islands as now are, and heretofore have been, within the limits of the said province of Nova Scotia.

Art. III. It is agreed that the people of the United States shall continue to enjoy unmolested the right to take fish of every kind on the Grand Bank, and on all the other Banks of Newfoundland; also in the Gulph of St. Lawrence, and at all other places in the sea, where the inhabitants of both countries used at any time heretofore to fish; and also that the inhabitants of the United States shall have liberty to take fish of every kind on such part of the coast of Newfoundland as British fishermen shall use (but not to dry or cure the same on that island) and also on the coasts, bays, and creeks, of all other of his Britannic Majesty's dominions in America; and the American fishermen shall have liberty to dry and cure fish in any of the unsettled bays, harbours, and creeks, of Nova Scotia, Magdalen Islands,

and Labrador, so long as the same shall remain unsettled; but so soon as the same or either of them shall be settled, it shall not be lawful for the said fishermen to dry or cure fish at such settlement, without a previous agreement for that purpose with the inhabitants, proprietors, or possessors of the ground.

Art. IV. It is agreed that creditors on either side shall meet with no lawful impediment to the recovery of the full value in sterling money, of all bona fide debts heretofore contracted.

Art. V. It is agreed that the Congress shall earnestly recommend it to the legislatures of the respective States, to provide for the restitution of all estates, rights, and properties, which have been confiscated, belonging to real British subjects, and also of the estates, rights, and properties of persons resident in districts in the possession of his Majesty's arms, and who have not borne arms against the said United States. And that persons of any other description shall have free liberty to go into any part or parts of any of the Thirteen United States, and therein to remain twelve months unmolested in their endeavours to obtain the restitution of such of their estates, rights, and properties, as may have been confiscated; and that Congress shall also earnestly recommend to the several states a reconsideration and revision of all acts or laws regarding the premises, so as to render the said laws or acts perfectly consistent not only with justice and equity, but with that spirit of conciliation which, on the return of the blessings of peace, should universally prevail. And that Congress shall also earnestly recommend to the several states, that the estates, rights, and properties of such last-mentioned persons shall be restored to them; they refunding to any persons who may be now in possession the bona fide price (where any has been given) which such persons may have paid on purchasing any of the said lands or properties since the confiscation.

And it is agreed, That all persons who have any interest in confiscated lands, either by debts, marriage settlements, or otherwise, shall meet with no lawful impediment in the prosecution of their just rights.

Art. VI. That there shall be no future confiscations made, nor any prosecutions commenced against any person or persons for or by reason of the part which he or they may have taken in the present war; and that no person shall, on that account, suffer any future loss or damage, either in his person, liberty, or property; and that those who may be in confinement on such charges at the time of the ratification of the treaty in America, shall be immediately set at liberty, and the prosecutions so commenced be discontinued.

Art. VII. There shall be a firm and perpetual peace between his Britannic Majesty and the said States, and between the subjects of the one and the citizens of the other; wherefore all hostilities both by sea and land shall then immediately cease. all prisoners on both sides shall be set at liberty; and his Britannic Majesty shall, with all convenient speed, and without causing any destruction, or carrying away any negroes, or other property of the American inhabitants, withdraw all his armies, garrisons, and fleets, from the said United States, and from every port, place, and harbour within the same; leaving in all fortifications the American artillery that may be therein: and shall also order, and cause all archives, records, deeds, and papers, belonging to any of the said States, or their citizens, which in the course of the war may have fallen into the hands of his officers, to be forthwith restored and delivered to the proper States and persons to whom they belong.

Art. VIII. The navigation of the Mississippi, from its source to the ocean, shall for ever remain free and open to the subjects of Great Britain and the citizens of the United States.

Art. IX. In case it should so happen that any place or territory belonging to Great Britain or the United States should be conquered by the arms of either from the other before the arrival of these articles in America, it is agreed that the same shall be restored without difficulty, and without requiring any compensation.

Done at Paris the 13th day of November, in the year 1782.

RICHARD OSWALD, (L. S.)
JOHN ADAMS, (L. S.
B. FRANKLIN, (L. S.)
JOHN JAY, (L. S.)
HENRY LAURENS. (L. S.)

Witness,
CALEB WHITEFOORD,
Secretary to the British Commission.

W. S. FRANKLIN,
Secretary to the American Commission.

44

Notes, 1782

1. That is, the Netherlands. St. Eustatius was captured by Rodney in February 1781, the islands of St. Martin and Saba surrendered shortly after, followed by the Dutch settlements in Guiana. A valuable Dutch West India convoy was taken after the fall of St. Eustatius, and in August an engagement with a Dutch squadron in the North Sea was claimed as a British victory.

2. News of the Yorktown surrender reached London on 25 November 1781.

3. Richard Rigby.

4. Constantine John Phipps (1744–92), M.P. for Huntingdon, 1776–84; succeeded his father as 2nd Baron Mulgrave in the Irish peerage in 1775; created 1st Baron Mulgrave in the English peerage in 1790. A Lord of the Admiralty, 1777–March 1782, he was an adherent of Sandwich and supported the Government line on the American war, acting as spokesman in the House on Admiralty matters after 1778.

5. Edward Hawke, 1st Baron Hawke (1705–81), Admiral and First Lord of the Admiralty, 1766–71.

6. That is, Viscount Weymouth and Viscount Stormont.

7. Henry Dundas (see "Notes, 1775," n. 54) had been a valuable Government supporter, but was angry at North's failure to secure him the office of Keeper of the Signet for life and began to express doubts about continuing the American war.

8. William Henry, Duke of Clarence (1765–1837), the future William IV, began a career in the navy in 1779 in Digby's flagship, *Prince George;* in this vessel, he was at New York from March through April 1782.

9. William Pitt (1759–1806), second son of the Earl of Chatham, M.P. for Appleby, 1781–84; his maiden speech on 26 February 1781 in support of Burke's economical reform bill was widely acclaimed, and his two other speeches in this session were received with general congratulations.

10. Welbore Ellis (1713–1802), M.P. for Weymouth and Melcombe Regis, 1774–90; held office from 1747 to 1765; joint Vice-Treasurer of Ireland, 1770–77; Treasurer of the Navy, 1777–82; and Secretary of State for America, February–March 1782. A narrow conservative, he supported coercion toward America, and the war.

11. Sir William Mayne (see "Notes, 1775," n. 45) became Baron Newhaven in the Irish peerage in 1776.

12. Richard Kempenfelt (1718–82), Rear-Admiral 1780. On 12 December, his squadron sighted Guichen's superior fleet in the Atlantic and managed to capture some of its transports before prudently retreating to harbour. The King believed Kempenfelt should have attempted an attack: "... for as *every* admiral now seems to expect that an English fleet must be equal in numbers to a French one, or else not risk an action, we must eternally go on without a decisive naval blow, which alone can put us again upon our legs." George III to Sandwich, 18 December 1781, *The Private Papers of John, Earl of Sandwich, First Lord of the Admiralty, 1771–1782*, eds. G. R. Barnes and J. H. Owen, 4 vols. (London: 1932–38), vol. 4, p. 78.

13. 14 February.

14. Isaac Hayne (1745–81) was captured in the fall of Charleston in 1780. He was released on parole but was ordered, as a British subject, to join the British forces in 1781. Regarding his parole broken by the British, he resumed a militia command. In July 1781, he captured the American General, Andrew Williamson, who had defected to the British, but was himself promptly taken by a force sent to recapture Williamson. His execution as an insurrectionist became a *cause célèbre*.

15. Henry Lee put the case differently: "Colonel Hayne was certainly either a prisoner of war, or a British subject. If the latter, he was amenable to the law, and indisputably entitled to the formalities and aids of a trial; but if the former, he was not responsible to the British government, or its military commander, for his lawful conduct in the exercise of arms." *Memoirs of the War in the Southern Department of the United States*, rev. ed. (New York, 1869, pp. 456–67).

16. Francis Hastings, 10th Earl of Huntingdon (1728–89).

17. Dundas and Rigby forced the resignation of Germain, and he was replaced by Welbore Ellis on 17 February; Germain went to the Lords as Viscount Sackville.

18. George Augustus Eliott (1717–90), Lieutenant-General in 1763, Commander-in-Chief of Gibraltar from 1775. He successfully defended the Rock through a siege which began on 11 July 1779 and lasted until 6 February 1783. James Murray (?1719–94), Lieutenant-General, 1772, Governor of Minorca from 1774, defended Fort St. Philip against a Franco-Spanish force in a seven-month siege which was to terminate in a British surrender in February 1782.

19. Welbore Ellis.

20. George John Spencer (1758–1834), styled Lord Althorpe, 1765–83; succeeded his father as Earl Spencer in 1783; M.P. for Northampton, 1780–April 1782, Surrey, April 1782–October 1783; Lord of the Treasury, March–July 1782.

21. James Wallace (1729–83), M.P. for Horsham, 1770–83; Attorney-General, 1780–April 1782, and from May 1783 to his death.

22. James Brydges, 3rd Duke of Chandos (1731–89).

23. Shelburne, in the Lords on 7 February. *Parliamentary History*, vol. 22, 1004.

24. Shelburne stated in the Lords on 7 February that "... he never would consent, under any possible given circumstances, to acknowledge the independency of America." *Parliamentary History*, vol. 22, 987. On the same day, in the Lords debate over Germain's elevation to the peerage, Shelburne claimed "... he had not the smallest objection to the King's being his own minister. He did not know, but the King's having an opinion of his own and feeling his interest in the management of the affairs of the realm, might be better for the general weal than his remaining a type of a mere King of Mahrattas ... a mere nominal monarch." Ibid., 1003–04.

25. William Adam (1751–1839), M.P. for Wigtown Burghs, 1780–85, consistent advocate of coercion toward America and a loyal supporter of North.

26. Charles Fox.

27. The vote was 226 to 210.

28. Alexander Stewart (?1741–94), Lieutenant-Colonel of the 31st Regiment.

29. The redoubtable Captain Robert Kirkwood (1730–91), commanded an elite unit of Delaware Continentals. The reputation of both the unit and its commander were among the best in the Continental Army.

30. Jethro Sumner (?1735–85), served in the Virginia militia in the Seven Years War; was commissioned Colonel of the 3rd North Carolina Battalion; and promoted to Brigadier-General in 1779. He retired in October 1780 but returned at Greene's request in February 1781.

31. A consensus of estimates suggests Greene's forces totalled about 2,200 (Stewart's between 1,800 and 2,000).

32. Greene's forces began to disintegrate when they overran the British camp and stopped to loot it of food and liquor; failure to dislodge the British position at the "brick house" was followed by a counterattack from its defenders, who forced back the American assault and routed the looters.

33. The official report gives 139 killed, 375 wounded, and 8 missing.

34. Lord George Gordon (1751–93), third son of the Duke of Gordon, M.P. for Ludgershall, 1774–80; served in the navy in America, 1766–69; retired from the service in 1777. He showed signs of mental disturbance in his incoherent speeches in the House after May 1779. His fanatical anti-Roman Catholic utterances helped precipitate the riots in London of June 1780, the most serious civil disturbances of the century. He was acquitted of treasonably instigating the riots in February 1781 but continued to bombard leading public figures with letters on various subjects, most of which indicated his megalomania. This relatively restrained example still reveals his belief in a huge public following. Gordon was sentenced to five years' imprisonment for libel in 1788 and he died in prison.

35. M.P.s not hitherto identified: George Byng (?1735–89), M.P. for Middlesex, 1780–84, a Rockingham supporter; Sir Joseph Mawbey (1736–98), M.P. for Surrey, 1775–90, created Baronet 1765, a faintly ridiculous figure who consistently voted with the Opposition; and Nathaniel Polhill (1723–82), M.P. for Southwark, 1774–August 1782, regularly opposed North's government. The Lord Mayor of London 1782–83 was Nathaniel Newnham (c. 1741–1809), M.P. for London, 1780–90; he was often in opposition and consistently condemned the American war.

36. The whole letter may be found in J. C. Fitzpatrick, *The Writings of George Washington*, vol. 24, pp. 243–44. Carleton inherited the Huddy-Asgill affair (see "Notes, 1783," n. 32) from Clinton, and the enclosures with the letter forwarded by Washington to Congress include details of several American atrocities. As a gesture of willingness to behave generously, Carleton mentions that he has released Henry Brockholst

Livingston (1757–1823), son of William Livingston (1723–90), Governor of New Jersey. Henry became secretary to John Jay in 1779 and was captured by the British on returning to America in 1782.

37. Dr. Maurice Morgan, Carleton's secretary.

38. That is, flags of truce permitting direct contact between members of the opposing armies, here to allow the passage of despatches.

39. Louis Le Begue de Presle du Portail (1743–1802), sent by France to join the Continental Army in 1777, appointed Brigadier-General and Chief of Engineers. Claude-Louis, Comte de St. Germain (1707–78), Secretary of State for War, 1775–78.

40. Alleyne Fitzherbert (1753–89), created Baron St. Helens in 1801; British Ambassador at Brussells, 1777–82; negotiator for the preliminary treaty with France and Spain.

41. Pedro Pablo Abarca de Bolea, Conde de Aranda (1719–98), President of the Council of Castile.

42. Richard Oswald (1705–84), a wealthy Scots merchant, former army contractor and slave trader with connections in America. He had business dealings with Henry Laurens.

43. John Jay (1745–1829), New York delegate to the Continental Congress, 1774–79; President, 1778–79; Chief Justice of New York, 1776–79; American Minister to Spain, 1779–82; Secretary of State for Foreign Affairs, 1784–90; and Chief Justice of the Supreme Court, 1789–94. Jay achieved little in Spain after Congress appointed him to the American negotiating committee for peace terms in June 1781. He reached Paris a year later and on 5 October produced the first draft of the preliminary treaty.

44. Caleb Whitefoord (1734–1810), writer and wit, was a neighbour of Franklin's during the latter's stay in London. On the strength of this acquaintance, Shelburne appointed him secretary to Oswald, to assist the negotiations. William Temple Franklin, grandson and personal secretary of Benjamin Franklin, appointed secretary to the American peace commission.

1783

Introduction

The ending of the war and the establishment of a peace settlement did not restore political tranquility and stability in Britain. On the contrary, during 1783 the Shelburne ministry collapsed and there was a prolonged constitutional crisis before the King was forced to accept the superficially unlikely coalition of Fox and North. The King detested that Government from the outset and helped destroy it at the end of the year. Moreover, although America had ceased to be an imperial problem, India and Ireland posed fundamental political questions.

During the Christmas recess, as Shelburne concentrated on completing peace preliminaries with France and Spain, his ministry started to disintegrate. On 4 January, Richmond and Keppel announced that they could not countenance the concessions made to Britain's enemies. Keppel resigned on the twenty-third, and Richmond withdrew from the Cabinet (though he kept his post at the Ordnance). Shelburne had already begun to realise that he must broaden the base of his parliamentary support if his administration was to survive; in effect this meant securing an alliance with either Fox or North. Shelburne's discussions with North collapsed at the end of the month, since Pitt made it clear that he would not serve with North in any major office, while North suspected that his only reward would be the obligation to support a peace treaty whose terms he deplored. On 10 February, Fox, the last resort, brusquely informed Pitt that he would never serve with Shelburne. These rejections not merely doomed Shelburne, they also threw together Fox and North. They discussed the basis of an alliance on 13 February and three days later agreed on tactics for the debate on the peace preliminaries.

Parliament had resumed sitting on 21 January and immediately dealt with a bill supplementing the Irish legislation of the previous year.[1] The peace preliminaries with France and Spain and the provisional treaty with America were laid before Parliament on 27 January; the debate was scheduled for 17 February. In a crowded House of Commons, Thomas Pitt moved the address, to assure the King that the House "had considered" the peace terms and "to express their satisfaction" with them. Lord John Cavendish promptly moved an amendment that the House give the terms "serious and full attention" and report the results of its investigation. North began the attack, particularly criticising the Government's desertion of the Loyalists. He was followed by Fox, who defended his new alliance with North, which William Pitt then sarcastically ridiculed. At the division, the Cavendish motion carried 224 to 208. In the Lords, Carlisle moved to condemn the peace terms, and there the debate centred on the American treaty. Particular attacks were made on the fate of the Loyalists and the cession of the trans-Appalachian lands. Shelburne's involved defence won the division by 72 to 59 in the most heavily attended debate since George III's accession. The debate resumed on 21 February with Shelburne full of doubts, for Grafton had left the Cabinet on the seventeenth, and Camden and Pitt had then advised Shelburne to resign. Pitt brilliantly defended the peace terms condemned by the Cavendish motion, but the Government lost the division 207 to 190. Shelburne recognised that general hostility made it impossible for him to continue, and he offered his resignation on 24 February; it was accepted on the twenty-sixth.[2]

A five-week crisis ensued. Shelburne first recommended to the King that Pitt succeed to the leadership. But after two days of brooding, Pitt decided he could not rely on the

1. Irish suspicion that the repeal of 5 Geo. I c. 5 in 1782 was intended as an empty gesture resulted in a new act affirming Irish legislative independence and another denying the right of appeal from Irish to English courts.
2. J. Cannon, *The Fox-North Coalition: Crisis of the Constitution, 1782–84* (Cambridge, 1969), p. 58, n. 4.

essential votes of North's group and he declined. The King turned next (inevitably) to Gower but on 2 March began serious negotiations with North, agreeing to accept Fox in office if the leadership were held by a neutral peer. Fox, however, would serve only under the Duke of Portland. The King detested Portland as much as he disliked Fox and so this negotiation collapsed. The King was now desperate and cast about in all directions. A major constitutional point was now at issue, the King's right to choose his ministers conflicted directly with the ministry's need to command a parliamentary majority. Specifically, George III's concept of the royal prerogative clashed head-on with Fox's notion of party government. By 12 March, the King was prepared to accept Portland at the head of a Fox-North combination, but the Rockingham group imposed a series of difficulties over the disposal of offices, and the negotiations became deadlocked. The King hoped Pitt would become his saviour. However, the Commons debate of 24 March, on a motion begging the King to appoint a ministry which had the confidence of the nation, produced no obvious signs that the independents were averse to the Fox-North alliance. Consequently, Pitt refused the role; indeed he resigned from the Cabinet on 31 March. After again contemplating abdication, the King finally capitulated to "... the most daring and unprincipled faction that the annals of this kingdom ever produced"[3] and accepted the Fox-North coalition on 1 April.[4]

The new government dealt first with the problem of trade with America. Shelburne hoped to secure a special commercial relationship with the United States and, on the basis of the agreed peace preliminaries, produced a bill which granted trading privileges to the Americans until a true commercial reciprocity treaty could be made.

3. Bonamy Dobrée, ed. *The Letters of King George III* (London, 1935), p. 169, n. 35.
4. The most detailed analysis of the crisis is that in J. Cannon, *The Fox-North Coalition*, ch. 4. The new Cabinet had Portland as First Lord of the Treasury, North as Home and Colonial Secretary, Fox as Foreign Secretary. Lord John Cavendish returned as Chancellor of the Exchequer and Keppel as First Lord of the Admiralty; Stormont became Lord President of the Council and the Earl of Carlisle, Lord Privy Seal. Conway was out of the Cabinet but remained Commander-in-Chief; Thurlow was dismissed from the post of Lord Chancellor, and the Great Seal put in Commission. Outside the Cabinet, Burke returned as Paymaster-General.

The American intercourse bill was introduced in the Commons by Pitt on 3 March, after Shelburne's resignation but before the formation of the coalition government. The bill was opposed by Fox and Burke, who advocated caution, but the decisive criticism came from William Eden, who convincingly pointed to the danger in giving the Americans an opportunity to dominate the Atlantic trade and to monopolise trade with the West Indies.[5] The merchant community was anxious to resume trade with America, which was still illegal under the legislation of 1775, but public opinion was sharply divided over the amount of concessions to be granted the Americans. Therefore on 9 April Fox moved to postpone consideration of the American intercourse bill on 9 April and then effectively killed it. He proposed instead repeal of the Prohibitory Acts and abolition of other formal restrictions on American vessels trading to British ports. Eden proposed an amendment which gave the Crown powers to deal with trade restrictions at discretion, and on this basis the legislation was passed. David Hartley was then despatched to Paris to negotiate a commercial treaty with the United States and also to conclude a definitive peace treaty. However, the use of the Crown's discretionary power by Orders in Council to make ad hoc regulations for the American trade (particularly the order of 2 July excluding the Americans from the West Indies) effectively wrecked the negotiations, and the proposed commercial treaty fell through.[6]

The coalition then turned to problems which required immediate solutions (for example, the Exchequer was unable to meet current requests for payment). First, in order to restore the nation's finances, Cavendish raised a loan on poor terms and gained acceptance for an unpopular budget which raised taxation levels. The ministry then fended off an Opposition attempt, led by Pitt, to introduce a new parliamentary reform measure and endured an

5. *Parliamentary History*, vol. 23, 602–14.
6. See V. T. Harlow, *The Founding of the Second British Empire 1763–1793*, vol. 1: *Discovery and Revolution* (London, 1952), ch. 9. Harlow argues that "after a violent controversy among themselves, the British declined to modify the Navigation Acts, even for the sake of good relations with the United States, with whom in other respects they hoped and intended to co-operate so extensively" because ". . . the Navigation Acts were about to be employed to build up the British mercantile marine . . . as the necessary instrument of a world-wide commerce." Ibid., p. 491.

embarrassing attack over Burke's treatment of allegations of corruption in the paymaster's office. More serious, a sudden quarrel with George III over arrangements for providing an establishment for the Prince of Wales revealed the King's implacable hostility toward the coalition. Two additional problems were simmering. The Irish Volunteer movement began a campaign to reform the Dublin parliament, and Indian affairs required detailed attention despite the Government's rejection of a regulating bill proposed by Dundas. The summer recess, beginning on 16 July, therefore gave the Government a welcome breathing space.

Parliament resumed sitting on 11 November with one vestige of the war yet to be considered—the definitive peace treaties. The Government had promised to accept the preliminary articles of peace agreed upon in February and was thus left with little room to improve the terms. A slight change in the French share of the Newfoundland fishery and in the British share of the West African gum trade was all that could be managed in concluding the treaty with France. Negotiations with the Dutch advanced very slowly; only the provisional articles were agreed upon by the end of September, and a definitive treaty was not signed until May 1784. The Netherlands obstinately insisted on restoration of British territorial conquests, compensation for ships seized, and recognition of neutral rights on the principle of "free ships, free goods." France supported the Dutch on restoration, since she was most anxious that Britain not retain Ceylon as a naval base from which to control the coasts of India. Britain and France finally agreed on terms, which were eventually reluctantly accepted by the Dutch. France gave up the Cape of Good Hope, and Britain returned Trincomalee and Ceylon, but kept Negapatam, secured trading rights in the East Indies, and refused any compensation. The definitive treaties with America, France, and Spain were laid before Parliament at the start of the session and produced a desultory debate. In the debate on the address in reply to the speech from the throne, Pitt ridiculed the Government for now approving treaties which its members had condemned when they were in opposition.[7] The

7. In the 1784–85 combined volume, the *Register* devotes about twenty-five lines to the announcement of the definitive treaties. *AR*, 1784–85, p. 58]. The *State Papers* gives the speech from the throne and the addresses of both Houses in reply (pp. [305–]307). This section also includes the congressional ratification of the peace, with its "recommendation" to the states on treatment of the Loyalists (p. 318]–319]).

treaties, however, were a dead issue, and interest now centred on other problems.

The issue which dominated the pre-Christmas session involved India. Fox introduced on 18 November a bill for the reorganisation of the East India Company which would have drastically reduced the independence of the company. The Opposition saw the bill as an attempt to capture permanent control of the company's patronage for the factions then in office. The furious debates which followed resulted in the bill's passage in the Commons but its rejection in the Lords, for the intense struggle over the bill had provided a key group of politicians an opportunity to topple the ministry. William Pitt, Charles Jenkinson, Dundas, and North's defecting secretary, Robinson, combined to take advantage of the furore and on 10 December informed the King that they were prepared to form a government.[8] The next day the King let it be known that he would regard any peer who voted for the bill as an enemy. The House of Lords rejected the bill on 17 December by a majority of nineteen. Late the following night, the King dismissed Fox and North and, despite his control of less than a third of the votes in the House of Commons, a new ministry was formed with Pitt as First Lord of the Treasury and chancellor of the Exchequer. From that point, America was of minor significance in British politics until the War of the French Revolution.

Despite the hope expressed in the preface to the 1782 volume that the end of the war would reduce the amount of material to be written up, and thus result in more prompt publication, the *Register* for 1783 was not published until December 1785. The increasing delay was an apparently insoluble problem; even when a single volume was issued for 1784–85, the subsequent volume was fifteen months late, and the situation worsened in succeeding years until Otridge and Rivington, each claiming to be the legitimate successor of Dodsley's *Annual Register*, published rival volumes for 1791. The historical article for 1783 was reduced to 180 pages. Of the eight chapters, the first four, comprising 118 pages, give a blow-by-blow account of the conflict in India, beginning with a resumé of the East India Company's problems in Bengal in 1781, and ending with the close of hostilities in the Carnatic in June 1783. It is difficult to avoid the conclusion that the attention the *Register* devotes to Indian affairs in this

8. Lucy S. Sutherland, *The East India Company in Eighteenth-Century Politics* (Oxford, 1952), pp. 392–406.

much-delayed volume is directly related to the central role India played in British politics in 1783 and 1784 and to the information which must have been compiled by Burke as preparation for his contribution to Fox's bill and his speeches in Parliament.[9]

Chapter V covers the last stages of the war in the Caribbean, Carleton's problems as Commander-in-Chief with ending hostilities in America, and, briefly, the provisional treaty with America and the preliminary articles of peace with France and Spain. The last three chapters deal with affairs in Parliament, as usual from the pre-Christmas session to the summer recess. Chapter VI discusses Shelburne's position, the breach with the Foxites, and Shelburne's overtures to North. It then provides an excellent account of the debates in December, and concludes with the January legislation for Ireland. Chapter VII reports equally well the February debates on the peace preliminaries. The final chapter covers Shelburne's resignation, the ensuing "ministerial interregnum," the emergence of the Fox-North coalition, and the activities of the new government to the end of the session in July, including the abandonment of the American intercourse bill and the legislation which replaced it.

The parts of Chapter V dealing with Carleton's efforts to settle affairs in America and with the preliminary articles of peace, parts of Chapter VI dealing with the December debates, the whole of Chapter VII, and the reference in Chapter VIII to the legislation affecting American commerce are extracted here.

The *Appendix to the Chronicle* for 1783 includes twenty-eight items, with a special section on "Remarkable Actions at Sea." The documents relating to the Asgill case; a memorial to Carleton from Loyalist officers indicating their fears for the future in view of Britain's recognition of American independence; letters from Carleton to the secretary to the Committee for Foreign Affairs and to Congress; Washington's famous circular letter to the state governors announcing his resignation as Commander-in-

---

9. Burke was the main architect of the bill. See Sutherland, *The East India Company*, p. 400. His three-hour defence of the bill in the debate of 1 December was a masterly survey of the details of the Indian problem and was regarded by one contemporary as the finest speech he had heard in the whole of his period as an M.P. *The Historical and Posthumous Memoirs of Sir Nathaniel William Wraxall*, ed. H. B. Wheatley, 5 vols. (London, 1884), vol. 3, p. 173.

Chief and advising those basic policies "... essential to the well-being, I may even venture to say, to the existence of the United States, as an independent power"; his farewell letter to the Continental Army and the reply are all extracted here. *State Papers* contains twenty-four items, including the definitive treaties with America and Spain and the preliminary articles of peace with the Netherlands. Extracted here are the speeches from the throne at the close of the summer session in 1782 and at the opening of the following session; the definitive peace treaty between Britain and the United States; and a translation of the agreement between France and America on the repayment of French loans since 1778.

In consequence of the resolutions of the British parliament for an accommodation with the American colonies, and the powers granted to the crown for negotiating and concluding a general or particular peace or truce, with the whole, or with any part of that people, and for suspending and setting aside all former laws, whose operations were in contravention to that purpose, instructions had been dispatched to Sir Guy Carleton (who succeeded Sir Henry Clinton in the command of the army, and the government of New York) to use his endeavours for carrying these dispositions into effect.

Upon these advices, Sir Guy Carleton, pretty early in the month of May, 1782, dispatched a letter to General Washington, informing him of the proceedings of parliament, of the dispositions prevalent both in that body and the British government, and of his own consequent instructions; accompanied with such written or printed documents, as were necessary to illustrate and authenticate what he had stated; and requiring, at the same time, a passport for Mr. Morgan, his secretary, who he wanted to dispatch on the same subject to congress. Washington, as usual, evading to act from himself in the business, referred the matter of the passport to congress; and that bo-

dy, on the 14th of the same month, issued a public resolution, forbidding the commander in chief to grant the passport.

This idea of opening separate negotiations with particular governments or bodies of men, or even of attempting to open a treaty with congress without the concurrence of its allies, caused no small alarm, and was much resented by the several states. They were perhaps equally apprehensive of it, producing a schism among themselves, and of its exciting the jealousy of France. Resolutions from the general assemblies of Maryland, New Jersey, Pensylvania, and Virginia, were accordingly speedily issued, in which they declared, that a proposition from the enemy, to all or any of the United States, for peace or truce, separated from their allies, was insidious and inadmissible. That a proposition for treating with any assembly or body of men in America, other than the congress, was insidious and inadmissible. That they (the respective assemblies) would not listen to any proposition, nor suffer any negotiation, inconsistent with their national faith and federal union. And, that they would exert the utmost power of their respective states to carry on the war with vigour and effect, until peace should be obtained in

a manner consistent with their national faith and federal union.

The council of Pensylvania went farther than the general assemblies in their zeal upon this occasion. They declared, that all men, or bodies of men, who should presume to enter into any separate or partial convention or agreement with Great Britain, ought to be considered and treated as open and avowed enemies of the United States of America. That any propositions which might be made by the court of Great Britain, tending, in any manner whatsoever, to violate the treaty between them and their illustrious ally, ought to be treated with every mark of indignity and contempt. They seemed even to entertain some jealousy with respect to the integrity of the general representative of the States, or at least to manifest a disposition to restrain its authority, by a resolution in which they declared, That the congress had no power, authority, or right, to do any act, matter, or thing, whatever, that might have a tendency to yield up, or abridge, the sovereignty and independence of that state, without its consent previously obtained.

The congress likewise passed a resolution, That the United States could not, with propriety, hold any conference or treaty with any commissioners on the part of Great

Britain, unless they should, as a preliminary thereto, either withdraw their fleets and armies, or else, in positive and express terms, acknowledge the independence of the said States.

Resolutions to a similar amount were generally passed by the other States. In fact, the Americans were too young a people, and had too much depending upon the establishment of a favourable and equitable character with other nations, to venture, at the very threshold of their emancipation, and just entering into the rank and confideration of a sovereign state, upon any violation of their public faith; particularly, to abandon those who had just faved them from the fubjugation, if not vengeance, of the parent country, would have been a degree of perfidy too flagrant, to be admitted under any laxity of moral ties, or almost justified by any change of political fituation.

It was probably fome jealoufy on this subject, expressed or apprehended on the fide of France, that occasioned congress, so long after as the month of October, to issue a public declaration, in which, after reciting that France and they were equally bound by the conditions of their alliance, that neither should conclude either peace or truce with Great Britain, without the confent of the other; and obferving, that their minifters in Europe were vested with full power and authority, in their behalf, and in concert with their allies, to negotiate and conclude a general peace; they then proceed to declare in the strongest terms (in order, as they fay, to extinguifh ill-founded hopes, to frustrate infidious attempts, and to manifest to the whole world the purity of their intentions) their fixed and unalterable determination, inviolably to adhere to the treaty of alliance with his Moft Chriftian Majesty, and to conclude neither a feparate peace nor truce with Great Britain: nor, that they would not enter in-

to the discussion of any overtures for pacification, but in confidence and in concert with his Moft Chriftian Majesty.

The concluding article of this document fufficiently fhews the apprehenfions they entertained of a fchifm among themfelves upon the fubject of peace; that is, that fome one or more of the ftates might be fo lured, by the advantages to be derived from an early and feparate accommodation, that neither the bonds of federal union, nor of their foreign alliance, would be able to withftand the ftrong temptations of felf-intereft that might be held out to them. It was undoubtedly upon this principle, and perhaps, likewife, under an apprehenfion of popular commotions, if the people were to become fully acquainted with the extent of the advantages that might be offered, that they ftrongly urged the respective ftates (in order, as they faid, to guard against the fecret artifices and machinations of the enemy) to be vigilant and active in detecting and feizing all Britifh emiffaries and fpies, that they might be brought to condign punifhment: that the officers of all departments, who might be charged with perfons coming from the enemy under the protection of flags of truce, fhould be enjoined to take efpecial care, that fuch perfons might not abufe their privileges, but be reftrained from all intercourfe with the country and inhabitants, which was not neceffary for transacting the public bufinefs on which they might be fent: and, that no fubject of his Britannic Majesty, coming directly or indirectly from any part of the Britifh dominions, fhould be admitted into any of the United States during the war.

While the Americans were thus oftentatioufly difplaying their public fidelity, and endeavouring even to cut off the poffibility of temptation, by fhutting out every overture towards a feparate accommodation, we are to look to the mea-

fures that were purfuing in Europe, for the attainment of a general peace between all the parties concerned in the war.

Two of the firft powers in Europe, the Emprefs of Ruffia and the Emperor of Germany, were the mediators in this great bufinefs; the difficulties of which feemed in no fmall degree to be done away, by the difpofition of granting independence to America which prevailed in England. With refpect to France, indeed, as the attainment of that point was her only avowed object in the war, its being granted feemed at once to remove the very ground of contention; and to leave no farther obftacles in the way of an accommodation; than thofe which arofe merely from the circumftances of the war itfelf; nor did the adjuftment of thefe feem exceedingly difficult; for though her acquifitions in the Weft-Indies were undoubtedly confiderable and valuble, yet her loffes in the Eaft left the means of a reafonable equivalent in the hands of England; without even confidering the ifland of St. Lucia, upon the fpot, which was a poffeffion of fuch importance, with refpect to its fize, ftrength, harbours, fituation, and capability of unbounded improvement, as could not but weigh heavily in every political fcale of eftimation.

As to Spain, if her conduct and motives could at all be clearly comprehended, fhe entered into the war, rather as an auxiliary, and in confequence of the family compact, than as a principal, or as acting at all upon national principles. The eftablifhment of an independent empire in America was to her the moft alarming meafure in point of precedent, and the moft dangerous in its probable and natural confequences, that could poffibly have happened, the emancipation of Mexico and Peru from her own government only excepted. It feems probable, that fhe did not apprehend (though the defign was avowed) that this event would have taken place, at the time she was led into the war; unlefs indeed it is fuppofed, that she was fo dazzled by the fplendid objects of Jamaica and Gibraltar, as to be blind to all others. The acquifition of thefe, as well as of Minorca, however unlikely at that time to be attained, was artfully held out by France, not only as a lure to the ambition of the king, but as impofing an opinion on the people that they had a national intereft in view, and that they were not plunged madly into a war, which was not only entirely *Bourbon*, but highly dangerous and deftructive in its principle and defign to themfelves. The ill fortune of England in the war, or, perhaps, it may be faid, the defect of wifdom and ability in the direction and application of the immenfe powers and the exhauftlefs ftock of valour which she poffeffed, enabled Spain to recover Minorca, and to fubdue Weft Florida. As the war afforded no equivalent on the other fide to propofe for thefe, it was reafonably to be expected that they should continue in the hands of Spain, affording in one inftance a diftant frontier againft the enterprize of that future enemy, which she had herfelf taken fo much pains in creating, and in the other, a confiderable facrifice to royal and national vanity. But neither the embarraffed ftate of her finances, the repeated failure of all her defigns upon Jamaica, her late fignal defeat at Gibraltar, nor any other circumftances of her prefent condition, feemed to afford any folid ground to Spain, upon which she could reafonably attempt to eftablish further claims. We have laid no ftrefs in this ftatement upon the Bahama iflands, (though they were eftimated at a high rate in the negotiation) as they could not have been retained by Spain, and they were in fact moft honourably and gallantly recovered by a handful of private adventurers, before any thing of the peace was known.

The republic of Holland, unfortunately fallen and degraded in a degree which she had never before experienced, from the firft general acknowledgment of her independency to the prefent æra, was, of courfe and of neceffity, reduced to depend entirely upon the favour, generofity and protection of France, as well in the conclufion of a peace, as she had through the progrefs of the war.

With refpect to the general circumftances of the contending parties, the moft fuccefsful members of the alliance, great and formidable as it was, fcarcely ftood much lefs in need of peace than England, notwithftanding all her loffes, and expofed as she had fo long been, as a common but, to withftand fingly all their attacks in every quarter. For it is probable that France had never been engaged, for the time of its continuance, in a more expenfive war than the prefent. Her extraordinary exertions[3] at fea, the oppofite extremes of the globe in which they were made, the great and frequent loffes fuftained in the fupply, the immenfe current charges to which it was fubjected, by the greatnefs of the diftance, along with the conftant two-fold drain, by loan and otherwife, of her treafure by America, may well be fuppofed all together, in point of expence, abundantly to fupply the place of thofe vaft armies which she had heretofore ufually fupported, and even of the fubfidies which she had been in the habit of paying, in the courfe of her continental wars. It is to be allowed, that her commerce had flourished to a degree, in the prefent war, which she had never before experienced in any conteft with England; but neither the advantages arifing from this circumftance, nor from the admirable financial regulations and reforms adopted during the prefent reign, were equivalent to the fupply of the continual demands, and of the numberlefs deficiencies produced by the war. Succeeding

events have shewn, that even a peace was not fufficient to prevent that nation from fuffering no fmall derangement of her monied and financial concerns, and which was accordingly attended with its ufual effect upon public credit.

Under thefe general circumftances of the contending powers, the independence of America being granted, there did not feem to be any mighty impediment remaining in the way to the reftoration of the public tranquillity.

The new adminiftration in England fpeedily adopted this bufinefs upon their coming into power; and Mr. Grenville had been[4] for fome time in Paris, in order to fettle the neceffary preliminaries, and to fmooth the way for opening a negociation in due form. Thefe matters being fettled, Mr. Fitz-Herbert, the minifter at Bruffels, proceeded to Paris, he being appointed, on the part of England, as plenipotentiary, to negotiate and conclude a treaty of peace with the minifters of France, Spain, and Holland. Mr. Ofwald, a merchant, was likewife difpatched to the fame place, as commiffioner from his Britannic majefty, for treating of peace with John Adams, Benjamin Franklin, John Jay, and Henry Laurens, four of the commiffioners appointed for the fame purpofe on the part of the United States of America.

The differences with America were much fooner fettled (fo far at leaft as their dependence on the main treaty could at prefent admit) than thofe with the European powers. On the 30th of November, 1782, provifional articles were figned on both fides, which were to be inferted in, and to conftitute a future treaty of peace, to be finally concluded between the parties, when that between Great Britain and France took place.

By this provifional treaty, the freedom, fovereignty, and independence, of the Thirteen United States was, individually by name, and in the fulleft and moft exprefs terms, acknowledged, and all claims to their government, propriety and territorial rights, for ever relinquished by the crown of Great Britain. To prevent all future disputes about boundaries, several imaginary lines were drawn, which interfecting immense countries, lakes, and rivers, threw vast tracts of land and water into the hands of the Americans to which they had no prior claim. Besides the fertile and extensive countries on the Ohio and Mississippi, which came within this defcription thefe limits trenched deeply on the boundaries both of Canada and Nova Scotia: and the fur trade was faid to be in a great meafure relinquifhed, by the forts, paffes, carrying places, and waters, which were now to be furrendered. It was likewife faid, that four or five-and-twenty Indian nations were by this arrangement given up to America; among whom, befides the Cherokees, were the celebrated Five Nations, who, through fo long a courfe of years, had held fo ftrict an alliance with England.

On the fea coafts, as the Britifh forces were to be withdrawn from all the territories of the United States, New York, Long Ifland, Staten Ifland, Charleftown, in South Carolina, and Penobfcot, in the borders of New England and Nova Scotia, with their dependencies, were of courfe to be given up. Savannah in Georgia, had already been evacuated by the Britifh troops. An unlimited right of fifhery on the Banks of Newfoundland, in the gulph of St. Lawrence, and all other places where both nations had heretofore been accuftomed to fifh, was likewife granted or confirmed to the Americans. We omit the articles with refpect to the loyalifts, as they will appear in the parliamentary difcuffions on that fubject.

The preliminary articles of peace between England and France were figned at Verfailles, on the 20th of January, 1798, by Mr. Alleyne [5]

Fitz-Herbert on the part of the one, and by the Count de Vergennes, on that of the other; as the preliminary articles between England and Spain were, on the fame day, by the firft of thefe gentlemen, and by the Count D'Aranda, on the part of the Catholic king. The preliminary articles with Holland were not yet fettled.

By the preliminary treaty with France, in the place of the narrow limits to which the latter had been reftrained by the laft peace, England now extends her rights of fifhery at Newfoundland to a long extent of coaft, reaching from Cape St. John, in about 50 degrees of north latitude, on the eaftern fide of the ifland, round by the north, to Cape Raye, on the weftern coaft, in 47 degrees and 50 minutes latitude.—England likewife ceded the iflands of St. Pierre and Miquelon in full right to France,[6] and confequently without any reftriction in point of fortification.

In the Weft Indies, England reftored to France the ifland of St. Lucia, and ceded and guaranteed to her the ifland of Tobago.—On the other hand, France reftores to Great Britain the iflands of Grenada, and the Grenadines, with thofe of St. Vincent, Dominica, St. Chriftopher's, Nevis, and Montferrat.

In Africa, England cedes and guarantees, in full right to France, the river of Senegal, and its dependencies, with the forts of St. Louis Podor, Galam, Arguin, and Portendie; and likewife reftores the ifland of Goree.—And, on the other hand, France guarantees to Great Britain the poffeffion of Fort James, and of the river Gambia. Certain new regulations with refpect to the gum trade were likewife to take place in this part of the world.

In the Eaft, England reftored every thing to France with confiderable additions, and without the poffibility of an equivalent in that quarter, which fhe had loft during

the war. All her eftablifhments in Bengal, and on the coaft of Orixa, were to be reftored, and liberty given for furrounding Chandenagor with a ditch for draining the waters. Pondicherry and Karical were likewife to be reftored and guaranteed to France; and his Britannic majefty was bound to procure, from the princes whofe property they were, certain fpecified neighbouring diftricts round thefe places, which were to be annexed to them as dependencies. And to fum up the account under this head, France was to regain poffeffion of Mahé, and of the Comptoir at Surat. For the conditions in favour of her commerce in India, and what relates to the allies on both fides in that quarter, we muft refer to the treaty.

In Europe, as if it were to complete in its parts this unequal fcene of ceffion, conceffion, and humiliation on the fide of England, fhe confented to the abrogation and fuppreffion of all the articles relative to Dunkirk, from the treaty of peace concluded at Utrecht in 1713, inclufively to the prefent time. [7]

By the preliminary treaty with Spain, befides relinquifhing all right and claim to Minorca and Weft Florida, England ceded to his Catholic majefty the province of Eaft Florida; while the Bahama iflands were the only reftitution or equivalent on the other fide. The affairs of the logwood-cutters, which had been fhamefully neglected in former treaties, were now left in a ftate of greater uncertainty and infecurity than ever.

• • •

In the mean time the negotiations for a general peace were advancing towards a conclufion. On the 23d of November letters were fent by the fecretary of ftate to the lord mayor of London and the governors of the Bank, acquainting them " for the information of the public, and to prevent the mifchiefs arifing from fpeculations in the

Nov. 23d.

funds, that the negotiations carrying on at Paris were brought so far to a point, as to promise a decisive conclusion, either for peace or war, before the meeting of parliament, which on that account was to be prorogued to the 5th of December."

On that day the session Dec. 5th. was opened by a speech 1782. from the throne of a very unusual length, and comprehending almost every possible topic of political disquisition. It set out with assuring both houses, that since the close of the last session, his majesty's whole time had been employed in the care and attention, which the important and critical conjuncture of affairs required

It next stated, that no time had been lost in putting an end to the prosecution of offensive war in North America; and after informing them that he had offered to declare those colonies free and independent states, and that provisional articles were actually agreed upon, to take effect whenever terms of peace should be finally concluded with the court of France, it was made to proceed as follows—" In " thus admitting their separation " from the crown of these king- " doms, I have sacrificed every " consideration of my own to the " wishes and opinion of my peo- " ple. I make it my humble and " earnest prayer to Almighty God, " that Great Britain may not feel " the evils, which might result " from so great a dismemberment " of the empire; and that Ame- " rica may be free from those ca- " lamities which have formerly " proved, in the mother country, " how essential monarchy is to the " enjoyment of constitutional li- " berty."

The defence and relief of Gibraltar, and the subsequent conduct of the fleet, were next mentioned in terms of the highest panegyric, as were also the proofs of public spirit that had been given by the city of London and private individuals.

The negotiations for a general peace were announced to be considerably advanced, and likely to be brought, in a very short time, to an honourable conclusion. At the same time a perfect confidence was expressed, that if these expectations should be frustrated, the most vigorous efforts would be used in the further prosecution of the war.

The members of the House of Commons were next assured of the endeavours that had been used to diminish the burthens of the people; of the better œconomy that was to be introduced into the expenditure of the army; of the reductions made in the civil list expences, as directed by an act of the last session; and of further reforms in other departments. By these means his establishments were said to be so regulated, that the expence should not in future exceed the income. The payment of the debt still remaining on the civil list, and the relief of the American sufferers, were recommended to their consideration.

Their attention was also called to the regulations that had been adopted in the incidental expences, fees, and other emoluments of office; to the landed revenue of the crown, and the management of its woods and forests; to the department of the mint; to the general state of the public receipts and expenditure, and of the public debt; and to such a mode of conducting future loans as to promote the means of its gradual redemption. The practice of payment by navy, ordnance, and victualling bills, was strongly reprobated; and a more correct method of making up the estimates for the service of the year was promised.

The high price of corn was next adverted to; the frequency of theft and robbery were mentioned; and the prevention of those crimes, by correcting the prevailing vices of the times, earnestly recommended.

The liberality with which the rights and commerce of Ireland had been established was highly extolled; a revision of our whole trading system upon the same comprehensive principles was recommended; and, lastly, some fundamental regulation of our Asiatic territories was earnestly called for.

A general profession of regard to the constitution, and a promise on all occasions to advance and reward merit in every profession, were held forth at the conclusion; at the same time, temper, wisdom, and disinterestedness in parliament, collectively and individually, were represented as necessary, to ensure the full advantage of a government conducted on such principles. It ended with telling both houses, that the people expected these qualifications of them, and that his Majesty called for them.

An address in the usual style was moved in both houses of parliament, and carried, nemine contradicente, after a long and desultory conversation. It was remarked, that the friends of administration begun thus early to lay the groundwork for the defence of the peace, the merits of which would necessarily become the subject of parliamentary discussion, by expatiating on the miseries and vicissitudes of war, by lamenting the hazardous state of public credit, and by depreciating the importance of the late successes. These, it was said, though brilliant, were not likely to be followed by any solid advantage that could either compensate the calamities of war, or balance the enormous expence that must necessarily attend the further prosecution of it.

In the House of Commons a [8] young member, supposed on this occasion to be in the confidence of administration, made some pointed allusions to the cession of Gibraltar, with a view, as was imagined, of discovering in what manner such a measure would be received by the house. The alarm and dissatisfaction which this intimation spread was very considerable; and as it was generally believed that the minister was at this time treating with the court of Spain for the exchange of that important fortrefs, it is probable that he was deterred from his purpofe by the declaration of feveral members of great weight in the houfe, that they confidered it as a poffeffion almost invaluable to this country.

But though the addreffes were voted without a diffentient voice, and even without any amendment being propofed, yet the fpeech did not efcape a moft fevere examination. The three firft paragraphs were objected to, as conveying a falfe and injurious imputation on the members of the late cabinet, that orders for putting an end to offenfive war in North America had not been iffued till after the recefs of parliament. Mr. Fox took this occafion to enter into a minute explanation of the caufe of[9] his retiring from the cabinet. Some time before his refignation, he faid that he had written, by the king's orders, to Mr. Grenville, then at Paris, to authorize him to offer to the American agents, " *to re-cognize the independence of the United States in the firft instance, and not to referve it as a condition of peace.*" At the fame time an official letter, for the fame purpofe, was fent by the Earl of Shelburne to Sir Guy Carlton in America. Mr. Fox fufpecting that this meafure, though confented to in the cabinet, had not the entire approbation of fome of his colleagues, had, in order to prevent any mifconception, purpofely chofen the moft forcible expreffions that the Englifh language could fupply; and he confeffed that his joy was fo great, on finding that the Earl of Shelburne, in the letter to Sir Guy Carleton, had repeated his very words, that he carried it immediately to the Marquis of Rockingham, and told him that their diftruft and fufpicions of that noble lord's intentions had been groundlefs, and were now done away— " Judge then," faid he, " of my grief

and aftonifhment, when, during the illnefs of my noble friend, another language was heard in the cabinet, and the noble earl and his friends began to confider the above letters as containing offers only of a conditional nature, to be recalled, if not accepted as the price of peace. Finding myfelf thus enfnared and betrayed, and all confidence deftroyed, I quitted a fituation in which I found I could not remain either with honour or fafety."

The next paragraph of the fpeech was condemned with great feverity, as an infidious and unmanly attempt to throw all the blame of the difmemberment of the empire on parliament. The calamities of the war, it was faid, were not taken into the account; the circumftances of the country, and the impoffibility of acting otherwife, were all overlooked, in order to charge it upon that houfe alone. It was, in fact, to make his majefty fay, that he did it againft wifdom, againft good fenfe, againft policy, againft neceffity, in conftrained obedience to the advice of an ill-judging Houfe of Commons. It was afked, what minifters meant by making the king fay, that he had confiderations of his own, feparate from the wifhes and opinion of his people? Such language, it was faid, was as new, as it was improper and unconftitutional. The prayer which follows was equally condemned, as a piece of unfeafonable, unmeaning, and hypocritical cant, played off at the expence of parliament. Much furprife was alfo expreffed, at finding benevolences praifed in a fpeech, the production of a cabinet, in which fat a * learned lord, who, when a commoner, had in that very houfe moved a refolution that fuch benevolences were illegal.

The call for wifdom, in the concluding paragraph, was ridiculed with infinite humour: and the call for difinterestednefs reprefented as an audacious infult on parlia-

ment. The folly and dangerous tendency of thefe and other parts of the fpeech were expofed with uncommon ability by a right honourable gentleman †, whofe fpeeches in this debate were greatly diftinguifhed by a happy mixture of the moft brilliant wit and pointed argument. He concluded with declaring, that he confidered the whole as a compound of hypocrify, felf-commendation, duplicity, and abfurdity; abounded with principles of a dangerous and unconftitutional nature, which, if unanimity was not fo abfolutely neceffary at the prefent crifis, parliament would have been bound to have reprobated in the moft exemplary manner.

In the upper houfe, the converfation principally turned on that part of the fpeech which related to America. The *irrevocable and unconditional* recognition of the independence of the United States, was condemned in the feverest terms by a noble vifcount, who had held a high office in a former adminiftration *. It was well known, he faid, that the French themfelves had at different times declared, that they did not think it poffible to wreft all the thirteen provinces from Great Britain; and yet an unqualified furrender was made of the whole, without obtaining a truce, or even a ceffation of hoftilities, as the price of fo lavifh a conceffion. In the moft abject and unfortunate reign that Spain ever knew (that of Philip III.) the negotiators of that prince retained ten out of feventeen of the revolted provinces, and detached the reft from their alliance with France. An act of indemnity and oblivion in favour of its partizans, was at leaft what the conceding party was bound by faith and juftice to procure. But here no ftipulations whatever had been made, fo far as

* Lord Afhburton.

† Mr. Burke.
* Lord Stormont.

could be collected from the king's speech, in favour of those wretched men who had hazarded their lives and sacrificed their fortunes to their attachment to the mother country.

The legality of the recognition of American independance, was also questioned; and it was absolutely denied, that the sense either of parliament or of the people had been collected on that subject.

In reply to this attack, the first lord of the treasury denied, that the offer of independance was irrevocable; the words of the speech, he said, clearly proved it was conditional; and if fair and equal terms could not be obtained from France, the ally of America, the offer might be withdrawn, and would cease and determine.

On the following day, Dec. 6th. when the report from the committee of the House of Commons appointed to draw up the address was read, several members got up to express their uneasiness at the explication given in the other house by the minister, of that paragraph of the speech which announced the provisional treaty with America; the unanimity, they said, with which the motion for an address had been suffered to pass, arose from a persuasion that the independence of the colonies was recognized irrevocably; so that though the treaty negotiating with the court of France should not terminate in a peace, yet the provisional treaty would remain in full force, to take place whenever the former event should happen. His majesty's servants were therefore called upon to clear up these doubts, and satisfy the minds of such as were of opinion that the unconditional recognition of independence, by making it the interest of America to put an end to the war as speedily as possible, would tend essentially to accelerate a general peace. In consequence of this appeal, the secretary of state, the chancellor of the exchequer, and the commander in chief, severally rose, and declared, that the articles [10] were only so far provisional, that they depended upon the single contingency of peace being concluded with France; but whenever that event took place, the independence of America stood recognized without any reserved condition whatever.

Dec. 13th. This contrariety of opinion amongst the members of the cabinet, occasioned a second debate on the same subject in the House of Lords. On the 13th, the Earl Fitzwilliam re-[11]marked, that these contradictions, being public and notorious, might lead to consequences of the utmost importance, and therefore demanded an immediate explanation. During the progress of negotiations with artful and jealous enemies, every appearance of duplicity, or even ambiguity in our councils, ought most anxiously to be avoided. In order therefore to rescue government from the suspicions under which it lay; in order to satisfy the country that the subjugation of America could not, under any possible circumstances, be again attempted; in order to secure confidence to administration both at home and abroad, he begged leave to propose the following question to the noble earl at the head of his majesty's treasury.

" Is it to be understood that the
" independence of America is ne-
" ver again to become a subject of
" doubt, discussion, or bargain;
" but is to take effect absolutely
" at any period, near or remote,
" whenever a treaty of peace is
" concluded with the court of
" France, though the present trea-
" ty should entirely break off?
" Or, on the contrary, is the in-
" dependence of America merely
" contingent; so that if the parti-
" cular treaty now negotiating
" with that court should not ter-
" minate in a peace, the offer is
" to be considered as revoked, and
" the independence left to be de-
" termined by circumstances, and
" the events of war."

To the question, thus put, the minister positively refused to give any answer, and was supported by the Dukes of Richmond and Chandos. It was urged in vain, that he had already, on the first day of the session, avowed his sentiments in a full and explicit manner; that the present question was only put on account of doubts that had arisen from the contradictory assertions of others of his majesty's servants; that it was the language of ministers, and not the secrets of the treaty, of which an explanation was desired; that the fact must necessarily be known to all the parties concerned in the subsisting negotiations; that it was a secret to the British parliament alone; and that no possible mischief could arise from his giving the satisfaction required. The noble earl persisted in his refusal; declaring that the whole house should not force an answer from him, which he conceived he could not give without violation of his oath as a privy counsellor. Declaring war and making peace, were, he said, the undoubted prerogative of the crown, and ought to be guarded from all incroachment with the most particular care. If the popular parts of the constitution thought themselves better adapted for carrying on negotiations of this sort, he would advise them to go the king at once, and tell him that they were tired of the monarchical establishment, that they meant to do the business of the crown themselves, and had no farther occasion for his services. No man, he added, could be more anxious than himself to have the world know what he had done, and to receive the judgment of parliament and of the people of England upon his proceedings; and that for this purpose, so soon as prudence and policy should warrant, he would not lose a moment in laying the treaty before them. With respect to the assertion that had so frequently been made, that no mischief would arise from giving the answer required, he said it was a little extraordinary that those who knew not what the treaty was, should be so positive in declaring there could be no secrets in it, whilst those who did know its contents as positively asserted there were.

Dec. 16th. On the 16th Mr. Fox gave notice of his intention to move, on the first convenient day, for the provisional treaty to be laid before the house, or such parts of it as related to the recognition of American independence. At the same time, as a proof that he had no design to embarrass government, or throw any impediment in the way of the minister's negotiations, he declared that if the secretary of state would pledge himself to the house, that the treaty in question contained particulars, which, if discovered earlier than the moment ministers might choose for laying it before parliament, would be attended with mischievous consequences, and materially affect the negotiations then carrying on, he would desist from his purpose altogether. The minister refusing to pledge himself in the manner proposed, Mr. Fox made the following motion on the 18th.

18th. "That an humble address be presented to his "majesty that he will be graciously "pleased to give directions that "there be laid before this house "copies of such parts of the pro-"visional articles as relate to the "independence of America."

The motion was opposed by the ministers and their friends, as both unseasonable and unnecessary. The moment of negotiation was said to be of all others that in which parliament ought to place confidence in ministers, and to abstain from interfering by its advice in measures, with the delicate situation of which it must necessarily be unacquainted. Whatever construc-

tion the treaty might bear, whatever contrariety of opinions might be entertained respecting it, it was signed, and could not be altered; and, what was most material, had given perfect satisfaction to the party that had accepted it. The mischiefs that might arise from discussing subjects of this nature in the house were strongly insisted on; and the ministers were advised to keep a total silence with respect to the matter in debate.

These objections were supported by Lord North in a speech full of irony and sarcastic observation. He said he entirely approved of the advice that had been given to ministers to keep silent, but wished the injunction had been laid upon them a little earlier; much trouble would then have been saved, much unseasonable discussion of characters stopped; and, if the new doctrine of a privy counsellor's oath were solid, something very like perjury prevented.

The motion before the house he understood was made for the purpose, either of satisfying them that the American treaty was irrevocable, or of declaring it to be so if it should appear doubtful. Now, as he neither wished nor believed it to be of that nature, he certainly could not vote with the right honourable mover.

It had been pleasantly remarked, that he should vote that day with the ministers, not because he agreed with them, but because they disagreed with each other. This, he said, was in some measure true; but it was a matter not of choice but of necessity; and as he wished to strengthen their government, he should be very happy if he could be instructed how he could support them collectively.

Differences, he admitted, undoubtedly existed, and of a very essential nature, in the cabinet; and those differences might certainly have an effect with foreign powers, but they were not likely to be reconciled within those walls.

The cabinet consisted of eleven persons of great genius, long experience, and invariable constancy; they had employed almost an equal number of commissioners at Paris in this important business; and if all these personages had not been able to fix a precise meaning to a treaty that was declared to be concluded, could it be expected that an unanimous explanation of it should be given in that house?

He then proceeded to state the grounds of the meaning he had affixed to the treaty. It was a maxim, he said, with casuists, that the support of one grave doctor was enough to make an opinion probable;—now he had the opinion of two grave doctors, two cabinet ministers, that the treaty was not irrevocable. He next examined the contradictory explanations that had been given; and after commenting on them for some time, argued that if, from so many contradictions, any thing certain could be deduced, it must be, that the provisional articles meant nothing fixed. In this opinion he was confirmed by the speech from the throne. To this edition of the treaty, printed on royal paper, he should certainly give the preference over the many that had since been published, and enriched *cum notis variorum*. In that it was said, in the first place, that independence had been *offered*; secondly, that this article was dependent on another treaty, in which it was *to be inserted*; and, thirdly, it is there styled only a *provisional* treaty, which clearly implied that it was conditional, and therefore revocable.

Having stated the grounds of his opinion, he added, that it could not be expected he should concur in a motion, the design of which was to affix a meaning on the treaty of which he could not approve. If, says he, the right honourable gentleman should succeed in that attempt, would not the ministers of France argue thus with our negociator, "You have told us, that the Englifh nation would fubmit with great unwillingnefs to the recognition of American independence, and you demand fome facrifice from us as an equivalent for that conceffion. You fee now that parliament has none of the difficulties you made account of; we therefore muft alter our terms, there being no reafon why we fhould now make the facrifice you require."

In fupport of the motion it was urged, that the production of a treaty, pending the negotiation, was perfectly parliamentary, and not unprecedented; and that none of his Majefty's fervants would venture to affert, that, in the prefent inftance, it would be dangerous or unfafe. The difficulties under which our negotiators muft unavoidably labour, fo foon as the contradictory language of minifters at home was known abroad, and the neceffity of relieving them from this embarraffment, was ftrongly infifted on. It was not from any abfurd idea of reconciling the contradictions of minifters that the prefent motion was brought forward, but that parliament might put fuch a clear, diftinct, and definitive conftruction on the treaty, as might fatisfy both foreign powers and the people at home of its true meaning and purpofe. Minifters could then no longer fluctuate in their explanations of it, and might recover that confidence abroad which at prefent it was ridiculous for them to expect. They had themfelves confeffed, that the infinuations that had been propagated refpecting the infincerity of the noble earl at the head of the treafury had materially impeded their negotiations; and was it likely that thefe fufpicions would be removed by what had paffed in parliament fince the firft day of the feffion?

It was not denied that the defign of the motion was to induce parliament to come to an explicit and unconditional acknowledgment of the independence of America; and this, it was argued, was the beft po-

licy we could adopt. To grant it as the price of peace, at the requifition of France, would be bafe and degrading. Should the French minifter infult us with an offer, he fhould be told, "We will not fell the independence of America to you at any price; we will freely prefent her with that which you fhall not procure her, offer what bargain you pleafe."

The motion was at length rejected on previous queftions, by a majority of 219 to 46; and both houfes adjourned on the 23d to the 21ft of the following month.

. . .

THE preliminary articles of peace between Great Britain and France, and between Great Britain and Spain, were figned at Verfailles on the 20th of January; and on the 27th copies of the fame, and of the provifional treaty with the United States of America, were laid before both houfes of parliament, and after a fhort debate, ordered to be printed. Monday the 17th of February was appointed for taking them into confideration; and in the intermediate time feveral motions were made for fuch papers and documents as might affift the houfe in deciding on their merits. On the day appointed upwards of four hundred and fifty members were affembled. After the papers were read, a motion was made by Mr. Thomas Pitt, and feconded by Mr. Wilberforce, " that an ad- [12] " drefs of thanks fhould be pre- " fented to the King for his gra- " cious condefcenfion in ordering " the preliminary and provifional " articles of the feveral treaties " which his Majefty had conclud- " ed to be laid before them; and " to affure his Majefty that they " had confidered them with that " attention that fo important a " fubject required. To exprefs " their fatisfaction that his Ma- " jefty had, in confequence of the " powers entrufted to him, laid the " foundation, by the provifional " articles with the States of North

" America, for a treaty of peace, " which they trufted would enfure " perfect reconciliation and friend- " fhip between both countries. " And that, in this confidence, " they prefumed to exprefs their " juft expectations, that the fe- " veral States of North America " would carry into effectual and " fatisfactory execution thofe mea- " fures which the congrefs was fo " folemnly bound by the treaty " to recommend, in favour of fuch " perfons as had fuffered for the " part they had taken in the war; " and that they fhould confider " this circumftance as the fureft " indication of returning friend- " fhip.

" To acknowledge their due " fenfe of that wife and paternal " regard for the happinefs of his " fubjects, which induced his Ma- " jefty to relieve them from a bur- " thenfome and expenfive war; " and to affure his Majefty they " would encourage every exertion " of his fubjects of Great Britain " and Ireland, in the improvement " of thofe refources which muft " tend to the augmentation of the " public ftrength, and the profpe- " rity of his dominions."

Of this addrefs an amendment was moved by Lord John Cavendifh, to leave out all that part after the words, " to affure his Ma- " jefty," and to infert inftead thereof the following—" His faithful " commons will proceed to con- " fider the fame with that ferious " and full attention which a fub- " ject of fuch importance to the " prefent and future interefts of " his Majefty's dominions deferves. " That in the mean time they en- " tertain the fulleft confidence of " his Majefty's paternal care, that " he will concert with his parlia- " ment fuch meafures as may be " expedient for extending the " commerce of his fubjects.

" That whatever may be the " fentiments of his faithful com- " mons on the inveftigation of the " terms of pacification, they beg

" leave to affure his Majefty of
" their firm and unalterable refo-
" lution to adhere inviolably to
" the feveral articles for which
" the public faith is pledged, and
" to maintain the bleffings of
" peace, fo neceffary to his Ma-
" jefty's fubjects and the general
" happinefs of mankind."

A fecond amendment was afterwards moved by Lord North, to
infert after the words, " commerce
" of his fubjects," the following—
" And his Majefty's faithful com-
" mons feel that it would be fu-
" perfluous to exprefs to his Ma-
" jefty the regards due from the na-
" tion to every defcription of men,
" who, with the rifque of their
" lives and the facrifice of their
" properties, have diftinguifhed
" their loyalty and fidelity during
" a long and calamitous war."

In the following account of the
important debate which thefe motions gave rife to, we have thought
it more advifeable, for the fake of
diftinctnefs and precifion, to follow the arrangement of the arguments ufed on both fides the queftion, than the order of fpeakers.
With refpect to the latter therefore it may fuffice to mention,
that the original addrefs was fupported by the fecretary of ftate,
the chancellor of the exchequer,
the treafurer of the navy, the foli-
citor general, and by Mr. Powis,
Mr. Banks, and fome other country gentlemen; the amendments
by Lord North, Mr. Fox, Mr.
Burke, Governor Johnftone, Lord
Mulgrave, Sir Henry Fletcher,
Mr. Sheridan, Mr. Adam, and[13]
alfo by feveral of the country gentlemen.

The defence of the peace was
undertaken on three grounds; firft,
on the weak and impoverifhed ftate
of this country; fecondly, on the
merits of the articles themfelves;
and laftly, on an attempt to difarm the arguments and objections
on the other fide of their force
and effect, by throwing on the oppofite party the odium of acting
entirely, on his occafion, from
interefted motives; and of having
entered into an unnatural coalition,
merely for the purpofe of difplac-
ing his Majefty's minifters by inducing parliament to cenfure the
peace.

On the firft of thefe heads, Mr.
Thomas Pitt entered into a circumftantial detail of the deplorable
ftate of the *finances* of this country,
taken from the report of a committee appointed to enquire into
the ftate of the funds, of which he
had been chairman. By this he
made it appear, that the national
debt, funded and unfunded, a-
mounted to upwards of 250 millions. That the annual intereft
on it would fall little fhort of nine
millions and a half. That this
enormous intereft, being added to
the civil lift, and to a moderately
calculated peace eftablifhment, our
annual expences, in feafons of profound peace, would (according to
his detailed calculations) amount
at leaft to 14,793,137l. That the
amount of the enormous load of
taxes under which the landed intereft was finking, did not exceed
all together 12,500,000l. So that
there remained an annual fum of
near 2,300,000l. to be raifed by
frefh burthens.—From thefe facts it
was demanded, whether the continuance of the war could end in
any thing lefs than certain ruin?

This ftate of our finances, it was
faid, ought to be kept conftantly
in view in difcuffing the merits of
the peace; and whenever it was
argued that conceffions had been
improvidently made, or that greater
advantages might have been obtained, members fhould fairly afk
themfelves, whether fuch an object, under uch circumftances,
was worth the expence and hazard
of another campaign?

It would doubtlefs be urged that
the other belligerent powers felt
an equal degree of diftrefs; but to
what a confequence would fuch a
mode of reafoning lead the houfe?
What man was fo defperate as to
advife the continuance of a war,
which might end in the bankruptcy
of public faith, a bankruptcy which
would almoft diffolve the bands of
government, and this merely on a
furmife, that probably one of the
adverfe powers might experience
an equal diftrefs.

The *navy*, the fecond great engine of war, was reprefented to be
in a condition fcarcely adequate
to the purpofes of defence, and (in
a competition of ftrength) greatly
inferior to that of the enemy.
From the papers on the table it
appeared that the whole Britifh
force, fit for fervice, fcarcely
amounted to one hundred fail of
the line. Of thefe many were un-
dermanned, feveral unclean and in
a mouldering ftate, and the greateft
part had been long and actively
employed on foreign ftations. Our
magazines were in an exhaufted
condition; and with the moft diligent exertions not more than fix
fail could have been added to this
catalogue in March. The force of
France and Spain amounted to one
hundred and forty fail of the line.
Thirteen new fhips would have
been added to the fleet of France
in the courfe of the enfuing fpring.
The Dutch fleet would have
amounted to twenty-five fail of
the line, and it was uncertain
what acceffion the Spanifh force
would have received at the fame
time.

With fo glaring an inferiority,
what hopes of fuccefs could we
derive, either from the experience
of the laft campaign, or from any
new diftribution of our force in
that which would have followed?
In the Weft-Indies we could not
have had more than forty-fix fail
to oppofe to forty, which on the
day that the peace was figned lay
in the harbour of Cadiz with
16,000 troops on board, ready to
fail for that quarter of the world,
where they would have been joined
by twelve fhips of the line from
the Havannah, and by ten from St.
Domingo, with 25,000 men on

board. A defenfive war, it was univerfally acknowledged, muft terminate in certain ruin; and it was afked, whether Admiral Pigot,[14] with fuch an inferiority could have undertaken any offenfive operations againft the iflands of the enemy; thofe iflands on which Lord Rodney flufhed with victory, could not attempt to make an impreffion? Could Admiral Pigot have regained by arms what the minifters had recovered by treaty? Could he, in the fight of a fuperior fleet, have captured Grenada, Dominique, St. Kitt's, Nevis, and Montferrat? Or might we not too reafonably apprehend, that the campaign in the Weft Indies would have clofed with the lofs of Jamaica itfelf, the avowed object of this immenfe armament?

In the Eaft our profpects were not brighter. A mere defenfive refiftance had entitled Sir Edward Hughes to the thanks of parliament;[15] but his fuccefs, if it might be termed a victory, had not prevented the enemy from landing a greater European force than we actually poffefs in that country, and which, in conjunction with Hyder Ally, was at that inftant fubduing or defolating the Carnatic. In the enfuing campaign, after the junction with Commodore Bickerton, the French fleet would at leaft[16] be equal to our ours.

If we looked forward to the probable operations in the channel, and in the northern feas, in a future campaign, it was faid to be clear, from the papers laid before the houfe, that the combined fleets of the houfe of Bourbon and of Holland, would at leaft have doubled our force in our own feas.

With refpect to the *army*, it was afferted, that we were in want of thirty thoufand men to complete its eftablifhments, and that levies could fcarcely be torn, on any terms, from a depopulated country. That after the moft careful inveftigation, it had appeared, that only three thoufand men could have been

fpared with fafety to this country, for any offenfive duty. The foreign troops in garrifon at New-York we had no power to embark on any other than American fervice; befides, if a new treaty had been entered into with the German princes, no tranfports could have been affembled for an early embarkation; and, even when embarked, where could they have directed their courfe, in the face of an enemy's fleet cruizing with undifputed fuperiority in every part of the weftern world?

From this view of our total inability to engage in another campaign, with any profpect of bringing it to a more favourable conclufion than the laft, it was argued, that peace on any terms, by breaking the powerful confederacy that was againft us, and giving us time to recruit our wafted ftrength, was preferable to a continuance of the war. But it was afferted, in the fecond place, that the peace did not ftand in need of fuch a defence, and that the terms obtained were fair and honourable, and adequate to the juft expectations of the nation.

By the 3d and 4th articles of the treaty with the court of France, we had ceded the exclufive right of fifhery on a certain part of the coaft of *Newfoundland*. But at the fame time we have alfo eftablifhed an exclufive right to the moft valuable banks. The concurrent fifhery formerly exercifed was a fource of endlefs ftrife. The French were now confined to a certain fpot: it was almoft nothing, when compared to the extent we poffefs, and befides is fituated in the leaft productive part of the coaft. In proof of thefe facts, the opinions of Admiral Edwards, of Captain Levefon Gower, and of Lieutenant Lane, who took an accurate furvey of the whole, were confidently appealed to.[17]

By the 5th article the iflands of *St. Pierre* and *Miquelon* were ceded to the French. Thefe iflands had

formerly belonged to that crown, but were retained, in the pride of our fuperiority, at the treaty of Paris, in 1762; and furely there could be no juft ground of complaint now, if France, in her afcendancy, fhould require the reftitution of them. If it fhould be alledged, that thefe places might be fortified fo as to annoy us in a future war, and even endanger our fifheries, the anfwer was at hand; —the moft fkilful engineers had certified, that neither ifland would admit the conftruction of a fortrefs which would ftand the attack of the fmalleft of our frigates.

In the *Weft-Indies*, by the 7th article, the ifland of St. Lucia was reftored, and Tobago ceded to the French; but in return, by the 8th, his Moft Chriftian Majefty had reftored to Great Britain the iflands of Grenada and the Grenadines, of St. Vincent, Dominica, St. Chriftopher, Nevis, and Montferrat. It was afferted, that the ifland of Dominica, confidered as a place of obfervation and ftrength, was as valuable to this country, if not more fo, than St. Lucia. The importance of the latter ifland, it was faid, might fairly be eftimated by the value fet upon it at the laft peace. It was then ours by conqueft; and if it had been thought of fuch ineftimable confequence, as was now pretended, why was it not then retained? The ifland of Tobago had alfo been extorted from France at the peace of Paris, and therefore might now be equitably re-demanded. Its importance to our cotton manufactory had been greatly exaggerated. If this manufacture had rifen to a flourifhing ftate before we ever poffeffed that ifland, why might it not remain fo now? The fact was, that cotton, whether in the hands of friend or foe, would always find its way to our door, in preference to that of thofe who cannot meet it with fuch a purfe.

In *Africa*, by the 9th article, the King of Gritain Britain cedes the river of Senegal, with its dependencies and forts, and restores the Island of Goree. On the other side, Fort James and the river Gambia is guaranteed to Great Britain, by the 10th; and by the 11th and 12th, the gum trade is[18] put on the same footing as in the year 1755. By these articles, it was said, we secure (as much as we ever had secured) a share in the gum trade; and were freed from the necessity of making that coast a grave for our fellow-subjects, thousands of whom were annually sent there to watch an article of trade which we in vain endeavoured to monopolize.

The four following articles relate to the *East Indies*. By these, Pondicherry and Karical, with suitable dependencies, the possession of Mahé, and the Comptoir of Surat, are restored, and guaranteed to France, together with all the establishments which belonged to that kingdom at the commencement of the war, on the coast of Orixa, and in Bengal, with liberty to surround Chandernagor with a ditch for draining the waters. These concessions were allowed to be very considerable, and they were defended by the advocates for the peace on two very different and opposite grounds. Some of them asserted, that the Company's affairs were in every respect in so deplorable a state, that the continuance of the war there must have brought on their irretrievable destruction; whilst others, in order to remove any apprehension that might be entertained from the re-establishment of the French power in India, contended, that their affairs were in so prosperous a train, as would speedily put them out of the reach of injury from any rival whatever.

The abrogation of all the articles relative to Dunkirk, which had been inserted in any former treaty of peace, formed the 17th article of the present. During all the administrations which have

passed away since the demolition of that harbour was first stipulated, those articles had never been inforced. This negligence, it was said, was a sufficient proof of the little account in which that matter was held; and the fact was, that all the art and cost that France could bestow on the bason of Dunkirk, could not render it in any degree formidable to Great Britain. France wished for the suppression of those articles, merely as a point of honour; and surely no sober man would continue the war to thwart a fancy so little detrimental to us. At former periods England had dictated the terms of peace to submissive nations; but the visions of her power and pre-eminence were passed away, and she was under the mortifying necessity of employing a language that corresponds with her true condition.

To the King of Spain, the possession of Minorca and West Florida was guaranteed, and East Florida ceded. With respect to the first-mentioned place, it was urged, that it was kept at an immense and useless expence in peace, and was never tenable in war; and as to the Floridas, that the possession of them was by no means so important as might be imagined, and that we had gained an equal advantage by the restoration of Providence and the Bahama islands. The imports of both the Floridas did not exceed 70,000l. and the exports amount to about 120,000l. It certainly was not desirable to take so much from the commerce of the nation; but it was a favourite object with Spain, and amidst the millions of our trade, it surely was not worth contending for at the hazard of continuing the war.

The treaty with the United States of America, as far as regarded their independence, had in some measure been previously formed by parliament; the only points therefore that remained for discussion

were the fixing of the boundaries, the settlement of the fisheries, and the terms stipulated for the loyalists.

By the line of boundaries, all the back settlements, and the whole country between the Allegany Mountains and the Mississippi were ceded to the United States. To have retained the large tract behind them, for the purpose of planting it with persons of different political principles, would have been little better than laying the foundation of new war and new disturbances. The free navigation of the Mississippi was however reserved.

To the northward, the line of division was carried through the centre of the lakes, and by that means a participation of the fur trade was secured to both countries, with a small advantage in favour of Great Britain; as it was well known to all men conversant in the nature of that trade, that its best resources lay to the northward. But supposing the entire fur trade was sunk in the sea, what was the detriment to this country? Let this and every other part of the treaties be examined by the fair value of the district ceded, drawn from the amount of the exports and imports, by which alone we could judge of its importance. The exports of this country to Canada, then, were only 140,000l. and the imports not more than 50,000l. Was this an object for Great Britain to continue a war, of which the people of England had declared their abhorrence? Surely it was not: and much less would it appear so, when it was recollected that the preservation of this annual importation of 50,000l. has cost the country for several years past, on an average, 800,000l. a year. A few interested Canadian merchants might complain; for merchants would always love monopoly, without considering that monopoly, by destroying rivalry, which was the very essence of the well-being of trade, was in fact detrimental to it.

The ceffion of Penobfcot had been objected to, as depriving us of a fupply of mafts, which that place is faid to furnifh in wonderful abundance. But in oppofition to this affertion, it was proved, they faid, by the certificate of Captain Twifs, one of the ablest furveyors[19] in the fervice, that there was not a tree there capable of being made a maft.

By the 3d article of the provifional treaty, the freedom of fifhing on all the banks of Newfoundland, and alfo on all the coafts of our dominions in America, was given to the fubjects of the United States. And why?—Becaufe in the firft place, t ey could, from their locality, have exercifed a fifhery in that quarter, in the firft feafon (for there are two) without our confent, nd in fpite of all our efforts to repel them. The firft feafon commences in February, and that is entirely at their difcretion : for our people have never, and can never take their ftation there fo foon. With regard to the other feafon, the principle on which the fur trade had been regulated was again reverted to; though we had not a monopoly, we poffeffed fuch fuperior advantages in the article of curing our fifh for market, from the exclufive command of the contiguous fhores, that a rivalry would only whet our induftry, to make the moft of thofe benefits which our fituation put within our power. It might be afked, why we had not ftipulated for a reciprocity of fifhing in the American harbours and creeks ? The anfwer was obvious—becaufe we had abundant employment in our own.

The laft article objected to, was the terms procured for the loyalifts. On this point but one alternative offered itfelf; either to accept from congrefs their recommendation to the provincial ftates in favour of thofe unhappy people, or to continue the war: and who was bold enough to ftep forward, and fay that we ought on that account to

have broken off the treaty ? But the fact was, that they could do no more than recommend. It was neceffary to be cautious in wording the treaty, left they fhould give offence to the new States In all their meafures, fince their firft conftitution, for providing either money or men, they have ufed the word *recommendation* to the provincial affemblies ; and it had always been paid refpect to. But to fuppofe the worft, that after all, this eftimable fet of men could not be received into the bofom of their own country; was England fo loft to gratitude and honour, as not to afford them an afylum ? Without one drop of blood fpilt, with one fifth of the expence of one campaign, happinefs and eafe might be given to the loyalifts in as ample a manner as thofe bleflings were ever in their enjoyment.

Such were the arguments urged in favour of the articles of the feveral treaties of peace : an indirect defence of it was alfo attempted, by endeavouring to throw odium on the characters of thofe who, it was faid, pretended to difapprove of it, and were defirous, from interested motives, of inducing parliament to pafs a cenfure upon it. A coincidence in opinion between a noble lord who had formerly been at the head of adminiftration, and the perfons who moved and fupported the amendment to the addrefs, was the ground of this accufation. So unnatural an alliance, between the lofty affertors of regal prerogative, and the humble worfhippers of the majefty of the people ; the determined advocate of the influence of the crown, and the great purifiers of the conftitution ; could not, it was faid, originate from any but the moft bafe and fordid views. It was not the peace, which, it was afferted, was unimpeachable, but the offices of the minifters, that was the object of their purfuit. On this occafion every art was ufed to inflame the minds of the public, and to incite

their own friends to revolt againft what was reprefented as a moft barefaced attempt to abufe their confidence : all the moft virulent expreffions of enmity and abufe, which during their long and violent contefts had fallen from either party in the heat of debate were induftrioufly brought forward : their junction was urged as a proof of a total dereliction of principle, and as an atrocious attempt to overbear the juft prerogative of the crown, and to feize on the adminiftration of public affairs by force.

On thefe grounds was the defence of the peace undertaken : it now remains that we ftate thofe arguments which induced the majority of the houfe to adopt the amendments, already recited, and on a following day to vote, " that " the conceffions granted by the " peace to the enemies of Great " Britain were greater than they " were entitled to, either from the " actual fituation of their refpective " poffeffions, or from their comparative ftrength."

On the firft head, viz. the inability of the country, from the fituation of public credit, and the ftate of its finances, to continue the war, it was faid, that fpeculative politicians had in all times been fond of circumfcribing the bounds of public credit, and drawing a line, beyond which they imagined it could not be ftretched; but that repeated experience had fhewn that fuch ideas were for the moft part imaginary and chimerical. But in whatever degree we may fuppofe the refources of this country to be exhaufted, we were well affured that thofe of the enemy were equally fo, and that their burthens were lefs cheerfully fupported ; witnefs the feveral fpirited memorials from the States of Britanny, and other places, againft the war ; the loud murmurs of the whole Spanifh nation ; and the refufal of moft of the provincial ftates in America to pay the laft tax ordered to be levied by congrefs. If the apprehenfion of bankruptcy made peace defirable, or even neceffary to Great Britain, it made it equally fo to the other belligerent powers; and where the reafons for defiring peace were equal, no argument could be adduced why the terms fhould not be equal and reciprocal. It was urged, befides, that this argument, if allowed, would prove too much. The ftate of our finances, from their public nature, being as well known to our enemies as to ourfelves, it might fairly be afked, how they came to grant us, knowing we were not able to profecute the war, even thofe terms that had been procured? Was it owing to the magnanimity of France that we are allowed to retain our poffeffions in the Eaft and Weft Indies? Had the court of Spain at once forgot thofe objects, on account of which it had engaged in the war, the reftoration of Gibraltar and Jamaica? Was it from the remains of a filial regard in the United States, that Canada and Nova Scotia were not claimed, in addition to the reft of our territories furrendered in America?—No; it arofe from their knowledge that this nation, however diftreffed, would not bear the impofition of fuch conditions. They faw they had a miniftry to deal with that was confcious of their own tottering fituation. Tho' equally defirous of peace, they perceived it was the happy moment for their demands, and our conceffion; but at the fame time their policy would not let them go farther than they have now ventured.

With refpect to the navy, it was affirmed to be in a flourishing and vigorous ftate, and that we had the happieft profpects before us for the next campaign. The noble vifcount*, who had lately retired from his high and refponfible office at the head of the admiralty, becaufe, as he declared, he would not fubfcribe to the terms of the peace,

had afferted in the other houfe that the British fleet confifted of 109 line of battle fhips, and that the united force of the houfe of Bourbon did not exceed 125. With refpect to their condition, he declared, that, from the beft information he could procure, ours was greatly fuperior. During the courfe of laft year, when our inferiority was infinitely more apparent, our navy had increafed (and principally by captures) feventeen in its number, whilft that of France alone had fuffered a diminution of thirteen fhips of the line. It was likewife affirmed, that Admiral Pigot would, at the time of action, have had 54 fail of the line in the Weft Indies; a force abundantly fufficient for every offenfive or defenfive purpofe, and which our enemies could not have met with any profpect of advantage. It was declared by the noble vifcount alluded to above, that he moft earneftly wifhed the fleet that was collected at Cadiz had failed, as he had not the fmalleft doubt that a decifive blow would have been given in the enfuing campaign in the Weft Indies to the marine of the Houfe of Bourbon.

In the Eaft Indies, it had been allowed, on the other fide, that our force in point of number of guns was equal to that of the enemy; but in other refpects, it was now afferted to be much fuperior; and that the poffeffion of Trincomale gave us a decided advantage in all our naval operations in that quarter.

For the channel fervice there remained thirty-four fail of the line. This force, though allowed to be inferior to that of the enemy, yet was afferted to be fufficient for the fecurity of our trade, and adequate to all the purpofes of home-defence.

An appeal had been made to the experience of the late campaign.—On this point it was demanded, whether the navy had been inadequate to any fervice on which it

was difpatched? And, whether there had been any one offenfive or defenfive meafure declined, in confequence of its being incompetent to the duty?—On the proof of either of thefe propofitions, Mr. Fox offered to reft the fate of the queftion before the houfe.

With refpect to the army, it was faid, that the argument drawn from the depopulated ftate of the country, did not deferve a ferious anfwer. It was afferted that tranfports might eafily have been procured for carrying the German troops to the Weft Indies; and above all, it was contended, that the American war, the mill-ftone that hung about our necks, being at an end, the nation would have foon emerged from its dejection, and recovered its ufual high tone of thinking and acting.

It had been faid, that peace on any terms, by breaking the alliance confederated againft us, and giving us time to breathe, was preferable to the continuance of the war under our prefent circumftances. In anfwer to that it was obferved, that improvident conceffions could never tend to the fecurity of peace; but by weakening the power that made them, rendered it more liable to future infults. It was further urged, that if any inability to profecute the war really exifted, it was not likely we fhould reap much benefit from the breathing time, which had been procured at fo great and certain a lofs. It was not probable that the national debt would be fpeedily reduced; and it was a doubt whether we could build fhips fafter in time of peace than the courts of France and Spain. On the other hand, a variety of obvious circumftances, and more efpecially the brilliant fucceffes of the late campaign, ferved to prove, that the prefent was the moment for pufhing our fortune, if peace could not be obtained on equal and honourable terms. That fuch terms have not been obtained, was the next

* Lord Vifcount Keppel.

point that was undertaken to be proved.

In every negotiation for peace, it is obvious that some point muſt be fixed for the baſis of the treaty. Two principles are uſually reſorted to for this purpoſe - either that of leaving each party in the actual ſtate of their poſſeſſions at the time of the treaty, which is commonly called that of *uti poſſidetis*; or that of reciprocal and general reſtitution. The latter principle directs a negotiation, when the belligerent powers have equal deſire and reaſon for concluding the war. It is then they find it their intereſt to reinſtate each other reciprocally in the poſſeſſions they have loſt. The *uti poſſidetis* is the principle of negotiation, when either of the belligerent powers has obtained a ſuperiority in the war over the other. It is then the party worſted is obliged to ſubmit to the loſs of its poſſeſſions; for, not having the power of enforcing, it aſſumes not the pretence of demanding reſtitution.

Allowing we were in a ſituation to treat on the principle of mutual reſtitution, to which, from the actual ſtate of our poſſeſſions, and our comparative ſtrength, it was contended we had fair pretenſions; the articles of reſtoration on our part could not have exceeded thoſe contained in the preſent treaty, the ſettlement on the river Gambia alone excepted, for which we had ceded and given up to France the iſlands of St. Pierre and Miquelon, and the right of fiſhery on an extenſive part of the coaſt of Newfoundland, the iſland of Tobago, the river Senegal, with its dependencies and forts, and the abrogation of all former articles relative to Dunkirk: To Spain, the iſland of Minorca, and the provinces of Eaſt and Weſt Florida.

If it ſhould be thought that the ſcale of fortune had turned in favour of our enemies, and that we were not entitled to inſiſt on a general reſtitution, yet ſtill, on the moſt unfavourable ground (that of *uti poſſidetis*) we ſhould have loſt, to France, only the iſlands of Grenada, St. Vincent, Tobago, Dominica, St. Chriſtopher, Nevis, and Montſerrat, the two latter of little importance, either in point of extent or quality; while, on the other hand, we ſhould have retained the very valuable iſland of St. Lucia, in the Weſt Indies, all their continental ſettlements in the Eaſt, together with their forts and trade, as well as our own, on the coaſt of Africa.

With theſe poſſeſſions, it was maintained that we might have ſtood on the ground of *uti poſſidetis*, without any material, or probably any diſadvantage. The iſland of St. Lucia, in how little eſtimation ſoever it might have been held at the peace of Paris, was now found by experience, and univerſally acknowledged to be, of the utmoſt importance; and, together with the other ſettlements mentioned, might be conſidered as a fair and full equivalent for the Weſt India iſlands reſtored to Great Britain.

In the treaty with Spain, ſuppoſing it likewiſe to have been conducted on the principle of *uti poſſidetis*, the province of Eaſt Florida had been exchanged for the iſland of Providence and the Bahamas. With reſpect to the merits of this exchange, it was ſaid that the value of Eaſt Florida, whether in point of ſituation, or of commercial produce, had been either little underſtood, or had been deſignedly under-rated. It poſſeſſed one of the fineſt harbours in the world, called the *Bay of Tampa*, or *Eſpiritu Santo*, ſituated in a healthy climate, and where ſhips were ſafe from the annoyance of worms. Beſides, the coaſt of that province was covered with ſmall iſlands, from whence privateers might run to ſea, and attack our Jamaica trade, as it paſſed the gulf of Florida. And this was the more to be feared in a future, than it would have been in any preceding war, from the loſs of Georgia, whoſe harbours formerly ſerved both to protect our trade and to ſhelter it from tempeſts.— As a further proof of the raſhneſs and improvidence of this exchange, an addreſs lately preſented by the provincial aſſembly of that country was read, in which, after ſetting forth their thriving ſituation, and expreſſing their abhorrence both of the rebellion in America, and of the Spaniſh government, they conclude " with profeſſions of the ſtrong- " eſt attachment to the Houſe of " Brunſwick, under whoſe protec- " tion they remained, convinced " that their civil and religious rights " would be ſecure to the lateſt poſ- " terity."

But granting that theſe exchanges had been equitably and prudently made, there ſtill remained to be accounted for the important conceſſions made to the court of France, of which no defence had been attempted, excepting that the houſe of Bourbon had a right to expect ſome compenſation for the humiliating terms impoſed upon her by the peace of 1762.

The firſt of theſe was an excluſive right of fiſhery on a conſiderable part of the coaſt of Newfoundland. It had been ſaid, that in return we had eſtabliſhed an excluſive right on the remaining and more advantageous parts. In anſwer to this, it was obſerved, that the propoſal having evidently originated from France, it was abſurd to ſuppoſe that ſhe had choſen for herſelf the worſt ſtations.— The contrary was aſſerted to be the fact; and that the conceſſion was of a new and important nature, the conſequences of which it was not perhaps eaſy at preſent to foreſee.[20]

The ceſſion of St. Pierre and Miquelon followed, together with the right of fortifying them. Heretofore, as ſoon as ever hoſtilities commenced between Great Britain and France, we were enabled, as had been the caſe in the preceding war, to seize upon her fisheries and her seamen, because they were unprotected. Hereafter, this important advantage would no longer exist; for, by fortifying the two ceded islands, France would be as capable of carrying on the fishery in time of war, as in time of peace, and at the same time would have it in her power to annoy and distress us exceedingly. This article therefore materially affected the whole of the Newfoundland fishery, and rendered the stipulations in that particular infinitely more important and more advantageous to France, than they had ever been by former treaties. It was farther observed, that these islands, if once fortified, would command the entrance of the river St. Lawrence.

The value and importance of the island of Tobago, the cession that followed next in order, was strongly insisted on; and, in answer to the arguments used on the other side, the misc-ievous consequences were stated, of leaving an article so essential to our manufactures as cotton, in the hands of a rival power, to be taxed or prohibited at its pleasure.

The cession of Senegal and Goree, it was said, was not less mischievous and improvident. If ministers had referred to the negotiation for the last peace, they would have seen that France explicitly states, that without one of these places the gum trade could not exist; and on this principle, admitted by us, they were then divided. Now that they are united, our trade is held at the pleasure of France. It had been urged, that the trade was an object of trifling importance; but the want of it would destroy two great branches of our manufacture, that of printed linens, and that of silks and gauzes. If a war should break out, we might be deprived of it entirely, and in peace we should buy it at the French price.

The last concession made to France, was the abrogation of all former articles relative to Dunkirk. It was allowed, that much difference of opinion existed with respect to the importance of this harbour; but what it wanted in other respects was abundantly made up by the peculiar advantages of its situation. The bason, when opened and repaired, would be capable of containing twenty or thirty ships of a considerable size and burthen.—These, issuing out at all seasons, would annoy our trade in its very centre, and counterbalance, in some measure, the advantages of our local situation for commerce.—At the same time, it would be of no use to the French, but in a war with England; so that it was of all others the greatest temptation that could be thrown in their way for commencing fresh hostilities.

To these great and extraordinary concessions, ought to be added the restoration of their settlements, and other important advantages secured to the French in the East Indies. The addition of territory to Pondicherry and Karical, might be treated as a trifling matter; but it was not thought so in the negotiations for the treaty of Paris.—Great art was employed, and pressing solicitations made, to carry that point; but the ministers then were well informed of the value M. du Pleix put upon that territory; and that he held it to be a firm foundation for the re-establishment of the power of France, and for an effectual opposition to the English influence on the coast of Coromandel.

The grant of a free and undefined trade, such as the French East India Company enjoyed, without specifying at what period, might not only raise a contest about duties; but, taken in its full extent, would make Chandenagore a place of arms. It was well known, that the French East India Company, prior to our acquisitions in Bengal, was encouraged to carry arms into that country; but,

during the last peace, their vessels had been visited, and no arms had been permitted to be brought in.—Would France now submit to such examinations? And if that restraint was intended to be given up, Chandenagore would soon be a most powerful post in the centre of our government.

On the whole of the treaty with the court of France, it was contended, that at a time when we had the command of the East Indies; when we had excluded France from the coasts of India, of Africa, and the banks of Newfoundland; when we were relieved from the pressure of the American war, and had nothing to apprehend in Europe, after having captured so many sail of their line, and without the disgrace of having a single ship of our line in the possession of the enemy; we had restored her to all her power, and given her a controul and check upon us in every quarter of the globe.

The American treaty, to which the principles already laid down were not strictly applicable, was reserved for a separate discussion.—The necessity or the policy of acknowledging the independence of the United States being admitted, it followed of course that they were to be considered merely in the same view as any other power at war with Great Britain. The first thing therefore to be looked at, in estimating the terms of peace, was the known situation of each at the time of the treaty.

At this time Great Britain possessed the strongest posts on the coast of North America; all the back country, and the river St. Lawrence; the fur trade and fisheries were entirely hers; a great party in the country were uneasy at the continuance of the war, and dissatisfied with the new government; and many were zealously attached to our interests. Under these favourable circumstances, it was demanded, whether we were under the necessity of accepting such conditions as the enemy chose to offer? or, whether we had not a right to infist on fair and honourable terms?

By the provifional articles we had given up Charleftown, New York, Long Ifland, Penobfcot, and all the back fettlements. Twenty-five nations of Indians, who had entered into offenfive alliances with us againft the States, were given up, without any conditions being ftipulated for their fecurity. A tranfaction of itfelf fufficient to ftigmatize the framers of the treaty on our part with indelible difgrace.

By the line of boundaries to the northward, all our fettlements, carrying places, and forts on the lakes, including the principal forts of Niagara, Michilimakinac, and Detroit, the erection of which had coft this country immenfe furns of money, were gratuitoufly transferred to the Americans, without even affuming the merit of making fo important a ceffion.

Together with our fettlements on the lakes, a confiderable part of the peltry trade, perhaps indeed the whole of it, was for ever transferred to the fubjects of the United States. An attempt had been made to defend this ceffion by an abfurd invective againft monopoly, and by a long encomium upon open and free trade. How this applied to the point in queftion, it was not eafy to conceive. We had a monopoly of the fur trade, in the fame manner that every country has a monopoly of its own produce. The fur trade was ours, becaufe we held the country that fupplies it. How was the trade laid open by transferring that country to the Americans.

The Canadian merchants had been at an enormous expence in erecting forts and ftorehoufes on the banks of the lakes. They too are accufed of being anxious for their own interefts, and not underftanding the benefit of fharing, or rather of having their profits transferred to others; and a new æra of trade on new principles is announced. It was well known to what height the purfuit of the old and plain maxims of trade had raifed this country; but it was not fo eafy to comprehend the benefits that would refult from the new fyftem, fo magnificently defcribed.

The argument drawn from the amount of exports and imports, would better conclude for the entire ceffion of Canada. And, indeed, without the interior trade of the country, it was a mockery to keep the two forts of Montreal and Quebec, to be fupported from this kingdom with much expence, and a fufficient fubject for future war. But the balance had been unfairly ftated; for the charge was in a great degree to be placed to the account of the war; and the profit would have been very great in peace, had we not given away the moft valuable part of the province.

By the 3d article, the fifhery on the fhores retained by Great Britain is, again, not ceded, but recognized as a right inherent in the Americans, which they are to continue to enjoy unmolefted; whilft, on the other hand, no right is referved to Britifh fubjects to approach their fhores, tho' the treaty profeffes in its preamble to proceed on principles of mutual advantage and reciprocity.

Again, in the 7th article, all the American artillery we had in our garrifons and fortified places on that continent were to be left behind us; whereas no fuch ftipulation was to be found in this reciprocal treaty for reftoring any Britifh artillery poffeffed by the Americans.

Even in the article for the ceffation of hoftilities, the period, which in every other treaty that had ever yet been made was always reciprocal, commenced on our part immediately; on the part of the Americans, confifcation, profcription, imprifonment, and captures at fea, were not to determine till after the ratification in America of the definitive treaty.

After fuch extraordinary and boundlefs conceffions on one part, it was natural, in a treaty defigned to exclude "partial advantages," and to be formed on the bafis of "liberal equity and reciprocity," to look for the equivalent benefits granted by the other. Two articles of this defcription prefented themfelves: that by which free navigation of the Miffiffippi for ever was ftipulated; and that by which congrefs was bound to recommend the cafe of the loyalifts to the feveral provincial ftates.

With refpect to the free navigation, it was thus circumftanced:—The northern boundary excluded us from all accefs to the courfe of it by that way. The eaft fide of the river was poffeffed by the Americans. To the weft all the country had been ceded by the peace of Paris to the French, and fince by them to Spain; and now each fhore of the mouth of it, by the prefent peace, came into the poffeffion of the Spaniards; fo that in what manner we were to avail ourfelves of this free navigation, remained yet to be explained.

The article refpecting the loyalifts met with a more fevere, and with almoft a general reprobation. Thofe whom it pretends to favour, could receive, it was faid, no benefit from it; for fince the recent refolutions of fome of the provincial affemblies*, what was the purport of a recommendation? But to thofe the moft entitled to our regard, the brave and unhappy men, who, bound by their oaths of allegiance, called on by the Britifh parliament, encouraged by the proclamations of our generals, and invited under every national affurance

---

* The province of Virginia, a fhort time before the peace, had come to an unanimous refolution, "that all demands or requefts of the Britifh court for the " reftoration of property confifcated by that ftate, were wholly inadmiffible; and " that their delegates fhould be inftructed to move congrefs that they fhould direct the deputies for adjufting a peace, not to agree to any fuch reftitution."

of security, had not only given up their property, but risked their lives in our cause, the distinction admitted to their prejudice was cruel in the extremest degree.

In defence of this article, it was said, that the commissioners, or even congress, had no power to undertake further. Why, then, treat without fuller powers. The first question Mr. Oswald should have put to the American commissioners, ought to have been, Are you empowered to treat upon and conclude a general amnesty and restitution of goods to all loyalists, without exception?

But, admitting the necessity of treating with persons not fully empowered, were no means left to secure just and honourable terms?—Could not all the surrenders we were to make; the surrender of Charlestown, of New York, of Long Island, Staten Island, Penobscot, and Savannah, purchase security for those meritorious persons? or why were they not retained as pledges, till such security was ratified? The inhabitants of those very places were armed with us in defence of their own estates; these estates by recent act had been confiscated; and when we evacuate those places, we shall give up the houses, goods, and even the persons of our friends, to the resentment of their enemies.

Was it possible to suppose that the States of America, unable to raise a farthing to carry on the war which was in the heart of their country, were so determined not to allow of any stipulation in favour of those unhappy men, that they would rather have continued the war, even with the possibility of being in this instance deserted by their allies? If we had implored the aid of France and Spain, there could be no doubt but the generosity of two great and respectable states would have interposed in favour of the men we have deserted. The fidelity of the loyalists to their king and country, however obnoxious to their hostile pursuits in A-

merica while the war lasted, could never have been felt by any honest mind as a crime that excluded them from any conditions of peace.

But it was said, that there was even a horrible refinement in the cruelty of this article. They are told that one year is allowed them to solicit from the lenity of their persecutors that mercy, which their friends neglected to secure; to beg their bread of those by whom they had been stripped of their all; to obtain, if they can, leave to re-purchase what it was known they had no money to pay for.

The conduct of other states in similar circumstances was contrasted with that of the ministers of Great Britain. At the peace of Munster, a general act of indem-[21]nity was passed, without exception of place or person; and the adherents of the Spanish monarch, whose effects and estates had been confiscated, had them either restored, or were paid interest for them at the rate of $6\frac{1}{4}$ per cent. on the purchase money. When the Catalonians revolted from Spain, and at one time put themselves under the protection of France, and again when they put themselves under the protection of England; in both cases, at the peace of the Pyrenees, and at the peace of Utrecht,[22] not only their lives and properties, but even their privileges, were preserved. No war was ever more marked by personal animosities and party hatred than that carried on in Ireland, after the abdication of James II.; yet in the articles of Limerick, there was no[23] difficulty of admitting the most favourable terms for the catholics engaged against king William. In short, it was said, that in ancient or modern history no instance could be found of so shameful a desertion of men, who had sacrificed all to their duty, and to their reliance upon our faith. No circumstances of distress, no degree of necessity, could be conceived sufficient to oblige a state to subscribe to an

article, which, unless marked by the just indignation of parliament, would blast for ever the honour of this country.

After so many demonstrative proofs of the weak, rash, and ignorant, of the ruinous and disgraceful conduct of the framers of the peace, it was asked whether a coincidence of opinion amongst members, however distinguished by different party connections, in their judgment upon it, deserved the name of an unnatural alliance? and whether it was not more to be wondered, how there could possibly exist two opinions in the House concerning it? Was it from the character of the noble lord, who had taken the lead in this business, that the nation was to be taught to consider it as a mere contest for power?—a character, which if it had any blemish to foil its eminent virtues, it was that of receding from those places where his abilities and integrity might essentially promote the interests of his country. Was it not necessary, in order to preserve the reputation and character of the nation from eternal disgrace, that parliament should express their utter disapprobation of a treaty, which rather deserved the name of an ignominious capitulation of the glory and essential interests of a powerful country?—Was it not their duty to lay before the throne their humble sense of the misconduct of ministers, who had so shamefully abused his Majesty's confidence? Was it not also their duty to shew those very ministers that they had forfeited the confidence of parliament by a criminal abuse of the trust reposed in them?

It was not denied that this coincidence of opinion might possibly lead to some future permanent connection. If, as it was reasonable to expect, the dismission of his Majesty's present ministers should be the consequence of the censure of that House, it was asked where another administration could be formed, sufficiently possessed of the confidence of the people, and of parliament, to undertake the direction of the affairs of the empire at so arduous a conjuncture with vigour and effect, without a coalition of parties? Had not the nation already suffered enough of evil from the weakness and impotence of government? and was it not a flagitious attempt, to endeavour to rouse the prejudices, and inflame the minds of the people against a measure, so necessary to heal its divisions, and to ensure the advantages of firm and permanent counsels?

Those who were at all conversant in the history of this island, must know, that such coalitions had frequently become necessary; and that, from the very nature of our constitution, which giving rise to various political parties, they sometimes became so equally balanced, as to preclude the possibility of a permanent administration, except by their union. Such had been the case in the year 1757,[24] when the country was as much distracted by violent parties as it had ever been before or since. What was done then? Men of all parties saw the necessity of uniting. The several factions forgot their animosities, and out of different sets of men an administration was formed that carried this nation to an unrivalled pitch of glory.

Such coalitions did not imply any inconsistency of conduct or desertion of principle. Persons differing in opinion on speculative political subjects, might yet be honestly and firmly united in the executive conduct of government? Private friendship and conformity of sentiment was undoubtedly the best basis of political connection. But where the nature of the case required a deviation from this rule, public characters, so far from being culpable, deserved the highest praise for sacrificing private resentments and personal animosities at the altar of public safety.

That the very persons who had so invidiously brought forward these objections, did not give them any credit, was clear, because they themselves had formed a junction in every respect equally liable to the same exceptions. The only difference was, that the coalition now censured consisted of the first and principal characters in both parties, and therefore was the most likely to answer the purpose of commanding the confidence of the nation, and putting an end to our divisions, by forming a firm and effective administration; whereas the other, being made out of the shreds and fragments of all parties, had proved destitute of every requisite that could entitle it to support.

Such were the arguments urged on both sides the House in support of their respective motions. The debate lasted till near eight o'clock in the morning, when on a division there appeared for the amendments 224, against them 208; so that the ministers lost the question in the House of Commons by a majority of sixteen.

In the House of Lords, the following address was moved by the Earl of Carlisle, in lieu of that which had been originally proposed by the Earl of Pembroke.—" To[25] " return our thanks to his Majesty " for the communication of the " preliminary articles of peace, and " for having put a stop to the cala- " mities of war by a peace, which " being concluded, we must consi- " der as binding, and not to be in- " fringed without a violation of the " national faith.

" To assure his Majesty, that we " feel in the strongest manner the " obligation of affording every re- " lief that can alleviate the dif- " tresses of those deserving subjects " who have exposed their lives " and fortunes for the support of " Great Britain; and at the same " time, that we cannot help la- " menting the necessity which bids " us subscribe to articles, which,

" considering the relative situation " of the belligerent powers, we " must regard as inadequate to our " just expectations, and derogatory " to the honour and dignity of " Great Britain."

The original address was supported by the Marquis of Carmarthen, Lord Hawke, the Dukes of Chandos and Grafton, Lord Grantham, Lord Howe, the Earl of Shelburne, and the lord chancellor. The speakers on the other side were the lords Walsingham, Dudley, Townshend, Keppel, King, Stormont, Sackville, and Loughborough, the last of whom distin-[26] guished himself by a most brilliant display of eloquence. The arguments were nearly the same with those made use of in the lower House, and, on the division, the amendment was negatived by 72 against 59.

On the 21st, the day fixed for taking into Feb. 21st. further consideration the articles of peace, Lord John Cavendish moved the four following resolutions:

1st. " To assure his Majesty that " his faithful Commons, in confi- " deration of the public faith so- " lemnly pledged, would inviola- " bly sustain and preserve the peace " agreed upon by the provisional " articles and preliminary treaties."

2dly. " That the House, deeply " affected by his Majesty's paternal " care, at all times displayed to his " people, would use their utmost en- " deavours to improve the blessings " of peace."

3dly. " That his Majesty's ac- " knowledgment of the indepen- " dence of America was in perfect " compliance with the necessity of " the times, and in conformity with " the sense of parliament."

4thly. " That the concessions " granted to the adversaries of " Great Britain were greater than " they were entitled to, either from " the actual state of their respective " possessions, or from their compa- " rative strength."

The two first resolutions were agreed to without any oppofition.— On the third a fhort debate took place, occafioned by doubts having arifen in the minds of feveral members, refpecting the nature of the power vefted in the King, by which he had acknowledged the independence of the United States. It was demanded, whether it was done by virtue of his royal prerogative, or by powers granted by ftatute ; and, if the latter, by what ftatute ?

In anfwer to thefe queftions, the gentlemen of the long robe were[27] unanimoufly of opinion, that the ftatute paffed laft year, to enable the King to make a peace or truce with the colonies in North America, *any law, ftatute, matter, or thing to the contrary not-withftanding*, gave him full power to recognize their independence ; tho' fuch words had not been inferted in the act, for reafons fufficiently obvious. Other members, who agreed with them in opinion as far as it refpected the acknowledgment of independence, did not think the ftatute in queftion granted him any authority to cede to them any part of the province of Canada and Nova Scotia.

With refpect to the powers of the prerogative, Mr. Wallace and Mr. Lee maintained that the King[28] could not abdicate a part of his fovereignty, or declare any number of his fubjects free from obedience to the laws in being. The contrary was afferted by the attorney general ; and each party pledged himfelf, if the matter fhould come regularly into difcuffion, to make good his opinion. A challenge to the fame effect had paffed in the Houfe of Peers between Lord Loughborough and the Lord Chancellor.[29]

At length it was propofed to alter the refolution into the following form : " That his Majefty, in " acknowledging the independence " of the United States of America, " *by virtue of the powers vefted in him* " *by an act of the laft feffion of parlia-* " *ment, entitled,* An act to enable " his Majefty to conclude a peace " or truce, &c. *has acted,* &c." when it paffed without a divifion.

The fourth refolution occafioned a long and vehement debate, in which the fame ground was gone over as on the 17th, and on a divifion it was carried by a majority of 207 to 190.

...

The firft object of importance[30] that engaged the attention of parliament after the change of adminiftration was the opening a commercial intercourfe with the States of North America. By the prohibitory acts which had paffed during the rebellion, all communication with that country, in the way of trade, had been entirely cut off ; and though it was the prevailing opinion in parliament, that thofe acts were virtually repealed by the acknowledgment of the independence of the United States, yet in their new character they became fubject to other reftrictions, which it was neceffary to relax and modify ; a bill for this purpofe had been brought into the Houfe of Commons by the late miniftry ; but during the great variety of difcuffions which it underwent, difficulties of fo complicated and important a nature had arifen that it never got through the committee.

In the mean time, no regulations whatever having been ftipulated by the treaty of peace, the commercial interefts of the country were fuffering very materially ; for not only a number of veffels, richly freighted for America, were detained in harbour, but there was great danger of having the market pre-occupied by our rivals. In this emergency the new minifters thought it moft advifeable to drop the old bill for the prefent, and to pafs two fhort bills, one to repeal all the prohibitory acts ; the other to remove the neceffity of requiring manifefts or other documents, and to lodge in the King and council, for a limited time, a power to make fuch other regulations as might be ex-[31]pedient.

Letters and Papers relating to Captain Afgill's *Cafe, written by his Mother,* Lady Afgill ; *the Comte de* Vergennes, *Prime Minifter of France ;* the American Congrefs ; *and General* Wafhington.[32]

Copy of a Letter from Lady Afgill *to Comte de* Vergennes, *dated* London, *July* 18, 1782.

SIR,

IF the politenefs of the French court will permit an application of a ftranger, there can be no doubt but one in which all the tender feelings of an individual can be interefted, will meet with a favourable reception from a nobleman whofe character does honour not only to his own country, but to human nature. The fubject, Sir, on which I prefume to implore your affiftance, is too heart-piercing for me to dwell on, and common fame has, moft probably, informed you of it, it therefore renders the painful talk unneceffary. My fon, an only fon, as dear as he is brave, amiable as he is deferving to be fo, only nineteen, a prifoner under articles of capitulation of York Town, is now confined in America, an object of retaliation. Shall an innocent fuffer for the guilty ! Reprefent to yourfelf, Sir, the fituation of a family under thefe circumftances, furrounded as I am by objects of diftrefs ; diftracted with fear and grief ; no words can exprefs my feeling, or paint the fcene. My hufband given over by his phyficians, a few hours before the news arrived, and not in a ftate to be informed of the misfortune ; my daughter feized with a fever and delirium, raving about her brother, and without one interval of reafon, fave to hear heart-alleviating circumftances — Let your feelings, Sir, fuggeft and plead for my inexpreffible mifery. A word from you, like a voice from heaven, will fave us from diftraction and wretchednefs. I am well informed General

Washington reveres your character; say but to him you wish my son to be released, and he will restore him to his distracted family, and render him to happiness. My son's virtue and bravery will justify the deed. His honour, Sir, carried him to America. He was born to affluence, independence, and the happiest prospects. Let me again supplicate your goodness; let me respectfully implore your high influence in behalf of innocence, in the cause of justice, of humanity; that you would, Sir, dispatch a letter to General Washington, from France, and favour me with a copy of it, to be sent from hence. I am sensible of the liberty I take in making this request; but I am sensible, whether you comply with it or not, you will pity the distress that suggests it; your humanity will drop a tear on the fault, and efface it. I will pray that heaven may grant you may never want the comfort it is in your power to bestow on

ASGILL.

Copy of a Letter from Comte Ver-gennes to General Washington, dated Versailles, the 29th of July, 1782.

SIR,

IT is not in quality of a king, the friend and ally of the United States, though with the knowledge and consent of his majesty, that I now have the honour to write to your excellency. It is as a man of sensibility, and a tender father who feels all the force of paternal love, that I take the liberty to address to your excellency my earnest solicitations in favour of a mother and family in tears. Her situation seems the more worthy of notice, on our part, as it is to the humanity of a nation, at war with her own, that she has recourse, for what she ought to receive from the impartial justice of her own generals.

I have the honour to inclose your excellency a copy of a letter which Mrs. Asgill has just wrote to me. I am not known to her, nor was I acquainted that her son was the unhappy victim, destined by lot to expiate the odious crime that a former denial of justice obliges you to revenge. Your excellency will not read this letter, without being extremely affected; it had that effect upon the king and upon the queen, to whom I communicated it. The goodness of their majesties hearts induce them to desire that the inquietudes of an unfortunate mother may be calmed, and her tenderness reassured. I feel, Sir, that there are cases where humanity itself exacts the most extreme rigour; perhaps the one now in question may be of the number; but allowing reprizals to be just, it is not less horrid to those who are the victims; and the character of your excellency is too well known for me not to be persuaded that you desire nothing more than to be able to avoid the disagreeable necessity.

There is one consideration, Sir, which, though it is not decisive, may have an influence upon your resolution. Capt. Asgill is doubtless your prisoner, but he is among those whom the arms of the king contributed to put into your hands at York-Town. Although this circumstance does not operate as a safeguard, it however justifies the interest I permit myself to take in this affair. If it is in your power, Sir, to confider and have regard to it, you will do what is very agreeable to their majesties; the danger of young Asgill, the tears, the despair of his mother, affect them sensibly, and they will see with pleasure the hope of consolation shine out for these unfortunate people.

In seeking to deliver Mr. Asgill from the fate which threatens him, I am far from engaging you to seek another victim; the pardon, to be perfectly satisfactory,

must be entire. I do not imagine it can be productive of any bad consequences. If the English general has not been able to punish the horrible crime you complain of, in so exemplary a manner as he should, there is reason to think he will take the most efficacious measures to prevent the like in future.

I sincerely wish, Sir, that my intercession may meet success; the sentiment which dictates it, and which you have not ceased to manifest on every occasion, assures me, that you will not be indifferent to the prayers and to the tears of a family which has recourse to your clemency through me. It is rendering homage to your virtue to implore it.

I have the honour to be, with the most perfect consideration, Sir, yours, &c.

(Signed)   DE VERGENNES.

Copy of the Order of Congress for releasing Capt. Asgill.

By the United States in Congress assembled, Nov. 7, 1782.

ON the report of a committee to whom was referred a letter of the 19th of August, from the commander in chief, a report of a committee thereon, and motion of Mr. Williamson and Rutledge relative thereto, and also another letter of the 25th of October from the commander in chief, with a copy of a letter from the Count de Vergennes, dated the 29th of July last, interceding for Capt. Asgill,

Resolved, that the commander in chief be directed, and he is hereby directed, to set Capt. Asgill at liberty.

CHARLES THOMSON, Sec.

Copy of a Letter from General Washington, to Capt. Asgill, covering the above Resolve.

Head Quarters; Nov. 13.

" SIR,

" IT affords me fingular pleafure to have it in my power to tranfmit you the inclofed copy of an act of Congrefs of the 7th inft. by which you are releafed from the difagreeable circumftances in which you have fo long been. Suppofing you would wifh to go to New-York as foon as poffible, I alfo inclofe a paffport for that purpofe.

" Your letter of the 18th of October came regularly to my hands; I beg you to believe that my not anfwering it fooner did not proceed from inattention to you, or a want of feeling for your fituation; I daily expected a determination of your cafe, and I thought it better to await that, than to feed you with hopes that might in the end prove fruitlefs. You will attribute my detention of the inclofed letters, which have been in my hands about a fortnight, to the fame caufe.

" I cannot take leave of you, Sir, without affuring you, that in whatever light my agency in this unpleafing affair may be received, I never was influenced through the whole of it by fanguinary motives, but by what I conceived a fenfe of my dury, which loudly called upon me to take meafures, however difagreeable, to prevent a repetition of thofe enormities which have been the fubject of difcuffion; and that this important end is likely to be anfwered without the effufion of the blood of an innocent perfon, is not a greater relief to you than it is to, Sir, your moft obedient and humble fervant,

(figned) G. WASHINGTON."

When Capt. Afgill arrived at New-York the Swallow packet having failed without him, he followed her in a boat, but did not overtake her till fhe had got upwards of four leagues to fea. The confequence was, that he came over without fervant or baggage.

* * *

To his Excellency Sir Guy Carleton, Knight of the moft Honorable Order of the Bath, General and Commander in Chief of all his Majefty's Forces in North-America, within the Colonies lying on the Atlantic Ocean from Nova Scotia to Weft Florida inclufive, &c. &c.*

The officers commanding his Majefty's Provincial Regiments, for themfelves, and in behalf of others his Majefty's Faithful Subjects in America, now ferving in his Provincial Forces, beg leave to reprefent,

THAT the offer of independence to the American colonies by Great Britain, and the probability that the prefent conteft will terminate in the feparation of the two countries, has filled the minds of his majefty's provincial troops with the moft alarming apprehenfions.

That, from the pureft principles of loyalty and attachment to the Britifh government, they took arms in his majefty's fervice, and relying on the juftice of their caufe, and the fupport of their fovereign and the Britifh nation, they have perfevered with unabated zeal through all the viciffitudes of a calamitous and an unfortunate war.

That their hearts ftill glow with loyalty to their fovereign, and the fame enthufiaftic attachment to the Britifh conftitution, which firft ftimulated them to action; and nothing can ever wean their affections from that government under which they formerly enjoyed fo much happinefs.

That their deteftation to that republican fyftem, which the leaders of the rebellion are aiming to eftablifh, the fatal effects of which are already felt, is unconquerable.

That whatever ftipulations may be made at a peace for the reftoration of the property of the loyalifts, and permiffion for them to return home; yet, fhould the American provinces be fevered from the Britifh empire, it will be utterly impoffible for thofe who have ferved his majefty in arms in this war to remain in the country. The perfonal animofities that arofe from civil diffenfions, have been fo heightened by the blood that has been fhed in the conteft, that the parties can never be reconciled.

That the officers of his majefty's provincial forces have facrificed not only their property, but many of them very lucrative profeffions, and all their expectations from their rank and connections in civil fociety.

That numbers of them entered very young into the king's fervice, and have grown up in the army; and having no other profeffion, and no family expectations, or homes to go to, their friends being all involved in the common ruin, they look forward to the day of their being difbanded with extreme folicitude.

That many of them have wives, who, born to the faireft expectations, and tenderly brought up, have been unaccuftomed to want; and children about them, for whofe education and future happinefs they feel the moft anxious concern.

That many who have ferved his majefty in his provincial troops, in fubordinate capacities, during this war, have been refpectable yeomen; of good connections, and poffeffed of confiderable property,

---

* This memorial of the commanding officers of his majefty's provincial regiments and corps in North America, was prefented to Sir Guy Carleton in March 1783, and was by him tranfmitted to the fecretary of ftate, with a letter ftrongly recommending the cafe of the provincial officers to their gracious fovereign.

which from princ ples of loyalty, and a fenfe of duty, they quitted, and in the courfe of this conteft have fhewn a degree of patience, fortitude, and bravery, almoft without example.

That there are ftill remaining in the provincial line a great number of men, who from wounds, and from diforders contracted in fervice, are rendered totally unable to provide for their future fubfiftence; they therefore look up to that government, in whofe fervice they have fuffered, with all the anxiety of men who have no other hope left; many of them have helplefs families who have feen better days.

That the widows and orphans of the provincial officers and foldiers, who have loft their lives in the king's fervice, are many of them reduced to extreme poverty and diftrefs, and have no profpect of relief but from the juftice and humanity of the British government.

Thefe, Sir, are the difficulties and the apprehenfions under which his majefty's provincial troops now labour; and to your excellency they look up for affiftance.

Relying on the gracious promife of their fovereign to fupport and protect them, and placing the fulleft confidence in your excellency's benevolent interpofition, and favourable reprefentation of their faithful fervices, they are induced to afk—

That grants of lands may be made to them in fome of his majefty's American provinces, and that they may be affifted in making fettlements, in order that they and their children may enjoy the benefits of the British government.

That fome permanent provifion may be made for fuch of the non-commiffioned officers, and private foldiers, as have been difabled, from wounds, and from diforders contracted in his majefty's fervice, and for the widows and orphans of the deceafed officers and foldiers.

That as a reward for their faithful fervices, the rank of the officers may be permanent in America, and that they all may be entitled to half pay upon the reduction of their regiments.

Signed by the commanding officers of fourteen provincial corps.

New York, March 14, 1783.

The following are Copies of Letters from General Carleton *and Admiral* Digby, *in Anfwer to thofe difpatched by* Robert R. Livingfton, *Efq. Secretary for Foreign Affairs, on Arrival of the* Triumph *Sloop of War, Lieutenant* Duquefne, *from* Cadiz. 34

New York, March 26, 1783.

SIR,

I Have received your letter of the 24th inftant, inclofing a refolution of congrefs of the fame date, taken in confequence of the arrival of the cutter Triumph, commanded by Lieutenant Du Quefne, with orders of the 10th of February laft, given at Cadiz by Vice admiral D'Eftaing, for him to put to fea, and cruife on fuch ftations as he fhall judge moft likely to meet with fhips of his nation, and inform them of the happy reconciliation of the belligerent powers, and to order all their fhips of war to ceafe hoftilities againft thofe of Great Britain; the preliminary articles of a general peace being figned the 20th of January. You therefore are pleafed to exprefs your expectation, that I would think the information thus conveyed, " fufficiently authentic to juftify my taking immediate meafures to ftop the farther effufion of blood."

For my own part, I have hitherto abftained from all hoftilities; and this conduct I mean to continue, fo far as our own fecurity would permit; but how great foever my defire is to put an entire ftop to the calamities of war, and whatever refpect this information may deferve, yet I do not find myfelf thereby juftified in recommending meafures, which might give facility to the fleets and armies menacing any part of the king's poffeffions, to carry their hoftilities into execution. To adopt a meafure of this importance, it is neceffary I fhould receive orders from home, which I may reafonably expect every hour, as a cruifer fent out on other purpofes is already arrived at Philadelphia; and I affure you, Sir, I only wait the official certainty of this great event, to affume the language, and the fpirit too, of the moft perfect conciliation and peace.

I perceive, Sir, by the refolution inclofed in your letter, that congrefs has thought fit to confider this information as authentic, and thereupon has taken one confiderable ftep towards the carrying the terms of peace into immediate execution. Another, not lefs important, I prefume has been taken, or is taking. With the ceffation of hoftilities, I perceive is connected, in the feventh article of the provifional treaty, an agreement, that " all prifoners, on both fides, fhall be fet at liberty." Of this event, therefore, I hope likewife fpeedily to receive the very neceffary and welcome notice, as I fhall find the higheft fatisfaction in feeing releafed on all fides, men upon whom the evils and calamities of war have more peculiarly fallen.

I am, Sir,

Your moft obedient,

humble fervant,

GUY CARLTON.

Robert R. Livingston, Esq.

New York, March 23, 1783.

SIR,

I Have received your letter, inclosing me the resolve of congress, with a copy of a letter to his excellency Sir Guy Carleton; but as I have as yet received no official accounts from England, I must wait till you on your side relieve our prisoners, before I give that general relief to yours I so much wish. There can be no reason for detaining our prisoners one moment, as congress must suppose the peace signed. I shall take every precaution in my power, consistent with my duty, to stop any further mischief upon the seas; but should recommend the preventing any vessels sailing, as I have not yet received sufficient authority to enable me to withdraw my cruisers.

I am, Sir,

Your very obedient,

humble servant,

ROBERT DIGBY.

To Robert Livingston, Esq. &c. &c.

Copy of a Letter from his Excellency Sir Guy Carleton, K. B. &c. &c. &c. to the President of the American Congress.

New York, Aug. 17, 1783.

SIR,

THE June packet lately arrived, has brought me final orders for the evacuation of this place; be pleased, Sir, to inform congress of this proof of the perseverance of the court of Great Britain, in the pacific system expressed by the provisional articles, and that I shall lose no time, as far as depends upon me, in fulfilling his majesty's commands.

But notwithstanding my orders are urgent to accelerate the total evacuation, the difficulty of assigning the precise period for this event is of late greatly increased.

My correspondence with General Washington, Governor Clinton, and Mr. Livingston (your late secretary for foreign affairs) early suggested the impediments, tending to retard this service. A letter to Mr. Livingston of the 6th of April, two more to General Washington of the 10th of May and 10th of June, with several to Governor Clinton, stating many hostile proceedings within the sphere of his authority, are those to which I refer; copies of some of these letters I enclose, though I am doubtless to presume, the congress to be informed of all transactions material to the general direction of their affairs.

The violence in the Americans, which broke out soon after the cessation of hostilities, increased the number of their countrymen to look to me for escape from threatened destruction; but these terrors have of late been so considerably augmented, that almost all within these lines conceive the safety both of their property and of their lives, depend upon their being removed by me, which renders it impossible to say when the evacuation can be completed. Whether they have just ground to assert, that there is either no government within your limits for common protection, or that it secretly favours the committee in the sovereignty they assume, and are actually exercising, I shall not pretend to determine; but as the daily gazettes and publications furnish repeated proofs, not only of a disregard to the articles of peace, but as barbarous menaces from committees formed in various towns, cities, and districts, and even at Philadelphia, the very place which the congress had chosen for their residence, I should shew an indifference to the feeling of humanity, as well as to the honour and interest of the nation whom I serve, to leave any of the loyalists that are desirous to quit the country, a prey to the violence they conceive they have so much cause to apprehend.

The congress will hence discern how much it will depend on themselves and the subordinate legislatures, to facilitate the service I am commanded to perform, by abating the fears they will hereby diminish the number of the emigrants. But should these fears continue and compel such multitudes to remove, I shall hold myself acquitted from every delay in the fulfilling my orders and the consequences which may result therefrom; and I cannot avoid adding, that it makes no small part of my concern, that the congress have thought proper to suspend to this late hour, recommendations stipulated by the treaty, and in the punctual performance of which, the king and his ministers have expressed such entire confidence.

I am, Sir, your excellency's

Most obedient, and

Most humble servant,

GUY CARLETON.

His excellency Elias Boudinot, Esq.

A circular Letter from his Excellency George Washington, Commander in Chief of the Armies of the United States of America, dated June 18, 1783.

Head Quarters, Newburgh, June 18, 1783.

SIR,

THE great object for which I had the honour to hold an appointment in the service of my country, being accomplished, I am now preparing to resign it into the hands of congress, and return to that domestic retirement, which, it is well known, I left with the greatest reluctance; a retirement for which I have never ceased to sigh through a long and painful absence, in which (remote from the noise and trouble of the world) I meditate to pass the remainder of life in a state of undisturbed repose; but before I carry this resolution into effect, I think it a duty incumbent on me to make this my last official communication, to congratulate you on the glorious events which heaven has been pleased to produce in our favour, to offer my sentiments respecting some important subjects, which appear to me to be intimately connected with the tranquillity of the United States, to take my leave of your excellency as a public character, and to give my final blessing to that country in whose service I have spent the prime of my life; for whose sake I have consumed so many anxious days and watchful nights; and whose happiness, being extremely dear to me, will always constitute no inconsiderable part of my own.

Impressed with the liveliest sensibility on this pleasing occasion, I will claim the indulgence of dilating the more copiously on the subject of our mutual felicitation. When we consider the magnitude of the prize we contended for, the doubtful nature of the contest, and the favourable manner in which it has terminated; we shall find the greatest possible reason for gratitude and rejoicing; this is a theme that will afford infinite delight to every benevolent and liberal mind, whether the event in contemplation be considered as a source of present enjoyment, or the parent of future happiness; and we shall have equal occasion to felicitate ourselves on the lot which Providence has assigned us, whether we view it in a natural, a political, or moral point of view.

The citizens of America, placed in the most enviable condition, as the sole lords and proprietors of a vast tract of continent, comprehending all the various soils and climates of the world, and abounding with all the necessaries and conveniences of life, are now, by the late satisfactory pacification, acknowledged to be possessed of absolute freedom and independency; they are from this period to be considered as the actors on a most conspicuous theatre, which seems to be peculiarly designed by Providence for the display of human greatness and felicity: here they are not only surrounded with every thing that can contribute to the completion of private and domestic enjoyments, but heaven has crowned all its other blessings, by giving a surer opportunity for political happiness, than any other nation has ever been favoured with. Nothing can illustrate these observations more forcibly than a recollection of the happy conjuncture of times and circumstances, under which our republic assumed its rank among the nations. The foundation of our empire was not laid in a gloomy age of ignorance and superstition, but at an epocha when the rights of mankind were better understood and more clearly defined, than at any former period: researches of the human mind after social happiness have been carried to a great extent; the treasures of knowledge acquired by the labours of philosophers, sages, and legislators, through a long succession of years, are laid open for use, and their collected wisdom may be happily applied in the establishment of our forms of government; the free cultivation of letters, the unbounded extension of commerce, the progressive refinement of manners, the growing liberality of sentiment, and, above all, the pure and benign

light of revelation, have had a meliorating influence on mankind, and increased the blessings of society. At this auspicious period the United States came into existence as a nation, and if their citizens should not be completely free and happy, the fault will be entirely their own.

Such is our situation, and such are our prospects; but notwithstanding the cup of blessing is thus reached out to us, notwithstanding happiness is ours, if we have a disposition to seize the occasion, and make it our own; yet it appears to me, there is an option still left to the United States of America, whether they will be respectable and prosperous, or contemptible and miserable as a nation; this is the time of their political probation; this is the moment, when the eyes of the whole world are turned upon them; this is the moment to establish or ruin their national character for ever; this is the favourable moment to give such a tone to the fœderal government, as will enable it to answer the ends of its institution; or this may be the ill-fated moment for relaxing the powers of the union, annihilating the cement of the confederation, and exposing us to become the sport of European politics, which may play one state against another, to prevent their growing importance, and to serve their own interested purposes. For, according to the system of policy the states shall adopt at this moment, they will stand or fall;—and, by their confirmation or lapse, it is yet to be decided, whether the revolution must ultimately be considered as a blessing or a curse;—a blessing or a curse, not to the present age alone, for with our fate will the destiny of unborn millions be involved.

With this conviction of the importance of the present crisis, silence in me would be a crime; I will therefore speak to your excellency the language of freedom and sincerity, without disguise. I am aware, however, those who differ from me in political sentiments, may, perhaps, remark, I am stepping out of the proper line of my duty; and they may possibly ascribe to arrogance or ostentation, what I know is alone the result of the purest intention; but the rectitude of my own heart, which disdains such unworthy motives; the part I have hitherto acted in life; the determination I have formed of not taking any share in public business hereafter; the ardent desire I feel and shall continue to manifest, of quietly enjoying in private life, after all the toils of war, the benefits of a wise and liberal government, will, I flatter myself, sooner or later, convince my countrymen, that I could have no sinister views in delivering, with so little reserve, the opinions contained in this address.

There are four things which I humbly conceive are essential to the well being, I may even venture to say, to the existence of the United States, as an independent power.

1st. An indissoluble union of the states under one federal head.

2dly. A sacred regard to public justice.

3dly. The adoption of a proper peace establishment. And,

4thly. The prevalence of that pacific and friendly disposition among the people of the United States, which will induce them to forget their local prejudices and policies, to make those mutual concessions which are requisite to the general prosperity, and, in some instances, to sacrifice their individual advantages to the interest of the community.

These are the pillars on which the glorious fabric of our independency and national character must be supported. Liberty is the basis—and whoever would dare to sap the foundation, or overturn the structure, under whatever specious pretexts he may attempt it, will merit the bitterest execration, and the severest punishment, which can be inflicted by his injured country.

On the three first articles I will make a few observations, leaving the last to the good sense and serious consideration of those immediately concerned.

Under the first head, although it may not be necessary or proper for me in this place to enter into a particular disquisition of the principles of the union, and to take up the great question which has been frequently agitated, whether it be expedient and requisite for the states to delegate a large proportion of power to congress, or not; yet it will be a part of my duty, and that of every true patriot, to assert, without reserve, and to insist upon the following positions: That unless the states will suffer congress to exercise those prerogatives they are undoubtedly invested with by the constitution, every thing must very rapidly tend to anarchy and confusion. That it is indispensible to the happiness of the individual states, that there should be lodged somewhere, a supreme power, to regulate and govern the general concerns of the confederated republic, without which the union cannot be of long duration.

That there must be a faithful and pointed compliance on the part of every state with the late proposals and demands of congress, or the most fatal consequences will ensue. That whatever measures have a tendency to dissolve the union, or contribute to violate or lessen the sovereign authority, ought to be considered as hostile to the liberty and independency of America, and the authors of them treated accordingly. And lastly, that unless we can be enabled by the concurrence of the states to participate of the fruits of the revolution, and enjoy the essential benefits of civil society, under a form of government so free and uncorrupted, so happily guarded against the danger of oppression, as has been devised and adopted by the articles of confederation, it will be a subject of regret, that so much blood and treasure have been lavished for no purpose; that so many sufferings have been encountered without a compensation, and that so many sacrifices have been made in vain. Many other considerations might here be adduced to prove that without an entire conformity to the spirit of the union, we cannot exist as an independent power. It will be sufficient for my purpose to mention but one or two, which seem to me of the greatest importance. It is only in our united character, as an empire, that our independence is acknowledged, that our power can be regarded, or our credit supported among foreign nations. The treaties of the European powers, with the United States of America, will have no validity on the dissolution of the union. We shall be left nearly in a state of nature; or we may find by our own unhappy experience, that there is a natural and necessary progression from the extreme of anarchy to the extreme of tyranny; and that arbitrary power is most easily established on the ruins of liberty abused to licentiousness.

As to the second article, which respects the performance of public justice, congress have, in their late address to the United States, almost exhausted the subject; they have explained their ideas so fully, and have enforced the obligations the states are under to render complete justice to all the public creditors, with so much dignity and energy; that in my opinion, no real friend to the honour and independency of America can hesitate a single moment respecting the propriety of complying with the just and honourable measures proposed; if their arguments do not produce conviction, I know of nothing that will have greater influence, especially when we reflect that the system referred to, being the result of the collected wisdom of the continent, must be esteemed, if not perfect, certainly the least objectionable of any that could be devised; and that, if it shall not be carried into immediate execution, a national bankruptcy, with all its deplorable consequences, will take place, before any different plan can possibly be proposed or adopted; so pressing are the present circumstances, and such is the alternative now offered to the states.

The ability of the country to discharge the debts, which have been incurred in its defence, is not to be doubted. An inclination, I flatter myself, will not be wanting; the path of our duty is plain before us; honesty will be found, on every experiment, to be the best and only true policy. Let us then, as a nation, be just; let us fulfil the public contracts which congress had undoubtedly a right to make for the purpose of carrying on the war, with the same good faith we suppose ourselves bound to perform our private engagements. In the mean time let an attention to the chearful performance of their proper business, as individuals, and as members of society, be earnestly inculcated on the citizens of America; then will they strengthen the bands of government, and be happy under its protection. Every one will reap the fruit of his labours; every one will enjoy his own acquisitions, without molestation and without danger.

In this state of absolute freedom and perfect security, who will grudge to yield a very little of his property to support the common interests of society, and ensure the protection of government? Who does not remember the frequent declarations at the commencement of the war, that we should be completely satisfied, if at the expence of one-half, we could defend the remainder of our possessions? Where is the man to be found, who wishes to remain indebted for the defence of his own person and property to the exertions, the bravery, and the blood of others, without making one generous effort to pay the debt of honour and of gratitude? In what part of the continent shall we find any man, or body of men, who would not blush to stand up, and propose measures purposely calculated to rob the soldier of his stipend, and the public creditor of his due? And were it possible that such a flagrant instance of injustice could ever happen, would it not excite the general indignation, and tend to bring down, upon the authors of such measures, the aggravated vengeance of heaven? If, after all, a spirit of disunion, or a temper of obstinacy and perverseness should manifest itself in any of the states; if such an ungracious disposition should attempt to frustrate all the happy effects that might be expected to flow from the union; if there should be a refusal to comply with the requisitions for funds to discharge the annual interest of the public debts, and if that refusal should revive all those jealousies, and produce all those evils which are now happily removed, congress, who have in all their transactions shewn a great degree of magnanimity and justice, will stand justified in the sight of God and man! And that state alone, which

puts itself in opposition to the aggregate wisdom of the continent, and follows such mistaken and pernicious councils, will be responsible for all the consequences.

For my own part, conscious of having acted, while a servant of the public, in the manner I conceived best suited to promote the real interest of my country; having, in consequence of my fixed belief, in some measure, pledged myself to the army, that their country would finally do them complete and ample justice; and not willing to conceal any instance of my official conduct from the eyes of the world, I have thought proper to transmit to your excellency the inclosed collection of papers, relative to the half pay and commutation granted by congress to the officers of the army: from these communications, my decided sentiment will be clearly comprehended, together with the conclusive reasons, which induced me at an early period, to recommend the adoption of this measure in the most earnest and serious manner. As the proceedings of congress, the army, and myself, are open to all, and contain, in my opinion, sufficient information to remove the prejudice and errors which may have been entertained by any, I think it unnecessary to say any thing more, than just to observe, that the resolutions of congress, now alluded to, are as undoubtedly and absolutely binding upon the United States, as the most solemn acts of confederation or legislation.

As to the idea, which I am informed, has in some instances prevailed, that the half pay and commutation are to be regarded merely in the odious light of a pension, it ought to be exploded for ever: that provision should be viewed, as it really was, a reasonable compensation offered by congress, at a time when they had nothing else to give to officers of the army, for services then to be performed: it was the only means to prevent a total dereliction of the service: it was a part of their hire. I may be allowed to say, it was the price of their blood, and of your independency; it is therefore more than a common debt, it is a debt of honour; it can never be considered as a pension or gratuity, nor cancelled until it is fairly discharged.

With regard to the distinction between officers and soldiers, it is sufficient that the uniform experience of every nation of the world, combined with our own, proves the utility and propriety of the discrimination. Rewards in proportion to the aid the public draws from them, are unquestionably due to all its servants. In some lines, the soldiers have perhaps generally had as ample compensation for their services, by the large bounties which have been paid them, as their officers will receive in the proposed commutation; in others, if besides the donation of land, the payment of arrearages of clothing and wages (in which articles all the component parts of the army must be put upon the same footing) we take into the estimate, the bounties many of the soldiers have received, and the gratuity of one year's full pay, which is promised to all, possibly their situation (every circumstance being duly considered) will not be deemed less eligible than that of the officers. Should a farther reward, however, be judged equitable, I will venture to assert, no man will enjoy greater satisfaction than myself, an exemption from taxes for a limited time (which has been petitioned for in some instances) or any other adequate immunity or compensation granted to the brave defenders of their country's

cause; but neither the adoption or rejection of this proposition will, in any manner affect, much less militate against the act of congress, by which they have offered five years full pay, in lieu of the half pay for life, which had been before promised to the officers of the army.

Before I conclude the subject on public justice, I cannot omit to mention the obligations this country is under to that meritorious class of veterans, the non-commissioned officers and privates, who have been discharged for inability, in consequence of the resolution of congress, of the 23d of April, 1782, on an annual pension for life: their peculiar sufferings, their singular merits and claims to that provision need only to be known, to interest the feelings of humanity in their behalf; nothing but a punctual payment of their annual allowance can rescue them from the most complicated misery; and nothing could be a more melancholy and distressing sight, than to behold those who have shed their blood, or lost their limbs in the service of their country, without a shelter, without a friend, and without the means of obtaining any of the comforts or necessaries of life, compelled to beg their daily bread from door to door. Suffer me to recommend those of this description, belonging to your state, to the warmest patronage of your excellency and your legislature.

It is necessary to say but a few words on the third topic which was proposed, and which regards particularly the defence of the republic. As there can be little doubt but congress will recommend a proper peace establishment for the United States, in which a due attention will be paid to the importance of placing the militia of the union upon a regular and respectable footing; if this should be the case, I should beg leave to

urge the great advantage of it in the strongest terms.

The militia of this country must be considered as the palladium of our security, and the first effectual resort in case of hostility: it is essential, therefore, that the same system should pervade the whole; that the formation and discipline of the militia of the continent should be absolutely uniform; and that the same species of arms, accoutrements, and military apparatus, should be introduced in every part of the United States. No one, who has not learned it from experience, can conceive the difficulty, expence, and confusion which result from a contrary system, or the vague arrangements which have hitherto prevailed.

If, in treating of political points, a greater latitude than usual has been taken in the course of the address, the importance of the crisis, and the magnitude of the objects in discussion, must be my apology: it is, however, neither my wish nor expectation, that the preceding observations should claim any regard, except so far as they shall appear to be dictated by a good intention: consonant to the immutable rules of justice; calculated to produce a liberal system of policy, and founded on whatever experience may have been acquired by a long and close attention to public business. Here I might speak with more confidence, from my actual observations; and if it would not swell this letter (already too prolix) beyond the bounds I had prescribed myself, I could demonstrate to every mind, open to conviction, that in less time, and with much less expence than has been incurred, the war might have been brought to the same happy conclusion, if the resources of the continent could have been properly called forth; that the distresses and disappointments which have very often occurred, have, in too many inftances, refulted more from a want of energy in the continental government, than a deficiency of means in the particular ftates; that the inefficacy of the meafures, arifing from the want of an adequate authority in the fupreme power, from a partial compliance with the requifitions of congrefs in fome of the ftates, and from a failure of punctuality in others, while they tended to damp the zeal of thofe who were more willing to exert themfelves, ferved alfo to accumulate the expences of the war, and to fruftrate the beft concerted plans; and that the difcouragement occafioned by the complicated difficulties and embarrassments, in which our affairs were by this means involved, would have long ago produced the diffolution of any army, lefs patient, lefs virtuous, and lefs perfevering, than that which I have had the honour to command. But while I mention thofe things, which are notorious facts, as the defects of our federal conftitution, particularly in the profecution of a war, I beg it may be underftood, that as I have ever taken a pleafure in gratefully acknowledging the affiftance and fupport I have derived from every clafs of citizens; fo fhall I always be happy to do juftice to the unparalleled exertions of the individual ftates, on many interefting occafions.

I have thus freely difclofed what I wifhed to make known before I furrendered up my public truft to thofe who committed it to me: the tafk is now accomplifhed; I now bid adieu to your excellency, as the chief magiftrate of your ftate; at the fame time I bid a laft farewell to the cares of office, and all the employments of public life.

It remains, then, to be my final and only requeft, that your excellency will communicate thefe fentiments to your legiflature, at their next meeting; and that they may be confidered as the legacy of one who has ardently wifhed, on all occafions, to be ufeful to his country, and who, even in the fhade of retirement, will not fail to implore the divine benediction upon it.

I now make it my earneft prayer, that God would have you, and the ftate over which you prefide, in his holy protection; that he would incline the hearts of the citizens to cultivate a fpirit of fubordination and obedience to government; to entertain a brotherly affection and love for one another, for their fellow-citizens of the United States at large; and particularly for their brethren who have ferved in the field; and finally, that he would moft gracioufly be pleafed to difpofe us all to do juftice, to love mercy, and to demean ourfelves with that charity, humility, and pacific temper of the mind, which were the characteriftics of the divine Author of our bleffed religion; without an humble imitation of whofe example, in thefe things, we can never hope to be a happy nation.

I have the honour to be, with much efteem and refpect, Sir,

Your excellency's moft obedient, and moft humble fervant,

G. WASHINGTON.

His Excellency William Greene, Efq.[36] *Governor of the State of Rhode Ifland.*

General Wafhington's *farewell Orders to the Armies of the United States.*

Rocky Hill, near Princeton, Nov. 2, 1783.

THE United States in congrefs affembled, after giving the moft honourable teftimony to the merits of the federal armies, and prefenting them with the thanks of their country, for their long eminent and faithful fervice, having thought proper, by their proclamation bearing date the 18th of October laft, to difcharge fuch part of the troops as were engaged for the war, and to permit the officers on furlough to retire from fervice, from and after to-morrow, which proclamation having been communicated in the public papers for the information and government of all concerned;—it only remains for the commander in chief to addrefs himfelf once more, and that for the laft time, to the armies of the United States (however widely difperfed individuals who compofed them may be), and to bid them an affectionate, a long farewell.

But before the commander in chief takes his final leave of thofe he holds moft dear, he wifhes to indulge himfelf a few moments in calling to mind a flight review of the paft:—he will then take the liberty of exploring, with his military friends, their future profpects, of advifing the general line of conduct which in his opinion ought to be purfued; and he will conclude the addrefs, by expreffing the obligations he feels himfelf under for the fpirited and able affiftance he has experienced from them, in the performance of an arduous office.

A contemplation of the complete attainment (at a period earlier than could have been expected) of the object for which we contended againft fo formidable a power, cannot but infpire us with aftonifhment and gratitude.—The difadvantageous circumftances on our part, under which the war was undertaken, can never be forgotten.—The fingular interpofitions of Providence in our feeble condition, were fuch as could fcarcely efcape the attention of the moft unobferving—while the unparalleled perseverance of the armies of the United States, through almost every possible suffering and discouragement, for the space of eight long years, was little short of a standing miracle.

It is not the meaning, nor within the compass of this address, to detail the hardships peculiarly incident to our service, or to describe the distresses which in several instances have resulted from the extremes of hunger and nakedness, combined with the rigours of an inclement season;—nor is it necessary to dwell on the dark side of our past affairs. Every American officer and soldier must now console himself for any unpleasant circumstances which may have occurred, by a recollection of the uncommon scenes in which he has been called to act no inglorious part, and the astonishing events of which he has been a witness; events which have seldom, if ever before, taken place on the stage of human action, nor can they probably ever happen again. For who has before seen a disciplined army formed at once from such raw materials? Who that was not a witness could imagine that the most violent local prejudices would cease so soon, and that men who came from the different parts of the continent, strongly disposed by the habits of education to despise and quarrel with each other, would instantly become but one patriotic band of brothers? Or who that was not on the spot, can trace the steps by which such a wonderful revolution has been effected, and such a glorious period put to all our warlike toils?

It is universally acknowledged, that the enlarged prospects of happiness, opened by the confirmation of our independence and sovereignty, almost exceed the power of description: and shall not the brave men who have contributed so essentially to these inestimable acquisitions, retiring victorious from the field of war to the field of agriculture, participate in all the blessings which have been obtained? In such a republic, who will exclude them from the rights of citizens, and the fruits of their labours? In such a country, so happily circumstanced, the pursuits of commerce, and the cultivation of the soil, will unfold to industry the certain road to competence. To those hardy soldiers, who are actuated by the spirit of adventure, the fisheries will afford ample and profitable employment; and the extensive and fertile regions of the West will yield a most happy asylum to those who, fond of domestic enjoyment, are seeking for personal independence. Nor is it possible to conceive that any one of the United States will prefer a national bankruptcy, and the dissolution of the union, to a compliance with the requisitions of congress, and the payment of its just debts, so that the officers and soldiers may expect considerable assistance, in recommencing their civil occupations, from the sums due to them from the public, which must and will most inevitably be paid.

In order to effect this desirable purpose, and to remove the prejudices which may have taken possession of the minds of any of the good people of the states, it is earnestly recommended to all the troops, that, with strong attachments to the union, they should carry with them into civil society the most conciliating dispositions; and that they should prove themselves not less virtuous and useful as citizens, than they have been persevering and victorious as soldiers.—What though there should be some envious individuals, who are unwilling to pay the debt the public has contracted, or to yield the tribute due to merit; yet let such unworthy treatment produce no invective, or any instance of intemperate conduct;—let it be remembered, that the unbiassed voice of the free citizens of the United States has promised the just reward, and given the merited applause;—let it be known and remembered, that the reputation of the federal armies is established beyond the reach of malevolence; and let a consciousness of their atchievements, and fame, still excite the men who composed them to honourable actions, under the persuasion, that the private virtues of œconomy, prudence, and industry, will not be less amiable in civil life, than the more splendid qualities of valour, perseverance and enterprize, were in the field:—every one may rest assured that much, very much of the future happiness of the officers and men will depend upon the wise and manly conduct which shall be adopted by them, when they are mingled with the great body of the community. And although the general has so frequently given it as his opinion, in the most public and explicit manner, that unless the principles of the federal government were properly supported, and the powers of the union increased, the honour, dignity, and justice of the nation, would be lost for ever; yet he cannot help repeating on this occasion so interesting a sentiment; and leaving it as his last injunction to every officer and every soldier who may view the subject in the same serious point of light, to add his best endeavours to those of his worthy fellow-citizens, towards effecting these great and valuable purposes, on which our very existence as a nation so materially depends.

The commander in chief conceives little is now wanting to enable the soldier to change the military character into that of a citizen, but that steady and decent tenour of behaviour, which has generally diftinguifhed not only the army under his immediate command, but the different detachments and feparate armies, through the courfe of the war. From their good fenfe and prudence he anticipated the happieft confequences : and while he congratulates them on the glorious occafion which renders their fervices in the field no longer neceffary, he wifhes to exprefs the ftrong obligations he feels himfelf under for the affiftance he has received from every clafs, and in every inftance. He prefents his thanks, in the moft ferious and affectionate manner, to the general officers, as well for their counfel on many interefting occafions, as for their ardour in promoting the fuccefs of the plans he had adopted ; to the commandants of regiments and corps, and to the officers for their zeal and attention in carrying his orders promptly into execution ; to the ftaff, for their alacrity and exactnefs in performing the duties of their feveral departments ; and to the non-commiffioned officers and private foldiers, for their extraordinary patience in fuffering, as well as their invincible fortitude in action. To various branches of the army the general takes this laft and folemn opportunity of profeffing his inviolable attachment and friendfhip.—He wifhes more than bare profeffions were in his power, that he was really able to be ufeful to them all in future life.—He flatters himfelf, however, they will do him the juftice to believe, that whatever could with propriety be attempted by him, has been done.—And being now to conclude thefe his laft public orders, to take his ultimate leave, in a fhort time, of the military character,—and to bid a final adieu to the armies he has fo long had the honour to command, he can only again offer, in their behalf,

his recommendations to their grateful country, and his prayers to the God of armies.—May ample juftice be done them here, and may the choiceft of heaven's favours, both here and hereafter, attend thofe who, under the divine aufpices, have fecured innumerable bleffings for others ! With thefe wifhes, and this benediction, the commander in chief is about to retire from fervice.—The curtain of feparation will foon be drawn—and the military fcene to him will be clofed for ever.

EDW. HAND, Adjutant-general.

The Addrefs of his Officers to his Excellency General Wafhington, Commander in Chief of the armies of the United States of America.

WE, the officers of the part of the army remaining on the banks of the Hudfon, have received your excellency's ferious and farewell addrefs, to the armies of the United States. We beg you to accept our unfeigned thanks for the communication, and our affectionate affurances of inviolable attachment and friendfhip. If your attempts to enfure to the armies the juft, the promifed rewards, of their long, fevere, and dangerous fervices, have failed of fuccefs, we believe it has arifen from caufes not in your excellency's power to controul. With extreme regret do we reflect on the occafion which called for fuch endeavours. But while we thank your excellency for thefe exertions in favour of the troops you have fo fuccefsfully commanded, we pray it may be believed, that in this fentiment our own particular interefts have but a fecondary place ; and that even the ultimate ingratitude of the people (were that poffible) could not fhake the patriotifm of thofe who fuffer by it. Still with plea-

fing wonder and with grateful joy fhall we contemplate the glorious conclufion of our labours. To that merit in the revolution which, under the aufpices of heaven, the armies have difplayed, pofterity will do juftice ; and the fons will blufh whofe fathers were their foes.

Moft gladly would we caft a veil on every act which fullies the reputation of our country—never fhould the page of hiftory be ftained with its difhonour—even from our memories fhould the idea be erafed. We lament the oppofition to thofe falutary meafures which the wifdom of the union has planted ; meafures which alone can recover and fix on a permanent bafis the credit of the ftates ; meafures which are effential to the juftice, the honour, and intereft of the nation. While fhe was giving the nobleft proofs of magnanimity, with confcious pride we faw her growing fame ; and regardlefs of prefent fufferings, we looked forward to the end of our toils and dangers, to brighter fcenes in profpect.—There we beheld the genius of our country dignified by fovereignty and independence, fupported by juftice, and adorned with every liberal virtue. There we faw patient Hufbandry fearlefs extend her cultured fields, and animated Commerce fpread her fails to every wind. There we beheld fair Science lift her head, with all the Arts attending in her train. There, bleft with freedom, we faw the human mind expand ; and throwing afide the reftraints which confined it to the narrow bounds of country, it embraced the world. Such were our fond hopes, and with fuch delightful profpects did they prefent us. Nor are we difappointed. Thofe animating profpects are now changed and changing to realities ; and actively to have contributed to their production is our pride, our glory.—But justice alone can give them stability. In that justice we still believe. Still we hope that the prejudices of the misinformed will be removed, and the arts of false and selfish popularity, addressed to the feelings of avarice, defeated: or in the worst event, the world, we hope, will make the just distinction: we trust the disingenuousness of a few will not sully the reputation, the honour, and dignity, of the great and respectable majority of the states.

We are happy in the opportunity just presented of congratulating your excellency on the certain conclusion of the definitive treaty of peace. Relieved at length from long suspence, our warmest wish is to return to the bosom of our country, to resume the character of citizens; and it will be our highest ambition to become useful ones. To your excellency this great event must be peculiarly pleasing: for while at the head of her armies, urged by patriot virtues and magnanimity, you persevered, under the pressure of, every possible difficulty and discouragement, in the pursuit of the great objects of the war—the freedom and safety of your country;—your heart panted for the tranquil enjoyments of peace. We cordially rejoice with you that the period of indulging them has arrived so soon. In contemplating the blessings of liberty and independence, the rich prize of eight years hardy adventure, past sufferings will be forgotten; or if remembered, the recollection will serve to heighten the relish of present happiness. We sincerely pray God this happiness may long be your's; and that when you quit the stage of human life, you may receive from the unerring Judge, the rewards of valour exerted to save the oppressed, of patriotism and disinterested virtue.

West Point,
15th November, 1783.
• • •

His Majesty's most gracious Speech to both* Houses of Parliament, on the closing of the Session, July 11, 1782.

My Lords and Gentlemen,

THE unwearied assiduity with which you have persevered in the discharge of your duty in parliament, during so long a session, bears the most honourable testimony to your zeal and industry in the service of the public; for which you have provided with the clearest discernment of its true interests; anxiously opening every channel for the return of peace; and furnishing with no less vigilance the means of carrying on the war, if that measure should be unavoidable.

The extensive powers with which I find myself invested to treat for reconciliation and amity with the colonies which have taken arms in North America, I shall continue to employ in the manner most conducive to the attainment of those objects, and with an earnestness suitable to their importance.

The zeal which my subjects in Ireland have expressed for the public service, shows that the liberality of your proceedings towards there is felt there as it ought; and has engaged their affections, equally with their duty and interest, in the common cause.

The diligence and ardour, with which you have entered upon the consideration of the British interests in the East-Indies, are worthy of your wisdom, justice, and humanity. To protect the persons and fortunes of millions in those distant regions, and to combine our prosperity with their happiness, are objects which amply repay the utmost labour and exertion.

Gentlemen of the House of Commons.

I return you my particular thanks for the very liberal supplies which you have granted with so much chearfulness and zeal for the service of the current year. I reflect with extreme regret upon the heavy expence which the circumstances of public affairs unavoidably call for. It shall be my care to husband your means to the best advantage; and, as far as depends on me, to apply that œconomy which I have endeavoured to set on foot in my civil establishment, to those more extensive branches of public expenditure, in which still more important advantages may be expected.

My Lords and Gentlemen,

The important successes, which, under the favour of Divine Providence, the valour of my fleet in the West Indies hath obtained, promise a favourable issue to our operations in that quarter. The events of war in the East Indies have also been prosperous. Nothing however can be more repugnant to my feelings, than the long continuance of so complicated a war.

My ardent desire of peace has induced me to take every measure which promised the speediest accomplishment of my wishes; and I will continue to exert my best endeavours for that purpose. But if, for want of a corresponding disposition in our enemies, I should be disappointed in the hope I entertained of a speedy termination of the calamities of war, I rely on the spirit, affection, and unanimity of my parliament and people to support the honour of my crown, and the interests of my kingdoms; not doubting that the blessing of heaven, which I devoutly implore upon our arms, employed as they are in our just and necessary defence, will enable

---

* This speech ought to have been inserted in the State Papers of the Annual Register for 1782, but was by mistake omitted.

me to obtain fair and reasonable terms of pacification. The most triumphant career of victory would not excite me to aim at more; and I have the satisfaction to be able to add, that I see no reason which should induce me to think of accepting less.

His Majesty's most gracious Speech to both Houses of Parliament, on the opening of the Session, December 5, 1782.

My Lords and Gentlemen,

SINCE the close of the last session I have employed my whole time in the care and attention which the important and critical conjuncture of public affairs required of me.

I lost no time in giving the necessary orders to prohibit the further prosecution of offensive war upon the continent of North America. Adopting, as my inclination will always lead me to do, with decision and effect, whatever I collect to be the sense of my parliament and my people; I have pointed all my views and measures, as well in Europe as in North America, to an entire and cordial reconciliation with those colonies.

Finding it indispensable to the attainment of this object, I did not hesitate to go the full length of the powers vested in me, and offered to declare them free and independent states, by an article to be inserted in the treaty of peace. Provisional articles are agreed upon, to take effect whenever terms of peace shall be finally settled with the court of France.

In thus admitting their separation from the crown of these kingdoms, I have sacrificed every consideration of my own to the wishes and opinion of my people. I make it my humble and earnest prayer to Almighty God, that Great Britain may not feel the evils which might result from so great a dismemberment of the empire; and, that America may be free from those calamities which have formerly proved in the mother country how essential monarchy is to the enjoyment of constitutional liberty.——Religion—language — interest——affections, may, and I hope will yet prove a bond of permanent union between the two countries: to this end, neither attention nor disposition shall be wanting on my part.

While I have carefully abstained from all offensive operations against America, I have directed my whole force by land and sea against the other powers at war, with as much vigour, as the situation of that force, at the commencement of the campaign, would permit. I trust that you feel the advantages resulting from the safety of the great branches of our trade. You must have seen with pride and satisfaction the gallant defence of the governor and the garrison of Gibraltar; and my fleet, after having effected the object of their destination, offering battle to the combined force of France and Spain on their own coasts; those of my kingdoms have remained at the same time perfectly secure, and your domestic tranquillity uninterrupted. This respectable state, under the blessing of God, I attribute to the entire confidence which subsists between me and my people, and to the readiness which has been shewn by my subjects in my city of London, and in other parts of my kingdoms, to stand forth in the general defence. Some proofs have lately been given of public spirit in private men, which would do honour to any age, and any country.

Having manifested to the whole world, by the most lasting examples, the signal spirit and bravery of my people, I conceived it a moment not unbecoming my dignity, and thought it a regard due to the lives and fortunes of such brave and gallant subjects, to shew myself ready on my part, to embrace fair and honourable terms of accommodation with all the powers at war.

I have the satisfaction to acquaint you, that negociations to this effect are considerably advanced, the result of which, as soon as they are brought to a conclusion, shall be immediately communicated to you.

I have every reason to hope and believe, that I shall have it in my power in a very short time to acquaint you, that they have ended in terms of pacification, which, I trust, you will see just cause to approve. I rely however with perfect confidence on the wisdom of my parliament, and the spirit of my people, that if any unforeseen change in the dispositions of the belligerent powers should frustrate my confident expectations, they will approve of the preparations I have thought it adviseable to make, and be ready to second the most vigorous efforts in the further prosecution of the war.

• • •

The definitive Treaty of Peace and Friendship, between his Britannic Majesty, and the United States of America, signed at Paris the 3d Day of September, 1783.

In the Name of the Most Holy and Undivided Trinity.

IT having pleased the divine Providence to dispose the hearts of the most serene and most potent prince George the Third, by the grace of God, king of Great Britain, France and Ireland, defender of the faith, Duke of Brunswick and Lunenburg, arch-treasurer and prince elector of the holy Roman empire, &c. and of the United States of America, to forget all past misunderstandings and differences that have unhappily interrupted the good correspondence and friendship which they mutually wish to restore, and to establish such a beneficial and satisfactory intercourse between the two countries upon the ground of reciprocal advantages and mutual convenience as may promote and secure to both perpetual peace and harmony; and having for this desirable end already laid the foundation of peace and reconciliation by the provisional articles signed at Paris on the 30th of November, 1782, by the commissioners empowered on each part, which articles were agreed to be inserted in and to constitute the treaty of peace proposed to be concluded between the crown of Great Britain and the said United States, but which treaty was not to be concluded until terms of peace should be agreed upon between Great Britain and France, and his Britannic majesty should be ready to conclude such treaty accordingly: and the treaty between Great Britain and France having since been concluded, his Britannic majesty and the United States of America, in order to carry into full effect the provisional articles above-mentioned, according to the tenor thereof, have constituted and appointed, that is to say, his Britannic majesty on his part, David Hartley, Esq. member of the parliament of Great Britain; and the said United States on their part, John Adams, Esq. late a commissioner of the United States of America at the court of Versailles, late delegate in congress from the state of Massachusetts, and chief justice of the said state, and minister plenipotentiary of the said United States to their high mightinesses the States General of the United Netherlands; Benjamin Franklin, Esq. late delegate in congress from the state of Pennsylvania, president of the convention of the said state, and minister plenipotentiary from the United States of America at the court of Versailles; and John Jay, Esq. late president of congress, and chief

justice of the state of New York, and minister plenipotentiary from the said United States at the court of Madrid; to be the plenipotentiaries for the concluding and signing the present definitive treaty; who after having reciprocally communicated their respective full powers, have agreed upon and confirmed the following articles:

Art. I. His Britannic majesty acknowledges the said United States, viz. New Hampshire, Massachusetts Bay, Rhode Island and Providence Plantations, Connecticut, New York, New Jersey, Pennsylvania, Delaware, Maryland, Virginia, North Carolina, South Carolina, and Georgia, to be free, sovereign, and independent states; that he treats with them as such, and for himself, his heirs and successors, relinquishes all claims to the government, propriety, and territorial rights of the same, and every part thereof.

II. And that all disputes which might arise in future on the subject of the boundaries of the said United States may be prevented, it is hereby agreed and declared, that the following are and shall be their boundaries, viz. From the north-west angle of Nova Scotia, viz. that angle which is formed by a line drawn due north from the source of St. Croix river to the Highlands, along the said Highlands, which divide those rivers that empty themselves into the river St. Laurence, from those which fall into the Atlantic ocean, to the north-westernmost head of Connecticut river; thence down along the middle of that river to the forty-fifth degree of north latitude; from thence by a line due west on said latitude, until it strikes the river Irroquois or Cataraquy; thence along the middle of said river into Lake Ontario; through the middle of said lake until it strikes the communication

by water between that lake and Lake Erie; thence along the middle of the said communication into Lake Erie, through the middle of said lake, until it arrives at the water communication between that lake and Lake Huron; thence through the middle of said lake to the water communication between that lake and Lake Superior; thence through Lake Superior northward of the Isles Royal and Philipeaux to the Long Lake; thence through the middle of said Long Lake and the water communication between it and the Lake of the Woods, to the said Lake of the Woods; thence through the said lake to the most north-westernmost point thereof, and from thence on a due west course to the river Mississippi; thence by a line to be drawn along the middle of the said river Mississippi until it shall intersect the northernmost part of the thirty first degree of north latitude. South, by a line to be drawn due east from the determination of the line last mentioned in the latitude of thirty-one degrees north of the equator, to the middle of the river Apalachiola or Catahouche; thence along the middle thereof to its junction with the Flint River; thence straight to the head of St. Mary's River, and thence down along the middle of St. Mary's River to the Atlantic ocean. East, by a line to be drawn along the middle of the river St. Croix from its mouth in the Bay of Fundy to its source, and from its source directly north to the aforesaid highlands which divide the rivers that fall into the Atlantic ocean from those which fall into the river St. Laurence, comprehending all islands within twenty leagues of any part of the shores of the United States, and lying between lines to be drawn due east from the points where the aforesaid boundaries between Nova Scotia on the one part, and East

Florida on the other, shall respectively touch the Bay of Fundy and the Atlantic ocean, excepting such islands as now are or heretofore have been within the limits of the said province of Nova Scotia.

Art. III. It is agreed that the people of the United States shall continue to enjoy unmolested the right to take fish of every kind on the Great Bank, and on all the other banks of Newfoundland; also in the Gulf of St. Laurence, and at all other places in the sea where the inhabitants of both countries used at any time heretofore to fish. And also that the inhabitants of the United States shall have liberty to take fish of every kind on such part of the coast of Newfoundland as British fishermen shall use (but not to dry or cure the same on that island), and also on the coasts, bays, and creeks, of all other of his Britannic majesty's dominions in America; and that the American fishermen shall have liberty to dry and cure fish in any of the unsettled bays, harbours, and creeks of Nova Scotia, Magdalen islands and Labrador, so long as the same shall remain unsettled; but so soon as the same or either of them shall be settled, it shall not be lawful for the said fishermen to dry or cure fish at such settlement, without a previous agreement for that purpose with the inhabitants, proprietors, or possessors of the ground.

Art. IV. It is agreed that the creditors on either side shall meet with no lawful impediment to the recovery of the full value in sterling money of all bona fide debts heretofore contracted.

Art. V. It is agreed that congress shall earnestly recommend it to the legislatures of the respective states, to provide for the restitution of all estates, rights, and properties, which have been confiscated, belonging to real British subjects; and also of the estates, rights, and properties, of persons resident in districts in the possession of his majesty's arms, and who have not borne arms against the said United States; and that persons of any other description shall have free liberty to go to any part or parts of any of the thirteen United States, and therein to remain twelve months unmolested in their endeavours to obtain the restitution of such of their estates, rights, and properties, as may have been confiscated; and that congress shall also earnestly recommend to the several states a reconsideration and revision of all acts or laws regarding the premises, so as to render the said laws or acts perfectly consistent not only with justice and equity, but with that spirit of conciliation which on the return of the blessings of peace should universally prevail: and that congress shall also earnestly recommend to the several states, that the estates, rights, and properties, of such last mentioned persons, shall be restored to them, they refunding to any persons who may be now in possession of the bona fide price (where any has been given), which such persons may have paid on purchasing any of the said lands, rights, or properties, since the confiscation.

And it is agreed that all persons who have any interest in confiscated lands, either by debts, marriage settlements, or otherwise, shall meet with no lawful impediment in the prosecution of their just rights.

Art. IV. That there shall be no future confiscations made, nor any prosecutions commenced against any person or persons for or by reason of the part which he or they may have taken in the present war; and that no person shall on that account suffer any future loss or damage either in his person, liberty, or property, and that those who may be in confinement on such charges at the time of the ratification of the treaty in America, shall be immediately set at liberty, and the prosecutions so commenced be discontinued.

Art. VII. There shall be a firm and perpetual peace between his Britannic majesty and the said United States, and between the subject of the one and the citizens of the other; wherefore all hostilities both by sea and land shall from henceforth cease; all prisoners on both sides shall be set at liberty, and his Britannic majesty shall, with all convenient speed, and without causing any destruction, or carrying away any negroes or other property of the American inhabitants, withdraw all his armies, garrisons, and fleets, from the said United States, and from every post, place and harbour, within the same; leaving in all fortifications the American artillery that may be therein; and shall also order and cause all archives, records, deeds, and papers belonging to any of the said states, or their citizens, which in the course of the war may have fallen into the hands of his officers, to be forthwith restored and delivered to the proper states and persons to whom they belong.

Art. VIII. The navigation of the river Mississippi, from its source to the ocean, shall for ever remain free and open to the subjects of Great Britain and the citizens of the United States.

Art. IX. In case it should so happen that any place or territory belonging to Great Britain, or to the United States, should have been conquered by the arms of either from the other, before the arrival of the said provisional articles in America, it is agreed that the same shall be restored without difficulty, and without requiring any compensation.

Art. X. The solemn ratifications of the present treaty, expedited in good and due form, shall be exchanged between the contracting parties in the space of six months, or sooner, if possible, to be computed from the day of the signature of the present treaty.

In witness whereof we the under-signed, their ministers plenipotentiary, have in their name, and in virtue of our full powers, signed with our hands the present definitive treaty, and caused the seals of our arms to be affixed thereto.

Done at Paris, this third day of September, in the year of our Lord one thousand seven hundred and eighty-three.

David Hartley. (L. S.) [37]
John Adams. (L. S.)
B. Franklin. (L. S.)
John Jay. (L. S.)

• • •

Transcript of the Treaty between France and the United States of America, together with the Ratification of the same by Congress.

THE United States, assembled in congress, to all who shall see these presents greeting. Whereas Benjamin Franklin, our minister plenipotentiary, by virtue of full powers vested in him, has made, with Charles Gravier de Vergennes, counsellor of the king in all his councils, commander of his orders, minister and secretary of state, vested also with full powers by his most Christian majesty for that purpose, concluded and signed a contract between his said most Christian majesty and the United States of North America, in the terms following ;

Contract between the King and the thirteen United States of North America, concluded by Mr. de Vergennes and Dr. Franklin.

As it has pleased the king to comply with the requests made to him in the name, and on the part of the United Provinces of North America, by assisting them in the war and invasion under which they have groaned during several years ; and his majesty, after having concluded a treaty of amity and commerce with the said confederated provinces, on the 6th of February, 1778, having had the goodness to succour them, not only by his sea and land-forces, but also by means of advancing them money, as bountifully as in its consequence efficaciously, at a time when their affairs were in a very critical situation ; it has been judged proper and necessary to fix the exact amount of these advances, the conditions upon which the king has made them, the different periods at which the congress of the United States have agreed to pay them into his majesty's royal treasury ; and finally, to regulate this matter so, that no difficulties may hereafter arise to interrupt that good harmony which his majesty is resolved to support on his part with the United States. For the purpose, therefore, of accomplishing so desirable an end, and with a view of strengthening those bonds of amity and commerce which subsist between his majesty and the United States : we Charles Gravier de Vergennes, &c. counsellor to the king and all his councils, commander of his orders, minister and secretary of state to his command and finances, vested with full powers by his majesty : and we Benjamin Franklin, minister plenipotentiary of the United States of North America, vested equally with full powers by the congress of the said states, after having each communicated our respective powers, have agreed upon the following articles :

Art. I. It is agreed upon and certified, that the sums advanced by his majesty to the congress of the United States, under the title of a loan, in the years 1778, 1779, 1780, 1781, and in the present year 1782, amount together to the sum of eighteen millions of livres, of French money, as appears by the twenty-one receipts following, signed by the said minister of the congress, and given by virtue of his full powers ; namely,

1.—28 Feb. 1778		750,000
2.—19 May	.	750,000
3.— 3 Aug.	.	750,000
4.— 1 Nov.	.	750,000
		3,000,000
5.—10 June, 1779		250,000
6.—16 Sept.	.	250,000
7.— 4 Oct.	.	250,000
8.—21 Dec.	.	250,000
		1,000,000
9.—29 Feb. 1780		750,000
10.—27 May		750,000
11.—21 June	.	750,000
12.— 3 Oct.	.	1,000,000
13.—27 Nov.	.	750,000
		4,000,000
14.—15 Feb. 1781		750,000
15.—15 May	.	750,000
16.—15 Aug.	.	750,000
17.— 1 Oct.	.	1,000,000
18.—15 Nov.	.	750,000
		4,000,000
19.—10 April, 1782		1,500,000
20.— 2 July	.	1,500,000
21.— 5	.	3,000,000
		6,000,000
Total		18,000,000

By which receipts, the said minister has promised, in the name of the congress, on the part of the thirteen United States to cause to be paid and reimbursed to the king's royal treasury, on the 1st of January, 1788, at the house of his principal banker at Paris, the above sum, with the interest due thereon, at the rate of five per cent. per annum.

Art. II. Upon consideration, however, that the payment of so large a capital at one stipulated period, namely, the 1st of January, 1788, may be exceedingly inconvenient to the finances of the congress of the United States, and that it might, perhaps, be even impracticable, it has pleased his majesty on that account to release them from the tenor of those receipts given by their minister for the eighteen millions of livres, Tournois, mentioned in the preceding article; and he has consented that the reimbursement of the capital in yearly money to his royal treasury shall be made in twelve equal payments, of 1,500,000 livres each, and in twelve years, to begin the third year after the peace.

Art. III. Although the receipts of the minister of the congress of the United States, mention, that " the 18,000,000 of livres above mentioned, shall be paid into the royal treasury with five per cent. interest ;" his majesty, desirous of giving a fresh proof to the said United States, of his friendship, has been pleased to make them a present of the arrears of interest to this day, and also to remit it from this time to the day of the date of the treaty of peace ; a favour which the minister of congress acknowledges as proceeding purely from the king's bounty, and which he accepts in the name of the United States with the most profound and lively gratitude.

Art. IV. The payment of the said 18,000,000 of livres shall be made in ready money to his majesty's royal treasury at Paris, in twelve equal payments, and at the period stated in the second article above. The interest on the said sum, at the rate of five per cent. to run from the date of the treaty of peace ; the payment of it shall be made at the time of each of the partial reimbursements of the capital, and shall diminish in proportion in the reimbursements ; the congress are nevertheless at liberty to free themselves from this obligation sooner, by anticipating payments, in case the state of their finances should permit.

Art. V. Although the loan of 5,000,000 of the Dutch florins, granted by the States General of the United Provinces of the Netherlands, on the terms of the obligation passed on the 5th of November, 1781, has been made in his majesty's name, and he has pledged himself for the payment of it ; it is nevertheless acknowledged by these presents, that the said loan has been made in reality on account of, and for the service of the United States of North America ; and that the capital amounting, according to a moderate valuation, to the sum of 10,000,000 livres Tournois, has been paid to the United States, agreeable to receipt given for the payment of the said sum by the undersigned minister of congress, on the 7th of last June.

Art. VI. By the said convention of the 5th of November, 1781, it has pleased the king to promise and to engage himself to furnish and to pay to the general office of the States General of the Netherlands the capital of the said loan, together with the interest of five per cent. without any charge or deduction whatsoever to the lenders, so that the said capital be entirely reimbursed within the space of five years, the payments to be made at ten equal periods, the first to begin the sixth year after the date of the loan, and from that time, during every year till the final payment of the said sum ; but it is likewise acknowledged by the present act, that this engagement has been entered into by the king, on the entreaty of the underwritten ministers of the United States, and upon the promise made by him in the name of the congress, and on the part of the thirteen United States to reimburse and pay into the royal treasury of his majesty at Paris, the capital, interest, and expences of the said loan, agreeable to the conditions and terms, fixed by the convention of the 5th of November, 1781.

Art. VII. It has been agreed upon and regulated in consequence, that the said sum of ten millions of livres Tournois, making, at a moderate estimate, five millions of Dutch florins as above mentioned, shall be reimbursed and paid into his majesty's royal treasury at Paris, with the interest at five per cent. in ten equal payments of one million each, and at the several periods, the first of which shall be made on the 5th of November, 1787, and thus from year to year till the final payment of the said sum of ten millions, the interest diminishing in proportion with the partial payments of the capital. But from the regard which his majesty bears to the United States, he has been pleased to take upon himself the expence of the commission, and of banking, attending the said loan, of which expence his majesty makes a present to the said United States ; and their underwritten minister accepts, with thanks, in the name of the congress, as an additional proof of his majesty's generosity, and of his friendship for the United States.

Art. VIII. With respect to the interest on the said loan, as the king had engaged to pay, during the five years preceding the first reimbursement of the capital, four per cent. on the whole, into the general office of the States General of the Netherlands, annually, from the 5th of November, 1781, agreeable to the convention entered into on that day, the minister of congress acknowledges, that the reimbursements of the said interest is due to his majesty from the United States; and he engages, in the name of the said states, to cause the payment thereof to be made at the same rate into the royal treasury of his majesty; the interest of the first year to be paid on the 4th of next November, and so on annually during the five years preceding the first payment of the capital, fixed on as above, for the 5th of November, 1787.

The high contracting parties reciprocally bind themselves to the faithful observance of this contract, the ratifications of which shall be exchanged within the space of nine months from the date hereof, if possible. In faith of which, we the said plenipotentiaries of his most Christian majesty, and of the thirteen United States of North America, by virtue of our respective powers, have signed these presents, and have thereto put the seal of our arms.

Given at Versailles, the 16th of July, 1782.

(Signed)
C. G. De Vergennes. (L. S.)
B. Franklin. (L. S.)

Be it known to all and every one, that we the said United States assembled in congress, penetrated with the most lively ideas of the generosity and affection manifested by his most Christian majesty in the above contract, have ratified and confirmed it; and by these presents we do ratify and confirm the said contract, and every article and clause therein. And we do by these presents authorise our minister plenipotentiary at the court of Versailles, to remit our present act of ratification, in exchange for the ratification of the said contract on the part of his most Christian majesty.

In faith of which we have caused our seal to be affixed hereunto, in presence of his excellency Elias Bourdinot, president, this 22d of January, in the year of grace, 1783, and the 7th of our sovereignty and independence.

Notes, 1783

1. Congress learned from the French minister on 28 May 1782 details of British attempts to make a separate peace with France, and passed a resolution on 31 May to assure France of "... a reciprocal and equal resolution to adhere, in every event, to the principles of the alliance, and to hearken to no propositions of peace which are not perfectly conformable thereto." *Journals of the Continental Congress 1774–1789*, ed. W. C. Ford, 34 vols. (Washington, D.C., 1904–37), vol. 22, pp. 302–05, 312–13. The resolution of 4 October was prompted by letters from John Jay and Lafayette indicating French doubts. Ibid., vol. 23, pp. 637–39.

2. France and Britain competed throughout the century for control of St. Lucia, partly for its value as a sugar island but mostly for its strategic position in the Windward Islands.

3. The cost of the war has been estimated at between 1,800 million and 2,000 million livres, or £90 million to £100 million; this would represent about half the cost of all wars fought by France from 1733 to 1783.

4. During the short-lived Rockingham administration (March–July 1782), the rivalry between Shelburne as Secretary for both Home and Colonial Affairs and Fox as Foreign Secretary resulted in both producing negotiators for Britain in France. Shelburne sent Oswald to Paris for discussions with Franklin; Fox, aiming to deal with Vergennes, sent a close friend, Thomas Grenville (1755–1846), M.P. for Buckinghamshire, 1779–84, brother of George Grenville, the younger.

5. Misprint for 1783.

6. These two tiny islands, ten miles off Newfoundland, were valued by France as local bases for her share of the fisheries. They were ceded to France in 1763, but devastated by the British in a raid in 1778.

7. That is, the prohibition of the erection of fortifications around the town or harbour and the right to maintain a British commissary there.

8. Henry Bankes (1756–1814), M.P. for Corfe Castle, 1780–1826; he opposed the American war, voted consistently against North, and was now an adherent of Pitt.

9. Fox resigned on 4 July; he learned on 30 June that Shelburne and others in the Cabinet were reconsidering an offer of unconditional independence to America.

10. Thomas Townshend, Home Secretary, July 1782–April 1783; William Pitt, Chancellor of the Exchequer, July 1782–April 1783; and General Conway, Commander-in-Chief, March 1782–December 1783.

11. William Fitzwilliam, 2nd Earl Fitzwilliam (1748–1833), nephew of the Marquis of Rockingham and his heir.

12. Thomas Pitt (1737–93), M.P. for Old Sarum, 1774–84, nephew of the

The Annual Register—1783

Earl of Chatham and a respected independent, created Baron Camelford in 1784. William Wilberforce (1759–1833), M.P. for Hull, 1780–84; a friend and adherent of Pitt; opposed North in the last stages of that ministry and supported Shelburne in 1783.

13. Sir Henry Fletcher (c. 1727–1807), M.P. for Cumberland, 1768–1806, a Rockingham supporter; as Chairman of the East India Company 1782–83, he supported Shelburne's peace terms for the benefits likely to be gained by the company from the settlement in India. Richard Brinsley Sheridan (1751–1816), M.P. for Stafford, 1780–1806; Under-Secretary for Foreign Affairs, April–July 1782; Secretary to the Treasury, April–December 1783; one of Fox's followers.

14. Hugh Pigot (?1721–92), Rear-Admiral, 1775; Admiral and Lord of the Admiralty, 1782; succeeded Rodney as Commander-in-Chief in the West Indies.

15. Sir Edward Hughes (?1720–94), Rear-Admiral and Knight of the Bath in 1778; Commander-in-Chief in the East Indies, 1773–77 and 1778–83.

16. Sir Richard Bickerton (1727–92), knighted 1773, created Baronet in 1778, Commodore, 1781; served in the East Indies 1782–84; later, Commander-in-Chief in the West Indies, 1786–87, and Vice-Admiral, 1790. The details of these events in India are covered in *AR*, 1783, ch. II, pp. 40]–54].

17. John Leveson-Gower (1740–92), younger son of the 1st Earl Gower, Captain in 1760, and Rear-Admiral, 1787; appointed Lord of the Admiralty by Howe in January 1783; dismissed in July and reappointed in December; M.P. for Appleby, 1784–90. ?Richard Lane, Lieutenant, 1781, Captain, 1794.

18. Gum senegal, a variety of gum arabic produced from the West African acacia tree, used in cloth finishing and in some medicines.

19. Not identified.

20. The teredo worm, a marine boring mollusc, attacked ships' timbers unless prevented by copper-bottoming the hull; the worst variety was said to be found in tropical waters.

21. The Treaty of Munster, in 1648, granted the Netherlands independence from Spain.

22. The Catalan revolt of 1640 permitted a French intervention which was not ended until the Treaty of the Pyrenees in 1659. In 1705, the Catalans supported Archduke Charles of Austria, the candidate for the Spanish throne supported by the Grand Alliance against Louis XIV, and secured concessions at the Treaty of Utrecht in 1713.

23. The Treaty of Limerick in 1691 ended William III's campaign to subdue Ireland; the penal code which was imposed after 1691 however is notorious for its treatment of the Irish Catholics.

24. In July 1757, after a protracted period of ministerial instability, the Elder Pitt and the Duke of Newcastle formed a coalition which permitted the successful prosecution of the Seven Years War until Pitt's resignation in September 1761.

25. Henry Herbert (1734–94), 9th Earl of Pembroke and 7th Earl of Montgomery, was deprived of his Lord Lieutenancy of Wiltshire in 1780 for voting in opposition, but the office was restored in 1782, when he was promoted to General.

26. Lord Ward (see "Notes, 1776," n. 32). George Townshend (1724–1807), former M.P. for Norfolk, 1747–64; succeeded his father as 4th Viscount Townshend in 1764; created Marquis Townshend in 1787; supported North and was Master-General of the Ordnance 1772–82. Peter King (1736–93) succeeded his father as 6th Baron King of Ockham in 1779; Alexander Wedderburn was created Baron Loughborough in June 1780.

27. That is, the Crown law officers.

28. John Lee (?1733–93), M.P. for Clitheroe, 1782–90; Solicitor-General, April–July 1782, April–November 1783, and Attorney-General November–December 1783; a friend of Rockingham and a critic of Shelburne's peace.

29. Thurlow was Lord Chancellor until April 1783, when the seal went into commission; he was reappointed in December and held the post until 1792.

30. Shelburne resigned on 24 February; after a five-week crisis, the Fox-North coalition took office, on 2 April.

31. 23 Geo. III c. 26 and 23 Geo. III c. 39.

32. As a reprisal for the hanging of an American officer by the Board of Associated Loyalists in April 1782 (see "Notes, 1781," n. 1), Washington, having received unsatisfactory replies from Clinton regarding the punishment of those responsible, ordered a British officer of the same rank who had surrendered without conditions to be selected by lot and executed. The officer in charge of prisoners at Lancaster, Pennsylvania, selected Charles Asgill (1762/3–1823), Captain in the 1st Foot Guards. Asgill, however, was a prisoner from the Yorktown surrender and was protected by the terms of Cornwallis's capitulation. Washington was thus placed in an embarrassing position and finally referred the matter to Congress. A solution became possible as a result of a direct appeal to Vergennes by Asgill's mother. Vergennes showed her letter to the King and Queen and interceded with Washington; Congress approved Asgill's release and Washington ordered it on 13 November.

33. Hugh Williamson (1735–1819), North Carolina delegate to the Continental Congress, 1782–85 and 1787–88. John Rutledge (1739–1800), brother of Edward Rutledge, South Carolina delegate to the Congress, 1774–75 and 1782–83, Governor of South Carolina, 1779–82.

34. Robert R. Livingston (1746–1813), New York delegate to the Continental Congress, 1775–76, 1779–81, 1784–85; first Secretary to the Department of Foreign Affairs in 1781; later, Minister to France and responsible for organising the purchase of Louisiana in 1801. Duquesne, not identified.

35. Elias Boudinot (1740–1821), Commissary General of Prisoners from June 1777; New Jersey delegate to the Continental Congress, 1778, 1781–83; President, 1782.

36. William Greene (1731–1809), Governor of Rhode Island, 1777–86.

37. Hartley was sent to Paris in April 1783 to negotiate the definitive treaty with America.

Index

Numbers in italics refer to editor's introductions; numbers in roman type refer to *Register* text. References to footnotes include footnote number in parentheses.